HANDBOOK OF SPORT PSYCHOLOGY

SECOND EDITION

Edited by

**ROBERT N. SINGER, HEATHER A. HAUSENBLAS,
and CHRISTOPHER M. JANELLE**

John Wiley & Sons, Inc.

New York • Chichester • Weinheim • Brisbane • Singapore • Toronto

This book is printed on acid-free paper. ∞

This publication is designed to provide accurate and authoritative information in
regard to the subject matter covered. It is sold with the understanding that the
publisher is not engaged in rendering professional services. If legal, accounting,
medical, psychological or any other expert assistance is required, the services of
a competent professional person should be sought.

Designations used by companies to distinguish their products are often claimed
as trademarks. In all instances where John Wiley & Sons, Inc. is aware of a
claim, the product names appear in initial capital or all capital letters. Readers,
however, should contact the appropriate companies for more complete
information regarding trademarks and registration.

Library of Congress Cataloging-in-Publication Data:

Handbook of sport psychology / Robert N. Singer, Heather A. Hausenblas, Christopher M. Janelle,
editors—2nd ed.
    p. cm.
  Rev. ed of: Handbook of research on sport psychology. c1993.
  Includes bibliographical references and index.
  ISBN 0-471-37995-6 (cloth : alk. paper)
  1. Sports—Psychological aspects. 2. Sports—Research. I. Singer, Robert N. II.
Hausenblas, Heather A. III. Janelle, Christopher M. IV. Handbook of
research on sport psychology.
GV706.4.H37 2001
796'.01—dc21   00-042291

Printed in the United States of America.

10 9 8 7 6 5 4 3 2

Contributors

Bruce Abernethy
School of Human Movement Studies
The University of Queensland
Brisbane, Queensland, Australia

Shawn M. Arent
Exercise Science and Physical Education
Arizona State University
Tempe, Arizona

Megan L. Babkes
Department of Psychology
International Center for Talent Development
University of California–Los Angeles
Los Angeles, California

Amy Baltzell
Boston University
Boston, Massachusetts

Bonnie G. Berger
Director of the School of Human Movement, Sport, and
    Leisure Studies
Bowling Green State University
Bowling Green, Ohio

Stuart J.H. Biddle
Department of Physical Education, Sports Science and
    Recreation Management
Loughborough University
Loughborough, England

Lawrence R. Brawley
Department of Kinesiology
Faculty of Applied Health Sciences
University of Waterloo
Waterloo, Ontario, Canada

Brenda Light Bredemeier
Center for Sport, Character and Culture
University of Notre Dame
Notre Dame, Indiana

Britton W. Brewer
Center for Performance Enhancement and
    Applied Research
Department of Psychology
Springfield College
Springfield, Massachusetts

Robert J. Brustad
School of KPE
University of Northern Colorado
Greeley, Colorado

Damon Burton
Division of HPERD
University of Idaho
Moscow, Idaho

Chris Button
Department of Physical Education, Sport, and
    Leisure Studies
University of Edinburgh
Edinburgh, England

Albert V. Carron
School of Kinesiology
University of Western Ontario
London, Ontario, Canada

Craig J. Chamberlin
Department of Kinesiology and PE
University College of the Fraser Valley
Abbotsford, British Columbia, Canada

Mick Court
Research Institute for Sport and Exercise Sciences
Liverpool John Moores University
Liverpool, England

Debra J. Crews
Department of Exercise Science and Physical Education
Arizona State University
Tempe, Arizona

S. Nicole Culos-Reed
Department of Kinesiology
University of Waterloo
Waterloo, Ontario, Canada

Keith Davids
Psychology Research Group
Department of Exercise and Sport Science
Manchester Metropolitan University
Alsager, England

Joan L. Duda
School of Sport and Exercise Sciences
The University of Birmingham
Edgbaston, England

Natalie Durand-Bush
University of Ottawa
Ottawa, Ontario, Canada

Paul A. Estabrooks
Department of Kinesiology
Kansas State University
Manhattan, Kansas

Deborah L. Feltz
Michigan State University
East Lansing, Michigan

Jere D. Gallagher
Department of HPRE
University of Pittsburgh
Pittsburgh, Pennsylvania

Lise Gauvin
GRIS & Department of Social and Preventive Medicine
University of Montreal
Montreal, Quebec, Canada

Nancy C. Gyurcsik
Department of Kinesiology and Office of
    Community Health
Kansas State University
Manhattan, Kansas

Craig R. Hall
School of Kinesiology
The University of Western Ontario
London, Ontario, Canada

Howard Hall
School of Physical Education Sport and Leisure
DeMontford University
Bedford, England

Stephanie J. Hanrahan
School of Human Movement Studies
The University of Queensland
Brisbane, Queensland, Australia

Lew Hardy
School of Sport, Health, and PE Sciences
University of Wales–Bangor
Bangor, England

Bradley D. Hatfield
Department of Kinesiology
University of Maryland
College Park, Maryland

Werner Helsen
Motor Learning Laboratory
Katholieke Universiteit Leuven
Leuven, Belgium

Charles H. Hillman
Department of Kinesiology
University of Illinois at Urbana-Champaign
Urbana, Illinois

Bernie Holliday
Division of HPERD
University of Idaho
Moscow, Idaho

Nicola J. Hodges
Department of Human Kinetics
University of British Columbia
Vancouver, British Columbia, Canada

Rachel Jack
Department of Kinesiology
McMaster University
Hamilton, Ontario, Canada

Paul Karoly
Department of Psychology
Arizona State University
Tempe, Arizona

Daniel M. Landers
Arizona State University
Tempe, Arizona

Timothy D. Lee
Department of Kinesiology
McMaster University
Hamilton, Ontario, Canada

Lucie Lévesque
GRIS
University of Montreal
Montreal, Quebec, Canada

Cathy D. Lirgg
University of Arkansas
Fayetteville, Arkansas

Marc R. Lochbaum
Texas Tech University
Department of HPER
Lubbock, Texas

Richard A. Magill
Department of Kinesiology
Louisiana State University
Baton Rouge, Louisiana

Penny McCullagh
Department of Kinesiology and Applied Physiology
California State University
Hayward, California

Robert Motl
Department of Exercise Science
The University of Georgia
Athens, Georgia

Sarah Naylor
Division of HPERD
University of Idaho
Moscow, Idaho

Kurt Nys
Faculty of Physical Education and Physiotherapy
Sport and Exercise Psychology
Katholieke University Leuven
Leuven, Belgium

Bruce C. Ogilvie
Los Gatos, California

David M. Paskevich
Faculty of Kinesiology
University of Calgary
Calgary, Alberta, Canada

Lucie Richard
GRIS & Faculty of Nursing
University of Montreal
Montreal, Quebec, Canada

François L. Rousseau
Department of Psychology
University of Quebec at Montreal
Montreal, Quebec, Canada

Randy Rzewnicki
Faculty of Physical Education and Physiotherapy
Katholieke University Leuven
Sport and Exercise Psychology
Leuven, Belgium

John H. Salmela
School of Human Kinetics
University of Ottawa
Ottawa, Ontario, Canada

Christopher N. Sellars
Department of Clinical and Health Sciences
School of Human and Health Sciences
University of Huddersfield
West Yorkshire, England

David Light Shields
Center for Sport, Character, and Culture
University of Notre Dame
Notre Dame, Indiana

John M. Silva III
University of North Carolina
Chapel Hill, North Carolina

Alan L. Smith
Department of HKLS
Purdue University
West Lafayette, Indiana

Janet L. Starkes
Department of Kinesiology
McMaster University
Hamilton, Ontario, Canada

Jim Taylor
San Francisco, California

Gershon Tenenbaum
Department of Educational Research
College of Education
Florida State University
Tallahassee, Florida

Jerry R. Thomas
Department of Health and Human Performance
Iowa State University
Ames, Iowa

Katherine Thomas Thomas
Department of Health and Human Performance
Iowa State University
Ames, Iowa

Robert J. Vallerand
Department of Psychology
University of Quebec at Montreal
Montreal, Quebec, Canada

Veerle Van Mele
Faculty of Physical Education and Physiotherapy
Katholieke University Leuven
Sport and Exercise Psychology
Leuven, Belgium

Yves Vanden Auweele
Faculty of Physical Education and Physiotherapy
Katholieke University Leuven
Sport and Exercise Psychology
Leuven, Belgium

Robin S. Vealey
PHS Department, Phillips Hall
Miami University
Oxford, Ohio

Maureen R. Weiss
Linda K. Bunker Professor of Education
Director, Health and Physical Education
Curry School of Education
University of Virginia
Charlottesville, Virginia

Jean M. Williams
Department of Psychology
College of Social and Behavioral Sciences
University of Arizona
Tucson, Arizona

Mark Williams
Research Institute for Sport and Exercise Science
School of Human Sciences
Liverpool John Moores University
Liverpool, England

Tim Woodman
School of Sport, Health, and PE Sciences
University of Wales–Bangor
Bangor, England

Craig A. Wrisberg
University of Tennessee
Knoxville, Tennessee

Leonard D. Zaichkowsky
Boston University
Boston, Massachusetts

Preface

In the preface to the original *Handbook of Research on Sport Psychology,* published in 1993, editors Robert Singer, Milledge Murphey, and Keith Tennant stated that they looked forward to its next publication. They predicted that a second edition of the *Handbook* would be even better due to an increase not only in number but also in sophistication of research efforts. As editors of the second edition of the *Handbook,* it is safe to say that their premonition was indeed accurate.

Because the interest in sport psychology has grown considerably in the past decade, undertaking the immense task of a second edition to the *Handbook* was both warranted and logical. Determining the text's content required the use of multiple decision criteria. First, to our definite advantage, the content of the original *Handbook* was available. After discussing changes in the field, such as the decline in research interests in certain areas and increases in others, we mapped out a tentative table of contents. Despite changes in specific chapters, the major divisions of the *Handbook* have remained the same as the original: skill acquisition, psychological characteristics of high level performance, motivation, psychological techniques for individual performance, life span development, exercise and health psychology, and future directions.

The fundamental difference between the first and second edition is in the nature and amount of new information included in the present *Handbook.* Although the chapters in this volume might appear at first glance to be similar to the original publication, they have profited considerably from new research, new insights, and renewed enthusiasm in a growing field. Most notable are new chapters and material dealing with the areas of exercise psychology, expertise, and psychophysiology. These divisions represent the expanding research interests in the effects of physical activity on psychological well-being, the interaction of physiology and psychology on performance, and the question of what makes someone an expert in his or her chosen domain.

We were committed to producing an authoritative book. With this in mind, once the content was agreed upon, we approached the leading experts on each topic and, with few exceptions, they agreed enthusiastically to contribute. These experts were issued the challenge of providing a succinct yet comprehensive current summary of their area, highlighting what is known and not known.

In the course of attempting to coordinate such an effort, we were faced with numerous editorial decisions and contentions. Perhaps the most critical involved how to provide the most contemporary research in the field to the reader. We recognize that the scope of sport psychology is changing rapidly and that current information is essential to teaching, training, counseling, and research. We vowed to make this book timely. This was a challenge given the large number of contributors. However, we established and met an aggressive schedule, due mainly to the dedicated efforts of our colleagues.

A second editorial decision was how to manage overlap in content across chapters. The primary issue was whether to edit and delete redundancy or not. We chose to maintain a certain degree of overlap among chapters for two main reasons. First, there is considerable insight to be gained when the same issue is addressed from multiple perspectives. Second, the overlap enables the chapters to stand on their own as thorough reviews of each topic, thereby increasing their individual effectiveness for teaching purposes.

The *Handbook* is a joint enterprise that has depended on the efforts of over 80 people. We are extremely grateful for the dedicated endeavors of the individuals who worked with us to make this text a reality. Chapter authors, with complex and demanding schedules, were generous in sharing their time, expertise, and knowledge. In addition, we sincerely appreciated the efforts of our secretarial staff: June Masters, Diane Williams, Susie Weldon, Judy Hopper, Louise Hubert, and Kim Hatch for their assistance with the editing processes. Their enthusiasm for the project was evidenced in their promptness and thoroughness in "fine-tuning" the chapters. We are also grateful to the staff at John Wiley & Sons, especially Tracey Belmont and Nancy Land, for their eagerness to see the book completed, promptness in meeting our goals, and quick feedback and praise for the exceptional quality of the chapters. Also, we would like to thank the University of Florida in general, and more specifically, the Department of Exercise and Sport Sciences, for their encouragement and resources during the project. We are honored, once again, that the International Society of Sport Psychology (ISSP) has officially endorsed the *Handbook*. We thank the chapter authors, to whom this book is dedicated. For two of us (Heather and Chris) this was our first attempt at book editing. We were forewarned by our veteran co-editor (Bob) about the trials and tribulations that awaited us, many of which were minimized by the cooperation, flexibility, and professionalism of the authors. Finally, our heart-felt gratitude is extended to our respective families, whose patience, encouragement, unyielding support, and words of advice are deeply appreciated.

We hope that in bringing together the material in this volume we have produced a useful and comprehensive *Handbook*. By ensuring an extensive text, our wish is that the reader will be exposed to the most current information on the majority of topics in the area of sport and exercise psychology. Our goal is that professionals, students, researchers, and the public in general will be as stimulated by reading this book as we were by editing it. Furthermore, it is our aspiration that the 33 chapters in the *Handbook* will serve to introduce readers to the complexity as well as the practical and theoretical significance of sport and exercise psychology as we enter the new millennium. In closing, as the editors of the original *Handbook* anxiously awaited its predecessor, so do we of the third edition. It is our hope that this text will stimulate even more interest among sport and exercise psychology researchers over the next decade.

Robert N. Singer
Heather A. Hausenblas
Christopher M. Janelle

October 2000

Contents

Prologue   xiii

PART I   SKILL ACQUISITION

1 | **Levels of Performance Skill: From Beginners to Experts**   3
Craig A. Wrisberg

2 | **Motor Development and Skill Acquisition during Childhood and Adolescence**   20
Katherine Thomas Thomas, Jere D. Gallagher, and Jerry R. Thomas

3 | **Attention**   53
Bruce Abernethy

4 | **Augmented Feedback in Motor Skill Acquisition**   86
Richard A. Magill

5 | **Practice**   115
Timothy D. Lee, Craig J. Chamberlin, and Nicola J. Hodges

6 | **An Integrative Modeling Approach to the Study of Intentional Movement Behavior**   144
Keith Davids, Mark Williams, Chris Button, and Mick Court

7 | **Expert Performance in Sport and Dance**   174
Janet L. Starkes, Werner Helsen, and Rachel Jack

PART II   PSYCHOLOGICAL CHARACTERISTICS OF HIGH-LEVEL PERFORMANCE

8 | **Modeling: Considerations for Motor Skill Performance and Psychological Responses**   205
Penny McCullagh and Maureen R. Weiss

9 | **Personality and the Athlete**   239
Yves Vanden Auweele, Kurt Nys, Randy Rzewnicki, and Veerle Van Mele

10 | **The Development of Talent in Sport**   269
Natalie Durand-Bush and John H. Salmela

11 | **Stress and Anxiety**   290
Tim Woodman and Lew Hardy

12 | **Arousal and Performance**   319
Leonard D. Zaichkowsky and Amy Baltzell

13 | **Self-Efficacy Beliefs of Athletes, Teams, and Coaches**   340
Deborah L. Feltz and Cathy D. Lirgg

14 | **The Psychophysiology of Sport: A Mechanistic Understanding of the Psychology of Superior Performance**   362
Bradley D. Hatfield and Charles H. Hillman

PART III   MOTIVATION

15 | **Intrinsic and Extrinsic Motivation in Sport and Exercise: A Review Using the Hierarchical Model of Intrinsic and Extrinsic Motivation**   389
Robert J. Vallerand and François L. Rousseau

16 | **Achievement Goal Theory in Sport: Recent Extensions and Future Directions**   417
Joan L. Duda and Howard Hall

17 | **Attributions: Past, Present, and Future**   444
Stuart J.H. Biddle, Stephanie J. Hanrahan, and Christopher N. Sellars

18 | **Group Cohesion in Sport and Exercise**   472
David M. Paskevich, Paul A. Estabrooks, Lawrence R. Brawley, and Albert V. Carron

PART IV   PSYCHOLOGICAL TECHNIQUES FOR INDIVIDUAL PERFORMANCE

19 | **Goal Setting in Sport: Investigating the Goal Effectiveness Paradox**   497
Damon Burton, Sarah Naylor, and Bernie Holliday

20 | **Imagery in Sport and Exercise**   529
Craig R. Hall

21 | **Understanding and Enhancing Self-Confidence in Athletes**   550
Robin S. Vealey

22 | **Self-Regulation: Concepts, Methods, and Strategies in Sport and Exercise**   566
Debra J. Crews, Marc R. Lochbaum, and Paul Karoly

PART V   LIFE SPAN DEVELOPMENT

23 | **Moral Development and Behavior in Sport**   585
David Light Shields and Brenda Light Bredemeier

24 | **Youth in Sport: Psychological Considerations**   604
Robert J. Brustad, Megan L. Babkes, and Alan L. Smith

25 | **Physical Activity and Quality of Life**   636
Bonnie G. Berger and Robert Motl

26 | **Career Termination among Athletes**   672
Jim Taylor and Bruce C. Ogilvie

PART VI   EXERCISE AND HEALTH PSYCHOLOGY

27 | Using Theories of Motivated Behavior to Understand Physical Activity: Perspectives on Their Influence   695
S. Nicole Culos-Reed, Nancy C. Gyurcsik, and Lawrence R. Brawley

28 | Helping People Initiate and Maintain a More Active Lifestyle: A Public Health Framework for Physical Activity Promotion Research   718
Lise Gauvin, Lucie Lévesque, and Lucie Richard

29 | Physical Activity and Mental Health   740
Daniel M. Landers and Shawn M. Arent

30 | Psychology of Injury Risk and Prevention   766
Jean M. Williams

31 | Psychology of Sport Injury Rehabilitation   787
Britton W. Brewer

32 | A Social-Cognitive Perspective of Perceived Exertion and Exertion Tolerance   810
Gershon Tenenbaum

PART VII   FUTURE DIRECTIONS

33 | Current Trends and Future Directions in Sport Psychology   823
John M. Silva III

Author Index   833
Subject Index   863

Prologue: A Brief History of Research in Sport Psychology

Sport psychology is frequently described as a young specialization. Its existence, with potential for research as well as practical applications, is becoming increasingly realized by young and enthusiastic would-be sport psychologists worldwide. In many ways, the foundation, depth, and scope of sport psychology are in the process of being established. Exciting research directions are being framed. Yet, one might ask how new sport psychology actually is?

Well-designed academic programs in this specialization are a recent development. Before the 1970s, courses related to the psychology of sport were offered, primarily to physical education students, in a small number of universities. No comprehensive and cohesive body of knowledge existed. Despite the lack of a scientific foundation and programs of study in sport psychology, pioneer scholars in many countries made major contributions earlier in the century. As Vanek and Cratty (1970) pointed out, between World War I and II, such physical educators and psychologists were particularly active in Russia, Germany, and the United States. Professional societies formed in the 1960s and organized congresses that helped to generate interest and offer a medium for the exchange of scholarly ideas. Journals solely for the purpose of providing an opportunity for the presentation of research in sport psychology were published shortly thereafter.

Research that could be considered to be sport psychology in theme appeared just prior to the twentieth century. The first publication of this nature is typically associated with Triplett in 1897–1898. He was interested in determining the effect of others on one's performance. Two conditions were used. One involved demonstrating skill in a laboratory reel-winding task while the other examined performance in cycling. His interest was to determine whether the influence of an audience was positive or negative on performance. Later, this type of approach would be considered to be an important contribution to research efforts testing social facilitation theory in the 1960s.

Throughout the early 1900s, there was research interest dedicated to understanding practice conditions leading to improved learning and retention. On occasion, sport skills, such as javelin throwing and archery, served as the object in this research. Massed versus distributed practice schedules and various practice conditions were manipulated to determine effects on achievement. Other themes appeared as well. As to what constitutes sport psychology research, much depends on a point of view that is either more restrictive or broadly interpretive. Books and research articles appeared on topics that could be construed as motor learning, pedagogy, motor development, and/or sport psychology. Wiggins (1985) provided a very insightful look into a variety of studies conducted by American psychologists and physical educators in those early years. The conceptualization of the nature of sport psychology and corresponding research also varies widely in emphasis from country to country.

In the United States, Coleman Griffith is recognized as becoming quite influential as a result of two books he wrote (*Psychology of Coaching* in 1926 and *Psychology and Athletics* in 1928). These were based on research he and others had conducted (Singer, 1989). In addition, he was involved in laboratory and field research related to sport psychology at the University of Illinois and was also a consultant for a professional baseball team. Because most of his work did not involve colleagues or students, it was not continued after he assumed another position at the university. Although interesting developments were occurring in some other countries, communication and language barriers prevented them from being widely disseminated. Vanek and Cratty's (1970) book provided valuable insights into these international developments.

World War II is associated with many profound changes and effects on practical research and the conceptual framing of skilled behaviors. For example, psychologists were called upon to determine underlying factors contributing to those perceptual-motor skills required to be performed in military operations. They were asked to design batteries of tests predictive of success in specialized tasks. Also of concern was how to train to improve or to maintain skill. The word *skill* suddenly had new meaning, especially with regard to person-machine interfaces. Cybernetics, hierarchical control, and communication models to explain skill evolved and replaced behavioristic ways of describing behavior (Singer, 1980). In later years, such thinking spawned much interest to pursue motor learning and motor control research, as well as that aspect of sport psychology associated with the acquisition of skill and the attainment of expertise. General research topics prior to the 1960s most attuned to sport psychology dealt with personality and success, abilities and achievement, motivation, and social process dynamics. Many of these and other initiatives could probably be related today to academic areas of study related to psychology. Examples would be social, cognitive, occupational/organization, developmental, and clinical/counseling (see Kremer & Scully, 1994).

THE 1960s AND 1970s

The 1960s is associated most with the scientific and professional identity of sport psychology, cross-country interactions, and the beginnings of public awareness. Knowledge about research in different countries, the ability to share ideas, and the possibility to develop a foundation for sport psychology were realized by the formation of the International Society of Sport Psychology in 1965. This was due primarily to the vision and efforts of Italian psychiatrist Ferruccio Antonelli and other European colleagues (Salmela, 1992). During the same year, the first International Congress of Sport Psychology was held in Rome, Italy. Many research presentations were made by scientists from all parts of the world. The next congress was held in 1968 in Washington, DC. Following the 1973 congress in Spain, one has been held every four years in various locations worldwide.

The North American Society for the Psychology of Sport and Physical Activity (NASPSPA) and FEPSAC (Fédération Européan de Psychologie du Sport et Activité Corporelle), which is the European Society of Sport Psychology, were formed and their first conference organized in 1967. Meetings have been conducted on a regular basis since then. Special invited lecturers, research presentations, symposia, and poster sessions constitute the respective programs.

Other major developments occurred in the 1970s that also made a major impact on the scientific and body of knowledge foundation of sport psychology. Once again, credit is given to Antonelli for his vision and determination in advancing sport psychology, this time with the creation of the *International Journal of Sport Psychology* (IJSP) in 1970. The *Journal,* although under the sponsorship of the International Society of Sport Psychology, had insufficient funding. Antonelli pledged his own monies to circulate and maintain the *Journal.* He convinced his friend, Liugi Pozzi, to add the *Journal* to his list of publications (Salmela, 1999). Even though research articles associated with sport psychology had been published earlier in psychology journals and the *Research Quarterly* (now the *Research Quarterly for Exercise and Sport*), the *IJSP* was the first journal to be dedicated solely to publishing empirical and review articles dedicated to research associated with the scholarly aspects of sport psychology. Although published in Italy, the articles were and are still presented in English, with abstracts in French, Spanish, and German. In 1979, the *Journal of Sport Psychology* (presently the *Journal of Sport & Exercise Psychology*) was produced under the leadership of Rainer Martens (a prominent sport psychologist) who founded the Human Kinetics Publishing Company. The *Journal* has enjoyed an outstanding reputation for the quality of the articles published.

Sport psychology grew up in other ways in the 1970s. University academic departments began offering solid graduate programs at the masters and doctoral levels as the scholarly substance of the specialization was being created. Student interest was stimulated. Respectability of departments and programs is very important in institutions of higher learning. Consequently, an earnest attempt was made in academia to develop and refine serious academic sport psychology programs and to produce research appreciated by peer educators/scholars. In later years, this direction was to be criticized by those who felt that this type of research direction was too academic and not sufficiently meaningful in the real world. As interests and directions have expanded in sport psychology, individuals committed to contributing primarily to the body of knowledge research or practical research have learned to co-exist. Both orientations are important.

1980s TO THE EARLY 1990s

More and more countries initiated their own sport psychology organizations, with meetings held annually. Increasing opportunities were afforded for those who wished to present their research. In the United States, the Association for the Advancement of Applied Sport Psychology (AAASP) was formed in 1985 under the inspiration of John Silva. In contrast to NASPSPA, it is more specifically directed to professional/practical issues and more applied sport psychology research. Research articles are published in the *Journal of Applied Sport Psychology,* which is sponsored by AAASP. Likewise, *The Sport Psychologist,* first published in 1986, also focuses on more applied research themes and professional issues papers. More and more sport science journals arose in different countries, with opportunities for sport psychologists to share their research.

The growth in the substance/depth and breadth of research themes was remarkable in the 1980s and early 1990s. Likewise, qualitative research (as compared to classical experimental methodology with resultant quantitative data) gained much greater endorsement than in previous years. Multidisciplinary, conceptually-driven research, with multiple dependent measures, also became customary. Applied research efforts answered critical questions concerning achievement and fulfillment in sport and exercise programs, while demonstrating the most scientifically acceptable methodology. Whereas researchers' interests in applied topics in general prior to the 1970s produced noncohesive and atheoretical research, systematic and more meaningful modes of inquiry were the norm in the 1980s and early 1990s and continue to be so today. Each of these advances led to the formation of a unique yet universally applicable body of research. This growing body of literature specific to sport psychology prompted publication of the first edition of the *Handbook of Research on Sport Psychology* by Singer and colleagues (1993).

SPORT PSYCHOLOGY FROM 1993 TO 2001

Since the publication of the first *Handbook of Research on Sport Psychology,* many developments have occurred that signal a scholarly maturing of the field. Examples include the broad range of contemporary research topics, the complexity of the research methodology, as well as the recognition that practice must be rooted in strong scientific principles. The immediate past and present represent a time of vast expansion in sport psychology research, as well as opportunity to continue to forge a unique, respected, and influential niche within the larger fields of psychology and exercise and sport sciences.

Sport Psychology Orientations

The current climate of research in sport psychology in North America is one of increasing orientation to the social

psychology of sport. Many of the early pioneers in sport psychology, most of whom emanated from traditional motor behavior backgrounds, have diversified in recent years to conduct research that has more of a social cognitive flavor. This polarization is somewhat ironic considering that the consensus father of North American sport psychology, Coleman Griffith, devoted almost half (seven chapters) of his famous book *Psychology of Athletics,* to topics that would be considered typical of present-day motor control and learning.

In contrast to the North American situation, sport psychology still tends to include motor learning/control topics in Australia and in many countries in Europe and Asia. Abernethy (1999) has emphasized that the motor learning/control and sport psychology fields have much shared history, and likewise, much to offer each other. In his 1997 keynote address at the annual conference of the Association for the Advancement of Applied Sport Psychology, Abernethy stressed that, "While sport psychology's divergence from motor control in the 1960s and 1970s to establish an independent field was undoubtedly important for the field's identity and maturation, continued divergence may well be counterproductive" (1999, p. 130). Topics of interest to motor learning/control and sport psychology researchers still hold common ground in many ways, especially with respect to the processes that underlie the mind-body interactions that form the foundation for each of these disciplines. The fact that Abernethy, a noted researcher of motor learning/control issues, was invited to give a keynote address at one of the more applied conferences in the field, is certainly indicative of an effort to maintain ties between sport psychology and its roots. The current state of science and practice in many scientific fields is one of increasing collaboration and unification. Hopefully, individuals specializing in sport psychology and motor learning/control will continue to reverse the trend toward fragmentation and overspecialization.

Signs that collaboration, not segmentation, is again desirable have begun to arise in various pockets of research germane to sport and exercise psychology and motor learning/control. Indeed, sport psychology research and practice is recognized as useful to psychologists, physical therapists, and sport medicine specialists, among others. For instance, recent work has been initiated in which sport psychology interventions, as well as principles developed from the motor learning literature dealing with practice scheduling and composition, are being applied to clinical populations; and the effectiveness of these interventions on psychological and physiological well-being is being evaluated (e.g., Page, Martin, & Wayda, 2000). Similarly, research efforts in the collective fields of sport psychology, motor behavior, and exercise psychology have been increasingly recognized by funding agencies interested in, for example, the rehabilitation and treatment of cancer patients and in the development of interventions to help improve the mental health of aging populations.

Although the relative usefulness of sport psychology principles and training is currently being scrutinized outside of sports, it is paradoxical that within the sport context, the viability, reliability, and validity of performance enhancement interventions are rarely evaluated in an empirical manner. Surprisingly, despite the increasing emphasis on and desire for applied experiences in sport psychology, the amount of applied research in which performance enhancement outcomes are examined is notably scarce (Vealey, 1994). With the increasing popularity of sport psychology worldwide, and the proliferation of sport psychology service-providers, the development of a knowledge base that includes evaluative statements concerning the effectiveness of the popular interventions used is critical for the maintenance of credibility and effectiveness in delivering them. Establishing the efficacy of different interventions with various populations must be a primary objective of sport psychology research in the new millennium.

Finally, a mission for sport psychology researchers is to generate unique and useful theories. Perhaps these theories will be meaningful to other subdisciplines in psychology. In this regard, nontraditional approaches to understanding the coordination of perception and action advanced in many forms by ecological theorists has certainly been driven in large part by those who would be considered sport psychologists or motor behaviorists (cf., Turvey, 1994). In addition to influencing the scientific community in psychology in general, this unique line of inquiry and investigation is also beginning to change how practitioners interested in improving the learning of motor skills develop guidelines for doing so (see Chapter 14). Likewise, theoretical advances made by sport psychologists to understand the epidemiology of athletic injuries, the psychological precursors to injuries, as well as the rehabilitation process, are significantly influencing the methods by which physicians and therapists approach injuries and illnesses in athletes and non-athletes alike. It is anticipated that the future of sport psychology research is one in which the theories that emanate from sport psychology will influence thinking in other fields to an even greater extent than is the case today. Almost 20 years ago, Landers (1982) titled a chapter "What ever happened to theory testing in sport psychology." Although atheoretical research is published (and is

often pragmatically valuable), contemporary sport psychology research tends to be conceptually grounded. Indeed, if sport psychology is to continue to emerge and mature as a scientific discipline, and as a respected applied field of endeavor, at the heart of these advances must be a foundation of theory-based research.

The primary focus in the past has been to understand and perhaps influence conditions and behaviors leading to an athlete's or group's achievement in sports. Lesser involvement, but of equal significance, has been in understanding movement (sport, dance, recreation, and the like) therapy for special populations (e.g., the severely depressed, the elderly, the handicapped). Likewise an increased interest has been shown in the psychology of recovery from injury in sport. For example the first *Handbook of Research on Sport Psychology* attempted to cover these and other topics of interest to sport psychology researchers. However, it was almost impossible to do justice in one book to the expanding research directions and contributions to society. The task is equally if not more daunting today. Furthermore, understanding how to help one to realize potential, to achieve, and/or to be fulfilled is not a unique consideration in sport settings.

Proliferation of Exercise Psychology Research

In addition to the obvious collaboration and corroboration that traditionally characterizes the relationship between sport psychologists and motor learning/control researchers, a similar relationship exists among exercise psychologists and sport psychologists. Indeed, many exercise psychologists initially received formal training in sport psychology or motor learning/control and then applied their research focus to questions more pertinent to exercise psychology. A major focus is on the physical activity, health, and lifestyles of people of all ages. Beginning in the 1970s, people were strongly encouraged to become fit, sweat, eat well, and in general, realize greater longevity and a better quality of life. Exercise/health psychologists have played an increasingly active role in generating research having to do with the psychological antecedents and consequences of involvement in physical activity programs.

Research and interest in exercise psychology did not proliferate until the late 1980s. Reasons for the relatively slow development of exercise psychology as a science, compared to sport psychology, included: (1) the early popularity of sport rather than physical activity within the general population and (2) the recent acknowledgment of the importance of physical activity for disease prevention and the maintenance of general health (Rejeski & Thompson, 1993;

USDHHS, 1996). When research in exercise psychology began to increase in the 1980s, the focus was on gaining an understanding of human attitudes, cognitions, and behaviors for physical activity. Evidence of this is provided by the most prevalent topics of investigations which include: (1) the effects of acute and chronic exercise on mental health and cognitions (e.g., depression, anxiety, self-esteem, body image, dependence, mood, stress), (2) examining subjective perceptions of physical function during acute exercise bouts, (3) identification of determinants of involvement in physical activity and interventions to increase exercise, and (4) social factors related to exercise (Carron, Hausenblas, & Mack, 1996; Gauvin & Spence, 1996; Rejeski & Thompson, 1993).

Perspectives

Researchers with very different professional and scientific orientations study such questions. The results of research conducted with exercisers and those who contemplate exercising, or with highly-skilled athletes, serious recreational athletes, or leisure athletes, frequently contribute to understanding many other human endeavors. Likewise,

scientific work in areas other than sport psychology has had a profound influence on the thinking of sport psychology scholars as to ideas for research, conceptual frameworks, research methodology, and potential practical applications. Certainly there are far more researchers in many academic specializations than there are in sport psychology. Sport psychologists have been affected greatly by the research of others, but in contemporary times, are reversing the process. A balance between influencing and being influenced is probably desirable.

Figure P.1 provides a fairly broad overview of the areas in which sport and exercise psychologists are actively engaged, for purposes of research and/or practical applications. The structure is laid out for convenience in identifying major themes. However, many investigations cut across categories, and it is impossible to generate all of the possible combinations.

The focus on *Learning, Performance, and Skill* is directed to how learning cognitive and perceptual processes work, how practice conditions might be most favorable for the beginner to the highly skilled, and differences between experts and beginners in the way cognitive operations

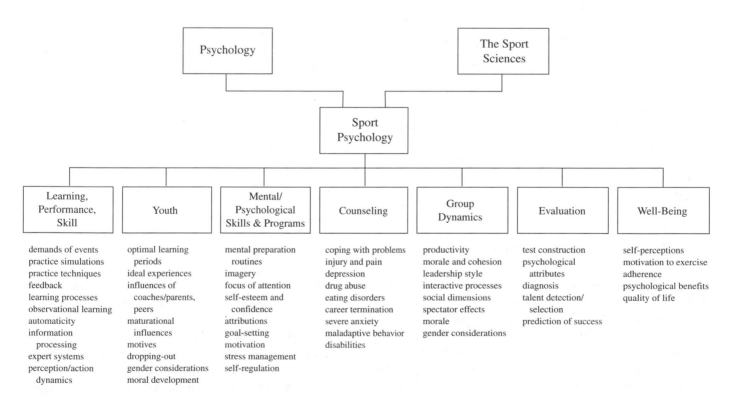

Figure P.1   The influence of psychology and the sport sciences on the many dimensions associated with sport psychology. From R.N. Singer (1996). Future of sport and exercise psychology. In J.L. VAn Raalte & B.W. Brewer (Eds.), *Exploring sport and exercise psychology* (pp. 451–468). Washington, DC: American Psychological Association.

function. An interest in *youth sport* participants and program encompasses understanding children, capabilities, motives, and the types of support systems that promote beneficial psychological and performance outcomes. *Mental/Psychological Skills and Programs* have been identified and studied to determine those procedures that can best improve personal resources that contribute to performance achievement and excellence.

Counseling typically applies to those who are trained in clinical or counseling psychology, or psychiatry, and are professionally prepared to help athletes under duress, with maladaptive behaviors and disorders that can undermine coping with the demands of athletic competition as well as life in general. Because athletes typically compete in some form of team structure, *group dynamics* research is conducted about organizational structures and systems in order to provide guidelines as to how groups or teams can best function to attain ideal goals. Those scholars who develop sport-specific psychological tests for purposes of assessment, advisement, and perhaps talent detection are concerned with *evaluation*. Finally, exercise/health psychologists are dedicated to the *well-being* of everyone, and the psychological antecedents and consequences of involvement in physical activity.

With increasing spectatorship in big-time sports, individual interest in recreational pursuits, the public's concern about health, and the potential for the quality of life to be improved through movement experiences, sport and exercise/health psychology research appears to have a glamorous future. Major contributions can be made in a variety of ways. Quality research paves the way to understandings and improvements. The myriad of topics covered in this book suggests many contemporary research foci in sport and exercise psychology, but is by no means comprehensive. Nonetheless, we hope that the nature and scope of research is covered in a reasonable manner so as to educate the nonfamiliar and to stimulate the enthusiasm and efforts of those intending to be scholars as well as those who are established scholars.

The overall credibility of an academic discipline is truly distinguished by the quality of its research. The current state of research in sport psychology is as sophisticated and diversified as virtually any other scientific field. From the instrumentation used in psychophysiological investigations, to the development of unique and innovative analyses for the purpose of coding and interpreting qualitative data, the scientific methods and merits of sport psychology researchers are quite impressive. Although other opinions

certainly exist, and may be expressed elsewhere (see the final chapter in the *Handbook*), the value of research, both basic and applied, cannot be overstated. Despite the ever-changing landscape that characterizes the science and practice of sport psychology, this attitude continues to be the dominant orientation of sport psychology scholars, thus providing the necessary motivation and content for this revised version of the *Handbook*.

REFERENCES

Abernethy, B. (1999). The 1997 Coleman Roberts Griffith address: Movement expertise: A juncture between psychology theory and practice. *Journal of Applied Sport Psychology, 11,* 126–141.

Carron, A.V., Hausenblas, H.A., & Mack, D. (1996). The social influence and exercise: A meta-analysis. *Journal of Sport & Exercise Psychology, 18,* 1–17.

Gauvin, L., & Spence, J.C. (1996). Psychological research on exercise and fitness: Current research trends and future challenges. *The Sport Psychologist, 9,* 434–446.

Kremer, J., & Scully, D. (1994). *Psychology in sport.* East Sussex, England: Psychology Press.

Landers, D.M. (1982). Whatever happened to theory testing in sport psychology? In L.M. Wankel & R.B. Wilberg (Eds.), *Psychology of sport and motor behavior: Research and practice* (pp. 88–104). Edmonton, Canada: University of Alberta.

Page, S.J., Martin, S.B., & Wayda, V.K. (2000). Attitudes toward seeking sport psychology consultation among elite wheelchair basketball players. *Research Quarterly for Exercise and Sport, 71,* 109.

Rejeski, W.J., & Thompson, A. (1993). Historical and conceptual roots of exercise psychology. In P. Seraganian (Ed.), *Exercise psychology: The influence of physical exercise on psychological processes* (pp. 3–39). New York: Wiley.

Salmela, J.H. (Ed.). (1992). *The world sport psychology sourcebook* (2nd ed.). Champaign, IL: Human Kinetics.

Salmela, J.H. (1999). The Antonelli era of sport psychology: Inspiration, improvisation, and angst. In R. Lidor & M. Bar-Eli (Eds.), *Sport psychology: Linking theory and practice* (pp. 3–12). Morgantown, WV: Fitness Information Technology.

Singer, R.N. (1980). *Motor learning and human performance* (3rd ed.). New York: Macmillan.

Singer, R.N. (1989). Applied sport psychology in the United States. *Journal of Applied Sport Psychology, 1,* 61–80.

Triplett, N. (1897–1898). The dynamogenic factors in pacemaking and competition. *American Journal of Psychology, 9,* 507–533.

Turvey, M.T. (1994). From Borelli (1680) and Bell (1826) to the dynamics of action and perception. *Journal of Sport & Exercise Psychology, 16,* S128–S157.

U.S. Department of Health and Human Services. (1996). *Physical activity and health: A report of the surgeon general.* Altanta, GA: Center for Disease Control and Prevention.

Vanek, M., & Cratty, C.J. (1970). *Psychology and the superior athlete.* London: Macmillan.

Vealey, R.S. (1994). Knowledge development and implementation in sport psychology: A review of *The Sport Psychologist,* 1987–1992. *The Sport Psychologist, 8,* 331–348.

Wiggins, D.K. (1985). The history of sport psychology in North America. In J.M Silva & R.S. Weinberg (Eds.), *Psychology foundations of sport* (pp. 9–22). Champaign, IL: Human Kinetics.

PART I

Skill Acquisition

CHAPTER 1

Levels of Performance Skill
From Beginners to Experts

CRAIG A. WRISBERG

> If you think of physical genius as a pyramid, with, at the bottom, the raw components of coordination, and above that, the practice that perfects those particular movements, then this faculty of imagination is the top layer. This is what separates the physical genius from those who are merely very good.
>
> Malcolm Gladwell (1999, August 2)

Even the most casual observations of elite athletic performance prompt speculation as to the possible factors that distinguish the knowledge and behaviors of experts from those of good or average performers. For years the prevailing opinion of coaches has been that the best athletes possess certain physical traits or perceptual-motor abilities that allow them to achieve extraordinary performance levels. Not surprisingly, tests (e.g., McDavid, 1977) or profiles (e.g., Rodionov, 1978) for predicting athletic superiority have emphasized the "hardware" attributes of individuals (e.g., eye-hand coordination, movement speed) that presumably contribute to their success in sports. Persons scoring higher on such tests or demonstrating more of the abilities associated with the "ideal" profile are expected to be the better performers.

In addition to the popular notion that superior athletes possess more elegant neuromuscular systems than their lesser-skilled counterparts (Sternberg, 1996; Winner, 1996), there is a growing body of research literature indicating that much of the performance advantage experts enjoy is due to domain-specific perceptual capabilities or functional knowledge (i.e., software) developed over many years of sporting experience. (See Abernethy, 1999a; Singer & Janelle, 1999; Starkes, Deakin, Allard, Hodges, & Hayes, 1996, for more detailed discussions.)

In this chapter, an attempt is made to summarize the literature that addresses possible factors differentiating the performance of individuals of different skill levels, from beginners to experts. The chapter is divided into several sections dealing with the stages of practice notion, experimental approaches used by sport scientists to explain or examine skill level differences, factors that contribute to differences in levels of performance skill, and implications of the available evidence for sport psychology consultants.

THE STAGES OF PRACTICE NOTION

One approach to the examination of differences in the skill levels of individuals has been to compare the characteristics of performers at various stages of practice. The notion of practice stages is not a new one. In fact, anyone who has ever attempted to learn a sport skill can probably recall the different types of experiences they had at different times during the course of practice.

Theoretical discussions of the stages of practice notion have typically centered on two (Adams, 1971; Gentile, 1972) or three (Anderson, 1982; Fitts & Posner, 1967) relatively distinct stages. All of these theorists seem to be in agreement that the initial stage of practice is characterized by the performer's attempts to acquire a general idea of the task. Many strategies are implemented and retained, modified, or discarded; errors are frequent; and the consistency of responding is quite low. However, once the individual achieves a rough notion of performance requirements, practice advances to a second stage, during which skill refinement occurs. In this stage, movements are performed with more precision and consistency and environmental cues appropriate to successful performance are processed more effectively and efficiently (Gentile, 1972). Many individuals never progress beyond an intermediate stage of learning. However, a few advance to yet another level, characterized by seemingly effortless execution of the correct action. Performers in this stage are able to produce their movements almost automatically (Anderson, 1982; Fitts & Posner, 1967). Since very little conscious thought is required for performance, attention can be devoted to other aspects of the skill environment (e.g., actions of an opponent, speed and trajectory of an approaching object, movement style, competitive strategies).

Based on the stages of practice notion, it might be inferred that beginning, intermediate, and advanced performers generally exhibit characteristics associated with the cognitive, associative, and autonomous stages of practice, respectively (Fitts & Posner, 1967). However, because skill development is usually a continuous process, some overlap among the various stages is to be expected at most times. In addition, performers in the autonomous stage (i.e., experts) may be expected to continue refining their skills, even after years of practice (Crossman, 1959).

Researchers have attempted to determine the extent to which the amount of "deliberate practice" contributes to the level of a person's performance skill or expertise. Stimulated by the theorizing of Ericsson, Krampe, and Tesch-Romer (1993), sport scientists have begun to examine the role of deliberate practice on the development of athletic skills. According to Ericsson et al. (1993), deliberate practice involves (1) the practice of a well-defined task that is challenging to the performer, (2) the presence of relevant feedback, and (3) the opportunity for repetition and error correction. The primary components of deliberate practice include the total number of hours spent practicing, the presence of effort, determination, and concentration, and the lack of inherent enjoyment. Based on research with experts in other domains (e.g., chess, music), Ericsson (1996) contends that both the quantity and quality of deliberate practice are essential ingredients for skill development and that, in most cases, 10 years of deliberate practice is required for an individual to achieve expertise.

To date, sport scientists have experienced difficulty producing empirical support for Ericsson's proposal (e.g., Baker & Abernethy, 1999). Salmela (1999) suggests that this lack of success may be due to qualitative differences in the nature of competitive sport and other performance domains (e.g., music). For example, the age at which sport performers achieve expertise is often different for different activities (e.g., younger for gymnastics and older for golf). In addition, improvements in athletic skill are often due to factors other than the amount and quality of deliberate practice (e.g., transfer of skill from other activities, the availability of coaches and other resources). Thus, the extent to which Ericsson et al.'s (1993) strict conceptualization of deliberate

practice is generalizable to the development of sport expertise remains at the present time unclear.

In the following sections, the experimental approaches used to examine differences in the level of people's performance skill are discussed and the primary research findings emanating from studies using these approaches are summarized.

EXPERIMENTAL APPROACHES

Researchers have favored a number of experimental approaches in an attempt to identify factors contributing to differences in the skill level of individuals. Two approaches (i.e., the individual differences approach and the information processing approach) dominated the research literature during the 1960s and 1970s. Scientists used the first to determine the degree of relationship between people's relatively permanent abilities (such as eye-hand coordination, reaction time, and movement speed) and their perceptual-motor performance (e.g., Fleishman, 1978, 1982; Fleishman & Hempel, 1955). Researchers employed the second approach in an attempt to isolate the processes individuals use when dealing with sundry types of information found in the performance environment (e.g., Kerr, 1973; Marteniuk, 1976). These two approaches produced considerable data on a variety of populations and offered insights into some of the factors that might distinguish the performance level of individuals on novel laboratory tasks at various stages of practice. Sport scientists have utilized a third approach (i.e., the expert-novice paradigm) that involves the comparison of various characteristics of beginning or average performers with those of experts (see Abernethy, 1994 for a review). Taken together, the results of investigations incorporating these three approaches provide a rather comprehensive picture of a number of factors that seem to contribute to differences in the levels of people's performance skill.

It is important to point out that comparisons between the skill levels of experimental participants who have practiced novel laboratory tasks for several days (which has generally been the case in studies using the first two approaches) and that of athletes who have practiced a specific skill for many years (as in studies employing the expert-novice approach) are probably inappropriate. Moreover, it is clear from even a surface perusal of the available literature that considerable variation exists in researchers' operational definitions of skill level or level of expertise. For example, "experts" have been variously defined as adult members of a national team (e.g., Kioumourtzoglou, Kourtessis, Michalopoulou, & Derri, 1998) and as children rated high in skill level by their coaches (e.g., French,

Spurgeon, & Nevett, 1995). Therefore, rather than emphasize the possible linkages or discrepancies between the three experimental approaches, the remainder of this chapter is devoted to a discussion of the cognitive, perceptual, and motor characteristics that appear to distinguish individuals possessing different levels of performance skill.

The Individual Differences Approach

Since the advent of the scientific method, investigators have typically employed an approach to experimentation that isolates various factors for the purpose of determining their influence on the performance of groups of participants. However, a few researchers have deviated from this approach in an attempt to identify inherited abilities or traits (i.e., hardware characteristics) that distinguish the performance of individuals on a variety of tasks. (See Schmidt & Lee, 1999, for a more detailed discussion of differences in the experimental and differential approaches to scientific inquiry.) Most prominent have been the efforts of Fleishman and colleagues (e.g., Fleishman, 1972, 1978; Fleishman & Bartlett, 1969; Fleishman & Hempel, 1955; Fleishman & Rich, 1963) and in the 1980s, Keele and associates (Keele & Hawkins, 1982; Keele, Ivry, & Pokorny, 1987; Keele, Pokorny, Corcos, & Ivry, 1985).

Abilities are typically considered to be relatively stable characteristics of individuals, the levels of which change little over time or practice. Thus, it is assumed that persons possessing high levels of the abilities important to the performance of a particular task will have a greater probability of success or, in light of the present discussion, demonstrate a higher level of skill. The approach that has generally been adopted to identify abilities underlying task performance involves the testing of many individuals on many tasks. Statistical correlations are then calculated between the various possible pairs of scores or occasionally among larger groups of scores to determine which tasks are highly related. Those tasks producing higher correlations are presumed to depend on similar underlying abilities.

Following the development of test batteries, relationships between the performance of individuals on those tests and on some new task may be determined. For example, scores on a test measuring an ability called "eye-foot coordination" might be expected to correlate highly with the performance of certain tasks required of a soccer goalie (e.g., receiving a pass from a teammate, making a kick save). If this were the case, elite soccer goalies would be predicted to score higher on tests of eye-foot coordination than would novice or non-elite athletes. If the notion of ability groupings is a valid one, then it should be possible to assess an individual's potential for task success by determining the level of task-relevant abilities the person possesses (e.g., McDavid, 1977).

The Information-Processing Approach

In addition to the fact that performers may differ with respect to the abilities (i.e., hardware characteristics) they bring to a task situation, there is also the likelihood that individuals respond with different levels of proficiency to information contained in the skill environment. The most important contributions to an understanding of how humans handle environmental information come from studies adopting an information-processing approach. An important assumption of this approach is that serial and non-overlapping processing stages exist between a stimulus and a response. Much of the research supporting this assumption has utilized a reaction-time (RT) paradigm. With this paradigm, it is assumed that slower decision times (i.e., slower RT) reflect longer delays in information processing in one or more of the stages. (See Schmidt & Lee, 1999, for a more complete discussion of the information-processing approach in motor behavior research.)

The results of many laboratory studies suggest the existence of at least three processing stages that comprise the interval between a stimulus and a response. The first stage, termed *stimulus identification,* involves the activation of *perceptual processes,* such as stimulus detection and pattern recognition. In this stage the performer's task is to make sense of the stimulus. Not surprisingly, variables that influence the duration of this stage include the intensity, clarity, and familiarity of the stimulus (e.g., Posner, 1964; Swets, 1964). In the second stage, *response selection* takes place and *decision processes* are activated. At this point, the performer has presumably identified the important features of the stimulus and must decide on an appropriate response. Factors that influence the duration of decision processing include the number of stimulus-response alternatives and the compatibility of the stimulus and response (e.g., Fitts & Seeger, 1953; Hick, 1952). In the third stage, *effector processes* are used to determine the correct spatial-temporal pattern of the movement that has been selected. The primary task of the performer in this stage is to decide which motor commands to issue in order to assure accurate *response execution.* The factors that influence the duration of this stage include movement complexity, the number of movement parts, the accuracy demands of the movement, and movement duration (e.g., Christina, 1992; Henry & Rogers, 1960; Klapp & Erwin, 1976; Sidaway, Sekiya, & Fairweather, 1995). Generally, more complex movements, those comprised of a greater number of parts, those requiring greater accuracy, and those of longer duration take longer to initiate than do actions that are simpler, require less accuracy, and are of shorter duration.

Later in this chapter, some of the research findings are discussed that illustrate how the efficiency of information processing in each of the three stages may be improved with practice and how elite performers may be able to perform more quickly and accurately than beginning or average performers by bypassing and/or expediting the activities of certain stages.

The Expert-Novice Approach

The most direct approach to examining differences in the skill level of individuals is to compare the proficiency of beginners, average performers, and experts on various characteristics of perceptual-motor performance. Pioneered originally by Chase and Simon (1973) with chess players, this paradigm has been adopted by investigators interested in expert-novice differences in a variety of perceptual-cognitive and motor characteristics of sport performers.

Studies of this nature typically involve comparisons of the perceptual processing capabilities, sport-specific knowledge, or mechanical efficiency of elite athletes and non-elite athletes. The results of these investigations indicate that more skilled athletes encode/retrieve game structure information differently and/or more quickly (e.g., Allard, Graham, & Paarsalu, 1980; Christensen & Glencross, 1993), structure their visual search of the environment differently (e.g., Abernethy, 1991; Bard & Fleury, 1981), selectively attend to different kinds of information in the sport environment (e.g., Allard & Starkes, 1980; Tenenbaum & Summers, 1996), and demonstrate different kinematic profiles for the movements they produce (Berg & Greer, 1995; Temprado, Della-Grasta, Farrell, & Laurent, 1997) than do less-skilled performers.

SYNTHESIS OF RESEARCH FINDINGS

Research examining differences in the skill levels of individuals has been extensive (see the references concluding this chapter). In this section, the important findings that have been obtained to this date are summarized.

The Role of General Abilities

The notion of general abilities falls somewhere between the older view of a single general ability, that was presumed to distinguish the performance of persons for all types of motor tasks (i.e., "he/she sure has a lot of *ability*"), and the hypothesis that every task has a constellation of abilities that are unique to the performance of that task and completely unlike those required for any other task (Henry,

1968). According to the general motor ability view, correlations between the performance of a large group of people on any two motor tasks should be quite high, with those individuals possessing more "general ability" doing better on both tasks and those with less ability doing worse. By way of contrast, a strict "specificity" interpretation postulates that intertask correlations should be extremely low since performance on one task is presumed to require an entirely different set of abilities than those needed for performance on any other task.

The available evidence from studies using general populations of research participants and novel laboratory tasks demonstrates consistent support for the specificity notion (Bachman, 1961; Henry, 1961; Lotter, 1960; J. Parker & Fleishman, 1960). However, while most intertask correlations reported in these studies have tended to be uniformly low and statistically nonsignificant, they have *not* been zero. This fact is perhaps best illustrated in a study by J. Parker and Fleishman (1960) comparing the performance of individuals on 50 different novel motor tasks. The results of this experiment indicated that tasks that were more similar in nature (e.g., squat, twist, touch and bend, twist, touch) correlated more highly than tasks that were less similar (e.g., squat, twist, touch and ball balance). Thus, it might be presumed that tasks containing similar requirements have at least some common underlying abilities. If such a proposal is correct (i.e., certain abilities are important to the performance of particular types of tasks), then individuals possessing high levels of the "necessary" abilities would be predicted to achieve greater success on a given task or sport than would persons possessing lower levels of the abilities.

In the 1980s, Keele and his associates (Keele & Hawkins, 1982; Keele et al., 1987; Keele et al., 1985) reasoned that since entire tasks typically share some, but not all, processes, the contribution of a shared process (e.g., attention switching) may be masked by a variety of other "unshared" processes (e.g., decision making) if the performance of individuals on entire tasks were correlated. Thus, Keele's group adopted an information-processing approach that allowed them to derive scores that reflected only the process being shared by two tasks. The correlations they obtained proved to be uniformly higher than those reported in earlier studies, suggesting the existence of several general timing abilities, such as maximum rate of repetitive movements (Keele & Hawkins, 1982), timing control (Keele et al., 1985), and force control (Keele et al., 1987). Subsequent researchers (Franz, Zelaznik, & Smith, 1992; Ivry & Hazeltine, 1995) have provided additional support for the notion of a general timing ability (although see Robertson et al., 1999, and

Zelaznik, Spencer, & Doffin, 2000, for possible exceptions) and offers an encouraging new direction for movement scientists interested in identifying abilities that distinguish levels of performance skill for various classes of motor tasks (e.g., jumping, throwing, striking, balancing).

While the majority of researchers exploring the notion of general abilities have used novel tasks and general populations in their experiments, some have attempted to identify general abilities possessed by elite athletes that distinguish their performance from that of beginning, average, or good performers. Extensive investigation of the relationship of specific abilities to athletic performance probably originated with Soviet researchers. (See Vanek & Cratty, 1970 for a more detailed historical perspective.) Studies of this nature often included attempts to identify traits such as will power, concentration, and the feeling of the water by swimmers. For example, during the National Championship in Leningrad in 1963, an effort was made to determine the relationship of concentration time (i.e., time prior to a performance attempt) and the high-jumping performance of the world-class athlete, Valeri Brumel. Summarizing the findings of this experiment, Vanek and Cratty (1970) reported that "concentration time, when coupled with performance scores (i.e., height jumped), purportedly reveals important relationships between preperformance activation and optimum effort" (p. 18). A significant outgrowth of this type of research was the development of models of the "ideal" athlete for a variety of sport disciplines (Rodionov, 1978). In addition, psychobiological profiles called "sportprofessiograms" were constructed by Soviet sport psychologists that detailed the important traits required for optimum performance by athletes in various activities (Schneidman, 1979).

Sport scientists in Europe and North America were not as successful in demonstrating a strong relationship between general abilities and athletic prowess. Much of this research involved the investigation of visual-perceptual factors and their relationship to performance. For example, depth perception (i.e., the ability to judge the relative distance of objects) was for some time assumed to be keener for elite athletes than for their lesser skilled counterparts or for non-athletes. In an early study, Bannister and Blackburn (1931) found that the interpupillary distance of rugby players was greater than that of nonplayers and concluded that the more advantageous angle of visual convergence of the players promoted superior depth perception that enhanced their athletic prowess. Similar studies reported that higher caliber athletes were superior to average athletes or non-athletes on visual attributes such as depth perception (Graybiel, Jokl, & Trapp, 1955; Miller, 1960; Montebello,

1953; Olsen, 1956), distance estimation (Cockerill, 1981), dynamic visual acuity (Morris & Kreighbaum, 1977), and peripheral vision (Olsen, 1956; Williams & Thirer, 1975), as well as on other abilities like velocity judgments (H. Parker, 1981), reaction time (Olsen, 1956; Wilkinson, 1958), movement time (Keller, 1940; Pierson, 1956), spatial perception (Meek & Skubic, 1971), and kinesthetic sensitivity (Wiebe, 1954). However, the results of most correlational analyses examining the relationship between perceptual-motor attributes and sport performance were statistically nonsignificant (Dickson, 1953; Montebello, 1953; Olsen, 1956; Ridini, 1968; Winograd, 1942).

Not surprisingly, very little of this type of research has been conducted in North America in the past 30 years. An exception is a study by Landers, Boutcher, and Wang (1986) in which certain physical, perceptual-motor, and psychological characteristics were found to be rather accurate predictors of archery performance. However, more recent work by Abernethy (1999b) revealed no differences in the visual "hardware" of skilled and novice sporting clay shooters. In fact, all shooters were found to demonstrate visual characteristics (e.g., static and dynamic visual acuity, depth perception, ocular balance) that fell within the expected range of scores of the normal population.

Information-Processing Characteristics of Performers at Various Stages of Practice

While the contribution of general abilities to perceptual-motor performance remains somewhat equivocal, there are a number of information-processing capabilities and cognitive processes that have been found to be associated with skill level (Starkes & Deakin, 1984). Most likely, superior skill in any activity is attributable to the functioning of a variety of processes. For example, the elite performer might excel because she/he (1) recognizes the stimulus sooner (perceptual processing), (2) has a variety of appropriate responses ready for execution (decision processing), and/or (3) issues movement commands more rapidly (effector processing). The expert may also be able to respond more efficiently by "speeding up" certain aspects/stages of information processing. For example, the baseball batter who recognizes a particular mannerism of a pitcher as a signal that a fastball is coming would have a reduced perceptual processing demand associated with the recognition of pitch speed. Thus, the batter could prepare an appropriately timed swing in advance.

In the following section, research is presented that demonstrates that elite performers select, process, and retrieve information more effectively and efficiently than beginning or average performers. Separate discussion is devoted to literature dealing with each of the three categories of information processing—perceptual processing, decision processing, and effector processing.

Perceptual Processing

The perceptual processing aspect of information processing deals with the reception and interpretation of environmental or movement-related cues. Most of the laboratory research conducted in this area has focused on two perceptual subprocesses, stimulus detection and pattern recognition. The former process pertains to the pick up of environmental information while the latter concerns the recognition of performance-relevant aspects of selected cues.

The two variables that seem to exert the greatest influence on stimulus detection are stimulus intensity and stimulus clarity (e.g., Posner, 1964; Swets, 1964). Specifically, the more intense and clearly presented the stimulus, the more rapidly it is detected. (See Schmidt & Lee, 1999, for a more detailed discussion.) Since intensity and clarity in a given sport situation is theoretically the same for all performers regardless of their skill level, it might be predicted that the superior stimulus detection capability of expert performers is due to the *ways* they search the performance environment for relevant sources of information.

Exactly which aspects of the environment experts direct their attention to has been the focus of several studies. For example, Allard and Starkes (1980) found that skilled volleyball players were able to detect the presence of the ball in slides of briefly presented volleyball situations faster than were nonplayers. Years earlier, Hubbard and Seng (1954) photographed the eye movements of professional baseball batters and speculated that they began their stride at the moment the pitcher released the ball and varied the duration of their stride according to the speed of the pitch. Using more sophisticated eye-movement apparatus, Bard and Fleury (1981) found that a greater proportion of the ocular fixations of expert ice hockey goaltenders were on the stick of the shooter. This aspect of expert visual fixation presumably allowed these goalies to anticipate the type of shot that was about to be taken and to initiate their blocking movements earlier than novice goalies who were found to fixate more on the puck. Similarly, Shank and Haywood (1987) found that the visual fixations of expert collegiate baseball batters prior to ball release were on the pitcher's release point and then shifted, 150 ms after ball release, to the ball. In contrast, novices demonstrated excessive eye movements or random fixations (e.g., on the pitcher's head) prior to ball release and exhibited no fixations after release. These data suggest that expert performers

visually fixate in ways that are different than beginners, allowing them to pick up environmental information at the earliest possible moment. Please see Chapter 3 of the *Handbook* for further discussion of this topic.

Some researchers have not found the visual search patterns of experts and novices to be significantly different (Abernethy & Russell, 1984, 1987b; Bard & Fleury, 1976; Tyldesley, Bootsma, & Bomhoff, 1982). However, as Adams (1966) warns, "the principal difficulty in using eye movements for inferring observing responses is that they measure looking, not seeing. Thus, they fail as a primary measure of an observing response which functions to provide the discriminating stimuli for the criterion response" (p. 177). In spite of Adams' point, it might be argued that the *product* of the advanced performer's attentional focus (i.e., the extraction of task-relevant information) is what differentiates experts' visual processing from that of beginning or average performers.

Another technique for determining either the type of visual cues individuals attend to or the time at which they attend to such cues is the *occlusion paradigm*. In studies adopting a *temporal occlusion* approach, vision of the movements of a videotaped or filmed performer is blocked at various times in the action sequence and the observer is instructed to predict the possible outcome of the movement. For example, Starkes and Deakin (1984) employed a temporal occlusion procedure to determine the shot prediction accuracy of national team, varsity, and less-experienced field hockey players. Participants viewed (from the perspective of a goalie) a videotape of an approaching offensive player who variously shot or passed the ball high or low to the right, left, or straight ahead. Vision of the player was occluded 1/20 sec prior to impact on half of the trials and 1/6 sec after impact on the other half. The results revealed that national team players predicted shot placement more accurately than the other groups under both occlusion conditions and were the only group that performed better than chance when they were forced to rely only on advance visual cues (i.e., when occlusion occurred 1/20 sec prior to impact).

Earlier, Jones and Miles (1978) reported that expert tennis players were better than novices at predicting the position of ball landing for a tennis serve, even when vision of the serve was occluded prior to ball impact. Similar results were obtained by Abernethy and Russell (1984, Experiment 2) who found that skilled cricket batsmen extracted advance information from the movements of bowlers more so than did lesser skilled batsmen. Abernethy and Russell (1987a, Experiment 1) and Abernethy (1989) also demonstrated that expert badminton players were superior to novices in predicting the landing location of approaching badminton shots when occlusion of the shot occurred prior to racquet-shuttle contact. Work by Howarth, Walsh, Abernethy, and Snyder (1984) similarly revealed that advanced squash players made their initial anticipatory movements prior to ball contact by an opponent, suggesting the usage of preshot visual cues. In that study, average players did not begin their movements until after the opponent contacted the ball. Taking a slightly different approach, Salmela and Fiorito (1979) discovered that predictions about the horizontal direction of an approaching shot were facilitated for young ice hockey goaltenders when preshot information about the shooter's movements was *not* occluded. Thus, these researchers deduced that the goalies must have been using preshot cues to enhance their predictions of shot direction.

In an attempt to determine the *types* of visual cues performers utilize during perceptual processing, several investigators have employed a different occlusion paradigm in which various aspects of the environmental display are "masked" or obscured. If a participant's response accuracy is diminished when a particular cue is occluded (i.e., masked), it is assumed that the individual normally processes that cue in order to predict an upcoming event. Generally, the results of *event occlusion* studies have revealed that advanced performers perceptually process different patterns of environmental information than do novice or average performers. For example, Abernethy and Russell (1987a, Experiment 1) found that expert badminton players attended to the arm action of an opponent more than did novice performers.

Later, Abernethy observed that expert badminton (Abernethy, 1988) and squash (Abernethy, 1990) players used both racquet and arm information to predict the location of an opponent's shot while novices used only racquet information. Goulet, Bard, and Fleury (1989) observed that, compared to novices, expert tennis players focused more on the server's shoulder and trunk during the preparatory phase of the action and on the server's racquet during the execution phase. In summary, then, the results of studies employing occlusion procedures suggest that, compared to average or novice performers, elite athletes perceptually process different patterns of visual information and do so earlier in the time course of environmental events.

One reason advanced performers are able to process environmental information more effectively than less-expert individuals is because they possess a more sophisticated knowledge of salient characteristics of the performance

environment (Tenenbaum & Summers, 1996). Differences in the recognition accuracy of domain-specific knowledge was perhaps first demonstrated in studies comparing the ability of chess experts and novices in reconstructing game situations from briefly-presented configurations (e.g., Chase & Simon, 1973). Of greater relevance to sport situations are experiments that have demonstrated superior recall of game-structure information by advanced basketball (Allard, Graham, & Paarsalu, 1980), rugby (Nakagawa, 1982), volleyball (Borgeaud & Abernethy, 1987), and field hockey (Christensen & Glencross, 1993; Starkes, 1987) players than by average or beginning players.

Of particular significance is a study by Starkes (1987) in which a multiple regression technique was used to determine which of a number of factors differentiated the performance of three groups of field hockey players varying in expertise. Of the nine possible predictor variables (simple reaction time, coincidence anticipation, ball detection speed and accuracy, shoot/dribble/dodge decision accuracy and speed, accuracy of shot prediction before and after view of ball impact, and recall accuracy of structured game positions) the only significant predictors were recall of game structured information and shot prediction accuracy following view of ball impact. In light of these results, Starkes concluded that advanced "tuning" of the visual search process is an important factor differentiating the performance of highly skilled and average performers. She further suggested that the tuning of visual search is characterized by three processes: "generalization" (i.e., broadening of the applicability of rules), "discrimination" (i.e., narrowing of rules), and "strengthening" (i.e., fortifying of better rules and weakening of poorer ones).

With practice, performers also become more aware of the sensory consequences of their movements, representing a slightly different form of perceptual processing. Using a simple movement time task and a general college student population, Schmidt and White (1972) found that, with practice, the error detection capabilities of participants improved along with improvements in movement production. The notion that elite athletic performers are also more adept than average or novice performers at evaluating the quality of their movements was demonstrated in a study by Henderson (1975). In this experiment, skilled darts throwers estimated the location of dart landing in the absence of visual feedback more accurately than average performers. This finding suggests that the skill level of advanced performers may be distinguished from that of average or beginning performers by the degree to which integration of effector and perceptual processing is achieved. Compared to less-skilled performers, advanced performers are more capable of effectively constructing the motor commands necessary to produce a movement and evaluating the sensory consequences and response outcomes associated with that movement.

In summary, the available research indicates that perceptual processing capability, particularly the type that deals with attention to and recognition of salient cues, is an important factor that differentiates highly skilled and less-skilled performers. Such processing is particularly advantageous for athletes performing skills requiring the continuous monitoring of environmental cues. By knowing what to look for, experts are able to extract meaningful information from the environment and quickly prepare appropriate responses (Adams, 1966).

Decision Processing

Once performers have completed perceptual processing of environmental information, they must decide on an appropriate response. Research by Abernethy and Russell (1984) revealed that skilled cricket batsmen were more accurate in their response selection decisions than were less-skilled batsmen. In this study, participants were asked to watch a filmed presentation of a bowler's run-up and then produce a key-press response when they had decided which stroke they would play. In all cases, the type of action selected by expert batsmen was a general movement designed to place their body in the best position to complete a successful response. Such generalized preparation might be likened to the preparatory movements of elite baseball batters who initiate the stride phase of their batting response when the ball is released from the pitcher's hand but do not begin their swing until they estimate the speed of the pitch (Hubbard & Seng, 1954).

Two factors that have been demonstrated to influence the response selection process in laboratory studies with general student populations are the number of stimulus-response choices and the compatability of stimuli and responses. Generally speaking, the results of these experiments show that the greater the number of stimulus-response choices and the less compatible the stimulus and response, the longer it takes performers to select the appropriate response (Fitts & Peterson, 1964; Hick, 1952; Hyman, 1953). Although these principles might be expected to hold for athletes as well as for laboratory participants, it must be pointed out that elite sport performers sometimes select responses that are, in their view, the most appropriate even though the responses may not be the most "compatible" with a stimulus. For example, a setter in volleyball may attempt to hit the ball directly over the net

(less compatible) rather than set up the outside hitter for a spike (more compatible) if she or he suddenly sees that the opponent has left an area of the floor uncovered. Thus, it should be remembered that the decision processing of athletes is sometimes contingent on factors other than those dealing with the number of stimulus-response choices or stimulus-response compatibility.

Another important issue concerning the response selection process of athletes is that both the number and the compatibility of stimulus-response combinations may differ for different sports activities. For example, badminton players may have a larger number of possible responses in their repertoire and deal with more levels of stimulus-response compatibility than do racquetball players. In one study, Housner (1981) obtained verbal reports from expert and novice badminton players and then observed their play in competitive situations. He found that experts not only possessed a greater number of strategies than did novices but also applied them more appropriately and with greater flexibility. Thus, differences in levels of performance skill for this sport appear to be associated with the rapid selection of the most appropriate (i.e., compatible) of a number of possible responses (i.e., shots) in the face of a variety of possible stimuli (i.e., returns) by an opponent.

By way of contrast, racquetball players probably have fewer possible responses and employ them more predictably than do badminton players. In support of this proposition, Alain and Girardin (1978) found no difference in the amount of uncertainty conveyed by the shots of expert and novice racquetball players, suggesting that successful execution (i.e., effector processing) of the shot was more crucial than response selection which, in racquetball, is generally predictable (e.g., kill shots are usually hit from the front court area while ceiling or passing shots are typically produced from the rear court area).

While the results of laboratory studies using novel tasks repeatedly indicate that extensive practice with difficult stimulus-response arrangements reduces performers' decision time (e.g., Mowbray & Rhoades, 1959), it is likely that the greater skill of more highly practiced athletes is also due to a more sophisticated knowledge of event probabilities (Alain & Proteau, 1980; Rosenbaum, 1980). In an investigation of the preparatory responses of racquet sport players (e.g., badminton, racquetball, squash, tennis), Alain and Proteau (1978) found that the greater the perceived probability of an anticipated event (i.e., certainty of the player as to what he thought an opponent's shot was going to be) the higher the proportion of effective anticipatory movements. More recently, investigations have revealed that advanced performers in the sports of baseball (French,

Nevett, Spurgeon, Graham, Rink, & McPherson, 1996; French & Thomas, 1987; Paull & Case, 1994), tennis (McPherson, 1999), and field hockey (Christensen & Glencross, 1993) possess superior knowledge of event probabilities compared to novice or average performers.

An enhanced appreciation of event probabilities with increased task experience has also been demonstrated in laboratory studies. For example, Larish and Stelmach (1982) found that the reactions of participants to highly probable stimuli became faster over practice while participants' reactions to less probable stimuli became slower. For elite athletes, faster reactions to highly probable events are occasionally "paid for" by an increased susceptibility to false information presented by an opponent in the form of fakes or infrequent variations of a familiar play. In a Super Bowl game a number of years ago, an important touchdown was scored when a defensive player vacated a zone he was assigned to protect. This happened because the player falsely assumed the movements of an opponent indicated that the offensive play would be going in the same direction that it had on every previous situation in which the opponent made those types of movements. The point is that early response selection may have costs as well as benefits associated with it.

In summary, it might be concluded that the response selection capabilities of expert performers are another factor that contributes to their exceptional demonstrations of skill. Effective decision processing may be one reason the movements of elite athletes rarely appear to be hurried or rushed. Knowledge of event probabilities and the responses that are most appropriate for a particular situation undoubtedly contributes to experts' rapid responses (Tyldesley, 1981). As in the case of perceptual processing, speeded decision processing is particularly advantageous for the open skill performer who must quickly select a response that meets the demands of changing environmental conditions.

Once decision processing has taken place, the remaining information processing demand, effector processing, must be satisfactorily met. How the process of response production is carried out by individuals differing in skill level is the focus of the next section.

Effector Processing

Over practice both the quality and consistency of movement production improves. Moreover, an increased automatization of movement execution occurs that enables the performer to produce movements with very little cognitive involvement. Or, as elite athletes sometimes say, to "just let it happen." An excellent illustration of the way performers increasingly automate their movements and diminish the demands of effector processing may be found in a laboratory study by Pew (1966). In this experiment, participants attempted to keep a constantly moving dot of light centered on an oscilloscope screen by alternately depressing two keys with their index fingers. Depression of the right key accelerated the movement of the dot to the right and depression of the left key caused the dot to accelerate to the left.

Early in practice, participants appeared to control the dot by intermittently observing the direction it was moving and then depressing the key required to reverse its direction before it exited the screen. After several weeks of practice, however, participants adopted a control style that involved a rapid succession of alternating right and left key presses to keep the dot centered. This more-automated response mode was only interrupted if the dot began to drift off-center. On such occasions, one of two correction strategies was implemented. Participants either stopped their movements to institute a single correction with one of the keys and then resume the pattern of alternate depression or they continued in the rapid mode but slowly returned the dot to the center by depressing one of the keys for a slightly longer time than the other.

A major point of this study is that by shifting to a more automated (i.e., open-loop) form of control over practice, participants required the use of vision only to make periodic corrections of the action rather than to monitor each individual movement. While an advanced performer in a task such as that employed by Pew can hardly be compared to an athlete who has achieved performance stability over hundreds of hours of practice, it is likely that elite athletes similarly shift the control of their movements to "automatic" in order to devote attention to important environmental information (e.g., the speed and spin of an approaching shot in tennis or the moves of an opponent in wrestling).

The results of several laboratory studies indicate that while the attention demands of effector processing diminish over practice (Wrisberg & Shea, 1978), movements are never performed attention-free (Stelmach & Hughes, 1983). Recent research with athletes suggests that this phenomenon may also exist for the performance of sport tasks. Smith and Chamberlin (1992) found that the time it took soccer players to run through a slalom course was slower when players were required to perform additional secondary tasks (e.g., dribbling a ball). However, the amount of slowing was not as great for expert players as it was for beginning and intermediate players. Thus, it is probably safe to say that differences in the effector processing of advanced and average or beginning performers lies in the *degree* to which automation is achieved (Leavitt, 1979).

Obviously, the greater the extent that performers are able to program or automate a to-be-performed movement, the more attention they can devote to other aspects of the competitive environment (Allport, Antonis, & Reynolds, 1972). This capability is especially crucial for athletes who must be able to process environmental cues during the course of movement execution (e.g., a point guard in basketball who is attempting to break a full-court press while dribbling). However, it is also possible that closed-skill performers enjoy the benefits of automated movements by being able to add stylistic flair to their actions (e.g., the figure skater who can express spontaneous creativity during the execution of a programmed routine).

The majority of findings from laboratory studies using novel tasks suggests that automation is particularly difficult when movements are more complex (Christina, 1992; Christina, Fischman, Vercruyssen, & Anson, 1982; Henry & Rogers, 1960; Klapp, 1977, 1996) or of longer duration (Klapp & Erwin, 1976; Quinn, Schmidt, Zelaznik, Hawkins, & McFarquhar, 1980). These factors have not been systematically explored in investigations with athletes. However, it might be expected that the duration factor is of little consequence in the case of rapid (i.e., < 500 ms duration) sporting movements (e.g., jumping, kicking, striking, throwing) that are likely controlled in an open-loop fashion (i.e., in the absence of feedback-based corrections). As an example, Hubbard and Seng (1954) reported that movement time during the swing phase (i.e., duration) of the standard batting action was extremely short and tended to vary little with the speed of the pitch.

If it may be assumed that movement duration is not a crucial factor in the effector processing of most sporting actions, it follows that differences in the skill levels of athletes may be associated more with the way individuals deal with the movement complexity factor. One way skilled performers appear to reduce the complexity of movements over practice is to progressively "chunk" (i.e., cluster or subjectively organize) multiple components of an action, as in the case of concert pianists who are able to run off long sequences of notes in rapid fashion (Shaffer, 1981). Another strategy involves the programming of individual components of larger movements or movement sequences, as dancers may do for certain parts of dance routines or as elite batters seem to do for the swing phase of the total hitting action (Hubbard & Seng, 1954).

Some recent theorists have advocated the use of an ecological perspective to explain the control of skilled actions (Haken, 1990; Turvey, 1990). According to these theorists, improvements in skill level are the result of natural physical transitions from one dynamical state of the musculo-skeletal system to another. Some contend that natural physical systems deal with the issue of movement complexity through the activity of coordinative structures that constrain the numerous muscles and limbs to act as a single unit (Fitch, Tuller, & Turvey, 1982; Turvey, 1977). While this notion has not been extensively applied to the performance of athletes on highly practiced sport tasks, it is reasonable to assume that some of the efficiency evident in the movements of elite performers is due to the activity of natural physical systems.

Any increase in the automation of motor acts means that higher centers are freed up to attend to the more global aspects of performance. (See Greene, 1972 for a thorough discussion of the concept of hierarchical control.) In fact, ecological psychologists contend that skill development is the result of an ongoing interaction of perceptual and motor processes. Evidence from studies with jugglers (Beek & van Santvoord, 1992), field hockey players (Burgess-Limerick, Abernethy, & Neal, 1991), table tennis players (Bootsma & van Wieringen, 1990), and volleyball players (Sardinha & Bootsma, 1993) suggests some support for this view. In their experiment, Beek and van Santvoord (1992) found that, with increased practice, jugglers were able to produce movements that were more accurate, consistent, and flexible, and that, in some instances, performers were able to add a stylistic "flair" to their actions.

That the movement characteristics of performers differ as a function of skill level is well substantiated in the scientific literature. Kinematic and/or kinetic analysis of the movements of individuals in the sports of long jumping (Berg & Greer, 1995; Scott, Li, & Davids, 1997), triple jumping (Maraj, Elliott, Lee, & Pollock, 1993), volleyball (Temprado et al., 1997), and youth baseball (French et al., 1995) has revealed differences in various components of the actions of expert and novice performers (e.g., relative timing patterns, spatial variability, and kinematics). As people's skill level improves, the patterns of their movements become more effective and efficient in achieving task requirements (McDonald, van Emmerik, & Newell, 1989).

In summary, it appears that another important contributor to differences in the skill levels of advanced and beginning, average, or even good performers is a capability to produce movements that are appropriate to situational demands. With practice, effector processing is probably improved by an enhanced organization of movement components and an increased automatization of motor commands. This in turn is reflected in a variety of changes in the quality of resulting movements; such as increased accuracy and consistency of kinematics (Marteniuk & Romanow, 1983), improved mechanical and energy efficiency (Sparrow & Irizarry-Lopez,

1987), and greater coordination (Moore & Marteniuk, 1986; Southard & Higgins, 1987; Vorro, Wilson, & Dainis, 1978).

SUMMARY AND CONCLUSION

Compared to beginning and intermediate performers, experts appear to be able to interpret environmental cues more accurately (i.e., perceptual processing), select appropriate responses more rapidly (i.e., decision processing), and execute their movements more effectively and efficiently (i.e., effector processing). In these ways, advanced performers accomplish the intended goal of their actions to a greater extent as well as more consistently than their lesser-skilled counterparts.

RECOMMENDATIONS FOR FUTURE RESEARCH

In this chapter, some of the research literature addressing factors that contribute to differences in the skill levels of advanced, intermediate, and beginning performers has been presented. In so doing, particular attention has been devoted to the role of general abilities (i.e., hardware characteristics) and information processing capabilities (i.e., software characteristics) in the performance of skilled movements. In light of the foregoing discussion, two general recommendations for future research are offered. The first deals with some possible ways of assessing factors that contribute to differences in the skill level of performers. The second concerns a possible approach researchers might use to identify the role of various information processes in the performance of athletes in different sports.

The assessment of behavior in any context is always an extremely difficult task because performance is based on such a large constellation of variables. Indeed, a prevalent theme suggested by the literature reviewed in this chapter is that no *single* factor, ability, or behavioral characteristic can account for all of the differences observed in the performance skill of individuals. Therefore, it behooves researchers to consider as many sources of variance as possible when attempting to locate the particular grouping of factors that contributes most to skillful behavior. Perhaps Fisher (1984) put it best when he contended that "to seriously begin understanding athletes' behavior, and to improve or predict performance outcomes, the reciprocal interaction between the athlete as a person and the specific sport environment must be considered" (p. 731). Key terms for anyone interested in maximizing predictions of skill would appear to be *interaction* and *multidimensional*. Put simply, sport psychology researchers must incorporate multivariate approaches when studying differences in the levels of people's performance skill.

More investigations are needed that adopt an approach similar to that of Starkes (1987), where a variety of predictor variables are simultaneously examined to determine which combination best differentiates the performance skill of athletes. Using this approach, Allard and Starkes (1991) found that one distinguishing feature of experts is their adeptness at both "knowing" what to do (i.e., perceptual and decision processing) *and* "doing" it (i.e., effector processing). While persons may achieve a degree of success in one or the other of these capabilities they are unable to "link" the two (e.g., the experienced reserve player who completely understands the nuances of a sport but is unable to produce the appropriate movements skillfully or the athlete who demonstrates skillful movements in practice but produces them at inappropriate moments in actual competition). Allard and Starkes have obtained additional support for a linkage between knowing and doing in experiments with videogame players, an oral surgeon, and baseball batters, all of whom possessed considerable experience in their respective activities. The results of these studies also suggest that it is the *appropriate linking* of doing to the present state of knowing (i.e., *flexibility* in linking rather than the establishment of stable condition-action links) that is crucial to successful performance.

In addition to measuring psychological/behavioral factors, researchers should probably include physical and physiological parameters in their assessments of performance skill. One example of this type of research is a study by Landers and his associates (1981) in which a variety of physical, psychological, and psychophysiological characteristics of competitive shooters were examined in order to determine which groupings of factors most clearly differentiated the performance of elite and subelite athletes.

While approaches such as this have obvious utility for the assessment of differences between individuals, sport psychology researchers might also consider using such methods to determine which performance characteristics are important for certain situations and tasks. In tennis, for example, accurate visual tracking of the ball is probably crucial for producing effective service returns, volleys, and groundstrokes but not as essential for executing effective serves. Although it is likely that a player must keep his or her eyes on the ball while serving, inferior performance of this action is less likely due to inaccurate visual tracking than it is to other factors (e.g., inconsistent ball toss, deficiency of interlimb coordination, excessive muscle tension levels). By determining those tasks (and task components) that pose consistent difficulties for the athlete, researchers may be able to identify the possible factors that are most in need of the performer's attention/improvement.

A second research implication of the present review deals with the issue of how the information processes most crucial to performance skill in different sports might be determined. Perhaps the most thorough theoretical discussion of information processing considerations in the learning and performance of motor skills was provided by Marteniuk (1976), who devotes particular attention to the mechanisms of perceptual, decision, and effector processing that contribute to the performance of motor skills. Fundamental to an information-processing approach to task analysis is an identification of the types of demands inherent in the task. One important consideration in the determination of task demands is whether the performer must deal with environmental uncertainty or not. A performance environment that is "open" or less predictable would impose a greater demand on perceptual and decision processing than one that is "closed" or stable (Poulton, 1957). For example, an option quarterback in American football must deal with a greater number of stimulus-response pairs and less stimulus-response compatibility than a sprinter in track. Therefore, the practice experiences of the quarterback should include opportunities to view the various types of circumstances he can expect to see when running the option play. In this way the athlete is able to learn which types of responses are most appropriate for each situation. With sufficient practice, the quarterback should be able to recognize defensive patterns and select the most appropriate response in the shortest time possible, thereby elevating his skill level. Similarly, levels of volleyball skill should improve as the performer becomes more adept at resolving the spatial, temporal, and event uncertainties inherent in the competitive environment. On the other hand, the skill of a gymnast performing in a relatively stable environment is primarily determined by her/his ability to produce a consistent movement (i.e., effector processing).

Preliminary analysis of the demands of various tasks allows the researcher to determine the types of processing requirements performers must deal with and perhaps ascertain those that are limiting an individual's skill performance. A useful method for assessing the demands of different tasks has been suggested by Salmela (1974, 1976); although, to date, this technique has not gained popularity with researchers. Fundamental to Salmela's approach is the identification of important task components, the assessment of athlete aptitude, and the provision of training experiences that target the components most in need of the performer's attention. It is assumed that perfor-

mance deficiencies can be due to the ineffectual functioning of one or more information processes. For example, inconsistent spiking performance of a volleyball player may be caused by a misinterpretation of the spatial-temporal path of the ball from the setter (perceptual processing), uncertainty about where to direct the spike given the type of set and configuration of the opponent's block (decision processing), and/or improper mechanics (effector processing). To determine which of these various processes may be impairing an individual's task performance, a process of *component isolation* could be employed. For the volleyball spike, isolation of the player's mechanics (reflecting the quality of effector processing) could be evaluated by requiring the individual to spike a ball that is suspended in a fixed position. If he or she is able to execute mechanically correct spikes toward a variety of target locations under these conditions, then it may be presumed that the problem is due more to difficulties associated with perceptual and/or decision processing than to those of effector processing. Progressive isolation of the other processing components would allow determination of the source(s) of the difficulty. Once the problem is identified, appropriate drills or practice experiences could be created to enable the athlete to develop those skills that produce the greatest performance improvements.

An excellent example of a training protocol designed to improve the speed and accuracy of an individual performer's decision processing was described in a case study by Christina, Barresi, and Shaffner (1990). The athlete in this study was an American collegiate football player who had demonstrated the tendency to respond quickly but inaccurately during various types of game situations. After consulting with the player's coaches, Christina and colleagues developed a videotape presentation of a series of simulated competitive scenarios. During several weeks of video training, the athlete practiced producing rapid and accurate responses to each of the scenarios. By the end of the training period the player's decision accuracy (i.e., percentage of correct responses) had increased from 25% to over 95% correct.

Since skill improvement is an ongoing challenge for all athletes, it is important to identify as many factors as possible that might limit such improvement. Once this is done, practice experiences can be created that allow the individual to sharpen the skills that will produce the biggest gains in performance. Hopefully in the future, sport scientists will be better able to determine which constellation of factors contributes the most to high levels of performance skill and identify strategies any performer can use to improve his or her respective skill level.

REFERENCES

Abernethy, B. (1988). The effects of age and expertise upon perceptual skill development in a racquet sport. *Research Quarterly for Exercise and Sport, 59*, 210–221.

Abernethy, B. (1989). Expert-novice differences in perception: How expert does the expert have to be? *Canadian Journal of Sport Sciences, 14*, 27–30.

Abernethy, B. (1990). Anticipation in squash: Differences in advance cue utilization between expert and novice players. *Journal of Sport Sciences, 8*, 17–34.

Abernethy, B. (1991). Visual search strategies and decision making in sport. *International Journal of Sport Psychology, 22*, 189–210.

Abernethy, B. (1994). The nature of expertise in sport. In S. Serpa, J. Alves, & V. Pataco (Eds.), *International perspectives on sport and exercise psychology* (pp. 57–68). Morgantown, WV: FIT Press.

Abernethy, B. (1999a). Movement expertise: A juncture between psychology theory and practice. *Journal of Applied Sport Psychology, 11*, 126–141.

Abernethy, B. (1999b). Visual characteristics of clay target shooters. *Journal of Science and Medicine in Sport, 2*, 1–19.

Abernethy, B., & Russell, D.G. (1984). Advance cue utilisation by skilled cricket batsmen. *Australian Journal of Science and Medicine in Sport, 16*, 2–10.

Abernethy, B., & Russell, D.G. (1987a). Expert-novice differences in an applied selective attention task. *Journal of Sport Psychology, 9*, 326–345.

Abernethy, B., & Russell, D.G. (1987b). The relationship between expertise and visual search strategy in a racquet sport. *Human Movement Science, 6*, 283–319.

Adams, J.A. (1966). Some mechanisms of motor responding: An examination of attention. In E.A. Bilodeau (Ed.), *Acquisition of skill* (pp. 169–200). New York: Academic Press.

Adams, J.A. (1971). A closed-loop theory of motor learning. *Journal of Motor Behavior, 3*, 111–150.

Alain, C., & Girardin, Y. (1978). The use of uncertainty in racquetball competition. *Canadian Journal of Applied Sport Sciences, 3*, 240–243.

Alain, C., & Proteau, L. (1978). Étude des variables relatives au traitement de l'information en sports de raquette [A study of variables related to information processing in racquet sports]. *Journal Canadien des Sciences Appliqués aux Sports, 3*, 27–35.

Alain, C., & Proteau, L. (1980). Decision making in sport. In C.H. Nadeau, W.R. Halliwell, K.M. Newell, & G.C. Roberts (Eds.), *Psychology of motor behavior and sport* (pp. 465–477). Champaign, IL: Human Kinetics.

Allard, F., Graham, S., & Paarsalu, M.E. (1980). Perception in sport: Basketball. *Journal of Sport Psychology, 2*, 14–21.

Allard, F., & Starkes, J.L. (1980). Perception in sport: Volleyball. *Journal of Sport Psychology, 2*, 22–33.

Allard, F., & Starkes, J.L. (1991). Motor skill experts in sports, dance and other domains. In K.A. Ericsson & J. Smith (Eds.), *Toward a general theory of expertise* (pp. 123–152). Cambridge, MA: Cambridge University Press.

Allport, D.A., Antonis, B., & Reynolds, P. (1972). On the division of attention: A disproof of the single channel hypothesis. *Quarterly Journal of Experimental Psychology, 24*, 225–235.

Anderson, J.R. (1982). Acquisition of cognitive skill. *Psychological Review, 89*, 369–406.

Bachman, J.C. (1961). Specificity vs. generality in learning and performing two large muscle motor tasks. *Research Quarterly, 32*, 3–11.

Baker, J., & Abernethy, B. (1999). *The role of sport-specific training in attaining expertise in team ball sports.* Paper presented at the annual conference of the Association for the Advancement of Applied Sport Psychology, Banff, Canada.

Bannister, H., & Blackburn, J.H. (1931). An eye factor affecting proficiency at ball games. *British Journal of Psychology, 21*, 382–384.

Bard, C., & Fleury, M. (1976). Analysis of visual search activity during sport problem situations. *Journal of Human Movement Studies, 3*, 214–222.

Bard, C., & Fleury, M. (1981). Considering eye movement as a predictor of attainment. In I.M. Cockerill & W.W. MacGillivary (Eds.), *Vision and sport* (pp. 28–41). Cheltenham, England: Stanley Thornes.

Beek, P.J., & van Santvoord, A.A.M. (1992). Learning the cascade juggle: A dynamical systems analysis. *Journal of Motor Behavior, 24*, 85–94.

Berg, W.P., & Greer, N.L. (1995). A kinematic profile of the approach run of novice long jumpers. *Journal of Applied Biomechanics, 11*, 142–162.

Bootsma, R.J., & van Wieringen, P.C.W. (1990). Timing an attacking forehand drive in table tennis. *Journal of Experimental Psychology: Human Perception and Performance, 16*, 21–29.

Borgeaud, P., & Abernethy, B. (1987). Skilled perception in volleyball defense. *Journal of Sport Psychology, 9*, 400–406.

Burgess-Limerick, R., Abernethy, B., & Neal, R.J. (1991). Experience and backswing movement time variability. *Human Movement Science, 10*, 621–627.

Chase, W.G., & Simon, H.A. (1973). Perception in chess. *Cognitive Psychology, 4*, 55–81.

Christensen, S.A., & Glencross, D.J. (1993). Expert knowledge and expert perception in sport. In G. Tenenbaum & T. Raz-Liebermann (Eds.), *Second Maccabiah-Wingate International Congress on Sport and Coaching Sciences: Proceedings* (pp. 142–150). Netanya, Israel: Wingate Institute for Physical Education and Sport.

Christina, R.W. (1992). The 1991 C.H. McCloy Research lecture: Unraveling the mystery of the response complexity effect in skilled movements. *Research Quarterly for Exercise and Sport, 63,* 218–230.

Christina, R.W., Barresi, J.V., & Shaffner, P. (1990). The development of response selection accuracy in a football linebacker using video training. *The Sport Psychologist, 4,* 11–17.

Christina, R.W., Fischman, M.G., Vercruyssen, M.J.P., & Anson, J.G. (1982). Simple reaction time as a function of response complexity: Memory drum theory revisited. *Journal of Motor Behavior, 14,* 301–321.

Cockerill, I.M. (1981). Peripheral vision and hockey. In I.M. Cockerill & W.W. MacGillivary (Eds.), *Vision and sport* (pp. 54–63). Cheltenham, England: Stanley Thornes.

Crossman, E.R.F.W. (1959). A theory of the acquisition of speed skill. *Ergonomics, 2,* 153–166.

Dickson, J.F. (1953). *The relationship of depth perception to goal shooting in basketball.* Unpublished doctoral dissertation, University of Iowa, Iowa City.

Ericsson, K.A. (1996). The acquisition of expert performance: An introduction to some of the issues. In K.A. Ericsson (Ed.), *The road to excellence: The acquisition of expert performance in the arts and sciences, sports, and games* (pp. 1–50). Mahwah, NJ: Erlbaum.

Ericsson, K.A., Krampe, R.T., & Tesch-Römer, C. (1993). The role of deliberate practice in the acquisition of expert performance. *Psychological Review, 100,* 363–406.

Fisher, A.C. (1984). New directions in sport personality research. In J.M. Silva & R.S. Weinberg (Eds.), *Psychological foundations of sport* (pp. 70–80). Champaign, IL: Human Kinetics.

Fitch, H.L., Tuller, B., & Turvey, M.T. (1982). The Bernstein perspective: III. Tuning of coordinative structures with special reference to perception. In J.A.S. Kelso (Ed.), *Human motor behavior: An introduction* (pp. 271–281). Hillsdale, NJ: Erlbaum.

Fitts, P.M., & Peterson, J.R. (1964). Information capacity of discrete motor responses. *Journal of Experimental Psychology, 67,* 103–112.

Fitts, P.M., & Posner, M.I. (1967). *Human performance.* Belmont, CA: Brooks/Cole.

Fitts, P.M., & Seeger, C.M. (1953). S-R compatibility: Spatial characteristics of stimulus and response codes. *Journal of Experimental Psychology, 46,* 199–210.

Fleishman, E.A. (1972). On the relationship between abilities, learning, and human performance. *American Psychologist, 27,* 1017–1032.

Fleishman, E.A. (1978). Relating individual differences to the dimensions of human tasks. *Ergonomics, 21,* 1007–1019.

Fleishman, E.A. (1982). Systems for describing human tasks. *American Psychologist, 37,* 821–834.

Fleishman, E.A., & Bartlett, C.J. (1969). Human abilities. *Annual Review of Psychology, 20,* 349–380.

Fleishman, E.A., & Hempel, W.E. (1955). The relationship between abilities and improvement with practice in a visual discrimination reaction task. *Journal of Experimental Psychology, 49,* 301–311.

Fleishman, E.A., & Rich, S. (1963). Role of kinesthetic and spatial-visual abilities in perceptual motor learning. *Journal of Experimental Psychology, 66,* 6–11.

Franz, E.A., Zelaznik, H.N., & Smith, A. (1992). Evidence of a common timing process in the control of manual, orofacial, and speech movements. *Journal of Motor Behavior, 24,* 281–287.

French, K.E., Nevett, M.E., Spurgeon, J.H., Graham, K.C., Rink, J.E., & McPherson, S.L. (1996). Knowledge representation and problem solution in expert and novice youth baseball players. *Research Quarterly for Exercise and Sport, 67,* 386–395.

French, K.E., Spurgeon, J.H., & Nevett, M.E. (1995). Expert-novice differences in cognitive and skill execution components of youth baseball performance. *Research Quarterly for Exercise and Sport, 66,* 194–201.

French, K.E., & Thomas, J.R. (1987). The relation of knowledge development to children's basketball performance. *Journal of Sport Psychology, 9,* 15–32.

Gentile, A.M. (1972). A working model of skill acquisition with application to teaching. *Quest, 17,* 3–23.

Gladwell, M. (1999, August 2). The physical genius. *The New Yorker, LXXVI,* 57–65.

Goulet, C., Bard, C., & Fleury, M. (1989). Expertise differences in preparing to return a tennis serve: A visual information processing approach. *Journal of Sport & Exercise Psychology, 11,* 382–398.

Graybiel, A., Jokl, E., & Trapp, C. (1955). Russian studies of vision in relation to physical activity and sports. *Research Quarterly, 26,* 212–223.

Greene, P.H. (1972). Problems of organization of motor systems. In R. Rosen & F.M. Snell (Eds.), *Progress in theoretical biology* (Vol. 2, pp. 303–338). New York: Academic Press.

Haken, H. (1990). Synergetics as a tool for the conceptualization and mathematization of cognition and behaviour: How far can we go? In H. Haken & M. Stadler (Eds.), *Synergetics of cognition* (pp. 2–31). Berlin, Germany: Springer-Verlag.

Henderson, S.E. (1975). Predicting the accuracy of a throw without visual feedback. *Journal of Human Movement Studies, 1,* 183–189.

Henry, F.M. (1961). Reaction time-movement time correlations. *Perceptual and Motor Skills, 12,* 63–66.

Henry, F.M. (1968). Specificity vs. generality in learning motor skill. In R.C. Brown & G.S. Kenyon (Eds.), *Classical studies on physical activity* (pp. 331–340). Englewood Cliffs, NJ: Prentice-Hall.

Henry, F.M., & Rogers, D.E. (1960). Increased response latency for complicated movements and the "memory drum" theory of neuromotor reaction. *Research Quarterly, 31,* 448–458.

Hick, W.E. (1952). On the rate of gain of information. *Quarterly Journal of Experimental Psychology, 4,* 11–26.

Housner, L.D. (1981). Expert-novice knowledge structure and cognitive processing differences in badminton [Abstract]. *Psychology of motor behavior and sport–1981* (p. 1). Proceedings of the annual meeting of the North American Society for the Psychology of Sport and Physical Activity, Asilomar, CA.

Howarth, C., Walsh, W.D., Abernethy, B., & Snyder, C.W. (1984). A field examination of anticipation in squash: Some preliminary data. *Australian Journal of Science and Medicine in Sport, 16,* 7–11.

Hubbard, A.W., & Seng, C.N. (1954). Visual movements of batters. *Research Quarterly, 25,* 42–57.

Hyman, R. (1953). Stimulus information as a determinant of reaction time. *Journal of Experimental Psychology, 45,* 188–196.

Ivry, R., & Hazeltine, R.E. (1995). Perception and production of temporal intervals across a range of durations: Evidence for a common timing mechanism. *Journal of Experimental Psychology: Human Perception and Performance, 21,* 3–18.

Jones, C.M., & Miles, T.R. (1978). Use of advance cues in predicting the flight of a lawn tennis ball. *Journal of Human Movement Studies 4,* 231–235.

Keele, S.W., & Hawkins, H.L. (1982). Explorations of individual differences relevant to high level skill. *Journal of Motor Behavior, 14,* 3–23.

Keele, S.W., Ivry, R.I., & Pokorny, R.A. (1987). Force control and its relation to timing. *Journal of Motor Behavior, 19,* 96–114.

Keele, S.W., Pokorny, R.A., Corcos, D.M., & Ivry, R.I. (1985). Do perception and motor production share common timing mechanisms: A correlational analysis. *Acta Psychologica, 60,* 173–191.

Keller, L.P. (1940). *The relation of quickness of bodily movement to success in athletics.* Unpublished doctoral dissertation, New York University, New York.

Kerr, B. (1973). Processing demands during mental operations. *Memory and Cognition, 1,* 401–412.

Kioumourtzoglou, E., Kourtessis, T., Michalopoulou, M., & Derri, V. (1998). Differences in several perceptual abilities between experts and novices in basketball, volleyball, and water polo. *Perceptual and Motor Skills, 83,* 899–912.

Klapp, S.T. (1977). Reaction time analysis of programmed control. *Exercise and Sport Sciences Reviews, 5,* 231–253.

Klapp, S.T. (1996). Reaction time analysis of central motor control. In H.N. Zelaznik (Ed.), *Advances in motor learning and control* (pp. 13–35). Champaign, IL: Human Kinetics.

Klapp, S.T., & Erwin, C.I. (1976). Relation between programming time and duration of the response being programmed.

Journal of Experimental Psychology: Human Perception and Performance, 2, 591–598.

Landers, D.M., Boutcher, S.H., & Wang, M.Q. (1986). A psychobiological study of archery performance. *Research Quarterly for Exercise and Sport, 57,* 236–244.

Landers, D.M., Christina, R.W., Hatfield, B.D., Daniels, F.S., Wilkinson, M.O., Doyle, L.A., & Feltz, D.L. (1981). A comparison of elite and subelite competitive shooters on selected physical, psychological, and psychophysiological tests. In G.C. Roberts & D.M. Landers (Eds.), *Psychology of motor behavior and sport–1980* (p. 93). Champaign, IL: Human Kinetics.

Larish, D.D., & Stelmach, G.E. (1982). Preprogramming, programming, and reprogramming of aimed hand movements as a function of age. *Journal of Motor Behavior, 14,* 322–340.

Leavitt, J. (1979). Cognitive demands of skating and stick-handling in ice hockey. *Journal of Applied Sport Sciences, 4,* 4–55.

Lotter, W.S. (1960). Interrelationships among reaction times and speeds of movement in different limbs. *Research Quarterly, 31,* 147–155.

Maraj, B.K., Elliott, D., Lee, T.D., & Pollock, B. (1993). Variance and invariance in expert and novice triple jumpers. *Research Quarterly for Exercise and Sport, 64,* 404–412.

Marteniuk, R.G. (1976). *Information processing in motor skills.* New York: Holt, Rinehart and Winston.

Marteniuk, R.G., & Romanow, S.K.E. (1983). Human movement organization and learning as revealed by variability of movement, use of kinematic information and Fourier analysis. In R.A. Magill (Ed.), *Memory and control of action* (pp. 167–197). Amsterdam: North Holland.

McDavid, R.F. (1977). Predicting potential in football players. *Research Quarterly, 48,* 98–104.

McDonald, P.V., van Emmerik, R.E.A., & Newell, K.M. (1989). The effects of practice on limb kinematics in a throwing task. *Journal of Motor Behavior, 21,* 245–264.

McPherson, S.L. (1999). Expert-novice differences in performance skills and problem representations of youth and adults during tennis competition. *Research Quarterly for Exercise and Sport, 70,* 233–251.

Meek, F., & Skubic, V. (1971). Spatial perception of highly skilled and poorly skilled females. *Perceptual and Motor Skills, 33,* 1309–1310.

Miller, D.M. (1960). *The relationships between some visual-perceptual factors and the degree of success realized by sports performers.* Unpublished doctoral dissertation, University of Southern California, Los Angeles.

Montebello, R.A. (1953). *The role of stereoscopic vision in some aspects of baseball playing.* Unpublished master's thesis, Ohio State University, Columbus.

Moore, S.P., & Marteniuk, R.G. (1986). Kinematic and electromyographic changes that occur as a function of learning a time-constrained aiming task. *Journal of Motor Behavior, 18,* 397–426.

Morris, G.S.D., & Kreighbaum, E. (1977). Dynamic visual acuity of varsity women volleyball and basketball players. *Research Quarterly, 48,* 480–483.

Mowbray, G.H., & Rhoades, M.U. (1959). On the reduction of choice reaction times with practice. *Quarterly Journal of Experimental Psychology, 11,* 16–23.

Nakagawa, A. (1982). A field experiment on recognition of game situations in ball games—in the case of static situations in rugby football. *Japanese Journal of Physical Education, 27,* 17–26.

Olsen, E.A. (1956). Relationship between psychological capacities and success in college athletics. *Research Quarterly, 27,* 79–89.

Parker, H.E. (1981). Visual detection and perception in netball. In I.M. Cockerill & W.W. MacGillivary (Eds.), *Vision and sport* (pp. 42–53). Cheltenham, England: Stanley Thornes.

Parker, J.F., & Fleishman, E.A. (1960). Ability factors and component performance measures as predictors of complex tracking behavior. *Psychological Monographs, 74*(Whole No. 503).

Paull, G., & Case, I. (1994). *Ecological validity in sports research through videosimulation.* Paper presented at the conference on Mathematics and Computers in Sports, Bond University, Queensland, Australia.

Pew, R.W. (1966). Acquisition of hierarchical control over the temporal organization of a skill. *Journal of Experimental Psychology, 71,* 764–771.

Pierson, W.R. (1956). Comparison of fencers and nonfencers by psychomotor, space perception and anthropometric measures. *Research Quarterly, 27,* 90–96.

Posner, M.I. (1964). Uncertainty as a predictor of similarity in the study of generalization. *Journal of Experimental Psychology, 63,* 113–118.

Poulton, E.C. (1957). On prediction in skilled movements. *Psychological Bulletin, 54,* 467–478.

Quinn, J.T., Schmidt, R.A., Zelaznik, H.N., Hawkins, B., & McFarquhar, R. (1980). Target-size influences on reaction time with movement time controlled. *Journal of Motor Behavior, 12,* 239–261.

Ridini, L.M. (1968). Relationships between psychological functions tests and selected sport skills of boys in junior high school. *Research Quarterly, 39,* 674–683.

Robertson, S.D., Zelaznik, H.N., Lantero, D.A., Bojczyk, K.G., Spencer, R.M., Doffin, J.G., & Schneidt, T. (1999). Correlations for timing consistency among tapping and drawing tasks: Evidence against a single timing process for motor control. *Journal of Experimental Psychology: Human Perception and Performance, 25,* 1316–1330.

Rodionov, A.V. (1978). *Psikholoqiia sportivnoi deiatel'nosti [The psychology of sport activity].* Moscow: Government Press.

Rosenbaum, D.A. (1980). Human movement initiation: Specification of arm, direction, and extent. *Journal of Experimental Psychology: General, 109,* 444–474.

Salmela, J.H. (1974). An information processing approach to volleyball. *CVA Volleyball Technical Journal, 1,* 49–62.

Salmela, J.H. (1976). Application of a psychological taxonomy to sport performance. *Canadian Journal of Applied Sport Sciences, 1,* 23–32.

Salmela, J.H. (1999). *Some thoughts on the relative contribution of deliberate practice to the development of sport expertise.* Paper presented at the annual conference of the Association for the Advancement of Applied Sport Psychology, Banff, Canada.

Salmela, J.H., & Fiorito, P. (1979). Visual cues in ice hockey goal tending. *Canadian Journal of Applied Sport Sciences, 4,* 56–59.

Sardinha, L.F., & Bootsma, R.J. (1993). Visual information for timing a spike in volleyball. In S. Serpa, J. Alves, V. Ferreira, & A. Paula-Brito (Eds.), *Proceedings of the 8th World Congress of Sport Psychology* (pp. 977–980). Lisbon, Portugal: International Society of Sport Psychology.

Schmidt, R.A., & Lee, T.D. (1999). *Motor control and learning: A behavioral emphasis* (3rd ed.). Champaign, IL: Human Kinetics.

Schmidt, R.A., & White, J.L. (1972). Evidence for an error detection mechanism in motor skills: A test of Adams' closed-loop theory. *Journal of Motor Behavior 4,* 143–153.

Schneidman, N.N. (1979). Soviet sport psychology in the 1970s and the superior athlete. In P. Klavora & J.V. Daniel (Eds.), *Coach, athlete, and the sport psychologist* (pp. 230–247). Champaign, IL: Human Kinetics.

Scott, M.A., Li, F., & Davids, K. (1997). Expertise and the regulation of gait in the approach phase of the long jump. *Journal of Sports Sciences, 15,* 597–605.

Shaffer, L.H. (1981). Performances of Chopin, Bach, and Beethoven: Studies in motor programming. *Cognitive Psychology, 13,* 326–376.

Shank, M.D., & Haywood, K.M. (1987). Eye movements while viewing a baseball pitch. *Perceptual and Motor Skills, 64,* 1191–1197.

Sidaway, B., Sekiya, H., & Fairweather, M. (1995). Movement variability as a function of accuracy demand in programmed serial aiming responses. *Journal of Motor Behavior, 27,* 67–76.

Singer, R.N., & Janelle, C.M. (1999). Determining sport expertise: From genes to supremes. *International Journal of Sport Psychology, 30,* 117–150.

Smith, M.D., & Chamberlin, C.J. (1992). Effect of adding cognitively demanding tasks on soccer skill performance. *Perceptual and Motor Skills, 75,* 955–961.

Southard, D., & Higgins, T. (1987). Changing movement patterns: Effects of demonstration and practice. *Research Quarterly for Exercise and Sport, 58,* 77–80.

Sparrow, W.A., & Irizarry-Lopez, V.M. (1987). Mechanical efficiency and metabolic cost as measures of learning a novel gross motor task. *Journal of Motor Behavior, 19,* 240–264.

Starkes, J.L. (1987). Skill in field hockey: The nature of the cognitive advantage. *Journal of Sport Psychology, 9,* 146–160.

Starkes, J.L., & Deakin, J.M. (1984). Perception in sport: A cognitive approach to skilled performance. In W.F. Straub & J.M. Williams (Eds.), *Cognitive sport psychology* (pp. 115–128). Lansing, NY: Sport Science Associates.

Starkes, J.L., Deakin, J.M., Allard, F., Hodges, N.J., & Hayes, A. (1996). Deliberate practice in sports: What is it anyway? In K.A. Ericsson (Ed.), *The road to excellence: The acquisition of expert performance in the arts and sciences, sports, and games* (pp. 81–106). Mahwah, NJ: Erlbaum.

Stelmach, G.E., & Hughes, B.G. (1983). Does motor skill automation require a theory of attention? In R.A. Magill (Ed.), *Memory and control of action* (pp. 67–92). Amsterdam: North Holland.

Sternberg, R.J. (1996). Costs of expertise. In K.A. Ericsson (Ed.), *The road to excellence: The acquisition of expert performance in the arts and sciences, sports, and games* (pp. 347–354). Mahwah, NJ: Erlbaum.

Swets, J.A. (1964). *Signal detection and recognition by human observers.* New York: Wiley.

Temprado, J., Della-Grasta, M., Farrell, M., & Laurent, M. (1997). A novice-expert comparison of (intra-limb) coordination subserving the volleyball serve. *Human Movement Science, 16,* 653–676.

Tenenbaum, G., & Summers, J. (1996). Recall and attention: Essentials for skilled performance in strategic-type tasks. In R. Lidor, E. Eldar, & I. Harari (Eds.), *Windows to the future: Bridging the gaps between disciplines, curriculum, and instruction–Proceedings of the 1995 AIESEP World Congress* (pp. 152–158). Netanya, Israel: Zinman College.

Turvey, M.T. (1977). Preliminaries to a theory of action with reference to vision. In R. Shaw & J. Bransford (Eds.), *Perceiving, acting, and knowing* (pp. 211–265). Hillsdale, NJ: Erlbaum.

Turvey, M.T. (1990). The challenge of a physical account of action: A personal view. In H.T.A. Whiting, O.G. Meijer, & P.C.W. van Wieringen (Eds.), *The natural-physical approach to movement control* (pp. 57–93). Amsterdam: Free University.

Tyldesley, D.A. (1981). Motion perception and movement control in fast ball games. In I.M. Cockerill & W.W. MacGillivary (Eds.), *Vision and sport* (pp. 91–115). Cheltenham, England: Stanley Thornes.

Tyldesley, D.A., Bootsma, R.J., & Bomhoff, G.T. (1982). Skill level and eye-movement patterns in a sport oriented reaction time task. In H. Rieder, K. Bös, H. Mechling, & K. Reischle (Eds.), *Motor learning and movement behavior: Contribution to learning in sport* (pp. 290–296). Cologne, Germany: Hofmann.

Vanek, M., & Cratty, B.J. (1970). *Psychology and the superior athlete.* Toronto, Canada: Macmillan.

Vorro, J., Wilson, F.R., & Dainis, A. (1978). Multivariate analysis of biomechanical profiles for the coracobrachialis and biceps brachii (caput breve) muscles in humans. *Ergonomics, 21,* 407–418.

Wiebe, V.R. (1954). A study of tests of kinesthesis. *Research Quarterly, 25,* 222–230.

Wilkinson, J.J. (1958). *A study of reaction-time measures to a kinesthetic and a visual stimulus for selected groups of athletes and nonathletes.* Unpublished doctoral dissertation, Indiana University, Bloomington.

Williams, J.M., & Thirer, J. (1975). Vertical and horizontal peripheral vision in male and female athletes and nonathletes. *Research Quarterly, 46,* 200–205.

Winner, E. (1996). The rage to master: The decisive role of talent in the visual arts. In K.A. Ericsson (Ed.), *The road to excellence: The acquisition of expert performance in the arts and sciences, sports, and games* (pp. 271–302). Mahwah, NJ: Erlbaum.

Winograd, S. (1942). The relationship of timing and vision to baseball performance. *Research Quarterly, 13,* 481–493.

Wrisberg, C.A., & Shea, C.H. (1978). Shifts in attention demands and motor program utilization during motor learning. *Journal of Motor Behavior, 10,* 149–158.

Zelaznik, H.N., Spencer, R.M., & Doffin, J.G. (2000). Temporal precision in tapping and circle drawing movements at preferred rates is not correlated: Further evidence against timing as a general purpose ability. *Journal of Motor Behavior, 32,* 193–199.

CHAPTER 2

Motor Development and Skill Acquisition during Childhood and Adolescence

KATHERINE THOMAS THOMAS, JERE D. GALLAGHER, and JERRY R. THOMAS

Human motor performance changes significantly during a lifetime. Movement performance improves during childhood and adolescence, remains relatively stable during the early adult years, and gradually deteriorates with aging. These age-related trends apply to many tasks, from simple reaction time to complex sport skills. Improvement in motor performance is called *skill acquisition*. To understand movement, sport, and exercise, one must understand the acquisition, development, maintenance, and deterioration of skill across the life span. Other chapters in this *Handbook* (Chapters 24, 25, and 29) discuss life span development of skill and exercise in adult and elderly populations. This chapter focuses on descriptions of, and explanations for, changes in motor performance that occur during childhood and adolescence. These changes are rapid and attributable to several sources:

- Biological factors (e.g., genetics, puberty, maturation, and growth);
- Environmental factors (e.g., practice, experience, opportunity, and encouragement); and
- The interaction of biological and environmental factors (e.g., practice and experience during periods of development).

Using a developmental skill acquisition model as a theoretical approach, two questions are asked: How do children and adolescents acquire and/or control skillful movements? What roles do factors such as cognitive development, growth, heredity, and environmental characteristics play? For example, how does sport and movement expertise develop across childhood and adolescence in concert with cognitive development, growth, and maturation (for overviews see Gallagher, French, Thomas, & Thomas, 1996; J. Thomas, 2000; J. Thomas, French, & Humphries,

1986; K. Thomas & Thomas, 1999)? A competing theoretical perspective is action systems (dynamical systems) that emphasize the direct perception-environment connection. (For a developmental overview see Clark, 1995; Woollacott & Shumway-Cook, 1989.) Both views are useful in the study of the development of expertise. For example, developmental skill acquisition relies on a central nervous system representation (e.g., a motor program) to explain selection, planning, execution, and controlling of complex movements. However, this literal a view is probably not an accurate representation of skilled behavior. The dynamical systems perspective addresses two of the major weaknesses of all central representations of movement:

1. How does the system reduce the "degrees of freedom" problem associated with a complex movement?
2. How does the system maintain the flexibility to deal with changing environmental demands found in sports?

Complex sport performance demands cognitive functions such as abstract representation and decision making. Dynamical systems theory does not effectively address decision making, and therefore, is unlikely to be an accurate representation of complex sport behavior. The proponents of both theories have tended to choose movement tasks compatible with their perspective. For example, researchers have examined sport skills in the sport environment (e.g., baseball by French, Nevett, & Spurgeon, 1995; basketball by French & Thomas, 1987; tennis by McPherson, 1999; soccer by A. Williams & Davids, 1998). The selection of these motor activities allows the determination of the complex cognitive components of expertise that are essential to success. Dynamical systems theorists often select phylogenetic skills—that naturally "unfold" with maturation—

such as locomotion (e.g., walking; J. Jensen, Ulrich, Thelen, Schneider, & Zernichke, 1994, 1995; Ulrich, Jensen, Thelen, Schneider, & Zernichke, 1994; Whitall, 1991; Wollacott & Shumway-Cook, 1989) or underlying motor characteristics such as balance and eye-hand coordination (Assaiante, Thomachot, Aurenty, & Amblard, 1998; Rosblad, 1997). These actions require minimal cognitive activity by the participants. The solution to understanding the development of human movement requires both perspectives and possibly the merging of the two approaches. Methodological issues when studying children's movement are addressed next and models for studying motor skill performance are presented.

METHODOLOGICAL ISSUES IN STUDYING MOTOR SKILL ACQUISITION

Studying skill acquisition in children presents unique methodological challenges. For example, the experimental treatment is likely to be the only explanation for improvement in an adult. However, for children, growth and maturation may also contribute to improvement; in adults product variables (outcome data) may be linear to the processes that produce them, while in children one may change while the other is stable. The challenge for developmental experimental research is to control many variables that are not the target variables so that results can be attributed to the treatment. Thus, developmental research must be based on a broad understanding of many aspects of human development, and researchers must carefully select questions worthy of investigation as well as determine relevant dependent variables to assess. Examples of the complex methodological issues in developmental research are discussed next, including measurement issues as well as the selection of appropriate sample population, dependent variables, and tasks.

Measurement Issues

Children are inherently more variable in performances than adults, which yields methodological issues unique to developmental research (J. Thomas, 1984c). Four of these issues are: (1) careful selection of age groups, (2) selection of dependent variables that are sensitive to experimental manipulation, (3) identifying short- and long-term effects by separating learning from performance, and (4) that the child understands what is required and has given his or her typical performance.

Selection of age groups for a developmental study should be determined based on the theory for the research project. Weiss and Bredemeier (1983) highlighted a problem with

sport psychology research when participants were selected within wide age bands. For example, 6-year-olds respond differently from 12-year-olds, but data are reported as the average for the two age groups. Therefore, the differences are masked and the data do not represent most of the children in the group. J. Thomas (1980) suggested narrow and distinct age groups (e.g., 6 to 7-year-olds and 11 to 12-year-olds, rather than 6 to 12-year-olds) with the actual ages selected because of a particular characteristic of the age group.

Age differences in processing speed and perceptual sensitivity (also called difference limens or just noticeable differences) must also be considered. The speed of processing influences memory and learning. Young children think differently from adults, therefore instructions should be modified for all participants to have equal comprehension. Otherwise, children's performance may be influenced before the experimental manipulation rather than by the experimental manipulation. Perceptual differences need to be considered as well. For example, K. Thomas and Thomas (1987) found that when using standard movement lengths from a common starting point but at slightly different angles, young children compared to older children and adults needed three times the difference between angles to consistently determine that the movement directions were different. Thus, when using movement tasks to evaluate movement differences in adults and children, differences must be greater than both groups perceptual threshold to detect experimental effects.

When wide age ranges are selected, such as 5-year-olds and 19-year-olds, task selection becomes critical. The situation could be that a task which 5-year-olds are unable to successfully complete (floor effect) can be completed by all 19-year-olds (ceiling effect). Here an artificial developmental difference would be responsible for performance variability. Consequently, tasks must be carefully selected to capture the wide range of developmental performance.

A final measurement problem relates to the issue of performance versus learning effects. As reviewed by Schmidt and Lee (1998), to determine learning effects, a retention interval needs to be included such that the participants are required to perform the task without the experimental variable present. Gallagher and Thomas (1980) manipulated feedback characteristics and gave children 3, 6, or 12 seconds to process the knowledge of results. At the end of 36 trials, they concluded that the young children, when given 12 seconds to process the information, were able to perform similarly to adults. However, Gallagher and Thomas did not include a retention interval and were therefore unable to determine whether these effects were temporary or lasting.

Most developmental research is cross-sectional and experimental. Longitudinal research can provide valuable information but is expensive to conduct. In addition, attrition rates are high in longitudinal research. Furthermore, the commitment to a long-term treatment in longitudinal experiments is problematic because new technology and/or information may make a treatment unethical or obsolete before the child is mature. These factors explain why most of the research on children is cross-sectional and primarily descriptive or quasi-experimental in nature. Selection of participants is also an important issue in developmental research, especially with regard to age and gender.

Motor skill acquisition and performance may reflect movement characteristics (process) and movement outcome. Movement outcome has been the traditionally favored measurement, which is based on achievement of the goal for the task. The current focus of study has been concentrated more toward the process of motor skill performance, which describes movement characteristics using one or more measures such as kinematics, electromyograph (EMG), and ground reaction forces. Many process measurements must be undertaken in the laboratory, whereas measuring movement outcome can often be undertaken in the field (e.g., child's school). The type of measurement is dependent on the research question, and often both measurements are used. Typical outcome and process measures are discussed next.

Movement Outcome

When evaluating movement outcome, three measurements (Schmidt & Lee, 1998) are generally recorded: error, time, and response magnitude. Error measurement describes deviations from the desired goal. For example, if consistency of performance is important, then variable error (VE) should be selected, or when response biasing is important then constant error (CE) or absolute constant error (ACE) should be used. Schmidt and Lee (1998) provide a comprehensive review of these and other error scores. In developmental studies, VE is often important because for many tasks human motor performance becomes less variable within participants during the developmental years and as a result of practice (however, the difference between participants may become more variable over the years and with practice). For example, the forehand shot of a child in tennis may become more consistent with practice; however, the difference between two children in their forehand shots may become greater with practice. Response bias is also important in developmental studies because bias could be a

result of the variable being studied or due to an extraneous variable such as children being smaller than adults.

A second type of outcome measure is time, which is directly related to and often measured as speed. Reaction time (RT) and movement time (MT) are traditional examples. Simple RT is both used to represent cognitive time and is the time from a signal to the initiation of a response. RT can be fractionated into premotor (an estimate of decision time) and motor time (the latency time from when a muscle receives the signal to move and is actually able to begin a movement). MT is the time from the initiation of the movement (i.e., the end of reaction time) to the end of the movement. Of developmental interest are cognitive time (premotor) and motor time that result from fractionating reaction time. Cognitive time decreases during childhood, that is, children take less time to make a decision. The simplest form of a decision is to respond (reaction time). Motor time is indicative of the neurological (e.g., increased myelinization and neuromotor maturation) changes observed with increased age. Therefore, both cognitive and motor time decrease during childhood and explain a portion of the age-related differences in motor performance of children. The third movement outcome measurement is response magnitude, and examples include how far the ball is thrown, or how many sit-ups an individual can complete.

Movement Characteristics

Movement characteristics (process) measurements provide information about the quality of the movement—how the child moves. Researchers who have described fundamental motor pattern development assess movement characteristics. When describing movement characteristics, three types of measurement are generally made: kinematic, EMG, and ground reaction forces. Kinematic measurement describes the movement of the limbs and/or entire body by recordings of locations, velocities, and acceleration (e.g., Yan, Thomas, Stelmach, & Thomas, 2000). Kinematic measures used to understand children's motor control include:

- Velocity information (speed of the limb/body across positions used to determine the timing of the movement, and to locate pauses or hesitation in the action),
- Acceleration (the change in velocity at each position which indicates change in force generation of the body/limb),
- Jerk (a derivation of movement displacement, which reflects the smoothness of movement and is sensitive to changes in movement speed, direction, and timing),

- Movement linearity (the temporal coordination of related joints and is a measure of the average deviation between the actual and ideal movement),

- Time to peak velocity (the time between the beginning of the movement and the fastest point of the movement), and

- Intersegment interval (the time required to change the movement direction).

Often the purpose of these measurements is to make inference about a process, which can not be directly observed. Therefore, the measurements have little meaning except as indicators of underlying mechanisms of skill acquisition. For example, these measurements can be used to examine age differences in the execution of movements. Other process measures have been derived to examine specific types of movement, for example, error root mean square (a deviation measure) and index-of-smoothness have been used to examine balance control in children and adults.

Ground reaction force, as determined by use of a force platform, is also used to measure movement characteristics. Fortney (1983) determined that, when running, young children produced peak and impact forces three times greater than their body weight, an extremely high value when compared to adults. Findings like these suggest why children may sometimes have greenstick leg fractures.

EMG recordings measure the involvement of a muscle in the movement by recording the electrical activity associated with contraction. The EMG tracing provides records of the temporal patterning of the movement segments and the intensity of the action. Using a combination of kinematics and EMG technology, Whitney (1991) investigated postural response differences between children who had experience with balance in a variety of movements (5-year-old gymnasts) and children who did not have extensive experience with balance (5-year-old swimmers). Both measurements were integrated to determine sequencing of the muscular contractions with overt movement. Even at 5 years of age, the nongymnast had more lateral sway and greater electrical activity in the legs during normal standing than gymnasts.

Factors like growth, maturation, and learning may influence a child's skill acquisition. For example, it is clear that older children run faster than younger children—an outcome measure. However, by looking at process measures, one can observe that stride-rate does not change across childhood and adolescence, but leg length and strength do change and contribute to better running efficiency.

Interventions, Longitudinal, and Cross-Sectional Research

Training of motor skills has been used to examine two questions: First, the influence of nature (genetics/maturation) and nurture (environment/learning), and second, whether the benefit of practice is retained over time. One issue, which has confounded the findings of training studies, is the type of skill. Phylogenetic skills (e.g., motor milestones) are not very responsive to training based on time of onset or efficiency of movement. Consequently, training (and deprivation) studies, which have examined these skills, suggest training does not work (Dennis, 1935; Dennis & Dennis, 1940). However, studies in which practice is applied to ontogenetic skills (learned skills) tend to show short-term positive benefits of training (McGraw, 1935). Unfortunately longitudinal investigations are necessary to examine the long-term influence of practice on skill performance and there are very few longitudinal training studies. To date, the skills of running, jumping, and throwing (Glassow & Kruse, 1960; Halverson, Roberton, & Langendorfer, 1982; Rarick & Smoll, 1967) have been investigated longitudinally but only to determine if the year-to-year correlation between the skills are high. This has been done to evaluate whether the skills maintain a stable order within the participants tested. They generally have not, with correlations being below 0.5.

Clarke (1967) reported a longitudinal study of coaches' ranking of boys when they were in elementary and junior high school, 25% were stars (picked on all-star teams) at both levels. Forty-four percent of the boys were rated as "stars" during elementary school but not in junior high school, while 30% were "stars" during junior high school but were not "stars" in elementary school. Data were not collected during the high school years, but one would expect a significant change in those selected as the "stars." Early maturing boys tend to be larger, giving them a size advantage at younger ages. Thus, a possible explanation of this data is that the elementary school stars were early maturing. However, with the onset of adolescence, the early-maturing boys no longer exhibit a size advantage. The relationship of growth and maturation to performance will be discussed at length in the section on growth.

APPROACHES TO THE STUDY OF SKILL DEVELOPMENT

Five of the most common approaches for studying motor skill development are stage, dynamical systems, information processing, expertise, and readiness. Each of these approaches makes an important contribution to the understanding of the influence of development on motor skill acquisition. A brief description of each is appropriate before discussing the results of research using these frameworks.

Stages of Development

The stages of development idea (e.g., Piaget, 1952) uses specific behaviors or clusters of behaviors to describe typical patterns that progress in an orderly, linear, and invariant manner. Stages have appeal for both application and research. Being able to classify participants into groups based on a common characteristic rather than chronological age or grade level is intuitively appealing and essential in many research paradigms. The two difficulties of stages are dealing with individuals who are in transition between stages and accurately classifying individuals into the stages. The use of broadly defined stages increases the risk of inaccurate classification, however, narrow and specific stages often demand definitions for each skill or class of skill which is less than pleasing (J. Thomas, 1980). Fitts and Posner (1967) and Piaget (1952) present stages of learning that have been used in motor skill acquisition research. These are briefly described next.

Fitts and Posner (1967) described motor skill learning as having three stages that reflected the characteristics of the performer. In the initial stage, the cognitive stage, the performer is "getting the idea" of the task. Performance is characterized by cognitively organizing the task, resulting in large and variable errors during the execution of the movement. In the second stage, the associative stage, error is less, with the learner making the same error repeatedly, rather than many different errors. The final stage, the autonomous stage, is marked by fewer and smaller errors which the learner can detect and correct. Thus, the learner does not think about the movement during execution—only when selecting the movement and when the movement is completed.

Piaget's (1952) stages of development were produced as a result of observing his two daughters. There were four stages: sensorimotor, pre-operational, concrete operations, and formal operations. Stages were identified by the ability or inability to solve certain tasks. The solution to the task became the definition and the criteria for the stage. For example, pre-operational children could sort items on one characteristic, but could not conserve or sort by two characteristics (Flavell, 1977). Concrete operators were characterized by their need to adhere to a strict set of rules and

to rely on those rules for decision making. Piagetian stages have two major strengths:

1. *Authenticity*—developed from direct observation of children for children.
2. *Eloquence*—describes development in a simple straight forward manner.

However, there are three limitations to Piaget's theory:

1. Tasks were difficult to quantify in terms of the cognitive abilities demanded in the task, therefore, performances were judged as pass or fail.
2. Exact changes in cognitive processing were difficult to assess.
3. Transition from stage to stage was attributed to maturation.

Pascual-Leone (1970) devised a solution to the first two problems, called *Neo-Piagetian Theory*. He proposed a numerical formula to identify the amount of capacity demanded by each task. This system allowed researchers to show differences between children within a stage and to better study differences between stages. The system involved the use of philosophical logic for task analysis of discrete skills; an approach that did not lend itself effectively to continuous tasks like movements. Thus, few researchers were able to master the system. The third problem—attributing stage transition to maturation—simply leaves the reason for the change as an unexplained variable. This perspective indicates that interventions and experimental manipulations will have minimal influence for performance by a child on a task beyond the current stage of development. Many scholars reject the notion that development of cognitive and motor skills are significantly limited by stages; rather they prefer and select approaches that attribute a greater proportion of behavior and performance to environmental characteristics such as practice and opportunity.

Information Processing

During the 1970s with the growth in computer literacy and usage, an explanation of cognitive behavior using the computer metaphor was framed. Atkinson and Shiffrin (1968) and Shiffrin and Schneider (1977) developed detailed models that simulated computer hardware and software to explain human thinking. Following this, Ornstein and Naus (1985), Chi (1976, 1978, 1982), and Kail (1986) sought to explain development in a similar way. They tried to build an adult processing system by studying children's processing of information. The theory allowed for different levels of performance by examining each component of processing separately.

The information processing model worked quite well and focused on memory span, speed of processing, short-term memory processes (encoding, rehearsal, retrieval, organization), and meta-memory (knowing about knowing and strategies). Considerable research on motor skills has been done using these paradigms (see J. Thomas, 1980, 1984a, for summaries). These studies used experimental manipulations from which two unique concepts resulted:

1. When given a solution to a task, young children could often use the solution effectively and perform like older children (Gallagher & Thomas, 1984, 1986; J. Thomas, Thomas, Lee, & Testerman, 1983; Winther & Thomas, 1981).
2. Younger children performed better than older children when the task related to one specific content area with which the younger children had greater experience.

The second point leads to the notion of expertise, which will be described next.

Expertise

Studies conducted within the information processing framework produced consistent findings that demonstrated that knowledge increased linearly with age during childhood. The increase in knowledge was attributed to experience and learning. However, some young children demonstrate more knowledge in specific content areas than older children or adults (e.g., chess, dinosaurs, baseball). In general, knowledge across most content areas increases with age so that older individuals have more knowledge than younger individuals. Knowledge usually increases with experience, so more experienced individuals have more knowledge than less experienced individuals. An intriguing observation which led to the early research on expertise was that within a category of knowledge that had been practiced by younger children, they could use the more sophisticated strategies expected of older children and adults. Intuitively, knowledge should increase with age and experience, however it is counter-intuitive that content area knowledge would result in younger children adopting more sophisticated strategies, even within the content area, than older children. Expertise research began as a result of this finding (Chase & Simon, 1973; Chi, 1978; Chiesi, Spilich, & Voss, 1979).

Studies of child experts revealed that the use of strategies was limited to the content of the area of expertise and did not generalize to other content areas. The notion that experience, rather than maturation alone may drive the changes in information processing, was an important shift in perspective. Initially case studies were used, followed by quasi-experimental designs to study expertise. Research on information processing and motor skill acquisition used novel tasks to eliminate experience, the focus on expertise demanded that researchers examine the specific contributions of experience and characteristics of experts. Sport researchers have advocated two perspectives for studying experts, the perception-action model (dynamical systems) and the cognitive model. (See Abernethy, Thomas, & Thomas, 1993 for a discussion of research methodology in sport expertise.)

An alternative way to study expertise would be to use a longitudinal model, following the same children as they developed expertise. The problem is predicting who will become experts. Because no reliable method has been developed to predict which children will become experts, researchers have been forced to use cross-sectional studies and retrospective inquiry.

Dynamical Systems

Those who study motor development from a dynamical systems approach view movement as patterns of motor coordination that self-organize in response to task-specific information. (For recent reviews see Ulrich, 1997, and Davids et al., Chapter 6 of this *Handbook*.) Three characteristics unique to the dynamical systems approach are that:

1. Movements are not symbolically represented in the brain,
2. Skilled movement does not develop as a function of maturation, and
3. Skilled movement behavior results from the interaction of multiple intrinsic and extrinsic subsystems.

Intrinsic subsystems include physical and physiological structures such as the muscular, neural, cardiovascular, and motivational systems, while extrinsic subsystems refer to the task and the environmental conditions. Dynamical systems theory explains potentially complex movements using as few degrees of freedom as possible (Heriza, 1991). For any given task, the system has numerous ways to move or act, yet movement is organized into a few simple patterns. New patterns emerge through the destabilization of existing stable forms. Change from one pattern to the next occurs because some component(s) of the system change and the current pattern no longer works as well. When the old pattern no longer works well, the motor system explores other alternatives and self-organizes based on the new configuration of subsystems. Variability of performance is great as the individual moves from one stable pattern to the next. Thelen and Ulrich (1991) provide an example of the emergence of a walking pattern in an infant. Due to the scaling of subsystems such as strength and postural control, the infant eventually abandons a creeping or rolling pattern and a walking pattern emerges.

The power of the dynamical systems model for studying motor development has been demonstrated in several experiments related to body control and walking in infants and toddlers. For example, J. Jensen and her colleagues (1994) showed the influence of gravity as postures change from supine to angled to vertical in 3-month-old infants. Gravitational influence was greater in the vertical position resulting in a decreased relationship between joints that influence leg kicking (hip and knee). In a subsequent study, J. Jensen et al. (1995) reported an age progression in infants at 2 weeks, 3 months, and 7 months that showed proximal to distal organization as well as better modulation of kick phases. Ulrich et al. (1994) reported that the treadmill stepping pattern in 7-month-old infants was stable when the infant was held in a vertical position, suggesting that the action was self-organized. Finally, with respect to toddlers, Assaiante et al. (1998) reported that balance was organized in young children (11 to 19 months) from the center of gravity (hip) to the shoulders and head; a proximal to distal organization if the center of gravity is considered the starting point for controlling balance. For phylogenetic skills, like walking, that develop as the individual matures, a view of the motor system as self-organizing is intuitively appealing and is consistent with the data in the studies previously cited.

Readiness

Readiness implies that the learner is in a position to acquire new skills when three prerequisites or precursors merge (Magill & Anderson, 1996). The first precursor is maturation, hence the individual has to possess the physical, cognitive, and emotional maturation to perform the skill. For example, the child has to have sufficient strength and balance to perform the hop; she or he needs to be able to attend to the appropriate cues to acquire the hop; and he or she must have the emotional maturity level to work in a group of other children. The second component of readiness is to analyze the task to insure that the learner has

acquired the prerequisite skills. For example, the child must be able to hop before he can learn to skip. The final component of readiness relates to motivation of the individual to acquire the skill. However, Passer (1996) pointed out the difficulties in determining readiness. For example, a child is ready to develop sport skills at 4 to 5 years of age, but a child cannot understand competition (e.g., role taking, attribution) until 11 to 12 years of age. Therefore, being ready based on one characteristic may not mean being ready on another characteristic, which complicates the use of readiness as a concept. One precursor of readiness, and an important factor in dynamical systems, is maturation and growth. The next section relates maturation and growth changes to skill performance, and important research findings related to growth and maturation are presented.

AGE-RELATED CHANGES AND GENDER DIFFERENCES IN GROWTH

Growth and maturation impact motor performance and skill acquisition in children. Therefore, an understanding of growth and maturation is necessary when studying children, even when they are not the variables of primary interest. Two categories of research will be briefly reviewed in this section: (1) general body development (e.g., height, weight or mass, fatness) and (2) gender/cultural differences. To plan, explain, and apply developmental research effectively, we must understand the influence of growth and maturation. For example, we might assume that practice and instruction would not improve the performance of young girls as much as the same training would improve the performance of young boys. However, this would be a poor assumption since prior to puberty, males and females are similar. Furthermore, both the performance and biological differences between young boys and girls are influenced significantly by environmental variables, such as physical activity, practice, and encouragement. The influence of physical parameters on motor skill performance will be discussed in greater detail in the section on motor skill performance.

Many of the components of growth—height, biacromial (shoulder) and bicristal (hip) breadths, location of fat, shoulder-to-hip and standing-to-sitting height ratios—are susceptible to relatively little environmental influence. Others (fat, body circumferences, muscle) are relatively difficult to change. However, all of these factors must be considered when studying skilled performance because these factors change across time in childhood and can explain some differences between children and adults (Malina, 1975). This point will be made clear in the discussion of the influence of growth on performance.

General Body Development

While growth and development are continuous and orderly, the systems of the body do not grow at equal rates. Scammon (1930) showed this by plotting the different developmental patterns for the reproductive, endocrine, neural, and general body systems (e.g., height and weight). The most rapid rate of growth is from birth to 2 years of age for height and weight; then the rate slows, but the child continues to gain both height and weight during childhood (Malina, 1975). The rate increases dramatically at puberty; then both rate and actual growth slow until the child stops growing at adulthood. Figure 2.1 presents a comparison of the distance and velocity curves for height and weight demonstrating the variation in rate and the linear increases in body growth.

Body proportions change as a result of the differences in rates of growth for different body parts (Malina, 1984). The torso and head grow relatively slowly, while the extremities grow at a faster rate. This means that the center of gravity moves downward, and the head accounts for less of the body mass. The greater the length of time the body grows the more these relationships are influenced. The bones grow in length then breadth and mass. The body

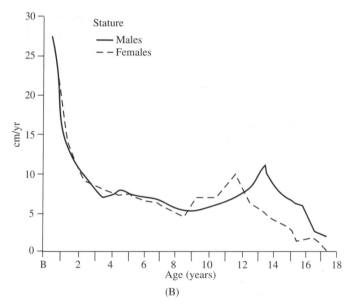

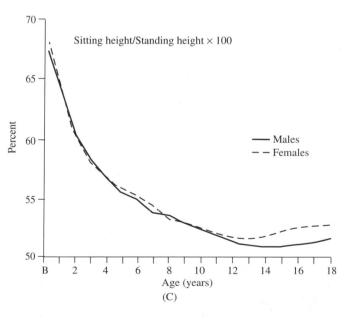

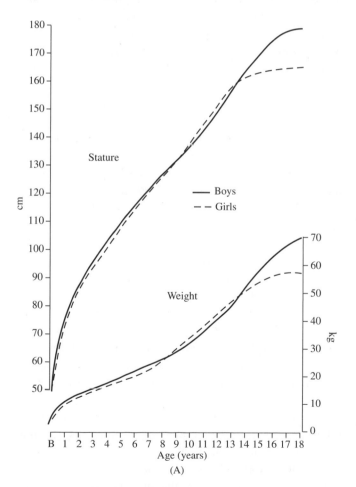

Figure 2.1   (A) Average height and weight distance curves, (B) velocity curve for height, and (C) average standing height/sitting height for American boys and girls.

gains lean tissue faster than fat tissue. In addition, breadths and circumferences increase across childhood as a result of bone growth with muscle and fat also contributing to increases in circumferences (Figure 2.2).

From birth to school age, the nervous system develops rapidly in three ways (H. Williams, 1983): (1) the neurons grow to match the physical lengthening of the body; (2) myelin becomes thicker (and longer) to protect the speed and fidelity of the neural transmissions; and (3) the number of synapses increase, allowing better communication between neurons. Both myelin and synapses continue to develop during the maturational process but in the motor neurons, development is nearly complete by school age. Some aspects of the central nervous system are still developing until the beginning of the third decade of life.

The maturation of the reproductive system influences anthropometric factors such as height, weight, body segment proportions, fatness, and growth rate. This influence is seen in robust gender differences and in cultural differences in anthropometric data.

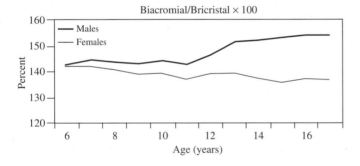

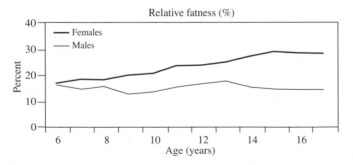

Figure 2.2 Average proportions, shoulder/hip, relative fat for boys and girls. Redrawn with permission of J.R. Thomas, from R.M. Malina (1984), *Physical Growth and Maturation*. In J.R. Thomas, *Motor development in childhood and adolescence* (pp. 2–26).

Gender Differences in Growth

While the means for height and weight favor males from birth through the lifespan, the differences during childhood are small, and the overlap between males and females is great (Malina, 1975). Thus, most boys and girls are similar in height and weight prior to puberty. Since girls usually enter puberty between 11 and 12 years of age and boys follow at 13 to 14 years of age, girls have their prepubescent growth spurt before boys (Figure 2.1). Girls also stop growing before boys do. The only time when the average height and weight for girls is greater than for boys is during the girls' growth spurt. There is great variation within each gender for height and weight, which is reflected in the considerable overlap of male and females in these dimensions.

The fact that males grow for a greater length of time, combined with the fact that the legs grow at a faster rate during childhood, means that males have relatively longer legs than females (Malina, 1984). Males' shoulders (biacromial breadth) grow more rapidly and for longer than females' shoulders. The growth curves for hip breadth (bicristal breadth) have similar slopes for males and females, after puberty males have slightly larger hip bone breadths than females. This means that the shoulder-hip ratio is greater for males after puberty (Figure 2.2). Like males, females have greater biacromial (shoulder) breadth than bicristal (hip) breadth, however, the ratio is greater in males because their shoulders tend to be considerably wider. Males also gain less fat and more lean tissue than females resulting in a higher percent of body fat (relative fatness) for females than males (Figure 2.2).

Physiques have been described in terms of three somatotypes; endomorph (pear-shaped, more body fat), mesomorph (muscular with large bones), and ectomorph (linear, tall, and lean) (Carter, 1980; Malina, 1984). Early maturing females tend to be endomorphic, early maturing males tend to be mesomorphic, and late maturing children tend to be ectomorphic. Most people have balanced physiques (moderate ratings in each of the components), however, some individuals have extreme physiques representing one of the somatotypes.

Today, children are maturing at an earlier age and are taller and heavier than preceding generations (Malina, 1975). Children in different cultures mature at varying rates, with extremes such as Norway (late maturing) and the United States (early maturing). Varying maturation influences growth, as does genetics. Gender differences are similar across cultures, and growth trends are similar within cultures.

An understanding of the relationship between growth and motor performance is important to explain the variability in motor development. In the next section, the changes in fundamental motor patterns (e.g., run, throw) across age are described. This is followed by a discussion of the relationship between growth and motor skill.

GENDER AND AGE-RELATED CHANGES IN MOTOR SKILL AND FITNESS

To undertake the task of describing age-related changes in skilled motor performance in less than a book (or at least several chapters of a book, e.g., Branta, Haubenstricker, & Seefeldt, 1984; Haubenstricker & Seefeldt, 1986; Seefeldt & Haubenstricker, 1982) is impossible. In fact, motor development books (e.g., Haywood, 1993; Payne & Isaacs, 1998) include significant sections and chapters to accomplish this purpose. Other books devote their total focus to specific aspects of motor development—posture and gait (Woolocott & Shumway-Cook, 1989) or eye-hand coordination (Bard, Fleury, & Hay, 1990). In lieu of these limitations, this section relates through theory and illustration the developmental nature of motor performance as it is influenced by specific factors such as gender, cognitive development, expertise, and growth. Reference will frequently be made to more complete reports and explanations for the phenomenon being described.

Figure 2.3 is an overview of how the skill process develops during childhood and adolescence. The idea represented by the pyramid is that later phases of movement development are built on earlier phases. Gallahue's (1989) conception provides a pictorial view of this process. However, the evidence available to support this orderly sequence is limited. More specifically, the evidence collected does not refute it, but limited research data are available.

Many motor skills have been described in terms of process and outcome, and both measures show improvement with age for most skills. Quantitative data have often been presented as normative data in tests of motor performance. Qualitative descriptions of skilled movement have a long history (e.g., overhand throwing; Wild, 1938). Numerous studies have provided data on the developmental nature of fundamental skills that have been summarized and explained by Wickstrom (1983) and in other motor development books (e.g., Eckert, 1987; Haywood, 1993; Payne & Isaacs, 1998; J. Thomas, 1984b; H. Williams, 1983). Despite the large

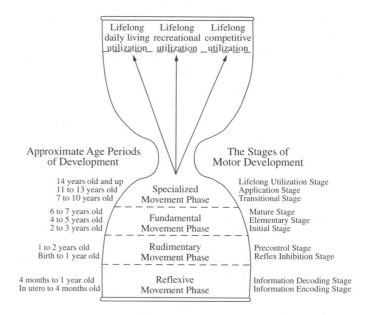

Figure 2.3 The phases of motor development. Redrawn with permission from D.L. Gallahue and J.L. Ozmun (1989). *Understanding Motor Development,* p. 81, Boston, Massachusetts: McGraw Hill.

body of research in the area, controversy concerning the level and nature of these qualitative analyses is replete in the literature.

For example, Seefeldt and Haubenstricker (1982) have argued for whole body descriptions of the levels or stages of qualitative skill analysis, while Roberton (1982) presents a case for the need to analyze the components of the movement (e.g., arm action, trunk action, and leg action in throwing). Either approach is certainly useful for teachers and coaches because movement analysis is done at a level the eye can observe (or at least can be recorded and observed on a video camera). However, if the purpose is to understand the nature of the movement and how it is influenced by growth, gender, implements (e.g., ball size/weight), practice, fatigue, or any number of other characteristics, a more detailed and quantitative biomechanical analysis is needed (e.g., high-speed video from several cameras). Additionally, if the purpose of the analysis is understanding skill and characteristics that influence skill rather than providing a basis for visual skill analysis, related measures such as muscle EMG and ground reaction forces must be considered.

Two skills have been selected for discussion rather than trying to present all skills. One is a locomotor skill (running), the other is a manipulative skill (throwing); both skills are important in many sports. Figure 2.4 (Seefeldt & Haubenstricker, 1982) provides an overview of the age (in months) that 60% of boys and girls are able to perform eight fundamental motor skills with proficiency. As an example, most boys can throw overhand with a fairly mature pattern (the number 5 above the solid line represents the accomplishment of the mature pattern) at about 60 months of age (5 years), but most girls are 102 months of age (8.5 years) before they exhibit a mature pattern. For running, the 60% criteria is reached about one year apart, 48 months for males and 60 months for females. Small differences favoring the females are observed for catching, hopping, and skipping, and small differences favoring the males are present for jumping, kicking, and striking.

Running: Quantitative Changes

Figure 2.5 (from a Michigan State study; see Branta, Haubenstricker, & Seefeldt, 1984) reflects two sets of longitudinal data, one set for boys and girls from 5 to 10 years of age, and a second set for boys and girls from 8 to 14 years of age. Girls and boys steadily increase in running

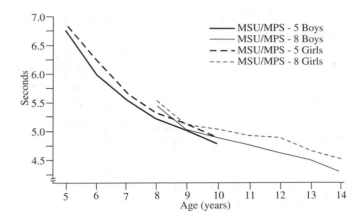

Figure 2.5 Means of 30-yard dash performance for four groups of children, measured longitudinally from 5 to 10 or 8 to 14 years of age. Reprinted with permission of D.C. Heath, from C. Branta, J. Haubenstricker, & V. Seefeldt (1984). Age changes in motor skills during childhood and adolescence. In R.L. Terjung (Ed.), *Exercise and sport sciences reviews* (Vol. 12, p. 485).

speed over the age ranges reported, and boys run slightly faster (on the average) at each age. Note that the differences in running speed between boys and girls becomes slightly greater beginning at about 11 to 12 years of age. (Gender differences are discussed in greater detail in a subsequent part of this chapter.)

While the mean running speed of boys is faster than girls at every age level, there is considerable overlap in the distributions. In fact, it is very common in an elementary physical education class or on a young coeducational age group sport team to observe that the fastest person is a girl. As children pass puberty and reach adolescence, less overlap in the distributions of running speeds between boys and girls is seen. However even in high school, a girl, particularly one on a sport team where speed is important, is often faster than many boys.

Some of the change in running speed across childhood and adolescence is a result of increased leg length. As presented in the previous section, when children grow taller, their legs increase in length and make up a proportionately greater percentage of total stature (Malina, 1975). This probably accounts for the stride length data seen in Figure 2.6. Observe that the stride rate per second during running remains fairly constant across the age ranges; however, stride length increases as age increases, probably reflecting changes in leg length.

Running: Qualitative Changes

Not all of the change in running speed during childhood is due to increased leg length. Improved running form

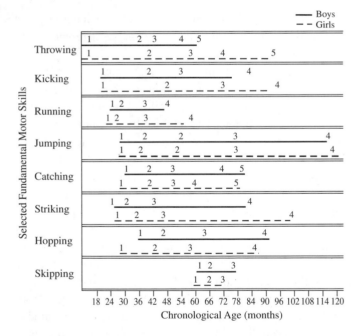

Figure 2.4 The age at which 60 percent of the boys and girls were able to perform at a specific developmental level for selected fundamental motor skills. Redrawn with permission of John Wiley & Sons, from V. Seefeldt & J. Haubenstricker (1982). Patterns, phases, or stages: An analytical model for the study of developmental movement. In J.A.S. Kelson & J.E. Clark (Eds.), *The development of movement control and coordiantion* (p. 314).

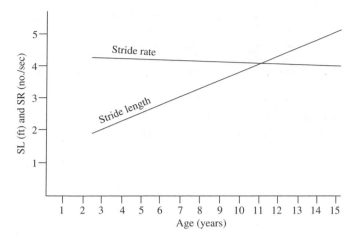

Figure 2.6 Longitudinal changes in five children in stride length (SL) and stride rate (SR). From S. Smith (1977). *Longitudinal changes in stride length and stride rate during sprint running.* Unpublished master's thesis, University of Wisconsin–Madison.

also accounts for increases in speed. We have chosen to present the component view (Roberton, 1982) of qualitative analysis, although the Seefeldt and Haubenstricker, (1982) approach is equally useful. Table 2.1 provides a description of the changes in running form that occur across childhood. This work by Roberton (1984) is divided into the levels of development for leg action and arm action (note that these are based on analyses that have not gone through the complete sequence of examination that Roberton uses). Increasingly higher levels represent more mature patterns that are likely to be present in older and more skillful children.

The increase in running speed across childhood is a result of maturation (e.g., growth) and environment (e.g., practice, strength). Individual differences among children are then a result of both environmental and innate factors. While it is known that motor skill outcomes improve across age, and that some of the difference is due to growth, why efficiency in motor patterns changes is unclear. Is it due to learning variables (e.g., feedback, instruction) or would the skills improve due to practice alone? This presents an interesting question for theory testing and future research.

Overhand Throwing: Quantitative Changes

Figure 2.7 is a sample of data depicting throwing performance for boys and girls across childhood and adolescence. The data (from Espenschade, 1960) are typical, showing steady increases in performance across childhood. Boys throw farther than girls, and the differences become larger

Table 2.1   Development Sequences for Running*

Leg Action Component

Level 1   Run is flat-footed, with minimal flight. Swing leg is slightly abducted as it comes forward. When seen from overhead, path of swing leg curves out to side during movement forward (Wickstrom, 1977). Foot eversion gives toeing-out appearance to swinging leg (Wickstrom, 1977). Angle of knee of swing leg is greater than 90 degrees during forward motion.

Level 2   Swing thigh moves forward with greater acceleration, causing 90 degrees of maximal flexion in knee. Viewed from rear, foot is no longer toed out nor is thigh abducted. Sideward swing of thigh continues, however, causing foot to cross body midline when viewed from rear (Wickstrom 1977). Flight time increases. After contact, which may still be flat-footed, support knee flexes more as child's weight rides over his foot (Seefeldt, Reuschlein, & Vogel, 1972).

Level 3   Foot contact is with heel or ball of foot. Forward movement of swing leg is primarily in sagittal plane. Flexion of thigh at hip carries knee higher at end of forward swing. Support leg moves from flexion to complete extension by takeoff.

Arm Action Component

Level 1   Arms are held in high to middle guard position, as described in development of walking (Seefeldt, Reuschlein, & Vogel, 1972).

Level 2   Spinal rotation swings arms bilaterally to counterbalance rotation of pelvis and swing leg. Frequently oblique plane of motion plus continual balancing adjustments give flailing appearance to arm action.

Level 3   Spinal rotation continues to be prime mover of arms. Now elbow of arm swinging forward begins to flex, then extend, during backward swing. Combination of rotation and elbow flexion causes arm rotating forward to cross body midline and arm rotating back to abduct, swinging obliquely outward from body.

Level 4   Humerous (upper arm) begins to drive forward and back in sagittal plane, independent of spinal rotation. Movement is in opposition to other arm and to leg on same side. Elbow flexion is maintained, oscillating through approximately 90-degree angle during forward and backward arm swings.

* These sequences have not been validated.

Used with permission from Roberton, M.A. (1984). Changing motor patterns during childhood. In J.R. Thomas (Ed.), *Motor development during childhood and adolescence.* Minneapolis, MN: Burgess. References in the table are from this source.

with each passing year, particularly after puberty. The overlap between the distributions of girls and boys is less than in running (and most other fundamental skills).

Overhand Throwing: Qualitative Changes

Overhand throwing patterns have been one of the more studied areas of fundamental movements (e.g., Branta et al., 1984; Roberton, 1984). Table 2.2 is from Roberton's work and uses the component model of preparatory arm backswing, upper arm action, forearm action, trunk action,

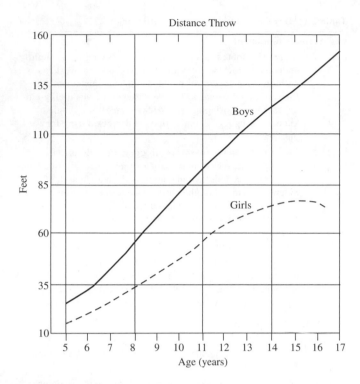

Figure 2.7 Distance throw for boys and girls. Used with permission of Harper & Row, from A.S. Espenschade (1960). Motor development. In W.R. Johnson (Ed.), *Science and medicine of exercise and sports* (pp. 419–439).

Table 2.2 Development Sequences for the Overhand Throw for Force*

Preparatory Arm Backswing Component

Level 1 No backswing. Ball in hand moves directly forward to release from its position when hand first grasped ball.

Level 2 Elbow and humeral flexion. Ball moves away from intended line of flight to position behind or alongside head by upward flexion of humerus and concomitant elbow flexion.

Level 3 Circular, upward backswing. Ball moves away from intended line of flight to position behind head via circular overhead movement with elbow extended, or oblique swing back, or vertical lift from hip.

Level 4 Circular, downward backswing. Ball moves away from intended line of flight to position behind head via circular, down, and back motion that carries hand below waist.

Humerus (Upper Arm) Action Component

Level 1 Humerus oblique. Humerus moves forward for ball's release in plane that intersects trunk obliquely above or below horizontal line of shoulders. Occasionally during backswing, humerus is placed at right angle to trunk, with elbow pointing toward target. It maintains this fixed position during throw.

Level 2 Humerus aligned but independent. Humerus moves forward for ball's release in plane horizontally aligned with shoulder, forming right angle between humerus and trunk. By time shoulders (upper spine) reach front facing, humerus (elbow) has moved independently ahead of outline of body (as seen from side) via horizontal adduction at shoulder.

Level 3 Humerus lags. Humerus moves forward for ball's release and is horizontally aligned, but at moment shoulders (upper spine) reach front facing, humerus remains within outline of body (as seen from side). No horizontal adduction of humerus occurs before front facing.

Forearm Action Component

Level 1 No forearm lag. Forearm and ball move steadily forward to release throughout throwing action.

Level 2 Forearm lag. Forearm and ball appear to lag (i.e., to remain stationary behind the child or to move downward or backward in relation to this body). Lagging forearm reaches its farthest point back, deepest point down, or last stationary point before shoulders (upper spine) reach front facing.

Level 3 Delayed forearm lag. Lagging forearm delays reaching its final point of lag until moment of front facing.

Trunk (Pelvis-Spine) Action Component

Level 1 No trunk action or forward-backward movements. Only arm is active in throw. Sometimes forward thrust of arm pulls trunk into passive left rotation (assuming a right-handed throw), but no twist-up precedes that action. If trunk action occurs, it accompanies forward thrust of arm by flexing forward at hips. Preparatory extension sometimes precedes forward hip flexion.

Level 2 Upper trunk rotation or total trunk block rotation. Spine and pelvis both rotate away from intended line of flight and then simultaneously begin forward rotation, acting as unit or block. Occasionally, only upper spine twists away and then twists toward direction of force. Pelvis then remains fixed, facing line of flight, or joins rotary movement after forward spinal rotation has begun.

Level 3 Differentiated rotation of trunk. Pelvis precedes upper spine in initiating forward rotation. Child twists away from intended line of ball flight and then begins forward rotation with pelvis while upper spine is still twisting away.

Foot Action Component

Level 1 No movement. Child throws from whatever position feet happen to be in.

Level 2 Child steps with foot on same side as throwing hand.

Level 3 Child steps with foot on opposite side from throwing hand.

Level 4 Child steps with opposite foot a distance of over half his standing height.

* Validation studies (Roberton, 1977, 1978; Roberton & Langendorfer, 1980; Roberton & DiRocco, 1981; Halverson et al., 1982) support these sequences with the exception of the Preparatory Arm Backswing and Foot Action Components.

and foot action to describe the overhand throwing movement as it develops across levels of performance. (This sequence has been validated using Roberton's standards.) The throwing sequence goes from the very crude dart board or shot put motion seen in young children (using the same hand and foot with little trunk rotation) to the smooth and coordinated action seen in more expert performers.

Gender Differences in Overhand Throwing

Seefeldt and Haubenstricker (1982) and Roberton (1984) suggest that girls simply lag behind boys in the development of a quality overhand throwing pattern. However, making these claims is tenuous from qualitative analyses where the observational categories are rather crude and one camera is used (e.g., rotational components cannot be estimated accurately, variables such as step length and ball velocity cannot be estimated accurately unless they are absolutely perpendicular to the camera lens). In fact, based on the work of J. Nelson (J. Nelson, Thomas, Nelson, & Abraham, 1986), K. Nelson, Thomas, and Nelson (1991), J. Thomas and Marzke (1992), Yan et al. (2000), Yan et al. (2000) it is apparent that expert male and female throwing patterns are different; thus, the patterns developed by young females are not just lagging behind the patterns used by young males, but are developing toward a different pattern (see the next section on gender differences). This view represents a very different theoretical explanation from the view presented by Roberton (1984) and Seefeldt and Haubenstricker (1982).

GENDER DIFFERENCES

As infants, male and female babies display reflexes and reactions and perform motor skills quite similarly. However with development gender differences become apparent in motor performance, motor activity, and physical fitness across childhood and adolescence and it is a common topic in motor development books (Haywood, 1993; Payne & Isaacs, 1998). Many studies have been conducted examining the development of gender differences in motor performance, motor activity, and physical fitness. Summaries of these studies have been reported in qualitative reviews (e.g., Eaton, 1989; J. Thomas & Thomas, 1988). However, three particularly interesting quantitative evaluations of the developmental nature of this literature have been done: a meta-analysis of gender differences in motor performance (J. Thomas & French, 1985); a meta-analysis of sex differences in motor activity (Eaton & Enns, 1986); and a secondary analysis of gender differences (J. Thomas, Nelson, & Church, 1991) based on the data from the normative study (National Children and Youth Fitness Study-Ross & Gilbert, 1985; J. Ross & Pate, 1987) on the physical fitness of U.S. children. The results of these three large-scale analyses will be used to discuss this topic along with some individual papers to identify possible explanations.

Gender Differences in Motor Performance

J. Thomas and French (1985) conducted a meta-analysis of gender differences across age for 20 motor performance tasks. This analysis was based on 64 previous studies yielding 702 effect sizes from 31,444 participants. Effect size were calculated by dividing the difference between the male and female mean scores on a motor performance task by the pooled (e.g., average) standard deviation. The development of gender differences was related to age in 12 of the 20 tasks: balance, catching, dash, grip strength, long jump, pursuit rotor tracking, shuttle run, sit-ups, tapping speed, distance throw, throwing velocity, and vertical jump. Five of those tasks (dash, sit-ups, long jump, grip strength, and shuttle run) have a similar profile across age. Figure 2.8 shows this profile for the dash (e.g., running, from J. Thomas and French, 1985) where the solid line represents the standardized performance difference between girls and boys where 0 is no difference, plus values represent better performance for boys, and minus values represent better performance for girls. Dotted lines are the confidence intervals for each data point. Thus, running speed shows an effect size of about 0.5 (standard deviation units) from 3 to 9 or 10 years of age. After 10, boys become increasingly faster than girls during the adolescent years.

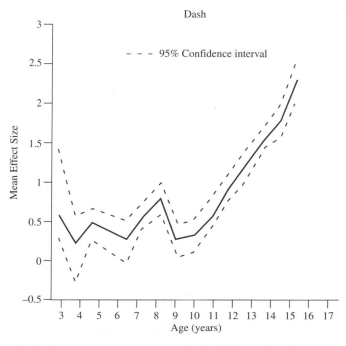

Figure 2.8 Gender differences in the dash. Used with permission, from J.R. Thomas, & K.E. French (1985). Gender differences across age in motor performance: A meta-analysis. *Psychological Bulletin,* pp. 260–282.

J. Thomas and French suggested that differences following this pattern type are likely caused by environmental factors (encouragement, practice, parental/peer norms) prior to puberty, but after puberty the biological factors previously suggested (e.g., boys now have longer legs and greater muscle mass than girls) interact with the same environmental characteristics to produce the rapid increase in performance differences. However, Smoll and Schutz (1990) reported a large study (2,142 students, ages 9, 13, and 17 years) in which they found the degree of body fatness to be a significant factor in physical performance (including running) at pre- and postpuberty. While the degree of fatness is a biological variable, Smoll and Schutz (1990) readily acknowledge that it is influenced by environmental characteristics (e.g., amount of exercise, type of diet); thus confounding the issue of environment versus heredity. Regardless, the gender differences in running prior to puberty are relatively small but become greater postpuberty. Differences this small are probably produced by varying environmental demands placed on children. The large differences postpuberty are likely not produced completely by growth/biological variables. Environment plays a major role in its interaction with biology. This view is supported by data on adults performing at the world class level, where gender differences are smaller than observed in the general population (Ransdell & Wells, 1999). In other words, when females have access to training and are motivated, they perform more like males.

Another way to consider how a fundamental task varies across age is to consider the stability of the same children's performance as they become older. Branta, Haubenstricker, and Seefeldt (1984) summarized stability data from several studies (including their own) and found that the year-to-year correlations for running speed become smaller with a greater number of intervening years. For example, the values with one intervening year range from the high 0.50s to 0.80, but are similar for boys and girls. Correlations decrease as more years intervene, particularly for girls (at least in Branta et al., 1984); thus, correlations decrease to the 0.40s and 0.50s for boys and 0.20s to 0.40s for girls. Tasks with correlations of 0.50 or higher across one year have been called stable (Bloom, 1964). Thus, running would be considered a stable task. Stable tasks might be considered as having a strong hereditary component.

Of the seven remaining tasks that J. Thomas and French (1985) reported as related to gender differences across age, five (balance, catching, pursuit rotor tracking, tapping, and vertical jump) have patterns like running. One exception is that they begin at a relatively similar level (about 0.0 effect size). Then they show an increasing effect size up to about 0.5 across childhood, followed by the rapid rise in gender differences typically, associated with puberty (up to 1.0–1.5 standard deviation units). As with the first five tasks discussed, explanations appear to be similar: mostly environmental effects prior to puberty with an environmental-biological interaction following puberty.

Explanations for Gender Differences in Throwing

Throwing (distance and velocity) was a task very different from the other 19 in the J. Thomas and French (1985) analysis (see Figure 2.9). Gender differences are as large as 1.5 standard deviation units at ages 3 to 5 years and show a nearly linear increase up to 3.0 to 3.5 standard deviation units by 16 to 18 years of age. These data reflect minimal overlap in the female-male distribution prior to puberty and practically no overlap after puberty (at 3.0 to 3.5 standard deviation units, just the extreme tails of the distributions overlap; or, to put it another way, the average boy's distance throw is greater than the 99th percentile for girls).

Because the gender differences in throwing for distance are so much larger than those for other motor tasks,

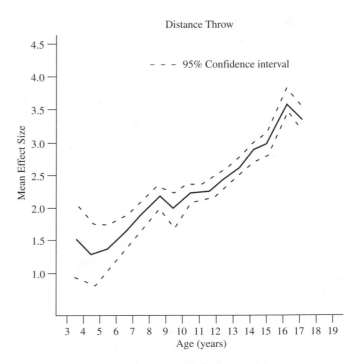

Figure 2.9 Gender differences in throwing distance. Used with permission, from J.R. Thomas, & K.E. French (1985). Gender differences across age in motor performance: A meta-analysis. *Psychological Bulletin, 98,* pp. 260–282.

Nelson and colleagues (J. Nelson et al., 1986; K. Nelson et al., 1991) completed two follow-up studies attempting to identify explanations for this finding. In the first study (J. Nelson et al., 1986), 5-year-old girls threw only 57% as far as 5-year-old boys (4.8 vs. 8.4 m). However, when these differences were corrected taking into account a series of biological variables (joint diameters, shoulder/ hip ratio, and sum of skinfolds), girls' corrected performance was 69% of boys' (5.4 vs. 7.8 m).

In a longitudinal follow-up study, K. Nelson et al. (1991) tested the same children when they were 9 years old. The girls now only threw 47% of the distance thrown by boys (8.8 vs. 18.7 m). Boys increased the distance thrown by 11 m (143%) over the 3+ years while girls increased by 4.6 m (109%). The correlation between throwing performance over the time period was 0.43 for girls and 0.44 for boys. Roberton, Halverson, Langendorfer, and Williams (1979) found the year-to-year correlations for throwing velocity to be higher, 0.65 to 0.78, suggesting that throwing is also a stable task. When considering throwing form, K. Nelson et al. indicated that by age 9, boys had reached the ceiling on the scale for rating form, but girls showed minimal improvement. This is somewhat different from the data reported in Figure 2.4, where Seefeldt and Haubenstricker (1982) reported that 60% of the girls reach mature form between 8 and 9 years of age. Few of the 9-year-old girls in the K. Nelson et al. study demonstrated mature form using Roberton's criteria (Table 2.2).

Why are gender differences in throwing performance so much greater than those for any of the other tasks reviewed by J. Thomas and French (1985)? Very little data are directly available to explain this finding. No evidence has been published to suggest that the throwing kinematics, ground-reaction forces, or muscle EMGs of expert males and females are either similar or different. A vital question is: Do expert females and males use the same movement pattern resulting from the same sequence of muscle contractions to generate force in throwing? Some preliminary evidence (J. Thomas & Marzke, 1992) suggests that the answer is "No." Upon careful examination of the stick drawings of overhand throwing sequences (throwing a tennis ball with maximum force) in Figure 2.10, it becomes evident that:

• Patterns are dissimilar for the two experts; and
• The movement pattern for the 5-year-old boy resembles the expert male's pattern more than the expert female's pattern resembles the expert male's pattern.

Adult Male (a)

Adult Female (b)

Child Male (c)

Child Female (d)

Figure 2.10   Stick figures of throwing: (a) adult male, (b) adult female, (c) child male, (d) child female.

The data on the angle of twist (angle in degrees between the shoulders and hips) from the two experts (male and female) suggests differences in three characteristics:

1. Timing in maximum angle of twist—200 msec before ball release for the male, 300 msec before ball release for the female.
2. Slope (angular velocity) of the twist just before ball release—the male's slope is nearly twice as large as the female's.

3. Continuation of the twist following release—the male continued counterclockwise rotation after ball release, the female maintained a constant twist after release (100 msec) and then begin to rotate back.

Figure 2.11 shows the internal/external rotational angular velocity (the rate of rotation of the humerus about its long axis at the shoulder) for the same expert male and female. Note that the male had nearly twice the throwing angular velocity of the female (2,100 deg/s vs. 1,100 deg/s) at or immediately following the ball release.

Is the development of the overhand throwing pattern for males and females across age moving toward a different final pattern? The thought is provocative. Data from the field of human evolution provide some support for this idea. Bipedal locomotion (McHenry, 1982; Washburn & Moore, 1980), the use of sharp-edged tools (Tobias, 1968; Washburn & Moore, 1980) and overhand throwing (Isaac, 1987) may have played significant roles in human evolution. Isaac (1987) suggest that "... skilled overarm throwing of missiles deserves a similar scrutiny, since it is possible that it developed into a behavior of adaptive importance with repercussions far beyond the simple scoring of a hit" (pp. 3–4). Calvin (1982, 1983) and Darlington (1975) have indicated that overhand throwing is a prime candidate in evolution to explain rapid increases in brain size, redundancy, and lateralization because the task involves a three-factor problem: (a) the location of the person throwing, whether moving or stationary; (b) the location of the target, moving or stationary; and (c) the trajectory velocity of the object being thrown.

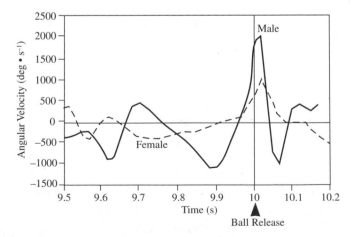

Figure 2.11   Internal/external angular velocity (of the humerus) in overhand throwing for an expert male and female.

Even if throwing is important in human evolution, why should males have developed greater throwing skill than females? Males were more likely to be the hunters and warriors, resulting in greater reproductive selection for those who threw effectively. If women provided more child care such as carrying a young child rather than leaving him or her unattended, did that inhibit their throwing action (e.g., there was minimal differentiated trunk rotation)? After a substantial review of the anthropological and historical records on throwing, Isaac (1987, p. 15) concluded, "It will have been noted by the reader that all historical instances so far quoted related to throwing by males. . . . The implications of this will not be pursued here, but they are not unimportant."

Gender Differences in Motor Activity Level

Eaton and Enns (1986) have provided an extensive meta-analysis of sex differences in human motor activity level based on 90 citations. (We have used the term gender differences because of the role of environment, especially with children past infancy; Eaton and Enns use sex differences because some of their data are prior to and immediately following birth where biology is more important.) Motor activity level reflects energy expenditure through movement using instruments designed to measure motor activity, ratings, and observations. Included are very specific measures such as arm movements and global measures such as how many different marked areas the child entered. They reported that males were more active than females (effect size = 0.49), but greater differences were found in studies with older samples. (Citations were limited for ages beyond late adolescence, restricting these findings to an upper age of about 15 years.) This finding suggests that social influence enlarges the gender differences across age.

However, significant sex differences were present in infants (under 12 months), with males being more active than females (effect size × 0.29). In addition, males were more active than females (effect size = 0.33) in six prenatal studies, although this difference was not significant or conclusive because of the small number of studies conducted. These findings at least suggest that the social differences hypothesis may only serve to magnify those sex differences in level of motor activity that are already present (perhaps because of genetics). As an aside, Schachar, Rutter, and Smith (1981) reported in a large sample of British children, the rate of hyperactivity for boys to girls was 2 to 1.

Even though Eaton and Enns (1986) found gender differences in motor activity to increase with age, the absolute amount of motor activity decreases with age (e.g., Eaton & Yu, 1989). Since girls are known to be relatively more mature than boys at every age (Tanner, 1978), Eaton and Yu (1989) attempted to determine if sex differences in motor activity were a function of sex differences in maturation rate. Using relative maturity (percent of estimated adult height) as a potential moderator variable, differences in motor activity were determined for 5- to 8-year-old boys and girls ($N = 83$). While the sex differences were reduced by relative maturity, girls were still less active than boys.

Thus, while absolute amount of motor activity tends to decrease with increasing age, gender differences become larger in motor activity across age. This effect is found as early as infancy (with some evidence of it prenatally), suggesting a genetic component, and is partially moderated by maturation rate. However, the steady increase across childhood and adolescence suggests a social/environmental explanation.

Gender Differences in Health-Related Physical Fitness

The finding that girls show a lower motor activity level than boys at every age suggests that they might maintain lower levels of health-related physical fitness. Evidence from a secondary analysis (J. Thomas et al., 1991) of the National Children and Youth Fitness Study (J. Ross & Gilbert, 1985; J. Ross & Pate, 1987) indicates that this hypothesis is correct. (For additional support see Smoll & Schutz, 1990.) The National Children and Youth Fitness Survey reported a nationwide sample from 6,800 boys and 6,523 girls where sampling and testing were carefully controlled.

Figure 2.12 is a plot from this data converted to effect sizes for the mile (half-mile for children under 8 years of age), chin-ups (modified pull-ups for children under 10 years of age), and sit-ups. The open squares in the figure are unadjusted differences while the solid markings have been adjusted for biological and environmental characteristics. All of the health-related measures in Figure 2.12 show a linear increase in the differences between boys and girls across age. The increase in differences is greatest for the chin-ups and least for the sit-ups. This might be anticipated, because chin-ups are most likely to be influenced by the increased strength and muscle mass associated with puberty in boys and the increased level of fat in girls. However, adjusting for the degree of fatness before puberty and for the degree of fatness and amount of exercise outside the school setting following puberty generally reduced the differences between males and females at each age.

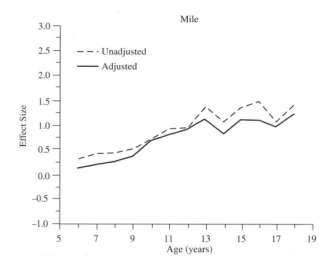

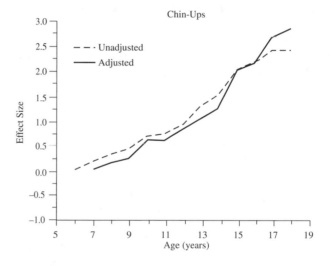

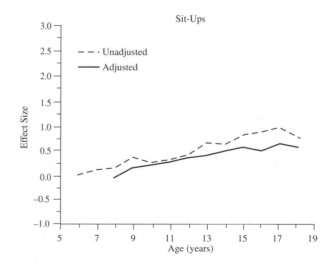

Figure 2.12 Results of secondary analysis of the National Children and Youth Fitness Study (Thomas, Nelson, & Church, 1991).

These findings are consistent with those reported in other large-scale studies for similar tasks: motor activity level (Eaton & Enns, 1986), motor performance (J. Thomas & French, 1985), and physical performance (Smoll & Schutz, 1990). Environmental characteristics (e.g., social situations, amount of exercise, peers, parents, teachers, opportunities, encouragement, practice) are the major factors in producing gender differences. However, biological variables (e.g., maturation, fatness) seem to mediate this difference. In a few instances (e.g., motor activity, throwing) there is some circumstantial evidence of the influence of heredity in producing some part of the differences observed. But even in those instances, environmental characteristics enhance and amplify these initial differences.

RELATIONSHIP OF GROWTH TO MOVEMENT

The relationship of growth to performance has been observed in many tasks, however, reporting of the *relative age effect* has highlighted the importance of growth and maturation as factors in performance. The relative age effect means that the oldest children in a group, who are typically largest and most mature, are identified by coaches as the most skilled (Baxter-Jones, Helms, Maffull, Baines-Preece, & Preece, 1995; Boucher & Mutimer, 1994; Brewer, Balsom, Davis, & Ekblom, 1992). For example, the oldest children in age group sports are over-represented on all star teams and as the best players, while younger children within the age group are typically under-represented. Although this phenomenon is rather short lived, and the age advantage disappears after puberty (K. Thomas & Thomas, 1999), there are several repercussions of the relative age effect. Most importantly, younger children have less opportunity to practice and less encouragement, so they will be more likely to drop out of the sport. The relative age effect has been used as one explanatory factor in studies of the development of expertise. Ironically, there is considerable evidence that late maturing children have an advantage in many sports after puberty. As previously mentioned, the somatotype associated with late maturing males and females is ectomorphy, which is also associated with higher levels of athletic performance (Malina, 1984).

A related question has been whether late maturing individuals select certain sports (gymnastics, ballet, track and field) or whether participation in those sports causes the later maturing (Broekoff, 1985; Malina, 1984). In either case, the relationship between maturation and performance is evident at the extremes of both performance and maturation. This means that for world-class athletes, later

maturing is observed in certain sports, but could be a result of or caused by participation.

Specific physiques and greater size are often advantageous in a motor skill achievement. Greater height, weight, muscle mass, or shoulder-hip ratio positively impacts on performance in many skills—especially those where lever length or strength is important. Some of the improvement observed across age in motor skill performance is due to greater size and accompanying strength. In addition, the change in body proportions (e.g., sitting height/standing height ratio) also has an impact on motor performance. Consider a static balance task—the infant has a head which is 25% of body height, while the adult's head is only 12.5% of body height. Imagine trying to maintain your balance with two heads above your shoulders if your head was 25% of your height! The moment of inertia and the amount of resistance to acceleration of a body part also change with growth. R. Jensen (1981) tracked growth and moment of inertia in boys. The findings indicated that over a 12-month time period the growth-related constraint on the boy's ability to accelerate increased by 27.7%, which far exceeded their increase in actual size. Children have difficulty maintaining increases in strength to generate the expanding force necessary to move larger body parts. The amount of force needed is disproportionately greater than the actual physical increase in size.

Related to these disparities is the notion that children often practice particular skills during a related sport season, then continue to grow in the off-season. When the season begins again, whatever information was learned and stored about the movement pertained to a very different body—with different ratios and moments of inertia. With practice, a motor program has developed to control the movement given the specific size characteristics of the child. If a skill has not been performed for a period of time during which substantial growth has occurred, invariant characteristics of the motor program such as relative force and timing will be inappropriately specified for the increased size of the child.

The physical parameters that change during the growth process influence performance more at the extremes. For example, performers who carry a substantial amount of fat may be adversely affected; but for those who fall within the average range of fatness, having somewhat more or less fat probably does not correlate to performance (Malina, 1975). While certain body types tend to be associated with excellent sport performance, those relationships are less clear than once believed (Malina, 1984). Taller children tend to be stronger, which is usually an advantage, while heavier children show no consistent pattern for performance. Heavier children are better throwers, but worse at running and jumping. Physical parameters also have less influence as age (and skill) increases (Espenschade, 1963). Body size (height and weight) has even less impact on performance for girls.

The amount of variation in performance accounted for by physical parameters is a unique way to examine gender differences in performance. Using an overhand throwing task, J. Nelson, Thomas, Nelson, and Abraham (1986) found that physical parameters (joint diameters, shoulder-hip ratios, and sums of skinfolds) accounted for 12% of the differences between 5-year-old boys and girls in throwing distance. Because those parameters are relatively similar at age 5, 12% is a meaningful contribution, however, the differences not accounted for by growth factors are equally meaningful. Some of the children were tested three years later (K. Nelson et al., 1991). The throwing distance and physical size increased for girls, but their throwing patterns did not change. This suggests that growth explained most of the improved performance for girls.

Considering the impact of exercise and/or activity on growth is a very interesting proposition. While there is apparently some minimal amount of exercise necessary for "normal" growth, the definition of minimal is elusive (Broekoff, 1985). To describe the optimal levels of exercise for growth is even more difficult. Early studies of the relationship have been criticized for lack of experimental control—specifically, the failure to match the exercise and non-exercise groups before the exercise programs. In other investigations, exercise has not been quantified. Results of more recent and less controversial research indicates that regular exercise and intensive training does not increase stature. While lack of activity may result in decreased bone density, intense training may increase skeletal thickness and bone density. Activity is an important factor in regulating body weight muscle hypertrophy, and bone growth, density, mineralization (Malina, 1986).

Taken together, the results of studies on physical growth, maturation, motor activity, physical fitness, and fundamental motor skills provide valuable background information necessary to plan, interpret, and apply research findings where males and females are participants. Unfortunately, the perception has been that gender differences were large and primarily biological. The implications for skill acquisition research are significant. The key findings are:

- Most of the gender difference before puberty is due to the different treatment of males and females.

- After puberty, gender differences are due to the interaction of biology and environment (e.g., treatment).

- In world-class adult athletes, 10% to 20% of the gender difference in performance can be attributed to biology (Ransdell & Wells, 1999).

Considering these findings, research and application expectations for young girls should be similar to young boys. When large differences are observed, environmental factors should be explored. It is reasonable to expect increasing gender differences after puberty, but not at the magnitude that has traditionally been accepted.

DEVELOPMENTAL CONTROL OF MOVEMENT

As children get older, their control of movements improves. One of the areas in which this can best be observed is with eye-hand coordination for fast and accurate movements. These movements are important in children's sport and every day life—overhand throwing, striking, reaching and grasping, controlling a joystick in computer games, and writing/drawing/coloring. Attention has been given to this topic in adults (for reviews see Meyer, Abrams, Kornblum, Wright, & Smith, 1988; Plamondon & Alimi, 1997), but little empirical work has been devoted to children, who differ from adults with regard to velocity and acceleration patterns underlying movements (Stelmach & Thomas, 1997).

Typically, during rapid hand movements to a target, the initial part of the movement is ballistic and is often assumed to be controlled by a central mechanism (e.g., a motor program). Adjustments are seen in the final stages of the movement because hitting the target requires feedback-based adjustments. For adults, Fitts' law (1954) on the speed-accuracy trade-off predicts the difficulty of the task based on the size of the target and the length of the movement. Numerous authors (e.g., Burton, 1987; Hay, Bard, Fleury, & Teasdale, 1991; Kail, 1991; J. Thomas, 2000) have reported that children, when compared to adults, take longer to process information, make more errors, and use more feedback-based adjustments as the target is approached in these tasks.

Yan et al. (2000) reported a comprehensive developmental study indicating for a rapid aiming task (point-to-point movement of about 20 cm), young children used ballistic control for about 25% of the movement and used corrective feedback during the movement to hit the target during the remaining 75% of the movement. Older children had greater ballistic control of the movement (about 50%) but were substantially below adults' proportion (about 80%) of ballistic control. Younger children's movements were also less smooth (as estimated by jerk costs) than older children's movements who were less smooth than adults' movements. A longer ballistic phase of the movement produced a smoother and more coordinated movement.

In a subsequent study, J. Thomas, Yan, and Stelmach (2000) reported that when younger children practiced a rapid aiming movement, they increased the proportion of the movement under ballistic control considerably more than older children and adults, although adults improved as a function of practice. In addition to the ballistic phase of the movement taking up a greater proportion of the total movement, the smoothness of the movement during the ballistic phase increased (jerk costs went down). Children's movement profiles (velocity and acceleration) looked more similar to adult profiles following practice. These findings provide substantial support for the hypothesis that children can increase the underlying control of the movement with practice, just as adults do. Thus, for eye-hand coordination tasks like these, lack of practice rather than a maturational deficit seems the more likely explanation for why children perform poorly.

COGNITIVE ASPECTS OF MOTOR SKILLS PERFORMANCE

In this section, general information is presented about the development of cognitive function as well as ways in which cognitive functioning relates to motor and sport skill performance. In particular, strategic knowledge is emphasized, and declarative and procedural knowledge are discussed in subsequent sections. This topic is important because children use cognitive processes as they perform, learn, and control motor and sport skills.

In many ways, cognitive processes operate in movement as they do for any type of skill or knowledge to be acquired or performed. But movements are clearly different in at least one way: Knowing and doing are not necessarily perfectly correlated. If a child knows how to solve a math problem, the solution is nearly always correct. However, knowing how to solve a movement problem (e.g., fielding a ground ball in baseball and throwing the runner out at first) is often unrelated to the skill necessary to execute the solution. So while discussing cognition and motor performance, it should be realized that knowing and executing are not the same thing (K. Thomas, 1994). Again, the need for understanding the role and impact of skill execution as described earlier in the chapter is emphasized.

In the following sections, cognitive features of processing are discussed as if they were relatively independent functions. Of course they are not, but they are presented in this way to address the large volume of literature on this topic. Focus will be on the movement and sport-related literature in these sections. However, by necessity, research on the development of cognitive processes from more generic sources such as developmental psychology and child development will be incorporated in the discussion. The presentation will be organized around age-related issues involving such topics as speed of processing, perceptual development, memory, and learning.

Speed of Processing

As children age, they are able to process the same information more quickly, or process more information in the same amount of time. Consistent results have been found with tasks such as simple reaction time (J. Thomas, Gallagher, & Purvis, 1981), the processing of feedback (Gallagher & Thomas, 1980; J. Thomas, Solmon, & Mitchell, 1979), anticipation timing (Dunham & Reid, 1987), Fitts' tapping task (Burton, 1987; Kerr, 1985; Salmoni & Pascoe, 1979), and decision making (Newell & Kennedy, 1978). Thus, when the processing interval is reduced, children's motor performance will be hindered because they have not been given enough time to "think" about what they need to do (Gallagher & Thomas, 1980). Researchers have focused on whether the speed of processing differences is due to structural or functional limitations. Information-processing theorists have attributed the cause to functional differences such as memory strategy usage (Chi, 1977; Lindberg, 1980) and knowledge base differences (Chi, 1982), while researchers adopting Piagetian theory have attributed differences to increases in memory capacity (Pascual-Leone, 1970; Tudor, 1979).

Although an increase in the physical aspects of memory (myelinization, brain size) cannot be completely eliminated as a causal factor in the developmental increase in memory performance, the contributions appear to be minimal. However, the amount of information in long-term memory and mnemonic strategies plays a greater role. Gallagher (1980, Experiment 1; Gallagher & Fisher, 1983) demonstrated the importance of memory strategy use for remembering movements. When asked to recall simple linear movements of varying amplitudes, children performed as accurately as adults; however, their performance was impaired when the complexity of the task increased.

Chi and Gallagher (1982) reviewed the developmental literature to determine the source of speed-of-processing differences. After separating the information-processing interval into four components—encoding, manipulation, response selection, and motor response—they determined differences between adults and children in manipulation and response selection. Children used different movement strategies to perform the tasks (McCracken, 1983; Sugden, 1980). In addition, they appeared to use different muscle groups and/or increased EMG activity to accomplish the tasks, possibly causing a time delay in responding. Therefore, movement-time differences do not appear to be caused by a developmental change in the capacity of the motor system (Burton, 1987; Chi & Gallagher, 1982; Kerr, 1985; Salmoni & Pascoe, 1979).

Speed-of-processing differences has focused on the relative contribution of two hypotheses that can explain changes in processing speed with age (Kail, 1986, 1988, 1991):

1. Improvements within a specific process, task, or domain (Kail, 1988); for example, as children get older, they acquire more task efficient strategies, additions to the content knowledge base, and accessibility of information in long-term memory (Dempster, 1988).
2. Use of more efficient allocation of processing resources such as attention and mental effort in older than younger children (Kail, 1988).

Next specific factors that elucidate age-related changes in speed of processing, including changes in perception, memory strategy use, and knowledge base are addressed.

Perceptual Development

The use and interpretation of the information in sensory store is termed perception (Thomas, 2000). Some researchers have suggested that a developmental shift occurs in the hierarchy of the dominant sensory systems, with intrasensory discrimination increasing (K. Thomas & Thomas, 1987) and intersensory integration improving (H. Williams, 1983). A shift from initial reliance on kinesthetic information to the more reliable visual information has been suggested (Williams, 1983). Williams noted that 4-year-olds are dependent on tactile-kinesthetic (bodily) cues in performing motor acts and, therefore, cannot fully and effectively use specific visual cues to regulate behavior successfully. Visual information dominates by 7 or 8 years of age. On the basis of such findings, she has suggested that sensory-perceptual development in the young child is characterized by a shift from relying on tactile kinesthetic or somatosensory information to relying on information from the visual system as a basis

for regulating or mediating motor behavior. This transition to visual dominance represents a shift from the use of input from sensory systems with relatively crude information-processing capacities to the use of input from a more refined sensory system (H. Williams, 1983).

An increase in intrasensory discrimination has been documented supporting Williams' ideas. With age, children are more accurate with positioning a limb (K. Thomas & Thomas, 1987; H. Williams, Temple, & Bateman, 1979), tactile point discrimination (VanDyne, 1973), and anticipation timing (Dunham & Reid, 1987; J. Thomas et al., 1981). Improved discrimination within a sensory system gives the individual higher quality information on which to make decisions for motor program selection, parameterization of the program, or detection and correction of errors.

K. Thomas and Thomas (1987) found children's movement performance improved with age, due not only to memory factors but also to perception. Young children (5-year-olds) needed nearly three times the distance of adults to differentiate a well-learned movement from a new but different one. Thomas and Thomas concluded that one should not assume children perceive the same level of information as an adult. The result is that a child may think the movement has been effectively reproduced, when in fact it has not. After the information has been perceived, the individual must manipulate that information, select a response, and attempt to move. Manipulation of the information occurs as an interaction of short- and long-term memory.

Memory

Memory and attention are also critical factors that must be considered from a developmental perspective. Attention is a global term that has been used to address a variety of processes ranging from concentration and vigilance to mental set and arousal (Abernethy, 1993). Selective attention serves in the perceptual encoding of task-appropriate cues and as a control process to continually maintain relevant information in working memory (Gallagher et al., 1996). Research on selective attention has moved from a description of the development of selective attention strategies (Ross, 1976) to determining the mechanisms of selective attention and the relationship between attention and perception (Barrett & Shepp, 1988; Shepp, Barrett, & Kolbert, 1987; Tipper, MacQueen, & Brehaut, 1988). Finally, researchers have examined the changing capabilities of young children to distribute their attentional resources in a dynamic environment.

Children's ability to attend to environmental information develops across age. According to A. Ross (1976) selective attention strategies are not used spontaneously until the beginning of adolescence, around 11 years of age. Attention develops in stages, where during the first stage (over-exclusive mode) children as young as one year of age are attracted to a single stimuli. By the time a child reaches the first grade, they can be classified as reaching the second stage, the overinclusive mode. Over-inclusive attention is when a child is overwhelmed by the environment and attends to numerous features while at the same time not being able to separate relevant from irrelevant information. The tendency to be over-inclusive is perhaps best illustrated by the child who is learning to catch a ball. The young child tends to look at the face of the thrower instead of focusing on the ball. This is an example of young children's poor use of selective attention strategies, and how they are more inclined to distractions by environmental cues. Selective attention, reached during early adolescence, is when young individuals are able to select the relevant information while disregarding what is irrelevant from a variety of displays in the environment (A. Ross, 1976).

Cognitive strategies can be defined as processes used in working memory to store, retrieve, and/or reorganize information in long-term memory (Chi, 1976; J. Thomas, 1980). A strategy related to the development of selective attention is *labeling*. Labels according to J. Thomas, Lee, and Thomas (1988) are defined as "attaching a name as an aid to memory" (p. 54). The development of selective attention to task appropriate information has focused on the use of labeling skill cues or environmental information that helps the child remember the location of the movement, assists in getting the "idea of the movement," or in sport to recognize as certain "plays" develop. Researchers have demonstrated that the use of task-appropriate cues has facilitated children's selective attention during performance for recall of movement location (Winther & Thomas, 1981), motor skill learning (handstand and forward roll: Masser, 1993; throwing: Fronske, Blakemore, & Abendroth-Smith, 1997), recalling movement sequences (Miller, 1990; Weiss, 1983; Weiss & Klint, 1987), balancing (deOliveria, Gallagher, & Smiley-Oyen, 1999), and selection of dynamic environmental information (Ladewig & Gallagher, 1994; Ladewig, Gallagher, & Campos, 1994). Labeling has also been beneficial for learning-disabled 7-year-olds (Miller, 1990).

These findings demonstrated that the use of cues positively influenced children's performance by focusing of attention to the relevant aspects of the skill or in focusing on appropriate environmental information. Winther and

Thomas (1981) used familiar names to recall patterns of an arm movement. Masser (1993) used kinematic cues to teach a handstand and forward roll while Fronske, Blakemore, and Abendroth-Smith (1997) provided kinematic cues to aid children's learning to throw. Weiss (1983) and Weiss and Klint (1987) used names of skills to assist children in recalling a movement sequence. Using a static cue but a continuous task (walking) and increasing task complexity (on a line, on a beam, over an object on a line or beam) deOliveria, Gallagher, & Smiley-Oyen (1999) required children to focus on a spot at the end of the path. Inexperienced 6-year-olds benefit from the use of a cue to focus attention as did the 11-year-olds and adults. Smoothness of walking for the inexperienced participants using a cue was similar to the experienced gymnasts.

Research manipulating levels of interference during practice has been conducted by Hagen and West (1970), Ladewig and Gallagher (1994), Stratton (1978), and J. Thomas and Stratton (1977). The basic concept behind these studies was to provide the participants with two different levels of task interference (i.e., distractors) during learning, and then to measure later performance. Participants were exposed to high amounts of interference (i.e., many distractors) at the beginning of the task and then exposed to lower levels of interference (i.e., fewer or no distractors), or they started the task in the reverse order. After a retention interval, performance was measured. The results from these studies (Hagen & West, 1970; J. Thomas & Stratton, 1977) suggested that when participants were exposed to high interference introduced late in practice, their performance during acquisition improved while participants exposed to high levels of interference early in practice demonstrated inferior performance. However, when participants from both conditions performed retention tests under high levels of interference, a reversal occurred. Those participants exposed to high levels of interference early in practice improved their performance during retention. These findings demonstrated that as long as the participants received some type of cues to assist them in focusing their attention to the relevant aspects of the task, high interference early in practice seems to benefit task performance.

Rehearsal is an important strategy needed to maintain information in memory. The importance of active rehearsal was demonstrated in a study by Gallagher and Thomas (1984). Given a series of eight movements, 5- and 7-year-old children chose to rehearse on an instance-by-instance basis, while 11- and 19-year-old participants grouped the movements for recall. When forced to rehearse in an adult fashion, the performance of the 5- and 7-year-olds improved. Reid (1980) found similar results for mentally retarded children in the IQ range of 43 to 83 as did Schroeder's (1981) using severely mentally retarded participants.

Organization is a strategy used to combine information in a meaningful way to reduce cognitive demands. Instead of thinking of separate pieces of information, the individual groups and recodes the information into one unit. Using a series of eight movements, and manipulating the degree of organization in the material, Gallagher and Thomas (1986) found that 5-year-old children were unable to increase performance regardless of organization strategy or input of information. The 7-year-old children were able to use organized input to facilitate recall, but the strategy failed to transfer to a new task. The 11-year-old children used organized input and showed some transfer of strategy. However, they could not restructure the information or provide self-generated organization. The 19-year-old participants organized the information regardless of input.

Integrating the studies on rehearsal and organization of input, Gallagher and Thomas (1986) indicated that forcing the use of the strategies was of greater importance to younger children, but it had less effect on older children and adults (Figure 2.13). The older children and adults used the strategies when not forced to do so, whereas younger children did not. Even though the 5-year-old children were given organizational cues, they failed to recall the movements in order (from short to long). Forcing rehearsal, on the other hand, aided recall for the 5-year-old children. The 7-year-old children used the organizational strategy to recall eight movements. The older children and adults in the self-determined strategy group were similar in recall to the organizational strategy group. They rehearsed spatially similar groups of movement.

In summary, there is evidence that even 4-year-olds behave strategically when asked to remember, but that younger children do not spontaneously use memory strategies. As Chi (1982) has suggested, this could be due to an inefficient knowledge base. Children's earliest successful memory strategies begin with highly familiar information as does successful training efforts. The automation of these strategies occurs as a result of practice and experience, and it leads to a functional increase of the space available in working memory for the handling of information-processing operations.

Knowledge Base

Knowledge base is also referred to as *long-term memory.* Knowledge base theorists postulate that knowledge is

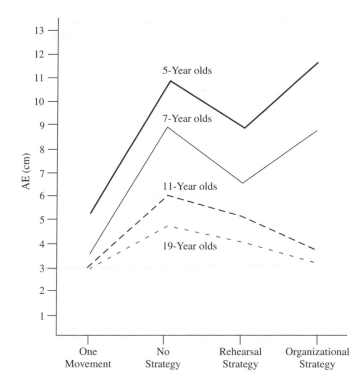

Figure 2.13   Summary of effects from rehearsal and organization of movement performance. Used with permission from J.D. Gallagher & J.R. Thomas (1986). Development effects of grouping and recoding on learning a movement series. *Research Quarterly for Exercise and Sport, 57,* 117–127.

represented more elaborately with increased practice. Children who possess a greater amount of knowledge in a given domain have shown that knowledge plays a salient role in the performance of domain-related tasks. Chi and Koeske (1983) documented that a 4-year-old child used a sophisticated organizational strategy to recall well-learned dinosaurs. The strategy to recall unfamiliar dinosaurs was typical for the age group. Other research has suggested that domain-specific knowledge may reduce the capacity limitations of working memory (Chase & Simon, 1973), reduce the attentional demands of certain tasks (Leavitt, 1979), and facilitate the effective use of memory strategies (Ornstein & Naus, 1985). Thus, information is accessed with less mental effort, leaving more of their mental resources available for the execution of strategies. Chi (1985) suggests that the relationship between strategy and knowledge is interdependent.

Knowledge can be represented as one of three types: declarative, procedural, and strategic (French & Thomas, 1987; K. Thomas, 1994). Declarative knowledge is the knowledge of factual information while procedural knowledge is the knowledge of how to do something (Abernethy et al., 1993). Both declarative knowledge and procedural knowledge are task-specific within a given knowledge domain. Strategic knowledge is knowledge of general rules (i.e., memory strategies such as rehearsal) that may be generalized across all knowledge domains.

LEARNING: PRACTICE AND FEEDBACK

The goal of learning at a high level of proficiency is to automate fundamental skills. Automaticity is consistent with the Stages of Learning model (Fitts & Posner, 1967) and motor programs. While performance is how a task is executed at a given time, learning is a relatively permanent change in the level of performance. Two of the most powerful variables in learning are feedback and practice.

Feedback

Young children tend to ignore feedback, but when forced to use feedback, task performance improves (Gallagher & Thomas, 1980; J. Thomas, Solmon, & Mitchell, 1979). Research on feedback has typically investigated knowledge of results (KR), which is outcome information; less research has been done on knowledge of performance (KP) which is process-related feedback. Knowledge of performance is important for beginners, young children and real world tasks, however KR is easier to study and equal to KP for more skilled performers. Often the two terms are used interchangeably or referred to simply as *feedback*.

Newell and Barclay (1982) have identified two factors a person learns and remembers about their actions: (1) the association between the movement and its consequences, and (2) a knowledge of variables or factors that affect outcome. Younger children need more time to process KR (Newell & Kenedy, 1978), and are not able to process precise KR as well as older children and adults (J. Thomas et al., 1979). Feedback is considered an important variable in skill acquisition (Schmidt & Lee, 1998). Therefore, the feedback processing differences among younger and older children, and adults is another factor which likely explains some of the age-related differences in motor performance.

Practice

Contextual interference and practice variability are robust learning variables. Similar tasks or a task with varying environmental conditions can be presented under different conditions. The same task or conditions present on every trial is termed *constant* practice. If several tasks

or conditions are presented in groups the practice is called *blocked*. When various tasks or conditions are presented so that a different condition occurs on adjacent trials, the practice is said to be *random*.

In a meta-analysis examining variability of practice for relatively closed movement tasks, the greatest benefit from random practice was to the youngest children (Yan, Thomas, & Thomas, 1998). Polkis (1990) found that under closed-skill conditions, young children were able to use random practice, but for an open environment, young children's performance was hindered under random practice schedules. Younger children may have been overwhelmed by open and random practice, two more difficult forms of practice. Many tasks require continual adjustments from one performance to the next. To adjust to a changing environment, the learner must practice under a variety of circumstances and detect the relationship between the parameters selected and performance outcome.

Thus, feedback and practice conditions seem to benefit children but with some variations relative to age. Younger children often do not use the feedback information available to them unless they are forced to do so, while older children are more similar to adults. Practice benefits children in similar ways to adults as long as tasks and conditions do not become overly complex.

EXPERTISE AND SKILLED PERFORMANCE

The development of expertise is studied in many content areas. The focus can be on the cognitive processes that form the basis for expertise, or the applied and context-specific aspects of expertise [see Abernethy, 1988b, for a review of visual search and selective attention, or Starkes, Helsen, & Jack (Ch. 7) or K. Thomas & Thomas, 1994, for a review of decision making and expertise]. The present focus is on the development of knowledge structures (declarative, procedural, strategic) and sport performance. The study of the development of expertise in sport is appropriate because:

- The knowledge base, skills, and game performance are context-specific and can be circumscribed (J. Thomas, French, & Humphries, 1986).
- Sports often stress the cognitive processing system because time constraints on decisions are encountered (Abernethy, 1990; K. Thomas & Thomas, 1994).
- In sports, knowing when and how to execute a skill is not synonymous with executing the skill (McPherson & Thomas, 1989; K. Thomas & Thomas, 1994).

The study of expertise, as a content area and paradigm, evolved from the information-processing research, specifically with respect to the knowledge base. How knowledge is represented and differs between experts and novices has been investigated in various sports including badminton (Abernethy, 1988a), baseball (Chiesi, Spilich, & Voss, 1979; French et al., 1996; French, Spurgeon, & Nevett, 1995; Nevett & French, 1997), basketball (Allard, Graham, & Paarsalu, 1980; French & Thomas, 1987), field hockey (Starkes, 1987; Starkes & Deakin, 1984), figure skaters (Deakin & Allard, 1991), squash (Abernethy, 1990), ballet (Starkes, Deakin, Lindley, & Crisp, 1987), and tennis (McPherson 1999; McPherson & Thomas, 1989). In the following sections two aspects of expertise are addressed: (a) its development across childhood and adolescence; and (b) the relations among decision making, skills, and performance (a more theoretical basis for this discussion can be found in Abernethy et al., 1993; Gallagher et al., 1996; J. Thomas et al., 1986; or K. Thomas & Thomas, 1994).

Development of Sport Knowledge, Skill, and Performance

The fact that older children perform better than younger children in sport skills is not new information. How expertise changes the developmental nature of this finding is the focus of this section. French and Thomas (1987) and McPherson and Thomas (1989) showed that for basketball and tennis knowledge (declarative and procedural), skills, and game performance (decisions and executions), younger experts (8 to 11 years of age) not only perform better than the same-age novices, but better than older novices (11 to 13 years of age).

More recent research has moved from simulated game situations to evaluation during actual game competition. French, Spurgeon, and Nevett (1995) found that baseball skill execution during game play discriminated levels of expertise. French et al. (1996) and Nevett and French (1997) linked task-specific practice to athlete's response selection during actual baseball game competition. The young baseball players represented the game situations at a more advanced level than their novice peers but less advanced than the older youth and high school players. French et al. also noted that younger players had less opportunity for practice during the game (e.g., they were placed in the outfield) or less game time than older players. Experience and maturation (e.g., the relative age effect) are possible explanations for this finding.

McPherson (1999) examined tennis performance skills and problem representations during singles competition for expert and novice 10- and 12-year olds and adults. Player's level of competition rather than age influenced their task performance. Regardless of age, experts were able to make more forceful tennis shots (e.g., executions) during the competition and monitored the success of their actions with the intention of developing solutions or making modifications. The behavioral data indicated that the experts made similar percentages of sophisticated response selections however the verbal data demonstrated that the adult expert's response selections were more sophisticated than the youth experts. The youth experts has less tactical action plans, used fewer support strategies and relied less on evaluation of the current context. A major implication from the findings was it appeared that adult experts used cognitive flexibility in their approach to game situations. Adults differed from children regardless of level of expertise because they used more regulatory strategies (monitoring performance) than the youth. Thus, perhaps the adults used a generalized learning strategy. Regardless of age, the novices did not use statements about the execution of the motor skills suggesting they were beginning to get the concept of tennis competition rather than focusing on learning motor skills.

Relations among Sports Knowledge, Skill, and Performance

Both French and Thomas (1987) and McPherson and Thomas (1989) found significant multivariate relationships between knowledge and skill as one component and game performance as the other. In both instances, the canonical correlation was above 0.70. For basketball, knowledge and skills (shooting and dribbling) related significantly to game performance (decisions and execution). For tennis, knowledge and ground strokes related significantly to game performance (decisions and execution). Thus, the relations between knowledge, skill, and game performance were consistent across the two sports for children ages 8 to 13 years. French and Thomas (1987) followed the younger children (both experts and novices) over the course of a basketball season and measured knowledge, skill, and game performance at the end of the season. Only basketball knowledge improved over the season; skill did not. The only game-performance measure to improve over the season was decisions (more good ones). At the end of the season, knowledge and decisions were the only variables that remained significantly correlated. Thus, the cognitive components of performance (knowledge about basketball and decisions during the game) appear to be improving in advance of skill components (dribbling, shooting, execution).

French and Thomas (1987) suggest that this result may be caused by what the coaches emphasized in practice (cognitive aspects of the game rather than skill), as indicated by coaches' and children's self-reports.

Children in studies by French and Thomas (1987) and McPherson and Thomas (1989) were interviewed to assess their procedural knowledge about basketball and tennis. Tapes of these interviews were coded according to specific criteria for analysis. The results suggested that experts have a larger, more complex, and better organized knowledge base than novices in basketball and tennis. The concept that procedural knowledge is more developed in experts is supported by their greater and more varied use of IF-THEN statements in both sports and the lack of their use by novices. In addition, McPherson and Thomas (1989) provided support for the idea that sports experts develop IF-THEN-DO productions. They show that level of expertise is what matters in the relation between THEN and DO. Younger experts had more disagreements between their ability, to select an action (THEN) and execute it (DO) than did novices. This was because experts selected more complex and difficult actions to execute. Older experts had fewer disagreements between actions selected and executed than did younger experts demonstrating that skill level was continuing to increase with practice and experience. We might speculate that the successful incorporation of the DO part into a single unit IF-THEN-DO loop is the real mark of expertise. That is, greater expertise results in a greater number of agreements between the "condition/action selection" and "execution" phases of performance. In this instance automaticity might well mean a "bonded" IF-THEN-DO loop.

Finally, the role of experience specifically practice has been examined in experts and the development of expertise. Practice alone does not guarantee expertise. For example, ballet dancers with similar amounts of experience and practice demonstrated markedly different levels of expertise (Starkes et al., 1987). The quality of practice has been hypothesized as one factor facilitating expertise (Ericsson & Charness, 1994; Helson, Starkes, & Hodges, 1998; K. Thomas & Thomas, 1999). Although 10,000 hours of practice seems a critical point in the quantity of practice, describing the critical components of quality is more difficult.

FUTURE RESEARCH

Research indicates that all children do not develop at the same rate, and the rates vary across characteristics (e.g.,

growth, cognition) and within children. Mean performances show trends that are smooth and linear. Within individuals, there is day-to-day variation and times when change is rapid or slow. Some of the underlying causes of individual differences and of age-related increases are beginning to be understood. Early research in motor development focused on description, while recent research has often used experimental or quasi-experimental designs to allow some manipulation of characteristics. While being able to influence development by manipulation is desirable, much can be learned by careful description and observation. As McCall (1977) suggested:

> Developmental psychologists should accord description the esteem other disciplines do because much has been learned at its hand: Consider the theory of evolution, the plate theory of continental drift, and our knowledge of the early evolution of Homosapiens. Paleontology, geology, and astronomy seem to be alive and well without manipulating fossils, continents, or heavenly bodies. (p. 337)

In addition, there is a complex interaction of factors that influence performance during childhood including: growth, cognition, motor patterns, and practice. While development can be described within those factors, it cannot be understood without looking across them. Individuals vary greatly, and the causes of those variations are of critical interest. As with gender, even though there are individual differences and each child is unique, children are more alike than different. All children move in a linear manner toward maturity through childhood, but all children exhibit variability in rate between and across factors of development.

Where should research on the developmental nature of skill acquisition go from here? We believe that the challenge, but also the essence of developmental research, will continue to be a more interdisciplinary approach to studying the questions of motor development. Clearly these are not new ideas, but to provide new information and insight, a move should be made away from typical descriptive and cross-sectional studies. Longitudinal and multiple studies, with factors from several areas, will be needed to answer these questions. Studies of experts, as well as the use of technology and dependent variables from several areas (e.g., biomechanics, neurophysiology), indicate the benefits from novel approaches to studying developmental issues. Efforts must be combined, searching for the best explanations from a variety of theories and paradigms, rather than adhering to the egocentric view, which sees these as competitive.

Crosscultural and gender studies can contribute to the understanding of the roles of genetics and environment. Studies of parents and siblings may help to understand those factors that limit performance. Studies following the same children across childhood and measuring the many contributors to performance may be informative as to how performance is enhanced (or limited) and how participation is encouraged. All of these efforts are costly, time consuming, and ambitious. Progress can be made through smaller projects that study varying combinations of fewer factors. In addition, a shift from descriptive research to experimental research or to the kind of descriptive research that uses multiple dependent variables is desirable. Behavior is complex, and this complexity must be captured within appropriate research designs.

REFERENCES

Abernethy, B. (1988a). The effects of age and expertise upon perceptual skill development in a racquet sport. *Research Quarterly for Exercise and Sport, 59,* 210–221.

Abernethy, B. (1988b). Visual search in sport and ergonomics: Its relationship to selective attention and performer expertise. *Human Performance, 1,* 205–235.

Abernethy, B. (1990). Expertise, visual search, and information pick-up in squash. *Perception, 18,* 63–77.

Abernethy, B. (1993). Attention. In R. Singer, M. Murphey, & L.K. Tennant (Eds.), *Handbook of research on sport psychology* (pp. 127–170). New York: Macmillan.

Abernethy, B., Thomas, K.T., & Thomas, J.R. (1993). Strategies for improving understanding of motor expertise (or mistakes we have made and things we have learned!). In J.L. Starkes & F. Allard (Eds.), *Cognitive issues in motor expertise* (pp. 317–358). Amsterdam: Elsevier.

Allard, F., Graham, S., & Paarsalu, M.E. (1980). Perception in sport: Basketball. *Journal of Sport Psychology, 2,* 14–21.

Assaiante, C., Thomachot, B., Aurenty, R., & Amblard, B. (1998). Organizational balance control in toddlers during the first year of independent walking. *Journal of Motor Behavior, 30,* 114–129.

Atkinson, R.C., & Shiffrin, R.M. (1968). Human memory: A proposed system and its control process. In K.W. Spence & J.T. Spence (Eds.), *The psychology of learning and motivation* (Vol. 2, pp. 90–197). New York: Academic Press.

Bard, C., Fleury, M., & Hay, L. (Eds.). (1990). *Development of eye hand coordination across the life span.* Columbia: University of South Carolina.

Barrett, S.E., & Shepp, B.E. (1988). Developmental changes in attentional skills: The effect of irrelevant variations on encoding and response selection. *Journal of Experimental Child Psychology, 45,* 382–399.

Baxter-Jones, A., Helms, P., Maffull, N., Baines-Preece, J., & Preece, M. (1995). Growth and development of male gymnasts, swimmers, soccer and tennis players: A longitudinal study. *Annals of Human Biology, 22,* 381–394.

Bloom, B.S. (1964). *Stability and change in human characteristics.* New York: Wiley.

Boucher, J., & Mutimer, B. (1994). The relative age phenomenon in sport: A replication and extension with ice-hockey players. *Research Quarterly for Exercise and Sport, 65,* 377–381.

Branta, C., Haubenstricker, J., & Seefeldt, V. (1984). Age changes in motor skills during childhood and adolescence. In R.L. Terjung (Ed.), *Exercise and sport sciences reviews* (Vol. 12, pp. 467–520). Lexington, MA: Heath.

Brewer, J., Balsom, P., Davis, J., & Ekblom, B. (1992). The influence of birth date and physical development on the selection of a male junior international soccer squad. *Journal of Sports Sciences, 10,* 561–562.

Broekoff, J. (1985). The effects of physical activity on physical growth and development. In G.A. Stull & H.M. Eckert (Eds.), *The academy papers: Effects of physical activity on children* (pp. 75–87). Champaign, IL: Human Kinetics.

Burton, A.W. (1987). The effect of number of movement components on response time. *Journal of Human Movement Studies, 13,* 231–247.

Calvin, W.H. (1982). Did throwing stones shape hominid brain evolution? *Ethology and Sociobiology, 3,* 115–124.

Calvin, W.H. (1983). A stone's throw and its launch window: Timing precision and its implications for language and hominid brains. *Journal of Theoretical Biology, 104,* 121–135.

Carter, J.E.L. (1980). *The Heath-Carter Somatotype method.* San Diego, CA: San Diego State University Syllabus Service.

Chase, W.G., & Simon, H.A. (1973). Perception in chess. *Cognitive Psychology, 4,* 55–81.

Chi, M.T.H. (1976). Short-term memory limitations in children: Capacity of processing deficits? *Memory and Cognition, 4,* 559–572.

Chi, M.T.H. (1977). Age differences in memory span. *Journal of Experimental Child Psychology, 23,* 266–281.

Chi, M.T.H. (1978). Knowledge structures and memory development. In R.S. Siegler (Ed.), *Children's thinking: What develops?* (pp. 73–105). Hillsdale, NJ: Erlbaum.

Chi, M.T.H. (1982). Knowledge development and memory performance. In M. Friedman, J.P. Das, & N. O'Connor (Eds.), *Intelligence and learning* (pp. 221–230). New York: Plenum Press.

Chi, M.T.H. (1985). Interactive roles of knowledge and strategies in the development of organized sorting and recall. In S.F. Chipman, J.W. Segal, & R. Glaser (Eds.), *Thinking and learning skills: Research and open questions* (Vol. 2, pp. 457–483). Hillsdale, NJ: Erlbaum.

Chi, M.T.H., & Gallagher, J.D. (1982). Speed of processing: A developmental source of limitation. *Topics of Learning and Learning Disabilities, 2,* 23–32.

Chi, M.T.H., & Koeske, R.D. (1983). Network representation of a child's dinosaur knowledge. *Developmental Psychology, 19,* 29–39.

Chiesi, H.L., Spilich, G.J., & Voss, J.F. (1979). Acquisition of domain related information in relation to high and low domain knowledge. *Journal of Verbal Learning and Verbal Behavior, 18,* 257–273.

Clark, J.E. (1995). Dynamical systems perspective on gait. In R.L. Craik & C.A. Oates (Eds.), *Gait analysis: Theory and application* (pp. 79–86). St. Louis, MO: Mosby.

Clarke, H. (1967). Characteristics of the young athlete: A longitudinal look. In *AMA proceedings of the eighth annual conference on the Medical Aspects of Sports–1966* (pp. 49–57). Chicago: American Medical Association.

Darlington, P.J., Jr. (1975). Group selection, altruism, reinforcement, and throwing in human evolution. *Proceedings of the National Academy of Science, USA, 72,* 3748–3752.

Dempster, F.N. (1988). Short-term memory development in childhood and adolescence. In C.J. Brainerd & M. Pressley (Eds.), *Basic processes in memory development: Progress in cognitive development research* (pp. 209–248). New York: Springer-Verlag.

Dennis, W. (1935). The effect of restricted practice upon the reaching, sitting, and standing of two infants. *Journal of Genetic Psychology, 47,* 17–32.

Dennis, W., & Dennis, M.G. (1940). The effect of cradling practices upon the onset of walking in Hopi children. *Journal of Genetic Psychology, 56,* 77–86.

deOliveria, A., Gallagher, J., & Smiley-Oyen, A. (1999). The influence of experience and selective attention on the development of balance control. *Journal of Sport & Exercise Psychology, 21,* S37.

Dunham, P., & Reid, D. (1987). Information processing: Effect of stimulus speed variation on coincidence-anticipation of children. *Journal of Human Movement Studies, 13,* 151–156.

Eaton, W.O. (1989). Childhood sex differences in motor performance and activity level: Findings and implications. In B. Kirkcaldy (Ed.), *Normalities and abnormalities in human movement* (pp. 58–75). Basel, Switzerland: Karger.

Eaton, W.O., & Enns, L.R. (1986). Sex differences in human motor activity level. *Psychological Bulletin, 100,* 19–28.

Eaton, W.O., & Yu, A.P. (1989). Are sex differences in child motor activity level a function of sex differences in maturational status? *Child Development, 60,* 1005–1011.

Eckert, H.M. (1987). *Motor development* (3rd ed.). Indianapolis, IN: Benchmark.

Ericsson, K.A., & Charness, N. (1994). Expert performance: Its structure and acquisition. *American Psychologist, 49,* 725–747.

Espenschade, A.S. (1960). Motor development. In W.R. Johnson (Ed.), *Science and medicine of exercise and sports* (pp. 419–439). New York: Harper & Row.

Espenschade, A.S. (1963). Restudy of relationships between physical performances of school children and age, height, and weight. *Research Quarterly, 34,* 144–153.

Fitts, P.M. (1954). The information capacity of the human motor system in controlling the amplitude of movements. *Journal of Experimental Psychology, 47,* 381–391.

Fitts, P.M., & Posner, M.I. (1967). *Human Performance.* Belmont, CA: Brooks/Cole.

Flavell, J.H. (1977). *Cognitive development.* Englewood Cliffs, NJ: Prentice-Hall.

Fortney, V.L. (1983). The kinematics and kinetics of the running pattern of 2-, 4-, and 6-year-old children. *Research Quarterly for Exercise and Sport, 54,* 126–135.

French, K.E., Nevett, M.E., Spurgeon, J.H., Graham, K.C., Rink, J.E., & McPherson, S.L. (1996). Knowledge representation and problem solution in expert and novice youth baseball players. *Research Quarterly for Exercise and Sport, 67,* 386–395.

French, K.E., Spurgeon, J.H., & Nevett, M.E. (1995). Expert-novice differences in cognitive and skill execution components of youth baseball performance. *Research Quarterly for Exercise and Sport, 66,* 194–201.

French, K.E., & Thomas, J.R. (1987). The relation of knowledge development to children's basketball performance. *Journal of Sport Psychology, 9,* 15–32.

Fronske, H., Blakemore, C., & Abendroth-Smith, J. (1997). The effect of critical cues on overhand throwing efficiency of elementary school children. *Physical Educator, 54,* 88–95.

Gallagher, J.D. (1980). *Adult-child motor performance differences: A developmental perspective of control processing deficits.* Unpublished doctoral dissertation, Louisiana State University, Baton Rouge.

Gallagher, J.D., & Fisher, J. (1983). A developmental investigation of the effects of grouping on memory capacity. In C. Branta & D. Feltz (Eds.), *Psychology of motor behavior and sport* [Abstracts from NASPSPA and CSPSLP, p. 160]. East Lansing: Michigan State University.

Gallagher, J.D., French, K.E., Thomas, K., & Thomas, J.R. (1996). Expertise in youth sport: The relationship between knowledge and skill. In F.L. Smoll & R.E. Smith (Eds.), *Children and youth sport: A biopsychosocial perspective* (pp. 338–358). Dubuque, IA: Brown & Benchmark.

Gallagher, J.D., & Thomas, J.R. (1980). Effects of varying post-KR intervals upon children's motor performance. *Journal of Motor Behavior, 12,* 41–46.

Gallagher, J.D., & Thomas, J.R. (1984). Rehearsal strategy effects on developmental differences for recall of a movement series. *Research Quarterly for Exercise and Sport, 55,* 123–128.

Gallagher, J.D., & Thomas, J.R. (1986). Developmental effects of grouping and recoding on learning a movement series. *Research Quarterly for Exercise and Sport, 57,* 117–127.

Gallahue, D.L. (1989). *Understanding motor development: Infants, children, adolescence* (2nd ed.). Indianapolis, IN: Benchmark.

Glassow, R., & Kruse, P. (1960). Motor performance of girls age 6 to 14 years. *Research Quarterly, 31,* 426–433.

Hagen, J., & West, R. (1970). The effects of a pay-off matrix on selective attention. *Human Development, 13,* 43–52.

Halverson, L.E., Roberton, M.A., & Langendorfer, S. (1982). Development of the overarm throw: Movement and ball velocity changes by seventh grade. *Research Quarterly for Exercise and Sport, 53,* 198–205.

Haubenstricker, J., & Seefeldt, V. (1986). Acquisition of motor skills during childhood. In V. Seefeldt (Ed.), *Physical activity and well-being* (pp. 41–102). Reston, VA: American Alliance for Health, Physical Education, Recreation, and Dance.

Hay, L., Bard, C., Fleury, M., & Teasdale, N. (1991). Kinematics of aiming in direction and amplitude: A developmental study. *Acta Psychologica, 77,* 203–215.

Haywood, K.M. (1993). *Life span motor development* (2nd ed.). Champaign, IL: Human Kinetics.

Helsen, W.F., Starkes, J.L., & Hodges, N.J. (1998). Team sports and the theory of deliberate practice. *Journal of Sport & Exercise Psychology, 20,* 12–34.

Heriza, C.B. (1991). Implications of a dynamical systems approach to understanding infant kicking behavior. *Physical Therapy, 71,* 222–235.

Isaac, B. (1987). Throwing and human evolution. *African Archaeological Review, 5,* 3–17.

Jensen, J.L., Ulrich, B.D., Thelen, E., Schneider, K., & Zernichke, R.F. (1994). Adaptive dynamics of the leg movement patterns of human infants: I. The effects of posture on spontaneous kicking. *Journal of Motor Behavior, 26,* 303–312.

Jensen, J.L., Ulrich, B.D., Thelen, E., Schneider, K., & Zernichke, R.F. (1995). Adaptive dynamics of the leg movement patterns of human infants: III. Age-related differences in limb control. *Journal of Motor Behavior, 27,* 366–374.

Jensen, R.K. (1981). The effect of a 12-month growth period on the body movements of inertia of children. *Medicine and Science in Sport and Exercise, 13,* 238–242.

Kail, R. (1986). Sources of age differences in speed of processing. *Child Development, 57,* 969–987.

Kail, R. (1988). Developmental functions for speeds of cognitive processes. *Journal of Experimental Child Psychology, 45,* 339–364.

Kail, R. (1991). Processing time declines exponentially during childhood and adolescence. *Developmental Psychology, 27,* 259–266.

Kerr, R. (1985). Fitts' law and motor control in children. In J. Clark & H.H. Humphrey (Eds.), *Motor development: Current selected research* (pp. 45–53). Princeton, NJ: Princeton Book.

Ladewig, I., & Gallagher, J. (1994). Cue use to enhance selective attention. *Research Quarterly for Exercise and Sport, 65,* S64.

Ladewig, I., Gallagher, J., & Campos, W. (1994). Development of selective attention: Relationship of dynamic cue use to varying levels of task interference. *Journal of Sport & Exercise Psychology, 16,* S75.

Leavitt, J. (1979). Cognitive demands of skating and stick handling in ice hockey. *Canadian Journal of Applied Sport Science, 4,* 46–55.

Lindberg, M.A. (1980). Is the knowledge base development a necessary and sufficient condition for memory development? *Journal of Experimental Child Psychology, 30,* 401–410.

Magill, R.A., & Anderson, D.I. (1996). The concept of readiness applied to the acquisition of motor skills. In F.L. Smoll & R.E. Smith (Eds.), *Children and youth in sport: A biopsychosocial perspective* (pp. 57–72). Dubuque, IA: Brown & Benchmark.

Malina, R.M. (1975). *Growth and development: The first twenty years in man.* Minneapolis, MN: Burgess.

Malina, R.M. (1984). Physical growth and maturation. In J.R. Thomas (Ed.), *Motor development during childhood and adolescence* (pp. 1–26). Minneapolis, MN: Burgess.

Malina, R.M. (1986). Physical growth and maturation. In V. Seefeldt (Ed.), *Physical activity and well-being* (pp. 3–38). Reston, VA: American Alliance for Health, Physical Education, Recreation, and Dance.

Masser, L.S. (1993). Critical cues help first-grade students' achievement in handstands and forward rolls. *Journal of Teaching in Physical Education, 12,* 302–312.

McCall, R.B. (1977). Challenges to a science of developmental psychology. *Child Development, 48,* 333–344.

McCracken, H.D. (1983). Movement control in a reciprocal tapping task: A developmental study. *Journal of Motor Behavior, 15,* 262–279.

McGraw, M.B. (1935). *Growth: A study of Johnny and Jimmy.* New York: Appleton-Century-Crofts.

McHenry, H.M. (1982). The pattern of human evolution: Studies in bipedalism, mastication and encephalization. *American Review of Anthropology, 11,* 151–173.

McPherson, S.L. (1999). Expert-novice differences in performance skills and problem representations of youth and adults during tennis competition. *Research Quarterly for Exercise and Sport, 70,* 233–251.

McPherson, S.L., & Thomas, J.R. (1989). Relation of knowledge and performance in boys' tennis: Age and expertise. *Journal of Experimental Child Psychology, 48,* 190–211.

Meyer, D.E., Abrams, R.A., Kornblum, S., Wright, C.E., & Smith, J.E.K. (1988). Optimality in human motor performance: Ideal control of rapid aimed movements. *Psychological Review, 95,* 340–370.

Miller, M.B. (1990). *The use of labeling to improve movement recall involving learning disabled children.* Unpublished doctoral dissertation, University of Pittsburgh, PA.

Nelson, J.K., Thomas, J.R., Nelson, K.R., & Abraham, P.C. (1986). Gender differences in children's throwing performance: Biology and environment. *Research Quarterly for Exercise and Sport, 57,* 280–287.

Nelson, K.R., Thomas, J.R., & Nelson, J.K. (1991). Longitudinal changes in throwing performance: Gender differences. *Research Quarterly for Exercise and Sport, 62,* 105–108.

Nevett, M.E., & French, K.E. (1997). The development of sport-specific planning, rehearsal, and updating of plans during defensive youth baseball game performance. *Research Quarterly for Exercise and Sport, 68,* 203–214.

Newell, K.M., & Barclay, C.R. (1982). Developing knowledge about action. In J.A.S. Kelso & J.E. Clark (Eds.), *The development of movement control and co-ordination* (pp. 175–212). New York: Wiley.

Newell, K.M., & Kennedy, J.A. (1978). Knowledge of results and children's motor learning. *Developmental Psychology, 14,* 531–536.

Ornstein, P.A., & Naus, M.J. (1985). Effects of knowledge base on children's memory strategies. In H.W. Reese (Ed.), *Advances in child development and behavior* (pp. 113–148). New York: Academic Press.

Pascual-Leone, J. (1970). A mathematical model for the transition rule in Piaget's developmental stages. *Acta Psychologica, 32,* 301–345.

Passer, M.W. (1996). At what age are children ready to compete? Some psychological considerations. In F.L. Smoll & R.E. Smith (Eds.), *Children and youth sport: A biopsychosocial perspective* (pp. 73–82). Dubuque, IA: Brown & Benchmark.

Payne, G.V., & Isaacs, L.D. (1998). *Human motor development: A lifespan approach.* Mountain View, CA: Mayfield.

Piaget, J. (1952). *The origins of intelligence in children.* New York: International Universities.

Plamondon, R., & Alimi, A.M. (1997). Speed/accuracy trade-offs in target-directed movements. *Behavioral and Brain Sciences, 20,* 279–303.

Polkis, G.A. (1990). *The effects of environmental context and contextual interference on the learning of motor skills: A developmental perspective.* Unpublished doctoral dissertation, University of Pittsburgh, PA.

Ransdell, L.B., & Wells, C.L. (1999). Sex differences in athletic performance. *Women in Sport and Physical Activity, 8,* 55–81.

Rarick, G.L., & Smoll, F. (1967). Stability of growth in strength and motor performance from childhood to adolescence. *Human Biology, 39,* 295–306.

Reid, G. (1980). The effects of motor strategy instruction in the short-term memory of the mentally retarded. *Journal of Motor Behavior, 12,* 221–227.

Roberton, M.A. (1977). Stability of stage categorizations across trials: Implications for the "stage theory" of overarm throw development. *Journal of Human Movement Studies, 3,* 49–59.

Roberton, M.A. (1978). Longitudinal evidence for developmental stages in the forceful overarm throw. *Journal of Human Movement Studies, 4,* 161–175.

Roberton, M.A. (1982). Describing "stages" within and across motor tasks. In J.A.S. Kelso & J.E. Clark (Eds.), *The development of movement control and co-ordination* (pp. 294–307). New York: Wiley.

Roberton, M.A. (1984). Changing motor patterns during childhood. In J.R. Thomas (Ed.), *Motor development during childhood and adolescence* (pp. 48–90). Minneapolis, MN: Burgess.

Roberton, M.A., & DiRocco, P. (1981). Validating a motor skill sequence for mentally retarded children. *American Corrective Therapy Journal, 35,* 148–154.

Roberton, M.A., Halverson, L.E., Langendorfer, S., & Williams, K. (1979). Longitudinal changes in children's overarm throw ball velocities. *Research Quarterly for Exercise and Sport, 50,* 256–264.

Rosblad, B. (1997). Roles of visual information for control of reaching movements in children. *Journal of Motor Behavior, 29,* 174–182.

Ross, A. (1976). *Psychological aspects of learning disabilities and reading disorders.* New York: McGraw-Hill.

Ross, J.G., & Gilbert, G.G. (1985). The national children and youth fitness study: A summary of findings. *Journal of Physical Education, Recreation and Dance, 56,* 45–50.

Ross, J.G., & Pate, R.R. (1987). The national children and youth fitness study: II. A summary of findings. *Journal of Physical Education, Recreation and Dance, 58,* 51–56.

Salmoni, A.W., & Pascoe, C. (1979). Fitts reciprocal tapping task: A developmental study. In G.C. Roberts & K.M. Newell (Eds.), *Psychology of motor behavior and sport—1978* (pp. 355–386). Champaign, IL: Human Kinetics.

Scammon, R.E. (1930). The measurement of the body in childhood. In J.A. Harris, C.M. Jackson, D.G. Jackson, & R.E. Scammon (Eds.), *The measurement of man* (pp. 171–215). Minneapolis: University of Minnesota.

Schachar, R., Rutter, M., & Smith, A. (1981). The characteristics of situationally and pervasively hyperactive children: Implications for syndrome definition. *Journal of Child Psychology and Psychiatry, 22,* 375–392.

Schmidt, R.A., & Lee, T.D. (1998). *Motor control and learning: A behavioral emphasis* (3rd ed.). Champaign, IL: Human Kinetics.

Schroeder, R.K. (1981). *The effects of rehearsal on information processing efficiency of severely/profoundly retarded normal individuals.* Unpublished doctoral dissertation, Louisiana State University, Baton Rouge.

Seefeldt, V., & Haubenstricker, J. (1982). Patterns, phases, or stages: An analytical model for the study of developmental movement. In J.A.S. Kelso & J.E. Clark (Eds.), *The development of movement control and co-ordination* (pp. 309–318). New York: Wiley.

Seefeldt, V., Reuschlein, S., & Vogel, P. (1972, March). *Sequencing motor skills withing the physical education curriculum.* Paper presented to the National Convention of the American Association for Health, Physical Education and Recreation, Houston, TX.

Shepp, B.E., Barrett, S.E., & Kolbet, L.K. (1987). The development of selection attention: Holistic perception versus resources allocation. *Journal of Experimental Child Psychology, 43,* 159–180.

Shiffrin, R.M., & Schneider, W. (1977). Controlled and automatic human information processing: II. Perceptual learning, automatic attending, and a general theory. *Psychological Review, 84,* 121–190.

Smoll, F.L., & Schutz, R.W. (1990). Quantifying gender differences in physical performance: A developmental perspective. *Developmental Psychology, 26,* 360–369.

Starkes, J.L. (1987). Skill in field hockey: The nature of the cognitive advantage. *Journal of Sport Psychology, 9,* 146–160.

Starkes, J.L., & Deakin, J.M. (1984). Perception in sport: A cognitive approach to skilled performance. In W.F. Straub & J.M. Williams (Eds.), *Cognitive sport psychology* (pp. 115–128). Lansing, NY: Sport Science Associates.

Starkes, J.L., Deakin, J.M., Lindley, S., & Crisp, F. (1987). Motor versus verbal recall of ballet sequences by young expert dancers. *Journal of Sport Psychology, 9,* 222–230.

Stelmach, G.E., & Thomas, J.R. (1997). What's different in speed/accuracy trade-offs in young and elderly subjects. *Behavioral and Brain Sciences, 20,* 321.

Stratton, R. (1978). Information processing deficits in children's motor performance: Implications for instruction. *Motor Skills: Theory into Practice, 3,* 49–55.

Sugden, D.A. (1980). Movement speed in children. *Journal of Motor Behavior, 12,* 125–132.

Tanner, J.M. (1978). *Fetus into man: Physical growth from conception to maturity.* Cambridge, MA: Harvard University Press.

Thelen, E., & Ulrich, B.D. (1991). Hidden skills: A dynamic systems analysis of treadmill stepping during the first year. *Monographs of the Society of Research in Child Development, 56*(1, Serial No. 223).

Thomas, J.R. (1980). Acquisition of motor skills: Information processing differences between children and adults. *Research Quarterly, 50,* 158–173.

Thomas, J.R. (1984a). Children's motor skill development. In J.R. Thomas (Ed.), *Motor development during childhood and adolescence* (pp. 91–104). Minneapolis, MN. Burgess.

Thomas, J.R. (1984b). *Motor development during childhood and adolescence.* Minneapolis, MN: Burgess.

Thomas, J.R. (1984c). Planning "Kiddie" research: Little "Kids" but big problems. In J.R. Thomas (Ed.), *Motor development during childhood and adolescence* (pp. 260–273). Minneapolis, MN: Burgess.

Thomas, J.R. (2000). C.H. McCloy lecture: Children's control, learning, and performance of motor skills. *Research Quarterly for Exercise and Sport, 71,* 1–9.

Thomas, J.R., & French, K.E. (1985). Gender differences across age in motor performance: A meta-analysis. *Psychological Bulletin, 98,* 260–282.

Thomas, J.R., French, K.E., & Humphries, C.A. (1986). Knowledge development and sport skill performance: Directions for motor behavior research. *Journal of Sport Psychology, 8,* 259–272.

Thomas, J.R., Gallagher, J.D., & Purvis, G. (1981). Reaction time and anticipation time: Effects of development. *Research Quarterly for Exercise and Sport, 52,* 359–367.

Thomas, J.R., Lee, A.M., & Thomas, K.T. (1988). *Physical education for children, concepts into practice.* Champaign, IL: Human Kinetics.

Thomas, J.R., & Marzke, M. (1992). The development of gender differences in throwing: Is human evolution a factor? In R. Christina & H. Eckert (Eds.), *The academy papers: Enhancing human performance in sport* (pp. 60–76). Champaign, IL: Human Kinetics.

Thomas, J.R., Nelson, J.K., & Church, G. (1991). A developmental analysis of gender differences in health related physical fitness. *Pediatric Exercise Science, 3,* 28–42.

Thomas, J.R., Solmon, M.A., & Mitchell, B. (1979). Precision knowledge of results and motor performance: Relationship to age. *Research Quarterly for Exercise and Sport, 50,* 687–698.

Thomas, J.R., & Stratton, R. (1977). Effect of divided attention on children's rhythmic response. *Research Quarterly, 48,* 428–435.

Thomas, J.R., & Thomas, K.T. (1988). Development of gender differences in physical activity. *Quest, 40,* 219–229.

Thomas, J.R., Thomas, K.T., Lee, A.M., & Testerman, E. (1983). Age differences in use of strategy for recall of movement in a large scale environment. *Research Quarterly for Exercise and Sport, 54,* 264–272.

Thomas, J.R., Yan, J.H., & Stelmach, G.E. (2000). Movement substructures change as a function of practice in children and adults. *Journal of Experimental Child Psychology, 75,* 228–244.

Thomas, K.T. (1994). The development of expertise: From Leeds to legend. *Quest, 46,* 199–210.

Thomas, K.T., & Thomas, J.R. (1987). Perceptual development and its differential influence on limb positioning under two movement conditions in children. In J.E. Clark (Ed.), *Advances in motor development research* (pp. 83–96). Baltimore: AMS Press.

Thomas, K.T., & Thomas, J.R. (1994). Developing expertise in sport: The relation of knowledge and performance. *International Journal of Sport Psychology, 25,* 295–312.

Thomas, K.T., & Thomas, J.R. (1999). What squirrels in the trees predict about expert athletes. *International Journal of Sport Psychology, 30,* 221–234.

Tipper, S.P., MacQueen, G.M., & Brehaut, J.C. (1988). Negative priming between response modalities: Evidence for the central locus of inhibition in selective attention. *Perception and Psychophysics, 43,* 42–52.

Tobias, P.V. (1968). Cultural hominization among the earliest African Pleistocen hominids. *Proceedings of the Prehistoric Society, 33,* 367–376.

Tudor, J. (1979). Developmental differences in motor task integration: A test of Pascual-Leone's Theory of constructive operators. *Journal of Experimental Psychology, 28,* 314–322.

Ulrich, B. (1997). Dynamic systems theory and skill development in infants and children. In K.J. Connolly & H. Forssberg (Eds.), *Neurophysiology and neuropsychology of motor development* (pp. 319–345). Cambridge, MA: MacKeith Press.

Ulrich, B.D., Jensen, J.L., Thelen, E., Schneider, K., & Zernichke, R.F. (1994). Adaptive dynamics of the leg movement patterns of human infants: II. Treadmill stepping in infants and adults. *Journal of Motor Behavior, 26,* 313–324.

VanDyne, H.J. (1973). Foundations of tactical perception in three- to seven-year olds. *Journal of the Association of Perception, 8,* 1–9.

Washburn, S.L., & Moore, R. (1980). *Ape into human.* Boston: Little, Brown.

Weiss, M.R. (1983). Modeling and motor performance: A developmental perspective. *Research Quarterly for Exercise and Sport, 54,* 190–197.

Weiss, M.R., & Bredemeier, B.J. (1983). Developmental sport psychology: A theoretical perspective for studying children in sport. *Journal of Sport Psychology, 5,* 216–230.

Weiss, M.R., & Klint, K.A. (1987). "Show and tell" in the gymnasium: An investigation of developmental differences in modeling and verbal rehearsal of motor skills. *Research Quarterly for Exercise and Sport, 58,* 234–241.

Whitall, J. (1991). The developmental effects of concurrent cognitive and locomotor skills: Time-sharing from a dynamical perspective. *Journal of Experimental Child Psychology, 51,* 245–266.

Whitney, S. (1991). *Development of postural control in young children.* Unpublished doctoral dissertation, University of Pittsburgh, PA.

Wickstrom, R.L. (1983). *Fundamental motor patterns* (3rd ed.). Philadelphia: Lea & Febiger.

Wild, M.R. (1938). The behavior pattern of throwing and some observation concerning its course of development in children. *Research Quarterly, 9,* 20–24.

Williams, A.M., & Davids, K. (1998). Visual search strategy, selective attention and expertise in soccer. *Research Quarterly for Exercise and Sport, 69,* 111–128.

Williams, H., Temple, J., & Bateman, J. (1979). A test battery to assess intrasensory and intersensory development of young children. *Perceptual and Motor Skills, 48,* 643–659.

Williams, H.G. (1983). *Perceptual and motor development.* Englewood Cliffs, NJ: Prentice Hall.

Winther, K.T., & Thomas, J.R. (1981). Developmental differences in children's labeling of movement. *Journal of Motor Behavior, 13,* 77–90.

Woollacott, M.H., & Shumway-Cook, A. (Eds.). (1989). *Development of posture and gait across the life span.* Columbia: University of South Carolina Press.

Yan, J.H., Hinrichs, R.N., Payne, V.G., & Thomas, J.R. (2000). Normalized jerk: A measure to capture development characteristics of young girls' overarm throwing. *Journal of Applied Biomechanics, 16,* 196–203.

Yan, J.H., Payne, V.G., & Thomas, J.R. (2000). Developmental kinematics of young females' overarm throwing. *Research Quarterly for Exercise and Sport, 71,* 92–98.

Yan, J.H., Thomas, J.R., Stelmach, G.E., & Thomas, K.T. (2000). Developmental features of rapid aiming arm movements across the lifespan. *Journal of Motor Behavior, 32,* 121–140.

Yan, J.H., Thomas, J.R., & Thomas, K.T. (1998). Children's age moderates the effect of practice variability: A quantitative review. *Research Quarterly for Exercise and Sport, 69,* 210–215.

CHAPTER 3

Attention

BRUCE ABERNETHY

Attention is fundamental to skilled motor performance. Indeed, it is difficult to imagine that there can be anything more important to the learning and performance of sports skills than paying attention to the task at hand. The anecdotal reports of athletes who have performed poorly because they were not quite prepared (e.g., the 100-meter sprinter who "missed" the gun), lost concentration (e.g., the pistol shooter whose thoughts wandered away from the target to internal thoughts of hunger and fatigue), became distracted (e.g., the basketball player who was disturbed at the free throw line by crowd noise), or became confused (e.g., the defensive player in football who was disoriented by the sheer complexity of the opposition's offensive pattern), all bear testimony to the importance of the optimal, selective, and sustained allocation of attention. At a superficial level, the notion of paying attention (or concentrating) would appear to be a rather straightforward one, yet psychologists have long grappled with the intricacies and complexities of this intuitive notion.

Interest in the concept of attention is at least as old as the field of experimental psychology itself (see Boring, 1970 for a review) with the early works having their origins in phenomenology. Hamilton (1859), James (1890), Jastrow (1891), Wundt (1905), Pillsbury (1908), and Titchener (1908) wrote about the concept of attention from introspective perspectives. However, such essentially philosophical works were supplemented by some, now classical, empirical examinations of divided attention by Binet (1890), Bliss (1892–1893), Solomons and Stein (1896), and Welch (1898). Of the early works by the phenomenologists, the most enduringly influential is undoubtedly the work of William James. His famous definition of attention is among the most-cited quotes in psychology. In reading any contemporary piece on attention one is inevitably presented with James' (1890) quote:

> Everyone knows what attention is. It is the taking possession by the mind, in clear and vivid form, of one out of what seem several simultaneously possible objects or trains of thought. Focalization, concentration, of consciousness, are of its essence. It implies withdrawal from some things in order to deal effectively with others. (pp. 403–404)

Given that James' insight into the phenomenon of attention was gained through introspection, it is perhaps not surprising to see his close linkage of the concept of attention to notions of consciousness. Indeed, our own naive impressions are that our consciousness determines our thoughts and our choices of action.

There are, however, at least two major problems with defining attention in terms of consciousness. First, attention may be equally the product of apparently automatic processes that selectively direct thinking and behavior without conscious awareness (e.g., see Underwood, 1982). Indeed, the contemporary study of attention is as much directed at understanding these so-called automatic processes, which operate below the level of consciousness, as it is at understanding attentional control processes that are voluntary and within the realm of awareness (e.g., Shiffrin & Schneider, 1977). Second, introspections about consciousness are notoriously inaccurate and sufficiently prone to situational bias to make the relationship between self-reported consciousness and behavior an unreliable one (e.g., Nisbett & Wilson, 1977; Posner, 1973, 1978). Such observations cast doubt on the credibility of consciousness as a basis upon which to ground a scientific theory of attention, although some authors (e.g., Stelmach & Hughes, 1983) argue that consciousness should be the centerpiece of any definition of attention. It remains possible that the experience of consciousness is reliable, but that the inaccuracies that are observed arise in the reporting of this experience to others (White, 1982). Nevertheless, the problem remains that if consciousness cannot be reliably and unambiguously linked to attention, an operational definition of attention in terms of consciousness is likely to be fraught with all manner of measurement problems.

Therefore, despite James' assertion, what attention is may not be necessarily known (see also Stelmach & Hughes, 1983). Certainly, scientists have not reached unanimous agreement on how to define it. In the modern study of perception, cognition, and action, attention has become a ubiquitous concept, being used in a range of diverse and only loosely related ways (Nougier, Stein, & Bonnel, 1991). Some time ago, Posner and Boies (1971) identified three major uses of the term attention in the psychology literature:

1. Attention as *alertness,* including concerns with the development and both short- and long-term maintenance of optimal sensitivity and readiness (or preparedness) for responding.
2. Attention as a *limited capacity* or *resource,* as examined in studies of divided attention aimed at isolating capacity and/or resource limitations in information processing.
3. Attention as *selectivity,* as examined in studies of selective attention requiring the preferential processing of information from a particular modality, spatial location, or context in the face of competition from other items and sources of distraction.

Attention, in the first context of alertness or preparedness, is directly dependent upon arousal and the associated construct of anxiety. Arousal, anxiety, and attention in this context are covered in detail elsewhere in this book and were given extensive treatment in the previous edition (Abernethy, 1993, Chapter 6). In this chapter, the focus is upon attention (1) as a limited capacity or resource, and (2) as selectivity. Each dimension is treated essentially independently. Each is discussed, with respect to:

- The definition of attention and its importance to sports performance and instruction;
- Major paradigms of study and principal measures of the key concepts, including the use of measures derived from a number of different levels of analysis;
- Performance limitations imposed by attention;
- Theoretical explanations and the evidence supporting and refuting given theories;
- Changes in attention which accompany skill acquisition (through consideration of research from training studies and expert-novice comparisons); and

- Practical implications of the available research for skill acquisition, instruction, and the design of practice for sport.

ATTENTION AS A LIMITED CAPACITY OR RESOURCE

It has long been known that humans have some very real limitations in their ability to perform two or more tasks simultaneously. In the late nineteenth century, Binet (1890) was able to demonstrate that performing a mental arithmetic task interfered with the capability to squeeze a rubber ball at a regular rate (see Keele, 1973) while Welch (1898) showed that hand-grip strength deteriorated during the performance of concurrent mental tasks, including arithmetic. Two tasks performed simultaneously may cause selective decrements in the performance of either one of the two tasks or general decrements in both of the tasks, although in some cases apparently no interference exists. The nature of the observed interference, if any, appears to depend on a number of factors but, as a general rule, newly acquired or difficult tasks appear less able to be performed in parallel with other tasks than well-learned or simple tasks. Adults (with some notable exceptions) have little difficulty walking and chewing gum at the same time. However, the slightest imposition of a second task to a toddler is generally sufficient to cause them to either stop walking or, in most cases, to lose balance. Skilled basketball players are able to carefully monitor the position of all teammates and opponents while dribbling the ball, whereas a novice trying to do the same thing will inevitably either lose control of the ball or be forced to rapidly switch attention between the two tasks.

Attention in this context, therefore, is equated with notions of limited information processing space (Keele, 1973), capacity (Moray, 1967), or resources (Wickens, 1992), such that difficult tasks performed together are conceived to have cumulative processing requirements that may exceed the available space, capacity, or resources. In such instances, the processing of information relevant to one or both of the tasks will be either incomplete or delayed and this, in turn, causes the observed performance decrements. The limited capacity or space perspective of attention draws an analogy between attention and the fixed capacity of storage devices such as the available memory in a computer (Moray, 1967). The available processing capacity is fixed but may be partitioned to different tasks in any way the performer decides. When demand exceeds supply, performance on one or both tasks must suffer. The resource analogy is similarly grounded but adds a second constraint that different tasks and processes may require access to different types of resources. Under either model, the pattern of interference that is observed between different tasks provides vital clues for understanding the nature of the underlying control processes and about the capacity or resources available to different individuals.

As the performance of many sports (especially team ball games like soccer, water polo, field and ice hockey, and football) frequently require the concurrent performance of two or more skills (e.g., carrying the ball while visually scanning for teammates to pass to), understanding more about attention in this particular context is important for the sport psychologist, coach, and athlete alike. In this section, an attempt is made to determine, among other things, to what extent information processing capacities and resources are limited and how skilled performers manage to alleviate some of the attentional constraints which are apparent in the performance of novices. The discussions lead into considerations of the *attention demands* of different tasks and component processes and onward to examination of the possibility of *automatic* processes which require apparently no attentional capacity or resources.

Paradigms for Studying Capacity/Resource Limitations and Divided Attention

The assessment of the mental workload of particular tasks requires access to measures displaying (1) *sensitivity* to alterations in capacity/resource demand, (2) *selective* influence only to factors affecting resource demand, (3) *diagnosticity* in terms of identifying which capacities or resources are being taxed, (4) *unobtrusiveness* in the sense of not interfering with the performance of the task of interest, and (5) *reliability* (Sheridan & Stassen, 1979; Wickens, 1992). The available behavioral, cognitive, and physiological measures of mental workload vary in the extent to which they satisfy each of these, occasionally competing, criteria (Wickens, 1979).

The Dual Task Paradigm

It follows logically from the preceding discussion that the most direct means of determining the extent and the nature of the limitations imposed by different tasks on different individuals may be to have them perform two (or more) tasks concurrently and measure how successfully they manage to divide attention between the competing tasks. In the dual task paradigm, the task for which an assessment of attention demand is sought, is termed the *primary task,* while the *secondary task* provides the principal performance measure from which the implications regarding primary task demand are derived. A large range of secondary

tasks have been described in the literature (Ogden, Levine, & Eisner, 1979; Wickens, 1992) but the most popular are simple reaction time (RT) tasks (usually referred to in the dual task configuration as probe reaction time—PRT).

Different instructional sets may be used to alter the priorities people are required to assign to the two tasks. In the simplest case, participants are required to give attentional priority to the primary task (so that primary task performance remains at a comparable level in the dual situation to when the task is performed in isolation). Changes in secondary task performance in this instance can be directly linked to attentional fluctuations in the demands of the primary task. Such an instructional set is most likely to be used if the researcher's interest is principally in understanding more about the primary task. An alternative instructional set, which might be employed if the principal interest is in understanding the capability of individuals to switch attention and time share between concurrent tasks rather than the attentional demands of the primary task per se, involves simply instructing subjects to perform both tasks to the best of their capability. Ogden et al. (1979) have suggested that the term secondary task paradigm be used to describe the first of these instructional sets and the term dual task paradigm be reserved for use with the latter. In the majority of the published literature, the terms have been used interchangeably.

If we assume (1) an instructional set that places priority on the primary task and (2) the pre-existence of a finite information processing capacity (Figure 3.1), then it seems reasonable to posit that secondary task performance will be a direct reflection of the residual processing capacity that remains after the demands of the primary task have been met. Poor secondary task performance would be expected to accompany difficult primary tasks (for which the demands on processing capacity are substantial) whereas secondary task performance with response latencies or error rates essentially unchanged from those evident when the secondary task is performed in isolation would be expected to accompany primary tasks that are simple and that tap little of the performer's limited processing capacity. Secondary task performance (relative to control levels) therefore reflects the attention demand of the primary task and its component processes. The total absence of secondary task decrements for secondary tasks known to be sensitive to primary task demands may indicate that the primary task is performed automatically, requiring none of the available processing capacity.

There are at least four major methodological concerns that need to be addressed by the researcher using the dual task paradigm (Abernethy, Summers, & Ford, 1998). The

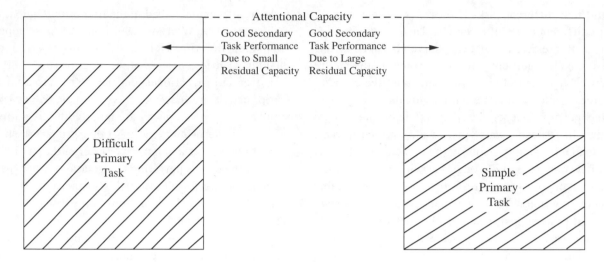

Figure 3.1 Fundamental notions underlying the dual-task measure of attention.

first of these concerns relates to the question of task selection. When the dual task method is applied to understanding attentional demands in sports, the sport task of interest automatically becomes the primary task. The vexing methodological question then becomes what secondary task from the enormous range of possible secondary tasks should be coupled with the primary task. Issues to be considered in secondary task selection include deciding between continuous and discrete measures and deciding between tasks that create or apparently avoid structural interference. *Structural interference* is interference caused by the simultaneous use of common processes by both tasks whereas *capacity interference* is interference which arises when the cumulative attentional demand of the two tasks exceeds the available central processing capacity (Kahneman, 1973). Interference between two concurrent tasks requiring the same perceptual system (e.g., simultaneous target shooting and peripheral visual detection) or the same response production system (e.g., simultaneous manual aiming and tapping) is obviously largely structural in origin. In contrast, interference in tasks that share no common perceptual or output processes is most likely of a capacity origin.

Continuous or temporally co-extensive secondary tasks (Heuer & Wing, 1984) have the advantage of keeping the cumulative (primary plus secondary) demands relatively constant throughout the task but are limited in terms of how much they can help the researcher equate attentional fluctuations with specific phases in the primary task (secondary task errors may cumulate with continuous secondary tasks). For this reason, discrete secondary tasks like PRT are

greatly favored if the precise localization of attentional demands is sought.

The decision of whether or not to seek secondary tasks that may cause structural rather than capacity interference depends largely on the purpose of the study. If the principal interest is in determining how well performers can cope with specific resource overloads of the type normally encountered in the natural setting then simulation of the precise structural interference of the "real world" setting is obviously desirable. If the interest is rather to develop a general measure of the residual attention remaining after the attentional needs of a particular primary task are met, then care should be taken to ensure that the secondary task utilizes different sensory and response modalities to those used by the primary task. The difficulty here is that structural interference may arise in subtle and unexpected ways, as in the case of tasks requiring bimanual responses (McLeod, 1977) or tasks sharing a common timing structure (e.g., Kelso, Tuller, & Harris, 1983). Perhaps more alarming is the possibility that a single, common, general-purpose central processing capacity may not exist. (Or, even if it does exist, its total capacity may be variable, Kahneman, 1973.) Rather, a finite number of special-purpose resource pools may exist that make the search for general measures of spare attention fruitless endeavours (Allport, 1980a; Navon & Gopher, 1979).

A second methodological problem relates to the control of temporal uncertainty in the presentation of the secondary task. If discrete secondary tasks such as PRT are used, care needs to be taken to ensure that the probability of the probe stimulus occurrence remains consistent throughout the duration of the primary task. Random presentations of the secondary task stimuli result in increased stimulus probability across the primary task extent. The longer the primary task proceeds without the probe stimulus occurring the more probable it becomes and this probability change can influence PRT independent of the concurrent primary task attentional demands. The inclusion of frequent *catch trials* (primary task trials without secondary stimuli) within the dual testing conditions provides one potential means of alleviating this problem (Salmoni, Sullivan, & Starkes, 1976).

Generating appropriate baseline measures for the primary and secondary task presents a third major methodological concern. Dual task data are only interpretable through comparison of the performance of both the primary and secondary task when they are completed together with their level of performance in isolation. Single-to-dual comparisons of primary task performance provide an indication of the extent to which the participants adhere to the imposed instructional set or attempt to time-share between the two tasks. Single-to-dual comparisons of secondary task performance provide a measure of the attentional demand of the primary task. Given the uses to which the secondary task data in particular are put, it is essential that the baseline (single) conditions match exactly the dual conditions with respect not only to the stimulus-response configurations used but also with respect to the spacing and relative frequency of stimuli. Measurement of baseline levels of the secondary task under conditions with a higher relative frequency of stimuli than in the dual setting may result in artificially low control values of PRT and, in turn, an inflated estimate of the attention demands of the primary task.

Finally, it should be noted that there are problems within the dual task paradigm in precisely localizing attentional demands. A common practice in many studies concerned with plotting the time course of attentional fluctuations in specific primary tasks and concerned with precisely locating attentional peaks and troughs in given tasks (e.g., Posner & Keele, 1969) is to plot PRT as a function of the time of probe stimulus presentation during the primary task and to then equate attention levels directly with events and processes occurring at the time of stimulus presentation. The inaccuracy in this approach is that attention may remain elevated beyond the time of probe presentation until the time at which the response to the probe is actually completed. Plotting attention demand relative to stimulus presentation may therefore place peak attentional demands systematically too early in the primary task, a bias that can be eliminated by also plotting PRT relative to the point of response completion (McLeod, 1980). When such plotting procedures are used, more conservative, but nevertheless more accurate, estimates of the location of attentional peaks in the primary task can be derived (Girouard, Laurencelle, & Proteau, 1984).

The dual task technique offers potential for insight into attention demand differences within and between different movement tasks, and between different individuals performing the same movement tasks. A relatively common application of the dual task technique has been to use PRT measurements to determine attention demand fluctuations within particular motor tasks, especially simple limb movements. The results from such studies have been somewhat mixed, although high attention demands are typically observed at the start of the movement, and attributed to pre-programming (e.g., Ells, 1973; Glencross, 1980), as well as at the end of movement, and attributed to error correction (e.g., Zelaznik, Shapiro, & McClosky, 1981). The middle, ballistic phase of simple positioning movements appears to place relatively low demands on available processing capacity/resources (Posner & Keele, 1969) although these conclusions now appear at least partially dependent on the modality used for stimulus presentation or response initiation (Girouard et al., 1984; McLeod, 1980). Schmidt and Lee (1999), in reviewing the available evidence, argue for increasing attention demands as information processing moves beyond stimulus identification and approaches the response programming stage.

Studies examining PRT changes throughout the performance of laboratory coincidence-timing tasks (e.g., Nettleton, 1979) suggest a time-course of attentional changes similar to those revealed in the control of simple linear aiming movements. Attention demands appear greatest during the initial and final stages of observation of the approaching motion, with monitoring in the middle, essentially redundant, phase being relatively attention-free. Studies of simple catching tasks indicate that attention demands are greatest in the later stages of ball flight when the initiation of the grasping response is being undertaken (Populin, Rose, & Heath, 1990; Starkes, 1986). Comparisons of the attention demands of a diverse range of sports tasks (volleyball, tennis, 100 m sprinting, and hurdling) by Castiello and Umilta (1988) demonstrate the presence of a high-degree of specificity in the demands different athletic events place on human attentional capacities and resources, indicating, among other things, the need for an expanded database on the patterns of attention within specific sport tasks. The limited evidence currently available from the studies mentioned previously, as well as those with tasks such as rifle shooting (Landers, Wang, & Courtet, 1985; Rose & Christina, 1990), badminton (Abernethy, 1988a), and high jumping (Girouard, Perreault, Vachon, & Black, 1978) do not permit simple categorization of sport tasks on the basis of patterns of attentional demands.

Although comparisons between different tasks are commonplace in the ergonomics field as a means of assessing relative workloads (Wickens, 1992), systematic comparisons between the attention demands of different sport tasks do not appear to have been undertaken to date. However, two particular applications appear worthy of pursuit: (1) the use of dual task comparisons between "real world" tasks and laboratory simulations as a means of assessing the extent to which simulations are successful in replicating the processing demands of the natural setting; and (2) the use of dual task comparisons of different lead-up activities for particular sports skills as a means of objectively ordering the presentation of the activities in terms of ascending complexity/attentional demand. With this information available, a more suitable matching of training activities to learner capability may be achieved than when this matching is done purely on the basis of performance scores on the (primary task) activities.

One of the most powerful applications of the dual task technique, and the one particularly relevant to sports coaches, involves the use of dual task techniques to determine the relative workloads given tasks impose on different individuals. The technique offers an objective means of determining attentional effort and the extent of spare (residual) attentional capacity. It provides an avenue for isolating differences in untapped performance potential between two individuals, even when their performance levels on the primary task may be indistinguishable. The existing evidence on expert-novice differences in attentional loads is considered later in this section when the links between attentional capacities, resources, and skill acquisition are discussed.

An emerging focus of recent dual task studies has been on determining the attentional costs associated with changing and sustaining different movement patterns (e.g., Lajoie, Teasdale, Bard, & Fleury, 1993, 1996). Applied in this context, the dual task method can assist in determining the extent to which central "effort" is required to sustain a particular pattern of coordination as opposed to the movement pattern being sustained largely by the intrinsic musculoskeletal dynamics of the movement (e.g., Summers, Byblow, Bysouth-Young, & Semjen, 1998; Temprado, Zanone, Monno, & Laurent, 1999).

Other Measures of Divided Attention and Mental Workload

The dual task method can be cumbersome to use and/or imprecise in measuring attentional workload. As a consequence, alternatives have been examined. One simple means of estimating the mental workload imposed by any particular task or combination of tasks is to have the individual performing the task self-report or rate the mental load he or she experiences (Moray, 1982). A number of scales for the subjective rating of mental workload have been developed for use in ergonomic settings, among the most popular being the NASA Task Load Index (TLX) (Hart & Staveland, 1988) and the Subjective Workload Assessment Technique (SWAT) (Reid & Nygren, 1988). Although such measures are convenient in the sense that they can be easily administered without disrupting primary task performance, the ever-present concern is that the performer's verbal estimates may not accurately reflect the actual demand placed on available processing resources. Perhaps because the predictive, concurrent, and construct validity of these subjective workload assessment instruments has not been strongly established (Nygren, 1991), such methods for assessing task demands have not, as yet, become popular in the sport psychology literature.

The dual task technique may actively alter the nature of primary task performance and may, in most cases, provide only a discontinuous measure of attentional fluctuations on a task. Physiological measures of information processing load, on the other hand, have the advantage of being generally continuous and, in some cases, non-intrusive. However, the collective disadvantage of the available physiological measures of information processing load is that by their very nature they are indirect measures of the phenomenon of capacity or resource limitations that we seek to understand (Wickens, 1992). Further, it can be argued that the inconvenience and constraints imposed by the presence of recording electrodes and other equipment may, in fact, affect the nature of primary task performance. Nevertheless, pupil diameter, cardiac acceleration/deceleration and variability, and EEG event-related potentials have been used at various times to provide markers of information processing load.

Small changes in pupil diameter appear to provide a reasonable indication of the resource demands of particular cognitive tasks (Beatty, 1982). Pupil dilations occur systematically with the imposition of arithmetic, memory, or problem-solving tasks (e.g., Beatty & Wagoner, 1978) although the changes themselves provide little illumination as to the nature/location of the underlying resource limitations. Pupil dilation also occurs with increased arousal and therefore arousal level changes between tasks or between individuals may act to confound and limit the types of comparisons justifiable from pupillometry.

Although absolute heart rate (HR) levels do not appear to be reliable indicators of task workload across a range of tasks (Wierwille & Connor, 1983; Wierwille, Rahimi, & Casali, 1985), at least two other HR measures may be related to the attentional demands of tasks. Jennings, Lawrence, and Kasper (1978) have argued that cardiac acceleration/deceleration (as assessed from relative changes in interbeat interval) may be systematically related to available processing capacity. Jennings et al. have demonstrated that while absolute HR is affected more by the overall response requirements of the task (a RT task in their case), the relative acceleration/deceleration patterns in HR relate closely to PRT measures. HR deceleration appears to accompany, and index, the presence of spare capacity or attentional reserves whereas HR acceleration is more prevalent in conditions of processing overload. This approach is used occasionally in the sport context (e.g., Crews, 1989), although clearly this, like other potential cardiac measures of attention, can only be of use in those activities where the performer remains essentially stationary.

An increasingly popular measure of mental workload within the ergonomics literature is HR *variability*. Across a range of different methods of calculating variability, including, more recently, spectral (e.g., Meshkati, 1988) and nonlinear (Sammer, 1998) analyses, heart rate variability appears to decrease with increasing attentional demands of tasks (Vincente, Thornton, & Moray, 1987), making it one of the more promising physiological indicators of attentional workload or effort. However, like the pupil diameter measure, HR variability appears to reflect more the total demand on all available processing resources than the specific competition between processing resources (Wickens & Derrick, 1981) and therefore may have limitations as a diagnostic device (Wickens, 1992). Heart rate variability has received little or no usage in assessing the attentional demands of different sports tasks, probably because the cardiac changes associated with any form of physical activity will confound and "swamp" the relatively small effects due to cognitive processing. Nevertheless, the measure may be useful in sports (such as the aiming ones) where the maintenance of body stability during preparation is important to performance. However, all peripheral physiological measures of nervous system activity (such as heart rate variability and pupillometry) are necessarily limited in

their utility in measuring attention to the extent that they are frequently: (1) too slow or late, (2) too remote from the processes that are of primary interest, (3) too nonspecific, and (4) too closely influenced by activity and emotion (Näätänen, 1992).

Event-related (or evoked) potentials (ERPs) within the electroencephalogram (EEG) may potentially provide valuable measures of attention and attentional workload. The typical ERP is composed of two types of components: (1) *exogenous components,* that are always present regardless of how the particular evoking stimulus is to be processed, and (2) *endogenous components,* that vary according to the type of information processing that is required. A number of endogenous ERP components appear to be related to the demands placed by tasks upon available processing capacity and resources. [See Hatfield & Hillman (this volume) for a more detailed treatment of this topic.] The N200 component (components are typically named with respect to their polarity and time of appearance relative to stimulus presentation) appears to reflect modality-specific processes but the later P300 appears to be nonmodality specific (Snyder, Hillyard, & Galambos, 1980) and therefore a potentially promising general marker of attention. The P300 *latency* appears to be sensitive to the memory load imposed by the primary task (Kramer & Strayer, 1988) although reported correlations between P300 latency and RT vary considerably in their strength (Donchin, 1984; Donchin, Ritter, & McCallum, 1978). More importantly, the *amplitude* of the P300 component appears sensitive to the resource demands of different processes with the P300 amplitude decreasing as secondary task demands are increased (e.g., Kramer, Wickens, & Donchin, 1983). The P300 measure has an important advantage over other physiological measures of attentional demand in that it provides a measure that is graded to perceptual/cognitive lead, and therefore may have some diagnostic value in isolating specific resource limitations (Wickens, 1992). The downside for sport psychologists is the relative inaccessibility and expense of the required recording technology, the task constraints that are imposed by the recording electrodes, and the necessity for athlete stillness to avoid movement artifacts in the recordings.

Concordance among behavioral, cognitive, and physiological measures of attention are not always high. For this reason, the question of determining the best single measure of attention demand is one that clearly depends on the use to which the collected measures are to be put and, to a lesser extent, the nature of the task(s) and individual(s) under examination. The use of multiple measures from a number of different levels of analysis appears to be a logical strategy for assessing attentional workload (Abernethy, Summers, & Ford, 1998; Wilson & O'Donnell, 1988); the physiological and cognitive measures in particular complementing well the strengths and weaknesses of each other. The movement toward greater use of multiple measures from different levels of analysis within the measurement of attention in movement tasks is consistent with the emerging predominance of multilevel measurement and theorizing in other areas of psychology (e.g., Cacioppo & Berntson, 1992; Cowen, 1995; McLeod & Driver, 1993).

Performance Limitations Imposed by Limited Processing Capacity and Resources

Substantial research on cognition and some on action using the dual task technique (e.g., see Eysenck, 1984 for a review) makes it clear, as coaches of young athletes will well recognize, that human information processing resources do indeed have finite limits and these limits can be sufficiently restrictive in some situations to make errors and performance decrements inevitable. A *complementarity principle* (Norman & Bobrow, 1975) appears to be in effect wherein resource (or capacity) availability determines performance and increases in the allocation of resources to one task produces a commensurate reduction in the availability of resources to other tasks or processes being performed at the same time. The resource allocation-performance relationship need not necessarily be a linear one, however, as measurement artifacts, such as ceiling effects (Heuer & Wing, 1984), and performance limiting factors other than resources (Norman & Bobrow, 1975) may be present. The magnitude of the errors observed on secondary tasks depends on a number of factors. Performance decrements are generally greatest for anxious, untrained subjects performing two or more complex tasks simultaneously and least for experienced subjects performing two apparently simple tasks together (e.g., an experienced motor racer driving a civilian vehicle in light traffic while conducting a conversation with a passenger). If it is assumed for the moment that available attention exists in the form of a general, undifferentiated capacity, then there are at least three major factors that will determine the capability to perform a secondary task. These factors are depicted schematically in Figure 3.2 and described in more detail next.

The Total Available Capacity as a Limiting Factor

The total available attentional capacity may depend on the alertness/arousal of the individual performer or athlete with greatest information processing capacity being available

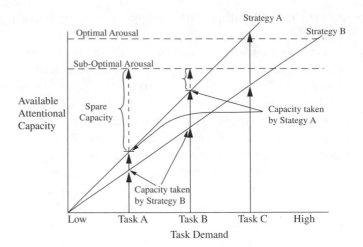

Figure 3.2 Primary task demand, absolute capacity, and time-sharing strategies as influences of secondary task performance. Adapted from *Psychology and sport* by D.J. Glencross, 1978, p. 87. Copyright 1978 by McGraw-Hill Book Company. Reprinted by permission.

when the person is optimally aroused (Kahneman, 1973). All the factors known to affect alertness, including individual differences in personality, may therefore affect available processing capacity and, in turn, secondary task performance.

The Primary Task Demand as a Limiting Factor

Secondary task performance depends strongly on the proportion of the available capacity that is consumed by the primary task and this in turn depends on the extent to which the primary task (or processes within it) can be performed automatically. Influential work by Schneider and Shiffin (1977) and Shiffrin and Schneider (1977) drew distinction between two fundamentally, and qualitatively, different forms of information processing. The term *controlled processing* was used to describe processing that was (1) attention demanding or effortful (in the sense of causing and experiencing interference with other concurrent tasks), (2) serial in nature, (3) slow, and (4) volitional, in the sense of being able to be consciously altered or prevented. Such processing was expected (and observed) in situations where the nature of the task and type of processing required were constantly changing (what Shiffrin and Schneider operationalized through *variable stimulus-response mapping* conditions).

In contrast, what Shiffrin and Schneider (1977) termed *automatic processing,* and what has been variously described elsewhere as "involuntary" (Kimble & Perlmutter,

1970), "obligatory" (LaBerge, 1975), "mindless" (Norman, 1976), "non-strategic" (Klein, 1978), and "mandatory" (Navon & Gopher, 1979), appears to be (1) largely without attention demand or effort (in the sense that other concurrent processes do not interfere with it), (2) parallel in nature, (3) fast, and (4) inevitable, in the sense that processing of this type does not appear to be consciously alterable or preventable. Shiffrin and Schneider (1977) maintain that such processing develops with practice when people repetitively experience the same stimulus and response patterns (e.g., *consistent mapping* conditions). While distinct, controlled and automatic processing can interact and cause interference effects in a host of circumstances, including the reproduction of skilled movement (Imanaka, Abernethy, & Quek, 1998; Rossetti, in press).

The notion of automatic processing is a particularly appealing one in terms of explaining the apparent release from effortful processing that accompanies skill acquisition and in explaining errors made in daily activities (Norman, 1981; Reason, 1979). However, its operationalization as a theoretical concept is confused by the range of different features and dimensions used to distinguish it from controlled processing. The difficulty is that there is a lack of internal consistency between the various features used to distinguish controlled and automatic processing (Phillips & Hughes, 1988) such that some processes that are considered to be beyond voluntary control, for example, may still be slow or elicit interference. The lack of consistent distinction between controlled and automatic processing has been the principal source of challenge to the dichotomous views of processing such as those posited by Shiffrin and Schneider (1977) and others (e.g., see Broadbent, 1982; Neumann, 1984).

Strategies for Attentional Switching and Time-Sharing as a Limiting Factor

A third factor influencing secondary task performance is the strategy individuals use to share resources and switch attention between the primary and secondary tasks (see Figure 3.2). Clear evidence exists that the allocation of attentional capacity and resources can be apportioned between two or more tasks in a flexible manner (e.g., Gopher & Navon, 1980; Schneider & Fisk, 1982) and an improved capability to share attentional resources and time between the concurrent tasks is an important component of skill acquisition in multitask situations (Adams, 1966; Klein, 1976). Damos and Wickens (1980), for example, demonstrated improvements in multitask performance which were a function of improved time-sharing rather than decreasing

attention demands (improved automation) of the primary task. The strategies people adopt to dual tasks are apparently not always fixed ones and may vary as the demands of the primary task alter (Sperandio, 1978).

If limiting attention consists not of a single capacity but rather a multiple set of relatively specific resources, each with their own unique capacity limits (e.g., Navon & Gopher, 1979; Wickens, 1980), then consideration of a fourth factor, the specific resources demanded by given combinations of tasks, also needs to be made in order to understand secondary task performance. Such a view also challenges some of the more fundamental assumptions upon which the dual task method in particular is based. These contrasting capacity and resource views of attention are considered in more detail in the next section.

Theories of Attentional Capacity and Resources

Attention as a Fixed Capacity with Structural Constraints: The Single-Channel Theory and Related Views

The earliest fixed-capacity theory of attention was the *single-channel theory* in which the processing of information from sensation to the production of action was conceived as occurring through a single processing channel limited to the sequential handling of either one signal at a time (Welford, 1952, 1967) or a finite number of bits of information per second (Broadbent, 1958). The principal support for the single-channel theory came from RT studies using a double stimulation paradigm in which participants were required to respond to two stimuli presented in rapid succession (each stimulus having its own unique response requirement). Of interest within this paradigm was the extent to which the RT to the second stimulus was elevated beyond normal control levels—the extent of any delay being known as the psychological refractory period (PRP). PRP effects are well known to sports performers; offensive players in a number of sports use fakes in an attempt to fool their opponents into processing incorrect information which, if successful, delays their opponent's response to their imperative move.

Early PRP studies revealed an essentially linear relationship between the extent of the PRP delay and the length of the interstimulus interval (ISI) for ISIs less than the duration of the first RT. The PRP delay disappeared when the length of the ISI exceeded the duration of the RT to the first stimulus (e.g., Davis, 1959; Welford, 1967). Reduced PRP delays were found when the RT to the first stimulus was fast rather than slow (e.g., Broadbent & Gregory,

1967). (See Figure 3.3.) Such evidence was consistent with the view that the processing of the second signal could not be commenced until the channel had been cleared of the demands imposed by the first signal. Unfortunately, the supportive evidence was gathered primarily from studies in which both stimuli were presented to the same sensory system (e.g., vision, audition), therefore potentially creating structural interference by overloading specific processors (Kahneman, 1973). When different stimulus and response modes were used for the two RT tasks consistent violations of the expected 45-degree slope between PRP and ISI were obtained (e.g., Greenwald & Schulman, 1973). RT to the second stimulus was frequently found to remain elevated after the channel in theory should have been cleared (e.g., Karlin & Kestenbaum, 1968). Finally the nature and difficulty of the second task was found to unexpectedly influence the RT to the first stimulus (e.g., Barber, 1989). The presence of these contradictory data, along with evidence from dual task paradigms for parallel processing in the early stages of visual search and memory retrieval (e.g., Keele, 1973; LaBerge, 1981), resulted in general abandonment of a global single channel view and the search for those specific processes within the information processing chain that appeared to be limited to serial, single-channel, kinds of processing.

Attempts to locate the so-called bottlenecks in human information processing (i.e., the points at which processing alters from a parallel mode to a serial mode and signals are forced to queue) also proved far from fruitful. Different bottlenecks appeared to exist dependent on task combinations, and on the attention- and time-sharing strategies used by the subjects (Barber, 1989), arguing against the presence of fixed structural constraints to processing capacity.

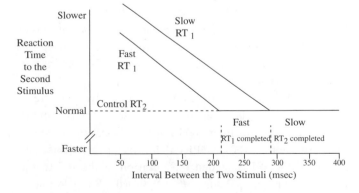

Figure 3.3 Relationships between RT_2, ISI, and the duration of RT_1 as predicted by single-channel theory.

Attention as a General, Flexible Capacity

On the basis of these inconsistent data concerning the location of the limited processing channel within the information processing chain, Moray (1967), and later Kahneman (1973), proposed that attention be more appropriately viewed as a flexible commodity that, while having finite overall limitations, can be flexibly allocated between concurrent tasks in any manner the subject chooses. Flexible allocation of a limited resource provides a reasonable explanation of why different bottlenecks emerge for different individuals and for different task combinations. As Allport (1980a) observed, the natural analogue for this type of capacity is not a passive, structurally fixed container but rather a limited power supply. Once the task demands fully load the system, additional "power consumption" at any point in the system can only be offset by reductions somewhere else, regardless of the use to which the power is to be put. Within this model ". . . interference is nonspecific, and depends only on the (combined) demands of both the tasks" (Kahneman, 1973, p. 11).

Like their predecessors (the fixed-capacity theories), the variable allocation theory of attention has also proven to be flawed, although it nevertheless retains a number of influential supporters (e.g., Kantowitz, 1985). The most damaging evidence against the variable allocation theory comes from observations of inconsistent interference when different secondary tasks are coupled with the same primary task. This ironically turns out not to be a new finding, but one that has been evident since the early studies of the late 1800s (see Keele, 1973). If attention really exists in the form of a large, undifferentiated general capacity, then different secondary tasks performed in conjunction with a common primary task should reveal consistent conclusions regarding the attention demand of the primary task. Yet, such does not appear to be the case (e.g., Wakelin, 1967).

Attention as Multiple-Resource Pools

The difficulties with viewing attention as a general-purpose, limited-capacity, central processor were clearly articulated by Navon and Gopher (1979) and Allport (1980a), and a major theoretical reformulation was set in place in the early 1980s. The newer view of attention is as a series of resource pools (Gopher & Sanders, 1984; Wickens, 1992), multiprocessors (Allport, 1980b), or specialized modules (Allport, 1989), each with their own unique capacities and resource-performance relationships. Within such a theory of attention, capacity is seen not to be centralized but rather distributed throughout the nervous system. The interest, therefore, becomes not that of measuring the limits of central processing capacity but rather isolating the specific, special purpose (dedicated or informationally encapsulated; Fodor, 1983) modular subsystems that collectively compose the resource pool. Autonomous visual mechanisms for the pick-up of time-to-contact information, for example, have been proposed as examples of such modules (McLeod, McLaughlin, & Nimmo-Smith, 1985). Evidence in support of the resource model of attention comes from a number of sources (Stelmach & Hughes, 1983) including: (1) the mutual interference increases when tasks share common sensory or output modalities (e.g., Mcleod, 1977), (2) the absence of secondary task decrements under some unique conditions of dissimilarity between the two tasks (e.g., Allport, Antonis, & Reynolds, 1972), and (3) the minimal commonality in time-sharing strategies across altered task combinations (e.g., Wickens, Mountford, & Schreiner, 1981).

A number of propositions have been advanced as to the composition of some of the many processing resources. Wickens (1992) has proposed that resources may be defined in terms of the subcells formed by the combination of a number of simple dichotomous dimensions, including stage of processing (e.g., early versus late processes), input and output modalities (e.g., visual versus auditory input; manual versus vocal output), and processing codes (e.g., spatial versus visual). (See Figure 3.4.) Interference can then be explained in terms of the extent to which the two tasks tap common resource features (or cells). An alternative means of identifying resources is in terms of the

capabilities of each of the cerebral hemispheres (e.g., Friedman & Polson, 1981); the advantage in this case being that manual and vocal control asymmetries can be used as markers of resource usage.

There remain acknowledged difficulties with the resource theories as currently formulated, especially with respect to the persistence of some minimal interference effects when tasks apparently share no specific resource demands in common (Barber, 1989). However, clearly, the greatest difficulty and future challenge for multiple resource theories lies in the specific identification of the different resource pools and the testing of their concordance with known patterns of interference from dual task studies (Neumann, 1987). The testing of resource theories is complicated by the possibility that performance, in all cases, may be limited by factors other than resources (e.g., see Norman & Bobrow, 1975, for a useful distinction of *resource-limited* and *data-limited* processing).

Attention with Connectionist Models

The notion of distributed capacity within resource models of attention is consistent in part with the development in cognitive science of parallel distributed processing models (or connectionist models) (e.g., Rumelhart & McClelland, 1986). These models offer a computational viewpoint based on the complex and plastic networking of simple processing units rather than fixed structures with known capacities and limits. Importantly, attention (and knowledge) in these models is not address-specific and describable in terms of the properties of individual units, structures, or resources, as the traditional models suggest, but is an integral property of performance which is understandable and definable only by considering the whole operation of the network. (See Rumelhart, Hinton, & McClelland, 1986 for further details.) Such a perspective is generally consistent with emerging data from imaging and neurophysiological studies of the brain (e.g., Posner & Dehaene, 1994).

Changes in Capacity and Resource Allocation That Accompany Skill Acquisition

Evidence and Mechanisms for Improved Dual Task Performance with Practice

Both training studies and expert-novice comparisons clearly indicate that the performance of two or more concurrent tasks can be improved with practice and that a capacity for handling concurrent task demands is an important ingredient of expert performance in many activities. It has been known that dual task performance can be

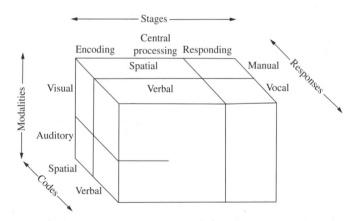

Figure 3.4 Some potential processing resources and their structure. From "Processing resources in attention" by C.D. Wickens. In R. Parasuraman & R. Davies (Eds.), *Varieties of attention,* 1984, p. 81. Copyright by Academic Press Inc. Reprinted by permission.

improved with practice since the time of Solomons and Stein's (1896) introspections on concurrent reading and writing, although the most widely cited empirical demonstration of the extent of improvement that is possible is a latter-day replication and extension of the Solomons and Stein work by Spelke, Hirst, and Neisser (1976). Spelke et al. gave two people five hours of training a week for four months on a range of tasks, including concurrent reading for comprehension and written dictation. After initially experiencing great difficulty with the concurrent tasks, the two participants acquired the combined skill to the point where the reading for comprehension task showed no single-to-dual task decrement although their memory for the dictation task remained poorer in the dual condition than it was when performed alone. These findings, demonstrating comprehensively that interference between tasks is not fixed but is readily modifiable with practice, are supported by a host of more recent studies (e.g., Damos, Bittner, Kennedy, & Harbeson, 1981).

Comparisons of the dual task performance of experts and novices in a range of ergonomic tasks (e.g., Brouwer, Waterink, Van Wolffelaar, & Rothengatter, 1991; Crosby & Parkinson, 1979; Korteling, 1994) and in some selected sports tasks (e.g., Leavitt, 1979; Parker, 1981; Vankersschaver, 1984) have clearly revealed systematic secondary task performance superiority for expert performers even in instances where expert-novice differences are not apparent on the primary task.

Parker's (1981) study of the concurrent performance of a ball catching and throwing task (the primary task) and a peripheral visual detection task (the secondary task) by netball players of different skill levels provides a good example of such a study delivered from a sports setting. The tasks selected for inclusion in this study mimicked fairly closely the demands of the actual game situation where players are required to perform basic skills, like passing and catching, under severe time constraints while simultaneously monitoring, through peripheral vision primarily, the movements of teammates and opponents. The primary task required the players to complete as many passes to a designated target and return as many catches as possible in a 30-second period. Analysis of primary task performance revealed (1) no significant differences in the number of passes and catches successfully completed between the A, B, and C grade players; and (2) some decrements in task performance for all the groups of subjects when they were required to perform the passing and catching task in conjunction with a secondary task. Secondary task performance, as assessed by the number of errors in detecting the

illumination of peripherally located lights during the performance of the primary task, was, however, sensitive to the skill level of the players with the high skilled (A grade) players making fewer detection errors than the lesser skilled (B and C grade) players (see Figure 3.5).

The expert players apparently have more "spare" capacity or resources to allocate to the secondary task, or stated alternatively, need less capacity or resource to perform the primary task than the lesser skilled players. These data also provide an important demonstration of one of the great advantages of the dual task paradigm, namely, the capability of the technique to isolate differences in attention demand between individuals even when primary task capabilities *appear* equivalent (cf. Glencross, 1978). Players who require relatively large amounts of their limited attentional capacity or resources to be allocated to the performance of basic game skills are those more likely to display "tunnel vision" during game situations, missing

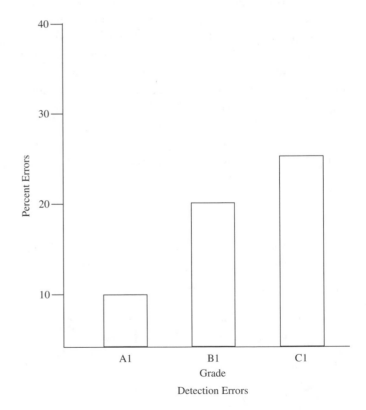

Figure 3.5 Secondary task performance on a visual detection task by A, B, and C grade netball players. From "Visual detection and perception in netball" by H. Parker. In I.M. Cockerill & W.W. MacGillivary (Eds.), *Vision and sport,* 1981, p. 49. Copyright 1981 by Stanley Thornes Publishers. Reprinted by permission.

opportunities to pass to free teammates and to "read" the developing patterns of play.

Eysenck (1984) suggests that there are at least three potential mechanisms through which dual task performance may be improved. These are:

1. The attentional demands of one or both tasks may be reduced (presumably through a complete or partial transition from controlled processing to automatic processing (cf. Shiffrin & Schneider, 1977);

2. New time-sharing and attentional-switching strategies may be developed that allow intertask interference to be reduced; and

3. A more economical mode of functioning may be established that either decreases the number of processing resources required (Norman & Bobrow, 1975) or spreads the processing requirements so that both tasks avoid using resources which are required by the other (Allport, 1980a).

Consideration of Figure 3.2 also suggests a fourth potential mechanism through which dual task performance may be improved, namely, increased availability of capacity or resources through optimization of arousal. The possibility of automaticity will be considered in further detail here because of the extent of attention it has attracted in the research literature and because empirical investigations (e.g., Brown & Carr, 1989) argue that increased intratask automaticity, rather than improved deployment of resources through attentional-switching strategies, is the principal mechanism through which dual task performance is enhanced with practice.

Evidence and Mechanisms for Increased Automaticity with Practice

As noted earlier, the most influential arguments to date for an automatic mode of processing have been advanced by Shiffrin and Schneider (1977). Shiffrin and Schneider base their arguments for automaticity on evidence that, when extensive practice is given under conditions of consistent stimulus-response mapping, RT becomes essentially independent of the number of items within the memory set that needs to be scanned (see Figure 3.6). Nevertheless, when RT is plotted against memory set size, small positive slopes remain that suggest that the memory scanning process is still not completely automatic (Logan, 1979). Similar effects can be seen in older studies on choice RT (Mowbray & Rhoades, 1959) where the slope of the RT-number of

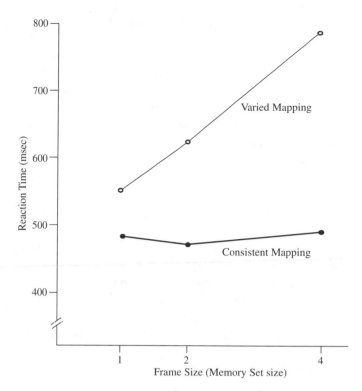

Figure 3.6 RT as a function of memory set size over consistent and varied practice. Adapted from "Controlled and automatic human information processing: I: Detection, search, and attention" by W. Schneider and R.M. Shiffrin, 1977, *Psychological Review, 84,* p. 20. Copyright 1977 by American Psychological Association. Reprinted by permission.

choices plot decreases with practice but never quite reaches a zero value. Likewise, although the single-to-dual differences in secondary task performance decrease with practice, secondary task decrements of zero, as a strict notion of automaticity requires, are rarely, if ever, found in dual task experiments, even for highly practiced subjects (Hoffman, Nelson, & Houck, 1983). Spelke et al.'s (1976) subjects, for example, still showed poorer performance in the dictation test when performed in tandem with the reading task than when performed alone and Parker's (1981) A grade netball players made errors in the secondary detection task that they would not have committed had the detection task been performed alone (Figure 3.5).

These data, which appear to indicate that there are some inevitable costs associated with performing two tasks together (Navon & Gopher, 1979), argue against the existence of automaticity in its strictest sense, as defined by Shiffrin and Schneider (1977) and Näätänen (1988), and suggest a more sensible way to conceive of controlled-automatic processing may be as a continuum rather than as a dichotomy (Logan, 1985). In line with this kind of view, Navon and Gopher (1979), Norman and Shallice (1986), and Kahneman and Treisman (1984) have made arguments for the recognition of different levels of automaticity, the latter authors suggesting that meaningful distinction can be drawn between *strong automaticity* (in which processing is neither facilitated by volition or impaired by distraction), *partial automaticity* (in which processing is normally non-volitional but can be facilitated by volition) and *occasional automaticity* (in which processing generally demands attention but can be sometimes completed without it). It is important to recognize that some component processes within a given task may be strongly automated and others only occasionally automated (Jonides, Naveh-Benjamin, & Palmer, 1985), although the general transition with practice appears to be away from controlled processing toward strongly automated processing (Schneider, 1985). Even with these modifications to Shiffrin and Schneider's (1977) original notion of automatic processing, the concept of increased automaticity with practice remains an appealing one and one with particular relevance to sport. One particularly interesting by-product of increased automaticity is a decreased ability of performers to self-report on the control processes they use and this frequently presents particular problems to expert sports performers who find themselves in the position of attempting to coach or instruct learners.

It is not quite clear what mechanisms are responsible for the emergence of automaticity with practice but a number of propositions appear feasible. Improved recognition and utilization of redundancies available in the perception of stimulus patterns and in the production of stereotyped movement responses may facilitate automation of processing through reducing the information processing load imposed on the performer. On the perceptual side, improved recognition of task-relevant sources of information and, on the response side, the feedback redundancy which supports the transition from closed-loop to open-loop movement control (Schmidt & McCabe, 1976) provide possible mechanisms for decreasing the processing demands of tasks, presumably allowing attentional resources to be freed up. The more efficient self-organizational strategies (Fowler & Turvey, 1978) people discover for resource-sharing between tasks also undoubtedly lays an important foundation for automaticity. Indeed, some authors (e.g., Heuer, 1984) have argued that what is observed and labeled as automaticity may be simply the result of a displacement in resource demands. Some claims have been made for attention-switching between tasks being a generalizable ability (Keele & Hawkins, 1982), and therefore a potentially useful advance predictor of success on tasks requiring divided

attention. However this generalizability seems limited (Wickens, 1992) and perhaps a methodological artifact (Ackerman, Schneider, & Wickens, 1984).

Evidence and Mechanisms for Reduced PRP Delays with Practice

As noted previously in discussing the single channel theory, people experience considerable delays in responding to two signals presented in rapid succession, and this has potentially devastating effects on the performance of defensive players in some sports. How might the potential problem of PRP delays be overcome by skilled performers? Practice in laboratory tasks reduces but does not eliminate PRP delays (Gottsdanker & Stelmach, 1971) suggesting that the benefits of practice may be primarily due to faster processing of the first stimulus. The only sure way to eliminate the PRP delays confronted in sports tasks is not to respond to the first (false) stimulus. Indeed, one of the distinguishing attributes of skilled performers, which will be discussed in the next section, appears to be this general ability to selectively attend to only the most relevant sources of information.

Implications for Skill Acquisition, Instruction, and the Design of Practice

Given that interference effects appear very task-specific and that the development of strategies for attentional sharing between tasks is an integral part of skill acquisition, it follows that training situations must afford the opportunity for the performer to practice the specific attention-switching and resource-sharing strategies required in the natural skill. Practice, consequently, is only likely to be effective if it is *content-specific* (Allport, 1980a). Evidence of long-term improvements in dual task performance (e.g., Spelke et al., 1976) suggests that there may be value in using progressively more difficult dual task combinations as a continued stimulus for primary task automation in performers at all skill levels (see also Schneider, 1985). As there appears little evidence to suggest that skill development ever ceases, even after millions of trials of practice (e.g., Crossman, 1959), continued attentional overload in practice (either through the addition of a more demanding secondary task or the addition of a third concurrent task) may be a useful method for maintaining skill improvements even in expert performers.

Dual task measures appear to offer particular benefits as measures of skill learning and consideration should be given by teachers and coaches to inclusion of measures of this type in skill assessment and talent identification. The real advantage of dual task measures, as was illustrated in

Figure 3.5, is that they allow differences in skill acquisition to be uncovered when such differences are not apparent from observation of the primary task alone. In using dual task measures in this way, however, it should be emphasized that performance may be determined by a range of factors in addition to resource allocation and availability (e.g., see Ackerman & Schneider, 1985). Knowledge of the attentional demands of different phases and types of movement also has important implications for how instruction might best proceed in sport skills. Magill (1998) provides a range of examples from the learning of sport skills illustrating how instruction and practice should focus selectively on those aspects of the skill that are initially attention-demanding but that ultimately need to be executed with little or no demand for attention.

ATTENTION IN THE CONTEXT OF SELECTIVITY

In the previous section, the existence of substantial limitations in human attentional capacity or resources has been documented. Given the enormous amount of information that bombards each and every individual every second of the day (from both external and internal sources) it becomes essential for performance efficiency that only the most relevant (or pertinent) information actually gets processed. *Selective attention* is the general term used to describe this process by which certain information is preferentially selected for detailed processing while other information is ignored.

In fast ball sports, where the time constraints are such that response selection decisions must frequently be made purely on the basis of information available prior to ball flight (Glencross & Cibich, 1977), selective attention to only the most relevant sources of information is clearly fundamental to successful performance. The success of the boxer trying to anticipate his opponent's punches, the baseball batter trying to predict the forthcoming pitch, the pole vaulter or golfer trying to avoid distractions from crowd noise, or the fullback in rugby trying to field a high kick while being stormed by opposing tacklers, all depend on the extent to which they can attend to only relevant information and exclude attending to irrelevant or distracting events. Distracting information may come not only from external sources (e.g., crowd noise, the fakes of an opponent) but also from within (e.g., subjective feelings of fatigue or excessive thinking about past successes or failures).

The important issues to address in furthering understanding of selective attention, especially as it applies to sports tasks, are therefore:

1. What stimulus events are sufficiently informative (and hence relevant) to warrant detailed processing and, equally, what stimuli (both internal and external) should be ignored? Identifying relevant sources of information for particular sport skills is vital as a means of providing a principled basis for instruction in these activities.

2. Through what mechanism(s) are processing resources selectively allocated to relevant rather than irrelevant stimuli?

3. How might attentional allocation to only relevant sources of information be improved with practice?

It is worth noting that attentional selectivity is not an insular concept nor one completely removed from the notions of attention as alertness and attention as a limited processing resource. The peripheral narrowing effects of heightened arousal, for instance, impact on the breadth of cue processing the player can partake in, while processing resource limitations ultimately constrain the extent to which simultaneous attention to different information sources is possible (Janelle, Singer, & Williams, 1999).

Paradigms for Studying Selective Attention

Paradigms for Examining Fundamental Theories of Selective Attention

Early investigations on selective attention utilized a dichotic listening paradigm which, in essence, was a laboratory analogue for the selective listening that occurs at many social gatherings (the so-called "cocktail party phenomenon"; Cherry, 1953). In this paradigm, people were presented with separate messages to the left and right ears and were required to verbally repeat (or *shadow*) the message presented to one of the ears. The shadowing task was assumed to cause attention to be allocated preferentially to the message that was to be repeated and the interest was in determining to what extent selective attention to only the shadowed message was complete. Measurement was then made of how much, and what, features of the message presented to the other ear could be reported. Studies of this kind (e.g., Cherry, 1953; Mowbray, 1953) consistently indicated that people processed very little of the information from the unshadowed message, apparently being able to selectively process only that information that was relevant to the task at hand, although some particular physical characteristics of the unshadowed message (such as a change from a male to a female voice or the insertion of a high frequency tone) were regularly detected, suggesting preferential (arguably automatic) processing of this kind of information.

Because many more of the selective attention problems encountered in sport involve selecting between competing visual signals rather than auditory signals, selective-looking rather than selective-listening paradigms may be more appropriate. Neisser and Becklen (1975) have presented one such paradigm by superimposing videotapes of separate games on the same television monitor (see Figure 3.7). In this case, the task is to follow one of the games only and to detect the occurrence of a particular event (e.g., a ball being thrown or caught). Despite changes in the stimulus modalities used, the same basic conclusions emerge regarding selective attention from studies using this visual analogue, that is, people can effectively selectively attend to only one of the images with relative ease, even when the competing displays are quite similar (Neisser, 1979), and even unusual events in the other display are only rarely noticed.

Methods for Determining the Direction and Breadth of Selective Attention

In sport psychology, the examination of attentional direction and breadth has been dominated by self-report measures. A popular psychological inventory for assessing individual attentional strengths and weaknesses in a range of performance settings, including sport, is the Test of Attentional and Interpersonal Style (TAIS) (Nideffer, 1976).

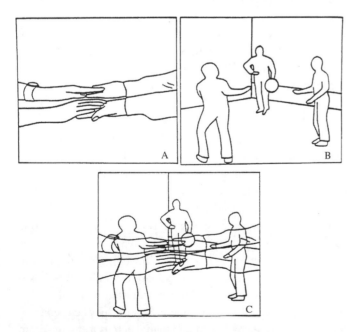

Figure 3.7 Sample single (A and B) and combined (C) video images from a selective looking experiment. From "Selective looking: Attending to visually specified events" by U. Neisser and R. Becklen, 1975, *Cognitive Psychology, 7,* p. 485. Copyright 1975 by Academic Press. Reprinted by permission.

The TAIS is a 144-item paper-and-pencil test structured on two basic theoretical premises. The first is that the attentional requirement of tasks can be adequately represented along two independent dimensions—a width dimension, which refers to the number of concurrent stimuli that can be effectively attended to, and a direction dimension, which refers to the extent to which attention is directed externally to environmental stimuli or internally to cognitions and emotions. Collectively, these dimensions allow the attentional requirements of different tasks to be positioned in one of four possible quadrants (see Nideffer, 1979, for examples). The second premise is that individuals, like tasks, can be classified with respect to some enduring attentional styles as well as with respect to their flexibility to change attentional style to match the situational demands. Measurement of these attentional styles is sought primarily through six scales within the TAIS, three measuring elements of effective attention and three complementary aspects of ineffective attention.

Despite its persistent use by sports psychologists, both the construct and predictive validity of the TAIS have been queried by a number of researchers (see Abernethy, Summers, & Ford, 1998 for a review). Factor analyses of data collected from the TAIS on sports groups do not appear to reveal the two-dimensional structure of attention on which the TAIS was developed, and the subscales are not independent (Ford & Summers, 1992). The attentional breadth (or bandwidth) dimension in particular appears to be multidimensional rather than unidimensional (e.g., Summers & Ford, 1990; Van Schoyck & Grasha, 1981). Further, although some gains in predictive validity may be achieved through the use of sport-specific rather than general test items (Albrecht & Feltz, 1987; Summers, Miller, & Ford, 1991; Van Schoyck & Grasha, 1981), the TAIS is generally a poor discriminator of experts and novices in sports in which selective attention is known to be important (e.g, Landers, Boutcher, & Wang, 1986; Zaichkowsky, Jackson, & Aronson, 1982). When expert-novice differences have been observed they have often been on subscales other than those presupposed to be important for the particular activity (Jackson, 1981). Moreover, the expected relationships between given subscales and specific behavioral tests of different aspects of attention (e.g., dual task and visual search tests) are also rarely observed (e.g., Dewey, Brawley, & Allard, 1989; Vallerand, 1983), casting further doubt on the validity of the measure. Although refutation of much of this contradictory evidence has been attempted (e.g., see Nideffer, 1990), the empirical evidence indicates that the test must be interpreted with caution. Concerns of the type outlined above have lead a number of researchers (e.g., Boutcher, 1992) to seek more objective behavioral and physiological measures or selective attention.

The dual task methods described earlier for assessing peripheral/attentional narrowing provide a potential objective means of assessing attentional breadth but not direction (e.g., see Landers et al., 1985). Decreased awareness or slowed responses to peripheral stimuli while performing a demanding task utilizing central vision may be directly indicative of a transition in attentional focus from broad to narrow. The reduced awareness of fatigued athletes to events occurring around them is a practical example of the kind of attentional breadth changes quantifiable by dual task methods in which the secondary task taps peripheral awareness.

Physiological measures offer some prospect for improved validity for measurement of attentional breadth and direction. For example, J. Lacey's (1967) intake-rejection hypothesis posits a direct relationship between HR changes and attentional direction. Lacey proposed that HR deceleration accompanies the intake of environmental information (i.e., an external focus of attention) whereas in situations where environmental information is rejected in order to focus on internal processes HR acceleration is observed. The intake-rejection hypothesis has received considerable empirical support (e.g., Martin & Venables, 1980), especially with visual RT tasks showing cardiac deceleration (e.g., B. Lacey & Lacey, 1970) and mental arithmetic tasks showing HR increases (e.g., Sharit, Salvendy, & Deisenroth, 1982). Although J. Lacey's (1967) hypothesis is consistent with the HR deceleration which occurs immediately prior to response initiation in a number of sport tasks, other explanations of this phenomenon, which do not involve an attentional direction notion, are also possible (e.g., Van der Molen, Somsen, & Orlebeke, 1985). For instance, research on golf putting by Crews (1989) suggests that an explanation of cardiac changes based on an attentional direction notion is at least partially viable. Crews argued that sensory awareness creates the cardiac deceleration pattern while cognitive elaboration acts to inhibit this effect. These suggestions, like those of Ray and Cole (1985) that spontaneous EEG alpha activity is sensitive to the internality-externality of attentional focus, clearly still require greater empirical verification, especially from examinations conducted in sport-specific settings.

Methods for Determining the Relevance of Specific Cues/Information Sources

One obvious means of attempting to determine what cues are important in a particular sports task is to simply ask expert performers what information they look for or place priority on. The difficulty with this self-report approach is that performers may not have direct verbal access to their control processes (Nisbett & Wilson, 1977), especially if these processes are automated ones. As a consequence they may tend to report the usage of cues that they expect to be important (or have been told are important), rather than the ones they actually use. For example, many tennis players and baseball batters report that they watch the ball right up to the point of contact with the racquet or bat and report seeing the ball actually hit the racquet or bat, yet objective measures of their visual tracking behavior make it clear that visual fixation on the ball is discontinued well before actual contact (Bahill & LaRitz, 1984; Stein & Slatt, 1981). The great difficulty with the study of selective attention is that improvements occur through recognition of stimulus patterns of which the performers are themselves not consciously aware (e.g., Nissen & Bullemer, 1987; Pew, 1974). As Sharp (1978) notes:

> The fact that top-level performers sometimes cannot recount and describe how it is they perform so skillfully . . . suggests that they may be operating at a "pre-attentive" level of processing having predicted the situation through contextual information and expectations derived from experience. (p. 5)

There is clear evidence, from a number of domains, of dissociation between what experts say they do and what they actually do (Annett, 1986; Saxe & Gearhart, 1990; Speelman, 1998). Indeed the capacity of expertise and knowledge to develop in the absence of conscious attention has caused enormous recent interest in the whole domain of implicit expertise and implicit knowledge (Kirsner et al., 1998). A major challenge for sport psychologists and others interested in expert performance is to understand more about the mechanisms of implicit perception (Milner & Goodale, 1995; Rossetti, in press) and implicit learning (e.g., Berry, 1994; Curran & Keele, 1993) and to locate alternative means of probing this knowledge base. It is clear that if self-report techniques are to be used to determine the relevance of different cue sources, they clearly must be used cautiously and preferably in tandem with other, more objective, measures. In this respect, one technique that has received considerable use in the sport and motor expertise literature is the technique of cue occlusion.

Selectively occluded performer's visibility to specific information sources in the display provides a viable and sensitive means of determining the importance of different environmental cues for performance. In the occlusion techniques, the visual display (often the action of an opposing player in sports such as tennis, soccer, and ice hockey) is typically simulated by filming from the performer's normal viewing position. Then, this film is selectively edited to either mask out visibility to specific time periods of environmental information (*temporal occlusion*) or specific spatial regions of the display (*spatial occlusion*). The performer's task in these instances may be to make either a perceptual decision (e.g., "where will the ball land?") or a response-selection decision (e.g., "what stroke should be played?") on the basis of the information available.

In the temporal occlusion technique the emphasis is upon discovering those time periods (or time windows) in which response accuracy is rapidly improved, indicating the pick-up of information from the display. By scanning the display for principal events occurring during these time windows, implications can be drawn as to probable cue usage. The technique has been used quite extensively to demonstrate the value of advance cues for anticipating the action of an opponent in many ball sports. Film simulations have generally been used (see Abernethy, Wann, & Parks, 1998 for a review), but "real-world" analogues using occluding visors (e.g., Starkes & Lindley, 1994) and electronically controlled glasses (e.g., Starkes, Edwards, Dissanayake, & Dunn, 1995) are also possible. In the spatial occlusion technique, cue importance can be assessed directly from the response decrements that occur when visibility of a given cue is occluded. Provided realistic display simulations can be developed, both these occlusion techniques are very useful ones for determining patterns of selective information pick-up by different performers, especially when both procedures are applied to the same activity to provide confirmatory checks (see Abernethy & Russell, 1987a, for a sample application).

Another popular means of attempting to ascertain patterns of information pick-up or cue usage in sports tasks is to monitor where players look through the use of sophisticated eye movement recording devices (e.g., see Vickers, 1992; A. Williams, Davids, Burwitz, & Williams, 1994). People constantly move their eyes in order to maintain high visual clarity on features of interest and information is, as a rule, only actively picked up during fixations (periods when the eye remains relatively stationary). Fixation locations, nevertheless, may also be selected in order to help optimise the pick up of information from the periphery. Consequently, information about the location, duration, and order of fixations in a given player's visual search pattern *may* be insightful with respect to their selective attention. Although at a global level visual search pattern analyses may be revealing, there are limitations in

the eye movement approach that need to be recognized and differences between visual search and selective attention that need to be highlighted (Abernethy, 1988c). The major limitations with the eye movement recording approach are:

1. As attention can be moved around the visual field without making eye movements, visual fixation and attention are therefore not one and the same (e.g., Remington, 1980; Shulman, Remington, & McLean, 1979);

2. Visual orientation (as shown through fixations) does not necessarily guarantee information pick-up (e.g., Stager & Angus, 1978) or, in other words, "looking" does not equate with "seeing";

3. Eye movement recording techniques are only informative with respect to central vision; they reveal nothing about the important pick-up of information for orienting, locating stimuli, and judging speed of motion and orientation, much of which occurs through peripheral vision (e.g., Leibowitz & Post, 1982);

4. The substantial trial-to-trial variability (Noton & Stark, 1971) and task specificity (Yarbus, 1967) of eye movement patterns makes it difficult to reach reliable conclusions about the importance of different display features; and

5. The data collection technique is in itself difficult and the recording devices are potentially disruptive to a persons' normal allocation of attention and information pick-up (e.g., Megaw & Richardson, 1979).

More detailed consideration of these constraints and the general value of eye movement recording approaches in sports are provided elsewhere (Abernethy, 1988c). Like the verbalization procedures, eye movement recording approaches to determining cue usage in sports may be most effective when used in combination with other methods (e.g., Helsen & Pauwels, 1993).

Performance Limitations Imposed by Selective Attention

Selective attention is a double-edged phenomenon—it is a blessing in terms of helping the performer overcome potential distractions but a curse in situations where attention needs to be simultaneously divided between more information sources than the person is able to concurrently process. A useful metaphor for describing these strengths and limitations of selective attention is in terms of a searchlight (Watchel, 1967) or zoom lens (Eriksen,

1990). The intent in using a searchlight is to focus the light only on that which is important (as everything within the beam of light comes under attention regardless of whether it is important or not). The breadth of the beam in this sense has to be adjusted according to the range of information that has to be picked up and the position of the beam may need to be constantly adjusted if important information exists at a number of different spatial locations. Further, just as the searchlight is only a guide to its user, varied visual attention is only a guide to the human brain. The brain then interprets the information available with regard to past experiences, contexts, and plans.

The searchlight metaphor is useful in describing the three main types of error associated with attentional selectivity, for example:

- Failure to focus all attention on the limited essential elements for task success ("having the searchlight too broad");
- Being distracted from relevant information by irrelevant information ("having the searchlight pointed in the wrong direction"); and
- Being unable to divide attention between all the stimuli that need to be processed concurrently ("having the searchlight beam too narrow or being unable to move the searchlight rapidly enough from one spot to the next").

The archer who performs poorly through directing attention in only the general direction of the target rather than concentrating intently on the precise point on the target he or she wishes to hit provides an example of the first type of error. The basketball player who falls for an opponent's head fake rather than watching his or her trunk for cues, or the golfer who is distracted from the task at hand by thoughts about previous shots, commit errors of the second type. Errors of the third type arise in situations where there is simply too much relevant information to process in too short a time. The beginner soccer player may have concurrent processing demands for relevant visual information (regarding the position of teammates, opponents, the sidelines, and goal posts), kinesthetic information (to help in the control of the dribbled ball), and auditory information (verbal instructions from the coach, captain, and teammates). Yet, some of this information will not be able to be processed in the time available and errors such as losing possession of the ball will inevitably arise. Switching attention between different stimulus modalities also appears to be a time-consuming process and delays in processing of

the order of 100 ms may occur if this switching is unanticipated (Moray & Fitter, 1973).

In sports situations, a number of factors will influence the efficiency of the selective attention process. In addition to limitations posed by the amount of irrelevant information (and its discernability from relevant information sources) and by the extent of attentional switching required by the task, the three principal factors influencing the effectiveness of the selective attention process will be (1) the total amount of information in the display, (2) the time required to pick up and process the essential information, and (3) the ability of the player (Jones, 1972).

Theories and Models of Selective Attention

The older formal theories of selective attention, which still tend to dominate the selective attention literature, have typically assumed the existence of fixed structural limitations to the parallel processing of input information (an assumption that was noted in the previous section on resources may not be justifiable). These older theories have varied mainly in terms of where the selection process is thought to take place, and hence where the bottleneck between parallel and serial processing is located (Shiffrin, Craig, & Cohen, 1973). (See Figure 3.8.)

Filter Models of Selective Attention

Broadbent (1958) attempted to explain the findings from the dichotic listening experiments of Cherry (1953) and others by proposing the existence of an early filter mechanism that selects incoming signals for further processing on the basis of some physical characteristics. Selected information was assumed to receive further detailed (resource-intensive) processing while the nonselected information was assumed, in the absence of further processing, to be subject to rapid decay and loss. The difficulty for this theory was in demonstrating that some apparently irrelevant information nevertheless appears to receive further and detailed processing. Some aspects of the nonshadowed message in dichotic listening tasks, for example, manage to gain access to the limited processing resource(s) and to consciousness. In the visual domain, the Stroop phenomenon (Stroop, 1935) provides a powerful demonstration of the interference effects of irrelevant stimulus features on RT (e.g., Keele, 1973). To account for these effects, Deutsch and Deutsch (1963) proposed that the selective filter was located much later in the information processing chain; at the completion of the perceptual analysis stage rather than at the completion of the stimulus encoding stage. The question of early versus late selection has

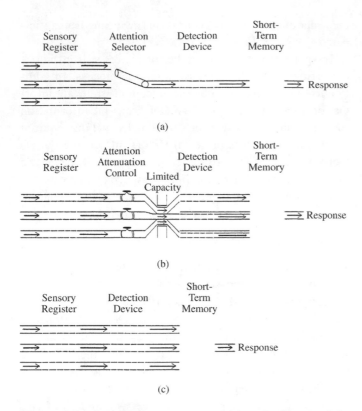

Figure 3.8 Comparative structure of (a) early filter models, (b) attentuation models, and (c) late selection models of selective attention. From "On the degree of attention and capacity limitations in tactile processing" by R.M. Shiffrin, J.C. Craig, & E. Cohen, 1973, *Perception and Psychophysics, 13,* p. 329. Copyright 1973 by The Psychonomics Society, Inc. Reprinted by permission.

remained a persistently interesting one to cognitive psychologists (e.g., see Broadbent, 1982) and, more recently, to physiological psychologists (e.g., Näätänen, 1988).

The Attenuation Model of Selective Attention

An alternative way of explaining how some, apparently irrelevant, stimuli manage to gain access to limited processing resources without necessitating a late selection filter of the type proposed by Deutsch and Deutsch (1963), is to assume that all incoming stimuli are subject to a series of increasingly complex signal analysis tests. The attenuation model of Treisman (1969) proposed a series of tests (the first based on physical properties of the stimuli, the second based on collective stimulus patterns, and the third based on semantics) with irrelevant information being progressively attenuated at each of these levels of analysis. The attenuation model therefore differs from the filter model in two principal ways: (1) it proposes selection is based on

elements in addition to the simple physical properties of the incoming stimuli; and (2) it proposes that the analyses that guide selection of stimuli for further processing (the so-called *pre-attentive analyses;* Neisser, 1967) occur in an essentially continuous rather than discrete fashion. The advantage of the attenuation model conceptually is that it provides a mechanism for reducing the inefficiency that would occur if all signals were to be processed through a full perceptual analysis (as a late selection model requires). Its apparent disadvantage is its complexity (e.g., Wessells, 1982), although this in itself should not be a reason for discarding the theory. Empirical evidence available to compare the two approaches appears more consistent with the attenuation model than a filter model of late selection (Eysenck, 1984).

Pertinence-Based Models of Selective Attention

An attractive model in terms of explaining selective attention in natural settings is the pertinence-based model presented by Norman (1968). In keeping with Deutsch and Deutsch's (1963) approach, Norman's model assumes late selection takes place, with short-term memory rather than the stimulus encoding process being the effective locus of selectivity. Signal pertinence, derived largely from the performer's past experiences and contextual knowledge of similar situations, is assumed to be the foundation upon which the discrimination between those signals for further processing and those to be ignored is based (see Figure 3.9).

Signals arriving at the sensory receptors are believed to be initially subjected to feature analysis, the result of which is automatic representation in short-term memory. In many cases, representations for given signals pre-exist through activation based on expectations of importance (pertinence) derived from past experience. Selection for further, attention-demanding, processing is conceived to be determined on the basis of the overall level of memory activation arising from the joint inputs from the current sensory analysis and the expectancies arising from prior, remembered experiences. The input signals most likely to be selected for continued processing within this model are therefore those which are both preconceived as being of high pertinence and which are also revealed by the sensory analyses as being physically present. The selection in this context is therefore conceived of as being both *data-driven* (by the current sensory information) and *conceptually-driven* (by the experiential input). The model is limited in terms of its use of fixed capacity assumptions (cf. Kahneman, 1973; Wickens, 1992) and its failure to provide

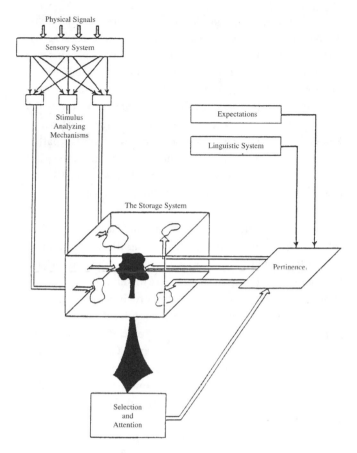

Figure 3.9 Norman's pertinence-based model of selective attention. From *Memory and attention* by D.A. Norman, 1976, 2nd ed., p. 31. Copyright 1976 by John Wiley & Sons. Reprinted by permission.

any explicit statement about how the control of action proceeds (Allport, 1980a). Nevertheless, it provides a very useful framework from within which to consider the changes in selective attention which accompany skill acquisition.

Neuropsychological Models of Selective Attention

The study of various disorders in visual selective attention that accompany different types of brain damage have provided some alternative insights into the way in which selective attention typically functions. On the basis of neuropsychological evidence, Posner and Petersen (1990) have proposed that for visual selective attention there are at least three independent underlying abilities: (1) the ability to *disengage* attention from a particular visual stimulus, (2) the ability to *shift* attention from one visual stimulus to another, and (3) the ability to *engage* attention on a new stimulus. Different areas of the brain appear to be implicated in each element. Disengagement of attention from a

stimulus appears to involve the parietal lobe primarily, shifting of attention appears to involve the midbrain, and the pulvinar nucleus appears to be centrally involved in the pick-up of information from a particular location. While a fuller understanding of brain mechanisms underpinning selective attention is now possibly within reach (with the increasing sophistication of brain imaging and other neurophysiological techniques now becoming available) the evidence to date is certainly sufficient to demonstrate that selective attention is a distributed function involving numerous functionally specific structures. Models of attention that are based around a single structure are clearly inconsistent with the majority of evidence emerging from neuropsychological studies of visual attentional deficits.

Changes in Selective Attention That Accompany Skill Acquisition

Even in simple motor tasks, selective attention can apparently be improved considerably with practice although much of this improvement may well occur below the level of consciousness. In the motor skills literature, persistent claims have been made regarding differences in the selective attention capabilities of expert and novice sports performers. Knapp (1963), for example, suggested that:

> The unskilled performer may notice a number of stimuli but he will be unable to perceive which are the important ones or what the responses should be. He will tend not to perceive any pattern to the stimuli and since the capacity to take in information is limited the number of stimuli to which he can pay attention will be relatively few. The skilled person on the other hand possesses a mental framework which takes into account a large number of the stimuli that have occurred before. He notices small changes from the expected display and is therefore able to react to them quickly. (p. 160)

Norman's (1968) selective attention model suggests at least two potential avenues for improvements in selective attention with practice (and hence expert-novice differences in selective attention):

1. There may be changes in the manner in which the available current perceptual analysis is conducted; and
2. There may be changes in the assignment of pertinence arising as a consequence of the learner's expanding experiential base.

In the subsections that follow, the existing evidence (primarily from within the visual modality) for differences between expert and novice sports performers on these two aspects of the selective attention process is briefly presented. For further, and more detailed, commentary, see Starkes et al. (Chapter 7).

Expert-Novice Differences in Performing the Current Perceptual Analysis

A useful distinction, in considering expert-novice differences in performing perceptual analyses, can be drawn between the concepts of visual "hardware" and "software" (Starkes & Deakin, 1984). This distinction, which has obvious origins in the information processing model of human performance, is between physical characteristics of the performer's visual systems (as determined from generalized optometric measures, for example) and specific information-processing capabilities (as determined from sports-specific tests). Although there have been some reports of differences between expert and novice sports performers on some optometric parameters (e.g., Graybiel, Jokl, & Trapp, 1955; J. Williams & Thirer, 1975) and on measures such as simple reaction time (e.g., Bhanot & Sidhu, 1979), the evidence is largely equivocal. While there appears little evidence to indicate that the visual hardware of the highly skilled players is systematically superior to that of the general population, there are increasingly clear demonstrations of expert-novice differences in the ability to perform selective attention tasks in which the opportunity for using acquired situation-specific strategies (or software) is present (Abernethy, Wann, & Parks, 1998; Starkes, 1987). The strongest, systematic evidence for a perceptual basis for sports expertise exists with respect to expert advantage on anticipation tasks and on pattern recognition tasks.

Systematic evidence exists, primarily through the use of the temporal occlusion paradigm, to demonstrate in a range of fast-ball sports that (1) information available prior to ball flight (often referred to as advance cues) is of use in predicting the direction and speed of forthcoming ball flight (predictions made on the basis of advance information are in excess of chance levels, usually for novices as well as experts), and (2) experts are superior to novices in their ability to pick up this early information from the action of the opponent or opposing team. (See Abernethy, Wann, & Parks, 1998, for a review of this literature.) Further, through the use of both temporal and spatial occlusion paradigms in conjunction with eye movement recordings, it has been demonstrated that these observable differences in anticipatory performance are related to differences in selective attention.

Expert players in racquet sports, for example, attend more to earlier occurring, more proximal sources of ad-

vance information (specifically, arm and racquet cues) than do novices (who use racquet cues alone) (Abernethy & Russell, 1987a). A systematic transition to using these earlier cues accompanies skill development through practice (Abernethy, 1988b). Experts also appear to attend more effectively to the essential kinematic details in their opponent's movement patterns than do novices (Abernethy, 1996). Expert-novice differences in visual search patterns occur less systematically, being observed in some sports activities (e.g., Vickers, 1992; A. Williams et al., 1994) but not in others (e.g., Abernethy, 1990; Abernethy & Russell, 1987b; Helsen & Pauwels, 1993). The latter observations of search pattern similarities in the face of expertise-related differences in cue usage highlight the potential difficulties of using eye movement recording alone as an indicator of individual differences in selective attention. It should be noted, however, that there is some evidence to suggest that differences in visual search rate in sports tasks *may* exist, with experts making fewer fixations each of longer duration (e.g., Bard, Fleury, Carrière & Hallé, 1980). This effect, if it indeed exists, may be explicable in terms of either the experts' lower total processing load (the *variable processing rate hypothesis* of Teichner & Krebs, 1974) or their need for fewer perceptual cues in order to construct the whole event (the *perceptual automatizing hypothesis* of Furst, 1971; Abernethy, 1988c).

The obvious advantage of selectively attending to advance cues which are useful in anticipating the action of an opponent or opposing team members is that not only does this allow responses to be initiated earlier, hence allowing experts to give the impression of ". . . having all the time in the world . . ." (Bartlett, 1947, p. 836), but the recognition of redundancy in the display also decreases the information processing load. The reduced processing load frees up processing resources and therefore may also contribute to the apparent ease that characterizes skilled sports performance. The transition to attending to different (earlier) information sources, which occurs with experience, as the distinctive features of the display are learned and the relationship between display features is acquired, is typical of most types of perceptual learning (E. Gibson, 1969).

Allied with the expert-novice differences in selective attention to different advance cues is a large body of evidence indicating expert superiority in the pick-up of complex structure of the type that exists in the stimulus patterns provided by many team sports. Using a paradigm initially developed by De Groot (1965) and Chase and Simon (1973) for examining chess skill, Allard and Burnett (1985); Allard, Graham, and Paarsalu (1980); Starkes (1987); and Starkes and Allard (1983) have been able to demonstrate that expert basketball and field hockey players are superior to novices in their recall of the position of the players within briefly presented slides of structured game situations (such as an offensive pattern in basketball). However, these differences disappear if the slides fail to depict structured events (e.g., a time-out in basketball), indicating that experts do not have larger general memory capacities than novices (a hardware difference). Rather, they have a superiority that relates to the ability to selectively attend to structure which is inherent within their particular sports (a software difference). There appears, therefore, to be objective evidence for skilled players having a superior ability to "read" patterns of play and this, in all probability, is a consequence of selective attention differences from novices. The superior recognition of embedded stimulus patterns also reveals itself in superior performance by experts in re-sequencing tasks where the images are drawn from their domain of sport expertise (e.g., Vickers, 1986).

Accurate processing of information from the flight of an approaching ball or equivalent is obviously a crucial part of successful performance in many sports. It may be reasonable to also expect expert-novice differences in selective attention to key visual variables which inform about the position and time-of-arrival of the ball. Although coincidence-timing tasks that use apparent motion rather than real ball flight generally do not discriminate expert from novice performers (e.g., Del Rey, Whitehurst, Wughalter, & Barnwell, 1983), the timing of interceptive tasks such as hitting and catching performed in response to real ball flight indicate significant proficiency-related differences (e.g., Savelsbergh & Bootsma, 1994; Savelsbergh, Whiting, & Pijpers, 1992). Selective attention differences to critical optical control variables may well account for these observed differences between experts and novices in timing accuracy (Bootsma & Peper, 1992; Bootsma & van Wieringen, 1990).

For selective attention to operate effectively in sports situations, it is imperative that, just as processsing resources must be allocated to relevant cues, distracting sources of information must receive no detailed processing. To date there have been few studies directed toward assessing this using behavioral measures, although some older paper-and-pencil tests such as Witkin, Dyk, Faterson, Goodenough, and Karp's (1962) field dependence/independence (or perceptual style) test, have been used, albeit with limited success. The field dependence/independence, or perceptual style test, examines the capabilities of performers to locate a particular figure (usually a regular geometric shape) within a background field full of distractions of different kinds. The assumption is that those individuals who can ignore the irrelevant background information in order to focus only on the characteristics of the target item (classified as field independent individuals) will also be better equipped to avoid distractions in natural tasks of the type which exist in sport. Although there are some studies demonstrating the expected greater prevalence of field independence amongst elite athletes (e.g., Pargman, Schreiber, & Stein, 1974) proficiency differences on this measure are rarely found (e.g., see MacGillivary, 1981). The absence of sports-specific stimuli and the attendant losses of ecological validity from within tests of this type have undoubtedly contributed to the failure to demonstrate clear expert-novice differences.

Expert-Novice Differences in the Assignment of Pertinence to Different Events and Sources of Information

In laboratory selective attention tasks, the sampling of different information sources becomes more optimal as the participants gain sufficient experience to generate an accurate statistical model of the environment (Senders, 1964). Knowledge of the probabilities of different events occurring in sports settings may be advantageous both in the reduction of RT (e.g., Alain & Proteau, 1980) and in the optimization of available attentional resources. In sport tasks, the non-equiprobability of different events provides a basis for facilitating RT to the more probable event (Alain & Proteau, 1980) although in laboratory simulations large deviations from equiprobability for two events, in the order of 9:1, are needed before RT to the more probable stimulus is significantly decreased (e.g., Dillon, Crassini, & Abernethy, 1989). There is limited evidence to suggest that the subjective estimates of event probabilities developed by experts in sport may more closely approximate actual event probabilities than the estimates novices use as a basis for their selective attention and decision making (e.g., see Cohen & Dearnaley, 1962; Whiting, 1979). Advancement of knowledge in this area still seems to be restricted substantially by the absence of a suitable investigative paradigm (Paull & Glencross, 1997).

Implications for Skill Acquisition, Instruction, and the Design of Practice

Isolation of the relevant cues used by performers in specific sports tasks is an essential element for improved and informed practice and instruction. Until the relevant cues for expert performance in a given activity are known, the effectiveness of instruction and of practice drills aimed at enhancing performance will be necessarily limited.

In sports where the relevant cues for expert performance have been isolated, skill acquisition may be enhanced by highlighting these cues in practice. Some evidence exists to suggest anticipation and pattern recognition can be improved through specific perceptual training (e.g., Abernethy, Wood, & Parks, 1999; Farrow, Chivers, Hardingham, & Sasche, 1998; Starkes & Lindley, 1994), but not through generalized visual training (e.g., Wood & Abernethy, 1997); nonetheless, clear demonstrations of the efficacy of the perceptual training approaches to improve actual sports performance rather than mere perceptual performance are still needed. Psychological skills training (as described elsewhere in this *Handbook*) may prove effective in enhancing selective attention although clearly the chances of these programs being effective will increase substantially if the optimal pattern of cue usage needed for maximal performance in the particular sport is known. Although there is little empirical evidence available to date to determine the effectiveness of these types of training programs (Singer, Cauraugh, Tennant, Murphey, Chen, & Lidor, 1991), what is available indicates that multicomponent attentional training that provides athletes with skills in relaxation, visualization, and focusing and refocusing may be helpful in maintaining performance in the face of external and unexpected distractors (Singer, Cauraugh, Murphey, Chen, & Lidor, 1991).

Because of the implicit nature of much of perceptual expertise, approaches that provide the opportunity to practice in the absence of specific attention to the task of interest may yet prove the most advantageous (e.g., Magill, 1994; Singer, Lidor, & Cauraugh, 1993). More evidence-based comparisons of practice regimes varying in their attentional focus (e.g., Green & Flowers, 1991; Masters, 1992; Wulf & Weigelt, 1997) are desperately needed to advance understanding of the selective attention-skill acquisition nexus beyond its current state.

SUMMARY AND CONCLUSIONS

Attention is clearly a broad and multifacetted psychological construct that impacts on sports performance and learning in a large number of quite diverse ways. In its various contexts of alertness, limited processing resources, and selectivity, attention imposes constraints on human performance that can only be partially offset by strategic planning. Knowing more about the sports-specific constraints imposed on performance by attention and knowing more about how these constraints are either alleviated or exploited by skilled performers is fundamental to the development of principled approaches to coaching and instruction of all types and at all skill levels. Given the long history of research interest in the topic of attention, the limited nature of existing knowledge about attention in "real world" tasks like those required in sport is somewhat disappointing. The limited emergence of knowledge about attention that is of direct practical significance to the sport psychologist is, however, a reflection of a general failure of cognitive psychology to satisfactorily resolve three fundamental issues in the study of attention: (1) the clear delineation of the *function(s) of attention;* (2) the development of *plausible, global theories of attention;* and (3) clearer understanding of the role of implicit, automatic and unattended processes in skilled performance.

Failure to satisfactorily delineate the function(s) of attention has been largely a consequence of the historical pre-occupation with the determination of capacity limitations and the discovery of processing bottlenecks; endeavors that have turned out to be largely fruitless. Coupled with this structural mindset has been a predominant use of simple laboratory task that place demands on attention which are far removed from the kinds of demands which exist in the natural tasks for which explanation is ultimately sought. A particular concern, given that (one of) the prime function(s) of attention may be in selectivity of perceptual-motor control (selection-for-action) (Allport, 1989), is the decoupling, in experimental settings, of the normal functional links between perception and action. The importance of studying perception and action (and hence also attention) in natural tasks is now recognized, thanks largely to the impact in the past decades of ecological psychology, grounded in the writings of J. Gibson (1979) on perception and Bernstein (1967) on action. Only by studying action in such settings may the true and complete functional importance of attention be revealed.

The development of plausible, generic theories of attention has been limited by the enduring assumption that attention is somehow a unitary process controlled by a single system. Such a view, as studies of neuropsychology now clearly reveal (Posner & Petersen, 1990), is unjustified. As Allport (1993, pp. 203–204) notes:

> There is no one uniform function, or mental operation (in general, no causal mechanism) to which all so-called attentional phenomena can be attributed. . . . It seems no more plausible that there should be one unique mechanism, or computational resource, as the causal basis of all attentional phenomena than that there should be a unitary causal basis for thought, or perception, or of any other traditional category of folk psychology.

Development of function-specific modules of attention appears the sensible way forward.

A major issue that must be addressed satisfactorily in order to advance understanding of attentional phenomena in general, and those that impinge upon learning and performance in particular, is the question of how implicit learning, knowledge, and perception operates and how it interacts with more explicit forms of knowledge and learning. The past decade in particular has seen a growing awareness of the significance and centrality of implicit processes to all types of perception, cognition, and action with new findings emerging that challenge significantly traditional views on attention and the implications that might be drawn for practice. Researchers in motor control and sports psychology need to position themselves at the forefront of research on implicit processes given the integral role automaticity and instruction play in the skill learning and competitive sports environments.

REFERENCES

Abernethy, B. (1988a). Dual-task methodology and motor skills research: Some applications and methodological constraints. *Journal of Human Movement Studies, 14,* 101–132.

Abernethy, B. (1988b). The effects of age and expertise upon perceptual skill development in a racquet sport. *Research Quarterly for Exercise and Sport, 59,* 210–221.

Abernethy, B. (1988c). Visual search in sport and ergonomics: Its relationship to selective attention and performer expertise. *Human Performance, 1,* 205–235.

Abernethy, B. (1990). Expertise, visual search, and information pick-up in squash. *Perception, 19,* 63–77.

Abernethy, B. (1993). Attention. In R.N. Singer, M. Murphey, & L.K. Tennant (Eds.), *Handbook of research on sport psychology* (pp. 127–170). New York: Macmillan.

Abernethy, B. (1996). Training the visual-perceptual skills of athletes: Insights from the study of motor expertise. *American Journal of Sports Medicine, 24,* 589–592.

Abernethy, B., & Russell, D.G. (1987a). Expert-novice differences in an applied selective attention task. *Journal of Sport Psychology, 9,* 326–345.

Abernethy, B., & Russell, D.G. (1987b). The relationship between expertise and visual search strategy in a racquet sport. *Human Movement Science, 6,* 283–319.

Abernethy, B., Summers, J.J., & Ford, S. (1998). Issues in the measurement of attention. In J.L. Duda (Ed.), *Advancements in sport and exercise psychology measurement* (pp. 173–193). Morgantown, WV: FIT Press.

Abernethy, B., Wann, J.P., & Parks, S.L (1998). Training perceptual-motor skills for sport. In B. Elliott (Ed.), *Training in sport: Applying sport science* (pp. 1–68). Chichester, England: Wiley.

Abernethy, B., Wood, J.M., & Parks, S.L. (1999). Can the anticipatory skills of experts be learned by novices? *Research Quarterly for Exercise and Sport, 70,* 313–318.

Ackerman, P.L., & Schneider, W. (1985). Individual differences in automatic and controlled processing. In R.F. Dillon (Ed.), *Individual differences in cognition* (Vol. 2, pp. 35–66). New York: Academic Press.

Ackerman, P.L., Schneider, W., & Wickens, C.D. (1984). Deciding the existence of a time-sharing ability: A combined methodological and theoretical approach. *Human Factors, 26,* 71–82.

Adams, J.A. (1966). Some mechanisms of motor responding: An examination of attention. In E.A. Bilodeau (Ed.), *Acquisition of skill* (pp. 169–200). New York: Academic Press.

Alain, C., & Proteau, L. (1980). Decision making in sport. In C.H. Nadeau, W.R. Halliwell, K.M. Newell, & G.C. Roberts (Eds.), *Psychology of motor behavior and sport–1979* (pp. 465–477). Champaign, IL: Human Kinetics.

Albrecht, R.R., & Feltz, D.L. (1987). Generality and specificity of attention related to competitive anxiety and sport performance. *Journal of Sport Psychology, 9,* 231–248.

Allard, F., & Burnett, N. (1985). Skill in sport. *Canadian Journal of Psychology, 39,* 294–312.

Allard, F., Graham, S., & Paarsalu, M.L. (1980). Perception in sport: Basketball. *Journal of Sport Psychology, 2,* 14–21.

Allport, D.A. (1980a). Attention and performance. In G. Claxton (Ed.), *New directions in cognitive psychology* (pp. 112–153). London: Routledge & Kegan Paul.

Allport, D.A. (1980b). Patterns and actions: Cognitive mechanisms are content-specific. In G. Claxton (Ed.), *New directions in cognitive psychology* (pp. 26–64). London: Routledge & Kegan Paul.

Allport, D.A. (1989). Visual attention. In M.I. Posner (Ed.), *Foundations of cognitive science* (pp. 631–682). Cambridge, MA: MIT Press.

Allport, D.A. (1993). Attention and control: Have we been asking the wrong questions? A critical review of twenty-five years. In D.E. Meyer & S.M. Kornblum (Eds.), *Attention and performance XIV* (pp. 183–218). Cambridge, MA: MIT Press.

Allport, D.A., Antonis, B., & Reynolds, P. (1972). On the division of attention: A disproof of the single channel hypothesis. *Quarterly Journal of Experimental Psychology, 24,* 225–235.

Annett, J. (1986). On knowing how to do things. In H. Heuer & C. Fromm (Eds.), *Generation and modulation of action patterns* (pp. 187–200). Berlin, Germany: Springer-Verlag.

Bahill, A.T., & LaRitz, T. (1984). Why can't batters keep their eyes on the ball? *American Scientist, 72,* 249–253.

Barber, P.J. (1989). Executing two tasks at once. In A.M. Colley & J.R. Beech (Eds.), *Acquisition and performance of cognitive skills* (pp. 217–245). Chichester, England: Wiley.

Bard, C., Fleury, M., Carrière, L., & Hallé, M. (1980). Analysis of gymnastics judges' visual search. *Research Quarterly for Exercise and Sport, 51,* 267–273.

Bartlett, F.C. (1947, June 14). The measurement of human skill. *British Medical Journal,* 835–838, 877–880.

Beatty, J. (1982). Task-evoked pupillary responses, processing load, and the structure of processing resources. *Psychological Bulletin, 91,* 276–292.

Beatty, J., & Wagoner, B.L. (1978). Pupillometric signs of brain activation vary with level of cognitive processing. *Science, 199,* 1216–1218.

Bernstein, N. (1967). *The co-ordination and regulation of movements.* Oxford, England: Pergamon Press.

Berry, D.C. (1994). Implicit learning: Twenty-five years on. A tutorial. In C. Umilta & M. Moscovitch (Eds.), *Attention and performance XV: Conscious and nonconscious information processing* (pp. 755–782). Cambridge, MA: MIT Press.

Bhanot, J.L., & Sidhu, L.S. (1979). Reaction time of Indian hockey players with reference to three levels of participation. *Journal of Sports Medicine and Physical Fitness, 19,* 199–204.

Binet, A. (1890). La concurrence des états psychologiques [Competition in psychology]. *Revue Philosophique de la France et de l'étranger, 24,* 138–155.

Bliss, C.B. (1892–1893). Investigations in reaction time and attention. *Studies of the Yale Psychological Laboratory, 1,* 1–55.

Bootsma, R.J., & Peper, C.E. (1992). Predictive visual information sources for the regulation of action with special emphasis on catching and hitting. In L. Proteau & D. Elliott (Eds.), *Vision and motor control* (pp. 285–314). Amsterdam: North Holland.

Bootsma, R.J., & van Wieringen, P.C. (1990). Timing an attacking forehand drive in table tennis. *Journal of Experimental Psychology: Human Perception and Performance, 16,* 21–29.

Boring, E.G. (1970). Attention: Research and beliefs concerning the concept in scientific psychology before 1930. In D.I. Mostofsky (Ed.), *Attention: Contemporary theory and analysis* (pp. 5–8). New York: Appleton-Century-Crofts.

Boutcher, S.H. (1992). Attention and athletic performance: An integrated approach. In T.S. Horn (Ed.), *Advances in sport psychology* (pp. 251–265). Champaign, IL: Human Kinetics.

Broadbent, D.E. (1958). *Perception and communication.* New York: Pergamon Press.

Broadbent, D.E. (1982). Task combination and selective intake of information. *Acta Psychologica, 50,* 253–290.

Broadbent, D.E., & Gregory, M. (1967). Psychological refractory period and the length of time required to make a decision. *Proceedings of the Royal Society, 168B,* 181–193.

Brouwer, W.H., Waterink, W., Van Wolffelaar, P.C., & Rothengatter, T. (1991). Divided attention in experienced young and older drivers: Lane tracking and visual analysis in a dynamic driving simulator. *Human Factors, 33,* 573–582.

Brown, T.L., & Carr, T.H. (1989). Automaticity in skill acquisition: Mechanisms for reducing interference in concurrent performance. *Journal of Experimental Psychology: Human Perception and Performance, 15,* 686–700.

Cacioppo, J.T., & Berntson, G.G. (1992). Social psychological contributions to the decade of the brain: Doctrine of multilevel analysis. *American Psychologist, 47,* 1019–1028.

Castiello, U., & Umilta, C. (1988). Temporal dimensions of mental effort in different sports. *International Journal of Sport Psychology, 19,* 199–210.

Chase, W.G., & Simon, H.A. (1973). Perception in chess. *Cognitive Psychology, 4,* 55–81.

Cherry, E.C. (1953). Some experiments on the recognition of speech, with one and with two ears. *Journal of the Acoustical Society of America, 25,* 975–979.

Cohen, J., & Dearnaley, E.J. (1962). Skill and judgement of footballers in attempting to score goals. *British Journal of Psychology, 53,* 71–88.

Cowen, N. (1995). *Attention and memory: An integrated framework.* New York: Oxford University Press.

Crews, D.L. (1989). *The influence of attentive states on golf putting as indicated by cardiac and electrocortical activity.* Unpublished doctoral dissertation, Arizona State University, Tempe.

Crosby, J.V., & Parkinson, J.R. (1979). A dual task investigation of pilots' skill level. *Ergonomics, 22,* 1301–1313.

Crossman, E.R.F.W. (1959). A theory of the acquisition of speed skill. *Ergonomics, 2,* 153–166.

Curran, T., & Keele, S.W. (1993). Attentional and nonattentional forms of sequence learning. *Journal of Experimental Psychology: Human Perception and Performance, 19,* 189–202.

Damos, D.L., Bittner, A.C., Kennedy, R.S., & Harbeson, M.M. (1981). Effects of extended practice on dual-task tracking performance. *Human Factors, 23,* 627–632.

Damos, D.L., & Wickens, C.D. (1980). The identification and transfer of timesharing skills. *Acta Psychologica, 46,* 15–39.

Davis, R. (1959). The role of "attention" in the psychological refractory period. *Quarterly Journal of Experimental Psychology, 11,* 211–220.

De Groot, A.D. (1965). *Thought and choice in chess.* The Hague: Mouton.

Del Rey, P., Whitehurst, M., Wughalter, E., & Barnwell, J. (1983). Contextual interference and experience in acquisition and transfer. *Perceptual and Motor Skills, 57,* 241–242.

Deutsch, J.A., & Deutsch, D. (1963). Attention: Some theoretical considerations. *Psychological Review, 70,* 80–90.

Dewey, D., Brawley, L.R., & Allard, F. (1989). Do the TAIS attentional-style scales predict how visual information is processed? *Journal of Sport & Exercise Psychology, 11,* 171–186.

Dillon, J.M., Crassini, B., & Abernethy, B. (1989). Stimulus uncertainty and response time in a simulated racquet-sport task. *Journal of Human Movement Studies, 17,* 115–132.

Donchin, E. (1984). Dissociation between electrophysiology and behavior: A disaster or a challenge? In E. Donchin (Ed.), *Cognitive psychophysiology: Event-related potentials and the study of cognition* (pp. 107–118). Hillsdale, NJ: Erlbaum.

Donchin, E., Ritter, W., & McCallum, C. (1978). Cognitive psychophysiology: The endogenous components of the ERP. In E. Callaway, P. Tueting, & S. Koslow (Eds.), *Brain event-related potentials in man* (pp. 349–441). New York: Academic Press.

Ells, J.G. (1973). Analysis of temporal and attentional aspects of movement control. *Journal of Experimental Psychology, 99,* 10–21.

Eriksen, C.W. (1990). Attentional search of the visual field. In D. Brogan (Ed.), *Visual search* (pp. 3–19). London: Taylor & Francis.

Eysenck, M.W. (1984). *A handbook of cognitive psychology.* London: Erlbaum.

Farrow, D., Chivers, P., Hardingham, C., & Sasche, S. (1998). The effect of video based perceptual training on the tennis return of serve. *International Journal of Sport Psychology, 29,* 231–242.

Fodor, J. (1983). *The modularity of mind: An essay on faculty psychology.* Cambridge, MA: MIT Press.

Ford, S.K., & Summers, J.J. (1992). The factorial validity of the TAIS attentional style subscales. *Journal of Sport & Exercise Psychology, 14,* 283–297.

Fowler, C.A., & Turvey, M.T. (1978). Skill acquisition: An event approach with special reference to searching for the optimum of a function of several variables. In G.E. Stelmach (Ed.), *Information processing in motor control and learning* (pp. 1–40). New York: Academic Press.

Friedman, A., & Polson, C.M. (1981). Hemispheres as independent resource systems: Limited-capacity processing and cerebral specialization. *Journal of Experimental Psychology: Human Perception and Performance, 7,* 1031–1058.

Furst, C.J. (1971). Automatizing of visual attention. *Perception and Psychophysics, 10,* 65–70.

Gibson, E.J. (1969). *Principles of perceptual learning and development.* New York: Appleton-Century-Crofts.

Gibson, J.J. (1979). *An ecological approach to visual perception.* Boston: Houghton Mifflin.

Girouard, Y., Laurencelle, L., & Proteau, L. (1984). On the nature of the probe reaction-time to uncover the attentional demands of movement. *Journal of Motor Behavior, 16,* 442–459.

Girouard, Y., Perreault, R., Vachon, L., & Black, P. (1978). Attention demands of high jumping [Abstract]. *Canadian Journal of Applied Sport Sciences, 3,* 193.

Glencross, D.J. (1978). Control and capacity in the study of skill. In D.J. Glencross (Ed.), *Psychology and sport* (pp. 72–96). Sydney, Australia: McGraw-Hill.

Glencross, D.J. (1980). Response planning and the organization of speed movements. In R.S. Nickerson (Eds.), *Attention and performance VIII* (pp. 107–125). Hillsdale, NJ: Erlbaum.

Glencross, D.J., & Cibich, B.J. (1977). A decision analysis of games skills. *Australian Journal of Sports Medicine, 9,* 72–75.

Gopher, D., & Navon, D. (1980). How is performance limited: Testing the notion of central capacity. *Acta Psychologica, 46,* 161–180.

Gopher, D., & Sanders, A.F. (1984). S-Oh-R: Oh stages! Oh resources! In W. Prinz & A.F. Sanders (Eds.), *Cognition and motor processes* (pp. 231–253). Berlin, Germany: Springer-Verlag.

Gottsdanker, R., & Stelmach, G.E. (1971). The persistence of psychological refractoriness. *Journal of Motor Behavior, 3,* 301–312.

Graybiel, A., Jokl, E., & Trapp, C. (1955). Russian studies of vision in relation to physical activity. *Research Quarterly, 26,* 480–485.

Green, T.D., & Flowers, J.H. (1991). Implicit versus explicit learning processes in a probabilistic, continuous fine-motor catching task. *Journal of Motor Behavior, 23,* 293–300.

Greenwald, A.G., & Shulman, H.G. (1973). On doing two things at once: II. Elimination of the psychological refractory period. *Journal of Experimental Psychology, 101,* 70–76.

Hamilton, W. (1859). *Lectures on metaphysics and logic.* Edinburgh, Scotland: Blackwood.

Hart, S.G., & Staveland, L.E. (1988). Development of NASA-TLX (Task Load Index): Results of empirical and theoretical research. In P.A. Hancock & N. Meshkati (Eds.), *Human mental workload* (pp. 139–183). Amsterdam: North Holland.

Helsen, W., & Pauwels, J.M. (1993). The relationship between expertise and visual information processing in sport. In J.L. Starkes & F. Allard (Eds.), *Cognitive issues in motor expertise* (pp. 109–134). Amsterdam: Elsevier.

Heuer, H. (1984). Motor learning as a process of structural constriction and displacement. In W. Prinz & A.F. Sanders (Eds.), *Cognition and motor processes* (pp. 295–305). Berlin, Germany: Springer-Verlag.

Heuer, H., & Wing, A.M. (1984). Doing two things at once: Process limitations and interactions. In M.M. Smyth & A.M.

Wing (Eds.), *The psychology of human movement* (pp. 183–213). London: Academic Press.

Hoffman, J.E., Nelson, B., & Houck, M.R. (1983). The role of attentional resources in automatic detection. *Cognitive Psychology, 15,* 379–410.

Imanaka, K., Abernethy, B., & Quek, J.J. (1998). The locus of distance-location interaction in movement reproduction: Do we know any more 25 years on? In J. Piek (Ed.), *Motor control and human skill: A multi-disciplinary perspective* (pp. 29–55). Champaign, IL: Human Kinetics.

Jackson, C.W. (1981). The relationship of swimming performance to measures of attentional and interpersonal style (Doctoral dissertation, Boston University, 1980). *Dissertations Abstracts International, 41,* 3353–A.

James, W. (1890). *Principles of psychology.* New York: Holt.

Janelle, C.M., Singer, R.N., & Williams, A.M. (1999). External distraction and attentional narrowing: Visual search evidence. *Journal of Sport & Exercise Psychology, 21,* 70–91.

Jastrow, O. (1891). The interference of mental processes. *American Journal of Psychology, 4,* 219–223.

Jennings, J.R., Lawrence, B.E., & Kasper, P. (1978). Changes in alertness and processing capacity in a serial learning task. *Memory and Cognition, 6,* 43–53.

Jones, M.G. (1972). Perceptual characteristics and athletic performance. In H.T.A. Whiting (Ed.), *Readings in sports psychology* (pp. 96–115). London: Kimpton.

Jonides, J., Naveh-Benjamin, M., & Palmer, J. (1985). Assessing automaticity. *Acta Psychologica, 60,* 157–171.

Kahneman, D. (1973). *Attention and effort.* Englewood Cliffs, NJ: Prentice-Hall.

Kahneman, D., & Treisman, A. (1984). Changing views of attention and automaticity. In R. Parasuraman & D.R. Davies (Eds.), *Varieties of attention* (pp. 29–61). London: Academic Press.

Kantowitz, B.H. (1985). Channels and stages in human information processing: A limited analysis of theory and methodology. *Journal of Mathematical Psychology, 29,* 135–174.

Karlin, L., & Kestenbaum, R. (1968). Effects of number of alternatives on psychological refractory period. *Quarterly Journal of Experimental Psychology, 20,* 167–178.

Keele, S.W. (1973). *Attention and human performance.* Pacific Palisades, CA: Goodyear.

Keele, S.W., & Hawkins, H.L. (1982). Explorations of individual differences relevant to high level skill. *Journal of Motor Behavior, 14,* 3–23.

Kelso, J.A.S., Tuller, B.H., & Harris, K.S. (1983). A "dynamic pattern" perspective on the control and coordination of movement. In P. MacNeilage (Ed.), *The production of speech* (pp. 137–173). New York: Springer-Verlag.

Kimble, G.A., & Perlmutter, L.C. (1970). The problem of volition. *Psychological Review, 77,* 361–383.

Kirsner, K., Speelman, C., Mayberry, M., O'Brien-Malone, A., Anderson, M., & MacLeod, C. (Eds.). (1998). *Implicit and explicit mental processes.* Mahwah, NJ: Erlbaum.

Klein, R.M. (1976). Attention and movement. In G.E. Stelmach (Ed.), *Motor control: Issues and trends* (pp. 143–173). New York: Academic Press.

Klein, R.M. (1978). Automatic and strategic processes in skilled performance. In G.C. Roberts & K.M. Newell (Eds.), *Psychology of motor behavior and sport–1977* (pp. 270–287). Champaign, IL: Human Kinetics.

Knapp, B.N. (1963). *Skill in sport.* London: Routledge & Kegan Paul.

Korteling, J.E. (1994). Effects of aging, skill modification, and demand alternation on multiple-task performance. *Human Factors, 36,* 27–43.

Kramer, A.F., & Strayer, D.L. (1988). Assessing the development of automatic processing: An application of dual-task and event-related brain potential methodologies. *Biological Psychology, 26,* 231–267.

Kramer, A.F., Wickens, C.D., & Donchin, E. (1983). An analysis of the processing demands of a complex perceptual-motor task. *Human Factors, 25,* 597–622.

LaBerge, D. (1975). Acquisition of automatic processing in perceptual and associative learning. In P.M.A. Rabbitt & S. Dornic (Eds.), *Attention and performance V* (pp. 50–64). London: Academic Press.

LaBerge, D. (1981). Automatic information processing: A review. In J. Long & A. Baddeley (Eds.), *Attention and performance IX* (pp. 173–186). Hillsdale, NJ: Erlbaum.

Lacey, B.C., & Lacey, J.I. (1970). Some autonomic-central nervous system interrelationships. In P. Block (Ed.), *Physiological correlates of emotion* (pp. 50–83). New York: Academic Press.

Lacey, J.I. (1967). Somatic response patterning and stress: Some revision of activation theory. In M.H. Appley & R. Trumbull (Eds.), *Psychological stress: Issues in research* (pp. 170–179). New York: Appleton-Century-Crofts.

Lajoie, Y., Teasdale, N., Bard, C., & Fleury, M. (1993). Attentional demands for static and dynamic equilibrium. *Experimental Brain Research, 97,* 139–144.

Lajoie, Y., Teasdale, N., Bard, C., & Fleury, M. (1996). Upright standing and gait: Are there changes in attentional requirements related to normal aging? *Experimental Aging Research, 22,* 185–198.

Landers, D.M., Boutcher, S.H., & Wang, M.Q. (1986). A psychobiological study of archery performance. *Research Quarterly for Exercise and Sport, 57,* 236–244.

Landers, D.M., Wang, M.Q., & Courtet, P. (1985). Peripheral narrowing among experienced and inexperienced rifle shooters under low- and high-time stress conditions. *Research Quarterly for Exercise and Sport, 56,* 122–130.

Leavitt, J.L. (1979). Cognitive demands of skating and stick handling in ice hockey. *Canadian Journal of Applied Sport Sciences, 4,* 46–55.

Leibowitz, H.W., & Post, R.B. (1982). The two modes of processing concept and some implications. In J. Beck (Ed.), *Organization and representation in perception* (pp. 343–363). Hillsdale, NJ: Erlbaum.

Logan, G.D. (1979). On the use of a concurrent memory load to measure attention and automaticity. *Journal of Experimental Psychology: Human Perception and Performance, 5,* 189–297.

Logan, G.D. (1985). Skill and automaticity: Relations, implications, and future directions. *Canadian Journal of Psychology, 39,* 367–386.

MacGillivary, W.W. (1981). The contribution of perceptual style to human performance. In I.M. Cockerill & W.W. MacGillivary (Eds.), *Vision and sport* (pp. 8–16). Cheltenham, England: Stanley Thornes.

Magill, R.A. (1994). Is conscious awareness of environmental information necessary for skill learning? In J.R. Nitsch & R. Seiler (Eds.), *Movement and sport. Psychological foundations and effects: Motor control and learning* (Vol. 2, pp. 94–103). Sankt Augustin, Germany: Academia Verlag.

Magill, R.A. (1998). *Motor learning: Concepts and applications* (5th ed.). Dubuque, IA: Brown.

Martin, I., & Venables, P.H. (1980). *Techniques in psychophysiology.* London: Wiley.

Masters, R.S.W. (1992). Knowledge, knerves and know-how: The role of explicit versus implicit knowledge in the breakdown of complex motor skill under pressure. *British Journal of Psychology, 83,* 343–358.

McLeod, P. (1977). A dual-task response modality effect: Support for multiprocessor models of attention. *Quarterly Journal of Experimental Psychology, 29,* 651–667.

McLeod, P. (1980). What can probe RT tell us about the attentional demands of movement? In G.E. Stelmach & J. Requin (Eds.), *Tutorials in motor behavior* (pp. 579–589). Amsterdam: North Holland.

McLeod, P., & Driver, J. (1993). Filtering and physiology in visual search: A convergence of behavioural and neurophysiological measures. In A. Baddeley & L. Weiskrantz (Eds.), *Attention: Selection, awareness, and control* (pp. 72–86). Oxford, England: Clarendon Press.

McLeod, P., McLaughlin, C., & Nimmo-Smith, I. (1985). Information encapsulation and automaticity: Evidence from the visual control of finely timed actions. In M.I. Posner & O. Marin (Eds.), *Attention and performance XI* (pp. 391–406). Hillsdale, NJ: Erlbaum.

Megaw, E.D., & Richardson, J. (1979). Eye movements and industrial inspection. *Applied Ergonomics, 10,* 145–154.

Meshkati, N. (1988). Heart rate variability and mental workload assessment. In P.A. Hancock & N. Meshkati (Eds.), *Human mental workload* (pp. 101–115). Amsterdam: North Holland.

Milner, A.D., & Goodale, M.A. (1995). *The visual brain in action.* New York: Oxford University Press.

Moray, N. (1967). Where is attention limited? A survey and a model. *Acta Psychologica, 27,* 84–92.

Moray, N. (1982). Subjective mental workload. *Human Factors, 23,* 25–40.

Moray, N., & Fitter, M. (1973). A theory and the measurement of attention: Tutorial review. In S. Kornblum (Ed.), *Attention and performance IV* (pp. 3–19). New York: Academic Press.

Mowbray, G.H. (1953). Simultaneous vision and audition: The comprehension of prose passages with varying levels of difficulty. *Journal of Experimental Psychology, 46,* 365–372.

Mowbray, G.H., & Rhoades, M.U. (1959). On the reduction of choice reaction times with practice. *Quarterly Journal of Experimental Psychology, 11,* 16–23.

Näätänen, R. (1988). Implications of ERP data for psychological theories of attention. *Biological Psychology, 26,* 117–163.

Näätänen, R. (1992). *Attention and brain function.* Hillsdale, NJ: Erlbaum.

Navon, D., & Gopher, D. (1979). On the economy of the human processing system. *Psychological Review, 86,* 214–255.

Neisser, U. (1967). *Cognitive psychology.* New York: Appleton-Century-Crofts.

Neisser, U. (1979). The control of information pick-up in selective looking. In A.D. Pick (Ed.), *Perception and its development: A tribute to Eleanor J. Gibson* (pp. 201–219). Hillsdale, NJ: Erlbaum.

Neisser, U., & Becklen, R. (1975). Selective looking: Attending to visually specified events. *Cognitive Psychology, 7,* 480–494.

Nettleton, B. (1979). Attention demands of ball-tracking skills. *Perceptual and Motor Skills, 49,* 531–534.

Neumann, O. (1984). Automatic processing: A review of recent findings and a plea for an old theory. In W. Prinz & A.F. Sanders (Eds.), *Cognition and motor processes* (pp. 256–293). Berlin, Germany: Springer-Verlag.

Neumann, O. (1987). Beyond capacity: A functional view of attention. In H. Heuer & A.F. Sanders (Eds.), *Perspectives on perception and action* (pp. 361–394). Hillsdale, NJ: Erlbaum.

Nideffer, R.M. (1976). The test of attentional and interpersonal style. *Journal of Personality and Social Psychology, 34,* 394–404.

Nideffer, R.M. (1979). The role of attention in optimal athletic performance. In P. Klavora & J.V. Daniel (Eds.), *Coach, athlete and sport psychologist* (pp. 99–112). Toronto, Canada: University of Toronto.

Nideffer, R.M. (1990). Use of the Test of Attentional and Interpersonal Style (TAIS) in sport. *The Sport Psychologist, 4,* 285–300.

Nisbett, R.E., & Wilson, T.D. (1977). Telling more than we can know: Verbal reports on mental processes. *Psychological Review, 84,* 231–259.

Nissen, M.J., & Bullemer, P. (1987). Attentional requirements of learning: Evidence from performance measures. *Cognitive Psychology, 19,* 1–32.

Norman, D.A. (1968). Toward a theory of memory and attention. *Psychological Review, 75,* 522–536.

Norman, D.A. (1976). *Memory and attention* (2nd ed.). New York: Wiley.

Norman, D.A. (1981). Categorization of action slips. *Psychological Review, 88,* 1–15.

Norman, D.A., & Bobrow, D. (1975). On data-limited and resource-limited processing. *Cognitive Psychology, 7,* 44–60.

Norman, D.A., & Shallice, T. (1986). Attention to action: Willed and automatic control of behaviour. In R.J. Davidson, G.E. Schwartz, & D. Shapiro (Eds.), *The design of everyday things* (Vol. 4). New York: Doubleday.

Noton, D., & Stark, L. (1971). Eye movements and visual perception. *Scientific American, 224,* 34–43.

Nougier, V., Stein, J.F., & Bonnel, A.M. (1991). Information processing in sport and orienting of attention. *International Journal of Sport Psychology, 22,* 307–327.

Nygren, T.E. (1991). Psychometric properties of subjective workload measurement techniques: Implications for their use in the assessment of perceived mental workload. *Human Factors, 33,* 17–33.

Ogden, G.D., Levine, J.M., & Eisner, E.J. (1979). Measurement of workload by secondary tasks. *Human Factors, 21,* 529–548.

Pargman, D., Schreiber, L.E., & Stein, F. (1974). Field dependence of selected athletic sub-groups. *Medicine and Science in Sports, 6,* 283–286.

Parker, H. (1981). Visual detection and perception in netball. In I.M. Cockerill & W.W. MacGillivary (Eds.), *Vision and sport* (pp. 42–53). London: Stanley Thornes.

Paull, G., & Glencross, D.J. (1997). Expert perception and decision making in baseball. *International Journal of Sport Psychology, 28,* 35–56.

Pew, R.W. (1974). Levels of analysis in motor control. *Brain Research, 71,* 393–400.

Phillips, J.G., & Hughes, B.G. (1988). Internal consistency of the concept of automaticity. In A.M. Colley & J.R. Beech (Eds.), *Cognition and action in skilled behaviour* (pp. 317–331). Amsterdam: North Holland.

Pillsbury, W.B. (1908). *Attention.* New York: Macmillan.

Populin, L., Rose, D.J., & Heath, K. (1990). The role of attention in one-handed catching. *Journal of Motor Behavior, 22,* 149–158.

Posner, M.I. (1973). *Cognition: An introduction.* Glenview, IL: Scott, Foresman.

Posner, M.I. (1978). *Chronometric explorations of mind.* Hillsdale, NJ: Erlbaum.

Posner, M.I., & Boies, S.J. (1971). Components of attention. *Psychological Review, 78,* 391–408.

Posner, M.I., & Dehaene, S. (1994). Attentional networks. *Trends in Neuro Science, 17,* 75–79.

Posner, M.I., & Keele, S.W. (1969). Attention demands of movements. *Proceedings of the 17th International Congress of Applied Psychology.* Amsterdam: Swets & Zeitlinger.

Posner, M.I., & Petersen, S.E. (1990). The attention system of the brain. *Annual Review of Neuroscience, 13,* 25–42.

Ray, W.J., & Cole, H.W. (1985). EEG alpha activity reflects attentional demands, and beta activity reflects emotional and cognitive processes. *Science, 228,* 750–752.

Reason, J.T. (1979). Actions not as planned: The price of automatization. In G. Underwood & R. Stevens (Eds.), *Aspects of consciousness: Psychological issues* (Vol. 1, pp. 67–89). London: Academic Press.

Reid, G.B., & Nygren, T.E. (1988). The subjective workload assessment technique: A scaling procedure for measuring mental workload. In P.A. Hancock & N. Meshkati (Eds.), *Human mental workload* (pp. 185–218). Amsterdam: North Holland.

Remington, R.W. (1980). Attention and saccadic eye movements. *Journal of Experimental Psychology: Human Perception and Performance, 6,* 726–744.

Rose, D.J., & Christina, R.W. (1990). Attention demands of precision pistol-shooting as a function of skill level. *Research Quarterly for Exercise and Sport, 61,* 111–113.

Rossetti, Y. (in press). Implicit perception in action: Short-lived motor representations of space. In P.G. Grossenbacher (Ed.), *Finding consciousness in the brain: A neurocognitive approach.* Amsterdam: Benjamins.

Rumelhart, D.E., Hinton, G.E., & McClelland, J.L. (1986). A general framework for parallel distributed processing. In D.E. Rumelhart & J.L. McClelland and the PDP Research Group (Eds.), *Parallel distributed processing: Explorations in the microstructure of cognition* (pp. 45–76). Cambridge, MA: MIT Press.

Rumelhart, D.E., & McClelland, J.L. (Eds.). (1986). *Parallel distributed processing.* Cambridge, MA: MIT Press.

Salmoni, A.W., Sullivan, J.J., & Starkes, J.L. (1976). The attentional demands of movement: A critique of the probe technique. *Journal of Motor Behavior, 8,* 161–169.

Sammer, G. (1998). Heart period variability and respiratory changes associated with physical and mental load: Non-linear analysis. *Ergonomics, 41,* 746–755.

Savelsbergh, G.J.P., & Bootsma, R.J. (1994). Perception-action coupling in hitting and catching. *International Journal of Sport Psychology, 25,* 331–343.

Savelsbergh, G.J.P., Whiting, H.T.A., & Pijpers, J.R. (1992). The control of catching. In J.J. Summers (Ed.), *Approaches to the study of motor control and learning* (pp. 313–342). Amsterdam: North Holland.

Saxe, G.B., & Gearhart, M. (1990). A developmental analysis of everyday topology in unschooled straw weavers. *British Journal of Developmental Psychology, 8,* 251–258.

Schmidt, R.A., & Lee, T.D. (1999). *Motor control and learning: A behavioral emphasis* (3rd. ed). Champaign, IL: Human Kinetics.

Schmidt, R.A., & McCabe, J.F. (1976). Motor program utilization over extended practice. *Journal of Human Movement Studies, 2,* 239–247.

Schneider, W. (1985). Towards a model of attention and the development of automatic processing. In M.I. Posner & O. Marin (Eds.), *Attention and performance XI* (pp. 475–492). Hillsdale, NJ: Erlbaum.

Schneider, W., & Fisk, A.D. (1982). Concurrent automatic and controlled visual search: Can processing occur without cost? *Journal of Experimental Psychology: Learning, Memory, and Cognition, 8,* 261–278.

Schneider, W., & Shiffrin, R.M. (1977). Controlled and automatic human information processing: I. Detection, search, and attention. *Psychological Review, 84,* 1–66.

Senders, J. (1964). The human operator as a monitor and controller of multidegree of freedom system. *IEEE Transactions on Human Factors in Electronics, HFE-5,* 2–6.

Sharit, J., Salvendy, G., & Deisenroth, M.P. (1982). External and internal attentional environments: I. The utilization of cardiac deceleratory and acceleratory response data for evaluating differences in mental workload between machine-paced and self-paced work. *Ergonomics, 25,* 107–120.

Sharp, R.H. (1978). Visual information-processing in ball games: Some input considerations. In F. Landry & W.A.R. Orban (Eds.), *Motor learning, sport psychology, pedagogy and didactics of physical activity* (pp. 3–12). Quebec, Canada: Symposia Specialists.

Sheridan, T., & Stassen, H. (1979). Definitions, models and measures of human workload. In N. Moray (Ed.), *Mental workload: Its theory and measurement* (pp. 219–233). New York: Plenum Press.

Shiffrin, R.M., Craig, J.C., & Cohen, E. (1973). On the degree of attention and capacity limitation in tactile processing. *Perception and Psychophysics, 13,* 328–336.

Shiffrin, R.M., & Schneider, W. (1977). Controlled and automatic human information processing: II. Perceptual learning, automatic attending, and a general theory. *Psychological Review, 84,* 127–190.

Shulman, G.L., Remington, R.W., & McLean, J.P. (1979). Moving attention through visual space. *Journal of Experimental Psychology: Human Perception and Performance, 5,* 522–526.

Singer, R.N., Cauraugh, J.H., Murphey, M., Chen, D., & Lidor, R. (1991). Attentional control, distractors, and motor performance. *Human Performance, 4,* 55–69.

Singer, R.N., Cauraugh, J.H., Tennant, L.K., Murphey, M., Chen, D., & Lidor, R. (1991). Attention and distractors: Considerations for enhancing sport performances. *International Journal of Sport Psychology, 22,* 95–114.

Singer, R.N., Lidor, R., & Cauraugh, J.H. (1993). To be aware or not aware? What to think about while learning and performing a motor skill. *The Sport Psychologist, 7,* 19–30.

Snyder, E., Hillyard, S.A., & Galambos, R. (1980). Similarities and differences in P3 waves to detected signals in three modalities. *Psychophysiology, 17,* 112–122.

Solomons, L., & Stein, G. (1896). Normal motor automatism. *Psychological Review, 3,* 492–512.

Speelman, C. (1998). Implicit expertise: Do we expect too much of our experts? In K. Kirsner, C. Speelman, M. Mayberry, A. O'Brien-Malone, M. Anderson, & C. MacLeod (Eds.), *Implicit and explicit mental processes* (pp. 135–147). Mahwah, NJ: Erlbaum.

Spelke, E., Hirst, W., & Neisser, U. (1976). Skills of divided attention. *Cognition, 4,* 215–230.

Sperandio, J.C. (1978). The regulation of working methods as a function of workload among air traffic controllers. *Ergonomics, 21,* 193–202.

Stager, P., & Angus, R. (1978). Locating crash sites in simulated air-to-ground visual search. *Human Factors, 20,* 453–466.

Starkes, J.L. (1986). Attention demands of spatially locating the position of a ball in flight. *Perceptual and Motor Skills, 63,* 1327–1335.

Starkes, J.L. (1987). Skill in field hockey: The nature of the cognitive advantage. *Journal of Sport Psychology, 9,* 146–160.

Starkes, J.L., & Allard, F. (1983). Perception in volleyball: The effects of competitive stress. *Journal of Sport Psychology, 5,* 189–196.

Starkes, J.L., & Deakin, J.M. (1984). Perception in sport: A cognitive approach to skilled performance. In W.F. Straub & J.M. Williams (Eds.), *Cognitive sport psychology* (pp. 115–128). Lansing, NY: Sport Science Associates.

Starkes, J.L., Edwards, P., Dissanayake, P., & Dunn, T. (1995). A new technology and field test of advance cue usage in volleyball. *Research Quarterly for Exercise and Sport, 66,* 162–167.

Starkes, J.L., & Lindley, S. (1994). Can we hasten expertise by video simulations? *Quest, 46,* 211–222.

Stein, H., & Slatt, B. (1981). *Hitting blind: The new visual approach to winning tennis.* Ontario, Canada: Mussen.

Stelmach, G.E., & Hughes, B. (1983). Does motor skill automation require a theory of attention? In R.A. Magill (Ed.), *Memory and control of action* (pp. 67–92). Amsterdam: North Holland.

Stroop, J.R. (1935). Studies of interference in serial verbal reactions. *Journal of Experimental Psychology, 18,* 643–662.

Summers, J.J., Byblow, W.D., Bysouth-Young, D.F., & Semjen, A. (1998). Bimanual circle drawing during secondary task loading. *Motor Control, 2,* 106–113.

Summers, J.J., & Ford, S.K. (1990). The test of attentional and interpersonal style: An evaluation. *International Journal of Sport Psychology, 21,* 102–111.

Summers, J.J., Miller, K., & Ford, S.K. (1991). Attentional style and basketball performance. *Journal of Sport & Exercise Psychology, 8,* 239–253.

Teichner, W.H., & Krebs, M.J. (1974). Visual search for simple targets. *Psychological Bulletin, 81,* 15–28.

Temprado, J.J., Zanone, P.G., Monno, A., & Laurent, M. (1999). Attentional load associated with performing and stabilizing preferred bimanual patterns. *Journal of Experimental Psychology: Human Perception and Performance, 25,* 1579–1594.

Titchener, E.B. (1908). *Lectures on the elementary psychology of feeling and attention.* New York: Macmillan.

Treisman, A. (1969). Strategies and models of selective attention. *Psychological Review, 76,* 282–299.

Underwood, G. (1982). Attention and awareness in cognitive and motor skills. In G. Underwood (Ed.), *Aspects of consciousness: Awareness and self-awareness* (Vol. 3, pp. 111–145). London: Academic Press.

Vallerand, R.J. (1983). Attention and decision-making: A test of the predictive validity of the Test of Attentional and Interpersonal Style (TAIS) in a sport setting. *Journal of Sport Psychology, 5,* 449–459.

Van der Molen, M.W., Somsen, R.J.M., & Orlebeke, J.F. (1985). The rhythm of the heart beat in information processing. In P.K. Ackles, J.R. Jennings, & M.G.H. Coles (Eds.), *Advances in psychophysiology* (pp. 1–88). Greenwich, CT: JAI Press.

Vankersschaver, J. (1984). Capacités de traitement des informations dans une habileté sensori-motrice: L'exemple d'une habileté sportive [Information processing capacities in a sensory-motor skill: A sport skill example]. *Le Travail Humain, 47,* 281–286.

Van Schoyck, S.R., & Grasha, A.F. (1981). Attentional style variations and athletic ability: The advantages of a sport-specific test. *Journal of Sport Psychology, 3,* 149–165.

Vickers, J.N. (1986). The resequencing task: Determining expert-novice differences in the organization of a movement sequence. *Research Quarterly for Exercise and Sport, 57,* 260–264.

Vickers, J.N. (1992). Gaze control in putting. *Perception, 21,* 117–132.

Vincente, K.J., Thornton, D.C., & Moray, N. (1987). Spectral analyses of sinus arrhythmia: A measure of mental effort. *Human Factors, 29,* 171–182.

Wakelin, D.R. (1967). The role of the response in psychological refractoriness. *Acta Psychologica, 40,* 163–175.

Watchel, P. (1967). Conceptions of broad and narrow attention. *Psychological Bulletin, 68,* 417–429.

Welch, J.C. (1898). On the measurement of mental activity through muscular activity and the determination of a constant of attention. *American Journal of Physiology, 1,* 253–306.

Welford, A.T. (1952). The psychological refractory period and the timing of high-speed performance: A review and a theory. *British Journal of Psychology, 43,* 2–19.

Welford, A.T. (1967). Single channel operation in the brain. *Acta Psychologica, 27,* 5–22.

Wessells, M.G. (1982). *Cognitive psychology.* New York: Harper & Row.

White, P.A. (1982). Beliefs about conscious experience. In G. Underwood (Ed.), *Aspects of consciousness: Awareness and self-awareness* (Vol. 3, pp. 1–25). London: Academic Press.

Whiting, H.T.A. (1979). Subjective probability in sport. In G.C. Roberts & K.M. Newell (Eds.), *Psychology of motor behavior and sport–1978* (pp. 3–25). Champaign, IL: Human Kinetics.

Wickens, C.D. (1979). Measures of workload, stress, and secondary tasks. In N. Moray (Ed.), *Mental workload: Its theory and measurement* (pp. 79–99). New York: Plenum Press.

Wickens, C.D. (1980). The structure of attentional resources. In R. Nickerson & R. Pew (Eds.), *Attention and performance VIII* (pp. 239–257). Hillsdale, NJ: Erlbaum.

Wickens, C.D. (1984). Process resources in attention. In R. Parasuraman & R. Davies (Eds.), *Varieties of attention* (p. 81). New York: Academic Press.

Wickens, C.D. (1992). *Engineering psychology and human performance* (2nd ed.). New York: HarperCollins.

Wickens, C.D., & Derrick, W. (1981). Workload measurement and multiple resources. *Proceedings of the IEEE Conference on Cybernetics and Society.* New York: Institute of Electrical and Electronics Engineers.

Wickens, C.D., Mountford, S.J., & Schreiner, W. (1981). Multiple resources, task-hemispheric integrity, and individual differences in time-sharing. *Human Factors, 23,* 211–229.

Wierwille, W.W., & Connor, S.A. (1983). Evaluation of 20 workload measures using a psychomotor task in a moving-base aircraft simulator. *Human Factors, 25,* 1–16.

Wierwille, W.W., Rahimi, M., & Casali, J.G. (1985). Evaluation of 16 measures of mental workload using a simulated flight task emphasizing mediational activity. *Human Factors, 27,* 489–502.

Williams, A.M., Davids, K., Burwitz, L., & Williams, J.G. (1994). Visual search strategies in experienced and inexperienced soccer players. *Research Quarterly for Exercise and Sport, 65,* 127–135.

Williams, J.M., & Thirer, J. (1975). Vertical and horizontal peripheral vision in male and female athletes and non-athletes. *Research Quarterly, 46,* 200–205.

Wilson, G.F., & O'Donnell, R.D. (1988). Measurement of operator workload with the neuropsychological workload test battery. In P.A. Hancock & N. Meshkati (Eds.), *Human mental workload* (pp. 63–100). Amsterdam: North Holland.

Witkin, H.A., Dyk, R., Faterson, H.F., Goodenough, D.R., & Karp, S.A. (1962). *Psychological differentiation.* New York: Wiley.

Wood, J.M., & Abernethy, B. (1997). An assessment of the efficacy of sports vision training programs. *Optometry and Vision Science, 74,* 646–659.

Wulf, G., & Weigelt, C. (1997). Instructions about physical principles in learning a complex motor skill: To tell or not to tell. *Research Quarterly for Exercise and Sport, 68,* 362–367.

Wundt, W. (1905). *Grundriss der psychologie [Foundations of Psychology].* Leipzig: Engelmann.

Yarbus, A.L. (1967). *Eye movement and vision.* New York: Plenum Press.

Zaichkowsky, L.D., Jackson, C., & Aronson, R. (1982). Attentional and interpersonal factors as predictors of elite athletic performance. In T. Orlick, J.T. Partington, & J.H. Salmela (Eds.), *Mental training for coaches and athletes* (pp. 103–104). Ottawa, Canada: Coaching Association of Canada.

Zelaznik, H.N., Shapiro, D.C., & McClosky, D. (1981). Effects of secondary task on the accuracy of single aiming movements. *Journal of Experimental Psychology: Human Perception and Performance, 7,* 1007–1018.

CHAPTER 4

Augmented Feedback in Motor Skill Acquisition

RICHARD A. MAGILL

When the term *feedback* is used in reference to performing a motor skill, it refers to performance-related information the individual receives during and after executing the skill. There are two general types of feedback in motor skill performance situations. One is the sensory-perceptual information available to the person as a natural part of performing the skill. In this chapter, this type of performance-related feedback is referred to as *task-intrinsic feedback*. For example, if a person throws a dart at a target on the wall, he or she receives visual task-intrinsic feedback from seeing the flight of the dart and where it lands on the target. The performer can also obtain proprioceptive task-intrinsic feedback from the movement of his or her body posture along with arm and hand movement, as when preparing to throw the dart and as the dart is thrown. Other sensory systems can also provide task-intrinsic feedback, such as hearing the dart hit, or not hit, the target.

The second general type of performance feedback is the performance-related information a person receives *in addition to* task-intrinsic feedback. This type of feedback is not always available. Although various terms have been used in the research literature to identify this feedback, the term that will be used in this chapter is *augmented feedback* (see also Swinnen, 1996). This term is appropriate because the adjective "augmented" refers to adding to or enhancing something, which in this case involves adding to or enhancing task-intrinsic feedback. Consider the dart-throwing task described in the preceding paragraph: The task-intrinsic feedback could be augmented in several ways. For example, a person who is standing by the dartboard could tell the performer the dart's location on the target, or a teacher or coach may tell the person something about his or her arm movement that led to the dart location on the dartboard. Although the additional information

could be redundant with task-intrinsic information, this possible redundancy is not a concern with respect to definition purposes. However, the redundancy issue will be considered later in this chapter.

TYPES OF AUGMENTED FEEDBACK

The research literature concerning augmented feedback and motor skill acquisition refers to two types of augmented feedback: *knowledge of results* (KR) and *knowledge of performance* (KP). Gentile (1972) can be credited with the initial use of these terms as a means of distinguishing between the distinct types of performance information that augmented feedback can provide. KR refers to augmented information about the *outcome* of performing a skill. To continue with the dart-throwing example, the scorekeeper would give KR when he or she tells the performer the location and/or point value of a throw. On the other hand, KP refers to augmented information about the *movement characteristics* associated with performing the skill. For dart throwing, a coach or teacher could give verbal KP by telling the performer something about the arm movement during the throw. KP can also be provided through the use of technology, such as by providing a videotape replay of a throw or a computer-generated display of the kinematics of the arm movement and dart release.

KR and KP can be presented after a person performs a skill, which is referred to as *terminal,* and/or during the performance itself, which is referred to as *concurrent.* The augmented feedback examples described for the dart-throwing task were terminal presentations. An example of concurrent augmented feedback would be the availability of electromyography (EMG) information about a specific muscle the person was instructed to activate during the dart throw. Additional examples of both terminal and concurrent presentations of augmented feedback are found throughout this chapter.

Finally, it is important to note that the term KR is not always used in the research literature to refer to a specific type of augmented feedback. In fact, there are numerous instances where KR refers to task-intrinsic feedback, such as when a person can see the outcome (i.e., result) of his or her own movement or performance (e.g., Annett & Kay, 1957; Liu & Wrisberg, 1997). Although an argument could be generated for the use of the term KR in this way, to do so adds to the confusion of an area of study already beset by a lack of understanding of the roles of various sources and types of information in skill acquisition.

THE ROLES OF AUGMENTED FEEDBACK IN SKILL ACQUISITION

Augmented feedback plays two important roles in the skill learning process. One is to provide the learner with performance-related information about the skill being performed, or just performed. As will be discussed later in more detail, this information may be very general and indicate that the performance was or was not successful, or it may be specific and inform the learner about errors and the corrections that are needed. When presented in this latter form, augmented feedback is high in information value about the performance itself and can help the learner plan how to perform the next attempt.

The second role is to motivate the learner to continue striving toward a performance achievement goal. Although the feedback provides performance-related information in this role, its primary purpose is to provide information that will allow the learner to compare his or her present achievement level with a specific achievement goal. This comparison process can help the learner to determine whether to strive toward the established goal, to stop working toward the goal, or to change the goal to one that is more achievable within the constraints of the situation.

In early research concerning augmented feedback, this motivation role was considered to play an important part in the skill learning process. One of the earliest examples of this research is an experiment reported by Elwell and Grindley (1938) in which participants practiced a two-hand coordination task with augmented feedback provided. After 200 trials, the augmented feedback was removed, which resulted in an immediate drop in performance. The experimenters interpreted the performance decline as evidence that the participants had lost interest in the task,

which they also based on the increase in participants' complaints and late arrivals for experimental sessions after the augmented feedback was removed.

Little and McCullagh (1989) provided an interesting alternative approach to investigating the motivational aspects of augmented feedback on skill learning. They considered motivation from the perspective of the learner's goal orientation as it related to learning a skill. Some people, whom the experimenters referred to as intrinsic mastery motivated, prefer to figure out how to perform a skill on their own and tend to focus on their own practice attempts and movement performance. Others, referred to as extrinsic mastery motivated, prefer guidance from an expert, such as a teacher or coach. During practice, they tend to focus on external sources of information to judge their performance. Little and McCullagh reasoned that the most effective type of augmented feedback for a person learning a skill may relate to the person's type of goal orientation. More specifically, they hypothesized that intrinsic mastery learners would more likely be influenced by KP because it provides information about movement performance characteristics, whereas extrinsic mastery learners would more likely be influenced by KR because it provides information about movement outcome. The experiment developed to test this hypothesis involved 12- to 15-year-old female novice tennis players who practiced the forehand ground stroke for three days. Four groups were formed on the basis of their intrinsic or extrinsic mastery orientation and whether they received KP or KR after each practice trial. Although the results only partially supported the hypothesis, the experiment yielded sufficient evidence to suggest that the relationship between goal orientation and the type of augmented feedback received is an issue worthy of consideration and further research efforts.

Another approach researchers have taken to investigate the motivational role of augmented feedback in skill acquisition comes from the physical education pedagogy area of study. This research has investigated the relationship between augmented feedback and students' engagement in practicing a skill. The results (e.g., Silverman, Woods, & Subramaniam, 1998) have consistently shown that there is a relatively strong relationship between the appropriateness of the feedback provided by teachers and the amount of time students engage in practice during class time.

In addition, augmented feedback has been shown to be influential in motivating people to adhere to exercise and rehabilitation programs (e.g., Annesi, 1998; Dishman, 1993). Although the focus of the investigation of the motivational role of augmented feedback in these types of programs is not on skill acquisition, this type of research provides evidence that augmented feedback also plays a motivational role in other important motor skill performance contexts.

The motivational role of augmented feedback is important in skill acquisition contexts and should be investigated more extensively. However, for purposes of this chapter, the focus is on augmented feedback as a source of information to help a person learn a skill. More specifically, the primary emphasis is on the information provided by augmented feedback that the learner can use to evaluate an ongoing or just completed practice attempt and to plan the next attempt. This delimitation will keep this within reasonable limits for a review chapter (for more complete discussions of the motivational role of augmented feedback in skill performance, see Little & McCullagh, 1989; Locke, Cartledge, & Koeppel, 1968; and Silverman, Tyson, & Krampitz, 1992).

HOW ESSENTIAL IS AUGMENTED FEEDBACK FOR SKILL ACQUISITION?

Some of the more popular theories of motor learning (e.g., Adams, 1971, 1978; Schmidt, 1975) have promoted the view that beginners (i.e., novices) *need* augmented feedback to learn motor skills. However, the research literature indicates that the need for augmented feedback to learn a skill depends on certain characteristics of a skill or learning environment. There are four distinct effects of augmented feedback on skill learning: some types of skills do indeed require augmented feedback to learn them; to learn other types of skills, augmented feedback may not be needed; augmented feedback may help a person to learn a skill more quickly or to perform to a higher level; or it may actually lead to some skills being learned more poorly than without augmented feedback. An important feature for distinguishing situations with regard to the need for augmented feedback is the degree to which task-intrinsic feedback provides the necessary information to determine the performance error for a trial that can be used to plan the next performance trial.

Augmented Feedback Can Be Essential for Skill Acquisition

For certain skills and skill performance situations, the critical task-intrinsic information needed to determine the appropriateness of a movement is not available or cannot be used by the learner. As a result, task-intrinsic feedback must be augmented. For example, if a person is learning to throw a ball at a target as accurately as possible but cannot see the target, then critical visual task-intrinsic feedback is not available to the person. Or, if a person is learning to throw a ball at a specific rate of speed and cannot determine the rate of speed of a throw because of a lack of experience, task-intrinsic feedback is not sufficient to provide critical information the person needs to learn the skill. In each of these situations, augmented feedback is essential to enable the learner to acquire the skill. The motor learning literature contains a great deal of research evidence that establishes the need for augmented feedback in these situations. In fact, some of the earliest experiments investigating augmented feedback and motor skill acquisition included skill learning situations like the examples just described. Two specific types of skill learning situations have consistently shown the need for augmented feedback to learn a motor skill.

In the first situation, critical task-intrinsic feedback is not available to the learner. Two classic experiments provide examples of the research evidence that establishes this type of situation as one in which augmented feedback is needed to learn the skill. In one of the earliest studies investigating augmented feedback and motor skill acquisition, Trowbridge and Cason (1932) asked blindfolded participants to learn to draw a line of a certain length. Many years later, Bilodeau, Bilodeau, and Schumsky (1959) asked blindfolded participants to learn to move a lever to a target location. The results of both experiments showed that participants needed augmented feedback (as KR) to learn the tasks, and that they could not learn the tasks without it. However, note that KR was a substitute for the visual task-intrinsic feedback that was not available to participants. Participants needed the augmented feedback about performance outcome to assess the correctness of their performance on each trial.

The second type of skill learning situation in which augmented feedback is essential for skill learning involves having the critical task-intrinsic feedback available to the learner, but the learner has difficulty using this information to improve performance. This type of situation often characterizes beginning learners. Newell (1974) reported one of the earliest experiments demonstrating this type of situation. The task required participants to learn to make a 24 cm lever movement in 150 msec. Although they could see their arms, the lever, and the target, they did not have an adequate sense of the duration of a millisecond, especially as it related to speed of arm movement. As a result, participants needed KR about their movement time accuracy to help them acquire this knowledge, which would then allow them to perform the skill correctly. When they received KR on each of 52 or 75 practice trials, they learned to perform the lever movement very accurately on later trials with no KR. However, when participants received KR only on the first 2 trials, they showed no improvement in their movement time accuracy for the remaining 73 trials. Thus, KR was necessary to help the learners establish a referent for 150 msec. After establishing this referent, which took a certain amount of practice with KR, they no longer needed KR to perform the skill and could effectively use the task-intrinsic feedback to evaluate their performance of the skill.

Augmented Feedback May Not Be Needed for Skill Acquisition

In contrast to the situations described previously, some motor skills provide sufficient task-intrinsic feedback to enable people to learn the skills *without* augmented feedback. As a result, augmented feedback is redundant with the task-intrinsic feedback. Experiments by Magill, Chamberlin, and Hall (1991) provide a laboratory example of this situation. Participants learned a coincidence-anticipation timing skill that simulated the striking of a moving ball, such as batting a pitched baseball or hitting a moving tennis ball. Ball movement was simulated as a series of sequentially lighted light emitting diodes (LEDs) on a 281-cm-long trackway. The participant faced the trackway at eye level with the LEDs lighting from their left to right at a preset speed. Directly in front of their eyes was the target LED. A small wooden barrier was located directly under the target, which the participant was instructed to use a handheld bat to strike and knock down coincident with the lighting of the target. KR was presented as the number of msec before or after the participant target struck the barrier with respect to the illumination of the target LED. Similar to the Newell (1974) experiment, groups of participants received KR for a specified number of practice trials. Results of four experiments consistently showed that regardless of the number of trials on which KR was given, participants significantly improved their anticipation performance during practice and maintained their learned level of performance on retention or transfer trials. Thus, the number of trials on which participants received KR did *not* influence learning the skill, indicating KR was not necessary to learn the skill.

Other types of skill learning situations have shown similar augmented feedback redundancy results. For example, people can learn various types of tracking tasks without receiving augmented feedback. Although much of this research was reported in the 1950s and 1960s (see Armstrong, 1970, for a review of this research), it is relevant

for the present discussion. A representative example of this research is an experiment by Goldstein and Rittenhouse (1954). Participants learned to perform the Pedestal Sight Manipulation Test (PSMT), which requires the use of a joystick to manipulate a cursor dot to track a target aircraft. In addition, participants were required to make "ranging adjustments" by framing the wingtips of the aircraft within a ring of small diamond shapes, which were visible around the target cursor. It is important to note that this task provides good visual task-intrinsic feedback for the aircraft tracking, but poor visual feedback for the ranging-adjustment part of the task. Task-intrinsic feedback was augmented in one of three ways: sounding a buzzer when both tracking and ranging were being done accurately, verbally telling the participants the proportion of on-target time and how that compared to other trials, or combining the first two conditions. Retention and transfer test results indicated that augmented feedback during practice did *not* benefit learning this skill compared to practice without augmented feedback.

These two motor skills did not require augmented feedback to learn them. Both skills have in common the characteristic that the task-intrinsic feedback involves a detectable external referent, which a person can use to evaluate performance correctness. For the anticipation-timing task, the external referents were the target and other LEDs, which learners could see when they contacted the barrier. For the PSMT task, the external referents for the ranging component were the aircraft wings and the ring that the participant adjusted; the external referents for the tracking component were the aircraft and target cursor. For each PSMT task component, participants could see the relationship between their own movements and the goal of those movements. It is important to note here that although performers may have been able to "see" the external referents in relation to their own performance, they *may not have been consciously aware* of this relationship. Both the sensory and motor control systems operate in these situations in a way that does not require the person's conscious awareness of the performance–external referent relationship (see Magill, 1998a). Thus, to enhance these external referents by augmenting them in some way does not influence the learning of the skill.

Finally, investigations of the use of teacher feedback in physical education classes have consistently found low correlations between teacher feedback and student achievement (e.g., Lee, Keh, & Magill, 1993; Silverman, Tyson, & Krampitz, 1992; Silverman, Tyson, & Morford, 1988). This finding is relevant to the present discussion because it indicates that in physical education class settings, augmented feedback plays a relatively small role in motor skill learning. In addition, it suggests that the amount and quality of teacher feedback does not influence skill learning in class environments to the degree that teacher educators have traditionally taught. However, it is important to caution that these results should not be interpreted as indicating that augmented feedback does not play an important role in effective teaching. Silverman and his colleagues have shown that teacher feedback influences skill learning in physical education class settings by influencing the amount of successful practice trials in which students will engage during a class (e.g., Silverman et al., 1992; Silverman et al., 1998). As a result, teacher feedback is an important mediating variable for skill learning in class settings, with the amount of successful practice as the more critical variable.

Augmented Feedback Can Enhance Skill Acquisition

There are some types of skills that people can learn without augmented feedback, but they will learn these skills more quickly, or at a higher level, if augmented feedback is provided. For these types of skills, augmented feedback is neither essential nor redundant, but it *enhances* skill learning. One of the types of skills that research has shown to have this characteristic is when the person must learn to move a limb as fast as possible. Classic research related to this situation was reported by Stelmach (1970). Participants practiced a three-segment arm movement task that required contact with a target at the end of each segment and a movement reversal at the end of the first and second segments. The goal was to complete the task as quickly as possible. Participants received KR as the movement time for completing the task. Results indicated that although participants who did not receive KR improved during the practice trials, participants who received KR reached the same performance level more rapidly and eventually achieved a higher level of performance than those who did not receive KR. Similarly, Newell, Quinn, Sparrow, and Walter (1983) demonstrated the same type of results for an arm movement task that had the same move-as-fast-as-you-can goal. Without KR, performance improved only to a certain level and then showed no further improvement. Alternatively, participants who received KR continued to improve beyond that level of performance.

Learning to perform the one-hand basketball set shot also benefits from the provision of augmented feedback. Wallace and Hagler (1979) asked beginners to practice a one-hand set shot with the nondominant hand from a distance of 3.03 m from the basket and 45 degrees to the left side of the basket. One group received KP, which was specific performance-error information about stance and limb movement during each shot. A second group did not receive this information, but received verbal encouragement statements after each shot, such as "Good shot," "You can do it," "Try harder next time," and so on. After 25 practice attempts, both groups performed at similar levels. But beyond that point, the verbal encouragement group showed no further improvement, whereas the KP group continued to improve. More important, the KP group continued to outperform the verbal-encouragement group on transfer-test trials on which neither KP nor verbal encouragement was given.

For the two types of tasks used in these experiments, participants could use task-intrinsic feedback during practice to help them improve their performance, but only to a limited extent. The question of interest here is why KR or KP would enable them to improve at a faster rate or to a higher level. One answer can be found in a psychophysics principle that is related to the detection of differences between two measurable levels of a variable. For example, if a person is asked to indicate which of two levels of sound is louder, there are some differences that are easier to detect than others. The psychophysical principle, which evolves out of Weber's Law, is that the detection of differences is more likely when the two levels are greater than the just-noticeable-difference (j.n.d.) value for the variable. This means that to detect the difference in loudness between two sounds, the difference needs to be greater than a certain decibel value (which can be mathematically calculated). If the actual difference is within the j.n.d., people will judge the two sounds as being the same level of loudness. When applied to the skill learning situation, this principle suggests that early in practice, when performance differences and errors tend to be rather large, learners can successfully determine if a just completed performance is better than a previous one. Furthermore, they can readily determine what to do on a succeeding trial to improve their performance. However, after performance improves to a certain level, learners have a more difficult time determining the movement-related changes they need to make to improve performance because the performance differences between two trials are difficult to detect. It is at this point that augmented feedback helps them continue to improve.

Augmented Feedback Can Hinder Skill Acquisition

There are some skill learning situations in which augmented feedback may lead to more negative rather than positive learning outcomes. The most common of these occurs when the learner becomes dependent on augmented feedback. This dependence can occur in several different ways. One that is relatively common is when augmented feedback is presented *concurrently* while performing a skill, especially if the learner can substitute performance information received from augmented feedback for a critical task-intrinsic feedback feature. In such a situation, the person learns to rely on the augmented feedback, which is easier to use to improve performance, rather than learn to process the task-intrinsic feedback, which can be difficult to use to improve performance. Examples of concurrently presented augmented feedback will be presented and discussed in later sections of this chapter.

The most prevalent hypothesis proposed to explain the deterioration effect found in these types of skill learning situations is that when task-intrinsic feedback is minimal or difficult to interpret, learners will attend to the augmented feedback rather than to the relevant task-intrinsic feedback. The result is that they become dependent on the augmented feedback to perform the skill and do not learn to use task-intrinsic feedback critical to performing it without augmented feedback (e.g., Adams, 1964; Lintern, Roscoe, & Sivier, 1990).

It is also worth noting that deterioration of practice performance achievement during transfer tests has been found in research related to questions concerning augmented feedback frequency (e.g., Winstein & Schmidt, 1990). Because this frequency issue will be discussed later, it will not be considered further here. However, it is important to point out, as in the case of concurrently presented augmented feedback, that learners also can become dependent on terminal augmented feedback when it is presented too frequently.

THE INFORMATION PROVIDED BY AUGMENTED FEEDBACK

The discussion in the preceding section indicated that augmented feedback can be categorized as KR, which provides information about the outcome of the performance of a skill, or KP, which provides information concerning movement characteristics associated with that performance outcome. Each of these categories includes various kinds of information and means of presentation. A relevant question for both motor learning theory and motor skill instruction concerns how these various kinds of information and means of presentation influence skill learning. In this section, research that has addressed this question will be discussed in terms of specific issues related to the content of augmented feedback.

KR versus KP

Because KR and KP provide different kinds of information to the learner, it is reasonable to ask whether KR and KP influence skill learning in similar or different ways. Interestingly, very little empirical study of this question has been reported. Instead, researchers have tended to focus on the use of various types of KR or KP. Two examples of exceptions to this tendency are experiments by Brisson and Alain (1997), which involved the learning of a laboratory task, and Zubiaur, Oña, and Delgado (1999), which involved the learning of a volleyball serve.

Participants in the Brisson and Alain (1997) experiment practiced a complex spatiotemporal arm movement pattern in which they had to learn a pattern to connect four targets on the computer monitor within a criterion amount of time. One group received KP after each trial as the displacement profile for that trial. Another group received the same KP but also saw a superimposed image of the most efficient spatial pattern. A third group received KP (without the superimposed pattern) and KR, which was the total absolute timing and amplitude error for the trial. Finally, a fourth group saw the KP with the superimposed pattern and KR. Results showed that KR was an influential variable for learning the criterion pattern, as both groups that received KR in addition to KP learned the pattern better than those who did not receive KP. The authors concluded that participants used KR as a reference for interpreting KP.

Zubiaur, Oña, and Delgado (1999) asked university students with no previous volleyball experience to learn the overhead serve in volleyball. KP was specific information about the most important error to correct as it related either to action before hitting or in hitting the ball. KR referred to the outcome of the hit in terms of the ball's spatial precision, rotation, and flight. Using a multiple-baseline within-subjects design, the experiment involved participants in four sets of practice trials on each of two days: 10 baseline trials, 10 trials of either KR or KP, another 10 baseline trials, and finally 10 trials of the opposite information received on the second set of trials. Results showed that although there were some individual differences, KP was more influential in serving score improvement than KR.

A different but insightful way to look at the comparative influences of KR and KP on skill learning is to compare how each relates to students engaging in successful or unsuccessful practice trials during a physical education class. Silverman, Woods, and Subramaniam (1998) observed eight middle school physical education teachers teach two classes each, which involved skill instruction in various sport-related activities. KR, which the researchers labeled as teacher feedback about performance outcome, and KP about a particular part of a skill performance, both showed relatively high correlations with engaging in successful practice of .64 and .67, respectively. Interestingly, KP about multiple components of a skill performance correlated notably lower at .49. These results suggest that KR and KP, especially when specific to one part of a skill, relate to the number of successful trials students will experience during a class session.

A second issue of interest concerning the comparison of KR and KP is which is more related to the type of augmented feedback instructors give in real-world instruction settings. The relevance of this issue is that it has implications for laboratory-based researchers in terms of which of these two variables should receive greater emphasis in their investigations. Most of the evidence addressing this issue comes from the study of physical education teachers in actual class situations. The best example is a study by Fishman and Tobey (1978). They observed teachers in 81 classes teaching a variety of physical activities. Their results showed that the teachers overwhelmingly gave KP (94% of the time), of which 53% of the statements were appraisals of students' performance, 41% involved instructions on how to improve performance on the next trial, and 5% were praise or criticism statements.

The Fishman and Tobey (1978) study appears to be representative of other studies that have reported the comparative amounts of KR and KP statements teachers give during class sessions (see Lee et al., 1993). Given the pervasiveness of the use of KP over KR in real-world settings, why has KR been the predominant type of augmented feedback studied in laboratory research? The most likely answer is that teachers, coaches, therapists, and others provide feedback that they consider to be information that the student, athlete, or patient could not obtain on their own. KR is most likely redundant with task-intrinsic feedback for most skills involved in these contexts. Unfortunately, there are no empirical studies to support this hypothesis, but its investigation could prove very insightful. In the laboratory, however, the focus on KR rather than KP can most likely be attributed to technology. Until computer availability became widespread in laboratories, it was difficult for researchers to assess the movement components of performing a skill. Performance outcome was much easier to measure, which led to the investigation of KR. Now that the technology is readily available to assess KP-related aspects of skill performance, we are beginning to see more research

published that investigates various types of KR. But the challenge to researchers is to determine if principles related to KP and skill learning are similar to or different from those that have been established for KR (see Schmidt & Lee, 1999, chap. 12, for a discussion of this point).

The Precision of Augmented Feedback

One information content issue that has generated research activity concerns how precise augmented feedback should be in reference to a person's performance of a skill. The information provided can range from very general to very specific. One example of augmented feedback that is not precise is qualitative KR, such as when an instructor tells a student in a tennis class that a particular serve was "good" or "long." An example of providing KR that is not precise is when the tennis instructor tells the student, "You made contact with the ball too early." On the other hand, the instructor would provide very precise information by telling the student, "The serve was long by 5 cm" or "You made contact with the ball about 1/2 sec too early." In each of these situations, augmented feedback contains different, but related, information about the outcome or characteristics of the serve performed. The primary difference is the degree of precision, or specificity, of the information. Although these examples involve verbal KR and KP, other forms of KR and KP can also be considered in terms of their information precision. The important question for motor learning is, How does the degree of precision of augmented feedback influence skill learning?

The investigation of augmented feedback precision and its effect on skill learning has a long history in motor learning research. Unfortunately, much of this research has violated an important research design principle for the assessment of the effect of practice-related variables on skill learning. That is, to validly assess effects of a variable on learning, experiments should include retention or transfer tests (see Magill, 1998b; Salmoni, Schmidt, & Walter, 1984; Schmidt & Lee, 1999). The purpose of these tests is to allow the observation of postpractice performance without the influence of any transitory effects of the variable on practice performance. Although influential learning theorists noted this issue in the 1930s and 1940s (e.g., Hull, 1943; Tolman, 1932), it was generally ignored in experimental designs of much of the post–World War II motor learning research. But a reawakening of this issue occurred when Salmoni, Schmidt, and Walter (1984) published a review of the KR research literature that provided empirical evidence of the significance of the assessment of learning based on retention or transfer tests. They showed that when experiments investigating KR-related issues included retention and transfer tests, many of the traditionally accepted "principles" of KR were not supported. As a result, there was a resurgence of KR research to reevaluate some of the traditional principles of KR. The study of KR precision was one of those rejuvenated research directions.

The traditional view about the precision of KR and skill learning had been that more precise information leads to better skill learning than less precise information, especially when the comparison was between qualitative and quantitative KR (e.g., Smoll, 1972; Trowbridge & Cason, 1932). However, two studies (Magill & Wood, 1986; Reeve & Magill, 1981) have reported evidence that suggests that although this traditional view is generally valid, it requires an important modification. In the Magill and Wood experiment, participants practiced a complex arm movement task in which they moved their arm through a series of small wooden barriers to produce a specific six-segment pattern. Their goal was to perform each of the segments in a specified movement time. At the end of each trial, they received for each segment either qualitative KR (i.e., "too fast," "too slow," or "correct") or quantitative KR (i.e., the number of msec too fast or too slow). The results showed that during the first 60 trials, there was no performance difference between the two groups. However, during the final 60 trials, and then on 20 no-KR retention trials, the quantitative KR condition yielded better performance. Thus, although quantitative KR led to better skill learning, learners performed at similar levels early in practice with either quantitative or qualitative KR.

The Magill and Wood (1986) results suggest that a more appropriate guideline for motor skill learning situations is that compared to qualitative augmented feedback, quantitatively precise augmented feedback benefits learning only after a sufficient amount of practice. Prior to that time, learners need less precise (i.e., more general) information about their performance. Although the quantitative group in the Magill and Wood experiment received information about the number of msec of error they made on each trial, it is important to note that they also received the same qualitative "too fast" or "too slow" information as the qualitative group. But, the results suggest that before the quantitative KR group could effectively use the more precise timing error information, they needed to understand the meaning (in movement terms) of the qualitative terms "too fast" and "too slow."

In terms of applying the guideline described in the preceding paragraph to sport skill learning situations, the beginner learning any sport skill will receive limited benefit from augmented feedback that provides information that is more specific than he or she is capable of using. For example, to tell a beginner in tennis "You contacted the ball 10 cm too far in front of you" very likely provides no more information than "You contacted the ball too far in front of you." This point is also relevant for the use of sophisticated movement-analysis information as augmented feedback for beginners, an issue that will be discussed more fully below.

Augmented Feedback Based on Errors versus Correct Performance

Another important augmented feedback content question concerns whether a person should give a learner information about performance errors or correct aspects of the performance. Unfortunately, there is little research evidence on which to base an answer. The few studies that have addressed this question, which were reported in the 1950s and 1960s, provide general support for the conclusion that augmented feedback about performance errors is the more effective means for helping people to learn motor skills.

For example, Gordon and Gottlieb (1967) had participants practice a rotary-pursuit task, which required them to hold a stylus and maintain stylus contact for as long as possible on a small target located on a disk. The disk rotated at specified speed. One group received KR about correct performance on each trial by seeing a yellow light illuminate the entire apparatus when they were on-target (i.e., correct). A second group received KR about their performance error by seeing the light illuminate the apparatus when they were off-target. A control group received no augmented feedback. The results showed that the two augmented feedback groups performed better than the no-augmented feedback group, and the off-target feedback led to better learning than the on-target feedback. Similar off-target augmented feedback benefits have been reported for other tasks, such as a compensatory tracking task (Williams & Briggs, 1962) and a force production task (Annett, 1959).

It is notable that the research described in the previous paragraph supports Annett's (1959) hypothesis that experience with error-based feedback is needed for skill acquisition in tasks that benefit from augmented feedback because repetition of a correct movement is not sufficient to produce learning. Lintern and Roscoe (1980) added to this hypothesis by stating that when task-intrinsic feedback is relatively obscure, augmented feedback related to performing the skill correctly can create a strong dependency on the augmented information, which will lead to poor performance when the augmented feedback is not available.

However, before any degree of certainty can be achieved about whether error or correct performance augmented feedback is better for skill learning, much research remains to be done, especially in instructional settings in which complex skills must be learned. The goal of this research should be to establish general guidelines for practitioners. An important related question concerns whether certain combinations of error and correct-performance feedback during practice sessions would be more beneficial than providing only one or the other type of information. Although some sport pedagogues have indicated that these types of combinations are desirable (e.g., Docheff, 1990), no published empirical evidence supports the benefit of these combinations. Thus, the challenge is to investigate this important issue and to provide evidence on which to base instructional decisions.

Augmented Feedback Based on Performance-Based Bandwidths

Closely related to the question of whether to provide augmented feedback that indicates correct performance or the errors in a performance is the question of *how much error* a person should make before he or she receives augmented feedback. This question has distinct practical appeal because it reflects a common strategy used in teaching and coaching situations, especially when large groups are involved. Because augmented feedback cannot be given for every error each student makes, it seems reasonable to provide feedback only for errors that are large enough to warrant attention. When using this strategy the instructor creates a *performance-based bandwidth,* or performance tolerance range, to determine when to provide augmented feedback. If the student is performing within the limits of that bandwidth, augmented feedback is not given. But, if the student makes a performance error that is outside the bandwidth, the instructor gives augmented feedback.

Although not often cited in this context, an early experiment by Thorndike (1927) was the first empirical use of a performance-based bandwidth basis for providing augmented feedback. In this experiment, qualitative KR was compared to no KR in terms of their relative effects on learning to draw lines of criterion lengths while blindfolded. When viewed from the perspective of KR bandwidths, the qualitative condition was actually a performance-based bandwidth condition, because participants were told that a drawing attempt was "right" only when it was within 0.25 in. of the line-length goal, and "wrong" if the length of the line was longer than this limit. The results showed that the performance-based bandwidth KR group improved considerably more than the no-KR condition.

Two important issues arise from Thorndike's (1927) research. First, the experiment did not include a retention or transfer test, which leads to the problems described earlier

with regard to generalizing results to skill learning. Second, because there was only one level of bandwidth KR, it is not possible to assess how the results would compare to the effects of various sizes of bandwidths. Although the first issue is easy to empirically address, the question about quantitative KR has a unique complexity that makes it difficult to investigate. When the presentation of quantitative KR is based on a performance-based bandwidth, both qualitative and quantitative KR are involved. That is, when a person performs within the bandwidth, no KR is given, which indicates to the performer that the performance was "correct." But when the person makes an error that exceeds the bandwidth, he or she receives quantitative KR. Cauraugh, Chen, and Radlo (1993) addressed this second issue by including a condition in which quantitative KR was given when performance error was within the bandwidth, and qualitative KR was given when performance error was outside the bandwidth. Their results showed that when KR was based on a performance bandwidth, either qualitative or quantitative KR led to better learning than KR that was not based on a performance-based bandwidth. However, a more recent study by Wright, Smith-Munyon, and Sidaway (1997) found that for the learning of a task that required participants to squeeze a handgrip with a criterion amount of force, quantitative KR for errors outside the performance bandwidth led to better retention performance for both performance accuracy and consistency.

Sherwood (1988) reported the first investigation of the relationship between quantitative KR and a performance-based KR bandwidth. Participants practiced a rapid elbow-flexion task, where the goal was to make the movement in 200 msec. One group received KR about movement time error after every trial, regardless of the amount of error (0% bandwidth). Two other groups received KR only when their movement time error exceeded bandwidths of 5% and 10% of the 200 msec goal movement time, respectively. The results of a no-KR retention test showed that the 10% bandwidth condition resulted in the best learning, and the 0% condition resulted in the poorest learning. Sherwood's results were later replicated by Lee, White, and Carnahan (1990).

Subsequent research has addressed the KR bandwidth question in various ways. One of the more interesting has been to consider the relationship between the size of the bandwidth and the amount of practice on a task. For example, Goodwin and Meeuwsen (1995) compared a 0% and a 10% bandwidth for all practice trials with expanding (0–5–10–15–20%) and contracting (20–15–10–5–0%) bandwidths for learning a golf putting task. Results showed that the expanding bandwidth and the constant

10% conditions produced similar performance on a 48-hour retention test and were superior to the performance of the other conditions. Lai and Shea (1999a) provided evidence that a 15% bandwidth was better than a 0% bandwidth for learning a multisegment task that required the achievement of a relative timing goal. Interestingly, switching from a 15% bandwidth to a 0% bandwidth midway through the practice trials did not affect learning the skill. This question concerning the size of the bandwidth and amount of practice will be discussed further in a later section concerning the use of the bandwidth technique as a means of reducing augmented feedback frequency.

Another way the bandwidth technique has been investigated is with respect to its relationship to instructions about the bandwidth procedure. Because no augmented feedback is given when performance is within the bandwidth of acceptable performance, receiving no augmented feedback is in actuality a nonverbal form of the qualitative statement "Correct." The instruction-related question here is: Is it important that the learner explicitly be told this information, or will the learner implicitly learn this information during practice? Butler, Reeve, and Fischman (1996) investigated this question by telling one group of participants that when they received no KR after a trial, their performance was "essentially correct." A second group was not told this information. The task required a two-segment arm movement to a target in a criterion movement time. The results showed that the bandwidth technique led to better learning when the participants knew in advance that not receiving KR meant they were essentially correct.

At this point, there is sufficient laboratory-based research to support the claim that the use of a performance-based bandwidth can be an effective way to determine when to administer augmented feedback. Additionally, it is notable that this research supports the important point discussed earlier that error information is not always needed to learn a skill. Much remains to be known about the bandwidth technique, which makes it a viable issue for future research. In addition to the need for researchers to address the questions raised in this discussion, an important question that remains to be investigated concerns the effectiveness of the use of a performance-based bandwidth strategy in sport and physical education skill learning contexts. That is, are the laboratory-based findings about the bandwidth technique generalizable to these real-world settings?

Erroneous Augmented Feedback When Augmented Feedback Is Not Needed

Earlier, situations were described where motor skill learning could occur without augmented feedback. In these situations, augmented feedback was redundant with the information available from task-intrinsic feedback and did not lead to better learning than receiving no augmented feedback. A question that arises in these redundancy situations concerns whether the learner ignores the augmented feedback or actually uses it in some way. One way to address this question is to consider the influence of erroneous augmented feedback. The hypothesis is that if the learner ignores the augmented feedback, then the erroneous information should have no effect on learning the skill because the task-intrinsic feedback provides sufficient information to enable the learner to acquire the skill. But, if the learner uses the augmented feedback, then the erroneous information will influence learning in such a way that it will bias the learner to perform according to the erroneous augmented feedback.

The first test of this hypothesis was reported by Buekers, Magill, and Hall (1992). Participants practiced an anticipation timing task similar to the one used by Magill, Chamberlin, and Hall (1991) in experiments described earlier in this chapter. An important feature of this task is that KR about movement time error is redundant with task-intrinsic feedback and therefore not needed to learn the task. Participants practiced the anticipation timing skill for 75 trials. KR about the direction and amount of timing error was given after every trial for three of four groups. For one of these groups, KR was correct. But for another group, KR was erroneous by indicating that performance on a trial was 100 msec later than it actually was. The third KR group received correct KR for the first 50 trials, but then received the erroneous KR for the last 25 trials. A fourth group did not receive KR during practice. All four groups performed 25 trials without KR one day later, and then 25 more no-KR trials one week later. The results showed two important findings. First, the correct-KR and the no-KR groups did not differ during the practice or the retention trials, which confirmed the KR redundancy results of the Magill, Chamberlin, and Hall (1991) experiments. Second, the erroneous KR information led participants to perform according to the KR rather than according to the task-intrinsic feedback. This latter result suggested that the participants used KR even though it was erroneous information. Even more impressive was that the erroneous KR influenced the group that had received correct KR for 50 trials and then was switched to the erroneous KR. After the switch, this group began to perform similarly to the group that had received the incorrect KR for all the practice trials. And the erroneous information not only influenced performance when it was available, it also influenced retention performance one day and one week later, when no KR was provided. A subsequent experiment (McNevin, Magill, & Buekers, 1994) demonstrated that the erroneous KR also influenced performance on a no-KR transfer test in which participants were required to respond to a faster or slower speed than they practiced.

More recent investigations have focused on the basis for the effect of erroneous KR on learning a skill for which KR is redundant information. The most likely reason may be that beginners rely on augmented feedback to help them deal with their uncertainty about what the task-intrinsic feedback is telling them about their performance, which may exist because task-intrinsic feedback for the anticipation timing task is difficult to consciously observe, interpret, and use. Evidence for an uncertainty-based explanation was demonstrated in experiments by Buekers, Magill, and Sneyers (1994) and Buekers and Magill (1995). In an experiment by Buekers, Magill, and Sneyers, participants received various ratios of no-KR to erroneous-KR trials. The erroneous KR effect occurred when the ratio was low (1:1 and 4:1) but not when it was high (9:1). Using a different approach to test the uncertainty hypothesis, Buekers and Magill found that the erroneous KR effect could be eliminated in two ways. First, the effect was eliminated after participants had practiced the anticipation timing task for 400 trials with correct KR and then unexpectedly switched to erroneous KR. Second, the effect was eliminated when participants were told prior to practice about the possibility of erroneous KR.

Additionally, it is interesting to note that when beginners receive erroneous KR while practicing the anticipation timing task, they adjust the timing of the initiation of their movement rather than the movement component of the task (Van Loon, Buekers, Helsen, & Magill, 1998). This suggests that even when augmented feedback is redundant with task-intrinsic feedback, beginners use augmented feedback. For the anticipation timing task, they use it to interpret, or calibrate, the visual task-intrinsic feedback. This means that if these two sources of feedback give the performer the same information, beginners use augmented feedback to confirm their visual task-intrinsic feedback. But if there is a conflict between these two sources of feedback, beginners resolve the conflict in favor of augmented feedback.

The important message for practitioners here is that people who are in the early stage of learning a motor skill will use augmented feedback when is available, whether it is correct or not. This is especially the case for skills for which the task-intrinsic feedback is difficult for beginners to interpret and use to improve performance. Because of their uncertainty about how to use or interpret task-intrinsic feedback, beginners rely on augmented feedback as a critical source of information on which to base movement corrections on future trials. As a result, instructors need to be certain that they provide correct augmented feedback, and establish a means for beginners to learn to use task-intrinsic feedback in a way that will enable them to eventually perform without augmented feedback. Beginning learners are of particular concern here because they will ignore their own sensory feedback sources and adjust future performance attempts on the basis of the information the instructor provides to them, even though it may be incorrect.

From a learning theory perspective, this reliance on augmented feedback by learners in the early stage of learning suggests that cognitive information can override the perception-action link, which suggests that the perceptual-motor control system does not "automatically" use task-intrinsic feedback appropriately. The perceptual component of this system appears to require some calibration. If augmented feedback is available, the learner uses this information to carry out this calibration process. However, if augmented feedback is not available, and if the task is one where augmented information is not necessary for learning the skill, then this calibration process appears to occur by means of trial-and-error experience occurring during practice.

The Use of Technology as a Source for Augmented Feedback

Pedagogical research related to the teaching of sport skills indicates that the most common means of providing augmented feedback to students is verbal (e.g., Eghan, 1988; Fishman & Tobey, 1978). This is undoubtedly due to the convenience of providing verbal feedback as well as to the limited availability of alternative means for providing feedback. However, the use of technology to provide performance-related information as augmented feedback has become increasingly more prevalent, especially as the various types of equipment used for this purpose have become less expensive and more readily available.

Videotape

Having athletes or students view videotaped replays of their performance of a skill is a commonly used instructional strategy in sport and physical education contexts. In fact, it is common to find articles in professional journals that offer guidelines and suggestions for the use of videotape replays (e.g, Franks & Maile, 1991; Jambor & Weekes, 1995;

Trinity & Annesi, 1996). Despite its frequent use, very little empirical research exists that establishes the effectiveness of videotape replays as an aid for skill acquisition. In fact, the most recent extensive review of the research literature related to the use of videotape replay as a source of augmented feedback in skill learning situations was published many years ago by Rothstein and Arnold (1976). Their review included over 50 studies that involved 18 different sport activities, including archery, badminton, bowling, gymnastics, skiing, swimming, and volleyball. In most of these studies, the students were beginners, although some included intermediate and advanced performers.

Despite the age of the review, current research and practice related to the use of videotape as augmented feedback tends to follow or be based on its general conclusions. Overall, Rothstein and Arnold (1976) reported that the results of the studies they reviewed were mixed with regard to the effectiveness of videotape as a means of providing augmented feedback. However, two points stood out as consistent across the various studies. First, the skill level of the student rather than the type of activity was the critical factor for determining the effectiveness of videotape as an instructional aid. That is, for beginners to benefit from videotape replay, they required the assistance of an instructor to point out critical information. Advanced or intermediate performers did not appear to need instructor aid as frequently, although anecdotal evidence from skilled athletes suggests they could receive greater benefit from observing replays when some form of attention-directing instructions are provided, such as verbal cues and checklists. Second, videotape replays were most effective when used repeatedly for an extended period of time. Rothstein and Arnold reported that in the studies they reviewed, the most beneficial effects of videotape replays resulted when they were used for at least five weeks. In studies in which replays were used for a shorter amount of time, they were ineffective as a form of augmented feedback to aid learning.

Research since the time of the Rothstein and Arnold review has provided additional information about the use of videotape replay as a source of augmented feedback. An important point from this research is that videotape replays transmit certain types of performance-related information to the learner more effectively than other types. A good example of support for this point is an experiment by Selder and Del Rolan (1979). They compared videotape replays and verbal augmented feedback (in the form of KP) in a study in which 12–13-year-old girls learned to perform a balance beam routine. All the girls used a checklist to

critically analyze their own performance after each trial. The verbal augmented feedback group used verbal KP to complete the checklist; the videotape feedback group completed the checklist after viewing videotape replays of each trial. Two results are especially noteworthy. After four weeks of practice, performance scores for the routine did not differ between the two groups. But at the end of six weeks of practice, the videotape group scored significantly higher on the routine than the verbal feedback group. Second, when each factor of the total routine score was evaluated, the videotape group scored significantly higher on only four of the eight factors: precision, execution, amplitude, and orientation and direction. The two groups did not differ on the other four: rhythm, elegance, coordination, and lightness of jumping and tumbling. The importance of these results is that they demonstrate that although videotape replay can be an effective means of giving augmented feedback to aid skill learning, it does not facilitate the learning of all aspects of a complex motor skill. The results of the Selder and Del Rolan study suggest that videotape replay facilitates the learning of those performance features that the performer can readily observe and determine how to correct on the basis of the videotape replay. However, for performance features that are not as readily discernible, videotape replay is not as effective as verbal KP. Finally, it is important to add that these conclusions about the informational component and effectiveness of videotape replays have been supported for the learning of other skills, such as the tennis serve (Rikli & Smith, 1980) and overarm throwing accuracy (Kernodle & Carlton, 1992).

A more recent study by Hebert, Landin, and Menickelli (1998) offered interesting evidence concerning the information provided by videotape replay and the steps skilled athletes go through to use this information. In a single-case, multiple-baseline study, skilled college female tennis players practiced improving their attacking stroke. The players observed videotape replays of their practice sessions for four, two, or no days. Results showed that the players who observed the videotape replays showed noticeably more improvement than the players who did not observe the replays. In addition, evidence from recordings of players' comments during videotape observation sessions and the researchers' fieldnotes showed that they progressed through four stages of information use while observing the replays. During the first stage, players familiarized themselves with observing themselves on videotape and made general observations about how they looked on videotape as well as their technique. In the next stage, players recognized specific technical errors. The third stage was more analytical, as the players made connections between technique and outcome. In the fourth and final stage, players began to show evidence of the use of their previous observations of replays by correcting their technique errors. As a result of this final stage, the players acknowledged what they considered to be the important key points related to successfully hitting the attack shot.

Finally, Starek and McCullagh (1999) have shown that another effective use of videotape replays is to use them in a combination as a source of augmented feedback and for self-modeling to facilitate the learning of correct technique. In their study, adult beginning swimmers were shown 3-minute videotape replays of their swimming performance during the lesson of the previous day. The replay showed four swimming behaviors they had performed correctly and four they had trouble performing. During the following two days, some students saw their own successfully performed skills from the previous day, and other students saw a skilled swimmer successfully perform these skills. The results showed that swimmers who saw their own videotaped performance performed better than those who saw the same skills performed by someone else.

Movement Kinematic Information

With the widespread availability of computer software capable of providing sophisticated kinematic analysis of movement, it has become increasingly common to find sport skill instruction situations in which students can view graphically presented kinematic representations about their performances as a form of feedback. Unfortunately, as was the case with the use of videotape replays, there is very little empirical evidence concerning the effectiveness of this means of providing augmented feedback. However, the few studies that have been reported provide some insight into the use of this form of augmented feedback.

An early, non-computer-based study by Lindahl (1945) involved machine operator trainees in industry. They were trained to precisely and quickly cut thin disks of tungsten with a machine that required fast, accurate, and rhythmic coordination of the hands and feet. Traditionally, training for this job was by trial and error. To test an alternate training method, Lindahl created a mechanism that would make a paper tracing of the foot movement pattern during the cutting of each disk, which was then shown to the trainees after each trial. The results indicated that the trainees who received the tracing of their foot movement pattern as augmented feedback achieved production performance levels in 11 weeks that had taken other trainees 20 weeks to achieve. In addition, these trainees reduced their percentage of broken cutting wheels to almost zero in 12 weeks, a level not achieved by those trained with the traditional method in less than 36 weeks. In this case, graphically presenting kinematic information as augmented feedback not only helped workers achieve desired performance levels, it also helped them achieve these levels in significantly less time.

Newell, Quinn, Sparrow, and Walter (1983) provided further support for the effectiveness of the use of movement kinematic displays as augmented feedback. In their laboratory-based study, which was an extension of an earlier experiment by Hatze (1976), participants practiced moving a lever as fast as possible to a target. Participants received KR verbally, in terms of their movement time, or graphically, as a display on the computer monitor of their movement velocity-time trace. A third group received no KR during practice. Results indicated that the group that saw the kinematic display performed best, followed by the verbal-KR condition and then the no-KR condition. It is interesting to note that participants in the no-KR condition showed improvement for the first 25 trials, but then their performance reached a steady state without further improvement, whereas the two KR conditions led to additional improvements. The difference between the two types of KR became more pronounced as practice continued.

More recently, Swinnen and his colleagues have reported the results of several experiments that showed the effectiveness of kinematic information as augmented feedback (Swinnen, Walter, Lee, & Serrien, 1993; Swinnen, Walter, Pauwels, Meugens, & Beirinkx, 1990). Participants in these experiments practiced a bimanual coordination task that required them to move two levers at the same time, but with each lever requiring a different spatiotemporal movement pattern. Kinematic information was presented as augmented feedback in the form of the angular displacement characteristics for each arm superimposed over the criterion displacements. In several experiments, the kinematic augmented feedback was compared with various other forms of augmented feedback. The results consistently demonstrated the effectiveness of the displacement information as augmented feedback.

The study of the use and benefit of movement kinematic displays as augmented feedback needs more attention by researchers (see Schmidt & Young, 1991; Young & Schmidt, 1992, for discussions concerning this issue). As computers and movement analysis systems as evaluative tools become more commonplace, the application of this type of movement-related information as KP will increase.

As a result there is an increased need to know more about the effective implementation of movement analysis information as augmented feedback to enhance skill learning and performance. Newell and his colleagues (e.g., Newell & McGinnis, 1985; Newell, Morris, & Scully, 1985), along with Fowler and Turvey (1978), have presented some initial attempts at providing theory-based guidelines for the effective use of this type of information as augmented feedback. However, further theoretical and empirical work is needed to develop guidelines that will lead to the most effective use of movement-related information as augmented feedback, especially in terms of the learning of nonlaboratory tasks.

Biofeedback

The term *biofeedback* refers to an augmented form of the activity of physiological processes, such as heart rate, blood pressure, and muscle activity. Several forms of biofeedback have been used in motor skill learning situations. The most common is EMG biofeedback, which provides information about muscle activity. Most of the research concerning EMG biofeedback has been undertaken in physical rehabilitation settings (e.g., Beckham, Keefe, Caldwell, & Brown, 1991; Moreland & Thomson, 1994; Sandweiss & Wolf, 1985; Wolf, 1983). Another form of biofeedback, which has been used primarily in physical rehabilitation for balance training, is a visual presentation on a computer monitor of a person's center of pressure and/or center of gravity (e.g., Shumway-Cook, Anson, & Haller, 1988; Simmons, Smith, Erez, Burke, & Pozos, 1998). Finally, a rather unique type of biofeedback in motor skill learning contexts has been applied in the training of competitive rifle shooters (Daniels & Landers, 1981). Heart-rate biofeedback was presented auditorally to help these athletes learn to squeeze the rifle trigger between heartbeats, which is a characteristic of elite shooters.

In general, research evidence has supported the effectiveness of biofeedback as a means of facilitating motor skill learning. However, debate continues concerning the specific situations in which the use of biofeedback is an effective and preferred form of augmented feedback (Moreland & Thomson, 1994). In addition, biofeedback is usually presented as concurrent augmented feedback, which leads to concerns related to the development of a dependency on the availability of the augmented feedback to maintain an acquired level of performance. This dependency issue, as it relates to the concurrent presentation of augmented feedback, will be discussed more specifically later in this chapter.

FREQUENCY OF PRESENTING AUGMENTED FEEDBACK

Another important issue related to the use of augmented feedback is the question of how frequently it should be given to a person who is learning a motor skill. Since the late 1980s, this frequency question has been one of the most investigated issues in the study of augmented feedback. Three issues have predominated. The first concerns whether the frequency of providing augmented feedback is important for skill learning, and if so, is there an optimal frequency? The second relates to the effects of various methods of reducing the frequency of augmented feedback during practice. Finally, researchers have investigated the predominant hypothesis proposed to explain the frequency effect on skill learning. Each of these concerns will be addressed below.

The Reduced Frequency Effect

The first issue that must be resolved when discussing the question of the role of the frequency of presenting augmented feedback concerns whether the primary focus should be on "absolute" or "relative" frequency. Absolute frequency refers to giving augmented feedback for a specific number of practice trials. Relative frequency, on the other hand, refers to the percentage of total practice trials on which KR is given. For example, if a person were to practice a skill for 80 trials and received KR on 20 of them, the absolute frequency would be 20, but the relative frequency would be 25%. The question is, which is more important for learning?

Prior to the Salmoni et al. (1984) reassessment of the augmented feedback research literature, the generally accepted conclusion was that absolute frequency was more important, and that more frequency is better than less (e.g., Bilodeau & Bilodeau, 1958a). Proponents of this view argued that augmented feedback is essential for learning, and the learner would not benefit from practice trials without augmented feedback. However, more recent research, in which absolute frequency was varied and where a learning test was included in the experiment (which was not done in the Bilodeau and Bilodeau experiment), has shown that absolute frequency of KR is *not* the critical factor for learning (e.g., Ho & Shea, 1978; Winstein & Schmidt, 1990). In addition, this research has demonstrated that augmented feedback on every trial (i.e., 100% frequency) is not a necessary condition to establish optimal learning.

If 100% frequency of augmented feedback does not establish an optimal learning situation, is there a relative frequency that does? Winstein and Schmidt (1990) reported an important study that addressed this question. Notably, their study has stimulated much of the augmented feedback frequency research since that time. Until their experiments, investigations of the frequency question typically reported that relative frequencies of less than 100% were not different from 100% relative frequency. But Winstein and Schmidt provided a breakthrough by using a "fading" technique, which had been reported to optimize the learning of word lists (Landauer & Bjork, 1978). The fading technique involved the systematic decrease of the number of trials on which augmented feedback was provided during practice. More specifically, Winstein and Schmidt systematically reduced the augmented feedback frequency from 100% early in practice to 25% later in practice, which yielded an average frequency of 50%. In their experiment, participants practiced producing a complex waveform pattern on a computer monitor by moving a lever on a tabletop that manipulated a cursor on the monitor. Augmented feedback was given as KP and KR by displaying the criterion movement pattern on the monitor along with the participant's pattern and overall error score. During two days of practice, participants received KP and KR after either 100% or 50% of the trials. On a no-KP/KR retention test given one day later, the group that had experienced the "faded" 50% frequency condition performed better than the group that received KP and KR on every practice trial. In fact, the retention test performance by participants in the 100% frequency condition resembled their performance early on the first day of practice.

Research on the frequency effect since the Winstein and Schmidt (1990) study has focused not only on providing additional empirical support for the reduced frequency benefit, but also on whether or not an optimal frequency exists to enhance skill learning (e.g., Lai & Shea, 1998, 1999b; Wulf, Lee, & Schmidt, 1994; Wulf, Schmidt, & Deubel, 1993). Two interesting conclusions have resulted from these research efforts. First, although a reduced frequency of augmented feedback can benefit motor skill learning, it does *not* benefit the learning of all motor skills. Second, an "optimal" relative frequency for the learning of all skills probably does not exist. As in the case for reduced relative frequency, the optimal relative frequency appears to be specific to the skill being learned.

These two conclusions lead to the question, What are the skill-related characteristics that would predict relative frequency effects? Wulf, Shea, and Matschiner (1998) proposed two. One is the *complexity* of the skill being learned. In investigations that found that reduced augmented feedback frequency is better than, or as effective as, 100%

frequency, the tasks were relatively simple. For example, they have involved simple ballistic movements for which the goal was to move in a specified amount of time (e.g., Lai & Shea, 1999b, Exp. 1), the ballistic striking of a pad with a specified amount of force (e.g., Kohl & Guadagnoli, 1996), or the moving of a lever to produce a specific spatiotemporal movement pattern (e.g., Winstein & Schmidt, 1990; Lai & Shea, 1999b, Exp. 2). On the other hand, studies that have reported that a reduced augmented feedback frequency does not benefit skill learning typically have involved relatively complex skills, such as a slalom ski simulator (e.g., Wulf et al., 1998).

One interpretation of this task complexity issue is to consider complexity in terms of the number of components of the task about which augmented feedback could be given. This interpretation would lead to the hypothesis that when the task and the performance measure are isomorphic, as exists when a lever must be moved in a specified amount of time or a pad must be struck with a specified amount of force, people do not require augmented feedback on every practice trial. But when the task involves several possible performance charactcristics about which augmented feedback can be given, more frequent augmented feedback may be required. The expectation for this latter case is that the performance characteristic about which augmented feedback would be given would be varied from trial to trial. However, Weeks and Kordus (1998) presented evidence that contradicts this interpretation of task complexity. In their experiment, 12-year-old boys who had no soccer experience practiced the soccer throw-in skill. KP was provided as one of eight technique-related errors, with a specific statement about the most critical error made on a trial. One group received one KP statement after every practice trial (100% frequency); a second group received one KP statement after every three trials (33% frequency). Results showed that both groups received the same relative distribution of the eight possible statements, but the 33% frequency group performed with better technique on both a 24-hour no-KP retention test and a transfer test that required a modification of the practiced throw-in skill.

The second task characteristic proposed by Wulf, Shea, and Matschiner (1998) relates to the motor control construct known as the generalized motor program (see Schmidt, 1975), which Schmidt proposed as an abstract memory representation of a class of movements that is responsible for the control of voluntary movement. Wulf et al. proposed that when multiple skill variations must be learned, and the variations are under the control of different generalized motor programs (i.e., the skills represent different movement classes), reduced relative frequencies lead to better learning of the variations. But when the skill variations are parameter modifications of the same generalized motor program, reduced relative frequencies do not benefit learning, and sometimes hinder it (e.g., Wulf et al., 1994; although see Wrisberg & Wulf, 1997, for contrary evidence).

Techniques for Altering the Frequency of Augmented Feedback

In addition to specifying less than 100% of trials on which to give augmented feedback during practice, researchers have investigated several other techniques for altering the frequency of presenting augmented feedback. Because these various techniques can be somewhat confusing, a brief comparison of each should be an instructive introduction. Three of these techniques (performance-based bandwidths, the average technique, and self-selected frequency) reduce both the number of times during practice that augmented feedback is presented and the number of practice trials about which the performer receives augmented feedback. For the performance-based bandwidth technique, the learner receives augmented feedback only when performance error on a trial is greater than a specified "acceptable" amount. The average technique involves presenting the average performance for a certain number of trials. The learner receives augmented feedback for performance on a trial for the self-selected technique only when he or she requests it. One other technique that will be discussed does not reduce the number of practice trials about which the performer receives augmented feedback, but reduces the number of times during practice that augmented feedback is presented. The summary technique involves presenting augmented feedback after a certain number of trials, but feedback about each trial since the previous presentation is included in the summary.

Performance-Based Bandwidths

Earlier, research evidence was discussed that showed that skill learning can be enhanced with augmented feedback only when performance is not within a preestablished tolerance limit (i.e., bandwidth). If the bandwidth issue is considered together with the augmented feedback frequency issue, it is possible to see an interesting relationship between them. That is, if augmented feedback is based on a performance bandwidth, then feedback will be provided with less frequency than when feedback is given regardless of the magnitude of the performance error.

Lee, White, and Carnahan (1990) investigated this relationship by yoking individual participants in the 5% and 10% bandwidth conditions with individual participants who would receive KR only on the trials on which the bandwidth participants received KR. The reason for the yoking of participants was to control for the possibility that the performance-based bandwidth benefit for learning was due to a reduced KR frequency. Thus, KR frequency was the same for the bandwidth and yoked groups, but the KR frequency for the bandwidth groups depended on performance criteria. Participants practiced a ballistic two-segment limb movement task. Results showed that the bandwidth-based KR conditions led to better retention performance than the yoked frequency KR conditions, which led to the conclusion that the performance-based bandwidth effect is more than a frequency effect. Lee, White, and Carnahan proposed that the bandwidth effect is due to combining KR with what the motor control system is capable of doing. That is, early in practice, the system is not capable of correcting errors with the precision required if errors must be corrected within a 5% or 10% tolerance limit. Thus a bandwidth-based KR delivery allows the control system to adapt to the demands of the task and to develop appropriate error-correction processes needed to perform the skill correctly and increase performance consistency.

An interesting characteristic of the bandwidth technique is that augmented feedback frequency reduces as a person continues to practice and improve performance. In effect, then, the bandwidth procedure could be considered a performance-based form of the fading technique described earlier. One way to determine if this performance-based frequency reduction works similarly to the experimenter-determined frequency reduction of the fading technique is to compare constant bandwidths throughout practice with those that change in size at different stages of practice. The effect of changing bandwidth sizes would be to allow augmented feedback frequency to remain relatively constant throughout practice.

Two experiments described earlier are examples of research that has addressed this issue. In the Goodwin and Meeuwsen (1995) experiment, which involved learning to putt a golf ball a criterion distance, 0% and 10% error bandwidth conditions were compared with those that were systematically expanded (0–5–10–15–20%) and contracted (20–15–10–5–0%) during practice. Results showed that retention performance did not differ between the expanded and 10% conditions, although both were better than the 0% and contracted bandwidth conditions. More recently, Lai and Shea (1999a) reported a similar finding by showing that a 15% error bandwidth led to better learning of a complex spatiotemporal movement pattern than either a 0% bandwidth or switching from 15% to 0% bandwidths midway through the practice trials. Thus, the reduced frequency of augmented feedback created by a specific performance-based bandwidth benefits learning in a manner similar to the fading technique in which the experimenter determines the frequencies.

From an applied perspective, the bandwidth procedure can be a useful means of individualizing the systematic reduction of the frequency of augmented feedback in practice situations. As suggested by Winstein and Schmidt (1990), because the weaning of individuals from the need for augmented feedback is beneficial for learning, administering augmented feedback on the basis of performance-based bandwidths creates a systematic means of reducing augmented feedback frequency. Because the bandwidth is related to individual performance, the "weaning" process becomes one that is specific to the individual's own performance.

Summary Technique

Another way to reduce augmented feedback frequency is to provide a summary of the augmented feedback after a certain number of practice trials. For example, rather than the presentation of augmented feedback after every trial, an alternative is to provide a listing of five trials of feedback statements after every fifth trial. The interesting feature of this technique is that the learner receives the same amount of information as if he or she were given augmented feedback after every trial, but the frequency with which the learner receives the information is reduced. It is also worth noting that this technique can be considered a variation of the "trials delay of KR" procedure, which will be discussed later in this chapter.

In addition to being a means of reducing augmented feedback frequency, the summary technique provides a useful method for providing augmented feedback for practice situations in which it would not be practical, or possible, to give it after every trial. For example, if a person is practicing a shooting skill where he or she cannot see the target because of the distance involved, efficiency of practice could be increased by giving the person KR after every 10 shots rather than after each. Although the summary technique may have practical appeal, the important question is How does it affect learning? Does the summary technique function similar to a reduced frequency situation, or does the summary provide too much information at one time, rendering it ineffective?

Schmidt, Young, Swinnen, and Shapiro (1989) investigated the effectiveness of the summary technique by extending earlier studies (Baker & Young, 1960; Lavery,

1962), which had not been given much attention by motor learning researchers. Participants practiced moving a lever along a trackway to achieve a specified movement time. One group received KR (as movement time) after every trial; the other three groups received KR summaries after 5, 10, or 15 trials. Results showed few differences among the groups during practice or on a 10-minute no-KR retention test. But on another no-KR retention test two days later, the 15-trial summary group performed the best, and the group that had received KR after every trial performed the worst.

Since Schmidt et al. (1989), numerous studies have been published concerning the summary technique. Although evidence supports the summary technique benefit (e.g., Guay, Salmoni, & Lajoie, 1999; Schmidt, Lange, & Young, 1990; Wright, Snowden, & Willoughby, 1990), many questions remain. One concerns the relationship between the summary technique and the reduced relative frequency effect on skill learning. This relationship becomes evident by noting that the largest summary length involves the lowest frequency of augmented feedback presentations (although all summary lengths include information about all trials, the number of times the information is presented during practice varies according to summary length). The question of interest here is whether there is something about the summarizing of augmented feedback for one presentation after a certain number of trials, or if the benefit observed for the summary technique is primarily due to the reduced frequency of presenting augmented feedback. Sidaway, Moore, and Schoenfelder-Zohdi (1991) investigated this question by holding KR frequency constant but manipulating the number of trials summarized. They concluded that the positive effects of summary KR are not due to the number of trials summarized, which argues against the notion of an "optimal summary length." Instead, they argued that the summary effect is related to either the frequency of KR presentation or the temporal delay in presenting KR.

In addition, others have found that the effectiveness of the summary technique interacts with other variables. For example, Guadagnoli, Dornier, and Tandy (1996) reported that task-related experience and task complexity interact with the effectiveness of summary KR. They found that shorter summaries were more beneficial than longer ones for beginners and for more complex tasks, but just the opposite was the case for more experienced performers and for simple tasks. Furthermore, Guay, Salmoni, and Lajoie (1999) reported that if a task has both spatial and temporal goals, the summarizing of KR influences temporal accuracy but not the spatial component, which was influenced more by the spacing of KR presentations.

Average Technique

A variation of the summary technique involves providing an average performance score for a series of trials rather than all the performance scores for the trials. Thus, the learner receives one score, which is representative of all trials in a series. Young and Schmidt (1992) appear to have been the first to investigate the use of the average KR technique. They found that for the learning of a coincident-anticipation timing task, average KR led to better learning than KR after every trial. Using a more complex task, Wulf and Schmidt (1996) concluded that for the learning of three spatiotemporal movement patterns, average KR was no better or worse than KR after every trial or after every third trial for learning the fundamental movement pattern underlying all three patterns, but worse than the other KR frequencies for learning to parameterize the amplitude characteristic of the patterns.

However, Weeks and Sherwood (1994) noted that for learning to produce a specific static force, average KR and summary KR conditions were not different from each other, although both were better than KR after every trial. Yao, Fischman, and Wang (1994) reported similar results for the learning of an aiming task that required both spatial and temporal accuracy. Guay, Salmoni, and Lajoie (1999) extended the Yao et al. study and observed that the summary and average KR conditions were not different only for the temporal accuracy component of the task, but not the spatial component.

The varied results of the use of the average KR technique makes it difficult to make definitive conclusions about its relationship to other techniques for reducing augmented feedback frequency. The similarity of results when compared to the summary technique suggests that learners may actually "calculate" an average when they are presented with a summary of KR for a certain number of trials. However, there is sufficient evidence to indicate that the average KR technique can be an effective means of reducing the presentation frequency of augmented feedback. Additional research must be done to determine the parameters of its effectiveness.

Self-Selected Frequency Technique

An interesting technique that reduces augmented feedback frequency and facilitates skill learning involves having the learner ask for feedback rather than having the person teaching the skill determine when to give augmented feedback. The basis for this technique comes from research that has shown the learning benefits derived from actively engaging the learner in the learning process. Researchers who study the learning of cognitive skills have shown that one effective means of actively engaging the learner is the "self-regulation" of the use of strategies to learn (e.g., Schneider & Pressley, 1989, Siegler, 1991).

Janelle, Kim, and Singer (1995) applied the concept of self-regulation to motor skill learning by engaging learners in the self-regulation of receiving augmented feedback. In their experiment, participants practiced an underhand ball toss to a target. Results showed that compared to practice conditions in which KP was presented as a summary every 5 trials, on every other trial, or not at all, the participant-controlled KP schedule led to the most accurate throwing performance on a retention test.

Janelle substantiated and extended these results in a later study in which videotape replay was a source of augmented feedback in addition to verbal KP (Janelle, Barba, Frehlich, Tennant, & Cauraugh, 1997). Although several conditions were included in the experiment, three are most relevant to the present discussion. One group received a summary form of KP and videotape replay after each block of 10 trials, a self-regulated group controlled the augmented feedback schedule by requesting KP at will during 200 practice trials, and individuals in another group were yoked to participants in the self-regulated condition to receive KP on the same trials, but without requesting it. This yoked condition was important to control for the possibility that the effect of self-regulation of augmented feedback is due only to reduced frequency. Results showed that participants in the self-regulated condition learned the throwing accuracy task with more accuracy and better throwing technique than both the summary KP and yoked conditions.

The results of Janelle's experiments indicate that a self-controlled schedule of augmented feedback benefits skill learning. In terms of augmented feedback frequency, it is interesting to note that in the Janelle, Kim, and Singer (1995) experiment, participants in the self-controlled condition requested KP on only 7% of the practice trials, and 11% in the Janelle et al. (1997) experiment. These low frequencies indicate that there is some relationship between the self-controlled procedure and the reduced relative frequency of augmented feedback. However, because the self-controlled conditions in both experiments led to better performance on retention tests than the frequency-yoked conditions, the benefit of the self-controlled situation is more than a simple frequency effect.

Janelle et al. (1997) described several hypotheses to account for this learning benefit. One is that a self-controlled learning environment allows a person to process important skill-related information at a deeper level (Watkins, 1984). Another is that the self-controlled situation encourages the learner to engage in more effective learning strategies (Chen & Singer, 1992). Some suggest that being able to control their own learning environment increases learners' confidence in their capability to perform the skill (i.e., self-efficacy) when they experience improvement (Zimmerman, Bonner, & Kovach, 1996). However, the specific reason for the learning benefit of a self-regulated schedule for receiving augmented feedback has yet to be established.

The Guidance Hypothesis Explanation of Reduced Frequency Effects

The several different augmented feedback presentation scheduling techniques just discussed have in common the finding that motor skill learning does *not* depend on learners receiving augmented feedback on every practice trial. What is the explanation for this finding? The predominant hypothesis is the "guidance hypothesis," which was proposed and has been generally supported by Schmidt and his colleagues (Salmoni et al., 1984; Winstein & Schmidt, 1990; Wulf, Lee, & Schmidt, 1994). According to this hypothesis, the learner is involved in fundamentally different learning processes when augmented feedback is presented with 100% frequency than with less frequency. When learners receive augmented feedback on every trial, they use the feedback as an effective "guide" to enable them to perform correctly. Although the guidance is a positive feature of 100% frequency, there is a negative aspect to it as well. Learners can develop such a dependency on the augmented feedback that when the skill must be performed without augmented feedback, performance deteriorates. The dependency on the augmented feedback may be due to the augmented feedback having become a part of what was learned during practice (Proteau, Marteniuk, & Levesque, 1992), or the learner did not adequately learn the critical task-intrinsic feedback that would allow performance of the task without augmented feedback. At the present time, research results are rather mixed with respect to support for the guidance hypothesis (see Swinnen, 1996, for an excellent discussion). However, sufficient evidence exists to warrant consideration of the hypothesis as a valid view of reduced frequency effects for various schedules of presentation of augmented feedback, although additional research is needed.

An important practical implication of the finding that less than 100% frequency leads to learning that is better than, or as good as, 100% frequency is that it reduces the demand on the instructor to provide feedback. It should be comforting to the instructor to realize that he or she will not cause the student or athlete harm by failing to provide feedback after every practice attempt. In fact, if Schmidt's guidance hypothesis is correct, then the instructor could actually be negatively influencing learning by giving feedback after every practice attempt. It is noteworthy in this regard that sport pedagogy research has typically shown that teachers and coaches of sport skills in situations involving groups of students or athletes do not provide augmented feedback with 100% frequency. In these types of teaching and coaching situations, augmented feedback is provided about one or two times per minute, where the same student rarely receives more than a few feedback statements throughout a class session or practice period (e.g., Eghan, 1988; Fishman & Tobey, 1978; Silverman, Tyson, & Krampitz, 1992). However, if a teacher or coach is working with a person individually, it is much easier to give feedback after every trial. But, based on the research literature, it appears that this would not be an optimal strategy and that less frequent feedback would be preferable. However, before proposing specific guidelines about optimal strategies for providing augmented feedback in teaching and coaching contexts, more research is needed that investigates the frequency issue in these types of contexts. In the meantime, the general conclusion that reduced augmented frequency is preferred over 100% frequency can serve as a guideline.

THE TIMING OF AUGMENTED FEEDBACK

Several issues relate to the timing aspects of augmented feedback. The first concerns whether it is better to provide augmented feedback concurrently during a practice attempt, or to give it terminally at the end of a practice attempt. The other issues relate specifically to terminal augmented feedback and concern two intervals of time that occur between the end of one practice attempt and the beginning of the next. The interval of time between the end of a practice attempt and the presentation of augmented feedback is typically referred to as the KR-delay interval. The interval that follows augmented feedback and the next practice trial is the post-KR interval. It is important to note that although the terms used to describe these two intervals refer to KR, they apply to KP as well.

Concurrent Augmented Feedback

When augmented feedback is given concurrently, it usually involves the enhancement of task-intrinsic feedback. This enhancement can take many forms and usually relates to characteristics of the task being learned. Consider the following four examples: (1) When the task requires movement accuracy, such as shooting at a target, a manual aiming task, a precision tracing task, or a pursuit tracking task, concurrent augmented feedback could be given by providing a visible or audible signal that lets the performer know when a movement is on- or off-target. (2) When the task involves the performance of a complex coordination task, concurrent augmented feedback could be given by using a computer to calculate and show the performer the displacement characteristics of the limbs as he or she performs the task. (3) When the task requires the person to learn to produce a specific force-time curve, the curve could be shown to the person on a computer monitor or oscilloscope as the person performed the task. (4) When the task requires learning to use a physiological feature or process in a specific way, such as learning to activate a specific muscle group to help relearn to step up on a stair-step, or to learn to time the trigger pull to shoot a rifle between heartbeats, biofeedback can be used as a means of providing concurrent augmented feedback.

Research evidence has shown two general types of effects for the use of concurrent augmented feedback in skill learning situations. The more common is that performance is very good when the concurrent augmented feedback is available, but then declines on transfer trials during which the augmented feedback is removed (e.g., Annett, 1959, 1970; Fox & Levy, 1969; Patrick & Mutlusoy, 1982; Verschueren, Swinnen, Dom, & DeWeert, 1997). In these situations, the concurrent augmented feedback appears to influence learners to direct their attention away from the critical task-intrinsic feedback and direct it toward the augmented feedback. The result is that the augmented feedback becomes a substitute for critical task-intrinsic feedback cues, which allows the augmented feedback to become an integral part of what is learned and therefore necessary for future performance (e.g., Karlin & Mortimer, 1963; Lintern, 1991; Lintern & Roscoe, 1980).

The second general effect is that concurrent augmented feedback enhances skill learning. One situation in which this positive effect has been consistently found is in the training of flight skills for airplane pilots (e.g., Lintern, 1991; Lintern, Roscoe, Koonce, & Segal, 1990; Lintern et al., 1990). In these experiments, concurrent augmented feedback enhanced relevant features of the instrumentation on the control panel of the aircraft. Results of the use of this visual augmentation of feedback have shown specific benefits for training pilots to perform landing and bombing skills. Another skill learning situation in which this positive effect has been found involves laboratory tasks that require the learning of new bimanual limb coordination relationships (e.g., Swinnen et al., 1993) and physical rehabilitation tasks that require the activation of specific muscles or muscle groups (e.g., Beckham et al., 1991).

Because concurrent augmented feedback can have either a negative or a positive effect on skill learning, it is important to identify the factors or conditions that will lead to one or the other of these effects. Two hypotheses have been forwarded to address this issue. Lintern and his colleagues (Lintern, 1991; Lintern et al., 1990) argued that practicing with augmented feedback will benefit learning to the extent that the feedback sensitizes the learner to properties or relationships in the task that specify how the system being learned can be controlled. Although their terminology relates to the control of aircraft systems, it applies to other types of skill learning as well. That is, for concurrent augmented feedback to be effective, it must facilitate the learning of the critical characteristics or relationships in the task as specified by the task-intrinsic feedback. Negative learning effects will result when the augmented feedback distracts attention from these features. But positive learning effects will result when the augmented feedback directs attention to these features.

Annett (1959, 1969, 1970) proposed a related hypothesis by contending that augmented feedback should be considered in terms of its information value, which he related to the "informativeness" of the task-instrinsic feedback and the augmented feedback. When the informativeness of task-intrinsic feedback is low and the informativeness of the augmented feedback is high, concurrent augmented feedback can lead to a dependency on the augmented feedback.

Terminal Augmented Feedback Time Intervals

The KR-Delay Interval

The interval of time between the completion of a movement and the presentation of augmented feedback traditionally has been termed the KR-delay interval, primarily because the vast majority of research addressing this interval of time has involved KR rather than KP. Differing views have been expressed concerning the importance of this interval for motor skill learning. For example, Ammons (1958) proposed that lengthening this interval would lead to poorer learning because the information value of the KR would diminish over time. However, Adams (1971) concluded that the delay of KR has little or no effect on skill learning. Since the time of these two conclusions, researchers have provided a clearer picture of the actual influence of various manipulations that can be associated with this interval. To discuss this interval appropriately, it is necessary to consider two KR-delay interval characteristics that are commonly manipulated in experiments investigating its role in skill learning: time (i.e., the length of the interval) and activity during the interval.

The Length of the KR-Delay Interval. One of the early outcomes of studying the KR-delay interval was that a distinction must be made between human and animal learning (see Adams, 1987). Human research established that KR was more than a reward, because it has informational value to humans for the solving of problems, which includes learning a motor skill. Research with humans made it evident that the effect on skill learning of delaying KR led to different results than occurred in animal learning when rewards were delayed. Animal learning studies showed that delaying reward led to decreased learning (e.g., Roberts, 1930), but human skill learning studies showed that delaying KR did not influence learning. Perhaps the most striking example of this latter finding is a study by Bilodeau and Bilodeau (1958b) in which they reported five experiments that required participants to learn spatial limb and finger positioning tasks. The KR-delay interval was varied from a few seconds to seven days. The consistent results in all of these experiments was that KR delays, even of up to one week, did not affect learning these skills.

Although the delaying of the presentation of KR does not appear to affect skill learning, there does seem to be a *minimum* amount of time that must pass before KR is given. For example, Swinnen, Schmidt, Nicholson, and Shapiro (1990) reported evidence that giving KR *too soon* after a movement was completed had a negative effect on learning. In two experiments involving the learning of ballistic movements with movement time goals, when KR was given "instantaneously" (i.e., the participants saw their score immediately on the completion of the required movement), they learned the skills with less accuracy than did those for whom KR was delayed for 3.2 or 8 seconds after completing the movement. The authors proposed that the degrading effect of providing KR too soon was due to the need for learners to engage in the subjective analysis of response-produced (i.e., task-intrinsic) feedback, which is essential for developing appropriate error-detection capabilities. Delaying KR by only a few seconds appeared to enable participants to develop this capability.

Activity During the KR-Delay Interval. Investigations of the effects of activity during the KR-delay interval have provided a variety of results. In some cases, activity has had no effect on skill learning; in other cases, activity has been shown to hinder learning or to benefit learning. However, rather than establishing a confusing state of affairs, these different results have provided insights into the learning processes in which a learner engages during the KR-delay interval, which have provided distinct implications for teaching strategies.

The most common effect of activity during the KR-delay interval is that it has *no influence* on skill learning. Experiments investigating the activity effect have demonstrated this result for over 20 years (e.g., Bilodeau, 1969; Boulter, 1964; Marteniuk, 1986). For example, Marteniuk had participants practice a complex arm movement that required them to move a lever to produce a specific spatiotemporal pattern. A control group received KR within a few seconds after completing the movement and engaged in no activity during the KR-delay interval. Another group had a 40-second KR-delay interval, but did not engage in activity during the interval. The third group also had a 40-second KR-delay interval, but engaged in an arm-movement task in which they attempted to reproduce a movement pattern the experimenter had just performed. The results indicated that during acquisition trials and on a no-KR retention test, there were no differences among the groups.

An example of an experiment in which activity during the KR-delay interval *hinders* learning is one that was part of the Marteniuk (1986) study. Marteniuk reasoned that reproducing an arm-movement pattern produced by another person did not interfere with learning because this activity did not demand the same type of learning processes as learning the arm-movement task. He hypothesized that to interfere with learning, KR-delay interval activity would have to interfere with the same learning processes as those required by the task being learned. In two additional experiments, he included in the KR-delay interval conditions in which participants had to learn either another arm-movement skill or a cognitive skill that involved a number-guessing task. In both experiments, the results indicated that learning another skill during the KR-delay interval interfered with learning the primary skill. This interference effect has also been reported by Shea and Upton (1976), who had participants engage in short-term memory tasks during the KR-delay interval, and by Swinnen (1990) in two experiments in which participants were required to estimate the movement-time error of the experimenter's lever movement performed during the KR-delay interval.

Finally, there have been experiments reported indicating that at least two types of activities during the KR-delay interval can *benefit* learning. One activity is having the learner verbally estimate his or her own error, referred to as *subjective error estimation*. Hogan and Yanowitz (1978) reported the first evidence of the beneficial effect of this activity. Participants practiced a task where the goal was to move a handle along a trackway a specified distance of 47 cm in 200 msec. One group did not engage in any activity before receiving KR, and participants in a second group verbally estimated their own error for each trial before receiving KR for that trial. The results showed that the group that had engaged in the verbal error-estimation activity performed significantly better on retention trials with no KR. It is important to note that these same error-estimation benefits have been reported in subsequent studies by Swinnen (1990) and Liu and Wrisberg (1997).

The second type of activity during the KR-delay interval that benefits learning is the performing of one or more additional practice trials before KR is given for a trial, referred to as the *trials-delay of KR*. For example, if KR is delayed for one trial, a person would perform a trial without KR, then perform a second trial but receive KR for trial 1, then perform a third trial but receive KR for trial 2, and so on. Although there is not an abundance of published research about the trials-delay of KR procedure, the few studies that have been reported have shown consistent evidence supporting its learning benefit. More specifically, Lavery and Suddon (1962) and Suddon and Lavery (1962) found that a 5-trial delay led to better learning of a simple force production task; Lavery (1964) showed that a 1-trial delay led to better learning of a ball tossing task; and Anderson, Magill, and Sekiya (1994) reported that a 2-trial delay led to better learning of a blind line-drawing task.

What do these various effects of activity in the KR-delay interval reveal about learning processes that occur during the interval of time, and why these activities would differentially affect learning? Swinnen (1990; Swinnen et al., 1990) hypothesized that during the KR-delay interval the learner actively uses task-intrinsic feedback to engage in the processing of movement information and the detecting of movement errors. Thus, activities that encourage the learner to actively attend to task-intrinsic feedback and to engage in movement error detection activities would be expected to benefit future performance of the skill without the availability of augmented feedback (see also Anderson et al., 1994). When viewed from this perspective it is reasonable to expect the three different effects of activity during the KR-delay interval. When learners are encouraged to engage in these types of activities, learning will benefit due to the enhancement of the learner's error-detection capability. However, if during the KR-delay interval learners engage in attention-demanding activity that does not permit attention to task-intrinsic feedback or the

self-generation of error estimation, then learning will be hindered. Finally, if the activity engaged in during this interval is not attention demanding to the degree that the learner can engage in some processing of task-intrinsic feedback but not in error-detection enhancement activity, then learning will not be influenced.

For instructional purposes, the most significant implication of these results is that students can engage in beneficial activity following the completion of performing a skill and before a teacher or coach gives them augmented feedback. Before they are given augmented feedback, they should verbally describe what they think they did wrong that led to a less than desired performance outcome. Based on the research evidence, this type of activity will have a positive influence on skill learning because it forces the learner to subjectively evaluate the task-intrinsic feedback in relation to the performance of the skill. Additionally, according to what we know about the motivational role of augmented feedback, especially in terms of its influence on self-esteem, having students occasionally describe what they think they did correctly should also benefit skill learning.

The Post-KR Interval

The interval of time between the presentation of augmented feedback and the beginning of the next trial or practice attempt is commonly called the post-KR interval. Research interest in this interval of time increased following research and comments by the Bilodeaus (e.g., Bilodeau, 1969, Bilodeau & Bilodeau, 1958b) and Adams (1971) that this interval may be the "most important" interval of time during skill acquisition. The basis for this view was that the post-KR interval involves the period of time during which the learner has both task-intrinsic feedback and augmented feedback about the just-completed performance, and he or she must use this information to develop a plan of action for the next trial. Accordingly, the interval of time available for this processing activity would appear to be very critical for skill learning. To evaluate whether this logic is valid or not, the discussion of the research that has investigated this interval of time needs to follow the same organization as the preceding discussion of the KR-delay interval.

Post-KR Interval Length. The questions and expectations about the influence of the time length of the post-KR interval on skill learning are similar to those for the KR-delay interval. In other words, is there an optimal range of time during which the next trial should occur after augmented feedback is given? If so, then when the next trial begins too soon (i.e., the interval is too short), the important processing activities would not have sufficient time to be carried out. Conversely, if the next trial begins too late (i.e., the interval is too long), then some forgetting will occur and the performance on the next trial will not be as good as it would have been otherwise. This reasoning seems logical and indeed has been stated before by others (e.g., Adams, 1971). However, similar to findings for the KR-delay interval, the only empirical support for these expectations relates to the "too early" end of the time continuum. This evidence was reported by Weinberg, Guy, and Tupper (1964); they demonstrated that for learning a limb-positioning movement, a 1-second post-KR interval led to poorer acquisition than did a 5-, 10-, or 20-second interval. None of these latter three interval lengths revealed any differences.

Rogers (1974) also reported results that indicated the need for a minimum post-KR interval length. What is particularly noteworthy in this study is the interaction between the length of the post-KR interval and the precision of KR. The task involved learning to move a micrometer dial to a criterion setting, which the participants had to discover by trial and error and by using KR. When KR was given as direction and quantity of error to the nearest thousandth of a unit, a post-KR interval of 7 seconds led to acquisition as poor as when only direction of error was given. However, a 14-second post-KR interval enabled participants who received the same precise KR to learn the skill better than those who had received the qualitative KR related only to the direction of error. Interestingly, Gallagher and Thomas (1980) reported similar results for children. Thus, similar to the KR-delay interval, there appears to be some minimum amount of time needed to engage in the learning processes that occur during the KR-delay interval if optimal learning is to be achieved. What is not known, and awaits further research, is how this minimum amount of time changes as a function of the skill being learned or as a function of the stage of learning of the learner.

With respect to the opposite end of the optimum range of time for the next trial to begin following KR, there is no evidence indicating that too long a delay will hinder learning. An example of the type of research addressing this question was reported by Magill (1977), who compared post-KR interval lengths of 10 and 60 seconds for participants learning three limb positions on a curvilinear positioning device. Results showed no differences between these two interval lengths.

Activity During the Post-KR Interval. Here again the effect of engaging in activity is similar to what was seen for the KR-delay interval. Depending on the kind of activity, the effect may be no influence on learning, interference with learning, or enhanced learning. It is important to note that these various effects are not in line with traditional predictions of the effect of activity during the post-KR interval. Earlier views (e.g., Adams, 1971; Bilodeau, 1969; Newell, 1976) suggested that because so many important information-processing activities occur during this interval, engaging in other activity during this time would interfere with learning. But more recent evidence has shown that this is only one of three possible effects.

That activity during the post-KR interval has *no effect* on skill learning has clearly been the most common finding. An example is an experiment by Lee and Magill (1983), in which participants practiced moving one arm through a series of three small wooden barriers in 1,050 msec. During the post-KR interval, one group performed a motor activity that involved the learning of the same movement in 1,350 msec, another group performed a cognitive activity that involved number guessing, and a third group engaged in no activity. At the end of the practice trials, the two activity groups showed poorer performance than the nonactivity group. However, on a no-KR retention test, the three groups did not differ from each other.

Results indicating *detrimental effects* of activity during the post-KR interval have been reported by several researchers (e.g., Benedetti & McCullagh, 1987; Boucher, 1974; Hardy, 1983; Swinnen, 1990, Exp. 3). Of these experiments, only those by Benedetti and McCullagh (1987) and Swinnen (1990) included an appropriate test for learning. In both of these experiments, the interfering activity was a cognitive activity. Participants in the experiment by Benedetti and McCullagh engaged in a mathematics problem-solving task; in the experiment by Swinnen, participants estimated the movement-time error of a lever movement made by the experimenter at the beginning of the interval.

Only one experiment demonstrated *beneficial effects* for activity in the post-KR interval. Magill (1988) reported an experiment in which participants practiced a two-component arm movement in which each component had its own criterion movement time. During the post-KR interval, one group practiced two additional two-component arm movements, one group practiced a mirror-tracing task, and a third group engaged in no activity. Results showed different effects for retention and transfer. The three groups did not differ on a no-KR retention test given one day after practice. However, on a transfer test where participants had to perform a new but related two-component task, the two post-KR interval activity groups performed better than the no-activity group.

These beneficial transfer effects were proposed to be due to the increased problem-solving activity experience during practice by the post-KR interval activity groups, which enabled them to transfer more successfully to a situation that required new problem-solving activity of a kind similar to that experienced in practice.

Research is critically needed to further explore the post-KR interval. At present, only logical argument exists to support the nature of the processing activity that occurs during this interval. Although different effects on learning have been reported for different types of activity during this interval, it is not yet clear what produces these different effects nor what the implications are of these different effects for determining the processing activity characterizing the post-KR interval.

In terms of instructional implications, the evidence related to this interval suggests that it is not an interval that needs to be given much direct concern in teaching settings. Although there appears to be a minimum post-KR interval length, this minimum does not seem problematic when applied to the typical teaching situation. Furthermore, although some activities have been found to be both detrimental and beneficial to skill learning, more evidence is needed to address these effects before instruction applications can be made with confidence.

A Potential Confound: The Intertrial Interval

One of the problems facing researchers interested in studying influences of the KR-delay and/or post-KR intervals is that to vary the length of one while holding the length of the other varies the length of the intertrial interval. The problem here is that without some control of intertrial interval length, two intervals vary in the experimental procedures, which can make the attribution of effects to the KR-delay or post-KR interval confounded by the intertrial interval length. Although this concern was raised by researchers in the early days of investigations of the KR intervals (Bilodeau & Bilodeau, 1958b), there is little evidence that the intertrial interval influences effects related to the KR-delay or post-KR intervals. Intertrial interval effects that have been reported involve practice trials without KR (see Salmoni et al., 1984; Schmidt & Lee, 1999).

CONCLUSION

In this chapter, diverse issues related to augmented feedback and skill learning and performance have been discussed. At present, there is little argument concerning the importance of augmented feedback as a variable that can influence motor skill learning. But considerable controversy exists with regard to how important it is and why it is important. The review and reevaluation of research by Salmoni et al. (1984) represented an important milestone in the advancement of our understanding of several key issues related to augmented feedback. But their primary focus was on research design problems that characterized much of the older research, which had been the basis for many traditional principles of augmented feedback. Although that focus was a necessary first step, it has become evident from the research reported since their influential publication that another important step must be taken to allow for confidence in principles of augmented feedback with respect to skill learning.

The next step should be to investigate currently proposed principles of augmented feedback in skill learning contexts in which complex skills are learned. The need for this focus was discussed in various parts of this chapter. For example, Wulf and her colleagues concluded in several studies that many of the empirical results concerning augmented feedback that are based on the use of simple motor skills do not generalize well to the learning of more complex skills (e.g., Wulf et al., 1998). Swinnen (1996) raised a similar concern with regard to the assessment of the validity of the guidance hypothesis that has been proposed to account for the reduced frequency effects. In addition, more research is needed to assess the effectiveness of methods of presenting augmented feedback other than verbal. In the discussions in this chapter related to the use of videotape, biofeedback, movement kinematics, and kinetics, the consistent concern was the lack of sufficient research evidence addressing the effectiveness of and the development of guidelines for the use of these means of augmented feedback delivery.

At the theoretical level, controversies continue concerning the role of cognition in motor skill learning and performance (e.g., Lee, 1998; Meijer & Roth, 1988). The investigation of the role of augmented feedback in motor skill learning has much to contribute to help resolve some of this controversy. There appears to be agreement that the performer cognitively processes the information that augmented feedback provides. Investigating the influence augmented feedback can have, or not have, on the learning of skills can provide insight into the manner in which cognitive processes are involved in skill acquisition. Unfortunately, few studies have provided this focus. One reason may be that researchers who investigate augmented feedback as a learning variable have been more interested in relating their investigations to empirical rather than theoretical issues. Some evidence for this attitude is revealed by a review of the past several years of research addressing augmented feedback issues. For example, researchers have placed a greater emphasis on determining the number of trials that should be in a summary KR statement than on relating the findings from this research to their implications for increasing our understanding of cognitive processes in motor skill acquisition.

Finally, more research remains to be done in the investigation of applied issues. Because augmented feedback is such a common part of the instructional process for skill learning, it is essential that confidence is increased in our knowledge about the most effective ways to implement it in skill learning contexts. For example, if augmented feedback can be overused, as was suggested in various parts of this chapter, then it is important to identify alternatives that will provide more effective learning environments. And, as suggested here, in addition to the need for research that involves complex skills, researchers should assess the generalization of laboratory-based research to real-world instructional environments.

REFERENCES

Adams, J.A. (1964). Motor skills. In P.R. Farnsworth (Ed.), *Annual review of psychology* (pp. 181–202). Palo Alto, CA: Annual Reviews.

Adams, J.A. (1971). A closed-loop theory of motor learning. *Journal of Motor Behavior, 3,* 111–149.

Adams, J.A. (1978). Theoretical issues for knowledge of results. In G.E. Stelmach (Ed.), *Information processing in motor control and learning* (pp. 229–240). New York: Academic Press.

Adams, J.A. (1987). Historical review and appraisal of research on learning, retention, and transfer of human motor skills. *Psychological Bulletin, 101,* 41–74.

Ammons, R.B. (1958). Le mouvement. In G.H. Steward & J.P. Steward (Eds.), *Current psychological issues* (pp. 146–183). New York: Henry Holt.

Anderson, D.I., Magill, R.A., & Sekiya, H. (1994). A reconsideration of the trials-delay of knowledge of results paradigm in motor skill learning. *Research Quarterly for Exercise and Sport, 65,* 286–290.

Annesi, J.J. (1998). Effects of computer feedback on adherence to exercise. *Perceptual and Motor Skills, 87,* 723–730.

Annett, J. (1959). Learning a pressure under conditions of immediate and delayed knowledge of results. *Quarterly Journal of Experimental Psychology, 11,* 3–15.

Annett, J. (1969). *Feedback and human behavior.* Baltimore: Penguin.

Annett, J. (1970). The role of action feedback in the acquisition of simple motor responses. *Journal of Motor Behavior, 11,* 217–221.

Annett, J., & Kay, H. (1957). Knowledge of results and "skilled performance." *Occupational Psychology, 31,* 69–79.

Armstrong, T.R. (1970). *Feedback and perceptual-motor skill learning: A review of information feedback and manual guidance training techniques* (Tech. Rep. No. 25). Ann Arbor: University of Michigan, Human Performance Center.

Baker, C.H., & Young, P. (1960). Feedback during training and retention of motor skills. *Canadian Journal of Psychology, 14,* 257–264.

Beckham, J.C., Keefe, F.J., Caldwell, D.S., & Brown, C.J. (1991). Biofeedback as a means to alter electromyographic activity in a total knee replacement patient. *Biofeedback and Self-Regulation, 16,* 23–35.

Benedetti, C., & McCullagh, P.M. (1987). Post-knowledge of results delay: Effects of interpolated activity on learning and performance. *Research Quarterly for Exercise and Sport, 58,* 375–381.

Bilodeau, E.A., & Bilodeau, I.M. (1958a). Variable frequency of knowledge of results and the learning of a simple skill. *Journal of Experimental Psychology, 55,* 379–383.

Bilodeau, E.A., & Bilodeau, I.M. (1958b). Variation of temporal intervals among critical events in five studies of knowledge of results. *Journal of Experimental Psychology, 55,* 603–612.

Bilodeau, E.A., Bilodeau, I.M., & Schumsky, D.A. (1959). Some effects of introducing and withdrawing knowledge of results early and late in practice. *Journal of Experimental Psychology, 58,* 142–144.

Bilodeau, I.M. (1969). Information feedback. In E.A. Bilodeau (Ed.), *Principles of skill acquisition* (pp. 225–285). New York: Academic Press.

Boucher, J.L. (1974). Higher processes in motor learning. *Journal of Motor Behavior, 6,* 131–137.

Boulter, L.R. (1964). Evaluations of mechanisms in delay of knowledge of results. *Canadian Journal of Psychology, 18,* 281–291.

Brisson, T.A., & Alain, C. (1997). A comparison of two references for using knowledge of performance in learning a motor task. *Journal of Motor Behavior, 29,* 339–350.

Buekers, M.J.A., & Magill, R.A. (1995). The role of task experience and prior knowledge for detecting invalid augmented feedback while learning a motor skill. *Quarterly Journal of Experimental Psychology, 48A,* 84–97.

Buekers, M.J.A., Magill, R.A., & Hall, K.G. (1992). The effect of erroneous knowledge of results on skill acquisition when augmented information is redundant. *Quarterly Journal of Experimental Psychology, 44A,* 105–117.

Buekers, M.J.A., Magill, R.A., & Sneyers, K.M. (1994). Resolving a conflict between sensory feedback and knowledge of results while learning a motor skill. *Journal of Motor Behavior, 26,* 27–35.

Butler, M.S., Reeve, T.G., & Fischman, M.G. (1996). Effects of the instructional set in the bandwidth feedback paradigm on motor skill acquisition. *Research Quarterly for Exercise and Sport, 67,* 355–359.

Cauraugh, J.H., Chen, D., & Radlo, S.J. (1993). Effects of traditional and reversed bandwidth knowledge of results on motor learning. *Research Quarterly for Exercise and Sport, 64,* 413–417.

Chen, D., & Singer, R.N. (1992). Self-regulation and cognitive strategies in sport participation. *International Journal of Sport Psychology, 23,* 277–300.

Daniels, F.S., & Landers, D.M. (1981). Biofeedback and shooting performance: A test of disregulation and systems theory. *Journal of Sport Psychology, 3,* 271–282.

Dishman, R.K. (1993). Exercise adherence. In R.N. Singer, M. Murphey, & L.K. Tennant (Eds.), *Handbook of sport psychology* (pp. 779–798). New York: Macmillan.

Docheff, D.M. (1990, November/December). The feedback sandwich. *Journal of Physical Education, Recreation, and Dance, 61,* 17–18.

Eghan, T. (1988). *The relation of teacher feedback to student achievement in learning selected tennis skills.* Unpublished doctoral dissertation, Louisiana State University, Baton Rouge.

Elwell, J.L., & Grindley, G.C. (1938). The effect of knowledge of results on learning and performance. *British Journal of Psychology, 29,* 39–54.

Fishman, S., & Tobey, C. (1978). Augmented feedback. In W.G. Anderson & G. Barrette (Eds.), What's going on in gym: Descriptive studies of physical education classes [Monograph]. *Motor Skills: Theory into Practice, 1,* 51–62.

Fowler, C.A., & Turvey, M.T. (1978). Skill acquisition: An event approach for the optimum of a function of several variables. In G.E. Stelmach (Ed.), *Information processing in motor control and learning* (pp. 2–40). New York: Academic Press.

Fox, P.W., & Levy, C.M. (1969). Acquisition of a simple motor response as influenced by the presence or absence of action visual feedback. *Journal of Motor Behavior, 1,* 169–180.

Franks, I.M., & Maile, L.J. (1991). The use of video in sport skill acquisition. In P.W. Dowrick (Ed.), *Practical guide to using video in the behavioral sciences* (pp. 105–124). New York: Wiley.

Gallagher, J.D., & Thomas, J.R. (1980). Effects of varying post-KR intervals upon children's motor performance. *Journal of Motor Behavior, 12,* 41–46.

Gentile, A.M. (1972). A working model of skill acquisition with application to teaching [Monograph]. *Quest, 17,* 3–23.

Goldstein, M., & Rittenhouse, C.H. (1954). Knowledge of results in the acquisition and transfer of a gunnery skill. *Journal of Experimental Psychology, 48,* 187–196.

Goodwin, J., & Meeuwsen, H. (1995). Using bandwidth knowledge of results to alter relative frequencies during motor skill acquisition. *Research Quarterly for Exercise and Sport, 66,* 99–104.

Gordon, N.B., & Gottlieb, M.J. (1967). Effect of supplemental visual cues on rotary pursuit. *Journal of Experimental Psychology, 75,* 566–568.

Guadagnoli, M., Dornier, L.A., & Tandy, R.D. (1996). Optimal length for summary knowledge of results: The influence of task-related experience and complexity. *Research Quarterly for Exercise and Sport, 67,* 239–248.

Guay, M., Salmoni, A., & Lajoie, Y. (1999). The effects of different knowledge of results spacing and summarizing techniques on the acquisition of a ballistic movement. *Research Quarterly for Exercise and Sport, 70,* 24–32.

Hardy, C.J. (1983). The post-knowledge of results interval: Effects of interpolated activity on cognitive information processing. *Research Quarterly for Exercise and Sport, 54,* 144–148.

Hatze, H. (1976). Biomechanical aspects of a successful motion organization. In P. Komi (Ed.), *Biomechanics V-B* (pp. 5–12). Baltimore: University Park Press.

Hebert, E., Landin, D., & Menickelli, J. (1998). Videotape feedback: What learners see and how they use it. *Journal of Sport Pedagogy, 4,* 12–28.

Ho, L., & Shea, J.B. (1978). Effects of relative frequency of knowledge of results on retention of a motor skill. *Perceptual and Motor Skills, 46,* 859–866.

Hogan, J., & Yanowitz, B. (1978). The role of verbal estimates of movement error in ballistic skill acquisition. *Journal of Motor Behavior, 10,* 133–138.

Hull, C.L. (1943). *Principles of behavior.* New York: Appleton-Century-Crofts.

Jambor, E.A., & Weekes, E.M. (1995, February). Videotape feedback: Make it more effective. *Journal of Physical Education, Recreation, and Dance, 66,* 48–50.

Janelle, C.M., Barba, D.A., Frehlich, S.G., Tennant, L.K., & Cauraugh, J.H. (1997). Maximizing performance feedback effectiveness through videotape replay and a self-controlled learning environment. *Research Quarterly for Exercise and Sport, 68,* 269–279.

Janelle, C.M., Kim, J., & Singer, R.N. (1995). Subject-controlled performance feedback and learning of a closed motor skill. *Perceptual and Motor Skills, 81,* 627–634.

Karlin, L., & Mortimer, R.G. (1963). Effect of verbal, visual, and auditory augmenting cues on learning a complex motor skill. *Journal of Experimental Psychology, 65,* 75–79.

Kernodle, M.W., & Carlton, L.G. (1992). Information feedback and the learning of multiple-degree-of-freedom activities. *Journal of Motor Behavior, 24,* 187–196.

Kohl, R.M., & Guadagnoli, M.A. (1996). The scheduling of knowledge of results. *Journal of Motor Behavior, 28,* 233–240.

Lai, Q., & Shea, C.H. (1998). Generalized motor program (GMP) learning: Effects of reduced frequency of knowledge of results and practice variability. *Journal of Motor Behavior, 30,* 51–59.

Lai, Q., & Shea, C.H. (1999a). Bandwidth knowledge of results enhances generalized motor program learning. *Research Quarterly for Exercise and Sport, 70,* 79–83.

Lai, Q., & Shea, C.H. (1999b). The role of reduced frequency of knowledge of results during constant practice. *Research Quarterly for Exercise and Sport, 70,* 33–40.

Landauer, T.K., & Bjork, R.A. (1978). Optimal rehearsal patterns and name learning. In M.M. Gruneberg, P.E. Morris, & R.N. Sykes (Eds.), *Practical aspects of memory* (pp. 625–632). New York: Academic Press.

Lavery, J.J. (1962). Retention of simple motor skills as a function of type of knowledge of results. *Canadian Journal of Psychology, 16,* 300–311.

Lavery, J.J. (1964). The effect of a one-trial delay in knowledge of results on the acquisition and retention of a tossing skill. *American Journal of Psychology, 77,* 437–443.

Lavery, J.J., & Suddon, F.H. (1962). Retention of simple motor skills as a function of the number of trials by which KR is delayed. *Perceptual and Motor Skills, 15,* 231–237.

Lee, A.M., Keh, N.C., & Magill, R.A. (1993). Instructional effects of teacher feedback in physical education. *Journal of Teaching in Physical Education, 12,* 228–243.

Lee, T.D. (1998). On the dynamics of motor learning research. *Research Quarterly for Exercise and Sport, 69,* 334–337.

Lee, T.D., & Magill, R.A. (1983). Activity during the post-KR interval: Effects upon performance or learning. *Research Quarterly for Exercise and Sport, 54,* 340–345.

Lee, T.D., White, M.A., & Carnahan, H. (1990). On the role of knowledge of results in motor learning: Exploring the guidance hypothesis. *Journal of Motor Behavior, 22,* 191–208.

Lindahl, L.G. (1945). Movement analysis as an industrial training method. *Journal of Applied Psychology, 29,* 420–436.

Lintern, G. (1991). An informational perspective on skill transfer in human-machine systems. *Human Factors, 33,* 251–266.

Lintern, G., & Roscoe, S.N. (1980). Visual cue augmentation in contact flight simulation. In S.N. Roscoe (Ed.), *Aviation psychology* (pp. 227–238). Ames: Iowa State University Press.

Lintern, G., Roscoe, S.N., Koonce, J.M., & Segal, L.D. (1990). Transfer of landing skills in beginning flight training. *Human Factors, 32,* 319–327.

Lintern, G., Roscoe, S.N., & Sivier, J. (1990). Display principles, control dynamics, and environmental factors in pilot training and transfer. *Human Factors, 32,* 299–317.

Little, W.S., & McCullagh, P. (1989). Motivation orientation and modeled instruction strategies: The effects on form and accuracy. *Journal of Sport & Exercise Psychology, 11,* 41–53.

Liu, J., & Wrisberg, C.A. (1997). The effect of knowledge of results delay and the subjective estimation of movement form on the acquisition and retention of a motor skill. *Research Quarterly for Exercise and Sport, 68,* 145–151.

Locke, E.A., Cartledge, N., & Koeppel, J. (1968). Motivational effects of knowledge of results: A goal-setting phenomenon. *Psychological Bulletin, 70,* 474–485.

Magill, R.A. (1977). The processing of knowledge of results for a serial motor task. *Journal of Motor Behavior, 9,* 113–118.

Magill, R.A. (1988). Activity during the post-knowledge of results interval can benefit motor skill learning. In O.G. Meijer & K. Roth (Eds.), *Complex motor behaviour: "The" motor-action controversy* (pp. 231–246). Amsterdam: North Holland.

Magill, R.A. (1998a). Knowledge is more than we can talk about: Implicit learning in motor skill acquisition. *Research Quarterly for Exercise and Sport, 69,* 104–110.

Magill, R.A. (1998b). *Motor learning: Concepts and applications* (5th ed.). Madison, WI: McGraw-Hill.

Magill, R.A., Chamberlin, C.J., & Hall, K.G. (1991). Verbal knowledge of results as redundant information for learning an anticipation timing skill. *Human Movement Science, 10,* 485–507.

Magill, R.A., & Wood, C.A. (1986). Knowledge of results precision as a learning variable in motor skill acquisition. *Research Quarterly for Exercise and Sport, 57,* 170–173.

Marteniuk, R.G. (1986). Information processes in movement learning: Capacity and structural interference. *Journal of Motor Behavior, 18,* 249–259.

McNevin, N., Magill, R.A., & Buekers, M.J.A. (1994). The effects of erroneous knowledge of results on transfer of anticipation timing. *Research Quarterly for Exercise and Sport, 65,* 324–329.

Meijer, O.G., & Roth, K. (Eds.). (1988). *Complex motor behaviour: "The" motor-action controversy.* Amsterdam: North Holland.

Moreland, J., & Thomson, M.A. (1994). Efficacy of electromyographic biofeedback compared with conventional physical therapy for upper-extremity function in patients following stroke: A research overview and meta-analysis. *Physical Therapy, 74,* 534–547.

Newell, K.M. (1974). Knowledge of results and motor learning. *Journal of Motor Behavior, 6,* 235–244.

Newell, K.M. (1976). Knowledge of results and motor learning. In J. Keogh & R.S. Hutton (Eds.), *Exercise and sport sciences reviews* (Vol. 4, pp. 196–228). Santa Barbara, CA: Journal Publishing Affiliates.

Newell, K.M., & McGinnis, P.M. (1985). Kinematic information feedback for skilled performance. *Human Learning, 4,* 39–56.

Newell, K.M., Morris, L.R., & Scully, D.M. (1985). Augmented information and the acquisition of skill in physical activity. In R.J. Terjung (Ed.), *Exercise and sport sciences reviews* (Vol. 13, pp. 235–261). New York: Macmillan.

Newell, K.M., Quinn, J.T., Jr., Sparrow, W.A., & Walter, C.B. (1983). Kinematic information feedback for learning a rapid arm movement. *Human Movement Science, 2,* 255–269.

Patrick, J., & Mutlusoy, F. (1982). The relationship between types of feedback, gain of a display and feedback precision in acquisition of a simple motor task. *Quarterly Journal of Experimental Psychology, 34A,* 171–182.

Proteau, L., Marteniuk, R.G., & Lévesque, L. (1992). A sensori-motor basis for motor learning: Evidence indicating specificity of practice. *Quarterly Journal of Experimental Psychology, 44A,* 557–575.

Reeve, T.G., & Magill, R.A. (1981). Role of components of knowledge of results information in error correction. *Research Quarterly for Exercise and Sport, 52,* 80–85.

Rikli, R., & Smith, G. (1980). Videotape feedback effects on tennis serving form. *Perceptual and Motor Skills, 50,* 895–901.

Roberts, W.H. (1930). The effect of delayed feeding on white rats in a problem cage. *Journal of Genetic Psychology, 37,* 35–38.

Rogers, C.A. (1974). Feedback precision and post-feedback interval duration. *Journal of Experimental Psychology, 102,* 604–608.

Rothstein, A.L., & Arnold, R.K. (1976). Bridging the gap: Application of research on videotape feedback and bowling. *Motor Skills: Theory into Practice, 1,* 36–61.

Salmoni, A.W., Schmidt, R.A., & Walter, C.B. (1984). Knowledge of results and motor learning: A review and reappraisal. *Psychological Bulletin, 95,* 355–386.

Sandweiss, J.H., & Wolf, S.L. (Eds.). (1985). *Biofeedback and sports science.* New York: Plenum Press.

Schmidt, R.A. (1975). A schema theory of discrete motor skill learning. *Psychological Review, 82,* 225–260.

Schmidt, R.A., Lange, C., & Young, D.E. (1990). Optimizing summary knowledge of results for skill learning. *Human Movement Science, 9,* 325–348.

Schmidt, R.A., & Lee, T.D. (1999). *Motor control and learning: A behavioral emphasis* (3rd ed.). Champaign, IL: Human Kinetics.

Schmidt, R.A., & Young, D.E. (1991). Methodology for motor learning: A paradigm for kinematic feedback. *Journal of Motor Behavior, 23,* 13–24.

Schmidt, R.A., Young, D.E., Swinnen, S., & Shapiro, D.C. (1989). Summary knowledge of results for skill acquisition: Support for the guidance hypothesis. *Journal of Experimental Psychology: Learning, Memory, and Cognition, 15,* 352–359.

Schneider, W., & Pressley, M. (1989). *Memory development between 2 and 20.* New York: Springer-Verlag.

Selder, D.J., & Del Rolan, N. (1979). Knowledge of performance, skill level and performance on a balance beam. *Canadian Journal of Applied Sport Sciences, 4,* 226–229.

Shea, J.B., & Upton, G. (1976). The effects on skill acquisition of an interpolated motor short-term memory task during the KR-delay interval. *Journal of Motor Behavior, 8,* 277–281.

Sherwood, D.E. (1988). Effect of bandwidth knowledge of results on movement consistency. *Perceptual and Motor Skills, 66,* 535–542.

Shumway-Cook, A., Anson, D., & Haller, S. (1988). Postural sway biofeedback: Its effect on reestablishing stance stability in hemiplegic patients. *Archives of Physical Medicine and Rehabilitation, 69,* 395–399.

Sidaway, B., Moore, B., & Schoenfelder-Zohdi, B. (1991). Summary and frequency of KR presentation effects on retention of a motor skill. *Research Quarterly for Exercise and Sport, 62,* 27–32.

Siegler, R.S. (1991). *Children's thinking* (2nd ed.). Englewood Cliffs, NJ: Prentice-Hall.

Silverman, S., Tyson, L.A., & Krampitz, J. (1992). Teacher feedback and achievement in physical education: Interaction with student practice. *Teaching and Teacher Education, 8,* 222–344.

Silverman, S., Tyson, L.A., & Morford, L.M. (1988). Relationships of organization, time, and student achievement in physical education. *Teaching and Teacher Education, 4,* 247–257.

Silverman, S., Woods, A.M., & Subramanian, P.R. (1998). Task structures, feedback to individual students, and student skill level in physical education. *Research Quarterly for Exercise and Sport, 69,* 420–424.

Simmons, R.W., Smith, K., Erez, E., Burke, J.P., & Pozos, R.E. (1998). Balance retraining in a hemiparetic patient using center of gravity biofeedback: A single-case study. *Perceptual and Motor Skills, 87,* 603–609.

Smoll, F.L. (1972). Effects of precision of information feedback upon acquisition of a motor skill. *Research Quarterly, 43,* 489–493.

Starek, J., & McCullagh, P. (1999). The effect of self-modeling on the performance of beginning swimmers. *The Sport Psychologist, 13,* 269–287.

Stelmach, G.E. (1970). Learning and response consistency with augmented feedback. *Ergonomics, 13,* 421–425.

Suddon, F.H., & Lavery, J.J. (1962). The effect of amount of training on retention of a simple motor skill with 0- and 5-trial delays of knowledge of results. *Canadian Journal of Psychology, 16,* 312–317.

Swinnen, S.P. (1990). Interpolated activities during the knowledge-of-results delay and post-knowledge-of-results interval:

Effects on performance and learning. *Journal of Experimental Psychology: Learning, Memory, and Cognition, 16,* 692–705.

Swinnen, S.P. (1996). Information feedback in motor skill learning: A review. In H.N. Zelaznik (Ed.), *Advances in motor learning and control* (pp. 37–66). Champaign, IL: Human Kinetics.

Swinnen, S.P., Schmidt, R.A., Nicholson, D.E., & Shapiro, D.C. (1990). Information feedback for skill acquisition: Instantaneous knowledge of results degrades learning. *Journal of Experimental Psychology: Learning, Memory, and Cognition, 16,* 706–716.

Swinnen, S.P., Walter, C.B., Lee, T.D., & Serrien, D.J. (1993). Acquiring bimanual skills: Contrasting forms of information feedback for interlimb decoupling. *Journal of Experimental Psychology: Learning, Memory, and Cognition, 19,* 1321–1344.

Swinnen, S.P., Walter, C.B., Pauwels, J.M., Meugens, P.F., & Beirinkx, M.B. (1990). The dissociation of interlimb constraints. *Human Performance, 3,* 187–215.

Thorndike, E.L. (1927). The law of effect. *American Journal of Psychology, 39,* 212–222.

Tolman, E.C. (1932). *Purposive behavior of animals and men.* New York: Century.

Trinity, J., & Annesi, J.J. (1996, August). Coaching with video. *Strategies, 9,* 23–25.

Trowbridge, M.H., & Cason, H. (1932). An experimental study of Thorndike's theory of learning. *Journal of General Psychology, 7,* 245–258.

Van Loon, E.M., Buekers, M.J., Helsen, W., & Magill, R.A. (1998). Temporal and spatial adaptations during the acquisition of a reversal movement. *Research Quarterly for Exercise and Sport, 69,* 38–46.

Verschueren, S.M.P., Swinnen, S.P., Dom, R., & DeWeert, W. (1997). Interlimb coordination in patients with Parkinson's disease: Motor learning deficits and the importance of augmented information feedback. *Experimental Brain Research, 113,* 497–508.

Wallace, S.A., & Hagler, R.W. (1979). Knowledge of performance and the learning of a closed motor skill. *Research Quarterly, 50,* 265–271.

Watkins, D. (1984). Students' perceptions of factors influencing tertiary learning. *Higher Education Research and Development, 3,* 33–50.

Weeks, D.L., & Kordus, R.N. (1998). Relative frequency of knowledge of performance and motor skill learning. *Research Quarterly for Exercise and Sport, 69,* 224–230.

Weeks, D.L., & Sherwood, D.E. (1994). A comparison of knowledge of results scheduling methods for promoting motor skill acquisition and retention. *Research Quarterly for Exercise and Sport, 65,* 136–142.

Weinberg, D.R., Guy, D.E., & Tupper, R.W. (1964). Variations of post-feedback interval in simple motor learning. *Journal of Experimental Psychology, 67,* 98–99.

Williams, A.C., & Briggs, G.E. (1962). On-target versus off-target information and the acquisition of tracking skill. *Journal of Experimental Psychology, 64,* 519–525.

Winstein, C.J., & Schmidt, R.A. (1990). Reduced frequency of knowledge of results enhances motor skill learning. *Journal of Experimental Psychology: Learning, Memory, and Cognition, 16,* 677–691.

Wolf, S.L. (1983). Electromyographic biofeedback applications to stroke patients: A critical review. *Physical Therapy, 63,* 1448–1455.

Wright, D.L., Smith-Munyon, V.L., & Sidaway, B. (1997). How close is too close for precise knowledge of results? *Research Quarterly for Exercise and Sport, 68,* 172–176.

Wright, D.L., Snowden, S., & Willoughby, D. (1990). Summary KR: How much information is used from the summary? *Journal of Human Movement Studies, 19,* 119–128.

Wrisberg, C.A., & Wulf, G. (1997). Diminishing the effects of reduced frequency of knowledge of results on generalized motor program learning. *Journal of Motor Behavior, 29,* 17–26.

Wulf, G., Lee, T.D., & Schmidt, R.A. (1994). Reducing knowledge of results about relative versus absolute timing: Differential effects on learning. *Journal of Motor Behavior, 26,* 362–369.

Wulf, G., & Schmidt, R.A. (1996). Average KR degrades parameter learning. *Journal of Motor Behavior, 28,* 371–381.

Wulf, G., Schmidt, R.A., & Deubel, H. (1993). Reduced feedback frequency enhances generalized motor program learning but not parameterization learning. *Journal of Experimental Psychology: Learning, Memory, and Cognition, 19,* 1134–1150.

Wulf, G., Shea, C.H., & Matschiner, S. (1998). Frequent feedback enhances complex skill learning. *Journal of Motor Behavior, 30,* 180–192.

Yao, W.X., Fischman, M.G., & Wang, Y.T. (1994). Motor skill acquisition and retention as a function of average feedback, summary feedback, and performance variability. *Journal of Motor Behavior, 26,* 273–282.

Young, D.E., & Schmidt, R.A. (1992). Augmented kinematic feedback for motor learning. *Journal of Motor Behavior, 24,* 261–273.

Zimmerman, B.J., Bonner, S., & Kovach, R. (1996). *Developing self-regulated learning: Beyond achievement to self-efficacy.* Washington, DC: American Psychological Association.

Zubiaur, M., Oña, A., & Delgado, J. (1999). Learning volleyball serves: A preliminary study of the effects of knowledge of performance and results. *Perceptual and Motor Skills, 89,* 223–232.

CHAPTER 5

Practice

TIMOTHY D. LEE, CRAIG J. CHAMBERLIN, and NICOLA J. HODGES

Many situations occur in which only a limited amount of instruction and practice are provided for motor skill learning. The novice golfer may take lessons from a pro or enroll in a three-week course. A company may want to retrain some employees to operate a new piece of equipment. A physical therapy client enters rehabilitation to try to regain motor skill capabilities. In each of these situations the goal for the learner is to make a significant and permanent improvement in skill during the limited period of time in which instruction and practice are provided. The goal for the instructor is to create a learning environment that optimizes the opportunity for the learners to achieve their goal. *Augmented feedback* is one important tool that the instructor has available for this purpose, and the research principles underlying the use of this tool are reviewed elsewhere by Magill (Chapter 4 in this volume). *Practice,* and the conditions under which it is conducted, has an equally important influence on learning, and is the focus of this present chapter.

Our review will be divided into two general types of practice conditions: *on-task* and *off-task* (Lee, Schmidt, & Young, in press). On-task conditions of practice are concerned with factors that influence how the learner directly interacts with the task or practices the skill to be learned. This type of practice condition involves factors that influence how practice is organized. Off-task conditions of practice are concerned with factors that predispose the learner to changes in skill as a function of practice that is conducted away from the specific task or skill to be learned.

PERFORMANCE, LEARNING, AND SKILL DEFINED

To understand how practice conditions influence skill acquisition, it is critical to underscore a fundamental principle in motor learning research: the distinction among *performance, skill,* and *learning.* The importance of this distinction is much more than a simple theoretical argument, for the failure to appreciate its implications can result, at best, in a misunderstanding of the research evidence and, at worst, in the potential to apply principles of practice arrangements that are in disagreement with the scientific evidence.

The distinction among performance, skill, and learning is an old one in psychology, and reminders of it have been made elsewhere by Schmidt (e.g., Schmidt, 1971, 1972). *Performance* is the motor behavior exhibited on a task that can be measured. In contrast, *skill* refers to an underlying capability or potential to perform at a certain level. Performance refers to a precise, quantitative assessment of ability that may or may not accurately reflect the more abstract, qualitative assessment that we refer to as skill. Many factors can affect performance that have no bearing on how skill would be judged. For example, wind conditions may affect the performance of an archer. Would a good performance on a calm day, followed by a relatively poor performance on a windy day, be evidence that the archer has lost some skill? Silly arguments about temporary losses or gains in skill can be avoided by remembering that performance can be quite variable and extremely sensitive to conditions that have little or no bearing at all on the assessment of skill.

The distinction between performance and learning follows a similar logic. *Learning* can be defined as an improvement in skill that is brought about as a function of *practice* (e.g., Magill, 1998b; Schmidt & Lee, 1999). Learning is not a change in performance per se, but rather in an improved capability or potential to perform at a skill level that is higher than the skill level before practice was undertaken. And, as environmental conditions (such as wind) can confuse the issue of performance and skill, so too can certain conditions of practice confuse the issue of performance and learning. Certain practice conditions (e.g., blocked vs. random practice) can create either temporary boosts or temporary decrements to performance. But do these boosts or decrements mean that the performer has gained or lost skill? As well, most off-task conditions of practice make no assessment of performance (e.g., mental practice). Does this mean that learning is not occurring?

Essentially, distinguishing between performance and learning requires determining when and how to assess skill. The assessment of someone's skill level requires that the measurement be *reliable*. Further, to assess learning, the improvement in skill must be relatively permanent and unaffected by factors (such as practice conditions) that might otherwise provide a temporary boost or decrement to performance. For these and other reasons (see Schmidt & Lee, 1999, for further discussion), measures of learning are most often accumulated from tests of *retention* (the same task) and *transfer* (a variation of the task). One important feature of these tests is that they are conducted after a period of time during which no further practice on the task is conducted in order to examine the relative permanence of the changes in skill that were brought about by practice. Another important feature is that, if various experimental groups have received different practice conditions, then retention and transfer represent *common* bases to assess skill. These concepts of performance, skill, and learning are important to remember when discussing various factors in the remainder of this chapter.

ON-TASK CONDITIONS OF PRACTICE

Practice that is conducted on the task to be learned represents, by far, the bulk of motor learning research. In this section, we discuss the research issues concerning the following topics: amount of practice, variability of practice, contextual interference, and part- versus whole-task practice.

Amount of Practice

Generally, researchers examining learning provide the participant with a limited amount of practice time and experience. Primarily for practical reasons (i.e., time constraints), there has not been much research examining practice over extended periods of time. A notable exception to this observation, however, is an early study conducted by Snoddy (1926), who provided participants in a mirror drawing task with 100 days of practice. More recently, interest

has resurged as to the effects of practice over extended periods due to both practical and theoretical considerations. In the skill acquisition literature, empirical evidence showing an increased dependence on information sources as a function of extended practice has served to question some basic assumptions about what is learned as a function of time (e.g., Proteau, 1992). Additionally, detailed analyses of expert practice patterns have shed light on the nature and significance of amount of practice hours in achieving elite levels of performance. Some of the influential studies that have provided insight into these practice issues and areas will be reviewed.

There have been a number of extremely notable investigations that have involved the extensive study of the skill acquisition process at different time scales throughout the learning process. Two studies in particular are cited considerably in the motor learning literature: the work of Bryan and Harter (1897, 1899; see Lee & Swinnen, 1993) and the work of Crossman (1959). Bryan and Harter conducted extensive investigation on the learning and performance of telegraphic skill (both sending and receiving), comparing both expert and novice telegraphers, as well as graphing the progress of novice telegraphers over months of practice. One of their particularly interesting and controversial findings was that of performance plateaus during the learning process for some of the telegraphers. That is, periods of time occurred where few or no detectable improvements in performance were observed. This finding has continually faced challenges due to a number of studies that have demonstrated almost linear relationships between amount of practice and performance.

Most notable is an investigation conducted by Crossman (1959) on cigar rolling, where it was found that the time to roll a cigar (i.e., performance) was a decreasing function of the number of cigars that had been rolled in the past (i.e., practice experience; see Figure 5.1). At the high ends of performance experience (where the practice curve appears to level off), the cigar rollers had been working at the factory for seven years or more and had arguably reached a performance ceiling due to the performance limits of the machinery itself. These somewhat incongruent findings may be a result of comparing individual performance data (i.e., Bryan & Harter, 1899) to data grouped across individuals (i.e., Crossman, 1959). In the latter case, variability in performance curves, both within and between individuals, may be masked by averaging across a number of participants, such that the data appear nearly linear. These considerations are important given the implications that these curves have for theories of learning.

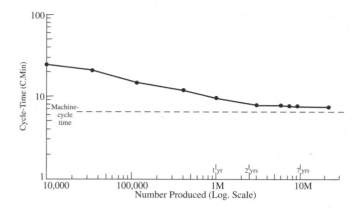

Figure 5.1 Cigar-rolling performance over seven years of practice (from Crossman, 1959).

Both the *type* and *amount* of practice that contribute to expert performance have been examined using retrospective recall procedures and diary studies to validate these estimates. Practice, rather than being viewed merely as a mediating variable in achieving high levels of performance, has been proposed to be *causative* and therefore given a primary role in the attribution of success. This interest in the examination of practice has been spearheaded by the work of Ericsson, Krampe, and Tesch-Römer (1993), who developed and provided empirical support for their theory of "deliberate practice." Ericsson has explored expertise since the early 1980s (e.g., Chase & Ericsson, 1981, 1982), most notably the specificity of memory performance as a function of the type and amount of practice (e.g., Ericsson, Chase, & Faloon, 1980; Ericsson & Polson, 1988). Based on these studies, he has concluded that supposed limits in performance (such as memory capacity; see Miller, 1956) can be circumvented by deliberate practice. In addition to this work, other researchers examining expertise have suggested a minimum number of years of practice (i.e., 10) as being necessary to achieve what typically is defined as expertise or exceptional performance (for examples, see Bloom, 1985). The implication is that extended periods of practice, rather than innate talent, is primarily, or possibly, wholly responsible for high levels of performance skill (see also Howe, Davidson, & Sloboda, 1998, and commentaries; Singer & Janelle, 1999, for different views on this topic).

One of the most significant findings to emerge from this analysis is that cumulative hours spent in *deliberate practice* over the course of a musician's career (i.e., practice defined as effortful, relevant to improving performance, and not inherently enjoyable) are monotonically related to performance level. Since the original study by Ericsson and colleagues, a number of studies have been conducted in a wide variety of domains ranging from chess (Charness, Krampe, & Mayr, 1996) to individual and team sports (e.g., Helsen, Starkes, & Hodges, 1998; Hodges & Starkes, 1996; Starkes, Deakin, Allard, Hodges, & Hayes, 1996).

On the whole, these studies have provided strong support for the deliberate practice hypothesis, although controversy exists as to what constitutes deliberate practice and whether a generic definition can be found to encompass a general theory of practice. Collecting practice data "retrospectively" also has its limitations (especially with respect to reliability), and longitudinal studies are needed to verify these estimates. Regardless of these concerns, the deliberate practice hypothesis does serve to refocus the practitioner's attention onto the importance of practice rather than "natural talent" when identifying individuals as potentially future experts.

Currently, work is being undertaken to examine practice past peak performance (e.g., among master athletes) to determine how much practice can stave off the normal declines in aging (see Starkes, Weir, Singh, Hodges, & Kerr, 1999). Additionally, the practice patterns of participants who engage in multisport events, such as triathlons, are being studied, where the scheduling of activities becomes an extremely important consideration when practice has to be divided among three sports rather than one (Kerr, Hodges, & Starkes, 1999). This type of analysis should also help elucidate how specific or general practice effects are to the actual event (e.g., comparison of a triathlete's training schedule and performance times at swimming, as compared to a person who only swims competitively, yet engages in many types of practice activities).

Variability of Practice

A key decision in practice concerns the amount, or *breadth,* of variability that is introduced into a practice regime. Should practice be concentrated on a single condition, type of play or shot, and so on, or should it be distributed among various conditions, types of plays or shots, and so on? For example, should a person who is practicing free throws always perform these attempts from the same spot on the court (i.e., from the free throw line), or is there any gain from practicing from different spots on the floor? In golf, should one always try to hit a 4-iron the same way every time while practicing on the driving range, or should one try different types of shots with the 4-iron? In many respects, an important consideration in the decision regarding how much variability to introduce into practice will be the variability in the types of conditions that will be experienced when the skills that have been practiced are performed in a game situation. Is there any advantage to practicing under a variety of practice conditions when the game situation for the application of that skill is constant or unchanging (e.g., the free throw), compared to situations that might require a novel variation in the skill (e.g., a low fade of a 4-iron out of the rough)? These two questions present the essence of research conducted to address the variability of practice question: (1) Does variability of practice affect the *retention* of one specific skill? and (2) Does variable practice affect the *transfer* of skill to a situation that has not specifically been practiced before?

Much of the theoretical impetus underlying this research issue was generated by *schema theory* (Schmidt, 1975), which provided a clear, testable prediction that variable practice would produce the type of skill learning that is superior to constant practice when a novel variation of the skill is required. The results of the research have been less than unequivocal, however, in the sense that the effects depend on a number of other factors, a full discussion of which is beyond the scope of this chapter (e.g., see Shapiro & Schmidt, 1982; van Rossum, 1990). Is variable practice always preferred to nonvariable (or constant) practice conditions? The simple answer is no. However, this simple answer must also be considered in light of the finding that when differences in retention and transfer have been found, they almost always have been in favor of variable practice conditions. Rarely have constant practice conditions been found to be superior to variable conditions, even when the retention of the constant practice conditions has been the criterion test for learning.

Retention Effects

As an example of variability of practice benefits for retention performance, consider the study reported by Shea and Kohl (1991, Exp. 1). Participants were asked to learn to squeeze a hand dynamometer with a certain amount of force, with the criterion test conducted in retention being a force of 150 Newtons. Three groups were compared in this retention test, which differed in terms of the amount of variability of practice that had been experienced during practice. Two of these groups practiced *only* at the very criterion that was tested in retention (150 N). One group practiced the task for 100 trials and the other group for 340 trials. The third group experienced the variable practice condition in which the criterion task (150 N) was practiced for 100 trials. As well, this group performed 240 trials on goal forces that surrounded the criterion task (at 100, 125, 175, and 200 N goals), for a total of 340 practice trials. The results were very clear. Performance in acquisition favored the two constant practice groups. However,

retention was much better for the variable practice group. Perhaps what makes this result even more remarkable is the fact that the variable group outperformed the practice group that had the same number of total practice trials (340) but that were concentrated solely on the very task that was performed in the retention test. Clearly, results such as these would not be expected unless the variable practice condition had a long-term effect on the memory of what had been practiced.

Transfer Effects

A similar type of experimental design adopted by Shea and Kohl (1991) had been used some years before by McCracken and Stelmach (1977) to examine variability of practice effects in transfer. Rather than a force production task, however, McCracken and Stelmach asked participants to learn to produce movements that were completed as close to 200 msec as possible, with variable practice conditions arranged by changing the amplitude of the movement. The constant condition group always practiced its timed trials at one of four distances (subgroups being used at each distance). The variable group performed a quarter of its practice trials at each of four distances. Compared to the Shea and Kohl study, the main difference in the design of the McCracken and Stelmach experiment was the assessment of learning, as transfer to a novel variation of the timing task (i.e., a new distance) was the criterion test condition that followed the practice sessions. The results were similar to the findings reported by Shea and Kohl, in that variable practice conditions were superior for transfer over constant practice.

Modifying Variables

A number of variables seem to modify the potential benefits of variable practice. For instance, if the participant has some experience in the task involved in the investigation, the potential for differences to emerge as a function of the variability may be reduced. This explanation has received support from the observation that variability of practice effects are generally larger in younger children than in older children or adults when the experimental conditions have been assessed across various age groups (Shapiro & Schmidt, 1982; Yan, Thomas, & Thomas, 1998). Complex tasks or those that need to be performed rapidly also show generally larger variability of practice effects than simple tasks or those that can be performed slowly (Yan et al., 1998).

Another modifying variable appears to be *how* variable practice conditions are organized during the practice session. A review of the variable of practice literature by Lee,

Magill, and Weeks (1985) presented evidence that simply having variable practice experiences may not be sufficient to produce variability of practice effects. These experiences need to be *organized* in a manner that maximizes the benefits of the variable practice conditions, as discussed in the next section.

Contextual Interference

Perhaps the easiest way to understand the contextual interference effect is to describe the pioneering study of Shea and Morgan (1979), which, together with the theorizing of Battig (1966, 1979), represents the landmark work in this area of research. Shea and Morgan asked two groups of university-age participants to practice three variations of a rapid arm-reversal task. The task required them, on seeing a stimulus light, to pick up a tennis ball, knock over 3 out of 6 wooden barriers, and then to place the tennis ball in a final rest position. Three movement patterns were defined in terms of the order of the three barriers to be knocked over. Each pattern was illustrated in full view of the participant during the acquisition trials and was paired with a specific colored stimulus light. The goal was to complete the movement pattern as fast as possible while remaining accurate.

All participants performed 18 practice trials with each of the three movement patterns, for a total of 54 acquisition trials. The two groups of participants were defined in terms of the order by which their practice trials were arranged. The *blocked* group performed its first 18 acquisition trials on one of the movement patterns. Another movement pattern was practiced next for 18 trials, and so on. The *random* group was equivalent to the blocked group in terms of the number of practice trials conducted for each of the movement patterns. However, the random group's acquisition period proceeded such that after every set of 18 trials, each pattern had been practiced 6 times, and no one pattern had been practiced for more than 2 consecutive trials. Retention and transfer tests were conducted 10 minutes and 10 days later in both blocked and random orders.

The results of the Shea and Morgan (1979) study are illustrated in Figure 5.2 (note that the retention and transfer data are averaged over the 10-minute and 10-day retention tests). During acquisition, the performance of the blocked group was better than the performance of the random group. However, during retention, the random group performed better than the blocked group. Two additional features of the retention data are worth noting. The performance of the random group was maintained at about the same level as that achieved by the end of acquisition. However, the performance of the blocked group

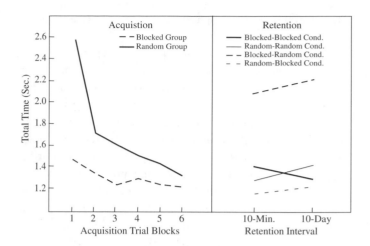

Figure 5.2   Acquisition and retention performance as a function of blocked and random schedules (from Shea & Morgan, 1979).

was not maintained and, in fact, reverted to a very poor level of performance during the randomly ordered retention trials. The other important feature of these data is that the advantage of the random group occurred on both the random and blocked-ordered retention trials.

The contextual interference effect demonstrated by Shea and Morgan (1979) sparked considerable research interest for several reasons. Perhaps foremost, the findings posed a paradox: How could a variable have such a potent effect on acquisition performance, and an equally potent but *opposite* effect on retention and transfer? Subsequent research was generated to resolve this question. Another area of research has been to extend the findings of Shea and Morgan by considering various factors that might interact with these results (e.g., participant and task characteristics). Finally, the research has also been driven by the obvious pedagogical interest and implications for teaching.

Theoretical Issues

More than 20 years and many empirical studies later, the theoretical issues underlying the contextual interference effect remain substantially unresolved. Of the handful of hypotheses that have been suggested, two have received the most empirical attention. One position, the *distinctive and elaborative processing* hypothesis, suggests that the effect emerges because of the nature of processing that is engaged when one task is practiced in the "context" of another task (Shea & Morgan, 1979). In blocked practice, for example, performance on one task is preceded and succeeded by performance on the same task. Thus, the opportunity to learn from the *comparative* and *contrastive* information by performing different tasks on successive trials is minimized.

The availability of comparative and contrastive information for the random group, which has an interfering effect on performance, becomes advantageous when learning is later assessed in retention and/or transfer. Verbal report data, acquired during practice trials of blocked and random participants, verify that the nature of elaborative and distinctive processing undertaken by blocked practice participants is severely impoverished compared to random practice participants (Shea & Zimny, 1983, 1988). Further support for the hypothesis has been provided by Wright (1991) and Gabriele, Hall, and Lee (1989), who showed that the impoverished processing of blocked practice could be enhanced by between-trial, cognitive manipulations that encourage elaborative and distinctive processing.

The other main theoretical explanation of contextual interference suggests that the active involvement of movement planning on each trial is the key processing factor underlying the effect (Lee & Magill, 1983, 1985). According to the *forgetting and reconstruction* view, random practice on successively different tasks requires that a previously constructed movement plan be abandoned to prepare a movement plan that is appropriate for the next task introduced in the practice sequence. When the task for which an action plan had formerly been constructed is reintroduced by the practice sequence, the memory of the previously constructed plan has been forgotten, requiring that the participant construct a new plan of action. The key feature is that random practice forces the individual to practice the process of action planning, a feature that is *not* forced on participants in a blocked practice sequence, who can use the same action plan from trial to trial because the task to be performed remains the same. Support for this position has been provided by experiments in which nonspecific, forgetting-induced conditions inserted during blocked practice trials have resulted in "randomlike" acquisition and retention effects (e.g., Magill, 1988; Young, Cohen, & Husak, 1993). Additional support using the opposite approach, a very strong guidance procedure that effectively obviates the need for active movement planning during random practice, eliminated both the performance deficit and retention advantage of this guided random practice group, compared to blocked practice (Lee, Wishart, Cunningham, & Carnahan, 1997).

Modifying Variables

Random and blocked orders of practice represent the opposite ends of a scheduling continuum, and variations of these practice orders have produced mixed results. Shea, Ho, and Morgan (cited by Shea & Zimny, 1983) combined one or more periods of random and blocked practice orders within the same acquisition period, and compared retention and performance of these mixed schedules to completely random and completely blocked schedules. Using the Shea and Morgan task (1979), they found that learning was facilitated relative to an entirely blocked practice schedule, regardless of how the mixed periods of random and blocked practice were alternated. Lee and Magill (1983) devised a serial practice order by rotating the task variations in an orderly manner on every trial (e.g., a serial order of three task variations might be ABCAB-CABC . . .). In both acquisition and retention, the performance of the serial group was identical to the performance of the random group (Lee & Magill, 1983, Exp. 2). However, the results of serial practice on a timing task (Lee & Magill, 1983, Exp. 3) and on learning three badminton serves (Goode & Magill, 1986) were no better than blocked practice. A variation of random practice that provides for two or more consecutive trials on the same task appears to be a promising compromise, as performance in acquisition is not as detrimental as in random practice, although there remained a positive benefit to retention (Al-Ameer & Toole, 1993).

Most studies of contextual interference have involved university-age participants, with no particular inclusion or exclusion criteria. However, Magill and Hall (1990) suggest that variations in the contextual interference effect may be seen when different participant samples are considered. A mixed pattern of results appears to emerge when children serve as participants. Del Rey, Whitehurst, and Wood (1983) examined the acquisition and retention performance of 6- to 10-year-olds under either a random or a blocked practice schedule. Unlike the performance of adults, the performance of the blocked group of children was better than the random group during both acquisition and retention. Pigott and Shapiro (1984) found no differences during acquisition and transfer between the blocked and random groups. However, they did observe that a group of participants that received random blocks of trials outperformed all others during acquisition and transfer. On the other hand, clear benefits following random practice have been demonstrated in 7-year-old children in retention (Pollock & Lee, 1997), and in 6-year-old children in transfer (Edwards, Elliott, & Lee, 1986). In neither of these latter two studies, however, were there acquisition differences between the random and blocked groups of children. Contextual interference effects have also been observed in individuals who are cognitively challenged (Edwards et al., 1986; Heitman & Gilley, 1989).

Initial research on the contextual interference effect was conducted on laboratory tasks that were rather simple in nature. Interest that these effects could have potential application to influence training procedures for the acquisition of sport and industrial skills as well as activities of daily living were tempered by the absence of experiments using tasks with greater complexity or that involved real-world skills. Some experiments have now been conducted, and though not unequivocal, the results generally support the benefit of random practice schedules. For example, contextual interference effects have been found in such sports as baseball, badminton, kayaking, volleyball, and rifle shooting (see Schmidt & Lee, 1999, for a review). Although much research still remains to be conducted, the application of contextual interference research to training regimes in the acquisition of skills appears warranted.

Part-Task versus Whole-Task Practice

The learning and performance of complex motor skills presents a significant information processing challenge to the performer. This situation is exaggerated when the performer is a beginner, bringing a limited capacity for attention to the performance of a task that has no automated components to ease the information processing load. Confronted with this situation, instructors must find ways to reduce the cognitive load so that effective learning of the task can occur. One common way to achieve this goal is to present the performer with a learning challenge that encompasses acquiring a part of the whole task. The basic assumption is that learning one part of the task will transfer positively to performing the whole task.

Several reviews of the part-task practice literature exist (e.g., Chamberlin & Lee, 1993; Wightman & Lintern, 1985), and most textbooks in motor behavior contain a section dedicated to a discussion of effective part-task practice. In these sources, it has been noted that the equivocal empirical findings from the part practice literature can be explained by considering the essential relation among the component parts. In general, tasks that by nature have parts that are highly interdependent for effective performance do not lend themselves well to part-task practice. This idea stems from Naylor and Briggs's (1963) hypothesis that tasks that are high in organization and low in complexity cannot be effectively acquired using a part-task training technique. Part practice is most effective for low-organization, high-complexity tasks. However, this basic rule does not address component practice on tasks that may fall somewhere between these two categories (e.g., high-organization, high-complexity).

Although determining component interdependence through the use of task analysis would appear to be the central principle on which to base the decision for using part practice (see Proctor & Dutta, 1995), a closer look at the research literature indicates that this may not be a complete picture. Normally, studies investigating part practice have compared the acquisition performance that results from part practice to a whole-task practice regime and a control group (no practice). Greater positive transfer to the whole task from part practice occurs when component interdependence is reduced. However, regardless of the degree of component interdependence, part practice is generally found to result in positive transfer (superior acquisition performance when compared to the control group). To our knowledge, only one study has produced negative part practice transfer acquisition performance worse than control group performance (Lersten, 1968), but positive transfer (albeit low) was noted for all except a single component of the task's performance. In other cases, tasks with highly interdependent components have been found to produce significant amounts of positive transfer, for example, playing the *Space Fortress* game (Mané, 1984) and in the acquisition of bimanual polyrhythms (Summers & Kennedy, 1992).

Component interdependence may not be telling the whole story. Component interdependence probably interacts with part practice techniques and learner characteristics to determine the effectiveness of incorporating part practice into the training regime. In effect, most motor skills can be acquired to some extent using part practice. Given the information processing demands placed on a beginner and the assumption that these demands normally exceed the capacity of the beginner to perform the task effectively, it becomes necessary to reduce processing demands by invoking some variant of part-task practice. The question becomes not whether part- or whole-task practice should occur, but *which part practice technique* should be applied.

To gain insight into this interaction, it is necessary to understand component interdependence from the control processes necessary to support effective task performance. Tasks with highly interdependent component parts place a strong emphasis on the coordination for skilled performance; to perform well, a highly integrated control mechanism (such as a motor program or a coordinative structure) should be developed. Klapp, Nelson, and Jagacinski (1998) provide evidence for an integrated sensorimotor representation as a control mechanism for the performance of a complex, restricted polyrhythm. Conditions of part practice that enhance the development of an integrated control mechanism for these types of movements would create strong positive transfer to the whole task. Conditions of practice that are neutral, or prevent the development of integrated control, would result in less positive transfer and, in some cases, create a negative transfer situation.

Different techniques for achieving part practice have been proposed. Wightman and Lintern (1985) suggested three basic part practice techniques: *segmentation, fractionation,* and *simplification.* Recently, a fourth technique has been suggested, *attention cuing* (see Magill, 1998b; Rose, 1997). These techniques will be considered separately, identifying the experimental results achieved with each and speculating on the nature of the control structure that may develop under each technique.

Segmentation

The most common of the part practice techniques, and the one that is used most frequently in studies investigating part practice, is segmentation or the partitioning of a task along a spatiotemporal dimension into component parts. In general, parts that have temporal distinctiveness in the performance of the task are subject to decomposition and presented to the participant for practice according to one of several training schedules. In pure part practice, each component part is practiced separately to some criterion level, at which time all parts are assembled into the whole task. Repetitive and progressive part practice are modest variations of a chaining technique in which whole-task practice is achieved through practicing successively larger chunks of action by systematically combining parts. Progressive part practice requires the learner to practice the new part in isolation before adding it to the previously practiced part(s). For combined practice, the repetitive part always has the new part being practiced in combination with the previously practiced part(s).

Repetitive or progressive part practice can be achieved by either *forward chaining* (practice of parts progressing in a logical temporal sequence from earliest performed part to last performed part) or *backward chaining* (practice of parts in a reverse temporal sequence from end part to beginning part). An example of forward chaining would be learning a piece on the piano by initially mastering the first measure of the score, then progressively adding the following measures in sequence. An example of backward chaining is teaching a layup in basketball where the end segment is taught first (the shot), then a step-shot combination, followed by a two step–shot combination, a dribble–two step–shot combination, and so on until the performer is executing several dribbles, steps, and shots in sequence for whole-task performance.

As mentioned, in the majority of studies investigating the effectiveness of part practice, the segmentation technique has been included. The subtask interdependence by degree of transfer interaction is clearly evident when this group of studies is taken into consideration. That is, part practice of a movement that has high subtask interdependence results in lower levels of positive transfer to performance of the whole task. From the perspective of developing an integrated control mechanism, this result makes sense. Part practice, particularly pure part practice, does not provide the learner with the opportunity to develop the necessary degree of coordination among the parts that is critical to successful whole-task performance.

However, some studies using tasks with a high degree of subtask interdependence have demonstrated effective application of segmented part practice for transfer to whole-task performance. For example, Ash and Holding (1990) had participants learn a musical score on the piano. Those using the forward chaining technique demonstrated superior acquisition performance of the task. The key here was the application of a segmentation technique that would enable the development of an integrated control mechanism.

It is also interesting to note that comparisons have been made between forward and backward chaining techniques. Wightman and Lintern (1985) reviewed four chaining studies and found that three of the four studies demonstrated superior transfer performance on the whole task for the backward chaining group. Ash and Holding (1990), however, found forward chaining to be a more effective part practice technique. The critical distinction here would appear to be the nature of the task. In all the studies that found evidence in support of a backward chaining technique, a common characteristic was the need for a high degree of end-point accuracy. The main function of the parts preceding the final segment is that of positioning the limbs correctly in support of the final segment movement execution. A layup in basketball is an example of this type of task. The ball dribble and steps serve to place the performer in a position to execute the key final segment: the actual shot. Landing an airplane on a carrier is another task requiring a high degree of end-point accuracy (Wightman & Sistrunk, 1987). However, in playing a musical score on the piano, each segment contributes equally to the overall quality of the performance; no one part can be considered more critical to successful performance than any other. It appears that for tasks of this nature, forward chaining would be more effective.

Fractionation

Fractionation is a part practice technique that separates practice parts normally executed simultaneously (Proctor & Dutta, 1995; Wightman & Lintern, 1985; Wightman & Sistrunk, 1987; but see Magill, 1998b, for a different interpretation of fractionation). A number of researchers have investigated the use of part practice for these types of tasks, which have included playing video games (Newell, Carlton, Fisher, & Rutter, 1989), tapping polyrhythms (Klapp et al., 1998), performing bimanual aiming tasks (Sherwood, 1994), juggling (Knapp & Dixon, 1952), tracking tasks (Briggs & Naylor, 1962), and controlling aircraft in flight (Briggs & Walters, 1958).

For most of these studies, the results have revealed that part practice is ineffective for creating significant levels of positive transfer to performance of the whole task (e.g., Briggs & Walters, 1958; Klapp et al., 1998; Knapp & Dixon, 1952), although some positive results have also occurred (Newell et al., 1989; Sherwood, 1994). It can be assumed that, by nature, simultaneously performed parts for a task require a high degree of coordination for the parts through an integrated control mechanism. The studies that have failed to find support for positive part practice have tended to include a pure part practice technique (each part practiced in isolation before transferring to whole-task performance). As mentioned previously, this type of practice would seem to prevent the development of the essential element of subtask integration control that is critical to performance success.

If this is true, why have some researchers observed positive transfer of part practice for these types of task? Participants in a study by Newell et al. (1989) acquired performance skill on the *Space Fortress* video game. Participants were required to maneuver a spaceship while evading mines and firing missiles at a rotating fortress. When playing the game, the parts that must be simultaneously performed were variable; that is, it could not be predetermined which parts would be used at different points throughout the game. Thus, success at the game was predicated on the ability to create integrated part performance on the spur of the moment rather than relying on a previously developed integrated control mechanism. Isolated practice on each element would result in a degree of automation for each part's performance, freeing up necessary mental capacity for creating the essential performance integrations.

Participants in a study by Sherwood (1994) performed a bimanual aiming task in which both arms performed a

reversal movement that varied in distance moved (either 20 or 60 degrees) but with a constant temporal dimension (200 msec movement to reversal point). In this study, he found that part practice of each movement was effective for acquisition of the whole (bimanual) task, but only if the long movement was practiced initially. In this case, the critical feature of bimanual task performance would be a velocity scaling factor, with the slower (shorter movement) limb using the movement of the faster (longer movement) limb for accomplishing the task goal. There is not a need for an integrated control mechanism for bimanual task performance; rather, a single control mechanism, established for one limb, is simply scaled for performance of the other limb. The results indicate that this scaling function works best if the control mechanism is established using practice on the more difficult component of the task. It should also be pointed out that this study was not a "true" part practice investigation in that transfer performance of the part practice groups was not compared to a control group that practiced the whole task or had no practice.

One study offering significant insight into the motor control representation issue was conducted by Klapp, Nelson, and Jagacinski (1998). Participants learned to tap a 3:2 bimanual polyrhythm (the right hand tapped three beats in a 1,800 msec interval while the left hand tapped two beats in 1,800 msec). The results demonstrated that the whole practice group acquired the task better than a part practice group. However, when asked to tap each rhythm independently following acquisition, the whole practice group performed poorly. Klapp et al. (1998) concluded that the whole practice group had acquired an integrated sensorimotor representation used to control performance of the task that did not specify each limb independently. In fact, the task was learned as a coordinated action involving both limbs rather than two limbs tapping independent rhythms. The findings led to interesting speculations relative to the application of part practice techniques to the learning of bimanual rhythmic tasks, such as in music. What can be concluded from the Klapp et al. (1998) study is that musical performances in which both limbs are creating rhythms should be acquired through whole-task practice. An example would be learning to play the drums (which requires an even more complex integration of limb when both upper and lower limbs are involved).

However, what is less clear is the best practice approach when each limb is not creating rhythms, such as in learning a piece on the piano where typically the left hand creates the rhythm and the right hand the melody. As Klapp et al. (1998) point out, it is still an open question whether learning of these types of tasks can be enhanced through part-task practice. Anecdotal evidence through the nonexperimental observation of children learning to play the piano has indicated that part-task practice of rhythmic and melodic aspects of performance is more effective for beginners. Once the basic elements of rhythm and melody have been acquired through the mastering of chord cadences and scales, part-task practice becomes less useful. Shaffer (1981) has indicated experimentally that independence of rhythm and melody is achieved in highly skilled musicians, which would suggest some efficacy of part-task practice. It seems apparent that further research in this area is required.

Another aspect of part-task practice for simultaneously performed components that remains unresolved is the predictions that can be derived from a connectionist/control architecture model as presented by Schneider and Detweiler (1988). As pointed out by Proctor and Dutta (1995), this model suggests that the mental workload necessary to support whole-task performance is a significant aspect of overall task coordination. This idea seems similar to Klapp et al.'s (1998) suggestion of an integrated sensorimotor representation that controls task performance. Part-task practice reduces this mental workload substantially. It can be predicted from the Schneider and Detweiler model that part-task practice of concurrent components would be more effective if done under conditions of high mental workload. So far, this prediction has not been put to an empirical test.

Simplification

Simplification is a part practice technique in which the difficulty of performing the whole task is reduced for initial task practice. Reduction of task difficulty can be achieved in a number of ways, such as in slowing the speed of movement, changing the nature of objects used in task performance to create easier interactions (e.g., scarves for juggling instead of balls, using an oversized plastic bat and ball for batting, or reducing degree of environmental instability), or using lead-up games that teach the essential principles of the activity, but in a simplified environment. As a teaching tool, simplification is ingrained in most education literature as a basic pedagogical principle, in that the majority of suggested teaching progressions incorporate an easy-to-difficult schedule for motor skill acquisition.

The results from the part practice literature in which a simplification technique has been used can be characterized as equivocal, at best. Wightman and Lintern (1985) concluded that despite simplification being a principle consistent with common practice in a variety of education and instructional environments, the empirical data have shown little evidence to support this practice. The majority of studies they reviewed resulted in generally positive but less than 100% transfer to the whole task, which indicates that simplification is less effective than whole-task practice. However, recent research has provided some support for simplification as an effective part practice technique (e.g., Hautala, 1988; Mané, Adams, & Donchin, 1989; Summers & Kennedy, 1992). Clearly, further research is required to understand the application of simplification as a useful part practice technique.

From a motor control perspective, it could be concluded that simplification of a task that maintains the essential nature of control for performance of the whole task would be effective, whereas simplification that creates a distinct control dynamic would be ineffective. Slowing the speed of a task would seem to serve as a case in point. For example, in the Mané et al. (1989) study, practicing a version of the *Space Fortress* video game that had slower speed of movement was found to transfer positively to performance of the game at regular speed. However, there was a limit to how slow the speed could be reduced. There appears to be an optimal minimum speed of movement, beyond which further slowing changes the essential nature of the component interactions required for successful task performance. This would seem to serve as a caution for learners who routinely incorporate slower speed of movement into their practice settings.

In a similar vein, Mathiowetz and Wade (1995) investigated the use of a miming technique for teaching activities of everyday living to healthy adults and adults with multiple sclerosis. One technique of miming that they investigated was with the objects removed, which appears to be analogous to the shadowing techniques common in sport settings (such as in practicing the golf swing without a club in hand, or a ball for contact). Their study indicated clearly that distinct kinematic profiles emerged for real task and mimed performances, suggesting distinct characteristics of performance for each task. Mimed, or shadowed, performances can be speculated to have motor control characteristics that are different from real task performance and would most likely be ineffective as a practice technique. Again, more research in this area is required before a definitive principle can emerge.

Attention Cuing

Although not strictly a part practice technique, attention cuing is an approach to practice that incorporates elements of part practice into whole-task performance. Using this technique, the performer practices the whole task, but directs attention to specific parts of the overall task performance, such as focusing on the follow-through of a tennis ground stroke or the reversal point in the golf swing. Attention research has clearly indicated that a selective focus of attention during task performance can be achieved.

The advantage to this type of practice performance is that emphasis can be placed on a particular critical aspect of performance for improvement while maintaining successful whole-task execution. Very little empirical research has investigated this approach. Gopher, Weil, and Siegel (1989) had participants practice the *Space Fortress* video game and compared the performance of several groups who were directed to attend to a particular component of the overall task with a control group that engaged in uncued whole-task practice. The results indicated that the attention-cued groups acquired the task more effectively than did the uncued group. However, the instructions provided to the cued groups directed attention to strategic elements of game play. It would be interesting if similar results could be obtained when attention is directed to motoric elements of task execution.

OFF-TASK CONDITIONS OF PRACTICE

Practice that is executed away from the actual task to be learned can be conducted in a wide range of formats and contexts. In this next section, the following off-task practice research issues are considered: imagery and mental practice, prepractice instruction and demonstrations, and simulated reality.

Imagery and Mental Practice

At times, when it is either inconvenient, impractical, or impossible to physically practice a motor skill, a common technique used in training is *mental practice*. Although there may be some neuromuscular activation associated with mental practice, the common view is that it involves practice of a task in the absence of overt movement. *Imagery* is a common type of mental practice and involves a visual representation of performance from either an internal or an external perspective. However, other forms of mental practice are possible in which the performer focuses on the processing of other channels of movement-related feedback, such as proprioceptive and auditory feedback.

Until recently, the role of imagery in motor performance had been difficult to assess due to the absence of an overt score following an imagined performance. However,

experimenters recently devised various means to overcome this problem, revealing that imagery is a powerful behavioral tool. For example, participants who were asked to start and stop a timer when walking to targets of varying distances produced similar times when they started and stopped the timer while mentally imaging walking to the same targets (Decety, Jeannerod, & Prablanc, 1989). Similar effects on movement time (i.e., actual and imagined times) have been found for the time taken to write or imagine writing a sentence (Decety & Michel, 1989), when performing or imaging tapping tasks that differ in terms of Fitts index of difficulty (Kohl & Fisicaro, 1995), and when imagining walking through gates with different Fitts indices of difficulty (Decety & Jeannerod, 1996). Moreover, evidence has recently accumulated through physiological measurements of brain activity (e.g., PET) that similar motor pathways are activated when imaging an action as when actually performing the action (see Jeannerod, 1999, for a review). Thus, the evidence appears to support the contention that mental practice, and imagery in particular, can represent the production of action in the absence of overt movement. But what about learning?

A meta-analysis conducted by Feltz and Landers (1983) concluded that mental practice was positively related to improvements in motor learning experiments, particularly so when the tasks emphasized cognitive components rather than strength components. In some cases, the mental practice benefits can be very large. For instance, in a study by Kohl, Ellis, and Roenker (1992), participants practiced a pursuit rotor tracking task under conditions of actual practice (18 trials), all-imagery practice (18 trials), or alternating conditions of practice and imagery (9 trials each) or practice and rest (9 trials each). The retention test performance revealed that the all-imagery and alternating practice + rest groups outperformed a control, no practice group, thereby confirming that imagery practice alone can facilitate some learning. However, the best learning results were produced by the all-physical practice group and the alternating physical + imagery group, which themselves were not different in retention. Thus, when alternating physical practice trials were replaced by imagery trials, there was no decrement to the learning experience (see also Hird, Landers, Thomas, & Horan, 1991).

Other evidence suggests that when mental or imagery practice is combined in studies of contextual interference (see earlier section), there is a substantial influence on the effect of random and blocked practice orders. As discussed earlier, blocked practice is usually found to produce better acquisition performance but poorer retention performance than random practice. However, Wright (1991) showed that retention performance could be substantially enhanced in blocked practice if the just-performed task was mentally contrasted with the other tasks in the learning set during the between-trial interval. A similar result was found by Gabriele, Hall, and Lee (1989), who asked blocked and random practice groups to image either the same or a different movement task as had just been performed. The effects on acquisition revealed that performance was worse when blocked practice was supplemented with random imagery than with blocked imagery (i.e., imagining the same task as had just been performed). The retention results were even more dramatic: Retention was facilitated by random imagery, regardless of whether it had been combined with blocked or random physical practice trials.

Findings from studies of mental practice and imagery are quite consistent in revealing positive benefits for learning. Although physiological measures of brain mechanisms that accompany these learning benefits do not appear to have been published, this should be a very fruitful area for continued research. See the chapter in this *Handbook* authored by C.R. Hall for a broad discussion of imagery and mental rehearsal.

Prepractice Instruction and Demonstration

Invariably in coaching situations, some sort of instruction and typically a movement demonstration is provided prior to any practice of a new motor skill. Indeed, most coaches would agree that providing instruction and/or using skilled demonstrations is one of the most important variables in facilitating the acquisition process. Instruction may be provided that specifies to the learner an optimal movement pattern, or in the form of feedback regarding errors in relation to specific task goals. As well, instruction can be presented in a number of different modalities and in a number of different ways. For example, a visual demonstration or verbal instruction relating to either the whole skill or specific aspects of the skill can be presented, in addition to changes in the temporal provision of instruction, that is either before any physical practice or at a later stage during or after practice. This instruction may also be independent of or dependent on the learner's performance (which has been termed augmented feedback). The focus in this section will be on information that is manipulated prior to practice and that is independent of the learner's performance.

Typically, instruction and demonstration supplement physical practice by providing the learner with information concerning how to perform a specific action and/or

the goal of the action. In addition, demonstrations are usually of a limited number, detailing a supposed correct way of attaining the task goal. Although it is acknowledged that verbal and visual instruction (such as a demonstration) may have differential effects on learning (i.e., the old adage that a picture is worth a thousand words), they will not be treated differently in this section. This is primarily because studies that have demonstrated differences have typically been limited to the developmental literature and as such have been related to memorial differences between different age groups and special populations (e.g., Minas, 1977).

Until quite recently, there was very little empirical research examining the role of instructional provision prior to practice and its effects on the skill acquisition process. One of the main reasons for this lack of research in motor learning was the type of laboratory tasks that have been used to examine learning. Typically, these tasks have not required any new learning as such, that is, acquiring new relations among body segments. Rather, only a rescaling of a previously acquired action has been necessary, for example, achievement of a specified movement time for a sequence of key presses (see Newell, 1989; Scully & Newell, 1985; Whiting, 1980, 1984, who differentiated novel movement pattern tasks from existing movement pattern tasks). In the latter cases, instructions that specify to the individual how to move limbs to attain the task goal have been unnecessary. Although some learning situations have required the individual to achieve the task goal in a particular way (i.e., match a movement template; e.g., Newell & McGinnis, 1985), the instruction is then isomorphic with the task goal. In other words, it is difficult to determine whether instruction concerning how to perform an action has a role in motor learning beyond making it clear to the learner the nature of the task requirements.

Early work by Singer and colleagues (Singer & Gaines, 1975; Singer & Pease, 1976) showed similar performance advantages for an instructed, guidance learning group (response-cued) as compared to a discovery learning group (trial and error). In their studies, participants were required to manipulate, in a predetermined sequence, a number of hand or foot operated items. Performance times, however, failed to show advantages for the guided group in retention. In fact, Singer and Pease (1976) showed that the non-guided participants were significantly faster. Additionally, transfer performance, at least on earlier trials was significantly improved for the non-guided participants in both studies. This work lends support to the suggestion that instructions and/or a demonstration of the correct movement sequence is necessary, but that continued instruction, or guidance during learning may decrease the cognitive effort devoted to the learning process which will lead to decrements in retention and transfer performance.

The question of whether there are benefits to be gleaned from watching a demonstration of the act before practice proceeds, or receiving instruction concerning underlying principles or expert strategies, has only recently begun to receive systematic attention in the motor learning literature. In the remainder of this section, the various task situations in which instruction has been examined will be reviewed, and an attempt will be made to reach some conclusions with respect to the benefits of instruction during the acquisition of motor skills.

The Role of Movement/Criterion Templates

Common practice in the study of motor skills is to differentiate between two different classes of movement (see Gentile, 1972, 1987): open and closed (although they are commonly viewed to lie on a continuum). One way to distinguish closed skills is the fact that the goal of the task *is* the manner by which the task goal is to be achieved. Typical examples of closed skills are diving and gymnastics, in which the nature of the movement itself is the task goal. In contrast, open skills commonly have conflicting goals, whereby the goal of the task and the way it is to be achieved are not compatible; for example, there may be many ways to reach a particular motor solution in open skills (e.g., scoring a goal in soccer and returning a serve in volleyball). In spite of this distinction, it is common practice for sport skill instructors to attempt to turn what have been defined as open skills into closed skills by the provision of optimal movement templates, or criterion movement patterns. In this situation, the instructor has to be aware that the goal of the task does not become confused (see Gentile, 1972; Whiting & den Brinker, 1982), such that achieving the task in a specified way gains precedence over attaining the task goal (e.g., achieving a certain hip, leg, and foot stance when kicking a ball, but not achieving the required movement distance).

The provision of movement templates has also been shown to increase task consistency (e.g., Newell, Carlton, & Antoniou, 1990). Although this is necessary for performing closed skills, it may be at the expense of developing a response repertoire (Gentile, 1972) necessary for the performance of skills in open, nonpredictable, and continually changing environments. Additionally, increased task consistency is beneficial to performance only if the skill

is being performed correctly. During the initial stages of learning, when preexisting behaviors or bad habits may dominate the action, increased variability in the early movements of the performer may be preferable to facilitate acquisition of a new movement pattern (see, e.g., Hodges & Lee, 1999, for an earlier discussion of variability in practice).

The concept of an optimal performance template in open skills is, itself, a contentious issue. Although there appear to be characteristic invariances across skilled performers (e.g., Wulf, Shea, & Matschiner, 1998), there is often considerable variability in the achievement of even the most simple movement skills (see Latash, 1996). Given the physiological, morphological, and biomechanical differences among individuals, the search for optimal movement templates that apply across individuals of varying skill and physical makeup may not be possible or, even if they are determined, may not be useful learning tools for unskilled individuals. For example, although Young and Schmidt (1992) found initial evidence suggesting an optimal movement pattern for a simple coincident timing task, on closer examination, Brisson and Alain (1996) failed to verify these findings. In addition, they found that compared to a "best" subject's template, individual movement profiles were equally as facilitatory for task performance, if not more so, especially for maintaining movement consistency.

Newell et al. (1990) have also examined criterion templates in situations where the goal of the movement and the manner in which it is achieved are the same. Over a series of experiments, the authors concluded that a criterion template specifying how a movement is to be produced is important for learning only when the goal of the task is unfamiliar to the performer. In addition, feedback regarding performance in relation to the criterion template (i.e., information concerning both the goal and how it was achieved) was found to facilitate learning more than providing either criterion information or feedback in isolation. These findings lead to the conclusion that as long as the performer knows what is required in terms of the task goal, additional information specifying the optimal way to achieve this goal may be redundant, or at least not as beneficial as feedback or instruction relating to one's own performance.

Learning Movement Sequences

As can be inferred from the experiments reviewed in the previous section, instructions have an important role in terms of specifying to the individual the task goal requirements. In addition, for tasks that require the coordination of movements that are already part of a person's movement repertoire (e.g., a specific sequence of key presses in a laboratory task, or a series of gymnastic moves in a floor routine), instructions and demonstrations likely have a special role to play. For example, Carroll and Bandura (1982, 1985, 1987) found benefits for a group learning a sequence of actions when it had been able to watch a demonstration of the actions prior to practice. These findings lead to the suggestion that prepractice information serves to enhance the memorial representation of the required sequence of movements.

Howard, Mutter, and Howard (1992) have shown that serial pattern knowledge can be acquired from observing a skilled performer respond in a key-pressing task where certain stimuli are presented in invariant sequences. Similarly, Ross, Bird, Doody, and Zoeller (1985) and Doody, Bird, and Ross (1985) examined the learning of a barrier knock-down task under various information manipulations, including auditory and visual models and videotape feedback. Again, modeling was found to facilitate performance when measured in delayed retention, and this was suggested to be due to the development of a stronger template of the required movement sequence. Arguably, these types of tasks may create more of a cognitive, memory problem for the individual, rather than having a high, novel, motoric component, such that movement demonstrations are particularly beneficial in these situations to facilitate learning. Similar conclusions were reached by Scully and Newell (1985), who, on reviewing the early modeling literature, proposed that systematic benefits for demonstrations were found only for tasks involving existing movement patterns, as compared to tasks requiring the learning of novel movement patterns.

Theoretical Rationale Underlying Instructional Provision

From a theoretical perspective, models and theories of skill acquisition have led researchers to propose that the early stages of learning are characterized by high demands on cognitive processes. For example, Fitts and Posner (1967) proposed that learning is characterized by a transition from a cognitive learning phase to a more autonomous final phase, where the skill is performed with very little cognitive involvement. Similar progressions in skill development have been proposed by Adams (1971), Anderson (1982), and Shiffrin and Schneider (1977). Both rationale and support for these models have been obtained from the cognitive learning literature whereby rules for solving puzzles and problems become more proceduralized with practice (e.g., Anderson, Conrad, & Corbett, 1989; Larkin, 1981; Newell, 1991). Anecdotal evidence suggests that learning proceeds in this manner. For example, when learning to drive a manual car, the gear stick shift, clutch, and brake control become proceduralized so that they are performed somewhat autonomously as a single unit.

As well, Fleishman and colleagues (see Fleishman, 1972, for a review), through a comprehensive examination of individual differences on a variety of cognitive and motor aptitude tests, have demonstrated that certain abilities are more or less predictive of performance capabilities at different stages of skill acquisition. Of particular relevance here are the findings of Fleishman and Hempel (1954, 1955), who noted that during the early stages of skill acquisition, the best performers were generally those who performed well on tests that were presumed to assess spatial-verbal ability, but that with increased practice, the importance of performance on these tests decreased and psychomotor abilities, such as reaction time, became better predictors.

Although the above rationale seems to offer some reason to assume that instruction will be most useful during the early stages of learning, there is little to suggest what type of information would be most useful. Indeed, it may be the case that because early stages of skill acquisition are proposed to be cognitively demanding (e.g., Schneider, 1985; Shiffrin & Schneider, 1977), rather than overloading the individual with augmented information and detailed instruction, it may be preferable to keep the cognitive demands low during this stage. This would allow attention to be more fully directed to solving the motor task and processing feedback, rather than additional processing that is required to understand and implement instructions or copy a movement demonstration.

Implicit and Explicit Learning

Work in the cognitive literature examining how instructions and explicit knowledge impact on the learning process for complex problem-solving tasks has served to question traditional views of learning. Reber (1967) showed that individuals were able to generalize their learning of artificial letter strings to correctly predict the grammaticality of newly presented sequences. Interestingly, however, these individuals were unable to explicitly verbalize *how* they were able to do this; they could not explain the rule or method. Based on these findings, Reber argued that learning could proceed at an unconscious level, what he termed *implicit learning,* which is characterized by the acquisition of abstract knowledge. Broadbent and colleagues (e.g., Berry & Broadbent, 1984; Broadbent & Aston, 1978; Broadbent, Fitzgerald, & Broadbent, 1986) have expanded on this work, specifically exploring the learning of computer interactive tasks, governed by a known or unknown complex algorithm or rule. Contrary to intuition, individuals were able to learn to control these complex systems more effectively if they had *not* received instruction in the form of the general rule underlying performance. As before, participants were often quite unaware as to how they had managed to correctly perform the computer task, again demonstrating knowledge without explicit awareness. These findings serve to question traditional theories of skill acquisition that propose a transition from a cognitive, verbal-like stage of learning to a final autonomous, less attention-demanding stage, as well as questioning the benefits of instructional provision.

As with the learning of cognitive tasks in an implicit manner (i.e., without awareness of the rules or regularities governing performance), there has been evidence that some motor tasks may be acquired in a similar manner. For example, early work on tracking by Pew (1974) showed that individuals were able to demonstrate improved performance on a regularly repeated segment during a tracking task without demonstrating any awareness that this segment had been repeated. This work has been extended by Green and Flowers (1991) using a visual-motor coordination task involving joystick manipulations, and Magill and colleagues (Magill, 1998a; Magill & Clark, 1997; Magill, Schöenfelder-Zohdi, & Hall, 1990; Magill, Sekiya, & Clark, 1995) with a tracking paradigm similar to the one used by Pew. In addition to observing learning of repeated segments in the tracking study and decreased error in the visual-motor coordination task of Green and Flowers, both sets of researchers failed to show any benefits of providing instruction concerning the repeated segment, or when using predictable stimulus-response pairings.

In the past, several researchers have associated implicit learning with motor learning (see Seger, 1994, for a review). This was because a number of experiments demonstrating learning without awareness had been those designed for tasks requiring some sort of motor response, or what has frequently been referred to as procedural skill learning (e.g., Lewicki, Hill, & Bizot, 1988; Stadler, 1989). Indeed, in a recent book discussing the nature of implicit learning (Berry, 1997), the suggestion was raised that perhaps implicit learning was merely "learning" (Cleeremans, 1997) or the default learning mechanism (see Manza & Reber, 1997; Reber, 1993). *Explicit learning* (i.e., learning

that is intentional and consciously driven) was proposed to be an additional learning process that may not always be appropriate, especially if the nature of the test environment does not require explicit recall of knowledge.

Recently, Gentile (1998) proposed a model of motor skill learning that defines learning as two distinct yet interdependent processes, consisting of both explicit and implicit processes. She suggests that the explicit process is directed toward acquiring the movement pattern and is achieved by forming a mapping between the performer and the environment. Accordingly, processing of information is active and effortful and therefore the information requires attention to be used effectively. The additional attention given to explicit processes by Gentile is due to the emphasis on functional, goal-relevant tasks. In the past, tasks such as serial reaction time or pursuit rotor have shown learning without awareness (i.e., implicit learning); subsequently, a significant role for implicit, not explicit, learning processes has been advanced (especially in the psychology literature). In contrast to the explicit process, the implicit process is not available to conscious awareness and is concerned with the effective generation and use of forces within and between individuals and their environment. The implicit process may be similar to the process of learning discussed by Polanyi (1958), who cites the example of an experienced cyclist who was never taught how to ride a bike in terms of mechanical principles necessary for maintaining equilibrium and who was still unaware of these principles at a high level of performance skill. Polanyi discusses this type of learning as the manner "by which we *feel our way* to success and may continue to improve on our success without specifically knowing how we do it" (1958, p. 62).

Despite the similarities in findings to the work of Reber, it has been suggested (see Buchner & Wippich, 1998) that tasks such as the ones used by Broadbent and colleagues are not good examples of implicit tasks, as participants know from the outset that they are expected to "solve" the problem and therefore actively search for the system invariances. In this manner, they are not *incidental,* which is a characteristic usually deemed necessary for implicit learning. Berry (1994) agrees that explicit processes may play a more significant role in these tasks than originally believed, whereby participants adopt explicit hypothesis-testing strategies to try to uncover the rules or regularities underlying task attainment. This situation is comparable to most motor learning contexts, where the individual is usually directed to discovering a motor solution that will lead to the production of a certain movement (e.g., hit a golf ball in the fairway). It is this functional, goal-directed nature of action that has led Gentile to propose a significant role for explicit processes in motor skill acquisition.

Learning Novel Motor Patterns

Given that motor learning often requires intentional learning of some kind (and therefore is more explicit), it is interesting that recent experiments requiring the learning of complex actions have also not shown benefits as a result of explicit instruction. Wulf and Weigelt (1997) provided instruction based on expert movement strategies involved in the learning of fast and wide movements on a ski simulator, and Hodges and Lee (1999) provided participants with instruction detailing how to perform a novel movement pattern in a bimanual coordination task. In both these experiments, performance was superior (as assessed in retention and transfer tests) for *discovery* learning groups that were not given any additional information prior to practice concerning the optimal or correct method for performing the task. Even when instruction was administered after three days of practice, Wulf and Weigelt still failed to show any advantage for explicit instruction. In fact, the participants demonstrated performance *decrements* in the three trials following instructional provision.

Interestingly, in the bimanual coordination task of Hodges and Lee (1999), the differences between the instructed participants and noninstructed participants were most pronounced under attention-demanding conditions. That is, the instructed participants appeared to regress to performing at a lower skill level under additional attentional constraints. It was suggested that this may be related to the shared processes required of the primary and secondary task, such that learning with instructions may pose greater cognitive demands on the learner, as opposed to learning without instructions. The instructed participants, however, were also the most variable at the end of practice and this in itself may be the reason for regressing back to a more stable level of performance when a cognitively demanding secondary task was added (see Kelso, 1994, who suggests that a cognitive load may have similar effects on performance as that of a physical, inertial load). These findings show that explicit knowledge specifying how to coordinate the limbs to acquire a complex motor task may not facilitate acquisition and indeed may be detrimental to the learning process.

Another interesting finding to evolve from this study was that the group that performed the best during retention and transfer testing (both in terms of accuracy and variability) also performed with the most variability at the start of acquisition. A similar observation was reported by Green and Flowers (1991), where participants who had

explicit knowledge withheld during learning showed more movements on the joystick than the explicit knowledge groups. These findings lead to the suggestion that variability in performance, in addition to gaining experience of the task dynamics, may be an important factor in facilitating motor skill acquisition during the early stages of learning. Recent progress in the area of dynamic pattern theory and its application to human movement (see Kelso, 1995, for a review) also speaks to the importance of variability as a catalyst for behavioral change (as well as an important index of performance stability).

The significance of variability in facilitating behavior change has also been emphasized by researchers who have studied "discovery learning" (see van Emmerik, den Brinker, Vereijken, & Whiting, 1989; Vereijken, 1991; Vereijken & Whiting, 1988). These researchers examined how movement demonstrations and attention-directing instructions affected the learning of slalom-type ski movements on a ski simulator task, as compared to discovery learning conditions where no instruction or feedback was provided. They, too, found that discovery learning resulted in performance that was equally as effective as instruction that directed attention to factors such as movement amplitude, frequency, or fluency. Additionally, this type of learning was more beneficial than instruction that directed attention to movement frequency or fluency when overall performance was evaluated. In subsequent experiments, Whiting, Bijlard, and den Brinker (1987) also showed that providing a dynamic model during acquisition failed to facilitate performance in any dependent measure compared to a control condition and, in fact, was detrimental to movement frequency (see also Anderson, Dialameh, Hilligan, Wong, & Wong, 1998).

The researchers suggest that these effects are primarily mediated by attentional focus toward factors or variables that may retard learning (e.g., trying to copy the form of the movement, at the expense of achieving the task goal). These specific performance effects as a result of instructional provision are quite pervasive in the motor skill literature and are important considerations in the design of experiments. For example, Maraj, Allard, and Elliott (1998) examined triple-jump performance in terms of variability of foot placements under instructional manipulations that emphasized either accuracy of take-off or distance jumped. Not surprisingly, according to the instructions, the skilled triple-jumpers traded accuracy for distance, if distance was emphasized in the instruction. Similarly, distance was traded for accuracy if the importance of not producing a foul jump was emphasized. These results underscore the attention-directing nature of instructions. They should also serve to caution against providing specific instructions if performance is to be assessed by a number of measures (such as both amplitude and frequency) or if the task is relatively complex. In the latter case, directing attention to one specific information source may be to the detriment of attending to other important factors or variables for performing the task.

Implicit motor learning has also been manipulated by requiring participants to focus attention on a secondary task during acquisition, with the supposition that the high cognitive demands would prevent the acquisition of verbalizable rules and thus prevent explicit learning. Masters (1992) and Hardy, Mullen, and Jones (1996) showed that although implicit learning delayed the acquisition of a golf putting skill, under conditions of pressure the implicit learning groups continued to improve, whereas the explicit learning groups did not. In addition, the control group (i.e., discovery learning) did not continue to show any learning effects when the task was performed under the stress-inducing conditions. However, the control groups in these studies scored the highest number of putts throughout acquisition and retention, supporting the idea that golf putting at least can be acquired in a noninstructional manner without detrimental effects on performance, relative to groups who receive detailed instruction.

Analysis of verbal protocols after practice also showed that participants in the discovery learning groups had acquired explicit knowledge of the rules governing golf putting. These findings support the suggestion that learning a motor skill in an explicit, rule-based manner may, in some situations, be detrimental to performance, especially if the task has to be conducted in a stressful situation or in conjunction with other attention-demanding tasks. The challenge for the coach or instructor is perhaps to minimize this explicit, rule-based search on the part of the learner and encourage learning that is less explicit, without incurring the performance losses realized by participants in the implicit learning conditions during acquisition of the skills.

Recently, Maxwell, Masters, Eves, and MacMahon (1999) found that the differences between implicit and explicit learning groups remained even after extended practice (i.e., 3,000 practice trials). Although the discovery learning group demonstrated significantly more rules with respect to putting than the implicit learning group, the number of rules acquired for this group correlated with scores on a scale that was proposed to assess a person's predisposition to focus attention inward toward the limbs, or the mechanics of the movement (Masters, Polman, & Hammond, 1993). Scores on this scale were shown to be negatively correlated with putting performance (a high

score was related to poorer performance), again supporting the idea that learning in an explicit, rule-based fashion may be harmful to motor learning.

These findings also support recent studies by Wulf and colleagues who suggest that an inward attentional focus may be the primary mechanism mediating negative instructional effects. Wulf and Weigelt (1997) proposed that the negative effects of instructions in the ski simulator task may have been the result of an increased focus of attention onto the limbs (as a result of trying to exert force on the ski simulator after it has passed the center), at the expense of a more global focus of attention onto the distal effects of the action. Subsequently, Wulf, Höss, and Prinz (1998) manipulated instructional information creating either an internal focus of attention onto the participant's limbs (i.e., the feet), or an external focus of attention toward the wheels on the apparatus. As predicted, the researchers found that a focus of attention onto the external effects of the action led to significantly better performance than instructions promoting an internal focus of attention during acquisition and retention. The fact that the control group (no instructions) was not significantly different from the internal focus of attention group during retention testing, at least for measures of movement amplitude, suggests that an external focus of attention provides an additional benefit for learning that is not realized when this instruction is withheld. Further evidence for the positive effects of external focus instructions versus internal focus instructions has also been demonstrated by Wulf and colleagues in performing a backhand shot in tennis and putting a golf ball (Maddox, Wulf, & Wright, 1999; Wulf, Lauterbach, & Toole, 1998). However, both of these studies failed to provide a control condition to evaluate whether an external focus of attention facilitates learning, or whether an internal focus is detrimental to learning relative to noninstructed learning conditions.

Despite the negative effects of internal focus of attention suggested by these researchers, Hodges and Franks (1999) did not find that instructions that directed attention toward the arms during learning in a bimanual coordination task was always detrimental to performance. Rather, the effects were somewhat dependent on how performance was assessed during practice (i.e., with or without feedback). Although the internal instruction group demonstrated more error at the start of practice, all instructions provided in addition to a movement demonstration (regardless of attentional focus) were beneficial to learning. This was particularly pronounced when learning was assessed in the absence of concurrent feedback, as compared to the performance of a demonstration-only group. It was proposed that these additional instructions served to direct attention onto other aspects required to perform the task, such as the processing of kinesthetic feedback. In this way, the detrimental effects associated with the removal of visual information were reduced. Interestingly, the control group (no instruction, no movement demonstration) performed as well as the instructed groups. This finding is similar to those discussed earlier with respect to discovery learning. Specifically, leaving the individual to his or her own methods for solving the task may be preferable to providing a demonstration without any additional instruction that directs attention to additional factors that may facilitate learning.

Current theoretical beliefs concerning movement control also accord well with recent findings with respect to attention. In particular, Latash (1993, 1996) proposed that the control focus of a performer in a movement task is directed toward the end-point of the action, what has been referred to as the *working end-point*. This has been defined as the most important point for executing a task and may include such working end-points as the fingertips when grasping or the trajectory of a basketball free throw (see Latash, 1993). In comparison to other points that are involved in the movement, the working point demonstrates the greatest invariance across trials. This finding leads to the suggestion that control strategies are somehow related to the working point, not with the details of the rest of the motor system (i.e., attending to limb positioning or the actual movement). This lack of awareness of limb positioning has been observed, both anecdotally and experimentally, in expert athletes. For example, Lee, Lishman, and Thomson (1984) observed that long jumpers were using information specifying time-to-contact to adjust the final footfalls in their run-up, without being aware of this adjustment strategy.

Further support for this nonawareness type strategy, even at the earlier stages of learning, is provided by Singer, Lidor, and Cauraugh (1993). They found that acquiring a self-paced motor task using a nonawareness (5-step) strategy during task execution was a preferable strategy to consciously attending to the act itself. However, a subsequent study by Bouchard and Singer (1998) looking at the acquisition of a sport task (i.e., learning a tennis serve) failed to show advantages for this strategy over a control condition. The authors suggested that this was because participants in the control condition adopted similar strategies to that encouraged by the 5-step strategy. Leaving participants to their own devices when acquiring new motor skills may be as beneficial (and maybe more so) to learning than providing some sort of explicit instruction beyond making the task requirements clear to a person.

Perspectives

The studies reviewed in this section lead to the conclusion that prepractice information should not be administered liberally and without concern for the type of motor skill that requires learning. Instructions and demonstrations have frequently been found not to provide the learner with any additional information beyond specifying the goal of the task, whether this requires matching a movement template or criterion, focusing on a particular movement variable, or remembering a movement sequence. Although there is a suggestion that instruction directing attention to the external or distal effects of the action may have benefits for learning over contexts that promote an inward focus of attention (at least when performance is assessed under the same conditions of learning), the benefits of this type of instruction compared to a no-instruction, control condition are equivocal and await further study. Recent advances in dynamics, particularly investigating the learning of new patterns of coordination, may offer new insights into the role instructions play in facilitating behavioral change. For example, work by Zanone and Kelso (1992, 1997) demonstrating different routes to learning depending on a person's preexisting coordination tendencies may have implications for instructions that either build on or avoid preexisting patterns or habits during learning.

Simulated Reality

A rapidly growing trend in the training of motor skill expertise is the use of simulated environments as a critical adjunct to practicing the goal task in the real world, or typical, performance context. Although a simulation can be achieved through manipulation of the cognitive and emotional climate of the practice session, the focus here will be on the development and application of engineered devices and apparati that can be used to create the simulated environment. (However, simulation can also be achieved through the use of human actors who model a desired behavior; see Collins & Harden, 1998.)

Typically, simulation is achieved through the use of *simulators* or *virtual environments*. The difference between the two tends to be in the creation of the response environment. A simulator establishes an environment for responding that is physically present, often as a very realistic depiction of the goal task's performance environment. Virtual environments are just that, a response environment that is computer-generated and exists in cyberspace with a response apparatus that may not be reflective of what is used in the real world, such as a data glove. In both cases, however, simulation is achieved and practice undertaken in an environment separate from the typical performance context. Because the lines of research investigating the use of each simulation technique for the development of motor skill expertise have evolved somewhat distinctly, each will be considered separately next.

Simulators

The use of simulators in training is widespread. Perhaps the area with the longest tradition of simulator development and use is aviation, although other areas such as driver education, medicine, nuclear power plant operation, and sports incorporate simulator use in training programs. It is interesting to note that in most areas of application, simulators have been subjected to a significant amount of empirical scrutiny. A notable exception is in sports, where the use of various simulators such as tackling dummies and blocking sleds in football, pitching machines in baseball, video golf, and other such devices are recommended with little understanding of the transfer relationship between performance on the simulator and performance in a game. Despite this lack of sport simulator research, however, the extensive empirical investigations of simulator use in other areas offer the opportunity to develop insight into the use of simulators for motor skill training.

Due to the acceptance and integration of simulator use in aviation, the vast majority of simulator research has been focused in this area. Other areas in which simulators have been developed for training often use the aviation model for integration of simulators (e.g., see Higgins, Merill, Hettinger, Kaufman, Champion, & Satava, 1997, for a discussion of the applicability of the principles derived from aviation simulator research and development to surgical training). The earliest aviation simulators were developed in the 1910s and 1920s, with the advent of the Link Trainer, and successive generations of increasingly complex simulators have evolved since then (see Koonce & Bramble, 1998, for a historical discussion of aviation simulator development). Several excellent reviews of simulator development and application in the aviation industry exist (e.g., a 1998 special issue of the *International Journal of Aviation Psychology*).

Simulator use is most often justified for training due to three major characteristics: (1) They offer a safe environment for skill development; (2) they are flexible, in that a variety of training scenarios can be offered in a compressed time frame; and (3) they are cost-effective (Higgins et al., 1997). It is interesting to note that positive transfer of training from the simulator to the real task performance is often assumed and not always measured. In fact, positive transfer of training has been an elusive goal in simulator research

and, in one case, negative transfer has occurred (Hughes, Brooks, Graham, Sheen, & Dickens, 1982).

In general, development and application of simulators in aviation have occurred within the identical elements transfer-of-training theoretical framework (Thorndike, 1914), invoking Osgood's (1949) transfer surface concept in which high amounts of positive transfer are best achieved through a close match of the features of the simulator and the task being simulated (Dennis & Harris, 1998). The result has been to develop simulators that offer increasingly higher degrees of fidelity (degree of similarity between the simulated and real devices), with as much realism as technically possible.

Because of this emphasis, simulation design and application have become largely a technological problem, with less emphasis on the learning that has occurred. The guiding principle has been to simulate reality, with the expectation (hope?) that learning will follow. Salas, Bowers, and Rhodenizer (1998) offer an eloquent discussion of this issue, calling for a paradigm shift in simulation research away from the technological questions of simulating reality and toward the design of "human-centered training systems that support the acquisition of complex skills" (p. 199). It is important, as stated by Salas et al., that consideration be given to the instructional features embedded in the simulation exercise, not simply to recreate the performance context in a highly realistic way. As has become apparent from the motor learning literature, practice in and of itself does not make perfect, any more than simply using a highly realistic simulator will make perfect without some structure to the practice context.

In fact, the pursuit of increasingly higher levels of fidelity may be detrimental to the understanding of simulator effectiveness as a training system for complex motor skills. Several divergent areas of investigation converge to provide what may be a clearer picture of effective simulator use. First, simulator research has indicated that the most effective training with simulators occurs in the acquisition of procedures (Chamberlin & Lee, 1993; Higgins et al., 1997; Koonce & Bramble, 1998; Schmidt & Lee, 1999). Successful simulator application has been undertaken in the development of aviation skills such as combat maneuvering in instrument training, decision making, and crew resource management (Salas et al., 1998) and in medical skills such as cardiac life support, anesthesiology, surgery, and bedside physical examination (Gordon, Issenberg, Mayer, & Felner, 1999). All of these tasks tend to emphasize procedures, implying that learning with a simulator is more successful when the task is more cognitive than motor in nature.

Second, recent advancements toward understanding transfer have indicated that transfer may have more to do with the similarity of cognitive processing that supports motor performance than with the physical similarity of tasks (see Lee, 1988). Support for this notion can be found in the simulator literature from several sources. Gopher, Weil, and Bareket (1994) demonstrated improved pilot performance after having practiced on the video game *Space Fortress*. Dennis and Harris (1998) found that student pilots trained on a low-fidelity desktop simulator, who had a realistic airplane control panel for responding, were not reliably different when measured in actual flight performance from a group of students who trained on the same system but used the computer keyboard for responding. Both groups, however, did demonstrate significantly better flight performance than a control group. Ortiz (1994, 1995) observed a similar result in that students trained on a flight simulator exhibited better actual flight performance than a control group, despite flying a plane that had a completely different flight control system than the one used on the simulator. This would indicate that simulator training was not causing a transfer of the neuromuscular details of the motor skill, but rather a transfer of the cognitive processes that underlie successful motor skill performance. Gopher et al. (1994) proposed that transfer in their study was due to the development of attention control (controlling attention under high concurrent demands), an important element in the acquisition and performance of flight skills.

Third, dynamical systems theory proposes an ecological perspective for the control of motor skills that hypothesizes a direct link between perception and action. Successful movement control is achieved through the interaction of environmental invariants that are perceived and a self-organizing action system that operates according to the principles of nonlinear dynamics. Learning involves the acquisition of knowledge regarding these "perceptual invariants." Koonce and Bramble (1998) describe perceptual invariants as "properties of the information flow that remain constant as other information changes and are linked to properties of the task to be learned" (p. 287). Lintern (1991) has argued that the acquisition of perceptual invariants is the key to effective transfer of training from simulator to the real task. Thus, highly realistic simulations may present irrelevant stimuli that distract the learner's attention and prevent the acquisition of knowledge critical to successful transfer of training.

Simulator use for the development of motor skill expertise should be most effective for the development of procedural skills and prove useful for learning serial tasks,

strategies, and teamwork. The simulator should be developed in a way that emphasizes the perceptual invariants of the performance context and minimizes irrelevant or distracting stimuli. Simulator fidelity may not be the critical factor in determining simulator effectiveness, as numerous studies have produced positive transfer results using lower fidelity fixed training devices and PC-based desktop simulators (e.g, Lintern, Roscoe, Koonce, & Segal, 1990; see also Jentsch & Bowers, 1998) Use of the simulator should be embedded within sound instructional practice with significant consideration being given to the learning process and less emphasis on technological advancement. The value of simulator training is in the maximizing of real-task practice by creating a knowledge or awareness of the performance context and procedural requirements of action production. Dennis and Harris (1998) suggest that for pilot training, simulators should be used to review previous in-flight practice and preview upcoming in-flight practice.

Limiting the capability of developing exact principles to guide simulator use has lead to experimental design issues that have made the study of simulator effectiveness difficult. For example, critical to the research effort in understanding the relative merits of simulators for the development of motor skills has been the evaluation approaches utilized in determining the training effectiveness of simulators. Bell and Waag (1998) identify three major categories of evaluation used: utility evaluations, in-simulator learning, and transfer of training. Central to any evaluation of training effectiveness should be transfer of training. Does practice with a simulator cause significant positive transfer to performance of the real task? In simulator research, transfer of training studies tend to be in the minority. Much of this is due to the majority of research having been undertaken on simulator use in aviation and the difficulties inherent in conducting transfer of training studies in this particular environment (such as cost of actual flight time, lack of environmental control, and measurement of pilot performance). In response to this, several researchers have made use of a transfer paradigm between two different task simulations, a technique termed *quasi-transfer* (Lintern, Roscoe, & Sivier, 1990; Taylor & Lintern, 1993). In this technique, transfer is made to a higher-fidelity simulation than that used in training. However, the obvious issue here is whether a similar degree of transfer can be expected between a simulated task and a real task as was found between two simulated tasks.

In a direct comparison of how well quasi-transfer predicts transfer of training effects, Taylor, Lintern, Koonce, Kaiser, and Morrison (1991) were able to offer only partial support for the use of a quasi-transfer paradigm. They investigated the influence of scene detail on the landing skill of students and found there was only a moderate correspondence between results predicted by quasi-transfer and those found in a transfer of training study, leaving the question of quasi-transfer experiments open to criticism. Other evaluation approaches can be similarly criticized. Utility evaluations rely mostly on subjective data by having experts in the performance of a particular task (subject matter experts: SMEs) perform the task on a simulator and provide ratings as to the effectiveness of the simulator for training of the task. Although the expert's acceptance of a simulator would seem to be useful, the best approaches to training are not necessarily those that have the most appeal to the performer. For example, in a study by Baddeley and Longman (1978) investigating distribution of practice, the subjectively "preferred" practice schedule actually demonstrated the worst levels of performance and learning. These findings are representative of a growing literature that suggests that metacognitive assessments of learning are notoriously unreliable (Bjork, 1998).

In-simulator learning is used to provide evidence that improvement in performance occurred across practice on the simulator. Although Bell and Waag (1998) argue that improvement in performance is a necessary condition to establish training effectiveness, the motor learning literature contains a number of examples where superior practice performance does not always indicate effective training conditions (see earlier discussion of contextual interference).

It appears that sport applications may be a fruitful area for investigating simulator effectiveness. Many of the difficulties encountered in the area of aviation training, particularly with respect to measurement, evaluation, and cost issues, are lessened or minimized in sport performance. There are a variety of simulators in use and the sport context offers a good environment to quantify performance. It remains a curiosity that more effort has not been forthcoming in investigating the application of simulators to the development of sport skills.

Virtual Reality

Recent advances in computer technology have produced powerful systems capable of creating virtual environments (VEs) that can be devised for most if not all possible response scenarios. In most cases, VEs produce simulations that consist of some type of device that presents a simulated perceptual context coupled with a simulated effector system. The computer integrates the response created within the simulated perceptual context to produce an expected consequence of the action. Not only can a single

user perform within the VE, but networked systems can integrate multiple users within the same VE in real time. And, unlike the earlier virtual reality systems, the integration of powerful microchips in desktop computers has made access to VEs quite affordable.

The rapid advances in computer technology have been both the boon and bane of virtual reality application. The possibilities seem endless, particularly for application to the training of motor skills, but most research in the area seems to still be at the "Wow! Look what I can do" stage. As in other areas, the technology seems to have overwhelmed the application, and the majority of research in the area is being conducted by computer scientists, rather than by scientists investigating learning issues. The most common application of virtual reality at present tends to be in the entertainment industry.

This is not to say that the application of VEs to motor skill acquisition does not hold some promise. Multiple applications have been developed in a variety of motor skill performance contexts. These areas include baseball batting (Andersson, 1993), table tennis (Todorov, Shadmehr, & Bizzi, 1997), navigation of burning buildings by firefighters (Bliss, Tidwell, & Guest, 1997), astronaut training for Hubble space telescope repair (Cater & Huffman, 1995), and diagnostic and therapeutic care of casualties in combat environments (Chi, Clarke, Webber, & Bodler, 1996). However, in most cases, the research has focused on the development of technological capability, with the authors generally speculating on the application to performance in the real world but offering no transfer of training data that would support their claims.

The results of transfer of training studies have been somewhat equivocal. In the Todorov et al. (1997) study, transfer of the table tennis skill to real-world execution was undertaken and positive evidence of transfer was found. It is interesting to note that the Todorov et al. study embedded the use of VE in a learning study that was investigating the manipulation of augmented feedback for motor skill acquisition. This would seem to be supportive of Salas et al.'s (1998) call for merging of technology advancements with principles from training research. However, a second study by Kozak, Hancock, Arthur, and Chrysler (1993) that had participants acquire a speeded grasp-and-place action failed to find any advantage for initial exposure to the task in a VE over a control group with no previous task exposure.

What is apparent from a survey of the virtual reality literature is that an understanding of the technology and the application of this technology to the development of motor skill expertise is very much in its infancy. An integrated and comprehensive program of research is required that is directed at understanding the multiple potential applications of VEs for the training of motor skills. Speculations are that the findings that would result from this research effort will have much in common with the work done on simulator application. That is, it is likely that VEs will be most effective for the development of procedural skills, decision-making tasks, and judgment tasks, and less effective for the acquisition of the neuromuscular details of movement production.

In undertaking this research program, two issues in particular will need to be addressed. The first issue relates to the concept of *presence*. VEs are immersive technologies; the degree to which the user experiences the sensation of immersion is the presence. Some researchers have speculated that an increased sense of presence may be necessary to maximize the training and performance effect of VEs (Carlin, Hoffman, & Weghorst, 1997; Sheridan, 1992). However, Stanney and Salvendy (1998) argue that presence may be an epiphenomenon of VE and not related to training. If it is, then a causal connection between presence and training may result in a negative performance gain by incurring an internal focus of attention (see earlier discussion on focus of attention and instruction). Clearly, an understanding of the connection between presence and training is critical to the application of VEs for motor skill acquisition.

A second concern that must be addressed in virtual reality application is the occurrence of aftereffects that are quite commonly noted following VE immersion. Researchers have indicated that immersion in three-dimensional simulated environments create motion-sickness-like symptoms (e.g., eyestrain, ataxia, fatigue, drowsiness) and aftereffects such as visual flashback, disorientation, and balance disturbances, which can last up to 12 hours during the readaptation to normal environments (Kennedy, Lanham, Drexler, & Massey, 1997; Stanney & Salvendy, 1998). The health and safety concerns of such effects are readily apparent. This issue needs to be adequately addressed before widespread use of immersion technology is attempted.

The potential application of VE to the development of decision-making skills in sports is very exciting. In a recent article, Rickel and Johnson (1999) describe the development of a virtual reality system called STEVE (Soar Training Expert for Virtual Environments). They conclude that the training of complex tasks requires hands-on experience with the motor responses, mentoring, and the development of teamwork. STEVE is a three-dimensional, interactive simulation of a performance environment to promote training. The multiple actors that must integrate their actions for effective task performance can be represented simultaneously in the virtual workspace but do not have to be physically present in the same location. A mentor can observe and interact with the actors during the execution of the task, providing guidance and feedback. Although developed and applied in industrial settings, it is not difficult to envision a similar application in the development of teamwork skills in sports, which rely heavily on effective decision making and judgment.

Perspectives

The application of simulated environments in the training of motor skill performance is relatively widespread. Most common is the creation of simulation through the use of simulators; however, rapid advancements in computer technology have made access to VEs for training purposes more realistic. Despite this widespread use and acceptance, research and development of simulation tends to be technology-based and not learning-based. Little direct evidence exists that would suggest significant positive transfer of training from simulation to real-world performance.

This lack of direct evidence may not necessarily be due to simulators' ineffectiveness for motor skill acquisition; rather, it may be due to research design limitations. Currently, simulation design has been driven by the desire to create maximum realism in the simulation, based on an identical elements theoretical framework for transfer. Sufficient evidence has been acquired indicating that emphasizing realism may be misguided. The need is to understand simulation from a learner-centered approach, where the simulation technique is applied within a skill acquisition context. The strongest indications from the research are that simulation is most effective for cognitive learning, leading to the need to design simulations focused on the acquisition of procedures and decision-making capability. Placed within a transfer-appropriate processing and dynamic systems perspective, effective simulation is most likely achieved by designing simulations that allow the learner to explore in a relatively uncluttered environment what will be present in real-world performance contexts.

SUMMARY

If anything is certain in motor learning it is that there is no better, faster, more efficient way of achieving it than with practice. However, practice in and of itself can take many forms. In this chapter, we have described some of the factors related to practice that influence learning, with particular emphasis on the activity of the learner in this process. Though not an exhaustive list, the major activities of current research interest have been reviewed regarding the conditions, types, and forms of practice for motor learning. The result is a mixture of factors that influence learning in both early and later stages. Looking ahead, we wonder what issues will be discussed in a review of the research on practice in 10 or 20 years? Consistent with history, the issues of interest will probably be driven by theory, practical relevance, and methodology. In the absence of theoretical development, some of today's "hot topics" may no longer be of research interest, as seen earlier, for example, in the demise of research on distribution of practice effects (Adams, 1987). New theoretical interests will no doubt replace some areas that have currently captured the attention of motor learning researchers.

Certain research focused on practice effects in motor learning will probably continue to be driven by relevance to issues of practical application. Historically, there has been a close association between motor learning and physical education, sports, and ergonomics. Although these associations should continue to be of importance, more research will no doubt be conducted on practice effects for motor learning in the field of rehabilitation, and this appears to be an area for continued advancement. New technologies are evolving that will also foster continued research growth and offer exciting avenues of empirical study for the motor learning researcher. The emerging field of virtual environments has been discussed in this chapter as one in which research is being driven largely by technological interests and developments.

Another area that offers potential for the future of motor learning research is brain imaging. In fact, Williamham and colleagues have recently made dramatic advances in understanding the neuropsychological bases of motor control, and have even proposed that learning grows directly out of motor control processes (cf., Willingham, 1997a, 1997b, 1998, 1999). As technological advances permit more precise examinations of brain processes, there may well be an opportunity to define the nature of neurological change that accompanies practice and the attainment of skill.

In conclusion, research directed toward understanding how to best train athletes and other performers has been a dominant focus for motor behaviorists and sport psychology researchers alike. However, traditional questions remain concerning how to best structure and administer practice for optimal motor skill acquisition, and contemporary issues continue to engage in this area, ensuring that the study of practice will continue to be a ripe topic for future inquiry.

REFERENCES

Adams, J.A. (1971). A closed-loop theory of motor learning. *Journal of Motor Behavior, 3,* 111–150.

Adams, J.A. (1987). Historical review and appraisal of research on the learning, retention, and transfer of human motor skills. *Psychological Bulletin, 101,* 41–74.

Al-Ameer, H., & Toole, T. (1993). Combinations of blocked and random practice orders: Benefits to acquisition and retention. *Journal of Human Movement Studies, 25,* 177–191.

Anderson, D.I., Dialameh, N., Hilligan, P., Wong, K., & Wong, R. (1998). Learning a slalom-ski-simulator task with a template of correct performance and concurrent or terminal videotape feedback. *Journal of Sport & Exercise Psychology, 20,* S69.

Anderson, J.R. (1982). Acquisition of cognitive skill. *Psychological Review, 89,* 369–406.

Anderson, J.R., Conrad, F.G., & Corbett, A.T. (1989). Skill acquisition and the LISP tutor. *Cognitive Science, 13,* 467–506.

Andersson, R.L. (1993). A real experiment in virtual environments: A virtual batting cage. *Presence: Teleoperators and Virtual Environments, 2,* 16–33.

Ash, D.W., & Holding, D.H. (1990). Backward versus forward chaining in the acquisition of keyboard skill. *Human Factors, 32,* 139–146.

Baddeley, A.D., & Longman, D.J.A. (1978). The influence of length and frequency of training session on the rate of learning to type. *Ergonomics, 21,* 627–635.

Battig, W.F. (1966). Facilitation and interference. In E.A. Bilodeau (Ed.), *Acquisition of skill* (pp. 215–244). New York: Academic Press.

Battig, W.F. (1979). The flexibility of human memory. In L.S. Cermak & F.I.M. Craik (Eds.), *Levels of processing in human memory* (pp. 23–44). Hillsdale, NJ: Erlbaum.

Bell, H.H., & Waag, W.L. (1998). Evaluating the effectiveness of flight simulators for training combat skills: A review. *International Journal of Aviation Psychology, 8,* 223–242.

Berry, D.C. (1994). Implicit learning: Twenty-five years on a tutorial. In C. Umilta & M. Moscovitch (Eds.), *Attention and performance XV* (pp. 755–782). Cambridge, MA: MIT Press.

Berry, D.C. (1997). *How implicit is implicit learning?* New York: Oxford University Press.

Berry, D.C., & Broadbent, D.E. (1984). On the relationship between task performance and associated verbalisable knowledge. *Quarterly Journal of Experimental Psychology, 36,* 209–231.

Bjork, R.A. (1998). Assessing our own competence: Heuristics and illusions. In D. Gopher & A. Koriat (Eds.), *Attention and performance XVII. Cognitive regulation of performance: Interaction of theory and application* (pp. 435–459). Cambridge, MA: MIT Press.

Bliss, J.P., Tidwell, P.D., & Guest, M.A. (1997). The effectiveness of VR for administering spatial navigation training to firefighters. *Presence: Teleoperators and Virtual Environments, 6,* 73–86.

Bloom, B.S. (1985). *Developing talent in young people.* New York: Ballantine Books.

Bouchard, L.J., & Singer, R.N. (1998). Effects of the five step strategy with videotape modeling on performance of the tennis serve. *Perceptual and Motor Skills, 86,* 739–746.

Briggs, G.E., & Naylor, J.C. (1962). The relative efficiency of several training methods as a function of transfer task complexity. *Journal of Experimental Psychology, 64,* 505–512.

Briggs, G.E., & Walters, L.K. (1958). Training and transfer as a function of component interaction. *Journal of Experimental Psychology, 56,* 492–500.

Brisson, T.A., & Alain, C. (1996). Should common optimal movement patterns be identified as the criterion to be achieved? *Journal of Motor Behavior, 28,* 211–223.

Broadbent, D.E., & Aston, B. (1978). Human control of a simulated economic system. *Ergonomics, 21,* 1035–1043.

Broadbent, D.E., Fitzgerald, P., & Broadbent, M.H. (1986). Implicit and explicit knowledge in the control of complex systems. *British Journal of Psychology, 77,* 33–50.

Bryan, W.L., & Harter, N. (1897). Studies in the physiology and psychology of the telegraphic language. *Psychological Review, 4,* 27–53.

Bryan, W.L., & Harter, N. (1899). Studies on the telegraphic language: The acquisition of a hierarchy of habits. *Psychological Review, 6,* 345–375.

Buchner, A., & Wippich, W. (1998). Differences and commonalties between implicit learning and implicit memory. In M.A. Stadler & P.A. Frensch (Eds.), *Handbook of implicit learning* (pp. 3–46). Thousands Oaks, CA: Sage.

Carlin, A.S., Hoffman, H.G., & Weghorst, S. (1997). Virtual reality and tactile augmentation in the treatment of spider phobia: A case report. *Behavior Research and Therapy, 35,* 153–158.

Carroll, W.R., & Bandura, A. (1982). The role of visual monitoring in observational learning of action patterns: Making the unobservable observable. *Journal of Motor Behavior, 14,* 153–167.

Carroll, W.R., & Bandura, A. (1985). Role of timing of visual monitoring and motor rehearsal in observational learning of action patterns. *Journal of Motor Behavior, 17,* 269–281.

Carroll, W.R., & Bandura, A. (1987). Translating cognition into action: The role of visual guidance in observational learning. *Journal of Motor Behavior, 19,* 385–398.

Cater, J.P., & Huffman, S.D. (1995). Use of the remote access virtual environment network (RAVEN) for coordinated IVA-EVA astronaut training and evaluation. *Presence: Teleoperators and Virtual Environments, 4,* 103–109.

Chamberlin, C.J., & Lee, T.D. (1993). Arranging practice conditions and designing instruction. In R.N. Singer, M. Murphey, & K. Tennant (Eds.), *Handbook of research in sport psychology* (pp. 213–241). New York: Macmillan.

Charness, N., Krampe, R.T., & Mayr, U. (1996). The role of practice and coaching in entrepreneurial skill domains: An international comparison of life-span chess skill acquisition. In K.A. Ericsson (Ed.), *The road to excellence: The acquisition of expert performance in the arts and sciences* (pp. 51–80). Mahwah, NJ: Erlbaum.

Chase, W.G., & Ericsson, K.A. (1981). Skilled memory. In J.R. Anderson (Ed.), *Cognitive skills and their acquisition* (pp. 141–189). Hillsdale, NJ: Erlbaum.

Chase, W.G., & Ericsson, K.A. (1982). Skill and working memory. In G.H. Bower (Ed.), *The psychology of learning and motivation* (Vol. 16, pp. 1–58). New York: Academic Press.

Chi, D.M., Clarke, J.R., Webber, B.L., & Bodler, N.I. (1996). Casualty modelling for real-time medical training. *Presence: Teleoperators and Virtual Environments, 5,* 359–366.

Cleeremans, A. (1997). Principles for implicit learning. In D.C. Berry (Ed.), *How implicit is implicit learning?* (pp. 195–234). New York: Oxford University Press.

Collins, J.P., & Harden, R.M. (1998). AMEE medical education guide No. 13: Real patients, simulated patients and simulators in clinical examinations. *Medical Teacher, 20,* 508–521.

Crossman, E.R.F.W. (1959). A theory of acquisition of speed-skill. *Ergonomics, 2,* 153–166.

Decety, J., & Jeannerod, M. (1996). Mentally simulated movements in virtual reality: Does Fitts's law hold in motor imagery? *Behavioural Brain Research, 72,* 127–134.

Decety, J., Jeannerod, M., & Prablanc, C. (1989). The timing of mentally represented actions. *Behavioural Brain Research, 34,* 35–42.

Decety, J., & Michel, F. (1989). Comparative analysis of actual and mental movement times in two graphics tasks. *Brain and Cognition, 11,* 87–97.

Del Rey, P., Whitehurst, M., & Wood, J.M. (1983). Effects of experience and contextual interference on learning and transfer by boys and girls. *Perceptual and Motor Skills, 56,* 581–582.

Dennis, K.A., & Harris, D. (1998). Computer-based simulation as an adjunct to flight training. *International Journal of Aviation Psychology, 8,* 261–276.

Doody, S.G., Bird, A.M., & Ross, D. (1985). The effect of auditory and visual models on acquisition of a timing skill. *Human Movement Science, 4,* 271–281.

Edwards, J.M., Elliott, D., & Lee, T.D. (1986). Contextual interference effects during skill acquisition and transfer in Down's syndrome adolescents. *Adapted Physical Activity Quarterly, 3,* 250–258.

Ericsson, K.A., Chase, W.G., & Faloon, S. (1980). Acquisition of memory skill. *Science, 208,* 1181–1182.

Ericsson, K.A., Krampe, R.T., & Tesch-Römer, C. (1993). The role of deliberate practice in the acquisition of expert performance. *Psychological Review, 100,* 363–406.

Ericsson, K.A., & Polson, P.G. (1988). An experimental analysis of a memory skill for dinner-orders. *Journal of Experimental Psychology: Learning, Memory, and Cognition, 14,* 305–316.

Feltz, D.L., & Landers, D.M. (1983). The effects of mental practice on motor skill learning and performance: A meta-analysis. *Journal of Sport Psychology, 5,* 25–57.

Fitts, P.M., & Posner, M.I. (1967). *Human performance.* Belmont, CA: Brooks/Cole.

Fleishman, E.A. (1972). On the relationship between abilities, learning and human performance. *American Psychologist, 27,* 1017–1032.

Fleishman, E.A., & Hempel, W.E. (1954). Changes in factor structure of a complex psychomotor test as a function of practice. *Psychometrika, 19,* 239–252.

Fleishman, E.A., & Hempel, W.E. (1955). The relationship between abilities and improvement with practice in a visual discrimination reaction task. *Journal of Experimental Psychology, 49,* 301–311.

Gabriele, T.E., Hall, C.R., & Lee, T.D. (1989). Cognition in motor learning: Imagery effects on contextual interference. *Human Movement Science, 8,* 227–245.

Gentile, A.M. (1972). A working model of skill acquisition to teaching. *Quest, 17,* 3–23.

Gentile, A.M. (1987). Skill acquisition: Action, movement, and the neuromotor processes. In J.H. Carr, R.B. Shepard, I Gordon, A.M. Gentile, & J.M. Hind (Eds.), *Movement science: Foundations for physical therapy in rehabilitation* (pp. 93–154). Rockville, MD: Aspen Press.

Gentile, A.M. (1998). Implicit and explicit processes during acquisition of functional skills. *Scandinavian Journal of Occupational Therapy, 5,* 7–16.

Goode, S., & Magill, R.A. (1986). Contextual interference effects in learning three badminton serves. *Research Quarterly for Exercise and Sport, 57,* 308–314.

Gopher, D., Weil, M., & Siegel, D. (1989). Practice under changing priorities: An approach to training of complex skills. *Acta Psychologica, 71,* 147–177.

Gopher, L.D., Weil, M., & Bareket, T. (1994). Transfer of skill from a computer game trainer to flight. *Human Factors, 36,* 387–405.

Gordon, M.S., Issenberg, S.B., Mayer, J.W., & Felner, J.M. (1999). Developments in the use of simulators and multimedia computer systems in medical education. *Medical Teacher, 21,* 32–36.

Green, T.D., & Flowers, J.H. (1991). Implicit versus explicit learning processes in a probabilistic, continuous fine-motor catching task. *Journal of Motor Behavior, 23,* 293–300.

Hardy, L., Mullen, R., & Jones, G. (1996). Knowledge and conscious control of motor actions under stress. *British Journal of Psychology, 87,* 621–636.

Hautala, R.M. (1988). Does transfer of training help children learn juggling? *Perceptual and Motor Skills, 67,* 563–567.

Heitman, R.J., & Gilley, W.F. (1989). Effects of blocked versus random practice by mentally retarded subjects on learning a novel skill. *Perceptual and Motor Skills, 69,* 443–447.

Helsen, W., Starkes, J.L., & Hodges, N. (1998). Team sports and the theory of deliberate practice. *Journal of Sport & Exercise Psychology, 20,* 13–35.

Higgins, G.A., Merill, G.L., Hettinger, L.J., Kaufman, C.R., Champion, H.R., & Satava, R.M. (1997). New simulation technologies for surgical training and certification: Current status and future projections. *Presence: Teleoperators and Virtual Environments, 6,* 160–172.

Hird, J.S., Landers, D.M., Thomas, J.R., & Horan, J.J. (1991). Physical practice is superior to mental practice in enhancing cognitive and motor task performance. *Journal of Sport & Exercise Psychology, 13,* 281–293.

Hodges, N.J., & Franks, I.M. (1999). *Instructions and coordination bias on the learning of a novel bimanual coordination pattern.* Paper presented at the annual conference of the Canadian Society for Psychomotor Learning and Sport Psychology, Edmonton, Alberta, Canada.

Hodges, N.J., & Lee, T.D. (1999). The role of augmented information prior to learning a bimanual visual-motor coordination task: Do instructions of the movement pattern facilitate learning relative to discovery learning? *British Journal of Psychology, 90,* 389–403.

Hodges, N.J., & Starkes, J.L. (1996). Wrestling with the nature of expertise: A sport specific test of Ericsson, Krampe, and Tesch-Römer's (1993) theory of "Deliberate Practice." *International Journal of Sport Psychology, 27,* 1–25.

Howard, J.H., Jr., Mutter, S.A., & Howard, D.V. (1992). Serial pattern learning by event observation. *Journal of Experimental Psychology: Learning, Memory, and Cognition, 18,* 1029–1039.

Howe, M.J.A., Davidson, J.W., & Sloboda, J.A. (1998). Innate talents: Reality or myth? *Behavioral and Brain Sciences, 21,* 399–442.

Hughes, R., Brooks, R.B., Graham, D., Sheen, R., & Dickens, T. (1982). Tactical ground attack: On the transfer of training from flight simulator to operational Red Flag exercise. *Proceedings of the 4th Interservice/Industry Training Conference* (Vol. 1, pp. 127–130). Washington, DC: National Security Industrial Association.

Jeannerod, M. (1999). The 25th Bartlett lecture. To act or not to act: Perspectives on the representation of actions. *Quarterly Journal of Experimental Psychology, 52A,* 1–29.

Jentsch, F., & Bowers, C.A. (1998). Evidence for the validity of PC-based simulations in studying aircrew coordination. *International Journal of Aviation Psychology, 8,* 243–260.

Kelso, J.A.S. (1994). The informational character of self-organized coordination dynamics. *Human Movement Science, 13,* 393–413.

Kelso, J.A.S. (1995). *Dynamic patterns: The self-organization of brain and behavior.* Cambridge, MA: MIT Press.

Kennedy, R.S., Lanham, D.S., Drexler, J.M., & Massey, C.J. (1997). A comparison of cybersickness incidences, symptom profiles, measurement techniques, and suggestions for further research. *Presence: Teleoperators and Virtual Environments, 6,* 638–644.

Kerr, T., Hodges, N.J., & Starkes, J.L. (1999). *Unpublished data.* Burnaby, Canada: Simon Fraser University.

Klapp, S.T., Nelson, J.M., & Jagacinski, R.J. (1998). Can people tap concurrent bimanual rhythms independently? *Journal of Motor Behavior, 30,* 301–322.

Knapp, C.G., & Dixon, W.R. (1952). Learning to juggle: II. A study of whole and part methods. *Research Quarterly, 23,* 398–401.

Kohl, R.M., Ellis, S.D., & Roenker, D.L. (1992). Alternating actual and imagery practice: Preliminary theoretical considerations. *Research Quarterly for Exercise and Sport, 63,* 162–170.

Kohl, R.M., & Fisicaro, S.A. (1995). Imaging goal-directed movement. *Research Quarterly for Exercise and Sport, 66,* 17–31.

Koonce, J.M., & Bramble, W.J., Jr. (1998). Personal computer-based flight training devices. *International Journal of Aviation Psychology, 8,* 277–292.

Kozak, J.J., Hancock, P.A., Arthur, E.J., & Chrysler, S.T. (1993). Transfer of training from virtual reality. *Ergonomics, 36,* 777–784.

Larkin, J. (1981). Enriching formal knowledge: A model for learning how to solve textbook physics problems. In J.R. Anderson (Ed.), *Cognitive skills and their acquisition* (pp. 311–334). Hillsdale, NJ: Erlbaum.

Latash, M.L. (1993). *Control of human movement.* Champaign, IL: Human Kinetics.

Latash, M.L. (1996). The Bernstein problem: How does the central nervous system make its choices? In M.L. Latash & M.T. Turvey (Eds.), *Dexterity and its development* (pp. 277–303). Hillsdale, NJ: Erlbaum.

Lee, D.N., Lishman, J.R., & Thomson, J.A. (1984). Regulation of gait in long jumping. *Journal of Experimental Psychology: Human Perception and Performance, 8,* 448–459.

Lee, T.D. (1988). Transfer-appropriate processing: A framework for conceptualizing practice effects in motor learning. In O.G. Meijer & K. Roth (Eds.), *Complex movement behaviour: "The" motor-action controversy* (pp. 201–215). Amsterdam: Elsevier.

Lee, T.D., & Magill, R.A. (1983). The locus of contextual interference in motor-skill acquisition. *Journal of Experimental Psychology: Learning, Memory, and Cognition, 9,* 730–746.

Lee, T.D., & Magill, R.A. (1985). Can forgetting facilitate skill acquisition? In D. Goodman, R.B. Wilberg, & I.M. Franks (Eds.), *Differing perspectives in motor learning, memory, and control* (pp. 3–22). Amsterdam: Elsevier.

Lee, T.D., Magill, R.A., & Weeks, D.J. (1985). Influence of practice schedule on testing schema theory predictions in adults. *Journal of Motor Behavior, 17,* 283–299.

Lee, T.D., Schmidt, R.A., & Young, D.E. (in press). Skill learning: Conditions of training. In W. Karwowski (Ed.), *International encyclopedia of ergonomics and human factors.* London: Taylor & Francis.

Lee, T.D., & Swinnen, S.P. (1993). Three legacies of Bryan and Harter: Automaticity, variability and change in skilled performance. In J.L. Starkes & F. Allard (Eds.), *Cognitive issues in motor expertise* (pp. 295–315). Amsterdam: Elsevier.

Lee, T.D., Wishart, L.R., Cunningham, S., & Carnahan, H. (1997). Modeled timing information during random practice eliminates the contextual interference effect. *Research Quarterly for Exercise and Sport, 68,* 100–105.

Lersten, K.C. (1968). Transfer of movement components in a motor learning task. *Research Quarterly, 39,* 575–581.

Lewicki, P., Hill, T., & Bizot, E. (1988). Acquisition of procedural knowledge about a pattern of stimuli that cannot be articulated. *Cognitive Psychology, 20,* 24–37.

Lintern, G. (1991). An informational perspective on skill transfer in human-machine systems. *Human Factors, 33,* 251–266.

Lintern, G., Roscoe, S.N., Koonce, J.M., & Segal, L. (1990). Transfer of landing skills in beginning flight training. *Human Factors, 32,* 319–327.

Lintern, G., Roscoe, S.N., & Sivier, J.E. (1990). Display principles, control dynamics, and environmental factors in pilot training and transfer. *Human Factors, 32,* 299–317.

Maddox, M.D., Wulf, G., & Wright, D.L. (1999). The effect of an internal vs. external focus of attention on the learning of a tennis stroke. *Journal of Sport & Exercise Psychology, 21,* S78.

Magill, R.A. (1988). Activity during the post-knowledge of results interval can benefit motor skill learning. In O.G. Meijer & K. Roth (Eds.), *Complex movement behaviour: "The" motor-action controversy* (pp. 231–246). Amsterdam: Elsevier.

Magill, R.A. (1998a). Knowledge is more than we can talk about: Implicit learning in motor skill acquisition. *Research Quarterly for Exercise and Sport, 69,* 104–110.

Magill, R.A. (1998b). *Motor learning: Concepts and applications.* Boston: McGraw-Hill.

Magill, R.A., & Clark, R. (1997). *Implicit versus explicit learning of pursuit-tracking patterns.* Paper presented at the annual meeting of the North American Society for the Psychology of Sport and Physical Activity, Denver, CO.

Magill, R.A., & Hall, K.G. (1990). A review of the contextual interference effect in motor skill acquisition. *Human Movement Science, 9,* 241–289.

Magill, R.A., Schönfelder-Zohdi, B., & Hall, K.G. (1990). *Further evidence for implicit learning in a complex tracking task.* Paper presented at the 31st annual meeting of the Psychonomics Society, New Orleans, LA.

Magill, R.A., Sekiya, H., & Clark, R. (1995). *Amplitude effects on implicit learning in pursuit tracking* [Abstract]. Paper presented at the annual meeting of the North American Society for the Psychology of Sport and Physical Activity, Monterey, CA.

Mané, A.M. (1984). Acquisition of perceptual-motor skill: Adaptive and part-whole training. In *Proceedings of the Human Factors Society 28th annual meeting* (pp. 522–526). Santa Monica, CA: Human Factors Society.

Mané, A.M., Adams, J.A., & Donchin, E. (1989). Adaptive and part-whole training in the acquisition of a complex perceptual-motor skill. *Acta Psychologica, 71,* 179–196.

Manza, L., & Reber, A.S. (1997). Representing artificial grammars: Transfer across stimulus forms and modalities. In D.C. Berry (Ed.), *How implicit is implicit learning?* (pp. 73–106). New York: Oxford University Press.

Maraj, B., Allard, F., & Elliott, D. (1998). The effect of nonregulatory stimuli on the triple jump approach run. *Research Quarterly for Exercise and Sport, 69,* 129–135.

Masters, R.S.W. (1992). Knowledge, knerves and know-how. *British Journal of Psychology, 83,* 343–358.

Masters, R.S.W., Polman, R.C.J., & Hammond, N.V. (1993). "Reinvestment": A dimension of personality implicated in skill breakdown under pressure. *Personality and Individual Differences, 14,* 655–666.

Mathiowetz, V., & Wade, M.G. (1995). Task constraints and functional motor performance of individuals with and without multiple sclerosis. *Ecological Psychology, 7,* 99–123.

Maxwell, J., Masters, R., Eves, F., & MacMahon, K. (1999). From novice to no know-how: A longitudinal study of implicit motor learning [Communications to the third annual congress of the European College of Sport Science]. *Journal of Sports Sciences, 17,* 608.

McCracken, H.D., & Stelmach, G.E. (1977). A test of the schema theory of discrete motor learning. *Journal of Motor Behavior, 9,* 193–201.

Miller, G.A. (1956). The magical number seven, plus or minus two: Some limits on our capacity for processing information. *Psychological Review, 63,* 81–97.

Minas, S.C. (1977). Memory coding for movement. *Perceptual and Motor Skills, 45,* 787–790.

Naylor, J.C., & Briggs, G.E. (1963). Effects of task complexity and task organization on the relative efficiency of part and whole training methods. *Journal of Experimental Psychology, 65,* 217–224.

Newell, K.M. (1989). On task and theory specificity. *Journal of Motor Behavior, 21,* 92–96.

Newell, K.M. (1991). Motor skill acquisition. *Annual Review of Psychology, 42,* 213 -237.

Newell, K.M., Carlton, M.J., & Antoniou, A. (1990). The interaction of criterion and feedback information in learning a drawing task. *Journal of Motor Behavior, 22,* 8–20.

Newell, K.M., Carlton, M.J., Fisher, A.T., & Rutter, B.G. (1989). Whole-part training strategies for learning the response dynamics of microprocessor driven simulators. *Acta Psychologica, 71,* 197–216.

Newell, K.M., & McGinnis, P.M. (1985). Kinematic information feedback for skilled performance. *Human Learning, 4,* 39–56.

Ortiz, G.A. (1994). Effectiveness of PC-based flight simulation. *International Journal of Aviation Psychology, 4,* 285–291.

Ortiz, G.A. (1995). PC-based training: Cost effectiveness. In N. Johnston, R. Fuller, & N. McDonald (Eds.), *Aviation psychology: Training and selection* (pp. 209–214). Aldershot, England: Avebury Aviation.

Osgood, C.E. (1949). The similarity paradox in human learning: A resolution. *Psychological Review, 56,* 132–143.

Pew, R.W. (1974). Levels of analysis in motor control. *Brain Research, 71,* 393–400.

Pigott, R.E., & Shapiro, D.C. (1984). Motor schema: The structure of the variability session. *Research Quarterly for Exercise and Sport, 55,* 41 45.

Polanyi, M. (1958). *Personal knowledge: Towards a post-critical philosophy.* Chicago: University of Chicago Press.

Pollock, B.J., & Lee, T.D. (1997). Dissociated contextual interference effects in children and adults. *Perceptual and Motor Skills, 84,* 851–858.

Proctor, R.W., & Dutta, A. (1995). *Skill acquisition and human performance.* Thousand Oaks, CA: Sage.

Proteau, L. (1992). On the specificity of learning and the role of visual information for movement control. In L. Proteau & D. Elliott (Eds.), *Vision and motor control* (pp. 67–103). Amsterdam: Elsevier.

Reber, A.S. (1967). Implicit learning of artificial grammars. *Journal of Verbal Learning and Verbal Behavior, 6,* 855–863.

Reber, A.S. (1993). *Implicit learning and tacit knowledge: An essay on the cognitive unconscious.* New York: Oxford University Press.

Rickel, J., & Johnson, W.L. (1999). Animated agents for procedural training in virtual reality: Perception, cognition, and motor control. *Applied Artificial Intelligence, 13,* 343–382.

Rose, D.J. (1997). *A multilevel approach to the study of motor control and learning.* Boston: Allyn & Bacon.

Ross, D., Bird, A.M., Doody, S.G., & Zoeller, M. (1985). Effect of modeling and videotape feedback with knowledge of results on motor performance. *Human Movement Science, 4,* 149–157.

Salas, E., Bowers, C.A., & Rhodenizer, L. (1998). It is not how much you have but how you use it: Toward a rational use of simulation to support aviation training. *International Journal of Aviation Psychology, 8,* 197–208.

Schmidt, R.A. (1971). Retroactive interference and amount of original learning in verbal and motor tasks. *Research Quarterly, 42,* 314–326.

Schmidt, R.A. (1972). The case against learning and forgetting scores. *Journal of Motor Behavior, 4,* 79–88.

Schmidt, R.A. (1975). Schema theory of discrete motor skill learning. *Psychological Review, 82,* 225–260.

Schmidt, R.A., & Lee, T.D. (1999). *Motor control and learning: A behavioral emphasis* (3rd ed.). Champaign, IL: Human Kinetics.

Schneider, W. (1985). Training high-performance skills: Fallacies and guidelines. *Human Factors, 27,* 285–300.

Schneider, W., & Detweiler, M. (1988). The role of practice in dual-task performance: Towards workload modelling in a connectionist/control architecture. *Human Factors, 30,* 539–566.

Scully, D.M., & Newell, K.M. (1985). Observational learning and the acquisition of motor skills: Toward a visual perception perspective. *Journal of Human Movement Studies, 11,* 169–186.

Seger, C.A. (1994). Implicit learning. *Psychological Bulletin, 115,* 163–196.

Shaffer, L.H. (1981). Performances of Chopin, Bach, and Beethoven: Studies in motor programming. *Cognitive Psychology, 13,* 326–376.

Shapiro, D.C., & Schmidt, R.A. (1982). The schema theory: Recent evidence and developmental implications. In J.A.S. Kelso & J.E. Clark (Eds.), *The development of movement control and co-ordination* (pp. 113–150). New York: Wiley.

Shea, C.H., & Kohl, R.M. (1991). Composition of practice: Influence on the retention of motor skills. *Research Quarterly for Exercise and Sport, 62,* 187–195.

Shea, J.B., & Morgan, R.L. (1979). Contextual interference effects on the acquisition, retention, and transfer of a motor skill. *Journal of Experimental Psychology: Human Learning and Memory, 5,* 179–187.

Shea, J.B., & Zimny, S.T. (1983). Context effects in memory and learning movement information. In R.A. Magill (Ed.), *Memory and control of action* (pp. 345–366). Amsterdam: Elsevier.

Shea, J.B., & Zimny, S.T. (1988). Knowledge incorporation in motor representation. In O.G. Meijer & K. Roth (Eds.), *Complex movement behaviour: "The" motor-action controversy* (pp. 289–314). Amsterdam: Elsevier.

Sheridan, T. (1992). Musings on telepresence and virtual presence. *Presence: Teleoperators and Virtual Environments, 1,* 120–126.

Sherwood, D.E. (1994). Hand preference, practice order, and spatial assimilation in rapid bimanual movement. *Journal of Motor Behavior, 26,* 535–542.

Shiffrin, R.M., & Schneider, W. (1977). Controlled and automatic human information processing: II. Perceptual learning, automatic attending and a general theory. *Psychological Review, 84,* 127–190.

Singer, R.N., & Gaines, L. (1975). Effect of prompted and trial-and-error learning on transfer performance of a serial motor task. *American Educational Research Journal, 12,* 395–404.

Singer, R.N., & Janelle, C.M. (1999). Determining sport expertise: From genes to supremes. *International Journal of Sport Psychology, 30,* 117–150.

Singer, R.N., Lidor, R., & Cauraugh, J.H. (1993). To be aware or not aware? What to think about while learning and performing a motor skill. *The Sport Psychologist, 7,* 19–30.

Singer, R.N., & Pease, D. (1976). A comparison of discovery learning and guided instructional strategies on motor skill learning, retention, and transfer. *Research Quarterly, 47,* 788–796.

Snoddy, G.S. (1926). Learning and stability: A psychophysical analysis of a case of motor learning with clinical applications. *Journal of Applied Psychology, 10,* 1–36.

Stadler, M. (1989). On learning complex procedural knowledge. *Journal of Experimental Psychology: Learning, Memory, and Cognition, 15,* 1061–1069.

Stanney, K., & Salvendy, G. (1998). Aftereffects and sense of presence in virtual environments: Formulation of a research and development agenda. *International Journal of Human-Computer Interaction, 10,* 135–187.

Starkes, J.L., Deakin, J.M., Allard, F., Hodges, N.J., & Hayes, A. (1996). Deliberate practice in sports: What is it anyway? In K.A. Ericsson (Ed.), *The road to excellence: The acquisition of expert performance in the arts and sciences, sports and games* (pp. 81–106). Hillsdale, NJ: Erlbaum.

Starkes, J.L., Weir, P.L., Singh, P., Hodges, N.J., & Kerr, T. (1999). Aging and the retention of sport expertise. *International Journal of Sport Psychology, 30,* 283–301.

Summers, J.J., & Kennedy, T.M. (1992). Strategies in the production of a 5:3 polyrhythm. *Human Movement Science, 11,* 101–112.

Taylor, H.L., & Lintern, G. (1993). Quasi-transfer as a predictor of transfer from simulator to airplane. *Journal of General Psychology, 120,* 257–276.

Taylor, H.L., Lintern, G., Koonce, J.M., Kaiser, R.H., & Morrison, G.A. (1991). Transfer of training and quasi-transfer of scene detail and visual augmentation guidance in landing training. *Proceedings of training transfer: Can we trust flight simulation?* (pp. 6.1–6.4). London: Royal Aeronautical Society.

Thorndike, E.L. (1914). *Educational psychology.* New York: Columbia University Press.

Todorov, E., Shadmehr, R., & Bizzi, E. (1997). Augmented feedback presented in a virtual environment accelerates learning of a difficult motor task. *Journal of Motor Behavior, 29,* 147–158.

van Emmerik, R.E.A., den Brinker, B.P.L.M., Vereijken, B., & Whiting, H.T.A. (1989). Preferred tempo in the learning of a gross cyclical action. *Quarterly Journal of Experimental Psychology, 41A,* 251–262.

van Rossum, J.H.A. (1990). Schmidt's schema theory: The empirical base of the variability of practice hypothesis. A critical analysis. *Human Movement Science, 9,* 387–435.

Vereijken, B. (1991). *The dynamics of skill acquisition.* Meppel, The Netherlands: Kripps Repro.

Vereijken, B., & Whiting, H.T.A. (1989). In defence of discovery learning. In P.C.W. van Wieringen & R.J. Bootsma (Eds.), *Catching up: Selected essays of H.T.A. Whiting* (pp. 155–169). Amsterdam: Free University Press.

Vereijken, B., Whiting, H.T.A., & Beek, W.J. (1992). A dynamical systems approach to skill acquisition. *Quarterly Journal of Experimental Psychology, 45A,* 323–344.

Whiting, H.T.A. (1980). Dimensions of control in motor learning. In G.E. Stelmach & J. Requin (Eds.), *Tutorials in motor behavior* (pp. 537–550). Amsterdam: North Holland.

Whiting, H.T.A., Bijlard, M.J., & den Brinker, B.P.L.M. (1987). The effect of the availability of a dynamic model on the acquisition of a complex cyclical action. *Quarterly Journal of Experimental Psychology, 39A,* 43–59.

Whiting, H.T.A., & den Brinker, B.P.L.M. (1982). Image of the act. In J.P. Das, R.F. Mulcahy, & A.E. Wall (Eds.), *Theory and research in learning disabilities* (pp. 217–235). New York: Plenum Press.

Wightman, D.C., & Lintern, G. (1985). Part-task training for tracking and manual control. *Human Factors, 27,* 267–283.

Wightman, D.C., & Sistrunk, F. (1987). Part-task training strategies in simulated carrier landing final-approach training. *Human Factors, 29,* 245–254.

Willingham, D.B. (1997a). Implicit and explicit memory do not differ in flexibility: Comment on Dienes and Berry (1997). *Psychonomic Bulletin and Review, 4*(4), 587–591.

Willingham, D.B. (1997b). Response-to-stimulus interval does not affect implicit motor sequence learning, but does affect performance. *Memory and Cognition, 25*(4), 534–542.

Willingham, D.B. (1998). A neuropsychological theory of motor skill learning. *Psychological Review, 105*(3), 558–584.

Wright, D.L. (1991). The role of intertask and intratask processing in acquisition and retention of motor skills. *Journal of Motor Behavior, 23,* 139–145.

Wulf, G., Höss, M., & Prinz, W. (1998). Instructions for motor learning: Differential effects of internal vs. external focus of attention. *Journal of Motor Behavior, 30,* 169–179.

Wulf, G., Lauterbach, B., & Toole, T. (1998). *Learning benefits of an external focus of attention in golf.* Paper presented at the annual meeting of the North American Society for the Psychology of Sport and Physical Activity, Denver, CO.

Wulf, G., Shea, C.H., & Matschiner, S. (1998). Frequent feedback enhances complex motor skill learning. *Journal of Motor Behavior, 30,* 180–192.

Wulf, G., & Weigelt, C. (1997). Instructions in learning a complex motor skill: To tell or not to tell. *Research Quarterly for Exercise and Sport, 68,* 362–367.

Yan, J.H., Thomas, J.R., & Thomas, K.T. (1998). Children's age moderates the effect of practice variability: A quantitative review. *Research Quarterly for Exercise and Sport, 69,* 210–215.

Young, D.E., Cohen, M.J., & Husak, W.S. (1993). Contextual interference and motor skill acquisition: On the processes that influence retention. *Human Movement Science, 12,* 577–600.

Young, D.E., & Schmidt, R.A. (1992). Augmented kinematic feedback for motor learning. *Journal of Motor Behavior, 24,* 261–273.

Zanone, P.G., & Kelso, J.A.S. (1992). Evolution of behavioral attractors with learning: Nonequilibrium phase transitions. *Journal of Experimental Psychology: Human Perception and Performance, 18,* 403–421.

Zanone, P.G., & Kelso, J.A.S. (1997). Coordination dynamics of learning and transfer: Collective and component levels. *Journal of Experimental Psychology: Human Perception and Performance, 23,* 1454–1480.

CHAPTER 6

An Integrative Modeling Approach to the Study of Intentional Movement Behavior

KEITH DAVIDS, MARK WILLIAMS, CHRIS BUTTON, and MICK COURT

Developing an understanding of the processes involved in movement coordination, control, and skill acquisition has been a key challenge for motor behavior theorists for decades (for historical reviews, see Glencross, Whiting, & Abernethy, 1994; Williams, Davids, Burwitz, & Williams, 1992; Williams, Davids, & Williams, 1999). Once the processes behind motor behavior are understood, the nature of interventions to enhance sport performance may be clarified. Motor behavior modeling, generally, falls into two broad categories: structural and phenomenological (Beek, Peper, & Stegeman, 1995). Structural modeling involves the search for dedicated neural structures and mechanisms underlying movement behavior. This type of work is typically undertaken by neuropsychologists who collate and synthesize empirical research on the human nervous system (e.g., Arbib, Érdi, & Szentágothai, 1998; Milner & Goodale, 1995; Willingham, 1998). Phenomenological modeling seeks the development of laws and principles of motor behavior, without necessarily making explicit reference to the mechanisms and structures of the human nervous system.

In the past few decades, two significant phenomenological models of movement coordination and control have been proposed (see Meijer & Roth, 1988; Summers, 1992; Van Gelder, 1998; Williams et al., 1999). In cognitive science accounts of movement coordination and control, the base metaphor views the mind as a kind of computer capable of forming symbolic representations in the central nervous system (CNS) during goal-directed behavior. Computational accounts are typically hierarchical in organization and implement a level of functional modeling between analysis of nervous system structure and movement system dynamics. Functional computational modeling purports to capture the putative information processing basis of

perception and action, how motor behavior is determined by cognitions, intentions, emotions, and memories, and how representations are acquired to control movements (e.g., Arbib et al., 1998; Proteau, Tremblay, & DeJaeger, 1998; Schmidt & Lee, 1999; Willingham, 1998). Alternatively, there are a group of interrelated theories forming the ecological approach[1] that take physical processes of self-organization as a basis for the emergence of coordination and control in biological movement systems (see Kelso, 1995; Michaels & Beek, 1996). An important distinction is that, in the ecological approach, the role of cognitions and intentions is viewed as setting up self-assembly (i.e., leading to the emergence of self-organized behavior), not explicitly controlling such processes during movement coordination (Meijer, 1988). In this respect, dynamic self-assembly of natural systems is constrained but not determined by cognitive processes such as intentions, perceptions, and memories (Carello, Turvey, Kugler, & Shaw, 1984).

In this chapter, we argue that explanatory accounts of the processes of coordination and control in human movement systems will require an integrative approach, in which structural and phenomenological modeling are mutually constraining. We argue that an integrative approach provides an excellent platform for understanding how cognition and dynamics support goal-directed movement behavior. The aim is to build on recent discussions of the potential for integration of ideas from cognitive science

---

[1] For brevity, we use the encompassing term "ecological approach" to describe concepts and ideas from dynamical systems theory, coordination dynamics, ecological psychology, and synergetics.

and dynamical systems theory (e.g., Bongaardt, 1996; Colley, 1989; Davids, Handford, & Williams, 1994; Pressing, 1998; Summers, 1992, 1998; van Wieringen, 1988).

This endeavor was exemplified by Colley (1989), who proposed three different routes in the nervous system for perception and action. The first route, mediated by processes in working memory, is used in instances such as learning and cognitively mediated behavior. The second, more automatic route, is used during well-rehearsed tasks and is apparently subserved by internal representations. The final route is capable of exploiting the design of the nervous system, facilitating direct links between the perceptual and action subsystems. A tight coupling among these subsystems emerges with experience and practice, with cognitive constraints typically playing a minimal role in supporting action.

The arguments proposed in these early integrative modeling attempts have been strengthened by recent work on the neurophysiological basis of perception and action (e.g., Harris & Jenkin, 1998; Milner & Goodale, 1995). Progress in neuroscience research during the past decade is beginning to have considerable influence in developing understanding of the relationship between cognition and self-organization in the movement system. For example, Goodale and Humphrey's (1998) work on the visual system highlighted a possible avenue for integration through consideration of two different cortical pathways for visual perception (see also Goodale & Milner, 1992). The first has associations with brain areas related to memory and may be considered to support the idea of cognitive constraints on goal-directed behavior. The second has cortical connections with the motor areas of the brain and is harmonious with the perception-action coupling route highlighted by Colley (1989).

Discussions are advanced by posing the guiding question: How can an integrated framework for understanding processes of movement coordination and control be informed by recent developments in the key subdisciplines of dynamical systems theory, ecological psychology, cognitive science, and the neurosciences? Interestingly, an integrative approach is not new. Perhaps the most influential figure in the study of coordination in movement systems, Bernstein (1967), disliked dichotomization of the theoretical field of movement science and sought to provide coherence among different approaches (see Bongaardt, 1996). To achieve integration, Newell's (1986) constraints model will be discussed as an important framework for sport psychologists and motor behaviorists interested in merging concepts such as self-organization, emergence under

constraint, intentionality, cognitions, perception, action, and processes of pattern formation and selection in the CNS (see also Davids, Bennett, Handford, & Jones, 1999; Handford, Davids, Bennett, & Button, 1997; Williams et al., 1999). The links between recent work on intentionality and variability in movement systems, within the constraints-led framework, will also be explored. Finally, the implications of an integrated approach for practical applications in sport including skill acquisition will be explored.

Perhaps the key question in the study of coordination and control concerns what proportion of movement behavior is controlled through the implementation of internalized movement representations, and how much is due to self-organization arising among motor system components (Meijer, Wagenaar, & Blankendaal, 1988). In the first part of this chapter, this issue is examined by exploring the validity of the computational approach to motor behavior. In the second part, arguments are fleshed out concerning how the question raised originally will be revealed through the development of an integrated modeling approach. However, to begin, two recently perceived weaknesses in the ecological approach are highlighted to open up an evaluation of computational cognitive science.

PERCEIVED WEAKNESSES IN THE ECOLOGICAL APPROACH TO MOVEMENT COORDINATION AND CONTROL

The first potential weakness of the ecological approach was identified by Summers (1998) as the lack of contact between concepts of pattern formation in dynamical system theory and knowledge about the neurophysiology of movement. As Carson and Riek (1998) put it, "In practice, contemporary dynamical accounts of coordination are expressed via phenomenological modeling schemes in which few assumptions are made regarding levels of observation beyond the behavioral" (p. 209). This is surprising given that Bernstein (1967) proposed that a full account of coordination in movement systems would need to consider mechanical, anatomical, and physiological mechanisms. As long ago as the 1940s, he recognized the need for phenomenological modeling to constrain and be constrained by knowledge of nervous system function. He argued that attempts to understand brain function should be "rooted in the evolution of morphology and behavior, dominated by the action of large populations of neurons acting as collectives, and regulated by modulatory systems" (Spoorns & Edelman, 1998, p. 283). More recently, it has been argued that claims in important dynamical models, such as coordination dynamics, to have a fundamentally abstract basis, may no longer be sustainable once the evolutionary development of neurophysiological mechanisms in the human movement system have been fully revealed (Carson & Riek, 1998).

The second perceived weakness is that important theoretical concepts such as self-organization and constraints are poorly defined. For example, Beek et al. (1995) remarked, "Unfortunately, the notion of self-organization is interpreted by some movement scientists as a kind of mystical ability, according to which movements come out of the blue. This is giving an incorrect ontological twist to the concept" (p. 577). Advances in mathematics, physics, and chemistry have demonstrated how internal and external constraints on behavior can lead to pressure for change and the emergence of spontaneous pattern formation in inanimate systems (e.g., Kauffmann, 1993, 1995; Kelso, 1995). These theoretical developments can help motor behavior theorists understand how order, available in nature "for free," can be exploited by intending biological systems (e.g., humans engaged in goal-directed activity during sport) needing to adapt to more immediate constraints on behavior (Kauffmann, 1993, 1995; Kugler, Shaw, Vicente, & Kinsella-Shaw, 1990). In the coming years, the challenge for sport psychologists will be to gain a greater understanding of the broad range of constraints on human movement behavior, including situational constraints such as intentions, cognitions, emotions, and instructions. What is needed is an explanatory account of the relationship between fundamental processes of self-organization at all levels of the movement system and the specific situational constraints on athletes in different sport contexts.

Taken together, these issues in the ecological framework point to the need to provide a meaningful explanation of processes of movement coordination and control, incorporating a multidisciplinary perspective, emphasizing the latest developments in the related research areas of cognitive science, dynamical systems theory, the neurosciences, and ecological psychology. This proposal is an advance on the position advocated in an earlier review paper (Davids et al., 1994), which has recently received increasing support (e.g., see Carson & Riek, 1998; Summers, 1998). But what exactly does integrated modeling mean? An integrated modeling approach to the study of brain processes and movement behavior is grounded in the view that the provision of an adequate theoretical account must be constrained by neuroscientific knowledge of the CNS and enriched by phenomenological modeling (see Bruce, Green, & Georgeson, 1996). Arbib et al. (1998) proposed that such an integrated, multilevel analysis is required to help interpret the structure, function, and dynamics of brain and behavior.

The goal of mapping mental processes to specific brain structures in the neurosciences needs to be supplemented with the provision of a theoretical framework for understanding how such processes are achieved by humans (Kelso, 1995; McCrone, 1999). Indeed, Freeman (1997) recently expressed his frustration at the way "most researchers still try to find memories in the temporal lobe, emotions in the amygdala, cognitive maps in the hippocampus, linguistic operations in Broca's and Wernicke's areas, holistic thinking in the right hemisphere . . . and so on" (p. 292). This form of reductionism is detrimental to the development of a coherent theoretical framework for explaining the processes involved in movement behavior.

In cognitive science, this weakness is beginning to be tackled, and integrative modeling has been implemented in the development of recent computational models of perceptual-motor behavior (e.g., Arbib et al., 1998). However, a major difficulty with computational functional modeling that is putatively constrained by neuroscientific advances is the lack of clarity in the definition of how key terms, such as "coding," "representations," and "computation," may be operationalized in the study of nervous system processes. To exemplify these arguments, one recent attempt to relate structure, function, and dynamics in a computational framework, Willingham's (1998) control-based learning theory (COBALT) of motor learning, will be examined.

THE COMPUTATIONAL BASIS OF COGNITIVE SCIENCE EXPLANATIONS OF MOTOR BEHAVIOR: THE EXAMPLE OF COBALT

Willingham (1998) proposed COBALT as an attempt to provide a motor learning theory constrained by knowledge of motor control processes. In COBALT, current knowledge of neural processes has been linked with computational constructs to explain the roles of imagery and observational learning in practice as well as the effects of emotions on cognitions during motor performance. According to COBALT, motor learning results in the acquisition of a number of different types of representations in the brain based on features of the world, intentions, or sequential patterns of spatial locations or specific muscle forces. In cognitive science explanations of motor learning, according to Willingham (1998), the nature of the representation in the CNS implies a "copy theory of knowledge" in which information about the world can be symbolically represented and stored. To exemplify this point, it was argued that performance of a sequence of movements, such as during a tennis serve, is based on a learned egocentric representation of the "knowledge of a sequence of locations to which one should respond" (Willingham, 1998, p. 574).

According to Globus (1995), computational theories of mind, brain, and behavior are "functionalist." Functionalism, in this sense, refers to the equivalence believed to exist between the brain's neural tissue and the hardware components (e.g., transistors and silicon chips) of a computer. In computational accounts, the brain is the hardware of the information processing system and mental processes are system software that logically operate on representations of the world (Johnson-Laird, 1993). But how well does this type of functional modeling stand up to scrutiny? How relevant is it to the study of nervous system processes in biological movement systems? In the following sections, computational functional modeling is subjected to critical analysis, focusing particularly on the extent to which it has been constrained by advances in the neurosciences. An alternative idea that will be considered is that mental life in humans evolves from physical, biological, psychological, and social processes acting as constraints, and is not produced by special substances composing representations and codes (Keil & Davids, 2000).

THE COMPUTATIONAL BASIS OF COGNITIVE SCIENCE: A CRITICAL EVALUATION

In many early cognitive science theories of brain and behavior, the process of representational transformation assumes computation to be "largely independent of the structure and mode of development of the nervous system" (Edelman, 1992, p. 13; see also Globus, 1995). Computational-based cognition involves manipulating symbols in an abstract and rule-governed manner according to a syntax (Edelman, 1992; Globus, 1992, 1995). Computers exemplify "digital thinking" in which the world can be neatly reduced to objectively understood symbols, exemplified by the use of terms such as "coding" and "computation" in COBALT. The concept of a computational brain implies that cognitions, perception, and action operate according to a rule-governed process in which internalized representations are transformed during learning (Blumberg & Wasserman, 1995; Edelman, 1992; Globus, 1995; Kelso, 1995; Pickering, 1997). Like a computer, the brain "reads" symbolic representations semantically.

In computational neuroscience, although it is claimed that the cognitive science assumption of the distinctiveness between brain and computer processes is not made, the evidence does not always support such arguments. For instance, Globus (1992, 1995) has highlighted as "paradigmatic" in cognitive neuroscience the assumption that brains perform computations on symbolic representations. He pointed out that the stated purpose of the *Journal of Cognitive Neuroscience* is to "bridge the gap between descriptions of information processing and specifications of brain activity" (Globus, 1992, p. 299). The view that this goal is key for many neuroscientists seems to be borne out by frequent references to such an enterprise in the literature. This assumption was captured by Sejnowski, Koch, and Churchland (1988), who described the study of brain and behavior as a concerted effort to "explain how electrical and chemical signals are used in the brain to represent and process information" (p. 1299). Jeannerod (1997) also referred to the "neurophysiologist's dream" as that of studying "a representing brain," from which it can be deduced how "motor actions are neurally represented and coded." Finally, the idea that both minds and machines are programmable was captured by Arbib et al. (1998) in their proposal that "a schema is like a computer program but with the special property that its instances can be combined with other simultaneously active programs to provide the ability of an organism or robot to perceive, or act within, its world" (p. 41). In the following sections, it is argued that functional computational modeling does not provide an empirically verifiable account of how motor control processes underpin motor learning. The biggest weakness in this approach seems to be that it is underconstrained by understanding of the evolution of the nervous system (Keil & Davids, 2000).

Functional Computational Modeling

In theories like COBALT, a fundamental issue concerns the tradition of accepting the existence of internalized representations as mechanisms of motor control a priori to scientific verification. Some motor learning theorists do not necessarily view this weakness as anything more than a temporary "glitch." For example, with reference to the widespread use of representations in traditional motor behavior theory, Weeks and Proctor (1991) acknowledged that the "approach afforded by the information processing framework provides only tentative explanations for behavioral phenomena" (p. 292). However, their argument is tempered with the notion that sport psychologists interested in motor behavior should be willing to "evaluate the inclusion of mental representations 'as if' they had construct validity" (p. 294). This process has occurred in other scientific subdisciplines. For example, in statistical mechanics in the physical sciences, hypothetical constructs were needed to initiate and build up phenomenology to the level of magnets or thermodynamics. The fundamental question to be considered is: Why should cognitive neuroscience be different?

Superficially, a computer might seem a useful analogy for how brains perceive and act in complex information-rich environments such as sport. However, just because, in the engineering and computer sciences, an algorithm can be written for a machine to act as a sensing device does not constitute an explanation for perception and action in biological systems (Edelman, 1992; Kelso, 1995). This type of traditional black-box modeling of computation in motor learning processes, exemplified in COBALT, suffers from a lack of conceptual definition. Problems occur due to the lack of an explicit and detailed theoretical framework with which to interpret terms like coding and transformation, and with which to specify the role of computations and representations.

In COBALT, explanations of how processes like coding and computation intervene during motor learning seem to be captured in the view that existing "behavioral and neural studies have provided a broad framework that is more or less agreed upon" (Willingham, 1998, p. 559). The implication is that there is little need to define the meaning of such terms because of the broad level of conceptual agreement in psychology concerning motor control processes. Willingham (1998) is correct in highlighting the broad agreement among most motor behavior theorists that the key processes to explain are intentionality, cognitions, perception, and action. However, as shall be outlined later, many diverse theoretical approaches exist to explain how these processes support motor behavior, some of which reject the computer metaphor in preference to neurobiological explanations.

Are Brains Like Computers?

At one level of description, the brain does appear to resemble a kind of organic computing device. The on-off nature of neuronal activity, coupled with the seemingly point-to-point architecture, imply a digital character. But what is the evidence from biology for the view that comparisons of the brain with the hardware and software of electronic computers are inadequate? First, it is apparent that biological nervous systems develop in highly variable ways. They are perhaps best understood as embedded, complex, "open"

systems whose microcomponents are continually modifying and adapting their structural organization in response to a range of constraints (Davids & Bennett, 1998; Freeman, 1999, 2000a, 2000b). The hardware components of the neural landscape are variable and emergent, being dynamically modified in the form of continuous cell migration, death, adherence, and differentiation.

However, there is also a high degree of individual variability in the anatomical structure of different regions of the human brain (Edelman, 1992). A population of neurons may vary in both structure and function, with microanatomical differentiation occurring in size, shape, position, and connective patterning. At the biochemical level of analysis, the dynamics of neural transmission can also be affected by variations in the flow of ions such as sodium and potassium through channel "gates" (Kelso, 1995). Edelman (1992) has termed the variability in the cortical substrate in individual brains "degeneracy." A degenerate anatomical structure in the population of cortical neurons underlies an adaptive capacity to learn how to perceive and act in complex, dynamically changing environments. Flexibility and novelty of behavior is enhanced by degeneracy in the CNS in many ways. For example, variant groups of neurons can support the performance of similar behavioral functions more or less well, a concept that has been termed "equifinality" (e.g., Kelso, 1995). Moreover, there is a huge degree of integration in the nervous system, as evidenced by the response of structures to neural activity originating in many sensory modalities. Indeed, it appears that even regions previously conceived as unimodal respond to the convergence of sensory inputs from different perceptual systems (Walsh, 2000; Stoffregen & Bardy, 2001).

Clearly, representational accounts based on symbolic information storage do not sit well in such a dynamic, integrated description of the nervous systems of cognitive agents. The dynamic nature of the constraints on biological nervous systems makes it virtually impossible to isolate digital inputs and to trace the symbolic transformation of information within the system. Electrochemical communication between directly (point-to-point) and indirectly (via the vast network of integrated feedback loops) connected neurons, involving states of polarization or depolarization, resembles a form of "pseudo-digitality" in biological nervous systems. Rather, it will be argued that stabilities and instabilities, critical fluctuations, and pattern formation in the interconnected neural landscape under constraint favors a dynamical systems perspective for cognitive functions such as memories, perception, and attention (Kelso,

1995). This argument is exemplified in the next section, where the relationship between computation and representational coding in the CNS is deconstructed.

Coding

Brains and computers are believed to be logical devices, both of which use codes to compute transformations to existing representations of objects and events. In the functionalist approach, the mechanics of how brain tissue actually computes, encodes, and transforms representations is of little concern (Globus, 1995). In COBALT, the coding process is exemplified with reference to the task constraints of reaching and grasping. A spatially coded representation of an object in allocentric space (i.e., a coordinate system based on relative spatial location in the environment) is transformed into a representation in egocentric space (i.e., perception of the object's location relative to an effector in the individual's movement system). A final transformation occurs as the egocentric representation is encoded into a dynamic representation of the specific muscle forces needed to reach and grasp the object. The details of how spinal interneurons actually compute the transformation of a spatially encoded representation of an object to a representation of the specific muscle forces required for reaching to grasp it are not a primary concern.

Willingham (1998) proposed the setting of movement goals or engaging in intentional behavior as the "coding of behavioral significance" (p. 560). It was argued that movement goals are "coded" into representations at the different levels of the hierarchically organized CNS. For example, movement planning is apparently coded in allocentric space in the dorsolateral frontal cortex. It was also argued that, in the primary motor cortex, movements are spatially coded into an egocentric representation as perceptual-motor processes transform the allocentric representation of intended movement. During growth and development, this transformational process operates continually to allow children to cope with the rapidly changing scale of their limbs. The result is that presumably "there must be some adjustment of the transformation between behavioral goals (which are represented in allocentric space) and spatial targets (which are represented in egocentric space)" (p. 565).

During learning, the sequencing of a movement is tuned continually as an action is completed. Using a tennis serve, for example, Willingham (1998) hypothesized that during the sequencing process, "the goal is to stereotype the stroke; one would like the movements to be identical every time it is executed" (p. 565). At the spinal interneurons, the specific pattern of muscle forces needed to achieve a movement goal needs to be represented by a different code understood by the musculature. Willingham proposed, "It is clear that eventually the neural code must be in terms of muscle commands" (p. 562), and because the primary motor cortex projects to the spinal interneurons, it is claimed that this is the site of the transformation of the spatially coded representation to a motor representation. Thus, in regard to reaching in space, Willingham proposed that "interneurons seem to have the property of acting as networks that translate desired endpoints in space into patterns of muscle forces (through motoneurons) that move an effector to a spatial location" (p. 562).

Is the Concept of Coding Neurally Plausible?

There are a number of general issues surrounding functional computational modeling accounts of coding transformation in the CNS. These issues are related to the problem in cognitive science of developing functional models that are computationally tractable and constrained by neuroscientific knowledge. This point was well captured by Bugmann (1997), who suggested that, in traditional computational modeling, "Generally, there has not been careful verification that abstract computational units are decomposable into simpler functions compatible with biological neurons" (p. 12). For example, in COBALT, there is a need for a tractable, well-constrained representational account specifying how translation could plausibly occur between different sensory pathways in biological movement systems. Although the claim in COBALT is that it is constrained by neuroscientific understanding, processes such as coding in biological nervous systems are somewhat ill-defined. The transformation of codes used in constructing different types of representations, such as the perceptual and motor variety, has been neglected in cognitive neuroscience as much as it was in cognitive science.

To exemplify, a specific question in COBALT is: How does the neural code get changed from the spatial coding of movement location to the coding of the specific muscle forces used in a movement pattern? Willingham (1998) argued, "It is clear that eventually the neural code must be in terms of muscle command" (p. 562). The black-box approach to this thorny question, adopted by Willingham, allocated a role as code translator to interneurons at the level of the spinal cord. Somehow, it seems that interneurons transform the representation coding spatial location of objects to be grasped into a representation of the muscle forces for achieving the grasp. The process of changing codes is never clarified. Moreover, a further issue with this explanation is that the evidence on which the coding conjecture is based is rather weak and tentative. This point was recognized by Willingham, who stated that the data "are from amphibia and must be treated with caution in consideration of human movement" (p. 562). An additional problem with hypothetical accounts of how intentions become translated into actions is that often several types of representations and codes are required in the CNS, implying the need for "translators" and "controllers" in the CNS (e.g., Arbib et al., 1998).

It appears that COBALT is an example of a weak computation theory, which Globus (1995) distinguishes from strong computation theory by the manner in which it "vacuously skirts the issue of how the computation is actually done and thus is divorced from neuroscience" (p. 61). Weak computational theories dominate cognitive science, a bias that adds to the general lack of clarity on the putative role of representations and on how different codes are translated by structures within the CNS as representations. An example of this attitude may be observed in Marks' (1999) recent review of the main drawbacks of cognitive theories of imagery. Marks proclaimed that cognitive theories tended to represent cognitive processes as if they were disembodied. He also highlighted the fact that, typically, no attempt is made to integrate processes of imagery and cognition with a theory of action. The underlying weakness in the arguments he proposed, however, is captured in the rationale for the selection of research studies to critique. It was proposed that "For theoretical reasons, an experiential rather than a behavioral or physiological perspective is taken" (Marks, 1999, p. 567), and only those studies examining the subjective reports of imagery experience were evaluated.

Another recent example of the liberal introduction of hypothetical constructs in explaining functionality in brain and behavior is captured in Arbib et al.'s (1998) proposal of schema as a unit of functional analysis intervening between the neural structure and movement system dynamics. The original conceptualization of schema as "a product . . . of pure a priori imagination" proposed by Kant (1781/1929, p. 182) was rejected for a description of them as "biologically rooted entities that evolve and develop" (Arbib et al., 1998, p. 37). However, the well-known issue of establishing the location of the schema in biological nervous systems was side-stepped by presenting "schema theory as a framework for the rigorous analysis of behavior that requires no prior commitment to hypotheses on the localization of each schema" (p. 33).

The Question of Abstractness in Cognitive Science and Dynamical Systems Modeling

Thus far, we have proposed arguments that computational accounts of processes of brain and behavior suffer from a lack of conceptual definition due to unconstrained functional modeling and the implementation of concepts and ideas that are difficult to empirically verify. However, theorists who adhere to a cognitive science approach to understanding perception and action might contend that dynamical systems theorists are equally abstract in their theoretical orientations. That is, terms such as self-organization, intentionality, attractor states, state space, invariants, and affordances, to name but a few, at first glance appear to be equally abstract in conception to terms such as coding, transformation, and representation.

However, there are good reasons for distinguishing between the abstractness in concepts from cognitive science and that in dynamical systems theory. In cognitive science theories, the abstractness is based on the need for complementary modeling in which a separate layer of conceptualization is needed to functionally model the role of cognitive processes in movement system behavior (Meijer & Bongaardt, 1992; Pattee, 1979). An implicit assumption is that one model cannot describe all these major features of human behavior. The dualist philosophical basis of cognitive science supports the introduction of a level of functional modeling between nervous system structure and movement dynamics, which is complementary in the sense of incorporating hypothetical computational constructs as nervous system constraints. The belief is that complementary models are needed in modeling processes of brain and movement behavior in the study of intending systems (e.g., Meijer & Bongaardt, 1992; Pattee, 1979). Complementarity refers to the "mutual exclusiveness of the models that are needed to capture all the relevant appearances of a thing or a process" (Bongaardt, 1996, p. 11). It is this implicit assumption that provides the rationale for the implementation of schema-based modeling as an additional functional level of explanation between the structural and system levels (e.g., Arbib et al., 1998). To integrate dynamical and structural levels of analysis, functional computational models resort to classical black-box modeling and use of hypothetical constructs such as representations and programs.

In dynamical systems theory, the abstractness of the conceptualization is predicated on the mathematical basis of the modeling that typifies the theoretical work. That is, the laws governing the behavior of biological movement

systems as dynamical systems are specific instantiations of more general physical laws, which the language of mathematics is used to formalize. The application of the principles of nonlinear dynamics to the study of complex biological systems is feasible because, as Yates (1979) argued, biological systems are in essence physical systems. He stated, "The ontological reduction of biology to physics claims that at the level of atoms and molecules living systems obey laws of physics (and chemistry) and have no new laws of their own" (p. 65). The lawful basis of the conceptualization of a movement system as a dynamical system opens the way to rigorous modeling and experimental testing of coordination processes in the brain and musculoskeletal subsystem. There is little need for complementary modeling, thus avoiding the complexity of making huge assumptions in the modeling process, captured metaphorically as "loans" and "mortgages" in the extant literature (Williams et al., 1999).

The Embodied Brain

The tendency of the computational approach to view the mind and body as functionally separate entities, and the lack of reference to physiological and environmental constraints, have been proposed as major weaknesses in theory development in cognitive science (Neisser, 1994; Williams et al., 1999). In the phenomenological framework of cognitive science, complementary modeling has been prevalent because the functional modeling of internal structures and hypothetical mental processes purported to underlie movement behavior has typically been underconstrained by neuropsychology. The relationship of cognitive processes with other systems in the body and the typical environments in which cognitive agents perceive information for action has also been conspicuously ignored (Neisser, 1994). What is needed is a theory allowing cognitions and intentions to be "embodied" (Edelman, 1992; Globus, 1995). Despite the pervasiveness of the computational view of brain function, neurobiologists have failed to provide reliable evidence for an architecture suited to symbolic manipulation and syntactical communication within biological nervous systems. Daugman (1990) summarized this argument against the computer metaphor: "Surprisingly, given the pervasive popularity of this metaphor, there remains today no well-established evidence of symbolic manipulation or formal logical rules at the neurobiological level in animal physiology" (p. 15). He also reminded psychologists that the computer metaphor should be regarded as "hypothetical, and historical, conjecture about the brain," characterizing it as a "bandwagon phenomenon" (p. 15).

The problem is that computers work by being discrete and modular. They break information down, package it up and pigeon-hole it, so that they can run in logical isolation of the world (McCrone, 1999). An important function of representations is to stand in for things external to the system to support independent function (Bechtel, 1998; Fodor, 1980). In this respect, computational accounts appear "claustrophobic" in highlighting symbol manipulation, hypothetical internal representations, and mental processes in explaining how intending agents acquire knowledge about their environments (Heft, 1989; Reed, 1993). Cognitions and intentions toward environmental objects are better understood in a biological context. They are not static, discrete, and private affairs. They are characterized by goal-directed, striving, persistent physical activity in relation to environmental surfaces, objects, and events. For Reed, intentions in natural cognitive agents are based in the real world and are constrained by mind, body, social, and biological contexts. According to this position, a more appropriate theory of motor behavior should have a biological rather than an engineering basis (Edelman, 1992; Globus, 1995).

A comprehensive theory of motor behavior in humans should have the capacity to explain natural cognition (Van Gelder, 1998). Natural cognitive agents are evolved biological agents operating within specific cultural contexts. To explain motor behavior, a computational approach needs to embed the brain three times: in the CNS, the body, and the environment (Edelman, 1992; Globus, 1995; Van Gelder, 1998; Varela, Thompson, & Rosch, 1991). A successful theory of motor behavior will have to explain how coordination and control are constrained by all three interacting influences on brain and behavior. This approach contrasts with the traditional tendency to focus modeling effort solely on hypothetical mental functions and representations to model interactions between nervous system and movement system components during goal-directed activity (e.g., Schmidt & Lee, 1999; Willingham, 1998). The embedding signifies that brain function is influenced by many different organismic and environmental constraints in modeling processes like cognition, perception, memory, and learning.

To summarize so far, a significant point in this chapter is that, although some researchers have purported to provide a computational account constrained by neurosciences, there is still a tendency to use ill-defined computational constructs that date back to a symbolic representational framework of cognitive science. What is needed is a theoretical framework that provides concepts and tools to explain

processes of pattern formation and coordination among many different microcomponents of an evolving biological nervous system (Keil & Davids, 2000). As was demonstrated in the analysis, an integrative modeling approach, which seeks to also incorporate ideas from dynamical systems theory, ecological psychology, and the neurosciences, may provide a more appropriate theoretical platform for explaining motor behavior processes in biological movement systems under the constraints of cognitive and social interactions. In the following section, an existing model of constraints in the motor behavior literature is highlighted because it neatly fits the demand for a multiply embedded brain. The main idea under exploration is whether Newell's (1986) model of constraints can provide a theoretical framework rich enough to integrate findings from cognitive science, ecological psychology, dynamical systems theory, and the neurosciences.

INTEGRATIVE MODELING OF MOVEMENT SYSTEMS: MULTIPLE CONSTRAINTS ON BRAIN AND BEHAVIOR

Newell (1986) argued for three main classes of constraints related to the performer (organismic), the specific performance context (task), and background factors (environmental). There is a rich tradition in physics, biology, and chemistry in conceptualizing constraints on system behavior (e.g., Kauffmann, 1993, 1995; Prigogine & Stengers, 1984; Yates, 1979). The problem for any complex system in nature is to constrain the number of microcomponents involved in system behavior. In the movement sciences, this goal is known as Bernstein's problem (e.g., Turvey, 1990). In the study of brain processes, the umbrella term for the study of self-organization under constraint in the huge arrays of nervous system cells has been termed "neurodynamics" (Arbib et al., 1998; Freeman, 2000a, 2000b; Freeman & Nunez, 2000). The important point in the study of the embodied brain is that constraints are specific to biological niches and can be found at many different levels of a system or the environment in which it functions. Constraints have been defined as boundaries or features that limit the form achieved by the system or subsystem seeking a stable state of organization (Kugler, Kelso, & Turvey, 1980; Newell, 1986).

At the species level, constraints are allied to selection as part of the optimizing evolutionary process that guides biological organisms toward functionally appropriate behaviors in a particular niche or habitat (Kauffmann, 1993, 1995). Constraints operate in a Darwinian process by favoring some emergent features of behavior rather than others. At the time scale of perception and action, constraints shape the behavior of movement systems during goal-directed activity. That is, selected coordination patterns in the human movement system emerge under constraint as less functional states of goal-directed behavior are destroyed. There are many classes of constraints capable of affecting human movement behavior, and it remains an important empirical task for motor behavior theorists to identify them (see Handford et al., 1997; also see the later section on manipulating constraints during skill acquisition).

Constraints on the Processes of Self-Organization in Animate and Inanimate Systems

The theoretical biologist Yates (1979) modeled how the transition between states of organization (known as order-order transitions) could occur in intending systems engaged in goal-directed activity (see also Kugler et al., 1990). In intending movement systems, as energy flows in the environment undergo critical changes, "A mode of marginally-stable behavior emerges, and holds until an outside cue creates a transient switch state (a bifurcation), and the system moves into another marginally stable mode, entrained by the environmental cue" (Yates, 1979, p. 65). What this means, according to Yates, is that "many of the apparent command-control 'algorithms' of living systems actually reside in the interaction between the environment, and their plant structures. These interactions initiate the trajectories from one marginally-stable dynamic mode (out of a very limited set) to another" (p. 65). Therefore, structurally stable states of ordered behavior, known as attractors (e.g., Kauffmann, 1993; Kelso, 1995), are destroyed by a critical variation in the energy sources in the perceptual field, allowing an organism to switch to other functional modes of behavior.

An important implication of this idea for motor behavior and sport psychology is that the development of neurodynamic models "is likely to lead to the discovery that much animal behavior, previously thought to be the province of mental states, is in fact the province of hydrodynamics/thermodynamics states and transitions" (Yates, 1979, pp. 66–67). Although the model proposed shows immediate contact between structural analyses of biological nervous systems and the movement system dynamics, not even the subdiscipline of social psychology may be excluded from such an analysis. Some neuroscientists (e.g., Freeman, 1995) have attempted to extend understanding of psychological processes such as consciousness, thought, perception, emotion, and memory, as "shared events within

tribal, family, and community groups." For instance, Goerner and Combs (1998) have argued "that the human brain did not evolve in isolation, but in the community of other such brains. Thus, it would seem that we need to seek a more complete understanding of social systems, from dyads to civilizations, in the context of the informational systems that nest conscious experience of individual minds within much larger dynamic community systems" (p. 126). Their view was that subcomponents of complex systems (e.g., individual brains) exhibit their own behavior but also contribute to the greater totality of system behavior (society). Thus, social systems that constrain the development of brain and behavior are called supraliving systems. Such social constraints fall into the category of Newell's (1986) environmental constraints. In this type of theorizing on social psychological phenomena, there is little need for an intervening level of functional modeling based on computational constructs such as schema or other forms of internal representations.

More Recent Neurodynamic Theories of Processes of Brain and Behavior

More recent examples of how dynamics and neuroscientific information on CNS structure have been integrated to explain mental life exist in Edelman's (1992) neurobiological theory of neuronal group selection (for detailed reviews, see Thelen & Smith, 1994, and Williams et al., 1999, and Freeman's 2000a model of stochastic chaos in the brain).

The main tenet of Edelman's (e.g., 1992) theory is that the brain is a dynamic organ containing vast banks of interconnecting neurons selected into variant groups under genetically and environmentally imposed constraints. Specific actions, cognitions, and emotions are characterized by patterns of interconnecting neurons within variant groups, which arise under constraint. Connecting the activity of such subsystems as they contribute to functionally different movement patterns are long-range (pyramidal) neurons, which form an essential component of Edelman's theory. A model integrating a Hebbian synaptic paradigm, with principles of dynamical systems theory, could explain how the strengthening of a network of neurons can occur when they are simultaneously excited by a stimulus at the time of learning. Synapses strengthened in this way are often referred to as Hebbian synapses because the synapses follow the Hebb rule. Simply put, synchronous activation of interconnected neurons will strengthen synapses. An assembly of neurons can, therefore, become associated with a particular stimulus through strengthening of the Hebbian synapses. On presentation of the stimulus activating any

part of the assembly, a rapid firing of the rest of the assembly is produced. This strengthening, involving "modulator" chemicals released from the brain stem, alters the postsynaptic sensitivity, thereby increasing the gain of the neuron and increasing the dendritic current (Freeman, 1997). Such an account of nervous system activity is a biologically plausible explanation for how cognitions, emotions, and actions arise in human behavior.

Freeman (1999, 2000a), in his model of stochastic chaos in the brain, argued that most neuroscientists reject the evidence from EEG and MEG studies which focuses on wave potentials or pulse trains of single neurons. Instead, the unit of analysis of CNS activity should be focused on the organized activity of arrays of neurons. He termed this an example of "mass action" in the nervous system. Brains basically work with huge masses of neurons having low amounts of shared variance, not with selected small numbers in networks with high covariance. According to Freeman (2000a), this distorted view of how neural networks function came about because of the techniques used for recording the activity of neurons. The concept of a neural network was derived from the Golgi studies of cerebral cortical neurons by Lorente de No, who provided the anatomical support for the concepts of computational neural nets and nerve cell assemblies. In fact, each neuron receives and gives stimulus to thousands of other neurons in very close approximation (<1 mm). The result is that population thinking is better for describing the behavior of neurons than is the concept of networks (see also Edelman, 1992).

Perhaps the most significant property of large groupings of neurons is the capacity for undergoing immediate and repeated global state changes. Freeman (2000a) highlighted some examples relevant to the motor behavior theorist, particularly "the abrupt reorganizations manifested in the patterns of neural activity in the brain and spinal cord by the transitions between walking and running, speaking and swallowing, sleeping and waking, and more generally the staccato flow of thoughts and mental images" (p. 11). These massive-scale pattern changes appear to be incompatible with systems dominated by noise, as traditional information processing accounts of brain behavior would have it. Crucially, current neural network models are inadequate for explaining the emergence of mass action in the nervous system. Because neurons are excitatory and can mutually excite each other, they are capable of providing the sustained aperiodic activity that is needed for them to flourish and develop. Unlike static transistors in an electronic machine, according to Freeman (2000a), "Neurons have a short shelf life if they are isolated and left inactive" (p. 12). Thus, there is clearly a biological need for a continuous amount of "self-sustaining, randomized, steady state background activity [as a] source of activity from which ordered states of macroscopic neural activity emerge" (p. 12). In summary, brain states leading to ideas, thoughts, images, perceptions, and actions are created from stochastic chaos because "it arises from and feeds on the randomized activity of myriads of neurons, and it provides the basis for self-organization [in the brain]" (p. 13). There are many advantages identified with such a dynamic model of stochastic chaotic processes in the human nervous system. These include enhancing the fitness of neurons, minimizing the tendency to create parasitic phase locking, providing unstructured activity to drive the formation of Hebbian synapses during learning, and creating new basins of attraction instead of reinforcing existing attractors in the landscape. All of these advantages promote functional behaviors such as formative creativity and exploration in movement systems during learning, and help avoid stereotypical, unvarying responses that are maladaptive during goal-directed behavior (Globus, 1995; Slifkin & Newell, 1999).

As shall be highlighted in the following sections, these advantages fit well with ideas of the emergence of patterns of organized activity in the brain and motor system under different types of constraints. They have important implications for developing an integrative modeling approach and for understanding the nature of processes involved in motor learning, including practicing. In the following sections, the integrative analysis is developed by focusing on recent modeling of situational and intentional constraints on emergent movement behavior. Dynamic interceptive actions are used as the vehicle for discussion.

SITUATIONAL CONSTRAINTS IN THE CONTEXT OF AN INTEGRATED APPROACH TO MOTOR BEHAVIOR

Sport provides a unique environment for the human performer to adapt and reorganize stable coordinative modes in response to numerous situational constraints in effecting highly skilled movements. Situational constraints arising within biological and environmental systems serve as boundary conditions within which human movement emerges (Davids et al., 1994). They include organismic processes such as attention and memory, emotions such as anxiety, and task constraints such as specific instructions or models to observe (Newell, 1991). A line of research currently gaining

momentum within dynamical systems theory is the examination of situational constraints from higher-order cognitive processes that influence coordination patterns. Due to the putative universal applicability of dynamical systems theories, researchers currently analyzing human movement propose that the same synergetic principles incorporating the notion of self-organization also govern the development of cognitive (Thelen, 1995) and emotional (Camras, 1992) activity within the CNS. The value of this fledgling line of empirical investigation to the proposed integrative modeling approach is becoming apparent. Some researchers have advocated that cognition should be considered an embodied subsystem of the dynamic human organism, capable of modifying the intrinsic dynamics of the movement system (Abernethy, Burgess-Limerick, & Parks 1994; Summers, 1998; Thelen, 1995). If the ecological approach is to provide an encompassing theory of motor behavior, the current challenge is to understand how the cognitive subsystem affects the production of emergent coordinated movement patterns. Recent work outlining a distinction between nonspecific and specific control parameters promises to help clarify the relationship between situational and cognitive constraints in shaping goal-directed behavior.

Nonspecific and Specific Control Parameters

A major aim of researchers in coordination dynamics has been to identify two intrinsically stable rhythmical modes of coordination (antiphase-asymmetrical movements and inphase-symmetrical movements) under boundary conditions at the level of the order parameter: relative phase. These two patterns were originally shown to emerge in investigations as participants cycled their index fingers or forearms at increasing movement frequencies (Kelso, 1981, 1984). As the movement frequency does not prescribe any information to participants, but simply leads them through different coordinative states, it has been termed a nonspecific control parameter (Schöner & Kelso, 1988a). Movement frequency was originally modeled as a nonspecific control parameter in the now widely accepted model of phase transitions in rhythmic bimanual coordination named after Haken, Kelso, and Bunz (1985).

A second aim has been to identify biological boundary conditions or situational constraints that serve as specific control parameters arising from higher-order cognitive processes (Kelso, 1994; Schöner, 1995; Summers, Byblow, Bysouth-Young, & Semjen, 1998) or environmental information sources (Schöner & Kelso, 1988a, 1988b). Specific control parameters provide extraneous behavioral information that cooperates or competes with intrinsically stable modes of system organization (Schöner & Kelso, 1988a, 1988b). Identifying specific control parameters related to sport performance is essential for understanding how behavioral information destabilizes or stabilizes the athlete's existing coordination dynamics, or "forces" the emergence of previously learned or new behavioral patterns. This critical task forms the basis of the argument that situational constraints set up self-organization processes in the movement system that can be exploited by the sport performer (Meijer, 1988). Recent attempts to examine this function of situational constraints, including intentional and attentional processes, volitional control, and anxiety, within dynamical movement systems are discussed in turn in the next section.

Intentional Constraints on Movement Coordination

One of the main difficulties facing movement scientists exploring intentionality is how such a concept should be defined (Davids et al, 1999; Freeman, 1997; Kelso, 1995; Schöner, 1990). Freeman described intentionality in behavioral terms as "a thought, action, or speech [that] has a purpose, goal, or intent, which is both outwardly directed towards manipulating objects in the world and inwardly directed toward satisfying biological drives, needs, or instincts" (p. 293). A traditional tendency in the field of human movement behavior has been to confuse the generation of an intention to move with a mental representation specifying a motor pattern (i.e., motor programs or schema) embedded within the CNS (e.g., Decety, 1996; Decety & Grèzes, 1999; Decety et al., 1994; Schmidt & Lee, 1999; Willingham, 1998). The assumption is that, if such representations were to be identified within the neural structure of the CNS, it would be possible to gain a better understanding of how movements are coordinated and learned.

With the advent of more sophisticated neurological techniques over the past 20 years, such as positron emission tomography (PET) scanning, functional magnetic resonance imaging (fMRI), and magnetoencephalographic (MEG) techniques, researchers have been able to advance toward this goal. In perhaps the first study to examine the neural basis of volitional control of motor behavior, Frith, Friston, Liddle, and Frackowiak (1991) asked participants to perform verbal and motor tasks under conditions in which responses were either generated internally or specified by external sensory stimulation. Using PET scans, they found evidence of increased blood flow in the prefrontal cortex under task constraints of generating intentions to act in one way rather than another. Their

conclusion was that a "representation held in memory" (p. 244) forms the basis of intentional behavior under dynamic task constraints. In a similar way, it has been suggested that the Bereitschaftpotential (or "readiness potential") recorded in the supplementary motor area (SMA) prior to movement onset might represent the neural correlate of an intention to move (for a review, see Deecke, 1990). Further, data showing changes in regional cerebral blood flow (rCBF) to the SMA prior to movement initiation have been assumed to indicate its role in programming movements (e.g., Decety, 1996; Decety & Grèzes, 1999).

However, the difficulty in interpreting these data as support for the motor programming perspective is evident in the confusion of intentionality and movement programming. For example, it has been argued that, "whereas the SMA exhibits preferential activity during internally-guided tasks, premotor neurons are more active during externally guided movements" (Decety, 1996, p. 47). This distinction between neural activity in the SMA and in premotor neurons is purported to support the proposition of the generation and reliance on an internal representation to control movement in the former area of the brain, compared information-regulated movement predominantly occurring in the latter. Clearly, experiencing an intention to move appears to have been confused with retrieving a movement program from memory and initiating it prior to acting (see also Arbib et al., 1998), given that a motor program has been defined as "an abstract representation that, when initiated, results in the production of a coordinated movement sequence" (Schmidt & Lee, 1999, p. 417). Thus, while the work of Deecke (1990) on motor learning was purported to indicate the composition of "anticipatory postural adjustment into motor programs" (p. 613), it was also claimed that the Bereitschaftpotential in the SMA plays "motivational, intentional or timing" (p. 612) roles in the initiation of volitional action, particularly in the "timing of single movements in motor sequences" (p. 612).

How can these different descriptions be reconciled? The problem is that it is somewhat misleading to refer to the internal generation of a willed voluntary action as if intentional behavior could exist in a vacuum. It makes little sense to propose such a hierarchical relationship between intentions and actions because it is not possible to separate the influence on movement system behavior of the "inextricable causal web of perception, action, and cognition" (Thelen & Smith, 1994, p. xxii). The conceptualization of the human nervous system as a natural biological system eschews the view of the brain as a processor of information. Brains process meaning rather than information (Freeman,

1997, 1999, 2000b). Neural activity patterns have no direct or immediate relationship to patterns of sensory information, a concept that Bernstein (1967) termed "nonunivocality." There is no one-to-one mapping between a specific source of sensory stimulation, an idea, an image, or a thought and a movement activity (Freeman, 1997, 1999, 2000b).

Rather, neural patterning during movement behavior is shaped by the perceptions and intentions of individuals as they pursue specific task goals. This idea was supported by a study using a MEG technique to investigate the relationship between brain processes and actual motor behavior (Kelso et al., 1998). Using a finger flexion and extension task, the investigators found that neural activity patterns significantly mirrored the movement derivative or velocity. Dynamic patterns of cortical activity were task-specific, however, in that large differences were found in the time course of cortical activity under different task constraints of synchronization and syncopation to the beat of a metronome. The interacting influence of intentionality, perception, and action is underpinned by the fact that the same movement coordination pattern (finger tapping) under different task constraints (i.e., constrained by the information of the metronomic beat) was correlated with completely different neural patterns.

Connectionism Does Not Imply Representations

There is an inordinate amount of confusion over the idea that highlighted patterns of connections among brain structures imply the existence of a representation. The computations performed in this model of the representing brain may be considered to be subsymbolic rather than symbolic. Nevertheless, input functions are mapped onto output functions in a process of state transition traditionally described by linear algebra (Globus, 1992). The use of representations in subsymbolic connectionist modeling implies the computation of state transitions described "in terms of the information transformed, represented and stored" (Sejnowski et al., 1988, p. 48). It is worth noting that a subsymbolic connectionist type of model was used by Decety et al. (1994) in interpreting their data on imagined and observed movements. In a comparison of rCBF data during imagined and observed prehension movements in six participants, they argued that "consciously representing an action involves a pattern of cortical and subcortical activation similar to that of intentionally executed action" (p. 601).

The implementation of concepts from a computational functional modeling framework need not be invoked at all,

as evident in the interpretation of neural data on perception and action by Frith et al. (1991). They noted that their study demonstrated the efficacy of PET scanning in showing how the prefrontal cortex interacts with other parts of the brain. A key proposal from their data was that the "same neural network is used to generate responses internally as is used to identify stimuli" (p. 245). That is, intending, perceiving, imagining, and acting are processes that assemble the neural pattern implemented in a specific task context. However, the pattern is never identical from moment to moment. Depending on the extent to which situational and task constraints dictate how each process intervenes, the neural network that is assembled will vary (Calvin, 1996; Edelman, 1992; Globus, 1995). As noted later, such a view has implications for the implementation of performance intervention techniques in motor behavior.

Intentional Movement Behavior: Noncomplementary Modeling

If neural activity in the SMA is not to be considered an intention generating an internal movement representation, then how is the role of intentionality within a noncomplementary framework to be interpreted? An early attempt to conceptualize intentional movement behavior within a unitary model was outlined by Kugler et al. (1990) within the dynamical systems framework. Intentions were considered goal-state attractors arising through the dynamic interplay of both organismic and environmental energy exchanges. In dynamical systems theory, attractor states are temporary, stable patterns of behavior that underpin the self-organizing tendencies of a complex system (Williams et al., 1999). In terms of intentional dynamics, attractors can be considered choice points, in that there is insufficient information in the state space (i.e., the total hypothetical number of coordination possibilities available to an individual movement system) to uniquely define a future path for the organism. These decisions emerge for the system depending on fluctuations in the initial task conditions and any higher-order goals impinging on action.

Soccer Goalkeeping

Consider an example from sport to help contextualize the concept of an embedded brain and the intricate and tangled relationship among intentions, perception, and action. A goalkeeper in soccer receives visual information from a ball crossed into the penalty area. He or she could use intentional information to choose whether to catch the ball and retain possession or punch the ball away from the goal. There are also organismic constraints related to the specific task of soccer goalkeeping in the form of tactics and rules, memories, and knowledge of opponents, which serve to shape the movement system dynamics. Such organismic constraints emerge as the individual brain assembles a solution to the performance problem. The key point is that intentions are not stored in the goalkeeper's CNS but emerge under the multitude of constraints related to the specific performance context. Intentions are more stable patterns of connections in the CNS, acting as attractors, which influence the motor task solutions assembled by the goalkeeper during performance. There are many attractors residing in the CNS, analogized as a landscape of possibilities. Because the brain is a hermeneutic device (i.e., it is a device that is constantly engaging in the interpretation of information, events, and ongoing behavior), goal-directed actions are assembled from the multitude of internal and external constraints impinging on the goalkeeper at any one instant (see Érdi, 1996; Globus, 1995).

The resulting behavior of the goalkeeper will depend, not only on various environmental factors such as the proximity of attacking players and the flight of the ball, but also on past experience and memories, as well as the strength of intentional information that he or she brings to the situation. If punching the ball forms a more stable attractor state than catching it, then that will be the most likely course of action that emerges for the goalkeeper. From this perspective, intentional information acts in the same state space as the movement system's coordination dynamics, either stabilizing or destabilizing the system organization to attain specific task goals (Scholz & Kelso, 1990; Williams et al., 1999). An intention to move is influenced by the instantaneous movement capabilities of the system, which in turn are constrained by intentions. This represents a radically different approach to intentionality. It is viewed as an important constraint that contributes to the self-organizing properties of the human movement system (i.e., an organizational mode in which any consituent subsystem can drive system behavior) rather than hierarchical control (i.e., a top-down mode of organization; see Davids & Button, 2000).

The Distinction between Intending Systems and Systems Exhibiting Intentions

Kugler et al. (1990) argued that a unique property of intending agents is that they are able to resist the gradients (i.e., changes in attractor level) specified by the informational field. Whereas self-organization processes in an inanimate object (e.g., a molecule of matter in rock) are causally restricted to force gradients (e.g., wind pressure

that can erode the rock formation), animate objects are not merely at the mercy of energy flows in the environment. Their states of organization can be influenced by both force fields (i.e., externally generated forces by wind, water, another individual) and informational fields (i.e., specific energy flows acting as unique information stheces to attract the dynamics of the system, for example, the scent of a pheromone for an insect or optical energy reflected from an ice puck traversing a rink). As a system moves from primitive behavior to higher-order intentions, the focus of constraints shift from the force fields to the information fields as goals become more sophisticated and more information is required to interact with complex, dynamic environments. Intentions can act in the informational field to guide the system to resist force field gradients, but at an energy cost. For example, in sport, an athlete can take the least energy-efficient option and intentionally attract movement system dynamics to less stable coordination solutions. That is, one can "showboat."

It is important, at this point, to distinguish between natural systems that merely have intentions and those that are intending systems. For instance, the example of nest-building termites has been used in the literature as a complex self-organizing system (Kugler, 1986). However, such a natural system is more accurately categorized as a complex system that exhibits intentions (i.e., it can exhibit goal-directed behavior without having the ability to formulate intentions as conceptualized in cognitive science). It can self-organize without being able to intend. The key point is that the termites do not make explicit choices or goals, whereas "intending systems" select from all possible attractor locations, a specific final state as the goal.

The focus of Kugler et al.'s (1990) ideas is that intentions identify a higher mode of system organization leading to the emergence of a new, more stable attractor. In other words, intentions may be perceived as one of the most important constraints on goal-directed dynamics (Kelso, 1995). Nevertheless, it needs to be recognized that intentions are just one of many influences shaping system behavior. Utilizing the physical model of escapement processes popular in dynamical systems theory, control decisions must arise at those points along a trajectory at which the system must inject a sustaining squirt of energy from the interior field potential. In other words, Kugler et al. have demonstrated how it is possible to view the human movement system as capable of sustaining a movement pattern by utilizing reactive forces (due to gravity, friction, anatomical design, momentum). The way expert sport performers can utilize these forces exemplifies how humans are able to exploit the "order for free" in nature that Kauffmann (1993, 1995) points to as the basis of self-organization in nature.

However, there comes a time when more than just reactive forces are needed to sustain physical activity. Sport performers can use energy systems specified in physiology for the purposes of injecting on-board sources of energy (e.g., ATP) to achieve task goals. These time points are choice points for the sport performer because there is insufficient information in the field to define uniquely the future path of movement. Viewed this way, it is possible to see how intentions set up self-organization processes in expert performers as they exploit energy sources available for free. The influence of intentionality, as a source of specific behavioral information on the emergence of coordinated movement, was captured in the model developed by Schöner (1990). The model depicts the numerical simulation of a discrete reaching task to a static location in space with point attractors (i.e., specific locations of stable coordination in the state space) at both the start and the termination of the movement. The trajectory of the arm between the attractors was modeled as one half of a limit cycle oscillator (see Figure 6.1).

Despite this modeling effort, empirical work on the concept of intentionality in dynamical movement systems represents an interesting challenge for motor behaviorists. One potential line of empirical work is to focus investigative effort on a more fine-grained level of movement behavior. Traditional approaches to motor behavior have tended to examine behavioral outcomes as indirect indices of motor

control processes (e.g., Schmidt & Lee, 1999). Modern approaches, on the other hand, have tended to focus on differences in coordination patterns emerging under different task constraints, in which intentions have been manipulated. Next, some recent work that has adopted such an approach is reviewed.

Experimental Work on Intentionality in Dynamical Movement Systems: Mechanical Perturbation of the Movement System

The use of a mechanical perturbation to the movement system is becoming a prevalent tool in attempting to identify stable patterns of movement behavior during goal-directed activity (e.g., Button, Davids, Bennett, & Tayler, in press; Haggard & Wing, 1995; Polman, Whiting, & Savelsbergh, 1996).

Prehension

Haggard and Wing (1995) studied the coordination of reach and grasp components in prehension when the participant's arm was unexpectedly pulled back with a linear actuator. In this experiment, participants commonly exhibited reversals in the direction of hand transport when perturbed, which were followed (in 67.5% of trials) by compensatory reversals in hand aperture. Such adaptive behavior may be viewed as evidence of "motor equivalence" (Saltzman & Kelso, 1987), whereby skilled performers are capable of finding alternative routes to a given goal if a preferred or current route is unexpectedly blocked. Such findings also have important implications for the analysis of intentional dynamics. The concept of motor equivalence indicates that movement systems may exhibit similar intentions from trial to trial, but can still exploit numerous mechanical degrees of freedom in the body in different ways to achieve a task goal. Goal-directed activity (even in tightly constrained tasks like prehension) could result in greater-than-expected levels of between-participant and between-trial variability, although task outcomes may still be reliably achieved (Davids et al., 1999).

Haggard and Wing (1995) also suggested that, as the perturbations in their experiment were delivered in a random fashion, the aperture reversals exhibited by participants indicated that information was exchanged between the aperture and transport components continuously during the movement rather than merely at an antecedent planning stage. Such a suggestion highlights the notion that there is constant interplay between intentional information and intrinsic dynamics. The generation of an intention for setting up self-organizing dynamics in the motor system must not

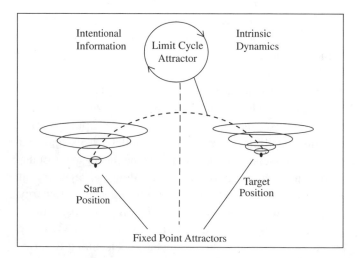

Figure 6.1 Graphical representation of intentionality as a constraint on the emergence of coordinated reaching movements formalized in the mathematical simulations of G. Schöner (1990).

be confused with the initiation of a motor representation for controlling the whole movement (see the earlier discussion). An interesting question to arise from the Haggard and Wing study concerned how (or if) participants' coordination pattern would change if they knew they were about to be perturbed. A comparison between conditions in which perturbations to movements were expected and unexpected would permit the exploration of the relationship between preplanned adaptive strategies and the emergent, self-organizing properties of the system. Examples of motor equivalence can be observed among skilled catchers when catching a moving ball (e.g., consider the many different ways in which baseball players often make catches in a game).

Ball Catching

Unfortunately, there has been only a small amount of experimental research examining the fine-grained kinematics of ball catching when an external perturbation has been applied. In a study by Polman, Whiting, and Savelsbergh (1996), participants sat at a table with their right arm constrained in an arm rest and were required to grasp a ball attached to a pendulum approaching in the sagittal plane. Temporal task constraints were manipulated by springloading the fingers of the grasping hand during the interceptive action to examine the stability of movement system dynamics. Perturbation of the grasp action was achieved by attaching flexible wires to the fingers of a glove worn by participants in a springloaded system. They started with their fingers closed and were required to time the opening of their hand as the ball on the pendulum approached. Two masses (0.6kg and 1.6kg) were used to manipulate the perturbing force to be resisted, in addition to a baseline (nonperturbed) condition. Nine kinematic variables were recorded as dependent measures. The only significant differences observed between baseline and perturbed conditions were for two grasp variables: the extent of the hand aperture at the time of catching (baseline < both perturbed conditions), and the maximal closing velocity of the fingers (baseline condition significantly faster than the 0.6kg condition only). It was concluded that the control pattern underlying discrete interceptive actions remained relatively invariant in both baseline and perturbed conditions.

Although the data of Polman et al. (1996) extended understanding of the effects of mechanical perturbations on the movement system to discrete interceptive actions, a number of interesting questions arise from their work. First, the design implemented by Polman et al. (1996) allowed them to perturb only the grasp phase of the one-

handed interceptive action. Second, the specific type of interceptive task they used permitted perturbation only of temporal task constraints, due to the fixed position of the wrist and the pendular trajectory of the ball. It is not clear to what extent the significant differences in grasp variables, noted between perturbed and nonperturbed conditions, may have simply been a function of this specific experimental version of an interceptive action. Third, and crucially, the methodology employed by Polman et al. resulted in the perturbation being either on or off across conditions. Although the springloaded system resulted in the perturbation being applied at different stages of the ongoing interceptive action, it remained constant over trials in the perturbed conditions. The participants also always knew when a movement was going to be perturbed beforehand. It is not clear whether individual participants might have adopted a specific type of movement strategy to deal with the perturbation. A key observation was that the "increased hand aperture at the moment of the catch could also indicate that participants used a qualitatively different grasp action altogether in the springloaded conditions" (Polman et al., 1996, p. 57). Due to the lack of random application of perturbations, it was not apparent to what extent these outcomes were a function of intentional constraints on the part of individual participants or the task constraints imposed by the added load to the fingers during the grasp.

Recently, Button et al. (in press) examined responses to an external pertubation during a one-handed catching task. The perturbation was in the form of a resistive force (12 N.m) applied to the wrist via a piece of cord attached to a mechanical brake. Skilled catchers were asked to catch tennis balls projected by a ball machine at approximately 8 m.s⁻¹. The trial blocks consisted of 10 nonperturbed trials (baseline) and a block of 54 trials, of which 20 trials were chosen at random for perturbation. In the kinematic data on the grasp and transport phases, a great deal of between-participant variability in the responses to the perturbations was shown. During trials where the perturbation was expected, participants initiated movements earlier (198 ms ± 32) than in randomly perturbed trials (217 ms ± 28) (p < .05). Furthermore, individuals tended to catch the ball later in its trajectory when they knew a perturbation was going to occur (p < .01). This intentional strategy was supported by a general trend for participants to reach maximal wrist velocity earlier in relation to the time of hand-ball contact in perturbed trials (309 ms (± 61) before contact) than in the baseline trials (237 ms (± 68) before contact) (see Figure 6.2). The analysis of individual coordination profiles revealed that four out of six participants were able

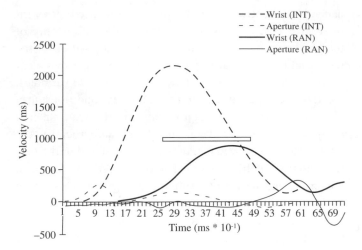

Figure 6.2   The kinematics of a skilled catcher described in relation to the intentional dynamics of the movement system. This typical participant intentionally initiated a change in coordination under conditions when a perturbation to the wrist was expected. N.B.: Different conditions were: INT = perturbation expected; RAN = perturbation not expected. Horizontal bar in mid-figure depicts the time of perturbation from start to finish. Data from C. Button et al. (in press).

to intentionally change the relative timing of the grasp phase to adapt to specific changes in task constraints. The large amount of between-participant variability lends support to the notion of skilled performers exhibiting motor equivalence to successfully achieve a task. In support of the finding by Polman et al. (1996), the relative moment of final hand closure parameter (approximately 70% of overall movement time) remained invariant despite the perturbation.

These data imply that the timing of the grasp specifies a stable attractor that is resistant to the influence of intentional information (see also Wallace & Weeks, 1988). By manipulating the timing of perturbation in a catching task, it would be possible to gain more direct evidence regarding the stability of this parameter. Indeed, Button et al. (in press) suggested that the momentum of the limb at the point of perturbation could also influence the degree of adaptation necessary for the rest of the movement. If the catching arm was perturbed as it was beginning to move, one might predict that the perturbation would have a greater effect than if it occurred as the arm was moving more quickly, later in the movement.

The studies overviewed in this section suggest that non-complementary modeling of intentions, perceptions, and movement dynamics represents a viable research avenue for

future work. From an integrated modeling perspective it appears that there is emerging evidence for (1) the difficulty in separating the influences of intentions, perception, and action during the regulation of ongoing movements; and (2) the role of intentionality in setting up and modifying the self-organizing dynamics of the movement system during goal-directed activity.

The role of intentional processes as setting up self-organization processes in the movement system may be best understood through the provision of behavioral information to attract the intrinsic dynamics toward a required behavioral pattern. This characterization of the notion of information is captured at the level of the collective variable relative phase that defines the intended pattern (Scholz & Kelso, 1990). For example, where intentional information cooperates with participants' intrinsic dynamics, its influence may be momentary, in simply forcing the system toward a required state of coordination. In contrast, where intentional information competes with participants' intrinsic dynamics, greater intentional effort may be required to force the system toward the desired pattern.

Following the intention to adopt a required coordination pattern, often the goal of the individual performer is to maintain a specific state of organization, such as during three-ball juggling or dribbling a hockey puck. The allocation of on-task "effort" or "energy" is needed to maintain a required pattern. Thus, while intentions set up processes of self-organization in the movement system, attentional processes may be considered ongoing specific parametric influences that continuously modify and stabilize intended patterns of coordination. We turn to discussion of attentional processes next.

Attentional Processes

Another important situational constraint receiving current empirical effort is attentional processes. They may be modeled as a specific control parameter providing behavioral information to constrain the dynamics of the human movement system, an issue initially investigated by Wuyts, Summers, Carson, Byblow, and Semjen (1996). Previous researchers indicated that erratic trajectories in the participants' nondominant hand during antisymmetrical movements caused a loss of stability and temporary transitions to an inphase mode as the control parameter oscillation frequency was increased (e.g., see Carson, Thomas, Summers, Walters, & Semjen, 1997; Semjen, Summers, & Cattaert, 1995). A proffered explanation for this imbalance was that participants preferentially allocated attention toward their dominant hand. Wuyts et al. hypothesized that intentionally directing attention to the nondominant hand would attenuate the imbalance of coupling, improving stability and reducing the formation of erratic trajectories.

In their study, participants performed a bimanual circle-tracking task that required completion of the contour of model circles at movement frequencies between 1.50 and 3.0 Hz at 0.25 Hz intervals, in symmetrical and antisymmetrical modes. Participants were required to consciously attend to either the dominant hand, nondominant hand, or a neutral reference position. It was found that consciously mediated attention strategies did not provide information that was relevant to changing the stability of behavioral patterns defined by the intrinsic dynamics at the level of the collective variable. However, differences in performance were observed at the level of the individual components, with the participants' nondominant hand oscillating more slowly, exhibiting greater circularity, lower variability, and less erratic behavior when attended to. Results were interpreted to suggest that directing attention to either the dominant or nondominant hand served to increase the degree of independence between the hands.

Using a bimanual circle-drawing task, Summers, Byblow, Bysouth-Young, and Semjen (1998) examined participants' ability to attend to a secondary-load counting task while performing symmetrical and asymmetrical bimanual circling movements with their index fingers. Results suggested that maintaining the antiphase mode at higher frequencies demanded greater mental effort, possibly due to resisting kinesthetic signals entraining the system toward the inphase mode of coordination. Of interest to an integrated modeling perspective, it was also proposed that a central control mechanism could have been a determinant of instability and pattern switches. Although participants were asked to act passively in response to the intrinsic dynamics of the movement system (Lee, Blandin, & Proteau, 1996), the findings of Summers et al. suggested that higher-order processes could have been involved in movement execution governing the stability of the order parameter dynamics. This perspective offers an explanation as to why variability is observed in the frequencies at which participants display transitions to the inphase mode, highlighting the need for appropriate instructions to be given to them during experiments on intrinsic dynamics.

Anxiety as a Situational Constraint

Within the sport psychology literature, the study of stress, arousal, and anxiety and their impact on motor performance retains a position of central importance (Gould & Krane, 1992). Explanations for the effects of anxiety on performance stemming from a traditional cognitive science background include Easterbrook's (1959) perceptual narrowing hypothesis, Baddeley and Hitch's (1974) attentional capacity and working memory theory, Eysenck's (1992) hypervigilance theory, and Eysenck and Calvo's (1992) processing efficiency theory. More recently, models of the arousal/anxiety–performance relationship such as multidimensional anxiety theory (Davidson & Schwartz, 1976) and a cusp catastrophe model (Fazey & Hardy, 1988) have also been advocated.

The catastrophe model of anxiety is interesting because it neatly fits into an integrated modeling framework and predicts sudden state transitions based on the interaction of cognitive anxiety, physiological arousal, and performance. Although the original catastrophe model (Thom, 1975) was formulated using tools of nonlinear dynamics, Fazey and Hardy's (1988) model makes little reference to concepts and methods from this framework. Thus, the validity of the predictions and concepts of Fazey and Hardy's model remain to be interpreted and evaluated from a dynamical systems perspective. Previous arguments that cognition is a subsystem embodied within the dynamic human performer highlights the view in dynamical systems theory that cognitive activity be considered neural patterns constantly self-organizing under the pressure of internal and external constraints (Edelman, 1992; Freeman, 1999). Ideas, thoughts, images, emotional reactivity, and actions can be thought of as emergent networks of neurons, and not stored symbolic representations in the mind.

Support for Edelman's (1992) approach of considering the brain as a dynamic organ comes from Huether's (1996) explanation of the individual's capacity to adapt to stressful situations. He argued that repeatedly successful cognitive responses mediate the effects of stress-inducing situations and optimally strengthen the neuronal circuitry and synaptic connectivity associated with a response. Neuronal circuitry is an example of an open biological system that can become unstable and can be reorganized in response to changing performance constraints (Williams et al., 1999). The interactive effect of internal and external constraints on sport performance may result in specific neuronal groups being selected that collectively yield cognitive or emotional patterns, such as those associated with anxiety. During sports performance, perceived anxiety may act as a control parameter constraining athletes toward meeting the requirements of imposed behavioral information, which could enhance or detract from the performance of required stable, learned patterns. If anxiety were to be successfully modeled as a control parameter, an alternative explanation is feasible for findings from the traditional cognitive literature, showing it to be sometimes debilitative or facilitative with respect to sport performance (e.g., Jones & Swain, 1992). It may be that the competition and cooperation between the performer's existing and required patterns of coordination dynamics could form the basis for explaining why effects are sometimes facilitating and sometimes debilitating. If the experienced anxiety produced perturbing effects that competed with the required patterns of movement coordination, then performance would be predicted to become more unstable and deteriorate. If, on the other hand, the effects complemented the required movement system dynamics, then improved performance would result. These ideas await confirmation.

A preliminary attempt to examine the possible specific or nonspecific parameteric effects of anxiety on participants' coordination dynamics was undertaken by Court, Bennett, Davids, and Williams (1998). Using the theoretical concepts and tools from the interdisciplinary field of synergetics, they examined the effects of anxiety on the intrinsic dynamics of the high trait-anxious participants during a rhythmic bimanual forearm coordination task. In a repeated-measures, multiple-case, staggered-baseline design, participants performed antiphase and inphase coordinative patterns at frequencies from 0.8 Hz to 2.8 Hz. From 12 testing sessions, 2 sessions were randomly selected during which participants were exposed to a social evaluation anxiety-inducing situation. For two participants, the mean time to the onset of fluctuations (SD of relative phase) and the transition from antiphase to inphase mode decreased in response to experimental treatments compared to baseline. This result suggested that anxiety destabilized the normally stable antiphase coordination pattern. For these participants, anxiety was interpreted to have acted as a nonspecific control parameter, leading them toward the inphase mode. For two further participants, the onset of fluctuations and the time to the transition from antiphase to inphase modes was delayed under experimental conditions. This result suggested that, when responding to the anxiety-inducing situation, participants adopted an intentional strategy to override their normally observed intrinsic dynamics (cf. Lee, Blandin, & Proteau, 1996). For these participants, anxiety was again interpreted as a specific control parameter, the perturbation of which they resisted by using intentional information to inhibit their predetermined intrinsic tendency to switch patterns (see Figures 6.3 and 6.4).

These initial findings suggest that the parametric effects of anxiety may be nonspecific or specific with respect to order parameter dynamics in the movement system. Fur-

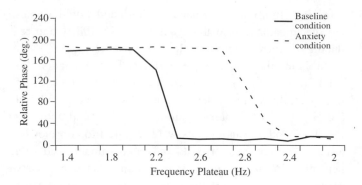

Figure 6.3   Mean relative phase during baseline and anxiety conditions for one participant (WB) in the experiment of Court et al. (1998). Note the higher mean transition frequency from the antiphase to the inphase mode during the anxiety condition.

thermore, it seems that (re)organization at a coordinative level may arise from participants' individual perceptions, appraisals, and responses to the surrounding environment. These results again indicate that the human performer is an intending system, capable of selecting different specific final states from equivalent environmental situations, and that behavior arises from a continuous interplay of intentions, perceptions, and actions. Attentional processes could operate to stabilize system dynamics in the face of the perturbing influence of anxiety as a control parameter.

In summary, the effects of situational constraints such as intentions, attention, and anxiety on participants' coordination dynamics are open to interpretation through a multidisciplinary synthesis of phenomenological and structural concepts within dynamical systems theory, neurobiology, and psychology. Like actions emerging from movement systems, by considering cognition and emotion as dynamical

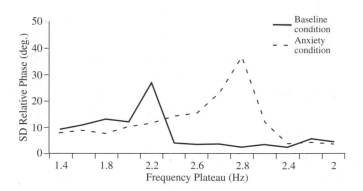

Figure 6.4   Mean SD of relative phase during baseline and anxiety conditions for one participant (WB) in Court et al. (1998). Note the greater level of fluctuations before the transition from the antiphase to the inphase mode during the anxiety condition.

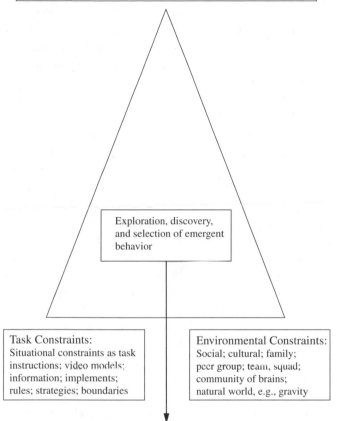

Organismic Constraints:
Brain as a hermeneutic device; cognitions; emotions; intentionality;
genes; levels of learning and experience; situational constraints,
e.g., attention, anxiety, memories; structural; anatomical, etc.

Exploration, discovery,
and selection of emergent
behavior

Task Constraints:
Situational constraints as task
instructions; video models;
information; implements;
rules; strategies; boundaries

Environmental Constraints:
Social; cultural; family;
peer group; team, squad;
community of brains;
natural world, e.g., gravity

Brain Processes and Movement Coordination and Control

Figure 6.5 Constraints on the emergence and selection of patterns in the CNS and movement apparatus. The model synthesizes the ideas of Newell (1986) and Edelman (1992) in describing the major constraints on coordinated behavior arising during goal-directed activity.

processes arising in the hermeneutic brain, an integrative modeling approach may be useful in extending current understanding beyond the polemics of the motor-action systems controversy (see Figure 6.5). In the final section of this chapter, we examine some of the implications of an integrative modeling approach for practical interventions in sport.

PRACTICE IN SPORT: SEARCHING FOR "VIRTUAL" SOLUTIONS TO MOVEMENT PROBLEMS

The central tenet of cognitive theories of motor skill learning is that learners develop internalized knowledge structures

and generalized motor programs that enable them to respond in an adaptive manner when confronted with a variety of related situations. Variable practice, high contextual interference practice conditions, and augmented feedback are presumed to be important in producing an expansive, generative rule to cope with a variety of similar but different instances (for recent reviews, see Abernethy, Kippers, Mackinnon, Neal, & Hanrahan, 1997; Magill, 1998; Schmidt & Lee, 1999). For example, contextual interference practice conditions are thought to benefit learners as a result of retroactive inhibition effects by forcing them to retrieve and parameterize a different generalized motor program on each occasion, or to undertake more elaborate processing of task-relevant cues (Brady, 1998). Furthermore, augmented feedback and guidance provided by coaches are seen as paramount, particularly during the early stages of learning.

An alternative approach, based on a constraints-led perspective to interventions in sport, is currently under development (e.g., Davids, in press; Davids, Bennett, Handford, & Jones, 1999). As with other aspects of integrated modeling, this approach has its roots in the framework of constraints espoused originally by Newell (1986; see Figure 6.1). It eschews symbolic representations in favor of theoretical explanations that view skill learning as the emergence of movement solutions based on various constraints on action. Organismic constraints refer to the unique characteristics of the performer and may manifest themselves in physical, physiological, cognitive, and emotional subsystems, among others. For example, body morphology, fitness levels, or technical proficiency as well as predisposition toward emotional states such as anxiety or achievement motivation act as pressures on the emergence of particular movement behaviors. Moreover, cognitive and intellectual factors related to "game intelligence" such as anticipation, decision making, and creativity could determine learners' intentions, guiding their search for virtual (optimal) task solutions. Task constraints relate to the goal of the task, any implements such as sticks or rackets that must be employed to satisfy the goal, and the rules, strategy, and tactics inherent to a sport. Such constraints have a powerful role to play in influencing intentional constraints on behavior. For instance, rules determine that the ball must be bowled overarm in cricket, whereas a goalkeeper may not handle the ball outside the penalty area in soccer. Similarly, strategy and tactics, which may be determined prior to performance and evolve as play progresses, are fundamental constraints on emergent behaviors. Environmental constraints refer to the energy flows such as visual and auditory information surrounding the performer, or the social contexts of behavior. Altitude, humidity, lighting, and other environmental features also act as structural (time-independent) constraints on emergent behavior (Newell, 1986).

Practice provides the opportunity to search for solutions to the movement problem in a perceptuomotor workspace that is generated by the combined constraints of the learner, task, and environment (McDonald, Oliver, & Newell, 1995; Newell, 1986, 1996). Newell's (1986) theory has significant implications for coaches in their perceptions of the role of variability in motor performance, in the manner with which they manipulate various constraints during instruction and practice, and in the scheduling of practice sessions. Practical implications from each of these areas are considered next.

Variability and Motor Behavior: The Need for Interpretation by Individual Profiling

Cognitive models of motor control view within-subject variability as a reflection of noise (task irrelevant or dysfunctional information) in the sensorimotor system (Kelso, 1992). System output is presumed to be deterministic and linearly related to input, with various sources of noise superimposed (Newell & Corcos, 1993). Due to these negative connotations, system noise is viewed as a performance-limiting factor that should be reduced or eliminated by extended and repetitive practice. Reduced variability is very often seen as a reflection of increased system stability and a characteristic of skilled sports performers. For example, relative timing and force invariance are commonly proposed as measures of stability in system dynamics that reflect the existence of centrally stored movement representations (see Schmidt & Lee, 1999). Although intuitively appealing, over the years, few studies have provided empirical support for this view of performance variability (e.g., see Burgess-Limerick, Neal, & Abernethy, 1992; Gentner, 1987; Maraj, Elliott, Lee, & Pollock, 1993). The evidence in favor of this proposal is typically restricted to tasks where reduced variability is the functional goal of performance, such as tracking or manual aiming (Slifkin & Newell, 1999).

Variability in Motor Behavior: An Inherent System Property

In tasks that involve many biomechanical degrees of freedom, such as pistol shooting, skiing, and soccer kicking, improved performance is often accompanied by an increase in movement variability at a segmental level of analysis (e.g., see Anderson & Sidaway, 1994; Arutyunyan, Gurfinkel, & Mirskii, 1968; Davids, Lees, & Burwitz, in press; Vereijken, van Emmerik, Whiting, & Newell, 1992; Williams, Alty, & Lees, in press). This increased variability in movement dynamics, which is due to the "unfreezing" or releasing of various system degrees of freedom (cf. Bernstein, 1967), has a compensatory effect in reducing outcome variability and is indicative of the performer's being able to exploit forces available as "order for free" in the environment.

An integrated modeling approach, incorporating the tools of nonlinear dynamics, and greater understanding of nervous system function, has opened the door to new ways of conceptualizing variability in motor behavior (Arbib et al., 1998; Newell & Corcos, 1993). Variability at all levels of the movement system is seen as playing an important functional role in adaptive behavior, an inherent determinative property rather than a peripheral, limiting factor. Because dynamical systems are inherently unstable and the constraints or working conditions underlying performance never identical, the learner has to continually search for regions of stability or attraction within the perceptuomotor workspace. The arguments against computational neuroscience presented earlier in this chapter suggest that practice is not intended to help the movement system write better motor programs (Conrad, 1989; Meijer, 1988). Instead, variability in practice and movement dynamics enhances this search process by increasing learners' exposure to varieties of task solutions (Newell & McDonald, 1991, 1992). Skill is enhanced because learners have the opportunity to more thoroughly search and discover the dynamical laws that organize information and action. By manipulating the different control variables underlying system dynamics, learners are able to move the system through different functional attractor states, continually probing the boundaries of their stability and providing a range of potential movement solutions. Experience of discovering various solutions to the task, whether successful or not, is essential in learning to explore and exploit system dynamics. Observations of variability in performance should not necessarily, therefore, be viewed negatively but as a reflection of the readiness or plasticity of the system to change. It is becoming clear that the structure of performance variability in a dynamical movement system needs to be measured over time and requires careful interpretation by the motor behavior specialist (Newell & Slifkin, 1998).

Implications for Coaches

In the early stages of skill learning, traditional approaches emphasize the importance of verbal instructions, specific practice, simple-to-complex progressions, and augmented feedback in prescribing strict compliance to a particular movement pattern. The difficulty with such a prescriptive approach is that coaches do not provide learners with the opportunity to search or explore the dynamics of the performance context. From an integrated modeling viewpoint, coaches are encouraged to value and exploit variability in practice by providing learners with the opportunity to search and explore the perceptuomotor workspace and to discover optimal solutions to the degrees of freedom problem posed by the skill (McDonald et al., 1995; Newell, 1996). For example, neo-Darwinian models of brain and behavior, which emphasize the emergence of stable, functionally relevant neuronal patterns of connections, support the argument that variability in practice should be exploited through the processes of "search and assemble under constraint." It has been shown that the search process allows the learner to assemble a coordination solution that eventually results in the establishment of a relatively stable pattern of connections between neurons in different parts of the brain (e.g., Spoorns & Edelman, 1998). Interestingly, a more adaptive approach to coaching has also been advocated recently in the cognitive science literature, as highlighted by contemporary research on variability of practice, contextual interference, and summary and bandwidth feedback (e.g., see Janelle, Barba, Frehlich, Tennant, & Cauraugh, 1997). Such instructional techniques cultivate a less prescriptive and more self-regulated or discovery-oriented approach to instruction, emphasizing the ideas of exploration within particular workspaces and increasing the learner's exposure to varieties of task solutions (e.g., see Davids et al., 1994).

In a more integrated approach to instruction, the key problem for the coach is to guide and constrain the search process such that exploratory activity occurs over an optimal area of the perceptuomotor workspace. An expansive workspace permits a more extensive search, probes different states of stability, and helps develop adaptive complex systems. Although prescriptive coaching strategies may produce temporary solutions and relatively stable neuronal connections in the brain for immediate performance effects, effective retention and transfer of movement skills require a less prescriptive "hands off" approach to coaching (Davids & Handford, 1994; Handford et al., 1997). Successful coaches achieve a balance between encouraging persistence and encouraging change, pushing the learner to probe various states of system stability, identifying the dynamic characteristics of the system, and discovering multiple task solutions. Coaches can create an appropriate

discovery environment by guiding exploration of the workspace through manipulation of task, environmental, and organismic constraints. Some examples of how constraints may be manipulated to limit the boundaries of the search are considered next.

Manipulating Constraints during Practice: Allowing Learners to Learn

There are many examples in sport of how coaches manipulate the constraints of the learning environment to facilitate skill acquisition. In soccer, coaches often use conditioned games to elicit certain types of behaviors from players. One- and two-touch practices constrain the learner to search for available passing opportunities prior to receiving the ball, and games that allow goals to be scored solely from crosses encourage teams to employ width in offensive play as well as developing the skills of heading and volleying. Other constraints that may be employed to promote discovery learning in team sports include the implementation of tight time constraints, the restriction of space through use of playing areas or zones, and the selective use of opponents to manipulate pressure (Davids, 1998). Similarly, in tennis, practice drills that require one player to stay at the net while an opponent remains on the baseline constrain the learner to play effective volleys or passing and lob shots, respectively (e.g., see Steinberg, Chaffin, & Singer, 1999). Preventing players from playing boast and drop shots during practice in squash promotes effective use of forehand and backhand drive shots, whereas constraining action to the forecourt region challenges learners to discover relatively unique ways of playing drop shots (e.g., see McKenzie, 1992).

Physical restraints may also constitute important task constraints on performance. For instance, in volleyball blocking, elasticized material is used to help learners acquire a functional bipedal coordination pattern for traversing the court at speed. In soccer, coaches use rope, secured to both posts and the goalkeeper, to constrain goalkeepers' positioning in restricting an attacker's view of the goal in one-on-one practice situations. Buoyancy aids and hand paddles in swimming and restraining harnesses in gymnastics and trampolining are other examples of how physical constraints can impact on skill acquisition in sport.

Although the majority of examples in sport relate to the manipulation of task constraints, plausible opportunities exist for innovative coaches to unlock potential through modifying organismic and environmental constraints. For example, emotional states such as anxiety may be manipulated in practice through use of induced competition or selected use of ego stressors (e.g., see Williams & Elliott, 1999). It is apparent that anxiety has a significant impact on several subsystems (e.g., physical, cognitive, perceptual), and learners in sport must be gradually exposed to it as a significant situational constraint on emergent behavior in sport (e.g., see Beuter & Duda, 1985; Bootsma, Bakker, Van Snippenberg, & Tdlohreg, 1992; Janelle, Singer, & Williams, 1999). Exposure to the situational constraint of anxiety allows the learner to practice strategies for stabilizing intrinsic movement system dynamics in the face of perturbations during competitive performance. These ideas have been supported by work on implicit and explicit learning in sport from a cognitive science perspective. For example, work by Masters and others (e.g., Masters, 1992) suggests that skills learned through implicit, self-directed approaches are less susceptible to the perturbing forces enforced by the organismic constraint of anxiety.

Coaches can manipulate the constraints of the learning environment equally effectively in self-paced as well as externally paced tasks. For example, in a self-paced task such as golf putting, the task constraints, such as distance to the hole, speed of the green, and the undulating nature of the terrain, can be effectively manipulated to encourage the development of movement system flexibility in adapting to a variety of performance conditions. Similarly, creative coaches may carefully manipulate various organismic (e.g., the learner's emotional and physiological state, such as anxiety, motivation, and fatigue) and environmental (e.g., weather conditions during practice, condition of the green, audience effects) constraints in an attempt to create variability in practice. Variability can also be introduced when learning more stable, self-paced skills such as archery and biathlon shooting. In such instances, variations in the background character of the learning context, such as the number and importance of the shots, crowd size/noise, and weather, may prove particularly effective.

The process of manipulating constraints during learning challenges coaches to be highly creative in designing games and practices that enable relevant skills to emerge in learners. A primary task for coaches is to master the specific and unique constraints underlying system behavior and how these can be manipulated for effective learning. Newell (1989) proposed that a "general theory of movement can be formulated only from a thorough grounding of the principles of task constraints" (p. 94). It is argued that this challenging task forms the basis of a principled constraints-led approach to practice in sport (Davids et al., in press). The problem with early approaches to this problem, according to Newell, is that previous attempts at the classification of tasks "have been closer to task description than to theoretical explanation" (p. 93).

Structural Organization of Practice: How Should Tasks Be Decomposed to Facilitate Learning?

Some skills are highly complex, and consequently, most coaches advocate part practice techniques to break down tasks into parts for rehearsal. Such techniques are frequently employed when teaching skills such as javelin throwing, long jumping, the tennis serve, and various gymnastic vaults. Three typical approaches to part practice include fractionization, segmentation, and simplification (see Wightman & Lintern, 1985). These procedures involve practicing parts of a skill separately, prior to adding other component parts for subsequent practice, or simplifying some aspect of the target skill during practice. From a cognitive science perspective, part practice is presumed to be effective provided there is no interaction among task components (Schmidt & Wrisberg, 2000) or if the skill is high in complexity and low in organization (Magill, 1998). The difficulty for coaches is that such evaluations are based purely on subjective assessment of skills, or at best on some limited form of task analysis. The use of part practice techniques in skill instruction may therefore be perceived as being rather tentative and unprincipled (Davids, Handford, & Williams, 1998).

Recent empirical findings from studies of volleyball serving have suggested that perception-action coupling may provide a more principled basis for determining whether tasks are amenable to part practice techniques (see Davids et al., 1999). In the overhead serve in volleyball, as well as in other related activities such as the tennis serve, the ball toss phase is often practiced independently of the service action. The assumption is that a successful serve is largely dependent on accurate ball placement. However, a recent study by Davids, Bennett, Court, Tayler, & Button (1997) showed significant variance in ball placement when elite volleyball players were required to complete a ball-placement-only task using their normal technique, but without striking the ball, compared with their customary full-service action. Three-dimensional film analysis indicated that there was less variability in the ball's position at the zenith and that the zenith was lower under full-service compared with ball-placement-only conditions. Ball placement was closely coupled with other phases of the action, particularly the initiation of forward movement at the hip. The servers were controlling the height of the ball zenith to ensure that the time remaining before contact was equivalent to the time required for the proximal-distal unfolding of the kinematic chain involved in the striking movement (Davids et al., 1999). The ball's zenith appears to act as an important functional constraint on emergent dynamics during the volleyball serve, suggesting that components of the skill should not be taught in isolation from each other. From a dynamical systems viewpoint, if the ball-placement phase is decoupled from the reach-and-contact phase during practice, it may disrupt important functional couplings between control and order parameters in self-paced, extrinsic-timing tasks. In line with Newell's (1989) suggestion for more work on understanding task constraints, an important role for sport psychologists, therefore, is to determine the specific information sources (e.g., perceptual invariants) that constrain movement dynamics in specific sport tasks. Understanding the nature of perception-action coupling in sport promotes awareness of how self-organization processes in the movement system can be exploited, and helps coaches manipulate key informational constraints to enhance skill acquisition.

From the perspective of integrated modeling, there is support emerging for employing the principle of perception-action coupling to constrain the way that sports actions are decomposed for subsequent practice, as evidenced in the neuroscience research of Milner and Goodale (1995). They argued that there are two separate pathways connecting visual and motor centers in the cortex. A ventral stream running from the striate cortex to the inferotemporal region is critical to the visual perception and identification of objects, and a dorsal root that runs from the striate cortex to the posterior parietal cortex mediates the required sensorimotor transformations for visually guided actions directed at those objects. This dedicated visuomotor pathway could provide a neurological basis for the concept of perception-action coupling and its implications for practice. The key point is that practice should be specific to the functional demands placed on perceptual and action systems during sports performance. In the case of the volleyball serve, practice on one component of the serve without the other prevents learners from exploring emerging relationships between perceptual information from the ball's trajectory and the functional muscle synergies of the striking system. A decoupling of the demands on the perceptual and motor systems during practice would therefore prevent learners from developing the cortical neural pathways underlying perception-for-action.

Further empirical effort is required to confirm the importance of information-movement coupling for skill acquisition and to identify other structure-function relations in the nervous system for guiding effective practice. Thus far, few studies have attempted to examine the neural basis

of motor learning, and integrative modeling approaches based on neuroscience and behavioral research are in their infancy (Worringham, Smiley-Oyen, & Cross, 1996). However, preliminary observations are promising, and guidelines based on principles of integrative modeling have already been proposed to guide practice during imagery and observational learning (e.g., see Decety & Grèzes, 1999) and the development of anticipation skill in sport (e.g., see Williams & Grant, 1999).

SUMMARY AND CONCLUSIONS

In this chapter, potential implications of a more integrated model of brain and behavioral processes on motor behavior theory development have been examined. Motor behavior theories are broadly concerned with the problem of how goals are selected during movement, as well as the processes involved in achieving these goals (e.g., Bernstein, 1967; Kelso, 1995; Schmidt & Lee, 1999; Willingham, 1998). Several shortcomings in traditional cognitive science models of motor behavior were identified. Potential advantages of an alternative framework based on ecological psychology, dynamical systems theory, and the neurosciences have been highlighted. The propositions of COBALT supported the main message from Willingham's argument that an integrated theoretical framework is needed to make sense of the neuropsychological research on brain processes and structures as it relates to motor behavior. However, the position that we have developed differs from Willingham's computational approach. It was argued that complementary modeling of structure-function relations in the CNS, with a computational basis, is difficult to sustain unless developments in the neurosciences more rigorously constrain theoretical developments. The implication is that the computer cannot be used as a metaphor for the study of organic material like the brain without reference to the physical laws and the social, historical, and biological constraints that influence its behavior (Penrose, 1994).

Given the inadequacies of digital electronics as the traditional computational framework for interpreting brain function during motor learning, the biophysical basis of the human nervous system as a complex system was explored. The role of cognitive science constructs such as representations, comparators, and controllers in the nervous system during motor behavior has never been verified directly by neurophysiological research, but has been implied through the associated black-box complementary modeling approach (Globus, 1995). Ingvaldsen and Whiting (1997) warned that this type of strategy could overdetermine research on motor behavior due to the use of an ill-defined theoretical framework that constrains the phenomena selected for investigation, the questions asked, and the methods utilized. In biological movement systems, the relationship among intentions, perceptions, and actions, under different task constraints during goal-directed behavior, is paramount. To gain a detailed understanding of these relationships, movement scientists are beginning to recognize the need to move beyond "strictly phenomenological models" (Carson & Riek, 1998, p. 209).

Viewing the brain as embedded in body and environment could require a multidisciplinary theoretical framework more akin to that required for studying pattern-forming dynamics in complex systems, rather than computing representational systems. The rejection of COBALT as a theoretical framework for the study of motor learning is in line with recent criticisms of the failure of computational theories to be appropriately constrained by neurophysiological evidence (e.g., Ingvaldsen & Whiting, 1997). In the discussion of the propositions of COBALT, it was suggested that the proliferation of computational theories of motor learning may have resulted from an overemphasis on the "how" questions concerned with specifying mechanisms and structures in modernist science. A more appropriate approach to the study of complex systems in biology may include a postmodern perspective and an equal emphasis on "why" questions, focusing on the teleological basis for the functional evolution of the dynamic nervous system.

In keeping with the chapter's overriding theme of integrative modeling in motor behavior research, an attempt was made to highlight the need for closer integration between behavioral and neural perspectives on motor learning. The lead for integrative modeling has already been provided in the motor control area, where behavioral and neuroscience perspectives are beginning to overlap. The challenge to identify structure-function relationships for motor learning, as for motor control, is likely to increase in importance in the future (Striedter, 1998; Worringham et al., 1996). Motor behaviorists may need to explore alternative theoretical frameworks, not merely the computational paradigm, to integrate ideas for functional modeling of neural and dynamical processes.

REFERENCES

Abernethy, B., Burgess-Limerick, R., & Parks, S. (1994). Contrasting approaches to the study of motor expertise. *Quest, 46,* 186–198.

Abernethy, B., Kippers, V., Mackinnon, L.T., Neal, R.J., & Hanrahan, S. (1997). *The biophysical foundations of human movement.* Champaign, IL: Human Kinetics.

Anderson, D.I., & Sidaway, B. (1994). Coordination changes associated with practice of a soccer kick. *Research Quarterly for Exercise and Sport, 65,* 93–99.

Arbib, M.A., Érdi, P., & Szentágothai, J. (1998). *Neural organization: Structure, function and dynamics.* Cambridge, MA: MIT Press.

Arutyunyan, G.H., Gurfinkel, V.S., & Mirskii, M.L. (1968). Investigation of aiming at a target. *Biophysics, 13,* 536–538.

Baddeley, A.D., & Hitch, G. (1974). Working memory. In G.H. Bower (Ed.), *The psychology of learning and motivation* (Vol. 8, pp. 179–201). London: Academic Press.

Bechtel, W. (1998). Representations and cognitive explanations: Assessing the dynamicist's challenge in cognitive science. *Cognitive Science, 22,* 295–318.

Beek, P.J., Peper, C.E., & Stegeman, D.F. (1995). Dynamical models of movement coordination. *Human Movement Science, 14,* 573–608.

Bernstein, N.A. (1967). *The coordination and regulation of movements.* Oxford, England: Pergamon Press.

Beuter, A., & Duda, J.L. (1985). Analysis of the arousal/motor performance relationship in children using movement kinematics. *Journal of Sport Psychology, 7,* 229–243.

Blumberg, M.S., & Wasserman, E.A. (1995). Animal mind and the argument from design. *American Psychologist, 50,* 133–144.

Bongaardt, R. (1996). *Shifting focus: The Bernstein tradition in movement science.* Amsterdam: Free University Press.

Bootsma, R.J., Bakker, F.C., Van Snippenberg, F.J., & Tdlohreg, C.W. (1992). The effects of anxiety on perceiving the reachability of passing objects. *Ecological Psychology, 4,* 1–16.

Brady, F. (1998). A theoretical and empirical review of the contextual interference effect and the learning of motor skills. *Quest, 50,* 266–293.

Bruce, V., Green, P.R., & Georgeson, M. (1996). *Visual perception: Physiology, psychology and ecology* (3rd ed.). London: Erlbaum.

Bugmann, G. (1997). Biologically plausible neural computation. *BioSystems, 40,* 11–19.

Burgess-Limerick, R., Neal, R.J., & Abernethy, B. (1992). Against relative timing invariance in movement kinematics. *Quarterly Journal of Experimental Psychology, 44A,* 705–722.

Button, C., Davids, K., Bennett, S.J., & Tayler, M. (in press). Mechanical perturbation of the wrist during one-handed catching. *Acta Psychologica.*

Calvin, W.H. (1996). *The cerebral code: Thinking a thought in the mosaics of the mind.* Cambridge, MA: MIT Press.

Camras, L.A. (1992). Expressive development and basic emotions. *Cognition and Emotion, 6,* 269–283.

Carello, C., Turvey, M.T., Kugler, P.N., & Shaw, R.E. (1984). Inadequacies of a computer metaphor. In M. Gazzaniga (Ed.), *Handbook of cognitive neuroscience* (pp. 229–248). New York: Plenum Press.

Carson, R.C., & Riek, S. (1998). Moving beyond phenomenology: Neuromuscular-skeletal constraints upon coordination dynamics. In J.P. Piek (Ed) *Motor behavior and human skill: A multidisciplinary approach* (pp. 209–230). Champaign, IL: Human Kinetics.

Carson, R.G., Thomas, J., Summers, J.J., Walters, M.R., & Semjen, A. (1997). The dynamics of bimanual circle drawing. *Quarterly Journal of Experimental Psychology, 50A,* 664–683.

Colley, A. (1989). Learning motor skills: Integrating cognition and action. In A. Colley & J. Beech (Eds.), *Acquisition and performance of cognitive skills* (pp. 167–189). Chichester, England: Wiley.

Conrad, D. (1989). Consciousness and the practice of science. *Journal of the Indian Council of Philosophical Research, 6,* 57–65.

Court, M.L.J., Bennett, S., Davids, K., & Williams, A.M. (1998). Effects of anxiety on bimanual coordination. *Journal of Sport & Exercise Psychology, 20,* S103.

Daugman, J.G. (1990). Brain metaphor and brain theory. In E.L. Schwartz (Ed.), *Computational neuroscience* (pp. 12–35). Cambridge, MA: MIT Press.

Davids, K. (1998). How much teaching is necessary for optimal learning of football skills? The role of discovery learning. *Insight: The Football Association Coaches Journal, 2,* 35–36.

Davids, K. (in press). Skill acquisition and the theory of deliberate practice: It ain't what you do it's the way that you do it! *International Journal of Sport Psychology.*

Davids, K., & Bennett, S.J. (1998). The dynamical hypothesis: The role of biological constraints on cognition. *The Behavioral and Brain Sciences, 21,* 636.

Davids, K., Bennett, S.J., Court, M., Tayler, M.A., & Button, C. (1997). The cognition-dynamics interface. In R. Lidor & M. Bar-Eli (Eds.), *Innovations in sport psychology: Linking theory and practice* (pp. 224–226). Netanya, Israel: International Society for Sport Psychology.

Davids, K., Bennett, S.J., Handford, C., & Jones, B. (1999). Acquiring coordination in self-paced, extrinsic timing tasks: A constraints-led perspective. *International Journal of Sport Psychology, 30,* 437–461.

Davids, K., & Button, C. (2000). The cognition-dynamics interface and intentionality in action. *International Journal of Sport Psychology*

Davids, K., & Handford, C.H. (1994). Perception and action in sport: The practice behind the theories. *Coaching Focus, 26,* 3–5.

Davids, K., Handford, C.H., & Williams, A.M. (1994). The natural physical alternative to cognitive theories of motor behavior: An invitation for interdisciplinary research in sports science? *Journal of Sports Sciences, 12,* 495–528.

Davids, K., Handford, C.H., & Williams, A.M. (1998). Evaluation, planning and organizing skill acquisition programmes in sport: The role of ecological sport psychologists. In H. Steinberg, I. Cockerill, & A. Dewey (Eds.), *What sport psychologists do* (pp. 94–100). Leicester, England: British Psychological Society.

Davids, K., Lees, A., & Burwitz, L. (in press). Understanding and measuring coordination and control in soccer skills: Implications for talent identification and skill acquisition. *Journal of Sports Sciences.*

Davidson, R.J., & Schwartz, G.E. (1976). The psychobiology of relaxation and related states: A multi process theory. In D.I. Mostofsky (Ed.), *Behavior control and modification of physiological activity* (pp. 399–442). Englewood Cliffs, NJ: Prentice-Hall.

Decety, J. (1996). Do imagined and executed actions share the same neural substrate? *Cognitive Brain Research, 3,* 87–93.

Decety, J., & Grèzes, J. (1999). Neural mechanisms subserving the perception of human actions. *Trends in Cognitive Sciences, 3,* 172–178.

Decety, J., Perani, D., Jeannerod, M., Bettinardi, V., Tadary, B., Woods, R., Mazziotta, J.C., & Fazio, F. (1994). Mapping motor representations with positron emission tomography. *Nature, 371,* 600–602.

Deecke, L. (1990). Electrophysiological correlates of movement initiation. *Reviews of Neurology, 146,* 612–619.

Easterbrook, J.A. (1959). The effect of emotion on cue utilisation and the organization of behavior. *Psychological Review, 66,* 183–201.

Edelman, G. (1992). *Bright air brilliant fire: On the matter of the mind.* London: Penguin.

Érdi, P. (1996). The brain as a hermeneutic device. *BioSystems, 38,* 179–189.

Eysenck, M.W. (1992). *The cognitive perspective.* Hove, England: Erlbaum.

Eysenck, M.W., & Calvo, M.G. (1992). Anxiety and performance: The processing efficiency theory. *Cognition and Emotion, 6,* 409–434.

Fazey, J.A., & Hardy, L. (1988). *The inverted-U hypothesis: A catastrophe for sport psychology.* (British Association of Sports Sciences Monograph, No. 1). Leeds, England: National Coaching Foundation.

Fodor, J.A. (1980). Methodological solopsism considered as a research strategy in cognitive psychology. *Behavioral and Brain Sciences, 3,* 63.

Freeman, W.J. (1995). *Societies of brains: A study in the neuroscience of love and hate.* Hillsdale, NJ: Erlbaum.

Freeman, W.J. (1997). Nonlinear neurodynamics of intentionality. *Journal of Mind and Behavior, 18,* 291–304.

Freeman, W.J. (1999). *How brains make up their mind.* London: Weidenfeld & Nicolson.

Freeman, W.J. (2000a). A proposed name for aperiodic brain activity: Stochastic chaos. *Neural Networks, 13,* 11–13.

Freeman, W.J. (2000b). *Neurodynamics: An exploration in mesoscopic brain dynamics.* London: Springer-Verlag.

Freeman, W.J., & Nunez, R. (2000). *Reclaiming cognition.* Thorverton, England: Imprint Academic.

Frith, C.D., Friston, K., Liddle, P.F., & Frackowiak, R.S.J. (1991). Willed action and the prefrontal cortex in man: A study with PET. *Proceedings of the Royal Society of London B., 244,* 241–246.

Gentner, D.R. (1987). Timing of skill in motor performance: Tests of the proportional duration model. *Psychological Review, 94,* 255–276.

Glencross, D., Whiting, H.T.A., & Abernethy, B. (1994). Motor control, motor learning and the acquisition of skill: Historical trends and future directions. *International Journal of Sport Psychology, 25,* 32–52.

Globus, G.G. (1992). Toward a noncomputational cognitive neuroscience. *Journal of Cognitive Neuroscience, 4,* 299–310.

Globus, G.G. (1995). *The postmodern brain.* Amsterdam: Benjamins.

Goerner, S., & Combs, A. (1998). Consciousness as a self-organizing process: An ecological perspective. *BioSystems, 46,* 123–127.

Goodale, M.A., & Humphrey, K.G. (1998). The objects of action and perception. *Cognition, 67,* 181–207.

Goodale, M.A., & Milner, A.D. (1992). Separate visual pathways for perception and action. *Trends in Neurosciences, 15,* 20–25.

Gould, D., & Krane, V. (1992). The arousal-athletic performance relationship: Current status and future directions. In T.S. Horn (Ed), *Advances in sport psychology* (pp. 119–142). Champaign, IL: Human Kinetics.

Haggard, P., & Wing, A. (1995). Coordinated responses following mechanical perturbation of the arm during prehension. *Experimental Brain Research, 102,* 483–494.

Haken, H., Kelso, J.A.S., & Bunz, H. (1985). A theoretical model of phase transitions in human hand movements. *Biological Cybernetics, 51,* 347–356.

Handford, C.H., Davids, K., Bennett, S., & Button, C. (1997). Skill acquisition in sport: Some applications of an evolving practice ecology. *Journal of Sports Sciences, 15,* 621–640.

Harris, L.R., & Jenkin, M. (1998). *Vision and action.* Cambridge, England: Cambridge University Press.

Heft, H. (1989). Affordances and the body: An intentional analysis of Gibson's ecological approach to visual perception. *Journal for the Theory of Social Behavior, 19,* 1–30.

Huether, G. (1996). The central adaptation syndrome: Psychosocial stress as a trigger for adaptive modifications of brain structure and function. *Progress in Neurobiology, 48,* 569–612.

Ingvaldsen, R.P., & Whiting, H.T.A. (1997). Modern views on motor skill learning are not "representative." *Human Movement Science, 16,* 705–732.

Janelle, C.M., Barba, D.A., Frehlich, S.G., Tennant, L.K., & Cauraugh, J.H. (1997). Maximizing feedback effectiveness through videotape replay and a self-controlled learning environment. *Research Quarterly for Exercise and Sport, 68,* 269–279.

Janelle, C.M., Singer, R.N., & Williams, A.M. (1999). External distraction and attentional narrowing: Visual search evidence. *Journal of Sport & Exercise Psychology, 21,* 70–91.

Jeannerod, M. (1997). *The cognitive neuroscience of action.* Oxford, England: Blackwell.

Johnson-Laird, P.N. (1993). *The computer and the mind: An introduction to cognitive science.* London: Fontana.

Jones, G., & Swain, A. (1992). Intensity and direction dimensions of competitive state anxiety and relationships with competitiveness. *Perceptual and Motor Skills, 74,* 467–472.

Kant, I. (1929). *Critique of pure reason (Norman Kemp Smith, Trans.).* London: Macmillan.

Kauffmann, S.A. (1993). *The origins of order: Self-organisation and selection in evolution.* New York: Oxford University Press.

Kauffmann, S.A. (1995). *At home in the universe: The search for laws of complexity.* London: Viking.

Keil, D., & Davids, K. (2000). Lifting the screen on neural organization: Is computational functional modeling necessary? *Behavioral and Brain Sciences, 23*(4), 102–103.

Kelso, J.A.S. (1981). On the oscillatory basis of movement. *Bulletin of the Psychonomic Society, 18,* 63.

Kelso, J.A.S. (1984). Phase transitions and critical behavior in human bimanual coordination. *American Journal of Physiology: Regulatory, Integrative and Comparative Physiology, 15,* R1000–R1004.

Kelso, J.A.S. (1992). Theoretical concepts and strategies for understanding perceptual-motor skill: From informational capacity in closed systems to self-organization in open, nonequilibrium systems. *Journal of Experimental Psychology: General, 121,* 260–261.

Kelso, J.A.S. (1994). The informational character of self-organised co-ordination dynamics. *Human Movement Science, 13,* 393–413.

Kelso, J.A.S. (1995). *Dynamic patterns: The self-organization of brain and behavior.* Cambridge, MA: MIT Press.

Kelso, J.A.S., Fuchs, A., Lancaster, R., Holroyd, T., Cheyne, D., & Weinberg, H. (1998). Dynamical cortical activity in the human brain reveals motor equivalence. *Nature, 392,* 814–818.

Kugler, P.N. (1986). A morphological perspective on the origin and evolution of movement patterns. In M. Wade & H.T.A. Whiting (Eds.), *Motor development in children: Aspects of co-ordination and control* (pp. 459–525). Dordrecht, The Netherlands: Martinus Nijhoff.

Kugler, P.N., Kelso, J.A.S., & Turvey, M.T. (1980). On the concept of coordinative structures as dissipative structures: I. Theoretical lines of convergence. In G.E. Stelmach & J. Requin (Eds.), *Tutorials in motor behavior* (pp. 3–47). Amsterdam: North Holland.

Kugler, P.N., Shaw, R.E., Vicente, K.J., & Kinsella-Shaw, J. (1990). Inquiry into intentional systems: Issues in ecological physics. *Psychological Research, 52*, 98–121.

Lee, T.D., Blandin, Y., & Proteau, L. (1996). Effects of task instructions and oscillation frequency on bimanual coordination *Psychological Research, 59*, 100–106.

Magill, R.A. (1998). *Motor learning: Concepts and applications* (5th ed.). Dubuque, IA: Brown.

Maraj, B.K.V., Elliott, D., Lee, T.D., & Pollock, B.J. (1993). Variance and invariance in expert and novice triple jumpers. *Research Quarterly for Exercise and Sport, 64*, 404–412.

Marks, D.F. (1999). Consciousness, mental imagery and action. *British Journal of Psychology, 90*, 567–585.

Masters, R.S.W. (1992). Knowledge, knerves and know-how: The role of explicit versus implicit knowledge in the breakdown of a complex motor skill under pressure. *British Journal of Psychology, 83*, 343–358.

McCrone, J. (1999). *Going inside.* London: Faber & Faber.

McDonald, P.V., Oliver, S.K., & Newell, K.M. (1995). Perceptual-motor exploration as a function of biomechanical and task constraints. *Acta Psychologica, 88*, 127–166.

McKenzie, I. (1992). *The squash workshop.* Marlborough, England: Crowood Press.

Meijer, O.G. (1988). *The hierarchy debate: Perspectives for a theory and history of movement science.* Amsterdam: Free University Press.

Meijer, O.G., & Bongaardt, R. (1992). Synergetics, self-simplification, and the ability to undo. In R. Friedrich & A. Wunderlin (Eds.), *Evolution of dynamical structures in complex systems* (pp. 272–298). Berlin, Germany: Springer-Verlag.

Meijer, O.G., & Roth, K. (1988). *Complex movement behaviour: "The" motor-action controversy.* Amsterdam: North Holland.

Meijer, O.G., Wagenaar, R.C., & Blankendaal, F.C.M. (1988). The hierarchy debate: Tema con variazioni. In O.G. Meijer & K. Roth (Eds.), *Complex movement behaviour: "The" motor-action controversy* (pp. 489–561). Amsterdam: North Holland.

Michaels, C.F., & Beek, P. (1996). The state of ecological psychology. *Ecological Psychology, 7*, 259–278.

Milner, D.A., & Goodale, M.A. (1995). *The visual brain in action.* Oxford, England: Oxford University Press.

Neisser, U. (1994). Multiple systems: A new approach to cognitive theory. *European Journal of Cognitive Psychology, 6*, 225–241.

Newell, K.M. (1986). Constraints on the development of coordination. In M. Wade & H.T.A. Whiting (Eds.), *Motor development in children: Aspects of coordination and control* (pp. 341–360). Dordrecht, The Netherlands: Martinus Nijhoff.

Newell, K.M. (1989). On task and theory specificity. *Journal of Motor Behavior, 21*, 92–96.

Newell, K.M. (1991). Motor skill acquisition. *Annual Review of Psychology, 42*, 213–237.

Newell, K.M. (1996). Change in movement and skill: Learning, retention and transfer. In M.L. Latash & M.T. Turvey (Eds.), *Dexterity and its development* (pp. 393–429). Hillsdale, NJ: Erlbaum.

Newell, K.M., & Corcos, D.M. (1993). Issues in variability and motor control. In K.M. Newell & D.M. Corcos (Eds.), *Variability and motor control* (pp. 1–12). Champaign, IL: Human Kinetics.

Newell, K.M., & McDonald, P.V. (1991). Practice: A search for task solutions. In R. Christina & H.M. Eckert (Eds.), *American Academy of Physical Education papers: Enhancing human performance in sport: New concepts and developments* (pp. 51–60). Champaign, IL: Human Kinetics.

Newell, K.M., & McDonald, P.V. (1992). Searching for solutions to the coordination function: Learning as exploration behavior. In G.E. Stelmach & J. Requin (Eds.), *Tutorials in motor behavior II* (pp. 517–531). Amsterdam: North Holland.

Newell, K.M., & Slifkin, A.B. (1998). The nature of movement variability. In J.P. Piek (Ed.), *Motor behavior and human skill: A multidisciplinary approach* (pp. 143–160). Champaign, IL: Human Kinetics.

Pattee, H.H. (1979). Complementation vs. reduction as an explanation of biological complexity. *American Journal of Physiology, 5*, 241–246.

Penrose, R. (1994). *Shadows of the mind: On consciousness, computation and the new physics of the mind.* Oxford, England: Oxford University Press.

Pickering, J. (1997). Beyond cognitivism: Mutualism and postmodern psychology. In P. Pylkkanen, P. Pylkko, & A. Hautamaki (Eds.), *Brain, mind and physics* (pp. 183–204). Amsterdam: IOS Press.

Polman, R.C.J., Whiting, H.T.A., & Savelsbergh, G.J.P. (1996). The spatio-temporal structure of control variables during catching in different load conditions. *Experimental Brain Research, 109*, 483–494.

Pressing, J. (1998). Referential behavior theory: A framework for multiple perspectives on motor control. In J.P. Piek (Ed.), *Motor behavior and human skill: A multidisciplinary approach* (pp. 357–384). Champaign, IL: Human Kinetics.

Prigogine, I., & Stengers, I. (1984). *Order out of chaos.* New York: Bantam Books.

Proteau, L., Tremblay, L., & DeJaeger, D. (1998). Practice does not diminish the role of visual information in on-line control of a precision walking task: Support for the specificity of practice hypothesis. *Journal of Motor Behavior, 30,* 143–150.

Reed, S.K. (1993). A schema-based theory of transfer. In D.K. Detterman & R.J. Sternberg (Eds.), *Transfer on trial: Intelligence, cognition, and instruction* (pp. 39–67). Newark, NJ: Ablex.

Saltzman, E.L., & Kelso, J.A.S. (1987). Skilled actions: A task-dynamic approach. *Psychological Review, 94,* 84–106.

Schmidt, R.A., & Lee, T.D. (1999). *Motor control and learning: A behavioral emphasis.* Champaign, IL: Human Kinetics.

Schmidt, R.A., & Wrisberg, C.A. (2000). *Motor learning and performance: A problem-based learning approach.* Champaign, IL: Human Kinetics.

Scholz, J.P., & Kelso, J.A.S. (1990). Intentional switching between patterns of bimanual co-ordination is dependent on the intrinsic dynamics of the patterns. *Journal of Motor Behavior, 22,* 98–124.

Schöner, G. (1990). A dynamic theory of coordination of discrete movement. *Biological Cybernetics, 63,* 257–270.

Schöner, G. (1995). Recent developments and problems in human movement science and their conceptual implications. *Ecological Psychology, 7,* 291–314.

Schöner, G., & Kelso, J.A.S. (1988a). Dynamic patterns of biological coordination: Theoretical strategy and new results. In J.A.S. Kelso, A.J. Mandell, & M.F. Schlesinger (Eds.), *Dynamic patterns in complex systems* (pp. 77–102). Singapore: World Scientific Singapore.

Schöner, G., & Kelso, J.A.S. (1988b). A dynamic pattern theory of behavioral change. *Journal of Theoretical Biology, 135,* 501–524.

Sejnowski, T., Koch, C., & Churchland, P. (1988). Computational neuroscience. *Science 241,* 1299–1306.

Semjen, A., Summers, J.J., & Cattaert, D. (1995). Hand coordination in bimanual circle drawing. *Journal of Experimental Psychology: Human Perception and Performance, 21,* 1139–1157.

Slifkin, A.B., & Newell, K.M. (1999). Noise, information transmission, and force variability. *Journal of Experimental Psychology: Human Perception and Performance, 25,* 837–851.

Spoorns, O., & Edelman, G.M. (1998). Bernstein's dynamic view of the brain: The current problems of modern neurophysiology (1945). *Motor Control, 2,* 283–305.

Steinberg, G.M., Chaffin, W.M., & Singer, R.N. (1998). Mental quickness training: Drills that emphasize the development of anticipation skills in fast-paced sports. *Journal of Physical Education, Recreation & Dance, 69,* 37–41.

Stoffregren, T.A., & Bardy, B.G. (in press). On specification and the senses. *Behavioral and Brain Sciences.*

Striedter, G.F. (1998). A comparative perspective on motor learning. *Neurobiology of Learning and Memory, 70,* 189–196.

Summers, J.J. (Ed.). (1992). *Approaches to the study of motor control and learning.* Amsterdam: North Holland.

Summers, J.J. (1998). Has ecological psychology delivered what it promised? In J.P. Piek (Ed.), *Motor behavior and human skill: A multidisciplinary approach* (pp. 385–402). Champaign, IL: Human Kinetics.

Summers, J.J., Byblow, W.D., Bysouth-Young, D.F., & Semjen, A. (1998). Bimanual circle drawing during secondary task loading. *Motor Control, 2,* 106–113.

Thelen, E. (1995). Time-scale dynamics and the development of an embodied cognition. In R.F. Port & T. Van Gelder (Eds.), *Mind as motion: Explorations on the dynamics of cognition* (pp. 32–51). Cambridge, MA: MIT Press.

Thelen, E., & Smith, L.B. (1994). *A dynamic systems approach to the development of cognition and action.* Cambridge, MA: MIT Press.

Thom, R. (1975). *Structural stability and morphogenesis.* New York: Addison-Wesley.

Turvey, M.T. (1990). Coordination. *American Psychologist, 45,* 938–953.

Van Gelder, T. (1998). The dynamical hypothesis. *Behavioral and Brain Sciences, 21,* 636–644.

van Wieringen, P.C.W. (1988). Kinds and levels of explanation: Implications for the motor systems versus action systems controversy. In O.G. Meijer & K. Roth (Eds.), *Complex movement behaviour: "The" motor-action controversy* (pp. 87–119). Amsterdam: North Holland.

Varela, F., Thompson, E., & Rosch, E. (1991). *The embodied mind.* Cambridge, MA: MIT Press.

Vereijken, B., van Emmerik, R.E.A., Whiting, H.T.A., & Newell, K.M. (1992). Free(z)ing degrees of freedom in skill acquisition. *Journal of Motor Behavior, 24,* 133–142.

Wallace, S.A., & Weeks, D.L. (1988). Temporal constraints in the control of prehensile movement. *Human Movement Science, 13,* 255–289.

Walsh, V. (2000). Neuropsychology: The touchy, feely side of vision. *Current Biology, 10,* 34–35.

Weeks, D., & Proctor, R. (1991). Ecological and process approaches to skill acquisition. *Journal of Human Movement Studies, 20,* 291–296.

Wightman, D.C., & Lintern, G. (1985). Part-task training for tracking and manual control. *Human Factors, 27,* 267–283.

Williams, A.M., Alty, P., & Lees, A. (in press). Effects of practice and knowledge of performance on the kinematics of ball kicking. In W. Spinks & T. Reilly (Eds.), *Science and Football IV.* London: E. & F.N. Spon.

Williams, A.M., Davids, K., Burwitz, L., & Williams, J.G. (1992). Perception and action in sport. *Journal of Human Movement Studies, 22,* 147–204.

Williams, A.M., Davids, K., & Williams, J.G. (1999). *Visual perception and action in sport.* London: Routledge & Kegan Paul.

Williams, A.M., & Elliott, D. (1999). Anxiety, expertise and visual search in karate. *Journal of Sport & Exercise Psychology, 21,* 362–376.

Williams, A.M., & Grant, A. (1999). Training perceptual skill in sport. *International Journal of Sport Psychology, 30,* 194–220.

Willingham, D.B. (1998). A neuropsychological theory of motor skill learning. *Psychological Review, 105,* 558–584.

Worringham, C.J., Smiley-Oyen, A.L., & Cross, C.L. (1996). Neural basis of motor learning in humans. In H.N. Zelaznik (Ed.), *Advances in motor learning and control* (pp. 67–86). Champaign, IL: Human Kinetics.

Wuyts, I.J., Summers, J.J., Carson, R.G., Byblow, W.D., & Semjen, A. (1996). Attention as a mediating variable in the dynamics of bimanual coordination. *Human Movement Science, 15,* 877–897.

Yates, F.E. (1979). Physical biology: A basis for modeling living systems. *Journal of Cybernetics and Information Science, 2,* 57–70.

CHAPTER 7

Expert Performance in Sport and Dance

JANET L. STARKES, WERNER HELSEN, and RACHEL JACK

In the past decade, the issue of expert performance has generated tremendous interest. This was not always the case. During the 1970s through the mid-1980s, there was a great reluctance by the sport establishment (athletes, coaches, and researchers) to perceive expert athletes as anything but an assemblage of physical prowess and extensive knowledge of the sport. It was difficult to convince those connected with the sport world that the development of sport-specific psychomotor capabilities and the refined used of these skills played a significant role in the acquisition of expert sport performance. Likewise, though the role of cognition was readily acknowledged in more esoteric areas such as chess and bridge, sport was never viewed as a very cognitively rich area. As a result, research on sport experts was often seen as falling between the cracks: too cognitive for sport enthusiasts, too physical for psychological study. Nevertheless, some psychologists have always thought sport was an important medium in which to study cognitive processes. In the early 1970s, Simon was convinced of the highly cognitive nature of sport and initiated verbal protocol analyses with field athletes (discus throwers). This work was put aside, however, as he continued to concentrate on chess research (H. Simon, personal communication, April 29, 1995). Long before Simon, many sport "psychologists" acknowledged the role of cognitive processes.

The relatively recent acceptance of the role of cognitive processes in determining expert sport performance has led to a substantial accumulation of literature in the area. Now, when one searches for information on sport experts, the research is likely to be published equally in sport journals and mainstream psychology journals and books. During the past five years, three special issues of the *International Journal of Sport Psychology* (1994, 1999, in press) have focused on expert-novice research in sport. Likewise, in 1994, *Quest* published a special issue on sport expertise. In the past decade, a number of books have also emerged with the theme of expertise; these have either included sections on sport or were entirely devoted to sport (Ericsson, 1996; Ericsson & Smith, 1991; Starkes & Allard, 1993; Williams, Davids, & Williams, 1999).

One of the early criticisms of the sport expertise research was the reliance on recipient paradigms from psychology (Abernethy, Thomas, & Thomas, 1993). The suggestion was that if cognitive paradigms proved successful in the study of chess or bridge playing, the paradigm could automatically be extrapolated to sport research. This was not entirely appropriate nor comprehensive in scope because expert performance in certain sports requires complex, time-constrained adaptive movements. In chess and bridge playing, the actual movement execution is a minor part of decision making and performance. To some extent, this criticism was valid. Many paradigms were simply lifted from psychology with little rationale for their applicability to sport. Yet, in the 1990s, sport expertise research often led the way in developing new approaches to examining both cognitive and movement expertise. For example, kinematic analyses of movement, eye movement registration techniques, the use of film occlusion, and the influence of dynamical systems are four areas where sport expertise research has benefited dramatically from technology development, but also proceeded in new, innovative directions. Whatever the reasons, research on expert performance in sport has grown substantially in interest, technique, and importance.

Over the past 20 years, an impressive body of literature has accumulated in the sport and dance domains with the use of the expert-novice paradigm termed "the expertise approach." The goal has been to determine those behaviors that best differentiate experts from less skilled individuals and to identify common features that may occur in more than just one sport, or even across domains. For example, in which sports/domains is it necessary for experts to have good recall of highly structured information? To date, research would suggest that this is important in areas as diverse as basketball, field hockey, soccer, dance, chess, and working as a waiter. High- and low-skilled athletes in a wide range of sports have been compared on mental chronometric, perceptual, cognitive, metacognitive, strategic, and game performance skills. Although the end goal has generally been to determine those aspects of skilled performance that cross domains, along the way a significant amount has been learned about what contributes to being an expert in activities such as tennis, badminton, karate, wrestling, kickboxing, table tennis, ballet, and modern dance. Team sports have also been the focus of much research (i.e., basketball, volleyball, field hockey, soccer, handball, and water polo). Within the confines of one chapter, it is impossible to outline all relevant sources of information. However, an attempt will be made here to indicate benchmarks within the literature, to discuss limitations and recent developments, and to pose questions for future consideration.

There are a number of research questions in the sport expertise literature that have been pursued extensively and for which there are consistent findings. In this section, a number of areas are outlined in which characteristic differences between expert and novice athletes have been demonstrated. For some characteristics there is a large body of literature and discussion of these areas in this chapter is more extensive. Less space is devoted to those characteristics for which there is a limited amount of research, or those areas where the findings are relatively straightforward.

PERCEPTION, COGNITION, AND STRATEGIES DIFFERENTIATE EXPERTS

The finding that experts in a particular sport are better than novices, not merely at physical skills but also on the underlying perceptual, cognitive, and strategic components of sport, is robust in both laboratory and field research. It has been demonstrated that within a specific domain, somewhere on the order of 10 years experience or 10,000 hours of practice is necessary to differentiate expert performance (Bloom, 1985; Ericsson, Krampe, & Tesch-Romer, 1993; Helsen, Starkes, & Hodges, 1998; Starkes, in

press). Support for this 10-year phenomenon has been found in domains as diverse as chess (Charness, Krampe, & Mayr, 1996), music (Ericsson, 1996; Ericsson et al., 1993; Sloboda, 1996), soccer (Helsen, Starkes, & Hodges, 1998), field hockey (Helsen, Starkes, & Hodges, 1998), figure skating (Starkes, Deakin, Allard, Hodges, & Hayes, 1996), wrestling (Hodges & Starkes, 1996), and surgery (Starkes, 1990), and in a host of scientific disciplines (Simonton, 1994, 1996). Simonton's work is of particular interest for those in academia. He has developed a mathematical model that predicts the output rate of creative products over the course of one's academic career and demonstrates that one's first publications begin after approximately 10 years' training and publication continues for roughly 20 years. This is true across nine different scientific disciplines with only slight variation.

The primary importance of the "10-year rule" is that it seems to hold up regardless of domain investigated. As such, it is one of the most robust findings in expertise research to date. Nevertheless, there are limitations to the rule. First, as most coaches and motor learning specialists would attest, the quality of practice is critical to skill development. Thus, although the 10-year finding is important, it does not assume all practice is of equal benefit. Practice time could potentially be shortened by high-quality practice conditions or lengthened by lesser-quality practice. Second, simpler tasks are acquired in less than 10 years; for example, we would not expect it to take someone 10 years to learn how to ride a bicycle. The assumption is that the 10-year descriptor is probably more representative of complex, strategic tasks and domains.

Understanding *what* practice is best and *how* practice should be carried out are even more important questions than *how much*. Although all of the studies cited as supportive of the 10-year rule initially set out to examine the types of practice in which subjects engaged, this observation has been largely ignored and these studies are more often cited for the 10-year finding. Several of the researchers (Ericsson et al., 1993; Helsen, Starkes, & Hodges, 1998; Hodges & Starkes, 1996; Starkes et al., 1996) have observed that those activities most related to real-world performance in music and sport also require the greatest mental concentration in practice. Data from sport studies also indicate that those practice activities that require the greatest physical effort and mental concentration are ultimately the most enjoyable. For example, jumps are the most demanding but enjoyable aspect of figure skating practice, and sparring the most important and enjoyable in wrestling (Starkes et al., 1996). More recent research has begun to focus on the quality of both practice and instruction by considering the "microstructure" of practice at varying skill levels, using time-motion studies of athletes in practice (Cullen & Starkes, 1997; Starkes, in press).

Singer and Janelle (1999) suggest that an abundance of attention has been directed toward the determination of the amount of deliberate practice necessary at the expense of focusing on the content and quality of practice sessions. Most efforts to date have centered on the issue of monotonicity of practice and performance. As a result, the focus has been on career practice patterns and logging amounts of practice. Probably more crucial is what is practiced, how it is practiced, and, from a developmental perspective, when. These are issues that may provide more enlightening information for coaches and mentors than simply knowing how much practice is necessary (Durand-Bush & Salmela, 1995; Salmela, 1996; Singer & Janelle, 1999; Starkes, in press; Starkes et al., 1996). Singer and Janelle also suggest that how one's genotype influences and potentially determines responsiveness to practice and training is an important issue worthy of examination. To date, this question has been inadequately addressed in the expertise literature.

Accessing Expertise through Laboratory Tasks

To measure expert performance, it is necessary to design laboratory tasks that tap the same expert behavior required on the field or court, but under laboratory conditions. Often, it has proven difficult to determine laboratory tasks that simulate the same requirements as in the real world of competitive sport. This has spurred the move toward life-size video simulations (cf. Helsen & Pauwels, 1993c) or on-court measurement of actual play (Singer et al., 1998). Still, skilled behaviors can often be elicited with relatively simple simulations, such as schematic plays (Allard, Graham, & Paarsalu, 1980) or slides (Allard & Starkes, 1980). Thus, physical fidelity with the real-world task has not always been necessary in designing laboratory tasks that adequately assess expert performance. As Ericsson and Smith (1991) indicate, this ability to scale actual levels of expertise based on laboratory tasks that utilize the same underlying components as the domain is critical to the development of a more general theory of expertise and is a cornerstone of the expertise paradigm.

HARDWARE, SOFTWARE, AND THE MULTITASK APPROACH

Research generally indicates that expertise can be more readily predicted by performance in sport-specific, "soft-

ware"-related tasks than in tasks that presumably measure "hardware" components of performance. Several reviews outline the evidence for this finding (Abernethy, 1993; Allard & Starkes, 1991; Helsen & Starkes, 1999a; Starkes & Allard, 1993; Starkes & Deakin, 1984; Williams, Davids, & Williams, 1999). Hardware-oriented tasks assess performance in such general areas as visual acuity, depth perception, peripheral visual range, reaction time, nerve conduction time, and coincidence-anticipation time. The assumption is that hardware is a fixed commodity. Software tasks are related to those skills that are the result of domain-specific practice and learning. These include error detection, recall and recognition or signal detection of structured game information, verbal reports of strategies, mental chronometry, eye-movement responses, and the use of advance cues as assessed by film occlusion techniques. Software measures tend to be sport-specific and improvements may be due to use of appropriate strategies. The hardware-software dichotomy is somewhat simplistic because, for example, *rate* of learning of declarative information (software) could be biologically limited within an individual. Nevertheless, the dichotomy has proven useful in categorizing the kinds of activities most likely to underlie expert performance.

Helsen and Pauwels (1993c) have outlined the various methods used to test expert-novice differences with such techniques as recognition or recall of game structure information, the use of advance visual cues (as tested through temporal and spatial film occlusion), and the tracking of eye movements. They discuss the advantages and disadvantages of the various techniques. They have also provided a chart summary of references available on hardware and software features of different sports. Their summary was complete to 1992; however, in the past eight years a substantial amount of research has been published. Table 7.1 provides an updated chart summary of research on hardware issues. Table 7.2 provides a similar chart of research currently available on software-oriented tasks.

Unfortunately, in the vast majority of studies to date, only single factors have been examined. A significant expert-novice difference, though interesting, does not help to determine the relative importance of that factor in overall performance. In spite of Wrisberg's (1993) call for a multitask approach to the assessment of skill, both hardware and software skills have hardly been researched in skilled subjects to determine their relative contributions to expertise. To date, only four studies have contained a multitask approach. Starkes (1987) assessed a number of different prediction factors (simple reaction

Table 7.1 Studies of "Hardware" Using the Expert/novice paradigm in Individual and Team Sports

Sport	Verbal Reports	Error Detection	Recall	Recognition	Signal Detection	Film Occlusion	Mental Chronometry	Eye-Movement Registration
Athletics	Pinheiro (1993)							Möckel & Heemsoth (1984)
Badminton	Abernethy & Russell (1987a)					Abernethy (1986a, 1988, 1989) Abernethy & Russell (1987a, 1987b)	Abernethy (1986b) Abernethy & Russell (1987b)	
Ballet			Starkes et al. (1987)					
Baseball	French et al. (1996) McPherson (1993) Nevett & French (1997)		Chiesi et al. (1979) Spilich et al. (1979)	Burroughs (1984)		Burroughs (1984) Glencross & Paull (1993) Paull & Fitzgerald (1993) Paull & Glencross (1997)	French et al. (1995) Kioumourtzoglou et al. (1998) Oudejans et al. (1997)	Hubbard & Seng (1954) Hubbard (1955) Shank & Haywood (1987)
Basketball	French & Thomas (1987)		Allard (1982) Allard & Burnett (1985) Allard et al. (1980) Millslagle (1988)	Allard et al. (1980)	Doody et al. (1987) Millslagle (1988) Tenenbaum et al. (1999)			Bard (1982) Bard & Carrière (1975) Bard & Fleury (1976a, 1976b, 1976c, 1978, 1981) Bard et al. (1975, 1987) Carriè (1978) Helsen, Pauwels, & Boutmans (1986) Helsen, Pauwels, & Van Outryve d'Ydewalle (1986)
Boxing							Ripoll et al. (1993a, 1993b)	Ripoll et al. (1993a, 1993b) Ripoll et al. (1995)
Castleball							Helsen, Pauwels, & Boutmans (1986) Pauwels & Helsen (1986)	
Cricket						Abernethy (1984) Abernethy & Russell (1984) Houlston & Lowes (1993)		

(continued)

Table 7.1 (Continued)

Sport	Verbal Reports	Error Detection	Recall	Recognition	Signal Detection	Film Occlusion	Mental Chronometry	Eye-Movement Registration
Dance	Poon & Rodgers (in press)		Jack et al. (1999) Poon & Rodgers (in press) Smyth & Pendleton (1994) Starkes et al. (1987, 1990)					Petrakis (1987)
Fencing								Bard (1982) Bard et al. (1981, 1987) Haase & Mayer (1978) Papin et al. (1984)
Field hockey	Christensen & Glencross (1993)		Starkes (1987) Starkes & Deakin (1984)		Doody et al. (1987) Starkes & Deakin (1984) Starkes (1987)	Starkes & Deakin (1984)	Starkes (1987)	Lyle & Cook (1984)
Figure skating			Deakin (1987)					
Golf								Vickers (1992)
Gymnastics	Côté et al. (1995)		Tenenbaum et al. (in press)	Imwold & Hoffman (1983) Vickers (1986, 1988)			Bard (1982) Bard et al. (1975, 1980) Neumaier (1982) Vickers (1988)	
Handball			Tenenbaum et al. (1994)				Lidor et al. (1998)	Deridder (1985)
Ice hockey		Leavitt (1979)				Salmela & Fiorito (1979)	Thiffault (1974, 1980)	Bard (1982) Bard & Fleury (1980, 1981) Bard et al. (1987)
Karate			Hodge & Deakin (1998)					A. Williams & Elliott (1997)
Netball					Parker (1981)			
Rugby				Nakagawa (1982)				
Sailing	Saury & Durand (1998)							

Sport							
Soccer	McMorris & Graydon (1997)	McMorris & Beazeley (1997) A. Williams & Davids (1995) M. Williams et al. (1993)	A. Williams & Davids (1995) M. Williams et al. (1993)		McMorris et al. (1993) Patrick & Spurgeon (1978) A. Williams & Burwitz (1993)	Helsen & Pauwels (1988) Helsen & Starkes (1999a) McMorris & Graydon (1997) A. Williams & Davids (1995)	Helsen & Pauwels (1990, 1991, 1993a, 1993b, 1993c) Helsen & Starkes (1999a) Tyldesley et al. (1982) A. Williams & Davids (1995) A. Williams et al. (1993, 1999)
Squash	Rutt Leas & Chi (1993)				Abernethy (1993)		Abernethy (1990a, 1990b)
Swimming						Kioumourtzoglou et al. (1998)	
Table tennis						Ripoll & Latiri (1997)	Ripoll (1988b)
Tennis	Armstrong & Hoffman (1979)	Haskins (1965)	Day (1980) Enberg (1968) Jones & Miles (1978)	Buckholz et al. (1988) Gouet et al. (1989, 1990) Isaacs & Finch (1983) Jackson (1986)	Tenenbaum et al. (1996, 1999)		Bard et al. (1987) Buckholz et al. (1988) Cauraugh et al. (1993) Fleury et al. (1986) Goulet et al. (1988, 1989, 1990) Petrakis (1986, 1993) Ritzdorf (1982, 1983) Singer et al. (1998)
Volleyball	McPherson (1999) McPherson & French (1991) McPherson & Thomas (1989)	Borgeaud & Abernethy (1987)		Allard & Starkes (1980) Starkes & Allard (1983)	Kioumourtzoglou et al. (1998) Soulière & Salmela (1982) Wright et al. (1990)	Kioumourtzoglou et al. (1998) Soulière & Salmela (1982)	Neumaier (1983) Ripoll (1988a)

Table 7.2 Studies of "Software" Using the Expert/Novice Paradigm in Individual and Team Sports

Sport	Visual Acuity	Depth Perception	Peripheral Visual Range	Visual Reaction Time	Visual Correction Time	Nerve Conduction Time	Coincidence Anticipation Time
Athletics		Graybiel et al. (1955) Olsen (1956)	Williams & Thirer (1975)	Burley (1944) Burpee & Stroll (1936) Westerlund & Tuttle (1931) Yandell & Spirduso (1981) Youngen (1959)	Yandell & Spirduso (1981)		
Badminton					Abernethy & Russell (1987b) Bartz (1967) Cohen & Ross (1977) Shank & Haywood (1987) Yoshimoto et al. (1982)		
Ballgames	J. Miller (1958) Sanderson & Whiting (1974, 1978)	Bannister & Blackburn (1931) Doil & Binding (1986) Davids (1984, 1988)	Davids (1984, 1988) Doil & Binding (1986)	Burke (1972)			
Baseball	Winograd (1942) Trachtman (1973)	Olsen (1956) Ridini (1968) Winograd (1942)	Ridini (1968)	McLeod (1987) Olsen (1956) Ridini (1968)			Bowers & Stratton (1993) Dunham (1989)
Basketball	Tussing (1940) Morris & Kreigbaum (1977)	Beals et al. (1971) Olsen (1956) Ridini (1968)	Stroup (1957) Ridini (1968) Mizusawa et al. (1983)	Olsen (1956) Ridini (1968)	Kioumourtzoglou et al. (1998)		
Boxing				Joch (1980)			
Cricket				Sanderson & Holton (1980)			
Fencing				Pierson (1956) Singer (1968)			
Field hockey	Starkes (1987)	Cockerill (1981b) Olsen (1956)	Cockerill (1981a, 1981b, 1981c)	Bhanot & Sidhu (1980) Starkes (1987) Starkes & Deakin (1984)			Starkes (1987)

Sport						
Football		Cockerill & Callington (1981) Deshaies & Pargman (1976)	Cockerill & Callington (1981) Deshaies & Pargman (1976)	Beise & Peaseley (1937)		
Golf		Cockerill & Calington (1981)				
Gymnastics						Gangemi et al. (1993)
Ice hockey				Olsen (1956)		
Soccer	Helsen & Starkes (1999a) Tussing (1940)	Helsen & Starkes (1999a) Olsen (1956) Ridini (1968)	Helsen & Starkes (1999a) Ridini (1968) Mizusawa et al. (1983)	Helsen & Starkes (1999a) Olsen (1956) Ridini (1968)	Helsen & Starkes (1999a)	Kuhn (1993)
Softball				R. Miller & Shay (1964)		
Squash				Nessler (1973)		
Table tennis	Hughes et al. (1993) Sanderson & Whiting (1972)					Benguigui & Ripoll (1998) Ripoll & Latiri (1997)
Tennis				Beise & Peaseley (1937) Blundell (1984) Tenenbaum et al. (1999)		Chen et al. (1993) Isaacs & Finch (1983)
Volleyball		Ridini (1968)	Ridini (1968) Sonneschein & Sonneschein (1981)	Ridini (1968)	Kioumourtzoglou et al. (1998)	
Waterpolo					Kioumourtzoglou et al. (1998)	
Wrestling				Rasch et al. (1961) Rasch & Pierson (1963)		

time, coincidence-anticipation, speed and accuracy of ball detection, shoot/dribble/dodge complex decision speed, accuracy of shot prediction with varying amounts of advance information, and recall of game structured and non-structured information). The only significant predictors of expertise were recall of game structured information and shot prediction accuracy following view of ball impact. Together these two domain-specific factors accounted for 69% of the variance ($R = .83$).

Recently, Helsen and Starkes (1999a) examined soccer experts and assessed both hardware elements (the relative contributions of simple and peripheral reaction time, visual correction time, optometric and perimetric parameters) and software (complex decision speed and accuracy, number of visual fixations, fixation duration, and fixation location in solving game problems). A stepwise discriminant function analysis of both hardware and software components yielded a squared canonical correlation of .84, derived all from software variables. Response accuracy ($r^2 = .42$), number of visual fixations in solving tactical problems ($r^2 = .42$), and ball-contact time during the kicking response ($r^2 = .19$) were all demonstrative of expert performance.

Abernethy, Neal, and Koning's (1994) study of expertise in snooker also revealed the importance of only domain-specific skills. Kioumourtzoglou, Kourtessis, Michalopoulou, and Derri (1998) performed multitask analyses of basketball, volleyball, and water polo. Although the results are interesting and suggestive of the importance of software variables, no multivariate analyses were conducted either within or between sports to determine the relative contribution of the many tasks assessed. (Were this done, this might have been the first study with the potential to compare the relative contribution of the same tasks both within and across sport domains.)

The Role of Game Structure in Recall and Recognition

The best athletes are able to recognize, recall, and retain more information about plays or structured game information than less skilled athletes. This has been demonstrated in basketball (Allard et al., 1980; Kioumourtzoglou et al., 1998), field hockey (Starkes, 1987), volleyball (Allard & Starkes, 1980; Ripoll, 1988a), soccer (Helsen & Pauwels, 1993b, 1993c; Williams, Davids, Burwitz, & Williams, 1993), karate (Hodge & Deakin, 1998), and figure skating (Deakin, 1987; Deakin & Allard, 1992). Likewise, expert dancers and gymnasts are better at recalling sequences of movements. Not only is recall better in experts, but recalled information deteriorates less quickly and is less susceptible to disruption from secondary tasks (Poon & Rodgers, in press; Smyth & Pendleton, 1994; Starkes, Caicco, Boutilier, & Sevsek, 1990; Starkes, Deakin, Lindley, & Crisp, 1987; Tenenbaum, Tehan, Stewart, & Christensen, in press).

Verbal Protocols and Sport Knowledge

Verbal protocols obtained from expert athletes reveal that they have greater declarative, procedural, and strategic knowledge about their particular sport than novices (French, Spurgeon, & Nevett, 1995; French & Thomas, 1987; McPherson, 1993, 1994; McPherson & Thomas, 1989; Rutt Leas & Chi, 1993). Young experts who exhibit rich declarative knowledge bases also benefit from advanced metacognition and more accurate estimates of their own knowledge base and recall abilities (Glaser, 1996; Schneider & Bjorklund, 1992).

Is Expertise a Function of Mere Exposure?

Because experts have typically been involved in their sport for many years, the question has been asked whether it is mere exposure to structured game information or the requirement to interact within that environment that fosters the development of expertise. A couple of very innovative studies have demonstrated that the knowledge experts have about a sport is a constituent skill, the result of actual participation and practice. Athletes do not acquire skill as a by-product of exposure to the domain or from simply watching the sport (Allard, Deakin, Parker, & Rodgers, 1993; Williams & Davids, 1995). Referees, coaches, and athletes may have quite different sets of knowledge and skills (Allard et al., 1993). Likewise, soccer expertise is attained by interacting within the game structure and cannot be gained by simply watching the event for an equal amount of time (Williams & Davids, 1995). Finally, one's ability to actually execute a skill influences the content and structure of the tactical knowledge used to derive the solution to the movement problem. In other words, if one cannot execute a particular move, it will not even be accessed as a potential tactic in a game (French, Nevett, Spurgeon, Graham, Rink, & McPherson, 1996).

The Use of Advance Visual Cues and Probability Estimates

Experts deal with information in their domain more quickly and efficiently than novices. One way this is accomplished is through the use of advance visual cues in making decisions (Abernethy & Russell, 1984; Goulet, Bard, & Fleury, 1989; Starkes, Edwards, Dissanayake, &

Dunn, 1995; Williams & Davids, 1998a, 1998b; Wright, Pleasants, & Gomez-Mesa, 1990). For example, in receiving a tennis or volleyball serve or preparing to hit a pitch in baseball, experts use early visual cues from the server's body position and movement during execution, even prior to release of the ball. In this way, they are able to gauge the kind of serve or pitch, as well as predict the destination of the ball with accuracy. Research on eye-movement registration has also demonstrated use of early visual information and expert-novice distinctions in number of fixations, fixation location, duration, and scan paths of experts (Abernethy & Russell, 1987a; Bard & Fleury, 1976a; Goulet et al., 1989; Helsen & Pauwels, 1993a, 1993b; Helsen & Starkes, 1999a, 1999b; Ripoll, 1988a; Ripoll, Kerlirzin, Stein, & Reine, 1995; Rodrigues, 1999). Despite relative consistency across sport domains with respect to expert advantages in focusing on relevant cues, the findings concerning search rate remain equivocal. More specifically, there is still controversy over whether experts have higher search rates (more fixations of shorter duration) (Williams & Davids, 1998b) or fewer fixations of longer duration (the result of superior selective attention or integrative viewing within a single fixation) (Helsen & Starkes, 1999a; Ripoll, 1991). Presumably, this may be due to the sport and task demands of the specific situation assessed with the eye-movement task. For example, one might speculate that athletes are likely to scan less in a fast-moving ballgame to avoid the loss of information that occurs from suppression of saccadic information during the change of fixation location. Likewise, if the visual field is extremely complex, longer fixations may be necessary to derive all the information necessary to elicit a response.

Nevertheless, some researchers have demonstrated that in visual search, the critical issue is not so much the manner in which the information is overtly searched but how readily the performer can make use of that information (Abernethy & Russell, 1987a, 1987b; Paull & Glencross, 1997). This has led to the conclusion that training the reproduction of expert scan paths or patterns is not a viable way of increasing expert perception (Abernethy & Russell, 1987a, 1987b).

One way of overcoming the severe time constraints imposed in fast-action sports such as volleyball, tennis, or baseball hitting is the use of probability estimates. When strategic information about the game context is provided, probability judgments are more accurate and presumably benefit performance (Alain & Sarrazin, 1990; Alain, Sarrazin, & Lacombe, 1986; Paull & Glencross, 1997).

Family Resources in the Development of Young Experts

Bloom's (1985) seminal research and longitudinal study on the development of young musicians, athletes, artists, and scientists has demonstrated that substantial family resources (both social and financial) are needed to provide access to coaches and mentors and an environment that promotes the development of skill. More recent research (Côté, in press; Csikszentmihalyi, Rathunde, & Whalen, 1993; Rowley, 1995) confirms the importance of the family and social milieu in determining self-esteem, motivation, competence, and eventual achievement levels. Parental behaviors, including emotional and tangible support of the child's skill level, modeling, expectations of the child, direction, and belief in the child, are critical to achievement (Côté & Hay, in press). On the other hand, in a study of Dutch athletes, van Rossum and van der Loo (1997) found no favorable difference in functionality of the family structure for very skilled athletes in comparison with ordinary athletes. They suggest that the results may reflect cross-cultural differences.

MORE CONTROVERSIAL ISSUES IN THE STUDY OF EXPERTISE

Who Is an Expert?

Throughout the expertise literature, there have been calls for better operational definitions of expertise and a clearer delineation of who can be considered an expert and what amount of experience and skill are inherent to the expert level of performance (Salthouse, 1991; Sloboda, 1991; Starkes, 1993). Originally, this issue stemmed from the tendency to call the most skilled subjects in any one study "experts." At times, these may have been university varsity athletes, or national team athletes, or professional athletes. On the other end of the expertise range, novices may have been those who had never participated in the sport or those who had participated only for a limited number of years. For many reasons, it is helpful when researchers are as descriptive as possible in their operational definitions of the characteristics of their selected groups, skill level, and experience. However, the actual designation of individuals as experts, highly skilled, moderately skilled, or novices is in the end a moot point. There is really only one end of the spectrum that is absolute: those who have never participated. All other levels of skill are probably best characterized as lying somewhere on a wide continuum. For this reason, it has also been most useful when investigators have included groups at three or more designated levels of skill because, realistically, more groups represent a broader range of behaviors in that sport and change due to experience.

Do Generalized Visual Training Programs Improve Athlete Performance?

In recent years, visual training programs to improve abilities such as depth perception, visual acuity, peripheral vision, and reaction time have become popular. Often, they are marketed for their purported effectiveness in improving sport performance. In their excellent review of this question, Williams and Grant (1999) note that all such programs are based on three underlying assumptions: first, that expert athletes have superior visual abilities to those less skilled; second, that visual function can be improved through these programs; and third, that this improvement transfers to the actual game situation. Both Williams et al. (1999) and others (Abernethy & Wood, in press; Helsen & Starkes, 1999b; Starkes & Lindley, 1994; Wood & Abernethy, 1997) noted that the weight of the empirical evidence does not support the notion that the best athletes have better visual function. Relatively speaking, the last two assumptions have had few empirical tests. There is evidence that those with pathological visual function show larger benefits from visual training than those with normal function, which leads one to wonder whether there are ceiling effects for the benefits of such programs (Williams & Grant, 1999).

Where appropriate, control and transfer studies have been conducted. In the clinically based studies of sport vision training by Wood and Abernethy (1997), the results are not overwhelming. They found some significant changes in visual and perceptual skill, but these were not dependent on the training program. Returning to one of the most robust findings in the expertise literature, that hardware does not differentiate between experts and novices, one might wonder how an argument can be made for improving visual hardware through vision training. Because these training programs are not sport-specific, they are also not likely to transfer well to specific sport domains.

In general, research points in two directions. First, "Caveat emptor" or "Buyer beware" before undertaking such programs. Often, these programs are highly marketed and direct a subject to train vision or reaction time on a particular apparatus. Performance improvements are seen on the apparatus that are simply the result of task-specific learning. If the promise is made that these improvements will transfer and enhance performance in a real-world skill, this is not likely to happen. Second, there is a dearth of training studies in which well-controlled, double-blind procedures have been implemented, with appropriate transfer tests to assess the efficacy of such programs. Improvement will probably not occur with visual training or, if it is shown, will probably not carry over to real-world performance.

Are Sport-Specific Perceptual Training Programs Likely to Improve Performance?

Perceptual training programs differ from the previous visual training programs in that they are sport-specific and generally designed to improve one's knowledge base in a sport, thereby allowing the athlete to perceptually decipher game information more quickly and accurately. Typically, the simulations used in perceptual training are prepared from actual game film or video, in the hopes of enhancing both specificity of learning and transfer to the real sport context. Perceptual training programs of this kind are often designed to assist decision making or aid recognition and recall of actual game information. In general, these programs are likely to be more successful in preparing athletes because they are aimed at training sport-specific software, which, as noted earlier, does differentiate expert from novice performers.

The results of these sport-specific perceptual training programs have typically been more promising than those derived from the use of generalized visual training programs. Usually these programs involve assessment of skill pre- and posttraining and may or may not involve a postassessment of transfer to the actual game. Williams and Grant (1999, Table 1) provide a very useful summary of all perceptual training studies to date and key findings. Among the studies that have included transfer tasks, perceptual training has benefited either response accuracy/speed of decisions or visual tracking of information (Adolphe, Vickers, & La Plante, 1997; Franks & Hanvey, 1997; Grant & Williams, 1996; Helsen & Starkes, 1999b; Singer et al., 1994; Starkes & Lindley, 1994). On the very important issue of whether these skill improvements transfer to game performance, the results are less clear. In part, this is because even if studies are well designed and include experimental and control groups, it is still difficult to implement the transfer phase of the design. First, the question arises of what is the most appropriate performance measure in the sport context to measure changes that result from perceptual training. Second, if one were to compare subjects' actual game performance pre- and post-perceptual-training, any improvements could equally well be attributed to the additive effects of perceptual training + continued regular practice throughout the test period. Alternatively, if treatment and control groups are employed and only the treatment group is exposed to perceptual training, any resultant improvements may be more related to the Hawthorne effect than perceptual training per se.

Some questions remain with regard to perceptual training programs: What age groups and skill levels offer the best candidates for training? What is the optimal scheduling of perceptual practice? Where is training likely to have its largest impact (i.e., decision accuracy, speed, eye movements, recall)? Is physical or psychological fidelity of the simulation important? How can transfer of performance improvements to the actual context be best assessed? Perceptual training programs are intuitively appealing, but a substantial amount of research is still required before they will be implemented effectively.

How Does Early Talent Influence the Development of Expertise?

One way of addressing this issue is to consider the relative importance of nature versus nurture. Ericsson et al. (1993) have suggested that expertise is almost entirely the result of practice (a nurturist view), and that physical and psychological adaptations that result from practice lead to expertise. They have cited investigations that show no reliable heritabilities for elite performance in Olympic athletes. Indeed, Ericsson and Lehmann (1996) have gone so far as to suggest that "the influence of innate, domain-specific basic capacities (talent) on expert performance is small, possibly even negligible" (p. 281). Their argument has been supported by Howe, Davidson, and Sloboda (1998), who also found little evidence for innate talents in the development of musical expertise. Others recognize the huge value of practice, yet continue to feel that genetic predispositions, biological limitations/advantages, and access to facilities and coaching are probably more interactive in their contributions to success (Durand-Bush & Salmela, 1995; Singer & Janelle, 1999; Starkes, in press; Starkes et al., 1996).

There is one way in which early "talent" has had a very direct impact on who is likely to be given the opportunities to become an expert. In young children, very often what coaches term "talent" is most likely the advantage afforded by early maturation, probably within the context of a sport's age grouping and eligibility year. Most sports age-group children in two-year categories (as in pee-wee, bantam, and midget hockey) and have a date that marks the beginning of the eligibility year. If January 1 is the date, then a child with a January birthday has a huge chronological and physical advantage over a child born in December, and certainly over a child almost two years younger.

According to Barnsley, Thompson, and Legault (1992), "relative age" refers to the difference in ages between children in the same-age group resulting from their different birthdates throughout the year. For example, a 12-year-old boy who is a relatively early maturer with a January birthdate could have as much as a 9-inch height and 40-pound weight advantage over a late maturer the same age. An average 12-year-old with January birthdate still has a 2-inch height and 8-pound weight advantage over his December-born counterpart (Payne & Isaacs, 1995). In sports, it has repeatedly been found that children selected to all-star teams or designated as "talented" are children with this relative age advantage. This has been demonstrated from minor leagues through professional leagues in a number of sports, including soccer (Barnsley et al., 1992; Brewer, Balsom, & Davis, 1995; Dudink, 1994; Helsen, Starkes, & Van Winckel, 1998; Verhulst, 1992), football (Glamser & Marciani, 1990), baseball (Schulz, Musa, Staszewski, & Siegler, 1994; Thompson, Barnsley, & Stebelsky, 1991), hockey (Barnsley & Thompson, 1988; Barnsley, Thompson, & Barnsley, 1985; Boucher & Mutimer, 1994), and cricket (Edwards, 1994).

Recently, Helsen, Starkes, and Van Winckel (1998) examined the relationship between birth month and number of participants at various levels in soccer. They found that youth players born between August and October (the early part of the selection year, as August 1 was the eligibility date), beginning in the 6–8-year age group, were more likely to be identified as talented and to be exposed to higher levels of coaching. These children were also significantly taller and heavier than average. Eventually, these players were more likely to be transferred to top teams, to play for national teams, and to become involved professionally. Equally important, they found that players from the age of 12 who dropped out were more likely to have birthdates in the last quartile and often fell below the 25th percentile in height and weight for their age. Ironically, and sadly, even though taller, heavier players are designated and selected as talented, there is very little relationship between physical size and motor skill level (Beunen, Ostyn, Renson, Simons, & Van Gerven, 1978).

Prior to 1997, the International Football Association used August 1 as the eligibility date; in 1997, the date was changed to January 1. In a second study (Helsen, Starkes, & Van Winckel, in press), the changes in birthdate distributions throughout youth categories were compared prior to the date change and after (1996–1997 versus the 1997–1998 competitive year). Birthdates were considered for national youth league players, ages 10–12, 12–14, 14–16, and 16–18 years. The results indicated that from 1996 to 1997, youth players born between January and March (the early part of the new selection year) were more likely to be identified as talented. In comparison, players born late in the new selection year (August to October) were assessed as talented in significantly lower proportions.

Therefore, early maturers and those with a relative age advantage are more often selected as talented and provided better access to competition, coaching, and facilities. They also end up more likely to be experts. There is no way of knowing whether children disadvantaged by birthdate or physical size might well become equally skilled athletes if they were afforded equivalent opportunities.

Is Deliberate Practice Necessary and Sufficient to Become an Expert?

The question of the role of "deliberate practice" stems from the work of Ericsson et al. (1993), who first coined the term. Their studies of the career practice patterns of expert pianists and violinists led them to conclude that extended deliberate practice and the body's adaptive responses to that practice can largely explain who becomes an expert. According to Ericsson and colleagues' nurturist approach, talent does not play a role in the development of expertise. Their delineation of what constitutes deliberate practice included all effortful activity motivated by the goal of improving performance, but did not include observational learning. Deliberate practice requires effort and attention from the learner, could involve coach-selected activities, does not lead to immediate social or monetary rewards, and is not inherently enjoyable. The model of deliberate practice is extensively discussed in a number of articles by these authors (Ericsson, 1996; Ericsson & Charness, 1994; Ericsson et al., 1993; Ericsson & Lehmann, 1996).

Since its inception, much of the research directed at the issue of deliberate practice in sport has centered on the validity of the definition and how well the notion of deliberate practice fits the sport experience. Several researchers have found complementary results with respect to deliberate practice. Whether one examines wrestling (Hodges & Starkes, 1996), figure skating (Starkes et al., 1996), karate (Hodge & Deakin, 1998), soccer, or field hockey (Helsen, Hodges, Van Winckel, & Starkes, in press; Helsen, Starkes, & Hodges, 1998), there is a monotonic relationship between the amount of practice in which one has engaged throughout one's career, and one's eventual athletic success. In this regard, the research is supportive of Ericsson et al. (1993). However, unlike the practice patterns of musicians, a certain base level of practice for all sports entails activities designed to maintain fitness level, individual forms of practice, and team practice. Also, contrary to Ericsson's original proposal, those activities seen as most

practiced and most related to performance are also highly enjoyable to athletes (Helsen, Starkes, & Hodges, 1998; Hodge & Deakin, 1998; Hodges & Starkes, 1996; Starkes et al., 1996; Young & Salmela, in press).

Although many aspects of the model of deliberate practice have been supported, it has also been criticized on a number of levels. First, the model is not likely to be disproven because it is largely untestable. To disprove its assertions one would need to find instances of complex strategic domains where individuals have attained expert performance with little practice. Alternatively, one would need evidence of extreme amounts of concentrated deliberate practice with no resultant change in performance. Still, if the former were found, the argument could always be made that the task was too easy. And it is unlikely that the latter could be found because practice would be so demotivating that the learner would not likely continue to practice.

One way to test the model would be to expose individuals very early in life to the same "doses" of deliberate practice on a task. Any resultant difference between subjects at the end of the allotted practice would be attributable to other factors besides deliberate practice.

Finally, the research on deliberate practice has demonstrated that regardless of whether beginning wrestling or field hockey at age 13 or figure skating, violin, piano, or soccer at age 5, the course of one's practice career is likely to follow the same pattern of increase. Whereas previously it may have been felt that 5-year-olds practice less because of short attention span or control, it is now known that these changes in practice patterns are not necessarily developmentally limited (Starkes, in press).

What is not determined by this model, but is absolutely crucial, is the role that motivation plays in determining who will put in the necessarily huge amounts of practice to become an expert. Early commitment, motivation, and retention are areas largely ignored but nevertheless fundamental to the study of expertise. In the end, it appears that deliberate practice is probably necessary for the attainment of expertise. Whether it is sufficient or whether the underlying mechanisms that induce deliberate practice are biologically/genetically influenced are still at issue.

Does Expertise in Dance and Martial Arts Differ from What Is Known about Sport Expertise?

A relatively new focus in the area of expertise is those domains that require memory for movement sequences. These include dance, gymnastics, figure skating, tai chi, and karate. Many of these studies have focused on replicating the expert-novice interaction first reported by Chase and Simon (1973a, 1973b). Their paradigm examined expertise through the structured and unstructured recall of domain-specific information from chess. Studies examining expertise in domains with movement sequences have attempted to follow the structured and unstructured dichotomy by using the structure provided by choreography. In a domain such as gymnastics, a choreographed routine on the balance beam is considered structured. A random sequence would use steps from the subjects' repertoire but combined in a random pattern. Subjects are required to replicate a movement sequence defined as choreographed (structured) or random (unstructured). Originally, it was hypothesized that dance experts would follow the same pattern that has been shown for experts in sports such as basketball and soccer. Elite dancers would recall choreographed sequences better than novices but show no advantage on random sequences.

Starkes et al. (1987) first examined experts in the area of movement sequences by looking at young expert ballet dancers. Expert and novice ballet dancers were presented with choreographed and random movement sequences. They were then asked to recall the sequences either verbally or physically. As predicted, young experts (mean age = 11.3 years) had superior recall of choreographed sequences. A second part of this study examined the use of music as a cue in enhancing recall. Sequences were always presented with music; however, recall was performed either with or without music. Unfortunately, this second task showed a ceiling effect for recall with music. A decrease in recall in the no-music condition was observed but only on the last steps.

The investigators also reported that the expert dancers had trouble separating verbal and motor recall conditions. For example, when asked to recall a sequence physically, the dancer would also verbally label the steps. Finally, experts demanded a short time to mentally rehearse the sequence before performing, whereas the novice dancers recalled steps immediately. From these initial observations, differences in expert and novice dancers seemed to go beyond the mere recall of structured movements. In figure skaters (Deakin, 1987; Deakin & Allard, 1992), the results more closely followed the traditional expertise literature.

Expert and novice figure skaters were shown a choreographed and randomly structured routine. Similar to the young dancers in the Starkes et al. study (1987), the skaters were asked to recall the elements either physically or verbally. Expert skaters were able to recall more elements of a choreographed figure skating sequence regardless of how they responded (verbally or physically). Subsequent tests also revealed that expert skaters were able

to encode more elements in the same amount of time as novice skaters and that interpolated tasks did not affect the encoding of either group. This implicated the use of long-term memory that has been seen in other experts (e.g., in chess). Expert and novice skaters did not differ in the type of encoding they used but rather the degree to which they were able to encode skating elements in a sequence. Finally, expert skaters were shown to have faster access to semantic memory by performing a recognition task quicker and with fewer errors than novice skaters. Most of these results for experts in dance and figure skating followed the pattern of results seen in other areas of expertise; however, some variances did occur in whether both primacy and recency or only primacy effects were seen in the accuracy of recall of sequences. It has been suggested that in movement recall tasks, improved recall toward the end of the sequence, or recency effects, may be decreased because of the actual time required to perform movements or because of the potential interference created by the actual recall performance (Starkes et al., 1987). In other words, the process of producing recalled movements in a sequence may cause one to forget subsequent movements.

Still, there is reason to believe that experts in movement sequences are different because often they are required to combine novel movements and choreography. Many variables in the learning environment are manipulated, such as music, the routine, the other athletes/artists worked with, the choreographer, the number of performers, and the limitations of the performing space. Dancers may be required to dance alone, with a partner, or in a group. They are also required to learn many forms and styles of dance, depending on the choreographer's preference. In light of this, expert dancers and figure skaters might be expected to be able to encode random sequences as well as choreographed sequences because their training constantly requires learning of new movement sequences in varying environments.

Findings from Smyth and Pendleton (1994) support the idea that this flexibility in encoding is a precursor to expertise. Expert and novice ballet dancers learned ballet and nonsense movements. Expert dancers did not show a superior recall for ballet items, but instead had enhanced encoding of movement items in general. This resulted in longer movement spans for both known and unknown movement sequences. The data suggest that unlike experts in other fields, dancers are more efficient encoders of movement in general than nondancers, even when the movements are not meaningful within their domain of expertise.

A study by Starkes et al. (1990) had earlier shown such effects in modern dancers. Expert and novice modern dancers were asked to recall movement sequences that were structured or unstructured. Due to the obscurity of the movement styles required in modern dance, it is not surprising that expert dancers had an increased ability to recall movements classed as both meaningful and non-meaningful. In this case, it could be argued that the open structure of creative modern dance requires experts to have different memory strategies from those of traditional dancers. A second argument is that the dancers in this study were simply better at memory tasks than the novice group. Both explanations seem relatively weak, however, in light of the Smyth and Pendleton study (1994).

To this point, there is conflicting evidence about the ability of expert dancers to recall unstructured information. Although Starkes et al. (1987) observed young expert ballet dancers to conform to the traditional findings, it is possible that their age and experience skewed the results. Due to their youth, the young ballet dancers may not yet have developed the strategies available to more experienced dancers that gave the latter the ability to recall unstructured sequences. It is also probable that the young experts had not yet developed the movement repertoire of an older dancer. This may explain their inability to remember random sequences. Support for this idea comes from Tenenbaum, Tehan, Stewart, and Christensen (in press), who studied young (6 to 8 years) and older (14 to 16 years) skilled and novice gymnasts' ability to recall floor routines. Their results indicated that serial recall improved with both age and experience and that older experienced gymnasts outperformed all other groups. This issue of the relative contribution of age and experience is far more crucial in gymnastics than dance because of the truncated age range of successful female gymnasts.

Current dance research has continued to look at movement sequence recall but has moved away from the traditional paradigm. A study by Poon and Rodgers (in press) focused on the learning and remembering strategies of novice and advanced jazz dancers for skill-level-appropriate dance routines. Participants learned an easy and a difficult jazz routine from video. They were also interviewed and asked to recall strategies they used to learn and remember the dance. Experts overall were superior to novices in their ability to combine strategies. These included counting music while verbally labeling the steps, as well as using bigger chunks of movements in phrases (phrasing implies that the movement commonly followed the music or a major change in the routine).

Ferrari (1999) examined metacognitive differences between experts and novices on a motor skill transfer task. Experts and novices in karate learned a 25-step tai chi movement sequence from video. Although the subjects were unfamiliar with tai chi, the movement skills of the two disciplines are closely related and require the transfer of existing expertise in karate. Experts did not show any increase in the number of steps they were able to remember when compared to novices, but they did report many more metacognitive experiences. These included possible strategies for learning the sequence or the need to redefine their objectives.

Dance and martial arts require movement sequences, but expertise in these areas has been relatively unexplored. Traditional methods of examining expertise may not be the most appropriate paradigms in these cases. Many other factors must still be addressed, such as the role music plays in recall, the importance of consolidation time, the use of verbal labels, and the application of metacognitive strategies in self-learning.

RESEARCH: WHERE TO FROM HERE?

Assessing Live Game Performance and Strategies

One drawback to expertise research has always been the difficulty of assessing decision making and strategies in performances in real sport situations. The past five years have seen significant advances in this direction. Three examples will serve to illustrate this point.

First, those studies that have examined visual search patterns of experts have invariably been forced to examine eye movements while subjects were looking at schematic diagrams, slides, film, or video. The ecological validity of these designs has always been in question. Singer et al. (1998) recently examined patterns of visual search in live tennis situations. The eye-movement measurement system they employed is a video-based monocular system that measures point of gaze via infrared reflection. Although similar systems had been used previously (Goulet et al., 1989; Helsen & Starkes, 1999a, 1999b; Williams et al., 1993) and visual search has been monitored in more stationary live tasks such as golf putting (Vickers, 1992) and basketball free throws (Vickers & Adolphe, 1997), recording search during more active responses, in this case a tennis service return, is unique.

Recently, Rodrigues (1999) analyzed return of service in table tennis by skilled and less skilled players. His goal was to determine whether "quiet eye," a phenomenon previously discussed by Vickers and Adolphe (1997), occurs much earlier and is of longer duration in skilled table tennis players. He was able to time-synchronize data collected independently from eye movements (through infrared technology), head movements (through magnetic tracking), and movement of the arm (through high-speed video). This represents the first synchronized collection of data from the eye, head, and arm in a real-world skill with normal time constraints on the movement response. This is a very real step forward in the analyses of skilled performance under closely simulated real-world conditions. Not only were eye and head movements tracked, but it was possible for the first time to perform kinematic analyses of the arm during return of the serve.

A second example has to do with the use of advance visual cues in sport. Again, all of the literature in this area has involved temporally or spatially occluded film or video as the perceptual stimulus. Starkes et al. (1995) were able to temporally occlude vision of an actual volleyball serve by having athletes in the service reception area wear visual occlusion goggles. Vision of the service was occluded either prior to or immediately after ball contact on the serve and athletes then predicted landing position of the serve. The visual stimuli were actual serves as performed in a game. This is another example of live game stimuli used to assess the use of advance visual cues in expert athletes. Interestingly, the results of this study closely mirror those found previously with temporal occlusion studies using film or video.

Finally, in the area of protocol analysis, McPherson (1994, 1999), French and McPherson (1999), and Nevett and French (1997) have made great strides in validating the collection of verbal protocols during actual competition, either during point breaks in tennis or between pitches to baseball batters. As a result, they have been able to determine goal, condition, and action concepts, thereby assessing both knowledge content and the use of strategies in developing as well as skilled tennis and baseball players. This is another way in which assessment of live performance becomes crucial to an understanding of the development of both declarative and strategic knowledge. Research in the future is destined to involve more live-action performance analysis. As technology improves, these types of studies will also become more feasible.

Master Athletes and the Retention of Expertise

Almost all knowledge of expertise is based on the advancement of average performance to peak level. There is a dearth of information on what happens to experts postpeak and how readily expert levels of performance can be retained. This is increasingly important as baby boomers age and pass prime levels of performance yet want to continue

in competitive performance. Worldwide participation rates in masters competition is increasing at surprising levels, and athletes make great time commitments to training (Hastings, Kurth, & Schloder, 1996). Track and field has masters-level competition throughout North America and Europe. International competitive structures exist, such as the World Association of Veteran Athletes (WAVA) and the Nike World Games for Masters Track and Field. In Canada, where registration for children's minor league hockey has been declining, registration for older men's hockey teams has recently surpassed 500,000 and is steadily climbing. At this time, there are more senior men participants in hockey than minor league participants in Canada.

In chess, it has been determined that performance at age 63 is roughly equivalent to that at 21 years and that after age 40 there is an average loss of 1 Elo point per year, although this shows high between-subject variability (Elo points are a standard metric used to assess chess performance; Grand Masters are those with 2,500+ Elo ratings). Chess players typically peak around age 30 years (Charness et al., 1996). In contrast, very little is known about declines in sport performance with age. Starkes, Weir, Singh, Hodges, and Kerr (1999) recently examined the career and current practice patterns of 40 masters track athletes and found that most had run for over 29 years on average and continued to train 6.5 hours per week. Life stage plays an important role in other activities. As athletes age they tend to sleep less and spend less time in active and nonactive leisure and much more time working than younger athletes. They have less access to coaching and training facilities and yet maintain performance quite well.

One of the major questions with older athletes is whether the normal physical declines associated with aging tend to result in linear decreases in performance with age or a positively decelerating quadratic relationship (i.e., performance can be retained well until about age 60, and then the decline accelerates). From examination of cross-sectional data, there is evidence to suggest that the decline appears to be almost twice as steep as in longitudinal data (Starkes et al., 1999; Stones & Kozma, 1981). To date, however, these analyses have been hampered by the lack of longitudinal data available on expert performers. This is an area in need of much more research.

The Need for Longitudinal Research

Longitudinal research is important not merely from the perspective of understanding the maintenance and retention of expertise. Much of the work available on deliberate practice is based on retrospective recall of practice patterns. Although several techniques are now available to help track the validity and reliability of these types of data (Ericsson et al., 1993; Helsen, Starkes, & Hodges, 1998; Hodges & Starkes, 1996), the best method is to have actual longitudinal evidence, through the use of either athletes' training records, coaches' logs, or other means (Young & Salmela, in press).

Longitudinal research is also critical to an understanding of the development of expertise (Abernethy et al., 1993; French & Nevett, 1993; Housner & French, 1994a; Thomas & Thomas, 1994, 1999). McPherson and French (1991), in one of the few longitudinal studies to date, examined the effects of timing and integration of tactical and skill instruction on the performance of adult beginners in tennis. They measured declarative knowledge base, tennis skill, and game performance on three occasions: prior to instruction, in the middle of a semester of instruction, and at the end of the semester. In beginners, response selection was more readily learned than the actual movement execution. McPherson and French suggest that a sufficient amount of practice time is necessary to develop consistent motor patterns and increase declarative knowledge, and this should be followed by the introduction of tactics and finally actual game play.

Gender Issues in Expertise Research

Interestingly, gender issues have never been addressed in the expertise literature. Subject groups have frequently included both male and female subjects, but equally often groups have been composed of only males or females. If there are differences in how each gender attains expert levels of performance, or the rates of change in performance, these have not been examined to date. This is surprising, as gender differences are often noted elsewhere in areas where perception and cognition have been measured. There may be potential areas of gender difference in sport situations involving recall of spatial information, verbal protocols, and the like. There are also likely to be gender differences in the maintenance of expertise over the life span and the likelihood of continuance of training past one's peak level of performance.

Understanding the What and How of Practice

One advantage of the deliberate practice approach has been that it has returned focus to the quality and quantity of extended practice as a means of realizing a higher level of proficiency. Because a substantial body of research demonstrates how much practice is necessary to attain excellence,

it is time to focus on what should be practiced, how it should be practiced, and how knowledge is best conveyed. Because sport is unique in that it is always movement-based, the challenge is to understand how knowledge should be integrated with motor skill development.

It is important to understand the "microstructure of practice," or what the best athletes do in practice and at what stage of their career (Hastings et al., 1996; Starkes, in press; Starkes et al., 1999). Earlier forms of research, such as time-motion studies of practice content (Cullen & Starkes, 1997; Starkes, in press), are helpful in determining how much of practice is spent active and what form of practice may be best at what age and stage of development. More investigations are needed to continue the work of McPherson and French (1991), to determine what teaching strategies and practice organization function best with individuals at particular skill levels. Further insight might be gained by understanding what the best coaches do to be successful, what works and, more important, why (Côté, Salmela, Trudel, Baria, & Russell, 1995; Durand-Bush & Salmela, 1995; Salmela, 1996; Saury & Durand, 1998; Starkes et al., 1996; Thomas & Thomas, 1994, 1999). New and revisited techniques broaden the scope and applicability of traditional sport expertise research.

Examining Other Paradigms

Scholars have noted that the bulk of sport expertise research has been influenced by methods derived from information processing and cognitive psychology. Approaches other than these may provide advantages that have not been extensively pursued (Abernethy, Neal, et al., 1994; Abernethy et al., 1993; Thomas & Thomas, 1999). Abernethy, Burgess-Limerick, and Parks (1994) present the case for an application of ecological psychology to the study of experts. Abernethy (1993) provides an excellent example of how an ecological approach may broaden an understanding of expert perception. His goal was to determine the minimal essential information that experts could take advantage of with skilled perception. Point light displays of expert squash players were created, and then novice and expert squash players' prediction of ball placement was recorded, when they were provided information either by temporally occluded film or just point light displays. Because point light displays provide only kinematic information about a movement, if expert differences persist, this is an indication that judgments may be based on far more minimal information than once thought. Indeed, experts retain their perceptual skill advantage, even with only point light information. Thus, the actual features resulting from movement production (kinematics) are useful. Abernethy suggests that the ultimate aim must be to determine how information sources in both perception and action are linked and how the coupling of perceptual and motor variables is affected by or reflective of changes in skill.

The efficacy of different approaches has also been noted elsewhere. Starkes (1993) discusses the model of symbolic connectionism and the potential insights it could offer to the study of experts. Housner and French (1994b) note that the study of implicit and explicit learning has been productive elsewhere yet has had little impact on the study of expertise.

SUMMARY AND CONCLUSION

Although the study of sport expertise is an important area and great strides have been made both technologically and theoretically over the past few years, it bears remembering that the area is still in its infancy. A number of areas in which there is a body of research available have been outlined in this chapter. For example, experts require large amounts of high-quality practice to reach peak performance, and they differ from novices both in their ability to perceive sport-specific information and to make the best use of it. This expertise comes only from interacting as an athlete within the sport environment, not simply from watching sport. Expertise is influenced by the family's support of that goal.

The fact that many controversial questions exist means sport expertise is both a fertile area for research and often the subject of popular debate. Ericsson and colleagues' (1993) model of deliberate practice sparked the debate on whether top athletes are "made" through practice or "born." In the end, the answer is likely to be "both," but along the way it is important to determine what forms of practice and how much practice are likely to be important.

Very often, advertisements are made for perceptual training systems that purport to increase performance in sport. It's important to examine what attributes are likely to improve using a particular system and whether these skills transfer directly back to the sport context. Empirical tests of these programs are necessary, and consumers need to be both informed and aware of the results.

Although sport expertise research was initially more focused on traditional team sports, researchers in dance and martial arts have begun to ask whether the principles of skill acquisition in sport expertise adequately describe their experience. Both sport and dance will be stronger as a result of investigations into recall of movement sequences

and the role of metacognition. In the long term, the goals of studying expert-novice differences remain the same: to understand the development of expertise, to shorten the journey on the road to expertise, and to lengthen one's ability to perform at a peak level on a number of occasions.

REFERENCES

Abernethy, B. (1984). Skill in cricket batting: Laboratory and applied evidence. In M.L. Howell & B.D. Wilson (Eds.), *Proceedings of the 7th Commonwealth and International Conference on Sport, Physical Education, Recreation and Dance: Kinesiological Sciences* (pp. 35–50). Brisbane, Australia: University of Queensland.

Abernethy, B. (1986a). Perceptual strategies in a racquet sport. In J. Watkins, T. Reilly, & C. Burwitz (Eds.), *Sports science commonwealth and international conference on sport, physical education, dance, recreation and health* (pp. 325–330). London: E. & F.N. Spon.

Abernethy, B. (1986b). Visual search characteristics of expert and novice racquet sport players. In J. Watkins, T. Reilly, & C. Burwitz (Eds.), *Sports science commonwealth and international conference on sport, physical education, dance, recreation and health* (pp. 331–336). London: E. & F.N. Spon.

Abernethy, B. (1988). The effects of age and expertise upon perceptual skill development in a racquet sport. *Research Quarterly for Exercise and Sport, 59,* 210–221.

Abernethy, B. (1989). Expert-novice differences in perception: How expert does the expert have to be? *Canadian Journal of Sport Sciences, 14,* 27–30.

Abernethy, B. (1990a). Anticipation in squash: Differences in advance cue utilization between expert and novice players. *Journal of Sport Sciences, 8,* 17–34.

Abernethy, B. (1990b). Expertise, visual search and information pick-up in squash. *Perception, 19,* 63–77.

Abernethy, B. (1993). The nature of expertise in sport. In S. Serpa, J. Alves, V. Ferreira, & A. Paula-Brito (Eds.), *Sport psychology: An integrated approach. Proceedings of the 8th World Congress on Sport Psychology* (pp. 18–22). Lisboa, Portugal: University of Lisboa Press.

Abernethy, B., Burgess-Limerick, R., & Parks, S. (1994). Contrasting approaches to the study of motor expertise. *Quest, 46,* 186–198.

Abernethy, B., Neal, R.J., & Koning, P. (1994). Visual-perceptual and cognitive differences between expert, intermediate and novice snooker players. *Applied Cognitive Psychology, 8,* 185–211.

Abernethy, B., & Russell, D.G. (1984). Advance in cue utilisation by skilled cricket batsmen. *Australian Journal of Science and Medicine in Sport, 16,* 2–10.

Abernethy, B., & Russell, D.G. (1987a). Expert-novice differences in an applied selective attention task. *Journal of Sport Psychology, 9,* 326–345.

Abernethy, B., & Russell, D.G. (1987b). The relationship between expertise and visual search strategy in a racquet sport. *Human Movement Science, 6,* 283–319.

Abernethy, B., Thomas, J., & Thomas, K. (1993). Strategies for improving understanding of motor expertise. In J. Starkes & F. Allard (Eds.), *Cognitive issues in motor expertise* (pp. 317–356). Amsterdam: Elsevier.

Abernethy, B., & Wood, J.M. (in press). Do generalized visual training programs for sport really work? An experimental investigation. *Journal of Sports Sciences.*

Adolphe, R.M., Vickers J.N., & LaPlante, G. (1997). The effects of training visual attention on gaze behaviour and accuracy: A pilot study. *International Journal of Sports Vision, 4,* 28–33.

Alain, C., & Sarrazin, C. (1990). Study of decision-making in squash competition: A computer simulation approach. *Canadian Journal of Sport Science, 15,* 193–200.

Alain, C., Sarrazin, C., & Lacombe, D. (1986). The use of subjective expected values in decision making in sport. In D.M. Landers (Ed.), *Sport and elite performers* (pp. 1–6). Champaign, IL: Human Kinetics.

Allard, F. (1982). Cognition, expert performance and sport. In J.H. Salmela, J.T. Partington, & T. Orlick (Eds.), *New paths of sport rearing and excellence* (pp. 22–26). Ottawa: Coaching Association of Canada.

Allard, F., & Burnett, N. (1985). Skill in sport. *Canadian Journal of Psychology, 39,* 294–312.

Allard, F., Deakin, J., Parker, S., & Rodgers, W. (1993). Declarative knowledge in skilled motor performance: Byproduct or constituent? In J.L. Starkes & F. Allard (Eds.), *Cognitive issues in motor expertise* (pp. 95–107). Amsterdam: North Holland.

Allard, F., Graham, S., & Paarsalu, M. (1980). Perception in sport: Basketball. *Journal of Sport Psychology, 2,* 14–21.

Allard, F., & Starkes, J.L. (1980). Perception in sport: Volleyball. *Journal of Sport Psychology, 2,* 22–23.

Allard, F., & Starkes, J.L. (1991). Motor skill experts in sports, dance, and other domains. In K.A. Ericsson & J. Smith (Eds.), *The study of expertise: Prospects and limits* (pp. 126–153). Cambridge, England: Cambridge University Press.

Armstrong, C.W., & Hoffman, S.J. (1979). Effects of teaching experience, knowledge of performer competence, and knowledge of performance outcomes on performance error identification. *Research Quarterly, 50,* 318–327.

Banister, H., & Blackburn, J.M. (1931). An eye factor affecting proficiency at ball games. *British Journal of Psychology, 21,* 382–384.

Bard, C. (1982). La prise d'information visuelle et la préparation à l'action [The nature of visual information and the preparation for action]. In G. Azemar & H. Ripoll (Eds.), *Neurobiologie des comportements moteur [Neurobiology of motor control]* (pp. 181–200). Paris: INSEP.

Bard, C., & Carrière, L. (1975). Etude de la prospection visuelle dans des situations problèmes en sport [A study of visual search in sport problem situations]. *Mouvement [Movement], 10,* 15–23.

Bard, C., & Fleury, M. (1976a). Analysis of visual search activity during sport problem situations. *Journal of Human Movement Studies, 3,* 214–222.

Bard, C., & Fleury, M. (1976b). Analysis of visual search activity during sport problem situations. In U. Simri (Ed.), *Motor learning in physical education and sport* (pp. 127–139). Netanya, Israel: Wingate Institute for Physical Education and Sport.

Bard, C., & Fleury, M. (1976c). Perception visuelle et sports collectifs [Visual perception and team sports]. *Mouvement [Movement], 11,* 22–38.

Bard, C., & Fleury, M. (1978). Manipulation de l'information visuelle et complexité de la prise de décision [Manipulation of visual information and complexity on the nature of decisions]. In F. Landry & W. Orban (Eds.), *Apprentisage moteur, psychologie du sport et aspects pédagogiques de l'activité physique [Motor learning, psychology of sport and pedagogical aspects of physical activity]* (pp. 77–85). Québec, Canada: Symposia Specialists.

Bard, C., & Fleury, M. (1980). Analyse des comportements perceptuels des gardiens de but experts et non-experts en hockey sur glace [An analysis of perceptual decisions of expert and non-expert ice hockey goaltenders]. In G. Marcotte & C. Thiffault (Eds.), *Tactique individuelle et collective au hockey sur glace [Individual and team tactics in ice hockey]* (pp. 111–115). Québec, Canada: Pélican.

Bard, C., & Fleury, M. (1981). Considering eye movements as a predictor of attainment. In I.M. Cockerill & W.W. MacGillivary (Eds.), *Vision and sport* (pp. 28–41). Cheltenham, England: Stanley Thornes.

Bard, C., Fleury, M., & Carrière, L. (1975). La stratégie perceptive et la performance sportive [Perceptual strategy and sport performance]. *Mouvement. Actes du 7° symposium en apprentisage psycho-moteur et psychologie du sport [Movement. Proceedings of the 7th symposium on Psycho-Motor Learning and Sport Psychology], 10,* 163–183.

Bard, C., Fleury, M., Carrière, L., & Hallé, M. (1980). Analysis of gymnastic judges' visual search. *Research Quarterly for Exercise and Sport, 51,* 267–273.

Bard, C., Fleury, M., & Goulet, C. (1987). *Relationship between visual search strategies and response adequacy and accuracy in sport situations.* Paper presented at the Eye-Movement Symposium, SCAPPS 10th annual conference, Banff, Canada.

Bard, C., Guézennec, Y., & Papin, J.P. (1981). Escrime: Analyse de l'exploration visuelle [Writing: An analysis of visual search]. *Médecine du Sport [Sport Medicine], 55,* 22–29.

Barnsley, R.H., & Thompson, A.H. (1988). Birthdate and success in minor hockey: The key to the NHL. *Canadian Journal of Behavioral Science, 20,* 167–176.

Barnsley, R.H., Thompson, A.H., & Barnsley, P.E. (1985). Hockey success and birthdate: The relative age effect. *Canadian Association for Health, Physical Education, and Recreation Journal, 51,* 23–28.

Barnsley, R.H., Thompson, A.H., & Legault, P. (1992). Family planning: Football style. The relative age effect in football. *International Review for the Sociology of Sport, 27,* 77–87.

Bartz, A.E. (1967). Fixation errors in eye movements to peripheral stimuli. *Journal of Experimental Psychology, 75,* 444–446.

Beals, R.P., Mayyasi, A.M., Templeton, A.E., & Johnston, W.L. (1971). The relationship between basketball shooting performance and certain visual attributes. *American Journal of Optometry, 48,* 585–590.

Beise, D., & Peaseley, V. (1937). The relation of reaction time, speed and agility of big muscle groups to certain sport skills. *Research Quarterly, 8,* 133–142.

Benguigui, N., & Ripoll, H. (1998). Effect of tennis practice on the coincidence timing accuracy of adults and children. *Research Quarterly for Exercise and Sport, 69,* 217–223.

Beunen, G., Ostyn, M., Renson, R., Simons, J., & Van Gerven, D. (1978). Motor performance related to chronological age and maturation. In R.J. Shephard & H. Lavalle (Eds.), *Physical fitness assessment: Principles, practice and application* (pp. 229–237). Springfield, IL: Thomas.

Bhanot, J.L., & Sidhu, L.S. (1980). Reaction time of hockey players with reference to their field positions. *Journal of Sports Medicine and Physical Fitness, 20,* 423–430.

Bloom, B.S. (Ed.). (1985). *Developing talent in young people.* New York: Ballantine Books.

Blundell, N.L. (1984). Critical visual-perceptual attributes of championship level tennis players. In M.L. Howell & B.D. Wilson (Eds.), *Proceedings of the 7th Commonwealth and International Conference on Sport, Physical Education, Recreation and Dance: Kinesiological Sciences* (Vol. 7, pp. 51–59). Brisbane, Australia: University of Queensland.

Borgeaud, P., & Abernethy, B. (1987). Skilled perception in volleyball defense. *Journal of Sport Psychology, 9,* 400–406.

Boucher, J., & Mutimer, B. (1994). The relative age phenomenon in sport: A replication and extension with ice hockey. *Research Quarterly for Exercise and Sport, 65,* 377–381.

Bowers, T.D., & Stratton, R.K. (1993). Relationship of anticipation timing to batting experience. *Journal of Sport & Exercise Psychology, 15,* 57.

Brewer, J., Balsom, P., & Davis, J. (1995). Seasonal birth distribution amongst European soccer players. *Sports Exercise and Injury, 1,* 154–157.

Buckholz, E., Prapavessis, H., & Fairs, J. (1988). Advance cues and their use in predicting tennis passing shots. *Canadian Journal of Sport Sciences, 13,* 20–30.

Burke, T.R. (1972). Athletes, athletic performance, and conditions in the environment. *Quest, 17,* 56–60.

Burley, L.R. (1944). A study of the reaction time of physically trained man. *Research Quarterly, 15,* 232–239.

Burpee, R.H., & Stroll, W. (1936). Measuring reaction time of athletes. *Research Quarterly, 7,* 110–118.

Burroughs, W.A. (1984). Visual simulation training of baseball batters. *International Journal of Sport Psychology, 15,* 117–126.

Carrière, L. (1978). Les effets de la compétition des réponses et du contexte sur la prise de décisions dans les situations problèmes [The effects of competition, responses, and context on the nature of decisions in problem situations]. In F. Landry & W.A.R. Orban (Eds.), *Motor learning, sport psychology, pedagogy and didactics of physical activity* (pp. 77–84). Québec, Canada: Symposia Specialists.

Cauraugh, J.H., Singer, R.N., & Chen, D. (1993). Visual scanning and anticipation of expert and beginner tennis players. In S. Serpa, J. Alves, V. Ferreira, & A. Paula-Brito (Eds.), *Sport psychology: An integrated approach. Proceedings of the 8th World Congress on Sport Psychology,* (pp. 336–340). Lisboa, Portugal: University of Lisboa Press.

Charness, N., Krampe, R., & Mayr, U. (1996). The role of practice and coaching in entrepreneurial skill domains: An international comparison of life-span chess skill acquisition. In K.A. Ericsson (Ed.), *The road to excellence: The acquisition of expert performance in the arts and sciences, sports and games* (pp. 51–80). Mahwah, NJ: Erlbaum.

Chase, W.G., & Ericsson, K.A. (1982). Skill and working memory. *Psychology of Learning and Motivation, 16,* 1–58.

Chase, W.G., & Simon, H.A. (1973a). The mind's eye in chess. In W.G. Chase (Ed.), *Visual information processing* (pp. 215–281). New York: Academic Press.

Chase, W.G., & Simon, H.A. (1973b). Perception in chess. *Cognitive Psychology, 4,* 55–81.

Chen, D., Singer, R.N., Cauraugh, J.H., & Kashdan, M.S. (1993). Tennis skill level and coincidence anticipation. *Research Quarterly for Exercise and Sport, 64,* 72.

Chiesi, H.L., Spilich, G.J., & Voss, J.F. (1979). Acquisition of domain-related information in relation to high and low domain knowledge. *Journal of Verbal Learning and Verbal Behavior, 18,* 257–274.

Christensen, S.A., & Glencross, D.J. (1993). Expert knowledge and expert perception in sport: Anticipating a field hockey goal shot. In S. Serpa, J. Alves, V. Ferreira, & A. Paula-Brito (Eds.), *Sport psychology: An integrated approach. Proceedings of the 8th World Congress on Sport Psychology* (pp. 340–344). Lisboa, Portugal: University of Lisboa Press.

Cockerill, I.M. (1981a). Distance estimation and sports performance. In I.M. Cockerill & W.W. MacGillivary (Eds.), *Vision and sport* (pp. 116–125). Cheltenham, England: Stanley Thornes.

Cockerill, I.M. (1981b). Peripheral vision and hockey. In I.M. Cockerill & W.W. MacGillivary (Eds.), *Vision and sport* (pp. 54–63). Cheltenham, England: Stanley Thornes.

Cockerill I.M. (1981c). Use the eyes to control your putting. In I.M. Cockerill, & W.W. MacGillivary (Eds.), *Vision and sport* (pp. 17–27). Cheltenham, England: Stanley Thornes.

Cockerill, I.M., & Callington, B.P. (1981). Visual information processing in golf and association football. In I.M. Cockerill & W.W. MacGillivary (Eds.), *Vision and sport* (pp. 126–138). Cheltenham, England: Stanley Thornes.

Cohen, M.E., & Ross, L.E. (1977). Saccade latency in children and adults: Effects of warning interval and target eccentricity. *Journal of Experimental Child Psychology, 23,* 539–549.

Côté, J. (in press). Family influences on youth sport performance and participation. In J.M. Silva & D. Stevens (Eds.), *Psychological foundations of sport* (2nd ed.). Boston: Merrill.

Côté, J., & Hay, J. (in press). Children's involvement in sport: A developmental perspective. In J.M. Silva & D. Stevens (Eds.), *Psychological foundations of sport* (2nd ed.). Boston: Merrill.

Côté, J., Salmela, J.H., Trudel, P., Baria, A., & Russell, S. (1995). The coaching model: A grounded assessment of expert gymnastic coaches' knowledge. *Journal of Sport & Exercise Psychology, 17,* 1–17.

Csikszentmihalyi, M., Rathunde, K., & Whalen, S. (1993). *Talented teenagers: The roots of success and failure.* New York: Cambridge University Press.

Cullen, J., & Starkes, J. (1997). *Deliberate practice in ice hockey.* Paper presented at the Canadian Society for Psychomotor Learning and Sport Psychology, Niagara Falls, Canada.

Davids, K. (1984). The role of peripheral vision in ballgames: Some theoretical and practical notions. *Physical Education Review, 7,* 26–40.

Davids, K. (1988). Developmental differences in the use of peripheral vision during catching performance. *Journal of Motor Behavior, 20,* 39–51.

Day, L.J. (1980). Anticipation in junior tennis players. In J. Groppel & R. Sears (Eds.), *Proceedings of the international symposium on the effective teaching of racquet sports* (pp. 107–116). Champaign: University of Illinois Press.

Deakin, J.M. (1987). *Cognitive components of skill in figure skating.* Unpublished doctoral dissertation, University of Waterloo, Canada.

Deakin, J.M., & Allard, F. (1992). *An evaluation of skill and judgement in basketball officiating.* Paper presented at the meeting of the North American Society for the Psychology of Sport and Physical Activity, Pittsburgh, PA.

Deridder, M. (1985). Enregistrement et analyse des comportements exploratoires visuels du gardien de but en situation de penalty [Recording and analysis of visual search patterns of goaltenders in penalty situations]. In M. Laurent & P. Therme (Eds.), *Recherches en activités physiques et sportives [Research in physical activity and sport]* (pp. 259–272). Aix-Marseille, France: UEREPS.

Deshaies, P., & Pargman, D. (1976). Selected visual abilities of college football players. *Perceptual and Motor Skills, 43,* 904–906.

Doil, W., & Binding, M. (1986). Peripheres Sehen als Voraussetzung für die Orientierung in Sportspielen [Peripheral vision skills for orienteering in sport]. *Medicin und Sport [Medicine and Sport], 26,* 55–58.

Doody, S.G., Huddleston, S., Beavers, C., & Austin, M. (1987). Detection of task-relevant cues in field hockey. *Journal of Sport Psychology, 9,* 74–78.

Dudink, A. (1994). Birth date and sporting success. *Nature, 368,* 592.

Dunham, P. (1989). Coincidence-anticipation performance of adolescent baseball players and non-players. *Perceptual and Motor Skills, 68,* 1151–1156.

Durand-Bush, N., & Salmela, J.H. (1995). Nurture over nature: A new twist to the development of expertise. *Avante, 2,* 1–19.

Edwards, S. (1994). Born too late to win? *Nature, 370,* 186.

Enberg, M.L. (1968). Assessing perception of object directionality in tennis. (Unpublished doctoral dissertation, Purdue University, 1968). *Dissertation Abstracts International, 29,* 806–A.

Ericsson, K.A. (Ed.). (1996). *The road to excellence: The acquisition of expert performance in the arts and sciences, sports and games.* Mahwah, NJ: Erlbaum.

Ericsson, K.A., & Charness, N. (1994). Expert performance: Its structure and acquisition. *American Psychologist, 49,* 725–747.

Ericsson, K.A., Krampe, R.T., & Tesch-Römer, C. (1993). The role of deliberate practice in the acquisition of expert performance. *Psychological Review, 100,* 363–406.

Ericsson, K.A., & Lehmann, A.C. (1996). Expert and exceptional performance: Evidence of maximal adaptation to task constraints. *Annual Review of Psychology, 47,* 273–305.

Ericsson, K.A., & Smith, J. (Eds.). (1991). Prospects and limits of the empirical study of expertise: An introduction. *Towards a general theory of expertise* (pp. 1–38). Cambridge, England: Cambridge University Press.

Ferrari, M. (1999). The influence of expertise on the intentional transfer of motor skill. *Journal of Motor Behavior, 31,* 79–85.

Fleury, M., Goulet, C., & Bard, C. (1986). Eye fixations as visual indices of programming of service return in tennis. *Psychology of Motor Behavior and Sport abstracts* (p. 17). Scottsdale, AZ: North American Society for the Psychology of Sport and Physical Activity.

Franks, I.M., & Hanvey, T. (1997). Cues for goalkeepers: High-tech methods used to measure penalty shot response. *Soccer Journal,* 30–38.

French, K.E., & McPherson, S.L. (1999). Adaptations in response selection processes used during sport competition with increasing age and expertise. *International Journal of Sport Psychology, 30,* 173–193.

French, K.E., & Nevett, M.E. (1993). The development of expertise in youth sport. In J.L. Starkes & F. Allard (Eds.), *Cognitive issues in motor expertise* (pp. 255–270). Amsterdam: Elsevier.

French, K.E., Nevett, M.E., Spurgeon, J.H., Graham, K.C., Rink, J.E., & McPherson, S.L. (1996). Knowledge representation and problem solution in expert and novice youth baseball performance. *Research Quarterly for Exercise and Sport, 66,* 194–201.

French, K.E., Spurgeon, J.H., & Nevett, M.E. (1995). Expert-novice differences in cognitive and skill execution components of youth baseball performance. *Research Quarterly for Exercise and Sport, 66,* 194–201.

French, K.E., & Thomas, J.R. (1987). The relation of knowledge development to children's basketball performance. *Journal of Sport Psychology, 9,* 15–32.

Gangemi, P.F., Zaccara, G., Bordiga, M., Caldarone, G., Minneo, L., Messori, A., Parigi, A., & Luzzi, S. (1993). Oculomotor and manual tracking in a group of Olympic gymnasts. In G. d'Ydewalle & J. Van Rensbergen (Eds.), *Perception and cognition: Advances in eye movement research* (pp. 149–157). Amsterdam: North Holland.

Glamser, F.D., & Marciani, L.M. (1990, October). *The importance of relative age to college football participation.* Paper presented at the annual meeting of the Mid-South Sociological Association, Hot Springs, AR.

Glaser, R. (1996). Changing the agency for learning: Acquiring expert performance. In K.A. Ericsson (Ed.), *The road to excellence: The acquisition of expert performance in the arts and sciences, sports and games* (pp. 303–311). Hillsdale, NJ: Erlbaum.

Glencross, D.J., & Paull, G. (1993). Expert perception and decision making in baseball. In S. Serpa, J. Alves, V. Ferreira, & A. Paula-Brito (Eds.), *Sport psychology: An integrated*

approach. Proceedings of the 8th World Congress on Sport Psychology (pp. 356–359). Lisboa, Portugal: University of Lisboa Press.

Goulet, C., Bard, C., & Fleury, M. (1989). Expertise differences in preparing to return a tennis serve: A visual information processing approach. *Journal of Sport & Exercise Psychology, 11,* 382–398.

Goulet, C., Bard, C., & Fleury, M. (1990). Visual search strategies and information processing in a racquet sport situation. In D. Brogan (Ed.), *Visual search* (pp. 185–192). London: Taylor & Francis.

Goulet, C., Fleury, M., Bard, C., Yerlès, M., Michaud, D., & Lemire, L. (1988). Analysis of visual cues from tennis serves. *Canadian Journal of Sport Sciences, 13,* 79–87.

Grant, A., & Williams, A.M. (1996). *Training cognitive decision-making in intermediate youth soccer players.* Unpublished manuscript, Liverpool, England, John Moores University.

Graybiel, A., Jokl, E., & Trapp, C. (1955). Russian studies in vision in relation to physical activity and sports. *Research Quarterly, 26,* 480–485.

Haase, H., & Mayer, H. (1978). Optische Oriëntierungsstrategieën von Fechtern [Optical strategies from fencing]. *Leistungssport, 8,* 191–200.

Haskins, M.J. (1965). Development of a response-recognition training film in tennis. *Perceptual and Motor Skills, 21,* 207–211.

Hastings, D.W., Kurth, S.B., & Schloder, M. (1996). Work routines in the serious leisure career of Canadian and U.S. Masters swimmers. *Avante, 2,* 73–92.

Helsen, W., Buekers, M., & Pauwels, J.M. (1986). The registration of eye-movements in sport games. In L.E. Unestahl (Ed.), *Contemporary sport psychology* (pp. 94–102). Orebro, Sweden: Veje.

Helsen, W., Hodges, N.J., Van Winckel, J., & Starkes, J. (in press). The roles of talent, physical maturation and practice in the development of soccer expertise. *Journal of Sport Sciences.*

Helsen, W., & Pauwels, J.M. (1988). The use of a simulator in evaluation and training of tactical skills in football. In T. Reilly, A. Lees, K. Davids, & W.J. Murphy (Eds.), *Science and football* (pp. 493–497). London: E. & F.N. Spon.

Helsen, W., & Pauwels, J.M. (1990). Analysis of visual search activity during tactical game problems. In D. Brogan (Ed.), *Visual search* (pp. 177–184). London: Taylor & Francis.

Helsen, W., & Pauwels, J.M. (1991). Visual search in solving tactical game problems. In R. Daugs, H. Mechling, K. Blischke, & N. Olivier (Eds.), *Sportmotorisches Lernen und Techniktraining [Sport motor learning and technical training]* (pp. 199–202). Schorndorf, Germany: Hofmann.

Helsen, W., & Pauwels, J.M. (1993a). A cognitive approach to skilled performance and perception in sport. In G. d'Ydewalle & J. Van Rensbergen (Eds.), *Perception and cognition: Advances in eye movement research* (pp. 127–139). Amsterdam: North Holland.

Helsen, W., & Pauwels, J.M. (1993b). A cognitive approach to visual search in sport. In D. Brogan, A. Gale, & K. Carr (Eds.), *Visual search* (Vol. 2, pp. 379–388). London: Taylor & Francis.

Helsen, W., & Pauwels, J.M. (1993c). The relationship between expertise and visual information processing in sport. In J. Starkes & F. Allard (Eds.), *Cognitive issues in motor expertise* (pp. 109–134). Amsterdam: Elsevier.

Helsen, W., Pauwels, J.M., & Boutmans, J. (1986). Decision making in sport games: The use of a game simulator in evaluation and training. In *Proceedings of FISU/CESU Conference* (pp. 354–359). Kobe, Japan: FISU University Group.

Helsen, W., Pauwels, J.M., Van Outryve, D., & d'Ydewalle, G. (1986). Analysis of visual search patterns during sports games. In R. Andresen (Ed.), *Beiträge zur Sportspielforschung [Contribution in applied sport research]* (pp. 69–81). Hamburg, Germany.

Helsen, W., & Starkes, J. (1999a). A multidimensional approach to skilled perception and performance in sport. *Applied Cognitive Psychology, 13*, 1–27.

Helsen, W., & Starkes, J. (1999b). A new training approach to complex decision making for police officers in potentially dangerous situations. *Journal of Criminality and Criminal Justice, 27*, 395–410.

Helsen, W., Starkes, J., & Hodges, N.J. (1998). Team sports and the theory of deliberate practice. *Journal of Sport & Exercise Psychology, 20*, 12–34.

Helsen, W., Starkes, J., & Van Winckel, J. (1998). The influence of relative age on success and dropout in male soccer players. *American Journal of Human Biology, 10*, 791–798.

Helsen, W., Starkes, J., & Van Winckel, J. (in press). Effect of a change in selection year on success in male soccer players. *American Journal of Human Biology.*

Hodge, T., & Deakin, J.M. (1998). Deliberate practice and expertise in the marital arts: The role of context in motor recall. *Journal of Sport & Exercise Psychology, 20*, 260–279.

Hodges, N., & Starkes, J.L. (1996). Wrestling with the nature of expertise: A sport specific test of Ericsson, Krampe & Tesch-Römer's theory of deliberate practice. *International Journal of Sport Psychology, 27*, 1–25.

Houlston, D.R., & Lowes, R. (1993). Anticipatory cue utilisation processes amongst expert and non-expert wicketkeepers in cricket. *International Journal of Sport Psychology, 24*, 59–73.

Housner, L.D., & French, K.E. (1994a). Expertise in learning, performance, and instruction in sport and physical activity [Special issue]. *Quest, 46*, 241–246.

Housner, L.D., & French, K.E. (1994b). Future directions for research on expertise in learning, performance, and instruction in sport and physical activity. *Quest, 46*, 241–246.

Howarth, C., Walsh, W.D., Abernethy, B., & Snijder, W. (1984). A field examination of anticipation in squash: Some preliminary data. *Australian Journal of Science and Medicine in Sport, 16*, 7–11.

Howe, M.J.A., Davidson, J.W., & Sloboda, J.A. (1998). Innate talents: Reality or myth? *Behavioural and Brain Sciences, 21*, 399–442.

Hubbard, A.W. (1955). Rebuttal to above comments on "visual movements of batters." *Research Quarterly, 26*, 366–368.

Hubbard, A.W., & Seng, C.N. (1954). Visual movements of batters. *Research Quarterly, 25*, 42–57.

Hughes, P.K., Blundell, N.L., & Walters, J.M. (1993). Visual and psychomotor performance of elite, intermediate and novice table tennis competitors. *Clinical and Experimental Optometry, 76*, 51–60.

Imwold, C.H., & Hoffman, S.J. (1983). Visual recognition of a gymnastics skill by experienced and inexperienced instructors. *Research Quarterly for Exercise and Sport, 54*, 149–155.

Isaacs, L.D., & Finch, A.E. (1983). Anticipatory timing of beginning and intermediate tennis players. *Perceptual and Motor Skills, 57*, 451–454.

Jack, R., Kirshenbaum, N., Poon, P., Rodgers, W., & Starkes, J. (1999). Metacognitive differences in experts and novices in self-directed learning. *Journal of Sport & Exercise Psychology, 21*, S61.

Jackson, M. (1986). Sportspersons' use of postural cues in rapid decision-making. In J. Bond & J.B. Gross (Eds.), *Sports psychology* (pp. 74–79). Canberra, Australia: Australian Sport Commission Press.

Joch, V.W. (1980). Zum Reaktionsvermögen von Boxern [Reaction time in boxing]. *Deutsche Zeitschrift für Sportmedizn [German Journal for Sport Medicine], 1*, 4–8.

Jones, C.M., & Miles, T.R. (1978). Use of advance cues in predicting the flight of a lawn tennis ball. *Journal of Human Movement Studies, 4*, 231–235.

Kioumourtzoglou, E., Kourtessis, T., Michalopoulou, M., & Derri, V. (1998). Differences in several perceptual abilities between experts and novices in basketball, volleyball and water-polo. *Perceptual and Motor Skills, 86*, 899–912.

Kuhn, W. (1993). Testing the ability of anticipation-coincidence of soccer players. In T. Reilly, J. Clarys, & A. Stibbe (Eds.), *Science and football* (Vol. 2, pp. 244–249). London: E. & F.N. Spon.

Leavitt, J. (1979). Cognitive demands of skating and stick handling in ice hockey. *Canadian Journal of Applied Sport Sciences, 4*, 46–55.

Lidor, R., Argov, E., & Daniel, S. (1998). An exploratory study of perceptual-motor abilities of women: Novice and skilled players of team handball. *Perceptual and Motor Skills, 86,* 279–288.

Lyle, J., & Cook, M. (1984). Non-verbal cues and decision-making in games. *Momentum, 9,* 20–25.

McLeod, P. (1987). Visual reaction time and high-speed ball-games. *Perception, 16,* 49–59.

McMorris, T., & Beazeley, A. (1997). Performance of experienced and inexperienced soccer players on soccer specific tests of recall, visual search and decision making. *Journal of Human Movement Studies, 33,* 1–13.

McMorris, T., Copeman, R., Corcoran, D., Saunders, G., & Potter, S. (1993). Anticipation of soccer goalkeepers facing penalty kicks. *Journal of Sport Sciences, 7,* 79–80.

McMorris, T., & Graydon, J. (1997). The effect of exercise on the decision-making performance of experienced and inexperienced soccer players. *Research Quarterly for Exercise and Sport, 67,* 109–114.

McPherson, S.L. (1993). The influence of player experience on problem solving during batting preparation in baseball. *Journal of Sport & Exercise Psychology, 15,* 304–325.

McPherson, S.L. (1994). The development of sport expertise: Mapping the tactical domain. *Quest, 46,* 223–240.

McPherson, S.L. (1999). Tactical differences in problem representations and solutions in collegiate varsity and beginner women tennis players. *Research Quarterly for Exercise and Sport, 70,* 369–384.

McPherson, S.L., & French, K.E. (1991). Changes in cognitive strategy and motor skill in tennis. *Journal of Sport & Exercise Psychology, 13,* 26–41.

McPherson, S.L., & Thomas, J.R. (1989). Relation of knowledge and performance in boys' tennis: Age and expertise. *Journal of Experimental Child Psychology, 48,* 190–211.

Miller, J.W. (1958). Study of visual acuity during the ocular pursuit of moving objects. *Journal of the Optical Society of America, 48,* 799–802.

Miller, R.G., & Shay, C.T. (1964). Relationship of reaction time to the speed of a softball. *Research Quarterly, 35,* 433–437.

Millslagle, D. (1988). Visual perception, recognition, recall and mode of visual search control in basketball involving novice and experienced basketball players. *Journal of Sport Behavior, 11,* 32–44.

Mizusawa, K., Sweeting, R.L., & Knouse, S.B. (1983). Comparative studies of color fields, visual acuity fields, and movement perception limits among varsity athletes and non-varsity groups. *Perceptual and Motor Skills, 56,* 887–892.

Möckel, W., & Heemsoth, C. (1984). Maximizing information as a strategy in visual search: The role of knowledge about the stimulus structure. In A.G. Gale & F. Johnson (Eds.), *Theoretical and applied aspects of eye movement research* (pp. 335–341). Amsterdam: Elsevier.

Morris, D., & Kreighbaum, E. (1977). Dynamic visual acuity of varsity women volleyball and basketball players. *Research Quarterly, 48,* 480–483.

Nakagawa, A. (1982). A field experiment on recognition of game situations in ball games: The case of static situations in rugby football. *Japanese Journal of Physical Education, 27,* 17–26.

Nessler, J. (1973). Length of time necessary to view a ball while catching it. *Journal of Motor Behavior, 5,* 179–185.

Neumaier, A. (1982). The function of watching behavior in the visual perception process in sport. *Sportwissenschaft, 12,* 78–91.

Neumaier, A. (1983). Beobachtungsstrategiën und antizipation bei der abwehr von volleyball angriffen [Observation strategies and anticipation in offensive volleyball attacks]. *Leistungssport, 13,* 5–10.

Nevett, M.E., & French, K.E. (1997). The development of sport-specific planning, rehearsal and updating of plans during defensive youth baseball game performance. *Research Quarterly for Exercise and Sport, 68,* 203–214.

Olsen, E.A. (1956). Relationship between psychological capacities and success in college athletics. *Research Quarterly, 27,* 79–89.

Oudejans, R.R.D., Michaels, C.F., & Bakker, F.C. (1997). The effects of baseball experience on movement initiation in catching fly balls. *Journal of Sports Sciences, 15,* 587–595.

Papin, J.P., Condon, A., & Guezennec, Y. (1984). Evolution de la stratégie de l'exploration visuelle d'enfants apprenant escrime [The evolution of visual search strategy in children learning to write]. *Medecine du Sport [Sport Medicine], 58,* 27–35.

Parker, H. (1981). Visual detection and perception in netball. In I.M. Cockerill & W.W. MacGillivary (Eds.), *Vision and sport* (pp. 42–53). Cheltenham, England: Stanley Thornes.

Patrick, J., & Spurgeon, P. (1978). The use of the body cues in the anticipation of the direction of a ball. *Physical Education Review, 10,* 5–16.

Paull, G., & Fitzgerald, D. (1993). Addressing ecological validity through interactive video simulation. In S. Serpa, J. Alves, V. Ferreira, & A. Paula-Brito (Eds.), *Sport psychology: An integrated approach. Proceedings of the 8th World Congress on Sport Psychology* (pp. 175–179). Lisboa, Portugal: University of Lisboa Press.

Paull, G., & Glencross, D. (1997). Expert participation and decision making in baseball. *International Journal of Sport Psychology, 28,* 35–56.

Pauwels, J.M., & Helsen, W. (1986). Relationship of static and dynamic displays of game problems. In R. Andresen (Ed.), *Beiträge zur sportspielforschung [Contributions in applied sport research]* (pp. 90–99). Hamburg, Germany.

Payne, V.G., & Isaacs, L.D. (1995). *Human motor development* (3rd ed.). Mountain View, CA: Mayfield.

Petrakis, E. (1986). Visual observation patterns of tennis teachers. *Research Quarterly for Exercise and Sport, 57*, 254–259.

Petrakis, E. (1987). Analysis of visual search patterns of dance teachers. *Journal of Teaching in Physical Education, 6*, 149–156.

Petrakis, E. (1993). Analysis of visual search patterns of tennis teachers. In G. d'Ydewalle & J. Van Rensbergen (Eds.), *Perception and cognition: Advances in eye movement research* (pp. 159–168). Amsterdam: Elsevier.

Pierson, W.R. (1956). Comparison of fencers and nonfencers by psychomotor, space perception, and anthropometric measures. *Research Quarterly, 27*, 90–96.

Pinheiro, V. (1993). Chunking: Perceptual advantage in motor skill diagnosis. In S. Serpa, J. Alves, V. Ferreira, & A. Paula-Brito (Eds.), *Sport psychology: An integrated approach. Proceedings of the 8th World Congress on Sport Psychology* (pp. 375–378). Lisboa, Portugal: University of Lisboa Press.

Poon, P.L., & Rodgers, W.M. (in press). Learning and remembering strategies of novice and advanced jazz dancers for skill level appropriate dance routines. *Research Quarterly for Exercise and Sport.*

Rasch, P.S., & Pierson, W.R. (1963). Reaction and movement time of experience karateka. *Research Quarterly, 34*, 416–419.

Rasch, P.S., Pierson, W.R., O'Connell, E.R., & Hunt, M.B. (1961). Response time of amateur wrestlers. *Research Quarterly, 32*, 416–419.

Ridini, L.M. (1968). Relationships between psychological functions tests and selected sport skills of boys in junior high school. *Research Quarterly, 39*, 674–683.

Ripoll, H. (1988a). Analysis of visual scanning patterns of volleyball players in a problem solving task. *International Journal of Sport Psychology, 19*, 9–25.

Ripoll, H. (1988b). Utilisation d'un dispositif vidéo-oculographique d'enregistrement de la direction du regard en situation sportive [Use of slides in the recording of direction of gaze in sport situations]. *Science et Motricité, 2*, 26–31.

Ripoll, H. (1991). The understanding-acting process in sport: The relationship between the semantic and sensorimotor visual function. *International Journal of Sport Psychology, 22*, 221–243.

Ripoll, H., Kerlirzin, Y., & Stein, J.F. (1993a). Cognition and decision making in externally-paced sport situation: French boxing. In S. Serpa, J. Alves, V. Ferreira, & A. Paula-Brito (Eds.), *Sport psychology: An integrated approach. Proceedings of the 8th World Congress on Sport Psychology* (pp. 383–386). Lisboa, Portugal: University of Lisboa Press.

Ripoll, H., Kerlirzin, Y., & Stein, J.F. (1993b). Decision making and visual strategies of boxers in a simulated problem solving situation. In G. d'Ydewalle & J. Van Rensbergen (Eds.), *Perception and cognition: Advances in eye movement research* (pp. 141–147). Amsterdam: Elsevier.

Ripoll, H., Kerlirzin, Y., Stein, J.F., & Reine, B. (1995). Analysis of information processing, decision making, and visual strategies in complex problem solving sport situations. *Human Movement Science, 14*, 325–349.

Ripoll, H., & Latiri, I. (1997). Effect of expertise on coincident-timing accuracy in a fast ball game. *Journal of Sports Sciences, 15*, 573–580.

Ritzdorf, W. (1982). Visuele wahrnehmung und antizipation [Visual perception and anticipation]. *Schriftenreihe des bundesinstituts für sportwissenschaft [National Institute for Sport] 45*, 270.

Ritzdorf, W. (1983). Antizipation im sportspiel: Dargestellt am beispiel des tennisgrundschlags [Anticipation in sport: Mapping examples from tennis ground strokes]. *Leistungssport, 13*, 5–9.

Rodrigues, S.T. (1999). *Visuo-motor coordination in table tennis.* Unpublished doctoral dissertation, University of Calgary, Alberta, Canada.

Rowley, S. (1995). Identification and development of talent in young athletes. In J. Freeman, P. Span, & H. Wagner (Eds.), *Actualizing talent: A lifelong challenge* (pp. 128–143). London: Cassell.

Rutt Leas, R., & Chi, M.T.H. (1993). Analyzing diagnostic expertise of competitive swimming coaches. In J.L. Starkes & F. Allard (Eds.), *Cognitive issues in motor expertise* (pp. 75–94). Amsterdam: Elsevier.

Salmela, J.H. (1996). *Great job coach: Getting the edge from proven winners.* Ottawa, Canada: Potentium.

Salmela, J.H., & Fiorito, P. (1979). Visual cues in ice hockey goaltending. *Canadian Journal of Applied Sport Sciences, 4*, 56–59.

Salthouse, T.A. (1991). Expertise as the circumvention of human processing limitations. In K.A. Ericsson & J. Smith (Eds.), *Towards a general theory of expertise* (pp. 286–300). Cambridge, England: Cambridge University Press.

Sanderson, F.H., & Holton, J.N. (1980). Relationships between perceptual motor abilities and cricket batting. *Perceptual and Motor Skills, 51*, 138.

Sanderson, F.H., & Whiting, H.T.A. (1972). The effect of exercise on the visual and auditory acuity of table-tennis players. *Journal of Motor Behavior, 4*, 163–169.

Sanderson, F.H., & Whiting, H.T.A. (1974). Dynamic visual acuity and performance in a catching task. *Journal of Motor Behavior, 6*, 87–94.

Sanderson, F.H., & Whiting, H.T.A. (1978). Dynamic visual acuity: A possible factor in catching performance. *Journal of Motor Behavior, 10*, 7–14.

Saury, J., & Durand, M. (1998). Practical knowledge in expert coaches: On-site study of coaching in sailing. *Research Quarterly for Exercise and Sport, 69,* 254–266.

Schneider, W., & Bjorklund, D.F. (1992). Expertise, aptitude and strategic remembering. *Child Development, 63,* 461–473.

Schulz, R., Musa, D., Staszewski, J., & Siegler, R.S. (1994). The relationship between age and major league baseball performance: Implications for development. *Psychology of Aging, 9,* 274–286.

Shank, M.D., & Haywood, K.M. (1987). Eye movements while viewing a baseball pitch. *Perceptual and Motor Skills, 64,* 1191–1197.

Simonton, D.K. (1994). *Greatness: Who makes history and why.* New York: Guilford Press.

Simonton, D.K. (1996). Creative expertise: A life-span developmental perspective. In K.A. Ericsson (Ed.), *The road to excellence: The acquisition of expert performance in the arts and sciences, sports and games* (pp. 227–253). Hillsdale, NJ: Erlbaum.

Singer, R. (1968). Speed and accuracy of movement as related to fencing success. *Research Quarterly, 39,* 1080–1083.

Singer, R.N., Cauraugh, J.H., Chen, D., Steinberg, G.M., Frehlich, S.G., & Wang, L. (1994). Training mental quickness in beginning/intermediate tennis players. *The Sport Psychologist, 8,* 305–318.

Singer, R.N., & Janelle, C.M. (1999). Determining sport expertise: From genes to supremes. *International Journal of Sport Psychology, 30,* 117–150.

Singer, R.N., Williams, A.M., Frehlich, S.G., Janelle, C.M., Radlo, S.J., Barba, D.A., & Bouchard, L.J. (1998). New frontiers in visual search: An exploratory study in live tennis situations. *Research Quarterly for Exercise and Sport, 69,* 290–296.

Sloboda, J.A. (1991). Musical expertise. In K.A. Ericsson & J. Smith (Eds.), *Toward a general theory of expertise* (pp. 153–171). Cambridge, England: Cambridge University Press.

Sloboda, J.A. (1996). The acquisition of musical performance expertise: Deconstructing the "talent" account of individual differences in musical expressivity. In K.A. Ericsson (Ed.), *The road to excellence: The acquisition of expert performance in the arts and sciences, sports and games* (pp. 107–126). Hillsdale, NJ: Erlbaum.

Smyth, M.M., & Pendleton, L.R. (1994). Memory for movement in professional ballet dancers. *International Journal of Sport Psychology, 25,* 282–294.

Sonneschein, G., & Sonneschein, I. (1981). Wahrnemung im volleyball. *Volleyball Journal, 16,* 207–208.

Soulière, D., & Salmela, J.H. (1982). Indices visuels, stress temporel et performance motrice au volleyball [Visual indices, temporal stress and motor performance in volleyball]. In J.H. Salmela, J.T. Partington, & T. Orlick (Eds.), *New paths of sport learning and excellence* (pp. 27–28). Ottawa, Canada: Sport in Perspective.

Spilich, G.J., Vesonder, G.T., Chiesi, H.L., & Voss, J.F. (1979). Text processing of domain-related information for individuals with high and low domain knowledge. *Journal of Verbal Learning and Verbal Behavior, 18,* 275–290.

Starkes, J.L. (1987). Skill in field hockey: The nature of the cognitive advantage. *Journal of Sport Psychology, 9,* 146–160.

Starkes, J.L. (1990). Eye-hand coordination in experts: From athletes to microsurgeons. In C. Bard, M. Fleury, & L. Hay (Eds.), *Development of eye-hand coordination across the life span* (pp. 309–326). Columbia: University of South Carolina Press.

Starkes, J.L. (1993). Motor experts: Opening thoughts. In J.L. Starkes & F. Allard (Eds.), *Cognitive issues in motor expertise* (pp. 3–16). Amsterdam: Elsevier.

Starkes, J.L. (in press). The road to expertise: Is practice the only determinant? *International Journal of Sport Psychology.*

Starkes, J.L., & Allard, F. (1983). Perception in volleyball: The effects of competitive stress. *Journal of Sport Psychology, 5,* 189–196.

Starkes, J.L., & Allard, F. (Eds.). (1993). *Cognitive issues in motor expertise.* Amsterdam: Elsevier.

Starkes, J.L., Caicco, M., Boutilier, C., & Sevsek, B. (1990). Motor recall of experts for structured and unstructured sequences in creative modern dance. *Journal of Sport & Exercise Psychology, 12,* 317–321.

Starkes, J.L., & Deakin, J.M. (1984). Perception in sport: A cognitive approach to skilled performance. In W.F. Straub & J.M. Williams (Eds.), *Cognitive sport psychology* (pp. 115–128). Lansing, NY: Sport Science Associates.

Starkes, J.L., Deakin, J.M., Allard, F., Hodges, N.J., & Hayes, A. (1996). Deliberate practice in sports: What is it anyway? In K.A. Ericsson (Ed.), *The road to excellence: The acquisition of expert performance in the arts and sciences, sports and games* (pp. 81–106). Hillsdale, NJ: Erlbaum.

Starkes, J.L., Deakin, J.M., Lindley, S., & Crisp, F. (1987). Motor versus verbal recall of ballet sequences by young expert dancers. *Journal of Sport Psychology, 9,* 222–230.

Starkes, J.L., Edwards, P., Dissanayake, P., & Dunn, T. (1995). A new technology and field test of advance cue usage in volleyball. *Research Quarterly for Exercise and Sport, 65,* 1–6.

Starkes, J.L., & Lindley, S. (1994). Can we hasten expertise by video simulations? *Quest, 46,* 211–222.

Starkes, J.L., Weir, P.L., Singh, P., Hodges, N.J., & Kerr, T. (1999). Aging and the retention of sport expertise. *International Journal of Sport Psychology, 30,* 283–301.

Stones, M.J., & Kozma, A. (1981). Adult age trends in athletic performance. *Experimental Aging Research, 17,* 269–280.

Stroup, F. (1957). Relationship between measurements of field of motion perception and basketball activity in college men. *Research Quarterly, 28,* 72–76.

Tenenbaum, G. (Ed.). (1999). The development of expertise in sport: Nature and nurture [Special issue]. *International Journal of Sport Psychology, 30,* 2.

Tenenbaum, G., Levy-Kolker, N., Bar-Eli, M., & Weinberg, R. (1994). Information recall of younger and older skilled athletes: The role of display complexity, attentional resources and visual exposure duration. *Journal of Sports Sciences, 12,* 529–534.

Tenenbaum, G., Levi-Kolker, N., Sade, S.S., Lieberman, D., & Lidor, R. (1996). Anticipation and confidence of decisions related to skilled performance. *International Journal of Sport Psychology, 27,* 293–307.

Tenenbaum, G., Stewart, E., & Sheath, P. (1999). Detection of targets and attentional flexibility: Can computerized simulation account for developmental and skill-level differences? *International Journal of Sport Psychology, 30,* 261–282.

Tenenbaum, G., Tehan, G., Stewart, G., & Christensen, S. (in press). Recalling a floor routine: The effect of skill and age on memory for order. *Applied Cognitive Psychology.*

Thiffault, C. (1974). Tachistoscopic training and its effect upon visual perceptual speed of ice hockey players. *Proceedings of the Canadian Association of Sport Sciences.* Edmonton: Canada.

Thiffault, C. (1980). Construction et validation d'une mesure de la rapidité de la pensée tactique des joueurs de hockey sur glace [Construction and validation of a measure of speed of tactical thinking in ice hockey players]. In C.H. Nadeau, W.R. Haliwell, K.M. Newell, & G.C. Roberts (Eds.), *Psychology of motor behavior and sport* (pp. 643–649). Champaign, IL: Human Kinetics.

Thomas, K.T., & Thomas, J.R. (1994). Developing expertise in sport: The relation of knowledge and performance. *International Journal of Sport Psychology, 25,* 295–312.

Thomas, K.T., & Thomas, J.R. (1999). What squirrels in the trees predicts about expert athletes. *International Journal of Sport Psychology, 30,* 221–234.

Thompson, A.H., Barnsley, R.H., & Stebelsky, G. (1991). Born to play ball: The relative age effect and major league baseball. *Sociology of Sport Journal, 8,* 146–151.

Trachtman, J.N. (1973). The relationship between ocular motilities and batting averages in Little Leaguers. *American Journal of Optometry and Archives of the American Academy of Optometry, 50,* 914–919.

Tussing, L. (1940). The effect of football and basketball on vision. *Research Quarterly, 11,* 16–18.

Tyldesley, D.A., Bootsma, R.J., & Bomhoff, G.T. (1982). Skill level and eye-movement patterns in a sport oriented reaction time task. In H. Rieder, K. Bös, H. Mechling, & K. Reischle (Eds.), *Motorik und bewegungsforschung: Ein beiträge zum lernen im sport [Motor research: A contribution for sport learning]* (pp. 290–296). Schorndorff, Germany: Hofmann.

van Rossum, J.H.A., & van der Loo, H. (1997). Gifted athletes and complexity of family structure: A condition for talent development? *High Ability Studies, 8,* 19–30.

Verhulst, J. (1992). Seasonal birth distribution of West European soccer players: A possible explanation. *Medical Hypotheses, 38,* 346–348.

Vickers, J.N. (1986). The resequencing task: Determining expert-novice differences in the organization of a movement sequence. *Research Quarterly for Exercise and Sport, 57,* 260–264.

Vickers, J.N. (1988). Knowledge structures of expert-novice gymnasts. *Human Movement Science, 7,* 47–72.

Vickers, J.N. (1992). Gaze control in putting. *Perception, 21,* 117–132.

Vickers, J.N., & Adolphe, R.N. (1997). Gaze behavior during a ball tracking and aiming skill. *International Journal of Sports Vision, 4,* 18–27.

Westerlund, J.H., & Tuttle, W.W. (1931). Relationship between running events in track and reaction time. *Research Quarterly, 2,* 95–100.

Williams, A.M., & Burwitz, L. (1993). Advance cue utilization in soccer. In T. Reilly, J. Clarys, & A. Stibbe (Eds.), *Science and football* (Vol. 2, pp. 239–243). London: E. & F.N. Spon.

Williams, A.M., & Davids, K. (1995). Declarative knowledge in sport: A byproduct of experience or a characteristic of expertise? *Journal of Sport & Exercise Psychology, 17,* 259–278.

Williams, A.M., & Davids, K. (1998a). Perceptual expertise in sport: Research, theory and practice. In H. Steinberg, I. Cockerill, & A. Dewey (Eds.), *What sport psychologists do* (pp. 48–57). Leicester, England: British Psychological Society.

Williams, A.M., & Davids, K. (1998b). Visual search strategy, selective attention, and expertise in soccer. *Research Quarterly for Exercise and Sport, 69,* 111–128.

Williams, A.M., Davids, K., Burwitz, L., & Williams, J.G. (1993). Visual search strategies in experienced and inexperienced soccer players. *Research Quarterly for Exercise and Sport, 65,* 127–135.

Williams, A.M., Davids, K., & Williams, J.G. (1999). *Visual perception and action in sport.* London: E. & F.N. Spon.

Williams, A.M., & Elliott, D.W. (1997). Visual search in karate kumite: A function of expertise and anxiety. In R. Lidor & M. Bar-Eli (Eds.), *Innovations in sport psychology: Linking theory and practice. Proceedings of the International Society for Sport Psychology 9th World Congress of Sport Psychology* (pp. 99–102). Netanya, Israel: Wingate Institute for Physical Education and Sport.

Williams, A.M., & Grant, A. (1999). Training perceptual skill in sport. *International Journal of Sport Psychology, 30,* 194–220.

Williams, H.G., & Thirer, J. (1975). Vertical and horizontal peripheral vision in male and female athletes and non-athletes. *Research Quarterly, 46,* 200–205.

Winograd, S. (1942). The relationship of timing and vision to baseball performance. *Research Quarterly, 13,* 481–493.

Wood, J.M., & Abernethy, B. (1997). An assessment of the efficacy of sports vision training programs. *Optometry and Vision Science, 74,* 646–659.

Wright, D., Pleasants, F., & Gomez-Mesa, M. (1990). Use of advance cue sources in volleyball. *Journal of Sport & Exercise Psychology, 12,* 406–414.

Wrisberg, C.A. (1993). Levels of performance skill. In R. Singer, M. Murphey, & K. Tennant (Eds.), *Handbook of sport psychology* (pp. 61–72). New York: Macmillan.

Yandell, K.M., & Spirduso, W.W. (1981). Sex and athletic status as factors in reaction latency and movement time. *Research Quarterly for Exercise and Sport, 52,* 495–504.

Yoshimoto, T., Fujita, A., Fukami, K., & Kondoh, A. (1982). The effect of athletic activity upon the development of motor coordination viewed from selective eye-head coordination reaction time. In J.H. Salmela, J.T. Partington, & T. Orlick (Eds.), *New paths of sport learning and excellence* (pp. 37–38). Ottawa, Canada: Sport in Perspective.

Young, B., & Salmela, J. (in press). Perceptions of deliberate practice and middle distance runners. *International Journal of Sport Psychology.*

Youngen, L. (1959). A comparison of reaction and movement times of woman athletes and non-athletes. *Research Quarterly, 30,* 349–355.

PART II

Psychological Characteristics of High-Level Performance

CHAPTER 8

Modeling
Considerations for Motor Skill Performance and
Psychological Responses

PENNY MCCULLAGH and MAUREEN R. WEISS

The adage "A picture is worth a thousand words" is reflective of the notion that action portrays information more efficiently than verbal instructions, and may explain why demonstrations are often employed as a means of imparting information to learners. Beyond the provision of information for skill learning, psychologists have acknowledged modeling "to be one of the most powerful means of transmitting values, attitudes, and patterns of thought and behaviors" (Bandura, 1986, p. 47). Thus, modeling or observational learning, as the phenomenon is alternatively called, is a pervasive topic that encompasses a variety of disciplines. It is an especially appropriate topic for the *Handbook* because it spans learning, developmental, and psychological issues related to movement and sport skills.

The purpose of this chapter is to review theories and related research that might contribute to understanding contemporary developments in observational learning. We build on our own previous reviews (McCullagh, 1993; McCullagh, Weiss, & Ross, 1989; Weiss, Ebbeck, & Wiese-Bjornstal, 1993) as well as reviews by others (Dowrick, 1999; Gould & Roberts, 1981; Newell, Morris, & Scully, 1985; Williams, 1993). However, the present chapter is arranged considering the wide range of sport and exercise behaviors that modeling may impact. The influence of a host of modeling variables on the acquisition and retention of motor skills is described. Research is also presented that examines the influence of modeling on psychological variables such as decision making and self-efficacy, as well as theory and research that speaks to developmental issues

and modeling. As will become evident, research on modeling and motor skills and psychological responses has expanded phenomenally since our first review of the literature over 10 years ago.

THEORETICAL AND CONCEPTUAL CONSIDERATIONS

Over the past century, a variety of explanations were proposed to account for imitative behavior, and these explanations typically concurred with the psychological orientation of the era. Thus, cognitive, information processing, and direct perception approaches have all been considered as viable explanations for observational learning. Many of the early theories were extensively reviewed in the previous edition of this chapter (McCullagh, 1993) and will not be repeated here. Rather, the more recent theories and conceptualizations that have typically been used as either a backdrop or to generate empirical hypotheses for observational learning of motor and psychological skills will be discussed.

The Social Cognitive Approach

Sheffield (1961) postulated that demonstrations were stored as symbolic representations, and Bandura (1969) advanced these concepts further. Bandura suggested that verbal or imaginal representations mediate observers' responses and allow learners to acquire a behavior before it is actually enacted. In contrast to Sheffield's position, Bandura's early writings asserted that responses can be acquired without overt practice; this has been labeled "no-trial learning" (Bandura, 1965). Through his progressive reformulations, Bandura (1965, 1969, 1971, 1986, 1997) has maintained that overt action is not necessary for the acquisition of responses, especially behaviors that are social

The authors would like to thank Nilam Ram for his assistance in researching materials for this chapter, and Steve Wallace for his comments on a preliminary draft.

or cognitive in nature. In fact, Bandura stated that "most human behavior is learned by observation through modeling" (1986, p. 47). According to Bandura, modeling is primarily an information processing activity that is governed by four subprocesses.

Attention is the first component of the observational learning process and is influenced by characteristics of the modeled event as well as observer characteristics. Thus, the complexity, discriminability, and saliency of the modeled event will influence the observer's attention level. If the behavior to be modeled is complex, then attention-directing aids may need to accompany the demonstration so the observer can extract "generative rules." According to Bandura, absorption of the sensory events provided by a demonstration is not the sole determinant of the attention phase. Rather, attributes such as observers' cognitive capabilities, arousal level, and expectations influence the perceptual process. Bandura suggested that a number of cues can be used to enhance the attention phase of observational learning. Emphasizing salient features of the modeled action, providing verbal cues, and alternating good and poor performances are all mechanisms that may help the learner distinguish important performance cues.

The second phase in the observational learning process is *retention*. The basic premise of this phase is that once a behavior is demonstrated it must be retained in representational form in memory if the behavior is to be enacted without repeated modeling. The representation is presumed to be either visual or verbal in nature and need not contain all aspects of the demonstration. Rather, it is an abstraction of relevant features. Imaginal or visual memory is especially important in early developmental stages when verbal skills are not fully developed, or for movement behaviors that require spatial and temporal coordination because such skills may be difficult to represent verbally. Thus, "a golf swing is much better visualized than described" (Bandura, 1986, p. 58).

The second representation system used to retain modeled acts is verbal in nature. Certain information types may be more amenable to verbal than visual coding. For example, the sequencing of right and left turns to follow a specified route may be better retained in verbal as opposed to imaginal form. In addition to organizing modeled acts, it is postulated that both cognitive and enactment rehearsal (practice) influence the retention phase of observational learning (Carroll & Bandura, 1985). Bandura (1986) recognized the potency of mental rehearsal for enhancing motor skills but questioned whether it primarily influenced cognitive set, attention mechanisms, or perceived self-efficacy. Interestingly, Bandura suggested that the symbolic representations

derived from modeled behaviors "serve as the internal models for response production and standards for response correction" (p. 51).

Production is the third subprocess and was not well developed in Bandura's original writings because he was interested primarily in the acquisition of social behaviors, which could be dichotomous in nature (i.e., the behavior was either exhibited or not). However, when assessing motor skills, researchers may be interested not only in exhibition of the behavior, but in movement quality. Indeed, numerous experiments have shown that demonstrations can modify both the spatial aspects of movements (e.g., Carroll & Bandura, 1982, 1985, 1987, 1990) and the timing of movement sequences (Adams, 1986; McCullagh & Caird, 1990). According to Bandura (1986), the behavioral production of modeled acts involves a conception-matching process wherein the feedback from the response is compared to the representation. Based on the comparison process, modifications to performance are made. Though the correctness of this process is typically inferred from performance, Bandura suggests alternative means for assessing the degree of observational learning, such as verbal production, recognition, and comprehensive tests.

The final subprocess is *motivational* in nature and has received the most focused attention in the mainstream psychology literature. Simply expressed, one may attend to and remember the modeled behavior and have the physical skills to execute the skill, but if not sufficiently motivated, behavioral enactment will not occur. Thus, Bandura (1986) recognized the role of external, vicarious, and self-incentives in the observational learning process.

A final consideration within Bandura's (1986) formulation is the influence of these four subprocesses on differential aspects of observational learning. Bandura hypothesized that attention and retention subprocesses influence the *learning* of responses, whereas production and motivation subprocesses affect *performance* indices. Distinction between learning and performance effects is made by motor learning researchers, but has received only limited attention in the sport psychology literature (e.g., McCullagh, 1986, 1987).

The Role of Self-Efficacy in Observational Learning

Bandura's most recent explanation of observational learning appears in his book on self-efficacy (Bandura, 1997), which promotes the view that efficacy beliefs are a major basis of action. According to Bandura, "Perceived self-efficacy refers to beliefs in one's capabilities to organize and execute the courses of action required to produce given attainments" (p. 3). Individual beliefs about self-efficacy are derived from four major sources of information: enactive mastery experiences, vicarious experiences, verbal persuasion, and affective and physiological states. Enactive mastery experiences indicate one's capabilities. Vicarious experiences can alter beliefs by indicating competencies in comparison with the capabilities of others. Verbal persuasion can act to modify the perception of one's capabilities, and finally physiological states can influence personal beliefs in capabilities or can influence interpretations of vulnerability to maladaptive behaviors. Observational learning or modeling could therefore influence an individual's self-efficacy by operating through any of these sources of information. Bandura suggests that the information one receives through these sources becomes important for modifying behavior only if the individual cognitively processes the information and reflectively acts on it. Thus, he recognizes personal, social, and situational factors that influence experiences if they are cognitively interpreted.

The two sources of information that undoubtedly have the most applicability to observational learning are enactive mastery experiences and vicarious experiences. According to Bandura (1986), enactive mastery experiences provide the most robust source of efficacy information because they are authentic information about one's ability to execute a particular behavior. Although much of the literature relating mastery experiences to efficacy has focused on cognitive variables, Bandura clearly recognizes that "research on self modeling provides evidence that efficacy is enhanced by selective focus on personal attainments" (1997, p. 86). A much needed research base in the motor skill literature needs to clearly establish the relationship between self-modeling and performance and psychological responses.

The second most powerful source of efficacy is vicarious experience, which by definition includes modeling. Bandura (1986) notes that for many tasks, the outcome is readily identifiable (e.g., time in a race) and therefore serves as a form of mastery experience. However, for many activities, individuals must determine their own capabilities in relation to observing others. Bandura clearly highlights that the more similar people perceive themselves to be to the model or demonstrator, the greater the influence of the model on behavior.

Motor Learning Theories

Although modeling is also referred to as observational learning, motor learning researchers did not focus on this topic until recently, and typically did not use Bandura's

(1986) conceptual framework in their research. Demonstrations are a form of information provided to learners *before* they execute responses. Historically, motor learning researchers focused on information provided to learners *after* action, and thus the role of knowledge of results (KR) was of primary interest. For years, two theories published in the 1970s held the attention of motor learning researchers.

The first theory was proposed by Adams (1971) and was based on empirical data, generated primarily from slow-positioning responses. Adams contended that the principles generated from these data could be generalized to other types of motor responses. Labeled *closed-loop theory,* Adams hypothesized that feedback obtained during movement execution is compared to an internal reference labeled the perceptual trace. The perceptual trace, which develops from practice and the corresponding proprioceptive feedback, serves as the reference for correctness, and the ability of the learner to perform is dependent on the strength of the perceptual trace. To establish if the perceptual trace is correct, it is expected that participants receive sensory feedback and KR. If either source of feedback is less than optimal, then the perceptual trace will not be as accurate and learning will be impaired. Once the movement is completed, participants compare the sensory feedback to the perceptual trace and the discrepancy, termed subjective reinforcement, could later help maintain performance without KR. In addition to the memory mechanism that evaluated the correctness of movements (i.e., the perceptual trace), Adams suggested that a second memory mechanism was essential to initiate the movement. The rationale for two memory mechanisms was an important contribution by Adams because it was recognized that the same memory state could not both produce and evaluate the correctness of a response.

Adams's (1971) notions generated a great deal of research but were countered and complemented by Schmidt's (1975) *schema theory.* Although Schmidt agreed with Adams's proposal of two memory states and the notion of subjective reinforcement, he argued for more open-loop control of movements. According to schema theory, when individuals make a response they store a number of items in memory: (1) the initial conditions of the movements, (2) the characteristics of the generalized motor program, (3) the result of the movement and accompanying KR, and (4) the sensory consequences of the movement. Rather than specifically storing these four sources indefinitely, the learner abstracts the information into two generalized schemas. The recall schema is concerned with response production, and the recognition schema is concerned with response evaluation. According to Schmidt, if any of these four sources of information are missing, the schemas will be degraded and less learning will occur.

A primary difference between the two theories relates to the variability of practice a learner receives. According to Adams's (1971) theory, practice should be correct to develop a strong perceptual trace. According to Schmidt (1975), both correct and incorrect responses can aid learning because they contribute to the development of a schema. Although Schmidt believed his theory could explain more about learning motor skills than Adams's theory, he also recognized a number of limitations in his theory (see Schmidt, 1988).

While observational learning theory (Bandura, 1986) and traditional motor learning theories (Adams, 1971; Schmidt, 1975) have not been intertwined, it seems reasonable to draw from both theoretical camps to explain how skills are acquired. Essentially, observational learning theory suggests that from watching others perform, a cognitive representation is formed that both initiates subsequent responses and serves as a reference to determine the correctness of these responses. In opposition to this notion, motor learning theories propose that error information after action (KR) is the primary variable affecting learning and suggests that two independent memory mechanisms are essential in the learning process. Thus, a primary difference in these two approaches to learning is the distinction between (1) the presence of recall memory (initiation of action) and recognition memory (standard of correctness) in motor learning theories, and (2) no differentiation of these as separate memory states in observational learning theory. The lack of such a distinction theoretically is surprising, considering that Bandura, in some of his own work (Carroll & Bandura, 1982, 1985, 1987, 1990), empirically distinguished these two processes and clearly recognized that "people do not always enact everything they learn" (1990, p. 85). Some of the confusion may arise from how the terms *recall* and *recognition* are used and assessed in the two different approaches. A further elaboration of this point will be discussed when recall and recognition are revisited later in the chapter.

From a theoretical and practical standpoint, it is important to determine if individuals can indeed develop recognition memory from demonstrations. Adams's (1971) original notions suggest that proprioceptive feedback is necessary to develop the perceptual trace, an information source that is obviously missing when another individual is merely observed. However, many practical examples arise of individuals who can clearly distinguish errors in other individuals, even though their own level of performance may be quite minimal. Supervisors of manual workers, teachers, coaches, or anybody who evaluates movement patterns of performers (e.g., judges and referees) need to be able to detect appropriate responses in others even if they are not required to execute these responses themselves.

Direct Perception Interpretation

For some researchers, it became apparent that the notions of Bandura (1986) could not sufficiently explain how people acquired skills through observation. Bandura himself noted that there was a need to accurately perceive movement (p. 51), and thus a few researchers attempted to extract what critical components observers derived from demonstrations (e.g., Scully & Newell, 1985; Whiting, 1988). Newell et al. (1985) were critical of the modeling research because most studies addressed *how* the demonstration should be conveyed but not *what* was conveyed. These authors (Scully, 1986, 1987; Scully & Newell, 1985) argued for an action perception approach to observational learning.

In this perspective, the action itself is directly perceived and there is no need for a cognitive mediation to turn observation into action. The idea is that observers perceive the invariant movement patterns (information about the relationships among components) and not the specific movement characteristics being demonstrated. Evidence to support this notion comes from experiments indicating that human motion can be accurately detected from limited point-light displays showing the relationships among movement components (Scully, 1986, 1987; Williams, 1989). Still pictures, in contrast, provide little information regarding the coordination of movement patterns to be learned. Other research employing a direct perception approach has shown that modeling leads to better performance than verbal instruction in the acquisition of complex motor skills (Schoenfelder-Zohdi, 1992). Williams, Davids, and Williams (1999), in their chapter on observational learning in sport, review the direct perception literature and recognize that translating perception of action into movement is not yet fully understood. These researchers argue that the dynamic perspective of modeling is promising, however, because this approach considers coordination and control, two critical elements in learning. They suggest that "a major prediction of this perspective is that visual demonstrations are facilitative at the coordination stage, but not the control stage" of learning (Williams et al., 1999, p. 347).

Bandura (1997) has responded to the direct perception approach by suggesting that observational learning is not that simple. He suggests that "cognitive sets guide what people look for, what they extract from observations, and how they interpret what they see. Extracting information is necessary but not sufficient for observational learning" (p. 370). Thus, he returned to his original ideas that once the information is extracted, it must be retained and individuals must be motivated to perform. It seems that both *how* the information is delivered and *what* is conveyed are essential ingredients of modeling.

Summary

Many theoretical and conceptual approaches have been used to explain how people acquire skills and behaviors through observation. Bandura's (1986) social cognitive interpretations have received the most attention in the literature and have attempted to show the relationship between a host of modeling variables and performance and psychological responses. Although these notions are popular, many scholars have not adopted them because the theory provides an indirect perception-action explanation. Empirical work that has tested one theory against another or combined two interpretations to provide a more parsimonious explanation of observational learning could be identified in the literature. In the remainder of this chapter, the breadth of the modeling phenomenon and how it has been studied from motor learning, developmental, and sport psychology perspectives is discussed.

BEHAVIORAL AND PSYCHOLOGICAL RESPONSES TO MODELING

In Bandura's initial formulation of modeling, little consideration was given to motor reproduction or the actual assessment of the skill. Because the theory was originally designed for the acquisition of social behaviors, many of the response categories were assessed based on whether the behavior was either exhibited or not. In this section of the chapter, we review the primary responses that humans may evoke to modeling stimuli: (1) outcome and process, (2) recall and recognition, (3) learning and performance, and (4) perceptual and psychological responses. Of primary interest in this chapter are behaviors relevant to sport and physical activity settings.

Outcome and Process

When providing learners with a demonstration, at least two important aspects of the skill can be conveyed and assessed. First, the observer can view the outcome of the skill or the end goal to be achieved. Second, the observer can learn the movement pattern or process that can be used to achieve the desired outcome. After the demonstration, both of these

movement characteristics can be assessed. Many investigators have determined the potency of modeling effects by assessing the movement outcome and not whether the learner exhibited the same movement form as the model. However, some researchers have attempted to assess movement form components as well (e.g., Carroll & Bandura, 1982, 1985, 1987, 1990; Feltz, 1982; Little & McCullagh, 1989; McCullagh, 1987).

McCullagh (1987) measured both outcome and form and found that control group participants (i.e., no model) could reach the same level of performance outcome as demonstration group participants, but that they did not exhibit the desired form. Early evidence by Martens, Burwitz, and Zuckerman (1976) supported this same conclusion. Recent evidence by Sidaway and Hand (1993) indicated that modeling enhanced outcome scores even though learners only observed an expert demonstrate the correct form. They argued that few sport skills measure form and that good outcome is the result of good form. In many studies, judges assess the degree to which the form of learners approximates a model's form.

It is also possible to assess numerous movement parameters through the use of two- or three-dimensional kinematic analysis (i.e., displacement velocity and acceleration profiles). For example, Southard and Higgins (1987) investigated the role of demonstrations and physical practice in altering the form of a racquetball serve. They found that participants receiving physical practice or a combination of demonstrations and practice changed their limb configurations from the first to fifth test day. Those receiving demonstrations without practice were no better than control participants in successfully altering their movements. The researchers concluded that providing a demonstration was not sufficient for changing constrained movement patterns, whereas practice facilitated the adoption of the appropriate kinematic characteristics. An interesting addition to this experiment would have been the assessment of outcome or accuracy.

Contrary to this finding, Whiting, Bijlard, and den Brinker (1987) used kinematic analysis and determined that performance on a ski simulation task was enhanced for participants who viewed demonstrations as compared to those who did not. The model's performance was videotaped and the frequency, amplitude, and fluency of the movements were recorded using a motion analysis system. The results indicated that none of the participants reached the same performance level as the model, but the demonstration group was significantly more fluent and produced more consistent movements than the physical practice group.

The goal of the task should probably determine what parameters are most appropriate to focus on for enhancing performance. A recent paper by Shea and Wulf (1999) highlights this issue while testing the importance of type of feedback. Based on previous studies that had shown the advantages of an external focus while learning (e.g., focus on club during golf swing) as opposed to internal focus (e.g., swing of arms), they reasoned that feedback relating to the external aspects of the task should enhance performance more than internal feedback. The data testing these notions with participants learning a balance task supported their predictions. An extension of this finding to modeling could support the idea of external focus in that a demonstration is external to the learner. If the feedback principle is generalizable, then the focus of demonstrations should be carefully considered (e.g., golf club versus arm swing).

How modeling influences behavior might also be related to task type. A survey of the modeling literature indicates a wide range of tasks from simple one-dimensional laboratory tasks to highly complex sport skills performed in the real world. Williams et al. (1999) are highly critical, however, of drawing conclusions about learning from single-level outcome measures. A task analysis of modeling effects might well help provide some consistency to the varied findings in the literature. Gentile (1987) proposed a task classification model that divided movement skills into 16 categories. Skills are categorized on the basis of action function (both body transportation and object manipulation) and environmental context (regulatory conditions and intertrial variability). The task analysis was originally developed for physical therapists to help evaluate movements and then select appropriate rehabilitation activities. However, as noted by Magill (1998), the task analysis has direct application for teachers of motor and sport skills as well because it may help define task goals and corresponding errors and, therefore, help determine appropriate feedback. In fact, the task analysis scheme could prove a useful tool for evaluating the types of skills most amenable to modeling effects.

Recall and Recognition

Earlier in the chapter, a comparison of motor learning theories (Adams, 1971; Schmidt, 1975) and the social-cognitive approach (Bandura, 1986) was made. One difference in the approaches is the distinction between recall and recognition. Both Adams and Schmidt posit two separate memory states: one that produces the movement (recall) and one that evaluates the outcome (recognition). Bandura suggests that the cognitive representation generated by observing a model "provides the internal model for response production and the standard for response correction" (p. 64). Thus, Bandura assumes a common mechanism for recall and recognition. Motor learning researchers have for years attempted to experimentally differentiate recall and recognition, and a review of the observational learning literature suggests that modeling may differentially affect these processes. In a series of experiments, Carroll and Bandura (1982, 1985, 1987, 1990) have consistently assessed the effects of modeling on recall and recognition and found differential effects.

A primary difference may exist in the definition and measurement of recall and recognition in the psychological and motor learning literature. For example, Carroll and Bandura (1987) assessed recall through reproduction accuracy of a nine-component wrist-arm paddle motion. Recognition was assessed by showing participants photographs of correct and incorrect components of the movement and requiring them to identify the correct components. In addition, they were asked to arrange the components in order. The experimental manipulation of whether participants concurrently or separately matched their movements with the model, and whether they could visually monitor their own movements, had an effect on reproduction accuracy (i.e., recall) but not on recognition measures. The correlations between recognition measures and reproduction accuracy ($r = .34$ to $.64$) were not extremely high, suggesting that recall and recognition did not develop at the same rate.

In the traditional motor learning literature, recall is typically measured by error after movement reproduction. Recognition is the difference between learners' subjective estimate of their movement error and actual movement errors. Such a measure might be quite distinct from choosing the correct sequencing of movements from still photographs. Although this type of recognition does provide some information, it does not reveal anything about recognition of temporal aspects of movements. Comparing photographs of identical twins is an analogy: Although it may be difficult to differentiate these individuals from still photographs, the comparison might become easier if they were asked to walk or run. Thus, an important development in this area is creation of appropriate measures to assess recognition and recall.

Newell (1976) was primarily interested in determining the independence of recall and recognition but used an observational learning paradigm. The results indicated that increasing the number of auditory demonstrations increased recognition memory, but because demonstration participants were also accurate in their first movement reproduction, he concluded that providing a demonstration also enhanced recall. With empirical testing of the effects of demonstrations on recall and recognition, it may become necessary to modify Bandura's original ideas if independence of these mechanisms within an observational learning paradigm can be shown.

Recently, Laugier and Cadopi (1996) were interested in the recognition and reproduction (i.e., recall) of both concrete and abstract dance movements. Their participants were able to recognize the order and number of movement elements in the demonstrated dance sequence. However, their findings clearly showed that the movement reproduction or recall performance of observers was different from the performance of their expert model. This led the authors to highlight the important distinction between qualitative and quantitative aspects of performance. Their conclusions were based on the finding that observers could quantitatively remember the movement components (as assessed by the photo recognition tests) but could not qualitatively reproduce the movement with a high degree of accuracy.

If it can be clearly documented that demonstrations can enhance recognition memory even though recall or reproduction does not improve, the finding would have clear implications for practitioners. By providing learners with correct demonstrations and feedback, perhaps recognition of one's own errors could be enhanced (McCullagh, Burch, & Siegel, 1990). Within the observational learning paradigm, participants are typically required to perform this conception-matching process based on their memory of the correct demonstration *and* the movements they have performed. McCullagh (1993) suggested that through enhanced technology of split-screen techniques, the conception-matching process could be explored.

In a recent study by Laguna (1996), this split-screen notion was put to a test. Participants attempted to learn an arm-sequencing task similar to the Carroll and Bandura (1982, 1985, 1987, 1990) task after viewing either a correct model, a self model, a split-screen model (correct and self), or no model. Both performance accuracy (recall) and cognitive representation (recognition) were assessed. Laguna found some evidence that the type of modeling intervention differentially affected the strength of the cognitive representation and response production. For recognition, the correct and split-screen groups evidenced the best performance, followed by the self-modeling group and finally the no-model condition. For recall, kinematic analyses of elbow displacement showed that the correct and split-screen conditions were similar and evidenced less error than the self- and no-model conditions, which had similar results.

Downey, Neil, and Rapagna (1996) assessed expert and novice recall accuracy, recall quality, and recognition responses to two dance sequences. For novices, recognition in the photo-sequencing task was related to performance

accuracy but not performance quality. Due to a small sample size in the expert group, this relationship was not investigated. Furthermore, because the correlations between the recognition and recall measures were low to moderate, the researchers sided with Bandura (1986), contending that "the cognitive representation acquired solely from observation is incomplete and by itself does not account for skillful overt performance" (Downey et al., 1996, p. 60). The performance accuracy scores were higher than the cognitive representation scores, suggesting that learners could do more than they reported they could do.

Learning and Performance

Bandura (1965, 1969, 1971) made a distinction between learning and performance in his early writings. Although motor learning researchers are typically familiar with the distinction between temporary and long-term performance effects (e.g., Ross, Bird, Doody, & Zoeller, 1985) and empirically examine the effect of variables on learning and performance, few studies examining social psychological variables make this distinction. Schmidt (1988) has clearly outlined the procedures for using retention and transfer designs to assess whether the effects of variables are relatively transient (performance) or rather long term (learning). To empirically make this distinction, it is necessary to manipulate the independent variables during an initial acquisition phase, followed by performance under a common level of the independent variable (usually the absence of the intervention) during the retention phase. The retention phase, which should occur after the independent variable has had time to dissipate, occurs anywhere from a few minutes to days after the acquisition phase. Some experimenters add an additional transfer phase to examine the generalizability of learning. Under these circumstances, individuals attempt a skill that is similar yet distinct from the initially acquired skill.

A few studies on social psychological effects of modeling have attempted to make this learning-versus-performance distinction. McCullagh (1986, 1987) examined the influence of model status and model similarity on both performance and learning. Supporting previous investigations (Gould & Weiss, 1981; Landers & Landers, 1973), model characteristics were found to influence performance. However, in both experiments, the effects of modeling were found to be rather short-lived because group differences did not maintain themselves through the retention phase. Most motor learning–based studies attempt to make this learning-versus-performance distinction; it would be a useful paradigm for examining the influence of social psychological or developmental variables as well.

Perceptual Responses to Modeling

There is an entire body of literature on developing expertise that is relevant to observational learning processes, although demonstrations are not the central focus of this research. Rather, the issue in this literature asks how individuals can develop or train perceptual processes and decision making. A recent review by Williams and Grant (1999) clearly illustrates that videos are often used to train participants on a wide variety of perceptual and performance tasks. Many studies on cognitive skill development include slides with sport-specific plays, but occasionally film or video is favored to perceptually train athletes (e.g., Abernethy, 1988; Abernethy & Russell, 1987; Burroughs, 1984; Jones & Miles, 1978; Londeree, 1967; Salmela & Fiorito, 1979). Although these studies are not labeled modeling studies, they often compare different types of visual displays and can therefore shed some light on observational learning processes.

For example, Starkes and Lindley (1994) reviewed an investigation from their laboratory that compared the effectiveness of slides with video on perceptual responses and game performance. Both slide (static) and video (dynamic) training enhanced decision-making accuracy relative to a control group, but neither type of training produced performance differences during play. The authors acknowledged "the difficulty of creating a veridical transfer test with appropriate experimental controls to assess on-court performance" (p. 219). Chamberlin and Coelho (1993) suggested that visual video training may be lacking the auditory and tactile information in real action and thus cannot be completely successful as a training technique. Although virtual reality environments may help enhance some modalities missing from video training, a review of virtual reality environments (Hancock, Arthur, & Andre, 1993) does not show enhanced learning.

Christina, Barresi, and Shaffner (1990) conducted an interesting case study using video. The issue centered on whether video training could enhance response selection accuracy without sacrificing speed in a football linebacker. A single participant who was responding quickly in games, but often selecting the incorrect response, viewed a video showing plays from a same-angle perspective. He practiced responding to these plays over 16 training/test sessions. The player increased his response selection accuracy from about 25% to nearly 100% over the training sessions and did so without sacrificing the speed of his responses. Because the player became injured, it was difficult to assess whether these improvements in the laboratory transferred to the actual game situation. As noted by Starkes and Lindley (1994), transfer is often problematic in perceptual training studies.

Weeks (1992) argued that most observational learning studies focused on movement patterns and avoided externally paced skills, where the learner needs to respond to constantly changing environmental demands. He suggested that training learners on both the perceptual and movement demands of the task may enhance observational learning. Thus, he compared three modeling conditions on the acquisition of a coincident-timing task. One group received modeling based on the perceptual demands of the task, one group received modeling based on the motoric task demands, and a third modeling group received both. A control group received no modeling. Results illustrated the positive benefits of perceptual modeling because the two groups receiving this training performed better than the other groups. Weeks suggested that for externally paced skills such as batting, learners should be trained on movement patterns as well as the perceptual characteristics of ball flight. A subsequent study by Weeks and Choi (1992) provided further evidence for the importance of perceptual modeling. The research on perceptual responses to modeling has received scant attention in the literature but may explain a crucial link between observation and action.

Psychological Responses to Modeling

Probably the most extensive body of literature related to modeling comes from mainstream psychology. Although much of this literature is outside the realm of this chapter because it does not relate to movement behaviors, a brief mention of psychological responses that are susceptible to modeling effects is warranted. Research on psychological effects of modeling that directly relates to motor or sport skill performance is reviewed in subsequent sections of the chapter.

The expanse of the literature on modeling and psychological responses is reflected in Bandura's (1997) recent analysis of self-efficacy. He clearly highlights the importance of self-beliefs in modifying a wide range of behaviors, including cognitive, health, clinical, organizational, and athletic functioning. Two of the major sources of self-efficacy, enactive mastery experiences and vicarious experiences, can both be regarded as observational learning variables (i.e., seeing yourself or seeing others). It is apparent that modeling can indeed have profound effects not only on performance but also on psychological variables (e.g., anxiety, fear, affect) that may impact physical activity patterns (Feltz, Landers, & Raeder, 1979; McAuley, 1985). Interesting studies in the sport psychology literature have included models as a stimulus for effecting some type of psychological change. Although not explicitly identified as observational learning studies, researchers nevertheless employed models as an intervention technique.

For example, Rejeski and Sanford (1984) examined affective responses of feminine-typed females after watching one of two models perform on a bicycle ergometer. The intolerant model portrayed difficulty with the task by grimacing, squinting, and displaying exaggerated movement while exhibiting low confidence. The tolerant model showed similar physical responses but to a much lesser extent and displayed optimism and confidence. The intolerant model group reported greater negative affect for the upcoming exercise test and higher ratings of perceived exertion. Model type clearly affected the psychological responses of the observers.

Crawford and Eklund (1994; Eklund & Crawford, 1994) were interested in the relationship between social physique anxiety and exercise attitudes, preferences, and behaviors among college-age women. Participants viewed two videos of aerobic class participants. In one video, the exercisers wore aerobic-style attire that emphasized body physique; in the other video they wore shorts and T-shirts that deemphasized the physique. Crawford and Eklund found a positive association between social physique anxiety and attitudes toward the T-shirt video, and a negative association with attitudes toward the aerobics attire video. It is conceivable that model-observer similarity may have been an important factor in participants' ratings of favorability toward the videos. Eklund and Crawford did not replicate this finding with a more active sample of women.

These studies clearly show that modeling can have an effect on a wide array of psychological responses. Typically, demonstrations are used as a way to modify physical performance. However, it is clear that observation can have pervasive effects on a number of psychological and social outcomes as well.

MODEL CHARACTERISTICS THAT INFLUENCE MOTOR SKILL PERFORMANCE AND PSYCHOLOGICAL RESPONSES

Numerous studies have been conducted in the motor learning and sport psychology literature that have been directed toward observational learning effects. In the next three sections of the chapter, three broad phenomena that have been shown to impact performance and psychological responses after observation are reviewed. The first section speaks to characteristics of the person demonstrating, or

the *model*. The second section addresses characteristics of the *demonstration* itself, and preexisting characteristics of the individual *observer* are explored in the third section. Some of these characteristics are clearly linked to development and will be covered in a subsequent section of the chapter.

Model Skill Level

A primary concern when providing demonstrations is the skill level of the model. Although it is intuitively appealing to assume that a skilled model helps to develop the most accurate cognitive representation of a skill, and therefore leads to best performance, an examination of the literature does not necessarily validate this notion. For example, Martens et al. (1976) tested the idea that participants would learn more by watching someone learn a skill than by observing either a correct or incorrect model. It was hypothesized that observers would be able to discriminate pertinent information in the learning condition as opposed to identical repetitions by a correct model. Results from three experiments failed to clearly support this hypothesis. Observing a correct or learning model produced initial performance increments over incorrect or control conditions on a skill with low cognitive demands, but these effects were relatively short-lived. On a more cognitively demanding task, it was clear that participants were adapting to the strategies displayed by correct models, suggesting that it is best to show learners a model demonstrating the correct movement form or strategy if this is an important component to be learned.

Not much attention had focused on learning models until Adams (1986) approached the issue. He recognized that learning theories had emphasized KR at the expense of other paradigms, and combined observational learning and KR within one paradigm. Adams proposed that observational learning could be enhanced if participants viewing a model also received the model's KR. It was his contention that participants would become actively, instead of passively, involved in the learning process and this would lead to higher performance. To empirically test this idea, participants either viewed a model learning a skill and received the model's KR, viewed a model learning the skill but did not receive model KR, or physically practiced the skill and received their own KR. The results produced slight advantages for the group that viewed a model and also received model KR over the other two groups.

Though Adams's research posed interesting questions, it also left many issues unanswered. The retention of the skill over a longer period of time would determine whether the effects were relatively stable. Moreover, the lack of a correct model condition precluded determining whether performance by a skilled model would have produced a better cognitive representation and superior performance than would a learning model condition.

McCullagh and Caird (1990) extended Adams's (1986) experiment by examining observers' ability to learn without ever receiving KR about their own movements. Therefore, participants viewed either a correct model, a learning model along with the model's KR, or a learning model with no model KR. The control group practiced and received KR. Comparable or superior performance by any of the demonstration groups would call into question the long-held view that KR is the most potent variable for learning because only the practice control group received KR about their own movements. Participants who viewed a learning model and were privy to the model's KR performed as well as participants who physically practiced and received KR. This finding generalized across acquisition, immediate and delayed retention, and transfer to a new task. Therefore, the view that KR about one's own movements is the most critical variable for learning was called into question.

Hebert and Landin (1994) investigated the impact of learning models with a complex sport skill. Inexperienced tennis students watched a correct video demonstration of the forehand stroke that included verbalizations of key movement elements. Then they were assigned to one of four groups that received combinations of individual and model feedback. The group that watched a model and received the model's feedback, and then received feedback about their own movements evidenced the best form and outcome performance. Interestingly, however, the group that watched a learning model and received only model feedback performed as well as the group that received feedback only about its own movements. Findings support the notions previously expressed by McCullagh and Caird (1990) that learning models can be an excellent tool, as in teaching situations where students have the opportunity to watch other learners perform *and* to hear the teacher's skill corrections.

McCullagh and Meyer (1997) extended McCullagh and Caird's (1990) research by examining modeling effects using a free-weight squat, one in which form components could be assessed. The control group physically practiced and received feedback about their own movements. A correct model group observed correct demonstrations and heard verbal feedback about the model's squat. One learning model group watched a model and heard the model's feedback. A second learning model group watched a model but did not receive model feedback. Acquisition data on

form and outcome revealed improvements over trials but no group effects. Retention data revealed that both the correct and the learning model groups that received model feedback produced better form scores than the other two groups. Differences compared to the previous study (McCullagh & Caird, 1990) may have been due to the type of task and feedback cues. Thus, richer feedback provided through knowledge of performance (KP) may have provided additional cues that aided the correct model group.

Lee and colleagues (Lee, Swinnen, & Serrien, 1994; Lee & White, 1990) offered some explanations as to why observing an unskilled or learning model may be an appropriate learning technique. First, agreeing with Adams (1986), they suggested that if the participant views an unskilled model and also receives the model's KR, he or she becomes actively involved in the problem-solving process that should lead to better learning. Thus, the amount of cognitive effort an individual puts into the acquisition process will have an influence on learning through observation. Second, though some might argue that learning is impaired if errors are made during acquisition, others suggest this is not the case (Schmidt, 1975). It seems reasonable that observers can learn from watching others make errors, especially if KR is provided in the process. Pollock and Lee (1992), however, found no differences between viewing a skilled and an unskilled model on computer game performance.

Weir and Leavitt (1990) made some interesting arguments about information conveyed by unskilled models in the acquisition of an aiming task. They noted that other researchers had purportedly manipulated the model's skill level (e.g., Landers & Landers, 1973; Martens et al., 1976), and they argued that the models were really skilled at the task, but feigned low skill in the appropriate experimental conditions. Weir and Leavitt argued that demonstrators were possibly executing the same movement patterns in both skilled and unskilled conditions and altered only the movement outcome. Although this is a valid criticism, it is essential to compare form scores of the model and the learner. Unfortunately, Weir and Leavitt did not do this. They did, however, make some improvements over previous research by incorporating additional control groups to balance for task exposures and also by examining initial trial performance to eliminate the confound of experimental conditions on practice. Participants viewed a skilled or unskilled model and received or did not receive the model's KR. Analysis of first trial performance indicated that outcome performance of participants who viewed an unskilled model and the model's KR was not affected. However, those viewing a skilled model needed the model's KR to perform as accurately as the unskilled model groups.

Analysis of the first block of trials upheld the skill level but not model KR effect. Participants performed better after viewing an unskilled model than a skilled model. Although this experiment raises some interesting issues, its primary limitation is the lack of improvement for any groups with practice. Also, because form was not assessed, one of the major study purposes that related to movement patterns exhibited by skilled and unskilled models could not be addressed.

Darden (1997) highlighted the importance of providing observers with learning models in a practical article for educators. He applied research findings to practical examples to explain why expert models may not be the best choice for teaching motor skills to students. For example, Darden was critical of the commercially produced SyberVision videos because they repeatedly show correct performances by experts and the research literature does not support the use of experts. He also focused on the role of cognitive effort in learners (Lee et al., 1994) and offered some practical suggestions for using demonstrations in ways that cognitive effort could be increased. He also reviewed a recently developed visual instruction system (Seat & Wrisberg, 1996) that offers effective strategies for teachers to enhance skill development through modeling.

Coping and Mastery Models

Coping models can be likened to the learning models discussed earlier, in that they do not repeatedly display exemplary behaviors. Rather, coping models demonstrate the negative cognitions, affects, and behaviors that may precede or accompany performance on tasks that are perceived as difficult or fearful (e.g., water activities, gymnastics skills). Through repeated trials, coping models gradually verbalize more positive thoughts and emit more positive affect and correct performance. Thus, these models show a progression of low ability to cope with the demands of the task to exemplary performance. According to Schunk (1987), coping models are similar to observers (i.e., fear, low confidence, low ability) but provide information (e.g., problem solving) and motivation (e.g., self-efficacy statements) to help observers gradually engage in approach behaviors and skilled performance.

Schunk, Hanson, and Cox (1987) compared mastery and coping models for children having difficulty learning mathematics. The mastery model demonstrated exemplary or errorless performance, and the coping model verbalized low-confidence and -ability statements but gradually improved over trials. Coping models led to higher self-efficacy and better performance than did mastery models. This finding provides support for the psychological and

behavioral benefits of coping models. The logical extension of this work to the sport or motor skill domain is that coping models may be especially useful in high-fear situations or when the task to be learned is extremely difficult.

Although coping models have been used extensively in therapeutic settings (e.g., Kulik & Mahler, 1987; Thelen, Fry, Fehrenbach, & Frautschi, 1979), the idea of coping models in sport, exercise, and athletic rehabilitation settings has received only limited attention (Flint, 1991, 1993; Weiss & Troxel, 1986; Wiese & Weiss, 1987). Flint (1991) examined the role of coping models compared to no models on psychological factors in athletic rehabilitation after anterior cruciate ligament reconstruction. The coping model video showed athletes similar in age, basketball position, and type of injury progressing through the rehabilitation process all the way to full recovery. At three weeks post-surgery, athletes who had watched the coping model had greater self-efficacy than the control group, and two months later reported higher perceived athletic competence. Model participants were able to identify with at least one of the coping models in the videos, confirming the role of model-observer similarity in the coping model procedure.

Lewis (1974) studied coping models with children who were fearful of swimming. They were assigned to either a coping-model-plus-participation group, a coping-model-only group, a participation-only group, or a control group. In the coping model conditions, they watched a videotape of same-gender children similar in age and race, who portrayed coping verbalizations and performance. Immediately after intervention, the coping-model-plus-participation group had a greater reduction in avoidance behavior than the other groups.

Nearly 25 years later, Weiss, McCullagh, Smith, and Berlant (1998) extended Lewis's (1974) findings. They analyzed modeling effects on fearful children's swimming skills, fear, and self-efficacy. All children participated in swim lessons over a three-day period in addition to one of three modeling conditions: peer mastery, peer coping, or control (irrelevant models). Coping models showed gradual improvement of swim skills and verbalized increasingly positive statements related to task difficulty, attitude, self-efficacy, and ability. Mastery models verbalized and performed the skills in an exemplary manner. Peer coping and mastery models produced better performance, higher self-efficacy, and lower fear from pre- to posttest compared to the control group. Performance and self-efficacy effects remained significant at retention four days after the posttest. Coping models had a stronger effect on self-efficacy than mastery models. Effect sizes were strong, suggesting that the addition of a peer model with swim lessons is an effective and cost-efficient means of instructing children who are fearful of the water.

Model Status

In Bandura's (1986) theory, model characteristics are hypothesized to influence the attention phase of observational learning. He hypothesized that a high-status model would command more attention than a low-status model and, thus, lead to greater learning. Although there have been few direct tests of this hypothesis, numerous studies have found performance differences dependent on model characteristics, such as competence (Baron, 1970), prestige (Mausner, 1953), status (McCullagh, 1986), social power (Mischel & Grusec, 1966), similarity (Gould & Weiss, 1981; McCullagh, 1987), and skill level.

McCullagh (1986, 1987) conducted two studies investigating the attention–model characteristic relationship. In the first experiment, participants viewed a filmed model who was construed to be of either high or low status. Half of the participants were precued regarding the status variable, whereas the other half viewed the demonstration and were then informed of model status (postcued). The assumption was that participants in the precued condition would differentially focus their attention and thereby perform dependent on model status, whereas the attention phase would be over by the time postcued participants became aware of model status. Results indicated that participants performed better after viewing a high- as opposed to low-status model irrespective of the cueing manipulations, thus suggesting a lack of differential attention. A second experiment (McCullagh, 1987) extended the earlier study by manipulating model similarity and assessing both outcome and strategy. Individuals who observed a similar model were more likely to evidence a similar form or strategy compared to the dissimilar condition. These experiments question the influence of model characteristics on attention and further reinforce the importance of assessing form and outcome performance.

Self-Modeling

One rudimentary form of viewing oneself is through videotape replay. An early review of over 50 studies employing replay as a skill-enhancement technique (Rothstein & Arnold, 1976) found little evidence to support this use of videotapes. However, as noted by Newell (1981), poor experimental designs may have led to the equivocal findings; a detailed analysis of what was shown on the videos would need to occur. For example, Bradley (1993) indicated that viewing one's own deficiencies has a detrimental effect on

performance, and many of these early studies may have shown exactly such deficiencies. Although not labeled self-modeling studies, the previously discussed experiments by Carroll and Bandura (1982, 1985, 1987, 1990) frequently used monitoring of one's own performance as a successful guidance technique.

A different and more controlled form of self-modeling has been developed by Dowrick (1991, 1999; Dowrick & Biggs, 1983), who defined self-modeling as "the behavioral change that results from the repeated observation of oneself on videotapes that show only desired target behavior" (Dowrick & Dove, 1980, p. 51) Thus, self-modeling is clearly different from videotape feedback, wherein all skill attempts are shown. In experiments that have used videotape of one's own movements, both desirable *and* undesirable actions were shown to participants (e.g., Carroll & Bandura, 1990; McCullagh, Burch, & Siegel, 1990). Dowrick referred to this type of manipulation as unstructured video replay. Thus, the primary difference between self-modeling and video replay is that errors are eliminated in self-modeling. The basis for using such a technique is that correct approximations will enhance self-efficacy and subsequently lead to enhanced performance. Most of the research on self-modeling has been done with small therapeutic samples. In his early review on self-modeling, Dowrick (1983) made some applications to the realm of physical skills, although empirical verification of the effectiveness of this technique was minimal. Theoretically, it is important to determine whether individuals can learn from an approach in which they see only successful performances of a skill they are having difficulty performing.

Dowrick (1999) recently published a review identifying approximately 150 studies that used the self-modeling technique. Although many researchers have employed videotapes as the source of self-modeling, Dowrick clearly recognized that audiotapes, imagery, role playing, or still photographs can be used as interventions within the self-modeling paradigm. Dowrick has also been instrumental in identifying two distinct forms of self-modeling: positive self-review and feedforward. Positive self-review includes "images of adaptive behavior as fine-tuned examples of the best the individual has been able to produce thus far" (p. 25). In sport, such videos would probably be referred to as highlight videos, where videotapes are edited so that errors or poor performance are removed from the intervention. Dowrick notes that B.F. Skinner had actually suggested this procedure for baseball players in a hitting slump.

The second type of self-modeling is known as feedforward. The learner might already possess the skills but may not have previously executed them in the particular order shown or in the particular context. By editing the video, it is possible to construct a behavior that is possible but has not yet occurred. For example, an individual may be able to perform well under practice conditions but not in game situations. Such a process may allow an individual to capture the adaptive behaviors during the practice and then reconstruct the environment so it appears as though these same behaviors occur during a game. Although most of the literature that Dowrick reviewed did not emanate from the motor skill literature, it can provide some directives for individuals who want to make applications of self-modeling to the motor learning, developmental, or sport psychology domains.

In the sport literature, Maile (cited in Franks & Maile, 1991) used self-modeling to train a nationally ranked power lifter. Maile produced edited videotapes that made it appear as though the athlete was lifting more weight than she actually had done previously. Performance gains were significant using this technique, even though the athlete was aware of the editing. Winfrey and Weeks (1993) examined whether videotapes that were edited to show only successful gymnastics performance would enhance self-efficacy and performance beyond that achieved by a control group with no self-modeling. No significant differences emerged for either self-efficacy or performance. However, those who viewed the self-modeling tapes had a more realistic judgment about their own performance capabilities than those who did not have the opportunity to view themselves. A major limitation recognized by the authors was that the same video was shown over a six-week period, so the "models" did not display skill improvement.

Starek and McCullagh (1999) recently compared the effects of self-modeling with peer modeling on the performance, self-efficacy, and anxiety of beginning adult swimmers. Baseline performance skills were assessed and individual self-modeling videos were developed for each participant based on personal skill level. After a series of lessons using one of the treatment interventions, self-modeling led to better performance compared to peer modeling despite the lack of differences in either anxiety or self-efficacy. Participants who watched themselves as opposed to peers had a more accurate estimation of their performance. This finding suggests that it is perhaps the accuracy of self-efficacy rather than the estimation of self-efficacy that influences performance changes.

The use of self-modeling videos seems widespread in the sports world. Anecdotal reports from athletes often cite the use of highlight videos that repeatedly show superior performances in an effort to motivate athletes or help them end performance slumps. Limited research has attempted to validate the effectiveness of such videos (Halliwell, 1990; Templin & Vernacchia, 1995), although there are examples of coaches and sport psychologists using such techniques in practical settings.

Model Similarity

One underlying variable that might help explain why certain model characteristic variables influence performance is the perceived similarity of the observer to the model. The power of model similarity was recognized early in the observational learning literature (Rosenthal & Bandura, 1978), and in fact many of the model characteristics just discussed may produce their impact through the mechanism of perceived model-observer similarity. For example, individuals may perform better after watching a learning or coping model because they perceive themselves to be similar to the model. Model status may also be linked to model-observer similarity. And who could argue that watching oneself ensures the highest level of similarity?

Gould and Weiss (1981) examined the effects of model similarity on self-efficacy and performance of a muscular endurance task. Female participants observed either a similar (nonathletic female) or dissimilar (athletic male) model demonstrate the skill. Observing a similar model led to higher self-efficacy and performance than watching a dissimilar model. Over 10 years later, George, Feltz, and Chase (1992) determined whether model gender (male, female) or model ability (athletic, nonathletic) was the most salient variable explaining performance effects in the Gould and Weiss study. Using the same leg extension task, they found that participants performed better after viewing a similar-ability model, but self-efficacy did not differ between athletic and nonathletic model groups. Model sex did not produce significant performance differences, suggesting that model ability was the more salient cue.

In the experiment by Schunk et al. (1987) previously discussed, the similarity notion was directly tested. Coping models led to higher self-efficacy and math performance, which could be attributed in part to the fact that children perceived themselves as more similar to the coping models. In general, findings of observer's perceived similarity to the model might provide some answers as to why certain model characteristics are likely to positively influence performance and self-efficacy. Perhaps the underlying key as to why skill level, coping, and status impact modeling is because observers perceive more similarity, which enhances self-efficacy and motivation to perform like the model. Manipulation checks for perceived similarity would help determine whether this is the key model characteristic influencing research findings.

DEMONSTRATION CHARACTERISTICS THAT INFLUENCE MOTOR SKILL PERFORMANCE AND PSYCHOLOGICAL RESPONSES

Practice Variables

Scheduling of Practice

Contextual interference (CI) deals with performance and learning differences attributable to blocked (i.e., practice all trials of one task, then move on to another) and random (i.e., practice a trial or two of one task, then another, and so on) practice schedules. The typical finding is that blocked practice during acquisition leads to better performance during acquisition. However, during retention, individuals who have practiced under random conditions typically perform better than those who received a blocked schedule (Shea & Morgan, 1979; see Lee, Chamberlin, & Hodges, in this volume). Lee and White (1990) reasoned that if observers engage in the same cognitive processes as the models they are observing, then observation of blocked and random schedules should produce the CI effect. Although observational learning effects were achieved, the model's practice schedule did not impact the observer's performance levels. The researchers concluded that observational learning was robust enough to overcome the deficiencies typically attributable to blocked practice, and that observing a model facilitated acquisition. This last conclusion needs clarification beyond that provided by the authors. Perhaps the observers performed well because the KR provided a goal to be achieved. Because only outcome was measured and not movement form it may be that observers were motivated to outperform the models. Of course, an additional control group that received only outcome information would be needed to assess this motivational explanation. Also, a retention test would be necessary to adequately test CI effects.

Other studies (Blandin, Proteau, & Alain, 1994; Lee, Wishart, Cunningham, & Carnahan, 1997; Wright, Li, & Coady, 1997) showed disparate findings regarding modeling and CI effects. Collectively, these studies raise questions as to whether CI is clearly produced by observation. Future research is necessary to determine whether these two constructs are linked.

Another way to organize the scheduling of demonstrations is to provide a variety of demonstrations as opposed to repeating the same one. The hypothesis that variability of practice will lead to enhanced performance over constant practice stems from Schmidt's (1975) schema theory.

Bird and Rikli (1983) extended this notion to the observational learning paradigm by comparing variable and constant modeling and physical practice. Surprisingly, they found that participants performed as well under variable demonstration as under constant physical practice despite the fact that they had not overtly practiced the skill.

Spacing and Timing of Demonstrations

How the demonstration is initially presented to participants may have an important impact on how they encode and subsequently rehearse the information. Questions such as how often a demonstration should be given and when it is introduced in the learning sequence have received scant attention both empirically and theoretically. A number of issues could be addressed here. For example, it may be best to view a demonstration before attempting to learn a new skill, or it may be best to physically practice the skill and then be provided with demonstrations. With the former sequence, it could be argued that the learner would have a better idea of what aspects of the skill are important.

Bird, Ross, and Laguna (1983) systematically manipulated the ratio of demonstrations and physical practice during the acquisition phase for learning a timing response. Seven experimental groups were formed and participants received either 100% physical practice, 100% demonstrations, or a combination of physical practice and demonstrations. Skill retention was superior for those participants who spent a greater proportion of their time observing as opposed to physically practicing with KR. Performance, however, was poor for those who spent all of their time observing. Thus, some amount of practice with KR was needed to form an accurate cognitive representation. Future research is needed to determine the importance of relative and absolute numbers of demonstrations in combination with and without KR.

Sidaway and Hand (1993) were interested in whether the frequency of modeling had a similar effect on the acquisition and retention of skills as shown in previous research on frequency of KR. They expected that greater relative frequency of demonstrations would lead to greater acquisition performance but poorer performance during retention and transfer due to the guidance effect, which has been shown in KR experiments. They chose a wiffle golf ball task, where it was expected that good form would lead to the best outcome. Participants were assigned to a 100%, 20%, or 10% relative frequency of demonstration condition, or to a control group. Contrary to expectations, there were no group differences during acquisition, and the 100% modeling group led to better performance during retention and a trend toward better performance during transfer. The researchers concluded that modeling and KR do not act in the same fashion. This study suggests that frequent demonstrations interspersed with practice leads to greater learning.

Weeks, Hall, and Anderson (1996) extended Lee et al.'s (1994) notion that greater cognitive effort should lead to greater learning. If an individual concurrently practices a skill while it is demonstrated, less cognitive effort would be expended than if he or she receives delayed imitations (i.e., first observed and later physically executed the skill). In line with previous research on other learning variables, they reasoned that concurrent observation should lead to better performance during acquisition. During retention, the increased cognitive effort required by delayed observation should lead to better performance. Participants were assigned to one of three groups to learn the manual alphabet. Results for immediate retention recall displayed no significant group effects, but by long-term retention the performance of the delayed observation group was significantly better than that of the concurrent group, with the combination group falling in between. Recognition scores revealed similar effects.

Using the same manual alphabet task, Richardson and Lee (1999) examined whether demonstrations were given before (proactive) or after (retroactive) performance. Acquisition data revealed that the proactive demonstrations led to better performance than retroactive demonstrations. Retention results showed a drop in performance for the proactive demonstrations and an increase in performance for the retroactive demonstrations. Richardson and Lee attribute the enhanced performance of retroactive groups during retention to the greater cognitive effort required to learn the letters during acquisition. The researchers concluded that observation could either enhance or debilitate performance and learning dependent on temporal placement.

Practicing in Dyads

Learning in the presence of others is not a new phenomenon. In fact, at the turn of the century, Triplett (1898) researched this phenomenon. A review of the motor performance literature (Landers & McCullagh, 1976) clearly indicates that learning tasks simultaneously with another person (coaction) can modify performance. In the human factors literature (Shebilske, Regian, Arthur, & Jordan, 1992), learning with another individual has been labeled active interlocked modeling (AIM). In this protocol, individuals attempt to learn a complex video game wherein one individual controls the joystick and the other controls the keyboard. On alternate trials they watch their partner practice components so that by the end of acquisition they have practiced a skill half the time and observed their partner practice the other

half of the time. A control group physically practices both components for the same number of trials throughout acquisition. During transfer, performance of the entire task is required. Interestingly, although individuals in the AIM group had only half as much direct practice with the task, their performance matched that of individuals who practiced the whole task themselves. In terms of training time efficiency, learning in dyads was more efficient.

A subsequent test of the AIM protocol (Arthur, Day, Bennett, McNelly, & Jordan, 1997) sought to determine if AIM learning and individual learning would lead to differential skill loss and reacquisition. For a computer task, no differences during acquisition, skill retention after eight weeks, or reacquisition were found for the individual versus AIM training protocols. The investigators suggest that the robustness of their findings "provides strong support and justification for the ongoing use of innovative dyadic protocols for the training of pilots and navigators in both military and nonmilitary settings" (p. 790). This holds for both acquisition and retention of skills when individuals may be precluded from practicing for a long period of time.

Shea, Wulf, and Whitacre (1999) extended these findings by embellishing the AIM protocol. Instead of merely passively observing a partner during acquisition, Shea et al. reasoned that dialogue between partners might enhance learning. Therefore, participants were assigned to one of three experimental conditions to learn a balance task. One group practiced individually. In the dyad-alternate-dialogue group, one individual practiced for a trial while the other watched, and then they switched positions and alternated practicing and watching. However, after each one had executed a trial, they had a chance to discuss task strategies. In the dyad-control group, the dyads alternated practicing and observing each other, but they did not discuss strategies until the end of acquisition. Both dyad groups evidenced larger errors than the individual group on the first trial, but only the dyad-control group had larger errors than the other groups through the end of acquisition. At retention, the dyad-alternate-dialogue group produced smaller errors throughout retention than the other two groups. The other two groups performed similarly during retention. These findings suggest that learning in pairs is an efficient strategy, especially if learners have a chance to verbalize and share strategies. Two can learn as much as one in the same amount of time!

Viewing Angle

How a demonstrator positions himself or herself when providing demonstrations is indeed a practical concern for effective learning but one that has not received much attention in the literature. If one demonstrates facing learners, then observers have to mentally rotate the image before they can enact the movement. If one faces away, no such rotation is required. Think of yourself in an aerobics class. Can you perform equally well in both situations? Early accounts of human learning by Fleishman and Gagné (1954) recognized the importance of the angle of viewing. Work by Roshall included in the Lumsdaine (1961) text on programmed instruction also spoke to the value of considering viewing angle.

Ishikura and Inomata (1995) reasoned that the level of cognitive processing required might influence the amount of learning when viewing angle is altered. Thus, subjective viewing or viewing a model from the rear does not require learners to reverse information. Observers who view a mirror demonstration need to make one reversal of the information, whereas observers who view an objective demonstration (front angle) need to make two reversals (front/rear and left/right). Therefore, these researchers assumed that the more reversals, the deeper the cognitive processing and the better the learning. Data from acquisition trials supported the hypothesis. Objective modeling led to greater immediate recall than a mirror condition, which outperformed a subjective model condition.

Augmented Information

Augmented information is typically described as feedback, but can be thought of in its broadest sense as additional information that may enhance learning (Newell et al., 1985). Feltz and Landers (1977) attempted to determine the role of augmented information in comparison to modeling. They reasoned that if people watched a demonstration, they would receive task-relevant information, but if they also heard the model's task score announced, they would also obtain motivational cues. They found that demonstrations enhanced performance relative to no demonstrations, but that announcing the model's score did not change performance levels. Because the task outcome was highly evident from the demonstration, it may have been difficult to separate the informational and motivational components of modeling. What additional augmented information might enhance visual demonstrations? For example, what is the role of other modalities, such as audition in modeling, and does the provision of verbal cues along with demonstrations enhance skill learning? Finally, what are the similarities between modeling and imagery, and can imagery enhance observational learning effects?

Audition

Although the visual modality is typically considered primary when presenting demonstrations, it may also be possible to learn from the auditory modality. This notion was clearly documented in an experiment by Newell (1976) that examined the ability to develop recognition memory for auditory demonstrations in the absence of movement practice. Increasing the number of auditory demonstrations led to the development of better recognition memory for ballistic movements despite the absence of physical practice. This finding is one in need of replication as well as extension to more complex movement skills.

Doody, Bird, and Ross (1985) were interested in the effect of auditory, visual, and auditory-plus-visual modeling on the acquisition and retention of a timing skill. Acquisition data indicated that the combination of auditory and visual demonstrations produced better performance than either visual demonstrations or control conditions. The superior performance by all experimental groups during retention led the researchers to conclude that demonstrations were more effective for learning than physical practice with KR. Caution, however, must accompany such an interpretation. All participants in the experiment received KR during the acquisition phase. Thus, the superior performance of the demonstration groups was due to a combination of modeling and physical practice with KR, not modeling alone. Also, the physical practice with KR control group had only 10 task exposures during acquisition, whereas modeling groups had 63 task exposures.

A subsequent experiment by McCullagh and Little (1989) attempted to determine the potency of auditory and visual demonstrations in the absence of KR. Participants practiced a timing skill interspersed with either visual, auditory, or visual-plus-auditory demonstrations. The control group received the same number of task exposures as well as KR on half its trials. In opposition to Doody et al.'s (1985) findings, KR was superior to modeling during immediate transfer. Contradictory findings in these two studies point to the necessity of assessing modeling effects independent of other potent performance modifiers. Both of these experiments, as well as Newell's (1976), discussed earlier, indicate the strong role of auditory models in skill learning, at least for timing tasks. Perhaps the modality of presentation interacts with the type of task to be learned. Visual information may be superior to auditory information if the task requires position or spatial components (Newell, 1976), whereas audition may be a more important modality for timing tasks.

Wuyts and Buekers (1995) tested the influence of model modality on a dance task requiring rhythmical synchronization. They predicted that an auditory model would enhance rhythmical timing over that of a visual model. Participants were asked to reproduce a rhythmical movement sequence after receiving both a visual and auditory demonstration, an auditory demonstration with auditory cues, a visual demonstration, or an auditory demonstration. The treatment groups did not demonstrate any differences in rhythmical timing. However, for synchronization, the auditory-auditory group produced the lowest errors during acquisition. No retention differences were found between the groups. The researchers suggested that the movement pattern was quite regular and thus visual demonstrations were sufficient to provide the necessary performance information.

Verbalization

In addition to providing a visual demonstration, verbal cues or prompts are often used to enhance the demonstration (Roach & Burwitz, 1986). These verbal cues may be delivered in conjunction with demonstrations, or they may be used as a rehearsal strategy after the demonstration is shown. For example, Bandura and Jeffery (1973) attempted to assess the role of symbolic coding and rehearsal processes by assigning either numeric or letter codes to movements. They found that allowing participants to verbally rehearse these codes led to better retention than if rehearsal was not allowed. The role of verbal cues and rehearsal has been examined in a number of studies with children, and these will be reviewed later in the chapter. Recent reviews by Magill (1993) and Landin (1994) on the role of verbal cues in skill learning recognize the importance of verbal cues in conjunction with demonstrations. Magill acknowledged that modeling and verbal cues may be redundant but may also possess unique characteristics that offer different information. A critical issue may be to examine whether a picture truly is worth a thousand words.

Magill and Schoenfelder-Zohdi (1996) compared performances after observing an expert model or a detailed verbal description of a rhythmic gymnastics rope skill. In addition, learners were provided with KP or no KP. Modeling led to better performance than no modeling, and KP led to better performance than no KP during acquisition. The no-modeling and no-KP group performed worse than all the groups. These findings were maintained during the transfer phase trials. A combination of both modeling and KP did not lead to better performance than only one or the other of these information sources. Observational learning effects may be dependent on whether learners are attempting to develop new movement patterns or scale existing ones. An analysis of the KP statements given to individuals in each group provided some interesting data to support these ideas.

Physical Practice

Shea, Wright, Wulf, and Whitacre (2000) reasoned that, during observation, learners are capable of determining general task characteristics but not specific response characteristics. They proposed that physical practice and observation might share some common cognitive operations but that physical practice additionally possesses activity at the muscle level that may contribute to acquisition. Participants in a first experiment were assigned to a physical practice, observational practice, or control group to learn a computer task. During retention, the physical practice group showed the fewest errors, followed by the observation group and then the control group. However, performance during transfer was similar for the physical practice and observation groups but significantly worse for the control group. Because the transfer task required the same coordination pattern but different timing characteristics than the acquisition task, the investigators concluded that observation is as good as physical practice for learning the coordination patterns of movement.

In a second experiment, they found that combining physical and observational practice led to some unique learning opportunities beyond physical practice alone. Shea et al. (2000) concluded that these findings support the notions expressed by Scully and Newell (1985). Shea et al. stated, "Observers are able to recognize and process the relative characteristics of the task in such a way that they can be translated into effective coordination patterns. Because observers do not have direct access to output processing and the associated feedback, however, they are less likely to be able to accurately calibrate the motor system." They believe that a combination of physical and observational practice allows the individual to calibrate the system, thereby explaining the superior performance of the combination group during transfer in Experiment 2.

Imagery

What is learned from watching a demonstration? Martens et al. (1976) suggested that the strategies or cognitive task components are more critical than the motor components. This cognitive versus motor distinction has been supported in the mental imagery literature (Feltz & Landers, 1983; Ryan & Simons, 1981, 1983). Although to date, researchers have not empirically verified a correspondence between imagery and modeling, innuendoes have been made that the processes may be similar (Druckman & Swets, 1988; Feltz & Landers, 1983; Housner, 1984a, 1984b; Ryan & Simons, 1983). In the observational learning paradigm, a demonstration is received, encoded, and rehearsed, and then a response is produced. In the imagery paradigm, an image is created, the image is rehearsed, and then a response is produced. White and Hardy (1995) suggested that external imagery and modeling are essentially the same because individuals view themselves or others from an external perspective. If modeling can be viewed as a form of covert rehearsal that primarily influences performance due to symbolic coding and subsequent rehearsal, and these internal representations serve as the internal standard for response production, then it may be reasonable that modeling and imagery are similar.

Hall and Erffmeyer (1983) compared an imagery and relaxation group to a group that received imagery, relaxation, and modeling. They referred to this latter condition as a visuomotor behavior rehearsal (VMBR) treatment, although it actually included modeling. For basketball foul shooting, they observed pronounced performance improvements for the group that received modeling in addition to relaxation and imagery. Subsequent studies (Gray, 1990; Gray & Fernandez, 1989; Li-Wei, Qi-Wei, Orlick, & Zitzelberger, 1992) found limited evidence to support the combination of imagery and modeling. To improve on previous experimental designs, Onestak (1997) added a third experimental group to the ones previously formed by Hall and Erffmeyer. Participants relaxed and visually rehearsed the basketball free throw (VMBR group), watched a video demonstration (modeling only), or received a combination of both treatments. Whether individuals had been classified as high or low ability did not support the advantage of modeling in combination with VMBR. Perhaps the arbitrary definition of some players as high ability or the extended practice received throughout the study may have masked some of the beneficial effects of the treatments.

Rushall (1988) used a covert modeling procedure with a world-ranked wrestler suffering from confidence problems when he competed in international meets. In covert modeling, initially other models are imagined, and then gradually the model becomes the participant. Eventually, the target behaviors should be performed under real-world circumstances. The intervention was deemed successful, as the wrestler practiced the covert modeling outside of consultations, reduced his negative self-statements, and was able to substitute himself as the model. Most important, his international wrestling performances improved considerably as a result of the modeling/imagery procedure.

Hall, Moore, Annett, and Rodgers (1997) examined the effectiveness of imagery, verbal mediators, and a combination of these strategies on the retention of movements. They chose a movement pattern task that had been shown to be highly amenable to imagery but not to verbal labeling. Participants received the movement stimulus either through a guided movement pattern or through demonstration. They imaged, labeled, imaged and labeled, or received

no treatment before movement production. Demonstrations were more effective than passive guidance for retention. The investigators suggested that the demonstration condition lured participants into paying more attention, leading to better performance.

In another study that combined imagery and modeling, Atienza, Balaguer, and Garcia-Merita (1998) compared a physical practice condition with a physical-practice-plus-video group, and a physical-practice-and-video-plus-imagery condition with experienced tennis players 9 to 12 years of age. Speed, accuracy, and techniques of the tennis serve were assessed. For service placement and technique, groups that included modeling plus imagery or modeling only performed similarly, and better than those in the physical-practice-only group. The researchers recognized that a factorial design combining imagery and modeling would have provided more definitive conclusions as to which intervention contributed most importantly to performance.

Although not labeled as a modeling study, Kim, Singer, and Tennant (1998) employed demonstrations as stimuli in their experiment. A visual imagery group watched a 10-minute video of a golf putt interspersed with imagery; an auditory imagery group received verbal instructions and then practiced imagery; and a kinesthetic imagery group listened to verbal instructions and kinesthetically imaged producing the golf-putting task. An irrelevant imagery group and a control group (prevented from rehearsing prior to task execution) were also included in the study. The group that received verbal instruction and then imaged performed better than the other groups during retention. Because modeling was combined with the visual imagery group, it is difficult to determine the relative contribution of each intervention.

Bouchard and Singer (1998) felt that a modeling intervention might enhance the five-step strategy previously developed by Singer to assist in the learning and performance of self-paced motor tasks. The strategy involves readying, imaging, focusing, executing, and evaluating performance. They compared learning of a tennis serve after presentation of the five-step strategy by verbal instruction, video modeling, or a no-strategy control condition. Although not significant, there was a tendency for better performance in the video modeling group during acquisition, and this group continued to improve during the retention period.

Theoretical approaches to imagery have suggested various ways in which information is stored in memory (Finke, 1986; Lang, 1979; Paivio, 1971). Verbal codes are thought to represent auditory information, whereas visual codes store spatial information. This idea parallels Bandura's

(1986) notion that information from demonstrations is symbolically transferred into images or verbal symbols that guide action, and these representations are especially important during the early stages of learning. However, Bandura also contends that "imaginal representations are abstractions of events, rather than simply mental pictures of past observances" (p. 56). Because imagery has been found to benefit cognitive more than motor skills (Feltz & Landers, 1983; Ryan & Simons, 1981, 1983), it may be productive to introduce modeling in situations where cognitive components of the skill are emphasized.

Vogt (1995) approached imagery and observational learning from a motor control perspective. In a series of three experiments, he examined the effects of observational, mental, and physical practice on the performance of cyclical movement sequences. The primary purpose was to determine if the three forms of practice involved a common process. Similar performance results were obtained across the three conditions, leading Vogt to suggest that the processes were indeed similar. Some might question the generalizability of these data to more complex tasks that have greater motor components or to simpler tasks that require less visual perception.

In a recent review from a neuropsychological perspective, Willingham (1998) applied principles of motor control to motor skill learning. He proposed that the observational learning and mental imagery literature cause some problems for traditional learning theories because learning has been shown to take place even when proprioceptive information is not available. He argued that most theoretical interpretations of learning require the use of proprioceptive feedback, whereas during imagery or observational learning, there is no proprioceptive feedback. He provided limited research support for his views, but perhaps his ideas will stir further research.

OBSERVER CHARACTERISTICS THAT INFLUENCE MOTOR SKILL PERFORMANCE AND PSYCHOLOGICAL RESPONSES

Motivational Orientation

Little research has been published examining the relationship between motivational orientation and modeling effects. In 1985, Weiss, Bredemeier, and Shewchuk designed a youth sport motivation scale based on Harter's (1981) intrinsic/extrinsic scale. The mastery subscale differentiated children who prefer to figure out skills on their own (intrinsic) from children who prefer guidance from external sources (extrinsic). The importance of motivational orientation lies not only in the task the child may choose to attempt, but also in the manner the child may be best primed for instruction. Extending this idea to the modeling domain, Little and McCullagh (1989) reasoned that more intrinsically motivated children would focus on their own movements, and more extrinsically motivated children would depend on external information to judge their performance. In teaching a new skill, it was hypothesized that focusing on KP (form or process) would be best for children who are more intrinsically motivated, whereas focusing on KR (outcome) would be best for more extrinsically motivated children. To test this notion, children who were high in intrinsic or extrinsic motivational orientation received observational learning training that was either form- or outcome-focused. The results provided limited support for the hypotheses but pointed to the importance of motivational orientation when considering modeling techniques.

Berlant and Weiss (1997) were interested in exploring the relationship between goal orientation and modeling. Specifically, they were interested in whether individuals who varied on task and ego orientation would differentially focus on the process or outcome of modeled actions. All participants were shown a video with correct demonstrations that included both form and outcome of the tennis forehand stroke. The recognition videotape contained a combination of correct and incorrect demonstrations as well as partially correct demonstrations. In addition to responding to recognition videos, participants were required to verbally recall specific form and outcome characteristics of the strokes they had observed. No relationship emerged between goal orientation and a differential focus on outcome and form. Thus, no support was found for the possibility that the observer's goal orientation is associated with a differential focus on form or outcome of a skill.

Learner Expertise

Much research has been conducted on expert/novice differences and has primarily focused on how information is represented in memory, processed, and then translated into action (e.g., Abernethy, 1989; Allard, Graham, & Paarsalu, 1980; Allard & Starkes, 1980; Deakin & Allard, 1991; McPherson & Thomas, 1989; Starkes & Deakin, 1984; Thomas, French, & Humphries, 1986). Because videos are often used as a means of displaying events and because cognitive processes are clearly linked to observational learning, the expert/novice literature may provide some insight regarding modeling. If experts who observe movements need less environmental information and can search displays faster than novices, then observational learning may be more effective for experts. On the other hand, experts may have acquired skills that allow them to gain more information from visual displays.

A study by Starkes, Deakin, Lindley, and Crisp (1987) is illustrative of how modeling stimuli are employed in novice/expert research. They equated observers for years of experience, but chose novice or expert ballet dancers to learn either a structured or unstructured dance sequence from a video. Both experts and novices performed similarly on unstructured sequences, but the experts clearly outperformed the novices on structured sequences. Thus, experts and novices may glean different amounts of information from visual demonstrations based on their domain-specific knowledge structures.

Downey et al. (1996) reasoned that learner expertise might influence the effectiveness of modeling because experts possess a stronger domain-specific knowledge base than do novices. This knowledge base should help experts perceive and execute movements more effectively after watching a demonstration. They examined the influence of demonstrations interspersed with both imagery and practice on recognition, as well as recall accuracy and quality among expert and novice dancers. Recall and recognition measures were moderately related for novices, but this relationship could not be determined for experts because of the small sample size. Further research is necessary before a clear link can be established between learner expertise and modeling.

Another key observer characteristic is age or cognitive development. Surprisingly, this observer characteristic has been neglected in comparison to characteristics of the model or the demonstration itself. However, in recent years, there has been increasing interest in the role of modeling on children's acquisition of motor and psychological skills. Thus, the theory and research related to developmental effects of observational learning are discussed next.

DEVELOPMENTAL CONSIDERATIONS IN MODELING

Theoretical Background

Bandura's (1969, 1977) social learning theory of modeling is the instrumental framework on which the vast amount of empirical research on observational learning effects is based. Interestingly, Bandura's subprocesses that are essential for modeling behavior to occur—attention, retention, production, and motivation—are all developmental in nature, yet age-related factors in the modeling process were largely neglected in his early writings. This is surprising

because social-cognitive theory highlights the importance of observer characteristics in the modeling process. For example, observers must be able to symbolically code and rehearse modeled actions to subsequently translate them into successful behavioral outcomes. Although control processes such as coding, grouping, labeling, and rehearsing are within adult capabilities, children are cognitively less mature to process information in the same ways (see Gallagher, French, Thomas, & Thomas, 1996). In fact, Bandura noted that a visual model plus concurrent verbalizing of modeled actions was superior to a visual model only for matching responses on novel play behaviors in 6- to 8-year-old children (Bandura, Grusec, & Menlove, 1966).

Yando, Seitz, and Zigler (1978) expressed strong support for Bandura's conceptualizations but asserted that developmental factors should be given greater attention in his theory. Because social learning theory emphasizes cognitive and physical abilities as well as motivational characteristics of learners, the theory could easily incorporate age-related considerations. Consequently, Yando et al. developed a two-factor developmental theory of imitation by synthesizing aspects of Bandura's social learning theory with Piaget's cognitive-developmental formulations. They also integrated aspects of cognitive and motivation development from theorists such as Flavell (1970) on the verbal self-regulation of behavior and Harter (1978) on effectance motivation in children.

According to Yando et al.'s (1978) developmental modeling theory, the observer's cognitive-developmental level and motivational system compose the two critical factors influencing children's observational learning of physical and social skills. Cognitive-developmental level includes attention span, memory capacity, symbolic coding capabilities, verbal rehearsal skills, and physical abilities, which correspond to Bandura's first three subprocesses. Motivational system was described as the intrinsic and extrinsic motives guiding children's attempts to reproduce observed behaviors, such as the desire to develop and demonstrate competence and social and tangible reinforcement, respectively. This factor corresponds to Bandura's motivation subprocess. The two-factor theory is thus quite similar to Bandura's formulations, differing only in its emphasis on developmental factors in the modeling process.

Yando et al.'s (1978) own extensive experiments with children age 4, 7, 10, and 13 provided strong empirical support for the explicit importance they assigned to the observer's cognitive-developmental level and motivational orientation in observational learning. For example, 4-year-old children were much less likely to recall and physically reproduce demonstrated actions than 7-year-olds, who were less successful than the 10- and 13-year-olds. Moreover, 4-year-old children modeled as many irrelevant as relevant task cues, whereas the three older groups modeled more task-relevant than -irrelevant cues. In follow-up interviews, only 42% of the 4-year-olds correctly remembered experimental instructions as compared to 80% or more of the three older groups. Yando et al. concluded that observed age differences were due to better-developed memory storage and retrieval systems, ability to discriminate task-relevant from -irrelevant cues, and more mature physical ability to reproduce modeled actions on the part of the older groups.

In the motor performance domain, several researchers have demonstrated strong support for developmental differences in a number of cognitive abilities, such as selective attention, rehearsal strategies, coding capabilities, decision making, and knowledge base (e.g., French & Thomas, 1987; Gallagher et al., 1996; McPherson, 1999; Nevett & French, 1997). These cognitive-developmental characteristics are essential for children's ability to successfully learn from visual and verbal models and to subsequently translate their perceptions to action. Findings show that children do not fully mature in selective attention, visual processing speed, and control processes (i.e., labeling, rehearsal, organization) until about age 12. Child novices possess less sport-specific knowledge (i.e., declarative, procedural, strategic) than child experts, who demonstrate less sophisticated cognitive representations than adults with the same level of expertise. These differences in knowledge base relate to children's ability to use self-regulated learning strategies (e.g., labeling, rehearsal, problem representation) to produce successful motor skill execution. Thus, efforts to facilitate task-relevant attention, rehearsal strategies, and knowledge development in children under 12 are paramount to effective motor skill instruction. Observational learning is key to the instruction of new skills and modification of learned skills, and these cognitive-developmental factors must be considered in the modeling process with children.

It was not until 1986 that Bandura explicitly and thoroughly integrated developmental factors into his formulations of observational learning. By this time, several researchers in the motor performance domain had already imposed their own developmental translation of his conceptualizations, with the help of Yando et al.'s (1978) writings and the research described previously on children's cognitive and memory development. The remainder of this section is organized to systematically present developmental modeling research. This research focuses on children's adoption of physical skills through observational learning, and developmental factors related to social psychological effects of modeling in educational contexts.

Early Research on Children's Modeling of Motor Skills

One of the earliest studies of children's modeling and motor performance was conducted by Donna and Daniel Landers (Landers, 1975; Landers & Landers, 1973). They were interested in the effects of model type (peer, teacher) and model skill level (skilled, unskilled) on children's (age 10 to 11) performance on a balance task. They found that performance scores were best after viewing a skilled teacher but not significantly different from viewing an unskilled peer. The researchers explained these unexpected findings in terms of the familiarity of the peer model (a classmate), whom observers may have been motivated to outperform. It is very likely that, given the age of the observers, the peer model was probably used as a source of social comparison or competition rather than for observational learning (Butler, 1989; Passer, 1996). In a replication and extension of this study, Lirgg and Feltz (1991) used unfamiliar peer models and found that model skill was the key variable explaining variations in performance outcome and form scores, with skilled teacher *and* peer models eliciting more successful behavioral responses than the other two groups.

Landers (1975) examined the temporal spacing of demonstrations on children's (age 11 to 13) motor performance. Demonstrations were given either before, midway through, or interspersed between practice trials. Children in the before and interspersed conditions performed generally better than those in the midway condition, suggesting that these conditions helped observers develop a cognitive representation of the skills to be executed. Thomas, Pierce, and Ridsdale (1977) extended Landers's study by examining the temporal spacing of demonstrations on balance performance in 7- and 9-year old girls. Children viewed demonstrations either before or midway through practice trials, or not at all (verbal instructions only). A model shown before learners performed the task was facilitative for both age groups. However, a model shown midway through practice trials was equally effective as the beginning model for 9-year-olds but detrimental to the performance of 7-year-olds. Thomas et al. attributed these findings to the older children's more mature information processing capabilities and their larger repertoire of motor abilities.

Anderson, Gebhart, Pease, and Ludwig (1982) replicated the study by Thomas et al. (1977) with boys rather than girls, and used videotaped rather than live demonstrations. Contrary to the previous study, Anderson et al. found that 9-year-olds performed superior to 7-year-olds only in the no-model condition. They conjectured that boys have more experience with gross motor skills that may have aided their performance. To test their notion, Anderson, Gebhart, Pease, and Rupnow (1983) examined the effects of age, gender, and temporal model placement on 7- and 9-year-old boys and girls attempting a ball-striking task. Children, regardless of age and gender, performed better in the beginning and middle model conditions than in the no-model condition. The discrepant findings across these studies on temporal spacing of demonstrations may perhaps be attributed to lack of selection criteria in the age groups chosen. According to Yando et al. (1978), developmental modeling studies should be designed so observers can be differentiated on cognitive-developmental or motivational criteria.

Feltz (1982) compared children (grades 4 and 5) and adults on performance outcome and form on a balance task after viewing zero or several task demonstrations. Adults achieved better performance on outcome and two of the five form components than did children. The majority of children were able to correctly describe only one component of form, whereas adults correctly identified three form components. Thus, outcome and form, and prompts to recall features of the demonstration, discriminated children's and adults' performance. However, though comparing children and adults maximizes observational learning effects, it does not sufficiently address cognitive-developmental differences in children's modeling of motor skills.

Weiss (1983; Weiss & Klint, 1987) responded to the need for developmentally based studies in a series of experiments on children's performance on a sequential motor task. Weiss chose 4–5- and 7–8-year-old children based on cognitive-developmental criteria, specifically verbal regulation of behavior or verbal self-instruction (Flavell, 1970). Children in each age group were randomly assigned to verbal, silent, or no model groups, and prompted or not prompted to use overt self-instruction as they performed the motor skills. Older children performed equally well under silent and verbal model conditions, and younger children performed significantly better after viewing a verbal model. Weiss concluded that a verbal or "show and tell" model, who concurrently shows and says what needs to be

executed, is especially helpful for younger children, who do not selectively attend to task-relevant cues or spontaneously use verbal rehearsal strategies to remember instructions.

Weiss and Klint (1987) followed with a study in which model type (verbal, no) and verbal rehearsal (yes, no) were combined to determine effects on 5–6- and 8–9-year-old children's motor performance. Children of both age groups performed better in the verbal-rehearsal (model or no model) than the verbal-model-only and no-model conditions. Thus, verbal rehearsal of skills was essential to help children selectively attend and remember the specific order in which skills are executed. Although no age differences were found on performance outcome as a function of modeling and rehearsal, children in the two age groups remembered the order of skills in distinctly different ways. When asked after the experiment, "How did you try to remember the order of the skills?" older children named planful strategies such as "I thought about what I had already done and what yet was to be done"; "Saying it over in my mind"; and "I pictured in my mind the order of the skills." Younger children frequently responded with "I thinked in my head"; "I thinked hard"; and "Used my brain." Children's behaviors during task instructions were another source of information on rehearsal strategies. Older children used some type of overt rehearsal strategy such as grouping skills, mouthing the names of the skills, or repeating instructions aloud with the researcher. In contrast, younger children overtly rehearsed *only after* their last trial of instructions was repeated—if they did at all. Kowalski and Sherrill (1992) replicated and extended Weiss and Klint's findings with 7- to 8-year-old children with learning disabilities. Participants in a verbal rehearsal condition (in combination with a silent or verbal model) performed better on a motor skill sequence than those who did not receive verbal rehearsal training.

Meaney and Edwards (1996) also extended Weiss and Klint's (1987) investigation of modeling and verbal rehearsal effects in children who were native or nonnative English speakers (i.e., Hispanic). Studying modeling effects among bilingual populations is important because many children in bilingual education programs receive instruction in academic courses in their native language but courses such as physical education and music are taught in English. Children (age 9.6 to 10.6 years) were randomly assigned to model type (show-and-tell model, no model) and verbal rehearsal (rehearsal, no rehearsal) conditions and subsequently assessed on performance outcome on a motor skill obstacle course. English-speaking children performed equally well under model and no-model conditions, but

Hispanic children were more successful in the show-and-tell model condition. As well, native speakers recorded higher scores in the verbal-rehearsal than no-rehearsal condition, but Hispanic children performed equivalently in the two rehearsal conditions. Therefore, presenting a visual-plus-verbal representation of skills facilitated Hispanic children's performance much more than did a verbal rehearsal strategy.

The studies reported so far were important in that they involved empirical tests of modeling theory as it pertains to children's performance on movement skills. Several practical implications could thereby be drawn, such as the necessity of using attention directing and memory strategies when teaching young children (McCullagh et al., 1989; Weiss, 1982). However, with the hindsight of advancements in conceptual and methodological knowledge, these studies contained certain limitations. As discussed earlier in this chapter, there are three major considerations in understanding behavioral responses to modeling: (1) outcome and process, (2) learning and performance, and (3) recall and recognition.

In many studies, observational learning was evaluated by performance outcome rather than form or technique measures (e.g., time on balance, number of trials to achieve criterion). To determine more accurately what children glean from observing a demonstration, assessing qualitative features of enacting physical skills is essential. Practically, teachers and coaches are more concerned that their students produce the desired technique parameters of sport skills that will eventually result in consistent and successful performance outcomes. Moreover, children are able to approximate technical aspects of a skill before they can execute successful performance outcomes (e.g., Wiese-Bjornstal & Weiss, 1992, underhand softball pitch). Therefore, the desired *goal* and *process* of motor performance are both essential to assessing observational learning effects.

Each of the studies previously described included an assessment of performance at a single point in time. This limits conclusions to the immediate and not more enduring effects of modeling. To gain a more accurate representation of the degree of *learning* from observing demonstrations, study designs must include retention or transfer tests in the absence of modeling interventions. If performance is sustained during a no-model retention phase, then observational effects on learning or relatively permanent, rather than temporary, performance changes can be inferred.

Finally, degree of observational learning was primarily determined by asking children to perform the actions as the model conveyed them. Because children learn more from a model early in learning than they can physically reproduce, Bandura (1986) recommended using cognitive measures of observational learning such as verbal production, recognition, and comprehension tests. Verbal production requires children to recall features of the modeled actions (e.g., name the stance, leg action, and follow-through of a basketball shot). Recognition means that children can distinguish between correct and incorrect alternatives of a skill demonstration (e.g., same versus opposite foot forward on the shot). Finally, comprehension entails explaining the "why" of modeled behavior, such as the rule underlying the need to bend one's legs when executing a basketball shot.

In the second wave of developmental modeling studies, described next, researchers responded to these early limitations by including one or more behavioral response variables. Specifically, researchers were intent on measuring outcome *and* form, performance *and* learning, and physical *and* cognitive measures related to observational learning of motor skills.

Contemporary Developmental Modeling Studies

Over the past 10 years, knowledge about the type of models that facilitate children's motor performance has advanced considerably. These studies were primarily designed to replicate and extend earlier studies. For example, McCullagh, Stiehl, and Weiss (1990) extended Weiss and Klint's (1987) investigation by assessing the effects of modeling (verbal, no) and verbal rehearsal (yes, no) on children's (age 5 to 6.5 and 7.5 to 9) sequential and form performance during acquisition and retention phases. For both age groups, the no-model condition (with or without verbal rehearsal) was best for performing the correct order of skills, but the verbal-model condition (with or without verbal rehearsal) was more desirable for reproducing correct form. Therefore, the show-and-tell model enhanced qualitative aspects of performance, and verbal instructions were sufficient in eliciting the sequencing of the motor task. These findings held for both performance and learning. Results contrasted those of Weiss and Klint, who found that verbal rehearsal groups (with or without a visual model) were superior for sequencing performance. The different protocol used by McCullagh et al. (i.e., provision of KR, single rehearsal trial, scoring of dependent variables) may have contributed to contradictory findings.

Weiss, Ebbeck, and Rose (1992) also expanded on Weiss and Klint's (1987) research by assessing children's (age 5 to 6 and 8 to 9) performance quality and sequential ordering during initial acquisition and delayed retention trials.

Modeling conditions included verbal-model only, rehearsal only (no model), and verbal-model-plus-rehearsal conditions. For older children, any of the model type conditions were equally effective for sequence and form scores during performance *and* learning phases. For younger children, the verbal-model-plus-rehearsal group was more effective for reproducing the order of skills than the other groups early during acquisition trials. However, the model-only group caught up with practice and recorded equivalent scores during later acquisition and retention trials. For form scores, children in the verbal-model-plus-rehearsal and model-only groups were superior to those in the verbal-rehearsal-only group at all performance and learning trials. Thus, a show-and-tell model or one combined with verbal rehearsal was equally effective for quantitative and qualitative performance among younger children. In contrast, older children benefited equally from a visual model and/or verbal rehearsal of the skills during performance and learning trials. These results underscore that model effectiveness depends on the age of the observer, the performance measure employed, and immediate performance versus long-term learning effects.

Meaney (1994) extended previous modeling studies in several ways. Children (age 9 to 11) were compared to adults on a novel physical activity (juggling scarves) for which participants had no previous experience. Performance was assessed during acquisition, retention, *and* transfer phases to determine whether knowledge could be applied to a new performance situation (juggling bean-bags). Observers in each age group were randomly assigned to one of four modeling conditions: visual model, visual model plus cues, visual model plus verbal rehearsal, and visual model plus cues plus rehearsal. Children who were exposed to a model plus verbal rehearsal or model combined with rehearsal and cues performed better than the other two conditions during acquisition trials. In contrast, adults performed equally well regardless of model type. At retention, children did not differ in juggling scores based on model type, but adults performed better in the model-plus-cues condition than in the other three groups. Only age differences were found during transfer, with adults performing significantly better than children. Assessment of observable transfer strategies indicated that adults used more strategies than children, and observers in the model-plus-rehearsal and model-with-rehearsal-and-cues groups used more strategies than individuals in the other conditions.

In contrast to using cognitive criteria for selecting children, Roberton, Halverson, and Harper (1997) examined the effect of visual and verbal modeling on children's hopping performance as a function of motor developmental level. All children were 6 years old and were assessed for modeling effects based on a competency-based approach (Bandura, 1986). Variation in hopping developmental level (i.e., levels 2 to 5 on arm action, levels 2 to 4 on leg action) was the observer characteristic of interest, and the main hypothesis was that children would respond differently to the model based on their hopping developmental level. They were pretested and classified according to arm and leg action levels of hopping. The teacher then demonstrated and verbalized cues for the advanced hop (level 4 leg action and level 5 arm action), followed by children's attempts to practice demonstrated skills. Contrary to previous studies, the show-and-tell model produced major disruptions in children's motor performance. Of the 100 children in the study, 55 showed regression in the arm action and 58 in the leg action. These surprising results were explained in terms of cognitive overload (i.e., dissecting the leg action, then the arm action) and what exactly children perceived to be the salient aspects of the demonstration (e.g., relative motion of legs and arms). Children's cognitive-developmental level (e.g., selective attention, memory strategies) combined with brief exposure to a model and practice (6 to 7 minutes) may have constrained their ability to produce responses that approximated the teacher's demonstration. It would have been interesting to include recognition and verbal recall tests to determine what children gleaned from observing the model.

Wiese-Bjornstal and Weiss (1992) investigated developmental differences in modeling by integrating knowledge from such areas as motor learning and control (visual and attention mechanisms), motor development (physical and cognitive capabilities), social psychology of sport (motivation and reinforcement), and biomechanics (mechanically effective techniques). The study was grounded in Bandura's (1986) social-cognitive theory as well as Scully's (1986; Scully & Newell, 1985) alternative hypothesis that demonstrations convey information about the relative motion pattern in the skills (i.e., movement of body parts in relation to one another). If observers are able to approximate the patterns of coordination, one can conclude that the skill has been modeled. Examining relative motion patterns, however, requires a more fine-grained analysis of performance. Wiese-Bjornstal and Weiss employed biomechanical techniques to quantify kinematic parameters of children's movements in relation to the model. In addition to a precise analysis of those cues children picked up from a model, the researchers also measured cognitive forms of learning using recognition and verbal production tests as recommended by Bandura (1986). Three key questions were addressed: (1) After viewing a model, do learners know what they are supposed to do (i.e., conception)? (2) If so, can they do it (i.e., action)? and (3) If they can do it, how well do they achieve the goal (i.e., outcome)?

Girls 7 to 9 years of age were selected because this is a transitional period in which children are developing in their ability to selectively attend to, rehearse, and organize information, but do not yet possess mature strategies (Gallagher & Hoffman, 1987). A modified softball fast pitch was selected as a novel, yet realistic, self-paced sport skill. Children were randomly assigned to one of three experimental conditions that varied in the number of trial blocks of visual model only and visual model plus verbal cues. Girls in all modeling conditions increasingly matched performance *form* to that of the model (i.e., stride length, starting shoulder angle, release body angle) but did not improve performance *outcome* (i.e., angle of release, ball velocity, absolute error). In addition, categorical form variables (e.g., starting with both feet on the white line, taking one step with the left foot) showed an increasing match to that of the model, especially in the trial block immediately following the first presentation of verbal cues. For the recognition test, children were asked to select the correctly executed softball pitch from among four alternative videotaped segments. There was an increasing trend toward selection of the correct model across trial blocks. The girls learned important information about the performance of the skill from viewing the correct model and improved in their ability to recognize and evaluate the outcome. Finally, a verbal production test at the end of the experiment requested girls to say what they were thinking about as they were pitching. Quotes such as "Try to look like you," "Arm straight out and going back," and "Step on my left leg, my arm falls back to my side" reflected many of the same verbal cues given by the demonstration and focused on performance form rather than outcome. In sum, many children learned the modeled skills based on both cognitive (recognition, recall) and physical enactment (increased matching of form kinematics) measures.

Cadopi, Chatillon, and Baldy (1995) compared 8- and 11-year-old children in producing a series of modeled ballet movements. In ballet, sequential and spatial properties of movement (form, position, trajectory) and kinematic and kinetic properties (quality of movements) constrain observers' ability to emulate what they view from demonstrations. The researchers conjectured that visual imagery would be most appropriate for retaining spatial movements, and visual and verbal rehearsal (e.g., temporal labels, sound codes) should be conducive to maximizing qualitative aspects of movement. Novice performers ages 8 and 11 years were chosen based on transitional periods in developing the ability to form visual images and verbal coding abilities.

After viewing an expert model, children were assessed on spatial and kinematic dimensions of three dance movements. The 11-year-old participants requested more observations of the model prior to indicating their readiness to perform the dance sequence. Moreover, 58% of the 11-year-olds compared to 33% of the 8-year-olds successfully completed the movement series. Form did not differentiate age groups, but quality of performance did. Moreover, form and quality were weakly related ($r = .39$) among 8-year-olds but more strongly related ($r = .61$) among the older dancers, suggesting that 11-year-olds were simultaneously encoding spatial and kinematic properties of movements. Postexperiment questions indicated that the 8-year-olds mentioned visual imagery more frequently than did the 11-year-olds, who used verbal coding much more frequently. In sum, many older children demonstrated more mature cognitive and physical abilities in performing spatial and qualitative aspects of the ballet skill. Older children may have also brought more varied experiences to the situation and engaged in more self-regulated learning strategies (e.g., verbal self-instruction, covert self-talk) that benefited production of modeled skills compared to the younger children.

Bouffard and Dunn (1993) were specifically interested in understanding children's use of self-regulated learning strategies in response to observing demonstrations. That is, what do children spontaneously do, in the absence of teacher or coach guidance, to enhance their chances of reproducing the sequencing and quality of movement skills? For example, in the Cadopi et al. (1995) study described earlier, older children may have requested more observations of the model in order to selectively attend to and rehearse components not well remembered on previous trials. Observations of children's behaviors during instructions in the Weiss and Klint (1987) study indicated that older, but not younger, children used self-regulated learning strategies (e.g., mouthing names of the skills, pointing at the mats).

Bouffard and Dunn (1993) assessed children's (age 6 to 7 and 9 to 10) use of self-regulatory strategies to learn a series of American sign language gestures that were longer than, but adjusted to, their memory span. These ages were chosen based on cognitive-developmental abilities to spontaneously engage in self-regulatory learning strategies.

Experimental conditions allowed participants to study the items for as long as they wanted and do whatever they wanted to recall the list. In addition to recall of the movement series, children's overt learning strategies were coded while watching the demonstration and during the period between viewing sequences. As hypothesized, older children viewed the sequences more frequently and displayed a greater and more varied number of strategies for learning the sequences. Such differential strategies included miming the gestures, rehearsing movements, anticipation (performing a gesture prior to viewing it on the video), and lip movements during the viewing phase. Thus, superior recall of the movement sequences by the 11-year-olds could be associated directly with their greater likelihood to use effective self-regulated learning strategies as a form of checking the accuracy of their performance. Given findings from earlier studies (e.g., McCullagh et al., 1990; Weiss et al., 1992; Wiese-Bjornstal & Weiss, 1992), it is clear that effective learning strategies can be taught to young nonverbalizers as a means of prompting overt or covert rehearsal strategies, ultimately resulting in improved motor performance.

Self-regulated learning in children's modeling of motor and psychosocial skills has recently received considerable attention (Ferrari, 1996; Schunk & Zimmerman, 1997). Self-regulation is defined as "processes that activate and sustain cognitions, behaviors, and affects, and that are oriented toward goal attainment" (Schunk & Zimmerman, 1997, p. 195). Self-regulated learning consists of three processes: self-observation, self-judgment, and self-reaction in relation to one's motor skill performance. *Self-observation* refers to attending to or monitoring one's own behavior, and is closely linked to *self-judgment,* which refers to comparing current performance to some goal standard, whether an objective or social means of comparison. Comparing one's performance against a standard provides information about progress or the conception-matching process in modeling. Finally, *self-reaction* entails an evaluative response to judgments of one's performance (i.e., good/bad, acceptable/unacceptable). Evaluative responses are important because they are influenced by observers' beliefs about their capabilities, or self-efficacy, to perform the skill and thus determine future motivated behavior on the particular task or activity.

Schunk (1987, 1989a, 1989b; Schunk & Zimmerman, 1997) contends that observational learning is an antecedent of self-regulation skills in children (i.e., self-observation, self-judgment, self-reaction). This helps explain findings in several previously described studies (Bouffard & Dunn, 1993; Cadopi et al., 1995; Starkes et al., 1987; Weiss & Klint, 1987). Models not only convey

information that allows observers to emulate problem-solving strategies to increase their self-regulation and motor skills, but are often characterized by similar model-observer qualities that enhance self-efficacy and motivate observers to persist in learning skills. Such model characteristics include peer models, coping models, and self-modeling. The effect of peer, coping, and self-models on children's motor and psychological responses in the physical domain is an important topic to consider.

Developmental Issues and Social Psychological Effects of Modeling

Typically in sport contexts, teachers or coaches demonstrate the motor skills they desire students and athletes to reproduce. Lirgg and Feltz (1991) determined that model skill, regardless of whether a teacher or peer demonstrated, was the key quality affecting motor performance and self-efficacy in 11- to 12-year-old children learning a balance task. However, other studies have shown that model-observer similarity (e.g., age, gender, athlete/nonathlete, injury status) is an important characteristic that can strongly impact motor and psychosocial responses (e.g., Flint, 1991; Gould & Weiss, 1981; McCullagh, 1987). Educational and sport psychology researchers suggest that peer models can effectively promote positive behavioral and psychological responses in children, especially with activities or in situations where children have experienced difficulties or are uncertain about their capabilities (Lewis, 1974; Schunk & Hanson, 1985; Schunk, Hanson, & Cox, 1987; Weiss et al., 1998).

In an extensive review of the peer modeling literature, Schunk (1987) contends that similar-age peers serve as an important source of information for conveying behavioral appropriateness, formulating outcome expectations, and assessing self-efficacy for performing tasks. A study by Feltz (1980) supports these contentions, in showing that a peer model (in combination with participant modeling) was effective in teaching a modified forward dive to a 12-year-old boy with mental challenges. Only four sessions of 30 minutes each were required to reach the target behavior, and a follow-up test three weeks later verified that the boy could still produce the dive successfully and without hesitation.

Developmental differences in children's use of social comparison may be an important consideration in peer modeling of motor and psychological skills. Research in academic settings (Stipek & MacIver, 1989) and sport (Horn & Harris, 1996) consistently show that during late childhood and early adolescence, peers become increasingly important as a source of information for assessing self-abilities, replacing successful task completion, parental feedback, and positive affect as key competence sources. Moreover, Butler (1989) has shown that children under the age of 8 years primarily look to peers for *observational learning* cues, and children older than 8 years use peers primarily as cues for *appraising one's relative ability* in a particular achievement domain. For example, children averaged 6 years of age in Weiss et al.'s (1998) study of peer modeling effects on swim skills, self-efficacy, and fear. Peer model conditions (coping or mastery) were superior on all variables to the condition in which children received swim lessons only, and peer coping models surpassed peer mastery models on self-efficacy. No differences between peer coping and mastery model groups were found for swim skill performance and fear of swimming. Given developmental differences in children's use of peer comparison, it is highly conceivable that children used both the peer mastery and coping models as sources of information for how to perform the skills rather than for assessing relative ability. It would be interesting to examine motor learning and psychological effects of peer modeling in children younger *and* older than 8 years of age to determine whether observational learning or peer ability comparison emerge. It is probable that, in the Landers and Landers (1973) study reported earlier, peer comparison or competition may have accounted for the 10-year-old children's relatively lower scores in the skilled peer model and higher scores in the unskilled peer model conditions.

Schunk and his colleagues (Schunk, 1987, 1989b; Schunk & Hanson, 1985, 1989a; Schunk et al., 1987) have extensively studied the influence of peer coping and mastery models on children's self-efficacy and academic achievement. Schunk maintains that peer coping models should be especially beneficial for children who experience difficulties with learning specific activities and who possess self-doubts about their capabilities for performing in such situations. The hypothesized mechanism underlying the influence of peer coping models is the perceived similarity between observer and model. The model's verbalizations and learning rates approximate those of the observer, which should raise self-efficacy and promote mastery behaviors. In contrast, a mastery model's flawless performance and confident verbalizations would be atypical of observers who may be experiencing learning difficulty and low self-confidence.

In several experiments, Schunk (Schunk & Hanson, 1985, 1989a; Schunk et al., 1987) examined the influence of peer coping models on children's self-efficacy and math achievement. Schunk and Hanson found that either a peer coping or mastery model was superior to teacher or no-model conditions for solving math problems. Lack of differences between peer coping and mastery models was

attributed to the children's not being anxious about doing math problems. Instead, they may have focused on the models' successful problem-solving rather than learning rates or negative verbalizations. In Weiss et al.'s (1998) study, the participants were, in fact, fearful and anxious of swimming. Robust findings for self-efficacy in favor of peer coping models were uncovered, which support Schunk's notion that peer coping models might be especially effective in therapeutic situations.

Schunk et al. (1987) revealed further information about the influence of peer models. In Experiment 1, low-achieving math students were assigned to a male or female peer coping or mastery model condition. Children viewing peer coping models scored significantly higher in self-efficacy and math skill, supporting the notion that peer coping models maximize model-observer similarity and result in higher efficacy and performance. In Experiment 2, children viewed single mastery, multiple mastery, single coping, or multiple coping models. The single and multiple coping as well as multiple mastery groups demonstrated higher self-efficacy and skill than did the single mastery group participants. Observing several children successfully solve the skills despite their rate of learning increased the probability that children identified with at least one of the models and that successful mastery of the task was realistic. In Weiss et al.'s (1998) study of peer models and fear of swimming, children had access to multiple models not only on video but also in their swim lesson groups, which may have had the same effect as the multiple mastery models in Schunk et al.'s experiment. In light of findings by Schunk and Weiss and colleagues on the efficacy of peer models with children experiencing difficulty or anxiety with particular activities, more research exploring the use of peer and coping models in the physical domain is warranted.

Finally, Dowrick (1999) has been prolific in demonstrating the widespread success of self-modeling in a variety of domains, including sport, and with populations spanning children through older adults. To date, only one self-modeling study with children in the physical domain was located (Winfrey & Weeks, 1993). However, Schunk and Hanson (1989b) examined the use of self-models in children's arithmetic skill learning. Over three experiments, they found that self-models were better than videotape controls and equally effective as peer models for skill acquisition and self-efficacy. Given the success of self-models in children's cognitive learning, it seems logical that self-modeling is likely to be efficacious for positively influencing children's motor performance and psychosocial responses, especially in situations where learning difficulties or doubts in self-confidence are paramount. These hypotheses await empirical testing.

SUMMARY AND CONCLUDING REMARKS

The purpose of this chapter was to review the literature on modeling as it relates to motor skill performance and psychological responses. There is little doubt that modeling is indeed a potent modifier of a wide range of movement-related behaviors, self-perceptions, affective reactions, and motivation. Numerous theoretical and conceptual approaches have been employed to explain the observational learning phenomenon. This should not be surprising because researchers in diverse fields, such as motor learning/control and developmental and social psychology, have attempted to determine optimal conditions for modeling. Characteristics of the model, demonstration, and observer were emphasized as correlates or moderators of modeling effectiveness. A considerable amount of empirical work has focused on these issues since the last review (McCullagh, 1993), yet much remains to be clarified and elaborated. It seems unlikely that one approach or theory will be able to parsimoniously explain all modeling effects. Rather, an integrated approach seems warranted wherein researchers from different subdisciplines cooperate in examining factors that maximize the effectiveness of observational learning as an educational or psychological intervention.

In reviewing the literature, we did not cover a vast array of data that speak to issues such as role modeling and gender-role stereotyping (see Signorielli, 1990) that exists in the psychological literature. These areas have direct observational learning applications, but were outside the realm of the current review. There is also literature on the impact of mass media (e.g., television) that definitely falls within the topic of modeling and that may provide insight on behavior within physical activity settings. For example, Marcus and her associates (Marcus, Owen, Forsyth, Cavill, & Fridinger, 1998) addressed the role of mass media interventions on physical activity levels. Unfortunately, this literature has not referred to or utilized observational learning research that could offer ideas for effective interventions for enhancing physical activity participation.

Although modeling has received increased attention in the motor behavior literature over the past decade, there are still many issues that remain unclear, untapped, or unanswered. Although the diverse approaches to the topic increase the generalizability of the phenomenon, integrating the findings and agreeing on appropriate research questions are difficult challenges. One suggestion encouraged

in this chapter is to analyze the wide range of modeling behaviors through a task analysis. Such an approach as well as integrative research may help provide coherency to this diverse literature.

REFERENCES

Abernethy, B. (1988). The effects of age and expertise upon perceptual skill development in a racquet sport. *Research Quarterly for Exercise and Sport, 59,* 210–221.

Abernethy, B. (1989). Expert-novice differences in perception: How expert does the expert have to be? *Canadian Journal of Sport Sciences, 14,* 27–30.

Abernethy, B., & Russell, D.G. (1987). The relationship between expertise and visual search strategy in a racquet sport. *Human Movement Science, 6,* 283–319.

Adams, J.A. (1971). A closed-loop theory of motor learning. *Journal of Motor Behavior, 3,* 111–150.

Adams, J.A. (1986). Use of the model's knowledge of results to increase the observer's performance. *Journal of Human Movement Studies, 12,* 89–98.

Allard, F., Graham, S., & Paarsalu, M.E. (1980). Perception in sport: Basketball. *Journal of Sport Psychology, 2,* 14–21.

Allard, F., & Starkes, J.L. (1980). Perception in sport: Volleyball. *Journal of Sport Psychology, 2,* 22–33.

Anderson, D.F., Gebhart, J.A., Pease, D.G., & Ludwig, D.A. (1982). Effects of age and temporal spacing of a model on children's performance on a balance task. *Perceptual and Motor Skills, 55,* 1263–1266.

Anderson, D.F., Gebhart, J.A., Pease, D.G., & Rupnow, A.A. (1983). Effects of age, sex, and placement of a model on children's performance on a ball-striking task. *Perceptual and Motor Skills, 57,* 1187–1190.

Arthur, W., Jr., Day, E.A., Bennett, W., McNelly, T.L., & Jordan, J.A. (1997). Dyadic versus individual training protocols: Loss and reacquisition of a complex skill. *Journal of Applied Psychology, 82,* 783–791.

Atienza, F.L., Balaguer, I., & Garcia-Merita, M.L. (1998). Video modeling and imaging training on performance of tennis service of 9- to 12-year-old children. *Perceptual and Motor Skills, 87,* 519–529.

Bandura, A. (1965). Vicarious processes: A case of no-trial learning. In L. Berkowitz (Ed.), *Advances in experimental social psychology* (Vol. 2, pp. 1–55). New York: Academic Press.

Bandura, A. (1969). *Principles of behavior modification.* New York: Holt, Rinehart and Winston.

Bandura, A. (1971). Analysis of modeling processes. In A. Bandura (Ed.), *Psychological modeling: Conflicting theories* (pp. 1–62). Chicago: Adline-Atherton.

Bandura, A. (1977). *Social learning theory*. Englewood Cliffs, NJ: Prentice-Hall.

Bandura, A. (1986). *Social foundations of thought and action: A social cognitive theory*. Englewood Cliffs, NJ: Prentice-Hall.

Bandura, A. (1997). *Self-efficacy: The exercise of control*. New York: Freeman.

Bandura, A., Grusec, J.E., & Menlove, F.L. (1966). Observational learning as a function of symbolization and incentive set. *Child Development, 37*, 499–506.

Bandura, A., & Jeffery, R.W. (1973). Role of symbolic coding and rehearsal processes in observational learning. *Journal of Personality and Social Psychology, 26*, 122–130.

Baron, R.A. (1970). Attraction toward the model and model's competence as determinants of adult imitative behavior. *Journal of Personality and Social Psychology, 14*, 345–351.

Berlant, A.R., & Weiss, M.R. (1997). Goal orientation and the modeling process: An individual's focus on form and outcome. *Research Quarterly for Exercise and Sport, 68*, 317–330.

Bird, A.M., & Rikli, R. (1983). Observational learning and practice variability. *Research Quarterly for Exercise and Sport, 54*, 1–4.

Bird, A.M., Ross, D., & Laguna, P. (1983). *The observational learning of a timing skill*. ERIC Database (1982–1991), ED 269 370.

Blandin, Y., Proteau, L., & Alain, C. (1994). On the cognitive processes underlying contextual interference and observational learning. *Journal of Motor Behavior, 26*, 18–26.

Bouchard, L.J., & Singer, R.N. (1998). Effects of the five-step strategy with videotape modeling on performance of the tennis serve. *Perceptual and Motor Skills, 86*, 739–746.

Bouffard, M., & Dunn, J.G.H. (1993). Children's self-regulated learning of movement sequences. *Research Quarterly for Exercise and Sport, 64*, 393–403.

Bradley, R.D. (1993). *The use of goal-setting and positive self-modeling to enhance self-efficacy and performance for the basketball free throw shot*. Unpublished doctoral dissertation, University of Maryland, College Park.

Burroughs, W.A. (1984). Visual simulation training of baseball batters. *International Journal of Sport Psychology, 15*, 117–126.

Butler, R. (1989). Mastery versus ability appraisal: A developmental study of children's observations of peers' work. *Child Development, 60*, 1350–1361.

Cadopi, M., Chatillon, J.F., & Baldy, R. (1995). Representation and performance: Reproduction of form and quality of movement in dance by eight- and 11-year-old novices. *British Journal of Psychology, 86*, 217–225.

Carroll, W.R., & Bandura, A. (1982). The role of visual monitoring in observational learning of action patterns: Making the unobservable observable. *Journal of Motor Behavior, 14*, 153–167.

Carroll, W.R., & Bandura, A. (1985). The role of timing of visual monitoring and motor rehearsal in observational learning of action patterns. *Journal of Motor Behavior, 17*, 269–281.

Carroll, W.R., & Bandura, A. (1987). Translating cognition into action: The role of visual guidance in observational learning. *Journal of Motor Behavior, 19*, 385–398.

Carroll, W.R., & Bandura, A. (1990). Representational guidance of action production in observational learning: A causal analysis. *Journal of Motor Behavior, 22*, 85–97.

Chamberlin, C.J., & Coelho, A.J. (1993). The perceptual side of action: Decision-making in sport. In J.L. Starkes & F. Allard (Eds.), *Cognitive issues in motor expertise* (pp. 135–158). Amsterdam: Elsevier.

Christina, R.W., Barresi, J.V., & Shaffner, P. (1990). The development of response selection accuracy in a football linebacker using video training. *The Sport Psychologist, 4*, 11–17.

Crawford, S., & Eklund, R.C. (1994). Social physique anxiety, reasons for exercise, and attitudes toward exercise settings. *Journal of Sport & Exercise Psychology, 16*, 70–82.

Darden, G.F. (1997). Demonstrating motor skills: Rethinking that expert demonstration. *Journal of Physical Education, Recreation & Dance, 68*, 31–35.

Deakin, J.M., & Allard, F. (1991). Skilled memory in expert figure skaters. *Memory and Cognition, 19*, 79–86.

Doody, S.G., Bird, A.M., & Ross, D. (1985). The effect of auditory and visual models on acquisition of a timing task. *Human Movement Science, 4*, 271–281.

Downey, P.J., Neil, G.I., & Rapagna, S. (1996). Evaluating modeling effects in dance. *Impulse, 4*, 48–64.

Dowrick, P.W. (1983). Self-modelling. In P.W. Dowrick & S.J. Biggs (Eds.), *Using video: Psychological and social applications* (pp. 105–124). New York: Wiley.

Dowrick, P.W. (Ed.). (1991). *Practical guide to using video in the behavioral sciences*. New York: Wiley.

Dowrick, P.W. (1999). A review of self-modeling and related interventions. *Applied and Preventive Psychology, 8*, 23–39.

Dowrick, P.W., & Biggs, S.J. (1983). *Using video: Psychological and social applications*. New York: Wiley.

Dowrick, P.W., & Dove, C. (1980). The use of self-modeling to improve the swimming performance of spina bifida children. *Journal of Applied Behavior Analysis, 13*, 51–56.

Druckman, D., & Swets, J.A. (1988). *Enhancing human performance: Issues, theories and techniques*. Washington, DC: Academy Press.

Eklund, R.C., & Crawford, S. (1994). Active women, social physique anxiety and exercise. *Journal of Sport & Exercise Psychology, 16*, 431–448.

Feltz, D.L. (1980). Teaching a high-avoidance motor task to a retarded child through participant modeling. *Education and Training of the Mentally Retarded, 15*, 152–155.

Feltz, D.L. (1982). The effects of age and number of demonstrations on modeling of form and performance. *Research Quarterly for Exercise and Sport, 53,* 291–296.

Feltz, D.L., & Landers, D.M. (1977). Informational-motivational components of a model's demonstration. *Research Quarterly, 48,* 525–533.

Feltz, D.L., & Landers, D.M. (1983). The effects of mental practice on motor skill learning and performance: A meta-analysis. *Journal of Sport Psychology, 5,* 25–57.

Feltz, D.L., Landers, D.M., & Raeder, U. (1979). Enhancing self-efficacy in high avoidance motor tasks: A comparison of modeling techniques. *Journal of Sport Psychology, 1,* 112–122.

Ferrari, M. (1996). Observing the observer: Self-regulation in the observational learning of motor skills. *Developmental Review, 16,* 203–240.

Finke, R.A. (1986). Mental imagery and the visual system. *Scientific American, 254,* 88–95.

Flavell, J.H. (1970). Developmental studies of mediated memory. In H.W. Reese & L.P. Lipsitt (Eds.), *Advances in child development and behavior* (Vol. 5, pp. 181–211). New York: Academic Press.

Fleishman, E., & Gagné, R.M. (1954). *Psychology and human performance: An introduction to psychology.* New York: Holt.

Flint, F.A. (1991). *The psychological effects of modeling in athletic injury rehabilitation.* Unpublished doctoral dissertation, University of Oregon, Eugene.

Flint, F.A. (1993). Seeing helps believing: Modeling in injury rehabilitation. In D. Pargman (Ed.), *Psychological bases of sport injuries* (pp. 183–198). Morgantown, WV: Fitness Information Technology.

Franks, I.M., & Maile, L.J. (1991). The use of video in sport skill acquisition. In P.W. Dowrick (Ed.), *Practical guide to using video in the behavioral sciences* (pp. 231–243). New York: Wiley.

French, K.E., & Thomas, J.R. (1987). The relation of knowledge development to children's basketball performance. *Journal of Sport Psychology, 9,* 15–32.

Gallagher, J.D., French, K.E., Thomas, K.T., & Thomas, J.R. (1996). Expertise in youth sport: Relations between knowledge and skill. In F.L. Smoll & R.E. Smith (Eds.), *Children and youth in sport: A biopsychosocial perspective* (pp. 338–358). Madison, WI: Brown & Benchmark.

Gallagher, J.D., & Hoffman, S. (1987). Memory development and children's sport skill acquisition. In D. Gould & M.R. Weiss (Eds.), *Advances in pediatric sport sciences* (pp. 187–210). Champaign, IL: Human Kinetics.

Gentile, A.M. (1987). Skill acquisition: Action, movement and neuromotor processes. In J.H. Carr, J. Shephard, J. Gordon, A.M. Gentile, & J.M. Held (Eds.), *Movement science: Foundations for physical therapy* (pp. 93–154). Rockville, MD: Aspen.

George, T.R., Feltz, D.L., & Chase, M.A. (1992). Effects of model similarity on self-efficacy and muscular endurance: A second look. *Journal of Sport & Exercise Psychology, 14,* 237–248.

Gould, D.R., & Roberts, G.C. (1981). Modeling and motor skill acquisition. *Quest, 33,* 214–230.

Gould, D.R., & Weiss, M.R. (1981). The effects of model similarity and model talk on self-efficacy and muscular endurance. *Journal of Sport Psychology, 3,* 17–29.

Gray, S.W. (1990). Effect of visuomotor rehearsal with videotaped modeling on racquetball performance of beginning players. *Perceptual and Motor Skills, 70,* 379–385.

Gray, S.W., & Fernandez, S.J. (1989). Effects of visuomotor behavior rehearsal with videotaped modeling on basketball shooting performance. *Psychology: A Journal of Human Behavior, 26,* 41–47.

Hall, C., Moore, J., Annett, J., & Rodgers, W. (1997). Recalling demonstrated and guided movements using imaginary and verbal rehearsal strategies. *Research Quarterly for Exercise and Sport, 68,* 136–144.

Hall, E.G., & Erffmeyer, E.S. (1983). The effect of visuomotor behavior rehearsal with videotaped modeling on free throw accuracy of intercollegiate female basketball players. *Journal of Sport Psychology, 5,* 343–346.

Halliwell, W. (1990). Providing sport psychology consultant services in professional hockey. *The Sport Psychologist, 4,* 369–377.

Hancock, P.A., Arthur, E.J., & Andre, A.D. (1993). Learning in virtual environments. *Journal of Sport & Exercise Psychology, 15,* S40.

Harter, S. (1978). Effectance motivation reconsidered. *Human Development, 21,* 34–64.

Harter, S. (1981). A new self-report scale of intrinsic versus extrinsic orientation in the classroom: Motivational and informational components. *Developmental Psychology, 17,* 300–312.

Hebert, E.P., & Landin, D. (1994). Effects of a learning model and augmented feedback in tennis skill acquisition. *Research Quarterly for Exercise and Sport, 65,* 250–257.

Horn, T.S., & Harris, A. (1996). Perceived competence in young athletes: Research findings and recommendations for coaches and parents. In F.L. Smoll & R.E. Smith (Eds.), *Children and youth in sport: A biopsychosocial perspective* (pp. 309–329). Madison, WI: Brown & Benchmark.

Housner, L.D. (1984a). The role of imaginal processing in the retention of visually presented sequential motoric stimuli. *Research Quarterly for Exercise and Sport, 55,* 24–31.

Housner, L.D. (1984b). The role of visual imagery in recall of modeled motoric stimuli. *Journal of Sport Psychology, 6,* 148–158.

Ishikura, T., & Inomata, K. (1995). Effects of angle of model demonstration on learning of a motor skill. *Perceptual and Motor Skills, 80,* 651–658.

Jones, C.M., & Miles, T.R. (1978). Use of advance cues in predicting the flight of a lawn tennis ball. *Journal of Human Movement Studies, 4,* 231–235.

Kim, J., Singer, R.N., & Tennant, L.K. (1998). Visual, auditory and kinesthetic imagery on motor learning. *Journal of Human Movement Studies, 34,* 159–174.

Kowalski, E.M., & Sherrill, C. (1992). Motor sequencing of boys with learning disabilities: Modeling and verbal rehearsal strategies. *Adapted Physical Activity Quarterly, 9,* 261–272.

Kulik, J.A., & Mahler, H.I. (1987). Effects of preoperative roommate assignment on preoperative anxiety and recovery from coronary bypass surgery. *Health Psychology, 6,* 525–543.

Laguna, P.L. (1996). The effects of model demonstration strategies on motor skill acquisition and performance. *Journal of Human Movement Studies, 30,* 55–79.

Landers, D.M. (1975). Observational learning of a motor skill: Temporal spacing of demonstrations and audience presence. *Journal of Motor Behavior, 7,* 281–287.

Landers, D.M., & Landers, D.M. (1973). Teacher versus peer models: Effects of model's presence and performance level on motor behavior. *Journal of Motor Behavior, 5,* 129–139.

Landers, D.M., & McCullagh, P. (1976). Social facilitation of motor performance. In J.F. Keogh (Ed.), *Exercise and sports sciences reviews* (pp. 125–162). Santa Barbara, CA: Journal Publishing Affiliates.

Landin, D. (1994). The role of verbal cues in skill learning. *Quest, 46,* 299–313.

Lang, P.J. (1979). A bio-informational theory of emotional imagery. *Psychophysiology, 16,* 495–512.

Laugier, C., & Cadopi, M. (1996). Representational guidance of dance performance in adult novices: Effect of concrete vs. abstract movement. *International Journal of Sport Psychology, 27,* 91–108.

Lee, T.D., Swinnen, S.P., & Serrien, D.J. (1994). Cognitive effort and motor learning. *Quest, 46,* 328–344.

Lee, T.D., & White, M.A. (1990). Influence of an unskilled model's practice schedule on observational motor learning. *Human Movement Science, 9,* 349–367.

Lee, T.D., Wishart, L.R., Cunningham, S., & Carnahan, H. (1997). Model timing information during random practice eliminates the contextual interference effect. *Research Quarterly for Exercise and Sport, 68,* 100–105.

Lewis, S. (1974). A comparison of behavior therapy techniques in the reduction of fearful avoidance behavior. *Behavior Therapy, 5,* 648–655.

Lirgg, C.D., & Feltz, D.L. (1991). Teacher versus peer models revisited: Effects on motor performance and self-efficacy. *Research Quarterly for Exercise and Sport, 62,* 217–224.

Little, W.S., & McCullagh, P. (1989). Motivational orientation and modeled instructional strategies: The effects on form and accuracy. *Journal of Sport & Exercise Psychology, 11,* 41–53.

Li-Wei, Z., Qi-Wei, M., Orlick, T., & Zitzelsberger, L. (1992). The effect of mental-imagery training on performance enhancement with 7- to 10-year-old children. *The Sport Psychologist, 6,* 230–241.

Londeree, B. (1967). Effect of training with motion pictures versus flash cards upon football play recognition. *Research Quarterly, 38,* 202–207.

Lumsdaine, A.A. (Ed.). (1961). *Student responses in programmed instruction.* Washington, DC: Academy of Sciences: National Research Council.

Magill, R.A. (1993). Modeling and verbal feedback influences on skill learning. *International Journal of Sport Psychology, 24,* 358–369.

Magill, R.A. (1998). *Motor learning: Concepts and applications.* New York: McGraw-Hill.

Magill, R.A., & Schoenfelder-Zohdi, B. (1996). A visual model and knowledge of performance as sources of information for learning a rhythmic gymnastics skill. *International Journal of Sport Psychology, 27,* 7–22.

Marcus, B.H., Owen, N., Forsyth, L.H., Cavill, N.A., & Fridinger, F. (1998). Physical activity interventions using mass media, print media, and information technology. *American Journal of Preventive Medicine, 15,* 362–378.

Martens, R., Burwitz, L., & Zuckerman, J. (1976). Modeling effects on motor performance. *Research Quarterly, 47,* 277–291.

Mausner, B. (1953). Studies in social interaction: III. Effect of variation in one partner's prestige on the interaction of observer pairs. *Journal of Applied Psychology, 37,* 391–393.

McAuley, E. (1985). Modeling and self-efficacy: A test of Bandura's model. *Journal of Sport Psychology, 7,* 283–295.

McCullagh, P. (1986). Model status as a determinant of attention in observational learning and performance. *Journal of Sport Psychology, 8,* 319–331.

McCullagh, P. (1987). Model similarity effects on motor performance. *Journal of Sport Psychology, 9,* 249–260.

McCullagh, P. (1993). Modeling: Learning, developmental, and social psychological considerations. In R.N. Singer, M. Murphey, & L.K. Tennant (Eds.), *Handbook of research on sport psychology* (pp. 106–125). New York: Macmillan.

McCullagh, P., Burch, C.D., & Siegel, D.I. (1990). *Correct and self-modeling and the role of feedback in motor skill acquisition.* Paper presented at the annual meeting of the North American Society for the Psychology of Sport and Physical Activity, Houston, TX.

McCullagh, P., & Caird, J.K. (1990). Correct and learning models and the use of model knowledge of results in the acquisition and retention of a motor skill. *Journal of Human Movement Studies, 18,* 107–116.

McCullagh, P., & Little, W.S. (1989). A comparison of modalities in modeling. *Human Performance, 2,* 101–111.

McCullagh, P., & Meyer, K.N. (1997). Learning versus correct models: Influence of model type on the learning of a free-weight squat lift. *Research Quarterly for Exercise and Sport, 68,* 56–61.

McCullagh, P., Stiehl, J., & Weiss, M.R. (1990). Developmental modeling effects on the quantitative and qualitative aspects of motor performance. *Research Quarterly for Exercise and Sport, 61,* 344–350.

McCullagh, P., Weiss, M.R., & Ross, D. (1989). Modeling consideration in motor skill acquisition and performance: An integrated approach. In K.B. Pandolf (Ed.), *Exercise and sport science reviews* (pp. 475–513). Baltimore: Williams & Wilkins.

McPherson, S.L. (1999). Expert-novice differences in performance skills and problem representations of youth and adults during tennis competition. *Research Quarterly for Exercise and Sport, 70,* 233–251.

McPherson, S.L., & Thomas, J.R. (1989). Relation of knowledge and performance in boy's tennis: Age and expertise. *Journal of Experimental Child Psychology, 48,* 190–211.

Meaney, K.S. (1994). Developmental modeling effects on the acquisition, retention, and transfer of a novel motor skill. *Research Quarterly for Exercise and Sport, 65,* 31–39.

Meaney, K.S., & Edwards, R. (1996). Ensenanzas en un gimnasio: An investigation of modeling and verbal rehearsal on the motor performance of Hispanic limited English proficient children. *Research Quarterly for Exercise and Sport, 67,* 44–51.

Mischel, W., & Grusec, J. (1966). Determinants of the rehearsal and transmission of neutral and aversive behaviors. *Journal of Personality and Social Psychology, 3,* 197–205.

Nevett, M.E., & French, K.E. (1997). The development of sport-specific planning, rehearsal, and updating of plans during defensive youth baseball game performance. *Research Quarterly for Exercise and Sport, 68,* 203–214.

Newell, K.M. (1976). Motor learning without knowledge of results through the development of a response recognition mechanism. *Journal of Motor Behavior, 8,* 209–217.

Newell, K.M. (1981). Skill learning. In D. Holding (Ed.), *Human skills* (pp. 203–226). New York: Wiley.

Newell, K.M., Morris, L.R., & Scully, D.M. (1985). Augmented information and the acquisition of skills in physical activity. In R.L. Terjung (Ed.), *Exercise and sport sciences reviews* (pp. 235–261). New York: Macmillan.

Onestak, D.M. (1997). The effect of visuomotor behavior rehearsal (VMBR) and videotaped modeling (VM) on the free-throw performance of intercollegiate athletes. *Journal of Sport Behavior, 20,* 185–198.

Paivio, A. (1971). *Imagery and verbal processes.* New York: Holt, Rinehart and Winston.

Passer, M.W. (1996). At what age are children ready to compete? Some psychological considerations. In F.L. Smoll & R.E. Smith (Eds.), *Children and youth in sport: A biopsychosocial perspective* (pp. 73–86). Madison, WI: Brown & Benchmark.

Pollock, B.J., & Lee, T.D. (1992). Effects of the model's skill level on observational motor learning. *Research Quarterly for Exercise and Sport, 63,* 25–29.

Rejeski, W.J., & Sanford, B. (1984). Feminine-typed females: The role of affective schema in the perception of exercise intensity. *Journal of Sport Psychology, 6,* 197–207.

Richardson, J.R., & Lee, T.D. (1999). The effects of proactive and retroactive demonstrations on learning signed letters. *Acta Psychologica, 101,* 79–90.

Roach, N.K., & Burwitz, L. (1986). Observational learning in motor skill acquisition: The effect of verbal directing cues. In J. Watkins, T. Reilly, & L. Burwitz (Eds.), *Sports science: Proceedings of the 8th Commonwealth and International Conference on Sport, Physical Education, Dance, Recreation and Health* (pp. 349–354). London: E. & F.N. Spon.

Roberton, M.A., Halverson, L.E., & Harper, C.J. (1997). Visual/verbal modeling as a function of children's developmental levels in hopping. In J.E. Clark & J.H. Humphrey (Eds.), *Motor development: Research and reviews* (Vol. 1, pp. 122–147). Reston, VA: National Association for Sport and Physical Education.

Rosenthal, T.L., & Bandura, A. (1978). Psychological modeling: Theory and practice. In S.L. Garfield & A.E. Bergin (Eds.), *Handbook of psychotherapy and behavior change: An empirical analysis* (2nd ed., pp. 621–658). New York: Wiley.

Ross, D., Bird, A.M., Doody, S.G., & Zoeller, M. (1985). Effect of modeling and videotape feedback with knowledge of results on motor performance. *Human Movement Science, 4,* 149–157.

Rothstein, A.L., & Arnold, R.K. (1976). Bridging the gap: Application of research on videotape feedback and bowling. *Motor Skills: Theory into Practice, 1,* 35–62.

Rushall, B.S. (1988). Covert modeling as a procedure for altering an elite athlete's psychological state. *The Sport Psychologist, 2,* 131–140.

Ryan, E.D., & Simons, J. (1981). Cognitive demand, imagery, and frequency of mental rehearsal as factors influencing acquisition of motor skills. *Journal of Sport Psychology, 3,* 35–45.

Ryan, E.D., & Simons, J. (1983). What is learned in mental practice of motor skills: A test of the cognitive-motor hypothesis. *Journal of Sport Psychology, 5,* 419–426.

Salmela, J.H., & Fiorito, P. (1979). Visual cues in ice hockey goaltending. *Canadian Journal of Applied Sport Sciences, 4,* 56–59.

Schmidt, R.A. (1975). A schema theory of discrete motor skill learning. *Psychological Review, 82,* 225–260.

Schmidt, R.A. (1988). *Motor control and learning: A behavioral emphasis.* Champaign, IL: Human Kinetics.

Schoenfelder-Zohdi, B.G. (1992). *Investigating the informational nature of a modeled visual demonstration.* Unpublished doctoral dissertation, Louisiana State University, Baton Rouge.

Schunk, D.H. (1987). Peer models and children's behavioral change. *Review of Educational Research, 57,* 149–174.

Schunk, D.H. (1989a). Self-efficacy and achievement behaviors. *Educational Psychology Review, 1,* 173–208.

Schunk, D.H. (1989b). Social cognitive theory and self-regulated learning. In B.J. Zimmerman & D.H. Schunk (Eds.), *Self-regulated learning and academic achievement: Theory, research, and practice* (pp. 83–110). New York: Springer-Verlag.

Schunk, D.H., & Hanson, A.R. (1985). Peer models: Influence on children's self-efficacy and achievement. *Journal of Educational Psychology, 77,* 313–322.

Schunk, D.H., & Hanson, A.R. (1989a). Influence of peer-model attributes on children's beliefs and learning. *Journal of Educational Psychology, 81,* 431–434.

Schunk, D.H., & Hanson, A.R. (1989b). Self-modeling and children's cognitive skill learning. *Journal of Educational Psychology, 81,* 155–163.

Schunk, D.H., Hanson, R.A., & Cox, P.D. (1987). Peer-model attributes and children's achievement behaviors. *Journal of Educational Psychology, 79,* 54–61.

Schunk, D.H., & Zimmerman, B.J. (1997). Social origins of self-regulatory competence. *Educational Psychologist, 32,* 195–208.

Scully, D.M. (1986). Visual perception of technical execution and aesthetic quality in biological motion. *Human Movement Science, 5,* 185–206.

Scully, D.M. (1987). *Visual perception of biological motion.* Unpublished doctoral dissertation. University of Illinois, Urbana-Champaign.

Scully, D.M., & Newell, K.M. (1985). Observational learning and the acquisition of motor skills: Toward a visual perception perspective. *Journal of Human Movement Studies, 11,* 169–186.

Seat, J.E., & Wrisberg, C.A. (1996). The visual instruction system. *Research Quarterly for Exercise and Sport, 67,* 106–108.

Shea, C.H., Wright, D.L., Wulf, G., & Whitacre, C. (2000). Physical and observational practice afford unique learning opportunities. *Journal of Motor Behavior, 32,* 27–36.

Shea, C.H., & Wulf, G. (1999). Enhancing motor learning through external-focus instruction and feedback. *Human Movement Science, 18,* 553–571.

Shea, C.H., Wulf, G., & Whitacre, C. (1999). Enhancing training efficiency through the use of dyad training. *Journal of Motor Behavior, 31,* 119–125.

Shea, J.B., & Morgan, R.L. (1979). Contextual interference effects on the acquisition, retention, and transfer of a motor skill. *Journal of Experimental Psychology, Human Learning and Memory, 5,* 179–187.

Shebilske, W.L., Regian, J.W., Arthur, W., Jr., & Jordan, J.A. (1992). A dyadic protocol for training complex skills. *Human Factors, 34,* 369–374.

Sheffield, F.N. (1961). Theoretical considerations in the learning of complex sequential tasks from demonstrations and practice. In A.A. Lumsdaine (Ed.), *Student response in programmed instruction* (pp. 13–32). Washington, DC: National Academy of Sciences.

Sidaway, B., & Hand, M.J. (1993). Frequency of modeling effects on the acquisition and retention of a motor skill. *Research Quarterly for Exercise and Sport, 64,* 122–125.

Signorielli, N. (1990). Children, television, and gender roles: Messages and impact. *Journal of Adolescent Health Care, 11,* 50–58.

Southard, D., & Higgins, T. (1987). Changing movement patterns: Effects of demonstration and practice. *Research Quarterly for Exercise and Sport, 58,* 77–80.

Starek, J., & McCullagh, P. (1999). The effect of self-modeling on the performance of beginning swimmers. *The Sport Psychologist, 13,* 269–287.

Starkes, J.L., & Deakin, J.M. (1984). Perception in sport: A cognitive approach to skilled performance. In W.F. Straub & J.M. Williams (Eds.), *Cognitive sport psychology* (pp. 115–128). Lansing, NY: Sport Science Associates.

Starkes, J.L., Deakin, J., Lindley, S., & Crisp, F. (1987). Motor versus verbal recall of ballet sequences by young expert dancers. *Journal of Sport Psychology, 9,* 222–230.

Starkes, J.L., & Lindley, S. (1994). Can we hasten expertise by video simulations? *Quest, 46,* 211–222.

Stipek, D., & MacIver, D. (1989). Developmental change in children's assessment of intellectual competence. *Child Development, 60,* 521–538.

Templin, D.P., & Vernacchia, R.A. (1995). The effect of highlight music videotapes upon the game performance of intercollegiate basketball players. *The Sport Psychologist, 9,* 41–50.

Thelen, M.H., Fry, R.A., Fehrenbach, P.A., & Frautschi, N.M. (1979). Therapeutic videotape and film modeling: A review. *Psychological Bulletin, 86,* 701–720.

Thomas, J.R., French, K.E., & Humphries, C.A. (1986). Knowledge of developmental and sport skill performance: Directions for motor behavior research. *Journal of Sport Psychology, 8,* 259–272.

Thomas, J.R., Pierce, C., & Ridsdale, S. (1977). Age differences in children's ability to model motor behavior. *Research Quarterly, 48,* 592–597.

Triplett, N. (1898). The dynamogenic factors in pacemaking and competition. *American Journal of Psychology, 9,* 507–533.

Vogt, S. (1995). On relations between perceiving, imagining and performing in the learning of cyclical movement sequences. *British Journal of Psychology, 86,* 191–216.

Weeks, D.L. (1992). A comparison of modeling modalities in the observational learning of an externally paced task. *Research Quarterly for Exercise and Sport, 63,* 373–380.

Weeks, D.L., & Choi, J. (1992). Modelling the perceptual component of a coincident-timing skill: The influence of frequency of demonstration. *Journal of Human Movement Studies, 23,* 201–213.

Weeks, D.L., Hall, A.K., & Anderson, L.P. (1996). A comparison of imitation strategies in observational learning of action patterns. *Journal of Motor Behavior, 28,* 348–358.

Weir, P.L., & Leavitt, J.L. (1990). Effects of model's skill level and model's knowledge of results on the performance of a dart throwing task. *Human Movement Science, 9,* 369–383.

Weiss, M.R. (1982). Developmental modeling: Enhancing children's motor skill acquisition. *Journal of Health, Physical Education, Recreation, and Dance, 53,* 49–50, 67.

Weiss, M.R. (1983). Modeling and motor performance: A developmental perspective. *Research Quarterly for Exercise and Sport, 54,* 190–197.

Weiss, M.R., Bredemeier, B.J., & Shewchuk, R.M. (1985). An intrinsic/extrinsic motivation scale for the youth sport setting: A confirmatory factor analysis. *Journal of Sport & Exercise Psychology, 7,* 75–91.

Weiss, M.R., Ebbeck, V., & Rose, D.J. (1992). "Show and tell" in the gymnasium revisited: Developmental differences in modeling and verbal rehearsal effects on motor skill learning and performance. *Research Quarterly for Exercise and Sport, 63,* 292–301.

Weiss, M.R., Ebbeck, V., & Wiese-Bjornstal, D.M. (1993). Developmental and psychological skills related to children's observational learning of physical skills. *Pediatric Exercise Science, 5,* 301–317.

Weiss, M.R., & Klint, K.A. (1987). "Show and tell" in the gymnasium: An investigation of developmental differences in modeling and verbal rehearsal of motor skills. *Research Quarterly for Exercise and Sport, 58,* 234–241.

Weiss, M.R., McCullagh, P., Smith, A.L., & Berlant, A.R. (1998). Observational learning and the fearful child: Influence of peer models on swimming skill performance and psychological responses. *Research Quarterly for Exercise and Sport, 69,* 380–394.

Weiss, M.R., & Troxel, R.K. (1986). Psychology of the injured athlete. *Athletic Training, 21,* 104–109, 154.

White, A., & Hardy, L. (1995). Use of different imagery perspectives on the learning and performance of different motor skills. *British Journal of Psychology, 86,* 169–180.

Whiting, H.T.A. (1988). Imitation and the learning of complex cyclical actions. In O.G. Meijer & K. Roth (Eds.), *Complex motor behavior: "The" motor-action controversy* (pp. 381–401). Amsterdam: North Holland.

Whiting, H.T.A., Bijlard, M.J., & den Brinker, B.P.L.M. (1987). The effect of the availability of a dynamic model on the acquisition of a complex cyclical action. *Quarterly Journal of Experimental Psychology, 39A,* 43–59.

Wiese, D.M., & Weiss, M.R. (1987). Psychological rehabilitation and physical injury: Implication for the sports medicine team. *The Sport Psychologist, 1,* 318–330.

Wiese-Bjornstal, D.M., & Weiss, M.R. (1992). Modeling effects on children's form, kinematics, performance outcome, and cognitive recognition of a sport skill: An integrated perspective. *Research Quarterly for Exercise and Sport, 63,* 67–75.

Williams, A.M., Davids, K., & Williams, J.G. (1999). *Visual perception and action in sport.* London: E. & F.N. Spon.

Williams, A.M., & Grant, A. (1999). Training perceptual skill in sport. *International Journal of Sport Psychology, 30,* 194–220.

Williams, J.G. (1989). Visual demonstrations and movement production: Effects of timing variations in a model's action. *Perceptual and Motor Skills, 68,* 891–896.

Williams, J.G. (1993). Motoric modeling: Theory and research. *Journal of Human Movement Studies, 24,* 237–270.

Willingham, D.B. (1998). A neuropsychological theory of motor skill learning. *Psychological Review, 105,* 558–584.

Winfrey, M.L., & Weeks, D.L. (1993). Effects of self-modeling on self-efficacy and balance beam performance. *Perceptual and Motor Skills, 77,* 907–913.

Wright, D.L., Li, Y., & Coady, W. (1997). Cognitive processes related to contextual interference and observational learning: A replication of Blandin, Proteau and Alain. *Research Quarterly for Exercise and Sport, 68,* 106–109.

Wuyts, I.J., & Buekers, M.J. (1995). The effects of visual and auditory models on the learning of a rhythmical synchronization dance skill. *Research Quarterly for Exercise and Sport, 66,* 105–115.

Yando, R., Seitz, V., & Zigler, E. (1978). *Imitation: A developmental perspective.* Hillsdale, NJ: Erlbaum.

CHAPTER 9

Personality and the Athlete

YVES VANDEN AUWEELE, KURT NYS, RANDY RZEWNICKI, and VEERLE VAN MELE

In contrast with mainstream psychology, where interesting ideas and methodologies have developed, personality research in sport psychology in the 1990s seems to be a moribund field and personality a dirty word. The paradigmatic and methodological fluctuations found in mainstream personology in the 1970s and 1980s were, soon after, incorporated in sport personology (Morgan, 1980). However, there is currently very little activity in this area.

Personality is an old line of research in sport psychology, which dominated the field from the 1950s to the 1970s and remained important in the early 1980s (Aguerri, 1986). A large number of studies and reviews on the topic of sport personology accumulated until the mid-1980s (Landers, 1983; Silva, 1984; Van den Auweele, De Cuyper, Van Mele, & Rzewnicki, 1993; Vealey, 1989, 1992). From the mid-1980s to the present, researchers never stopped studying personality-related concepts (e.g., traits, dispositions, states). Some personality-relevant conceptual progress has been made on the complex relations among constructs, multidimensionality, contextual embedding, and the hierarchical structure of the concepts under consideration (Fox, 1998; Hanin, 1997; Vallerand, 1997). However, little explicit attention is given nowadays to personality research. In those rare articles, few, if any, references are made to the discussions and controversies of earlier decades (e.g., Davis & Mogk, 1994; Gat & McWhirter, 1998; Hassmén, Koivula, & Hansson, 1998). In this review, some vague references were found, but no specific suggestions or proposals for conceptual or methodological progress.

Before writing this chapter, we asked ourselves an important question: what can be added to the seminal major reviews of sport personology research in the past two decades? Bakker, Whiting, and van der Brug (1990), Carron (1980), Fisher (1984), Martens (1975), Morgan (1980), Van den Auweele et al. (1993), and Vealey (1989, 1992) have not left much more to say. Or have they? It is our goal to stimulate sport personality research, so our intention is to go beyond lamenting the limitations and oversimplifications of the past decades. In fact, more explicit attention will be given to the interface between mainstream personality and sport personology. Where possible, reflection on the tacit assumptions of the scientific practice in sport psychology will be undertaken. Our view is that personality is a meaningful concept and the measurement of it a useful tool. It can be used to sharpen thinking on the complex interplay of athletes, competitive situations, and their behaviors and practices. In the quest to be scientific, researchers may have lost sight of a goal to understand psychological processes in sport (Strean & Roberts, 1992). Therefore, the focus of this chapter is on theories and concepts and how well they can answer relevant sport psychological questions, rather than on any technical sophistication of new research methods and statistics.

The mere listing of errors in previously used methodologies and interpretations of data, though necessary, does not markedly improve the quality of personology research. Corrective suggestions have been published previously (e.g., Carron, 1980; Martens, 1975). There is also the possibility that the criticisms of personology research are somewhat exaggerated (Landers, 1983; Martens, 1987). In this chapter, a brief overview is presented of the paradigmatic and methodological trends and evolutions from the 1950s to the 1980s in both mainstream psychology and sport personology. Then research is reevaluated in the light of the more sophisticated integration tools now available as well as a more differentiated view of the underlying trait paradigms. The third and main purpose is to identify and to operationalize new paradigms and strategies in mainstream personality research that can be integrated in the objectives of sport psychology research. In addition, an example of a new technique used in a sport setting for elite athletes is elaborated on.

CONCEPTUAL FRAMEWORK FOR THE STUDY OF PERSONALITY

Although many attempts have been made to establish the boundaries of research by defining personality, the focus here is on two fundamentally different conceptions. They are crucial to understanding directions in personality research and history in both mainstream psychology and sport psychology. Furthermore, the flow (interface) of new ideas should be facilitated. In the past, research was based mainly on the long-standing conception of personality in terms of behavioral dispositions or traits that predispose individuals to activate relevant behaviors. The purpose of research based on this definition has been the identification of the personality traits of elite athletes compared to nonelite athletes (Van den Auweele et al., 1993; Vealey, 1992).

Research has also been framed within a process conception of personality (see Magnusson & Törestad, 1993; Mischel & Shoda, 1995). In this orientation, personality is defined as a system of conscious and unconscious mediating processes whose interactions are manifested in predictable or coherent patterns of functioning in individuals. Personality as such is an abstraction. What exists is a living, active, and purposeful organism, functioning and developing as an integrated being. Based on this view, personality research is defined as the study of how and why individuals think, feel, act, and react as they do. The question here is How does a particular athlete function? rather than Which qualities remain invariant across situations and are distinctive for that athlete? The focus is, for example, on the meaningful patterns that characterize the functioning of top-level athletes, especially when they are performing optimally, and on the processes that underlie those patterns (Jackson, 1995; Jackson & Roberts, 1992).

Elite Performance in Relation to Predictability, Lawfulness, and Functionality

The criteria used to describe a successful performer are related to the trait and process conceptions of personality, the role of prediction, and the definition of functionality. The prediction of behavior as well as why, when, and how certain mediating processes affect behavior and the outcome of behavior have been major concerns in psychology. According to Magnusson and Törestad (1993), the concept of prediction is closely connected with a trait orientation toward personality and a mechanistic and deterministic model of human behavior. In contrast, in their process interpretation of personality, the term *lawfulness* is introduced to describe individual functioning that proceeds according to a set of identifiable principles but is not necessarily predictable (much as chaos theory describes dynamic processes that are lawful but unpredictable).

Neither predictability nor lawfulness of behavior or of functioning offer information on the functionality of behavior in a certain situation. However, in sport psychology, the definition, identification, and measurement of the functionality of predictable or lawful behaviors of individual athletes are of major importance (Apitzsch & Berggren, 1993; Hanin, 1997; Schlattmann & Hackfort, 1991; Van den Auweele, Depreeuw, Rzewnicki, & Ballon, 1999). Functionality implies the identification of relationships among personality characteristics or patterns, whether defined in terms of dispositions or processes, and some criterion of success. Functionality also implies the identification of the nature of such characteristics or patterns, whether determined by or related to genetic or environmental factors. For example, the relation between emotions and functionality seems to be a complex one. Hanin (1997) distinguished two independent factors: positivity-negativity and optimality-dysfunctionality. Both positive and negative emotions can be functional, optimal, and helpful, or dysfunctional and harmful to the athlete's performance. A discussion with a coach can generate anger and deteriorate the working relationship but can be functional to the athlete's training motivation and determination.

In research, an outcome or process criterion has been used to define success (Van den Auweele et al., 1999). The widely used interpretation is based on the deterministic model and the outcome criterion. Elite athletes are those who are eligible for competition at the national, international, or Olympic level, or are engaged in professional sports. This definition includes athletes who may not actually compete at this level, but who are described as eligible for such competitions (e.g., Johnson, 1972). Less research is based on the process conception of personality and on a process criterion (i.e., how the athlete acts and feels in competitive situations). Success of an athlete is defined here in reference to personal standards. These can be optimal for him or her or can be damaging, substandard, or even potentially threatening. Examples can be found in research on the functionality of task- versus ego-orientations

(Duda, 1998) (e.g., zone of optimal functioning, Hanin, 1997) and on peak performances (e.g., Jackson, 1995; Jackson & Roberts, 1992; Singer, 1988). In this chapter, research on both criteria is reviewed. Both are valid in realizing sport psychology objectives, such as diagnosis and eventual intervention (counseling, selection, psychological skills training, and behavioral modification) to help athletes enhance performance or come closer to realizing their potential and well-being.

Personology and Related Areas

Until the 1980s, most research reported in the sport psychology literature concerning the psychological attributes of the elite performer had been placed under the heading *sport personology* or *personality research*. Recently, however, important theories, concepts, methodologies, and data related to other psychological research areas that implicitly refer to personology (traits, stability, uniqueness, hierarchical structure, etc.) have been introduced in the study of the recreational and elite athlete. Evidence has converged from diverse studies on self-perceptions, personal beliefs about performance outcomes, self-efficacy, perceived control, motivation, goal orientation, attentional and attributional styles, affect, and emotions. Vealey (1992) suggests that much of what is studied in sport psychology could be called the study of personality in sport.

These topics can be explicitly integrated or included in the process conception of personality elaborated by Magnusson and Törestad (1993) and Mischel and Shoda (1995). Although various concepts and data from many research areas are related to conceptions of personality, they are addressed only briefly here. The reasons are threefold: First, they are covered in other chapters; second, it would be an encyclopedic task to review the recent developments for each of these topics; third and most important, the accumulation of all these fragments would not increase the knowledge on how athletes *integrate and organize* thoughts and emotions and show *coherent patterns* of behavior in various situations. The main task of personality research is to focus on the ongoing interplay of all the above-mentioned aspects and processes in the athlete's functioning in relation to types of competitive situations.

Overview of Major Paradigmatic and Methodological Trends from 1950 to the Mid-1980s

The emerging field of sport psychology has gone through various stages of inquiry into the nature of personality, and the trait and state debate has continued. Sport psychologists have debated which personality paradigm is the most

efficacious to understand, explain, and predict behaviors in sport situations (Vealey, 1989). For personality psychologists, the trait concept has been a central within-person construct intended to predict future behavior. Traits have been defined as "stable internal structures that serve as pre-dispositions to behavior and could therefore be used as adequate predictors of behavior" (Sherman & Fazio, 1983, p. 310). Individual differences can be subdivided into competencies (e.g., technical sport talent), affective-dynamic traits (e.g., sensation seeking, goal-orientation, trait anxiety), and cognitive traits (e.g., beliefs). According to traditional formal trait theories, each individual can be characterized by his or her position in a number of so-called common traits, or universal personality dimensions on which all individuals can be situated (e.g., introversion-extroversion).

Many personality questionnaires have been constructed to detect the position of individuals on those dimensions with the intent "to learn how a person might be expected to react and to behave in various situations" (Singer, 1988, p. 89). The prototypical questionnaire is a self-report consisting of a number of personality adjectives (e.g., I am accurate, or adventurous, or sentimental), where respondents have to make a judgment on the degree to which each item is applicable to themselves. The traditional nomothetic trait psychologies share three assumptions: (1) Individuals are cross-situationally consistent; (2) behavior represents a temporal stability; and (3) there is a co-occurrence of behavioral manifestations referring to the same underlying trait.

From a different perspective, the importance of situational factors in predicting behavior is undisputed among major trait theorists (Pervin, 1985). Mischel reviewed empirical evidence concerning the basic assumptions of the common trait theories. His 1968 book, *Personality and Assessment,* is widely accepted as marking the onset of a period questioning the utility of the trait concept. He repeated weak correlations (between .20 and .50 with a mean of .30) between traits (measured by questionnaires) and some behavioral criteria. Mischel introduced the term *personality coefficient* to indicate the low predictability of behavior by personality variables. Many personality psychologists, convinced that traits could not serve as predictors of future behavior, abandoned trait research and turned to research on the predictability of behavior from situational variables. However, despite the fundamental criticism of the trait concept, research to determine the basic dimensions of personality has never stopped. Moreover, there is much contemporary interest in trait research. In the early 1990s, factor analysis allowed the "discovery" of the five basic dimensions of personality (Costa & McCrae, 1992; Goldberg, 1992): surgency, agreeableness, conscientiousness, emotional stability versus neuroticism, and openness to experience (John, 1990). Digman (1990), in reviewing the research, supported the emergence of the five personality factors. However, other researchers remain critical of trait theory.

In the 1970s, several research directions and strategies appeared with the common message that they could present a way out of the crisis without abandoning trait psychology. The most widely accepted strategy in the disposition approach is to acknowledge the low cross-sectional consistency found from situation to situation. Then an individual's behavior is aggregated on a given dimension (e.g., anxiety) over many different situations to estimate an overall true score or act-trend (Buss & Craik, 1983; Epstein, 1979; Mischel & Peake, 1982). Such aggregation, carried out with the correlational analysis, provides evidence that people differ significantly on a given dimension (e.g., anxiety) and demonstrate stable overall individual differences. Other strategies have suggested the use of moderator variables, which specify the conditions under which the trait concept remains useful. This research has been summarized by Sherman and Fazio (1983). Some of these conditions (moderator variables) and different research directions in conservative support of trait theory will be briefly described here.

One interpretation of the literature in favor of trait theory is that the behavior of a relatively small number of people is presumably predictable from measures of traits. Only individuals low in self-monitoring (Snyder, 1979, 1983) or those with a high degree of private self-consciousness (Fenigstein, Scheier, & Buss, 1975) should show consistency between self-reports of traits and actual overt behavior.

Second, some traits are useful for describing and predicting people. There are two versions of this position. Some scholars suggest the existence of stable versus unstable traits. The stable trait perspective suggests that people should show high trait-behavior consistency, but only for stable traits, such as punctuality (McGowan & Gormly, 1976). The unstable trait perspective is that the behavior of individuals will be predictable only for those traits that are relevant for the particular individual. A substantial trait-behavior consistency may exist only for traits that are identified by the person as important (Kenrick & Stringfield, 1980; Markus, 1977). Another line of research defending trait theory stresses that trait-behavior consistency will vary as a function of the situation. To the extent that there

are strong situational pressures and/or that situations are norm-regulated, individual differences will be minimized and the correlation between the trait and the corresponding behavior will be small. Proposed is that trait measurements could serve as predictors of future behavior only in situations low in constraint (Price & Bouffard, 1974) or weak in pressures to conform (Monson, Hesley, & Chernick, 1982).

A consequence of the moderator approach is that general conclusions are limited to those people for whom the moderator variable is applicable. For example, implications can be drawn for low self-monitoring individuals who guide their behavioral choices on the basis of information from relevant internal states. Conclusions cannot be drawn for high self-monitors when relationships between behavior and underlying characteristics should be minimal because the influence of situational and interpersonal cues of social appropriateness is too strong. Theoretically, it should be possible to specify many moderator variables in a large multivariate design (Bem, 1983; Krahé, 1992) to obtain a generalized system. However, that would require large groups of people (Brody, 1988), which, in elite sport, is unrealistic. Moreover, the question remains why traits or situations should be predictable for some people and not for others.

The lack of empirical support for cross-situational stability, which is a basic assumption of trait theory, has promoted the adoption of an interactionistic position. However, the concept of interactionism has different meanings (e.g., Claeys, 1980). In some publications, the person-situation interactionism seems nothing more than a statement that the person and the situation are codeterminers of behavior. This is a trivial statement: No psychologist (and no trait theorist) has ever doubted that behavior is a function of environmental as well as person variables. As Fisher (1977, p. 190) stated: "Trait theorists really are not so naive as to discount environmental influences." According to Claeys (1980), analysis of the publications of modern interactionists reveals the existence of three interpretations of a person-situation interaction: organismic, statistical, and dynamic.

Organismic interactionism stresses the reciprocal causal interaction between personality factors and situational characteristics. On the one hand, the actual behavior is a function of the situation as perceived and interpreted by the individual. This perception and interpretation is influenced by preexisting cognitive-dynamic person variables (e.g., attitudes). On the other hand, those personality characteristics are seen as the result of the exposure to past situations, which is an adoption of a social learning view. Proponents of dynamic interactionism argue that the exposure of the individual to certain situations is a function of the personality characteristics of that individual. By his or her overt behavior, the person can create a situation that, in combination with personality traits, elicits ensuing behavior. Snyder is convinced that individuals have a good deal of latitude to choose the kinds of situations they engage in and also the ability to alter situations they have entered, except in artificial settings (as in laboratory studies) and other unique cases. His experiments (e.g., Snyder & Gangestad, 1982) support the position that individuals may choose settings and will try to alter situations in ways that reflect their traits (see Magnusson & Törestad, 1993; Mischel & Shoda, 1995).

Sport Personology

As in mainstream psychology, there was a cry for abandoning research on person factors or at least for discarding the trait concept in the sport psychology literature (Landers, 1983; Morgan, 1978). The development of new types of measurements, the selection of relevant traits to examine, and a plea for an interactionistic approach were proposed. Early research in sport psychology was characterized by a tradition of between-groups comparisons; specifically, athletes were compared with nonathletes, successful athletes with less successful ones, and athlete groups representing different sports were compared. Some scholars speculated that such data could be useful for talent detection, prediction, and selection. By comparing the personality profile of an athlete with the profile of an elite performer in a particular sport, it was thought that one might be able to answer such questions as: Is this youngster a good investment who merits placement in an intensive training program? Will this individual excel in high-level competitions, as elite performers do, due to the right temperament and motivation (see Durand-Bush and Salmela, this volume)?

The tests typically used were nomothetic trait inventories, such as the 16 Personality Factors (16PF; Institute for Personality and Ability Testing, 1986) and the Eysenck Personality Inventory (EPI; Eysenck & Eysenck, 1964, 1975). According to Fisher (1984), more than 1,000 sport personality studies were published during the 1960s and 1970s. Aside from some moderate evaluations—as presented in Singer's (1988) report that conclusive evidence is lacking, or in Browne and Mahoney's conclusion: "A few hints garnered from this research were interesting, though they held no great surprises" (1984, p. 610)—contrasting evaluations can be observed.

Some sport personality researchers, such as Martens (1975) and Rushall (1975), wrote that general trait measures were worthless for the purpose of predicting relevant sport behavior. Conversely, Morgan (1980) consistently defended a contrasting viewpoint. He argued that existing research favorable to the hypothesis that traits are useful was excluded from those pessimistic reviews, and he presented optimistic evidence that elite athletes do display unique personality characteristics. Morgan reported that his mental health model was effective in predicting success in athletics. According to him, there was substantial empirical support for this mental health model, as displayed in the "Iceberg Profile." "An athlete who is neurotic, depressed, anxious, schizoid, introverted, confused, fatigued, and scores low on psychic vigor will tend to be unsuccessful in comparison to an athlete who is characterized by the absence of such traits" (Morgan, 1980, p. 62).

In several publications, successful athletes were characterized by such traits as emotional stability, high need for achievement, assertion, and dominance (Alderman, 1974; Cooper, 1969; Kane, 1964; Ogilvie, 1976). Concerning the logic behind such findings, Fisher spoke of the "survival of the fittest" (1977, p. 92). Nevertheless, discrepancies in the interpretation of research existed. They can be explained, at least in part, by difficulties in interpreting data. As Martens (1981, p. 493) observed: "Perhaps the most fundamental reason for the inconclusive findings is that the trait approach has not been based on any conceptual or theoretical framework." And as Singer (1988, p. 92) noted, "So many and varied psychological tests are available and have been used, with varied groups of subjects." The negative evaluation of the atheoretical use of the personality measurements in the studies on the characteristics of athletes was unanimous, as illustrated by Ryan: "The research in this area has been the 'shot gun' variety. By that I mean the investigators grabbed the nearest and most convenient personality test, and the closest sport group, and with little or no theoretical basis for their selection fired into the air to see what they could bring down. It isn't surprising that firing into the air at different times and at different places, and using different ammunition, should result in different findings. In fact it would be surprising if the results weren't contradictory and somewhat confusing." (Qtd. in Straub, 1977, p. 177)

Although the atheoretical character or the lack of any conceptual framework in the sport personology research can be considered its most fundamental deficiency, serious methodological shortcomings have been identified as well (Carron, 1980; Hardman, 1973; Heyman, 1982; Martens,

1975; Morgan, 1980; Silva, 1984). The problems most commonly mentioned included:

1. Little or no concern for clear definitions and/or operationalizations. Crucial variables such as elite and nonelite athletes and successful and unsuccessful athletes should be carefully defined in advance. An a priori rationale for the proposed relationship between the predictors being considered and successful athletic performance should be provided. Several inventories were included, for example, an anxiety scale; however, this does not mean that those anxiety operationalizations are equivalent, or refer to the same construct.

2. The use of poor sampling techniques. For convenience, intact teams of athletes were selected, with considerable heterogeneity of skill level and homogeneity of environmental influences. This makes generalizations of the conclusions to other teams limited.

3. The use of inappropriate statistical analyses. Critics mention the reliance on univariate statistical analyses when multivariate procedures are appropriate, and the reliance on average scores representing no individual athlete in the sample because extreme scores often dramatically affect the mean.

4. The misuse of personality measurements. Tests were selected without regard for their origin or for the rationale of their development. The Minnesota Multiphasic Personality Inventory (MMPI), for example, was not developed for measuring the normal person's personality. The inappropriate use of that particular test for analyzing the personality of normal athletes invalidates conclusions of the research.

5. Where the data of between-group comparisons are relational, some researchers have assumed them to be causal.

It is impossible to assess the extent to which sport psychology researchers reacted to the pessimism about the early sport personality investigations when they advocated situationistic research. However, when research is associated with a situationistic perspective, when behavior is exclusively seen as the product of environmental variables, there is consequently no belief in the utility of assessing personality traits. As Martens (1975, p. 18) notes: "The central assumption of situationism is that individuals behave differently across situations and that behavior across subjects is minimally different within similar situations." In other words, situationists renounce the whole concept of personality.

It is evident that the studies in which a situational approach was used were not included in Vealey's content analysis (1989) of the sport personality research between 1974 and 1987. Several quotations, however, suggest that pure situationism, with its total neglect of interindividual differences and its exclusive reliance on external variables, has not seen much success in sport psychology. Situationism is seen as "an overreaction to trait psychology" (Martens, 1975, p. 19), or as "an antithesis of personologism . . . going too far to the other extreme" (Horsfall, Fisher, & Morris, 1975, p. 61). It seems reasonable that the rebuff of the situationistic paradigm by sport psychologists was influenced by the rejection of the central assumption of situationism in mainstream psychology. The influence of the negative evaluation of the situationistic model by personality researchers in mainstream psychology is illustrated in the theoretical viewpoint of Rushall (1978, pp. 98–99): "The reactionary approach away from general, trans-situational theories of personality to pure situational considerations was also found to be deficient. The proposal that behavior was controlled solely by circumstantial contingencies was shown to be limited in its accountability for behavior predictions." Undoubtedly, it was interactionism that was recommended by the leading sport psychologists to replace the trait paradigm (Straub, 1977).

To summarize, noteworthy attempts were made to defend trait psychology by aggregating the individual's behavior across situations and by specifying the conditions under which the trait concept remained useful. Sport personology shifted paradigmatically from a trait approach, through a flirtation with the situationistic approach, to interactionism. The most fundamental deficiencies of the past sport personology research have been its atheoretical character, the lack of useful hypotheses, and methodological shortcomings.

PERSONALITY OF ELITE PERFORMERS AND THE PREDICTION OF SUCCESS

Aggregation Using Visual Inspection and Meta-Analysis

Hardman (1973) suggested using visual inspection to compare the results of studies in which the same test (measuring the same trait) was administered to comparable athlete samples, with the appropriate (population) norms. Carron (1980) recommended a continuation of the work Hardman had begun. Landers's (1983) suggestion to go beyond a mere inspection of comparable data and to report more statistically integrated results on the topic of personality and performance was evidenced by the increased popularity of meta-analysis (Cooper, 1990; Halliwell & Gauvin, 1982; Wolf, 1986). To exemplify these aggregation procedures, studies from two topics will be described. In one, the existence of extroversion trait differences was analyzed (Eysenck, Nias, & Cox, 1982). Research on mood differences, as determined by the Iceberg Profile (Morgan, 1985), when comparing elite and nonelite athletes and the elite and nonathletes will also be presented (Renger, 1993b).

Extroversion

Vanden Auweele et al. (1993) tested the extroversion hypothesis with meta-analysis using the data that Hardman (1973) reported to test his hypothesis with visual inspection. The data collected for this analysis covered 25 studies on 1,042 elite performers. The hypothesis was that there would be no difference between athletes and the normal population on extroversion as measured by 16PF, EPI, or EPQ (Eysenck Personality Questionnaire). Results revealed that elite athletes did not differ from the normal population on extroversion. Open and closed skill sport athletes compared to population norms also revealed no differences.

Eysenck et al. (1982) stated that differences could be expected between types of sport, between team and individual sports, and even within the same sport. However, visual inspection of the data in the Van den Auweele et al. (1993) study showed that the sport did not seem to account for any difference in extroversion. Positive difference scores were obtained with athletes engaged in distance running, rowing, shooting, wrestling, rugby, swimming, track and field, and sailing. Negative scores were associated with distance running, table tennis, badminton, wrestling, fencing, hockey, rodeo, cycling, shooting, and sailing.

The Iceberg Profile of Mood States (POMS)

Using visual inspection of 18 studies, Van den Auweele et al. (1993) determined whether elite athletes differ from nonathletes (population norms) on the POMS. They concluded that elite American athletes displayed the Iceberg Profile especially during training periods before competition and that none of the studies contained irrefutable results contradicting the existence of a profile for elite athletes in comparison with the general population. Rowley, Landers, Kyllo, and Etnier (1995) conducted a meta-analysis with 33 POMS studies to find out whether the Iceberg Profile could differentiate between successful and less successful athletes. They found an overall effect size of 0.15, which was significantly different from zero but accounted for only 1% of the variance. These results suggest that across different sports, successful athletes possess a mood profile only slightly more positive than less successful athletes. This means that the utility of the POMS in predicting athletic success is more than questionable.

Multivariate Analysis, Multidimensional Models, and Multimethodologies in Research on the Elite Athlete

Paradigmatic and Methodological Considerations

Most researchers who have examined the psychological characteristics of elite athletes have conducted univariate techniques of analysis within a unidimensional approach, (i.e., examining only psychological variables). The use of multivariate techniques, multidimensional designs, and multimethod approaches has been recommended to enhance the possibilities of performance prediction, whether performance has been operationalized in terms of differences between elite/successful/qualifier versus nonelite/nonsuccessful/nonqualifier or in terms of some direct measurement of ability (e.g., Marsh, Richards, Johnson, Roche, & Tremayne, 1994). (See Table 9.1 for variables used with elite athletes.) The use of multivariate statistical techniques such as multiple regression, discriminant analysis, and factor and cluster analysis has been proposed to examine the interrelations among predictor variables. Path analysis and structural equation modeling have been suggested to test complex, hierarchical models and causal relationships (Dishman, 1982; Landers, 1989; Morgan, 1980; Régnier, Salmela, & Russell, 1993; Tanaka, Panter, Winborne, & Huba, 1990). Using these types of analyses, predictor variables, which are correlated with the performance criterion but not with each other, will account for more of the variance. The structural equation modeling technique allows for more theoretically conceived research in which hypothesized causal relationships between selected variables and a performance or other functionality criterion (Reeds, 1985; Tanaka et al., 1990) can be tested with multivariate procedures.

Since the early 1970s, some scholars have strongly advocated the use of psychobiological and multidimensional models. In addition to psychological variables, such models include physiological (e.g., heart rate, blood lactate), morphological (e.g., weight, body fat), and skill (e.g., skating speed, stick handling) variables. The use of these models has been suggested in order to deal more adequately with the complex nature of human functioning and the multifactorial determination of performance (Deshaies, Pargman,

Table 9.1 Psychological Variables Used in Multivariate, Multidimensional Research with Elite Athletes[1]

Trait Measures[2]	Sport-Specific State Measures[2]
Anxiety and neuroticism-related traits (high-low anxiety)	Arousal/anxiety-related variables
• Emotional stability: 16PF-C (1,R) (4,H)	• Tension: POMS-t (5,W)
• Trait anxiety: STAI-DY2 (9,DR)	• Anger: POMS-a (5,W)
• Hypochondriasis: MMPI-Hs (2a,R)	• Global mood: POMS (9,DR)
• Lie scale: MMPI (2a,R)	• Specific state anxiety patterns:
• F-scale (frequency): MMPI (2a,R)	STAI-DY1 (10,At)
• Confident-apprehensive: 16PF-O (4,H)	MA (6,D)
• Trusting-suspicious: 16PF-L (4,HI)	• Sport-specific anxiety:
	MA (6, W) (6,D) (8,At)
Tough-poise/tender-minded	• Motivation: MA (8,At)
• Tough-minded/tender-minded: 16PF-I (1,R) (4,H)	• Mental preparation/psych-up:
• Sober-enthusiastic: 16PF-F (4,H)	MA (3,W) (8,At)
• Psychopathic deviate: MMPI-Pd (2a,R)	• Self-talk: MA (3,W) (6,W) (6,D)
	• Load-carrying capacity: (10,At)
Extroversion/introversion	
• (Social) Introversion-extroversion:	Feelings related to the appraisal of concordance/discordance between task difficulty and own capacity
MMPI-Si (2a,R)	• Self-confidence: MA (3,W) (8,At) (11,Ar)
EPI (2b,R)	• Role performance: MA (3,W)
• Group-dependent/self-sufficient:	• Feeling close to maximum potential: MA (3,W)
16PF-Q2 (1,R)	
• Shy-bold: 16PF-H (4,H)	Interpersonal relationships
	• Relation athlete-parents: (10,At)
Cognitive factors	• Relation athlete-trainer: (10,At)
• Intelligence: 16PF-B (3,H)	
	Cognitive factors
	• Thoughts: MA (3,W) (6,W) (6,D)
	• Performance attributions: Ma (6,W) (6,D) (11,Ar)
	• Concentration: MA (3,W) (6,W) (8,At)
	• Dreams: MA (3,W)
	• Distraction: MA (3,W)
	• Cognitive coping: MA (3,W) (6,D)
	• Blocking: MA (3,W)

[1] Only significant measures are reported here. The titles of the tests are indicated following each item. For identification of sports and studies, see legend, Figure 9.1.
[2] The trait variables are categorized according to the second-order factors (16PF). Sport-specific and state variables are categorized according to their similarity in denotation.

& Thiffault, 1979; Feltz, 1992; Landers et al., 1986b; Morgan, 1973; Prapavessis, Grove, McNair, & Cable, 1992; Silva, Shultz, Haslam, & Murray, 1981; Singer, 1988; Williams, 1978). Similarly, Feltz (1987, 1989), Brewer and Hunter (1989), and Vealey (1992) have also advocated the planned use of several methods or instruments (multimethod) to compensate for weaknesses in the research. Vealey (1994) reported in her review of *The Sport Psychologist* from 1987 to 1992 that 14% of the articles included multiple methods. (See also Van Mele, Van den Auweele, & Rzewnicki, 1995, for an example of the combined use of questionnaires, interviews, and grid methodology.) Although some studies have empirically demonstrated the superiority of the psychobiological approach by producing greater overall prediction accuracy than either a physiological or a psychological model (Deshaies et al., 1979; Landers et al., 1986b; Morgan, 1973; Silva et al., 1981),

there is still a paucity of research using multidimensional models.

In 1984, Silva questioned why, a decade after Morgan's (1973) suggestion to use psychobiological models, the further refinement and development of sport-specific multidimensional models had not been pursued to a greater extent. Presently, there has been no change in research approaches. Most of the recent research is of a unidimensional or unidisciplinary psychological nature. The explanation may be the trend toward specialization, not toward multidisciplinary research. Exercise physiologists attempt to explain performance in biological terms, whereas sport psychologists rely on psychological constructs. Although this is undoubtedly a promising line of research, there are some problems. One of the difficulties is the existence of disparate findings in multivariate research conducted with elite athletes (Highlen & Bennett, 1983; Renger, 1993a).

Also, there is the situation where the overall prediction accuracy is perhaps too impressive in some studies. For example, Nagle, Morgan, Hellickson, Serfass, and Alexander (1975) and Silva et al. (1981) found classification accuracy of 80% and 93.33%, respectively, in wrestlers. One might therefore advise at least a little caution in generalizing the results, as well as careful reflection on the conclusiveness of the studies. In addition to the methodological shortcomings mentioned earlier in this chapter (e.g., the criteria used to distinguish elite athletes), Landers et al. (1986a), Highlen and Bennett (1983), Haase (1984), and Renger (1993a) have identified two other methodological issues that may be partly responsible for these disparate findings.

First, the small sample sizes relative to the number of variables examined is often questionable. Researchers are frequently limited to small samples for practical reasons and opt to enter all possible predictors in a stepwise regression analysis. In so doing, they avoid the responsibility of having to make a priori predictors that are theoretically hypothesized to be more related to athletic success. An inadequate subject-to-variable ratio is associated with instability of the data, poor statistical power, and an overestimation of the amount of explained variance.

Second, the existence of a unique set of characteristics for high-level athletes across all sports is questionable. Highlen and Bennett (1983) argue that the converse assumption, that each sport requires its own unique set of characteristics, seems equally untenable. They suggest a typological hypothesis that there are types of sports that are similar to each other on psychological features. To explain disparate findings between elite wrestlers and gymnasts, they conducted research on open- and closed-skill athletes. They suggested similar research on contact versus noncontact sport athletes and in sports requiring different types of motor coordination, such as skating and golf.

Tentative Conclusions Based on Multivariate/Multidimensional Research

Certain multivariate/multidimensional/multimethod studies help integrate points made previously in this chapter:

1. The trait position has not been abandoned, although researchers have become progressively more selective in measuring traits according to their assumed relationship to performance in a specific sport (Landers et al., 1986a; Morgan, 1978; Reeds, 1985; Renger, 1993a; Silva et al., 1981; Van den Auweele et al., 1993).

2. More sport-specific instruments and personality dimension–specific instruments have been constructed (e.g., anxiety: Martens, Burton, Vealey, Bump, & Smith, 1990; attention: Nideffer, 1990; goal orientation: Duda & Whitehead, 1998; self-confidence: Vealey, Hayashi, Garner-Holman, & Giacobbi, 1998). Sports can be grouped according to their physical, psychomotor, and psychological demands, including open- versus closed-skill, direct or contact versus parallel or noncontact, and team versus individual. This can be considered an expression of the organismic interactionist position (Grove & Heard, 1997; Highlen & Bennett, 1983; Mahoney, Gabriel, & Perkins, 1987; Newcombe & Boyle, 1995).

3. There is interest in the longitudinal and sequential aspects of psychological variables, including their measurement prior to and during competition (Highlen & Bennett, 1983; Renger, 1993a; Van Mele et al., 1995). This area will be discussed in a later section concerning new directions in sport personology.

4. Limitations of self-report measures in psychological assessment have been acknowledged (Mahoney et al., 1987; Van Mele et al., 1995).

5. Some scholars, although aware of the limited value of psychological factors in predicting performance, see no need to be masochistic: "Any variable that accounts for 20–45% of the variance should theoretically be useful in predicting behavior or utilized in concert with other dependent variables" (Morgan, 1980, p. 72). Others (Reeds, 1985) even argue that in research on superior athletes, psychological factors might be the most important consideration. The rationale is that top-level athletes in a specific sport are, to a great extent, homogeneous with regard to physiological, technical, and tactical parameters. Therefore, differentiation in performance might be attributed mostly to psychological factors. But, as can be observed regularly in sport personality research, the opposite has also been concluded. Van Ingen Schenau, De Koning, Bakker, and De Groot (1996) warned that given the small number of significant correlations, the benefit of this type of research is limited. It is also apparent from the work of Silva, Shultz, Haslam, and Murray (1981) that physiological measures have greater discriminatory power than psychological profiles, even among physiologically homogeneous samples. Hence, where physical variations are substantial, it is entirely unreasonable to expect mood to predict achievement.

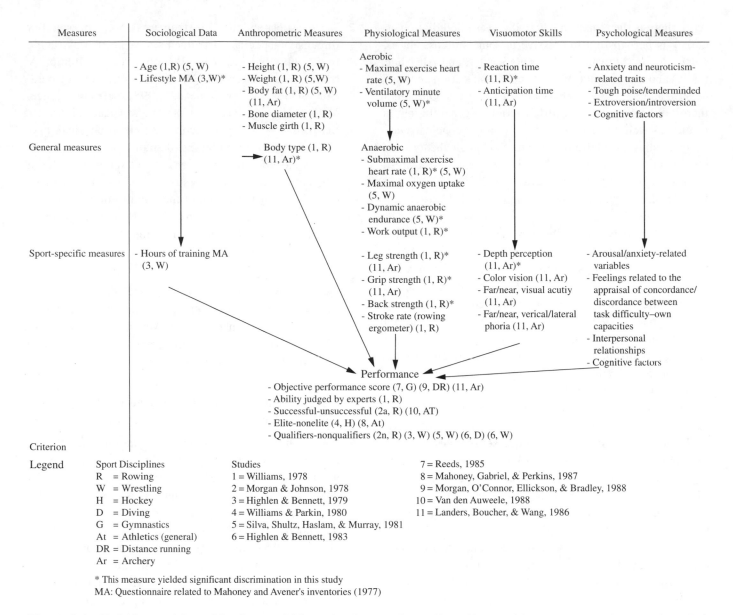

Figure 9.1 Variables used in multivariate, multidimensional research on elite athletes, with arrows suggesting a path-analytic design.

6. To identify some characteristics that have been reported to distinguish elite and nonelite athletes, we selected, for the 1993 edition of this chapter, 11 multidimensional, multivariate studies according to the stringent criteria mentioned earlier. See Figure 9.1 for a pathanalytical design of the results, which is consistent with requests for an integrated multidimensional model. The multivariate studies reviewed were designed to test relationships between some general and/or sport-specific psychological, physiological,

anthropometric, and skill variables and some criterion of performance, or to test mutual relationships among these variables.

In Figure 9.1, the numbers following each variable identify the researchers, and the letters indicate the sport sample examined. A star indicates that the variable has shown a significant contribution to discriminate between elite and nonelite groups or that it correlated significantly with a performance criterion. Arrows indicate the relationships tested.

NEW DEVELOPMENTS IN PERSONOLOGY AND SPORT PERSONOLOGY

The situation regarding personality research in the 1990s is ambiguous. On the one hand, the personality field has been abandoned by leading researchers, who have directed their attention and efforts to more specific themes and constructs, such as attributions, goal orientations, self-confidence, motivation, anxiety, and attention (Duda, 1998; Singer, 1994). The criticisms of personality research were a major impetus to search for sound theoretical foundations and sophisticated statistical tools. On the other hand, researchers have continued using personality-related concepts (e.g., traits, dispositions, states), and in their constructs, they have elaborated concepts (e.g., hierarchical structures, contextual-related dispositions) that fit in the new *process* conception of personality.

Recent theoretical developments in mainstream personology and in psychological methodology have converged because of these applied interests. For example, how should an athlete's development toward excellence in performance be monitored? What needs to change? What are the ambitions, the values, the priorities, and the goals of the athlete? What kind of stressor causes what sort of response, in which kind of athlete, in what types of situations?

This section describes some paradigmatic and methodological developments that have been selected because of their relevance in the context of mental training and counseling. First, a description of four developments is given, and for each, an appropriate research methodology is indicated. Then some of the attempts to apply these new concepts and methods in sport psychology are reviewed. Finally, Mischel's cognitive-affective system theory (e.g., Mischel & Shoda, 1995) is described, with special attention to those aspects that show either the link or the contrast between traditional and new concepts in personality research.

One new development is related to the emphasis on behavioral assessment rather than self-description techniques, such as questionnaires and projective techniques (Barlow & Hersen, 1984; Barrios & Hartmann, 1986; Hartmann, Roper, & Bradford, 1979; Nelson & Hayes, 1986; Staats, 1986). Second, there is interest in intraindividual versus interindividual research, or for idiographic versus nomothetic research (Barlow & Hersen, 1984; Killpatrick & Cantrill, 1960; Runyan, 1983). The intraindividual/idiographic approach is concerned with the psychological structure within the individual, such as in the interaction among different behavioral components (i.e., cognitions, emotions,

and overt behavior). Furthermore, there is interest in the life history of the individual.

A third development is that the deterministic model has been abandoned in favor of a probabilistic model. The deterministic model assumes that each behavior (e.g., an excellent performance) is predictable if all relevant antecedents can be identified. With the probabilistic, or stochastic model, a more flexible concept of causality is advocated. The rationale of the model is that in a specific situation, an individual can react in different ways and that only the probability of each of these reactions can be predicted (Schlicht, 1988). For example, it should be possible to predict the probability that a series of behaviors belonging to an athlete's repertoire is likely to occur in a specific situation.

Finally, to some scholars, the fundamental issue is no longer whether there are cross-situational consistencies in behavior, but how broad or generalized these consistencies are (Buss & Craik, 1983; Hampson, John, & Goldberg, 1986; Murtha, Kanfer, & Ackerman, 1996). Broad and global constructs should enable one to predict diverse behaviors at moderate levels of accuracy, whereas narrow and specific constructs should enable one to predict with high accuracy within a very limited range of behaviors. Acknowledging that issue in sport psychology, Vealey (1992) differentiates between trait and disposition concepts, with the difference appearing to be one of degree versus kind. Mischel and Peake (1982) and Hampson, John, and Goldberg (1986) propose searching for consistencies in behavior at different levels of abstraction to be represented in a hierarchical structure. In addition, Murtha, Kanfer, and Ackerman (1996) suggest linking categories of behaviors structured hierarchically with situation categories likewise structured hierarchically in what they call an interactionist situational-dispositional taxonomy of personality. According to them, the reason interactionists have not assuaged the tensions between trait theorists and situationist theorists is that they did not succeed in developing taxonomies that incorporate both situational and trait effects.

Behavioral Assessment

In mainstream personality research, there has been an evolution toward the construction of behavioral assessment techniques in reaction to Mischel's (1968) arguments against traditional approaches to personality assessment.

In the argument against personality as a reflection of underlying traits, the crucial fact is that traits are inferred from questionnaires and those questionnaires are essentially based on self-descriptions. That limitation should partly be responsible for the low predictive value of questionnaires. For example, an individual's self-description that he or she is a punctual person seems to be related only to a small degree to actual behavioral punctuality. Inaccuracy of self-knowledge and/or self-defensiveness may be the most obvious reasons for inappropriate self-analyses (Kenrick & Dantschik, 1983; Verstraeten, 1987). Alternative methods to questionnaires include intraindividual or idiographic studies, direct methods (behavioral observation), natural environment and field studies, the sequential aspect of assessment, sport-specific measures and variables, and the use of data in a way that is more compatable with the actual concerns with the elite athlete. Mental training and counseling to enhance performance are of greater interest than classification and prediction.

Of special interest to psychologists working with elite athletes is an alternative technique suggested by Hartmann, Roper, and Bradford (1979) and Barrios and Hartmann (1986) for the evaluation of test scores. A persistent problem in the psychological measurement of highly skilled performers is the ambiguous meaning of test scores due to the lack of concrete referents for the assessment scales from which the scores were derived. With the psychometric or norm-referenced approach, scores are interpreted by comparing them with a standard or norm that is based on the performance of a suitable reference group. Scores that express an individual's performance in relation to the performance of other individuals on the same measuring device illustrate this method. Norm-referenced assessment thus implies interindividual research.

Because it is by definition difficult to find a suitable reference group in which standardized norms have been established for an elite athlete, the alternative method of criterion-referenced testing may be more valuable. Also, perhaps it is more in keeping with the actual performance-enhancement-focused approach of concern to the elite performer. This technique of evaluation is illustrated by the use of percent correct scores on well-defined performance objectives or target behaviors (Hawkins, 1986).

Sport psychologists working with elite performers are typically interested in knowing the degree to which they can execute precisely defined skills effectively at a particular moment in time. Behavioral procedures have been used to assess sport-specific target behaviors, to modify behaviors (e.g., behavioral modification, behavioral coaching), and to measure the effects of applied behavioral techniques on these target behaviors (Allison & Ayllon, 1980; Donahue, Gillis, & King, 1980; Martin & Hrycaiko, 1983; Rushall, 1975; Rushall & Smith, 1979; Smith, Smoll, & Hunt, 1977; Trudel, Coôté, & Sylvestre, 1996; Van Raalte, Brewer, Rivera, & Petitpas, 1995; Vealey & Garner-Holman, 1998; Williams, 1982). Until recently, only a few researchers, limiting their studies to very few sports, have undertaken studies in this area. Vealey and Garner-Holman (1998) conducted a survey and found that consultants used interviews the most (57.2%), followed by behavioral observation (21.2%) and questionnaires (17.3%).

Interindividual versus Intraindividual Research

The heading of this section could as easily be "Nomothetic versus Idiographic Research" or "Research on Groups versus Single-Subject Research" (Jaccard & Dittus, 1990). The nomothetic-idiographic debate in psychology is very old (Allport, 1937). Idiography means the description of the unique characteristics of an individual. It is important to notice that single-case research is not necessarily idiographic. Each individual has, besides unique features, characteristics in common with at least some others. Therefore, he or she can be described and compared with these others (nomothetic research). Allport defined idiography as research on the psychological structure within an individual in a moment in time as well as in the life history of that particular individual. He introduced both the aspect of consistency and the aspect of change as a research topic (Runyan, 1983).

One of the main criticisms of the idiographic approach is that there is no such thing as a unique trait or element. In fact, when a characteristic of an individual can be defined, that individual can be essentially compared with others on that characteristic. Runyan (1983, p. 420) answered the cry "How can you generalize from an idiographic study?" with the response "How can you particularize from that group or population study?" The purpose here is neither to discuss the philosophy of science nor mere terminological questions. In the context of interest in diagnosis of and intervention with elite athletes, one point needs to be made clear. Because the study of the elite performer is the study of a small number of individuals and, moreover, as it is the study of performance fluctuations of these high-achievers (e.g., poor versus peak performances), the possibility of conducting meticulous idiographic research is highly relevant.

Elite performers on occasion want help to overcome a less than ideal presence of a particular behavior (e.g., high anxiety) at a particular moment in reference to competition. Or they may desire assistance to cope with general or sport-specific problems that could impair their performance. These examples show the need to understand an individual's unique organization of characteristics as well as his or her unique process of changing behavior related to more skillful performance (Browne & Mahoney, 1984; Butt, 1987; Martens, 1987; Ravizza, 1984). For such goals, interindividual nomothetic research has severe limitations, which justifies the use of single-case designs.

First, when intializing research in this area, the investigator is confronted with the difficulty of having available a large number of superior athletes. Locating athlete subjects with the same background and the same performance deficiencies causes almost insuperable problems. Second, the statistical handling of group data can obscure relevant individual changes in behavior due to a particular interviewing technique. In group comparisons, results are usually averaged and within-group variability is interpreted as an error term. This way of examining data does not reflect individual performance or individual fluctuations, but a nonexistent average person and error variance. Moreover, in many experimental studies, much emphasis is placed on significance level, sample size, and other factors. Unfortunately, there is often little relationship between what is statistically significant and what is practically significant. In single-case studies, on the contrary, the emphasis is on intuitive clinical significance or relevance.

Research on elite athletes through in-depth interviews and case studies has grown. Bull (1989), for example, reported a case of an ultradistance runner. Mace, Eastman, and Carroll (1986) studied a young female gymnast, and Mace and Carroll (1986) undertook a case study of two squash players. The studies by Gould, Jackson, and Finch (1993), Scanlan, Stein, and Ravizza (1989), Scanlan, Ravizza, and Ravizza (1991), and Jackson (1992) are must readings for those who work with elite figure skaters, as are the studies on Olympic gold medalists by Jackson, Dover, and Mayocchi (1998) and Jackson, Mayocchi, and Dover (1998). The text on psychological preparation and elite athletes by Hardy, Jones, and Gould (1996) is also recommended; these authors reported the diagnosis, intervention, and evaluation of their work with athletes.

Shifting from Deterministic to Probabilistic Models

Another line of research can be seen in the shift from deterministic to probabilistic models. Probabilistic or stochastic models seem to be more flexible and therefore better for describing psychological processes than deterministic approaches. In the deterministic model, the attempt is made to predict a certain probability structure, instead of assuming the total predictability of an event

(Verstraeten, 1987). Changes thus can be incorporated more easily in a model where there is a certain possibility (probability) of variables having changing values (Schlicht, 1988).

A small example of the application of a probabilistic diagnostic model in a sport psychological context is from Bar-Eli and Tenenbaum (1988a, 1988b, 1989). They investigated the probability of an individual psychological crisis during a basketball game. A crisis was defined as the moment at which the athlete's internal equilibrium is disturbed so much by psychological stress that he or she can no longer optimally control personal behaviors. They studied the effect of game standings on the vulnerability of a basketball player. Experts rated probabilistically the relevance of the game standing with regard to the development of an individual psychological crisis. The Bayesian likelihood ratio was applied to these estimates. For each single moment along the time axis of the competition, a specific position on the athlete's momentary inverse U function can be plotted, reflecting vulnerability to psychological crisis at each moment (Bar-Eli & Tenenbaum, 1989).

In some methods of data analysis, the element of probability is integrated in the results. In the hierarchical analysis, a goodness-of-fit index is computed. This index, always representing a less than perfect fit to the data, indicates to what degree an item is a good example of a class of feelings or behaviors and how well it fits into the pattern of the class. In predictions, given a certain situation, it can reflect the probability of the appearance of a feeling or behavior. These examples show that in addition to traditional deterministic models, more flexible stochastic ways of behavior prediction are being used in sport psychology to study fluctuations in athletes' behavior.

Interactionist Situational-Dispositional Taxonomy of Personality

A line of research that could constitute a guiding theoretical perspective in the study of the athlete is the development in the conceptual and empirical elaboration of a real interactionist situational-dispositional taxonomy of personality. Hampson, John, and Goldberg (1986) and Murtha, Kanfer, and Ackerman (1996) pointed out that the fundamental issue is no longer whether there are cross-situational consistencies but how generalized these behavioral consistencies are in relation to groups of situations, which may differ also in breadth. This personality conception implies the principles of construct breadth of traits and hierarchical class-inclusion relations. Eysenk (cited in Hampson, John, & Goldberg, 1986) used these principles as early as 1947 in his trait model of extroversion. What is new is the linking of behavioral classes with situational classes differing in both breadth and hierarchical organization.

The first principle is that trait constructs (classes of behavior) and situational constructs (classes of situations) differ from each other either in breadth, generality, inclusiveness, or abstractness. For example, extroversion is a construct that is viewed as broad, whereas "talkative" is a narrow construct within extroversion. The Big Five traits are broad constructs, which need to be completed by more narrowly delineated constructs to fully represent the structure underlying the variability in behavior. The second principle suggests that relations between these constructs may be represented within a hierarchical structure. Hierarchy is defined generally as a sequence of classes (or sets) at different levels in which each class except the lowest includes one or more subordinate classes. Hierarchy implies an asymmetric class inclusion, which requires that all properties of a concept at a lower level in the hierarchy also apply to the hierarchically higher concept, the reverse not necessarily being true. For example, in the hierarchical structure proposed by Fehr and Russel (1984), emotion is the concept at the superordinate level, and anger, anxiety, happiness, sadness, pride, and envy the concepts at the middle level. Types of anger (e.g., annoyance, indignation, rage) or anxiety (e.g., alarm, dread, panic) are situated at the subordinate level.

Recently, an interactionist representation of personality that integrates both hierarchical organized traits and situational factors has been proposed. To conceptualize the context or the situation, Shoda, Mischel, and Wright (1994) made a distinction between nominal situations and situations characterized in terms of active psychological features. Nominal situations are defined by the setting in which they occur. Competitions or training sessions are examples of nominal situations in a sport setting. Active psychological features are situational characteristics that have an impact on behavior or that determine the meaning of the situation. For example, active psychological features in a sport setting could be whether or not the coach is shouting during the game, whether a basketball player made a mistake or five shots consecutively, and whether one's opponent is appraised as performing on a higher or lower level.

Shoda et al. (1994) argued that it is psychologically more useful to investigate situations in terms of their active psychological features. Individual differences in relation to specific nominal situations, even if highly stable, would be of limited generalizability. However, if situations are defined in terms of their basic psychological features, then information about a person's behavioral tendencies

that are specific to those situations might be used to predict behavior across a broad range of situations that contain the same psychological features. In terms of a model that links hierarchically structured personalities and situational classes, it would thus be recommended to group situations according to their functional equivalence. Situations would be related to the same functionally equivalent types of behavior, presumably because of common active psychological features.

In sport psychology, little research has been done with the identification and classification of the psychological features of the relevant situations of athletes as the explicit purpose (Gould et al., 1993; Jackson, 1995; Russell, 1990; Van Mele, 1996). However, research on the influence of some features of competitive situations on other variables (performance, performance expectations, dropout, stress, and enjoyment) also yields interesting information (Gould, Horn, & Spreeman, 1983; Gould et al., 1993; Moore & Brylinsky, 1993; Robinson & Carron, 1982; Scanlan & Lewthwaite, 1984, 1985, 1986; Scanlan et al., 1989, 1991; Wankel & Kreisel, 1985a, 1985b). For example, results related to the causes of competitive stress reveal the following compelling psychological features of competitive situations: mistakes, the perception of inappropriate behavior, loss of control, social pressure, and social evaluation. Features of noncompetition-related situations include conflict-filled interpersonal relationships, personal problems, and traumatic experiences. Psychological features of situations related to enjoyment are related to performance (perception of competence, esteem from relevant others, winning) or to social factors (belonging to a team, good interpersonal relationships).

In terms of the counseling of an elite athlete and consequently of the linkage of a set of situations, emotions, and behavioral reactions, all of which are hierarchically organized and relevant to this particular athlete, the problem was to find a methodology that could analyze the data. An algorithm, HICLAS, that can handle this complex interplay within one person (idiographic), is consistent with the principles of category breadth and hierarchical structure, and is probabilistic in nature (De Boeck, Rosenberg, & Van Mechelen, 1993) will be elaborated on later.

FUTURE RESEARCH DIRECTIONS

Mischel and Shoda's theory (1995), integrates both the past research and the new developments in sport psychology. An important theoretical consideration is to reveal beyond a formal representation the psychological mechanisms underlying the principles described previously. Even a sophisticated interactionist situational-dispositional linkage does not answer the question as to what the psychological mechanisms are behind it. Mischel and Shoda proposed a cognitive-affective system theory to deal with this particular question. Using Mischel and Shoda's theory in a sport psychological context, a theory of athletic functioning will be described next.

A Cognitive-Affective System Theory of Personality

Guided by the conception of personality in terms of dispositions, for decades researchers pursued cross-situational consistency as evidence of a basic coherence in the individual's underlying personality dispositions. The research results for this type of consistency were discouraging (Mischel, 1968). Instead of abandoning the field, Mischel and colleagues (Mischel, 1990; Mischel & Shoda, 1995; Shoda, Mischel, & Wright, 1993, 1994) have conceptualized a fundamentally different type of behavioral coherence than cross-situational consistency. In the behavioral disposition conception, the variability within each person on a certain dimension (e.g., anxiety) across situations is seen as error and averaged out in a true test score to get the best approximation of the underlying stable trait. The goal is to obtain for each individual a single average score of the amount of presence of the disposition (e.g., trait anxiety). According to Mischel and colleagues, this information is important but ignores when and where two individuals differ in their unique pattern with regard to the particular dimension of behavior (e.g., stress coping).

Referring to a resurgence of mediating process models in personality and social psychology, Shoda, Mischel, and Wright (1994) propose another type of personality invariance or coherence in a process conception of personality. According to them, clues about the person's underlying invariant qualities may be seen especially considering when, where, and which type of a behavior is manifested. Mischel and Peake (1982) found that the cross-situational consistency in the behavior of college students was not significantly greater for those who considered themselves consistent (stable trait people) than it was for those who perceived themselves as variable (low in self-monitoring). However, self-perceived consistency was related to the temporal stability of their relevant behavior within particular types of situations. The question to ask is whether an individual's distinctive if-then situation-behavior relations within a particular domain of behavior are stable and meaningful. If so, the intraindividual patterns of situation-behavior relationships shown by a person might be a possible key

to uniqueness and personality coherence, rather than an error source.

Mischel and Shoda (1995) argued that individual differences in if (situation)–then (behavior) profiles constitute a kind of behavioral signature that reflects the Cognitive-Affective Person System (CAPS). This system contains cognitive-affective units that mediate between the context or situation and the person's behavioral manifestations. Personality itself is to be considered a complex organization of cognitive-affective units. Mischel and Shoda (1995) outlined five types of mental mediating cognitive-affective units that need to be hypothesized in the processing system of personality. Many of these have been documented in the past few decades (see Mischel & Shoda, 1995). These basic types include encodings (e.g., of self, other people, situations), affects and emotions, expectancies and beliefs (about outcomes, one's own efficacy), subjective values, competencies and self-regulatory strategies, and plans in the pursuit of goals.

These cognitive-affective units are not static components. They are organized into subjective equivalence classes that interact and influence each other reciprocally, and it is this complex hierarchical organization that forms the core of the personality structure. Individuals differ in how they selectively focus on different features of situations, how they categorize and encode them cognitively and emotionally, and how these encodings activate and interact with other cognitions and affects in the personality system. Individual differences may occur because persons have different *thresholds* for the activations of cognitions and affects and have a different *organization* of cognitive-affective units.

Some individuals focus more on the potentially threatening features of a situation. Others interpret the same situational features as challenging. Some are more prone to experience irritability or differ in a stable way in the goals and experiences they value and pursue most persistently or more readily encode ambiguous situations negatively. The task for the personality psychologist in this conception is to identify the relevant underlying cognitive and affective units (and thresholds) in relation to types of situations relevant for that person. Once identified, one can try to reveal the relations, including the hierarchical ones, between these units and then whether and when these units become in various degrees activated, deactivated, or are not influenced by each other. By relating the if-then rules of the formal model, reformulated into rules such as if (situational feature)–then (behavioral or emotional feature) and interpreted as being related, not deterministically, but probabilistically, to the relevant cognitive and affective units, one may be able to discover the dynamics of an individual athlete.

Essentials of the CAPS Theory

Mischel and Shoda's (1995) CAPS theory contributes to understanding both the stable differences among people in their overall characteristic levels of types of behavioral dispositions (traditional personality research) and, concurrently, their stable (coherent if-then) profiles of situation-behavior variability as essential expressions of the same personality system. Their theory incorporates the conception of situations elaborated previously, stressing the perception and encoding of the acquired meaning of situational features by the individual. It incorporates also the hierarchically structured complexity of thoughts, planning, imagination, moods, and the everyday stream of experience and feeling of the individual (Cantor, Mischel, & Schwartz, 1982).

The CAPS theory can also be linked with practice-oriented sport psychological questions such as Why should an athlete selectively focus on specific features of competitive situations? How should the athlete encode them cognitively and emotionally? How should those encodings activate and interact with other cognitions and affects and eventually generate plans and actual competitive behavior? How functional are these behaviors in the competitive situation at hand?

In summary, in this process theory of personality, the following elements are especially interesting for sport psychology; included are articles from the recent sport psychological literature that have acknowledged the various elements:

1. The clear reference to the importance of the subjective decoding, both cognitive and emotional, of the context or the situation in which the behaviors occur (Gould et al., 1993; Vealey, 1992).
2. The inclusion of cognitions (encodings, self-perceptions, beliefs, expectancies), emotions and affects, and overt behaviors (see Duda, 1998), as well as acknowledgment of the complex (hierarchical) relationships and the iterative sum of pathways among these processes (Curry, Snyder, Cook, Ruby, & Rehm, 1997; Grove & Heard, 1997; Hardy et al., 1996; Singer, 1997, Van den Auweele et al., 1999).
3. The acknowledgment of meaningful patterns of stability (coherence) within a person.

4. The conditional if-then approach in which the unit of observation is the conditional occurrence of a certain type of behavior given types of situations.
5. The assumption that the situation types as well as the behavior types are *prototype*-based categories with elements that vary from highly central to more peripheral category members.
6. The assumption that the linking rules between those categories are not necessarily deterministic but more probabilistic in nature (Vanden Auweele et al., 1993; Van Mele et al., 1995).

SITUATION-RELATED INTRAINDIVIDUAL PERSONALITY DIAGNOSIS: THE CASE OF INGRID

Although especially useful in an idiographic approach, neither Mischel and Shoda's (1995) CAPS theory nor the formal interactionistic models necessarily imply an idiographic approach. This was clearly demonstrated by Vansteelandt and Van Mechelen (1998), who worked out a triple typology model characterizing not a single person but *types* of persons in terms of different sets of situations and behaviors.

In this section, research conducted to demonstrate a model that simultaneously describes both a set of situations and emotions/behaviors and the associated method of data analysis called HICLAS is described (De Boeck, 1989; De Boeck & Rosenberg, 1988; De Boeck et al., 1993). Although the model originated in the field of social perception (Gara & Rosenberg, 1979), it is formulated in a general sense and is applicable to all kinds of binary matrices (i.e., grids), for example, person-by-test-item data, person-by-person sociometric data, and in other circumstances. Of special interest is that the model and the method used to fit the model to a given data set can be linked with many of the aforementioned developments (e.g., with the main features of the CAPS and with the requirements of the sport psychological objectives). This analysis method was introduced to the field of sport psychology by Van den Auweele in 1988.

In the following study of a single elite athlete, most of the important new concepts and methodologies described in the prior section are operationalized: the intraindividual approach, dynamic-interactionism, a focus on emotional and behavioral reactions (mediating units) in a relevant sport context, the use of a probabilistic model within the goals of intervention and counseling, and the inclusion of the principles of category breadth, prototype-based elements, and hierarchy. Idiographic data are collected, structured, and interpreted according to the grid technique developed by De Boeck and Rosenberg (1988).

Data Collection

Guided by the process conception of personality, the first step in the data collection phase is to compile the athlete's repertoire of emotional and behavioral reactions in situations she reports as relevant to her in order to know how she functions in them. Probably competitive contexts would be of special importance to top athletes, but the situations examined could include anything the athlete and counselor found relevant.

Ingrid is a 20-year-old female athlete. She was a frequent Belgian age-group champion middle-distance runner. In an interview, Ingrid was asked to list a number of situations, incidents, and events that had occurred during her sports career. The purpose of the interview is to identify the active psychological features of the situations and not the nominal situations (Shoda et al., 1994). These situations had to be described as concretely as possible (see Figures 9.2 and 9.3). For every situation, the athlete had to specify how she perceived it and which emotions she experienced at the time. These emotional reactions are called *emotional characteristics*. The athlete was also asked to describe her overt behavior in each situation. These reactions are called *behavioral characteristics*. The exact wording of the athlete is retained as far as possible to obtain a high degree of recognition (face validity) for the athlete.

In the second step, two grids are constructed on the basis of the information collected during the interview. The grid in Figure 9.2 displays the relevant situations versus the emotional characteristics, and the grid in Figure 9.3 represents the same situations versus the behavioral characteristics.

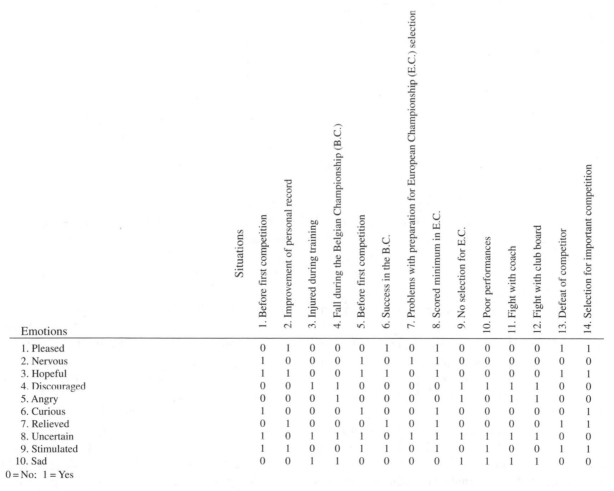

Emotions	1. Before first competition	2. Improvement of personal record	3. Injured during training	4. Fall during the Belgian Championship (B.C.)	5. Before first competition	6. Success in the B.C.	7. Problems with preparation for European Championship (E.C.) selection	8. Scored minimum in E.C.	9. No selection for E.C.	10. Poor performances	11. Fight with coach	12. Fight with club board	13. Defeat of competitor	14. Selection for important competition
1. Pleased	0	1	0	0	0	1	0	1	0	0	0	0	1	1
2. Nervous	1	0	0	0	1	0	1	1	0	0	0	0	0	0
3. Hopeful	1	1	0	0	1	1	0	1	0	0	0	0	1	1
4. Discouraged	0	0	1	1	0	0	0	0	1	1	1	1	0	0
5. Angry	0	0	0	1	0	0	0	0	1	0	1	1	0	0
6. Curious	1	0	0	0	1	0	0	1	0	0	0	0	0	1
7. Relieved	0	1	0	0	0	1	0	1	0	0	0	0	1	1
8. Uncertain	1	0	1	1	1	0	1	1	1	1	1	1	0	0
9. Stimulated	1	1	0	0	1	1	0	1	0	1	0	0	1	1
10. Sad	0	0	1	1	0	0	0	0	1	1	1	1	0	0

0 = No; 1 = Yes

Figure 9.2   Grid used to represent Ingrid's rating of the applicability of emotions to each situation.

Behaviors	Situations	1. Before first competition	2. Improvement of personal record	3. Injured during training	4. Fall during the Belgian Championship (B.C.)	5. Before first competition	6. Success in the B.C.	7. Problems with preparation for European Championship (E.C.) selection	8. Scored minimum in E.C.	9. No selection for E.C.	10. Poor performances	11. Fight with coach	12. Fight with club board	13. Defeat of competitor	14. Selection for important competition
1. Contacted my coach		1	1	0	0	1	1	1	0	0	0	0	0	1	0
2. Refused to do something against my will		0	0	0	0	0	0	0	0	0	0	1	1	0	0
3. Did my best		0	0	0	0	1	1	1	0	1	1	0	0	1	1
4. Contacted friends		1	0	0	1	1	0	0	0	0	0	0	0	0	0
5. Persevered		0	0	1	0	0	0	1	0	1	1	0	0	0	0
6. Stopped training		0	0	0	0	0	0	0	0	0	0	1	1	0	0
7. No longer participated in competitions		0	0	0	0	0	0	0	0	0	0	1	1	0	0
8. Did not give up		0	0	1	0	0	0	1	0	1	1	0	0	0	0
9. Prepared with others		1	1	1	0	1	0	1	0	1	1	0	0	1	1
10. Trained harder		0	1	0	0	1	1	1	0	0	0	0	0	1	1
11. Trained intensively		0	1	1	0	1	1	1	1	1	1	0	0	1	1

0 = No; 1 = Yes

Figure 9.3 Grid used to represent Ingrid's rating of the applicability of behaviors to each situation.

A guideline for the size of the grid is to list at least 15 situations and 15 emotions or behaviors, which is required by the mathematical algorithm that underlies the HICLAS method (De Boeck & Rosenberg, 1988). The more the grid looks like a square, the better (e.g., 15 × 15 is better than 18 × 13). An explanation of this algorithm is beyond the scope of this chapter and is not necessary to know how to use and interpret HICLAS. In the third step, the athlete has to rate each of the situations, evaluating to what degree the emotional and behavioral characteristics listed actually occur or are relevant in each situation. Ingrid's scores appear in Figures 9.2 and 9.3.

After the construction of a grid (emotions and behaviors versus situations), it is presented to the athlete for completion; this becomes in fact an extension of the interview. Whereas in the interview the athlete spontaneously reports only a few emotions and behavioral reactions for each particular situation, while completing the grid she is now confronted with her whole repertoire of emotions and behaviors and has to score the applicability of each in all the situations she reported. The respondent uses a rating scale of 0 to 10. Three anchors are defined explicitly: 0 indicates that the particular reaction (behavioral or emotional) does not apply to a certain situation at all, 10 indicates that the reaction is perfectly applicable to the situation, and 5 means that the reaction is just applicable to the particular situation. The respondent thus evaluates the applicability of her entire cognitive-affective reaction-repertoire in every relevant situation. The completed grid is the data input for the subsequent analysis performed by the HICLAS statistical technique. Data from the completed grid is first dichotomised (usually ratings of 0–4 = 0 and 5–10 =1) and then input for the analysis performed by the HICLAS statistical technique.

Data Analysis by Means of Hierarchical Class Analysis

Although other methods of analysis could be used, such as factor or cluster analysis and multiple regression analysis (see Van den Auweele, 1988), hierarchical class analysis was chosen because it simultaneously yields a hierarchical structure of situations and the emotional characteristics as well as a hierarchical structure of situations and behavioral characteristics. Examples of these structures can be seen in the results of the hierarchical class analysis completed on data about Ingrid and shown in Figures 9.4 and 9.5.

HICLAS is performed by means of software using a rather complex algorithm that is based on Boolean algebra. Detailed information can be found in De Boeck and Rosenberg (1988), De Boeck and Van Mechelen (1990), De Boeck, Rosenberg, and Van Mechelen (1993) and Van Mechelen, De Boeck, and Rosenberg (1995). Here we aim only to provide a clear explanation of the rationale and terminology used in the HICLAS context.

Classes, Equivalence within a Class, Hierarchy between Classes

Figures 9.4 and 9.5 contain the results of the HICLAS analysis. Such displays reveal classes of situations characterized by a similar pattern of reactions as well as for classes of emotional and behavioral characteristics with a similar pattern of situations. The search for these relationships makes up the basis of this form of analysis. The degree of correspondence of characteristics to a similar pattern is called equivalence within the class. Equivalence scores (range .58 to 1.00) appear as decimal numbers to the right of each emotion and behavior in Figures 9.4 and 9.5. These equivalence scores can also be considered goodness-of-fit scores for each item, and these terms will be used interchangeably. The element with the highest goodness-of-fit score is the best prototype of its class (see earlier discussion of goodness-of-fit index).

The concepts of equivalence within a class and hierarchy between classes are the bases of hierarchical class

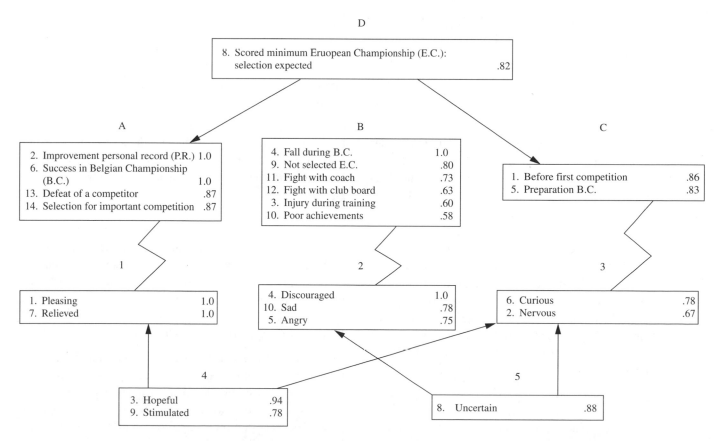

Figure 9.4   Hierarchical class analysis of situations and emotions with goodness-of-fit scores. Hierarchical relationships indicated by arrows, associative connections by zigzag lines. This chart is derived from Ingrid's scores.

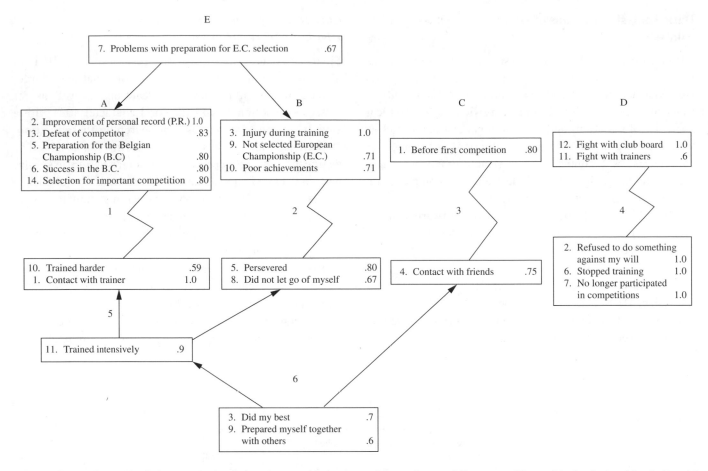

Figure 9.5   Hierarchical class analysis of situations and behaviors with goodness-of-fit scores. Hierarchical relationships indicated by arrows, associative connections by zigzag lines. This chart is derived from Ingrid's scores.

analysis. If a class of situations is hierarchically in a higher position than another class (e.g., in Figure 9.4, class D is in a higher position than class A), this means that all the characteristics pertaining to the lower class (e.g., A) also pertain to the higher class (e.g., D). But this higher class (e.g., D) has even more characteristics, because it is also connected hierarchically to other lower classes (e.g., B and C). The relationships between the class of emotional and behavioral characteristics can thus be interpreted as follows: If the emotions or behaviors of a lower class (e.g., 1) are present in a certain class of situations (e.g., A), then the emotions or behaviors of the hierarchically higher class are also present (e.g., 4). This hierarchy is always indicated with an arrow from the higher to the lower class.

Graphic Display

A simultaneous graphic representation of both hierarchies can be given by making use of a symmetric association relation between them. In Figures 9.4 and 9.5 the situations

hierarchy (upper side) and the emotions or behaviors hierarchy (upside down) can clearly be seen. The zigzag line indicates the connection between the two structures. The zigzag line indicates that a situation class is associated with the emotion/behavior class with which it is connected and vice versa. Both aspects, classification and hierarchy, represent important features of the structural organization of an athlete's personality. The final result or output is a hierarchical structure of classes (groups) of situations and of classes of emotions and behaviors.

Rank and Complexity of the Structure

The result of the HICLAS analysis includes different solutions that represent a variable complexity of the structure, which is expressed by the term *rank* (comparable to factor analysis). A solution with a low rank (1 or 2) is simple but yields less accurate representation and a low goodness-of-fit value of the data of the original grid. A solution with a higher rank has a more complex structure, but matches the original data better as indicated by a high goodness-of-fit value. One can conclude that in the more complex structures (with higher ranks), there is less loss of information. To select the optimal rank or complexity, criteria that are also used in other statistical contexts (e.g., factor analysis) apply here. Usually, one can see quite a steep improvement of goodness-of-fit as one moves from the lower to higher ranks, but after a while, the well-known law of diminishing returns can be observed. The gain in goodness-of-fit value becomes more and more negligible, whereas the structure becomes more and more complex. A goodness-of-fit value of .60 or higher for any one model is considered acceptable. Other criteria used to select the ideal rank can include the total number of items lost to the null class (thus not included in the model) and the relative importance of such lost items to the athlete, the researcher, or the interviewer, and the goals of the analysis.

Interpretation

To interpret the results, it is best to start with the graphic representation. Although often the data found in the rating grid can also provide some information, this information is mostly limited to one situation or emotion or behavior at a time. De Boeck and Maris (1990) state that the interpretation is more than an enumerative description of the graphical representation and should be considered as a whole of hypothetical statements that can be inspiring for further investigation or for the planning of an intervention.

First, one looks at the *degree of integration* of the structure. Are there classes that are unconnected with other classes? If many items are in the null class, this automatically means that the structural model (or rank) lacks integration. A second point is the *complexity of the structure.* As stated, complexity is indicated by the rank and the goodness-of-fit (the number of discrepancies). High goodness-of-fit and a low rank point in the direction of a simple structure, whereas a low goodness-of-fit and a high rank are the mark of a complex structure.

Each class contains elements that are more or less equivalent, otherwise they would be in different classes. Thus, to interpret a class it is important to seek *the common features of the different elements in the class.* De Boeck and Maris (1990) advise starting with the basic classes, as these are normally the most homogeneous. The higher classes include ipso facto the aspects from the connected lower classes.

Another point to consider is *the level of a class:* The higher the specific emotions and behaviors classes are situated in the hierarchy, the more this is an indicator of a

stable characteristic (traitlike element) of the athlete. Finally, the goodness-of-fit value (prototypicality) indicates how well the element fits in a class.

Ingrid's Results

Figure 9.4 is a representation of the results of the hierarchical class analysis in rank 3 for the data in Figure 9.2 (emotional matrix). In the upper half of Figure 9.4 (above the zig zags), the four classes of situations are rendered in relation to each other. Bottom class A includes a number of success or achievement situations, of which the best prototype is "A considerable improvement in my personal record." The emotional pattern that corresponds with this class of situations includes all classes of emotional reactions connected with it downwards (i.e., class 1 "pleasing; relieved" and class 4 "hopeful; stimulated"). One can also observe the relationship between bottom classes 2 and 3 and the associated emotions.

There is one hierarchically higher class of situations, class D, which includes "Scored the minimum for the European Championship (E.C.): selection expected." D combines the emotional patterns of bottom classes A and C and is consequently associated with the emotions "pleasing; relieved" (class 1), "curious; nervous" (class 3), "hopeful; stimulated" (class 4), and "uncertain" (class 5).

The lower half of Figure 9.4 (below the zig zags) represents the structure of the set of emotional characteristics. This structure consists of three basic classes (1, 2, and 3) and two hierarchically higher classes (4 and 5). Class 4 is associated with all situations related to classes 1 and 3. When the athlete feels pleasant and relieved as well as when she is curious and nervous, she is also hopeful and stimulated. Class 5 is associated with the classes of situations of classes 2 and 3 in the same manner.

Tension and stress are felt in the precompetitive situations used in classes C and D: "Before my first official competition," "Preparation for the B.C. (Belgian Championships)," and "Scored the minimum for the E.C.: selection expected." Consequently, especially in these emotionally straining situations, it is important to observe the athlete's overt behavioral reactions.

The results of the hierarchical class analysis in rank 3 for the data in Figure 9.3 (behavioral matrix) are resented in Figure 9.5 (above the zig zags). In the upper half, five classes of situations appear. Basic class A in the behavioral analysis includes three success situations as well as the situation "Preparation for the B.C." The behavioral pattern associated with class A contains exclusively functional behavioral reactions: "trained harder; contacted my coach" (class 1), "trained intensively" (class 5), and "did my best; preparation with others" (class 6). These behavioral reactions occur in all success situations with the emotional pattern "pleasing, hopeful."

In a number of situations, the athlete shows some very functional behavioral reactions, although the situations also evoke very negative emotions, such as discouraged, sad, angry, and uncertain. In these situations, the athlete is able to cope positively with this strain. Class C includes only one element ("before the start of the competition"), which corresponds with the emotional pattern "curious, nervous, uncertain." The behavioral reactions associated with this situation are "contacted friend" (class 3) and "did my best; preparation with others" (class 6). Only the situations in class D, which is not connected to the rest of the structure ("fight with trainer; fight with club board"), seem to trigger dysfunctional behavioral reactions ("refused to do something against my will; stopped training; no longer participated in competition"; class 4). It is remarkable that situations that have a similar emotional affect (see class B and 2 in Figure 9.4) can be related to entirely different behavioral reactions. Apparently, the athlete's coping behavior fails in interpersonal conflict situations.

There is one hierarchically higher class of situations, class E, combining the behavioral patterns of classes A and B. The only element in class E is "Problems with the preparation for the E.C. selection," with the corresponding behavioral pattern "trained harder; contacted my coach" (class 1), "persevered; did not give up" (class 2), "trained intensively" (class 5), and "did my best; preparation with others" (class 6).

Discussion and Conclusions of the Case Study

When the athlete is involved in interpersonal conflicts, negative emotional reactions occur, accompanied by a dysfunctional behavioral reaction. To coach her for successful career development, the first priority is to help her learn to avoid or tackle these interpersonal problems. The athlete's behavior is functional in all other situations, though a number of other situations are also experienced as very stressful, such as "injuries; not being selected; and poor performances" (see Figure 9.5, bottom class B). Although the athlete is discouraged and uncertain in these situations (see Figure 9.5, classes 2, 5, and 6), she manages to cope with them positively. We hope it is clear how this type of information lends itself to generating advice specifically relevant to this athlete.

When these data and the related suggestions were presented to the athlete and her coach, their reactions were positive. The athlete felt her uniqueness was well-understood. She endorsed the interpretations about her reaction patterns and said that this procedure had enhanced her self-knowledge. The coach expressed surprise at the many things revealed that he had not previously recognized, both the competition situations that had impacted on the athlete and her way of coping with them.

By combining different relevant aspects of Ingrid's functioning as an athlete (i.e., situations, emotions, behaviors, underlying constants, and if-then patterns of situations and emotional and behavioral reactions), idiosyncratic information can be obtained objectively and relatively quickly. The situations and responses mentioned were all important to her, so no time was wasted answering questions about irrelevant topics. This method also avoided drawing hypothetical conclusions from situations and responses of limited relevance to the elite athlete. Furthermore, detailed and subtle information was obtained that could not have been obtained by questionnaires.

Importantly, this information led to an approach to advising this athlete that would not have been possible following an evaluation with, for example, an anxiety questionnaire. In fact, Ingrid's Sport Competition Anxiety Text (SCAT) anxiety score was very high, which could have led to the suggestion to learn relaxation or other anxiety-reducing strategy. However, our recommendations did not include such, as the intraindividual data show that Ingrid can cope with her anxiety most of the time, but does not have adequate coping behavior in some very specific interpersonal situations. Relaxation seems to be, therefore, less necessary than some communications skill training or another intervention related to her interpersonal relationships. One could even argue that, generally, Ingrid's anxiety is functional (Hanin, 1997) and that, as such, any suggestion to modify it could have had deleterious effects on her functioning in competition.

Most of the important new directions described earlier have been concretized in this case study. The behavioral assessment approach is incorporated, as the athlete is asked for her overt behavioral reactions in relevant situations; the interactional approach has been illustrated; the cognitive and affective-emotional encoding and processing of the situation is highlighted; the intraindividual coherence between the different personality components (cognitions, emotions, and overt behavior) in their hierarchical structure has been operationalized; and the interaction between the individual and her situation, as well as the changes and the constants in this interaction, have been attended to. This is a prime example of the intraindividual approach, as only one athlete has been investigated without making any comparisons to others. Finally, recall that the hierarchical class model provides a goodness-of-fit index, which can be used probabilistically in making predictions about future feelings and behaviors.

CONCLUSIONS

The major reason for studying personality in sports has been the possibility of predicting future success in sport more accurately. According to this supposition, successful performers display a personality profile that differs from less successful performers. The successful personality profile presumably includes sociability, emotional stability, ambitions, dominance, responsibility, leadership, self-confidence, persistency, and trait anxiety. On the other hand, skeptical sport psychologists have minimized the relevance of personality information in predicting future success in sport. According to them, no incontestable scientific evidence has been produced to support the existence of a substantial relation between personality characteristics and success in sport.

In fact, the majority of published research suffers serious deficiencies in procedural aspects, including research design, sampling and testing procedures, analyses, and interpretation. Moreover, the question remains whether scientifically sound personality research could predict more than a trivial amount of the relevant variance in competition. In any case, even based on a solid research methodology, the trait approach of personality has failed to provide the conclusions that were expected in other areas of psychology. Personality psychologists have not had much success in predicting behavior in complex situations. Utilizing questionnaire data that are considered indicators of some underlying personality traits, the maximal validity coefficients obtained were on average about .30, which accounts for only about 10% of the relevant behavioral variance.

These serious doubts concerning the predictive power of psychological variables, based on both empirical evidence and conceptual considerations, led to the pessimistic conclusion that personality diagnosis is ineffective in sports. However, it has also helped to precipitate a critical reexamination of the field, from which has emerged a more cautious and precise approach to the prediction of behavior and performance. This includes the specification of the conditions under which the trait concept remains useful

(some people are predictable; only some traits are useful; only in situations with low constraints or weak in pressures to conform). A more accurate definition has been the development of variants of interactionism (e.g., organismic, dynamic, statistical interaction). Newer and sophisticated techniques such as meta-analysis and structural equation modeling are being used. The combination of psychological, physiological, anthropometric, and visuomotor skill data is being examined in large multidimensional designs in an attempt to explain more behavioral variance.

When generating conclusions in this area, caution is a good scientific attitude. Keep in mind the history of the POMS, once vaunted as a prime example of evidence for the existence of psychological differences between elite and other athletes as well as athletes and nonathletes. Elite athletes may display a specific pattern of mood states and differ from lesser athletes in self-confidence, anxiety, motivation, and cognitive variables. However, closer inspection of the totality of the evidence in support of these notions reveals that it is not very impressive.

Nonetheless, the new directions in sport psychological research and in mainstream personology are more important and promising than the attempts to enhance the predictive power of psychological variables or to increase the proportion of explained behavioral variance within the trait conception of personality. These new directions have emerged in sport psychology due to the shift in goals from prediction to mental training and counseling. From the attempt to validate personality constructs in a sports setting, present emphasis is on the multivariate testing of sport psychological models. The shift toward the study of relevant sport psychological phenomena implied the need for a process conception of personality, which is being developed in mainstream personology. Furthermore, a need has been expressed for a methodology that is able to handle complex hierarchical interactions and is sensitive enough to register fluctuations and changes, which has also been developed recently.

De Boeck and Rosenberg (1993), De Boeck and Van Mechelen (1990), and De Boeck, Rosenberg, and Van Mechelen (1993), Magnusson and Törestad (1993), and Shoda, Mischel, and Wright (1993, 1994) offer a theoretical and methodological framework that is simultaneously able to link both the traditional and the new developments in paradigms, empirical research, and methodologies. They offer new impetus to research that currently is disregarded in sport psychology. They suggest that processes such as perceptions, cognitions, emotions, motives, values, and plans take their meaning from the role they play in the total functioning of the individual. Thus, these research topics are said to be basic to personality research and have to be studied in relation to each other in the context of an integrated model of human functioning (Strean & Roberts, 1992). For a full understanding of how and why individuals think, feel, act, and react as they do, personality theory must incorporate knowledge from research in many areas, including perception, cognition, emotion, values, and goals (Magnusson & Törestad, 1993).

At the beginning of this chapter, it was mentioned that to be accepted by the sport psychological establishment, both the relevance to sport psychology and the scientific credibility of those new developments had to be demonstrated. Some of the new advances have already been integrated and are used in sport psychological contexts. Danziger (1990) suggested that more may be needed than relevance and scientific status to transform the knowledge claims of new ideas into accepted knowledge. Ideas have to be recognized and validated by the authorities working within the scientific sport psychological framework. We believe this touches a core element explaining the difficult phase personality research is going through. It was beyond the scope of this chapter to investigate the role of the scientific sport psychological framework in the establishment and the maintenance of this situation. But it would be interesting to investigate, as Danziger (1990) did for early psychological research, the influence of the politics and power of the sport psychological associations, journals, prominent scientists, reviewers, and textbook writers on the evolution of the field. Is science at least partly a political process in which alliances have to be formed, competitors defeated, programs formulated, recruits won, power captured, and organizations formed (Biddle, 1995; Danziger, 1990)?

Keeping in mind the plea for a healthy scientific field and a sound balance between theoretical and applied research (Landers, 1983; Vealey, 1994), far from being the moribund field some critics maintain, personality research will emerge as a phoenix from its crisis period to again become an exciting area of research in sport psychology.

REFERENCES

Aguerri, P. (1986). The development of sport psychology as seen through the analysis of the first fifteen years of the *Journal*. *International Journal of Sport Psychology, 17,* 87–99.

Alderman, R.B. (1974). *Psychological behavior in sport.* Philadelphia: Saunders.

Allison, M.G., & Ayllon, T. (1980). Behavioral coaching in the development of skills in football, gymnastics, and tennis. *Journal of Applied Behavior Analysis, 13,* 297–314.

Allport, G.W. (1937). *Personality: A psychological interpretation.* New York: Holt, Rinehart and Winston.

Apitzsch, E., & Berggren, B. (1993). *The personality of the elite soccer player.* Lund, Sweden: Lund University, Department of Applied Psychology.

Bakker, F.C., Whiting, H.T.A., & van der Brug, H. (1990). *Sport psychology: Concepts and applications.* Chichester, England: Wiley.

Bar-Eli, M., & Tenenbaum, G. (1988a). The interaction of individual psychological crisis and time phases in basketball. *Perceptual and Motor Skills, 66,* 523–530.

Bar-Eli, M., & Tenenbaum, G. (1988b). Time phases and the individual psychological crisis in sports competition: Theory and research findings. *Journal of Sports Sciences, 6,* 141–149.

Bar-Eli, M., & Tenenbaum, G. (1989). Game standings and psychological crisis in sport: Theory and research. *Canadian Journal of Sports Science, 4,* 31–37.

Barlow, D.H., & Hersen, M. (1984). *Single case experimental designs: Strategies for studying behavior change.* New York: Pergamon Press.

Barrios, B., & Hartmann, D.P. (1986). The contributions of traditional assessment: Concepts, issues, and methodologies. In R.O. Nelson & S.C. Hayes (Eds.), *Conceptual foundations of behavioral assessment* (pp. 81–110). New York: Guilford Press.

Bem, D.J. (1983). Constructing a triple typology: Some (second) thoughts on nomothetic and idiographic approaches to personality. *Journal of Personality, 51,* 566–577.

Biddle, S.J.H. (1995). Editorial: Applied sport psychology in Europe. *The Sport Psychologist, 9,* 127–129.

Brewer, J., & Hunter, A. (1989). *Multimethod research: A synthesis of styles.* Newbury Park, CA: Sage.

Brody, N. (1988). *Personality: In search of individuality.* San Diego, CA: Academic Press.

Browne, M.A., & Mahoney, M.J. (1984). Sport psychology. *Annual Review of Psychology, 35,* 605–625.

Bull, S.J. (1989). The role of the sport psychology consultant: A case study of ultra-distance running. *The Sport Psychologist, 3,* 254–264.

Buss, D.M., & Craik, K.H. (1983). The act frequency approach to personality. *Personality Review, 90,* 105–126.

Butt, D.S. (1987). *Psychology of sport: The behavior, motivation, personality, and performance of athletes.* New York: Van Nostrand-Reinhold.

Cantor, N., Mischel, W., & Schwartz, J.C. (1982). A prototype analysis of psychological situations. *Cognitive Psychology, 14,* 45–77.

Carron, A. (1980). *Social psychology of sport.* Ithaca, NY: Mouvement.

Claeys, W. (1980). Het modern interactionisme in de persoonlijkheidspsychologie (Modern interactionism in personality psychology). In J.R. Nuttin (Ed.), *Gedrag, dynamische relatie en betekeniswereld* (pp. 221–237). Leuven, Belgium: University of Leuven.

Cooper, H. (1990). Meta-analysis and the integrative research review. In C. Hendrick & M.S. Clark (Eds.), *Research methods in personality and social psychology (Review of personality and social psychology 11)* (pp. 142–163). Newbury Park, CA: Sage.

Cooper, L. (1969). Athletics, activity and personality: A review of the literature. *Research Quarterly, 40,* 17–22.

Costa, P.T., Jr., & McCrae, R.R. (1992). The five-factor model of personality and its relevance to personality disorders. *Journal of Personality Disorders, 6,* 343–359.

Curry, L.A., Snyder, C.R., Cook, D.L., Ruby, B.C., & Rehm, M. (1997). Role of hope in academic and sport achievement. *Journal of Personality and Social Psychology, 73,* 1257–1267.

Danziger, K. (1990). *Constructing the subject: Historical origins of psychological research.* Cambridge, England: Cambridge University Press.

Davis, C., & Mogk, J.P. (1994). Personality correlates of interest excellence in sport. *International Journal of Sport Psychology, 25,* 131–143.

De Boeck, P. (1989). *Brief user's guide for the HICLAS program on PC, version 1.1.* Unpublished manuscript, University of Leuven, Belgium, Department of Psychology.

De Boeck, P., & Maris, E. (1990). *Individueel roosteronderzoek en hiërarchische klasse-analyse: Basisprincipes en leidraad voor toepassingen [Individual grid analysis and hierarchical class analysis: Basic principles and guide for applications] (manual).* Leuven, Belgium: University of Leuven.

De Boeck, P., & Rosenberg, S. (1988). Hierarchical classes: Model and data analysis. *Psychometrika, 53,* 361–381.

De Boeck, P., Rosenberg, S., & Van Mechelen, I. (1993). The hierarchical classes approach: A review. In J. Hampton, R.S. Michalski, & P. Theunis (Eds.), *Categories and concepts: Theoretical views and inductive data analysis* (pp. 265–286). London: Academic Press.

De Boeck, P., & Van Mechelen, I. (1990). Traits and taxonomies: A hierarchical classes approach. *European Journal of Personality, 4,* 147–156.

Deshaies, P., Pargman, D., & Thiffault, C. (1979). A psychobiological profile of individual performance in junior hockey players. In G.C. Roberts & K.M. Newell (Eds.), *Psychology of motor behavior and sport–1978* (pp. 36–50). Champaign, IL: Human Kinetics.

Digman, J.M. (1990). Personality structure: Emergence of the five factor model. *Annual Review of Psychology, 41,* 417–440.

Dishman, R.K. (1982). Identity crisis in North American sport psychology: Academics in professional issues. *Journal of Sport Psychology, 5,* 123–134.

Donahue, J.A., Gillis, J.H., & King, K. (1980). Behavior modification in sport and physical education: A review. *Journal of Sport Psychology, 2,* 311–328.

Duda, J.L. (1998). Introduction. In J.L. Duda (Ed.), *Advances in sport and exercise psychology measurement* (pp. xxi-xxiii). Morgantown, WV: Fitness Information Technology.

Duda, J.L., & Whitehead, J. (1998). Measurement of goal perspectives in the physical domain. In J.L. Duda (Ed.), *Advances in sport and exercise psychology measurement* (pp. 21–48). Morgantown, WV: Fitness Information Technology.

Epstein, S. (1979). The stability of behavior: I. On predicting most of the people much of the time. *Journal of Personality and Social Psychology, 37,* 1079–1126.

Eysenck, H.J., & Eysenck, S.B.G. (1964). *Manual of the Eysenck Personality Inventory.* London: University of London Press.

Eysenck, H.J., & Eysenck, S.B.G. (1975). *Manual of the Eysenck Personality Questionnaire.* Kent, England: Hodder & Stoughton.

Eysenck, H.J., Nias, D.K.B., & Cox, D.N. (1982). Sport and personality. *Advances in Behavior Research and Therapy, 1,* 1–56.

Fehr, B., & Russel, J.A. (1984). Concept of emotion viewed from a prototype perspective. *Journal of Experimental Psychology: General, 113,* 464–486.

Feltz, D.L. (1987). Advancing knowledge in sport psychology: Strategies for expanding our conceptual frameworks. *Quest, 39,* 243–254.

Feltz, D.L. (1989). Theoretical research in sport psychology: From applied psychology toward sport science. In J.S. Skinner, C.D. Corbin, D.M. Landers, P.E. Martin, & C.L. Wells (Eds.), *Future directions in exercise and sport science research* (pp. 435–452). Champaign, IL: Human Kinetics.

Feltz, D.L. (1992). The nature of sport psychology. In T.S. Horn (Ed.), *Advances in sport psychology* (pp. 3–11). Champaign, IL: Human Kinetics.

Fenigstein, A., Scheier, M.F., & Buss, A.H. (1975). Public and private self-consciousness: Assessment and theory. *Journal of Consulting and Clinical Psychology, 43,* 522–527.

Fisher, A.C. (1977). Sport personality assessment: Facts, fallacies, and perspectives. *Motor Skills: Theory into Practice, 1,* 87–97.

Fisher, A.C. (1984). New directions in sport personality research. In J.M. Silva & R.S. Weinberg (Eds.), *Psychological foundations of sport* (pp. 70–80). Champaign, IL: Human Kinetics.

Fox, K.R. (1998). Advances in the measurement of the physical self. In J.L. Duda (Ed.), *Advances in sport and exercise psychology measurement* (pp. 295–310). Morgantown, WV: Fitness Information Technology.

Gara, M., & Rosenberg, S. (1979). The identification of persons as supersets and subsets in free-response personality descriptions. *Journal of Personality and Social Psychology, 37*, 2161–2170.

Gat, I., & McWhirter, B.T. (1998). Personality characteristics of competitive and recreational cyclists. *Journal of Sport Behavior, 21*, 408–420.

Goldberg, L.R. (1992). The development of marker variables for the big five factor structure. *Psychological Assessment, 4*, 26–42.

Gould, D., Horn, T., & Spreeman, J. (1983). Sources of stress in junior elite wrestlers. *Journal of Sport Psychology, 5*, 159–171.

Gould, D., Jackson, S.A., & Finch, L.M. (1993). Life at the top: The experiences of U.S. national champion figure skaters. *The Sport Psychologist, 7*, 354–374.

Grove, J.R., & Heard, N.P. (1997). Optimism and sport confidence as correlates of slump-related coping among athletes. *The Sport Psychologist, 11*, 400–410.

Haase, H. (1984). Selection of "talents" for high performance sports: A venture beyond hope? *Studia Psychologica, 26*, 271–277.

Halliwell, W.L., & Gauvin, L. (1982). Integrating and interpreting research findings: A challenge to sport psychologists. In J.T. Partington, T. Orlick, & J.H. Salmela (Eds.), *Sport in perspective* (pp. 77–122). London: Kimpton.

Hampson, S.E., John, O.P., & Goldberg, L.R. (1986). Category breadth and hierarchical structure in personality: Studies of asymmetries in judgments of trait implications. *Journal of Personality and Social Psychology, 51*, 37–54.

Hanin, Y. (1997). Emotions and athletic performance: Individual zones of optimal functioning model. *European Yearbook of Sport Psychology, 1*, 29–72.

Hardman, K. (1973). A dual approach to the study of personality and performance in sport. In H.T.A. Whiting, K. Hardman, L.B. Hendry, & M.G. Jones (Eds.), *Personality and performance in physical education and sport* (pp. 77–122). London: Kimpton.

Hardy, L., Jones, G.J., & Gould, D. (1996). *Understanding psychological preparation for sport: Theory and practice of elite performers.* Chichester, England: Wiley.

Hartmann, D.P., Roper, B.L., & Bradford, D.C. (1979). Some relationships between behavioral and traditional assessment. *Journal of Behavioral Assessment, 1*, 3–21.

Hassmén, P., Koivula, N., & Hansson, T. (1998). Precompetitive mood states and performance of elite male golfers: Do trait characteristics make a difference? *Perceptual and Motor Skills, 86*, 1443–1457.

Hawkins, R.P. (1986). Selection of target behaviors. In R.O. Nelson & S.C. Hayes (Eds.), *Conceptual foundations of behavioral assessment* (pp. 331–385). New York: Guilford Press.

Heyman, S.R. (1982). Comparisons of successful and unsuccessful competitors: A reconsideration of methodological questions and data. *Journal of Sport Psychology, 4*, 295–300.

Highlen, P.S., & Bennett, B.B. (1983). Elite divers and wrestlers: A comparison between open- and closed-skill athletes. *Journal of Sport Psychology, 5*, 390–409.

Horsfall, J.S., Fisher, A.C., & Morris, H.H. (1975). Sport personality assessment: A methodological re-examination. In D.M. Landers (Ed.), *Psychology of sport and motor behavior* (pp. 61–69). College Station: Pennsylvania State University Press.

Institute for Personality and Ability Testing. (1986). *Administrators manual for the 16 personality factor questionnaire.* Champaign, IL: Author.

Jaccard, J., & Dittus, P. (1990). Idiographic and nomothetic perspectives on research and data analysis. In C. Hendrick & M.S. Clark (Eds.), *Research methods in personality and social psychology (Review of personality and social psychology 11)* (pp. 312 351). Newbury Park, CA: Sage.

Jackson, S.A. (1992). Athletes in flow: A qualitative investigation of flow states in elite figure skaters. *Journal of Applied Sport Psychology, 4*, 161–180.

Jackson, S.A. (1995). Factors influencing the occurrence of flow state in elite athletes. *Journal of Applied Sport Psychology, 7*, 138–166.

Jackson, S.A., Dover, J., & Mayocchi, L. (1998). Life after winning gold: I. Experiences of Australian Olympic gold medalists. *The Sport Psychologist, 12*, 119–136.

Jackson, S.A., Mayocchi, L., & Dover, J. (1998). Life after winning gold: II. Experiences of Australian Olympic gold medalists. *The Sport Psychologist, 12*, 137–155.

Jackson, S.A., & Roberts, G. (1992). Positive performance states of athletes: Towards a conceptual understanding of peak performance. *The Sport Psychologist, 6*, 156–171.

John, O.P. (1990). The "big five" factor taxonomy: Dimensions of personality in the natural language and in questionnaires. In L. Pervin (Ed.), *Handbook of personality: Theory and research* (pp. 66–100). New York: Guilford Press.

Johnson, P.A. (1972). A comparison of personality traits of superior skilled women athletes in basketball, bowling, field hockey and golf. *Research Quarterly, 43*, 409–415.

Kane, J.E. (1964). Personality and physical ability. In K. Kato (Ed.), *Proceedings of international congress of sport sciences* (pp. 201–208). Tokyo: Japanese Union of Sport Sciences.

Kenrick, D.T., & Dantschik, A. (1983). Interactionism, idiographics, and the social psychological invasion of personality. *Journal of Personality, 51,* 286–307.

Kenrick, D.T., & Stringfield, D.O. (1980). Personality traits and the eye of the beholder: Crossing some traditional philosophical boundaries in the search for consistency in all of the people. *Psychological Review, 87,* 88–104.

Killpatrick, F.P., & Cantrill, H. (1960). Self-anchoring scale: A measure of the individual's unique reality world. *Journal of Individual Psychology, 16,* 158–170.

Krahé, B. (1992). *Personality and social psychology: Towards a synthesis.* London: Sage.

Landers, D.M. (1983). Whatever happened to theory testing in sport psychology? *Journal of Sport Psychology, 5,* 135–151.

Landers, D.M. (1989). Sport psychology: A commentary. In J.S. Skinner, C.D. Corbin, D.M. Landers, P.E. Martin, & C.L. Wells (Eds.), *Future directions in exercise and sport science research* (pp. 475–486). Champaign, IL: Human Kinetics.

Landers, D.M., Boutcher, S.H., & Wang, M.Q. (1986a). The history and status of the *Journal of Sport Psychology:* 1979–1985. *Journal of Sport Psychology, 8,* 149–163.

Landers, D.M., Boutcher, S.H., & Wang, M.Q. (1986b). A psychobiological study of archery performance. *Research Quarterly for Exercise and Sport, 57,* 236–244.

Mace, R., & Carroll, D. (1986). Stress inoculation training to control anxiety in sport: Two case studies in squash. *British Journal of Sports Medicine, 20,* 115–117.

Mace, R., Eastman, C., & Carroll, D. (1986). Stress inoculation training: A case study in gymnastics. *British Journal of Sports Medicine, 20,* 139–141.

Magnusson, D., & Törestad, B. (1993). A holistic view of personality: A model revisited. *Annual Review of Psychology, 44,* 427–452.

Mahoney, M.J., Gabriel, T.J., & Perkins, T.S. (1987). Psychological skills and exceptional athletic performance. *The Sport Psychologist, 1,* 181–199.

Markus, H. (1977). Self-schemata and processing information about the self. *Journal of Personality and Social Psychology, 35,* 63–78.

Marsh, H.W., Richards, G.E., Johnson, S., Roche, L., & Tremayne, P. (1994). Physical self-description questionnaire: Properties and a multitrait-multimethod analysis of relations to existing instruments. *Journal of Sport & Exercise Psychology, 16,* 270–305.

Martens, R. (1975). The paradigmatic crisis in American sport personology. *Sportwissenschaft, 5,* 9–24.

Martens, R. (1981). Sport personology. In G.R.F. Lüschen & G.H. Sage (Eds.), *Handbook of social science of sport* (pp. 492–508). Champaign, IL: Stipes.

Martens, R. (1987). Science, knowledge, and sport psychology. *The Sport Psychologist, 1,* 29–55.

Martens, R., Burton, D., Vealey, R.S., Bump, L.A., & Smith, D.E. (1989). The Competitive State Anxiety Inventory–2 (CSAI–2). In D. Burton & R. Vealey (Eds.), *Competitive anxiety* (pp. 117–213). Champaign, IL: Human Kinetics.

Martin, G., & Hrycaiko, D. (1983). Effective behavioral coaching: What's it all about? *Journal of Sport Psychology, 5,* 8–20.

McGowan, J., & Gormly, J. (1976). Validation of personality traits: A multicriteria approach. *Journal of Personality and Social Psychology, 34,* 791–795.

Mischel, W. (1968). *Personality and assessment.* New York: Wiley.

Mischel, W. (1990). Personality dispositions revisited and revised: A view after three decades. In L.A. Pervin (Ed.), *Handbook of personality: Theory and research* (pp. 111–134). New York: Guilford Press.

Mischel, W., & Peake, P.K. (1982). Beyond déjà vu in the search for cross-situational consistency. *Psychological Review, 89,* 730–755.

Mischel, W., & Shoda, Y. (1995). A cognitive-affective system theory of personality: Reconceptualizing situations, dispositions, dynamics, and invariance in personality structure. *Psychological Review, 102,* 246–268.

Monson, T.C., Hesley, J.W., & Chernick, L. (1982). Specifying when personality traits can and cannot predict behavior: An alternative to abandoning the attempt to predict single-act criteria. *Journal of Personality and Social Psychology, 43,* 385–399.

Moore, J.C., & Brylinsky, J.A. (1993). Spectator effect on team performance in college basketball. *Journal of Sport Behavior, 16,* 77–84.

Morgan, W.P. (1973). Efficacy of psychobiologic inquiry in the exercise and sport sciences. *Quest, 20,* 39–47.

Morgan, W.P. (1978). Sport personology: The credulous-skeptical argument in perspective. In W.F. Straub (Ed.), *Sport psychology: An analysis of athlete behavior* (pp. 330–339). Ithaca, NY: Mouvement.

Morgan, W.P. (1980). The trait psychology controversy. *Research Quarterly for Exercise and Sport, 51,* 50–73.

Morgan, W.P. (1985). Selected psychological factors limiting performance: A mental health model. In D.H. Clarke & H.M. Eckert (Eds.), *Limits of human performance* (pp. 70–80), Champaign, IL: Human Kinetics.

Morgan, W.P., O'Connor, P.J., Ellickson, A.E., & Bradley, P.W. (1988). Personality structure, mood states and performance in elite male distance runners. *International Journal of Sport Psychology, 19,* 247–263.

Murtha, T.C., Kanfer, R., & Ackerman, P.L. (1996). Toward an interactionist taxonomy of personality and situations: An integrative situational-dispositional representation of personality traits. *Journal of Personality and Social Psychology, 71,* 193–207.

Nagle, F.J., Morgan, W.P., Hellickson, R.O., Serfass, R.C., & Alexander, J.F. (1975). Spotting success traits in Olympic contenders. *Physician and Sportsmedicine, 3,* 31–34.

Nelson, R.O., & Hayes, S.C. (1986). The nature of behavioral assessment. In R.O. Nelson & S.C. Hayes (Eds.), *Conceptual foundations of behavioral assessment* (pp. 3–41). New York: Guilford Press.

Newcomb, P.A., & Boyle, G.J. (1995). High school students' sports personalities: Variations across participation level, gender, type of sport, and success. *International Journal of Sport Psychology, 26,* 277–294.

Nideffer, R.M. (1990). Use of the Test of Attentional and Interpersonal Style (TAIS) in sport. *The Sport Psychologist, 4,* 285–300.

Ogilvie, B. (1976). Psychological consistencies within the personality of high-level competitors. In A.C. Fisher (Ed.), *Psychology of sport: Issues and insights* (pp. 335–358). Palo Alto, CA: Mayfield.

Pervin, L.A. (1985). Personality: Current controversies, issues, and directions. *Annual Review of Psychology, 36,* 83–114.

Prapavessis, H., Grove, J.R., McNair, P.J., & Cable, N.T. (1992). Self-regulation training, state anxiety, and sport performance: A psychophysiological case study. *The Sport Psychologist, 6,* 213–229.

Price, R.H., & Bouffard, D.L. (1974). Behavioral appropriateness and situational constraint as dimensions of social behavior. *Journal of Personality and Social Psychology, 30,* 579–586.

Ravizza, K. (1984). Qualities of the peak experience in sport. In J.M. Silva & R.S. Weinberg (Eds.), *Psychological foundations of sport* (pp. 452–461). Champaign, IL: Human Kinetics.

Reeds, G.K. (1985). The relationship of personality and anxiety to performance among elite male and female gymnasts. *Canadian Association of Health and Physical Education Record Journal, 51,* 5–7.

Régnier, G., Salmela, J., & Russell, S.J. (1993). Talent detection and development in sport. In R.N. Singer, M. Murphey, & L.K. Tennant (Eds.), *Handbook of research on sport psychology* (pp. 290–313). New York: Macmillan.

Renger, R. (1993a). Predicting athletic success: Issues related to analysis and interpretation of study findings. *The Sport Psychologist, 7,* 262–274.

Renger, R. (1993b). A review of the Profile of Mood States (POMS) in the prediction of athletic success. *Journal of Applied Sport Psychology, 5,* 78–84.

Robinson, T.T., & Carron, A.V. (1982). Personal and situational factors associated with dropping out versus maintaining participation in competitive sport. *Journal of Sport Psychology, 4,* 364–378.

Rowley, A., Landers, D., Kyllo, L., & Etnier, J. (1995). Does the iceberg profile discriminate between successful and less successful athletes? A meta-analysis. *Journal of Sport & Exercise Psychology, 17,* 185–199.

Runyan, W.M. (1983). Idiographic goals and methods in the study of lives. *Journal of Personality, 51,* 413–437.

Rushall, B.S. (1975). Alternative dependent variables for the study of behavior in sport. In D.M. Landers, D.V. Harris, & R.W. Christina (Eds.), *Psychology of sport and motor behavior* (Vol. 2, pp. 49–55). State College: Pennsylvania State University Press.

Rushall, B.S. (1978). Environment specific behavior inventories: Developmental procedures. *International Journal of Sport Psychology, 9,* 97–110.

Rushall, B.S., & Smith, K.C. (1979). The modification of the quality and quantity of behavior categories in a swimming coach. *Journal of Sport Psychology, 1,* 138–150.

Russell, S.J. (1990). Athletes' knowledge in task perception, definition, and classification. *International Journal of Sport Psychology, 21,* 85–101.

Scanlan, T.K., & Lewthwaite, R. (1984). Social psychological aspects of competition for male youth sport participants 1: Predictors of competitive stress. *Journal of Sport Psychology, 6,* 208–226.

Scanlan, T.K., & Lewthwaite, R. (1985). Social psychological aspects of competition for male youth sport participants 3: Determinants of personal performance expectancies. *Journal of Sport Psychology, 7,* 389–399.

Scanlan, T.K., & Lewthwaite, R. (1986). Social psychological aspects of competition for male youth sport participants 4: Predictors of enjoyment. *Journal of Sport Psychology, 8,* 25–35.

Scanlan, T.K., Ravizza, K., & Ravizza, K. (1991). An in-depth study of former elite figure skaters 3: Sources of stress. *Journal of Sport & Exercise Psychology, 13,* 103–120.

Scanlan, T.K., Stein, G.L., & Ravizza, K. (1989). An in-depth study of former elite figure skaters 2: Sources of enjoyment. *Journal of Sport & Exercise Psychology, 11,* 65–83.

Schlattmann, A., & Hackfort, D. (1991). Attributions of functional meanings of "positive" emotions in acting in sport. In D. Hackfort (Ed.), *Research on emotions in sport* (pp. 1–20). Köln, Germany: Bundesinstitut für Sportwissenschaft, Sport und Buch Straus.

Schlicht, W. (1988). Einzelfallanalyse im Hochleistungssport: Zum Verlauf und zur Wirkung selbstbezogener Aufmerksamkeit im 400-Meter-Hürdenlauf [Single-case analysis in elite sport: About the process of paying attention to oneself in 400m hurdles]. Schorndorf, Germany: Hofmann.

Sherman, S.J., & Fazio, R.H. (1983). Parallels between attitudes and traits as predictors of behavior. *Journal of Personality, 51,* 308–345.

Shoda, Y., Mischel, W., & Wright, J.C. (1993). The role of situational demands and cognitive competencies in behavior organization and personality coherence. *Journal of Personality and Social Psychology, 65,* 1023–1035.

Shoda, Y., Mischel, W., & Wright, J.C. (1994). Intraindividual stability in the organization and pattering of behavior: Incorporating psychological situations into the ideographic analysis of personality. *Journal of Personality and Social Psychology, 67,* 674–687.

Silva, J.M. (1984). Personality and sport performance: Controversy and challenge. In J.M. Silva & R.S. Weinberg (Eds.), *Psychological foundations of sport* (pp. 59–69). Champaign, IL: Human Kinetics.

Silva, J.M., Shultz, B.B., Haslam, R.W., & Murray, D. (1981). A psychophysiological assessment of elite wrestlers. *Research Quarterly for Exercise and Sport, 52,* 348–358.

Singer, R.N. (1988). Psychological testing: What value to coaches and athletes? *International Journal of Sport Psychology, 19,* 87–106.

Singer, R.N. (1994). Sport psychology: An integrated approach. In S. Serpa, J. Alves, & V. Pataco (Eds.), *International perspectives on sport and exercise psychology* (pp. 1–20), Morgantown, WV: Fitness Information Technology.

Singer, R.N. (1997). Persistence, excellence, and fulfillment. In R. Lidor & M. Bar-Eli (Eds.), *Innovations in sport psychology: Linking theory and practice: Proceedings of the 9th World Congress of Sport Psychology* (pp. 629–631). Netanya, Israel: Wingate Institute for Physical Education and Sport.

Smith, R.E., Smoll, F.L., & Hunt, E. (1977). A system for the behavioral assessment of athletic coaches. *Research Quarterly, 48,* 401–407.

Snyder, M. (1979). Self-monitoring processes. *Advances in Experimental Social Psychology, 12,* 85–128.

Snyder, M. (1983). Choosing friends as activity partners: The role of self-monitoring. *Journal of Personality and Social Psychology, 45,* 1061–1072.

Snyder, M., & Gangestad, S. (1982). Choosing social situations: Two investigations of self-monitoring processes. *Journal of Personality and Social Psychology, 43,* 123–135.

Staats, A.W. (1986). Behaviorism with a personality: The paradigmatic behavioral assessment approach. In R.O. Nelson & S.C. Hayes (Eds.), *Conceptual foundations of behavioral assessment* (pp. 243–296). New York: Guilford Press.

Straub, W.F. (1977). Approaches to personality assessment of athletes: Personologism, situationism and interactionism. In R.E. Stadulis & C.O. Dotson (Eds.), *Research and practice in physical education* (pp. 176–187). Champaign, IL: Human Kinetics.

Strean, W.B., & Roberts, G.C. (1992). Future directions in applied sport psychological research. *The Sport Psychologist, 6,* 55–65.

Tanaka, J.S., Panter, A.T., Winborne, W.C., & Huba, G.J. (1990). Theory testing in personality and social psychology with structural equation models: A primer in 20 questions. In C. Hendrick & M.S. Clark (Eds.), *Research methods in personality and social psychology (Review of personality and social psychology 11)* (pp. 217–242). Newbury Park, CA: Sage.

Trudel, P., Côté, J., & Sylvestre, F. (1996). Systematic observation of youth ice hockey coaches during games. *Journal of Sport Behavior, 19,* 50–65.

Vallerand, R.J. (1997). Intrinsic and intrinsic motivation in sport: Implications from the hierarchical model. In R. Lidor & M. Bar-Eli (Eds.), *Innovations in sport psychology: Linking theory and practice: Proceedings of the 9th World Congress of Sport Psychology* (pp. 45–47). Netanya, Israel: Wingate Institute for Physical Education and Sport.

Van den Auweele, Y. (1988). Personality diagnosis in young toplevel athletes. In P. Kunath, S. Müller, & H. Schellenberger (Eds.), *Proceedings of the 7th congress of the European Federation of Sports Psychology 2* (pp. 507–525). Leipzig, Germany: Deutsche Hochschule für Körperkultur.

Van den Auweele, Y., De Cuyper, B., Van Mele, V., & Rzewnicki, R. (1993). Elite performance and personality: From description and prediction to diagnosis and intervention. In R.N. Singer, M. Murphey, & L.K.Tennant (Eds.), *Handbook of research on sport psychology* (pp. 257–289). New York: Macmillan.

Van den Auweele, Y., Depreeuw, E., Rzewnicki, R., & Ballon, F. (1999). Optimal functioning versus dysfunctioning of athletes: A comprehensive model for the practice of sport psychology. In *European Yearbook of Sport Psychology* (pp. 1–37).

Van Ingen Schenau, G.J., De Koning, J.J., Bakker, F.C., & De Groot, G. (1996). Performance-influencing factors in homogeneous groups of top athletes: A cross-sectional study. *Medicine and Science in Sport and Exercise, 28,* 1305–1310.

Van Mechelen, I., De Boeck, P., & Rosenberg, S. (1995). The conjunctive model of hierarchical classes. *Psychometrika, 60,* 505–521.

Van Mele, V. (1996). *Intra-individuele, kwantitatieve persoonlijkheidsdiagnostiek bij de begeleiding van atleten [Intra-individual, quantitative personality diagnosis in counselling athletes].* Unpublished doctoral dissertation, University of Leuven, Belgium.

Van Mele, V., Vanden Auweele, Y., & Rzewnicki, R. (1995). An integrative procedure for the diagnosis of an elite athlete: A case study. *The Sport Psychologist, 9,* 130–147.

Van Raalte, J.L., Brewer, B.W., Rivera, P.M., & Petitpas, A.J. (1995). Behavioral assessment of self-talk and gestures during competitive tennis. In J. Viitasalo & U. Kujala (Eds.), *The way to win: Proceedings of the International Congress on Applied Research in Sports* (pp. 341–343). Helsinki: Finnish Society for Research in Sport and Physical Education.

Vansteelandt, K., & Van Mechelen, I. (1998). Individual differences in situation-behavior profiles: A triple typology model. *Journal of Personality and Social Psychology, 75,* 751–765.

Vealey, R.S. (1989). Sport personology: A paradigmatic and methodological analysis. *Journal of Sport & Exercise Psychology, 11,* 216–235.

Vealey, R.S. (1992). Personality and sport: A comprehensive view. In T.S. Horn (Ed.), *Advances in sport psychology* (pp. 25–59). Champaign, IL: Human Kinetics.

Vealey, R.S. (1994). Knowledge development and implementation in sport psychology: A review of *The Sport Psychologist,* 1987–1992. *The Sport Psychologist, 8,* 331–348.

Vealey, R.S., & Garner-Holman, M. (1998). Applied sport psychology: Measurement issues. In J.L. Duda (Ed.), *Advances in sport and exercise psychology measurement* (pp. 433–446). Morgantown, WV: Fitness Information Technology.

Vealey, R.S., Hayashi, S.W., Garner-Holman, M., & Giacobbi, P. (1998). Sources of sport-confidence: Conceptualization and instrument development; *Journal of Sport & Exercise Psychology, 20,* 54–80.

Verstraeten, D. (1987). Persoonlijkheidsonderzoek en meten van verandering: Een terugblik over twintig jaar [Personality research and the measurement of change: A review over twenty years]. *Tijdschrift voor Klinische Psychologie, 17,* 232–253.

Wankel, L.M., & Kreisel, P.S.J. (1985a). Factors underlying enjoyment of youth sports: Sport and age group comparisons. *Journal of Sport Psychology, 7,* 51–64.

Wankel, L.M., & Kreisel, P.S.J. (1985b). Methodological considerations in youth sport motivation research: A comparison of open-ended and paired comparison approaches. *Journal of Sport Psychology, 7,* 65–74.

Williams, L.R.T. (1978). Prediction of high-level rowing ability. *Journal of Sports Medicine, 18,* 11–17.

Williams, L.R.T. (1982). Innovations in behavioural research: Implications for elite performance. *New Zealand Journal of Health, Physical Education and Recreation, 15,* 19–26.

Wolf, F.M. (1986). *Meta-analysis: Quantitative methods for research synthesis.* Beverly Hills, CA: Sage.

CHAPTER 10

The Development of Talent in Sport

NATALIE DURAND-BUSH and JOHN H. SALMELA

The Chinese bamboo plant takes 10 years to grow six inches. It then grows 10 feet in six months. Ask yourself: Did the plant grow 10 feet in six months or 10 feet and six inches in 10 years and six months?

The above observation is central to any discussion regarding the nature of talent in sport. In a previous overview of this topic (Régnier, Salmela, & Russell, 1993), the predominant thinking of the era in sport psychology was not as sensitive to the developmental issues and the nature-nurture debate regarding talent in sport. Quite simply, the individual contribution and relationship between environmental and genetic factors was believed to be of unknown magnitude. More important, the precise definition of the talent concept was not addressed at the time, but the highly skilled athlete was believed to be "talented" and had to call on some inherited "gift" or innate ability to excel. In this way, the state of affairs in the study of talent in sport was analogous to seeing only the rapid growth of the Chinese bamboo plant without considering the 10-year period of gestation and development.

The belief that innate talent is, in fact, a primary construct for exceptional athletic performance is reinforced daily in almost every sport telecast, where the word "talented" is used as a synonym for "highly skilled" athlete. However, some researchers now argue that contrary to this belief, exceptional performance is more the result of extended amounts of high-quality practice and that innate abilities play a minimal role (Ericsson, Krampe, & Tesch-

Preparation of this chapter was supported by a standard research grant from the Social Sciences and Humanities Research Council of Canada (SSHRC Grant #410-97-0241). The authors are grateful to Mike Stevenson for his helpful comments in the preparation of this chapter.

Römer, 1993; Howe, Davidson, & Sloboda, 1998). This view has definitely revived the nature-nurture debate.

Furthermore, Ericsson and Lehmann (1996) challenged the scientific community by highlighting the fact that in sport, athletes winning Olympic marathon performances early in the century are now surpassed by amateur senior citizens, which brings to question whether or not innate talent can increase in magnitude. Indeed, the assumptions regarding the notion of talent have been severely scrutinized by a number of scholars who have critically reconsidered how exceptional performance develops in the arts, music, sciences, mathematics, chess, and sport (Ericsson & Charness, 1994; Ericsson et al., 1993; Ericsson & Lehmann, 1996; Hodges & Starkes, 1996; Howe et al., 1998; Salmela & Durand-Bush, 1994; Singer & Janelle, 1999).

The purpose of this chapter is to provide an overview of traditional and contemporary views on the development of talent, particularly in the domain of sport. Controversial questions are raised and innovative ideas are generated that could potentially influence the thinking of researchers and practitioners in the future. The first part of the chapter focuses on providing a definition of talent. The second part summarizes traditional approaches to talent development, which were centered around the concept of talent detection and selection. Concerns regarding talent detection procedures are also discussed. The third part of the chapter presents more contemporary views on talent development, including those of Bloom (1985), Ericsson and colleagues (1993), Côté (1999), and Csikszentmihalyi, Rathunde, and Whalen (1993). The last part focuses on unresolved issues pertaining to talent, based on one of the most interesting and at times heated debates that developed around a recent target article written by Howe and colleagues (1998). Also discussed are relevant concerns raised in the 30 open peer commentaries of noted international scholars of varying epistemological orientations that accompanied the article.

DEFINING TALENT

There have been numerous attempts over the past century to define "talent." Although the use of this term is very common across domains, its meaning substantially changes depending on the particular perspective of the users. Howe et al.'s (1998) perspective is that performers become highly successful as a result of environmental factors such as intense training rather than innate abilities. They believe that people often label performers as being talented because it helps them explain their success, and that such early assessments or "talent accounts" can be either very influential or prejudicial to the ultimate performance outcomes of these individuals. Howe and colleagues suggested: "The talent account has important social implications. A consequence of the belief that innate gifts are a precondition for high achievement is that young people who are not identified as having innate talents in a particular domain are likely to be denied the help and encouragement they would need to attain high levels of competence" (p. 399).

Howe and colleagues (1998) clearly adopted a view opposed to the "talent account," which refers to the notion that the attainment of exceptional performance depends on a special genetic potential that can be identified in certain children. Before presenting arguments for and against this talent account, they found it was important to provide an explicit definition of the concept of talent that respected most of the criteria typically acknowledged by the scientific community. They assigned the five following properties to talent: "(1) It originates in genetically transmitted structures and hence is at least partly innate. (2) Its full effects may not be evident at an early stage, but there will be some advance indications, allowing trained people to identify the presence of talent before exceptional levels of mature performance have been demonstrated. (3) These early indications of talent provide a basis for predicting who is likely to excel. (4) Only a minority are talented, for if all children were, there would be no way to predict or explain differential success. Finally, (5) talents are relatively domain specific" (pp. 399–400).

Howe and colleagues (1998) stated that by adopting this definition, the scientific and lay communities would be more likely to assess the concept of talent from a less intuitive stance. However, scholars who were asked to respond to the article varied in receptivity to the idea. Although a number were supportive of the environmentally deterministic position (Charness, 1998; Eisenberger, 1998; Ericsson, 1998; Irvine, 1998; Lehmann, 1998; Simonton, 1998; Starkes & Helsen, 1998; Tesch-Römer, 1998; Weisberg, 1998), others questioned its radical nature, which excluded innate talent as a determinant of exceptional performance (Baltes, 1998; Csikszentmihalyi, 1998; Detterman, Gabriel, & Ruthsatz, 1998; Feldman & Katzir, 1998; Gagné, 1998; Heller & Ziegler, 1998; Plomin, 1998; Rowe, 1998; Rutter, 1998; Schneider, 1998; Sternberg, 1998; Trehub & Schellenberg, 1998; Winner, 1998; Zohar, 1998). To better understand the history behind such opposing viewpoints, both traditional and more recent orientations that have guided the research on talent will be reviewed next, particularly in the domain of sport, beginning with traditional orientations.

TRADITIONAL TALENT DEVELOPMENT ORIENTATIONS

European-based research, predominantly in the 1970s, was concerned with "sport talent detection." During this period, it was well-known that coaches and sport scientists in East Germany and the Soviet Bloc countries scoured elementary schools for young children who demonstrated aptitudes that were supposedly going to lead to success in sport. Researchers attempted to predict performance across various periods of time by measuring psychological aptitudes, alone or in combination with other physical, physiological, or technical abilities. To this day, talent detection refers to the attempt to determine (1) the congruency among a variety of performer characteristics, which could be either innate or subject to the effect of learning or training, and (2) the task demands of a given sport activity to ensure the highest probability of maximum performance outcome (Régnier et al., 1993).

Talent detection and talent selection were seen as interrelated processes in traditional sport science. According to Régnier et al. (1993), talent selection takes place over a shorter period of time and is focused on choosing individuals who can best carry out the tasks within a specific sport context, for example, the Olympic Games. Talent selection can be viewed as "very short-term talent detection," as it is concerned with assessing which athletes will perform best in two months or sometimes even in two weeks (Blahüs, 1975; Hay, 1969). In that this is not so much a process as it is a punctual task within the more global processes of talent detection and talent development, talent selection will not be covered separately in this section.

The attempts to detect talent in sport have been numerous (Ackland, Bloomfield, Elliott, & Blanksby, 1990;

Bar-Or, 1975; Bartmus, Neumann, & de Marées, 1987; Bulgakova & Voroncov, 1978; Geron, 1978; Gimbel, 1976; Harre, 1982; Havlicek, Komadel, Komarik, & Simkova, 1982; Jones & Watson, 1977; Kerr, Dainty, Booth, Gaboriault, & McGavern, 1979; Montpetit & Cazorla, 1982; Régnier & Salmela, 1983; Régnier, Salmela, & Alain, 1982; Salmela & Régnier, 1983). Traditionally, researchers were concerned with developing talent detection models; thus, an overview of these is described in the next section. They are also reassessed in light of more recent thinking on the issue of talent.

Overview of Talent Detection Models

Several sport-specific talent detection models have been developed over the years. One model was proposed by Bar-Or (1975), who provided a detailed operational procedure for sport talent detection using a five-step approach: (1) Evaluate children on a series of morphological, physiological, psychological, and performance variables; (2) weigh the results with a "development index" to account for biological age; (3) test their reaction to training with exposure to a brief training program; (4) evaluate family history (e.g., height, sport activities); and (5) use a multiple regression analysis model to predict performance from results on the first four steps. Though plausible, this model was not submitted to any longitudinal field study across sports.

Shortly after, Jones and Watson (1977) developed a procedure to predict performance from psychological variables. Even though they did not present a talent detection model as such, their work was considered valuable because they provided information on performance prediction. Their steps to predict performance included (1) determining the target performance, (2) selecting a criterion to represent the target performance, (3) selecting potential performance predictors and verifying their predictive power, and (4) applying the results.

Gimbel (1976) embraced both the nature and nurture perspectives and assumed that talent should be analyzed from three perspectives: (1) physiological and morphological variables, (2) trainability, and (3) motivation. Talent was divided into internal factors (genetics) and external factors (environment). According to Gimbel, genetic factors were essential in the development of expert performance, but performance was minimized if environmental conditions were not favorable. It was highlighted that in most sports, top-level performances were reached by the time athletes were between 18 and 20 years of age, and that 8 to 10 years of training were required to develop champions. Furthermore, promising athletes had to be identified

at 8 to 9 years of age, before their growth spurt began. To prevent excluding late bloomers, Gimbel proposed a one-year "recovery period" for uncertain cases so that those not initially identified could be reintegrated into training after having made significant improvement in performance.

Gimbel (1976) also addressed the question of "false positives," that is, individuals identified as talented who never fulfilled their predicted potential. Three explanations for this phenomenon were suggested: (1) Tests used to predict performance were not sufficiently valid, reliable, and objective; (2) it was impossible to accurately predict performance from such tests because of biological age differences among children; and (3) contributions from psychological variables were neglected in predictive models.

Geron (1978) developed a talent detection model similar to the one proposed by Gimbel (1976) and later refined by Montpetit and Cazorla (1982). The model comprised the following procedures: (1) the determination of an "elite athlete" profile in a given sport, (2) the identification through longitudinal studies of variables strongly related to success and highly dependent on heredity, and (3) the determination of age periods when the genetic dimension of selected factors are the most powerful. Geron found that profiles of top-level athletes, or "sportograms," were not sufficient to predict talent. She underlined the difference between simply enumerating factors predicting performance and identifying the constituent success elements in a given sport. In other words, there is a difference between the early qualities required for athletes to become champions and the characteristics of champions.

An improved version of Gimbel's (1976) model was developed by Montpetit and Cazorla (1982) and used for talent detection in swimming. Procedures were added to identify morphological variables on which predictions should rest. The first step in the model entailed sketching a "top-level swimmer profile" for each event based on conventional physiological testing procedures. The second step consisted of verifying the stability of the variables in the profile through longitudinal studies. Using stability indices and developmental rates of variables best describing swimming champions, Montpetit and Cazorla suggested that the evolution of underlying performance factors, and thus performance itself, could be predicted.

Another talent detection model constructed by Harre (1982) was based on the assumption that it is only through training that one can determine if a child possesses the required attributes to succeed. Consequently, it was postulated that the first step in talent detection is to put as many children as possible through training programs. They can then be tested during the early years of training to assess their level of performance, rate of improvement, stability of performance, and reaction to training demands.

Havlicek et al. (1982) recognized the multidimensional nature of sport performance and adopted a multidisciplinary approach to talent detection. They also underscored the importance of heredity-dependent and performance-related factors in talent detection, such as height and general morphology. Contrary to Harre (1982), they stated that it would be a mistake to rely only on such factors. Their research took into consideration the degree of heredity of various multidisciplinary variables believed to be related to sport performance. The concept of "priorizing" the predictive contribution of each factor based on its respective stability was one way of dealing with the heredity question. For example, although height is highly correlated to the stature of parents and to the gymnastics performance of young athletes, it is not correlated with the performance of mature gymnasts (Régnier, 1987).

Régnier (1987) proposed a conceptual model for sport talent detection that provided a general framework around which research and professional efforts in sport talent detection could be organized to develop detection instruments for any sport setting. This model was based on the four steps of performance prediction postulated by Jones and Watson (1977). A fifth step was added based on Blahüs's (1975) suggestion to validate performance predictors by testing the stability of any precision model found with regression analyses through cross-validating with other samples of athletes taken from the same population from which it was originally developed. Régnier's model was used to guide talent detection research in gymnastics (Jancarik & Salmela, 1987; Régnier & Salmela, 1987; Salmela, Régnier, & Proteau, 1987) and baseball (Régnier, 1987). Due to the model's broad multidisciplinary and multivariate nature, sport scientists as well as experts from each sport discipline (i.e., coaches) could be involved.

Concerns Regarding Talent Detection Models

The attempts described in developing talent detection models and procedures were considered innovative and appropriate at the time. However, in light of more recent thinking, their validity and usefulness are questionable. Two of the criteria ascribed by Howe and colleagues (1998) to a contemporary definition of talent were that, first, there are early indications of talent that will allow trained professionals to detect it before exceptional performance is achieved, and second, these indications provide a basis for predicting who is likely to achieve

exceptional performance. Yet, many scholars have stated that talent, innate or acquired, cannot be used to predict future levels of performance (Bartmus, Neumann, & de Marées, 1987; Bloom, 1985). This does not imply that innate talent does not exist and does not have any influence on the development of performance. The interaction between the genetic makeup of athletes and numerous environmental factors makes it very difficult, in fact, most likely impossible at this time, to determine the longitudinal effects of talent on sport performance. A number of researchers have argued against the detection of talent and talent-based predictions of performance.

For example, Seefeldt (1988), after reviewing the literature on the prediction of the rate of motor skill acquisition, concluded: "Virtually all of the investigators . . . reported the retrospective prediction of success, often through the use of regression equations that were obtained from cross-sectional studies or computed at the termination of longitudinal studies. None of the investigators attempted to predict the success of individuals in motor performance prior to their involvement in activity programs, nor did they conduct a longitudinal follow-up to determine the accuracy of the original predictions. In no case were the predictive equations applied to other samples as a test of their validity" (pp. 49–50).

Although this approach promoted by Seefeldt (1988) is a rigorous one, it also has the important drawback of being very time-consuming. The delays involved in producing and testing a detection instrument are so significant that by the time one becomes operational, it might very well be obsolete. This holds especially true for sports characterized by the frequent introduction of new trends, such as judgment sports (e.g., gymnastics, figure skating, diving) and some team sports, after which the relative importance of the qualities required to achieve success shifts. This might explain why Seefeldt did not locate any studies in which a strict application of this procedure was reported for the prediction of motor skill acquisition.

It can be seen from the overview of the models that talent detection based on a scientific approach is an arduous process. The issues involved are so complex that more and more questions are being raised concerning the feasibility of this process in general. Several scholars at a symposium on talent detection reported by Bartmus et al. (1987) expressed such skepticism. In his introduction, de Marées, the chairman of the symposium, emphasized that "many questions are still unanswered despite numerous investigations during the second half of the seventies" (p. 415).

Bartmus et al. (1987) reported the results of a longitudinal study of 100 tennis players. Their conclusion was that "no uniform tennis performance ability exists: Deficiencies in one area of performance can be compensated for by a high level in others" (p. 415). These results imply that talent detection cannot be based on only one set of supposed prerequisites of excellence. The compensation phenomenon is one of the factors that make one-shot long-term performance predictions difficult.

However, the use of multilayered longitudinal task analyses that incorporate a variety of sport science variables, ranging from "hard" morphological measures to "softer" psychological ones, can provide flexible tools to control the phenomenon. For example, Régnier and Salmela (1987) found that with a population of gymnasts, measures of speed, power, and strength were adequate for predicting performance results in athletes younger than 12 years of age because these variables accounted for 100% of the variance. However, factors such as perceptual awareness and spatial orientation, as well as psychological variables such as anxiety, had to be included to differentiate among 20-year-old gymnasts at the upper levels of performance. The fact that different factors predicted performance at different age levels appears to preclude the notion that there are uniform abilities that could be labeled "talent" and that might be used to project the performance of athletes.

Other findings suggesting that performance cannot be predicted based on a requisite set of abilities stemmed from Russell's (1990) study in which highly skilled athletes were asked to define their sport tasks situations. These elite athletes emphasized metacognitive knowledge and skills rather than the physical and technical aspects of their sport performance. Russell suggested that performers of different skill levels focus on different aspects of their sport tasks: "Novices, for example, may stress the physical demands of training, while middle-level performers might focus on technical skills, and highly skilled athletes emphasize metacognitive task components" (p. 93). It is thus difficult to define the factors most significant in predicting performance, particularly in the early years when athletes have not yet reached physical, psychological, and emotional maturity.

Talent is also difficult to predict in the later years because as time progresses, the population of "successful" athletes becomes smaller and more homogeneous with respect to both their physical and psychological profiles (Régnier, 1987). Those who have not developed the sport-specific prototype (e.g., being a short gymnast) tend to

drop out of the sport. Csikszentmihalyi and Robinson (1986) described this phenomenon common to all fields of excellence: "The youngsters who were not performing at the top in a previous stage are usually no longer in contention for 'gifted' status by the time that status and its attendant support change in *ways* that might benefit them. In highly competitive domains, such as music, math, or sports, the way down is always much broader than the way up. Year by year, it becomes more difficult to catch up, and dropping out becomes increasingly easy" (p. 275).

Another concern regarding talent detection models emerged from a five-year longitudinal study conducted with alpine skiers (Willimczik, 1986). This study was presented at the symposium on talent detection (Bartmus et al., 1987), where it was concluded that "talent search with respect to individual sports disciplines hardly seems possible; only scientifically based support of already identified athletes appears to be indicated" (p. 415). The circular nature of identifying highly skilled athletes as being talented is again evident from these conclusions and limits the advancement of research in this domain (Howe et al., 1998).

Mocker (cited in Bartmus et al., 1987) took a similar stance by stating that scientifically valid methods do not exist in the field of talent search and that the judgment of qualified coaches is preferred. He described the system of sport schools in which children who were favored by coaches from the former East German regime had to achieve a fixed set of norms to progress toward higher levels of training and support. Ulmer (cited in Bartmus et al., 1987) also believed that conducting a scientifically based talent search was problematic. His studies led him to believe that the selection of athletes for success in competition should be at best based on the observation of skilled coaches.

The ability of skilled physical education teachers to have an eye for "talent" was studied by Thomas and Thomas (1999). They reported that expert physical education teachers who reflected on the early career characteristics of two athletes who eventually became all-stars indicated that they practiced more and had a significantly better work ethic than other students. These qualities were deemed more important than other talent-related qualities such as quickness and coordination.

In sum, it is noteworthy that some evidence has been advanced to substantiate the ability of expert observers to note special characteristics and attitudes of future champions at an early stage (Thomas & Thomas, 1999). However, experts in the sport sciences are skeptical about whether or not traditional a priori sport-science-based methods, some of which involve the use of expert observers, are capable of predicting who can become outstanding athletes. The forging of "talent" in sport through detection programs must therefore be reconsidered. In view of the difficulty of the talent detection process, Bartmus et al. (1987) suggested that research efforts be shifted from talent detection to talent guidance and development, or what could be called "talent surveillance." The following section presents some of the more recent and modern research that has been conducted on the development of talent and exceptional performance.

MODERN TALENT DEVELOPMENT ORIENTATIONS

In the 1980s, there were epistemological and methodological shifts in some of the research on the development of talent and expertise. Martens (1987) led this movement in the field of sport psychology. He critically analyzed various sources of knowledge and made some persuasive arguments regarding the benefits of not subscribing strictly to the precepts of orthodox science. He contended that the field of experiential knowledge was rich in useful information and might be best approached nontraditionally, using idiographic approaches, introspective methods, and field studies to complement the methods of orthodox science. The work of researchers who adopted holistic, nontraditional approaches to study talent and expertise in sport is synthesized next.

Bloom's Stages of Talent Development

Benjamin Bloom (1985) conducted a four-year longitudinal study on the career evolution of 120 talented athletes, musicians, artists, and scientists, and largely contributed to the advancement of knowledge in the field of expertise. He was particularly concerned with the process of talent development in children, beginning with their early involvement and culminating with the achievement of expertise in their respected fields. Contrary to popular opinion, talent in this context was not used to refer to innate aptitudes or special gifts. Bloom clearly indicated his viewpoint on the nature-nurture debate by stating that, despite the "initial characteristics (or gifts) of the individuals, unless there is a long and intensive process of encouragement, nurturance, education, and training, the individuals will not attain extreme levels of capability in these particular fields" (p. 3).

Bloom (1985) was innovative in that he identified three critical stages of talent development and provided important

insights on how Olympic swimmers, world-class tennis players, concert pianists, sculptors, research mathematicians, and research neurologists became exceptional in their chosen endeavors. One important conclusion was that talent development requires years of commitment to learning, and that the amount and quality of support and instruction children receive from parents, teachers, or coaches is central to this process. Bloom identified three distinct stages of talent development. However, he indicated that these are only "signposts along a long and continuous learning process" (p. 537). The stages provide excellent guidelines for performers who are going through this process, as well as for teachers and parents, who play an important role throughout the career of these performers.

Early Years and Stage of Initiation

Bloom (1985) discovered that the participants in his study first went through an initiation stage, in which they were engaged in fun, playful activities. As children, they were excited about their participation at this stage and relied heavily on their teacher or coach for guidance and support. It was predominantly during this early stage that parents and/or teachers noticed certain children appearing to be gifted, talented, or "special" in some way. These attributions of special qualities affected both the expectations for the children and the methods used for teaching.

Teachers or coaches generally adopted a process-oriented approach in their teaching, and thus encouraged and rewarded the young children for the process of effort rather than the outcome of achievement. Although teachers and coaches were not necessarily technically advanced at this stage, they provided the love and positive reinforcement the children needed to keep learning and performing activities. Bloom (1985) found that parents also played a very important role in the development of their children's talents. As a result of their interest in a particular field or activity, the parents were often responsible for initially stimulating their children's interest in that same field or activity. In sharing their excitement, as well as being positive and supportive of their children, parents were an excellent source of energy and motivation.

Middle Years and Stage of Development

Eventually, the participants moved on to a stage of development where they became, as Bloom (1985) termed it, "hooked" on their particular activity. For example, they were "gymnasts" rather than "children who did gymnastics." Their pursuits evolved to a more serious nature and consequently, higher levels of dedication to succeed were witnessed. Teachers or coaches were usually more technically skilled than those at the previous level. They emphasized the development of proper technique, provided children with opportunities to evaluate their performance and expected results through discipline and a hard work ethic. Bloom found that teachers and coaches took a strong personal interest in the participants at this stage, and the loving relationship the children had with them during the initial stage was subsequently replaced by one of respect.

Practice time was significantly increased at this stage. The participants became more achievement-oriented and competition became the yardstick for measuring progress. Sacrifices had to be made on the part of not only the performers but also the parents. As a result of the crucial demands at this level, parents had to provide both moral and financial support to sustain their children's involvement in their chosen activity. They also helped in restricting outside activities such as work and outings with friends, while still showing concern for the total development of their children.

Late Years and Stage of Perfection

According to Bloom (1985), it was in the final stage, the one of perfection, that these individuals became experts. The participants were radically obsessed by their chosen activity, which dominated their lives at this point. The emphasis was now placed on the development of very high-level skills, and the participants were willing to invest the necessary time and effort required to achieve their ultimate performance goals. Furthermore, there was a shift in the responsibility for training and competition from the teachers or coaches to the performers. The performers had to be autonomous and extremely knowledgeable. Bloom revealed that because the mentors or master teachers at this level placed enormous demands on the performers, they sometimes became feared, but always were respected. The parents played a lesser role at this stage because the participants were completely immersed in their actions and assumed total responsibility for them.

In summary, Bloom (1985) provided a valuable framework for studying the development of expertise. He elicited data on the global process of talent development from the early childhood years to the later, more highly demanding years of talent perfection. His viewpoint on this process can be best summarized as follows: "There are many years of increasingly difficult stages of talent development before the mature and complex talent will be fully attained. No matter how precocious one is at age ten or eleven, if the individual doesn't stay with the talent development process over many years, he or she will soon be outdistanced by others who do continue. A long-term commitment to the talent field and an increasing passion for the talent development are essential if the individual is to attain the highest levels of capability in the field" (p. 538).

Other researchers have followed in Bloom's (1985) footsteps and attempted to provide more information on the evolution of outstanding performance. Côté (1999) was particularly interested in studying the influence of the family on the development of talent in sport. His research, combined with that of others, led him to postulate three stages of sport participation from early childhood to late adolescence. These stages are discussed next.

Côté's Stages of Sport Participation

Côté and colleagues (Abernethy, Côté, & Baker, 1999; Côté, 1999; Côté & Hay, in press) recently studied the career development of elite Canadian and Australian athletes in rowing, gymnastics, basketball, netball, and field hockey. In one study, Côté (1999) attempted to shed more light on the role of the family in the development of young athletes. More specifically, he was interested in investigating how family members support children in their initiation and development of high-level performance. He also attempted to determine whether patterns of family dynamics that contributed to the success of athletes existed at different stages of development.

Côté (1999) interviewed 15 members of four different families in which at least one child was intensely involved in sport. Four athletes, four mothers, three fathers, and four siblings were asked to discuss the dynamics of their family as they related to motivational, effort, and resource constraints inherent in the development of exceptional performance (Ericsson et al., 1993). All four athletes were 18 years of age, and three of them (one man and two women) were part of the Canadian national junior rowing team; the other was a male tennis player competing at a national level in Canada. The advantage of gathering data during this developmental training period was that the participants had superior recollections of past and current events, making them more accurate.

As a result of his research, Côté (1999) suggested three distinct stages of participation in sport: the sampling, the specializing, and the investment years. It is noteworthy that at each level, athletes have the potential to move to another level, drop out of sport, or enter the recreational years.

Sampling Years

The sampling years consisted of a period during which children and siblings were encouraged by their parents to experiment with different sports and games for pure pleasure, rather than for attaining specific goals. Côté (1999) revealed that the children were not pressured to choose one sport discipline in preference over another, but rather they were motivated to sample the benefits of various activities. They were also usually introduced to organized sport during this period, whereby their participation was active, voluntary, pleasurable, intrinsically motivating, and provided immediate gratification. Côté and Hay (in press) referred to this type of involvement in sport and games as "deliberate play." More specifically, deliberate play was characterized as being intentional and involving an implicit or explicit set of rules, depending on the level of organization of the sport and activities.

During the sampling years, parents and coaches were concerned with providing children with opportunities to have fun and develop fundamental motor skills, positive identities, motivations, values, and beliefs about sport and physical activity. The families of aspiring athletes in Côté's (1999) study revealed that play was more predominant than practice or training during this period. The emphasis was on enjoyment rather than competition. Of particular interest is that parents in three out of the four families revealed that they felt their child had a special gift for sport during the sampling years. This could have led to increased supportive behaviors, such as encouragement and positive reinforcement for skill and effort. This suggests that parents' beliefs can reinforce their children's self-beliefs, which, according to Dweck (1986), are determinants of progress and persistence.

Specializing Years

During the specializing years, the athletes narrowed their focus on one or two sport disciplines. They typically made this choice around the age of 13, and their decision was often influenced by the social support and encouragement they received from coaches, older siblings, and parents, as well as by the intrinsic enjoyment and success they experienced within their sport. At this level, the development of sport-specific skills was emphasized through more structured practice, although fun and excitement still remained central elements in the process. Côté and Hay (in press) suggested that to prevent children from becoming disinterested and dropping out, there should be a balance between deliberate play and practice during the specializing years.

It is noteworthy that parents in all four families attributed more importance to achievement in school than to that in sport. However, because school and sport were priorities in their children's lives, they did not expect them to work outside the home. Parents also developed an interest in their children's sport and thus got involved at differing degrees, from spectator to coach. They also invested considerable time and money to support their children's participation. In terms of older siblings, Côté (1999) found that they often acted as role models and had a positive influence on the work ethic of the children.

Investment Years

The investment years were characterized by the pursuit of an elite level of performance usually in one or two specific sports. Children typically reached this level around the age of 15; however, this could vary depending on the sport. Similar to Bloom's (1985) stage of perfection, the investment years were notably more intense in terms of the time and effort the participants dedicated to training. The main focus was on the development of skills and strategies for competition; thus, deliberate play was replaced by extensive amounts of deliberate practice.

As was the case in the specializing years, the parents showed great interest in their children's career and provided emotional and financial support to sustain their involvement in sport. They also helped their children cope with setbacks such as injuries, failure, and lack of motivation. Due to the high-level sport participation of one child, there was an uneven distribution of resources within the family, which often created tension and jealousy among siblings. Although parents were consciously aware of this, their belief in their talented child was enough to justify their actions toward all of their children.

Recreational Years

Côté (1999) included the "recreational years" in his model to account for children or athletes who cannot or choose not to invest the necessary resources to participate at a high level or do not want to focus on a single sport. The recreational years consist of a period in which individuals practice several sports and activities to experience enjoyment and personal growth, remain physically active, and maintain a healthy lifestyle.

Côté's stages of sport participation were evident in a recent study conducted by Durand-Bush (2000) in which 10 expert athletes having won at least two gold medals at separate Olympics and World Championships were interviewed to investigate how they became champions. Results indicated that the athletes followed patterns of sport participation similar to those described by Côté (1999). However, Durand-Bush postulated another stage, Maintenance Years, to characterize the period after which athletes achieved the highest level in their sport; that is, after they won a gold medal at the Olympics or World Championships.

In the maintenance years, there was usually more pressure from outside sources for athletes to perform, as they were the best in their sport. This created additional stress, but fortunately, they developed personal strategies to deal with distractors. Most athletes revealed that, at this level, they needed to be innovative in attempts to stay motivated and also to avoid being "copied" by competitors. Furthermore, the focus of their training shifted from quantity to quality. The athletes did not necessarily increase the hours of training during this period—in fact, some decreased them—but they made a conscious effort to improve every microscopic aspect of their performance (Durand-Bush, 2000).

In sum, the aforementioned stages of participation provide guidelines for nurturing and monitoring talent in children and young adults. Côté and Hay (in press) revealed that skill development and enjoyment were the most important factors for keeping children involved in sport and helping them progress through the levels of development. Knowing this, appropriate environments can be created for them to experience fun and success at each level, but more particularly when they are young and perhaps more sensitive to various elements of participation in sport. It is noteworthy that young children can be provided such opportunities regardless of whether or not they show "promise" or "talent" in a particular activity or sport.

Ericsson's Notion of Deliberate Practice

The research of Bloom (1985) and Côté and colleagues (Abernethy et al., 1999; Côté, 1999; Côté & Hay, in press) demonstrated the important role of environmental factors in the development of talent and expertise. Ericsson and collaborators (Ericsson & Faivre, 1988; Ericsson et al., 1993; Ericsson & Lehmann, 1996) also provided evidence in this regard. Adopting an extreme environmental position, they proposed a theory of expertise predominantly based on what they termed "deliberate practice."

In their studies of expert performers, Ericsson et al. (1993) observed that even when individuals had access to similar training environments, large differences in performance often occurred. They also found that experience in a domain was a weak predictor of performance. Rather than accepting these facts as evidence for innate differences in

ability, they attempted to identify training activities that were most closely related to improvements in performance. They found that improvements were generally manifested when performers engaged in well-defined tasks with appropriate difficulty levels, informative feedback, and opportunities for repetition and corrections for errors. Ericsson and collaborators subsequently used the term deliberate practice to characterize these activities. More specifically, they used this term to refer to any highly structured, goal-directed activity aimed exclusively at improving performance. It is noteworthy that these activities are distinct from recreation and spontaneous play, competition, work, and other forms of experience in a domain. Because they are effortful, Ericsson et al. postulated that they are generally not inherently motivating or enjoyable.

The nurture aspect of performance was strongly advocated and expertise as the result of an extended process of skill development involving interactions between individuals and their environment was postulated. At any stage of development, performance is presumably significantly influenced by environmental factors that either facilitate or constrain the developmental process. Ultimately, the achievement of exceptional skills reflects the ongoing long-term adaptation to the demands and constraints of deliberate practice within a particular domain. This finding has since been replicated within the sport domain, more specifically with soccer players (Helsen, Starkes, & Hodges, 1998), wrestlers, (Starkes, Deakin, Allard, Hodges, & Hayes, 1996), and middle-distance runners (Young, 1998).

Constraints that prevent athletes from engaging in maximum amounts of deliberate practice pertain to resources, motivation, and effort. First, individuals striving to excel must overcome resource constraints. They must have adequate time and energy, as well as access to competent teachers, training materials, and facilities. Second, because practicing in a deliberate fashion is believed to be neither pleasant nor immediately rewarding and does not lead to immediate social and monetary rewards, individuals have to overcome motivational constraints. Ericsson and collaborators (1993) suggested that individuals who engage in deliberate practice are in part motivated by the fact that practice leads to improved performance. Finally, because deliberate practice is mentally and physically demanding, individuals must overcome effort constraints. The process in which performers are able to supply the effort required to achieve outstanding performance and balance their effort with appropriate recovery periods to prevent exhaustion and burnout has often been referred to as "learned industriousness" (Eisenberger, 1998). Ericsson et al. stated:

"Disregard of the effort constraint on deliberate practice leads to injury and even failure. In the short term, optimal deliberate practice maintains equilibrium between effort and recovery. In the long term, it negotiates the effort constraint by slow, regular increases in amounts of practice that allow for adaptation to increased demands" (p. 371).

According to Ericsson and Charness (1994), the number of hours of deliberate practice accumulated in a domain is a significant determinant of the level of expertise attained. In fact, research with novices and experts in various disciplines suggests that the amount of accumulated practice is monotonically related to the achieved level of expert performance. This implies that an individual's level of performance will be severely constrained if sufficient time is not invested in high-quality training.

Researchers have found that experts invest more hours of practice per week compared to novices and start engaging in deliberate practice at younger ages. However, the amount of daily deliberate practice does not appear to be constant throughout the career of expert performers. When individuals start practicing in a domain, the weekly amount of practice is minimal and is slowly increased to maximal levels in later stages of their developmental path (Ericsson, 1996; Krampe, 1994; Starkes et al., 1996). Interestingly, it was revealed that it is impossible for individuals with less accumulated practice at a given age to catch up with the best individuals who started deliberate practice earlier and maintained optimal levels of practice that did not lead to either exhaustion or burnout.

Given that late starters receive the same amount of support and resources and engage in the same amounts of deliberate practice over the years, why would they not reach levels similar to those of early starters? Ericsson's (1996) contention that children who start training later cannot attain the same level of expertise as those starting at a younger age is questionable, at least in the domain of sports. More research needs to be conducted to verify the accuracy of this observation. Despite this, one must keep in mind that in sport, there is generally a critical age span during which peak performances can be attained because of limiting physical and physiological factors (Bouchard, Malina, & Pérusse, 1997). If athletes do not respect this age span, it might make it more difficult for them to achieve exceptional performance.

In striving to develop talent to its full potential, Ericsson (1996) argued that it is important to consider that performers typically spend at least 10 years or 10,000 hours practicing before reaching expert status. This 10-year rule has been found to hold in the domains of chess (Simon &

Chase, 1973), sport (Kalinowski, 1985; Monsaas, 1985; Starkes et al., 1996), mathematics (Gustin, 1985), and music (Sosniak, 1985). Ericsson indicated that experience or the number of years spent in a chosen field does not accurately reflect the level of expertise attained. The 10-year rule of preparation refers to 10 years or 10,000 hours of *deliberate practice,* and not simply 10 years of experience. Spending 10 years in a specialization is a necessary but not sufficient condition to achieve expertise.

Ericsson and colleagues (1993) have put forth an interesting framework to study the development of expertise. However, their claim that deliberate practice is *most* accountable for expert levels has led to some disagreement and controversy. In a recent article, Singer and Janelle (1999) stated the following regarding this 10-year rule: "A chief concern is the abundance of attention directed toward the amount of deliberate practice (i.e., 'the 10-year rule') as well as the general characteristics of deliberate practice, at the expense of focussing on the content and quality of practice sessions. It is intuitively obvious that practice over a long period of time during which arduous levels of concentration, effort, and determination are expended, will result in the development of expertise if practice is conducted in an effective manner on critical performance skills. . . . Given the emerging evidence of innate contributions to success in sport . . . the primary issue to be resolved is not how long or how hard to practice, but how and what to practice" (p. 134).

In their review of current nature-nurture perspectives on the development of sport expertise, Singer and Janelle (1999) reported that practicing 10 years or more does not guarantee expertise or even near-expertise. They suggested that athletes' trainability of skills and adaptability to practice is greatly influenced by genetic factors. It appears that "the more favorable the genetic disposition, the more likely that dedicated practice will result in intended outcomes" (p. 134).

Ericsson et al. (1993) did not attribute an important role to innate abilities in the achievement of expertise, which, according to findings in the literature, is a topic far from being resolved (T.J. Bouchard, 1984; C. Bouchard & Malina, 1984; C. Bouchard, Malina, & Pérusse, 1997; Singer & Janelle, 1999). Ericsson and colleagues did, however, state the following: "Several 'personality' factors, such as individual differences in activity levels and emotionality may differentially predispose individuals toward deliberate practice as well as allow these individuals to sustain very high levels of it for extended periods" (p. 393). Furthermore, they suggested it was possible for early signs of natural ability or talent to be the cause for engaging in deliberate practice in early childhood, but that characteristics having long been assumed to be a result of innate talent are the result of deliberate practice. However, who is to say that innate abilities do not play a role throughout the developmental process? To date, no one has proved nor disproved this possibility. Perhaps the genetic composition of athletes does play a role at the most elite level, enabling them to win medals at the Olympics and World Championships. It is possible that athletes are able to sustain extensive and arduous hours of deliberate practice because they were born with a certain predisposition to do so. It is also possible for athletes who are not born with this predisposition to learn to motivate themselves to endure the required training.

This leads the discussion to another issue regarding the framework of Ericsson and colleagues (1993). One has to question the degree to which the significance of feedback and monitoring of goals is emphasized with only superficial discussion regarding the role of teachers and coaches. This refers to the "what" and "how" to practice raised by Singer and Janelle (1999). The latter scholars raised another important point: "One of the key concerns when considering deliberate practice is the implicit assumption that deliberate practice is directed toward practicing the correct skills, and is done in a manner that will lead to expert performance" (p. 136). Obviously, coaches play a significant role in determining which techniques and strategies must be trained, and how they must be trained. Salmela (1996) interviewed 22 expert coaches on the topic of expertise development and found that one of their main goals was to create an environment that was most conducive to improving performance. These coaches invested considerable effort and time into planning and structuring practices so that the highest quality of training could occur.

However, similar to what was found by Bloom (1985), Côté (1999), and Durand-Bush (2000), some coaches revealed that their role changed as athletes reached higher levels of performance (Salmela, 1996). They were concerned with creating opportunities for athletes to become more autonomous and self-directed. This is illustrated by the following quote from an expert basketball coach: "The idea is you want to develop independent thinking, creative, responsible individuals who can make decisions when they leave. Clearly, it's incumbent upon athletes to develop self-discipline and properly manage their time and priorities. There will be ups and downs, pitfalls along the way but in the end, if they've survived a rigorous, demanding, and intense athletic involvement, and if they've also done well academically, achieving their degree, what more rewarding experiences could you ask for?" (qtd. in Salmela, 1996, p. 50).

At an elite stage, there is a reduced dependence on external human resources and athletes become more responsible for the course of their learning and actions. To best prepare athletes to engage in self-directed learning, coaches provide them with opportunities to exert control over their training environment, starting in early stages of talent development. Singer and Janelle (1999) stated: "The learner is more inclined to be actively involved in self-instruction when given the opportunity to do so. . . . Also, by directly involving the learner in the learning process, responsibility for acquiring the skill is assumed by the learner, leading to greater effort, persistence, and satisfaction" (p. 138). Effort, persistence, and satisfaction are all important for athletes to engage in extensive amounts of deliberate practice. However, it is as important that athletes derive continuous enjoyment from their activities if they are to remain committed to developing their talent. Ericsson et al.'s (1993) finding that deliberate practice is not inherently enjoyable is debatable, at least when it is considered in the domain of sport, where athletes have reported that some deliberate practice activities are both highly relevant and enjoyable (Starkes et al., 1996; Young, 1998).

Young (1998) studied the development of 81 Canadian national, provincial, and club-level middle-distance runners. Referring to the training diaries they kept over the years, the runners identified their practice patterns and performance levels for the initial nine years of their career. In particular, they rated lists of track practice activities, track-related activities, and everyday activities according to their relevance for improving performance, the amount of effort and concentration required to perform them, and also according to how enjoyable they were. Contrary to Ericsson et al.'s (1993) contention that deliberate practice is not enjoyable, it was found that the two most relevant and effortful activities in middle-distance running were perceived to be highly enjoyable compared to all other practice activities.

Although athletes' motives for enjoying deliberate practice activities remain unclear, the current findings are not that surprising considering that several researchers found that enjoyment is an antecedent of participation in sport (Scanlan, Carpenter, Schmidt, Simons, & Keeler, 1993). Furthermore, athletes reported that enjoyment was a reason they remained involved in their chosen sport over an extensive period of time (Côté, 1999; Csikszentmihalyi et al., 1993; Durand-Bush, 2000). In fact, Csikszentmihalyi and colleagues stated that "no teenager will develop talent unless he or she enjoys working in the talent area" (p. 148). Young (1998) suggested that if practice is relatively enjoyable, then the very nature of deliberate practice may facilitate the continued commitment and persistence of athletes in sport.

Evidently, future research is necessary to clarify the enjoyment dimension and hedonic states associated with deliberate practice, at least in the domain of sport. Ericsson and colleagues' (1993) theory was mainly tested in the field of music with expert and novice pianists and violinists, so perhaps their findings cannot be entirely generalized to sport. As can be seen thus far, several researchers have attempted to expand the understanding of the development of talent and expert performance. The research of Csikszentmihalyi, Rathunde, and Whalen (1993) has also been influential in this field and is discussed next.

Csikszentmihalyi's View on Talented Teenagers

Csikszentmihalyi and colleagues (1993) were particularly interested in studying the thoughts, behaviors, and experiences of individuals who had reached what Bloom (1985) called the "middle years" and Côté (1999) called the "investment years." Their study was conducted over a period of four years with 208 high school students excelling in the domains of athletics, arts, mathematics, music, and science. Variables such as personality traits, family interactions, education, and the social environment were examined to determine their impact on talent development. Another important objective was to identify factors involved in the loss of achievement potential over the years.

Csikszentmihalyi and collaborators (1993) were guided by a unique theoretical approach in their study. Their perspective was based on the assumption that "the development of talent requires a peculiar mind-set, based on habits cultivated in one's early environment that eventually become so ingrained that they end up forming something like a personality trait . . . this mind-set [is called] a complex attentional structure, or a complex consciousness, or a complex self" (p. 11). This complex attentional structure was further defined using a dialectical model that included two opposing processes: integration and differentiation. Csikszentmihalyi et al. believed that these processes were concurrently interrelated because only when combined did they best explain the development of expertise. Another term that was used to refer to this dialectical model was "the flow model of optimal experience."

Csikszentmihalyi and colleagues (1993) suggested that flow is related to the growth of talent. They defined it as a subjective state experienced when individuals are completely connected to a task, to the point of losing track of time and being unaware of fatigue and everything else besides the activity itself. Flow is relatively rare in everyday life; however, it can occur if both external and internal conditions, including one's complex attentional structure, are at optimal levels.

However exhilarating it may be, it was indicated that flow eventually makes training and performing more complex because to keep enjoying an activity, individuals need to seek new challenges to avoid boredom and perfect new skills to avoid anxiety. Therefore, people need to *differentiate* new challenges in the environment and also *integrate* new abilities in their repertoire of skills. Csikszentmihalyi et al. (1993) summarized flow in the following way: "The reason for expecting that the flow experience will be involved in the development of talent is that flow usually begins when a person takes on challenges that are just above her or his skills. This is the phase of change or differentiation; to be enjoyable, this phase must be followed by a stabilizing or integrating phase when skills appropriate to the challenge are developed. The completion of the activity, at the conclusion of a cycle of differentiation and integration, results in stretching or extending the person's being" (p. 16). Interestingly, there is a link between Ericsson and collaborators' (1993) definition of deliberate practice and Csikszentmihalyi et al.'s interpretation of the flow process. The latter postulated that the result of flow is to extend one's limits, knowledge, or skills, which is also the goal and result of deliberate practice. Despite this similarity, there is a discrepancy between the two concepts in that flow is believed to be an enjoyable experience whereas deliberate practice is not, at least, according to Ericsson and colleagues.

To continue the comparison, the notion of deliberate practice could be best accommodated in the initial part of the flow process, the phase of differentiation, in which individuals accept challenges that are beyond their perceived skills to improve performance. However, if we extend Ericsson et al.'s (1993) notion of deliberate practice and incorporate Csikszentmihalyi et al.'s (1993) phase of integration, in which an activity is enjoyable because the skills being performed are appropriate to the challenge, a new dimension is added to the concept of deliberate practice. From this perspective, engaging in deliberate practice could be an enjoyable experience. In fact, according to Csikszentmihalyi and colleagues, individuals do not extend themselves until they go through a cycle of both differentiation and integration, that is, until they perfect or learn a new skill *and* also experience or derive some enjoyment from it.

It is important to note that although enjoyment and fun are part of the process of talent development, talented people do not constantly live pleasurable moments. It was found that "what characterizes people who use their skills to the utmost is that they enjoy the hardships and the challenges of their task" (Csikszentmihalyi et al., 1993, p. 8). Experts do not necessarily encounter more enjoyable experiences, but they tend to view difficult situations as positive and challenging.

Perhaps one of the most important findings of this study was that when individuals experience flow, the likelihood that they will continue to develop their talent is significantly increased. Even though talented individuals do not always experience enjoyment, it remains one of the most important determinants of talent development. Csikszentmihalyi et al. (1993) stated that talent is essentially made up of three elements: "Individual traits, which are partly inherited and partly developed as a person grows up; cultural domains, which refer to systems of rules that define certain ranges of performance as meaningful and valuable; and social fields, made up of people and institutions whose task is to decide whether a certain performance is to be considered valuable or not" (p. 23). Like Bloom (1985) and other researchers who endorse the nature perspective, Csikszentmihalyi and colleagues maintained that aside from cultural domains and social fields in which parents, teachers, and coaches play an important role, there is a genetic component to talent. Inevitably, we are all born with genes that direct the development of our abilities to a certain degree. However, although some people are born with greater gifts, such as perfect pitch or superior spatial visualization, it is not the size of the initial gift that counts, but what an individual makes of it. Csikszentmihalyi et al. see talent as a dynamic process that evolves over a long period of time rather than a trait that is inherited and remains unchanged for the rest of an individual's life.

In summary, whether children or teenagers become top experts in a domain depends on many factors. Some factors are external, such as the society and culture in which they live; these factors affect their access to knowledge, expertise, resources, and support. Other factors are more internal, such as personal qualities; for example, skills related to attention and motivation can be learned and modified, and can thus make a difference in the levels of expertise attained. The following section focuses on psychological characteristics that have been found to be associated with the development of talent.

Psychological Characteristics Involved in the Development of Talent

We often hear statements like "This athlete has a natural drive" or "This athlete can focus naturally." Whether athletes are born with abilities to motivate themselves, to persevere in the face of adversity, or to focus under the most stressful conditions is still a mystery. However, there are psychological characteristics and skills that are associated with high-level performance and differentiate between exceptional and less skilled performers.

Orlick and Partington (1988) provided empirical evidence on the importance of psychological skills in sport. They found that in terms of the physical, technical, and mental preparation of 235 Canadian Olympians, only the latter variable could significantly predict actual Olympic placings. What was unique in this particular study was that it was primarily concerned with psychological skills rather than traits, which were underscored in previous decades. Orlick and Partington identified certain mental skills termed "success elements" that distinguished successful from unsuccessful athletes. These elements were related to commitment and quality training, including the daily use of imagery and goal setting, and simulation training. Other success elements pertained to the mental preparation of athletes for competition, including the development of competition focusing and refocusing plans and postcompetition evaluation plans.

Mahoney, Gabriel, and Perkins (1987) also attempted to uncover some of the mental skills linked to exceptional athletic performance. Based on their work with collegiate and Olympic athletes, they developed the Psychological Skills Inventory for Sport (PSIS) and administered it to 713 male and female athletes. Selected across 23 different sports, these athletes were competing at either an elite, a pre-elite, or a nonelite collegiate level. The authors reported that concentration, anxiety management, self-confidence, mental preparation, and motivation were important in differentiating the skill level of elite and nonelite athletes. It is important to note that the results of this study have to be interpreted with caution, as problems were identified with the validity and reliability of the PSIS (Chartland, Jowdy, & Danish, 1992).

In another study, Grove and Hanrahan (1988) assessed the psychological strengths and weaknesses of 39 interstate- and international-level field hockey players training at the Australian Institute of Sport using the Self-Analysis of Mental Skills questionnaire (SAMS). Participants had to rank-order the following six general scales from what they did best to what they did worst: concentration, emotional control, self-confidence, control of nervousness or tension, use of imagery, and planning or analysis. They ranked control of nervousness or tension and concentration as their best mental skills, and use of imagery and self-confidence as their worst.

Of interest was that five coaches who had daily contact with these athletes were also asked to rank the same skills as the athletes, based on their perception of the players' strengths and weaknesses. Significant discrepancies were found between the rankings of the athletes and those of the coaches. Coaches perceived athletes to be good at maintaining self-confidence, whereas these athletes perceived the opposite. Coaches also perceived their players to be poor at controlling emotions and tension, yet the athletes reported themselves as being proficient at these skills. Results from Grove and Hanrahan's (1988) study also have to be interpreted with caution because no evidence was provided on the validity and reliability of the SAMS questionnaire and on the effectiveness of using a rank-order format rather than a continuous scale.

Other mental skills, perspectives, and techniques that have been perceived to be important for consistently performing at a high level in sport include goal-setting (Burton, 1993; Locke & Latham, 1985; Weinberg, Stitcher, & Richardson, 1994), commitment (Ericsson et al., 1993; Orlick, 1992; Scanlan, Stein, & Ravizza, 1989), and self-confidence, (Orlick, 1992; Vealey, 1986). After 20 years of research and applied work with exceptional performers, Orlick postulated (in his model of human excellence) that commitment and self-confidence were the most important psychological variables associated with elite performance.

Bota (1993) obtained similar findings after conducting analyses with the Ottawa Mental Skills Assessment Tool (OMSAT), an instrument developed to measure a broad range of mental skills. Bota found that self-confidence, commitment, and goal setting were the best-discriminating scales between elite and less elite athletes. As a result, he suggested that goal setting be considered another fundamental element of success.

Mental skills and perspectives associated with the regulation of intensity or arousal have also been linked to consistent high-level performance (Landers & Boutcher, 1998). More specifically, stress and fear control (Rotella & Lerner, 1993; Selye, 1974; Smith & Smoll, 1990; Smith, Smoll, & Weichman, 1998), relaxation (Jacobson, 1930; Williams & Harris, 1998), and activation (Williams & Harris, 1998; Zaichkowsky & Takenaka, 1993) have been identified as important psychological skills to develop to excel in sport.

Several researchers have also examined the nature and importance of concentration and distraction control (Boutcher, 1993; Nideffer & Sagal, 1998; Orlick, 1992; Orlick & Partington, 1988). In fact, Nideffer and Sagal

stated that "concentration is often the deciding factor in athletic competition" (p. 296). Athletes must be able not only to focus effectively but also to refocus their attention when distracted by internal or external stimuli (Boutcher, 1993; Orlick, 1992). Orlick (1996) noted that although distraction control or refocusing is an extremely important skill, it is often the least practiced by athletes.

Other psychological skills relevant to the improvement of athletic performance include imagery and mental practice (Feltz & Landers, 1983; Orlick, 1992; Vealey & Greenleaf, 1998). Although imagery and mental practice are related and often used interchangeably, research has shown that the two constructs should be differentiated (Murphy & Jowdy, 1993). Whereas imagery refers to a *mental process* involving quasi-sensory and quasi-perceptual experiences, mental practice relates to a *technique* used by individuals to engage in introspective or covert rehearsal. Mental practice can but does not necessarily have to involve imagery. According to Murphy and Jowdy, imagery and mental practice can facilitate skill acquisition and maintenance, as well as help athletes increase their self-awareness and confidence, regulate their arousal, emotions, and pain, and enhance their competition-planning strategies.

Competition planning is certainly another valuable skill in the achievement of exceptional performance. In their study conducted with 235 Canadian Olympic athletes, Orlick and Partington (1988) found that the athletes had clearly established competition plans that helped them prepare to focus and refocus before and during events, as well as evaluate their performance after events. In another study, Gould, Eklund, and Jackson (1992) revealed that Olympic wrestling champions adhered to their mental preparation plans and precompetition routines and were better able to cope with distractions and unforeseen circumstances than nonmedalists.

Spink (1990) reviewed studies in which successful and less successful athletes were differentiated based on their psychological characteristics in gymnastics (Mahoney & Avener, 1977), wrestling (Gould, Weiss, & Weinberg, 1981; Highlen & Bennett, 1979), and racquetball (Meyers, Schleser, Cooke, & Cuvillier, 1979). Gymnasts competing at different levels were distinguished on the basis of two psychological factors: psychological recovery and self-confidence. Once again, self-confidence is a significant factor associated with elite athletic performance.

In a study following that of Bota (1993), Durand-Bush, Salmela, and Green-Demers (in press) also identified certain mental skills that significantly differentiate between elite and competitive athletes. The Ottawa Mental Skills

Assessment Tool (OMSAT-3), which comprises 12 mental skills scales grouped under three broader conceptual components (foundation, psychosomatic, and cognitive skills), was administered to 335 athletes from 35 different sports. In comparing the scores of the two groups of athletes on goal setting, self-confidence, commitment, stress reactions, fear control, relaxation, activation, imagery, mental practice, focusing, refocusing, and competition planning, results indicated that elite athletes scored significantly higher than their competitive counterparts on the commitment, self-confidence, stress reactions, focusing, and refocusing scales. A confirmatory factor analysis indicated that the instrument is an acceptable psychometric tool (Durand-Bush et al., in press).

In a related study, Wilson (1999) assessed the level and use of mental skills of elite and nonelite athletes in the environments of training and competition in an attempt to determine if there were any significant differences. A modified version of the OMSAT (OMSAT-3*; Durand-Bush et al., in press) was administered to 158 female synchronized skaters. A multivariate analysis of covariance indicated that, as hypothesized, elite synchronized skaters reported using more mental skills in both training and competition than nonelite synchronized skaters. Furthermore, although mental skills for training and competition were rated as equally important, both groups used mental skills more in competition than in training.

Stevenson (1999) administered the OMSAT-3* to 249 male and female athletes categorized in either a provincial or a development group in an attempt to determine if there were any gender differences. No significant gender differences were found, which suggests that both male and female athletes had acquired similar levels of mental skills. On the other hand, results showed that provincial-level athletes scored significantly higher than developing athletes on the goal-setting, commitment, competition planning, focusing, and refocusing scales.

To summarize this section: Research has shown that elite athletes possess significantly higher levels of mental skills than do less elite athletes. The development and maintenance of psychological skills in sport is obviously important for the evolution of talent. It is noteworthy that commitment and self-confidence have consistently been found to be associated with high-level performance. In other words, expert athletes are extremely confident and dedicated individuals who are willing to do anything to become the best, even if this means sacrificing other important activities for a certain period of their lives (Ericsson et al., 1993; Mahoney et al., 1987; Orlick, 1996; Orlick &

Partington, 1988). These variables should definitely be given special attention in future research attempting to further investigate the concept of talent. Also, from a practical standpoint, coaches, parents, educators, and sport psychologists should help athletes develop adequate levels of commitment and self-confidence, which could enhance the process of talent development. Logically, this should occur in the earliest stages of their development.

So far, several issues, models, and characteristics related to talent in sport have been discussed, yet there are still many questions that remain unanswered. Many reviews of this topic have been done in the past and they have helped us increase our understanding of the talent process. One of the latest reviews was published by Howe, Davidson, and Sloboda (1998) and, to no surprise, it generated much controversial discussion. The last section focuses on relevant points and unresolved issues raised in Howe et al.'s article and the accompanying open peer commentaries.

UNRESOLVED ISSUES RELATED TO TALENT IN SPORT

Unmistakably, "talent" is a word with many interpretations. It was apparent in reviewing the literature that scholars are still debating whether there is such a thing called talent. Beliefs regarding this disputed topic largely depend on how the term is defined. Many definitions have been put forth, but unfortunately, there is no universally accepted criteria used to characterize the concept. Howe and colleagues (1998) attempted to define talent in their recent article; some scholars were in agreement with their view and others refuted it.

Howe et al. (1998) must be commended for providing an elaborate and clear definition of the concept of talent, even though it was not well received by everyone. It is also interesting that they referred to the concept as "innate talent" rather than just talent. The mere adjective "innate" appears to limit the concept to genetically transmitted structures. However, several researchers used the term in a more holistic way. For example, Csikszentmihalyi (1998) indicated that talent involves personal qualities based not only on innate differences, but also on social opportunities, supports, and rewards. Therefore, when using the term talent, he implied that there were two dimensions involved: inherited and learned abilities.

In reviewing the commentaries to Howe et al.'s (1998) article, it was obvious that some researchers were at one end of the continuum and endorsed the "nature" or "innate talent" account, whereas others were at the opposite end and advocated the "nurture" or "environmental" account, almost to the exclusion of the former. The perspectives of researchers such as Csikszentmihalyi (1998), Detterman, Gabriel, and Ruthsatz (1998), Feldman and Katzir (1998), and Freeman (1998) were more realistic and appealing because they embraced the mutual importance of the two dimensions. Csikszentmihalyi best summarized the state of the nature-nurture debate the following way: "At this point, there is no conclusive support for either account, and it is doubtful that talent could be explained exclusively by one of them" (p. 411).

There is empirical support for both the innate talent and environmental accounts. In terms of the former, various cognitive and physical characteristics were found to be influenced by genetics (Baltes, 1998; Plomin, 1998; Rowe, 1998; Zohar, 1998). One example is height, a variable that largely contributes to the success of athletes in sports like basketball. Olivier (1980) found that the heritability of stature is approximately 95% when different environments are accounted for and equalized. Furthermore, Lykken (1982) found that monozygotic twins correlated approximately .94 in height, even when considering age and gender, whereas, a correlation of .50 was obtained with dizygotic twins.

Height is only one of several genetically determined characteristics that can contribute to the talent of athletes. According to C. Bouchard and colleagues (1997), body composition and morphology are also influenced by genetics. These authors revealed that body size and proportion, physique, skeletal lengths and breadths, limb circumferences, and bone mass are in part genetically influenced. Furthermore, there is evidence showing that aerobic capacity, adaptability or responsiveness to training, and the composition of muscle tissue are influenced by heredity (Cowart, 1987).

In a recent review of empirical findings related to the genetics of fitness and physical performance, C. Bouchard et al. (1997) raised the fact that the true contribution of genetics in human performance is far from understood. However, with respect to talent in sport, they postulated the following: "First, the elite athlete is probably an individual with a favorable profile in terms of the morphological, physiological, metabolic, motor, perceptual, biomechanical, and personality determinants of the relevant sport. Second, the elite athlete is a highly responsive individual to regular training and practice" (p. 366). Their research suggests that some athletes have an advantage because they are more able to adapt to and benefit from intense training. Also, some athletes possess a higher distribution of slow-twitch muscle fibers that makes them more prone to suc-

cess in endurance sports. On the other hand, athletes having a higher percentage of fast-twitch fibers are more likely to excel in sports involving sprinting. According to Simoneau and Bouchard (1995), the distribution of muscle fibers has a heritability (h^2) of approximately 40% to 50%, although it has now been shown that this distribution can be modified with training.

Indeed, characteristics contributing to the development of talent are partly inherited, but they can be modified with extensive practice as well. There is evidence indicating that many human anatomical and physiological characteristics, such as size of the heart, number of capillaries supplying blood to muscles, and, as previously mentioned, metabolic properties of fast- and slow-twitch muscles, are alterable with intense practice. Other studies have shown that several perceptual, motor, and cognitive abilities can also be developed with practice (Keele & Ivry, 1987; Schlaug, Jäncke, Huang, & Steinmetz, 1995; Takeuchi & Hulse, 1993). Azar (1996) reported that brain studies have shown that repetitive motor sequences can trigger changes in the parts of the brain that accept sensory information and control motor function. It thus appears that the brain can alter its circuitry and reorganize it as individuals develop advanced motor skills.

Psychological skills can be learned, but they are also influenced by genetics. Plomin, Owen, and McGuffin (1994) reported a heritability of cognitive ability of approximately 50%. Also, Saudino (1997) concluded that 20% to 50% of the variance in personality traits (i.e., impulsivity, aggression, depression, thrill seeking, neuroticism, extroversion, and shyness) within a population is due to genetic differences. These traits can enhance or inhibit athletic performance depending on the level at which they are expressed and the demands of the sport.

The extent to which personality traits contribute to the development of talent in sport is becoming clearer. Research conducted in the early 1970s suggested that personality, as assessed by traditional personality tests, was not a significant factor in sport (Martens, 1975; Rushall, 1970). However, contemporary researchers have been studying sport personality using a more interactional approach that is based on both personal and situational factors. They have found that elite athletes compared to less elite athletes do in fact possess certain personality-related characteristics and skills that help them in their pursuit of excellence. The most compelling evidence of this was provided by Morgan, O'Connor, Ellickson, and Bradley (1988), who demonstrated that successful athletes exhibit an "Iceberg Profile" that is indicative of positive mental health.

Regardless of the extensive research demonstrating the heritability of several human attributes, researchers such as Howe and colleagues (1998) still believe that innate talent does not exist. These authors stated in their article, "Innate talents are, we think, a fiction, not a fact" (p. 437). They argued that if innate talent does exist, there should be early indicators that enable experts to detect it before exceptional levels of mature performance are manifested. They also postulated that talent should serve as a basis to predict who is likely to excel. However, as previously discussed in this chapter, talent detection is very complex and often irrelevant because the performance of early-identified individuals cannot be accurately predicted.

But even if it is difficult to accurately detect and predict talent, this does not mean that innate abilities do not exist. Howe and colleagues (1998) once again disagree with this. They believe that early superior performance is not the result of innate differences but rather differences in training, motivation, and self-confidence. They stated that "early ability is not evidence of talent unless it emerges in the absence of special opportunities to learn" (p. 402).

This seems a strict and even unrealistic observation to make. Csikszentmihalyi (1998) argued that talent cannot develop without opportunities to learn. It can, on the other hand, manifest itself in some children's ability to learn more, given equal opportunities to do so. According to Csikszentmihalyi, a more plausible explanation is that children may have a neurological composition that makes them more sensitive to sounds, for example, which would motivate them to pay more attention to auditory cues and stimulation, be self-confident in listening and singing, and likely to seek training in music. The same could be said about children having innate sensitivities to light or kinesthetic movement.

In sum, it is disconcerting that after decades of debates, the academic community is still questioning whether talent is genetically determined. Many would argue that the question is irrelevant because every characteristic of the human body is influenced to some degree by genetic predispositions as well as by gene and environment interactions. However, as long as it is not proven through the isolation of specific genes, researchers like Howe and colleagues (1998) will continue to advocate that innate talent is nonexistent.

CONCLUSION

The purpose of this chapter was to provide a broad overview of the research on talent and expertise and to discuss traditional and modern views on this topic. Various accounts of the multidimensionality and dynamic nature of talent were provided. Some questions were illuminated, others remain ambiguous or unexplained. Every scholar mentioned in this chapter added a piece to the puzzle; many of them came from different schools of thought and therefore used different protocols to conduct their research. This shows that there is definitely more than one way to examine the concept of talent.

Our review of the topic suggests that talent is not an all-or-none phenomenon. It is a dynamic manifestation that appears to be determined by both innate and environmental factors. The extent to which these different factors influence the development of performance seems irrelevant. We cannot change our genetic makeup, but we can change our environment to make it as conducive as possible to improving performance. Extensive and meaningful practice, familial support, competent coaches and teachers, and adequate physical resources were found to play a significant role in the achievement of exceptional performance. Researchers and practitioners should focus their attention on determining how these factors can be maximized in the lives of athletes wishing to develop their talent to its full potential, rather than focusing on proving the mere existence of innate talent.

Regardless of the amount of research that will be conducted in the near future, the nature-nurture debate will not be resolved any time soon. We do hope, however, that some of the evidence and perspectives highlighted in this chapter will generate ideas for subsequent studies and continue to fuel interesting and challenging discussions that will help athletes of all levels reach their ultimate abilities in sport.

REFERENCES

Abernethy, B., Côté, J., & Baker, J. (1999). *Expert decision-making in sport.* Canberra: Australian Institute of Sport Publication.

Ackland, T.R., Bloomfield, J., Elliott, B.C., & Blanksby, B.A. (1990). Talent identification for tennis and swimming. *Journal of Sport Sciences, 8,* 161–162.

Azar, B. (1996, January). Why is it that practice makes perfect? *Monitor: American Psychological Association,* p. 18.

Baltes, P.B. (1998). Testing the limits of the ontogenetic sources of talent and excellence. *Behavioral and Brain Sciences, 21,* 407–408.

Bar-Or, O. (1975). Predicting athletic performance. *Physician and SportsMedicine, 3,* 81–85.

Bartmus, U., Neumann, E., & de Marées, H. (1987). The talent problem in sports. *International Journal of Sports Medicine, 8,* 415–416.

Blahüs, P. (1975). For the prediction of performance capacity in the selection of youth talented for sports. *Téorie a Praxe Telesne Vycsbovy, 24,* 471–477.

Bloom, B.S. (1985). *Developing talent in young people.* New York: Ballantine Books.

Bota, J.D. (1993). *Development of the Ottawa Mental Skills Assessment Tool (OMSAT).* Unpublished master's thesis, University of Ottawa, Canada.

Bouchard, C., & Malina, R.M. (1984). Genetics and Olympic athletes: A discussion of methods and issues. In J.E.L. Carter (Ed.), *Kinanthropology of Olympic athletes* (pp. 28–38). Basel, Switzerland: Karger.

Bouchard, C., Malina, R.M., & Pérusse, L. (1997). *Genetics of fitness and physical performance.* Champaign, IL: Human Kinetics.

Bouchard, T.J., Jr. (1984). Twins reared together and apart: What they tell us about human diversity. In S.W. Fox (Ed.), *Individuality and determinism: Chemical and biological bases* (pp. 147–178). New York: Plenum Press.

Boutcher, S.H. (1993). Attention and athletic performance: An integrated approach. In T.S. Horn (Ed.), *Advances in sport psychology* (pp. 251–265). Champaign, IL: Human Kinetics.

Bulgakova, N.S., & Voroncov, A.R. (1978). How to predict talent in swimmers using longitudinal studies. *Teoriza y Practika, 7,* 37–40.

Burton, D. (1993). Goal setting in sport. In R.N. Singer, M. Murphey, & L.K. Tennant (Eds.), *Handbook of research on sport psychology* (pp. 467–491). New York: Macmillan.

Charness, N. (1998). Explaining exceptional performance: Constituent abilities and touchstone phenomena. *Behavioral and Brain Sciences, 21,* 410–411.

Chartland, J.M., Jowdy, D.P., & Danish, S.J. (1992). The psychological skills inventory for sports: Psychometric characteristics and applied implications. *Journal of Sport & Exercise Psychology, 14,* 405–413.

Côté, J. (1999). The influence of the family in the development of talent in sport. *The Sport Psychologist, 13,* 395–417.

Côté, J., & Hay, J. (in press). Children's involvement in sport: A developmental perspective. In J.M. Silva & D. Stevens (Eds.), *Psychological foundations of sport* (2nd ed.). Boston: Merrill.

Cowart, V.S. (1987). How does heredity affect athletic performance? *Physician and SportsMedicine, 15,* 134–140.

Csikszentmihalyi, M. (1998). Fruitless polarities. *Behavioral and Brain Sciences, 21,* 411.

Csikszentmihalyi, M., Rathunde, K., & Whalen, S. (1993). *Talented teenagers: The roots of success and failure.* New York: Cambridge University Press.

Csikszentmihalyi, M., & Robinson, R.E. (1986). Culture, time and development of talent. In R.J. Sternberg & J.E. Davidson (Eds.), *Conceptions of giftedness* (pp. 264–284). New York: Cambridge University Press.

Detterman, D.K., Gabriel, L.T., & Ruthsatz, J.M. (1998). Absurd environmentalism. *Behavioral and Brain Sciences, 21,* 411–412.

Durand-Bush, N. (2000). *The development and maintenance of expert performance: Perceptions of Olympic and world champions.* Unpublished doctoral dissertation, University of Ottawa, Canada.

Durand-Bush, N., Salmela, J.H., & Green-Demers, I. (in press). The Ottawa Mental Skills Assessment Tool (OMSAT-3*). *The Sport Psychologist.*

Dweck, C.S. (1986). Motivational processes affecting learning. *American Psychologist, 41,* 1040–1048.

Eisenberger, R. (1998). Achievement: The importance of industriousness. *Behavioral and Brain Sciences, 21,* 412–413.

Ericsson, K.A. (1996). *The road to excellence: The acquisition of expert performance in the arts and sciences, sports and games.* Mahwah, NJ: Erlbaum.

Ericsson, K.A. (1998). Basic capacities can be modified or circumvented by deliberate practice: A rejection of talent accounts of expert performance. *Behavioral and Brain Sciences, 21,* 413–414.

Ericsson, K.A., & Charness, N. (1994). Expert performance: Its structure and acquisition. *American Psychologist, 49,* 725–747.

Ericsson, K.A., & Faivre, I.A. (1988). What's exceptional about exceptional abilities? In I.K. Obler & D. Fein (Eds.), *The exceptional brain: Neuropsychology of talent and special abilities* (pp. 436–473). New York: Guilford Press.

Ericsson, K.A., Krampe, R.T., & Tesch-Römer, C. (1993). The role of deliberate practice in the acquisition of expert performance. *Psychological Review, 100,* 363–406.

Ericsson, K.A., & Lehmann, A.C. (1996). Expert and exceptional performance: Evidence of maximal adaptation to task constraints. *Annual Review of Psychology, 47,* 273–305.

Feldman, D.H., & Katzir, T. (1998). Natural talents: An argument for the extremes. *Behavioral and Brain Sciences, 21,* 414.

Feltz, D.L., & Landers, D.M. (1983). The effects of mental practice on motor skill learning and performance: A meta-analysis. *Journal of Sport Psychology, 5,* 25–57.

Freeman, J. (1998). Inborn talent exists. *Behavioral and Brain Sciences, 21,* 415.

Gagné, F. (1998). A biased survey and interpretation of the nature-nurture literature. *Behavioral and Brain Sciences, 21,* 415–416.

Geron, E. (1978). Psychological assessment of sport giftedness. In U. Simri (Ed.), *Proceedings of the international symposium* on *psychological assessment in sport* (pp. 216–231). Netanya, Israel: Wingate Institute for Physical Education and Sport.

Gimbel, B. (1976). Possibilities and problems in sports talent detection research. *Leistungssport, 6,* 159–167.

Gould, D., Eklund, R.C., & Jackson, S.A. (1992). 1998 U.S. Olympic wrestling excellence: I. Mental preparation, precompetitive cognition and affect. *The Sport Psychologist, 6,* 358–382.

Gould, D., Weiss, M., & Weinberg, R. (1981). Psychological characteristics of successful and nonsuccessful Big Ten wrestlers. *Journal of Sport Psychology, 3,* 69–81.

Grove, J.R., & Hanrahan, S.J. (1988). Perceptions of mental training needs by elite field hockey players and their coaches. *The Sport Psychologist, 2,* 222–230.

Gustin, W.C. (1985). The development of exceptional research mathematicians. In B.S. Bloom (Ed.), *Developing talent in young people* (pp. 270–331). New York: Ballantine Books.

Harre, D. (1982). *Trainingslehre.* Berlin, Germany: Sportverlag.

Havlicek, I., Komadel, L., Komarik, E., & Simkova, N. (1982, June). *Principles of the selection of youth talented in sport.* Paper presented at the International Conference on the Selection and Preparation of Sport Talent, Bratislava, Czechoslovakia.

Hay, J.G. (1969). Rowing: An analysis of the New Zealand Olympic selection tests. *Research Quarterly for Exercise and Sport, 40,* 83–90.

Heller, K.A., & Ziegler, A. (1998). Experience is no improvement over talent. *Behavioral and Brain Sciences, 21,* 417–418.

Helsen, W., Starkes, J.L., & Hodges, N.J. (1998). Team sports and the theory of deliberate practice. *Journal of Sport & Exercise Psychology, 20,* 13–25.

Highlen, P.S., & Bennett, B.B. (1979). Psychological characteristics of successful and unsuccessful elite wrestlers: An exploratory study. *Journal of Sport Psychology, 1,* 123–137.

Hodges, N.J., & Starkes, J.L. (1996). Wrestling with the nature of expertise: A sport specific test of Ericsson, Krampe and Tesch-Römer's (1993) theory of "deliberate practice." *International Journal of Sport Psychology, 27,* 400–424.

Howe, M.J.A., Davidson, J.W., & Sloboda, J.A. (1998). Innate talents: Reality or myth? *Behavioral and Brain Sciences, 21,* 399–442.

Irvine, S.H. (1998). Innate talents: A psychological tautology. *Behavioral and Brain Sciences, 21,* 419.

Jacobson, E. (1930). *Progressive relaxation.* Chicago: University of Chicago Press.

Jancarik, A., & Salmela, J.H. (1987). Longitudinal changes in physical, organic and perceptual factors in Canadian elite male gymnasts. In B. Petiot, J.H. Salmela, & T.B. Hoshizaki (Eds.), *World identification systems for gymnastic talent* (pp. 151–159). Montreal, Canada: Sport Psyche Editions.

Jones, M.B., & Watson, G.G. (1977). Psychological factors in the prediction of athletic performance. In U. Simri (Ed.), *Proceedings of the International Symposium on Psychological Assessment in Sport* (pp. 89–102). Netanya, Israel: Wingate Institute for Physical Education and Sport.

Kalinowski, A.G. (1985). The development of Olympic swimmers. In B.S. Bloom (Ed.), *Developing talent in young people* (pp. 139–192). New York: Ballantine Books.

Keele, S.W., & Ivry, R.I. (1987). Modular analysis of timing in motor skill. In G.E. Bower (Ed.), *The psychology of learning and motivation* (pp. 183–228). New York: Academic Press.

Kerr, R., Dainty, D., Booth, M., Gaboriault, G., & McGavern, R. (1979). Talent identification for competitive diving. In P. Klavora & K.A.W. Wipper (Eds.), *Psychological and sociological factors in sport* (pp. 270–276). Toronto, Canada: University of Toronto, School of Physical and Health Education.

Krampe, R.T. (1994). *Maintaining excellence: Cognitive-motor performance in pianists differing in age and skill level.* Berlin, Germany: Max-Planck-Institut fur Bildungsforschung.

Landers, D.M., & Boutcher, S.H. (1998). Arousal-performance relationships. In J.M. Williams (Ed.), *Applied sport psychology: Personal growth to peak performance* (3rd ed., pp. 197–218). Mountainview, CA: Mayfield.

Lehmann, A.C. (1998). Historical increases in expert performance suggest large possibilities for improvement of performance without implicating innate capacities. *Behavioral and Brain Sciences, 21,* 419–420.

Locke, E.A., & Latham, G.P. (1985). *A theory of goal setting and task performance.* Englewood Cliffs, NJ: Prentice-Hall.

Lykken, D.T. (1982). Research with twins: The concept of emergenesis. *Psychophysiology, 19,* 361–373.

Mahoney, M.J., & Avener, M. (1977). Psychology of the elite athlete: An exploratory study. *Cognitive Therapy and Research, 1,* 135–141.

Mahoney, M.J., Gabriel, T.J., & Perkins, T.S. (1987). Psychological skills and exceptional athletic performance. *The Sport Psychologist, 1,* 189–199.

Martens, R. (1975). The paradigmatic crisis of American sport psychology. *Sportwissenschaft, 5,* 9–24.

Martens, R. (1987). Science, knowledge, and sport psychology. *The Sport Psychologist, 1,* 29–55.

Meyers, W.A., Schleser, R., Cooke, C.J., & Cuvillier, C. (1979). Cognitive contributions to the development of gymnastic skills. *Cognitive Therapy and Research, 3,* 75–85.

Monsaas, J.A. (1985). Learning to be a world class tennis player. In B.S. Bloom (Ed.), *Developing talent in young people* (pp. 211–269). New York: Ballantine Books.

Montpetit, R., & Cazorla, G. (1982). La détection du talent en natation. *La Revue de l'Entraîneur, 5,* 26–37.

Morgan, W.P., O'Connor, P.J., Ellickson, K.A., & Bradley, P.W. (1988). Personality structure, mood states, and performance in elite distance runners. *International Journal of Sport Psychology, 19,* 247–269.

Murphy, S.M., & Jowdy, D.P. (1993). Imagery and mental practice. In T.S. Horn (Ed.), *Advances in sport psychology* (pp. 221–250). Champaign, IL: Human Kinetics.

Nideffer, R.M., & Sagal, M. (1998). Concentration and attention control. In J.M. Williams (Ed.), *Applied sport psychology: Personal growth to peak performance* (3rd ed., pp. 296–315). Mountainview, CA: Mayfield.

Olivier, G. (1980). The increase in stature in France. *Journal of Human Evolution, 9,* 645–649.

Orlick, T. (1992). The psychology of personal excellence. *Contemporary Thought on Performance Enhancement, 1,* 109–122.

Orlick, T. (1996). The wheel of excellence. *Journal of Performance Education, 1,* 3–18.

Orlick, T., & Partington, J. (1988). Mental links to excellence. *The Sport Psychologist, 2,* 105–130.

Plomin, R. (1998). Genetic influence and cognitive abilities. *Behavioral and Brain Sciences, 21,* 420–421.

Plomin, R., Owen, M.J., & McGuffin, P. (1994). The genetic basis of complex human behaviors. *Science, 264,* 1733–1739.

Régnier, G. (1987). *Un modèle conceptuel pour la détection du talent sportif [A conceptual model for talent detection].* Unpublished doctoral dissertation, University of Montreal, Canada.

Régnier, G., & Salmela, J.H. (1983). Détection du talent au baseball [Talent detection in baseball]. *Revue de l'Entraîneur, 6,* 13–20.

Régnier, G., & Salmela, J.H. (1987). Predictors of success in Canadian male gymnasts. In B. Petiot, J.H. Salmela, & T.B. Hoshizaki (Eds.), *World identification systems for gymnastic talent* (pp. 143–150). Montreal, Canada: Sport Psyche Editions.

Régnier, G., Salmela, J.H., & Alain, C. (1982). Strategie für Bestimmung und Entdeckung von Talenten im Sport. *Leistungssport, 12,* 431–440.

Régnier, G., Salmela, J.H., & Russell, S.J. (1993). Talent detection and development in sport. In R.N. Singer, M. Murphey, & L.K. Tennant (Eds.), *Handbook of research in sport psychology* (pp. 290–313). New York: Macmillan.

Rotella, R.J., & Lerner, J.D. (1993). Responding to competitive pressure. In R.N. Singer, M. Murphey, & L.K. Tennant (Eds.), *Handbook of research on sport psychology* (pp. 528–541). New York: Macmillan.

Rowe, D.C. (1998). Talent scouts, not practice scouts: Talents are real. *Behavioral and Brain Sciences, 21,* 421–422.

Rushall, B.S. (1970). An evaluation of the relationship between personality and physical performance categories. In G.S. Kenyon (Ed.), *Contemporary psychology of sport* (pp. 157–165). Chicago: Athletic Institute.

Russell, S.J. (1990). Athletes' knowledge in task perception, definition, and classification. *International Journal of Sport Psychology, 21,* 85–101.

Rutter, M. (1998). What can we learn from highly developed special skills? *Behavioral and Brain Sciences, 21,* 422–423.

Salmela, J.H. (1996). *Great job coach! Getting the edge from proven winners.* Ottawa, Canada: Potentium.

Salmela, J.H., & Durand-Bush, N. (1994). La détection des talents ou le développement de l'expertise en sport? [Talent detection or the development of expertise in sport?] *Enfance, 2/3,* 233–245.

Salmela, J.H., & Régnier, G. (1983, October). A model for sport talent detection. *Science Periodicals on Research and Technology in Sport.* Ottawa: Coaching Association of Canada.

Salmela, J.H., Régnier, G., & Proteau, L. (1987). Analyse biobehaviorale des déterminants de la performance gymnique [Behavioral analysis of the determinants of gymnastics performance]. In B. Petiot, J.H. Salmela, & T.B. Hoshizaki (Eds.), *World identification systems for gymnastic talent* (pp. 126–142). Montreal, Canada: Sport Psyche Editions.

Saudino, K.J. (1997). Moving beyond the heritability question: New directions in behavioral genetic studies of personality. *Current Directives in Psychological Science, 4,* 86–90.

Scanlan, T.K., Carpenter, P.J., Schmidt, G.W., Simons, J.P., & Keeler, B. (1993). An introduction to the sport commitment model. *Journal of Sport & Exercise Psychology, 15,* 1–15.

Scanlan, T.K., Stein, G.L., & Ravizza, K. (1989). An in-depth study of former elite figure skaters: II. Sources of enjoyment. *Journal of Sport & Exercise Psychology, 11,* 65–83.

Schlaug, G., Jäncke, L., Huang, Y., & Steinmetz, H. (1995). In vivo evidence of structural brain asymmetry in musicians. *Science, 267,* 699–701.

Schneider, W. (1998). Innate talent or deliberate practice as determinants of exceptional performance: Are we asking the right question? *Behavioral and Brain Sciences, 21,* 423–424.

Seefeldt, V. (1988). The concept of readiness applied to motor skill acquisition. In F.L. Smoll, R.A. Magill, & M.J. Ash (Eds.), *Children in sport* (3rd ed., pp. 45–52). Champaign, IL: Human Kinetics.

Selye, H. (1974). *Stress without distress.* New York: New American Library.

Simon, H.A., & Chase, W.G. (1973). Skill in chess. *American Science, 61,* 394–403.

Simoneau, J.A., & Bouchard, C. (1995). Genetic determinism of fiber type proportion in human skeletal muscle. *Journal of the Federation of the American Societies of Experimental Biology, 9,* 1091–1095.

Simonton, D.K. (1998). Defining and finding talent: Data and a multiplicative model? *Behavioral and Brain Sciences, 21,* 424–425.

Singer, R.N., & Janelle, C.M. (1999). Determining sport expertise: From genes to supremes. *International Journal of Sport Psychology, 30,* 117–150.

Smith, R.E., & Smoll, F.L. (1990). Athletic performance anxiety. In H. Leitenberg (Ed.), *Handbook of social and evaluation anxiety* (pp. 417–454). New York: Plenum Press.

Smith, R.E., Smoll, F.L., & Weichman, S.A. (1998). Measurement of trait anxiety in sport. In J.L. Duda (Ed.), *Advances in sport and exercise psychology measurement* (pp. 105–127). Morgantown, WV: Fitness Information Technology.

Sosniak, L.A. (1985). Learning to be a concert pianist. In B.S. Bloom (Ed.), *Developing talent in young people* (pp. 19–67). New York: Ballantine Books.

Spink, K.S. (1990). Psychological characteristics of male gymnasts: Differences between competitive levels. *Journal of Sport Sciences, 8,* 149–157.

Starkes, J.L., Deakin, J.M., Allard, F., Hodges, N.J., & Hayes, A. (1996). Deliberate practice in sport: What is it anyway? In K.A. Ericsson (Ed.), *The road to excellence: The acquisition of expert performance in the arts and science, sports and games* (pp. 81–106). Mahwah, NJ: Erlbaum.

Starkes, J.L., & Helsen, W. (1998). Practice, practice, practice: Is that all it takes? *Behavioral and Brain Sciences, 21,* 425.

Sternberg, R.J. (1998). If the key's not there, the light won't help. *Behavioral and Brain Sciences, 21,* 425–426.

Stevenson, M. (1999). *The use of mental skills by male and female athletes.* Unpublished master's thesis, University of Ottawa, Canada.

Takeuchi, A.H., & Hulse, S.H. (1993). Absolute pitch. *Psychological Bulletin, 113,* 345–361.

Tesch-Römer, C. (1998). Attributed talent is a powerful myth. *Behavioral and Brain Sciences, 21,* 427.

Thomas, K.T., & Thomas, J.R. (1999). What squirrels in the trees predict about expert athletes. *International Journal of Sport Psychology, 30,* 221–234.

Trehub, S.E., & Schellenberg, E.G. (1998). Cultural determinism is no better than biological determinism. *Behavioral and Brain Sciences, 21,* 427–428.

Vealey, R.S. (1986). Conceptualization of sport-confidence and competitive orientation: Preliminary investigation and instrument development. *Journal of Sport Psychology, 8,* 221–246.

Vealey, R.S., & Greenleaf, C.A. (1998). Seeing is believing: Understanding and using imagery in sport. In J.M. Williams (Ed.), *Applied sport psychology: Personal growth to peak performance* (3rd ed., pp. 237–269). Mountainview, CA: Mayfield.

Weinberg, R.S., Stitcher, T., & Richardson, P. (1994). Effects of seasonal goal setting on lacrosse performance. *The Sport Psychologist, 8,* 166–175.

Weisberg, R.W. (1998). Creativity and practice. *Behavioral and Brain Sciences, 21,* 429–430.

Williams, J.M., & Harris, D.V. (1998). Relaxation and energizing techniques for regulation of arousal. In J.M. Williams (Ed.), *Applied sport psychology: Personal growth to peak performance* (3rd ed., pp. 219–236). Mountainview, CA: Mayfield.

Willimczik, K. (1986). Scientific support in the search of talents in sport. In L.E. Unesthal (Ed.), *Sport psychology theory and practice* (pp. 95–105). Orebro, Sweden: Veje.

Wilson, K.R. (1999). *The use of mental skills in training and competition by synchronized skaters: Are there differences?* Unpublished master's thesis, University of Ottawa, Canada.

Winner, E. (1998). Talent: Don't confuse necessity with sufficiency, or science with policy. *Behavioral and Brain Sciences, 21,* 430–431.

Young, B.W. (1998). *Deliberate practice and skill acquisition in Canadian middle distance running.* Unpublished master's thesis, University of Ottawa, Canada.

Zaichkowsky, L., & Takenaka, K. (1993). Optimizing arousal level. In R.N. Singer, M. Murphey, & L.K. Tennant (Eds.), *Handbook of research on sport psychology* (pp. 511–527). New York: Macmillan.

Zohar, A.H. (1998). Individual differences in some special abilities are genetically influenced. *Behavioral and Brain Sciences, 21,* 431–432.

CHAPTER 11

Stress and Anxiety

TIM WOODMAN and LEW HARDY

It doesn't take much technique to roll a 1.68 inch ball along a smooth, level surface into, or in the immediate vicinity of, a 4.5 inch hole. With no pressure on you, you can do it one-handed most of the time. But there is always pressure on the shorter putts...90 percent of the rounds I play in major championships, I play with a bit of a shake. (Jack Nicklaus on golf putting, qtd. in Patmore, 1986, p. 75)

As illustrated in this quote, athletes who participate in competitive sport invariably have to deal with a great deal of pressure. This pressure is most often associated with elevated levels of stress and anxiety, which form an integral part of high-level sport (Gould, Eklund, & Jackson, 1992a, 1992b; Gould, Jackson, & Finch, 1993a, 1993b; Patmore, 1986; Scanlan, Ravizza, & Stein, 1989; Scanlan, Stein, & Ravizza, 1991). In this chapter, the current state of research in stress and anxiety in sport is reviewed and some guidelines for future research in this area are offered.

One of the problems that has plagued stress and anxiety research has been a lack of clarity of the terms stress, anxiety, arousal, and activation. It is important to be clear about what these terms mean with regard to theory, research methodology, and conclusions. Consequently, a clarification of these terms forms the basis of the first section of this chapter. The second section comprises a brief review of the measurement of anxiety in sport. The third section focuses on research that has investigated the sources of stress and anxiety. The fourth section discusses theories, hypotheses, and models of anxiety and sports performance. In the fifth section, measurement issues in competitive anxiety research are revisited in light of the research reviewed in section four, and in the sixth section, the mechanisms by which anxiety might affect performance are explored using theories from mainstream psychology. In the final section, the applied implications of the

research to date are discussed and future research directions and questions are offered.

DEFINING TERMS

Arousal

Arousal has typically been referred to as the intensity of behavior as a unitary construct encompassing both psychological and physiological aspects of behavior. For example, Duffy (1962) defined arousal as "the extent of release of potential energy, stored in the tissues of the organism, as this is shown in activity or response" (p. 179). Although this definition will be accepted here as a working hypothesis, it will be criticized and revised later in the chapter.

Stress

Jones (1990) defined stress as a state in which some demand is placed on the individual, who is then required to react in some way to be able to cope with the situation. This definition implies that stress may or may not place a "strain" on the individual (Jick & Payne, 1980; Lazarus, 1966); it will depend on one's perceived ability to cope with the stressor. Thus, it is the individual's cognitive appraisal of the situation that is central to the stress process (T. Cox, 1978; Lazarus, 1966; Sanders, 1983; Welford, 1973). If one doubts one's ability to cope with the stressor, then feelings of anxiety will likely ensue.

Anxiety

Anxiety is generally accepted as being an unpleasant emotion. There are two rather discordant views on the role of cognition in the generation of emotions. Some researchers (e.g., Zajonc, 1980, 1984) argue that the affective evaluation of stimuli involves basic processes that do not always require the involvement of the cognitive system. Other researchers (e.g., Eysenck, 1992; Lazarus, 1982) propose that an emotional reaction will be triggered only in the presence of cognitive processing, even though such processing might be at differing levels of accessibility to consciousness. Espousing such a view, Lazarus stated, "Cognitive appraisal (of meaning or significance) underlies and is an integral feature of all emotional states" (p. 1021). If one accepts that anxiety is an emotion, and that some level of cognitive processing necessarily precedes emotions, then it is necessary to consider cognitive processes to fully understand the mechanisms underlying anxiety.

State and Trait Anxiety

Spielberger (1966) defined *state anxiety* as "subjective, consciously perceived feelings of tension and apprehension, associated with . . . arousal of the autonomic nervous system" (p. 17). Such feelings of apprehension are normally relatively transitory and relate to a particular event. As such, state anxiety is the individual's response to a *specific* threatening situation. *Trait anxiety* is a *general* disposition to respond to a variety of situations with high levels of state anxiety.

Although early researchers investigated anxiety from a unidimensional perspective, with no differentiation being made between different components of anxiety (e.g., Lowe & McGrath, 1971; Scanlan & Passer, 1978; Simon & Martens, 1977), researchers in mainstream psychology have suggested that anxiety might have at least two distinguishable components (e.g., Davidson & Schwartz, 1976; Liebert & Morris, 1967): a mental component normally termed *cognitive anxiety* or *worry,* and a physiological component normally termed *somatic anxiety* or *physiological arousal.* However, as will be made clearer later, somatic anxiety and physiological arousal are related yet also unique constructs.

In their development of the Competitive State Anxiety Inventory 2 (CSAI-2), Martens, Burton, Vealey, Bump, and Smith (1990) used Morris, Davis, and Hutchings's (1981) definition of cognitive anxiety. Morris et al. defined cognitive anxiety as "negative expectations and cognitive concerns about oneself, the situation at hand, and potential consequences" (p. 541). Morris et al. defined somatic anxiety as "one's perception of the physiological-affective elements of the anxiety experience, that is, indications of autonomic arousal and unpleasant feeling states such as nervousness and tension" (p. 541). In their definition of state somatic anxiety (A-state), Martens et al. stated: "Somatic A-state refers to the physiological and affective elements of the anxiety experience that develop directly from autonomic arousal. Somatic A-state is reflected in such responses as rapid heart rate, shortness of breath, clammy hands, butterflies in the stomach, and tense muscles" (p. 121).

There appears to be ambiguity as to whether somatic anxiety refers to one's perception of one's physiological symptoms (cf. Morris et al., 1981) or refers directly to these physiological symptoms (cf. Martens et al., 1990). It is assumed here that somatic anxiety refers to the perception of one's physiological arousal symptoms (Morris et al., 1981). As such, levels of somatic anxiety can be determined with the use of a self-report measure, whereas, if Martens and associates's definition is adopted, somatic anxiety could not be directly assessed by self-report measures.

THE MEASUREMENT OF ANXIETY

Since Spielberger's (1966) distinction between trait anxiety and state anxiety, researchers have constructed scales to measure these two constructs separately (e.g., Spielberger, Gorsuch, & Lushene, 1970). Following the lead of researchers who developed measures specific to particular settings (e.g., Sarason, Davidson, Lighthall, Waite, & Ruebush, 1960; Watson & Friend, 1969), Martens (1977) constructed the Sport Competition Anxiety Test (SCAT), a sport-specific measure of trait anxiety. Also, Martens and associates (Martens, Burton, Rivkin, & Simon, 1980) developed the CSAI, a sport-specific measure of state anxiety.

Following the distinction between cognitive anxiety and somatic anxiety (e.g., Davidson & Schwartz, 1976), sport psychology researchers developed sport-specific multidimensional measures of trait and state anxiety. For example, Smith, Smoll, and Schutz (1990) constructed the Sport Anxiety Scale (SAS), which contains three trait measures: worry, somatic anxiety, and concentration disruption. Also, Martens et al. (1990) developed the CSAI-2, which contains three relatively independent state subscales: cognitive anxiety, somatic anxiety, and self-confidence. The CSAI-2 has become almost the sine qua non for researchers undertaking research in precompetition state anxiety.

SOURCES OF STRESS AND ANXIETY

Sources of Stress

Many studies on stress and anxiety have included participants from a wide range of ability levels; as nonelite populations are typically more accessible for researchers, this is not surprising. However, to further our understanding of elite performance, information must be gleaned from top-level performers, yet studies with such individuals are fairly limited. In an attempt to unveil some of the pertinent sources of stress and anxiety experienced by elite performers, researchers have begun to employ interview methods (Gould, Eklund, & Jackson, 1991; Gould et al., 1993a, 1993b; Hardy & Woodman, 1999; Scanlan et al., 1989; Scanlan et al., 1991; Woodman & Hardy, 1999).

Scanlan et al. (1991) interviewed 26 former national championship figure skaters to identify the stressors encountered during the most competitive phase of their career. The interviews were analyzed for content and the sources of stress were categorized under five headings: negative aspects of competition (e.g., experiencing competition worries); negative significant-other relationships (e.g., not getting along with others); demands/costs of skating (e.g., dealing with family's financial sacrifice); personal struggles (e.g., experiencing the consequences of having an injury); and traumatic experiences (e.g., having significant others die). Gould et al. (1993a) extended Scanlan et al.'s research by interviewing 17 current and former U.S. national champion figure skaters. The sample included three skaters who had won a World Championship and seven skaters who had won a medal either at the World Championships or at the Olympic Games. The sources of stress revealed in Gould et al.'s study were similar to those revealed by Scanlan and her colleagues. An example of some of the pressure with which elite performers can be confronted is: "He could not handle the frustration, and he would really freak out and blame me for my injury. That was a really hard thing to deal with. It's like, 'Yes, of course I know we are supposed to be training hard, and yes, I want to defend the title too, but I don't need you putting more stress on me'" (U.S. pairs ice skating champion, qtd. Gould et al., 1993a, pp. 140–141).

Interview studies dealing with sources of stress in top-level performers have begun to unearth some of the organizational issues they face. Interviews also formed the basis of Hardy and Woodman's (1999; Woodman & Hardy, 1999) study of organizational stress in 15 elite performers. Their findings, together with those of Gould et al. (1993a, 1993b) and Scanlan et al. (1991), suggest that organizational stress might be an important issue in preparing for major international competitions. For example, coach and teammate problems, selection procedures, and financial issues that are poorly managed will likely result in competition preparation that is far from ideal. To date, there is no research directly investigating the effects of organizational stress on subsequent performance. Although a challenging area, organizational

stress in high-level sport is likely to be a fruitful area of research in the future.

The research outlined above suggests that top-level performers can face a wide spectrum of stressors. These include interpersonal problems (with teammates or coaches), financial concerns, injury problems, issues arising from selection procedures, lack of social support, traumatic experiences, and other personal issues. In view of the vast array of stressful issues that the athlete may face in preparation for a major competition, it is likely that sport psychology consultants working with elite performers will need to possess skills that go beyond the application of mental skills training. Indeed, the array of psychological skills that currently form the typical sport psychologist's arsenal is not likely to prove particularly useful for addressing such issues as a lack of social support, problematic selection criteria, or traumatic experiences.

Antecedents of Anxiety

Gould, Petlichkoff, and Weinberg (1984) argued that if the causes of debilitating anxiety in a competitive setting could be identified, then sport psychologists would be well-equipped to help athletes avoid the sources of their anxiety. Clearly, research in this area is seriously constrained by the ethical dilemma of manipulating variables that are thought to cause anxiety. Researchers have typically circumvented this issue by investigating the correlation between factors that are thought to cause anxiety and the intensity of the anxiety response. These factors have typically been called *antecedents* of state anxiety.

In an attempt to identify some of the antecedents of anxiety, most researchers in earlier years did not differentiate between the cognitive and the somatic components of anxiety. Also, many of these earlier investigations included only young samples. For example, Scanlan and Passer (1978) reported that trait anxiety, self-esteem, and performance expectancies were all significant predictors of state anxiety in a sample of competitive female youth soccer players between 10 and 12 years old. Furthermore, Lowe and McGrath (1971) found the importance of a game in a season to be a significant predictor of physiological arousal. More specifically, the critical and important games were associated with higher levels of physiological arousal. Finally, Hanson's (1967) study revealed that, when they were at bat, young baseball players' physiological arousal was significantly higher than at any other phase of the game.

Investigations of the differential antecedents of cognitive and somatic anxiety in a sport setting were first conducted by Gould et al. (1984) in their study with wrestlers. Gould et al. reported years of experience to be the strongest (negative) predictor of cognitive anxiety. Furthermore, they found trait anxiety to be the only antecedent of somatic anxiety. Jones, Swain, and Cale (1990) conducted a similar, albeit more in-depth study with male middle-distance runners. In Jones et al.'s study, the major predictors of cognitive anxiety were performers' perceptions of readiness, their attitude toward previous performances, and their use of outcome goals. However, somatic anxiety was not related to any of the variables considered in their study. In a follow-up study, Jones, Swain, and Cale (1991) found evidence for different cognitive anxiety antecedents between men and women. Specifically, they observed that the cognitive anxiety of the women was mainly predicted by their readiness to perform and the importance of doing well. However, the cognitive anxiety of the men was predicted by their opponent's ability in relation to themselves and their perceived probability of winning.

In determining different antecedents for the different anxiety components, researchers have provided further evidence for the need to distinguish between cognitive and somatic anxiety. Indeed, if the antecedents of cognitive and somatic anxiety are sometimes different, this would seem to indicate that they are, at least partially, independent constructs. Investigations of how cognitive and somatic anxiety change over time have typically shown that the components of anxiety fluctuate differently prior to a competition (Gould et al., 1984; Jones & Cale, 1989; Krane & Williams, 1987; Parfitt & Hardy, 1987). More precisely, these studies have typically indicated that cognitive anxiety remains fairly high and stable prior to a competition, whereas somatic anxiety remains fairly low up to one or two days before a competition and then increases steadily up to the competition (e.g., Gould et al., 1984). Researchers who have examined physiological arousal and somatic anxiety separately have determined that these two variables follow similar temporal patterns (e.g., Parfitt, Jones, & Hardy, 1990). Jones and his colleagues (Jones & Cale, 1989; Jones et al., 1991) concluded that women's precompetition anxiety differed from that of the men in a variety of team sports. Whereas men's cognitive anxiety remained stable prior to a competition, women's cognitive anxiety increased steadily up to the competition. Furthermore, women's somatic anxiety increased earlier than did that of the men.

In summary, although most early researchers identified antecedents of unidimensional anxiety in youth participants, more recent findings indicate differences between the antecedents of cognitive and those of somatic anxiety in wrestlers and middle-distance runners. Furthermore, antecedents of cognitive and somatic anxiety can be different for male and female middle-distance runners, suggesting that gender differences may pervade various sports.

STATE ANXIETY AND PERFORMANCE

In mainstream psychology, Broadhurst (1957) and Hebb (1955) proposed that the relationship between arousal and performance can best be explained by the inverted-U hypothesis (Yerkes & Dodson, 1908). The inverted-U hypothesis proposes that the relationship between arousal and performance will be in the form of a symmetrical inverted U, such that increases in arousal will result in increases in performance up to a point (optimal arousal), beyond which further increases in arousal will result in a gradual decrement in performance (see Figure 11.1). Sport psychology researchers (Anshel, 1990; R. Cox, 1990; Gill, 1986; Landers, 1994; Landers & Boutcher, 1986) adopted the inverted U as the dominant explanation of arousal-performance relationships in sport. Subsequently, many researchers (e.g., Gill, 1986) have used the inverted U as an explanation of the relationship between arousal and performance, stress and performance, and anxiety and performance. However, the use of the inverted U as an explanation of such relationships has been extensively and severely criticized by many researchers (e.g., Hardy, 1990; Hockey & Hamilton, 1983; Jones, 1990; Krane, 1992; Neiss, 1988).

One major problem with the inverted-U hypothesis as an explanation of arousal-performance relationships lies in the operationalization of arousal and activation. Following Duffy's (1962) definition (see the beginning of this chapter), arousal has been regarded as a unidimensional activation response that prepares the organism for action. This response has been viewed as lying on a continuum

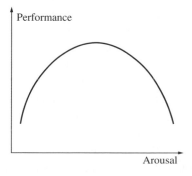

Figure 11.1   The inverted-U hypothesis.

from deep sleep to extreme excitement (Malmo, 1959). Thus, according to this view, arousal is conceptualized as a simple unitary construct accounting for behavioral, physiological, and cognitive factors. However, many researchers have argued that this is a simplistic conceptualization of more complex relationships (Hardy, 1990; Hockey & Hamilton, 1983; Jones & Hardy, 1989; Lacey, 1967; Neiss, 1988). Also, research conducted by Lacey presented strong evidence for three distinct forms of activation (arousal): electrocortical (electric activity in the cortex measured by EEG), autonomic (physiological activity measured by skin conductance, heart rate, etc.); and behavioral (overt activity).

A number of researchers (e.g., Hockey & Hamilton, 1983; Näätänen, 1973; Neiss, 1988; Parfitt et al., 1990) have suggested that it is necessary to view arousal in a more detailed fashion by investigating the systems that are involved in different aspects of performance. According to this position, arousal is best viewed as a patterning of various physiological parameters. If this patterning is appropriate for the task at hand, then performance will likely be maintained; if the patterning is not appropriate, then performance will likely be impaired (cf. Neiss, 1988).

Other researchers (e.g., Hardy, Jones, & Gould, 1996; Pribram & McGuinness, 1975) have advocated a clearer distinction between arousal and activation. For example, Pribram and McGuinness proposed that activation is the cognitive and physiological activity geared toward preparing a planned response that is appropriate to the task; arousal is defined as the cognitive and physiological activity that occurs in response to some new and external input to the system. Hardy, Jones, et al. provided the example of a gymnast immediately before performing a beam routine in an important international competition. If the gymnast has prepared well, having performed the routine over 100 times in training and various competitions, she probably has the appropriate activation state for performing this routine. However, if a balloon bursts loudly the very moment she is about to land on the springboard for a complex mount, the gymnast may experience an involuntary startle (arousal) response, leading to a disruption of her activation pattern. With this different activation pattern, she misses her mount. Thus, *activation* (e.g., the appropriate state for performing a beam routine) refers to the cognitive and physiological activity that is geared toward the preparation of a *planned response* to an anticipated situation. *Arousal* (e.g., an involuntary startle) refers to the cognitive and physiological activity that takes place *in response to some new input* (Pribram & McGuinness, 1975).

The utilization of the inverted-U hypothesis as an explanation of complex relationships among arousal, anxiety, stress, and sport performance has been criticized on a number of additional points. Perhaps the most salient criticism of the hypothesis is that it offers no explanation of *how* arousal affects performance. Also, it does not allow for an individual's cognitive appraisal of the situation and consequently is "an impediment to the understanding of individual differences" (Neiss, 1988, p. 353); and its symmetrical shape is not realistic of a competitive sport situation when a performer who has gone "over the top" is unlikely to be able to regain an optimal level of performance with only a slight reduction in physiological arousal (Hardy, 1990).

In summary, the application of the inverted-U hypothesis to sport is a description of the relationship between unidimensional arousal and performance. Given that arousal and anxiety are distinct constructs, this relationship is unlikely to be useful as a description, let alone as an explanation, of the effects of anxiety on performance. In an attempt to address the shortcomings of the inverted-U hypothesis, various theorists have formulated alternative hypotheses, theories, and models. These will be elaborated on in the following section.

Individualized Zones of Optimal Functioning

The individualized zone of optimal functioning (IZOF) hypothesis was developed by Yuri Hanin in the 1970s and published in the English language in the 1980s (1980, 1986). The central tenet of the IZOF hypothesis is that each athlete has his or her own optimal zone of preperformance anxiety within which he or she is more likely to attain optimal performance. If the anxiety level lies outside of this zone, performance will be impaired. Contrary to earlier attempts at classifying optimal levels of anxiety based on task characteristics and experience (e.g., Oxendine, 1970, 1984), the IZOF approach simply purports that a person's optimal level of anxiety is specific to that particular individual.

Hanin (1986) has claimed that IZOFs can be derived either by direct and repeated measurement of anxiety levels and subsequent performance, or by recall of anxiety levels prior to a past peak performance. There is some evidence that IZOFs can be determined by recall of past optimal levels of anxiety (Hanin, 1986; Morgan, O'Connor, Sparling, & Pate, 1987; Raglin & Morgan, 1988). Also, research generally supports the contention that anxiety levels that are within individualized zones correspond to higher levels of performance (Gould, Tuffey, Hardy, & Lochbaum, 1993;

Hanin & Kopysov, 1977, cited in Hanin, 1980; Krane, 1993; Randle & Weinberg, 1997; Turner & Raglin, 1991; Woodman, Albinson, & Hardy, 1997). For example, Turner and Raglin found that track and field athletes who competed with anxiety levels within their estimated IZOF performed significantly better than those who competed with anxiety levels outside their estimated IZOF. Also, in an investigation employing a multidimensional framework, Woodman et al. observed that 10-pin bowling performance was better when bowlers' combined cognitive anxiety and somatic anxiety scores were within their IZOF compared to when they were outside this multidimensional IZOF.

Gould and Udry (1994) proposed that anxiety is unlikely to be the only emotion that affects performance and that researchers would do well to consider other emotions (e.g., anger, disappointment, frustration, excitement, joy, etc.). They suggested that a recipe of emotions for a performer is likely to account for larger proportions of variance than anxiety alone. Certainly, preliminary investigations that have included other emotions to derive IZOFs have supported the applicability of the IZOF concept to a wider range of emotions (Hanin & Syrjä, 1995a, 1995b).

From a more theoretical perspective, Gould and Tuffey (1996) and Hardy, Jones, et al. (1996), noted that Hanin's IZOF hypothesis lies on barren ground for two reasons. First, Hanin's (1980) original hypothesis was based on a unidimensional conceptualization of anxiety. However, this shortcoming has recently been overcome by research that has investigated IZOFs within a multidimensional framework (Gould et al., 1993; Krane, 1993; Randle & Weinberg, 1997; Thelwell & Maynard, 1998; Woodman et al., 1997). Second, and more seriously, Hanin's IZOFs constitute what is essentially an individual difference "theory" without any individual difference variables (Gould & Tuffey, 1996; Hardy, Jones, et al., 1996). Gould and Tuffey offered two possible explanations accounting for the effects of state anxiety on performance. First, based on Easterbrook's (1959) cue-utilization theory, a number of researchers have stated that an athlete's perceptual field will narrow as a result of increased anxiety (e.g., Eysenck, 1992; Landers & Boutcher, 1993). In essence, Easterbrook's theory states that an athlete will perform optimally when he or she is attending to all those cues that are relevant to the task at hand, and to those cues only. Any deviation from this optimal focus (i.e., a focus that either takes in too many cues or too few) will result in suboptimal performance. Second, Gould and Tuffey cited research showing that increases in anxiety can be accompanied by increased muscular tension and cocontraction, which are associated with inferior

performance (Weinberg & Hunt, 1976). Although both of these explanations are fairly tenable, they do not account for the *individual differences* revealed in various IZOF studies. Consequently, despite encouraging applied data, IZOF remains an intuitive applied tool that, as yet, has little theoretical value.

Multidimensional Anxiety Theory

Multidimensional anxiety theory hypothesizes that the antecedents of cognitive and somatic anxiety are different and that these anxiety components are differentially related to performance. More specifically, cognitive anxiety is hypothesized to have a negative linear relationship with performance. This hypothesis is largely based on early theories of attention (e.g., Wine, 1971, 1980). The premise is that cognitive resources are taken up by worrying thoughts and so are not available for the task at hand. Consequently, the more athletes are worried, the less well they will perform.

Somatic anxiety is hypothesized to have a quadratic (inverted-U-shaped) relationship with performance, whereby performance is expected to be optimal at moderate levels of somatic anxiety. The rationale for this hypothesized relationship between somatic anxiety and performance is unclear. It appears that it is largely an extension of the hypothesized inverted-U-shaped relationship between arousal and performance (Broadhurst, 1957). In attempting to explain why somatic anxiety might affect performance in this fashion, Martens et al. (1990) cited the research of Weinberg (1978) suggesting that too much muscular tension might lead to a deterioration in performance. If this is the case, it is unclear why somatic anxiety, and not physiological arousal, was used in Martens et al.'s theory of multidimensional anxiety. Indeed, if physiological arousal is expected to directly affect motor performance, then measuring a performer's *perception* of this physiological arousal might not be the most effective manner in which to test for such effects. Certainly, in light of the research that has found no significant relationships between perceived physiological arousal and indicators of physiological arousal (e.g., Karteroliotis & Gill, 1987; Yan Lan & Gill, 1984), it appears that somatic anxiety might well be, at best, only a very crude indicator of the physiological component of anxiety. Clearly, a *theory* that offers a relationship between somatic anxiety and performance, and yet does not offer an *explanation* of this relationship, remains a weak theory.

Multidimensional anxiety theory also proposes that self-confidence will have a positive linear relationship with performance. It is worth explaining here how self-confidence became part of a theory on multidimensional *anxiety*. In the factor analysis of the items composing the CSAI-2, Martens et al. (1990) found that cognitive anxiety effectively separated into two factors: one that included negatively phrased items and one that included positively phrased items. These factors were subsequently labeled cognitive anxiety and self-confidence, respectively. Therefore, what was originally intended to be an anxiety scale comprising the two subscales of cognitive anxiety and somatic anxiety ended up also including a self-confidence subscale. Given that self-confidence and cognitive anxiety emerged as orthogonal (i.e., independent) factors, it is rather surprising that Martens et al. should appear to view them as interdependent. In the discussion of their factor analyses, Martens et al. stated: "These findings suggest that cognitive A-state and state self-confidence represent opposite ends of a cognitive evaluation continuum, state self-confidence being viewed as the absence of cognitive A-state, or conversely, cognitive A-state being the lack of state self-confidence" (p. 129). This conclusion has been supported neither in independent research (Gould et al., 1984; Hardy, 1996a; Jones & Cale, 1989) nor in Martens et al.'s own analyses, both of which have demonstrated the relative independence of cognitive anxiety and self-confidence. Also, the research conducted by Jones et al. (1990, 1991) on the antecedents and temporal patterning of cognitive anxiety and self-confidence provided additional evidence for their relative independence. Finally, Hardy's study of golfers revealed that self-confidence accounted for performance variance over and above the performance variance accounted for by cognitive and somatic anxiety. In light of these findings, it follows that cognitive anxiety and self-confidence do not lie at opposite ends of the same continuum.

Empirical support for multidimensional anxiety theory has been somewhat equivocal. Burton's (1988) study with swimmers yielded support for all three multidimensional anxiety theory predictions. That is, the relationship between cognitive anxiety and swimming performance was negative and linear, the relationship between somatic anxiety and performance was in the form of an inverted U, and the relationship between self-confidence and performance was positive and linear. However, in Raglin's (1992) review of eight studies reporting relationships between CSAI-2 subscales and sport performance, Burton's was the only study that supported all of the predictions of multidimensional anxiety theory. Of the seven remaining studies reviewed by Raglin, three provided partial support

and four provided no support for any of the hypothesized relationships between the CSAI-2 components and performance. In a more recent review, Burton (1998) classified studies based on the level of support (strong, moderate, or weak) that they provided for the predictions of the CSAI-2. Of the 16 studies reviewed, 2 provided strong support,[1] 6 provided moderate support, and 8 provided weak support for the CSAI-2 predictions. The inconsistencies in these findings might be attributable to a number of factors, notably inappropriate performance measures and individual differences.

To control for individual differences, Gould, Petlichkoff, Simons, and Vevera (1987) and Burton (1988) standardized all anxiety and performance scores within subjects, such that each individual's anxiety and performance scores were expressed relative to his or her mean scores. When utilizing this procedure, Gould et al. identified no significant relationship between cognitive anxiety and pistol shooting performance, and a negative linear relationship between self-confidence and pistol shooting performance. As already stated, Burton found support for all three relationships proposed in multidimensional anxiety theory. In both studies, a significant inverted-U-shaped relationship between somatic anxiety and performance was revealed.

In his critique of these intraindividual procedures, Raglin (1992) correctly pointed out that median or mean scores do not necessarily reflect moderate scores. Therefore, when transforming raw scores to standardized scores, a high score simply reflects a score that is *higher than normal* for that individual rather than a score that is high in absolute terms. The fact that both Gould et al. (1987) and Burton (1988) found a significant quadratic relationship between somatic anxiety and performance, *despite* this potential confound, adds support for the hypothesized inverted-U-shaped relationship between somatic anxiety and performance in these instances.

Another possible reason for the inconsistent support for multidimensional anxiety theory is the terminology used in the CSAI-2. This is particularly the case for cognitive anxiety. Indeed, in an effort to reduce potential social desirability, Martens et al. (1990) replaced cognitive anxiety statements starting with "I am worried" with statements starting with "I am concerned." The verb "concern" is

---

[1] In Burton (1998), presumably due to a typographical error, Burton's (1988) study was not classified. It is assumed here that Burton (1998) would have classified his 1988 study as providing strong support for the CSAI-2 predictions.

clearly less evaluative than "worry," and as such, might well be more open to divergent interpretation by different performers. This point is not semantic pedantry. Rather, it is central to a number of issues that have recently been debated in the competitive state anxiety literature (cf. Burton & Naylor, 1997; Hardy, 1997; Jones, Hanton, & Swain, 1994). These points will be elaborated on later in the chapter.

In summary, multidimensional anxiety theory has allowed researchers to move anxiety research beyond the inverted-U arousal-performance hypothesis. Multidimensional anxiety theory hypothesizes that athletes will perform their best at low levels of cognitive anxiety, high levels of self-confidence, and moderate levels of somatic anxiety. Research in support of these hypothesized relationships has been equivocal or, at best, mildly supportive. Furthermore, no theoretical reason has been offered for why somatic anxiety should affect performance in the manner hypothesized by multidimensional anxiety theory. Finally, the proposition that cognitive anxiety and self-confidence are codependent has been refuted in a number of studies (for a more detailed discussion of this issue, the reader is referred to Hardy, Jones, et al., 1996).

Catastrophe Models of Anxiety and Performance

One of the major shortcomings of multidimensional anxiety theory identified by Hardy and his colleagues (Hardy, 1990; Hardy & Fazey, 1987; Hardy & Parfitt, 1991) is that it attempts to explain the potentially complex four-dimensional relationship among cognitive anxiety, somatic anxiety, self-confidence, and performance in a series of *independent* two-dimensional relationships. The cusp catastrophe model of anxiety and performance was developed and proposed by Hardy and associates as a result of their dissatisfaction with such explanations of anxiety-performance relationships. As catastrophe models are at least three-dimensional in nature, they allow for the illustration of *interactions* between the anxiety components and performance.

The cusp catastrophe model originally proposed by Hardy and Fazey (1987) illustrated a three-dimensional relationship among cognitive anxiety, physiological arousal, and performance (see Figure 11.2). In this model, cognitive anxiety is termed the splitting factor, and physiological arousal is termed the asymmetry (or normal) factor. The splitting factor (i.e., cognitive anxiety) determines whether the effect of the asymmetry factor (i.e., physiological arousal) will be smooth and small, large and catastrophic, or somewhere in between these two extremes.

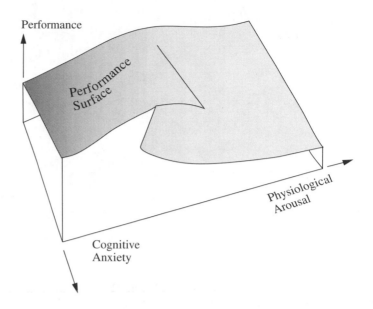

Figure 11.2   Two-surface catastrophe model [reproduced from Hardy, Jones, et al. (1996) with permission].

The cusp catastrophe model predicts that increases in cognitive anxiety will be beneficial to performance under conditions of low physiological arousal (see the left edge of Figure 11.2), but will be detrimental to performance under conditions of high physiological arousal (see the right edge of Figure 11.2). Also, under conditions of low cognitive anxiety, changes in physiological arousal should result in small and continuous changes in performance in the form of a mild inverted-U (see the back face of Figure 11.2). Under conditions of high cognitive anxiety, physiological arousal can either be facilitating or debilitating to performance, depending on the level of physiological arousal experienced (see the front face of Figure 11.2). Furthermore, under conditions of high cognitive anxiety, changes in physiological arousal can result in large and discontinuous changes in performance in the form of hysteresis. That is to say, the path that performance follows is different depending on whether physiological arousal is increasing or decreasing (see Figure 11.3). Under these elevated levels of cognitive anxiety, when physiological arousal increases continually from a fairly low level, performance will also increase up to a point. However, if physiological arousal increases beyond this point, performance will suffer a large drop (i.e., a catastrophe). Once a catastrophe has occurred, a considerable reduction in physiological arousal is required before the upper performance surface can be regained.

To date, apart from Hardy and his associates, researchers appear to have been fairly reticent in testing the

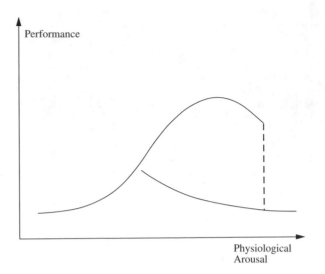

Figure 11.3 Hysteresis [reproduced from Hardy, Jones, et al. (1996) with permission].

catastrophe model of cognitive anxiety, physiological arousal, and performance. This may well be due to the perceived complexity of the model (Gill, 1994). However, as Hardy (1996b) stated, "Complexity is an insufficient reason for rejecting any theory or model" (p. 140). Indeed, research in anxiety would not have advanced beyond the inverted-U hypothesis had it not been for theorists' challenging of simplistic conceptualizations of anxiety (Lacey, 1967; Martens et al., 1990; Neiss, 1988). To render research on the catastrophe model more readily accessible, Hardy provided a number of ways of testing the various aspects of the model, notably: (1) methods that explore the interactive effects between cognitive anxiety and physiological arousal, (2) methods that explore the facilitative versus the debilitative effects of cognitive anxiety, (3) surface-fitting procedures, and (4) examination of the frequency distributions of raw data. It is beyond the scope of this chapter to explore each of these predictions in full, and the interested reader is referred directly to Hardy.

The research conducted to date has generally provided some support for the cusp catastrophe model (e.g., Edwards & Hardy, 1996; Hardy, 1996a; Hardy & Parfitt, 1991; Hardy, Parfitt, & Pates, 1994; Krane, 1990; Woodman et al., 1997; Woodman, Hardy, Hanton, Jones, & Swain, 1999). For example, Hardy and Parfitt found evidence for a hysteresis effect with a sample of basketball players. Specifically, they found that the relationship between physiological arousal (as measured by heart rate) and performance followed a mild inverted-U path under conditions of low cognitive anxiety (during training), but a hysteresis

path under conditions of high cognitive anxiety (prior to an important match). Also, there is some fairly conclusive evidence for interactive effects between cognitive anxiety and somatic anxiety/physiological arousal (Deffenbacher, 1977; Edwards & Hardy, 1996; Hardy et al., 1994; Woodman et al., 1997; Woodman et al., 1999). However, the interactions revealed in these studies generally have not been in precisely the form predicted by the cusp catastrophe model originally proposed by Hardy and his colleagues. Furthermore, those studies that tested the hysteresis effect using direct physiological arousal measures (e.g., Hardy & Parfitt, 1991; Hardy et al., 1994) manipulated heart rate by means of physical exercise rather than anxiety.

To date, no studies have investigated the catastrophe model by manipulating anxiety-induced physiological arousal. This could be a serious limitation in the studies that have tested the hysteresis effect, as the mechanisms underlying exercise-induced physiological arousal could be quite different from those underlying anxiety-induced physiological symptoms. For example, in a study conducted by Williams, Taggart, and Carruthers (1978), rock climbers' level of adrenaline was significantly higher after their climb than before. In contrast, there were no significant differences in noradrenaline levels before and after the climb. In the Williams et al. study, the climbs "required minimal physical effort, but they engendered considerable anxiety owing to the steepness of the rock face and its slippery nature caused by rain which continued all day" (p. 126). Considering that noradrenaline levels rise as a function of exercise (Wilmore & Costill, 1994), these results suggests that noradrenaline secretion differs depending on whether the physiological response is triggered by anxiety or exercise. Thus, although anxiety-induced physiological arousal might be similar to exercise-induced physiological arousal when measured by heart rate, the two states will likely differ when measured using other physiological indicators.

Two additional points about catastrophe models are worth mentioning at this juncture. First, Hardy and associates' cusp catastrophe model of cognitive anxiety, physiological arousal, and performance is a model; it is not a theory. This distinction is important because the mechanisms via which cognitive anxiety and physiological arousal might interact in their effects on performance are not *explained* in the model. Theories that might explain the mechanisms underlying anxiety-performance relationships and catastrophe models are discussed later. Second, the nature of catastrophe models is such that they can be rotated, stretched, or bent (although not torn) into a variety of different shapes and positions (Zeeman, 1976). It follows that the cusp catastrophe model originally presented by Hardy and Fazey (1987) reflects only one of a plethora of subtly different forms and shapes that a cusp catastrophe model might take. Consequently, it is unlikely to be the only catastrophe model of cognitive anxiety, physiological arousal, and performance. For example, Hardy et al. (1994) suggested that, under certain conditions, the original model should be tilted either about the cognitive anxiety axis or the physiological arousal axis. Also, Hardy (1996b) surmised that the performance surface might be tilted forward about the physiological arousal axis for tasks that require more fine motor control and touch (e.g., golf putting), but not so for tasks that require more anaerobic power (e.g., slam dunking in basketball). Of course, it is likely that individual differences will further moderate these models. If the model were tilted far enough forward, cognitive anxiety would be detrimental to performance regardless of the level of physiological arousal. However, the crucial prediction of the models is that this debilitating effect should be greater under high levels of physiological arousal when compared to low levels of physiological arousal.

As Hardy (1996b) has indicated, physiological arousal (rather than somatic anxiety) was an astute choice for the asymmetry factor in the catastrophe model. The rationale for this choice was that physiological arousal can exert both direct and indirect effects on performance, whereas somatic anxiety can exert only indirect effects. This is because somatic anxiety is simply the *perception* of one's physiological symptoms (cf. Morris et al., 1981). Physiological arousal, on the other hand, can affect performance both indirectly (i.e., through one's perception) and directly through changes in one's activation state (Hockey & Hamilton, 1983; Humphreys & Revelle, 1984; Parfitt et al., 1990). For example, a gymnast might perceive himself to be fairly relaxed physically even though his muscular tension reflects a high level of physiological arousal. In such a case, the gymnast's pommel horse routine might suffer because of tight shoulders, even though, in terms of somatic anxiety, he was not aware of this tightness, and thus might have reported a low level of somatic anxiety. Conversely, if somatic anxiety were used as the asymmetry factor, then the underlying assumption would be that physiological arousal exerts no direct effects on performance; only its perception is important. This does not fit at all well with documented views of the experiences of high-level performers (e.g., Gould et al., 1993, 1993b).

In support of the differentiation between somatic anxiety and physiological arousal, Yan Lan and Gill (1984) and Karteroliotis and Gill (1987) found no relationship between somatic anxiety and physiological arousal as measured by heart rate and blood pressure. Furthermore, Parfitt, Hardy, and Pates (1995) found performance on an anaerobic task to be more strongly related to physiological arousal than to somatic anxiety. Finally, research on individuals' perceptions of their bodily symptoms has shown that, unless trained to do so, people can be fairly poor at reading their own physiological symptoms to any degree of accuracy (e.g., Yamaji, Yokota, & Shephard, 1992). Consequently, it is important to consider both the potential direct and indirect effects of physiological arousal on performance.

Higher-Order Catastrophe Models

Although the cusp catastrophe model is the most often cited, there exist higher-order catastrophe models of anxiety and performance. The most commonly used higher-order catastrophe model is the butterfly catastrophe (cf. Hardy, 1990; Zeeman, 1976). This model allows for the incorporation of two further control dimensions: a bias factor and a butterfly factor. A detailed discussion of higher-order catastrophe models is beyond the scope of this chapter, and the interested reader is referred directly to Hardy (1990) and Zeeman (1976). However, in essence, the addition of a bias factor to a cusp catastrophe model has the effect of swinging the front face of the model either to the right or to the left.

Fazey and Hardy (1988) proposed that task difficulty might act as a bias factor. However, this proposal was largely dismissed by Hardy (1990), who proposed that self-confidence would form a better bias factor in a catastrophe model of anxiety and performance. According to this proposal, under high levels of cognitive anxiety, highly self-confident performers might withstand higher levels of physiological arousal before suffering a sudden drop in performance than their less self-confident counterparts. Using Guastello's (1982) method of dynamic differences to test the catastrophe model's fit to putting performance data from eight golfers over 18 holes, Hardy (1996a) offered some empirical support for self-confidence acting as a bias factor. However, there is a clear need for further research that tests the proposition that self-confidence might moderate the interactive effects of cognitive anxiety and physiological arousal on performance.

Although the cusp catastrophe model proposed by Hardy and his associates accounts for some of the inconsistencies in the research, it does not offer any theoretical explanation for the interactive effects of cognitive anxiety and physiological arousal on performance. For example, Why does cognitive anxiety sometimes have a positive effect on performance? Why do performers sometimes suffer dramatic drops in performance when they are cognitively anxious? It is important for researchers to address such questions if further understanding is to be achieved with respect to the mechanisms underlying anxiety-performance relationships.

In summary, research to date generally provides support for an interaction between cognitive anxiety and physiological arousal. Also, there is encouraging support for the notion of hysteresis under high levels of cognitive anxiety. However, a number of issues need addressing with regard to catastrophe models of anxiety and performance. These include clarifications of (1) the interaction between cognitive anxiety and physiological arousal, (2) the possible mediating and moderating variables within catastrophe models, and (3) the importance of differentiating between anxiety-induced physiological arousal and exercise-induced physiological arousal in tests of the hysteresis effect. Despite these limitations, at present, Hardy and associates' catastrophe models are the only models of anxiety and performance that predict an interaction between cognitive anxiety and physiological arousal and, as such, appear worthy of further investigation.

Reversal Theory

Multidimensional anxiety theory (Martens et al., 1990) proposes that the relationship between somatic anxiety and performance is in the form of an inverted U. As such, high levels of perceived physiological arousal are always associated with poor performance. Other theories suggest that high somatic anxiety might not always be perceived as detrimental. Reversal theory (Apter, 1982; Kerr, 1990) is one such theory. Reversal theory is based on the concept of "metamotivational states." A metamotivational state is a "phenomenological state which is characterized by a certain way of interpreting some aspect(s) of one's own motivation" (Kerr, 1990, p. 129). Reversal theory postulates that there are four possible pairs of metamotivational states. These are telic-paratelic, negativism-conformity, autic-alloic, and sympathy-mastery. The telic-paratelic pair has received the most attention in a sporting context. In a telic state (i.e., a state in which individuals are goal-oriented and express purpose), individuals tend to be fairly serious, with a preference for low arousal. Conversely, in a paratelic state (i.e., a state in which individuals are oriented toward the sensations associated with their behavior), individuals tend to be fairly spontaneous, with a preference for high arousal. According to reversal theory (e.g., Kerr, 1990), if performers are in a telic state, they will interpret high physiological arousal as anxiety; if they

are in a paratelic state, they will experience high physiological arousal as excitement.

Reversal theory further posits that performers can rapidly change (reverse) from one metamotivational state to another. Consequently, a performer in a telic state who is experiencing a high level of arousal as unpleasant (anxiety) might suddenly change to a paratelic state and perceive this high level of arousal as pleasant (excitement). In reversal theory, this perceived pleasure is known as "hedonic tone." Thus, one's hedonic tone can be either pleasant (i.e., perceiving a low level of arousal as relaxation and a high level of arousal as excitement) or unpleasant (i.e., perceiving a low level of arousal as boredom and a high level of arousal as anxiety).

Despite its intuitive appeal, the application of reversal theory to sport has been limited by its lack of hypothesized relationships with performance. Recent research by Kerr and associates (Kerr, Yoshida, Hirata, Takai, & Yamazaki, 1997; Males, Kerr, & Gerkovich, 1998) has started to address this limitation. For example, Kerr et al. (1997) investigated the effects of the different combinations of metamotivational states (telic or paratelic) and felt arousal (high or low) on archery performance. They hypothesized that the combined high hedonic tone group (telic-low, paratelic-high) would perform better than the combined low hedonic tone group (telic-low, paratelic-high). That is to say, the archers who perceived their arousal (low or high) as pleasant were hypothesized to perform better than those archers who perceived their arousal as unpleasant. Although this hypothesis was not supported, the study does offer a method for examining the effects of hedonic tone on performance. However, the question still remains: Why should hedonic tone affect performance? Indeed, there does not appear to be an obvious theoretical reason for proposing that pleasant feelings about one's level of physiological arousal should lead to better performance.

In summary, although the notion of reversals is interesting, reversal theory has been limited by its lack of theory in relation to performance. Although recent studies have begun to investigate the relationships among metamotivational states, hedonic tone, and performance, the theoretical rationale for this relationship remains unclear. As such, reversal theory does not offer a great deal in terms of explaining *how* and *why* anxiety might affect motor performance.

Interpretation of Anxiety States

The proposition that anxiety can be perceived as facilitating is not new. Indeed, as early as 1960 in the test anxiety literature, such effects were brought to light by Alpert and

Haber (1960). Whereas other anxiety instruments measured the debilitating component of anxiety, the Achievement Anxiety Test (AAT) introduced by Alpert and Haber measured a facilitating component of anxiety as well as a debilitating component of anxiety. This distinction resulted in two fairly simple predictions: students with high debilitating anxiety were expected to do poorly in an examination setting and students with high facilitating anxiety were expected to do well in an examination setting. Alpert and Haber provided support for this prediction with a significant negative correlation between debilitating test anxiety and grade-point average (GPA) and a significant positive correlation between facilitating test anxiety and GPA. In a subsequent examination of the factor structure of Alpert and Haber's measure, Couch, Garber, and Turner (1983) found that facilitative and debilitative factors could be distinguished for both males and females. In this study, Couch et al. revealed that a combined measure of facilitating and debilitating test anxiety was a better predictor of GPA than either measure of test anxiety alone.

In the sport psychology literature, Mahoney and Avener (1977) were the first to report that performers could interpret their anxiety in different ways. In their study of gymnasts, Mahoney and Avener found that the more successful gymnasts (those who qualified for the 1976 U.S. Olympic team) tended "to 'use' their anxiety as a stimulant to better performance" (p. 140). Conversely, those gymnasts who were less successful (those who did not qualify for the Olympic team) seemed "to arouse themselves into near-panic states" (p. 140).

Following research conducted in test anxiety and Mahoney and Avener's (1977) observations with gymnasts, Jones and his colleagues (Jones, 1991; Jones & Swain, 1992) developed the notion of "directional interpretation of anxiety" in sport psychology. Jones's (1995) subsequent model of facilitative and debilitative competitive anxiety (see Figure 11.4) was largely based on Carver and Scheier's (1988) control model of anxiety, which predicted that perceived control over coping and goal attainment was an important mediator of anxiety interpretation. More specifically, in Jones's model, anxiety is interpreted as facilitative when expectations of control are positive, and as debilitative when expectations of control are negative.

To measure directional interpretation (i.e., facilitative versus debilitative), Jones and Swain (1992) modified Martens et al.'s (1990) CSAI-2 to include a direction scale next to each of the 27 items. Thus, in this modified version of the CSAI-2, performers are asked to respond to their experience of each symptom in the normal fashion from 1 (not at all) to 4 (very much so). After each response, performers

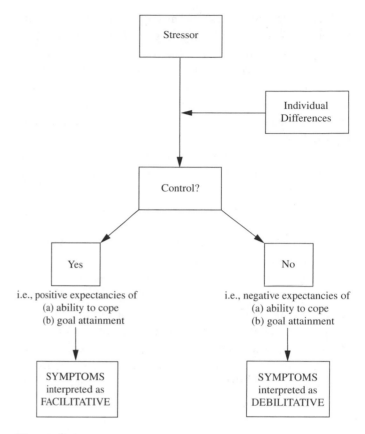

Figure 11.4 A model of facilitative and debilitative competitive anxiety [reproduced from Jones (1995) with permission].

are asked to rate the perceived effect of this feeling on an interpretation scale from −3 (very debilitative) to +3 (very facilitative). For example, a performer might respond with a maximum score of 4 to the statement "I am concerned about this competition," indicating that she is very concerned about the pending competition. If this performer then rates this concern as +3 on the interpretation scale, she is essentially saying that she feels this concern is likely to have a beneficial effect on her upcoming performance.

Using this modified scale, Jones and his colleagues have demonstrated the need to differentiate between performers' perceived level of anxiety ("intensity") and the concomitant interpretation of these symptoms ("direction"). For example, Jones, Swain, and Hardy (1993) reported no significant differences between high-performance and low-performance gymnasts for cognitive anxiety intensity, somatic anxiety intensity, and somatic anxiety direction scores. However, the high-performance gymnasts' cognitive anxiety was more facilitative than their low-performance counterparts'. Similarly, although Jones et al. (1994) found no significant differences between elite and nonelite swimmers for anxiety intensity, the elite swimmers reported both their cognitive anxiety and their somatic anxiety to be more facilitative than the nonelite swimmers. This finding is similar to that of Perry and Williams (1998), who administered the modified CSAI-2 to advanced, intermediate, and novice tennis players. Consistent with Jones et al.'s (1994) results, the advanced players reported significantly more positive interpretations for cognitive and somatic anxiety than their intermediate and novice counterparts. Finally, in attempting to predict basketball performance, Swain and Jones (1996) found direction scores to be better predictors of performance than intensity scores for both anxiety components.

Other studies of the antecedents and precompetition temporal patterning of anxiety intensity and direction have also supported the need to differentiate between intensity and direction dimensions of anxiety (e.g., Lane, Terry, & Karageorghis, 1995; Wiggins, 1998). For example, in Lane et al.'s path analysis of the antecedents of anxiety, state anxiety responses, and triathlon performance, the antecedents of anxiety intensity and anxiety direction were determined to be different. Specifically, anxiety intensity was predicted by perceived readiness and perceived difficulty of race goals, whereas anxiety direction was predicted by perceived readiness, coach's influence, and recent form.

In addition to the interpretations of anxiety, the frequency with which performers experience anxiety symptoms has received research interest, albeit to a far lesser extent. For example, Swain and Jones (1993) observed that, although cognitive anxiety remained stable throughout the precompetition period in accordance with past research (e.g., Jones & Cale, 1989; Parfitt & Hardy, 1987), cognitive anxiety symptoms were experienced progressively more frequently as the competition approached.

Taken together, the findings to date regarding the interpretation of anxiety imply that the intensity-alone approach to anxiety-performance relationships in sport is likely to be limiting when attempting to account for larger proportions of performance variance. It follows from this research that anxiety researchers should employ intensity, interpretation, and frequency paradigms to investigate the mechanisms underlying anxiety-performance relationships.

MEASUREMENT ISSUES

As indicated, early researchers in competitive anxiety used unidimensional measures of precompetitive anxiety. Such measures typically developed from Spielberger et al.'s

(1970) State-Trait Anxiety Inventory (STAI). For example, from the state anxiety component of the STAI, Martens et al. (1980) developed the CSAI. However, as anxiety theorists (e.g., Davidson & Schwartz, 1976; Liebert & Morris, 1967) had already started to conceptualize anxiety as a multidimensional construct, the CSAI was soon superseded by the CSAI-2 (Martens et al., 1990). Although some researchers continue to argue that anxiety is best measured as a unidimensional construct (e.g., Landers, 1994), most theorists accept that anxiety contains at least a cognitive and a physiological component. Consequently, since 1983 (when Martens et al., 1990, originally constructed the CSAI-2), research in competitive anxiety has largely employed the CSAI-2 as a measure of cognitive and somatic anxiety. In this section, the CSAI-2 is discussed in some depth, perhaps to the partial detriment of other measures. There are two main reasons for this. First, although other measures of competitive anxiety in sport do exist, the CSAI-2 has been, and continues to be, the choice of predilection for most researchers with an interest in competitive state anxiety. Second, almost all of the issues associated with the CSAI-2 that are discussed in this section apply equally well to other measures.

The CSAI-2 (Martens et al., 1990) was developed as a measure of cognitive anxiety, somatic anxiety, and self-confidence. As mentioned previously, Jones and Swain (1992) modified the original CSAI-2 to include a direction scale, whereby performers are asked to rate how debilitating or facilitating they perceive their anxiety symptoms to be. The terminology given to this debilitation-facilitation continuum has varied from "direction" to "interpretation" to "directional interpretation." Regardless of the terminology employed, this scale was designed to measure the extent to which an individual perceives that his or her state anxiety is either debilitating or facilitating to subsequent performance. Since the development of the modified CSAI-2, there has been an increasing interest in the concept of "facilitative anxiety" (e.g., Burton & Naylor, 1997; Hardy, 1997; Jones et al., 1994). Indeed, many studies have revealed that directional interpretation of anxiety symptoms is a better predictor of performance than measures of anxiety intensity. With respect to understanding the effects of anxiety on performance, two fundamental questions are posed here: Can anxiety facilitate performance? Does the CSAI-2 measure cognitive anxiety or some other construct? These two questions are addressed in the next few paragraphs.

The question, "Is cognitive anxiety really facilitative?" was the title of a recent article by Burton and Naylor

(1997). This question formed the basis of a reaction to Hardy's (1997) proposal that cognitive anxiety is not always detrimental to performance. In line with Jones et al. (1994), Burton and Naylor argued that "anxiety" symptoms that are perceived as being facilitative are unlikely to be labeled as anxiety at all. Indeed, it seems perfectly plausible that a performer who is experiencing facilitative anxiety might also feel self-confident, for example. However, Burton and Naylor stated that "the challenge confronting anxiety researchers is to develop a conceptually more explicit definition of anxiety that separates negative affective states (e.g., anxiety) that have debilitating effects on performance from positive affective states (e.g., challenge, excitement or self-confidence) that facilitate performance" (p. 299). Herein lies an assumption that seemingly has come to be accepted as self-evident. That is, a negative emotion will always have a negative effect on performance. The question remains: Why should a negative emotion *always* have a negative effect on performance? Also, why should a positive emotion *always* have a positive effect on performance? In fact, Gould et al.'s (1987) study with pistol shooters revealed a significant *negative* correlation between self-confidence and pistol shooting performance, thus providing evidence that a positive emotion (i.e., self-confidence) can, in fact, be negatively related to performance. As the present chapter's focus is on anxiety, the assumption that anxiety will always have a negative effect on performance is discussed in more detail here.

In justifying the hypothesized negative relationship between cognitive anxiety and performance, Martens et al. (1990) used an explanation based on reduced attentional resources (e.g., Wine, 1971). That is, a performer who is worried will use up valuable resources that would otherwise be directed toward the task at hand. Although this is a reasonable theoretical standpoint for predicting that cognitive anxiety will have a negative effect on performance, there is empirical evidence that contradicts it. For example, Hardy and Parfitt (1991) found that basketball players' best performance was significantly better, and their worst performance significantly worse, when they were cognitively anxious than when they were not. Hardy et al. (1994) replicated this finding with crown green bowlers. These results provide evidence that a negative emotion (e.g., cognitive anxiety) can have a positive relationship with performance and that it does not, perforce, debilitate performance. In addition to the studies conducted by Hardy and associates, other theories suggest that a negative emotion (e.g., cognitive anxiety) might sometimes have a positive influence on performance. Processing efficiency

theory is one such theory (Eysenck, 1992) that will be discussed later.

A second issue that competitive anxiety researchers need to address is the measurement of precompetition anxiety using the CSAI-2. It is fairly clear from the research discussed earlier that performers can interpret statements in the CSAI-2 quite differently. If this is the case, the construct validity of the CSAI-2 must be at least questioned. In other words, does the CSAI-2 measure what it purports to measure, or is it possible for two different performers with different cognitive states to report the same values? To illustrate this point, let us consider two performers, Performer A and Performer B. If Performer A scores 25 (out of a possible 36) on the cognitive anxiety subscale and feels worried beyond repair, she is likely to be feeling rather different from Performer B, who also scores 25 on the cognitive anxiety subscale and yet feels excited about her upcoming event. It is interesting to note that, of the three CSAI-2 subscales, it is the cognitive anxiety subscale that has revealed the most consistent differentiation between intensity and direction (cf. Jones et al., 1993). This might well be an artifact of the terminology used for the cognitive anxiety statements in the inventory. Indeed, eight of the nine cognitive anxiety statements have the prefix "I am concerned" or "I'm concerned." It could be argued that "concern" is not necessarily a reflection of worry or cognitive anxiety, but rather a perception of the importance of the upcoming event. This feature was highlighted in a study conducted by Barnes, Sime, Dienstbier, and Plake (1986). In their study of college swimmers, Barnes et al. felt obliged to remove the first item from the CSAI-2 because of the confusion it created among the swimmers. The statement "I am concerned about this competition" was interpreted in one of two ways: "(1) The swimmer thought it was asking if he was worried about the competition, or (2) the swimmer thought it [w]as asking if the event was important to him" (p. 368). It is fairly clear that other statements in the CSAI-2 could as easily be differentially interpreted. For example, the statement "I am concerned about reaching my goal" is open to the same kind of interpretation. Indeed, Athlete A might interpret this statement as "I am so worried that I will not achieve my goal that I cannot stop thinking about failing." Athlete B might interpret the same statement as "I am worried about not doing very well in this competition, so I had better get myself up for it right now." Athlete C might interpret the same statement as "I have worked really hard to achieve this goal and it means a lot to me." Clearly, the same statement can be interpreted quite differently.

There are two main issues here. First, it is clear that statements in the CSAI-2 can be interpreted ambiguously, to the point that they might, at times, not be measuring anxiety at all. It follows that the construct validity of the inventory as one purporting to measure anxiety needs further investigation. Second, if one considers the interpretations of Athlete A and Athlete B, one can see that seemingly similar anxiety states can be interpreted quite differently. These interpretations are not dissimilar to those revealed by Mahoney and Avener (1977). The first interpretation (Athlete A) is one of impending failure, whereas the second interpretation (Athlete B) is one that reflects a degree of perceived readiness. In light of the latter interpretation, a possible reply to Burton and Naylor's (1997) question "Is anxiety really facilitative?" is Yes, for some people, sometimes.

Furthermore, as Hardy (1997) pointed out, there is much anecdotal evidence of people performing incredible feats under extremely threatening circumstances. For example, there are accounts of mothers exhibiting extreme strength in their attempt to save their baby's life. In a sport context, the following quote from Hemery (1976), an Olympic athlete, illustrates how performers can perform exceptionally well (i.e., breaking a World record) even when they are under extreme pressure:

> Standing behind my blocks, I put my hands on my knees and tried to take as deep a breath as I could. I could not completely fill my lungs. There was a cold constriction between my stomach and my throat. My mouth and throat were dry, it was impossible to swallow . . . I wished I could be anywhere else. Why was I doing this anyway? I had never before felt such dreadful pressure. I walked forward to put my hands on the track in front of my blocks. Take your marks! No turning back. I kicked each leg out and placed it against the block. Still I felt weak. Did I feel ready to run the fastest quarter of my life? I was not sure. (David Hemery, prior to his World Record and Olympic-winning 400-meter hurdles run at the Mexico City Olympics in 1968, p. 4)

Other issues with the CSAI-2 appear to warrant further investigation. Indeed, the items that were originally chosen by Martens et al. (1990) might not reflect the most important aspects of precompetition anxiety for some athletes. For example, whereas the statement "I have self-doubts" might reflect a particular athlete's worry about her upcoming competition, the statement "I am concerned about losing" might not appear relevant, particularly for some female athletes (cf. Jones et al., 1991). Similarly, whereas the statement "My heart is racing" might reflect one athlete's somatic anxiety, the statement "I feel jittery" might not appear relevant. If athletes can interpret their scores on these items as reflecting different states, then measurements of precompetition anxiety utilizing the CSAI-2 are unlikely to account for large proportions of performance variance. For example, a 100-meter sprinter is likely to respond somewhat more calmly than a gymnast or a rock climber to a high score on the statement "My hands are clammy" because the consequences of having clammy hands are not the same for these individuals; indeed, whereas clammy hands are not likely to (directly) affect a sprinter's performance to a great extent, they might well affect a gymnast's or a climber's performance. Such possible differences suggest a need for the development of anxiety measures that are specific to particular sports, if not particular individuals. Furthermore, in light of the fairly modest proportion of performance variance accounted for in most anxiety studies, Gould and Udry (1994) called for researchers to consider a wider range of emotions to better understand the relation between different emotions and performance. However, apart from IZOF studies (e.g., Hanin & Syrjä, 1995a, 1995b), research in this area has not been particularly forthcoming.

A recent confirmatory factor analysis of the CSAI-2 (Lane, Sewell, Terry, Bartram, & Nesti, 1999) has questioned its structural validity. Lane et al. split their sample of 1,213 athletes into two samples. The results of their analyses revealed that all fit indices for the original CSAI-2 model were below the thresholds for acceptable fit; this was the case for both samples. For example, the Robust Comparative Fit Indices (RCFI) were 0.82 and 0.84 for the two samples. As a result of this confirmatory factor analysis, Lane et al. concluded, "Investigators of anxiety responses to sport competition cannot have faith in data obtained using the CSAI-2 until further validation studies have been completed and possible refinements to the inventory have been made" (p. 511). In light of the results obtained by Lane et al., this conclusion certainly seems reasonable.

In summary, although many researchers appear to believe that cognitive anxiety *necessarily* has a debilitating effect on performance, research suggests that this assumption may be misleading. Also, in light of past research, the construct validity of the CSAI-2 (in particular the cognitive anxiety measure) has been questioned here. The arguments presented here have been strengthened by the results of a recent confirmatory factor analysis of the CSAI-2 revealing its relatively weak factor structure. Finally, researchers might need to investigate other emotions to account for larger percentages of performance variance in a sporting context.

HOW ANXIETY AFFECTS PERFORMANCE: POSSIBLE EXPLANATIONS

Humphreys and Revelle's Information Processing Model

Humphreys and Revelle's (1984) information processing model is an attempt to explain the relationship among personality, stress, and performance. More specifically, the model proposes that performance (at the level of information processing) is predicted by the combined effects of (1) selected personality dimensions (i.e., achievement motivation, trait anxiety, and impulsivity); (2) situational moderators (i.e., stressors); and (3) motivational states (i.e., approach motivation, avoidance motivation). The model integrates two systems, termed arousal and on-task effort. Humphreys and Revelle used the notion of arousal as "a conceptual dimension defined as that factor common to various indicants of alertness" (p. 158). This is essentially a unidimensional view of arousal similar to that of Duffy (1962). Rather than simply "trying hard," on-task effort was defined by Humphreys and Revelle as the allocation of available resources to the task at hand. Although this definition of arousal could be viewed as simplistic, their model is included here as it was the first explicitly to include

personality, motivational, situational, and cognitive variables in a single arousal model. A simplified version of Humphreys and Revelle's model is illustrated in Figure 11.5. A detailed discussion of this model would be beyond the scope of this chapter and only its central features are discussed here. For a more in-depth discussion of the model, the reader is referred either directly to Humphreys and Revelle or to Jones and Hardy (1989) and Jones (1990).

In the Humphreys and Revelle (1984) model, performance is predicted on two types of tasks: sustained information transfer (SIT) tasks and short-term memory (STM) tasks. SIT tasks involve rapid throughput of information with no attempt at retaining this information in memory (e.g., a net rally in tennis). STM tasks require information either to be maintained in an available state or to be retrieved when it has not been attended to for a short while (e.g., deciding which serve to deliver next in a tennis match). One of the major predictions of the model is that performance on these two tasks is differentially affected by arousal.

Performance on SIT tasks is predicted to be a monotonically increasing function of arousal (i.e., the greater the level of arousal, the better the performance), whereas performance on STM tasks is predicted to be a monotonically

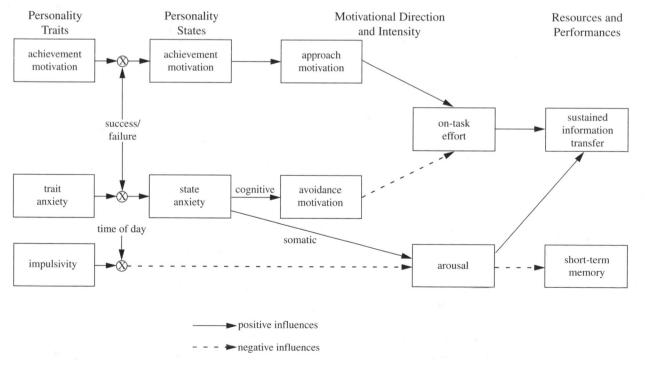

Figure 11.5 Conceptual structural model of the effects of personality, situational moderators, and motivational states on information processing and cognitive performance [reproduced from Jones & Hardy (1989) with permission].

decreasing function of arousal (i.e., the greater the level of arousal, the poorer the performance). In this way, performance may either be enhanced or impaired by arousal, depending on the nature of the task. For example, increased arousal might affect tennis performance in different ways depending on the demands of the task and different points in the match. If the rally were predominantly a fast exchange of volleys at the net, requiring rapid throughput of information, then increased arousal would likely help the tennis player. However, if the player was serving a second serve, she might have to recall a number of aspects from previous returns of serve. As such a task is more dependent on short-term memory, higher levels of arousal will more likely be detrimental to performance. Of course, if a task contained elements of both SIT and STM, then arousal could either enhance or impair performance, possibly accounting for an inverted-U relationship between arousal and performance (Humphreys & Revelle, 1984).

Despite Humphreys and Revelle's (1984) commendable attempt to move beyond theories that emphasize the role of worry, their model has three main limitations. First, it adopts a unidimensional view of arousal, whereas most researchers accept that arousal comprises at least two components (e.g., Hardy, Jones, et al., 1996; Pribram & McGuinness, 1975). Second, there is no differentiation between arousal and activation (see earlier section on state anxiety and performance). Third, the database of knowledge gleaned from research is as yet insufficient to sustain such a complex model of interactions between personality variables and task characteristics (Eysenck, 1986).

With its dual-system approach, Humphreys and Revelle's (1984) information processing model is quite possibly an advance over theories that emphasize worry to the exclusion of other systems. However, the model has a number of limitations, particularly the limited database on which such complex interactions might be based.

Processing Efficiency Theory

After the initial work of Eysenck (1979, 1982, 1983, 1986), Eysenck and Calvo (1992) proposed the processing efficiency theory. Although processing efficiency theory was developed in cognitive psychology, it may have important relevance for sport psychology. The theory emerged from Eysenck's dissatisfaction with theorists' simplistic conceptualization of anxiety-performance relationships. In essence, most anxiety theories are based on anxiety-induced cognitive interference, such that anxiety uses up attentional resources. These theories typically predict that high-anxious individuals will perform less well than low-

anxious individuals (e.g., Deffenbacher, 1980; Easterbrook, 1959; Mandler & Sarason, 1952; Sarason, 1984, 1988). Eysenck (1992) argued that such theories are limited because they exaggerate the effects of self-preoccupation and worry. Indeed, Eysenck cited numerous studies in which high-anxious individuals did not perform less well than low-anxious individuals (e.g., Blankstein, Flett, Boase, & Toner, 1990; Blankstein, Toner, & Flett, 1989; Calvo, Alamo, & Ramos, 1990; Calvo & Ramos, 1989). For example, Blankstein et al. (1989) found support for the notion that high-anxious individuals have more negative thoughts about themselves than low-anxious individuals. However, no differences were noted between high-anxious and low-anxious individuals in performance on an anagram task.

Eysenck (1992) argued that cognitive anxiety serves two principal functions. First, consistent with cognitive interference theories, worry will consume some of the individual's attentional resources, such that the attentional capacity for the task will be reduced. Second, worry signals the importance of the task to the individual and, as such, serves a monitoring function. In this way, anxious individuals will invest more effort if they perceive their performance to be below their expectations. However, Eysenck (1982) argued that this increase in effort will occur only when individuals perceive that they have at least a moderate probability of succeeding. In other words, if performers are reasonably confident, they will invest more effort in the task when their anxiety increases. Therefore, processing efficiency theory states that cognitive anxiety (a negative emotion) can have a negative cognitive effect (reduced attentional capacity) while serving *a positive motivational function* (increased effort).

In processing efficiency theory (Eysenck, 1992; Eysenck & Calvo, 1992), an important distinction is made between processing efficiency and performance effectiveness. Processing efficiency refers to the speed and ease with which information is processed. Performance effectiveness is, in essence, the quality of performance. Consequently, an increase in anxiety will likely result in a decrease in processing efficiency because of the extra effort invested in performance and the reduced attentional resources. However, performance effectiveness could be maintained or improved as a result of this extra effort, or it could be impaired.

As cognitive anxiety is hypothesized to tax working memory, the effects of elevated anxiety are likely to be fairly positive if the task does not overwhelm working memory. However, if the task is cognitively demanding, then performance may be impaired by elevated anxiety due to the limited remaining resources available for the task at hand. Research on processing efficiency theory has generally been supportive of its predictions using various procedures to tax working memory. For example, Eysenck (1985) used a letter transformation task to manipulate task difficulty. In these tasks, participants are asked to transfer a series of letters into another series of letters by converting the letters by a certain amount. For example, a participant might be asked to add 4 to the series ADG. The correct answer would then be EHK (A+4, D+4, G+4). When Eysenck (1985) increased the number of letters to be transformed, he found no differences between high-anxious and low-anxious individuals on performance when the task was fairly simple (one or two letters). However, a significant interaction indicated that the differences in performance between the two groups increased as a function of task difficulty. That is to say, the high-anxious individuals' performance was increasingly worse than their low-anxious counterparts as task difficulty increased. As processing efficiency theory predicts that performance impairment is caused by overloads to working memory, it follows that the performance of tasks that do not tax working memory to any great extent will not be affected by anxiety because performers can increase their effort to maintain or improve performance. However, if the cognitive demand is beyond a certain threshold, performers will lose confidence in being able to achieve the task, effort will likely be withdrawn, and performance will suffer.

Although processing efficiency theory emanated from cognitive psychology, its central tenets appear particularly relevant to some of the seemingly conflicting findings in competitive anxiety research, particularly the negative and positive effects of cognitive anxiety. Despite its natural extension from other theories in cognitive psychology (e.g., Wine's, 1971, theory of attention and interference), processing efficiency theory differs considerably in its dual-system approach. Indeed, rather than viewing the cognitive system as one passive mechanism (i.e., less cognitive resources = poorer performance), it allows for a positive moderating influence (i.e., effort) that might attenuate the negative effects of reduced resources.

Although Martens et al.'s (1990) multidimensional anxiety theory does not allow for any such compensatory mechanisms, Hardy and associates' cusp catastrophe model (Hardy, 1990, 1996b; Hardy & Fazey, 1987; Hardy & Parfitt, 1991) appears to fit well into a processing efficiency theory framework. For example, consider the proposed hysteresis effect illustrated earlier (see Figure 11.3).

Under conditions of high worry (cognitive anxiety), the cusp catastrophe model proposes that increases in physiological arousal will result in increases in performance up to some optimal point, beyond which further increases in physiological arousal will result in a dramatic drop in performance. In processing efficiency theory, individuals are predicted to monitor their performance: When performers are anxious, they are expected to respond to the possibility of unsatisfactory performance with increases in effort to maintain performance effectiveness (at the cost of processing efficiency); however, if the performance demands are beyond a certain threshold, the anxious individual will likely perceive the task demands to be too great, lose confidence, and withdraw effort. A withdrawal of effort is likely to be accompanied by a significant drop in performance as reflected in the cusp catastrophe model under conditions of high cognitive anxiety.

It is worth giving further consideration to the role that self-confidence and expectancies of success might play in processing efficiency theory. For example, Carver and Scheier (1988) suggested that anxiety will enhance performance when people are able to maintain a favorable expectancy regarding goal attainment. Also, Hardy (1990, 1996b) proposed that self-confidence might play a buffering role in protecting performers against the potential debilitating effects of elevated cognitive anxiety. For example, Hardy (1996b) postulated that high self-confidence might result in the front face of the catastrophe model shifting toward the right. The result of such a shift would be higher levels of physiological arousal being tolerated before a dramatic drop in performance occurred. Similarly, Hardy (1996b) proposed that low levels of self-confidence would result in the front face of the model shifting toward the left, such that only fairly low levels of physiological arousal could be tolerated before a dramatic drop in performance occurred. If these propositions, in the context of processing efficiency theory, are combined, it is quite conceivable that anxious performers who are self-confident (and therefore have favorable goal attainment expectancies) will increase their effort for a longer period of time in their attempt to achieve their goal. This proposition seems to accord with anecdotal reports of athletes performing exceptionally well under conditions of extreme pressure (e.g., breaking world records at major international events). Conversely, anxious performers with relatively low levels of self-confidence are more likely to withdraw their effort and "give up." If such a proposition were supported, then one would expect highly self-confident performers to exert more effort under conditions of elevated cognitive anxiety.

This would result in enhanced performance under conditions of high (i.e., "higher than normal") cognitive anxiety, but impaired performance if performers lost their self-confidence because task conditions changed (cf. Hardy & Parfitt, 1991; Hardy et al., 1994). Based on these propositions, exploration of the interaction among cognitive anxiety, effort, and self-confidence appears likely to be a fruitful area for future research.

The majority of research on processing efficiency theory has been conducted in laboratory settings using test anxiety measures such as Spielberger et al.'s (1970) STAI. As such, it would be crude to suggest that findings from test anxiety research could be applied en bloc to a competitive sport context. However, more recent research within a sport environment has also lent credence to processing efficiency theory. Hardy and Jackson's (1996) examination of rock climbers is one such example. In this study, experienced rock climbers led and seconded high- and low-anxiety rock climbs.[2] Climbers performed better and exerted more cognitive and physiological effort when they were cognitively anxious (leading) compared to when they were not cognitively anxious (seconding). In another study, with golfers, Mullen, Hardy, and Tattersall (1999) also found more effort was exerted when performers were anxious in a golf-putting task. Interestingly, Mullen et al.'s study did not reveal any significant changes in golf-putting performance. Golf putting differs from rock climbing in that although golfers and rock climbers are both required to react to a changing environment, the rock climber constantly has to make important decisions with respect to the changing nature of the climb as it evolves, including the risk of injury. In view of the likely different demands on working memory, it is possible that a contrived golf-putting task will not tax working memory as much as rock climbing. Consequently, the stakes might have to be perceived as very high before anxiety significantly affects performance. Australian golfer Greg Norman's demise[3] at the 1996 Masters is a case where such conditions might apply.

In summary, processing efficiency theory overcomes the shortcomings of many previous theories of anxiety and performance by incorporating a monitoring system, whereby anxious individuals will invest more effort if they perceive their performance to be threatened and they are reasonably confident of achieving their goal. A distinction is made between processing efficiency and performance effectiveness, such that an increase in effort will allow an individual to maintain performance effectiveness, albeit at a cost in terms of processing efficiency. Processing efficiency theory has received support in test anxiety. Also, recent research in a sporting environment suggests that processing efficiency theory may be applicable in competitive anxiety research, particularly in those sports that tax working memory. However, because of the obvious differences between test anxiety and competitive anxiety in sport, further research examining the theory in a sporting context is much needed. Processing efficiency theory appears to dovetail rather well with catastrophe models, particularly with respect to the role that self-confidence might play in buffering the debilitating effects of elevated cognitive anxiety. As such, self-confidence might allow anxious individuals to invest more effort in their performance due to their elevated anxiety. Consequently, performers who enjoy high levels of self-confidence might well be expected to perform better under conditions when they feel more anxious. Research investigating the interaction among cognitive anxiety, physiological arousal, effort, and sport performance will undoubtedly clarify the applicability of processing efficiency theory to a sport environment.

Conscious Processing Hypothesis

The conscious processing hypothesis (Masters, 1992) states that performers who are experiencing increased anxiety attempt to control their performance by consciously controlling their movements using explicit "rules" to perform the task, rather than simply "doing it automatically" as they would normally. Baumeister (1984) suggested that performers have a tendency to focus on the process of performing in competitive situations because they are highly motivated to do well. Thus, performers who are normally capable of executing a task "without thinking about it" will lapse into conscious monitoring and control of their performance under conditions of stress. As conscious control is relatively crude compared to automatic control (Keele, 1973; Langer & Imber, 1979), performance should suffer when conscious control is exerted over a skill that is normally executed automatically.

Masters (1992) tested the conscious processing hypothesis with a sample of novice golfers. These novices were taught a golf-putting task either under explicit learning conditions or under implicit learning conditions. Golfers in the explicit learning group were given instructions on the correct method of putting and were asked to use this technical information during their practice sessions. The implicit

---

[2] When rock climbers lead a climb, they run the risk of serious injury. When climbers second a climb, the technical difficulty remains the same, but the risk is largely removed.

[3] Greg Norman had a six-shot lead going into the final round of the 1996 Masters; he eventually lost by five.

learning golfers were asked to perform a random-letter generation task during their practice sessions to prevent them from forming or using any explicit rules on how to putt a golf ball. After an extended practice period, both groups were asked to perform the putting task under high-stress conditions. These conditions were induced by using both social evaluation and financial incentive. Under stressful conditions, the implicit learning group continued to improve, whereas the explicit learning group did not.

Hardy, Mullen, and Jones (1996) argued that Masters's (1992) results did not necessarily support the conscious processing hypothesis because the implicit learning group was not asked to continue their random-letter-generation task in the high-stress condition. As such, the continued improvement in the implicit learning group could be attributable to a decrease in task difficulty. However, when Hardy, Mullen, et al. (1996) controlled for this possible confound, their results also supported the conscious processing hypothesis. Bright and Freedman (1998) partially replicated Masters's study but failed to produce the same results as Masters and Hardy, Mullen, et al. However, Bright and Freedman introduced their stress intervention after only 160 putting trials, as opposed to the other two studies, which made their intervention after 400 trials. As such, the lack of significance in Bright and Freedman's study could be attributable to the participants' earlier stage of learning. That is to say, the participants in Bright and Freedman's explicit learning group were likely still at the cognitive stage of learning when performance is normally controlled by conscious processes (cf. Schneider, Dumais, & Shiffrin, 1984) and so did not experience any decrement in performance when they performed under conscious control.

These investigations in support of the conscious processing hypothesis have important practical implications. At present, many practitioners and researchers advocate the use of process goals as important methods of retaining or regaining focus during performance (Bull, Albinson, & Shambrook, 1996; Kingston & Hardy, 1994b, 1997; Kingston, Hardy, & Markland, 1992). It could be argued that process goals encourage the use of explicit knowledge to control movements and should therefore increase the likelihood of a breakdown in automatic processing. Based on our current knowledge, it is plausible that holistic process goals that encourage a focus on global aspects of performance will be beneficial because they encourage automaticity rather than a dechunking of the skill into parts (Kingston & Hardy, 1994a, 1997).

The conscious processing hypothesis could dovetail rather well with Hardy and colleagues' cusp catastrophe model, particularly if the basic tenets of processing efficiency theory were also included. For example, when performers are cognitively anxious, Eysenck (1992) argued they are likely to invest more effort in the task at hand provided they perceive that they have at least a moderate chance of succeeding. Under these conditions of high cognitive anxiety, performance is likely to be fairly good. However, if performers increase their effort to such a degree that they lapse into conscious processing (cf. Masters, 1992), then their performance will likely suffer dramatically. Hence, a performance catastrophe (cf. Hardy, 1990) could be explained either by a withdrawal of effort or by an effort-induced lapse into conscious processing, or both. Thus, under elevated cognitive anxiety, an increase in effort might be beneficial to performance up to a point, beyond which a further increase in effort will lead to a catastrophic drop in performance due to a lapse into conscious processing.

At an applied level, this suggests that any effort invested under conditions of elevated cognitive anxiety will be best directed through the use of holistic process goals rather than through the dechunking of an otherwise automatic skill. There is some evidence to suggest that some elite performers do tend to use such holistic process goals (Jones & Hardy, 1990; Orlick & Partington, 1988). The following quote, from an Olympic pairs kayaker, reported by Orlick and Partington (1988), exemplifies such an approach:

> My focus was very concentrated throughout the race. We have a start plan, and in it I concentrate only on the first few strokes. . . . Then I concentrate on the next little bit of the race. . . . Then it's getting to the end, we have to really push. Almost every 3 seconds or so toward the end I'd have to say, 'Relax,' and I'd let my shoulders and my head relax, and I'd think about putting on the power, and then I'd feel the tension creeping up again so I'd think about relaxing again, then power, then relax . . . (p. 116)

In summary, the conscious processing hypothesis predicts that performers whose cognitive anxiety is elevated are more likely to lapse into the conscious controlling of a normally automatic skill. Although there is a need for more corroborating evidence for the conscious processing hypothesis in sport settings, the research to date has generally supported its central features both in laboratory and sport settings. At an applied level, the hypothesis implies that process goals should be used wisely so as not to encourage the breakdown of a normally automated skill.

Theory of Ironic Processes of Mental Control

The theory of ironic processes of mental control was developed by Wegner (1989, 1994, 1997) from the observation that it is difficult not to think about something when this is one's explicit desire. For example, if one explicitly tries not to think of a white bear, one will have difficulty not bringing the image of a white bear to mind (Wegner, 1989). Wegner postulated that mental control is accomplished by the interaction of two processes: an intentional operating process and an ironic monitoring process. The *operating process* is conscious, effortful, and interruptible. The *monitoring process* is unconscious, less effortful, and uninterruptible. The operating process consciously seeks mental components that are consistent with the intended state of mind, whereas the monitoring process searches for those mental components that signal a failure to create the intended state of mind. Wegner (1997) suggested that the operating process and the monitoring process function together as a feedback unit in an attempt to produce mental control. For example, prior to a tennis player's second serve, the operating process might look for any signs that will allow the player successfully to execute the second serve. Such signs might include picking a target spot on the court, reminding oneself of the opponent's weak backhand return, or remembering the last successful second serve. At the same time, the monitoring process might look for signs that will result in a double fault. These might include recalling where the ball went on one's previous double fault, remembering the opponent's powerful forehand return, focusing on the point of impact of the first serve.

When working in an adaptive fashion, the monitoring process will ensure that threats to the operating process are registered and dealt with accordingly. In the example above, the monitoring process might register the opponent's strong forehand return and, under normal circumstances, the tennis player should be able to concentrate on delivering an appropriate serve to the opponent's backhand. However, the monitoring process is called an *ironic* monitoring process because it increases the accessibility of those thoughts that are the most undesirable. Under normal conditions, the operating process outweighs the monitoring in its consumption of processing capacity (Wegner, 1989, 1994, 1997). However, when mental load increases (e.g., under various types of pressure, including high levels of stress or anxiety), the monitoring process begins to outweigh the operating process and mental control backfires by attending to those thoughts that are precisely the most undesirable. In the case of the tennis player, the place on the net where the last double fault was made becomes the fixated thought. The thought "Whatever you do, do not put the ball in the net" results in the player's hitting the ball into the net and committing a double fault. As Wegner, Schneider, Carter, and White (1987) suggested,

suppression of a thought induces the monitoring process to search for that very thought. Thus, if the reader is instructed not to pay attention to the period at the end of this sentence (something one would normally not pay attention to), the monitoring process will be primed to attend to it (Wegner, 1989).

Research that has directly tested the theory of ironic effects has received limited attention in sport psychology. However, there is some evidence that supports its central thesis. For example, Wegner, Broome, and Blumberg (1997) found that people who attempted to relax under conditions of mental load demonstrated an increase in symptoms of anxiety and physiological arousal. Also, in their study of auto race simulation, Janelle, Singer, and Williams (1999) found that when participants were more anxious, they were more inclined to focus on and process irrelevant internal and external information. Finally, in Wegner, Ansfield, and Pilloff's (1998) golf-putting experiment investigating ironic effects, players were instructed not to hit the ball past the hole. However, when players were under mental load, the propensity to hit the ball past the hole increased significantly.

Interestingly, it appears rather difficult to discriminate between the theory of ironic effects and the conscious processing hypothesis (Masters, 1992), particularly in terms of the hypothesized effects of stress on performance. Indeed, under increased levels of stress, both the theory of ironic effects and the conscious processing hypothesis predict that individuals will focus on thoughts that will be detrimental to their performance. One difference between the two predictions may be in the precise way in which these breakdowns in performance occur. For example, according to the conscious processing hypothesis, performance might break down in a number of ways (i.e., by consciously processing information that is normally processed automatically), whereas according to the theory of ironic effects, performance will break down in precisely the way that is to be avoided (i.e., by focusing on the cues to be avoided).

At an applied level, there are likely countless instances where ironic processes might be responsible for poor performance. For example, a golfer might think "Whatever you do, don't hit the ball in the lake" and subsequently proceed to hit the ball into the center of the lake (Janelle, 1999). Despite initial research in support of the theory, there has been little encouragement with respect to changing or preventing ironic processes (Shoham & Rohrbaugh, 1997). Janelle suggested that one way to interrupt ironic processes is to render the functioning of the monitoring process useless or irrelevant through paradoxical interventions. Such interventions encourage a person to focus on the threatening situation, thus rendering the monitoring process less debilitative. For example, an athlete who is experiencing debilitative precompetition anxiety might choose to focus on these feelings. As a consequence of focusing on these negative feelings, the monitoring system would search for cues that are incompatible with the anxious state, and the athlete should be able to reduce the level of debilitative anxiety through the identification of anxiety-reducing cues. Of course, as Janelle and Hall, Hardy, and Gammage (1999) pointed out, such paradoxical interventions should probably be viewed with great caution because of their counterintuitive quality and the lack of supporting research. If such interventions were revealed as sometimes being helpful, the question remains: When should an athlete abandon attempts at mental control in favor of the ironic monitoring process? Indeed, presumably, such a threshold exists (Wegner, 1997). If this were the case, then the skillful intervention would be in deciding whether this threshold had been crossed: If so, then the athlete should probably abandon attempts at mental control in favor of the ironic monitoring process; if not, then the athlete should attempt to redeem mental control with astute rebuilding of the operating process. However, these points remain conjectural until further research is conducted on the theory of ironic processes.

In summary, the theory of ironic processes of mental control (Wegner, 1989, 1994, 1997) suggests that mental control is achieved via the interaction of an intentional operating process and an ironic monitoring process. When mental load is elevated, the monitoring process outweighs the operating process and leads individuals to focus on that aspect of behavior that they precisely intended to avoid. Although initial research on the theory of ironic processes has been encouraging, the implications for applied interventions are yet to be elucidated.

APPLIED IMPLICATIONS

Antecedents of Stress and Anxiety

The sources of stress and anxiety revealed in the research include readiness and performance problems, interpersonal problems with teammates and coaches, financial and time constraints, selection procedures, lack of social support, injury struggles, traumatic experiences, and other personal issues. Many of these areas can be influenced by the coach. For example, if coaches encourage athletes to

have attainable goals and to prepare sufficiently well to perceive these goals as attainable, these athletes are likely to maintain a reasonably positive precompetition affective state. Conversely, if coaches try to pressure them to goals that are not really attainable, then negative precompetition affective states might well follow.

Useful strategies will likely be those that encourage automatic responses with respect to mental and physical preparation for competition. One such strategy that is widely used, particularly in team situations, is to have athletes generate "What if" scenarios (e.g., "What if my sports bag is stolen?"). In such cases, the coach, sport psychologist, and athlete can work together to come up with contingency plans when the competition does not run as smoothly as planned. Personal experience and discussions with coaches, athletes, and practicing sport psychologists suggest a competition rarely runs as smoothly as planned. Consequently, strategies that prepare one for numerous (not necessarily positive) eventualities will likely be beneficial.

State Anxiety and Performance

The relationship between state anxiety and performance arguably has been one area in sport psychology that has received a great deal of attention. However, the research to date allows only for informed speculations to be made about how state anxiety might affect performance. Consequently, any implications for best practice can only reflect this relatively limited state of knowledge.

Based on the empirical work presented in this chapter, there appears to be fairly sound evidence that cognitive anxiety can be either detrimental or beneficial to performance. If physiological arousal is not too high, and if performers perceive that they have a fairly reasonable chance of achieving their goal, then cognitive anxiety is likely to act as a motivator before and during performance. Conversely, if physiological arousal is elevated, and if athletes perceive that they have little chance of achieving their goal, then cognitive anxiety is likely to be detrimental to performance. Furthermore, when athletes suffer a decrement in performance under high levels of cognitive anxiety, the decrement is likely to be large, sudden, and difficult to recover from.

Ideally, performers will not suffer such a drop. One way to reduce the chance of such occurrences is by establishing truly attainable goals in conjunction with the coach. However, if a large drop in performance occurs, and if athletes are competing in a sport where recovery time is possible, then a combination of physical relaxation and cognitive restructuring might be helpful. More specifically, in relation to the cusp catastrophe model, athletes could physically relax and then cognitively restructure to regain the upper performance surface. Only then would recommencing one's preperformance routine (e.g., mental rehearsal) be recommended. Of course, in view of the relatively limited amount of research directly investigating catastrophe models of anxiety and performance, these recommendations remain fairly speculative.

In summary, from the research to date, the applied implications for coaches and athletes are these:

1. "Psyching up" strategies should be employed with great caution, as it is difficult for athletes to recover from a large drop in performance.
2. Stress management strategies that enable athletes to target cognitive anxiety and physiological arousal separately should be learned and practiced.
3. Truly attainable goals should be agreed between the coach and the athlete. If the goal is unrealistic (regardless of perceptions), athletes will start to fail sooner or later. Once this failure has occurred, the impact on self-efficacy will likely be disastrous because they were previously convinced that the goal *was* attainable.
4. Athletes should have well-practiced and effective self-talk and cognitive restructuring strategies. For athletes who typically experience anxiety as debilitative, such cognitive restructuring strategies might include changing their cognitive appraisal to a more facilitating state, such as excitement or challenge.

SUMMARY AND FUTURE DIRECTIONS

This chapter has included a review of research on the antecedents of competitive anxiety, the effects of anxiety on performance, and various hypotheses, models, and theories that can be used to describe and explain the effects of anxiety on performance. Despite the criticism leveled at multidimensional anxiety theory here and elsewhere, it is fairly clear that this theory has allowed researchers to progress from the rather simplistic inverted-U hypothesis.

Researchers in mainstream psychology have long accepted the interaction between cognition and emotionality or physiological arousal (Deffenbacher, 1977; Marañon, 1924; Schachter, 1964; Schachter & Singer, 1962), whereas researchers in sport psychology, perhaps rather surprisingly, have been slower to examine this notion. Future researchers interested in the effects of anxiety or other emotions on performance (or performance-related variables) will need to adopt interactive paradigms if they are

to take research in the field of sport psychology to the next level. Some research questions that are particularly worthy of attention are these:

- What are the organizational issues that impinge on athletes' preparation for competition, and how can these be best addressed and, at least partially, resolved?
- How do cognitive anxiety and physiological arousal (or somatic anxiety) exert their influence on performance (or performance-related variables)?
- What role, if any, does effort play in delaying drops in performance or in curtailing the magnitude of such decrements?
- Does effort moderate the effects of cognitive anxiety on performance?
- Which personality and individual variables influence IZFOs?
- What moderating role, if any, does self-confidence play in the effects of cognitive anxiety and physiological arousal on performance?
- How do other emotions (e.g., excitement and anger) affect performance?

Sport psychology research on anxiety has made significant advances over the past couple of decades. The inverted-U hypothesis is now discussed in most textbooks only as an introduction and to bring attention to its limitations. Although multidimensional anxiety theory has undoubtedly allowed anxiety research to move beyond simplistic notions of arousal, anxiety, and performance, the research on the interpretation of anxiety suggests that current operationalizations of anxiety need to be reconsidered and that anxiety and other emotions need to be investigated through different viewpoints. Even though the cusp catastrophe model is probably not *the* model of anxiety and performance, it has encouraged an understanding of the interactive effects of different anxiety components on performance. Also, with the possibilities that processing efficiency theory, the conscious processing hypothesis, and the theory of ironic processes of mental control can offer, these are exciting times for those who are eager to embrace the challenge of furthering knowledge and science in the study of anxiety.

REFERENCES

Alpert, R., & Haber, R.N. (1960). Anxiety in academic achievement situations. *Journal of Abnormal and Social Psychology, 61,* 207–215.

Anshel, M.H. (1990). Toward a validation of a model for coping with acute stress in sport. *International Journal of Sport Psychology, 21,* 58–83.

Apter, M.J. (1982). *The experience of motivation: The theory of psychological reversal.* London: Academic Press.

Barnes, M.W., Sime, W., Dienstbier, R., & Plake, B. (1986). A test of construct validity of the CSAI–2 questionnaire on male elite college swimmers. *International Journal of Sport Psychology, 17,* 364–374.

Baumeister, R.F. (1984). Choking under pressure: Self-consciousness and paradoxical effects of incentives on skillful performance. *Journal of Personality and Social Psychology, 46,* 610–620.

Blankstein, K.R., Flett, G.L., Boase, P., & Toner, B.B. (1990). Thought listing and endorsement measures of self-referential thinking in test anxiety. *Anxiety Research, 2,* 103–112.

Blankstein, K.R., Toner, B.B., & Flett, G.L. (1989). Test anxiety and the contents of consciousness: Thought-listing and endorsement measures. *Journal of Research in Personality, 23,* 269–286.

Bright, J.E.H., & Freedman, O. (1998). Differences between implicit and explicit acquisition of a complex motor skill under pressure: An examination of some evidence. *British Journal of Psychology, 89,* 249–263.

Broadhurst, P.L. (1957). Emotionality and the Yerkes-Dodson law. *Journal of Experimental Psychology, 54,* 345–352.

Bull, S.J., Albinson, J.G., & Shambrook, C.J. (1996). *The mental game plan: Getting psyched for sport.* Eastbourne, England: Sports Dynamics.

Burton, D. (1988). Do anxious swimmers swim slower? Re-examining the elusive anxiety-performance relationship. *Journal of Sport Psychology, 10,* 45–61.

Burton, D. (1998). Measuring competitive state anxiety. In J.L. Duda (Ed.), *Advances in sport and exercise psychology measurement* (pp. 129–148). Morgantown, WV: Fitness Information Technology.

Burton, D., & Naylor, S. (1997). Is anxiety really facilitative? Reaction to the myth that cognitive anxiety always impairs sport performance. *Journal of Applied Sport Psychology, 9,* 295–302.

Calvo, M.G., Alamo, L., & Ramos, P.M. (1990). Test anxiety, motor performance and learning: Attentional and somatic interference. *Personality and Individual Differences, 11,* 29–38.

Calvo, M.G., & Ramos, P.M. (1989). Effects of test anxiety on motor learning: The processing efficiency hypothesis. *Anxiety Research, 2,* 45–55.

Carver, C.S., & Scheier, M.F. (1988). A control perspective on anxiety. *Anxiety Research, 1,* 17–22.

Couch, J.V., Garber, T.B., & Turner, W.E. (1983). Facilitating and debilitating test anxiety and academic achievement. *Psychological Report, 33,* 237–244.

Cox, R.H. (1990). *Sport psychology: Concepts and applications.* Dubuque, IA: Brown & Benchmark.

Cox, T. (1978). *Stress.* London: Macmillan.

Davidson, R.J., & Schwartz, G.E. (1976). The psychobiology of relaxation and related states: A multiprocess theory. In D. Mostofsky (Ed.), *Behavioral control and modification of physiological activity* (pp. 399–442). Englewood Cliffs, NJ: Prentice-Hall.

Deffenbacher, J.L. (1977). Relationship of worry and emotionality to performance on the Miller analogies test. *Journal of Educational Psychology, 69,* 191–195.

Deffenbacher, J.L. (1980). Worry and emotionality in test anxiety. In I.G. Sarason (Ed.), *Test anxiety: Theory, research, and applications* (pp. 111–128). Hillsdale, NJ: Erlbaum.

Duffy, E. (1962). *Activation and behavior.* New York: Wiley.

Easterbrook, J.A. (1959). The effect of emotion on cue utilization and the organization of behavior. *Psychological Review, 66,* 183–201.

Edwards, T., & Hardy, L. (1996). The interactive effects of intensity and direction of cognitive and somatic anxiety and self-confidence upon performance. *Journal of Sport & Exercise Psychology, 18,* 296–312.

Eysenck, M.W. (1979). Anxiety, learning, and memory: A reconceptualization. *Journal of Research in Personality, 13,* 363–385.

Eysenck, M.W. (1982). *Attention and arousal: Cognition and performance.* Berlin, Germany: Springer.

Eysenck, M.W. (1983). Anxiety and individual differences. In G.R.J. Hockey (Ed.), *Stress and fatigue in human performance* (pp. 273–298). Chichester, England: Wiley.

Eysenck, M.W. (1985). Anxiety and cognitive-task performance. *Personality and Individual Differences, 6,* 579–586.

Eysenck, M.W. (1986). Individual differences in anxiety, cognition and coping. In G.R.J. Hockey, A.W.K. Gaillard, & M.G.H. Coles (Eds.), *Energetics and human information processing* (pp. 255–269). Dordrecht, The Netherlands: Martinus Nijhoff.

Eysenck, M.W. (1992). *Anxiety: The cognitive perspective.* Hove, England: Erlbaum.

Eysenck, M.W., & Calvo, M.G. (1992). Anxiety and performance: The processing efficiency theory. *Cognition and Emotion, 6,* 409–434.

Fazey, J.A., & Hardy, L. (1988). *The inverted-U hypotheses: A catastrophe for sport psychology* (British Association of Sport Sciences Monograph No. 1). Leeds, England: National Coaching Foundation.

Gill, D.L. (1986). *Psychological dynamics of sport.* Champaign, IL: Human Kinetics.

Gill, D.L. (1994). A sport and exercise psychology perspective on stress. *Quest, 44,* 20–27.

Gould, D., Eklund, R.C., & Jackson, S.A. (1991). *An in-depth examination of mental factors and preparation techniques associated with 1988 U.S. Olympic team wrestling success.* Grant report to USA Wrestling, Colorado Springs, CO.

Gould, D., Eklund, R.C., & Jackson, S.A. (1992a). 1988 U.S. Olympic wrestling excellence I: Mental preparation, precompetitive cognition and affect. *The Sport Psychologist, 6,* 358–362.

Gould, D., Eklund, R.C., & Jackson, S.A. (1992b). 1988 U.S. Olympic wrestling excellence II: Thoughts and affect occurring during competition. *The Sport Psychologist, 6,* 383–402.

Gould, D., Jackson, S.A., & Finch, L.M. (1993a). Life at the top: The experiences of U.S. national champion figure skaters. *The Sport Psychologist, 7,* 354–374.

Gould, D., Jackson, S.A., & Finch, L.M. (1993b). Sources of stress in national champion figure skaters. *Journal of Sport & Exercise Psychology, 15,* 134–159.

Gould, D., Petlichkoff, L., Simons, J., & Vevera, M. (1987). Relationship between Competitive State Anxiety Inventory–2 subscale scores and pistol shooting performance. *Journal of Sport Psychology, 9,* 33–42.

Gould, D., Petlichkoff, L., & Weinberg, R.S. (1984). Antecedents of, temporal changes in, and relationships between CSAI–2 subcomponents. *Journal of Sport Psychology, 6,* 289–304.

Gould, D., & Tuffey, S. (1996). Zones of optimal functioning research: A review and critique. *Anxiety, Stress, and Coping, 9,* 53–68.

Gould, D., Tuffey, S., Hardy, L., & Lochbaum, M. (1993). Multidimensional state anxiety and middle distance running performance: An exploratory examination of Hanin's (1980) zone of optimal functioning hypothesis. *Journal of Applied Sport Psychology, 5,* 85–95.

Gould, D., & Udry, E. (1994). Psychological skills for enhancing performance: Arousal regulation strategies. *Medicine and Science in Sports and Exercise, 26,* 478–485.

Guastello, S.J. (1982). Moderator regression analysis and the cusp catastrophe: Application of a two-stage personnel selection, training, therapy and policy evaluation. *Behavioral Science, 27,* 259–272.

Hall, C.R., Hardy, J., & Gammage, K.L. (1999). About hitting balls in the water: Comments on Janelle's (1999) article on ironic processes. *The Sport Psychologist, 13,* 221–224.

Hanin, Y.L. (1980). A study of anxiety in sport. In W.F. Straub (Ed.), *Sport psychology: An analysis of athletic behavior* (pp. 236–249). Ithaca, NY: Mouvement.

Hanin, Y.L. (1986). State trait anxiety research on sports in the USSR. In C.D. Spielberger & R. Diaz (Eds.), *Cross-cultural anxiety* (Vol. 3, pp. 45–64). Washington, DC: Hemisphere.

Hanin, Y.L., & Syrjä, P. (1995a). Performance affect in junior ice hockey players: An application of the individual zones of optimal functioning model. *The Sport Psychologist, 9,* 169–187.

Hanin, Y.L., & Syrjä, P. (1995b). Performance affect in soccer players: An application of the IZOF model. *International Journal of Sports Medicine, 16,* 260–265.

Hanson, D.L. (1967). Cardiac response on participation in Little League baseball competition as determined by telemetry. *Research Quarterly, 38,* 384–388.

Hardy, L. (1990). A catastrophe model of anxiety and performance. In J.G. Jones & L. Hardy (Eds.), *Stress and performance in sport* (pp. 81–106). Chichester, England: Wiley.

Hardy, L. (1996a). A test of catastrophe models of anxiety and sports performance against multidimensional theory models using the method of dynamic differences. *Anxiety, Stress, and Coping: An International Journal, 9,* 69–86.

Hardy, L. (1996b). Testing the predictions of the cusp catastrophe model of anxiety and performance. *The Sport Psychologist, 10,* 140–156.

Hardy, L. (1997). Three myths about applied consultancy work. *Journal of Applied Sport Psychology, 9,* 277–294.

Hardy, L., & Fazey, J. (1987, June). *The inverted-U hypothesis: A catastrophe for sport psychology?* Paper presented at the annual conference of the North American Society for the Psychology of Sport and Physical Activity, Vancouver, Canada.

Hardy, L., & Jackson, B. (1996). Effect of state anxiety upon effort and performance. *Journal of Sports Sciences, 14,* 31–32.

Hardy, L., Jones, J.G., & Gould, D. (1996). *Understanding psychological preparation for sport.* Chichester, England: Wiley.

Hardy, L., Mullen, R., & Jones, G. (1996). Knowledge and conscious control of motor actions under stress. *British Journal of Psychology, 87,* 621–636.

Hardy, L., & Parfitt, C.G. (1991). A catastrophe model of anxiety and performance. *British Journal of Psychology, 82,* 163–178.

Hardy, L., Parfitt, C.G., & Pates, J. (1994). Performance catastrophes in sport: A test of the hysteresis hypothesis. *Journal of Sports Sciences, 12,* 327–334.

Hardy, L., & Woodman, T. (1999). *A case study of organizational stress in elite sport II: Environmental and personal issues.* Manuscript submitted for publication.

Hebb, D.O. (1955). Drives and the CNS (conceptual nervous system). *Psychological Review, 62,* 243–254.

Hemery, D. (1976). *Another hurdle.* London: Heinemann.

Hockey, G.R.J., & Hamilton, P. (1983). The cognitive patterning of stress states. In G.R.J. Hockey (Ed.), *Stress and fatigue in human performance* (pp. 331–362). Chichester, England: Wiley.

Humphreys, M.S., & Revelle, W. (1984). Personality, motivation and performance: A theory of the relationship between individual differences and information processing. *Psychological Review, 91,* 153–184.

Janelle, C.M. (1999). Ironic mental processes in sport: Implications for sport psychologists. *The Sport Psychologist, 13,* 201–220.

Janelle, C.M., Singer, R.N., & Williams, A.M. (1999). External distraction and attentional narrowing: Visual search evidence. *Journal of Sport & Exercise Psychology, 21,* 70–91.

Jick, T., & Payne, R.L. (1980). Stress at work. *Exchange: The Organizational Behavior Teaching Journal, 5,* 50–53.

Jones, J.G. (1990). A cognitive perspective on the processes underlying the relationship between stress and performance in sport. In J.G. Jones & L. Hardy (Eds.), *Stress and performance in sport* (pp. 17–42). Chichester, England: Wiley.

Jones, J.G. (1991). Recent developments and current issues in competitive state anxiety research. *The Sport Psychologist, 4,* 152–155.

Jones, J.G. (1995). More than just a game: Research developments and issues in competitive anxiety in sport. *British Journal of Psychology, 86,* 449–478.

Jones, J.G., & Cale, A. (1989). Relationship between multidimensional competitive state anxiety and cognitive and motor subcomponents of performance. *Journal of Sports Sciences, 7,* 129–140.

Jones, J.G., Hanton, S., & Swain, A.B.J. (1994). Intensity and interpretation of anxiety symptoms in elite and non-elite sports performers. *Personality and Individual Differences, 17,* 657–663.

Jones, J.G., & Hardy, L. (1989). Stress and cognitive functioning in sport. *Journal of Sports Sciences, 7,* 41–63.

Jones, J.G., & Hardy, L. (1990). Stress in sport: Experiences of some elite performers. In J.G. Jones & L. Hardy (Eds.), *Stress and performance in sport* (pp. 247–277). Chichester, England: Wiley.

Jones, J.G., & Swain, A.B.J. (1992). Intensity and direction dimensions of competitive anxiety and relationships with competitiveness. *Perceptual and Motor Skills, 74,* 467–472.

Jones, J.G., Swain, A.B.J., & Cale, A. (1990). Antecedents of multidimensional competitive state anxiety and self confidence in elite intercollegiate middle distance runners. *The Sport Psychologist, 4,* 107–118.

Jones, J.G., Swain, A.B.J., & Cale, A. (1991). Gender differences in precompetition temporal patterning and antecedents of anxiety and self confidence. *Journal of Sports & Exercise Psychology, 13,* 1–15.

Jones, J.G., Swain, A.B.J., & Hardy, L. (1993). Intensity and direction dimensions of competitive state anxiety and relationships with performance. *Journal of Sports Sciences, 11,* 525–532.

Karteroliotis, C., & Gill, D. (1987). Temporal changes in psychological and physiological components of state anxiety. *Journal of Sport Psychology, 9,* 261–274.

Keele, S.W. (1973). *Attention and human performance.* Pacific Palisades, CA: Goodyear.

Kerr, J.H. (1990). Stress in sport: Reversal theory. In J.G. Jones & L. Hardy (Eds.), *Stress and performance in sport* (pp. 107–131). Chichester, England: Wiley.

Kerr, J.H., Yoshida, H., Hirata, C., Takai, K., & Yamazaki, F. (1997). Effects on archery performance of manipulating metamotivational state and felt arousal. *Perceptual and Motor Skills, 84,* 819–828.

Kingston, K.M., & Hardy, L. (1994a). Factors affecting the salience of outcome, performance and process goals in golf. In A.J. Cochran & M.R. Farrally (Eds.), *Science and golf II: Proceedings of the Second World Scientific Congress of Golf* (pp. 244–249). London: E. & F.N. Spon.

Kingston, K.M., & Hardy, L. (1994b). When are some goals more beneficial than others? *Journal of Sports Sciences, 12,* 198–199.

Kingston, K.M., & Hardy, L. (1997). Effects of different types of goals on processes that support performance. *The Sport Psychologist, 11,* 277–293.

Kingston, K.M., Hardy, L., & Markland, D. (1992). Study to compare the effects of two different goal types on the number of situationally relevant performance subcomponents. *Journal of Sports Sciences, 10,* 610–611.

Krane, V. (1990). *Anxiety and athletic performance: A test of the multidimensional anxiety and catastrophe theories.* Unpublished doctoral thesis, University of North Carolina, Greensboro.

Krane, V. (1992). Conceptual and methodological considerations in sport anxiety research: From the inverted-U hypothesis to catastrophe theory. *Quest, 44,* 72–87.

Krane, V. (1993). A practical application of the anxiety-performance relationship: The zone of optimal functioning hypothesis. *The Sport Psychologist, 7,* 113–126.

Krane, V., & Williams, J.M. (1987). Performance and somatic anxiety, and confidence changes prior to competition. *Journal of Sport Behavior, 10,* 47–56.

Lacey, J.I. (1967). Somatic response patterning of stress: Some revisions of activation theory. In M. Appley & R. Trumbell (Eds.), *Psychological stress in research* (pp. 14–37). New York: Appleton.

Landers, D.M. (1994). Performance, stress and health: Overall reaction. *Quest, 46,* 123–135.

Landers, D.M., & Boutcher, S.H. (1986). Arousal-performance relationships. In J.M. Williams (Ed.), *Applied sport psychology:*

Personal growth to peak performance (pp. 170–184). Palo Alto, CA: Mayfield.

Landers, D.M., & Boutcher, S.H. (1993). Arousal-performance relationships. In J.M. Williams (Ed.), *Applied sport psychology: Personal growth to peak performance* (2nd ed., pp. 170–184). Palo Alto, CA: Mayfield.

Lane, A.M., Sewell, D.F., Terry, P.C., Bartram, D., & Nesti, M.S. (1999). Confirmatory factor analysis of the Competitive State Anxiety Inventory–2. *Journal of Sports Sciences, 17,* 505–512.

Lane, A.M., Terry, P.C., & Karageorghis, C.I. (1995). Path analysis examining relationships among antecedents of anxiety, multidimensional state anxiety, and triathlon performance. *Perceptual and Motor Skills, 81,* 1255–1266.

Langer, E.J., & Imber, L.G. (1979). When practice makes imperfect: Debilitating effects of overlearning. *Journal of Personality and Social Psychology, 37,* 2014–2024.

Lazarus, R.S. (1966). *Psychological stress and coping process.* New York: McGraw-Hill.

Lazarus, R.S. (1982). Thoughts on the relation between emotion and cognition. *American Psychologist, 37,* 1019–1024.

Liebert, R.M., & Morris, L.W. (1967). Cognitive and emotional components of test anxiety: A distinction and some initial data. *Psychological Reports, 20,* 975–978.

Lowe, R., & McGrath, J.E. (1971). *Stress, arousal and performance: Some findings calling for a new theory.* Project Report, AF 1161–67, AFOSR.

Mahoney, M.J., & Avener, M. (1977). Psychology of the elite athlete: An exploratory study. *Cognitive Therapy and Research, 1,* 135–141.

Males, J., Kerr, J.H., & Gerkovich, M.M. (1998). Metamotivational states during canoe slalom competition: A qualitative analysis using reversal theory. *Journal of Applied Sport Psychology, 10,* 185–200.

Malmo, R.B. (1959). Activation: A neuropsychological dimension. *Psychological Review, 66,* 367–386.

Mandler, G., & Sarason, S.B. (1952). A study of anxiety and learning. *Journal of Abnormal and Social Psychology, 47,* 166–173.

Marañon, G. (1924). Contribution à l'étude de l'action émotive de l'adrénaline [Contribution to the study of the emotional effects of adrenaline]. *Revue Française d'Endocrinologie, 2,* 301–325.

Martens, R. (1977). *Sport Competition Anxiety Test.* Champaign, IL: Human Kinetics.

Martens, R., Burton, D., Rivkin, F., & Simon, J. (1980). Reliability and validity of the Competitive State Anxiety Inventory (CSAI). In C.H. Nadeau, W.C. Halliwell, K.M. Newell, & G.C. Roberts (Eds.), *Psychology of motor behavior and sport–1979* (pp. 91–99). Champaign, IL: Human Kinetics.

Martens, R., Burton, D., Vealey, R.S., Bump, L.A., & Smith, D.E. (1990). Development and validation of the Competitive State Anxiety Inventory–2. In R. Martens, R.S. Vealey, & D. Burton (Eds.), *Competitive anxiety in sport* (pp. 117–190). Champaign, IL: Human Kinetics.

Masters, R.S.W. (1992). Knowledge, knerves, and know-how. *British Journal of Psychology, 83,* 343–358.

Morgan, W.P., O'Connor, P.J., Sparling, P.B., & Pate, R.R. (1987). Psychological characterization of the elite female distance runner. *International Journal of Sports Medicine, 8,* 124–131.

Morris, L., Davis, D., & Hutchings, C. (1981). Cognitive and emotional components of anxiety: Literature review and revised worry-emotionality scale. *Journal of Educational Psychology, 75,* 541–555.

Mullen, R., Hardy, L., & Tattersall, A.J. (1999). State anxiety and motor performance: The role of heart rate variability as an index of effort. *Journal of Sports Sciences, 17,* 62–63.

Näätänen, R. (1973). The inverted-U relationship between activation and performance: A critical review. In S. Kornblum (Ed.), *Attention and performance IV* (pp. 155–174). New York: Academic Press.

Neiss, R. (1988). Reconceptualizing arousal: Psychobiological states in motor performance. *Psychological Bulletin, 103,* 345–366.

Orlick, T., & Partington, J. (1988). Mental links to excellence. *The Sport Psychologist, 2,* 105–130.

Oxendine, J.B. (1970). Emotional arousal and motor performance. *Quest, 13,* 23–32.

Oxendine, J.B. (1984). *Psychology of motor learning.* Englewood Cliffs, NJ: Prentice-Hall.

Parfitt, C.G., & Hardy, L. (1987). Further evidence for the differential effects of competitive anxiety upon a number of cognitive and motor sub-systems. *Journal of Sports Sciences, 5,* 62–63.

Parfitt, C.G., Hardy, L., & Pates, J. (1995). Somatic anxiety and physiological arousal: Their effects upon a high anaerobic, low memory demand task. *International Journal of Sport Psychology, 26,* 196–213.

Parfitt, C.G., Jones, J.G., & Hardy, L. (1990). Multidimensional anxiety and performance. In J.G. Jones & L. Hardy (Eds.), *Stress and performance in sport* (pp. 43–80), Chichester, England: Wiley.

Patmore, A. (1986). *Sportsmen under stress.* London: Stanley Paul.

Perry, J.D., & Williams, J.M. (1998). Relationship of intensity and direction of competitive trait anxiety to skill level and gender in tennis. *The Sport Psychologist, 12,* 169–179.

Pribram, K.H., & McGuinness, D. (1975). Arousal, activation and effort in the control of attention. *Psychological Review, 82,* 116–149.

Raglin, J. (1992). Anxiety and sport performance. *Exercise and Sport Science Review, 20,* 243–274.

Raglin, J., & Morgan, W. (1988). Predicted and actual precompetition anxiety in college swimmers. *Journal of Swimming Research, 4,* 5–7.

Randle, S., & Weinberg, R. (1997). Multidimensional anxiety and performance: An exploratory examination of the zone of optimal functioning hypothesis. *The Sport Psychologist, 11,* 160–174.

Sanders, A.F. (1983). Towards a model of stress and human performance. *Acta Psychologica, 53,* 64–97.

Sarason, I.G. (1984). Stress, anxiety, and cognitive interference: Reactions to tests. *Journal of Personality and Social Psychology, 46,* 929–938.

Sarason, I.G. (1988). Anxiety, self-preoccupation and attention. *Anxiety Research, 1,* 3–7.

Sarason, S.B., Davidson, K.S., Lighthall, F.F., Waite, R.R., & Ruebush, B.K. (1960). *Anxiety in elementary school children.* New York: Wiley.

Scanlan, T.K., & Passer, M.W. (1978). Factors related to competitive stress among male youth sport participants. *Medicine and Science in Sport, 10,* 103–108.

Scanlan, T.K., Ravizza, K., & Stein, G.L. (1989). An in-depth study of former elite figure skaters: 1. Introduction to the project. *Journal of Sport & Exercise Psychology, 11,* 54–64.

Scanlan, T.K., Stein, G.L., & Ravizza, K. (1991). An in-depth study of former elite figure skaters: 3. Sources of stress. *Journal of Sport & Exercise Psychology, 13,* 102–120.

Schachter, S. (1964). The interaction of cognitive and physiological determinants of the emotional state. In L. Berkowitz (Ed.), *Advances in experimental social psychology* (Vol. 1, pp. 49–80). New York: Academic Press.

Schachter, S., & Singer, J. (1962). Cognitive, social, and physiological determinants of emotional state. *Psychological Review, 69,* 379–399.

Schneider, W., Dumais, S.T., & Shiffrin, R.M. (1984). Automatic and controlled processing and attention. In R. Parasuraman & R. Davies (Eds.), *Varieties of attention* (pp. 1–270). Orlando, FL: Academic Press.

Shoham, V., & Rohrbaugh, M. (1997). Interrupting ironic processes. *Psychological Science, 8,* 151–153.

Simon, J.A., & Martens, R. (1977). SCAT as a predictor of A-states in varying competitive situations. In D.M. Landers & R.W. Christina (Eds.), *Psychology of motor behavior and sport–1976* (Vol. 2, pp. 146–156). Champaign, IL: Human Kinetics.

Smith, R.E., Smoll, F.L., & Schutz, R.W. (1990). Measurements and correlates of sport-specific cognitive and somatic trait anxiety. *Anxiety Research, 2,* 263–280.

Spielberger, C.D. (1966). Theory and research on anxiety. In C.S. Spielberger (Ed.), *Anxiety and behavior* (pp. 3–20). New York: Academic Press.

Spielberger, C.D., Gorsuch, R.I., & Lushene, R.L. (1970). *Manual for the State-Trait Anxiety Inventory.* Palo Alto, CA: Consulting Psychologists.

Swain, A.B.J., & Jones, J.G. (1993). Intensity and frequency dimensions of competitive state anxiety. *Journal of Sports Sciences, 11,* 533–542.

Swain, A.B.J., & Jones, J.G. (1996). Explaining performance variance: The relative contribution of intensity and direction dimensions of competitive state anxiety. *Anxiety, Stress and Coping: An International Journal, 9,* 1–18.

Thelwell, R.C., & Maynard, I.W. (1998). Anxiety-performance relationships in cricketers: Testing the zone of optimal functioning hypothesis. *Perceptual and Motor Skills, 87,* 675–689.

Turner, P.E., & Raglin, J.S. (1991). Anxiety and performance in track and field athletes: A comparison of ZOF and inverted-U theories. *Medicine and Science in Sport and Exercise, 23,* S119.

Watson, G.G., & Friend, R. (1969). Measurement of social-evaluative anxiety. *Journal of Consulting and Clinical Psychology, 33,* 448–457.

Wegner, D.M. (1989). *White bears and other unwanted thoughts: Suppression, obsession, and the psychology of mental control.* New York: Viking.

Wegner, D.M. (1994). Ironic processes of mental control. *Psychological Review, 101,* 34–52.

Wegner, D.M. (1997). Why the mind wanders. In J.D. Cohen & J.W. Schooler (Eds.), *Scientific approaches to consciousness* (pp. 295–315). Hillsdale, NJ: Erlbaum.

Wegner, D.M., Ansfield, M., & Pilloff, D. (1998). The putt and the pendulum: Ironic effects of the mental control of action. *Psychological Science, 9,* 196–199.

Wegner, D.M., Broome, A., & Blumberg, S.J. (1997). Ironic effects of trying to relax under stress. *Behavior Research and Therapy, 35,* 11–21.

Wegner, D.M., Schneider, D.J., Carter, S., & White, L. (1987). Paradoxical effects of thought suppression. *Journal of Personality and Social Psychology, 53,* 5–13.

Weinberg, R.S. (1978). The effects of success and failure on the patterning of neuromuscular energy. *Journal of Motor Behavior, 10,* 53–61.

Weinberg, R.S., & Hunt, V. (1976). The interrelationships between anxiety, motor performance, and electromyography. *Journal of Motor Behavior, 8,* 219–224.

Welford, A.T. (1973). Stress and performance. *Ergonomics, 16,* 567–580.

Wiggins, M.S. (1998). Anxiety intensity and direction: Preperformance temporal patterns and expectations in athletes. *Journal of Applied Sport Psychology, 10,* 201–211.

Williams, E.S., Taggart, P., & Carruthers, M. (1978). Rock climbing: Observations on heart rate and plasma catecholamine concentrations and the influence of oxprenolol. *British Journal of Sports Medicine, 12*(3), 125–128.

Wilmore, J.H., & Costill, D.L. (1994). *Physiology of sport and exercise.* Champaign, IL: Human Kinetics.

Wine, J.D. (1971). Test anxiety and direction of attention. *Psychological Bulletin, 76,* 92–104.

Wine, J.D. (1980). Cognitive-attentional theory of test anxiety. In I.G. Sarason (Ed.), *Test anxiety: Theory, research and applications* (pp. 349–385). Hillsdale, NJ: Erlbaum.

Woodman, T., Albinson, J.G., & Hardy, L. (1997). An investigation of the zone of optimal functioning hypothesis within a multidimensional framework. *Journal of Sport & Exercise Psychology, 19,* 131–141.

Woodman, T., & Hardy, L. (1999). *A case study of organizational stress in elite sport II: Leadership and team issues.* Manuscript submitted for publication.

Woodman, T., Hardy, L., Hanton, S., Jones, J.G., & Swain, A. (1999). *Anxiety and self-confidence: An investigation of the mechanisms underlying their relationship.* Manuscript in preparation.

Yamaji, K., Yokota, Y., & Shephard, R.J. (1992). A comparison of the perceived and the ECG measured heart rate during cycle ergometer, treadmill and stairmill exercise before and after perceived heart rate training. *Journal of Sports Medicine and Physical Fitness, 32,* 271–281.

Yan Lan, L., & Gill, D. (1984). The relationships among self-efficacy, stress responses, and a cognitive feedback manipulation. *Journal of Sport Psychology, 6,* 227–238.

Yerkes, R.M., & Dodson, J.D. (1908). The relation of strength of stimulus to rapidity of habit formation. *Journal of Comparative Neurology and Psychology, 18,* 459–482.

Zajonc, R.B. (1980). Feeling and thinking: Preferences need no inferences. *American Psychologist, 35,* 151–175.

Zajonc, R.B. (1984). On the primacy of affect. *American Psychologist, 39,* 117–123.

Zeeman, E.C. (1976). Catastrophe theory. *Scientific American, 234,* 65–82.

CHAPTER 12

Arousal and Performance

LEONARD D. ZAICHKOWSKY and AMY BALTZELL

Like so many psychological constructs, the concept of arousal is complex and lacks a universally accepted definition (Gould & Krane, 1992; Venables, 1984). Yet, arousal regulation is one of the most frequently discussed issues in applied sport psychology textbooks and, in general, is a topic of great interest for sport psychologists (Gould & Udry, 1994). Many anecdotal reports highlight both the facilitating and debilitating effects of arousal on sport performance but there is little empirical research. It is ironic that coaches and sport psychologists are trying to help athletes achieve appropriate arousal levels for competition, but are doing so with few empirically supported theoretical perspectives. There is ambiguity about the specific nature of arousal and how to measure it. Current research also points to the need to carefully operationalize performance to best understand the arousal-performance relationship (Edwards & Hardy, 1996; Gould & Krane, 1992).

The term *arousal,* which Webster's simply defines as "to excite to action from a state of rest" (1960, p. 49) has not been consistently operationalized in research, varying within and among the domains of psychology. For example, in sport psychology research, arousal has been used interchangeably with the following constructs: *anxiety, activation, emotion, tense,* and *psyched-up* (Sage, 1984). Other terms convey similar ideas, such as *motivated, psychic energy, excited, vigilant,* and *mentally ready.*

The interchange of the terms arousal and anxiety, in particular, has created conceptual confusion. Because anxiety often results in increased central and autonomic nervous system activity (arousal), it (unfortunately) has been used synonymously with arousal. Numerous researchers refer to arousal but instead use anxiety scales and discuss the findings as though arousal were measured (Klavora, 1979;

Sage & Bennett, 1973; Sonstroem & Bernardo, 1982). There have been efforts over the decades to differentiate between the terms. For instance, Fenz and Epstein's (1967) study of sport parachutists distinguished anxiety and arousal by arguing that physiological arousal was distinct from psychological fear and anxiety. Other researchers differentiate these constructs by defining anxiety as a form of excess arousal (feelings of tension and nervousness) that negatively affects performance (Koob, 1991; Wann, Brewer, & Carlson, 1998).

Recently, the term "emotion" has added additional conceptual confusion to discussions on arousal and how arousal relates to performance. In his popular book, *Emotional Intelligence,* Goleman (1995, p. 289) answers the question, "What is emotion?" in the following way: "I take emotion to refer to a feeling and its distinctive thoughts, psychological and biological states and range of propensities to act." He then lists a number of primary emotions as well as "families" of emotions, including anger, sadness, fear, enjoyment, love, surprise, disgust, and shame. Like Lazarus (1993) and Plutchik (1993), we would add the emotions of pride, passion, and confidence. Goleman's writing is based primarily on the empirical work of Levenson, Ekman, and Friesen (1990), and Lazarus. Reading Goleman, one could easily substitute the word "arousal" for "emotion."

Yuri Hanin's recent book, *Emotions in Sport,* (2000) describes his over 30 years of research on emotions in sport and how they relate to performance. But Hanin did not refer to emotions in his early work. Instead, he referred to anxiety (1978). In 1993, he shifted from writing about anxiety to writing about arousal; as he states in the introduction of his book, "We also present recent developments that have extended the model beyond anxiety to incorporate both positive and negative affect and to examine the influences of affect during as well as prior to performance" (Hanin, 2000, p. xi). Hanin's model, which he termed the individualized zone of optimal functioning (IZOF), is discussed in greater detail later in this chapter. The point here is that much of the writing on arousal in sport psychology includes terms such as anxiety and emotions that convey similar meaning. Clearly, there is a call to stabilize the meaning and use of arousal for the purposes of theory and practice.

The purpose of this chapter is to review the theories and research in sport psychology and related fields that lead to an understanding of the arousal construct and how it relates to performance in sport. Specifically, the focus will be to (1) define the arousal construct, (2) review neurophysiological aspects of arousal, (3) determine typical measurements of arousal and performance, (4) provide an overview of arousal-performance theories and related research, and (5) discuss the issue of arousal regulation in sport and exercise.

DEFINING THE AROUSAL CONSTRUCT

As stated earlier, many terms are associated with the concept of arousal, including both generalized and specific types and levels of excitement. Excitement, or levels of elevated energy, are thought to be reflected in sexual and physical activation and/or behaviors, positive and negative emotional responses, and cognitive activity. Prior to turning to the current debate and potential future direction of the usability of the arousal construct, a brief historical review of the use of arousal in the field of psychology is presented.

The study of arousal began in response to the difficulties associated with the study of emotion, drive, and motive. Arousal superseded these constructs given its early appeal of simplicity and the ease of empirically measuring physiological responses (Neiss, 1988a; 1988b). Early researchers viewed arousal as a unidimensional phenomenon, specifically energy mobilization along a continuum with concomitant psychophysiological responses (Cannon, 1932; Hebb, 1955; Malmo, 1959). The initial study of the arousal construct represented the organism's physiological and energy mobilization in response to physical threats (Cannon, 1932). Duffy (1934, 1941, 1957, 1962), one of the first psychologists to address arousal, viewed it as a behavior that varied along two dimensions, intensity and direction, which interestingly is consistent with the study of motivation. Specifically, Duffy (1962, p. 179) defined arousal as "the extent of release of potential energy, stored in the tissues of the organism, as this is shown in activity or response."

Motor behaviorists drew on motivation as the theoretical foundation for the arousal construct. Specifically, Sage (1984) operationalized arousal as an energizing function (1) reflecting the intensity of the motivation and (2) directing behavior toward a specific goal. Magill (1989) viewed arousal as synonymous with activation. He stated that "to motivate an individual is, in effect, to arouse or activate that person in such a way as to prepare himself or herself for the task at hand" (p. 485). R. Cox (1990) emphasized the "readiness" or alertness of an individual solely as a function of a physiological state of readiness. Currently, some sport psychology texts operationalize arousal within the framework of motivation. For example, Landers and Boutcher (1998, p. 198) define arousal as "an energizing function that is responsible for the harnessing of the body's resources for intense and vigorous activity."

Some researchers suggest that arousal represents only the intensity dimension of motivation (Smith, Smoll, & Wiechman, 1998), which is consistent with Brehm and Self's (1989) term "motivational arousal" used to describe the intensity of motivation, primarily the sympathetic nervous system response. In general, with motivation as the theoretical framework for arousal, arousal is viewed as varying on a continuum from extremely low levels (e.g., sleep) to very high levels (e.g., excitement) that occur in threatening (e.g., flight or fight) or incentive (e.g., sexual activity) situations. The motivational explanation of arousal suggests that the sympathetic nervous system is most reflective of motivational arousal.

Criticism has been levied against operationalizing arousal as a unidimensional construct, and strong support has been provided for arousal as a (1) multidimensional physiological construct (Hockey & Hamilton, 1983; Jones & Hardy, 1989; Lacey, 1967; Stankard, 1990; Ursin, 1988) and (2) a multidimensional construct with physiological, behavioral, cognitive, and/or affective dimensions (Adam, Teeken, Ypelaar, Verstappen, & Paas, 1997; Gould & Krane, 1992; Gould & Udry, 1994; Hardy, Jones, & Gould, 1996; Koob, 1991; Raedeke & Stein, 1994; Stankard, 1990; Wann, 1997). Lacey provided early evidence that it was possible to distinguish among three types of physiological arousal, including electrocortical, autonomic, and behavioral, with results indicating that these dimensions of arousal could covary independently from one another. Ursin pointed out that arousal is not identical to changes in heart rate, galvanic skin response, rise in plasma cortisol or growth hormone, or increases in metabolism. Each of these physiological changes constitutes only a part of the arousal response. He added that any of these factors can be altered without affecting the others.

Today, the majority of researchers conceptualize arousal as a complex, multidimensional construct including a physiological dimension paired/grouped with cognitive, affective, and/or behavioral dimensions. This multidimensional conceptualization of the athlete's competitive experience in sport is similar to that of McGrath's (1970) model of stress. This model has been relied on heavily by sport psychologists for the past 40 years in their effort to understand how elevated levels of cognitive, emotional, and physiological factors influence outcome behavior, such as "choking" and injury.

Currently, extensive support for a multidimensional arousal construct is present in research and theory. Adam et al.'s (1997) study determined how different arousal levels affected human information processing. Results indicated that physiological arousal was positively related to improvements in decision time in short-term memory tasks. In another investigation of arousal, Parfitt, Hardy, and Pates (1995) studied 32 basketball and volleyball players using the Competitive State Anxiety Inventory–2 (CSAI-2), heart rate measures, and performance based on Sargent jump performance (height jumped). Results supported a multidimensional arousal construct. Specifically, cognitive anxiety did not affect performance; however, increased physiological and somatic arousal were positively related to height jumped.

Koob (1991), using a neuropsychological perspective, indicated that arousal is multidimensional and includes physiological and behavioral dimensions. Wann (1997, p. 133) likewise defined arousal as a multidimensional construct, with physiological and cognitive dimensions, "a nonemotional physiological state of readiness to perform physically, intellectually, or perceptually." Hardy et al. (1996, p. 118) provided a definition of arousal that is consistent with yet more specific than that of Wann in an effort to distinguish arousal from activation: "Arousal . . . refers to cognitive and physiological activity which takes place in response to some new input to the system." Their definition of arousal highlights some of the challenges associated with interpretation. They argue that cognitive and physiological states underlie arousal and that anxiety is a "metacognitive emotion" that should be clearly distinguished from arousal. Indeed, strong opinions have emerged regarding the current valence of the arousal construct.

Martens (1987), in expressing his dislike for the term arousal, chose the term "psychic energy," for which he referred only to cognitive arousal. He asserted that terms such as arousal, drive, and activation confuse psychic energy with physical energy. His choice of the term psychic energy specifically reflects the activation of the mind, a term that he suggested would be more readily received by coaches given the frequently used colloquial terms "psyching up" and "psyching out." Martens stated that psychic energy is the "vigor, vitality and intensity with which the mind functions and is the bedrock of motivation" (p. 92). His efforts to dismiss the term arousal in an effort to better understand cognitive aspects of the athlete's motivation contributes to the confusion regarding efforts to operationalize the concept of arousal. However, his argument is of great value given that it highlights the relationship between cognitive arousal and athletic performance.

Neiss (1988a, 1988b, 1990) has been another strong critic of the arousal construct and, in fact, proposed abandoning the term. He (1990) suggested that studying arousal minimally contributes to understanding the arousal-performance relationship. He (1988a, p. 346) stated, "It is unduly reductionistic to focus on the physiological construct of arousal and to ignore the psychological variables. Such a focus is a hold-over from the era of behaviorism." He noted that debilitating anxiety and optimal state of readiness may include equivalent levels of arousal. Neiss (1990) reasoned that the study of discrete psychobiological states and their independent relationship to sport performance would better serve research. He concluded that it would be of most value to abandon arousal and to promote the study of unnamed discrete psychobiological states, which include physiological, cognitive, and affective dimensions.

Although controversy remains over the meaning of arousal, most contemporary researchers in sport psychology operationalize arousal as a condition that ranges along the sleep–high excitation continuum and finds expression in physiological, psychological (cognitive and affective), and behavioral terms (Adam et al., 1997; Gould & Krane, 1992; Gould & Udry, 1994; Hardy et al., 1996; Raedeke & Stein, 1994; Wann, 1997). Gould and Udry expand on this multidimensional explanation of arousal: "It is a mistake to conceptualize arousal as a unitary construct. Instead, arousal should be viewed as a multidimensional construct that contains a physiological arousal component and a cognitive interpretation-appraisal component. Furthermore, the cognitive interpretation-appraisal component consists of a cognitive appraisal of one's physiological arousal (somatic state anxiety), negative affect associated with one's cognitive appraisal of increased arousal (cognitive state anxiety) and positive affect associated with one's cognitive appraisal of increased arousal (paratelic state of excitement)" (p. 479).

The current trend to operationalize arousal as a multidimensional construct including physiological, cognitive, and affective interacting dimensions as it pertains to understanding the relationship of arousal to performance is also supported by Bandura (1997, p. 107).

> The information conveyed by physiological states and reactions is not, by itself, diagnostic of personal efficacy. Such information affects perceived self-efficacy through cognitive processing. A number of factors—including cognitive appraisal of the sources of physiological activation, its intensity, the circumstances under which the activation occurs, and construal bias—affect what is made of physiological conditions. The presumed diagnosticity of emotional arousal for performance enhancement or impairment is also an important factor in the cognitive processing of somatic efficacy information.

After tracing the history of the study of arousal and related phenomena, it appears that the perspective taken by Gould and Udry (1994) and Hardy, Jones, and Gould (1996) is correct, that arousal is a multidimensional construct. As is represented in Figure 12.1, arousal contains a physiological component that can be represented in a multitude of ways: through muscle tension, cortical activity, cardiovascular activity, electrodermal activity, and biochemistry. There is, however, a cognitive interpretation-appraisal component that influences the physiological component. Additionally, human affect interacts with thoughts to also influence physiological responses. Presented next is a brief overview of the neurophysiology of arousal, or what happens in the nervous system when one makes the transition from a condition of rest to the excitement of action.

NEUROPHYSIOLOGY OF AROUSAL

Malmo (1959) and Duffy (1962) undoubtedly made the seminal contributions to understanding brain mechanisms, autonomic nervous system activity, and other behaviors that accompany changes in physiological arousal. Structures of the central nervous system (CNS) that are closely related to arousal include the cortex of the brain, the reticular formation, the hypothalamus, and the limbic system. Figure 12.2 provides a simplified illustration of how the nervous system is involved in regulating physiological arousal. Table 12.1 summarizes the nervous system structures as well as their location and function.

The meticulous work of LeDoux (1993) has contributed much to an understanding of events that take place within the nervous system during emotional episodes. According to LeDoux, thoughts and feelings about competition trigger the reticular activating system (RAS), which increases neuronal activity along a vast network of neurons to the cortex. It appears that the RAS organizes sensorimotor behavior through its interconnections with the cortex

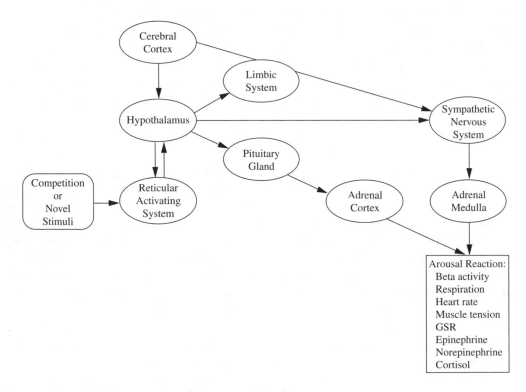

Figure 12.1 Conceptual model of the arousal-performance relationship.

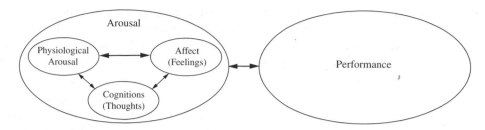

Figure 12.2 Nervous system and arousal reaction.

hypothalamus, and nervous system. The cerebral cortex becomes activated, characterized by rapid, low-amplitude asynchronous patterns known as beta waves. The hypothalamus receives input from higher brain centers in the nervous system as well as internal organs of the body. As such, it is involved in integrating messages from the cortex and internal organs. For many years, it has been known that the limbic system (or "primitive" brain structure) is involved in the development of emotions, but the recent work of LeDoux has more clearly mapped out the mechanisms,

and in particular, the role of the amygdala in regulating emotions.

The hypothalamus, located at the level of the midbrain, is involved with regulating the sympathetic nervous system and the pituitary gland. It stimulates the adrenal medulla to release adrenalin and noradrenalin. The pituitary gland is in close proximity to the hypothalamus, and releases adrenocorticotropin hormone (ACTH) into the blood, stimulating the adrenal cortex to release cortisol (Dienstbier, 1989).

Table 12.1   Nervous System Structures Involved in Arousal

Structure	Location	Function
Reticular formation	Part of brain stem that continues out of medulla and pons.	Involved in sleep, waking, alertness, and optimal brain arousal.
Hypothalamus	Between the thalamus and midbrain.	Involved in appetitive and sexual behavior, regulation of sympathetic nervous system and pituitary gland.
Limbic system	Series of structures, including the hypocampus and amygdala, located near the border between the cerebral hemisphere and the brain stem. The hypothalamus is sometimes considered part of the limbic system.	Primarily concerned with emotional behavior. Amygdala appears to be involved in aggression.
Cerebral cortex	Convoluted outer layer of the human brain.	Highest center involved in learning, remembering, planning, and performing motor acts.
Sympathetic nervous system	A branch of the autonomic nervous system (ANS) with nerve fibers originating in thoracic and lumbar regions of the spinal cord.	Activates glands and smooth muscles during arousal.
Parasympathetic nervous system	A branch of the ANS, with nerve fibers originating in the brain stem and sacral regions of the spinal cord.	Maintains appropriate internal states in times of relaxation.
Adrenal cortex	Outer layer of two small endocrine glands just above the kidneys.	Secretes cortisol that regulates metabolism and stress response.
Adrenal medulla (Closely related to the ANS, but technically not part of the nervous system)	Inner layer of two small endocrine glands just above the kidneys.	Secretes adrenaline (epinephrine) and noradrenaline (norepinephrine), both involved in increased activation of the body.
Pituitary gland	Deep inside brain, just below hypothalamus.	Releases adrenocorticotropic hormone (ACTH) that stimulates adrenal cortex to release cortisol.

The nervous system contains two major divisions, the peripheral nervous system (PNS), which innervates the skeletal muscles of the body, and the autonomic nervous system (ANS), which innervates the smooth muscles and glands of the body. The ANS is itself divided into two divisions: the sympathetic and the parasympathetic. The sympathetic division is primarily responsible for psychophysiological exchanges associated with arousal. These changes include increased heart rate, pupil dilation, increased respiration, release of glucose for the liver, and decreased kidney output. The sympathetic division also releases catecholamines, known as adrenalin and noradrenalin, at the site of the gland or smooth muscles (with the exception of palmar sweat glands). The parasympathetic division of the ANS produces hypoarousal effects and, in general, a return of bodily function to a state of homeostasis.

MEASURING THE AROUSAL CONSTRUCT

Arousal can be measured in a variety of ways, including physiological recordings, self-reports, self-ratings, and behavioral observations (Smith et al., 1998). Measurement technique is based on the definition used by the researcher and, as previously discussed, has been operationalized as both solely and combinations of physiological, cognitive, affective, and behavioral constructs. Traditionally, arousal is measured as a function of changes in physiological systems as well as at the biochemical level. These changes are presented in Table 12.2. Additionally, researchers attempt to assess levels of physiological arousal and other psychological aspects of arousal by using self-report inventories or questionnaires. Most of these scales are designed to

Table 12.2 Neurophysiological Indicators of Increased Arousal

Indicator	Response
Electroencephalogram (EEG) brain waves	Increase from sleep/theta waves to excitement (beta waves)
Electrocardiogram (EKG) heart rate	Generally increases in heart rate with increased arousal
Electromyogram (EMG) muscle tension	Generally increases in muscle tension as arousal increases
Respiration	Generally increases with increased arousal
Blood pressure	Generally increases with increased arousal
Galvanic skin response (GSR)	Increase in arousal results in palmar sweating and a decrease in skin resistance of GSR
Biochemical	Increase in adrenalin and noradrenaline with increases in arousal

measure anxiety, with the arousal construct then measured using the same scale because it was presumed the effects of arousal, if not identical, are at least similar. The State-Trait Anxiety Inventory (Spielberger, Gorsuch, & Lushene, 1970) is the most widely used scale for this purpose. The Activation Deactivation Adjective Checklist (Thayer, 1967) and the Somatic Perception Questionnaire (Landy & Stern, 1971) have also been used frequently. Finally, Martens's (1977) Sport Competition Anxiety Test, although a trait measure, has been used to measure anxiety in sport-specific environments.

A trend in the construction of inventories has been the creation of multidimensional self-report instruments. The Cognitive-Somatic Anxiety Questionnaire developed by Schwartz, Davidson, and Goleman (1978) was the first multidimensional tool, dividing anxiety into cognitive and somatic aspects. Martens and colleagues developed a sport-specific scale, the Competitive State Anxiety Inventory–2 (CSAI-2; Martens, Burton, Vealey, Bump, & Smith, 1990), which has cognitive and somatic state anxiety subscales as well as a self-confidence scale. Smith, Smoll, and Schutz's (1990) Sport Anxiety Scale (SAS) is also sport-specific and assesses somatic and cognitive anxiety. These scales partition anxiety into a somatic component (e.g., "How tense are the muscles in your body?") and a cognitive component (e.g., "Do you worry a lot?"). However, assessing only somatic anxiety in the effort to assess physiological arousal is limiting and problematic. Raedeke and Stein (1994) noted the importance of assessing the positive-negative continuum of perceived arousal. They stated, "Arousal includes perceptions of arousal independent of whether those perceptions are associated with positive or negative affective states, whereas somatic anxiety refers only to the perceptions of arousal associated with negative affect" (pp. 365–366). It is important for future researchers to develop assessment tools that consider both negative and positive aspects of perceived physiological arousal.

In addition, Parfitt et al. (1995) and Raedeke and Stein (1994) emphasize the importance of differentiating perceived physiological state and actual physiological state. Research has indicated that these states do not systematically covary. As shown in Table 12.2, a number of physiological indices have been used to measure actual physiological arousal. Recognizing the complexity of arousal, Cattell (1972) suggested 30 years ago that a minimum of six physiological indices should be taken if arousal is to be measured meaningfully. Test batteries have in fact been developed and tend to show stability over time

(Berman & Johnson, 1985). Physiological measures should include those traditionally used with arousal-discriminating properties, such as respiration rate, blood pressure, heart rate, electrodermal activity, brain waves, and electromyography from various sites.

Biochemical responses have also been used to assess arousal. According to Dienstbier (1989), sympathetic nervous system arousal features the hypothalamus stimulating the adrenal medulla to release adrenalin and noradrenalin. Pituitary adrenal-cortical arousal, on the other hand, causes the pituitary gland to release ACTH so that the cortex is stimulated to release cortisol. The work of Ursin et al. (1978) and Vaernes, Ursin, Darragh, and Lamb (1982) verified the belief that there are two different arousal responses (catecholamine and cortisol) to stressful situations. To date, researchers in sport psychology have rarely included biochemical measures of arousal in studies dealing with this topic.

Researchers who have studied what they called emotion have also contributed to knowledge about measuring arousal. Much of the research on the study of emotion focuses on anxiety, which represents only a small portion of the affective spectrum. In sport psychology research, the use of the Profile of Mood States (POMS; McNair, Lorr, & Droppleman, 1971) and Hanin's (2000) study of the emotion-performance relationship with the IZOF model are two ways in which emotion has been assessed. The POMS inventory has made significant contributions to an understanding of precompetitive mood states and performance. In particular, superior elite performance is related to high levels of vigor and low levels of the remaining affective measures. The POMS is limited in furthering the understanding of how emotion influences performance because this inventory primarily assesses the presence of negative affect, with the exception of the item "vigor." The IZOF model developed by Hanin (1978, 2000), which focused on a spectrum of positive and negative emotions, is significant in the measurement of emotional arousal and holds great promise for future research.

One of the frustrations experienced by researchers is the low correlations between self-report scales and biochemical indicators of arousal, as well as low correlations among the various physiological/biological indicators. There are a number of reasons for these low intercorrelations. Lacey and Lacey (1958) suggested that autonomic response stereotypy may be one explanation. That is, individuals differ widely in how they reflect arousal. One athlete may demonstrate arousal increase via elevated heart rate, whereas another may demonstrate increases in muscle tension or an increased sweat response; still others may reflect arousal in a more cognitive manner. Errors in measurement may also contribute to this problem. In the case of questionnaires, social desirability may override the scale's ability to discriminate among different levels of arousal. Because of the low intercorrelations among physiological measures, as well as difficulty in easily obtaining these measures, and cost considerations, a majority of the research regarding the arousal-performance relationship has relied heavily on questionnaires. The recent literature makes it clear that arousal is a multidimensional construct and as such it is imperative, in future research, to consider physiological (multiple measures), affective, and cognitive measures.

MEASUREMENT OF PERFORMANCE

Much arousal-performance research has been directed toward problems associated with assessing the arousal construct. However, current research points to the need to measure performance carefully and precisely (Edwards & Hardy, 1996; Gould, Petlichkofff, Simons, & Vevera, 1987; Parfitt, Jones, & Hardy; 1990; Prapavessis & Grove, 1991). Performance is generally measured solely in terms of competition outcome (Prapavessis & Grove, 1991). Gould and colleagues (Gould & Krane, 1992; Gould et al., 1987) note that a number of studies include measures of performance as a function of win/loss without taking into consideration the role of team members or team member performance (e.g., Gould, Petlichkoff, & Weinberg, 1984).

In an effort to understand the arousal-performance relationship, Gould and Krane (1992) suggested that researchers either "standardize" performance environments to establish accurate and reliable measures of performance, or use "process measures" to assess performance. In Gould, Tuffey, Hardy, and Lochbaum's (1993) study, in which process measures were used to assess performance, highlighted was the difficulty of quantifying performance. They stated, "A multitude of factors that affect race performance . . . need to be accounted for in order to have a valid, accurate measure of performance" (p. 93). Clearly, precise measures of performance are necessary to best understand the arousal-performance relationship. Another problem with measuring performance in sport is the use of laboratory tasks. Although laboratory tasks allow for greater precision in measuring performance and hence have high internal validity, they most likely do not relate to "real-life" sport performance and as such lack external validity.

THEORIES OF THE AROUSAL-PERFORMANCE RELATIONSHIP

A number of theories have attempted to explain the arousal-performance relationship; however, not one has decisively explained and predicted this relationship. Until recently, two main orientations have been advanced and tested: drive theory and the inverted-U hypothesis. The IZOF concept, reversal theory, catastrophe model, and the multidimensional anxiety theory have become popular perspectives in contemporary times. (For review of the catastrophe model and the multidimensional anxiety theory, see Woodman & Hardy, this volume.)

Drive Theory

Drive theory was derived from the learning theory work of Hull (1943) and later modified by Spence and Spence (1966). It predicted that performance (P) was a multiplicative function of drive state (D) and habit strength (H), or $P = D \times H$. Hull saw drive as physiological arousal and habit as the dominance of correct or incorrect responses. Simply stated, drive theory maintained that there is a positive linear relationship between arousal and performance (see Figure 12.3).

After an extensive review of the literature, Martens (1971) concluded that drive theory did not provide an adequate explanation for the relationship between arousal and performance in sport. This theory has faded from prominence for several reasons. First, it is difficult to test in the area of motor performance. For example, determining habit hierarchies (i.e., dominance of correct or incorrect responses) for complex motor skills is nearly impossible. Second, the few studies conducted in this framework have failed to support the predictions of drive theory (i.e., increased performance with increased arousal). Third, anecdotal

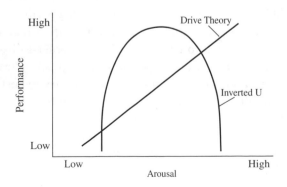

Figure 12.3 Drive theory and the inverted-U hypothesis.

reports from athletes and other performers strongly suggest that excessive arousal disrupts performance.

Oxendine (1984), however, argues that linear relationships between arousal and performance do exist for gross motor activities that involve strength, endurance, and speed. These tasks are typically overlearned and do not require extensive information processing and motor control. Examples include lifting a heavy weight or sprinting. There seems to be some anecdotal support for this position because numerous examples exist showing highly aroused individuals lifting unusually heavy weights or running rapidly for short periods of time. Although these tasks are overlearned and require little information processing, the reports typically come from situations where high performance was necessary because of emergency life-threatening situations. The rush of epinephrine would be expected to result in superior performance, but it is unlikely to occur in sport. So-called simpler gross motor tasks such as a bench press still require a great deal of motor control. There have also been studies outside the realm of sport psychology that provide support for drive theory, such as one by Thompson and Perlini (1998). This study dealt with simplistic, unpracticed tasks such as serial reaction and digit span. Current sport psychology research, however, does not support drive theory.

Inverted-U Hypothesis

Another theory regarding the arousal-performance relationship is popularly known as the inverted-U hypothesis. This position, derived from the animal work of Yerkes and Dodson (1908), is also known as the Yerkes–Dodson Law. It posits a curvilinear relationship between arousal and performance. That is, as physiological arousal increases, there is a corresponding increase in performance until an optimal level is reached; Further increases in arousal result in performance decrement (see Figure 12.3). Yerkes and Dodson also demonstrated that, for laboratory animals, optimal arousal varied across different tasks. This was later supported by Broadhurst (1957). It was concluded that achievement in tasks with higher cognitive demands required lower levels of arousal than tasks with low cognitive demands. Many studies using both laboratory tasks and field measures provided support for the inverted-U hypothesis. One of the early human studies supporting this hypothesis was by Stennett (1957). He showed that performance on auditory tasks associated with very high or low levels of physiological function was inferior to tracking performance associated with moderate levels of physiological functioning.

Studies by Levitt and Gutin (1971) and Sjoberg (1968) have demonstrated that reaction time performance resembles an inverted U after participants were activated through exercise that had varying levels of intensity and duration. The study conducted by Lansing, Schwartz, and Lindsley (1956) on reaction time also supported the notion of the inverted U. Martens and Landers (1970) assigned high, moderate, and low trait-anxious junior high school boys to three different stress conditions while performing a steadiness task. Questionnaire data plus heart rate and palmar sweat responses confirmed three distinct levels of arousal. Results showed that moderate trait-anxious participants performed significantly better than low and high trait-anxious participants, thus providing support for the inverted-U hypothesis. Later, Weinberg and Ragan (1978) manipulated three levels of trait anxiety and stress. Their results showed that high trait-anxious participants performed a throw for accuracy task best under low stress, and low trait-anxious participants performed best under high stress, thus confirming inverted-U hypothesis predictions, at least when arousal was operationally defined and measured as anxiety.

Because of the possible limited external validity of laboratory tasks for testing the inverted-U hypothesis, a number of researchers have undertaken field studies. The often-cited work of Fenz and his colleagues has provided indirect support for the inverted-U hypothesis (Fenz & Epstein, 1967; Fenz & Jones, 1972). These researchers compared heart rate and respiratory rate of experienced and novice parachute jumpers. They noted that technically good jumpers, regardless of experience, had increased levels of arousal prior to jump time and then reduced arousal immediately before executing the jump. Conversely, technically poor jumpers did not reduce their levels of arousal prior to executing their jump. In an interesting study of 11- and 12-year-old baseball players, Lowe (1971) investigated the inverted-U hypothesis using batting performance and changes in heart rate and subjective behavioral ratings. He also factored in the "criticality" or importance of the situation. Arousal levels increased as criticality of the situation increased. It was concluded that when the data were averaged, players hit their best in games of moderate critical situations and less well under low and high criticality. Also, players varied considerably in optimal levels of arousal, and task difficulty (quality of pitching) influenced the inverted-U relationship.

Klavora (1979) examined the validity of the inverted-U hypothesis by testing 145 Canadian high school basketball players. Participants completed the Spielberger State-Trait Anxiety Inventory prior to each game and coaches evaluated the performance of each player after each game. Results supported the inverted-U hypothesis in showing that the best performances occurred under moderate levels of state anxiety, average performance under conditions of slight under- or overarousal, and poor performance under either very low or high levels of anxiety. Using a paper-and-pencil test of anxiety as a measure of arousal/anxiety, Sonstroem and Bernardo (1982) demonstrated that an inverted-U relationship existed between basketball performance and arousal/anxiety. They assessed the composite performance scores of female university players and plotted these scores against arousal/anxiety scores. They concluded that a moderate level of arousal/anxiety was associated with the highest level of performance. Once again, interpretation of these studies becomes problematic given the synonymous use of arousal and anxiety.

More recent studies have also provided support for the inverted-U relationship between somatic arousal and performance. Burton's (1988) study indicated an inverted-U relationship between somatic arousal and performance in the sports of pistol shooting and swimming. Gould et al.'s (1987) study assessing pistol shooting performance indicated similar results. Support for the inverted-U relationship was again based solely on measures of somatic anxiety (physiological aspect) and excluded cognitive and/or affective factors.

Not all studies support the inverted-U hypothesis. In investigations where arousal was manipulated by electric shock, performance did not vary as a function of level of arousal. This was demonstrated in a variety of tasks, such as balancing on a stabilometer (Carron, 1968; Ryan, 1961, 1962), simulated guided missile tracking performance (Bergstrom, 1970), and pursuit rotor tasks (R. Cox, 1983; Marteniuk & Wenger, 1970; Sage & Bennett, 1973). Several studies also failed to show an inverted-U relationship between reaction time and various indicators of arousal (Paller & Shapiro, 1983; Stern, 1976; Wankel, 1972). One could argue, however, that reaction time, although important to motor performance, is considerably different from complex motor performance. Giabrone (1973) failed to show a relationship between Big Ten college basketball players' free throw shooting and levels of arousal. Basler, Fisher, and Mumford (1976), L. Murphy (1966), and Pinneo (1961) also failed to support the inverted-U hypothesis in their studies.

Though there remains theoretical support for the inverted-U hypothesis (Landers & Boutcher, 1998; Yancey, Humphrey, & Neal, 1992), there has been strong criticism levied against it (Gould & Udry, 1994; Neiss, 1988a, 1988b, 1990; Raedeke & Stein, 1994). From a theoretical perspective, the hypothesis is primarily descriptive and does not provide an adequate explanation for the arousal-performance relationship. Another criticism of the hypothesis is that arousal is not viewed as multidimensional (Gould & Udry, 1994; Raedeke & Stein, 1994). For example, high levels of arousal can be associated with both optimal and poor performance. Therefore, concomitant cognitions and affect related to "psyched up" and "psyched out" must be considered in the effort to best understand the arousal-performance relationship (Neiss, 1988a; Raedeke & Stein, 1994).

In his extensive critical review, Neiss (1988a) proposed that not only should the arousal construct be abandoned but so should the proposition of the inverted-U relationship between arousal and human performance. Neiss sees four major problems with the inverted-U hypothesis: It (1) cannot function as a causal hypothesis, (2) is essentially non-falsifiable, (3) has trivial value if true, and (4) hinders understanding of individual differences. Measuring arousal is unquestionably the greatest deterrent to adequate testing of the inverted-U hypothesis.

Anderson (1990) challenged Neiss's (1988a, 1988b) objections to the inverted-U hypothesis. She presented evidence refuting Neiss's arguments and suggested that arousal as a construct and the inverted-U hypothesis are useful for predicting behaviors in a variety of contexts. Anderson's data, however, are largely derived from studies on cognitive performance. Although the inverted-U hypothesis does indeed have difficulties, the reasons cited by Neiss do not warrant his radical solution, such as abandoning the notion altogether. What is needed is a refinement of the idea (creating "zones"), much like that proposed by Martens (1987) and Hanin (2000), as well as the utilization of current psychophysiological measurement techniques. Raedeke and Stein (1994) also support this need. They stated, "The interaction of arousal, thoughts, and feelings needs consideration to more fully understand the arousal-performance relationship" (p. 361). A positive outcome that has resulted from criticism of the inverted-U hypothesis is the development of alternative theories and hypotheses.

The Concept of Optimal Zones

One alternative to the inverted-U hypothesis is the Zone of Optimal Functioning (ZOF) Norton proposed by Hanin, although researchers such as Martens (1987) and Csikszentmihalyi (1975) have also used the idea of "zones" in describing optimal performance. Over the past 30 years,

Hanin has collected considerable idiographic data on top Soviet and, more recently, Finnish athletes to better understand emotional states and optimal performance. Throughout this period (1978–2000), he has developed the ZOF model. The measurement of the ZOF was based on a Russian version of the Spielberger et al. (1970) STAI to determine optimal anxiety levels. Hanin uses the construct Optimal S-anxiety (S-opt) to represent the idiosyncratic level of anxiety that is related to personal best performances of each athlete. From prestart and retrospective measures of anxiety associated with successful previous performance as measured by the STAI, Hanin developed ZOF. Because of possible errors in reporting one's anxiety, Hanin added and subtracted four points from the athlete's prestart S-anxiety level. Thus, each athlete had a "bandwidth" zone of precompetitive "anxiety" where performance was optimally facilitated. Not surprisingly, Hanin discovered large individual differences in optimal anxiety scores, which ranged from scores of 26 to 67 on the STAI. The ZOF model is primarily focused on task-specific patterns of optimal emotion (negative and positive) that reflect individual optimal levels of performance.

Hanin's ZOF theory differs from the inverted U hypothesis in the following ways: It (1) is idiographic, (2) is a bandwidth, not a single point, and (3) can occur along any segment of the arousal-anxiety continuum. In addition, the ZOF model is focused specifically on the self-report emotional aspect of arousal compared to the generalized, unidimensional arousal construct of the inverted-U hypothesis. There has been modest support for the ZOF model in research in demonstrating an idiographic relationship between types of emotion and specific tasks as a strong predictor of athletic performance (Imlay, Carda, Stanbrough, Dreiling, & O'Connor, 1995; Morgan, O'Connor, Ellickson, & Bradley, 1988; Morgan, O'Connor, & Pate, 1987; Prapavessis & Grove, 1991).

Although most researchers have used the STAI to assess precompetitive state anxiety, they have also adapted alternatives measures. Two popular tools are the Body Awareness Scale (BAS) and the CSAI-2. Morgan et al. (1987), using the BAS, found that optimal zones of functioning existed for elite distance runners. Recently, there has been interest in the use of the CSAI-2 to assess optimal zones of functioning. Gould et al. (1993) conducted a study of 11 middle and distance runners' ZOF, based on retrospective reports using the CSAI-2. Results indicated that the distance from each runner's ZOF was correlated with poorer performance. However, it remains uncertain whether the CSAI-2 is a reliable instrument to determine optimal zones of functioning. The use of the CSAI-2 to determine ZOF was strongly supported by Harger and Raglin's (1994) study of collegiate track-and-field athletes, whereas support was not provided by Annesi (1997) in a study of young and adolescent female gymnasts and field hockey players.

In the past decade, Hanin has significantly revised his ZOF model to the individual zones of optimal functioning (IZOF) model, in which a spectrum of emotions are measured in addition to anxiety (Hanin & Syrjä, 1995). Despite these advances, the IZOF model is and has been theoretically limited for a number of reasons. Hanin initially conceptualized arousal in terms of a unidimensional anxiety construct as measured by the non-sport-specific STAI. However, more recently, the IZOF model has broadened the conceptualization of anxiety to that of a multidimensional construct, and research here has been limited to date. A second criticism of the model is that the IZOF theory is an individual differences theory without individual differences variables (Gould & Tuffey, 1996; Hardy et al., 1996). Hardy et al. argue that the IZOF model lacks a theoretical explanation for the idiosyncratic nature of zones of optimal functioning.

In addition, given an understanding of the multidimensional aspects of arousal, it would have been more appropriate to obtain additional measures of arousal, particularly physiological indices. Several investigators have, in fact, experimented with this approach to learning more about zones of optimal functioning. Davis (1991), in his work with professional hockey players, attempted to help players become aware of their ZOF using a heart rate monitor. Zaichkowsky, Hamill, and Dallis (1995) also collected extensive heart rate data on elite and youth sport athletes representing a number of different sports to help them learn their ZOF. Hamill (1996) has provided perhaps the best test, to date, of Hanin's IZOF model, integrating psychological and physiological measures. Hamill determined that there were heart rate correlates of positive negative affect among elite male and female tennis players and the ranges of intensity were related to effective and ineffective performance outcomes.

Optimal Arousal States: Flow

A number of scholars have provided their own special labels to describe superior performance or intense experience related to arousal. Privette (1983) described flow and peak performance; Maslow (1970) and Ravizza (1977) wrote about peak experience; and Csikszentmihalyi (1975) proposed the concept of flow. Perhaps Csikszentmihalyi offered the most insightful view on the concept of flow state. His observations were based on the study of

accomplished rock climbers, surgeons, artists, pianists, and athletes. Csikszentmihalyi (1990) found a number of qualities common to the flow state:

"A challenging activity that requires skills" (p. 49).

"The merging of action with awareness" (p. 53). Performers are aware of their actions when performing, but not aware of their awareness. They act and do not have to think about what they are going to do.

"Clear goals and feedback" (p. 54). The activity provides performers with clear, unambiguous feedback.

"Concentration on the task at hand" (p. 58). Performers' attention is focused entirely on what they are doing.

"The paradox of control" (p. 59). Performers feel in control of their actions.

"The loss of self-consciousness" (p. 62). Performers lose their self-consciousness or egos, so that there is no evaluation of their doing well or poorly.

"The transformation of time" (p. 66). Performers require no goals or external rewards because the process itself is intrinsically rewarding.

Csikszentmihalyi's flow concept leads to a generalizable, two-dimensional model that highlights the importance of the skill of the individual meeting the challenge of the situation such that optimal levels of performance for all levels and types of activities can be achieved. By definition, the flow state, or flow channel, reflects an absence of stress, anxiety, and boredom. Pleasant feelings or exhilaration describe optimal arousal. The notion of the flow state or zone is illustrated in Figure 12.4.

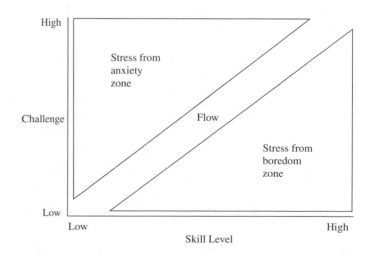

Figure 12.4 Optimal energy or flow zone.

The study of flow has been an area of increasing interest to sport psychology researchers. Jackson and colleagues have made strides to develop inventories (Flow State Scale and Flow Trait Scale) designed to measure Csikszentmihalyi's flow construct (Jackson & Marsh, 1996; Marsh & Jackson, 1999). There have been a number of studies regarding the correlates of flow, with a focus both on cognitive and behavioral factors. Jackson, Kimiecik, Ford, and Marsh (1998) found, for 398 nonelite World Masters Games athletes, a moderate relationship among perceived ability, anxiety, intrinsic motivation, and dispositional flow states (state and trait). Catley and Duda's (1997) correlational study of recreational golfers (*n* = 163) indicated that both skill level and preperformance psychological states, including preround confidence, positive thinking, motivation, level of relaxation, mental focus, and physical readiness, were significantly related to flow (intensity and frequency). Researchers have also indicated that for circuit trainers (*n* = 96), flowlike states increase from early to later in circuit exercises, and that there is a greater change for those with relatively higher hypnotic susceptibility (Grove & Lewis, 1996). Jackson and Robert (1992) found that flow was strongly related to mastery-oriented focus and high perceived ability. In Jackson and Roberts' qualitative study, 16 national champion figure skaters retrospectively reported factors they perceived as helping them achieve optimal flow states during performance. These factors included (1) a positive mental attitude, (2) positive precompetitive and competitive affect, (3) maintenance of appropriate focus, and (4) physical readiness.

There have been a few studies in which expected correlates of flow were not significantly related. For example, in the Stein, Kimiecik, Daniels, and Jackson (1995) study, the conclusion was that goals, competence, and confidence did not predict the flow experience.

Reversal Theory

The reversal theory developed by Apter (1982, 1984) provides an alternative explanation for the relationship between arousal and performance. It attempts to grapple with the complexities of human behavior and offer explanations for inconsistencies associated with human emotion, cognition, and subsequent motivation. Apter (1982) proposed that motivation is influenced by quick changes or reversals between four paired, opposite metamotivational states. Metamotivational states are conceptualized as alternative mental states in which the individual can alternate between motives at any moment in time. These changes are called reversals and provide the origin of the theory's title. In essence, high or low levels of arousal can be perceived as pleasant one moment but unpleasant the next. Performance is expected to be optimized when there is minimal difference between preferred and actual arousal state.

Kerr (1993) adapted reversal theory to sport. The telic-paratelic pairing, which represents the individual's felt arousal and is used to describe emotional intensity, has received the most attention in sport psychology research. In particular, the theory suggests that with high arousal levels, anxiety is experienced when the athlete is in an evaluative or telic state and, in contrast, excitement when the athlete is in a nonevaluative or paratelic state. Conversely, with low arousal levels, the athlete will experience relaxation in a telic state and boredom in paratelic state. Using Figure 12.5, one can determine that high levels of arousal can be interpreted by the individual in two ways: as feelings of anxiety or feelings of excitement. Similarly, low levels of arousal can be interpreted two different ways: as relaxation or as boredom (Kerr, 1989).

Initial research in sport psychology has provided inconsistent support for the reversal theory, most of which has been provided by Kerr and colleagues (T. Cox & Kerr, 1989; Kerr, 1987; Kerr & Vlaswinkel, 1993; Kerr, Yoshida, Hirata, Takai, & Yamazaki, 1997; Males & Kerr, 1996; Males, Kerr, & Gerkovich, 1998). Males and Kerr examined the relationship between precompetitive affect and performance for best and worst performances of nine elite slalom canoeists. There was no statistical support for the hypothesis that best performances would precede worst performances based on higher levels of pleasant mood. Kerr et al. (1997) hypothesized that archery performance would be superior under telic-low arousal conditions.

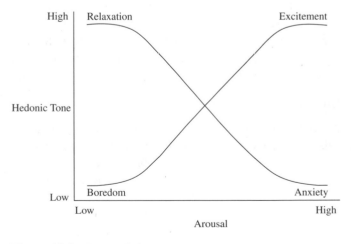

Figure 12.5 Reversal theory.

However, this prediction was not confirmed. In contrast, Males et al. provided support for the reversal theory in their structural qualitative analysis study. Fifty postevent interviews were conducted with nine elite male slalom canoeists regarding metamotivational states during competition. Results indicated that (1) paratelic-autic-mastery states occurred more frequently for above average performances, and (2) participants experienced "reversals" during competition. In addition, Raedeke and Stein (1994) conducted a correlational study based on the tenets of the reversal theory and reported that high positive arousal was related to better perceived performance.

The telic-paratelic metamotivational pairing of the reversal theory provides a valuable theoretical foundation for current and future sport psychology research, though additional research is needed. Based on this pairing, the theory suggests that both high somatic and cognitive anxiety result in anxiety (deter performance) and that high somatic and low cognitive anxiety result in excitement (enhance performance). Kerr (1993) suggests that the most effective intervention would therefore be to help the athlete change interpretation of the situation such that a cognitive reversal occurs, whereby cognitive anxiety is minimized and high arousal can be experienced as excitement.

FACTORS THAT MEDIATE AROUSAL AND PERFORMANCE

Although it is not possible to determine the precise level of arousal for optimal performance in sport for a given athlete, some generalizations can be made about factors that influence arousal and performance. Currently, theory indicates that the arousal-performance relationship is primarily mediated by (1) task complexity, (2) skill level of the performer, and (3) personality differences. Unfortunately, the data supporting these generalizations are not voluminous and in some cases are based on assumptions rather than data themselves.

Task Complexity

Yerkes and Dodson (1908) originally proposed that as tasks increased in difficulty, peak performance is achieved with less arousal. This proposition was based on their finding that mice made fewer performance errors when an electric shock of medium intensity was applied than when shocks of low or high intensity were used. Testing this hypothesis in the motor domain has been difficult. In addition to the problem of defining high and low arousal, there is the problem of defining simple and complex tasks. An approach to defining task complexity was offered by Billing (1980), who suggested that task complexity should be based on information processing demands and complexity of the motor response. Using this classification, it can be inferred that motor tasks requiring concentration, judgment, discrimination, and fine motor control are best performed under low or moderate states of arousal. In contrast, motor tasks requiring strength, endurance, speed, or ballistic movements require higher levels of arousal.

Using the idea of task complexity, Oxendine (1970) speculated about the optimal level of arousal for various sports. He suggested that skills such as the golf putt and the basketball free throw would require relatively lower arousal in comparison with the throwing skills of baseball pitchers and football quarterbacks, which would require slightly more arousal. The next level of arousal (moderate) would be suitable for gymnasts and boxers. Higher levels of arousal would be needed for swimmers and wrestlers, and extremely high levels of arousal would be needed for football tackling, weight lifting, and sprinting (see Table 12.3).

Though there is an intuitive appeal to matching a specific level of arousal with a particular sport, Jones and colleagues have levied criticism against Oxendine's theoretical supposition that the nature of the task mediates that arousal-performance relationship (Hardy et al., 1996; Jones, 1990; Jones & Hardy, 1989). Specifically, Oxendine's classification has been criticized for being too simplistic. Though it does make an attempt to differentiate optimal arousal levels with some sports, such as slight arousal for football quarterbacking and extreme arousal for football tackling, the classification system does not acknowledge the need to change arousal levels within a particular task and performance. There also has been strong criticism against Oxendine's classification for not taking into consideration the varying cognitive requirements or

Table 12.3   Hypothesized Optimal Arousal Levels for Selected Sport Skills

Slight	Slight +	Moderate	High	Extreme
golf putting, basketball	baseball pitching, football quarterbacking	gymnastics, boxing	swimming, wrestling,	football tackling, weight lifting, sprinting

Source: Adapted from Oxendine, 1970.

the information processing demands for different tasks (Hardy et al., 1996), specifically, perceptual and decision-making tasks (Weinberg, 1989). Oxendine's classification of tasks as simple or complex was based on the physiological, unidimensional understanding of arousal. However, in addition to the gross or fine motor demands of a given task, there are cognitive demands and affective responses that must be taken into consideration in the effort to understand or predict optimal arousal levels in sport.

Skill Level of the Performer

It is also assumed that optimal arousal is dependent on the skill level of the performer. This view comes largely from observations indicating that novice or low-skilled athletes perform poorly under pressure conditions when arousal is high, whereas experienced or highly skilled athletes tend to excel when pressure in highest (and arousal is modest). R. Cox (1990, p. 99), in discussing skill level and arousal, suggests the application of the following principle: "Highly skilled athletes and athletes performing simple tasks need a moderately high level of arousal for maximum performance. Less skilled athletes and athletes performing a complex task require a relatively low level of arousal for maximum performance."

The limited empirical research on this topic comes under the heading of social facilitation and tests of Zajonc's (1965) general theory of social facilitation. According to Zajonc, the crucial factor that determines whether an audience will enhance or inhibit performance is whether the dominant response is correct or incorrect. Correctness of response is determined by the interaction of three factors: Task difficulty, skill level, and type of audience. Simply, when novices perform a difficult task before an audience, they will perform poorly, whereas experts will perform well. Limited research in sport has addressed this theory; however, anecdotal evidence and practice conditions developed by coaches suggest that this proposition is accepted as being correct.

Individual Differences

According to Ebbeck and Weiss (1988), for any given task there is no single optimal level of arousal. Individual differences prevail. There is strong support for individual differences being a mediator of the arousal-performance relationship (Hardy et al., 1996). Besides individual differences in skill level, personality differences, particularly trait anxiety, and introversion-extroversion affects arousal and performance (Thompson & Perlini, 1998).

Mahoney (1979, p. 436) emphasized the importance of individual differences: "It seems apparent that absolute

level of arousal may be only one factor in athletic performance. The person's reactions to that arousal may be a significant determinant of its course and its effect on performance." Neiss (1990) also stressed the importance of individual differences in his discussion of arousal. He described "clutch players," who excelled in pressure situations, and what he referred to as "choke artists," or those who failed in pressure situations. Neiss also noted that in actual emergency situations, individual differences can be even more striking, with some people freezing in panic and others exhibiting almost superhuman coping resources.

Spielberger (1989), in discussing anxiety, stated that there are large individual differences in trait anxiety as well as how people report their state anxiety. In general, people high in state anxiety respond to evaluative situations with greater amounts of arousal than people low in trait anxiety. These different levels of arousal presumably lead to individuals performing differently in similar situations. Individuals high in trait anxiety tend to perform better than individuals with normally low arousal levels on simple tasks. Conversely, high-anxious individuals tend to do poorly on complex tasks, particularly if novel responses are required. Several studies have shown that high-anxious participants performed motor tasks best in low-stress situations, whereas low-anxious participants performed best under high-stress conditions (Carron, 1968; Weinberg & Hunt, 1976; Weinberg & Ragan, 1978). Hamilton (1986) also found significant differences in performance, favoring low-anxious over high-anxious participants in cognitive and reaction time tasks; however, these differences did not covary with heart rate and electrodermal activity. Variability in performance and self-reported anxiety could not be explained by differences in physiological arousal. Studies from the test anxiety and performance literature also support the importance of individual differences because high- and low-test-anxious participants do not differ on measures of heart rate and electrodermal activity (Holroyd, Westbrook, Wolf, & Badhorn, 1978).

Attentional Processes

Although related to individual differences and skill level, attentional processes deserve special consideration as a factor mediating arousal and performance. Several writers have suggested that attention and cue utilization may be the crucial factor in understanding anxiety/arousal and performance. Easterbrook's (1959) cue utilization theory was one of the first cognitive theories of arousal and performance. Arousal was theorized to reduce the range of attentional cues. Initially, the narrowing of attention improved performance by rejecting irrelevant cues. However, with further arousal increases, attentional narrowing would lead to bypassing relevant cues, resulting in a performance decrement. Landers (1978, 1980), consistent with Easterbrook, hypothesized that as performance anxiety increases, perceptual selectivity also increases. At optimal levels of arousal, better perceptual selectivity should occur through the elimination of task-irrelevant cues. At low levels of arousal, an athlete may fail to eliminate irrelevant stimuli due to an uncritical perceptual focus, whereas at high levels of arousal, the perceptual range may narrow to the point of eliminating valuable cues. Nideffer (1976, 1989) has offered the most systematic analysis of the role of attention in sport, particularly as it relates to arousal and performance.

Much of the current applied research, which has been quasi-experimental in nature, strongly suggests that attentional focus is a mediator of performance. Johnston and McCabe's (1993) study of a simulated golf task ($n = 90$) indicated that changing attentional focus with an appropriate mental strategy during a stressful experience can enhance performance. Janelle, Singer, and Williams's (1999) auto racing simulation study ($n = 48$) of distraction and attentional narrowing indicated that with higher levels of anxiety, visual search patterns became more peripheral and less accurate, and thus performance declined. Lohasz and Leith's (1997) study of mental preparation strategies ($n = 45$) indicated that enhancing attention by means of three interventions—self-efficacy, attentional focus, and self-determined group—positively affected performance.

Cognitive Appraisal

Cognitive appraisal is another individual differences factor that influences arousal level and performance. In particular, elevated levels of anxiety/arousal can be interpreted as facilitative or debilitative to performance (Hanton & Jones, 1999). Jones, Hanton, and Swain's (1994) study noted that elite performers had higher levels of facilitative versus debilitative cognitive and somatic anxiety symptoms (85:15%) compared to nonelite counterparts (53:47%). How one interprets the demands of a task, the resources, the consequences of performance, and perceptions of bodily reactions clearly differs among individuals. Under identical situations, one athlete may appraise the competitive situation as physically and mentally impossible and thus display high anxiety (debilitative anxiety); another athlete may appraise the situation positively. In this case, optimal physiological arousal will be present, but anxiety will be absent (facilitative arousal).

In the search for optimal levels of arousal for optimal performance, researchers have confirmed that this rela-

tionship is complex. Activation of the different systems of the body are influenced by thoughts and feelings. In turn, they are mediated by factors such as the skill level of the performer and the difficulty of the task or level of competition. There are large individual differences in how athletes cope with excessive arousal, and excessive arousal negatively affects attentional processes. Dysfunctional attention in turn affects performance. Coping with or regulating arousal is a major research topic and of practical concern for sport psychologists. It is the focus of the next section.

COMMENTS ON THE REGULATION OF AROUSAL

This section is purposely brief. Although it follows that research on arousal regulation techniques should accompany a discussion of arousal, we have determined that a careful evaluation of the research on arousal regulation techniques is beyond the scope of this chapter. One could argue that most, if not all, interventions used by sport psychologists in their work with athletes are designed to regulate arousal (either maintain, increase, or decrease it). Entire books or sections of books cover arousal regulation techniques as part of "psychological skills training." This would mean a thorough evaluation of the research on topics such as those listed in Table 12.4, thus adding to an already lengthy chapter. Also, some arousal regulation techniques have been reviewed in other chapters of this *Handbook,* and this would create redundancy. It is also true that although coaches and sport psychologists teach arousal regulation techniques to

Table 12.4   Arousal Regulation Strategies

Techniques for Decreasing Arousal	Techniques for Increasing Arousal
Controlled breathing	Quick, shallow breathing
Progressive muscle relaxation	Stretching and exercise
Meditation	Precompetitive workout
Transcendental Meditation (TM)	Drawing energy from environment (4–10 hours before)
Relaxation response (RR)	
Self-talk	Pep talks
Imagery	Energizing imagery
Zen meditation	Energizing self-talk (e.g. "energy")
Goal setting (realistic)	Goal setting
Biofeedback	Distraction (from fatigue)
Music	Transferring energy (e.g. negative to positive)
Yoga	
	Bulletin boards
	Music/video

athletes, little quality empirical research has been conducted supporting their efficacy and effectiveness. The one exception is in the area of imagery, where considerable original research has been undertaken and reviewed. Murphy and Jowdy (1992) provided one of the most comprehensive reviews of theory, research, and practice related to imagery. The most recent detailed review of the literature was conducted by S. Martin, Moritz, and Hall (1999). Druckman and Bjork (1991), in their National Research Council report to the Army Research Institute, were properly critical of the sparse research literature on performance-enhancing techniques. This criticism can be extended to research on arousal regulation techniques.

Most coaches and athletes would agree that performance fluctuations in sport are often related to being either excessively over- or underaroused. A variety of strategies have been utilized for arousal regulation by coaches, athletes, and sport psychologists. Regulation strategies can be categorized as either self-regulation (e.g., the athlete) or external agent regulation (e.g., the coach or the sport psychologist). Additionally, self-regulation approaches are often referred to as either somatic (e.g., progressive muscular relaxation and respiration control) or cognitive (e.g., imagery and self-talk) in nature (Davidson & Schwartz, 1976). Table 12.4 categorizes the major techniques used to regulate arousal and includes somatic as well as cognitive-behavioral approaches. It should be noted that many of these techniques can be used to both increase and decrease arousal depending on instructions given to the athlete. For example, slow, deep, diaphragmatic breathing is prescribed to reduce arousal; however, rapid, shallow breathing from the chest area is used to increase arousal.

SUMMARY

In this chapter, the history of the arousal construct and related theoretical and research perspectives have been traced. Currently, arousal is understood to be a multidimensional construct with physiological, cognitive, and affective dimensions. The construct based on prevailing thoughts of the 1990s was operationally defined. Discussed then was how the nervous system (central and autonomic) functions during different levels of arousal and how arousal is typically measured. The importance of the measurement of performance was briefly addressed. Traditional theoretical views of arousal and their relationship to performance (drive theory and inverted-U hypothesis) were presented, as well as variations in thinking about the inverted-U hypothesis, namely, the concept of zones of

optimal functioning and the reversal theory. Finally, arousal regulation was briefly discussed.

It is clear that the arousal construct is multidimensional, reflecting interacting physiological, cognitive, and affective responses. Measuring all of these components accurately, particularly physiological measures, in a sport context is becoming a reality as more sport psychologists develop expertise in the neurosciences. These methodological advances lead us to not only a better understanding of the relationship between arousal and performance, but also will help teach athletes and coaches about optimal arousal states and how to attain them.

REFERENCES

Adam, J., Teeken, J., Ypelaar, P., Verstappen, F., & Paas, F. (1997). Exercise-induced arousal and information processing. *International Journal of Sport Psychology, 28,* 217–226.

Anderson, J.A. (1990). Arousal and the inverted-U hypothesis: A critique of Neiss's "Reconceptualizing arousal." *Psychological Bulletin, 107,* 96–100.

Annesi, J. (1997). Three-dimensional state anxiety recall: Implications for individual zones of optimal functioning research and application. *The Sport Psychologist, 11,* 43–52.

Apter, M.J. (1982). *The experience of motivation: The theory of psychological reversals.* London: Academic Press.

Apter, M.J. (1984). Reversal theory and personality: A review. *Journal of Research in Personality, 18,* 265–288.

Bandura, A. (1997). *Self-efficacy: The exercise of control.* New York: Freeman.

Basler, M.L., Fisher, A.C., & Mumford, N.L. (1976). Arousal and anxiety correlates of gymnastic performance. *Research Quarterly, 47,* 586–589.

Bergstrom, B. (1970). Tracking performance under threat-induced stress. *Scandinavian Journal of Psychology, 11,* 109–114.

Berman, P.S., & Johnson, H.J. (1985). A psychophysiological assessment battery. *Biofeedback and Self-Regulation, 10,* 203–221.

Billing, J. (1980). An overview of task complexity. *Motor skills: Theory into practice, 4,* 18–23.

Brehm, J.W., & Self, E.A. (1989). The intensity of motivation. *Annual Review of Psychology, 40,* 109–131.

Broadhurst, P.L. (1957). Emotionality and the Yerkes–Dodson Law. *Journal of Experimental Psychology, 54,* 345–352.

Burton, D. (1988). Do anxious swimmers swim slower? Reexamining the elusive anxiety-performance relationship. *Journal of Sport & Exercise Psychology, 10,* 45–61.

Cannon, W.B. (1932). *The wisdom of the body.* New York: Norton.

Carron, A.V. (1968). Motor performance under stress. *Research Quarterly, 39,* 463–469.

Catley, D., & Duda, J. (1997). Psychological antecedents of the frequency and intensity of flow in golfers. *International Journal of Sport Psychology, 28,* 309–322.

Cattell, R.B. (1972). The nature and genesis of mood states: A theoretical model with experimental measurements concerning anxiety, depression, arousal, and other mood states. In C.D. Spielberger (Ed.), *Anxiety: Current trends in theory and research* (pp. 115–183). New York: Academic Press.

Csikszentmihalyi, M. (1975). *Beyond boredom and anxiety.* San Francisco: Jossey-Bass.

Csikszentmihalyi, M. (1990). *Flow: The psychology of optimal experience.* New York: Harper & Row.

Cox, R.H. (1983). Consolidation of pursuit rotor learning under conditions of induced arousal. *Research Quarterly for Exercise and Sport, 54,* 223–228.

Cox, R.H. (1990). *Sport psychology: Concepts and applications.* Dubuque, IA: Brown & Benchmark.

Cox, T., & Kerr, J. (1989). Arousal effects during tournament play in squash. *Perceptual and Motor Skills, 69,* 1275–1280.

Davidson, R.J., & Schwartz, G.E. (1976). The psychobiology of relaxation and related states: A multi-process theory. In D.I. Mostofsky (Ed.), *Behavioral control and modification of physiological activity* (pp. 399–442). Englewood Cliffs, NJ: Prentice-Hall.

Davis, H. (1991). Passive recovery and optimal arousal in ice hockey. *Perceptual and Motor Skills, 72,* 1–2.

Dienstbier, R.A. (1989). Arousal and physiological toughness: Implications for mental and physical health. *Psychological Review, 96,* 84–100.

Druckman, D., & Bjork, R.A. (Eds.). (1991). *In the mind's eye: Enhancing human performance.* Washington, DC: National Academy Press.

Duffy, E. (1934). Emotion: An example of the need for reorientation in psychology. *Psychological Review, 41,* 184–198.

Duffy, E. (1941). The conceptual categories of psychology: A suggestion for revision. *Psychological Review, 48,* 177–203.

Duffy, E. (1957). The psychological significance of the concept of "arousal" or "activation." *Psychological Review, 41,* 265–275.

Duffy, E. (1962). *Activation and behavior.* New York: Wiley.

Easterbrook, J. (1959). The effect of emotion on cue utilization and the organization of behavior. *Psychological Review, 66,* 183–201.

Ebbeck, V., & Weiss, M.R. (1988). The arousal-performance relationship: Task characteristics and performance measures in track and field athletics. *The Sport Psychologist, 2,* 13–27.

Edwards, T., & Hardy, L. (1996). The interactive effects of intensity and direction of cognitive and somatic anxiety and self-confidence upon performance. *Journal of Sport & Exercise Psychology, 18,* 296–312.

Fenz, W.D., & Epstein, S. (1967). Gradients of physiological arousal in parachutists as a function of approaching jump. *Psychosomatic Medicine, 29,* 33–51.

Fenz, W.D., & Jones, G.B. (1972). Individual differences in physiologic arousal and performance in sport parachutists. *Psychosomatic Medicine, 34,* 1–8.

Giabrone, C.P. (1973). *Effect of situation criticality on foul shooting.* Unpublished master's thesis, University of Illinois, Urbana.

Goleman, D. (1995). *Emotional intelligence.* New York: Bantam Books.

Gould, D., & Krane, V. (1992). The arousal-athletic performance relationship: Current status and future directions. In T. Horn (Ed.), *Advances in sport psychology* (pp. 119–142). Champaign, IL: Human Kinetics.

Gould, D., Petlichkoff, L., Simons, J., & Vevera, M. (1987). The relationship between Competitive State Anxiety Inventory–2 subscale scores and pistol shooting performance. *Journal of Sport Psychology, 9,* 33–42.

Gould, D., Petlichkoff, L., & Weinberg, R. (1984). Antecedents of, temporal changes in, and relationships between CSAI–2 subcomponents. *Journal of Sport Psychology, 6,* 289–304.

Gould, D., & Tuffey, S. (1996). Zones of optimal functioning research: A review and critique. *Anxiety, Stress and Coping: An International Journal, 9,* 53–68.

Gould, D., Tuffey, S., Hardy, L., & Lochbaum, M. (1993). Multidimensional state anxiety and middle distance running performance: An exploratory examination of Hanin's (1980) zones of optimal functioning hypothesis. *Journal of Applied Sport Psychology, 5,* 85–95.

Gould, D., & Udry, E. (1994). Psychological skills for enhancing performance: Arousal regulation strategies. *Medicine and Science in Sports and Exercise, 26,* 478–485.

Grove, R., & Lewis, M. (1996). Hypnotic susceptibility and the attainment of flow-like states during exercise. *Journal of Sport & Exercise Psychology, 18,* 380–391.

Hamill, G. (1996). *Psychological and physiological correlates of the individual zones of optimal functioning.* Unpublished dissertation, Boston University.

Hamilton, V. (1986). A cognitive model of anxiety: Implications for theories of personality and motivation. In C.D. Spielberger & I.G. Sarason (Eds.), *Stress and anxiety* (Vol. 10, pp. 229–250). Washington, DC: Hemisphere.

Hanin, Y.L. (1978). A study of anxiety in sports. In W.F. Straub (Ed.), *An analysis of athlete behavior* (pp. 236–249). Ithaca, NY: Mouvement.

Hanin, Y.L. (1993). Optimal performance emotions in top athletes. In S. Serpa, J. Alves, V. Ferreira, & A. Paula-Brito (Eds.), *Sport psychology: An integrated approach. Proceedings from the 8th World Congress of Sport Psychology* (pp. 229–232). Lisbon, Portugal: International Society of Sport Psychology.

Hanin, Y.L. (Ed.). (2000). *Emotions in sport.* Champaign, IL: Human Kinetics.

Hanin, Y.L., & Syrjä, P. (1995). Performance affect in junior ice hockey players: An application of the individual zones of optimal functioning model. *The Sport Psychologist, 9,* 169–187.

Hanton, S., & Jones, G. (1999). The acquisition and development of cognitive skills and strategies: I. Making the butterflies fly in formation. *The Sport Psychologist, 13,* 1–21.

Hardy, L., Jones, G., & Gould, D. (1996). *Understanding psychological preparation for sport: Theory and practice of elite performers.* New York: Wiley.

Harger, G., & Raglin, J. (1994). Correspondence between actual and recalled precompetition anxiety in collegiate track and field athletes. *Journal of Sport & Exercise Psychology, 16,* 206–211.

Hebb, D. (1955). Drives and the CNS (conceptual nervous system), *Psychological Review, 62,* 243–254.

Hockey, G., & Hamilton, P. (1983). The cognitive patterning of stress states. In G. Hockey (Ed.), *Stress and fatigue in human performance* (pp. 331–362). New York: Wiley.

Holroyd, K.A., Westbrook, T., Wolf, M., & Badhorn, E. (1978). Performance, cognition, and physiological responding in test anxiety. *Journal of Abnormal Psychology, 87,* 442–451.

Hull, C.L. (1943). *Principles of behavior.* New York: Appleton-Century-Crofts.

Imlay, G., Carda, R., Stanbrough, M., & Dreiling, A. (1995). Anxiety and athletic performance: A test of optimal functioning theory. *International Journal of Sport Psychology, 26,* 295–306.

Jackson, S., Kimiecik, J., Ford, S., & Marsh, H. (1998). Psychological correlates of flow in sport. *Journal of Sport & Exercise Psychology, 20,* 358–378.

Jackson, S., & Roberts, G. (1992). Positive performance states of athletes: Toward a conceptual understanding of peak performance. *The Sport Psychologist, 6,* 156–171.

Jackson, S.A., & Marsh, H.W. (1996). Development and validation of a scale to measure optimal experience: The Flow State Scale. *Journal of Sport & Exercise Psychology, 18,* 17–35.

Janelle, C., Singer, R., & Williams, M. (1999). External distraction and attentional narrowing: Visual search evidence. *Journal of Sport & Exercise Psychology, 21,* 70–91.

Johnston, B., & McCabe, M. (1993). Cognitive strategies for coping with stress in a simulated golfing task. *International Journal of Sport Psychology, 24,* 30–48.

Jones, G. (1990). A cognitive perspective on the processes underlying the relationship between stress and performance in sport. In G. Jones & L. Hardy (Eds.), *Stress and performance in sport* (pp. 17–42). Chichester, England: Wiley.

Jones, G., Hanton, S., & Swain, A. (1994). Intensity and interpretation of anxiety symptoms in elite and non-elite sports performers. *Personality and Individual Differences, 17,* 657–663.

Jones, G., & Hardy, L. (1989). Stress and cognitive functioning in sport. *Journal of Sports Sciences, 7,* 41–63.

Kerr, J. (1987). A new perspective for sports psychology. In M.J. Apter, D. Fontana, & S. Murgatroyd (Eds.), *Applications and developments* (pp. 89–102). Cardiff, Wales: University College Cardiff Press.

Kerr, J. (1989). Anxiety, arousal, and sport performance. In D. Hackfort & C. Spielberger (Eds.), *Anxiety in sports: An international perspective* (pp. 137–151). New York: Hemisphere.

Kerr, J. (1993). An eclectic approach to psychological interventions in sport: Reversal theory. *The Sport Psychologist, 7,* 400–418.

Kerr, J., Yoshida, H., Hirata, C., Takai, K., & Yamazaki, F. (1997). Effects on archery performance of manipulating metamotivational state and felt arousal. *Perceptual and Motor Skills, 84,* 819–828.

Kerr, J.H., & Vlaswinkel, E.H. (1993). Self reported mood and running under natural conditions. *Work and Stress, 7,* 161–178.

Klavora, P. (1979). Customary arousal for peak athletic performance. In P. Klavora & J. David (Eds.), *Coach, athlete, and the sport psychologist* (pp. 155–163). Toronto, Canada: University of Toronto.

Koob, G. (1991). Arousal, stress, and inverted U-shaped curves: Implications for cognitive function. In R. Lister & H. Weingartner (Eds.), *Perspectives on cognitive neuroscience* (pp. 300–313). New York: Oxford University Press.

Lacey, J.I. (1967). Somatic response patterning of stress: Some revisions of activation theory. In M.H. Appley & R. Trumbell (Eds.), *Psychological stress, issues in research* (pp. 160–208). New York: Appleton.

Lacey, J.I., & Lacey, B.C. (1958). Verification and extension of the principle of autonomic response-stereotype. *American Journal of Psychology, 71,* 50–73.

Landers, D. (1978). Motivation and performance: The role of arousal and attentional factors. In W.F. Straub (Ed.), *Sport psychology: An analysis of athletic behavior* (pp. 75–87). Ithaca, NY: Mouvement.

Landers, D. (1980). The arousal-performance relationship revisited. *Research Quarterly for Exercise and Sport, 51,* 77–90.

Landers, D., & Boutcher, S. (1998). Arousal-performance relationship. In J. Williams (Ed.), *Applied sport psychology:*

Personal growth to peak performance (pp. 197–236). Mountain View, CA: Mayfield.

Landy, F., & Stern, R. (1971). Factor analysis of a somatic perception questionnaire. *Journal of Psychosomatic Research, 15,* 179–181.

Lansing, R.W., Schwartz, E., & Lindsley, D.B. (1956). Reaction time and EEG activation. *American Psychologist, 11,* 433.

Lazarus, R.S. (1993). From psychological stress to the emotions: A history of changing outlooks. *Annual Review of Psychology, 44,* 1–21.

LeDoux, J.E. (1993). Emotional networks in the brain. In M. Lewis & J. Haviland (Eds.), *Handbook of emotions* (pp. 109–118). New York: Guilford Press.

Levenson, R.W., Ekman, P., & Friesen, W.V. (1990). Voluntary facial action generates emotion-specific autonomous nervous system activity. *Psychophysiology, 27,* 363–384.

Levitt, S., & Gutin, B. (1971). Multiple choice reaction time and movement time during physical exertion. *Research Quarterly, 42,* 405–410.

Lohasz, P., & Leith, L. (1997). The effect of three mental preparation strategies on the performance of a complex response time task. *International Journal of Sport Psychology, 28,* 25–34.

Lowe, R. (1971). *Stress, arousal, and task performance of Little League baseball players.* Unpublished doctoral dissertation, University of Illinois, Urbana.

Magill, R.A. (1989). *Motor learning: Concepts and applications.* Dubuque, IA: Brown.

Mahoney, M.J. (1979). Cognitive skills and athletic performance. In P.C. Kendale & S.D. Hollon (Eds.), *Cognitive-behavioral interventions: Theory, research, and procedures* (pp. 423–443). New York: Academic Press.

Males, J., & Kerr, J. (1996). Stress, emotion, and performance in elite slalom canoeists. *The Sport Psychologist, 10,* 17–43.

Males, J., Kerr, J., & Gerkovich, M. (1998). Metamotivational states during canoe slalom competition: A qualitative analysis using reversal theory. *Journal of Applied Sport Psychology, 10,* 185–200.

Malmo, R.B. (1959). Activation: A neurophysiological dimension. *Psychological Review, 66,* 367–386.

Marsh, H., & Jackson, S. (1999). Flow experience in sport: Construct validation of multidimensional, hierarchical state and trait responses. *Structural Equation Modeling, 6,* 343–371.

Marteniuk, R.G., & Wenger, H.A. (1970). Facilitation of pursuit rotor learning by induced stress. *Perceptual and Motor Skills, 31,* 471–477.

Martens, R. (1971). Anxiety and motor behavior: A review. *Journal of Motor Behavior, 3,* 151–179.

Martens, R. (1977). *Sport Competition Anxiety Test.* Champaign, IL: Human Kinetics.

Martens, R. (1987). *Coaches' guide to sport psychology.* Champaign, IL: Human Kinetics.

Martens, R., Burton, D., Vealey, R., Bump, L., & Smith, D. (1990). Development and validation of Competitive State Anxiety Inventory–2. In R. Martens, R. Vealey, & D. Burton (Eds.), *Competitive anxiety in sport* (pp. 117–190). Champaign, IL: Human Kinetics.

Martens, R., & Landers, D.M. (1970). Motor performance under stress: A test of the inverted-U hypothesis. *Journal of Personality and Social Psychology, 16,* 29–37.

Martin, M., Moritz, S., & Hall, C. (1999). Imagery use in sport: A literature review and applied model. *The Sport Psychologist, 13,* 245–268.

Maslow, A. (1970). *Motivation and personality.* New York: Harper & Row.

McGrath, J. (1970). Major methodological issues. In J.E. McGrath (Ed.), *Social and psychological factors in stress* (pp. 19–49). New York: Holt, Rinehart and Winston.

McNair, D., Lorr, M., & Droppleman, L. (1971). *Manual for the Profile of Mood States.* San Diego, CA: Educational and Industrial Testing Services.

Morgan, W., O'Connor, P., Ellickson, K., & Bradley, P. (1988). Personality structure, mood states, and performance in elite male distance runners. *International Journal of Sport Psychology, 19,* 247–263.

Morgan, W., O'Connor, P., & Pate, R. (1987). Psychological characterization of elite female distance runners. *International Journal of Sports Medicine, 8,* 124–131.

Murphy, L.E. (1966). Muscular effort, activation level, and reaction time. In E. Mallinoff (Ed.), *Proceedings of the 74th annual convention of the American Psychological Association* (pp. 1–2). Washington, DC: America Psychological Association.

Murphy, S.M., & Jowdy, D.P. (1992). Imagery and mental practice. In T. Horn (Ed.), *Advances in sport psychology* (pp. 221–250). Champaign, IL: Human Kinetics.

Neiss, R. (1988a). Reconceptualizing arousal: Psychobiological states in motor performance. *Psychological Bulletin, 103,* 345–366.

Neiss, R. (1988b). Reconceptualizing relaxation treatments: Psychobiological states in sport. *Clinical Psychology Review, 8,* 139–159.

Neiss, R. (1990). Ending arousal's reign of error: A reply to Anderson. *Psychological Bulletin, 107,* 101–105.

Nideffer, R.M. (1976). Test of attentional and interpersonal style. *Journal of Personality and Social Psychology, 34,* 394–404.

Nideffer, R.M. (1989). Anxiety, attention, and performance in sports: Theoretical and practical considerations. In D. Hackfort & C.D. Spielberger (Eds.), *Anxiety in sports: An international perspective* (pp. 117–136). New York: Hemisphere.

Oxendine, J.B. (1970). Emotional arousal and motor performance. *Quest, 13,* 23–30.

Oxendine, J.B. (1984). *Psychology of motor learning.* Englewood Cliffs, NJ: Prentice-Hall.

Paller, K., & Shapiro, D. (1983). Systolic blood pressure and a simple reaction time task. *Psychophysiology, 20,* 585–592.

Parfitt, G., Hardy, L., & Pates, J. (1995). Somatic anxiety and physiological arousal: Their effects upon a high anaerobic, low memory demand task. *International Journal of Sport Psychology, 26,* 196–213.

Parfitt, G., Jones, G., & Hardy, L. (1990). Multi-dimensional anxiety and performance. In G. Jones & L. Hardy (Eds.), *Stress and performance in sport* (pp. 43–80). Chichester, England: Wiley.

Pinneo, L.R. (1961). The effects of induced muscle tension during tracking on level of activation and on performance. *Journal of Experimental Psychology, 62,* 523–531.

Plutchik, P. (1993). Emotions and their vicissitudes: Emotions and psychopathology. In M. Lewis & J. Haviland (Eds.), *Handbook of emotions* (pp. 53–66). New York: Guilford Press.

Prapavessis, H., & Grove, R. (1991). Precompetitive emotions and shooting performance: The mental health and zone of optimal function models. *The Sport Psychologist, 5,* 223–234.

Privette, G. (1983). Peak experience, peak performance, and flow: A comparative analysis of positive human experiences. *Journal of Personality and Social Psychology, 45,* 1361–1368.

Raedeke, T., & Stein, G. (1994). Felt arousal, thoughts/feelings, and ski performance. *The Sport Psychologist, 8,* 360–375.

Ravizza, K. (1977). Peak experiences in sport. *Journal of Humanistic Psychology, 17,* 35–40.

Ryan, E.D. (1961). Motor performance under stress as a function of the amount of practice. *Perceptual and Motor Skills, 13,* 103–106.

Ryan, E.D. (1962). Effects of stress on motor performance and learning. *Research Quarterly, 33,* 111–119.

Sage, G.H. (1984). *Motor learning and control: A neurophysiological approach.* Dubuque, IA: Brown.

Sage, G.H., & Bennett, B. (1973). The effects of induced arousal on learning and performance of a pursuit motor skill. *Research Quarterly, 44,* 140–149.

Schwartz, G.E., Davidson, R.J., & Goleman, D. (1978). Patterning of cognitive and somatic processes in the self-regulation of anxiety: Effects of meditation versus exercise. *Psychosomatic Medicine, 40,* 321–328.

Sjoberg, L. (1968). Unidimensional scaling of multidimensional facial expressions. *Journal of Experimental Psychology, 78,* 429–435.

Smith, R., Smoll, F., & Schutz, R.W. (1990). Measurement and correlates of sport specific cognitive and somatic trait anxiety: The Sport Anxiety Scale. *Anxiety Research, 2,* 263–280.

Smith, R., Smoll, F., & Wiechman, S. (1998). Measurement of trait anxiety in sport. In J. Duda (Ed.), *Advances in sport and exercise psychology measurement* (pp. 105–127). Morgantown, WV: Fitness Information Technology.

Sonstroem, R.J., & Bernardo, P. (1982). Individual pregame state anxiety and basketball performance: A re-examination of the inverted-U curve. *Journal of Sport Psychology, 4,* 235–245.

Spence, J.T., & Spence, K.W. (1966). The motivational components of manifest anxiety: Drive and drive stimuli. In C.D. Spielberger (Ed.), *Anxiety and behavior* (pp. 291–326). New York: Academic Press.

Spielberger, C.D. (1989). Stress and anxiety in sports. In D. Hackfort & C.D. Spielberger (Eds.), *Anxiety in sports: An international perspective* (pp. 3–17). New York: Hemisphere.

Spielberger, C.D., Gorsuch, R.L., & Lushene, R.E. (1970). *STAI manual for the State-Trait Anxiety Inventory.* Palo Alto, CA: Consulting Psychologists.

Stankard, W. (1990). Arousal gradient and performance. *Perceptual and Motor Skills, 71,* 935–946.

Stein, G., Kimiecik, J., Daniels, J., & Jackson, S. (1995). Psychological antecedents of flow in recreational sport. *Personality and Social Psychology Bulletin, 21,* 125–135.

Stennett, R.C. (1957). The relationship of performance level to level of arousal. *Journal of Experimental Psychology, 54,* 54–61.

Stern, R.M. (1976). Reaction time between the get set and go of simulated races. *Psychophysiology, 13,* 149–154.

Thayer, R.E. (1967). Measurement of activation through self-report. *Psychological Reports, 20,* 663–679.

Thompson, R., & Perlini, A. (1998). Feedback and self-efficacy, arousal and performance of introverts and extroverts. *Psychological Reports, 82,* 707–716.

Ursin, H. (1988). The instrumental effects of emotional behavior: Consequences for the physiological state. In V. Hamilton, G.H. Bower, & N.H. Frijda (Eds.), *Cognitive perspectives on emotion and motivation* (pp. 221–237). Dordecht, The Netherlands: Kluwer Academic.

Ursin, H., Baade, E., & Levine, S. (1978). *Psychobiology of stress: A study of coping men.* New York: Academic Press.

Vaernes, R., Ursin, H., Darragh, A., & Lamb, R. (1982). Endocrine response patterns and psychological correlates. *Journal of Psychosomatic Research, 26,* 123–131.

Venables, P.H. (1984). Arousal: An examination of its status as a concept. In M.G.H. Coles, J.R. Jennings, & J.A. Stern (Eds.), *Psychobiological perspectives: Festschrift for Beatrice and John Lacey* (pp. 134–142). New York: Van Nostrand-Reinhold.

Wankel, L.M. (1972). Competition in motor performance: An experimental analysis of motivational components. *Journal of Experimental Social Psychology, 8,* 427–437.

Wann, D. (1997). *Sport psychology.* Upper Saddle River, NJ: Prentice Hall.

Wann, D., Brewer, K., & Carlson, J. (1998). Focus of attention and sport spectators: Beliefs about causation. *Perceptual and Motor Skills, 87,* 35–41.

Weinberg, R. (1989). Anxiety arousal and motor performance: Theory, research and applications. In D. Hackfort & C.D. Speilberger (Eds.), *Anxiety in sports: An international perspective* (pp. 95–115). New York: Hemisphere.

Weinberg, R.S., & Hunt, U.V. (1976). The relationship between anxiety, motor performance, and electromyography. *Journal of Motor Behavior, 8,* 219–224.

Weinberg, R.S., & Ragan, J. (1978). Motor performance under three levels of stress and trait anxiety. *Journal of Motor Behavior, 10,* 169–176.

Yancey, G., Humphrey, E., & Neal, K. (1992). How perceived incentive, task confidence, and arousal influence performance. *Perceptual and Motor Skills, 74,* 279–285.

Yerkes, R.M., & Dodson, J.D. (1908). The relation of strength of stimulus to rapidity of habit formation. *Journal of Comparative Neurology and Psychology, 18,* 459–482.

Zaichkowsky, L.D., Hamill, G., & Dallis, B. (1995, June). *Physiological and psychological correlates of the zone of optimal functioning.* Paper presented at the twelfth annual conference on Counseling Athletes, Springfield, MA.

Zajonc, R.B. (1965). Social facilitation. *Science, 149,* 269–274.

CHAPTER 13

Self-Efficacy Beliefs of Athletes, Teams, and Coaches

DEBORAH L. FELTZ and CATHY D. LIRGG

The self-efficacy construct is one of the most influential psychological constructs thought to affect achievement strivings in sport (Feltz, 1988). In fact, Gould and his colleagues found that self-efficacy and team efficacy were chief among factors that U.S. Olympic athletes reported to influence their performance at the Nagano Olympic Games (Gould, Greenleaf, Lauer, & Chung, 1999). The term *self-efficacy,* as it is being used here, is the belief one has in being able to execute a specific task successfully (e.g., a pitcher striking out a batter) to obtain a certain outcome (e.g., self-satisfaction or coach recognition) (Bandura, 1977, 1986, 1997). Since the first publication of the self-efficacy concept by Bandura (1977), there have been over 60 research articles published on the topic related specifically to sport performance (Moritz, Feltz, Fahrbach, & Mack, in press). This chapter provides an overview of the self-efficacy concept and its measurement, a review of relevant research on athletes, athletic teams, and coaches, and future directions for research in this field.

SELF-EFFICACY THEORY

Bandura's (1977) theory of self-efficacy was developed within the framework of social-cognitive theory. Although the theory was originally proposed to account for the different results achieved by diverse methods used in clinical psychology for the treatment of anxiety, it has since been expanded and applied to other domains of psychosocial functioning, including health and exercise behavior (McAuley, 1992; McAuley & Mihalko, 1998; O'Leary, 1985) and sport and motor performance (Feltz, 1988).

Self-efficacy beliefs are not judgments about one's skills, objectively speaking, but rather are judgments of what one can accomplish with those skills (Bandura,

1986). In other words, self-efficacy judgments are about what one thinks one can do, not what one has done. These judgments are a product of a complex process of self-appraisal and self-persuasion that relies on cognitive processing of diverse sources of efficacy information (Bandura, 1990). Bandura (1977, 1986) categorized these sources as past performance accomplishments, vicarious experiences, verbal persuasion, and physiological states. Others have added separate categories for emotional states and imaginal experiences (Maddux, 1995; Schunk, 1995).

Performance accomplishments are the most influential source of efficacy information because they are based on one's own mastery experiences (Bandura, 1997). One's mastery experiences affect self-efficacy beliefs through the cognitive processing of such information. If one has repeatedly viewed these experiences as successes, self-efficacy beliefs will increase; if these experiences are viewed as failures, self-efficacy beliefs will decrease. Furthermore, the self-monitoring or focus on successes should provide more encouragement and enhance self-efficacy more than the self-monitoring of one's failures. One must be careful, however, not to become complacent by success. Bandura suggests that letdowns after easy successes and intensifications after failure are common sequences in competitive struggles. The continued setting of challenging goals and the positive reactions to substandard performances help to elevate the intensity and level of motivation.

The influence of past performance experiences on self-efficacy beliefs also depends on the perceived difficulty of the performance, the effort expended, the amount of guidance received, the temporal pattern of success and failure, and the individual's conception of a particular "ability" as a skill that can be acquired versus an inherent aptitude (Bandura, 1986; Lirgg, George, Chase, & Ferguson, 1996).

Bandura has argued that performance accomplishments on difficult tasks, tasks attempted without external assistance, and tasks accomplished with only occasional failures carry greater efficacy value than tasks that are easily accomplished, tasks accomplished with external help, or tasks in which repeated failures are experienced with little sign of progress. Miller (1993) found a negative relationship between high self-efficacy perceptions of competitive swimmers and their motivation when they were given unchallenging goals.

Efficacy information can also be derived through a social comparison process with others. This process involves observing the performance of one or more other individuals, noting the consequence of their performance, and then using this information to form judgments about one's own performance (Maddux, 1995). Vicarious sources of efficacy information are thought to be generally weaker than performance accomplishments; however, their influence on self-efficacy can be enhanced by a number of factors. For example, the less experience people have had with performance situations, the more they will rely on others in judging their own capabilities. The effectiveness of modeling procedures on one's self-efficacy judgments has also been shown to be enhanced by perceived similarities to a model in terms of performance or personal characteristics (George, Feltz, & Chase, 1992; Weiss, McCullagh, Smith, & Berlant, 1998).

One particular mode of modeling influence that has been suggested to enhance one's sense of efficacy and performance in sport is self-modeling (Dowrick, 1991; Franks & Maile, 1991). Self-modeling consists of the individual repeatedly observing the correct or best parts of his or her own past performance, and using that as a model for future performance (Dowrick & Dove, 1980). Bandura (1997) suggests that self-modeling affects performance through its impact on efficacy belief. The little research in sport on this topic is equivocal (Singleton & Feltz, 1999; Winfrey & Weeks, 1993). Winfrey and Weeks found no effects on self-efficacy for balance beam performance using self-modeling videotapes with female gymnasts. However, they did not measure self-efficacy according to Bandura's recommended procedures and had a very small sample. Singleton and Feltz, using a five-item, skill-specific self-efficacy scale, found that collegiate hockey players exposed to several weeks of self-modeling videotapes showed greater shooting accuracy and higher self-efficacy for game performance compared to controls.

Persuasive techniques are widely used by coaches, managers, parents, and peers in attempting to influence an athlete's self-perceptions of efficacy. These techniques include verbal persuasion, evaluative feedback, expectations by others, self-talk, positive imagery, and other cognitive strategies. Self-efficacy beliefs based on persuasive sources are also likely to be weaker than those based on one's accomplishments, according to the theory. However, Bandura (1997) indicates that the debilitating effects of persuasory information are more powerful than the enabling effects. Individuals tend to avoid challenging activities in which they have been persuaded that they lack the capabilities or they give up quickly. It is harder to instill strong beliefs of self-efficacy by persuasory means only. The extent of the persuasive influence on self-efficacy has also been hypothesized to depend on the prestige, credibility, expertise, and trustworthiness of the persuader. Coaches are usually believed to be credible sources of their athletes' capabilities. In addition to providing inspirational messages, effective coaches also structure activities for their athletes that bring success and avoid placing them prematurely in situations that are likely to bring repeated failures (Bandura, 1997). Credible coaches also encourage their athletes to measure their successes in terms of self-improvement rather than outcome.

In addition, efficacy information can be obtained from a person's physiological state or condition. Physiological information includes autonomic arousal that is associated with fear and self-doubt or with being psyched up and ready for performance, as well as one's level of fitness, fatigue, and pain (in strength and endurance activities). Physiological information has been shown to be a more important source of efficacy information with respect to sport and physical activity tasks than in the case of nonphysical tasks (Chase, Feltz, Tully, & Lirgg, 1994; Feltz & Riessinger, 1990). Similar to physiological information, one's emotional state can be a supplementary source of information in forming efficacy perceptions. Positive affect, characterized by happiness, exhilaration, and tranquility, is more likely to enhance efficacy judgments than are negative affective states, such as sadness, anxiety, and depression (Maddux & Meier, 1995; Treasure, Monson, & Lox, 1996). Schunk (1995) suggested that emotional symptoms that signal anxiety might be interpreted by an individual to mean that he or she lacks the requisite skills to perform a certain task, which in turn influences efficacy judgments.

Finally, Maddux (1995) introduced imaginal experiences as a separate source of efficacy information. People can generate efficacy beliefs by imagining themselves or others behaving successfully or unsuccessfully in anticipated performance situations. Bandura (1997) refers to this as cognitive self-modeling (or cognitive enactment) and describes it as a form of modeling influence. Imagining oneself winning against an opponent has been shown to raise efficacy judgments and endurance performance (Feltz & Riessinger, 1990). Other cognitive simulations, such as mental rehearsal strategies, have also been shown to enhance competition efficacy beliefs and competitive performance (Garza & Feltz, 1998).

These categories of efficacy information, based on Bandura's theory of self-efficacy (1977, 1986, 1997), are not mutually exclusive in terms of the information they provide, though some are more influential than others. How various sources of information are weighted and processed to make judgments on different tasks, in different situations, and for individuals' skills is still unknown. The consequences of these judgments, however, have been shown to determine people's levels of motivation, as reflected in the challenges they undertake, the effort they expend in the activity, and their perseverance in the face of difficulties (Bandura, 1997). In addition, individuals' self-efficacy judgments also have been shown to influence certain thought patterns (e.g., goal intentions, worries, causal attributions) and emotional reactions (e.g., pride, shame, happiness, sadness) that also influence motivation (Bandura, 1997).

Furthermore, the relationship between self-efficacy judgments and performance accomplishments is believed to be temporally recursive: "Mastery expectations influence performance and are, in turn, altered by the cumulative effect of one's efforts" (Bandura, 1977, p. 194). Bandura (1990) has emphasized the recursive nature of the relationship between self-efficacy and thought patterns as well. Figure 13.1 presents the relationships among the major sources of efficacy information, efficacy judgments, and consequences as predicted by Bandura's theory and the additional determinants proposed by Maddux (1995).

Bandura (1977, 1986, 1997) has provided some qualifiers to the predictiveness of self-efficacy judgments. Self-efficacy beliefs are a major determinant of behavior only when people have sufficient incentives to act on their self-perception of efficacy and when they possess the requisite skills. Self-efficacy beliefs will exceed actual performance when there is little incentive to perform the activity or when physical or social constraints are imposed on performance. Some people may have the necessary skill and high self-efficacy beliefs, but no incentive to perform. According to Bandura, discrepancies between efficacy beliefs and performance will also occur when tasks or circumstances are ambiguous or when one has little information on which to base efficacy judgments, such as when one is first learning a skill.

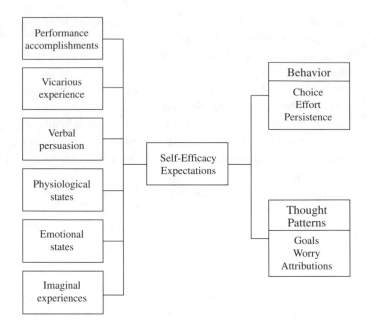

Figure 13.1 Relationships among sources of efficacy information, efficacy judgments, and consequences. From *Advances in sport and exercise psychology measurement* (p. 66), by J.L. Duda (Ed.), 1998, Morgantown, WV: Fitness Information Technology. Copyright by Fitness Information Technology. Adapted with permission.

Self-efficacy expectations should not be confused with outcome expectations. Outcome expectancies are defined as the belief that certain behaviors will lead to certain outcomes. Self-efficacy, on the other hand, is the belief in one's ability to perform the behavior successfully (Bandura, 1977). In essence, outcome expectations are concerned with beliefs about one's environment, and efficacy expectations are concerned with beliefs about one's competence. Some sport psychology researchers confuse performance markers, such as winning an event, with an outcome expectation. Bandura (1997) describes the three major forms that outcome expectations can take: physical effects, social effects, and self-evaluative effects. He writes, "Behavior and the effects it produces are different classes of events" (p. 22). That is, examples of physical outcome effects are positive/negative sensory experiences; examples of social outcome effects are approval/disapproval and monetary compensation/deprivation of privileges; and examples of self-evaluative outcome effects are self-sanctions/self-satisfaction. An athlete's position in a competition or winning does not fit this class of effects. An athlete's position in a competition (first, second, third, etc.) is a performance marker. Feltz and Chase (1998) have labeled this "competitive" or "comparative" efficacy. An outcome expectation of winning a competitive event might be a high level of self-satisfaction, approval from one's coach, and money or a trophy. Although both self-efficacy beliefs and outcome expectations can influence behavior in sport situations, according to Bandura (1997), outcome expectations are highly dependent on self-efficacy judgments and thus do not predict much beyond what is predicted by self-efficacy.

Research has supported a consistent positive relationship between self-efficacy beliefs and performance from divergent domains of functioning and with the use of different research designs (Bandura, 1997). However, the measurement of self-efficacy beliefs has not been consistent across research studies nor always appropriate. Therefore, some attention to the measurement of self-efficacy is warranted.

MEASUREMENT OF SELF-EFFICACY

Bandura (1977, 1986, 1997) advocates the use of self-efficacy measures that are specific to particular domains of functioning rather than ones that assess global expectations of performance. This means using a microanalytic approach that requires a detailed assessment of the level, strength, and generality of self-efficacy beliefs. Level of self-efficacy is defined as one's belief about the magnitude or level of performance possible. Strength is defined as the certainty that one can attain a given level of performance. Generality refers to the number of domains in which an individual believes he or she is efficacious. Measures of generality of self-efficacy are rarely included in research studies on sport. A microanalytic approach allows one to analyze the degree of congruence between self-efficacy and performance at the level of individual tasks (Bandura, 1997). Analyzing the degree of congruence involves a computation of the percentage of items for which an efficacy judgment and performance agree. As Wurtele (1986) noted, this type of analysis has not been conducted in studies in sport psychology. Rather, researchers have typically correlated aggregate self-efficacy level or strength scores with aggregate performance scores (Feltz & Chase, 1998).

In sport studies, self-efficacy measures typically are constructed by listing a series of tasks that vary in difficulty, complexity, or stressfulness. These are called hierarchical self-efficacy measures. Participants are asked to designate (yes or no) the tasks they believe they can perform (efficacy level). For each task designated as yes, they rate their degree of certainty (efficacy strength) that they can execute it on a near-continuous scale from total uncertainty to total certainty; scales range from 0 to 10 in one-unit increments, or 0 to 100 in 10-unit increments. Most hierarchical scales are constructed by listing tasks in increasing order of difficulty, such as landing your most difficult figure skating jump from 1 out of 10 to 10 out of 10 times (Garza & Feltz, 1998).

In constructing nonhierarchical scales, a conceptual analysis of the subskills needed to perform in a given domain is conducted, along with a contextual analysis of the level of situational demands. Such a scale for wrestling might include the following items: escape, get reversal, get back points, pin opponent, not get take down, get take down by throw, get take down single leg, ride opponent, get take down double leg, and not be pinned (Treasure et al., 1996). Researchers using nonhierarchical scales should determine and report the internal consistency if they are using an aggregated score to represent self-efficacy (Feltz & Chase, 1998).

Some researchers have used one-item questions in which participants rate how certain they are of their performance or of beating an opponent's performance. These one-item scales have been subject to problems with reliability and validity, especially in competitive situations when several factors influence the outcome (Feltz & Chase, 1998). In such situations, the correlations between self-efficacy and performance outcome have been shown to be much smaller than when using multiple items (Moritz et al., in press).

Although most of the self-efficacy scales have been constructed for a specific study, Ryckman and his colleagues (Ryckman, Robbins, Thornton, & Cantrell, 1982) constructed the Physical Self-Efficacy Scale (PSE), which contains two subscales, to provide a more generalized measure of self-efficacy in the sport and physical activity realm. The Perceived Physical Ability subscale (PPA) measures perceptions about one's general physical ability, and a Physical Self-Presentation Confidence subscale (PSC) reflects perceived efficacy in the display of physical skills. Rather than being on a probability scale, items are on a 6-point Likert scale, with response alternatives ranging from *strongly agree* to *strongly disagree*. Although predictive validity has been found for the PSE in competitive sports contexts (Gayton, Matthews, & Borchstead, 1986), others have found task-specific scales to be better predictors of specific tasks (LaGuardia & Labbé, 1993; McAuley & Gill, 1983; Slanger & Rudestam, 1997). The concept of the PSE as a self-efficacy measure has also been questioned because the items were not developed within a goal-striving context and seem to represent more of a self-concept measure (Feltz & Chase, 1998; Maddux & Meier, 1995).

Two other measures that have been used to tap self-appraisals of capability in sport are Vealey's (1986) sport confidence measure and the self-confidence subscale of the Competitive Sport Anxiety Inventory–2 (CSAI-2: Martens, Burton, Vealey, Bump, & Smith, 1990). Sport confidence is a more broadly defined concept that assesses one's trait and state perceptions to be successful in a sport. Self-confidence as measured by the CSAI-2 also has a broader focus regarding one's capability to perform successfully in competition. Details regarding the use of these measures are described in Vealey (Ch. 21) and Woodman and Hardy (Ch. 11), of this *Handbook*.

Regardless of how the self-efficacy measure is constructed, it is most useful in explaining motivated behavior and sport performance when the measures have been constructed within the tenets of the theory. Thus, research participants should have the proper incentives to perform, measures that are specific to the performance domain should be used, self-efficacy and performance measures should be concordant, and self-efficacy and performance measures should be assessed closely in time. Of particular importance, Bandura (1997) stated that a proper assessment of the structure of the relationship between efficacy beliefs and action requires that both measures tap similar capabilities. In other words, they should be concordant. In a meta-analysis of the relationship between self-efficacy and sport performance, Moritz et al. (in press) found that when the self-efficacy and performance measures were not concordant, the correlations between the two variables were not as strong ($r = .26$) as when both measures tapped similar capabilities ($r = .43$). A lack of concordance would be evident if one assessed wrestling moves microanalytically (e.g., escapes, reversals, pins) but then used the wrestler's overall score as the performance measure.

The time lapse from self-efficacy assessment to performance is also important (Bandura, 1986). If self-efficacy and performance measures are not assessed closely in time, one's efficacy beliefs could be altered by an intervening experience (Bandura, 1986). Wiggins (1998) found, however, that efficacy expectations for athletes remained very stable within 24 hours to competition.

In summary, a number of measurement factors have been described that may affect the predictiveness of self-efficacy on performance. Feltz (1992) argued that in studies where self-efficacy has not been shown to be a significant predictor of performance, this had more to do with measurement problems of the study than with the conceptual soundness of the theory. For a more thorough discussion on how to construct self-efficacy scales and the measurement issues surrounding self-efficacy, the reader is directed to Feltz and Chase (1998).

SELF-EFFICACY RESEARCH CONDUCTED WITH ATHLETES

Much of the evidence for the effectiveness of self-efficacy as an influential mechanism in sport performance comes from studies using nonathlete populations and contrived settings (Feltz, 1992). That research has demonstrated consistent evidence that people's perceptions of their performance capability significantly affect their motivation and performance (Feltz, 1994). The research reviewed in this section contains only studies in which the self-efficacy of athletes was examined with self-efficacy scales. Studies in which solely sport confidence (Vealey, 1986) or CSAI-2 measures were reported are not included here because they are covered in other chapters of this *Handbook*. Of the 45 studies that were reviewed in the Moritz et al. (in press) meta-analysis on self-efficacy, only 10 were concerned with the self-efficacy and sport performance relationship with athletes. An additional 15 studies were located that either included children and youth (Moritz et al. did not include samples under 16 years of age), did not employ a performance measure, or were published after the meta-analysis was conducted. A summary of the 25 studies is contained in Table 13.1.

Studies ranged from a focus on youth and high school athletes to extreme sport athletes to athletes with disabilities. Feltz and Chase (1998) caution researchers about the format and appropriateness of measures used in assessing self-efficacy in children. The typical format with measures of strength and level of self-efficacy may be too difficult for children under 9 years of age. In addition, children under 9 years are not as accurate in their self-assessments of capabilities as older children and adults (Lee, 1982, 1986; Watkins, Garcia, & Turek, 1994; Weiss, Wiese, & Klint, 1989; Winfrey & Weeks, 1993).

In terms of the measures of self-efficacy, all but two studies (Gayton et al., 1986; Ryckman & Hamel, 1993) used task-specific scales. However, in approximately half of the studies, researchers measured self-efficacy in accord with Bandura's (1977) recommendations and administered them within 24 hours of performance measures. For studies in which performance was of interest, 11 reported competitive outcomes, such as finish times, win/loss percentages, and scores on judged competitions. In other studies, specific contests were constructed, such as penalty shooting, in which the number of shots made constituted the performance. Most of the researchers ($n = 18$) who investigated self-efficacy beliefs of athletes examined the self-efficacy–performance relationship (see Table 13.1).

Table 13.1   Self-Efficacy Research Studies Conducted with Athletes

Study	Sample	Purpose	Self-Efficacy Measure	Performance Measure	Results
Barling & Abel (1983)	32 league & 8 nonleague tennis athletes; *M* age = 26.6 yrs.; USA	Examine relationship among SE, response-outcome, valence, and tennis performance.	10-item SE strength on 5-pt. scale for tennis skills (α = N/A); TTP: 3 hr after performance rating	37-item external rating scale, 12 categories	1. Efficacy strength related to 12 performance categories. 2. Lower correlations with response-outcome and valence.
Garza & Feltz (1998)	27 female members of U.S. Figure Skating Association; prepreliminary–novice; *M* age = 12.37 yrs.; USA	Intervention to compare effectiveness of MP techniques on SE, competition self-confidence (CSAI-2), and performance.	Three 10-item SE strength on 11-pt. probability scales (jumps, spins, moves) (hierarchical); TTP: 1 week after competition	3 external 6-pt. rating scales: 16-item jump scale, 10-item spin scale, 5-item moves scale	1. Both MP techniques improved performance and competitionce. 2. All groups improved in SE.
Gayton et al. (1986)	33 marathon runners (22 men, 11 women); *M* age = 38.6 yrs.; USA	Test the validity of the PSE.	PSE and PPA (α = N/A); TTP: less than 1 hr.	Finish time	PSE and PPA were related to finish time.
George (1994)	25 collegiate and 28 high school baseball athletes; *M* age = 20.7 yrs. college; 17.3 yrs. high school; USA	Examine SE-performance relationship and cognitive and somatic state anxiety (CSAI-2) over 9-game period.	4-item SE strength on 11-pt. probability scale for hitting (hierarchical); TTP: 15–20 min.	Contact percentages for 9 games	1. SE predicted hitting performance in 5 games. 2. Performance predicted SE in 6 games. 3. Anxiety and SE predicted performance in game 1. 4. Lower levels of anxiety were related to stronger SE in 7 games (used path analysis).
Geisler & Leith (1997)	40 male current and former collegiate soccer athletes; *M* age = 23.8 yrs.; Canada	Examine self-efficacy, self-esteem, and audience effects on soccer penalty shooting performance.	1-item SE on 10-pt. scale on comparative ability in penalty shots; TTP: several weeks	10 penalty shots against a goal keeper	1. Dichotomized SE had no effect on performance. 2. Dichotomized self-esteem had no effect on performance. 3. No audience effect on performance.
Haney & Long (1995)	178 female athletes; *M* age = 18.7yrs.; 20.4 yrs. (basketball, field hockey/soccer); Canada	Examine a model of coping effectiveness: relationships among SE, control, somatic anxiety (CSAI-2), engagement and disengagement coping, and performance.	Two 4-item SE strength on 101-pt. probability scales for shots listed for field hockey/soccer and basketball (hierarchical); TTP: 5 min.	Shooting contest (2 rounds): 1. Number of free throws or penalty shots 2. Performance satisfaction	1. Years playing experience predicted SE and perceived control. 2. SE predicted round 1 performance, but not round 2. 3. Round 1 performance predicted control and SE (used path analysis).

(continued)

Table 13.1 (Continued)

Study	Sample	Purpose	Self-Efficacy Measure	Performance Measure	Results
Kane et al. (1996)	216 high school wrestlers; M age = N/A; USA	Examine the relationships among SE, personal goals, and wrestling performance.	10-item SE strength on 7-pt. scale for wrestling moves (α = .80); TTP: N/A	1. Prior performance 2. Win percentage 3. Overtime sudden death performance 4. Performance satisfaction	1. Prior performance predicted SE. 2. SE did not predict win percentage. 3. SE predicted overtime performance and satisfaction (used path analysis).
LaGuardia & Labbé (1993)	47 club runners (33 men, 14 women), 16 college track athletes (10 men, 6 women); M age = N/A (all over 19 yrs.); USA	Compare predictive power of task-specific SE, general SE, predicted time, and training mileage on running performance and examine the anxiety (STAI)-SE relationship.	1. 14-item SE on 7-pt. probability scale for running; 2. PSE and PPA (α = N/A); TTP: 1 hr.	Pace times for 3 races (1 mile to 10K)	1. Running SE, but not PSE, predicted pace times in all 3 races. 2. PSE, but not running SE, was related to STAI.
Lee (1982)	14 female gymnasts; M age = 9.7 yrs.; Australia	Compare predictive power of SE and previous competitive scores on competition performance.	Public estimation of score on each of 5 apparatus (1–10 pts.); TTP: 7 days prior	M score of best 3 apparatus performances on 10-pt. scales.	1. Gymnasts' expectancies related to performance more than previous performance. 2. Coaches' expectancies related to performance more than gymnasts' expectancies.
Lee (1986)	16 female gymnasts; M age = 10.9 yrs.; Australia	Compare predictive power of SE, previous competition score, and training performance on competition performance.	Public estimation of score (1–10 pts.) on uneven bars; TTP: 2 weeks prior	Judged score on 10-pt. scale on uneven bars	1. Training performance related to competition score. 2. SE and previous score not related to competition score.
Lee (1988)	96 college female field hockey athletes on 9 teams; M age = 21 yrs.; USA	Examine relationships among SE, goal setting, and team performance.	Number of items: N/A; 10-pt. probability scale for SE strength and level for hockey skills (α = N/A); TTP: Distant	Team won/lost percentage	1. SE strength, but not level, related to team winning percentage. 2. Team goal setting had stronger direct relationship with winning percentage than SE strength level.
Martin & Gill (1991)	73 male high school middle and long distance runners; M age = 16 yrs.; USA	Examine relationships among SE, competitive orientation (SOQ and COI), sport confidence (TSCI and SSCI), cognitive anxiety (CSAI-2), and performance.	1. 6-item placement SE (strength) on 101-pt. probability scale; 2. 6-item performance time SE (strength) on 101-pt. scale (hierarchical); TTP: 25–35 min.	1. Finish time for ½, 1, or 2 mile, standardized across events 2. Finish place	1. TSCI predicted placement SE. 2. Only placement SE predicted finish time and finish place. 3. Competitive orientation (SOQ) was weak predictor of performance time SE.
Martin & Gill (1995a)	86 high school distance runners (38 women, 48 men); M age = 16 yrs.; USA	Examine relationships among SE, competitive orientation (SOQ), goal importance, goal thoughts, and performance.	1. 6-item placement SE on 101-pt. probability scale; 2. 6-item performance time SE on 101-pt. scale (hierarchical); TTP: 25–35 min.	1. Finish time for ½, 1, or 2 mile, standardized across events 2. Finish place	1. Win orientation and place goal importance predicted placement SE. 2. Time goal importance predicted performance time SE. 3. Placement SE predicted finish place (used path analysis).

Study	Sample	Purpose	Measures	Performance	Results
Martin & Gill (1995b)	41 male marathon runners; *M* age = 32.2 yrs.; Philippines	Examine relationships among SE, sport confidence (TSCI), competitive orientation (SOQ), and goal importance.	1. 6-item placement SE on 101-pt. probability scale; 2. 6-item performance time SE on 101-pt. scale (hierarchical); TTP: 1–3 days	None	1. TSCI correlated with placement SE. 2. Placement SE correlated with place and time goal importance. 3. Time SE correlated with time goal importance.
Martin & Mushett (1996)	78 athletes with disabilities competing at cerebral palsy games in England (34 women, 44 men); *M* age = 23.4 yrs.; Australia, Canada, Great Britain	Examine relationships among social support, SE, and athletic satisfaction.	1-item SE on 101-pt. probability scale for ability to train to achieve one's potential	None	SE correlated with listening support, emotional support, and technical challenge support.
McAuley & Gill (1983)	52 female collegiate gymnasts; *M* age = N/A; USA	Compare predictive power of task-specific and general SE on gymnastic performance.	1. 4 SE strength scales (vault, beam, floor, bars), each with 7 items (hierarchical); 2. PSE ($\alpha = .72$) Subscales: PPA ($\alpha = .76$); PSPC ($\alpha = .42$); TTP: less than 1 hr.	Individual scores for each event on 10-pt. scale	Task-specific SE scales were better predictors of performance than PSE scales.
Miller (1993)	84 club-level competitive swimmers (42 men, 42 women); *M* age = 14.38 yrs.; Canada	Compare SE, skill level, and motivation on swimming performance in experimental design, manipulating SE into high and low levels; and examine the SE-motivation relationship	SE strength on 100-pt. probability scale; number of items = N/A ($\alpha = N/A$); TTP: 3 min.	200m individual medley. Simulated competition	1. High SE faster than low SE swimmers. 2. No effect on performance for skill level or motivation. 3. Negative relationship between high SE and motivation.
Okwumabua (1986)	90 marathon runners (82 men, 8 women); *M* age = 35.5 yrs.; USA	Examine relationships among SE, associative cognitive strategy use, expected pain, training history, past performance, and race performance.	9-item SE strength and level on a 100-pt. probability scale for the marathon task (hierarchical); TTP: approx. 3 days	Finish time	1. SE strength was the strongest predictor of finish time, followed by past performance, expected pain, and training history. 2. SE strength and level were related to training history and past performance.
Ryckman & Hamel (1993)	123 grade 9 high school athletes (61 women, 62 men); *M* age = 14.34 yrs.; USA	Examine PPA and sport participation motives.	PPA	None	High PPA athletes rated skill development, team affiliation, and having fun as more important reasons for sport participation than low PPA athletes.

(continued)

Table 13.1 (Continued)

Study	Sample	Purpose	Self-Efficacy Measure	Performance Measure	Results
Singleton & Feltz (1999)	23 male ice hockey athletes; M age = N/A (range = 18–23); USA	Intervention to examine effect of self-modeling on SE and goal-shooting performance.	5-item SE strength on 10-pt. probability scale for performing shooting skills in competition (α = .80); TTP: immediate	5 backhand shots at each of four targets in each corner of goal; total shots = 20 at each of 3 time periods	Self-modeling group showed greater shooting accuracy and stronger SE than control.
Slanger & Rudestam (1997)	40 male participants in extreme sports of skiing, rock climbing, white water kayaking, stunt flying (20 extreme risk takers, 20 high risk takers) (20 trained athletes in moderate risk sports); M age = N/A	Compare extreme, high risk sports, and moderate risk sports participants on general SE, task-specific SE, sensation seeking, death anxiety, and repression/sensitization.	1. Physical risk SE strength scale (α = .91) with 3 error focused subscales: trivial, harmful, fatal; Each scale contained 6 items on 101-pt. probability scale. trivial (α = .90); harmful (α = .89); fatal (α = .92); 2. PSE; 3. SES; TTP: not relevant	None	Physical risk SE was the only variable that distinguished between extreme and high risk participants.
Treasure et al. (1996)	70 male high school wrestlers; M age = 16.03 yrs.; USA	Examine the relationships among SE, performance, anxiety (CSAI-2), and affect prior to competition.	10-item SE strength on 101-pt. probability scale on wrestling maneuvers (α = N/A); TTP: 15 min.	1. Win-loss; 2. Number of points scored	1. SE significantly related to precompetition positive affect and anxiety. 2. SE significantly related to both performance measures. 3. SE was only significant predictor of winners and losers compared with positive affect, anxiety, wrestling experience, and age.
Watkins et al. (1994)	205 male youth baseball players at sports camp; M age = 12.5 yrs.; USA	Examine the relationship between SE and baseball hitting performance.	6-item SE strength on 10-cm visual analog scale (hierarchical); TTP: immediate	Hitting performance in batting cage over 4 trials	1. SE did not predict performance. 2. Previous performance predicted SE and subsequent performance.
Weiss et al. (1989)	22 male youth gymnasts at state tournament; M age = 11.5 yrs.; USA	Examine the relationships among SE, competitive anxiety (CSAI-C), worry cognitions, experience, and performance.	Estimation of score on each of 6 apparatus; TTP: 2 hr.	Judges' scores on high bar, horse, floor, bars, rings, vault, and all-around	SE only significant predictor of performance.
Winfrey & Weeks (1993)	11 female youth gymnasts, intermediate level; M age = N/A (range = 8–13 yrs.); USA	Intervention to examine effect of self-modeling on SE and balance beam performance.	9-item SE on 9-pt. scale for balance beam, modified from SSCI (α = .82–.97); TTP: immediate	Judged balance beam skill tests across 4 time periods	No effect for SE or performance.

COI = Competitive Orientation Inventory (Vealey, 1986). CSAI-2 = Competitive State Anxiety Inventory–2 (Martens et al., 1990). CSAI-C = Competitive State Anxiety Inventory–Children (Martens, Burton, Rivkin, & Simon, 1980). MP = Mental practice. N/A = Not available. PPA = Perceived Physical Ability Subscale (Ryckman et al., 1982). PSE = Physical Self-Efficacy Scale (Ryckman et al., 1982). PSC = Physical Self-Presentation Confidence Subscale (Ryckman et al., 1982). SE = Self-efficacy. SOQ = Sport Orientation Questionnaire (Gill & Deeter, 1988). SSCI = State Sport Confidence Inventory (Vealey, 1986). STAI = State-Trait Anxiety Inventory (Spielberger, Gorsuch, & Lushene, 1970). TSCI = Trait Sport Confidence Inventory (Vealey, 1986). TTP = Time to performance.

Some of these studies also included comparisons with other predictors of performance. Most of the studies showed a significant and at least moderate relationship between self-efficacy and performance. Investigations in which low correlations between the two measures were reported either used a nontraditional measure of self-efficacy, had a long time-lag between measures, or had a low concordance between the self-efficacy and performance measures. For instance, in the Lee (1988) study of collegiate female hockey players, there was an unspecified time period between self-efficacy and performance, self-efficacy was not assessed prior to matches, and the self-efficacy scale (based on individual hockey skills) was not concordant with the performance measure (based on team winning percentage).

In addition to examining the relationship of self-efficacy to performance, 14 studies also compared self-efficacy beliefs with other predictors of performance. Various other predictors included general self-efficacy measures, response outcome, valance, anxiety, worry, affect, perceived control, personal goals and goal importance, competitive orientation, sport confidence, and past performance/experience/training history. Most of these studies indicated that self-efficacy beliefs had predictive superiority over other variables or had similar predictive strength. For instance, George (1994) found self-efficacy and anxiety (cognitive and somatic) to equally predict hitting performance in the first of a nine-game series. Kane, Marks, Zaccaro, and Blair (1996) found that prior performance predicted the percentage of wrestling matches won, but that self-efficacy contributed most strongly to overtime performance. LaGuardia and Labbé (1993) demonstrated that runners' predicted times, training mileage, and self-efficacy beliefs predicted pace times for three races.

In only three studies were other variables noted to be stronger predictors of performance than self-efficacy beliefs. Lee (1982) found that although gymnasts' self-efficacy was more related to performance than was previous performance, only the coach's estimate of the gymnast's performance and, to a lesser extent, the number of previous competitions were significant predictors of performance score. Wurtele (1986, p. 292), however, pointed out a number of methodological problems with the study that limit generalizations: "(1) Subjects were quite young (ages 7–12 years) and may not have understood the task; (2) not all of the subjects had been in previous competition; (3) only subjects' strength was assessed, and not level of self-efficacy; and (4) self-efficacy judgments were made 1 week prior to competition." Although the measurement of self-efficacy level (or magnitude) is not essential (Feltz & Chase, 1998), the use of a public estimation of one's performance score as a measure of self-efficacy strength is of questionable validity.

In a subsequent study, Lee (1988) found team goal setting to have a stronger direct relationship with the teams' winning percentages than players' self-efficacy beliefs. In addition to the problems noted earlier in this chapter with the way self-efficacy was measured, Feltz and Lirgg (1998) demonstrated that team performance is more strongly related to team beliefs than to individual beliefs. Last, Watkins et al. (1994) did not determine self-efficacy beliefs of youth baseball players to predict batting cage performance as well as previous performance. Baseball hitters in this study performed under invariant conditions for four trials. As Bandura points out (1997), the predictiveness of prior performance is inflated under this condition and is not realistic to batting under competitive conditions. When batting was performed in baseball games, George (1994) concluded that self-efficacy beliefs, not prior performance, predicted subsequent performance.

Some studies have examined the antecedents of self-efficacy judgments. Performance variables such as prior performance, training history, and playing experience have been investigated as predictors of self-efficacy expectations in accord with Bandura's (1986, 1997) predictions. Other measures have included cognitive variables such as anxiety, affective states, competitive orientation, goal importance, and trait sport confidence. Where performance variables were tested as predictors of self-efficacy, strong relationships were found between the two measures (George, 1994; Haney & Long, 1995; Kane et al., 1996; Okwumabua, 1986; Watkins et al., 1994). In addition, researchers who have measured this relationship over trials through path analysis (e.g., George, 1994; Haney & Long, 1995; Kane et al., 1996) have indicated support for the recursive pattern that Bandura (1977) emphasized between performance and self-efficacy. Even so, performance variables typically were found to be stronger predictors of self-efficacy than self-efficacy was of performance, which supports the results of previous path analyses with nonathletes (e.g., Feltz, 1982; Feltz & Mugno, 1983) and corroborates the findings in the meta-analysis by Moritz et al. (in press). Given the complex nature of sport performance, however, self-efficacy should not be expected to be as strong a variable in the efficacy-performance relationship (Bandura, 1986, 1990). If performance measures are used where factors beyond one's control are partially responsible for the performance score, such as contact percentage (in baseball), winning percentage, and finish place, self-efficacy will not be as strong a predictor of performance as performance is of self-efficacy (Feltz, 1992).

The cognitive variables most strongly associated with self-efficacy expectations of athletes are anxiety, positive and negative affective states, goal orientation to win, and trait sport confidence. George (1994) and Treasure et al. (1996) found significant negative relationships between self-efficacy and state anxiety (cognitive and somatic). Treasure and his colleagues also found self-efficacy to be negatively correlated with negative affect (e.g., jittery, nervous, upset) and positively correlated with positive affect (e.g., alert, determined, inspired). Thus, not only do more efficacious athletes have lower levels of cognitive and somatic anxiety prior to competition, but they maintain a more positive affective state (Treasure et al., 1996).

The competitive orientations of athletes (i.e., desire to win or perform better than others or perform well relative to one's own standard) have been thought to be related to their efficacy expectations (Martin & Gill, 1991, 1995a, 1995b). In particular, outcome goals, based on a win orientation, are reasoned to undermine self-efficacy expectations because they are considered less controllable and flexible than performance goals. Performance goals, based on a goal orientation, are suggested to enhance efficacy expectations (Martin & Gill, 1991). In a series of studies, Martin and Gill examined the competitive orientations and self-efficacy beliefs for placing (outcome) and for finish time (performance) of distance runners. They found that a win orientation was positively associated with efficacy beliefs for placing, whereas a goal orientation was positively associated with beliefs for finish time. However, the outcome efficacy–win orientation relationship was much stronger than the performance efficacy–goal orientation. In their second study (Martin & Gill, 1995b), they observed that runners with a strong win orientation chose important place goals that also predicted outcome efficacy beliefs. The results suggest that rather than outcome goals being negatively associated with self-efficacy, they may be based on realistic appraisals of one's capability compared with other competitors. The researchers also admit that their performance time efficacy measure was not conceptually consistent with their goal importance measure.

Finally, only three studies were located in which interventions were provided to athletes to enhance self-efficacy expectations. Interventions are typically based on one or more sources of efficacy information in Bandura's (1977) theory. Singleton and Feltz (1999) investigated the use of self-modeling techniques to enhance the self-efficacy beliefs and backhand shots of collegiate hockey players. As mentioned earlier, they found that players exposed to several weeks of self-modeling videotapes showed greater shooting accuracy and higher self-efficacy for game performance compared to controls. A second study, with a much smaller sample, also investigated the use of self-modeling techniques with gymnasts, but did not reveal self-efficacy or performance effects (Winfrey & Weeks, 1993). The researchers also failed to measure self-efficacy appropriately.

The third study involved the use of two selected mental practice techniques in an effort to enhance the self-efficacy beliefs, competition confidence, and performance ratings of competitive figure skaters (Garza & Feltz, 1998). Junior figure skaters, who were members of the U.S. Figure Skating Association, were randomly assigned to one of two mental practice interventions (drawing one's freestyle routine on paper or walking through one's routine on the floor) or a stretching control group. The home-based interventions took place over four weeks and included procedural reliability and manipulations checks. On completion of the intervention training, the skaters competed in their club's annual competition. Coaches rated their skaters' skating ability prior to the intervention and after the competition. Self-efficacy was measured by constructing individualized figure skating self-efficacy scales to emphasize the skaters' own skating ability levels in jumps, spins, and steps/connecting moves. Skaters were asked "What is the most difficult jump or combination jump, spin or spin combination, and step/connecting move in your skating routine?" Skaters were then asked to rate their confidence in performing each skill from 1 out of 10 to 10 out of 10 times on an 11-point probability scale. Competition self-confidence was measured using the self-confidence subscale of the CSAI-2.

Both mental practice groups significantly improved their performance ratings and their competition confidence compared to the stretching control group. All groups improved in their self-efficacy judgments, including the stretching group, but the walk-through group showed higher improvements in spin self-efficacy compared to the other two groups. The investigators noted that self-efficacy assessment was not concordant with the treatment intervention. That is, the intervention was designed to improve one's entire freestyle routine rather than just jumps, spins, and connecting moves.

It is surprising that so few intervention studies have been conducted with self-efficacy as a dependent variable. Perhaps the reason is the emphasis on performance as the primary variable in competitive sport. Nonetheless, research is needed to examine other promising interventions to enhance and maintain self-efficacy beliefs over time. As

Schunk (1995) noted, studies are typically conducted over brief periods and may not be designed to examine maintenance of self-efficacy beliefs. Overall, the research on the self-efficacy beliefs of athletes has shown self-efficacy to be a reliable predictor of sport performance and useful in combination with other cognitive and training variables in accounting for performance variance. High self-efficacy expectations have also been shown to be accompanied by low precompetitive anxiety, positive affect, strong goal importance, high personal goals, and high trait sport confidence in athletes. In studies where self-efficacy was not found to be a significant predictor of performance and where interventions were not fully successful in enhancing efficacy beliefs, measurement problems were readily apparent.

COLLECTIVE EFFICACY RESEARCH CONDUCTED WITH TEAMS: AN EXTENSION OF SELF-EFFICACY THEORY

Although many researchers have examined the relationship between a performer's self-efficacy and subsequent performance, only recently has the relationship between a group's collective confidence and its performance been studied. Sport coaches and spectators alike are often baffled by teams who are composed of talented individuals but who perform poorly. In contrast, some overachieving teams frequently are characterized by a togetherness that overshadows any individual performer. Other overachieving teams win in spite of within-group problems. The confidence group members have in their collective abilities (collective efficacy) may begin to explain these inconsistencies.

Definitions

Conceptual distinctions need to be made between collective efficacy as defined by Bandura (1997) and other related constructs. Bandura defines collective efficacy as a group's shared beliefs in its capacities to organize and execute actions to produce a desired goal. Therefore, collective efficacy, as well as self-efficacy, is seen as task-specific. Bandura asserts that merely summing a group's individual assessments of personal efficacy is insufficient to represent the coordinative dynamics of its members. In other words, groups may be composed of high- or low-efficacious persons; however, how members perceive their group's ability as a whole is more salient than how they perceive their individual capabilities. According to Zaccaro, Blair, Peterson, and Zazanis (1995), because

groups inherently require coordination, interaction, and integration, a summing of individuals' judgments about their individual abilities ignores these components. Collective efficacy refers not only to how well each and every group member can use his or her individual resources, but also to how well those resources can be coordinated and combined.

Although Bandura (1997) considers perceptions of a team's capability to perform a task to encompass the coordination and interaction influences operating within a team, some scholars consider these resources to measure separate factors of collective efficacy perceptions (Mischel & Northcraft, 1997; Paskevich, 1995; Zaccaro et al., 1995). Mischel and Northcraft, for instance, define *collective task efficacy* as "members' beliefs that their group has the task-related knowledge, skill, and abilities (KSAs) to successfully perform a specific task," and *collective interdependence efficacy* as "members' beliefs that their group has the knowledge, skills, and abilities (KSAs) to interact effectively in performing a specific task" (p. 184). These separate dimensions are also hypothesized to be influenced by different moderators. Perceived task complexity is proposed to moderate collective task efficacy, whereas perceived task interdependence is proposed to moderate collective interdependence efficacy.

A concept related to collective efficacy, group potency, has been defined as the shared belief of a group that it can be effective (Guzzo, Yost, Campbell, & Shea, 1993). However, group potency suggests generalized beliefs, whereas collective efficacy is task-specific (Mulvey & Klein, 1998). Although collective efficacy is typically a measure of individuals, those individuals are, by necessity, influenced by other group members. Collective efficacy, then, may have both individual- and group-level components (Kenny & La Voie, 1985; Zaccaro, Zazanis, Diana, & Greathouse, 1994).

Because Bandura (1997) places the construct of collective efficacy at the group level, the averaging of individual data for use as group means is arguable. For example, Gibson, Randel, and Earley (1996) use the term "group efficacy" to denote a group's consensus about that group's abilities. Group efficacy, in this sense, would comprise one rating, agreed on by all members of the group. The drawback to this method is that social persuasion by a few leaders within the group may lead to a forced consensus that is not representative of most of the members (Bandura, 1997). However, Rousseau (1985) suggests that perceptions at the level of the individual can be aggregated to a higher-level construct and the mean used to represent this collective interpretation when the two variables are functionally equivalent. This condition is met when perceptual consensus has been demonstrated (James, 1982; Kozlowski & Hattrup, 1992). Perceptual consensus exists when group members perceive the team or their abilities within the team to function in the same way. Within-group differences in collective efficacy may be the result of self-efficacy beliefs, personalities of the individuals in the group, or different perceptions or exposure to group stimuli within the group (Watson & Chemers, 1998). If within-group variabilities are not taken into account, aggregating data at the individual level to represent a higher level of analysis may result in aggregation bias (James, 1982). Therefore, studies in collective efficacy should first consider the research question to determine the proper level of analysis. Consensus should be demonstrated if a group-level analysis is deemed appropriate (see Feltz & Chase, 1998, for a complete discussion of measurement issues for collective efficacy).

However, Bandura (1997) suggests that in groups where interdependence among group members is low (e.g., a golf team), an aggregate of individual efficacies may have sufficient predictive power for group outcomes. When interdependence is high (e.g., a basketball team), an aggregate of individuals' judgments about group efficacy would be the better predictor. Some evidence, using sport tasks, exists to support this contention (Moritz, 1998). Bandura also contends that individuals who play different positions in the group may view that group's efficacy differently. It would be rare for a group to have unanimity of beliefs across members. However, as the group continues sharing experiences and outcomes, collective efficacy beliefs should reflect group consensus over time.

Zaccaro et al. (1994) suggest that the degree to which collective efficacy is made at the group level is dependent on whether team members have a sufficient base of common experiences. Results from the Zaccaro et al. study support this premise. They assigned U.S. Army soldiers to teams of 10 to 12 persons and asked them to complete a series of physical exercises that required substantial coordination of movement. Results showed that collective efficacy beliefs become more homogeneous within the teams over their life span. In sport, there may be new team members from season to season, but brand new teams form much less frequently. Thus, most sport teams have some shared congruence at the onset of a season. For example, Watson and Chemers (1998) studied 28 Division III basketball teams and found collective efficacy to be stable from beginning to end of season, but they also noted smaller within-group variance at the end of the season than at the beginning.

Sources of Collective Efficacy

Because collective efficacy is rooted in self-efficacy (Bandura, 1997), at least some of the sources of collective efficacy should be similar to self-efficacy. Of course, these sources should be focused at the group level. Thus, enactive mastery experiences would be based on team masteries; vicarious experience might involve watching a similar team in a similar situation; verbal persuasion would be directed to the group; and physiological and affective states might involve perceptions of the group's nervousness. Although these may indeed affect individuals' perceptions of their team's efficacy, other influences may be important.

Watson and Chemers (1998) suggest that three group-level influences are most important: group composition, previous group experiences, and leader's effectiveness. First, the group's composition may contribute to high or low perceptions of collective efficacy. Large groups may experience coordination difficulties and those difficulties may be reflected in low perceived collective efficacy. However, large groups may also contain more resources, which may strengthen collective efficacy beliefs. If coordination is the problem, collective efficacy may increase across a season as the team learns to work together (Watson & Chemers, 1998; Zaccaro et al., 1994). Past experience has been shown to be the strongest source of efficacy for individuals. Likewise, a group's previous experiences should have a powerful effect on a team's collective efficacy. Using structural equation modeling, Riggs and Knight (1994) tested the effects of a group's success or failure in a work environment on personal and collective efficacy as well as personal and collective outcome expectancy. They found that success/failure played a direct and dominant role in all four variables, suggesting that "success breeds success and that failure must surely be difficult to overcome" (p. 762).

Watson and Chemers (1998) added leader effectiveness to the list of sources of collective efficacy. They suggest that a group's collective efficacy will be influenced by exceptional leadership (Shamir, House, & Arthur, 1992). Leaders have the opportunity to contribute to their team's smooth functioning and to eliminate or minimize coordination problems for performance. They can also enhance efficacy by modeling confidence. A well-respected leader may verbally be able to persuade his or her teammates that they indeed have the resources necessary to achieve a goal. By contrast, a negative coach could demoralize a team by constantly belittling the group.

George and Feltz (1995) stated that spectators or the media may similarly provide relevant feedback to teams that may influence their collective efficacy. A booing home crowd or negative hometown newspaper article may be as demoralizing as the coach who constantly berates his or her team. In contrast, a supportive home crowd, even in times where the going is tough, may lift that team's confidence. It is obvious that research in discerning sources of collective efficacy is needed so that coaches can use such information to potentially strengthen their team's confidence levels.

Collective Efficacy Research in Sport

To date, only a few studies have been conducted for the specific purpose of determining the relationship between collective efficacy and performance in sport. In the most extensive study, Feltz and Lirgg (1998) followed six intercollegiate male ice hockey teams across the season. Individual and collective efficacy were assessed before each game; team performance statistics from each game were also obtained. Results were in agreement with Bandura's (1997) suggestion that collective efficacy, rather than aggregated self-efficacy, should hold more predictive power in relation to team performance for highly interdependent teams, because collective efficacy emerged as the stronger predictor of team performance. In addition, when wins and losses were analyzed across a season, collective efficacy but not self-efficacy was affected by performance outcome: Team efficacy increased after a win and decreased after a loss.

Spink (1990) was primarily interested in the relationship between team cohesion and collective efficacy. He recruited volleyball players competing in a tournament for either elite or recreational teams. They were asked to complete the Group Environment Questionnaire (Widmeyer, Brawley, & Carron, 1985), a cohesion measure, as well as responding to questions devised to measure collective efficacy. Individuals were asked what placing they expected for their teams and how confident they were in those placings. Elite and recreational teams were similarly confident in their ratings. Results showed that, for elite teams only, high collective efficacy teams scored higher on Individual Attractions to the Group Task (e.g., an individual's feelings toward involvement with the group's task, productivity, goals, and objectives) and the shared social interests of the team than did low-efficacy teams. No differences between high and low collective efficacy groups were found among the recreational players. Spink also found that high collective efficacy teams placed higher than did low collective efficacy teams. He argued that the difference in the finding between elite and recreational teams could have been a result of the greater emphasis on winning by the elite teams (the reward was monetary for the elite tournament only). He suggested that group goals may moderate the relationship between collective efficacy and team cohesion.

Paskevich (1995) also examined the collective efficacy and cohesion relationship to performance in volleyball teams. His eight collective efficacy scales were more elaborate than Spink's (1990), and efficacy values were measured over the course of a season. Results showed that perceived collective efficacy and cohesion increased over the course of the season and that collective efficacy mediated the relationship between task-oriented cohesion and team performance at early season but not later season. There was also evidence for the independent effects of collective efficacy and cohesion on performance. The mediation effect supports Bandura's (1986, 1997) contention that collective efficacy acts as a mediator between cohesion and performance. However, as Paskevich noted, the independent effects of these variables on performance at different points in the season suggest that a more complex relationship was operating.

Watson and Chemers (1998) measured 28 male and female intercollegiate basketball team members concerning their collective efficacy and self-efficacy beliefs and their optimism. Team captains, or other team leaders, were also asked to rate their leadership confidence. Measures were taken before the season began and before postseason play. Previous team performance (the previous year's won-loss record), season team and individual performances, and leader evaluations made by team members were also examined. Before the season, players who had higher optimism scores also had higher collective efficacy beliefs. By the end of the season, this relationship was not apparent. Also, at the beginning of the season, collective and self-efficacy were positively related, but only for high self-efficacy teams. Low self-efficacy teams showed a negative relationship between collective and self-efficacy. However, at the end of the season, this relationship was positive. Beginning-of-season collective efficacy predicted end-of-season collective efficacy. In addition, Watson and Chemers also found that beginning efficacy expectations predicted end-of-season performance. Finally, leader evaluation was positively related to collective efficacy, but more so for teams that were unsuccessful in the previous season; in previously unsuccessful teams, players who believed they had effective leaders were more confident in their teams. This last finding may be especially relevant to coaches who find themselves inheriting losing teams. If leadership abilities are apparent to team members, they may also increase collective efficacy.

Three additional studies on collective efficacy included contrived teams or tasks to examine experimentally the collective efficacy and performance relationship. Using a novel physical task, Hodges and Carron (1992) assigned individuals to teams and gave bogus feedback on a hand dynamometer task concerning the team's ability. One team was led to believe that it was inferior in team strength to a confederate group; the other team was led to believe that it was superior. Team members were then shown the competitive task in which they would participate: a medicine ball task where groups would be asked to hold the ball with one arm as long as possible with that arm fully extended at shoulder level. A manipulation check confirmed that this bogus manipulation was sufficient to affect collective efficacy, as the inferior team recorded lower collective efficacy scores than did the superior team before the task was even attempted. After one trial of the task, both teams were told that they had been beaten by their respective confederate teams. However, after this failure, the high collective efficacy team actually improved their performance on a second trial, whereas the low collective efficacy team showed a decrement in performance. Similar to self-efficacy, high-efficacious teams may be more likely to put forth more effort in the face of failure to achieve a goal than would low-efficacious teams.

Lichacz and Partington (1996) also manipulated collective efficacy. They created three- and four-member groups composed either of members of basketball or rowing teams (true teams) or ad hoc groups (nonteam members). Subjects were asked to participate in a rope-pulling task, where individual pulls and group pulls could be recorded. Collective efficacy was manipulated by telling teams that their collective pulls were either 10% below standards set by high-level athletes (low efficacy) or 10% above standards set by nonathletes (high efficacy). Results showed that high-efficacy groups rated their collective efficacy higher than did low-efficacy groups. In terms of performance, an interaction between group history (true versus ad hoc teams) and performance feedback was found. For all groups, except the rowers, high-efficacy teams outperformed low-efficacy teams. However, the two groups of rowers (high and low collective efficacy) did not differ in performance. The researchers suggest that a task that is both salient and challenging to experienced performers may, in fact, motivate them to do their best work. That is, in terms of task characteristics, pulling may be more similar to rowing performance than to basketball performance. However, it is possible that preexisting efficacy beliefs may not have been tapped, especially in the case of the row-

ers, and those beliefs may have influenced the results of this study.

In an effort to examine the relationships among self-efficacy, collective efficacy, and team performance in both more and less interdependent tasks, Moritz (1998) randomly assigned participants in bowling classes to two-person teams. For half of the teams, the team score was represented by the sum of their two scores (less interdependent). The other half of the teams performed "Scotch bowling," where bowlers alternated balls and the team scores were reflected by one score for the team (more interdependence). However, each bowler started in alternating frames, whether or not he or she was the last person to bowl in the previous frame. The performance measure used in the analyses was the average number of pins dropped on each first ball divided by 10 frames. Individual efficacy was an aggregate measure of both bowlers' efficacy scores. Consensus analyses were conducted to ensure that this aggregation was justified. For collective efficacy (or "group efficacy," as used by Gibson et al., 1996), both bowlers together agreed on a team efficacy rating. Results showed that the predictiveness of collective efficacy to performance was moderated by task type (i.e., bowling condition). For the less interdependent condition, collective efficacy was not a predictor of team performance; however, it was for the more interdependent condition. Task type did not moderate the relationship between aggregated self-efficacy and team performance. For more interdependent tasks, then, collective efficacy is a stronger predictor of team performance than it is for less interdependent tasks, at least with two-person teams.

In summary, the examination of collective efficacy in sport is still in its infancy. Researchers are struggling with varying definitions of the construct as well as appropriate procedures to measure it. Collective efficacy appears to be a more complex construct than self-efficacy and may be dependent on the degree of interdependence of team members. Although somewhat similar, the sources used to build collective efficacy beliefs likewise appear to be more complex than those used to determine self-efficacy beliefs. However, preliminary studies seem to suggest that the confidence one places in one's team may predict team performance more than will the confidence one has in one's own individual abilities. Also, though the study of team cohesion and collective efficacy seems to make conceptual sense, the exact influences of each or their interaction on performance has yet to be established. Clearly, collective efficacy research holds much promise in understanding team dynamics in sport.

SELF-EFFICACY RESEARCH CONDUCTED WITH COACHES

In addition to the paucity of research on collective efficacy in sport, few studies have investigated the role that coaches play in building the efficacy beliefs of their athletes and teams nor the efficacy beliefs of coaches themselves to carry out their roles. Three groups of investigators have examined the strategies that coaches use most to develop self-efficacy in athletes (Gould, Hodge, Peterson, & Giannini, 1989; Weinberg, Grove, & Jackson, 1992; Weinberg & Jackson, 1990). At the elite level, intercollegiate wrestling coaches and U.S. national coaches reported encouraging positive as opposed to negative self-talk, modeling confidence themselves, using instruction and drills to ensure performance improvements, and using rewarding statements liberally to be the most effective ways to enhance self-efficacy in their athletes (Gould et al., 1989). High school and age-group coaches reported using similar techniques to enhance self-efficacy. They also reported using verbal persuasion as an efficacy-enhancing technique (Weinberg et al., 1992; Weinberg & Jackson, 1990). These strategies are all based on the major sources of efficacy information as identified in Bandura's (1977) theory: performance accomplishments, vicarious experiences (modeling), and verbal and self-persuasion. As the researchers noted, however, observations of coaches were not conducted to determine the actual use of the self-efficacy techniques or whether these techniques were effective in enhancing the confidence of their athletes and improving performance.

The coaches' efficacy expectations of the athlete or team may also play a role in determining the efficacy beliefs of their athletes. When U.S. Olympic athletes were asked to list the best coaching actions to enhance athletes' performance, providing support and confidence was ranked second (Gould et al., 1999). Chase, Lirgg, and Feltz (1997) specifically examined the relationship between coaches' efficacy for their teams and team performance. Coaches of four intercollegiate women's basketball teams were queried before their games as to their confidence in their team's ability to perform specific basketball skills (i.e., shoot field goals and free throws, rebound, commit turnovers, etc.). Coaches were also asked to rate the importance they placed on these skills, the perceived control they felt over the outcome, and opponent ability. Coaches who had higher efficacy beliefs for their teams perceived themselves to have higher control over their teams' outcomes. Also, the higher the perceived ability of the opponent, the lower the

coach's efficacy in her team. In terms of coach's efficacy in the team and team performance, only free throws and turnover performance could be predicted.

A second purpose of the study was to determine what coaches used as a basis in forming efficacy judgments of their teams. Inductive content analysis was used to identify both high and low efficacy sources. Factors that resulted in high efficacy expectations included good past game and practice performances, favorable comparison with opponents, return of an injured player, and hearing negative comments from players on the opposing team. Coaches also identified good performance preparation by either themselves, their staff, or their players as contributing to high efficacy expectations in their teams. One interesting finding was that many coaches cited past poor performance as a reason they were confident in their teams because they believed in their team's ability to bounce back. Low-efficacy factors were similar to high-efficacy factors: past poor game and practice performance, injured or tired players, and comparisons to better opponents. Other factors that contributed to coaches' low efficacy expectation for their team included their perceptions that the players themselves had low efficacy and a team's inconsistent prior performances. The researchers reasoned that if indeed players are aware of the efficacy expectations coaches have for their teams, a situation similar to the *Pygmalion Effect* might occur. According to this effect, a coach first forms expectations of his or her team. He or she then acts in ways that are consistent with those expectations. Athletes then perceive and interpret those actions and respond in a way that reinforces the original expectations. If this happens, coaches with low efficacy expectations for their teams may inadvertently contribute to low player efficacy and those who believe their teams are capable may contribute to high efficacy.

Another line of research is the examination of the efficacy beliefs of coaches with regard to their own coaching ability. As Bandura (1997) suggests, the development of resilient self-efficacy in athletes is heavily influenced by the managerial efficacy of coaches. Coaching efficacy has been defined as the extent to which coaches believe they have the capacity to affect the learning and performance of their athletes (Feltz, Chase, Moritz, & Sullivan, 1999). Feltz et al. conceptualized a model of coaching efficacy based on Bandura's (1977, 1986, 1997) writings and Denham and Michael's (1981) model of teacher efficacy. Their concept of coaching efficacy comprised four dimensions: motivation, technique, game strategy, and character building efficacy. Motivation efficacy was defined as the confidence coaches have in their ability to affect the psychological skills and motivational states of their athletes. Technique efficacy was defined as the belief coaches have in their instructional/diagnostic skills. Game strategy efficacy was defined as the confidence coaches have in their ability to coach during competition and lead their team to a successful performance. Last, character building efficacy involved the confidence coaches have in their ability to influence a positive attitude toward sport in their athletes.

In line with Bandura's concept of self-efficacy, Feltz et al. (1999) proposed that the four dimensions of coaching efficacy are influenced by one's past performance and experience (e.g., coaching experience, coaching preparation, previous won-lost record), the perceived ability of one's athletes, and perceived social support (e.g., school, community, and parents). They also proposed, in turn, that coaching efficacy has an influence on one's coaching behavior, player satisfaction with the coach, the performance of one's athletes (as measured by winning percentage in their study), and player efficacy levels. Figure 13.2 illustrates the model of coaching efficacy as conceptualized by Feltz et al.

In addition to the model, Feltz et al. (1999) developed the Coaching Efficacy Scale (CES) to measure the multidimensional aspects of coaching efficacy. They concluded that the psychometric properties of the CES were sound. The confirmatory factor analysis supported the four-factor solution structure and marginal support was found for one overall coaching efficacy factor using various global fit indices. Feltz et al. also tested the proposed sources and outcomes of CES using high school basketball coaches. Support was identified for their model of coaching efficacy, in that

past winning percentage, years in coaching, perceived team ability, community support, and parental support were significant predictors of coaching efficacy. The most important sources of coaching efficacy were years of coaching experience and community support. They also found that higher-efficacy coaches had significantly higher winning percentages, had greater player satisfaction, used more praise and encouragement behaviors, and used fewer instructional and organizational behaviors than lower-efficacy coaches. However, the sources of coaching efficacy accounted for only 13% of coaching efficacy beliefs, and the correlational design in the study did not allow for tests of causal effects between any of the variables within the model.

This investigation was followed by two studies that provided support for the concept of coaching efficacy (Chase, Hayashi, & Feltz, 1999; Malete & Feltz, in press). In the first study, 12 of 30 high school basketball coaches observed in the "outcome" portion of the Feltz et al. (1999) study were randomly selected from the high and low efficacy groups and interviewed to identify sources of coaching efficacy information from a coach's perspective. Major sources of efficacy themes supported and delineated the sources presented in the Feltz et al. model. Basketball coaches reinforced the importance of coaching development in terms of education, preparation, philosophy, experience, and knowledge of the game. Coaches also identified information supplied by their players in terms of players' confidence in them, players' enjoyment of the sport, and player development. A coach's past success or performance accomplishments may be more related to player development, which is more under the coach's control, than to won-lost records. The third major efficacy source theme was self-assessment, in terms of analyzing one's own coaching performance and one's leadership skills. This supports Bandura's (1997) contention that past performance by itself does not provide sufficient information to judge one's ability. Self-appraisal of one's effectiveness includes assessments of one's effort, task difficulty, and situational circumstance. This requires the integration of multiple sources of efficacy information.

Although Feltz et al. (1999) assessed coaching experience in terms of years in coaching, they did not measure the extent of coaching preparation. Malete and Feltz (in press) examined the effect of participation in a 12-hour coaching education program on coaches' perceived coaching efficacy. Results showed a small but significant improvement in coaching efficacy based on the educational program compared to the efficacy levels of control coaches. This study adds further support for coaching preparation as a

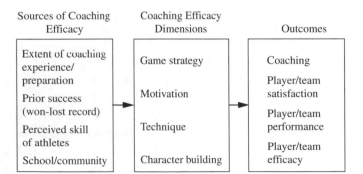

Figure 13.2 Conceptual model of coaching efficacy. From "A conceptual model of coaching efficacy: Preliminary investigation and instrument development," by D.L. Feltz, M.A. Chase, S.E. Moritz, and P.J. Sullivan, 1999, *Journal of Educational Psychology, 91,* p. 2. Copyright 1999 by the American Psychological Association.

source of coach efficacy information. The most effective coaching education programs should use approaches that help increase one's confidence in coaching (e.g., mastery experiences, challenging and reachable goals, observational learning, and simulated learning components).

Barber (1998) also examined the sources of coaching efficacy information and coaching efficacy levels of male and female high school coaches within a perceived competence framework. Using a Sources of Coaching Competence Information Scale and a Perceived Coaching Competence Questionnaire, developed specifically for the study, Barber found few gender differences in preferences for sources of coaching competence information. Female coaches placed greater importance on the improvement observed in their athletes and improvement they observed in their own coaching skills as sources of coaching competence than did male coaches, but all coaches viewed these as the top two sources. In terms of perceived coaching competence, of the seven competency areas surveyed, the only gender difference was in teaching sport skills, where female coaches perceived themselves to be more competent than male coaches.

Barber (1998) was also interested in coaches' perceptions of factors that might influence a future decision to discontinue coaching. Of the three categories of reasons offered, "time demands," "perceptions of coaching competence," and "lack of administrative support," gender differences were found for two of them. Males cited "lack of administrative support" as a more important reason for retiring from coaching, whereas females reported "low perceived coaching competence" as more important. This finding suggests the importance of developing and maintaining coaching efficacy in terms of coaching motivation, especially for women.

Similar to collective efficacy research, efficacy research on coaches is just beginning. The first steps of this research have been to understand how coaches determine their own coaching efficacy levels and the methods they use to increase their athletes' efficacy levels. Future research that specifically focuses on a coach's efficacy should be enhanced by the recent development of the CES.

FUTURE DIRECTIONS FOR RESEARCH

Ever since Feltz's (1992) commentary on self-efficacy and motivation in sport, more research has moved from laboratory to field settings with athletes in competition. However, as previously called for, more research is needed concerning how athletes process multidimensional efficacy information; the study of efficacy beliefs over time and in

different situations; efficacy beliefs regarding the cognitive and emotional aspects of performance; the resiliency of efficacy beliefs; how various interventions can enhance efficacy beliefs; and a comprehensive examination of efficacy beliefs in teams that would include individual beliefs, team beliefs, and beliefs of coaches and leaders (Feltz, 1992, 1994).

Research has not been conducted on how athletes process multidimensional efficacy information and the heuristics they use in weighting and integrating these sources of information in forming their efficacy perceptions. Athletes across situations and in different sports may vary in the importance they place on various sources of efficacy information. For instance, as mentioned earlier in this chapter, physiological information was a more important source of efficacy information for female collegiate athletes than was social comparison or persuasive information (Chase et al., 1994). However, how these athletes derived the weightings of their sources and how they integrated them into an efficacy judgment were not determined. That is, was the information available used in an additive way? Did some information override other sources? Answers to such questions as whether or how a coach's persuasive techniques can outweigh an athlete's or team's previous performance defeats in forming efficacy expectations for subsequent performance would be of great importance to coaches. The use of qualitative analyses may be necessary to determine some of these answers.

The majority of the research on self- and collective efficacy in sport has been approached in a static way. Athletes, however, usually perform over time and across seasons. Many athletes are also members of teams, which are dynamic in nature (Carron & Hausenblas, 1998). The sources of efficacy information may change over time for individual athletes and teams, and the influence of self- and collective efficacy perceptions, in combination with other cognitions, may change. For instance, a recent gold medalist at the Nagano Olympic Games reported that knowing he was the strongest and fittest person in the event had always been his source of efficacy information in the past, but that was not the case at these Olympic Games. Therefore, he worked on his mental skills to provide him with the level of efficacy needed (Gould et al., 1999).

Athletic performance is influenced by cognitive and emotional skills as well as physical skills. Some athletes have stronger perceptions of efficacy than others in the mental aspects of performance. As Bandura (1997) noted, athletic efficacy involves control of disruptive thinking and affective states as well as physical performance. Furthermore, Gould and his colleagues (1999) found that successful Olympic performance required extensive planning and flexibility to deal with numerous unexpected events and distractions. Research is needed to examine the influence on performance of efficacy beliefs regarding one's attention/concentration skills, one's ability to set and work toward goals, one's ability to manage stress and disruptive thought processes, and one's ability to make the right decisions unhesitatingly.

Bandura (1997) also suggested that athletes must have a resilient sense of self-efficacy to sustain perseverant effort in the face of failure and competitive pressure. According to Bandura, experience with failures and setbacks helps in developing this robust sense of personal efficacy. Future research might examine how different patterns of success and failure influence the development of a robust sense of efficacy. In addition, Bandura notes that some individuals and teams recover from setbacks more quickly than others. Knowing how and why some individual athletes and teams are able to regain their sense of efficacy more quickly than others would be valuable information for designing interventions to help efficacy recovery.

As stated previously, few intervention studies have been conducted with athletes and teams to enhance their efficacy perceptions in their physical or mental performance. Two procedures based on Bandura's (1977) sources of efficacy information are worthy of examination. One uses computer technology and the other is based on social comparison information. The use of computer graphics and virtual reality technology is becoming more popular as a teaching tool among coaches. However, whether these techniques can enhance and maintain efficacy beliefs over time has not yet been investigated. Before athletic programs invest large sums of money in expensive equipment, they should determine if the technology has any lasting influence on efficacy beliefs. The use of social comparison information also has not been investigated with athletes. Whether upward comparisons have a negative effect on self-efficacy beliefs or a motivating and challenging effect to surpass the comparative standard has not been tested. Evidence from nonathletes suggests that upward comparisons have negative effects (George et al., 1992). However, athletes, who generally have a more robust sense of efficacy, may use the upward comparative information as a challenge. There is some evidence that high self-esteem individuals are more likely to make upward comparisons (Collins, 1996). Coaches and sport psychologists would benefit from knowing what specific models or comparative others athletes rely on to build their confidence when left to their own choices, and how they use that information.

In terms of collective efficacy specifically, a comprehensive examination of efficacy beliefs in teams that would include individual beliefs, team beliefs, and beliefs of coaches and leaders is needed along with other team-related variables to better understand the group dynamics. Sources of collective efficacy that are unique at the level of the team need further investigation, as does how the collective efficacy beliefs of team members change when team leadership or membership changes (Mischel & Northcraft, 1997). In addition, the concepts of collective task and collective interdependence efficacy as separate dimensions could be examined in relation to their proposed moderators: task complexity and task interdependence perceptions (Mischel & Northcraft).

Further research could include other conceptual and theoretical perspectives of group motivation. For example, relationships between collective efficacy and team attributions, desire for team success, team goals, communication in teams, and team cohesion have received little to no attention. These variables should be examined over the course of a competitive season. Finally, the influence of coaches on the collective efficacy judgments of athletic teams warrants further investigation. What characteristics of coaches and what coaching behaviors provide the strongest efficacy beliefs in athletes and teams? In addition to the confidence that coaches have in their players and teams, their own perceived managerial efficacy may influence the team's performance. Research outside of sport suggests that there is evidence for this influence (Wood & Bandura, 1989).

SUMMARY

In this chapter, an overview of self-efficacy theory and measurement has been provided, along with a review of relevant research conducted with athletes, teams, and coaches, and future directions for research in the field. Self-efficacy beliefs are based on the processing of multidimensional sources of information. When measured and tested within the confines of the theory, self-efficacy has shown a consistent and positive relationship to athletic performance. These relationships have been found with athletes of various ages and abilities, with teams, and with coaches. However, research conducted at the team and coach levels is still in its infancy. The most informative research of the future will include how athletes and teams process multidimensional efficacy information, how sources of information changes over the course of a season, and how efficacy beliefs at the levels of individual, coach, and team interact to influence performance.

REFERENCES

Bandura, A. (1977). Self-efficacy: Toward a unifying theory of behavioral change. *Psychological Review, 84,* 191–215.

Bandura, A. (1986). *Social foundation of thought and action: A social cognitive theory.* Englewood Cliffs, NJ: Prentice-Hall.

Bandura, A. (1990). Perceived self-efficacy in the exercise of personal agency. *Journal of Applied Sport Psychology, 2,* 128–163.

Bandura, A. (1997). *Self-efficacy: The exercise of control.* New York: Freeman.

Barber, H. (1998). Examining gender differences in sources and levels of perceived competence in interscholastic coaches. *The Sport Psychologist, 12,* 237–252.

Barling, J., & Abel, M. (1983). Self-efficacy beliefs and tennis performance. *Cognitive Therapy and Research, 7,* 265–272.

Carron, A.V., & Hausenblas, H.A. (1998). *Group dynamics in sport* (2nd ed.). Morgantown, WV: Fitness Information Technology.

Chase, M.A., Feltz, D.L., Tully, D.C., & Lirgg, C.D. (1994). Sources of collective and individual efficacy in sport. *Journal of Sport & Exercise Psychology, 16,* S18.

Chase, M.A., Hayashi, S., & Feltz, D.L. (1999). *Sources of coaching efficacy: The coaches' perspectives.* Unpublished manuscript, Michigan State University, East Lansing.

Chase, M.A., Lirgg, C.D., & Feltz, D.F. (1997). Do coaches' efficacy expectations for their teams predict team performance? *The Sport Psychologist, 11,* 8–23.

Collins, R.L. (1996). For better or worse: The impact of upward social comparison on self-evaluations. *Psychological Bulletin, 119,* 51–69.

Denham, C.H., & Michael, J.J. (1981). Teacher sense of efficacy: A definition of the construct and a model for further research. *Educational Research Quarterly, 5,* 39–63.

Dowrick, P.W. (1991). *Practical guide to using video in the behavioral sciences.* New York: Wiley.

Dowrick, P.W., & Dove, C. (1980). The use of modeling to improve the swimming performance of spina bifida children. *Journal of Applied Behavior Analysis, 13,* 51–56.

Feltz, D.L. (1982). Path analysis of the causal elements in Bandura's theory of self-efficacy and an anxiety-based model of avoidance behavior. *Journal of Personality and Social Psychology, 42,* 764–781.

Feltz, D.L. (1988). Self-confidence and sports performance. In K.B. Pandolf (Ed.), *Exercise and sport sciences reviews* (pp. 423–457). New York: Macmillan.

Feltz, D.L. (1992). Understanding motivation in sport: A self-efficacy perspective. In G.C. Roberts (Ed.), *Motivation in sport and exercise* (pp. 107–128). Champaign, IL: Human Kinetics.

Feltz, D.L. (1994). Self-confidence and performance. In D. Druckman & R.A. Bjork (Eds.), *Learning, remembering,*

believing (pp. 173–206). Washington, DC: National Academy of Sciences.

Feltz, D.L., & Chase, M.A. (1998). The measurement of self-efficacy and confidence in sport. In J.L. Duda (Ed.), *Advancements in sport and exercise psychology measurement* (pp. 63–78). Morgantown, WV: Fitness Information Technology.

Feltz, D.L., Chase, M.A., Moritz, S.E., & Sullivan, P.J. (1999). Development of the multidimensional coaching efficacy scale. *Journal of Educational Psychology, 91,* 765–776.

Feltz, D.L., & Lirgg, C.D. (1998). Perceived team and player efficacy in hockey. *Journal of Applied Psychology, 83,* 557–564.

Feltz, D.L., & Mugno, D.A. (1983). A replication of the path analysis of the causal elements in Bandura's theory of self-efficacy and the influence of autonomic perception. *Journal of Sport Psychology, 5,* 263–277.

Feltz, D.L., & Riessinger, C.A. (1990). Effects on in vivo emotive imagery and performance feedback on self-efficacy and muscular endurance. *Journal of Sport & Exercise Psychology, 12,* 132–143.

Franks, I.M., & Maile, L.J. (1991). The use of video in sport skill acquisition. In P.W. Dowrick (Ed.), *Practical guide to using video in the behavioral sciences* (pp. 231–243). New York: Wiley.

Garza, D.L., & Feltz, D.L. (1998). Effects of selected mental practice on performance, self-efficacy, and competition confidence of figure skaters. *The Sport Psychologist, 12,* 1–15.

Gayton, W.F., Matthews, G.R., & Borchstead, G.N. (1986). An investigation of the validity of the physical self-efficacy scale in predicting marathon performance. *Perceptual and Motor Skills, 63,* 752–754.

Geisler, G.W.W., & Leith, L.M. (1997). The effects of self-esteem, self-efficacy, and audience presence on soccer penalty shot performance. *Journal of Sport Behavior, 20,* 322–337.

George, T.R. (1994). Self-confidence and baseball performance: A causal examination of self-efficacy theory. *Journal of Sport & Exercise Psychology, 16,* 381–399.

George, T.R., & Feltz, D.L. (1995). Motivation in sport from a collective efficacy perspective. *International Journal of Sport Psychology, 26,* 98–116.

George, T.R., Feltz, D.L., & Chase, M.A. (1992). The effects of model similarity on self-efficacy and muscular endurance: A second look. *Journal of Sport & Exercise Psychology, 14,* 237–248.

Gibson, C.B., Randel, A., & Earley, P.C. (1996). *Understanding group efficacy: An empirical test of multiple assessment models.* Paper presented at the Society for Industrial and Organizational Psychology Conference, San Diego, CA.

Gill, D.L., & Deeter, T.E. (1988). Development of the Sport Orientation Questionnaire. *Research Quarterly for Exercise and Sport, 59,* 191–202.

Gould, D., Greenleaf, C., Lauer, L., & Chung, Y. (1999). Lessons from Nagano. *Olympic Coach, 9,* 2–5.

Gould, D., Hodge, K., Peterson, K., & Giannini, J. (1989). An exploratory examination of strategies used by elite coaches to enhance self-efficacy in athletes. *Journal of Sport & Exercise Psychology, 11,* 128–140.

Guzzo, R.A., Yost, P.R., Campbell, R.J., & Shea, G.P. (1993). Potency in groups: Articulating a construct. *British Journal of Social Psychology, 32,* 87–106.

Haney, C.J., & Long, B.C. (1995). Coping effectiveness: A path analysis of self-efficacy, control, coping, and performance in sport competitions. *Journal of Applied Social Psychology, 25,* 1726–1746.

Hodges, L., & Carron, A. (1992). Collective efficacy and group performance. *International Journal of Sport Psychology, 23,* 48–59.

James, L.R. (1982). Aggregation bias in estimates of perceptual agreement. *Journal of Applied Psychology, 67,* 219–229.

Kane, T.D., Marks, M.A., Zaccaro, S.J., & Blair, V. (1996). Self-efficacy, personal goals, and wrestlers' self-regulation. *Journal of Sport & Exercise Psychology, 18,* 36–48.

Kenny, D.A., & La Voie, L. (1985). Separating individual and group effects. *Journal of Personality and Social Psychology, 48,* 339–348.

Kozlowski, S., & Hattrup, K. (1992). A disagreement about within-group agreement: Disentangling issues of consistency versus consensus. *Journal of Applied Psychology, 77,* 161–167.

LaGuardia, R., & Labbé, E.E. (1993). Self-efficacy and anxiety and their relationship to training and race performance. *Perceptual and Motor Skills, 77,* 27–34.

Lee, C. (1982). Self-efficacy as a predictor of performance in competitive gymnastics. *Journal of Sport Psychology, 4,* 405–409.

Lee, C. (1986). Efficacy expectations, training performance, and competitive performance in women's artistic gymnastics. *Behaviour Change, 3,* 100–104.

Lee, C. (1988). The relationship between goal setting, self-efficacy, and female field hockey team performance. *International Journal of Sport Psychology, 20,* 147–161.

Lichacz, F.M., & Partington, J.T. (1996). Collective efficacy and true group performance. *International Journal of Sport Psychology, 27,* 146–158.

Lirgg, C.D., George, T.R., Chase, M.A., & Ferguson, R.H. (1996). Impact of conception of ability and sex-type of task on male and female self-efficacy. *Journal of Sport & Exercise Psychology, 18,* 426–443.

Maddux, J.E. (1995). Self-efficacy theory: An introduction. In J.E. Maddux (Ed.), *Self-efficacy, adaptation, and adjustment: Theory, research, and application* (pp. 3–33). New York: Plenum Press.

Maddux, J.E., & Meier, L.J. (1995). Self-efficacy and depression. In J.E. Maddux (Ed.), *Self-efficacy, adaptation, and adjustment: Theory, research, and application* (pp. 143–172). New York: Plenum Press.

Malete, L., & Feltz, D.L. (in press). The effect of a coaching education program on coaching efficacy. *The Sport Psychologist.*

Martens, R., Burton, D., Rivkin, F., & Simon, J. (1980). Validity and reliability of the Competitive State Anxiety Inventory–1. In C.H. Nadeau, W.R. Haliwell, K.M. Newell, and G.E. Roberts (Eds.), *Psychology of motor behavior and sport—1979* (pp. 91–99). Champaign, IL: Human Kinetics.

Martens, R., Burton, D., Vealey, R.S., Bump, L., & Smith, D.E. (1990). Competitive State Anxiety Inventory–2. In R. Martens, R.S. Vealey, & D. Burton, *Competitive anxiety in sport* (pp. 117–213). Champaign, IL: Human Kinetics.

Martin, J.J., & Gill, D.L. (1991). The relationships among competitive orientation, sport-confidence, self-efficacy, anxiety, and performance. *Journal of Sport & Exercise Psychology, 13,* 149–159.

Martin, J.J., & Gill, D.L. (1995a). Competitive orientation, self-efficacy and goal importance in Filipino marathoners. *International Journal of Sport Psychology, 26,* 348–358.

Martin, J.J., & Gill, D.L. (1995b). The relationships of competitive orientations and self-efficacy to goal importance, thoughts, and performance in high school distance runners. *Journal of Applied Sport Psychology, 7,* 50–62.

McAuley, E. (1992). Self-referent thought in sport and physical activity. In T.S. Horn (Ed.), *Advances in sport psychology* (pp. 101–118). Champaign, IL: Human Kinetics.

McAuley, E., & Gill, D. (1983). Reliability and validity of the physical self-efficacy in a competitive sport setting. *Journal of Sport Psychology, 5,* 185–191.

McAuley, E., & Mihalko, S.L. (1998). Measuring exercise-related self-efficacy. In J.L. Duda (Ed.), *Advancements in sport and exercise psychology measurement* (pp. 371–390). Morgantown, WV: Fitness Information Technology.

Miller, M. (1993). Efficacy strength and performance in competitive swimmers of different skill levels. *International Journal of Sport Psychology, 24,* 284–296.

Mischel, L.J., & Northcraft, G.B. (1997). "I think we can, I think we can . . .": The role of efficacy beliefs in group and team effectiveness. In B. Markovsky, M.J. Lovaglia, & E.J. Lawler (Eds.), *Advances in group processes* (Vol. 14, pp. 177–197). Greenwich, CT: JAI Press.

Moritz, S.E. (1998). *The effect of task type in the relationship between efficacy beliefs and performance.* Unpublished doctoral dissertation, Michigan State University, East Lansing.

Moritz, S.E., Feltz, D.L., Fahrbach, K., & Mack, D. (in press). The relation of self-efficacy measures to sport performance: A meta-analytic review. *Research Quarterly for Exercise and Sport.*

Mulvey, P.W., & Klein, H.J. (1998). The impact of perceived loafing and collective efficacy on group goal processes and group performance. *Organizational Behavior and Human Decision Processes, 74,* 62–87.

Okwumabua, T.M. (1986). Psychological and physical contributions to marathon performance: An exploratory investigation. *Journal of Sport Behavior, 8,* 163–171.

O'Leary, A. (1985). Self-efficacy and health. *Behavior Therapy and Research, 23,* 437–452.

Paskevich, D.M. (1995). *Conceptual and measurement factors of collective efficacy in its relationship to cohesion and performance outcome.* Unpublished doctoral dissertation, University of Waterloo, Canada.

Riggs, M.L., & Knight, P.A. (1994). The impact of perceived group success-failure on motivational beliefs and attitudes: A causal model. *Journal of Applied Psychology, 79,* 755–766.

Rousseau, D.M. (1985). Issues in organizational research: Multilevel and cross level perspectives. *Research in Organizational Behavior, 7,* 1–37.

Ryckman, R.M., & Hamel, J. (1993). Perceived physical ability differences in the sport participation motives of young athletes. *International Journal of Sport Psychology, 24,* 270–283.

Ryckman, R., Robbins, M., Thornton, B., & Cantrell, P. (1982). Development and validation of a physical self-efficacy scale. *Journal of Personality and Social Psychology, 42,* 891–900.

Schunk, D.H. (1995). Self-efficacy and education and instruction. In J.E. Maddux (Ed.), *Self-efficacy, adaptation, and adjustment: Theory, research, and application* (pp. 281–303). New York: Plenum Press.

Shamir, B., House, R.J., & Arthur, M.B. (1992). The motivational effects of charismatic leadership: A self-concept based theory. *Organizational Science, 4,* 577–594.

Singleton, D.A., & Feltz, D.L. (1999). *The effect of self-modeling on shooting performance and self-efficacy among intercollegiate hockey players.* Unpublished manuscript, Michigan State University, East Lansing.

Slanger, E., & Rudestam, K.E. (1997). Motivation and disinhibition in high risk sports: Sensation seeking and self-efficacy. *Journal of Research in Personality, 31,* 355–374.

Spielberger, C.D., Gorsuch, R.L., & Lushene, R.E. (1970). *Manual for the State-Trait Anxiety Inventory (Self-Evaluation Questionnaire).* Palo Alto, CA: Consulting Psychologists.

Spink, K.S. (1990). Group cohesion and collective efficacy of volleyball teams. *Journal of Sport & Exercise Psychology, 12,* 301–311.

Treasure, D.C., Monson, J., & Lox, C.L. (1996). Relationship between self-efficacy, wrestling performance, and affect prior to competition. *The Sport Psychologist, 10,* 73–83.

Vealey, R.S. (1986). Conceptualization of sport-confidence and competitive orientation: Preliminary investigation and instrument development. *Journal of Sport Psychology, 8,* 221–246.

Watkins, B., Garcia, A.W., & Turek, E. (1994). The relation between self-efficacy and sport performance: Evidence from a sample of youth baseball players. *Journal of Applied Sport Psychology, 6,* 21–31.

Watson, C.B., & Chemers, M.M. (1998). *The rise of shared perceptions: A multilevel analysis of collective efficacy.* Paper presented at the Organizational Behavior Division for the Academy of Management Meeting, San Diego, CA.

Weinberg, R., Grove, R., & Jackson, A. (1992). Strategies for building self-efficacy in tennis players: A comparative analysis of Australian and American coaches. *The Sport Psychologist, 6,* 3–13.

Weinberg, R.S., & Jackson, A. (1990). Building self-efficacy in tennis players: A coach's perspective. *Journal of Applied Sport Psychology, 2,* 164–174.

Weiss, M.R., McCullagh, P., Smith, A.L., & Berlant, A.R. (1998). Observational learning and the fearful child: Influence of peer models on swimming skill performance and psychological responses. *Research Quarterly for Exercise and Sport, 69,* 380–394.

Weiss, M.R., Wiese, D.M., & Klint, K.A. (1989). Head over heels with success: The relationship between self-efficacy and performance in competitive youth gymnastics. *Journal of Sport & Exercise Psychology, 11,* 444–451.

Widmeyer, W.N., Brawley, L.R., & Carron, A.V. (1985). *The measurement of cohesion in sport teams: The Group Environment Questionnaire.* London, Canada: Sports Dynamics.

Wiggins, M.S. (1998). Anxiety intensity and direction: Preperformance temporal patterns and expectations in athletes. *Journal of Applied Sport Psychology, 10,* 201–211.

Winfrey, M.L., & Weeks, D.L. (1993). Effects of self-modeling on self-efficacy and balance beam performance. *Perceptual and Motor Skills, 77,* 907–913.

Wood, R., & Bandura, A. (1989). Impact of concept of ability on self-regulatory mechanisms and complex decision making. *Journal of Personality and Social Psychology, 56,* 407–415.

Wurtele, S.K. (1986). Self-efficacy and athletic performance: A review. *Journal of Social and Clinical Psychology, 4,* 290–301.

Zaccaro, S.J., Blair, V., Peterson, C., & Zazanis, M. (1995). Collective efficacy. In J.E. Maddux (Ed.), *Self-efficacy, adaptation and adjustment: Theory, research, and application* (pp. 308–330). New York: Plenum Press.

Zaccaro, S.J., Zazanis, M., Diana, M., & Greathouse, C. (1994). *The antecedents of collective efficacy over a team's lifespan.* Paper presented at the Society for Industrial and Organizational Psychology Conference, Nashville, TN.

CHAPTER 14

The Psychophysiology of Sport
A Mechanistic Understanding of the Psychology of
Superior Performance

BRADLEY D. HATFIELD and CHARLES H. HILLMAN

J. Williams and Krane (1998) described the ideal performance state that athletes typically report in conjunction with the experience of a peak performance as follows:

- Absence of fear—no fear of failure.
- No thinking about or cognitive analysis of performance.
- A narrow focus of attention concentrated on the activity itself.
- A sense of effortlessness—an involuntary experience.
- A sense of personal control.
- A disorientation of time and space, in which the perception of time is slowed.

The ideal performance state represents the ultimate goal that applied sport psychologists attempt to achieve when delivering performance enhancement services to athletes. In phenomenological terms, the ideal performance state is characterized by an absence of negative self-talk (Meichenbaum, 1977), high self-efficacy (Feltz, 1984), an adaptive focus on task-relevant cues during the negotiation of the challenge (Landers, 1980), and a similarity to the concept of flow, as outlined by Csikszentmihalyi (1975). Such psychological constructs represent foundational issues in the scientific study of sport psychology. Attainment of the ideal performance state increases the probability that the high-level athlete will perform effectively and in a state of automaticity as defined by Fitts and Posner (1967), without interference from irrelevant cognitive and affective processes. Walter Payton, one of the premiere running backs in the history of the National Football League, reported an example of this psychological state that richly reinforces the concept of efficiency discussed throughout this chapter:

I'm Dr. Jekyll and Mr. Hyde when it comes to football. When I'm on the field sometimes I don't know what I am doing out there. People ask me about this move or that move, but I don't know why I did something, I just did it. I am able to focus out the negative things around me and just zero in on what I am doing out there. Off the field I become myself again. (qtd. in Attner, 1984, pp. 2–3).

This state seems to be characterized by efficient allocation of psychological resources such that the athlete's thoughts are limited to task-relevant processes. Conceptually, it is important to note that the mental state described earlier relies largely on activation of appropriate parts of the nervous system and on a consistent basis. It is generally agreed that expertise results from an extended duration of deliberate practice (Ericsson, Krampe, & Tesch-Römer, 1993). Furthermore, expertise appears to result from the long-term changes or adaptations in the manner in which the brain (Elbert, Pantev, Weinbruch, Rockstroh, & Taub, 1995; Issacs, Anderson, Alcantara, Black, & Greenough, 1992) and other relevant systems of the body (Selye, 1976) respond to situations. Additionally, the physical changes that result from training and conditioning, as well as the experiences of success and failure achieved in practice and competition, alter higher-level psychological constructs such as the self-image and confidence of the performer (Breger, 1974; Feltz, 1984). These phenomenological alterations may, in turn, influence the concomitant changes accruing in the central nervous system (CNS). As such, there appear to be reciprocal interrelationships among psychobiological variables at different levels of analysis that result in an optimal mental state during performance.

Such deliberate practice and effort over an extended period of time can fundamentally alter and specifically shape the involved neural processes (Bell & Fox, 1996;

Smith, McEvoy, & Gevins, 1999). Again, the fundamental neurobiological changes may emerge on a phenomenological level of analysis as a significant contributor to the confident and focused psychological state typically reported by the superior performer. Additionally, the reciprocal influences between factors at the different levels of analysis (i.e., neural and psychological) would ultimately manifest themselves in the nature of the involved motor control processes and the quality of the neuromuscular, autonomic, and endocrine action during the skilled performance (see Figure 14.1). Accordingly, an environmental challenge results in changes in cortical activity which, in turn, influences the emergent psychological state (e.g., self-efficacy, focus, mood). The psychological state then alters the resultant motor control processes (which are mediated by the motor loop), autonomic, and endocrine system functions, resulting in changes in the quality of physiological state and the resultant movement outcome.

Importantly, the changes achieved with expertise are guided by a process of adaptation that can generally be described as efficient (Sparrow, 1983). The attainment of such adaptations directly influences the quality of expression of the resultant outcome (i.e., physical performance). Therefore, one purpose of this chapter is to articulate and offer evidence for such a concept. The evidence offered herein is of a psychophysiological nature and is based primarily on electroencephalographic (EEG) studies of skilled athletes as well as participants in research who were asked to master novel psychomotor tasks. Additional

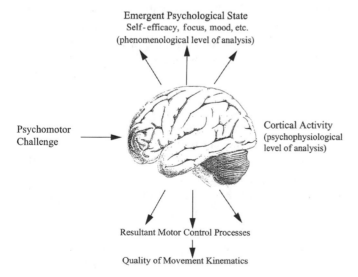

Figure 14.1   Illustration of the relationship among the neurobiological response to challenge, the emergent psychological state, and the resultant psychological processes.

studies that report peripheral measures of the psychological state (e.g., eye movement, autonomic, electromyographic) are also presented in an attempt to provide convergent evidence for the efficient psychological state.

SPECIFICITY OF ADAPTATION

To illustrate the principle by which changes in the brain of the expert performer may occur, analogies are offered that are based on the changes or adaptations known in other biophysical systems. The process of adaptation revolves around the principle of specificity, which suggests physiological conformity to the particular overload imposed by the constraints of a given training process (McArdle, Katch, & Katch, 1986). The goal of conformity is to achieve an efficient physiological system capable of meeting the demands of the particular task with economy of effort and reduced stress on the system. Researchers have shown that athletes conditioned for a specific aerobic activity (e.g., running) are not equally fit (as indicated by VO_2 max) for other endurance activities (e.g., cycling) when challenged with sport-specific tests of their aerobic capacity that mimic those different activities (Hoffman et al., 1993; Withers, Sherman, Miller, & Costill, 1981).

Specific metabolic adaptations also occur in the muscles recruited for the sport or exercise pursued. These adaptations are not only sport-specific (e.g., differentially involve the primary muscles involved in cycling versus running) but are metabolically specific as well (i.e., aerobic and anaerobic). McArdle et al. (1986) listed a number of physiological changes that occur in the process of aerobic training. Among these changes are an increase in capillarization, mitochondrial density and size, and oxygen extraction capability with a concomitant increase in the capacity to generate adenosine triphosphate (ATP). Furthermore, there are increases in the ability to mobilize and oxidize fat and carbohydrates as energy substrate, as well as increases in heart size (i.e., both weight and volume), stroke volume, and cardiac output. Different adaptations occur with anaerobic training. All of the aerobic and anaerobic adaptations occur with overload training so as to create a more efficient system that is uniquely capable of responding to a specific demand with the most adaptive resources possible, while reducing strain on the system. Such a process also occurs in the brain.

Accordingly, in terms of central neural structures, Isaacs and colleagues (1992) noted a differential angiogenic effect in rats' cerebellum based on the type of physical activity involvement to which they were customarily subjected. Specifically, they noted that aerobically trained rats (i.e., engaged in treadmill and wheel running) exhibited shorter diffusion distances from blood vessels in the molecular layer of the paramedian lobule relative to sedentary controls and acrobatically trained rats (i.e., engaged in obstacle maneuvering and motor skill learning). The latter group experienced an increase in the volume of the molecular layer per Purkinje neuron that was complemented by a vascularization effect that maintained the diffusion distance. Elbert et al. (1995) also noted a fundamental neural difference in the contralateral motor cortex between the brains of highly skilled violinists and controls such that the neural resources available for fine motor control were increased in the musicians for the hand that specifically controlled the strings of the instrument.

The process of specificity of adaptation may also extend to the psychological level of analysis. The precise matching or pairing of neural resources with task demand may help to optimize the athlete's behavioral transaction with the environment. For example, the psychological state experienced during competition may differ significantly from that associated with the practice environment. This difference may be due to novel stimuli introduced during the contest relative to the more familiar routines associated with practice. Some athletes may perform better under practice conditions because they have adapted to the familiar routines. During competition, when the stress of performance evaluation is exaggerated, the cognitive-affective state may be different from the typical style of attentional resources allocation such that the athlete is indecisive (Baumeister, 1984; Landers, 1980).

The concept of specific adaptation in the psychological realm can be extended to other areas, such as the nature of the task with which the athlete is confronted. For example, the challenges faced by a starting pitcher may differ greatly from those associated with a relief pitcher. The former role is typically characterized by a higher degree of perceived control and the latter by a lower degree of perceived control and increased uncertainty of outcome. These differences in perception may further relate to specific adaptations in cognitive management and resource allocation by the two athletes. That is, when challenged with a very uncertain and potentially critical situation in regard to the outcome of the game, the relief pitcher may be experienced in the suppression or inhibition of distracting cues. He or she may effect a matching of relevant neural resources (e.g., visual-spatial processes) with the demands of his or her position as compared to athletes who typically negotiate situations characterized by a higher degree of certainty in outcome. The precise pairing of resources with

demand would serve to optimize the behavioral transaction with the environment, and the relief pitcher would be described as focused.

On the other hand, the starter may likely engage in increased verbal-analytic processing because of the novelty of the situation (i.e., one to which he or she has not specifically adapted). Self-talk, accruing from self-doubt or the overanalysis of skill execution, would likely be inconsistent with the task demands (Williams & Krane, 1998). Such a response could be described as a nonspecific allocation of neural resources to the task at hand. Furthermore, the misappropriation of resources could result in interference with the normal patterns of neural activity that precede the execution of the motor commands to the muscles involved in the execution of the pitch. This interference could alter the timing and sequencing of motor unit recruitment in the agonistic, antagonistic, and synergistic muscles so as to alter the quality of the performer's movement. To deal more effectively with the anxiety-provoking situations, it would follow from the previous discussion that the athlete would need to repeatedly confront such situations while attempting to inhibit the attendant distractions (i.e., adaptive suppression). Therefore, repeated challenge may result in reduced novelty and increased familiarity with task demands to promote a more efficient transaction with the environment.

THE PRINCIPLE OF PSYCHOMOTOR EFFICIENCY

Efficiency, which is the conservation of effort to accomplish a given interaction with the environment, would appear to be a fundamental organizing principle of the human condition. In the field of physics, efficiency is defined as:

$$\text{Efficiency} = \frac{\text{Work}}{\text{Effort}}$$

This formula has significant psychological implications when considering the nature of efficiency as the minimization of resources to successfully negotiate a challenge. It is this conservative manner that enables the organism to respond to any new or additional demands placed on it. In extreme instances, this conservation of resources acts to preserve coping resources for "surprise" demands and could result in the survival of the organism. Accordingly, any principle of behavior that is adaptive for survival would appear foundational to our nature and, therefore, exert its influence across a broad expanse of situations. Additionally, efficient allocation of resources serves to reduce strain or wear and tear on the organism. For example, in the physiological domain, efficiency is an adaptive process that is promoted by the effortful training of various physiological systems. Kraemer (1994, p. 137) discussed this notion using muscle endurance training as an example:

> Adaptations in the nervous system play a role in the early stages of endurance training. At the outset, efficiency is increased and fatigue of the contractile mechanisms delayed. The level of motor unit activation in the prime movers needed to maintain a given submaximal force decreases as skill is acquired. Additionally, improved endurance performance may also result in rotation of neural activity among synergists and among motor units within a muscle. Thus, the athlete produces more efficient locomotion during the activity with lower energy expenditure.

DeVries and Housh (1994) also subscribed to the efficiency principle when explaining the action of motor unit recruitment as a result of resistance training. That is, training was shown to result in a decrement in motor unit recruitment (as measured by integrated electromyographic activity [EMG]) when negotiating a given absolute workload relative to the magnitude of recruitment in the untrained state (DeVries, 1968). As stated earlier, this basic organizing principle can be extended to other biophysical systems as well (Sparrow, 1983). For example, Kelso, Tuller, and Harris (1983) postulated that in the nervous system, even the simplest of human movements involved many neuromuscular events overlapping in time. They suggested a need for some type of organizing principle that allowed for the appropriate sets of muscles to be activated in proper sequence, and for correct amounts of facilitation and inhibition to be applied to specific muscles for coordinated action. The coordinative structure or synergy was not viewed as merely a set of similar muscle actions at a joint, or as a reflex mechanism. Rather, it was defined as the functional grouping of muscles that spanned several joints and constrained to act as a single unit. Thus, a complex action characterized by many degrees of freedom was simplified or organized in a more efficient manner.

It should be noted that the activity that accompanies superior physical performance may not always be expressed in terms of efficiency per se but, rather, as adaptivity. As such, some performance states may be marked by relatively high levels of effort but still precisely matched or titrated to the demands of the challenge. For example, a runner sprinting for the finish at the end of a 10K competition may move in such a manner as to precisely and preferably activate the Type II fast-twitch fibers to accomplish the desired outcome. Although effort is not minimized in an absolute sense, as energy expenditure is higher than that during the earlier phases of the race, it may still be economical relative to an untrained individual who is attempting such a sprint. Furthermore, the effort is "minimized" relative to the work output at that stage of the race. Of course, during most of the competition (i.e., prior to sprinting to the finish line), the most efficient runner with the appropriate physical typology would be able to conserve motor units in such a manner as to economize motor unit recruitment relative to running pace and, therefore, maintain maximal steady-state effort. Daniels (1985) and others (D. Morgan, Daniels, Carlson, Filarski, & Landle, 1991) have discussed the adaptive notion of running economy in endurance performers in which minimization of O_2 consumption relative to absolute work is characteristic of superior endurance performers.

In terms of the application of the adaptivity and efficiency principles to the brain of the superior athlete, one can conceptualize the brain as a system of various resources and neural generators that process information in functional ways with a great diversity of function. That is, the brain has a great repertoire of resources, some for visual-spatial processing, some for logical-sequential processing, some for affective-response orchestration, and some for the spectrum of motor control resources. There are many degrees of freedom regarding the selection of mental resources. However, when the individual precisely matches the appropriate neural resources with environmental demand, an adaptive allocation of neurophysiological resources occurs that may underlie the phenomenological experience of being focused. The process of mental adaptation can be defined as the progressive psychological conformity to a given set of constraints with a concomitant reduction in apprehension, self-doubt, and any habitual cognitive tendencies incongruent with the task. Such a notion is consistent with the concept of the Iceberg Profile advanced by W. Morgan, O'Connor, Ellickson, and Bradley (1988).

The idea of mental adaptation traces its lineage back to the early theoretical position of William James (1977), who posited that learning involves the formation of habits that manifest themselves in new neural pathways of discharge through which all incoming stimuli are processed to a specific end. It is hypothesized that not only is there a formation of new neural pathways in the genesis of mental adaptation, but with this psychological conformity comes a unique reduction or inhibition of the maladaptive processes (i.e., neural noise) that act to hinder one's progress toward an adaptive task focus. Hence, the definition of efficiency in terms of minimization of neural noise during psychomotor performance can be more specifically stated as:

$$\text{Efficiency} = \frac{\text{Psychomotor behavior}}{\text{Neural resource allocation}}$$

The conceptual framework derived by Hans Selye (1976), the general adaptation syndrome (GAS), provides an ideal example of the development of such an attribute. Selye described three universal stages of response to any environmental, physical, or psychological challenge (i.e., stressor). These stages included the alarm, resistance, and exhaustion stages. The alarm stage was defined as a disruption in homeostasis. Resistance was defined by the changes or adaptations that occurred in the organism in response to repetitive challenges. The goal of such adaptive change was to minimize the disruption in homeostasis. Importantly, during the second stage of adaptation, changes occur to help the organism deal with challenges in a more efficient manner. The process of efficient allocation of resources serves to reduce the strain on the organism. Lastly, the exhaustion stage referred to a burned-out phase in which excessive chronic engagement with the stressor exceeded the adaptive capacity of the organism. In the sport sciences, D. Morgan and colleagues (1991) have studied the exhaustion stage in competitive swimmers in terms of overtraining. That is, with excessive challenge, in terms of volume and intensity of training, heightened cortisol secretion occurs, which promotes a catabolic or degradative effect on the muscles and other tissues of the body. This process results in a weakened physical state.

Extension of the GAS principle to a neurophysiological level implies that an organism, when initially confronted with a specific challenge, will respond with global neural activation involving both relevant and irrelevant cortical connections. This results in an overflow of neural communication that is relatively inefficient. With repeated challenge or increased skill level, neural organization becomes more refined. That is, relevant neural pathways are activated while irrelevant pathways are suppressed during this adaptive or learning process (Greenough, Black, & Wallace, 1987). Bell and Fox (1996) have described this phenomenon as a pruning process. Specifically, they suggested that prior to crawling onset in infants, there was an "overproduction of synapses in expectation of behavioral change" (p. 552). However, with experience, pruning of unnecessary synapses occurs, resulting in a more efficient neural adaptation. Busk and Galbraith (1975) also supported this notion with adults involved with learning a novel psychomotor task (i.e., mirror tracing). The participants in their study exhibited a high degree of cortical coherence between the visual and premotor areas of the brain during the early stages of skill acquisition. At that stage, the participants showed a high degree of similarity among different cortical regions of the brain (i.e., as measured by increased coherence or homogeneity of the EEG time series recorded at the different electrode locations). However, relative heterogeneity of regional cortical activity was observed after practice, suggesting that increased specialization occurred in cortical regions. This adaptation would allow for "less" of the cortex to negotiate the task.

In terms of organismic behavior, the physical movements of a great athletic performer, described by sportswriters and adoring fans as fluid, graceful, and smooth, can also be described on another level as efficiently matching motor unit recruitment in an optimal manner with environmental demand and behavioral intention. Furthermore, the adaptive processes that lead to brain or cerebral cortical efficiency may be captured by the phenomenological experiences reported by some athletes. Illustrating this concept is the following quote provided by Zimmerman (1979, p. 40), who reported the psychological state of an NFL running back: "No, even though I'm not thinking, I'm aware of everything. I may run sixty yards without a thought, but when I get to the end zone I can tell you where everybody was and who blocked who. And not just the guys near me but all over the field." One possible interpretation of this quote is that the athlete is experiencing specific and exclusive activation of the relevant visual-spatial resources in a virtually automatic manner to negotiate the movement of the body down the field. This primary task is accomplished while surrounded by a dynamic, potentially distracting multisensory array. It would appear that self-talk and logical analytical processing are minimized (perhaps even actively inhibited) while kinesthetic awareness and any relevant visual-motor generators are allocated and activated.

Hence, the goal of sport psychology as a behavioral science is to measure mental phenomena and attempt to relate these measures to parsimonious theoretical perspectives. In this regard, psychophysiology has been a valuable tool in unobtrusively measuring the psychological correlates of performance in real time, and psychomotor efficiency can provide a useful framework to predict the nature of the brain electrical activity in superior performers.

ELECTROENCEPHALOGRAPHY AND SKILLED PSYCHOMOTOR PERFORMANCE

A large body of empirical evidence for the principle of psychomotor efficiency can be acquired from an analysis of psychophysiological research. A wide variety of studies have examined hemispheric lateralization and regional specificity, cortical event-related potentials (ERPs), and other cortical phenomena obtainable from EEG and cortical-mapping techniques. These measures have been acquired during execution of specific skills across a broad range of behaviors and in the preparatory period just prior to execution of a self-paced task. In addition to the relative unobtrusiveness of psychophysiological measures, they provide an unbiased, objective index of psychological processes. In the first published study of this kind in the sport psychology literature, Hatfield, Landers, and Ray (1984) examined left-hemispheric and right-hemispheric activity in world-class competitive marksmen as they aimed at a target and prepared to execute shots. Hatfield et al. demonstrated that the analytical left hemisphere decreased its activation level during the preparatory sighting phase, whereas the right hemisphere (involved in visual-spatial processing) remained at a relatively higher activation level. In essence, these highly skilled athletes experienced an overall quieting of the forebrain accompanied by a shift in relative hemispheric dominance. Although the specific requirements of rifle marksmanship differ from those of other sports, marksmen are particularly useful for studying such attentive states with EEG technology because they are motionless, yet highly engaged psychologically.

Walter Payton's assertion "I don't know why I did something, I just did it" would seem consistent with the hemispheric shift phenomenon. Although it would appear, on one level, that he thought about "nothing" during a given play (i.e., analytical processing), activation of visual-spatial systems was apparently considerable. The running back position requires the ability to constantly change direction due to the changing environment on the field, and simultaneously requires the ability to allocate the fixed or limited attentional resources to process a wide array of spatially oriented cues. Such a state would enable the athlete to effectively react to changing conditions on the field. Obviously, in the case of skilled performers, it would seem that they would not need to "think about" or analyze their actions (Fitts & Posner, 1967). Such a high degree of skill may minimize engagement in negative or worrisome self-talk as well. The allocation of attention to process only the cues and cognitive activity that relate specifically to the athlete's challenge illustrates the concept of mental/psychological efficiency.

Basic Properties of Electroencephalography

To assist in understanding the available EEG literature, a brief introduction to the measure is provided here. More extensive sources of information are available elsewhere

(Coles, Gratton, & Fabiani, 1990; Lawton, Hung, Saarela, & Hatfield, 1998; Ray, 1990). Neural activity in the cerebral cortex produces electrical potentials at the scalp, and the EEG is obtained as a recorded time series of the fluctuating voltages. The placement of electrodes on the scalp conforms to a standard system of locations called the international 10–20 system (Jasper, 1958). The nomenclature of the electrode sites corresponds to the underlying gross neuroanatomy of the brain. The capital letters F, T, C, P, and O, for example, designate scalp placements that correspond to frontal, temporal, central, parietal, and occipital lobes of the brain, respectively.

Functionally, each of the lobes is associated with specific processes. The frontal lobes are associated with higher-order functions such as language, emotion, and motor planning. The temporal lobes house auditory processing and concept formation. The central region mainly involves motor execution. The parietal lobes are associated with sensorimotor function as well as cognition and perception, and the occipital lobes regulate basic visual processes. These cortical locations are further distinguished by subscripts. Sites designated with the subscript letter z are situated on the midline of the scalp (i.e., proceeding from rostral to caudal). Sites designated with numerical subscripts indicate lateral locations. Odd numbers indicate left hemisphere sites and even numbers indicate right hemisphere sites. Higher numbers indicate greater distance from the midline (see Figure 14.2).

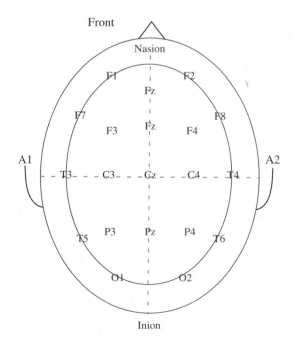

Figure 14.2 International 10-20 standard electrode placements for EEG data collection.

The EEG represents a record or time series of continuously fluctuating changes in electrical potentials across time. The recording represents the instantaneous difference in electrical potentials between two electrodes, with one of the electrodes situated on an area of the scalp overlying the brain and the other placed on a "neutral" or reference area (e.g., the ear lobe or the mastoid). Sometimes, the reference is achieved by linking two neutral sites (e.g., the two ears) to provide an averaged reference. Such a recording convention is termed a "monopolar" record, as only one of the inputs to the amplifier is obtained from an active cortical site (i.e., the other is a reference). At other times, the EEG is recorded in a "bipolar" manner, in that both inputs to the amplifier are obtained from active sites. Bipolar montages are typically employed in clinical applications. When all of the recording sites are commonly referenced to a single active site, the montage is referred to as "referential" as opposed to bipolar (Lawton et al., 1998). The reason for the differential amplification process is based on the concept of common mode rejection or CMR. By employing CMR, any signal that is common to the two recording sites (e.g., active and reference in the case of a monopolar recording) would imply that it is noncortical in origin. Accordingly, it is automatically canceled or subtracted from the records of the two recording channels by the differential amplifier such that the resultant record is considered to represent "true" bioelectrical activity from the cerebral cortex.

The resultant time series, or plot of cortical activity, has two basic properties: frequency and amplitude. In terms of amplitude, the EEG is measured in microvolts or millionths of a volt. The EEG signal typically fluctuates with total or peak-to-peak amplitude smaller than 100 μV. As a consequence, EEG recording requires high levels of amplification, typically with gain factors from 20,000 to 50,000. Additionally, the signal is characterized by a range or spectrum of frequencies from .01 to 50 Hz, although some investigators examine frequencies up to 80 Hz.

The voltage fluctuations of the continuous analog signal are sampled at fixed time intervals, and the rate at which the analog signal is sampled and recorded determines the precision with which the resultant digital time series represents the analog signal. According to a basic principle of digital signal processing called the Nyquist principle (Challis & Kitney, 1991), the analog sample requires a sampling rate that is at least double the highest frequency component of interest to "capture" the range without distortion or aliasing (Newland, 1993; Porges & Bohrer, 1990; Ramirez, 1985).

Muscle movements, especially the movements of large muscles, produce electrical signals that can be confounded with EEG. Even small muscular movements including tension in the neck and face can create artifacts. The ability to reduce such unwanted noise is accomplished by means of filtering. Eye movements can also produce large electrical signals that can mask or distort electrical activity from the cortex. Usually, records of eye movement and blinks are recorded simultaneously with EEG in the form of an electrooculogram (EOG). The EOG allows the investigator to identify segments of the EEG record that are accompanied by eye movements or blinks and to either remove the data from further consideration or correct them statistically. Once the "clean" EEG time series has been achieved, it is decomposed into its constituent frequencies by a process termed spectral analysis that is achieved by computing fast Fourier transforms (FFT). The frequencies are grouped according to bands with the traditionally defined categories: delta (1–4 Hz), theta (4–7 Hz), alpha (8–12 Hz) beta (13–36 Hz), and gamma (36–44 Hz). Delta and theta activation has reflected low levels of arousal. Alpha activity relates to a relaxed, conscious state, and beta and gamma activation are directly related to activation. Much of EEG research that has focused on psychomotor performance has examined the alpha and beta bands.

Previously, many studies in this area of research have been confined to an examination of EEG alpha power, which is believed to largely result from thalamic input to the cortex (Lopes da Silva, 1991). Pfurtscheller, Stancak, and Neuper (1996) offered an interpretation of EEG alpha that is useful in relating it to cortical function. In their review, increases in the amplitude of alpha power or event-related synchronization (ERS) are explained as disengagement of cortical structures with a given task or event. Because the EEG electrode senses neural activity over several square centimeters, it is believed that relative inactivity in the involved networks causes them to be more similar and, therefore, more synchronous, resulting in higher amplitude low-frequency recordings. As an analogy, each of the many neuronal columns or assemblies act like the members of a choir singing in unison, such that the volume for a particular passage is loud. Conversely, the size and magnitude of event-related desynchronization (ERD; i.e., decreases in alpha power) reflect the mass of neural networks involved in the performance of a specific task at a given moment. For instance, task complexity increases the magnitude of ERD. In terms of the analogy described above, think of the neuronal assemblies as disjointed members of a choir who are not in unison, such that the volume achieved for a passage is relatively low. Higher levels of alpha power within a recorded time series imply a reduction in cortical involvement in the area of the scalp (brain) from which the recording was obtained and have been referred to by Pfurtscheller et al. (1996) as indicative of "cortical idling." Sterman and Mann (1995, p. 116) offer additional information regarding EEG alpha: "The thalamic generation of localized EEG rhythmic patterns is known to reflect changes in neuronal membrane potentials associated with the attenuation of impulse conduction within a given functional system (Anderson & Andersson, 1968; Kuhlman, 1978; Steriade, Gloor, Llinas, Lopes da Silva, & Mesulam, 1990). Conversely, the suppression of these patterns with task engagement is associated with electrophysiological and metabolic evidence for active processing within these systems (Mazziotta & Phelps, 1985; Pfurtscheller & Klimesch, 1991; Thatcher & John, 1977)."

Neurophysiological Basis of Electrocortical Activation

Initially, psychophysiologists subscribed to the notion that EEG alpha and beta activation were simple indices of relaxation and activation, respectively, and that the two were inversely related. This perspective was first advanced in the early reports of Adrian and Matthews (1934). However, alternative views of the neurophysiological basis of EEG have been advanced, suggesting that the view of Adrian and Matthews may be incomplete (Nunez, 1995; Ray & Cole, 1985; Smith et al., 1999). For example, Ray and Cole proposed that EEG alpha activity indexes attentional demands, whereas beta activity is more related to cognitive processes. This view differs from that of Adrian and Matthews in that alpha and beta are not inversely related; rather, they are indicative of differential processes and may even covary depending on the psychological strategies employed. Furthermore, the attribution of unique psychological processes to different bands within the EEG spectrum has been extended, on a more fundamental level, to unique neurological processes. Specifically, Nunez suggested that alpha power reflects more global cortico-cortico interaction, whereas higher frequencies are more indicative of localized activation, further suggesting the possibility of covariation between differential frequency bands depending on task demands and resource allocation. That is, cortico-cortico interaction refers to communication between different locations within the cortex. However, his position does not rule out the possibility that alpha and beta power can be inversely related in response to a different set of constraints than those that would require covariation.

More recently, Smith et al. (1999) also endorsed the notion that EEG is related to neural communication and networking during skill acquisition and visual-spatial challenge. Specifically, they interpreted increased alpha with skill acquisition as indicative of a change in the neural organization processes that reflect a more refined and task-specific adaptation to demands. That is, specific neural pathways are enhanced while others undergo a pruning process such that the remaining active pathways are those that are specific to the demands. This concept is described by Smith et al. (1999, p. 390):

> Increases in performance accuracy and decreases in reaction times between the beginning and the ending portions of a testing session were accompanied by increased power and parietal alpha and 'frontal midline' (Fm) theta EEG spectral components. The improvements in performance are consistent with prior results from cognitive studies of skill acquisition which suggest that practice yields an increase in the efficiency with which procedural skills operate on information in working memory. The accompanying changes in EEG signals might be related to the neural reorganization that accompany skill acquisition.

Taken together, Nunez (1995) and Smith et al. (1999) provide an alternative explanation for the nature of alpha activation from simple relaxation (Adrian & Matthews, 1934) to that of neural reorganization. Importantly, the reorganization is characterized by both a relaxation of irrelevant resources and an increased allocation of relevant resources and functional pathways. By deduction, Earle (1988) also advanced the position that alpha increases are indicative of relaxation or inhibition of irrelevant resources that may be characterized by the establishment of new and more adaptive pathways. Other researchers have employed functional magnetic resonance imaging (fMRI) to detect changes in specific areas of the cortex during skill acquisition (Elbert et al., 1995). They compared the cortical representation of the fingers of skilled musicians to those of nonmusical controls. Results indicated that cortical representations were related to the level of use, and that these representations were specifically adapted to the current needs and experiences of the individual (Elbert et al., 1995).

In this regard, a well-established principle in the exercise physiology literature has been the specific adaptation to imposed demand (SAID), describing the chronic change that an organism undergoes in response to training. It would appear that this principle is gaining empirical support in the psychophysiological literature as well. Additional support for this notion is offered by Haier, Siegel, Tang, Abel, and

Buchsbaum (1992), who noted reductions in cerebral glucose metabolism in individuals on attainment of a cognitive skill. Such change epitomizes the notion that the brain is characterized by a more efficient adaptive state. That is, the reorganization of neural resources is an adaptive state that provides increased matching between resource and demand resulting in greater efficiency. As stated earlier, this neural change may influence the phenomenological experience of focus, confidence, and peak performance reported by expert performers.

Spectral EEG and Regional Cortical Specificity

As previously mentioned, psychophysiological measurement of the brain in sport performance began with a series of experiments by Hatfield and his colleagues (Hatfield et al., 1984; Hatfield, Landers, & Ray, 1987; Hatfield, Landers, Ray, & Daniels, 1982). Specifically, competitive marksmen were studied to gain insight into cognitive states associated with skilled performance. The use of marksmen for psychophysiological testing was based on the intense level of concentration and psychological engagement accompanied by the minimization of movement. The assessment of hemispheric differences within the brain using electrocortical measurement (EEG) allowed for a contrast between the preparatory state preceding shot execution and known psychological states associated with verbal-analytic and visual-spatial processing. Such an approach established a new paradigm that provided an opportunity to examine the cognitive concomitants of skilled performance in real time in a relatively unobtrusive manner.

Based on a preliminary report by Pullum (1977) that indicated superior marksmanship was associated with an enhanced alpha state, a more stringent psychophysiological assessment was undertaken by Hatfield and colleagues (1982). Specifically, the cortical processes of elite marksmen were examined during the preparatory periods immediately prior to each of 40 shots in the standing position while they aimed at a target at a distance of 50 feet. The results revealed a hemispheric lateralization effect in the brain such that increased alpha power was apparent in the left compared to the right hemisphere, as the time to trigger pull approached. These results were replicated and extended by Hatfield et al. (1984) with a different group of elite marksmen performing the same task. Using a referential montage with a common vertex reference, their results indicated that increased alpha power was observed across three successive 2.5-s epochs over all electrode locations (left [T3] and right [T4] temporal and left [O1] and right [O2] occipital). In other words, the cortex was becoming

progressively "quieted." In addition, hemispheric differences in the temporal region were observed with increased alpha power at T3, and relative stability was found at T4 across the three successive 2.5-s epochs leading up to trigger pull. To highlight changes in hemispheric dominance across the epochs, an alpha ratio for the homologous temporal leads (i.e., T4/T3) was computed (see Figure 14.3). A significant decrease in the magnitude of these ratios was observed up to the trigger pull, indicating decreased alpha power in the right hemisphere. Further, this effect was found to be consistent across the four blocks of 10 shots.

Collectively, these results suggested that right-hemispheric processing became increasingly important over the time to trigger pull while a progressive decrease in left cerebral activation was noted. This finding was interpreted as a reduction of verbal-analytic processes such as self-talk while visual-spatial processing was enhanced. To further support this interpretation, elite marksmen were also presented with two known psychological challenges: arithmetic calculation and verbal comprehension to engage the left hemisphere, and matching geometric forms and Moonie faces to engage the right. Similar to the Rorschach test, Moonie faces are vague stimuli that require increased perceptual processing to assemble the image of a face. The hemispheric dominance associated with shooting was more similar to that associated with the right-hemispheric tasks than for those observed in response to the left-hemispheric tasks (Hatfield et al., 1984). Furthermore, the dominance

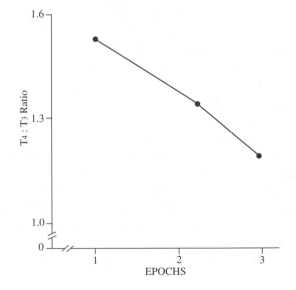

Figure 14.3   Changes in EEG alpha activity ratios (T4:T3) over successive epochs. Decreasing ratios indicate a trend toward relatively greater right-hemispheric processing.

effect evoked by the shooting task was remarkably lateralized even in comparison to the right-hemispheric tasks. Figure 14.4 illustrates this finding.

Corroborating the findings of Hatfield et al. (1984), Rebert, Low, and Larsen (1984) assessed central, temporal, and parietal hemispheric asymmetry during visual-spatial challenge. EEG activity was assessed during 10-s epochs preceding an error using the video game *Pong*. Their results showed a progressive increase in right-hemispheric dominance at the temporal and parietal regions and an opposing left-hemispheric dominance in the central region. During the time between rallies, when the brain was not actively challenged, alpha power was relatively undifferentiated between hemispheres in all regions. The results suggested that psychomotor performance of a visual-spatial task (e.g., video game rallies, shooting) preferentially engages the right hemisphere as decreased alpha power (i.e., ERD) was found in the right compared to the left hemisphere. Figure 14.5 illustrates the results obtained by Rebert et al. The hemispheric differences were most pronounced in the temporal region (Hatfield et al., 1984; Rebert et al., 1984) and appeared to lessen posteriorly. That is, decreased lateralization was evident in the parietal region (Rebert et al., 1984) and altogether absent from the occipital region (Hatfield et al., 1984). Collectively, these findings suggest that EEG recordings during performance are sensitive to the specific cognitive challenges involved with the task. Such regional specificity may be similar in kind to the metabolic and musculoskeletal resources that are differentially engaged in different types of motor performance (McArdle et al., 1986) and may contribute to the experience of a focused state.

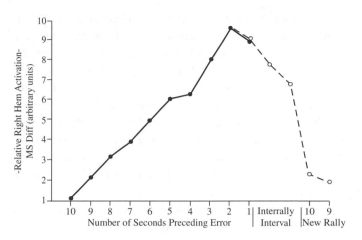

Figure 14.5 Changes in EEG alpha power asymmetry during *Pong* rallies and interrally intervals recorded from temporal leads.

Crews and Landers (1993) extended the finding of differential hemispheric engagement during psychomotor performance using another closed motor task, the golf putt. Again, a relative increase in left-hemispheric alpha power was noted during the preparatory period leading to the golf putt. This finding was accompanied by relative stability of the right hemisphere. Furthermore, there was a significant decrease in left-hemispheric beta I activity (i.e., 13–20 Hz), whereas no change was observed in the beta II band (i.e., 21–31 Hz). These results can also be interpreted as a reduction of verbal-analytic processes in a highly skilled population, not only because of increased alpha power in the left hemisphere, but also due to the ipsilateral decrease in beta power. Hatfield et al. (1984) similarly reported a relative reduction of beta power in the left compared to that in the right hemisphere in elite marksmen.

EEG Spectral Differences in Expert-Novice Paradigms

In an attempt to ascertain the changes in electrocortical activity that accompany skill development, comparative analyses between highly skilled and true novice shooters were conducted by Haufler, Spalding, Santa-Maria, and Hatfield (2000). When compared with the highly skilled marksmen, who were characterized by relative automaticity (Fitts & Posner, 1967), novices were predicted to be more effortfully and verbal-analytically engaged during the preparatory aiming period. To test this hypothesis, the participants were provided shooting, verbal, and spatial challenges. The latter two tasks were administered in a

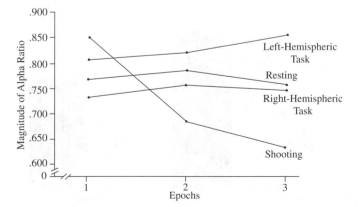

Figure 14.4 Relative changes in EEG alpha activity ratios (T4:T3) over successive epochs for four different cognitive-demand conditions.

manner similar to that used by Hatfield et al. (1984) to achieve psychological inference of the mental state during sharpshooting. Specifically, it was hypothesized that novice performers would exhibit relatively higher left hemispheric activation while preparing to shoot and would evidence an EEG activity profile more similar, with regard to alpha spectral power, to that observed during the execution of the verbal task. In sum, decreased alpha power was expected in the left relative to the right hemisphere during shooting, an effect opposite that expected in the expert performers.

Consistent with expectations, novices, when compared to highly skilled marksmen, showed reduced levels of alpha power (10–11 Hz) in the left hemisphere and increased levels of beta and gamma activity. However, no such differences were observed in the right hemisphere. These results imply that the true novices were less efficient in their resource allocation to accomplish the task. No such group differences were observed for the verbal or spatial tasks that were equally novel for both groups. Furthermore, in novices, a similar level of right hemisphere alpha power was noted for both the shooting and the novel spatial challenge. Interestingly, skilled marksmen showed higher alpha power across all sites relative to that observed in the novices; this effect was particularly noticeable at the T3 site. Again, such a finding suggests an increase in efficiency for experts with specific activation in the cortical area that would appear most relevant to the task demands.

Additional comparative research, also with highly skilled marksmen and noncompetitive shooters as participants, was conducted by Janelle et al. (2000) to examine differences in specific engagement of resources based on skill level. This research was also guided by the hypothesis that less-skilled shooters would exhibit differential hemispheric dominance and activation relative to that observed in highly skilled marksmen. Specifically, noncompetitive less-skilled shooters were predicted to show decreased alpha power in the left hemisphere compared to highly skilled marksmen.

Findings were in opposition to the stated hypotheses, as increased alpha power across both hemispheres was found in the less-skilled group. One possible interpretation of this finding is that the less-skilled participants were unable to actively engage the relevant cortical resources to the same degree as the experts. When considering the notions of Pfurtscheller et al. (1996), the less-skilled shooters may have been characterized by a relative degree of cortical idling, as they may have lacked the requisite experience to focus on the task-relevant cues. According to the notion of

psychomotor efficiency, one would expect increased alpha power to be displayed in the more highly skilled group. However, the lack of support may be explained by the nature of the less-skilled athletes. These athletes were not at the novice stage of skill, as was the group examined by Haufler et al. (2000), and it is possible that they had progressed beyond the stage characterized by effortful processing. A "high" level of alpha power would be consistent with such a post hoc explanation. Furthermore, the results revealed an increased level of hemispheric lateralization in the highly skilled marksmen. Specifically, Janelle et al. (2000) noted increased alpha (i.e., 8–12 Hz) and beta (i.e., 13–20 Hz) power in the left hemisphere of the experts concomitant with a relative decrease in alpha and beta power in the right hemisphere as compared to the less-skilled. Therefore, the magnitude of difference in band power between the two hemispheres was greater than that observed in the noncompetitive shooters (see Figure 14.6). This latter finding may imply an increased level of hemispheric specificity (i.e., specialization) in the highly skilled marksmen, suggesting a more efficient match between neural resource allocation and task demand.

Although the cross-sectional studies comparing experts and novices are informative, they are problematic in the sense that the observed group differences in spectral power may be due to a number of competing explanations beyond those of a neurocognitive nature. For example, any differences in the morphology of the skull (e.g., skull thickness) as well as any differences in cortical neuroanatomy (e.g., orientation of the gyri and sulci) between the groups could

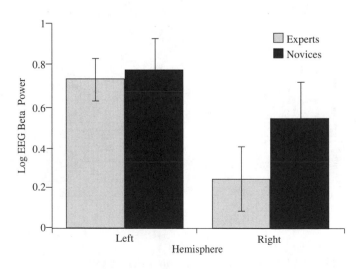

Figure 14.6 Group × hemispheric interaction for EEG beta spectral power for expert and novice marksmen.

affect the amplitude or power of the derived spectral content. Moreover, the few studies that have been reported in the literature of EEG change in association with skill development (i.e., intervention studies) are brief in training duration, typically involving repeated trials within only one session (Busk & Galbraith, 1975; Etnier, Whitwer, Landers, Petruzzello, & Salazar, 1996).

In an attempt to overcome these problems, Landers and his colleagues (1994) conducted a longitudinal investigation with beginning-level archers who participated in a semester-long physical education class. Results showed that novice archers significantly increased alpha power in the left hemisphere during a 14-week performance training course such that increased cerebral asymmetry was observed at the posttest compared to the pretest (see Figure 14.7) as performance improved. These findings strongly suggest that EEG asymmetries as related to psychomotor performance are learned patterns, and that they may facilitate task-specific environmental transactions. Although a comparative control group was not formed in the study, the results appear to provide support for enhanced cortical efficiency because the increased synchronization in the left hemisphere would imply a reduction in irrelevant processing (e.g., verbal-analytical) along with a maintenance of right-hemispheric visual-spatial involvement.

In a similar attempt to causally relate electrocortical activity with performance, Landers et al. (1991) used an EEG biofeedback intervention with pre-elite archers to facilitate skill acquisition and improve performance outcome. Experienced archers were placed in one of three groups: correct biofeedback (i.e., greater left hemisphere slow potential negativity), incorrect biofeedback (i.e., greater right hemisphere slow potential negativity), and a no-feedback control. Results showed that the correct feedback group significantly increased shooting accuracy from pre- to posttest (as measured by the score achieved over 27 shots). The incorrect group decreased performance, and the control group showed no change after one 45- to 75-minute session of biofeedback training (Landers et al., 1991). Additionally, the incorrect feedback group revealed increased beta power in the right hemisphere in the 13–31 Hz range, whereas the other two groups showed no such effect. This heightened power observed in the right hemisphere may be interpreted as more effortful processing or reduced efficiency compared to the other two groups. Figure 14.8 illustrates this finding.

Intrasubject Variability in EEG and Performance Outcome

In another investigation of electrocortical responses of skilled athletes (i.e., elite archers), Salazar and his colleagues (1990) found support for the hemispheric asymmetry effect reported in the literature with golfers (Crews & Landers, 1993) and marksmen (Hatfield et al., 1984). Twenty-eight elite archers completed 16 shots in one of four conditions: normal archery shooting with 14–22-kg bow at full draw; holding the bow at full draw while looking at the target; holding a 2-kg bow while looking at the target; and rest, EEG was monitored at sites T3 and T4 during the final 3 seconds of the aiming period. The four comparative conditions were created to ascertain the relative influence of the physical exertion involved in the task, as opposed to the neurocognitive processes, on the

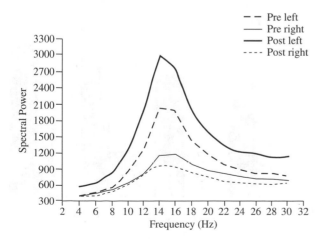

Figure 14.7 Pretest and posttest EEG differences for the left and right hemispheres.

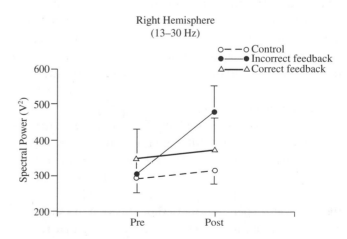

Figure 14.8 Absolute spectral power estimates (V^2) for right hemisphere EEG (13–30 Hz).

recorded EEG. Across all conditions, a significant difference in hemispheric power was noted in the final second prior to arrow release such that the left hemisphere exhibited significantly higher levels at 10, 12, and 24 Hz, whereas relative stability was shown in the right hemisphere over the 3-s aiming period. Worth noting is that the highest level of synchronization of spectral power was observed during the condition characterized by the highest level of ecological validity. Interestingly, this condition represented the situational challenge to which the participants were most adapted. Furthermore, the observed EEG differences were associated with performance variability (i.e., comparison of the four best and worst shots), again supporting the concept that lateralization levels may affect performance levels. The findings indicated increased power in the left hemisphere at 6, 12, and 28 Hz for the worst shots compared to that observed for the best (Salazar et al., 1990). No such performance-related differences in EEG power were noted in the right hemisphere. Although one would expect from the preceding discussion that higher levels of alpha power would be associated with better performance, the heightened levels associated with poorer performance might be indicative of excessive synchronization. That is, the relatively inactive left hemisphere may have been inappropriately disengaged. Salazar et al. caution that the lack of spatial resolution in this investigation (i.e., only two recording sites) precludes definitive insights as to the neurocognitive basis for the observed findings.

Using a denser electrode array to characterize intraindividual differences in electrocortical activity with greater spatial resolution, findings similar to those of Salazar et al. (1990) were obtained by Hillman, Apparies, Janelle, and Hatfield (2000). Using a within-subjects design, EEG alpha and beta activity assessed during the preparatory period prior to executed and rejected trials were compared in highly skilled marksmen. Shot rejection trials referred to those when the shooter would aim his or her rifle at the target and then withdraw without firing a shot. EEG was measured at sites F3, F4, T3, C3, C4, T4, P3, and P4 with a referential montage employing the vertex (i.e., Cz) as the common active site. Based on the model described by Hatfield et al. (1984), Hillman et al. (2000) hypothesized that decreased alpha power in the left hemisphere would accompany the rejected shots. More specifically, they predicted that left hemispheric dominance would characterize the preparatory period prior to shot rejection. As such, they subscribed to an interference model positing that relative left-hemispheric activation would be incompatible with the execution of the task.

Contrary to expectations, the comparison of the EEG during the preparatory periods that preceded shot execution and rejection revealed increased alpha and beta power for the latter. Moreover, the increased power for rejected shots was observed at all regions, with the greatest power at the temporal sites and the least power at the central sites. Furthermore, this effect interacted with time, as increased power was observed for rejected shots while power remained stable during executed shots (i.e., the magnitude of difference increased as the time to trigger pull approached; see Figure 14.9). These results are consistent with the cortical idling explanation advanced by Pfurtscheller et al. (1996). That is, prior to shot rejection, the marksman may have failed to engage the relevant cortical processes to the extent that they were recruited prior to execution. The ERD

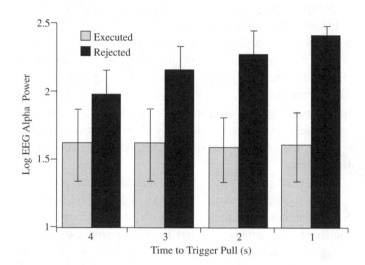

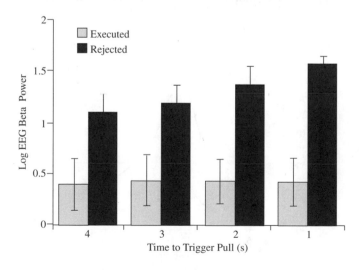

Figure 14.9 Alpha and beta spectral power for the trial type × epoch interaction.

noted in the "successful" state would imply greater engagement of the relevant resources in cortex with challenge.

Failure to appropriately engage task-relevant resources during the performance of a novel task has also been observed in research beyond psychomotor performance. For example, Earle (1988) measured alpha power in temporal and parietal regions in individuals engaged in visual-spatial problem solving and noted increased alpha power in those individuals who experienced greater difficulty negotiating the task. He also contended that the increased alpha power was due to a failure to activate task-relevant neural resources. Taken together, the results of Janelle et al. (2000), Hillman et al. (2000), and Earle are consistent with the notion that less-experienced individuals, or skilled individuals who are not in an ideal performance state, fail to efficiently allocate task-specific neurobiological resources as they struggle with task demands.

Affective Correlates of Psychomotor Skill

Previous investigators have confined their assessment of the electrocortical correlates of skilled performance to the cognitive and motor domains. However, Saarela (1999) attempted to extend the psychophysiological assessment of this state to the affective domain by manipulating time pressure with skilled marksmen who were given varying amounts of time to complete a regulation shooting match in the standing position. That is, marksmen were given the regulation 80 minutes to complete 40 shots. They also experienced a temporal perturbation such that they were required to complete an additional round of 40 shots in half of the time it actually took them to complete the first round. To assess the emotional states associated with these conditions and their relationship to performance, Saarela measured frontal asymmetry (i.e., F3, F4), an established index of affect (Davidson, 1988). Davidson and colleagues (Davidson, Ekman, Saron, Senulis, & Friesen, 1990) have provided evidence that relative left frontal activation (i.e., decreased alpha power at F3 relative to F4) is associated with approach-related behaviors and pleasant affect, and relative right frontal activation (i.e., decreased alpha power at F4 relative to F3) indexes withdrawal-related behaviors and unpleasant affect. Saarela et al. hypothesized that increased right frontal dominance would be found as a result of temporal perturbation along with a deterioration in performance compared to the nonstressed condition. Their findings indicated that marksmen did exhibit greater right frontal activation (i.e., reduced alpha power at F4) in conjunction with poorer performance under temporal stress relative to that under normal shooting conditions in which

relative left frontal activation was observed (Saarela et al., 1999). Moreover, a strong correlation was noted between frontal asymmetry and performance outcomes in the hypothesized direction. Accordingly, the approach orientation associated with the nonstressed shooting condition can be considered an active engagement with the task or high degree of focus that may explain the superior performance. Conversely, the temporal perturbation influenced the emotional state and subsequent performance in a negative direction. Importantly, the prefrontal area, which is involved in the emotional state, is also intricately related to the motor control centers of the brain (Bear, Connors, & Paradiso, 1996). Therefore, the variability in affect could potentially cause variability in the motor pathways, resulting in alterations in the quality of performance.

In an attempt to further assess the influence of emotional states on performance, Kerick, Iso-Ahola, and Hatfield (2000) examined frontal asymmetry in novice shooters by providing them with false feedback. That is, positive feedback was manipulated to generate psychological momentum that was hypothesized to enhance task engagement or approach-related behavior. Alternatively, negative feedback was hypothesized to decrease task engagement. Although the differences in frontal asymmetry were not significantly different, a trend was found in the hypothesized direction. Because the performers were at the novice stage of skill, the failure to achieve significance may have been due to the inherent variability in the cognitive-affective processes associated with the preparatory state. From a speculative point of view, the variability of a beginning performer may be due to inconsistent allocation of neural resources. Furthermore, such inexperienced individuals may not have efficiently adapted to meet task demands (Smith et al., 1999). That is, they may be struggling effortfully to negotiate the challenges, a style that could contribute to their lack of consistency in negotiating the challenge and concomitant cortical activity.

Event-Related Potentials and Skilled Motor Performance

Beyond the information provided by examination of the EEG spectral domain, ERPs offer an additional tool in understanding performance, as they are indicative of specific temporal processes. Coles et al. (1990) defined the ERP as a manifestation of brain activities that occur in preparation for or in response to discrete events. That is, ERPs represent cortical activation that is time-locked to a specific stimulus. Additionally, ERPs are derived from the average of multiple responses to increase the signal-to-noise ratio.

Generally, ERPs are measured in terms of the direction of peak amplitude (i.e., positive or negative) and latency of the cortical waveform. For example, a positive peak that occurs approximately 300 ms after stimulus presentation would be referred to as P3.

In the field of sport performance, a number of investigators have used such measures to study attentional processes in the moments leading up to the execution of a self-paced motor performance. Konttinen and Lyytinen (1992) reported their findings from examination of slow potential (SP) negative shifts (recorded from sites Fz, C3, C4, and Oz) in national-level marksmen and nonpracticed participants. SPs refer to a specific type of ERP that indexes slow shifts in cortical activation related to stimulus processing. Increasing negativity was observed across the sites prior to trigger pull, implying an increasing level of "readiness" to execute the shot. The less successful shots were preceded by a significantly larger shift at the Fz site. Based on these data, Konttinen and Lyytinen theorized that the level of arousal preceding the poorer shots was excessive, and a more economical cortical activity profile was associated with superior performance.

In a subsequent investigation, Konttinen and Lyytinen (1993) reported the individual variability of SP activity in skilled sharpshooters during the 7.5-s preparatory period prior to trigger pull. Recording of SP activity was obtained from the midline (Fz, Cz, Pz) and central lateral (C3, C4) sites. Konttinen and Lyytinen hypothesized that individual marksmen would evidence consistent SP profiles that were reflective of an overlearned automatic cognitive and attentional strategy. Furthermore, individual differences were hypothesized to exist among marksmen, suggesting unique adaptations to the challenge of sharpshooting. The results were consistent with their hypotheses. Importantly, intrasharpshooter variability occurred between high- and low-scoring shots. These findings suggest that variability in electrocortical activity, which underlies the psychological approach, influences performance outcome (see Figure 14.10).

In an attempt to more clearly relate cortical activity to behavior, Konttinen, Lyytinen, and Era (1999) used a psychobiomechanistic approach to explain differences in sharpshooting performance. Specifically, they compared elite (i.e., Finnish Olympic team) and nonelite (i.e., nationally ranked but without international competitive experience) shooters in terms of SP activity (Fz, C3, C4 sites) and postural sway behavior. Participants fired 200 shots in the standing position on an indoor 18-meter range and were instructed to hold the aiming period for at least 7 to 8 seconds prior to the trigger pull to provide a constant time period for SP recording. SP positivity was predicted to be

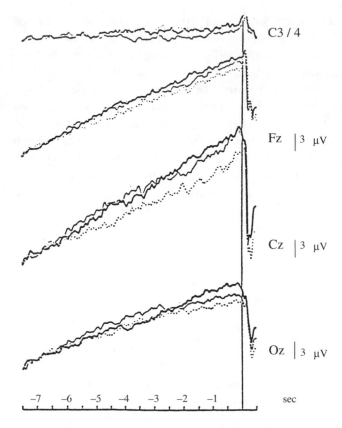

Figure 14.10 The grand averages from the SP calculated across high (687 trials), medium (716), and low (724) score shots. The time window is −7500 to 1500 ms.

heightened prior to poorer performance compared to more accurate trials. This increase would imply elevated psychomotor effort to inhibit irrelevant motor activity and override the SP negativity associated with arousal regulation and visual-spatial processing (i.e., a less efficient state; Konttinen et al., 1999). The results revealed that the elite group showed a reduction in the amplitude of body sway that coincided with a reduction in frontal positivity, and the nonelite group evidenced a different association between the cortical and biomechanical variables. That is, both the amplitude of sway and sway velocity in the anteroposterior plane were related to lateralization in SP central negativity. It is remarkable that such differences emerged in light of the approximation in skill level between the two groups. These results are consistent with the principle of psychomotor efficiency in that superior performance was characterized by decreased cortical effort (as indicated by the reduced amplitude of SP positivity), which, in turn, resulted in reduced sway behavior in the elite group.

In the broader context of attention (i.e., within the reactive task domain), a number of investigators have examined how individuals shift attention in dynamic, fast-paced, and unpredictable environments. The implications for this research are paramount to sport, as athletes are often challenged with a complex visual-spatial array in which they must focus on relevant cues while preparing for the unexpected. Attentional flexibility has been described as the ability to quickly disengage, move attention, and then engage attention again on different aspects of a task. It has been empirically assessed through the use of Posner's (1980) cued attentional paradigm. According to Posner's paradigm, an individual must react to one of two imperative stimuli (i.e., choice RT) preceded by a directional warning stimulus (i.e., an arrow pointing to the left or right of a visual display). The imperative stimulus (S2) follows a warning stimulus (S1) that either correctly or incorrectly cues the subject as to the position of the imperative stimulus that is about to appear. Higher levels of attentional flexibility are characterized by a reduction in attention cost concomitant with an equivalent or greater attention benefit. Attentional cost is defined as slower RT to an imperative stimulus that is preceded by an invalid cue (relative to an uncued RT), and attentional benefit is defined as faster RT in response to an imperative stimulus preceded by a valid warning cue relative to noncued stimuli. This view of attentional flexibility is referred to as location shift. Alternatively, some investigators prefer the term attentional flexibility to refer to the ability to quickly vary or shift the span of visual attention from a focal to a diffuse mode and vice versa (Eriksen & Yeh, 1985). Accordingly, attention is conceived as a "scarce" processing resource that can vary from uniform distribution over the entire visual field to highly focused concentration. When spatial information is provided, the system switches to its focused mode, thus concentrating all resources on a circumscribed area, and processing is allocated to objects falling within the focused area.

In studies of athletic populations, a number of investigators have provided behavioral evidence (i.e., as operationalized by RT) that athletes are characterized by greater attentional flexibility than nonathletes. Castiello and Umilta (1992) compared the RTs of volleyball players to nonathletes. Their results showed that attention benefit did not differ between the two groups, but that attention cost was smaller in the athletic group, thus providing support for the notion that athletes have greater attentional flexibility from the location shift perspective. Conversely, the results of other studies have shown that both attention benefit and cost were smaller in athletes compared to nonathletes (Nougier, Ripoll, & Stein, 1989; Nougier, Stein, & Azemar, 1990; Nougier, Stein, & Bonnel, 1991).

In an attempt to resolve the contradictory findings, the cued attention paradigm (Posner, 1980) has also been used to study attention benefit and cost with ERPs (Hillyard, Luck, & Mangun, 1994; Mangun & Hillyard, 1991; Mangun, Hillyard, & Luck, 1993; Van Voorhis & Hillyard, 1977). Use of this paradigm may provide an opportunity to determine some aspects of the covert strategic neurocognitive processes. Because the paradigm is presented visually, occipitally recorded visual ERPs can be recorded from participants as they negotiate the challenge. The amplitude of constituent components (i.e., P1, a positive waveform component that occurs approximately 70–110 ms after stimulus presentation, and N1, a negative component that occurs approximately 125–170 ms after the stimulus) can then be used as indices of attention allocation. Investigators (Eimer, 1994; Hillyard et al., 1994; Mangun & Hillyard, 1991) have found that the amplitudes of both P1 and N1 were greater in response to the imperative stimulus in the valid cueing condition. Although the neuroanatomical source of N1 is not clear, its maximal amplitude distribution over the posterior area of the brain, and its sensitivity to the cueing effect, make it an ideal candidate for studying attentional flexibility. Therefore, one would expect that the amplitudes of P1 and N1 would show a similar pattern of attentional benefit and cost to that indicated by RT. According to the location shift perspective, a person with greater attentional flexibility would exhibit a similar or greater amplitude enhancement under valid cueing conditions relative to the neutral condition, whereas the amplitude reduction under invalid cueing conditions would not be as severe.

Hung, Santa-Maria, and Hatfield (1999) administered Posner's cued attention task to determine attention flexibility and motor preparedness in 15 table tennis players and 15 nonathletes. Table tennis players were hypothesized to have greater attention benefit and reduced attention cost compared to nonathletes. The variables were measured by means of RT and ERPs (i.e., P1, N1, and the contingent negative variation, CNV). The CNV is an SP wave that is defined between a fixed S1–S2 interval (e.g., a warning and imperative stimulus, respectively). ERPs were recorded from scalp sites C3, C4, O1, and O2 to obtain visual ERPs from the occipital sites and a lateralized CNV recorded from the central sites over the motor cortex. The amplitude of N1 was used as an index of visual attentional resource allocation, and the amplitude of the CNV served as an index of the magnitude of resources allocated to motoric preparedness. Their results revealed that the athletes were faster in terms of RT and were characterized by an inverse N1 cueing effect (i.e., amplitude of N1 to the invalid condition was greater than in the valid condition). Interestingly, this result suggests that the table tennis players directed their limited attentional resources to the less likely location in order to prepare for the unexpected. The reactive-task athletes were also found to have greater motor preparedness, as indicated by greater amplitude of the CNV prior to movement initiation. As such, it may be that skilled psychomotor performers adopt specific strategies to optimize speeded behavioral responses in uncertain or ambiguous situations by allocating attention to the lower probability event while motorically preparing for the event associated with the higher expected probability. Such an adaptation would appear to be ideally suited to the minimization of maladaptive responses to unexpected challenges.

Electrocortical Activity and the Quiet Eye Period

To better understand electrocortical differences between skilled and unskilled psychomotor performance in a convergent methodology, gaze behavior has been studied concurrently with EEG recording based on the underlying assumption that the eye is a "window to the brain." Of specific interest has been the "quiet eye period," which has been hypothesized to index the time needed to organize the visual parameters prior to task execution (Vickers, 1996a, 1996b; Vickers & Adolphe, 1997). Vickers (1996a) explained the quiet eye period by incorporating the work of Posner and Raichle (1991), who postulated the involvement of three critical neural networks. These include the posterior (i.e., orienting) and anterior (i.e., executive) attention networks, as well as one for the coordination of the anterior and posterior systems, the vigilance network. The orienting network directs attentional resources to the most critical environmental cues for the planning of responses. The executive attention network is involved with the recognition of specific cues that relate to goal achievement. Once the pertinent cues have been identified, the vigilance network maintains focused attention. Accordingly, longer quiet eye periods allow performers to extend programming duration for specific targets without disruption from other environmental cues. In line with this view, the quiet eye duration indexes the organization of critical neural networks necessary for optimal control of visual attention.

From a behavioral perspective, Vickers (1996b) and colleagues (Vickers & Adolphe, 1997) have found differences in quiet eye duration based on skill level in both open (e.g., volleyball) and closed (i.e., basketball free throw shooting) sports. Furthermore, Janelle and colleagues (2000) examined the relationship between EEG and quiet eye duration in highly skilled and less-skilled shooters. The specifics of their methods and the design employed were described in an earlier section of this chapter. Experts showed longer quiet eye duration and reduced alpha and beta band power compared to the less-experience shooters. Additionally, lower levels of alpha and beta power were observed in the right hemisphere of the experts, indicative of superior organization of the visual-spatial parameters needed for effective performance. Subscribing to the framework provided by Nunez (1995), the reduced EEG power may imply decreased cortico-cortico communication, which, in turn, may imply reduced activation of irrelevant neural pathways. These findings suggest a more focused state from both measurement perspectives, in that longer quiet eye duration and decreased spectral power in skilled marksmen may relate to quiescence of irrelevant neural activity. The pruning of irrelevant resources may provide an opportunity for more pronounced involvement of task-specific neural activation and the observed activation pattern may underlie greater attentional focus.

In sum, multiple psychophysiological measures reveal different patterns of cortical activity based on expertise. That is, the combined measures (e.g., EEG, ERPs, quiet eye) have enabled investigators to index elite performance, compare skill levels (i.e., expert-novice), and observe differences within individual performance states. Collectively, these studies have attempted to address the differences in cognitive strategies associated with different levels of skill and during different performance states.

NEURAL PROCESSES AND THE MOTOR SYSTEM

With regard to motor control and performance, the efficient allocation of neural resources at one level (i.e., cognitive, affective, and attentional) would appear to be intimately related to the organization and quality of efferent motor outflow. Specifically, integral interactions occur between the higher association areas of the brain, such as the prefrontal cortex and the motor loop (Bear et al., 1996). Higher cortical structures, such as the parietal cortex and the prefrontal area, are directly involved in initiating the signal sent to the motor cortex to "launch a movement." Once the signal leaves the higher cortical structures, it is sent to the basal ganglia that act on the thalamus to trigger the motor cortex. The signal is then sent from the motor cortex via the corticospinal tract to the relevant skeletal muscles (Bear et al., 1996). Hence, task difficulty and effortful cognitive processing may have a strong negative influence on the quality and consistency of the resultant movement by increasing the "noise" input to the motor loop. Conversely, a skilled athlete performing a familiar task would be expected to exhibit decreased noise in the motor loop, which may result in increased quality and consistency of movement (see Figure 14.11).

To illustrate this concept, the example of a place kicker faced with a critical situation in the final moments of a critical football game is provided. In this situation, the opposing team usually calls a time-out to make the athlete "think too much" and overly analyze the challenge with which he is faced. In a sense, the brain of the athlete could be characterized as busy or "noisy" in the cognitive-affective domain. This altered psychological state may then cause disregulation (i.e., excess activation or alteration in the sequencing of events) within the motor loop (Kandel & Schwartz, 1985). Accordingly, the activation of the involved agonistic muscles (hip flexors) and the attendant coordination of the antagonists (gluteal and upper hamstring groups) may also be disregulated, resulting in an alteration of the kinematics of the motion involved in the actual kick. Such processes may underlie the following real-life occurrence: "With only eight seconds on the clock and a chance to tie the game, Mowrey ensured instead that he will be remembered as a copycat killer of Seminole hopes. When Florida State had a chance to beat the Hurricanes in Tallahassee last year, Gerry Thomas saw his last-second kick sail wide right too. New goat, same result" (Murphy, 1992, p. 14).

Of interest to sport psychologists is the question of how elite athletes coordinate cognitive and motor functions to produce the optimal movements required for their sport. To understand this, the organizing principles associated with skilled movement must first be understood. One theoretical perspective that relates well to the principle of psychomotor efficiency for explaining the control and coordination of movement is that of dynamical systems. The dynamical

systems perspective views movement as the result of many control parameters, including the interaction of neural maturation and physical growth. Thelen, Kelso, and Fogel (1987) believe that it is this interaction, along with the intrinsically self-organizing properties of the sensorimotor system, that produces movements that are appropriate within the context of the prevailing environmental conditions.

Bernstein (1967, p. 185) stated that "motor acts demand the most precise intercorrelations of a multiplicity of muscles acting together and of the entire interconnected musculature, with uncontrollable external and reactive forces making up the variable force field in which a movement is carried out." He proposed that coordination of movement was a process of mastering the redundant degrees of freedom of the moving organism and that this process converts the system from a multivariable system into a more simplified one. Rather than having each element of the movement controlled by the CNS, a relationship is formed among the various elements of the system to constrain the vast complexity or degrees of freedom. Gel'fand, Gurfinkel, Fomin, and Tsetlin (1971) view the function of the nervous system in a similar manner. They emphasize the principle of "least interaction": that a system works expediently in some external environment if it minimizes its interaction with that environment.

Considering the role of the CNS, this principle means that minimal input is needed by the higher centers for movement production while control is shifted to lower centers. Thus, the complexity or degrees-of-freedom problem presented to the cortex was solved by apportioning relatively few responsibilities to the executive level and many to the lower levels of the CNS, whose activity the cortex regulates. Therefore, the forming of movements becomes more automatic as opposed to requiring cognitive effort, allowing for the execution of motor skill in an efficient manner. It would appear that there is abundant evidence to support the notion that the organizing principle of neuro-cognitive efficiency extends to the periphery as well. In this regard, the next three sections of the chapter concern the efficient regulation of muscular, cardiovascular, and metabolic activity in higher-ability individuals or participants in research characterized by lower levels of emotional arousal. This generalizability to the periphery relates to the concept of the mind-body link that was illustrated in Figure 14.1.

Electromyographic Correlates of Psychomotor Performance

In addition to electrocortical activation, the measurement of electrical activity within specific muscles has been useful

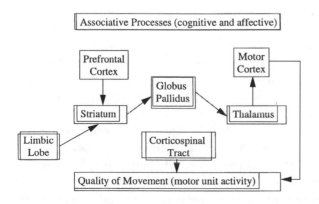

Figure 14.11 The influence of cognitive-affective processes on the motor loop.

in understanding the psychological states associated with skilled performance. Weinberg (1978) used EMG and the Sport Competition Anxiety Test (SCAT; Martens, 1977) to determine how high and low state/trait anxiety, under success or failure feedback conditions, affected the expenditure of neuromuscular energy on an overarm throwing task. EMG was measured from both the biceps and triceps brachii, antagonist muscle groups of the upper arm. These measures were obtained to assess the quality of neuromuscular activation. Results revealed that high trait-anxious subjects, before and after feedback, activated more motor units than the low-anxious subjects before, during, and after the throw. Presumably, individuals who move in a certain manner over time develop a neuromuscular pattern, which is reflective of their cognitive interpretation of the situation. Further, the highly anxious participants viewed the performance situation as threatening; therefore, their movement patterns reflected this by being constrained and inhibited. In terms of positive feedback presented to the participants, Weinberg stated that "the important point is that a successful experience helped high-anxious subjects become more efficient in their quality of movement" (p. 59). Again, this finding supports the interactive relationship between mental and physical efficiency.

EMG has also been used to study the preparatory state associated with large-muscle gross motor performance. Brody, Hatfield, Spalding, Frazer, and Caherty (2000) measured integrated EMG activity and force in 15 strength-trained men during maximal isometric actions of the biceps brachii, with the elbow in a position of $90°$, immediately following 20-s periods of mental preparation, reading aloud, and mental arithmetic. Bipolar recordings of EMG were obtained from the agonistic and antagonistic muscles involved in the task. The reading aloud and mental arithmetic conditions were employed as attentional distractions. Perceived arousal and attentional focus ratings for the mental preparation conditions were significantly greater than those obtained for reading aloud and mental arithmetic, which were undifferentiated. However, perceived effort, average biceps and triceps EMG, and maximal force did not differ across the conditions. These findings indicate that relatively stable neuromuscular adaptations were achieved in trained individuals that are robust to attentional perturbation. Of course, such activation and force-production stability may not occur in relatively inexperienced individuals for whom the alterations in emotional state (i.e., psyching vs. calm) may result in drastic performance alterations.

Cardiovascular Psychophysiology

In addition to the cortical influence on the voluntary nervous system and subsequent neuromuscular activity, the brain is intimately interconnected with the autonomic nervous system. This interrelationship has been extensively examined during psychomotor performance in the cardiovascular domain. Early research by Landers, Christina, Hatfield, Daniels, and Doyle (1980) revealed that elite marksmen fired their shots between heartbeats, an effect not found for less-experienced shooters. Remarkably, of the 400 shots executed by the 10 elite marksmen examined in this study (i.e., each took 40 shots from the standing position), only 6 shots coincided with ventricular contraction (Landers et al., 1980). This phenomenon, which was unconscious to the performer, seemed to serve as an adaptive influence by decreasing reverberatory movement associated with ventricular ejection and enhanced quality of performance.

Research by Hatfield et al. (1987) revealed that, in addition to a top-down perspective, the activity of the heart may also influence the activation level of the cortex. Specifically, they noted an overall chronotropic pattern (i.e., faster heart rate) during the 3-second period preceding the trigger pull that followed a phasic heart rate response, characterized by a preliminary acceleration followed by the deceleratory phase. Framing this work within the broader context of basic psychophysiology may be useful for understanding the significance of the changes in cardiac activity. Accordingly, Lacey and Lacey (1978) postulated that cardiac deceleration facilitated sensorimotor efficiency by increasing the sensitivity of the CNS to environmental stimuli. In their words, cardiac deceleration was related to "intake of environmental stimuli." Alternatively, cardiac acceleration was associated with "environmental rejection" and internal cognitive elaboration (Lacey & Lacey, 1978). Therefore, a circular regulatory process was posited in which the orientation of attention influences cardiac activity that, in turn, facilitates the attentive processes (and, eventually, the performance outcome).

Hatfield et al. (1987) did, in fact, provide evidence that cardiac activity is related in an influential manner to cortical activity during skilled psychomotor performance. Specifically, they tested a centralist model maintaining that cortical activity (i.e., EEG alpha power) would influence subsequent cardiac activity (i.e., heart rate), versus a peripheralist model that held that cardiac activity would influence subsequent EEG activity. Findings supported the peripheralist model such that heart rate activity during the periods preceding trigger pull was related to the subsequent EEG alpha power during the later epochs just prior to trigger pull (Hatfield et al., 1987). This finding suggested that skilled performance is associated with a complex integrated systems adaptation that aids in arousal regulation—one that may help to shape the specific pattern of cortical activation in the highly skilled performer.

Fenz (1975) also studied the relationship between autonomic arousal and psychological state during a high-risk activity, sport parachuting. In the classic work of Fenz and Epstein (1967), two groups of parachuters that were equally experienced but differed in skill level were monitored during the events leading up to the final altitude prior to sky diving. Specifically, heart rate (in beats per minute, bpm) progressively climbed from the time they arrived at the airport until they entered the aircraft. However, the groups exhibited a divergent heart rate pattern from the time they entered the aircraft until they reached final altitude. Poorer performers continued a progressive increase in cardiac activity (reaching a mean above 120 bpm), whereas the superior performers revealed a cardiac deceleration pattern during this same period (mean of approximately 90 bpm; Fenz & Epstein, 1967). Subscribing to Lacey and Lacey's (1978) intake-rejection model of attention, the divergent cardiac patterns were also associated with different psychological profiles. Fenz observed that superior jumpers were more externally focused and task-oriented, whereas the less-skilled jumpers were characterized by excessive cognitive rumination, thoughts of fear, and general rejection of the environment. In this manner, the task-oriented or intake perspective of the superior performer was considered to influence cardiac deceleration, which would, in turn, facilitate performance by increasing sensorimotor efficiency or the processing of task-relevant cues. Again, on a different level of analysis than that conducted by Hatfield et al. (1987), the adaptive regulation of arousal seems to be characterized by a complex interactive system.

In another illustration of the significance of efficiency within psychophysiology, Porges and colleagues (Porges, Doussard-Roosevelt, Stifter, McClenny, & Riniolo, 1999) have extensively researched the role of the vagus nerve (i.e., the tenth cranial nerve responsible for the majority of parasympathetic outflow) in behavioral transactions with the environment. They determined that vagal tone (i.e., as indexed by heart rate variability) is involved in adaptive coupling between the brain and the metabolic state of the organism. This coupling may manifest itself as an efficient transaction between the nervous system and the environment when metabolic activity of the organism is matched to environmental challenge.

PSYCHOLOGICAL STATES AND METABOLIC EFFICIENCY

Reviewing the concepts presented thus far, it becomes obvious how influential physical efficiency is in determining the outcome of a performance. It is also important to note that physical efficiency, in many instances, may be achieved as a result of being mentally efficient. There is a constant interaction between the psychological and physiological domains such that the effects of one on the other may be beneficial or destructive. W. Morgan (1985) reviewed a number of studies that supported the influence of psychogenic factors on physiological and metabolic factors during exercise. Additionally, T. Williams, Krahenbuhl, and Morgan (1991) administered the Profile of Mood States (POMS) to moderately trained runners performing at 50%, 60%, and 70% of VO_2 max to examine the effects different mood states had on running economy. Collectively, findings demonstrated that those who experienced mood states that were low in negative affect had a lower oxygen consumption rate for a given amount of work.

Hatfield et al. (1992) also conducted a study to determine how cognitive orientation influences physiological economy. They attempted to determine whether there was a causal influence of the association and disassociation strategies as originally noted in endurance athletes by W. Morgan and Pollock (1977). Interestingly, W. Morgan and Pollock determined that elite U.S. distance runners tended to focus on their bodily efforts during competition, whereas less accomplished runners tended to block out or disassociate the effort associated with exertion. Hatfield et al. reasoned that biofeedback, a strategy that can help one to attenuate physiological responses, appeared similar in principle to such associative strategies and disassociation was similar to distraction. Therefore, in a controlled laboratory setting, they examined whether physiological feedback (ventilatory effort and EMG activity) and distraction (a coincident timing task) would differentially affect the physiological economy of competitive distance runners performing immediately below ventilatory threshold. Daniels (1985) had earlier established the importance of running economy to performance outcome in endurance athletes. The results revealed a measurable effect on ventilatory effort (V_E/VO_2) for the biofeedback condition as compared to the distraction and control (i.e., no manipulation) conditions, although oxygen consumption did not differ. That is, during the feedback condition, the runners were able to maintain a similar oxygen consumption level while breathing a reduced volume of air. These findings lend strong support to the interactive relationship between mental and physical efficiency by showing how a specific cognitive strategy (i.e., associative) may alter the physiological state. It is possible that such an effect could result in a more physically efficient performance.

FUTURE RECOMMENDATIONS

Several key concerns should be addressed in future performance psychophysiological research. Technologically, most EEG research has involved only two to four electrode sites. One such development that may advance our understanding of the psychology of performance is increased spatial resolution. To date, up to 256 electrode locations have been employed to measure electrocortical activity. Although such detailed resolution may be excessive for many of the questions in performance psychology, denser electrode arrays are needed to capture the activity of the brain in a more representative manner. Another concern in this area of research is the lack of consistency in recording strategies across studies. The diversity of methodologies in kinesiological psychophysiology is problematic. Specifically, different referencing strategies (e.g., linked ears, averaged ears, vertex) can alter the spectral estimates that are derived from the recorded EEG waves. Although the specific reference used in a given study will be determined on the basis of the question being addressed by the investigators, it would seem that some reasonable degree of standardization would result in greater comparability of results across studies.

Also of concern when studying the psychology of skilled psychomotor performance is the lack of consistency in the labeling of the participants as "skilled" and "unskilled" or "expert" and "novice." It would appear problematic that different investigators assign different levels of ability to categories that are characterized by the same name. In other words, skilled performers in one investigation may not be similar in ability to those who are labeled skilled in another study. It would be helpful, when possible, to describe skill in terms of absolute behavioral criteria as opposed to the relative rankings of the groups that are included in a given study. Subscription to such an approach would resolve possible contradictions that may emerge in the results of various studies.

Finally, it would appear of major importance for future studies to determine cognitive activity from EEG by employing experimental designs that incorporate appropriate comparison conditions. In this regard, the participants should be challenged with "known" psychological tasks so that the recorded time series can then be compared to those that are obtained during psychomotor performance. Such a strategy will allow for reasonable cognitive inferences so that the psychophysiological recordings can be related to higher-level psychological functioning.

CONCLUSIONS

Generally, the psychophysiological measures that have been used in performance psychology are sensitive to both intersubject and intrasubject differences. That is, expert and novice as well as skilled and unskilled performers exhibit different electrophysiological profiles. Further, performance variability within participants is also associated with specific patterns of psychophysiological activity. These physiological distinctions have been observed in both the cognitive and affective domains and, importantly, have been associated with performance state.

Efficiency of psychomotor performance may provide a conceptual framework within kinesiological psychology to guide both research efforts and interventions employed by applied sport psychologists. The acquisition of skilled performance may undergo an adaptive process that prunes task-irrelevant processes, resulting in a more economical or efficient allocation of neural resources. Such processes may contribute significantly to the phenomenological experiences or psychological states that are central to this area of research. Because the integration of motor control and psychological processes occurs in the brain, the psychophysiological level of measurement holds promise for understanding how cognitive-affective factors influence the quality of motor behavior.

REFERENCES

Adrian, E.D., & Matthews, B.H.C. (1934). Berger rhythm: Potential changes from the occipital lobes of man. *Brain, 57,* 355–385.

Anderson, P., & Andersson, S.A. (1968). *Physiological basis of the alpha rhythm.* New York: Appleton-Century-Crofts.

Attner, P. (1984, October 1). Payton vs. Harris vs. Brown. *Sporting News, 198,* pp. 2–3.

Baumeister, R.F. (1984). Choking under pressure: Self-consciousness and paradoxical effects of incentives on skillful performance. *Journal of Personality and Social Psychology, 46,* 610–620.

Bear, M.F., Connors, B.W., & Paradiso, M.A. (1996). *Neuroscience: Exploring the brain* (pp. 374–401). Baltimore: Williams & Wilkins.

Bell, M.A., & Fox, N.A. (1996). Crawling experience is related to changes in cortical organization during infancy: Evidence from EEG coherence. *Developmental Psychobiology, 29,* 551–561.

Bernstein, N. (1967). *The coordination and regulation of movements.* London: Pergamon Press.

Breger, L. (1974). *From instinct to identity: The development of personality.* Englewood Cliffs, NJ: Prentice Hall.

Brody, E.B., Hatfield, B.D., Spalding, T.W., Frazer, M.B., & Caherty, F.J. (2000). The effect of a psyching strategy on neuromuscular activation and force production in strength-trained men. *Research Quarterly for Exercise and Sport, 71,* 162–170.

Busk, J., & Galbraith, G.C. (1975). EEG correlates of visual-motor practice in man. *Electroencephalography and Clinical Neurophysiology, 35,* 415–422.

Castiello, U., & Umilta, C. (1992). Orienting of attention in volleyball players. *International Journal of Sport Psychology, 23,* 301–310.

Challis, R.E., & Kitney, R.I. (1991). Biomedical signal processing (in four parts). Part 3: The power spectrum and coherence function. *Medical and Biological Engineering and Computing, 29,* 225–241.

Coles, M.G.H., Gratton, G., & Fabiani, M. (1990). Event-related brain potentials. In J.T. Cacioppo & L.G. Tassinary (Eds.), *Principles of psychophysiology: Physical, social and inferential elements* (pp. 413–455). New York: Cambridge University Press.

Crews, D.J., & Landers, D.M. (1993). Electroencephalographic measures of attentional patterns prior to the golf putt. *Medicine and Science in Sports and Exercise, 25,* 116–126.

Csikszentmihalyi, M. (1975). *Beyond boredom and anxiety.* San Francisco: Jossey-Bass.

Daniels, J.T. (1985). A physiologist's view of running economy. *Medicine and Science in Sport and Exercise, 17,* 332–338.

Davidson, R.J. (1988). EEG measures of cerebral asymmetry: Conceptual and methodological issues. *International Journal of Neuroscience, 39,* 71–89.

Davidson, R.J., Ekman, P., Saron, C.D., Senulis, J., & Friesen, W.V. (1990). Approach-withdrawal and cerebral asymmetry: Emotional expression and brain physiology I. *Journal of Personality and Social Psychology, 58,* 330–341.

DeVries, H.A. (1968). Efficiency of electrical activity as a physiological measure of the functional state of muscle tissue. *American Journal of Physical Medicine, 47,* 10–22.

DeVries, H.A., & Housh, T.J. (1994). *Physiology of exercise for physical education, athletics, and exercise science.* Dubuque, IA: Brown & Benchmark.

Earle, J.B. (1988). Task difficulty and EEG alpha asymmetry: An amplitude and frequency analysis. *Neuropsychobiology, 20,* 96–112.

Eimer, M. (1994). An ERP study of visual spatial priming with peripheral onsets. *Psychophysiology, 31,* 154–163.

Elbert, T., Pantev, C., Weinbruch, C., Rockstroh, B., & Taub, E. (1995). Increased cortical representation of the fingers of the left hand. *Science, 270,* 305–307.

Ericsson, K.A., Krampe, R.T., & Tesch-Römer, E. (1993). The role of deliberate practice in the acquisition of expert performance. *Psychological Review, 100,* 363–406.

Eriksen, C.W., & Yeh, Y.Y. (1985). Allocation of attention in the visual field. *Journal of Experimental Psychology: Human Perception and Performance, 11,* 583–597.

Etnier, J.L., Whitwer, S.S., Landers, D.M., Petruzzello, S.J., & Salazar, S.J. (1996). Changes in electroencephalographic activity associated with learning a novel motor task. *Research Quarterly for Exercise and Sport, 67,* 272–279.

Feltz, D.L. (1984). Self-efficacy as a cognitive mediator of athletic performance. In W.F. Straub & J.M. Williams (Eds.), *Cognitive sport psychology* (pp. 191–198). Lansing, NY: Sport Sciences Associates.

Fenz, W.D. (1975). Coping mechanisms in performance under stress. In D.M. Landers, D.V. Harris, & R.W. Christina (Eds.), *Psychology of sport and motor behavior II* (pp. 3–24). University Park: Pennsylvania State University Health, Physical Education and Recreation Series.

Fenz, W.D., & Epstein, S. (1967). Changes in gradients of skin conductance, heart rate, and respiration rate as a function of experience. *Psychosomatic Medicine, 29,* 33–51.

Fitts, P.M., & Posner, M.I. (1967). *Human performance.* Belmont, CA: Brooks/Cole.

Gel'fand, I.M., Gurfinkel, V.S., Fomin, V., & Tsetlin, M.L. (1971). *Models of the structural-functional organization of certain biological systems.* Cambridge, MA: MIT Press.

Greenough, W.T., Black, J.E., & Wallace, C. (1987). Effects of experience on brain development. *Child Development, 58,* 540–559.

Haier, R.J., Siegel, B.V., Tang, C., Abel, L., & Buchsbaum, M.S. (1992). Intelligence and changes in regional cerebral glucose metabolic rate following learning. *Intelligence, 16,* 415–426.

Hatfield, B.D., Landers, D.M., & Ray, W.J. (1984). Cognitive processes during self-paced motor performance. *Journal of Sport Psychology, 6,* 42–59.

Hatfield, B.D., Landers, D.M., & Ray, W.J. (1987). Cardiovascular-CNS interactions during a self-paced, intentional attentive state: Elite marksmanship performance. *Psychophysiology, 24,* 542–549.

Hatfield, B.D., Landers, D.M., Ray, W.J., & Daniels, F.S. (1982). An electroencephalographic study of elite rifle shooters. *American Marksmen, 7,* 6–8.

Hatfield, B.D., Spalding, T.W., Mahon, A.D., Slater, B.A., Brody, E.B., & Vaccoro, P. (1992). The effect of psychological strategies upon cardiorespiratory and muscular activity during treadmill running. *Medicine and Science in Sport and Exercise, 24,* p. 218–225.

Haufler, A.J., Spalding, T.W., Santa Maria, D.L., & Hatfield, B.D. (2000). Neurocognitive activity during a self-paced visuospatial task: Comparative EEG profiles in marksmen and novice shooters. *Biological Psychology.*

Hillman, C.H., Apparies, R.J., Janelle, C.M., & Hatfield, B.D. (2000). An electrocortical comparison of executed and rejected shots in skilled marksmen. *Biological Psychology, 52,* 71–83.

Hillyard, S.A., Luck, S.J., & Mangun, G.R. (1994). The cueing of attention to visual field locations: Analysis with ERP recording. In H.J. Heinze, T.F. Munte, & G.R. Mangun (Eds.), *Cognitive electrophysiology* (pp. 1–25). Boston: Birkhauser.

Hoffman, J.J., Loy, S.F., Shapiro, B.I., Holland, G.J., Vincent, W.J., Shaw, S., & Thompson, D.L. (1993). Specificity effects of run versus cycle training on ventilatory threshold. *European Journal of Applied Physiology, 67,* 43–47.

Hung, T.M., Santa Maria, D.L., & Hatfield, B.D. (1999). *Attentional flexibility and motor preparedness in fast-action sport athletes: An electroencephalographical study of table tennis players.* Manuscript submitted for publication.

Isaacs, K.R., Anderson, B.J., Alcantara, A.A., Black, J.E., & Greenough, W.T. (1992). Exercise and the brain: Angiogensis in the adult rat cerebellum after vigorous physical activity and motor skill learning. *Journal of Cerebral Blood Flow and Metabolism, 12,* 110–119.

James, W. (1977). Psychology (briefer course). In J.J. McDermott (Ed.), *The writings of William James* (pp. 9–21). Chicago: University of Chicago Press. (Original worked published 1892)

Janelle, C.M., Hillman, C.H., Apparies, R.J., Murray, N.P., Meili, L., Fallon, E.A., & Hatfield, B.D. (2000). Expertise differences in cortical activation and gaze behavior during rifle shooting. *Journal of Sport & Exercise Psychology, 22,* 167–182.

Jasper, H.H. (1958). Report of the committee on methods of clinical examination in electroencephalography. *Journal of Electroencephalography and Clinical Neurophysiology, 10,* 370–375.

Kandel, E.R., & Schwartz, J.H. (1985). *Principles of neural science.* New York: Elsevier.

Kelso, J.A.S., Tuller, B., & Harris, K.S. (1983). A "dynamic pattern" perspective on the control and coordination of movement.

In P. MacNeilage (Ed.), *The production of speech* (pp. 137–173). New York: Springer-Verlag.

Kerick, S.E., Iso-Ahola, S.E., & Hatfield, B.D. (2000). Psychological momentum in target shooting: Cortical, cognitive-affective, and behavioral responses. *Journal of Sport & Exercise Psychology, 22,* 1–20.

Konttinen, N., & Lyytinen, H. (1992). Physiology of preparation: Brain slow waves, heart rate, and respiration preceding triggering in rifle shooting. *International Journal of Sport Psychology, 23,* 110–127.

Konttinen, N., & Lyytinen, H. (1993). Individual variability in brain slow wave profiles in skilled sharpshooters during the aiming period in rifle shooting. *Journal of Sport & Exercise Psychology, 15,* 275–289.

Konttinen, N., Lyytinen, H., & Era, P. (1999). Brain slow potentials and postural sway behavior during sharpshooting performance. *Journal of Motor Behavior, 31,* 11–20.

Kraemer, W.J. (1994). General adaptations to resistance and endurance training programs. In T.R. Baechle (Ed.), *Essentials of strength training and conditioning* (pp. 127–150). Champaign, IL: Human Kinetics.

Kuhlman, W.N. (1978). Functional topography of the human mu rhythm. *Electroencephalography and Clinical Neurophysiology, 43,* 83–93.

Lacey, B.C., & Lacey, J.L. (1978). Two-way communication between the heart and the brain: Significance of time within the cardiac cycle. *American Psychologist, 33,* 99–113.

Landers, D.M. (1980). The arousal-performance relationship revisited. *Research Quarterly for Exercise and Sport, 51,* 77–90.

Landers, D.M., Christina, R.W., Hatfield, B.D., Daniels, F.S., & Doyle, L.A. (1980). Moving competitive shooting into the scientist's lab. *American Rifleman, 128,* 36–37, 76–77.

Landers, D.M., Han, M., Salazar, W., Petruzzello, S.J., Kubitz, K.A., & Gannon, T.L. (1994). Effect of learning on electroencephalographic and electrocardiographic patterns in novice archers. *International Journal of Sport Psychology, 22,* 56–71.

Landers, D.M., Petruzzello, S.J., Salazar, W., Crews, D.J., Kubitz, K.A., Gannon, T.L., & Han, M. (1991). The influence of electrocortical biofeedback and performance in pre-elite archers. *Medicine and Science in Sports and Exercise, 23,* 123–129.

Lawton, G.W., Hung, T.M., Saarela, P., & Hatfield, B.D. (1998). Electroencephalography and mental states associated with elite performance. *Journal of Sport & Exercise Psychology, 20,* 35–53.

Lopes da Silva, F. (1991). Neural mechanisms underlying brain waves: From neural membranes to networks. *Electroencephalography and Clinical Neurophysiology, 79,* 81–93.

Mangun, G.R., & Hillyard, S.A. (1991). Modulations of sensory-evoked brain potentials indicate changes in perceptual processing during visual-spatial priming. *Journal of Experimental Psychology: Human Perception & Performance, 17,* 1057–1074.

Mangun, G.R., Hillyard, S.A., & Luck, S.J. (1993). Electrocortical substrates of visual selective attention. In D.E. Meyer & S. Kornblum (Eds.), *Attention and performance XIV: Synergies in experimental psychology, artificial intelligence, and cognitive neuroscience* (pp. 219–243). Cambridge, MA: MIT Press.

Martens, R. (1977). *Sport Competition Anxiety Test.* Champaign, IL: Human Kinetics.

Mazziotta, J.C., & Phelps, M.E. (1985). Metabolic evidence of lateralized cerebral function demonstrated by positron emission tomography in patients with neuropsychiatric disorders and normal individuals. In D.F. Benson & E. Ziabel (Eds.), *The dual brain: Hemispheric specialization in humans* (pp. 181–192). New York: Guilford Press.

McArdle, W.D., Katch, F.I., & Katch, V.L. (1986). *Exercise physiology: Energy, nutrition, and human performance.* Philadelphia: Lea & Febiger.

Meichenbaum, D. (1977). *Cognitive-behavior modification: An integrative approach.* New York: Plenum Press.

Morgan, D., Daniels, J., Carlson, P., Filarski, K., & Landle, K. (1991). Use of recovery VO_2 to predict running economy. *European Journal of Applied Physiology, 62,* 420–423.

Morgan, W.P. (1985). Psychogenic factors and exercise metabolism: A review. *Medicine and Science in Sports and Exercise, 17,* 309–316.

Morgan, W.P., O'Connor, P.J., Ellickson, K.A., & Bradley, P.W. (1988). Personality structure, mood states, and performance in elite distance runners. *International Journal of Sport Psychology, 19,* 247–269.

Morgan, W.P., & Pollock, M.L. (1977). Psychologic characterization of the elite distance runner. *Annals of the New York Academy of Sciences, 301,* 482–503.

Murphy, A. (1992, October 12). Same old story. *Sports Illustrated, 77,* 13–16.

Newland, D.E. (1993). *An introduction to random vibrations, spectral, and wavelet analysis.* New York: Longman Scientific and Technical.

Nougier, V., Ripoll, H., & Stein, J. (1989). Orienting of attention with highly skilled athletes. *International Journal of Sport Psychology, 20,* 205–223.

Nougier, V., Stein, J., & Azemar, G. (1990). Covert orienting of attention and motor preparation processes as a factor of studying fencing. *Journal of Human Movement Study, 19,* 251–272.

Nougier, V., Stein, J., & Bonnel, A. (1991). Information processing in sport and orienting of attention. *International Journal of Sport Psychology, 22,* 307–327.

Nunez, P.L. (1995). Neuromodulation of neocortical dynamics. In P.L. Nunez (Ed.), *Neocortical dynamics and human EEG rhythms* (pp. 591–627). New York: Oxford University Press.

Pfurtscheller, G., & Klimesch, W. (1991). Event-related desynchronization during motor behavior and visual information processing. *Event-Related Brain Research, 42*(EEG Suppl.), 58–65.

Pfurtscheller, G., Stancak, A., & Neuper, C. (1996). Event-related synchronization (ERS) in the alpha band: An electrophysiological correlate of cortical idling. A review. *International Journal of Psychophysiology, 24,* 39–46.

Porges, S.W., & Bohrer, R.E. (1990). The analysis of periodic processes in psychophysiological research. In J.T. Cacioppo & L.G. Tassinary (Eds.), *Principles of psychophysiology: Physical, social and inferential elements* (pp. 708–753). New York: Cambridge University Press.

Porges, S.W., Doussard-Roosevelt, J.A., Stifter, C.A., McClenny, B.D., & Riniolo, T.C. (1999). Sleep state and vagal regulation of heart period patterns in the human newborn: An extension of the polyvagal theory. *Psychophysiology, 36,* 14–21.

Posner, M.I. (1980). Orienting of attention. *Quarterly Journal of Experimental Psychology, 32,* 3–25.

Posner, M.I., & Raichle, M. (1991). *Images of mind.* New York: Scientific American Books.

Pullum, B. (1977). Psychology of shooting. *Schiessportschule Dialogues, 1,* 1–17.

Ramirez, R.W. (1985). *The FFT: Fundamentals and concepts.* Englewood Cliffs, NJ: Prentice-Hall.

Ray, W.J. (1990). The electrocortical system. In J.T. Cacioppo & L.G. Tassinary (Eds.), *Principles of psychophysiology: Physical, social and inferential elements* (pp. 385–412). New York: Cambridge University Press.

Ray, W.J., & Cole, H.W. (1985). EEG alpha activity reflects attentional demands, and beta activity reflects emotional and cognitive processes. *Science, 228,* 750–752.

Rebert, C.S., Low, D.W., & Larsen, F. (1984). Differential hemispheric activation during complex visuomotor performance: Alpha trends and theta. *Biological Psychology, 19,* 159–168.

Saarela, P. (1999). *The effects of mental stress on cerebral hemispheric asymmetry and psychomotor performance in skilled marksmen.* Unpublished doctoral dissertation, University of Maryland, College Park.

Salazar, W., Landers, D.M., Petruzzello, S.J., Han, M., Crews, D.J., & Kubitz, K.A. (1990). Hemispheric asymmetry, cardiac response, and performance in elite archers. *Research Quarterly for Exercise and Sport, 61,* 351–359.

Selye, H. (1976). *The stress of life.* New York: McGraw-Hill.

Smith, M.E., McEvoy, L.K., & Gevins, A. (1999). Neurophysiological indices of strategy development and skill acquisition. *Cognitive Brain Research, 7,* 389–404.

Sparrow, W.A. (1983). The efficiency of skilled performance. *Journal of Motor Behavior, 15,* 237–261.

Steriade, M., Gloor, P., Llinas, R.R., Lopes da Silva, F.H., & Mesulam, M.M. (1990). Basic mechanisms of cerebral rhythmic activities. *Electroencephalography and Clinical Neurophysiology, 76,* 481–508.

Sterman, M.B., & Mann, C.A. (1995). Concepts and applications of EEG analysis in aviation performance evaluation. *Biological Psychology, 40,* 115–130.

Thatcher, R.W., & John, E.R. (1977). The genesis of alpha rhythms and EEG synchronizing mechanisms. In E.R. John & R.W. Thatcher (Eds.), *Foundations of cognitive processes* (Vol. 1, pp. 53–82). Hillsdale, NJ: Erlbaum.

Thelen, E., Kelso, J.A.S., & Fogel, A. (1987). Self-organizing systems and infant motor development. *Developmental Review, 7,* 39–65.

Van Voorhis, S., & Hillyard, S.A. (1977). Visual evoked potentials and selective attention to points in space. *Perception and Psychophysics, 22,* 54–62.

Vickers, J.N. (1996a). Control of visual attention during the basketball free throw. *American Journal of Sports Medicine, 24,* S93–S97.

Vickers, J.N. (1996b). Visual control while aiming at a far target. *Journal of Experimental Psychology: Human Perception and Performance, 22,* 342–354.

Vickers, J.N., & Adolphe, R.M. (1997). Gaze behavior during a ball tracking and aiming skill. *International Journal of Sports Vision, 4,* 18–27.

Weinberg, R.S. (1978). The effects of success and failure on the patterning of neuromuscular energy. *Journal of Motor Behavior, 10,* 53–61.

Williams, T.J., Krahenbuhl, G.S., & Morgan, D.W. (1991). Mood state and running economy in moderately trained male runners. *Medicine and Science in Sport and Exercise, 23,* 727–731.

Williams, J.M., & Krane, V. (1998). Psychological characteristics of peak performance. In J.M. Williams (Ed.), *Applied sport psychology* (pp. 158–170). Mountain View, CA: Mayfield.

Withers, R.T., Sherman, W.M., Miller, J.M., & Costill, D.L. (1981). Specificity of the anaerobic threshold in endurance trained cyclists and runners. *European Journal of Applied Physiology, 47,* 93–104.

Zimmerman, P. (1979, November 26). All dressed up: Nowhere to go. *Sports Illustrated, 51,* 38–40.

PART III

Motivation

CHAPTER 15

Intrinsic and Extrinsic Motivation in Sport and Exercise
A Review Using the Hierarchical Model of Intrinsic
and Extrinsic Motivation

ROBERT J. VALLERAND and FRANÇOIS L. ROUSSEAU

If athletes are to meet successfully the many challenges they encounter, they need the psychological strength to help them sustain their drive toward excellence in sport. Motivation represents an important ingredient underlying this psychological force (Vallerand & Losier, 1999), and it comes as no surprise that elite athletes and coaches alike underscore its importance in sport (Gould, 1982).

The concept of motivation has been defined as "the hypothetical construct used to describe the internal and/or external forces that produce the initiation, direction, intensity, and persistence of behavior" (Vallerand & Thill, 1993, p. 18; translated from French). Over the years, several theoretical positions have been formulated in the field of motivation (see Ford, 1992). Two major traditions can be identified. One posits that individuals are passive organisms that are moved by instincts (Freud, 1940/1969), by primary and secondary drives (Hull, 1943), or by a history of stimulus-reinforcement conditioning (Skinner, 1953). This represents a mechanistic position to the study of motivation that assumes that individuals are passive and cannot take matters into their own hand. They only react to either internal or external stimuli (Weiner, 1972). On the other hand, a second position proposes that individuals are very active in their interaction with the environment (e.g., White, 1959). Indeed, according to this perspective, individuals can decide by themselves to explore their environment without internal or external prodding. These two camps have led to the study of intrinsic and extrinsic motivation.

Intrinsic motivation pertains to behaviors performed due to interest and enjoyment. For example, a woman who engages in roller skating because of the fun she experiences while doing so displays intrinsic motivation. In contrast, extrinsic motivation refers to behaviors carried out to attain contingent outcomes that lie outside the activity itself (Deci, 1971; Vallerand & Ratelle, in press). Athletes who engage in competitive sports for the prestige and honors they may derive from their participation represent examples of extrinsic motivation. A third motivational concept, amotivation, has been posited recently by theorists (Deci & Ryan, 1985) to capture the relative absence of motivation. Athletes who stop training because they believe that it will not help them in the upcoming event display a high level of amotivation. Much research has shown that intrinsic and extrinsic motivation, as well as amotivation, represent useful concepts leading to a better understanding of motivational processes in sport and exercise settings (see Ryan, Vallerand, & Deci, 1984; Vallerand, Deci, & Ryan, 1987; Vallerand & Reid, 1990).

Since the first intrinsic motivation experiment (Deci, 1971), over 800 publications have focused on the concept of intrinsic/extrinsic motivation (Vallerand, 1997). Close examination of the research conducted over the years reveals that these investigations can be grouped into three major categories (Vallerand, 1997). The first group of studies is associated with the link between a global motivational

Preparation of this chapter was facilitated through grants from the Social Sciences and Humanities Research Council of Canada (SSHRC), Le Fonds pour la Formation des Chercheurs et l'Aide à la Recherche (FCAR Québec), and the Université du Québec à Montréal (UQAM) to the first author and SSHRC and UQAM fellowships to the second author. Reprint requests and any information concerning this article may be addressed to Robert J. Vallerand, Laboratoire de Recherche sur le Comportement Social, Département de Psychologie, Université du Québec à Montréal, C.P. 8888, Station "Centre-Ville," Montréal, QC, Canada H3C 3P8, e-mail: vallerand.robert_J@uqam.ca.

orientation (similar to a personality trait) and psychological correlates. For instance, Vallerand and Blanchard (1998b) reported a negative correlation between global intrinsic motivational orientation and negative affectivity in exercise participants. The second group of studies has dealt with the determinants and consequences of generalized levels of intrinsic and extrinsic motivation toward specific life contexts, such as education, interpersonal relationships, and leisure/sport. For example, Pelletier et al. (1995) have shown that when coaches allow for the active engagement of their players (providing choice within reasonable limits), athletes' general intrinsic motivation toward their sport is enhanced. The third group of studies is related to the immediate effects of situational variables such as feedback, rewards, and surveillance on one's current level of intrinsic and/or extrinsic motivation. An example is the study by Weinberg and Ragan (1979), in which it was shown that competition can undermine intrinsic motivation toward a laboratory task.

Various conceptual frameworks have been advanced to explain the major findings (e.g., Csikszentmihalyi & Nakamura, 1989; Deci & Ryan, 1985, 1991; Harter, 1978; Lepper & Greene, 1978). For instance, self-determination theory (SDT; Deci & Ryan, in press) describes the conditions under which social-contextual factors will promote intrinsic motivation and internalized forms of extrinsic motivation. Furthermore, the theory posits that it is these types of motivation that will produce positive outcomes.

Although the above theories, especially SDT, have led to breakthroughs in the understanding of intrinsic and extrinsic motivational processes, they do not provide an integrated framework of the relations among the three levels of motivation discussed above. Recently, Vallerand (1997, in press; Vallerand & Blanchard, 1999; Vallerand & Grouzet, in press; Vallerand & Perreault, 1999; Vallerand & Ratelle, in press) has posited a model that proposes such an integration. This model takes into consideration the variety of ways motivation is represented in the individual, the relationships among these representations, and their determinants and consequences. The model is presented in Figure 15.1.

The purpose of this chapter is to present this model, called the hierarchical model of intrinsic and extrinsic motivation, to review and derive implications from sport and exercise research. The model provides a coherent framework to conduct such a review. In addition, it will be shown that the model also leads to new perspectives on the study of intrinsic and extrinsic motivation. Furthermore, the model embraces several of the elements of SDT (Deci & Ryan, 1985, 1991). In the following three sections, reference is made to

the model to review research with respect to the determinants and consequences of situational, contextual, and global motivation. The subsequent section contains a review of studies that have involved the testing of either the interplay between motivation at different levels in the hierarchy or an integrative causal sequence.

A HIERARCHICAL MODEL OF INTRINSIC AND EXTRINSIC MOTIVATION

The hierarchical model of intrinsic and extrinsic motivation provides a framework that seeks to integrate the findings on intrinsic and extrinsic motivation research. It comprises five postulates and five corollaries. Taken together, these postulates and corollaries explain (1) the motivational determinants and consequences at three levels of generality, and (2) the interactions among motivation at the three levels of generality, while taking into account the complexity of human motivation. The model is described next.

Multidimensional Perspective of Motivation

The first issue of interest is that humans are motivationally complex. For that reason, Postulate 1 in the hierarchical model proposes that a complete analysis of motivation must include three important concepts: intrinsic motivation, extrinsic motivation, and amotivation.

Intrinsic motivation refers to performing an activity for itself and the pleasure and satisfaction derived from participation (Deci, 1971). Vallerand and his colleagues (Vallerand, Blais, Brière, & Pelletier, 1989; Vallerand et al., 1992, 1993) posited the existence of three types of intrinsic motivation: intrinsic motivation to know, intrinsic motivation to accomplish, and intrinsic motivation to experience stimulation. Intrinsic motivation to know refers to engaging in an activity for the pleasure and satisfaction that one experiences while learning, exploring, or trying to understand something new. Basketball players who practice because they enjoy learning new ways to apply pressure defense as a team display intrinsic motivation to know. Intrinsic motivation to accomplish pertains to engaging in a given activity for the pleasure and satisfaction experienced while one is *attempting* to accomplish or create something, or to surpass oneself. Thus, the important aspect is the process of trying to accomplish something and not the outcome per se. Tennis players who work on their serve for the pleasure they experience while *trying* to hit an ace display intrinsic motivation to accomplish. Finally, intrinsic motivation to experience stimulation is at work when one engages in an activity to experience pleasant sensations

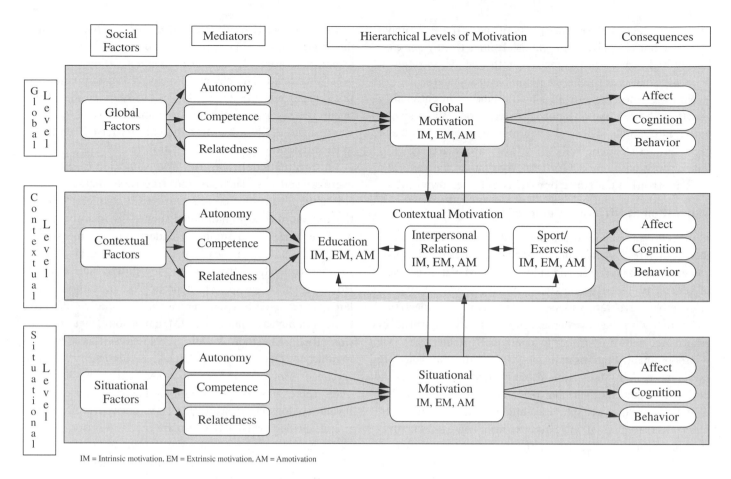

IM = Intrinsic motivation, EM = Extrinsic motivation, AM = Amotivation

Figure 15.1   The hierarchical model of intrinsic and extrinsic motivation as applied to sport and exercise. From Vallerand (in press).

associated mainly with one's senses (e.g., sensory and aesthetic pleasure). Swimmers who swim because they enjoy the pleasant sensations they experience while their body glides through water display this type of intrinsic motivation. This tripartite distinction highlights the different fashions in which intrinsic motivation may be experienced in sport and exercise. In addition, it can lead to the enhanced prediction of behavior because research has shown that engagement in specific sport activities is related to the three types of intrinsic motivation (Vallerand & Brière, 1990).

Extrinsic motivation refers to engaging in an activity as a means to an end and not for its own sake. There are different types of extrinsic motivation, some of which are more self-determined in nature (Deci & Ryan, 1985, 1991; Ryan, Connell, & Grolnick, 1992; Vallerand, 1997). In other words, individuals may choose to perform an activity even though they do not do it for pleasure. Deci and Ryan (1985) have proposed four types of extrinsic motivation. External regulation refers to behavior that is regulated through external means, such as rewards and constraints.

For instance, an athlete might say "I'm going to today's practice because I want the coach to let me play tomorrow." With introjected regulation, individuals begin to internalize the reasons for their actions. However, this type of extrinsic motivation is not self-determined because individuals still experience pressure, although the pressure is self-imposed (e.g., through guilt and anxiety). An example of introjected regulation is when athletes go to a practice because they would feel guilty if they missed it. It is only with identified regulation that behavior is emitted out of choice. When they display identified regulation, athletes highly value an activity, judge it to be important, and choicefully engage in it. The activity is then performed freely even if it is not pleasant in itself. An example of identified regulation is a soccer player who does not like weight lifting but who nevertheless chooses to do it because she knows that building her strength will allow her to become a better player. Finally, integrated regulation also involves emitting an activity choicefully; however, in this case, the choice represents a harmonious part of the individual. In other words, people's choices are made as a function of their coherence with other aspects of the self. An example is the ice hockey player who gladly decides to stay home on Friday night instead of going out with friends, in order to be in top shape for the big game on Saturday night.

Finally, amotivation refers to the lack of intentionality and thus the relative absence of motivation. When amotivated, individuals experience feelings of incompetence and expectancies of uncontrollability. They are relatively without purpose with respect to the activity and therefore have little motivation (intrinsic or extrinsic) to perform it.

Motivation at Different Levels of Generality

A second issue of interest is that motivation must be examined at different levels. Thus, Postulate 2 states that intrinsic and extrinsic motivation and amotivation exist at three levels of generality: global, contextual, and situational. Motivation at the global level refers to a general motivational orientation to interact with the environment in an intrinsic, extrinsic, or amotivated way. It is similar to a personality trait, where one is predominantly intrinsically or extrinsically motivated, or even amotivated. Motivation at the contextual level is an individual's usual motivational orientation toward a specific context, or a "distinct sphere of human activity" (Emmons, 1995). Research on intrinsic and extrinsic contextual motivation has typically focused on three contexts: education or work, interpersonal relationships, and leisure (of which sport is an important part; see Vallerand, 1997). Finally, motivation at the situational level refers to motivation individuals experience when engaging in a specific activity at a specific moment in time. Situational motivation refers to a motivational state. It is important to distinguish among these three different levels, as such a conceptualization provides a more refined understanding of motivational processes involved in human behavior.

Postulate 2 underscores the fact that it is insufficient to discuss general motivation. Instead, reference needs to be made to a collection of motivations that vary in levels of generality (and in types). Thus, to gain a better understanding of motivation displayed by individuals, it is essential to look at different types of motivation (Postulate 1) and motivation at the three levels of generality (Postulate 2; Vallerand, 1997).

Assessing Motivation

It is important to highlight recent methodological advances that have led to the development of scales to assess the different motivations at the situational, contextual, and global levels. At the situational level, the Situational Motivation Scale (SIMS; Guay, Vallerand, & Blanchard, 2000), which measures intrinsic motivation (IM; without distinguishing the three types of IM), identified and external types of external motivation (EM), as well as amotivation (AM), has been developed. The choice to measure only four motivational types was dictated by the need to keep the scale brief to capture situational motivation in many lab and field situations. Indices of reliability and validity have been found to be satisfactory (Guay et al., 2000).

Other situational measures have been used in sport and exercise settings, such as the free-time measure (also called the free-choice period; Deci, 1971), which measures the amount of time an individual spends on an activity during free time. The assumption underlying this measure is that individuals intrinsically motivated toward an activity will return to the activity when they do not have to do it. However, this measurement approach is not without problems, as research has shown that the free-choice measure, besides being associated with IM, can also reflect introjection (Ryan, Koestner, & Deci, 1991) as well as identified regulation (Deci, Eghrari, Patrick, & Leone, 1994). The Intrinsic Motivation Inventory (McAuley & Tammen, 1989) represents another situational measure. However, the inventory does not measure the different types of motivation described previously (see Vallerand & Fortier, 1998).

Scales assessing motivation at the contextual level have also been developed. Because research revealed that college students rated education, leisure, and interpersonal relationships as their three main life contexts (Blais, Vallerand, Gagnon, Brière, & Pelletier, 1990), scales were developed to measure motivation in these contexts. The Academic Motivation Scale (AMS; Vallerand et al., 1989, 1992, 1993) assesses contextual motivation toward education; the Interpersonal Motivation Inventory (IMI; Blais, Vallerand, Pelletier, & Brière, 1994) assesses contextual motivation in interpersonal relationships; and the Leisure Motivation Scale (LMS; Pelletier, Vallerand, Green-Demers, Blais, & Brière, 1996) measures contextual motivation toward leisure activities. Because sport represents an important type of leisure activity, a scale to assess sport motivation both in French (the Echelle de Motivation dans les Sports; EMS; Brière, Vallerand, Blais, & Pelletier, 1995) and English (Sport Motivation Scale; SMS; Pelletier et al., 1995) was developed. All of these scales assess the seven motivational constructs described earlier (the three types of intrinsic motivation; identified, introjected, and external regulation; and amotivation. Integrated regulation has not been assessed because it does not seem to be present in young adults). Indices of reliability and validity are adequate for the scales (Li & Harmer, 1996; Vallerand, 1997).

Other scales assessing contextual motivation toward sport include the Motivation for Physical Activity Measure–Revised (e.g., Frederick, in press) and the Motivational Orientation in Sport Scale (Weiss, Bredemeier, & Shewchuk, 1985). However, these scales do not assess the different types of motivation proposed by Vallerand et al. (1989, 1992) and Deci and Ryan (1985).

One should also note that scales such as the Behavioural Regulation in Exercise Questionnaire (BREQ; Mullan, Markland, & Ingledew, 1997) and the Exercise Motivation Scale (EMS; Li, 1999) have been developed to assess contextual motivation toward exercise. These scales measure the various constructs described earlier and have shown high levels of validity and reliability (see Li, 1999; Mullan et al., 1997).

Finally, at the global level, the Global Motivation Scale (GMS; Guay, Blais, Vallerand, & Pelletier, 1999) has been developed. It assesses the three different types of IM and the identified, introjected, and external types of EM, as well as AM toward life in general. Results with the GMS indicate that the scale is both reliable and valid. Furthermore, the different subscales of the GMS were found to be unrelated to social desirability (as assessed by the Social Desirability Scale; Crowne & Marlowe, 1960).

A final element to be mentioned with respect to the assessment of intrinsic and extrinsic motivation and amotivation is that, sometimes, researchers combine the different subscales into a self-determination index (e.g., Fortier, Vallerand, & Guay, 1995; Grolnick & Ryan, 1987; Vallerand & Bissonnette, 1992; Vallerand, Fortier, & Guay, 1997). This is done by specifically weighting and adding the scores of the subscales so as to derive a single score. Because the various types of motivation are theoretically posited to lie on a continuum of self-determination from intrinsic motivation to integrated, identified, introjected, and external regulation, and to amotivation (Deci & Ryan, 1985, 1991), weights are given to the motivational items according to their respective placement on this continuum.[1]

Obviously, the higher the scores on the self-determined forms of motivation (i.e., intrinsic motivation and integrated and identified regulation) and the lower the scores on the non-self-determined forms of motivation (i.e., amotivation and external and introjected regulation), the more self-determined the overall index. Individuals with a high positive score are described as having a self-determined motivational profile; those who have a negative score are portrayed as having a non-self-determined motivational profile. This index, which has been used in some of the studies reviewed in this chapter, displays high levels of reliability and validity (e.g., Blais et al., 1990; Fortier, Vallerand, & Guay, 1995; Grolnick & Ryan, 1987; Ryan & Connell, 1989; Vallerand & Bissonnette, 1992; Vallerand, Fortier, & Guay, 1997).

Motivation as a Social Phenomenon

A third issue of interest is that motivation is a social phenomenon. Corollary 3.1 of the hierarchical model states that motivation can result from social factors that are either global, contextual, or situational, depending on the level of generality. Global social factors are so pervasive that they are present in most aspects of a person's life. An example of a global factor would be a residence for adolescent elite athletes. Contextual social factors are present on a general or recurrent basis in one specific life context but not in another. For example, a controlling coach would influence an adolescent's motivation toward sport but not toward education. Finally, situational social factors are present at a given point in time but not on a permanent basis (e.g., receiving positive feedback from the coach after completing a great catch in baseball).

Corollary 3.2 is closely related to Corollary 3.1. In line with the work of several theorists (deCharms, 1968; Deci & Ryan, 1985; White, 1959), it states that the impact of social factors on motivation is mediated by perceptions of competence, autonomy, and relatedness. This means that motivation is not influenced by social factors per se, but by

[1] The self-determination index is calculated as follows: Intrinsic motivation, integrated, and identified regulation items are assigned the weights of +3, +2, and +1, respectively, because they represent self-determined forms of motivation (Deci & Ryan, 1985). Amotivation, external, and introjected regulation items, because they are conceptualized as less self-determined forms of motivation, are assigned the weights of −3, −2, and −1, respectively. All three types of intrinsic motivation are given the same weight (+3). The total for the three types of intrinsic motivation is divided by 3 to make it comparable to the other scales.

If integrated regulation is not used in the index, intrinsic motivation and identified regulation are respectively given the weights of +2 and +1, and amotivation is given the weight of −2. Introjected and external regulation are then added up, divided by 2, and given the weight of −1. In both self-determination indices, the total score reflects the person's relative level of self-determined motivation. A positive score indicates that the person's motivational profile is relatively self-determined, whereas a negative score reflects the presence of a relatively non-self-determined motivational profile.

the way individuals *interpret* those factors in terms of facilitating their needs for competence (feeling efficient), autonomy (feeling free to make choices), and relatedness (feeling connected to significant others). These needs are essential for individuals because they allow them to flourish and to experience psychological growth (see Deci & Ryan, in press). People will then be inherently motivated to engage in activities that facilitate these needs. Thus, motivation is posited to be influenced by social factors at each of the three levels of the hierarchy (Corollary 3.1). That relationship, however, is mediated by perceptions of competence, autonomy, and relatedness (Corollary 3.2).

Motivation as an Intrapersonal Phenomenon

Motivation is also an intrapersonal phenomenon. According to Corollary 3.3, motivation at one level of the hierarchy also results from top-down effects of motivation at the proximal level higher up in the hierarchy. Thus, having a high level of intrinsic motivation toward sport (at the contextual level) should lead an athlete to be intrinsically motivated toward his or her sport at one given point in time (at the situational level).

Moreover, the dynamic nature of the relationship among motivation at different levels can result not only in top-down effects, but also in bottom-up effects. Thus, Postulate 4 states that there is a recursive bottom-up relationship between motivation at a given level and motivation at the next higher level in the hierarchy. For example, an athlete repeatedly experiencing situational intrinsic motivation in a particular sport should eventually develop a higher contextual intrinsic motivation toward sports in general.

Corollary 3.3 and Postulate 4 show that intrapersonal phenomena are important to consider when dealing with the prediction of motivation. Such effects can take place from top to bottom (Corollary 3.3) or from bottom to top (Postulate 4). As such, these theoretical propositions allow for a more comprehensive integration of the personality perspective in the prediction of motivation changes and development.

Motivational Consequences

A final point of interest with respect to motivation is that it leads to three important consequences: affective, cognitive, and behavioral (Postulate 5; Vallerand, 1997). According to Corollary 5.1, consequences (of the three types) are decreasingly positive from intrinsic motivation to amotivation.

This influence of motivation on consequences can occur at all three levels of the hierarchical model. Thus,

Corollary 5.2 states that the degree of generality of the consequences depends on the level of the motivation that has produced them. For instance, consequences at the contextual level may vary from context to context as a function of the relevant contextual motivation. An individual may generally experience positive consequences (e.g., fun and enjoyment) from his or her engagement in school and interpersonal activities, but experience negative consequences in sport (e.g., frustration, lack of concentration) because his or her motivation in sport is extrinsic (external regulation) in nature. Therefore, as research reveals (e.g., Amabile, 1985), motivation does not appear to be an epiphenomenon because it can lead to important outcomes.

In summary, the hierarchical model of intrinsic and extrinsic motivation deals with at least two important elements. First, it identifies the psychological mechanisms underlying motivational changes. Of particular interest is the demonstration of the need to (1) consider different types of motivation (i.e., intrinsic and extrinsic motivation and amotivation); (2) examine motivation at three levels of generality (i.e., situational, contextual, and global); and (3) take into account the dynamic relationships among motivation at different levels of the hierarchical model (e.g., top-down and bottom-up effects). Moreover, the hierarchical model also provides a better understanding of motivational consequences. Table 15.1 summarizes the postulates and corollaries of the hierarchical model.

Second, the hierarchical model also provides a rich framework to make sense of existing knowledge on intrinsic and extrinsic motivation. It is this same framework that will be used in this chapter to review the literature on intrinsic and extrinsic motivation in sport and exercise. More specifically, research will be reviewed according to each of the three levels of motivation: situational, contextual, and global. Moreover, at each level of generality, studies concerned with motivational determinants will be presented first, followed by the studies examining motivational consequences. Integrative studies will be presented in the final section. Two types of integrative studies will be reviewed: (1) those examining motivation at two or more levels of generality, and (2) those that deal with the "social factors → motivation → consequences" sequence proposed by the hierarchical model.

RESEARCH ON MOTIVATION AT THE SITUATIONAL LEVEL

As discussed previously, situational motivation refers to the motivation individuals experience while engaging in a

Table 15.1   Postulates and Corollaries of the Hierarchical Model of Intrinsic and Extrinsic Motivation

Postulate 1	A complete analysis of motivation must include intrinsic and extrinsic motivation and amotivation.
Postulate 2	Intrinsic and extrinsic motivation exist at three levels of generality: global, contextual, and situational.
Postulate 3	Motivation is determined by social factors and top-down effects from motivation at the proximal level higher up in the hierarchy.
Corollary 3.1	Motivation can result from social factors that are either global, contextual, or situational depending on the level of generality.
Corollary 3.2	The impact of social factors on motivation is mediated by perceptions of competence, autonomy, and relatedness.
Corollary 3.3	Motivation results from top-down effects from motivation at the proximal level higher up in the hierarchy.
Postulate 4	There is a recursive bottom-up relationship between motivation at a given level and motivation at the next higher level in the hierarchy.
Postulate 5	Motivation leads to important consequences.
Corollary 5.1	Consequences are decreasingly positive from intrinsic motivation to amotivation.
Corollary 5.2	Motivational consequences exist at the three levels of the hierarchy, and the degree of generality of the consequences depends on the level of the motivation that has produced them.

given activity at a specific point in time. Vallerand (1997, in press) refers to situational motivation as a motivational state rather than a trait. This means that an individual's situational motivation for an activity could be intrinsic one day, but extrinsic (e.g., external regulation) the next. An example would be the tennis player who is practicing her backhand at 3:00 P.M. on a Saturday for the sheer pleasure of executing the movement and feeling her racket hit the ball. Although at that specific moment she is intrinsically motivated, she may have been extrinsically motivated to practice the same movement the previous day (she may have felt coerced by her coach to do it). In this section, the studies dealing with the determinants and consequences of situational motivation in sport and exercise are reviewed.

Determinants

Much laboratory research involving nonsport and nonphysical activity tasks has shown that social factors such as rewards (e.g., Deci, 1971; Ryan, Mims, & Koestner, 1983; deadlines (e.g., Amabile, DeJong, & Lepper, 1976; Dollinger & Reader, 1983), evaluation (e.g., Benware & Deci, 1984; Harackiewicz, Manderlink, & Sansone, 1984), surveillance (e.g., Lepper & Greene, 1975; Pittman, Davey,

Alafat, Wetherill, & Kramer, 1980), and competition (e.g., Deci, Betley, Kahle, Abrams, & Porac, 1981; Reeve & Deci, 1996) can undermine situational intrinsic motivation. Laboratory research involving tasks associated with sport or exercise has yielded similar findings. Thus, athletes or participants who engage in a particular sport-related activity to receive a trophy or a reward display a decrease in situational intrinsic motivation as assessed by self-report scales (e.g., Halliwell, 1978; Thomas & Tennant, 1978) and the free-choice measure (Orlick & Mosher, 1978).

Another social factor that has been found to affect situational motivation is competition. Competition is an integral part of sport. It allows athletes to measure their abilities against others in a particular activity. Consequently, in the context of competitive sport, the focus is often on beating the opponent and not on the task itself (e.g., running in the 100-meter run). Initial research using a cognitive task has shown that such a focus undermines intrinsic motivation (Deci, Betley, et al., 1981). Vallerand, Gauvin, and Halliwell (1986b) showed that this conclusion also applies to sport-related tasks. In their laboratory study, 10- to 12-year-old children who engaged in a balancing task (i.e., the stabilometer) with the explicit goal to beat other participants displayed lower levels of intrinsic motivation than participants who simply tried to do their best. Thus, competition undermined children's intrinsic motivation toward the motor task.

Winning or losing a competition represents another potent social determinant of motivation. Research in sport reveals that winners (e.g., Vallerand, Gauvin, & Halliwell, 1986a; Weinberg & Ragan, 1979) and those who subjectively feel that they have done well in competition (McAuley & Tammen, 1989) display higher levels of intrinsic motivation than losers and those who feel that they have not done well. Clearly, competition represents a potent social factor that can influence sport motivation.

Finally, receiving positive and negative performance feedback (Vallerand & Reid, 1984, 1988; Whitehead & Corbin, 1991b) has also been found to influence participants' situational motivation. By providing athletes with feedback about their strengths and weaknesses, coaches, fitness instructors, and physical education teachers may modify athletes' situational intrinsic motivation. For example, Thill and Mouanda (1990) hypothesized that handball players receiving bogus negative verbal feedback (indicating failure) after performing suspension throws (a task they are familiar with) would report lower levels of situational intrinsic motivation than players receiving bogus positive verbal feedback (indicating success). Results supported the hypothesis.

Why do factors such as rewards, competition, and performance feedback influence athletes' intrinsic and extrinsic motivation? According to the hierarchical model and SDT (Deci & Ryan, 1985, 1991), situational social factors influence motivation through their impact on one's perceptions of competence, autonomy, and relatedness. Because individuals experience the needs to feel competent (the need to interact effectively with the environment), autonomous (a desire to engage in activities of one's own choosing), and connected to significant others in their interaction with their environment (feeling that one belongs in a given social milieu), activities that allow them to satisfy these needs will be engaged in choicefully and on a regular basis.

The relationship among success or failure, perceived competence, and intrinsic motivation has been reported in several sport-related studies (e.g., Anshel, Weinberg, & Jackson, 1992; Goudas, Biddle, & Fox, 1994; McAuley & Tammen, 1989; Prong, Rutherford, & Corbin, 1992; Rutherford, Corbin, & Chase, 1992; Sinnott & Biddle, 1998; Vallerand et al., 1986a; Weinberg, 1979; Weinberg & Jackson, 1979; Weinberg & Ragan, 1979). For instance, McAuley and Tammen showed that among participants who took part in a one-on-one basketball jump-shooting competition, winners and participants who felt successful *even if they had lost* reported greater intrinsic motivation (as assessed by the Intrinsic Motivation Inventory; McAuley & Tammen, 1989) than losers and those who felt unsuccessful. These results underscore the importance of considering athletes' perceptions of competence for a better understanding of the effects of success and failure on situational intrinsic motivation.

Similarly, research in sport and exercise reveals that autonomy plays a role in the impact of situational factors on motivation (Vallerand & Perreault, 1999). For example, Dwyer (1995) examined the impact of autonomy-supportive instructions on situational intrinsic motivation and perceived autonomy toward aerobics. Adult females individually performed a 25-minute session of aerobics. Results showed that after the aerobics sessions, participants who had been given the opportunity to select the songs they wanted to hear while exercising experienced higher levels of intrinsic motivation than participants in the control condition, even though both groups heard the same songs. Similar findings have also been reported with respect to physical education classes (Goudas, Biddle, Fox, & Underwood, 1995). Thus, it appears that perceptions of autonomy need

to be considered when charting the psychological processes involved in intrinsic motivation changes.

However, full support for the hierarchical model (and especially Corollary 3.2) is realized only if perceptions of competence, autonomy, and relatedness are empirically shown to mediate the impact of social factors on motivation. Reeve and Deci (1996) looked at the mediating role of perceptions of competence and autonomy on influencing intrinsic motivation in a laboratory study involving various elements of a competitive situation. Participants were asked to perform a task consisting of solving spatial-relations puzzles. The instructions and feedback provided to participants were manipulated to influence their perceptions of competence and autonomy. Results from a path analysis showed that receiving positive feedback (i.e., winning) increased perceptions of competence, which in turn increased intrinsic motivation. Moreover, feeling pressured to do well decreased perceptions of autonomy, which in turn decreased intrinsic motivation. Thus, Reeve and Deci's results support the mediating role of both perceptions of competence and perceptions of autonomy in a competitive situation. Although competition studies conducted in the realm of sport and exercise have supported the role of autonomy (Vallerand et al., 1986b) and competence (Vallerand et al., 1986a; Weinberg & Jackson, 1979), no study on competition has demonstrated the mediating role of such perceptions in sport. Future research is thus needed to replicate the Reeve and Deci findings within the sport/exercise arena.

In the domain of sport, Blanchard and Vallerand (1996a) were interested in assessing the role of the psychological mediators of competence, autonomy, and relatedness within the confines of the same study. The researchers asked basketball players to complete measures of situational perceptions of personal and team performance, objective indicators of team performance (win/loss record), and situational motivation immediately after a game. In addition, participants were asked to complete measures of situational mediators (perceptions of competence, autonomy, and relatedness). Based on the hierarchical model, the authors hypothesized that both individual and team performance would determine the psychological mediators that in turn would influence self-determined motivation. In line with the hierarchical model, results from a path analysis provided support for the hypothesized sequence and thus the proposed mediating effects.

Results from the Blanchard and Vallerand study (1996a) illustrate that perceptions of autonomy, competence, and relatedness are important mediators in the social factors–

motivation relation. Of particular interest is the mediating role played by perceived relatedness because research on perceived relatedness is still very recent. Therefore, the results of Blanchard and Vallerand show that in addition to playing an important role in the domain of interpersonal relationships (Baumeister & Leary, 1995), perceived relatedness may also be an important factor in sport and exercise. These findings are in line with anecdotal evidence associated with professional athletes who reveal that one of the most difficult aspects of retirement is the absence of teammates and the camaraderie they shared in the locker room (Baillie, 1993).

So far in this section, the impact of social factors on situational motivation has been examined. However, intrapersonal factors can also affect motivation. Corollary 3.3 posits that there is a top-down effect from motivation at the contextual level on motivation at the situational level. For example, an athlete who usually plays her favorite sport, tennis, because of intrinsic motivation (contextual sport motivation characterized by a high level of intrinsic motivation) should be predisposed to display high levels of intrinsic motivation at a given moment (high level of situational intrinsic motivation) while playing tennis.

Corollary 3.3 is in line with recent conceptual work on self-regulatory processes that has shown that global properties of the self can influence more specific aspects of the self (Brown, 1993; Brown & Dutton, 1997; Sansone & Harackiewicz, 1996). However, little research has specifically tested Corollary 3.3. In fact, only three studies have tested Corollary 3.3 in sport/exercise settings with respect to the influence of contextual motivation on situational motivation. In one study, Blanchard and Vallerand (1998) showed that contextual motivation toward exercise was an important predictor of situational motivation toward exercise. As predicted, the more self-determined the contextual motivation, the more self-determined the situational motivation toward exercising. In two other studies, the link between contextual motivation and situational motivation was assessed in sport settings. Blanchard, Vallerand, and Provencher (1998) found that contextual motivation toward basketball in general, as assessed either just prior to (Study 1) or several weeks before (Study 2) a game, predicted situational motivation experienced during the basketball game. Thus, the more self-determined the athletes' contextual motivation toward basketball, the more self-determined their situational motivation. Overall, in accord with Corollary 3.3, it appears that motivation at the contextual level can produce top-down effects on situational motivation. Although the results of these studies are

encouraging, they involved correlational designs. Thus, additional research is needed to test this hypothesis from an experimental perspective.

In summary, the studies reviewed show that social factors such as rewards, competition, and feedback can influence individuals' levels of situational motivation (see Vallerand & Losier, 1999). Moreover, as hypothesized by Corollary 3.2, perceived competence, autonomy, and relatedness have been shown to mediate the impact of social factors on situational motivation. Although most studies examining the mediating role of human needs so far have focused on perceived competence (e.g., Vallerand & Reid, 1984, 1988; Whitehead & Corbin, 1991a, 1991b), recent studies indicate that perceived autonomy and perceived relatedness also represent important mediators of situational motivation in sport and exercise (e.g., Blanchard & Vallerand, 1996a). Finally, support for Corollary 3.3 on the top-down effect has been found in studies in both sport (Blanchard et al., 1998) and exercise (Blanchard & Vallerand, 1998).

Consequences

According to the hierarchical model, situational motivation leads to situational consequences (outcomes that are experienced at one specific point in time and with respect to a specific activity) that can be affective, cognitive, and behavioral in nature (Vallerand, 1997). In addition, the most positive consequences should be produced by the most self-determined forms of motivation (i.e., intrinsic motivation and identified regulation), and the least self-determined forms of motivation (i.e., external regulation and especially amotivation) should lead to the most negative consequences (Corollary 5.1). Introjection should lead to intermediate effects.

In line with the hierarchical model and SDT (Deci & Ryan, 1985, 1991), several studies in sport and exercise have shown that intrinsic motivation predicts the occurrence of positive affect in sports as diverse as basketball (e.g., McAuley & Tammen, 1989) and figure skating (Scanlan & Lewthwaite, 1986). More recent research has focused on the impact of the different types of situational motivation on affect. For example, Blanchard and Vallerand (1996c) asked basketball players to complete the SIMS (Guay et al., 2000) as well as scales assessing affective consequences immediately after a basketball game. Results showed that intrinsic motivation and identified regulation were positively associated with positive emotions, and external regulation and amotivation were negatively associated with positive emotions.

In another study, Blanchard and Vallerand (1998) examined the relationship between situational motivation and affective consequences (i.e., positive emotions and enjoyment) with individuals engaged in a weight-loss program based on exercise. Results revealed that positive emotions and enjoyment were positively correlated with intrinsic motivation, followed by identified regulation, whereas correlations with external regulation and amotivation were either negative or nonsignificant. The Blanchard and Vallerand (1996c, 1998) studies provide further support for the hierarchical model by showing that higher levels of self-determined motivation lead to increased positive affect.

Recently, Kowal and Fortier (1999) examined the relationships between situational intrinsic motivation and flow (an affective consequence). Flow refers to the feeling that one experiences while being totally immersed in an activity (Csikszentmihalyi, 1975). Some of the characteristics used to define flow refer to the affect individuals experience, such as the enjoyable nature of the experience (Csikszentmihalyi, 1990; Jackson & Marsh, 1996). Kowal and Fortier hypothesized that self-determined motivation should lead to flow, whereas non-self-determined motivation should detract from it. The researchers asked 203 swimmers from eight swimming clubs to complete the SIMS (Guay et al., 2000) and the Flow State Scale (Jackson & Marsh, 1996) following a swimming practice. Results showed that swimming for intrinsic reasons was associated with the highest levels of flow during practice, followed decreasingly by identified regulation, external regulation, and amotivation (the latter two scales yielded mostly negative correlations).

Situational motivation can also influence cognitive outcomes. For instance, Blanchard and Vallerand (1996c, 1998) found that higher levels of self-determined situational motivation was associated with higher levels of concentration during activity engagement. Similarly, in the Kowal and Fortier (1999) study with swimmers, higher levels of self-determined motivation was positively related to better concentration on the task at hand. These results may be explained by the fact that individuals who display a self-determined motivational profile focus more on the task and are not bothered as much by external distractions (e.g., behaviors from the coach, teammates, or the crowd), and thus can devote all their attention and concentration to the task. These hypothesized mediating processes nevertheless remain to be empirically supported.

Finally, the hierarchical model also posits that higher levels of self-determined situational motivation should result in positive behavioral consequences at a specific moment in time. However, although research in nonsport areas has shown that situational intrinsic motivation leads to behaviors such as persistence at the task (e.g., Deci, 1971) and choice of behavior (e.g., Swann & Pittman, 1977), very little research in sport or exercise has looked at the link between self-determined motivation and behavior. This represents an important agenda for the future. More particularly, the relationship between motivation and performance should be of special interest to researchers, coaches, and athletes (Gould, 1982). Based on Corrolary 5.1 of the hierarchical model, self-determined motivation should lead to better performance than non-self-determined motivation. (Possible exceptions to this hypothesis will be presented in the section on contextual consequences.)

In summary, research shows that situational motivation leads to several consequences that can be grouped in three categories: affective, cognitive, and behavioral. Furthermore, higher levels of self-determined motivation result in more positive situational outcomes, and lower levels of self-determined motivation result in less positive situational outcomes (Corollary 5.1). Thus, findings on consequences at the situational level provide support for the hierarchical model as well as SDT (Deci & Ryan, 1985, 1991). The next section focuses on studies that have examined intrinsic and extrinsic motivation at the second level of the hierarchical model, the contextual level.

RESEARCH ON MOTIVATION AT THE CONTEXTUAL LEVEL

According to the hierarchical model, contextual motivation "refers to one's usual motivational orientation toward a specific context" (Vallerand, 1997, p. 290). As indicated previously, context refers to a life domain as characterized by a specific type of activity (Emmons, 1995). Research on contextual motivation has focused on three contexts: education or work, interpersonal relationships, and leisure (see Vallerand, 1997). Because sport and exercise represent significant leisure activity, much research has been devoted to these contexts (see Vallerand, in press; Vallerand & Grouzet, in press). In the present section, studies on contextual intrinsic and extrinsic motivation in sport and exercise are reviewed.

Determinants

Several social factors influence individuals' situational motivation. In a similar fashion, it is hypothesized that contextual social factors influence athletes' contextual motivation.

Contextual social factors are those that are present on a general or recurrent basis in one life context, but not in another (Vallerand, 1997). For example, students' contextual motivation in education is influenced by contextual factors such as type of school (e.g., Matthews, 1991), curriculum (e.g., Senécal, Vallerand, & Pelletier, 1992), and teachers' interactive style (e.g., Deci, Schwartz, Sheinman, & Ryan, 1981). However, such factors should have little impact on athletes' motivation because they are not directly pertinent to the realm of sports. With respect to the domain of sport and exercise, several contextual factors have been found to influence athletes' contextual motivation toward sport.

A first contextual factor is that of the coach (or exercise/fitness instructor). Two dimensions of coaching behavior have been examined: coaches' interactional style with their athletes, and the way coaches provide instructions to their athletes. With respect to the first aspect of coaching, it has been shown that the way coaches and instructors typically interact with their athletes can influence greatly athletes' motivation (e.g., Cadorette, Blanchard, & Vallerand, 1996; Goudas et al., 1993, as cited in Goudas & Biddle, 1994; Thompson & Wankel, 1980). One dimension of the interactive style that appears important with respect to coaching is the "control/autonomy support" dimension (Deci & Ryan, 1987; Deci, Schwartz, et al., 1981). Coaches provide autonomy support when they allow their athletes to make choices within reasonable limits. On the other hand, coaches are controlling when they force or coerce their athletes to behave as they see fit. Research reveals that athletes who feel that their coaches are controlling tend to report less intrinsic motivation and identified regulation and more amotivation and external regulation than those who feel that their coaches and instructors are autonomy-supportive (Brière et al., 1995; Pelletier, Fortier, Vallerand, & Brière, 2000; Pelletier et al., 1995).

If coaches' interactional style influences athletes' motivation, then helping coaches modify their style to become more autonomy-supportive should lead to increases in athletes' intrinsic motivation. Using this rationale, Pelletier and his colleagues (Pelletier, Brière, Blais, & Vallerand, 2000) developed an intervention program to help swim coaches in becoming autonomy-supportive and consequently facilitating their athletes' motivation. This 18-month intervention program focused on: (1) helping coaches to adopt a more autonomy-supportive strategy, thereby allowing them to foster competence and autonomy in their athletes, and (2) teaching athletes how to deal with the increased autonomy and to become more proactive in their sport environment. Results revealed that the program

was highly effective, because at the end of the intervention, athletes perceived their coach as less controlling and more autonomy-supportive. Of greater importance, athletes' level of perceived competence and intrinsic motivation toward swimming showed significant increases. These differences were also significant when compared to a control group (swim teams not receiving the intervention). Results from the Pelletier et al. study reveal that by modifying social factors, it becomes possible to change motivation, thereby providing support for Corollary 3.1.

Coaches can also influence athletes' motivation through the way they transmit their instructions. For instance, Beauchamp, Halliwell, Fournier, and Koestner (1996) examined the impact of different types of instructions on the contextual motivation of novice golfers in a 14-week golf program. Three groups were formed: a cognitive-behavioral group (CBG), a physical skills group (PSG), and a control group (CG). Participants in the CBG received information about the right technique for putting, the importance of psychological skills before and during putting, stress management, motivation (including goal setting), and self-monitoring of the preputt routines. Participants in the PSG received information about the importance of physical skills in golf and the mechanics of putting. Finally, participants in the CG followed a regular golf instructional program where they received no instruction in putting and were told that it was a highly individual skill. Moreover, they had no exposure to putting prior to the execution of the four putting test sessions. Results showed that at the end of the program, participants in the CBG reported experiencing more intrinsic motivation and less introjection (as assessed by the SMS; Pelletier et al., 1995) than participants in the other groups. According to Beauchamp et al., the instructions given to the participants in the CBG (e.g., goal setting, self-monitoring) were more autonomy-supportive than the information given to the participants in the PSG or CG because participants in the CBG were taught to use self-set goals rather than imposed goals and to focus on the process rather than the outcome of the activity. These types of instructions (i.e., self-set goals and process-oriented approach) may have led participants to feel more autonomous and, as a result, to experience self-determined motivation. Thus, the Pelletier, Brière, et al. (2000), Pelletier, Fortier, et al. (2000), and Beauchamp et al. studies show that coaches and instructors can influence athletes' intrinsic motivation through their coaching style and the types of instructions they give to their athletes. In addition, results from the Pelletier, Brière et al. study indicate that coaches' style can be modified to the benefit of athletes' motivation.

If coaches or instructors can influence athletes' contextual motivation toward their sport, nonhuman contextual factors must also be considered. One such factor is scholarships. The purpose of scholarships is to reward athletes for their effort and good performance and to provide more time for training. Unfortunately, scholarship recipients may feel that they are training more for money than for pleasure and self-fulfillment. As a result, they may feel controlled and less intrinsically motivated. In a study with basketball players, Wagner, Lounsbury, and Fitzgerald (1989) found that athletes who received scholarships reported lower levels of intrinsic motivation than players who did not receive scholarships. Similar findings have also been obtained in previous studies (e.g., Ryan, 1977, 1980). The issue of scholarships is extremely interesting and several avenues for future research exist. For instance, it is necessary to establish that it is the scholarships that undermine athletes' motivation and that the effect is not due simply to a selection bias (athletes who are already lower in intrinsic motivation receive the scholarships). In addition, the psychological processes through which this undermining effect takes place must be identified: Is it a loss of perceived autonomy as predicted by SDT and the hierarchical model? Finally, if gender differences exist, they also need to be explained.

Another nonhuman contextual factor is sport structures, which refer to the organizational pattern that is inherent in athletic leagues. Certain leagues may foster competitive structures, whereas others may instill a more relaxed climate where self-improvement is the goal. These should lead to different effects on sport motivation. Sport structures are important because they convey an implicit message through which athletes' motivational processes are set in motion. If the message conveyed to athletes is that winning is the only thing, they are likely to experience lower levels of intrinsic and self-determined motivation, and as a result have less fun. However, if the structures help athletes focus on self-improvement at the expense of winning, they are likely to experience higher levels of intrinsic and self-determined motivation, and consequently more enjoyment.

These hypotheses were tested by Fortier, Vallerand, Brière, and Provencher (1995) with a sample of 399 Canadian athletes (M age = 19 years). These authors hypothesized that athletes in highly competitive leagues (collegiate sports) would report experiencing lower levels of self-determined motivation than athletes in recreational leagues. Results supported the hypothesis. Athletes playing in competitive leagues reported less intrinsic motivation to accomplish and to experience stimulation, as well as more amotivation than recreational athletes. These results suggest that when the sport structures emphasize competition and performance over simple participation, athletes may feel that they are taking part in their sport for reasons other than the pleasure they get out of practicing. This may result in lower levels of self-determined motivation. Similar results have been found in other sport studies with different motivational measures (e.g., Cornelius, Silva, & Molotsky, 1991; Frederick & Morrison, 1996).

A final nonhuman social factor likely to influence motivation is the motivational climate (e.g., Lloyd & Fox, 1992; Mitchell, 1996; Papaioannou, 1994, 1995; Seifriz, Duda, & Chi, 1992; Theeboom, De Knop, & Weiss, 1995). Motivational climate refers to the general team ambience that exists and the message it may convey to athletes. Coaches, teammates, administrators, and parents play an important role in determining the type of climate that will prevail in a given team or club. There are two main types of motivational climate: mastery and competitive (see Roberts, 1992). A mastery climate encourages participants to perform an activity to improve their skills; a competitive climate leads athletes to believe that they must outperform other athletes, including their teammates. It should then be hypothesized that a mastery climate should be more conducive to the growth of self-determined forms of motivation, and the opposite should occur with a competitive climate. Using college students enrolled in beginning tennis classes, Kavussanu and Roberts (1996) found that both male and female participants who perceived the motivational climate of their classes to be mastery-oriented reported higher levels of intrinsic motivation than participants who perceived the climate to be competitive. Of interest are the findings of Cadorette et al. (1996), who found that the general ambience that exists in a fitness center had an indirect influence on participants' motivation through the feelings of relatedness it fostered. It may be that the motivational climate also influences perceptions of relatedness in addition to those of competence and autonomy. Future research on this issue is warranted.

As explained earlier, Corollary 3.2 posits that the impact of social factors on motivation should be mediated by perceptions of autonomy, competence, and relatedness. With respect to the contextual level, this means that individuals' general perceptions of competence, autonomy, and relatedness toward their sport should mediate the relationship between contextual social factors (e.g., feedback) and their contextual motivation toward sport.

Athletes' perceptions of their successes, failures, skills, and abilities have been shown to be related to their contextual motivation (Duda, Chi, Newton, Walling, & Catley, 1995). Several studies have highlighted the importance of perceived competence for intrinsic motivation (e.g., Goudas, Biddle, & Underwood, 1995; Markland & Hardy, 1997; Mobily et al., 1993; Weigand & Broadhurst, 1998; Whitehead & Corbin, 1991a). For example, Ryckman and Hamel (1993) found that adolescent athletes with high perceived physical ability rated intrinsic factors (e.g., skill development and having fun) as more important reasons for participating in sports than athletes with low perceived physical ability. Similarly, research in sport and exercise settings has repeatedly shown that perceived competence is positively associated with self-determined forms of motivation, and non-self-determined forms are negatively related to perceived competence (Brière et al., 1995; Cadorette et al., 1996; Li, 1999; Pelletier et al., 1995). Similar findings have been obtained with respect to perceptions of autonomy (e.g., Carroll & Alexandris, 1997; Goudas, Biddle, Fox, et al., 1995; Goudas, Biddle, & Underwood, 1995; Markland & Hardy, 1997) and relatedness (i.e., Blanchard & Vallerand, 1996b; Cadorette et al., 1996).

However, a complete test of the role of perceived competence, autonomy, and relatedness in motivation as posited by the hierarchical model involves testing their mediating role in the social factors–motivation relationship. At least two studies have examined the contextual level in the sport/exercise domain. With a sample of 208 adult exercisers, Cadorette et al. (1996) explored the relationships among participants' perceptions of the fitness leader's style (autonomy support), the ambience of the fitness center, participants' perceptions of competence, autonomy, and relatedness, and contextual motivation toward exercising. Results from a path analysis showed that perceiving their fitness leader as being autonomy-supportive and the fitness center as promoting a positive ambience induced perceptions of competence, autonomy, and relatedness, which in turn led to higher levels of self-determined motivation. These findings were replicated in a second study involving basketball players (Blanchard & Vallerand, 1996b). Results from this study indicated that perceptions of autonomy support from the coach as well as team cohesion predicted perceptions of competence, autonomy, and relatedness (however, the team cohesion–perceived competence link was not significant). In turn, these perceptions predicted contextual self-determined motivation (with the perceived competence–motivation link not being significant).

A final type of motivational determinant comes from the top-down effect of the motivation at the next higher level on motivation at the next lower level. Thus, as presented earlier, Corollary 3.3 posits that there is a top-down effect from motivation at the global level on motivation at the contextual level. For example, an individual who has a predisposition to do things due to intrinsic motivation (a high level of global intrinsic motivation) should be likely to display high levels of intrinsic motivation toward sport in general (high level of contextual intrinsic motivation).

A number of studies in areas other than sports have shown that global motivation is related to contextual motivation. For example, Vallerand, Guay, and Blanchard (2000, Study 1) demonstrated that the more self-determined the global motivation, the more college students displayed self-determined contextual motivations toward education, interpersonal relationships, and leisure. These findings have been replicated in a three-month prospective study involving contextual motivation toward the leisure context (Vallerand et al., 2000, Study 2). Finally, one study determined the role of global motivation in contextual motivation toward exercise (Blanchard & Vallerand, 1998). The researchers first assessed adults' global motivation; four weeks later, they assessed adults' contextual motivation toward exercise. Results showed that global motivation influenced contextual motivation toward exercise. As in past studies, the more self-determined the global motivation, the more self-determined the motivation toward exercising in general.

In summary, studies reviewed in this section indicate that contextual self-determined motivation toward sport is influenced by several social factors, including sport structures, scholarships, coaches' behavior, and the team's climate (or fitness center ambience). Furthermore, the relationships between those social factors and contextual self-determined motivation toward sport or exercise are mediated by individuals' general sense of competence, autonomy, and relatedness toward sport or exercise. Finally, global motivation has been found to predict contextual motivation. Overall, these results provide further support for several of the postulates and corollaries of the hierarchical model as applied to sport and exercise (Vallerand, in press; Vallerand & Grouzet, in press; Vallerand & Perreault, 1999).

Consequences

The hierarchical model argues that contextual motivation leads to contextual consequences of three types (i.e., affective, cognitive, and behavioral). Much research in sport has been designed to examine the relationship between contextual intrinsic motivation and affective consequences. For instance, in the Beauchamp et al. (1996) study described earlier, participants with higher levels of intrinsic motivation (i.e., in the cognitive-behavioral program) reported greater pleasure and enjoyment toward golf lessons compared to those in the two other conditions (the physical skills and control groups). Similarly, Brustad (1988) showed that the strongest predictor of enjoyment regarding one's participation in basketball over the season for both boys and girls age 9 to 13 years was intrinsic motivation toward basketball in general (i.e., contextual intrinsic motivation). Other studies have shown that intrinsic motivation is positively associated with a variety of affective variables, such as satisfaction with the activity (Brière et al., 1995; Frederick, Morrison, & Manning, 1996; Pelletier et al., 1995), interest (Brière et al., 1995; Li, 1999), and positive emotions (Brière et al., 1995).

Researchers have also examined Corollary 5.1 of the hierarchical model, which posits that affective consequences are decreasingly positive moving down the self-determination continuum from intrinsic motivation toward amotivation. For example, several studies have shown that the more self-determined forms of motivation (e.g., intrinsic motivation and identified regulation) are more positively related to positive affect, enjoyment, interest, and satisfaction than the less self-determined forms (amotivation and external regulation), which are typically negatively related to these outcomes (Brière et al., 1995; Li, 1999). In contrast, amotivation and external regulation have been found to correlate positively to contextual anxiety, and intrinsic motivation and identified regulation were unrelated to anxiety (Brière et al., 1995).

In a study of 398 athletes participating in swimming, triathlon, cycling, and track and field at the World Masters Games, Jackson, Kimiecik, Ford, and Marsh (1998) showed that contextual intrinsic motivation predicted contextual (or trait) experiences of flow. The other types of motivation (as assessed by the SMS) did not predict flow. Of additional interest is that Jackson et al. found that only intrinsic motivation toward stimulation predicted flow. It would thus appear that this type of intrinsic motivation is conducive to flow experiences. Additional research is needed to further test the potential role of the other types of intrinsic motivation (to know and to accomplish) in the occurrence of flow experiences.

Recently, researchers have examined the link between motivation and affective consequences with different populations of sport participants. Perreault and Vallerand (1998) looked at the impact of sport motivation as assessed by the French version of the SMS (EMS; Brière et al.,

1995) on sport coping skills as assessed by the Athletic Coping Skills Inventory 28 (Smith, Schutz, Smoll, & Ptacek, 1995) among wheelchair basketball players. Results showed that the more self-determined the motivation, the better coping abilities reported by the athletes. It would thus appear that athletes with self-determined forms of motivation are better equipped to deal with the stress and anxiety of competition through the buffer effect provided by their more effective coping skills. These findings help shed light on those of Gottfried (1990), who reported a negative correlation between intrinsic motivation and anxiety in students. It is possible that being intrinsically motivated facilitates the use of adaptive coping skills, which in turn leads to lower levels of anxiety. Future research is needed to test this hypothesis.

Other studies have focused on intellectually challenged children taking part in sport and physical activities (Reid, Poulin, & Vallerand, 1994; Reid & Vallerand, 1998). To assess the motivation of this population, these researchers developed and validated the Pictorial Motivation Scale. This scale assesses four types of motivation: intrinsic motivation, identified regulation, external regulation, and amotivation. Each scale is composed of four items; each item is presented with a drawing that helps children understand the item. Results of factor and item analyses revealed that the scale displays a four-factor structure and has acceptable levels of internal consistency (Reid et al., 1994; Reid & Vallerand, 1998). In two studies, it was found that Canadian children's motivation was related to indices of interest and positive affect as perceived by their physical education teacher. Results showed that higher levels of self-determined motivation were associated with more positive affect and interest. Of additional interest is the fact that these data were obtained even though the affective scales were completed by the children's teacher. It would appear that the link between motivation and affective consequences is robust.

Finally, Losier, Gaudette, and Vallerand (1997) were interested in assessing affective consequences derived from coaches' levels of motivation. Losier et al. developed and validated a scale based on the SMS to assess coaching motivation. This scale assesses the same seven types of motivation as the SMS (intrinsic motivation to know, to accomplish, and to experience stimulation, and external, introjected, and identified regulation, and amotivation) with four items per scale. Results from preliminary analyses supported the factor structure and reliability of the scale. Correlations were also conducted between the different motivations and coaching satisfaction. As expected, results revealed that the more self-determined the coaches' motivation, the more satisfied they were with their interpersonal relationships with their athletes and the more satisfied they were with coaching in general.

The Perreault and Vallerand (1998), Reid et al. (1994), Reid and Vallerand (1998), and Losier et al. (1997) studies are important for at least three reasons. First, support was obtained for the hierarchical model and for the proposed relationship between motivation and affective consequences as described in Corollary 5.1. Second, these results provide a better understanding of sport motivation with relatively untested populations. For instance, few researchers have examined the role of motivation among athletes with physical or psychological disabilities; yet these populations represent an important number of participants with the same zest and enthusiasm as "regular" athletes. Scientific research with these special populations is extremely important to determine if the same psychological processes associated with athletes operate in these other sport and exercise participants. Preliminary evidence reveals that it is the case; however, much more research is needed before a firm conclusion can be offered. Finally, results from such research point toward interesting future research. For example, is it possible that coaches' own motivation influence that of their athletes? If so, through which mechanisms do these effects operate?

Contextual motivation can also produce consequences at the cognitive level. One important cognitive outcome is concentration. Being able to concentrate fully on the task at hand may yield important benefits with respect to performance. In line with Corollary 5.1 of the hierarchical model, it is predicted that the most self-determined forms of motivation (i.e., intrinsic motivation and identified regulation) should lead to the highest levels of concentration. Conversely, the least self-determined forms of motivation (i.e., amotivation and external regulation) are expected to yield the lowest levels of concentration. Correlations with introjection are expected to lie between these extremes. Research in sport has supported Corollary 5.1 with athletes from a variety of sports (Brière et al., 1995; Pelletier et al., 1995). Of additional interest is a study that replicated these findings with adult exercisers (Vallerand & Blanchard, 1998a). Finally, it should be underscored that this pattern of results has also been replicated with intellectually challenged children with a concentration scale completed by the children's physical education teacher (Reid et al., 1994). Overall, it appears that the link between motivation and cognitive outcomes is very robust, in that it has been obtained with various populations in both sport and exercise settings.

Finally, contextual motivation can also lead to behavioral consequences. For instance, several studies have shown that there is a relationship between contextual motivation and effort. More specifically, the most self-determined forms of motivation have been found to be positively associated with increased effort invested in the sport (Pelletier et al., 1995; Williams & Gill, 1995) or type of exercise engaged in (e.g., Fortier & Grenier, 1999; Li, 1999; Reid & Vallerand, 1998), whereas the non-self-determined forms of motivation have been negatively related to effort.

Intentions to participate in sport and exercise have also been found to be influenced by motivation. For example, Oman and McAuley (1993) conducted a study with adults who participated in 12 aerobic sessions. Results showed that participants with higher levels of intrinsic motivation were more confident in their intentions to continue exercising than participants with lower levels of intrinsic motivation. These findings were replicated in other studies with athletes and exercise participants (e.g., Goudas, Biddle, & Underwood, 1995; Pelletier et al., 1995). Finally, in a study with ice hockey coaches, Losier et al. (1997) showed that higher levels of self-determined motivation toward coaching were positively associated with intentions to pursue coaching in the future.

Motivation has not only been related to behavioral intentions but also to *actual decisions* to continue participating in exercise and sport. Thus, with respect to exercise, using the Exercise Motivations Inventory 2 (Markland & Ingledew, 1997), Ingledew, Markland, and Medley (1998) examined the relationship between exercise motives that can be intrinsic (e.g., enjoyment) or extrinsic (e.g., competition) and stages of change (precontemplation, contemplation, preparation, action, and maintenance) in exercise among 247 British government employees. The higher the stage (e.g., action and maintenance stages), the more active the engagement in exercise (see Marcus, Selby, Niaura, & Rossi, 1992). The results showed that participants in earlier stages of exercise adoption (e.g., precontemplation) reported more extrinsic motives (i.e., appearance and weight management), and those in later stages of exercise adoption (e.g., maintenance) reported more intrinsic motives (i.e., enjoyment and revitalization).

Similarly, Fortier and Grenier (1999) examined the relationship between motivation and adherence to an exercise program among 40 participants age 17 to 75 years who were members of a sports complex. Results showed that higher levels of self-determined motivation at Time 1 were associated with higher levels of adherence one month later.

Similar findings have been obtained by R. Ryan, Frederick, Lepes, Rubio, and Sheldon (1997), who concluded that adherence was associated with intrinsic motives but unrelated to extrinsic motives. These studies reveal that although both extrinsic and intrinsic motivation can be important reasons to join in an activity (Drummond & Lenes, 1997), higher levels of self-determined motivation are essential to continue engaging in regular exercise.

Similar findings have been obtained in sport settings. For instance, in the intervention study mentioned earlier, Pelletier, Brière, et al. (2000) also assessed the effects of their intervention on dropout rate. Results revealed that their intervention not only increased the swimmers' intrinsic motivation but also increased their attendance rate at practices and decreased their dropout rate. Results showed that before the program was implemented, an average of only 12.6 of the 22 swimmers on the team showed up for practices. At the end of the program, presence at practice increased to an average of 19.7 swimmers. Annual dropout rates in swimmers went down from 35% to 4.5% (they remained at 35% in other clubs serving as control groups). These changes were still evident two years later. In another study (Pelletier, Fortier, et al., 2000), it was also noted that self-determined and non-self-determined motivation were, respectively, positively and negatively associated with persistence over a two-year period. It appears that the motivation-persistence relationship is well supported at the contextual level both in exercise and sport settings.

Another type of outcome from a self-determined motivational profile is a positive sportspersonship orientation, or the tendency to respect the rules and sport participants (see Vallerand, Deshaies, Cuerrier, Brière, & Pelletier, 1996; Vallerand & Losier, 1994). Indeed, it seems plausible that athletes who display a self-determined motivational profile should be more likely to show respect for others and less likely to cheat than athletes who want to win trophies and medals at all costs (a non-self-determined motivational orientation). Some evidence from the education domain supports such an interpretation. For instance, Lonky and Reihman (1990) found that students who displayed a self-determined motivational profile cheated less than students who had a non-self-determined motivational profile.

A similar relationship seems to exist in sports. Vallerand and Losier (1994) examined the relationship between self-determined motivation and sportspersonship orientations over time. Two weeks into the hockey season, adolescent elite players completed a questionnaire measuring both their levels of self-determined motivation (the SMS) and their sportspersonship orientations (the Multidimensional Sportspersonship Orientations Scale; Vallerand,

Brière, Blanchard, & Provencher, 1997). Five months later, participants completed the questionnaires again. Results from regression analyses revealed that, over time, self-determined motivation and sportspersonship orientations had a positive bidirectional relation. However, self-determined motivation had a greater influence on sportspersonship than sportspersonship had on self-determined motivation. These findings have been replicated with coaches (Losier et al., 1997). Their results showed that the more coaches had a self-determined motivation toward coaching, the more they reported having positive forms of sportspersonship. Overall, these results suggest that self-determined motivation represents a crucial determinant of sportspersonship orientations. Thus, why you play (or coach) the game determines how you play (or coach) it.

A final motivational outcome is performance. Because self-determined forms of contextual motivation have been found to facilitate persistence at a sport activity (Biddle et al., 1996; Biddle & Brooke, 1992; Fortier & Grenier, 1999; Ingledew et al., 1998; Pelletier, Brière et al., 2000; Pelletier, Fortier, et al., 2000; R. Ryan et al., 1997), given equal ability and coaching, additional practice should lead to increased performance. Thus, self-determined motivation should be associated with enhanced performance. In the Beauchamp et al. (1996) study presented earlier, performance was also monitored. Results did indeed reveal that higher levels of intrinsic motivation and performance were obtained in the cognitive-behavioral group.

Similarly, in the Pelletier, Brière, et al. (2000) intervention study discussed earlier, performance was also assessed. Results revealed that immediately following the first year of the program, athletes in the program, compared to those in the control group, felt more competent and more intrinsically motivated. The program also improved the swimmers' performance. At the beginning of the program, only two swimmers had met the national standards for their age group. By the end of the third year, 22 athletes had done so, four athletes were selected to the Olympic team, and one won a silver medal at the Seoul Olympics. Combined, the Beauchamp et al. (1996) and Pelletier, Brière, et al. studies tend to suggest that changes in intrinsic motivation lead to increased performance. However, because neither study contained a true experimental design, alternative hypotheses exist. Additional research is needed to more fully identify the psychological processes involved in such performance increases.

Although intrinsic motivation tends to result in the most positive consequences, some exceptions have been found. For instance, identified regulation has been shown to lead to more positive consequences than intrinsic motivation with respect to certain types of activities, including politics (e.g., Koestner, Losier, Vallerand, & Carducci, 1996) and protecting the environment (Pelletier, Tuson, Green-Demers, Noels, & Beaton, 1996). One possible explanation proposed by Vallerand (1997) deals with the nature of the activity. When the task to be performed is perceived as interesting, intrinsic motivation should lead to the most positive outcomes. However, when the task is uninteresting, then identified regulation may become a more important determinant of positive consequences than intrinsic motivation. Indeed, if a task is dull and unappealing, intrinsic motivation may be insufficient to engage in it. Rather, what is needed is a motivational force to engage in the activity despite the fact that it is not interesting. Identified regulation can provide such a force.

In the context of sport and exercise, such findings might occur if some of the activities to be performed are not interesting. For instance, ice hockey athletes may enjoy playing in a game. However, they may not enjoy the off-ice exercises, such as lifting weights and jogging. For these activities to be completed, a hockey player may need to have a strong identified regulation. It should come as no surprise if identified regulation may at times lead to more positive consequences in important but uninteresting tasks in sport (e.g., stretching or lifting weights). At this point, however, no empirical support for this idea is available. Thus, future research is recommended on this issue.

Research has also shown that non-self-determined motivation may sometimes be more beneficial than self-determined forms of motivation. For instance, Chantal, Guay, Dobreva-Martinova, and Vallerand (1996) found that non-self-determined types of motivation (external and introjected regulation) were conducive to better performance in high-elite adult athletes in a controlling culture (the former communist regime in Bulgaria). Therefore, it could be that in a controlling context, less self-determined forms of motivation can facilitate performance, whereas self-determined forms of motivation are necessary in autonomy-supportive contexts. Perhaps a person-environment fit exists and influences how motivation leads to various consequences. For example, in a study on psychological adjustment in old age, O'Connor and Vallerand (1994) found that elderly individuals with a self-determined motivational profile who lived in autonomy-supportive residences (as assessed by judges) reported higher levels of psychological adjustment than self-determined individuals living in controlling residences. On the other hand, non-self-determined elderly individuals living in controlling residences fared better than non-self-determined individuals living in autonomy-supportive residences. Future research

is needed to test this person-environment hypothesis within the realm of sport.

Although non-self-determined forms of motivation may lead to positive consequences (e.g., Chantal et al., 1996) and a person-environment fit may exist (O'Connor & Vallerand, 1994), such gains may take place mainly in the short term. If athletes and fitness participants are to reap the full benefits of their participation, their need for autonomy must be fostered. If not, they may start feeling like pawns (DeCharms, 1968) and at some point become amotivated. Future research is needed to look into this matter.

In summary, the studies reviewed in this section on intrinsic and extrinsic motivation at the contextual level provide strong support for the hierarchical model. First, as posited by Corollary 3.1, several social factors that are present in the context of sport and exercise (e.g., coaches' style, motivational climate) have an impact on the contextual motivation of various types of participants (e.g., athletes, coaches, exercise participants, intellectually challenged individuals). Moreover, in line with Corollary 3.2, the social factors–motivation relation is mediated by perceptions of competence, autonomy, and relatedness. Finally, in accord with Corollary 5.1, motivation has been found to be associated with a host of consequences (i.e., affective, cognitive, and behavioral), with higher levels of contextual self-determined motivation resulting in more positive contextual outcomes.

RESEARCH ON MOTIVATION AT THE GLOBAL LEVEL

Motivation at the global level represents a predisposition to interact with the environment with a given motivational orientation (Guay et al., 1999; Vallerand, 1997). At this level, it is proposed that global factors can affect global motivation. Global factors refer to social factors that are present in most contexts of the person's life on a relatively permanent basis and shape global motivation. As is the case with situational and contextual motivation, global motivation is also expected to lead to specific consequences of three types (i.e., affective, cognitive, and behavioral). Although research on global motivation is at the beginning stage, results reveal its importance in providing a better understanding of motivational processes in sport and exercise.

Determinants

No research appears to have examined how global social factors may affect global motivation. However, research by Vallerand and O'Connor (1991) with elderly individuals has revealed that the type of residence they live in seems to impact on their global motivation. Elderly people living in residences that provided autonomy support reported higher levels of contextual self-determined motivation toward most aspects of their lives (across six life contexts) compared to those living in controlling residences. Thus, although Vallerand and O'Connor did not measure global motivation per se, it does appear that spending most of one's life in a controlling or autonomy-supportive residence may represent a global social factor likely to influence global motivation.

Similar research could be conducted in sports. For instance, the motivational impact of living in sports residences, as is the case in Europe with teenagers who enroll in sports boarding schools (see Riordan, 1977), could be studied. Assessing the role of global social factors on global motivation in the arena of sports represents an important task for the future. Indeed, such research might suggest the nature of psychological processes through which motivational dispositions at the personality level develop and, once developed, continue to evolve and change.

Consequences

As is the case at the other two levels of generality, global motivation is expected to influence global types of consequences. Examples are life satisfaction and general positive and negative affect. Quite clearly, such types of outcomes are not sport-specific. However, they still can be studied when experienced by athletes or exercise participants. The little research that has been done at this level supports this aspect of the hierarchical model. For instance, using the GMS, Guay et al. (1999) found that life satisfaction was positively related to global intrinsic motivation, but negatively related to global external regulation and amotivation.

An important point to be made with respect to consequences deals with the element of specificity. Corollary 5.2 posits that the degree of generality of the various consequences depends on the level of motivation that engenders them. More specifically, global motivation should lead to global consequences (e.g., life satisfaction); contextual motivation should lead to contextual consequences (i.e., consequences specific to a given context such as sport or education); and situational motivation should lead to situational consequences related to the activity being performed at a given point in time.

At this point, only one study has directly examined the validity of Corollary 5.2. Vallerand and Blanchard (1998b) investigated the consequences associated with motivation at all three levels. They asked exercise participants to complete measures of motivation and motivational consequences on three different occasions. At Time 1, participants completed the GMS (Guay et al., 1999) and the contextual motivation scale toward exercise adapted from the French form of the SMS (EMS; Brière et al., 1995). Four weeks later (Time 2), participants completed the SIMS (Guay et al., 2000) and measures of situational consequences related to concentration and positive emotions. Finally, another four weeks later (Time 3), participants completed measures of motivational consequences at the global level (i.e., general negative affect; Watson, Clark, & Tellegen, 1988) and at the contextual level (i.e., satisfaction with exercise, positive attitudes toward exercise, and enrolling in another exercise program in a fitness center). Results from regression analyses revealed that motivational consequences at each level were best predicted by motivation at the same level. Therefore, global motivation was the strongest predictor of global consequences, contextual motivation was the best predictor of contextual consequences, and situational motivation was the strongest predictor of situational consequences. In addition, as posited by Corollary 5.1, higher levels of self-determined motivation resulted in more positive outcomes at all three levels. Therefore, in line with the hierarchical model, results from the Vallerand and Blanchard study provide evidence for Corollary 5.2 on the specificity of motivational consequences.

In summary, little research has been done at the global level. Further research is needed to gain a better understanding of the motivational determinants and consequences at this level. However, the results from the studies conducted to date (Blanchard & Vallerand, 1998; Vallerand & Blanchard, 1998b) are very encouraging. Potential studies related to sport could examine global motivation and its determinants and consequences among children and adolescents who spend many years in an environment shaped around a particular sport. In addition, one could also ascertain the impact of several years of sport engagement on the development of a self-determined global motivation. If Postulate 4 on the recursive effect is supported, it would be expected that experiencing a self-determined contextual motivation toward sports on a long-term basis should lead over time to the development of a self-determined global motivation. Should such findings be obtained, they would clearly justify participation in sport and exercise.

RESEARCH ON INTEGRATIVE STUDIES

The studies reviewed so far provide support for several of the postulates and corollaries of the hierarchical model.

However, two limitations are present in the studies reviewed: (1) Within the confines of a given study, motivation has been examined at only one level of generality (except for Vallerand & Blanchard, 1998b, presented in the previous section), and (2) motivational determinants and consequences typically have been studied separately. The studies reviewed in the present section do not suffer from these limitations, and therefore provide a more comprehensive perspective on intrinsic and extrinsic motivation processes in sport and exercise.

Motivation at Two or Three Levels of Generality

The studies reviewed in this section have examined motivation at two or three levels of generality simultaneously. A good point to begin with in the hierarchical model is the interplay between two levels in the hierarchy. As described earlier with Corollary 3.3, a top-down effect is proposed. For instance, in the Blanchard et al. (1998) study, it was found that contextual motivation toward exercise was an important predictor of situational motivation toward exercise. As predicted, the more self-determined the contextual motivation, the more self-determined the situational motivation toward exercising. These findings were replicated by Blanchard et al. in two studies dealing with basketball as well as by Goudas, Biddle, Fox, and Underwood (1995) in physical education classes.

It is further proposed with Postulate 4 that a bottom-up effect can also take place over time. More specifically, motivation experienced at a lower level (e.g., the situational level) can over time produce a recursive effect on motivation at the next higher level (e.g., contextual motivation toward sport). For example, an individual who would repeatedly experience intrinsic motivation at the situational level could develop an intrinsic motivation at the contextual level. Thus, the interplay of the situational and contextual levels helps explain changes in contextual motivation.

Blanchard et al. (1998) conducted a study to test this interplay between the contextual and situational levels leading to the change in contextual motivation of basketball players participating in a tournament. Measures of contextual motivation (using the EMS) were obtained before the first and second games of the tournament and 10 days after the tournament. Moreover, measures of situational motivation (using the SIMS) were obtained immediately after the two games of the tournament. Finally, players' assessment of personal and team performance as well as objective results of the games were collected to test the role of situational factors in the prediction of situational motivation. Results from a path analysis showed that contextual motivation for basketball predicted situational motivation during each of the two games during the tournament. Moreover, situational motivation for both basketball games was also predicted by the situational factors (team and personal performance). In turn, situational motivation influenced contextual motivation subsequent to each game, as well as 10 days after the tournament. Figure 15.2 presents the results from the path analyses.

The results from the Blanchard et al. (1998) investigation are important because they demonstrate that there is an interplay of influences between motivation at two adjacent levels (e.g., the contextual and situational). These results also provide strong support for the hierarchical model, especially as it pertains to Corollary 3.1 (the motivational effect of social factors—personal and team performance), Corollary 3.3 (the top-down effect of contextual motivation on situational motivation), and Postulate 4 (the recursive effect of situational motivation on contextual motivation). It appears that the interplay among motivations at different levels of the hierarchy is responsible for the occurrence of motivational changes over time.

So far, the focus has been on how contextual and situational motivation can influence each other through top-down and bottom-up effects. However, little attention has been devoted to the interplay of different contextual motivations and their influence on situational motivation. For example, a student involved with a tedious algebra assignment who thinks about the soccer game she could participate in is likely to experience motivational conflict. Her situational motivation will then be a function of her contextual motivations toward both school and sports. The relative strength of each contextual motivation will dictate which of these two contexts will have the most prevalent effect on situational motivation. To the extent that the student's contextual motivation toward school (and algebra) is less self-determined than that toward sports (and soccer in particular), she should experience a drop in IM toward her assignment. Results from a recent study (Ratelle, Rousseau, & Vallerand, 1999) provided support for this hypothesis. Specifically, participants who were led to think about an interesting leisure activity experienced significant drops in IM toward the educational task. These results indicate that experiencing a conflict between two motivations (e.g., motivation toward education and motivation toward leisure) can lead to negative consequences, especially if one has to remain engaged in the less interesting activity. Future research should build on these preliminary findings and assess whether the opposite can also occur, that is, if other life contexts can undermine motivation toward sport and exercise motivation.

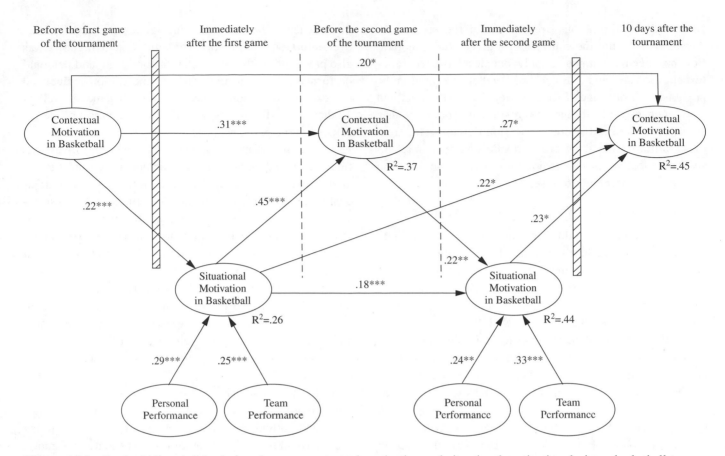

Figure 15.2 On the bidirectional relations between contextual motivation and situational motivation during a basketball tournament: results from the path analysis. Numbers are the Beta weights and R^2 is the percentage of explained variance ($*p < .10$, $**p < .01$, $***p < .001$). From Blanchard, Vallerand, & Provencher (1998).

Another promising area of research involving the dynamic interplay between contextual motivations is that of motivational compensation. From the model's perspective, losses in self-determined motivation in one context can lead a person to compensate by becoming more intrinsically motivated in another context. A preliminary study by Blanchard et al. (1998) supports such compensatory effects. Basketball players completed scales assessing their contextual motivation toward education (the AMS) and sport (specifically basketball; the SMS) and their perceptions of competence toward education and basketball on two separate occasions. They were also asked to rate their school performance at Time 2 (and thus drops in academic perceived competence and self-determined motivation). Individuals who experienced failure in the academic context at Time 2 and who perceived themselves as competent in basketball at Time 1 reported a small increase in contextual self-determined motivation toward basketball over time. No other group experienced an increase in contextual sport motivation over time. Losses of competence and self-determined motivation in

one domain (school) may have motivated individuals to restore their sense of self and, consequently, to experience an increase in self-determined motivation toward the other context (sport). However, such an effect seems to take place in life domains in which people feel competent. More research on this issue is needed.

Other studies have integrated motivation at the three levels of the hierarchy. For instance, Vallerand and Blanchard (1998b) have tested the interplay among motivations at the three levels of the hierarchy with participants in a fitness program. Based on Corollary 3.3 (the top-down effect), the researchers hypothesized that global motivation measured with the GMS (Guay et al., 1999) at the beginning of the fitness program would influence contextual motivation toward exercise (as assessed by a measure adapted from the SMS) four weeks later. In turn, contextual motivation toward exercise would influence situational motivation, which in turn would determine situational consequences of concentration and enjoyment while exercising. Results from structural equation modeling supported the model. These findings have been replicated in the context of education (see Vallerand et al., 2000).

The results from these studies (Vallerand & Blanchard, 1998a; Vallerand et al., 2000) are important for at least two reasons. First, they provide support for several postulates and corollaries of the hierarchical model. They support Postulate 2 (of the existence of the different types of motivation at the three levels of generality) and Corollaries 3.3 (on the top-down effect), 5.1 (on the increasing positive effect of self-determined motivation on consequences), and 5.2 (on the motivation-consequences link at the proper level of specificity). In addition, these results reveal that the interplay of motivation at the three levels of the hierarchy takes place as predicted in the realm of sport and exercise.

A "Determinants → Motivation → Consequences" Sequence

Most studies have examined motivational determinants and motivational consequences separately. However, some researchers have assessed how motivation relates to determinants and consequences (e.g., Beauchamp et al., 1996; Brière et al., 1995; Brustad, 1988; Li, 1999; McAuley & Tammen, 1989; Pelletier et al., 1995; Weinberg, 1979). Unfortunately, because these data were correlational, the issue of the "social determinants → self-determined motivation → consequences" sequence proposed by the hierarchical model was not addressed. It should be noted that this sequence can take place at all three levels of the hierarchy.

A recent study in sport by Pelletier, Fortier, et al. (2000) provides support for the proposed sequence of the hierarchical model at the contextual level. In this study, 368 competitive swimmers were asked to complete various questionnaires including perceptions of the coach's interactive style dealing with autonomy support and control, and contextual motivation (using the SMS). For two years, athletes were followed to determine those who persisted and those who dropped out of swimming. Results from structural equation modeling analyses revealed that perceptions of the coach's autonomy-supportive behavior were positively related to intrinsic motivation and identified regulation, but negatively related to external regulation and amotivation. On the other hand, the coach's controlling behavior was negatively related to intrinsic motivation and identified regulation, but positively related to external regulation and amotivation (perceptions of the coach's autonomy-supportive and controlling behavior were unrelated to introjection). In turn, amotivation and intrinsic motivation, respectively, had the most negative

and positive impact on persistence over the two years. Furthermore, the impact of some types of motivation varied over time. Thus, the impact of external regulation on persistence was negligible the first year but negative the second, and that of introjected regulation was positive the first year but negligible the second.

In addition to providing support for the sequence proposed by the hierarchical model, the Pelletier et al. (2000) study charts the social psychological processes involved in the process of dropping out. It would appear that coaches' behavior triggers motivational changes that evolve over time and that ultimately lead to the decision to drop out of sports. Additional research is needed to determine if these findings are replicated in other sports (and in exercise) and with different age groups. However, the causal sequence appears robust, as it has been supported in the education context with high school students (Vallerand, Fortier, & Guay, 1997) and university graduate students (Losier et al., 1996).

CONCLUSIONS

The purpose of this chapter was to review the extant literature on intrinsic and extrinsic motivation in sport and exercise using the hierarchical model of intrinsic and extrinsic motivation (Vallerand, 1997, in press; Vallerand & Blanchard, 1999; Vallerand & Grouzet, in press; Vallerand & Perreault, 1999; Vallerand & Ratelle, in press). The model provides a framework for organizing and understanding the basic mechanisms underlying intrinsic and extrinsic motivational processes associated with sport and exercise settings. Specifically, the postulates and corollaries of the model provide a more refined analysis of the determinants and consequences of motivation. Thus, in support of Corollary 3.1, a host of social factors such as rewards, competition, feedback (at the situational level) and sport structures, coaching behavior, and team cohesion and fitness center ambience (at the contextual level) have been shown to influence motivation toward sport and/or exercise.

Furthermore, these effects have largely been found to be mediated by participants' perceptions of competence, autonomy, and relatedness, as proposed by Corollary 3.2. However, the influence of global factors on the global motivation of athletes or exercise participants has not been reported in any one study. Finally, in line with Corollary 3.3., it was found that motivation at a higher level (e.g., contextual sport motivation) represents an important determinant of motivation at the lower level (e.g., situational motivation toward a given sport activity). Research on motivational consequences has shown that outcomes can be of three types: cognitive (e.g., concentration), affective (e.g., satisfaction), and behavioral (e.g., effort and persistence). In support of Corollary 5.1, it was found that the more positive consequences were the result of the more self-determined forms of motivation. Furthermore, research has also supported Corollary 5.2 as to the specificity of motivational outcomes: Situational motivation influences situational outcomes, contextual motivation determines contextual consequences, and global motivation predicts global outcomes.

The model also leads to novel and testable hypotheses. Indeed, suggestions for future research were made throughout the chapter. From a conceptual standpoint, the hierarchical model provides a comprehensive framework to study motivation from a multidimensional perspective. It is now made explicit that sport and exercise participants are not simply intrinsically or extrinsically motivated, or even amotivated, but all of the above to various degrees depending on the task at hand. For instance, the basketball player who is intrinsically motivated to play in games may be externally regulated to do situps and pushups. Furthermore, it is important to pay attention to motivation at multiple levels of generality (the situational, contextual, and global levels). Though social factors do play a role in motivation, intrapersonal forces (motivation in the individual) also have an effect on motivation through both top-down effects (Corollary 3.3) or recursive (bottom-up) effects (Postulate 4). By considering the interplay between the interpersonal and intrapersonal forces, social psychological and personality perspectives can be used for a better understanding of motivation in athletes and exercise participants. Focusing on this dialectic in the study of motivation should lead to several conceptual advances.

The hierarchical model also suggests that it is desirable to progress from the mere study of athletes (or exercise participants) to that of whole individuals who, in addition to being athletes (or exercise participants), are also students (or workers) and part of a social matrix. This means that if we are to better understand an individual's sport (or exercise) motivation, we need to know more about his or her motivations in other life contexts such as education (or work) and interpersonal relationships. Indeed, research has revealed that what happens in one life context (e.g., education) can influence what happens in another (e.g., sport; Blanchard, Vallerand, & Provencher, 1996; Provencher & Vallerand, 1995; Ratelle et al., 1999).

In summary, the present review has shown that the hierarchical model of intrinsic and extrinsic motivation

represents a useful organizing and integrating theoretical framework to make sense of motivation in sport and exercise settings. Future research framed with this model should lead to a more comprehensive understanding of the psychological processes underlying motivational phenomena that take place in sport and exercise settings.

REFERENCES

Amabile, T.M. (1985). Motivation and creativity: Effects of motivational orientation on creative writers. *Journal of Personality and Social Psychology, 48,* 393–399.

Amabile, T.M., DeJong, W., & Lepper, M.R. (1976). Effects of externally imposed deadlines on subsequent intrinsic motivation. *Journal of Personality and Social Psychology, 34,* 92–98.

Anshel, M.H., Weinberg, R., & Jackson, A. (1992). The effect of goal difficulty and task complexity on intrinsic motivation and motor performance. *Journal of Sport Behavior, 15,* 159–176.

Baillie, P.H.F. (1993). Understanding retirement from sports: Therapeutic ideas for helping athletes in transition. *Counseling Psychologist, 21,* 399–410.

Baumeister, R.F., & Leary, M.R. (1995). The need to belong: Desire for interpersonal attachments as a fundamental human motivation. *Psychological Bulletin, 117,* 497–529.

Beauchamp, P.H., Halliwell, W.R., Fournier, J.F., & Koestner, R. (1996). Effects of cognitive-behavioral psychological skills training on the motivation, preparation, and putting performance of novice golfers. *The Sport Psychologist, 10,* 157–170.

Benware, C., & Deci, E.L. (1984). Quality of learning with an active versus passive motivational set. *American Educational Research Journal, 21,* 755–765.

Biddle, S., Akande, D., Armstrong, N., Ashcroft, M., Brooke, R., & Goudas, M. (1996). The Self-Motivation Inventory modified for children: Evidence on psychometric properties and its use in physical exercise. *International Journal of Sport Psychology, 27,* 237–250.

Biddle, S., & Brooke, R. (1992). Intrinsic versus extrinsic motivational orientation in physical education and sport. *British Journal of Educational Psychology, 62,* 247–256.

Blais, M.R., Vallerand, R.J., Gagnon, A., Brière, N.M., & Pelletier, L.G. (1990). Significance, structure, and gender differences in life domains of college students. *Sex Roles, 22,* 199–212.

Blais, M.R., Vallerand, R.J., Pelletier, L.G., & Brière, N.M. (1994). *Construction et validation de l'Inventaire des Motivations Interpersonnelles [Construction and validation of the Interpersonal Motivations Inventory].* Unpublished manuscript, Université du Québec à Montréal, Canada.

Blanchard, C., & Vallerand, R.J. (1996a). *The mediating effects of perceptions of competence, autonomy, and relatedness on the social factors–self-determined situational motivation relationship.* Unpublished manuscript, Université du Québec à Montréal, Canada.

Blanchard, C., & Vallerand, R.J. (1996b). *Perceptions of competence, autonomy, and relatedness as psychological mediators of the social factors–contextual motivation relationship.* Unpublished manuscript, Université du Québec à Montréal, Canada.

Blanchard, C., & Vallerand, R.J. (1996c). *On the relations between situational motivation and situational consequences in basketball.* Raw data, Université du Québec à Montréal, Canada.

Blanchard, C., & Vallerand, R.J. (1998). *On the relations between situational motivation and situational consequences toward exercise.* Raw data, Université du Québec à Montréal, Canada.

Blanchard, C., Vallerand, R.J., & Provencher, P.J. (1996, August). *Une analyse motivationnelle des mécanismes de compensation et de contagion du soi [A motivational analysis of the compensation and contagion mechanisms of the self].* Paper presented at the first annual conference on social psychology in the French language, Montreal, Canada.

Blanchard, C., Vallerand, R.J., & Provencher, P.J. (1998). *Une analyse des effets bidirectionnels entre la motivation contextuelle et la motivation situationnelle en milieu naturel [An analysis of the bi-directional effects between contextual and situational motivation in a natural setting].* Unpublished manuscript.

Brière, N.M., Vallerand, R.J., Blais, M.R., & Pelletier, L.G. (1995). Développement et validation d'une mesure de motivation intrinsèque, extrinsèque et d'amotivation en contexte sportif: L'échelle de Motivation dans les Sports (ÉMS) [On the development and validation of the French form of the Sport Motivation Scale]. *International Journal of Sport Psychology, 26,* 465–489.

Brown, J.D. (1993). Self-esteem and self-evaluation: Feeling is believing. In J. Suls (Ed.), *Psychological perspectives on the self* (Vol. 4, pp. 27–58). Hillsdale, NJ: Erlbaum.

Brown, J.D., & Dutton, K.A. (1997). Global self-esteem and specific self-views as determinants of people's reactions to success and failure. *Journal of Personality and Social Psychology, 73,* 139–148.

Brustad, R.J. (1988). Affective outcomes in competitive youth sport: The influence of intrapersonal and socialization factors. *Journal of Sport & Exercise Psychology, 10,* 307–321.

Cadorette, I., Blanchard, C., & Vallerand, R.J. (1996, October). *Programme d'amaigrissement: Influence du centre de conditionnement physique et du style de l'entraîneur sur la motivation des participants [Weight loss program: Effects of the fitness center and the instructor on participants' motivation].* Paper presented at the annual conference of the Quebec Society for Research in Psychology, Trois-Rivières, Canada.

Carroll, B., & Alexandris, K. (1997). Perception of constraints in strength of motivation: Their relationship to recreational sport participation in Greece. *Journal of Leisure Research, 29,* 279–299.

Chantal, Y., Guay, F., Dobreva-Martinova, T., & Vallerand, R.J. (1996). Motivation and elite performance: An exploratory investigation with Bulgarian athletes. *International Journal of Sport Psychology, 27,* 173–182.

Cornelius, A.E., Silva, J.M., & Molotsky, E.J. (1991). *Motive structures for engaging in regular exercise.* Unpublished manuscript.

Crowne, D.P., & Marlowe, D. (1960). A new scale of social desirability independent of psychopathology. *Journal of Consulting Psychology, 24,* 349–354.

Csikszentmihalyi, M. (1975). *Beyond boredom and anxiety.* San Francisco: Jossey-Bass.

Csikszentmihalyi, M. (1990). *Flow: The psychology of optimal experience.* New York: Harper & Row.

Csikszentmihalyi, M., & Nakamura, J. (1989). The dynamics of intrinsic motivation: A study of adolescents. In C. Ames & R. Ames (Eds.), *Motivation in education: Goals and cognitions* (Vol. 3, pp. 45–71). New York: Academic Press.

deCharms, R.C. (1968). *Personal causation: The internal affective determinants of behavior.* New York: Academic Press.

Deci, E.L. (1971). Effects of externally mediated rewards on intrinsic motivation. *Journal of Personality and Social Psychology, 18,* 105–115.

Deci, E.L., Betley, G., Kahle, J., Abrams, L., & Porac, J. (1981). When trying to win: Competition and intrinsic motivation. *Personality and Social Psychology Bulletin, 7,* 79–83.

Deci, E.L., Eghrari, H., Patrick, B.C., & Leone, D.R. (1994). Facilitating internalization: The self-determination theory perspective. *Journal of Personality, 62,* 119–142.

Deci, E.L., & Ryan, R.M. (1985). *Intrinsic motivation and self-determination in human behavior.* New York: Plenum Press.

Deci, E.L., & Ryan, R.M. (1987). The support of autonomy and the control of behavior. *Journal of Personality and Social Psychology, 53,* 1024–1037.

Deci, E.L., & Ryan, R.M. (1991). A motivational approach to self: Integration in personality. In R. Dienstbier (Ed.), *Nebraska symposium on motivation: Perspectives on motivation* (Vol. 38, pp. 237–288). Lincoln: University of Nebraska Press.

Deci, E.L., & Ryan, R.M. (in press). The "What" and "Why" of goal pursuits: Human needs and the self-determination of behavior. *Psychological Inquiry.*

Deci, E.L., Schwartz, A.J., Sheinman, L., & Ryan, R.M. (1981). An instrument to assess adults' orientations toward control versus autonomy with children: Reflections on intrinsic motivation and competence. *Journal of Educational Psychology, 83,* 642–650.

Dollinger, S.J., & Reader, M.J. (1983). Attributions, deadlines, and children's intrinsic motivation. *Journal of General Psychology, 109,* 157–166.

Drummond, J.L., & Lenes, H.S. (1997). The fitness facility membership questionnaire: A measure of reasons for joining. *Perceptual and Motor Skills, 85,* 907–916.

Duda, J.L., Chi, L., Newton, M.L., Walling, M.D., & Catley, D. (1995). Task and ego orientation and intrinsic motivation in sport. *International Journal of Sport Psychology, 26,* 40–63.

Dwyer, J.J.M. (1995). Effect of perceived choice of music on exercise intrinsic motivation. *Health Values, 19,* 18–26.

Emmons, R.A. (1995). Levels and domains in personality: An introduction. *Journal of Personality, 63,* 341–364.

Ford, M.E. (1992). *Motivating humans: Goals, emotions and personal agency beliefs.* Newbury Park, CA: Sage.

Fortier, M.S., & Grenier, M.N. (1999). Les déterminants personnels et situationnels de l'adhérence à l'exercise: Une étude prospective [Personal and situational determinants of exercise adherence]. *STAPS, 48,* 25–37.

Fortier, M.S., Vallerand, R.J., Brière, N.M., & Provencher, P.J. (1995). Competitive and recreational sport structures and gender: A test of their relationship with sport motivation. *International Journal of Sport Psychology, 26,* 24–39.

Fortier, M.S., Vallerand, R.J., & Guay, F. (1995). Academic motivation and school performance: Toward a structural model. *Contemporary Educational Psychology, 20,* 257–274.

Frederick, C.M. (in press). Self-Determination Theory and participation motivation research in the sport and exercise domain. In E.L. Deci & R.M. Ryan (Eds.), *Handbook of self-determination research.* Rochester, NY: University of Rochester Press.

Frederick, C.M., & Morrison, C.S. (1996). Social physique anxiety: Personality constructs, motivations, exercise attitudes, and behaviors. *Perceptual and Motor Skills, 82,* 963–972.

Frederick, C.M., Morrison, C.S., & Manning, T. (1996). Motivation to participate, exercise affect, and outcome behaviors toward physical activity. *Perceptual and Motor Skills, 82,* 691–701.

Freud, S. (1969). *An outline of psycho-analysis.* New York: Norton. (Original work published 1940)

Gottfried, A.E. (1990). Academic intrinsic motivation in young elementary school children. *Journal of Educational Psychology, 82,* 525–538.

Goudas, M., & Biddle, S. (1994). Intrinsic motivation in physical education: Theoretical foundations and contemporary research. *Educational and Child Psychology, 11,* 68–76.

Goudas, M., Biddle, S., & Fox, K. (1994). Achievement goal orientations and intrinsic motivation in physical fitness testing with children. *Pediatric Exercise Science, 6,* 159–167.

Goudas, M., Biddle, S., Fox, K., & Underwood, M. (1995). It ain't what you do, it's the way that you do it! Teaching style affects children's motivation in track and field lessons. *The Sport Psychologist, 9,* 254–264.

Goudas, M., Biddle, S., & Underwood, M. (1995). A prospective study of the relationships between motivational orientations and perceived competence with intrinsic motivation and achievement in a teacher education course. *Educational Psychology, 15,* 89–96.

Gould, D. (1982). Sport psychology in the 1980's: Status, direction and challenge in youth sports research. *Journal of Sport Psychology, 4,* 203–218.

Grolnick, W.S., & Ryan, R.M. (1987). Autonomy in children's learning: An experimental and individual difference investigation. *Journal of Personality and Social Psychology, 52,* 890–898.

Guay, F., Blais, M.R., Vallerand, R.J., & Pelletier, L.G. (1999). *The Global Motivation Scale.* Unpublished manuscript, Université du Québec à Montréal, Canada.

Guay, F., Vallerand, R.J., & Blanchard, C.M. (2000). *On the assessment of situational intrinsic and extrinsic motivation: The Situational Motivation Scale (SIMS).* Manuscript submitted for publication.

Halliwell, W. (1978). The effect of cognitive development on children's perceptions of intrinsically and extrinsically motivated behavior. In D. Landers & R. Christina (Eds.), *Psychology of motor behavior and sport–1977* (pp. 403–419). Champaign, IL: Human Kinetics.

Harackiewicz, J.M., Manderlink, G., & Sansone, C. (1984). Rewarding pinball wizardry: Effects of evaluation and cue-valence on intrinsic interest. *Journal of Personality and Social Psychology, 47,* 287–300.

Harter, S. (1978). Effectance motivation reconsidered: Toward a developmental model. *Human Development, 1,* 34–64.

Hull, C.L. (1943). *Principles of behavior: An introduction to behavior theory.* New York: Appleton-Century-Crofts.

Ingledew, D.K., Markland, D., & Medley, A.R. (1998). Exercise motives and stages of change. *Journal of Health Psychology, 3,* 477–489.

Jackson, S.A., Kimiecik, J.C., Ford, S.K., & Marsh, H.W. (1998). Psychological correlates of flow in sport. *Journal of Sport & Exercise Psychology, 20,* 358–378.

Jackson, S.A., & Marsh, H.W. (1996). Development and validation of a scale to measure optimal experience: The flow state scale. *Journal of Sport & Exercise Psychology, 18,* 17–35.

Kavussanu, M., & Roberts, G.C. (1996). Motivation in physical activity contexts: The relationship of perceived motivational climate to intrinsic motivation and self-efficacy. *Journal of Sport & Exercise Psychology, 18,* 264–280.

Koestner, R., Losier, G.F., Vallerand, R.J., & Carducci, D. (1996). Identified and introjected forms of political internalization: Extending self-determination theory. *Journal of Personality and Social Psychology, 70,* 1025–1036.

Kowal, J., & Fortier, M.S. (1999). Motivational determinants of flow: Contributions from Self-Determination Theory. *Journal of Social Psychology, 139,* 355–368.

Lepper, M.R., & Greene, D. (1975). Turning play into work: Effects of adult surveillance and extrinsic rewards on children's intrinsic motivation. *Journal of Personality and Social Psychology, 31,* 479–486.

Lepper, M.R., & Greene, D. (1978). Overjustification research and beyond: Toward a means-ends analysis of intrinsic and extrinsic motivation. In M.R. Lepper & D. Greene (Eds.), *The hidden costs of reward: New perspectives on the psychology of human motivation* (pp. 109–148). Hillsdale, NJ: Erlbaum.

Li, F. (1999). The Exercise Motivation Scale: Its multifaceted structure and construct validity. *Journal of Applied Sport Psychology, 11,* 97–115.

Li, F., & Harmer, P. (1996). Testing the simple assumption underlying the Sport Motivation Scale: A structural equation modeling analysis. *Research Quarterly for Exercise and Sport, 67,* 396–405.

Lloyd, J., & Fox, K.R. (1992). Achievement goals and motivation to exercise in adolescent girls: A preliminary intervention study. *British Journal of Physical Education Research Supplement, 11,* 12–16.

Lonky, E., & Reihman, J.M. (1990). *Self-regulation and moral reasoning as mediators of moral behavior.* Unpublished manuscript.

Losier, G.F., Gaudette, G.M., & Vallerand, R.J. (1997, October). *Une analyse motivationnelle des orientations à l'esprit sportif auprès d'entraîneurs certifiés du Nouveau-Brunswick [A motivational analysis of the sportpersonship orientations of certified coaches from New Brunswick].* Paper presented at the annual conference of the Quebec Society for Research in Psychology, Sherbrooke, Canada.

Losier, G.F., Vallerand, R.J., Provencher, P.J., Fortier, M.S., Senécal, C.B., & Rinfret, N. (1996). *Persistence in graduate school: A motivational analysis.* Unpublished manuscript, Université de Moncton, Canada.

Marcus, B.H., Selby, V.C., Niaura, R.S., & Rossi, J.S. (1992). Self-efficacy and the stages of exercise behavior change. *Research Quarterly for Exercise and Sport, 63,* 60–66.

Markland, D., & Hardy, L. (1997). On the factorial and construct validity of the Intrinsic Motivation Inventory: Conceptual and operational concerns. *Research Quarterly for Exercise and Sport, 68,* 20–32.

Markland, D., & Ingledew, D.K. (1997). The measurement of exercise motives: Factorial validity and invariance across gender of a revised Exercise Motivations Inventory. *British Journal of Health Psychology, 2,* 361–376.

Matthews, D.B. (1991). The effects of school environment on intrinsic motivation of middle-school children. *Journal of Humanistic Education and Development, 30,* 30–36.

McAuley, E., & Tammen, V.V. (1989). The effects of subjective and objective competitive outcomes on intrinsic motivation. *Journal of Sport & Exercise Psychology, 11,* 84–93.

Mitchell, S.A. (1996). Relationships between perceived learning environment and intrinsic motivation in middle school physical education. *Journal of Teaching in Physical Education, 15,* 369–383.

Mobily, K.E., Lemke, J.H., Ostiguy, L.J., Woodard, R.J., Griffee, T.J., & Pickens, C.C. (1993). Leisure repertoire in a sample of Midwestern elderly: The case for exercise. *Journal of Leisure Research, 25,* 84–99.

Mullan, E., Markland, D., & Ingledew, D.K. (1997). A graded conceptualisation of self-determination in the regulation of exercise behaviour: Development of a measure using confirmatory factor analytic procedures. *Personality and Individual Differences, 23,* 745–752.

O'Connor, B.P., & Vallerand, R.J. (1994). Motivation, self-determination, and person-environment fit as predictors of psychological adjustment among nursing home residents. *Psychology and Aging, 9,* 189–194.

Oman, R., & McAuley, E. (1993). Intrinsic motivation and exercise behavior. *Journal of Health Education, 24,* 232–238.

Orlick, T.D., & Mosher, R. (1978). Extrinsic awards and participant motivation in a sport related task. *International Journal of Sport Psychology, 9,* 27–39.

Papaioannou, A. (1994). Development of a questionnaire to measure achievement orientations in physical education. *Research Quarterly for Exercise and Sport, 65,* 11–20.

Papaioannou, A. (1995). Differential perceptual and motivational patterns when different goals are adopted. *Journal of Sport & Exercise Psychology, 17,* 18–34.

Pelletier, L.G., Brière, N.M., Blais, M.R., & Vallerand, R.J. (2000). *When coaches become autonomy-supportive: Effects on intrinsic motivation, persistence, and performance.* Manuscript in preparation, University of Ottawa, Canada.

Pelletier, L.G., Fortier, M.S., Vallerand, R.J., & Brière, N.M. (2000). *Associations between perceived autonomy support, forms of self-regulation, and persistence: A prospective study.* Manuscript submitted for publication.

Pelletier, L.G., Fortier, M.S., Vallerand, R.J., Tuson, K.M., Brière, N.M., & Blais, M.R. (1995). Toward a new measure of intrinsic motivation, extrinsic motivation, and amotivation in sports: The Sport Motivation Scale (SMS). *Journal of Sport & Exercise Psychology, 17,* 35–53.

Pelletier, L.G., Tuson, K.M., Green-Demers, I., Noels, K., & Beaton, A.M. (1996). *Why are you doing things for the environment? The Motivation Towards the Environment Scale (MTES)*. Unpublished manuscript, University of Ottawa, Canada.

Pelletier, L.G., Vallerand, R.J., Green-Demers, I., Blais, M.R., & Brière, N.M. (1996). Vers une conceptualisation motivationnelle multidimensionnelle du loisir: Construction et validation de l'Échelle de Motivation vis-à-vis des Loisirs (EML) [Construction and validation of the Leisure Motivation Scale]. *Loisir et Société, 19*, 559–585.

Perreault, S., & Vallerand, R.J. (1998). *On the relationship between sport motivation and coping abilities of wheel-chair basketball players*. Manuscript in preparation, Université du Québec à Trois-Rivières, Canada.

Pittman, T.S., Davey, M.E., Alafat, K.A., Wetherill, K.V., & Kramer, N.A. (1980). Informational versus controlling verbal rewards. *Personality and Social Psychology Bulletin, 6*, 228–233.

Prong, T., Rutherford, W.J., & Corbin, C.B. (1992). Physical fitness testing: The effects of rewards and feedback on intrinsic motivation. *Physical Educator, 49*, 144–151.

Provencher, P.J., & Vallerand, R.J. (1995, October). *Facteurs situationnels et motivation situationnelle: Un test de l'effet de spécificité [Situational factors and situational motivation: A test of the specificity effect]*. Paper presented at the annual conference of the Quebec Society for Research in Psychology, Ottawa, Canada.

Ratelle, C.F., Rousseau, F.L., & Vallerand, R.J. (1999). *The affective, cognitive, and behavioral consequences of a motivational conflict: Implications for the hierarchical model of intrinsic and extrinsic motivation*. Manuscript in preparation, Université du Québec à Montréal, Canada.

Reeve, J., & Deci, E.L. (1996). Elements of the competitive situation that affect intrinsic motivation. *Personality and Social Psychology Bulletin, 22*, 24–33.

Reid, G., Poulin, C., & Vallerand, R.J. (1994, June). *A pictorial motivational scale in physical activity for people with a mental disability: Development and initial validation*. Paper presented
at the annual conference of the North American Society for the Psychology of Sport and Physical Activity.

Reid, G., & Vallerand, R.J. (1998). *The development and validation of the Pictorial Motivation Scale in physical activity*. Unpublished manuscript, McGill University, Canada.

Riordan, J. (1977). *Sport in Soviet society*. Cambridge, MA: Cambridge University Press.

Roberts, G.C. (1992). Motivation in sport and exercise: Conceptual constraints and convergence. In G.C. Roberts (Ed.), *Motivation in sport and exercise* (pp. 3–29). Champaign, IL: Human Kinetics.

Rutherford, W.J., Corbin, C.B., & Chase, L.A. (1992). Factors influencing intrinsic motivation towards physical activity. *Health Values, 16*, 19–24.

Ryan, E.D. (1977). Attribution, intrinsic motivation, and athletics. In L.I. Gedvilas & M.E. Kneer (Eds.), *Proceedings of the National College of Physical Education Association for Men/National Association for Physical Education of College Women, national conference* (pp. 346–353). Chicago: University of Illinois, Office of Publications Services.

Ryan, E.D. (1980). Attribution, intrinsic motivation, and athletics: A replication and extension. In C.H. Nadeau, W.R. Halliwell, K.M. Newell, & G.C. Roberts (Eds.), *Psychology of motor behavior and sport–1979* (pp. 19–26). Champaign, IL: Human Kinetics.

Ryan, R.M., & Connell, J.P. (1989). Perceived locus of causality and internalization: Examining reasons for acting in two domains. *Journal of Personality and Social Psychology, 57*, 749–761.

Ryan, R.M., Connell, J.P., & Grolnick, W.S. (1992). When achievement is not intrinsically motivated: A theory and assessment of self-regulation in school. In A.K. Boggiano & T.S. Pittman (Eds.), *Achievement and motivation: A social-developmental perspective* (pp. 167–188). Cambridge, MA: Cambridge University Press.

Ryan, R.M., Frederick, C.M., Lepes, D., Rubio, N., & Sheldon, K.M. (1997). Intrinsic motivation and exercise adherence. *International Journal of Sport Psychology, 28*, 335–354.

Ryan, R.M., Koestner, R., & Deci, E.L. (1991). Ego-involved persistence: When free-choice behavior is not intrinsically motivated. *Motivation and Emotion, 15*, 185–205.

Ryan, R.M., Mims, V., & Koestner, R. (1983). Relation of reward contingency and interpersonal context to intrinsic motivation: A review and test using cognitive evaluation theory. *Journal of Personality and Social Psychology, 45*, 736–750.

Ryan, R.M., Vallerand, R.J., & Deci, E.L. (1984). Intrinsic motivation in sport: A cognitive evaluation theory interpretation. In W. Straub & J. Williams (Eds.), *Cognitive sport psychology* (pp. 231–242). Lansing, NY: Sport Science Associates.

Ryckman, R.M., & Hamel, J. (1993). Perceived physical ability differences in the sport participation motives of young athletes. *International Journal of Sport Psychology, 24*, 270–283.

Sansone, C., & Harackiewicz, J.M. (1996). "I don't feel like it": The function of interest in self-regulation. In L. Martin & A. Tesser (Eds.), *Striving and feeling: Interactions between goals and affect* (pp. 203–228). Hillsdale, NJ: Erlbaum.

Scanlan, T.K., & Lewthwaite, R. (1986). Social psychological aspects of competition for male youth sport participants: IV. Predictors of enjoyment. *Journal of Sport Psychology, 8*, 25–35.

Seifriz, J.J., Duda, J.L., & Chi, L. (1992). The relationship of perceived motivational climate to intrinsic motivation and beliefs about success in basketball. *Journal of Sport & Exercise Psychology, 14,* 375–391.

Senécal, C.B., Vallerand, R.J., & Pelletier, L.G. (1992). Les effets du type de programme universitaire et du sexe de l'étudiant sur la motivation académique [Effects of type of curriculum and student gender on academic motivation]. *Revue des Sciences de l'Éducation, 18,* 375–388.

Sinnott, K., & Biddle, S. (1998). Changes in attributions, perceptions of success and intrinsic motivation after attribution retraining in children's sport. *International Journal of Adolescence and Youth, 7,* 137–144.

Skinner, B.F. (1953). *Science and human behavior.* New York: Macmillan.

Smith, R.E., Schutz, R.W., Smoll, F.L., & Ptacek, J.T. (1995). Development and validation of a multidimensional measure of sport-specific psychological skills: The Athletic Coping Skills Inventory–28. *Journal of Sport & Exercise Psychology, 17,* 379–398.

Swann, W.B., & Pittman, T.S. (1977). Initiating play activity of children: The moderating influence of verbal cues on intrinsic motivation. *Child Development, 48,* 1128–1133.

Theeboom, M., De Knop, P., & Weiss, M.R. (1995). Motivational climate, psychological responses, and motor skill development in children's sport: A field-based intervention study. *Journal of Sport & Exercise Psychology, 17,* 294–311.

Thill, E., & Mouanda, J. (1990). Autonomy or control in the sports context: Validity of cognitive evaluation theory. *International Journal of Sport Psychology, 21,* 1–20.

Thomas, J.R., & Tennant, L.K. (1978). Effects of rewards on children's motivation for an athletic task. In F.L. Smoll & R.E. Smith (Eds.), *Psychological perspectives in youth sports* (Vol. 1, pp. 123–144). Washington, DC: Hemisphere.

Thompson, C.E., & Wankel, L.M. (1980). The effect of perceived activity choice upon frequency of exercise behavior. *Journal of Applied Social Psychology, 10,* 436–443.

Vallerand, R.J. (1997). Toward a hierarchical model of intrinsic and extrinsic motivation. In M.P. Zanna (Ed.), *Advances in experimental social psychology* (Vol. 29, pp. 271–360). New York: Academic Press.

Vallerand, R.J. (in press). A hierarchical model of intrinsic and extrinsic motivation in sport and exercise. In G. Roberts (Ed.), *Advances in motivation in sport and exercise* (2nd ed.). Champaign, IL: Human Kinetics.

Vallerand, R.J., & Bissonnette, R. (1992). Intrinsic, extrinsic, and amotivational styles as predictors of behavior: A prospective study. *Journal of Personality, 60,* 599–620.

Vallerand, R.J., Blais, M.R., Brière, N.M., & Pelletier, L.G. (1989). Construction et validation de l'Échelle de motivation en éducation (EME) [On the construction and validation of the French form of the Academic Motivation Scale]. *Canadian Journal of Behavioural Science, 21,* 323–349.

Vallerand, R.J., & Blanchard, C.M. (1998a). *A prospective test of the hierarchical model of intrinsic and extrinsic motivation in an exercise setting.* Unpublished raw data, Université du Québec à Montréal, Canada.

Vallerand, R.J., & Blanchard, C.M. (1998b). *A test of the motivation-consequences relationship at three levels of generality.* Unpublished raw data, Université du Québec à Montréal, Canada.

Vallerand, R.J., & Blanchard, C.M. (1999). Éducation permanente et motivation: Contribution du modèle hiérarchique de la motivation intrinsèque et extrinsèque [Continuing education and motivation: Contribution of the Hierarchical Model of Intrinsic and Extrinsic Motivation]. *Éducation Permanente, 136,* 15–36.

Vallerand, R.J., & Brière, N.M. (1990). *Développement et validation d'un instrument de mesure par questionnaire de motivation intrinsèque, extrinsèque, d'amotivation pour le domaine des sports [Validation of the French form of the Sport Motivation Scale].* Final report presented to the Canadian Fitness and Lifestyle Research Institute, Ottawa, Canada.

Vallerand, R.J., Brière, N.M., Blanchard, C.M., & Provencher, P.J. (1997). Development and validation of the Multidimensional Sportspersonship Orientations Scale. *Journal of Sport & Exercise Psychology, 19,* 197–206.

Vallerand, R.J., Deci, E.L., & Ryan, R.M. (1987). Intrinsic motivation in sport. In K. Pandolf (Ed.), *Exercise and sport science reviews* (Vol. 15, pp. 389–425). New York: Macmillan.

Vallerand, R.J., Deshaies, P., Cuerrier, J.-P., Brière, N.M., & Pelletier, L.G. (1996). Toward a multidimensional definition of sportsmanship. *Journal of Applied Sport Psychology, 8,* 89–101.

Vallerand, R.J., & Fortier, M.S. (1998). Measures of intrinsic and extrinsic motivation in sport and physical activity: A review and critique. In J. Duda (Ed.), *Advancements in sport and exercise psychology measurement* (pp. 83–100). Morgantown, WV: Fitness Information Technology.

Vallerand, R.J., Fortier, M.S., & Guay, F. (1997). Self-determination and persistence in a real-life setting: Toward a motivational model of high school dropout. *Journal of Personality and Social Psychology, 72,* 1161–1176.

Vallerand, R.J., Gauvin, L., & Halliwell, W.R. (1986a). Effects of zero-sum competition on children's intrinsic motivation and perceived competence. *Journal of Social Psychology, 126,* 465–472.

Vallerand, R.J., Gauvin, L., & Halliwell, W.R. (1986b). Negative effects of competition on children's intrinsic motivation. *Journal of Social Psychology, 126,* 649–657.

Vallerand, R.J., & Grouzet, F.M.E. (in press). Pour un modèle hiérarchique de la motivation intrinsèque et extrinsèque dans les pratiques sportives et l'activité physique [For a hierarchical model of intrinsic and extrinsic motivation in sport and physical activity]. In F. Curry, P. Sarrazin, & J.P. Famose (Eds.), *Théories de la motivation et pratiques sportives* [Theories of motivation and sport practices]. Paris: Presses Universitaires de France.

Vallerand, R.J., Guay, F., & Blanchard, C.M. (2000). *Self-regulatory processes in human behavior: A test of the hierarchical model of intrinsic and extrinsic motivation.* Manuscript submitted for publication, Université du Québec à Montréal, Canada.

Vallerand, R.J., & Losier, G.F. (1994). Self-determined motivation and sportsmanship orientations: An assessment of their temporal relationship. *Journal of Sport & Exercise Psychology, 16,* 229–245.

Vallerand, R.J., & Losier, G.F. (1999). An integrative analysis of intrinsic and extrinsic motivation in sport. *Journal of Applied Sport Psychology, 11,* 142–169.

Vallerand, R.J., & O'Connor, B.P. (1991). Construction et validation de l'Échelle de Motivation pour les personnes âgées (EMPA) [Construction and validation of the French form of the Elderly Motivation Scale]. *International Journal of Psychology, 26,* 219–240.

Vallerand, R.J., Pelletier, L.G., Blais, M.R., Brière, N.M., Senécal, C., & Vallières, E.F. (1992). The Academic Motivation Scale: A measure of intrinsic, extrinsic, and amotivation in education. *Educational and Psychological Measurement, 52,* 1003–1019.

Vallerand, R.J., Pelletier, L.G., Blais, M.R., Brière, N.M., Senécal, C., & Vallières, E.F. (1993). On the assessment of intrinsic, extrinsic, and amotivation in education: Evidence on the concurrent and construct validity of the Academic Motivation Scale. *Educational and Psychological Measurement, 53,* 159–172.

Vallerand, R.J., & Perreault, S. (1999). Intrinsic and extrinsic motivation in sport: Toward a hierarchical model. In R. Lidor & M. Bar-Eli (Eds.), *Sport psychology: Linking theory and practice* (pp. 191–212). Morgantown, WV: Fitness Information Technology.

Vallerand, R.J., & Ratelle, C.F. (in press). Intrinsic and extrinsic motivation: A Hierarchical model. In E.L. Deci & R.M. Ryan (Eds.), *Handbook of self-determination research.* Rochester, NY: University of Rochester Press.

Vallerand, R.J., & Reid, G. (1984). On the causal effects of perceived competence on intrinsic motivation: A test of cognitive evaluation theory. *Journal of Sport Psychology, 6,* 94–102.

Vallerand, R.J., & Reid, G. (1988). On the relative effects of positive and negative verbal feedback on males' and females' intrinsic motivation. *Canadian Journal of Behavioural Sciences, 20,* 239–250.

Vallerand, R.J., & Reid, G. (1990). Motivation and special populations: Theory, research and implications regarding motor behavior. In G. Reid (Ed.), *Problems in motor control* (pp. 159–197). New York: North Holland.

Vallerand, R.J., & Thill, E.E. (1993). Introduction au concept de motivation [Introduction to the concept of motivation]. In R.J. Vallerand & E.E. Thill (Eds.), *Introduction à la psychologie de la motivation* [Introduction to the psychology of motivation] (pp. 3–39). Laval, Canada: Éditions Études Vivantes.

Wagner, S.L., Lounsbury, J.W., & Fitzgerald, L.G. (1989). Attribute factors associated with work/leisure perceptions. *Journal of Leisure Research, 21,* 155–166.

Watson, D., Clark, L.A., & Tellegen, A. (1988). Development and validation of brief measures of positive and negative affect: The PANAS scales. *Journal of Personality and Social Psychology, 54,* 1063–1070.

Weigand, D.A., & Broadhurst, C.J. (1998). The relationship among perceived competence, intrinsic motivation, and control perceptions in youth soccer. *International Journal of Sport Psychology, 29,* 324–338.

Weinberg, R.S. (1979). Intrinsic motivation in a competitive setting. *Medicine and Science in Sports, 11,* 146–149.

Weinberg, R.S., & Jackson, A. (1979). Competition and extrinsic rewards: Effect on intrinsic motivation and attribution. *Research Quarterly, 50,* 494–502.

Weinberg, R.S., & Ragan, J. (1979). Effects of competition, success/failure, and sex on intrinsic motivation. *Research Quarterly, 50,* 503–510.

Weiner, B. (1972). *Theories of motivation: From mechanism to cognition.* Chicago: Markham.

Weiss, M.R., Bredemeier, B.J., & Shewchuk, R.M. (1985). An intrinsic/extrinsic motivation scale for the youth sport setting: A confirmatory factor analysis. *Journal of Sport Psychology, 7,* 75–91.

White, R.W. (1959). Motivation reconsidered: The concept of competence. *Psychological Review, 66,* 297–333.

Whitehead, J.R., & Corbin, C.B. (1991a). Effects of fitness test type, teacher, and gender on exercise intrinsic motivation and physical self-worth. *Journal of School Health, 61,* 11–16.

Whitehead, J.R., & Corbin, C.B. (1991b). Youth fitness testing: The effect of percentile-based evaluative feedback on intrinsic motivation. *Research Quarterly for Exercise and Sport, 62,* 225–231.

Williams, L., & Gill, D.L. (1995). The role of perceived competence in the motivation of physical activity. *Journal of Sport & Exercise Psychology, 17,* 363–378.

CHAPTER 16

Achievement Goal Theory in Sport
Recent Extensions and Future Directions

JOAN L. DUDA and HOWARD HALL

During the past decade, achievement goal theory (Ames, 1992a, 1992b; Dweck, 1986, 1999; Nicholls, 1984, 1989) has become a major theoretical paradigm in sport psychology research around the world for investigating the antecedents and consequences of sport motivation. Since the previous review of this literature in the first edition of the *Handbook on Research in Sport Psychology* (Duda, 1993), a plethora of studies have been conducted concerning the achievement-related implications of variations in goal perspectives (see Duda & Whitehead, 1998). Indeed, given the myriad research directions and findings concerning achievement goals in the physical domain (i.e., sport, physical education, and exercise), it is no longer possible to do justice to this body of literature in one chapter.

Consequently, major trends in current work on goal perspectives is the focus in this chapter (particularly those that have evolved since previous reviews; see also Duda, 1992; Roberts, Treasure, & Kavussanu, 1997). Further, the studies addressed in this chapter are primarily those conducted in athletic settings. Before reviewing recent lines of investigation on achievement goals in sport, advances in and challenges facing measurement in this area of inquiry are highlighted. Finally, we conclude with future directions for sport studies grounded in achievement goal theory.

REVIEW OF MAJOR THEORETICAL CONSTRUCTS AND TENETS

The Conceptualization of Achievement Goals

The central tenet of achievement goal theory is that achievement behavior is a function of the personal meaning an individual assigns to perceived success and failure (Maehr & Braskamp, 1986). Thus, it is assumed that the choice to invest in any activity, the amount of effort expended on a task, the level of persistence shown toward a challenge, and the cognitions and affective responses associated with the resulting behaviors emanate from the meaning that is attached to one's achievement striving.

Most achievement goal theorists (Ames, 1992b; Duda, 1993; in press-a; Dweck, 1999; Dweck & Leggett, 1988; Maehr & Braskamp, 1986; Nicholls, 1984, 1989; Roberts, 1992, 1997) suggest that in any achievement context, individuals give meaning to their investment through the achievement goals they endorse. Those embracing this school of thought consider achievement goals to be the critical determinants of behavioral intention because they reflect the purposes underlying people's actions in achievement settings (such as the classroom, sport, and physical education). Once endorsed, an achievement goal defines an integrated pattern of beliefs, attributions, and affect that underpins different approach and avoidance strategies, different levels of engagement, and different responses to achievement outcomes (Kaplan & Maehr, 1999). That is, achievement goals are presumed to be the organizing principle influencing how we interpret, feel about, and react to our achievement-related endeavors.

Nicholls (1984, 1989) further argued that individuals adopt different achievement goals as a direct consequence of the way in which they construe competence. His research identified two specific achievement goals to which he attached the labels "task" and "ego." Although other theorists (e.g., Ames, 1992b; Dweck, 1986, 1999) utilize other names for these two goal perspectives, Nicholls's terminology is employed in this chapter. According to Nicholls (1984, 1989), a task goal reflects a focus on the development of competence; an ego goal reflects an underlying concern with the demonstration of competence or the avoidance of being judged incompetent.

The experiences associated with endorsing each of these achievement goals are held to be qualitatively different (Ames, 1992b; Dweck, 1999; Dweck & Leggett, 1988). When endorsing a task goal, there is a fundamental belief that ability and effort covary (Ames, 1992b; Dweck, 1999; Nicholls, 1989), such that when effort is applied, competence will increase. A task goal will thus orient an individual toward the development of potential, which can be measured through personal improvement, learning, and mastery of the task. When targeting task goals, individuals are assumed to become immersed in the intrinsic value of learning and a quest to discover strategies to meet the demands of the activity and further enhance their competence. Because perceptions of success and failure tend to be based on self-referenced standards, it is suggested that a focus on task goals will lead to greater absorption in the process of improving and less preoccupation with proving to others how good one is.

In contrast, when endorsing an ego goal, both the demonstration of one's high ability and the avoidance of demonstrating comparative low ability are of major concern. This focus has enormous implications for the public presentation of self, and is assumed to result in heightened self-awareness (Ames, 1992b; Dweck, 1999; Kaplan & Maehr, 1999; Nicholls, 1989). For individuals centered on an ego goal, a positive validation of one's competence can only occur if one's performance compares favorably with that of others. Unlike those endorsing a task goal, those who hold an ego goal are less likely to consider effort to be an important cause of success. Rather, they tend to believe that success stems primarily from the possession of comparatively high ability. However, individuals emphasizing an ego goal are acutely aware that the utilization of effort is of critical importance to both the demonstration of competence and the avoidance of a judgment of low ability. That is, when adopting an ego goal perspective, it becomes possible to demonstrate greater competence if one is successful with little effort. Similarly, one can avoid demonstrating incompetence if failure can be attributed to not trying hard. In essence, what becomes most threatening to those holding ego goals is the thought of expending maximal effort only for it to result in failure. Under these circumstances, all that can be demonstrated is a lack of competence. Consequently, when holding an ego goal, effort becomes a "double-edged sword," in that it tends to be strategically expended or withheld to enhance or protect self-worth (Covington, 1992; Dweck, 1999). Although rescinding effort may enable people to avoid demonstrating incompetence, it should also hinder learning and skill development and ultimately lead to individuals failing to live up to their potential.

Goals as Antecedents of Adaptive and Maladaptive Patterns of Motivation

In achievement domains such as the classroom, it has been noted that the endorsement of a task goal frequently results in adaptive achievement striving for individuals regardless of level of perceived competence (Ames, 1992b; Dweck, 1999; Dweck & Leggett, 1988; Kaplan & Maehr, 1999; Nicholls, 1989). Because task-goal-focused individuals hold a belief that effort is a critical determinant of success and are less concerned about "looking good," they tend to try hard and be more persistent when faced with obstacles and difficulty. It has been noted that, when emphasizing task goals, individuals are more likely to develop and employ effective strategies to improve their performance by planning, monitoring, and regulating their efforts. They also tend to maintain a fervent and optimistic belief that success is possible (Dweck, 1999; Pintrich, 1989). Furthermore, when given the choice, such individuals are expected to prefer challenging rather than easy activities. This is because it is their self-referenced progress, stemming from maximum exerted effort, that informs task-focused individuals of their competence gains. In this case, immense satisfaction may be experienced when it can be seen that trying hard to overcome difficult challenges results in success.

In contrast, the endorsement of an ego goal is assumed to spur individuals to display their ability rather than focus on its development. When an ego goal predominates, adaptive achievement striving will result only when the goal is accompanied by the individual's holding a comparatively high perception of competence (Nicholls, 1989). Fortunately, for those who have confidence that their competence is comparatively high, there is a reasonable probability that success will occur (Bandura, 1990). Under these conditions, an individual's sense of self is unlikely to be threatened. Another important tenet of achievement goal theories, however, is that perceptions of sufficiently high ability are fragile when ego goals are stressed (Dweck, 1999; Nicholls, 1989). This is because, when adopting ego goals, perceptions of competence involve social comparison processes and entail a consideration of the observed performance and exerted effort of others. It is not easy to always be the best.

When those endorsing an ego goal have reason to question their ability (e.g., when facing a challenge and/or possibility of not demonstrating superiority; Dweck, 1999), their sense of self comes under threat. Maladaptive patterns of achievement behavior are held to result because these individuals become preoccupied about whether their ability is adequate. This preoccupation may result in anxiety and may subsequently lead to task-irrelevant thoughts rather than focused attention on the task at hand. Performance debilitation and diminished persistence are expected to ensue as a consequence of such negative cognitions and affect.

The major contributor to the expected adaptive and maladaptive patterns associated with task and ego goals of motivation appears to lie in the source of control (Biddle, 1999). For those who endorse task goals, the arbitration over subjective success lies within themselves. As such, these individuals can choose to focus on any aspect of the performance process (including the outcome; see Duda, 1996, in press-a) to evaluate whether self-referenced success has occurred. In contrast, when evaluating personal achievement, those who endorse ego goals tend to rely on facets of performance that lie outside of their control. These individuals are more likely to look to the performance of others to judge their own competence.

In Nicholls's thinking (1984, 1989), the endorsement of task and ego goals is manifested in people's states of involvement. That is, while engaging in achievement tasks, degree of task and ego involvement is varied. Nicholls (1984, 1989) and later Dweck (1991, 1999) have pointed out that there are individual differences in the proneness to adopt task or ego goals (or tendencies to exhibit task and ego involvement) while engaged in achievement tasks. Accordingly, people vary in their degree of task and ego orientation (Duda, 1992; Nicholls, 1989).

According to Nicholls (1989), individual differences in goal orientations are inextricably intertwined with people's beliefs about the causes of success. In fact, he proposes that the interdependencies between task orientation and the belief that effort leads to success and ego orientation and the view that ability is a prerequisite to achievement constitute two distinct and independent personal theories (Duda & Nicholls, 1992). These goal-belief dimensions or personal theories reflect what is deemed important in achievement activities (i.e., personal goals) and people's ideas about how achievement activities operate (i.e., personal beliefs about success).

For Dweck (1991, 1999), achievement goal orientations are coupled with personal theories of intelligence/ability. More specifically, an ego goal orientation is presumed to be linked with the "theory" that intelligence or ability is fixed (i.e., an entity view). In contrast, a task goal orientation is expected to be associated with the endorsement of an incremental theory of intelligence/ability. When individuals hold the latter personal theory, they tend to believe that intelligence/ability can be increased via the exertion of effort, learning, and other factors.

The Prediction of Achievement Patterns

As suggested in the previous discussion, achievement goal theories (Ames, 1992a, 1992b; Dweck, 1986, 1999; Nicholls, 1984, 1989) center not only on the prediction of performance variability. Other achievement behaviors, such as the exertion of effort, task choice preference (in terms of difficulty), and sustained involvement versus a lack of persistence are presumed to be impacted by the differential adoption of achievement goals (and perceptions of and commitment to demonstrate ability). Thus, the achievement goal framework has implications for the prediction of immediate achievement behaviors and the forecasting of behavioral patterns over time. Indeed, achievement goal theorists have placed particular significance on understanding what contributes to long-term accomplishment along with short-term successes (Nicholls, 1989). Finally, at the heart of achievement goal conceptualizations is the aim of gaining insight into the constellation of beliefs, cognitions, and emotions that are differentially tied to task and ego goal adoption and held to underpin behavioral variability. Thus, this theoretical framework pivots around the prediction of motivational processes rather than motivation-related outcomes exclusively.

Situational Influences: The Role of the Climate

Both Dweck (1986, 1999) and Nicholls (1989) point to the importance of situational factors in influencing whether individuals are more likely to be task- or ego-involved in achievement activities. For the most part, they refer to features of the objective environment. However, Ames (1992a, 1992b; Ames & Archer, 1988) especially contributed to the operationalization and awareness of the motivational significance of perceptions of the situationally emphasized goal perspectives operating in achievement settings. According to Ames (1992b), the perceived structure of the achievement environment, or motivational climate, makes task and ego goals differentially salient. She holds that this climate is multidimensional. Differential structures such as the standards, methods, and criteria underlying evaluation, the nature of recognition and the manner in which it is expressed, the source of authority, the way tasks are structured, and the manner in which individuals are grouped are held to constitute the overriding climate operating in achievement settings. Another important contribution of Ames's work (1992a) is that it provided straightforward (although not necessarily easy to meet) strategies for fostering task involvement and reducing ego involvement in achievement situations. That is, in Ames's research (1992b), the goal is to work with the significant other and modify the various components underpinning a task in contrast to ego-involving climate.

MEASUREMENT OF SPORT ACHIEVEMENT GOALS

Before examining the antecedents and consequences of achievement goals in sport settings, it is paramount that sound measures of dispositional, situational, and state goal perspectives be available. It has been suggested that the development of assessment tools has mirrored the application and extension of achievement goal theories in sport and other physical activity domains (Duda, in press-a). Although more work is needed, considerable efforts have been made to develop reliable and valid assessments of goal orientations and perceptions of the motivational climate pertinent to the athletic milieu. More limited but equally important attempts to measure goal involvement in sport are also evident in the literature. This research is briefly highlighted next (for a more extensive review, see Duda & Whitehead, 1998).

Goal Orientations

With respect to constructs embedded in achievement goal theories, the development of assessments specific to the sport setting initially centered on the measurement of individual differences in the proneness for task and ego involvement. The first to be developed was the Task and Ego Orientation in Sport Questionnaire (TEOSQ; Duda, 1989) and the second was the Perceptions of Success Questionnaire (POSQ; Roberts & Balague, 1991; Roberts, Treasure, & Balague, 1998). Congruent with Nicholls's (1989) ideas regarding the measurement of achievement goal orientations, both the TEOSQ and POSQ determine athletes' differential emphasis on achievement-related criteria underlying subjective success. That is, individuals are requested to consider the stem "I feel successful in sport when . . ." and then indicate their agreement with a series of items reflecting task or ego criteria. Also aligned with Nicholls, the task and ego orientation scales of the TEOSQ and POSQ have generally been found to be orthogonal (Chi & Duda, 1995; Roberts, Treasure, & Kavussanu, 1996). When they are found to be associated (e.g., Li, Harmer, Chi, & Vongjaturapat, 1996), the observed correlation is usually low to moderate and positive. Both instruments have been successfully translated into a variety of languages (e.g., the

Spanish version of the TEOSQ, Balaguer, Castillo, & Tomas [1996], and the French version of the POSQ, Cury, Biddle, Famose, Goudas, Sarrazin, & Durand [1996]). A considerable amount of work has been done examining the factorial and construct validity as well as reliability of these instruments (see Duda & Whitehead, 1998, for a detailed review). Support for the sound psychometric features of the TEOSQ and POSQ has been garnered.

Questions have been raised in the literature concerning the operationalization of goal orientations as epitomized in the TEOSQ and POSQ. In some cases, there is perplexity about what these two instruments measure. In other cases, discontent has been expressed regarding whether the TEOSQ and POSQ adequately assess individual differences in goal perspectives. With respect to the former issue, dispositional goal orientations have been errantly equated to measures of goal setting style (i.e., whether individuals tend to set process or outcome goals; see Duda, 1997; Duda, in press-a; Hardy, 1997) and competitive orientations that have not been grounded in the contemporary achievement goal framework (such as Vealey's [1986] Competitive Orientation Inventory; see Duda, 1992, 1996, in press-a). There has also been some confusion about whether the TEOSQ and POSQ measure conceptions of ability (i.e., self-referenced and effort-based as well as normative conceptions; see Harwood & Hardy, 1999) or subjective criteria for success. As indicated previously, they were designed to tap the latter (see Duda, in press-a). In terms of potential shortcomings in the predictive utility of the TEOSQ and POSQ, recent work (Harwood & Hardy, 1999) has suggested that more specific assessments of goal orientations (e.g., specific to the current sport event, measures that target competition versus training) may be more useful than general sport goal orientation measures in terms of the prediction of situationally specific responses of athletes.

This, however, does not reflect a limitation of the TEOSQ or POSQ. Rather, such a consideration points to the importance of ensuring a level of congruence (from more general to more situational or task-specific) in the measurement tools used to examine particular relationships between independent and dependent variables (Papaioannou, 1999; Vallerand, 1997). The TEOSQ and POSQ were developed to assess how individuals tend to define success in sport overall (or in a targeted sport) across particular competitive events and training periods. Neither measure was designed to assess momentary change in the meaning of achievement. Future psychometric development may work toward this aim.

Motivational Climate

The available assessments of the perceived motivational climate in sport have primarily drawn from the work of Ames (1992a, 1992b) and centered on the determination of the motivational atmosphere created by the coach (Ntoumanis & Biddle, 1999b; Seifriz, Duda, & Chi, 1992; Walling, Duda, & Chi, 1993). A number of investigations have examined the motivation-related correlates of scores on the Perceived Motivational Climate in Sport Questionnaire (PMCSQ; Walling et al., 1993). Research has also been done regarding the measurement of the motivational climate deemed to be emphasized by parents with respect to the learning of sport skills (White, 1996, 1998; White, Duda, & Hart, 1992). In both cases, it seems that the task- and ego-involving features of the social environment surrounding individuals in sport can be distinguished. That is, studies have provided evidence for task and ego climate dimensions that tend to be slightly inversely related (see Duda & Whitehead, 1998, and Ntoumanis & Biddle, 1999b, for a review).

Furthermore, research using the PMCSQ indicates that there is variability in how athletes on one team see the climate manifested (Duda, Newton, & Yin, 1999). This is particularly true in terms of the ego-involving facets of the climate. However, research by Duda and her colleagues involving 46 female volleyball teams also indicated that there is significant within-team interdependence in perceptions of the motivational atmosphere. More specifically, although they don't all "see eye to eye," athletes on one team are more similar in how they view the coach-created environment than are athletes from different teams.

Recently, investigators of the perceived motivational climate on sport teams (as created by the coach) have attempted to develop and test a hierarchically structured PMCSQ (Newton, 1994; Newton, Duda, & Yin, in press). The measurement model hypothesized to underlie the PMCSQ-2 holds that there are two overriding climate dimensions (i.e., a task-involving and an ego-involving climate dimension). It is also assumed, congruent with the thinking of Ames (1992a, 1992b), that there are particular and differential situational structures that lay the foundation for athletes' overall perceptions of a task and ego climate. These structures are targeted by specific subscales of the PMCSQ-2. For example, a component of a perceived task-involving environment would be the athletes' views that the coach shows how each player contributes to the team's performance. In contrast, a component of an ego-involving climate would be that the coach treats the high-ability players differentially and preferentially.

Evidence in support of the hypothesized hierarchical structure of the PMCSQ-2 has been acceptable but not compelling (Newton et al., in press). The internal reliability of some of the current subscales needs to be improved (e.g., increase items on the problematic subscales). Moreover, future research should help to determine whether all the salient structures underpinning the perceived coach-created motivational climate are captured by the PMCSQ-2.

Existing measures of the motivational climate manifested in the physical domain, such as the PMCSQ-2, were designed to tap the prevailing and prototypical (Kaplan & Maehr, 1999) atmosphere created by particular significant others that envelope an athlete. As indicated in previous sport research, however (e.g., Harwood & Swain, 1998; Swain & Harwood, 1996), there are contextual factors that occur "at the moment" in athletes' training and competitive encounters. An interesting avenue for subsequent work might be to formulate a sound assessment of current environmental factors that are influencing an athlete's goal state at a particular point in time.

Goal States

A critical but especially challenging line of inquiry centers on the measurement of goal states (i.e., states of task and ego involvement) in the sport domain. The work that has been completed has taken one of two approaches. One has been to take existing measures of dispositional goal orientations such as the TEOSQ or POSQ and examine athletes' state goal orientations (e.g., Hall & Kerr, 1997; Hall, Kerr, & Matthews, 1998; Williams, 1998). A second has been to present athletes with single-item measures, having them indicate their differential emphasis on achieving a personal standard or beating others in the forthcoming contest (Harwood & Swain, 1998; Swain & Harwood, 1996). Both types of assessment strategies have generally been found to be more predictive of athletes' cognitions and affect related to the competition than measures of dispositional goal orientations (such as the TEOSQ and POSQ). This might be another illustration of the "congruence in level of measurement" principle (general-specific) referred to previously in this chapter.

Recently, Duda (in press-a) has questioned whether such single-item or modified dispositional goal measures capture states of task and ego involvement as operationalized by Nicholls (1989) and Dweck (1999). That is, in the view of the latter two achievement goal theorists, task and ego involvement seem to have a cognitive component (e.g., What is the person concerned about at the moment: The task or exhibiting superiority/avoiding the demonstration of low ability?), an attentional aspect (e.g., Is one attending to task-relevant cues or attending to someone/something else?), and an affective facet (e.g., Is the person enjoying the moment? Is he or she anxious?). In essence, as proposed by Duda and Whitehead (1998), task and ego involvement in sport settings might represent two distinct and multidimensional motivational processes that can ebb and flow throughout each competitive and practice situation. In other words, they may be more than an athlete's subjective criteria of success at the moment.

Similar conceptual reasoning has been utilized in educational contexts by Kaplan and Maehr (1999). They argue that achievement goals may operate as social schemas. That is, in any context, they provide a broad framework for filtering information, construing the nature and meaning of given situations, and they provide both a stimulus and a guide for actions and feelings. Kaplan and Maehr also suggest that goals might be considered "self-primes" in that each goal may underpin a differential awareness of self. When an ego goal is endorsed, it focuses attention on who one is, what one can be, or what one can do. As task involvement cannot be sustained under conditions of self-awareness, adaptive motivation often becomes undermined. In contrast, self-awareness is minimal when an individual endorses a task goal in a particular situation, and thus is able to maintain a state of task involvement and demonstrate more adaptive patterns of achievement behavior.

RESEARCH FINDINGS: GOALS AND THEIR MOTIVATIONAL IMPLICATIONS IN SPORT

Goals and Behavior

It is fair to say that the majority of sport research on achievement goals to date has focused on the prediction of beliefs, values, cognitions, and emotional responses associated with task and ego goals. Relatively less has been done regarding the examination of theoretically expected links to behavior, especially objective rather than self-reported behavioral indices (Duda & Whitehead, 1998). Overall, the research conducted has been consonant with theoretical predictions.

With reference to the prediction of performance, the research points to a positive association between task orientation and performance outcomes (e.g., Chi, 1993; Kingston & Hardy, 1997; Sarrazin, Cury, & Roberts, 1999; Solmon & Boone, 1993; VanYperen & Duda, 1999). A negative association between ego orientation and sport-related performance, as suggested by the theory, has emerged

when perceived ability is low and/or individuals' task orientation is not strong (e.g., Chi, 1993; Kingston & Hardy, 1997; Sarrazin et al., 1999).

Recently, researchers have investigated the implications of achievement goals for persistence in sport (Andree & Whitehead, 1996; Guillet & Sarrazin, 1999; LeBars & Gernigon, 1998). To address such a question, longitudinal studies are necessary. The findings from the limited research that has been conducted has been consonant with achievement goal theory. For example, in a study of 138 male and female (13 to 17 years old) British club sport participants, Andree and Whitehead (1996) examined the significance of goal orientations, the perceived motivational climate, and perceptions of ability in distinguishing between persisters and nonpersisters across two years of involvement. Importantly, these researchers also realized that there are those who don't persist from one season to the next because of "involuntary" reasons. These athletes were not considered part of the nonpersister or dropout group. Andree and Whitehead found that those who did not continue participation perceived their ability to be low and viewed their sport environment as highly ego-involving.

Guillet and Sarrazin (1999) examined the role of the perceived motivational climate in the prediction of dropping out of sport among 600 French female handball players. They found that a perceived task-involving climate operating on one's team positively related to greater perceived progress and perceptions of an ego-involving atmosphere corresponded to lower perceived autonomy. Perceived progress and perceived autonomy emerged as two strong, positive predictors of self-determined motivation. When the handball players' motivation to participate in their sport was more self-determined, they reported lower intentions to drop out. Those athletes who reported stronger intentions to quit handball were significantly more likely to do so at the end of the season.

More work is needed on the relationship of both dispositional and situationally emphasized goals to behavioral patterns in the sport domain. Thankfully, however, the existing literature provides some insight into the cognitive and affective reasons why variability is seen in performance, skill development, and persistence in relation to achievement goals.

Reviewed next are five areas of research that foster understanding of why and how task and ego goals may correspond to different achievement behaviors. The first three (i.e., the interdependencies between goal perspectives and beliefs about success, the perceived purposes of sport, and enjoyment and intrinsic motivation) are particularly informative with respect to explaining links between achievement goals and sustained, quality involvement in sport. The latter two (i.e., the relationship of goal perspectives to strategy use and anxiety) seem especially enlightening in terms of performance effects (which, of course, over time may have implications for sport persistence). Because it is a central variable in the sport psychology literature and the focus of a number of interesting, contemporary studies on goal perspectives in sport, more attention is given in this chapter to the role of dispositional and situational achievement goals with respect to the stress process.

Goals, Beliefs, and Values

A cogent body of literature has evolved regarding the link between goal orientations and athletes' beliefs about the determinants of success. Overall, this work suggests that there is a logical congruence between the purposes of athletes' sport participation (i.e., which goals they emphasize) and their views about what is necessary to achieve success. A plethora of studies have supported the hypothesized link between task orientation and the beliefs that one must work hard and work with others to be successful in sport (Biddle, Akande, Vlachopoulos, & Fox, 1996; Duda, Fox, Biddle, & Armstrong, 1992; Duda & Nicholls, 1992; Duda & White, 1992; Gano-Overway & Duda, in press; Guivernau & Duda, 1994; Hom, Duda, & Miller, 1993; Newton & Duda, 1993; Newton & Fry, 1998; Roberts & Ommundsen, 1996; Seifriz, Duda, & Chi, 1992; Treasure & Roberts, 1994, 1998; VanYperen & Duda, 1999; White & Duda, 1993). Research has also provided support for the predicted association between an ego orientation and the belief that being athletically able is a critical antecedent to sport achievement. Ego orientation has not been found to correlate with the view that the exertion of effort leads to sport success. This pattern of results has emerged across different sports, national origins, and competitive levels.

Thus, goals and beliefs about the causes of success seem to be aligned in a way that makes conceptual sense. As Nicholls (1989) has suggested, these two related constructs form the backbone of individuals' personal theories of sport achievement. That is, the observed goal-belief dimension is informative about what is important to the person (lays the basis for subjective success) and his or her ideas regarding how the sport in question functions. More needs to be known, however, about how different beliefs about success correspond to different ways in which individuals process their sport experience. For example, an interesting direction for future work would be to examine the interdependencies between overall beliefs about sport success and

athletes' attributional style or their specific attributions for good and poor performances following a competitive event. A second intriguing avenue for subsequent research would be to determine whether effort and ability beliefs about the determinants of sport achievement differentially relate to perceptions of control (Biddle, 1999; Kim & Duda, 1999) in accordance with theoretical predictions (Dweck, 1999; Nicholls, 1984, 1989). Finally, what is the role of views about the causes of sport failure in terms of motivation-related processes?

Extending the work of Nicholls (1989) in the classroom to the athletic milieu, previous investigations have also examined the interdependencies between goal orientations and athletes' views about the purposes of sport involvement. In this case, the focus is not on athletes' ideas about how sport functions but rather their conceptions of what should be the function(s) of athletic participation. In total, this line of investigation suggests that the desired consequences of sport are deemed more or less intrinsic or extrinsic depending on the goal orientation manifested by athletes.

Research involving youth sport through college-age participants (Duda, 1989; Roberts, Hall, Jackson, Kimiecik, & Tonymon, 1995; Roberts & Ommundsen, 1996; Roberts, Treasure, & Balague, 1998; Treasure & Roberts, 1994) has generally revealed a positive association between task orientation and the perceptions that sport should contribute to character development, a strong work ethic, and lifetime health. The major trend with respect to ego orientation is that this dispositional goal perspective seems to correspond to the view that sport should enhance one's social status and sense of self-importance. In their work involving high-level football players from the UK, however, Carpenter and Yates (1997) reported a positive link between ego orientation and the perception that an important purpose of soccer is to enhance levels of physical fitness. This purpose seems more intrinsic in nature. Aligned with Nicholls (1989) and the achievement goal framework, though, a pronounced task orientation and low ego orientation were negatively related to the perceptions that involvement in soccer should result in financial remuneration and aggressive behaviors. High task and low ego orientation also were coupled with the belief that an athlete should be higher in sportspersonship after competing in soccer. Moreover, Carpenter and Yates observed a positive relationship between ego orientation and the view that soccer should prove profitable for the participants.

A recent study by Ommundsen and Roberts (1999) examined the interrelationships between perceptions of the motivational climate and perceptions of the purposes of sport. The participants in this investigation were 148 Norwegian university students who had participated and/or were currently participating in a team sport. Results indicated that athletes who perceived their sport environment as being highly ego-involving and less task-involving were less likely to endorse the view that sport should foster social responsibility and the development of lifetime skills. Based on their findings, Ommundsen and Roberts argued that the perceived purposes of sport could be considered more "adaptive" as long as the task-involving features of the climate were strong.

Although the existing research suggests that there is a conceptual congruence between achievement goals and perceptions of the purposes of sport engagement, other potential antecedents and consequences of these latter perceptions have not been examined in the athletic domain. There are a number of interesting questions to be tackled here. For example, are the socialization (via sport) experiences of athletes endorsing a more intrinsic or extrinsic view of the functions of sport involvement inherently different (Shields & Bredemeier, 1995)? Do various views regarding the purposes of athletic participation correspond to athletes' degree of intrinsic and extrinsic motivation? The observed associations between achievement goals and indices of intrinsic and extrinsic motivation is discussed next.

Goals, Enjoyment, and Intrinsic Motivation

Research that has examined the relationship among achievement goals, enjoyment, and intrinsic interest in sport and physical activity has reported findings that are conceptually consistent with the predictions made by both achievement goal theory and cognitive evaluation theory (Duda, in press-a; Roberts, Treasure, & Kavussanu, 1997). That is, both task goals and perceived motivational climates that foster task involvement are associated with constructs reflecting positive affect, such as enjoyment, satisfaction, and interest (Boyd & Callaghan, 1994). In contrast, ego goals and perceived ego-involving atmospheres are more often than not negatively related or unrelated to these variables. However, when a positive relationship is observed, it is usually accompanied by high perceptions of ability. Therefore, although it is possible for individuals endorsing an ego orientation to experience positive affect as a result of their investment, it will most likely result from the experience of successful performance outcomes rather than from any intrinsic aspect of the investment process.

Achievement goal theory suggests that the development of intrinsic motivation is most likely when task involvement is encouraged (Nicholls, 1989). It is proposed that when endorsing a task goal or when task-involved, an individual invests in an activity for its own sake and thus, considers it to be an end in itself (Nicholls, 1989). When in a state of task involvement, individuals become focused on the task demands and work hard to overcome challenges. It is these intrinsic aspects of the investment process that become most pertinent in helping to define success rather than the extrinsic dimensions typically associated with performance outcomes. In contrast, when endorsing an ego goal, investment becomes a means to an end. The performance outcome rather than the process of performing becomes most salient to these individuals, and heightened self-awareness often occurs because self-worth is inextricably linked to the demonstration of superior ability. Thus, it is predicted that ego involvement can lead to an undermining of intrinsic motivation (Nicholls, 1989; Ryan, 1982).

The most fundamental tenets of cognitive evaluation theory (Deci & Ryan, 1985) offer further explanatory detail for the predictions made by achievement goal theory. Cognitive evaluation theory holds that intrinsic motivation is a consequence of a need to feel both competent and self-determining. When endorsing a task goal, individuals' perceptions of competence are self-referenced and an undifferentiated concept of ability tends to be utilized. Consequently, sustained effort on the part of an individual that results in mastery, learning, or improvement will provide positive information about competence, and, thus, greater levels of intrinsic motivation will accrue. Even those who lack ability at an activity can benefit as they recognize that their efforts result in competence gains. Furthermore, because achievement is self-referenced, it is considered to lie within the individual's control and, thus, is more self-determined.

In contrast, those endorsing an ego goal utilize a differentiated concept of ability and consider that success is achieved only when comparative ability has been demonstrated, thus reducing the probability that intrinsic motivation will be forthcoming. This is because, first, the opportunities to demonstrate competence are more limited, and, second, the ensuing behavior tends to be more externally regulated and successful outcomes are less within the person's volitional control (Duda, Chi, Newton, Walling, & Catley, 1995).

Much of the research that has provided support for the association between task involvement and intrinsic motivation

(Biddle & Soos, 1997; Dobrantu & Biddle, 1997; Duda et al., 1995; Hall, Humphrey, & Kerr, 1997; Kavussanu & Roberts, 1996; Lintunen, Valkonen, Leskinen, & Biddle, 1999; Newton & Duda, 1999; Seifriz et al., 1992) has utilized the Intrinsic Motivation Inventory (IMI; Ryan, 1982). This instrument comprises four subscales and assesses perceptions of competence, effort exertion and the importance placed on an activity, the degree to which individuals find an activity enjoyable and interesting, and reported tension and pressure experienced during participation. The first three subscales are considered to reflect positive components of intrinsic motivation and the fourth subscale represents an undermining factor. In two studies reported by Duda and colleagues (1995), the consistent finding was that a task orientation was positively related to enjoyment and interest in both tennis and physical education. In the sample of physical education students, a task orientation was linked to effort and task importance, whereas in a sample of novice tennis participants, an ego orientation was negatively related to enjoyment and interest in tennis.

A number of studies have attempted to examine the separate and combined relationships of dispositional goals and the perceived achievement climate to the constructs assessed by the IMI (Kavussanu & Roberts, 1996; Newton & Duda, 1999; Seifriz et al., 1992). For example, in a sample of basketball players, Seifriz et al. found that a high task-involving and moderately low ego-involving climate was related to greater enjoyment and interest. However, when both dispositional goals and the achievement climate were entered into a hierarchical regression analysis as predictors of the IMI dimensions, Seifriz and his associates found that dispositional goals contributed the greatest amount of behavioral variance to the prediction of enjoyment, effort/importance, and competence, whereas the climate contributed most to the prediction of the pressure/tension dimension.

Kavussanu and Roberts (1996) found similar results in a sample of novice tennis players. Specifically, they reported that a strongly task-involving climate that was low in its ego-involving features corresponded to greater enjoyment, effort/importance, and perceived competence. Consistent with the tenets of achievement goal theory, the lowest level of intrinsic motivation was exhibited among the tennis players who perceived a highly ego-involving environment and perceived their tennis ability to be low.

Newton and Duda (1999; Newton, 1994) attempted to examine the separate and interactive effects of dispositional goals, perceptions of the achievement climate, and perceived competence on intrinsic motivation. With a sample of 345 volleyball players, they used moderated hierarchical regression to predict the different dimensions of intrinsic motivation (as measured by the IMI). The results indicated that a high task-involving climate, low ego orientation, and high perceived competence each contributed to the prediction of enjoyment and interest in volleyball. In addition, a low ego and a high task orientation positively predicted perceived effort exerted when participating in volleyball and the importance of the sport for the athlete. Although they did not find any significant interaction effects with respect to the prediction of dimensions of intrinsic motivation, Newton and Duda concluded that the climate variables appeared to be the best predictors of affective responses, whereas the dispositional goals seemed to be the best predictors of self-reported effort.

A parallel body of literature linking achievement goals with intrinsic motivation has utilized the interest/satisfaction scale developed by Duda and Nicholls (1992). This is an eight-item scale with two dimensions assessing satisfaction/enjoyment and boredom. The findings from research using this instrument are largely supportive of those using the IMI and, in addition, are conceptually consistent with the tenets of cognitive evaluation theory (Duda et al., 1992; Duda & Nicholls, 1992; Hom et al., 1993; Roberts et al., 1996; Standage, Butki, & Treasure, 1999). For example, Duda and colleagues, in a study of British children, reported that task goals were positively related to enjoyment and interest and negatively related to boredom. In contrast, an ego orientation was found to be positively associated with boredom.

Not all studies in sport settings have demonstrated that an ego orientation undermines positive affective responses. One study that has found evidence of positive affect being linked to an ego orientation was conducted by Hom et al. (1993). In an investigation of young athletes enrolled in a summer basketball camp, these researchers reported that both dispositional task and ego goal perspectives were positively related to satisfaction and enjoyment. This apparent conceptual anomaly was explained by the fact that the participants also perceived their ability to be high. Moreover, because the athletes who were predominantly ego-oriented tended to perceive that external factors are an important determinant of success, it remains questionable whether the enjoyment or satisfaction associated with an ego orientation was truly intrinsic in this study.

Roberts et al. (1996) reported findings similar to those of Hom and associates (1993) in an investigation of 333 undergraduate physical activity students. That is, canonical correlation analysis revealed that a high task and low ego orientation were related to moderate satisfaction/interest and moderately low levels of boredom. However, a high ego orientation and a moderate task orientation corresponded to high satisfaction and interest and moderately low boredom.

When the task-involving and ego-involving dimensions of the achievement climate have been used to predict satisfaction, interest, and boredom, the results have largely been consistent with the tenets of the achievement goal and cognitive evaluation theories. For example, in a study of Norwegian athletes, Ommundsen, Roberts, and Kavussanu (1997) reported that over and above the effects of dispositional goals, a perceived ego-involving climate was a significant and negative predictor of the degree of satisfaction experienced during performance. Similarly, Carpenter and Morgan (1999) found that a highly task-involving climate and a moderately low ego-involving climate were associated with greater satisfaction and lower boredom scores among children engaged in physical education lessons.

Consistent with the findings of studies focused on dispositional goals, however, research on the achievement climate has also indicated that positive affective responses can be associated with perceptions of an ego-involving atmosphere. For example, although Treasure (1997) found that a high ego-involving climate and a low task-involving climate was related to boredom, an environment marked by moderate task-involving features and moderate ego-involving attributes was positively associated with satisfaction.

In total, these findings suggest that there is a large degree of consistency in reported relationships among dispositional goals, perceptions of the motivational climate, and intrinsic motivation. Simply examining the correlates of intrinsic motivation may not permit a comprehensive understanding of the motivational processes involved. What may be most useful is to look beyond the simple associations between achievement goals and dimensions of intrinsic motivation (whether assessed by the IMI or the interest/satisfaction scale developed by Duda & Nicholls, 1992) and adopt more integrated perspectives. To address the latter, the intrinsic and extrinsic facets of motivation must be considered multidimensional and/or variables should be examined that are theoretically expected to moderate or mediate the relationships among goals, the perceived climate, and intrinsic/extrinsic motivation.

A study by Hall, Humphrey, and Kerr (1997) utilized Eccles's model of achievement motivation (Eccles & Harold, 1991), which assumes that the effects of goals on intrinsic motivation and other achievement cognitions and behavior would be mediated by the expectancy of success and the value of the activity to the individual. In a sample of 308 youth sport participants from 26 different sports, Hall et al. found that, although the influence of task goals was moderated by the value of the task and the expectancy of success, the largest contribution of task orientation to intrinsic motivation was through a direct path. In contrast, a direct negative path was found from ego orientation to intrinsic motivation.

A study by Lintunen, Valkonen, Leskinen, and Biddle (1999) tested a different path model that considered how sport ability beliefs might be related to goal orientations, perceived competence, and intrinsic motivation. They found that athletes' beliefs that ability is a function of learning and that ability can be developed incrementally had a direct positive influence on intrinsic motivation. These beliefs were also found to be positively related to a dispositional task orientation. In contrast, athletes' belief that ability is a stable entity had a direct negative influence on intrinsic motivation. Furthermore, the effects of both dispositional task and ego goals on intrinsic motivation were mediated by sport competence, a finding that only partially supports achievement goal theory.

Although many of the relationships reported here support the tenets of cognitive evaluation theory, recent innovative work by Vallerand (e.g., 1997; Vallerand & Losier, 1999) has been framed in self-determination theory (Deci & Ryan, 1985, 1992) to propose that athletes' intrinsic motivation is not a direct function of social factors inherent in sport, but that the motivational impact of these social factors is mediated by perceptions of autonomy, competence, and relatedness. Self-determination theory holds that individuals are seeking to achieve particular goals through their sport involvement, and that investment to fulfill these goals is further energized by three psychological needs. The needs for competence, self-determination, and a connection with/to others are considered to facilitate personal growth, and thus, it is assumed that individuals will be intrinsically motivated to approach situations that will satisfy these needs.

Another important contribution of self-determination theory (Deci & Ryan, 1985) was the premise that intrinsic motivation, extrinsic motivation, and amotivation (i.e., when the person has no reason for doing an activity) are multidimensional constructs that vary along a self-determination continuum. The least self-determined form of motivation is amotivation; in this case, involvement in an activity is seen as completely outside the individual's control. Reflecting lower to more self-determined regulation, there are three subdimensions to extrinsic motivation: external regulation (when people behave to achieve external rewards), introjected regulation (when external pressures/contingencies regarding participation are internalized), and identified regulation (when the person volitionally chooses to participate, but not because of the intrinsic enjoyment of the activity). Finally, it is held that intrinsic motivation is itself multifaceted (Vallerand, 1997). That is, athletes may participate in sport for intrinsic reasons such as to know/learn/understand, to accomplish things, and/or to experience stimulation. In each case, participation is grounded in the intrinsic pleasure of the activity and behavior is self-determined.

Although Vallerand (1997) presents indirect evidence from achievement goal theory to support his extensions of self-determination theory (Deci & Ryan, 1985, 1992), few empirical examinations have, to date, been conducted testing the two conceptual models conjointly. One recent study that has examined the relationship among dispositional goals, dimensions of the perceived achievement climate, and the degree of self-determined motivation to participate in sport was conducted by Petherick and Weigand (in press). In a sample of junior swimmers, they found that dispositional task goals and a perceived task-involving climate were consistent predictors of internally regulated forms of motivation, whereas an ego orientation and the perception of an ego-involving performance climate predicted externally regulated forms of behavior. Brunel (1999a) reported similar findings with a sample of French physical activity students.

Treasure, Standage, and Lochbaum (1999) examined the relationship between perceptions of the motivational climate and situational motivation among 439 elite male youth soccer players from the United States Canonical correlation analysis revealed that a highly perceived task-involving and low negative perceived ego-involving climate was associated with higher intrinsic motivation and identified regulation and lower external regulation and amotivation. In contrast, a strong perceived ego-involving and low task-involving environment corresponded to higher external regulation, identified regulation, and amotivation.

In a study of the potential mediators between achievement goals and intrinsic motivation, Biddle and Soos (1997) employed a path model to predict the intrinsic motivation and future exercise intentions among Hungarian schoolchildren. Specifically, they found that both perceived competence and autonomy mediated the relationship between dispositional task goals and intrinsic

motivation (as measured by the IMI). On the other hand, ego orientation was unrelated to autonomy, but its effect on intrinsic motivation was mediated by athletes' perceptions of competence. The latter finding is congruent with the tenets of achievement goal theory.

A further study that has attempted to test Vallerand's extension of self-determination theory (see Vallerand & Rousseau, this volume) was conducted by Hall, Kerr, and Greenshields (1998). These investigators sought to determine the relationship between perceptions of the motivational climate and self-determination and ascertain whether this relationship was mediated by perceived competence. Hierarchical regression analyses using a sample of 130 youth sport athletes did not provide evidence for the full mediational effects of perceived ability. However, consistent with self-determination theory (Deci & Ryan, 1985, 1992), a task climate predicted self-regulated aspects of motivation and an ego orientation predicted externally regulated forms of motivation.

Such recent studies are indicative of a fruitful line of further investigation. They suggest that achievement goals do differentially relate to motivational processes that foster or undermine intrinsic motivation or encourage or impede extrinsic motivation and, perhaps, even amotivation. Surely, for a more complete understanding of human striving in the sport milieu, it is important that researchers turn to models of motivation that complement and extend each other and are conducive to testing in a synthesized fashion. It appears that achievement goal theory and the self-determination framework (including Vallerand's [1997] extensions) are two such conceptualizations of motivated behavior.

Goals and Strategy Use

Achievement goal theorists (Ames, 1992b; Dweck, 1986, 1999; Nicholls, 1989) have proposed that task, in contrast to ego involvement, corresponds to the tendency to employ adaptive or maladaptive learning and performance-related strategies. A number of studies in the educational domain have supported a positive association between a focus on task goals and the use of cognitive and metacognitive strategies for learning and self-regulation (e.g., Ford, Smith, Weissbein, Gully, & Salas, 1998; Meece, Blumenfeld, & Hoyle, 1988; Nolen, 1988; Pintrich & De Groot, 1990). The first to address the question of goals and strategy used in the sport context were Lochbaum and Roberts (1993). They found task orientation to be positively related to the reported employment of more positive strategies (e.g., trying to understand what the coach is saying in his or her instruction) by athletes in both competitive and practice situations. Thill and Brunel (1995), in a study of varsity soccer players engaged in a soccer shooting task, reported a positive association between task orientation and the use of spontaneous, deep-processing strategies during task engagement. In contrast, ego orientation was coupled with a tendency to evoke more "surface" or superficial task strategies.

Roberts and Ommundsen (1996) looked at the relationship of goal orientations and perceptions of the motivational climate to reported strategy use in practice and competition among Norwegian team sport participants. Task orientation and perceptions of a task-involving climate were positively associated with the reported reliance on training to facilitate learning and negatively linked to the strategy of avoiding practice. When the athletes were high in ego orientation and perceived the climate to be ego-involving, their perspective on practice seemed to be contradictory. That is, these athletes were likely to endorse the strategy of seeking out additional training but also felt that a viable alternative was to avoid practice.

In a recent study of Norwegian college-age students involved in team sports, Ommundsen and Roberts (1999) examined the interdependencies between perceptions of the motivational climate and strategy use. The latter variable comprised three subdimensions: the strategy to avoid practice, the strategy to learn from and persist in practice situations, and the strategy to seek practice with the aim of improving. When their team environment was deemed more task-involving (and low in its ego-involving characteristics), the athletes were less likely to endorse avoiding practice as a viable strategy.

Cury and associates (Cury, Famose, & Sarrazin, 1997; Cury & Sarrazin, 1998) recently examined the interdependencies between achievement goals and individuals' strategic decisions regarding what type of feedback they would prefer following task completion (and subsequent to further task engagement). In a study of French boys engaged in a series of climbing tasks, Cury and Sarrazin found that the boys who were high ego-oriented and low in task orientation and doubted their ability were more likely to reject task-related or objective performance-related feedback. The authors suggested that these latter posttask strategies were probably not conducive to skill development with respect to the particular climbing activities at hand.

In two related investigations (Cury et al., 1997), 12 to 14-year-old French boys were requested to engage in timed tests of basketball dribbling ability. The boys were divided into one of four groups based on their goal orientation and perceptions of ability: those who were predominantly task-oriented with high perceived ability, those who were strongly ego-oriented with high perceived ability, those who were low in task orientation with low perceived ability and those low in ego orientation with low perceived ability. While performing the dribbling tests, the boys were presented with task-related instructions that were consistent with their prevailing goal orientation. Cury and his colleagues found that the boys who were high in ego orientation and perceived ability sought out normative information and reject objective feedback posttest. Those who were strongly ego-oriented and doubted their competence were more likely to request no feedback or discard task or objective information regarding their dribbling task performance.

In total, the limited literature to date suggests that there is a theoretically consonant relationship between achievement goal emphasis and the strategies individuals employ during and following participation in sport activities. The former evidence in sport environments, regarding reported strategy employment during training and competition events, is not as compelling as the latter, as it is based primarily on cross-sectional survey studies. Clearly, more work is warranted with respect to the links between achievement goals and strategy formulation and selection in athletic settings. With such information in hand, there will be greater insight into how achievement goals may influence performance execution and skill development.

Goals and the Stress Process

Although goal theorists have argued that goals provide a framework for understanding athletes' cognitions, affect, and behavior, only a few sport researchers have examined the specific role that goals play in underpinning heightened competitive anxiety responses in athletes. This relative dearth of attention is a bit paradoxical, as the topic of stress (its measurement, social psychological antecedents, and behavioral consequences) is a mainstay in the contemporary sport psychology literature.

One of the first researchers to suggest that knowledge of an athlete's achievement goals would permit a better understanding of competitive anxiety was Roberts (1986). Although he made no explicit reference to the appraisal process, Roberts proposed that individual differences in athletes' dispositional goals would render them more or less likely to experience anxiety prior to competition, while performing in an event, and once the competition had concluded. Roberts argued that athletes who endorse a task goal, and thus view achievement in self-referent terms, would be less likely to experience competitive anxiety because they perceive competition as a challenge to be overcome rather than as a threat. Furthermore, he suggested that because these individuals view effort as a personally controllable means for goal achievement, both in-event and postevent anxiety would be lessened when athletes perceive that they are meeting or have met their own personal standards for performance through maximal effort. In contrast, Roberts argued that when athletes adopt an ego goal, the meaning of achievement is very different: Success and failure are viewed in comparative terms so that competence becomes a quality that is valued and is reflective of one's self-worth. Thus, when ego-involved individuals begin to doubt that their ability compares favorably with others, precompetitive anxiety may become more likely.

The earliest empirical tests of Roberts's (1986) conceptualization were conducted by Vealey and Campbell (1988) with a sample of adolescent figure skaters and by Gould, Eklund, Petlichkoff, Peterson, and Bump (1991) with junior elite wrestlers. Due in part to the measurement technology adopted (i.e., Ewing's [1981], a critical incident technique employed to measure dispositional goal perspectives), the findings from these early studies were equivocal. For example, Vealey and Campbell found evidence of a negative relationship between a task orientation and a unidimensional measure of state anxiety. Roberts's predictions regarding an ego orientation, however, were unsubstantiated.

Newton and Duda (1995) attempted to overcome the problem of weak assessment by utilizing the TEOSQ (Duda, 1989) to measure the achievement goals of individuals enrolled in a tennis class. In addition to the TEOSQ, three single items measuring outcome expectations, the importance of doing better than others, and the importance of winning were used to predict the multidimensional state anxiety responses of participants who were about to compete in a class tennis tournament. The results indicated that 26% of the variance in participants' cognitive anxiety was predicted by a view that outdoing one's opponents and winning were important in conjunction with low expectations of success. Furthermore, 9% variance in somatic anxiety was predicted by a consideration that winning was important. Contrary to the hypothesized relationships, neither task nor ego goals predicted any behavioral variance in cognitive or somatic state anxiety. However, a negative relationship was reported between an ego orientation and confidence.

The failure to find further support for goals underpinning negative affect may have been a function of the competitive context in which the participants were asked to perform in the Newton and Duda (1995) study. An inspection of the state anxiety scores indicated that few, if any, of the participants found the class tournament to be anxiety-producing.

Some researchers interested in the influence of motivational variables on state anxiety have attempted to utilize contexts where athletes clearly have a personal stake in the encounter. Hall and Kerr (1997) examined how the achievement goals of competitive junior fencers impacted on the temporal patterning of anxiety prior to a fencing tournament. The results of both bivariate and multivariate correlational analyses provide some initial evidence to support the view that individuals who evaluate their self-worth on the basis of comparative judgments of their ability (i.e., are high in ego orientation) are the ones most at risk of experiencing excessive anxiety, particularly when they perceive their ability to be low. Further evidence was found to support the view that those who adopt a more self-referent focus (i.e., are predominantly task-oriented) are less prone to debilitating anxiety even when ability is questioned.

More specifically, Hall and Kerr's (1997) results indicated that over and above the effects of perceived ability, an ego orientation was positively related to cognitive anxiety on two out of four occasions when anxiety was measured prior to performance. At no point prior to performance was a task orientation found to be a significant predictor of cognitive anxiety. However, when goals measured immediately prior to the event were included as predictors, a task orientation was found to be negatively related to somatic anxiety and positively related to confidence. A similar and more pronounced pattern was highlighted when a sample of athletes who were classified as having low perceived ability was identified.

More recently, Hall, Kerr, and Matthews (1998) attempted to replicate the results with a sample of high school runners. Unfortunately, the data demonstrated little support in this context and indicated that dispositional goals measured one week prior to the event failed to predict either cognitive anxiety or confidence at any time to competition after perceived ability had been entered into a regression analysis. However, when the athletes' goals were assessed within 30 minutes of performing, it was found that an ego orientation emerged as a significant predictor of cognitive anxiety and a task orientation as a significant predictor of confidence. These findings suggest that the personal meaning of the achievement context may have changed for some of the athletes with the onset of competition. This situationally specific change of meaning was more intimately linked with their precompetition stress responses.

The fact that the meaning of achievement can change from moment to moment has been highlighted as an important facet of both transactional models of stress and anxiety (Folkman, 1984; Lazarus, 1993) and recent perspectives on achievement motivation (Ames, 1992b; Duda, in press-a; Dweck, 1999; Ntoumanis & Biddle, 1998). A limited body of research has begun to develop examining the effects of the perceived motivational climate on anxiety responses in young athletes. Underlying this research is the belief that the achievement climate in which athletes are participating may have an influence on their appraisal process, depending on how the cues within the achievement context are interpreted.

One of the initial pieces of research to examine the influence of the climate on competitive anxiety was conducted by Ntoumanis and Biddle (1998). They examined the role of task and ego goals and perceptions of ego-involving and task-involving environments on intensity and direction of cognitive and somatic anxiety in student athletes. The intensity of anxiety was calculated as the reported score on the Competitive State Anxiety Inventory 2 (CSAI-2) multidimensional anxiety instrument, and the direction was measured by asking the athletes whether they considered each item on the scale to be facilitative or debilitative to performance. The results demonstrated some consistency with the research reported earlier. Specifically, neither task goals nor a task-involving climate was related to the intensity or direction of cognitive or somatic anxiety. In contrast, an ego-involving atmosphere and an ego orientation were found to correlate with both the intensity and direction of cognitive and somatic anxiety. Aligned with the assumptions of achievement goal theory, these latter relationships were mediated by the athletes' confidence.

Papaioannou and Kouli (1999) examined the influence of achievement goals and the perceived climate initiated by the physical education teacher on the state anxiety responses of children in Greek physical education classes. They found that neither goals nor the perceived climate predicted cognitive anxiety. As was the case in the Newton and Duda (1995) study, this may be due to the possibility that the physical education classes were not perceived as highly evaluative contexts that threatened the self-worth of the students. However, Papaioannou and Kouli did find that when teachers emphasized a learning orientation in the classroom (i.e., the class was more task-involving), it was negatively related to somatic anxiety. Furthermore, they

reported evidence that when teachers emphasized competition within the classroom (i.e., the class was more ego-involving), this was positively related to somatic anxiety. In addition to state anxiety, Papaioannou and Kouli also measured three constructs related to flow. They found that both a dispositional task orientation and a perception that the climate was task-involving were positively related to concentration, autotelic experiences, and loss of self-consciousness within the physical education lesson. The results of the Papaioannou and Kouli investigation have implications. Namely, it appears that a task focus or a task-involving climate not only reduces the probability of experiencing elevated state anxiety, but it can lead to students maintaining greater levels of attention. Similar associations were reported by Newton and Duda (1993), who found that though a task orientation was negatively related to anxiety, it was positively related to concentration on a bowling task.

Although task goals appear to facilitate concentration, it is clear from the research presented in this section that ego goals are generally implicated in elevated levels of cognitive anxiety in sport participants. Pertinent to the former relationship, Hatzigeorgeadis and Biddle (1999) measured the relationship among achievement goals, perceived ability, and task-irrelevant and self-preoccupied thinking in a sample of snooker and tennis players. The degree of cognitive interference was measured using the Thought Occurrence Questionnaire (TOQ; Sarason, Sarason, Keefe, Hayes, & Shearin, 1986), which assesses the frequency that certain thoughts come to mind during performance. Consistent with achievement goal theory, the findings indicated that regardless of perceived competence, task goals were negatively associated with thoughts of escape. In contrast, a positive relationship was found between ego goals and thoughts of escape in low-perceived-ability athletes. However, this relationship was not found with high-perceived-ability athletes.

Thus, it appears that an examination of dispositional or perceived situational goal perspectives is informative in terms of predicting variations in anxiety responses. As situational factors have been found to impact the associations between dispositional goal orientations and affect (Ntoumanis & Biddle, 1999a), future work should consider analyzing the possible interplay between dispositional goals and the perceptions of the motivational climate on anxiety. Although it is assumed that achievement goals may color key cognitions in the stress process, such as individuals' perceptions of the demands of the activity, their ability to meet those demands, and the salience of "failure," it is important to test whether such perceptions mediate the goal-anxiety relationship.

Other work on achievement goals suggests that there may be additional links between the purposes of sport-related striving and stress. For example, dispositional goal orientations have been found to relate to other individual difference factors that seem to set the stage for achievement-related appraisals to be more anxiety-provoking. Moreover, Lazarus (1993) has proposed that the coping resources and choices made by individuals play a role in the occurrence of stress. Recent sport research has revealed conceptually consistent relationships between achievement goals and the reported employment of coping strategies among athletes, which is reviewed next.

Goal Orientations and Other Personality Factors Related to Stress

Why is there a propensity for those high in ego orientation (or surrounded by an ego-involving climate) to exhibit higher stress? One reason is that dispositional goal orientations seem to be associated with other personality characteristics that are predictive of anxiety responses. First, studies that have examined the relationship between goals and competitive trait anxiety are reviewed. A more detailed discussion, however, centers on how goals may link with perfectionism in sport.

A large body of research has indicated that competitive trait anxiety is predictive of athletes' state anxiety responses before, during, and following competition (Smith, Smoll, & Wiechman, 1998). White and Zellner (1996) administered the TEOSQ and a measure of multidimensional trait anxiety (i.e., the Sport Anxiety Scale; Smith, Smoll, & Schutz, 1990) to male and female high school, intercollegiate, and recreational athletes. A high ego orientation coupled with low task orientation was predictive of a stronger dispositional tendency for athletes to experience cognitive anxiety when they compete. White (1998), in a study of female and male adolescent athletes, also found higher trait anxiety scores among those who were high in ego orientation and low in task orientation.

In an investigation of 136 young Norwegian athletes, Ommundsen and Pedersen (1999) investigated the relationship between achievement goal orientations and indices of cognitive and somatic trait anxiety. Ego orientation was not associated with a dispositional tendency to be either cognitively or somatically anxious in sport competition. Task orientation and perceived ability, however, emerged as negative predictors of cognitive trait anxiety (although the percentage of variance accounted for was small). Further

analyses indicated that perceptions of ability did not mediate or moderate the observed interdependencies between task orientation and the tendency to report high cognitive anxiety.

A second individual difference factor that seems fundamental to variations in the stress process is perfectionism. Individuals who are more negatively perfectionistic tend to exhibit higher state and trait anxiety (e.g., Flett, Hewitt, Endler, & Tassone, 1998). How might task and ego goal perspectives correspond to differences in perfectionistic tendencies?

It should be clear from the evidence presented earlier that achievement goal theorists consider that adaptive forms of achievement behavior in sport are most frequently associated with the endorsement of a dispositional task goal, or participation in an environment in which strong mastery cues are perceived. Across many achievement domains, adaptive achievement behavior seems to be characterized by a focus on striving toward excellence. It requires that individuals put forth effort under conditions of extreme challenge to overcome barriers, and it also demands that individuals persist following mistakes or perceived failures.

Covington (1992) has noted, however, that some individuals who appear to show all the qualities of adaptive achievement striving also appear to be riddled with self-doubt when faced with immediate challenges. He has classified these individuals as overstrivers, and their continual striving can be seen as having maladaptive consequences. In essence, overstrivers appear to have an intense desire to achieve success and avoid failure. They are often driven to pursue greater and greater accomplishments, and eventually, these challenges become an intolerable burden (Covington, 1992). Intrinsic satisfaction from such achievement endeavors is rarely experienced, and working to reach the next, even more demanding goal can become psychologically debilitating for overstrivers (Burns, 1980). The term used by clinical and counseling psychologists to describe this excessive achievement striving is "perfectionism" (Blatt, 1995; Burns, 1980).

The concept of perfectionism was originally defined by Hamacheck (1978) and was considered to have two forms. The first was normal perfectionism; this described individuals who set high standards of achievement and who derived pleasure from doing something well. The second was neurotic perfectionism; this described individuals who were unable to experience pleasure as a result of their efforts because they never considered that their accomplishments were adequate.

The conceptual links between perfectionism and the endorsement of ego goals are readily apparent. What appears important to predominantly ego-oriented individuals is the demonstration of competence and the incessant pursuit of self-validation. Dykman (1998) has confirmed this in his work, indicating that individuals who are disposed toward validation seeking as opposed to growth seeking in their goals seem prone to anxiety, depression, and maladaptive functioning because they have a sense of contingent self-worth. That is, they feel worthy only when they succeed and worthless when they fail.

Contemporary thinking holds perfectionism to be a composite of different characteristics. One popular assessment of this personality characteristic is Frost, Marten, Lahart, and Rosenblate's (1990) Multidimensional Perfectionism Scale (F-MPS). This instrument assesses six key facets of perfectionism: an intense concern over making mistakes, the endorsement of high personal standards, a perception that parents currently or in the past have expressed high expectations for achievement and performance, a further perception that parents have been critical of one's efforts and achievements, a nagging doubt about the quality of one's actions, and a preference for precision, order, and organization.

Specific to the academic domain, Ablard and Parker (1997) considered how the motivational goals of parents related to the dimensions of perfectionism exhibited by their children. They found that children whose parents typically endorsed ego goals were more likely to exhibit dysfunctional forms of perfectionism than those whose parents endorsed task goals. Dysfunctional perfectionists were characterized by high scores on the dimensions of concern about mistakes, doubts about action, parental expectations, and parental criticism.

Frost and Henderson (1991) were some of the first researchers to examine perfectionism specifically in the context of sport. They reported that female athletes high in neurotic perfectionism exhibited higher levels of trait anxiety and were less self-confident than those considered to be low on this dimension. In addition, neurotic perfectionists were found to have a distinct failure orientation toward sports, reacted more negatively toward mistakes, and engaged in more negative thoughts in the 24 hours before competition began. These athletes also reported more images of failure, had greater attentional difficulties, and expressed more worries about audience responses than those who were less concerned with mistakes.

Hall, Kerr, and Matthews (1998) examined the combined influence of perfectionism and achievement goals on the temporal patterning of state anxiety in adolescent runners in the leadup to a meet. Interestingly, although achievement goals had little influence on cognitive anxiety, elements of neurotic perfectionism seemed to impact on the negative affect experienced by the athletes as the event approached. The results indicated that overall perfectionism underpinned achievement anxiety as it emerged as a consistent predictor of cognitive anxiety prior to performance. Furthermore, when the individual subscales of perfectionism were entered into separate regression analyses as predictors of state anxiety, concern over mistakes and doubts about action (which are considered to be elements of neurotic perfectionism) contributed most to the prediction of cognitive anxiety.

Hall, Kerr, and Matthews (1998) also examined the interplay between facets of perfectionism and achievement goals. They reported that a combination of high ego orientation and moderate task orientation related to each dimension of perfectionism (as assessed by F-MPS). However, a strong task orientation (coupled with a low ego orientation) was negatively associated with two of the dimensions considered to reflect neurotic perfectionism (i.e., concern about mistakes and parental criticism). According to Hall et al., these findings indicate that the greatest amount of overlap appears to be between the constructs of ego orientation and perfectionism. A reasonably robust level of task orientation, in this case, did not diminish the perfectionistic tendencies of highly ego-oriented athletes.

Researchers should continue to investigate the interdependencies between achievement goals and perfectionism and explore ideas emanating from the work of Frost and Marten (1990) concerning the relevance of evaluative threat to this relationship. Furthermore, in extending the work of Hall and colleagues (1998), researchers might seek to determine if the potentially debilitating effects of neurotic perfectionism can be prevented by evoking a strong task goal emphasis in athletes. Engineering the motivational climate to be more task-involving has been found to be an effective way of fostering more adaptive patterns of achievement cognition, affect, and behavior in both educational and sporting contexts (Ames, 1992b; Ames & Archer, 1988; Treasure & Roberts, 1995). Therefore, it seems prudent to ask whether similar manipulations of the achievement climate can reduce the potentially debilitating impact of neurotic perfectionism on achievement striving in sport.

Interrelationships with Coping Strategies

Another way goals may influence anxiety responses is via their influence on coping behaviors. According to Lazarus

(1993), the effect of stress is dependent on how individuals appraise the stressor *and* the coping strategies employed to counter the stress. In those situations where the stressor is controllable, active and problem-solving strategies are assumed to be the most productive in terms of handling the stressful situation and reducing associated negative affective responses. A number of studies have examined the associations between goal orientations and coping strategies (e.g., Gano-Overway & Duda, 1999; Martin, Pease, & Zhang, 1999; Pensgaard & Roberts, 1997). In general, a task orientation has been found to positively relate to the use of problem-solving coping behaviors. Ego orientation, on the other hand, has been linked to a greater reported employment of avoidance and/or emotional-focused coping strategies.

Ntoumanis, Biddle, and Haddock (1999) framed their research with achievement goal theory and tested the theoretical assumptions embedded in Lazarus's (1993) and Folkman's (1984) work on emotion and coping. In particular, they examined the interrelationships among motivational factors (i.e., goal orientations and perceptions of the motivational climate), coping strategies, positive and negative affective responses, and perceptions of control over the situation. The participants in this investigation were 356 British college-level athletes. Consistent with the findings reported earlier, both task orientation and perceptions of a task-involving climate were positively associated with the reported use of problem-focused coping strategies (i.e., increased effort and the suppression of competing activities). On the other hand, ego orientation and perceptions of an ego-involving atmosphere were coupled with emotion-focused coping and a tendency to disengage during stressful situations. The employment of problem-focused coping behaviors was linked to positive affect, and behavioral engagement and the venting of emotions were associated with negative affect. Moreover, coping strategies were found to mediate the relationship between dispositional and perceived situational goals and affective responses. Postcoping positive affect was linked with greater perceived control over the situation. The reverse was true for reported negative affect following the employment of coping strategies. Overall, the findings of Ntoumanis and colleagues indicated that reported coping strategy use was more strongly related to the perceived motivational climate in contrast to the athletes' dispositional goal orientations.

Also with an eye toward integrating Lazarus's (1993) transactional model of stress and coping and the achievement goal framework, Kim and Duda (1998, under review)

examined the degree to which dispositional goals, perceptions of ability, beliefs about the determinants of success, the perceived motivational climate, and the interrelationships among these variables were predictive of important components of the stress process among athletes. The first study (Kim & Duda, under review) involved 318 U.S. intercollegiate athletes from a variety of sports. The stressor in this investigation was the experience of psychological difficulties during competition, which was leading to performance problems. The athletes indicated the frequency with which they experienced such psychological difficulties, their perceptions of control over this situation, and the ways they coped. For the male athletes, a positive relationship between perceptions of an ego-involving atmosphere and reported psychological difficulties during competition was revealed. Athletes who experienced psychological difficulties often were more likely to mentally withdraw and/or try to avoid the situation as a way of coping. When male and female competitors felt they had greater control over the stressor, they were more likely to have higher perceived ability and endorse the belief that effort leads to success. The task orientation and effort belief coupling so typical of the achievement goal literature once again was evident. Perceived controllability emerged as a positive predictor of the use of more active and problem-focused coping strategies. Finally, a direct path between perceptions of a task-involving climate and more active and problem-focused coping was observed.

A similar study was conducted with a sample of 404 Korean intercollegiate athletes (Kim & Duda, 1998). Replicating the research with U.S. athletes, perceptions of a task-involving climate positively related to the employment of active and problem-focused coping behaviors. A perceived task-involving environment also was coupled with greater perceived controllability over the stressor. Perceptions of an ego-involving climate, however, corresponded to a higher incidence of psychological difficulties during competition and a greater use of avoidance/mental withdrawal strategies when trying to counter this stressor.

Consistent with the work of Ntoumanis and cohorts (1999), the findings from the Kim and Duda (1998, under review) studies indicate that achievement goals, particularly those manifested in sport environments, are associated with appraisals endemic to the stress process. In particular, it appears that a differential emphasis on task and ego goals is predictive of the degree to which sport is stressful, athletes' views about what they can do about that stress, and their typical ways of trying to reduce that stress. The integration of achievement goal theory with current conceptualizations of stress and coping appears to be a promising direction for sport research.

NEW DIRECTIONS

The past several years have been an exciting time in the evolution of goal perspective research in sport. New extensions and applications of the theory and existing empirical literature seem to be emerging at a fast and furious pace. Although such popularity can pose some problems (see Duda, in press-a), the existing enthusiasm for achievement goal frameworks can only enhance our comprehension of variability in motivational processes in athletic settings. Our hope and expectations are further fueled by the fact that some of the most current research directions have just started to scratch the surface. Indeed, there is still much to learn about the antecedents and consequences of achievement goals in the sport domain. For example, researchers have recently begun to examine the linkages between the achievement goal framework and the investigation of moral behavior (e.g., Bredemeier, 1999; Duda, Olson, & Templin, 1991; Shields & Bredemeier, 1995), group dynamics and leadership behaviors (e.g., Balaguer, Crespo, & Duda, 1996; Carron & Hausenblas, 1998; Chi & Lu, 1995; Duda & Balaguer, 1999), health-related behavior and indices of psychological and physical health (e.g., Biddle & Goudas, 1996; Duda, 1999, in press-b; Dykman, 1998; Lintunen et al., 1999), emotions and mood (Ntoumanis & Biddle, 1999a), and elite sport performance (e.g., Pensgaard & Roberts, 1997).

In this last section of the chapter, two promising new approaches are described that have implications across a wide array of topics in the study of achievement goals. First, new directions in and the challenges associated with the consideration of possible interactions between dispositional and perceived environmental goals are discussed. Then, recent work that has centered on the potential motivational significance of other goals, in particular "avoidance" as well as "approach" goal perspectives, is presented.

Goal Orientations and Situational Goals: An Interactionist Perspective

Achievement goal theorists proffer that both person-related factors (i.e., goal orientations) and situational factors (i.e., objective and subjective environmental characteristics) influence goal involvement. The interplay between these variables, though, is not well specified by Nicholls (1989) or Ames (1992a, 1992b). Dweck and Leggett (1988), on the other hand, have provided some detail regarding how personal goals and situations may inter-

act to influence the goals adopted and resulting achievement- related patterns. In particular, they propose that differences in goal orientations will influence the probability of individuals being focused on task or ego goals and that environmental characteristics can alter that probability. Furthermore, they suggest that if dispositional goal perspectives are strong, then the situation at hand should have less impact on goal involvement. However, if individuals' goal orientations are moderate to low in strength, than a pronounced task- or ego-involving environment will be more effectual in terms of the degree to which task and ego involvement is evident.

In earlier sport work considering both dispositional and perceived situationally emphasized goals (Kavussanu & Roberts, 1996; Ommundsen et al., 1997; Seifriz et al., 1992), the aim was on identifying the best predictor of the dependent variables targeted in each respective study. In these studies, task and ego orientations were entered in the first step of a hierarchical multiple regression and perceptions of a task- and ego-involving climate on the second step (and then vice versa) to see whether goal orientations or the perceived environment captured more variance. Overall, the findings from such investigations were aligned with the suggestions of Duda and Nicholls (1992). That is, which factors emerged as the best predictor(s) depended on what one was predicting. If the dependent variable was more state-like and/or situationally specific, then the perceived motivational atmosphere was more salient. When the dependent variable was more dispositional in nature (such as athletes' beliefs about the causes of success in sport in general), then goal orientations emerged as the best predictor.

Other research that has tapped both goal orientations and perceptions of the climate with respect to the prediction of motivational indices has employed structural equation modeling (e.g., Cury et al., 1996; Kim & Duda, 1998, under review; Ntoumanis & Biddle, 1998). In this work, paths between dispositional goal perspectives and respective components of the climate are usually expected. Then goal orientations and perceptions of the motivational atmosphere are presumed to impact the dependent variables in question either directly or via potential mediators such as perceived ability. To date, however, researchers have generally not considered the possibility that individual differences in and perceived situationally emphasized goals may interact.

Possible interactions between personal and situational goals have been the focus of contemporary goal perspective research. Multiple regression analyses are also employed in such studies, but in this case, interaction terms are entered as possible predictor variables. In some of these investigations, no support for the interplay between dispositional and environmental goals emerges. For example, Newton (1994; Newton & Duda, 1999), in her research on female volleyball players from 46 different teams, examined whether there were significant interactions among goal orientations, the perceived motivational climate, and perceived ability with respect to the athletes' beliefs about success and facets of intrinsic motivation (i.e., the effort/importance placed on the sport, the enjoyment of and interest in volleyball, the amount of pressure/tension experienced). Although task and ego orientations and perceptions of the task- and ego-involving team environment related to these motivational indices in theoretically expected ways, no significant interaction terms emerged.

In a study of female basketball players conducted by Treasure and Roberts (1998), however, views about the determinants of success and sources of satisfaction were predicted by the interaction between personal and situational goal perspectives. Walker, Roberts, and Nyheim (1998) also reported a significant P X S goal perspective effect with respect to the prediction of enjoyment and beliefs about success. When significant interactions do not emerge, authors often point to insufficient sample sizes or limited variability in the independent variables (e.g., Newton & Duda, 1999). Overcoming the former limitation becomes even more challenging when considering adding differences in perceived ability as one of the independent variables assumed to interact with dispositional goals and perceptions of the climate. Furthermore, subsequent empirical research aiming to predict achievement-related responses exhibited in a particular competition or training session seems to necessitate a large sample of study participants. That is, it has been suggested that the situational goals perceived to be operating in the immediate setting (besides perceptions of the typical motivational climate on one's team) may need to be considered as part of the mix as well (Kaplan & Maehr, 1999; Swain & Harwood, 1996).

Clearly, potential interactive effects among goal orientations, the perceived motivational environment (immediate and/or overall), and perceived ability should be further explored in subsequent research. When utilizing nomothetic methodologies, a large number of study participants and adequate variance in independent variables are needed. Perhaps another strategy would be to employ more ideographic and qualitative methods (see Georgiadis, Biddle, & Van den Auweele, 1999; Krane, Greenleaf, & Snow, 1997).

Other Goal Perspectives

As the previous discussion indicates, the majority of sport research on achievement goals has centered on the motivational implications of task and ego goal perspectives. In the educational domain, and to a lesser degree in terms of sport activities, other goals have started to receive notice. Urdan and Maehr (1995) have called for an examination of different types of social goals, such as the goals to gain approval from others, to experience affiliation and develop relationships with others, and to bring honor to and foster solidarity in one's group. Nicholls and others (1989; Duda & Nicholls, 1992; Thorkildsen, 1988) have examined the motivational correlates of cooperation goals in sport and the classroom. In this case, the purpose of one's achievement striving is to collaborate and work with others.

The goal of effort reduction, namely work avoidance, has garnered some attention in the literature (Duda & Nicholls, 1992; Thorkildsen, 1988). Kaplan and Maehr (1999) have discussed the potential significance of extrinsic goals within a comprehensive motivation framework. Gano-Overway and Duda (1999), in their recent work on White and African American athletes, have identified the goal of expressive individualism. In this case, the focus is on demonstrating one's performance style. This goal has been found to be bidimensional: One facet concerns the importance placed on improvisation, creativity, and personal expression through one's movements; the second component centers on the expression of a unique appearance or physical image of oneself via sport performance.

In their research focused on academic achievement and engagement, Middleton and Midgley (1997) have pointed out that achievement motivation has traditionally been characterized with respect to approach and avoidance tendencies. The conceptualization and measurement of task and ego goal perspectives as described above, though, are reflective of approach tendencies. In the former instance, the focus is on improving, in the latter case, the concern is with proving one's ability. However, as Nicholls (1989) has emphasized in his work, those focused on ego goals are concerned with demonstrating superior competence *and* avoiding the display of inferior ability. That is, as Skaalvik (1997) has argued, there may be two dimensions of ego orientation. Depending on which nomenclature is adopted (Elliot & Church, 1997; Middleton & Midgley, 1997; Skaalvik, 1997), one dimension is approach/offensive/self-enhancing and the other is avoidance/defensive/self-defeating in nature.

Incorporating approach (termed mastery-approach and performance-approach) and avoidance (labeled performance-avoidance) goal perspectives, Elliot and Church (1997) have put forward an integrated model of achievement motivation that seeks to examine how classic approach/avoidance motives might underpin these different types of achievement goals. Their efforts come full circle to the groundbreaking theoretical contributions of the work of McClelland and Atkinson regarding the nature and determinants of achievement motivation (McClelland, Atkinson, Clark, & Lowell, 1953). The conceptual model proposed by Elliot and Church argues that goals are mid-level constructs that mediate the relationship between global motivational dispositions and specific achievement behaviors. Goals are considered to be both cognitive and dynamic manifestations of two underlying competence motives that have been labeled "achievement motivation" (or the motive to achieve) and "fear of failure." Unlike the traditional achievement goals approach in which the goals themselves are considered to be the critical determinants of achievement cognition, affect, and behavior, Elliot and Church's model considers that it is the dispositional motives that energize an individual's achievement striving. That is, the motives are held to be the critical antecedents to goal adoption. Consequently, their effects on subsequent motivational processes are believed to be indirect.

Another important conceptual difference between this approach and traditional views on achievement goal theory (Ames, 1992b; Dweck, 1999; Nicholls, 1989) lies in the role of perceived competence. Rather than considering perceived competence to play a mediating role between goals and achievement outcomes, Elliot and Church (1997) consider competence expectancies to be another antecedent of achievement goals.

The integrated model of Elliot and Church (1997) predicts that both mastery and performance-approach goals will be underpinned by those with high competence expectancies, whereas low competence expectancies will underpin performance-avoidance goals. Mastery approach goals are also considered to lead to adaptive achievement striving and positive affective responses to the same extent that task goals do because they are underpinned by a fundamental desire to approach challenge, and this seems to be untainted by fear of failure or threats to self-worth. In contrast, performance-avoidance goals have their foundations in both fear of failure and low performance expectancies. As a result, performance avoidance goals are predicted to have a uniformly negative influence on achievement-related affect and tend to promote maladaptive forms of achievement striving.

In Elliot and Church's (1997) model, performance-approach goals can be underpinned by either the motive to achieve or the fear of failure. Because of this, the psychological processes that are operating will often be antagonistic, and therefore any positive achievement affect that may result from investment will not be as strong as when mastery-approach goals are endorsed. However, the fact that performance-approach goals are also underpinned by high competence expectations means that individuals will exhibit high levels of persistence with the aim of achieving some externally generated ideal standard and/or avoid failure by succeeding on challenging goals. Thus, Elliot and Church predict that although performance-approach goals can lead to positive achievement striving and elevated performance, high levels of positive affect are unlikely to emanate from such investment.

To date, attempts to test this model in the context of sport have been scarce. One notable exception has been the work of Cury, Laurent, De Tonac, and Sot (1999) with French athletes. They validated three scales to measure the different approach-avoidance goals in sport and found evidence confirming the predictions made by Elliot and Church (1997). Specifically, they found that mastery approach goals were positively associated with intrinsic motivation in sport, and performance-avoidance goals were negatively associated with intrinsic motivation and positively associated with self-handicapping strategies.

Clearly, the integrated model not only requires further empirical validation in the context of sport, but future studies must begin to examine the conceptual similarities and differences between this model and other theoretical frameworks focused on achievement motivation. An important question for subsequent research will be to further explore whether the determinants and ramifications of task, approach-ego, and avoidance-ego goals vary in the sport setting. More work on the development of psychometrically sound assessments of these different goals within the sport domain is warranted as well.

CONCLUSIONS

In a review of achievement goal research, Kaplan and Maehr (1999) have recently concluded that the origin of task and ego goals and their measurement is a domain of inquiry where there is still considerable disagreement. They argue that a number of key constructs have yet to be integrated into a comprehensive framework that combines the findings from differing paradigms and begins to untangle what appear to be conflicting views on motivation. They also suggest that the roles played by context and social processes are areas clearly in need of attention, and call for other methodologies (such as constructivist and qualitative approaches) besides survey-based studies and experimental protocols. Finally, Kaplan and Maehr, debating whether goal orientations are particular manifestations of needs, values, or schemas impacting how people view and respond to their worlds, pose the following question for future study: "How and when do goal orientations become relevant in a particular instance?"

With specific reference to the study of achievement goals in the physical domain, these are important issues to resolve and directions to consider. Not only would further work in this area mean that sport motivation research maintains a position on the cutting edge, but more important, it would offer an opportunity to expand conceptual understanding of motivational processes and achievement behavior in this context.

REFERENCES

Ablard, K.E., & Parker, W.D. (1997). Parents' achievement goals and perfectionism in their academically talented children. *Journal of Youth and Adolescence, 26,* 651–667.

Ames, C. (1992a). Achievement goals, motivational climate, and motivational processes. In G. Roberts (Ed.), *Motivation in sport and exercise* (pp. 161–176). Champaign, IL: Human Kinetics.

Ames, C. (1992b). Classrooms: Goals, structures, and student motivation. *Journal of Educational Psychology, 84,* 261–271.

Ames, C., & Archer, J. (1988). Achievement goals in the classroom: Students' learning strategies and motivation processes. *Journal of Educational Psychology, 80,* 260–267.

Andree, K.V., & Whitehead, J. (1996, June). *The interactive effect of perceived ability and dispositional or situational achievement goals on persistence in young athletes.* Paper presented at the annual meetings of the North American Society for the Psychology of Sport and Physical Activity, Asilomar, CA.

Balaguer, I., Castillo, I., & Tomas, I. (1996). Analisis de las Questionario de Orientacion al Ego y a la Tarea en el Deporte (TEOSQ) en su traduccion al Castellano. *Psicologia, 17,* 71–87.

Balaguer, I., Crespo, M., & Duda, J.L. (1996). The relationship of motivational climate and athletes' goal orientations to perceived/preferred leadership style. *Journal of Sport & Exercise Psychology, 18,* S13.

Bandura, A. (1990). Conclusion: Reflections on nonability determinants of competence. In R.J. Sternberg & J. Kolligan (Eds.), *Competence considered* (pp. 315–362). New Haven, CT: Yale University Press.

Biddle, S., & Goudas, M. (1996). Analysis of children's physical activity and its association with adult encouragement and social cognitive variables. *Journal of School Health, 66,* 75–78.

Biddle, S., Soos, I., & Chatzisarantis, N. (1999). Predicting physical activity intentions using a goal perspective approach: A study of Hungarian youth. *Scandanavian Journal of Medicine and Science in Sports, 9,* 353–357.

Biddle, S.J.H. (1999). Motivation and perceptions of control: Tracing its development and plotting its future in exercise and sport psychology. *Journal of Sport & Exercise Psychology, 21,* 1–23.

Biddle, S.J.H., Akande, A., Vlachopoulos, S., & Fox, K.R. (1996). Toward an understanding of children's motivation for physical activity: Achievement goal orientations, beliefs about the causes of success, and sport emotion in Zimbabwean children. *Psychology & Health, 12,* 49–55.

Biddle, S.J.H., & Soos, I. (1997). Social cognitive predictors of motivation and intention in Hungarian children. In R. Lidor & M. Bar-Eli (Eds.), *Innovations in sport psychology: Linking theory and practice. Proceedings of the 9th World Congress of Sport Psychology: Part I* (pp. 121–123). Netanya, Israel: Ministry of Education, Culture and Sport.

Blatt, S.J. (1995). The destructiveness of perfectionism: Implications for the treatment of depression. *American Psychologist, 50,* 1003–1020.

Boyd, M., & Callaghan, J. (1994). Task and ego goal perspectives in organized youth sport. *International Journal of Sport Psychology, 22,* 411–424.

Boyd, M., & Yin, Z. (1996). Cognitive-affective sources of sport enjoyment in adolescent sport participants. *Adolescence, 31,* 283–295.

Bredemeier, B.L. (1999). Character in action: Promoting moral behavior in sport. In R. Lidor & M. Bar-Eli (Eds.), *Innovations in sport psychology: Linking theory and practice* (pp. 247–260). Morgantown, WV: Fitness Information Technology.

Brunel, P. (1996). The relationship of task and ego orientation to intrinsic and extrinsic motivation. *Journal of Sport & Exercise Psychology, 18,* S59.

Brunel, P. (1997). Toward an integrative approach to sport motivation. In R. Lidor & M. Bar-Eli (Eds.), *Innovations in sport psychology: Linking theory and practice. Proceedings of the 9th World Congress in Sport Psychology: Part I* (pp. 160–162). Netanya, Israel: Ministry of Education, Culture and Sport.

Brunel, P. (1999a). Predicting cognitions and strategies to cope with the situation: Influence of motivational climate and goal orientation. *Journal of Sport & Exercise Psychology, 21,* S22.

Brunel, P. (1999b). Relationship between achievement goal orientations and perceived motivational climate on intrinsic motivation. *Scandanavian Journal of Medicine and Science in Sports, 9,* 365–374.

Burns, D.D. (1980, November). The perfectionist's script for self-defeat. *Psychology Today,* 34–51.

Carpenter, P., & Yates, B. (1997). Relationship between achievement goals and the perceived purposes of soccer for semiprofessional and amateur players. *Journal of Sport & Exercise Psychology, 19,* 302–312.

Carpenter, P.J., & Morgan, K. (1999). Motivational climate, personal goal perspectives, and cognitive and affective responses in physical education classes. *European Journal of Physical Education, 4,* 31–44.

Carron, A.V., & Hausenblas, H.A. (1998). *Group dynamics in sport* (2nd ed.). Morgantown, WV: Fitness Information Technology.

Chi, L. (1993). *Prediction of achievement-related cognitions and behaviors in the physical domain: A test of the theories of goal perspective and self efficacy.* Unpublished doctoral dissertation, Purdue University, West Lafayette, IN.

Chi, L., & Duda, J.L. (1995). Multi-group confirmatory factor analysis of the Task and Ego Orientation in Sport Questionnaire. *Research Quarterly for Exercise and Sport, 66,* 91–98.

Chi, L., & Lu, S.-E. (1995, June). *The relationships between perceived motivational climates and group cohesiveness in basketball.* Paper presented at the annual meetings of the North American Society for the Psychology of Sport and Physical Activity, Clearwater, FL.

Covington, M.V. (1992). *Making the grade: A self-worth perspective on motivation and school reform.* Cambridge, MA: Cambridge University Press.

Cury, F., Biddle, S., Famose, J.P., Goudas, M., Sarrazin, P., & Durand, M. (1996). Personal and situational factors influencing intrinsic interest of adolescent girls in school physical education: A structural equation modeling analysis. *Educational Psychology, 16,* 305–315.

Cury, F., Biddle, S., Sarrazin, P., & Famose, J.P. (1997). Achievement goals and perceived ability predict investment in learning a sport task. *British Journal of Educational Psychology, 67,* 293–309.

Cury, F., Famose, J.P., & Sarrazin, P. (1997). Achievement goal theory and active search for information in a sport task. In R. Lidor & M. Bar-Eli (Eds.), *Innovations in sport psychology: Linking theory and practice. Proceedings of the 9th World Congress in Sport Psychology: Part I* (pp. 218–220). Netanya, Israel: Ministry of Education, Culture and Sport.

Cury, F., Laurent, M., De Tonac, A., & Sot, V. (1999). An unexplored aspect of achievement goal theory in sport: Development and predictive validity of the Approach and Avoidance Achievement in Sport Questionnaire (AAASQ). In V. Hosek, P. Tilinger, & L. Bilek (Eds.), *Psychology of sport and exercise: Enhancing the quality of life. Proceedings of the 10th European Congress of Sport Psychology–FEPSAC* (pp. 153–155). Prague, Czech Republic: Charles University Press.

Cury, F., & Sarrazin, P. (1998). Achievement motivation and learning behaviors in sport tasks. *Journal of Sport & Exercise Psychology, 20,* S11.

Deci, E., & Ryan, R. (1985). *Intrinsic motivation and the self-determination of human behavior.* New York: Plenum Press.

Deci, E.L., & Ryan, R.M. (1992). The initiation and regulation of intrinsically motivated learning and achievement. In A.K. Boggiano & T.S. Pittman (Eds.), *Achievement and motivation: A social-developmental perspective* (pp. 9–36). Cambridge, MA: Cambridge University Press.

Dempsey, J.M., Kimiecik, J.C., & Horn, T.S. (1993). Parental influence on children's moderate to vigorous physical activity participation: An expectancy-value approach. *Pediatric Exercise Science, 5,* 151–167.

Dobrantu, M., & Biddle, S.J.H. (1997). The influence of situational and individual goals on intrinsic motivation of Romanian adolescents towards physical education. *European Yearbook of Sport Psychology, 1,* 148–165.

Duda, J.L. (1989). The relationship between task and ego orientation and the perceived purpose of sport among male and female high school athletes. *Journal of Sport & Exercise Psychology, 11,* 318–335.

Duda, J.L. (1992). Sport and exercise motivation: A goal perspective analysis. In G. Roberts (Ed.), *Motivation in sport and exercise* (pp. 57–91). Champaign, IL: Human Kinetics.

Duda, J.L. (1993). Goals: A social cognitive approach to the study of motivation in sport. In R.N. Singer, M. Murphey, & L.K. Tennant (Eds.), *Handbook on research in sport psychology* (pp. 421–436). New York: Macmillan.

Duda, J.L. (1996). Maximizing motivation in sport and physical education among children and adolescents: The case for greater task involvement. *Quest, 48,* 290–302.

Duda, J.L. (1997). Perpetuating myths: A response to Hardy's 1996 Coleman Griffith address. *Journal of Applied Sport Psychology, 9,* 307–313.

Duda, J.L. (1999). The motivational climate and its implications for motivation, health, and the development of eating disorders in gymnastics. *Revista de Psicologia Social Aplicada, 9,* 7–24.

Duda, J.L. (in press-a). Goal perspective research in sport: Pushing the boundaries and clarifying some misunderstandings. In G.C. Roberts (Ed.), *Advances in motivation in sport and exercise.* Champaign, IL: Human Kinetics.

Duda, J.L. (in press-b). Goal perspectives and their implications for health-related outcomes in the physical domain. In F. Cury, P. Sarrazin, & F.P. Famose (Eds.), *Advances in motivation theories in the sport domain.* Paris: Presses Universitaires de France.

Duda, J.L., & Balaguer, I. (1999). Toward an integration of models of leadership with a contemporary theory of motivation. In R. Lidor & M. Bar-Eli (Eds.), *Sport psychology: Linking theory and practice* (pp. 213–230). Morgantown, WV: Fitness Information Technology.

Duda, J.L., Chi, L., Newton, M.L., Walling, M.D., & Catley, D. (1995). Task and ego orientation and intrinsic motivation in sport. *International Journal of Sport Psychology, 26,* 40–63.

Duda, J.L., Fox, K.R., Biddle, S.J.H., & Armstrong, N. (1992). Children's achievement goals and beliefs about success in sport. *British Journal of Educational Psychology, 62,* 313–323.

Duda, J.L., Newton, M.L., & Yin, Z. (1999). *The perceived motivational climate in sport: Within-team member variability/ interdependence and the correspondence to perceptions held by the coach.* Manuscript submitted for publication.

Duda, J.L., & Nicholls, J.G. (1992). Dimensions of achievement motivation in schoolwork and sport. *Journal of Educational Psychology, 84,* 1–10.

Duda, J.L., Olson, L., & Templin, T. (1991). The relationship of task and ego orientation to sportsmanship attitudes and the perceived legitimacy of injurious acts. *Research Quarterly for Exercise and Sport, 62,* 79–87.

Duda, J.L., & White, S.A. (1992). The relationship of goal perspectives to beliefs about success among elite skiers. *The Sport Psychologist, 6,* 334–343.

Duda, J.L., & Whitehead, J. (1998). Measurement of goal perspectives in the physical domain. In J. Duda (Ed.), *Advances in sport and exercise psychology measurement* (pp. 21–48). Morgantown, WV: Fitness Information Technology.

Durand, M., Cury, F., Sarrazin, P., & Famose, J.P. (1996). Le Questionnaire de Perception du Succes en Sport: Validation Française du "Perception of Success Questionnaire." *International Journal of Sport Psychology, 27,* 251–268.

Dweck, C.S. (1986). Motivational processes affecting learning. *American Psychologist, 41,* 1040–1048.

Dweck, C.S. (1991). Self-theories and goals: Their role in motivation, personality, and development. In R.A. Dienstbler (Ed.), *Nebraska Symposium on Motivation–1990* (pp. 199–235). Lincoln: University of Nebraska Press.

Dweck, C.S. (1999). *Self-theories and goals: Their role in motivation, personality, and development.* Philadelphia: Taylor & Francis.

Dweck, C.S., & Leggett, E.L. (1988). A social-cognitive approach to personality and motivation. *Psychological Review, 95,* 256–273.

Dykman, B.M. (1998). Integrating cognitive and motivational factors in depression: Initial tests of a goal orientation approach. *Journal of Personality and Social Psychology, 74,* 139–158.

Eccles, J., & Harold, R.D. (1991). Gender differences in sport involvement: Applying the Eccles' expectancy-value model. *Journal of Applied Sport Psychology, 3,* 7–35.

Elliot, A.J., & Church, M.A. (1997). A hierarchical model of approach and avoidance achievement motivation. *Journal of Personality and Social Psychology, 72,* 1–15.

Ewing, M.E. (1981). *Achievement motivation and sport behavior of males and females.* Unpublished doctoral dissertation, University of Illinois, Urbana-Champaign.

Flett, G.L., Hewitt, P.L., Endler, N.S., & Tassone, C. (1998). Perfectionism and components of state and trait anxiety. *Current Psychology, 13,* 326–350.

Folkman, S. (1984). Personal control and stress and coping processes: A theoretical analysis. *Journal of Personality and Social Psychology, 46,* 839–852.

Ford, J.K., Smith, E.M., Weissbein, D.A., Gully, S.M., & Salas, E. (1998). Relationships of goal orientation, metacognitive activity, and practice strategies with learning outcomes and transfer. *Journal of Applied Psychology, 83,* 218–233.

Frost, R.O., & Henderson, K.J. (1991). Perfectionism and reactions to athletic competition. *Journal of Sport & Exercise Psychology, 13,* 323–335.

Frost, R.O., & Marten, P.A. (1990). Perfectionism and evaluative threat. *Cognitive Therapy and Research, 14,* 559–572.

Frost, R.O., Marten, P.A., Lahart, C., & Rosenblate, R. (1990). The dimensions of perfectionism. *Cognitive Therapy and Research, 14,* 449–468.

Gano-Overway, L.A., & Duda, J.L. (1999). Interrelationships between expressive individualism and other achievement goal orientations among African and European American athletes. *Journal of Black Psychology, 25*(4), 544–563.

Gano-Overway, L.A., & Duda, J.L. (in press). Goal perspectives and their relationship to beliefs and affective responses among African and Anglo American athletes. *International Journal of Sport Psychology.*

Georgiadis, M., Biddle, S., & Van den Auweele, Y. (1999). *Cognitive, emotional, and behavioural connotations of task and ego orientation profiles: An ideographic approach using hierarchical class analysis.* Manuscript submitted for publication.

Goudas, M., Fox, K., Biddle, S., & Armstrong, N. (1992). Children's task and ego goal profiles in sport: Relationship with perceived competence, enjoyment, and participation. *Journal of Sport Sciences, 10,* 606–607.

Gould, D., Eklund, R., Petlichkoff, L., Peterson, K., & Bump, L. (1991). Psychological predictors of state anxiety and performance in age group wrestlers. *Pediatric Exercise Science, 3,* 198–208.

Guillet, E., & Sarrazin, P. (1999). L'influence du climate de l'extraineur sur le processus motivationnel de l'abandon: Un test du modele hierarchique deVallerand (1997). In the *Proceedings of the 8th International Congress of the Association for Research on Physical Activity and Sport (ACAPS)* (pp. 110–112). Macolin, Switzerland: Universities of Geneva and Lausanne.

Guivernau, M., & Duda, J.L. (1994). Psychometric properties of a Spanish version of the Task and Ego Orientation in Sport Questionnaire (TEOSQ) and Beliefs about the Causes of Success Inventory. *Revista de Psicologia del Deporte, 5,* 31–51.

Hall, H.K., Humphrey, E., & Kerr, A. (1997). Understanding and enhancing children's intrinsic motivation in sport: Adopting the tenets of Eccles' Expectancy-Value Model. In R. Lidor &

M. Bar-Eli (Eds.), *Innovations in sport psychology: Linking theory and practice. Proceedings of the 9th World Congress in Sport Psychology: Part I* (pp. 309–311). Netanya, Israel: Ministry of Education, Culture and Sport.

Hall, H.K., & Kerr, A.W. (1997). Motivational antecedents of precompetitive anxiety in youth sport. *The Sport Psychologist, 11,* 24–42.

Hall, H.K., Kerr, A.W., & Greenshields, H. (1998, July). *The influence of dispositional goals and the achievement climate on self determination in sport and physical activity.* Paper presented at the International Association of Applied Psychology Congress, San Francisco.

Hall, H.K., Kerr, A.W., & Matthews, J. (1998). Precompetitive anxiety in sport: The contribution of achievement goals and perfectionism. *Journal of Sport & Exercise Psychology, 20,* 194–217.

Hamacheck, D.E. (1978). Psychodynamics of normal and neurotic perfectionism. *Psychology, 15,* 27–33.

Hardy, L. (1997). Three myths about applied consultancy work. *Journal of Applied Sport Psychology, 9,* 277–294.

Harwood, C., & Hardy, L. (1999). Achievement goals in competitive sport: A critique of conceptual and measurement issues. *Proceedings of the 10th European Congress of Sport Psychology* (pp. 241–243). Prague, Czech Republic: Charles University Press.

Harwood, C., & Swain, A. (1998). Antecedents of precompetition achievement goals in elite junior tennis players. *Journal of Sports Sciences, 16,* 357–371.

Hatzigeorgeadis, A., & Biddle, S. (1999). The effects of goal orientation and perceived competence on cognitive interference during tennis and snooker performance. *Journal of Sport Behavior, 22.*

Hewitt, P.L., & Plett, G.L. (1991). Perfectionism in the self and social contexts: Conceptualization, assessment, and association with psychopathology. *Journal of Personality and Social Psychology, 60,* 456–470.

Hom, H., Duda, J.L., & Miller, A. (1993). Correlates of goal orientations among young athletes. *Pediatric Exercise Science, 5,* 168–176.

Kaplan, A., & Maehr, M.L. (1999). *Achievement motivation: The emergence, contributions, and prospects of a goal orientation theory perspective.* Unpublished manuscript, Ben Gurion University, Beer Sheva, Israel.

Kavussanu, M., & Roberts, G.C. (1996). Motivation in physical activity contexts: The relationship of perceived motivational climate to intrinsic motivation and self-efficacy. *Journal of Sport & Exercise Psychology, 18,* 254–280.

Kim, M.-S., & Duda, J.L. (1998). Achievement goals, motivational climates, and occurrence of and responses to psychological difficulties and performance debilitation among Korean athletes. *Journal of Sport & Exercise Psychology, 20,* S124.

Kim, M.-S., & Duda, J.L. (1999). *Predicting coping responses: An integration of Lazarus' transactional theory of psychological stress and coping and goal perspective theory.* Manuscript submitted for publication.

Kingston, K.M., & Hardy, L. (1997). *Do goal orientation profiles impact upon competition performance?* Unpublished manuscript.

Krane, V., Greenleaf, C.A., & Snow, J. (1997). Reaching for gold and the price of glory: A motivational case study of an elite gymnast. *The Sport Psychologist, 11,* 53–71.

Lazarus, R.S. (1993). From psychological stress to the emotions: A history of changing outlooks. *Annual Review of Psychology, 44,* 1–21.

Le Bars, H., & Gernigon, C. (1998). Perceived motivational climate, dispositional goals, and participation withdrawal in judo. *Journal of Sport & Exercise Psychology, 20,* S58.

Li, F., Harmer, P., Chi, L., & Vongjaturapat, S. (1996). Cross-cultural validation of the Task and Ego Orientation Questionnaire. *Journal of Sport & Exercise Psychology, 18,* 392–407.

Lintunen, T., Valkonen, A., Leskinen, E., & Biddle, S. (1999). Predicting physical activity intentions using a goal perspective approach: A study of Finnish youth. *Scandanavian Journal of Medicine and Science in Sports, 9,* 344–352.

Lochbaum, M., & Roberts, G.C. (1993). Goal orientations and perceptions of the sport experience. *Journal of Sport & Exercise Psychology, 15,* 160–171.

Locke, E.A., & Latham, G.P. (1990). *A theory of goal setting and task performance.* Englewood Cliffs, NJ: Prentice-Hall.

Maehr, M.L., & Braskamp, L. (1986). *The motivation factor: A theory of personal investment.* Lexington, MA: Lexington Books.

Martin, J.W., Pease, D.G., & Zhang, J.J. (1999, October). *Relationship of athlete goal orientations and coping strategies.* Paper presented at the annual meetings of the Association for the Advancement of Applied Sport Psychology, Banff, Canada.

Meece, J.L., Blumenfeld, P.C., & Hoyle, R.H. (1988). Students' goal orientations and cognitive engagement in classroom activities. *Journal of Educational Psychology, 80,* 514–523.

Middleton, M.J., & Midgley, C. (1997). Avoiding the demonstration of lack of ability: An underexplored aspect of goal theory. *Journal of Educational Psychology, 89,* 710–718.

Newton, M.L. (1994). *The relationship of perceived motivational climate and dispositional goal orientations to indices of motivation among female volleyball players.* Unpublished doctoral dissertation, Purdue University, West Lafayette, IN.

Newton, M.L., & Duda, J.L. (1993). Elite adolescent athletes' achievement goals and beliefs concerning success in tennis. *Journal of Sport & Exercise Psychology, 15,* 437–448.

Newton, M.L., & Duda, J.L. (1995). The relationship of goal orientations and expectations on multi-dimensional state anxiety. *Perceptual and Motor Skills, 81,* 1107–1112.

Newton, M.L., & Duda, J.L. (1999). The interaction of motivational climate, dispositional goal orientation and perceived ability in predicting indices of motivation. *International Journal of Sport Psychology, 30,* 63–82.

Newton, M.L., Duda, J.L., & Yin, Z. (in press). The Perceived Motivational Climate in Sport Questionnaire–2: A test of the hierarchical factor structure. *Journal of Sport Sciences.*

Newton, M.L., & Fry, M.D. (1998). Senior Olympians' achievement goals and motivational responses. *Journal of Aging and Physical Activity, 6,* 256–270.

Nicholls, J.G. (1984). Achievement motivation: Conceptions of ability, subjective experience, task choice, and performance. *Psychological Review, 91,* 328–346.

Nicholls, J.G. (1989). *The competitive ethos and democratic education.* Cambridge, MA: Harvard University Press.

Nolen, S. (1988). Reasons for studying: Motivational orientations and study strategies. *Cognition and Instruction, 5,* 269–287.

Ntoumanis, N., & Biddle, S. (1998). The relationship between competitive anxiety, achievement goals, and motivational climates. *Research Quarterly for Exercise and Sport, 69,* 176–187.

Ntoumanis, N., & Biddle, S.J.H. (1999a). Affect and achievement goals in physical activity: A meta-analysis. *Scandanavian Journal of Medicine and Science in Sports, 9,* 315–332.

Ntoumanis, N., & Biddle, S.J.H. (1999b). A review of motivational climate in physical activity. *Journal of Sport Sciences, 17,* 643–665.

Ntoumanis, N., Biddle, S.J.H., & Haddock, G. (1999). The mediating role of coping strategies on the relationship between achievement motivation and affect in sport. *Anxiety, Stress, and Coping, 12,* 299–327.

Ommundsen, Y., & Pedersen, B.H. (1999). The role of achievement goal orientations and perceived ability upon somatic and cognitive indices of sport competition trait anxiety: A study of young athletes. *Scandanavian Journal of Medicine and Science in Sports, 9,* 333–343.

Ommundsen, Y., & Roberts, G.C. (1996). Goal orientations and perceived purposes of training among elite athletes. *Perceptual and Motor Skills, 83,* 463–471.

Ommundsen, Y., & Roberts, G.C. (1999). Effect of motivational climate profiles on motivational indices in team sport. *Scandanavian Journal of Medicine and Science in Sports, 9,* 389–397.

Ommundsen, Y., Roberts, G.C., & Kavussanu, M. (1997). Perceived motivational climate and cognitive and affective correlates among Norwegain athletes. In R. Lidor & M. Bar-Eli (Eds.), *Innovations in sport psychology: Linking theory and practice. Proceedings of the 9th World Congress in Sport Psychology: Part II* (pp. 522–524). Netanya, Israel: Ministry of Education, Culture and Sport.

Papaioannou, A. (1999). Towards multidimensional hierarchical models of motivation. In V. Hosek, P. Tilinger, & L. Bilek (Eds.), *Psychology of sport and exercise: Enhancing the quality of life* (pp. 45–52). Prague, Czech Republic: Charles University Press.

Papaioannou, A., & Kouli, O. (1999). The effect of task structure, perceived motivational climate, and goal orientations on students' task involvement and anxiety. *Journal of Applied Sport Psychology, 11,* 51–71.

Pensgaard, A.M., & Roberts, G.C. (1997). The interaction between goal orientations and use of coping strategies among elite sport participants. In R. Lidor & M. Bar-Eli (Eds.), *Innovations in sport psychology: Linking theory and practice. Proceedings of the 9th World Congress of Sport Psychology* (pp. 552–554). Netanya, Israel: Ministry of Education, Culture, and Sport.

Petherick & Weigand, D.A. (in press). Goals, motivational climates and motivation. *International Journal of Sport Psychology.*

Pintrich, P. (1989). The dynamic interplay of student motivation and cognition in the college classroom. In M.L. Maehr & C. Ames (Eds.), *Advances in motivation and achievement: Motivation enhancing environments* (Vol. 6, pp. 117–160). Greenwich, CT: JAI Press.

Pintrich, P., & De Groot, E.V. (1990). Motivational and self-regulated learning components of classroom academic performance. *Journal of Educational Psychology, 82,* 33–40.

Roberts, G.C. (1986). The perception of stress: A potential source and its development. In M.R. Weiss & D.R. Gould (Eds.), *Sport for children and youths* (pp. 119–126). Champaign, IL: Human Kinetics.

Roberts, G.C. (1992). In G. Roberts (Ed.), *Motivation in sport and exercise: Conceptional constraints and convergence* (pp. 3–29). Champaign, IL: Human Kinetics.

Roberts, G.C. (1997). Future research directions in understanding the motivation of children in sport: A goal orientation perspective. In R. Lidor & M. Bar-Eli (Eds.), *Innovations in sport psychology: Linking theory and practice. Proceedings of the 9th World Congress in Sport Psychology: Part II* (pp. 576–580). Netanya, Israel: Ministry of Education, Culture and Sport.

Roberts, G.C., & Balague, G. (1991, September). *The development and validation of the Perception of Success Questionnaire.* Paper presented at the FEPSAC Congress, Cologne, Germany.

Roberts, G.C., Hall, H., Jackson, S., Kimiecik, J., & Tonymon, P. (1995). Implicit theories of achievement and the sport experience: The effect of goal orientations on achievement strategies and perspectives. *Perceptual and Motor Skills, 81,* 219–224.

Roberts, G.C., & Ommundsen, Y. (1996). Effects of achievement goal orientations on achievement beliefs, cognitions, and strategies in team sport. *Scandanavian Journal of Medicine and Science in Sport, 6,* 46–56.

Roberts, G.C., Treasure, D.C., & Balague, G. (1998). *Journal of Sports Sciences.*

Roberts, G.C., Treasure, D.C, & Kavussanu, M. (1997). Motivation in physical activity contexts: An achievement goal perspective. In M.L. Maehr & P.R. Pintrich (Eds.), *Advances in motivation and achievement* (Vol. 10, pp. 413–447). Greenwich, CT: JAI Press.

Roberts, G.C., Treasure, D.C., & Kavussanu, M. (1996). Orthogonality of achievement goals and its relationship to beliefs about success and satisfaction in sport. *The Sport Psychologist, 10,* 398–408.

Ryan, R.M. (1982). Control and information in the interpersonal sphere: An extension of cognitive evaluation theory. *Journal of Personality and Social Psychology, 43,* 450–461.

Ryan, R.M., Connell, J.P., & Grolnick, W.S. (1992). When achievement is not intrinsically motivated: A theory of assessment of self-regulation in school. In A.K. Boggiano & T.S. Pittman (Eds.), *Achievement and motivation: A social developmental perspective* (pp. 167–188). Cambridge, MA: Cambridge University Press.

Sarason, I.G., Sarason, B.R., Keefe, D.E., Hayes, B.E., & Shearin, E.N. (1986). Cognitive interference: Situational determinants and traitlike characteristics. *Journal of Personality and Social Psychology, 51,* 215–226.

Sarrazin, P., Cury, F., & Roberts, G. (1999). Exerted effort in climbing as a function of achievement goals, perceived ability, and task difficulty. In V. Hosek, P. Tilinger, & L. Bilek (Eds.), *Psychology of sport and exercise: Enhancing the quality of life. Proceedings of the 10th European Congress on Sport Psychology–FEPSAC* (pp. 138–140). Prague, Czech Republic: Charles University Press.

Seifriz, J., Duda, J.L., & Chi, L. (1992). The relationship of perceived motivational climate to intrinsic motivation and beliefs about success in basketball. *Journal of Sport & Exercise Psychology, 14,* 375–391.

Shields, D., & Bredemeier, B.J. (1995). *Character development and physical activity.* Champaign, IL: Human Kinetics.

Skaalvik, E.M. (1997). Self-enhancing and self-defeating ego orientation: Relations with task and avoidance orientation, achievement, self-perceptions, and anxiety. *Journal of Educational Psychology, 89,* 71–81.

Smith, R.E. (1996). Performance anxiety, cognitive interference, and concentration strategies in sports. In I.G. Sarason, G.R. Pierce, & B.R. Sarason (Eds.), *Cognitive interference:*

Theories, methods, and findings (pp. 261–283). Mahwah, NJ: Erlbaum.

Smith, R.E., Smoll, F., & Wiechman, S. (1998). Measuring sport trait anxiety. In J.L. Duda (Ed.), *Advances in sport and exercise psychology measurement* (pp. 105–128). Morgantown, WV: Fitness Information Technology.

Solmon, M., & Boone, J. (1993). The impact of student goal orientation in physical education classes. *Research Quarterly for Exercise and Sport, 64,* 418–424.

Standage, M., Butki, B.D., & Treasure, D.C. (1999). Predicting satisfaction/interest and boredom in the context of physical activity: Achievement goal orientations, situational motivation, and perceived ability. *Journal of Sport & Exercise Psychology, 21*(Suppl.), S103.

Swain, A., & Harwood, C. (1996). Antecedents of state goals in age-group swimmers: An interactionist perspective. *Journal of Sports Sciences, 14,* 111–124.

Swain, A.B.J. (1996). Social loafing and identifiability: The mediating role of achievement goal orientations. *Research Quarterly for Exercise and Sport, 67,* 337–344.

Thill, E.E. (1993). Conceptions differenciees et non differenciees de l'effort et de la competence en fonction de l'age: Consequences sur les affects et les strategies d'autohandicap. *International Journal of Sport Psychology, 26,* 81–97.

Thill, E.E., & Brunel, P.C. (1995). Ego-involvement and task-involvement: Related conceptions of ability, effort, and learning strategies among soccer players. *International Journal of Sport Psychology, 26,* 81–97.

Thorkildsen, T. (1988). Theories of education among academically precocious adolescents. *Contempory Educational Psychology, 13,* 323–330.

Treasure, D.C., & Roberts, G.C. (1994). Cognitive and affective concomitants of task and ego goal orientations during the middle school years. *Journal of Sport & Exercise Psychology, 16,* 15–28.

Treasure, D.C., & Roberts, G.C. (1995). Applications of achievement goal theory to physical education: Implications for enhancing motivation. *Quest, 47,* 45–489.

Treasure, D.C., & Roberts, G.C. (1998). Relationships between children's achievement goal orientations, perceptions of the motivational climate, beliefs about success, and sources of satisfaction in basketball. *International Journal of Sport Psychology, 29,* 211–230.

Treasure, D.C., Standage, M., & Lochbaum, M. (1999, October). *Perceptions of the motivational climate and situational motivation in elite youth sport.* Paper presented at the annual meetings of the Association for the Advancement of Applied Sport Psychology, Banff, Canada.

Vallerand, R.J. (1997). Toward a hierarchical model of intrinsic and extrinsic motivation. In M.P. Zanna (Ed.), *Advances in experimental social psychology* (pp. 271–360). New York: Academic Press.

Vallerand, R.J., & Losier, G.F. (1999). An integrative analysis of intrinsic and extrinsic motivation in sport. *Journal of Applied Sport Psychology, 11,* 142–169.

VanYperen, N.W., & Duda, J.L. (1999). Goal orientations, beliefs about success, and performance improvement among young elite Dutch soccer players. *Scandanavian Journal of Medicine and Science in Sports, 9,* 358–364.

Vealey, R.S. (1986). Conceptualization of sport-confidence and competitive orientation: Preliminary investigation and instrument development. *Journal of Sport Psychology, 8,* 221–246.

Vealey, R.S., & Campbell, J.L. (1988). Achievement goals of adolescent skaters: Impact on self-confidence, anxiety, and performance. *Journal of Adolescent Research, 3,* 227–243.

Walker, B.W., Roberts, G.C., & Nyheim, M. (1998). Predicting enjoyment and beliefs about success in sport: An interactional perspective. *Journal of Sport & Exercise Psychology, 20*(Suppl.), S59.

Walling, M., Duda, J.L., & Chi, L. (1993). The Perceived Motivational Climate in Sport Questionnaire: Construct and predictive validity. *Journal of Sport & Exercise Psychology, 15,* 172–183.

White, S.A. (1996). Goal orientations and perceptions of the motivational climate initiated by parents. *Pediatric Exercise Science, 8,* 122–129.

White, S.A. (1998). Adolescent goal profiles, perceptions of the parent-initiated motivational climate, and competitive trait anxiety. *The Sport Psychologist, 12,* 16–28.

White, S.A., & Duda, J.L. (1993). Dimensions of goal-beliefs about success among disabled athletes. *Adapted Physical Activity Quarterly, 10,* 125–136.

White, S.A., Duda, J.L., & Hart, S. (1992). An exploratory examination of the Parent-Initiated Motivational Climate Questionnaire. *Perceptual and Motor Skills, 75,* 875–880.

White, S.A., & Zellner, S. (1996). The relationship between goal orientation, beliefs about the causes of sport success, and trait anxiety among high school, intercollegiate, and recreational sport participants. *The Sport Psychologist, 10,* 58–72.

Williams, L. (1998). Contextual influences and goal perspectives among female youth sport participants. *Research Quarterly for Exercise and Sport, 69,* 47–57.

CHAPTER 17

Attributions
Past, Present, and Future

STUART J.H. BIDDLE, STEPHANIE J. HANRAHAN, and CHRISTOPHER N. SELLARS

Research on attributions and attribution-related processes in sport and exercise is reviewed in this chapter. First, a brief historical perspective and a summary of "classical" theories of attribution are provided. Second, attributions in physical activity contexts, mainly sport, are discussed in terms of antecedent factors, attributional style, biases, actor-observer differences, spontaneous causal thinking, and measurement issues, including new ways of investigating "naturally occurring" attributions in sport. Third, the consequences of making attributions, such as expectancies, emotions, and behavior, including learned helplessness, beliefs concerning the nature of ability, and attribution retraining are described. Finally, a theoretical analysis of attributional constructs is undertaken using Skinner's (1995, 1996) agent-means-ends analysis of perceived control.

A REVISION OF BASIC CONCEPTS

This section deals briefly with basic concepts of attributions. Because the topic of attributions in social psychology is so well documented, it is assumed that the content serves as a review rather than a presentation of new material. Attributions are perceived causes or reasons people give for an event related either to themselves or others. The term "causal attribution" is often used. However, whether attributions are actually causal is a matter of debate. For this chapter, the term is avoided, although causal thinking and causal thought are appropriate related terms. Although a great deal has been said about attributions in achievement settings, including sport, the study of attributions has been diverse and includes applications in areas such as health, law, family therapy, social affiliation, and clinical psychology settings (Weary, Stanley, & Harvey, 1989). Similarly, attributional analyses have been used to examine and

explain behaviors at intrapersonal, interpersonal, intergroup, and societal levels of analysis (Hewstone, 1989).

The study of attributions in many areas of psychology, including sport and exercise psychology, has been popular since the early 1970s. Entire books have been devoted to attribution theories (Hewstone, 1989; Weiner, 1986), and substantial sections of books have appeared, including chapters in sport/exercise books. Similarly, the seminal book on social cognition by Fiske and Taylor (1991) included two chapters and over 13% of the total text on attributions. In an analysis of all motivation papers published in the *International Journal of Sport Psychology* and *Journal of Sport (& Exercise) Psychology* between 1979 and 1991, Biddle (1994) found that attribution papers were the most popular, accounting for 12.9% of 224 motivation publications.

Thus, attribution is a popular topic in sport and exercise psychology, although interest has declined recently. Reasons for the decline are discussed later. However, much of the attribution research in sport and exercise has been narrow if one compares it with the many approaches used in other domains of psychology, and thus the full scope of attribution theory has not been exploited (Biddle, 1993). Furthermore, we concur with Weary et al. (1989) when they state, "To us, the attributional approach is not a sacrosanct school of thought on the human condition. It is, rather, a body of ideas and findings that we find to be highly useful in our work" (p. vii).

Despite the recent upsurge of interest in cognitive and social cognitive paradigms in psychology, attribution theory can be traced back to the work of Heider (1944, 1958). Although later theories have had considerable impact on the field, many of these are based on Heider's theorizing. The perspectives put forward by Jones and Davis (1965), Kelley

(1967), and Weiner (1986; Weiner et al., 1972) have been dominant, although the works of Bem (1972), Kruglanski (1975), Schacter and Singer (1962), and Seligman and coworkers (Abramson, Seligman, & Teasdale, 1978) have had a significant influence on the theory and application of attributions. Although little use has been made in sport psychology research of some of the perspectives outlined in this section, it is important to provide a brief historical sketch here to understand the attribution processes that have been studied in sport contexts.

Heider is considered the founding father of attribution theory, and although his seminal book, *The Psychology of Interpersonal Relations* (1958), is often used as the benchmark against which other attribution perspectives are compared, it was some 14 years prior to this that his article in *Psychological Review* was published. This article should be cited as the beginning of the contemporary literature on attributions (Heider, 1944). In this paper, Heider suggested that the determination of the locality ("locus") of an attribution was related to the concept of "unit formation." By this he meant that both causes (origins) and effects constituted causal units and that by studying the similarity between origins and effects, inferences or attributions about the event could be made. Similarly, Heider suggested that "person" attributions were more likely than situational attributions because he believed that people were the "prototype of origins." Such suggestions have fueled a great deal of research into attribution errors and biases, as well as the attribution of responsibility. Developing these ideas in his book, Heider (1958) began formulating his "naive psychology" or what became known as the phenomenology of the layperson.

Three fundamental propositions stem from this approach. First, to understand the behavior of individuals, one must first understand how they perceive and describe their social environment. Second, Heider made the assumption that people seek a stable and predictable environment in their effort to control their surroundings and anticipate the behavior of others. Finally, he suggested that the processes of perceiving objects and people were similar and that to understand behavior, people will look toward the dispositional qualities of the individual.

In 1979, E.E. Jones commented that "getting from acts to dispositions, or more generally, making inferences from behavior about personality, is a ubiquitous activity of paramount significance for all of us" (p. 107). Some 14 years prior to this statement, Jones and Davis (1965) had formulated their theory of correspondent inferences in which they attempted to explain how people infer dispositions, or

personality characteristics, of individuals from their behavior. This approach, therefore, is one of social ("other person") attribution rather than the self-perception more commonly found in the sport psychology literature. For example, one might gain more information about an athlete's commitment by observing his or her enthusiasm for training in adverse conditions than one would when conditions were comfortable.

Kelley's (1967, 1972) perspective is not too dissimilar from that of Jones and Davis (1965). Using his principle of co-variation, Kelley suggested that people arrive at a cause for an event by processing information about whether accompanying conditions and circumstances vary or not as the event changes. This was considered analogous to experimental methods (mainly, the ANOVA model in statistics) in which the event or outcome (dependent variable) is studied in relation to associated conditions (independent variables). Hence, Kelley and Michela (1980, p. 462) said, "The effect is attributed to the factor with which it covaries."

Weiner's Theory of Achievement Attributions

Bernard Weiner's contribution to the field of attribution theory has been highly significant, nowhere moreso than in the area of attribution processes associated with achievement contexts (Weiner, 1979, 1980, 1985a, 1986, 1992, 1995; Weiner et al., 1972). Weiner's initial work centered on attributional responses to academic success and failure in the classroom. This area was extended into investigations on links between attributions and emotions, behavioral correlates of the attribution-emotion relationship, whether people make spontaneous attributions in everyday life, and the consequences of attributional thinking associated with social conduct. For a summary of Weiner's attributional theory of achievement motivation and emotion, see Figure 17.1. The theory is organized around the simple notions of certain outcomes generating attributional thinking, which, in turn, are organized into dimensions. These have particular psychological and behavioral consequences (Weiner, 1986, 1992, 1995).

This theory shows that an outcome may generate positive or negative emotion (attribution-independent affect) and a search for the reasons for the outcome. The latter is more likely in the case of negative, unexpected, or important outcomes. Various antecedent factors will affect the nature of these attributions. The attributions themselves are thought to be organized into key dimensions that, in turn, influence the psychological consequences of the attributions, such as expectancy change or emotional feeling

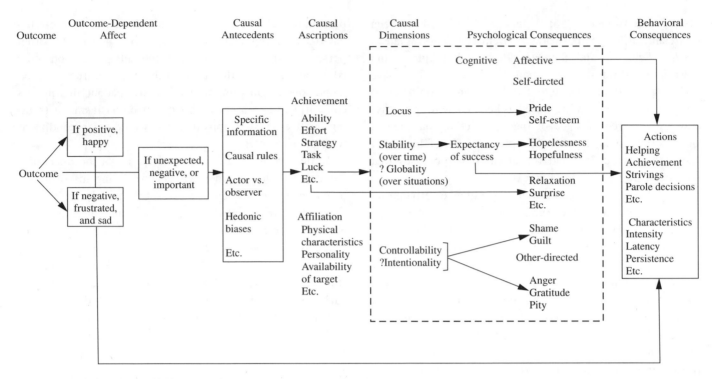

Figure 17.1   Weiner's attributional theory of motivation and emotion. From B. Weiner (1986), *An attributional theory of motivation and emotion.* New York: Springer-Verlag. Reprinted with permission.

(attribution-dependent affect). Finally, these consequences may affect behaviors such as offering help or achievement motivation. Aspects of Weiner's model have been tested in many different contexts, including achievement and affiliation settings. Central to the model is the belief that people organize their attributional thinking around dimensions of locus of causality, stability, and controllability.

ATTRIBUTION ANTECEDENTS AND ATTRIBUTIONS IN SPORT

Much of the sport psychology research in attribution theory has focused on the antecedent variables of attributions, such as individual differences or expectancies, and the nature of the attributions themselves (Biddle, 1993). Early studies were primarily descriptive. The approach adopted by Weiner et al. (1972) was used in early sport psychology attribution research. Based on Heider's theorizing, Weiner et al. identified four main attributions (attribution elements) related to achievement contexts: ability, effort, task difficulty, and luck. These attributions were not meant to be identified as the only attributions in achievement situations (Weiner, 1980). Nevertheless, two major criticisms can be made. First, the four factors were not derived through experimental research; second, many

sport psychology researchers adopted only these four factors in early studies.

Weiner et al. (1972) categorized these four elements into attributional dimensions. His original model is well-known, whereby attributions are classified along the dimensions of locus of control and stability. With respect to the locus dimension, attributions associated with the individual are internal (ability and effort), whereas those outside the individual are external (task difficulty and luck). Attributions related to enduring features are labeled stable (ability and task difficulty), whereas factors thought to be more variable are labeled unstable (effort and luck). Later, Weiner (1979) added the controllability dimension and relabeled the locus dimension "locus of causality." Controllability distinguished between factors that were perceived to be under one's control (e.g., effort) and those that were not (e.g., natural ability).

In one of the first studies of sport attributions, Iso-Ahola (1977), investigating Little League baseball players, proposed that effort has a different attributional meaning in the cases of success and failure. Results indicated that effort was associated with ability in the win situation, but with luck and task difficulty in the loss situation. Iso-Ahola interpreted this as meaning that effort is treated as an internal factor when winning, but as an external factor when losing. Other researchers also have questioned the fit of Weiner's basic four elements into dimensions. Carron (1984) suggested that ability associated with fitness might be viewed as relatively unstable rather than stable. Similarly, task difficulty may not always be stable (Deaux, 1976), as it may be dependent on the quality of the opponent or environmental conditions such as wind or temperature. Weiner (1983) also recognized the shortcomings of this classification system. He stated that ability, effort, and task difficulty can all be perceived as both internal and external to the person.

In addition to the traditional four elements not always fitting neatly into the dimensions of locus of control and stability, early sport research indicated that stringent use of these four elements is constraining. Iso-Ahola and Roberts (1977) included eight attribution elements in their study and found that lack of practice and "other" were more important external reasons for failure than the traditional reasons of task difficulty and luck. Similarly, Bukowski and Moore (1980) observed that task difficulty and luck were perceived by boys as having little importance in attributions for success and failure in athletic events. Additional studies in sport attributions have indicated that the traditional four elements make up less than half the attributions made by participants. For example, Roberts and Pascuzzi (1979) administered an open-ended questionnaire to American undergraduate students who were requested to respond to a variety of sports situations by providing possible attributions to several different scenarios. On coding the responses, they found that ability, effort, task difficulty, and luck were used only 45% of the time, suggesting that attribution research in sport relying on these four factors is overrestricted. However, in classifying these elements, the researchers were able to utilize the basic locus × stability model in placing all attributions.

Because of the diversity of attributions possible in sporting situations, some writers have suggested that research in sport should focus on causal dimensions rather than the four basic elements (Hanrahan, 1995). However, the nature of attribution dimensions in sport has not been studied extensively, and most sport psychology researchers have accepted uncritically the dimensions of locus, stability, and, more recently, controllability. In attribution theory, there has been some debate about the nature of attribution dimensions. For example, the internal/external distinction has been found to have some support, but other dimensions have been supported less consistently. Perhaps the greatest problem is that much of the research has been based on attribution researchers

determining the dimensional categorization of attributions rather than the participants stating how they perceive the attributions in terms of dimensional properties.

ASSESSMENT OF ATTRIBUTION ELEMENTS AND DIMENSIONS IN SPORT

In almost all attribution research, the events about which attributions are made are either positive, negative, or both. It is false to assume that the attributions someone makes for a positive event would be the same as those made for a negative event. Separate measurement of attributions about positive and negative events has been proposed (Tenenbaum, Furst, & Weingarten, 1984). These frequently concern success and failure in sport. It should be noted, however, that a person's perceptions of success and failure are distinct from objective outcomes of winning and losing. A loss will not always be considered by individuals to be a failure, and a win will not always be thought of as a success. Success and failure are psychological states based on an individual's subjective perception of the implications of the outcome on desirable personal qualities (Maehr & Nicholls, 1980). Therefore, subjective interpretations of success and failure should be used when measuring attributions.

When investigating attributions, researchers can use the participants' actual responses or the attributional dimensions that the responses may represent. As stated, the actual responses (elements) are the specific reasons people give for an event. Qualitative researchers may gain insight into responses to specific situations by content-analyzing the raw attributions given by participants. For example, it may be useful for coaches to understand the reasons officials give for making certain calls in specific situations. In-depth qualitative data may be more useful in this circumstance than ratings along attributional dimensions, such as locus of causality, stability, controllability, or globality. No research has been located using this approach in sport.

Problems can arise when researchers try to summarize attributions along dimensions or otherwise assume the dimensional categories of attributions (Russell, 1982). Weiner (1986) stated that ability, effort, and task difficulty can all be perceived as stable and unstable, and that luck can be considered both internal and external to the person. Therefore, if a participant states that the cause of an event was due to lack of effort, it is difficult for the researcher to know whether perception of that cause is stable or unstable. Similarly, if a participant indicates that the cause of a poor performance was that "the opposition played better defensively than we did," it cannot be known whether this is perceived to be an internal or external cause. Having participants rate their own attributions along causal dimensions avoids interpretation problems. The main question is then along which causal dimensions should individuals rate their attributions? Weiner's (1979) model involving the three attributional dimensions of locus of causality, stability, and controllability has been widely adopted in sport and exercise psychology. In many other attribution studies, the additional dimensions of globality and intentionality have also been proposed.

Whether the cause of an event is perceived to influence just that particular event (a specific attribution) or many different events (a global attribution) is the distinction represented by the globality dimension. Globality has been considered, along with locus of causality and stability, as one of the important attributional dimensions when studying "depressive attributional style" (Seligman, Abramson, Semmel, & vonBaeyer, 1979). This attributional style involves attributing uncontrollable negative events to internal, stable, and global causes. In a study examining attributions for a single, objectively defined loss in tennis, Prapavessis and Carron (1988) found that globality was a useful dimension when studying attributions in sport. Findings suggested that players who exhibited symptoms of learned helplessness attributed losses to internal, stable, and global factors to a greater extent than did players not exhibiting these symptoms.

Intentionality has been used as a causal dimension by a number of researchers. There is little agreement, however, on the meaning of intentionality. Elig and Frieze (1975) included the intentionality dimension in a coding scheme of causality they created. Intentional causes were defined as those under conscious control of the person. In this case, intentionality appears to be equivalent to controllability. Similarly, in Russell's (1982) original version of the Causal Dimension Scale (CDS), intentionality was one of the rating scales used to measure controllability. The theoretical interpretations of the intentionality dimension have been noted as being unclear (Kelley & Michela, 1980) and questionable (Weiner, 1986). Support for distinguishing between controllability and intentionality has also been provided by Hanrahan, Grove, and Hattie (1989). A confirmatory factor analysis of the Sport Attributional Style Scale (SASS) allowed reasonable confidence in using these two dimensions.

Confusion about the independence of controllability and intentionality is probably accentuated when attributions for positive events are considered. Attributions perceived to be controllable are likely to be perceived to be intentional as well. Hanrahan et al. (1989) found a correlation of .67 between these two dimensions when attributions were made for positive events. On the other hand, when attributions were made for negative events, the correlation between the two dimensions fell to .38. Therefore, the distinction between intentionality and controllability for negative events is most important. This is logical, as few athletes would tend to indicate that a poor performance was intentional. However, attributing a poor performance to a controllable factor suggests that future improvement is possible. Attributing a poor performance to the distracting behavior of spectators or other competitors is an example of an attribution that could be perceived as unintentional yet controllable.

Instruments for Assessing Attributions in Sport and Exercise

Few sport/exercise-specific inventories assess attributions (Biddle & Hanrahan, 1998). Those reported in the literature include the SASS (Hanrahan et al., 1989) and the Wingate Sport Achievement Responsibility Scale (Tenenbaum et al., 1984); both are trait attribution measures. In addition, the Performance Outcome Survey (POS; Leith & Prapavessis, 1989), a sport-specific version of the CDS, has been developed. Prapavessis and Carron (1988) have reported a sport-specific version of the Attributional Style Questionnaire.

Prior to the development of a psychometrically standardized scale, sport attribution researchers relied on a checklist approach for assessing individual attributions (Vallerand, 1987). These were then analyzed as individual attributions (Biddle & Hill, 1988) or coded into dimensions either by the researcher or through data-reduction procedures. In response criticisms discussed earlier, Russell (1982) developed the CDS based on Weiner's (1979) three-dimensional model of attributions. The CDS and its successor, the CDSII (McAuley, Duncan, & Russell, 1992), have been the most widely used state attribution measures in the past decade. The CDS was formulated on the basis of two premises. First, the measurement method should reduce or eliminate the possibility of making the fundamental attribution researcher error because the participant, not the researcher, decides on the dimensional properties of the attribution elements. Second, attributions can be classified into the three dimensions of locus of causality, stability, and controllability.

In the first of two studies, Russell (1982) identified three semantic differential scale items to reflect the locus dimension, three items for stability, and six for controllability.

Students then rated the scales in response to eight different hypothetical achievement scenarios. The participants were given a scenario and an associated attribution for the outcome. The attributions were stable effort, unstable effort, ability, mood, other's stable effort, other's unstable effort, task difficulty, and luck. Each scenario attribution was then rated on all of the 12 scales. For example, one of the locus items was anchored by *outside of you* and *inside of you,* one stability item was anchored by *permanent* and *temporary,* and one controllability item was anchored by *someone else is responsible* and *no one else is responsible.* All items were worded to reflect Weiner's (1979) three dimensions, although the controllability dimension was modified to include both internal and external causal factors. In other words, controllability could be reflected in control by the actor or control by others (e.g., athletic opponent).

Initial psychometric analyses provided evidence for validity for the locus and stability subscales. The discriminant validity of the controllability subscale, however, was not confirmed because of overlap with the locus scale. Only the "intentional or unintentional" item "was found to adequately measure controllability" (Russell, 1982, p. 1140). However, no test of factorial structure was undertaken in this first study. In his second study, Russell retained the six locus and stability items from Study 1 and added two new controllability items to the "intentionality" item mentioned previously. This produced a nine-item scale with three items for each attribution dimension. Psychometric evaluation was largely positive.

The use of the CDS has been prominent in sport and exercise psychology as a research tool but has not been subjected to rigorous psychometric scrutiny in the physical domain. McAuley and Gross (1983) reported its use by undergraduate students enrolled in physical education classes. The controllability subscale was found to have low internal consistency, whereas locus and stability subscales were adequate. Unfortunately, the sample size was not large enough for a factor analysis to be computed.

Other studies in sport and exercise have assessed attributions using the CDS. However, Van Raalte (1994) reported low internal consistency coefficients for the CDS subscales with undergraduate students for locus and controllability. Grove, Hanrahan, and McInman (1991), although not testing the psychometric properties of the CDS, reported the use of the CDS for players, officials, and spectators, suggesting that it is suitable to use across different sport settings. Finally, Morgan, Griffin, and Heyward (1996) reported satisfactory use of the CDS with a moderately large, ethnically diverse sample ($N = 755$) of track and field athletes.

The development of the CDS was a breakthrough in terms of assessing dimensions of attributions from the point of view of the participant. However, a number of potential problems were evident at the time of Russell's (1982) publication. First, the CDS was developed using only hypothetical achievement situations, and yet the assumption was that it could be used in real situations as well, although Russell did acknowledge this problem. Second, psychometric evidence for the CDS was based only on attributions provided for the participants. No work has been reported on the difference between free-response attributions and those supplied. The instructions for the CDS request that the individual "think about the reason or reasons you have written above." This can be problematic if more than one attribution is given or if the reason is not clear (Leith & Prapavessis, 1989). In addition, whether some people are able to accurately write down their causal thoughts at all or, indeed, whether they have given much thought to attributions is also open to question in some situations.

The first of Russell's (1982) studies on the CDS highlighted some problems with the items assessing controllability. In the final nine-item scale, the three controllability items refer to "controllability" (Item 2), "intentionality" (Item 4), and "responsibility" (Item 9). Criticism of this approach can be made on conceptual and empirical grounds. First, it is not at all clear whether intentionality and responsibility are conceptually related to controllability; second, evidence exists for the separation of these constructs (Biddle, 1988). In addition, the CDS was developed by having students respond to hypothetical achievement situations. It is not known whether the dimensions proposed, or the item wording, is appropriate across all settings or just achievement contexts. In addition, the interrelationship between dimensions, such as locus and controllability, may vary between situations.

Russell (1982) modified Weiner's (1979) definition of controllability to include both internal and external sources of control. This resulted in the three controllability items in the CDS including potentially confounding statements. Items 2 (controllability) and 4 (intentionality) refer to "you or other people," and item 9 refers to "no one" and "someone" being responsible. Being controllable by "you" may be quite different from being controlled by others. Similarly, "someone" being responsible may mean that I am responsible or my opponent is responsible—again quite different from each other. Moreover, Item 2 refers to whether the cause or reason is perceived to be controllable.

This may be different from believing that the cause was actually controlled. Although the development of the CDS was an important step forward in assessing causal dimensions from the viewpoint of the attributer and is seen as reducing the chance of making the fundamental attribution researcher error, a number of methodological issues remain. This prompted the development of the CDSII (McAuley et al., 1992), and this instrument has now been adopted in sport and exercise research.

McAuley et al. (1992) created and tested the CDSII in four studies, three of which involved sport and exercise contexts. The revision of the CDS focused on changes to the controllability items, with the items from the locus and stability subscales left unaltered. In Study 1, undergraduate students responded to the CDS after receiving their results of a psychology examination. The original CDS was used, plus an additional 10 items. These new items were added to reflect personal control and external control, with five items each. Three items were retained after analysis to represent the personal control subscale and three for external control. Of interest was the fact that all three of the original CDS controllability items were rejected. This process meant that the CDSII comprised four subscales of three items each.

To test for factorial validity of the CDSII, confirmatory factor analysis was used by collapsing data across studies. A good fit of the data to the hypothesized four-factor oblique model was obtained. In addition, tests of alternative two- and three-factor models were shown to fit the data less well. Given that three of the four studies used in the development of the CDSII by McAuley et al. (1992) were in the physical domain, the psychometric evidence in favor of the instrument in sport and exercise settings is quite strong. A modification of the CDSII for children (CDSII-C) aged 10 to 16 years has been constructed (Vlachopoulos, Biddle, & Fox, 1996). A four-factor eight-item scale was used in a study of attributions, goal orientations, and emotional reactions following an endurance run in a school physical education lesson, and the scale showed reasonably sound psychometric properties. Confirmatory factor analysis supported a four-factor oblique structure. All items had statistically significant factor loadings on their appropriate factors, but interitem correlations for the two items within each subscale were only small to moderate. Measuring attributions remains a central issue for researchers and some progress has been made. However, the experience of the authors in using the CDSII suggests that it can be difficult for adults to understand. In addition, the CDSII-C requires further testing before its utility is known.

Attributional Style

A tendency to make particular attributions across different situations and time has been termed "attributional style." Despite the attempt to measure this "trait" by Peterson and his colleagues (Peterson et al., 1982; Peterson & Villanova, 1988), it has not been accepted by all researchers as a meaningful or useful construct. For example, Cutrona, Russell, and Jones (1984) found that the Attributional Style Questionnaire (ASQ) developed by Peterson et al. (1982) did not predict attributions for actual negative events very well. However, a meta-analytic review by Sweeney, Anderson, and Bailey (1986) found support for the concept of attributional style in depression.

State measures of attributions typically involve participants making attributions about a common event. Trait measures, on the other hand, need to allow participants to make attributions about multiple events. Because it cannot be assumed that respondents have had identical experiences, questionnaires that measure attributional styles usually rely on hypothetical situations.

Probably the most frequently used measure of attributional style is the ASQ (Peterson et al., 1982), which consists of 12 hypothetical situations: 6 good outcomes and 6 bad outcomes. For each situation, respondents are asked to name the one major cause of the outcome described. Each cause is then rated on a seven-point scale for the degree of internality (locus of causality), stability, and globality. Peterson et al. studied the ASQ and found it to have good construct, criterion, and content validity. However, they also found the discrimination among the individual dimensions on the ASQ to be less than precise, especially for good events.

Measures of Attributional Style in Sport

Although attributional style is a trait measure, it requires domain-specific assessment (Cutrona et al., 1984). When investigating sport-related attributional style, therefore, it is appropriate to use a sport-specific measure rather than a general measure. One of the first instruments designed to measure enduring dispositions for appraising successful and unsuccessful sport outcomes was the Wingate Sport Achievement Responsibility Scale (WSARS; Tenenbaum et al., 1984). The WSARS was designed to measure perceived responsibility for sport-related outcomes, but considers only the locus of causality dimension.

The Sport Attributional Style Scale (SASS) was constructed by Hanrahan et al. (1989). Its development was based on the following premises: (1) Subjective interpretations of success and failure should be used instead of the objective outcome of win or loss; (2) the measure should allow for a variety of causal attributions; (3) attributions can be classified into five dimensions of locus of causality, stability, globality, controllability, and intentionality; (4) separate attributions should be allowed for positive and negative events (Corr & Gray, 1996; Xenikou, Furnham, & McCarrey, 1997), which should be matched for content; (5) it should not be assumed that researchers can accurately place causal attributions into causal dimensions; and (6) a multiple-item questionnaire should be used to measure attributional style.

The SASS initially involved 12 positive and 12 negative events in sport that were matched for content. The original situations were based on modifications to items appearing in other attributional style scales. Respondents are asked to provide the single most likely cause of each event if it happened to them and then rate the cause on seven-point scales measuring each of the dimensions.

Nearly 300 undergraduate physical education students completed the SASS in the initial study of the scale (Hanrahan et al., 1989). Confirmatory factor analysis provided reasonable support for the five dimensions for both positive and negative events. After further psychometric assessment, 16 items were retained.

Because research with the SASS involved university undergraduate physical education students as participants, an additional study determined the factor structure and internal consistency of the SASS when administered to athletes from outside the university environment (Hanrahan & Grove, 1990a). Confirmatory factor analysis supported the proposed factor structure of the SASS, with mean factor loadings actually stronger on 8 of the 10 subscales than in the original student sample. These results indicate that the SASS is appropriate for use with nonuniversity samples. As the 16-item version of the SASS takes between 20 and 30 minutes to complete, the feasibility of employing a shortened 10-item version was investigated (Hanrahan & Grove, 1990b). Using four different samples and three different versions of the 10-item form, correlations between 16-item and 10-item forms were found to be consistently high. Results suggest that all three versions of the short form could be used in research. Further coverage of attributional style is presented later in the chapter, when the role of attributions and attributional style in learned helplessness is discussed (Peterson, 1990).

The Self-Serving Bias

Support has been found for the self-serving bias in sport attribution research. This "hedonic bias" suggests that strategies operate to protect or enhance self-esteem. Typically, this is thought to involve taking credit for success but not taking the blame for failure. Hence, attributions may be distorted, such as externalizing the reasons for failure, to protect self-esteem. Alternatively, people may actually perceive themselves as being more responsible for successful or positive outcomes than unsuccessful ones. This distortion may be the result of motivational influences and is more likely to occur in situations considered important.

A review by Miller and Ross (1975) found that internal attributions were common under success conditions, but that self-protecting attributions in failure were not so common. Much of the work relevant to the self-serving bias in sport psychology has investigated the difference in attributions between winners and losers. For example, McAuley and Gross (1983), using the CDS, found that winners of table tennis matches were significantly higher on ratings of internal, unstable, and controllable attributions than were losers. Grove et al. (1991) addressed the self-serving issue from the standpoints of player, coach, and spectator. A modified version of the CDS was used to assess attribution dimensions given by males and females in each of the three categories of involvement for both winning and losing games of basketball. No effects were found for the gender or involvement category, but a significant effect was found for outcome. Winning situations produced more stable and controllable attributions than were found in losing situations. No difference was found between winning and losing attributions on the locus of causality dimension.

Mullen and Riordan (1988) reported a meta-analysis of attributions in sport settings with a particular focus on the self-serving bias. Moderate effect sizes (ES) were found for the internal/external dimension (ES = .33) and for ability attributions (ES = .31), with a smaller effect for effort (ES = .20). Little effect was found for task difficulty (ES = .09) or luck (ES = .10). Mullen and Riordan concluded that "the data are inconsistent with an intentional motivational explanation and that are more easily reconciled with an unintentional information processing perspective" (pp. 16–17). The reason for such a conclusion is that the magnitude of the self-serving effect for internal/ external and ability attributions increased with team size. Attributions to difficulty decreased with group size. Overall, effect sizes were larger for attributions to team performance in team sports and smaller for individual performance in individual sports. One factor of importance in studying the self-serving bias is that significant group differences often mask the extent of real differences. Sometimes, winners and losers report internal attributions, but winners may have significantly stronger ratings than losers. Reported internal-external differences may really be showing just degrees of internality.

Actor-Observer Differences in Attributions

There has been a bias in sport psychology research toward the study of self-attributions rather than attributions made by observers. Although the literature is extensive on the issue of "other person" attributions, sport psychology has not responded in the same way, despite suggestions that such an approach might prove fruitful in some fields (Biddle, 1986, 1993; Rejeski, 1979). Jones and Nisbett (1972) made a distinction between attributions made by the participant (actor) and those made by an observer for the behavior of the actor. This actor-observer distinction is sometimes referred to as the "divergent perspectives" hypothesis because it is believed that the two individuals process information about the same event in different ways and end up making different types of attributions.

Jones and Nisbett (1972) proposed that actors typically use situational attributions to explain their behavior, whereas observers report attributions that center on dispositions or traits of the individual. One reason for this tendency is that actors will have information about their own behavior across many past situations ("consistency" information; Kelley, 1972), whereas observers may have only the one situation in which to draw inferences about the event. Similarly, some researchers have suggested that perceptual factors account for the difference; that is, the actor's perceptual focus will naturally be more external toward the environment, whereas observers will be focused on the actor (Fiske & Taylor, 1991).

Sport psychology has not adopted this perspective a great deal, despite the obvious application to such areas as athlete-coach interaction. For example, Rejeski (1979) has suggested that the divergent perspectives approach allows for a greater understanding of attributional conflict between athlete and coach. Another application is in teacher-pupil interaction in physical education (PE). For example, Biddle and Goudas (1997) studied the preferences of teachers for pupils who differed in effort, ability, and outcome in PE. Specifically, Biddle and Goudas sampled student elementary school teachers who specialized (took extra credit) or did not specialize in PE, as well as a group of qualified secondary school PE teachers. They were asked to rate, on seven-point scales, the degree to which they would like to work with each of five hypothetical pupils who varied in their effort (high/low), ability (high/low), and outcome (success/failure) in PE. Results are shown in Figure 17.2 and reveal a clear preference for effort. Trying hard is socially valued. Research reported on attributions and emotions later in this chapter is also consistent with such an approach. Effort is valued because it

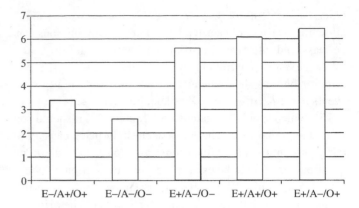

Figure 17.2   Preferences expressed by teachers for pupils who vary in effort, ability, and outcome. Date drawn from Biddle and Goudas (1997). Key: E = effort; A = ability; O = outcome; + = high/positive; − = low/negative.

is a controllable attribution. As such, teachers will feel greater pleasure at the success of the child if it is due to the child's own efforts. Similarly, they still value children who try hard when the outcome is "failure." Weiner's (1995) theory of social emotions shows that sympathy and pity will be elicited after heroic failure, but anger is more likely to be expressed toward high-ability pupils who fail.

In summary, the divergent perspectives hypothesis has not been studied extensively in sport, yet has potential to shed light on a number of important emotional and interpersonal issues. These include the reactions of teachers or coaches and the interactions between coaches and athletes.

Spontaneous Attributions in Sport

The initial studies in sport attribution research relied almost exclusively on having individuals rate attribution statements supplied by the experimenters. Although the results from these studies are reasonably consistent in showing that many attributions are strongly endorsed and that certain attributions are more likely to occur in one situation than in another, they raise the fundamental question of whether people actually engage in causal thought after sports events. Few studies can be located that have analyzed naturally occurring discourse in sport (see later section on analyzing attributions using qualitative methods).

The study of naturally occurring attributions, particularly in achievement situations, is not extensive. Weiner (1985b) located 17 published studies that investigated "spontaneous" attributional thought and found clear support for the proposition that attributions do occur as a part of everyday life. However, attributions were found to be more likely when a goal was not attained or when an outcome was unexpected. Assuming that participants in sport have some commitment to winning and playing well, it is likely that those who lose, especially unexpectedly, or those who are dissatisfied with their performance will engage in more attributional thought than others.

Measuring Naturally Occurring Attributions

In the study of attributions in sport, questionnaires have been the primary research tool; examples of such scales have been alluded to. Clearly, there are numerous advantages to these approaches, such as allowing a relatively easy application of a standardized measure and having data from which quantification is relatively easy. However, such approaches do have significant disadvantages, too. For example, the participant responds to questions or settings that are of interest to the researcher (and that are often hypothetical) rather than to participants themselves, and in a format chosen by the researcher. The response is "forced" in the sense that the questionnaire requires an answer at that time and in response to that particular question. Additionally, as Munton, Silvester, Stratton, and Hanks (1999) point out, items are usually considered in isolation from the context in which they operate (i.e., outcomes are usually part of a causal chain of events which is difficult to consider within a questionnaire framework). Perhaps of most significance, the use of questionnaires implies that the participant reaches a causal conclusion in isolation, a "private cognition" (p. 30), and that the purpose of the questionnaire is to expose these to the researcher. There is no opportunity to negotiate meaning, clarify explanations, and place causes within their contextual framework when using a questionnaire approach. "This method (questionnaires) fails to recognize the subtlety or complexity of the relationship between language and cognition or thought. Only when causal beliefs are located within entire sequences of natural discourse can they adequately be understood" (p. 181).

In response to the challenge of exposing attributions within their host context, Stratton and colleagues at the Leeds Family Therapy Research Center in England utilized a cognitive-behavioral perspective to develop the Leeds Attributional Coding System (LACS). This approach allows the exploration of attributions in qualitative material with quantitative analysis (Stratton, Munton, Hanks, Hard, & Davidson, 1988). This coding system is amenable to any qualitative material, ranging from naturally occurring dialogue (the LACS was initially devised to be used in a family therapy setting) to interviews, focus group discussion, and speech material. In this way, "public attributions" (attributions made in

conversation or in written form) can be examined within the context in which they are made. In sports settings, this has obvious advantages when considering social settings such as team meetings, coach-performer interactions, media interviews, and postevent analysis. It allows chains of causes and outcomes to be considered within the natural contexts in which they are set, without the necessity of a forced response to predetermined situations.

To describe the other advantages of this approach, it is necessary to explain how the LACS is used. Munton et al. (1999) discuss a six-part process: (1) Identify the sources of attributions; (2) extract attributions; (3) separate cause and outcome elements of the attribution; (4) identify the "speaker," "agent," and "target"; (5) code attributions on causal dimensions; and (6) analyze the data.

Identify the Sources of Attributions. Any verbatim material can be coded for use with the LACS. Usually, verbal material will be audiotaped and transcribed verbatim. For example, we used an open interview format with a number of coaches and their performers to explore the perceived causes of sporting outcomes in training and competition. Alternatively, written material (e.g., archive material, letters) can be analyzed.

Extract Attributions. An attribution is any answer to the question *why?* Having identified the material from which the analysis will be drawn, the specific attributions now need to be identified and extracted from the text.

Within an attribution will be a number of constituent parts that together relate one or more causes (C) with one or more outcomes (O) via some link or links (L). For example: *My performance was disappointing because of my poor preparation this week.* The outcome (*disappointing performance*) is linked to the cause (*my poor preparation*) by the obvious link word (*because*). It should be noted that attributions do not always contain obvious link words such as *because, due to,* or *as a result,* and indeed some causally related aspects of the attribution may be implied rather than stated explicitly. Furthermore, in naturally occurring speech, more than one cause and/or outcome may be included in the statement, and not always located within the same sentence. For example: *I didn't really care about the session, especially with the weather being so bad, so when it came to it, the times were below par and I didn't enjoy it at all, you know, with the slippery conditions as well.*

A number of related causes bring about a number of outcomes. Indeed, this is one of the advantages of the LACS; it allows long chains of causes and outcomes to develop in speech, permitting causes and their associated outcomes to be analyzed regardless of where they are located within the text, thus giving a rich contextual clarity to the analysis.

Separate Cause and Outcome Elements of the Attribution.   In the LACS, cause and outcome are dealt with separately. It is therefore helpful to identify these before coding begins. A number of conventions can be applied to the transcript data to make this aspect of the coding easier (see Munton et al., 1999). Whichever method is used, the coder needs to be able to clearly identify each outcome and the cause or causes that have brought this outcome about.

Identify Speaker, Agent, and Target.   For each attributional statement, it should be possible to identify a *speaker* (the person making the attribution), an *agent* (the person or circumstance that is bringing about the outcome), and the *target* (the person or circumstance affected by the cause and located in the outcome). At this stage, a set of codes needs to be developed for the speaker, agent, and target (the so-called SAT codes) that are of interest to the research question. It is sometimes helpful to identify common SATs from a subsample of the total interview data to include all those of relevance. For example, in ongoing studies of ours concerning coach-performer relationships, the following SAT codes were identified: (1) coach; (2) athlete; (3) other athletes (e.g., opposition); (4) conditions or specifics of the event; (5) athlete's performance (competition or training); (6) other people (not athletes or coach); (7) training program or aspect of it; (8) outcome (position); and (9) default.

Using the codes identified, the following extract made by a coach can be coded: *He [the athlete] tried his best and this showed in the improvement in times over the season:*

Speaker: Coach (1)

Agent: He (the athlete) (2)

Target: Athlete's performance (5)

It should be noted that the speaker, agent, and target might be the same person or different people or circumstances. This process now allows the researcher to consider causal dimensions in relation to each (e.g., when the agent or target is not the speaker).

Code Attributions on Causal Dimensions.   It is common when analyzing attributions to locate specific causes within a framework of causal dimensions (e.g., the CDS

using the attributional dimensions of locus, stability, and control). The LACS includes the dimensions of locus of causality, stability, controllability, universality, and globality. For purposes of statistical analysis, the LACS allocates one of three codes to each dimension: 0, 1, or 2 (undecoded). This is shown in Table 17.1. It should be stressed that all attributions are considered from the perspective of the speaker (e.g., does the *speaker* consider the outcome controllable by himself or herself, the agent, and/or the target?). The coder should then use the information in the statement and surrounding transcript material when making decisions concerning dimension codes.

It should be apparent from previous discussion that coding on some dimensions (locus of causality, controllability, and universality) is affected by whether the statement is

Table 17.1   Coding Naturalistic Attributions into Dimensions Using the LACS

Dimension	Scoring	Explanation
Locus of causality	Internal = 1 External = 0	Internal causes are believed to originate from within the person being coded and external causes from other people or circumstances; it is therefore coded by looking at the cause.
Stability	Stable = 1 Unstable = 0	Stable causes are those expected to have a continued influence on outcomes in the future (the precise timescale should be decided in advance and be appropriate to the study in question); stability is coded by looking at the cause.
Controllability	Controllable =1 Uncontrollable = 0	Controllability represents the speaker's belief that he or she could have influenced the outcome without exerting exceptional effort; it is coded by looking at all three elements (cause, link, and outcome).
Universality	Personal = 1 Universal = 0	Personal attributions say something unique or idiosyncratic about the person being coded; universality is coded by looking at all three elements.
Globality	Global = 1 Specific = 0	Global causes are deemed likely to have a significant effect on a number of outcomes; globality is coded by looking at the cause.

coded in relation to the speaker, the agent, or the target. For example, considering the following statement from a coach: *I arranged for him [the athlete] to do the session on grass for a change, but this made it impossible for him to produce the goods.* Here the speaker is the coach (1), the agent is the coach (1), and the target is the athlete's performance (5). The statement can be coded as:

Unstable (0): This was an unusual cause (the coach arranging for the session to be on grass *for a change*).

Specific (0): The cause (change of training venue) is unlikely to have many potential outcomes.

However, for the three dimensions, one must consider each in relation to speaker, agent, and target separately. Concerning locus of causality, for example:

In relation to the speaker (i.e., Is the cause internal to the speaker?): (Yes) Internal (1)

In relation to the agent (i.e., Is the cause internal to the agent?): (Yes) Internal (1)

In relation to the target (i.e., Is the cause internal to the target?): (No) External (0)

In addition to the dimension codes, other important aspects of the attributional statement can be coded using a set of content codes. This provides useful information concerning the context in which the statement is made. The examples shown in Table 17.2, are data pertinent to the study of coaches' and performers' perceptions of sporting outcomes.

LACS Data Analysis. Table 17.2 shows how the LACS enables coding and quantification of the qualitative data. It is now possible to develop a data sheet similar to the one in Table 17.3 and input these data into statistical packages.

Analyzing Naturally Occurring Attributions: Summary Comments

It is important to remember that one cannot always assume that attributions conveyed in public communications necessarily reflect internal thought processes. We may, for example, modify our expressed views when conveying them to others for a variety of reasons, such as to protect the feelings of others, to portray ourselves or others in a better light, or because we cannot find the words to adequately express our thoughts. Attribution is, after all, part of what Higgins (1981) refers to as "the communication game," where expressed cause and effect occurs in a variety of forms and is influenced by a variety of intrapersonal and interpersonal factors. However, what this method allows is an analysis of those messages conveyed to others across the media of spoken and written language and that may form the basis for how others respond or act in the future.

This system does rely on the coder's making subjective judgments regarding the values of attribution dimensions associated with each statement. Such a problem has been faced previously by researchers using questionnaire approaches and is the reason behind the development of the CDS. However, when using the LACS, the problem can be

Table 17.2   Examples of Additional Coding Characteristics Using the LACS

Coding Category	Coding Characteristics
Outcome	positive (1), negative (2), neutral (9)
Specificity of the event	specific event/session-related (1), non-event-related (2), default (9)
Statement related to dyadic partner	yes (1), no (2), default (9)
Expressed emotion	positive (1), negative (2), no emotion (9)
Time of season	out of season (1), early competitive phase (2), main competitive phase (3)
Speaker number	*Coach:* Sue (1), John (2), Peter D. (3), Don (4), John (5)
	Performer: Becky (11), Phillip (12), Elizabeth (21), Robin (31), Peter M. (32), Jayne (41), Anne (42), Helen (51)

Table 17.3   Example Data Table Based on Input from Table 17.1

Attribution Number	1	2	3	4	5	6
Speaker	2	3				
Agent	1	2				
Target	1	1				
Stable (1), Unstable (0)	1	1				
Global (1), Specific (0)	1	0				
Internal (1), External (0) Speaker	0	1				
Internal (1), External (0) Agent	0	0				
Internal (1), External (0) Target	0	0				
Personal (1), Universal (0) Speaker	1	0				
Personal (1), Universal (0) Agent	1	0				
Personal (1), Universal (0) Target	1	0				
Controllable (1), Uncontrollable (0) Speaker	0	1				
Controllable (1), Uncontrollable (0) Agent	0	0				
Controllable (1), Uncontrollable (0) Target	0	0				
Other content codes . . .						

Based on format proposed by Munton et al. (1999).

reduced with rigorous use of clear definitions for each dimension (e.g., what constitutes "stable" and "unstable" in a particular study) and making use of tests for intercoder reliability to enhance consistency.

The recording, transcribing, coding, and analyzing of naturally occurring material is not a quick process. It requires learning and protracted practice. However, the rewards in terms of the richness and depth of the data make it a useful tool for the sport and exercise psychologist and one that should be explored further.

Summary of Attribution Antecedents and Assessment

Research on attributions in sport has tended to be narrow in its focus. Indeed, Brawley and Roberts (1984) identified the following characteristics of sport attribution research in laboratory settings: (1) Participants were mainly university students or children; (2) the focus was almost exclusively on self-attributions; (3) the experimental tasks were usually novel; (4) the independent variables were usually outcome (i.e., win/loss) or prior wins and losses; (5) some attempts were made to manipulate ego involvement, but rarely was this checked for effectiveness; and (6) most participants were asked to choose attributions from a list provided by the experimenters. These attributions were predominantly ability, effort, task difficulty, and luck. Although more recent attribution studies in sport psychology have addressed some of these limitations, the diversity of methods has not matched that in some other areas of psychology. Consequently, sport attribution research has remained narrow, and much needs to be done to enhance knowledge in this area (Biddle, 1993).

CONSEQUENCES OF ATTRIBUTIONS

Three main areas of attribution consequences will be considered: expectancies, emotions, and beliefs.

Attributions and Expectancies

Weiner (1986) stated that people are guided by anticipations of expected rewards; this view reflects the shift from mechanistic to cognitive approaches to motivation (Weiner, 1982). Indeed, Heider (1958) suggested that expectations will result from the interaction of personal and environmental factors. For example, he proposed that expectations will be high on an easy task, especially for someone high in perceived ability who believes that he or she always tries hard. However, in his analysis of expectations and attributions, Weiner (1986) argued that it is much more difficult

to find the determinants of absolute expectancy levels because a number of factors are likely to be influential. Nevertheless, he says that changes in expectancy are related to attributions: "For many human endeavours, prediction of just the direction of expectancy shift . . . will facilitate our understanding of motivation and emotion" (p. 81).

In short, Weiner (1986) argued that the stability of the attribution is the most important factor in determining changes in expectancy. He proposed that research findings allow the statement of a fundamental psychological "law": "Changes in expectancy of success following an outcome are influenced by the perceived stability of the cause of the event" (p. 114). This law has three corollaries:

1. If the outcome of an event is ascribed to a stable cause, then that outcome will be anticipated with increased certainty, or with increased expectancy, in the future.
2. If the outcome of an event is ascribed to an unstable cause, then the certainty or expectancy of that outcome may be unchanged, or the future will be anticipated to be different from the past.
3. Outcomes ascribed to stable causes will be anticipated to be repeated in the future with a greater degree of certainty than outcomes ascribed to unstable causes. (Weiner, 1986)

Some sport psychological research has tackled attributions and the consequences these may have for expectations. For example, Singer and McCaughan (1978) found that male high school students showed more positive expectations after success than after failure, and these expectations were enhanced by attributions to stable factors. Rudisill (1989) noted that expectations, persistence, and performance were enhanced after failure feedback on a balance stabilometer task for those high in perceived competence and for those oriented toward attributions that were internal, controllable, but unstable. After failure, it would appear to be more beneficial to feel that future success is possible. This often will require, as shown by Rudisill (1988, 1989), attributions to controllable factors that, almost by definition, will also be relatively unstable. However, three studies reported by Grove and Pargman (1986) show quite clearly that it was effort rather than ability attributions that related to future expectancies. These findings suggest that it is the controllability, rather than the stability, of the attribution that is important.

Expectancies, therefore, can be influenced by many factors, including the stability of the attribution. However, the role of future expectancies and confidence has been addressed through other routes, such as self-efficacy. Indeed, Bandura (1990) argues that causal attributions and outcome expectancies are different motivational processes, although both operate through the anticipation of future behavior and performance. Bandura states that "causal attributions and self-efficacy appraisals involve bidirectional causation. Self-beliefs of efficacy bias causal attribution" (p. 141).

Attributions and Emotional Reactions

The study of attributions and emotions became popular in psychology in the 1980s (Weiner, 1986) and interest also developed in sport psychology (Biddle, 1993; McAuley & Duncan, 1990). Weiner proposed that two main types of emotion could be identified (see Figure 17.1). "Outcome-dependent" emotion was that associated with the outcome itself (success and failure) rather than with specific attributions. Weiner, Russell, and Lerman (1978) referred to these as a "general reaction" to the outcome, such as being pleased or happy. Second, they reported "attribution-dependent" emotion, which related to the stated causes or reasons for the outcome. Subsequent work by Weiner and colleagues has shown that the main attribution dimensions relate to emotions in different ways (Graham, Doubleday, & Guarino, 1984; Weiner, 1986; Weiner, Graham, & Chandler, 1982; Weiner & Handel, 1985; Yirmiya & Weiner, 1986). Results from these studies support the proposition that self-esteem emotions, such as pride, are associated with an internal causality dimension. Emotions related to expectancy, such as hope, are associated with the stability dimension of attributions, and social emotions, such as pity and guilt, are related to the controllability of the attribution. Social emotions, Weiner (1995) has suggested, can be self-directed, such as shame and guilt, or other-directed, such as anger and pity.

Research on Attributions and Emotions in Physical Activity

An early study in sport psychology in this area was reported by McAuley, Russell, and Gross (1983). They studied attribution-emotion relationships following table tennis matches. However, their study provided only weak support for attribution-emotion relationships for winners, and no relationships for losers. Biddle and Hill (1988, 1992a, 1992b) conducted a series of studies in which some support was given to the role of internal attributions in emotional reactions in competitive situations.

McAuley, Poag, Gleason, and Wraith (1990) studied the attributions middle-aged adults gave for dropping out of structured exercise programs, and how these were associated with the emotional reactions felt from ceasing exercise. Results showed that attributions were associated with emotional reactions, but only to a modest extent. For example, after controlling for the effects of other attribution dimensions, feelings of guilt and shame were predicted by internal attributions, displeasure by personally controllable attributions, and frustration by stable and uncontrollable attributions.

Vallerand (1987; Vallerand & Blanchard, 2000) has proposed an "intuitive-reflective appraisal model" of emotion in sport in which two types of emotional processing are suggested. First is the intuitive appraisal, or immediate and relatively automatic appraisal of the event; second is the reflective appraisal, where greater thought is given to the outcome, and attributional processing occurs. The intuitive appraisal appears to be similar to Weiner's (1986) notion of outcome-dependent, attribution-independent emotion, whereas the reflective appraisal is similar to attribution-dependent, outcome-independent emotion.

In one study, Vallerand (1987) asked basketball players to rate their intuitive appraisal by giving their general impression of whether they had had a "good or bad game today." Attributions and emotions were also assessed. For those players who perceived their performance as successful, Vallerand found that the best predictor of emotion was the intuitive appraisal, although this was augmented by attribution ratings. The results were weaker for those perceiving their performance as a failure. In drawing conclusions from two studies, Vallerand stated: (1) There was support for an intuitive-reflective appraisal model of emotion in sport; (2) the intuitive appraisal is an important antecedent of self-related emotion in both success and failure situations; (3) the intuitive appraisal has a greater impact on the objective outcome; and (4) attributional reflective appraisal is also related to emotion but to a lesser extent than the intuitive appraisal. Vallerand's proposals have been supported in other research (Biddle & Hill, 1992a, 1992b; Vlachopoulos & Biddle, 1997; Vlachopoulos, Biddle, & Fox, 1997).

For example, Vlachopoulos et al. (1997) studied the positive and negative affective reactions of 11 to 14-year-old boys and girls participating in either a 400m or endurance shuttle-run task in normal physical education lessons. Positive affective reactions were predicted best by perceptions of success and high task goal involvement, with internal attributions adding a small amount of additional variance. Negative affect was also negatively predicted by perceived success but not by attributions. They concluded that "the adoption of a task goal is important for the experience of positive emotional experiences in physical activity in children and . . . attributions play a secondary role" (p. 76).

Robinson and Howe (1989) arrived at three main conclusions from their study of attributions and emotions in young people: (1) Sport emotion was related to perceptions of performance and attributions, but also involves other cognitive antecedents; (2) Weiner's model received only partial support; and (3) the effect of the attribution dimensions on emotion was variable. Specifically, the locus dimension was found to have an augmenting influence in both success and failure conditions, the stability dimension was influential only under success conditions, and the control dimension only in failure conditions. Robinson and Howe and Vlachopoulos and colleagues (1996, 1997; Vlachopoulos & Biddle, 1997) support Vallerand (1987) in showing that a major predictor of emotion in physical activity is the intuitive appraisal (performance satisfaction or perceptions of success), but with attributions accounting for additional variance.

Learned Helplessness

Attributions have been used extensively in an effort to explain deficits in learning and performance after failure. The concept of "learned helplessness" (LH) has received a great deal of attention in psychology (Dweck & Leggett, 1988; Peterson, Maier, & Seligman, 1993) and has generated much literature, in clinical psychology in particular (Abramson et al., 1978; Alloy, Abramson, Metalsky, & Hartlage, 1988; Peterson & Seligman, 1984). Somewhat surprisingly, LH has generated little published output in sport psychology, although several discussion papers are available (Dweck, 1980; Martinek, 1996; Robinson, 1990) and unpublished research is cited by Peterson (1990).

The term learned helplessness was used first by researchers to describe deficits in learning exhibited by animals after uncontrollable failure. For example, when an animal failed to take advantage of an escape route during the administration of electric shock after previously having been in a situation when escape seemed uncontrollable, an apathetic response ensued. This failure was labeled learned helplessness and has been shown in animals and humans (Abramson et al., 1978). Dweck (1980, p. 2) defined LH as "the perception of independence between one's responses and the occurrence of aversive outcomes . . . that is, the belief that what you do will not affect the course of negative events, that you have no control over negative events." Although the nature of LH remains the subject of much debate (Alloy et al., 1988), one theme to have emerged in

recent years is the role attributions may play in the development, intensity, and persistence of LH deficits. These deficits may be manifested in terms of behavior (e.g., motivational deficits or withdrawal from a situation), cognition (e.g., negative self-statements or difficulties in learning that responses may be related to outcomes), and emotions (e.g., depressed affect or deficits in self-esteem). A meta-analysis of more than 100 studies involving over 15,000 participants has shown reliable associations between attributions and the depression symptoms of LH (Sweeney et al., 1986). Specifically, correlations weighted for sample size showed small to moderate effect sizes for depression when attributions for negative events were attributed to either internal, stable, or global factors. This was also the case when ability attributions were analyzed separately.

Abramson et al. (1978) made several reformulations to the original LH theory. First, they made a distinction between "personal helplessness" and "universal helplessness." Personal helplessness is when the event is seen as uncontrollable for oneself but not for others. Universal helplessness, on the other hand, is the belief that control is not possible for all people. Their second reformulation concerned the chronicity of LH. Specifically, they suggested that the stability of the attribution for failure will help determine whether the helplessness effects are short-lived (transient) or long-lived (chronic). Similarly, their reformulation stated that the specificity of the attribution would affect the helplessness response. They made a distinction between perceptions of helplessness in a narrow range of situations (specific) and helplessness across a wide range of situations (global). Clearly, the prediction is for greater negative cognitive, emotional, and behavioral effects following global attributions than following specific ones. Abramson et al., therefore, proposed that LH effects would be greatest when failure was perceived to be uncontrollable and attributions were made to internal, stable, and global factors.

Five studies that have addressed LH in the physical domain are summarized in Table 17.4 (see also Peterson, 1990). Although the trends clearly support the utility of studying LH in physical activity, the research designs are cross-sectional, and statements concerning causality are premature. In addition, true helplessness involves a severe state of apathy and demotivation. It is unlikely that any of the studies listed in Table 17.4 included people in this condition. One could argue that the studies merely show associations with a measure of mild demotivation or occasional failure, the long-term effect of which is unknown.

Table 17.4   Physical Activity Studies Investigating Learned Helplessness

Study	Sample and Research Design	Measures	Results	Comments
Prapavessis & Carron (1988)	Young elite tennis players from Canada ($N = 50$). Cross-sectional survey.	An attributional questionnaire to assess attributional style from a recalled unsuccessful event; Maladaptive Achievement Pattern Questionnaire (MAPQ): assessed cognitive, motivational, and emotional correlates of the failure event.	Those classified as "learned helpless" on the basis of MAPQ responses ($N = 11$) explained failure more in terms of internal, stable, and global attributions. Coaches provided independent ratings of persistence supporting the helplessness hypothesis.	The measure of attributions was not a measure of attributional style but rather how players assessed their recent failure. The event was recalled; need a replication assessing reactions immediately after an event.
Johnson & Biddle (1989)	British undergraduate sport studies students ($N = 30$). Quasi-experimental design with participants randomly assigned to "personal" and "universal" helplessness conditions based on contrived failure feedback on a balance board task.	"Persistence" on the task assessed by number of trials taken through free choice; "think aloud" attributions recorded during the task.	No effect for personal vs. universal helplessness manipulation. Participants split into "persisters" (P) and "nonpersisters" (NP) by median split. NP made more negative attributions and self-statements than P, mainly in terms of attributions to task difficulty and lack of ability. P made more attributions referring to task strategy.	Not a direct test of LH but shows likely importance of attributions in task persistence, itself an indicator of LH tendencies.
Seligman et al. (1990)	Members of highly ranked U.S. university swimming teams (Study 1, $N = 47$; Study 2, $N = 33$ from Study 1 sample). Study 1: cross-sectional survey; Study 2: quasi-experimental design.	*Study 1* Attributional Style Questionnaire (ASQ) administered to all swimmers; coaches' ratings of how well they thought the swimmer would perform after a defeat; ratings of each race swim by both coach and swimmer. *Study 2* False feedback given to create "slow" time in a race; swimmers raced the same distance 30 min. later.	*Study 1* Attributional style and coaches' judgments of swimmers' resilience after defeat predicted the number of "poor" swims in the season. *Study 2* Those with a pessimistic attributional style did worse in their second race; those with an optimistic style did not.	Attributional style predicted performance beyond that accounted for by measures of "talent."
Martinek & Griffith (1994)	U.S. elementary ($N = 14$) and high school ($N = 13$) students; cross-sectional field study of PE lessons.	Intellectual Achievement Responsibility (IAR) scale used to classify children into learned helplessness (LH) and mastery-oriented (MO) groups; children videotaped to assess task persistence in PE lessons; attributions assessed for "success" and "failure" on PE tasks.	Task persistence greater for MO children but only in the older age group. No differences between the younger LH and MO children on attributions for success and failure. Older LH children attributed failure more to lack of ability, MO children to lack of effort.	Only small effects detected; suggests age effects may be important. Because the PE classes were taught within a teacher education program, it is possible that all classes created positive "motivational" climates with little scope for significant demotivation.
Martinek & Williams (1997)	U.S. middle school students ($N = 32$); cross-sectional field survey of PE classes.	Modified IAR scale used to classify children into LH and MO groups; task and ego goal orientations (TEOSQ); children videotaped to assess task persistence in PE lessons.	Task persistence greater for LH students. LH children were lower on task and higher on ego goal orientation.	Goal orientation may be less important than goal involvement. The measure of persistence is situation-specific, therefore assessment of situational-specific goals might be informative. No assessment of attributions.

Beliefs about the Nature of Sport Ability

Central to the notion of LH is that the way we think about events can influence our subsequent reactions. Indeed, this is central to attribution theories in general. Although very few sport researchers have taken up the challenge of investigating LH, related themes have been investigated. For example, researchers in several subdisciplines of psychology, including educational, health, social, and sport and exercise, have investigated the role of beliefs concerning ability and competence. For example, historical trends show that a great deal of research has been published on self-confidence from a self-efficacy framework (Bandura, 1997), and perceptions of control from numerous frameworks (Skinner, 1996). The conceptual overlap between such approaches is clear to see; they focus on belief systems that operate, although quite often in different ways, to affect an individual's thoughts, emotions, and behaviors.

Recently, a more systematic approach to the study of beliefs underlying motivated behavior has emerged; it has close links to earlier work in LH, emotions, and attributions. Such an approach may be fruitful in extending current notions of attributional thinking in sport and physical activity. The way people construe the nature of ability, through self-referenced or externally referenced criteria, has been the approach adopted in achievement goal orientations research. This is currently popular in the educational (Nicholls, 1989) and sport psychology (Duda, 1993; see Duda & Hall, this volume) literatures. In addition, and stemming from notions of goal orientations, Dweck and her colleagues have proposed a model of individual differences centered on two major beliefs concerning human attributes (Dweck, 1996; Dweck, Chiu, & Hong, 1995).

Entity and Incremental Beliefs

Initially in the domain of intelligence, and more recently extended to include views of morality and stereotyping, Dweck and colleagues have proposed that two clusters of beliefs underpin people's judgments and actions (Dweck, 1992, 1996; Dweck et al., 1995; Dweck & Leggett, 1988; Levy, Stroessner, & Dweck, 1998; Mueller & Dweck, 1998). These beliefs center on the way people view the malleability of attributes. Those subscribing to the view that a particular attribute is fixed and relatively stable hold an "entity" view or theory and can be described as "entity theorists." Conversely, those seeing the attribute as changeable and open to development hold an "incremental" view or theory and can be described as "incremental theorists."

Researchers have shown that those holding an entity view are more likely to have negative reactions, such as helplessness, when faced with achievement setbacks (Dweck & Leggett, 1988). Entity theorists are more likely to endorse performance (ego) goals, whereas incremental theorists have been shown to endorse learning (task) goals more. In addition, Mueller and Dweck (1998) found that children praised for their intelligence, in contrast to those praised for their effort, more strongly endorsed the view that intelligence is fixed, suggesting that verbal feedback can affect such beliefs. Despite evidence in support of entity and incremental beliefs, Dweck et al. (1995, p. 267) state that "systematic effort is required on the part of behavioral scientists to identify them and to map out their effects." In addition, they argue that entity and incremental beliefs can be general and domain-specific. Beliefs in the domain of intelligence, for example, will not necessarily be related to those concerning moral behavior or athletic ability.

There has been little attention given to entity and incremental beliefs in the physical activity domain, although there are parallel research themes not necessarily wedded to Dweck's specific theorizing. For example, Jourden, Bandura, and Banfield (1991) provided evidence that self-efficacy and perceptual-motor performance are more positively affected by conceptions of ability associated with acquirable skill than when ability is viewed as an inherent aptitude. Specifically, the researchers induced the two different cognitive sets for students participating in a pursuit tracking task. Those taking part under the condition where the task was seen as an acquirable skill showed, in contrast to their counterparts, growth in perceived self-efficacy, more positive reactions, greater interest in the task, and a higher level of skill acquisition. Jourden et al. suggested that two possible mechanisms may account for such differences. First, those in the acquirable skill condition, with higher self-efficacy, are likely to have a higher interest. Hence, self-efficacy itself explains the effects. Second, the results could be accounted for through the more positive affective reactions experienced by the acquirable skill group. This may indicate greater intrinsic interest and motivation. The results also suggest that participants in the acquirable skill condition will make greater use of attributions associated with effort and personal mastery than their counterparts, although attributions were not assessed in this study.

In replicating the study by Dweck and Leggett (1988), Sarrazin et al. (1996), in the first study of such beliefs in the physical domain, found some support for the relationship between beliefs concerning the nature of athletic ability and the adoption of different goals in physical activity (specifically sport) for children age 11 to 12 years. Sarrazin et al. tested the link between goals and beliefs by modifying for the sport context an early scale designed to assess beliefs about the nature of intelligence (see Dweck, 1999). It was hypothesized that children preferring a "learning" (task) goal would be more likely to endorse incremental beliefs about sport ability than those adopting performance (ego) goals. Although the trends were less obvious than reported in the academic domain by Dweck and Leggett, this hypothesis was supported (see Figure 17.3). Given the well-documented association between a task goal orientation and the belief that success is caused more by effort than by ability (Biddle, Akande, Vlachopoulos, & Fox, 1996; Duda, 1993; Duda, Fox, Biddle, & Armstrong, 1992), these data reflect the likely use of effort and mastery-based attributions for those endorsing a task goal and incremental beliefs.

Biddle, Soos, and Chatzisarantis (1999) tested a model predicting intentions from perceived competence, achievement goals, and ability beliefs. They found that data from Hungarian youth fitted the model well when subdomains of entity beliefs (comprising beliefs that sport ability is general and a gift) were modeled to predict an ego goal orientation, and incremental beliefs (learning and changeable subdomains) were modeled to predict a task orientation. However, the path coefficients were generally small. In a parallel study with youth from Finland, Lintunen, Valkonen, Leskinen, and Biddle (1999) reported similar findings, although the magnitude of the relationships was slightly larger. In addition, they found that for girls,

changeable beliefs predicted higher perceptions of sport competence, and for boys, both changeable and learning beliefs predicted greater feelings of enjoyment. In a small-scale experiment, Kasimatis, Miller, and Macussen (1996) told students that athletic coordination was mostly learned, to create an incremental condition, and told others that coordination was genetically determined (entity condition). After initial success, participants were subjected to a difficult physical exercise task through video. Results showed that in the face of such difficulty, more positive responses were found for those in the incremental condition. Specifically, such participants reported higher motivation and self-efficacy and less negative affect, replicating the results of Jourden et al. (1991). Levy et al. (1998, Study 2) included a three-item domain-general measure ("implicit person theory measure") to assess whether university students endorsed generalized entity or incremental beliefs. They found that entity theorists agreed with the stereotype that African Americans were "more athletic" to a greater extent than did incremental theorists. In addition, the entity theorists supported the view that such athleticism was due to "innate-inherent" factors, whereas incremental theorists were more likely to explain it in terms of environmental factors.

Measuring Ability Beliefs in the Physical Domain

Physical activity research suggests that relationships exist between "lay" ability beliefs and motivation or behavior. However, the measurement of beliefs in the physical domain requires attention, and poor measurement technology may be hampering the identification of such links. Dweck and colleagues have used various scales assessing beliefs, and these have been modified to suit the domain of interest, such as intelligence or morality (Dweck, 1999; Dweck et al., 1995). Dweck et al. defend using only three items in some versions of their scales "because implicit theory is a construct with a simple unitary theme" (p. 269). More recently, scales of up to eight items have been proposed (see Dweck, 1999). However, although the assessment of such scales has met with support, one could argue that ability in physical activity is more complex than suggested. Nicholls (1992, p. 45) has said that "we cannot effectively study children's conceptions of intelligence or sport competence by simply asking . . . whether such skills are changeable or not. Intelligence can have many referents."

Sarrazin et al. (1996), therefore, proposed a multidimensional view of sport ability by referring to "scientific" and "lay" conceptions of ability, the former stemming from the motor behavior literature (Fleishman,

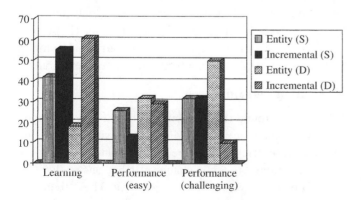

Figure 17.3 Choice of learning (task) or performance (ego) goals as a function of incremental and entity beliefs from academic (Dweck & Leggett, 1988) and athletic (Sarrazin et al., 1996) contexts. Data expressed as percentage of entity and incremental groups.

1964; Schmidt, 1982). In motor behavior, abilities are defined as relatively stable, genetically determined, and rather general, and are not easily modified by practice. Schmidt suggests that "abilities represent the collection of 'equipment' that one has at his or her disposal" (p. 395). As such, ability limits the effect of learning on performance. Skills, on the other hand, are seen as modifiable through practice and learning and are specific to a task or group of tasks (Sarrazin et al., 1996; Schmidt, 1982). In addition to the scientific conception of ability, Sarrazin et al. also argued that people hold lay beliefs about sport ability, such as those expressed by fans or journalists, an example being natural giftedness (see also Levy et al., 1998).

Sarrazin et al. (1996) proposed a multidimensional assessment of sport ability beliefs. Their Conceptions of the Nature of Athletic Ability Questionnaire (CNAAQ) contains 21 items assessing the six subdomains of *learning* (sport ability is the product of learning), *incremental/improvement* (sport ability can change), *specific* (sport ability is specific to certain sports or groups of sport), *general* (sport ability generalizes across many sports), *stable* (sport ability is stable across time), and *gift* (sport ability is a gift, i.c., "God-given"). Support for the six factors in the French version of the CNAAQ was derived from exploratory factor analysis (EFA). All subscales, except specific, exhibited satisfactory internal consistency. EFA and internal consistency statistics on a Hungarian version of the CNAAQ showed the specific and stable subscales to be problematic (Biddle, Soos, et al., 1999). Similar problems were reported by Lintunen et al. (1999) with a Finnish version.

Recently, the CNAAQ was tested with a national sample (N = 2,875) of 12- to 15-year-olds in England (Biddle, Wang, Chatzisrantis, & Spray, 1999). A hierarchical model was supported through confirmatory factor analysis. This showed that the higher-order factors of entity and incremental beliefs were underpinned by beliefs concerning learning and improvement (incremental) and stability and giftedness (entity). Low motivation was also predicted quite strongly by entity beliefs. An important point is that, although the evidence points to potential negative effects of holding entity beliefs, most people hold stronger incremental than entity beliefs. For example, Sarrazin et al. (1996) report high mean scores from five-point scales for incremental beliefs (above 4.00) and moderately low scores on entity beliefs for French children. Similar scores have been reported for British (Biddle, Wang, et al., 1999), Hungarian (Biddle, Soos, et al., 1999), and Finnish (Lintunen et al., 1999) youth. This said, it is the *relationships* between such beliefs and motivational indicators that appear important.

The link between sport ability beliefs and attributions has not yet been tested, although one could hypothesize that incremental beliefs will be associated with effort attributions. Recently, Hong, Chiu, Dweck, Lin, and Wan (1999) have shown such links outside of the physical domain. Hong et al. propose that attribution-based formulations of motivation are incomplete because they fail to take into account "the theories, belief systems, or conceptual frameworks people bring with them to a situation that can foster particular attributions" (p. 588). In their first study, Hong et al. found that incremental theorists, after negative feedback on a task purported to be a test of intelligence, were more likely to use effort attributions than entity theorists regardless of confidence levels.

In a second study, Hong et al. (1999) demonstrated that students in Hong Kong with a relatively low English-language grade were more willing to take a remedial course in English if they were incremental theorists. In their final study, they tested the causal relationship between incremental and entity beliefs and responses to setbacks while also investigating the role of effort attributions. Results indicated that when incremental and entity beliefs were experimentally induced and low-ability feedback was given, incremental theorists were more likely to take remedial action (a tutorial) for academic deficiencies. In addition, when given unsatisfactory feedback, those in the incremental condition made much stronger attributions to effort than those in the entity condition. Overall, Hong et al. concluded "that implicit theories create a meaning framework within which attributions occur. The present research supported the critical role of attributions in mediating coping but demonstrated how implicit theories set up those attributions" (pp. 597–598). The same argument could also be made for the link between achievement goals and attributions. Given the coverage of goals in other chapters of the *Handbook* (see Duda & Hall and Burton, Naylor, & Holliday), this topic will not be discussed further here.

Attribution Retraining

When it was found that attributions might play an important role in the reaction of individuals to success and failure, and in particular their recovery from failure, it was logical to attempt to try to change attributions so that subsequent behavior would be more positive. This "therapeutic" approach to attributions has become popular and is used widely in clinical psychology (Brewin, 1988). Similarly, attribution change, or "attribution retraining" programs, have been developed (Forsterling, 1988). These programs seek to alter attributions that are deemed unsuitable and that may lead to cognitive, emotional, or behavioral deficits, and then seek to develop more appropriate attributions that might suggest positive and future-oriented thoughts.

One of the first studies in this area was conducted by Dweck (1975) with 8- to 13-year-old children. She sought to determine whether "altering attributions for failure would enable learned helpless children to deal more effectively with failure" (p. 674). Dweck studied 12 children who had shown strong reactions to failure on problem-solving tasks and then gave them one of two treatments. One group was provided only with successful experiences, whereas the other was exposed to attribution retraining, such that the children were taught to attribute failure to low effort. The results showed that the success-only group continued to show negative reactions after subsequent failure, whereas the attribution retraining group maintained or improved their performance. Support has also been provided for attribution retraining in a number of other contexts, including students with learning disabilities (Okolo, 1992), self-worth-protective students (Thompson, 1994), and college freshmen (Wilson & Linville, 1985). Attribution retraining has been found to be successful not only with different populations, but in different areas of behavior. Although the majority of studies have dealt with academic performance, retraining also has been found to be useful in reducing aggression (Hudley et al., 1998) and depression (Green-Emrich & Altmaier, 1991).

Curtis (1992) found attribution retraining to be effective for physical therapists who were experiencing role strain (failure) in their professional interactions with physicians. Half of the therapists were randomly assigned to an attribution retraining intervention that trained them to attribute failure to poor choice of strategy (a controllable factor), rather than to uncontrollable factors such as low ability or physician bias. Relative to the control group, the therapists who participated in the attribution retraining program were more likely to endorse strategy attributions and had greater expectancies for future success when dealing with physicians. At six-month follow-up, a significantly greater percentage of therapists in the intervention group had received promotions than had those in the control

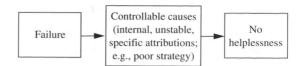

Figure 17.5 An attribution retraining sequence based on learned helplessness theory (Abramson et al., 1978).

group. Forsterling (1988) suggests at least three different ways of approaching attribution retraining: the attributional model (Weiner, 1986), the learned helplessness model (Abramson et al., 1978), and the self-efficacy model (Bandura, 1986). These are illustrated in Figures 17.4, 17.5, and 17.6.

Weiner's (1986) attribution theory suggests that attribution retraining should involve the creation of positive emotional states and expectancies after success and failure by avoiding ability attributions for failure (Figure 17.4). Promoting controllable attributions for failure that suggest positive expectations is favored. However, although lack of effort is usually suggested as the best attribution to give for failure (Dweck, 1975; Forsterling, 1988), there are dangers with this approach. Covington and Omelich (1979) highlight the importance placed on effort in achievement. If an individual tries hard but still fails, attributions to low ability are more likely. This double-edged sword of effort attributions means that instead of attributing failure to low effort, other controllable factors could be used in attribution retraining, such as changing the failed strategy (Sinnott & Biddle, 1998).

The LH model of retraining (Figure 17.5) is based on the principles of avoiding perceptions of lack of control and the changing of attributions for failure that are internal, stable, and global. Internal attributions can still be used in failure, but it is important that participants attribute failure to unstable, controllable, and specific factors. Finally, the self-efficacy model of attribution retraining (Figure 17.6) suggests that attributions lead to perceptions of efficacy for specific behaviors that, in turn, predict persistence and behavior.

Figure 17.4 An attribution retraining sequence based on Weiner's (1986) attribution theory.

Figure 17.6 An attribution retraining sequence based on Bandura's (1986) self-efficacy theory.

Attribution Retraining Studies in Sport

Researchers have only recently begun to investigate attribution retraining in sport situations. Indeed, it is surprising that few studies exist in the light of Hardy and Jones's (1992, p. 12) comment that investigating "ways in which attribution retraining . . . can be used to modify attributions" is a priority for future research in sport. The utility and effectiveness of attribution retraining in sport was also identified as a gap in knowledge by Biddle (1993).

Orbach, Singer, and Murphey (1997) randomly assigned recreational college basketball players to one of three groups: controllable and unstable attributional orientation (e.g., effort, strategy); uncontrollable and stable attributional orientation (e.g., innate ability); or a nonattributional orientation. Participants in the first group not only made more controllable and less stable attributions, they also outperformed the other groups on a basketball dribbling task. Using similar intervention groups with beginning tennis players, Orbach, Singer, and Price (1999) again found that those in the controllable and unstable attribution retraining group made more controllable and less stable attributions. In addition, this group had greater expectations for future success and experienced more positive emotions than the other two groups.

In an investigation with a younger age group, high school players received either feedback on basketball shooting technique combined with encouragement to attribute their performance to effort, or shooting technique feedback alone (Miserandino, 1998). Prior to the intervention there was no difference between the groups in terms of shooting performance or mastery orientation. After the four-week intervention, the attribution retraining group significantly improved their performance and had a stronger mastery orientation, whereas the feedback-only group had no significant improvement in shooting and had a weaker mastery orientation.

Attribution retraining has also been found to be useful for children. Sinnott and Biddle (1998) studied 12 children, age 11 to 12 years. Six rated their performance as poor on a ball dribbling task and had maladaptive attributions for their performance. They received 20 minutes of attribution retraining where the focus was on attributions to task strategy. The other six children who rated themselves successful on the task formed a no-training group. After a retest of the dribbling task, the no-training group showed little change in attributions or perceived success. The attribution retraining group, however, showed clear changes in attributions and a marked improvement in perceived success.

In fact, after the retest, the attribution retraining group had higher success perceptions and higher levels of intrinsic motivation than the initially successful no-training group.

Although the existing attribution retraining studies in sport support the efficacy of retraining attributions, many questions remain unanswered: What method of retraining is best? How durable are the effects of attribution retraining? How much do the effects of retraining generalize to other skills within the same sport and to other tasks outside of the targeted sport?

Summary of Attributional Consequences

Unlike research on the antecedents of attributions in the physical domain, there has been more progress in understanding attributional consequences. Researchers have shown that attributions are associated with expectancies and emotions. When studied jointly, emotions have been demonstrated to be more strongly associated with perceptions of success than have attributions. Nevertheless, similar trends have emerged from studies of youth, young adults, and middle-aged adults in sport, physical education, and exercise settings. The theoretical foundations for learned helplessness effects in sport and exercise have yet to be properly tested. However, studies are emerging and a strong literature in clinical psychology should be used for guidance. Researchers should investigate the role of entity and incremental beliefs as these appear to hold some promise for understanding attributional thinking and their effects on motivation in physical activity. Finally, the few attribution retraining studies in sport show a positive trend.

AN AGENT-MEANS-ENDS ANALYSIS OF ATTRIBUTIONS IN SPORT

This chapter has shown that new research on attributions in sport over the past 10 years has not been extensive. When one considers that attribution theory was the most popular research topic in sport psychology in the 1980s, this is even more remarkable. Why has this area declined in popularity? Does it reflect a waning in the perceived utility of the area? One way to better understand attributional theories, as well as other theories in motivation, is to analyze attributions using Skinner's (1995, 1996) agent-means-ends model (Biddle, 1999). This might allow for a more complete understanding of attributional concepts and partly explain why the topic has not been pursued so vigorously by researchers in recent years. Although such a framework is not new, as noted by Skinner, it may prove useful in judging some of the properties of attributions.

Skinner (1995, 1996) makes the point that one way to conceptualize the vast array of control constructs is to analyze them in relation to their place within the tripartite model of agent, means, and ends. This is illustrated in Figure 17.7. Agent-means connections involve expectations that the agent (self) has the means to produce a response (but not necessarily an outcome). This involves beliefs concerning whether the agent has the ability to produce the appropriate cause, referred to as capacity beliefs. For example, if effort is deemed important to produce success in distance running, then positive capacity beliefs must involve the belief "I can try hard in running." Self-efficacy research has adopted this approach and has become a major force in motivational research in exercise and sport psychology (Bandura, 1997; Schunk, 1995). Similarly, perceived competence approaches adopt the agent-means approach.

Means-ends connections involve beliefs about the link between potential causes and outcomes. This involves beliefs concerning the necessary availability of means to produce the desired outcomes and are referred to as strategy beliefs. For example, if trying hard is necessary in successful running, a strategy belief is "I need to try hard to be successful at running," thus contrasting with the capacity belief "I can try hard." Typically, means-ends relations involve attributional approaches, outcome expectancies, and locus of control. As Skinner (1995, p. 554) stated, "Connections between people and outcomes prescribe the proto-

typical definitions of control." Hence, this connection involves control beliefs, beliefs by agents that a desirable outcome is within their capability: "I can be successful at running if I want to." This has to involve both capacity *and* strategy beliefs.

Agent-ends connections are less easy to recognize in sport and exercise psychology. Some of Bandura's (1989, 1997) later writings suggest that self-efficacy can have an agent-ends connection as well as the more traditional agent-means connection. Similarly, outcome expectancies can involve agent-ends as well as means-ends. Behavioral regulations, as depicted in self-determination theory (Deci & Ryan, 1985), which is becoming popular in exercise (Chatzisarantis & Biddle, 1998; Mullan, Markland, & Ingledew, 1997) and sport (Vallerand & Blanchard, 2000; Vallerand & Fortier, 1998; Vallerand & Losier, 1999), may suit an agent-ends analysis.

Skinner (1995) proposes that humans have a need to seek competence. If this is the case, control-related beliefs can be analyzed within a system of competence seeking. Skinner refers to this as the "competence system" (Figure 17.8). Figure 17.8 shows that action is regulated by initial control beliefs. Action, in turn, produces some form of outcome that is evaluated and interpreted in respect of other beliefs (self, causes); these can lead to further control beliefs. Beliefs prior to action, therefore, are "regulative" beliefs. Those concerning the self and causes are "interpretive" beliefs because they function after the event has taken place.

Attributions primarily concern the interpretation of outcomes, the consequences of which may impact future

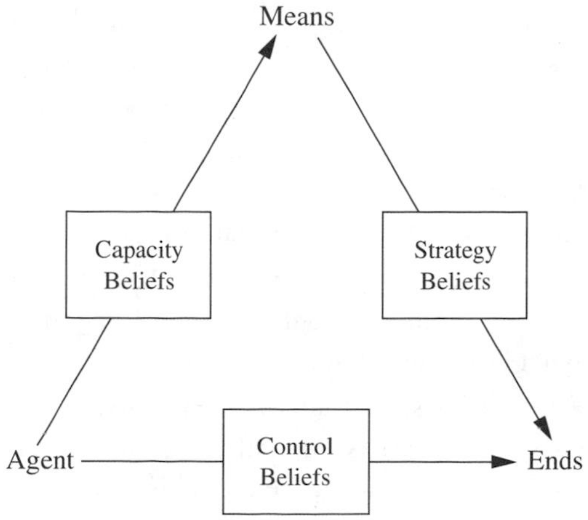

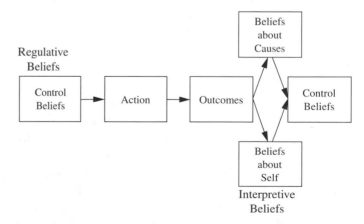

Figure 17.7 Skinner's (1995) agent-means-ends model showing different types of beliefs. Reprinted with permission of Sage Publishers, Inc.

Figure 17.8 Skinner's (1995) competence system model showing regulative and interpretive beliefs. Reprinted with permission of Sage Publishers, Inc.

regulative beliefs and actions (Weiner, 1986, 1995). They are, therefore, more distant from (future) actions and outcomes than most regulative beliefs such as locus of control. This may explain the difficulty researchers have had in demonstrating strong relationships between attributions and behavior in sport. Only prospective studies can test this, and these are sparse. It also assumes that little will change between making the attributions and subsequent behavior, yet we have not tested the longevity or consistency of attributions over time. Indeed, we have nearly always assessed attributions immediately after performance. Many coaches, athletes, and sport psychologists say, however, that attributions are an important part of the sport experience, are reflected in subsequent thoughts, feelings, and actions, and change with time.

Attributional processing reflects means-ends connections and therefore involves strategy, not capacity, beliefs. According to this perspective, attributional thinking looks to identify causes of outcomes (e.g., ability, effort, and luck) rather than appraising whether the individual (agent) has access to these causes (e.g., ability). In reality, one could argue that true attributional thinking, though primarily being about identification of causes, is also a response to questions such as "Why did *I* fail at this task?", thus necessitating control beliefs (i.e., strategy *and* capacity beliefs). Athletes, for example, will probably not be interested in whether a particular game strategy caused success unless they are also thinking about whether they can produce that strategy. If so, attributions are more central to control beliefs and will also involve agent-ends connections. True perceptions of control, through control beliefs, require a combination of competence and contingency (Skinner, 1995, 1996). Attributional processing involves both means-ends (contingency) and agent-ends (competence).

Although attributions traditionally are seen as means-ends connections, further support for attributions involving agent-ends processes comes from matching attributions against other agent-ends constructs. For example, outcome expectancies involve agent-ends connections, and attributions have been linked, mainly via the stability dimension, to beliefs concerning outcome expectancies. One reason why attribution research has declined in popularity in recent years in exercise and sport psychology may be associated with the belief that attributions do not predict behaviors particularly well due to their distal location from subsequent behavior in the competence system. However, they may act as both means-ends and agent-ends connections, thus embracing control beliefs and both competence and contingency—a true sense of perceived control. Further study is

required to tease out the relative importance of these beliefs. Given that effort and ability are central constructs both to the beliefs in Skinner's tripartite model and within attribution theories, continued linkage in research seems prudent.

CONCLUSIONS

Attribution research has a long and influential history in social psychology and remains an important area. However, although a popular topic in sport and exercise psychology during the 1970s and 1980s, interest has waned. Related topics, such as achievement goal orientations, have meant that the study of perceptions of effort and ability have remained central to sport and exercise psychology. In reviewing the past, present, and future perspectives of attributions, the following are concluded:

1. Weiner's (1986, 1992) attribution model has provided a useful framework for the study of attributions in sport. However, although the dominant attributions associated with ability, effort, task, and luck have been found in sport, it is thought that sport contexts encourage more diverse attributions to be made than are made in classroom settings. Nevertheless, attributions associated with ability and effort appear to be very important in sport.

2. Winners, or those perceiving success in sports events, tend to make attributions to internal and controllable factors more than do those losing or perceiving failure.

3. Attributional style has been shown to predict positive and negative reactions in sport and remains a concept worthy of further study in sport and other physical activity contexts.

4. The study of the differences in attributions between actors and observers provides a good foundation for investigating pupil-teacher and athlete-coach relationships. Preliminary evidence suggests that effort-based attributions made by the observer for the behavior of the actor elicits a favorable reaction by the observer.

5. The existence of a self-serving bias has been supported in sport research, although the underlying mechanisms have not been clearly identified.

6. Research shows that attributions are made spontaneously, can be assessed, and can be analyzed through qualitative and quantitative methods.

7. Attributions are more likely to be made when the outcome is unexpected or a goal is not reached.

8. The stability dimension of attributions is associated with the prediction of expectancy change.

9. Attributions are associated with emotional reactions, but perceived (subjective) performance is thought to be a more powerful predictor of emotion in sport than the attributions given for either outcome or performance.

10. Studies are now emerging showing the potential utility of attribution retraining in sport.

11. Beliefs concerning the nature of athletic ability have been shown to be associated with adaptive and maladaptive motivational responses in physical activity and require continued investigation, including their relationships with attributions.

12. An agent-means-ends analysis of attributions shows that they function either as means-ends strategy beliefs or as agent-ends control beliefs. Further analysis using this framework may allow researchers to make realistic predictions concerning the role of attributions in predicting behavior.

Attribution research in sport has adopted a narrow perspective, and there is still need to investigate wider issues making use of alternative theories and paradigms. In reviewing the research findings of attributions in sport and exercise psychology, the intention has been to show that related perspectives and methods, in addition to the typical achievement attribution paradigm, have value. Hopefully, attribution research will continue and thrive as we endeavor to understand motivation in physical activity.

REFERENCES

Abramson, L.Y., Seligman, M.E.P., & Teasdale, J.D. (1978). Learned helplessness in humans: Critique and reformulation. *Journal of Abnormal Psychology, 87,* 49–74.

Alloy, L.B., Abramson, L.Y., Metalsky, G.I., & Hartlage, S. (1988). The hopelessness theory of depression: Attributional aspects. *British Journal of Clinical Psychology, 27,* 5–21.

Bandura, A. (1986). *Social foundations of thought and action: A social cognitive theory.* Englewood Cliffs, NJ: Prentice-Hall.

Bandura, A. (1989). Perceived self-efficacy in the exercise of personal agency. *The Psychologist: Bulletin of the British Psychological Society, 10,* 411–424.

Bandura, A. (1990). Perceived self-efficacy in the exercise of personal agency. *Journal of Applied Sport Psychology, 2,* 128–163.

Bandura, A. (1997). *Self-efficacy: The exercise of control.* New York: Freeman.

Bem, D. (1972). Self-perception theory. In L. Berkowitz (Ed.), *Advances in experimental social psychology* (Vol. 6, pp. 1–62). New York: Academic Press.

Biddle, S. (1993). Attribution research and sport psychology. In R.N. Singer, M. Murphey, & L.K. Tennant (Eds.), *Handbook of research on sport psychology* (pp. 437–464). New York: Macmillan.

Biddle, S. (1994). Motivation and participation in exercise and sport. In S. Serpa, J. Alves, & V. Pataco (Eds.), *International perspectives on sport and exercise psychology* (pp. 103–126). Morgantown, WV: Fitness Information Technology.

Biddle, S., Akande, A., Vlachopoulos, S., & Fox, K. (1996). Towards an understanding of children's motivation for physical activity: Achievement goal orientations, beliefs about sport success, and sport emotion in Zimbabwean children. *Psychology & Health, 12,* 49–55.

Biddle, S., & Goudas, M. (1997). Effort is virtuous: Teacher preferences of pupil effort, ability and grading in physical education. *Educational Research, 39,* 350–355.

Biddle, S., & Hanrahan, S. (1998). Attributions and attributional style. In J.L. Duda (Ed.), *Advances in sport and exercise psychology measurement* (pp. 3–19). Morgantown, WV: Fitness Information Technology.

Biddle, S., Soos, I., & Chatzisarantis, N. (1999). Predicting physical activity intentions using a goal perspectives approach: A study of Hungarian youth. *Scandinavian Journal of Medicine and Science in Sports, 9,* 353–357.

Biddle, S.J.H. (1986). The contribution of attribution theory to exercise behaviour. In J. Watkins, T. Reilly, & L. Burwitz (Eds.), *Sports science* (pp. 285–290). London: E. & F.N. Spon.

Biddle, S.J.H. (1988). Methodological issues in the researching of attribution-emotion links in sport. *International Journal of Sport Psychology, 19,* 264–280.

Biddle, S.J.H. (1999). Motivation and perceptions of control: Tracing its development and plotting its future in exercise and sport psychology. *Journal of Sport & Exercise Psychology, 21,* 1–23.

Biddle, S.J.H., & Hill, A.B. (1988). Causal attributions and emotional reactions to outcome in a sporting contest. *Personality and Individual Differences, 9,* 213–223.

Biddle, S.J.H., & Hill, A.B. (1992a). Attributions for objective outcome and subjective appraisal of performance: Their relationship with emotional reactions in sport. *British Journal of Social Psychology, 31,* 215–226.

Biddle, S.J.H., & Hill, A.B. (1992b). Relationships between attributions and emotions in a laboratory-based sporting contest. *Journal of Sports Sciences, 10,* 65–75.

Biddle, S.J.H., Wang, J., Chatzisarantis, N.L.D., & Spray, C.M. (1999). *Entity and incremental beliefs concerning athletic ability: Measurement and relationships with physical activity motivation in youth.* Manuscript in preparation.

Brawley, L.R., & Roberts, G.C. (1984). Attributions in sport: Research foundations, characteristics and limitations. In

J. Silva & R. Weinberg (Eds.), *Psychological foundations of sport* (pp. 197–213). Champaign, IL: Human Kinetics.

Brewin, C.R. (1988). Editorial: Developments in an attributional approach to clinical psychology. *British Journal of Clinical Psychology, 27*, 1–3.

Bukowski, W.M., & Moore, D. (1980). Winners' and losers' attributions for success and failure in a series of athletic events. *Journal of Sport Psychology, 2*, 195–210.

Carron, A.C. (1984). Attributing causes to success and failure. *Australian Journal of Science and Medicine in Sport, 16*, 11–15.

Chatzisarantis, N., & Biddle, S.J.H. (1998). Functional significance of psychological variables that are included in the theory of planned behaviour: A self-determination theory approach to the study of attitudes, subjective norms, perceptions of control, and intentions. *European Journal of Social Psychology, 28*, 303–322.

Corr, P.J., & Gray, J.A. (1996). Structure and validity of the Attributional Style Questionnaire: A cross-sample comparison. *Journal of Psychology, 130*, 645–657.

Covington, M., & Omelich, C. (1979). Effort: The double-edged sword in school achievement. *Journal of Educational Psychology, 71*, 169–182.

Curtis, K.A. (1992). Altering beliefs about the importance of strategy: An attributional intervention. *Journal of Applied Social Psychology, 22*, 953–972.

Cutrona, C.E., Russell, D., & Jones, R.D. (1984). Cross-situational consistency in causal attributions: Does attributional style exist? *Journal of Personality and Social Psychology, 47*, 1043–1058.

Deaux, K. (1976). Sex: A perspective on the attribution process. In J.H. Harvey, W.J. Ickes, & R.F. Kidd (Eds.), *New directions in attribution research* (Vol. 1, pp. 335–352). Hillsdale, NJ: Erlbaum.

Deci, E.L., & Ryan, R.M. (1985). *Intrinsic motivation and self-determination in human behavior.* New York: Plenum Press.

Duda, J.L. (1993). Goals: A social cognitive approach to the study of achievement motivation in sport. In R.N. Singer, M. Murphey, & L.K. Tennant (Eds.), *Handbook of research on sport psychology* (pp. 421–436). New York: Macmillan.

Duda, J.L., Fox, K.R., Biddle, S.J.H., & Armstrong, N. (1992). Children's achievement goals and beliefs about success in sport. *British Journal of Educational Psychology, 62*, 313–323.

Dweck, C.S. (1975). The role of expectations and attributions in the alleviation of learned helplessness. *Journal of Personality and Social Psychology, 31*, 674–685.

Dweck, C.S. (1980). Learned helplessness in sport. In C.H. Nadeau, W.R. Halliwell, K.M. Newell, & G.C. Roberts (Eds.), *Psychology of motor behavior and sport–1979* (pp. 1–11). Champaign, IL: Human Kinetics.

Dweck, C.S. (1992). The study of goals in psychology. *Psychological Science, 3*, 165–167.

Dweck, C.S. (1996). Implicit theories as organizers of goals and behavior. In P. Gollwitzer & J. Bargh (Eds.), *The psychology of action* (pp. 69–90). New York: Guilford Press.

Dweck, C.S. (1999). *Self-theories: Their role in motivation, personality, and development.* Philadelphia: Taylor & Francis.

Dweck, C.S., Chiu, C.Y., & Hong, Y.Y. (1995). Implicit theories and their role in judgments and reactions: A world from two perspectives. *Psychological Inquiry, 6*, 267–285.

Dweck, C.S., & Leggett, E. (1988). A social-cognitive approach to motivation and personality. *Psychological Review, 95*, 256–273.

Elig, T., & Frieze, I.H. (1975). A multidimensional coding scheme for coding and interpreting perceived causality for success and failure events: The SCPC. [Ms No. 1069]. *Catalogue of Selected Documents in Psychology, 5*, 313.

Fiske, S.T., & Taylor, S.E. (1991). *Social cognition.* New York: McGraw-Hill.

Fleishman, E.A. (1964). *Structure and measurement of physical fitness.* Englewood Cliffs, NJ: Prentice-Hall.

Forsterling, F. (1988). *Attribution theory in clinical psychology.* Chichester, England: Wiley.

Graham, S., Doubleday, C., & Guarino, P.A. (1984). The development of relations between perceived controllability and the emotions of pity, anger and guilt. *Child Development, 55*, 561–565.

Green-Emrich, A., & Altmaier, E.M. (1991). Attribution retraining as a structured group counseling intervention. *Journal of Counseling and Development, 69*, 351–355.

Grove, J.R., Hanrahan, S.J., & McInman, A. (1991). Success/failure bias in attributions across involvement categories in sport. *Personality and Social Psychology Bulletin, 17*, 93–97.

Grove, J.R., & Pargman, D. (1986). Relationships among success/failure, attributions, and performance expectancies in competitive situations. In L.V. Velden & J.H. Humphrey (Eds.), *Psychology and sociology of sport: Current selected research I* (pp. 85–95). New York: AMS Press.

Hanrahan, S.J. (1995). Attribution theory. In T. Morris & J. Summers (Eds.), *Sport psychology* (pp. 122–142). Brisbane, Australia: Wiley.

Hanrahan, S.J., & Grove, J.R. (1990a). Further examination of the psychometric properties of the Sport Attributional Style Scale. *Journal of Sport Behavior, 13*, 183–193.

Hanrahan, S.J., & Grove, J.R. (1990b). A short form of the Sport Attributional Style Scale. *Australian Journal of Science and Medicine in Sport, 22*, 97–101.

Hanrahan, S.J., Grove, J.R., & Hattie, J.A. (1989). Development of a questionnaire measure of sport-related attributional style. *International Journal of Sport Psychology, 20*, 114–134.

Hardy, L., & Jones, G. (1992). *Future directions for perfor-mance-related research in sport psychology.* London: Sports Council.

Heider, F. (1944). Social perception and phenomenal causality. *Psychological Review, 51,* 358–374.

Heider, F. (1958). *The psychology of interpersonal relations.* New York: Wiley.

Hewstone, M. (1989). *Causal attribution: From cognitive pro-cesses to collective beliefs.* Oxford, England: Blackwell.

Higgins, E.T. (1981). The "communication game": Implications for social-cognition. In E.T. Higgins, C.P. Herman, & M.P. Zanna (Eds.), *Social cognition: The Ontario symposium* (Vol. 1, pp. 343–392). Hillsdale, NJ: Erlbaum.

Hong, Y.Y., Chiu, C.Y., Dweck, C.S., Lin, D.M.-S., & Wan, W. (1999). Implicit theories, attributions, and coping: A mean-ing system approach. *Journal of Personality and Social Psy-chology, 77,* 588–599.

Hudley, C., Britsch, B., Wakefield, W.D., Smith, T., Demorat, M., & Cho, S. (1998). The attribution retraining program to reduce aggression in elementary school students. *Psychology in the Schools, 35,* 271–282.

Iso-Ahola, S.E. (1977). Immediate attributional effects of suc-cess and failure in the field: Testing some laboratory hy-potheses. *European Journal of Social Psychology, 7,* 275–296.

Iso-Ahola, S.E., & Roberts, G.C. (1977). Causal attributions following success and failure at an achievement motor task. *Research Quarterly, 48,* 541–549.

Jones, E.E. (1979). The rocky road from acts to dispositions. *American Psychologist, 34,* 107–117.

Jones, E.E., & Davis, K.E. (1965). From acts to dispositions: The attribution process in person perception. In L. Berkowitz (Ed.), *Advances in experimental social psychology* (Vol. 2, pp. 219–266). London: Academic Press.

Jones, E.E., & Nisbett, R.E. (1972). The actor and the observer: Divergent perceptions of the causes of behavior. In E.E. Jones, D.E. Kanouse, H.H. Kelley, R.E. Nisbett, S. Valins, & B. Weiner (Eds.), *Attribution: Perceiving the causes of behav-ior* (pp. 79–94). Morristown, NJ: General Learning Press.

Jourden, F., Bandura, A., & Banfield, J.T. (1991). The impact of conceptions of ability on self-regulatory factors and motor skill acquisition. *Journal of Sport & Exercise Psychology, 13,* 213–226.

Kasimatis, M., Miller, M., & Macussen, L. (1996). The effects of implicit theories on exercise motivation. *Journal of Re-search in Personality, 30,* 510–516.

Kelley, H.H. (1967). Attribution theory in social psychology. In D. Levine (Ed.), *Nebraska symposium on motivation* (Vol. 15, pp. 192–240). Lincoln: University of Nebraska Press.

Kelley, H.H. (1972). Causal schemata and the attribution pro-cess. In E.E. Jones, D.E. Kanouse, H.H. Kelley, R.E. Nisbett,

S. Valins, & B. Weiner (Eds.), *Attribution: Perceiving the causes of behaviour* (pp. 1–26). Morristown, NJ: General Learning Press.

Kelley, H.H., & Michela, J. (1980). Attribution theory and re-search. *Annual Review of Psychology, 31,* 457–501.

Kruglanski, A.W. (1975). The endogenous-exogenous partition in attribution theory. *Psychological Review, 82,* 387–406.

Leith, L., & Prapavessis, H. (1989). Attributions of causality and dimensionality associated with sport outcomes in objec-tively evaluated and subjectively evaluated sports. *Interna-tional Journal of Sport Psychology, 20,* 224–234.

Levy, S.R., Stroessner, S.J., & Dweck, C.S. (1998). Stereotype formation and endorsement: The role of implicit theories. *Journal of Personality and Social Psychology, 74,* 1421–1436.

Lintunen, T., Valkonen, A., Leskinen, E., & Biddle, S.J.H. (1999). Predicting physical activity intentions using a goal perspectives approach: A study of Finnish youth. *Scandina-vian Journal of Medicine and Science in Sports, 9,* 344–352.

Maehr, M.L., & Nicholls, J.G. (1980). Culture and achievement motivation: A second look. In N. Warren (Ed.), *Studies in cross-cultural psychology* (Vol. 2, pp. 221–267). New York: Academic Press.

Martinek, T.J. (1996). Fostering hope in youth: A model for ex-plaining learned helplessness in physical activity. *Quest, 48,* 409–421.

McAuley, E., & Duncan, T.E. (1990). The causal attribution pro-cess in sport and physical activity. In S. Graham & V. Folkes (Eds.), *Attribution theory: Applications to achievement, men-tal health and interpersonal conflict* (pp. 37–52). Hillsdale, NJ: Erlbaum.

McAuley, E., Duncan, T.E., & Russell, D. (1992). Measuring causal attributions: The Revised Causal Dimension Scale (CDS-II). *Personality and Social Psychology Bulletin, 18,* 566–573.

McAuley, E., & Gross, J.B. (1983). Perceptions of causality in sport: An application of the Causal Dimension Scale. *Journal of Sport Psychology, 5,* 72–76.

McAuley, E., Poag, K., Gleason, A., & Wraith, S. (1990). Attri-tion from exercise programs: Attributional and affective per-spectives. *Journal of Social Behavior and Personality, 5,* 591–602.

McAuley, E., Russell, D., & Gross, J. (1983). Affective conse-quences of winning and losing: An attributional analysis. *Journal of Sport Psychology, 5,* 278–287.

Miller, D., & Ross, M. (1975). Self-serving biases in the attribu-tion of causality: Fact or fiction? *Psychological Bulletin, 82,* 213–225.

Miserandino, M. (1998). Attributional retraining as a method of improving athletic performance. *Journal of Sport Behavior, 21,* 286–297.

Morgan, L.K., Griffin, J., & Heyward, V.H. (1996). Ethnicity, gender, and experience effects on attributional dimensions. *The Sport Psychologist, 10,* 4–16.

Mueller, C.M., & Dweck, C.S. (1998). Praise for intelligence can undermine children's motivation and performance. *Journal of Personality and Social Psychology, 75,* 33–52.

Mullan, E., Markland, D., & Ingledew, D. (1997). A graded conceptualisation of self-determination in the regulation of exercise behaviour: Development of a measure using confirmatory factor analytic procedures. *Personality and Individual Differences, 23,* 745–752.

Mullen, B., & Riordan, C. (1988). Self-serving attributions for performance in naturalistic settings: A meta-analytic review. *Journal of Applied Social Psychology, 18,* 3–22.

Munton, A.G., Silvester, J., Stratton, P., & Hanks, H. (1999). *Attributions in action: A practical approach to coding qualitative data.* Chichester, England: Wiley.

Nicholls, J.G. (1989). *The competitive ethos and democratic education.* Cambridge, MA: Harvard University Press.

Nicholls, J.G. (1992). The general and the specific in the development and expression of achievement motivation. In G.C. Roberts (Ed.), *Motivation in sport and exercise* (pp. 31–56). Champaign, IL: Human Kinetics.

Okolo, C.M. (1992). The effects of computer-based attribution retraining on the attributions, persistence, and mathematics computation of students with learning disabilities. *Journal of Learning Disabilities, 25,* 327–334.

Orbach, I., Singer, R.N., & Murphey, M. (1997). Changing attributions with an attribution training technique related to basketball dribbling. *The Sport Psychologist, 11,* 294–304.

Orbach, I., Singer, R.N., & Price, S. (1999). An attribution training program and achievement in sport. *The Sport Psychologist, 13,* 69–82.

Peterson, C. (1990). Explanatory style in the classroom and on the playing field. In S. Graham & V.S. Folkes (Eds.), *Attribution theory: Applications to achievement, mental health, and interpersonal conflict* (pp. 53–75). Hillsdale, NJ: Erlbaum.

Peterson, C., Maier, S.F., & Seligman, M.E.P. (1993). *Learned helplessness: A theory for the age of personal control.* New York: Oxford University Press.

Peterson, C., & Seligman, M.E.P. (1984). Causal explanations as a risk factor for depression: Theory and evidence. *Psychological Review, 91,* 347–374.

Peterson, C., Semmel, A., vonBaeyer, C., Abramson, L.Y., Metalsky, G.I., & Seligman, M.E.P. (1982). The Attributional Style Questionnaire. *Cognitive Therapy and Research, 6,* 287–300.

Peterson, C., & Villanova, P. (1988). An expanded attributional style questionnaire. *Journal of Abnormal Psychology, 97,* 87–89.

Prapavessis, H., & Carron, A.V. (1988). Learned helplessness in sport. *The Sport Psychologist, 2,* 189–201.

Rejeski, W.J. (1979). A model of attributional conflict in sport. *Journal of Sport Behavior, 2,* 156–166.

Roberts, G.C., & Pascuzzi, D. (1979). Causal attributions in sport: Some theoretical implications. *Journal of Sport Psychology, 1,* 203–211.

Robinson, D.W. (1990). An attributional analysis of student demoralization in physical education settings. *Quest, 42,* 27–39.

Robinson, D.W., & Howe, B.L. (1989). Appraisal variable/affect relationships in youth sport: A test of Weiner's attributional model. *Journal of Sport & Exercise Psychology, 11,* 431–443.

Rudisill, M. (1988). The influence of causal dimensions orientations and perceived competence on adults' expectations, persistence, performance, and the selection of causal dimensions. *International Journal of Sport Psychology, 19,* 184–198.

Rudisill, M. (1989). Influence of perceived competence and causal dimension orientations on expectations, persistence, and performance during perceived failure. *Research Quarterly for Exercise and Sport, 60,* 166–175.

Russell, D. (1982). The Causal Dimension Scale: A measure of how individuals perceive causes. *Journal of Personality and Social Psychology, 42,* 1137–1145.

Sarrazin, P., Biddle, S., Famose, J.P., Cury, F., Fox, K., & Durand, M. (1996). Goal orientations and conceptions of the nature of sport ability in children: A social cognitive approach. *British Journal of Social Psychology, 35,* 399–414.

Schacter, S., & Singer, J.E. (1962). Cognitive, social and physiological determinants of emotional state. *Psychological Review, 69,* 379–399.

Schmidt, R.A. (1982). *Motor control and learning.* Champaign, IL: Human Kinetics.

Schunk, D.H. (1995). Self-efficacy, motivation, and performance. *Journal of Applied Sport Psychology, 7,* 112–137.

Seligman, M.E.P., Abramson, L.Y., Semmel, A., & vonBaeyer, C. (1979). Depressive attributional style. *Journal of Abnormal Psychology, 88,* 242–247.

Seligman, M.E.P., Nolen-Hoeksema, S., Thornton, N., & Thornton, K.M. (1990). Explanatory style as a mechanism of disappointing athletic performance. *Psychological Science, 1,* 143–146.

Singer, R.N., & McCaughan, L. (1978). Motivational effects of attributions expectancy, and achievement motivation during the learning of a novel motor task. *Journal of Motor Behavior, 10,* 245–253.

Sinnott, K., & Biddle, S. (1998). Changes in attributions, perceptions of success and intrinsic motivation after attribution retraining in children's sport. *International Journal of Adolescence and Youth, 7,* 137–144.

Skinner, E. (1995). *Perceived control, motivation, and coping.* Thousand Oaks, CA: Sage.

Skinner, E. (1996). A guide to constructs of control. *Journal of Personality and Social Psychology, 71,* 549–570.

Stratton, P., Munton, A.G., Hanks, H., Hard, D.H., & Davidson, C. (1988). *Leeds Attributional Coding System (LACS) manual.* Leeds, England: LFTRC.

Sweeney, P.D., Anderson, K., & Bailey, S. (1986). Attributional style in depression: A meta-analytic review. *Journal of Personality and Social Psychology, 50,* 974–991.

Tenenbaum, G., Furst, D., & Weingarten, G. (1984). Attribution of causality in sports events: Validation of the Wingate Sport Achievement Responsibility Scale. *Journal of Sport Psychology, 6,* 430–439.

Thompson, T. (1994). Self-worth protection: Review and implications for the classroom. *Educational Review, 46,* 259–274.

Vallerand, R.J. (1987). Antecedents of self-related affects in sport: Preliminary evidence on the intuitive-reflective appraisal model. *Journal of Sport Psychology, 9,* 161–182.

Vallerand, R.J., & Blanchard, C.M. (2000). The study of emotion in sport and exercise: Historical, definitional, and conceptual perspectives. In Y.L. Hanin (Ed.), *Emotions in sport* (pp. 3–37). Champaign, IL: Human Kinetics.

Vallerand, R.J., & Fortier, M.S. (1998). Measures of intrinsic and extrinsic motivation in sport and physical activity: A review and critique. In J.L. Duda (Ed.), *Advances in sport and exercise psychology measurement* (pp. 81–101). Morgantown, WV: Fitness Information Technology.

Vallerand, R.J., & Losier, G.F. (1999). An integrative analysis of intrinsic and extrinsic motivation in sport. *Journal of Applied Sport Psychology, 11,* 142–169.

Van Raalte, J. (1994). Sport performance attributions: A special case of self-serving bias? *Australian Journal of Science and Medicine in Sport, 26,* 45–48.

Vlachopoulos, S., & Biddle, S.J.H. (1997). Modeling the relation of goal orientations to achievement-related affect in physical education: Does perceived ability matter? *Journal of Sport & Exercise Psychology, 19,* 169–187.

Vlachopoulos, S., Biddle, S., & Fox, K. (1996). A social-cognitive investigation into the mechanisms of affect generation in children's physical activity. *Journal of Sport & Exercise Psychology, 18,* 174–193.

Vlachopoulos, S., Biddle, S., & Fox, K. (1997). Determinants of emotion in children's physical activity: A test of goal perspectives and attribution theories. *Pediatric Exercise Science, 9,* 65–79.

Weary, G., Stanley, M.A., & Harvey, J.H. (1989). *Attribution.* New York: Springer-Verlag.

Weiner, B. (1979). A theory of motivation for some classroom experiences. *Journal of Educational Psychology, 71,* 3–25.

Weiner, B. (1980). *Human motivation.* New York: Holt, Rinehart and Winston.

Weiner, B. (1983). Some methodological pitfalls in attributional research. *Journal of Educational Psychology, 75,* 530–543.

Weiner, B. (1985a). An attributional theory of achievement motivation and emotion. *Psychological Review, 92,* 548–573.

Weiner, B. (1985b). Spontaneous causal thinking. *Psychological Bulletin, 97,* 74–84.

Weiner, B. (1986). *An attributional theory of motivation and emotion.* New York: Springer-Verlag.

Weiner, B. (1992). *Human motivation.* Newbury Park, CA: Sage.

Weiner, B. (1995). *Judgments of responsibility.* New York: Guilford Press.

Weiner, B., Frieze, I.H., Kukla, A., Reed, L., Rest, S., & Rosenbaum, R.M. (1972). Perceiving the causes of success and failure. In E.E. Jones, D.E. Kanouse, H.H. Kelley, R.E. Nisbett, S. Valins, & B. Weiner (Eds.), *Attribution: Perceiving the causes of behavior* (pp. 95–120). Morristown, NJ: General Learning Press.

Weiner, B., Graham, S., & Chandler, C. (1982). Pity, anger, and guilt: An attributional analysis. *Personality and Social Psychology Bulletin, 8,* 226 232.

Weiner, B., & Handel, S. (1985). A cognition-emotion-action sequence: Anticipated emotional consequences of causal attributions and reported communication strategy. *Developmental Psychology, 21,* 102–107.

Weiner, B., Russell, D., & Lerman, D. (1978). Affective consequences of causal ascriptions. In J.H. Harvey, W. Ickes, & R.F. Kidd (Eds.), *New directions in attribution research* (Vol. 2, pp. 59–90). Hillsdale, NJ: Erlbaum.

Wilson, T.D., & Linville, P.W. (1985). Improving the performance of college freshmen with attributional techniques. *Journal of Personality and Social Psychology, 49,* 287–293.

Xenikou, A., Furnham, A., & McCarrey, M. (1997). Attributional style for negative events: A proposition for a more reliable and valid measure of attributional style. *British Journal of Psychology, 88,* 53–69.

Yirmiya, N., & Weiner, B. (1986). Perceptions of controllability and anticipated anger. *Cognitive Development, 1,* 273–280.

CHAPTER 18

Group Cohesion in Sport and Exercise

DAVID M. PASKEVICH, PAUL A. ESTABROOKS, LAWRENCE R. BRAWLEY,
and ALBERT V. CARRON

Historically, cohesion has been identified as *the* most important small-group variable (Golembieski, 1962; Lott & Lott, 1965). Indirect verification for this conclusion is available from a wide variety of settings. For example, a long-standing interest in cohesion has been shown by researchers in social psychology (Eisman, 1959; Zaccaro & Lowe, 1986), military psychology (e.g., Manning & Fullerton, 1988; McGrath, 1962), organizational psychology (e.g., Keller, 1986; Trist & Bamforth, 1951), counseling psychology (e.g., Peterroy, 1983; Roark & Sharah, 1989), and educational psychology (e.g., Festinger, Schachter, & Back, 1950; Shaw & Shaw, 1962). Also, cohesion has been the object of scientific scrutiny in both sport and exercise psychology.

The present chapter, which contains an overview of the scientific investigation of cohesion in sport and exercise groups, is composed of eight main sections. The first two present theoretical perspectives on cohesion: definitional, conceptual, and measurement considerations. In the next two sections, the results from cohesion research in the areas of sport and exercise psychology are summarized. The next section contains a discussion of topical issues that should be considered by researchers interested in examining the construct. Then, two sections provide suggestions for future research on cohesion in sport and exercise settings. Finally, an overview and recommendations are provided in the final section.

COHESION DEFINED

The term cohesion is derived from the Latin word *cohaesus*, which means to cleave or stick together. Mudrack (1989, p. 39) has pointed out that although cohesiveness "seems intuitively easy to understand and describe . . . this 'ease of description' has failed to translate into an 'ease of definition.'" Thus, like many social constructs, cohesion has been defined in a variety of ways by different authors. In one classic definition advanced by Festinger et al. (1950, p. 164), it was considered to be "the total field of forces that act on members to remain in the group." They also proposed that there are two general types of forces: the attractiveness of the group (which represents the social and affiliative aspects of a group) and means control (which represents the task, performance, and productive concerns of the group).

After citing the Festinger et al. (1950) definition, however, most early researchers ignored a number of important types of forces (e.g., normative forces that keep members from leaving a group as well as the forces that pull members to alternative groups). Instead, cohesion was treated simply as the attraction of the group for its members (Libo, 1953). Also, Mudrack (1989, p. 42) pointed out that although such a definition is easy to operationalize, it focuses "exclusively on *individuals* at the expense of the *group* and therefore may not entirely capture the concept of *group* cohesiveness." A second classic definition, one that does focus on the group, describes cohesiveness as the resistance of the group to disruptive forces (Gross & Martin, 1952). A group that is strongly united (to use Aesop's term) is better able to resist the disruptions and pressures that could tear it apart.

In sport psychology, Carron, Brawley, and Widmeyer (1998, p. 213) proposed that cohesion is "a dynamic process that is reflected in the tendency for a group to stick together and remain united in the pursuit of its instrumental objectives and/or for the satisfaction of member affective needs." This definition was intended to highlight the fact that cohesion in sport teams is:

Multidimensional: There is more than one factor underlying the unity/cohesiveness of sport teams.

Dynamic: It is not a trait, it changes over time.

Instrumental: It reflects the reason(s) for group formation and maintenance.

Affective: It is associated with positive affect.

The definition advanced by Carron et al. is linked with their conceptual model and operational definition that forms the basis for most of the research undertaken on cohesion in sport and exercise groups.

CONCEPTION AND MEASUREMENT OF GROUP COHESION

A Conceptual Model

The conceptual model for cohesion advanced by Carron, Widmeyer, and Brawley (1985) is based on the assumption that both individual and group aspects of cohesion are represented, in part, as multiple beliefs and perceptions of individual members of a group. The model proposes that each group member integrates the information from various aspects of the social world that are relevant and meaningful to the group such that a variety of perceptions and beliefs are generated. These beliefs/perceptions about ways the group and its members remain united in the pursuit of group goals and/or member affective needs can be classified into two broad categories within the conceptual model.

The first category is *Group Integration,* which concerns the beliefs and perceptions individual group members hold about the group (team) as a totality. The second category, *Individual Attractions to the Group,* relates to each group member's personal beliefs and perceptions about what both initially attracted and continues to attract him or her to the group. Each of these categories is further divided into *task* and *social* orientations. Thus, the conceptual model has four related dimensions concerning the multiple beliefs and perceptions that are part of the dynamic process of characterizing a group's or team's cohesiveness. These beliefs and perceptions are thought to act *together* in creating a group's and individual group member's sense of cohesiveness. Their integrated totality represents an indicant of the multidimensional construct of cohesion. The four related dimensions are (1) Group Integration–Task (GI-T); (2) Group Integration–Social (GI-S); (3) Individual Attractions to the Group–Task (ATG-T); and (4) Individual Attractions to the Group–Social (ATG-S). From a theoretical perspective, each dimension alone could be sufficient

to encourage athletes in a group to "stick together" or stay united in their group. However, given that group cohesion is characterized as a dynamic process, it seems more probable that some of each dimension will contribute to the team's overall level of cohesion.

The relative contribution of each dimension to cohesiveness is hypothesized to vary over time, depending on the impact of suspected moderator variables. For example, level of group development (e.g., months or years a team has been together; time of season) or nature of the group (their motivational base having a task or social focus) might influence the degree to which a particular dimension contributes to overall cohesion. Given that these moderators are part of what constitutes the social experience of the group and the individual members in the group, they are hypothesized to affect the beliefs and perceptions that are indicants of the four dimensions of cohesion. Therefore, for example, a group/team with a *task* focus as its motivational base may have more experiences occurring over time that contribute to stronger and greater numbers of task-related beliefs and perceptions (i.e., GI-T and ATG-T) in comparison to the number and strengths of experiences that contribute to social percepts of cohesiveness.

The changing nature of beliefs and perceptions over time is consistent with Carron et al.'s (1998) definition of cohesion and with the notion in group dynamics that as a group's characteristics increase or decrease in stability, so will the behaviors and beliefs of individual group members. The changes in behaviors and beliefs of individual members will correspond to changes that occur in matters of consequence to the whole group (Sherif & Sherif, 1969). Although various antecedents to and consequences of group process may influence the development of cohesion in dynamic fashion over time, their influence in the conceptual model is presumed to operate (at least in part) *through* the perceptions and beliefs of individual team members. Figure 18.1 schematically illustrates the conceptual model as it derives from the operation of internal and external factors on beliefs.

In summary, group members perceive and believe that their group can supply them with various task and social provisions that fulfill their needs. Believing in and receiving those provisions is thought to cause athletes to be attracted to their team (i.e., ATG-T and ATG-S). The perceptions of and beliefs in a team's united purpose to reach a group goal or objective, as well as the group's unity about being socially supportive for group task or social concerns (i.e., GI-T and GI-S), are motivations for an athlete to continue as a member of a team. Individual members both

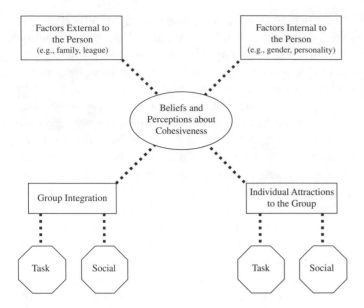

Figure 18.1   A conceptual model of cohesion.

observe behavior and confirm beliefs about the multiple aspects of cohesion, which, from the individual member's perspective, adds to and reinforces a sense that he or she does wish to remain with the team and that the team is united. The extent to which an individual group member can describe the strength of his or her perception about each of the four aspects of cohesion makes possible the measurement of each.

It is recognized that the four related dimensions concerning various perceptions of cohesion are likely a product of a complex person-environment interaction occurring as a team progresses through its season. It is assumed that the process of a team becoming cohesive is one that happens through social learning as team athletes interact with their environment. These notions are at the basis of the conceptual model, are related to the way the operational measure of cohesion (the Group Environment Questionnaire) was developed, and are associated with the procedures for measuring sport team cohesion.

The Group Environment Questionnaire

The specific procedures for the development of the Group Environment Questionnaire (GEQ) are described in detail elsewhere (Brawley, Carron, & Widmeyer, 1987, 1988; Carron et al., 1985, 1998; Widmeyer, Brawley, & Carron, 1985). The process evolved from the conceptual model described previously. The link between the concepts and the GEQ was facilitated not only by the model but also by involving members of teams in the development process. The phenomenology outlined by team members was examined to

ensure a face-valid instrument that linked each of the four dimensions of cohesion to their respective measurement. Through this protocol, the measures were meaningful to team athletes and free of items that would either reflect aspects of investigator bias or ignore the concept-operational definition link. The resulting GEQ is an 18-item, four-scale measure. Sample items from each of the four scales are presented in Table 18.1.

Research that has examined the psychometric properties of the GEQ has been discussed at length by Carron et al. (1998); consequently, that discussion is not repeated here. Suffice it to say that approximately 15 years of research has provided evidence that the GEQ is internally consistent and demonstrates face, concurrent, predictive, and factorial validity.

CORRELATES OF GROUP COHESION IN SPORT

Since the development of the GEQ (Carron et al., 1985), the body of literature that characterizes the research program undertaken with the GEQ has grown considerably (e.g., more than 30 published studies using the GEQ in a sport context). Thus, in this section, a portion of the literature that has examined correlates of the GEQ is summarized. This review of literature is not meant to be all-inclusive of the work done on cohesion in sport with the GEQ, and is primarily reflective of the research undertaken by the authors of this chapter and their research colleagues.

Over 13 correlates of cohesion in sport have been examined since the development of the GEQ. Correlates of cohesion typically have been categorized into one of four categories: (1) environmental factors (e.g., normative

Table 18.1   Sample Items from the Four Scales of the Group Environment Questionnaire

Dimension (Scale)	Sample Item
Individual Attractions to the Group–Task	"I do not like the style of play on this team."[1]
Individual Attractions to the Group–Social	"I am not going to miss the members of this team when the season ends."
Group Integration–Task	"Our team members have conflicting aspirations for the team's performance."
Group Integration–Social	"Our team members rarely party together."

[1]The items are negatively worded. Consequently, strong denial of the statement would represent a greater perception of group cohesion.

pressures), (2) personal factors (e.g., responsibility for negative outcomes), (3) leadership factors (e.g., task-oriented versus person-oriented behaviors), and (4) team factors (e.g., status congruency). Although this is convenient from an organizational perspective, in the final analysis, it must be remembered that many of the examined correlates could be included in more than one category. The following is a brief synopsis of selected correlates.

Environmental Factors

Level of Competition

In examining level of competition, Granito and Rainey (1988) assessed the cohesion of high school and college football teams. They administered the GEQ at the end of a season to 44 football players from a large high school, 25 players from a medium-size high school, and 52 players from a National Collegiate Athletic Association Division III university. It was hypothesized that high school teams would be more cohesive than the university team. Results indicated that task cohesion (ATG-T and GI-T) was in fact significantly greater in the high school teams.

Size of Team

Widmeyer, Brawley, and Carron (1990) carried out two studies that demonstrated team size was associated with cohesion. In their first study, participants in a 3-on-3 recreational basketball league were formed into teams consisting of either three, six, or nine members. Results indicated that as roster size increased, task cohesion decreased, whereas social cohesion was greatest in the six-member group. In the second study, Widmeyer and colleagues examined the relationship between group size and cohesion in a recreational volleyball league. Teams were comprised of either 3, 6, or 12 members and competed against like-size teams. The results showed that the level of cohesion was greatest in the three-member teams, and with increasing team size, there was a progressive decrease in cohesiveness. The association between group size and cohesion is not limited to sport teams. Mullen and Copper (1994), on the basis of their meta-analysis of cohesion research undertaken with a wide cross-section of groups, concluded that cohesiveness is greater in smaller groups.

Personal Factors

Social Loafing

The reduction in individual effort when people work in groups versus when they work alone has been referred to as social loafing (Latane, 1981; Latane, Williams, & Harkins, 1979; Williams, Harkins, & Latane, 1981). In their 1993

meta-analysis, Karau and Williams showed that even though social loafing is pervasive across task, gender, and culture, it may be reduced under certain conditions. The potential to identify individuals' outputs and the presence of a relationship among group members are two conditions that are thought to reduce social loafing (Karau & Williams, 1993; Williams, Nida, Baca, & Latane, 1989).

McKnight, Williams, and Widmeyer (1991) examined the impact of cohesion and identifiability on social loafing among swimmers who competed in relay teams of four versus swimming alone. By informing swimmers of their individual event and relay split times in the presence of teammates and spectators, a high-identifiability condition was created. For the low-identifiability condition, the swimmers were informed of their individual event times privately and only the total time for the team was given for the relay event. McKnight et al. found that when task cohesion was low, only the high-identifiability condition was effective in reducing social loafing. Thus, when swimmers were given their times privately, they socially loafed. In contrast, on relay teams that were characterized by high task cohesion, social loafing did not occur regardless of whether personal output was relayed to the swimmers in the private or public condition.

Adherence Behavior

Not surprisingly, cohesion has found to be related with adherence in sport teams (Brawley et al., 1988, Study 1; Prapavessis & Carron, 1997b; Widmeyer, Brawley, & Carron, 1988, Study 2). Athletes who held the perception that their team was more cohesive were more likely to be on time for practices, to be present at practices and games (Carron, Widmeyer, & Brawley, 1988, Study 1), and to feel that their team was better able to withstand the negative impact of disruptive events (Brawley et al., 1988, Study 1).

Leadership Factors

Two elements of leadership that are related to the development of group cohesion are the leader's behavior and decision style. Westre and Weiss (1991) examined the relationship between coaching behaviors and team cohesion with high school football players. They found that higher levels of training and instruction behavior, social support behavior, positive feedback, and a democratic style were associated with higher levels of task cohesion in athletes. Kozub (1993) has reported a similar finding in a study carried out with high school basketball teams. In the case of decisional style, stronger perceptions of cohesiveness are present when a more participative (democratic) approach is used to arrive at a decision. Brawley, Carron, and

Widmeyer (1993) determined that athletes who had greater participation in team goal setting possessed a stronger sense of task and social cohesion. It was also observed in the Westre and Weiss and Kozub studies that athletes who perceived that their coach used a democratic style perceived the group to be more task-cohesive.

Team Factors

Role Involvement

Role involvement is inextricably linked to team unity. In both team and individual sports, various aspects of role involvement and cohesion are strongly related, sharing from 13% to 40% of the common variance (Brawley et al., 1987; Dawe & Carron, 1990). For example, Brawley et al. reported correlations of .38, .49, and .43 between task cohesion (i.e., GI-T) and role clarity, role acceptance, and role performance for team sport athletes. For individual sport athletes, the comparable correlational values were .56, .63, and .57.

Group Norms

Research on cohesion and conformity to group norms has yielded a positive relationship. The higher the cohesion, the greater is the conformity to group norms. For example, Shields, Bredemeier, Gardner, and Boston (1995) observed that team cohesion was positively related to normative expectations that peers would cheat and aggress and that the coach would condone cheating. Additionally, Prapavessis and Carron (1997a) found that athletes positively related perceptions of task cohesion to the groups norms that were identified as important.

Collective Efficacy

A recent correlate of cohesion (i.e., in the past five years) has been collective efficacy (Paskevich, 1995; Paskevich, Brawley, Dorsch, & Widmeyer, 1997, 1999). Collective efficacy is the sense of shared competence held by team members that they can successfully respond to the demands of the situation (Zaccaro, Blair, Peterson, & Zazanis, 1995). It seems reasonable to assume that when cohesion is higher, the sense of collective confidence in a team would also be higher. In a series of studies by Paskevich and his colleagues (Dorsch, Widmeyer, Paskevich, & Brawley, 1995; Paskevich, 1995; Paskevich, Brawley, Dorsch, & Widmeyer, 1995; Paskevich et al., 1997, 1999), this relationship has been consistently demonstrated. Not surprisingly, task cohesion is the type of cohesiveness that has the strongest relationship with collective efficacy. A belief that the team holds similar perceptions on the style of play being used and the collective goals and objectives being pursued are associated with increased group confidence.

Paskevich (1995, Study 3) examined the interrelationships among collective efficacy, cohesion, and performance in 25 intercollegiate volleyball teams. He found that collective efficacy is a mediator between task cohesion and team performance (i.e., win-loss record). Thus, greater task cohesion contributed to greater collective efficacy, which, in turn, contributed to better team performance.

Dorsch, Paskevich, Widmeyer, and Brawley (1994) noted a relationship among such group-based perceptions as collective efficacy for aggressive behaviors, the team's acceptability of aggressive behaviors, and group cohesion. Furthermore, these relationships were influenced by the social context (i.e., level of hockey competition) in which the athletes were participating (Dorsch et al., 1995). As well, within the more elite Junior A levels of ice hockey, collective efficacy for aggression, three cohesion scales (ATG-T, GI-T, and GI-S), and norms for intimidating behaviors significantly discriminated between teams with high and low aggressive behaviors (Dorsch, Paskevich, Brawley, & Widmeyer, 1995).

Performance: Does a Cohesion-Performance or Performance-Cohesion Relationship Exist?

Although this issue has been addressed previously (cf. Widmeyer, Carron, & Brawley, 1993), it must be reemphasized that the research thus far has had limited success at providing a definitive answer to whether cohesion effects performance or performance effects cohesion. In an attempt to resolve inconsistencies in the research that have examined the cohesion-performance relationship, Mullen and Copper (1994) performed a meta-analysis using 49 studies from a wide variety of settings: work groups, military units, laboratory groups, and sport teams.

These studies produced 66 tests of the cohesiveness-performance effect relationships. Of the 66 hypotheses tested, 92% reported a small positive cohesiveness-performance effect. Thus, Mullen and Copper's (1994) findings indicated that the cohesiveness-performance relationship was highly significant and of small magnitude. Effect sizes were stronger among real groups (i.e., sport teams) than among artificial groups (i.e., laboratory group created for purpose of the study). Effect sizes were also stronger in smaller groups compared to larger groups and stronger in correlational studies than in experimental studies. Additionally, the cohesiveness-performance relationship is primarily due to a commitment to the task rather than to interpersonal attraction or group pride. Last, in regard to the temporal patterning in the cohesiveness-performance effect, the direction of the effect seems to be stronger from performance to cohesion than from cohesion to performance. However, this finding does not negate the point that cohesion can cause increases in performance. It does suggest, nonetheless, that the changes in cohesiveness brought about by increases in performance are likely to be even stronger than changes in performance that can be brought about by increases in cohesiveness.

In summary, on the basis of the research conducted to date, it is reasonable to conclude that many factors are positively related to group cohesion, and that cohesion is a factor that directly contributes to group maintenance and facilitates group locomotion. Additionally, even though relationships between cohesion and other variables were presented in an independent or unrelated fashion, it is important to bear in mind the dynamic, circular nature of group dynamics and that in real groups these factors are often interwoven. Thus, as stated previously, cohesion plays such an important role in the dynamics of all groups that some social scientists have called cohesion the most important small-group variable (Golembieski, 1962; Lott & Lott, 1965).

CORRELATES OF GROUP COHESION IN EXERCISE GROUPS/PROGRAMS

The literature examining the impact of group cohesion on exercise participation has also been based on the conceptual model of group cohesion developed by Carron et al. (1985). As exercise classes differ from sport teams in task, social, individual, and group level characteristics, the original GEQ was modified for use in the exercise domain (Carron et al., 1988). It should be noted that the modifications were minor and the operational definition of cohesion was still reflective of the four primary dimensions of cohesion. Carron et al. (1988, Study 1) were the first to examine the effect of cohesion on adherence and withdrawal from physical activity groups. Participants were fitness class adherers and nonadherers. The GEQ was administered to determine perceptions of the four cohesion constructs. The adherers and nonadherers were correctly classified (61%) by a function that included two cohesion measures, ATG-T and ATG-S. It was concluded that a relationship was present between cohesion and adherence in physical activity classes (Carron et al., 1988, Study 1).

Spink and Carron (1992) then examined the relationship between group cohesion and nonadherence (operationally defined as absenteeism and lateness) in females ($n = 171$)

participating in exercise classes. Four weeks of attendance and punctuality data were collected during Weeks 8 to 12 of a 13-week program. The GEQ was administered in Week 13. Two cohesion dimensions, ATG-T and ATG-S, were negatively associated with absenteeism. It was also found that ATG-T accounted for the greatest difference between those participants who were never late and those who were late four or more times. It was concluded that these results supplied initial support for the relationship between group cohesion and the adherence of female exercise participants.

Although these results were considered promising, each of these studies was retrospective in nature, with no clear direction of the relationship between group cohesion and exercise adherence. For this reason, Spink and Carron (1994) conducted two prospective studies to examine the predictive ability of group cohesion on exercise adherence. The purpose of Study 1 was to determine if perceptions of group cohesion assessed relatively early in an exercise program would predict subsequent participant adherence or dropout. Participants were 37 females who attended exercise classes offered one hour per day for three days each week at a major university. The GEQ was used to assess the four dimensions of cohesion in Week 3 of a 13-week program. Adherence was operationalized as attendance during the final four weeks of the program. The results showed that ATG-T discriminated between adherers and dropouts. A complete function that included ATG-T, GI-T, and GI-S successfully categorized 78% of the participants into adherers and dropouts (Spink & Carron, 1994).

Spink and Carron (1994, Study 2) then replicated Study 1 with one exception; it was conducted at a private fitness club rather than in a university setting. Participants again completed the GEQ during the third week of a 13-week program and attendance was monitored for the final four weeks of the program. The results showed that only two of the dimensions of group cohesion distinguished adherers from dropouts: individual ATG-S and GI-S. A function containing these two components successfully categorized 65% of the participants. On the basis of their two studies, Spink and Carron concluded that (1) cohesive feelings can develop early in group situations (within the first three weeks) and those feelings of cohesion are related to whether an individual adheres to a program; (2) the type of cohesion necessary for adherence to exercise classes is dependent on the exercise setting (e.g., a university versus a club setting); and (3) a team-building intervention strategy might be an effective modality for increasing individual exercise behavior.

Given the consistent findings from the descriptive studies outlined previously, a program of intervention (team-building) was developed by Carron and Spink (1993) to improve cohesion in exercise classes. The intervention focused on utilizing five group dynamic principles: (1) development of a feeling of distinctiveness, (2) assignment of group roles, (3) development of group norms, (4) provision of opportunities to make sacrifices for the group, and (5) development of interaction and communication within the group (Carron & Spink, 1993). To examine the efficacy of this team-building intervention for developing group cohesion in exercise classes, Carron and Spink randomly assigned university aerobics classes to a control ($n = 9$) or team-building ($n = 8$) condition. Assessments during the eighth week of a 13-week program showed that the scale ATG-T was significantly greater in the team-building condition. Similarly, in a second intervention study, team building also improved perceptions of ATG-T and was associated with fewer dropouts and late arrivals (Spink & Carron, 1993).

More recently, Estabrooks and Carron (1999b) analyzed the effectiveness of a similar team-building intervention on improving exercise adherence and return rates in classes for older adults. The exercise classes were offered twice a week for six weeks and return rates (following a 10-week hiatus) to the program were monitored. All participants in the study were first-time exercise class attendees and were assigned to a team-building, placebo, or control condition. Results showed that participants in the team-building condition (1) attended more classes than the control ($ES = 1.2$, $p < .05$) and placebo ($ES = 1.1$, $p < .05$) conditions, and (2) had a higher return rate following a 10-week hiatus (93%, 40%, 73%, respectively) although only the difference between the team-building and control conditions was significant.

Research concerning group cohesion in the exercise domain has also highlighted a number of cognitive correlates. Brawley et al. (1988, Study 2) explored the relationship between perceptions of cohesion and resistance to group-disruptive events in an exercise setting. Using extreme groups based on perceptions of the group's resistance to disruption, Brawley and his associates found that GI-T significantly discriminated between participants with high and low perceptions of the group's resistance to disruption. Courneya (1995) investigated the relationship between group cohesion and affect, in the form of feeling states, and found that higher perceptions of ATG-T, ATG-S, and GI-T were related to higher feeling states during exercise. The impact of cohesion in broader social cognitive frameworks has also been examined. For example, within the

framework of the theory of planned behavior (Ajzen, 1985), Estabrooks and Carron (1999) found that in a sample of older adults enrolled in a physical activity program, increases in ATG-T and ATG-S were associated with respective increases in perceived behavioral control and attitude toward exercise. Furthermore, self-efficacy has also been related to ATG-T and GI-T (Estabrooks & Carron, 2000).

In summary, on the basis of research conducted to date, it is reasonable to conclude that individuals who hold stronger beliefs about the cohesiveness of their exercise class will (1) attend more exercise classes, (2) be more likely to arrive on time, (3) be less likely to drop out, and (4) be more resistant to disruptions in the group. There is also preliminary evidence that individuals who have stronger beliefs about cohesiveness in their class will (1) be more likely to experience greater amounts of positive affect related to exercise, (2) have improved attitudes toward exercise, and (3) have stronger efficacy beliefs related to exercise.

ADVANCING COHESION RESEARCH

Four key issues must be addressed to advance cohesion research in sport and exercise psychology:

1. An understanding of the nature and scope of cohesion.
2. Consideration of the level of group development and the social context in which cohesion takes place.
3. Development of principles for linking the cohesion concept to its operational definition.
4. Necessary empirical data that will help to validate the conceptual model of cohesion and measure reflecting cohesion.

Each of these issues will be addressed in turn.

To conduct research based on a conceptual model, several aspects of the model need to be considered when investigators propose their research questions. These aspects are: (1) the multidimensional nature of the cohesion construct, (2) the level of group development, (3) the dynamic nature of cohesion, and (4) the main assumptions of the conceptual model. Sport psychology investigators should be aware of the implications that each aspect of the model has for their hypotheses, the research design of their study, and the measure necessary to test the hypotheses. To illustrate the importance of these aspects of the conceptual model to conduct cohesion research, they will be described in brief.

Multidimensional Nature of Cohesion

To detect a multifaceted phenomenon such as cohesion, a measure must reflect its multiple facets: hence the four aspects of cohesion that are measured by the GEQ. Investigators frequently expect all four aspects of assessed cohesion to be expressed by all groups (cf. Carron & Brawley, 2000; Carron et al., 1998). However, the cohesion phenomenon develops within the group through the process of social learning and group socialization (Levine & Moreland, 1991). Thus, it is unlikely that all groups will reflect all manifestations of cohesion at all times. Furthermore, the motivational base of a group governs its most central operations such that even when a group has been together for extended time periods, it may be unreasonable to assume that all aspects of cohesion will develop to equally strong levels. For example, a sport team spends frequent bouts of interactive time together, whereas an exercise group may spend only structured limited amounts of time together. It is not uncommon for the former group to interact both on and off the court/playing field. Task and social interactions occur with sufficient frequency over time such that different manifestations of cohesion emerge.

By contrast, the exercise group interacts within a structured context for limited amounts of time where the group's "performance" is adherence to the class and individual improvement in response to graded exercise training. Although there is a sense of group effectiveness when adherence is good and class members keep pace with instruction, the group disbands at the end of each class with few reasons to interact until the next in-exercise situation. The mode of interaction during the class is not dramatically different from time to time (i.e., no demand for changing task roles or for varying interaction) and such classes often end after three months (e.g., consistent with facility program offerings or semesters at a university). Thus, reliable manifestations of cohesion may primarily take the form of individual attractions to the group task. Other manifestations of an individual and group nature may be highly variable both within and between groups and dependent on the individual differences in the nature of similar exercise groups.

Investigators who examine the two examples offered above (i.e., team and exercise groups) should not advance arbitrary hypotheses about cohesion. Based on the conceptual model and its assumptions, a priori hypotheses could be made. In the team example, it would be hypothesized that new teams (i.e., weeks old) would be best characterized by task forms of cohesion, whereas teams of long-standing experience (i.e., years old) might exhibit all forms of cohesion. In the exercise group example, it would be hypothesized that a new class that has been together only three times per week for a month would be characterized by ATG-T (cf. Carron et al., 1998). By contrast, exercise groups composed of the same exercisers who have been repeating their registration in the same class every three months may reflect additional manifestations of cohesion (e.g., ATG-S).

To appreciate the influence of group development on the emergence of different aspects of cohesion, Sherif and Sherif (1969) offered a useful multifactored perspective about group formation. They noted that as groups form and develop, four basic factors impact on the emergence of the group's properties and how these properties stabilize over time. These factors are:

1. The motivational base of the group: the central task and related group goals—their reason for being—as in task goals for the season.

2. The roles, status, and power that develop and characterize the group's organizational structure: the task-related roles, their importance to the group, and the power to influence others, as in starting status.

3. The formal and informal rules, values, and norms regarding task and social behavior: formal rules related to the task; informal task rules and norms regarding effort or social rules regarding team travel.

4. The differential effects of the above properties on member cognitions and behavior in matters of consequence to the group: how these properties contribute to or detract from the degree of social interaction group members experience, the information they share, the consensus they reach and the group-related socialization processes that occur (e.g., differential effects on the sharing of beliefs within the group: cohesion, collective efficacy).

These factors are not uniformly influential but emerge and influence group members as they develop over time. Thus, group properties may not be equally stable as the group develops. Accordingly, the influence of these properties may not be equal in the way they contribute to group cohesion and its different facets of group cohesion (see Figure 18.2).

Figure 18.3 illustrates the differential development of various aspects of cohesion. Early in a group's life, its membership consists mainly of new members and its motivational base tends to govern the interactions of those new members. Thus, new sport and exercise groups tend to have

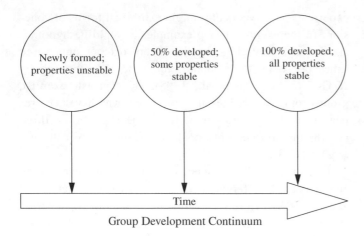

Figure 18.2   Group development continuum.

a task-oriented motivational base (e.g., competing, winning, and related practice/competition goals; fitness participation, cardiovascular fitness/strength goals). This task orientation is attractive to group members (i.e., one of the reasons they joined the group) and focuses the manner in which they integrate with respect to task-related matters of consequence to the group. As a group's properties gradually stabilize in relation to its motivational base, the primary efforts of group interaction are focused on accomplishing the task(s) effectively to the extent that it is within the group's control. As shown in Figure 18.3, this development takes time, is dynamic, and governs the emergence of task-related forms of cohesion.

However, as the group's properties and actions stabilize with respect to its task(s), members can devote their attention to more social interactions. Therefore, a group's social norms and roles emerge and develop in addition to existing

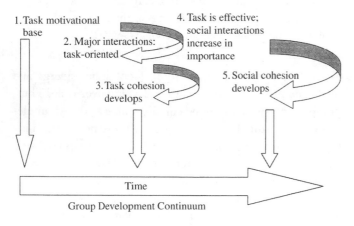

Figure 18.3   Differential development of various aspects of cohesion.

stable, task-related properties of the group. In Figure 18.3, the developmental sequence of task cohesion emerging first with social forms of cohesion following illustrates only one and perhaps the simplest of several dynamic sequences that characterize when different forms of cohesion develop. It is also likely that the development of these various forms of cohesion could occur in parallel with the task aspects of cohesion. The task aspects would be of primary importance and be more stable, and the social aspects of cohesion would be variable and of secondary importance to the group.

Figures 18.2 and 18.3 illustrate the dynamic aspect of cohesion development and underscore the challenge for measurement and the need for research questions to be focused. The practice of simply administering any cohesion measure with the view that cohesion is a traitlike group property similar to a group "personality trait" is doomed to failure. Clearly, the multifaceted and changing nature of cohesion is a manifestation of the outcomes of group development and group processes. Advancing hypotheses about the relation of group cohesion to other group phenomena (e.g., collective efficacy, group attributions, social loafing) or to group outcomes (e.g., performance, satisfaction, group goals) requires an understanding of the way groups develop, interact, and stabilize over time and an awareness of their properties, the longevity of the group, and the group's experience with their task.

Does the Conceptual Model of Cohesion Apply to Other Groups and Contexts?

Recently, Carron and Brawley (2000) pointed out the liabilities of arbitrarily applying their conceptual model and their measure of cohesion (GEQ) in different group domains without considering several factors. These factors are the nature of the social context and whether all aspects of their measure can be used or modified in various social contexts (e.g., the workplace, fitness groups, musical groups, the military). The GEQ measure was specifically developed to study adult recreational and competitive sport teams, and thus a simple prescription for modification of the instrument to other social contexts is not forthcoming. Simple modification of the GEQ by changing a few words is not the tactic to achieve generalizability of the measure. Although some success has been realized by using this method (e.g., see Carron et al., 1998: adult fitness groups, dormitory groups), a different starting point for investigating groups in a variety of social contexts is recommended.

A conceptual model or theory should be the starting point for the development of measures. Although there is evidence from more than 30 studies that the conceptual model is valid (cf. Carron et al., 1998), it is important to obtain the scientific opinions of other investigators in this regard. In their examination of cohesion in *Small Group Research,* Dion and Evans (1992) observed that the Carron et al. (1985) four-dimensional conceptual model and measurement method had broad applicability. They noted that it is unlikely that a single generic cohesion measure will be applicable in every social context without modification. However, they also emphasized that the conceptual model held promise for serving as a foundation for studying cohesion across many groups. Similarly, Cota, Evans, Dion, Kilik, and Longman (1995) believed that Carron et al. (1985) had identified the primary components of a multidimensional model of cohesion.

However, support for the generalizability of a conceptual model or theory must be shown across various social contexts and types of groups. Elsewhere, Carron et al. (1998) have pointed out that the initial measurement attempts of cohesion in various groups (i.e., sport, business, physical activity) and in different cultures have had mixed success with adaptations of the GEQ. Thus, it is necessary to suggest guidelines for using the conceptual model for the measurement of cohesion that are applicable across situations, social contexts, and cultures. These guidelines follow:

1. Using the four dimensions of the conceptual model as a guide, consider whether these dimensions are relevant to the social context and the groups being investigated. This may require pilot work and elicitation of examples of task and social attractions to the group and task and social group integration from members of target groups. If the constructs are recognized as relevant by group members, then step 2 follows.

2. Link the constructs of cohesion to the social context. The elicitation of situations, attractions, behaviors, and group coordination/integration examples that represent attractions to the group (task or social) and group integration (task or social) may help to develop the conceptual content. This content would be useful in developing operational definitions/measures of the four constructs as relevant to groups in the specific social context.

3. Use the original GEQ instrument to determine if any items are generic across groups and social contexts.

4. Develop new cohesion items specific to the group and social context from the elicitation pilot work in steps 1 and 2.

5. Follow normal psychometric procedures for using a larger item pool (i.e., larger than the final instrument's). These procedures include reducing the size of the item pool by revising wording, removing terminology not applicable to the social context, pilot-testing the new instrument with relevant groups to eliminate irrelevant or confounded items, and adding new/reworded items based on pilot testing.

6. Examine psychometric properties.

A new GEQ should not be developed for every different group in every social context. However, any adaptation of the GEQ or development of a new cohesion measure should be done on the basis of an analysis of the social context of the group and the manifestations of cohesion the group may express. Adaptations or new measurements should not be based solely on the researcher's assumptions.

Results of Using the Guidelines

In this section, several examples of new GEQ instrument developments are provided to illustrate the points made above. As a result of following the guidelines, investigators may find that their modified GEQ-type measure has more than 18 items to characterize the relevant dimensions being measured. As well, the guidelines allude to normal measurement development steps, iterations of items being taken to create a preliminary measure, and multiple validation approaches appropriate to the program of research (i.e., Is the measure a focal point of research or one of many measures?). If the research program primarily concerns cohesion in the social context being examined, then all possible validation procedures must be undertaken (cf. Nunnally, 1978). Conversely, focused tests of validity will be more appropriate if cohesion is more of a secondary measure or outcome (e.g., establishing face or concurrent validity).

Examples of Context-Specific Developments. To illustrate the development of different cohesion measures based on the conceptual model, a comparison of modified items may help. For example, the original GI-T item about goals is "Our team is united in trying to reach its goals for performance." Other examples of similar items that relate to goals and outcomes are:

Fitness revision: "Our exercise group is united in trying to reach its goals for fitness" (Carron et al., 1998).

Business revision: "Our office is united in trying to reach its goals for performance" (Doherty & Carron's study, as cited in Carron, Estabrooks, Paskevich, & Brawley, 1999).

Seniors fitness class revision: "Our group is united in its beliefs about the benefits of physical activities offered in this program" (Estabrooks & Carron, in press).

These items represent minor modifications to the original GEQ item because the concept of goals is fairly generic to most task-oriented groups.

However, not all GEQ concepts and items are as generic across social contexts. There may be other aspects of a given construct from the conceptual model for cohesion that are more relevant to groups in social contexts outside sport. Therefore, the following items serve to illustrate the point that new items may need to be developed that are unlike the conceptual dimensions of cohesion in a fashion valid for the social context being investigated. These example items represent context-appropriate forms of the cohesion dimension of GI-T. To illustrate, an original GI-T item from the GEQ is presented as a frame of reference:

Original GI-T item: "We all take responsibility for any loss or poor performance by our team."

Seniors fitness class new GI-T item: "Members of our group enjoy helping if work needs to be done to prepare for the activity sessions" (Estabrooks & Carron, in press).

Francophone walking club new GI-T item: "In our group, we believe the most important reason for walking together is to make us more fit and healthy" (Gauvin & Brawley, 1999, as cited in Brawley, Carron, Paskevich, & Estabrooks, 1999).

In the case of the two new items, the representation of GI-T is quite different from the original item used to represent part of the same construct to sport groups. However, the same process of careful elicitation of content and steps toward face validity and internal consistency were followed. The Francophone walking club example represents not only a new item appropriate to the study of cohesion in walking clubs, but also the challenge of developing or modifying a measure for use in a different culture. For the development of the instrument, Gauvin and Brawley (1999) first constructed "draft" items from background information and elicited items in the French language from walking clubs. Because the conceptual ideas about cohesion and the original GEQ was in English, they developed the first draft of the walking club measures in English to try to ensure a correct concept to an operational definition link. This English-language draft of the GEQ was then translated to a

French Canadian version and data were gathered. Thus, context- and culture/language-appropriate measures were used. Finally, psychometric procedures for reducing the draft item pool were employed and a "back-translation" step was used to determine that items from the translated French Canadian version retained the representation of the original English item construction. Further development and analysis work continues using this process, as well as recognized psychometric procedures. For an excellent discussion of measurement issues and cross-cultural research in sport, see Duda and Hayashi (1998). However, this example illustrates the nature of the measurement development work that needs to be done in cohesion-related research. Hopefully, the foregoing discussion serves to emphasize that the measurement of cohesion in different social contexts may involve more than the simple modification of a few words for specific items for the GEQ.

The borrowing and revising of items on the original GEQ and the development of new, context-appropriate representations of a cohesion construct should be accomplished after careful consideration of (1) the nature of the group that researchers wish to investigate, (2) the research question being examined, and (3) the guidelines for examining the conceptual model of cohesion in different social contexts. Given that investigators follow suggestions for the development of context-appropriate cohesion, it is important to emphasize that the validation process does not end with the construction of a context-relevant instrument. For example, some investigators consider factorial validity the sine qua non of the validation process (Schutz, Eom, Smoll, & Smith, 1994). However, this is but one step in a complex ongoing process if the researcher is interested in using a measure in a long-term program of research. To underscore the notion that validation of a measure and conceptual model is an ongoing process, a brief examination of some general and specific ideas about this process is presented for future cohesion research.

Validation as a Process

The final issue believed to be important for future cohesion research is that of validation. Although an estimate of validity can be obtained by conducting a single investigation, the validation of both a conceptual model and related measurement instrument must occur through multiple studies that examine the different types of validity (i.e., content, concurrent, divergent, convergent, predictive, construct, factorial).

Validation, Nunnally (1978) emphasized, is a process that may be reflected through a program of research. What are the research goals that future investigators should pursue to validate theory and related measures?

At the *level of the conceptual model,* the research questions that need to be addressed concern:

1. The support of predictions based on theory (e.g., task cohesion predicts team performance).
2. The identification of moderators that differentially influence predictions (e.g., group size moderates cohesion).
3. The identification of mediators of various proposed relationships: Which process variable or mediator is a focal point through which antecedent variables influence behavior (e.g., group attributions function through collective efficacy [mediator] to influence cohesion)?
4. Cumulative evidence to address confidence in the theory (i.e., series of studies supporting each type of validity or the various relationships proposed by the theory).

At the *measurement level,* the required evidence that evolves through validation is that:

1. The measure reflects the assumptions and the constructs of a conceptual model or theory.
2. Different types of validity are demonstrated (see earlier comments).
3. The bulk of the evidence supports the types of validity and is *reproducible* (e.g., repeated prediction of task performance by task cohesion).

If the foregoing goals for theory and measurement are considered general targets for future research, what specific type of evidence would need to be demonstrated (i.e., required evidence) and what type of study might generate that evidence? At this point in the evolution of theoretical propositions that Carron et al. (1998) offered in their conceptual model, there is evidence for several types of validity. However, some of the more complex issues regarding cohesion require attention. Two of these issues about cohesion are offered as future research challenges.

Becoming cohesive is a dynamic process. The required evidence to demonstrate this central aspect of this group phenomenon is sparse. The validation of the dynamics of multiple aspects of cohesion requires (1) data that suggest that any one or all four aspects of cohesion vary in importance over time (i.e., as they develop), and (2) that social context influences this differential importance (i.e., social context moderates the dynamic process). Thus, the types of studies that could provide this required evidence would be

(1) prospective, (2) those that examine the influence of different social contexts (e.g., those promoting task or social cohesion or both), and/or (3) those that are both prospective and of different social contexts. Figures 18.2 and 18.3 partly conceptualize the research challenge entailed in accomplishing the goal of studying a dynamic process and conducting the types of studies just suggested.

Cohesion is a belief shared by group members. The beliefs that members hold about their group develop as a function of socialization into the group and through intragroup interaction overtime. Indeed, some level of shared knowledge is necessary for a team to operate effectively. Rules, routines, and norms of the group environment encourage new group members to learn specific types of information about the group that is already shared among long-standing members (Levine & Moreland, 1991; Levine, Resnick, & Higgins, 1993). Consequently, members of cohesive groups or teams should reflect shared beliefs about cohesion. This is because the various forms of cohesion are manifestations of what the member has observed, experienced, and shared with group/team members over time regarding group unity.

Arguments have been presented elsewhere (cf. Carron & Brawley, 2000; Carron et al., 1998; Paskevich et al., 1999) that when team members respond to questions abut the group or what the group fulfills for them, their responses are not independent of one another. That is, each group member's response to a question about cohesion may reflect a group effect as well as that individual member's variability in response. Kenny and La Voie (1985) have noted that the interdependence associated with group member responses actually violates the normal statistical assumption of independent responses that is the basis for standard analysis procedures used to study individuals. Much of the sport group research, including that of Carron, Brawley, and Widmeyer until recently, has overlooked this statistical issue and the conceptual idea of examining shared beliefs. (Note: Elsewhere in the chapter, procedures to analyze shared beliefs are briefly introduced.) However, it is suggested that analyzing for group effects may prove to be another means of validating theoretical notions about cohesion (e.g., linking level of group development to the degree of a group effect that reflects sharing).

The required evidence to demonstrate the validity of shared beliefs is limited. Recently, Paskevich et al. (1999) have demonstrated that beliefs about cohesion and about collective efficacy are shared. In their examination of the relationships between these group constructs for elite volleyball teams, they used a procedure to detect shared response variability that was recommended by Kenny and La Voie (1985). The procedure involves the calculation of the intraclass correlation coefficient (ICC), which provides an estimate of whether the responses of a given team's members are alike or are no different from responses of nonmembers or of members of another team. Essentially, the similarity in response variability within and without the group is estimated. The ICC statistic of 1.00 reflects identical response variability. Thus, higher estimates reflect more of a group effect in team members' responses and lower estimates reflect more individual variation.

Validation that cohesive beliefs are shared is important evidence to confirm that cohesiveness is a psychological outcome encouraged by group processes. Therefore, future researchers should examine the shared beliefs notion by (1) analyzing the shared variability in responses to the GEQ dimensions as per procedures described by Kenny and La Voie (1985) or by Moritz and Watson (1998); (2) using the group as the unit of analysis to determine if the nature of the group effect (i.e., the sharing) makes a difference in the strength of relationships with other group variables (cf. unit of analysis discussion in this chapter; Carron et al., 1998; Moritz & Watson, 1998); (3) determining if the extent of sharing reflected by various statistical estimates is a function of the developmental level of the group; and (4) determining if the processing of information that relates to cohesion leads to responses that reflect group unity (see Hinsz, Tinsdale, & Vollrath, 1997). The types of studies to examine sharing could be both concurrent and prospective and should also consider variables that moderate sharing, including the influence of different social contexts.

Certainly, other avenues of research stemming from the conceptual relationships advanced about cohesion (e.g., in relation to performance effectiveness, group behavior, collective and role efficacy) are also tests of validity of the conceptual model and measure. However, research that addresses either of the future research challenges—cohesion as a dynamic process or cohesion reflecting shared beliefs—would contribute greatly to the validation process and to the cohesion literature in general.

FUTURE DIRECTIONS FOR RESEARCH ON COHESION IN SPORT TEAMS

Although there has been considerable research to date exploring the correlates of cohesion in sport teams, a number of unexplored issues remain. One of the general issues pertains to how cohesion is viewed by team members.

Certainly, the implicit assumption held by researchers, coaches, and athletes is that cohesion is universally considered by all group members to be a desirable quality. Generally this is a safe assumption. However, findings from research examining the relationship of team cohesion and self-handicapping behavior by individuals differing in the dispositional tendency (i.e., trait) raise some interesting questions (Carron, Prapavessis, & Grove, 1994; Hausenblas & Carron, 1996). Athletes high in self-handicapping rated the severity of impediments to their performance preparation prior to an important competition as high when they perceived that the cohesion of their team was high. When they perceived that their team was low in task cohesion, however, they rated the severity of impediments to preparation as low.

In an attempt to explain their findings, Carron et al. (1994) suggested that team cohesion might be viewed by athletes from two perspectives: as a psychological benefit (i.e., a more cohesive group provides the athlete with feelings of greater security and comfort), and/or as a psychological cost (i.e., a more cohesive group leaves the athlete with greater feelings of responsibility to teammates). Thus, the psychological costs alternative might have been more salient to those athletes high in the trait of self-handicapping. As a consequence, they engaged in greater self-handicapping behavior to protect their self-esteem in the event that they performed poorly in the important competition.

Whether these two contrasting perspectives of athlete perceptions of cohesion exist, as a psychological cost and/or as a psychological benefit, is unknown. Do athletes perceive a cohesive team as anything but positive? Or does the presence of high team cohesion leave athletes feeling pressured not to disappoint highly valued teammates? If athletes consider cohesion to have psychological costs and benefits, what is the nature of these costs and benefits? Subsequent research might shed light on these questions.

A second general, related issue pertains to the positive versus negative consequences of team cohesion. Again, the implicit assumption held by researchers, coaches, and athletes is that higher cohesion is associated with qualitatively better positive consequences for the group. This assumption does have considerable empirical support. Higher team cohesion does lead to better team performance (Mullen & Copper, 1994), greater collective efficacy (Paskevich, 1995), greater work output (Prapavessis & Carron, 1997a), less social loafing (McKnight et al., 1991), and so on. However, in a part tongue-in-cheek, part serious article written over 20 years ago, Buys (1978a, 1978b) proposed that humans would be better without groups. The basis for his claim was that there are a number of negative or destructive behaviors associated with group involvement. These consequences, behaviors such as conformity, groupthink, and deindividuation, for example, are more likely to be manifested when the group is highly cohesive. What about sport? Is greater cohesion in sport teams associated with antisocial or undesirable behavior? Although some research has been undertaken to examine the role that cohesion plays in conformity to undesirable group norms (Shields et al., 1995), these general questions have remained unexplored. One reason for this may be the implicit assumption that team cohesion is a "good thing," that is, a quality that should be developed and enhanced whenever possible.

Topical Analysis Issues in Cohesion Research

The Unit of Analysis

An important question that arises in the measurement of cohesion is What is the appropriate unit of analysis? In the study of group dynamic issues, three approaches have been used (Cota et al., 1995). In the first approach, the individual group member is used as the unit of analysis. The research of Spink and Carron (1993, 1994) of the relationship between individuals' perceptions of cohesiveness and individual exercise adherence behavior in exercise classes provides an example of this approach. For the second approach, researchers have used aggregated group variables (e.g., the group mean) as the unit of analysis. An example of this approach is reflected in Ball and Carron's (1976) research examining the relationship of cohesion to team success in ice hockey. The group average was used to represent the cohesiveness in each team, and performance outcome (i.e., win/loss percentage for each team) was used to represent team success. The third approach is to include the intact group as the unit of analysis. As an example, Widmeyer et al. (1993) focused on the communication, coordination, and cohesion in intramural basketball teams. From researcher observation of these teams, the total amount of communication and coordination among team members was recorded.

Of the three approaches, which one is best? There is no simple answer. When selecting the appropriate unit of analysis, three factors must be considered. The first is the nature of the research question. Some research questions are best answered when a specific level of analysis is selected. For example, if the research question is centered on the relationship of cohesiveness to individual behavior (e.g., adherence to exercise class), then the individual's cognitions about his or her group's cohesion is the primary consideration. In this instance, the individual can be the unit of analysis. The second factor to be considered is the nature of the theory being tested (Cota et al., 1995). For example, in social comparison theory, which is derived from the premise that individuals have a need to compare their behavior, cognitions, and attitudes with those of others to evaluate personal efficacy, the aggregate value can be the unit of analysis.

The third factor that impacts on the appropriate unit of analysis is empirical in nature. The comparison of relationships at the group versus individual level has important applications for theory. That is, in some instances, group level, individual level, or group and individual analyses would provide information of interest. In real groups, individual responses reflect group influences and are thus interdependent, a case of statistical nonindependence. Thus, investigators involved in group research must be sensitive to the issues of level of analysis and nonindependence of responses and use methods that allow the strategy of simultaneously studying the group and the individual.

Methodological Sophistication

Researchers face unique difficulties when they study individuals embedded in small groups. The recognition that individuals, groups, and organizations are not separate conceptual entities but parts of a whole, each affecting and being affected by the other, remains an issue that needs to be further addressed in small group research. A statistical dilemma that exists in group research that has received little attention is the fact that traditional analysis procedures (e.g., ANOVA) proceed from the assumption that observations are independent. As a result, individual effects are analyzed but group effects are ignored. In violating this assumption of independence of responses, estimates of error are biased because group effects make the scores of members more similar than different if a true group effect (i.e., cohesion) is present. Therefore, to avoid overlooking either individual or group effects when examining group cohesion, alternative approaches to the analysis of group data should be considered. These will be discussed next.

Separating Individual- and Group-Level Effects

A statistical technique that allows for the analysis of nonindependence of responses was introduced by Kenny and La Voie (1985). It provides an estimation of both individual- and group-level effects using a hierarchically nested design. Because a given measure may refer to both an individual- and a group-level construct, the simultaneous study of individual and group refers to the similarity and differences of processes at each level (Kenny & La Voie, 1985). By using a nested ANOVA design that treats individuals as members of their respective groups, the ICC provides this information. The ICC can be tested for statistical significance by an F test; if significantly different from zero, there are two levels: group and individual. If not significantly different from zero, then only individual scores can be analyzed. Additional approaches to separate individual- and group-level effects are the use of within-entity and between-entities analysis (WABA) and hierarchical linear modeling (HLM).

Using WABA, researchers may gain a more sophisticated approach when analyzing individual- and group-level effects (Moritz & Watson, 1998). To determine the level at which a phenomenon is occurring (i.e., within entities, between entities, both, or none), WABA uses an integration of different correlational, ANOVA, and analysis of covariance procedures (Dansereau, Alutto, & Yammarino, 1984; Moritz & Watson, 1998). Although WABA has advantages over conventional analysis procedures, there are several limitations when using this method: (1) Until recently WABA had been limited to bivariate relationships; (2) it is not possible to test for cross-level effects (e.g., context and compositional effects); and (3) researchers need to exercise caution when interpreting "mixed" results (i.e., when both individual-level and group-level effects are supported; Moritz & Watson, 1998).

HLM is ideally suited for analyzing many of the questions researchers wish to examine when dealing with small groups. Many sport teams have subgroups nested within their organizational structure (e.g., in football, there are offensive and defensive units, which can be further broken down into subunits). Additionally, much of sport research involves investigating the relationship between athlete outcomes and the characteristics of those groups. Many athletes are located within subgroups within larger groups, and factors at each level could affect performance. Using HLM allows the researcher to simultaneously test individual-level, group-level, and cross-level relationships. Thus, HLM has several advantages and potential uses for small group researchers in the sport and exercise domain (Arnold, 1992).

Consensus versus Consistency

If group members perceive that their team is cohesive, these perceptions should be cognitively held and expressed as shared beliefs (Bandura, 1986; Zaccaro et al., 1995). To determine if this sharing is reflected in the responses of team members, a measurement protocol designed to elicit such responses must be used and the data must be analyzed for the interdependence of responses characteristic of shared beliefs. Essentially, the data should reflect greater homogeneity in responses if beliefs are shared and, in contrast, considerable heterogeneity if they are not. However, commonality in cohesiveness beliefs does not indicate that every member is exactly the same with respect to the group function. Indeed, Bandura (1997) mentioned that complete uniformity would be rare. Empirical demonstrations of shared beliefs (cf. Watson & Chemers, 1998) are not the norm in small group research despite the existence of statistical techniques that allow investigators to detect homogeneity/heterogeneity of responses (cf. Kenny & La Voie, 1985).

One means of considering whether beliefs are shared is to examine the agreement of each group member. Thus, responses to the GEQ could be analyzed with respect to the degree to which members have similar responses, such as how much they agree. This concept has also been referred to as interobserver consensus (cf. Kozlowski & Hattrup, 1992; Moritz & Watson, 1998).

Distinctions between indices of consistency (ICC) and consensus (agreement index) have been made by Kozlowski and Hattrup (1992). Selection of an approach depends on the research question of the investigator (Mitchell, 1979). Consistency refers to the consistency of variance in response among members of a group; agreement refers to the extent to which group members provide the same response (i.e., the degree to which members' responses are interchangeable; Moritz & Watson, 1998). Both indices consider some aspect of sharing. Bandura (1997) noted that a criterion of a shared belief is agreement among group members, but he also notes that "commonality of *beliefs does not mean* that every member is of exactly the same view on every aspect of group functioning—complete uniformity would be rare. . . . A group belief, therefore, is best characterized by a representative value for the beliefs of its members and the degree of variability OR consensus around that central belief" (p. 479).

It is beyond the scope of this portion of the chapter to provide more than a brief summary of analysis strategies. The interested reader should further examine each of the listed procedures to become more fully aware of the benefits and limitations in their approach. However, researchers now have a choice to make in statistical procedures for resolving the unit-of-analysis issue in cohesion research. When this strategy is coupled with a strong rationale for the research question used, the real influence of group effects may be observed.

FUTURE DIRECTIONS FOR RESEARCH ON COHESION IN EXERCISE/PHYSICAL ACTIVITY

Although earlier conclusions made regarding the impact of group cohesion in the exercise domain are encouraging, there are a number of areas in need of future research. Four priority areas can be identified: (1) the examination of the model of group development in physical activity classes, (2) the clarification of the impact of group cohesion in the exercise domain, (3) the examination of the impact of group cohesion on both group and *individual* exercise behavior, and (4) the examination of measurement issues associated with group cohesion.

The model of group development proposed by Brawley and his associates (1987) suggests that an individual is typically drawn to a group due to his or her task motivational base (i.e., ATG-Task). Once involved with the group, task interactions occur, which leads to the development of the group's integration around the task. Once the group is able to manage the interactions around task-related goals, members may then take time to engage in social interactions, which may increase in importance (see issue section earlier in chapter and Figure 18.3). Finally, as the group increases in performing satisfying social interactions, the group members become integrated around those interactions. This model of group development, if present in exercise groups, leads to the hypothesis that the four dimensions of cohesion should have differential prediction over time. That is, the most salient predictor of adherence to a group should first be the ATG-T. Then, following group interaction around the task, GI-T should emerge as the salient predictor. Once the task goals have been managed, ATG-S should develop and become predictive, and finally, once the group integrates around these social interactions, GI-S should be the salient predictor of exercise group adherence.

Interestingly, no research has focused on testing the model of group development in an exercise class setting. Of particular interest would be to examine the natural rate of development of the particular dimensions of cohesion. Insofar as adherence has been examined, could the consistent finding of a relationship between ATG-T be the result of assessments in relatively short exercise programs? The effect of group cohesion on physical activity adherence has been examined in programs of short duration; the modal length of programs was 12 weeks. Further, typically, cohesion was used to describe/predict adherence behavior for only a 4-week block of time; relatively few researchers

have examined the impact of cohesion on long-term participation. Estabrooks and Carron (2000) provide some evidence of the developmental nature of groups described above. They found that GI-S was the best predictor of 4-week adherence in participants who were involved in the exercise group for longer than four months. However, 6 and 12 months later, GI-T was the only significant predictor of adherence. Clearly, research is still needed to determine the developmental nature of physical activity groups.

Once the developmental nature of exercise groups is established, the next research step would be to determine possible interventions to increase either the rate or the magnitude of cohesion development. Research may provide preliminary insight into effective group development interventions. In the exercise domain, it is essential that there is a clarification of the impact of group cohesion. Although the conceptualization of group development is well thought out and should guide adherence research in exercise groups, there is a lack of clear conceptualization regarding the relations between group cohesion and other individual and group outcomes. Figure 18.4 outlines a general heuristic for conceptualizing the impact of group cohesion on individual cognitions, group processes, quality of life, and adherence behavior. As described earlier, recent research has tied the dimensions of group cohesion to a number of individual cognitive variables (e.g., Estabrooks & Carron, 1999).

Although understanding the relation of group cohesion with other cognitive precursors to activity is necessary, other fruitful areas of research would analyze the impact of cohesion on group processes and vice versa. Surprisingly, beyond examining the relationship between group cohesion

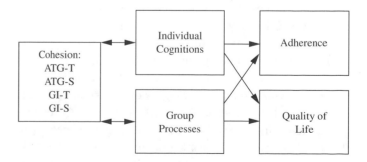

Figure 18.4 A general heuristic to understand the interplay among cohesion, individual cognitions, group processes, adherence behavior, and quality of life. *Note:* ATG-T = Individual Attractions to the Group–Task, ATG-S = Individual Attractions to the Group–Social, GI-T = Group Integration–Task, GI-S = Group Integration–Social.

and group structure (Carron & Spink, 1995), no other group processes have been observed in concert with cohesion in exercise groups. A further area in need of assessment is the relationship between group cohesion and quality of life. This line of inquiry may be more salient in populations where social isolation is a threat (e.g., AIDS carriers). It could be hypothesized that being a member of a cohesive exercise group could improve the quality of life of those involved. There is currently no framework from which to hypothesize the relations between group cohesion and these variables in an exercise group setting.

Although previous research has examined the effect of group cohesion on exercise behavior almost exclusively within the group, there is some evidence that group cohesion may impact both group and individual exercise behavior. Anecdotally, the popular television talk show host Rosie O'Donnell has developed an Internet "group" of exercisers. The individuals involved in the group enjoy interaction and communication back and forth over e-mail or in chat rooms; they set a group goal (to complete a 5-kilometer race) and gave themselves a distinctive name (the Chub Club). Clearly, most of the necessary components to categorize this club as a group were present. Interestingly, most physical activity behavior was done alone and away from the group. Therefore, one could argue that this is a group intervention to increase activity and that it is promoting individual activity. More empirically, Brawley and his associates (Brawley, Rejeski, & Lutes, 2000) found that a group-mediated intervention improved home-based exercise frequency. It is unfortunate that the impact of cohesion cannot be determined from either anecdotal or empirical support thus far. Hence, future research is necessary to determine what dimensions of cohesion are salient for promoting individual behavior away from the group.

Finally, although the conceptual model of cohesion, as outlined by Carron et al. (1985), may have universal application to different types of groups, there is some question regarding the universal applicability of the GEQ. In particular, in research examining older adults (Estabrooks & Carron, 1999b, 2000, in press), two persistent problems have arisen that question the utility of the GEQ for this population. First, there is issue with the psychometrics of the test. For example, for some samples, the internal consistency values for specific scales have been marginal, that is, < .70 (e.g., Estabrooks & Carron, in press a, Study 1). For other samples (e.g., Estabrooks & Carron, 1999b, Study 2), the entire data set was unusable because the internal consistency values on all scales were less than .60. Second, many participants expressed dissatisfaction, confusion, or

uncertainty when they completed the questionnaire. The GEQ contains a number of negatively worded items, for example, "This exercise group does not give me enough opportunities to improve my personal fitness." Thus, a greater perception of cohesion would be manifested in a stronger level of disagreement with the statement. However, many older participants find a negative item either difficult to interpret or are uneasy about considering their group in a negative light.

As a consequence, Estabrooks and Carron (in press b) developed the Physical Activity Environment Questionnaire to assess group cohesion in older adults. By following the protocol outlined by Carron and his associates (1985), the new measure was found to possess adequate reliability, and content, concurrent, and predictive validity. (For a complete description, see Estabrooks and Carron, in press b.) By following a documented protocol based on the conceptual model of group cohesion, measures for special populations can be developed. That is not to say that every researcher needs to develop a new measure for every different group or population, but when there are concerns regarding participant ability to complete the GEQ (e.g., preadolescents), a structured process exists whereby a new measure may be developed.

Other cohesion research advances relative to exercise and physical activity both relate to the measurement of cohesion in different social contexts. The two examples presented are from research in progress. The first study is an example of developing and using a measure to examine cohesion among Francophone walking clubs. The second study is an example of measuring cohesion as an indirect outcome of a group-motivated behavior change intervention. Both examples illustrate the use of the guidelines discussed as part of the issues section of this chapter.

Cohesion in Walking Clubs

As part of a larger study whose purpose was to examine exercise adherence in a French Canadian culture, Gauvin and Brawley (1999, as cited in Brawley et al., 1999) developed a Francophone measure of cohesion for walking clubs. The goal was to measure the cohesion in these unique physical activity groups to examine the possibility that cohesion was related to or was a potential determinant of exercise adherence. To follow a blueprint or framework for measurement development, the four-dimensional conceptual model of Carron et al. (1998) was used with the following rationale. Walking groups are developed through a club format for the specific purposes of obtaining exercise (task) in a supportive and social context (social).

These two core purposes for walking groups offer potential for the group to reflect all four dimensions of cohesion. Obviously, the walking clubs are attractive to potential group members for the provision of task fulfillment and social needs, such as the need to belong to a group where social opportunities are available (cf. Baumeister & Leary, 1995). In brief, the individual task and social needs of group members are satisfied (i.e., individual attractions to the group–task and social).

These clubs also provide the opportunity for members to unite around common goals of walking for personal fitness and accomplishing specific types of exercise sessions (e.g., variations in intensity, duration, routes, distances, and goals). Similarly, the unity around the group tasks provokes interactions among club members that may start to become more social once that it is obvious that the club's walking goals are being accomplished and members' task needs are being satisfied. Thus, unity may occur around group-oriented social interactions (e.g., club breakfasts, festive occasions, etc.). In summary, over time, the interactions of club members lead to common perceptions of group task and social unity (i.e., group integration–task and social).

The method to develop the walking club cohesion instrument followed the guidelines outlined earlier (also see Carron & Brawley, 2000; Carron et al., 1998). Briefly, the strategies used were: (1) expert input about cohesion, (2) development of manifestations of cohesion characteristic of group behavior within the walking club and of satisfactions with member needs, and (3) writing items reflecting these manifestations in French and then back-translating so that both language and cultural communication was correctly conveyed and meaning between English/French items was not lost. Because data gathering methods involved a phone interview protocol, both the questions about the walking club and the interview's presentation needed to be crystal clear and consistent.

Eleven clubs were sampled and ranged in membership size from 5 to 69 ($N = 250$). Larger clubs had subgroup members who walked together regularly. These groups varied in size from 3 to more than 30 members being active together at any one time. A 20-item instrument was the initially developed measure to which club members responded. Illustrated are the changes from original content of the GEQ for sport with the following English examples of items:

ATG-T: "I like walking with my group because I can walk at a challenging pace."

GI-T: "In my group, we believe that our walking speed satisfies group goals for health and fitness."

ATG-S: "I like walking with my group because there is a lot of camaraderie."

GI-S: "In my group, if someone misses sessions we believe a group member should contact that person."

Initial psychometric analyses suggested that four dimensions were perceived (as constructed) by group members. Preliminary factor analyses revealed loadings of items to dimensions. Recommended "rules of thumb" for retaining items (Tabachnick & Fidell, 1996), with a minimum loading value of greater than .40 resulted in 14 retained items (loadings exceeding .58). Interfactor correlations ranged between .29 and .53.

The walking club cohesion measure was used to examine a research question about the determinants of cohesion in this social setting. Therefore, the major hypothesized determinants, such as attitudes toward health outcomes, values of those outcomes, psychological well-being, and health expectancies, were used to predict the four aspects of cohesion that follow. Attitudes toward health outcomes and the value of social outcomes of walking were major predictors of GI-T (R^2 adj. – .25). Expectancies for health outcomes and task-related social support best predicted ATG-T (R^2 adj. – .10). Both of the task cohesion regression models were significant ($p < .01$), with the common link being attitudes and expectancies toward health-related task outcomes.

For the social aspect of cohesion, the values of social outcomes of being in the walking club and the psychological well-being that is found through walking were the best predictors of group integration–social (R^2 adj. = 42.0). Both of the social cohesion regression models were also significant ($p < .01$), with the most common predictors being the values of social outcomes of club membership and the psychological well-being achieved relative to walking. One suggested reason for the relationships of the predictors to cohesion may be that members of cohesion groups share beliefs related to the group (e.g., attitudes and values toward the health outcomes of physical activity/walking). The strength of each group member's individual beliefs have similarity that is developed as a function of interactions with other walking club members over time (cf. Hinsz et al., 1997).

Group-Mediated Behavior Change

Brawley et al. (2000) reported the results of a group-mediated intervention to promote adherence to independent physical activity in a sedentary healthy elderly population.

The group and each of its members were the targets of behavior change (i.e., increased physical activity). Both the group and its unity were systematically developed within the group to motivate members to learn how to change personal behavior. The researchers hypothesized that this intervention would maintain long-term adherence to independent physical activity six months after a three-month period of combined behavior change and exercise training. Further, they hypothesized that this maintenance would be better than that experienced by a group that received structured exercise training or a wait-list control group. The results of the study supported the hypothesis. At nine months, after three months of no staff contact or group interaction, the group-motivated intervention not only maintained postclinic exercise adherence but also increased individual home-based activity beyond that observed at the three-month level. Perceptions of health-related quality of life were also increased in both the intervention and the standard exercise training group in comparison to the sedentary wait-list control group.

One question that arises as a result of this research is: What were the specific group influences involved in the intervention? A logical focus of this question would be to examine the cohesiveness of the group as one of several process-oriented variables that might be related to the outcomes of adherence (see earlier discussions in this chapter). Although it was not the specific purpose of Brawley et al. (2000) to develop and measure cohesiveness as an outcome of their intervention, such a research goal would be a logical target for related research.

Building on the knowledge obtained in this intervention with asymptomatic elderly, Rejeski, Brawley, and Brubaker (in progress, as cited in Brawley et al., 1999) initiated a randomized clinical trial (RCT) that used a similar version of the Brawley et al. (2000) intervention with patients engaged in cardiac rehabilitation. The purpose of this RCT (Cardiac Health and Activity Maintenance Program: CHAMP) was to contrast the traditional three-month cardiac rehabilitation approach with an intervention that added a group-motivated lifestyle activity intervention to the clinical delivery of rehabilitation. Patients were elderly individuals who had cardiovascular disorders. The RCT had two arms, one offering standard care and the other offering the group-mediated intervention. Intervention patients experienced a three-month clinical phase where the primary aspects of the intervention and standard care were delivered. They then continued their rehabilitation in a three-month home-based phase where staff contact, and for the intervention, group contact, was gradually removed. Finally, patients continued their home-based rehabilitation and lifestyle change for six months, when they were completely independent. The hypothesis is that the group-mediated intervention will better maintain adherence to activity than the standard care condition.

Although this RCT is still underway (i.e., in its third of four years), one important issue is to confirm that group processes are functioning in the group intervention. Cohesion would be one overall manifestation of the types of manipulations being applied to the group and unity of common purpose (i.e., independent physical activity). Two of several key intervention group manipulations are to develop a group with a common goal accepted by each member (i.e., learning to be an independent exerciser), and group goal setting using the independent exercise of each patient as a contribution to the overall goal. If these manipulations and the development of the group are effective, the intervention group should be united around its task-oriented goals (i.e., be cohesive). Thus, the investigators developed a task cohesion measure based on the conceptual model described in this chapter. Although the RCT is still underway, this in-progress example illustrates a way in which cohesion can be examined beyond the context of a sport group using the same conceptual model.

SUMMARY

The research advances in cohesion are proceeding in many new directions in sport and, recently, in exercise and physical activity. The advances in this chapter have been illustrated with examples from the most recently published and in-progress studies. At the center of these advances is a common conceptual model of cohesion that serves as the foundation for new research questions, measurement development, and methodology. The model was used to outline the perspectives relevant to definitional, conceptual, and measurement considerations for current and future research. To provide a perspective for future research, a summary of past and present correlates of cohesion was presented in sport, categorized as personal, environmental, leadership, team, and performance correlates; and exercise, categorized as adherence, team-building, and social-cognitive correlates. Also discussed were the issues important to making research advances, such as the multi-dimensional nature of the cohesion construct, the level of development of the group, the social context in which the group exists, relevant links from concept to operational definition, and the type of validation data necessary for research to be considered an advancement.

Future directions and recent research examined as *common* to sport and exercise were new context-specific measures, the negative side of cohesion, and appropriate analyses of group and individual effects. Future directions examined as *specific* to exercise/physical activity were exercise–group development and the impact of cohesion. Also discussed was the impact of cohesion on individual exercise behavior and the consequences of cohesion such as enhanced quality of life. Other new directions described were group cohesion measures that take into account age-related goals and objectives of seniors' exercise groups, positive psychological consequences of being in specialized exercise groups (e.g., walking clubs), and group-mediated interventions designed to promote older adults' independent self-regulation of physical activity. For investigators to better understand the advantages and the liabilities of delivering physical activity in a group context, or how to encourage individuals to be active through the motivating forces of a group, more group research must be conducted in the context of physical activity. Examples provided should stimulate new thinking and at the same time emphasize the need for careful research based on sound models and measurement.

For research to advance, the simple description of the correlates of cohesion will not suffice. The processes that make groups powerful motivating agents that unite people around a common goal must be understood. Cohesion is a manifestation of group processes that may moderate desirable personal outcomes of being in a group and desirable group products. However, these outcomes will not be fully understood without research that focuses on these processes. Without such research advances, interventions that are designed to manipulate group processes to stimulate group cohesion have only a chance probability of success. This chapter describes new directions with clear paths for investigators to either challenge or follow. In 5 to 10 years, future reviews of cohesion research will determine if these paths are well traveled and if new "maps" of advances in cohesion research have been drawn.

REFERENCES

Ajzen, I. (1985). From intentions to actions: A theory of planned behavior. In J. Kuhl & J. Beckmann (Eds.), *Action-control from cognitions to behavior* (pp. 11–39). Heidelberg, Germany: Springer.

Arnold, C.L. (1992). An introduction to hierarchical linear models. *Measurement and Evaluation in Counseling and Development, 25,* 58–90.

Ball, J., & Carron, A.V. (1976). The influence of team cohesion and participation motivation upon performance success in intercollegiate ice hockey. *Canadian Journal of Applied Sport Sciences, 1,* 271–275.

Bandura, A. (1986). *Social foundations of thought and action.* Englewood Cliffs, NJ: Prentice-Hall.

Bandura, A. (1997). *Self-efficacy: The exercise of control.* New York: Freeman.

Baumeister, R.F., & Leary, M.R. (1995). The need to belong: Desire for interpersonal attachment as a fundamental human motivation. *Psychological Bulletin, 117,* 497–529.

Brawley, L.R., Carron, A.V., Paskevich, D.M., & Estabrooks, P. (1999, June). *Topical issues in cohesion research.* Paper presented at the North American Society for Psychology of Sport and Physical Activity conference, Clearwater Beach, FL.

Brawley, L.R., Carron, A.V., & Widmeyer, W.N. (1987). Assessing the cohesion of teams: Validity of the Group Environment Questionnaire. *Journal of Sport Psychology, 9,* 275–294.

Brawley, L.R., Carron, A.V., & Widmeyer, W.N. (1988). Exploring the relationship between cohesion and group resistance to disruption. *Journal of Sport & Exercise Psychology, 10,* 199–213.

Brawley, L.R., Carron, A.V., & Widmeyer, W.N. (1993). The influence of the group and its cohesiveness on perceptions of group-related variables. *Journal of Sport & Exercise Psychology, 15,* 245–260.

Brawley, L.R., Rejeski, W.J., & Lutes, L. (2000). A group-mediated cognitive behavioral intervention for increasing adherence to physical activity in older adults. *Journal of Applied Biobehavioral Research, 5,* 47–65.

Buys, C.J. (1978a). On "humans would do better without groups": A final note. *Personality and Social Psychology Bulletin, 4,* 568.

Buys, C.J. (1978b). Humans would do better without groups. *Personality and Social Psychology Bulletin, 4,* 123–125.

Carron, A.V., & Brawley, L.R. (2000). Cohesion: Conceptual and measurement issues. *Small Group Research, 31,* 89–106.

Carron, A.V., Brawley, L.R., & Widmeyer, W.N. (1990). The impact of group size in an exercise setting. *Journal of Sport & Exercise Psychology, 12,* 376–387.

Carron, A.V., Brawley, L.R., & Widmeyer, W.N. (1998). The measurement of cohesiveness in sport groups. In J.L. Duda (Ed.), *Advances in sport and exercise psychology measurement* (pp. 213–226). Morgantown, WV: Fitness Information Technology.

Carron, A.V., Estabrooks, P., Paskevich, D.M., & Brawley, L.R. (1999, June). *Advances in cohesion research: Issues, correlates, and new directions.* Paper presented at the North American Society for Psychology of Sport and Physical Activity Conference, Clearwater Beach, FL.

Carron, A.V., & Prapavessis, H. (1997). Self-presentation and group influence. *Small Group Research, 28,* 500–516.

Carron, A.V., Prapavessis, H., & Grove, J.R. (1994). Group effects and self-handicapping. *Journal of Sport & Exercise Psychology, 16,* 246–258.

Carron, A.V., & Spink, K.S. (1993). Team building in an exercise setting. *The Sport Psychologist, 7,* 8–18.

Carron, A.V., & Spink, K.S. (1995). The group-size cohesion relationship in minimal groups. *Small Group Research, 26,* 86–105.

Carron, A.V., Widmeyer, W.N., & Brawley, L.R. (1985). The development of an instrument to assess cohesion in sport teams: The Group Environment Questionnaire. *Journal of Sport Psychology, 7,* 244–266.

Carron, A.V., Widmeyer, W.N., & Brawley, L.R. (1988). Group cohesion and individual adherence to physical activity. *Journal of Sport & Exercise Psychology, 10,* 119–126.

Cota, A.A., Evans, C.R., Dion, K.L., Kilik, L., & Longman, R.S. (1995). The structure of group cohesion. *Personality and Social Psychology Bulletin, 21,* 572–580.

Courneya, K.S. (1995). Cohesion correlates with affect in structured exercise classes. *Perceptual and Motor Skills, 81,* 1021–1022.

Dansereau, F., Alutto, J.A., & Yammarino, F.J. (1984). *Theory testing in organizational behavior: The variant approach.* Englewood Cliffs, NJ: Prentice-Hall.

Dawe, S.W.L., & Carron, A.V. (1990, October). *Interrelationships among role acceptance, role clarity, task cohesion, and social cohesion.* Paper presented at the meeting of the Canadian Society for Psychomotor Learning and Sport Psychology, Windsor, Canada.

Dion, K.L., & Evans, C.R. (1992). On cohesiveness: Reply to Keyton and other critics of the construct. *Small Group Research, 23,* 242–250.

Dorsch, K.D., Paskevich, D.M., Brawley, L.R., & Widmeyer, W.N. (1996). Collective efficacy as shared beliefs: Implications for the group as the unit of analysis. *Journal of Sport & Exercise Psychology, 18,* S26.

Dorsch, K.D., Paskevich, D.M., Widmeyer, W.N., & Brawley, L.R. (1994, October). *Exploring relationships between cohesion, collective efficacy for, and acceptability of aggression in ice hockey.* Paper presented at the annual meeting of the Canadian Society for Psychomotor Learning and Sport Psychology, Hamilton, Canada.

Dorsch, K.D., Widmeyer, W.N., Paskevich, D.M., & Brawley, L.R. (1995). Collective efficacy: Its measurement and relationship to cohesion in ice hockey. *Journal of Applied Sport Psychology, 7,* S56.

Duda, J.L., & Hayashi, C.T. (1998). Measurement issues in cross-cultural research within sport and exercise psychology. In J.L. Duda (Ed.), *Advances in sport and exercise psychology measurement* (pp. 471–482). Morgantown, WV: Fitness Information Technology.

Eisman, B. (1959). Some operational measures of cohesiveness and their interrelations. *Human Relations, 12,* 183–189.

Estabrooks, P.A., & Carron, A.V. (1999a). Group cohesion in older adult exercisers: Prediction and intervention effects. *Journal of Behavioral Medicine, 22,* 575–588.

Estabrooks, P.A., & Carron, A.V. (1999b). The role of the group with elderly exercisers. *Small Group Research, 30,* 438–452.

Estabrooks, P.A., & Carron, A.V. (2000). Predicting self-efficacy in elderly exercisers: The role of recent experience and task cohesion. *Journal of Aging and Physical Activity, 8,* 41–50.

Estabrooks, P.A., & Carron, A.V. (in press). The Physical Activity Environment Questionnaire: An instrument for the assessment of cohesion in exercise classes. *Group Dynamics.*

Festinger, L., Schachter, S., & Back, K. (1950). *Social pressure in informal groups.* New York: Harper & Row.

Golembiewski, R. (1962). *The small group.* Chicago: University of Chicago Press.

Granito, V., & Rainey, D. (1988). Differences in cohesion between high school and college football teams and starters and nonstarters. *Perceptual and Motor Skills, 66,* 471–477.

Gross, N., & Martin, W. (1952). On group cohesion. *American Journal of Sociology, 57,* 533–546.

Hausenblas, H.A., & Carron, A.V. (1996). Group cohesion and self-handicapping in female and male athletes. *Journal of Sport & Exercise Psychology, 18,* 132–143.

Hinsz, V.B., Tinsdale, R.S., & Vollrath, D.A. (1997). The emerging conceptualization of groups as information processors. *Psychological Bulletin, 121,* 43–64.

Karau, S.J., & Williams, K.D. (1993). Social loafing: A meta-analytic review and theoretical integration. *Journal of Personality and Social Psychology, 65,* 681–706.

Keller, R.T. (1986). Predictors of the performance of project groups in R&D organizations. *Academy of Management Journal, 29,* 715–726.

Kenny, D.A., & La Voie, L. (1985). Separating individual and group effects. *Journal of Personality and Social Psychology, 48,* 339–348.

Kozlowski, S.W.J., & Hattrup, K. (1992). A disagreement about within-group agreement: Disentangling issues of consistency versus consensus. *Journal of Applied Psychology, 77,* 161–167.

Kozub, S.A. (1993). *Exploring the relationships among coaching behavior, team cohesion, and player leadership.* Unpublished doctoral dissertation, University of Houston, TX.

Latane, B. (1981). The psychology of social impact. *American Psychologist, 36,* 343–356.

Latane, B., Williams, K.D., & Harkins, S.G. (1979). Many hands make light the work: The causes and consequences of social loafing. *Journal of Personality and Social Psychology, 37,* 822–832.

Leary, M.J. (1992). *Understanding social anxiety.* Beverly Hills, CA: Sage.

Leary, M.J., & Kowalski, R.M. (1990). Impression management: A literature review and two component models. *Psychological Bulletin, 107,* 34–47.

Levine, J.M., & Moreland, R.L. (1991). Culture and socialization in work groups. In L.B. Resnick, J.M. Levine, & S.D. Teasley (Eds.), *Perspectives on socially shared cognition* (pp. 257–282). Washington, DC: American Psychological Association.

Levine, J.M., Resnick, L.B., & Higgins, E.T. (1993). Social foundations of cognition. *Annual Review of Psychology, 44,* 585–612.

Libo, L. (1953). *Measuring group cohesiveness.* Ann Arbor: University of Michigan Press.

Lott, A.J., & Lott, B.E. (1965). Group cohesiveness as interpersonal attraction: A review of relationships with antecedent and consequent variables. *Psychological Bulletin, 64,* 259–309.

Manning, F.J., & Fullerton, T.D. (1988). Health and well-being in highly cohesive units of the U.S. Army. *Journal of Applied Social Psychology, 18,* 503–519.

McGrath, J. (1962). The influence of positive interpersonal relations on adjustment and effectiveness in rifle teams. *Journal of Abnormal and Social Psychology, 65,* 365–375.

McKnight, P., Williams, J.M., & Widmeyer, W.N. (1991, October). *The effects of cohesion and identifiability on reducing the likelihood of social loafing.* Paper presented at the Association for the Advancement of Applied Sport Psychology annual conference, Savannah, GA.

Mitchell, S.K. (1979). Interobserver agreement, reliability, and generalizability of data collected in observational studies. *Psychological Bulletin, 86,* 376–390.

Moritz, S.E., & Watson, C.B. (1998). Levels of analysis issues in group psychology: Using efficacy as an example of a multilevel model. *Group Dynamics: Theory, Research, and Practice, 2,* 1–14.

Mudrack, P.E. (1989). Defining group cohesiveness: A legacy of confusion. *Small Group Behavior, 20,* 37–49.

Mullen, B., & Copper, C. (1994). The relation between group cohesiveness and performance: An integration. *Psychological Bulletin, 115,* 210–227.

Nunnally, J.C. (1978). *Psychometric theory.* New York: McGraw-Hill.

Paskevich, D.M. (1995). *Conceptual and measurement factors of collective efficacy in its relationship to cohesion and performance outcome.* Unpublished doctoral dissertation, University of Waterloo, Canada.

Paskevich, D.M., Brawley, L.R., Dorsch, K.D., & Widmeyer, W.N. (1995). Implications of individual and group level analyses applied to the study of collective efficacy and cohesion. *Journal of Applied Sport Psychology, 7,* S95.

Paskevich, D.M., Brawley, L.R., Dorsch, K.D., & Widmeyer, W.N. (1997, September). *Collective efficacy, cohesion, and performance: Evidence for reliable, strong effects.* Paper presented at the annual meeting of the Association for the Advancement of Applied Sport Psychology, San Diego, CA.

Paskevich, D.M., Brawley, L.R., Dorsch, K.D., & Widmeyer, W.N. (1999). Relationship between collective efficacy and team cohesion: Conceptual and measurement issues. *Group Dynamics: Theory, Research, and Practice, 3,* 210–222.

Peterroy, E.T. (1983). Cohesiveness development in an ongoing therapy group: An exploratory study. *Small Group Behavior, 14,* 269–272.

Prapavessis, H., & Carron, A.V. (1997a). Cohesion and work output. *Small Group Research, 28,* 294–301.

Prapavessis, H., & Carron, A.V. (1997b). The role of sacrifice in the dynamics of sport teams. *Group Dynamics, 1,* 231–240.

Roark, A.E., & Sharah, H.S. (1989). Factors related to group cohesiveness. *Small Group Behavior, 20,* 62–69.

Schutz, R.W., Eom, H.J., Smoll, F.L., & Smith, R.E. (1994). Examination of the factorial validity of the Group Environment Questionnaire. *Research Quarterly for Exercise and Sport, 65,* 226–236.

Shaw, M.E., & Shaw, L.M. (1962). Some effects of sociometric grouping on learning in a second grade classroom. *Journal of Social Psychology, 57,* 453–458.

Sherif, M., & Sherif, C.W. (1969). *Social psychology.* New York: Harper & Row.

Shields, D.L., Bredemeier, B.J., Gardner, D.E., & Boston, A. (1995). Leadership, cohesion, and team norms regarding cheating and aggression. *Sociology of Sport Journal, 12,* 324–336.

Spink, K.S., & Carron, A.V. (1992). Group cohesion and adherence in exercise classes. *Journal of Sport & Exercise Psychology, 14,* 78–86.

Spink, K.S., & Carron, A.V. (1993). The effects of team building on the adherence patterns of female exercise participants. *Journal of Sport & Exercise Psychology, 15,* 39–49.

Spink, K.S., & Carron, A.V. (1994). Group cohesion effects in exercise classes. *Small Group Research, 25,* 26–42.

Tabachnick, B.G., & Fidell, L.S. (1996). *Using multivariate statistics* (3rd ed.). New York: HarperCollins.

Trist, E., & Bamforth, K. (1951). Some social and psychological consequences of the long-wall method of coal mining. *Human Relations, 4,* 3–38.

Watson, C.B., & Chemers, M.M. (1998, August). *The rise of shared perceptions: A multi-level analysis of collective efficacy.* Paper presented at the annual convention of the Academy of Management, San Diego, CA.

Westre, K., & Weiss, M. (1991). The relationship between perceived coaching behaviors and group cohesion in high school football teams. *The Sport Psychologist, 5,* 41–54.

Widmeyer, W.N., Brawley, L.R., & Carron, A.V. (1985). *The measurement of cohesion in sport teams: The Group Environment Questionnaire.* London, Canada: Sports Dynamics.

Widmeyer, W.N., Brawley, L.R., & Carron, A.V. (1988). How many should I carry on my team? Consequences of group size. *Psychology of Motor Behavior and Sport: Abstracts 1988.* Knoxville, TN: North American Society for the Psychology of Sport and Physical Activity.

Widmeyer, W.N., Brawley, L.R., & Carron, A.V. (1990). Group size in sport. *Journal of Sport & Exercise Psychology, 12,* 177–190.

Widmeyer, W.N., Carron, A.V., & Brawley, L.R. (1993). The cohesion-performance outcome relationship with teams as the unit of analysis. *Journal of Sport & Exercise Psychology, 15,* S90.

Williams, K., Harkins, S., & Latane, B. (1981). Identifiability as a deterrent to social loafing: Two cheering experiments. *Journal of Personality and Social Psychology, 40,* 303–311.

Williams, K., Nida, S.A., Baca, L.D., & Latane, B. (1989). Social loafing and swimming: Effects of indentifiability on individual and relay performance of intercollegiate swimmers. *Basic and Applied Social Psychology, 10,* 73–81.

Zaccaro, S.J., Blair, V., Peterson, C., & Zazanis, M. (1995). Collective efficacy. In J. Maddux (Ed.), *Self-efficacy, adaptation, and adjustment* (pp. 305–328). New York: Plenum Press.

Zaccaro, S.J., & Lowe, C.A. (1986). Cohesiveness and performance on an additive task: Evidence of multidimensionality. *Journal of Social Psychology, 128,* 547–558.

PART IV

Psychological Techniques for Individual Performance

CHAPTER 19

Goal Setting in Sport
Investigating the Goal Effectiveness Paradox

DAMON BURTON, SARAH NAYLOR, and BERNIE HOLLIDAY

An exponential explosion of goal setting research in sport has occurred in the seven years since the first edition of the *Handbook* was published. A quick review of the suddenly extensive competitive goal literature prompts two inescapable conclusions: First, goals work well in sport, but not as well as in business; second, goal setting is a paradox because this simple technique is somewhat more complicated than it looks, at least if one hopes to maximize the effectiveness of setting goals to improve competitive performance. Recent studies of the goal setting patterns of adolescent, collegiate, and Olympic athletes (Burton, Weinberg, Yukelson, & Weigand, 1998; Burton, Weinberg, Yukelson, & Weigand, in preparation; Weinberg, Burke, & Jackson, 1997; Weinberg, Burton, Yukelson, & Weigand, 1993; Weinberg, Burton, Yukelson, & Weigand, in press) have confirmed that almost all athletes set goals, but on average, most of them rate goals as only moderately effective. Thus, athletes intuitively know goals can help, but they have trouble figuring out how to best set goals to maximize their effectiveness. The consensus of an extensive review of goal setting research in sport and physical activity also concludes that goal setting is an extremely effective strategy to enhance performance, but those results are considerably less consistent and robust than findings for the general goal setting literature. Although a number of explanations warrant attention, this chapter focuses on the role of goal implementation strategies as a major factor responsible for why goals are less effective in sport.

Therefore, the primary purpose of this chapter is to review existing theory and research on goal setting, with the intent of better understanding the goal setting process and how to maximize the effectiveness of setting goals in sport. In the first section, goal setting is defined, including clarification of what goals are, their primary psychological func-

tions, and the role of goals in such divergent constructs as motivation and stress. In the second section, theory and research on goal setting are reviewed, highlighting the role that goal attributes such as focus, specificity, difficulty, valence, proximity, and collectivity play in goal effectiveness. The third section describes explanations of why goals work less effectively in sport as compared to other domains. The major components of the goal setting process are delineated in the fourth section, including identification of problem areas that often limit goal setting effectiveness. Finally, the last section addresses future directions in goal setting research, highlighting six important issues that seemingly impact goal effectiveness

WHAT ARE GOALS?

William James prefaced his classic definition of attention by saying "Everyone knows what attention is" (1890, p. 455). It is tempting to define goal setting in a similar way, because it is one of the most commonly used performance-enhancement strategies in psychology, with both researchers and practitioners assuming that the concept has a straightforward meaning. Webster's *New World Dictionary* defines a goal as "an object or end that one strives to attain; an aim." The world's most prolific goal setting researcher, Edwin Locke, takes a similar approach in defining a goal simply as "what an individual is trying to accomplish; it is the object or aim of an action" (Locke, Shaw, Saari, & Latham, 1981, p. 126).

Locke's approach to goals is grounded in objectivism, emphasizing that behavior is purposeful and human beings are rational beings who have survived by using their intellect to govern their behavior. Although goal setting has been described by many terms, including "level of aspiration" in the early years and "management by objectives" in business contexts, the term "goal" is commonly used today in a vast array of disciplines and contexts to refer to these cognitive regulators of behavior. Ryan (1970, p. 18) noted that "to the layman it seems a simple fact that human behavior is affected by conscious purposes, plans, intentions, tasks, and the like." As easy as it might be to accept goals as the tools necessary to pursue goal-directed behavior, goals do not necessarily work at a conscious level all the time. Locke and Latham (1990a) emphasize that goals enter and recede from conscious awareness at different times. For example, focusing on winning a game may be disruptive to performance because it interferes with actions needed to reach the goal. Particularly with a skill that has become somewhat automated like a jump shot in basketball or a drop volley in tennis, goals help to initiate action, but once initiated, little conscious control is needed to pursue those goals effectively.

Every goal includes two basic components: direction and the amount or quality of the product. Direction implies choice, specifically the choice about how to direct or focus one's behavior, whereas amount or quality suggests a minimal standard of performance that must be attained. For example, when a high school athlete sets a goal to make the varsity basketball team, a choice is involved to pursue basketball instead of competing winter sports or other extracurricular activities. Moreover, it also connotes a commitment on the part of the athlete to work on developing basketball skills to a high enough level to be selected for the high school varsity team.

Thus, goals are cognitive mechanisms that describe what an individual is trying to accomplish, an aim or objective. Goals can enter or recede from consciousness at different times depending on the demands of the situation, and they have both direction and amount/quality dimensions that focus one's behavior and provide a minimal standard for performance to be attained.

Goal Mechanisms: How Goals Work

How do goals work? Goal theorists (e.g., Locke, 1968; Locke & Latham, 1990a) have recognized the importance of four mechanisms that underlie the goal setting process. According to Locke and his colleagues, goals enhance performance by (1) directing action by focusing attention on specific task(s), (2) increasing effort and intensity, (3) encouraging persistence in the face of failure or adversity, and (4) promoting the development of new task or problem-solving strategies. The direct, short-term motivational function of goals is most readily apparent with the first three goal mechanisms, whereas development of new task strategies is often a more indirect, long-term process

that may be necessary with complex tasks or when confronting failure or adversity. That is, as long as the task is relatively simple and straightforward and athletes can perform the skill effectively, the motivational benefits of goals should prompt direct improvement in the quantity and/or quality of performance. However, for highly complex tasks or when confronted with problems during the learning or execution of proper skill mechanics, direct motivational goal mechanisms designed to enhance the quantity and/or quality of performance may not be enough to ensure that athletes attain their goals. Developing new task strategies involves working smarter as well as longer and harder.

For example, a basketball coach whose team shoots free throws poorly may choose to set a goal designed to increase the team's competitive free throw percentage by developing an action plan that calls for players to shoot 500 free throws each day in practice. Regrettably, the motivational benefits of such a goal will probably be ineffective if the players have major flaws in their free throw mechanics, do not utilize the same routine shooting free throws in practice that they use in competition, or become distracted during stressful competitive free throw situations. Thus, developing new task strategies would focus on making desirable changes in shooting form, developing a consistent routine that is used in both practice and competition, and/or remaining focused on positive performance cues during pressure-packed free throw situations before using the motivational benefits of goals to automate new shooting fundamentals.

State and Trait Conceptions of Goals

The concept of goals is currently used in two major ways. First, industrial and organizational psychologists such as Locke and his colleagues (Locke & Latham, 1990a; Locke et al., 1981) view goals as direct, specific motivational strategies. In this context, goals function primarily like a psychological state, providing a specific standard that serves to motivate individuals to focus their attention and improve efforts at attaining a particular quantity or quality of performance. Similarly, stress researchers such as Lazarus and his colleagues (1991; Lazarus & Folkman, 1984) use the concept of specific goals as an important component of stress models, conceptualizing that stress will occur when individuals become challenged and/or threatened about their ability to attain important goals. In both cases, the state conception of goals focuses on attaining a goal in a particular situation for a specific purpose. In one case, the prospect of success should engender personal motivation, and in the other, the threat of failure should promote perceived stress.

Several contemporary motivation theorists (Dweck, 1980; Elliott & Dweck, 1988; Maehr & Braskamp, 1986; Maehr & Nicholls, 1980; Nicholls, 1984a, 1984b) use the notion of goals in a second way to suggest a more global purpose for involvement in particular activities. Goals in this context are more like personality traits, implying predispositions for participation based on underlying motives for what individuals want to attain or accomplish and how they view ability and define success and failure. Motivation theorists often label these more global goals "goal orientations" (e.g., Elliott & Dweck, 1988; Maehr & Braskamp, 1986; Maehr & Nicholls, 1980; Nicholls, 1984a, 1984b). Inherent in the idea of goal orientations is the premise that success and failure are subjective perceptions, not objective events. Thus, success can be attained in any situation in which individuals are able to either infer personally desirable characteristics, qualities, or attributes about themselves or attain personally meaningful objectives (Maehr & Braskamp, 1986). Dweck (1999) emphasizes that goal orientations reflect underlying theories of ability about what ability means as well as how it develops. Even though these two conceptions of goals have a different focus, they appear to be highly complementary, with discrete goals serving as the tools for achieving more global goal orientations.

GOAL SETTING THEORY AND RESEARCH

The primary question in assessing any intervention strategy is whether it works. Goal setting has been a topic of great interest to researchers and practitioners, with empirical interest centered around testing the efficacy of goals for enhancing performance in organization/industrial (Locke & Latham, 1990a) and sport settings (Burton, 1992, 1993; Kyllo & Landers, 1995; Weinberg, 1994). This section focuses on summarizing general and sport goal setting research, highlighting goal attribute research and drawing specific conclusions about the types of goals that should be most beneficial in sport and physical activity.

Overall Goal Setting Effectiveness

The consensus of over 500 goal setting studies (e.g., Burton, 1992, 1993; Kyllo & Landers, 1995; Locke & Latham, 1990a; Weinberg, 1994) confirms that specific, difficult goals prompt higher levels of performance than vague, do-your-best, or no goals. Of the 201 studies reviewed by Locke and Latham (1990a), goal setting effects were demonstrated totally or contingently in 183 studies, a 91% success rate. Moreover, five meta-analyses of the general goal setting research (Chidester & Grigsby, 1984;

Hunter & Schmidt, 1983; Mento, Steel, & Karren, 1987; Tubbs, 1986; Wood, Mento, & Locke, 1987), each containing from 17 to 53 goal setting studies and including from 1,278 to 6,635 participants, demonstrated mean effect sizes ranging from .42 to .80, representing performance increases of from 8.4% to 16%.

A comprehensive review of the goal setting literature convincingly demonstrates the generalizability of general and sport findings. Locke and Latham's (1990a) review of nearly 500 goal setting studies confirmed tremendous consistency for the frequency and magnitude of goal effects across different tasks, settings, performance criteria, and types of participants. Goal setting effects were documented across 90 tasks, ranging from simple laboratory experiments (e.g., listing nouns, computation) to complex tasks such as prose learning and management simulation, as well as across a great diversity of populations that varied in gender, age, race, socioeconomic status, and type of employment (e.g., loggers, factory workers, engineers and scientists, and college professors). Finally, goal setting benefits have been documented for time spans as short as one minute (Locke, 1982) and as long as 36 months (Ivancevich, 1974). Clearly, these data confirm that goal setting is both a highly consistent and effective performance-enhancement strategy that works almost universally for most people, for a wide variety of tasks, and across many diverse settings.

Goal Setting Research in Sport

A perusal of sport-specific goal research (Burton, 1992, 1993; Kyllo & Landers, 1995; Weinberg, 1994) indicates that setting goals is also an effective performance-enhancement technique in the physical activity domain. In the most comprehensive review to date, Kyllo and Landers identified 49 sport-related goal setting studies, 36 of which were appropriate for their meta-analysis. When compared to no goals or do-your-best goals, goal setting yielded a similar, although slightly smaller, effect size of .34 compared to effect sizes of .42 to .80 in the general goal literature. Our review, which focused only on published research, discounting unpublished theses and dissertations, found 67 goal setting publications, 56 of which were empirical investigations that met our inclusion criteria. Of those 56 published goal setting studies in sport and physical activity, 44 demonstrated moderate or strong goal setting effects, for a 78.6% effectiveness rate (see Table 19.1). The review for the earlier version of this chapter seven years ago uncovered 14 sport-related goal setting studies and revealed that goal setting effects were shown in approximately 66% of the studies. Thus, as more studies accumulate in sport, the consistency of goal

Table 19.1 Summary of Goal Research in Sport and Physical Activity

Study	Subjects	Results	Level of Support
General Goal Effectiveness (Goal versus no-goal/control conditions: 15 out of 19 studies strongly or partially supported general goal effectiveness)			
Anshel, Weinberg, & Jackson (1992)	54 undergraduate students	All goal conditions (easy, difficult, and self-set) performed better than a no-goal condition on a juggling task	Strong
Bar-Eli, Levy-Kolker, Tenenbaum, & Weinberg (1993)	184 army trainees	No differences between five goal setting conditions and no-goal condition on physical fitness tasks	Weak
Barnett (1977)	93 female high school students	No difference in juggling performance between two student-set goal conditions and three no-goal conditions	Weak
Barnett & Stanicek (1979)	30 university archery undergraduates	Goal condition resulted in superior archery performance compared to no-goal condition	Strong
Boyce & Wayda (1994)	252 female university weight training students	Self-set and assigned goal conditions performed better than no-goal condition	Strong
Burton, Weinberg, Yukelson, & Weigand (1998)	321 male and 249 female college athletes	Most college athletes reported setting goals, but found them to be only moderately effective	Moderate
Hollingsworth (1975)	90 junior high school students	No difference between performance goal condition, "do your best," condition, and no-goal condition on a juggling task	Weak
Humphries, Thomas, & Nelson (1991)	60 college males	Goal conditions led to superior mirror tracing performance compared to no-goal condition	Strong
Lerner, Ostrow, Yura, & Etzel (1996)	12 female basketball players	Goal setting condition resulted in superior free throw shooting improvement compared with goal setting + imagery condition and imagery condition	Moderate
Nelson (1978)	100 college males	Assigned goal condition performed better on a muscular endurance task compared to no-goal condition	Strong
Shoenfelt (1996)	12 female collegiate basketball players	Goals and feedback condition increased free throw accuracy more than did control condition	Strong
Smith & Lee (1992)	51 university students	Public and private goals improved performance during a novel motor task compared to a no-goal condition	Strong
Tenenbaum, Pinchas, Elbaz, Bar-Eli, & Weinberg (1991)	214 9th grade white Israeli students	Short-term, long-term, and short-term + long-term goal conditions performed better on sit-up task compared to no goal or "do your best" goal condition	Strong
Theodorakis (1995)	42 undergraduate physical education students	Setting goals significantly improved performance on swimming task trials compared to no-goal trials	Strong
Theodorakis (1996)	48 undergraduate physical education students	Self-efficacy and goal setting were found to be predictors of performance on a tennis service task	Moderate
Tzetzis, Kioumourtzoglou, & Mavromatis (1997)	78 boys associated with a basketball academy	Goal setting coupled with performance feedback on simple and complex basketball tasks improved performance more than feedback alone	Strong
Weinberg, Burton, Yukelson, & Weigand (1993)	678 intercollegiate male and female athletes	Nearly all subjects reported setting goals and perceived goals to be moderately to highly effective	Strong
Weinberg, Burton, Yukelson, & Weigand (in press)	185 male and 143 female Olympic athletes	All Olympic athletes set goals to enhance performance and they found their goals to be highly effective	Moderate
Weinberg, Garland, Bruya, & Jackson (1990)	87 undergraduate students in fitness courses	No difference between realistic, unrealistic, "do your best," and no-goal conditions on a sit-up task	Weak
Goal Difficulty (10 out of 19 studies supported or partially supported goal difficulty predictions)			
Anshel, Weinberg, & Jackson (1992)	54 undergraduate students	Difficult goals increased intrinsic motivation while easy goals decreased intrinsic motivation on a juggling task	Strong for goal difficulty
Bar-Eli, Levy-Kolker, Tenenbaum, & Weinberg (1993)	184 army trainees	No differences between easy, moderate, hard, very hard, "do your best," and control goal setting conditions on physical fitness tasks	Weak for goal difficulty

Study	Participants	Results	Support
Bar-Eli, Tenenbaum, Pie, Btesh, & Almog (1997)	364 male high school students	Difficult/realistic group exhibited the greatest increase in sit-up performance compared to the easy goal, "do your best" goal, and no-goal groups	Strong for difficult, yet realistic goals
Boyce (1990)	90 students in a rifle shooting contest	Only the specific/difficult condition (specific/difficult, specific/moderate, "do your best") was superior to the "do your best" condition on shooting task	Strong for goal difficulty
Boyce (1990)	135 university riflery class participants	Specific and difficult goal conditions performed better than "do your best") condition during a rifle shooting task	Strong for goal difficulty
Frierman, Weinberg, & Jackson (1990)	45 novice and 27 intermediate bowlers	Long-term, specific, and difficult goal conditions performed better than "do your best" condition	Strong for goal difficulty
Hall, Weinberg, & Jackson (1987)	94 college males	No difference in hand dynamometer performance between "improve by 40 seconds" goal condition and "improve by 70 seconds goal condition	Weak for goal difficulty
Humphries, Thomas, & Nelson (1991)	60 college males	No difference in minor tracing performance between attainable and unattainable goal conditions	Weak for goal difficulty
Jones & Cale (1997)	44 adult participants	Difficult goal condition performed better than "very easy" and "do your best" conditions on a series of perceptual speed trials	Strong for goal difficulty
Lerner & Locke (1995)	60 participants	Both medium and hard goal groups significantly outperformed the "do your best" condition on sit-up performance	Moderate for goal difficulty
Nelson (1978)	100 college males	Students in the fictitious goal/norm group (highly difficult suggested goal/norm) performed best, compared to two realistic norm/goal groups and a control group	Moderate for goal difficulty
Weinberg, Bruya, Jackson, & Garland (1986)	123 students enrolled in university fitness courses	No difference between extremely hard goals, highly improbable goals, and "do your best" goals on a sit-up task	Weak for goal difficulty
	30 students enrolled in university fitness courses	No difference between easy, moderate, and extremely hard goal conditions on a sit-up task	Weak for goal difficulty
Weinberg, Burke, & Jackson (1997)	224 youth tennis players	Athletes preferred setting moderately difficult goals	Moderate for goal difficulty
Weinberg, Burton, Yukelson, & Weigand (in press)	185 male and 143 female Olympic athletes	Olympic athletes preferred setting difficult goals that were somewhat higher than the athletes' current performance capabilities	Moderate for goal difficulty
Weinberg, Fowler, Jackson, Bagnall, & Bruya (1991)	114 boys and 135 girls from 3rd through 5th grades	No difference between easy, difficult, improbable, and "do your best" goal conditions on a sit-up task	Weak for goal difficulty
	50 college males and 50 college females	No difference between easy, moderately difficult, very difficult, highly improbable, and "do your best" goal conditions on a basketball shooting performance	Weak for goal difficulty
Weinberg, Garland, Bruya, & Jackson (1990)	87 undergraduate students in fitness courses	No difference between realistic, unrealistic, "do your best," and no-goal conditions on a sit-up task	Weak for goal difficulty
	120 participants	No difference between moderately difficult, difficult, unrealistic, and "do our best" goal conditions on a hand dynamometer task	Weak for goal difficulty

Goal Focus (9 out of 10 studies directly or indirectly supported the use of multiple goal-focus strategies)

Study	Participants	Results	Support
Burton (1989b)	29 collegiate swimmers	Setting performance goals more effectively enhanced both competitive cognitions and performance compared to a control condition	Strong for performance goals
Burton, Weinberg, Yukelson, & Weigand (1998)	321 male and 249 female college athletes	Athletes setting process goals found goal setting more beneficial than athletes who set outcome or product goals	Moderate for process goals
Filby, Maynard, & Graydon (1999)	40 adult participants	Multiple-goal strategies (outcome + performance + process goals) more effectively improved soccer performance compared to single-goal strategies	Strong for multiple goal-focus strategies

(continued)

Table 19.1 (Continued)

Study	Subjects	Results	Level of Support
Giannini, Weinberg, & Jackson (1988)	100 college male recreational basketball players	No difference between competitive, cooperative, and mastery goal conditions on a basketball task	Weak for goal focus differential effects
Jones & Hanton (1996)	91 competitive swimmers	When athletes set multiple focus goals, high expectations of goal attainment increased facilitative anxiety perceptions compared to lower goal expectations	Moderate for goal-anxiety relationship
Kingston & Hardy (1997)	37 club golfers	Both process goal and performance goal groups showed improvement in golf handicap, the process goal condition showed significant improvement more quickly	Strong for process and performance goals
Kinston, Kieran, & Hardy (1997)	37 club golfers	Both process goals and performance goals improved processes supporting performance, the process goal condition showed significant improvement more quickly	Strong for process and performance goals
Pierce & Burton (1998)	25 female adolescent gymnasts	Performance-oriented athletes improved more than success-oriented and failure-oriented athletes (respectively) during a goal setting training program	Strong for performance goals, weak for outcome goals
Weinberg, Burke, & Jackson (1997)	224 youth tennis players	Descriptive study findings identify three most important goals: To improve performance, to have fun, and to win	Moderate for process, performance, and outcome goals
Weinberg, Burton, Yukelson, & Weigand (1993)	678 intercollegiate male and female athletes	Males set more outcome goals and less performance goals compared to females, and both groups reported goals to be effective	Moderate for performance and outcome goals
Zimmerman & Kitsantas (1998)	50 female high school physical education students	Process goals led to improved dart throwing performance compared to product goals	Strong for process goals
Task Complexity (1 of 2 studies partially supported task complexity as a moderating variable of goal-setting effectiveness)			
Anshel, Weinberg, & Jackson (1992)	54 undergraduate students	All goal conditions (easy, difficult, and self-set) improved for both simple and difficult juggling tasks	Strong for both simple and difficult tasks
Burton (1989a)	16 male and 7 female college basketball students	Specific-goal condition outperformed general-goal condition on low but not on moderate or high complexity basketball tasks	Moderate support for task complexity distinction
Goal Specificity (15 out of 25 studies strongly or partially supported goal specificity predictions)			
Bar-Eli, Levy-Kolker, Tenenbaum, & Weinberg (1993)	184 army trainees	No differences between four specific goal conditions (easy, moderate, hard, very hard), "do your best" goal condition, and control condition on physical fitness tasks	Strong for goal specificity
Bar-Eli-Tenenbaum, Pie, Btesh, & Almog (1997)	364 high school students	All specific goal groups (easy, difficult/realistic, and improbable/unrealistic) performed better than non-specific goal groups on sit-up task	Strong for goal specificity
Boyce (1990)	90 students in a rifle shooting contest	Of three goal conditions (specific/difficult, specific/moderate, and "do your best"), specific/difficult condition was superior to "do your best" condition on shooting task	Moderate for specificity
Boyce (1990)	135 university riflery class participants	Specific and difficult goal conditions performed better than "do your best" condition during a rifle shooting task	Strong for goal specificity
Boyce (1992)	181 university students	Short-term goal, long-term goal, and short- + long-term goal conditions performed better on shooting task compared to "do your best" condition	Strong for goal specificity
Boyce (1992)	138 university riflery class participants	Both self-set and assigned goal conditions performed better than "do your best" condition during a rifle shooting task	Moderate for goal specificity
Boyce (1994)	30 experienced pistol shooters	No difference between instructor-set and "do your best" goal conditions on a pistol shooting task	Weak for goal specificity
Boyce & Bingham (1997)	288 college students performing a bowling task	No difference between self-set, assigned, and "do your best" goal conditions on bowling performance	Weak for goal specificity
Burton (1989a)	16 male and 7 female college basketball students	Specific-goal condition performed better on most basketball skills compared to general-goal condition	Moderate for goal specificity

Study	Sample	Findings	Conclusion
Erbaugh & Barnett (1988)	52 elementary school children	Both goal conditions (goals, goals/modeling) enhanced rope jumping performance compared to "do your best" condition	Strong for goal specificity
Frierman, Weinberg, & Jackson (1990)	45 novice and 27 intermediate bowlers	Of the four goal conditions (short-term, long-term, short- + long-term, and "do your best"), only the long-term goal condition improved more than the "do your best" condition	Moderate for goal specificity
Giannini, Weinberg, & Jackson (1988)	100 college male recreational basketball players	Only competitive goal condition (One of 3 specific-goal conditions) performed better than "do your best"–without-feedback condition on a basketball task	Weak for goal specificity
Hall & Byrne (1988)	43 male and 11 female college weight training students	The two long-term + intermediate goal conditions performed better than a "do your best" condition on an endurance task	Moderate for goal specificity
Hall, Weinberg, & Jackson (1987)	94 college males	The two specific goal conditions performed better than the "do your best" goal condition on a hand dynamometer endurance task	Strong for goal specificity
Hollingsworth (1975)	90 junior high school students	No difference between performance goal condition, "do your best" condition, and no goal condition on a juggling task	Weak for goal specificity
Jones & Cale (1997)	44 adult participants	"Do your best" goals improved performance more than "very easy" goals, but were less effective than "very hard" goals	Moderate for goal specificity
Lee & Edwards (1984)	93 5th grade physical education students	Specific goals (self-set and assigned) enhanced performance to a greater extent than did "do your best" goals on motor tasks	Strong for goal specificity
Lerner & Locke (1995)	60 participants	Both medium and hard goal groups significantly outperformed the "do your best" condition on sit-up performance	Moderate for goal specificity
Tenenbaum, Pinchas, Elbaz, Bar-Eli, & Weinberg (1991)	214 9th grade white Israeli students	Short-term + long-term goal condition performed better on sit-up task compared to "do your best" goal condition	Strong for goal specificity
Weinberg, Bruya, & Jackson (1985)	96 students enrolled in university fitness courses	No difference between short-term, long-term, short-term + long-term, and "do your best" conditions on a sit-up task	Weak for goal specificity
Weinberg, Bruya, Jackson, & Garland (1986)	123 students enrolled in university fitness courses	No difference between extremely hard goals, highly improbable goals, and "do your best" goals on a sit-up task	Weak for goal specificity
Weinberg, Bruya, Longino, & Jackson (1988)	130 boys and 125 girls from grades 4–6	Specific goals led to better performance on a sit-up endurance task compared to "do your best" goals	Moderate for goal specificity
Weinberg, Garland, Bruya, & Jackson (1990)	87 undergraduate students in fitness courses	No difference between realistic, unrealistic, "do your best," and no-goal condition on a sit-up task	Weak for goal specificity
	120 participants	No difference between moderately difficult, difficult, unrealistic, and "do your best" goal conditions on a hand dynamometer task	Weak for goal specificity
Weinberg, Stitcher, & Richardson (1994)	24 male Division III lacrosses players	No difference between specific and "do your best" goal conditions in lacrosse performance	Weak for goal specificity
Goal Collectivity (4 studies support or partially supported the setting of group goals)			
Brawley, Carron, & Widmeyer (1992)	167 college and recreational athletes	Group goals were general rather than specific, and while process goals predominated during practice, groups set both outcome and process goals during competition	Group goals exploratory study
Brawley, Carron, & Widmeyer (1993)	145 adult and college athletes	Participation in team goal setting was strongly related to "groupness" variables, such as cohesion	Strong for group goals
Johnson, Ostrow, Perna, & Etzel (1997)	36 male undergraduate bowling students	Of the three conditions (group goals, individual goals, and "do your best" goals), only the group goals condition improved bowling performance	Strong for group goals
Lee (1989)	9 women's field hockey teams (96 women)	Team goals were positively related to winning percentage	Strong for group goals
Widmeyer & DuCharme (1997)	Not applicable	Position paper on enhancing team cohesion through team goal setting	Not applicable

(continued)

Table 19.1 (Continued)

Study	Subjects	Results	Level of Support
Goal Participation (1 out of 7 studies partially supported self-set goals as superior to assigned goals)			
Boyce (1992)	138 university riflery class participants	No difference between self-set and assigned goal conditions on rifle shooting performance	Weak for goal setting participation
Boyce & Bingham (1997)	288 college students performing a bowling task	No difference between self-set, assigned, and "do your best" goal conditions on bowling performance	Weak for goal setting participation
Boyce & Wayda (1994)	252 female university weight training students	Assigned goal condition performed better than self-set goal condition	Weak for goal setting participation
Fairall & Rodgers (1997)	67 track and field athletes	No difference between participative, assigned, and self-set goal conditions	Weak for goal setting participation
Hall & Byrne (1988)	43 male and 11 female college weight training students	No difference between long term + instructor-set intermediate goal condition and long term + self-set intermediate goal condition on an endurance task	Weak for goal setting participation
Lambert, Moore, & Dixon (1999)	4 female gymnasts	Gymnasts with a more internal locus of control benefited from self-set goals, while external locus of control gymnasts benefited from coach-set goals	Moderate for goal setting participation
Lee & Edwards (1984)	93 5th grade physical education students	Assigned goals enhanced performance to a greater extent than did self-set goals on two out of three motor tasks	Weak for goal setting participation
Goal Interventions (6 out of 7 studies supported or partially supported goal-setting as an effective intervention technique)			
Anderson, Crowell, Doman, & Howard (1988)	17 male intercollegiate hockey players	Goal setting intervention increased hitting performance during hockey games	Strong for goal setting as an intervention strategy
Burton (1989b)	29 collegiate swimmers	Goal setting intervention enhanced competitive cognitions and performance for collegiate swimmers	Strong for goal setting as an intervention strategy
Galvan & Ward (1998)	5 collegiate tennis players	Goal setting, in part, reduced the number of inappropriate on-court behaviors immediately following the goal setting intervention	Strong for goal setting as an intervention strategy
Miller & McAuley (1987)	18 undergraduate students	No difference in free throw performance between goal-training and no-goal-training conditions	Weak for goal setting as an intervention strategy
Poag-DuCharme, Kimberley, & Brawley (1994)	99 adults enrolled in exercise classes	Participants set multiple goals and developed action plans and specific behavioral strategies for achieving the identified goals	Moderate for goal setting as an intervention strategy
Swain & Jones (1995)	4 male collegiate basketball players	Goal setting intervention enhanced basketball skills for three out of four subjects	Moderate for goal setting as an intervention strategy
Wanlin, Hrycaiko, Martin, & Mahon (1997)	4 female speed skaters	Goal setting intervention enhanced skating performance	Strong for goal setting as an intervention strategy
Weinberg, Stitcher, & Richardson (1994)	24 male Division III lacrosse players	Goal setting intervention failed to significantly improve performance, although researchers identified a positive trend toward improvement	Weak for goal setting as an intervention strategy
Goals and Self-Efficacy (7 out of 7 studies supported goal setting as an effective mediator or enhancer of self-efficacy)			
Kane, Marks, Zaccaro, & Blair (1996)	216 high school wrestlers	Outcome goals mediated self-efficacy performance relationship for wrestlers at camp	Strong for goals mediating efficacy and performance
Kinston, Kieran, & Hardy (1997)	37 club golfers	Both process goals and performance goals improved golfing self-efficacy, the process goal condition showed significant improvement more quickly	Strong for enhancing self-efficacy
Lee (1989)	9 women's field hockey teams (96 women)	Setting specific and challenging team goals mediated the effect of self-efficacy on team performance (won/loss record)	Moderate for enhancing self-efficacy
Miller & McAuley (1987)	18 undergraduate students	Goal-training condition reported higher free throw self-efficacy compared to no-goal-training condition	Strong for enhancing self-efficacy

Study	Sample	Findings	Support
Poag & McAuley (1992)	76 adult female community conditioning participants	Goal efficacy predicted perceived goal achievement at the end of the program	Strong for efficacy as a goal moderator
Theodorakis (1995)	42 undergraduate physical education students	Goals were found to be a mediator between self-efficacy and performance	Strong for goals mediating efficacy and performance
Theodorakis (1996)	48 undergraduate physical education students	Self-efficacy and goal setting were found to be predictors of performance on a tennis service task	Strong for efficacy as a predictor of performance

Goal Proximity (3 out of 8 studies supported or partially supported setting both short- and long-term goals)

Study	Sample	Findings	Support
Bar-Eli, Hartman, & Levy-Kolker (1994)	80 adolescents with behavior disorders	Although both conditions improved, the short- + long-term goal condition showed greatest increased in sit-up performance compared to the long-term only goal condition	Strong for setting both short- and long-term goals
Boyce (1992)	181 university students	No difference between short-term, long-term, and short-term + long-term conditions on shooting task performance	Weak for setting both short- and long-term goals
Frierman, Weinberg, & Jackson (1990)	45 novice and 27 intermediate bowlers	Of the four goal conditions (short-term, long-term, short- + long-term, and "do your best"), only the long-term goal condition improved more than "do your best" condition	Weak for setting both short- and long-term goals
Hall & Byrne (1988)	43 male and 11 female university weight training students	The two long-term + intermediate goal conditions performed better than long-term only goal condition on an endurance task	Moderate for setting both short- and long-term goals
Howe & Poole (1992)	115 male undergraduate physical education students	No difference between short-term, long-term, and short- + long-term goal conditions on basketball shooting performance	Weak for setting both short- and long-term goals
Tenenbaum, Pinchas, Elbaz, Bar-Eli, & Weinberg (1991)	214 9th grade white Israeli students	Short-term + long-term goal condition performed best on sit-up task compared to short-term only or long-term only goal conditions	Strong for setting both short- and long-term goals
Weinberg, Bruya, & Jackson (1985)	96 students enrolled in university fitness courses	No difference between short-term, long-term, short-term + long-term, and "do your best" conditions on sit-up task	Weak for setting both short- and long-term goals
Weinberg, Bruya, Longino, & Jackson (1988)	130 boys and 125 girls from grades 4–6	No difference between short-term, long-term, and short-term + long-term conditions on sit-up endurance task	Weak for setting both short- and long-term goals

Meta-Analyses and Reviews
Burton (1992)
Burton (1993)
Kylio & Landers (1995)
Weinberg (1994)

setting effects increases, although it is still well below similar figures for the general goal literature.

Goal Attribute Research

Although the overall effectiveness of goals is clearly the most extensively researched goal setting topic, goal attribute research has been a close second (Locke & Latham, 1990a). Goal attribute researchers focus on what types of goals are most effective, and this section highlights research dealing with the efficacy of six goal types frequently utilized in sport: goal focus, goal specificity, goal difficulty, goal valence, goal proximity, and goal collectivity.

Goal Focus

Goal focus is a term that has been almost exclusively a product of goal setting research in sport (Burton, 1989a, 1992, 1993; Kingston & Hardy, 1997; Kingston, Hardy, & Markland, 1992). Burton (1989a) pioneered the distinction between performance and outcome goals. Performance goals are defined in terms of their "process" focus, emphasizing form, technique, improvement, and attaining specific performance standards. Outcome goals are conceptualized as more "product"-oriented, focusing on social comparison and object outcome (i.e., place in a race, winning or losing; Burton, 1989a). Burton (1989a, 1992, 1993) argued that the superiority of performance goals is due to their greater flexibility and controllability compared to outcome goals. The flexibility of performance goals allows athletes of all ability levels to raise and lower goal difficulty levels to keep them challenging but realistic for athletes' "current performance capabilities," thus prompting higher motivation and more consistent success. Moreover, the controllability of performance goals should prompt performers to internalize credit for success as indicative of improved or high ability.

The consensus of sport goal research (Burton, 1989a; L. Hardy, Jones, & Gould, 1996; Kingston & Hardy, 1997; Kingston et al., 1992; Zimmerman, 1989) has generally indicated that performance goals are more effective than outcome goals. Further support for the superiority of performance goals has come from the goal orientation literature (e.g., Duda, 1992) and from anecdotal reports of sport psychology consultants (Gould, 1998; L. Hardy et al., 1996; Orlick, 1986). Although Kyllo and Landers's (1995) meta-analysis questioned this conclusion, the research they reviewed did not directly test goal focus. The effectiveness of performance compared to outcome goals has been attributed to several factors: (1) increased attentional focus (Kingston & Hardy, 1994, 1997), (2) enhanced concentration (Beggs,

1990; Boutcher, 1990; Hardy & Nelson, 1988), (3) automation of key skills (L. Hardy et al., 1996), and (4) improved self-efficacy due to higher levels of perceived control (Burton, 1989a; Hall & Byrne, 1988).

Recently, researchers (Singer, Lidor, & Cauraugh, 1993; Zimmerman, 1994; Zimmerman & Bonner, 1997) have proposed a developmental continuum extending from performance to outcome goals. During the skill acquisition and skill mastery phases of the learning process, performance goals are hypothesized to be more effective, whereas outcome goals should be more effective helping performers maintain focus and effort once skills have been successfully automated. Zimmerman and Kitsantas (1996) investigated the impact of performance versus outcome goals on skill acquisition and performance on a dart-throwing task. As predicted, novice performers using performance goals performed significantly better than did their counterparts using outcome goals, presumably because performance goals enhanced competitors' ability to focus on the technical elements of the task. However, Giannini, Weinberg, and Jackson (1988) found no difference between these types of goals.

Kingston and Hardy (1994, 1997) have recently clarified and broadened this goal focus distinction by splitting performance goals into two categories, performance goals and process goals. In this refined goal focus categorization, process goals refer to improving form, technique, and strategy, whereas performance goals refer solely to improving overall performance (e.g., running a faster time, throwing farther, or shooting a lower score). Kingston and Hardy's rationale for this reconceptualization is based on the argument that performance goals still focus on the end products of performance, although success is based on the attainment of absolute or self-referenced performance standards (e.g., shooting a 74 in a round of golf, running the 100 meters in 10.22, or scoring 25 points in a basketball game). Their new conceptualization of goal focus places these types of goals on a continuum, with outcome goals on the product end of the continuum, process goals on the opposite end of the continuum, and performance goals in between.

Clearly, this revised goal focus model makes a valuable addition to both the empirical and applied sport psychology literatures because process goals are definitely more flexible and controllable than are performance goals. In sport, where skills are highly complex and take lengthy practice intervals to master, process goals should function as the stepping stones to achieving required performance levels that will ultimately lead to desired outcomes. Moreover, some complex tasks require that performers first develop new or more effective task strategies for performing skills before the motivational benefits of goals can promote enhanced performance. Thus, process goals could obviously provide the framework for developing these new or improved task strategies that over time can be automated to raise performance to the levels necessary to attain desired outcomes.

Preliminary work by Kingston, Hardy, and their colleagues (Kingston et al., 1992; Kingston & Hardy, 1994, 1997) have supported the validity of this reconceptualization of goal focus, demonstrating several important benefits of process compared to performance goals. These benefits include: (1) helping athletes improve concentration because of more effective allocation of attentional resources (Hardy & Nelson, 1988; Kingston & Hardy, 1997); (2) enhancing self-efficacy because success at attaining process goals is more controllable (Kingston & Hardy, 1997); and (3) improving control of cognitive anxiety because process goals allow greater flexibility to set performance standards that are optimal for current performance capabilities, thus reducing stress prompted by unrealistically high goals (Kingston & Hardy, 1997; Kingston et al., 1992). Kingston and Hardy (1997) found no difference in overall improvement in golf performance between golfers setting process versus performance goals, although both goal setting groups improved significantly more than did a control group. However, the process goal group demonstrated their performance improvement more quickly than did their performance goal counterparts, suggesting some possible benefit in terms of speed of improvement. Our review of goal focus revealed that 9 out of 10 studies supported the efficacy of employing a combination of process, performance, and outcome goals compared to using any of these goals individually (see Table 19.1).

Most experts (Burton, 1989a; Gould, 1998) agree that outcome goals seem to be more popular or more emphasized in our modern sport culture, primarily because of the tremendous rewards available for winning (i.e., trophies, medals, recognition, fame, money, etc.). The popular sport literature is replete with examples in which winning is glorified and attainment of performance and/or process goals dismissed as unimportant (e.g., Super Bowl champions are glorified forever and their stars enshrined in the Hall of Fame, but the runner-up team is quickly forgotten). However, several recent goal practices survey studies (Burton et al., 1998; Burton et al., in preparation; Weinberg et al., 1993, 1997, in press) have confirmed that athletes do not necessarily follow this traditional goal setting wisdom. Surveys with collegiate athletes and youth tennis players

(Burton et al., 1998; Weinberg et al., 1993, 1997) revealed that both age groups of athletes set performance and outcome goals with virtually equal frequency and effectiveness. Moreover, research on the goal practices of Olympic athletes (Burton et al., in preparation; Weinberg et al., in press) indicates that elite performers set performance goals slightly more often and with slightly greater effectiveness compared to outcome goals, although these differences were nonsignificant. However, Olympic performers reported more frequently making outcome goals slightly more important than performance goals in competition. Thus, it might be concluded that athletes still value outcome goals, but they also have become more sophisticated about using process and performance goals as means to achieve these product-oriented ends.

Goal Specificity

Early reviews of the general goal specificity literature (Chidester & Grigsby, 1984; Latham & Lee, 1986; Locke et al., 1981; Mento et al., 1987; Tubbs, 1986) concluded that goal specificity, or precision, enhances performance. Locke and his colleagues found that 51 of 53 goal specificity studies partially or completely supported the premise that specific goals promote better performance than general or do-your-best goals or no goals, whereas Chidester and Grigsby's meta-analytic review of 22 studies confirmed that goal specificity consistently improved performance. Latham and Lee subsequently reviewed 64 studies with almost identical findings. In a broader-based meta-analysis, Mento and his colleagues revealed an effect size of .44 for goal specificity across 49 studies and over 5,800 participants, which translates into a nearly 9% increase in productivity.

However, Locke and Latham's (1990a) more recent revision of goal setting theory predicted that goal specificity is a less important goal attribute than goal difficulty and will contribute primarily to enhancing performance consistency more than performance quality. Locke and Latham hypothesized that making difficult goals specific will further enhance performance because specific goals make it more difficult to feel successful with performance that is lower than one's goal. They further argued that when goals are vague, it is easier for individuals to give themselves the "benefit of the doubt" in evaluating performance and rate a relatively lower level of performance as acceptable. For example, Kernan and Lord (1989) found that individuals with no specific goals generally evaluated their performance more positively than subjects with specific-hard goals when provided with varying types of negative feedback. Additionally, Mento, Locke, and Klein (1992) demonstrated that subjects with do-your-best goals anticipated more satisfaction from every level of performance than did performers with specific-hard goals.

Locke and Latham (1990a) concluded that goal specificity does not have a direct performance-enhancement effect; rather, goal specificity interacts with goal difficulty to influence performance. Thus, specific-easy goals may actually be less effective than vague-hard goals (Locke, Chah, Harrison, & Lustgarten, 1989). Locke and Latham (1990a) hypothesized that when goal difficulty is controlled, the major effect of goal specificity is to reduce performance variance. Because goal specificity reduces interpretative leeway in evaluating success, they argue that the range of performance variability should be reduced. In support of this prediction, Locke et al. (1989) separated the effects of goal difficulty and goal specificity and found that the more specific the goal, the lower the performance variance. Therefore, goal specificity seems to be an important attribute of effective goals, but its impact is most prominent when combined with goal difficulty to maintain more stringent standards for success, thereby enhancing performance consistency.

Interestingly, researchers interested in goal specificity in sport have not examined the effects of specificity independent of goal difficulty. Although approximately 15 out of 25 studies in sport (i.e., 60%) have documented that athletes setting specific goals performed significantly better than performers setting general, do-your-best goals or no goals, significant goal-setting effects were not found in the remaining four studies (see Table 19.1). However, it is unclear whether significant effects evident in the majority of studies would remain if goal difficulty effects were partialed out.

Goal Difficulty

Locke and Latham's (1990a) goal setting theory postulates a positive linear relationship between goal difficulty and performance, primarily because hard goals prompt greater effort and persistence than do easy goals. However, goal setting theory acknowledges that as individuals reach the upper limits of their ability at high goal difficulty levels, performance plateaus. Nevertheless, the consensus of nearly 200 general goal setting studies has provided strong support for this "goal difficulty hypothesis." Locke and Latham found that 91% of the 192 goal difficulty studies they reviewed yielded positive (140 studies) or contingently positive (35 studies) relationships between hard goals and performance. Moreover, four meta-analyses of goal difficulty research

(Chidester & Grigsby, 1984; Mento et al., 1987; Tubbs, 1986; Wood et al., 1987), each reviewing from 12 to 72 studies that utilized from 1,770 to 7,548 participants, demonstrated mean effect sizes ranging from .52 to .82, representing performance increments from 10.4% to 16.4%. Thus, the consensus of available enumerative and meta-analytic reviews in the general goal literature provides strong support for the goal difficulty hypothesis, and a number of subsequent studies (Chesney & Locke, 1991; Ruth, 1996; White, Kjelgaard, & Harkins, 1995; Wood & Locke, 1990) have further supported this prediction. However, limitations have been found with the proposed linear relationship between goal difficulty and performance (e.g., DeShon & Alexander, 1996; Earley, Connolly, & Ekegren, 1989). Specifically, as goals exceed individuals' performance capability, researchers have shown that excessively difficult goals will be abandoned in favor of more realistic self-set goals. In a test of this proposed limitation, Wright, Hollenbeck, Wolf, and McMahan (1995) found that when goals were operationalized in terms of absolute performance level, the traditional linear relationship between goal difficulty and performance resulted. Conversely, when goals are operationalized in terms of performance improvement, an inverted-U relationship emerged between goal difficulty and performance. Clearly, perceived ability seems to mediate the relationship between goal difficulty and performance.

Surprisingly, sport research generally contradicts the goal difficulty hypothesis (see Table 19.1). Initial goal difficulty research by Weinberg and his colleagues (Hall, Weinberg, & Jackson, 1987; Weinberg, Bruya, Jackson, & Garland, 1986) was the first to question the goal difficulty hypothesis. Hall et al. compared hand dynamometer endurance performance of participants randomly assigned to do-your-best, improve-by-40-seconds, and improve-by-70-seconds goal conditions. Although they confirmed that participants who were assigned to the two specific goal conditions performed better than did their do-your-best counterparts, they found no goal difficulty effects for the specific goal conditions. Similarly, Weinberg et al. demonstrated no goal difficulty effects for participants assigned to easy, moderate, and extremely hard goal conditions who performed a situp task for five weeks.

Our review found only 10 of 19 studies (i.e., 53%) supported goal difficulty (see Table 19.1). Not only have many studies failed to demonstrate hypothesized goal difficulty effects, but they also contradicted the prediction that unrealistically high goals will lead to performance decrements (see Table 19.1). Interestingly, Anshel, Weinberg, and

Jackson (1992) demonstrated that even in the absence of performance improvement, difficult goals significantly increased performers' level of intrinsic motivation. Researchers surveying goal practices in sport (Weinberg et al., 1993, in press) have demonstrated that moderately difficult, rather than very difficult, goals are preferred by the majority of collegiate and Olympic athletes, and more effective goal setters (Burton et al., 1998, in preparation) set moderately difficult goals more frequently than difficult ones. Moreover, reviews of sport research (Kyllo & Landers, 1995; Weinberg, 1994) have revealed that moderately difficult goals are more effective than difficult goals, accounting for an effect size of .53.

Several explanations are offered to account for the contradictory goal difficulty findings between sport and business settings. First, researchers' operationalization of goal difficulty may differ between general and sport domains. Locke (1991) suggests that a difficult goal is one that no more than 10% of participants can achieve, although there is little evidence that this criterion has been put to consistent use by researchers in either general or sport goal research. However, a goal that can be accomplished by only 5% to 10% of performers may be too difficult, prompting low goal acceptance and thereby motivating individuals to set more realistic goals on their own (i.e., spontaneous goal setting; Kyllo & Landers, 1995). A second explanation that may account for equivocal goal difficulty results in sport is ability (Kanfer & Ackerman, 1989; Weinberg et al., 1997). Goal setting theory predicts that goal difficulty has a positive linear relationship with performance until the upper limits of ability are reached, when performance levels off. However, goal theory assumes that individuals believe in their ability to achieve difficult goals. If goal attainment self-efficacy is low, a negative linear relationship is observed between goal difficulty and performance (Erez & Zidon, 1984), so that the more difficult the goal, the greater the reduction in performance. Theodorakis (1995, 1996) supported this prediction in sport, demonstrating that personal goal setting behaviors were predicted by perceived self-efficacy (see Bandura, 1977). Thus, self-efficacy seems to be a significant mediator of goal difficulty effects.

Recently, Campbell and Furrer (1995) suggested that the effects of goal difficulty can also be mediated by competition. Results investigating the effects of competition on goal setting performance in a math class demonstrated that across three goal conditions (i.e., easy, moderate, and difficult), participants performing in the noncompetitive environment significantly outperformed their counterparts in the competitive environment. Although there was no difference in the mean number of problems attempted across conditions, competitive participants made significantly more mistakes than did noncompetitive classmates. These findings suggest that competition reduces goal effects by increasing anxiety or reducing concentration. Interestingly, Lerner and Locke (1995) found that competition did not mediate goal effects on sport performance. Due to the competitive nature of athletics and the degree to which athletes compete in most situations, further investigation of the role of competition as a mediator of goal difficulty results seems warranted.

Goal Valence

Sport practitioners often encourage athletes to set goals in positive terms, focusing on what they want to accomplish (e.g., two hits in four at-bats) rather than what they hope to avoid (e.g., striking out or going 0 for 4; Gould, 1998). However, Kirschenbaum (1984) has suggested that this goal setting strategy may work only in certain situations. Kirschenbaum concluded from extensive self-regulation research that positively focused goals are most effective for new or difficult skills (e.g., Johnston-O'Connor & Kirschenbaum, 1984; Kirschenbaum, Ordman, Tomarken, & Holtzbauer, 1982), whereas negatively focused goals that emphasize minimizing mistakes are more effective for well-learned skills (e.g., Kirschenbaum, Wittrock, Smith, & Monson, 1984). This review was unable to find any sport studies that focused on goal valence. Additional research is clearly needed to test predictions and clarify goal valence effects.

Goal Proximity

Locke and Latham's (1990a) theory makes no specific predictions about the efficacy of short-term versus long-term goals, and existing reviews of goal proximity research (Kirschenbaum, 1985; Locke & Latham, 1990a) have revealed equivocal results, prompting confusion about what goal proximity recommendations to make to practitioners. Clinical researchers (e.g., Bandura, 1986) argue that short-term (ST) goals are more effective because they provide more frequent evaluation of success that stimulates development of self-confidence when goals are attained and motivation regardless of the outcome, thus preventing procrastination and premature discouragement. Burton (1989b) emphasizes other attributes of ST goals, contending that ST goals are more flexible and controllable. Because ST goals are more flexible, they can be readily raised or lowered to keep the level of challenge optimal. Moreover, the controllability of ST goals makes it easier for performers to take credit for success as indicative of high ability and a good work ethic.

Long-term (LT) goal proponents (e.g., Kirschenbaum, 1985) theorize that LT goals facilitate greater performance improvement than ST goals because they foster "protracted choice." These theorists argue that too frequent goal assessment may prompt excessive evaluation, making it difficult to remain focused on performance because social comparison concerns become more salient (Nicholls, 1984a), prompting performers to feel like "pawns" because goals are perceived as controlling rather than informational (e.g., deCharms, 1976; Deci & Ryan, 1985). Thus, LT goals would allow ST flexibility that prevents discouragement if individuals should fail to attain daily performance goals.

Locke and Latham's (1990a) review suggests that goal proximity has not been a popular topic for goal setting research. This limited research can be interpreted two ways: Either researchers believe that this goal attribute has limited impact on goal setting efficacy, or they have had difficulty identifying the optimal time span for ST and LT goals. In the latter case, goals that are set too often may become intrusive, distracting, and annoying, thus prompting their rejection. Conversely, goals set too infrequently may be viewed as unreal and not worthy of attention, thus failing to mobilize effort and persistence resources that are necessary to stimulate enhanced performance.

Early general goal studies (e.g., Bandura & Schunk, 1981; Bandura & Simon, 1977; Manderlink & Harackiewicz, 1984) revealed that ST goals led to better performance than LT goals. It is hypothesized that ST goals offer the performer more opportunities to assess success and correct effort levels or modify strategies, thereby enhancing self-efficacy and intrinsic motivation. However, subsequent self-regulation findings found that moderately specific planning and longer-term goals seem to facilitate behavioral change (Kirschenbaum, Tomarken, & Ordman, 1982). Although research conducted in both sport and nonsport settings (Bandura & Simon, 1977; Bar-Eli, Hartman, & Levy-Kolker, 1994; Borrelli & Mermelstein, 1994; Hall & Byrne, 1988; Kirschenbaum, 1985; Latham & Locke, 1991) suggested that LT goals are important to provide individuals with direction for their achievement strivings, these findings also confirmed that the motivational impact of LT goals depends on establishing ST goals to serve as intermediate steps in the achievement process (Bandura & Simon, 1977; Hall & Byrne, 1988; Locke, Cartledge, & Knerr, 1970).

In sport, goal proximity findings are equivocal, with the number of studies investigating LT versus ST goals again quite limited. Several goal proximity studies (Boyce, 1992b; Frierman, Weinberg, & Jackson, 1990) have confirmed that setting LT or ST goals facilitates performance more than does setting do-your-best goals, although differences between ST and LT goals were not found. Meanwhile, four investigations (Hall & Byrne, 1988; Howe & Poole, 1992; Weinberg, Bruya, & Jackson, 1985; Weinberg, Bruya, Longino, & Jackson, 1988) demonstrated no differences between LT and ST goals or a combination of the two. More recently, the consensus of sport goal research (e.g., Kyllo & Landers, 1995; Tenenbaum, Pinchas, Elbaz, Bar-Eli, & Weinberg, 1991) suggests that LT goals enhance performance most effectively when ST goals are used to mark progress. Kyllo and Landers's meta-analysis of the sport goal research demonstrated an effect size of .48 for the combined effect of ST and LT goals on performance. Our review found that 3 of 8 studies (i.e., 38%) demonstrated that a combination of ST and LT goals were superior to either type of goal individually. Extensive future goal proximity research seems needed to not only confirm the superiority of a combination of ST and LT goals, but also to identify the most effective time frames for ST and LT goals and to verify the relationship between these two goal proximity types.

Goal Collectivity

Group/team goals are objectives established for the collective performance of a group or team. According to Brawley, Carron, and Widmeyer (1992), team goals tend to be general rather than specific, and the focus of group goals often varies considerably between practice and competition. Moreover, they found that in practice situations, group goals were process-oriented (89.9%) rather than outcome-oriented (10.1%), focusing primarily on skill/strategy (66.1%), effort (29.3%), and fitness (4.6%). Conversely, competitive goals were shown to split evenly between outcome (53.1%) and process (46.9%), with specific goals focusing on skill/strategy (43.5%), outcome (41.5%), and effort (15%). Group goals have also been found to impact psychological variables such as team satisfaction, cohesion, and motivation as well as performance (Brawley, Carron, & Widmeyer, 1993).

Locke and Latham's (1990a) goal setting theory makes no predictions about the effectiveness of group/team versus individual goals, but available reviews of group goal setting research (Carroll, 1986; Kondrasuk, 1981; Locke & Latham, 1990a; Rodgers & Hunter, 1989) revealed that group goals enhance performance as effectively as individual goals. Locke and Latham reported that in the general goal literature, 38 out of 41 group goal setting studies

(93%) demonstrated positive or contingently positive performance enhancement effects, virtually the same success rate as individual goal setting findings. They concluded that group goals, in addition to or instead of individual goals, are necessary or at least facilitative when the task is a group/team rather than an individual one.

Positive goal collectivity results were further confirmed in several reviews of the management by objectives (MBO) literature (a goal setting approach to business management; Carroll, 1986; Kondrasuk, 1981; Locke & Latham, 1990a; Rodgers & Hunter, 1989). For example, Locke and Latham (1990b) reanalyzed Kondrasuk's review of 185 MBO studies and found that approximately 90% demonstrated positive or contingently positive results. Rodgers and Hunter subsequently conducted a meta-analysis of 68 MBO studies and demonstrated that 97% of them showed positive results; for the 28 studies in which effect size could be computed, the average performance improvement was a whopping 44%.

Although the efficacy of group/team goals has been confirmed, direct comparisons of the effectiveness of group/team versus individual goals have been relatively limited, both in sport and nonsport settings (Hinsz, 1995; Larey & Paulus, 1995; Shalley, 1995). Larey and Paulus assigned participants to no-goal, individual-goal, and interactive-goal conditions for a brainstorming task. Their results demonstrated that individual-goal performers set more difficult goals (i.e., number of ideas generated) than did their counterparts in the group/team goal condition. Low perceptions of other group members' ability were believed to lower the difficulty of group goals. In two additional studies (Hinsz, 1995; Shalley, 1995), similar decrements in performance were evident for group compared to individual goal conditions, with group performance decrements explained by (1) reduced goal difficulty due to an averaging of goal difficulty levels across performers, and (2) the distraction effect of other group members on the creative process.

All four of the studies reviewed contradicted general goal research on the efficacy of group/team versus individual goals. For example, Johnson and his colleagues (1997) examined the impact of do-your-best, individual, and team goal setting conditions on bowling performance. Contrary to general goal collectivity results, they found that group goals increased bowling performance more than either do-your-best or individual goal groups, in part because they were significantly harder goals than were set in either of the other two conditions. The authors put forth several explanations for these contradictory results: (1) the movement coordination of the task, (2) the high level of encouragement and feedback provided to bowlers by team members, and (3) the public nature of the team goal (i.e., all group members were aware of each bowler's personal and team goals). Similarly, Weldon, Jehn, and Pradham (1991) emphasized that group goals were mediated by three additional factors: the amount of effort exerted by team members toward team goals, the amount of team planning and strategy, and the degree of team members' concern for the quality of the overall team product.

Goal collectivity is probably not an either/or proposition because both team and individual goals probably make a valuable contribution to performance enhancement. Team goals offer direction for establishing appropriate types and levels of individual goals that are then responsible for the specific motivational benefits to individual performers. In fact, social loafing research (e.g., C. Hardy & Latane, 1988; Jackson & Williams, 1985; Latane, 1986; Latane, Williams, & Harkins, 1979) predicts that group/team goals, without accompanying individual goals, may reduce performance by prompting *social loafing*. Social loafing is a group performance phenomenon in which individuals working together on a task tend to exert less individual effort than when they perform the same task alone (Jackson & Williams, 1985). Although not extensively studied in sport settings, social loafing has been shown to occur for a variety of physically effortful tasks (e.g., Ingham, Levinger, Graves, & Peckham, 1974; Kerr & Brunn, 1981; Latane et al., 1979).

Interestingly, researchers have confirmed that social loafing is reduced or eliminated when individual performance is identifiable (Williams, Harkins, & Latane, 1981) and individuals perceive that they have made a unique contribution to the group effort or performed difficult tasks (Harkins & Petty, 1982). Thus, the implication of social loafing research for goal collectivity is that individuals setting group/team goals should be prone to loaf and perform below their capabilities unless they also set individual goals that hold each team member responsible for a specific level of performance, and these individual goals are perceived as indispensable for team success. Teams need to use the "role" concept for setting goals to maximize identifiability and accountability. Thus, goals are set based on the role that each player needs to attain to maximize team effectiveness. Regrettably, the prediction that a combination of group/team and individual goals should maximally enhance performance has not been tested adequately to allow firm conclusions to be drawn about group goal phenomena.

In summary, based on the research reviewed in this goal attribute section, the following recommendations are made for the types of goals that practitioners should set in sport. First, athletes should set a combination of process, performance, and outcome goals. Outcome goals should be used to enhance practice motivation, whereas performance and, especially, process goals should be focused on during competition. Second, to promote improvement in both performance quality and consistency goals should be specific, measurable, and difficult. Third, in the absence of contradictory evidence, goals should be positive and focus on desired behavioral outcomes rather than emphasizing performance problems or pitfalls to be avoided. Finally, although the research supporting these recommendations is still somewhat equivocal, practitioners should use a combination of short- and long-term goals and individual and team goals to foster maximal performance enhancement effects.

WHY GOALS WORK LESS EFFECTIVELY IN SPORT

The answer to why goals are less effective in sport than in business settings has been hotly debated, but definitive answers have proved elusive, prompting heated discussion among general and sport goal researchers (Burton, 1992, 1993; Locke, 1991, 1994; Weinberg & Weigand, 1993, 1996). The thrust of this point-counterpoint debate and rebuttal has been largely methodological in nature, with five key methodological issues highlighted as the crux of the problem: (1) participation motivation, (2) goal setting in do-your-best conditions, (3) feedback in do-your-best conditions, (4) personal goals, and (5) goal difficulty. Weinberg and Weigand (1993, 1996) contend that there are inherent differences between sport and business domains that affect motivation. Specifically, they argue that sport participants are more motivated because they have chosen to participate in the activity rather than being required to be involved. They contend that the higher motivation of participants in sport settings may account for why control participants do as well as their counterparts setting specific goals. Locke (1991, 1994) believes that control participants in general goal research are as highly motivated as their sport counterparts because they are largely college students volunteering as participants for extra course credit.

Locke (1991, 1994) also emphasizes that differential goal results across the two domains may be a function of do-your-best participants in the sport studies setting their own goals, making them virtually identical to their counterparts in the goal conditions. Weinberg and Weigand (1993, 1996) counter that preventing spontaneous goal

setting can be done in the lab but it does not accurately represent the goal practices of performers in real-world situations. They argue that if goal setting is a robust phenomenon, then individuals setting goals systematically should demonstrate performance superior to their counterparts' who spontaneously set goals.

Next, Locke (1991, 1994) argues that feedback should not be given in do-your-best conditions because without feedback it is difficult to spontaneously set goals. Weinberg and Weigand (1993, 1996) counter that such a design is flawed because conditions would differ due to two major variables: goals and feedback. Although Locke contends that this is not a problem because feedback without goals does not affect motivation, Weinberg and Weigand provide empirical evidence from the motor learning literature demonstrating that feedback is both informational and motivational. Further, they emphasize that it is extremely difficult to withhold feedback from sport performers in most real-world settings.

Further, Locke (1991, 1994) cautions that goal researchers must measure personal as well as assigned goals because participants often do not accept assigned goals, confounding results of goal setting studies by setting their own personal goals. Additionally, Locke reports empirical evidence that the relationship between assigned and personal goals is moderate at best ($r = .58$). As a result, he recommends that researchers regularly measure personal goals as a manipulation check and reassign participants to treatments if personal goals vary drastically with assigned goal conditions. Weinberg and Weigand (1993, 1996) agree and emphasize that personal goals normally impact performance improvement more than do assigned goals, highlighting the importance of measuring personal goals in all goal setting studies. Finally, Locke reiterates the need to make goals specific and difficult, emphasizing that difficult goals should produce better performance than do-your-best, easy, or moderate goals. Weinberg and Weigand counter that sport research has generally confirmed the superiority of moderately difficult goals, even though unrealistically high goals have not always reduced performance as Locke predicts.

Although this methodological debate has been entertaining, it has not succeeded in clarifying the issue of why goals are less effective in sport compared to business settings. As Weinberg and Weigand (1993, 1996) have indicated, if goal setting is a robust phenomenon that has a significant and practical impact on sport performance, then systematic goal setting programs should demonstrate performance superior to spontaneously set goals, despite these minor flaws in methodology. Several other recent findings also suggest that other, more influential factors many account for this discrepancy. First, recent goal practices surveys document that most collegiate and Olympic athletes (Burton et al., 1998, in preparation; Weinberg et al., 1993, in press) rate goals as only moderately effective. Comprehensive reviews of goal setting research (Burton, 1992, 1993; Kyllo & Landers, 1995; Weinberg, 1994) confirm that goal effects are less consistent and robust in sport and exercise. In the earlier edition of this chapter (Burton, 1993), five additional factors were posited as plausible explanations for the less consistent goal setting effects in sport: (1) small sample sizes of sport studies, (2) athletes operating closer to their performance potential, (3) highly complex skills being performed in sport, (4) individual differences that influence goal setting effectiveness, and (5) failure to employ appropriate goal implementation strategies.

Small Sample Size

One concern about the less consistent and robust goal setting effects in sport is that these findings reflect a lack of statistical power due to small sample size (Cohen, 1992). Kyllo and Landers (1995) argue that this is a viable reason for the divergent goal setting results across the two domains. They drew a random sample of 22 studies from the empirical research in both sport and business domains and generated mean cell sample sizes. Sport researchers typically had 26 participants per cell compared with 43 participants per cell in the general goal literature. A follow-up power analysis (Cohen, 1992) was performed on a sample of 8 studies from the sport goal literature, and results revealed a mean power of .53, a value well below the .80 Cohen recommends as minimal to reduce the risk of incurring Type II error. Thus, Kyllo and Landers concluded that small sample size is a possible reason for reduced goal setting effects in sport and exercise.

About 20% to 25% of the goal setting studies in sport have reported small samples (i.e., 30 or fewer subjects), and generally sample sizes in competitive goal setting studies have increased greatly in the past eight years (see Table 19.1). Because of the sensitivity of many inferential statistics to sample size, small samples may be responsible for the less consistent goal setting effects in sport. However, careful scrutiny of goal setting research in sport reveals that the average sample size across all goal attributes except goal collectivity was over 100 participants, and most goal conditions had a minimum of 20 participants (see Table 19.1). Both sample parameters appear large

enough to adequately demonstrate differences in goal setting effects, thus negating sample size as a prime explanation of the less consistent goal setting effects in sport.

Athletes Operating Closer to Their Performance Potential

The performance limits argument is consistent with Locke and Latham's (1990a) predictions for the moderating effects of ability on goal setting effectiveness. Locke and Latham present convincing evidence that the goal effectiveness curve flattens out as individuals approach the limits of their ability, in part because ability factors restrict the amount of improvement that can be made through goal setting. This explanation seems plausible for most of the nonsignificant studies in sport.

Task Complexity

The task complexity argument is also consistent with Locke and Latham's (1990a) theory, particularly the predictions for the moderating effects of task complexity on goal setting effectiveness. Wood and his colleagues (1987) performed a meta-analysis on 125 goal setting studies to assess the influence of task complexity as a moderator of goal setting; results revealed that task complexity predicted 6% of the variance in goal difficulty–performance effects and 95% of the variance in goal difficulty/specificity–performance results. Moreover, when separate meta-analyses were computed for studies with low, moderate, and high task complexity ratings, the effect sizes for both goal difficulty and goal difficulty/specificity were larger for simple as compared to more complex tasks. These findings confirm that task complexity does moderate goal setting effects, although the exact mechanism for how this happens remains speculative.

In sport, our review found one of two studies supported task complexity predictions (see Table 19.1). Burton (1989b) has confirmed that complex tasks involve a greater time lag to demonstrate goal setting effects because new task strategies often have to be developed to perform the skill more effectively, even though Anshel et al. (1992) found no task complexity effects. Only when individuals have developed effective task strategies can the motivational effects of goals stimulate performance increments by prompting greater effort and persistence. Because most sports involve the development of a large number of complex individual and team skills and strategies and due to the relatively short treatment length of many sport studies, this explanation again seems plausible for most of the nonsignificant goal setting studies in sport.

Individual Differences

Locke and Latham (1990a) suggest that individual differences, particularly self-efficacy, should have a significant impact on how individuals respond to goal setting, particularly for complex tasks and goal difficulty levels in the upper ranges of performers' ability. Specifically, they predict that when confronted with temporary failure on complex tasks, high self-efficacy performers will increase the quality of their task strategies and put forth elevated levels of effort and persistence to make those strategies work. Conversely, low self-efficacy competitors will normally display less functional task strategies and reduced effort and persistence.

In the first edition of this chapter (Burton, 1993), a competitive goal setting (CGS) model was proposed that focused on the role played by goal setting styles, a personality variable that is a combination of athletes' goal orientation and level of perceived ability, in the goal setting process. Regrettably, the CGS model and goal setting styles have received little empirical attention, even though the limited research testing the model is generally supportive of model predictions and the role that goal setting styles play in the goal setting process. Space limitations have precluded a review of the CGS model in this chapter, but interested readers are referred to the first edition of this chapter. Thus, although both self-efficacy and goal setting styles have been shown to influence goal effectiveness, individual differences have largely not been assessed or controlled in sport and nonsport goal setting research and remain a viable explanation for nonsignificant findings in goal setting research.

Failure to Employ Appropriate Goal Implementation Strategies

Locke and Latham (1990a) have emphasized that setting goals is only one component of the goal setting process. Although goal process variables have not received extensive empirical attention, the consensus (Kyllo & Landers, 1995; Locke & Latham, 1990a) is that strategies such as writing down and posting goals, developing action plans, and evaluating goal attainment enhance overall goal setting effectiveness. Recent collegiate and Olympic goal setting surveys (Burton et al., 1998, in preparation) have confirmed that more effective goal setters use all goal implementation strategies more frequently and with greater effectiveness than do less effective goal setters. Although goal implementation details are sketchy for some studies, making it difficult to determine the extent to which

appropriate strategies were utilized, many of the nonsignificant goal setting studies in sport have failed to use one or more of these key goal implementation strategies necessary to enhance performance.

In summary, the somewhat less consistent and robust goal setting results in sport may be attributable to five primary factors: small sample sizes, performers operating closer to their performance potential, athletes performing highly complex skills that make the demonstration of goal setting effects a more lengthy and difficult process, individual differences that prompt athletes to respond to goal setting programs in idiosyncratic ways, and failure to employ key goal implementation strategies. Although each of these explanations is intriguing in its own right, the role of goal implementation strategies in the goal setting process seems to have been largely neglected by previous goal setting researchers. Moreover, goal implementation strategies may also be responsible for practitioners' difficulty in achieving optimal effectiveness from setting goals.

THE GOAL SETTING PROCESS

Anecdotal and empirical evidence (Burton et al., 1998, in preparation) suggests that failure to systematically employ a number of key steps in the goal setting process may be responsible for many of the problems with goal effectiveness in sport. Process research has been dramatically underrepresented in the goal setting literature, making it an important focus of future research to identify how goals work and what strategies can be employed to foster greater goal effectiveness.

One of the biggest misconceptions about making goals work is that goal setting is more than merely setting goals. It is a comprehensive process comprising a series of systematic steps. Many individuals mistakenly believe that all they have to do is set a few goals and those goals will miraculously be attained. However, goal theory and research (e.g., Locke & Latham, 1990a) emphasize that goal setting is most effective when viewed as a process composed of seven key steps (see Figure 19.1). These implementation steps require athletes to: (1) set goals, (2) develop goal commitment, (3) evaluate barriers to goal attainment, (4) construct action plans, (5) obtain feedback, (6) evaluate goal attainment, and (7) reinforce goal achievement. The steps of the goal implementation process are described next, highlighting both ideas for enhancing the effectiveness with which practitioners set goals as well as identifying topics for future process research. However, research documenting each

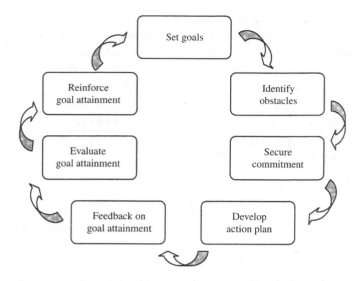

Figure 19.1   Goal setting implementation process.

step is extremely limited, so some recommendations represent "best practice" guidelines or ideas derived from related theory and research.

Step 1: Set Goals

The first step in the goal setting process is to set appropriate goals (see Figure 19.1). Locke and Latham (1990a) suggest that almost everyone who is trying to enhance their performance can benefit from setting goals. Goals should be set anytime individuals want to enhance their performance and strive for excellence, either formally after systematic evaluation of resources designed to determine appropriate long-term objectives, or informally on the spot to foster immediate focus and motivation. Goals can be set anywhere, including both practice and competition and in sport, academics, business, and other important achievement domains. Three important steps for setting effective goals include (1) developing goals systematically, (2) adjusting goals for practice and competition, and (3) optimizing goal difficulty.

Develop Goals Systematically

Most experts agree that goals should be developed systematically, preferably identified through a comprehensive needs assessment (e.g., performance profiling) that is part of the design of a periodized training program. First, athletes should develop long-term performance objectives. Next, they should conduct a systematic assessment of current capabilities for critical physical and psychological skills. Finally, using a systematic approach to varying volume and intensity of training, they should identify the

structure of long-term training as well as individual short-term workouts necessary to achieve long-term objectives. Long-term goals represent the top of the staircase, and short-term goals are depicted as specific individual steps that are important for developing specific attributes as well as to encourage athletes to progress systematically toward their long-term competitive objectives. Goals can emphasize increasing performance quantity, quality, or both. Unfortunately, there is often a quantity/quality trade-off. A basketball team that sets a goal to increase the number of shots taken may actually prompt players to take more bad shots, whereas conversely, goals that focus on improving shot quality may actually decrease the number of shots taken. Thus, in most cases, effective goals need to emphasize both quantity and quality of performance (i.e., improve the number of good shots taken by 10%) to maximize goal effectiveness.

Adjust Goals for Practice versus Competition

Goals often have different functions in practice and competition. Because practices are designed to enhance learning and promote skill development, evaluation pressure is normally low, making the motivational function of goals more salient to practice with purpose and intensity. However, because competition is designed to facilitate social comparison and outcome evaluation, performance pressure is elevated, encouraging athletes to emphasize the stress management function of goals to develop poise, maintain mental toughness, and perform optimally.

Burton (1999) emphasizes four critical differences that practitioners should keep in mind when setting goals in practice versus competitive situations: (1) goal focus, (2) psychological skills emphasized, (3) types of goals set, and (4) level of goal difficulty adopted. First, the focus of practice goals is on developing skills, whereas goals in competition must be oriented toward performing optimally and outperforming one's opponent. Second, the skill development nature of practice emphasizes the importance of such psychological skills as focus/concentration and motivation needed to work hard on skill refinement. The psychological skills targeted in competition include confidence and stress management. Thus, competitive goals must be kept realistic to enhance athletes' confidence and minimize stress about goal attainment. Third, practice goals need to be directed toward the development of complex skills (e.g., shooting in basketball, volleying in tennis) to enhance the quantity and quality of desired skill mechanics. Competitive goals are more susceptible to stress factors and function best when they stress effort-based skills and improving the quantity of specific behaviors (Riley, 1996). Finally, goal difficulty in practice should be kept challenging to push athletes beyond their comfort zone to maximize skill development. Practice goals should be moderately to very difficult to challenge performers to improve. Competitive goals are often set too high because they are set at the level needed to win or socially compare well, prompting stress because athletes worry that they cannot attain these unrealistic standards. Competitive goals must be kept realistic to reduce stress and promote self-confidence.

Optimize Goal Difficulty

As the goal difficulty research reviewed earlier in this chapter confirms, identifying the optimal goal difficulty levels for each athlete is an area of controversy. Although several experts have attempted to provide practitioners with strategies to determine appropriate levels of goal difficulty (e.g., O'Block & Evans, 1984), few goal setting studies have attempted to operationalize the goal difficulty level that will promote best performance. In one of the few studies to look at goal difficulty preferences, Burton, Daw, Williams-Rice, and Phillips (1989) found that high-perceived-ability performers set more difficult goals across all four skills ($Ms = 102–111\%$ of previous performance) than did low-perceived-ability classmates ($Ms = 94–103\%$ of previous performance).

What goal difficulty level should athletes choose? Self-change research (Kirschenbaum, 1984; Mahoney & Mahoney, 1976) suggests that the best and most lasting behavioral change occurs with small, slow, gradual, and systematic changes in underlying behavior patterns rather than large, quick, inconsistent, or haphazard behavioral adjustments. Thus, self-change models normally advocate moderate goal difficulty levels (5–10% above current performance capabilities). Orlick (1998) has pioneered another potentially valuable and practical goal setting strategy of using multiple goal difficulty levels for each performance goal. Instead of setting a single goal difficulty level of running the 400 meters in 50 seconds, a runner would actually set three goal difficulty levels: (1) "dream goal," (2) realistic goal, and (3) "self-acceptance goal." A dream goal would have high goal difficulty and reflect a level of performance that is achievable only if athletes perform at the top of their game (i.e., experience flow). A realistic goal would have a moderate difficulty level (i.e., lower than dream goals but higher than self-acceptance goals). Realistic goals reflect an accurate appraisal of a number of factors, such as current performance

capabilities, situational factors, and quality of mental preparation, and would be the performance standard that could be realistically expected with a good, but not great, performance. Finally, self-acceptance goals define the lowest level of performance that athletes can attain and still feel somewhat successful. These goals are designed to help athletes deal with those situations when they perform poorly, helping them to still take away positive things from a below-average performance.

Step 2: Develop Goal Commitment

For goals to have motivational value, individuals must develop a high degree of commitment to goal achievement (see Figure 19.1). Goal commitment is an important component of Locke's (1968) goal setting model; he emphasizes that unless individuals are committed to achieving their goals, they will probably not employ the necessary implementation strategies to achieve them. Moreover, Locke postulates that factors such as participation in setting the goal, incentives available for goal achievement, and the level of trust and supportiveness of others in the organization, including coaches, teammates, and parents, are important to the development of high commitment. In two meta-analyses, Locke and his colleagues (Locke, 1996; Locke, Latham, & Erez, 1988) noted two consistent findings for goal commitment. First, goal commitment is most important when goals are specific and difficult. Second, goal commitment is enhanced when the goal is perceived to be important yet attainable.

Interestingly, the mechanism by which commitment influences goal setting may be somewhat more complicated than it appears. For example, Locke and Latham (1990a) have identified an interesting interaction between level of commitment and goal difficulty. They argue that under low goal difficulty, low-commitment individuals probably will perform better than their high-commitment counterparts, whereas under high goal difficulty conditions, the opposite occurs. These predictions suggest that highly committed performers will attempt to make their performance conform to their goals, whether they are easy or difficult, more than will less-committed performers, thus highlighting the importance of setting difficult goals to enhance performance. General goal setting research has confirmed that a number of factors can improve commitment, including the authority of the individual assigning the goals (e.g., Latham, Erez, & Locke, 1988; Latham & Lee, 1986; Latham & Yukl, 1975; Oldham, 1975), peer influences (e.g., Matsui et al., 1987; Rakestraw & Weiss, 1981), competition (e.g., Locke & Shaw, 1984; Mitchell, Rothman, & Liden, 1985; Shalley, Oldham, & Porac, 1987), public disclosure of goals (e.g., Hayes et al., 1985; Hollenbeck, Williams, & Klein, 1989), incentives and rewards (e.g., Huber, 1985; Riedel, Nebeker, & Cooper, 1988; Terborg, 1976), and goal participation (e.g., Earley, 1985; Earley & Kanfer, 1985; Erez, 1986; Erez, Earley, & Hulin, 1985).

Interestingly, Locke and Latham's (1990a) review of the goal participation literature revealed that participation has a negligible impact on enhancing goal effectiveness through increased commitment. A number of studies (e.g., Boyce & Wayda, 1994; Earley & Kanfer, 1985; Erbaugh & Barnett, 1986; Hollenbeck et al., 1989; A. Lee & Edwards, 1984; Racicot, Day, & Lord, 1991) have demonstrated that assigned goals are more difficult and inspire higher levels of effort and commitment than do self-set goals. Interestingly, Hinsz (1995) found that despite the higher performance in the assigned goal condition, participants in the self-set goal condition had more positive affect toward setting goals. However, these results were far from unanimous, as three studies (Ludwig & Geller, 1997; Madden, 1996; Yearta, Maitlis, & Briner, 1995) yielded contradictory results.

Sport research on commitment tends to contradict general goal results. However, this finding is based on Kyllo and Landers's (1995) meta-analysis, in which they demonstrated a significantly larger effect size for self-set than assigned goals. These results much be questioned based on conclusions that found effect sizes of .62 for cooperative, .49 for self-set, and .32 for assigned goals because of extremely small sample sizes (i.e., 2 participants in the cooperative goal condition, 24 participants in the self-set condition, and 100 for the assigned condition). Consistent with the general goal literature, the present review with significantly more sport participation studies found that only one (Boyce, 1990b) of seven studies supported the efficacy of participation to enhance commitment or performance (see Table 19.1). Recent research with Olympic athletes (Weinberg et al., in press) indicates that commitment can be enhanced by a variety of factors, particularly (1) intrinsic factors (e.g., participation in setting goals and/or telling others), (2) extrinsic factors (e.g., rewards, sponsorship/endorsements, national team, and/or international medal), and (3) social support factors (e.g., support from others and/or help shaping goals). This research also confirmed that writing goals down and posting them were goal implementation strategies that fostered enhanced commitment. Moreover, more effective goal setters could be distinguished from less effective goal setters based on their commitment in two areas: social support from significant others and extrinsic rewards (Burton et al., in preparation).

Step 3: Evaluate Barriers to Goal Attainment

Once individuals become committed to their goals, the next step is to evaluate what obstacles and roadblocks might prevent goal attainment (Locke & Latham, 1990a; see Figure 19.1). Athletes encounter many obstacles and roadblocks to goal attainment, but three of the most common are situational factors, knowledge, and skill. Thus, for a team to attain their goal of enhancing their defensive rebounding, they may need to evaluate the factors that are currently preventing them from being a good rebounding team. A quick analysis may show that (1) little practice time is devoted to developing rebounding skills, (2) players do not have good knowledge of where they need to position themselves to rebound shots missed from specific locations on the court, and (3) players have insufficient upper body strength to block out opponents or pull down rebounds that they get their hands on. Thus, a series of subgoals may need to be developed to help overcome each of these barriers so the team can rebound more effectively.

The area of obstacles or barriers to goal attainment has not been extensively studied in the goal literature. In their recent study of the goal patterns of Olympic athletes, Weinberg et al. (in press) found that this group of elite athletes reported two types of goal barriers they commonly encountered in sport: internal/goal and external/social barriers. Internal/goal barriers included such factors as lack of confidence, deadlines too short, lack of physical skills, lack of feedback, vagueness of goals, unrealistically difficult goals, and too many or conflicting goals. External/social barriers included such factors as lack of time to properly train, work commitments, family and personal responsibilities, and lack of social support. Moreover, this research confirmed that more effective goal setters could be discriminated from less effective goal setters based on having fewer internal/goal and external/social barriers (Burton et al., in preparation).

Step 4: Construct Action Plans

Goals are more effective when a systematic plan is developed to guide attainment (Locke & Latham, 1990a; see Figure 19.1). Obviously, once obstacles have been identified, action plans must be developed to overcome these barriers, enabling goals to be attained. However, even in the absence of significant barriers, planning a systematic process by which goals are to be attained can speed up the process and make it more efficient.

The efficacy of action plans and their impact on goal effectiveness has received almost no attention in sport and nonsport goal research. However, constructing effective action plans clearly seems to require a systematic approach to problem solving, such as Mahoney and Mahoney's (1976) "personal science" process. In personal science, each letter in the word science represents a critical step in the problem-solving process: S = specify the problem, C = collect data, I = identify patterns, E = evaluate options, N = narrow and experiment, C = collect additional data to monitor progress, and E = extend or revise solutions that are not optimally effective. Each of the first five steps in the personal science process facilitates the development of effective action plans. For example, once the problem of improving a team's defensive rebounding has been identified, the next step would be to collect data on current rebounding performance, perhaps through a detailed evaluation of previous game tapes. Next, patterns have to be identified in the previous 10 games' worth of data that help or hurt rebounding effectiveness. For example, failure to make contact with opponents and lack of strength may be patterns that hurt rebounding performance, whereas strong jumping ability, good eye-hand coordination, and good anticipation seem to be patterns that help rebounding effectiveness. Then, a number of options need to be developed for solving the problem, emphasizing both practicality and creativity. Finally, a limited number of solutions (usually the three to five best) are selected for implementation to meet the demands of this situation.

In the three studies investigating action plans, Heckhausen and Strang (1988) demonstrated that performers who were more effective at developing action plans to modify exertion performed better on a simulated basketball task, particularly under stressful conditions, than did less action-oriented performers. Additionally, survey research with both collegiate and Olympic athletes (Burton et al., 1998, in preparation) revealed that more effective goal setters used action plans significantly more frequently and effectively than did less effective goal setters.

Step 5: Obtain Feedback

Locke and Latham's (1990a) goal theory contends that feedback is an essential part of the goal setting process and necessary for realizing performance-enhancement effects from setting goals (see Figure 19.1). In the most comprehensive review of the role of feedback on goal setting to date, Locke and Latham (1990a) reviewed 33 studies comparing the effectiveness of goals plus feedback with either goals or feedback individually. They found that 17 of 18 studies showed that the combination of goals and feedback was significantly better than goals alone, and 21 of 22 studies revealed that the combination was superior to feedback

alone. Moreover, Mento et al.'s (1987) meta-analysis of goal setting research reported that when feedback was added to goal setting, productivity increased an additional 17%. Thus, the consensus of the general goal setting literature is that feedback is an important and necessary moderator of goal setting effects.

Subsequent self-monitoring research (Earley, Northcraft, Lee, & Lituchy, 1990; Hutchison & Garstka, 1996; Locke, 1996; B. Martens, Hiralall, & Bradley, 1997; Mesch, Farh, & Podsakoff, 1994; Roberts & Reed, 1996; Shoenfelt, 1996; Tzetzis, Kioumourtzoglou, & Mavromatis, 1997; Vance & Colella, 1990; Zagumny & Johnson, 1992; Zimmerman & Kitsantas, 1996) has further confirmed the importance of feedback on goal attainment. Locke's (1996) meta-analysis revealed that goal setting is most effective when progress feedback is given. However, he cautions that feedback is only as effective as the individual's reaction. If feedback is viewed negatively, self-efficacy and effort expended toward the goal may be compromised. Similarly, Vance and Colella compared two types of feedback and concluded that when goal discrepancy feedback became too negative (i.e., individuals are far from reaching their goals), goals were abandoned. Interestingly, when performers were given feedback about how goals compare to both current and previous performance, they shifted their goal to exceeding past performance rather than achieving the more difficult current goal. Thus, it appears that individuals revert to a more ideographic form of comparison when objective goal difficulty is too high.

Step 6: Evaluate Goal Attainment

Evaluation may be the most critical step in the goal setting process (Locke & Latham, 1990a; see Figure 19.1). Only when athletes evaluate goals do the motivational and self-confidence benefits of goal setting become evident. The evaluation process involves a comparison of current performance with the original goal. If performance equals or exceeds the goal, then that positive discrepancy should be informational about competence, raising self-confidence and increasing intrinsic motivation. If performance fails to reach goal levels, then individuals should be motivated to work even harder to attain goals in the future. In either case, goal evaluation should promote increased motivation, and goal attainment, or even significant progress toward achieving a goal, should also foster increased self-confidence.

Locke and Latham (1990a) hypothesize similar but slightly more complex benefits from evaluation of goal feedback. They suggest that feedback prompts a complex appraisal process that influences goal mechanisms by providing information that either enhances self-efficacy and perceived ability (e.g., Bandura & Cervone, 1983; Locke, Frederick, Lee, & Bobko, 1984) or allows adjustment or improvement of task strategies (e.g., Latham & Baldes, 1975). If feedback evaluation indicates a small goal-performance discrepancy, individuals usually are satisfied and maintain a similar level of effort. However, if evaluation reveals a large goal-performance discrepancy that prompts dissatisfaction with goal progress, Locke and Latham predict that the motivational response will differ depending on individuals' level of self-efficacy. For high-self-efficacy individuals who set high goals, negative evaluation should prompt them to substantially increase their effort and persistence levels and the quality of their task strategies, usually enhancing performance. For low-self-efficacy performers who set low goals, negative evaluation should impair performance because it prompts reductions in effort and persistence and deterioration in task strategies (Locke & Latham, 1990a).

Kirschenbaum (1984) concluded that self-monitoring and self-evaluation are necessary but not sufficient conditions for maintaining effective self-regulation. Kirschenbaum and Tomarken (1982) argued that increasing self-awareness through self-monitoring and evaluation typically increases attempts to match behavior to goals. However, there seems to be an inherent trade-off in the self-monitoring/evaluation process. If monitoring and evaluation are too infrequent, athletes will have difficulty perceiving improvement in competence, a necessary condition to enhance intrinsic motivation (e.g., Deci & Ryan, 1985; Vallerand, Gauvin, & Halliwell, 1986). However, if monitoring and evaluation are too frequent, it may be difficult to maintain a performance orientation because extensive evaluation makes outcome concerns more salient (e.g., Nicholls, 1984b), making performers feel like pawns because goals are perceived as controlling rather than informational (e.g., deCharms, 1992; Deci & Ryan, 1985; Vallerand et al., 1986). These evaluation patterns are consistent with self-regulation research (e.g., Kirschenbaum, Tomarken, & Ordman, 1982) that suggests moderately specific and longer-term plans may facilitate self-control to a greater degree than specific, short-term plans. Indeed, anecdotal evidence confirms that maintaining the same goals for weekly intervals seems to facilitate improvement more than changing goals daily.

Step 7: Reinforce Goal Achievement

Reinforcement principles emphasize that reinforcing goal achievement should increase the quantity or quality of that behavior (Locke & Latham, 1990a; Smith, 1998; see Figure 19.1). Thus, reinforcing goal achievement should

further enhance motivation to set and reach new goals, prompting the goal setting process to be repeated. Using shaping procedures, skill acquisition is broken down into a series of realistic steps, each representing a specific goal. Athletes are rewarded for attaining the goal, using a reinforcement schedule that emphasizes immediate reinforcement on every attempt initially and moving to a delayed, variable schedule. Once the initial goal is attained consistently over a period of time, the next higher goal is set and the process is repeated until the athlete finally performs the skill with the desired level of proficiency. For example, teaching a young player to shoot a basketball may require breaking down the shooting process into five steps, each step representing a specific goal in the shaping process. Step 1 may be to consistently shoot with the elbow under the basketball. Regardless of what other form problems the player might have and whether the ball goes in the basket or not, each shot performed with the elbow in the correct position is reinforced immediately. Gradually, reinforcement on elbow position is delayed and provided more intermittently. Once consistent performance of elbow position mechanics has been attained, a new goal is set such as a high release point. Now execution of shooting mechanics with correct elbow position and release point is required for reinforcement. Again, reinforcement gradually moves from immediate to delayed and from constant to intermittent until consistency is attained on Goal 2. The process continues through as many additional steps/goals as necessary to attain consistently correct overall shooting mechanics.

In summary, one of the reasons that goal setting effects have been less consistent and robust in sport is the failure of researchers and practitioners to use all seven steps of the goal implementation process. A paucity of research has been conducted on many of these variables, but each step was discussed, highlighting critical implementation strategies for the practitioner and topics needing additional research. Clearly, the focus of future research in sport needs to switch from basic questions of whether goals work and what types work best to more conceptual, process-oriented questions about how goals work and the influence of key process variables on how athletes set goals. The next section highlights ideas for future directions in goal setting research in sport.

FUTURE DIRECTIONS IN GOAL SETTING RESEARCH IN SPORT

Although goal setting is one of the most heavily researched topics in sport psychology, a number of important issues still need to be resolved, particularly relating to the influence of key process variables on goal effectiveness. Six areas of future research seem to be critical if a better understanding of goal setting is to be obtained and goals are to become an even more effective performance enhancement tool in sport and exercise:

1. What is the optimal level of goal difficulty for specific individuals and particular situations?

2. What are the antecedents of goal commitment, and how can goal commitment be increased for less inherently attractive goals?

3. What is the role of self-monitoring and evaluation in the goal setting process, and how can the optimal amount and type of self-monitoring/evaluation be determined?

4. What is the role of action plans in goal setting effectiveness, and how can they be developed most successfully?

5. What role does task complexity play in goal setting effectiveness?

6. What type of generalization effects can be expected with goal setting, and how can generalization effects be maximized across people, tasks, and domains?

Optimal Goal Difficulty

Although Burton, Daw, et al. (1989) attempted to assess typical goal difficulty levels for different goal setting styles for learning basketball skills in a class situation, little is known about how well these goal difficulty ranges generalize to more competitive situations or other sports. Additional questions concerning how to optimize goal difficulty include: How should goal difficulty be adjusted when key situational factors such as importance of the competition change? How does an adjustment in personal goal difficulty levels influence performance? and Is the goal difficulty–performance relationship linear or curvilinear?

Components of Goal Commitment

For goals to have motivational value, individuals must have a high degree of commitment to attain them (Locke & Latham, 1990a). Goal commitment is an important component of Locke's goal setting model, which emphasizes that factors such as participation in setting the goal, incentives available for goal achievement, and the level of trust and supportiveness of others in the organization such as coaches, teammates, and parents arc important to the development of high commitment. Moreover, Locke and Latham have concluded that lack of goal commitment often significantly reduces the effectiveness of goal setting programs, a

conclusion supported by Kyllo and Landers (1995) in sport and exercise domains. As suggested earlier in this chapter, one important question needing further research is the impact of goal difficulty on goal commitment. Additional goal commitment questions needing further examination include: How does commitment relate to locus of control? What is the relationship between commitment and perceived threat? and How effective is identification as a motivational strategy for enhancing commitment?

Goal Monitoring and Evaluation

A major dilemma in maximizing goal setting effectiveness is that athletes do not like to make the time or put forth the effort to self-monitor and evaluate goals regularly. However, without these critical goal implementation steps, research confirms that goal setting effectiveness is reduced. Several goal monitoring and evaluation questions needing further research include: Does excessive self-evaluation lower perceived ability? If so, how frequently and through what mechanisms? What is the most effective way to provide feedback to enhance both self-confidence and motivation? Can social support (e.g., the buddy system) be used to facilitate self-monitoring? What strategies can enhance the enjoyment of and adherence to self-monitoring and self-evaluation? and What specific mechanisms are responsible for the positive impact of goal monitoring and evaluation on performance?

Environmental Engineering/ Developing Action Plans

Goal setting research assessing the moderating effects of task complexity (Mento et al., 1987) has suggested that the motivational benefits of goals work only when athletes are practicing skills correctly and have good action plans for long-term skill development (e.g., Burton et al., 1998, in preparation; Hall & Byrne, 1988). Thus, optimal skill development requires first developing a fundamentally sound technique and then practicing that skill until it becomes highly automated. For complex skills, competent coaches can help athletes develop correct technique. Moreover, coaches must also understand the basic principles of periodization of training so they can develop accurate action plans that help athletes adjust goals appropriately during different portions of the training or skill development cycle (Bompa, 1999; Burton, 1987).

One of the most difficult aspects of skill development is understanding when a learning strategy is appropriate and needs only systematic practice to automate skills and when it is limited or ineffectual and a new strategy must be developed to reach one's performance potential. Abandoning an effective strategy too soon is undesirable and will only lengthen the time necessary to automate skills. However, practicing an ineffective technique will prevent optimal skill development. Perhaps one of the talents that separates effective from ineffective coaches is the ability to understand the skill development process well enough to know which approach is needed in a particular situation. Clearly, goal setting is dramatically changed based on which approach is taken, so research is needed to investigate the effectiveness of each approach and key process variables responsible for those changes. Future research is needed on a number of environmental engineering/action plan questions: Does formal problem-solving training facilitate the development of new strategies necessary to enhance complex skills? What factors need to be included in effective action plans? and How detailed do actions plans need to be to maximize goal effectiveness?

Goal Setting for Complex Tasks

Locke and Latham (1990a) argue that the motivational effects of goals will not enhance performance on complex tasks if individuals are not using appropriate task strategies. Thus, task complexity should complicate and lengthen the process by which goals facilitate performance because individuals must first find or develop effective new task strategies and then use the motivational impact of goals (i.e., effort and persistence) to make these new task strategies work, a prediction confirmed by Burton (1989b) for learning basketball skills. Thus, task complexity questions include: How much longer does it take for complex tasks to demonstrate goal effects compared to simple tasks? Should the types of goals set be modified for complex tasks? and Do action plans need to be modified for more complex tasks?

Generalization of Goal Setting Effects

Kirschenbaum (1984) suggested that self-regulatory failure typically occurs because of the inability to generalize relevant behaviors to other settings, times, or conditions. Kirschenbaum emphasized that circumventing generalization problems requires an obsessive-compulsive behavior style in which vigilant self-monitoring and self-evaluation lead to appropriate changes in goals or goal levels. Not only do goals need to be set in sport to help athletes develop new skills and strategies, but goals also need to be established that focus on how skills and strategies must be adjusted in different competitions, at different times of the competitive season, and against different opponents. Some goal generalization questions that warrant further research include: What situational cues typically prompt athletes to

adopt similar versus dissimilar action plans for implementing goals? How can athletes be trained to successfully implement the goal setting process in the face of changing situational factors? and How can goal setting strategies learned in sport best be transferred to other achievement domains, such as academic and job domains?

CONCLUSIONS

This chapter reviewed goal setting research and arrived at two unmistakable conclusions. First, goal setting is an effective performance enhancement strategy, although goals demonstrate less consistent and robust performance enhancement effects in sport compared to business settings. Second, goal setting is somewhat of a paradox because this relatively simple technique seems to be more difficult to implement effectively than it initially appears. Goal attribute research reviewed six types of goals—goal focus, goal specificity, goal difficulty, goal valence, goal proximity, and goal collectivity—and recommended that practitioners set process, performance, and outcome goals that are specific, measurable, and difficult. Moreover, goals should also be focused positively on what athletes are trying to accomplish and include both short- and long-term goals and team and individual goals. Five plausible reasons were offered for why goal setting is less effective in sport than business settings: small sample sizes, athletes operating closer to their performance potential, task complexity, individual differences in goal preferences, and failure to employ appropriate goal implementation strategies. Based on a review of the sport goal literature, all five explanations were deemed plausible to explain this discrepancy. However, inappropriate use of goal implementation strategies also provided a realistic explanation for moderate goal effectiveness results in sport. The seven steps of the goal implementation process were described and the importance of each step for practitioners and researchers was highlighted. Finally, six areas of future research were identified, emphasizing the need to get away from simplistic questions (e.g., Do goals work? What types of goals are most effective?) and focus on key process variables such as goal implementation strategies to determine why and how goals work.

REFERENCES

Anderson, D.C., Crowell, C.R., Doman, M., & Howard, G.S. (1988). Performance posting, goal setting, and activity-contingent praise as applied to a university hockey team. *Journal of Applied Psychology, 73,* 87–95.

Anshel, M.H., Weinberg, R.S., & Jackson, A. (1992). The effect of goal difficulty and task complexity on intrinsic motivation and motor performance. *Journal of Sport Behavior, 15,* 159–176.

Bandura, A. (1977). Self-efficacy: Toward a unifying theory of behavioral change. *Psychological Review, 84,* 191–215.

Bandura, A. (1986). *Social foundations of thought and actions: A social cognitive theory.* Englewood Cliffs, NJ: Prentice Hall.

Bandura, A., & Cervone, D. (1983). Self-evaluative and self-efficacy mechanisms governing the motivational effects of goal systems. *Journal of Personality and Social Psychology, 45,* 1017–1028.

Bandura, A., & Schunk, D.H. (1981). Cultivating competence, self-efficacy, and intrinsic interest through proximal self-motivation. *Journal of Personality and Social Psychology, 41,* 586–598.

Bandura, A., & Simon, K.M. (1977). The role of proximal intentions in self-regulation of refractory behavior. *Cognitive Therapy and Research, 1,* 177–193.

Bar-Eli, M., Hartman, I., & Levy-Kolker, N. (1994). Using goal setting to improve physical performance of adolescents with behavior disorders: The effect of goal proximity. *Adapted Physical Activity Quarterly, 11,* 86–97.

Bar-Eli, M., Levy-Kolker, N., Tenenbaum, G., & Weinberg, R.S. (1993). Effect of goal difficulty on performance of aerobic, anaerobic and power tasks in laboratory and field settings. *Journal of Sport Behavior, 16,* 17–32.

Bar-Eli, M., Tenenbaum, G., Pie, J., Btesh, Y., & Almog, A. (1997). Effect of goal difficulty, goal specificity and duration of practice time intervals on muscular endurance performance. *Journal of Sports Sciences, 15,* 125–135.

Barnett, M.L. (1977). Effects of two methods of goal setting on learning a gross motor task. *Research Quarterly, 48,* 19–23.

Barnett, M.L., & Stanicek, J.A. (1979). Effects of goal-setting on achievement in archery. *Research Quarterly, 50,* 328–332.

Beggs, A. (1990). Goal setting in sport. In G. Jones & L. Hardy (Eds.), *Stress and performance in sport* (pp. 135–170). Chichester, England: Wiley.

Bompa, T.O. (1999). *Periodization training for sports.* Champaign, IL: Human Kinetics.

Borrelli, B., & Mermelstein, R. (1994). Goal setting and behavior change in a smoking cessation program. *Cognitive Therapy and Research, 18,* 69–83.

Boutcher, S. (1990). The role of performance routines in sport. In G. Jones & L. Hardy (Eds.), *Stress and performance in sport* (pp. 231–245). Chichester, England: Wiley.

Boyce, B.A. (1990a). Effects of goal specificity and goal difficulty upon skill acquisition of a selected shooting task. *Perceptual and Motor Skills, 70,* 1031–1039.

Boyce, B.A. (1990b). The effect of instructor-set goals upon skill acquisition and retention of a selected shooting task. *Journal of Teaching in Physical Education, 9,* 115–122.

Boyce, B.A. (1992a). Effects of assigned versus participant-set goals on skill acquisition and retention of a selected shooting task. *Journal of Teaching in Physical Education, 11,* 220–234.

Boyce, B.A. (1992b). The effects of goal proximity on skill acquisition and retention of a shooting task in a field-based setting. *Journal of Sport & Exercise Psychology, 14,* 298–308.

Boyce, B.A. (1994). The effects of goal setting on performance and spontaneous goal-setting behavior of experienced pistol shooters. *The Sport Psychologist, 8,* 87–93.

Boyce, B.A., & Bingham, S.M. (1997). The effects of self-efficacy and goal setting on bowling performance. *Journal of Teaching in Physical Education, 16,* 312–323.

Boyce, B.A., & Wayda, V.K. (1994). The effects of assigned and self-set goals on task performance. *Journal of Sport & Exercise Psychology, 16,* 258–269.

Brawley, L.R., Carron, A.V., & Widmeyer, W.N. (1992). The nature of group goals in sport teams: A phenomenological analysis. *The Sport Psychologist, 6,* 323–333.

Brawley, L.R., Carron, A.V., & Widmeyer, W.N. (1993). The influence of the group and its cohesiveness on perceptions of group goal-related variables. *Journal of Sport & Exercise Psychology, 15,* 245–260.

Burton, D. (1987, September). Integrating Psychological Skills Training (PST) into a periodized training program. In G. Dirkin (Chair), *Periodized training models: Implications for the sport psychologist.* Symposium conducted at the meeting of the Association for the Advancement of Applied Sport Psychology, Newport Beach, CA.

Burton, D. (1989a). The impact of goal specificity and task complexity on basketball skill development. *The Sport Psychologist, 3,* 34–47.

Burton, D. (1989b). Winning isn't everything: Examining the impact of performance goals on collegiate swimmers' cognitions and performance. *The Sport Psychologist, 3,* 105–132.

Burton, D. (1992). The Jekyll/Hyde nature of goals: Reconceptualizing goal setting in sport. In T. Horn (Ed.), *Advances in sport psychology* (pp. 267–297). Champaign, IL: Human Kinetics.

Burton, D. (1993). Goal setting in sport. In R.N. Singer, M. Murphey, & L.K. Tennant (Eds.), *Handbook of research on sport psychology* (pp. 467–491). New York: Macmillan.

Burton, D. (1999, June). *Goal-setting: Current findings and practical implications.* Paper presented at the second annual Sport Psychology Conference, National University of Madrid, Spain.

Burton, D., Daw, J., Williams-Rice, B.T., & Phillips, D. (1989, October). *Goal setting styles: The influence of self-esteem on goal difficulty preferences.* Paper presented at the meeting of the Canadian Society for Psychomotor Learning and Sport Psychology, Victoria, Canada.

Burton, D., Weinberg, R.S., Yukelson, D., & Weigand, D.A. (1998). The goal effectiveness paradox in sport: Examining the goal practices of collegiate athletes. *The Sport Psychologist, 12,* 404–418.

Burton, D., Weinberg, R.S., Yukelson, D., & Weigand, D.A. (1999). An elite perspective on the goal effectiveness paradox in sport: Surveying the goal practices of Olympic athletes. Manuscript in preparation.

Campbell, D.J., & Furrer, D.M. (1995). Goal setting and competition as determinants of task performance. *Journal of Organizational Behavior, 16,* 377–389.

Carroll, S.J. (1986). Management by objectives: Three decades of research and experience. In S.L. Rynes & G.T. Milkovich (Eds.), *Current issues in human resource management.* Plano, TX: Business Publications.

Chesney, A., & Locke, E. (1991). Relationships among goal difficulty, business strategies, and performance on a complex management simulation task. *Academy of Management Journal, 34,* 400–424.

Chidester, T.R., & Grigsby, W.C. (1984). A meta-analysis of the goal-setting-performance literature. In J.A. Pearce & R.B. Robinson (Eds.), *Academy of management proceedings* (pp. 202–206). Ada, OH: Academy of Management.

Cohen, J. (1992). A power primer. *Psychological Bulletin, 112,* 155–159.

DeCharms, R. (1976). *Enhancing motivation: Change in the classroom.* New York: Irvington.

DeCharms, R. (1992). Personal causation and the origin concept. In C.P. Smith, J.W. Atkinson, D.C. McClelland, & J. Veroff (Eds.), *Motivation and personality: Handbook of thematic content analysis* (pp. 325–333). New York: Cambridge University Press.

Deci, E.L., & Ryan, R.M. (1985). *Intrinsic motivation and self-determination in human behavior.* New York: Plenum Press.

DeShon, R.P., & Alexander, R.A. (1996). Goal setting effects on implicit and explicit learning of complex tasks. *Organizational Behavior and Human Decision Processes, 65,* 18–36.

Duda, J.L. (1992). Motivation in sport settings: A goal perspective approach. In G.C. Roberts (Ed.), *Motivation in sport and exercise* (pp. 57–92). Champaign, IL: Human Kinetics.

Dweck, C.S. (1980). Learned helplessness in sports. In C.H. Nadeau, W.R. Halliwell, K.M. Newell, & G.C. Roberts (Eds.), *Psychology of motor behavior and sport–1979* (pp. 1–12). Champaign, IL: Human Kinetics.

Dweck, C.S. (1999). *Self theories: Their role in motivation, personality, and development.* Philadelphia: Taylor & Francis.

Earley, P.C. (1985). Influence of information, choice, and task complexity upon goal acceptance, performance, and personal goals. *Journal of Applied Psychology, 70,* 481–491.

Earley, P.C., Connolly, T., & Ekegren, G. (1989). Goals, strategy development, and task performance: Some limits on the efficacy of goal setting. *Journal of Applied Psychology, 74,* 24–33.

Earley, P.C., & Kanfer, R. (1985). The influence of component participation and role models on goal acceptance, goal satisfaction, and performance. *Organizational Behavior and Human Decision Processes, 36,* 378–390.

Earley, P.C., Northcraft, G., Lee, C., & Lituchy, T. (1990). Impact of process and outcome feedback on the relation of goal setting to task performance. *Academy of Management Journal, 33,* 87–105.

Elliott, E.S., & Dweck, C.S. (1988). Goals: An approach to motivation and achievement. *Journal of Personality and Social Psychology, 54,* 5–12.

Erbaugh, S.J., & Barnett, M.L. (1986). Effects of modeling and goal-setting on the jumping performance of primary-grade children. *Perceptual and Motor Skills, 63,* 1287–1293.

Erez, M. (1986). The congruence of goal setting strategies with socio-cultural values, and its effect on performance. *Journal of Management, 12,* 585–592.

Erez, M., Earley, P.C., & Hulin, C.L. (1985). The impact of participation on goal acceptance and performance: A two-step model. *Academy of Management Journal, 28,* 50–66.

Erez, M., & Zidon, I. (1984). Effect of goal acceptance on the relationship of goal difficulty to performance. *Journal of Applied Psychology, 69,* 69–78.

Fairall, D.G., & Rodgers, W.M. (1997). The effects of goal-setting methods on goal attributes in athletes: A field experiment. *Journal of Sport & Exercise Psychology, 19,* 1–16.

Filby, W.C.D., Maynard, I.W., & Graydon, J.K. (1999). The effect of multiple-goal strategies on performance outcomes in training and competition. *Journal of Applied Sport Psychology, 11,* 230–246.

Frierman, S.H., Weinberg, R.S., & Jackson, A. (1990). The relationship between goal proximity and specificity in bowling: A field experiment. *The Sport Psychologist, 4,* 145–154.

Galvan, Z.J., & Ward, P. (1998). Effects of public posting on inappropriate on-court behaviors by collegiate tennis players. *The Sport Psychologist, 12,* 419–426.

Garland, H., Weinberg, R.S., Bruya, L., & Jackson, A. (1988). Self-efficacy and endurance performance: A longitudinal field test of cognitive mediation theory. *Applied Psychology: An International Review, 34,* 381–394.

Giannini, J.M., Weinberg, R.S., & Jackson, A.J. (1988). The effects of mastery, competitive, and cooperative goals on the performance of simple and complex basketball skills. *Journal of Sport & Exercise Psychology, 10,* 408–417.

Gould, D. (1998). Goal setting for peak performance. In J.M. Williams (Ed.), *Applied sport psychology: Personal growth to peak performance* (3rd ed., pp. 182–196). Mountain View, CA: Mayfield.

Hall, H.K., & Byrne, A.T.J. (1988). Goal setting in sport: Clarifying recent anomalies. *Journal of Sport & Exercise Psychology, 10,* 184–198.

Hall, H.K., Weinberg, R.S., & Jackson, A. (1987). Effects of goal specificity, goal difficulty, and information feedback on endurance performance. *Journal of Sport Psychology, 9,* 43–54.

Hardy, C.J., & Latane, B. (1988). Social loafing in cheerleaders: Effects of team membership and competition. *Journal of Sport & Exercise Psychology, 10,* 109–114.

Hardy, L., Jones, J.G., & Gould, D. (1996). *Understanding psychological preparation for sport: Theory and practice of elite performers.* Chichester, England: Wiley.

Hardy, L., & Nelson, D. (1988). Self-control training in sport and work. *Ergonomics, 31,* 1573–1585.

Harkins, S.G., & Petty, R.E. (1982). Effects of task difficulty and task uniqueness on social loafing. *Journal of Personality and Social Psychology, 43,* 1214–1229.

Hayes, S.C., Rosenfarb, I., Wulfert, E., Munt, E.D., Korn, Z., & Kettle, R.D. (1985). Self-reinforcement effects: An artifact of social standard setting? *Journal of Applied Behavior Analysis, 18,* 201–214.

Heckhausen, H., & Strang, H. (1988). Efficiency under record performance demands: Exertion control—An individual difference variable? *Journal of Personality and Social Psychology, 55,* 489–498.

Hinsz, V. (1995). Goal setting by groups performing an additive task: A comparison with individual goal setting. *Journal of Applied Social Psychology, 25,* 965–990.

Hollenbeck, J.R., Williams, C.R., & Klein, H.J. (1989). An empirical examination of the antecedents of commitment to difficult goals. *Journal of Applied Psychology, 74,* 18–23.

Hollingsworth, B. (1975). Effects of performance goals and anxiety on learning a gross motor task. *Research Quarterly, 46,* 162–168.

Howe, B., & Poole, R. (1992). Goal proximity and achievement motivation of high school boys in a basketball shooting task. *Journal of Teaching in Physical Education, 11,* 248–255.

Huber, V.L. (1985). Comparison of monetary reinforcers and goal setting as learning incentives. *Psychological Reports, 56,* 223–235.

Humphries, C.A., Thomas, J.R., & Nelson, J.K. (1991). Effects of attainable and unattainable goals on mirror-tracing performance and retention of a motor task. *Perceptual and Motor Skills, 72,* 1231–1237.

Hunter, J.E., & Schmidt, F.L. (1983). Quantifying the effects of psychological interventions on employee job performance and work force productivity. *American Psychologist, 38,* 473–478.

Hutchinson, S., & Garstka, M.L. (1996). Sources of perceived organizational support: Goal setting and feedback. *Journal of Applied Social Psychology, 26,* 1351–1366.

Ingham, A., Levinger, G., Graves, J., & Peckham, V. (1974). The Ringlemann effect: Studies of group size and group performance. *Journal of Experimental Social Psychology, 10,* 371–384.

Ivancevich, J.M. (1974). Changes in performance in a management by objectives program. *Administrative Science Quarterly, 19,* 563–574.

Jackson, J.M., & Williams, K.D. (1985). Social loafing on difficult tasks: Working collectively can improve performance. *Journal of Personality and Social Psychology, 49,* 937–942.

James, W. (1890). *The principles of psychology* (Vol. 2). New York: Holt.

Johnson, S.R., Ostrow, A.C., Perna, F.M., & Etzel, E.F. (1997). The effects of group versus individual goal setting on bowling performance. *The Sport Psychologist, 11,* 190–200.

Johnston-O'Connor, E.J., & Kirschenbaum, D.S. (1984). Something succeeds like success: Positive self-monitoring for unskilled golfers. *Cognitive Therapy and Research, 10,* 123–136.

Jones, G., & Cale, A. (in press). Goal difficulty, anxiety and performance. *Ergonomics.*

Jones, G., & Hanton, S. (1996). Interpretation of competitive anxiety symptoms and goal attainment expectancies. *Journal of Sport & Exercise Psychology, 18,* 144–157.

Kane, T.D., Marks, M.A., Zaccaro, S.J., & Blair, V. (1996). Self-efficacy, personal goals, and wrestlers' self-regulation. *Journal of Sport & Exercise Psychology, 18,* 36–48.

Kanfer, R., & Ackerman, P. (1989). Motivation and cognitive abilities: An integrative/aptitude-treatment interaction approach to skill acquisition. *Journal of Applied Psychology, 74,* 657–690.

Kernan, M.G., & Lord, R.G. (1989). The effects of explicit goals and specific feedback on escalation processes. *Journal of Applied Social Psychology, 19,* 1125–1143.

Kerr, N.L., & Brunn, S.E. (1981). Ringlemann revisited: Alternative explanations for the social loafing effect. *Personality and Social Psychology Bulletin, 7,* 224–231.

Kingston, K.M., & Hardy, L. (1994). Factors affecting the salience of outcome, performance, and process goals in golf. In A. Cochran & M. Farrally (Eds.), *Science and golf* (Vol. 2, pp. 144–149). London: Chapman-Hill.

Kingston, K.M., & Hardy, L. (1997). Effects of different types of goals on processes that support performance. *The Sport Psychologist, 11,* 277–293.

Kingston, K.M., Hardy, L., & Markland, D. (1992). Study to compare the effect of two different goal orientations and stress levels on a number of situationally relevant performance subcomponents. *Journal of Sports Sciences, 10,* 610–611.

Kirschenbaum, D.S. (1984). Self-regulation and sport psychology: Nurturing an emerging symbiosis. *Journal of Sport Psychology, 6,* 159–183.

Kirschenbaum, D.S. (1985). Proximity and specificity of planning: A position paper. *Cognitive Therapy and Research, 9,* 489–506.

Kirschenbaum, D.S., Ordman, A.M., Tomarken, A.J., & Holtzbauer, R. (1982). Effects of differential self-monitoring and level of mastery on sport performance: Brain power bowling. *Cognitive Therapy and Research, 6,* 335–342.

Kirschenbaum, D.S., & Tomarken, A.J. (1982). On facing the generalization problem: The study of self-regulatory failure. In P.C. Kendall (Ed.), *Advances in cognitive-behavioral research and therapy* (Vol. 1, pp. 121–200). New York: Academic Press.

Kirschenbaum, D.S., Wittrock, D.A., Smith, R.J., & Monson, W. (1984). Criticism inoculation training: Concept in search of a strategy. *Journal of Sport Psychology, 6,* 77–93.

Kondrasuk, J.N. (1981). Studies in MBO effectiveness. *Academy of Management Review, 6,* 419–430.

Kyllo, L.B., & Landers, D.M. (1995). Goal-setting in sport and exercise: A research synthesis to resolve the controversy. *Journal of Sport & Exercise Psychology, 17,* 117–137.

Lambert, S.M., Moore, D.W., & Dixon, R.S. (1999). Gymnasts in training: The differential effects of self- and coach-set goals as a function of locus of control. *Journal of Applied Sport Psychology, 11,* 72–82.

Larey, T.S., & Paulus, P.B. (1995). Social comparison and goal setting in brainstorming groups. *Journal of Applied Social Psychology, 25,* 1579–1596.

Latane, B. (1986). Responsibility and effort in organizations. In P. Goodman (Ed.), *Groups and organizations* (pp. 277–303). San Francisco: Jossey-Bass.

Latane, B., Williams, K.D., & Harkins, S.G. (1979). Many hands make light the work: The causes and consequences of social loafing. *Journal of Personality and Social Psychology, 37,* 822–832.

Latham, G.P., & Baldes, J.J. (1975). The "practical significance" of Locke's theory of goal setting. *Journal of Applied Psychology, 60,* 122–124.

Latham, G.P., Erez, M., & Locke, E.A. (1988). Resolving scientific disputes by the joint design of crucial experiments by the antagonists: Application to the Erez-Latham dispute regarding participation in goal setting. *Journal of Applied Psychology* (Monograph), *73,* 753–772.

Latham, G.P., & Lee, T.W. (1986). Goal setting. In E.A. Locke (Ed.), *Generalizing from laboratory to field settings: Research findings from industrial-organizational psychology, organizational behavior, and human resource management* (pp. 101–117). Lexington, MA: Heath.

Latham, G.P., & Locke, E.A. (1991). Self-regulation through goal setting. *Organizational Behavior and Human Decision Processes, 50,* 212–247.

Latham, G.P., & Yukl, G.A. (1975). Assigned versus participative goal setting with educated and uneducated woods workers. *Journal of Applied Psychology, 60,* 299–302.

Lazarus, R.S. (1991). *Emotion and adaptation.* New York: Oxford University Press.

Lazarus, R.S., & Folkman, S. (1984). *Stress, appraisal and coping.* New York: Springer.

Lee, A.M., & Edwards, R.V. (1984). Assigned and self-selected goals as determinants of motor skill performance. *Education, 105,* 87–91.

Lee, C. (1988). The relationship between goal setting, self-efficacy and female field hockey team performance. *International Journal of Sport Psychology, 20,* 147–161.

Lerner, B.S., & Locke, E.A. (1995). The effects of goal setting, self-efficacy, competition and personal traits on the performance of an endurance task. *Journal of Sport & Exercise Psychology, 17,* 138–152.

Lerner, B.S., Ostrow, A.C., Yura, M.T., & Etzel, E.F. (1996). The effects of goal-setting and imagery training programs on the free-throw performance of female collegiate basketball players. *The Sport Psychologist, 10,* 382–397.

Locke, E.A. (1968). Toward a theory of task motivation and incentives. *Organizational Behavior and Human Performance, 3,* 157–189.

Locke, E.A. (1982). Relation of goal level to performance with a short work period and multiple goal levels. *Journal of Applied Psychology, 67,* 512–514.

Locke, E.A. (1991). Problems with goal-setting research in sports—and their solution. *Journal of Sport & Exercise Psychology, 8,* 311–316.

Locke, E.A. (1994). Comments on Weinberg and Weigand. *Journal of Sport & Exercise Psychology, 16,* 212–215.

Locke, E.A. (1996). Motivation through conscious goal setting. *Applied and Preventative Psychology, 5,* 117–124.

Locke, E.A., Cartledge, N., & Knerr, C.S. (1970). Studies of the relationship between satisfaction, goal setting, and performance. *Organizational Behavior and Human Performance, 5,* 135–158.

Locke, E.A., Chah, D.O., Harrison, S., & Lustgarten, N. (1989). Separating the effects of goal specificity from goal level. *Organizational Behavior and Human Decision Processes, 43,* 270–287.

Locke, E.A., Frederick, E., Lee, C., & Bobko, P. (1984). Effect of self-efficacy, goals, and task strategies on task performance. *Journal of Applied Psychology, 69,* 241–251.

Locke, E.A., & Latham, G.P. (1990a). *A theory of goal setting and task performance.* Englewood Cliffs, NJ: Prentice-Hall.

Locke, E.A., & Latham, G.P. (1990b). Work motivation and satisfaction: Light at the end of the tunnel. *Psychological Science, 1,* 240–246.

Locke, E.A., Latham, G.P., & Erez, M. (1988). The determinants of goal commitment. *Academy of Management Review, 13,* 23–39.

Locke, E.A., & Shaw, K.N. (1984). Atkinson's inverse-U curve and missing cognitive variables. *Psychological Reports, 55,* 403–412.

Locke, E.A., Shaw, K.N., Saari, L.M., & Latham, G.P. (1981). Goal setting and task performance: 1969–1980. *Psychological Bulletin, 90,* 125–152.

Ludwig, T.D., & Geller, E.S. (1997). Assigned versus participative goal setting and response generalization: Managing injury control among professional pizza deliverers. *Journal of Applied Psychology, 82,* 253–261.

Madden, L.E. (1996). Motivating students to learn better through own goal-setting. *Education, 117,* 411–414.

Maehr, M.L., & Braskamp, L. (1986). *The motivation factor: A theory of personal investment.* Lexington, MA: Heath.

Maehr, M.L., & Nicholls, J.G. (1980). Culture and achievement motivation: A second look. In N. Warren (Ed.), *Studies in cross-cultural psychology* (pp. 341–363). New York: Academic Press.

Mahoney, M.J., & Mahoney, K. (1976). *Permanent weight control.* New York: Norton.

Manderlink, G., & Harackiewicz, J.M. (1984). Proximal versus distal goal setting and intrinsic motivation. *Journal of Personality and Social Psychology, 47,* 918–928.

Martens, B.K., Hiralall, A.S., & Bradley, T.A. (1997). A note to teacher: Improving student behavior through goal setting and feedback. *School Psychology Quarterly, 12,* 33–41.

Matsui, T., Kakuyama, T., & Onglatco, M.L. (1987). Effects of goals and feedback on performance in groups. *Journal of Applied Psychology, 72,* 407–415.

Mento, A.J., Locke, E.A., & Klein, H.J. (1992). Relationship of goal level to valence and instrumentality. *Journal of Applied Psychology, 77,* 395–405.

Mento, A.J., Steel, R.P., & Karren, R.J. (1987). A meta-analytic study of the effects of goal setting on task performance: 1966–1984. *Organizational Behavior and Human Decision Processes, 39,* 52–83.

Mesch, D., Farh, J., & Podsakoff, P. (1994). Effects of feedback sign on group goal setting, strategies, and performance. *Group and Organizational Management, 19,* 309–333.

Miller, J.T., & McAuley, E. (1987). Effects of a goal-setting training program on basketball free-throw self-efficacy and performance. *The Sport Psychologist, 1,* 103–113.

Mitchell, T.R., Rothman, M., & Liden, R.C. (1985). Effects of normative information on task performance. *Journal of Applied Psychology, 70,* 48–55.

Nelson, J.K. (1978). Motivating effects of the use of norms and goals with endurance testing. *Research Quarterly, 49,* 317–321.

Nicholls, J.G. (1984a). Achievement motivation: Conceptions of ability, subjective experience, task choice, and performance. *Psychological Review, 91,* 328–346.

Nicholls, J.G. (1984b). Conceptions of ability and achievement motivation. In R. Ames & C. Ames (Eds.), *Research on motivation in education: Student motivation* (Vol. 1, pp. 39–73). New York: Academic Press.

O'Block, F.R., & Evans, F.H. (1984). Goal setting as a motivational technique. In J.M. Silva & R.S. Weinberg (Eds.), *Psychological foundations of sport* (pp. 188–196). Champaign, IL: Human Kinetics.

Oldham, G.R. (1975). The impact of supervisory characteristics on goal acceptance. *Academy of Management Journal, 18,* 461–475.

Orlick, T. (1986). *Psyching for sport: Mental training for athletes.* Champaign, IL: Human Kinetics.

Orlick, T. (1998). *Embracing your potential.* Champaign, IL: Human Kinetics.

Pierce, B.E., & Burton, D. (1998). Scoring the perfect 10: Investigating the impact of goal-setting styles on a goal-setting program for female gymnasts. *The Sport Psychologist, 12,* 156–168.

Poag, K., & McAuley, E. (1992). Goal setting, self-efficacy and exercise behavior. *Journal of Sport & Exercise Psychology, 14,* 352–360.

Poag-DuCharme, K.A., & Brawley, L.R. (1994). Perceptions of the behavioral influence of goals: A mediational relationship to exercise. *Journal of Applied Sport Psychology, 6,* 32–50.

Racicot, B., Day, D., & Lord, R. (1991). Type A behavior pattern and goal setting under different conditions of choice. *Motivation and Emotion, 15,* 67–79.

Rakestraw, T.L., & Weiss, H.M. (1981). The interaction of social influences and task experience on goals, performance, and performance satisfaction. *Organizational Behavior and Human Performance, 27,* 326–344.

Riedel, J.A., Nebeker, D.M., & Cooper, B.L. (1988). The influence of monetary incentives on goal choice, goal commitment, and task performance. *Organizational Behavior and Human Decision Processes, 42,* 155–180.

Riley, P. (1996). *The winner within: A life plan for team players.* New York: Berkley Books.

Roberts, G., & Reed, T. (1996, Fall). Performance appraisal participation, goal setting and feedback. *Review of Public Personnel Administration,* 29–61.

Rodgers, R.C., & Hunter, J.E. (1989). *The impact of management by objectives on organizational productivity.* Unpublished manuscript, University of Kentucky, Lexington, School of Public Administration.

Ruth, W. (1996). Goal setting and behavior contracting for students with emotional and behavioral difficulties: Analysis of daily, weekly, and total goal attainment. *Psychology in the Schools, 33,* 153–158.

Ryan, T.A. (1970). *Intentional behavior: An approach to human motivation.* New York: Ronald Press.

Shalley, C. (1995). Effects of coaction, expected evaluation, and goal setting on creativity and productivity. *Academy of Management Journal, 38,* 483–503.

Shalley, C.E., Oldham, G.R., & Porac, J.F. (1987). Effects of goal difficulty, goal-setting method, and expected external evaluation on intrinsic motivation. *Academy of Management Journal, 30,* 553–563.

Singer, R., Lidor, R., & Cauraugh, J. (1993). To be aware or not aware? What to think about while learning and performing a motor skill. *The Sport Psychologist, 7,* 19–30.

Shoenfelt, E.L. (1996). Goal setting and feedback as a posttraining strategy to increase the transfer of training. *Perceptual and Motor Skills, 83,* 176–178.

Smith, M., & Lee, C. (1992). Goal setting and performance in a novel coordination task: Mediating mechanisms. *Journal of Sport & Exercise Psychology, 14,* 169–176.

Smith, R.E. (1998). A positive approach to sport performance enhancement: Principles of reinforcement and performance feedback. In J.M. Williams (Ed.), *Applied sport psychology: Personal growth to peak performance* (3rd ed., pp. 28–40). Mountain View, CA: Mayfield.

Swain, A., & Jones, G. (1995). Effects of goal-setting interventions on selected basketball skills: A single-subject design. *Research Quarterly for Exercise and Sport, 66,* 51–63.

Tenenbaum, G., Pinchas, S., Elbaz, G., Bar-Eli, M., & Weinberg, R.S., (1991). Effect of goal proximity and goal specificity on muscular endurance performance: A replication and extension. *Journal of Sport & Exercise Psychology, 13,* 174–187.

Terborg, J.R. (1976). The motivational components of goal setting. *Journal of Applied Psychology, 61,* 613–621.

Theodorakis, Y. (1995). Effects of self-efficacy, satisfaction, and personal goals on swimming performance. *The Sport Psychologist, 9,* 245–253.

Theodorakis, Y. (1996). The influence of goals, commitment, self-efficacy and self-satisfaction on motor performance. *Journal of Applied Sport Psychology, 8,* 171–182.

Theodorakis, Y., Malliou, P., Papaioannou, A., Beneca, A., & Filactakidou, A. (1996). The effect of personal goals, self-efficacy and self-satisfaction on injury rehabilitation. *Journal of Sport Rehabilitation, 5,* 214–223.

Tubbs, M.E. (1986). Goal setting: A meta-analytic examination of the empirical evidence. *Journal of Applied Psychology, 71,* 474–483.

Tzetzis, G., Kioumourtzoglou, E., & Mavromatis, G. (1997). Goal setting and feedback for the development of instructional strategies. *Perceptual and Motor Skills, 84,* 1411–1427.

Vallerand, R.J., Gauvin, L.I., & Halliwell, W.R. (1986). Effects of zero-sum competition on children's intrinsic motivation and perceived competence. *Journal of Social Psychology, 126,* 465–472.

Vance, R., & Colella, A. (1990). Effects of two types of feedback on goal acceptance and personal goals. *Journal of Applied Psychology, 75,* 68–76.

Wanlin, C.M., Hrycaiko, D.W., Martin, G.L., & Mahon, M. (1997). The effects of a goal-setting package on the performance of speed skaters. *Journal of Applied Sport Psychology, 9,* 212–228.

Weinberg, R.S. (1994). Goal setting and performance in sport and exercise settings: A synthesis and critique. *Medicine and Science in Sports and Exercise, 26,* 469–477.

Weinberg, R.S., Bruya, L.D., & Jackson, A. (1985). The effects of goal proximity and goal specificity on endurance performance. *Journal of Sport Psychology, 7,* 296–305.

Weinberg, R.S., Bruya, L.D., Jackson, A., & Garland, H. (1986). Goal difficulty and endurance performance: A challenge to the goal attainability assumption. *Journal of Sport Behavior, 10,* 82–92.

Weinberg, R.S., Bruya, L.D., Longino, J., & Jackson, A. (1988). Effect of goal proximity and specificity on endurance performance of primary-grade children. *Journal of Sport & Exercise Psychology, 10,* 81–91.

Weinberg, R.S., Burke, K.L., & Jackson, A. (1997). Coaches' and players' perceptions of goal setting in junior tennis: An exploratory investigation. *The Sport Psychologist, 11,* 426–439.

Weinberg, R.S., Burton, D., Yukelson, D., & Weigand, D.A. (1993). Goal setting in competitive sport: An exploratory investigation of practices of collegiate athletes. *The Sport Psychologist, 7,* 275–289.

Weinberg, R.S., Burton, D., Yukelson, D., & Weigand, D.A. (2000). Perceived goal setting practices of Olympic athletes: An exploratory investigation. *The Sport Psychologist, 14,* 279–295.

Weinberg, R.S., Fowler, C., Jackson, A., Bagnall, J., & Bruya, L. (1991). Effect of goal difficulty on motor performance: A replication across tasks and subjects. *Journal of Sport & Exercise Psychology, 13,* 160–173.

Weinberg, R.S., Garland, H., Bruya, L., & Jackson, A. (1990). Effect of goal difficulty and positive reinforcement on endurance performance. *Journal of Sport & Exercise Psychology, 12,* 144–156.

Weinberg, R.S., Stitcher, T., & Richardson, P. (1994). Effects of seasonal goal setting on lacrosse performance. *The Sport Psychologist, 8,* 166–175.

Weinberg, R.S., & Weigand, D.A. (1993). Goal setting in sport and exercise: A reaction to Locke. *Journal of Sport & Exercise Psychology, 15,* 88–96.

Weinberg, R.S., & Weigand, D.A. (1996). Let the discussions continue: A reaction to Locke's comments on Weinberg and Weigand. *Journal of Sport & Exercise Psychology, 18,* 89–93.

Weldon, E., Jehn, K., & Pradham, P. (1991). Processes that mediate the relationship between a group goal and improved group performance. *Journal of Personality and Social Psychology, 61,* 555–569.

White, P.H., Kjelgaard, M.M., & Harkins, S.G. (1995). Testing the contribution of self-evaluation to goal-setting effects. *Journal of Personality and Social Psychology, 69,* 69–79.

Widmeyer, W.N., & Ducharme, K. (1997). Team building through team goal setting. *Journal of Applied Sport Psychology, 9,* 97–113.

Williams, K.D., Harkins, S.G., & Latane, B. (1981). Identifiability as a deterrent to social loafing: Two cheering experiments. *Journal of Personality and Social Psychology, 40,* 303–311.

Wood, R.E., & Locke, E.A. (1990). Goal setting and strategy effects on complex tasks. In B.M. Shaw & L.L. Cummings (Eds.), *Research in organizational behavior* (Vol. 12, pp. 73–109). Greenwich, CT: JAI Press.

Wood, R.E., Mento, A.J., & Locke, E.A. (1987). Task complexity as a moderator of goal effects: A meta-analysis. *Journal of Applied Psychology, 72,* 416–425.

Wright, P.M., Hollenbeck, J.R., Wolf, S., & McMahan, G.C. (1995). The effects of varying goal difficulty operationalizations on goal setting outcomes and processes. *Organizational Behavior and Human Decision Processes, 61,* 28–43.

Yearta, S., Maitlis, S., & Briner, R. (1995). An exploratory study of goal setting in theory and practice: A motivational technique that works? *Journal of Occupational and Organizational Psychology, 68,* 237–252.

Zagummy, M., & Johnson, C. (1992). Using reinforcement and goal setting to increase proof reading accuracy. *Perceptual and Motor Skills, 75,* 1330.

Zimmerman, B. (1989). A social cognitive view of self-regulated academic learning. *Journal of Educational Psychology, 81,* 329–339.

Zimmerman, B. (1994, April). *The development of self-regulatory skill: A social cognitive view.* An invited address presented at the State University of New York, Albany, Sesquicentennial Celebratory Symposium in the Department of Educational Psychology and Statistics.

Zimmerman, B., & Bonner, S. (1997). A social cognitive view of strategic learning. In C. Weinstein & B. McCombs (Eds.), *Strategic learning: Skill, will and self-regulation.* Hillsdale, NJ: Erlbaum.

Zimmerman, B.J., & Kitsantas, A. (1996). Self-regulated learning of a motoric skill: The role of goal setting and self-monitoring. *Journal of Applied Sport Psychology, 8,* 60–75.

CHAPTER 20

Imagery in Sport and Exercise

CRAIG R. HALL

On initial consideration, imagery and motor performance may seem to be far removed from each other. Imagery is a psychological activity that is mostly inward, belonging to the class of "private events," whereas motor performance is more external and public in nature (Denis, 1985). Furthermore, imagery evokes the physical characteristics of an absent object that has been perceived in the past or may take place in the future. Motor activity is associated with the present; as people perform, they can be observed and objectively measured by others. Given these differences, why have researchers been investigating the relation between imagery and action for over 50 years? The answer is that many researchers believe actions are acquired and controlled, at least in part, at the cognitive level (e.g., Adams, 1990; Annett, 1996b). They argue that the learning and performance of motor skills are influenced by people's goals, what knowledge they possess, and the incorporation of new knowledge with old. Furthermore, an action representation system is valuable for interpreting the actions and intentions of others, and this system is on a par with the language system in facilitating communication (Annett, 1996a). This cognitive approach to skill acquisition and motor control supports the existence of functional relations between imagery and action.

Everyone has the ability to generate and use imagery. However, people sometimes choose not to use it even in situations in which it could be beneficial. Betts (1909) conducted one of the first studies on imagery use. He examined the spontaneous use of imagery in a variety of tasks, including simple association, logical thinking, mental multiplication, and discrimination judgments. He found that imagery is often used in doing these tasks, but that it is more helpful in some tasks than in others. One domain in which imagery is used extensively is sport. Whereas elite athletes report the extensive use of imagery in both training and competition, even nonelite athletes make considerable use of imagery (Barr & Hall, 1992; Hall, Rodgers, & Barr, 1990; Salmon, Hall, & Haslam, 1994). Recent evidence (Gammage, Hall, & Rodgers, in press; Hausenblas, Hall, Rodgers, & Munroe, 1999) indicates that participants in other forms of physical activity (e.g., aerobics, jogging) also use imagery regularly.

When asked about imagery, many people seem to have a relatively good understanding of what it entails (Hausenblas et al., 1999; Munroe, Giacobbi, Hall, & Weinberg, 2000). Over the years, researchers have defined imagery in a variety of ways. One fairly comprehensive definition was recently offered by White and Hardy (1998, p. 389): "Imagery is an experience that mimics real experience. We can be aware of 'seeing' an image, feeling movements as an image, or experiencing an image of smell, tastes, or sounds without actually experiencing the real thing. Sometimes people find that it helps to close their eyes. It differs from dreams in that we are awake and conscious when we form an image." Some researchers have considered imagery and mental practice to be one and the same in the literature (Singer, 1980). The way other authors have defined mental practice suggests that it involves more than just imagery. Marteniuk (1976, p. 224) defined mental practice as "improvement in performance that results from an individual's either thinking about a skill or watching someone else perform it." Clearly, this definition of mental practice encompasses not only imagery, but other processes such as observational learning. Hall (1985) suggested that imagery should be considered the major component of mental practice.

Most mental practice studies (sometimes termed mental rehearsal studies) have primarily been concerned with the effects of imagery on motor performance (e.g., Hird, Landers, Thomas, & Horan, 1991; Wrisberg & Ragsdale, 1979). Therefore, the definition of imagery suggested by White and Hardy (1998) is used in the present chapter and any mental practice studies that have focused on imagery effects are considered imagery research.

The aim of this chapter is to examine the role imagery plays in sport and exercise. The approach taken is one recently suggested by Munroe et al. (1999), namely, to look at four basic questions: *Where* is imagery used? *When* is imagery used? *Why* is imagery used? and *What* is being imagined? These questions are considered first in the context of competitive sport, then for exercise. An additional question as to *how* imagery actually operates in motor skill learning and performance will be considered. Next, variables determining the effectiveness of imagery are discussed. Finally, an approach to the practical application of imagery in sport and exercise is outlined and some directions for future research are recommended.

IMAGERY IN SPORT

Where Do Athletes Use Imagery?

Where athletes use imagery seems to be a fairly basic question. Of course, the answer is that athletes use imagery in practice and competition. However, it is not quite that simple. Although the majority of the imagery research (see Hall, Schmidt, Durand, & Buckolz, 1994) has considered practice situations (e.g., using imagery to facilitate skill learning), athletes report using imagery more in conjunction with competition than practice (Hall et al., 1990). Barr and Hall (1992) asked 348 high school, college, and national team rowers how much they used imagery in training and how much they used it in competition. They indicated their use of imagery on a 7-point Likert scale with 1 = never and 7 = always. The mean rating for imagery use in training was 4.47, and the mean rating for competition was 5.13. Given these findings, it can be argued that athletes are using imagery more for performance enhancement (i.e., competing effectively) than for skill learning. Athletes often report using imagery outside of practice and competition (Salmon et al., 1994). They use it in a variety of places, including school, work, and home. Some athletes (e.g., elite soccer players) have reported using more imagery outside of practice than during practice.

When Do Athletes Use Imagery?

Athletes use imagery immediately prior to competing more than at any other time. Hall et al. (1990) asked male and female participants in football, ice hockey, soccer, squash, gymnastics, and figure skating to rate their use of imagery before a competition, during a competition, and after a competition. The athletes indicated their use of imagery on a 7-point scale (1 = never, 7 = always). The mean rating for immediately prior to competing was 4.71, the mean rating for during competition was 3.80, and the mean rating for after competition was only 3.07. Corresponding results were found in the sport of rowing by Barr and Hall (1992), and in golf, softball, swimming, tennis, athletics, volleyball, and wrestling by Munroe et al. (1998). With respect to practice, athletes use imagery more during practice than before or after practice. The mean ratings given by the athletes in the Hall et al. study for these three practice situations were 3.48, 2.85, and 2.65, respectively. Outside of competition and practice, athletes use imagery during breaks in their daily activities (e.g., during school or work), and many regularly use imagery at night just before going to sleep (Hall et al., 1990; Rodgers, Hall, & Buckolz, 1991).

Researchers (Cupal, 1998; Green, 1992) have suggested that athletes should also use imagery when they are injured. Schwartz (1984) proposes that humans are systems in which there is a constant interchange between one's mental and physiological functions. Thus, an appropriate physiological change occurs within a person for every alteration in mental state, and for treatment to be effective and for full recovery to take place following an injury, body and mind must work together (Green, 1992).

Although the use of imagery by athletes during injury rehabilitation has received little investigation, Korn (1994) contends that imagery can be used to increase relaxation, decrease anxiety, aid in the management of depression, increase self-confidence, increase motivation, and facilitate in relieving pain. He further suggests that injured athletes should first imagine themselves being fully recovered and able to perform the way they did prior to becoming injured. Next, the athletes should imagine specific motor skills being executed, each being imagined in such a way as to bring the athletes closer to full recovery. Reasons for this type of approach are that such images will help the athletes obtain the mind-set required for a return to optimal levels of performance, and will help bring closure to the entire injury experience (Green, 1992).

Sordoni, Hall, and Forwell (2000) recently asked athletes about their use of imagery while injured. The participants were 71 athletes from a variety of sports. They ranged in age from 18 to 64 years and competed to various levels (e.g., recreational to international). The athletes were in the functional stage of injury rehabilitation and had attended a minimum of five physiotherapy appointments to ensure that they had the opportunity to use imagery as part of their rehabilitation program. Imagery was found to be used considerably less during injury rehabilitation than in association with competition and practice. In addition, the injured athletes indicated using imagery for two main reasons: to motivate themselves to recover and to rehearse their rehabilitation exercises. The reasons why athletes use imagery is addressed in detail in the next section.

Why Do Athletes Use Imagery?

Suppose basketball players are asked what they image when they activate processes associated with imagery. They might say that they are image-performing a well-executed jump shot from the top of the key. This will tell you something about what they image, or the *content* of their imagery; however, it will provide no indication of why they are imagining this shot. Their imagery could serve various *functions*. They might use imagery to help improve performance of this particular shot (i.e., increase learning), or to serve as a readiness procedure for an important game; imagery might provide a means to improve self-efficacy to make this shot, or it might function for all three of these purposes. When considering imagery use by athletes, it is often important to distinguish between the content of their images (i.e., what they image) and the function of their imagery (i.e., why they use imagery).

Paivio (1985) proposed a simple analytical framework of how imagery influences physical activity. He suggested that imagery serves two functions and that these two functions operate either at a specific or a general level. The cognitive function involves the rehearsal of skills (cognitive specific imagery) and strategies of play (cognitive general imagery). The motivational function, at the specific level, involves imagining one's goals and the activities required in achieving these goals (motivational specific imagery). At the general level (motivational general imagery), images relate to general physiological arousal and affect. Hall, Mack, Paivio, and Hausenblas (1998) identified two specific components of motivational general imagery: Motivational general–arousal imagery is associated with arousal and stress, and motivational general–mastery imagery is associated with being in control, self-confident, and mentally tough.

Cognitive Specific (CS) Imagery

In the majority of imagery studies (including the mental practice and mental rehearsal studies that have essentially been concerned with imagery), CS imagery has been examined. A cursory review of this literature indicates three

standard conditions: a physical practice condition, an imagery condition, and a control condition. Participants are randomly assigned to one of these conditions after completion of initial practice on a specific motor skill (e.g., basketball free-throws). Their performance on the skill is used as a baseline (pretest). Then the physical practice participants actually practice the skill for a set number of trials or a given amount of time. Those in the imagery condition mentally rehearse the skill (i.e., use CS imagery) for the same number of trials or amount of time that the physical practice participants actually practice. The control participants do not engage in any physical or imagery practice (i.e., they rest), or they practice an unrelated skill. All participants are then retested on the skill. Although Rawlings, Rawlings, Chen, and Yilk (1972) found that imagery practice is as effective as physical practice, most researchers have reported the order of performance from best to worst to be physical practice, imagery practice, and control conditions. Considering the results of these studies collectively, it is now generally accepted that CS imagery facilitates the learning and performance of motor skills (Driskell, Copper, & Moran, 1994; Hall et al., 1994), but not to the same extent as physical practice.

An extension of the above paradigm involves examining the effects of combining physical and imagery practice (e.g., 50% physical and 50% imagery) compared to 100% physical or 100% imagery practice. That is, some imagery practice is substituted for physical practice. Early research suggested that a combination of physical and imagery practice was better than physical or imagery practice alone. For example, McBride and Rothstein (1979) required participants to hit a solid whiffle golf ball at a target 10 feet away using a table tennis paddle. A forehand stroke with the nondominant hand was employed. Three groups of participants all practiced for 40 trials. The first group physically practiced the task. The second group was given a demonstration of the task, three physical practice trials, and then practiced 40 imagery trials. The third group experienced the following combination of physical and imagery trials: 10 physical, 10 imagery, 10 physical, and 10 imagery. For both immediate and delayed retention (one day later), the combination of physical and imagery practice trials resulted in superior performance compared to only physical or imagery practice.

Hird et al. (1991) challenged these findings. They investigated the effects of various combinations of physical and imagery practice on the acquisition of two tasks: a pursuit rotor task in which the target moved in a circular pattern at 45 rpm for 15 seconds, and a pegboard task in which participants placed as many round and square pegs in appropriately marked places as they could in 60 seconds. The combinations of physical and imagery practice were 75:25, 50:50, and 25:75. There was also a 100% physical practice condition, a 100% imagery practice condition, and a control condition. It was found that as the proportion of physical practice increased for both tasks, the level of posttest performance improved. Concluded was that a combination of physical and imagery practice is not more effective than physical practice alone.

Durand, Hall, and Haslam (1997) recently revisited the research combining physical and imagery practice. After considering most of the data available, they reached two noteworthy conclusions. First, consistent with Hird et al. (1991), they concluded that a combination of physical and imagery practice is usually no better than 100% physical practice. Second, it is often possible to substitute some CS imagery practice for physical practice without affecting learning and performance. This conclusion has important implications for athletes. Although athletes would not normally substitute imagery practice for physical practice, sometimes circumstances may make this necessary (e.g., injury, fatigue, travel, loss of practice facilities). In these situations, by using imagery, athletes may be able to maintain their usual levels of practice and obtain the positive effects associated with such practice.

The typical approach preferred by athletes is to incorporate CS imagery practice into their overall training program. That is, imagery practice supplements regular physical practice. How effective is the addition of CS imagery practice to the regular physical practice undertaken by athletes? Blair, Hall, and Leyshon (1993) investigated this question with nonelite and elite soccer players. Initially, the players were tested on a soccer task designed to incorporate some of the basic skills required in the sport (e.g., passing, dribbling, shooting). The players were then randomly assigned to either an imagery group or a control group with the only restriction being that equal numbers of nonelite and elite players were in each group. The imagery group received six weeks of imagery practice on the task, and the control group spent this time developing a competition strategy for soccer. During this period, all players also engaged in their regular soccer activities (e.g., team practices). After the six weeks, the players were again tested on the soccer task. The imagery group significantly improved its performance on the task, and the control group showed no change. The amount of improvement was about the same for both nonelite and elite players in the imagery group. These results suggest that athletes should supplement their regular physical practice with CS imagery practice.

One issue that remains to be determined is whether there is an optimum amount of CS imagery practice that should be added to physical practice. Research on the functional equivalence of imagery and action provides some direction with respect to this matter. The notion of functional equivalence can be rationalized in the context of performing motor skills because both types of activity are characterized by the need to reconstruct or generate a temporally extended event on the basis of memory. Accordingly, imagery may be seen as a process of "pure" event generation, whereas action necessarily requires the coupling of this generative process to the articulatory system (Vogt, 1995). The fact that in some movement imagery studies (Hale, 1982; Wehner, Vogt, & Stadler, 1984) muscular activation can be observed seems to indicate that such articulatory coupling is reduced, but not completely suppressed, during imagery.

Two general approaches have been used to investigate the functional equivalence issue. Some researchers have examined the neurophysiological basis of motor imagery. One of the first studies of this nature was conducted by Ingvar and Philipson (1977). They measured the regional cerebral blood flow (rCBF) in the dominant hemisphere of six patients in three conditions: at rest, during movements of the right hand, and during imagery of the same right-hand movements. During the imagery condition, the normal hyperfrontal resting blood flow changed and an increase of the hemisphere mean flow was recorded, especially in the frontal and temporal structures. This finding corresponds with others (e.g., Decety et al., 1994; Decety, Sjöholm, Ryding, Stenberg, & Ingvar, 1990) showing common neural mechanisms between imagery and motor preparation.

In addition to rCBF studies, Decety (1996) has reviewed mental chronometric studies and studies examining autonomic responses during motor imagery tasks. He contends that these studies "converge to support the notion that motor imagery shares the same neural mechanisms that are involved in motor control of actual actions" (p. 91). Other researchers (Marks & Isaac, 1995; Williams, Rippon, Stone, & Annett, 1995) have studied electroencephalography (EEG) activity accompanying motor imagery. Their results indicate that motor imagery involves some changes in EEG activity in both motor and sensory areas. Thus, research investigating the neurophysiological basis of motor imagery has provided considerable support for the functional equivalence of imagery and action.

The second approach to investigating functional equivalence has been to compare the effects of imagery practice and physical practice on learning and performance. The influence of CS imagery practice compared to physical practice on the acquisition of specific motor skills has been discussed previously, with the conclusion that the latter is usually more effective. Hall, Bernoties, and Schmidt (1995) argue that although CS imagery and physical practice do not produce identical results, they do produce similar results. Furthermore, they contend: "Given that there are a number of factors that influence how effective imaginary practice may be in a specific situation (let alone other factors that may be affecting physical practice), it is probably not surprising that imaginary practice and physical practice do not always produce identical results" (p. 182). The correspondence between imagery and physical practice has been even closer in studies in which interference effects have been of interest.

Johnson (1982) used a linear positioning task in which novel movements were interpolated between initial presentation and recall of a criterion movement length. These interpolated movements were either imagined or physically performed, and were either shorter or longer than the criterion movement. He found that imagery of movements and physically producing movements showed essentially the same characteristics with respect to both direction and error. That is, when either physically practicing or imagining an interpolated movement longer than the criterion movement, participants produced movements longer than the criterion movement. Participants physically practicing or imagining interpolated movements shorter than the criterion movement produced movements shorter than the criterion movement during recall. Johnson concluded that the biasing effects for imagery and actual movements on motor behavior are about the same.

Gabriele, Hall, and Lee (1989) investigated the effects of imaginary practice on another type of interference: contextual interference. To determine if the retention advantage of randomly practiced over blocked practice movements would be found for imagery as well as physical practice, a factorial combination of physical practice conditions with imagery practice conditions was administered. The actions to be learned were four patterns of arm movements that were different with respect to spatial layout, and each was to be completed in 700 ms. Each group of participants received a different ratio of physical practice interspersed with imagery practice. All groups practiced under their conditions until the criterion movement time was achieved. They were then given a delayed retention test. Randomly ordered imagery practice trials, combined with blocked or randomly ordered physical trials, facilitated retention compared to blocked imagery trials. In addition, random imagery practice was shown to cause as much interference during acquisition and as much benefit to retention as random physical practice.

In a more recent study examining interference effects of imagery on motor task performance, Hall et al. (1995) used a retroactive interference paradigm. Sixty participants performed a simple motor task that was to be completed in a criterion time of 700 ms. They were then randomly assigned to one of six groups that differed in the amount and type of interpolated practice they received. One group experienced interpolated activity involving physical practice of another motor task. The other physical practice group participated in two such sessions. A third group experienced imagery practice of the same interpolated motor task, while the (other) imagery group had two such sessions. A fifth group experienced a combination of physical practice and rest periods for two interpolated sessions, and the sixth group was a control group and did not have any interpolated activity sessions. Following the interpolated activity sessions, all groups were given a retention test on the original task. Imagery and physical practice during the interpolated activity sessions resulted in similar interference effects on retention. All groups demonstrated greater deviation from the 700 ms criterion time during retention than the control group, and these deviations were in the expected direction given the nature of the interpolated task. It was concluded that imagery practice and physical practice can be viewed as functionally similar.

Taken together, the results of the functional equivalence research strongly suggest that CS imagery practice should be treated similarly to physical practice. Work in the area of expertise (Ericsson, Krampe, & Tesch-Römer, 1993; Hodges & Starkes, 1996) indicates that elite performance is a product of a decade or more of effort to improve performance through an optimal distribution of deliberate practice. If large amounts of deliberate practice are recommended as the key to becoming an elite athlete, it follows that large amounts of imagery practice should produce maximum benefits. There is likely no optimal amount of CS imagery practice that should be added to regular physical practice. Rather, athletes should be encouraged to use as much CS imagery practice as possible, and to do so following the guidelines recommended for deliberate physical practice (Ericsson et al., 1993).

Cognitive General (CG) Imagery

In addition to using imagery to rehearse specific skills (i.e., CS imagery), athletes also report using imagery to rehearse entire game plans, strategies of play, and routines (e.g., a figure skater's long program; Madigan, Frey, & Matlock, 1992). This represents the cognitive general (CG) function of imagery. There have not been any controlled studies investigating the effects of CG imagery on the learning and performance of game plans, strategies of play, or entire routines. Case study reports, however, have supported the performance benefits of CG imagery for rehearsing slalom canoe races (MacIntyre & Moran, 1996), football plays (Fenker & Lambiotte, 1987), wrestling strategies (Rushall, 1988), gymnastic pommel horse routines (Mace, Eastman, & Carroll, 1987), and artistic gymnastic routines (White & Hardy, 1998). Together, these studies indicate that CG imagery can facilitate athletic performance.

Motivational Specific (MS) Imagery

When athletes imagine specific goals such as winning or being congratulated for a good performance, they are using motivational-specific (MS) imagery. Bandura (1997) notes that imagery may influence the self-standards against which performance is appraised and evaluated. When athletes parallel their performances with imaged representations, they may have more realistic self-standards and be less likely to give up when they fail to perfect a skill. Supporting evidence for these assertions comes from a study of beginner golfers (Martin & Hall, 1995). Participants assigned to a six-session imagery condition spent more time practicing a golf-putting task, set higher goals for themselves, and were more adherent to their training regimen than participants in an attentional control condition. Martin and Hall suggest, "When it comes to enhancing motivation, imagery and goals may go hand in hand" (p. 66). Stemming from interviews with varsity athletes, Munroe, Hall, and Weinberg (1999) take this even further. They argue that because goal setting is often the first step in an effective intervention program, the next logical step should be for athletes to use these goals as a basis for their imagery.

Motivational General–Mastery (MG-M) Imagery

Moritz, Hall, Martin, and Vadocz (1996) contend that if athletes want to develop, maintain, or regain sport confidence, they should imagine performing in a confident manner. In other words, they should use motivational general–mastery (MG-M) imagery. Moritz et al. administered the Sport Imagery Questionnaire (SIQ; Hall et al., 1998) and the State Sport Confidence Inventory (SSCI; Vealey, 1986) to participants at the Junior North American Roller Skating Championships. The SIQ was employed to measure the five functions of imagery (CS, CG, MS, MG-M, and MG-A), and the SSCI was administered to assess

sport confidence. The results revealed that high-sport-confident athletes used more MG-M imagery than low-sport-confident athletes. In addition, MG-M imagery accounted for the majority of variance in SSCI scores (20%).

The confidence-enhancing benefits of MG-M imagery have often been reported in applied sport psychology practice (e.g., Orlick, 1990; Rushall, 1988; Suinn, 1996). A recent intervention examining MG-M imagery in the sport of badminton provides some support for these reports (Callow, Hardy, & Hall, in press). With a single-subject multiple-baseline design, three elite badminton players completed the SSCI once a week for 20 weeks prior to a match. A baseline for sport confidence was determined and the MG-M imagery intervention was implemented for the three players at weeks 5, 7, and 9, respectively. The two-week, six-session intervention consisted of mastery imagery (i.e., imagery associated with self-confidence, control, and successful management of challenging situations). The intervention increased sport confidence for two of the players and stabilized the level of confidence of the third. It was concluded that an MG-M imagery intervention can improve sport confidence.

Bandura (1997) argues that confidence is a nondescript term that refers to strength of belief but fails to specify what the certainty is about. In contrast, self-efficacy is the belief in one's capabilities to organize and execute courses of action required to produce specific attainments. It includes both the affirmation of capability and the strength of that belief. Bandura has also proposed that positive visualizations enhance self-efficacy by preventing negative visualizations in situations where athletes may begin to question their own abilities. Two studies provide support for this proposal. Feltz and Riessinger (1990) demonstrated that participants who used MG-M imagery (i.e., imagined themselves feeling competent and being successful) on a muscular endurance task had higher and stronger efficacy expectations for their performance on the task than participants who did not use imagery. Mills, Munroe, and Hall (in press) administered the SIQ and a self-efficacy questionnaire to varsity athletes involved in wrestling, rowing, and track and field. They found that athletes who were high in self-efficacy in competition situations used more motivational imagery, especially MG-M imagery, than their low-self-efficacy counterparts.

Motivational General–Arousal (MG-A) Imagery

In the same way that MG-M imagery is related to self-confidence and self-efficacy, there is evidence that MG-A imagery is related to arousal and competitive anxiety.

Anecdotal reports and studies of athletes' favorite "psyching-up" strategies indicate that athletes use MG-A imagery to increase their arousal levels (Caudill, Weinberg, & Jackson, 1983; Munroe et al., 2000; White & Hardy, 1998). There is also empirical support for this finding. Hecker and Kaczor (1988) found athletes' heart rates significantly increased above baseline levels when they employed MG-A imagery. In addition to using imagery to psyche themselves up, athletes also report using it to bring themselves down (Cancio, 1991; Orlick, 1990; White & Hardy, 1998). Researchers who have considered arousal-reducing imagery have usually combined imagery with relaxation training (e.g., Cogan & Petrie, 1995), thus making it difficult to determine the exact role imagery plays in producing any treatment effects.

It has generally been accepted by sport psychologists that competitive anxiety can be influenced by the use of imagery (Gould & Udry, 1994; Orlick, 1990), but this has been difficult to empirically demonstrate. One possible reason why researchers have found no significant differences in preperformance state anxiety levels between control participants and those instructed to use imagery is because the imagery employed was either CS imagery (Terry, Coakley, & Karageorghis, 1995; Weinberg, Seabourne, & Jackson, 1981) or MG-M imagery (Carter & Kelly, 1997). Vadocz, Hall, and Moritz (1997) observed that MG-A imagery predicted competitive anxiety in a linear regression model, but CS and MG-M imagery failed to account for significant variance in athletes' anxiety. Even though further research is needed, it does appear that competitive anxiety can be influenced by the use of MG-A imagery.

In summary, research suggests that athletes use imagery for both cognitive and motivational reasons. Why they use imagery in a given situation depends on the outcome they are hoping to achieve. They might be attempting to rehearse specific skills or strategies of play, modify cognitions (e.g., increase their self-efficacy), or regulate their arousal or competitive anxiety levels. Of course, they could be using imagery for several of these purposes at the same time.

What Do Athletes Image?

The quality of an athlete's imagery is often a primary concern when examining image *content*. For example, researchers may be interested in the accuracy of the images. Is the imagined jump shot being correctly executed? Another consideration may be vividness. Is the athlete's imagery of the skill as clear and vivid as normal vision? When athletes are administered imagery ability tests, it is essentially the quality of their imagery content that is being assessed. Sometimes specific attributes of the images are measured, such as vividness (Isaac, Marks, & Russell, 1986), whereas at other times, more general measures of imagery quality are assessed (Hall, Pongrac, & Buckolz, 1985).

Does image quality make a difference in athletic performance? Isaac (1992) examined the influence of vividness as assessed by the Vividness of Movement Imagery Questionnaire (VMIQ; Isaac et al., 1986), on trampoline performance. Novice and experienced trampolinists were divided into an imagery and a control group, and both groups attempted to improve three trampoline skills over each of three six-week training periods. These athletes were also divided into high and low vividness groups depending on their VMIQ scores. Over the training periods, athletes in the imagery group, regardless of skill level, showed significantly more improvement than athletes in the control group. Furthermore, athletes with high vividness scores improved significantly more than those in the low vividness group. It was suggested, therefore, that athletes with high vividness scores and who engage in imagery practice are more likely to improve their physical skills.

Another approach researchers have taken when investigating imagery content is to compare positive imagery with negative imagery. One of the first studies on the effects of positive versus negative imagery practice was conducted by Powell (1973). Using a dart throwing task, participants in the positive imagery group were instructed to imagine the dart landing near the center of the target; those in the negative imagery group imagined a very poor performance outcome (e.g., the dart hitting the edge of the board). Scores were obtained from three blocks of 24 actual throws (blocks 1, 3, and 5), which were interspersed with blocks of imagery throws (blocks 2 and 4), either positive or negative. Participants in the positive group improved their performance scores from blocks 1 to 5 by an average of 28%, whereas the performance of the participants in the negative group deteriorated by an average of −3%. Powell concluded that what a participant imagines is liable to differentially affect later performance.

Woolfolk, Parrish, and Murphy (1985) also investigated positive versus negative imagery. They assigned college students to one of three groups: positive imagery, negative imagery, or a control. Golf putting was the task and the positive imagery group was instructed to imagine the ball going into the hole, whereas the negative imagery group was instructed to imagine the ball narrowly missing the hole. The control group performed without any imagery instructions. Participants in the positive imagery group improved significantly (30.4%) from their baseline accuracy scores over a period of six consecutive testing days. The group employing negative imagery showed a significant decline (21.2%) in performance accuracy relative to the control group, which showed a slight increase in accuracy (9.9%) over the same time period.

Studies such as these indicate that negative imagery can have a detrimental influence on motor performance. However, athletes usually imagine themselves performing their sport skills clearly and accurately (Barr & Hall, 1992; Hall et al., 1990). Furthermore, athletes often imagine themselves winning and seldom imagine themselves losing (Hall et al., 1990). Therefore, practitioners probably should not be overly concerned with negative imagery.

Researchers have also investigated the content of athletes' images by inquiring about the modality information constituting those images. There is evidence supporting a distinction in imagery along sensory lines, especially visual and kinesthetic (see Paivio, 1986, pp. 101–102). Hall et al. (1990) asked elite and nonelite athletes in both team and individual sports about their use of visual and kinesthetic imagery. All athletes reported the extensive use of both types of imagery and indicated employing them to about the same extent. In a follow-up study, Barr and Hall (1992) asked novice and elite rowers about their visual and kinesthetic imagery. As in other sports, all the rowers, but especially the elite ones, reported frequently using both types of imagery and did so with about equal frequency. Salmon et al. (1994), in their study of soccer players, not only considered visual and kinesthetic imagery, but also asked the players about their use of auditory imagery. The players reported some auditory imagery; however, they employed it considerably less than visual and kinesthetic imagery. Athletes in other sports may make greater use of auditory imagery than soccer players, and this possibility deserves investigation.

The fourth approach to examining imagery content has been to consider the visual imagery perspective of athletes. Sometimes athletes imagine themselves performing as if they were looking at themselves on a video; this is referred to as an external perspective. At other times, athletes imagine themselves performing as if they were looking at themselves through their own eyes (i.e., they imagine what they would see if they were physically executing the skill); this is referred to as an internal perspective. Initial studies suggested that elite athletes favor an internal perspective (Mahoney & Avener, 1977; Rotella, Gansneder, Ojala, & Billing, 1980), but other research (Hall et al., 1990; Highlen & Bennett, 1979) has failed to support this contention. More recently, Hardy and his colleagues (e.g., Hardy, 1997; White & Hardy, 1995) have argued that task

differences may influence the use of each perspective. They propose that the external perspective has superior effects on the acquisition and performance of skills that depend heavily on form for their successful execution, whereas the internal perspective is superior for the acquisition and performance of open skills that depend heavily on perception and anticipation for their successful execution.

Hardy and Callow (1999) recently investigated the relative efficacy of different imagery perspectives on the performance of tasks in which form was important. In the first of three experiments, karateists learned a new kata (simulated fighting forms) using either external or internal visual imagery. External visual imagery proved to be the more effective of the two. In the second experiment, participants learned a simple gymnastics floor routine in one of four conditions: external or internal visual imagery with or without kinesthetic imagery. Results indicated that once again external visual imagery was best, but there was no effect for kinesthetic imagery. The third experiment adopted the same paradigm as the second, but with high-ability rock climbers performing difficult boulder problems. Here the results showed that external visual imagery was best, and kinesthetic imagery was better than no kinesthetic imagery. These three experiments support the proposal that the external perspective has superior effects on the acquisition and performance of skills that depend on form for their successful execution. These results also provide some evidence for the notion of some researchers (Hall, 1997; White & Hardy, 1995) that regardless of which perspective athletes use, kinesthetic imagery can be effectively combined with both internal and external visual perspectives.

A recent study by Cumming and Ste-Marie (2000) confirmed and extended the findings of Hardy and Callow (1999). The effects of external and internal visual imagery training on the cognitive and motivational functions of imagery were examined in synchronized skating. Skaters participated in a five-week imagery training program that concentrated on the form and body shape of skating skills. The SIQ was employed to measure changes in the skaters' use of cognitive and motivational imagery as a result of the training program. Skaters who had used an external visual imagery perspective showed significant increases for the cognitive functions, whereas skaters who had used an internal visual perspective showed no gains. Neither group demonstrated any changes in the motivational functions of imagery. This is the first study to consider whether visual imagery perspective is related to the motivational functions of imagery. Additional research into this issue is warranted.

The four approaches to examining what athletes image have provided considerable information. Munroe et al. (2000) expanded this knowledge base through the use of in-depth interviews of 14 elite athletes participating in seven different sports. They found that the content of athletes' images could be categorized under the following headings: sessions, effectiveness, nature of imagery, surroundings, types of imagery, and controllability. With respect to sessions, the frequency and duration of athletes' imagery sessions varied considerably. During competition, the sessions were usually shorter than during practice, as there was simply less time to image. Athletes reported that their imagery was most effective during precompetition and practice. Comments on the nature of their images indicated that they were mainly positive and were usually accurate and very detailed. Any negative images they experienced most often occurred during competition. Athletes also reported imaging the surroundings in which they were going to compete. With respect to types of imagery, they indicated that they used primarily visual and kinesthetic imagery, and auditory and olfactory imagery to a lesser extent. Finally, athletes commented very little on the controllability of their images, suggesting that this was not a major concern.

Overall, the research examining what athletes image indicates that (1) their images are usually accurate and vivid; (2) they tend to be positive rather than negative; (3) they incorporate visual, kinesthetic, and sometimes auditory and olfactory information; and (4) they incorporate both internal and external perspectives. They image the skills and strategies they perform in their sport, but also image other things such as the surroundings in which they are going to compete.

IMAGERY IN EXERCISE

Only in recent years have researchers started to consider the role imagery plays in exercise. Hall (1995) was the first to suggest that exercise participants may use imagery. He proposed that imagery may be as powerful a motivator in exercise as it is in sport. He thought that regular exercisers may imagine themselves engaging in their chosen physical activity (e.g., aerobics, weightlifting), enjoying their workouts, and achieving their desired goals. Recent research, as discussed in the following sections, indicates he was at least partially correct.

Where Do Exercisers Image?

Hausenblas et al. (1999) asked 144 aerobic exercisers about their use of imagery. The majority of these participants were female, full-time university students. Although they were not directly asked where they used imagery, it is clear from their responses that they employed imagery in conjunction with exercising (i.e., just before, during, and just after). They also employ it in a variety of other places, such as home, school, and work.

When Do Exercisers Image?

Exercisers were specifically asked by Hausenblas et al. (1999) when they imagined themselves exercising. The most frequently given response was just before going to bed. Other times mentioned included when studying, when daydreaming, while eating, when listening to music, while watching TV, and when stressed. Although none of the exercisers reported using imagery when injured, it seems reasonable to assume that injured exercise participants could obtain benefits from using imagery rehabilitation similar to that of injured athletes.

Why Do Exercisers Use Imagery?

Two studies (Hausenblas et al., 1999; Rodgers, Hall, Blanchard, & Munroe, 2000) revealed that exercisers use imagery for three main reasons: (1) energy, which includes being energized and relieving stress; (2) appearance, relating both to physique and fitness; and (3) technique, which involves imagining correct form and body position during exercise. Of these three functions of imagery, appearance imagery is the most frequently employed (Gammage, Hall, & Rodgers, in press). In addition, appearance and energy imagery are considered motivational in nature, whereas technique imagery clearly has a cognitive function. Therefore, as in sport, imagery in exercise serves both a motivational and a cognitive role.

Given that exercisers use imagery for motivational purposes such as feeling good about themselves and becoming energized (Hausenblas et al., 1999), it follows that exercise imagery should be related to other social cognitive variables (e.g., self-efficacy and incentives for physical activity) known to influence exercise intention and behavior. Hall (1995) proposes that exercise imagery may be an important source of self-efficacy. Indeed, self-efficacy can be derived from numerous sources (i.e., actual and vicarious experiences, physiological arousal, verbal persuasion, and observing others), including imagery (Bandura, 1997). Rodgers et al. (2000) administered the Exercise Imagery Questionnaire (EIQ; Hausenblas et al., 1999) and a self-efficacy questionnaire to a large sample of exercisers and found that motivational imagery and self-efficacy were related. If future research can confirm the relationship between exercise imagery and self-efficacy and demonstrate that exercise imagery is also related to other social cognitive variables, this could have implications for intervention programs concerned with exercise participation and adherence. For example, if individuals commencing an exercise program can imagine completing all the physical activities successfully and achieving their exercise goals (e.g., becoming leaner and more fit), this may make them more motivated to adhere to the program either directly, or indirectly through increasing their self-efficacy.

What Do Exercisers Image?

The content of exercisers' imagery was also studied by Hausenblas et al. (1999). The participants in their study were asked "What do you imagine about exercising?" Their responses were organized into nine categories: body image, techniques/strategies, feel good about oneself, motivation, general exercise, fitness/health, music, goals, and maintaining focus. These results indicate that the content of exercisers' images are quite varied. Their content also reflects some of the reasons why they are using imagery (e.g., body image coincides with the appearance function of exercise imagery).

Much less is known about imagery in exercise than is known about imagery in sport, but hopefully this will change with additional exercise imagery research. The potential significance of this research stems directly from sport. The benefits athletes realize from using imagery are numerous and well documented. There is every reason to believe that exercisers can also gain significant benefits through using imagery.

HOW DOES IMAGERY WORK?

A number of explanations have been advanced over the years as to how imagery benefits motor performance. Not one of them is comprehensive enough to embody all the functions of imagery. For the most part, these explanations have focused on how CS imagery facilitates the learning and performance of skills.

Symbolic Learning Theory

Symbolic learning theory offers a cognitive explanation for how imagery works. It holds that actions are symbolically coded as "mental blueprints" (Vealey & Walter, 1993); imagery strengthens the mental blueprint, enabling actions to become more familiar and possibly automatic. According to the theory, skills that are more cognitive in nature (e.g., finger maze learning) are more easily coded than pure motor skills (e.g., strength tasks).

Sackett (1934) was the first to propose the symbolic learning theory after showing that imagery improved performance on a cognitive task (a finger maze) that could easily be symbolized. A number of early imagery studies seemed to provide support for this theory (Minas, 1978; Wrisberg & Ragsdale, 1979). For example, Ryan and Simons (1983) compared the acquisition of a task that was more difficult to perform (i.e., less cognitive) and a task that was easier to perform (i.e., more cognitive). For both tasks a Dial-a-Maze was used. That is, a stylus was moved through a maze pattern by turning two handles, one controlling vertical movement and the other controlling horizontal movement. The more difficult task required the two hands to work together to move the stylus in a diagonal direction through the maze. The easier task consisted of moving the stylus through the maze only in vertical and horizontal directions. These two tasks were practiced under conditions of physical practice, imagery practice, and no practice. Ryan and Simons predicted that if imagery is essentially a cognitive phenomenon, then learning a task that is cognitively oriented (i.e., the easy task) should benefit more from imagery than a task that is less cognitively oriented (i.e., the more difficult task). As predicted, imagery practice was found to be superior to no practice only for the easier task.

Symbolic learning theory leaves some questions unanswered. It explains how novice performers may benefit from using imagery: Imagery strengthens the mental blueprints of the new skills being learned. However, the theory does not explain how performance is enhanced in experienced performers who already have mastered the skills required. Furthermore, it is difficult to determine the size of the cognitive component in any motor task. What makes finger maze learning more cognitive than dart throwing or lifting a weight?

MacKay (1981, 1982) has proposed a theory of the acquisition of serial skills that is consistent with symbolic learning theory. The theory involves a hierarchy of interconnected nodes that are responsible for controlling an organized sequence of actions. The network ensures that the components of the skill are executed in the proper sequence. It is capable of learning so that the time to produce a proper sequence is reduced by practice. At the top of the hierarchy is a node representing the whole behavior, and nodes controlling individual muscles are at the bottom. Activation generally spreads from the top down through the network of nodes, and each node is primed when the nodes connected to it become active. Annett (1995) has illustrated how such a network might function for the serial skill of tying a bow versus imagining tying a bow. In the latter case, the triggering of muscle nodes is voluntarily inhibited but the other nodes are primed and activated in exactly the same way as happens when physically tying a bow. Mackay (1981) has provided some support for his theory with a speech production task, but other researchers (see Annett, 1988) have been less successful employing other serial skills.

Psychoneuromuscular Theory

This psychoneuromuscular theory posits that imagined actions produce low levels of impulses through the nerves from the brain to the muscles, similar in nature to those produced during the actual physical execution of actions. According to Jacobson (1931), motor imagery is essentially suppressed physical activity. Imagery can strengthen "muscle memory" (Vealey & Walter, 1993) for a motor skill by having the muscles fire in the correct sequence for an action, without actually physically executing the action.

Jacobson's (1931) research seemed to support this theory. When participants were asked to imagine bending their right arm or lifting a 10-pound weight, muscular activity appeared in the biceps in more than 90% of the trials. Support for EMG activity in the muscles of participants asked to imagine movements has since been provided by other researchers (e.g., Hale, 1982; Suinn, 1980). Moreover, Bird (1984) examined EMG recordings of athletes in various sports and showed a congruence between the EMG of their imagined sport activity and the EMG of their actual sport activity.

Some researchers (e.g., Feltz & Landers, 1983) have been critical of the research supporting psychoneuromuscular theory. They suggest that many of these studies have lacked appropriate controls. In addition, a methodological weakness of most of these experiments is that the EMG data reported have been confined to amplitude measures. Frequency and duration also need to be assessed to fully support the theory (Hale, 1994).

Bioinformational Theory

Bioinformational theory was proposed by Lang (1977, 1979) to explain the psychophysiology of imagery, especially with respect to phobia and anxiety disorders. Other researchers have extended the theory to the motor domain (e.g., Bakker, Boschker, & Chung, 1996; Hecker & Kaczor, 1988). Bioinformational theory holds that an image contains information about stimulus propositions and response propositions. The former transmit information about the imagined environmental stimuli; the latter relay information regarding behavioral activity. Because response propositions are modifiable and represent how an individual may react in a real-life situation, imaged response propositions can have a potent impact on subsequent overt behavior (Lang, Melamed, & Hart, 1970). For example, if a hockey player included the physical symptoms of arousal and tension while imagining taking a penalty shot, this should facilitate his actual performance in a game situation compared to when not including these symptoms (i.e., response propositions) in his imagery.

Imagery instructions that contain response propositions should elicit far more physiological responses than imagery instructions that contain only stimulus propositions (Bakker et al., 1996; Budney, Murphy, & Woolfolk, 1994). In addition, it has been argued that the differences between stimulus and response propositions are functionally similar to the differences between external and internal imagery (Hale, 1994). Evidence consistent with this proposal comes from the research of Hale (1982) and Harris and Robinson (1986), showing that imagery from an internal perspective produces more EMG activity than imagery from an external perspective. These EMG studies, however, have some methodological weaknesses, as discussed previously. Nevertheless, the notion that athletes' images should contain more than merely information about technique and form (i.e., CS imagery) fits well with what is known about why athletes use imagery. Thus, bioinformational theory seems to be an improvement over symbolic learning theory and psychoneuromuscular theory; however, it has a psychophysiology basis and explains relatively little about the motivational functions served by imagery. It also does not address the role of imagery in linking action with other forms of information processing such as language. Explanations dealing with this issue will be considered next.

Dual Coding Theory

Dual coding explanations of imagery have received extensive empirical investigation in cognitive psychology. Paivio (1986) has reviewed the research that converges to support the dual coding approach to memory and learning. More recently, Annett (1988, 1994) has proposed a dual coding model that is specific to the motor domain. His action-language-imagination (ALI) model is shown in Figure 20.1. In the model, there are two main routes by which a performer can acquire information about a skill; these correspond to demonstration and verbal instruction and are based on two independent channels or encoding systems. The first channel, the motor channel, is specialized for encoding human action; the second channel, the verbal

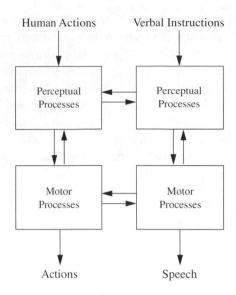

Figure 20.1   The ALI model, showing the relationships among action, language, and imagination [Hall et al. (1997)].

channel, encodes speech or linguistic gestures, including written language. There is a link between the two channels referred to as the action-language bridge. This bridge makes it possible to describe an action, generate an action, and act on verbal instructions. Annett (1990, 1996b) has provided evidence that images are essential to translate action from motor to verbal codes.

A basic tenet of dual coding theory is that encoding information in both the action and language systems should produce better learning than encoding the information in only one of the systems. As an example, a verbal mediator may prompt, via imagery, the performance of an action otherwise not remembered. Hall, Moore, Annett, and Rodgers (1997) provided some evidence for this tenet. They investigated the recall of movement patterns presented either by demonstration or guided movement with vision eliminated. Participants rehearsed the patterns using one of three strategies—imagery, verbal labeling, imagery and verbal labeling—or no rehearsal strategy (i.e., control condition). More patterns were recalled if a combination of imagery and verbal labeling was employed as a rehearsal strategy compared to using imagery alone.

Kim, Singer, and Tennant (1998) also provided some support for dual coding theory. They compared the relative effectiveness of auditory (i.e., verbal), visual, and kinesthetic imagery on learning a golf putting task. Auditory imagery, which would necessitate the dual coding of the information according to the ALI model, led to better retention performance accuracy than visual imagery, and was

also superior to kinesthetic imagery for one of the performance measures. Overall, dual coding theory offers a good explanation for how imagery links action and language. Like the other theories discussed, it is not comprehensive enough to explain all of the functions imagery serves in the motor domain, nor was it intended to. It is unlikely that a comprehensive theory explaining every aspect of motor imagery will be forthcoming in the near future.

VARIABLES INFLUENCING THE USE OF IMAGERY

A number of variables are known to influence how effective imagery will be when it is used by athletes and exercisers. The four variables covered in this section are type of activity, level of skill and activity, gender, and imagery ability. The instructions for using imagery given to athletes and exercisers is another variable often considered (e.g., Hall, Buckolz, & Fishburne, 1992; Janssen, & Sheikh, 1994), but the research concerning this variable is dealt with in other sections throughout this chapter.

Type of Activity

Of course, imagery use varies from activity to activity. One pronounced difference is the opportunity for imagery to occur. For example, in discrete tasks such as archery and bowling, participants can image before each attempt, whereas there is less opportunity to use imagery while competing in continuous tasks such as swimming and cycling. Another obvious difference is with respect to imagery content. The basic imagery content of a basketball player will consist of the skills needed to perform successfully in that sport, including shooting, passing, and dribbling; in contrast, a squash player will image forehands, backhands, and serves. Other aspects of image content may vary among activities in less obvious ways. As previously discussed, some research has indicated that an external visual perspective is better than an internal visual perspective for acquiring skills that depend heavily on form for their successful execution (e.g., gymnastics).

Early imagery researchers often considered the cognitive component involved in learning and performing a motor skill (e.g., Wrisberg & Ragsdale, 1979). Using meta-analytic techniques, Feltz and Landers (1983) found that the size of the effect produced by imagery was larger for more cognitive tasks such as finger maze learning than for tasks such as dart throwing. The latter, in turn, exceeded the effects in tasks in which strength was the major component. These findings, however, pertain exclusively to the use of cognitive specific imagery. Furthermore, determining the relative contribution of the cognitive component in performing any task is extremely difficult.

Rather than attempting to identify the cognitive component of a motor skill, the type of task analysis proposed by Paivio (1985) could be undertaken. For example, one may analyze whether the task involves a perceptual target, whether such a target is moving or stationary, and what the performer is doing in relation to the target. Paivio contends that such task distinctions must have implications for how imagery can be most effectively used.

When considering skill acquisition, Hall et al. (1994) believe it may be worthwhile to address how easy the skill is to image. They argue that the learning and performance of different motor skills will not benefit equally from using CS imagery because some skills are easier to imagine than others. Evidence supporting their argument comes from studies (Hall, 1980; Hall & Buckolz, 1981) demonstrating that different movements have different imagery values (i.e., a rating of how easily the movement can be imagined), and the easier a movement is to imagine (i.e., has a higher rating), the better it is remembered. Hall et al. recommend that if a motor skill is difficult to image, alternative strategies for helping to learn the skill might be useful, such as using verbal descriptions.

Recently, researchers have examined whether participants in various activities make differential use of cognitive and motivational imagery. Hall et al. (1998, Study 3) administered the SIQ to individuals competing in track and field and ice hockey. The hockey players reported greater use of MS imagery and MG-M imagery than the participants in track and field. The researchers speculated that team and individual sport athletes might employ the motivational and cognitive functions of imagery differently.

In a more comprehensive investigation, Munroe, Hall, Simms, and Weinberg (1998) administered the SIQ to 350 varsity athletes (111 women and 239 men) both early and late in their competitive seasons. These athletes participated in 10 different sports: badminton, basketball, field hockey, fencing, football, ice hockey, rugby, soccer, volleyball, and wrestling. The results indicated that the five functions of imagery (CS, CG, MS, MG-M, and MG-A) are used to different degrees in the various sports. Furthermore, imagery use changes over the competitive season, but this also depends on the sport. No support was found for systematic differences in imagery use between team and individual sports as proposed by Hall et al. (1998). Because sports can be classified in various ways (e.g., open vs. closed) other than team versus individual, it was suggested

that the relationship between sport classifications and imagery use deserves further investigation.

Gammage et al. (in press) examined whether type of activity influenced exercise participants' use of motivational and cognitive imagery. They administered the EIQ to 577 (312 women and 264 men) exercisers participating in aerobics, weight training, running, and swimming, and those using cardiovascular equipment such as a Stairmaster. The EIQ measures two motivational functions of imagery, appearance and energy, and one cognitive function of imagery, technique. They discovered some differences in imagery use across the various activities. Individuals who weight trained used more technique imagery than those who ran or used cardiovascular equipment. In addition, runners used less appearance imagery than those involved in weight training, aerobics, and the use of cardiovascular equipment.

There is a wealth of research demonstrating that imagery use and effectiveness are influenced by the type of activity in which athletes and exercisers participate. This is to be expected. What still needs to be determined is how to make imagery work better and in more situations. This requires answers to specific task-related questions and some of these have been provided in this section. For example, participants in weight training report using considerable technique imagery. Therefore, if individuals are starting to weight train, encouraging them to use technique imagery might have a positive effect on their adherence. Investigating how all the various types of physical activity can influence imagery may seem like a daunting task, but the potential benefits definitely make the effort worthwhile.

Level of Skill and Activity

One of the early topics addressed in the sport imagery literature was skill level. Researchers wanted to determine if imagery was more beneficial for novice or skilled performers. Some argued that imagery should be most effective in the early stages of learning, when cognitive processes (e.g., determining what to do) play a large role. Support for this position was offered by Wrisberg and Ragsdale (1979). They introduced imagery practice either early or later in the learning of a motor skill and demonstrated that the amount it facilitated performance decreased with the amount of physical practice participants had experienced. Other researchers alleged that imagery should be more effective for more elite performers because a strong internal representation of the skill is required for participants to form a clear, accurate image of what good task performance is like. Noel (1980) argued that mere experience at a skill to be imaged is not enough; proficiency is required. He examined high- and low-ability tennis players. A significant performance improvement was demonstrated in the high-ability players who used imagery, whereas a deterioration was evidenced in the low-ability players.

A limitation with these studies is that only CS imagery was considered; no examination of motivational imagery was undertaken. Furthermore, studies varied in how the amount of learning that occurred was determined. A novice might show improvements in performance accuracy by using CS imagery, but a more skillful performer might show improvements in consistency. Even elite performers sometimes work on learning new skills (e.g., a figure skater learning a quad jump), and often basic skills in a sport have to be put together in a new sequence (e.g., a gymnastics routine). Blair et al. (1993) investigated whether novice or elite soccer players benefited more from using CS imagery to acquire a task designed to include most of the basic soccer skills. Players were tested on the task both before and after six weeks of imagery practice. The amount of improvement was about the same for both the novice and elite players, suggesting that players of all skill levels can benefit from using CS imagery.

In the studies conducted by Hall and his colleagues (e.g., Barr & Hall, 1992; Hall et al., 1990, 1998) athletes at all skill levels reported the extensive use of both motivational and cognitive imagery. One of the most consistent findings, however, is that the higher the skill level of the athletes, the greater their use of imagery. For example, Salmon et al. (1994) examined the imagery use of soccer players at the national, provincial, and local levels. Although players at all three skill levels reported using imagery more for its motivational function than its cognitive function, the elite players reported more imagery than the nonelite players regardless of the function imagery served. The more extensive use of imagery by elite athletes is undoubtedly due to the greater commitment these athletes make to their sport.

With respect to exercise, the level (i.e., frequency) of exercise has been found to be an important consideration. Rodgers and Gauvin (1998) investigated the motivational features of two groups of women: those who exercised two or fewer times per week and those who exercised three or more times per week. They found that these two groups could be distinguished based on self-efficacy as well as incentives for stress reduction and aspects of mental health (e.g., energy and well-being). Godin, Desharnis, Valois, and Bradet (1995) also showed that these two groups differed on perceived behavioral control for exercise. Do these two groups also differ on their use of exercise imagery? Gammage et al. (in press) administered the EIQ to exercisers participating in a wide variety of activities. Of these participants, 287 reported exercising one to two times per week (the low-activity group) and 290 reported exercising three or more times per week (the high-activity group). The high-activity group claimed to use all three functions of exercise imagery (appearance, energy, and technique) more than the low-activity group. It was argued that because the high-activity group spend more time exercising, it is logical that they also spend more time thinking about exercise. Furthermore, these people are likely to be more concerned with exercise and its benefits and therefore spend more time thinking about and imagining these benefits.

Gender

There is no doubt that both men and women can benefit from imaging. A review of the motor skills imagery research provides no evidence for suggesting that imagery is more effective for one gender than the other. Furthermore, only minor differences have been noted between men and women on their reported use of imagery. Of all the variables they examined, Barr and Hall (1992) noted that male and female rowers differed significantly on their responses to only three items. The male rowers reported having better control of their external perspective and having more vivid internal visual images than women; the female rowers practiced imagery more regularly than the men. In most studies (e.g., Munroe et al., 1998; Salmon et al., 1994), differences are so minor between men and women on their reported use of motivational and cognitive imagery that gender is not included as a variable in any of the analyses.

In contrast with sport, gender does seem to be a determinant of exercise imagery use. Gammage et al. (in press) concluded that women use appearance imagery more frequently than men. This seems sensible given the pressures placed on women to maintain a physically ideal body. A second finding was that men use technique imagery more frequently than women. One explanation for this finding could be that more men than women in the study participated in weight training and this activity is very technical in nature (i.e., it requires proper form to be completed safely and effectively). A second explanation proposed by Gammage et al. is that men tend to exercise for more competitive reasons than women and the weight training culture tends to be very competitive. Men often attempt to lift more weight and work harder than others around them. With this type of exercise motive, men may imagine themselves perfecting their form and technique to lift more weight. Men and women show no difference in their use of energy imagery (Gammage et al., in press). This result is consistent with research showing no gender differences in psychological motives for exercise (Markland & Hardy, 1993; Mathes & Battista, 1985). Because men and women exercise for similar psychological reasons, it is not surprising to find that they use energy imagery similarly as well.

Imagery Ability

Although most athletes and exercisers report using imagery, there are differences in their abilities to do so. Individual differences in imagery ability have been of interest to psychologists for over a century. Paivio (1986) believes that these individual differences are a product of experience interacting with genetic variability. For researchers in the motor domain, one of the main issues has been whether it is possible to predict task performance from variations in imagery ability. The initial work on this issue produced mixed results.

Start and Richardson (1964) measured both the vividness and controllability of participants' imagery and found no relationship between these attributes of imagery ability and the learning and performance of a gymnastics skill. Similarly, Epstein (1980) was unable to demonstrate any relationship between individual differences in imagery and performance accuracy on a dart-throwing task. Ryan and Simons (1982), however, produced more positive results. Participants were classified according to the frequency with which they reported using imagery in everyday life and then assigned to one of six conditions: frequent imagers instructed to use imagery to learn a balance task, frequent imagers asked not to use imagery, nonfrequent imagers instructed to use imagery to learn the task, nonfrequent imagers asked not to use imagery, physical practice, and no practice (i.e., control condition). Following their performance on the task, participants using imagery completed a questionnaire on which they rated the amount and quality of any visual or kinesthetic imagery they had experienced. As would be expected, imagery practice was effective for learning the task, and those participants using imagery improved more than those not using imagery. More important, participants reporting strong visual images showed more improvement than those with weak visual images, and those reporting strong kinesthetic images improved more than those with weak kinesthetic images.

Why were these mixed results obtained? One explanation offered by Hall et al. (1985) was that these studies failed to specifically measure imagery ability for motor skills. Rather, imagery ability tests were administered that

classified individuals as high and low imagers based on their ratings of people, places, and scenes. Since that time, imagery questionnaires have been developed that are designed to assess movement imagery abilities (see Hall, 1998, for a review of these questionnaires). With these instruments, researchers have more consistently demonstrated a relationship between imagery ability and motor performance.

Goss, Hall, Buckolz, and Fishburne (1986) administered the Movement Imagery Questionnaire (MIQ; Hall & Pongrac, 1983) to study three imagery ability groups: low visual/low kinesthetic (LL), high visual/low kinesthetic (HL), and high visual/high kinesthetic (HH). Participants were required to learn simple movements to a criterion performance level and were then tested on their retention and reacquisition of these movements after one week. The results revealed that imagery ability is related to the learning of movements. The LL group took the most trials to learn the movements, the HL group required an intermediate number of trials, and the HH group learned the movements in the least number of trials. The same trend was found for the reacquisition of the movements one week later, but weaker support was provided for a relationship between imagery ability and retention.

In another study, Hall, Buckolz, and Fishburne (1989) also classified participants as low and high imagers based on their MIQ scores. They were then tested on how well they could remember movements using both recall and recognition tests. Although there were no performance differences on the tests between the two groups, when the physical accuracy with which the movements were reproduced was assessed, high imagers were more accurate than low imagers. These findings indicate that individual differences in imagery ability can influence the learning and performance of motor skills.

When addressing individual differences, researchers have typically considered imagery to be an ability. An ability in the strict sense of the meaning is quite stable. Athletes, however, spend considerable time and effort attempting to improve their imagery. In this regard, imagery is perceived more as a skill than an ability. If imagery is a skill, then imagery test scores should improve with practice. Rodgers et al. (1991) investigated this possibility by administering the MIQ to figure skaters both before and after a 16-week imagery training program. The skaters experiencing the training program showed improvements in their imagery scores, but the MIQ scores for a control group remained unchanged. These results suggest that imagery is a skill as well as an ability and, like any skill, can be improved through regular, deliberate practice.

APPLICATION AND FUTURE DIRECTIONS FOR IMAGERY RESEARCH

When it comes to imagery in sport and exercise, the issue is not motivating participants to image, but rather having them image most effectively. They may use imagery in one situation, such as psyching up for a practice or game, but may not think to use it in another, such as motivating themselves to do their rehabilitation exercises. One possible starting place for providing an imagery intervention as an instructor, coach, or sport psychologist is to ask athletes and exercisers about the four Ws of imagery use: *where, when, why,* and *what.*

Although all four questions are important, where and why might be more critical to ask than when and what. This is because the answers given to when and what are usually much more consistent across participants (Hausenblas et al., 1999; Munroe et al., 1999). For example, athletes use imagery most immediately prior to performing, and their images tend to be accurate, vivid, and positive (Barr & Hall, 1992; Hall et al., 1990). Because there is more variability in where and especially why athletes and exercisers use imagery, having a framework to guide the application of where and why to use imagery would have considerable utility for both practitioners and researchers. Martin, Moritz, and Hall (1999) have recently developed such a framework for athletes. Their organizational model was developed to "reduce the myriad of imagery-related variables that have been studied in applied sport contexts to the smallest possible set of theoretically meaningful factors" (p. 248). Four key components for the model were identified: (1) the situation (i.e., *where*), (2) the function of imagery (i.e., *why*), (3) imagery ability, and (4) outcomes associated with imagery use. Their ideas and some others pertaining to exercise imagery are captured in Figure 20.2.

In the model, two basic situations are distinguished: sport and exercise. One feature of sport that separates it from exercise is competition. Often with competition comes pressure, anxiety, and an emphasis on winning; these tend to be much less evident in exercise. However, with the exception of judged sports (e.g., figure skating), exercise tends to place a greater emphasis on appearance than does sport. Given these differences, some of the cognitive and motivational functions served by imagery in these two situations are bound to vary.

The second component of the model is imagery function. As already discussed at some length, research has demonstrated that athletes use imagery for five basic functions (CS, CG, MS, MG-M, and MG-A), and exercisers employ

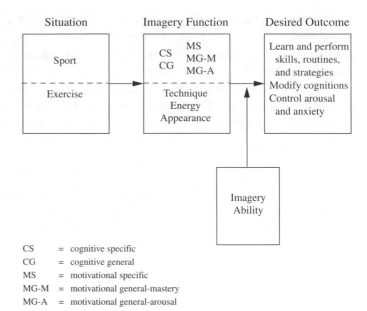

CS   = cognitive specific
CG   = cognitive general
MS   = motivational specific
MG-M = motivational general-mastery
MG-A = motivational general-arousal

Figure 20.2   A model describing how athletes and exercisers can use imagery to achieve a variety of outcomes [adapted from Martin et al. (1999)].

imagery for primarily three functions (appearance, energy, and technique). The third component of the model is the desired outcomes athletes and exercisers are hoping to achieve from using imagery. Three general categories of outcomes are (1) the learning and performance of skills, routines, and strategies; (2) the modification of cognitions (e.g., being more positive, increasing self-confidence); and (3) the regulation of arousal and anxiety levels. Martin et al. (1999) make very persuasive arguments for matching the function of imagery being used with the outcome desired. For example, if athletes want to increase their self-efficacy for performing a difficult skill, they should use MG-M imagery. Using another type of imagery (e.g., CS imagery) is likely to be less effective or not effective at all. Martin et al. stress that athletes (and exercisers) often have more than one outcome they hope to achieve from using imagery; therefore, their imagery should serve a number of functions and these functions can be prioritized within their imagery practice (e.g., a greater amount of MG-A imagery than CG imagery).

The fourth component of the model is imagery ability. It is conceptualized as a moderator variable and is included in the model because of the research showing a relationship between imagery ability and various motor performance outcomes. Some of the other variables (e.g., activity/skill level) also known to influence imagery use in sport and exercise, and discussed earlier in this chapter, could also be included in this component of the model. Overall, the model provides some general directions for instructors, coaches, and sport psychologists for undertaking imagery interventions with respect to the where and why of imagery use.

Significant strides have been made in the understanding of imagery in sport and exercise. This is especially true during the past 10 years or so as researchers have gone beyond examining mainly CS imagery. Nevertheless, the surface has only been scratched and there are many more questions left to be answered. In particular, we know very little about exercise imagery, yet it has tremendous potential as an intervention. Dishman (1994) has pointed out that despite continuing research addressing exercise adherence and the development and assessment of possible interventions, adherence rates have not appreciably increased from the late 1980s, suggesting that current interventions are not very effective. Given that exercise imagery has motivational functions (Hausenblas et al., 1999), researchers need to determine if imagery is an effective intervention to enhance exercise adherence.

Investigators are also encouraged to explore the relationships between exercise imagery and other variables that influence exercise participation and adherence. Although some initial research suggests exercise imagery is related to self-efficacy (Rodgers et al., 2000), this needs to be confirmed and extended to variables such as incentives for physical activity. It has also yet to be determined if imagery is directly related to exercise behavior, or if it influences such behavior indirectly through other variables (e.g., self-efficacy), as proposed by Hall (1995).

There has been considerable effort to determine the functions of imagery in sport and exercise. With the exception of CS imagery in sport, there is a lack of research on the effectiveness of these functions, and some (e.g., CG imagery) have received virtually no examination. Longitudinal studies are especially required to identify cognitive, affective, and behavioral changes associated with different functions of imagery. For example, does a greater use of MS imagery result in greater goal commitment? Adherence to imagery interventions is another issue that needs to be investigated. It is possible that adherence differs between interventions based on cognitive imagery and those based on motivational imagery.

When investigating the content of images, the typical approach has been to consider one attribute or dimension at a time (e.g., positive vs. negative imagery). Researchers are urged to design controlled experiments that examine several attributes concurrently. The work by Hardy and Callow (1999) is a good example of this type of research. They investigated the relative efficacy of different visual imagery perspectives, with and without kinesthetic imagery, on the performance of tasks in which form is important. It would also be valuable to vary imagery content and imagery function in the same experiment. Hardy and Callow varied content, but they evaluated only the CS function of imagery.

The model presented in Figure 20.2 not only offers some direction in consulting with athletes and exercisers, but can also be used as a guiding framework for designing imagery studies. The relationships proposed in the model can be tested, with the main prediction being that desired outcomes are best achieved by using specific functions of imagery. There are numerous questions about imagery in sport and exercise that need to be addressed. Only some of these are captured in the model; many more are left to the imagination of innovative researchers.

In summary, this chapter discussed the role imagery plays in sport and exercise. The approach taken was to consider the four Ws of imagery use: *where, when, why,* and *what.* The latter two have been the subject of most empirical investigations, yet all four are important in the development and implementation of imagery interventions. Although researchers have been investigating imagery in sport for over 60 years, their focus has been relatively narrow. The majority of studies have examined the role of imagery in the acquisition and performance of specific motor skills, with little attention given to the other functions imagery may serve, such as rehearsing strategies of play and increasing motivation. Fortunately, this situation is changing; researchers are currently studying motivational imagery and are also beginning to consider the possible roles imagery can have in exercise.

How imagery operates in motor skill acquisition was also discussed. Several theories have been advanced and have served to direct a considerable amount of research. However, these theories are limited in scope, pertaining primarily to the CS function of imagery (i.e., rehearsing specific motor skills). Until more comprehensive theories are developed, models for applying imagery in sport and exercise, such as proposed by Martin et al. (1999), can guide researchers in asking relevant and meaningful questions. These models also offer direction to practitioners when they are consulting with athletes and exercisers.

Both researchers and practitioners should be encouraged by some of the recent initiatives and approaches that are evident in the study of sport and exercise imagery.

Given the research described in the present chapter, the argument can easily be advanced that every year more progress is made in understanding imagery, the situations and variables that influence it, and how it can be most effectively applied. Undoubtedly, imagery will continue to be a major topic of interest in sport and exercise psychology.

REFERENCES

Adams, J.A. (1990). The changing face of motor learning. *Human Movement Science, 9,* 209–220.

Annett, J. (1988). Imagery and skill acquisition. In M. Denis, J. Engelkamp, & J.T.E. Richardson (Eds.), *Cognitive and neuropsychological approaches to mental imagery* (pp. 259–268). Dordrecht, The Netherlands: Martinus Nijhoff.

Annett, J. (1990). Relations between verbal and gestural explanations. In G.R. Hammong (Ed.), *Cerebral control of speech and limb movements* (pp. 295–314). Amsterdam: North Holland.

Annett, J. (1994). The learning of motor skills: Sports science and ergonomics perspectives. *Ergonomics, 37,* 5–15.

Annett, J. (1995). Motor imagery: Perception or action? *Neuropsychologia, 33,* 1395–1417.

Annett, J. (1996a). Imaginary actions. *The Psychologist, 9,* 25–29.

Annett, J. (1996b). On knowing how to do things: A theory of motor imagery. *Cognitive Brain Research, 3,* 65–69.

Bakker, F.C., Boschker, M.S.J., & Chung, T. (1996). Changes in muscular activity while imagining weight lifting using stimulus or response propositions. *Journal of Sport & Exercise Psychology, 18,* 313–324.

Bandura, A. (1997). *Self-efficacy: The exercise of control.* New York: Freeman.

Barr, K., & Hall, C. (1992). The use of imagery by rowers. *International Journal of Sport Psychology, 23,* 243–261.

Betts, G.H. (1909). *The distribution and functions of mental imagery.* New York: Columbia University, Teachers College.

Bird, E. (1984). EMG quantification of mental rehearsal. *Perceptual and Motor Skills, 59,* 899–906.

Blair, A., Hall, C., & Leyshon, G. (1993). Imagery effects on the performance of skilled and novice soccer players. *Journal of Sports Sciences, 11,* 95–101.

Budney, A.J., Murphy, S.M., & Woolfolk, R.L. (1994). Imagery and motor performance: What do we really know? In A.A. Sheikh & E.R. Korn (Eds.), *Imagery in sports and physical performance* (pp. 97–120). Amityville, NY: Baywood.

Callow, N., Hardy, L., & Hall, C. (in press). The effects of a motivational general-mastery imagery intervention on the sport confidence of high-level badminton players. *Research Quarterly for Exercise and Sport.*

Cancio, L.C. (1991). Stress and trance in free fall parachuting: A pilot study. *Journal of Clinical Hypnosis, 33,* 225–234.

Carter, J.E., & Kelly, A.E. (1997). Using traditional and paradoxical imagery interventions with reactant intramural athletes. *The Sport Psychologist, 11,* 175–189.

Caudill, D., Weinberg, R., & Jackson, A. (1983). Psyching-up and track athletes: A preliminary investigation. *Journal of Sport Psychology, 5,* 231–235.

Cogan, K.D., & Petrie, T.A. (1995). Sport consultation: An evaluation of a season-long intervention with female collegiate gymnasts. *The Sport Psychologist, 9,* 282–296.

Cumming, J.L., & Ste-Marie, D.M. (2000). *Cognitive and motivational effects from imagery training: A matter of perspective.* Manuscript submitted for publication.

Cupal, D.D. (1998). Psychological interventions in sport injury prevention and rehabilitation. *Journal of Applied Sport Psychology, 10,* 103–123.

Decety, J. (1996). Do imagined and executed actions share the same neural substrate? *Cognitive Brain Research, 3,* 87–93.

Decety, J., Perani, D., Jeannerod, M., Bettinardi, V., Tadary, B., Woods, R., Mazziotta, J.C., & Fazio, F. (1994). Mapping motor representations with PET. *Nature, 371,* 600–602.

Decety, J., Sjöholm, H., Ryding, E., Stenberg, G., & Ingvar, D. (1990). The cerebellum participates in mental activity: Tomographic measurements of regional cerebral blood flow. *Brain Research, 535,* 313–317.

Denis, M. (1985). Visual imagery and the use of mental practice in the development of motor skills. *Canadian Journal of Applied Sport Sciences, 10,* 4S–16S.

Dishman, R.K. (1994). Introduction: Consensus, problems, and prospects. In R.K. Dishman (Ed.), *Advances in exercise adherence* (pp. 1–28). Champaign, IL: Human Kinetics.

Driskell, J.E., Copper, C., & Moran, A. (1994). Does mental practice enhance performance? *Journal of Applied Psychology, 79,* 481–491.

Durand, M., Hall, C., & Haslam, I.R. (1997). The effects of combining mental and physical practice on motor skill acquisition: A review of the literature and some practical implications. *The Hong Kong Journal of Sports Medicine and Sports Science, 4,* 36–41.

Epstein, M.L. (1980). The relationship of mental imagery and mental rehearsal to performance of a motor task. *Journal of Sport Psychology, 2,* 211–220.

Ericsson, K.A., Krampe, R.T., & Tesch-Römer, C. (1993). The role of deliberate practice in the acquisition of expert performance. *Psychological Review, 100,* 363–406.

Feltz, D.L., & Landers, D.M. (1983). The effects of mental practice on motor skill learning and performance: A meta-analysis. *Journal of Sport Psychology, 5,* 25–57.

Feltz, D.L., & Riessinger, C.A. (1990). Effects of in vivo imagery and performance feedback on self-efficacy and muscular endurance. *Journal of Sport & Exercise Psychology, 12,* 132–143.

Fenker, R.M., & Lambiotte, J.G. (1987). A performance enhancement program for a college football team: One incredible season. *The Sport Psychologist, 1,* 224–236.

Gabriele, T.E., Hall, C.R., & Lee, T.D. (1989). Cognition in motor learning: Imagery effects on contextual interference. *Human Movement Science, 8,* 227–245.

Gammage, K.L., Hall, C.R., & Rodgers, W.M. (in press). More about exercise imagery. *The Sport Psychologist.*

Godin, G., Desharnis, R., Valois, P., & Bradet, R. (1995). Combining behavioral and motivational dimensions to identify and characterize the stages in the process of adherence to exercise. *Psychology & Health, 10,* 333–344.

Goss, S., Hall, C., Buckolz, E., & Fishburne, G. (1986). Imagery ability and the acquisition and retention of movements. *Memory and Cognition, 14,* 469–477.

Gould, D., & Udry, E. (1994). Psychological skills for enhancing performance: Arousal regulation strategies. *Medicine and Science in Sports and Exercise, 26,* 478–485.

Green, L. (1992). The use of imagery in the rehabilitation of injured athletes. *The Sport Psychologist, 6,* 416–428.

Hale, B.D. (1982). The effects of internal and external imagery on muscular and ocular concomitants. *Journal of Sport Psychology, 4,* 379–387.

Hale, B.D. (1994). Imagery perspectives and learning in sports performance. In A.A. Sheikh & E.R. Korn (Eds.), *Imagery in sports and physical performance* (pp. 75–96). Amityville, NY: Baywood.

Hall, C.R. (1980). Imagery for movement. *Journal of Human Movement Studies, 6,* 252–264.

Hall, C.R. (1985). Individual differences in the mental practice and imagery of motor skill performance. *Canadian Journal of Applied Sport Sciences, 10,* 17S–21S.

Hall, C.R. (1995). The motivational function of mental imagery for participation in sport and exercise. In J. Annett, B. Cripps, & H. Steinberg (Eds.), *Exercise addiction: Motivation for participation in sport and exercise* (pp. 15–21). Leicester, England: British Psychological Society.

Hall, C.R. (1997). Lew Hardy's third myth: A matter of perspective. *Journal of Applied Sport Psychology, 9,* 310–313.

Hall, C.R. (1998). Measuring imagery abilities and imagery use. In J.L. Duda (Ed.), *Advances in sport exercise and psychology measurement* (pp. 165–172). Morgantown, WV: Fitness Information Technology.

Hall, C.R., Bernoties, L., & Schmidt, D. (1995). Interference effects of mental imagery on a motor task. *British Journal of Psychology, 86,* 181–190.

Hall, C.R., & Buckolz, E. (1981). Recognition memory for movement patterns and their corresponding pictures. *Journal of Mental Imagery, 5,* 97–104.

Hall, C.R., Buckolz, E., & Fishburne, G.J. (1989). Searching for a relationship between imagery ability and memory of movements. *Journal of Human Movement Studies, 17,* 89–100.

Hall, C.R., Buckolz, E., & Fishburne, G.J. (1992). Imagery and the acquisition of motor skills. *Canadian Journal of Sport Sciences, 17,* 19–27.

Hall, C.R., Mack, D., Paivio, A., & Hausenblas, H. (1998). Imagery use by athletes: Development of the Sport Imagery Questionnaire. *International Journal of Sport Psychology, 29,* 73–89.

Hall, C.R., Moore, J., Annett, J., & Rodgers, W. (1997). Recalling demonstrated and guided movements using imaginary and verbal rehearsal strategies. *Research Quarterly for Exercise and Sport, 68,* 136–144.

Hall, C.R., & Pongrac, J. (1983). *Movement Imagery Questionnaire.* London, Canada: University of Western Ontario.

Hall, C.R., Pongrac, J., & Buckolz, E. (1985). The measurement of imagery ability. *Human Movement Science, 4,* 107–118.

Hall, C.R., Rodgers, W.M., & Barr, K.A. (1990). The use of imagery by athletes in selected sports. *The Sport Psychologist, 4,* 1–10.

Hall, C.R., Schmidt, D., Durand, M., & Buckolz, E. (1994). Imagery and motor skills acquisition. In A.A. Sheikh & E.R. Korn (Eds.), *Imagery in sports and physical performance* (pp. 121–134). Amityville, NY: Baywood.

Hardy, L. (1997). Three myths about applied consultancy work. *Journal of Applied Sport Psychology, 9,* 277–294.

Hardy, L., & Callow, N. (1999). Efficacy of external and internal visual imagery perspectives for the enhancement of performance on tasks in which form is important. *Journal of Sport & Exercise Psychology, 21,* 95–112.

Harris, D.V., & Robinson, W.J. (1986). The effects of skill level on EMG activity during internal and external imagery. *Journal of Sport Psychology, 8,* 105–111.

Hausenblas, H.A., Hall, C.R., Rodgers, W.M., & Munroe, K.J. (1999). Exercise imagery: Its nature and measurement. *Journal of Applied Sport Psychology, 11,* 171–180.

Hecker, J.E., & Kaczor, L.M. (1988). Application of imagery theory to sport psychology: Some preliminary findings. *Journal of Sport & Exercise Psychology, 10,* 363–373.

Highlen, P., & Bennett, B. (1979). Psychological characteristics of successful and non-successful elite wrestlers: An exploratory study. *Journal of Sport Psychology, 1,* 123–137.

Hird, J.S., Landers, D.M., Thomas, J.R., & Horan, J.J. (1991). Physical practice is superior to mental practice in enhancing cognitive and motor task performance. *Journal of Sport & Exercise Psychology, 8,* 281–293.

Hodges, N.J., & Starkes, J.L. (1996). Wrestling with the nature of expertise: A sport specific test of Ericsson, Krampe and Tesch-Römer's (1993) theory of "deliberate practice." *International Journal of Sport Psychology, 27,* 400–424.

Ingvar, D.H., & Philipson, L. (1977). Distribution of cerebral blood flow in the dominant hemisphere during motor ideation and motor performance. *Annals of Neurology, 2,* 230–237.

Isaac, A. (1992). Mental practice—does it work in the field? *The Sport Psychologist, 6,* 192–198.

Isaac, A., Marks, D., & Russell, E. (1986). An instrument for assessing imagery of movements: The Vividness of Movement Imagery Questionnaire (VMIQ). *Journal of Mental Imagery, 10,* 23–30.

Jacobson, E. (1931). Electrical measurement of neuromuscular states during mental activities. *American Journal of Physiology, 96,* 115–121.

Janssen, J.J., & Sheikh, A.A. (1994). Enhancing athletic performance through imagery: An overview. In A.A. Sheikh & E.R. Korn (Eds.), *Imagery in sports and physical performance* (pp. 1–22). Amityville, NY: Baywood.

Johnson, P. (1982). The functional equivalence of imagery and movement. *Quarterly Journal of Experimental Psychology, 34*(A), 349–365.

Kim, J., Singer, R.N., & Tennant, L.K. (1998). Visual, auditory and kinesthetic imagery on motor learning. *Journal of Human Movement Studies, 34,* 159–174.

Korn, E. (1994). Mental imagery in enhancing performance: Theory and practical exercises. In A.A. Sheikh & E.R. Korn (Eds.), *Imagery in sports and physical performance* (pp. 201–230). Amityville, NY: Baywood.

Lang, P.J. (1977). Imagery in therapy: An information-processing analysis of fear. *Behavior Therapy, 8,* 862–886.

Lang, P.J. (1979). A bio-informational theory of emotional imagery. *Psychophysiology, 16,* 495–512.

Lang, P.J., Melamed, B.G., & Hart, J.A. (1970). A psychophysiological analysis of fear modification using an automated desensitization procedure. *Journal of Abnormal Psychology, 76,* 229–234.

Mace, R.D., Eastman, C., & Carroll, C. (1987). The effects of stress inoculation training on gymnastics' performance on the pommel horse: A case study. *Behavioral Psychotherapy, 15,* 272–279.

MacIntyre, T., & Moran, A. (1996). Imagery use among canoeists: A worldwide survey of novice, intermediate, and elite slalomists. *Journal of Applied Sport Psychology, 8,* S132.

MacKay, D.G. (1981). The problem of rehearsal or mental practice. *Journal of Motor Behavior, 13,* 274–285.

MacKay, D.G. (1982). The problem of flexibility, fluency and speed-accuracy trade-off in skilled behavior. *Psychological Review, 89,* 483–506.

Madigan, R., Frey, R.D., & Matlock, T.S. (1992). Cognitive strategies of university athletes. *Canadian Journal of Applied Sport Sciences, 17,* 135–140.

Mahoney, M.J., & Avener, M. (1977). Psychology of the elite athlete: An exploratory study. *Cognitive Therapy and Research, 1,* 135–141.

Markland, D., & Hardy, L. (1993). The Exercise Motivations Inventory: Preliminary development and validity of a measure of individuals' reasons for participation in regular physical exercise. *Personality and Individual Differences, 15,* 289–296.

Marks, D.F., & Isaac, A.R. (1995). Topographical distribution of EEG activity accompanying visual and motor imagery in vivid and non-vivid imagers. *British Journal of Psychology, 86,* 271–282.

Marteniuk, R.G. (1976). *Information processing in motor skills.* New York: Holt, Rinehart and Winston.

Martin, K.A., & Hall, C.R. (1995). Using mental imagery to enhance intrinsic motivation. *Journal of Sport & Exercise Psychology, 17,* 54–69.

Martin, K., Moritz, S., & Hall, C. (1999). Imagery use in sport: A literature review and applied model. *The Sport Psychologist, 13,* 245–268.

Mathes, S.A., & Battista, R. (1985). College men's and women's motives for participation in physical activity. *Perceptual and Motor Skills, 61,* 719–726.

McBride, E.R., & Rothstein, A.L. (1979). Mental and physical practice and the learning and retention of open and closed skills. *Perceptual and Motor Skills, 49,* 359–365.

Mills, K.D., Munroe, K.J., & Hall, C.R. (in press). The relationship between imagery and self-efficacy in competitive athletes. *Imagination, Cognition and Personality.*

Minas, C.A. (1978). Mental practice of a complex perceptual-motor skill. *Journal of Human Movement Studies, 4,* 102–107.

Moritz, S., Hall, C., Martin, K., & Vadocz, E. (1996). What are confident athletes imagining? An examination of image content. *The Sport Psychologist, 10,* 171–179.

Munroe, K.J., Giacobbi, P.R., Jr., Hall, C., & Weinberg, R. (2000). The four w's of imagery use: Where, when, why, and what. *The Sport Psychologist, 14,* 119–137.

Munroe, K., Hall, C., Simms, S., & Weinberg, R. (1998). The influence of type of sport and time of season on athletes' use of imagery. *The Sport Psychologist, 12,* 440–449.

Munroe, K., Hall, C.R., & Weinberg, R.S. (1999, October). *The relationship of goal setting and imagery: A qualitative analysis.* Paper presented at the annual meeting of the Canadian Society for Psychomotor Learning and Sport Psychology, Edmonton, Canada.

Noel, R.C. (1980). The effect of visuomotor behavioral rehearsal on tennis performance. *Journal of Sport Psychology, 2,* 221–226.

Orlick, T. (1990). *In pursuit of excellence* (2nd ed.). Champaign, IL: Human Kinetics.

Paivio, A. (1985). Cognitive and motivational functions of imagery in human performance. *Canadian Journal of Applied Sport Sciences, 10,* 22S–28S.

Paivio, A. (1986). *Mental representations: A dual coding approach.* New York: Oxford University Press.

Powell, G.E. (1973). Negative and positive mental practice in motor skill acquisition. *Perceptual and Motor Skills, 37,* 312.

Rawlings, E.I., Rawlings, I.L., Chen, S.S., & Yilk, D. (1972). The facilitating effects of mental rehearsal in the acquisition of rotary pursuit tracking. *Psychonomic Science, 26,* 71–73.

Rodgers, W.M., & Gauvin, L. (1998). Heterogeneity of incentives for physical activity and self-efficacy in high active and moderately active women exercisers. *Journal of Applied Social Psychology, 28,* 1016–1029.

Rodgers, W.M., Hall, C.R., Blanchard, C.M., & Munroe, K.J. (2000). *Refinement and validation of the Exercise Imagery Questionnaire.* Manuscript submitted for publication.

Rodgers, W.M., Hall, C.R., & Buckolz, E. (1991). The effect of an imagery training program on imagery ability, imagery use, and figure skating performance. *Journal of Applied Sport Psychology, 3,* 109–125.

Rotella, R.J., Gansneder, D., Ojala, D., & Billing, J. (1980). Cognitions and coping strategies of elite skiers: An exploratory study of young developing athletes. *Journal of Sport Psychology, 2,* 350–354.

Rushall, B.S. (1988). Covert modeling as a procedure for altering an elite athlete's psychological state. *The Sport Psychologist, 2,* 131–140.

Ryan, E.D., & Simons, J. (1982). Efficacy of mental imagery in enhancing mental rehearsal of motor skills. *Journal of Sport Psychology, 4,* 41–51.

Ryan, E.D., & Simons, J. (1983). What is learned in mental practice of motor skills? A test of the cognitive-motor hypothesis. *Journal of Sport Psychology, 5,* 419–426.

Sackett, R.S. (1934). The influences of symbolic rehearsal upon the retention of a maze habit. *Journal of General Psychology, 10,* 376–395.

Salmon, J., Hall, C., & Haslam, I. (1994). The use of imagery by soccer players. *Journal of Applied Sport Psychology, 6,* 116–133.

Schwartz, G. (1984). Psychophysiology of imagery and healing: A systems perspective. In A. Sheikh (Ed.), *Imagination and healing* (pp. 38–50). Farmingdale, NY: Baywood.

Singer, R.N. (1980). *Motor learning and human performance.* New York: Macmillan.

Sordoni, C., Hall, C., & Forwell, L. (2000). *The use of imagery by athletes during injury rehabilitation.* Manuscript submitted for publication.

Start, K.B., & Richardson, A. (1964). Imagery and mental practice. *British Journal of Educational Psychology, 34,* 280–284.

Suinn, R.M. (1980). Body thinking: Psychology for Olympic champions. In R.M. Suinn (Ed.), *Psychology in sport: Methods and applications* (pp. 306–315). Minneapolis, MN: Burgess.

Suinn, R.M. (1996). Imagery rehearsal: A tool for clinical practice. *Psychotherapy in Private Practice, 15,* 27–31.

Terry, P., Coakley, L., & Karageorghis, C. (1995). Effects of intervention upon precompetition state anxiety in elite junior tennis players: The relevance of the matching hypothesis. *Perceptual and Motor Skills, 17,* 428–446.

Vadocz, E.A., Hall, C.R., & Moritz, S.E. (1997). The relationship between competitive anxiety and imagery use. *Journal of Applied Sport Psychology, 9,* 241–253.

Vealey, R.S. (1986). Mental imagery training for performance enhancement. In J.M. Williams (Ed.), *Applied sport psychology: Personal growth to peak performance* (pp. 209–234). Mountain View, CA: Mayfield.

Vealey, R.S., & Walter, S.M. (1993). Imagery training for performance enhancement and personal growth. In J.M. Williams (Ed.), *Applied sport psychology: Personal growth to peak performance* (2nd ed., pp. 200–224). Mountain View, CA: Mayfield.

Vogt, S. (1995). On relations between perceiving, imagining and performing in the learning of cyclical movement sequences. *British Journal of Psychology, 86,* 191–216.

Wehner, T., Vogt, S., & Stadler, M. (1984). Task-specific EMG-characteristics during mental practice. *Psychological Research, 46,* 380–401.

Weinberg, R.S., Seabourne, T.G., & Jackson, A. (1981). Effects of visuomotor behavioral rehearsal, relaxation, and imagery on karate performance. *Journal of Sport Psychology, 3,* 228–238.

White, A., & Hardy, L. (1995). Use of different imagery perspectives on the learning and performance of different motor skills. *British Journal of Psychology, 86,* 169–180.

White, A., & Hardy, L. (1998). An in-depth analysis of the uses of imagery by high-level slalom canoeists and artistic gymnasts. *The Sport Psychologist, 12,* 387–403.

Williams, J.D., Rippon, G., Stone, B.M., & Annett, J. (1995). Psychophysiological correlates of dynamic imagery. *British Journal of Psychology, 86,* 283–300.

Woolfolk, R.L., Parrish, M.W., & Murphy, S.M. (1985). The effects of positive and negative imagery on motor skill performance. *Cognitive Therapy and Research, 9,* 335–341.

Wrisberg, C.A., & Ragsdale, M.R. (1979). Cognitive demand and practice level: Factors in the mental rehearsal of motor skills. *Journal of Human Movement Studies, 5,* 201–208.

CHAPTER 21

Understanding and Enhancing Self-Confidence in Athletes

ROBIN S. VEALEY

The influence of self-confidence on sport performance is one of the most intriguing topics in sport psychology. After achieving peak performances, athletes often describe a strong, almost "shatterproof" sense of confidence that they believe allowed them to perform their best. Conversely, two of the most dreaded psychobehavioral occurrences in sport, choking under pressure and sudden performance slumps, are often attributed to "losing" one's confidence. Research has supported the notion that higher levels of self-confidence are related to success in sport (e.g., Feltz, 1988, 1994; Vealey, 1986, 1999). Coaches and sport psychology consultants, therefore, consider confidence a critical mental skill to be developed and enhanced in athletes.

However, despite the consensus that self-confidence is critical to athlete performance, research in sport psychology has barely scratched the surface in developing an understanding of this area. This may partly be attributed to the relative youth of the field of sport psychology, with the optimistic view taken that advances in the study of confidence in sport are an inevitable development as the field matures. Another perspective, however, is that significant advances in the study of self-confidence in sport await fresh conceptual frameworks and useful methodological vehicles to spur meaningful research questions that have relevance to the world of sport. For example, researchers have established that confidence is important to athletes' performance, and therefore research questions should now focus more on *why* and *how* confidence works to enhance performance. Knowledge gained from these types of questions would then provide meaningful and specific information to practitioners as to the nature of confidence and suggest ideas for quality intervention programs in sport psychology.

Thus, the purpose of this chapter is to discuss the nature of self-confidence in sport, and more important, to attempt to provide a conceptual framework from which research and practice related to confidence in sport may be extended in meaningful ways. The chapter begins with a brief historical summary of how the study of self-confidence has been approached in sport psychology. This summary then leads to a presentation of an integrated conceptual model of sport confidence to serve as the unifying framework for the chapter. The framework is used to overview what is known about confidence, as well as to offer suggestions about what could be known about confidence through the advancement of conceptual models and intervention research. Extending from the conceptual framework of confidence and research evidence/ideas related to this framework, intervention strategies for developing and enhancing confidence in athletes are discussed.

HISTORICAL BRIEF OF THE STUDY OF SELF-CONFIDENCE IN SPORT

Similar to other areas of study, self-confidence has been conceptualized and operationalized in many different ways in the sport psychology literature. Conceptual constructs related to the study of confidence in sport include sport confidence (Vealey, 1986; Vealey, Hayashi, Garner-Holman, & Giacobbi, 1998), self-efficacy (Bandura, 1986; Feltz, 1994), movement confidence (Griffin & Keogh, 1982), perceived competence (Harter, 1981), and performance expectancy (Corbin, 1981; Corbin, Landers, Feltz, & Senior, 1983; Corbin & Nix, 1979; Scanlan & Passer, 1979, 1981). It is counterproductive to debate the relative merits of each approach and how they differ, and especially to debate which approach is "right" or most useful. Rather, the knowledge base in sport psychology is broadened with an understanding of how these constructs form a constellation of approaches to the study of confidence, each providing bits of evidence to enhance our knowledge of the ubiquitous concept called self-confidence in sport.

The focus of this chapter is on the conceptual model of sport confidence based on its development as a theoretical framework dedicated to the specific study of confidence in sport. Self-efficacy, as a conceptualization of confidence developed in the general field of psychology, has been extensively reviewed by Feltz and Lirgg (this volume). However, several research findings and theoretical predictions from this area are mentioned again in this chapter due to their relevance to the understanding of confidence in sport.

Initial Conceptual Model of Sport Confidence

Building on work in the areas of self-efficacy, perceived competence, movement confidence, and expectancy theory, Vealey (1986) proposed a conceptual model of sport confidence and developed companion inventories to measure the key constructs in the model. A sport-specific construct of self-confidence, termed sport confidence, was defined as the belief or degree of certainty that individuals possess about their ability to be successful in sport (Vealey, 1986). Sport confidence is similar to self-efficacy, defined by Bandura (1986) as the belief one has about being able to execute a specific task successfully to obtain a desired outcome. However, the conceptualization of sport confidence and the development of measurement instruments related to this model were spurred by the need for a sport-specific conceptual framework and inventories to operationalize confidence in relation to the unique context of competitive sport.

The original model of sport confidence (Vealey, 1986) predicted that dispositional sport confidence (called trait sport confidence or SC-trait) interacts with competitive goal orientation to create a momentary sport confidence (called state sport confidence or SC-state) that directly influences behavior and performance. Competitive orientation was included in the model to account for the goal on which sport confidence is based, taken from the idea that success means different things to different people (Nicholls, 1989). The term competitive orientation was established to indicate a tendency for individuals to strive toward achieving a certain type of goal in sport. Vealey chose the two inherent goals of sport—performing well and winning—to represent the competitive orientations in the sport confidence model, because they seem likely to reflect

an athlete's belief that attainment of one of these goals demonstrates competence and success.

The competitive orientation construct is dispositional, meaning that over time, athletes develop a tendency to strive for a certain type of goal (either performance or outcome) and use this goal to define competence and success for themselves. Thus, athletes tend to be either performance-oriented or outcome-oriented, although in theory it is possible for a person to be high in both. This construct was viewed as a critical concomitant to confidence, meaning that understanding the influence of confidence on behavior and performance was facilitated by knowing what athletes were confident about (competitive goal orientation). To complete the model, various subjective outcomes (attributions, perceived success, emotions) were predicted to emanate from an athlete's behavior and feed back in the model to modify existing levels of SC-trait and types of competitive orientations.

To test the sport confidence model, three inventories were developed to operationalize key constructs in the theoretical framework: the Trait Sport Confidence Inventory (TSCI), the State Sport Confidence Inventory (SSCI), and the Competitive Orientation Inventory (COI). The TSCI and SSCI were developed to assess unidimensional constructs of SC-trait and SC-state, respectively. The COI produces a performance orientation score and an outcome orientation score for each individual completing the inventory. A multiphase research project in which over 1,000 participants were tested provided evidence to support the validity and reliability of the instruments, as well as to provide some support for the proposed model of sport confidence (Roberts & Vealey, 1992; Vealey, 1986, 1988b; Vealey & Campbell, 1988; Vealey & Sinclair, 1987).

Limitations of the Initial Sport Confidence Model

Although the original model of sport confidence carved out a sport-specific conceptual framework for the study of confidence in sport, it did not serve as a strong impetus for additional research. Several limitations of this initial conceptual framework may be identified to explain the lack of research in the area.

One weakness of the model seemed to be its dispositional-state approach in distinguishing SC-trait and SC-state, and hypothesizing that SC-state should be the best predictor of behavior/performance. This hypothesis was not supported, and interestingly, SC-trait emerged in various studies as a better predictor of sport behavior and performance than SC-state (Gayton & Nickless,1987; Roberts

& Vealey, 1992; Vealey, 1986). Certain theorists question the "arbitrary" distinction between personality dispositions and states, and it may be that this distinction has not enhanced the study of self-confidence in sport. Allen and Potkay (1981) state that the trait-state distinction in personality measurement has little conceptual or empirical viability. Mischel (1968) has argued that although the dispositional-state approach is conceptually logical, it is difficult to validate empirically. Problems in predicting sport behavior (particularly performance) using the trait-state approach have been discussed frequently in the literature (e.g., Burton, 1988; Gould, Petlichkoff, Simons, & Vevera, 1987). Therefore, it seemed fruitful to move beyond the arbitrary dichotomy of dispositions and states and think about sport confidence as being on a continuum from trait-like to state-like. In this way, consistency in confidence and behavior over time and situations could be examined in many different ways across the continuum, as opposed to thinking of confidence as being manifested statically in two dichotomous categories.

A second limitation of the initial sport confidence model was that it did not account for the impact of social and organizational factors on the development and manifestation of confidence in athletes. For example, most athletes would agree that such social factors as coaching behavior and expectancies of significant others influence their levels of confidence. This has been supported in research on gender differences in self-confidence, as the perceived cultural appropriateness of an activity has been shown to affect confidence levels of males and females (Clifton & Gill, 1994; Lirgg, 1991; Lirgg, George, Chase, & Ferguson, 1996). This research demonstrated that males were less confident than females on a perceived feminine task, and females were less confident than males on a perceived masculine task. Thus, there is a need to move beyond a narrow focus on self-confidence and performance to more broadly focus on how patterns of confidence are developed and continually influenced by social and cultural factors in society and the subculture of sport.

Reconceptualizing the Sport Confidence Model: A Social-Cognitive Emphasis

In 1998, a revised conceptual model of sport confidence was published with the intent to reconceptualize sport confidence based on social-cognitive theory, a conceptual shift that seemed warranted to enhance the study of confidence in sport (Vealey et al., 1998). Social-cognitive theory emphasizes the social origins of behavior, the importance of cognitive thought processes in human motivation, emotion,

and action, and the learning of complex individualized patterns of behavior in the absence of rewards (Pervin & John, 1997). In social-cognitive theory, behavior is situation-specific, and distinctive situation-behavior patterns are viewed as more defining of personality than the aggregate, cross-situational differences emphasized by dispositional theorists. For example, social-cognitive theorists emphasize that it is more important to know about the kinds of situations that enhance or decrease confidence in athletes, as well as the strategies used by athletes in different situations, than to assess athletes' overall levels of innate SC-trait relative to others.

Overall, the reconceptualized model of sport confidence based on a social-cognitive perspective included three new features: (1) a single sport confidence construct, as opposed to separate dispositional and state constructs; (2) the inclusion of organizational culture in the model to emphasize that sociocultural forces must be taken into account to understand how confidence is manifested in athletes in the unique subculture of competitive sport; and (3) the conceptualization of sources of confidence that are salient to athletes (Vealey et al., 1998). These three additions to the model are discussed next.

Deletion of Dispositional and State Confidence Constructs

The first modification to the model was the deletion of separate dispositional and state conceptualizations of sport confidence. Rather, sport confidence was viewed as a social-cognitive construct that can be more trait-like or state-like depending on the temporal frame of reference used (confidence about today's competition vs. confidence about the upcoming season vs. typical level of confidence over the past year). This modification was made in the model because the separate designations (and measures) of SC-trait and SC-state were not found to be useful predictors of behavior in the initial research in this area (Vealey, 1986).

Accounting for Influence of Organizational Culture

The second new feature of the sport confidence model was the inclusion of organizational culture as an influence on the sources and levels of sport confidence experienced by athletes. As discussed previously, psychological constructs such as self-confidence in sport must be studied in relation to the cultural forces that shape human cognition and behavior. Accounting for the sociocultural forces that are part of the organizational subculture of competitive sport is imperative to understanding self-confidence in a social-cognitive perspective due to the emphasis in this approach on the learning of behavior patterns within a specific cultural system.

Organizational culture factors that seem to influence the development and manifestation of confidence in athletes include level of competition, motivational climate, and the goals and structural expectations of particular sport programs. For example, the organizational culture of an elite gymnastics academy would differ from a local city gymnastics program for children in terms of goals, coaching behaviors, and expected levels of behavioral commitment from the participants. These social-structural-cultural factors are critical to consider when attempting to understand, assess, and enhance self-confidence in athletes of different ages, needs, and levels. Important organizational culture influences might also include stereotypical expectations for individuals' sport participation and behaviors based on ethnicity, class, gender, or sexual orientation. For example, in the United States, if an adolescent girl wanted to pursue competitive wrestling (traditionally a male sport), she would face a great deal of social disapproval, which would certainly influence her level of confidence as well as the sources that she uses to gain and maintain confidence. The main point is that psychological constructs such as sport confidence must be studied in relation to the cultural forces that shape human cognition and behavior.

Conceptualization of Sources of Sport Confidence

The third revision to the sport confidence model was the inclusion of sources of confidence based on a new line of research that identified nine sources of confidence salient to athletes in the sport environment (Vealey et al., 1998). Bandura (1990) states that advances in a field are best achieved when phenomena of interest are rooted in theories that specify their determinants or sources. As a social-cognitive theorist, Bandura emphasizes the need to understand the origins of critical human self-perceptions, such as confidence and self-efficacy, that are developed via social interactions with one's environment.

Most research in sport psychology on the sources of self-confidence has been conducted within the parameters of Bandura's (1986) self-efficacy theory. Bandura asserts that there are four sources of self-efficacy: performance accomplishments, vicarious experiences, verbal persuasion, and physiological states. The effects of these sources of self-efficacy on efficacy expectations and performance have been examined in experimental research in various motor and sport performance situations (see Feltz, 1994; Feltz & Lirgg, this volume). Descriptive research has

also supported the four sources of self-efficacy proposed by Bandura (Feltz & Riessinger, 1990). Bandura's self-efficacy theory has proved to be a fruitful theoretical framework within which to examine sources of confidence. The question remains, however, as to whether these sources are indeed the most salient to athletes within the unique sport context. Thus, this research line was pursued to examine the sources of confidence used by athletes based on the specific nature of competitive sport.

Nine Sources of Sport Confidence Supported by Research. A four-phase research project utilizing over 500 athletes from a variety of sports was conducted to identify relevant sources of confidence for athletes and to develop a reliable and valid measure of the sources of sport confidence (Vealey et al., 1998). Psychometric evidence supported the Sources of Sport Confidence Questionnaire (SSCQ) as a reliable and valid measure of nine sources of confidence in athletes. These sources are identified and defined in Table 21.1.

Mastery is a source of confidence derived from mastering or improving personal skills. *Demonstration of ability* becomes a source of confidence when athletes show off their skills to others or demonstrate more ability than their opponents. These two sources of sport confidence support Bandura's position that performance accomplishments are

Table 21.1 Sources of Sport Confidence

Source	Confidence derived from . . .
Mastery	Mastering or improving personal skills.
Demonstration of ability	Showing off skills to others or demonstrating more ability than one's opponent.
Physical/mental preparation	Feeling physically and mentally prepared with an optimal focus for performance.
Physical self-presentation	Perceptions of one's physical self (how one perceives one looks to others).
Social support	Perceiving support and encouragement from significant others in sport, such as coaches, family, and teammates.
Vicarious experience	Watching others, such as teammates or friends, perform successfully.
Coach's leadership	Believing coach is skilled in decision making and leadership.
Environmental comfort	Feeling comfortable in a competitive environment.
Situational favorableness	Feeling that the breaks of the situation are in one's favor.

an important source of self-confidence. However, the emergence of these two separate sources indicates that accomplishment is manifested in two ways in sport: mastering skills and demonstrating ability. The distinction between demonstrating ability and mastery as sources of confidence or perceived ability has also been supported by the work of Nicholls (1989), Horn and Hasbrook (1987), Duda (1992), and Gill, Dzewaltowski, and Deeter (1988).

Physical/mental preparation involves feeling physically and mentally prepared with an optimal focus for performance. This source of confidence has been supported by Gould, Hodge, Peterson, and Giannini (1989), who found that physical conditioning was one of the highest rated strategies utilized by coaches to develop self-confidence in athletes. Both Horn and Hasbrook (1987) and Williams (1994) also determined that effort was a source of competence information used by athletes. In addition, Bandura (1986) identified physiological arousal as a source of self-efficacy, which is similar to the popular sport concept of "psyching up" for optimal confidence and performance. Williams also noted that "pregame attitude" such as feeling relaxed or energized influences perceptions of competence.

Physical self-presentation is defined as athletes' perceptions of their physical selves, or body image. Previous research in self-efficacy has supported a construct of physical self-efficacy based on perceptions of one's body and physical conditioning (Ryckman, Robbins, Thornton, & Cantrell, 1982). Moreover, research has demonstrated that sport participants are often concerned with the appearance and evaluation of their bodies (Martin & Mack, 1996).

As a source of sport confidence, *social support* is similar to Bandura's (1986) verbal persuasion source of self-efficacy. Weinberg, Grove, and Jackson (1992) found that verbal persuasion was one of the most common strategies used by coaches to facilitate confidence in tennis players. Harter (1981) identified reinforcement from significant others as an important facilitator of perceived competence. Evaluative feedback from coaches, parents, and peers has been shown to be an important influence on children's perceptions of competence (Black & Weiss, 1992; Horn, 1985; Horn & Hasbrook, 1986, 1987; Horn & Weiss, 1991).

Vicarious experience involves gaining confidence from watching others, such as teammates or friends, perform successfully. Similarly, Bandura's (1986) self-efficacy theory predicts that seeing someone else perform successfully serves to enhance one's own confidence. Vicarious experience as a source of confidence has been supported in the sport psychology literature (Gould & Weiss, 1981; McAuley, 1985; Weinberg, Gould, & Jackson, 1979).

Coach's leadership is a source of confidence derived from believing in the coach's skills in decision making and leadership. This source has been supported by research establishing a link between coaching behavior and perceptions of competence in athletes (Horn, 1985).

Environmental comfort is a source of confidence that comes from feeling comfortable in a competitive environment, such as the particular gymnasium or pool, where competition will occur. The "home advantage," or finding that home teams in sport competitions win over 50% of the games played under a balanced home-and-away schedule (Courneya & Carron, 1992), is often anecdotally cited as a source of confidence for athletes. *Situational favorableness* involves gaining confidence by feeling that the breaks of the situation are in one's favor. For example, the popular notion of psychological "momentum" refers to athletes' perceptions that something has occurred that increases their probability of success, which typically creates a surge of confidence (Richardson, Adler, & Hankes, 1988).

It seems conceptually useful to consider the nine sources of sport confidence supported by the research as falling within three broad domains. First, athletes gain confidence from *achievement,* which includes both mastery and demonstration of ability. Second, athletes gain confidence from *self-regulation,* which includes physical/mental preparation and physical self-presentation. Third, athletes gain confidence from a positive and achievement-nurturing *social climate,* which includes the sources of social support, vicarious experience, coach's leadership, environmental comfort, and situational favorableness. That is, athletes gain self-confidence when they achieve their goals, engage in effective self-regulation of cognitions, emotions, and behavior, and train and compete in a competitive climate that is supportive, challenging, comfortable, and motivating. Practically, a clearer understanding of the sources underlying self-confidence and their relationships to other psychological constructs and behaviors may provide useful insight for interventions to enhance self-confidence in athletes. Potential practical implications and interventions are discussed later in the chapter.

Importance of Sources to Athletes.   Beyond the identification of salient sources of confidence in sport, it was also of interest to examine which sources were most important for athletes. For individual sport collegiate athletes, the top five sources of sport confidence were physical/mental preparation, social support, mastery, demonstration of ability, and physical self-presentation (Vealey et al., 1998). Physical self-presentation and social support were more important sources of confidence for females than for males, emphasizing that body image along with social approval from others is learned to be important for females when participating in sport. Female athletes learn that maintaining socially defined feminine qualities affords them social acceptance and approval due to the emphasis placed on how women look in our society. These findings are congruent with researchers who have found that the presence of social evaluation cues influences females' level of confidence more than males' (Lenney, 1977; Lirgg, 1991; Lirgg et al., 1996).

For high school basketball players, mastery, social support, physical/mental preparation, coach's leadership, and demonstration of ability were the top five sources of sport confidence. However, physical self-presentation was the least important source of sport confidence and did not differ based on gender for this sample (in contrast to the collegiate individual sport sample). Typically, greater emphasis is placed on body type and presentation in individual sports as compared to the team sport of basketball, thus physical self-presentation may be a more salient source for athletes in sports where body type is more highly scrutinized. Due to limitations in the samples of this study, an alternative explanation may also be that more elite college athletes place greater emphasis on their physical self-presentation and body image as compared to high school athletes. Future research is needed to more fully examine the nature of physical self-presentation as a source of confidence in different sports and age groups.

Similar to the results with college athletes, social support was a more important source of sport confidence for female than male high school athletes. In addition, male athletes in this sample indicated that demonstration of ability was a more important source of confidence than for female athletes. This finding is supported by research indicating that males experience extreme normative social comparison expectations with regard to sport prowess and participation (e.g., Duda, 1989; Eccles & Harold, 1991; Gill & Deeter, 1988). However, gender differences in demonstration of ability as a source of sport confidence were not found with college athletes, so additional research is needed to further examine whether this gender difference is influenced developmentally or based on level of sport participation.

Summary of Reconceptualized Sport Confidence Model

The initial sport confidence model published by Vealey in 1986 was reconceptualized within a social-cognitive perspective to include an emphasis on salient sources of confidence for athletes and the influence of sociocultural

factors on the manifestation of confidence in sport. In preparing this chapter, however, it became apparent that an even broader, more integrative model is needed to explicitly illustrate the critical psychosocial processes that influence the important yet fragile construct of self-confidence in sport. A chronic problem in sport psychology is the schism that exists between research and practice, which relates to the need for a unifying framework that is relevant to both researchers and practitioners with regard to the study and enhancement of confidence. In the next section, a preliminary integrative model for research and practice is offered. The main focus of the model does not differ radically from previous frameworks, but the objective was to illustrate a broader, more explicit, perspective of how confidence "works" in sport.

An Integrative Model of Sport Confidence for Research and Practice

The point of developing an integrative model of sport confidence is to serve two functions: The model should serve as an organizational framework to elicit meaningful extensions to the research examining confidence in sport, and it should also serve as a foundation for interventions designed to enhance confidence in athletes. Clearly, a model such as this represents only a point of departure for both researchers and practitioners; hopefully, the framework will mature and extend as the knowledge base grows from research and successful interventions. The integrative model of sport confidence is shown in Figure 21.1. In the following section, a description of the model is provided, and relevant research is reviewed to support the model.

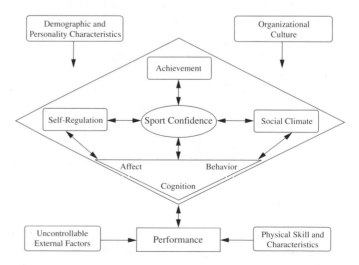

Figure 21.1 An integrated model of sport confidence for research and practice.

Core Psychosocial Constructs and Processes in the Model

The diamond shape in the center of the model contains the core psychosocial constructs and processes that define confidence, fuel its existence, and explain its mediating influence on sport performance. These include the sport confidence construct itself, the three domains representing sources of confidence for athletes (achievement, self-regulation, and social climate), and the ABC (affect, behavior, cognition) triangle, which is predicted to most directly influence athlete performance.

Sport Confidence.   Sport confidence is situated as the heart of the model; it is defined as the beliefs or degree of certainty that individuals possess about their ability to be successful in sport. Sport confidence is conceptualized as a social-cognitive construct that may be operationalized as more trait-like or state-like, depending on whatever temporal frame of reference is used. The social-cognitive nature of confidence is supported by Bandura's (1986) definition of self-efficacy as belief in one's capabilities to mobilize motivation, cognitive resources, and courses of action needed to exercise control over task demands. Thus, sport confidence, like self-efficacy, involves more than perceived competence. It is, rather, one's perceived competence to *do something*. That is, confidence is linked to a goal, or an outcome, that is perceived as success to the individual.

Unlike previous unidimensional operationalizations of sport confidence (Vealey, 1986), emerging theory and research supports confidence as a multidimensional construct (Maddux & Lewis, 1995). Preliminary results indicate that athletes possess multiple types of confidence, including confidence about one's ability to execute physical skills, psychological skills, perceptual skills such as decision making and adaptability, physical fitness and training status, and learning potential or ability to improve one's ability (Vealey & Knight, in progress). A new multidimensional Sport Confidence Inventory (SCI) requires researchers to provide respondents with a temporal frame of reference on which to base their responses (Vealey & Knight, in progress). Examples of temporal frames of reference for athletes' confidence that may be used in the SCI are shown in Table 21.2.

ABC Triangle.   The triangle shown directly below sport confidence in the model contains the ABCs of sport psychology: affect, behavior, and cognition. That is, the main focus in sport psychology is on how people feel, act,

Table 21.2   Sample Temporal Frames of Reference for the Sport Confidence Inventory (SCI)

Respond to each item based on . . .

1. How you feel RIGHT NOW about your abilities.
2. How you have felt about your abilities DURING THE PAST WEEK.
3. How you feel about your abilities in relation to the UPCOMING COMPETITION.
4. How you feel about your abilities in relation to YOUR TENNIS MATCH THIS COMING WEEKEND.
5. How you feel right now about your abilities in relation to the UPCOMING SEASON.
6. How you felt about your abilities DURING YOUR COMPETITIVE SEASON (retrospective assessment, after the season is over).
7. How you TYPICALLY feel about your abilities.

and think. In the social-cognitive perspective of psychology, the ABCs are termed the "domains of personal adjustment," or the feeling (affect), doing (behavior), and thinking (cognition) of human functioning (Maddux & Lewis, 1995). The ABCs are so interactive, or reciprocally determined (Bandura, 1978), that they are illustrated together within a triangle in Figure 21.1 to emphasize their continuous interactional reciprocity.

As a primary mediator of the ABCs of athletes, sport confidence may be considered the "mental modifier," meaning that confidence modifies how athletes feel about, respond to, and think about everything that happens to them in sport. This is the most critical link in the model because it represents the importance of understanding why and how sport confidence influences performance through its effect on how athletes feel, think, and act.

First, confidence arouses positive emotions ("A"), whereas a lack of confidence relates to negative affect such as anxiety, depression, and dissatisfaction (Martens, Vealey, & Burton, 1990; Roberts & Vealey, 1992; Vealey, 1986; Vealey & Campbell, 1988; Vealey et al., 1998). Thus, strong beliefs about personal competence and ability produce adaptive emotional states, whereas a lack of confidence (or beliefs about incompetence and lack of ability) are emotionally painful and lead to ineffective actions and thoughts (Maddux & Lewis, 1995). Interestingly, researchers have demonstrated that higher levels of confidence are associated with more positive perceptions of arousal and anxiety (Jones, Hanton, & Swain, 1994; Jones & Swain, 1995). Thus, confidence seems not only to enhance positive emotions, but also to provide a productive belief system in which emotions generally viewed as negative (e.g., anxiety) are reframed to be viewed as necessary and facilitative to athletic performance.

Second, self-confidence has been linked to productive achievement behaviors ("B") such as effort and persistence (Nelson & Furst, 1972; Ness & Patton, 1979; Weinberg, Yukelson, & Jackson, 1980). A strong sense of confidence leads athletes to set challenging goals, expend maximal effort, and persist in the face of obstacles in attempting to reach these goals, and thus to accomplish more as the result of these proactive behaviors (Bandura, 1986; Maddux & Lewis, 1995).

Third, confident individuals are more skilled and efficient in using cognitive resources ("C") that are necessary for sport success. Confident athletes have more productive attributional patterns, attentional skills, goal orientations, self-perceptions of success and ability, and coping strategies as compared to less confident athletes (Grove & Heard, 1997; Roberts & Vealey, 1992; Vealey, 1986, 1988b; Vealey & Campbell, 1988). Research has also demonstrated that highly confident athletes use more mastery and arousal imagery and have better kinesthetic and visual imagery ability than less confident athletes (Moritz, Hall, Martin, & Vadocz, 1996). Although not directly tested in the sport literature, Bandura and Wood (1989) have shown that confident individuals remain task-diagnostic by focusing on process solutions to problems in the face of obstacles, whereas less confident individuals are more likely to become self-diagnostic and focus on their perceived inadequacies. Remaining cognitively efficient via productive thinking is an essential skill for success in competitive sport, thus emphasizing the importance of self-confidence as a mental modifier of this cognitive efficiency.

Three Source Domains for Sport Confidence. Along with sport confidence and the ABC triangle, the other three constructs in the central diamond portion of the model represent source domains, or categories of factors that develop and/or enhance sport confidence in athletes. As explained previously, *achievement* represents the two sources of confidence used by athletes that are based on their past accomplishments. Specifically, research has shown that demonstrating ability and mastering sport skills are two of the most important sources of confidence for high school and college athletes (Vealey et al., 1998).

Self-regulation is the second source domain for confidence, emphasizing that the human ability to use self-reflection to plan and regulate behavior in pursuit of personal goals is paramount to developing confidence (e.g., Scheier & Carver, 1988). Vealey and colleagues (1998) found that physical and mental preparation were important sources of confidence in athletes, as well as positive self-perceptions about one's physical self.

The third source domain for sport confidence is the *social climate,* the myriad social processes that are typical to achievement situations. Social climate factors that have emerged as salient sources of confidence for athletes include social support, coach's leadership style and effectiveness, vicarious experience or available models, feelings of comfort and acclimation to the competitive environment, and an intuitive feeling of situational favorableness (Vealey et al., 1998). As discussed later, these source domains represent significant areas to target for intervention work on confidence.

Reciprocal Interactionism in the Central Sport Confidence Process. All constructs in the central process part of the sport confidence model (represented inside the diamond shape) interact continuously to influence performance. The three source domains are shown to directly influence athletes' level of sport confidence. Secondary arrows acknowledge the direct relationships between self-regulation and the ABC triangle and social climate and the ABC triangle. This means that although the focus of the model is on the determinants and consequences of sport confidence, self-regulatory forces and social climate factors also impact directly on how athletes think, feel, and respond in the competitive environment. The two-way arrows emphasize that all processes in the core of the model interact in a reciprocal manner.

Self-Confidence and Performance

The core of the model illustrates that, from a psychosocial perspective, the influence of confidence on performance is mediated by the ABC triangle. Specifically, performance is influenced by the thoughts, emotions, and behaviors of athletes. This is, of course, a major tenet of self-efficacy theory. Performance is ultimately shaped by the goals that athletes set, the behavioral choices they make, the effort they engage to pursue their goals, and the persistence they demonstrate when obstacles arise. Performance is also shaped by the ability of athletes to elicit productive emotions and thoughts, as well as their ability to manage and cope with counterproductive emotions and thoughts. As seen at the bottom of the model, performance is also influenced by the physical skill and characteristics of the athlete as well as uncontrollable external factors (e.g., weather, luck, opponents). It seems important to acknowledge these influences to indicate to athletes that they cannot control all things that influence their performance.

It is well established that self-confidence is facilitative to physical performance (Feltz, 1988, 1994; Roberts &

Vealey, 1992; Vealey, 1986). Feltz (1988) found that the correlations between self-confidence and subsequent performance in 28 studies ranged from .19 to .73, with a median of .54. Several correlational studies have demonstrated the importance of confidence in distinguishing between successful and less successful Olympic gymnasts (Mahoney & Avener, 1977), elite/collegiate wrestlers (Gould, Weiss, & Weinberg, 1981; Highlen & Bennett, 1979; Meyers, Cooke, Cullen, & Liles, 1979), swimmers (Jones et al., 1994), and athletes from a variety of sports (Mahoney, Gabriel, & Perkins, 1987). Thus, although multiple factors influence performance, overall it can be stated that one's self-perceptions of ability to succeed clearly influence motivated behavior and performance in physical activity and sport.

Organizational Culture

Organizational culture remains an important factor in the overall model of sport confidence. As shown in Figure 21.1 (and discussed previously), organizational culture represents the structural aspects of the sport subculture that influence the ways in which confidence is developed and manifested in athletes. For example, Olympic athletes report that the pressure and distractions in world-class competition such as the Olympic Games render their confidence level atypically "fragile" and vulnerable to instability (Gould, Guinan, Greenleaf, Medbery, & Peterson, 1999).

Demographic and Personality Characteristics

The final box in the model represents all the personality characteristics, attitudes, and values of individual athletes, as well as demographic characteristics such as age, experience, gender, and ethnicity. These characteristics are predicted to influence the development and manifestation of confidence in individuals as well as the sources that they use to gain confidence.

For example, competitive orientation, shown to be an important influence on sport confidence in Vealey's (1986) original model, is a personality characteristic that should influence levels and sources of sport confidence. Research has indicated that performance goal orientation was related to a more stable pattern of sport confidence for collegiate field hockey players over the course of a competitive season as compared to outcome goal orientation (Vealey & Sinclair, 1987). Also, competitive orientation has been shown to influence the sources of confidence that athletes use. Physical/mental preparation emerged as a more important source of confidence for performance-oriented athletes,

and demonstration of ability and environmental comfort were the preferred sources of confidence for outcome-oriented athletes. These findings suggest that performance-oriented athletes may use more personally controllable sources to fuel their confidence, whereas outcome-oriented athletes may focus on more uncontrollable sources of confidence such as normative social comparison and the social climate.

Gender is the main demographic characteristic that has been examined in relation to confidence in sport. A fairly consistent finding in the literature is that males tend to be higher in self-confidence than females (e.g., Lirgg, 1991). However, based on Lenney's (1977) now classic assertion that these confidence differences were based on perceived gender-appropriateness of the task (sport), research has shown that females are less confident than males on a perceived masculine task and that males are less confident than females on a perceived feminine task (Clifton & Gill, 1994; Lirgg, 1991; Lirgg et al., 1996). Vealey (1988b) found that although elite male athletes were more confident than male and female athletes at the high school and college levels, there was no difference in confidence between elite male and elite female athletes.

These findings suggest a strong sociocultural influence on the previously found gender differences in confidence. Females at an elite level of sport strongly believe they have the ability to succeed, and they feel this way no less than their male counterparts. An interesting question to address is whether they are selected into elite levels of sport because of their confidence (and ability), or whether they develop high levels of confidence from competing at an elite level. That is, it may be that elite athletes have deeply rooted confidence that is less affected by cultural constraints on acceptable gender behavior, or it could be that their elite status has helped them to develop greater confidence than females at lower levels of competition. However, it seems likely that gender differences in sport confidence have largely been misunderstood based on sport psychologists' neglect to more deeply understand the sociocultural influences on the possession and expression of confidence for females and males in sport.

STRATEGIES TO ENHANCE CONFIDENCE IN ATHLETES

The integrative model of sport confidence and review of literature based on the model provide a basic foundational framework for the development of intervention strategies to enhance confidence in athletes (see Figure 21.1).

Quality of Physical Training and Perceived Achievement

The most obvious point about developing confidence in athletes is that self-confidence must be earned through the development of physical skill and fitness to serve as a basic prerequisite for performance success. This is represented in the conceptual model as the link between achievement and sport confidence. Quality training to hone skills and fitness development are foundational achievements that serve as the basis for confidence building. Coaches clearly understand this, as they have rated physical conditioning as their top strategy in developing confidence in athletes (Gould et al., 1989). Athletes have also rated physical preparation as one of their top sources of confidence (Vealey et al., 1998), and successful world-class athletes have particularly emphasized the importance of *quality* training for their confidence and performance success (Orlick & Partington, 1988). This point should never be overlooked by sport psychology consultants. No mental training intervention can ever take the place of the physical skill and conditioning needed to perform in sport. Coaches and sport psychology consultants should work together to analyze practice methods and teaching strategies to enhance the quality and impact of physical training on athletes' confidence and performance levels. Examples of practice management to enhance confidence include simulation of pressure situations and creating unexpected situations to train adaptability.

Another basic foundation for athletes' confidence is their perception of their past achievement (Bandura, 1986; Vealey et al., 1998). The key here is the emphasis on perception, the point being that athletes must engage in productive attributional assessments of their achievement attempts and perceptions of success based on controllable factors (e.g., appropriate goal setting and evaluation). Higher levels of confidence in athletes have been shown to be related to focusing on sources or strategies that athletes personally control, such as mastery of physical skills, whereas lower levels of confidence were related to uncontrollable socially comparative or environmental sources (Vealey et al., 1998). Coaches and sport psychology consultants should help athletes define success in personally controllable ways, such as through the use of performance and process goals (e.g., Gould, 1998). Similarly, from a young age, athletes should learn to make productive attributions for their successes and failures to enhance their expectancies that they will be successful in the future.

As shown in Figure 21.1, personality characteristics interact with organizational culture to affect sources and levels of confidence in athletes. From an intervention standpoint, this interactional effect should be carefully assessed in relation to athletes' perceptions of their achievement and success. For example, perfectionism as well as certain personal identity issues have been related to youth athlete burnout, particularly in organizational sport subcultures where young athletes face high expectations of performance and professionalized attitudes about sport (Coakley, 1992; Gould, Udry, Tuffey, & Loehr, 1996). From a structural standpoint, sport researchers and administrators must lobby for institutional change in organizational subcultures that are counterproductive to the skill and confidence development of young athletes. Also, sport psychology consultants should carefully assess the personality of young athletes to identify those "at risk" for the development of negative self-perceptions or a lack of perceived success. Organizational/cultural factors dictate whether athletes perceive success and significant achievement, and these factors should be acknowledged and explained so that athletes become aware of their overriding social influence on their perceptions of competence.

Self-Regulation

Self-regulation has been identified as a significant source of confidence for athletes (Bandura, 1986; Vealey et al., 1998), and it is the central focus of interventions in sport psychology. To self-regulate means to manage one's behaviors, thoughts, and feelings, which is shown in the sport confidence model as a direct link between self-regulation and the ABC triangle. Self-regulation also is a direct source of confidence because it enhances athletes' beliefs in their abilities to be successful. Most mental training programs target confidence as a critical skill to develop and advocate several self-regulatory strategies to enhance confidence (e.g., Moore, 1998; Vealey, 1988a; Zinsser, Bunker, & Williams, 1998). Goal mapping, imagery, and self-talk are the three basic self-regulatory tools advocated by sport psychologists to enhance confidence.

Goal Mapping

The focused and persistent pursuit of goals serves as a basic regulator of human behavior; thus, it seems obvious that goal mapping is an important strategy to enhance the confidence and performance of athletes (see Burton, Naylor, & Holliday, this volume, for more detail on goal setting). A goal map is a personalized plan for an athlete that contains various types of goals and goal strategies as well as a systematic evaluation procedure to assess progress toward goals (e.g., Gould, 1998). Although athletes typically talk about the motivating qualities of outcome goals (winning, making the Olympic team), research indicates that performance and process goals are better sources of confidence (Burton, 1988; Kingston & Hardy, 1997). These types of goals seem to enhance confidence by allowing athletes to feel a sense of control over their performance and also by providing a specific task focus for productive concentration.

Imagery

Imagery, or visualization, is assumed to enhance confidence in two ways. First, visualizing oneself successfully performing in sport may, in an individualized vicarious sense, provide a perfect mental model for performance. Imagery in this sense serves a cognitive function to improve or refine the physical reproduction of a motor skill (Murphy, 1994; Paivio, 1985). Second, imagery may enhance confidence by influencing the athlete's ABCs through its motivational effect on behavior, creating a productive task focus of "what to do," and/or by creating positive emotion to energize confidence and performance (Vealey & Greenleaf, 1998). Researchers have shown that highly confident athletes tend to image the mastery and emotion associated with sport competition more than less confident athletes (Moritz et al., 1996). Thus, imagery interventions to enhance confidence should focus not only on the cognitive reproduction of skill execution, but also the emotional, attentional, and motivational aspects of performing in sport. Similar to simulation training advocated previously, imagery should simulate all social-environmental conditions and then program athletes' specific and productive emotional, behavioral, and cognitive responses to these various stimuli (Lang, 1979). By repeatedly imaging specific responses, imagery is thought to help athletes create a mental response set that is analogous to what is achieved via physical practice. Research has demonstrated that imagery training enhances sport confidence in athletes (Garza & Feltz, 1998).

Self-Talk

Managing thoughts, or self-talk, is advocated by applied sport psychology sources as an important key for self-confidence (e.g., Zinsser et al., 1998). Athletes who effectively manage their self-talk are, in essence, controlling how they think, as opposed to letting external events dictate how they think. This is essential due to the social-cognitive nature of sport confidence. That is, confidence is a belief system, a set of beliefs about one's ability to be successful in sport. Self-talk is representative of this belief system because what athletes say to themselves is

what they believe. The difficulty in managing self-talk lies in the automaticity and invisibility of athletes' thoughts that make up their belief systems. These belief systems are a product of past social interactions that have reinforced certain ideas about their abilities. These belief systems directly influence, and in fact define, one's self-confidence.

There are several variations of self-talk interventions that may serve to enhance confidence, including negative thought–stopping, countering, reframing, and the use of affirmations (Zinsser et al., 1998). Negative thought–stopping teaches athletes to recognize negative thoughts, self-monitor across time to learn individualized thought patterns in response to social stimuli, and habituate personal cues that allow them to stop negative thoughts from becoming internalized into their belief systems. Countering involves self-debate to understand how irrational and inappropriate beliefs create negative thinking. Rational emotive therapy (Ellis, 1981), as a form of countering negative self-talk, has been shown to enhance confidence in athletes (Elko & Ostrow, 1991). Reframing involves choosing to look at events in alternative ways, typically in more productive ways, and affirmations are a form of productive self-statement repeated over and over to internalize a belief or attitude. All of these interventions focus on the development and internalization of a positive belief structure about oneself; thus, all serve to enhance confidence.

Summary of Self-Regulation

Overall, self-regulation is based on the idea of choice. Athletes have the volition, or will, to choose how they act, think, and feel. Social conditioning clouds this perception and seduces individuals into believing that their thoughts and feelings are controlled by their social and physical environments. The key to consistent, healthy confidence in sport is the exercise of personal volition through self-regulation. Although this is difficult, particularly in the organizational culture of sport, it is possible to learn and enhance self-regulatory skills to maintain optimal self-confidence in sport.

Social Climate

Self-regulation has been hailed as an important and successful strategy to enhance confidence, yet coaches and sport psychology consultants must keep in mind that human behavior always takes place within a social climate. Intervention plans designed to enhance the motivational climate of educational settings have increased the motivation and confidence of learners (Ames, 1992;

Theeboom, De Knop, & Weiss, 1995). Examples of social climate factors that seem to influence confidence are leadership style, types of goal recognition and evaluation, social feedback sources and types, and availability and characteristics of models.

Confidence is enhanced when athletes are part of a productive and congruent social support network, which can be facilitated through team-building activities (Rosenfeld & Richman, 1997). The social influence of coaches' leadership style and feedback patterns have been shown to be important influences on athletes' perceptions of competence and confidence (Horn, 1985; Vealey et al., 1998). Horn and Harris (1996) advocate that coaches who display autonomous coaching styles that facilitate athletes' perceptions of control are more likely to enhance the confidence of their athletes, as compared to coaches who use more controlling leadership styles. Coaches can be more autonomous in their styles by providing contingent reinforcement and informative, as opposed to evaluative, feedback (Horn & Harris, 1996).

Based on the importance of vicarious experience as a source of confidence (Vealey et al., 1998), athletes should be provided effective models for not only skill execution, but also for achievement behaviors such as effort and persistence. Although environmental comfort emerged as a significant source of confidence for athletes, teaching athletes to rely on such external and uncontrollable factors to enhance their confidence seems problematic. Athletes should learn to base their confidence more on self-regulatory control of perceptions, emotions, and behaviors, so that they are not subject to the inconsistent type of self-confidence that is dependent on social and environmental confidence builders.

Summary of Intervention Strategies to Enhance Confidence

In summary, intervention strategies for confidence may be targeted from many different positions within the model of sport confidence. The reciprocal arrows throughout the model emphasize that confidence, although typically viewed as critical to performance, is also influenced *by* performance. Note that the ABC triangle of affect, behavior, and cognition mediates this reciprocal influence of performance on confidence. Thus, to enhance confidence, it may be more viable to focus interventions directly on the ABCs that relate so strongly to self-confidence. The idea is that by enhancing athletes' thoughts, feelings, and behaviors in relation to competitive demands, confidence may be enhanced.

FUTURE DIRECTIONS FOR THE STUDY AND ENHANCEMENT OF CONFIDENCE IN SPORT

An important objective for this chapter was to stimulate ideas for research and interventions in the area of confidence in sport. Hopefully, the predictions offered in the integrative model of sport confidence may serve as an initial conceptual vehicle to launch additional lines of research and confidence interventions.

One seemingly fruitful line of inquiry is research that attempts to explain how and why self-confidence facilitates performance. The literature contains ample evidence that confidence and successful performance are linked; thus, it seems important to turn our attention to an explanation of the processes or mechanisms by which this occurs. As illustrated in the sport confidence model, this would typically involve examining the affective, cognitive, and behavioral concomitants of confidence. Specifically, key ABCs such as persistence in goal striving, cognitive efficiency or the utilization of cognitive resources, and emotional adaptiveness should be examined in relation to self-confidence (Maddux & Lewis, 1995). Intervention research that evaluates the effectiveness of different types of self-regulation strategies in optimizing targeted affective, cognitive, and behavioral outcomes as well as subsequent levels of sport confidence is needed.

Another area that has not been examined is the nature of the expectancy construct in relation to confidence and performance. Expectancy is sometimes viewed as synonymous with confidence, in that athletes have beliefs about their abilities that lead them to expect to perform well and succeed. However, expectancy, as it relates to sport confidence, has not been extensively examined from a conceptual standpoint. As athletes and coaches can attest, expectancy often becomes a burden, especially when lofty and often unrealistic expectations are heaped onto young athletes. Moreover, a common belief in sport psychology is that flow, or peak performance, occurs best when athletes are in a state of automaticity and where there is an absence of any type of expectancy (Moore, 1998). Thus, the relationship between sport confidence and expectancy should be examined to provide a deeper understanding of this puzzling social phenomenon. Perhaps related to expectancy, the nature of overconfidence needs to be conceptually clarified to provide greater conceptual and practical insight into this popular term.

More research is needed to fully understand how self-confidence is manifested uniquely in the sport context, including the relevance of various dimensions, or types, of sport confidence (Vealey & Knight, in progress). Are certain types of confidence more critical to performance, and does this differ across sports and individuals? From an intervention perspective, different dimensions of confidence may be targeted by specific interventions, similar to the "matching hypothesis" applied in anxiety interventions to match the type of intervention to the specific type of anxiety (Martens et al., 1990). Also, the stability or fluctuation of confidence across time should be examined to better understand the factors that influence stability and change in different domains of sport confidence. The stability of confidence is important due to the often fleeting nature of confidence across competitive events.

The model of sport confidence advocated in this chapter was conceptualized to be integrative in nature, to provide a "big picture" of the plethora of constructs and processes that influence the complex relationship between confidence and performance. Future research should begin to account for this complexity by situating the study of confidence within the unique organizational subcultures represented in sport. Questions abound in relation to this point, including: What organizational and social structures work best to develop confidence in youth sport? How do athletes' sources and level of confidence develop, stabilize, and/or change developmentally as they move through the various organizational subcultures of sport? How do sources and level of confidence change over the course of a competitive season in relation to various factors in the social climate?

To enhance intervention work in building confidence in athletes, the development of applied assessment instruments related to confidence could be very useful. Most assessment tools that measure self-confidence were developed and validated as research tools, and these tools are not particularly useful for intervention work in sport psychology (Vealey & Garner-Holman, 1998). Obviously, sport psychology consultants have multiple ways of assessing confidence in athletes, such as by observation and interview/discussion. However, a fruitful area of future applied research would be the development of an applied confidence-assessment system to be used as a template to assess and monitor athletes' confidence and factors related to confidence.

Hopefully, the integrative model of sport confidence presented in this chapter will spark additional lines of inquiry and significant intervention ideas related to self-confidence in sport. Overall, researchers and practitioners are encouraged to remain mindful of the social-cognitive nature of confidence so as to account for the powerful influence of social learning and cultural factors on the manifestation of confidence in sport. It seems important to move beyond research that tests social psychological theories to see how well they "fit" in sport, to the pursuit of more socially valid research objectives based on the unique factors in sport that influence the development, stability, and change in the self-confidence of athletes over time.

REFERENCES

Allen, B.P., & Potkay, C.R. (1981). On the arbitrary distinction between states and traits. *Journal of Personality and Social Psychology, 41,* 916–928.

Ames, C. (1992). Classrooms: Goals, structures, and student motivation. *Journal of Educational Psychology, 84,* 261–271.

Bandura, A. (1978). The self system in reciprocal determinism. *American Psychologist, 33,* 344–358.

Bandura, A. (1986). *Social foundations of thought and action.* Englewood Cliffs, NJ: Prentice-Hall.

Bandura, A. (1990). Perceived self-efficacy in the exercise of personal agency. *Journal of Applied Sport Psychology, 2,* 128–163.

Bandura, A., & Wood, R.E. (1989). Effect of perceived controllability and performance standards on self-regulation of complex decision-making. *Journal of Personality and Social Psychology, 56,* 805–814.

Black, S.J., & Weiss, M.R. (1992). The relationship among perceived coaching behaviors, perceptions of ability, and motivation in competitive age-group swimmers. *Journal of Sport & Exercise Psychology, 14,* 309–325.

Burton, D. (1988). Do anxious swimmers swim slower? Reexamining the elusive anxiety-performance relationship. *Journal of Sport & Exercise Psychology, 10,* 45–61.

Clifton, R.T., & Gill, D.L. (1994). Gender differences in self-confidence on a feminine-typed task. *Journal of Sport & Exercise Psychology, 16,* 150–162.

Coakley, J. (1992). Burnout among adolescent athletes: A personal failure or social problem? *Sociology of Sport Journal, 9,* 271–285.

Corbin, C.B. (1981). Sex of subject, sex of opponent, and opponent ability as factors affecting self-confidence in a competitive situation. *Journal of Sport Psychology, 3,* 265–270.

Corbin, C.B., Landers, D.M., Feltz, D.L., & Senior, K. (1983). Sex differences in performance estimates: Female lack of confidence vs. male boastfulness. *Research Quarterly for Exercise and Sport, 54,* 407–410.

Corbin, C.B., & Nix, C. (1979). Sex-typing of physical activities and success predictions of children before and after cross-sex competition. *Journal of Sport Psychology, 1,* 43–52.

Courneya, K.S., & Carron, A.V. (1992). The home advantage in sport competitions: A literature review. *Journal of Sport & Exercise Psychology, 14*, 13–27.

Duda, J.L. (1989). Relationship between task and ego orientation and the perceived purpose of sports among high school athletes. *Journal of Sport & Exercise Psychology, 11*, 318–335.

Duda, J.L. (1992). Motivation in sport settings: A goal perspective approach. In G.C. Roberts (Ed.), *Motivation in sport and exercise* (pp. 57–91). Champaign, IL: Human Kinetics.

Eccles, J.S., & Harold, R.D. (1991). Gender differences in sport involvement: Applying the Eccles' expectancy-value model. *Journal of Applied Sport Psychology, 3*, 7–35.

Elko, P.K., & Ostrow, A.C. (1991). Effects of a rational-emotive education program on heightened anxiety levels of female collegiate gymnasts. *The Sport Psychologist, 5*, 235–255.

Ellis, A. (1981). *Rational emotive therapy and cognitive behavior therapy.* New York: Springer.

Feltz, D.L. (1988). Self-confidence and sport performance. In K.B. Pandolf (Ed.), *Exercise and sport science reviews* (pp. 423–457). New York: Macmillan.

Feltz, D.L. (1994). Self-confidence and performance. In D. Druckman & R.A. Bjork (Eds.), *Learning, remembering, believing: Enhancing human performance* (pp. 173–206). Washington, DC: National Academy Press.

Feltz, D.L., & Riessinger, C.A. (1990). Effects of in vivo emotive imagery and performance feedback on self-efficacy and muscular endurance. *Journal of Sport & Exercise Psychology, 12*, 132–143.

Garza, D.L., & Feltz, D.L. (1998). Effects of selected mental practice on performance, self-efficacy, and competition confidence of figure skaters. *The Sport Psychologist, 12*, 1–15.

Gayton, W.F., & Nickless, C.J. (1987). An investigation of the validity of the trait and state sport-confidence inventories in predicting marathon performance. *Perceptual and Motor Skills, 65*, 481–482.

Gill, D.L., & Deeter, T.E. (1988). Development of the Sport Orientation Questionnaire. *Research Quarterly for Exercise and Sport, 59*, 191–202.

Gill, D.L., Dzewaltowski, D.A., & Deeter, T.E. (1988). The relationship of competitiveness and achievement orientation to participation in sport and nonsport activities. *Journal of Sport & Exercise Psychology, 10*, 139–150.

Gould, D. (1998). Goal setting for peak performance. In J.M. Williams (Ed.), *Applied sport psychology: Personal growth to peak performance* (3rd ed., pp. 182–196). Mountain View, CA: Mayfield.

Gould, D., Guinan, D., Greenleaf, C., Medbery, R., & Peterson, K. (1999). Factors affecting Olympic performance: Perceptions of athletes and coaches from more and less successful teams. *The Sport Psychologist, 13*, 371–394.

Gould, D., Hodge, K., Peterson, K., & Giannini, J. (1989). An exploratory examination of strategies used by elite coaches to enhance self-efficacy in athletes. *Journal of Sport & Exercise Psychology, 11*, 128–140.

Gould, D., Petlichkoff, L., Simons, J., & Vevera, M. (1987). Relationship between Competitive State Anxiety Inventory-2 subscale scores and pistol shooting performance. *Journal of Sport Psychology, 9*, 33–42.

Gould, D., Udry, E., Tuffey, S., & Loehr, J. (1996). Burnout in competitive junior tennis players: I. A quantitative psychological assessment. *The Sport Psychologist, 10*, 322–340.

Gould, D., & Weiss, M.R. (1981). The effects of model similarity and model talk on self-efficacy and muscular endurance. *Journal of Sport Psychology, 3*, 17–29.

Gould, D., Weiss, M.R., & Weinberg, R.S. (1981). Psychological characteristics of successful and non-successful Big Ten wrestlers. *Journal of Sport Psychology, 3*, 69–81.

Griffin, N.S., & Keogh, J.F. (1982). A model for movement confidence. In J.A.S. Kelso & J. Clark (Eds.), *The development of movement control and coordination* (pp. 213–236). New York: Wiley.

Grove, J.R., & Heard, N.P. (1997). Optimism and sport confidence as correlates of slump-related coping among athletes. *The Sport Psychologist, 11*, 400–410.

Harter, S. (1981). A model of intrinsic mastery motivation in children: Individual differences and developmental change. In W.A. Collins (Ed.), *Minnesota symposium on child psychology* (Vol. 14, pp. 215–255). Hillsdale, NJ: Erlbaum.

Highlen, P.S., & Bennett, B.B. (1979). Psychological characteristics of successful and unsuccessful elite wrestlers: An exploratory study. *Journal of Sport Psychology, 1*, 123–137.

Horn, T.S. (1985). Coaches' feedback and changes in children's perceptions of their physical competence. *Journal of Educational Psychology, 77*, 174–186.

Horn, T.S., & Harris, A. (1996). Perceived competence in young athletes: Research findings and recommendations for coaches and parents. In F.L. Smoll & R.E. Smith (Eds.), *Children and youth in sport: A biopsychosocial perspective* (pp. 309–329). Dubuque, IA: Times Mirror.

Horn, T.S., & Hasbrook, C.A. (1986). Information components influencing children's perceptions of their physical competence. In M.R. Weiss & D. Gould (Eds.), *Sport for children and youths* (pp. 81–88). Champaign, IL: Human Kinetics.

Horn, T.S., & Hasbrook, C.A. (1987). Psychological characteristics and the criteria children use for self-evaluation. *Journal of Sport Psychology, 9*, 208–221.

Horn, T.S., & Weiss, M.R. (1991). A developmental analysis of children's self-ability judgments in the physical domain. *Pediatric Exercise Science, 3*, 310–326.

Jones, G., Hanton, S., & Swain, A.B.J. (1994). Intensity and interpretation of anxiety symptoms in elite and non-elite sports performers. *Personal Individual Differences, 17,* 657–663.

Jones, G., & Swain, A.B.J. (1995). Predisposition to experience debilitative and facilitative anxiety in elite and nonelite performers. *The Sport Psychologist, 9,* 201–211.

Kingston, K.M., & Hardy, L. (1997). Effects of different types of goals on processes that support performance. *The Sport Psychologist, 11,* 277–293.

Lang, P.J. (1979). A bio-informational theory of emotional imagery. *Psychophysiology, 16,* 495–512.

Lenney, E. (1977). Women's self-confidence in achievement settings. *Psychological Bulletin, 84,* 1–13.

Lirgg, C.D. (1991). Gender differences in self-confidence in physical activity: A meta-analysis of recent studies. *Journal of Sport & Exercise Psychology, 8,* 294–310.

Lirgg, C.D., George, T.R., Chase, M.A., & Ferguson, R.H. (1996). Impact of conception of ability and sex-type of task on male and female self-efficacy. *Journal of Sport & Exercise Psychology, 18,* 426–434.

Maddux, J.E., & Lewis, J. (1995). Self-efficacy and adjustment: Basic principles and issues. In J.E. Maddux (Ed.), *Self-efficacy, adaptation, and adjustment: Theory, research, and application* (pp. 37–68). New York: Plenum Press.

Mahoney, M.J., & Avener, M. (1977). Psychology of the elite athlete: An exploratory study. *Cognitive Therapy and Research, 1,* 135–141.

Mahoney, M.J., Gabriel, T.J., & Perkins, T.S. (1987). Psychological skills and exceptional athletic performance. *The Sport Psychologist, 1,* 181–199.

Martens, R., Vealey, R.S., & Burton, D. (1990). *Competitive anxiety in sport.* Champaign, IL: Human Kinetics.

Martin, K.A., & Mack, D. (1996). Relationships between physical self-presentation and sport competition trait anxiety: A preliminary study. *Journal of Sport & Exercise Psychology, 18,* 75–82.

McAuley, E. (1985). Modeling and self-efficacy: A test of Bandura's model. *Journal of Sport Psychology, 7,* 283–295.

Meyers, A.W., Cooke, C.J., Cullen, J., & Liles, L. (1979). Psychological aspects of athletic competitors: A replication across sports. *Cognitive Therapy and Research, 3,* 31–366.

Mischel, W. (1968). *Personality and assessment.* New York: Wiley.

Moore, W.E. (1998). Confidence. In M.A. Thompson, R.A. Vernacchia, & W.E. Moore (Eds.), *Case studies in applied sport psychology: An educational approach* (pp. 63–88). Dubuque, IA: Kendall/Hunt.

Moritz, S.E., Hall, C.R., Martin, K.A., & Vadocz, E. (1996). What are confident athletes imaging? An examination of image content. *The Sport Psychologist, 10,* 171–179.

Murphy, S.M. (1994). Imagery interventions in sport. *Medicine and Science in Sports and Exercise, 26,* 486–494.

Nelson, L., & Furst, M. (1972). An objective study of the effects of expectation on competitive performance. *Journal of Psychology, 81,* 69–72.

Ness, R.G., & Patton, R.W. (1979). The effects of beliefs on maximum weight-lifting performance. *Cognitive Therapy and Research, 3,* 205–211.

Nicholls, J.G. (1989). *The competitive ethos and democratic education.* Cambridge, MA: Harvard University Press.

Orlick, T., & Partington, J. (1988). Mental links to excellence. *The Sport Psychologist, 2,* 105–130.

Paivio, A. (1985). Cognitive and motivational functions of imagery in human performance. *Canadian Journal of Applied Sport Science, 10,* 22–28.

Pervin, L.A., & John, O.P. (1997). *Personality: Theory and research* (7th ed.). New York: Wiley.

Richardson, P.A., Adler, W., & Hankes, D. (1988). Game, set, match: Psychological momentum in tennis. *The Sport Psychologist, 2,* 69–76.

Roberts, W., & Vealey, R.S. (1992, October). *Attention in sport: Measurement issues, psychological concomitants, and the prediction of performance.* Paper presented at the Association for the Advancement of Applied Sport Psychology conference, Colorado Springs, CO.

Rosenfeld, L.B., & Richman, J.R. (1997). Developing effective social support: Team building and the social support process. *Journal of Applied Sport Psychology, 9,* 133–153.

Ryckman, R.M., Robbins, M.A., Thornton, B., & Cantrell, P. (1982). Development and validation of a physical self-efficacy scale. *Journal of Personality and Social Psychology, 42,* 891–900.

Scanlan, T.K., & Passer, M.W. (1979). Factors influencing the competitive performance expectancies of young athletes. *Journal of Sport Psychology, 1,* 212–220.

Scanlan, T.K., & Passer, M.W. (1980). Determinants of competitive performance expectancies of young male athletes. *Journal of Personality, 49,* 60–74.

Scheier, M.F., & Carver, C.S. (1988). A model of behavioral self-regulation: Translating intention into action. In L. Berkowitz (Ed.), *Advances in experimental social psychology* (Vol. 21, pp. 322–343). San Diego, CA: Academic Press.

Theeboom, M., De Knop, P., & Weiss, M.R. (1995). Motivational climate, psychological responses, and motor skill development in children's sport: A field-based intervention study. *Journal of Sport & Exercise Psychology, 17,* 294–311.

Vealey, R.S. (1986). Conceptualization of sport-confidence and competitive orientation: Preliminary investigation and instrument development. *Journal of Sport Psychology, 8,* 221–246.

Vealey, R.S. (1988a). Future directions in psychological skills training. *The Sport Psychologist, 2,* 318–336.

Vealey, R.S. (1988b). Sport-confidence and competitive orientation: An addendum on scoring procedures and gender differences. *Journal of Sport & Exercise Psychology, 10,* 471–478.

Vealey, R.S. (1999). Conceptual and psychometric advances in the study of sport-confidence. *Revista de Psicologia Social Aplicada, 9,* 71–84.

Vealey, R.S., & Campbell, J.L. (1988). Achievement goals of adolescent figure skaters: Impact on self-confidence, anxiety, and performance. *Journal of Adolescent Research, 3,* 227–243.

Vealey, R.S., & Garner-Holman, M. (1998). Measurement issues in applied sport psychology. In J.L. Duda (Ed.), *Advances in sport and exercise psychology measurement* (pp. 247–268). Morgantown, WV: Fitness Information Technology.

Vealey, R.S., & Greenleaf, C.A. (1998). Seeing is believing: Understanding and using imagery in sport. In J.M. Williams (Ed.), *Applied sport psychology: Personal growth to peak performance* (3rd ed., pp. 237–269). Mountain View, CA: Mayfield.

Vealey, R.S., Hayashi, S.W., Garner-Holman, G., & Giacobbi, P. (1998). Sources of sport-confidence: Conceptualization and instrument development. *Journal of Sport & Exercise Psychology, 20,* 54–80.

Vealey, R.S., & Knight, B. (2000). *Multidimensional sport-confidence: A conceptual and psychometric extension.* Unpublished manuscript, Miami University, Oxford, OH.

Vealey, R.S., & Sinclair, D.A. (1987, September). *The analysis and prediction of stability in sport-confidence.* Paper presented at the Association for the Advancement of Applied Sport Psychology conference, Newport Beach, CA.

Weinberg, R.S., Gould, D., & Jackson, A. (1979). Expectancies and performance: An empirical test of Bandura's self-efficacy theory. *Journal of Sport Psychology, 1,* 320–331.

Weinberg, R.S., Grove, R., & Jackson, A. (1992). Strategies for building self-efficacy in tennis players: A comparative analysis of Australian and American coaches. *The Sport Psychologist, 6,* 3–13.

Weinberg, R.S., Yukelson, D., & Jackson, A. (1980). Effect of public versus private efficacy expectations on competitive performance. *Journal of Sport Psychology, 2,* 340–349.

Williams, L. (1994). Goal orientations and athletes' preferences for competence information sources. *Journal of Sport & Exercise Psychology, 16,* 416–430.

Zinsser, N., Bunker, L., & Williams, J.M. (1998). Cognitive techniques for building confidence and enhancing performance. In J.M. Williams (Ed.), *Applied sport psychology: Personal growth to peak performance* (3rd ed., pp. 270–295). Mountain View, CA: Mayfield.

CHAPTER 22

Self-Regulation
Concepts, Methods, and Strategies in Sport and Exercise

DEBRA J. CREWS, MARC R. LOCHBAUM, and PAUL KAROLY

Among the most exciting domains of contemporary sport and exercise science is that which assumes (1) people are capable of self-regulated thought, action, and emotion in the service of their personal goals, and (2) such self-directive capabilities and their supportive mediational processes can be harnessed for the short- and long-term enhancement of learning, performance, and sustained task involvement. The label that fits this field of interest is *self-regulation*. Unfortunately, use of this term and associated terms (such as *volition, self-discipline, mental control,* and the omnibus term *motivation*) is not particularly clear or systematic in the sport and exercise science literature. The result is a collection of research that exploits the above noted assumptions, and does so in methodologically and theoretically diverse ways. In this chapter, the attempt is to organize the insights of self-regulation-based research, detailing both converging and discrepant pathways to understanding, and highlighting the need for greater integration of concepts, methods, and training strategies. To accomplish this attempt, self-regulation is discussed in terms of conceptions and research in both sport and exercise. From these discussions, conclusions and future research directions are advanced.

CONCEPTIONS OF SELF-REGULATION: SIMPLE TO COMPLEX

Definitions and Model

The broad question that self-regulation theories attempt to address can be stated simply: How do people navigate from their consciously stated or implied intentions (goals, desires, wants, etc.) in the present toward some satisfactory level of attainment in the future? For example, how might a person interested in taking up golf become a competent or, perhaps more important, satisfied golfer? How might a skilled athlete improve his or her abilities? How might a teacher assist a young boy with no apparent interest in exercise to value or prize physical fitness? These are a few of the questions that could be addressed profitably with a framework that has as its center the analysis of *psychological mechanisms underlying goal-directed movement.* Thus, this chapter focuses on the psychological mechanisms of self-regulated behavior and the biophysical interventions (i.e., biofeedback) and outcomes linked to these mechanisms.

In the psychological domain, the use of the term *self* implies that the future-directed movement is not under strong, unmodifiable external guidance, but that the individual is responsible for supplying the bulk (though certainly not *all*) of the incentives and instigators to action (cf. Bandura, 1986; Karoly, 1993). It is also suggested by many of the extant conceptual models of self-regulation that overt goal-directed movement across changing and/or challenging circumstances will not occur automatically (Bandura, 1986). Some form of *planning* and *decision making* is required, at least episodically. In truth, when most of us navigate through life, we do so as a result of a confluence of forces: a "dynamic interaction" of external, decisional, biogenetic, and automatic elements (Bandura, 1986; Bargh & Barndollar, 1996; von Bertalanfy, 1968). However, the focus of contemporary researchers and intervention agents (teachers, trainers, coaches, therapists, etc.) who operate from a self-regulatory vantage is on the internal, present- or future-directed, representational, self-conscious components of life navigation. Finally, it is imperative that those who employ the term self-regulation avoid the mistake of assuming that a self-regulatory process has occurred based purely on the observation that an individual has proceeded effectively toward a goal. Goal attainment cannot be used as a proxy for self-regulation. Nor can goal attainment failure be read as a failure of self-regulation if outcome and process are to be preserved as separate and distinct causal elements in empirical work.

Perhaps the most frequently cited depiction of the self-regulatory process derives from social-cognitive theories, with Bandura's (1986) three-dimensional model among the most notable. Bandura and other theorists in the social-learning and cognitive traditions have pointed out that, for people to mobilize their directional intentions, they must engage a series of self-focused mechanisms that include (1) self-observation (the monitoring and sometimes the recording of one's overt and/or covert activities), (2) evaluative judgments and/or judgments regarding the matching of one's actions to internally held standards or goals, and (3) self-reactions (both tangible and intangible; cf. Kanfer & Karoly, 1972; Kirschenbaum, 1984).

By contrast, individuals working in a control-systems, feedback-driven, or cybernetic tradition (Carver & Scheier, 1998; Miller, Galanter, & Pribram, 1960; Powers, 1973) tend to approach self-regulation as a process that pivots on knowledge of results (feedback), the hierarchical arrangement of standards (goals, intentions) within a system, and the online process of attention deployment. Meanwhile, investigators working within an industrial/organizational framework tend to emphasize the mechanisms of *goal setting* (Locke & Latham, 1990). Theories of self-regulation tend to vary in their emphasis on process, structure, or underlying mechanisms. Different perspectives (e.g., the cybernetic versus the social cognitive) take on a somewhat unique identity by virtue of their selective analytic foci. Yet, in fact, modern self-regulatory perspectives are more alike than they are divergent.

Emerging Complexities

Because self-regulation is most often thought of as an unfolding process, efforts have occasionally been made to describe its stages (phases), consistent with the view that successful regulation normally requires the sequential enactment of a series of interconnected subfunctions (Bandura, 1986; Ford, 1987). Twenty years ago, Karoly (1980) sought to outline an integrated, person-centered model of change and development in the context of psychotherapy. Built around the general "tasks" of therapy, the framework that emerged was an open-ended, five-element account of self-regulation consisting of (1) readiness for problem recognition; (2) decision, commitment, and/or motivational arousal (including expectancy and attribution factors); (3) acquisition and use of skills (instrumental and cognitive); (4) maintenance processes (including memory, self-administered consequences, and contextual management); and (5) transfer processes (including situational appraisal and the generalization of coping skills). Although Karoly made no mention of sport and exercise in his early account, Kirschenbaum (1984, 1987; Kirschenbaum & Wittrock, 1984) has suggested that a model structured around five similar elements (alternately labeled *problem recognition, commitment, execution, environmental management,* and *generalization*) holds considerable promise as a conceptual blueprint for the study of self-regulatory components in sport. Moreover, Kirschenbaum's writings have spurred empirical, sport-related applications of the five-stage model (e.g., Anshel & Porter, 1995).

Over the years, however, it has become apparent that investigating self-regulation is a formidable task due to the number of possible derailing or undermining factors. In addition, self-regulatory components may be examined singly or jointly and sequential operation in real time. The sheer complexity of the process, the nature of the dynamic interface between deliberate, conscious cognitive activity and nonconscious processing (i.e., automaticity) again hinders the examination of self-regulation (Bargh & Barndollar, 1996; Baumeister, Heatherton, & Tice, 1994; Karoly, 1998, 1999; Kirschenbaum, 1984, 1987).

For example, whether one thinks about self-regulation as occurring in 3, 5, or 25 stages, the fact remains that goal-directed movement does not conform easily to a categorical analysis. Researchers attempt to *describe* what they see without actually knowing how the performer is *strategically regulating* (cognitively and behaviorally) or how the environment is aiding or disrupting the process. Illustratively, Karoly's (1980) formulation of self-regulated change was not offered as an invariant stage model, but rather as a rough template for troubleshooting and planning, one that included personal, historical, and situational antecedents and environmental consequences that could modify the sought-after outcome. Similarly, Kirschenbaum (1984) warned that "corollaries or qualifiers" of the five-stage conception are necessary to flesh out real-world applications. Included among these important considerations were the role of individual differences, expectancies, emotional states, and the changing role of self-monitoring. Therefore, anyone interested in attempting to design a training program based on stage-like models of self-regulation would need to proceed with caution, keeping individual differences and situational affordances in mind, and avoiding the force-fitting of trainees into "lock-step" interventions (designed to work for the "average" person, but ill-fitting the majority of real participants).

As another illustration of emerging complexities, consider that one of the defining questions with which self-regulation theorists must grapple has to do with *directional persistence*. Myriad forces are at work that can potentially sidetrack, distract, temporarily block, or otherwise "demotivate" a person en route to a sport or exercise goal. The process of staying on track over extended periods of time (e.g., for Olympic athletes or committed exercisers) is certainly one that must be thoroughly understood. Although most of the theoretically derived self-regulatory mechanisms heretofore noted (e.g., self-observation, the setting of goals, attention to task feedback, efficacy and outcome expectancies, the self-administration of rewards) have been shown to relate to persistence over time, there is reason to doubt that empirical relations discovered in the context of a controlled laboratory study or a correlational study will be as clearly discernible in the real world of dynamic processes.

Self-Regulation Research: Organizing Assumptions

The lesson to be garnered from the discussion to this point is that self-regulation is a complex, time-dependent, multilevel process that may be approached from different theoretic vantage points. Any theory that one might elect to use in the design of research or in the creation of a strategic intervention is likely to represent but a piece of the whole fabric of self-regulation. Table 22.1 includes a partial listing of self-regulatory mechanisms or parameters derived from a broad sampling of theoretical formulations in the psychological literature.

Whether they derive from a general theory, specific hypotheses, or a broad-based model of self-regulation, it is important that investigators specify the mechanisms influencing the self-regulation and performance relationship. Identification of the mechanism(s) helps in the selection of independent variables to assess (descriptive studies) or manipulate (causal/predictive) and also guide the selection of the outcome variable(s). In addition to performance that is measured in almost all sport and exercise studies, it is important to include relevant cognitive and/or affective measures. For example, if sustained task involvement is a central issue, it would be wise to employ self-satisfaction as an outcome measure. The following review of self-regulation research in sport and exercise relates to this mechanism-centered framework in organizing and evaluating the empirical data. The studies reviewed in the corresponding chapter in the first edition of this *Handbook* are

not included in the present revision. Readers interested in the older literature are referred to the earlier edition.

REVIEW OF RESEARCH ON SELF-REGULATION

This chapter is limited to published data articles written in English. Thirty-four databased articles are reviewed, most published since 1990. Studies were considered appropriate if they included the word self-regulation or a regulatory subcomponent (i.e., self-monitoring, self-reward) in the report. Therefore, it is possible that all articles on a particular subject (i.e., association/dissociation) are not included, only those that purported to relate to self-regulation. It appears that three articles (Anshel, 1995; Anshel & Porter, 1995, 1996) were published from the same database. These are counted separately, as they attempted to address three different questions related to self-regulation.

Table 22.2 depicts the design characteristics of the 34 studies reviewed. It is apparent that the skill acquisition studies were predominately causal/predictive laboratory studies that included necessary controls. The majority of sport, physical activity, and exercise studies were conducted in the field rather than the laboratory. Overall, 15 studies used a control group, and 8 manipulation or training studies did not use a control group (2 were case studies). Manipulation checks were reported in 12 studies; 3 studies either did not use or did not report using a manipulation check when it would have been appropriate. Additional characteristics of the studies include the age, gender, skill level, and ethnicity of the samples. Participants varied in age from 6 to 70 years old. Whereas 22 studies included both male and female participants, only 2 studies reported significant gender effects. Six studies tested or included children in their samples and 2 specifically tested exercise in the elderly. Skill level differences were reported in 4 studies, and only 2 studies tested and 1 study found ethnic differences in self-regulation characteristics.

The empirical data are presented in two sections below based on the outcome focus: *task performance* or *sustained task involvement*. Task performance includes both sport ($n = 15$) and skill acquisition ($n = 6$) studies, and sustained task involvement research includes both exercise ($n = 7$) and physical activity ($n = 6$) studies. In these two sections, the seven categories of mechanisms are discussed. Although none of the authors specifically alluded to a self-regulating "mechanism" to guide them in the selection of measured or manipulated variables, an attempt was made to identify the mechanism(s) that served as the conceptual

Table 22.1   Hypothesized Mechanisms of Self-Regulation According to Contemporary Social-Cognitive Accounts

Account	Hypothesized Mechanisms
Awareness-based and metacognitive factors	Self-monitoring /self-observation. Knowledge of situational requirements (situation awareness). Knowledge of situation-specific sanctions and limitations. Awareness of the need to employ specific self-management strategies in context. Awareness of the need to employ personal performance standards (even if they conflict with those currently being promoted). Awareness of the need to and the ability to break up (unitize) one's performance aspirations into manageable subtasks. Unconscious motives. Intellectual skills.
Cognitive and imaginal factors	
Attentional Skills	Efficiency of scanning/listening. Sustained focal attention or self-initiated distraction. Distraction. Visualization/imagery.
Information-processing skills	Accuracy of time estimation. Accuracy of event sequencing. Habits of labeling. Storage and retrieval of task-relevant and background information.
Verbal skills	Self-instructional control over attention, listening, and motor responding. Verbal self-instruction. Expressive skills (communicating one's objectives to others).
Cognitive-imaginal competencies	Symbolic representation. Memory. Comprehension. Organization and rehearsal of complex thought/behavior sequences. Formation and control of visual imagery.
Goal-centered competencies	Goal formation. Goal alignment (organization of multiple goals). Goal valuation/commitment.
Instrumental competencies	Physical coordination. Sensorimotor capacities. Visual-motor capacities. Endurance and discomfort tolerance.
Motivation and emotional competencies/dispositions	Intrinsic vs. extrinsic motives. Emotion labeling. Emotion recognition. Recognition of the linkages among emotions, goal, and instrumental action. Emotion regulation (e.g., positive affect generation, negative affect suppression).
Planning and problem-solving skills	Problem identification. Alternative solution generation. Means-end thinking. Foresight. Sequential planning. Role taking. Hypothesis generation and testing.
Self-reaction and self-reward factors	Performance and self-efficacy attributions. Task-specific success/failure expectancies. Leniency/stringency of self-evaluative standards. Type of self-administered consequence (e.g., tangible, symbolic, linguistic, positive, negative). Social comparison process (upward vs. downward).

Table 22.2　Number of Studies Using Specific Design Characteristics

Characteristics	Task Performance		Sustained Task Involvement	
	Skill Acquisition ($n = 6$)	Sport ($n = 15$)	Physical Activity ($n = 10$)	Exercise ($n = 3$)
Tested theory/model	1	4	1	1
Referenced theory/model	2	1	6	1
Descriptive	1	4	4	1
Causal/predictive	5	5	6	1
Training	1	5	0	1
Control group	6	5	3	1
Manipulation check	6	3	1	2
Laboratory	6	3	2	1
Field	0	12	8	2

base of each study. The mechanism was derived from an examination of the theory or model mentioned in the study and the target variables selected to produce specific outcomes. The seven mechanisms included awareness-based, cognitive-imaginal, goal-centered, instrumental competence, intrinsic motivation-emotion, planning–problem solving, and self-reactive/self-reward. Studies are further differentiated as descriptive, causal/predictive, or training studies. Descriptive studies ($n = 10$) exist in both task performance ($n = 5$) and sustained task involvement ($n = 5$) research. Causal/predictive studies are defined as those studies with the intention to manipulate a self-regulation mechanism and predict either task performance or sustained task involvement. In some cases, these studies attempt to test a theory or model of self-regulation ($n = 7$), or may be one-shot ($n = 5$) or multiple training session ($n = 2$) studies. In other cases, these causal/predictive studies ($n = 16$) may use a regulatory theory or model to *support* their predictions ($n = 11$) about task performance or sustained task involvement. Finally, training studies ($n = 8$) are those conducted with the sole intention of improving performance based on the presumed validity of a theory or a model of self-regulation. The measured or manipulated variables are denoted as behavioral, cognitive, or affect/arousal measures, and the outcome variables as behavioral, cognitive, or affect/arousal.

The 34 studies revealed a broad and extensive array of measures used to assess one or more aspects of self-regulation (Table 22.3). These variables were either measured (descriptive studies) or manipulated (causal/predictive studies) to correlate with or predict performance or sustained task involvement. In some cases, these measures were linked to theories or models ($n = 17$). In the remaining studies ($n = 17$), measures were simply selected as variables of interest to describe or predict performance. The wide display of assessment devices suggests that the

field of sport and exercise psychology is more appropriately viewing self-regulation as an "umbrella" term rather than a strategy (i.e., self-monitoring) or set of strategies. As the field progresses, the continued use of theories, models, and mechanisms to guide the selection of the

Table 22.3　List of Measures Utilized in the Reviewed Studies

Attentional Focus Questionnaire
Autonomic Perception Questionnaire
Children's Arousal Scale–Adult Version Intention Questions
Children's Effort Rating Table
Cognitive Somatic Anxiety Inventory 2
Decision Balance Questionnaire
Electroencephalograph, electrocardiograph, electromyograph, breathing and temperature biofeedback
Episodic-Specific Interpretations of Exercise Inventory
Exercise Behavior Analysis
Exercise Benefits/Barriers Scale
Exercise diary form
Exercise Self-Regulation Questionnaire
General Interpretations of Exercise Inventory
Intention questions
Internalization Styles Scale
Intrinsic Motivation Inventory
Leisure Index of the Minnesota Heart and Health Program Physical Activity Questionnaire
Leisure-Time Exercise Questionnaire
Motivation for Physical Activity Measure
Passionate Interests Questionnaire
Personal and Health Characteristics Questionnaire
Processes of Change
Self-efficacy questions
Self-Regulation Questionnaire
Self-questionnaire
Short Form Activation-Deactivation Adjective Check List
Sport Motivation Scale
State of Change Instrument
Survey to test Kirschenbaum's model of self-regulation
Task and Ego Orientation in Sport Questionnaire
Test of Performance Strategies

most appropriate measures will advance research in self-regulation.

Task Performance Research

Theories and Models of Self-Regulation

The theories and models tested in the skill acquisition studies included self-regulated learning, goal setting, a trophotropic biasing model, a discriminating motor skills model, and a model of self-regulation. Those tested in the sport studies included goal setting, a self-regulation model, social-cognitive theory, self-determined motivation, and the zone of optimal functioning. A theory or model was *tested* in one skill acquisition study and in four sport studies, whereas a theory or model was *referenced* in two skill acquisition and one sport study. Thus, approximately half of the studies were theory-based.

Hypothesized Mechanisms

The hypothesized mechanisms for the task performance studies are depicted in Table 22.4. Over half of the studies could be referenced to more than one mechanism. It is the interaction of these mechanisms that likely explains the outcomes. The studies will be discussed relative to the mechanisms.

Awareness-Based and Metacognitive Factors. As indicated in Table 22.1, awareness-based and metacognitive factors include a variety of mechanisms that potentially underlie self-regulation. The studies primarily included self-monitoring (tally system), self-observation (biofeedback), and awareness of task and situation variables. These various components offer a means whereby individuals can track internal events or processes and the results of their overt expressive and instrumental activity. They provide a means of monitoring information, input, or disturbances. It is through this surveillance process that individuals are able to assess movement toward or away from a goal. Awareness also includes the recognition of the need to self-manage the interaction of these variables singly or in combination. Increasing awareness is commonly viewed as a first step in the long-term self-regulation process. What is important is that the participant is the one who tallies or observes, not the experimenter.

Two studies specifically examined self-monitoring and its relationship to performance. Martin and Anshel (1995) tested the effects of self-monitoring on 36 male and female students learning a computer game. They found that positive self-monitoring facilitated performance in difficult tasks, and negative self-monitoring improved easy task performance. This finding is commonly found in skill

Table 22.4 Mechanisms, Design, and Variables Identified for Task Performance Studies

Mechanisms	Design			Variables		
	D	C	T	B	C	A
Awareness						
Beauchamp et al. (1996)		X		Y	Y	Z
Blais & Vallerand (1986)		X			Y	Y
Blumenstein et al. (1995)		X			Y	Y
Cummings et al. (1984)			X		Y	Y
French (1978)			X		Y	
Kavussanu et al. (1998)			X		Y	Y
Kirschenbaum et al. (1998)		X		Y/Z	Y/Z	Y/Z
Martin & Anshel (1995)		X		Y	Y	
Prapavessis et al. (1992)		X		Y	Y	Y
Simek et al. (1994)			X	Y	Y	
Singer et al. (1993)		X		Y	Y	Y
Zimmerman & Kitsantas (1996)		X		Y/Z	Y	Z
Cognitive/Imaginal						
Cummings et al. (1984)			X		Y	Y
Hill & Borden (1995)		X			Y	
Prapavessis et al. (1992)		X		Y	Y	Y
Goal-Centered						
Beauchamp et al. (1996)		X		Y	Y	Z
Kane et al. (1996)		X		Y/Z		Y/Z
Kirschenbaum et al. (1998)		X		Y/Z	Y/Z	Y/Z
Instrumental Competence						
Sanderson (1987)		X		Y		
Svec (1982)			X	Y	Y	
Intrinsic Motivation						
Beauchamp et al. (1996)		X		Y	Y	Z
Green-Demers et al. (1998)		X		Z		Y/Z
Planning and Problem Solving						
Anshel & Porter (1996)	X			Y	Y	Y
Anshel (1995)	X			Y	Y	
Anshel & Porter (1995)	X			Y		Y
Kirschenbaum et al. (1999)		X				Y
Kirschenbaum et al. (1998)		X		Y/Z	Y/Z	Y/Z
Simek et al. (1994)			X	Y	Y	
Self-Reactive/Self-Reward						
Kane et al. (1996)	X			Y/Z		Y/Z
Kavussanu et al. (1998)			X		Y	Y
Kirschenbaum et al. (1999)		X				Y
Singer et al. (1993)		X		Y	Y	Y

X = design; Y = mediator variable; Z = outcome variable; D = descriptive design; C = causal design; T = training design; B = behavioral variable; C = cognitive variable; A = affective variable.

acquisition studies; however, self-monitoring of a well-learned, automatic process can be detrimental to performance (Karoly, 1993; Kirschenbaum, 1987).

Zimmerman and Kitsantas (1996) analyzed the effects of goal setting and self-monitoring on the skill of dart throwing among beginners. Self-monitoring was found to facilitate not only performance but also self-efficacy and positive self-reactions.

The effects of self-monitoring on golf performance were the focus of three studies. Beauchamp, Koestner, and Fournier (1996) used self-monitoring during a 14-week cognitive-behavioral program. Golf putting performance was improved along with positive motivational effects. Simek, O'Brien, and Figlerski (1994) conducted a *Total Golf* chaining-mastery program that included self-observation of skills. Golf scores improved, as will be discussed in more detail later. Kirschenbaum, Owens, and O'Connor (1998) required golfers to self-monitor directly on their scorecards relative to their focus of attention. This also was part of a total *Smart Golf* program. Positive outcomes included lower golf scores and handicaps, enhanced emotional control, and positive self-talk both posttraining and at a three-month follow-up assessment.

Singer, Lidor, and Cauraugh (1993) designed a study to determine the effect of three strategies on the learning and performance of the overhand throw to a target. Their Five-Step Approach to learning a motor skill and the "nonaware" condition produced the most positive performance outcomes. In the nonaware condition, participants were encouraged to preplan the skill and then "just do it." The Five-Step Approach is similar to nonawareness except that it has more preplanning steps.

The remaining studies using awareness as a potential mechanism are the biofeedback studies. They are noted here because it is the self-observation and self-monitoring of physiological signals that presumably influences the outcomes. These studies will be discussed separately as training studies.

Cognitive-Imaginal Factors.   Cognitive-imaginal mechanisms include a large set of thought- and imagery-based factors that potentially influence self-regulation. The subset relevant to these skill acquisition and sport performance studies includes attention, self-talk, visualization, imagery, and labeling. Hill and Borden (1995) studied the effect of an attentional cueing script on league bowling performance. The attentional script comprised of verbal cues (e.g., "Relax"), visualization, and imagery. The bowlers improved performance compared to a control group. Cummings, Wilson, and Bird (1984) and Prapavessis, Grove, McNair, and Cable (1992) added a relaxation/imagery and relaxation/thought-refocusing condition to their biofeedback study. Relaxation and biofeedback enhanced sprint performance and rifle shooting performance, respectively. Prapavessis et al. also found reduced anxiety and increased self-confidence.

Goal-Centered Competencies.   Goal-centered competency mechanisms include goal formation, alignment, value, and commitment. The most studied mechanism is goal setting. For example, Beauchamp et al. (1996); Kane, Marks, Zaccaro, and Blair (1996); and Kirschenbaum, O'Connor, and Owens (1999) included goal setting in a cognitive-behavioral training program and a model of self-regulation. Both golfers (Beauchamp et al., 1996; Kirschenbaum et al., 1999) and wrestlers (Kane et al., 1996) improved performance following training and testing. The Kirschenbaum et al. study taught golfers to set more appropriate goals for their tee shot in golf and thus improved performance.

Instrumental Competence.   Instrumental competence refers to the physical and sensory abilities of the performer, including the ability to endure and tolerate discomfort. Though this would appear to be an important self-regulating mechanism for skill acquisition and sport, only two studies attempted to influence these abilities. Sanderson (1987) used biofeedback to train pedaling style in cycling, and Svec (1982) examined pulling efficiency in swimming. Although neither study included an outcome measure of performance, both authors felt this was a viable training tool for sport.

Intrinsic Motivation.   The task performance studies in this section of mechanisms relate to intrinsic motivation. Organismic theories place great emphasis on basic human needs and their role as the "locus of initiation" of goal-directed activity. Autonomous action (internally caused) is believed to underlie extended self-regulatory effort, whereas extrinsic sources of motivation (e.g., external rewards) may undermine performance. A number of instruments designed to assess a person's "regulatory style" have been used in the sport context. Beauchamp et al. (1996) and Green-Demers, Pelletier, Stewart, and Gushue (1998) were interested in intrinsic motivation as an outcome measure in golf and figure skating, respectively. Intrinsic motivation increased with Beauchamp et al.'s cognitive-behavioral program and with Green-Demers et al.'s (1998) interest-enhancing strategies.

Green-Demers et al. (1998) actually proposed a model of "interest and motivation self-regulation" from the perspectives of self-determination theory. The model comprised three components: interest-enhancing strategies, interest, and motivation. The authors hypothesized that four proposed interest-enhancing strategies would improve interest in tasks of high and low interest. The model was tested among 36 recreational figure skaters and 84 competitive skaters. Intrinsic motivation increased with interest in tasks and with self-determined extrinsic motivation. The model was supported except that exploiting stimulation (cues external to the task) was negatively related to extrinsic motivation. Both studies highlight the value of increasing intrinsic motivation in addition to performance for sustained sport involvement.

Planning and Problem Solving.   Planning and problem-solving mechanisms include problem identification, sequential planning, and alternative solution generation. Kirschenbaum's five-stage model of self-regulation, comprised of problem recognition, commitment, execution, environment management, and generalization elements, highlights these mechanisms. In fact, the Anshel studies and the Kirschenbaum studies all attempted to use or test the five-stage model. Anshel and Porter (1996) developed a 100-item scale for their descriptive study to test Kirschenbaum's five-stage model of self-regulation among swimmers. Support was found for all stages of the model with the exception of generalization. Only the three stages of problem identification, commitment, and execution were differentiated by skill. Elite swimmers did not appear to need environmental management. Anshel (1995) further confirmed from previous research that elite performers engage in more self-regulatory behaviors than the less skilled. Finally, Anshel and Porter (1995) indicated gender differences in self-regulatory behaviors: Males tended to sacrifice more recreational time to swim and trained with more intensity after a disappointing performance than did females.

Kirschenbaum et al. (1999), as previously suggested, used goal theory and planning to improve the golf club selection for tee shots. A more conservative/realistic plan was implemented for second shots after 80% of the players used poor planning on the first shot. The Simek et al. (1994) study used a behavioral contingency contract and backward chaining to enhance golf performance. The behavioral contingency contract was established by pairing mastery of skills based on the backward chaining program to rewards such as free balls. Backward chaining is a teaching method in which golfers must demonstrate mastery of the short putt then work backwards until they have demonstrated mastery of all golf skills until the tee shot. The number of steps completed in the process explained 74% of the variance in golf scores.

Self-Reactive/Self-Reward.   Perhaps the most familiar self-regulatory mechanisms are self-efficacy and self-reward. However, social comparison and performance attributions are other self-reactive components that relate to the sport and exercise literature.

Kane et al. (1996) tested a self-regulation model that included the prior season's performance and junior varsity and varsity status, personal goals, self-efficacy, and performance. Multiple matches performed by high school wrestlers supported the role of self-efficacy as the only predictor of performance in highly competitive overtime matches. Kavussanu, Crews, and Gill (1998) conducted a biofeedback study to enhance basketball free-throw shooting performance. Again, the only measure that predicted performance was self-efficacy (60% at the pretest and 46% at the posttest). Kirschenbaum et al. (1999) included self-report as the fifth component in the *Smart Golf* program to enhance golf score performance. Golfers self-reported their golf scores for both balls played on the hole. The second ball score showed an .11 stroke improvement over the first ball score. Singer et al. (1993) included self-evaluation of performance as the final component in their Five-Step Approach to skill acquisition (ball throwing). This condition was equal to the unaware condition for enhancing target accuracy.

Mediator and Outcome Measures

Table 22.4 shows the number of behavioral, cognitive, and affective mediator variables identified in the 21 task performance studies (indicted by "Y"). The majority of studies used multiple combinations of measures (behavioral/cognitive = 8 studies, cognitive/affective = 4 studies, behavioral/cognitive/affective = 4 studies). It is not necessarily the case that "more is better" for selecting mediator and outcome measures in self-regulation research. It is preferable that the theory and, more specifically, the mechanism(s) reveal the most appropriate mediator and outcome variables.

Although all but the two instrumental competency studies (Sanderson, 1987; Svec, 1982) used an outcome behavioral measure of performance, it was of interest to determine other outcome measures that were included in task performance studies (Table 22.4, "Z" indicators). Five causal/predictive studies (Beauchamp et al., 1996; Green-Demers et al., 1998; Kane et al., 1996; Kirschenbaum et al., 1998; Zimmerman & Kitsantas, 1996) included a cognitive or affective/arousal outcome measure to performance. Zimmerman and Kitsantas (1996) and Kane et al. (1996) investigated self-satisfaction, Kirschenbaum et al. (1998) included positive reaction, and Beauchamp et al. (1996) and Green-Demers et al. (1998) researched motivation.

Task Performance Summary

Mechanisms explaining task performance, skill acquisition, and sport performance are summarized as follows.

Self-monitoring is clearly the variable most often assessed in the category of awareness-based and metacognitive factors. The results tend to be positive, particularly for beginners. Cognitive-imaginal factors tend to improve performance and to positively influence cognitive and affective outcome variables (i.e., self-confidence and anxiety). While it is well established that goal setting improves performance, Kirschenbaum et al. (1999) showed that more appropriate goals contributed to added success in golf. Instrumental competence studies need to be explored using a performance outcome measure to validate their contribution to sport. In addition, increases in intrinsic motivation were found to be a significant contributor to models of self-regulation. Planning and problem-solving techniques enhance task performance; however, skill and gender may differentially affect the outcomes. The self-reactive/self-reward mechanism demonstrated that self-efficacy appears to be the best predictor of performance; however, it was only measured in two studies and needs to be included in future self-regulation studies.

Sustained Task Performance Research

Theories and Models of Self-Regulation

The theories and models tested in physical activity and exercise studies included social learning theory, goal orientation, self-regulation theory, two-dimensional model of mood, the transtheoretical model, self-determination theory, attentional theory, the theory of reasoned action, and the theory of planned behavior. A theory or model was *tested* in one physical activity study and in one exercise study, and a theory or model for these studies was *referenced* in six physical activity and one exercise study. Thus, approximately two-thirds of these studies were theory-based.

Hypothesized Mechanisms

The hypothesized mechanisms for each study are depicted in Table 22.5. Approximately half of the studies could be referenced to more than one mechanism.

Awareness-Based and Metacognitive Factors. Once again, self-monitoring is a component of awareness that is commonly employed in physical activity and exercise studies. Three of the seven studies in this section used self-monitoring or self-observation as a means of influencing sustained task involvement. Madsen et al. (1993) studied families (adults and children) using self-monitoring, goal setting, and goal achievement over 12 training sessions. Adults improved diet behaviors, and children increased

Table 22.5 Mechanisms, Design, and Variables Identified for Sustained Task Involvement Studies

Mechanisms	Design			Variables		
	D	C	T	B	C	A
Awareness						
Cowden & Plowman (1999)		X			Y/Z	Y
Gorely & Gordon (1995)		X			Y	Y
Herald & Lucker (1995)	X				Y	
Kirkcaldy & Christen (1981)	X				Y	Y
LaGreca (1979)		X			Y	Y
Madsen et al. (1993)			X		Y	Y
Schneider et al. (1997)	X			Y	Y	Y
Thayer et al. (1992)		X				Y
Cognitive/Imaginal						
Bagozzi et al. (1995)	X			Y	Y	
Couture et al. (1994)		X		Y	Y	Y
Gorely et al. (1995)	X			Y	Y	
Wrisberg & Penn (1990)	X				Y	
Goal-Centered						
Goudas et al. (1994)		X			Y	Y
Madsen et al. (1993)			X		Y	Y
Intrinsic Motivation/Emotion						
Goudas et al. (1994)		X			Y	Y
Thayer et al. (1992)		X			Y	
Planning and Problem Solving						
Bagozzi et al. (1995)		X			Y	Y
Self-Reactive/Self-Reward						
Gorely et al. (1995)	X			Y	Y	
Hallam et al. (1998			X		Y/Z	Y

X = design; Y = mediator variable; Z = outcome variable; D = descriptive design; C = causal design; T = training design; B = behavioral variable; C = cognitive variable; A = affective variable.

fitness levels. The authors also conducted 3-, 12-, and 24-month follow-up assessments showing positive retention of behaviors. This study alluded to the difficulty of continued self-monitoring and recognized the need to fade self-monitoring during maintenance training sessions. Perhaps intermittent self-monitoring would be most beneficial in training studies and real-life performance.

La Greca and Ottinge (1979) conducted an interesting study of a 12-year-old girl with congenital cerebral palsy and a three-year history of avoiding physical therapy for her hip muscles. The child was treated with a combination of self-monitoring and relaxation procedures while increasing the frequency of therapeutic exercises. The frequency of therapeutic sessions increased from 0 to 2 sessions/week to 5 to 7 sessions/week, and this rate continued at three- and six-month follow-up assessments.

Thayer, Peters, Takahashi, and Birkhead-Flight (1993) had participants complete self-observations of smoking and snacking behavior on 12 separate occasions. The intervention was a five-minute brisk walk and the dependent measures were self-ratings of mood, energy, and desire to smoke or eat. Results supported the benefits of the brisk walks as a self-regulation strategy in that the time until the next cigarette was smoked and the next snack was eaten increased with the brisk walks. Although exercise was the intervention, the presumed change mechanism was the participants' self-observation of mood. This will be discussed further in the intrinsic motivation/emotion factors section.

The remaining studies listed in the awareness section involved biofeedback (Cowden & Plowman, 1999; Kirkcaldy & Christen, 1981) and increasing consciousness studies (Herald & Lucker, 1995; Schneider, 1997). One set of investigators sought to determine whether children could self-regulate exercise intensity or perceived effort during a physical education class (Cowden & Plowman, 1999). The children were 6 to 11 years of age and participated in a training study of five sessions, one each week. Children wore heart rate monitors with feedback regarding target heart rate zone and they also self-rated perceived effort. Results indicated that children were not successful at regulating intensity or perceived effort. Only 40% of the children maintained the target heart rate zone (130–186 bpm) over two days of exercise. The authors concluded that the children did not have the cognitive or perceptual capabilities at this age to self-regulate intensity or perceived effort.

EMG biofeedback (real feedback, false feedback, after-exercise feedback) was tested using an eight-minute cycling task in the laboratory (Kirkcaldy & Christen, 1981). Continuing EMG biofeedback after exercise produced significant reductions in EMG along with real feedback. The biofeedback was necessary to elicit changes in EMG when compared to a control condition.

Herald and Lucker (1995) tested the impact of gender and ethnicity on types of norm- or self-referenced information used in self-evaluation of exercise behavior. Participants, 484 Caucasian and Hispanic exercisers 18 to 52 years old, completed a self-evaluation questionnaire that assessed importance of sources of information used to judge personal performance following a 13-week aerobic, swimming, or weight training class. Twelve sources of information were examined (e.g., instructor feedback, personal attraction toward the activity) that were broadly classified as norm- or self-referenced information sources. Both gender and ethnicity differences emerged in self-evaluation, showing that males and Caucasians tended to use norm-referenced criteria for self-evaluation, whereas females and Hispanics used self-referenced criteria.

Schneider (1997) examined self-regulation of exercise behavior in 364 older women. Participants' self-regulation focused on exercise maintenance by way of episode-specific and general interpretations of the exercise experience. Episode-specific interpretations referred to immediate exercise experience, and general interpretations referred to accumulated information from proximal and distal exercise experiences. It was hypothesized that from these interpretations of the experience, exercisers would self-regulate future exercise behavior. Participants completed a battery of questionnaires to measure the above constructs as related to self-regulation of exercise maintenance and to assess exercise behavior. Hierarchical regression analysis revealed that episode-specific and general interpretations accounted for 20% of the variance in exercise behavior, with episode-specific interpretations accounting for the majority (15%) of the explained variance. The authors suggested the importance of episode-specific interpretations of the experience for regulating future exercise behavior.

Cognitive-Imaginal Factors. Attentional focus was a potential mechanism in two studies, one consisting of 40 soldiers (Couture et al., 1994) and one including 187 runners (Wrisberg & Pein, 1990). The previous version of this chapter suggested that novice exercisers tend to dissociate, whereas experienced exercisers associate to achieve enhanced performance. These two studies showed the opposite effects.

Couture et al. (1994) investigated the effects of associative and dissociative thinking on the ability of 40 soldiers to perform a weight-loaded march. The soldiers completed two weeks of mental training and then repeated the weight-loaded march. Results indicated that both mental training strategies improved the soldiers' abilities to estimate march time and heart rate control. However, neither the mental training intervention nor perceived exertion reduced perceived fatigue during the march.

Wrisberg and Pein (1990) examined the types of cues and thoughts that 115 male and 75 female college-age students attended to while jogging. The runners were given instructions to self-monitor their thoughts. The two broad styles of thoughts during jogging have been defined as inner mood (associative) or environmental cues (dissociative), and these two styles have been shown to influence perceived exertion during jogging. Wrisberg and Pein reported that self-monitoring style differed by runner experience, in that experienced runners tended to use more environmental cues, whereas inexperienced runners attended to inner mood while jogging. It appears that more studies are needed to understand the effects of self-monitoring cues on the reporting of associative and dissociative cognitive thought and cues.

Gorely and Gordon (1995) tested the structure of the transtheoretical model in relation to exercise behavior change among 583 adults (age $R = 50$ to 65 years). The model focuses on the dynamic nature of behavior change and postulates changes occurring through five stages. Within the five stages of precontemplation, contemplation, preparation, action, and maintenance, a variety of cognitive self-regulatory mechanisms emerged (i.e., self-reevaluation, consciousness rating). The authors found that half (5 of 10) of the processes of change, self-efficacy, and the pros and cons (cost-benefit analysis of exercising) measures made significant and unique contributions to discriminate among the five stages of change.

Bagozzi and Kimmel (1995) collected questionnaire data from 142 college students. The authors attempted to compare the ability of four theories (reasoned action, planned behavior, self-regulation, and trying) to explain the behaviors of exercising and eating. According to theories, intentions to exercise and exercise behavior can be predicted through a variety of variables (i.e., attitudes, social norms, perceived behavioral control, desires, past exercise behavior). Results indicated that attitudes significantly predicted intentions in all theories, and that desires had direct effects on intentions and also mediated most of the impact of attitudes on exercise and diet. When past behavior was taken into account, intentions did not predict the target acts and perceived behavioral control did not predict intentions or behavior, as the theory of planned behavior postulates. Further research is needed to assess the relative contribution of these theories to the self-regulation of sustained exercise behavior.

Goal-Centered Competencies.   Goal formulation, goal value, and goal commitment are also important mechanisms for both exercise (Goudas, Biddle, & Fox, 1994) and physical activity (Madsen et al., 1993). Goudas et al. reported that goal orientation (task, ego) directly affected intrinsic interest for both gymnastics and a soccer class. Task involvement increased intrinsic motivation in both activities. This study will be discussed in the section on intrinsic motivation/emotion factors. Madsen et al. combined self-monitoring with goal setting and goal achievement, as previously described. Adults improved diet behaviors and children improved exercise fitness levels. This study is a good example of the beneficial interaction of two mechanisms for change of behavior.

Intrinsic Motivation/Emotion Factors.   In addition to intrinsic motivation, emotions related to physical activity and exercise would seem important for sustained task involvement. Goudas et al. (1994) examined antecedents of 85 school-age students' intrinsic interests in physical education activities (soccer and gymnastics) and their intentions to stay actively involved in these activities. The antecedents examined were motivational orientations, intrinsic interests, and goal orientations. Specific to self-regulation, the motivation orientations relating to behavioral regulation were external, introjected, and identified, in addition to intrinsic motivation. Behavior that is initiated and sustained for external involvement is referred to as external regulation; introjected regulation refers to behaviors that are regulated by rules that the actor sets and controls; in identified regulation, the individual consciously values the goal or regulator. The investigators demonstrated that self-determination (represented by a continuum measure of perceived locus of causality) and task orientation directly affected intrinsic interest in both activities. The more self-determined and task-oriented the participants felt, the higher their level of intrinsic motivation. However, perceived competence was positively associated with soccer only. Thus, activity selection in physical education classes may be an important variable for enhancing sustained task involvement.

Thayer et al. (1993) regulated mood in an attempt to influence the self-regulation of smoking and eating behaviors. Smokers ($n = 16$) and snackers ($n = 18$) attempted to regulate mood via a five-minute brisk walk. Participants reported increased energy and decreased urge to smoke and snack. The walks nearly doubled the time to the next cigarette or snack. The mechanism of awareness is also important in this study, and it is likely that the interaction of awareness with the mechanism of mood is key to influencing the behavior change and sustained task involvement.

Planning and Problem Solving.   The only study for which planning was a potential mechanism to explain exercise behavior was the comparison of four theories applied to exercise: the theory of reasoned action, the theory of planned behavior, self-regulation theory, and trying (Bagozzi & Kimmel, 1995). As previously described, attitudes and desires had the strongest effects on intentions, and desires mediated most of the impact of attitudes. These findings were not consistent with past research; therefore, the potential of these theories to explain exercise behavior remains speculative. Additional causal/predictive studies are needed to understand the sustained task involvement relationship.

Self-Reaction/Self-Reward. Two studies tested the effects of self-efficacy on change in exercise behavior (Gorely & Gordon, 1995) and the effect of a four-session worksite intervention to increase exercise adherence (Hallam & Petosa, 1998). As previously discussed, Gorely and Gordon (1995) found that self-efficacy increased from precontemplation to maintenance along with decisional balance (pros and cons). It is a common finding in the exercise literature that self-efficacy increases with increased exercise behavior. However, its role in the self-regulation of exercise behavior is not completely clear at this time. For example, Hallam and Petosa (1998) tested the effects of self-efficacy, self-regulation skills, and outcome expectancy value for exercise among 86 employees. These measures were chosen because they are known to relate to exercise adherence. The worksite intervention program showed increases only in self-regulation skills and outcome expectancy scores, not self-efficacy, when compared to a control group. The effect on adherence was not reported. Self-efficacy is an important contributor to sustained task involvement, and perhaps further research will help to explain its role as a mechanism of self-regulation.

Mediator and Outcome Measures

As indicated in Table 22.5, 13 studies primarily reported the combinations of cognitive/affective (n = 6) and behavioral/cognitive/affective (n = 2) mediator variables. The first edition of this chapter reported primarily behavioral techniques for exercise studies; this edition verifies the increased use of multiple combinations of variables. Once again, if the mechanism directs the selection of mediator variables, it is likely that, for example, cognitive-imaginal mechanisms would require a cognitive mediator variable as one of its measures and an emotion mechanism would dictate the use of an affective variable.

The outcome measure for sustained task involvement was the behavioral measure of continued participation in either physical activity or exercise (Table 22.5, "Z" indicator). Only two studies included the cognitive measures of effort ratings (Cowden & Plowman, 1999) and outcome expectancy measures (Hallam & Petosa, 1998). Often, these other two categories of variables (cognitive and affective/arousal) are measured and manipulated in the study; however, they do not seem to be considered an important outcome variable. It seems that for sustained task involvement, cognitive and affect/arousal variables may be equally important to behavior (participation). For example, self-satisfaction may be equally if not more important as an outcome measure than adherence in an eight-week exercise program if the ultimate goal is sustained task involvement.

Sustained Task Performance Summary

The results of self-regulation mechanisms influencing sustained task performance are summarized. Although self-monitoring was the most frequently used awareness factor, one study suggested the use of fading self-monitoring techniques during maintenance stages of exercise to optimize effectiveness. Another study alluded to the questioned ability of children to effectively self-regulate, at least in reference to exercise. In addition, there may be gender and ethnic differences in self-evaluation style. The results of cognitive-imaginal factors, such as association/dissociation, appear to remain equivocal in their ability to influence exercise behavior. Theories attempting to explain exercise behavior (i.e., reasoned action, planned behavior) also continue to produce equivocal findings and need further testing. Specific goal orientation (task, ego) may differentially affect exercise and physical activity behaviors, and effective goal setting strategies may vary with the age of the participant. Whereas task performance research used only intrinsic motivation as a potential mechanism, sustained task performance adds emotion. Regulating emotion through exercise appears to influence behaviors such as smoking and snacking. Planning and problem solving were used in only one study, and the unclear results indicate the need for additional research. Once again, self-efficacy increased with increased exercise behavior, and further research is needed to clarify its role in self-regulation.

Training Studies

The eight training studies were conducted for the sole purpose of investigating the effects of self-regulation on performance (n = 7) or sustained task involvement (n = 1). Although these studies have already been discussed relative to theories and potential mechanisms, it is of interest to examine some of their unique contributions. Two of these were biomechanical studies, examining cycling (Sanderson, 1987) and swimming (Svec, 1982) technique to optimize performance. The remaining six studies used biofeedback to train and enhance performance or sustain performance, primarily through the use of EMG biofeedback.

Blumenstein, Bar-Eli, and Tenenbaum (1995) used biofeedback (EMG, heart rate, galvanic skin response, and breathing frequency) to enhance performance in the 100-meter sprint. Biofeedback exceeded the effects of autogenic training and imagery. However, Kavussanu et al. (1998) found that multiple signal biofeedback did not exceed the effects of single EMG biofeedback training on basketball free-throw shooting performance. This beneficial use of multiple biofeedback signals remains equivocal. Kavussanu et al. also found that those who performed the best in biofeedback increased self-efficacy, and this predicted 60% (Time 1) and 46% (Time 1 and 2) of variability in free-throw shooting scores.

Cummings et al. (1984) and Blais and Vallerand (1986) tested biofeedback training and added a test of retention and transfer, which are very important components of learning biofeedback. In addition, French (1978) found enhanced posttest effects with the use of biofeedback during the posttest (stabilometer) and added the outcome assessment of tension ratings. One of the criticisms of biofeedback training has been the ability to transfer the learned response to performance in the real world. These studies are attempting to facilitate retention and transfer for enhanced performance. Comparison studies are needed to determine the schedule of training that is optimal for retention and transfer.

Prapavessis et al. (1992) conducted an interesting case study of a 20-year-old small-bore rifle shooter with high competitive anxiety. A multidimensional six-week intervention program included relaxation training, thought stopping, refocusing, coping statements, and ECG biofeedback training. This multidimensional program was based on Kirschenbaum's (1984) model of self-regulation. Anxiety, self-confidence, and performance measures were recorded pre- and posttraining. Results indicated reductions in cognitive anxiety, somatic anxiety, gun vibration, and urinary catecholamines as well as increases in self-confidence and performance following training.

Training Studies Summary

Training studies, focused on improving performance or sustained task performance, showed positive effects primarily for biofeedback training. The inclusion of retention and transfer protocols also enhanced biofeedback effects on performance. Cognitive and affect outcome measures (self-confidence, anxiety) were also positively affected through the use of biofeedback training.

CONCLUSIONS

The first version of this chapter generated several recommendations for future research, some of which were addressed in the 34 studies reviewed. Advances in the study of self-regulation since the earlier version include:

- The use of multiple theories and models (other than cybernetic theory and control theory) viewing self-regulation as more than a strategy.
- An increase in use of control groups and manipulation checks.

- Implementing of retention and transfer following training.
- Long-term follow-up (e.g., 3 to 24 months).
- Using multiple outcome measures, not simply performance (to include cognitive and affect/arousal).
- Using advanced statistical analysis to assess relationships among variables.
- Examining various skill levels and cultural backgrounds as well as both genders.

It appears that the research community views self-regulation as more than a strategy evolving from more than two theoretical frameworks (cybernetic theory and control theory), as presented in the first version of this chapter. Numerous theories are being presented to study the concept of self-regulation. Researchers utilize theoretical frameworks to organize constructs that they believe to be important for the act of self-regulation, and thus attempt to find questionnaires to assess their models. When a study fails to support a model, it is not clear if the model or the means of assessment is at fault. The field is in need of a more systematic, unifying approach to the study of self-regulation. Perhaps the consideration of the mechanism(s) underlying self-regulation, as presented in this chapter, will facilitate the design, operational components, and interpretation of results in future studies.

Additional precautionary measures for future studies include the following:

- The value of defining the potential mechanism(s) before determining the variables to measure/manipulate.
- The need to incorporate more of the potential mechanisms (as listed in Table 22.1).
- The need to continue to study the mechanisms in combination.
- Because measured and manipulated variables are not outcome variables, they need to be distinct (i.e., self-efficacy is either an independent variable or a dependent variable).
- Assessment of positive self-monitoring among moderate and highly skilled performers.
- Importance of using multiple outcome variables in addition to the behavioral measure of performance (i.e., self-satisfaction may be more valuable for sustained task involvement).
- Possible use of intermittent self-monitoring to maximize performance and sustained task involvement.
- Continued use of control groups, randomization, and manipulation checks.

- The importance of the word "self" in self-regulation: participants (even children), not the experimenter, need to keep records.

Consider the following as an illustration of how to proceed in self-regulatory research. Most of the theoretical accounts noted thus far (and others discussed elsewhere in this *Handbook*) give a great deal of weight to the way a self-regulatory goal is cognitively represented. For example, few would deny that an individual with the goal of increasing his or her exercise activity would tend to act diligently in its pursuit to the degree that this aspiration was considered *important* (*urgent, valuable, necessary*). Goal importance is one of several goal appraisal dimensions that have proven useful as a predictor of eventual goal attainment (cf. Austin & Vancouver, 1996; Emmons, 1986; Karoly, 1999; Little, 1983). Likewise, *self-confidence* (or *self-efficacy* or *optimism*) would be expected to relate to task engagement over extended periods of time (Bandura, 1997).

Consequently, it might be predicted that task persistence (going to the gym every day) would vary directly with goal importance, and similarly, that task persistence would vary with confidence. Attempts might be to instill confidence and/or to elevate importance as a means of enhancing exercise self-regulation in a group of unreliable exercisers. Yet, Carver and Scheier (1998), basing their analysis on dynamical systems (chaos, catastrophe) theory, offer a treatment of the three-way relationship among *task engagement, confidence,* and *importance* that challenges what has come to be the conventional wisdom of social-cognitive theory.

Carver and Scheier (1998) discuss task engagement, confidence, and importance (task urgency) within the context of a *cusp catastrophe*. A cusp catastrophe model is one that links several (in this case, two) control parameters (x and z) to an outcome parameter (y) that represents the behavior of the system under study. This model has also been used to explain the relationship of anxiety and performance in sport. What is critical in this application is the depiction of the three-dimensional surface of the cusp catastrophe as one that has a fold toward the front end, such that the relation between x and y at high values of z becomes discontinuous (whereas the relation between x and y toward the back [low levels of z] appears familiarly linear). Therefore, as self-confidence (or x) increases, so does task engagement—y (a reflection of self-regulation)—in a linear fashion, but only at low levels of task urgency or importance (parameter z). When the z parameter, urgency or importance (labeled "pressure" by Carver and Scheier), reaches a high level, there is an abrupt turn that precipi-

tates a drop in task engagement (i.e., quitting). The important message is that if the relations among task engagement, self-confidence, and goal urgency operate in accordance with a dynamical catastrophe model (or in accordance with some other dynamic arrangement) rather than a set of simple linear models (such as the ones guiding the majority of behavioral science research in self-regulation), then predictions and interventions will likely miss their marks. How can a confident exerciser keep from disengaging from exercise behavior? According to Carver and Scheier, one possible answer is to keep him or her toward the back plane of the surface; this might mean doing something quite counterintuitive insofar as goal theory is concerned, namely, *devaluing the goal of exercise.*

Detailing the precise form of all the hypothesized self-regulatory components or mechanisms, the nature of their dynamic interplay with environmental and biological forces over time, and the best methods for accurately appraising these interacting elements has not been an easy task. The "solution" that many researchers (inside and outside of sport psychology) have employed is to operationalize self-regulation via attention to a relatively small number of defining ingredients, effectively ignoring (holding constant) the others as well as the role of time (or change). For example, an investigator might assess some aspect of performance-specific *self-efficacy* and then relate the self-efficacy scores to background dimensions (prior performance, athletic skill) as well as to indices of later sport performance, referring to the overall focus of the research as self-regulation. Such a research tactic (however useful) differs markedly from one in which a group of sport experts (elite athletes) is identified, along with a group of novices or beginners, with both then required to complete a battery of questionnaires that presumably gauge various aspects of self-regulation (broadly defined). The purpose of this latter approach is to *describe* putative differences in self-regulatory functioning among known groups who are, in fact, not engaging in any sport-related self-regulatory skills in real time. Anshel and Porter (1996) and Anshel (1995) attempted this approach with a 100-item questionnaire and found differences among elite and nonelite swimmers. Each of these research tactics has merit.

It is particularly important, therefore, that individuals delving into the self-regulation literature be mindful of the *type* of study they are encountering (*predictive* versus *descriptive*) as well as the nature of the *inactive process* being investigated, that is, *skill acquisition, task performance* (real time or simulated), or *sustained involvement* (*maintenance of interest*). Studies differ also in terms of whether the *target* and *outcome* measure of regulatory effort is behavior, aspects of thinking, or emotional arousal. Finally, although the self-regulation literature in sport and exercise is often motivated purely by the desire to *test hypotheses* about the empirical relations among parameters, investigators are increasingly conducting *training studies*, whose purpose is to evaluate the power of specific interventions (interventions that exploit specific self-regulatory mechanisms) for enhancing sport performance. And, of course, a most critical distinguishing characteristic of the research has to do with which *specific regulatory mechanism* is being explored or manipulated.

REFERENCES

Anshel, M.H. (1995). An examination of self-regulatory cognitive-behavioural strategies of Australian elite and non-elite competitive male swimmers. *Australian Psychologist, 30,* 78–83.

Anshel, M.H., & Porter, A. (1995). Self-regulatory characteristics of competitive swimmers as a function of skill level and gender. *Journal of Sport Behavior, 19,* 91–110.

Anshel, M.H., & Porter, A. (1996). Efficacy of a model for examining self-regulation with elite and non-elite male and female competitive swimmers. *International Journal of Sport Psychology, 27,* 321–336.

Austin, J.T., & Vancouver, J.B. (1996). Goal constructs in psychology: Structure, process, and content. *Psychological Bulletin, 120,* 338–375.

Bagozzi, R.P., & Kimmel, S.K. (1995). A comparison of leading theories for the prediction of goal-directed behaviours. *British Journal of Social Psychology, 34,* 437–461.

Bandura, A. (1986). *Social foundations of thought and action: A social-cognitive theory.* Englewood Cliffs, NJ: Prentice-Hall.

Bandura, A. (1997). *Self-efficacy: The exercise of control.* New York: Freeman.

Bargh, J.A., & Barndollar, K. (1996). Automaticity in action: The unconscious as repository of chronic goals and motives. In P.M. Gollwitzer & J.A. Bargh (Eds.), *The psychology of action* (pp. 457–481). New York: Guilford Press.

Baumeister, R.F., Heatherton, T.F., & Tice, D.M. (1994). *Losing control: Why people fail at self-regulation.* San Diego, CA: Academic Press.

Beauchamp, P.H., Koestner, R., & Fournier, J.F. (1996). Effects of cognitive-behavioral psychological skills training on the motivation, preparation, and putting performance of novice golfers. *The Sport Psychologist, 10,* 157–170.

Blais, M.R., & Vallerand, R.J. (1986). Multimodel effects of electromyographic biofeedback: Looking at children's ability to control precompetitive anxiety. *Journal of Sport Psychology, 8,* 283–303.

Blumenstein, B., Bar-Eli, M., & Tenenbaum, G. (1995). The augmenting role of biofeedback: Effects of autogenic, imagery and music training on physiological indices and athletic performance. *Journal of Sports Sciences, 13,* 343–354.

Carver, C.S., & Scheier, M.F. (1998). *On the self-regulation of behavior.* New York: Cambridge University Press.

Couture, R.T., Singh, M., Lee, W., Chahal, P., Wankel, L., Osen, M., & Wheeler, G. (1994). The effect of mental training on the performance of military endurance tasks in the Canadian infantry. *International Journal of Sport Psychology, 25,* 144–157.

Cowden, R.D., & Plowman, S.A. (1999). The self-regulation and perception of exercise intensity in children in a field setting. *Pediatric Exercise Science, 11,* 32–43.

Cummings, M.S., Wilson, V.E., & Bird, E.I. (1984). Flexibility development in sprinters using EMG biofeedback and relaxation training. *Biofeedback and Self-Regulation, 9,* 395–405.

Emmons, R.A. (1986). Personal strivings: An approach to personality and subjective well-being. *Journal of Personality and Social Psychology, 51,* 1058–1068.

Ford, D.H. (1987). *Humans as self-constructing living systems: A developmental perspective on behavior and personality.* Hillsdale, NJ: Erlbaum.

French, S.N. (1978). Electromyographic biofeedback for tension control during gross motor skill acquisition. *Perceptual and Motor Skills, 47,* 883–889.

Gorely, T., & Gordon, S. (1995). An examination of the transtheoretical model and exercise behavior in older adults. *Journal of Sport & Exercise Psychology, 17,* 312–324.

Goudas, M., Biddle, S., & Fox, K. (1994). Perceived locus of causality, goal orientations, and perceived competence in school physical education classes. *British Journal of Educational Psychology, 64,* 453–463.

Green-Demers, I., Pelletier, L.G., Stewart, D.G., & Gushue, N.R. (1998). Coping with the less interesting aspects of training: Toward a model of interest and motivation enhancement in individual sports. *Basic and Applied Social Psychology, 20,* 251–261.

Hallam, J., & Petosa, R. (1998). A worksite intervention to enhance social cognitive theory constructs to promote exercise adherence. *American Journal of Health Promotion, 13,* 4–7.

Herald, M.M., & Lucker, G.W. (1995). Ethnic and gender variations in the sources of information used to evaluate performance in the exercise setting. *Journal of Applied Social Psychology, 25,* 2180–2191.

Hill, K.L., & Borden, F. (1995). The effect of attentional cueing scripts on competitive bowling performance. *International Journal of Sport Psychology, 26,* 503–512.

Kane, T.D., Marks, M.A., Zaccaro, S.J., & Blair, V. (1996). Self-efficacy, personal goals, and wrestlers' self-regulation. *Journal of Sport & Exercise Psychology, 18,* 36–48.

Kanfer, F.H., & Karoly, P. (1972). Self-control: A behavioristic excursion into the lion's den. *Behavior Therapy, 3,* 398–416.

Karoly, P. (1980). Person variables in therapeutic change and development. In P. Karoly & J.J. Steffen (Eds.), *Improving the long-term effects of psychotherapy* (pp. 195–261). New York: Gardner Press.

Karoly, P. (1993). Mechanisms of self-regulation: A systems view. *Annual Review of Psychology, 44,* 23–52.

Karoly, P. (1998). Expanding the conceptual range of health self-regulation research: A commentary. *Psychology & Health, 13,* 741–746.

Karoly, P. (1999). A goal systems self-regulatory perspective on personality, psychopathology, and change. *Review of General Psychology, 3,* 264–291.

Kavussanu, M., Crews, D.J., & Gill, D. (1998). The effects of single versus multiple measures of biofeedback on basketball free throw shooting performance. *International Journal of Sport Psychology, 29,* 132–144.

Kirkcaldy, B.D., & Christen, J. (1981). An investigation into the effect of EMG frontalis biofeedback on physiological correlates of exercise. *International Journal of Sport Psychology, 12,* 235–252.

Kirschenbaum, D.S. (1984). Self-regulation and sport psychology: Nurturing an emerging symbiosis. *Journal of Sport Psychology, 6,* 159–183.

Kirschenbaum, D.S. (1987). Self-regulation of sport performance. *Medicine and Science in Sports and Exercise, 19,* S106–S113.

Kirschenbaum, D.S., O'Connor, E.A., & Owens, D. (1999). Positive illusions in golf: Empirical and conceptual analyses. *Journal of Applied Sport Psychology, 11,* 1–27.

Kirschenbaum, D.S., Owens, D., & O'Connor, E.A. (1998). Smart golf: Preliminary evaluation of a simple, yet comprehensive, approach to improving and scoring the mental game. *The Sport Psychologist, 12,* 271–282.

Kirschenbaum, D.S., & Wittrock, D.A. (1984). Cognitive-behavioral interventions in sport: A self-regulatory perspective. In J.M. Silva & R.S. Weinberg (Eds.), *Psychological foundations of sport* (pp. 81–90). Champaign, IL: Human Kinetics.

La Greca, A.M., & Ottinge, D.R. (1979). Self-monitoring and relaxation training in the treatment of medically ordered exercises in a 12-year-old female. *Journal of Pediatric Psychology, 4,* 49–54.

Little, B.R. (1983). Personal projects: A rationale and method for investigation. *Environment and Behavior, 15,* 273–309.

Locke, E.A., & Latham, G.P. (1990). *A theory of goal-setting and task performance.* Englewood Cliffs, NJ: Prentice-Hall.

Madsen, J., Sallis, J.F., Rupp, J.W., Senn, K.L., Patterson, T.L., Atkins, C.J., & Nadier, P.R. (1993). Relationship between self-monitoring of diet and exercise change and subsequent risk factor changes in children and adults. *Patient Education and Counseling, 21,* 61–69.

Martin, M.B., & Anshel, M.H. (1995). Effect of self-monitoring strategies and task complexity on motor performance and affect. *Journal of Sport & Exercise Psychology, 17,* 153–170.

Miller, G.A., Galanter, E., & Pribram, K.H. (1960). *Plans and the structure of behavior.* New York: Holt, Rinehart and Winston.

Powers, W.T. (1973). *Behavior: The control of perception.* Chicago: Aldine.

Prapavessis, H., Grove, R., McNair, R.J., & Cable, N.T. (1992). Self-regulation training, state anxiety, and sport performance: A psychophysiological case study. *The Sport Psychologist, 6,* 213–229.

Sanderson, D.J. (1987, February). Training with biofeedback: Real-time feedback improves pedaling style. *Biomechanics, 10–13.*

Schneider, J.K. (1997). Self-regulation and exercise behavior in older women. *Journal of Gerontology: Psychological Sciences, 52B,* 235–241.

Simek, T.C., O'Brien, R.M., & Figlerski, L.B. (1994). Contracting and chaining to improve the performance of a college golf team: Improvement and deterioration. *Perceptual and Motor Skills, 78,* 1099–1105.

Singer, R.N., Lidor, R., & Cauraugh, J.H. (1993). To be aware or not aware? What to think about while learning and performing a motor skill. *The Sport Psychologist, 7,* 19–30.

Svec, O.J. (1982, May/July). Biofeedback for pulling efficiency. *Swimming Technique, 38–46.*

Thayer, R.E., Peters, D.P., III, Takahashi, P.J., & Birkhead-Flight, A.M. (1993). Mood and behavior (smoking and sugar snacking) following moderate exercise: A partial test of self-regulation theory. *Personality and Individual Differences, 14,* 97–104.

von Bertalanfy, L. (1968). *General systems theory.* New York: Braziller.

Wrisberg, C.A., & Pein, R.L. (1990). Past running experience as a mediator of the attentional focus of male and female recreational runners. *Perceptual and Motor Skills, 70,* 427–432.

Zimmerman, B.J., & Kitsantas, A. (1996). Self-regulated learning of a motoric skill: The role of goal setting and self-monitoring. *Journal of Applied Sport Psychology, 8,* 60–75.

PART V

Life Span Development

CHAPTER 23

Moral Development and Behavior in Sport

DAVID LIGHT SHIELDS and BRENDA LIGHT BREDEMEIER

The view that sport can be a useful venue for developing character virtues has a venerable history. From the writings of Plato to the contemporary declarations of politicians, educators, and theologians, sport has been portrayed as a builder of character. This claim has found a place in popular folk wisdom and is reflected by the cultural adage "Sport builds character."

Can participation in sport really promote the development of good character? Despite the fact that educational sport programs are often justified by this claim, the question has received little empirical investigation. In this chapter, one aspect of the concept of character, namely, moral development, will be examined as it relates to sport. Moral development is not the totality of what is meant by character, but it is an important part. For purposes of this chapter, moral development is defined as the evolution of a person's grasp of the interpersonal rights and responsibilities that characterize social life.

In the first part of the chapter, two theoretical approaches to moral development, the social learning and structural developmental perspectives, are summarized. Because most recent research on sport morality has utilized a structural developmental approach, the two structural developmental theories most frequently used in sport research, those proposed by Kohlberg and Haan, are elaborated. In the remainder of the chapter, major findings about moral development and sport are presented in relation to eight organizing questions. The chapter concludes with some brief suggestions for future research directions.

THEORETICAL APPROACHES TO MORAL DEVELOPMENT

The Social Learning Approach

There are many variants to the social learning approach to moral development. Dispute among leading advocates of this approach focuses on a number of critical issues: (1) What are the primary vehicles through which learning occurs? (2) What are the most important outcomes or products of learning? and (3) How central are innate factors in producing individual differences (Rushton, 1982)? Eysenck (1977), for example, emphasizes classical conditioning as the primary learning vehicle, conditioned affect as the focal learning outcome, and innate differences in the "conditionability" of people's nervous system as the primary source of individual variation in learning. Thus, in the area of morality, Eysenck points to the utility of linking antisocial behavior to immediate punitive response, so that the behavior becomes associated with negative affect. An illustrative contrast is Bandura (1977), who emphasizes modeling and reinforcement as the major stimulants for learning and cognitive constructs as a major learning outcome with little attention paid to genetic predispositions. For Bandura, prosocial behavior can invariantly be traced to a social learning history in which that behavior was modeled and reinforced.

The trend in recent years has been toward a modified social learning theory that takes greater account of cognitive factors in the mediation of behavior. Bandura, for example, has abandoned the label "social learning theory" in favor of "social cognitive theory" (Bandura, 1986, 1991). Despite this increased appreciation for the cognitive mediation of behavior, the cognitive factors themselves are said to result from the standard set of social learning processes: conditioning, modeling, and reinforcement.

Though different social learning theorists offer varying interpretations of the learning process, there are a number of shared theoretical tenets that shape how they view the moral domain. First, social learning theorists view moral behavior as nondistinct from other types of behavior. The same learning principles that operate in the acquisition, maintenance, and modification of hand-washing behavior operate to control the exhibition of helping, sharing, or acting justly. Second, the degree to which a person acts "morally" is directly related to that person's previous learning history. In other words, a person is moral to the degree that he or she has learned to be so. Third, what constitutes morality is socially defined. Moral development is equivalent to a process of socialization through which the norms of one's society are internalized. Moral behavior is that behavior that conforms to the prosocial norms of a given society or cultural group. Thus, moral norms or principles are relative to the culture; no universal moral principles are acknowledged. Finally, social learning theorists are methodologically committed to a focus on overt behavior. What happens "in the mind" of people is viewed as fundamentally unknowable; only observable behavior can be subjected to reliable scientific investigation.

The Structural Developmental Approach

Like social learning theorists, structural developmentalists hold a number of basic assumptions in common while diverging in specific detail. The differences between two theories will be highlighted in the next section. The purpose of the present discussion is to indicate the points of convergence.

One major distinguishing feature of the structural developmental approach is the distinction between two levels of analysis. People's actions or thinking can be analyzed at the level of *content* or at the level of *structure*. What people think, how they behave, what answers they give on a questionnaire, how they respond to an experimental manipulation are all *contents* of thought or behavior.

Beneath or behind the specific, observable content is a more or less coherent psychological *structure* that generates the specific contents. The structure itself is outside of conscious awareness. For example, when one speaks, the specific verbal utterances are *contents,* but lying beneath them is a complex grammatical *structure* that the speaker

uses without even being aware of it. Few individuals could identify the grammatical rules that they effortlessly follow, yet their speech is generated from these organizing rules. Similarly, structural developmentalists believe that when people deal with such diverse issues as moral problems, mathematical puzzles, and decisions about social roles, their reasoning is generated from and reflects identifiable psychological structures (e.g., Piaget, 1970). The underlying structures arise from an innate psychological tendency to organize experience into coherent, meaningful patterns (Case, 1992; Piaget, 1971). One of the major theoretical tasks of the structural developmentalist is to make explicit the implicit structure of these diverse areas of human functioning. Thus, in contrast to social learning theorists, structural developmentalists have tended to focus more on moral thought than on moral action.

When structural developmentalists assess moral development, they are not analyzing the correctness of a person's moral beliefs. People who are equally mature may hold very different beliefs about moral issues. Although moral beliefs reveal something of the content of a person's moral convictions, structural developmentalists are interested in the relative adequacy of the *structure* that generates these beliefs. They are interested in the pattern of reasoning that a person uses to support his or her beliefs. From this notion emerges the second major theme held in common by structural developmentalists.

According to structural developmental theory, the structures that underlie a person's reasoning are not static: They change with development. Furthermore, they change in an orderly, progressive way from less adequate to more adequate (Kohlberg, 1981). As one's innate tendency to organize experience interacts with actual experience, the underlying structures of reasoning become more differentiated and integrated (Kohlberg, 1984). *Differentiation* refers to increased refinement in the psychological structure that enables the individual to recognize and respond appropriately to more complex and more subtle aspects of experience. *Integration* is the structural reorganization through which external phenomena are comprehended in a more integrated and parsimonious manner. It is presumed that as psychological structures become more differentiated and integrated, they also become more adequate.

In the following sections, two prominent theories about the developmental course that individuals follow in their march toward moral maturity are reviewed. With regard to each of these two theories, the following questions are addressed: What are the basic tenets underlying the theory? What prevents some people in some situations from acting on their most mature moral convictions? What are the mechanisms by which moral growth occurs that might be tapped for educational purposes?

Kohlberg's Theory of Moral Development

Kohlberg's (1981, 1984) groundbreaking theory of moral development is rooted in the cognitive developmental approach to psychology most prominently associated with Piaget. Accordingly, the concept of universal stages occupies a central place in Kohlberg's work. Within the Piagetian framework, stage progression is hypothesized to reflect an interactive process between the innate tendency of the developing child to actively organize information and an environment that demands accommodation to its features.

Basic Concepts.   Four key concepts can help to educate Kohlberg's theory of moral development: moral issues, orientations, principles, and stages. Kohlberg (1976) believed that certain moral issues or values are universally recognized as important; these include the values of life, property, truthfulness, civil liberties, conscience, rules and laws, affiliation, authority, contract, and trust. The content of moral thinking is about these moral values. Sometimes, however, one person's claim on a particular value may come into conflict with those of others. Kohlberg (1969, p. 401) wrote, "The area of conflicting claims of selves is the area of morality." Thus, for example, if a player is asked by a coach to violate a rule, the coach's claim of authority may conflict with the player's claim to rule obedience.

To clarify what is involved in moral thinking, Kohlberg (1976) turned to philosophy and isolated four basic types of orientations used by various traditions of moral philosophy. A moral orientation is a general approach for dealing with moral conflicts. Each moral orientation focuses on a critical element to help decide right and wrong. The first, the *normative order* orientation, focuses on prescribed rules and roles such that decision making is guided by a consideration of rules. The *consequence* orientation focuses on the impact of various actions on the welfare of others and/or the self. Thus, decision making is guided by beliefs about the outcome of various behavioral options. The *justice* orientation highlights relations of liberty, equality, reciprocity, and contract among people. Accordingly, this orientation is characterized by a concern for impartiality and fairness in making decisions. Finally, the *ideal self* orientation concentrates on an image of the actor as a good self, or as someone with conscience. Those who operate from this orientation seek to maintain personal

virtue or integrity and pure motives through their moral decisions.

It is not difficult to see how these basic moral orientations might all come into play in a sport setting. Certainly, rules hold a highly prominent place in sport, and many, probably most, decisions are based on the rules and prescribed roles. Concern for consequences, particularly the welfare implications for behaviors like aggression, constrain action in certain ways. The structure of the game is designed to ensure fairness and equal opportunity, and some players may rely on this dimension (i.e., the "spirit of the game") for their moral guidance. Finally, themes of sportspersonship are often tethered to images of the ideal athlete who exhibits virtues of politeness and good humor in the midst of fierce competition.

Kohlberg's (1981) theory is deeply embedded in his conviction that the justice orientation is the most adequate of the four. Only the justice orientation, Kohlberg maintained, can lead to the formulation of a moral principle that can be used to decide fairly among competing moral claims. Rules can conflict with one another. The consequences to one person or group may conflict with those of another and, furthermore, consequences often cannot be foreseen with clarity. Conscience, contrary to the popular adage, is too contaminated by cultural baggage to be the best guide. The justice orientation, however, can lead to "a mode of choosing which is universalizable, a rule of choosing which we want all people to adopt always in all situations" (Kohlberg, 1970, pp. 69–70).

To summarize, there are certain universal moral issues that can give rise to moral conflict. Moral conflict can be dealt with through the use of one of four major decision-making strategies, though one of these, the orientation to justice, is said to be the most adequate. Kohlberg's stage theory reflects his investigation into the developmental course by which people come to a mature understanding of justice.

Kohlberg hypothesized an invariant, culturally universal, six-stage sequence of moral development. A stage refers to the underlying deep structure of reasoning. Each moral stage is an integrated, coherent approach to problem solving that can be applied to whatever content is present in a moral situation. The details of Kohlberg's six stages are beyond the scope of this chapter, but the general course of development can be noted. In the first two stages, one approaches moral problems through an individualistic or egocentric perspective. Kohlberg calls this the *preconventional* level because the person does not yet comprehend the way social norms and rules impact on moral responsibility. The next two stages comprise the *conventional* level, during which time one approaches problems through the eyes of one's social group or society as a whole. Finally, at the *postconventional* level, one recognizes universal values that are not tied to the particular norms of any given society. Ultimately, according to Kohlberg, justice is identified as the single moral norm from which all others are derived.

Within each stage, Kohlberg also identified a Type A and Type B substage. These were derived from the four moral orientations. In Kohlberg's view, everyone uses all four orientations, but each person has a preference between using either a combination of the normative order and consequence orientations (called substage A), or a combination of the justice and ideal self orientations (called substage B). Thus, an emphasis on rules or consequences in response to moral problems is indicative of substage A reasoning within any of the stages. In contrast, reasoning at the B substage of each stage is associated with an emphasis on the justice and ideal self orientations (Kohlberg, 1984).

From Thought to Action.   Kohlberg's stage theory focuses on how people come to decide what they believe to be morally right behavior. But, clearly, people do not always behave in ways they think they should. An athlete, for example, may strike an opponent and later regret the action. Why is there a gap between moral thought and action?

The simplest model of the thought-action relationship suggests that ethical behavior can be accurately predicted from the stage of moral reasoning. Such a simple model, however, fails to address the complexity of the relationship. As Kohlberg (1984, p. 517) wrote, "The prediction from stages or principles to action requires that we take account of intermediary judgments that an individual makes." In Kohlberg's view, two critical intermediary judgments come into play: (1) a deontic judgment, or, simply stated, a judgment that a particular act is right or wrong, and (2) a judgment of responsibility, in which one considers the facts of the situation and the needs and motives of self and other in conjunction with one's deontic judgment to determine one's responsibility. For example, Athlete A, knowing a teammate is using performance-enhancing drugs, might believe that the player should be disqualified from competition (deontic judgment), but she may decide against turning the player in because she does not believe that her role on the team includes rule enforcement (responsibility judgment).

Whereas deontic decisions are prescriptive judgments of rightness, responsibility judgments are "an affirmation of the will to act in terms of that [deontic] judgment" (Kohlberg & Candee, 1984, p. 57) given the particular

facts of the real-life context. Blasi (1984, 1989) suggests that the selection of information to be factored into responsibility judgments is related to how salient moral considerations are to one's definition of who one is as a person. As moral concepts become more central to self-definition, responsibility judgments will be more influenced by critical moral issues as opposed to morally extraneous information.

Kohlberg (1984) pointed out that moral action often fails to keep pace with mature moral reasoning because people use various "quasi-obligations," or excuses, to avoid a judgment of responsibility that parallels their deontic choice. For example, the quasi-obligation of team loyalty may keep the above player from turning in her teammate. Kohlberg also has noted that reasoning reflecting substage B considerations contains fewer excusing complications, and fewer quasi-obligations, than does reasoning at substage A.

It is not difficult to see why sport action may depart from participants' best moral reasoning. The sport structure itself may encourage the use of substage A reasoning, replete with quasi-obligations. Players' judgments of self-responsibility are further discouraged by the generally accepted practice of concentrating moral authority in the roles of coaches and officials. Players often view their responsibility to opponents as limited to obeying the game rules or informal norms, avoiding officials' negative sanctions, or conforming to coaches' orders.

Moral Education.   Kohlberg's first approach to moral education was to devise hypothetical moral dilemmas that could be discussed in small groups in educational settings. The teacher's role was that of a Socratic facilitator; more specifically, the teacher asked questions to enable students to elaborate on their own reasoning and encouraged them to directly dialogue with one another. The approach built on the work of one of Kohlberg's students, Moshe Blatt, who found that such discussions could promote moral stage growth (Blatt & Kohlberg, 1975). The underlying mechanism responsible for growth was hypothesized to be cognitive conflict or disequilibrium. As students encountered moral reasoning slightly more mature than their own, they were attracted to it. However, their own moral reasoning had to change to incorporate the new patterns of reasoning. Change in the deep structure of reasoning is a slow process whereby an existent pattern of reasoning is disrupted, then reconstructed to meet new challenges.

In Kohlberg's later work (Higgins, Power, & Kohlberg, 1984; Kohlberg & Higgins, 1987; Power, Higgins, & Kohlberg, 1989), he substantially modified his approach to moral education. He became dissatisfied with the peer dialogue method because it was limited to a discussion of either hypothetical stories or relatively trivial real-life ones. Second, it was disconnected from moral action: It generated reasoning in a behavioral vacuum. To correct these difficulties, Kohlberg and his colleagues developed the *just community* approach to moral education. In brief, the just community approach involves the formation of a participatory democracy within the school. The just community seeks to foster a sense of community identity that becomes the vehicle through which collective moral norms are generated.

This movement into the just community approach necessitated a branching beyond Kohlberg's Piagetian roots. Rather than focus specifically on the individual as the focus of concern, Kohlberg began to see group norms as equally important (similar to Durkheim, 1973). Groups have moral norms that are sui generis; that is, they are not reducible to the sum of the individual's moral perspectives. The shared collective norms help to define the *moral atmosphere* of a group. Although group norms can change in important ways, including becoming more comprehensive and adequate from a moral standpoint, they are not developmental in the way individual moral stages are. Group life is too variable for the use of stringent developmental criteria. Nonetheless, helping groups progress in the development of their collective norms is vital, Kohlberg argued, because the group's moral atmosphere influences both individual moral growth and appropriate moral action by individuals and the group as a whole.

The concepts of moral atmosphere and collective norms have significant theoretical, empirical, and practical implications for sport and physical education. As an initial step in this direction, a checklist was developed to assess the moral atmosphere of physical activity contexts in the upper elementary school (Shields, Getty, & Bredemeier, 1991). Likewise, Shields et al. have begun to develop intervention strategies for sport teams based on a "team as moral community" model. The issue of moral atmosphere will be revisited in the concluding section of the chapter.

Haan's Theory of Moral Development

Kohlberg's theory has dominated the landscape of moral development inquiry for the past few decades, but a considerable amount of sport research has utilized a related theory of moral development, that of Haan. The major features of Haan's model are described following.

Basic Concepts.   Haan (1977b, 1978, 1983, 1991; Haan, Aerts, & Cooper, 1985) was less concerned than Kohlberg with how people reason about abstract moral issues.

Rather, she focused on how people in actual life situations believe moral agreements should be reached and moral disputes negotiated. Haan's (1978) basic constructs were derived from an analysis of moral action in the context of simulation games. Thus, the basic concepts of her theory describe the structure of interpersonal moral action.

There are three major concepts at the heart of Haan's model of moral development: moral balance, moral dialogue, and moral levels. The first concept, the *moral balance,* refers to an interpersonal state when all parties involved in a relationship are in basic agreement about respective rights, obligations, and privileges. From Haan's perspective, morality arises from the reality of human interdependence and the need to balance the give-and-take of any relationship. One can both "take" too much and "give" too much in a relationship. The appropriate balance of giving and taking needs to reflect the particular interests and needs of the parties involved and the vagaries of context and situation. When people are in moral balance, an agreement exists—usually informal and unstated—about what should or should not be done and who should do what to keep the relationship subjectively equalized. For example, in a game of basketball, competitors are in moral balance if they are in basic agreement about the informal norms of play and all parties are complying with those norms. Similarly, a player and a coach are in moral balance if they have a shared understanding about such issues as the amount of practice required, the type and quality of the coach's input, and the amount of the player's game time.

When two or more people disagree about mutual rights and obligations, the moral balance is disrupted and a state of moral imbalance follows. Moral imbalances occur frequently because interpersonal life is characterized by shifting expectations, selective perceptions, and subtle changes in mood and behavior.

When moral imbalances occur, people use a variety of means to try to reestablish moral balance. Haan collectively called these efforts *moral dialogue.* The most obvious and clear instance of moral dialogue is open, verbal negotiation. But moral dialogue can take many other forms. If a soccer player is tripped in violation of both the rules and informal player norms, the moral dialogue may take the form of the offended player's hitting the offending player with extra force during a later play to communicate "I didn't like what you did to me and don't do it again." If the communication succeeds at restoring shared understanding of appropriate behavior, the moral balance is restored. However, if the communication is unsuccessful at restoring balance, further "dialogue" may continue until balance is achieved or until the relationship ends. In sum, any communication—direct or indirect, verbal or nonverbal—intended to convey information about one's needs or desires in an effort to maintain or restore moral balance is an instance of moral dialogue.

According to Haan (1978), there are five *moral levels* in the development of moral maturity. Each level reflects a different understanding of the appropriate structuring of the moral balance. The first two levels comprise what can be called the *assimilation phase,* during which time the person believes that moral balances should be constructed that generally give preference to the needs and concerns of the self. This is not because the person is "selfish," but because the person, due to developmental limitations, is unable to comprehend with equal clarity and urgency the felt needs and desires of others. This situation is turned around during the *accommodation phase,* consisting of Levels 3 and 4. People reflecting these levels generally seek to give to the moral exchange more than they receive. Finally, at the *equilibration phase,* Level 5, the person gives equal recognition to all parties' interests.

Haan's model follows the same basic contour of development as Kohlberg's, but the two theorists differ significantly on their depiction of moral maturity. For Haan, no abstract principle of justice is adequate to deal with the intricately nuanced situations of everyday moral life. Instead, she maintained that the morally mature person recognizes that moral dialogue must meet certain procedural criteria for guaranteeing equality if a moral balance is to be considered adequate. Specifically, a fully adequate moral dialogue allows all parties equal access to relevant information, includes all those who will be affected by decisions reached, seeks to achieve unforced consensus through nondominated discussion, and reflects the particularities of the situation and the parties involved. Such stringent conditions are rarely, if ever, descriptive of actual moral dialogues, but are implicitly recognized by the morally mature person as defining the preconditions for establishing a situational moral "truth." The conclusions of all moral dialogues that do not meet these stringent criteria must be seen as provisional or tentative.

From Thought to Action. To help explain the discrepancy that often occurs between thought and action, Haan (1997a) placed her moral theory within a broader model of psychological functioning. This model highlights both psychological structures discussed previously and ego processes. Ego processes provide for two types of regulation: They are involved in the intrapsychic integration of outputs from different psychological structures, and they coordinate interchange between the person's ongoing psychological functioning and the environment. A crude analogy would hold that structures are like the processing chips of a computer and the ego processes are like the circuitry that connects the internal components and coordinates them with input from the keyboard, modem, or other external devices.

The ego processes can be subdivided into two sets: *coping* ego processes that reflect accurate and faithful intrapsychic coordinations and interchange with the environment, and *defending* processes which reflect a breakdown in accuracy. Coping processes, such as empathy, suppression, concentration, logical analysis, and sublimation, are analogous to properly functioning circuitry. In contrast, defensive processes, which include such mechanisms as projection, repression, denial, rationalization, and displacement, are like "bugs" that distort information.

For action to reflect a person's most mature moral capabilities, the person must remain coping in his or her ego processing. Sometimes, however, accuracy is abandoned for the sake of maintaining a coherent and positive sense of self. Particularly under stress, coping may give way to defending, and the quality of moral action may deteriorate. The role of acute stress in eliciting defensive ego processes is of special interest to sport psychologists, because competition often is associated with high levels of stress. It may be, for example, that when excessive emphasis is placed on performance outcome, the resultant stress may encourage temporary moral dysfunctions. This is a relatively unexplored area that is ripe for research.

Moral Education. Haan did not give extensive treatment to moral education. Her focus on moral action rather than moral cognition, however, led her to suggest that it is social disequilibrium, not cognitive disequilibrium, that is the primary vehicle for moral development (Haan, 1985). As an example of what she meant by social disequilibrium, let us imagine an elementary school child who refuses to share playground equipment. Repeated failure to share the balls and bats will lead, most probably, to robust problems in social relationships. Haan argued that it is these social disruptions, not disequilibrium in abstract cognitive structures, that provide the motivation for reexamining one's way of constructing moral exchange.

The educational implications of Haan's approach have been developed elsewhere (Shields, 1986). In brief, it is important to provide action contexts where dialogue and negotiation among interdependent parties can take place. The group leader can help participants use their coping processes by minimizing unnecessary stress and by monitoring and addressing signs of the use of defending processes. In addition, when participants deviate from the criteria for truth-identifying dialogues, these shortcomings can be discussed by the group.

In this section, two important theories of moral development have been discussed. The review has been selective rather than exhaustive. The important works of Piaget (1932), Gilligan (1982; Gilligan, Lyons, & Hanmer, 1990), and Rest (1986; Rest, Narvaez, Bebeau, & Thoma, 1999), for example, have not been reviewed because, to date, they have been seldom used by sport psychologists in their published research. The next section focuses on a review of the empirical research that has been done on sport and morality.

MORALITY AND SPORT: EMPIRICAL FINDINGS

Investigators with a variety of theoretical perspectives and research traditions have begun to tackle the complex issues involved in the moral psychology of sport. While reviewing the literature, the following questions are addressed:

How does sport influence the valuing of fairness relative to other sport values?

What is the relationship between sport participation and moral reasoning?

How does sport involvement relate to prescriptive moral judgments?

How do moral variables relate to other important constructs, such as achievement motivation?

Can personal variables be used to predict moral behavior?

Can a comprehensive model of moral action be developed?

How can sport-specific moral constructs, such as sportspersonship, be assessed?

How can physical education and sport experience be used to promote positive character development?

Sport and the Prioritizing of Moral Values

Two primary methods have been used to investigate the relationship between sport participation and the relative priority of moral values. One approach relies on the use of non-sport-specific value surveys, such as the Rokeach Values Survey (Rokeach, 1973). The other research tradition has employed Webb's (1969) Orientations toward Play Scale, often referred to simply as the Webb scale, or one of its variants.

Several researchers have used Rokeach's (1973) approach to assess the value orientation of athletes (Davis & Baskett, 1979; Lee, 1977, 1986, 1988). For example, Davis

and Baskett concluded that college athletes differed from nonathletes in terms of their terminal but not instrumental values. Lee (1977), however, found no difference between athletes and nonathletes, other than that athletes tended to place more value on being good at what they do. In recent work, Lee has employed more open-ended methodological strategies to identify the value structures of athletes (Lee & Cockman, 1995).

Webb (1969) developed a very simple instrument to assess the value priorities of sport participants. Respondents are asked to rank order the values of winning, playing fair, playing well, and having fun. The Webb scale and its variants have been used extensively by sport psychologists and sociologists (Blair, 1985; Card, 1981; Kidd & Woodman, 1975; Knoppers, Schuiteman, & Love, 1986, 1988; Loy, Birrell, & Rose, 1976; Maloney & Petrie, 1972; Mantel & Vander Velden, 1974; McElroy & Kirkendall, 1980; Nicholson, 1979; Nixon, 1980; Petrie, 1971a, 1971b; Sage, 1980; Snyder & Spreitzer, 1979; Theberge, Curtis, & Brown, 1982). Though there are methodological difficulties with the Webb scale (Bredemeier & Shields, 1998; Knoppers, 1985), a few conclusions have been sufficiently robust that they have become widely accepted. Most important, research in which the Webb scale and its variants have been used suggests that sport involvement tends to socialize away from a value orientation that places a premium on playing fair and having fun toward an orientation that centers on the values of winning (foremost) and playing well. How this shift relates to other variables, such as gender, age, type of athletic involvement, religion, and socioeconomic status, has been investigated (Blair, 1985; Card, 1981; Kidd & Woodman, 1975; Knoppers et al., 1986, 1988; Loy et al., 1976; Maloney & Petrie, 1972; Mantel & Vander-Velden, 1974; McElroy & Kirkendall, 1980; Nicholson, 1979; Nixon, 1980; Petrie, 1971a, 1971b; Sage, 1980; Snyder & Spreitzer, 1979; Theberge et al., 1982). However, results from these studies need to be viewed cautiously in light of methodological concerns. Future research in this area will need to improve on the original methodology if progress is to be made.

Sport Participation and Moral Reasoning

A few investigators have published empirical research guided by Kohlberg's theory of moral development to assess the maturity of sport participants' moral reasoning. Hall (1981), for example, found that collegiate basketball players' moral reasoning maturity was lower than their college peers. Using Rest's "objective measure" of moral development, derived from Kohlberg's model, Bredemeier and Shields (1984a) replicated Hall's finding in an exploratory study of moral reasoning and behavior among female and male basketball players at the college level.

Haan's (1977) model of moral development influenced Bredemeier and Shields (1986c), who extended the athlete-nonathlete comparisons by testing the reasoning maturity of male and female basketball players and nonathletes at both the high school and college level. They adapted the moral measure so that respondents reasoned about two hypothetical moral dilemmas set in everyday life contexts and two in sport-specific situations. This adaptation yielded two distinct scores: one for "life" moral reasoning, and one for "sport" moral reasoning. Among the 50 college students, the nonathletes were again found to have significantly more mature moral reasoning than the basketball players, a finding that held for both sport and life dilemmas. Among the 50 high school students, however, no reasoning differences between athletes and nonathletes were found.

Bredemeier and Shields (1986c) also discovered gender differences. Both college and high school females reasoned at a more mature level than did their male counterparts in response to the sport dilemmas. In response to the life dilemmas, the high school females, but not the college females, exhibited more mature reasoning than did the males.

To determine whether the same athlete-nonathlete relationship would hold for college athletes other than basketball players, Bredemeier and Shields (1986c) also examined the moral reasoning of 20 intercollegiate swimmers. The swimmers' mean scores for "life" and "sport" moral reasoning were between those of the nonathletes and the basketball players. "Life" reasoning differences only approached significance, but basketball players' "sport" reasoning was less mature than that of both the swimmers and the nonathletes; "sport" reasoning for the latter two groups did not significantly differ. This finding suggests that it is not experience in sport per se that is associated with less mature moral reasoning.

The Hahm-Beller Values Choice Inventory, a measure designed to assess the extent to which respondents embrace deontological ethics, was administered by Beller and Stoll (1995). They observed reasoning differences in secondary school students. Paralleling the finding reported by Bredemeier and Shields (1986c) with college students, Beller and Stoll noted that high school athletes displayed less adequate moral reasoning than their nonathlete counterparts. Ambiguities about the extent to which the Hahm-Beller Values Choice Inventory is developmental, however, raise questions about the meaning of these findings (Bredemeier & Shields, 1998).

The research on sport involvement and moral reasoning maturity raises a number of questions. Does the amount of physical contact, the length of involvement, the competitive level, or the type of interpersonal interaction in one's sport experience influence the development of moral reasoning? Alternatively, are people with more mature reasoning less interested in, or purposefully "selected out" of, some college athletic programs? What is the role of the coach? With regard to the observed gender differences, it is not too surprising that, given typical gender socialization and the traditional role of sport in the socialization process, males' moral reasoning may be more influenced by the egocentric aspects of competitive sport (Bredemeier, 1982, 1984). But more research is clearly desirable and improved methodologies will be needed to address some of these critical questions.

The research reported thus far has been focused on the relationship between sport involvement and stage or level of moral reasoning. Another line of research relevant to the sport involvement/moral reasoning relationship focuses on how people may actually change their way of thinking about or responding to moral issues when they enter the world of sport. To place this research in context, it should be emphasized that most structural developmental theorists have traditionally held that a person's moral reasoning level will remain fairly constant across different types of situations. This is because stages are thought to reflect structured wholes or integrated functional systems. Nonetheless, a few highly irregular situations have been shown to alter the person's level of moral reasoning. Research conducted in prisons (Kohlberg, Hickey, & Scharf, 1972), for example, has demonstrated that inmates use lower stages of reasoning in response to prison dilemmas than when they attempt to resolve standard hypothetical dilemmas. Kohlberg hypothesized that when a group's collective norms reflect a low stage of moral reasoning, the constraining "moral atmosphere" may inhibit more advanced moral functioning, even among those individuals capable of higher-stage thought (see Power et al., 1989).

Bredemeier and Shields (1985, 1986b; Shields & Bredemeier, 1984, 1995) have hypothesized that sport is one of those unusual contexts where moral reasoning undergoes a change in its underlying structure. This hypothesis was generated in light of the "set aside" character of sport activity. Sport is set apart from everyday life both spatially, through marked boundaries, and temporally, by designated playing periods replete with "time-outs." A variety of symbols—such as whistles, buzzers, flags, uniforms, and special rituals and ceremonies—are used to create and reinforce the world-within-a-world character of sport. The separated world of sport is governed by artificial rules and roles and is oriented toward a goal with no intrinsic meaning or value.

It was noted earlier that in several studies by Bredemeier and Shields, moral interviews were conducted that included both life and sport dilemmas. When they analyzed reasoning maturity scores, they found that the "life" scores were significantly higher than "sport" scores (Bredemeier & Shields, 1984a). This finding was quite robust, holding for athletes and nonathletes, swimmers and basketball players, college students and high school students, males and females. Similar analyses were conducted with 110 girls and boys in grades 4 through 7 (Bredemeier, 1995). It was found that sixth- and seventh-graders' "sport" reasoning was significantly lower than their "life" reasoning, and that this life-sport reasoning divergence was significantly greater than that for the younger children. The children below grade 6 did not demonstrate context-specific reasoning patterns.

Based on these findings, Bredemeier and Shields (1985, 1986a, 1986b; Shields & Bredemeier, 1984, 1995) have proposed a theory of *game reasoning*. The theory holds that the unique context of sport elicits a transformation in moral reasoning such that egocentrism, typically the hallmark of immature morality, becomes a valued and acceptable principle for organizing the moral exchange. In terms of moral reasoning, they hypothesized that sport offers a context for a "legitimated regression" (Shields, 1986; Shields & Bredemeier, 1984) to a form of moral reasoning that is similar to less mature moral reasoning.

Sport may allow for the temporary suspension of the typical moral obligation to equally consider the interests of all parties in favor of a more egocentric style of moral engagement as an enjoyable and nonserious moral deviation. There may be several reasons why such a moral transformation is culturally sanctioned and viewed as appropriate within the limits of sport. First of all, competition is premised on each party or team seeking self-gain. There is little room in sport for equally considering the desires, goals, and needs of opponents. While competition demands a degree of egocentrism, the unique protective structures of sport function to legitimate it. The carefully planned and rigorously enforced rules protect participants from many of the negative consequences that would typically ensue from egocentric morality. Furthermore, the continual presence of officials and coaches allows for the temporary transference of moral responsibility. Of course, sport is not a moral free-for-all: Players are people and moral responsibility cannot be

completely set aside. Bredemeier and Shields (1985, 1986a, 1986b; Shields & Bredemeier, 1984, 1995) suggest that just as sport may be a world-within-a-world, existing within and connected to the real world, so game reasoning does not completely displace or render inoperative basic moral understandings. To remain legitimate, one can only "play" at egocentrism. When the play character of game reasoning is lost, sport can deteriorate into a breeding ground for aggression, cheating, and other moral defaults.

The elaboration and validation of the theory of game reasoning awaits future research, and at this point there can be only speculation about potential implications for the theory. If sport does elicit its own special form of moral reasoning, it may help to shed light on some of the earlier findings. Consider, for example, the finding that for some college athletes, participation in sport is associated with lower levels of moral reasoning maturity. Perhaps for some college athletes, particularly those for whom sport is a highly salient experience, game reasoning may begin to lose its "set aside" character and have undue influence on moral reasoning beyond the bounds of sport. Several factors may account for why this is more true for participants in some sports than in others. Participation in elite sports, particularly those for which professional opportunities are available, often include external rewards contingent on performance. The infusion of "daily life" rewards (e.g., money or educational opportunity) into the sport experience may encourage a blurring of the distinction between sport and everyday life.

Sport and Prescriptive Moral Judgment

Another area of sport morality research deals with prescriptive judgments. Prescriptive judgments, also referred to as legitimacy judgments, are judgments made about the rightness or wrongness of particular acts. From a structuralist perspective, prescriptive judgments are aspects of moral content (not structure). The importance of studying prescriptive judgments stems from the fact that they may reflect intermediary processes between an underlying moral stage and actual behavior. For example, there is some evidence that Stage 2 moral reasoning is associated with higher levels of aggression than Stage 5 (Bredemeier & Shields, 1984a). But Stage 2 reasoning itself is neither consistent nor inconsistent with a belief that aggression is an appropriate game tactic. If data are also available about the particular judgments that an individual makes about the legitimacy of aggression under varying circumstances, a better set of aggression predictors is available than if moral stage alone is known.

Prescriptive judgments regarding aggression and gender stratification have been investigated in relation to moral variables. In one such study, Bredemeier (1985) again used hypothetical sport and life dilemmas with 40 female and male high school and college basketball players. In addition, participants made judgments about the legitimacy of six behaviors with varying implications. In terms of the actor's intention toward an opponent, the six acts, in order of severity, were (1) nonphysical intimidation, (2) physical intimidation, (3) make the opponent miss several minutes of play, (4) eliminate the opponent from the game due to injury, (5) make the opponent miss a season due to injury, (6) permanently disable the opponent.

The athletes made judgments under two conditions about the appropriateness of each of the six behaviors in this Continuum of Injurious Acts (CIA): (1) during a midweek interview session in which hypothetical dilemmas were discussed, and (2) during an interview session immediately following an important late-season game. In the first, hypothetical condition, the athlete focused on what acts he or she thought would be acceptable for a fictitious football player. In the second, engaged condition, the athlete made judgments about what would be appropriate in his or her own basketball play.

Results indicated an inverse relationship between players' level of moral reasoning and the number of intentionally injurious sport acts they judged to be legitimate. Those athletes with more mature moral reasoning accepted fewer acts as legitimate. Also, "sport" moral reasoning was a significantly better predictor than "life" moral reasoning of legitimacy judgments in both the hypothetical and engaged contexts. The relationship was strongest between "sport" moral reasoning and hypothetical judgments, and weakest between "life" moral reasoning and engaged judgments. This pattern suggests that the reasoning-judgment relationship can be most clearly predicted when the contexts are similar and when the judgments, like the moral interviews, pertain to a hypothetical actor.

Secondary issues examined in this study were differences in legitimacy judgments as a function of gender, school level, and judgment context. Male athletes were found to accept a greater number of CIA acts as legitimate than females, and college athletes a greater number than high school competitors. The gender finding is consistent with a considerable body of literature suggesting that males accept and express more aggression than females (Hyde, 1984). Similarly, the school level finding is consistent with the view that an in-sport socialization process tends to encourage the legitimation of aggression (Silva, 1983).

Results also indicated that athletes judged significantly more CIA acts as legitimate in the engaged condition than in the hypothetical condition, even though the latter context focused on football, a collision sport structured by rules permitting potentially injurious acts, and the former context focused on basketball, a sport in which relatively limited physical contact is normative. One interpretation of these results is that the stresses of competitive sport experience may erode a person's capacity to make clear judgments consistent with that person's most mature reasoning. Other interpretations are also possible and future research is needed to disentangle the influence of such factors as (1) the sport involved (football vs. basketball), (2) the timing of the interview (midweek vs. postgame), and (3) the subject of action (hypothetical other vs. self).

A second study on morality and legitimacy judgments focused on children in fourth through seventh grade. Bredemeier, Weiss, Shields, and Cooper (1987), using a methodology similar to that of Silva (1983), showed 78 children slides of potentially injurious sport behaviors and administered moral interviews. The slide series featured male athletes performing the following acts: legal boxing punch, legal football tackle, illegal basketball contact, illegal soccer tackle, legal baseball contact, illegal football tackle, illegal basketball trip, illegal soccer contact, and a legal baseball slide. Although some of the slides reflected activity within the rules of the sport, all involved action that was judged by the children to carry a high risk of injury. Children were asked to indicate approval or disapproval of the actions depicted. Results paralleled those with college students: Children with less mature reasoning judged a significantly greater number of potentially injurious acts to be legitimate than their more mature peers.

Solomon and her colleagues (Solomon, Bredemeier, & Shields, 1993) developed the Gender Stratification Interview (GSI) to assess children's prescriptive judgments about gender stratification in sport. The GSI consists of six brief sport scenarios, each depicting a situation of potential gender stratification. Solomon (Solomon & Bredemeier, 1999) administered the GSI to 160 children, age 6 to 11, and found that most children perceive sport as a context where gender stratification exists. Nearly two-thirds of the children, however, judged this stratification as inappropriate. Older children, girls, and children with more sport experience were more likely to be critical of gender stratification than were their counterparts.

In summary, the literature on prescriptive judgments has helped to clarify how moral reasoning relates to particular judgments. This is an important step. Within a structural developmental research paradigm, the logical progression will be to next investigate the relationships among moral reasoning maturity, legitimacy judgments under varying conditions, and actual behavior.

Moral Development and Related Constructs

Moral variables do not work in isolation and it is important to understand how they relate to and interact with other important psychological processes. To date, most attention has been given to the relationship between moral and motivational variables, particularly achievement motivation as conceptualized by Nicholls (1983, 1989, 1992).

Nicholls's work focuses on how the individual constructs the value of achievement activities. Two primary orientations are identified: For some people, motivation arises from a comparative stance toward others; for others, motivation is self-referenced. An *ego orientation* is one in which a person is motivated to display competence in relation to others, seeking to demonstrate superiority in the task at hand. In contrast, a *task orientation* is characterized by a concern for self-referenced personal achievement.

Nicholls (1989, p. 102) maintained that "different motivational orientations are not just different types of wants or goals. They involve different world views." He hypothesized that a person's goal orientation (task or ego) will correspond with a set of moral attitudes, beliefs, and values that are congruent with the trajectory of achievement calibration that the goal orientation defines. A person with a high ego orientation calibrates achievement through referencing self against others, and this approach to defining success is likely to correlate with a relative lack of concern for moral issues like justice or fairness. A person with a high task orientation, on the other hand, defines success in terms that are self-referenced and is likely, according to Nicholls, to emphasize such values as fairness and cooperation.

Duda (1989) empirically tested Nicholls's hypothesis. She examined the relationship between goal orientation in sport and beliefs about the purposes of sport participation among high school athletes. Her findings revealed a positive association between athletes' task orientation and their view that sport should teach people such values as trying hard, cooperation, rule obedience, and being good citizens. In contrast, athletes who were predominantly ego-orientated tended to believe that sport should increase one's social status and show people how to survive in a competitive world.

In another study, Duda, Olson, and Templin (1991) found a strong association between motivational orientation and behaviors perceived as legitimate in the pursuit of victory. Athletes who were more task-oriented endorsed less cheating behavior and expressed greater approval of

"sportsmanlike" actions. High ego orientation scores related to higher approval ratings of intentionally injurious behavior, a finding replicated with a sample of high school and college-level football players (Duda & Huston, 1997). Similar findings have been reported by Stephens and Bredemeier (1996) and Dunn and Dunn (1999).

Predicting Moral Action in Sport

Moral behavior is notoriously difficult to study. Clearly, there are ethical reasons not to subject people to a study in which moral failings may become evident. Additionally, behavior itself is open to varying interpretations. Because the motivation for a behavior is not necessarily self-evident from observing the behavior, it is difficult to draw conclusions about the moral meaning of particular observed behaviors. Despite these difficulties, some attempts have been made to research moral behavior, particularly aggression, in a sport context.

Preliminary evidence that moral reasoning is related to aggression in sport was reported in a basketball study (Bredemeier & Shields, 1984a), discussed previously. In addition to administering a moral maturity measure, Bredemeier and Shields asked the athletes' coaches to rate and rank their players on aggressive behavior on the court. They operationally defined aggression as the initiation of an attack with the intent to injure, distinguishing it from forceful, assertive play. Using the coaches' evaluations as a measure of players' aggression, significant relationships were found between stages of moral reasoning and tendencies to aggress. Specifically, athletes' preconventional moral reasoning was positively correlated with coaches' evaluations of high aggressiveness, and postconventional moral reasoning was associated with low aggression scores.

In a study with children in grades 4 through 7, Bredemeier (1994) administered four hypothetical moral dilemmas, together with pencil-and-paper measures designed to assess assertive, aggressive, and submissive action tendencies in both everyday life (Deluty, 1979, 1984) and sport. Assertion is a conflict resolution strategy that reflects a balancing of one's own needs with those of others, aggressive responses place personal interests above the needs or rights of others. Thus, it was hypothesized that assertion would be associated with more mature moral reasoning and aggression with less mature reasoning. Results supported the hypotheses. Children's moral reasoning scores were predictive of self-reported assertive and aggressive action tendencies in both sport and daily life.

In a related study, Bredemeier, Weiss, Shields, and Cooper (1986) examined the relationship of sport participation and interest with moral reasoning maturity and aggression tendencies among children in grades 4 through 7. Analyses revealed that boys' participation and interest in high-contact sports and girls' participation in medium-contact sports (the highest level of contact sport experience girls reported) were associated with less mature moral reasoning and greater tendencies to aggress. None of the remaining sport involvement–reasoning/behavior associations were significant. One probable explanation for the gender difference is that girls, having no direct experience in high-contact sports, perceived the meaning of physical contact in medium-contact sports in a way that is closer to how boys perceive high-contact sports. This perception typically will contrast with males' perceptions of the same medium-contact sports.

In another study, Stephens and Bredemeier (1996) extended Duda's investigation of motivational orientations to examine children's self-reported temptation to behave counter to moral norms. They administered a test battery to 214 female soccer players, age 10 to 14, that included a sport-specific achievement orientation scale, a measure of participants' perceptions of their coaches' motivational orientation, a sportspersonship inventory, and a self-report measure assessing participants' temptation to violate moral norms during a sport contest (lie to an official, hurt an opponent, and break one of the rules) (Stephens, Bredemeier, & Shields, 1997). Players who described themselves as experiencing high temptation to play unfairly differed significantly from those experiencing low temptation. Specifically, players who were more tempted were more ego- than task-oriented and perceived their coaches as being more ego-oriented and less task-oriented. Also, high temptation was associated with (1) greater approval of behaviors designed to obtain an unfair advantage over an opponent, (2) the belief that more of their teammates would play unfairly in the same situation, and (3) longer involvement with current team. This research points to the need to directly study the relationships among moral atmosphere variables (e.g., perceptions of coaches' goal orientation and beliefs about the likelihood of teammates engaging in unfair sport practices), moral reasoning level, motivational achievement orientation, and sport behavior.

Toward a Comprehensive Model of Moral Action in Sport

Moral behavior stems from a complex set of influences. Early moral research, both in general psychology and in sport psychology, focused on identifying stages of moral reasoning development and then how moral judgment re-

lated to other constructs of interest, but this was too confining an approach to encompass all of the components of moral functioning. To address these limitations, Rest (1984, 1986, 1994) proposed a broader model of moral functioning that has been influential in identifying and organizing the various determinants of moral behavior. Rest asked a simple question: What must happen psychologically for moral behavior to take place? In response, he identified four key components to moral functioning. For a person to behave morally, he or she must have (1) interpreted the situation, identifying the moral issues; (2) formed a moral judgment; (3) decided to act on the moral judgment rather than on some competing value; and (4) sustained that decision through the various action sequences needed to fulfill the moral intent.

To better understand the conceptual, theoretical, and empirical relations among the complex variables that interact in the production of moral action in a sport setting, Bredemeier and Shields (1994, 1996; Shields & Bredemeier, 1995) have proposed a 12-component model of moral action. Expanding on Rest's four processes (interpretation, judgment, choice, and implementation), Bredemeier and Shields specified three sets of influences that operate on each of the four processes: contextual influences, psychological competencies, and competence-performance mediators (such as ego processes). The resultant 12-component model suggests that moral action requires a complex coordination among numerous internal and external influences and that, correspondingly, moral failings can stem from any number of sources. A review of the theoretical and empirical literature relevant to each of the components of the model is developed in more detail in Shields and Bredemeier. A presentation of exemplars of each component within the model is presented in Table 23.1.

A focal feature of the Bredemeier and Shields model is the central importance it places on the interaction between contextual and personal influences. At the contextual level, influences include such potent forces as the goal or reward structure (e.g., competitive or cooperative), the prevailing group norms or moral atmosphere, the motivational climate, and the established power relationships.

Several studies illustrate the importance of the interrelationships between contextual variables and personal variables. Stuart and Ebbeck (1995), for example, investigated the influence of perceived social approval on the moral processes of judgment, reasoning, and behavioral intention. They found that for younger children (grades 4 and 5), when parents, coaches, and teammates disapprove of antisocial behavior, the children are better able to judge

Table 23.1   12-Component Model of Moral Action

Influence:	Process			
	1. Interpretation	2. Judgment	3. Choice	4. Implementation
Contextual	Goal structure	Moral atmosphere	Motivational climate	Power structure
Psychological Competence	Role-taking ability	Moral reasoning stage	Motivational orientation	Social problem-solving skills
Competence/Performance Mediators	Intraceptive ego processes	Cognitive ego processes	Affective impulse-regulating ego processes	Attention-focusing ego processes

Source: Adapted from Shields & Bredemeir, 1995.

situations involving such behavioral choices as presenting a moral problem. The children also developed concordant behavioral intentions. For adolescents, however, perceived social approval was inversely related to the main variables, particularly to the intent to exhibit moral behavior. Vallerand, Dehaies, and Cuerrier (1997), using behavioral intentions related to sportspersonship, also found social context effects.

Shields and his colleagues (Shields, Bredemeier, Gardner, & Bostrom, 1995) used the 12-component model of moral action to frame a study investigating the correlates of collective team norms sanctioning aggression and cheating. They found that age, year in school, and years playing baseball or softball all correlated positively with expectations of peer cheating and aggression and with the belief that the coach would sanction cheating if necessary to win. Vallerand, Dehaies, et al. (1997) have also conducted a study to examine context-person interaction within a moral framework. They demonstrated that team sport athletes have low levels of concern for the opponent, irrespective of the expected utility of behaving in a morally appropriate way. In contrast, individual sport athletes, though always showing more concern for the opponent than did the team sport athletes, were significantly more concerned for the opponent if the personal costs were not too high. Placed in the 12-component model of moral action (Shields & Bredemeier, 1995), this study can be interpreted as investigating how context, in the form of type of sport and expected utility, mediates the "choice" process.

Assessment of Sport-Specific Moral Constructs

Several instruments have been designed specifically to assess sport-specific moral constructs. Some of these have been mentioned already, such as Webb's (1969) Orientation toward Play Scale, the sport dilemmas used by Bredemeier and Shields (1985, 1986a, 1986b), and the Hahm-Beller Values Choice Inventory (Hahm, Beller, & Stoll, 1989).

Often, when people think of morality and sport, however, the construct that most readily comes to mind is sportsmanship (or sportspersonship).

Sportspersonship has been a topic of considerable, but intermittent, interest to sport psychologists, who have developed a large number of sportspersonship inventories over the years (Dawley, Troyer, & Shaw, 1951; Haskins, 1960; Haskins & Hartman, 1960; Johnson, 1969; Lakie, 1964; McAfee, 1955; Vallerand, Deshaies, Cuerrier, Brière, & Pelletier, 1996; Vallerand & Losier, 1994; Wright & Rubin, 1989). It is beyond our scope to review each of these instruments separately, nor is there need to do so. Very few have been used beyond pilot investigations, and most have significant shortcomings that limit their utility (Bredemeier & Shields, 1998).

To remedy some of the difficulties that have plagued sportspersonship research, Vallerand and his colleagues have undertaken a sophisticated research program to operationally define and measure sportspersonship. In the first phase of their investigation, they asked male and female athletes ($n = 60$) to present their definition of sportsmanship, and to offer examples (Vallerand et al., 1996). From these definitions and examples, 21 situations were identified that potentially exemplified the meaning of sportspersonship. These 21 items were then presented to a sample of 1,056 French Canadian athletes ranging in age from 10 to 18. The athletes then rated the extent to which each of the items dealt with sportspersonship. A factor analysis revealed five factors: (1) respect and concern for one's full commitment toward sport participation; (2) a negative approach toward sport; a "win at all costs" approach; (3) respect and concern for the rules and officials; (4) respect for social conventions found in sport; and (5) respect and concern for the opponent.

Based on this preliminary investigation, Vallerand et al. (1996) suggested that sportspersonship be conceptualized as encompassing a number of related yet distinct dimensions. To operationalize their multidimensional definition of sportspersonship, they developed the Multidimensional Sportspersonship Orientations Scale (MSOS) (Vallerand, Brière, Blanchard, & Provencher, 1997). Hopefully, future research will test the power of this instrument to yield new theoretical insights and empirical data.

Can Sport Build Character?

At one time, it was widely believed that sport was valuable because it develops the character of its participants (Spreitzer & Snyder, 1975), a belief that is no longer so widely shared (Martin & Dodder, 1993). If sport does not *automatically* build character, is it possible to develop interventions within a sport context that do, in fact, lead to improved social outcomes? Can sport build character? Unfortunately, relatively few studies have been conducted that address these questions. Research does exist to suggest that physical education can be structured so as to promote social and moral development, but research conducted within a physical education context cannot be generalized to sport. Nonetheless, this research will be reviewed because it may provide insights and direction for those working in a sport context.

Orlick (1981) used a social learning approach to investigate the possible positive effects of an alternative approach to physical education. Seventy-one 5-year-old children from two schools participated for 18 weeks in either a cooperative games program or a traditional games program. The dependent variable was children's sharing behavior, operationally defined as amount of candy donated to children in another class. Results were generally in the direction predicted, but were inconsistent. The cooperative games program fostered a significant increase in children's willingness to share in one school, but not in the other. Similarly, the traditional games program resulted in a significant decrease in willingness to share in one school, with no significant differences occurring in the other school.

Romance, Weiss, and Bockovan (1986) used a physical education context to investigate the effectiveness of interventions rooted in structural developmental theory. They found that an eight-week intervention program with fifth-grade children significantly improved their moral reasoning. Miller and his colleagues (Miller, Bredemeier, & Shields, 1997) used the Shields and Bredemeier (1995) model of moral action processes to design a physical education curriculum for upper elementary at-risk youth. The curriculum incorporates cooperative learning, building moral community, creating a mastery-oriented motivational climate, and promoting self-responsibility as primary

learning processes. Though a detailed presentation of outcomes is lacking from the published report, the authors provide anecdotal evidence of program effectiveness.

Gibbons, Ebbeck, and Weiss (1995) conducted a field experiment to test the efficacy of a particular fair play curriculum. Children in the fourth through sixth grade were randomly assigned to one of three conditions: control, fair play curriculum during physical education, or fair play curriculum during all school subjects. Dependent measures included assessments of various components of the moral action model proposed by Rest (1984) and a measure of prosocial behavior. Results suggested that both treatment groups were significantly higher than the control group at posttest on the moral measure but not the prosocial measure.

Over the past 20 years, Hellison has been working to develop and field-test a physical education model for teaching self-responsibility to delinquency-prone youth. Hellison and his colleagues (De Busk & Hellison, 1989; Hellison, 1978, 1983, 1985, 1995; Hellison, Lifka, & Georgiadis, 1990) report the successful use of physical education instruction with at-risk youth in promoting self-control, respect for the rights of others, and prosocial behavior. Hellison's fieldwork has yielded important insights for those engaged in physical education pedagogy, but more empirical research is needed to test instructional strategies and establish causal relationships. Similar points could be made about the work of Solomon (1997a, 1997b) who is, likewise, developing promising approaches to the teaching of physical education.

In a preliminary investigation to determine whether theoretically based instructional strategies can be efficacious in promoting moral growth in a sport context, Bredemeier, Weiss, Shields, and Shewchuk (1986) conducted a field experiment designed to explore the effectiveness of a moral development program in a summer sport camp. Children age 5 to 7 were matched and randomly assigned to one of three conditions: a control group, a social learning group, or a structural developmental group. After the six-week intervention program, both the social learning and structural developmental group showed improvement in moral reasoning.

Comprehensive approaches to promoting moral development through sport have not yet been developed and tested. Thompson (1993) and Beedy (1997), however, have published books on promising experimental sport programs that have incorporated moral development goals. Both authors identify coaches as critical influences on the quality of the sport experience and offer approaches to coaching that they believe will lead to positive character development among participants. Thompson and Beedy are theoretically eclectic, drawing insights from both social learning and structural developmental perspectives. Hopefully, in the near future, these and other models of sport leadership will benefit from thorough empirical investigation.

FUTURE DIRECTIONS FOR RESEARCH AND APPLICATION

It is clear that there is much work to be done before a clear understanding of how sport and physical education experiences relate to the many processes involved in moral thought and action is realized. To date, moral research in the context of sport has focused on only a very few sports, and it is difficult to generalize beyond that narrow base. A broader range of both sport and physical education experiences across varying conditions and structures needs to be explored. Moreover, sport morality research has been hampered by a lack of valid and reliable measures and other methodological difficulties (see Bredemeier & Shields, 1998). These difficulties must be overcome if this field of study is to advance. In addition, researchers need to move beyond their tendency to isolate aspects of moral functioning—such as moral reasoning maturity or prosocial behavior—to incorporate a more elaborate model of moral social psychology, such as that offered by Rest (1984, 1986).

The theory of game reasoning that has been tentatively put forward (Bredemeier & Shields, 1985, 1986a, 1986b; Shields & Bredemeier, 1995) needs to be refined, further tested empirically, and examined in relation to its potential consequences for moral behavior. Related to this project is the need to consider the role that group moral norms play in sport and physical education settings. It may be, for example, that game reasoning involves an accommodation to the prevailing moral atmosphere of a particular sport context more than an internal psychological shift in response to the sport structure itself. In turn, leadership styles and friendship groups may play a significant role in establishing and maintaining group moral norms. Conceptualizing the team as a moral community may open new avenues of theoretical and empirical investigation and practical intervention.

CONCLUSION

In this chapter, we offered empirical findings, theoretical suggestions, and practical implications derived from sport morality research. Most of this research has been rooted in a structural developmental perspective, and the influential theories of Kohlberg and Haan have been reviewed.

However, relatively few definitive statements about moral development and moral behavior in sport can be drawn from the empirical research to date. There is sufficient evidence, based on research employing the Webb scale or one of its variants, to conclude that there is a professionalization process that occurs as people move from lower levels of sport to higher levels. The longer one stays in sport, and the higher the competitive level reached, the more winning becomes the dominant value. There is also sufficient empirical evidence to warrant the conclusion that many athletes use a pattern of moral reasoning in sport that diverges from their more usual pattern of moral reasoning, and that athletes in at least some sports tend to score lower on moral reasoning assessments than their nonathlete counterparts. In most of this research, however, there have not been adequate controls for potential mediating variables, and thus interpretation of these findings remains problematic. Finally, there is ample evidence to support the claim that moral reasoning has implications for moral behavior in sport. The evidence is particularly strong in relation to aggression. In general, athletes with less mature moral reasoning patterns are more likely to use aggression as a game tactic than are athletes with more mature patterns of moral reasoning. Finally, there appears to be a strong relationship between moral variables and motivational orientation, though additional research is needed to further clarify this relationship.

REFERENCES

Bandura, A. (1977). *Social learning theory.* Englewood Cliffs, NJ: Prentice-Hall.

Bandura, A. (1986). *Social foundations of thought and action: A social cognitive theory.* Englewood Cliffs, NJ: Prentice-Hall.

Bandura, A. (1991). Social cognitive theory of moral thought and action. In W.M. Kurtines & J.L. Gewirtz (Eds.), *Handbook of moral behavior and development: Theory* (Vol. 1, pp. 45–103). Hillsdale, NJ: Erlbaum.

Beedy, J. (1997). *Sports PLUS: Developing youth sports programs that teach positive values.* Hamilton, MA: Project Adventure.

Beller, J., & Stoll, S. (1995). Moral reasoning of high school student athletes and general students: An empirical study versus personal testimony. *Pediatric Exercise Science, 7,* 352–363.

Blair, S. (1985). Professionalization of attitude toward play in children and adults. *Research Quarterly in Exercise and Sport, 56,* 82–83.

Blasi, A. (1984). Moral identity: Its role in moral functioning. In W. Kurtines & J. Gewirtz (Eds.), *Morality, moral behavior, and moral development* (pp. 128–139). New York: Wiley.

Blasi, A. (1989). The integration of morality in personality. In I.E. Bilbao (Ed.), *Perspectivas acerca de cambio moral: Posibles intervenciones educativas* (pp. 229–253). San Sebastian, Spain: Servicio Editorial Universidad del Pais Vasco.

Blatt, M.M., & Kohlberg, L. (1975). The effects of classroom moral discussion upon children's level of moral judgment. *Journal of Moral Education, 4,* 129–161.

Bredemeier, B.J. (1982). Gender, justice, and non-violence. *Perspectives, 9,* 106–113.

Bredemeier, B.J. (1984). Sport, gender and moral growth. In J. Silva & R. Weinberg (Eds.), *Psychological foundations of sport and exercise* (pp. 400–414). Champaign, IL: Human Kinetics.

Bredemeier, B.J. (1985). Moral reasoning and the perceived legitimacy of intentionally injurious sport acts. *Journal of Sport Psychology, 7,* 110–124.

Bredemeier, B.J. (1994). Children's moral reasoning and their assertive, aggressive, and submissive tendencies in sport and daily life. *Journal of Sport & Exercise Psychology, 16,* 1–14.

Bredemeier, B.J. (1995). Divergence in children's moral reasoning about issues in daily life and sport specific contexts. *International Journal of Sport Psychology, 26,* 453–463.

Bredemeier, B., & Shields, D. (1984a). Divergence in moral reasoning about sport and life. *Sociology of Sport Journal, 1,* 348–357.

Bredemeier, B., & Shields, D. (1984b). The utility of moral stage analysis in the understanding of athletic aggression. *Sociology of Sport Journal, 1,* 138–149.

Bredemeier, B., & Shields, D. (1985). Values and violence in sport. *Psychology Today, 19,* 22–32.

Bredemeier, B., & Shields, D. (1986a). Athletic aggression: An issue of contextual morality. *Sociology of Sport Journal, 3,* 15–28.

Bredemeier, B., & Shields, D. (1986b). Game reasoning and interactional morality. *Journal of Genetic Psychology, 147,* 257–275.

Bredemeier, B., & Shields, D. (1986c). Moral growth among athletes and non–athletes: A comparative analysis. *Journal of Genetic Psychology, 147,* 7–18.

Bredemeier, B., & Shields, D. (1994). Applied ethics and moral reasoning in sport. In J. Rest & D. Narváez (Eds.), *Moral development in the professions: Psychology and applied ethics* (pp. 173–187). Hillsdale, NJ: Erlbaum.

Bredemeier, B., & Shields, D. (1996). Moral development and children's sport. In F.L. Smoll & R.E. Smith (Eds.), *Children and youth in sport: A biopsychosocial perspective* (pp. 381–401). Madison, WI: Brown & Benchmark.

Bredemeier, B., & Shields, D. (1998). Moral assessment in sport psychology. In J.L. Duda (Ed.), *Advances in sport and exercise psychology measurement* (pp. 257–276). Morgantown, WV: Fitness Information Technology.

Bredemeier, B., Weiss, M., Shields, D., & Cooper, B. (1986). The relationship of sport involvement with children's moral reasoning and aggression tendencies. *Journal of Sport Psychology, 8,* 304–318.

Bredemeier, B., Weiss, M., Shields, D., & Cooper, B. (1987). The relationship between children's legitimacy judgments and their moral reasoning, aggression tendencies and sport involvement. *Sociology of Sport Journal, 4,* 48–60.

Bredemeier, B., Weiss, M., Shields, D., & Shewchuk, R. (1986). Promoting moral growth in a summer sport camp: The implementation of theoretically grounded instructional strategies. *Journal of Moral Education, 15,* 212–220.

Card, A. (1981, April). *Orientation toward winning as a function of athletic participation, grade level, and gender.* Paper presented at the annual meeting of the American Alliance for Health, Physical Education, Recreation, and Dance, Detroit, MI.

Case, R. (1992). *The mind's staircase.* Hillsdale, NJ: Erlbaum.

Davis, H., & Baskett, G. (1979). Do athletes and non-athletes have different values? *Athletic Administration, 13,* 17–19.

Dawley, D.J., Troyer, M.E., & Shaw, J.H. (1951). Relationship between observed behavior in elementary school physical education and test responses. *Research Quarterly, 22,* 71–76.

De Busk, M., & Hellison, D. (1989). Implementing a physical education self-responsibility model for delinquency-prone youth. *Journal of Teaching Physical Education, 8,* 104–112.

Deluty, R.H. (1979). Children's Action Tendency Scale: A self-report measure of aggressiveness, assertiveness, and submissiveness in children. *Journal of Consulting and Clinical Psychology, 47,* 1061–1071.

Deluty, R.H. (1984). Behavioral validation of the Children's Action Tendency Scale. *Journal of Behavioral Assessment, 6,* 115–130.

Duda, J.L. (1989). The relationship between task and ego orientation and the perceived purpose of sport among male and female high school athletes. *Journal of Sport & Exercise Psychology, 11,* 318–335.

Duda, J.L., & Huston, L. (1997). The relationship of goal orientation and degree of competitive sport participation to the endorsement of aggressive acts in American football. In R. Vanfraechem-Raway & Y. Vanden Auweele (Eds.), *9th European Congress on Sport Psychology Proceedings* (pp. 655–662). Brussels, Belgium: European Federation of Sports Psychology.

Duda, J.L., Olson, L.K., & Templin, T.J. (1991). The relationship of task and ego orientation to sportsmanship attitudes and the perceived legitimacy of injurious acts. *Research Quarterly for Exercise and Sport, 62,* 79–87.

Dunn, J.G.H., & Dunn J.C. (1999). Goal orientation, perceptions of aggression, and sportspersonship in elite male youth ice hockey players. *The Sport Psychologist, 13,* 183–200.

Durkheim, E. (1973). *Moral education: A study in the theory and application of the sociology of education.* New York: Free Press.

Enright, R. (1981). *A user's manual for the Distributive Justice Scale.* Madison: University of Wisconsin.

Eysenck, H.J. (1977). *Crime and personality* (3rd ed.). St. Albans, England: Paladin.

Gibbons, S., Ebbeck, V., & Weiss, M. (1995). Fair play for kids: Effects on the moral development of children in physical education. *Research Quarterly for Exercise and Sport, 66,* 247–255.

Gilligan, C. (1982). *In a different voice: Psychological theory and women's development.* Cambridge, MA: Harvard University Press.

Gilligan, C., Lyons, N., & Hanmer, T. (Eds.). (1990). *Making connections: The relational worlds of adolescent girls at Emma Willard School.* Cambridge, MA: Harvard University Press.

Haan, N. (1977a). *Coping and defending: Processes of self-environment organization.* New York: Academic Press.

Haan, N. (1977b). *A manual for interactional morality.* Unpublished manuscript, University of California, Berkeley, Institute of Human Development.

Haan, N. (1978). Two moralities in action contexts: Relationship to thought, ego regulation, and development. *Journal of Personality and Social Psychology, 36,* 286–305.

Haan, N. (1983). An interactional morality of everyday life. In N. Haan, R. Bellah, P. Rabinow, & W. Sullivan (Eds.), *Social science as moral inquiry* (pp. 218–250). New York: Columbia University Press.

Haan, N. (1985). Processes of moral development: Cognitive or social disequilibrium. *Developmental Psychology, 21,* 996–1006.

Haan, N. (1991). Moral development and action from a social constructivist perspective. In W.M. Kurtines & J.L. Gewirtz (Eds.), *Handbook of moral behavior and development: Theory* (Vol. 1, pp. 251–273). Hillsdale, NJ: Erlbaum.

Haan, N., Aerts, E., & Cooper, B.B. (1985). *On moral grounds: The search for a practical morality.* New York: New York University Press.

Hahm, C., Beller, J., & Stoll, S. (1989). *The Hahm-Beller Values Choice Inventory in the sport milieu.* Moscow: University of Idaho Press.

Hall, E. (1981). *Moral development of athletes in sport specific and general social situations.* Unpublished doctoral dissertation, Texas Women's University, Denton.

Haskins, M.J. (1960). Problem solving test of sportsmanship. *Research Quarterly, 31,* 601–606.

Haskins, M.J., & Hartman, B.G. (1960). *Action-choice tests for competitive sports situations.* Author.

Hellison, D. (1978). *Beyond balls and bats: Alienated (and other) youth in the gym.* Washington, DC: American Alliance for Health, Physical Education, Recreation, and Dance.

Hellison, D. (1983). Teaching self-responsibility (and more). *Journal of Physical Education, Recreation, and Dance, 54,* 23ff.

Hellison, D. (1985). *Goals and strategies for teaching physical education.* Champaign, IL: Human Kinetics.

Hellison, D. (1995). *Teaching responsibility through physical activity.* Champaign, IL: Human Kinetics.

Hellison, D., Lifka, B., & Georgiadis, N. (1990). Physical education for disadvantaged youth: A Chicago story. *Journal of Physical Education, Recreation and Dance, 61,* 36–46.

Higgins, A., Power, C., & Kohlberg, L. (1984). The relationship of moral atmosphere to judgments of responsibility. In W. Kurtines & J. Gewirtz (Eds.), *Morality, moral behavior, and moral development* (pp. 74–106). New York: Wiley.

Hyde, J.S. (1984). How large are gender differences in aggression? A developmental meta-analysis. *Developmental Psychology, 20,* 722–736.

Johnson, M.L. (1969). Construction of sportsmanship attitude scales. *Research Quarterly, 40,* 312–316.

Kidd, T., & Woodman, W. (1975). Sex and orientation toward winning in sport. *Research Quarterly, 46,* 476–483.

Knoppers, A. (1985). Professionalization of attitudes: A review and critique. *Quest, 37,* 92–102.

Knoppers, A., Schuiteman, J., & Love, B. (1986). Winning is not the only thing. *Sociology of Sport Journal, 3,* 43–56.

Knoppers, A., Schuiteman, J., & Love, B. (1988). Professional orientation of junior tennis players. *International Review for the Sociology of Sport, 23,* 243–254.

Kohlberg, L. (1969). Stage and sequence: The cognitive-developmental approach to socialization. In D.A. Goslin (Ed.), *Handbook of socialization theory and research* (pp. 347–480). Chicago: Rand McNally.

Kohlberg, L. (1970). Education for justice: A modern statement of the platonic view. In N.F. Sizer & T.R. Sizer (Eds.), *Moral education: Five lectures.* Cambridge, MA: Harvard University Press.

Kohlberg, L. (1976). Moral stages and moralization: The cognitive-developmental approach. In T. Lickona (Ed.), *Moral development and behavior: Theory, research and social issues* (pp. 31–53). New York: Holt, Rinehart and Winston.

Kohlberg, L. (1981). *Essays on moral development: The philosophy of moral development* (Vol. 1). San Francisco: Harper & Row.

Kohlberg, L. (1984). *Essays on moral development: The psychology of moral development* (Vol. 2). San Francisco: Harper & Row.

Kohlberg, L., & Candee, D. (1984). The relationship of moral judgment to moral action. In W. Kurtines & J. Gewirtz (Eds.), *Morality, moral behavior, and moral development* (pp. 52–73). New York: Wiley.

Kohlberg, L., Hickey, J., & Scharf, P. (1972). The justice structure of the prison: A theory and intervention. *Prison Journal, 51,* 3–14.

Kohlberg, L., & Higgins, A. (1987). School democracy and social interaction. In W. Kurtines & J. Gewirtz (Eds.), *Moral development through social interaction* (pp. 102–128) New York: Wiley.

Lakie, W.L. (1964). Expressed attitudes of various groups of athletes toward athletic competition. *Research Quarterly, 35,* 497–503.

Lee, M. (1977). *Expressed values of varsity football players, intramural football players, and non-football players.* Eugene, OR: Microform.

Lee, M. (1986). Moral and social growth through sport: The coach's role. In G. Gleeson (Ed.), *The growing child in competitive sport* (pp. 248–255). London: Hodder and Stoughton.

Lee, M. (1988). Values and responsibilities in children's sports. *Physical Education Review, 11,* 19–27.

Lee, M., & Cockman, M. (1995). Values in children's sport: Spontaneously expressed values among young athletes. *International Review for the Sociology of Sport, 30,* 337–351.

Loy, J., Birrell, S., & Rose, D. (1976). Attitudes held toward agonetic activities as a function of selected social identities. *Quest, 26,* 81–93.

Maloney, T.L., & Petrie, B. (1972). Professionalization of attitude toward play among Canadian school pupils as a function of sex, grade, and athletic participation. *Journal of Leisure Research, 4,* 184–195.

Mantel, R.C., & Vander Velden, L. (1974). The relationship between the professionalization of attitude toward play of preadolescent boys and participation in organized sport. In G. Sage (Ed.), *Sport and American society* (2nd ed., pp. 172–178). Reading, MA: Addison-Wesley.

Martin, D., & Dodder, R. (1993). A reassessment of the psychosocial foundations of sport scale. *Sociology of Sport Journal, 10,* 197–204.

McAfee, R. (1955). Sportsmanship attitudes of sixth, seventh, and eighth grade boys. *Research Quarterly, 26,* 120–121.

McElroy, M., & Kirkendall, D.R. (1980). Significant others and professionalized sport attitudes. *Research Quarterly for Exercise and Sport, 51,* 645–667.

Miller, S., Bredemeier, B., & Shields, D. (1997). Sociomoral education through physical education with at-risk children. *Quest, 49,* 114–129.

Nicholls, J.G. (1983). Conceptions of ability and achievement motivation: A theory and its implications for education. In S.G. Paris, G.M. Olson, & H.W. Stevenson (Eds.), *Learning and motivation in the classroom* (pp. 211–237). Hillsdale, NJ: Erlbaum.

Nicholls, J.G. (1989). *The competitive ethos and democratic education.* Cambridge, MA: Harvard University Press.

Nicholls, J.G. (1992). The general and the specific in the development and expression of achievement motivation. In G.C. Roberts (Ed.), *Motivation in sport and exercise* (pp. 31–54). Champaign, IL: Human Kinetics.

Nicholson, C. (1979). Some attitudes associated with sports participation among junior high school females. *Research Quarterly, 50,* 661–667.

Nixon, H. (1980). Orientation toward sports participation among college students. *Journal of Sport Behavior, 3,* 29–45.

Orlick, T. (1981). Positive socialization via cooperative games. *Developmental Psychology, 17,* 126–129.

Petrie, B. (1971a). Achievement orientations in adolescent attitudes toward play. *International Review of Sport Sociology, 6,* 89–99.

Petrie, B. (1971b). Achievement orientations in the motivation of Canadian university students toward physical activity. *Journal of the Canadian Association of Health, Physical Education, and Recreation, 37,* 7–13.

Piaget, J. (1932). *The moral judgment of the child.* London: Routledge & Kegan Paul.

Piaget, J. (1970). *Structuralism.* New York: Basic Books.

Piaget, J. (1971). *Biology and knowledge: An essay on the relations between organic regulations and cognitive processes.* Chicago: University of Chicago Press.

Power, F.C., Higgins, A., & Kohlberg, L. (1989). *Lawrence Kohlberg's approach to moral education.* New York: Columbia University Press.

Rest, J. (1984). The major components of morality. In W. Kurtines & J. Gewirtz (Eds.), *Morality, moral behavior, and moral development* (pp. 24–40). New York: Wiley.

Rest, J. (1986). *Moral development: Advances in research and theory.* New York: Praeger.

Rest, J. (1994). Background: Theory and research. In J. Rest & D. Narváez (Eds.), *Moral development in the professions: Psychology and applied ethics* (pp. 1–26). Hillsdale, NJ: Erlbaum.

Rest, J., Narváez, D., Bebeau, M., & Thoma, S. (1999). *Postconventional moral thinking: A neo-Kohlbergian approach.* Mahwah, NJ: Erlbaum.

Rokeach, M. (1973). *The nature of human values.* New York: Free Press.

Romance, T., Weiss, M., & Bockovan, J. (1986). A program to promote moral development through elementary school physical education. *Journal of Teachers of Physical Education, 5,* 126–136.

Rushton, J.P. (1982). Social learning theory and the development of prosocial behavior. In N. Eisenberg (Ed.), *The development of prosocial behavior* (pp. 77–105). New York: Academic Press.

Sage, G. (1980). Orientation toward sport of male and female intercollegiate athletes. *Journal of Sport Psychology, 2,* 355–362.

Shields, D. (1986). *Growing beyond prejudices.* Mystic, CT: Twenty-Third.

Shields, D., & Bredemeier, B. (1984). Sport and moral growth: A structural developmental perspective. In W. Straub & J. Williams (Eds.), *Cognitive sport psychology* (pp. 89–101). New York: Sport Science Associates.

Shields, D., & Bredemeier, B. (1995). *Character development and physical activity.* Champaign, IL: Human Kinetics.

Shields, D., Bredemeier, B., Gardner, D., & Bostrom, A. (1995). Leadership, cohesion and team norms regarding cheating and aggression. *Sociology of Sport Journal, 12,* 324–336.

Shields, D., Getty, D., & Bredemeier, B. (1991). *Moral Atmosphere Checklist.* Unpublished manuscript, University of California at Berkeley.

Silva, J. (1983). The perceived legitimacy of rule violating behavior in sport. *Journal of Sport Psychology, 5,* 438–448.

Snyder, E.E., & Spreitzer, E. (1979). Orientations toward sport: Intrinsic, normative, and extrinsic. *Journal of Sport Psychology, 1,* 170–175.

Solomon, G. (1997a). Character development: Does physical education affect character development in students? *Journal of Physical Education, Recreation and Dance, 68,* 38–41.

Solomon, G. (1997b). Fair play in the gymnasium: Improving social skills among elementary school students. *Journal of Physical Education, Recreation and Dance, 68,* 22–25.

Solomon, G., & Bredemeier, B. (1999). Children's moral conceptions of gender stratification in sport. *International Journal of Sport Psychology, 30,* 350–368.

Solomon, G., Bredemeier, B., & Shields, D. (1993). *Manual for the Gender Stratification Interview.* Unpublished manuscript, University of California, Berkeley.

Spreitzer, E., & Snyder, E. (1975). The psychosocial functions of sport as perceived by the general population. *International Review of Sport Sociology, 10,* 87–93.

Stephens, D., & Bredemeier, B. (1996). Moral atmosphere and judgments about aggression in girls' soccer: Relationships among moral and motivational variables. *Journal of Sport & Exercise Psychology, 18,* 158–173.

Stephens, D., Bredemeier, B., & Shields, D. (1997). Construction of a measure designed to assess players' descriptions and prescriptions for moral behavior in youth sport soccer. *International Journal of Sport Psychology, 28,* 370–390.

Stuart, M., & Ebbeck, V. (1995). The influence of perceived social approval on moral development in youth sport. *Pediatric Exercise Science, 7,* 270–280.

Theberge, N., Curtis, J., & Brown, B. (1982). Sex differences in orientation toward games: Tests of the sport involvement hypothesis. In A. Dunleavy, A. Miracle, & O.R. Rees (Eds.), *Studies in the sociology of sport* (pp. 285–308). Fort Worth: Texas Christian University Press.

Thompson, J. (1993). *Positive coaching: Building character and self-esteem through sports.* Dubuque, IA: Brown & Benchmark.

Vallerand, R.J., Brière, N.M., Blanchard, C., & Provencher, P. (1997). Development and validation of the Multidimensional Sportspersonship Orientations Scale (MSOS). *Journal of Sport & Exercise Psychology, 19,* 197–206.

Vallerand, R.J., Deshaies, P., & Cuerrier, J.P. (1997). On the effects of the social context on behavioral intentions of sportsmanship. *International Journal of Sport Psychology, 28,* 126–140.

Vallerand, R.J., Deshaies, P., Cuerrier, J.P., Brière, N.M., & Pelletier, L.G. (1996). Toward a multidimensional definition of sportsmanship. *Journal of Applied Sport Psychology, 8,* 123–135.

Vallerand, R.J., & Losier, G.F. (1994). Self-determined motivation and sportsmanship orientations: An assessment of their temporal relationship. *Journal of Sport & Exercise Psychology, 16,* 229–245.

Webb, H. (1969). Professionalization of attitudes toward play among adolescents. In G. Kenyon (Ed.), *Aspects of contemporary sport sociology* (pp. 161–179). Chicago: Athletic Institute.

Wright, W., & Rubin, S. (1989). The development of sportsmanship [Abstract]. *Proceedings of the 7th World Congress in Sport Psychology* (No. 155). Singapore.

CHAPTER 24

Youth in Sport
Psychological Considerations

ROBERT J. BRUSTAD, MEGAN L. BABKES, and ALAN L. SMITH

Organized sport participation for children is a social phenomenon. Tens of millions of children and adolescents around the world participate in some form of agency-sponsored or school-sponsored sport competition. Although it is difficult to obtain precise data on participation numbers in various countries around the world, participation estimates indicate that organized sport for children has a substantial and growing presence in many countries (De Knop, Engstrom, Skirstad, & Weiss, 1996). The extensive participatory involvement of children in organized sport programs has generated considerable attention and discussion in relation to the psychological effects of such participation. Fortunately, a growing body of systematic research has helped us to gain a much better perspective on psychological issues related to youth sport participation.

Since the publication of the previous edition of this chapter in *The Handbook of Research on Sport Psychology*, there has been a substantial amount of new research on the psychological dimensions of youth sport. The focus of much of this research has shifted to reflect contemporary perspectives in pediatric sport psychology. For example, the study of peer influence on children's sport participation is an area of research that has only begun to receive attention during this decade. Conversely, the study of participation motivation and attrition, which received close attention during the 1970s and 1980s, has not been heavily investigated of late. The organization of this chapter reflects current areas of emphasis in the youth sport knowledge base.

This chapter is organized into six sections. The first section focuses on theoretical perspectives on youth sport participation. Fortunately, recent research has typically utilized theoretically based approaches to the study of youth sport issues and theoretical limitations in our investigations no longer represent the same level of concern as was noted in the previous edition of this chapter. The second section focuses on the issue of psychological readiness. This issue revolves around concerns such as When are children ready to compete? and How will early sport involvement affect children? The third section addresses the participation motivation and attrition knowledge base. The knowledge in this area is fundamental to the understanding of children's participatory behavior. The fourth section focuses on children's affective outcomes in sport. The most common emotional outcomes of interest have been children's stress and anxiety responses and, in a more favorable light, their sport enjoyment characteristics. The fifth section addresses social influences on the psychological characteristics of children's sport involvement. Attention is directed toward understanding the role of parents, coaches, and peers in contributing to psychological outcomes for children. The final section of the chapter considers future directions for research in youth sport in those areas of study that receive the greatest current attention. Because children's ethical development in relation to organized sport participation receives full attention in the chapter by Shields and Bredemeier (this volume), this area of research is not addressed in this chapter.

It is important to note that most of the published research on psychological aspects of youth sport has been conducted in North America, particularly in the United States. Therefore, we urge caution in generalizing findings obtained in this cultural context to youngsters in other cultures or participating in sport programs differing substantially from those most common to North America. At minimum, however, the lines of investigation that have been pursued should prove useful in providing a framework from which to study youth sport in varying cultural settings.

THEORETICAL PERSPECTIVES ON YOUTH SPORT PARTICIPATION

The quality of sport involvement for youth is affected by social, psychological, and developmental influences. To best account for these diverse forms of influence, theoretical approaches are desirable, if not necessary, in providing a foundation from which youth sport issues can be examined and understood. Fortunately, most of the research conducted on psychological aspects of youth sport involvement has emerged from theory. Four different theoretical frameworks have been most commonly used: Harter's (1978, 1981) competence motivation theory, achievement goal orientation theory as applied to sport (Duda, 1992; Duda & Nicholls, 1992; Eccles & Harold, 1991; Nicholls, 1984, 1989), Eccles's expectancy-value theory (Eccles & Harold, 1991; Eccles-Parsons et al., 1983), and the sport commitment model (Scanlan & Simons, 1992; Scanlan, Simons, Carpenter, Schmidt, & Keeler, 1993). The major assumptions of each of these theories are described in this section, and specific studies using these theoretical frameworks are described in subsequent sections.

Competence Motivation Theory

Harter's (1978, 1981) competence motivation theory has been a popular theoretical framework from which to understand children's motivational and affective outcomes in sport. This theory is an extension of R. White's (1959) effectance motivation theory, which emerged in response to the popular behavioristic and reinforcement theories of motivation popular at the time. The fundamental precept of competence motivation theory is that individuals have an inherent desire to experience feelings of competence and these can be attained through mastery experiences in various achievement domains. Positive affective experiences (e.g., pride, satisfaction, pleasure) accompany feelings of mastery. In turn, these favorable emotional consequences fuel continued motivation. Harter's theory thus focuses attention on intrinsic sources of motivation that are demonstrated by desires to put forth effort, to seek challenges, and to display persistence even in the face of unsuccessful outcomes. However, these behaviors occur only when individuals perceive that they have the requisite competence and situational control to obtain desired outcomes. When they perceive that they lack the necessary competence to master an achievement challenge, or when they feel they have insufficient control over particular achievement outcomes, motivation toward mastery will be attenuated. In such circumstances, unfavorable affective experiences,

specifically anxiety, will be experienced in achievement circumstances. It is then unlikely that future mastery experiences will be pursued in the particular domain or that an extrinsic orientation toward achievement will be adopted.

A strength of Harter's theory is the integration of socialization and developmental considerations in the explanation of psychological, affective, and motivational outcomes for children. From a socialization perspective, parents are regarded as essential contributors in shaping children's self-perceptions of competence and control, their emotional responses to involvement in any particular domain, and the intrinsic or extrinsic nature of their subsequent motivation. The theory focuses particular attention on parents' responses to children's initial mastery strivings in any particular domain. From this perspective, if parents respond with encouragement and support to the child's attempts at mastery, they convey the idea that the child has natural capacity in this area and reinforce the child's motives toward competence. Conversely, if parents fail to provide support and encouragement for children's mastery strivings, particularly for the process of engaging in challenging achievement efforts, children are likely to infer that they lack ability in this area. Subsequently, these children will likely have low perceptions of competence and personal control, may experience anxiety in similar contexts, and will likely have less intrinsic motivation to pursue achievement tasks in that particular domain.

Developmental components of Harter's theory are also highly relevant to understanding socialization influence and motivational outcomes in sport. First, as Harter (1983) noted, the processes by which children and adolescents form perceptions of ability and the accuracy of these self-appraisals change in relation to age and cognitive development. These hypotheses have been supported by sport-related research (Horn, Glenn, & Wentzell, 1993; Horn & Weiss, 1991). Younger children rely more extensively on the feedback provided by significant adults, including parents and coaches, as well as game outcome in forming perceptions of their competence. During later childhood and through middle adolescence (ages 10 to 15 years), children place greater reliance on peer comparison and peer evaluation in forming these self-evaluations. Finally, during later adolescence (ages 16 to 18 years), individuals utilize self-referenced forms of information, including goal achievement, speed of skill improvement, effort exerted, and level of attraction to the sport or skill, as a means of formulating beliefs about their capacity in sport. This knowledge has implications for understanding the relative socialization influence of adults and peers in shaping motivational aspects of children in sport and accentuates the need to consider the nature and strength of parental and peer influence in relation to children's cognitive-developmental status (Brustad, 1996b).

Harter's theoretical perspective has been widely used in pediatric sport research. Her approach has been applied to the study of participation motivation and attrition (e.g., Klint & Weiss, 1987), children's sport-related self-perception characteristics (e.g., Horn & Hasbrook, 1987; Weiss, Ebbeck, & Horn, 1997; Williams, 1994), affective outcomes for children in sport (e.g., Brustad, 1988; Brustad & Weiss, 1987), parental influence on psychological dimensions of children's sport involvement (Babkes & Weiss, 1999; Weiss & Hayashi, 1995), and intrinsic and extrinsic motivational orientations toward sport involvement (Weiss, Bredemeier, & Shewchuk, 1985).

Achievement Goal Theory

Achievement goal theory (Duda, 1992; Duda & Nicholls, 1992; Nicholls, 1984, 1989) has been extensively used in sport psychology during the past decade for research on sport motivation and behavior. This theory shares common roots with other prominent cognitively based theoretical perspectives on achievement (e.g., Ames, 1992; Dweck, 1986; Harter, 1978) in that the theory places considerable emphasis on individuals' desire to experience feelings of competence as a fundamental incentive in human motivation. However, a primary contribution of achievement goal orientation theory is that it directs attention to individual differences in the subjective meaning of achievement to individuals. Specifically, achievement goal theory proposes that individuals can possess a self-referenced, or mastery-oriented, view on achievement in which the demonstration of competence is evidenced by personal improvement. Alternatively, individuals can adhere to an other-referenced, or ego-oriented, perspective on competence in which normative perceptions dominate an individual's appraisal of success or failure outcomes. From this perspective, competence is demonstrated when an individual outperforms others and is thus a social comparison process.

The effect of one's achievement goal orientation on motivationally related behaviors needs to be considered in combination with self-perceptions of ability. Ego-oriented individuals with high perceived competence are anticipated to approach achievement tasks with high motivation because they have the opportunity to demonstrate personal competence. However, ego-oriented individuals with low perceived competence are hypothesized to avoid achievement settings in which the demonstration of low ability is likely. Thus, we would anticipate that children with a

strong ego orientation and unfavorable perceptions of competence would be less inclined to participate in sport and more likely to consider quitting when involved (Roberts, 1993). However, task-oriented youngsters are less affected by perceptions of competence in relation to motivation. Because task-oriented participants assess achievement in relation to personal standards and improvement, their motivation should not be as strongly affected by lower perceptions of competence. Thus, children with a strong mastery orientation may have high motivation in sport contexts even if they possess low perceived sport competence.

Achievement goal theory is highly applicable to many important issues in youth sport. The theory has been applied to the understanding of children's beliefs about the purposes of sport involvement (Treasure & Roberts, 1994), children's participatory involvement and attrition (Whitehead, 1995), children's sport-related achievement-related beliefs (Duda, Fox, Biddle, & Armstrong, 1992; Treasure & Roberts, 1994), and parental socialization processes as they affect children's achievement orientations toward sport (Ebbeck & Becker, 1994; Hom, Duda, & Miller, 1993).

The developmental roots of achievement goal theory make it most amenable for use by youth sport researchers (Duda, 1987). Research conducted in academic (Nicholls, 1978; Nicholls & Miller, 1984) and sport (Fry & Duda, 1997) contexts suggests that children's understanding of achievement outcomes is affected by their capacity to understand the relative influence of task difficulty, effort, and ability in contributing to these outcomes. This line of research further indicates that children do not necessarily have a full adultlike capacity to differentiate among these forms of influence on achievement until late childhood. Cognitive-developmental status has implications for children's motivational characteristics in sport because younger children may lack the capacity to accurately appraise their capacity or ability. And because ability perceptions are fundamental to motivational processes, subsequent motivation may be affected. The reader is referred to Duda and Hall (this volume) for a more thorough account of achievement goal theory and for a review of research assessing the theory's fundamental contentions.

Eccles's Expectancy-Value Theory

Eccles's theoretical model (Eccles & Harold, 1991; Eccles-Parsons et al., 1983) attempts to explain children's motivational processes in relation to socialization influences, specifically parental belief systems. This theoretical model has roots in the expectancy-value motivational framework advanced by Atkinson (1964). A primary focus of Eccles's research has been on explaining gender differences in children's achievement-related characteristics, motivated behavior patterns, and activity choices (e.g., Eccles, 1987; Eccles & Harold, 1991). In Eccles's model, children's activity choices are related to their performance expectations, or activity-specific ability perceptions, and to the perceived value, or importance, of a particular area of achievement in relation to other possible pursuits. Thus, children's domain-specific perceptions of competence, in combination with the perceived value or importance of varying achievement domains, explain children's levels of interest, effort, and persistence in sport and other achievement contexts.

Children's success expectancies and perceptions of value are strongly related to parental beliefs and behaviors. From this viewpoint, parental beliefs about their child's aptitudes, temperament, and talents impact the types of opportunities the child is provided as well as the level of encouragement and support while involved. A particularly influential role of parents in the socialization process is in their function as interpreters of achievement outcomes for their children. In this regard, parents help to shape children's own perceptions of competence and subsequent expectations for achievement. Furthermore, parents assist children in forming attributions about the reasons underlying successful or unsuccessful achievement outcomes in various domains. Thus, in line with parental expectations, children may interpret their success and failure outcomes as attributable to ability (or lack of ability), effort, or task difficulty characteristics.

In Eccles's theory, parental beliefs and behaviors also shape children's perceptions of the relative value of various achievement domains. This occurs in relation to parents' own beliefs about the relative importance of various achievement areas as worthy of pursuit, and by parental gender-related stereotypes. For example, if parents have strong gender-related stereotypes, they may be less likely to encourage their daughter to achieve in sport or mathematics than would parents without strong stereotypical views. In essence, Eccles's model holds that parents' belief systems in relation to their perceptions of a child's natural abilities, in combination with parental views on the value or importance of various achievement domains, underlie parental socialization practices. Because children are likely to internalize their parents' belief systems, their perceived competence and value orientations may be fundamentally shaped by parental socialization processes.

Eccles's theory has been employed to help explain children's interest in sport in relation to gender and in comparison to other achievement areas (Eccles & Harold, 1991; Jacobs & Eccles, 1992). It also has been a primary socialization perspective utilized to explain differences in children's interest and involvement in physical activity behaviors in both sport and nonsport contexts (Brustad, 1993a, 1996a; Eccles & Harold, 1991; Kimiecik & Horn, 1998; Kimiecik, Horn, & Shurin, 1996). Such investigations have yielded support for the fundamental contentions of Eccles's theory.

Sport Commitment Model

A fourth theoretical model appropriate for the study of children's participatory behavior in sport is the sport commitment model (Scanlan, Carpenter, Schmidt, Simons, & Keeler, 1993; Scanlan & Simons, 1992). As with the preceding theories, the sport commitment model has roots elsewhere, in this case, social exchange theory (Kelley & Thibaut, 1978) and theories of commitment to interpersonal relationships (Rusbult, 1983). Sport commitment is considered to be a "psychological construct representing the desire and resolve to continue sport participation" (Scanlan & Simons, 1992, p. 201). In essence, sport commitment is synonymous with the level of psychological attachment individuals have to their sport involvement. And understanding psychological attachment can be useful in explaining individual differences in participation motivation and motivational levels.

Sport commitment is believed to be affected by five factors: sport enjoyment, involvement alternatives, personal investments, involvement opportunities, and social constraints. Sport enjoyment is the amount of pleasure, liking, or fun that the child experiences in sport. Involvement alternatives represent the attractiveness of competing activities. Personal investments are resources (e.g., time, money) that have been put into the activity that cannot be readily recovered if the child discontinues participation. Involvement opportunities are those benefits that accrue from sport participation that are not provided through other activities. Finally, social constraints represent normative expectations that contribute to feelings of obligation to remain in the activity. Parental expectations could constitute one form of social constraint. High levels of sport enjoyment, personal investment, involvement opportunities, and social constraints in combination with limited involvement alternatives should result in high levels of motivation for children to remain in sport.

The sport commitment model has been used to elucidate the motivational characteristics of young athletes (Scanlan, Carpenter, et al., 1993; Scanlan, Simons, et al., 1993). Research employing the sport commitment model has highlighted the importance of sport enjoyment, personal investments, and involvement opportunities as fundamental contributors to sport commitment in young athletes (Carpenter, Scanlan, Simons, & Lobel, 1993). In a recent investigation, Carpenter and Coleman (1998) assessed the relationship between hypothesized determinants of sport commitment across a season for elite young British cricket players, age 9 to 17 years. These authors found that changes in sport enjoyment and involvement opportunities were related to changes in sport commitment in the anticipated directions.

PSYCHOLOGICAL READINESS FOR SPORT COMPETITION

At what age is it appropriate for children to commence their participation in organized sport? In the United States, children can initiate their involvement in swimming and gymnastics at age 3 years; by age 5 in track and field, baseball, and wrestling; and by age 6 in soccer (Martens, 1986). Comparable opportunities for organized sport participation exist in many countries, as evidence indicates that similar early competitive involvement is available to youngsters in Canada, Australia, and Brazil, among other nations (Ferreira, 1986; Robertson, 1986; Valeriote & Hansen, 1986). Although precise data are not available for organized sport involvement levels prior to age 12 years in the United States (Ewing & Seefeldt, 1996) or other countries, a trend exists toward earlier and more specialized sport participation at younger ages. In response to concerns about potentially deleterious aspects of early specialization and the psychological and emotional risks that may result from intensive early participation, there has been a movement during the past decade toward placing age limits for youngsters in international and professional competitions in sports such as gymnastics and tennis. Whether we are discussing children's entry into organized sport or children's and adolescents' participation in sport at elevated levels of competition, concerns about the psychological and emotional readiness of children to compete have been at the forefront.

Readiness has been characterized as the level of maturation or experience needed for learning or some similar benefit to be realized (Seefeldt, 1996). The concept of readiness emerges out of developmental perspectives that recognize that children are not miniature adults with regard to their physical, cognitive, social, and emotional maturity. The issue of readiness should also be examined from a cost-benefit perspective. Specifically, in what ways might sport participation contribute to the child's development, and in what respects might such participation

negatively affect the child? At what age, or developmental level, is it appropriate for children to begin structured sport competition? These issues are subsumed by the general topic of psychological readiness.

The psychological readiness for children to compete has rarely been considered in establishing age-related standards for sport participation. For the most part, entry standards take into account only the typical physical size and motor skill characteristics of youngsters (Malina, 1986). Unfortunately, age-related standards are not able to accommodate the tremendous variability that exists in maturity of children at a given chronological age, nor are they established with a concern for the psychological and emotional consequences for children of premature participation. What are the most important dimensions of psychological readiness, and what are the criteria we should utilize in making judgments in relation to this issue? This issue can be addressed in relation to two important dimensions of readiness: motivational and cognitive readiness.

Motivational Readiness

Motivational readiness refers to the extent to which children are motivated to participate in sport because of their own interest in and attraction to the activity. In this regard, the relative roles of children and parents in contributing to the decision on the child's sport involvement need to be examined. Obviously, if the child's participation reflects primarily a parental decision, it might be assumed that the child is not necessarily motivationally ready to participate and, thus, might not experience all of the potential benefits.

A second component of motivational readiness for children relates to their developmentally related interest in comparing skills with others (Passer, 1996; Roberts, 1980; Scanlan, 1996). Social comparison processes represent a natural developmental occurrence by means of which children seek out opportunities to assess personal abilities in various areas of achievement in relation to the skills of others. This process has an important function, for as children gain a better appreciation for their abilities in various areas of achievement, they make subsequent participatory decisions based on these competency beliefs. From a developmental perspective, research indicates that children do not typically begin to show an interest in social comparison processes until at least age 5 or 6 years (Veroff, 1969), and that it is more common around age 7 and 8 years that children demonstrate an active interest in social comparison (Butler, 1989; Ruble, 1983). Thus, this aspect of motivational readiness is unlikely to be present for youngsters prior to age 7 or 8 years.

Cognitive Readiness

In relation to children's cognitive readiness, an important consideration involves children's capacity for abstract reasoning. The most popular participatory sports for youngsters are typically team sports such as soccer and basketball. These sports place unique cognitive demands on participants if the team is to function effectively. Specifically, team sports require participants to understand that unique roles, responsibilities, and relational characteristics exist within a team framework. As Coakley (1986) has argued, team sports require participants to have the role-taking capacities necessary to assume another's perspective. Role-taking abilities are particularly essential in team sports that involve large numbers of children participating in games that involve considerable amounts of teamwork and strategy in response to the actions of an opposing team. Children's role-taking limitations are particularly apparent when we see young children swarm to a soccer ball like bees to honey while ignoring their positional responsibilities on the field. Research suggests that children do not have the role-taking abilities necessary to fully understand another person's point of view until roughly 8 to 10 years of age (Selman, 1971, 1976). With regard to the readiness issue, the greatest potential drawback to premature sport participation occurs when coaches and parents expect more from children in team sport contexts than their cognitive maturational level would warrant. In such circumstances, children might experience considerable frustration and could lose interest in subsequent sport participation because they do not have the cognitive capacity to handle the demands placed on them. However, if children's fundamental abstract reasoning limitations are recognized by adults and unreasonable strategic expectations are not placed on them, then poorly coordinated team efforts such as "beehive soccer" are not necessarily of major concern as long as young athletes retain the enjoyment and excitement of participation.

A second important component of cognitive readiness for sport participation pertains to children's ability to understand the causes of performance outcomes. In sport, a large number of factors can contribute to achievement outcomes (e.g., effort, ability, opponent's ability, task difficulty, and luck). A body of knowledge suggests, however, that children do not effectively distinguish among these various contributors to achievement outcomes until around age 10 to 12 years (Fry & Duda, 1997; Nicholls, 1978; Nicholls, Jagacinski, & Miller, 1986). For example, Fry and Duda found that until about age 11 years, children do not make a clear distinction between effort and ability as

contributors to successful and unsuccessful performance outcomes. As such, children cannot accurately estimate their own ability, and this has motivational implications.

As a consequence of cognitive-developmental characteristics, children are heavily reliant on adult informational sources in shaping their beliefs about competence. Therefore, adults exert a powerful function in shaping children's self-perception characteristics and motivational processes. Thus, concerns about readiness for participation must also include the types of interactions anticipated between adults and children in any sport context.

If psychological readiness for competition is perceived as a match between the psychological capacities of the child and the demands of the sport, it would be wise to consider restructuring many youth sport programs to make them more compatible with children's developmentally related capacities during the years that correspond with peak sport involvement. Such a restructuring would place greater emphasis on the dimensions of fun, excitement, and skill development during the early and middle childhood years while reducing the emphasis on strategic elements and competitive outcomes. One modification that is quite easy to achieve is to reduce the number of players on sport teams so that there is less emphasis on strategic responsibilities and more opportunities for action. In general, emphasis on strategic and competitive elements should not be introduced prior to later childhood.

It is not possible to identify a single age at which competitive sport is appropriate for youngsters because children differ in their own levels of readiness and because various sports place unique demands on youngsters. Coakley (1986, p. 59) recommended that children should not begin competing prior to age 8 years but commented, "It is never too early to engage in expressive physical activities." As an expressive physical activity, youth sport should be structured so that it meets developmentally appropriate outcomes for its participants. By focusing on skill development and sport enjoyment goals during childhood rather than emphasizing competitive strategies, children will be more likely to attain the positive psychological outcomes they deserve.

PARTICIPATION MOTIVATION AND ATTRITION

Research related to children's motives for participation in sport and the factors underlying their decisions to discontinue sport involvement are two of the most important lines of investigation in pediatric sport psychology. Examination of the reasons why children choose to initiate and maintain involvement provides insight into the meaning of sport participation in the lives of children and in relation to peer cultures. Likewise, the exploration of why children decide to terminate their sport participation is an important research topic because of concerns that attrition, or dropout behavior, is the consequence of undesirable psychological, social, or affective experiences.

The study of participation motivation and attrition in youth sport is complex. Motives for participation in and reasons for disengagement from sport must be examined in light of the variety of social, psychological, and developmental factors that operate during childhood and adolescence. Furthermore, participatory involvement and discontinuance need to be considered from appropriate theoretical frameworks to make sense of these outcomes.

Participation Motivation Research

The most systematic attempts to ascertain age-related sport participation patterns among youth in North America were conducted during the late 1970s through the Michigan Youth Sport Institute (State of Michigan, 1976, 1978a, 1978b). These studies revealed that involvement levels in popular and traditional sports such as baseball, softball, swimming, and basketball increased dramatically for both girls and boys from age 5 to 11 years. Research findings from the same series of studies also suggested a sharp decline in participatory involvement between the ages of 11 and 13 years. More recently, findings from a study conducted by the Athletic Footwear Association (1990) support the results of previous research and indicate that a significant decrease in children's sport participation, in both school and nonschool contexts, begins around the age of 10 years and continues through the adolescent years. Overall, the best available estimates are that, on average, 35% of youth age 10 to 18 years choose to terminate their participation in sport each year (Gould, 1987). Although age-related participatory trends have rarely been subject to dispute, the underlying contributors to these outcomes is less understood.

In one of the original studies on the topic, Sapp and Haubenstricker (1978) assessed the participatory motives of over 1,000 male and female athletes age 11 to 18 years involved in agency-sponsored sport programs in the state of Michigan. They found that "having fun" and "improving skills" were cited by an overwhelming majority of participants as the primary motives for their sport involvement. Gill, Gross, and Huddleston (1985) examined motives for sport involvement in 1,100 young male and female sport camp participants. Their results indicated that children place a high value on having fun, improving their skills, learning new skills, playing for the challenge, and being physically fit as reasons for sport involvement. Gould, Feltz, and Weiss (1985) found that fun, fitness, skill improvement, the social atmosphere of the team, and a desire for challenge were the most highly rated factors associated with participation by young swimmers. Longhurst and Spink (1987), in their study of Australian children, found that the most frequently cited participatory motives for these youngsters were improving skills, being physically fit, enjoying competition, learning new skills, and the desire for challenge.

In their review of the participation motivation literature, Weiss and Petlichkoff (1989) concluded that the most commonly identified motives can be classified into four general categories: competence (learning and improving skills), affiliation (establishing and maintaining friendships), fitness, and fun. Although researchers have used a variety of measures and examined young athletes' motives across gender, culture, and sport type, these four categories seem to best represent children's reasons for sport participation. Furthermore, it should be recognized that most children cite multiple motives for their sport participation (Petlichkoff, 1996; Weiss & Petlichkoff, 1989).

Given the consistency of findings in relation to children's participatory motives, more recent research has begun to pursue other avenues of investigation. In a unique study, Brodkin and Weiss (1990) examined differences in participatory motives in relation to age among competitive swimmers throughout the life span. In their study, they found that younger children (age 6 to 9 years) rated fun as the most important component of involvement in competitive swimming, whereas older children and younger adolescents (age 10 to 14 years) and high school/college-age swimmers (age 15 to 22 years) rated social status to be the most important dimension of participation. Although affiliation opportunities were important to swimmers in all age groups, these findings highlight the increasing salience of social acceptance and favorable social evaluation during the late childhood and early adolescent years.

A related area of investigation involves children's attraction to physical activity in general, which can include both sport and nonsport forms of physical activity. Attraction is a construct that represents the extent to which children desire to participate in physical activity in accordance with the appeal of various aspects of involvement. Attraction is conceptualized as multidimensional in nature, and five dimensions of physical activity attraction have been identified in children age 6 to 12 years (Brustad, 1993a). These dimensions of attraction include children's interest in physical activity participation due to liking of games and sport, liking of vigorous exercise, perceived importance of sport and physical activity for health-related reasons, peer acceptance opportunities, and liking of physical exertion.

Sport Attrition Research

As with the research on children's sport participatory motives, the bulk of the research on children's discontinuance from sport was conducted during the late 1970s and early 1980s. Much of the initial research on children's withdrawal from competitive sport was sparked by concerns that children's discontinuation from competitive sport was the consequence of an overly stressful sport environment. Orlick's (1973, 1974) studies, in particular, were instrumental in contributing to the research attention devoted to this topic. Orlick interviewed youth sport participants, ranging in age from 7 to 18 years, about their intended future involvement in sport. He found that the majority of youngsters who decided that they would not continue their participation in sport during the following season cited negative aspects of involvement as the reasons for their intended withdrawal. These negative aspects included lack of playing time, the competitive emphasis of the program, and an overemphasis on winning. Orlick's findings suggested that the structure and climate of youth sport was inadequate in meeting children's needs and was responsible for dropout behavior.

Sapp and Haubenstricker's (1978) subsequent research painted a much less gloomy portrait of the youth sport attrition process. Overall, they found that the incidence of youth sport withdrawal was higher than had been anticipated, with 37% of youngsters in the 11- to 18-year age group and 24% of the children in the 6 to 10 age group indicating that they planned to not return to sport participation the following season. However, the negative experiences that were prevalent in Orlick's studies were infrequently reported by these youngsters. In fact, negative experiences were cited by fewer than 15% of the children as reasons for their sport withdrawal. The more frequently cited reasons were "work" by the older age group and "other reasons" by the younger children.

Gould, Feltz, Horn, and Weiss (1982) examined motives for attrition for 50 former swimmers, age 10 to 18 years. The most frequently cited reasons for withdrawal were "other things to do," "not enough fun," "wanted to participate in another sport," and "not as good as I wanted to be." Overall, 84% of the swimmers identified factors related to

conflict of interest as an important or very important motive for choosing to not remain involved in competitive swimming.

One of the major limitations of early research was that individuals in these studies were typically classified as either a "participant" or a "nonparticipant" when participation could actually be considered along a continuum of involvement (Weiss & Petlichkoff, 1989). Robinson and Carron's (1982) study diverged from the traditional approach by categorizing young football players as either dropouts, starters, or nonstarters. Findings from this study revealed that dropouts, in contrast to the starters and nonstarters, did not generally feel as much social support for their participation on the team, did not have favorable perceptions of their own ability, and were more likely to view the coach as an autocrat. Perhaps most important, this research encouraged future investigators to reconsider their approach to classifying individuals' participatory status.

Klint and Weiss (1986) examined the withdrawal motives of 37 former competitive gymnasts. Overall, the former gymnasts indicated that the major reasons for withdrawing from the sport were the desire to pursue other interests, feeling excessive pressure, not having enough fun, and the extensive time commitment required by their sport. The findings from this study suggested that the nature of the demands of particular sports are strongly related to the motives cited by youngsters for leaving that sport.

More recent research has examined attrition in relation to individual differences in level of sport involvement. Lindner, Johns, and Butcher (1991) provided a perspective on different types of sport dropouts. They distinguished among three different types of dropouts, which they referred to as the sampler dropout, the participant dropout, and the transfer dropout. They characterized the sampler dropout as a child who has not made a serious commitment to playing a particular sport and may in fact have participated for only a short period of time (i.e., one season). This type of individual is likely to be a younger participant because children are much more inclined to sample new activities than are adolescents or adults. The participant dropout is represented by a child who invested many years and likely competed at different levels of the sport, but subsequently discontinued participation because that sport no longer met the child's individual needs and goals. The transfer dropout is described as an individual who withdraws from one sport but participates in another sport. This individual often reenters sport at another level or participates in multiple sports simultaneously at various levels over time. Thus, it seems evident that many youngsters may discontinue sport involvement for entirely different reasons and that sport discontinuance should not necessarily be viewed as a negative occurrence.

Theoretical Perspectives on Children's Participatory Motivation and Attrition

Much of the initial participation motivation research was descriptive in nature and, thus, difficult to interpret in line with contemporary theoretical perspectives. Three theoretical frameworks were identified by Gould (1987) as highly appropriate for the examination of the study of participation motivation and attrition. These frameworks were competence motivation theory and achievement goal theory, which have been previously described, and Smith's (1986) model of sport withdrawal, which includes components from social exchange (Thibaut & Kelley, 1959) and cognitive-affective theories.

Competence motivation theory has been used on a number of occasions for the study of participation motivation. According to Harter's (1978, 1981) theory, when children believe they have adequate ability and situational control in a particular domain of achievement, they will engage in mastery behaviors. Thus, competence motivation theory predicts that sport participants will have higher perceptions of competence and control than nonparticipants and dropouts. Consistent with the contentions of the theory, Roberts, Kleiber, and Duda (1981) observed that sport participants, in contrast to nonparticipants, had more favorable self-perceptions of physical and cognitive competence. Similarly, Feltz and Petlichkoff (1983) found that active sport participants had higher levels of perceived competence than did sport dropouts.

Klint and Weiss (1987) investigated the relationship between competence perceptions and participatory motives in young gymnasts. This study revealed that gymnasts high in perceived physical competence were more motivated by skill development reasons than were their counterparts with lower perceived physical competence. Similarly, gymnasts with higher perceived social competence were more motivated by affiliation opportunities than their counterparts with lower social competence perceptions. Klint and Weiss contended that these findings were consistent with the predictions of competence motivation theory because the gymnasts were motivated to demonstrate competence in those areas in which they perceived themselves to possess high ability.

Similar to competence motivation theory, achievement goal theory regards self-perceptions of competence as critical components of motivated behavior. Achievement goal theory, however, also considers individual differences in the subjective meaning of achievement to be highly influential in affecting motivation. With regard to participatory behaviors and motivational patterns in achievement contexts, this theory proposes that ability perceptions and goal perspectives interact to influence behavior. Because task-involved individuals define success as personal improvement, they should select appropriately challenging tasks and display effort and persistence while engaged even if they possess a low perception of competence. Conversely, ego-oriented persons are concerned primarily with demonstrating competence relative to others; thus, if they perceive low personal ability, they will likely avoid activities that highlight the manifestation of this lack of ability. As applied to sport involvement and attrition, achievement goal theory proposes that task-oriented individuals should be motivated to participate, and remain, in sport as long as an appropriate level of challenge is present. In contrast, ego-oriented persons are likely to engage in sport only if they perceive that they have more ability than others and are, therefore, prone to terminate their sport involvement when they possess less ability than others.

Cognitive-developmental changes in children's appraisal of their competence may also have an effect on motivational processes in sport. Research suggests that, with age, youngsters become increasingly capable of differentiating the roles of ability and effort in contributing to success and failure outcomes (Nicholls, 1978; Nicholls et al., 1986). Cognitive-developmental processes also have implications for the persistence of youngsters in sport (Duda, 1987; Roberts, 1984). Roberts speculated that the high incidence of dropout occurring during late childhood and early adolescence might be partly attributable to children's increasing capacity to accurately appraise personal ability. He suggested that ego-oriented youngsters should be particularly predisposed to drop out of sport if it becomes apparent that they do not possess as much ability as others. Although many youngsters cite reasons unrelated to ability for dropping out, Roberts suggested that the stated reasons may be superficial and socially desirable explanations that mask underlying self-perceptions of low ability.

A few studies have turned to achievement goal theory to explore youth sport participation motivation. Petlichkoff (1988) examined the relationship between achievement goal perspectives and participatory behavior in 557 high school athletes during a basketball season. As a first step in this study, she categorized these youngsters according to their involvement status as either starters, survivors, cuttees, or dropouts. Results did not reveal a meaningful relationship between goal orientation and participatory status, but did find that youth who were task-oriented were more satisfied with their sport experiences than were ego-oriented youngsters. In this study, the perceived ability levels of the athletes and former athletes were not assessed.

Duda (1989) examined the relationship between goal perspectives and sport participation and persistence in 871 high school students. Subjects were categorized as (1) current participants in organized and recreational sport, (2) current organized-sport participants only, (3) current recreational-sport participants only, (4) sport dropouts, or (5) those never involved in sport. Findings from this study indicated that youth who were current participants in organized/recreational sport or organized sport reported stronger task and ego motivational orientations than the youth who were dropouts or nonparticipants.

Burton and Martens (1986) contrasted wrestlers and former wrestlers, age 7 to 17 years, on levels of perceived competence, significant other influence, and additional motivational factors. They found that current wrestlers demonstrated higher levels of perceived ability, more functional attributions, and more positive wrestling expectancies and valued wrestling success more than did the wrestlers who had dropped out. Although the wrestling dropouts demonstrated lower perceptions of competence than the current wrestlers, they rarely cited ability-related reasons as being responsible for their decision to discontinue wrestling. Although the findings of this research were discussed by the authors in light of achievement goal theory, interpretation of these findings is complicated because the goal orientations of the wrestlers were never directly assessed.

Smith's (1986) conceptual model of sport withdrawal is a third viable approach for the examination of youth sport attrition. Integral to this explanation of sport withdrawal processes is the distinction between sport *dropout* and sport *burnout*. Smith contends that sport dropout results largely from a change of interests or a logical cost-benefit analysis by the athlete, whereas burnout is withdrawal from the sport due to chronic stress. He incorporated two theoretical perspectives into this conceptual model to distinguish between dropout and burnout behavior.

With regard to sport dropout, Smith (1986) stated that the perspective provided by social exchange theory (Thibaut & Kelley, 1959) best explains the findings of the attrition research conducted to date. Social exchange theory maintains that behavior is motivated by the desire to maximize the probability of positive experiences and minimize the probability of negative experiences. According to social exchange theory, individuals will continue to engage in a given activity even when the costs outweigh the benefits until an appropriate alternative activity becomes available. This explanation of sport dropout is consistent with two patterns of findings in the attrition literature. First, the most frequently cited motive for sport dropout is "having other things to do." Because sport attrition rates are high during adolescence, and because youngsters do have many alternative opportunities available to them, it is logical from this perspective to expect high rates of sport attrition during adolescence. Second, because most youngsters cite multiple motives for both sport participation and attrition, it seems apparent that youngsters' participatory behavior is not the result of a single factor, but likely to be influenced by a weighing of the costs and benefits of continued participation. To the extent that youngsters engage in a rational cost-benefit analysis regarding their sport participation, social exchange theory may be a viable explanation of sport dropout.

Petlichkoff's (1988) research also included a cost-benefit analysis of sport dropout behavior. In her study of basketball players, findings revealed that starters and nonstarters had higher levels of satisfaction than did survivors, dropouts, or cuttees. The survivors, however, had lower levels of satisfaction than did the dropouts. These results suggested that the survivors either had fewer attractive alternative opportunities to pursue or perceived additional "costs" to dropping out. This conclusion was supported by the survivors' reports that they perceived a strong negative stigma to dropping out and that this "cost" was a factor in their decision to remain on the team.

Although Smith proposed that social exchange theory best explains sport dropout, he proposed an alternative explanation for the occurrence of youth sport burnout. Burnout is characterized by the desire to withdraw from sport because of a need to escape stressful experiences, rather than due to a cost-benefit appraisal. This rationale is best explained by cognitive-affective theories of stress (e.g., Lazarus, 1966). Currently, burnout is not considered a frequent occurrence among the majority of youth sport participants who choose to disengage from athletics. However, in circumstances of very intense sport involvement, this conceptual perspective may help to explain participant attrition.

Future Directions in Participation Motivation Research

Future research on youth sport participation and attrition should focus more on the processes underlying children's participatory experiences. Weiss and Petlichkoff (1989) proposed that longitudinal research on children's participation motivation would enhance the knowledge base on how motives change across various participatory phases of sport involvement. Similarly, Petlichkoff (1996) suggested that youth sport organizations could track their participants by administering pre- and postparticipation assessments that would identify the specific programmatic, social, and intrapersonal factors that affect participation motivation in youth sport. In addition, inductive methodologies may provide additional insight into the participatory experiences and sport withdrawal of youngsters.

Little attention has been directed to the influence of developmental factors in youngsters' descriptions of their motives. For example, both children and adolescents may report that they participate for fun, but a child may consider fun to be related to the play aspects of sport involvement, whereas the adolescent may view fun as the excitement of competition. Only Brodkin and Weiss (1990) have addressed developmental differences in motives for sport participation, and they found age-related differences in participatory motives for competitive swimmers across the life span. Future research needs to consider developmental characteristics that influence children's and adolescents' participatory behaviors.

An additional shortcoming has been that the majority of the research on youth sport participatory motivation has focused only on children's initial motives for becoming engaged in sport or examined these motives at only one point in time (Weiss & Chaumeton, 1992). This approach suggests that children's motives for participation in sport remain stable over time and assumes that these psychological characteristics are not continually reshaped by intrapersonal, developmental, and social influences during the course of involvement. Although considerable attention has been devoted to the study of participation motivation and attrition, there is a considerable amount of work to do to advance our understanding of these phenomena.

AFFECTIVE OUTCOMES FOR CHILDREN IN SPORT

Understanding children's emotional responses to organized sport competition has been one of the major areas of research interest for youth sport investigators over the past two decades. Much of the initial research on this topic was fueled by concerns that children's sport competition might be too stressful or provoke excessive anxiety in children. Further research explorations have concentrated on understanding factors that contribute to individual differences in children's affective response to sport as well as on identifying correlates and sources of positive affective outcomes. This line of research is important because the nature of

children's emotional experiences in sport is likely related both to their psychological well-being and to their desire to continue participation in the organized sport context.

Historically, there has been considerable concern expressed in the United States about the amount of psychological stress that children experience as a consequence of sport involvement (Wiggins, 1996). Various educational, medical, and recreational leaders have discouraged sport involvement for children because of beliefs that competitive youth sport was too stressful and resulted in unfavorable short- and long-term emotional and psychological outcomes (Brower, 1978; Smilkstein, 1980). Concern has also existed that high levels of stress and anxiety contribute to children's dropping out of sport at an early age (Orlick, 1974). Although the participation motivation literature is not strongly supportive of the notion that a large proportion of youngsters discontinue participation because of aversive psychological experiences, some studies have found that "too much stress" or "not having enough fun" are reasons cited by some youngsters for dropout (Klint & Weiss, 1986; Orlick, 1974).

Research on unfavorable affective outcomes for youngsters in sport has focused almost exclusively on anxiety outcomes. Anxiety has been examined in relation to both state and trait characteristics. Competitive trait anxiety is a stable, or enduring, characteristic of the individual that reflects a person's generalized tendency to perceive competition as threatening (Martens, 1977). In contrast, competitive state anxiety is a situation-specific form of anxiety that involves feelings of apprehension or tension "right now." It is important to note that competitive trait and state anxiety are related, as children with higher trait anxiety are more likely to perceive competitive situations as stressful and to experience greater state anxiety in various contexts (Gould, Horn, & Spreeman, 1983a; Scanlan & Lewthwaite, 1984).

Levels of Stress and Anxiety in Youth Sport

Understanding the extent of stress and anxiety for young athletes has been one of the most important undertakings for youth sport researchers. In addressing the question: How stressful is competitive youth sports?, the most important and conclusive study was conducted by Simon and Martens (1979). In this study, the investigators administered the Competitive State Anxiety Inventory (CSAI-C) to young males, age 9 to 14 years, across a variety of evaluative contexts. These evaluative conditions comprised the following situations: immediately prior to taking an academic test, while participating in physical education class competition, performing with the band in a solo role or as a member of the group, practicing with an organized sport team, or competing in any of seven different organized sports (baseball, basketball, tackle football, gymnastics, ice hockey, swimming, and wrestling).

Three major findings emerged from the Simon and Martens (1979) study. First, state anxiety levels were higher for boys during sport competition than during practice sessions. However, the rise in state anxiety from practice to competition was only slight to moderate. Second, the highest mean level of state anxiety in any condition was recorded by the band soloists, indicating that involvement in activities other than competitive sport can also provoke anxiety. Third, among athletes engaged in organized sports, wrestlers and gymnasts experienced higher levels of state anxiety than did team sport athletes. The authors concluded that competitive sport does not appear to be overly stress-invoking for youngsters but that circumstances that maximize the opportunity for social evaluation of the individual increase state anxiety. Thus, the solo band performance and competition in individual sports, such as wrestling and gymnastics, constituted conditions in which social evaluation opportunities were greatest.

The findings by Simon and Martens (1979) were important in discounting the idea that sport competition was inherently overly stressful for all participants. However, as noted by Gould (1996), as long as a substantial proportion of young athletes experience high levels of sport-related anxiety, understanding the causes and consequences of anxiety is an important undertaking to minimize the frequency of this occurrence.

Sources of Trait and State Anxiety in Young Athletes

What are the primary contributors to individual differences in anxiety responses? Cognitively based psychological theories hold that certain cognitive appraisal characteristics are likely to result in anxiety perceptions, whether referring to sport or nonsport contexts (e.g., Lazarus & Folkman, 1984; Leary, 1992). In youth sports, the cognitions most frequently examined in relation to competitive trait and state anxiety are self-perception characteristics, social evaluation concerns, and perception of goal endangerment.

Children's self-perception-related characteristics comprise an important, theoretically based antecedent to competitive anxiety. When individuals perceive that they lack the essential capacities to succeed in an achievement domain of importance, such as sport, they are more likely to

experience feelings of anxiety because of their perceived lack of sufficient personal resources to meet the demands of the task. This assumes that the child values success in the specific domain of achievement. In Harter's (1978, 1981) competence motivation theory, low perceived competence is explicitly linked to high achievement-related anxiety and the desire to avoid similar achievement contexts. Other important competence-related beliefs include children's performance-related expectancies because such expectancies reflect on their underlying perceptions of their capacities in relation to task demands. In addition, overall feelings of self-esteem have also been considered to be predictors of sport-related anxiety. Children with low self-esteem are hypothesized to feel less worthy or capable in more contexts, and this logically translates into greater achievement-related anxiety.

In general, there has been moderate support for the role of these intrapersonal perceptions in contributing to anxiety outcomes among young athletes. In Passer's (1983) study, children with lower expectations for personal performance also had higher competitive trait anxiety in sport. However, perceived sport competence was not predictive of trait anxiety levels for the participants in this study. Brustad and Weiss (1987) found that high competitive trait anxiety (CTA) boys were characterized by lower levels of self-esteem and also expressed more frequent worries about performance than did their low CTA counterparts. Self-esteem has been a significant predictor of precompetition state anxiety levels for young athletes. Research has found that low-self-esteem boys and girls have higher CTA levels than do high-self-esteem children (Scanlan & Passer, 1978, 1979). Brustad (1988) also found that high CTA male and female basketball players had lower self-esteem than did their low CTA counterparts.

Social evaluation concerns represent a second important contributor to competitive anxiety for many youngsters. Social evaluation concerns can be accentuated in sport contexts by the public nature of sport participation and by the importance of possessing sport ability within children's peer groups (Adler, Kless, & Adler, 1992; Chase & Dummer, 1992). Of considerable potential influence are children's concerns about living up to the expectations of their parents, and concern for this aspect of social evaluation may further augment anxiety levels. Because parents are heavily involved in the sport socialization of their children, youngsters' concerns about how sport involvement may affect the quality of their interactions with their parents can contribute to anxiety. Scanlan and Lewthwaite (1984) found that wrestlers who reported higher levels of parental pressure to participate experienced higher levels of prematch state anxiety. High state anxiety in these wrestlers was also predicted by the tendency to worry frequently about meeting parental and coach expectations. Weiss, Weise, and Klint (1989) found that the top two precompetition worries for their sample of young male gymnasts were worries about "what my parents will think" and about "letting my parents down."

A third contributor to anxiety may be goal endangerment, which reflects youngsters' concerns that they may not achieve personally valued goals. Lewthwaite (1990) examined the influence of perceived threat to personally valued goals in the frequency and intensity of competitive trait anxiety reported by 9- to 15-year-old male soccer players. As predicted, boys who perceived greater threat to personally valued goals also had higher levels of trait anxiety. Game or match importance is also related to precompetition state anxiety. Participating in championship competitions has been identified as a major source of stress by elite young wrestlers (Gould, Horn, & Spreeman, 1983b) and runners (Feltz & Albrecht, 1986). Gould et al. found that two major sources of prematch stress in their sample of young wrestlers were worries about performing up to their level of ability and about improving on their most recent performance. Similarly, Feltz and Albrecht (1986) found that young runners, age 9 to 15 years, reported that their major worries were about performing up to their level of ability and improving on their last performance.

From research findings on predictors of competitive stress and anxiety in young athletes, a relatively clear picture emerges in relation to contributors to these outcomes. High-anxious young athletes are likely to have less favorable perceptions of their sport ability, lower expectations of their capacity to achieve personally valued goals, and lower self-esteem than their less anxious colleagues. Furthermore, high-anxious children seem to worry more about incurring negative performance evaluations from others, particularly parents (Passer, 1983).

An additionally important contributor to sport anxiety for children may relate to peer acceptance concerns, although this line of investigation has not been examined to any depth. Sport participation may be inherently anxiety-provoking for many children because athletic ability is strongly linked to social status, particularly for boys (Adler et al., 1992; Chase & Dummer, 1992). Consequently, it may be very important for many youngsters to demonstrate athletic ability, or at least to avoid the demonstration of low ability, in the presence of their peers. This

dimension of social evaluation concern needs further examination.

Sport Burnout

Athlete burnout is a topic that has received much speculation but only a limited amount of empirical research. Coakley (1992) addressed the issue of sport burnout in relation to the structure of high-level sport participation. From his interviews with high-level adolescent athletes, Coakley concluded that sport burnout is the result of feelings of entrapment due to perceptions of low perceived personal control and an identity that is disproportionately focused on the athletic role.

Raedeke (1997) examined sport burnout within the framework of the sport commitment model. This researcher hypothesized that burnout can occur when athletes feel a level of entrapment in sport that outweighs their feelings of attraction to the sport. Participants in this study were 236 swimmers (age 13 to 18 years) participating in an intense swim program. On average, the swimmers trained 10.6 months of the year and devoted nearly 14 hours per week to training. Results from his study yielded four distinct clusters, or profiles, within the larger sample. In general, those athletes who demonstrated characteristics of sport entrapment had higher burnout scores than did those who were characterized by greater sport attraction.

Predictors of Sport Enjoyment

The flip side of research on the unfavorable aspects of sport involves understanding correlates and contributors to favorable emotional outcomes for young athletes. Scanlan and Lewthwaite (1986) examined correlates of season-long enjoyment in male age-group wrestlers, age 9 to 14 years. They found that greater enjoyment for these athletes was predicted by high parental satisfaction with performance, positive adult involvement and interactions, a lower frequency of negative maternal interactions, and high perceived ability. These researchers also found a relatively strong correlation ($r = .70$) between level of sport enjoyment and the extent to which these wrestlers wished to compete in the sport during the following season.

In a study of young basketball players, Brustad (1988) found that motivational characteristics and perceived parental pressure were predictive of season-long enjoyment levels for both male and female study participants. Specifically, an intrinsic motivational orientation, as demonstrated by a preference for challenging rather than easy tasks, and low perceived parental pressure were associated with greater enjoyment. An additionally important finding was that team win-loss records and actual levels of ability (as assessed by each player's coach) were not related to enjoyment levels.

Scanlan, Stein, and Ravizza (1989) conducted a retrospective study of sources of enjoyment for former elite figure skaters. Using open-ended interview techniques, these researchers found that five characteristics of enjoyment were most commonly reported by these former skaters. The first category was social and life opportunities, which reflected the enjoyment experienced by forming affiliations with others and/or having opportunities for unique experiences outside of the sport realm (e.g., travel). A second category was identified as perceived competence, which reflected satisfaction with one's level of sport achievement. Social recognition of competence was a third characteristic of enjoyment and referred to the satisfaction from having others recognize competence. A fourth theme was the act of skating itself, which referred specifically to the enjoyment resulting from the physical sensations and self-expression inherent in skating. The final category was identified as special cases and pertained to both a sense of personal uniqueness and the development of life coping skills that resulted from participation in the sport.

FUTURE DIRECTIONS IN RESEARCH ON AFFECTIVE OUTCOMES

Research on the affective outcomes experienced by young athletes reveals consistency in the type of influences that contribute to favorable and unfavorable emotional outcomes for youngsters. Overall, research indicates that when children have less favorable perceptions of their capacity to accomplish a desired outcome, in combination with concerns about incurring negative social evaluation from others, they are likely to experience anxiety. Conversely, high perceived ability and favorable parental support are linked to positive affective outcomes for young athletes. Given this knowledge, two avenues for future research are encouraged.

Because self-perception and social support influences are integrally related to children's affective experiences, a greater depth of understanding is needed to examine the processes through which children develop perceptions in each of these areas. In this regard, greater knowledge about intrapersonal, developmental, and social forms of influence on children's sport-related self-concept will enhance understanding of contributors to children's affective outcomes. Consequently, attempts can be made to structure youth sport interventions in a manner that

enhances self-perceptions. Similarly, an enhanced understanding of the specific means by which significant others shape children's evaluation and performance apprehension will provide additional depth of understanding to the knowledge base.

A second important dimension of future research is the relationship between children's affective responses to sport involvement and their continued motivation to participate. Implicitly, and in theoretical perspectives such as Harter's (1978, 1981), affect and motivation are related. However, little research exists to provide us with understanding of the strength of this relationship or of the influence of favorable affective experiences on children's ongoing motivation. Longitudinal studies in this regard would be particularly insightful.

SOCIAL INFLUENCE IN YOUTH SPORT

Youth sport takes place within a social context shaped by adults, peers, and the participants themselves. The influence of parents and coaches has generated considerable attention over the past two decades, but the role of peers has only recently been systematically addressed. The influence of adults in the youth sport arena is pervasive and easily recognized. Adults attend competitions, organize events, and may coach as a consequence of their child's interest and participation. However, peers are also extremely influential in shaping the psychological and social context of participation, particularly during later childhood and adolescence. Peers can influence children's self-perceptions, feelings of social support, and social status levels through sport. In this section, the knowledge base on adult and peer influence is addressed in relation to psychosocial and motivational outcomes for children.

Parental Influence

Parents are typically the primary sport socializers for children during their initial forays into sport (Brustad, 1996b; Greendorfer, Lewko, & Rosengren, 1996). This research base indicates that parents are primarily responsible for providing children with initial opportunities to play sport, for helping to maintain their sport involvement, and potentially, for affecting children's withdrawal from sport (Greendorfer, 1992). The extent to which parents become involved in their children's sport experiences is reflected in research on youth hockey in Canada. McPherson and Davidson (1980, cited in Smith, 1988) found that 80% of the players had parents who attended at least three-quarters of their games. An additional finding was that at least 25% of parents attended their children's practices at least two or three times a month.

Although concern for adult influence in youth sport has always existed, the nature of research questions in this regard has changed over time. Whereas initial research was largely concerned with understanding potentially unfavorable forms of parental influence, more recent research attention has been directed toward uncovering the nature of differences in parenting styles as such socialization practices contribute to favorable and unfavorable psychosocial outcomes for children. Thus, there has been much less recent interest in generalizing about parental influence in sport and much more concern for the nature of individual difference effects in outcomes for children in relation to parental involvement (Brustad, 1992). The most important forms of parental influence include their roles in affecting children's self-perceptions, motivational characteristics, and affective experiences in sport. Because current motivational theories highlight the influence of self-perceptions in shaping motivational characteristics, parental influence on self-perception and motivational processes will be discussed simultaneously and, subsequently, parental roles in shaping children's affective outcomes will be discussed.

It is also necessary to note an important methodological consideration in the parental socialization research. Almost all studies that have been conducted on parental influence have depended on children's perceptions of parental beliefs and practices rather than utilizing parents' own self-reports or third-party assessments. However, this tendency does not necessarily represent a limitation, as research exists that indicates that children's perceptions of parental influence are more strongly related to children's psychological and affective outcomes than are parents' own self-reports of their beliefs and behaviors (Babkes & Weiss, 1999; Gecas & Schwalbe, 1986).

Children's Self-Perceptions and Motivation

The nature of parental influence on children's self-perception and motivational characteristics is an important area of study in relation to children's participatory and attrition-related motives, as well as with regard to the intrinsic/extrinsic nature of children's sport motivation. During their sport involvement, children's self-perceptions are likely to be heavily influenced by adults for two reasons. First, adults are extensively involved in the youth sport domain and thereby provide a great deal of information to children about their personal capacities. Second, as a consequence of cognitive-developmental characteristics,

younger children prefer to use adult sources of feedback in assessing their abilities in achievement situations (Frieze & Bar-Tal, 1980; Horn & Hasbrook, 1986; Horn & Weiss, 1991). The research by Horn and colleagues reveals that children age 8 to 11 years prefer to use adult sources of information in judging their sport competence, whereas older children and adolescents (age 12 to 14 years) rely more heavily on peer-based social comparison processes. During later childhood and through adolescence, children become increasingly capable of and prefer using peer comparison, peer evaluation, and internal information sources.

Parental socialization influence on children's self-perception characteristics and subsequent motivational processes is addressed by both Harter's (1978, 1981) competence motivation theory and Eccles's (Eccles & Harold, 1991; Eccles-Parsons et al., 1983) expectancy-value theory. From Harter's perspective, parents exert the primary form of influence on children's developing self-perceptions of competence and control through the type of support and feedback they provide in relation to children's mastery strivings. Research indicates that children's perceptions of parental support are, in fact, related to self-esteem, positive affect, and intrinsic motivation levels of youngsters in classroom settings (Harter, 1988a).

Eccles's theory contends that parents influence the favorability of children's self-perceptions through the feedback they provide to children about their competence in various domains. In this role, parents serve to interpret competence-related information for children and thus shape their emerging achievement expectations. From Eccles's perspective, parents appraise their child's capacities in varying achievement arenas and provide differential levels of opportunity, encouragement, and support in relation to their underlying beliefs. The combination of parental belief characteristics, social support patterns, and provision of opportunities results in differing levels of perceived competence for children across achievement domains, as reflected by differences in their expectancies for success.

The relationship between parental influence and children's self-perceptions of ability has been a focus of academic research. Eccles-Parsons, Adler, and Kaczala (1982) found that children's perceptions of their math ability and their perceptions regarding the difficulty and level of effort required for success at mathematics were more strongly linked to their parents' beliefs about the child's capacity than to the child's own demonstrated level of ability. Phillips (1984, 1987) also examined the relationship between parental belief systems and the academic self-perceptions of third and fifth-grade students. Her research focused on highly competent students ranked in the upper 25% of their grade level on the basis of achievement test scores, but who differed in the favorability of their self-perceptions of academic ability. The children with lower self-perceptions of ability believed that their parents shared these low perceptions and that their parents had low expectations for their future level of achievement.

The research findings obtained from academic contexts highlight the influence of parents in shaping children's self-appraisals. This influence may be even greater in the sport domain because parents have more firsthand opportunities to participate in their children's sport experiences and to provide immediate, interpretive, and evaluative feedback to their children.

Felson and Reed (1986) found that parental judgments of upper elementary school children's abilities in athletics and academics were strongly related to children's self-appraisal of ability even when their level of actual ability was statistically controlled. These findings are consistent with those of Eccles-Parsons et al. (1982) and Phillips (1984, 1987) in that parental ability appraisals superseded actual ability information available to the child. Similarly, Scanlan and Lewthwaite (1984) found that young wrestlers who perceived greater parental satisfaction with their performance demonstrated higher general expectancies for their future wrestling performance.

In a test of the applicability of the expectancy-value model for the explanation of differences among children in their level of interest and participation in varied activities, Eccles and Harold (1991) conducted a three-year longitudinal study of parental belief characteristics in relation to children's self-perception characteristics and children's free-choice activity motivation. In this study, parents' perceptions of their child's competence (expectancy) and parental perceptions of the importance and usefulness (value) of each activity explained variability among children in children's own perceptions of competence and value. In turn, children's expectancy and value perceptions affected their own activity choices. Thus, these findings were consistent with theoretical expectations.

Eccles's expectancy-value model was also applied in two studies (Brustad, 1993a, 1996a) examining children's physical activity motivation. In these studies, it was found that children's perceptions of physical competence and levels of attraction to physical activity were related to their perceptions of parental encouragement for physical activity participation. These findings were in support of Eccles's theory because, from this perspective, it is believed that

parents provide greater encouragement for their children in those areas of achievement at which they are believed to possess high ability. Dempsey, Kimiecik, and Horn (1993) found that parental beliefs about their children's physical competence were associated with children's actual levels of physical activity participation. Furthermore, children's perceptions of their parents' beliefs about physical activity participation were found to be significantly related to children's own beliefs about physical activity involvement (Kimiecik et al., 1996).

Babkes and Weiss (1999) explored the relationship between parental attitudes and behaviors in competitive youth soccer players' (age 9 to 11 years) psychosocial responses to sport participation. Perceived parental attitudes and behaviors that were assessed included parental beliefs about their child's soccer competence, performance expectations, positive contingent performance responses, and level of involvement. Results revealed that mothers and fathers who were perceived by their child as having more favorable beliefs about their child's competency and who gave more frequent positive contingent responses to athletic performance success had children with more favorable perceptions of soccer competence and higher levels of intrinsic motivation than did fellow players who reported less favorable parental perceptions. Additionally, children who reported higher perceptions of soccer competence indicated that their fathers were more involved in their soccer participation but exerted lower amounts of pressure than did those children lower in perceived soccer competence. Those children who perceived their fathers to exert high amounts of pressure to perform well in soccer reported lower levels of intrinsic motivation as compared to their cohorts, who perceived less pressure from their fathers.

In one of the few studies to examine the congruence between perceived motives for sport participation from the perspective of both parents and children, McCullagh, Matzkanin, Shaw, and Maldonado (1993) examined the correspondence between parents' perceptions of their children's motives for participating in sport with children's own self-reported motives. They found a significant relationship between the motives identified by children for their sport participation with their parents' perceptions of their children's motives. These findings suggest that children's participatory motives are likely to be shaped by parents' perspectives on the primary benefits provided by youth sport participation.

Research on parental influence on the motivational processes of young athletes has also been framed within achievement goal theory (Duda & Hom, 1993; Ebbeck & Becker, 1994; S. White, 1996). From this perspective, parents can be instrumental in shaping the motivational context, or climate, within which children participate in sport. Ames and Archer (1987) proposed that parents could convey to children many beliefs that may impact children's own views on motivation. For example, parents may express their beliefs about the importance of personal improvement relative to doing well in comparison to others; may communicate their beliefs about the contribution of ability and effort to achievement outcomes; and may convey expectations about appropriate levels of challenge to select on achievement tasks. Of particular importance may be parental reward structures or the criteria that parents use to reinforce children's motivational and achievement outcomes. For example, reward structures may be based primarily on the child's demonstration of improvement or on the level of ability demonstrated relative to others. In this way, parents have the capacity to shape children's goal orientation characteristics by making certain cues, rewards, and expectations salient to the child. Similar to the perspectives held by Harter and Eccles, parents also provide evaluative feedback to children that communicates information about the parents' perceptions of the child's competence. Thus, in establishing a motivational climate and by providing competence-related information for the child, parents seem to influence the achievement goal orientation of their children in sport.

Duda and Hom (1993) examined the correspondence between parent and child goal orientations for participants in youth basketball. In this study, children assessed their own goal orientations toward basketball and reported their perceptions of their parents' goal orientations toward sport. Similarly, parents reported their sport-related goal orientations as well as their perceptions of their child's goal orientation in basketball. A moderate relationship was found between children's perceptions of their parents' degree of task orientation and the child's own task orientation. Children's perception of their parents' degree of ego orientation was also moderately to strongly related with children's rating of ego orientation. All other relationships were not significantly related (i.e., parents' self-reported goal orientation and child's goal orientation). In related research, Ebbeck and Becker (1994) found that young athletes' task and ego goal orientations were predicted, in part, by perceived parental task and ego goal orientations and by the child's perceptions of competence.

White (1996) investigated the relationship between perceived parent-initiated motivational climate and young female volleyball players' goal orientations. The specific focus of this study was to determine whether children's goal orientation characteristics were related to their perceptions of the goal orientations maintained by their parents. Results revealed that young volleyball players who perceived that their parents emphasized athletic success but without the demonstration of high effort were more likely to demonstrate an ego-oriented motivation. Conversely, findings revealed that athletes who felt their parents fostered a climate where learning and enjoyment were important were more likely to maintain a task orientation. Overall, research in this area has provided support for the relationship between parent and child goal orientation characteristics.

Escarti, Roberts, Cervello, and Guzman (1999) conducted a study that examined adolescent goal orientations in relation to perceptions of the criteria of success used by parents, peers, and coaches. In this study, the researchers found two distinct goal orientation profiles. One group of athletes was characterized by high levels of task (mastery) and ego orientation. The second group comprised individuals who were high only on task orientation. Athletes in the high task/high ego group perceived that parents, coaches, and peers shared similar criteria (high task and high ego) for success. However, the high task-oriented group of athletes perceived that parents and coaches adhered to an ego-oriented criteria of success, whereas peers were believed to possess a similar task-oriented view. The findings from this study support the view that it is important to consider both adult and peer forms of social influence during adolescence.

Children's Affective Outcomes

In addition to the research on parental socialization influence on children's self-perception and motivational characteristics in youth sport, the examination of the role of parents in contributing to the favorability of children's affective responses to sport participation has been an important arena of investigation. The majority of this research has examined children's perceptions of parental pressure, expectations, and evaluative characteristics in relation to these emotional outcomes. The affective responses of children that have been most frequently assessed have been trait and state anxiety and enjoyment. The most important findings in this line of research relative to parental influence will be summarized.

A growing body of knowledge supports the view that parents are extremely influential in shaping the emotional response of young athletes to their sport involvement.

Children's perceptions of "parental pressure" to participate in sport, concerns about unfavorable evaluation by their parents, as well as concerns about meeting their parents' expectation levels have been linked to unfavorable affective outcomes for children. Passer (1983) found that children high in competitive trait anxiety are characterized by the tendency to worry more frequently about incurring negative evaluations from significant others. Scanlan and Lewthwaite (1984) also found that young wrestlers who perceived high levels of parental pressure were more likely to have high state anxiety regarding wrestling competition. Hellstedt (1988) found that an elite group of young skiers reported that they were apprehensive about their parents' emotional responses after poor performances and indicated that they continued sport participation, in part, to please their parents. Lewthwaite and Scanlan (1989) reported that parental expectations and parental pressure to wrestle were sources of worry for elite young wrestlers. In similar research, Weiss et al. (1989) also found a relationship between precompetition worry and fear of negative evaluation from parents in their study of young male gymnasts. Prematch state anxiety in young wrestlers has also been linked to perceptions of parental pressure to compete in wrestling (Gould, Eklund, Petlichkoff, Peterson, & Bump, 1991).

In contrast, parental behaviors that are regarded by children as positive and supportive have been linked to favorable affective experiences for children in sport. Scanlan and Lewthwaite (1986) found that greater season-long enjoyment for young wrestlers was related to high levels of perceived parental satisfaction with performance, positive parental involvement and interactions, and a low frequency of negative maternal interactions. Brustad (1988) also determined that greater season-long enjoyment in young male and female basketball players was related to a lower perception of parental pressure to participate. Hellstedt (1988) concluded that young skiers who viewed their parents' involvement as positive and supportive reported more positive emotional responses, such as enthusiasm, for their sport involvement. In their study of competitive youth tennis players, Leff and Hoyle (1995) noted that perceptions of parental support, described as parental behavior aimed at facilitation of children's involvement in athletics, was positively associated with higher levels of enjoyment (and self-esteem) for both male and female tennis players. Finally, Babkes and Weiss (1999) found that competitive youth soccer players who perceived positive parental forms of influence and reported that their fathers were more involved in their participation but exerted less pressure to

perform well also experienced more enjoyment. This study is important because it suggests that a high level of parental involvement in sport can result in favorable outcomes for children and that children's perceptions of their parents' role is most likely to influence their affective experiences.

Of particular importance may be parental reward structures or the criteria that parents use to reinforce children's motivational and achievement outcomes. For example, reward structures may be based primarily on the child's demonstration of improvement or on level of ability demonstrated relative to others. In this way, parents have the capacity to shape children's goal orientation characteristics by making certain cues, rewards, and expectations salient to the child. Similar to the perspectives held by Harter and Eccles, parents also provide evaluative feedback to children that communicates information about their perceptions of the child's competence. Thus, in establishing a motivational climate and by providing competence-related information for the child, it is anticipated that parents influence the achievement goal orientation of their children in sport.

Future Directions for the Examination of Parental Influence in Youth Sport

The expansion of research on parental influence in youth sport in the past decade has provided a substantial contribution to the existing knowledge base on how adults impact young athletes' sport experiences. Yet, although this area of study within pediatric sport psychology has become increasingly systematic and insightful, additional room for growth exists.

First, it is recommended that future research on parental influence in youth sport build on prevailing theoretical perspectives to link parental socialization influence with children's self-perception characteristics, their motivational processes, and affective experiences. Harter's (1978, 1981) competence motivation theory, Eccles's (Eccles & Harold, 1991; Eccles-Parsons et al., 1983) expectancy-value model, and achievement goal theory (Duda, 1992; Duda & Nicholls, 1992; Nicholls, 1984, 1989) are all highly amenable to this work.

Second, greater precision in the definition and operationalization of key constructs would be helpful in establishing consistency across areas. To date, there is no single, consistently used measure of parental pressure, evaluation characteristics, expectational levels, and the like. Therefore, it is not certain that researchers are measuring the same constructs. For example, an item included on one measure as an index of parental pressure may, on another measure, be regarded as an index of parental expectations.

In relation to methodological concerns, almost all research conducted has asked children to report on the collective beliefs and behaviors of their parents without distinguishing between mothers' and fathers' beliefs. It would be useful to examine mothers and fathers separately as it is likely that one parent is a more important agent in the child's sport, and because parents are likely to manifest their influence in differing ways.

Coach Influence

Coaches assume an important role in shaping children's psychosocial experiences in the sport domain. The study of coaches' influence on young athletes has been one of the most systematically studied areas in pediatric sport psychology. In a series of well-designed and highly regarded studies, Smith, Smoll, and colleagues (Smith, Smoll, & Curtis, 1978, 1979; Smith, Smoll, & Hunt, 1977; Smith, Zane, Smoll, & Coppel, 1983) found that coaching behaviors substantially influence children's self-perception characteristics as well as their psychosocial and affective responses to sport participation. These studies will be discussed collectively because this line of research has been a progressively based effort to identify the coaching behaviors that are most influential in shaping children's psychological, motivational, and affective experiences in sport and subsequent intervention efforts have been grounded in this knowledge base.

The multiphase research on coach influence in youth sport conducted by Smith, Smoll, and colleagues established a solid foundation for the knowledge base on coach influence. In the first phase of their research, Smith et al. (1977) developed a system to categorize coaching behaviors. The Coaching Behavior Assessment System (CBAS) resulted from direct observation of youth sport coaches and yielded 12 behavioral categories that included reactive and spontaneous coaching behaviors to a variety of player behaviors (i.e., desirable performance, mistakes). At the conclusion of the sport season, players were interviewed in their homes about various aspects of their athletic experience. The findings of this study (Smith et al., 1978) indicated that relationships existed between coaching behaviors and children's psychological and affective outcomes in sport. In particular, it was found that players low in self-esteem appeared to be most affected by behavioral differences among coaches. Players who started the season with low self-esteem appeared to benefit most from playing for coaches who emphasized a "positive approach" in providing feedback to players. The empirical findings of this study led to the development of a set of behavioral recommendations and a training program for youth sport coaches.

The second phase of their research involved the implementation of an intervention program with 31 coaches of Little League baseball players, age 10 to 15 years (Smith et al., 1979). Eighteen of these coaches received preseason training in a program designed to help them in communicating more effectively with young athletes. The intervention program encouraged the coaches to increase the frequency of technical instruction, to provide a greater frequency of positive reinforcement, and to reduce the use of punishment. The remaining 13 coaches constituted the control group and did not receive any training. Results indicated that the training sessions enhanced the communication effectiveness of the coaches as intended. More important, children who played for the trained coaches exhibited a significant increase in self-esteem compared to the previous season, evaluated their coaches more favorably, and had a higher level of attraction to team members, even though win-loss record did not differ between teams with trained and untrained coaches. As hypothesized, low-self-esteem children benefited most from playing for trained coaches. The results of this study also revealed that children who played for coaches who had received coaching-effectiveness training identified a stronger desire to play baseball again the following season than did their peers who played for untrained coaches.

The relationship between coaching behaviors and children's self-perceptions and enjoyment in sport was further examined in a study of coaches and athletes in a youth basketball league (Smith et al., 1983). This research indicated that coaching behaviors were significantly, although weakly, related to children's self-esteem and team unity. However, differences in coaches' behaviors were strongly related to players' attitudes at the end of the season, accounting for over half of the variance in players' attitudes toward the coach and sport. Specifically, coaches who provided more mistake-contingent technical instruction, less general (nonspecific) feedback, and less punishment and who engaged in fewer "controlling" behaviors had athletes who evaluated them more highly and expressed higher levels of sport participatory interest.

In their intervention study, Smoll, Smith, Barnett, and Everett (1993) found that low-self-esteem children who played for trained coaches demonstrated a significant increase in self-esteem during the season, whereas low-self-esteem children who played for untrained coaches did not. R. Smith, Smoll, and Barnett's (1995) research indicated that children who played for trained coaches experienced less competitive anxiety in comparison to young athletes who played for untrained coaches. With regard to levels of sport dropout, Barnett, Smoll, and Smith (1992) assessed the dropout rates of young baseball players in relation to whether children played for trained or untrained coaches. Results revealed that 26% of the children who played for untrained coaches did not play the next season. Although somewhat alarming, this statistic was consistent with previous findings on youth sport attrition rates (Gould, 1987; Petlichkoff, 1996). More important, however, only 5% of the young athletes who played for trained coaches chose not to return for another season of baseball. Furthermore, these findings indicated that the high attrition rate among youth who played for untrained coaches was not attributable to differences in team win-loss records.

Horn (1985) explored relationships between coaching behaviors in practice and competitive settings with changes in adolescent female softball players' competence perceptions. Whereas the series of studies conducted by Smith, Smoll, and colleagues focused on coaches' communications to the team as a whole, Horn examined the effects of individually based coach feedback on individual team members. Previous research (Rejeski, Darracott, & Hutslar, 1979) indicated that there is considerable intrateam variability in the type of feedback received by young athletes according to differences in coach expectations for performance.

Horn found that although skill improvement was the primary contributor to positive changes in self-perceptions of ability for these athletes, certain behaviors of coaches in practice also contributed to the enhancement of these perceptions. Specifically, players who received the greatest frequency of verbal feedback from coaches following successful performance manifested lower perceptions of competence than their counterparts. In addition, those players who received a high frequency of criticism in response to performance errors reported higher perceptions of competence than did those players who received less criticism. Although these findings appeared to be contradictory to "commonsense" expectations about the effect of reinforcement in achievement situations, Horn noted that these results were consistent with research on the relationship between adult expectational levels and patterns of feedback provided to children in the academic domain (Cooper & Good, 1983). Generally, low-expectancy students are likely to receive more frequent, but less specific, feedback from teachers following success at a task. It is believed that the student who receives this type of feedback is likely to infer low ability because the teacher does not praise others who

have performed similarly on the task. Furthermore, because technical feedback conveys the impression that there is capacity for improvement on a skill, children who receive less technical feedback may be more prone to infer low ability.

In a study that was framed within Harter's (1978, 1981) competence motivation theory, Black and Weiss (1992) extended Horn's (1985) research on coach influence by examining the relationship between young swimmers' perceptions of their coaches' performance-contingent praise, encouragement, informational feedback, and criticism after both successful and unsuccessful athletic performances. For children younger than 11 years, no significant relationships were found between youngsters' perceptions of their coach's behaviors and the athlete's own self-perception variables. However, adolescent swimmers who perceived that their coach gave more frequent contingent praise and information following desirable performances and more frequent encouragement plus information following undesirable performances had higher scores on measures of enjoyment, challenge motivation, perceived success, and perceived competence.

Allen and Howe (1998) continued the line of research instigated by Horn (1985) and subsequently addressed by Black and Weiss (1992). The participants in Allen and Howe's study, female adolescents age 14 to 18 years, participated at a high level of competitive field hockey. The researchers were specifically interested in identifying contributors to these players' levels of perceived competence. They found that skill level was a significant contributor to the explanation of individual differences in perceived competence. However, coaching behaviors also contributed to this explanation. Specifically, more frequent praise by the coaches plus instruction was positively linked to the swimmers' competence perceptions. Conversely, more frequent encouragement plus instruction after skill errors was negatively related to perceived competence. This outcome was explained by the authors as attributable to the attention given to performance mistakes in a group setting, which highlights individuals' concerns about demonstrating low ability to others.

Future Directions for Research on Coach Influence

Given the systematic line of research conducted on coaching influence, particularly through the work of Smith, Smoll, and colleagues, our primary recommendation is an encouragement to continue further well-designed work of this nature. It should be recognized that, currently, research on coach influence does not receive attention proportionate to its importance to our field. An important content area to examine involves further understanding of the influence of specific coaching behaviors, leadership practices, and feedback patterns on psychosocial outcomes for children. Within this general area, understanding coaches' goals and views on the purposes of sport for children, particularly in relation to motivational and affective outcomes for young athletes, is an area of investigation that has yet to be pursued.

Peer Influence

A third important form of social influence involves peers. Research on peer influence in youth sport has lagged considerably behind research on parents and coaches. Peers become especially influential socializing agents as youth enter the school setting and move through important developmental milestones. During late childhood and early adolescence in particular, youth look to their peers for validation of worth and other forms of social and emotional support (Harter, 1998; Sullivan, 1953). Indeed, a youngster's relationships with peers can have an important impact on his or her psychosocial development. Therefore, given the extent of sport involvement in the United States, sport psychologists have begun to call for more direct research attention to peer relationships in youth sport (e.g., Brustad, 1996b; Weiss, Smith, & Theebom, 1996). Examining peer relationships in youth sport may provide a better understanding of participation patterns as well as psychosocial outcomes of sport involvement. This section details important considerations in the study of peer relationships. Specifically, the context-specific nature of peer relationships is discussed as well as the distinction between friendship and peer acceptance. Furthermore, this section discusses research evidence illustrating sport participation with popularity as well as the links among peer relationships and self-perceptions, affect, and moral development. Finally, future directions for research on peer relationship are suggested.

Context-Specific Examination of Peer Relationships

Despite extensive study of peer relationships in educational settings by developmental psychologists (e.g., see Berndt & Ladd, 1989; Bukowski, Newcomb, & Hartup, 1996), a dearth of research exists on peers in the sport context. To some degree this can be attributed to the challenges of pursuing research on peer groups and to lack of theory on peer relationships (Brustad, 1996b; Furman, 1993). Nonetheless, research on peer relationships can and should be pursued in the sport context.

Developmental and sport psychology researchers advocate examination of peer relationships with particular attention to the context of peer interaction (e.g., Bigelow, Lewko, & Salhani, 1989; Kunesh, Hasbrook, & Lewthwaite, 1992; Weiss et al., 1996; Zarbatany, Ghesquiere, & Mohr, 1992; Zarbatany, Hartmann, & Rankin, 1990). For example, Zarbatany et al. (1992) found that fifth- and sixth-grade boys and girls held different friendship expectations when interacting in different settings. When involved in sports and games, ego reinforcement, preferential treatment, and fair play were particularly important features of friendship to the youngsters. In the academic domain, however, considerateness and helping were most preferred. These differences can be tied to a number of factors, but the public nature and importance of sport ability to youth are particularly relevant. For example, excessive helping behavior can be perceived negatively in sport because of the competitiveness of the setting and because such behavior is a public reflection of one's lack of skills and capabilities (Zarbatany et al., 1992). On the other hand, preferential provision of opportunity to demonstrate valued skills followed by the proverbial pat on the back would serve to boost a youngster's perceptions of sport ability. In the school setting, which is more collaborative but typically less valued by youth, helping behavior is viewed in a positive light. An important implication of these findings is that researchers need to develop a database on the nature and function of peer relationships that is specific to sport contexts.

A comprehensive understanding of peer relationships will also require attention to the variety of settings that shape interactions within the sport context. Expectations of relationships and social interactions within competitive sport versus recreational sport, for example, may vary considerably. Kunesh et al. (1992) found that physical activity type (i.e., formal sport, informal play and games, exercise) and social setting (i.e., home vs. school) were associated with different types of peer interactions in 11- to 12-year-old girls. Specifically, they found that the girls enjoyed and were attracted to informal physical activity in their own neighborhood. Negative affect and poor treatment from boys were more consistent with formal, school-based sport experiences. Therefore, features specific to the sport context, and the variety of settings within it, need to be considered when pursuing peer relationships research in sport.

Friendship and Peer Acceptance

In addition to context, peer influence in youth sport should be examined with regard to types of peer relationship. One important category of relationships among peers is friendship.

Friendships are generally viewed as dyadic relationships characterized as close and mutual (Bukowski & Hoza, 1989). Research on youth friendships has stemmed largely from Sullivan's (1953) perspective regarding chumships. Sullivan identified intimacy as an important component of chumships and believed that intimate relationships bolster self-esteem of adolescents. His views have directed current empirical efforts toward the exploration of friendship components as well as psychosocial correlates of friendship (Berndt, 1996). For example, Weiss et al. (1996) explored perceptions of sport friendships among 8- to 16-year-old summer sport program participants. Participants were interviewed about their "best" sport friendship, and in response shared both positive and negative features of their relationships. Qualitative dimensions of friendship included companionship, self-esteem enhancement, prosocial behavior, loyalty, and conflict. This study highlights the multifaceted nature of sport-related friendships and also provides a context-specific database on which to pursue future sport friendship research. In particular, this study specifies what comprises friendship quality in sport. Hartup (1996) suggested that to fully understand the psychosocial implications of friendship for an individual, one must know whether that person has friends, who those friends are, and the quality of those relationships. Because sport is a setting where intense interpersonal relationships can be experienced, understanding these components of friendship in sport may foster a deeper understanding of sport socialization processes.

Contemporary research on peer relationships also addresses issues of peer acceptance. Peer acceptance pertains to one's experience of status within or liking by the peer group (Bukowski & Hoza, 1989). Rather than placing emphasis on dyadic interactions, researchers examining peer acceptance focus on actual (e.g., through sociometric methods) or perceived acceptance by a larger social group. Sullivan (1953) believed that peer acceptance could affect views toward competition and cooperation, personal attitudes, and other psychological, social, and emotional outcomes. Importantly, peer acceptance is considered complementary to friendship with regard to psychosocial development. Although peer acceptance and friendship are certainly related constructs, they have been associated with distinct contributions to psychosocial outcomes in both educational and physical activity contexts (e.g., Parker & Asher, 1993; Smith, 1999). This is consistent with Sullivan's theoretical contentions and suggests that both constructs must be explored to develop a comprehensive understanding of peer influence in sport.

Sport Involvement and Popularity

As mentioned earlier in the chapter, youth identify a wide array of motives when asked their reasons for sport participation (see Weiss & Chaumeton, 1992; Weiss & Petlichkoff, 1989). Examination of the most frequently cited motives suggests that youth participation is characterized by a desire to make friends and be affiliated with a team or group, to learn and improve skills, and to have fun. Not surprisingly, significant others, competence-related perceptions, and affect appear as key elements of motivational theoretical perspectives that have been used to understand youth sport motivation (e.g., Ames, 1992; Eccles-Parsons et al., 1983; Harter, 1978, 1981; Nicholls, 1984). These motivational elements are related to one another, and as such it is important to understand how youth conceptualize the ties among their relationships, competence perceptions, and feelings in sport. For example, do children view competence in sport as critical to obtaining status in their peer group? Do peers contribute to competence perceptions in sport? If a child has relatively low sport ability, but also has a good friend on his or her team, what are the affective (e.g., enjoyment) consequences of participation? Some research has been conducted in the sport domain that moves us toward answers to these questions.

The sport setting is ideal for the exploration of motivational and other psychosocial processes because it is a highly valued achievement context among youth. This value emanates, in part, from the belief that being good at sports makes one popular among one's peers. Numerous studies have examined youth perceptions of what makes them popular among their peers (e.g., Adler et al., 1992; Buchanan, Blankenbaker, & Cotton, 1976; Chase & Dummer, 1992; Eitzen, 1975; Feltz, 1978; Williams & White, 1983). Typically, gender differences have been observed, with boys placing greater importance on athletic ability in comparison to ability in other domains than do girls. However, both boys and girls believe they attain high status among peers through athletic accomplishment and rank athletics comparable to academic achievement. In their research, Chase and Dummer asked fourth- to sixth-grade youth to rank the importance of being good at sports, making good grades, being physically attractive, and having money in relation to their popularity with classmates. Boys ranked sports ability as most important to popularity, followed by physical appearance. Girls ranked appearance as most important, followed by sports ability. Also, as grade level increased, importance of sports and appearance to popularity also increased for both boys and girls. Interestingly, this corresponds with the ascendancy of peer comparison and evaluation as salient sources of physical competence information (see Horn & Amorose, 1998).

The belief that athletic capability is tied to popularity appears to be well founded. Investigations have shown that actual status among peers is associated with athletic status and ability (e.g., Buhrmann & Bratton, 1977; Evans & Roberts, 1987; Weiss & Duncan, 1992). For example, Buhrmann and Bratton assessed status among same-sex peers, status among opposite-sex peers, leading crowd status, and status with teachers of 551 high school girls. Athletes scored higher than nonathletes and good athletes scored higher than less skilled athletes on status ratings. Furthermore, the relationship between athletic participation and status remained when variables such as academic achievement and activity of friends were controlled. Thus, being an athlete, and in particular a good athlete, appears to enhance one's standing among peers. Weiss and Duncan also found that sport ability is associated with peer status among third- through sixth-grade boys and girls. Those who exhibited higher perceived and actual physical competence than their peers were rated higher by their teachers on peer acceptance and, importantly, also perceived greater acceptance from their peers. Sport participation, therefore, clearly has social and personal implications for youth.

Peers and Self-Perceptions

Although little research has been devoted specifically to understanding the influence of peer relationships on self-perceptions, preliminary efforts indicate that these variables are related to one another. Both friends and the larger peer group appear to play a role in the self-perceptions of youth sport participants. For example, in Weiss et al.'s (1996) investigation of sport friendships, self-esteem enhancement emerged as a key friendship dimension. Self-esteem enhancement was characterized by higher-order themes such as provision of positive reinforcement, accepting mistakes, and saying nice things. In brief, friends in sport appear to do and say things that enhance their sense of worth as well as their perceptions of athletic ability. With regard to the larger peer group, Weiss and Duncan's (1992) study clearly shows a positive relationship between perceptions of athletic competence and peer acceptance. Perceptions of athletic competence and peer acceptance are key dimensions of overall self-concept in both childhood and adolescence (see Harter, 1985, 1988a).

Corroborating Weiss and Duncan's (1992) findings, Smith (1999) found that perceived peer acceptance in physical activity contexts is related to physical self-worth. Physical self-worth represents one's satisfaction and confidence with the physical self (see Fox & Corbin, 1989) and therefore is a critical component of one's overall self-concept. The link between peer relationships and physical self-perceptions may be strongest during early adolescence, when sport involvement is most extensive. Although a developmental examination of this link has not been undertaken, research by Horn and colleagues suggests that peers are particularly important sources of physical competence information during early adolescence (Horn et al., 1993; Horn & Hasbrook, 1986, 1987; Horn & Weiss, 1991; Weiss et al., 1997). Collectively, these studies demonstrate that preference for adult sources of competence information in early childhood gives way to preference for peer evaluation and comparison in late childhood and early adolescence. As youth move into later adolescence, internal sources of information are most favored in assessing one's physical competence.

The shift to preference of peer comparison and evaluation as a source of competence information may, in part, contribute to the sharp declines in sport involvement evidenced in early adolescence. This may stem from the inability to fully differentiate the concepts of effort and ability prior to age 12 (Fry & Duda, 1997; Nicholls, 1978). As youth are able to make this distinction, they may choose to define success by using social comparison, come to recognize the existence of peers with higher sport ability, and realize the need to work harder to achieve the same degree of success as their more able peers in physical activities. This could, therefore, serve to lower physical self-perceptions and, in turn, one's motivation to pursue physical activities. Interestingly, Weiss et al.'s (1997) study uncovered a profile representative of youth in early adolescence (age 10 to 13) that was characterized by lower perceived competence, lower self-esteem, and higher competitive trait anxiety. These youth also exhibited a strong preference for peer comparison and evaluation by coaches and peers. This highlights early adolescence as a period when peers may play an important part in the development and expression of physical self-perceptions. The competitive trait anxiety findings also suggest that peers may contribute to affective predispositions and responses in the sport setting.

Peers and Affect

Although little research has directly examined how peers shape affective experiences for others in sport, without doubt peers are important contributors to the positive feelings that young athletes experience. Sullivan (1953) believed that peers contribute to youth affective experiences and developmental psychologists have shown peer relationships to impact both positive and negative affect (Newcomb & Bagwell, 1996; Parker & Asher, 1993). In the sport setting, a few investigations highlight the link between peers and affect. Scanlan et al. (1989) found that social and life opportunities were an important source of enjoyment among elite-level figure skaters. Over half of their interviewees saw the friendships afforded by skating as meaningful and positive sources of opportunity. Among middle-school-age youth, Duncan (1993) and Smith (1999) have demonstrated that higher perceptions of friendship relate to more positive affect in both physical education and physical activity contexts. Finally, pleasant play/association was a dimension of friendship quality that emerged in Weiss et al.'s (1996) study of youth sport friendships. Enjoyment and feelings of affection, among other themes, characterized this component of friendship quality.

Negative affect is also prevalent in the sport setting. The conflict dimension that emerged in Weiss et al.'s (1996) study demonstrates that there is potential for peer relationships to contribute to negative affective experiences. Youth reported that even best friends in sport say and do things that make each other angry. Some respondents also discussed excessive competitiveness of their best sport friend. There are likely a number of processes that contribute to negative affect in sport, including dispositional factors such as competitive trait anxiety or excessive ego orientation and environments that overemphasize social comparison (see Duda & Hall, this volume). Given the importance of peer evaluation and comparison to sport competence perceptions (Horn et al., 1993; Horn & Hasbrook, 1986, 1987; Horn & Weiss, 1991; Weiss et al., 1997), such dispositions and environments may exacerbate negative interactions among youth in late childhood and early adolescence. Negative interactions with peers, in turn, will unquestionably foster negative affective reactions in young athletes. However, more research is needed to fully understand how peers influence affect in the sport context. Some popular theoretical models (e.g., Eccles-Parsons et al., 1983; Harter, 1978, 1981) give considerable weight to significant others as contributors to affective and other psychosocial outcomes in achievement contexts, yet little research has used such frameworks to explore the role of peers in youngsters' affective responses to sport participation.

Peers and Moral Development

Sport is viewed as a context in which young athletes develop moral attitudes and behaviors (Shields & Bredemeier, 1995). The potential for peer contribution to these outcomes is evident in the two dominant theoretical approaches to moral development. In brief, the social learning perspective (Bandura, 1977, 1986) defines moral development as the extent to which one's behavior is in accord with social expectations or conventions. This perspective suggests that individuals learn socially accepted values and behavior through the mechanisms of modeling and reinforcement. Structural-developmental theoretical approaches (e.g., Haan, 1978; Kohlberg, 1969; Piaget, 1965; Rest, 1984) define moral development as the organization and structure of cognitions regarding the "rightness" or "wrongness" of a given situation. These theorists believe that moral reasoning results from an interaction between the individual and his or her environment (Shields & Bredemeier, 1995). Experiencing and discussing moral dilemmas or conflicts with others are believed to impact an individual's subsequent reasoning patterns. Thus, from both theoretical perspectives, peers can play an important role in moral development. Peers model or reinforce what is considered acceptable behavior in the sport setting. Likewise, verbal interactions among peers in sport contexts would be expected to influence attitudes regarding sport-related dilemmas such as cheating and aggression.

Youth sport research grounded within these theoretical approaches (e.g., Mugno & Feltz, 1985; Smith, 1979; Stuart & Ebbeck, 1995) suggests that peers contribute to moral attitudes and behaviors. Young football players in the Mugno and Feltz study ranked teammates as having the most influence on their decisions to use illegal aggressive behaviors, and youth hockey players in Smith's study perceived high teammate approval of fighting. Smith's study and research by Stuart and Ebbeck show that as youth move into and through adolescence, perceptions of teammate approval of illegal or harmful acts are heightened. Thus, as young athletes move through the competitive ranks, teammates have the potential to substantially shape moral attitudes and behaviors. Therefore, carefully engineering sport environments so teammates have a positive influence on youth athletes is critical.

Physical education and sport research assessing intervention programs grounded within structural developmental principles have shown that sport environments can be designed to enhance moral reasoning and behavior (e.g., Bredemeier, Weiss, Shields, & Shewchuck, 1986; Gibbons, Ebbeck, & Weiss, 1995; Romance, Weiss, & Bockovan, 1986). Because the structural developmental approach is steeped in dialogue and focuses on issues related to moral balance among individuals involved in a particular situation, intervention techniques within this perspective are typically peer-based. Teachers or coaches may create a dilemma by limiting available equipment or asking athletes to self-substitute during game play. On experiencing such dilemmas, youth are encouraged to discuss the situation, consider the perspectives of others, and find solutions that are satisfactory to all involved parties.

Future Directions in Peer Relationships Research

Peers clearly are important contributors to psychosocial outcomes in sport in relation to self-perceptions, affect, and moral development. However, specific research efforts designed to understand peer relationships in sport have been few. As a result, foundational work is needed to develop a database on peer relationships in sport and theoretical work is needed to help sport psychologists better understand how peers influence important outcomes such as performance and motivation. This research should draw from a variety of methods and approaches. Qualitative, sociometric, observational, and other methodologies will be necessary to help build a comprehensive knowledge base on peer relationships in sport. Examining change in peer relationships over time and in relation to developmental status will also be critical. Such suggestions are not unique when considering research needs in sport psychology, but they seem particularly important to the study of peers because of the complexity of social relationships. Peer relationships can be studied and understood at the individual, interactional, relational, or group level (Rubin, Bukowski, & Parker, 1998). As such, creative use of multiple methods will be necessary to improve understanding of peer influence in sport. Most of the work on peer relationships in sport to date, because of reliance on more typical "one-shot" studies using traditional methodological techniques, has focused on individual perceptions of peer relationships. This research is necessary and valuable, but illuminates only one dimension of peer influence.

Because the nature and function of peer relationships are linked to the specific context of peer interaction, future research efforts will need to carefully design or adapt measures of peer relationships. Weiss and Smith (1999) developed a measure of sport friendship quality through several steps, which included assessing the validity of a preexisting measure from the developmental psychology literature and drawing from their qualitative assessment of youth sport friendships (i.e., Weiss et al., 1996). Further work is needed that provides valid measurement of perceptions of peer acceptance in sport as well as interactional, relational, and group aspects of peer influence. Measures need to address both positive and negative aspects of peer relationships, and also may need to consider the developmental

level and gender of the athlete (Weiss & Smith, 1999). Such measures will allow researchers to examine psychosocial correlates of peer relationships. Also, when researchers use team building (e.g., Ebbeck & Gibbons, 1998) or structural developmental techniques (e.g., Gibbons et al., 1995) in their intervention efforts, such measures may allow better understanding of how peers serve as mechanisms of psychosocial change.

Finally, it is important to remember the simultaneous and interactive contributions of significant others to psychosocial outcomes. Sullivan (1953) theorized that the peer group and specific friendships were related, yet independent contributors, to psychosocial outcomes. Smith's (1999) work on youth physical activity motivation demonstrated this to be the case, and research in developmental psychology corroborates Sullivan's contentions (e.g., Parker & Asher, 1993). When possible, it is important to examine both sources of social influence in sport.

RECOMMENDATIONS FOR FUTURE DIRECTIONS IN YOUTH SPORT RESEARCH

In an effort to encourage continued exploration and growth of the knowledge base of psychological aspects of youth sport, three general recommendations are provided for future research. These recommendations pertain to theoretical approaches, methodological diversity, and the breadth of future research.

First, youth sport research should continue to be conducted from a theoretically driven approach within models that are suitable for use with children and adolescents. Although the importance of theory testing in pediatric sport psychology has been highlighted on earlier occasions, it is particularly important that theoretical efforts also consider the role of cognitive-developmental processes within these theoretical lines. In this regard, the contentions of the most highly relevant theoretical orientations can be addressed with closer attention to cognitive-developmental influence and patterns of developmental change. Developmental considerations based in theory are highly important in understanding issues in youth sport, particularly because the sport involvement of children is extensive during the years of rapid developmental change.

Second, future researchers are encouraged to employ a greater variety of methodological approaches to the understanding of sport behavior. Inductive and longitudinal forms of research could provide a greater depth of insight into the sport experience for youngsters. Qualitative research methodologies, including interviews and focus group approaches, remain a primary recommendation for further research on children's sport experiences. These qualitative approaches provide children a voice in explaining their sport experiences and provide additional depth of explanation. In addition, more process-product investigations, such as those conducted in the areas of coaching influence by Smith, Smoll, and colleagues, would be particularly warranted.

A third recommendation pertains to the breadth and content of the current research on youth sport. Particularly needed is further research from non–North American contexts. To date, most of the research in youth sport has been generated from similar populations in the United States and Canada. Although the body of knowledge is increasing, there is concern regarding generalizability to other cultures and contexts. A potentially fertile and currently unexplored area of pediatric sport research lies in the examination of the meaning and experiences of sport participation for youth from a wide range of culturally and ethnically diverse backgrounds, as well as those with cognitive disabilities, physical disabilities, and disadvantaged life situations. Such efforts, in conjunction with theoretically appropriate, methodologically diverse, and well-designed studies will enhance the relevance of future scholarly efforts.

REFERENCES

Adler, P.A., Kless, S.J., & Adler, P. (1992). Socialization to gender roles: Popularity among elementary school boys and girls. *Sociology of Education, 65,* 169–187.

Allen, J.B., & Howe, B. (1998). Player ability, coach feedback, and female adolescent athletes' perceived competence and satisfaction. *Journal of Sport & Exercise Psychology, 20,* 280–299.

Ames, C. (1992). Achievement goals, motivational climate, and motivational processes. In G. Roberts (Ed.), *Motivation in sport and exercise* (pp. 161–176). Champaign, IL: Human Kinetics.

Ames, C., & Archer, J. (1987). Mothers' beliefs about the role of ability and effort in school learning. *Journal of Educational Psychology, 79,* 409–414.

Amorose, A.J., & Weiss, M.R. (1998). Coaching feedback as a source of information about perceptions of ability: A developmental examination. *Journal of Sport & Exercise Psychology, 20,* 395–420.

Athletic Footwear Association (1990). *American youth sports participation.* North Palm Beach, FL: Athletic Footwear Association.

Atkinson, J.W. (1964). *An introduction to motivation.* Princeton, NJ: Van Nostrand.

Babkes, M.L., & Weiss, M.R. (1999). Parental influence on children's cognitive and affective responses to competitive soccer participation. *Pediatric Exercise Science, 11,* 44–62.

Bandura, A. (1977). *Social learning theory.* Englewood Cliffs, NJ: Prentice-Hall.

Bandura, A. (1986). *Social foundations of thought and action: A social cognitive theory.* Englewood Cliffs, NJ: Prentice-Hall.

Barnett, N.P., Smoll, F.L., & Smith, R.E. (1992). Effects of enhancing coach-athlete relationships on youth sport attrition. *The Sport Psychologist, 6,* 111–127.

Berndt, T.J. (1996). Exploring the effects of friendship quality on social development. In W.M. Bukowski, A.F. Newcomb, & W.W. Hartup (Eds.), *The company they keep: Friendship in childhood and adolescence* (pp. 346–365). New York: Cambridge University Press.

Berndt, T.J., & Ladd, G.W. (Eds.). (1989). *Peer relationships in child development.* New York: Wiley.

Bigelow, B.J., Lewko, J.H., & Salhani, L. (1989). Sport-involved children's friendship expectations. *Journal of Sport & Exercise Psychology, 11,* 152–160.

Black, S.J., & Weiss, M.R. (1992). The relationship among perceived coaching behaviors, perceptions of ability, and motivation in competitive age-group swimmers. *Journal of Sport & Exercise Psychology, 14,* 309–325.

Bredemeier, B.J., Weiss, M.R., Shields, D.L., & Shewchuk, R.M. (1986). Promoting moral growth in a summer sport camp: The implementation of theoretically grounded instructional strategies. *Journal of Moral Education, 15,* 212–220.

Brodkin, P., & Weiss, M.R. (1990). Developmental differences in motivation for participating in competitive swimming. *Journal of Sport & Exercise Psychology, 12,* 248–263.

Brower, J.J. (1978). Little League baseballism: Adult dominance in a "child's game." In R. Martens (Ed.), *Joy and sadness in children's sports* (pp. 39–49). Champaign, IL: Human Kinetics.

Brustad, R.J. (1988). Affective outcomes in competitive youth sport: The influence of intrapersonal and socialization factors. *Journal of Sport & Exercise Psychology, 10,* 307–321.

Brustad, R.J. (1992). Integrating socialization influences into the study of children's motivation in sport. *Journal of Sport & Exercise Psychology, 14,* 59–77.

Brustad, R.J. (1993a). Who will go out and play? Parental and psychological influences on children's attraction to physical activity. *Pediatric Exercise Science, 5,* 210–223.

Brustad, R.J. (1993b). Youth in sport: Psychological considerations. In R.N. Singer, M. Murphey, & L.K. Tennant (Eds.), *Handbook of research on sport psychology* (pp. 695–717). New York: Macmillan.

Brustad, R.J. (1996a). Attraction to physical activity in urban schoolchildren: Parental socialization and gender influences. *Research Quarterly for Exercise and Sport, 67,* 316–323.

Brustad, R.J. (1996b). Parental and peer influence on children's psychological development through sport. In F.L. Smoll & R.E. Smith (Eds.), *Children and youth in sport: A biopsychosocial perspective* (pp. 112–124). Madison, WI: Brown & Benchmark.

Brustad, R.J., & Weiss, M.R. (1987). Competence perceptions and sources of worry in high, medium, and low competitive trait-anxious young athletes. *Journal of Sport Psychology, 9,* 97–105.

Buchanan, H.T., Blankenbaker, J., & Cotton, D. (1976). Academic and athletic ability as popularity factors in elementary school children. *Research Quarterly, 47,* 320–325.

Buhrmann, H.G., & Bratton, R.D. (1977). Athletic participation and status of Alberta high school girls. *International Review of Sport Sociology, 12,* 57–69.

Bukowski, W.M., & Hoza, B. (1989). Popularity and friendship: Issues in theory, measurement, and outcome. In T.J. Berndt & G.W. Ladd (Eds.), *Peer relationships in child development* (pp. 15–45). New York: Wiley.

Bukowski, W.M., Newcomb, A.F., & Hartup, W.W. (Eds.). (1996). *The company they keep: Friendship in childhood and adolescence.* New York: Cambridge University Press.

Burton, D., & Martens, R. (1986). Pinned by their own goals: An exploratory investigation into why kids drop out of wrestling. *Journal of Sport Psychology, 8,* 183–197.

Butler, R. (1989). On the psychological meaning of information about competence: A reply to Ryan and Deci's comment of Butler (1987). *Journal of Educational Psychology, 79,* 474–482.

Carpenter, P.J., & Coleman, R. (1998). A longitudinal study of elite youth cricketeers' commitment. *International Journal of Sport Psychology, 29,* 195–210.

Carpenter, P.J., Scanlan, T.K., Simons, J.P., & Lobel, M. (1993). A test of the sport commitment model using structural equation modeling. *Journal of Sport & Exercise Psychology, 15,* 119–133.

Chase, M.A., & Dummer, G.M. (1992). The role of sports as a social status determinant for children. *Research Quarterly for Exercise and Sport, 63,* 418–424.

Coakley, J. (1986). When should children begin competing? A sociological perspective. In M.R. Weiss & D. Gould (Eds.), *Sport for children and youths* (pp. 59–63). Champaign, IL: Human Kinetics.

Coakley, J. (1992). Burnout among adolescent athletes: A personal failure or social problem? *Sociology of Sport Journal, 9,* 271–285.

Cooper, H., & Good, T. (1983). *Pygmalion grows up: Studies in the expectation communication process.* New York: Longman.

De Knop, P., Engstrom, L.M., Skirstad, B., & Weiss, M.R. (1996). *Worldwide trends in youth sport.* Champaign, IL: Human Kinetics.

Dempsey, J.M., Kimiecik, J.C., & Horn, T.S. (1993). Parental influence on children's moderate to vigorous physical activity participation: An expectancy-value approach. *Pediatric Exercise Science, 5,* 151–167.

Duda, J. (1987). Toward a developmental theory of children's motivation in sport. *Journal of Sport Psychology, 9,* 130–145.

Duda, J. (1989). Goal perspectives, participation, and persistence in sport. *International Journal of Sport Psychology, 20,* 42–56.

Duda, J. (1992). Sport and exercise motivation: A goal perspective analysis. In G. Roberts (Ed.), *Motivation in sport and exercise* (pp. 57–91). Champaign, IL: Human Kinetics.

Duda, J.L., Fox, K.R., Biddle, S.J.H., & Armstrong, N. (1992). Children's achievement goals and beliefs about success in sport. *British Journal of Educational Psychology, 62,* 313–323.

Duda, J.L., & Hom, H.L. (1993). Interdependencies between the perceived and the self-reported goal orientations of young athletes and their parents. *Pediatric Exercise Science, 5,* 234–241.

Duda, J.L., & Nicholls, J.G. (1992). Dimensions of achievement motivation in schoolwork and sport. *Journal of Educational Psychology, 84,* 290–299.

Duncan, S.C. (1993). The role of cognitive appraisal and friendship provisions in adolescents' affect and motivation toward activity in physical education. *Research Quarterly for Exercise and Sport, 64,* 314–323.

Dweck, C.S. (1986). Motivational processes affecting learning. *American Psychologist, 41,* 1040–1048.

Ebbeck, V., & Becker, S.L. (1994). Psychosocial predictors of goal orientations in youth soccer. *Research Quarterly for Exercise and Sport, 65,* 355–362.

Ebbeck, V., & Gibbons, S.L. (1998). The effect of a team building program on the self-conceptions of grade 6 and 7 physical education students. *Journal of Sport & Exercise Psychology, 20,* 300–310.

Eccles, J., & Harold, R. (1991). Gender differences in sport involvement: Applying the Eccles' expectancy-value model. *Journal of Applied Sport Psychology, 3,* 7–35.

Eccles, J.S. (1987). Gender roles and women's achievement-related decisions. *Psychology of Women Quarterly, 11,* 135–172.

Eccles-Parsons, J., Adler, T.F., Futterman, R., Goff, S.B., Kaczala, C.M., Meece, J.L., & Midgley, C. (1983). Expectancies, values, and academic behaviors. In J. Spence & R. Helmreich (Eds.), *Achievement and achievement motives: Psychological and sociological approaches* (pp. 75–146). San Francisco: Freeman.

Eccles-Parsons, J., Adler, T.F., & Kaczala, C.M. (1982). Socialization of achievement attitudes and beliefs: Parental influences. *Child Development, 53,* 310–321.

Eitzen, D.S. (1975). Athletics in the status system of male adolescents: A replication of Coleman's "The adolescent society." *Adolescence, 10*, 267–276.

Escarti, A., Roberts, G.C., Cervello, E.M., & Guzman, J.F. (1999). Adolescent goal orientations and the perception of criteria of success used by significant others. *International Journal of Sport Psychology, 30*, 309–324.

Evans, J., & Roberts, G.C. (1987). Physical competence and the development of children's peer relations. *Quest, 39*, 23–35.

Ewing, M.E., & Seefeldt, V. (1996). Patterns of participation and attrition in American agency-sponsored youth sports. In F.L. Smoll & R.E. Smith (Eds.), *Children in sport: A biopsychosocial perspective* (pp. 31–45). Madison, WI: Brown & Benchmark.

Felson, M.B., & Reed, M. (1986). The effect of parents on the self-appraisals of children. *Social Psychology Quarterly, 49*, 302–308.

Feltz, D.L. (1978). Athletics in the status system of female adolescents. *Review of Sport and Leisure, 3*, 98–108.

Feltz, D.L., & Albrecht, R.R. (1986). Psychological implications of competitive running. In M.R. Weiss & D. Gould (Eds.), *Sport for children and youth* (pp. 225–230). Champaign, IL: Human Kinetics.

Feltz, D.L., & Petlichkoff, L.M. (1983). Perceived competence among interscholastic sport participants and dropouts. *Canadian Journal of Applied Sport Sciences, 8*, 231–235.

Ferreira, M.B.R. (1986). Youth sport in Brazil. In M.R. Weiss & D. Gould (Eds.), *Sport for children and youths* (pp. 11–15). Champaign, IL: Human Kinetics.

Fox, K.R., & Corbin, C.B. (1989). The physical self-perception profile: Development and preliminary validation. *Journal of Sport & Exercise Psychology, 11*, 408–430.

Frieze, I., & Bar-Tal, D. (1980). Developmental trends in cue utilization for attributional judgments. *Journal of Applied Developmental Psychology, 1*, 83–94.

Fry, M.D., & Duda, J.L. (1997). A developmental examination of children's understanding of effort and ability in the physical and academic domains. *Research Quarterly for Exercise and Sport, 68*, 331–344.

Furman, W. (1993). Theory is not a four-letter word: Needed directions in adolescent friendships. In B. Laursen (Ed.), *Close friendships in adolescence* (pp. 89–103). San Francisco: Jossey-Bass.

Gecas, V., & Schwalbe, M.V. (1986). Parental behavior and adolescent self-esteem. *Journal of Marriage and the Family, 48*, 37–46.

Gibbons, S.L., Ebbeck, V., & Weiss, M.R. (1995). Fair play for kids: Effects on the moral development of children in physical education. *Research Quarterly for Exercise and Sport, 66*, 247–255.

Gill, D.L., Gross, J.B., & Huddleston, S. (1985). Participation motivation in youth sports. *International Journal of Sport Psychology, 14*, 1–4.

Gould, D. (1987). Understanding attrition in youth sport. In D. Gould & M.R. Weiss (Eds.), *Advances in pediatric sport sciences: Behavioral issues* (Vol. 2, pp. 61–85). Champaign, IL: Human Kinetics.

Gould, D. (1996). Sport psychology: Future directions in youth sport research. In F.L. Smoll & R.E. Smith (Eds.), *Children and youth in sport: A biopsychosocial perspective* (pp. 405–422). Madison, WI: Brown & Benchmark.

Gould, D., Eklund, R., Petlichkoff, L., Peterson, K., & Bump, L. (1991). Psychological predictors of state anxiety and performance in age-group wrestlers. *Pediatric Exercise Science, 3*, 198–208.

Gould, D., Feltz, D., Horn, T., & Weiss, M. (1982). Reasons for attrition in competitive youth swimming. *Journal of Sport Behavior, 5*, 155–165.

Gould, D., Feltz, D., & Weiss, M. (1985). Motives for participating in competitive youth swimmers. *International Journal of Sport Psychology, 16*, 126–140.

Gould, D., Horn, T., & Spreeman, J. (1983a). Competitive anxiety in junior elite wrestlers. *Journal of Sport Psychology, 5*, 58–71.

Gould, D., Horn, T., & Spreeman, J. (1983b). Sources of stress in junior elite wrestlers. *Journal of Sport Psychology, 5*, 159–171.

Greendorfer, S.L. (1992). Sport socialization. In T.S. Horn (Ed.). *Advances in sport psychology* (pp. 201–218). Champaign, IL: Human Kinetics.

Greendorfer, S.L., Lewko, J.H., & Rosengren, K.S. (1996). Family and gender-based influences in sport socialization of children and adolescents. In F.L. Smoll & R.E. Smith (Eds.), *Children and youth in sport: A biopsychosocial perspective* (pp. 89–111). Madison, WI: Brown & Benchmark.

Haan, N. (1978). Two moralities in action contexts: Relationship to thought, ego regulation, and development. *Journal of Personality and Social Psychology, 36*, 286–305.

Harter, S. (1978). Effectance motivation reconsidered. *Human Development, 21*, 34–64.

Harter, S. (1981). A model of intrinsic mastery motivation in children: Individual differences and developmental change. In W.A. Collins (Ed.), *Minnesota symposium on child psychology* (Vol. 14, pp. 215–255). Hillsdale, NJ: Erlbaum.

Harter, S. (1983). Developmental perspectives on the self-system. In E.M. Hetherington (Ed.), *Handbook of child psychology, socialization, personality, and social development* (pp. 275–385). New York: Wiley.

Harter, S. (1985). *Manual for the self-perception profile for children.* Denver, CO: University of Denver Press.

Harter, S. (1988). Causes, correlates and the functional role of global self-worth: A life-span perspective. In J. Kolligan & R. Sternberg (Eds.), *Perceptions of competence and incompetence across the life-span* (pp. 67–98). New Haven, CT: Yale University Press.

Harter, S. (1998). The development of self-representations. In N. Eisenberg (Ed.), *Handbook of child psychology* (5th ed., Vol. 3, pp. 533–617). New York: Wiley.

Hartup, W.W. (1996). The company they keep: Friendships and their developmental significance. *Child Development, 67,* 1–13.

Hellstedt, J.C. (1988). Early adolescent perceptions of parental pressure in the sport environment. *Journal of Sport Behavior, 13,* 135–144.

Hom, H.L., Duda, J.L., & Miller, A. (1993). Correlates of goal orientations among young athletes. *Pediatric Exercise Science, 5,* 168–176.

Horn, T.S. (1985). Coaches' feedback and changes in children's perceptions of their physical competence. *Journal of Educational Psychology, 77,* 174–186.

Horn, T.S., & Amorose, A.J. (1998). Sources of competence information. In J.L. Duda (Ed.), *Advances in sport and exercise psychology measurement* (pp. 49–63). Morgantown, WV: Fitness Information Technology.

Horn, T.S., Glenn, S.D., & Wentzell, A.B. (1993). Sources of information underlying personal ability judgments in high school athletes. *Pediatric Exercise Science, 5,* 263–274.

Horn, T.S., & Hasbrook, C.A. (1986). Informational components influencing children's perceptions of their physical competence. In M.R. Weiss & D. Gould (Eds.), *Sport for children and youths* (pp. 81–88). Champaign, IL: Human Kinetics.

Horn, T.S., & Hasbrook, C.A. (1987). Psychological characteristics and the criteria children use for self-evaluation. *Journal of Sport & Exercise Psychology, 9,* 208–221.

Horn, T.S., & Weiss, M.R. (1991). A developmental analysis of children's self-ability judgments in the physical domain. *Pediatric Exercise Science, 3,* 310–326.

Jacobs, J.E., & Eccles, J.S. (1992). The influence of mothers' gender-role stereotypic beliefs on mothers' and children's ability perceptions. *Journal of Personality and Social Psychology, 63,* 932–944.

Kelley, H.H., & Thibaut, J.W. (1978). *Interpersonal relations: A theory of interdependence.* New York: Wiley.

Kimiecik, J.C., & Horn, T.S. (1998). Parental beliefs and children's moderate-to-vigorous physical activity. *Research Quarterly for Exercise and Sport, 69,* 163–175.

Kimiecik, J.C., Horn, T.S., & Shurin, C.S. (1996). Relationships among children's beliefs, perceptions of their parents' beliefs, and their moderate-to-vigorous physical activity. *Research Quarterly for Exercise and Sport, 67,* 324–336.

Klint, K.A., & Weiss, M.R. (1986). Dropping in and dropping out: Participation motives of current and former youth gymnasts. *Canadian Journal of Applied Sport Sciences, 11,* 106–114.

Klint, K.A., & Weiss, M.R. (1987). Perceived competence and motives for participating in youth sports: A test of Harter's competence motivation theory. *Journal of Sport Psychology, 9,* 55–65.

Kohlberg, L. (1969). Stage and sequence: The cognitive-developmental approach to socialization. In D. Goslin (Ed.), *Handbook of socialization theory and research* (pp. 347–480). Chicago: Rand-McNally.

Kunesh, M.A., Hasbrook, C.A., & Lewthwaite, R. (1992). Physical activity socialization: Peer interactions and affective responses among a sample of sixth grade girls. *Sociology of Sport Journal, 9,* 385–396.

Lazarus, R.S. (1966). *Psychological stress and the coping process.* New York: McGraw-Hill.

Lazarus, R.S., & Folkman, S. (1984). *Stress, appraisal, and coping.* New York: Springer.

Leary, M.R. (1992). Self-presentation processes in exercise and sport. *Journal of Sport & Exercise Psychology, 14,* 339–351.

Leff, S.S., & Hoyle, R.H. (1995). Young athletes' perceptions of parental support and pressure. *Journal of Youth and Adolescence, 24,* 187–203.

Lewthwaite, R. (1990). Threat perception in competitive trait anxiety: The endangerment of important goals. *Journal of Sport & Exercise Psychology, 12,* 280–300.

Lewthwaite, R., & Scanlan, T.K. (1989). Predictors of competitive trait anxiety in male youth sport participants. *Medicine and Science in Sport and Exercise, 21,* 221–229.

Lindner, K.J., Johns, D.P., & Butcher, J. (1991). Factors in withdrawal from youth sport: A proposed model. *Journal of Sport Behavior, 14,* 3–18.

Longhurst, K., & Spink, K.S. (1987). Participation motivation of Australian children involved in organized sport. *Canadian Journal of Sport Sciences, 12,* 24–30.

Malina, R.M. (1986). Readiness for competitive sport. In M.R. Weiss & D. Gould (Eds.), *Sport for children and youths* (pp. 45–50). Champaign, IL: Human Kinetics.

Martens, R. (1977). *Sport competition anxiety test.* Champaign, IL: Human Kinetics.

Martens, R. (1986). Youth sport in the U.S.A. In M.R. Weiss & D. Gould (Eds.), *Sport for children and youths* (pp. 27–31). Champaign, IL: Human Kinetics.

McCullagh, P., Matzkanin, K., Shaw, S.D., & Maldonado, M. (1993). Motivation for participation in physical activity: A comparison of parent-child perceived competence and participation motives. *Pediatric Exercise Science, 5,* 224–233.

Mugno, D.A., & Feltz, D.L. (1985). The social learning of aggression in youth football in the United States. *Canadian Journal of Applied Sport Sciences, 10,* 26–35.

Newcomb, A.F., & Bagwell, C.L. (1996). The developmental significance of children's friendship relations. In W.M. Bukowski, A.F. Newcomb, & W.W. Hartup (Eds.), *The company they keep: Friendship in childhood and adolescence* (pp. 289–321). New York: Cambridge University Press.

Nicholls, J.G. (1978). The development of the concepts of effort and ability, perceptions of academic attainment, and the understanding that difficult tasks require more ability. *Child Development, 49,* 800–814.

Nicholls, J.G. (1984). Conceptions of ability and achievement motivation. In R. Ames & C. Ames (Eds.), *Research on motivation in education: Student motivation* (Vol. 1, pp. 39–73). New York: Academic Press.

Nicholls, J.G. (1989). *The competitive ethos and democratic education.* Cambridge, MA: Harvard University Press.

Nicholls, J., & Miller, A.T. (1984). The differentiation of the concepts of ability and difficulty. *Child Development, 54,* 951–959.

Nicholls, J.G., Jagacinski, C.M., & Miller, A.T. (1986). Conceptions of ability in children and adults. In R. Schwarzer (Ed.), *Self-related cognitions in anxiety and motivation* (pp. 265–284). Hillsdale, NJ: Erlbaum.

Orlick, T.D. (1973, January/February). Children's sport: A revolution is coming. *Canadian Association for Health, Physical Education and Recreation Journal,* 12–14.

Orlick, T.D. (1974, November/December). The athletic dropout: A high price for inefficiency. *Canadian Association for Health, Physical Education and Recreation Journal,* 21–27.

Parker, J.G., & Asher, S.R. (1993). Friendship and friendship quality in middle childhood: Links with peer group acceptance and feelings of loneliness and social dissatisfaction. *Developmental Psychology, 29,* 611–621.

Passer, M.W. (1983). Fear of failure, fear of evaluation, perceived competence and self-esteem in competitive trait-anxious children. *Journal of Sport Psychology, 5,* 172–188.

Passer, M.W. (1996). At what age are children ready to compete? Some psychological considerations. In F.L. Smoll & R.E. Smith (Eds.), *Children and youth in sport: A biopsychosocial perspective* (pp. 73–86). Madison, WI: Brown & Benchmark.

Petlichkoff, L.M. (1988). *Motivation for sport persistence: An empirical examination of underlying theoretical constructs.* Unpublished doctoral dissertation, University of Illinois, Urbana-Champaign.

Petlichkoff, L.M. (1996). The dropout dilemma in sport. In O. Bar-Or (Ed.), *Encyclopaedia of sports medicine: The child and adolescent athlete* (Vol. 6, pp. 418–430). Oxford, England: Blackwell Scientific.

Phillips, D. (1984). The illusion of incompetence among academically competent children. *Child Development, 55,* 2000–2016.

Phillips, D. (1987). Socialization of perceived academic competence among highly competent children. *Child Development, 58,* 1308–1320.

Piaget, J. (1965). *The moral judgment of the child.* Glencoe, IL: Free Press.

Raedeke, T.D. (1997). Is athlete burnout more than just stress? A sport commitment perspective. *Journal of Sport & Exercise Psychology, 19,* 396–417.

Rejeski, W., Darracott, C., & Hutslar, S. (1979). Pygmalion in youth sport: A field study. *Journal of Sport Psychology, 1,* 311–319.

Rest, J.R. (1984). The major components of morality. In W.M. Kurtines & J.L. Gerwitz (Eds.), *Morality, moral behavior, and moral development* (pp. 24–40). New York: Wiley.

Roberts, G.C. (1980). Children in competition: A theoretical perspective and recommendations for practice. *Motor Skills: Theory into Practice, 4,* 37–50.

Roberts, G.C. (1984). Toward a new theory of motivation in sport: The role of perceived ability. In J.M. Silva & R.S. Weinberg (Eds.), *Psychological foundations of sport* (pp. 214–228). Champaign, IL: Human Kinetics.

Roberts, G.C. (1993). Motivation in sport: Understanding and enhancing the motivation and achievement of children. In R.N. Singer, M. Murphey, & L.K. Tennant (Eds.), *Handbook of research on sport psychology* (pp. 405–420). New York: Macmillan.

Roberts, G.C., Kleiber, D., & Duda, J.L. (1981). An analysis of motivation in children's sport: The role of perceived competence in participation. *Journal of Sport Psychology, 3,* 206–216.

Robertson, I. (1986). Youth sports in Australia. In M.R. Weiss & D. Gould (Eds.), *Sport for children and youths* (pp. 5–10). Champaign, IL: Human Kinetics.

Robinson, T., & Carron, A.V. (1982). Personal and situational factors associated with dropping out versus maintaining participation in competitive sport. *Journal of Sport Psychology, 4,* 364–378.

Romance, T.J., Weiss, M.R., & Bockovan, J. (1986). A program to promote moral development through elementary school physical education. *Journal of Teaching in Physical Education, 5,* 126–136.

Rubin, R.H., Bukowski, B.H., & Parker, J.G. (1998). Peer interactions, relationships, and groups. In N. Eisenberg (Ed.), *Handbook of child psychology* (5th ed., Vol. 3, pp. 619–700). New York: Wiley.

Ruble, D.N. (1983). The role of social comparison processes in achievement-related self-socialization. In E.T. Higgins, D.N. Ruble, & W.W. Hartup (Eds.), *Social cognitions and* social development: A sociocultural perspective (pp. 134–157). New York: Cambridge University Press.

Rusbult, C. (1983). A longitudinal test of the investment model: The development (and deterioration) of satisfaction and commitment in heterosexual involvements. *Journal of Personality and Social Psychology, 45,* 101–117.

Sapp, M., & Haubenstricker, J. (1978). *Motivation for joining and reasons for not continuing in youth sport programs in Michigan.* Paper presented at the annual meeting of the American Alliance for Health, Physical Education, Recreation, and Dance, Kansas City, MO.

Scanlan, T.K. (1996). Social evaluation and the competition process: A developmental perspective. In F.L. Smoll & R.E. Smith (Eds.), *Children and youth in sport: A biopsychosocial perspective* (pp. 298–308). Madison, WI: Brown & Benchmark.

Scanlan, T.K., Carpenter, P.J., Schmidt, G.W., Simons, J.P., & Keeler, B. (1993). An introduction to the sport commitment model. *Journal of Sport & Exercise Psychology, 15,* 1–15.

Scanlan, T.K., & Lewthwaite, R. (1984). Social psychological aspects of competition for male youth sport participants: I. Predictors of competitive stress. *Journal of Sport Psychology, 6,* 208–226.

Scanlan, T.K., & Lewthwaite, R. (1986). Social psychological aspects of competition for male youth sport participants: IV. Predictors of enjoyment. *Journal of Sport Psychology, 8,* 25–35.

Scanlan, T.K., & Passer, M.W. (1978). Factors related to competitive stress among male youth sport participants. *Medicine and Science in Sports, 10,* 103–108.

Scanlan, T.K., & Passer, M.W. (1979). Sources of competitive stress in young female athletes. *Journal of Sport Psychology, 1,* 151–159.

Scanlan, T.K., & Simons, J.P. (1992). The construct of sport enjoyment. In G. Roberts (Ed.), *Motivation in sport and exercise* (pp. 199–215). Champaign, IL: Human Kinetics.

Scanlan, T.K., Simons, J.P., Carpenter, P.J., Schmidt, G.W., & Keeler, B. (1993). The sport commitment model: Measurement development for the youth sport domain. *Journal of Sport & Exercise Psychology, 15,* 16–38.

Scanlan, T.K., Stein, G.L., & Ravizza, K. (1989). An in-depth study of former elite figure skaters: II. Sources of enjoyment. *Journal of Sport & Exercise Psychology, 11,* 65–83.

Seefeldt, V. (1996). The concept of readiness applied to the acquisition of motor skills. In F.L. Smoll & R.E. Smith (Eds.), *Children and youth in sport: A biopsychosocial perspective* (pp. 49–56). Madison, WI: Brown & Benchmark.

Selman, R.L. (1971). Taking another's perspective: Role-taking development in early childhood. *Child Development, 42,* 1721–1734.

Selman, R.L. (1976). Social-cognitive understanding: A guide to educational and clinical practice. In T. Lickona (Ed.), *Moral

development and behavior* (pp. 299–316). New York: Holt, Rinehart and Winston.

Shields, D.L.L., & Bredemeier, B.J.L. (1995). *Character development and physical activity.* Champaign, IL: Human Kinetics.

Simon, J., & Martens, R. (1979). Children's anxiety in sport and nonsport evaluative activities. *Journal of Sport Psychology, 1,* 160–169.

Smilkstein, G. (1980). Psychological trauma in children and youth in competitive sport. *Journal of Family Practice, 10,* 737–739.

Smith, A.L. (1999). Perceptions of peer relationships and physical activity participation in early adolescence. *Journal of Sport & Exercise Psychology, 21,* 329–350.

Smith, M.D. (1979). Towards an explanation of hockey violence: A reference other approach. *Canadian Journal of Sociology, 4,* 105–124.

Smith, M.D. (1988). Interpersonal sources of violence in hockey: The influence of parents, coaches, and teammates. In F.L. Smoll, R.A. Magill, & M.J. Ash (Eds.), *Children in sport* (3rd ed., pp. 301–313) Champaign, IL: Human Kinetics.

Smith, R.E. (1986). Toward a cognitive-affective model of athletic burnout. *Journal of Sport Psychology, 8,* 36–50.

Smith, R.E., & Smoll, F.L. (1996). The coach as a focus of research and intervention in youth sports. In F.L. Smoll & R.E. Smith (Eds.), *Children and youth in sport: A biopsychosocial perspective* (pp. 125–141). Madison, WI: Brown & Benchmark.

Smith, R.E., Smoll, F.L., & Barnett, N.P. (1995). Reduction of children's sport performance anxiety through social support and stress-reduction training for coaches. *Journal of Applied Developmental Psychology, 16,* 125–142.

Smith, R.E., Smoll, F.L., & Curtis, B. (1978). Coaching behaviors in Little League baseball. In F.L. Smoll & R.E. Smith (Eds.), *Psychological perspectives on youth sports* (pp. 173–201). Washington, DC: Hemisphere.

Smith, R.E., Smoll, F.L., & Curtis, B. (1979). Coach effectiveness training: A cognitive behavioral approach to enhancing relationship skills in youth sport coaches. *Journal of Sport Psychology, 1,* 59–75.

Smith, R.E., Smoll, F.L., & Hunt, B. (1977). A system for the behavioral assessment of athletic coaches. *Research Quarterly, 48,* 401–407.

Smith, R.E., Zane, N.S., Smoll, F.L., & Coppell, D.B. (1983). Behavioral assessments in youth sports: Coaching behaviors and children's attitudes. *Medicine and Science in Sports and Exercise, 15,* 208–214.

Smoll, F.L., Smith, R.E., Barnett, N.P., & Everett, J.J. (1993). Enhancement of coaches' self-esteem through social support training for youth sport coaches. *Journal of Applied Psychology, 78,* 602–610.

State of Michigan. (1976). *Joint legislative study on youth sports programs: Phase I*. East Lansing: Michigan State University.

State of Michigan. (1978a). *Joint legislative study on youth sports programs: Phase II*. East Lansing: Michigan State University.

State of Michigan. (1978b). *Joint legislative study on youth sports programs: Phase III*. East Lansing: Michigan State University.

Stuart, M.E., & Ebbeck, V. (1995). The influence of perceived social approval on moral development in youth sport. *Pediatric Exercise Science, 7*, 270–280.

Sullivan, H.S. (1953). *The interpersonal theory of psychiatry*. New York: Norton.

Thibaut, J.W., & Kelley, H.H. (1959). *The social psychology of groups*. New York: Wiley.

Treasure, D.C., & Roberts, G.C. (1994). Cognitive and affective concomitants of task and ego goal orientations during the middle school years. *Journal of Sport & Exercise Psychology, 16*, 15–28.

Valeriote, T.A., & Hansen, L. (1986). Youth sport in Canada. In M.R. Weiss & D. Gould (Eds.), *Sport for children and youths* (pp. 17–20). Champaign, IL: Human Kinetics.

Veroff, J. (1969). Social comparison and the development of achievement motivation. In C.P. Smith (Ed.), *Achievement-related motives in children* (pp. 46–101). New York: Russell Sage Foundation.

Weiss, M.R., Bredemeier, B.J., & Shewchuk, R.M. (1985). An intrinsic/extrinsic motivation scale for the youth sport setting: A confirmatory factor analysis. *Journal of Sport Psychology, 7*, 75–91.

Weiss, M.R., & Chaumeton, N. (1992). Motivational orientations in sport. In T.S. Horn (Ed.), *Advances in sport psychology* (pp. 61–99). Champaign, IL: Human Kinetics.

Weiss, M.R., & Duncan, S.C. (1992). The relationship between physical competence and peer acceptance in the context of children's sports participation. *Journal of Sport & Exercise Psychology, 14*, 177–191.

Weiss, M.R., Ebbeck, V., & Horn, T.S. (1997). Children's self-perceptions and sources of competence information: A cluster analysis. *Journal of Sport & Exercise Psychology, 19*, 52–70.

Weiss, M.R., & Hayashi, C.T. (1995). All in the family: Parent-child socialization influences in competitive youth gymnastics. *Pediatric Exercise Science, 7*, 36–48.

Weiss, M.R., & Petlichkoff, L.M. (1989). Children's motivation for participation in and withdrawal from sport: Identifying the missing links. *Pediatric Exercise Science, 1*, 195–211.

Weiss, M.R., & Smith, A.L. (1999). Quality of youth sport friendships: Measurement development and validation. *Journal of Sport & Exercise Psychology, 21*, 145–166.

Weiss, M.R., Smith, A.L., & Theeboom, M. (1996). "That's what friends are for": Children's and teenagers' perceptions of peer relationships in the sport domain. *Journal of Sport & Exercise Psychology, 18*, 347–379.

Weiss, M.R., Wiese, D.M., & Klint, K.A. (1989). Head over heels with success: The relationship between self-efficacy and performance in competitive youth gymnastics. *Journal of Sport & Exercise Psychology, 11*, 444–451.

White, R.W. (1959). Motivation reconsidered: The concept of competence. *Psychological Review, 66*, 297–323.

White, S.A. (1996). Goal orientation and perceptions of the motivational climate initiated by parents. *Pediatric Exercise Science, 8*, 122–129.

Whitehead, J. (1995). Multiple achievement orientations and participation in youth sport: A cultural and developmental perspective. *International Journal of Sport Psychology, 26*, 431–452.

Wiggins, D.K. (1996). A history of organized play and highly competitive sport for American children. In F.L. Smoll & R.E. Smith (Eds.), *Children and youth in sport: A biopsychosocial perspective* (pp. 15–30). Madison, WI: Brown & Benchmark.

Williams, J.M., & White, K.A. (1983). Adolescent status systems for males and females at three age levels. *Adolescence, 18*, 381–389.

Williams, L. (1994). Goal orientations and athletes' preferences for competence information. *Journal of Sport & Exercise Psychology, 16*, 416–430.

Zarbatany, L., Ghesquiere, K., & Mohr, K. (1992). A context perspective on early adolescents' friendships expectations. *Journal of Early Adolescence, 12*, 111–126.

Zarbatany, L., Hartmann, D.P., & Rankin, D.B. (1990). The psychological functions of preadolescent peer activities. *Child Development, 61*, 1067–1080.

CHAPTER 25

Physical Activity and Quality of Life

BONNIE G. BERGER and ROBERT MOTL

Current research focusing on the complex interrelationships between physical activity and quality of life is reviewed and synthesized in this chapter. We have chosen the phrase "quality of life" to emphasize the diverse contributions of exercise to an individual's life. Quality of life depicts the health enhancement model of physical activity, such as increases in vitality, enhanced mood states, and personal enjoyment, rather than a disease-prevention model, with its typical focus on prevention of coronary artery disease, obesity, and cancer. "Subjective well-being" is closely related to quality of life and is theorized to be composed of three major constructs: the absence of negative affect, the presence of positive affect, and high levels of life satisfaction (Diener, 1994; Mroczek & Kolarz, 1998; Pavot & Diener, 1993). "Happiness," another commonly employed term in everyday conversation, is synonymous with well-being (Mroczek & Kolarz, 1998). Terminology such as quality of life, subjective well-being, and happiness emphasize the current focus in psychology on hedonic psychology, and especially on the phenomenon of "elevation" and the exploration of factors influencing "the good life" (Csikszentmihalyi, 1999; Ruark, 1999). In this chapter, several key areas in which exercise may contribute to the good life are explored—although ultimately the perception of life quality resides with the individual.

We express appreciation to Chris Brandt for his assistance in the preparation of this manuscript and to Robert N. Singer, Heather Hausenblas, and others for their helpful comments on an earlier version of this chapter.

QUALITY OF LIFE

The term "life quality" is similar to subjective well-being and happiness, but denotes an even broader range of components. For many purposes, however, the terms are interchangeable. Life quality reflects the harmonious satisfaction of one's goals and desires as defined in the current literature (e.g., Diener, 1994). The nebulous term quality of life also has been defined as your behavioral functioning ability, or being able to "do stuff" and living long enough to do it (Kaplan, 1994, p. 151). Quality of life emphasizes subjective experience or your perceptions and needs of the spirit, rather than objective conditions of life and affluence (A. Campbell, Converse, & Rogers, 1976; Diener, 1994; Mroczek & Kolarz, 1998). Bradburn (1969) describes life quality or happiness as abundance of positive affect and absence of negative affect. Quality of life also reflects the perceived degree to which individuals are able to satisfy their psychophysiological needs (Dalkey, Lewis, & Snyder, 1972). See Diener (e.g., 1984, 1994; Diener & Suh, 1999) for a discussion of the diverse structures, measurement considerations, and general influences on subjective well-being.

Factors Influencing Quality of Life

Quality of life is a global assessment of your life as a whole. Quality of life reflects an overall sense of well-being and accompanying positive and negative feelings, rather than a narrow focus on one or more life domains, such as work, love, and financial status. The importance of life quality is illustrated by the observation that the quest for understanding what happiness is goes back to the Golden Age of Greece. Aristotle and the Epicureans viewed happiness as the supreme good; all else in a person's life is a means to this end. Once an individual attains happiness, nothing else is desired (Diener, 1994).

Recent research on the quality of life as psychological and cognitive experiences illustrates the paradox that sociodemographic variables such as income, education, marital status, and age explain only a small portion of the differences in individuals' states of happiness (Mroczek & Kolarz, 1998). Individual differences in happiness and the quality of life are universally related to the following:

* *Personality characteristics,* such as extroversion, neuroticism, optimism, and self-esteem (e.g., Diener & Lucas, 1999);
* *Sociodemographic characteristics* of age, education, marital status, gender, income, social class, and social relationships (e.g., Argyle, 1999; Mroczek & Kolarz, 1998; Nolen-Hoeksema & Rusting, 1999);
* *Contextual and situational factors,* such as positive and negative affect (especially frequency rather than intensity), emotion, stress, and physical health (e.g., Morris, 1999); and
* *Subjective* life satisfaction (Diener & Diener, 1996; Oishi, Diener, Lucas, & Suh, 1999).

Cross-cultural influences such as individualistic and collectivist values and the financial status of the country also differentially predict global life satisfaction. For example, in poorer nations, financial satisfaction was more strongly associated with life satisfaction; in wealthy nations, home life satisfaction was more strongly related to life satisfaction and subjective well-being (Oishi et al., 1999). As concluded by Oishi and colleagues, "Universalist theories of SWB [subjective well-being] . . . need to be supplemented with theories that account for cross-cultural differences in values" (pp. 989–990). Among equally wealthy and individualistic nations, however, the factors of personality, sociodemographic variables, contextual variables, situational variables, and subjective experience are major influences on subjective well-being (Diener & Suh, 1999). Exercise programs can contribute to a person's quality of life primarily by influencing the contextual and situational variables of affect, perceived stress, physical health, and life satisfaction.

One approach to categorizing factors that influence the quality of life is depicted in Figure 25.1. In the introduction to their edited book on well-being, Kahneman, Diener, and Schwarz (1999) describe quality of life as including multiple factors and levels. The factors differ in level of

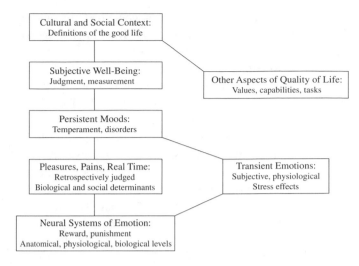

Figure 25.1   Factors of analysis in the quality of life. From *Well-being: The foundations of hedonic psychology* (p. x), by D. Kahneman, E. Diener, and N. Schwarz, 1999, New York: Russell Sage Foundation. Copyright 1999 by Russell Sage Foundation. Adapted with permission.

response to the question What makes for a "good life"? As illustrated in Figure 25.1, the factors include macro *cultural and social context* for both the person responding and the evaluator. Another factor for defining the good life includes *objective characteristics* such as crime rate, poverty, and pollution as well as *values, capabilities, and tasks. Subjective well-being* is another factor and involves judgments and comparisons with other people, your past, ideals, and aspirations. *Persistent mood states* that are loosely connected to daily events and *transient emotions* that include subjective and physiological stress effects are two additional contributors to your quality of life. *Pleasures and pains* and the *underlying neural systems of emotion* and biochemical, anatomical, and physiological processes also are integral components when determining your life quality (Kahneman et al., 1999).

Measuring the Quality of Life

Measures of life quality are as varied as are the definitions. In fact, over 300 scales have been developed to measure quality of life (Spilker, Molinek, Johnston, Simpson, & Tilson, 1990). A typical quality of life measure is the Delighted-Terrible Scale that asks a single question: "How do you feel about your life as a whole?" (Andrews & Withey, 1976). Participants base their responses to this question on the past year and expectations for the near future. As the name of the scale implies, the seven response options vary from "delighted" to "terrible." Single-item quality of life measures include a good/bad dimension, which has a natural zero point that is neither unpleasant nor pleasant (Kahneman et al., 1999).

One way to obtain accurate data on the quality of life is to collect multiple and immediate reports from people in real-life environments (Stone, Shiffman, & De Vries, 1999). In contrast to single-item scales, other quality of life measures reflect a global assessment of subjective well-being but include more than a single item. For example, the Satisfaction with Life Scale (SWLS) includes five items: (1) In most ways my life is close to my ideal; (2) The conditions of my life are excellent; (3) I am satisfied with my life; (4) So far I have gotten the important things I want in life; and (5) If I could live my life over, I would change almost nothing (Diener, Emmons, Larson, & Griffin, 1985). The SWLS is a valid and reliable measure that is appropriate for a wide range of age groups and has a high convergence with peer-reported subjective well-being (Pavot, Diener, Colvin, & Sandvik, 1991).

Some quality of life scales include measures of subjective well-being in specific subdomains that vary from measure to measure and reflect a general index of well-being as described by A. Campbell et al. (1976). Subdomains common to many measures include the biophysical area (health, comfort, food, shelter, exercise); work; self (humor, honesty, accomplishment, self-acceptance); primary social contacts (close relatives, friends); and secondary social components such as acceptance by others, recognition, and prestige. See A. Campbell et al. (1976), Diener (1984), and Flanagan (1978) for in-depth discussions of measuring subjective well-being and for reviews of specific inventories.

After comparing several different measurement strategies including single-item measures, multiple-item scales, and memory search procedures, Pavot and Diener (1993) conclude that the various types of self-report measures demonstrated good reliability across a one-month period, despite fluctuations in transient mood states and item placement within batteries of tests. Although single-item inventories are valid measures of subjective well-being, multi-item inventories are less susceptible to item placement and contextual factors. The self-report measures of subjective well-being also correlate highly with reports by peers, family members, and friends (Pavot & Diener, 1993). For additional measurement considerations such as comparisons of intensity and quality of subjective well-being across contexts, see Diener (1994), Kahneman et al. (1999), Schwarz and Strack (1999), Spilker et al. (1990), and Stone et al. (1999).

Quality of Life and Physical Activity

The time is ripe to devote additional resources to examining the psychological benefits of an active lifestyle. As human beings live longer, they are becoming concerned about their quality of life, particularly the quality of their later years. Funding agencies, academic and therapeutic institutions, and professional organizations also are increasing their awareness and support of the body-mind unity, implications of physical activity for the quality of life, and related programs and research.

Exercise directly influences the health and self subdomains of the quality of life, and it indirectly influences the primary and secondary social components. Because physical activity has been associated with mood benefits, more positive self-concept and self-esteem, increases in self-efficacy, decreases in psychological and physiological stress indices, and the experiences of joy, fun, enjoyment, flow, and other peak experiences, it can play a pivotal role in life quality (Argyle, 1999; Berger, 1994, 1996). In fact, active and participatory recreational activities were one of 15 quality of life components based on 6,500 critical incidents of satisfactory experiences collected from nearly 3,000 people of various ages, regions of the country, races, and backgrounds (Flanagan, 1978). Results indicate that 6 of the 15 components, one of which was active recreation, had the largest correlation coefficients with overall quality of life. Selected aspects of the relationship between life quality and physical activity explored in this chapter include the following themes: (1) the relationship between subjective well-being and exercise in members of "normal" populations, (2) proposed taxonomy for enhancing the psychological benefits of exercise, (3) peak moments in exercise and sport, and (4) the enjoyment of physical activity.

RELATIONSHIP BETWEEN SUBJECTIVE WELL-BEING AND PHYSICAL ACTIVITY IN MEMBERS OF "NORMAL" POPULATIONS

The relationship between physical activity and subjective well-being is complex. Contributing to this complexity is the fact that there are many types and forms of physical activity. Exercise and sport may refer to group or solitary activity, competitive and noncompetitive recreational physical activity, aerobic or anaerobic activity, acute and chronic exercise, and activities performed by individuals who differ greatly in fitness and skill levels. It is likely that the psychological benefits of physical activity, much like the physical benefits, differ across modalities and differ between exercise and sport. Even within a single activity, multitudes of factors vary, including the practice characteristics, the exercise environment, the participants, and the instructors. Another contributor to the complexity of the relationship between exercise and quality of life is that the type and extent of the psychological benefits (and decrements) of exercise also may differ for specific groups of people. These include participants who vary in age from preschoolers to the elderly, as well as individuals from normal and psychiatric populations. Further complicating the interrelationships, the term subjective well-being, as described earlier, includes many facets, such as the absence of negative affect, the presence of positive affect, and high levels of life satisfaction (Diener, 1994; Mroczek & Kolarz, 1998).

Despite such complexities, there is a strong consensus that habitual physical activity can be associated with enhanced subjective well-being or a sense of "feeling better." For in-depth information about the mental health benefits associated with exercise, see the chapters in this *Handbook* by Culos-Reed, Gyurcsik, and Brawley and by Landers and Arent, and reviews by Berger (1994, 1996), Craft and Landers (1998), Hays (1998, 1999), International Society of Sport Psychology (1991), Leith (1994), Morgan (1997), Long and van Stavel (1995), Mutrie and Biddle (1995), and Rostad and Long (1996). It is important to emphasize that the relationship between physical activity and well-being at the present time is one of association rather than cause. Many individuals feel better after exercising. However, the causes of these changes may be the exercise itself or many other influences such as having time out from one's daily hassles, being outside in nature, or interacting with friends (e.g., Berger, 1996). Each of the following generalizations about the relationships between exercise and subjective well-being are presented briefly as a framework for proposing more heuristic hypotheses that can guide future research endeavors.

Acute Mood States

Acute or short-term changes in the mood states of anxiety, depression, and anger have been associated primarily with single exercise sessions in members of the normal population (e.g., Berger, 1994, 1996; International Society of Sport Psychology, 1991; Morgan, 1997; Thayer, 1996). Immediately after exercising, many but not all people feel better than they did before exercising. However, as noted later in this chapter, mood changes have been in undesirable directions if, for example, an individual exercises at too high an intensity or for too long a duration. Thus, it is important

to maintain a balanced perspective on the benefits of physical activity.

Many participants in exercise and sport report the "Iceberg Profile" on the subscales of the Profile of Mood States (POMS; McNair, Lorr, & Droppleman, 1971, 1981, 1992). Morgan (1980) first identified the Iceberg Profile in his classic study investigating the mood states of athletes who hoped to quality for Olympic teams. Although the Iceberg Profile was developed from and based on the mood states of athletes, the profile also has been widely reported by exercisers (see Berger & Motl, 2000, for a review). This profile typically is characterized by Vigor scores that are elevated above a mean *T* score of 50, and by scores on the other POMS subscales of Tension, Depression, Anger, Fatigue, and Confusion that are submerged beneath the surface, or mean, of the normative population. See Figures 25.2a and 25.2b for representative profiles of individuals before and after exercise sessions. As reflected by the

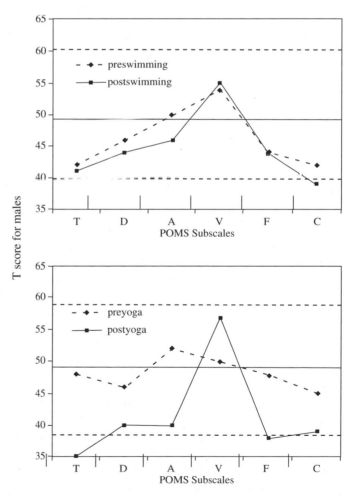

Figure 25.2a POMS scores of men before and after Hatha yoga and swimming sessions (Berger & Owen, 1992a).

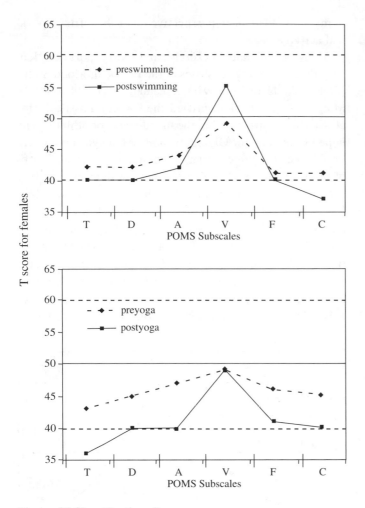

Figure 25.2b   (Continued).

swimmers and Hatha yoga participants in Figure 25.2a and 25.2b (Berger & Owen, 1992a), participants in physical activity often report decreases on the Tension, Depression, Anger, and Confusion subscales of the POMs. Changes on the Vigor and Fatigue subscales have been in both desirable and undesirable directions and seem to be related to intensity and duration of the physical activity. In comparison to chronic mood changes, the acute changes in mood are more clearly associated with the intervening activity of exercise (e.g., Berger, Friedman, & Eaton, 1988).

As reviewed in the next section, some types of physical activity are more likely to be associated with mood benefits than others. Specific physical activities associated with mood enhancement include aerobic dance, circuit training, country line-dancing, cycling, Hatha yoga, jogging, rock climbing, swimming, Tai Chi, and weight training. See Table 25.1 for a representative sample of studies in which these activities have been of interest. In addition to

mode of activity, training factors such as exercise intensity, frequency, and duration as well as various personal characteristics of the participants such as fitness level and age may be related to the direction and extent of the mood changes (Berger, 1996).

Among members of a normal population, acute changes in mood tend to last for at least two to four hours after exercising (Raglin & Morgan, 1987; Thayer, 1996). Although this may seem to be a short length of time, experiencing more positive moods for even this length of time may have a highly desirable influence on quality of life. During the two to four hours, the mood changes can influence an individual's social interactions with colleagues and friends, choice of work projects, and even work efficiency. These interactions and events then may spill over and affect the person's quality of life for even longer periods of time, especially when they are experienced on a daily basis.

Chronic Changes

There also may be chronic or longer-lasting benefits, as evidenced by stable changes in mood, especially in anxiety and depression. Chronic benefits may be associated with exercise programs lasting a few weeks, months, or as long as a year (e.g., Berger et al., 1988; Brown et al., 1995). Unfortunately, it is difficult to attribute the occurrence of such changes in the normal population to the exercise program itself. When measured prior to starting the exercise program and at the end of a lengthy exercise program, the changes may be due to the exercise itself or to other seasonal and life influences. Until more research data are available about chronic changes in mood for members of a normal population, claims for benefits need to be restricted to those reported immediately after exercise sessions. Members of psychiatric populations, however, tend to report more lasting or chronic changes in mood as their depression and/or anxiety levels decrease (e.g., Hays, 1998, 1999; Martinsen & Morgan, 1997). If a person is clinically anxious, depressed, or highly stressed, there is more opportunity for long-term mood improvement.

Moderating One's Stress Response

Too little stress (i.e., boredom) and too much stress have detrimental influences on the quality of life. Both too little and too much stress result in "distress," which is shortened to the word "stress" in everyday usage. Distress/stress detracts from one's zest for living and the quality of life (Berger, 1994). In contrast to stress, the term "eustress" denotes an optimal level of stress and refers to a highly desirable stress that is exhilarating, exciting, and challenging (see Berger, 1994, for a review). Experiencing optimal levels of stress contributes directly to the quality of everyday life. Stress, which has been referred to as the "spice of life" by Selye (1975, p. 83), is integrally related to subjective well-being, as individuals self-regulate its level along a continuum progressing from too little, to optimal, to too much.

Stress often is defined as "a relationship with the environment that the person appraises as significant for his or her well-being and in which the demands tax or exceed available coping resources" (Lazarus & Folkman, 1986, p. 63). Anxiety, a psychological characteristic that is malleable by exercise, is a common response to situations that are appraised as threatening to a person's well-being. Although individuals vary in optimal levels of stress, a personal appraisal of "too much stress" often is associated with physical illness, high blood pressure, and rapid pulse rate (see Seaward, 1997, for a review.) Too much stress also is associated with psychological distress, as reflected by anxiety, depression, hostility, and personal unhappiness in general (Avison & Gotlib, 1994). Various stress management techniques are useful in reducing the deleterious effects of stress, and one of these is exercise.

Physical activity is an effective stress management technique. Exercise and sport are multifaceted coping techniques that can assist participants in raising or lowering stress levels and, thus, move toward personally optimal levels. For example, physical activity serves as a technique for increasing stress levels as experienced in competitive and in high-risk physical activities such as rock climbing, downhill skiing, and scuba diving. Exercise also serves as a means for reducing stress levels, as experienced in noncompetitive, rhythmical physical activities that promote abdominal breathing, such as jogging, swimming, and Hatha yoga. Participants have "time out" from a busy day, time to think and problem-solve while exercising, and an opportunity to experience their bodies in movement.

Physical activity can play a key role in moderating psychological and/or physical stress symptoms. Together, the psychological and physical changes associated with exercise can interact to produce the "feeling better" sensation. Some of the psychological changes that habitual exercisers report include decreased levels of state and trait anxiety, increases in positive mood states, feelings of attractiveness, and a sense of being more sure of themselves (see studies in Table 25.1). Exercisers also tend to be more confident about their physical capabilities and have more positive self-concepts (Berger, 1994). As a result of these psychological changes, exercisers have greater psychological resources for coping with stressful

situations. As concluded by Rostad and Long (1996, p. 216) in a review of studies examining exercise as a stress management technique, results in the 46 studies reviewed indicated "some improvement on psychological and physiological variables."

Exercise directly addresses several components of Lazarus and Folkman's (1994) cognitive theory of stress and coping. As concluded by Rostad and Long (1996), exercise can serve as an emotional-focused coping strategy, as a problem-focused coping technique, or as an approach for enhancing one's personal resources. Exercise can facilitate emotion-based coping by reducing the undesirable stress-related emotions and moods of anxiety, depression, fatigue, and confusion. Reflecting the use of exercise as a problem-solving coping technique, participants can devise strategies while exercising to address stressful situations. Exercisers also may enhance their personal resources by increased experiencing of self-efficacy, self-confidence, and physical energy and/or fitness.

Results of studies examining the influence of acute and chronic exercise on psychological and physiological stress indices are difficult to interpret and to compare with one another. For example, results may differ according to the timing of a stressor in relation to exercise, the nature of stress tasks, and the type of exercise investigated. Despite these difficulties of interpretation, it seems that individuals who are fit and those who exercise habitually have reduced stress symptoms. These observations apply to individuals in both normal and clinical populations who have exercised for a six-week period or longer (Petruzzello, Landers, Hatfield, Kubitz, & Salizar, 1991; Rostad & Long, 1996). Additional research is needed to determine whether exercise is an effective stress management technique for individuals who are not particularly stressed, the role of expectancy in the exercise–stress management relationship, and the effectiveness of particular types of exercise. Despite remaining questions, there is a positive trend in the research supporting the effectiveness of exercise in reducing stress levels (Long & van Stavel, 1995; Rostad & Long, 1996). Habitual exercisers tend to recover from stress more rapidly (e.g., Sinyor, Schwartz, Peronnet, Brisson, & Seraganian, 1993), have attenuated (or more pronounced) psychophysical stress responses (e.g., Claytor, 1991; Dienstbier, 1989; Long, 1991; Rejeski, Thompson, Brubaker, & Miller, 1992), have less physical illness when experiencing many negative life events (e.g., Brown, 1991; Brown & Siegel, 1988), and occasionally increase their stress levels by overexercising and possibly trigger an immunosupressive response (Mackinnon, 1992).

Table 25.1 Acute Mood Changes in a Variety of Physical Activity Modes for Members of Normal Populations

Activities and Authors	Sex	Age (Years)	Duration/Intensity	POMS Subscale Changes[1]
Aerobic dance				
Dyer & Crouch (1988)	M/F	17 to 26	45 min./N/A	T, D, V, C
Maroulakis & Zervas (1993)	F	19 to 55; $M = 28.8$	30 min./60–80% $HR_{reserve}$	T, D, A, V, C
McInman & Berger (1993)	F	15 to 43; $M = 23.1$	45 min./N/A	T, D, A, V, C
Cycling				
Farrell et al. (1986)	M	$M = 24.2$	30 min./70% VO_{2max}	T
Steptoe & Cox (1988)	F	18 to 23; $M = 20$	8 min./25 watts	V
			100 watts	T, V, F
Steptoe et al. (1993)	M	20 to 35 Active $M = 26.4$ Inactive $M = 27.3$	20 min./50 & 70% VO_{2max}	T, V
Hatha Yoga				
Berger & Owen (1988)	M/F	$Ms = 22.8$ & 27.2	40 & 80 min./N/A	T, D, A, F, C
Berger & Owen (1992a)	M/F	$M = 28.4$	60 min./N/A	T, D, A, F, C
Jogging				
Berger et al. (1988)	M/F	$M = 20$	20 min./65–80% HR_{max}	T, D, A
Berger & Owen (1998)	M/F	$Ms = 20.7$ to 25.1	20 min./55, 75, & 79% HR_{max}	T, D, A, V, F, C
Berger et al. (1998)				
Study 1	M/F	18 to 51; $M = 21.39$	15 min./50, 65, & 80% HR_{max}	T, D, A, V, C (females only)
Study 2	M/F	18 to 45; $M = 22.22$	15 min./50, 65, & 85% HR_{max}	T, D, A, V, C
Boutcher & Landers (1988)	M	N/A	20 min./80 to 85% HR_{max}	No changes
Dyer & Crouch (1988)	M/F	17 to 26	30 min./N/A	T, D, A, V, F, C
Farrell et al. (1987)	M	$M = 27.4$	80 min./40% VO_{2max}	No change
			80 min./60% VO_{2max}	T
			40 min./80% VO_{2max}	T
Kraemer et al. (1990)	M/F	$Ms = 28.8$ to 31.5	30 min./80% HR_{max}	T, D, A, C, TMD
Rock climbing				
Motl et al. (in press)	M	18 to 38; $M = 25.5$	10 to 50 min./N/A	T, D, V, C
Berger et al. (1997)	M/F	12 to 20; $M = 14.6$		
			3,500–5,000 meters/N/A	T, D, C
			6,000–7,000 meters/N/A	V, F, TMD
Berger et al. (1993)	F	$M = 22.4$ CZ	60 min./N/A	T, D, A, V, C
		$M = 20.5$ U.S.	30 min./N/A	T, D, A, V, C
Berger & Owen (1988)	M/F	N/A	40 min./N/A	T, C
Berger & Owen (1992a)	M/F	$Ms = 20.3$ & 21.1	25 to 30 min./N/A	T, D, A, V, C
Tai Chi				
Jin (1992)	F	$M = 37.8$	60 min./N/A	V, TMD
	M	$M = 34.6$		
Walking				
Berger & Owen (1998)	M/F	$M = 22.3$	20 min./55, 75, & 79% HR_{max}	T, D, A, V, F, C
Jin (1992)	F	$M = 34.6$	60 min./6 km/hr.	TMD
	M	$M = 37.8$		
Weight training				
Dyer & Crouch (1988)	M/F	17 to 26	40 min./N/A	A, V, C

M = male and F = female; N/A = information not available; T = tension, D = depression, A = anger, V = vigor, F = fatigue, C = confusion, and TMD = total mood disturbance; POMS = profile of mood states; M = mean; CZ = Czechoslovakian; U.S. = United States.

[1]POMS subscale changes were in both desirable and in undesirable directions.

Source: Berger, B.G., & Motl, R.W. (2000). Exercise and Mood: A selective review and synthesis of research employing the Profile of Mood States. *Journal of Applied Sport Psychology.* Copyright 2000 by the Association for the Advancement of Applied Sport Psychology. Reprinted with permission.

In conclusion, there is accumulating evidence that physical activity is a multifaceted stress management technique that enables participants to increase as well as decrease their stress levels and move toward establishing optimal levels. Competitive physical activity and high-risk activities such as rock climbing, sky diving, and even football enable participants to increase their level of stress and perhaps experience feelings of eustress. Participation in noncompetitive and highly predictable exercise modes facilitates stress reduction. Although the specific stress-reduction mechanisms are unclear, they probably include opportunities for returning to environments that are within the participants' capabilities, time out from busy days, time for introspection, and experiences that nourish the soul. As concluded by Rostad and Long (1996) in a review of 46 preexperimental, quasi-experimental, and experimental research studies, there were improvements on the psychological or physiological stress variables in each of the studies. It seems that exercise can serve as a coping strategy for stress reduction by facilitating emotion-based coping, by providing opportunity for problem solving, and by enhancing personal resources.

Effectiveness of Exercise in Comparison to Other Approaches for Enhancing Subjective Well-Being

Although exercise is an effective stress management technique, it is important to recognize that it is only one of many possible approaches to enhancing one's quality of life. A particularly appealing aspect of the use of exercise to enhance one's subjective well-being, however, is that it simultaneously provides a variety of health benefits and desirable changes in appearance by increasing muscle definition and reducing body fat. Some of the other, less physically active mood enhancement techniques listed in Table 25.2 do not provide these additional health benefits. They do, however, have the appeal of ease and immediacy.

Exercise has been shown to be as effective as more traditional mood management and stress-reduction approaches such as reading, Benson's relaxation response, quiet rest, and eating a sugar snack in reducing anxiety, tension, depression, and anger (Bahrke & Morgan, 1978; Berger et al., 1988; Jin, 1992; Long, 1993; Long & van Stavel, 1995). These effects were particularly impressive because the participants in some of the studies were randomly assigned to treatment. Thus, exercise was stress-reducing even for individuals who were not self-selected exercisers. The observation that the benefits of exercise were comparable, but not superior, to the other mood management techniques emphasizes the need for realistic claims regarding the benefits of exercise. Further investigation is needed to clarify whether the psychological benefits of exercise and other stress management techniques differ in regard to the duration of the benefits, patterns of change on mood profiles, and possible underlying mechanisms.

A Need for Caution: Possible Mood Decrements

When examining the relationship between exercise and the quality of life, it is important to recognize that exercise also can have negative influences on mood in particular, and on quality of life in general. For example, exercise

Table 25.2 Procedures for Changing Negative into Positive Moods and for Maintaining Positive Moods

Procedure	Reference
Active mood management	
Exercise	Berger, 1996; Gallup & Castelli, 1989; Thayer, 1996; Thayer et al., 1994
Light therapy	Schwartz & Clore, 1983; Thayer, 1996
Music and guided imagery therapy	Campbell, 1997; McKinney, Antoni, Kumar, Tims, & McCabe, 1997
Prayer	Gallup & Castelli, 1989
Walking	Berger & Owen, 1998; Rippere, 1977; Thayer et al., 1994
Yoga	Berger & Owen, 1988, 1992a; Thayer, 1996
Distraction and seeking pleasurable activities	
Keeping busy, avoidance	Rippere, 1977; Thayer et al., 1994
Listening to music	Clark & Teasdale, 1985; Fried & Berkowitz, 1979; Rippere, 1977; Thayer et al., 1994
Social support	
Social interaction	Rippere, 1977; Thayer, 1996; Thayer et al., 1994
Passive mood management	
Coffee	Thayer, 1996; Thayer, et al., 1994
Food, especially good-tasting	Thayer, 1996; Thayer et al., 1994
Direct tension reduction	
Alcohol and recreational drug use	Thayer et al., 1994

compulsion or addiction, injuries, eating disorders, and even extreme competitiveness are not conducive to enhanced quality of life. Many individuals find that feeling physically inept, noting slow progress with one's physical skills, experiencing overtraining or burnout, encountering an overuse injury, and even losing a competitive match can be associated with undesirable psychological changes (e.g., Berger, Butki, & Berwind, 1995; Hays, 1999; O'Conner, 1997). Typical mood changes might include personal disappointment, fatigue, depression, anxiety, anger, and decreased energy. With acknowledgment of possible mood detriments in specific exercise settings, there are sufficient data to support the conclusion that habitual physical activity can be associated with desirable changes in subjective well-being (see references in Table 25.1).

Conclusions: Relationships between Physical Activity and Subjective Well-Being

Many exercisers have personally experienced the psychological benefits of physical activity, as reflected in the following observation of Sarah Ban Breathnach (1998), author of a best-selling book, *Something More: Excavating Your Authentic Self:* "A half hour of walking every other day increases your vitality and energy level and you find yourself less depressed. Suddenly you become more relaxed and fun to be around. You smile, maybe even laugh" (p. 86).

Despite the benefits of exercise as described by Breathnach in her best-seller, they are not guaranteed to occur. Sometimes, there are no mood changes; at other times, the changes are in an undesirable direction. It seems that some types and formats of exercise and sport are more likely to enhance the quality of life than others. A taxonomy to identify the essential attributes of physical activities that facilitate the enhanced subjective well-being of participants has been proposed to avoid investigating the psychological benefits of each type of physical activity individually. Such a taxonomy can serve as a useful guide for analyzing some of the underlying factors that facilitate the beneficial effects. A taxonomy would be of particular value to exercise psychologists, other mental health professionals, physical educators, sport scientists, and individuals in the general population who wish to use exercise for stress reduction and/or for enhancing the quality of life. In the next section, specific exercise parameters that seem to influence the mood benefits of exercise and other psychological benefits such as self-concept, flow, maintenance of zest and vitality throughout one's life, and personal enjoyment will be examined.

As emphasized throughout the chapter, the mental health benefits of physical activity are not automatic and depend on multiple factors. Extensive research is needed to better understand the interrelationships and to suggest appropriate guidelines to increase the psychological benefits of physical activity for recreational and athletic participants. A taxonomy is proposed that describes some potential relationships among type of physical activity, training factors, and psychological benefits.

PROPOSED TAXONOMY FOR ENHANCING THE PSYCHOLOGICAL BENEFITS OF PHYSICAL ACTIVITY

Although sport and motor skill classification systems were proposed and developed as long as 40 years ago, they have little relationship to the psychological benefits of exercise. There is a critical need to examine exercise characteristics and parameters that enhance mental health benefits due to an apparent assumption that the same well-established

guidelines for physiological functioning (e.g., American College of Sports Medicine, 1995) also apply to the psychological benefits of exercise. This assumption quite likely is incorrect, despite the body-mind relationship. Emphasizing the lack of guidelines for the psychological benefits of exercise, participants in a state-of-the-art conference on exercise and mental health concluded that there was a need to investigate "the optimal *mode, intensity, duration, and frequency* of exercise required to provide more effective responses to mental stress" (Morgan & Goldston, 1987, p. 157; italics added). Some progress in investigating these areas has been made in past years. However, there still is a great need for additional research, especially in the areas of exercise mode and duration.

Recognizing the need for a taxonomy to predict which types of physical activity will have the greatest psychological benefits of exercise, Berger and her colleagues (Berger, 1983/1984, 1996; Berger & McInman, 1993; Berger & Motl, 2000; Berger & Owen, 1988, 1992a, 1992b, 1998) have proposed such a taxonomy. It is presented here in detail, because it highlights some of the major issues in the relationship between subjective well-being and physical activity. Certain factors are based on replicable research; others are more speculative. The taxonomy will need revision as new relevant research is conducted. As illustrated in Figure 25.3, there are three primary components in the taxonomy: enjoyment of the activity, type of activity or mode characteristics, and practice requirements (Berger, 1996).

Pleasing and Enjoyable

Before discussing enjoyment, it is important to define what the term means. A detailed description of enjoyment was

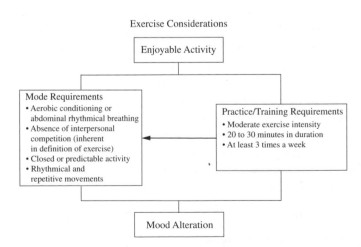

Figure 25.3 Tentative taxonomy for enhancing the psychological benefits of exercise.

offered earlier. Researchers often differ on the definition of enjoyment (e.g., Kimiecik & Harris, 1996; Scanlan & Simons, 1992; Wankel, 1997). For the purposes of the taxonomy, we accepted Kimiecik and Harris's definition: "An optimal psychological state (i.e., flow) that leads to performing an activity for its own sake and is associated with positive feeling states" (p. 256). Kimiecik and Harris continue, "Enjoyment is *not an affective product of experience,* but *a psychological process that is the experience*" (p. 257; italics added).

Enjoyment is the first component in the exercise taxonomy because it has primary importance over the other factors. This overriding requirement adjusts for individual differences and preferences of physical activity type and training characteristics. An activity that is mood-enhancing or stress-reducing for many participants may be stress-producing for others. For example, some might enjoy the social atmosphere when running on a treadmill in a health club in the presence of other club members; other individuals might find such an experience to be stress-producing. As concluded in the final section of this chapter, enjoyment seems to be an important consideration for exercisers who wish to maximize the psychological benefits of physical activity. If exercise is unpleasant, it is unlikely that participants will feel better after exercising. Thus, exercise participants who are seeking the psychological benefits of mood enhancement would be well-advised to seek alternate activities if some aspect of an activity is unpleasant (Berger, 1996). Activity "enjoyment" clearly is an individual phenomenon. Because enjoyment is related to exercise adherence (Scanlan & Simons, 1992; Wankel, 1993), it affects the potential long-term success of the use of exercise for elevating subjective well-being (Wankel & Berger, 1990).

Mode Characteristics

In addition to exercise enjoyment, the type, or mode, of exercise also seems to influence the relationship between exercise and subjective well-being. See Figure 25.1 for a listing of these potential mode considerations.

Rhythmical Abdominal Breathing or an Aerobic Quality

A large body of literature supports a relationship between aerobic types of exercise and subjective well-being (e.g., Berger et al., 1988; Berger & Owen, 1988; Long & van Stavel, 1995; Plante, Lantis, & Checa, 1998; Rostad & Long, 1996). Little research has been published that directly investigates the need for aerobic rather than other

types of exercise for the promotion of mood alteration. The psychological effects of less intense exercise, that is, below the aerobic training zone, have been investigated primarily as a control condition to contrast with aerobic training activities (e.g., Long & van Stavel, 1995).

Studies that have been focused on exercise modes with relatively little aerobic training benefit, such as weight training and Hatha yoga, support the possibility that diverse exercise modes are associated with psychological benefits (e.g., Berger & Owen, 1988, 1992a; Jin, 1992; O'Connor, Bryant, Veltri, & Gebhardt, 1993). As concluded by Leith (1994, p. 22), "Research has not yet identified one particular type of exercise as being superior in terms of its potential to reduce depression in the participant. *Both aerobic and anaerobic exercise sessions appear equally effective.*"

Rhythmical abdominal breathing (generated by aerobic exercise and other less intense types of exercise) may lead to enhanced subjective well-being. Recent psychological studies of Hatha yoga, Tai Chi, walking, and riding a bicycle ergometer at light workloads lend credence to the possibility that exercise-associated changes in breathing patterns, rather than the aerobic quality, are associated with psychological benefits (Berger & Owen, 1988, 1992a; Jin, 1992; Thayer, 1987). These activities meet the taxonomy requirements, except for the aerobic guideline. However, they do encourage participants to engage in abdominal rhythmical breathing. As suggested by Berger (1996), it may be abdominal, diaphragmatic, rhythmical breathing, a concomitant of aerobic exercise, that is conducive to enhanced subjective well-being.

Because the importance of rhythmical abdominal breathing in the mood benefits of exercise has generated little or no objective research, there is a strong need for studies to clarify the role of aerobic as well as less intense exercise in enhancing mental health. Kabat-Zinn, former director of the Stress Reduction Clinic at the University of Massachusetts Medical Center, emphasizes the importance of mindfully tuning in to one's breathing as a technique for stress reduction and pain control. Rather than the aerobic exercise, it may be the change in breathing patterns that often accompanies aerobic exercise that is associated with feelings of well-being. Kabat-Zinn's (1990) description of the breathing process in meditation can be an integral part of any exercise session. Rhythmical abdominal breathing tends to happen anatomically as a person exercises and tunes in to bodily changes resulting from physical exertion.

Consciously being aware of one's breathing patterns and changing them is basic in many stress management techniques, including yoga, biofeedback, and the relaxation response. Hatha yoga, the exercise form of yoga, helps the exerciser to balance mind, body, and spirit through physical activity (Seaward, 1997). Major benefits of Hatha yoga are feelings of calmness, increased flexibility, static muscle strength, muscle relaxation, increased bodily awareness, and an alert mind. Other types of exercise may accomplish the same objectives, but more research needs to focus on these benefits, which are considerably broader than mood alteration. Until recently, however, changes in breathing patterns have generated little objective research (Fried, 1993), and there still is a need for research in this area.

Relative Absence of Interpersonal Competition

Competition seems to be part of life in the United States and in many other developed and developing countries. Competition can add zest and excitement to one's life and is a major component in many types of physical activity. Taken to an extreme, however, and constantly competing in all domains of life, can be counterproductive to high life quality. Competitiveness can be stressful, associated with negative mood states, and provide the impetus to constantly strive to do "more." As emphasized in Gallwey's (1997) "inner game" approach, in very competitive situations, neither the present moment nor personal accomplishments may be savored. Some of Gallwey's suggestions for competing "well" include avoiding being judgmental, bringing harmony to mind and body, feeling the body in movement, and appreciating the obstacles presented by an opponent—since responding to them brings out a high level of performance in oneself. Due to the difficulty of adopting Gallwey's inner game approach to competitive forms of recreational physical activity by many members of Western society, the taxonomy in this chapter includes noncompetitive forms of physical activity. Physical activity that is noncompetitive (in reference to others and to oneself) is conducive to desirable mood alteration, stress reduction, and enhanced sense of accomplishment and physical prowess.

Emphasizing the importance of an absence of competition in his discussion of exercise characteristics leading to positive addictions, Glasser (1976) theorized that "positive addictions" (PA), in contrast to "negative addictions," lead to confidence, creativity, happiness, and health. As Glasser emphasized, "Not only must we not compete with others, we must learn not to compete with ourselves if we want to reach the PA state" (p. 57). In contrast to Glasser's theory that positive addictions enhance the quality of life, negative addictions detract from its quality. Physical activity detracts from quality of life if the person *must* exercise to maintain subjective well-being or if exercise interferes with other life obligations or physical health.

Supporting the need for less competition, recreational swimmers have reported more positive mood profiles than intercollegiate competitive swimmers who consistently participate in high-intensity, long-duration training (Riddick, 1984). More specifically, recreational swimmers and a group of sedentary controls were significantly lower in fatigue, depression, anger, and confusion than the competitive swimmers. These results must be regarded as tentative, because Riddick tested swimmers whenever they were available: before, during, and after swimming sessions. Whether they were tested before or after swimming could have had a direct influence on their mood states.

A relative absence of interpersonal competition can enhance the psychological benefits of physical activity for many reasons. For one, noncompetitive activities enable the participant to avoid the negative psychological effects of losing. Losing occurs in competitive recreational physical activity as well as in sport competition approximately 50% of the time. For many individuals, losing detracts from positive mood states such as joy and vigor. Losing also tends to detract from feelings of self-efficacy, pride, accomplishment, competency, and control. In addition, losing is associated with stress and higher scores on negative mood states than is winning (e.g., Berger et al., 1995; Grove & Prapavessis, 1992; Hassmén & Blomstrand, 1995; Kerr & Schaik, 1995). Game outcome seems to greatly affect the acute changes in pleasant and unpleasant moods associated with competitive physical activity.

Another reason (in addition to losing) why participants in competitive recreational physical activity and sport may not be associated with enhanced subjective well-being is that competitive participants tend to overtrain and to extend their physical competencies fully during competition. Overtraining especially to the beginning of staleness, and subsequent burnout are associated with undesirable mood states and decreased subjective well-being (O'Connor, 1997). As concluded by Morgan and colleagues (Morgan, Brown, Raglin, O'Conner, & Ellickson, 1987, p. 109), "Perhaps the most notable feature of this particular study is the apparent paradox observed in connection with the exercise-depression relationship. Whereas vigorous exercise is known to reduce depression in moderately depressed individuals . . . depression also seems to be a product of overtraining." Again, it is not clear in the studies reported by Morgan and colleagues exactly *when,* in reference to the actual swimming, the swimmers were tested. As suggested in a subsequent section on exercise intensity, high intensity exercise often associated with competitive forms of physical activity does not seem to be associated with desirable changes in mood states.

To test the possibility that physically taxing training aspects of competitive sport are related to mood decrements, Berger, Grove, Prapavessis, and Butki (1997) examined the relationship between training distance and mood alteration in age-group competitive swimmers. Results indicated a significant interaction between training distance and mood. Shortened, tapered practice sessions (3,500 to 5,000 meters), which typically were held prior to competition, were associated with acute decreases in total mood disturbance scores, depression, and confusion. However, during the more typical normal-distance practice sessions (6,000 to 7,000 meters), total mood disturbance significantly increased. The young swimmers reported increased fatigue and decreased vigor. Thus, competitive swimming practice was associated with mood benefits only when athletes swam practice distances that were shorter than usual. Many participants in recreational competitive activities as well as athletes complete training sessions that tax their maximal physical capabilities. It seems unlikely that competitive practice sessions are mood enhancing (Berger et al., 1997; Morgan et al.; Morgan, Costill, Flynn, Raglin, & O'Connor, 1988).

In conclusion, the relative absence or presence of competition in recreational physical activity is an important factor in the personal choice of an exercise mode. Some individuals find exercise without the competitive element to be boring, and thus competition is an appealing aspect of physical activity. Others find competition in recreational physical activity to be a continuation of an already competition-filled lifestyle. For these people, exercise, especially when performed in a noncompetitive manner, can provide a measured period of noncompetition, a respite from a typically hectic, often competitive day.

Closed, Predictable, and Temporally and Spatially Certain Activities

Jogging and swimming, two activities repeatedly associated with psychological benefits, are highly predictable, closed, and temporally and spatially certain activities (Berger, 1972; Gentile, 1972, 1992; Poulton, 1957; Singer & Gerson, 1981). Closed environments tend to occur in individual types of physical activity and allow participants to preplan their movements and patterns of energy expenditure. Participants tend to encounter few unexpected events

that require careful attention. Self-paced activities enable participants to tune out the environment and engage in free-association while they are exercising (Berger, 1980, 1994, 1996). Rybczynski's (1991) observations about the benefits of solitary reading also apply to closed, spatially certain physical activities. Closed sport activities, such as jogging and swimming, provide opportunity for solitude, contemplation, reflection, and withdrawal. This withdrawal can be from the world and withdrawal into oneself. Joggers and swimmers report appreciation of the solitude and periods of imagination and creativity of thought while exercising (e.g., Berger & Mackenzie, 1980; Paffenbarger & Olsen, 1996; Rimer, 1990). The opportunity to tune in to one's inner thoughts during this exercise time of peace and quiet may contribute to feelings of well-being. There also is the opportunity while exercising in closed predictable activities to have no thoughts at all.

Research evidence supports the psychological value of solitary time for thinking because it facilitates "mental stimulation." As theorized by Taylor and colleagues (Taylor, Pham, Rivkin, & Armor, 1998), some of the primary benefits of mental stimulation are the provision of opportunities to envision new solutions to problems and new possibilities. Mental stimulation during solitary periods as described by Taylor et al. also allows the exerciser to anticipate and manage emotions associated with such problems and possibilities, and then to develop plans of action to initiate and maintain problem-solving behavior.

Noting the importance of solitude when exercising and the accompanying creativity, George Sheehan (1990) commented, "Where once I found all my good thoughts on the run, I now find them in *other solitary movement* [italics added]. Given the choice I might walk rather than run—or choose to cycle over either one" (p. 210). Glass (1976, p. 93) supported the importance of predictability when he observed that activities which do not require great mental effort are likely to become positive addictions. In summary, having the opportunity to harness one's imagination while exercising is an important benefit of participating in closed predictable forms of exercise.

A near absence of thought can occur in closed activities and is highly valued in Eastern types of physical activity such as Hatha yoga. This is illustrated by a typical article about yoga entitled, "Awakening Spirit: The Power of Silence" (Shraddhananda, 1997). Although there is little or no research evidence to support the need of quiet time, the common personal descriptions of its importance highlight a need to investigate this area within exercise psychology. As noted by Shaddhananda, when thinking and worrying come to a stop, energy is no longer being fragmented or dispersed. In the silence that follows the ending of thought, we actually experience a gathering, an accumulation of energy.

Individuals who choose to participate in closed physical activities tend to enjoy the predictability and solitude of the activities and/or the opportunity not to attend to the immediate exercise situation. Some of the subjective well-being benefits of these predictable activities may be related to opportunities presented to harness the imagination, to problem-solve, and to experience related emotions associated with problems and other general plans of action. Participants in closed activities can preplan their movements and engage in free association while they exercise (Berger, 1994, 1996). Supporting the importance of predictable types of exercise, participants in Hatha yoga and joggers reported greater mood benefits on tension, depression, anger, fatigue, and confusion subscales of the POMS than did fencers. Fencing is a less predictable and more open activity than is yoga and jogging.

Despite the benefits, some people clearly do not enjoy closed types of exercise. These individuals tend to find that closed physical activities are boring and prefer the unpredictability of open exercise activities such as tennis, baseball, and basketball. There is little or no information available concerning the mental health benefits of these other types of activities (e.g., Berger, 1972). Because open physical activities usually involve competition against at least one other person, examination of acute mood effects associated with activity outcome is greatly needed. Open types of activities tend to be exhilarating and somewhat stress-producing. Clearly, various types of physical activity are associated with differing psychological changes that may be either desirable or undesirable to different individuals.

Rhythmical and Repetitive Movements

Repetitive and rhythmical movements, in addition to those that are closed, may be conducive to subjective well-being. Both types of exercise do not require much attention. Thus, the participant's mind is free to wander while exercising (Berger, 1980; Berger & Mackenzie, 1980). The rhythmicity of repetitive movements might encourage introspection or creative thinking during participation. Paffenbarger and Olsen (1996) speculated that rhythmical movements can have a hypnotic, relaxing effect and provide opportunities for wide-ranging thoughts. The repetitive monotony of these movements also might encourage introspective and/or creative thinking during participation. *"The routine rhythmic motion* of running or walking, in particular,

requires little thought or attention. Anyone who has run or walked regularly for even a few minutes knows how the *mind seems to open to a flood of thoughts and emotions;* solutions to nagging problems suddenly appear like flashing 100-watt bulbs. Fantasies arise. You find yourself thinking of all of the smart things you should have said to the cop who gave you that speeding ticket" (Paffenbarger & Olsen, 1996, p. 225).

Exercisers describe the psychological benefits associated with participating in rhythmical and repetitive movements, but the mental clarity, creativity, and feelings of peace are difficult to investigate. In a phenomenological study of the meaning of jogging to the participant, Berger and Mackenzie (1980) asked a woman jogger to keep a personal journal of her thoughts and emotions while completing 32 jogging sessions during a four-month period. In addition to the diary material, three weekly 50-minute interviews were held immediately after jogging. Interested in investigating the meaningfulness of physical activity to participants, the jogger was asked directly what she experienced while jogging. One of the four propositions emanating from the study was that repetitive and rhythmical types of exercise are conducive to introspection and to thinking in general.

In conclusion, it is clear that additional research is needed to explore the types of physical activity that are associated with self-insight, mood alteration, feelings of self-efficacy, and enhanced self-concept. Presently, it seems that exercise modes that promote rhythmical abdominal breathing, include relatively little competition against others and oneself, are closed or predictable, and are rhythmical and repetitive are likely to be associated with subjective well-being.

Practice Requirements

In this section, the practice conditions of exercise (see Figure 25.3) that may influence the relationship between quality of life and physical activity are examined. Physiologically, the training considerations of exercise intensity, frequency, and duration are clear (e.g., American College of Sports Medicine, 1995). However the parameters of these training requirements may change depending on the psychological benefits desired. The three training characteristics of intensity, duration, and frequency are labeled "practice requirements" to emphasize their relationship to subjective well-being and to contrast them with "training guidelines" that contribute to developing physiological capabilities such as cardiorespiratory fitness, strength, speed, and endurance.

Intensity: Moderate

The exercise intensity requirement for facilitating the participant's subjective well-being and quality of life is controversial. However, moderate exercise consistently seems to be associated with enhancing mental health (e.g., Berger & Motl, 2000; Berger & Owen, 1988, 1998; Steptoe, Kearsley, & Walters, 1993). Beyond a certain level, increasing exercise intensity may be counterproductive to feeling better. High-intensity physical activity promotes cardiorespiratory and metabolic training benefits, but high intensity is not always associated with desirable changes in mood (e.g., Berger & Owen, 1992b; Berger et al., 1999; Moses, Steptoe, Matthews, & Edwards, 1989; Motl, Berger, & Wilson, 1996; O'Connor, 1997). It should be noted, however, that other researchers have indicated that high-intensity exercise (e.g., 80% [VO_2max]) may be associated with reduced anxiety (e.g., Boutcher & Landers, 1988; Dishman, 1986; Morgan & Ellickson, 1989).

Researchers have directly investigated the mood changes associated with different exercise intensities. Steptoe and Cox (1988) reported that eight-minute trials of high intensity (100 watts on a bicycle ergometer) exercise was associated with acute increases in tension and fatigue as measured by a modified version of the POMS (McNair et al., 1971/1981/1992). Low-intensity exercise (25 watts) led to positive mood changes in vigor as measured by the POMS and in exhilaration (as measured by three items: invigorated, refreshed, and uplifted). An undesirable relationship between high-intensity exercise and mood was corroborated by Motl and colleagues (1996), who compared the acute changes associated with moderate, high, and maximal exercise intensities. Highly fit collegiate cyclists rode their bicycles on stationary trainers and reported mood benefits immediately after the moderate exercise, no changes after the high-intensity exercise, and undesirable changes after the maximal-intensity sessions. More specifically, moderate cycling at 69% of maximal heart rate (HR_{max}) was associated with decreases on the anger, vigor, fatigue, and confusion subscales of the POMS. Cycling at 89% of HR_{max} was associated with increases in fatigue but no other mood changes, and cycling at maximal heart rate (95% of HR_{max}) was associated with increases in depression, anger, fatigue, and confusion. Because exercise intensity was determined by a percentage of each participant's maximal heart rate, the mood changes associated with specific exercise intensities in athletes would seem applicable to recreational exercise participants. However, the relationship between exercise intensity and mood alteration needs further investigation.

As concluded by Berger and Motl (2000), there is little research available that focuses on the relationship between low-intensity exercise and mood alteration. Evidence, however, is beginning to accumulate that low- to moderate-intensity exercise such as brisk walking may be conducive to mood alteration (Berger & Owen, 1998; Jin, 1992; Thayer, 1987, 1996). Individual preferences for low-, moderate-, and high-intensity exercise also may influence the relationship between exercise and mood alteration (e.g., Mertesdorf, 1994). It is possible that preferred exercise intensity interacts with actual intensity levels when exercisers report how they feel after exercising. Until more research data are available concerning the mood benefits of low-intensity exercise, the possibility of an intensity threshold, and an apparent undesirable relationship between high-intensity exercise and mood, exercise participants who wish psychological benefits probably should maintain intensity in the moderate range (Berger, 1996).

Duration: At Least 20 to 30 Minutes

In addition to exercise intensity, the duration of physical activity also appears to be related to the psychological changes that tend to occur. Personal, introspective reports of experiences differ when exercising for various durations. Exercise experiences and subjective states may be different when exercising for 5 to 10 minutes, 20 to 30 minutes, and 60 minutes or longer. Complicating the relationship between duration of physical activity and quality of life, the mood states associated with specific exercise durations may be related to physical fitness levels, personality characteristics, and environmental factors. For example, the personality construct of hardiness has been related to the extent of mood decrements associated with an increase in exercise duration (Gross, 1994).

A characteristic of modern society is a feeling of having too little leisure time; thus, the possibility that exercising for a short period of time is appealing. Thayer (1987, 1996; Thayer, Peters, Takahashi, & Birkhead-Flight, 1993) repeatedly has reported that as little as 5 to 10 minutes of walking was mood-elevating as measured on the Activation-Deactivation Adjective Check List (Thayer, 1986). After walking briskly for 10 minutes, participants reported feeling calm-energy as reflected by more energy and less tension and tiredness after the exercise than before. These psychological changes were evident for 30, 60, and 120 minutes after conclusion of the walking session. More recently, running on a treadmill for either 10, 15, or 20 minutes was associated with increases in well-being and decreases in psychological distress (Butki & Rudolph,

1997). These benefits were reported at both 5 and 20 minutes after cessation of the exercise session.

The psychological changes associated with short exercise sessions require further investigation, as emphasized by Petruzzello and colleagues (1991) in their meta-analysis of the anxiety-reducing effects of acute and chronic exercise. When exercise sessions were between 0 and 20 minutes in length, the effect size was exceedingly small ($ES = .04$). Eliminating studies that employed exercise as a treatment modality for comparison with other anxiety-reduction treatments, the effect size for the 0- to 20-minute exercise duration was increased to .22. This larger effect size is significantly different from zero and no longer different from the other exercise durations (Petruzzello et al., 1991). It should be noted, however, that exercise sessions between 21 and 30 minutes had a more substantial effect size of .41 for the desirable changes in state anxiety.

There seems to be consensus that exercise sessions between 20 and 40 minutes in duration are conducive to acute psychological benefits (e.g., Berger, 1984/1997; Dishman, 1986; Petruzzello et al., 1991). However, the relationship between specific exercise durations and the psychological benefits has not been studied extensively. Thus, it is unclear whether there is a minimal duration or threshold as well as a maximal duration beyond which there are no additional psychological benefits. Until additional information about the relationship between subjective well-being and exercise duration, exercising for at least 20 minutes seems to be a cautious approach to using exercise to enhance one's mood states. It is possible that long exercise duration of 60 minutes or more may result in additional psychological advantages (e.g., Carmack & Martens, 1979; Mandell, 1979). Glasser (1976) has suggested 40 to 50 minutes to attain the "positive addiction" state in which the mind spins free.

> Then, sometime into the second hour comes the spooky time. Colors are bright and beautiful, water sparkles, clouds breathe, and my body, swimming, detaches from the earth. A loving contentment invades the basement of my mind, and thoughts bubble up without trails. I find the place I need to live if I'm going to live. (Mandell, 1979, pp. 50–57)

The relationship between exercise duration/distance and psychological benefits appears to be paradoxical. Until a certain point, exercise is mood-enhancing; beyond this point, increasing exercise duration can be detrimental to subjective well-being. Morgan and colleagues (Morgan, Costill, Flynn, Raglin, & O'Conner, 1988) illustrated the relationship in a study of chronic exercise in which training distance was purposely increased to examine possible

mood decrements. Distance swum was increased abruptly from 4,000 to 9,000 meters during a 10-day period. Exercise intensity also was unusually high (approximately 94% of VO$_2$max). As hypothesized, the highly trained collegiate swimmers reported significant increases in depression, anger, fatigue, and total mood disturbance. Recent evidence also suggests that exercising for an extended duration that often occurs with overload training has been associated with few benefits. Extended duration may be associated with either no mood changes (e.g., Berger et al., 1997; Hooper, Mackinnon, & Hanrahan, 1997) or with mood decrements (e.g., O'Connor, Morgan, & Raglin, 1991). Directly examining the relationship between swimming duration and mood change, Berger and colleagues reported that only shortened or tapered practices were associated with acute mood benefits as measured by the POMS for young age-group swimmers. As previously noted in this chapter, normal-distance practice sessions were associated with mood decrements. Beyond a certain distance, which may vary according to fitness level, increased exercise duration tends to be associated with negative mood states.

In conclusion, it seems that 20 to 30 minutes of exercise generates psychological benefits (see Table 25.1). Considerably more information is needed to understand the relationship between both short and very long exercise duration. Qualitative studies would be useful in examining possible differences in psychological states possibly associated with exercising for durations ranging from 10 to 60 minutes, 120 minutes, and longer.

Frequency: Regularly Included in a Weekly Schedule

By exercising regularly, but not so frequently as to incur an overuse injury or boredom, participants increase the likelihood of exercise enjoyment and overall quality of life. As exercisers become more physically fit with frequent participation, the discomfort often associated with the conditioning process recedes. Another way that frequent exercise sessions assist participants in decreasing physical discomfort is through a self-learning process. Habitual exercisers learn to interpret various physical sensations, to pace themselves, and to relax while exercising.

Examining a possible relationship between general fitness levels (i.e., frequent exercise participation) and the psychological benefits of exercise, Boutcher and Landers (1988) reported that a single, high-intensity (80–85% HR$_{max}$) session for a 20-minute period on a treadmill was associated with an acute reduction in state anxiety for those who habitually ran 30 miles or more per week for the past two years. Nonrunners who had no history of participation in any aerobic activity did not report any decreases in anxiety after the high-intensity exercise. Neither trained runners nor nonrunners reported any acute changes on the POMS. The high-intensity running at 80 to 85% of maximal heart rate may not have been an enjoyable activity, especially for the novice runners, who had little or no experience with high-intensity aerobic activity. Because other researchers have failed to produce evidence of a relationship between fitness level and acute mood changes associated with exercise (e.g., Blanchard & Rodgers, 1997), additional studies are needed to understand a possible relationship between fitness levels of participants or exercise frequency and mood changes associated with physical activity.

Especially when exercising at a high intensity, participants may need a minimal level of fitness to enjoy the physical activity and to feel better rather than worse after the exercise session. This possibility was supported in a meta-analysis of the relationship between physical activity and depression (North, McCullagh, & Tran, 1990). As North and colleagues reported, the mental health benefits associated with physical activity increased as the length of an exercise program (measured in weeks and sessions) increased. The decreases in depression may reflect chronic or accumulative changes associated with exercise, or they might reflect a need for physical conditioning. Frequent exercise and the accompanying increase in physical conditioning also enable the participant to devote less attention to the movement activity as it becomes more automatic. As frequent exercise participants become more fit, the activity becomes easier, less physically grueling, and more predictable.

Another reason to exercise on a regular basis is that the mental health effects tend to last at least two to four hours after exercising in members of normal populations (Morgan, 1987). As indicated in a classic study, the temporal duration of exercise-induced anxiety reduction and decreases in systolic blood pressure after exercise may last two to three hours longer than that of simple rest, which was short-lived (Raglin & Morgan, 1987). Recent evidence supports the likelihood that the psychological benefits remain beyond the exercise session itself (Bartholomew, 1997; Butki & Rudolph, 1997; Etnier et al., 1997; Thayer, 1987, 1996).

Conclusions

The mood benefits associated with exercise are not automatic. They may be reduced, eliminated, or even reversed by choosing inappropriate types of exercise or by not following appropriate practice guidelines. Throughout this section, it has been emphasized that it is "unlikely that all types, volumes, and settings of exercise will affect all aspects of mental health for all people" (Dishman, 1986, p. 328). The tentative physical activity taxonomy developed by Berger (1983/1984, 1994, 1996) still requires considerable development. It is presented here in detail because it includes many key considerations in maximizing psychological benefits associated with exercise participation. The taxonomy is not all-inclusive and does not disprove or discount the importance of other exercise considerations that might affect the mental health benefits of exercise. Therefore, the following conclusions are somewhat speculative.

An overriding requirement for enhancing the psychological benefits of exercise is that the activity is enjoyable or pleasant (Berger, 1996; Motl, Berger, & Leuschen, in press). In addition, it seems that the exercise mode should include as many of the following as possible: rhythmical abdominal breathing, noncompetition, closed or predictable activity, and rhythmical and repetitive movements (e.g., Berger & Owen, 1986, 1988, 1992a; Berger et al., 1995). Finally, training or practice conditions can further maximize or detract from the psychological benefits. Based on increasing research evidence, the activity should be of moderate intensity, at least 20 to 30 minutes in duration, and of a regular frequency to promote a minimal fitness level (e.g., Berger & Owen, 1992b; Berger et al., 1997).

PEAK MOMENTS IN EXERCISE AND SPORT

The opportunity to experience a peak moment is another way that exercise can add to the quality of one's life (Berger, 1996; Csikszentmihalyi, 1991, 1997). Peak moments, which include flow, peak performance, peak experience, and exercise high, are rewarding, memorable, and powerful experiences that can greatly enhance the quality of life (Berger, 1996; Csikszentmihalyi, 1991, 1993, 1997; Jackson, 1996; Jackson & Csikszentmihalyi, 1999; Privette & Bundrick, 1997). Fun, elation, outstanding performance, and utter contentment often characterize peak moments (Jackson & Csikszentmihalyi, 1999). The fullness and depth of such experiences can be tremendously fulfilling, profound, and rewarding (Csikszentmihalyi, 1991; Privette & Bundrick, 1997).

Peak moments often occur in exercise and sport (Csikszentmihalyi, 1991; McInman & Grove, 1991; Privette & Bundrick, 1987) and are special and rewarding bonuses of physical activity (Jackson & Csikszentmihalyi, 1999). When describing peak moments in sport and physical activity, individuals report a great deal of similarity in experiential, psychological, and performance states, which is impressive considering that peak moments are experienced in many types of physical activities. Specific conditions that are associated with peak moments, particularly flow, include:

Balance between challenge and skills

Merging of action and awareness

Clear goals

Unambiguous feedback

Concentration on the task at hand

Perception of control

Loss of self-consciousness

Transformation of time

Autotelic experience (Csikszentmihalyi, 1975, 1991, 1993, 1997; Jackson, 1992, 1996; Jackson & Csikszentmihalyi, 1999; Jackson & Marsh, 1996; Marsh & Jackson, 1999)

See McInman and Grove (1991) for a more detailed discussion of the characteristics of peak moments.

Theories and Models of Peak Moments

Another way to illustrate the richness and depth of peak moments is to review theories and models that account for peak moments in a wide variety of activities. Landsman (1969) developed the "positive experiences model," a three-category topology of self, external world, and interpersonal relationships. Using content and factor analyses of art- and music-based peak experiences of individuals in art galleries and concert locations, Panzarella (1980) proposed a "peak experiences model." The model included four major phenomenological categories: renewal ecstasy, motor-sensory ecstasy, fusion-emotional ecstasy, and withdrawal ecstasy. The model also included three stages: cognitive phenomena, such as aesthetic judgments and loss of self; climax-associated motor responses, such as locomotion, tachycardia, and shivers; and postclimax, which is similar to an afterglow and results in emotional and stimulus-specific responses. Thorne (1963) proposed a more detailed model that includes both positive and negative experiences forming a six-category classification system (sensual, emotional, cognitive, conative, self-actualization, and climax experiences). Thorne's model has been reported to be reliable by a number of other researchers (Allen, Haupt, & Jones, 1964; Ebersole, 1972).

Privette and Bundrick (1987, 1991, 1997) designed the "feeling and performance model" (Figure 25.4), which

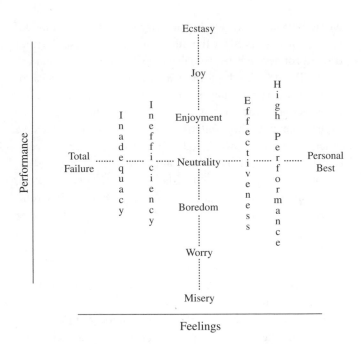

Figure 25.4   Experience model of feeling and performance. From "Measurement of experience: Construct and content validity of the Experience Questionnaire," by G. Privette and C.M. Brundrick, 1987, *Perceptual and Motor Skills, 65,* p. 318. Copyright 1987 by C.H. Ammons and R.B. Ammons. Adapted with permission.

classified peak moments on the two orthogonal dimensions of feeling and performance. The feeling dimension ranges from an extreme of misery, worry, and boredom to neutrality to enjoyment, joy, and ecstasy. Peak experience is located near ecstasy on the feeling dimension. The performance dimension ranges from total failure, inadequacy, and inefficiency to mediocrity to effectiveness, high performance, and personal best. Peak performance is located at the extreme of personal best performance. The two dimensions have been validated by Privette (1985; Privette & Bundrick, 1991, 1997).

Using this model, any experience can be classified according to the two dimensions of feelings and performance. For example, the bottom left corner is characterized by total failure and misery, which would describe an experience of an extremely bad performance and the accompanying negative feelings. The center of the figure is neutral and typifies everyday experience. Everday experiences are generally somewhere between enjoyment and boredom and between inefficiency and effectiveness. The top and right quadrants contain peak moments. When behavior is in the top right quadrant, the individual performs well and expresses positive feelings. Peak performance is located in the extreme right end of the performance continuum. From the center of the figure to the upper right-hand corner is an area that contains flow. Flow has fairly equal components of feeling and performance states. The intensity may mirror "microflow." The extreme top end of the feeling dimension describes peak experiences, which may or may not be accompanied by peak performance.

Based on extensive research, Csikszentmihalyi (1991, 1993, 1997) has proposed a flow model, which describes the occurrence of flow experiences in everyday life and physical activity. The model describes flow according to a delicate balance between skill level and task demands. If ability exceeds the demands of the task, the task is too easy and will result in boredom. If ability is inadequate to meet the demands of the task, the task will promote feelings of anxiety. The enjoyable, pleasurable, and rewarding experience of flow results when the task demands intense concentration and there is a match between personal ability and task demands.

To provide a catalyst for researchers interested in studying flow, Kimiecik and Stein (1992) suggested a person-by-situation framework to understand flow experiences in physical activity environments. The person-based factors can be separated into dispositional and state components. The dispositional components include goal orientation (i.e., task and ego orientations), attentional style, trait anxiety, trait confidence, and perceived sport competence. State-based person factors include game goals, concentration, state anxiety, self-efficacy, and perceived game ability. The situational components include type of sport (e.g., self-paced vs. other-dependent), competition importance, opponent ability, coach behavior and feedback, teammate interactions/behaviors, and competitive flow structure. The framework highlights personal and situational factors that may interact to promote flow experiences and perhaps other peak moments.

Peak Moments: Peak Performance, Flow, the Runner's High, and Peak Experience

Peak Performance

The defining characteristic of peak performance is exceptional functioning. In fact, Privette and Landsman (1983, p. 195) define peak performance as "behavior that goes beyond the level at which a person normally functions." Although it is not necessarily a world-record performance, it is rather exceptional functioning in a specific situation that transcends everyday capacity. Peak performance can result from a wide variety of activities, such as physical strength, athletic prowess, creative expression, intellectual

mastery, and even work (Privette & Bundrick, 1987, 1989, 1991, 1997). Peak performance can happen spontaneously or in response to a placebo, biofeedback, or hypnosis (Privette, 1983).

There are five characteristics that describe peak performances: clear focus, high level of performance, initial fascination with the task, spontaneity, and strong sense of self (Brewer, Van Raalte, Linder, & Van Raalte, 1991; Cohn, 1991; Jackson & Roberts, 1992; Privette & Bundrick, 1987, 1989, 1991, 1997; Privette & Landsman, 1983). Additional characteristics of peak performance may include awareness of power, fulfillment, temporality, and insufficiency of words to describe the moment (Privette & Bundrick, 1987, 1991). Peak performance may even trigger ecstasy and peak experience (Privette & Bundrick, 1997). Interestingly, participation with others may actually hinder the likelihood of experiencing a peak performance, perhaps because others may disrupt an individual's concentration (Privette & Landsman, 1983).

Flow

The concept of flow has been described and studied extensively (Csikszentmihalyi, 1991, 1993, 1997). Flow is an optimal and high-quality experience, a state "in which people are so involved in an activity that nothing else seems to matter; the experience itself is so enjoyable that people will do it even at great cost, for the sheer sake of doing it" (Csikszentmihalyi, 1991, p. 4). This optimal experiential state frequently results when skills match opportunities for action and when "psychic energy B or attention B is invested in realistic goals" (p. 8). Enjoyment is a central element in the flow state. In fact, flow is intrinsically enjoyable and fun, and people seek it out (Csikszentmihalyi, 1975, 1991, 1993; Jackson & Csikszentmihalyi, 1999; Marsh & Jackson, 1999; Stein, Kimiecik, Daniels, & Jackson, 1995).

Not all activities are optimally conducive to flow. When questioning university students ($N = 123$) between 20 and 50 years of age, Privette and Bundrick (1987, 1989) found that sport was a major source of flow experiences. Not one subject mentioned having a flow experience at school or work, in relationships or sickness, or in connection with religious events. These results, however, may reflect the particular study sample. Csikszentmihalyi (1991) and Jackson and Csikszentmihalyi (1999) reinforce the likelihood of flow in sport and exercise. The extensive work by Jackson and colleagues (Jackson, 1992, 1995, 1996; Jackson & Csikszentmihalyi, 1999; Jackson & Roberts, 1992; Marsh & Jackson, 1999) also highlights the likelihood of experiencing flow in the context of sport and exercise.

The Running or Exercise High

The runner's high may be a specialized example of a peak moment, particularly a peak experience. Terms commonly employed to describe the runner's high include euphoria, unusual strength and power, gracefulness, spirituality, sudden realization of one's potential, glimpsing perfection, moving without effort, and spinning out (Berger, 1996; Masters, 1992; Sachs, 1980, 1984). In light of the many terms to describe the runner's high, it has not been an easy construct to define. Some definitions are available, however, and highlight the characteristics and desirable nature of the runner's high. Sachs (1984) proposed a preliminary definition of the runner's high as "a euphoric sensation experienced during running, usually unexpected, in which the runner feels a heightened sense of well-being, enhanced appreciation of nature, and transcendence of barriers of time and space" (p. 274). Recently, Berger (1996) defined the runner's or exercise high as a specific type of peak experience characterized by euphoria, a heightened sense of well-being, feelings of psychological/physical strength and power, a glimpse of perfection, and even spirituality (p. 346).

The diversity of descriptions expressed by runners and other exercise participants is remarkable, but troublesome (e.g., Masters, 1992). Some descriptions are congruent with peak experiences; others are more characteristic of "an enhanced sense of well-being." Many runners report experiencing the runner's high, but closer examination of the personal descriptions has suggested widely different experiences, ranging from a generalized sense of well-being to a peak experience. Some runners, however, have defined the runner's high in ambivalent or even negative terms (Masters, 1992).

Dramatically different percentages of runners report experiencing a runner's high. Sachs (1984) estimated that between 9% and 78% of runners have experienced it. Among runners who have experienced a runner's high, the frequency of such an experience varies from rarely (i.e., only several times during their running careers) to an average of 29.4% of daily runs (Sachs, 1980). Very little is known about the runner's high. Clearly, researchers should conduct more research to further define, describe, and explain the runner's high. Researchers also need to identify factors that trigger the runner's or exercise high.

Peak Experience

Peak experiences are defined by strong affective states such as bliss, ecstasy, great joy, and/or illumination. Such episodes produce a strong sense of self and freedom from outer restrictions, and can be considered moments of highest happiness (Privette & Bundrick, 1987). Maslow (1968, 1970) considered peak experiences to be an individual's most exciting, fulfilling, and meaningful moments in life, suggesting that peak experiences greatly impact quality of life. Maslow also suggested that peak experiences are associated with fully functioning individuals (self-actualizers), and that such individuals tend to report more numerous peak experiences than less fully developed individuals.

Obviously, the occurrence of a peak experience through physical activity would be beneficial to the quality of life. Little is known, however, about peak experiences in exercise and sport. Peak experiences occur unexpectedly, and the percentage of people who report such an experience in general and in exercise is unknown. In a study of university students ($N = 214$), only three did not report having a peak experience (Allen et al., 1964), suggesting that peak experiences are common. In contrast, Keutzer (1978) reported that 61% of a national sample had not reported an experience that made them feel as though they were very close to a powerful, spiritual force that seemed to lift them out of themselves.

Linking Peak Performance, Flow, and Peak Experience to Quality of Life

"Peak performance" is superior functioning, "peak experiences" involve intense joy, and "flow" is an intrinsically enjoyable matching of ability and task difficulty (Berger, 1996; McInman & Grove, 1991; Privette, 1983, Privette & Bundrick, 1991, 1997). As summarized in Table 25.3, peak performance involves outstanding behavior. Thus, it is likely to promote perceptions of competence, excellence, mastery, and self-efficacy that permeate all aspects of an individual's life. Such perceptions will likely promote strong feelings of satisfaction and well-being, which are crucial to quality of life. Flow is fun, enjoyable, and results in feelings of control (Csikszentmihalyi, 1991, 1993, 1997; Jackson & Csikszentmihalyi, 1999; Privette, 1983) and is likely to promote feelings of happiness and well-being. Peak experience involves joy or cosmic and absolute ecstasy (Privette & Bundrick, 1987, 1991; Privette & Sherry, 1986). Perceptions of joy and ecstasy likely impact the perceptions of overall personal and life satisfaction, not to mention happiness and enhanced well-being. Clearly, the strong psychological and physical elements of peak moments have great potential to impact an individual's quality of life.

Table 25.3 Major Characteristics of Peak Moments

Peak Experience	Flow	Peak Performance
High level of joy (ecstasy)	Fun	Superior behavior
Transpersonal and mystical	Enjoyable	High level of performance
Passive (absorption)	Loss of ego	Clear focus
Feeling of unity and fusion	Playful	Strong sense of self
Loss of self	Feeling of control	Fulfillment
Spontaneous	Lost time and space	Not playful
Feeling of peak power	Intrinsic motivation	Intended action but spontaneous performance

Source: From "Peak experience, peak performance and flow: A comparative analysis of positive human experiences," by G. Privette, 1983, *Journal of Personality and Social Psychology, 45,* p. 1365. Copyright 1983 by the American Psychological Association. Reprinted with permission.

Facilitating Peak Moments

If peak moments influence quality of life and are associated with exercise and sport, then it is important to understand factors that promote peak moments in physical activity. Not surprisingly, researchers have increasingly become interested in facilitating peak moments in sport and exercise (e.g., Jackson & Csikszentmihalyi, 1999). In one study exploring possible correlates of flow, Jackson and Roberts (1992) examined the role of goal orientation and perceived ability in relation to self-reports of flow in Division 1 collegiate athletes ($N = 200$). The athletes were males and females between 17 and 25 years of age, and competed in gymnastics, swimming, golf, track, cross-country running, tennis, and diving. The athletes completed a goal orientation scale and flow scale, described best and worst performances, and described challenges and skill rankings of the performances. The results indicated that perceived ability and mastery orientations were predictors of flow, and flow was a predictor of peak performances. Thus, focusing on increasing perceptions of ability and structuring environments to promote mastery experiences may be one method of promoting flow and perhaps other peak moments.

In a qualitative study, Jackson (1995) interviewed 28 elite-level athletes about factors related to the experience of flow. Using content analysis, Jackson synthesized 361 themes to form 10 dimensions. The dimensions highlighted factors that influence the flow state. Some of the important factors influencing flow were physical and mental preparation, focus, perceptions of performance progression and feeling, and optimal motivation and arousal. The athletes also perceived the flow state and the factors influencing flow as controllable. These dimensions require quantitative confirmation to determine the impact on peak moments in sport and exercise settings.

Hypnotic susceptibility and experience may be associated with peak moments. Grove and Lewis (1996) examined hypnotic susceptibility and previous experience as correlates of flowlike states in a sample of individuals ($N = 96$) performing circuit training. Results indicated that self-reports of flowlike states increased across a 45- to 50-minute exercise session, and that the magnitude of change was related to hypnotic susceptibility. Participants high in hypnotic susceptibility reported greater increases in flowlike states than those low in hypnotic susceptibility. The individual's previous experience had an effect on self-reports of flowlike states that were similar to the effect of hypnotic susceptibility. This suggests that specific association/dissociation strategies and continued participation in physical activity to gain experience may promote flow and perhaps other peak moments.

To better identify the antecedents of flow in recreational athletes, Stein et al. (1995) examined goals, competence, and confidence as predictors of flow in tennis, basketball, and golf in a series of three studies. Tennis and golf were performed in competitive environments; basketball was performed in a learning environment. Results of the three studies indicated that goals, competence, and confidence did not predict the flow experience, but the sport context did influence perceptions of experience quality. In the competitive environment, participants in flow or boredom reported a better quality of experience than in apathy or anxiety. Additionally, in the learning environment, participants in flow reported greater enjoyment, satisfaction, concentration, and control than individuals experiencing boredom, apathy, or anxiety. Perhaps structuring physical activity settings may increase the likelihood of experiencing flow and peak moments.

Recently, Jackson and colleagues (Jackson, Kimiecik, Ford, & Marsh, 1998) examined the psychological correlates of flow in a sample of older adult athletes. The participants ($N = 398$) were athletes competing in the World Masters Games and the athletes completed dispositional measures of intrinsic motivation, goal orientation, perceived sport ability, competitive trait anxiety, and trait flow. The athletes also completed event-specific measures of perceived challenges and skills, perceived success, and flow. Results of correlation analyses indicated that perceived sport ability, anxiety, and intrinsic motivation scores were correlated with measures of both trait and state flow. Multiple linear regression indicated that perceived sport ability, intrinsic motivation, and anxiety were independent predictors of state and trait flow. Thus, developing perceptions of sport competence and focusing on sources of intrinsic motivation may promote flow in some environments.

We are not aware of research examining factors facilitating peak moments in sport and exercise environments. This is discouraging. Identifying factors that promote peak experience and the runner's high should become research priorities, because such factors may be linked to continued involvement and enjoyment of physical ability. Further, peak moments and perhaps the runner's high would greatly impact perceptions of life quality.

Measuring Peak Moments

The techniques utilized to measure peak moments have typically been a limiting factor in studying these exceptional moments. The most common method has been the experience sampling method (ESM), developed by Csikszentmihalyi and colleagues (Csikszentmihalyi & Larson, 1987; Larson & Csikszentmihalyi, 1983), to investigate the quality of experience in everyday life. The ESM involves interrupting an individual during daily activities via an electronic beeper and obtaining self-reports on an experience sampling form (ESF). The ESF includes items pertaining to current challenges and skills to identify flow and items pertaining to quality of the experience (i.e., thoughts and feelings) and the type of activity engaged at the moment of the signal.

Two measurement instruments for the study of peak moments include the Experience Questionnaire (EQ) and the Flow-State Scale (FSS). The EQ was developed and validated by Privette and colleagues (Privette, 1984; Privette & Bundrick, 1987, 1991; Privette & Sherry, 1986). It contains an initial question asking for a narrative description of a personal experience of peak performance, peak experience, flow, an average event, misery, or failure. The EQ contains 42 items rated on a 5-point Likert-type scale ranging from "much importance" to "no importance" according to importance in the narrative description of a personal experience. Additional items are included that pertain to the magnitude of performance, feelings, aftereffects, checking descriptors, and demographic variables (Privette & Sherry, 1986). The estimated reading level of the EQ is ninth to tenth grade, and it has been reported to contain reasonable item-level test-retest reliability. Evidence of construct

and content validity has been provided by Privette and Bundrick (1987). The EQ, as would be expected, has been a commonly employed tool to study peak moments.

The FSS is one of the best contributions to research on peak moments (Jackson & Marsh 1996; Marsh & Jackson, 1999). It is a multidimensional measure of flow in sport and physical activity settings, and was developed based on definitions of the nine proposed dimensions of flow (Csikszentmihalyi, 1991, 1993) and the qualitative studies of Jackson (1992, 1995). An initial pool of 54 items, 6 items per scale, was developed and presented to seven researchers for evaluation of content representativeness. The 54 items were then administered to 394 athletes from the United States and Australia, and the responses were subjected to confirmatory factor analysis (CFA). The CFA did not provide evidence for the 54-item, nine-factor model, but it did provide support for a 36-item, nine-factor model with 4 items per factor. It seems a single higher-order factor was superordinate to the nine first-order factors. The nine FSS scales possessed reasonable internal consistency. The factor structure and internal consistency of the FSS have been further tested in subsequent research (Marsh & Jackson, 1999; Vlachopoulos, Karageorghis, & Terry, 1999). Marsh and Jackson also provided initial evidence for the construct validity of the FSS using multitrait, multimethod techniques with CFA, and also have provided a trait measure of the flow experience.

Future Research Needs

The understanding of peak moments is limited by the difficult nature of studying these elusive and fleeting moments. Understanding the phenomenology, antecedents, and consequences of peak moments is a challenge because they are unplanned and unexpected phenomena. All methods of measurement require interrupting the experience or relying on retrospective reports. Peak moments also are not available to be studied using experimental designs and laboratory settings. In addition, neuroanatomical and neurobiological bases of peak moments are difficult to uncover. One potential method of understanding the neural mechanisms of peak moments involves the use of pharmacological approaches (i.e., drug comparison studies), in which researchers compare the self-reports of peak moments to drug-related experiences. However, even this design is limited to retrospective reports.

Despite these challenges, continued research into peak moments is warranted. Currently, there is limited progress in the understanding of peak performance, peak experience, and runner's high, especially with regard to exercise.

Peak moments are elusive in nature, difficult to define, and typically difficult to measure in research studies.

Recently, researchers have opted for quantitative research methodologies in studying peak moments (e.g., Grove & Lewis, 1996; Jackson & Marsh, 1996; Marsh & Jackson, 1999; Stein et al., 1995). However, such attempts to improve validity have shifted the emphasis away from what participation in such activities actually feels like for the individual (Kirk, 1986). Regardless of the methodology employed, the major difficulty lies in determining what questions to ask. Peak performance, flow, runner's high, and peak experience research is particularly prone to bias due to differences in the education levels of the participants. For instance, Wuthnow (1978) found that 65% of "high peakers" (individuals who experienced a peak experience that had a lasting influence on their life) attended college. Only 45% of the "nonpeakers" (individuals who had not had a peak experience, or had not had a peak experience that had changed their life) attended college. The percentage of people who have experienced a peak moment is unknown, and the frequency with which peak moments are experienced also is unclear. Some suggest that peak moments are a once-in-a-lifetime occurrence (Panzarella, 1980). Others suggest they can be experienced quite regularly (Csikszentmihalyi, 1991, 1997; Ravizza, 1984).

Many unanswered questions about peak moments in exercise and sport remain for the enterprising researcher. Some of the more obvious questions are as follows. What are the meanings and consequences of peak moments? For example, do peak moments in physical activity affect the mental health or quality of life of an individual? Does the likelihood of peak experiences differ across cultures? Do certain personality characteristics increase the occurrence of peak moments? Do older individuals have fewer peak experiences, as Maslow suggests? Do males and females differ in the types and numbers of peak moments? Do flow, the runner's high, peak performance, and peak moments result more frequently in specific types of sports and exercise? What are the exercise parameters (i.e., intensity, duration, and frequency) that promote the experience of a peak moment?

Conclusions

Peak moments are profound, rewarding, memorable, and moving experiences that can greatly enhance the quality of life. Peak performance, flow, runner's high, and peak experience are peak moments likely to deeply impact the physical activity experience and one's life. Researchers have accurately characterized peak moments, with the

exception of the runner's high, and it is now time to examine how and why peak moments occur. Examining peak moments in physical activity settings is worth pursuing, particularly with the recent advancements in measurement (Jackson & Marsh, 1996; Marsh & Jackson, 1999) and the potentially strong relationship to quality of life. Understanding the experience of peak moments may unlock the gate to the pursuit and promotion of exercise and sport as attractive and rewarding forms of recreation, activities that are directly and meaningfully pursued rather than avoided.

ENJOYMENT AND QUALITY OF LIFE

Another way that physical activity influences quality of life is by providing opportunities to experience enjoyment. Enjoyment seems to be integrally linked to quality of life by providing hedonic, interesting, rewarding, and truly memorable experiences (Kahneman et al., 1999). As recognized by Csikszentmihalyi (1991, p. 46), "When people ponder further about what makes their lives rewarding, they tend to move beyond pleasant memories and begin to remember other events, other experiences that overlap with pleasurable ones but fall into a category that deserves a separate name: enjoyment."

Enjoyment also may add zest to one's life. Experiences of enjoyment may produce feelings of accomplishment, euphoria, and happiness (Kendzierski & DeCarlo, 1991), which may add meaning and "zip" to one's daily routine. Another way that enjoyment influences quality of life is by improving one's mental health. For example, participating in an enjoyable activity may counterbalance the psychological stress associated with everyday hassles and demands (Berger, 1994, 1996; Sacks, 1996; Wankel, 1993). Enjoyment in life may reduce the likelihood of developing depression affect (Brenner, 1975). Enjoyment has been linked to positive affective states during leisure, school, and work (Csikszentmihalyi & LeFevre, 1989; Hewitt & Miller, 1981; Wheeler, 1985). Enjoyment of flow experiences has been associated with affective well-being, relaxation, and life satisfaction (Clarke & Haworth, 1994).

What Is Enjoyment?

Enjoyment is an ephemeral construct. We all know what enjoyment means, but it has been a difficult construct to define. Webster's Dictionary of the English Language (1992) defines enjoyment as "something that gives joy or satisfaction." This definition highlights the importance of enjoyment for improving life quality; experiences of enjoyment result in positive feelings and perceptions of satisfaction.

Some researchers have suggested that enjoyment is related to positive affective states. For example, Scanlan and Simons (1992, pp. 202–203) defined sport enjoyment as "a positive affective response to the sport experience that reflects generalized feelings such as pleasure, liking, and fun." Wankel (1993, p. 153) described exercise enjoyment as "a positive emotion, a positive affective state." Wankel (1997) further speculated that positive feeling states are a common element of physical activity and exercise enjoyment. Thus, some researchers agree that enjoyment involves positive affective states.

Other researchers have equated enjoyment with flow-type experiences and suggested that positive affect is a by-product of an enjoyable experience. According to Csikszentmihalyi (1991), enjoyment is an optimal experience, one of high quality, and serves as an end in itself. Enjoyment often occurs in autotelic (i.e., self-contained) activities that are intrinsically rewarding. The optimal experience of enjoyment seems to result in positive affective states such as happiness, vigor, pleasure, and relaxation (Clarke & Haworth, 1994; Csikszentmihalyi & LeFevre, 1989; Motl et al., in press). Based on these descriptions, enjoyment can be preliminarily defined as "an optimal psychological state (i.e., flow) that leads to performing an activity for its own sake and is associated with positive feeling states" (Kimiecik & Harris, 1996, p. 256).

The definition provided by Kimiecik and Harris (1996) sparked an issue with Wankel (1997) and perhaps other researchers. Wankel suggested that Kimiecik and Harris misinterpreted or inaccurately reported aspects of previous research (e.g., Wankel & Kreisel, 1985; Wankel & Sefton, 1989), utilized inconsistent logic in building a definition of enjoyment based on flow, and developed "strawperson" arguments to promote a self-directed definition of enjoyment. The commentary of Wankel and Kimiecik and Harris illustrates the lack of agreement and difficulty in defining enjoyment, and both articles deserve critical attention and consideration in enjoyment-based research.

Researchers in exercise and sport science have acquired a myopic view of enjoyment; discussing research from the study of emotion may provide new definitions and methods for understanding enjoyment in physical activity. Emotion theorists also have discussed the concepts of joy and enjoyment and consider them to be basic human emotions (Ekman & Davidson, 1993; Ekman, Davidson, & Friesen, 1990; M. Frank, Ekman, & Friesen, 1993). Like all positive and negative emotions, enjoyment has affective, behavioral, and physiological components (Frijda, 1999). Enjoyment is a positive emotion and reflects appetitive or approach action tendencies rather than aversive or avoidance action

tendencies. Enjoyment consists of distinct facial expressions (i.e., the Duchenne smile) associated with the contraction of eye muscles (i.e., orbicularis oculi and zygomatic major; M. Frank et al., 1993; M. Frank, Ekman, & Friesen, 1997). There also are specific physiological responses in the central (CNS) and peripheral nervous system associated with enjoyment, which include cerebral asymmetry in EEG activity reflecting more left-hemisphere activity in the anterior temporal region and autonomic nervous system (ANS) activation (Ekman et al., 1990; Ekman & Davidson, 1993; M. Frank et al., 1997).

The characteristics of enjoyment identified by emotion theorists, therefore, indicate that it is more than a simple positive affective state that is measurable by self-report. Enjoyment includes distinct facial expressions and physiological reactions in the CNS and ANS, and it undoubtedly has a neuroanatomical and neurobiological basis (LeDoux & Armony, 1999). Exercise and sport scientists should consider a broader definition of enjoyment that includes subjective feelings (i.e., positive affect), distinct facial expressions, and physiological responses in the CNS and ANS. The Facial Action Coding System (FACS), which is a method of classifying and quantifying facial expressions (i.e., movements and muscle actions; Bartlett, Hager, Ekman, & Sejnowski, 1999; Ekman & Friesen, 1978), may be one method of understanding enjoyment of physical activity.

Fun versus Enjoyment

It is important to distinguish between fun and enjoyment for both research and semantic purposes. Fun may not be synonymous with enjoyment (Podilchak, 1991). One possible difference is that fun is a descriptive state or affective component of an enjoyable experience, whereas enjoyment is a more encompassing experience characterized by affective, behavioral, and physiological responses. As noted by De Grazia (1962), fun is "the mood of anticipating pleasure" (p. 332) and it has an "orgiastic flare" (p. 337). Fun also may be a factor that promotes enjoyment. Researchers in sport and exercise psychology reported that having fun was a source of enjoyment in youth sport participants (Wankel & Kreisel, 1985; Wankel & Pabich, 1982).

Podilchak (1991, p. 123) described fun as "a social-emotional interactional process wherein persons deconstruct social-biographical inequalities to create a with-equal-other, social-human bond." Enjoyment, on the other hand, was conceptualized as a self-referential process that can be experienced in many contexts. Enjoyment, it seems, differs from fun in exercise, and sport scientists should recognize this distinction.

Measuring Enjoyment

Researchers have employed a variety of measures to examine enjoyment of sport and exercise. The measures have ranged from a single item (e.g., Garcia & King, 1991; Turner, Rejeski, & Brawley, 1997) to a set of items (e.g., Boyd & Yin, 1996; Carpenter & Coleman, 1998; Paxton, Browning, & O'Connell, 1997) to a validated questionnaire (e.g., Kendzierski & DeCarlo, 1991). The single-item measures include phrases commonly rated according to a Likert-type scale (e.g., "did not enjoy at all" to "enjoyed completely"; Turner et al., 1997). Others have employed measures of enjoyment that consist of multiple items pertaining to "happiness," "fun," and "liking," which also are rated on Likert-type (Carpenter & Coleman, 1998) or Harter-type (Boyd & Yin, 1996) scales and then summed to form an enjoyment score. These methods of measuring enjoyment, however, may not be reliable (i.e., single indicator measures) or valid, and the psychometric properties have not been thoroughly established.

The best example of an enjoyment questionnaire, the Physical Activity Enjoyment Scale (PACES), which is particularly applicable to sport and exercise, was developed by Kendzierski and DeCarlo (1991). The PACES consists of 18 items rated on a bipolar scale. The item scores are summed to form a unidimensional measure that seems to tap "the extent to which an individual enjoys physical activity." The items seem to encompass dimensions of "flow-like experiences" and "positive feeling states" (Crocker, Bouffard, & Gessaroli, 1995; Motl et al., in press), which correspond with the definitions of enjoyment provided by experts (e.g., Kimiecik & Harris, 1996; Scanlan & Simons, 1992; Wankel, 1993, 1997). Examples of items on the PACES are "I feel interested," "I am very absorbed in this activity," "It makes me happy," and "It's very exhilarating." The internal consistency, test-retest reliability, and factorial and predictive validity of the PACES also have been evaluated. The internal consistency was supported by an alpha value of .96 in two independent samples. The test-retest reliability has ranged between .60 and .93. Although the factorial validity of the PACES has not be universally supported (e.g., Crocker et al., 1995), the predictive validity has been established via successful differentiation between exercising in pleasant and unpleasant environments (Kendzierski & DeCarlo, 1991). Wankel (1993) suggested that the PACES is a promising instrument, but based on other research (i.e., Crocker et al., 1995; Motl, Bieber, & Berger, 1997) continued evaluation and refinement of the PACES is necessary to improve the factorial validity and invariance and the interpretation of score meaning.

Benefits of Enjoying Physical Activity

Adherence

As stated by Singer (1996, p. 249), "There's got to be a way to associate regular involvement in vigorous physical activity as something we look forward to and are dedicated to—something we miss when we don't do it." Perhaps the method of making physical activity enticing and desirable is increasing the likelihood of experiencing enjoyment. Enjoyment is a commonly cited reason for participating in exercise and sport (e.g., Berger, 1996; Carpenter & Coleman, 1998; Scanlan & Simons, 1992; Wankel, 1993; Welk, 1999). The anticipation of enjoyment may be important for initial attraction to physical activity (Welk, 1999), and its experience either during or following exercise and sport activities may be related to sustained commitment (Carpenter, 1995; Carpenter & Coleman, 1998; Carpenter, Scanlan, Simons, & Lobel, 1993) and involvement in physical activity. Very simply, activities that are perceived to be enjoyable are likely to be attractive, enticing, meaningful, rewarding, and worthwhile (Kahneman et al., 1999).

Researchers have examined enjoyment as a predictor of exercise and sport behavior in cross-sectional and longitudinal studies. Using cross-sectional research designs, enjoyment has been investigated in relation to sport commitment and physical activity in youth and adults (e.g., Bungum & Vincent, 1997; Carpenter et al., 1993; Paxton et al., 1997; Sallis, Prochaska, Taylor, Hill, & Geraci, 1999). Enjoyment also has been examined in relation to commitment or involvement in physical activity in adults and youth using longitudinal or intervention research designs (e.g., Carpenter & Coleman, 1998; DiLorenzo, Stucky-Rupp, Vander Wal, & Gothan, 1998; Garcia & King, 1991; Leslie, Owen, Salmon, Bauman, & Sallis, 1999; Sallis, Calfas, Alcaraz, Gehrman, & Johnson, 1999). For example, in a test of the sport commitment model in elite youth cricket players across a season, Carpenter and Coleman indicated that sport enjoyment along with recognition of competence and social opportunities significantly predicted sport commitment across the season. In another study, Sallis, Calfas, et al. reported that enjoyment of physical activity predicted physical activity levels across a 16-week course in college-age male students who were randomly assigned to an intervention.

Enhancement of Mental Health

Enjoyment may be linked to the psychological benefits associated with physical activity. Berger and Owen (1986) and Koltyn, Shake, and Morgan (1993) have provided indirect evidence of a relationship between enjoyment and acute mood enhancement. Berger and Owen reported a lack of mood changes on the POMS following a summer swim class and attributed it to extremely unpleasant water and air temperatures. More specifically, they examined the relationship between acute bouts of swimming and mood changes during fall and summer sessions. In the fall semester, college students enrolled in swim classes reported short-term improvements on a variety of POMS subscales. In the summer session, however, there was no evidence that swimming was related to mood alteration. Berger and Owen speculated that the lack of mood change during the summer was attributable to extremely unpleasant exercise conditions, which may have affected perceptions of enjoyment. Koltyn et al. found a similar effect of unpleasant exercise conditions on acute mood states. Helping to clarify the relationship between enjoyment of an environment and mood, Turner et al. (1997) indicated that enjoyment of exercising in bland or enriched physical activity environments was related to acute improvements in mood. Unpleasant environmental conditions may affect perceptions of enjoyment, which impact the mood changes associated with physical activity.

Enjoyment of physical activity has been more directly linked to short-term mood benefits in a recent study (Motl et al., in press). The researchers examined whether enjoyment was related to the acute mood changes reported by rock climbers and students in a health education class who listened to a lecture and watched a video on rock climbing. The rock climbers and students in a health education class completed the POMS pre- to postactivity, and the PACES only postactivity. Canonical correlation analysis indicated that both enjoyment and activity were related to acute changes in mood as measured by the POMS. Path analysis and a series of simple and multiple regression analyses suggested that enjoyment mediated the acute mood changes reported by rock climbers and students in a health education lecture class.

Sacks (1996), in an edited book on the mind-body connection, suggested that experiences of exercise enjoyment may help to counterbalance the psychological stress associated with everyday activities. Berger (1994, 1996) and Wankel (1993) also have discussed the importance of enjoyment during exercise in counterbalancing the mood disturbances resulting from stress and hassles of everyday life. Clearly, enjoyment plays a role in the mental health benefits associated with exercise.

Sources of Enjoyment

It is important to explore possible sources of enjoyment in exercise and sport to understand how to facilitate the occurrence of this desirable, hedonic, and rewarding experience. Unfortunately, little research has been conducted to examine sources of enjoyment in exercise settings or in adult populations. Many research studies have focused on college-age exercisers and youth sport participants. It is quite possible that sources of enjoyment may differ between youth and adult participants and between sport and exercise environments, but this possibility needs to be tested directly.

Youth Sport Participants

Researchers examining sources of enjoyment for youth sport participants have employed quantitative and qualitative designs. Using quantitative methodologies, three categories of enjoyment have been consistently identified: intrinsic, social, and extrinsic factors. Specific intrinsic factors include fun, accomplishment, challenge, improving skills, and excitement (Wankel & Kreisel, 1985; Wankel & Pabich, 1982; Wankel & Sefton, 1989). Social factors consist of being with friends and being on a team. The extrinsic factors include receiving awards and winning. The intrinsic sources have been rated as most important to enjoyment, followed by social and then extrinsic factors (Wankel & Pabich, 1982).

Examining sources of sport enjoyment in a large sample ($N = 1,342$) that was diverse in age, ethnicity, and gender, Scanlan and colleagues (1993) generated 37 items based on an extensive review of the sport enjoyment literature and evaluation of content validity by expert judges. The items were then administered to the sample of youth sport participants, and the responses were factor analyzed to identify the underlying constructs. These underlying constructs were sport enjoyment; perceived ability; positive team interactions and support; positive parental involvement, interactions, and performance satisfaction; effort and mastery; and positive coach support and seasonal performance satisfaction. Multiple regression indicated that effort and mastery, positive team interactions and support, and positive coach support and satisfaction with performance were significant sources of enjoyment. These three constructs surprisingly accounted for 47% of the variance in sport enjoyment.

Other factors also have been identified as contributing to enjoyment in youth sport participants. For example, enjoyment of sport has been linked to task orientation, perceived competence, learned helplessness, and years of sport participation, but not ego orientation in physical activity (Boyd & Yin, 1996). Enjoyment of sport also has been related to perceived ability/competence (Oman & McAuley, 1993; Ommundsen & Vaglum, 1991), perceived parent involvement, pressure, and satisfaction (e.g., Babkes & Weiss, 1999; Brustad, 1996; Ommundsen & Vaglum, 1991; Scanlan & Lewthwaite, 1986), and perceptions of success (Briggs, 1994).

Utilizing qualitative methodology, researchers have exposed some of the more diverse and elusive sources of enjoyment in youth sport participants. For example, Scanlan, Stein, and Ravizza (1989) interviewed elite figure skaters about important sources of enjoyment and then content analyzed the transcripts. Sources of enjoyment fit into four major themes: perceived competence, act of skating, social and life opportunities, and social recognition of competence. Perceived competence was characterized by factors such as skill mastery, performance accomplishment, and competitive achievement. Act of skating was best characterized by factors such as movement sensations, self-expressiveness, flow/peak experiences, and athleticism of skating. Factors such as making and having friends, and interactions with coaches, parents, and athletes characterized social and life opportunities. Social recognition of competence included performance acknowledgment and social recognition. Bakker, De Koning, Van Ingen Schenau, and De Groot replicated the results (1993), using nearly identical methodology and younger elite speed skaters.

In a qualitative analysis that included 14- and 15-year-old American and English pupils, Smith and Conkell (1999) examined factors contributing to enjoyment in physical education. They identified 11 factors influencing enjoyment and then categorized the factors into four main headings: the pupil, the teacher, the environment, and the activities. No cross-cultural differences in enjoyment were apparent, with one exception: English students reported that enjoyment derived from teachers was related to task differentiation; American students identified teaching styles.

In summary, researchers have identified intrinsic, social, and extrinsic factors as sources of enjoyment in youth sport and physical education participants. Intrinsic sources of enjoyment range from developing and improving skills to self-expression to simply having fun. Social sources also are important, and range from being on a team and making friends to parental involvement to positive interactions with coaches. The final category, extrinsic factors, is least important for enjoyment and includes receiving trophies and recognition. It remains to be determined whether the sources of enjoyment for youth are applicable to adult participants and across sport and exercise environments.

Adult Exercisers

Sources of enjoyment in adults also have been investigated with quantitative and qualitative methodologies. Utilizing a quantitative research design, Widmeyer, Carron, and Brawley (1990) examined the effects of group size in sports, with a focus of group size on perceptions of enjoyment in the second of two studies. The results revealed an inverse relationship between group size and enjoyment. Smaller groups (3 players) reported more enjoyment than larger groups (12 players). Within the small and moderate size (6 players) exercise groups, getting exercise and the positive feelings of fatigue associated with competition also were related to enjoyment scores. The best predictors of enjoyment in the larger group were perceptions of reduced influence and responsibility.

Leadership behavior also may influence exercise-induced feeling states, perceptions of self-efficacy, and enjoyment (Turner et al., 1997). This behavior consisted of the exercise instructor's forming either a socially enriched or a socially bland exercise environment. The results of this study that focused on 46 college-age women undertaking ballet indicated that the socially enriched environment which included frequent technical instruction, technical support, and positive feedback, was reported to be more enjoyable than the bland exercise condition. Enjoyment also was related to acute changes in mood, but it is uncertain whether enjoyment caused the mood changes or vice versa.

In two qualitative studies, Wankel (1985) interviewed adult males to determine personal and situational factors affecting continued exercise involvement and possibly enjoyment. Exercise "maintainers" reported that developing skills, going out with friends, releasing competitive drives, satisfying curiosity, mental and physical outcomes, and developing social relationships were important qualities of the exercise experience. These elements along with exercise intensity, exercise variability, and consistent leadership may influence enjoyment. Heck and Kimiecik (1993) interviewed male and female adult exercisers to define exercise enjoyment. The content analysis of the interviews identified social interaction and competition as important components of enjoyment. Other factors related to enjoyment included the exercise environment, flow experiences, emotional and physical outcomes, and outlet or distraction from daily hassles and demands.

Other Sources of Enjoyment

Examination of the interaction between personality characteristics and the exercise mode or environment may help to clarify why some people find exercise to be enjoyable and others do not. Clearly, not all types of exercise are enjoyable to a particular individual, and individuals differ in personal preferences for physical activities. For example, there may be a unique personality profile that enables enjoyment of swimming versus rock climbing. Motl et al. (1997) found that swimmers reported high trait-anxiety scores and low sensation-seeking scores, whereas rock climbers reported the opposite personality profile. The difference in personality may have influenced enjoyment of swimming and rock climbing.

Using an interactionist perspective, Walker, Roberts, Nyheim, and Treasure (1998) examined the relationship between dispositional achievement goals and the perceived motivational climate in predicting enjoyment. The participants were females and males participating in summer sport camps. Results indicated that the interaction of dispositional achievement goals and the perceived motivational climate predicted enjoyment scores to a greater extent than did each factor individually. The findings underscore the interaction between dispositional and situational factors in understanding enjoyment of sport in males and females.

The interaction between personality and the exercise environment may affect perceptions of enjoyment in other ways. For example, individuals with social physique anxiety may not enjoy exercising in gyms or aerobics classes, because these environments often present a strong physique-evaluative component that could produce anxiety rather than enjoyment (Hart, Leary, & Rejeski, 1989). Individuals with a high level of social physique anxiety may need to participate in physical activity environments that contain less of an evaluative component. Such environments may include the home, neighborhood, park, or even specifically designed exercise classes.

There are many other factors in exercise that may make it enjoyable, such as mood enhancement or feeling better, need for thrills and excitement, and peak moments. Other sources of enjoyment include testing one's ability, mind-body-spirit unity, communing with nature, escape, progress, and playfulness and frivolousness. The depth and breadth of factors contributing to enjoyment are as diverse as the array of personal meanings associated with physical activity (Berger, 1996; Berger & Mackenzie, 1980).

Models Describing the Experience of Enjoyment

Stein and Scanlan (1992) proposed and tested a conceptual framework to explain sources of enjoyment in athletes. The framework consists of two potential underlying mechanisms: goal attainment and nongoal occurrences. Goal attainment involves experiences in which an individual sets a desired goal or standard of achievement and then strives to achieve the standard. Two functional related goal levels exist within goal attainment (i.e., universal and general

goals), which form a goal hierarchy. Nongoal occurrences are environmental events that are unplanned and unexpected, and that transpire in the sports domain, but are outside of the athlete's a priori goal hierarchy. Using a sample of 181 male adolescent athletes, Stein and Scanlan tested the model and found support for predictive relationships between general goal attainment and universal goal attainment and general goal attainment and seasonal enjoyment. There were no apparent relationships among seasonal enjoyment, universal goal attainment, and nongoal occurrences. This conceptual framework is quite logical and requires further testing using structural equation modeling and in a variety of physical activity settings.

Conclusions

Enjoyment is linked to quality of life (Kahneman et al., 1999), and physical activity may be one way of experiencing enjoyment and improving quality of life. Enjoyment of physical activity also may influence exercise adherence and promote mental health benefits. Little is known about factors that maximize enjoyment, but progress has been made in highlighting some potential influences.

Considerable research is needed in the area of enjoyment. Although researchers have not examined enjoyment in the context established by emotion researchers, future studies of enjoyment should include a combination of self-report and behavioral and physiological measures such as the FACS or EEG activity. Studies also are needed to (1) test the multitude of benefits associated with exercise enjoyment, (2) explore new sources of enjoyment, and (3) develop new theoretical approaches for understanding the importance and determinants of physical activity enjoyment.

CONCLUDING OBSERVATIONS

This chapter focused on only four of a multitude of ways that exercise may affect the quality of life. Life quality emphasizes a state of excellence and/or an enhanced sense of well-being and is similar to the concepts of subjective well-being and happiness. Although the study of exercise/health psychology is still in its infancy, the research evidence reviewed in this chapter suggests that habitual exercise is related to life quality. The myriad interacting factors challenge researchers attempting to understand the somatopsychic and psychosomatic relationship, especially as related to the quality of life.

A. Frank (1991, p. 6) comments that serious illness "leaves no aspect of life untouched. . . . Your relationships, your work, your sense of who you are and who you might become, your sense of what life is and ought to be—these all change, and the change is terrifying." The major premise of this chapter is that the same can be said for physical activity. Physical activity, like illness, directly affects the body and thus our core. To paraphrase Frank, exercise leaves no aspect of life untouched: relationships, work, sense of who you are and who you might become, and your sense of what life is and ought to be. Although self-attuned exercisers know this on a phenomenological level, researchers need to gather empirical data that more fully describe, examine, and predict the relationships between physical activity and body-mind.

In summary, the research evidence reviewed in this chapter supports the following observations:

1. *Exercise is associated with subjective well-being in members of a "normal" population.* The benefits, especially for mood, most plausibly attributed to exercise tend to be acute or short term rather than chronic, long-term alterations. Chronic benefits tend to occur in populations with clinical psychological diagnoses. In addition to mood benefits, habitual physical activity is related to moderating one's stress response. Exercise provides opportunities for eustress as well as for decreasing ongoing levels of distress. Although exercise is only one of many ways to enhance one's subjective well-being, it is particularly appealing because it simultaneously provides a variety of health benefits and desirable changes in appearance. Further investigation is needed to clarify whether the psychological benefits of exercise differ in extent, duration, and specific qualities from those of other mood-elevating and stress management techniques. Presently, it seems that exercise is moderately comparable to other common techniques, such as those listed in Table 25.2. When examining the relationship between exercise and the quality of life, it is important to recognize that exercise can have negative influences if the participant habitually overtrains. Some of the undesirable changes include overuse injuries, exercise compulsion, and increased fatigue/decreased energy.

2. *To facilitate the desirable psychological changes associated with exercise, Berger and her colleagues proposed a taxonomy for enhancing the psychological benefits of exercise.* The taxonomy includes three sets of factors: enjoyment of the activity, mode characteristics, and practice requirements (Berger, 1983/1984, 1996; Berger & Motl, 2000; Berger & Owen, 1988, 1992a, 1992b,

1998). Taxonomy factors highlight some of the major issues in the relationship between physical activity and subjective well-being. *Enjoyment,* an optimal psychological state, is the first factor in the taxonomy because it adjusts for individual differences and preferences for physical activity. *Mode characteristics* include rhythmical abdominal breathing or an aerobic quality, a relative absence of interpersonal competition, closed exercise modes, and rhythmical and repetitive movements. The *practice factors* or training requirements include a moderate exercise intensity, a duration of at least 20 minutes, and frequent physical activity to establish minimum fitness levels to prevent personal and physical discomfort.

3. *The opportunity to experience peak moments is another way that physical activity can add to the quality and meaning of life.* Flow, peak performance, peak experience, and the running or exercise high are examples of different types of peak moments that exercise participants report. Although understanding peak moments is limited by the difficult nature of these elusive and fleeting moments, the current research on exercise adherence emphasizes a critical need to move beyond describing the experiences and to examine factors influencing this important psycho-social-physical factor. Understanding the experience of peak moments may be one piece of the puzzle for encouraging more people to be physically active. The experience of peak moments also may have a dramatic impact on quality of life.

4. *Another way that physical activity influences quality of life is by providing opportunities to experience personal enjoyment.* Enjoyment can be defined as "an optimal psychological state (i.e., flow) that leads to performing an activity for its own sake and is associated with positive feeling states" (Kimiecik & Harris, 1996, p. 257). Enjoyment is linked to quality of life by providing rewarding, interesting, and even hedonic experiences that truly are memorable. Daily doses of enjoyment may counterbalance the stress and hassles of everyday life, reduce the likelihood of developing depressive affect, and contribute to positive mood states. In physical activity, enjoyment appears to result from factors such as skill mastery, physical achievement, social interactions, body-mind integration, close interactions with the beauty of nature, increased self-awareness, and peak moments. Enjoyment, as well as peak moments, quite likely influences exercise adherence, the mental health benefits of physical activity, and a person's overall quality of life.

REFERENCES

Allen, R.M., Haupt, T.D., & Jones, W. (1964). An analysis of peak experiences reported by college students. *Journal of Clinical Psychology, 20,* 207–212.

American College of Sports Medicine. (1995). *ACSM's guidelines for exercise testing and prescription* (5th ed.). Baltimore: Williams & Wilkins.

Andrews, F.M., & Whithey, S.B. (1976). *Social indicators of well-being: America's perception of life quality.* New York: Plenum Press.

Argyle, M. (1999). Causes and correlates of happiness. In D. Kahneman, E. Diener, & N. Schwarz (Eds.), *Well-being: The foundations of hedonic psychology* (pp. 353–373). New York: Russell Sage Foundation.

Avison, W.R., & Gotlib, I.H. (Eds.). (1994). *Stress and mental health: Contemporary issues and prospects for the future.* New York: Plenum Press.

Babkes, M.L., & Weiss, M.R. (1999). Parental influence on children's cognitive and affective responses to competitive soccer participation. *Pediatric Exercise Science, 11,* 44–62.

Bahrke, M.S., & Morgan, W.P. (1978). Anxiety reduction following exercise and meditation. *Cognitive Therapy and Research, 2,* 323–333.

Bakker, F.C., De Koning, J.J., Van Ingen Schenau, G.J., & De Groot, G. (1993). Motivation of young elite speed skaters. *International Journal of Sport Psychology, 24,* 432–442.

Bartholomew, J.B. (1997). Post exercise mood: The effect of a manipulated pre-exercise mood state. *Journal of Sport & Exercise Psychology, 9,* S29.

Bartlett, M.S., Hager, J.C., Ekman, P., & Sejnowski, T.J. (1999). Measuring facial expressions by computer image analysis. *Psychophysiology, 36,* 253–263.

Berger, B.G. (1972). Relationships between environmental factors of temporal-spatial uncertainty, probability of physical harm, and nature of competition and selected personality characteristics of athletes. *Dissertation Abstracts International, 33,* 1014A. (University Microfilms No. 72–23689, 373)

Berger, B.G. (1980). The meaning of regular jogging: A phenomenological approach. In R. Cox (Ed.), *American Alliance for Health, Physical Education, and Recreation Research Consortium symposium papers* (Vol. 2, Bk. 2, pp. 40–44). Washington, DC: American Alliance for Health, Physical Education, Recreation, and Dance.

Berger, B.G. (1983/1984). Stress reduction through exercise: The mindbody connection. *Motor Skills: Theory into Practice, 7,* 31–46.

Berger, B.G. (1994). Coping with stress: The effectiveness of exercise and other techniques. *Quest, 46,* 100–119.

Berger, B.G. (1996). Psychological benefits of an active lifestyle: What we know and what we need to know. *Quest, 48,* 330–353.

Berger, B.G. (1984/1997). Running strategies for women and men. In M.L. Sachs & G.W. Buffone (Eds.), *Running as therapy* (pp. 23–62). Northvale, NJ: Aronson.

Berger, B.G., Butki, B.D., & Berwind (1995). Acute mood changes associated with competitive and non-competitive physical activities. *Journal of Applied Sport Psychology, 7,* S41.

Berger, B.G., Friedman, E., & Eaton, M. (1988). Comparison of jogging, the relaxation response, and group interaction for stress reduction. *Journal of Sport & Exercise Psychology, 10,* 431–447.

Berger, B.G., Grove, J.R., Prapavessis, H., & Butki, B.D. (1997). Relationship of swimming distance, expectancy, and performance to mood states of competitive athletes. *Perceptual and Motor Skills, 84,* 1199–1210.

Berger, B.G., & Mackenzie, M.M. (1980). A case study of a woman jogger: A psychodynamic analysis. *Journal of Sport Behavior, 3,* 3–16.

Berger, B.G., & McInman, A. (1993). Exercise and the quality of life. In R.N. Singer, M. Murphey, & L.K. Tennant (Eds.), *Handbook of research on sport psychology* (pp. 729–760). New York: Macmillan.

Berger, B.G., & Motl, R.W. (2000). Exercise and mood: A subjective review and synthesis of research employing the Profile of Mood States. *Journal of Applied Sport Psychology, 12,* 69–92.

Berger, B.G., Motl, R.W., Butki, B.D., Martin, D.T., Wilkinson, J.G., & Owen, D.R. (1999). Mood and cycling performance in response to three weeks of high-intensity, short-duration overtraining, and a two-week taper. *The Sport Psychologist, 13,* 466–479.

Berger, B.G., & Owen, D.R. (1986). Mood alteration with swimming: A re-evaluation. In L. Vander Velden & J.H. Humphrey (Eds.), *Current selected research in the psychology and sociology of sport* (Vol. 1, pp. 97–114). New York: AMS Press.

Berger, B.G., & Owen, D.R. (1988). Stress reduction and mood enhancement in four exercise modes: Swimming, body conditioning, Hatha yoga, and fencing. *Research Quarterly for Exercise and Sport, 59,* 148–159.

Berger, B.G., & Owen, D.R. (1992a). Mood alteration in yoga and swimming: Aerobic exercise not necessary. *Perceptual and Motor Skills, 75,* 1331–1343.

Berger, B.G., & Owen, D.R. (1992b). Preliminary analysis of a causal relationship between swimming and stress reduction: Intense exercise may negate the effects. *International Journal of Sport Psychology, 23,* 70–85.

Berger, B.G., & Owen, D.R. (1998). Relation of low and moderate intensity exercise with acute mood change in college joggers. *Perceptual and Motor Skills, 87,* 611–621.

Berger, B.G., Owen, D.R., & Man, F. (1993). A brief review of literature and examination of acute mood benefits in Czechoslovakian and United States swimmers. *International Journal of Sport Psychology, 24,* 130–150.

Berger, B.G., Owen, D.R., Motl, R.W., & Parks, L. (1998). Relationship between expectancy of psychological benefits and mood alteration in joggers. *International Journal of Sport Psychology, 29,* 1–16.

Blanchard, C., & Rodgers, W. (1997). The effects of exercise intensity and fitness level on mood states. *Journal of Sport & Exercise Psychology, 9,* S32.

Boutcher, S.H., & Landers, D.M. (1988). The effects of vigorous exercise on anxiety, heart rate, and alpha activity of runners and nonrunners. *Psychophysiology, 25,* 696–702.

Boyd, M.P., & Yin, Z. (1996). Cognitive-affective sources of sport enjoyment in adolescent sport participants. *Adolescence, 31,* 383–395.

Bradburn, N.M. (1969). *The structure of psychological wellbeing.* Chicago: Aldine.

Breathnach, S.B. (1998). *Something more: Excavating your authentic self.* New York: Warner Books.

Brenner, B. (1975). Enjoyment as a preventive of depressive affect. *Journal of Community Psychology, 3,* 346–357.

Brewer, B.W., Van Raalte, J.L., Linder, D.E., & Van Raalte, N.S. (1991). Peak performance and the perils of retrospective introspection. *Journal of Sport & Exercise Psychology, 8,* 227–238

Briggs, J.D. (1994). An investigation of participant enjoyment in the physical activity setting. *Journal of Physical Education, Recreation, and Dance, 65,* 213–221.

Brown, J.D. (1991). Staying fit and staying well: Physical fitness as a moderator of life stress. *Journal of Personality and Social Psychology, 60,* 555–561.

Brown, J.D., & Siegel, J.M. (1988). Exercise as a buffer of life stress: A prospective study of adolescent health. *Health Psychology, 7,* 341–353.

Brown, J.D., Wang, Y., Ward, A., Ebbeling, C.B., Fortalage, L., Puleo, E., Benson, H., & Rippe, J.M. (1995). Chronic psychological effects of exercise and exercise plus cognitive strategies. *Medicine and Science in Sports and Exercise, 27,* 765–775.

Brustad, R.J. (1996). Attraction to physical activity in urban school children: Parental socialization and gender influences. *Research Quarterly for Exercise and Sport, 67,* 316–323.

Bungum, T.J., & Vincent, M.L. (1997). Determinants of physical activity among female adolescents. *American Journal of Preventive Medicine, 13,* 115–122.

Butki, B.D., & Rudolph, D.L. (1997). Self-efficacy and affective responses to short bouts of exercise [Abstract]. *Journal of Sport & Exercise Psychology, 19,* S38.

Campbell, A., Converse, P.E., & Rogers, W.L. (1976). *The quality of American life: Perceptions, evaluations, and satisfactions.* New York: Russell Sage Foundation.

Campbell, D. (1997). *The Mozart effect: Tapping the power of music to heal the body, strengthen the mind, and unlock the creative spirit.* New York: Avon.

Carmack, M.A., & Martens, R. (1979). Measuring commitment to running: A survey of runners' attitudes and mental states. *Journal of Sport Psychology, 1,* 25–42.

Carpenter, P.J. (1995). Modification and extension of the sport commitment model. *Journal of Sport & Exercise Psychology, 17,* S37.

Carpenter, P.J., & Coleman, R. (1998). A longitudinal study of elite cricketeers' commitment. *International Journal of Sport Psychology, 29,* 195–210.

Carpenter, P.J., Scanlan, T.K., Simons, J.P., & Lobel, M. (1993). A test of the sport commitment model using structural equation modeling. *Journal of Sport & Exercise Psychology, 15,* 119–133.

Clark, D.M., & Teasdale, J.D. (1985). Constraints on the effects of mood on memory. *Journal of Personality and Social Psychology, 48,* 1595–1608.

Clarke, S.G., & Haworth, J.T. (1994). "Flow" experience in the daily lives of sixth-form college students. *British Journal of Psychology, 85,* 511–523.

Claytor, R.P. (1991). Stress reactivity: Hemodynamic adjustments in trained and untrained humans. *Medicine and Science in Sports and Exercise, 23,* 873–881.

Cohn, P.J. (1991). An exploratory study on peak performance in golf. *The Sport Psychologist, 5,* 1–14.

Craft, L.L., & Landers, D.M. (1998). The effect of exercise on clinical depression and depression resulting from mental illness: A meta-analysis. *Journal of Sport & Exercise Psychology, 20,* 339–357.

Crocker, P.R.E., Bouffard, M., & Gessaroli, M.E. (1995). Measuring enjoyment in youth sport settings: A confirmatory factor analysis of the Physical Activity Enjoyment Scale. *Journal of Sport & Exercise Psychology, 17,* 200–205.

Csikszentmihalyi, M. (1975). *Beyond boredom and anxiety.* San Francisco: Jossey-Bass.

Csikszentmihalyi, M. (1991). *Flow: The psychology of optimal experience.* New York: Harper & Row.

Csikszentmihalyi, M. (1993). *The evolving self.* New York: Harper & Row.

Csikszentmihalyi, M. (1997). *Finding flow: The psychology of engagement with everyday life.* New York: Basic Books.

Csikszentmihalyi, M. (1999). If we are so rich, why aren't we happy? *American Psychologist, 54,* 821–827.

Csikszentmihalyi, M., & Larson, R. (1987). Validity and reliability of the experience sampling method. *Journal of Nervous and Mental Disorders, 175,* 526–536.

Csikszentmihalyi, M., & LeFevre, J. (1989). Optimal experience in work and leisure. *Journal of Personality and Social Psychology, 56,* 815–822.

Dalkey, N.C., Lewis, R., & Snyder, D. (1972). *Studies of life quality.* Boston: Heath.

DeGrazia, S. (1962). *Of time, work, and leisure.* New York: Twentieth Century Fund.

Diener, E. (1984). Subjective well-being. *Psychological Bulletin, 95,* 542–575.

Diener, E. (1994). Assessing subjective well-being: Progress and opportunities. *Social Indicators Research, 31,* 103–157.

Diener, E., & Diener, C. (1996). Most people are happy. *Psychological Science 7,* 181–185.

Diener, E., Emmons, R.A., Larson, R.J., & Griffin, S. (1985). The Satisfaction with Life Scale. *Journal of Personality Assessment, 49,* 71–75.

Diener, E., & Lucas, R.E. (1999). Personality and subjective well-being. In D. Kahneman, E. Diener, & N. Schwarz (Eds.), *Well-being: The foundations of hedonic psychology* (pp. 213–229). New York: Russell Sage Foundation.

Diener, E., & Suh, E.M. (1999). National differences in subjective well-being. In D. Kahneman, E. Diener, & N. Schwarz (Eds.), *Well-being: The foundations of hedonic psychology* (pp. 434–450). New York: Russell Sage Foundation.

Dienstbier, R.A. (1989). Arousal and physiological toughness: Implications for mental and physical health. *Psychological Review, 96,* 84–100.

DiLorenzo, T.M., Stucky-Rupp, R.C., Vander Wal, J.S., & Gothan, H.J. (1998). Determinants of exercise among children: II. A longitudinal analysis. *Preventive Medicine, 27,* 470–477.

Dishman, R.K. (1986). Mental health. In V. Seefeldt (Ed.), *Physical activity and well-being* (pp. 304–341). Reston, VA: American Alliance for Health, Physical Education, Recreation, and Dance.

Dyer, J.B., III, & Crouch, J.G. (1988). Effects of running and other activities on moods. *Perceptual and Motor Skills, 67,* 43–50.

Ebersole, P. (1972). Effects of classification of peak experiences. *Psychological Reports, 30,* 631–635.

Ekman, P., & Davidson, R.J. (1993). Voluntary smiling changes regional brain activity. *Psychological Science, 4,* 342–345.

Ekman, P., Davidson, R.J., & Friesen, W.V. (1990). The Duchenne smile: Emotional expression and brain physiology II. *Journal of Personality and Social Psychology, 58,* 342–353.

Ekman, P., & Friesen, W.V. (1978). *The Facial Action Coding System: A technique for the measurement of facial movements.* Palo Alto, CA: Consulting Psychologists.

Etnier, J.L., Salazar, W., Landers, D.M., Petruzzello, S.J., Han, M., & Nowell, P. (1997). The influence of physical fitness and exercise upon cognitive functioning: A meta-analysis. *Journal of Sport & Exercise Psychology, 19,* 249–277.

Farrell, P.A., Gustafson, A.B., Garthwaite, T.L., Kalkhoff, R.K., Cowley, A.W., & Morgan, W.P. (1986). Influence of endogenous opioids on the response of selected hormones to exercise in humans. *Journal of Applied Physiology, 61,* 1051–1057.

Farrell, P.A., Gustafson, A.B., Morgan, W.P., & Pert, C.B. (1987). Enkephallins, catecholamines, and psychological mood alterations: Effects of prolonged exercise. *Medicine and Science in Sports and Exercise, 19,* 347–353.

Flanagan, J.C. (1978). A research approach to improving our quality of life. *American Psychologist, 33,* 138–147.

Frank, A.W. (1991). *At the will of the body.* Boston: Houghton Mifflin.

Frank, M.G., Ekman, P., & Friesen, W.V. (1993). Behavioral markers and recognizability of the smile of enjoyment. *Journal of Personality and Social Psychology, 64,* 83–93.

Frank, M.G., Ekman, P., & Friesen, W.V. (1997). Behavioral markers and recognizability of the smile of enjoyment. In P. Ekman & E.L. Rosenberg (Eds.), *What the face reveals: Basic and applied studies of spontaneous expression using the Facial Action Coding System (FACS)* (pp. 217–242). New York: Oxford University Press.

Fried, R. (with Grimaldi, J.). (1993). *The psychology and physiology of breathing in behavioral medicine, clinical psychology, and psychiatry.* New York: Plenum Press.

Fried, R., & Berkowitz, L. (1979). Math hath charms—and can influence helpfulness. *Journal of Applied Social Psychology, 9,* 199–208.

Frijda, N.H. (1999). Emotions and hedonic experience. In D. Kahneman, E. Diener, & N. Schwarz (Eds.), *Well-being: The foundations of hedonic psychology* (pp. 190–212). New York: Russell Sage Foundation.

Gallup, G., Jr., & Castelli, J. (1989). *The people's religion.* New York: Macmillan.

Gallwey, W.T. (1997). *The inner game of tennis* (2nd ed.). New York: Random House.

Garcia, A.W., & King, A.C. (1991). Predicting long-term adherence to aerobic exercise: A comparison of two models. *Journal of Sport & Exercise Psychology, 13,* 394–410.

Gentile, A.M. (1972). A working model of skill acquisition with application to teaching. *Quest, 17,* 3–23.

Gentile, A.M. (1992). The nature of skill acquisition: Therapeutic implications for children with movement disorders. In H. Forssberg & H. Hirschfeld (Eds.), *International Sven*

Jerring Sympotiu: Movement Disorders in Children, (pp. 31–40). Basel, Switzerland: Karger.

Glasser, W. (1976). *Positive addiction.* New York: Harper & Row.

Gross, J.D. (1994). Hardiness and mood disturbances in swimmers while overtraining. *Journal of Sport & Exercise Psychology, 16,* 135–149.

Grove, J.R., & Lewis, M.A.E. (1996). Hypnotic susceptibility and the attainment of flowlike states during exercise. *Journal of Sport & Exercise Psychology, 18,* 380–391.

Grove, J.R., & Prapavessis, H. (1992). Preliminary evidence for the reliability and validity of an abbreviated Profile of Mood States. *International Journal of Sport Psychology, 23,* 93–109.

Hart, E.A., Leary, M.R., & Rejeski, W.J. (1989). The measurement of social physique anxiety. *Journal of Sport & Exercise Psychology, 11,* 94–104.

Hassmén, P., & Blomstrand, E. (1995). Mood states relationships and soccer team performance. *The Sport Psychologist, 9,* 297–308.

Hays, K.F. (Ed.). (1998). *Integrating exercise, sports, movement and mind: Therapeutic unity.* New York: Haworth Press.

Hays, K.F. (1999). *Working it out: Using exercise in psychotherapy.* Washington, DC: American Psychological Association.

Heck, T.A., & Kimiecik, J.C. (1993). What is exercise enjoyment? A qualitative investigation of adult exercise maintainers. *Wellness Perspectives, 10,* 3–21.

Hewitt, J., & Miller, R. (1981). Relative effects of meditation vs. other activities on ratings of relaxation and enjoyment of others. *Psychological Reports, 48,* 395–398.

Hooper, S.L., Mackinnon, L.T., & Hanrahan, S. (1997). Mood states as an indication of staleness and recovery. *International Journal of Sport Psychology, 28,* 1–12.

International Society of Sport Psychology (1991, Fall). Physical activity and psychological benefits: An ISSP position statement. *Newsletter, 2,* 1–3.

Jackson, S.A. (1992). Athletes in flow: A qualitative investigation of flow in elite figure skaters. *Journal of Applied Sport Psychology, 4,* 161–180.

Jackson, S.A. (1995). Factors influencing the occurrence of flow state in elite athletes. *Journal of Applied Sport Psychology, 7,* 138–166.

Jackson, S.A. (1996). Toward a conceptual understanding of the flow experience in elite athletes. *Research Quarterly for Exercise and Sport, 67,* 76–90.

Jackson, S.A., & Csikszentmihalyi, M. (1999). *Flow in sports.* Champaign, IL: Human Kinetics.

Jackson, S.A., Kimiecik, J.C., Ford, S.K., & Marsh, H.W. (1998). Psychological correlates of flow in sport. *Journal of Sport & Exercise Psychology, 20,* 358–378.

Jackson, S.A., & Marsh, H.W. (1996). Development and validation of a scale to measure optimal experience: The Flow State Scale. *Journal of Sport & Exercise Psychology, 18,* 17–35.

Jackson, S.A., & Roberts, G.C. (1992). Positive performance states of athletes: Toward a conceptual understanding of peak performance. *The Sport Psychologist, 6,* 156–171.

Jin, P. (1992). Efficacy of Tai Chi, brisk walking, meditation, and reading in reducing mental and emotional stress. *Journal of Psychosomatic Research, 36,* 361–370.

Kabat-Zinn, J. (1990). *Full catastrophe living: Using the wisdom of your body and mind to face stress, pain, and illness.* New York: Delacorte Press.

Kahneman, D., Diener, E., & Schwarz, N. (Eds.). (1999). *Well-being: The foundations of hedonic psychology.* New York: Russell Sage Foundation.

Kaplan, R.M. (1994). The Ziggy theorem: Toward an outcomes-focused health psychology. *Health Psychology, 13,* 451–460.

Kendzierski, D., & DeCarlo, K.J. (1991). Physical Activity Enjoyment Scale: Two validation studies. *Journal of Sport & Exercise Psychology, 13,* 50–64.

Kerr, J.H., & Schaik, P. (1995). Effects of game venue and outcome on psychological mood states in rugby. *Personality and Individual Differences, 19,* 407–410.

Keutzer, C.S. (1978). Whatever turns you on: Triggers to transcendent experiences. *Journal of Humanistic Psychology, 18*(3), 77–80.

Kimiecik, J.C., & Harris, A.T. (1996). What is enjoyment? A conceptual/definitional analysis with implications for sport and exercise psychology. *Journal of Sport & Exercise Psychology, 18,* 247–263.

Kimiecik, J.C., & Stein, G.L. (1992). Examining flow experiences in sport contexts: Conceptual issues and methodological concerns. *Journal of Applied Sport Psychology, 4,* 144–160.

Kirk, D. (1986). The aesthetic experience in sport. *Journal of Human Movement Studies, 12,* 99–111.

Kolyton, K.F., Shake, C.L., & Morgan, W.P. (1993). Interaction of exercise, water temperature and protective body apparel on body awareness and anxiety. *International Journal of Sport Psychology, 24,* 297–305.

Kraemer, R.R., Dzewaltowski, D.A., Blair, M.S., Rinehardt, K.F., & Castracane, V.D. (1990). Mood alteration from treadmill running and its relationship to beta-endorphin, corticotrophin, and growth hormone. *Journal of Sports Medicine and Physical Fitness, 30,* 241–246.

Landsman, T. (1969). The beautiful person. *Futurist, 3,* 41–42.

Larson, R., & Csikszentmihalyi, M. (1983). The experience sampling method. In H.T. Reis (Ed.), *Naturalistic approaches to studying social interaction: New directions for methodology of social and behavioral sciences* (pp. 41–56). San Francisco: Jossey-Bass.

Lazarus, R.S., & Folkman, S. (1986). Cognitive theories of stress and the issue of circularity. In M.H. Appley & R. Trumbull (Eds.), *Dynamics of stress: Physiological, psychological, and social perspectives* (pp. 63–80). New York: Plenum Press.

Lazarus, R.S., & Folkman, S. (1994). *Stress, appraisal, and coping.* New York: Springer.

LeDoux, J., & Armony, J. (1999). Can neurobiology tell us anything about human emotion? In D. Kahneman, E. Diener, & N. Schwarz (Eds.), *Well-being: The foundations of hedonic psychology* (pp. 489–499). New York: Russell Sage Foundation.

Leith, L.M. (1994). *Foundations of exercise and mental health.* Morgantown, WV: Fitness Information Technology.

Leslie, E., Owen, N., Salmon, J., Bauman, A., Sallis, J.F., & Lo, S.K. (1999). Insufficiently active Australian college students: Perceived personal, social, and environmental influences. *Preventive Medicine, 28,* 20–27.

Long, B.C. (1991). Physiological and psychological stress recovery of physically fit and unfit women. *Canadian Journal of Behavioral Science, 23,* 53–65.

Long, B.C. (1993). Aerobic conditioning (jogging) and stress inoculation interventions: An exploratory study of coping. *International Journal of Sport Psychology, 24,* 94–109.

Long, B.C., & van Stavel, R. (1995). Effects of exercise training on anxiety: A meta-analysis. *Journal of Applied Sport Psychology, 7,* 167–189.

Mackinnon, L.T. (1992). *Exercise and immunology: Current issues in exercise science* (Monograph No. 2). Champaign, IL: Human Kinetics.

Mandell, A. (1979). The second second wind. *Psychiatric Annals, 9,* 57–68.

Maroulakis, E., & Zervas, Y. (1993). Effects of aerobic exercise on mood of adult women. *Perceptual and Motor Skills, 76,* 795–801.

Marsh, H.W., & Jackson, S.A. (1999). Flow experience in sport: Construct validation of multidimensional, hierarchical state and trait responses. *Structural Equation Modeling, 6,* 343–371.

Martinsen, E.W., & Morgan, W.P. (1997). Antidepressant effects of physical activity. In W.P. Morgan (Ed.), *Physical activity and mental health* (pp. 93–106). Washington, DC: Taylor & Francis.

Maslow, A.H. (1968). *Toward a psychology of being.* Princeton, NJ: Van Nostrand.

Maslow, A.H. (1970). *Motivation and personality* (2nd ed.). New York: Harper & Row.

Masters, K.S. (1992). Hypnotic susceptibility, cognitive dissociation, and runner's high in a sample of marathon runners. *American Journal of Clinical Hypnosis, 34,* 193–201.

McInman, A.D., & Berger, B.G. (1993). Self-concept and mood changes associated with aerobic dance. *Australian Journal of Psychology, 45,* 134–140.

McInman, A.D., & Grove, J.R. (1991). Peak moments in sport: A literature review. *Quest, 43,* 333–351.

McKinney, C.H., Antoni, M.H., Kumar, M., Tims, F.C., & McCabe, P.M. (1997). Effects of Guided Imagery and Music (GIM) therapy on mood and cortisol in healthy adults. *Health Psychology, 16,* 390–400.

McNair, D.M., Lorr, M., & Droppleman, L.F. (1971/1981/1992). *Profile of Mood States manual.* San Diego: Education and Industrial Testing Service.

Mertesdorf, F.L. (1994). Cycle exercising in time with music. *Perceptual and Motor Skills, 78,* 1123–1141.

Morgan, W.P. (1980). The trait psychology controversy. *Research Quarterly for Exercise and Sport, 51,* 50–76.

Morgan, W.P. (1987). Reduction of state anxiety following acute physical. In W.P. Morgan & S.E. Goldston (Eds.), *Exercise and mental health* (pp. 105–109). Washington, DC: Hemisphere.

Morgan, W.P. (Ed.). (1997). *Physical activity and mental health.* Washington, DC: Taylor & Francis.

Morgan, W.P., Brown, D.R., Raglin, J.S., O'Connor, P.J., & Ellickson, K.A. (1987). Psychological monitoring of overtraining and staleness. *British Journal of Sports Medicine, 21,* 107–114.

Morgan, W.P., Costill, D.L., Flynn, M.G., Raglin, J.S., & O'Connor, P.J. (1988). Mood disturbance following increased training in swimmers. *Medicine and Science in Sports and Exercise, 20,* 408–414.

Morgan, W.P., & Ellickson, K.A. (1989). Health, anxiety, and physical exercise. In D. Hackfort & C.D. Spielberger (Eds.), *Anxiety in sports: An international perspective* (pp. 165–182). New York: Hemisphere.

Morgan, W.P., & Goldston, S.E. (1987). Summary. In W.P. Morgan & S.E. Goldston (Eds.), *Exercise and mental health* (pp. 155–159). New York: Hemisphere.

Morris, W.N. (1999). The mood system. In D. Kahneman, E. Diener, & N. Schwarz (Eds.), *Well-being: The foundations of hedonic psychology* (pp. 169–189). New York: Russell Sage Foundation.

Moses, J., Steptoe, A., Matthews, A., & Edwards, S. (1989). The effects of exercise training on mental well-being in the normal population: A controlled trial. *Journal of Psychosomatic Research, 33,* 47–61.

Motl, R.W., Berger, B.G., & Leuschen, P.S. (in press). The role of enjoyment in the exercise-mood relationship. *International Journal of Sport Psychology.*

Motl, R.W., Berger, B.G., & Wilson, T.E. (1996). Exercise intensity and the acute mood states of cyclists. *Journal of Sport & Exercise Psychology, 18,* S59.

Motl, R.W., Bieber, S.L., & Berger, B.G. (1997). A multigroup invariance factor analysis of the Physical Enjoyment Scale: Comparison of enjoyment among rock-climbers, swimmers, and wellness students. *Journal of Applied Sport Psychology, 9,* S133.

Mroczek, D.K., & Kolarz, C.M. (1998). The effect of age on positive and negative affect: A developmental perspective on happiness. *Journal of Personality and Social Psychology, 75,* 1333–1349.

Mutrie, N., & Biddle, S.J.H. (1995). The effects of exercise on mental health in nonclinical populations. In S.J.H. Biddle (Ed.), *European perspectives on exercise and sport psychology* (pp. 50–70). Champaign, IL: Human Kinetics.

Nolen-Hoeksema, S., & Rusting, C.L. (1999). Gender differences in well-being. In D. Kahneman, E. Diener, & N. Schwarz (Eds.), *Well-being: The foundations of hedonic psychology* (pp. 330–350). New York: Russell Sage Foundation.

North, T.C., McCullagh, P., & Tran, Z.V. (1990). Effect of exercise on depression. In K.B. Pandolf & J.O. Holloszy (Eds.), *Exercise and sport sciences reviews* (Vol. 18, pp. 379–415). Baltimore: Williams & Wilkins.

O'Connor, P.J. (1997). Overtraining and staleness. In W.P. Morgan (Ed.), *Physical activity and mental health* (pp. 145–160). Washington, DC: Taylor & Francis.

O'Connor, P.J., Bryant, C.X., Veltri, J.P., & Gebhardt, S.M. (1993). State anxiety and ambulatory blood pressure following resistance exercise in females. *Medicine and Science in Sports and Exercise, 25,* 516–521.

O'Connor, P.J. Morgan, W.P., & Raglin, J.S. (1991). Psychobiological effects of 3 days of increased training in female and male swimmers. *Medicine and Science in Sports and Exercise, 23,* 1055–1061.

Oishi, S., Diener, E.F., Lucas, R.E., & Suh, E.M. (1999). Cross-cultural variations in predictors of life satisfaction: Perspectives from needs and values. *Personality and Social Psychology Bulletin, 25,* 980–990.

Oman, R.F., & McAuley, E. (1993). Intrinsic motivation and exercise behavior. *Journal of Health Education, 24,* 232–238.

Ommundsen, Y., & Vaglum, P. (1991). Soccer competitive anxiety and enjoyment in young boy players: The influence of perceived competence and significant others' emotional involvement. *International Journal of Sport Psychology, 22,* 35–49.

Paffenbarger, R.S., & Olsen, E. (1996). *Lifefit: An effective exercise program for optimal health and a longer life.* Champaign, IL: Human Kinetics.

Panzarella, R. (1980). The phenomenology of aesthetic peak experiences. *Journal of Humanistic Psychology, 20,* 67–85.

Pavot, W., & Diener, E.F. (1993). Review of the Satisfaction with Life Scale. *Psychological Assessment, 5,* 164–172.

Pavot, W., Diener, E.F., Colvin, C.R., & Sandvik, E. (1991). Further validation of the Satisfaction with Life Scale: Evidence for the cross-method convergence of well-being measures. *Journal of Personality Assessment, 57,* 149–161.

Paxton, S.J., Browning, C.J., & O'Connell, G. (1997). Predictors of exercise program participation in older women. *Psychology & Health, 12,* 543–552.

Petruzzello, S.J., Landers, D.M., Hatfield, B.D., Kubitz, K.A., & Salizar, W. (1991). A meta-analysis on the anxiety reducing effects of acute and chronic exercise: Outcomes and mechanisms. *Sports Medicine, 11,* 142–182.

Plante, T.G., Lantis, A., & Checa, G. (1998). The influence of perceived versus aerobic fitness on psychological health and physiological stress responsivity. *International Journal of Stress Management, 5,* 141–156.

Podilchak, W. (1991). Establishing the fun in leisure. *Leisure Sciences, 13,* 123–136.

Poulton, E.C. (1957). On prediction in skilled movements. *Psychological Bulletin, 54,* 467–478.

Privette, G. (1983). Peak experience, peak performance and flow: A comparative analysis of positive human experiences. *Journal of Personality and Social Psychology, 45,* 1361–1368.

Privette, G. (1984). *Experience Questionnaire.* Pensacola: University of West Florida.

Privette, G. (1985). Experience as a component of personality theory. *Psychological Reports, 56,* 263–266.

Privette, G., & Bundrick, C.M. (1987). Measurement of experience: Construct and content validity of the Experience Questionnaire. *Perceptual and Motor Skills, 65,* 315–332.

Privette, G., & Bundrick, C.M. (1989). Effects of triggering activity on construct events: Peak performance, peak experience, flow, average events, misery, and failure. *Journal of Social Behavior and Personality, 4,* 299–306.

Privette, G., & Bundrick, C.M. (1991). Peak experience, peak performance, and flow: Correspondence of personal descriptions and theoretical constructs. *Journal of Social Behavior and Personality, 6,* 169–188.

Privette, G., & Bundrick, C.M. (1997). Psychological processes of peak, average, and failing performance in sport. *International Journal of Sport Psychology, 28,* 323–334.

Privette, G., & Landsman, T. (1983). Factor analysis of peak performance: The full use of potential. *Journal of Personality and Social Psychology, 44,* 195–200.

Privette, G., & Sherry, D. (1986). Reliability and readability of questionnaire: Peak performance and peak experience. *Psychological Reports, 58,* 491–494.

Raglin, J.S., & Morgan, W.P. (1987). Influence of exercise and quiet rest on state anxiety and blood pressure. *Medicine and Science in Sports and Exercise, 19,* 456–463.

Ravizza, K. (1984). Qualities of peak experience in sport. In J.M. Silva & R.S. Weinberg (Eds.), *Psychological foundations of sport* (pp. 452–462). Champaign, IL: Human Kinetics.

Rejeski, W.J., Thompson, A., Brubaker, P.H., & Miller, H.S. (1992). Acute exercise: Buffering psychosocial stress responses in women. *Health Psychology, 11,* 355–362.

Riddick, C.C. (1984). Comparative psychology profiles of three groups of female collegians: Competitive swimmers, recreational swimmers, and inactive swimmers. *Journal of Sport Behavior, 7,* 160–174.

Rimer, S. (1990, April 29). Swimming for fitness and solitude. *New York Times magazine, Part 2: The Good Health magazine,* pp. 59–60, 83–84.

Rippere, V. (1977). "What's the thing to do when you're feeling depressed?" A pilot study. *Behavior Research and Therapy, 15,* 185–191.

Rostad, F.G., & Long, B.C. (1996). Exercise as a coping strategy for stress: A review. *International Journal of Sport Psychology, 27,* 197–222.

Ruark, J.K. (1999, February 12). Redefining the good life: A new focus in the social sciences. *Chronicle of Higher Education, 45*(23), A13–A15.

Rybczynski, W. (1991). *Waiting for the weekend.* New York: Viking.

Sachs, M.L. (1980). *On the tail of the runner's high: A descriptive and experimental investigation of characteristics of an elusive phenomenon.* Unpublished doctoral dissertation, Florida State University, Tallahassee.

Sachs, M.L. (1984). The runner's high. In M.L. Sachs & G.W. Buffone (Eds.), *Running as therapy* (pp. 273–287). Lincoln: Nebraska University Press.

Sacks, M.H. (1996). Exercise for stress control. In D. Goleman & J. Gurin (Eds.), *Mind/body medicine: How to use your mind for better health* (pp. 315–327). Yonkers, NY: Consumer Report Books.

Sallis, J.F., Calfas, K.J., Alcaraz, J.E., Gehrman, C., & Johnson, M.F. (1999). Potential mediators of change in a physical activity promotion course for university students: Project GRAD. *Annals of Behavioral Medicine, 21,* 149–158.

Sallis, J.F., Prochaska, J.J., Taylor, W.C., Hill, J.O., & Geraci, J.C. (1999). Correlates of physical activity in a national sample of girls and boys in grades 4 through 12. *Health Psychology, 18,* 410–415.

Scanlan, T.K., Carpenter, P.J., Lobel, M., & Simons, J.P. (1993). Sources of enjoyment for youth sport athletes. *Pediatric Exercise Science, 5,* 275–295.

Scanlan, T.K., & Lewthwaite, R. (1986). Social psychological aspects of competition for male youth sport participants: IV. Predictors of enjoyment. *Journal of Sport Psychology, 8,* 25–35.

Scanlan, T.K., & Simons, J.P. (1992). The construction of sport enjoyment. In G.C. Roberts (Ed.), *Motivation in sport and exercise* (pp. 199–215). Champaign, IL: Human Kinetics.

Scanlan, T.K., Stein, G.L., & Ravizza, K. (1989). An in-depth study of former elite figure skaters: II. Sources of enjoyment. *Journal of Sport & Exercise Psychology, 11,* 65–83.

Schwarz, N., & Clore, G.L. (1983). Mood, misattribution, and judgments of well-being: Informative and directive functions of affective states. *Journal of Personality and Social Psychology, 45,* 513–523.

Schwarz, N., & Strack, F. (1999). Reports of subjective well-being: Judgmental processes and their methodological implications. In D. Kahneman, E. Diener, & N. Schwarz (Eds.), *Well-being: The foundations of hedonic psychology* (pp. 61–84). New York: Russell Sage Foundation.

Seaward, B.L. (1997). *Managing stress: Principles and strategies for health and wellbeing* (2nd ed.). Boston: Jones & Bartlett.

Selye, H. (1975). *Stress without distress.* New York: Signet.

Sheehan, G. (1990). The ages of the runner. *Annals of Sports Medicine, 5,* 210.

Shraddhananda, S. (1997, February/March). Awakening spirit: The healing power of silence. *Yoga International, 34,* 21–23.

Singer, R.N. (1996). Moving toward the quality of life. *Quest, 48,* 246–252.

Singer, R.N., & Gerson, R.F. (1981). Task classification and strategy utilization in motor skills. *Research Quarterly for Exercise and Sport, 52,* 100–112.

Sinyor, D., Schwartz, S.G., Peronnet, F., Brisson, G., & Seraganian, P. (1993). Aerobic fitness level and reactivity to psychosocial stress: Physiological, biochemical, and subjective measures. *Psychosomatic Medicine, 65,* 205–217.

Smith, M.A., & Conkell, C. (1999). An examination of pupils' perceptions of enjoyment in physical education: A cross-cultural study. *Research Quarterly for Exercise and Sport, 70,* A100.

Spilker, B., Molinek, F.R., Jr., Johnston, K.A., Simpson, R.L., & Tilson, H.H. (1990). Quality of life bibliography and indexes. *Medical Care, 28*(Suppl.), DS1–DS77.

Stein, G.L., Kimiecik, J.C., Daniels, J., & Jackson, S.A. (1995). Psychological antecedents of flow in recreation. *Personality and Social Psychology Bulletin, 21,* 125–135.

Stein, G.L., & Scanlan, T.K. (1992). Goal attainment and nongoal occurrences as underlying mechanisms to an athlete's sources of enjoyment. *Pediatric Exercise Science, 4,* 150–165.

Steptoe, A., & Cox, S. (1988). Acute effects of aerobic exercise on mood. *Health Psychology, 7,* 329–340.

Steptoe, A., Kearsley, N., & Walters, N. (1993). Acute mood response to maximal and submaximal exercise in active and inactive men. *Psychology & Health, 8,* 89–99.

Stone, A.A., Shiffman, S.S., & De Vries, M.W. (1999). Ecological momentary assessment. In D. Kahneman, E. Diener, & N. Schwarz (Eds.), *Well-being: The foundations of hedonic psychology* (pp. 26–39). New York: Russell Sage Foundation.

Taylor, S.E., Pham, L.B., Rivkin, I.D., & Armor, D.A. (1998). Harnessing the imagination: Mental stimulation, self-regulation, and coping. *American Psychologist, 53,* 429–439.

Thayer, R.E. (1986). Activation-Deactivation Adjective Checklist: Current overview and structural analysis. *Psychological Reports, 58,* 607–614.

Thayer, R.E. (1987). Energy, tiredness, and tension effects of a sugar snack versus moderate exercise. *Journal of Personality and Social Psychology, 52,* 119–125.

Thayer, R.E. (1996). *The origin of everyday moods: Managing energy, tension, and stress.* New York: Oxford University Press.

Thayer, R.E., Peters, D.P., Takahashi, P.J., & Birkhead-Flight, A.M. (1994). Mood and behavior (smoking and sugar snacking) following moderate exercise: A partial test of self-regulation theory. *Personality and Individual Differences, 14,* 97–104.

Thorne, F.C. (1963). The clinical use of nadir experience reports. *Journal of Clinical Psychology, 19,* 248–250.

Turner, E.E., Rejeski, W.J., & Brawley, L.R. (1997). Psychological benefits of physical activity are influenced by the social environment. *Journal of Sport & Exercise Psychology, 19,* 119–130.

Vlachopoulos, S.P., Karageorghis, C.I., & Terry, P.C. (1999). Hierarchical confirmatory factor analysis of the Flow State Scale in an exercise setting. *Journal of Sport Science, 17,* 69–70.

Walker, B.W., Roberts, G.C., Nyheim, M., & Treasure, D.C. (1998). Predicting enjoyment and beliefs about success in sport: An interactionist perspective. *Journal of Sport & Exercise Psychology, 20,* S59.

Wankel, L.M. (1985). Personal and situational factors affecting exercise involvement: The importance of enjoyment *Research Quarterly for Exercise and Sport, 56,* 275–282.

Wankel, L.M. (1993). The importance of enjoyment to adherence and psychological benefits from physical activity. *International Journal of Sport Psychology, 24,* 151–169.

Wankel, L.M. (1997). "Strawpersons," selective reporting, and inconsistent logic: A response to Kimiecik and Harris's analysis of enjoyment. *Journal of Sport & Exercise Psychology, 19,* 98–109.

Wankel, L.M., & Berger, B.G. (1990). The psychological and social benefit of sport and physical activity. *Leisure Research, 21,* 167–182.

Wankel, L.M., & Kreisel, P.S.J. (1985). Factors underlying enjoyment of youth sports: Sport and age group comparisons. *Journal of Sport Psychology, 7,* 51–64.

Wankel, L.M., & Pabich, P. (1982). The minor sport experience: Factors contributing to or detracting from enjoyment. In J.T. Partington, T. Orlick, & J.H. Salmela (Eds.), *Mental training for coaches and athletes* (pp. 70–71). Ottawa, Canada: Sports in Perspective.

Wankel, L.M., & Sefton, J.M. (1989). A season-long investigation of fun in youth sports. *Journal of Sport & Exercise Psychology, 11,* 355–366.

Webster's Dictionary of the English Language (1992). New York: PMC Publishing.

Welk, G.J. (1999). The youth physical activity promotion model: A conceptual bridge between theory and practice. *Quest, 51,* 5–23.

Wheeler, B.L. (1985). Relationship of personal characteristics to mood and enjoyment after hearing live and recorded music and to musical taste. *Psychology of Music, 13,* 81–92.

Widmeyer, W.N., Carron, A.V., & Brawley, L.R. (1990). The effects of group size in sport. *Journal of Sport & Exercise Psychology, 12,* 177–190.

Wuthnow, R. (1978). Peak experiences: Some empirical tests. *Journal of Humanistic Psychology, 18,* 59–75.

CHAPTER 26

Career Termination among Athletes

JIM TAYLOR and BRUCE C. OGILVIE

Athletic participation is characterized by glorious peaks and debilitating valleys. The range of events and emotions experienced by athletes seems to be extreme compared to the normal population. Perhaps the most significant and potentially traumatic experience encountered by athletes is career termination. Moreover, termination from sports involves a variety of unique experiences that sets it apart from typical retirement concerns, including the early age of career termination, the need to find another career to pursue, and diverse ways in which athletes choose to or are forced to leave their sport.

The terms termination, retirement, and transition have been used in the study of the career-ending experiences of athletes (Blinde & Greendorfer, 1985; Ogilvie & Howe, 1982; J. Taylor & Ogilvie, 1998; Werthner & Orlick, 1982). To ensure consistency of meaning, termination and retirement are used interchangeably throughout this chapter because they are more widely used and do not relate to a specific theoretical explanation of this process. In addition, both terms are consistent with research outside of sport.

In response to the apparent significance of this issue, during the past 25 years, there has been a small but steady stream of anecdotal, theoretical, and empirical accounts of career termination among athletes (Botterill, 1982; Hoffer, 1990; Morrow, 1978; Ogilvie & Howe, 1982; Werthner & Orlick, 1982). These articles have brought attention to the potential difficulties of athletic retirement, provided explanations for the retirement process, and offered evidence of the nature of the athletic termination process.

Career termination has received considerable attention in the popular press. These reports typically are anecdotal accounts of professional athletes who had either a successful (Batten, 1979; White, 1974) or an unsuccessful (Alfano, 1982; Bradley, 1976; Elliott, 1982; Hoffer, 1990; Jordan, 1975; Kahn, 1972; Plimpton, 1977; P. Putnam, 1991; Stephens, 1984; Vecsey, 1980) career termination experience. Based on the large proportion of these articles that suggest termination difficulties, which include alcohol and drug abuse and criminal behavior, it might be concluded that career termination distress is a widespread phenomenon. However, because these accounts are anecdotal and have not employed the scientific method to determine the veracity and generalizability of their conclusions, it is impossible to make any conclusive judgments about the prevalence of termination difficulties among athletes.

Commensurate interest in athletic career termination began to grow in the sport psychology community. What resulted was a variety of scholarly articles by sport psychology professionals based on their own consulting experiences dealing with this issue, available research in the area, and literature from related fields (Botterill, 1982; Broom, 1982; McPherson, 1980; Ogilvie & Howe, 1982; Werthner & Orlick, 1982). These professionals concluded that athletic career termination can be a source of difficulties and, as a result, is an area worthy of further exploration.

Those individuals who have published their concerns about this issue have mainly been sport psychologists who provide services to elite-level athletes. Due to the dearth of empirical evidence in this area, it was unclear during this early period of exploration how far-reaching this problem may be in sport. Yet, there was consistent concern for the athletes throughout the sport world who experienced difficulties on career termination (J. May & Sieb, 1987; Ogilvie, 1982, 1983; Rotella & Heyman, 1986). The observations made by these professionals have raised important questions relative to career termination: What is the incidence of athletes who experience significant distress when leaving their sport? What level of athlete (e.g., high school, collegiate, professional) may be most prone to retirement difficulties?

The goal of this chapter is to provide an integrative view of career termination among athletes. This objective will be accomplished by considering the following areas: (1) historical and conceptual issues that will assist in the understanding of the growth of career termination as a meaningful avenue of inquiry; (2) theoretical perspectives of career termination; (3) a conceptual model that we proposed (J. Taylor & Ogilvie, 1994), which considers the causes of athletic career termination, factors that impact adaptation to career termination, available resources for responding to career termination, the quality of adaptation to career termination, and the prevention and treatment of career termination distress; and (4) avenues for future theoretical and empirical investigation into career termination in sports.

HISTORICAL AND CONCEPTUAL ISSUES

Career termination received little attention prior to 20 years ago. This may have been due in large part to the fact that elite athletes were more fully integrated into the basic fabric of society as compared to now (McPherson, 1980; Ogilvie, 1982, 1983). Specifically, due to limited technology, they did not receive a high level of media attention. In addition, salaries were not significantly higher than those in the nonsport population. Also, elite amateur athletes typically were either students or held full-time jobs away from their sports involvement. As a consequence, their transition to life as an "average" citizen was not as dramatic (Chartland & Lent, 1987).

The nature of the athlete development system in North America also may have contributed to the lack of concern and study of the postcareer adjustment problems experienced by elite athletes two decades ago. In particular, largely as a function of the sociopolitical system, athletic development in North America has occurred in a laissez-faire fashion. This approach emphasizes the self-responsibility of the athletes in their entrance into the sport and their development during their athletic career and, by extension, in their departure from the sport. Additionally, due to the large population of the United States, there was a constant influx of talented athletes who replaced those at the end of their career, thereby drawing attention away from the career termination of those athletes.

The nature of the relationship that sport psychologists had with elite athletes has also inhibited opportunities to address their career termination needs. Until recently, the team psychologist associated with a national governing body, collegiate team, or professional organization rarely had occasion to develop an extended relationship with team members. In fact, even at present, few sport psychologists have the chance to establish and maintain ongoing relationships with the athletes with whom they work. It has been our experience that this also holds true for athletes participating in individual sports. For example, typical involvement of a sport psychologist consists of periodic contact at training camps or competitions, or being called on for some form of performance or crisis intervention (Meyers, 1997). This type of contact rarely allows for the sport psychologist and athletes to communicate about issues related to career termination. Also, sports organizations often do not want the sport psychologist to address career termination and life after sport for fear of distracting the athletes from their competitive focus (J. Taylor, Ogilvie, Gould, & Gardner, 1990).

In contrast to the approach used in North America, the Eastern European nations over 10 years ago, accepted more responsibility for preparing their national athletes for life after sport (Ogilvie & Howe, 1986). This greater awareness would be expected because team psychologists often had long-term relationships with their team members. These professionals frequently established contact with the athletes at the inception of the structured selection process that was common in countries such as the former East Germany, the former Soviet Union, and China. Thus, relationships were initiated as early as preteens or early teens and often endured until the athlete's mid-thirties (Ogilvie & Howe, 1982). Moreover, education and vocational counseling were an integral part of the athletes' developmental process (Chartland & Lent, 1987). It is also true that a significant number of these athletes studied in areas that were related to their sports participation. Specifically, coaching, motor learning, exercise physiology, and physical therapy often became their areas of major interest and, subsequently, their chosen career following termination of their athletic career. Because the discrepancy between athletic and postathletic careers was relatively small and the athletes were able to combine their love of sport with a postathletic career, it seems reasonable to suggest that they would be less likely to exhibit problems of adaptation to life as a noncompetitor (Pawlak, 1984).

As a consequence, in clarifying the factors that contribute to difficulties in career termination, it is valuable to examine alternative systems, such as what we used in Eastern Europe. This knowledge contributes to an understanding of differences among athletes that might explain the divergent responses to career termination as a function of the country they represent and the nature of the system in which they developed.

Over the past 15 years, there has been an increasing awareness of the need for preretirement planning and counseling outside the sports domain (Kleiber & Thompson, 1980; Manion, 1976; Rowen & Wilks, 1987). Similarly, during the past decade, there has been a growing concern about career termination on several levels of elite sports. For example, in 1989, the United States Olympic Committee (USOC) developed a manual designed to assist elite athletes in understanding important issues related to career termination and to guide them in devising a plan for their postcompetition career (USOC, 1988). In addition, the USOC implemented career counseling training seminars for interested national athletes that were very well received (Murphy et al., 1989; Petitpas, Danish, McKelvain, & Murphy, 1990), and many sport psychologists currently working with U.S. Olympic Teams provide services related to career termination and planning (Gould, Tammen, Murphy, & May, 1989; May & Brown, 1989).

Professional sports in the United States also appear to be responding to this need (Dorfman, 1990). Specifically, the National Football League Players Association, the National Basketball Association Players Association, and the National Hockey League Players Association have developed similar programs for players whose careers are terminated (Ogilvie & Howe, 1982). And a survey of collegiate athletic advisors indicated that a portion of their responsibilities involved providing vocational counseling (Brooks, Etzel, & Ostrow, 1987). Unfortunately, there has been no empirical exploration of the extent to which these services have been used by the elite athletes.

This interest has spread to the coaching ranks. Traditionally, coaches have actively avoided career guidance programs based on the belief that such involvement would act as a distraction to the athletes that would detract from their focus on their performance (Taylor et al., 1990). However, this opposition appears to be softening as coaches at both the professional and elite amateur levels are realizing that providing such opportunities to mature athletes can contribute to the ultimate success of the athletic program (Blann, 1985; Ogilvie & Howe, 1982).

THEORETICAL PERSPECTIVES ON CAREER TERMINATION

During the past 25 years, as career termination attracted increasing attention from the sport scientific community, efforts have been made to develop theoretical conceptualizations to explain the process that athletes go through as their career comes to an end. Sport researchers examining this issue have sought formulations from outside of the sports world as a foundation for developing explanatory models for the athletic population (Hill & Lowe, 1974; Lerch, 1982; Rosenberg, 1981).

Thanatology

Rosenberg (1982) suggests that retirement from sport is akin to social death, which is characterized as social isolation and rejection from the former in-group. Social death focuses on how members treat an individual who has recently left the group. Ball (1976) suggested that a common reaction of teammates is to ignore the former athlete, resulting in embarrassment and anxiety (Rosenberg, 1982). From this perspective, retirement is seen as a singular, abrupt event (Blinde & Greendorfer, 1985).

Thanatology theory has received support from anecdotal accounts of athletes who have experienced such reactions on retirement (Bouton, 1970; Deford, 1981; Kahn, 1972). However, the concept of social death has also received considerable criticism. For example, Blinde and Greendorfer (1985) argue that, though the depictions of athletic retirement as social death are poignant and dramatic, the thanatological perspective may be an excessively negative characterization of career termination. In addition, Lerch (1982) questions the generality of social death beyond the few dramatic anecdotal cases. He bases this concern on data collected from a large sample of former professional baseball players (Lerch, 1981). Using in-depth interviews, the findings indicated that not one of the athletes made reference to death of any sort.

Social Gerontology

This perspective emphasizes the role of aging in the career termination process and considers life satisfaction as being dependent on characteristics of the sports experience. Greendorfer and Blinde (1985) suggested that four social gerontological approaches are most appropriate to the study of retirement from sports. The first approach, disengagement theory (Cummings, Dean, Newell, & McCaffrey, 1960), posits that society and the person withdraw from each other for the good of both, enabling younger people to enter the workforce and the retired individual to enjoy his or her remaining years. The second approach, activity theory (Havighurst & Albrecht, 1953), maintains that lost roles are exchanged for new ones, so that a person's overall activity level is sustained. The third approach, continuity theory (Atchley, 1980), suggests that, if people have varied roles, the time and energy from the previous role can be reallocated to the remaining roles. Finally, social breakdown theory (Kuypers & Bengston, 1973) proposes that retirement becomes associated with negative evaluation, which causes individuals to withdraw from the activity and internalize the negative evaluation. All four theories suggest that career termination is a circumscribed event rather than a process (Blinde & Greendorfer, 1985).

Despite the intuitive appeal of the social gerontology perspectives, they have been criticized as inadequate when applied to athletic retirement because retirement is conceived of as an abrupt event. Greendorfer and Blinde (1985) indicate that there is no empirical support for the relationship between sport-related factors and adjustment to retirement. Lerch (1981) tested continuity theory on a sample of professional baseball players and found that continuity factors were not associated with postretirement adjustment. Similar findings were reported by Arviko (1976) and Reynolds (1981) in their studies of professional athletes. The other social gerontology theories have not been empirically studied.

Termination as Transition

A criticism of both thanatology and social gerontology views is that they consider retirement as a singular, abrupt event (Blinde & Greendorfer, 1985). In contrast, other researchers characterize retirement as a process, rather than a discrete event, which involves development through life (Carp, 1972; C. Taylor, 1972).

An early view of athletic retirement as transition was delineated by Hill and Lowe (1974). These researchers applied Sussman's (1971) analytic model of the sociological study of retirement to termination from sport. Sussman, in his multidimensional conceptualization, asserts that perceptions about retirement will be influenced by the following factors: (1) individual (e.g., motives, values, goals, problem-solving skills); (2) situational (e.g., circumstances of retirement, preretirement planning, retirement income); (3) structural (e.g., social class, marital status, availability of social systems); (4) social (e.g., family, friends, extended social support); and (5) boundary constraints (e.g., societal definitions, economic cycles, employer attitudes). Schlossberg (1981) offered a similar model that emphasizes athletes' perceptions of the termination, characteristics of the pre- and posttermination environments, and the attributes of the individuals in their roles in adaptation to the termination.

Hopson and Adams (1977) proposed a seven-step model of termination that is similar to the grieving process: (1) immobilization (i.e., shock from the event); (2) minimization (i.e., negative emotions associated with a loss are downplayed); (3) self-doubt, in which self-esteem is threatened and depression may ensue; (4) letting go, where the individual works through feelings of loss, anger, and disappointment; (5) testing out, when groundwork for a new direction is laid; (6) searching for meaning, where the individual gains perspective on the difficulties of the earlier stages; and (7) internalization, when this insight is accepted and the termination is complete. Greendorfer and Blinde (1985) assert that the emphasis from this perspective is on the continuation rather than cessation of behaviors, the gradual alteration rather than relinquishment of goals and interests, and the emergence of few difficulties in adjustment.

Kübler-Ross's Human Grieving Model

The psychosocial process that athletes experience during career termination may be conceptualized within the framework of the human grieving model proposed by Kübler-Ross (1969). This model contains five distinct sequential stages in the grieving process: (1) denial against the initial trauma; (2) anger about the perceived injustice and lack of control; (3) bargaining to delay the inevitable; (4) depression over acceptance of the loss; and (5) full acceptance and a reorientation toward the future. Previous research has demonstrated the value of applying this model to nonsport employment issues (Winegardner, Simonetti, & Nykodym, 1984); it has also proven to be a useful means by which the experiences of terminated athletes may be understood in terms of the emotions they experience and the process by which they will work their way through termination (Ogilvie & Howe, 1986; Wolff & Lester, 1989).

CONCEPTUAL MODEL OF CAREER TERMINATION

J. Taylor and Ogilvie (1994) presented a five-stage conceptual model of athlete retirement that drew on past theoretical and empirical work to create a parsimonious and operationalizable framework that addresses critical issues throughout the duration of the career termination process (see Figure 26.1). The five stages are (1) causes of career termination, (2) factors that impact adaptation to career termination, (3) available resources that can facilitate the termination process, (4) the quality of adaptation to retirement, and (5) the prevention and intervention of career termination distress. Each of these stages is described in detail.

Causes of Career Termination among Athletes

Termination of an athletic career is usually the result of chronological age, deselection, and/or injury (Taylor &

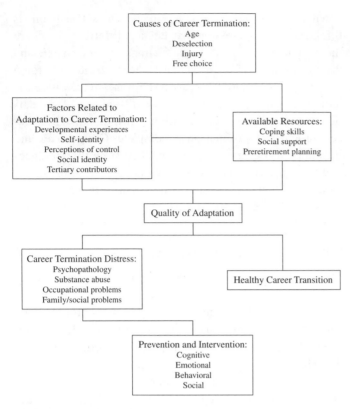

Figure 26.1   Conceptual model of athletic career termination (Taylor & Ogilvie, 1994).

Ogilvie, 1994). As these major factors are examined below, an attempt is made to clarify their psychological, social, and physical ramifications in the career termination process. In addition, these factors are scrutinized in terms of how they interact in the emergence of a crisis in the process of career termination.

Chronological Age

Age is typically considered to be a primary cause of athletic career termination. Anecdotal accounts of former elite athletes underscore the importance of age in career termination (Kahn, 1972; Kramer, 1969). Empirical research has also supported this relationship. For example, in a study of former Yugoslavian professional soccer players, 27% indicated that they were forced to retire because of their age (Mihovilovic, 1968). In addition, a study examining retired boxers reported similar findings (Weinberg & Arond, 1952). Also, Svoboda and Vanek (1982) showed that 13% of Czechoslovakian national team athletes terminated their career because of age. Allison and Meyer (1988) found that 10% of their sample of female tennis professionals retired due to age.

The age of the athletes as a contributor to career termination has physiological and psychological implications. Perhaps the most significant is the physiological influence of age. In particular, athletes' ability to compete at the elite level is largely a function of maintaining their physical capabilities at a commensurate level. Relevant physical attributes include strength, endurance, flexibility, coordination, and physical composition. A natural part of the maturation process is the slow deterioration of these attributes (Fisher & Conlee, 1979). Some physical deterioration can be slowed through intensive physical conditioning, experience, and motivation (Mihovilovic, 1968; Svoboda & Vanek, 1982). However, others, such as the ability to execute fine motor skills or changes in body composition, are not considered to be remediable.

These changes have implications for both young and old elite athletes. For athletes engaged in sports such as gymnastics and figure skating, the physical changes that accompany puberty, such as height and weight gain, can make it impossible for them to execute skills that were previously routine, thus contributing to the premature conclusion of their career. In response to these changes and their debilitating effects on performance, young athletes are most vulnerable to chemical remedies for maintaining or reducing body weight, such as cigarettes, cocaine, diuretics, and laxatives, resulting in eating disorders (Thornton, 1990). Similarly, among older athletes, loss of muscle mass or agility may contribute to career termination from sports such as football, tennis, and basketball (Fisher & Conlee, 1979).

Psychological components that accompany the aging process also influence career termination. For example, Werthner and Orlick (1986) found that as athletes become older, they may lose their motivation to train and compete, and they may conclude that they have reached their competitive goals. In addition, as athletes mature, their values may change. Svoboda and Vanek (1982) found that the values of Czechoslovakian world-class athletes shifted away from a self-focus involving winning and traveling toward an other-focus with an emphasis on family and friends.

Deselection

One of the most significant contributors to the incidence of difficulties in the career termination of athletes is the deselection process that occurs at every level of competitive sports (Svoboda & Vanek, 1982). Sports rely on the Darwinian philosophy of "survival of the fittest" that places great value on the individuals who survive, but pays little attention to those who are deselected (Ogilvie & Howe, 1982).

Furthermore, this same Darwinian philosophy prevails throughout high school, university, elite amateur, and professional sport, and the current deselection process is a natural consequence of such a philosophy. The process is clearly illustrated with statistics indicating the reality of attrition factors that operate within the competitive sports world (i.e., the proportion of athletes who successfully ascend succeeding rungs of the competitive ladder). For example, in the United States it is estimated that 5% of high school football players receive university scholarships and, of these, only 1% have an opportunity to play in the National Football League (Ogilvie & Howe, 1986). Similar statistics are found in basketball (Ogilvie & Howe, 1982). In addition, the average professional career span of basketball and football players is under five years (Ogilvie & Howe, 1986). From this perspective, to represent a career in professional football or basketball as a viable option for any child appears to be the height of deceit. As a result, it is important that the ramifications for those who have been deselected are explored, particularly for those who remain committed to participation.

To date, the only study that has specifically looked at the role of deselection among elite amateur and professional athletes was conducted by Mihovilovic (1968). In his study, 7% of the Yugoslavian professional soccer players indicated that they were forced out by younger players. Additionally, not being selected for a team was not rated as being a primary cause of career termination in a group of retired world-class athletes (Sinclair & Orlick, 1993). However, as will be discussed later, the theoretical and empirical evidence suggests that career termination difficulties are more likely to occur among these groups of athletes. As a consequence, it may be reasonable to assume that deselection is a significant issue for many athletes at the highest rung of the competitive ladder.

Injury

A variety of researchers have suggested that injuries may result in serious distress, manifested in depression, substance abuse, and suicidal ideation and attempts (Ogilvie & Howe, 1982; Werthner & Orlick, 1986). Furthermore, it is believed that career-ending injuries may cause athletes to experience an identity crisis (Elkin, 1981), social withdrawal (Lewis-Griffith, 1982), and fear, anxiety, and loss of self-esteem (Rotella & Heyman, 1986). Webb, Nasco, Riley, and Headrick (1998) reported that high school, collegiate, and professional athletes who were forced to retire due to an injury had the most difficult adjustment compared to athletes who had more control over their retirement.

Research has shown that injuries are a significant cause of career termination. Mihovilovic (1968) reported that 32% of the Yugoslavian professional soccer players indicated that sport-related injuries were the cause of their career termination. Werthner and Orlick (1986) found that 14% of a sample of 28 elite Canadian athletes were forced to retire due to injury. Also, Svoboda and Vanek (1982), in their study of Czechoslovakian national team members, indicated that 24% retired because of injury. Similar findings were reported by Weinberg and Arond (1952) and Hare (1971) in their investigations of former world-class professional boxers. In addition, 15% of the female tennis professionals studied by Allison and Meyer (1988) stated that they were forced to retire due to injury.

Exacerbating the impact of injury on career termination, elite athletes perform at such a high level that even a small reduction in physical capabilities may be sufficient to make them no longer competitive at the elite level. As a consequence, an injury need not be serious to have dramatic impact on athletes' performance and, in turn, their career. Moreover, when serious injury does occur, the considerable time and effort required for rehabilitation act as contributors to career termination (Feltz, 1986; Heil, 1988; Samples, 1987). This process not only affects athletes' return to previous competitive level, but also inhibits the normal improvement that occurs during the course of an athletic career. This event further increases the likelihood that the injury will be career-ending.

Free Choice

A neglected cause of career termination is free choice of the athlete (Blinde & Greendorfer, 1985; Coakley, 1983). The impetus to end a career freely is the most desirable of the causal factors. Reasons why athletes freely choose to retire may be a function of personal, social, or sport-related issues. On a personal level, athletes might wish to assume a new direction in life (Lavallee, Grove, & Gordon, 1997; Werthner & Orlick, 1986), to seek out new challenges and sources of satisfaction in other areas of life, or may have a change in values (Greendorfer & Blinde, 1985; Svoboda & Vanek, 1982). Socially, athletes may want to spend more time with family and friends or immerse themselves in a new social milieu (Svoboda & Vanek, 1982). In terms of the sport itself, athletes might simply find that sport participation no longer provides the enjoyment and fulfillment that it once did (Lavallee, Grove, et al., 1997; Werthner & Orlick, 1986).

There is some empirical evidence for free choice as a cause of career termination. Werthner and Orlick (1986) interviewed Olympic-caliber Canadian athletes and indicated that 42% of the ex-competitors retired for reasons that were within their control. In addition, another study of world-class athletes indicated that the two most prominent reasons for retiring were that they were tired of the lifestyle and that they had achieved their goals (Sinclair & Orlick, 1993), both reasons that were within the athletes' control. However, in the Mihovilovic (1968) study, only 4% of athletes freely chose to end their careers. No research has examined this issue among scholastic and collegiate populations. Therefore, conclusions cannot be drawn about the prevalence of free choice in athletic retirement among a wide range of athletic levels.

Voluntary career termination does not necessarily preclude athletes from experiencing distress. In a study of elite female gymnasts, Kerr and Dacyshyn (in press) found that several athletes who chose to retire still described their termination as difficult. They also suggested that "voluntary" retirement is not always clear-cut. Though athletes may choose to end their career, this decision may be due to a need to get out of an uncomfortable situation, such as conflict with a coach or the high stress of competition.

This issue relative to the precise definition of voluntary retirement is also illustrated in a study of Australian elite amateur athletes who described nine causes of career termination: work/study commitments, lost motivation, politics of sport, decrease in performance, finance, decrease in enjoyment, age, injury, and deselection (Lavallee, Grove, et al., 1997). The authors categorized the first six causes of retirement as voluntary and the last three as involuntary. However, based on the position taken by Kerr and Dacyshyn (in press), it could be argued that work/study commitments, politics of sport, decrease in performance, and finance could be considered involuntary causes of career termination because the athletes left their sport either out of dissatisfaction (politics of sport), a forced change in priorities (work/study commitments, finance), or a decline in ability to be competitive (decrease in performance). Thus, these athletes who seemingly voluntarily left their sport are more appropriately characterized as "reluctant dropouts" (Kerr & Dacyshyn, in press).

Other Causes of Career Termination

In addition to the causes discussed above, which have been found to be the predominant reasons for career termination, other factors have been either suggested or reported to contribute to retirement. These causes include family reasons (Mihovilovic, 1968), problems with coaches or the sports organization (Mihovilovic, 1968; Werthner &

Orlick, 1986), and financial difficulties (Lavallee, Grove, et al., 1997; Werthner & Orlick, 1986).

Factors Contributing to Adaptation to Career Termination

In considering the potential for distress following career termination, it is important to note that ending a career will not necessarily cause distress (Coakley, 1983; Greendorfer & Blinde, 1985). Rather, there are a number of factors that make individuals, including athletes, more vulnerable to difficulties in the termination process (Rosenkoetter, 1985).

Elite athletes, when faced with the end of their career, are confronted by a wide range of psychological, social, and financial/occupational threats. The extent of these threats will dictate the severity of the crisis they experience as a function of their career termination.

Self-Identity

Most fundamental of the psychological issues that influence adaptation to career termination is the degree to which athletes define their self-worth in terms of their participation and achievement in sports (Greendorfer & Blinde, 1985; Ogilvie & Howe, 1982; Svoboda & Vanek, 1982). Elite athletes who have been immersed in their sport to the exclusion of other activities will have a self-identity that is composed almost exclusively of their sports involvement (McPherson, 1980). This notion is derived from the early work of the ego psychologists (Ausubel & Kirk, 1977) and the more recent considerations involving self-esteem and self-identity (Wolff & Lester, 1989). Without the input from their sport, these athletes have little to support their sense of self-worth (Pearson & Petitpas, 1990).

Athletes who are heavily invested in their sports participation may be characterized as "unidimensional," meaning that their self-concept does not extend beyond the limits of their sport (Ogilvie & Howe, 1982). Moreover, these athletes often have provided themselves with few options of other activities in which they can invest their ego that can bring them similar satisfaction and ego gratification (McPherson, 1980). In support of this position, Erikson (1959) and Marcia (1966) suggest that the search for self-identity requires the examination of many potential alternatives as adulthood approaches. However, the structure of elite sports seldom provides athletes with sufficient time or opportunities for exploring options.

Athletes who had serious problems with the end of their career clung to their identity as athletes and were most fearful of how termination would impact their self-identity

(Ungerleiter, 1997). Grove, Lavallee, and Gordon (1997) reported that athletes who have a strong and exclusive identification with their role as athlete were most susceptible to career termination distress. They further indicate that the difficulties that highly identified athletes experience are more severe and take longer to adapt to than those of athletes less invested in their sports. Athletes in this situation typically experience career termination as something very important that is lost and can never be recovered (Werthner & Orlick, 1986). Furthermore, the finality of the loss seems impossible to bear, and herein lies a significant source of the distress associated with career termination. Finally, the ability of athletes to modify their identity in an adaptive manner following retirement is essential for a positive and healthy response to distress over career termination (Lavallee, Grove, et al., 1997).

Kerr and Dacyshyn (in press) emphasize the importance of identity formation in their study of elite female gymnasts. They suggest that the challenges of career termination are magnified for adolescent athletes because adolescence is normally a time during which identity is forming (Chickering, 1969; Erikson, 1963). But for young athletes who are ending their career, identity is actually deconstructed, which may interfere with or slow the identity formation process.

Kerr and Dacyshyn (in press) further indicate that career termination of young female athletes inhibits identity formation in several ways. Retirement at an early age limits athletes' abilities to experiment with different roles and relationships and learn about themselves. They also have little control over their athletic life, usually ceding control to a parent or coach, and often feel powerless when they leave their sport. This lack of control interferes with the development of perceptions of autonomy and decision-making skills that are essential to identity formation (Chickering & Reisser, 1993). An important part of identity formation for young women is acceptance of their bodies (Piphers, 1994). Because issues such as body weight, appearance, and eating habits play such a large role in the lives of gymnasts and other young female athletes in other sports, body image distortion can create uncertainty and insecurity that further constrain identity formation. These researchers concluded that all of these issues have the cumulative effect of stunting the creation of a mature self-identity in young athletes.

Social Identity

It has been suggested that retired individuals who experience the most doubt and anxiety are those who feel they are no longer important to others (Sheldon, 1977). Pollack (1956) and Tuckman and Lorge (1953) also associate retirement with a loss of status and social identity. Certainly, due to the high profile of elite athletes today, this issue is a significant concern for them (Gorbett, 1985). McPherson (1980) suggests that athletes define themselves in terms of their popular status. However, this recognition typically lasts only a few years and disappears following retirement. As a result, athletes may question their self-worth and feel the need to regain the lost public esteem. A significant fear that has been reported is a loss of attention (Ungerleiter, 1997).

In addition, athletes whose socialization process occurred primarily in the sport environment may be characterized as "role-restricted" (Ogilvie & Howe, 1986). That is, these athletes have learned to assume certain social roles specific to the athletic setting and are able to interact with others only within the narrow context of sports. As a result, their ability to assume other roles following career termination is severely inhibited (Greendorfer & Blinde, 1985).

Only one study to date has addressed the issue of role restriction specifically. Arviko (1976) found that former professional baseball players who had a substantial number of social roles during their competitive careers were better adjusted following retirement than those players who reported having limited social roles outside of baseball. It is also possible to infer support for this contention from other research. Specifically, Haerle (1975) reported that professional baseball players who continued their education or held meaningful jobs during the off-season had better occupational adjustment following career termination. In addition, Mihovilovic (1968) reported that if the athletes did not plan for another career following termination, the experience could be painful. Similar findings were described by Werthner and Orlick (1986). Educational and occupational preretirement planning can encourage the development of social roles outside of their sport that would enable athletes to better adapt to life after sport.

Perceptions of Control

At the heart of the issue of perceived control relative to career termination is whether athletes left their sport voluntarily or involuntarily (Kerr & Dacyshyn, in press; Lavallee, Grove, et al., 1997). Many athletes perceived a profound lack of control over the termination of their career (McPherson, 1980). Consideration of the three primary causes of career termination discussed above (i.e., age, deselection, and injury) indicates that all are occurrences outside the control of the individual athlete. As a result, this absence of control related to an event so intrinsically connected to athletes' self-identity creates a situation that is highly aversive and threatening (Blinde & Greendorfer, 1985; Szinovacz, 1987).

Strong empirical evidence supports the importance of control in career termination. Mihovilovic (1968) reports that 95% of the athletes attributed causes to the end of their career that were beyond their control, and 52% were forced to retire suddenly. Additionally, 29% of the Olympic-caliber Canadian athletes experienced a decrease in their sense of personal control following retirement (Werthner & Orlick, 1986). Similar results were found by Svoboda and Vanek (1982). Also, elite amateur athletes who were forced to end their career reported significantly more emotional and social adjustment difficulties than those who ended their career voluntarily (Lavallee, Grove, et al., 1997). Finally, Wheeler, Malone, VanVlack, and Nelson (1996) reported that, among a group of disabled athletes, those who retired voluntarily had fewer difficulties than those who were forced to retire.

Though the issue has not been addressed extensively in the sport literature, there is considerable research from the areas of clinical, social, and physiological psychology that demonstrates that perceptions of control are related to many areas of human functioning, including sense of self-competence (White, 1974), the interpretation of self (Kelley, 1967), and other information (Jones & Davis, 1965). In addition, perceptions of control may influence individuals' feelings of helplessness (Friedlander, 1984/1985), motivation (Wood & Bandura, 1989), physiological changes (Tache & Selye, 1985), and self-confidence (Bandura & Adams, 1977). Also, control has been associated with a variety of pathologies, including depression (Alloy & Abramson, 1982), anxiety (Garfield & Bergin, 1978), substance abuse (Shiffman, 1982), and dissociative disorders (F. Putnam, 1989).

Other Contributing Factors

The above factors have received substantial and consistent attention as potential contributors to adaptation to career termination. In addition, a number of other factors have been suggested to contribute to this process. These variables include socioeconomic status (Hare, 1971; Weinberg & Arond, 1952), financial dependency on the sport (Lerch, 1981; McPherson, 1980; Werthner & Orlick, 1986), minority status (Blinde & Greendorfer, 1985; Hill & Lowe, 1974), postathletic occupational potential (Haerle, 1975; Hill & Lowe, 1974), health (Gorbett, 1985; Hill & Lowe, 1974), and marital status (Svoboda & Vanek, 1982).

Available Resources for Career Termination Adaptation

The quality of adaptation that athletes experience during career termination depends on the resources they have available to overcome the challenges they will face as their athletic career ends. These resources can be categorized as personal, social, and practical. Personal resources focus on coping skills that enable athletes to address the specific change that impacts them individually and in terms of their lifestyle (Lazarus & Folkman, 1984; Meichenbaum, 1977). Social issues relate to the degree of support they get from other people in their lives, including family, friends, teammates, and the sport organizations with whom they were affiliated (Cohen & Wills, 1985; Sarason & Sarason, 1986; Smith, 1985). Practical resources include various forms of preretirement planning (Coakley, 1983; Hill & Lowe, 1974; Pearson & Petitpas, 1990).

Coping Strategies

Athletes who are faced with the end of their career must confront potentially significant obstacles to the continuation of their personal, social, and occupational lives. These challenges will impact their thinking, emotions, and actions. The presence of effective coping skills can reduce the distress that these changes can lead to and promote a healthy response to the career termination process.

Athletes whose careers are ending must be aware of how their beliefs and attitudes about the process will impact their self-identity, perceptions of control, and social identity (Bandura, 1977; Lazarus, 1975). Athletes can use a number of cognitive strategies to better assimilate the potentially stressful career termination process. Techniques they may employ include cognitive restructuring (Lazarus, 1972) and mental imagery (Smith, 1980) to redirect their thoughts more constructively, self-instructional training (Meichenbaum, 1977) to enhance focus and decision making, and goal setting to facilitate their determination and direction in their postathletic lives (Bruning & Frew, 1987). These methods have proven to be effective in encouraging healthy adjustment in a number of settings (Labouvie-Vief & Gonda, 1976; Meichenbaum & Cameron, 1973; Moleski & Tosi, 1976; Trexler & Karst, 1972).

Other strategies can be used to overcome the emotional and physiological demands of career termination, such as time-out (Browning, 1983), relaxation training (Bruning & Frew, 1987; Delman & Johnson, 1976; May, House, & Kovacs, 1982), and health (Savery, 1986) and exercise and nutritional counseling (Bruning & Frew, 1987).

Active steps can be taken to respond to the practical obstacles that athletes will face during the career termination process, including stress management training (Lange & Jakubowski, 1976), time management training (Bruning & Frew, 1987; King, Winett, & Lovett, 1986), and skills assessment and development (Bruning & Frew, 1987; Taylor, 1987).

Coping strategies suggested by retired world-class athletes include finding a new focus to direct their energies, keeping busy, maintaining a routine of training and exercise, social support, and staying in contact with their sport (Sinclair & Orlick, 1993). Another study of elite athletes reported that commonly used coping strategies included acceptance, positive reinterpretation, planning, active coping, and seeking social support (Grove et al., 1997). These researchers also found that athletes who had a strong athletic identity tended to use avoidance-based coping strategies such as denial, mental and behavioral disengagement, and venting of emotions, rather than more problem-focused techniques.

Social Support

Elite athletes' primary social support system is often derived from their athletic involvement (Coakley, 1983; Rosenfeld, Richman, & Hardy, 1989). In other words, the vast majority of their friends, acquaintances, and other associations are found in the sport environment and their social activities revolve primarily around their athletic life (Botterill, 1990; Svoboda & Vanek, 1982).

When the athletes' career ends, they are no longer an integral part of the team or organization. As a consequence, the social support they received previously may no longer be present. Moreover, due to their restricted social identity and the absence of alternative social support systems, they may become isolated, lonely, and unsustained socially, thus leading to significant distress (Greendorfer & Blinde, 1985; McPherson, 1980). In support of this notion, the findings of Remer, Tongate, and Watson (1978) suggest that a support system based entirely in the sport setting will limit athletes' ability to acquire alternative roles and assume a nonsport identity.

The ease of the career termination process may also depend on the amount of social support the athletes receive (Coakley, 1983). Werthner and Orlick (1986) report that Olympic-caliber Canadian athletes who received considerable support from family and friends had an easier termination than athletes who received little support from family and friends. In addition, the athletes who had the most difficulties indicated that they felt alone as their career ended and expressed the desire for support during that

period. Svoboda and Vanek (1982) found that social support was the most important factor mediating adaptation to career termination. Specifically, 37% indicated their family most often as a meaningful source of support, followed by colleagues in their new profession (12%), friends (8%), and their coach (3%).

Mihovilovic (1968) also demonstrated that social support was an important part of the career termination process. Specifically, he found that, according to the Yugoslavian soccer players he surveyed, 75% of their friends were from their sports club. Also, 60% of the athletes indicated that these friendships were maintained, but 34% said that the friendships ended after they retired. Moreover, 32% of the respondents stated that their circle of friends diminished following career termination. Additionally, Reynolds (1981) reported that, among a sample of retired professional football players, those athletes who received support from close friends and relatives demonstrated the highest level of satisfaction in their current job.

Ungerleiter (1997) reported that a sample of ex-Olympic athletes received support from coaches, parents, and significant others. In addition, the 20% of these athletes who reported experiencing serious difficulties following career termination received help from a mental health professional. Another study of retired world-class athletes indicated that they received considerable support from family and friends and little institutional support from the national governing body or their former coach (Sinclair & Orlick, 1993). In a study of retiring disabled athletes, Wheeler et al. (1996) found that retirement was facilitated by having family interests outside of sport.

Gorbett (1985) also recommends that, in addition to emotional support from family and friends, athletes must receive institutional support. However, Svoboda and Vanek (1982) found that athletes expressed considerable dissatisfaction over the support they received from their organization during the retirement process. Schlossberg (1981) found that employer support was critical for the termination to retirement outside of sport. Furthermore, Schlossberg (1981) and Manion (1976) suggest that institutional and interpersonal support can best be provided through preretirement counseling programs.

Preretirement Planning

A common theme that emerges from the literature on retirement outside of sport is the resistance on the part of individuals to plan for their life after the end of their career (Avery & Jablin, 1988; Chartland & Lent, 1987; Rowen & Wilks, 1987; Thorn, 1983). This finding is most evident among athletes with a strong and exclusive athletic identity

(Grove et al., 1997). This type of denial may be even more threatening for elite athletes because the immediate rewards are so attractive and the discrepancy between their current lifestyle and that which might occur on career termination is significant. As a consequence, any acknowledgment or consideration that their athletic career might end would be a source of significant anxiety, thus warranting avoidance of the issue altogether. Yet, it is likely that this denial of the inevitable will have serious, potentially negative, and extended implications for the athletes.

It has been widely asserted that an essential component of effective career termination is sound postathletic career planning (Coakley, 1983; Hill & Lowe, 1974; Pearson & Petitpas, 1990). Substantial research is supportive of this position. Haerle (1975) reported that 75% of the professional baseball players he surveyed did not acknowledge their postcareer life until the end of their career. He also found that the level of educational attainment, which may be considered a form of preretirement planning, was a significant predictor of postathletic occupational status. Arviko (1976) and Lerch (1981) reported similar findings in their studies of professional baseball and football players, respectively.

Perna, Ahlgren, and Zaichkowsky (1999) found that collegiate athletes who could state a postcollegiate occupational plan indicated significantly more life satisfaction than those who did not have such a plan. Similarly, a study of disabled athletes indicated that their retirement was easier if they had job interests outside of sport (Wheeler et al., 1996).

Svoboda and Vanek (1982) showed that 41% of the Czechoslovakian national team athletes admitted that they had paid no attention to the reality that their career would end, and 31% began to consider the future only immediately before termination. The athletes interviewed by Ungerleiter (1997) wished they had been more active in planning and developing needed skills before they retired. Similar comments were expressed by the Olympic-caliber Canadian athletes interviewed by Werthner and Orlick (1986). The most common recommendation from a survey of world-class athletes was to plan for retirement (Sinclair & Orlick, 1993).

In addition, research on former world-class professional boxers found a high incidence of difficulties following retirement (Hare, 1971; Weinberg & Arond, 1952). The authors conclude that, because the majority of their sample came from lower-socioeconomic-status environments, they lacked the education and experience to plan for the end of their career.

Quality of Adaptation to Career Termination

Despite the extensive amount of literature on the issue of career termination, there is still considerable debate about the proportion of athletes who experience distress due to retirement and how the distress is manifested. Some early writers such as Sussman (1971) believed professional athletes did not experience difficulties because they knew their sport career would be short and they prepared appropriately. In addition, he asserted that most professional athletes were assured of a second occupation on retirement. Other researchers, both within and outside of sport, drew similar conclusions. For example, outside of sport, Atchley (1980) and George (1980) suggested that retirement seemed to have little influence on personal adjustment and self-identity, and most people possess the necessary coping skills to overcome any problems that arise.

In the sports domain, others make similar arguments (Blinde & Greendorfer, 1985; Coakley, 1983; Greendorfer & Blinde, 1985). These investigators base their judgments predominantly on research at the scholastic and collegiate levels. In fact, substantial research has found little evidence of distress due to career termination among these athlete populations. Specifically, several studies of high school athletes indicate that, compared to nonathletes, they are more likely to attend college, obtain undergraduate and graduate degrees, achieve greater occupational status, and earn higher income (Otto & Alwin, 1977; Phillips & Schafer, 1971). In addition, Sands (1978), in a study of outstanding male scholastic athletes, found that the importance of sports to these athletes declined following high school and they defined their sports participation as a passing phase of life. Sands concluded that these athletes' departure from scholastic sports was not accompanied by trauma or identity crisis.

Less clear findings were reported from research involving collegiate athletes. Snyder and Baber (1979) found that there were no differences between former college athletes and nonathletes in terms of life satisfaction and attitudes toward work. Also, the former athletes effectively altered their interests and activities on graduation. Therefore, their findings do not support the argument that disengagement from collegiate sports is stressful for former athletes. Greendorfer and Blinde (1985) also judged that there were few adjustment difficulties among a large sample of male and female ex-college competitors. In support of their position, they indicated that 90% of the respondents looked forward to life after college and about 55% were very or extremely satisfied when their athletic career ended. However, the authors de-emphasize the finding that one-third of their sample indicated that they were very or extremely unhappy with their retirement and that 38% of the males and 50% of the females responded that they very much or extremely missed sport involvement.

Curtis and Ennis (1988) found few indications of distress among junior elite Canadian hockey players and nonathletes. Specifically, there were no differences in life satisfaction, employment, or marital status. Moreover, although 50% of the athletes indicated that retirement was difficult and 75% experienced a feeling of loss after leaving hockey, these perceptions did not appear to significantly impact the athletes at a practical level (e.g., educational, occupational, and family pursuits). Based on these results, the authors concluded that these findings reflect "a brief lament at having to give up hockey, and an occasional longing to relive the competition, camaraderie, and excitement" (p. 102).

Coakley (1983, p. 4), in a review of relevant literature, stated that "the termination out of intercollegiate sport seems to go hand-in-hand with the termination from college to work careers, new friendships, marriage, parenthood, and other roles normally associated with early adulthood." He further argued that the perception that distress is common is based on the biased sampling of male professional athletes participating in spectator sports (Greendorfer & Blinde, 1985) and accounts in the popular media (Coakley, 1983).

At the same time, another group of researchers developed an opposing view. Specifically, career termination may cause distress that manifests itself in a wide variety of dysfunctional ways. The majority of those who hold this view have focused on elite amateur and professional athletes. Anecdotal accounts of athletes with psychological difficulties include financial problems and drug abuse (Newman, 1991), attempted suicide (Beisser, 1967; Hare, 1971; Vinnai, 1973), and criminal activity (Hare, 1971; McPherson, 1980).

At a scholarly level, it has been asserted that retiring individuals experience a loss of status, identity crisis, and a loss of direction and focus (Ball, 1976; Pollack, 1956; Tuckman & Lorge, 1953). In addition, Ogilvie and Howe (1982) report experiences of working with retired athletes suffering from alcoholism and acute depression.

There is also some empirical evidence for the occurrence of distress. For example, Mihovilovic (1968) reported that the coaches and management of Yugoslavian professional soccer players believed that retired players drank excessively, resorted to illegal activities, were in a

serious psychic state, and had significant fears about the future. In questioning the players themselves, he found that 38% smoked cigarettes more and 16% drank more after their career ended. Arviko (1976) also found alcoholism to be present in his study of former professional baseball players. In a sample of retired Olympic athletes, almost 40% reported having serious or very serious problems adjusting to life after sport (Ungerleiter, 1997).

Svoboda and Vanek (1982) studied the ability of Czechoslovakian national team members to cope with the practical and psychological stress of adjustment to their new profession. Their results indicated that 30% were able to meet the new practical demands immediately and 58% were able to adjust within three years. However, psychological adjustment took much longer: 34% adapted immediately, but 17% had not adjusted at all.

In addition, Hallden (1965) found that 45% of retired Swedish athletes who were interviewed were concerned about their emotional adjustment following the end of their career. Also, Weinberg and Arond (1952) reported that retired professional boxers experienced severe emotional distress after leaving the boxing world. Unfortunately, neither study specified the nature of the emotional difficulties experienced by the athletes. One study found that athletes with strong athletic identities were most vulnerable to zeteophobia (i.e., anxiety associated with career termination decision making; Grove et al., 1997). In a summary of 11 empirical studies of career termination, Grove, Lavallee, Gordon, and Harvey (1998) indicated that, on average, 19% of the athletes sampled experienced considerable emotional distress in response to their retirement.

However, as indicated previously, one criticism of this research is that it is biased toward professional male athletes in team sports. In response to this issue, Allison and Meyer (1988) studied the effects of career termination on a sample of 20 female tennis professionals. Their findings indicate that 50% of the athletes perceived retirement as a relief and an opportunity to reestablish a more traditional lifestyle and felt a sense of satisfaction about their competitive careers. Furthermore, it should be noted that 75% remained actively involved in tennis as coaches or in business. The authors concluded that, rather than the social death concept suggested by Rosenberg (1982) and Lerch (1984), retirement may be considered social rebirth (Coakley, 1983). However, the researchers pay little attention to the finding that 30% of the athletes expressed feelings of isolation and loss of identity on retirement and 10%, who retired unexpectedly due to injury, felt that they had failed to achieve their competitive goals.

In addition, Kerr and Dacyshyn (in press) reported that 70% of their sample of elite female gymnasts experienced distress when their career ended. These athletes described feelings of disorientation, void, and frustration, and struggled with issues such as self-identity, personal control, and body image.

Prevention and Treatment of Crises of Career Termination

The phenomenon of career termination from sports can best be understood as a complex interaction of stressors. Whether the stressors are physical, psychological, social, or educational/occupational, their effects on athletes may produce some form of distress when athletes are confronted with career termination.

Researchers indicate that crises due to career termination occur less often among retiring scholastic and collegiate athletes (Greendorfer & Blinde, 1985; Otto & Alwin, 1977; Phillips & Schafer, 1971; Sands, 1978) and with greater frequency among elite amateur (Werthner & Orlick, 1986) and professional athletes (Mihovilovic, 1968; Weinberg & Arond, 1952).

The prevention of crises of career termination is the responsibility of individuals involved at all levels and in all areas of sports, including parents, educators, coaches, administrators, physicians, and psychologists (Werthner & Orlick, 1986). Moreover, participation of these people in fulfilling their role in this process can range from the earliest stages of sports participation to the termination process itself (Pearson & Petitpas, 1990).

Early Development

The often single-minded pursuit of excellence that accompanies elite sports participation has potential psychological and social dangers. As discussed above, these risks involve the development of a unidimensional person. The personal investment in and pursuit of elite athletic success, though a worthy goal, may lead to a restricted development.

Though there is substantial evidence demonstrating the debilitating effects of deselection on self-esteem among young athletes (Orlick, 1980; Scanlan, 1985; Smith, Smoll, & Curtis, 1979), little consideration has been given to changing this process in a healthier direction. Most organized youth programs still appear to place the highest priority on winning.

It is important that the indoctrination of a more holistic approach to sports development begins early in the life of the athlete (Pearson & Petitpas, 1990). This perspective relies on a model that emphasizes preventing problems prior to their occurrence. Considerable research indicates that primary preventive measures are a useful and efficient means of allocating resources (Conyne, 1987; Cowen, 1983). As a consequence, the first step in the prevention process is to encourage in parents and coaches involved in youth sport a belief that long-term personal and social development is more important than short-term athletic success (Ogilvie, 1987). This view is especially relevant because it has been asserted that developing athletes must often face issues that are unique and separate from the normal requirements of development (Remer et al., 1978).

It has been further argued that high school and college athletic programs restrict opportunities for personal and social growth (Remer et al., 1978; Schafer, 1971). Significant issues in this area include the development of self- and social identities, social roles and behaviors, and social support systems. Moreover, examples of this balance not being fostered include the low graduation rates of collegiate basketball and football players (Sherman, Weber, & Tegano, 1986). Efforts to maintain balance in athletes' lives and encouraging the development of roles other than that of athlete will facilitate the formation of a mature self-identity.

It is also important to emphasize that sport participation and development are not mutually exclusive. Sport participation may, in fact, become a vehicle through which general life skills may be learned (Scanlan, Stein, & Ravizza, 1989). In addition, sports may be the foundation on which children may develop the ability to take psychological and social risks in other areas of their life. Thus, a healthy sports environment may assist athletes to become more fully integrated personally and socially, thereby enabling them to function in a more diverse variety of situations.

Prior to and during Career Termination

In addition to the values, beliefs, and skills that can be instilled in developing athletes, there is much that can be done with the athletes who attain elite status and are currently in the midst of an elite athletic career. As discussed earlier, recognition of the inevitability of career termination and subsequent action in preparation for that eventuality are the best courses of action (Haerle, 1975; Pearson & Petitpas, 1990; Werthner & Orlick, 1986).

Preretirement planning that involves reading materials and workshops (Kaminski-da-Rosa, 1985; Manion, 1976; Thorn, 1983; USOC, 1988) are important opportunities for elite athletes to plan for and work toward meaningful lives following career termination. In addition, effective money management and long-term financial planning will provide athletes with financial stability following the conclusion of their career (Hill & Lowe, 1974). It should also be noted that organizational support of this goal is critical to the comfort and commitment experienced by the athletes (Gorbett, 1985; Pearson & Petitpas, 1990).

Therapeutically, an essential task in the termination process is to help athletes retain their self-worth during this period of personal upheaval and encourage the adaptation of a new self-identity that incorporates the strengths of their past athletic experience with the new life they are creating after sport. The fundamental objective of the termination process is to modify athletes' beliefs and attitudes about themselves in a way that will result in their being happy and productive people (Taylor & Ogilvie, 1994). Baillie (1993) suggests a combination of career counseling strategies and life development interventions to assist athletes in their adjustment to retirement.

Sport psychologists can assist athletes in working through any emotional distress they may experience during career termination (Kübler-Ross, 1969). Specifically, they may provide the athletes with the opportunity to express feelings of doubt, concern, or frustration relative to the end of their career (Gorbett, 1985). Also, athletes can explore ways of broadening their social identity and role repertoire (Ogilvie & Howe, 1982), thus taking on a new, nonsport identity and experiencing feelings of value and self-worth in this new personal conception. Additionally, athletes may be encouraged to expand their social support system to individuals and groups outside of the sports arena. Constantine (1995) reported that a group counseling experience comprised of supportive counseling techniques and psychoeducational exercises for retired female collegiate athletes who were experiencing adjustment difficulties indicated higher levels of satisfaction from participation in the group.

On a manifest level, the sport psychologist may help the athletes cope with the stress of the termination process (Gorbett, 1985). Traditional therapeutic strategies such as cognitive restructuring (Garfield & Bergin, 1978), stress management (Meichenbaum & Jaremko, 1987), and emotional expression (Yalom, 1980) may be used in this process.

Outside of sport, Brammer and Abrego (1981) offer an interactive model of coping with termination adapted from Moos and Tsu (1977). This model posits the need to intervene at a variety of levels, including the appraisal process, social support systems, internal support systems, emotional and physical distress, and planning and implementing change. In addition, within sport, Wolff and Lester (1989) propose a three-stage therapeutic process comprised of listening/confrontation, cognitive therapy, and vocational guidance to aid athletes in coping with their loss of self-identity and assist them in establishing a new identity.

There has been little empirical research examining the significant factors in this process. Outside of sport, Roskin (1982) found that the implementation of a package of cognitive, affective, and social support interventions in didactic and small-group settings significantly reduced depression and anxiety among a high-stress group of individuals composed partly of retirees.

In the most recent work to date examining intervention strategies for facilitating the career termination process, Grove et al. (1998) adapted Horowitz's (1986) model of coping with loss to retirement from sport. This conceptualization emphasizes the need for athletes to have a working-through process in the form of the construction of a narrative about the career termination experience, termed account making. This working-through story is composed of descriptions, attributions, memories, emotions, expectations, and plans for the future. This account enables athletes to gain a greater understanding of the retirement experience, allows them to produce closure on their athletic career, and fosters the development of a new and adaptive self- and social identity that will encourage growth in their postathletic life. Preliminary research indicates that account making was directly related to athletes' success in coping with career termination (Lavallee, Grove, et al., 1997).

The account-making model of coping involves seven steps that athletes will proceed through on the path to closure:

1. *Traumatic event:* shock and feeling overwhelmed and numb in response to the realization that their sports career is over.
2. *Outcry:* produces strong emotional reactions such as panic and despair.
3. *Denial:* focuses on escapism, avoidance, and isolation.
4. *Intrusion:* account making continues, with an emphasis on thought processes associated with career termination in the form of distraction and obsessive review.
5. *Working-through:* more intensive account making and initial attempts at sharing experiences with others.
6. *Completion:* finishing the narrative, letting go of the negative emotions related to the retirement experience, adoption of coping skills, improved mental and physical health, and a greater sense of control.
7. *Identity change:* closure occurs, identity evolves into a healthy postathletic form, and a solid foundation is put down for life after sports. (Grove et al., 1998)

Grove and his colleagues (1998) emphasize two key issues in this process. First, an important part of the working-through process is confiding in others, in which athletes share parts of the narrative with significant others and use their feedback to modify and refine their account. Second, the end of the process is often signaled by a shift in focus away from the athlete himself or herself and onto others who may be experiencing a similar plight. This change manifests itself as a concern for the welfare of others and a strong desire to assist those athletes who might benefit from their experiences and the lessons they learned from their working-through process (Grove et al., 1998).

AVENUES FOR FUTURE RESEARCH

The area of career termination among athletes has been receiving increasing attention in recent years. Moreover, there has been an increased shift toward research that is both theory-driven and programmatic (e.g., Lavallee and his colleagues, 1997). These investigations have provided a growing body of empirical evidence to support the positions held by the leading researchers in the area and have given the field a deeper and more comprehensive understanding of all facets of the athlete retirement process. Nonetheless, more research is needed to further delineate the theoretical foundations of career termination and to provide empirical support of the theoretical conceptualizations that have been offered.

Theoretical Development

The first area of research development should be in the theoretical domain. In particular, there is a need for continued refinement of the field's conceptual understanding of all aspects of the career termination process. Though, as discussed previously, attempts have been made to develop a conceptual model of career termination from work done outside of sport (Lerch, 1982; Rosenberg, 1982), these efforts have met with limited success (Blinde & Greendorfer, 1985; Greendorfer & Blinde, 1985).

The model of Taylor and Ogilvie (1994) was an initial attempt to delineate the career termination process. More recently, the conceptual model proposed by Grove et al. (1998) offers a theory-driven framework for intervention of athletes experiencing distress in response to the end of their sports career. Further efforts to refine the theoretical foundations of athlete reactions to career termination should consider these models and other relevant conceptualizations both within and outside of sport.

Empirical Development

Based on conceptual models such as those suggested by Taylor and Ogilvie (1994) and Grove et al. (1998), a

systematic program of research may be implemented that would progressively examine and generate data for each phase of the models. Such an organized approach would enable researchers to draw meaningful conclusions from sound theory-driven data gathering.

Pertinent empirical questions should be considered: Does the particular cause of career termination influence the nature of the response to retirement from the athletes? What are the underlying factors relative to these causes that differentiate athletes' responses to career termination (e.g., voluntary vs. involuntary; controllable vs. uncontrollable)? What are the specific factors that mediate the nature of the response to career termination? What preventive measures will moderate the distress of career termination? What strategies are most effective in the treatment of distress due to career termination?

In addition, other ancillary concerns are worth addressing: What issues in childhood development and early sports participation will influence the career termination process? What types of changes at the development level may mitigate potential trauma in the career termination process? Are there differences in the type of sport (e.g., individual vs. team, professional vs. amateur) with respect to the athletes' responses to career termination? Are there gender, age, and cultural differences in athletes' responses to career termination?

CONCLUSION

The purpose of this chapter was to provide an overview of relevant issues in the process of career termination among athletes. Another objective was to discuss the factors that contribute to distressful reactions to athlete retirement.

Based on this review, it is clear that career termination is an important issue worthy of study. It is hoped that the present integration of current information will act as an impetus for future theoretical and empirical inquiry.

REFERENCES

Alfano, P. (1982, December 27). When applause ends athletes face financial hurdles. *Ottawa Citizen*, p. 41.

Allison, M.T., & Meyer, C. (1988). Career problems and retirement among elite athletes: The female tennis professional. *Sociology of Sport Journal, 5*, 212–222.

Alloy, L.B., & Abramson, L.Y. (1982). Learned helplessness, depression, and the illusion of control. *Journal of Personality and Social Psychology, 42*, 1114–1126.

Arviko, I. (1976). *Factors influencing the job and life satisfaction of retired baseball players.* Unpublished master's thesis, University of Waterloo, Canada.

Atchley, R.C. (1980). *The social forces in later life.* Belmont, CA: Wadsworth.

Ausubel, D., & Kirk, D. (1977). *Ego psychology and mental disease: A developmental approach to psychopathology.* New York: Grune & Stratton.

Avery, C.M., & Jablin, F.M. (1988). Retirement preparation programs and organizational communication. *Communication Education, 37,* 68–80.

Baille, P.H. (1993). Understanding retirement from sports: Therapeutic ideas for helping athletes in transition. *Counseling Psychologist, 21,* 399–410.

Ball, D.W. (1976). Failure in sport. *American Sociological Review, 41,* 726–739.

Bandura, A. (1977). Self-efficacy: Toward a unifying theory of behavior change. *Psychological Review, 84,* 191–215.

Bandura, A., & Adams, N.E. (1977). Analysis of self-efficacy theory of behavioral change. *Cognitive Therapy and Research, 1,* 287–308.

Batten, J. (1979, April). After the cheering stops can athletes create new life in the business world? *Financial Post Magazine,* 14–20.

Beisser. (1967). *The madness of sports.* New York: Appleton-Century-Croft.

Blinde, E.M., & Greendorfer, S.L. (1985). A reconceptualization of the process of leaving the role of competitive athlete. *International Review of Sport Sociology, 20,* 87–94.

Botterill, C. (1982). What "endings" tell us about beginnings. In T. Orlick, J.T. Partington, & J.H. Salmela (Eds.), *Proceedings of the 5th World Congress of Sport Psychology* (pp. 164–166). Ottawa: Coaching Association of Canada.

Botterill, C. (1990). Sport psychology and professional hockey. *The Sport Psychologist, 4,* 358–368.

Bouton, J. (1970). *Ball four.* New York: Dell.

Bradley, B. (1976). *Life on the run.* New York: *New York Times,* Quadrangle.

Brammer, L.M., & Abrego, P.J. (1981). Intervention strategies for coping with terminations. *Counseling Psychologist, 9,* 19–35.

Bramwell, S.T., Masuda, M., Wagner, N.N., & Holmes, A. (1975). Psychological factors in athletic injuries: Development and application of the Social and Athletic Readjustment Rating Scale (SARRS). *Journal of Human Stress, 2,* 6–20.

Brooks, D.D., Etzel, E.F., & Ostrow, A.C. (1987). Job responsibilities and backgrounds of NCAA Division I athletic advisors and counselors. *The Sport Psychologist, 1,* 200–207.

Broom, E.F. (1982). Detraining and retirement from high level competition: A reaction to "Retirement from high level competition" and "Career crisis in sport." In T. Orlick, J.T. Partington, & J.H. Salmela (Eds.), *Proceedings of the 5th World Congress of Sport Psychology* (pp. 183–187). Ottawa: Coaching Association of Canada.

Browning, E.R. (1983). A memory pacer for improving stimulus generalization. *Journal of Autism and Developmental Disorders, 13,* 427–432.

Bruning, N.S., & Frew, D.R. (1987). Effects of exercise, relaxation, and management skills on physiological stress indicators: A field experiment. *Journal of Applied Psychology, 72,* 515–521.

Carp, F.M. (1972). Retirement as a terminational life stage. In F.M. Carp (Ed.), *Retirement* (pp. 1–27). New York: Behavioral Publications.

Chartland, J.M., & Lent, R.W. (1987). Sports counseling: Enhancing the development of the student athlete. *Journal of Counseling and Development, 66,* 164–167.

Chickering, A., & Reisser, L. (1993). *Education and identity* (2nd ed.). San Francisco: Jossey-Bass.

Coakley, J.J. (1983). Leaving competitive sport: Retirement or rebirth? *Quest, 35,* 1–11.

Cohen, N. (1989, January). The Sport 100 Salary Survey. *Sport,* 75–77.

Cohen, S., & Wills, T.A. (1985). Stress, social support, and the buffering hypothesis. *Psychological Bulletin, 98,* 310–357.

Constantine, M.G. (1995). Retired female athletes in transition: A group counseling intervention. *Journal of College Student Development, 36,* 604–605.

Conyne, R. (1987). *Primary preventive counseling.* Muncie, IN: Accelerated Development.

Cowen, R.L. (1983). Primary prevention in mental health: Past, present and future. In R. Felnes, I. Jason, J. Moritsuqu, & S. Farber (Eds.), *Preventive psychology: Theory, research, and practice* (pp. 11–25). New York: Pergamon Press.

Cummings, E., Dean, L.R., Newell, D.S., & McCaffrey, I. (1960). Disengagement: A tentative theory of aging. *Sociometry, 13,* 23.

Curtis, J., & Ennis, R. (1988). Negative consequences of leaving competitive sport: Comparative findings for former elite-level hockey players. *Sociology of Sport Journal, 5,* 87–106.

Deford, F. (1981). *Everybody's all-American.* New York: Viking.

Delman, R., & Johnson, H. (1976). Biofeedback and progressive muscle relaxation: A comparison of psychophysiological effects. *Psychophysiology, 13,* 181.

Dorfman, H.A. (1990). Reflections on providing personal and performance enhancement consulting services in professional baseball. *The Sport Psychologist, 4,* 341–346.

Duda, J.L., Smart, A.E., & Tappe, M.K. (1989). Prediction of adherence in the rehabilitation of athletic injuries. *Journal of Sport & Exercise Psychology, 11,* 318–335.

Eitzen, D.S., & Sage, G.H. (Eds.). (1982). *Sociology of American sport* (2nd ed.). Dubuque, IA: Brown.

Elkin, D. (1981). *The hurried child.* Reading, MA: Addison-Wesley.

Elliott, B. (1982, December 27). Transition into working world can take years in some cases. *Ottawa Citizen,* p. 41.

Erikson, E. (1959). *Identity and the life cycle: Selected papers* (Psychological Issues, Monograph No. 1). New York: Simon & Schuster.

Erikson, E. (1963). *Childhood and society.* New York: Norton.

Feldman, L. (1990, February). Fallen angel. *Gentleman's Quarterly,* 218–225.

Feltz, D.L. (1986). The psychology of sports injuries. In E.F. Vinger & P.F. Hoerner (Eds.), *Sports injuries: The unthwarted epidemic* (pp. 336–344). Littleton, MA: PSG.

Fisher, A.G., & Conlee, R.K. (1979). *The complete book of physical fitness* (pp. 119–121). Provo, UT: Brigham Young University.

Friedlander, S. (1984/1985). Learned helplessness in children: Perception of control and causal attributions. *Imagination, Cognition, and Personality, 4,* 99–116.

Garfield, S., & Bergin, A. (1978). *Handbook of psychotherapy and behavior change: An empirical analysis* (2nd ed.). New York: Wiley.

George, L.K. (1980). *Role terminations in later life.* Monterey, CA: Brooks/Cole.

Gorbett, F.J. (1985). Psycho-social adjustment of athletes to retirement. In L.K. Bunker, R.J. Rotella, & A. Reilly (Eds.), *Sport psychology: Psychological considerations in maximizing sport performance* (pp. 288–294). Ithaca, NY: Mouvement.

Gould, D., Tammen, V., Murphy, S., & May, J. (1989). An examination of U.S. Olympic sport psychology consultants and the services they provide. *The Sport Psychologist, 3,* 300–312.

Greendorfer, S.L., & Blinde, E.M. (1985). "Retirement" from intercollegiate sport: Theoretical and empirical considerations. *Sociology of Sport Journal, 2,* 101–110.

Greendorfer, S.L., & Blinde, E.M. (1987). Female sport retirement descriptive patterns and research implications. In L. Vander Velden & H. Humphrey (Eds.), *Psychology and sociology of sport* (pp. 167–176). New York: AMS Press.

Grove, J.R., Lavallee, D., & Gordon, S. (1997). Coping with retirement from sport: The influence of athletic identity. *Journal of Applied Sport Psychology, 9,* 191–203.

Grove, J.R., Lavallee, D., Gordon, S., & Harvey, J.H. (1998). Account-making: A model of understanding and resolving distressful reactions to retirement from sport. *The Sport Psychologist, 12,* 52–67.

Haerle, R.K., Jr. (1975). Career patterns and career contingencies of professional baseball players: An occupational analysis. In D. Ball & J. Loy (Eds.), *Sport and social order* (pp. 461–519). Reading, MA: Addison-Wesley.

Hallden, D. (1965). The adjustment of athletes after retiring from sports. In F. Antonelli (Ed.), *Proceedings of the 1st International Congress of Sport Psychology* (pp. 730–733). Rome, Italy.

Hare, N. (1971). A study of the Black fighter. *Black Scholar, 3,* 2–9.

Havighurst, R.J., & Albrecht, R. (1953). *Older people.* New York: Longmans, Green.

Heil, J. (1988, October). *Early identification and intervention with injured athletes at risk for failed rehabilitation.* Paper presented at the annual meetings of the Association for the Advancement of Applied Sport Psychology, Nashua, NH.

Henschen, K.P. (1986). Athletic staleness and burnout: Diagnosis, prevention and treatment. In J.M. Williams (Ed.), *Applied sport psychology: Personal growth to peak performance* (pp. 327–342). Palo Alto, CA: Mayfield.

Hill, P., & Lowe, B. (1974). The inevitable metathesis of the retiring athlete. *International Review of Sport Sociology, 4,* 5–29.

Hoffer, R. (1990, December 3). Magic's kingdom. *Sports Illustrated,* 106–110.

Hopson, B., & Adams, J. (1977). Toward an understanding of termination: Defining some boundaries of termination. In J. Adams & B. Hopson (Eds.), *Transition: Understanding and managing personal change* (pp. 3–25). Montclair, NJ: Allanheld, Osmun.

Horowitz, M.J. (1986). *Stress response syndromes* (2nd ed.). Northvale, NJ: Aronson.

Jones, E.E., & Davis, K.E. (1965). From cuts to dispositions: The attribution process in person perception. *Archives in Experimental Social Psychology, 2,* 219–266.

Jordan, P. (1975). *A false spring.* New York: Bantam Books.

Kahn, R. (1972). *The boys of summer.* New York: Harper & Row.

Kaminski-da-Rosa, V. (1985). Planning today for tomorrow's lifestyle. *Training and Development Journal, 39,* 103–104.

Kelley, H.H. (1967). Attribution in social psychology. In D. Levine (Ed.), *Nebraska symposium on motivation* (pp. 221–253). Lincoln: University of Nebraska Press.

Kerr, G., & Dacyshyn, A. (in press). The retirement experiences of elite, female gymnasts. *Journal of Applied Sport Psychology.*

King, A.C., Winett, R.A., & Lovett, S.B. (1986). Enhancing coping behaviors in at-risk populations: The effects of time-management instruction and social support in women from dual-earner families. *Behavior Therapy, 17,* 57–66.

Kleiber, D., & Thompson, S. (1980). Leisure behavior and adjustment to retirement: Implications for pre-retirement education. *Therapeutic Recreation Journal, 14,* 5–17.

Kramer, J. (1969). *Farewell to football.* New York: World Books.

Kraus, J.F., & Conroy, C. (1989). Mortality and morbidity from injuries in sport and recreation. *Annual Review of Public Health, 5,* 163–192.

Kübler-Ross, E. (1969). *On death and dying.* New York: Macmillan.

Kuypers, J.A., & Bengston, V.L. (1973). Social breakdown and competence: A model of normal aging. *Human Development, 16,* 181–120.

Labouvie-Vief, G., & Gonda, J. (1976). Cognitive strategy training and intellectual performance in the elderly. *Journal of Gerontology, 31,* 327–332.

Lange, A.J., & Jakubowski, P. (1976). *Responsible assertive behavior.* Champaign, IL: Research Press.

Lavallee, D., Gordon, S., & Grove, J.R. (1997). Retirement from sport and the loss of athletic identity. *Journal of Personal and Interpersonal Loss, 2,* 129–147.

Lavallee, D., Grove, J.R., & Gordon, S. (1997). The causes of career termination from sport and their relationship to post-retirement adjustment among elite-amateur athletes in Australia. *Australian Psychologist, 32,* 131–135.

Lazarus, A. (1972). *Behavior theory and beyond.* New York: McGraw-Hill.

Lazarus, R.S. (1975). The self regulation of emotion. In L. Levi (Ed.), *Emotions: Their parameters and measurement* (pp. 47–68). New York: Ravel.

Lazarus, R.S., & Folkman, S. (1984). *Stress, appraisal, and coping.* New York: Springer.

Lerch, S.H. (1981). The adjustment to retirement of professional baseball players. In S.L. Greendorfer & A. Yiannakis (Eds.), *Sociology of sport: Perspectives* (pp. 138–148). West Point, NY: Leisure.

Lerch, S.H. (1982). Athletic retirement as social death: An overview. In N. Theberge & P. Donnelly (Eds.), *Sport and the sociological imagination* (pp. 259–272). Fort Worth: Texas Christian University.

Lewis-Griffith, L. (1982). Athletic injuries can be a pain in the head. *Woman's Sports, 4,* 44.

Manion, U.V. (1976). Preretirement counseling: The need for a new approach. *Personnel and Guidance Journal, 55,* 119–121.

Marcia, J.E. (1966). Development and validation of ego-identity state. *Journal of Personality and Social Psychology, 3,* 551–558.

May, J.R., & Brown, L. (1989). Delivery of psychological services to the U.S. Alpine ski team prior to and during the Olympics in Calgary. *The Sport Psychologist, 3,* 320–329.

May, J.R., & Sieb, G.E. (1987). Athletic injuries: Psychosocial factors in the onset, sequelae, rehabilitation, and prevention. In J.R. May & M.J. Asken (Eds.), *Sport psychology: The psychological health of the athlete* (pp. 157–186). New York: AMS Press.

McPherson, B.P. (1980). Retirement from professional sport: The process and problems of occupational and psychological adjustment. *Sociological Symposium, 30,* 126–143.

Meichenbaum, D. (1977). *Cognitive-behavior modification.* New York: Plenum Press.

Meichenbaum, D., & Cameron, R. (1973). Training schizophrenics to talk to themselves: A means of developing attentional controls. *Behavior Therapy, 4,* 515–534.

Meichenbaum, D., & Jaremko, M. (1987). *Stress reduction and prevention.* New York: Plenum Press.

Meyers, A. (1997). Sport psychology service to the United States Olympic Festival: An experiential account. *The Sport Psychologist, 11,* 454–468.

Mihovilovic, M. (1968). The status of former sportsman. *International Review of Sport Sociology, 3,* 73–96.

Moleski, R., & Tosi, E.J. (1976). Comparative psychotherapy: Rational-emotive therapy versus systematic desensitization in the treatment of stuttering. *Journal of Consulting and Clinical Psychology, 44,* 309–311.

Moos, R., & Tsu, V. (1977). The crisis of physical illness: An overview. In R. Moos & V. Tsu (Eds.), *Coping with physical illness* (pp. 9–22). New York: Plenum Press.

Morrow, L. (1978, February 27). To an athlete getting old. *Time,* 45.

Murphy, S.M., Abbot, S., Hillard, N., Petitpas, A., Danish, S., & Holloway, S. (1989, September). *New frontiers in sport psychology: Helping athletes with career termination process.* Paper presented at the annual meeting of the Association for the Advancement of Applied Sport Psychology, Seattle, WA.

Newman, B. (1989). Striking the lode [Special issue]. *Sports Illustrated,* 282–285.

Newman, B. (1991, March 11). The last return. *Sports Illustrated,* 38–42.

Ogilvie, D.C. (1982). Career crises in sports. In T. Orlick, J.T. Partington, & J.H. Salmela (Eds.), *Proceedings of the 5th World Congress of Sport Psychology* (pp. 176–183). Ottawa: Coaching Association of Canada.

Ogilvie, B.C. (1983). When a dream dies. *Women's Sports Magazine, 5,* 5–7.

Ogilvie, B.C. (1987, October). *Traumatic effects of sports career termination.* Paper presented at the National Conference of Sport Psychology, Washington, DC.

Ogilvie, B.C., & Howe, M. (1982). Career crisis in sport. In T. Orlick, J.T. Partington, & J.H. Salmela (Eds.), *Proceedings of the 5th World Congress of Sport Psychology* (pp. 176–183). Ottawa: Coaching Association of Canada.

Ogilvie, B.C., & Howe, M. (1986). The trauma of termination from athletics. In J.M. Williams (Ed.), *Applied sport psychology: Personal growth to peak performance* (pp. 365–382). Palo Alto, CA: Mayfield.

Orlick, J. (1980). *In pursuit of excellence.* Ottawa: Coaches Association of Canada.

Orlick, T.D., & Botterill, C. (1975). *Every kid can win.* Chicago: Nelson-Hall.

Otto, L.B., & Alwin, D.F. (1977). Athletics, aspirations, and attainments. *Sociology of Education, 42,* 102–113.

Pawlak, A. (1984). The status and style of life of Polish Olympians after completion of their sports careers. *International Review of Sport Sociology, 19,* 169–183.

Pearson, R.E., & Petitpas, A.J. (1990). Transitions of athletes: Developmental and preventive perspectives. *Journal of Counseling and Development, 69,* 7–10.

Perna, F.M., Ahlgren, R.L., & Zaichkowsky, L. (1999). The influence of career planning, race, and athletic injury on life satisfaction among recently retired collegiate male athletes. *The Sport Psychologist, 13,* 144–156.

Peterson, C., Bettes, B.A., & Seligman, M.E. (1985). Depressive symptoms and unprompted causal attributions: Content analysis. *Behavior Research and Therapy, 23,* 379–382.

Petitpas, A.J., Danish, S., McKelvain, R., & Murphy, S.M. (1990, September). *A career assistance program for elite athletes.* Paper presented at the annual meetings of the Association for the Advancement of Applied Sport Psychology, San Antonio, TX.

Phillips, J.C., & Schafer, W.E. (1971). Consequences of participation in interscholastic sport. *Pacific Sociological Review, 14,* 328–338.

Piphers, M. (1994). *Reviving Ophelia: Saving the selves of adolescent girls.* New York: Ballantine Books.

Plimpton, G. (1977, January). The final season. *Harpers,* 63–67.

Pollock, O. (1956). *The social aspects of retirement.* Homewood, IL: Irwin.

Putnam, F.W. (1989). Pierre Janet and modern views of dissociation. *Journal of Traumatic Stress, 2,* 413–429.

Putnam, P. (1991, February 18). So long, Sugar. *Sports Illustrated,* 22–25.

Remer, R., Tongate, R.A., & Watson, J. (1978). Athletes: Counseling for the overprivileged minority. *Personnel and Guidance Journal, 56,* 622–629.

Reynolds, M.J. (1981). The effects of sports retirement on the job satisfaction of the former football player. In S.L. Greendorfer & A. Yiannakis (Eds.), *Sociology of sport: Perspectives* (pp. 127–137). West Point, NY: Leisure.

Rosenberg, E. (1981). Gerontological theory and athletic retirement. In S.L. Greendorfer & A. Yiannakis (Eds.), *Sociology of sport: Perspectives* (pp. 119–126). West Point, NY: Leisure.

Rosenberg, E. (1982). Athletic retirement as social death: Concepts and perspectives. In N. Theberge & P. Donnelly (Eds.), *Sport and the sociological imagination* (pp. 245–258). Fort Worth: Texas Christian University.

Rosenfeld, L.B., Richman, J.M., & Hardy, C.J. (1989). Examining social support networks among athletes: Description and relationship to stress. *The Sport Psychologist, 3,* 23–33.

Rosenkoetter, M.M. (1985). Is your older client ready for a role change after retirement? *Journal of Gerontological Nursing, 11,* 21–24.

Roskin, M. (1982). Coping with life changes: A preventive social work approach. *American Journal of Community Psychology, 10,* 331–340.

Rotella, R.J., & Heyman, S.R. (1986). Stress, injury, and the psychological rehabilitation of athletes. In J.M. Williams (Ed.), *Applied sport psychology: Personal growth to peak performance* (pp. 343–364). Palo Alto, CA: Mayfield.

Rowen, R.B., & Wilks, S. (1987). Pre-retirement planning: A quality of life issue for retirement. *Employee Assistance Quarterly, 2,* 45–56.

Samples, P. (1987). Mind over muscle: Returning the injured athlete to play. *Physician and Sportsmedicine, 15,* 172–180.

Sands, R. (1978). A socio-psychological investigation of the effects of role discontinuity on outstanding high school athletes. *Journal of Sport Behavior, 1,* 174–185.

Sarason, I.G., & Sarason, B.R. (1986). Experimentally provided social support. *Journal of Personality and Social Psychology, 50,* 1222–1225.

Savery, L.K. (1986). Stress and the employee. *Leadership and Organization Development Journal, 7,* 17–20.

Scanlan, T.K. (1985). Sources of stress in youth sport athletes. In M.R. Weiss & D. Gould (Eds.), *Sports for children and youth* (pp. 75–89). Champaign, IL: Human Kinetics.

Scanlan, T.K., Stein, G.L., & Ravizza, K. (1989). An in-depth study of former elite figure skaters: II. Sources of enjoyment. *Journal of Sport & Exercise Psychology, 11,* 65–83.

Schafer, W. (1971). *Sport socialization and the school.* Paper presented at the Third International Symposium on the Sociology of Sport, Waterloo, Canada.

Schlossberg, N. (1981). A model for analyzing human adaptation to termination. *Counseling Psychologist, 9,* 2–18.

Sheldon, R. (1977). Self-confidence in preparing for retirement. *Gerontologist, 17,* 28–38.

Sherman, T.M., Weber, L.J., & Tegano, C. (1986). Conditions for effective academic assistance programs for football student athletes. *Journal of Sport Behavior, 9,* 173–181.

Shiffman, S. (1982). A relapse-prevention hotline. *Bulletin of the Society of Psychologists in Substance Abuse, 1,* 50–54.

Sinclair, D.A., & Orlick, T.D. (1993). Positive terminations from high-performance sport. *The Sport Psychologist, 7,* 138–150.

Smith, R.E. (1980). A cognitive-affective approach to stress management training for athletes. In C. Dadeau, W. Halliwell, K. Newell, & G. Roberts (Eds.), *Psychology of motor behavior and sports* (pp. 55–71). Champaign, IL: Human Kinetics.

Smith, R.E. (1985). A component analysis of athletic stress. In M. Weiss & D. Gould (Eds.), *Competitive sports for children* and youths: *Proceedings of the Olympic Scientific Congress* (pp. 107–112). Champaign, IL: Human Kinetics.

Smith, R.E., Smoll, F.L., & Curtis, B. (1979). Coach effectiveness training: A cognitive-behavior approach to enhancing relationship skills in youth sport coaches. *Journal of Sport Psychology, 1,* 59–75.

Snyder, E., & Baber, L. (1979). A profile of former collegiate athletes and non-athletes: Leisure activities, attitudes toward work and aspects of satisfaction with life. *Journal of Sport Behavior, 2,* 211–219.

Stephens, L. (1984, May 11). After cheers fade away, hockey stars find life rough. *Ottawa Citizen,* p. 43.

Sussman, M.B. (1971). An analytical model for the sociological study of retirement. In F.M. Carp (Ed.), *Retirement* (pp. 29–73). New York: Behavioral Publications.

Svoboda, B., & Vanek, M. (1982). Retirement from high level competition. In T. Orlick, J.T. Partington, & J.H. Salmela (Eds.), *Proceedings of the 5th World Congress of Sport Psychology* (pp. 166–175). Ottawa: Coaching Association of Canada.

Szinovacz, M.E. (1987). Preferred retirement satisfaction in women. *International Journal of Aging and Human Development, 24,* 301–317.

Tache, J., & Selye, H. (1985). On stress and coping mechanisms. *Issues in Mental Health Nursing, 7,* 3–24.

Taylor, C. (1972). Developmental conceptions and the retirement process. In F.M. Carp (Ed.), *Retirement* (pp. 77–113). New York: Behavioral Publications.

Taylor, J. (1987, September). *The application of psychological skills for the enhancement of coaching effectiveness.* Presented at the Association for the Advancement of Applied Sport Psychology annual meetings, Newport Beach, CA.

Taylor, J., & Ogilvie, B. (1994). A conceptual model of adaptation to retirement among athletes. *Journal of Applied Sport Psychology, 6,* 1–20.

Taylor, J., & Ogilvie, B. (1998). Career transition among elite athletes: Is there life after sport? In J.M. Williams (Ed.), *Applied sport psychology: Personal growth to peak performance* (pp. 429–444). Mountain View, CA: Mayfield.

Taylor, J., Ogilvie, B., Gould, D., & Gardner, F. (1990, September). *The biggest mistake I ever made as a sport psychologist (and what I learned from it).* Paper presented at the Association for the Advancement of Applied Sport Psychology annual meeting, San Antonio, TX.

Thorn, I. (1983). Counseling and career development programs in an organization: Design, implementation, and evaluation. *International Journal for the Advancement of Counseling, 6,* 69–77.

Thornton, J.S. (1990). Feast or famine: Eating disorders in athletes. *Physician and Sportsmedicine, 18,* 116–121.

Trexler, L.D., & Karst, T.O. (1972). Rational emotive therapy, placebo, and no treatment effects on public speaking anxiety. *Journal of Abnormal Psychology, 79,* 60–67.

Tuckman, J., & Lorge, I. (1953). *Retirement and the industrial worker.* New York: Macmillan.

Ungerleiter, S. (1997). Olympic athletes' termination from sport to workplace. *Perceptual and Motor Skills, 84,* 1287–1295.

United States Olympic Committee. (1988). *Career assessment program for athletes: 1988–89 seminar workbook.* Colorado Springs, CO: Author.

Vecsey, G. (1980, October 28). Counseling helps many in 2nd career. *New York Times,* pp. A33, 36.

Vinnay, G. (1973). *Footballmania.* London: Orbach & Chambers.

Webb, W.M., Nasco, S.A., Riley, S., & Headrick, B. (1998). *Journal of Sport Behavior, 21,* 338–362.

Weinberg, K., & Arond, H. (1952). The occupational culture of the boxer. *American Journal of Sociology, 57,* 460–469.

Werthner, P., & Orlick, T. (1982). Retirement experiences of successful Olympic athletes. *International Journal of Sport Psychology, 17,* 337–363.

Werthner, P., & Orlick, T. (1986). Retirement experiences of successful Olympic athletes. *International Journal of Sport Psychology, 17,* 337–363.

Wheeler, G.D., Malone, L.A., VanVlack, S., & Nelson, E.R. (1996). Retirement from disability sport: A pilot study. *Adapted Physical Activity Quarterly, 13,* 382–399.

White, C. (1974). After the last cheers, what do superstars become? *Physician and Sportsmedicine, 2,* 75–78.

Williams, J.M., & Andersen, M.B. (1998). Psychosocial antecedents of sport injury: Review and critique of the stress and injury model. *Journal of Applied Sport Psychology, 10,* 5–25.

Winegardner, D., Simonetti, J.L., & Nykodym, N. (1984). Unemployment: The living death? *Journal of Employment-Counseling, 21,* 149–155.

Wolff, R., & Lester, D. (1989). A theoretical basis for counseling the retired professional athlete. *Psychological Reports, 64,* 1043–1046.

Wood, R., & Bandura, A. (1989). Social cognitive theory of organizational management. *Academy of Management Review, 14,* 361–384.

Yalom, I.D. (1980). *Existential psychotherapy.* New York: HarperCollins.

PART VI
Exercise and Health Psychology

Using Theories of Motivated Behavior to Understand Physical Activity

Perspectives on Their Influence

S. NICOLE CULOS-REED, NANCY C. GYURCSIK, and LAWRENCE R. BRAWLEY

One challenge of writing a chapter about theories of exercise behavior is the decision about which theories should be examined. An initial and important clarification is that there are no formal theories of exercise behavior. However, there are psychosocial theories of human behavior. Physical activity and exercise, like any other human behavior, can thus be considered from the numerous theoretical perspectives already developed in psychology. If all the perspectives that have been applied to studying physical activity and exercise were considered, this chapter could easily become a book with contributions from multiple authors. An example of such a text is Seraganian's (1993) *Exercise Psychology: The Influence of Physical Exercise on Psychological Processes.*

WHY A SPORT PSYCHOLOGIST SHOULD CONTINUE READING

A second challenge for this chapter is to convince sport psychologists interested in performance enhancement that they should continue reading. Does a chapter about the application of theory to exercise/physical activity have any relevance for individuals interested in performance enhancement? The answer to this question is yes, because of the practicality of using theory not only as the "blueprint" for research (cf. Brawley, 1993), but also as a blueprint in the applied practice of enhancing the performance of both physical activity and sport-related behavior.

Investigators interested in behavior change for health-related purposes have the same intent as sport psychologists interested in enhancing sport performance. For example, the outcomes in exercise/physical activity may be related to an improvement in physical function (i.e., cardiovascular or mobility), exercise adherence, or psychosocial function (i.e., reduced anxiety or depression), and the parallel outcomes in sport are more than win/loss. Additional sport outcomes are improvements in athletes' personal time standards, the quality of their athletic skills, or the coping abilities necessary to deal with their competitive anxiety. Additionally, in the sense that performance enhancement focuses on helping athletes to be consistent in their performance by training and competing regularly, the goal is also to improve adherence to training and competing.

Therefore, the answer to the question Why should a sport psychologist continue reading? is that lessons learned in one field can be helpful in another. Because the performance enhancement aspect of exercise and physical activity may involve many types of behavior change interventions, it seems probable that the mistakes, successes and lessons learned could be useful to advance knowledge in both fields. Kirschenbaum (1992) provided the field of sport psychology with an important message. He wrote about the tremendous difficulties of getting people to lose weight and maintain weight loss. Three central points were that: (1) the task was not easy, (2) sport psychologists interested in performance enhancement could avoid many of the mistakes they might make in conducting interventions if they learned lessons from the weight loss field, and (3) sport and exercise psychologists should learn to be humble about their role in enhancement. In other words, more needs to be learned about the magnitude of effect of interventions on any kind of performance (either sport or exercise). Armed with that knowledge, how can impact be improved?

It is contended that only a modest impact on performance has been made in the areas of both sport and physical activity. In this chapter, it is proposed that reliance on sound theory and on a better translation of theoretical variables into behavior change mechanisms (i.e., psychological/behavioral determinants of behavioral outcomes, such as improved end performance, or quality of life) is a route for scientific research *and* practice. This applies not only to physical activity research but also to sport performance enhancement.

QUESTIONS ABOUT EXERCISE THAT REFLECT RESEARCH DIRECTIONS

Much of the research about exercise-related psychosocial outcomes has been driven by many questions: Why does exercise seem to energize people? Why do people drop out of exercise? What are the reasons people engage in exercise or avoid exercise? Other exercise or physical activity questions have been related to public health issues: Why are people so inactive when they know inactivity is a major health risk factor? What amount of activity can be motivated in sedentary individuals to reduce their risk? How do interventions change lifestyle physical activity? How can motivation and behavior be altered to reduce dropout and promote exercise prescriptions? What are the psychosocial benefits of regular physical activity? No one volume has been devoted to answering all of these questions. However, recent books and journals have made major contributions in shedding light on at least some of these issues. For example, Dishman's (1994) volume on exercise adherence presented chapters that concerned the psychosocial aspects of exercise adherence; a special issue of the *American Journal of Preventive Medicine* (Blair & Morrow, 1998) was devoted to physical activity interventions, with many articles on psychosocial aspects of these interventions; and Biddle, Sallis, and Cavill (1998) examined physical activity for children and youth from biopsychosocial perspectives. Such literature confirms that there are many social science disciplines, and more specifically, psychological perspectives, that have been used to answer the questions raised previously.

SELECTING AND REVIEWING THEORIES FOR THIS CHAPTER

In writing this chapter, a conscious decision was made to discuss those theories that have a cross-cutting influence on the study of various types of physical activity as a motivated, healthy behavior for the young child to the older adult. These theories were selected for numerous reasons and reflected a number of different characteristics. The criteria were that they had (1) an impact on the scientific literature, (2) a consistent pattern of investigation in exercise/physical activity over a number of years, (3) clear measurement principles and measures, (4) stimulated reviews of the literature on exercise/health, (5) been used in studying health behaviors other than exercise behavior (i.e., generalizability), and (6) some form of perceived control included as part of the model or theory. The criteria for the inclusion of theories guaranteed that a large and systematically examined literature could be considered. Furthermore, the amount of research that has been conducted on a theoretical model has implications for the use of the theory in behavior change interventions (cf. Baranowski, Lin, Wetter, Resnicow, & Davis-Hearn, 1997).

The selection of theories does not imply that other theories and models are of lesser importance in the study of physical activity. A number of theories that have been used to investigate exercise-related questions have received relatively little attention compared to the theories selected for review. However, the other theories have been used in preliminary ways, for example, to bring order to areas of research that have equivocal findings, to provide an alternative to data-driven research, or to examine questions about exercise-induced psychosocial outcomes (other than behavior). Examples of these models and theories are the theory of personal investment (i.e., person X situation interaction model of motivation: Maehr & Braskamp, 1986; its application to exercise: Duda, Smart, & Tappe, 1989); perceived exertion models (cf. Noble & Robertson, 1996; Rejeski, 1981); attribution theory in the study of exercise barriers as excuses and reasons (Brawley, Martin, & Gyurcsik, 1998); models of affect in the study of exercise-induced effort (e.g., state-trait anxiety: Spielberger, Gorsuch, Luschene, Vagg, & Jacobs, 1983; positive and negative affect: Diener & Emmons, 1985); and theories about physical self-presentation (cf. health/physical activity, Leary, 1992; Schlenker, 1980). This list is by no means exhaustive.

Theories can be placed on a developmental continuum, where one end may be represented by a single hypothesis, the midpoint of the continuum by a conceptual model, and the opposite end by a fully developed theory. For the purposes of this chapter, the theories presented not only have met the aforementioned selection criteria, but also reflect a greater level of development (i.e., the range of the continuum that includes a conceptual model to a full theory). Thus, the theories selected are the theory of planned behavior (Ajzen, 1985), self-efficacy theory (Bandura, 1997), social-cognitive theory (Bandura, 1986), and the transtheoretical model.

In discussing perspectives about these influential theories, the following approach was used. First, for those theories that have a substantive research base and also reviews of this research base, the major reviews were used to develop the perspectives for the chapter. Rather than creating another literature analysis, the major reviews illustrate the common and unique conclusions related to theory-based exercise/health research. The two theories that received this treatment in the chapter are the theory of planned behavior and self-efficacy theory. Second, two theoretical perspectives were examined that have received less systematic testing but have been the theoretical foundations for numerous reports of physical activity interventions. These two theories are social-cognitive theory and the transtheoretical model.

Common Theoretical Assumptions and Elements

The four theories mentioned share certain assumptions about human beings. They assume that human beings are goal-directed and capable of rational decision making, forethought, and planning. Thus, people are capable of self-regulating their own actions. These theories also share certain common elements: (1) outcome expectancies (i.e., expected benefits and costs), (2) outcome value (i.e., reinforcement value, incentive value), (3) self-efficacy expectancy (i.e., part of perceived control), and (4) intentions (i.e., proximal goals). Together, these factors influence health-related decisions about exercise and behavior (cf. Maddux, Brawley, & Boykin, 1995). The theories presented either explicitly or implicitly acknowledge that experience, decision making, and self-regulation are part of a dynamic social learning process (cf. Bandura, 1986).

Consider exercise adherence as an example. Participants in either structured or unstructured physical activity experience both success and failure as they try to adhere over time. Based on these experiences, they generally try to adjust their goals/intentions and thus regulate their adherence efforts. Given the process of cognitive and behavioral adjustment that people make through social learning, it is not surprising that they vary the frequency, effort, duration, and type of their exercise behavior, and thus their adherence (cf. Brawley & Culos-Reed, 2000; Maddux & Lewis, 1995). To better understand the support behind these assumptions and common elements, it is instructive to consider the research evidence. Ajzen's (1985) theory of planned behavior is considered first.

THEORIES OF REASONED ACTION AND PLANNED BEHAVIOR

Two related theories that have been frequently applied to the investigation of health behaviors and specifically to exercise behavior are the theory of reasoned action (TRA; Ajzen & Fishbein, 1980, 1975) and the theory of planned behavior (TPB; Ajzen, 1985). Although both of these theories concern attitude-behavior relationships and assume that individuals are capable of forethought and make rational decisions about their behavior and its consequences, the focus of behavioral control differs.

Theory of Reasoned Action

The TRA was developed to explain volitional, or freely chosen, behavior. Thus, for exercise, behavior is determined by one's intentions to perform, or not perform, the exercise-related behavior. Intentions are the immediate and sole determinant of behavior in the TRA. In turn, the determinants of intentions are one's attitude about performing the exercise actions and the influence of normative social forces (i.e., subjective norms) on the individual performing the physical activity. These two factors are weighted because their impact on behavioral intention is a function of factors such as the individual's experience and the situational constraints. For example, the specific social context, the proximity of the action in time (e.g., immediate or in future), and the particular aspect of the activity (e.g., the specific exercise, sport, or other health behavior) are proposed to vary the weighted influence of both attitude and subjective norm on the individual's intention to attempt an activity (e.g., exercise).

The first determinant of intentions, attitudes (i.e., the individual's affective feelings) are a function of beliefs concerning the perceived consequences of performing a behavior and a personal evaluation of these consequences. For example, an individual who regularly engages in physical activity may believe that exercise is important for staying healthy, and highly values this lifestyle. The second determinant of intentions, subjective norms (i.e., the social pressures to behave in a specific manner), are a function of the perceived expectations of salient others (referred to as normative beliefs) and the motivation to comply with these expectations. In essence, it is an outcome expectation (cf. Maddux et al., 1995). For example, if individuals believe that their spouse wants them to remain active and they value the opinion of their spouse, their subjective norm for exercising will be high and thus will positively influence their intentions. As this theory concerns freely chosen behavior, both objective and subjective control are assumed to be high. In examining behaviors with this model, it must be assumed (rather than measured) that control is high. Indeed, Ajzen (1985) notes that when control is high, the TPB operates like the TRA. To understand this idea, a brief explanation of the TPB is provided.

The Theory of Planned Behavior

The TPB is an extension of the TRA with the addition of a single factor: perceived behavioral control (see Figure 27.1). The purpose of the addition of perceived behavioral control within the TPB was to provide an actual measurement of the control element, taking into account both real and perceived limitations to performing the behavior. This enabled researchers to move from an attitudinal-based theory (e.g., attitude, action) focused only on volitional behavior, to examining nonvolitional behaviors, or those not completely under the individual's control.

According to Ajzen (1991), perceived behavioral control is conceptualized as one's belief regarding how easy or difficult performance of the behavior is likely to be. Underlying this conceptualization are individuals' beliefs about their resources and capabilities. Perceived behavioral control is viewed as both an indirect and direct predictor of behavior. It is hypothesized that there is a direct link between perceived behavioral control and behavior for nonvolitional behaviors, such as exercise, where the individual may face real or perceived limitations to carrying out the physical activity. Thus, if the individual's perceived behavioral control is high, the exercise behavior is more likely to be performed. In contrast, when perceived control is low, the exercise behavior is not likely to occur. Perceived behavioral control is in turn influenced by control beliefs and by the perceived power of a particular control factor to facilitate or inhibit performance of the behavior. Similar to the influence of attitude and subjective norm on intentions, the precursors of perceived behavioral control are weighted and thus have an indirect weighted influence on behavioral intention and behavior.

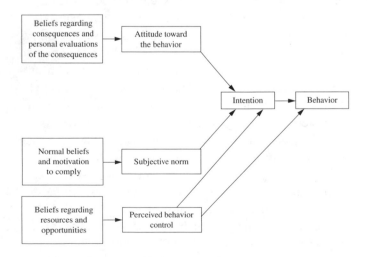

Figure 27.1 The theory of planned behavior.

A Review of the TPB

Although both the TRA and the TPB have been used in the physical activity domain, the TPB has been applied with more success. Research examining the TPB has thus been conducted at an increasing rate in recent years. A number of reviews have summarized this research and a sampling of the most recent is presented in Table 27.1. Information from each of the TPB reviews includes (1) the type of review (i.e., statistical or narrative), (2) the number of studies included in the review, (3) the search and inclusion/exclusion criteria used, (4) the results, (5) authors' conclusions, and (6) limitations to the review. These reviews vary in the number of studies covered, and some are more selective than others (i.e., only focus on physical activity or cover a variety of health behaviors). The physical activity study results are the focus of the review results presented here.

In addition to these reviews, Table 27.2 highlights some of the conceptual and measurement issues that have arisen along with the proliferation of research on the TPB. Information from the four papers in Table 27.2 includes (1) the focus of the paper (i.e., what TPB issue is being discussed), (2) number of studies reviewed (if applicable), (3) inclusion/exclusion criteria (if applicable), (4) results, and (5) authors' conclusions.

Next, the most recent research utilizing the TPB in exercise settings is highlighted, and discussion about the direction of this research and suggestions for future research is presented.

TPB Reviews

A number of reviews focused on research in exercise or physical activity have been conducted since 1980 utilizing the TPB as a conceptual framework (see Table 27.1). The reviews, which are primarily of two types, statistical and conceptual, offer overwhelming support for the TPB as a useful framework for examining physical activity or exercise behaviors. On average, the TPB variables of attitude, subjective norm, and perceived behavioral control explain 40% to 60% of the variance in behavioral intentions, and 20% to 40% of the variance in behavior. Within the support for the overall model, the TPB components that have received the strongest endorsement in the physical activity setting are perceived behavioral control and attitude. Whether this is largely due to the setting, the participants, the type of behavior being studied, or the nature of the measurement of these variables remains unclear.

The studies in the reviews were highly variable in a number of aspects. For example, the number of participants

Table 27.1 Reviews of the TPB in Exercise, Sport, and Physical Activity

Review and Type	Inclusion Criteria	Number of Studies; Search	Results	Main Conclusions	Limitations of Reviewed Studies
Hausenblas et al., 1997 Meta-analysis	Exercise focus; Used minimum of 2 TRA/TPB constructs; Able to calculate ES	31 Computer, manual, and journal searches	ES with BI and Att (1.22), BI and SN (.56), BI and PBC (.97); ES with B and BI (1.09), B and PBC (1.01), B and Att (.84), and B and SN (.18)	TPB superior to TRA for predicting B, and SN is less important for predicting exercise behavior	No examination of the quality of the TPB measures; ES likely overestimated due to interrelation between TRA and TPB
Godin & Kok, 1996 Narrative and quantitative	TPB information; Respect of causal associations underlying theory; PBC measured according to Ajzen's, Triandis's or Bandura's specifications	18 Journal searches since 1985 and contact with researchers known to study the TPB	Average correlation between BI and Att (.51), BI and SN (.30), BI and PBC (.50), between B and BI (.52), B and PBC (.41); Average R^2 to predict BI (.42), R^2 added by PBC (.17); Average R^2 to predict B (.36), R^2 added by PBC (.08)	PBC a significant contributor of both BI and B, but BI most important predictor of exercise behavior	Measurement of TPB variables by numerous methods, generating confusion in comparing and interpreting results
Sutton, 1998 Review of previous meta-analyses	None stated	9 reviews No search criteria stated	Average prediction of BI from Att, SN, and PBC (multiple correlations ranged from .63 to .71); Average prediction of B by BI (product moment correlations ranged from .44 to .62), from BI and PBC (multiple correlations ranged from .48 to .51)	Prediction of BI produces a large ES, whereas B is slightly lower at a medium to large ES; 9 reasons for poor prediction are presented	No knowledge of the studies used in the reviews that were included in this summary, therefore unaware of theoretical or measurement issues that might impact this review's conclusions
Godin, 1993 Narrative	None stated	8 None stated	PBC adds a significant portion of the variance explained in BI (4%–20%, average 8%); only 1 study examined B and found PBC accounted for an additional 3% of the variance	Partial support for the usefulness of the TPB over the TRA for studying exercise behavior; the inconsistency of PBC to predict B may be due to the population studied, the type of exercise, or other external factors	Small number of reviewed articles and the quality of the studies included was not ascertained

Note. ES = effect size; R^2 = multiple correlation; Att = attitudes; SN = subjective norms; PBC = perceived behavioral control; BI = behavior intentions; B = behavior; TPB = theory of planned behavior; TRA = theory of reasoned action.

Table 27.2 Reviews of Theoretical, Conceptual, and Measurement Issues with the TPB

Review and Type	Inclusion Criteria	Number of Studies/Search	Results	Main Conclusions
Connor & Armitage, 1998 Narrative	Studies must have examined a variable as an extension to the TPB	36 (9 on exercise) No search stated	6 variables showed impact as extensions to the TPB: belief salience, past behavior/habit, PBC versus self-efficacy, moral norms, self-identity, and affective beliefs	Depending on the behavior under study and the purpose, researchers may wish to include different combinations of the potential TPB extensions; two avenues for expansion are to study the spontaneous impact of Att on B and the impact of BI on B
Randall & Wolff, 1994 Meta-Analysis	Studies must have examined the BI-B link; statistics must have included bivariate correlations; and BI had to be assessed at an earlier time than B	60 (6 on exercise) Searched earlier review and journal articles	5 categories of the BI-B relationship emerged: less than 1 day, less than 1 week, less than 1 month, less than 1 year, and greater than 1 year; overall size-weighted correlation between BI and B was .45; only significant moderator of this relationship was type of behavior, explaining over 19% of the variance in the strength of the BI-B relationship	The BI-B relationship does not significantly decline over time, in contradiction to Fishbien and Ajzen's warning; there was no difference in the strength of this relationship when intention was measured as expectation; only type of behavior moderates the relationship
Ajzen, 1991 Narrative and quantitative	None stated; included several recent studies conducted within the TPB	4 exercise studies No search stated	Average multiple correlation for all studies in the prediction of B from BI and PBC was .51 (range from .20 to .78); average multiple correlation for all studies in the prediction of BI from Att, SN, and PBC was .71 (range from .43 to .94); no separate statistics on the exercise studies alone	Regression coefficients for PBC were significant in every study, indicating that the addition of PBC to the model considerably improved the prediction of BI; Att also clearly added to the prediction, but the pattern for SN was more variable; belief-based indices also examined in relation to their respective components (i.e., control beliefs and PBC), with preliminary results suggesting that the expectancy-value formulation may be inadequate for explaining how individual beliefs combine to produce the global response
Courneya & McAuley, 1993 Narrative	Examination of 2 issues within the BI-B relationship; intention versus expectation and scale correspondence	N/A	Only 1 study has achieved scale correspondence in the BI-B relationship, with the lack of correspondence decreasing the correlation between BI and B	Four possible methods of scale correspondence need to be addressed in future research, as does the measurement issue of intention versus expectation

Note. Att = attitudes; SN = subjective norms; PBC = perceived behavioral control; BI = behavioral intentions; B = behavior; TPB = theory of planned behavior; N/A = not applicable.

included in the studies in the Godin (1993) review ranged from 56 to 444. Sample size was not reported in any of the other three reviews. The settings of the physical activity studies were primarily fitness situations, but also included employment exercise programs and outdoor activities (e.g., jogging, biking, hiking). Participants were primarily university convenience samples; however, the elderly, disabled adults, pregnant women and employee populations were also included. Finally, in cases where multiple correlations were not calculated, other measures of the degree of the relationship, such as effect size, are reported in Table 27.1.

TPB Conceptual, Measurement, and Analysis Issues

Regardless of the consistent support of the TPB components for predicting exercise intentions and behavior, researchers continue to scrutinize the TPB and advocate improvements. More specifically, some of the research conducted using the TPB has violated theoretical and measurement assumptions, thus jeopardizing the validity and reliability of the physical activity findings (cf. Courneya & McAuley, 1993). For example, perhaps the single most important consideration that should be adhered to when conducting research within the framework of either the TRA or the TPB is the operationalization and measurement of the theoretical constructs (see reviews and descriptions by Brawley & Rodgers, 1993; Godin, 1993; Godin & Kok, 1996; Hausenblas, Carron, & Mack, 1997). In particular, it is important to define the action, context, type, and time elements of the behavior being investigated (Godin, 1993; Sutton, 1998).

The aforementioned reviews of the literature highlight two potential problems that occur when improper operationalization and measurement occur. First, the researcher may not be measuring what the theoretical construct proposes to measure. For example, including a perceived barriers measure such as "I do not like the way I feel when I exercise" may really be an indicator of the affective component of attitude and not of perceived behavioral control. The second problem that can arise from improper operationalization of the variables is that two different variables may be measuring the same construct. For example, if perceived behavioral control is operationalized as "I am determined to exercise three times per week for the next four weeks" and intention is operationalized as "I intend to try to exercise three times per week for the next four weeks" or "I will exercise three times per week for the next four weeks," a legitimate question can be raised with respect to the similarity of measurement.

An important consideration related to the operationalization of theoretical constructs is consistency across studies. This becomes important when compiling studies to assess the usefulness of various theories. Care must be taken to note the use of different measures of the same variable when comparing study results. This issue is best highlighted when considering the conceptualization and measurement of perceived behavioral control. Skinner (1996) has attempted to illustrate the many ways in which perceived control has been conceptualized and operationalized. Perceived control is a multidimensional construct. The issue for the TPB, however, is which measures provide a best representation of the construct for the test of the TPB. Currently, the theoretical construct of perceived behavioral control within the TPB has been operationalized most often in one of two ways. The first is to conceptualize perceived behavioral control using a measure of self-efficacy. This was suggested, but not examined, by Ajzen and Madden (1986). Thus, if a person's confidence in his or her ability to perform a behavior is high, it is taken as an indicant of greater perceived control.

A second operationalization of control is to use a measure of perceived barriers. This measure was used in early investigations based on the TPB. Thus, if the influence of perceived barriers to exercise was high, control was deemed low. Likewise, if the influence of perceived barriers was not limiting, perceived control for exercise behavior was high. Reviews of the literature suggest that if measured properly, either method for assessing perceived behavioral control has received some support (Brawley & Rodgers, 1993; Godin, 1993). However, once again, the method of measurement may have influenced the interpretation of the results (cf. measurement of barriers: Brawley et al., 1998).

Another measurement issue that has been a focus of attention more recently concerns the construct "subjective norm." Consistent throughout the physical activity literature, the TPB variables of attitude and perceived behavioral control/self-efficacy are significant predictors of behavioral intention. Subjective norm, however, is generally a weak predictor at best. One reason that has been offered for the inconsistent prediction by this construct concerns the type of behavior being studied. In other words, for physical activity or exercise behaviors, the role of significant others is not viewed to be important in encouraging participation by those people already involved in activity to some degree. Supportive of this view is the fact that subjective norm is a stronger predictor of behavioral intention for other health behaviors, such as contraceptive use, where the role of significant others is deemed to be more important for the decisions made and cannot be ignored.

However, a second reason for the weak contribution of subjective norm to the prediction of physical activity may lie in the operationalization of the construct. Is it the motivation to comply with the belief that important others wish an individual to exercise (i.e., subjective norm) that increases an individual's intention? Or is intent increased because of the support and praise from significant others that give the individual assurance about and confidence in trying an activity (i.e., social support)? Future researchers who examine this issue may help to uncover and delineate a clearer role of the social influence of significant others in exercise when using the TPB.

Finally, an analysis issue that is frequently discussed but rarely addressed is the idea of intention as a mediator of the relationship between perceived behavioral control and actual behavior. Baron and Kenny (1986) provide an excellent discussion of the conceptual distinction of what entails mediation and also provide the proper statistical testing necessary to determine mediation. Most simply, a series of hierarchical regression analyses, examining the relationships among perceived behavioral control, behavioral intention, and behavior, are conducted. If all the variables in the regression model are related, then a test of the mediation of intention can proceed. If intention is truly a mediator of the effects of the other TPB variables on behavior, intention will capture the lion's share of the variance in behavior, and the remaining TPB variables will not contribute significant variance to the regression model's prediction of behavior. This statistical test of intention as the theorized mediator has not occurred in the published exercise literature to date.

Beyond these conceptual, measurement, and analysis issues, suggestions have also been made for potentially improving the predictive ability of the theory by adding new components. For example, habit has been suggested as an independent predictor of behavioral intention and behavior, and thus is a potentially important construct to add to the existing TPB model. A selection of papers that have addressed the various measurement and conceptual issues specific to the TPB can be seen in Table 27.2. For example, researchers have highlighted factors that impact the predictive relationship among the TPB components of attitudes, subjective norms, perceived behavioral control, and behavioral intention, as well as the predictive relationship among perceived behavioral control, behavioral intention, and actual behavior. Additional issues, such as

scale correspondence or the inclusion of other variables into the TPB to improve prediction, are important to understand from a research perspective because they have been identified as key areas that will impact the prediction of behavioral intention and behavior. The papers included in Table 27.2 are not an exhaustive list of "issues" papers published on the TPB, but do provide a sampling of some of the more contentious areas of the theory and highlight needs for future research.

New Directions for TPB Research in Physical Activity

Despite the efforts by researchers to bring to attention limitations in earlier work, very little of the recent research specifically targets the TPB measurement issues that have been raised (e.g., Courneya, 1994 scale correspondence). Future initiatives in the TPB research should include attempts to examine some of these issues or, at the bare minimum, acknowledge the issues and discuss what was done to attempt to deal with them. However, research utilizing the TPB has developed in new areas (i.e., chronic disease research), and other research has examined TPB extensions. For example, Courneya and colleagues (Courneya & Friedenreich, 1997a, 1997b, 1997c; Courneya, Friedenreich, Arthur, & Bobick, 1999) have reattempted to analyze the usefulness of the TPB in examining exercise in cancer patients. Early results support the use of this theory and in particular highlight the importance of the attitude component. The TPB provides a framework for continued exploration of the role of physical activity for improving the quality of life of cancer survivors.

Conclusions

The TPB has proven to be useful as a tool for systematically examining physical activity intentions and actual behavior. Reviews conducted on research over the past 15 years have consistently shown a strong positive relationship among the TPB components of attitudes, subjective norms, perceived behavioral control, and behavioral intentions and behavior. The degree, or strength, of this relationship, however, has often varied, leading researchers to delve into issues that might help to explain the variability in the results. Areas of measurement and correspondence of the TPB components to behavior and intent, inclusion of other variables to improve prediction, and the changing role of the components depending on the behavior and participants under investigation represent areas in which questions have been raised. It is the role of investigators to consider such issues *as they are pertinent to their research question.* For the sport psychologist, the TPB may provide an ideal model to investigate areas to gather information that could be used to format later interventions with their athletes. The link between this well-supported theory and interventions is addressed in a later section in this chapter.

SELF-EFFICACY THEORY

Self-efficacy theory (Bandura, 1986, 1997) is another theory that has been frequently applied to the investigation of health behaviors. Self-efficacy is defined as beliefs in one's skills and abilities to organize and execute necessary courses of action that are required to produce a given attainment (Bandura, 1997). Efficacy beliefs are hypothesized to influence behavior through the choice of activity, the amount of effort exerted in the activity, and the amount of persistence exhibited in the face of obstacles and failures. For example, people who are efficacious in their skills and abilities in a particular behavioral domain will likely choose to engage in the behavior and exert greater effort and persistence compared to individuals who lack efficacy. In addition to influencing behavior, efficacy beliefs are hypothesized to influence individuals' affect, thought patterns, and motivation. For example, those with high efficacy in a particular domain will likely experience more positive affect, set higher goals, and have higher motivation to behave compared to individuals who lack efficacy.

According to self-efficacy theory, four main determinants are capable of altering self-efficacy beliefs: (1) enactive mastery experiences, (2) vicarious experiences, (3) verbal persuasion, and (4) physiological and affective states (Bandura, 1997). First, mastery experiences are obtained through performance accomplishments and are the most influential determinant of self-efficacy beliefs. Mastery experiences are so influential because they provide direct evidence of one's ability to successfully carry out effective courses of action. Second, vicarious experiences are obtained through modeling. The extent to which vicarious experiences influence self-efficacy depends on the individual's perceived similarity to the model. That is, the more similar the model is perceived to be, the more that self-efficacy will be influenced. Third, verbal persuasion reflects approaches used to convince individuals that they possess the capabilities to succeed in a given domain. Fourth, physiological and affective states produce somatic information that individuals rely on when appraising their self-efficacy in a given domain. For example, one may perceive that one's racing heart, profuse sweating, and

extreme feelings of nervousness when shooting a basketball free throw are indicants of one's inability to successfully shoot the ball.

Given that mastery experiences, which arise from successful behavioral performance, are determinants of self-efficacy and given that self-efficacy is a determinant of behavior, it is clear that a reciprocal relationship between self-efficacy and behavior exists. For example, individuals with high efficacy to perform fitness class moves (i.e., in-class self-efficacy; DuCharme & Brawley, 1995) will likely enroll and participate in a fitness class. They will also exert great effort and persistence, which should facilitate adherence, which is a type of mastery experience. In turn, this mastery experience enhances in-class self-efficacy beliefs. Recent reviews of self-efficacy and exercise behavior capture this reciprocal relationship. Specifically, some reviews examine self-efficacy as a determinant of exercise adherence (e.g., McAuley & Courneya, 1993), and other reviews analyze self-efficacy as an outcome of exercise adherence (e.g., McAuley, 1994).

Another important construct in self-efficacy theory is outcome expectations. Specifically, outcome expectations are defined as beliefs concerning the likely consequences that a behavior produces (Bandura, 1986, 1997). Thus, outcomes are not the behavioral performance itself, but the outcomes that result from the behavior. For example, lifting weights for an hour each day is the behavior, whereas the resultant muscle gain and weight loss are the outcomes. According to self-efficacy theory, outcome expectations take three major forms: (1) physical outcomes of the behavior, (2) social outcomes of the behavior, and (3) self-evaluative reactions to the behavior. Within each form, positive and negative expectations can exist and serve as either incentives or disincentives of behavioral performance.

A question that naturally arises is: When do outcome expectations and self-efficacy account for significant variation in behavior? According to self-efficacy theory, outcome expectations do not account for significant variation, beyond self-efficacy, when predicting behaviors that are highly contingent on the quality of performance. In these situations, how well an individual expects to perform (i.e., self-efficacy) also determines the outcomes an individual expects. For example, one who is highly confident that she can swim faster than any other competitor in the 200 meter backstroke at the Olympics will also expect to receive, if successful, certain outcomes (e.g., social outcomes such as recognition; monetary rewards such as product endorsement packages). Such outcomes occur directly as a result of the swimmer's performance, and thus would not significantly contribute to the prediction of swimming performance beyond self-efficacy.

In contrast to this situation, many outcomes in exercise and sport are not directly contingent on performance quality. Lack of contingency can occur in two ways. First, a lack of contingency can occur when extraneous factors, in addition to performance quality, impact sought-after outcomes. For example, an individual may cycle for an hour each day to lose weight and gain the outcome of social approval but not shed any pounds because he or she has maintained a high fat and caloric diet (i.e., the extraneous factor). Second, a lack of contingency can occur when no behavior can produce the desired outcomes. For example, an unranked college football team may play the best game of its season and still lose to a superior, number-one-ranked team. Thus, when a lack of contingency exists between performance quality and outcomes, outcome expectations may be an important predictor of behavior and account for significant variance in addition to self-efficacy (Bandura, 1986, 1997).

In the exercise domain, both outcome expectations and self-efficacy have been examined. However, no work has been done that summarizes the findings of both self-efficacy *and* outcome expectancy studies. Thus, the next section presents a sampling of the most recent reviews of self-efficacy in the exercise domain. In this section, reviews are presented that summarize the literature on (1) self-efficacy as a determinant of exercise behavior, (2) self-efficacy as an outcome of exercise adherence, and (3) the measurement of self-efficacy. This is followed by suggestions for future research, and then a brief section on outcome expectations.

Self-Efficacy Theory Reviews

Table 27.3 contains a sampling of the most recent reviews of the self-efficacy construct in the exercise/physical activity domain. Information contained in Table 27.3 includes (1) type of review (e.g., narrative), (2) study inclusion criteria, (3) number of studies included (if able to be determined), (4) focus of the review (e.g., self-efficacy as a determinant or outcome of exercise, measurement of self-efficacy), (5) main conclusions, and (6) limitations of the reviewed studies as cited by the authors.

As seen in Table 27.3, the most recent reviews of self-efficacy in the exercise domain are narrative in nature. To date, no meta-analytical reviews have been conducted on self-efficacy studies in the exercise domain. Despite this lack of a statistical summary of effect sizes, the narrative reviews indicate support for self-efficacy as a *determinant*

of exercise/physical activity behavior, and an *outcome* of exercise/physical activity behavior.

Specifically, three reviews report that self-efficacy is influential on exercise adherence in various populations (e.g., asymptomatic, diseased communities; Bandura, 1997; McAuley & Courneya, 1993; McAuley & Mihalko, 1998). However, only one review indicates the amount of variance accounted for in exercise adherence by self-efficacy. Specifically, McAuley and Mihalko reported that the reviewed studies had R^2s ranging from .04 to .26. These values represent small to moderate effect sizes (Green, 1991). Moreover, the reviews indicate that self-efficacy exerts differential impacts on exercise adherence over time. For example, McAuley and Mihalko concluded that self-efficacy exerts the greatest impact on adherence when individuals are initiating a regular exercise program or attempting long-term maintenance of regular exercise. Although not a primary focus of any of the reviews, it is suggested that certain variables may moderate the relationship between self-efficacy and exercise adherence (McAuley & Courneya, 1993). For example, one moderator may be gender. Specifically, males have been found to have higher perceptions of exercise self-efficacy at the onset of an exercise program compared to females (cf. McAuley & Courneya, 1993). Despite encouraging findings regarding moderators of this efficacy-adherence relationship, evidence is minimal, and thus, additional empirical evidence is required.

Recall that self-efficacy theory (Bandura, 1986, 1997) hypothesizes that self-efficacy is also a determinant of affect, thought patterns, intention, effort expenditure, and perseverance. McAuley and Mihalko (1998) briefly describe at least some of the relationships between self-efficacy and these outcomes in the exercise domain. Specifically, it is reported that self-efficacy is significantly related to the type of attributions (i.e., a type of thought pattern) provided for a behavioral outcome. That is, highly efficacious individuals indicate attributions of high personal control and stability. Efficacy beliefs have also shown consistent effects on exercise intention and effort expenditure (e.g., peak heart rate, ratings of perceived exertion). This latter effect is moderate in nature, typically ranging from R^2 of .30 to .53. In summary, many of the reviews included in Table 27.3 provide narrative support for the relationship between self-efficacy and various outcomes (e.g., exercise intention and behavior) as hypothesized by self-efficacy theory.

Self-efficacy theory (Bandura, 1986, 1997) also hypothesizes that self-efficacy is an *outcome* of exercise

Table 27.3 Self-Efficacy Reviews

Review and Type	Inclusion Criteria	Number of Studies	Focus	Main Conclusions	Limitations of Reviewed Studies
McAuley & Mihalko, 1998 Narrative	Studies in which self-efficacy was either a determinant or an outcome of exercise	85	Primarily on the measurement of SE. Brief summary on SE as a determinant and an outcome of exercise adherence	(1) Six types of SE measures have been used: behavioral, barriers, disease-specific/health behavior, perceived behavioral control, general, and other. (2) SE has a small to moderate relationship with exercise adherence. (3) SE influences various thought patterns (i.e., attributions, intrinsic motivation, optimism, self-esteem) and exercise intention. (4) SE has a moderate relationship with measures of effort expenditure (e.g., peak heart rate, perceived exertion ratings). SE related to physiological responses (e.g., peak treadmill heart rate). Most consistent findings in clinical populations (e.g., coronary heart disease, chronic obstructive lung disease). (5) Acute and long-term exercise programs influence specific and general SE beliefs.	Internal consistency of SE measures not frequently reported
Bandura, 1997 Narrative	Not stated	Not explicitly stated	SE as a *determinant* of exercise adoption and adherence.	(1) Efficacy in abilities to make exercise a habit fosters exercise adoption. (2) Self-regulatory efficacy is most relevant to sustaining adherence. (3) Dropouts from exercise programs are most likely individuals with low efficacy beliefs and high outcome expectations.	None stated
McAuley, 1994 Narrative	Selected studies in which (1) SE was the outcome; (2) exercise/physical activity was used in attempts to influence SE; (3) pre- and post-SE mean values were reported.	16	SE as an *outcome* of exercise/physical activity.	(1) Exercise/physical activity exerts consistent and robust effects on SE. (2) These effects are consistent across acute and long-term exercise, gender, age, and study designs.	(1) Diverse SE measures and methods used across studies. (2) Minimal longitudinal and randomized designs. (3) Minimal follow-up assessments. (4) Inconsistencies in methods, definitions, and measurements. (5) Some SE measures are conceptually and psychometrically suspect.
McAuley & Courneya, 1993 Narrative	Selected studies in three domains in the adult population: (1) SE and the behavioral epidemiology of exercise; (2) SE, exercise adherence, and diseased populations; (3) SE, exercise adherence, and asymptomatic populations.	Not explicitly stated	SE as a *determinant* of exercise behavior.	(1) Epidemiological evidence supports a positive relationship between SE and exercise adherence in symptomatic and normal populations. (2) SE influences physical activity performance and adherence in diseased populations. (3) SE consistently influences the adoption and maintenance of exercise behavior in asymptomatic populations.	(1) Cross-sectional designs. (2) Self-report measures of physical activity. (3) Lack of prospective designs. (4) Multitude of methods for assessing SE.

Note. SE = self-efficacy beliefs.

behavior (i.e., mastery experiences). The reviews included in Table 27.3 (i.e., McAuley, 1994; McAuley & Mihalko, 1998) provide narrative support for this relationship. Specifically, both acute (e.g., graded exercise tests) and long-term (e.g., fitness class programs) exercise has been found to enhance perceptions of efficacy. This increase in self-efficacy occurs in both females and males of various ages (e.g., younger to older healthy but sedentary adults; McAuley & Courneya, 1993).

In conclusion, this sampling of recent reviews provide robust narrative support for self-efficacy as a determinant of exercise behavior, and self-efficacy as an outcome of exercise behavior. The consistency of these relationships is encouraging considering the variable nature of the studies included in the reviews. For example, McAuley (1994) included studies in which the mean age ranged from 16 to 73 years and the sample sizes ranged from 27 to 119. Sample sizes were not included in any of the other reviews. In addition, study populations varied to a great extent. For example, in the McAuley and Mihalko (1998) review, the populations ranged from healthy to clinical (e.g., arthritic). Finally, the type of exercise behavior examined varied greatly across the reviewed studies. For example, studies examined adherence to exercise behavior such as walking, strength training, volleyball, exercise as part of a cardiac rehabilitation program, or aerobic dance.

Measurement Reviews of Self-Efficacy

One measurement review of self-efficacy in the exercise domain has been published (McAuley & Mihalko, 1998). After reviewing 85 studies, six categories of self-efficacy measures were identified: behavioral, barriers, disease-specific/health behavior, perceived behavioral control, general, and other. Despite this diversity of exercise-related self-efficacy measures, the relationship between self-efficacy and exercise behavior is consistent. This consistency once again supports the robustness of the self-efficacy–adherence relationship.

It is important to note that the diversity of exercise-related self-efficacy measures is not particularly surprising. Specifically, self-efficacy perceptions involve beliefs about specific skills and abilities needed for a given behavioral performance (Bandura, 1986, 1997). Taking exercise as an example, it may not be sufficient for individuals to simply have efficacy in their ability to perform a particular exercise (i.e., behavioral self-efficacy). Individuals may also have to be efficacious in their ability to overcome exercise-related barriers (i.e., barrier self-efficacy) and schedule the exercise session into the day (i.e., scheduling

self-efficacy). Clearly, assessing efficacy beliefs in all abilities important for performance of the exercise would be beneficial in accounting for a greater amount of variance in exercise behavior than when only one type of efficacy belief is assessed.

Future Research on Self-Efficacy

As outlined above, future researchers should assess a variety of efficacy beliefs when predicting the outcome of exercise behavior. This assessment should include specific type of efficacy beliefs as outlined by McAuley and Mihalko (1998) when applicable to the population of interest under investigation. Additional type(s) of efficacy beliefs that have been examined more recently should also be assessed when applicable. For example, Gyurcsik and Brawley (1999) found that inconsistent and beginner exercisers' confidence in their ability to cope with acute, or day-to-day, exercise-related thoughts (called coping self-efficacy) may be an important type of confidence to possess in the exercise domain. Specifically, coping self-efficacy was predictive of the case with which individuals made decisions to exercise.

When examining the self-efficacy–adherence relationship, future researchers should also address the limitations of the studies that were reviewed in Table 27.3. Limitations, as cited by the reviewers, include design and measurement issues. The design issues include a lack of prospective/longitudinal designs, randomized designs, and inadequate follow-up. The measurement issues include inconsistent interpretations of self-efficacy, which can lead to different operational definitions. This, in turn, makes it difficult to compare results across studies. Additional measurement issues include the use of psychometrically suspect measures of self-efficacy and the self-report nature of physical activity. Researchers should also analyze the reciprocal nature of the self-efficacy–adherence relationship. Specifically, the majority of past research has examined either self-efficacy as a determinant *or* as an outcome of exercise adherence. Through prospective study, future research would contribute to the existing knowledge in this area by unraveling the reciprocal nature of the relationship between self-efficacy and adherence.

Researchers should also determine potential moderators (e.g., gender) of the self-efficacy–adherence relationship. Specifically, at this time, a consistent and robust relationship has been found to exist between these two constructs. The next step in this research area should be to examine under what circumstances this relationship is the strongest. Finally, to provide a robust test of the self-efficacy construct in the exercise domain, it is prudent for researchers to include those outcomes that, in addition to exercise behavior, are hypothesized to be influenced by self-efficacy. Such outcomes should include affect, thought patterns, motivation, effort, and persistence.

Outcome Expectation Reviews

No comprehensive review of outcome expectations in the exercise domain exists to date. However, a recent edited book chapter by Dawson, Gyurcsik, Culos-Reed, and Brawley (in press) provided a selective review of such studies. They concluded that in studies where outcome expectations have been measured and studied in conjunction, but not confounded, with self-efficacy, outcome expectations predict behavioral *intentions* over and above the independent predictiveness of self-efficacy. Thus, although research on the predictiveness of outcome expectations on exercise *behavior* is relatively scant, the findings are promising. Within this selective review, Dawson et al. outline several issues related to outcome expectancy research in the exercise domain. First, it is unclear when outcome expectations exert a stronger influence on exercise intention and behavior than self-efficacy. According to self-efficacy theory (Bandura, 1986, 1997), when individuals are beginning an exercise program, outcome expectations should play a larger role than efficacy beliefs in helping to motivate the behavior. However, as an individual gains mastery experiences, efficacy beliefs should be more influential.

Second, it is unclear what specific types of outcome expectations are most influential of motivated exercise behavior over time (Dawson et al., in press). Recall that self-efficacy theory (Bandura, 1986, 1997) classifies outcome expectations into (1) pleasant or aversive physical outcomes, (2) positive or negative social outcomes, and (3) positive or negative self-evaluative reactions to the behavior. The specific type of expectancy that motivates people early in an exercise program may be different from the type that motivates them later in a program. For example, one may begin a regular program of walking because of expectations to gain the positive physical outcome of weight loss. However, once the desired weight is lost, it would be erroneous to assume that the weight loss expectation continues to motivate the person. Rather, it may be that other outcomes, such as praise through social recognition or feelings of less stress and increased energy after exercise, contribute to continued behavior.

A third issue focuses on the measurement of outcome expectations (Dawson et al., in press). Specifically, in the past, outcome expectations have not always been assessed because it was assumed that most exercise and sport behavior is highly motivated and thus incentives are always operating. From a prediction viewpoint, two alternatives are possible. The first alternative is where incentives are functioning somewhat like a constant with motivation from this source not varying and thus not contributing to the prediction of behavior. The second alternative is that other activities that compete for time with exercise may be more valued or have greater incentive than exercise. To assume there is no need to assess and predict using outcome expectations may be erroneous. Consider, for example, individuals who wish to begin an exercise program or initiate a new program. They may understand the likelihood of attaining certain outcomes (i.e., high outcome likelihood) associated with regular exercise but may value more highly the outcomes (i.e., high outcome value) associated with inactivity (e.g., socializing with friends, enjoyment that arises from having the time to watch a favorite television program) compared to exercise outcomes (e.g., weight loss, increased energy). Thus, outcome expectation might vary for this individual and others like him or her. By not measuring outcome expectation and value, it may be inaccurately concluded that outcome expectations are not predictive of exercise behavior and are valued, when in fact the outcomes are only moderately valued and thus unlikely to motivate behavior consistently. A valuable predictor of the variation in behavior may be overlooked.

Dawson et al. (in press) suggest that when assessing outcome expectations as a composite of outcome likelihood and outcome value, a statistical flag must be waved. Specifically, calculating an overall outcome expectancy value as a sum of all of the multiplicative outcome expectancy composites (i.e., sum of outcome likelihood X outcome value items) is problematic. The problem arises because the size of the correlation and thus the amount of variance accounted for in the criterion variable by the composite vary depending on the numerical scale used to measure each component (see Evans, 1991, for a full discussion).

As one solution, it was suggested to use a specific multiple regression analysis. This type of analysis involves calculating three predictor variables: (1) the sum of the first component variable (e.g., sum of five outcome likelihoods), (2) the sum of the second component variable (e.g., sum of five outcome values), and (3) an interaction term derived from multiplying these two summed variables. The next step is to regress the criterion on each of these three variables with the interaction term being entered last. This analysis is the same as testing for moderation (cf. Baron & Kenny, 1986). If the interaction term is significant, then the interaction of the two summed variables adds unique variance to the prediction of the criterion variable.

Future Research Using Outcome Expectancy

Future research employing the outcome expectancy construct should be longitudinal in nature. Such studies would help to determine when and what type of outcome expectations are influential on exercise intention and behavior over time. Researchers should also assess both outcome likelihood and outcome value and analyze the overall outcome expectancy construct appropriately. Finally, investigations should be directed toward assessing the influence of both outcome expectancy and self-efficacy on motivated exercise behavior. According to self-efficacy theory (Bandura, 1986, 1997), when outcomes are not directly contingent on performance quality, outcome expectations may explain further variation in motivation and behavior in addition to efficacy beliefs.

Conclusions

Self-efficacy theory (Bandura, 1986, 1997) has been used extensively to examine motivated exercise behavior. In this theory, the self-efficacy construct has been found to be a consistent determinant and outcome of exercise behavior across various study populations (e.g., healthy, diseased, middle-aged adults, older adults). Typically, the effect of the efficacy-adherence relationship has varied from small to moderate. Although research on the outcome expectancy construct in the exercise domain is relatively scant, the results are promising. Specifically, outcome expectations have been found to account for significant variation in exercise intention and behavior in addition to that accounted for by self-efficacy. Thus, researchers in both exercise and sport should consider including both outcome expectations and self-efficacy in their investigations. Understanding when each social cognition is predictive of intention and behavior over time may provide useful information to future interventionists who have the goal of enhancing adherence to motivated exercise or sport behavior.

Self-efficacy theory is concerned with the role of the person (personal cognitive factors) within the triadic interaction described in social-cognitive theory. As well, self-efficacy beliefs are pivotal in the causal structure of social-cognitive theory because they not only are independent determinants of behavior but they also influence other determinants of behavior in the theory. This theory is described next to clarify the relationship of efficacy to other social-cognitive constructs.

SOCIAL-COGNITIVE THEORY

Bandura's (1986) social-cognitive theory (SCT) is a broad theoretical framework for analyzing and understanding human cognitions, motivations, actions, and related emotions. Only the core premises are introduced in this chapter. SCT has as an important central assumption, the principle of *triadic reciprocal causation*. This principle stresses the interaction among cognition (personal factors: cognitive, emotional, biological), behavior, and environment in determining causation. The reciprocity inherent in this interaction suggests that each factor in the interaction may help to determine the others. It is important to realize that being reciprocal does not mean that the factors are influencing one another simultaneously or in equal strength.

Consider this brief description. Psychologists have demonstrated that humans respond in affective, cognitive, and behavioral ways to environmental circumstances. Through thought (cognition), we attempt to establish control over their own actions (behavior). Such thoughts and behaviors may influence the social environment and concurrently or subsequently impact on our affective, cognitive, and biological states. Note that everything in SCT does not influence everything else either equally and/or simultaneously, but all factors are important to understand behavior. Bandura's (1986) theory is not another name for social learning theory. It goes well beyond issues about learning to discuss self-regulation and motivation processes, and it includes psychosocial phenomena not examined by social learning theory. Learning, in SCT, is considered primarily as the acquisition of knowledge via cognitive processing of information. This contrasts with the perspective that social learning theory is a conditioning model of response acquisition.

SCT offers several important assumptions:

1. People have the capacity to symbolize, which allows them to internalize their experiences, develop new courses of action, predict outcomes by considering personal hypothesis testing, and communicate complex ideas and experiences.

2. People are self-reflective and can analyze their own thoughts/feelings. This is important for personal control of thoughts and behavior.

3. People are capable of self-regulation by means of directly controlling their own actions, being selective about entering situations that influence their behavior, or altering social-environmental conditions that influence their

behavior. People set their own standards for behavior and then self-evaluate their behavior versus these standards. People create personal incentives that motivate and guide their actions.

4. People learn vicariously by observing others (thereby reducing hit-or-miss attempts at learning).

SCT also assumes that behavior is goal-directed through anticipation and prediction. Bandura refers to this as "forethought." A person's capacity for forethought and intentional action is dependent on symbolizing capabilities (see 1 above). Self-efficacy theory suggests that all processes of psychological and behavioral change function through the alteration of a person's sense of mastery (i.e., self-efficacy beliefs about personal capabilities).

A number of main determinants of behavior in SCT are pointed out in the beginning of the chapter and have conceptual overlap with other theories (e.g., TRA and TPB). Bandura (1995) argues that SCT is the most comprehensive of the social psychological and health behavior theories. He notes that research designed to maximize explained variance in, for example, exercise-related functioning should use the full array of primary sociocognitive determinants hypothesized to contribute to behavioral causation. The array of determinants in SCT can be described as:

1. Self-efficacy beliefs that function as a central regulator in SCT because they influence cognition, behavior, and affect. However, they also are central because they are hypothesized to act on other determinants (e.g., aspirations, commitments, expected outcomes).

2. Outcome expectations, which Bandura classifies into physical, social, and self-evaluative types. These can be physically beneficial or detrimental, socially favorable or even adverse, and positive or negative assessments of self.

3. Cognized goals, which can be proximal (specific and more immediate) or distal (general and more long-range). The former goals tend to be more influential at present, thereby stimulating effort and action. Bandura points out that "intentions" and proximal goals are basically the same concept.

4. Impediments, which can be grouped as personal and situational as well as system-level in nature. The former are perceived barriers (e.g., perceived lack of time), whereas the latter are the absence of a needed resource (e.g., access to a nearby exercise facility).

The breadth of SCT is obvious. Bandura (1986) discusses SCT as applied to a multitude of broad psychosocial constructs such as anxiety, cognitive development, freedom and determinism, observational learning, and gender-role adoption. He points out that the time lag in the interaction of person, behavior, and environment is such that it allows for assessing segments of triadic interaction without assessing every possible interaction at the same time. Thus, "segments" of interaction within the causal processes can be experimentally considered. As well, the notion of reciprocal triadic interaction is useful when considering a model as the foundation for interactions.

Research Perspective: SCT

Perhaps a way to appreciate the varied use (or claims of use) of SCT is to examine its utilization with respect to the prediction of behavior and with respect to interventions to change physical activity. No attempt will be made to examine all possible studies that might have employed a social-cognitive framework. Instead, the focus here is specifically on reviews of physical activity research. The *American Journal of Preventive Medicine* (Blair & Morrow, 1998) reviews 12 different physical activity interventions. Seven of these reviews deal with different populations, settings, and intervention types. Three of the reviews, Baranowski, Anderson, and Carmack (1998), Marcus, Owen, Forsyth, Cavill, and Fridinger (1998), and Stone, McKenzie, Walk, and Booth (1998) clearly delineate the type of theory that served as the foundation for either predictive or intervention studies.

In the exercise/physical activity literature, there is more that can be said about the frequency of claimed use of SCT than about the support of the theory. This is not a criticism of the theory itself but speaks to the inconsistency in the way the theory and its constructs are operationalized. Few researchers operationalize a large core of social-cognitive factors (i.e., physical, social, self-evaluative outcome expectancies; proximal and distal goals; self-efficacy; personal and situational impediments, health or activity system impediments). The Baranowski et al. review (1998) contained 11 SCT interventions conducted with children or adults. Seven of these interventions examined mediating variables from SCT. Three of the interventions demonstrated an observed relationship between an SCT variable and the dependent variable of physical activity.

Regarding the SCT–physical activity predictive studies in the same review, 26 were examined. Few included the majority of SCT variables. Sixteen studies examined self-efficacy and intention (proximal goal); nine studies used barriers (impediments) as a predictor; and 11 studies used various outcome expectations as predictors. Results across the studies that reported findings about self-efficacy indicated that it was the most reliable predictor of the various forms of physical activity. In 9 of the 11 studies, barriers demonstrated significant beta weights for their contribution to the variance accounted for by the model (R^2). Mixed support was found for the contribution of outcome expectancy to the prediction of physical activity, but this could vary depending on whether participants were inactive or just beginning activity versus being an active participant (see the earlier section in this chapter regarding outcome expectancies and self-efficacy).

The review by Stone et al. (1998) focused on children and youth and reported 17 completed school and community interventions and 9 "in-progress" interventions in the same two areas ($n = 26$). The major goals of most interventions varied, but all included as a part that of increasing physical activity. Although the review was not designed to report on the SCT–physical activity link, it is noteworthy that 19 of the 26 interventions reported using SCT as a theoretical foundation. The review of Marcus et al. (1998) included 28 studies of media-based or media-based–plus–face-to-face interventions. They ranged in scope as follows: (1) the state through national level in promoting involvement in physical activity, (2) health care system, (3) workplace, and (4) community (including underserved populations). Nine of the 28 studies were based on SCT as a foundation for the intervention. Effects of the interventions were mixed. The review did not present an evaluation of whether SCT-mediating variables were measured and whether these mediators were linked to the primary study outcome (i.e., a demonstrated significant relationship). Therefore, definitive support for SCT cannot be concluded or refuted.

Although these three reviews of interventions and predictive studies are not all-encompassing, they do present a picture of the frequent use of SCT with some support for selected key relationships in the theory. The relationship most reliably observed across studies was the self-efficacy–physical activity relationship.

SCT Research and Physical Activity: Challenges

Systematic testing of large portions of the SCT remain a challenge for future research in exercise and physical activity. Given the reciprocal triadic interaction principle of the theory, it would be appropriate to consider prospective, longitudinal studies that would take into account the time lag that Bandura (1997) mentions will naturally occur for

various person, behavior, and environment interactions. Furthermore, different aspects of the theoretical links among efficacy, outcome expectations, goals, and impediments included in SCT could be examined systematically in physical activity and health situations without examining all of the SCT. At present, the most reliable relationship in the larger theory of SCT is the reciprocal relationship between self-efficacy and physical activity (cf. Bandura, 1997: health functioning, athletic functioning).

The SCT was a theory prominently featured in the reviews mentioned above. These same reviews included reports of the transtheoretical model. This model concerns behavior change and has great intuitive appeal to practitioners because of its promise for targeted intervention. An overview and critique of the transtheoretical model is presented next.

THE TRANSTHEORETICAL MODEL

The popularity of the transtheoretical model (TTM) in the health community, the exercise literature, and its use by practitioners far outweighs its objective research support. The popularity of the model can be attributed to a number of factors. First, the TTM's stages of readiness for change not only include people taking action, but also include most people who range from not thinking about taking action, to those who are unsure about taking action, to those taking initial action or maintaining a behavior. Second, the model acknowledges that change is dynamic, takes more than one attempt, and takes time. Third, because the model proposes that different processes influence an individual's readiness for change, it offers the potential to "match" an intervention to the state of readiness for change. This is perhaps the most intuitively appealing feature of the model. Fourth, the model emphasizes that multiple outcomes such as beliefs (e.g., self-efficacy, cost-benefit) are changing across the different stages of readiness, not just behavior.

The TTM (Prochaska, DiClemente, & Norcross, 1992) proposes that there are five discrete stages through which people pass in attempting health behavior change. The stages range from not thinking about any health behavior change (precontemplation) to a stage of maintaining successful change (maintenance). Each stage is progressive in the sense that the individual moves from a lack of awareness of the need for change to thinking actively about change, to making preparations for change, taking action, and eventually maintenance. Thus, the stages are logically named precontemplation, contemplation, preparation, action, and maintenance. The general description of stages that follows varies slightly with the exercise program (e.g., home-based or structured).

In the *precontemplation stage,* people have no intention for behavior change. They are not ready for change because there is no perceived need for it. An exercise-related criterion for estimating this stage is "currently inactive and do not intend to become active in the next six months."

Individuals in the *contemplative stage* are thinking about the need for change because they are aware of, for example, their level of physical inactivity and the risk associated with it. At this stage, however, people are not committed to the change they are contemplating. Important considerations they may think about are those strategies that might make change possible (e.g., joining a fitness club) and those outcomes that result from change (i.e., outcome expectancies). An exercise-related criterion for estimating this stage is "currently thinking about starting an exercise program, possibly within the next six months."

In the *preparation stage,* people make attempts to change and strongly intend to make more attempts in the future. Some effort has been made to change, particularly with those strategies that they contemplated would be feasible to enact change. Individuals may have strong incentive to change based on optimistic views about the outcomes from which they will benefit. Resources are assessed and action plans are made accordingly. An exercise-related criterion for estimating this stage is "currently preparing to initiate exercise or engage in recommended levels of activity within the next month."

In the *action stage,* individuals make deliberate attempts to surmount their perceived or real problems by changing their behavior, environmental circumstances, and experiences. Commitment to change is high and people monitor their efforts to change, often perceiving that they are trying hard. An exercise-related criterion for estimating this stage is "currently engaged in an activity program but for less than six months."

Finally, in the *maintenance stage,* people focus on their successes and try to avoid relapsing (e.g., stopping exercise, or becoming an irregular exerciser). Exercise is regular and people are confident in their ability to continue in this fashion. They tend to overcome obstacles to their regular activity. An exercise-related criterion for estimating this stage is "regularly active for more than six months."

The TTM also proposes 10 specific processes in which individuals engage as they move through the stages. The processes are both cognitive and behavioral. More of the cognitive-experimental processes are presumed to occur in the preparation stage, whereas more behavioral processes occur in the action and maintenance stages (cf. DiClemente, Fairhurst, & Piotrowski, 1995). The reader is referred to Prochaska et al. (1992) for a more detailed description about processes relative to addictive behaviors because there is very limited TTM process evidence in exercise research.

The TTM (also called the "stages of change" model) incorporates the idea that individuals change in a dynamic fashion but that this change is not necessarily a linear progression. Instead, it is proposed that people move in and out of stages in spiral fashion, circling in asymmetric behavioral patterns in and out of adjacent stages. This description sounds complex but really describes the cognitive and behavioral fluctuations people experience as they attempt to make a change and adjust according to their successes and failures at changing.

For example, individuals are thought to advance through the stages in sequential order, but relapse (i.e., failures or problems that may cause them to stop exercising) to a previous stage is possible. Thus, with attempts to make changes in their exercise/physical activity, they may experience regular progress from the contemplation to the preparation stage; however, progress may falter at the action stage (i.e., by exercising too hard or too frequently). Individuals who lapse may return to preparation to reconsider their strategies for change until they feel ready to gradually move toward action again. Similarly, individuals could move from the action to the maintenance stage, where their exercise is characterized by regular adherence. Adherence over time is frequently difficult for a host of reasons (cf. Dishman, 1994), and it is not uncommon for people to lapse back to the action stage (i.e., become more intermittent in their exercise patterns). In this example, they have to work harder, both cognitively and behaviorally, to regain the maintenance stage. Their readiness for change as well as their cognitive-experimental and behavioral processes are "characteristic" of the harder changes necessary to take regular action. Prochaska et al. (1992) argue that processes are related to the stages. Thus, certain processes are associated with earlier stages, and others are associated with later stages. This suggests that interventions should be matched to a given stage to address the processes and encourage "movement" from stage to stage.

The constructs of self-efficacy (Bandura, 1997) and decision balance from Janis and Mann's (1977) decision-making model are TTM components. Both constructs are thought to be useful in predicting movement through the stages. The construct of decision balance is operationalized to measure the relative importance an individual places on the advantages (pros) and disadvantages (cons) of, for example, engaging in exercise. When the cons are of greater importance than the pros, motivation to change behavior (i.e., move from being sedentary to engaging in exercise) is low. The converse is also assumed to be true. As would be expected in a stage model, the pro-versus-con balance is presumed to vary by stage.

Self-efficacy is presumed to reflect the confidence of individuals in their ability to change their behavior. Furthermore, this confidence should mediate attempts to change following the learning of self-regulation skills for a target behavior such as exercise. Self-efficacy is proposed to change with each stage, presumably increasing as individuals gain confidence, for example, through successful attempts to change their exercise behavior (i.e., mastery experience). Conversely, self-efficacy may decrease if individuals falter and spiral back to a prior behavioral stage.

Research Support for the TTM

If the health and physical activity literature were examined, it would be readily apparent that in the past decade, the number of TTM-related publications (i.e., journal articles, chapters, monographs) has been rapidly growing (the earliest publications began in approximately 1979; Joseph, Curtis, & Skinner, 1997). Much of the research, including the development/intervention of the model, was concerned with the addictions of tobacco and alcohol use (i.e., 44% of the TTM research as of 1997). However, the number of publications devoted to development/evaluation is small relative to studies applying or describing the TTM. Descriptive research frequently consisted of identifying the "stage" construct using a four- to five-item categorization algorithm that concerns an individual's intention to, for example, cease an addictive type behavior or to increase a health-promoting behavior (e.g., intent to be physically active). There are also multiple-item stage categorization instruments, but these are used infrequently in the exercise research.

The physical activity evidence claimed as support for the TTM ranges from (1) studies that link the stage categorization to the variables in another social-cognitive model (e.g., Courneya, 1995); to (2) studies that offer a cross-sectional description of exercisers where stages, pros and cons, and self-efficacy are the primary dependent measures (e.g., Marcus & Eaton, 1994); to (3) studies of physical activity interventions based on the model (e.g., Lombard, Lombard, & Winett, 1995).

In the *American Journal of Preventive Medicine* (Blair & Morrow, 1998) mentioned in the discussion of SCT, a num-

ber of TTM studies were reviewed (cf. Baranowski et al., 1998; Marcus et al., 1998). In these studies, the TTM was either the sole basis for planning the intervention or was used in combination with another theory (e.g., SCT). A careful scrutiny of the two reviews indicates that two of the four TTM-based physical activity interventions and three of the seven print- or telephone-mediated interventions offered what may be interpreted as partial support for the relationships proposed by the TTM. Evidence for the TTM in the former group of interventions would require measurement of mediating psychological mechanisms, as this is essential to link stage to mechanism. For example, contemplators would need to reflect lower efficacy and more cons (or fewer pros) than individuals in the preparation stage, or changes in mediating variables (e.g., processes, efficacy) would need to be predictive of changes in stage. Thus, partial support for TTM constructs and links can be claimed based on the data from the two studies that measured mediating variables.

Concerning the media-based interventions, the evidence for partial support indicated (1) that stage-matched print manuals produced greater change in stage progression than change produced by standard print materials given to a control group, and (2) that there was greater increased readiness of intervention subjects to adopt physical activity than controls after receiving treatments of face-to-face physician counseling followed by telephone contacts. Parallel behavioral evidence for this readiness was also demonstrated (i.e., walking).

Recall that in the physical activity review of theoretically based behavior change interventions (Baranowski et al., 1998), there was also a narrative review of studies where theoretical models were used to predict physical activity. The three findings from the TTM-based studies in this review can be summarized as follows. One study demonstrated expected cross-sectional differences between stages on minutes of self-reported physical activity (i.e., seven-day recall). A second study demonstrated that stage predicted minutes of self-reported activity (cross-sectional) as expected, but there was no predictive contribution from either pros/cons or self-efficacy. The third study employed a longitudinal design allowing for baseline prediction of six-month behavior. The predictor of baseline "stage" accounted for 28% of the variance in self-reported minutes of exercise at six months. As in the cross-sectional studies, baseline pros/cons and efficacy did not predict future exercise. In general, the effect sizes in these correlational studies ranged from an R^2 of .08 to .28, with the majority of the effects being small to moderate.

In light of the foregoing evidence, what can be concluded about the TTM and its support in the area of exercise and physical activity? Certainly, there are no complete tests of the entire TTM in physical activity. Thus, support must be considered only for certain hypotheses. The cross-sectional and longitudinal studies provide some modest evidence for the relationship between stage and activity. This support must be considered cautiously, however, because of the absence of a link between mediator variables (e.g., pros/cons, efficacy) and physical activity outcomes. Regarding the TTM interventions reported in both of the aforementioned reviews, fewer than half of the studies provided any test of the link between stage and mediating variables or between mediating variables and outcomes. In several cases, mediating (process) variables were not measured. At best, the evidence for relationships hypothesized by the TTM is mixed. This conclusion should be considered in concert with the fact that the TTM was the foundation for the intervention studies but its test was not the primary research objective. To appreciate what constitutes a test of the TTM or relationships within the model, it is necessary to consider both its strengths/advantages and weaknesses. The section that follows summarizes some of the major issues about the quality of current and future TTM research.

Critical Perspectives on the TTM

The TTM offers an intuitively appealing framework for tailoring interventions to an individual's readiness for behavior change. This appeal generates a "readiness" to adopt and use the model on the part of scientist and practitioner. Joseph et al. (1997) presented a variety of statistics on the TTM, such as rate of increase in publications over 15 years (i.e., 150 between 1979 and 1995), proportion of publications by field of inquiry (e.g., substance abuse constituted 45% compared to 17% for exercise), and publications by type of study. This last statistic indicated that the two main types of publication were description, which constituted 25% of the publications, and application, which comprised 44% of the publications. Thus, application types of publications outstripped all others, including theorizing (12%), testing the TTM (11%), and critiques (7%). There appears to have been a readiness to accept the TTM for application beyond any reasonable amount of validation evidence that would be expected for theories in behavioral science. This readiness includes an acceptance of any research evidence that favors the model and, conversely, for critics of the model, a readiness to reject any evidence that is not supportive of the entire model.

The following series of pros and cons about the TTM is instructive. Joseph et al. (1997) suggest these as pros of the TTM:

1. Dynamic nature.
2. Expansion of the potential to employ behavior change tactics across various states of readiness.
3. Emphasis on matching interventions to state of readiness.
4. Attempts to integrate concepts such as relapse, decision balance, and self-efficacy.
5. Flexibility to incorporate new constructs.

Prochaska and colleagues (1994) offered evidence in support of the TTM that can be described as a similar pattern of decision-balance changes across 12 different problem behaviors (including exercise). In a companion article, Prochaska (1994) also offered what he describes as strong and weak principles for the movement of individuals from precontemplation to action relative to the 12 problem behaviors. These studies are not presented here for reasons of brevity, yet the generality of the evidence (across 12 behaviors) seems compelling.

In contrast, if the cons of the TTM are considered, the evidence for the model is not as clear as claimed by supporters of the model. As is frequently the case when a model is comprehensive in scope, it is not examined in its entirety. The TTM is no exception. Joseph et al. (1997) summarized the cons of the TTM as follows:

1. Supporting evidence for distinct stages is weak and not consistent.
2. Evidence for the hypothesized relationship between the processes (cognitive-experiential and behavioral) and the stages is mixed (in the exercise domain, it is almost nonexistent).
3. The TTM is primarily descriptive rather than explanatory (e.g., characteristics within stages are described but causal processes are not tested).
4. The TTM fails to consider the impact of moderator variables such as individual differences (e.g., personality differences), comorbidities (i.e., different disease states experienced by the same individual: sedentary, obese, and diabetic), and social influences (i.e., socioeconomic status, culture).
5. Critics (e.g., Bandura, 1997) note that from a conceptual perspective, the model is at odds with itself.

Regarding the last criticism of the TTM, Bandura (1995) emphasizes that some of the borrowing and "integrating" of various models to construct the TTM places these borrowed models at odds with each other within the integrated TTM. Bandura also argues that the linkages between potential behavior change interventions and stages is debatable. Finally, he suggests that classifying a stage is done by how regularly an individual initiated or stopped a behavior or, in exercise, by an arbitrary six months duration of attempting or not attempting to exercise. Bandura's point is that this says nothing about which determinants of behavior are most influential at the point that would be useful to assist with the selection of a matched intervention.

Recently, Weinstein, Rothman, and Sutton (1998) discussed the conceptual and methodological aspects of the two most well-developed stage models of health behavior change: the TTM and the precaution-adoption-process model (cf. Weinstein & Sandman, 1992). In this article, Weinstein and colleagues critiqued their own precaution-adoption-process model as well as the TTM. Their conclusion, on reviewing the research in light of numerous conceptual/methodological issues, was that most of the evidence supporting both stage models was weak. Thus, Weinstein et al. offered on objective view of both models and provided suggestions for future research and better stage model tests.

THE DILEMMA FACING THEORETICALLY BASED INTERVENTIONS

For studying exercise and physical activity, a theoretical model has distinct advantages (Brawley, 1993). However, present theories do not account for large amounts of explained variance in health outcomes, even though reliable, but modest significant effects have been demonstrated.

Baranowski et al. (1998) argue that current theories do not completely predict behavior or behavior change. Second, they note that interventions do not appear to be creating substantial change in the mediating variables described by theory (e.g., mechanisms influencing behavior such as self-efficacy motivating persistence in following a diet). Consider the issues they present. Physical activity interventions are thought to function through mediating variables to influence the outcome of increased activity. An example would be an intervention that was designed to enhance self-efficacy (i.e., mediator), which, in turn, influences persistence and effort of behavior changes designed to encourage adherence. Baranowski et al. (1998) note that the intervention outcome is better adherence, but they would legitimately question whether it had been shown that self-efficacy had actually accounted for (i.e., in terms of a

demonstrated effect) the behavioral change in adherence as specified by the theory.

Current theories and models, such as those discussed in this chapter, do not predict behavior (account for the variability in target outcome) at a level much beyond an R^2 value of .30 to .40. For prediction, this effect size would be considered large according to effect size conventions in the social-behavioral sciences. However, to assess the effectiveness of interventions, a second portion of variance also requires examination. This portion is the amount of variance that the intervention creates in the mediator variable. Once again, based on the scientific evidence described in major literature reviews, it is clear that effect sizes are more often moderate than large (i.e., for reasons of measurement error, unassessed variables, and general error variance due to other factors).

Considered together, the intervention to mediator link and the mediator to outcome link describe the causal sequence or direct relationship between intervention and outcome. The less than perfect accounted for variance in the two portions of this sequence impose a limit on the variance that the intervention to outcome relationship can describe. Baranowski et al. (1997) statistically illustrate that the correlations that represent the indirect effects between the intervention to mediator and the mediator to outcome can be multiplied to reflect the direct effects of the intervention on the target outcome. Given that each of the first two correlations will invariably be less than R = 1.00, it follows that the direct product of the two correlations will be less than either one of these indirect effects.

For example, suppose (a) a social persuasion intervention produces an R of .50 in the mediator of self-efficacy and (b) self-efficacy is correlated with increased exercise adherence, R = .50. Baranowski et al. (1997, 1998) show that the cross-product of these two indirect effects leads to the direct R (a times b) of .25. Thus, the accounted for variance or $R(ab)^2$ would be 6.25% (.25 x .25 = .0625), indicating a modest amount of explained variability between intervention and outcome. The point of the example is that it clearly illustrates the need to improve the relationship demonstrated between theory and outcome and the impact of interventions on mediating variables.

Thus, in facing the acid test of the amount of explained variance in the intervention-mediator-outcome relationship, it appears that much more research is required. Baranowski et al. (1997) suggest that this emphasizes the critical importance of theory in the behavior change process. With this in mind, they offer a six-phase, task-oriented approach to developing an intervention. The first three phases dwell on behavior change theory development. However, the current practice of initially constructing comprehensive interventions for outcome evaluation does not follow a sequence of testing whether comprehensive interventions alter theoretically identified mediators or whether changes in these mediators affect the target health outcome. For the current practice to change, a necessary requirement should entail regular data gathering on mediating processes between baseline measurements and the eventual outcome assessment. For example, if the expected intervention outcome is improved aerobic capacity or exercise tolerance (i.e., a functional ability test), then the mediators assessed could be adherence to behavior change and self-efficacy for mastering regimens leading to those outcomes.

Theory development for the purpose of behavior change does not require the immediate discard of existing theories that have substantive predictive support such as the first two theories presented in this chapter. Instead, new ideas for intervention should be examined in the context of existing theories and established results.

In addition, Baranowski et al. (1997) suggest that existing data sets should be analyzed to establish the amount of behavior change that can be produced as a function of demonstrated increments in already identified mediating variables. For example, how much of a change in self-efficacy for adherence-related behaviors (mediator) and how much of a change in daily, moderate-level exercise adherence (mediator) is required to produce a measurable increase in the outcome of exercise tolerance of the older adult?

It is clear that investigators need to think more critically from a conceptual perspective about the unique challenges posed in both testing theory and using theory-driven interventions for behavior change. Scientifically demonstrating that theory-driven interventions work requires convincing evidence at several levels. However, if sport and exercise psychologists wish to avoid the limitations characteristic of interventions in other areas (e.g., community health; Baranowski et al., 1998), efforts must be directed toward facing the unique challenges described earlier. To continue the present course means conducting more interventions where the mechanism producing a desired outcome remains unclear and the chances of producing the outcome are no better than chance.

CONCLUSION

The issues raised at the beginning of this chapter related to the influence of specific social-cognitive theories for understanding physical activity and using physical activity to promote health. These theories were selected for discussion based on their current influence and/or their strong research base. Reliance on sound theory and on a better translation of theoretical variables into behavior change mechanisms that produce specific behavioral/psychosocial outcomes is a desirable mandate for scientific research and practice in sport and exercise/physical activity. However, it should be recognized from the discussion that improvements in science and practice are necessary to develop and validate these theories with regard to their integral place in changing exercise and physically active behavior. In reciprocal fashion, these theories are meant to be improved as a result of improved and intertwined science and practice. Baranowski et al. (1997, 1998) have offered an integrated framework for advancing on both fronts that spans the continuum from the experiment to the adoption of effective physical activity interventions in the community.

Armed with the knowledge that has been provided about these influential theories relative to physical activity, and with a framework for future research, can sport and exercise psychologists rise to the challenge of making improvements in their science and practice of motivating physically active behavior? Meeting the challenge over the next 10 years offers the promise of being less humble about our efforts to understand and intervene than has been (Kirschenbaum, 1992), and is currently the case. Meeting the challenge may make a difference in knowing how to motivate people to improve their own health using physical activity.

REFERENCES

Ajzen, I. (1985). From intentions to actions: A theory of planned behavior. In J. Kuhl & J. Beckmann (Eds.), *Action control: From cognition to behavior* (pp. 11–40). Berlin, Germany: Springer-Verlag.

Ajzen, I. (1991). The theory of planned behavior. *Organizational Behavior and Human Decision Processes, 50,* 179–211.

Ajzen, I., & Fishbien, M. (1980). *Understanding attitudes and predicting behavior.* Englewood Cliffs, NJ: Prentice Hall.

Ajzen, I., & Madden, T.J. (1986). Prediction of goal-directed behavior: Attitudes, intentions, and perceived behavioral control. *Journal of Experimental and Social Psychology, 22,* 453–474.

Bandura, A. (1986). *Social foundations of thought and action.* New York: Prentice-Hall.

Bandura, A. (1995, March). *Moving into forward gear in health promotion and disease prevention.* Keynote address presented at the annual meeting of the Society of Behavioral Medicine, San Diego, CA.

Bandura, A. (1997). *Self-efficacy: The exercise of control*. New York: Freeman.

Baranowski, T., Anderson, C., & Carmack, D. (1998). Mediating variable framework in physical activity interventions: How are we doing? How might we do better? *American Journal of Preventive Medicine, 15,* 266–297.

Baranowski, T., Lin, L.S., Wetter, D.W., Resnicow, K., & Davis-Hearn, M.D. (1997). Theory as mediating variables: Why aren't community interventions working as desired? *Annals of Epidemiology, 57,* 389–595.

Baron, R.M., & Kenny, D.A. (1986). The moderator-mediator variable distinction in social psychological research: Conceptual, strategic, and statistical considerations. *Journal of Personality and Social Psychology, 51,* 1173–1182.

Biddle, S., Sallis, J., & Cavill, N. (Eds.). (1998). *Young and active? Young people and health-enhancing physical activity: Evidence and implications.* London, England: Health Education Authority.

Blair, S.N., & Morrow, J.R. (Eds.). (1998). Theme issue: Physical activity interventions. *American Journal of Preventive Medicine, 15*(4).

Brawley, L.R. (1993). The practicality of using social psychological theory for exercise and health research and interventions. *Journal of Applied Sport Psychology, 5,* 99–115.

Brawley, L.R., & Culos-Reed, S.N. (2000). Studying adherence to therapeutic regimens: Overviews, theories, and recommendations. *Controlled Clinical Trials, 21.*

Brawley, L.R., Martin, K.A., & Gyurcsik, N.C. (1998). Problems in assessing perceived barriers to exercise: Confusing obstacles with attributions and excuses. In J.L. Duda (Ed.), *Advances in sport and exercise psychology measurement* (pp. 337–350). Morgantown, WV: Fitness Information Technology.

Brawley, L.R., & Rodgers, W.M. (1993). Social-psychological aspects of fitness promotion. In P. Seraganian (Ed.), *Exercise psychology: The influence of physical exercise on psychological processes* (pp. 254–298). New York: Wiley.

Conner, M., & Armitage, C.J. (1998). Extending the theory of planned behavior: A review and avenues for further research. *Journal of Applied Social Psychology, 28,* 1429–1464.

Courneya, K.S. (1994). Predicting repeated behavior from intention: The issue of scale correspondence. *Journal of Applied Social Psychology, 24,* 580–594.

Courneya, K.S. (1995). Understanding readiness for regular activity in older individuals: An application of the theory of planned behavior. *Health Psychology, 14,* 80–87.

Courneya, K.S., & Friedenreich, C.M. (1997a). Determinants of exercise during colorectal cancer treatment: An application of the theory of planned behavior. *Oncology Nursing Forum, 24,* 1715–1723.

Courneya, K.S., & Friedenreich, C.M. (1997b). Relationship between exercise during treatment and current quality of life among survivors of breast cancer. *Journal of Psychosocial Oncology, 15,* 35–57.

Courneya, K.S., & Friedenreich, C.M. (1997c). Relationship between exercise pattern across the cancer experience and current quality of life in colorectal cancer survivors. *Journal of Alternative and Complementary Medicine, 3,* 215–226.

Courneya, K.S., Friedenreich, C.M., Arthur, K., & Bobick, T.M. (1999). Understanding exercise motivation in colorectal cancer patients: A prospective study using the theory of planned behavior. *Rehabilitation Psychology, 44,* 68–84.

Courneya, K.S., & McAuley, E. (1993). Predicting physical activity from intention: Conceptual and methodological issues. *Journal of Sport & Exercise Psychology, 15,* 50–62.

Dawson, K.A., Gyurcsik, N.C., Culos-Reed, S.N., & Brawley, L.R. (in press). Perceived control: A construct that bridges theories of motivated behavior. In G.C. Roberts (Ed.), *Advances in motivation in sport and exercise.* Champaign, IL: Human Kinetics.

DiClemente, C.C., Fairhurst, S.K., & Piotrowski, N.A. (1995). Self-efficacy and addictive behaviors. In J.E. Maddux (Ed.), *Self-efficacy, adaptation and adjustment: Theory, research and application* (pp. 109–141). New York: Plenum Press.

Diener, E., & Emmons, R.A. (1985). The independence of positive and negative affect. *Journal of Personality and Social Psychology, 47,* 1105–1117.

Dishman, R.K. (Ed.). (1994). *Advances in exercise adherence.* Champaign, IL: Human Kinetics.

DuCharme, K.A., & Brawley, L.R. (1995). Predicting the intentions and behavior of exercise initiates using two forms of self-efficacy. *Journal of Behavioral Medicine, 18,* 479–497.

Duda, J.L., Smart, A.E., & Tappe, M.K. (1989). Predictors of adherence in the rehabilitation of athletic injuries: An application of personal investment theory. *Journal of Sport & Exercise Psychology, 11,* 367–381.

Evans, M.G. (1991). The problem of analyzing multiplicative composites: Interactions revisited. *American Psychologist, 46,* 6–15.

Godin, G. (1993). The theories of reasoned action and planned behavior: Overview of findings, emerging research problems and usefulness for exercise promotion. *Journal of Applied Sport Psychology, 5,* 141–157.

Godin, G., & Kok, G. (1996). The theory of planned behavior: A review of its applications to health-related behaviors. *American Journal of Health Promotion, 11,* 87–98.

Green, S.B. (1991). How many subjects does it take to do a regression analysis? *Multivariate Behavioral Research, 26,* 499–510.

Gyurcsik, N.C., & Brawley, L.R. (1999). Exercise and the power of positive thinking. *The Weight Control Digest, 9,* 865–867.

Hausenblas, H.A., Carron, A.V., & Mack, D.E. (1997). Application of the theories of reasoned action and planned behavior to exercise behavior: A meta-analysis. *Journal of Sport & Exercise Psychology, 19,* 36–51.

Janis, I.L., & Mann, L. (1977). *Decision-making: A psychological analysis of conflict, choice, and commitment.* New York: Free Press.

Joseph, J., Curtis, B., & Skinner, H. (1997). *Critical perspectives on the transtheoretical model and the stages of change* (Ontario Tobacco Research Unit: Working Papers Series No. 30). Toronto, Canada: Ontario Tobacco Research Unit.

Kirschenbaum, D.S. (1992). Elements of effective weight control programs: Implications for exercise and sport psychology. *Journal of Applied Sport Psychology, 4,* 77–93.

Lombard, D.N., Lombard, T., & Winett, R.A. (1995). Walking to meet health guidelines: The effect of prompting frequency and prompt structure. *Health Psychology, 14,* 164–170.

Leary, M.R. (1992). Self presentational processes in exercise and sport. *Journal of Sport & Exercise Psychology, 14,* 339–351.

Maddux, J.E., Brawley, L.R., & Boykin, A. (1995). Self-efficacy and healthy behavior: Prevention, promotion, and detection. In J.E. Maddux (Ed.), *Self-efficacy, adaptation, and adjustment: Theory, research, and application* (pp. 123–202). New York: Plenum Press.

Maddux, J.E., & Lewis, J. (1995). Self-efficacy and adjustment: Basic principles and issues. In J.E. Maddux (Ed.), *Self-efficacy, adaptation, and adjustment: Theory, research, and application* (pp. 37–68). New York: Plenum Press.

Maehr, M.L., & Braskamp, L.A. (1986). *The motivation factor: A theory of personal investment.* Lexington, MA: Lexington Books.

Marcus, B.H., & Eaton, C.A. (1994). Self-efficacy, decision-making, and stages of change: An integrative model of physical exercise. *Journal of Applied Social Psychology, 24,* 489–508.

Marcus, B.H., Owen, N., Forsyth, L.H., Cavill, N.A., & Fridinger, F. (1998). Physical activity interventions using mass media, print media, and information technology. *American Journal of Preventive Medicine, 15,* 362–378.

McAuley, E. (1994). Physical activity and psychosocial outcomes. In C. Bouchard, R.J. Shephard, & T. Stephens (Eds.), *Physical activity, fitness, and health: International proceedings and consensus statement* (pp. 551–568). Champaign, IL: Human Kinetics.

McAuley, E., & Courneya, K.S. (1993). Adherence to exercise and physical activity as health-promoting behaviors: Attitudinal and self-efficacy influences. *Applied and Preventive Psychology, 2,* 65–77.

McAuley, E., & Mihalko, S.L. (1998). Measuring exercise-related self-efficacy. In J.L. Duda (Ed.), *Advances in sport and exercise psychology measurement* (pp. 371–390). Morgantown, WV: Fitness Information Technology.

Noble, B.J., & Robertson, R.J. (1996). *Perceived exertion.* Champaign, IL: Human Kinetics.

Prochaska, J.O. (1994). Strong and weak principles for progressing from precontemplation to action based on twelve problem behaviors. *Health Psychology, 13,* 47–51.

Prochaska, J.O., DiClemente, C.C., & Norcross, J.C. (1992). In search of how people change: Applications in addictive behaviors. *American Psychologist, 47,* 1102–1111.

Prochaska, J.O., Velicier, W.F., Rossi, J.S., Goldstein, M., Marcus, B., Rakowski, W., Fiore, C., Harlow, L., Redding, C., Rosenbloom, D., & Rossi, S. (1994). Stages of change and decision balance for 12 problem behaviors. *Health Psychology, 13,* 39–46.

Randall, D.M., & Wolff, J.A. (1994). The time interval in the intention-behavior relationship: Meta-analysis. *British Journal of Social Psychology, 33,* 405–418.

Rejeski, W.J. (1981). Perception of exertion: A social psychobiological integration. *Journal of Sport Psychology, 3,* 305–320.

Schlenker, B.R. (1988). *Impression management: The self-concept, social identity, and interpersonal relations.* Monterey, CA: Brooks/Cole.

Seraganian, P. (1993). *Exercise psychology: The influence of physical exercise on psychological processes.* New York: Wiley.

Skinner, E.A. (1996). A guide to constructs of control. *Journal of Personality and Social Psychology, 71,* 549–570.

Spielberger, C.D., Gorsuch, R.L., Luschene, R., Vagg, P.R., & Jacobs, G.A. (1983). *Manual for the State-Trait Anxiety Inventory.* Palo Alto, CA: Consulting Psychologists.

Stone, E.J., McKenzie, T.L., Welk, G.J., & Booth, M.L. (1998). Effects of physical activity interventions in youth: Review and synthesis. *American Journal of Preventive Medicine, 15,* 298–315.

Sutton, S. (1998). Predicting and explaining intentions and behavior: How well are we doing? *Journal of Applied Social Psychology, 28,* 1317–1338.

Weinstein, N.D., Rothman, A.J., & Sutton, S.R. (1998). Stage theories of health behavior: Conceptual and methodological issues. *Health Psychology, 17,* 290–299.

Weinstein, N.D., & Sandman, P.M. (1992). A model of the precaution adoption process: Evidence from home radon testing. *Health Psychology, 11,* 170–180.

CHAPTER 28

Helping People Initiate and Maintain a More Active Lifestyle
A Public Health Framework for Physical Activity Promotion Research

LISE GAUVIN, LUCIE LÉVESQUE, and LUCIE RICHARD

In recent years, scientific and medical organizations have recognized that physical inactivity is a major risk factor for disease, and thus position statements regarding the promotion of physical activity for public health have been formulated (American College of Sports Medicine, 1991; Pate, et al., 1995). Notably, the Surgeon General of the United States released a report on the health benefits and promotion of physical activity (United States Department of Health & Human Services [USDHHS], 1996, 1999). In parallel, data on the prevalence of physical inactivity in most industrialized nations (Caspersen, Merritt, & Stephens, 1994) reveal that about two-thirds of the population is not active at frequency and intensity levels that are sufficient to result in health promotion or disease prevention effects.

It is generally agreed that to alleviate the burden of a risk factor, a public health approach that recognizes the complementary contributions of clinical and population approaches to prevention is required to effect significant changes (Glasgow, Wagner, et al., 1999; Jeffery, 1989; Rose, 1992; Vogt, 1993). As illustrated by Lichtenstein and Glasgow (1992), clinical approaches involve intensive, multisession interventions often delivered by health professionals in a medical or psychotherapeutic setting. By contrast, population approaches are less intensive, delivered by lay leaders or automated through the presence of particular environmental features, and unfold in natural life settings such as the workplace or the community. Although clinical approaches often lead to larger outcomes at the individual level than do population approaches, these latter approaches reach more people and result in a greater population impact (Rose, 1992). In the context of this chapter, the public health approach to understanding and investigating how people initiate and maintain a more active lifestyle is adopted.

In this regard, efforts to alleviate the public health burden of physical inactivity have focused on identifying the determinants of physical activity (Dishman, 1994). More important, researchers have studied the efficacy of interventions targeted to the individual and to the community (Blair & Morrow, 1998; King, 1991, 1994; Sallis et al., 1997; Schooler, 1995; USDHHS, 1999). Other investigators have either conceptually examined the value of policy advocacy intervention (King et al., 1995) or suggested public policy and legislative initiatives to enhance physical activity (Blair et al., 1996). As a result, there is a significant body of information on the impact of interventions designed to increase physical activity involvement. The term *intervention*, as it is used throughout this chapter, refers to health-promoting activities[1] that originate from a health promotion team with the intention of instilling or maintaining health-related attitudes, norms, and behaviors in a specific target (e.g., an individual or a group of individuals) within a particular setting.

Given the importance of developing clinical and population approaches to increase physical activity levels, there is consensus regarding the need for and relevance of conducting psychosocial research on physical activity *interventions* (Blair & Morrow, 1998). The purpose of this chapter is fourfold. The first goal consists of providing an overview of the vast research agenda facing investigators interested in conducting studies on promoting physically active lifestyles. In this regard, the physical activity requirements to achieve health benefits are summarized, the behavioral and self-regulatory implications of such public health recommendations are

---

[1] An activity is an interrelated sequence of actions targeting an individual or a group of individuals.

outlined, and the descriptive epidemiology of physical activity in the population is reviewed.

The second goal is to introduce a conceptual framework developed by Richard, Potvin, Kishchuk, Prlic, and Green (1996) that allows for a description of the breadth of intervention strategies available to fitness professionals, health professionals, and public health practitioners in promoting physical activity. This public health framework incorporates concepts from ecological models of health promotion and operationally classifies interventions as a function of their targets (e.g., individuals, small groups, organizations, communities, public policies), the relationship between targets (e.g., modifying the target vs. creating linkages between targets), and their delivery setting (e.g., workplaces, schools, communities, health care institutions). This public health framework is useful in understanding the array of interventions that have been used to promote physical activity and in orienting future research efforts. The third goal is to summarize what is known about the impact of physical activity interventions in effecting behavioral change. The fourth goal consists of identifying methodological challenges involved in conducting research on physical activity interventions. Rather than addressing methodology in a separate section, issues of research design and measurement are outlined throughout the chapter.

PROMOTING PHYSICAL ACTIVITY

Four parameters describe physical activity: type, frequency, intensity, and duration. Type of activity refers to the main physiological systems that are activated during activity. Activities are often characterized as taxing aerobic (cardiorespiratory), strength and endurance (musculoskeletal), or flexibility (extension of muscles and ligaments surrounding the joints) systems. Frequency designates the number of times a person engages in an activity over a predetermined period of time (e.g., weekly frequency of selected activities). Duration refers to the temporal length of an activity bout and is often quantified in minutes. Intensity is the degree of overload an activity imposes on selected physiological systems in comparison to resting states (e.g., mild, moderate, strenuous). Exercise physiology researchers have developed a series of indicators of physical activity and energy expenditure (Montoye, Kemper, Saris, & Washburn, 1996) that constitute useful constructs for studying the outcomes of physical activity interventions.

There are two complementary recommendations regarding the volume of physical activity required to achieve health benefits (USDHHS, 1996). Optimal benefits from physical activity can be achieved if people exercise aerobically 3 to 4 times per week for 20 to 30 minutes at 65% to 75% of maximal aerobic capacity (Pollock et al., 1998). However, significant public health benefits can be realized if sedentary people cumulate 30 minutes of moderate-intensity (around 50% of maximal capacity) physical activity on most, preferably all, days of the week (Pate et al., 1995). These recommendations emerged from consensus conferences wherein leading experts in exercise physiology, epidemiology, and public health integrated data pertaining to health benefits associated with different volumes of physical activity (i.e., dose-response relationships). It is generally accepted that the benefits gained from increasing volumes of physical activity increase at a rapid rate when people progress from being sedentary to moderately active and then taper off when people advance from being moderately to very active (see Haskell, 1994, for a more detailed discussion of dose-response relationships).

Population Prevalence and Demographic Trends of Physical Inactivity

Behavioral surveillance data show that approximately one third of the population in most industrialized countries is physically active at frequency and intensity levels sufficient to achieve some minimal health benefits (Caspersen et al., 1994; Sallis & Owen, 1999). When a more stringent definition of physical activity is used (i.e., high enough frequency and intensity levels to meet recommendations for optimal benefits), only 10% to 15% of the population can be considered sufficiently active (Canadian Fitness & Lifestyle Research Institute, 1996a).

Of greater concern is the fact that the prevalence of physical inactivity varies as a function of age, gender, socioeconomic status, and community size (Canadian Fitness and Lifestyle Research Institute, 1996a; Casperson et al., 1994; USDHHS, 1996, 1999). As age increases, activity levels tend to decrease. In most age categories, men display greater frequencies, intensities, and volumes of physical activity. As education and income rise, so do rates of involvement in physical activity. Also, persons living in larger communities tend to be more physically active than those living in smaller communities, although some data show that persons living in rural areas show greater readiness for physical activity in comparison to persons living in urban and suburban communities (Potvin, Gauvin, & Nguyen, 1997). Although rates of involvement in physical activity and readiness to become involved have generally increased over the past 15 years (Canadian Fitness and

Lifestyle Research Institute, 1996b; Stephens, 1987; Stephens & Craig, 1990), there has been no appreciable change in physical activity trends related to age, gender, socioeconomic status, and community size. In other words, physical inactivity is a risk factor that has a high prevalence rate and that is inequitably distributed throughout the population.

The existence of dose-response relationships, the relative complexity of defining optimal amounts of physical activity, and the existence of demographic trends pose several challenges for understanding and promoting physically active lifestyles. First, though there may be substantial agreement on what volumes of activity are required to achieve health gains, there has been only limited research on the *behavioral implications* (i.e., determination of the array of behavior patterns that allow people to engage in optimal volumes of physical activity on a daily basis) of the public health recommendations. Second and more important, researchers are only beginning to map out the *self-regulatory challenges* (i.e., those psychological variables and processes that are activated to produce each behavior pattern) that must be mastered to achieve public health recommendations for physical activity (American College of Sports Medicine, 1991; Pate et al., 1995; Pollock et al., 1998). These issues are discussed in the next section and are further highlighted in the discussion section on physical activity interventions.

Behavioral and Self-Regulatory Implications of Public Health Recommendations Regarding Optimal Volumes of Physical Activity

Blair, Kohl, and Gordon (1992) proposed that persons who are categorized as either sedentary, active via the incorporation of physical activity into their daily living, or active through more intense bouts of leisure physical activity adopt very different patterns of daily activities. For example, the person who participates in a workout over the lunch hour would have to initiate a different sequence of actions leading to physical activity involvement (e.g., bring workout clothes to work, promptly leave the workplace at noon, participate in the workout, quickly shower and return to work) in comparison to a person attempting to integrate activity into his or her daily life. This person would need to initiate a different sequence of behaviors (e.g., take stairs instead of riding on the escalator, get off the bus one stop earlier, take a brisk walk after dinner). Furthermore, the person exercising vigorously only once a day would need to devote a greater amount of effort in a short period of time to engage in higher-intensity activity, whereas the person

engaging in lifestyle activity would need comparatively smaller amounts of effort over longer periods of time to be involved in moderate-intensity activity. The behaviors undertaken by these two persons are therefore vastly different. Hence, the first challenge faced by a researcher studying the promotion of physical activity is to identify the specific behavior pattern that is the focus of a given intervention.

Equally important, once the specific physical activity behavior has been identified, there is a need to uncover and disentangle its self-regulatory requirements. As reviewed elsewhere in this *Handbook* (see Culos-Reed, Gyurcsik, & Brawley), several theories of how people control their own behavior have been applied to the understanding of physical activity behavior. For instance, if one were applying self-efficacy theory (Bandura, 1986, 1997) to understand behavior change, then exploring the respective combination of self-efficacy and outcome expectations for changing vigorous leisure-time physical activity in comparison to lifestyle activities might represent a useful way of identifying the self-regulatory requirements of a given behavioral choice. Similarly, the explanatory constructs of behavioral goals, self-monitoring, and mental effort (Baumeister, Heatherton, & Tice, 1994; Carver & Scheier, 1998; Karoly, 1993) for lifestyle activity versus structured leisure-time activity might be examined in an effort to describe the self-regulatory mechanisms of selected behaviors. As indicated by Culos-Reed et al. (this volume) and others (Maddux, Brawley, & Boykin, 1995), there is a substantial body of literature pertaining to the self-regulatory determinants of different forms of physical activity involvement, but there are still many gaps in the literature. The availability of such information is a critical starting point for the formulation of physical activity interventions because these psychosocial constructs represent targets for selected intervention activities (see Baranowski, Anderson, & Carmack, 1998; Baranowski, Lin, Wetter, Resnicow, & Davis-Hearn, 1997).

It should be noted that research supports the viability of changing both involvement in vigorous activity in a structured setting (e.g., fitness club) as well as engagement in moderate activity integrated into daily life (e.g., taking stairs rather than the elevator at work). For example, a meta-analysis by Dishman and Buckworth (1996) showed that a variety of interventions can influence vigorous leisure physical activity performed in a structured environment. In parallel, Dunn, Anderson, and Jakicic (1998) concluded that lifestyle activity programs can be effective in increasing activity involvement in sedentary adults and in obese children. Overall, researchers have only begun to explore the behavioral and self-regulatory underpinnings of public health recommendations for physical activity. If progress is to be made toward an understanding of the behavioral implications of public health recommendations regarding optimal amounts of health-related physical activity, then the behavioral and self-regulatory implications of different amounts of physical activity will require further research efforts.

Vastness of the Research Agenda

Theoretically based studies of the psychosocial correlates of the evolution of activity involvement across time represent a useful area of investigation. Qualitative studies of the meaning of different forms of involvement in physical activity represent a useful endeavor for future research, whereas studies of the life circumstances that are best suited to different forms of physical activity involvement across life stages represent another useful direction.

Above and beyond this, it should be noted that although population surveys provide a wealth of information on the relationship between demographic variables and physical activity involvement, there is general consensus emerging in the field of public health regarding the need for more multilevel descriptions of health behaviors in a variety of social contexts (Duncan, Jones, & Moon, 1993, 1996; Ewart, 1991). The basic premise of multilevel descriptions of health behaviors lies in the idea that a person's behavior must be understood as a function of the behavioral settings within which he or she lives (Aguirre-Molina & Gorman, 1996). McIntyre, MacIver, and Sooman (1993), for example, call for the need to assess the influence of compositional (i.e., the attitudes, norms, and behaviors displayed by people who evolve in the same life settings) and contextual (i.e., the features that characterize important life settings) factors. Thus, in addition to understanding the intrapersonal self-regulatory processes that bring about human behavior, there is a need to examine causal determinants of behavior that exist in the person's interpersonal, community, social, and cultural environments.

Applied to the understanding of physical activity behavior, this means that one must also examine the presence and influence of family, the workplace environment, important social groups, and the community not simply as correlates but as integrated features of prevalence estimates. There is also a need to understand the role of organizational structures (e.g., number, nature, diversity, and suitability of activity programs) and policies (e.g., extended lunch hours to exercise) influencing behaviors, as well as the influence

of community characteristics (e.g., number and accessibility of activity settings) on activity behavior.

Until recently, documenting the existence of compositional and contextual effects was problematic because software associated with the appropriate statistical models was not widely available to researchers. The advent of multilevel modeling software programs (HLM; Bryk & Raudenbush, 1992; Bryk, Raudenbush, & Congdon, 1996; MLwiN; Goldstein et al., 1998) have alleviated this concern. Hence, a new, very fruitful research direction pertains to documenting the extent to which physical activity behaviors are susceptible to compositional and contextual influences. This is critical information toward the formulation and planning of clinical and population interventions. This perspective represents the foundation of a public health framework for physical activity promotion research and is further developed in the following section.

ECOLOGICAL MODELS: TOWARD A PUBLIC HEALTH FRAMEWORK FOR PHYSICAL ACTIVITY PROMOTION RESEARCH

Building on the idea of multilevel conceptualizations of health behaviors, a new paradigm emerged in the field of public health over the past two decades. Often referred to as the new public health (Ashton & Seymour, 1988; Bunton & MacDonald, 1992; Kickbush, 1986), this paradigm evolved within the emergence of the health promotion movement, with its emphasis on an ecological approach to research and action (Schwab & Syme, 1997). Advocated by the World Health Organization as well as many governments, the ecological approach encourages a broadening of the vision of the determinants of health, which in turn results in a shift from an individual focus to a higher level of causality involving various facets of people's environment. The ecological approach has underscored the complexity of the interrelations among humans, their health, and the environment. Notions such as feedback, interaction, and reciprocal determinism (Bandura, 1986; Green, Richard, & Potvin, 1996; Stokols, 1992, 1996) have been put forward to describe the nature of these complex, multilevel relationships.

In line with this vision, practitioners have been urged to implement *multilevel interventions*[2] that simultaneously target intrapersonal factors (e.g., knowledge, attitudes,

---

[2] Multilevel intervention is defined as a set of interventions aimed at one or more targets within one or more settings, usually in an effort to modify a specific risk factor.

skills, and behaviors) as well as the physical and social surroundings thought to be determinants of health and health-related behaviors (Powell, Kreuter, & Stephens, 1991). The following section describes how the ecological approach to health promotion might serve as an integrative framework for physical activity promotion studies. To date, there have been only preliminary efforts to achieve such an integration in the area of physical activity (Powell et al., 1991; Sallis & Owen, 1997, 1999).

For instance, in their conceptual analysis, Powell et al. (1991) suggest that several dimensions of health promotion could be applied to the public health issue of physical activity, namely, the notion that programs should target not only the individual also but his or her social and physical environments. They also suggest that there is a need to develop a standardized and systematic format for describing physical activity promotion interventions and to collect more population data on the impact of such interventions. Specifically, they propose that "efforts to measure the outcomes of health promotion programs [designed to increase physical activity] are important but only half the task. Adequate descriptions of the [physical activity] programs are also necessary. This will be aided by efforts to identify and codify the individual elements of health promotion programs [designed to increase physical activity]" (p. 501).

The Ecological Approach: Description and Basic Tenets

It is generally agreed that the ecological approach casts the issue of intervention in a more comprehensive framework than the clinical, individual-level, intervention approach. In the face of mounting and unequivocal evidence that health problems are strongly associated with social structures and conditions (Evans, Barer, & Marmor, 1995), the ecological approach attempts to overcome some of the limitations of traditional clinical approaches often associated with victim blaming (Pearce, 1996). The victim-blaming approach refers to the tendency to impute lack of success in behavior change to lack of willpower or some failure on the part of the individual. Furthermore, in light of data showing that persons who belong to middle and upper socioeconomic classes achieve greater benefits from standard health education efforts than persons in lower echelons (Breslow, 1990), the ecological approach may be better suited to reaching disadvantaged populations (Raeburn & Beaglehole, 1989). More important, because they attempt to target variables in all relevant domains, intervention programs based on the ecological approach are thought to be more effective than more narrowly focused intervention programs (Sallis & Owen, 1997).

The ecological approach has raised a great deal of interest in the health promotion community. Many scholars have introduced the approach and illustrated its application in various contexts, such as injury prevention (D. Simons-Morton et al., 1989), nutrition (Glanz & Mullis, 1988; Sallis & Owen, 1997), and tobacco control (Richard, Potvin, Denis, & Kishchuk, 2000). The approach has also been touted as highly relevant to the promotion of physical activity, a domain where the dominance of educational and cognitive-behavioral approaches has been linked to poor long-term effects. Indeed, according to Sallis and Owen (1997), King et al. (1995), and the Surgeon General's Report (USDHHS, 1996), as long as little or no effort is made to modify the environmental factors that may be determinants of sedentary behaviors, physical activity promotion programs targeting individuals will bring about only limited and nonsustained changes in physical activity. Environmental barriers such as those related to the lack of social support or the inappropriateness of the natural or constructed environments definitively need to be addressed to encourage transition from a sedentary to an active lifestyle and to lead to long-lasting changes (USDHHS, 1999).

Early Theorizing Based on the Ecological Model

Despite the interest and enthusiasm raised by the principles underlying the ecological approach, designing ecological programs remains a challenge for planners and practitioners because the operationalization of conceptual models is difficult (Green et al., 1996). Toward this end, conceptual models of the ecological approach have been proposed. Another contribution is found in the formulation of useful working definitions of ecological concepts within the context of health promotion. More concretely, by providing detailed descriptions of programs deemed ecological, these models have provided useful heuristics for health promotion practitioners interested in ecological programming. Two of these models are presented next to help illustrate an ecological agenda of physical activity promotion.

In a paper that contributed greatly to the introduction of the ecological approach in health promotion, McLeroy, Bibeau, Steckler, and Glanz (1988) summarized the classes of factors that influence health-related behaviors. According to their model, health behaviors are determined by five classes of factors: (1) intrapersonal characteristics, (2) interpersonal processes and primary groups, (3) institutional factors, (4) community factors, and (5) public policy. These five levels of influence are conceptualized as targets for intervention programs. For McLeroy et al., the notion of target is pivotal to the understanding of an ecological approach in health promotion. Indeed, it is through an examination of the breadth of targets that a statement regarding the *ecologicalness* of a given program can be achieved. In other words, if the intervention program attempts to act on a variety of targets, then it is believed that a greater variety of determinants of health can be influenced. Consequently, an ecological program is one that includes activities targeted directly toward the individual and also, and perhaps more critically, at a variety of environmental targets such as those included in McLeroy et al.'s framework.

Sallis and Owen (1997) provided a useful application of the McLeroy model to the area of physical activity promotion. Noting that variables in all domains (e.g., intrapersonal, social, cultural, and physical) are related to physical activity in adults and in youth, they discuss and illustrate the potential role of each of the five classes of factors included. The first two classes of factors (i.e., intrapersonal and interpersonal) are the most studied in the empirically based intervention literature. Notably, a host of intrapersonal psychological variables such as intention, self-efficacy, and attitudes have been found to be predictive of this behavior (see Culos-Reed et al., this volume). And accordingly, many interventions have sought to increase the frequency of physical activity by acting on intrapersonal determinants (see Dishman & Buckworth, 1996). A similar picture emerges for interpersonal factors, where research and intervention data have shown the potent role of social support in helping people adopt and maintain physical activity behaviors (e.g., Chogohara, Cousins, & Wankel, 1998).

Variables related to the three other classes of factors in the McLeroy et al. (1988) model have been the focus of far less research. Yet, as discussed by Sallis and Owen (1997), they represent critical variables in understanding how to promote physical activity behaviors. Hence, several research directions can be reiterated. First, research examining the potential role of interventions that manipulate environmental features is required. For example, analysis of the impact of providing space devoted to physical activity in institutions such as schools and workplaces would be enlightening as to the power of environmental factors in helping people adopt and maintain an active lifestyle. Concurrently, the role of important actors evolving in these organizations (e.g., teachers, managers, etc.) should be the focus of future research. Notably, the extent to which these organizational figures send appropriate messages (see Rothman & Salovey, 1997) regarding physical activity and contribute to creating an organizational climate favorable to physical activity also needs to be considered.

Second, community factors constitute a particularly relevant class of potential determinants. How a community's physical design (e.g., lighting, parking facilities) and the availability of specific resources (e.g., recreation facilities or bicycling trails) influence levels of physical activity requires further description. Third, as it has been shown in the study of other health behaviors such as smoking (Brownson, Koffman, Novotny, Hughes, & Eriksen, 1995) and nutrition (Glanz et al., 1995), public policies and regulations might have an important impact as well. Sallis and Owen (1997) as well as King et al. (1995) have identified many relevant sectors for study in this respect, including transportation, building codes, education, and health care expenditures. For example, political decisions to invest massive resources in highway development at the expense of local walking and cycling paths might bear a negative impact on the level of physical activity in a community.

It is important to note that although there exists a rationale to link environmental factors to physical activity behavior, limited data are available regarding the exact processes underlying any relationships. In addition, the most effective methods for orchestrating environmental changes still remain to be identified (King et al., 1995). While advocating for the application of ecological models to health promotion programs, Sallis and Owen (1999) call for more research to guide cost-effective and rigorous intervention in this field.

Recent Developments in Relation to the Ecological Approach

The ecological perspective is useful for the formulation of more far-reaching intervention strategies, but until recently, a systematic tool for describing the degree of integration of the ecological perspective in health promotion programs has eluded researchers. This is particularly critical given the complexity of the ecological approach and the unlikely possibility that all of its complexity will be captured by a model including only one feature (i.e., targets). Similarly, the extent to which currently used interventions might be incorporated into an overriding framework has thus far not been achieved. To address these concerns, Richard et al. (1996) adopted a systemic view of health promotion programs and extended models by McLeroy et al. (1988) and D. Simons-Morton, Simons-Morton, Parcel, and Bunker (1988). Richard et al. proposed that to fully understand the ecological character of a health promotion program, there is a need to examine more than one dimension of health promotion programs (i.e., intervention targets), as proposed by McLeroy and his colleagues. Harnessing and illustrating the dynamic relationships between two dimensions is better suited to capturing the concept of *ecologicalness*. That is, in addition to examining intervention *targets,* Richard et al. propose that it is important to understand the *settings* in which interventions reach clients (i.e., the people targeted by intervention activities) and wherein interventions actually unfold. *An ecological program is one that includes interventions aimed at both environmental and individual targets and that delivers these interventions in a variety of settings.* The more a program integrates multitarget, multisetting interventions, the more ecological it is.

Intervention Setting

According to this framework, a health promotion program can be conceived as a social transformation process initiated to reach specific objectives (see Richard et al., 1996, for a detailed rationale). As such, programs can be conceptualized as organizations or social systems (Laszlo, 1975). Organizations are social systems that are a subclass of concrete, living open systems. Miller's theory of living systems (Miller, 1978; Miller & Miller, 1992) identifies eight levels of living systems, forming a nested hierarchy. In this hierarchy, the five most macro categories form social systems. These are groups, organizations, communities, societies, and supranational systems. Given the inclusive nature of the hierarchy, organizations such as health promotion programs may thus be located in any of the following settings: organizations, communities, societies, or supranational systems (see Table 28.1 for definitions and examples of physical activity for each of these levels). The setting(s) of a given intervention is (are) thus defined as the social system(s) in which clients are reached.

Intervention Target

A systemic vision helps define a second, independent dimension of the ecological approach: the target of the intervention. Systems theory states that open systems exchange energy, matter, and information with other systems in their environment. Activities and services are the most common forms of energy matter and information outputs of health promotion programs. Program outputs can be channeled to the ultimate targets (i.e., clients ultimately being targeted by an intervention), either directly without intermediary steps or through other systems before they reach the ultimate target. The McLeroy et al. (1988) model as well as other theoretical formulations (Green & Kreuter, 1999; D. Simons-Morton et al., 1988) are particularly useful in defining five types of targets for program outputs: the individual clients, other persons and small groups, organizations, communities, and political systems.

The five previously mentioned targets can be conceptualized as building blocks for a more complex entity: the intervention strategy. Prior to describing intervention strategies,

Table 28.1   Definitions and Examples of Physical Activity Intervention Settings

Setting	Definition	Example
Organizations	Systems with a formal multiechelon decision process operating in pursuit of specific objectives	Private fitness center Sports club School Community center Public health infrastructure Regional health and social services board
Communities	A restricted geographical area composed of persons and organizations (e.g., neighborhoods, cities, villages, groups of towns)	Municipality West end town
Societies	Larger systems possessing means to control several aspects of the lives and development of their constituent subsystems	Australia Canada Great Britain United States
Supranational systems	Associations composed of two or more societies	European Union Commonwealth

it is useful to define the two types of relationships that may exist between targets included in the intervention strategy. The first involves the direct transformation of a target or a series of targets and the second refers to the networking of two or more targets. Examples of a direct type of relationship include interventions that are directly aimed at modifying personal characteristics (e.g., knowledge and attitude) of the clients themselves. Health education classes designed to encourage workers to exercise are one example of such a relationship. Direct-type relationships between targets can also entail the modification of other targets in the clients' environment that will convey the health promotion intervention to them. For example, changes aimed at an organizational target could imply changes in the organizational structure or functioning or changes among influential decision-makers in an organization. For example, rather than instructing workers themselves, health promotion practitioners could work with senior managers to convince them to provide appropriate physical activity facilities in their workplace. A third example could involve health promotion practitioners lobbying elected officials to have them offer economic incentives to include appropriate physical activity facilities when new workplaces are planned (King et al., 1995). In this example, practitioners aim at a political target to bring about changes that should eventually impact on workers' level of physical activity. All of these examples involve the direct transformation of one or more targets by an intervention.

The second type of relationship involves the creation of a network among two or more targets. For example, networking interventions could involve the creation of a support group involving post–myocardial infarct clients who share ways to cope with their exercise prescription. A second example could involve networking among these clients' spouses, whereby they could exchange tips about how to help their partners comply with their exercise prescription. A third example could involve linking up organizations interested in promoting physical activity through the creation of a coalition.

Thus, an *intervention strategy* describes the transactions of a program with the different systems in its environment to affect the health or health behaviors of persons previously defined as clients. An intervention can be directly aimed at modifying personal characteristics of the clients themselves. A program can also entail the modification of other targets in the environment that will directly convey the health promotion intervention to the clients or involve the networking of targets. These networks can involve the clients themselves or other targets in their environment. The five targets can be used in numerous combinations to attain health objectives. Table 28.2 presents some examples of intervention strategies involving the five targets of the model. The list is not exhaustive nor exclusive but provides an illustrative overview of intervention strategies that can be used by health promotion practitioners to maintain or improve physical activity levels in clients. Table 28.2 also includes examples of activities that could be used either alone or in combination as constituent components of a physical activity intervention to promote physical activity initiation and maintenance.

To more concisely illustrate intervention strategies, a graphic notation system was developed. This system links programs and targets by a set of arrows, brackets, and abbreviations. Hence, potential targets are abbreviated as follows: (1) clients: IND, (2) interpersonal environment: INT, (3) organizations: ORG, (4) community: COM, and (5) political actors and processes: POL. A transformation relationship is illustrated by an arrow linking the program or intervention (HP) to its targets. For example, the previously alluded to intervention including health education classes is represented as follows: HP → IND. The example involving activities designed to influence elected officials is depicted HP → POL → IND. The establishment of a network is graphically illustrated by the use of brackets surrounding the targets to be networked. For example, self-help groups involving post–myocardial infarct clients are represented

by HP → [IND–IND], and self-help groups joining their spouses are depicted by HP → [INT–INT] → IND.

Emerging Perspectives

The ecological approach has contributed a framework for conceptualizing the vast array of interventions that can be used for promoting physical activity at the individual and population levels. Outlining the breadth of interventions in this way highlights three important points for physical activity interventions. First and foremost, multilevel physical activity interventions are in their infancy. The cornerstone of the ecological approach rests in attempting to simultaneously work on several levels of the hierarchy of a person's life settings. Second, there is a lack of description of activities, combinations of activities, and processes underlying physical activity interventions. As such, significant are the comments of Powell et al. (1991) and Schwartz and Goodman (2000), who call for more effort into intervention analysis and description. Evaluation studies involving archival analysis and in-depth interviews represent useful ways of achieving such descriptions.

Third, there is an absence of indicators of physical activity intervention outcomes at the interpersonal, organizational, community, and political levels. Several scholars have argued for the desirability of measuring mediating variables to understand how physical activity interventions achieve change (Baranowski et al., 1997, 1998). However, as others have shown (Sallis & Owen, 1997), there are a variety of measures that tap into physical activity behaviors and intrapersonal variables associated with physical activity at the individual level. Unfortunately, indicators of physical activity outcomes at the other levels of the ecological hierarchy (i.e., interpersonal, organizational, community, and political environments) are either limited in number (e.g., measures of social norms, social support) or absent in the literature (e.g., indicators of environmental features that are conducive to physical activity). Efforts in this direction are emerging in the literature (see Corti, Donovan, & Holman, 1997), for the development of this measurement technology is critical for the advancement of knowledge about physical activity interventions.

THE IMPACT OF PHYSICAL ACTIVITY INTERVENTIONS

A frequently articulated distinction in the health promotion literature pertains to *efficacy* versus *effectiveness*. According to Flay (1986, p. 451), *efficacy* trials "provide a test of whether a technology, treatment, procedure, or program does more good than harm when delivered under

Table 28.2   Descriptions and Examples of Components of Physical Activity Interventions

Intervention Target	Health Promotion Strategy	Examples of Intervention	Example of Potential Activities That Could Be Used in Varying Combinations to Produce an Intervention
IND	HP → IND	Activity classes	Class instruction
		Open use of exercise facilities	Reward systems, lotteries, contracts
		Personal training services	Visualization, positive thinking, mental self-control techniques
		Information sessions (e.g., lectures, classroom information sessions)	Education about health benefits of exercise, importance of nutrition
		Special events	Fitness appraisal and health risk assessment
		Web site	Exercise prescription
			Technical instruction
			Face-to-face counseling
			Cognitive-behavioral interventions
	HP → [IND – IND]	Services to link up clients to perform activities together (e.g., finding a partner for racquet sports, outdoors clubs)	Technical instruction
			Changing social norms within the group (e.g., putting more emphasis on health, making exercise a group priority)
		Support/discussion group to promote maintenance of physical activity	Social support systems (e.g., buddy systems, teaching people how to offer support)
			Group problem-solving techniques
			Reward systems, lotteries, contracts
			Education about health benefits of exercise, importance of nutrition
			Fitness appraisal and health risk assessment
			Exercise prescription
INT	HP → INT → IND	Activity classes for families, couples or small groups of friends	Technical instruction
			Developing interaction strategies
		Programs that involve spouses of exercisers (e.g., partners of pregnant women, spouses of cardiac patients)	Changing social norms (e.g., putting more emphasis on health, making exercise a family priority)
		Open use of exercise facilities for families, couples, or small groups	Social support systems (e.g., buddy system, teaching people how to offer support)
		Information sessions for families, couples, or small groups	Modeling (e.g., training peers to act as models for physical activity)
			Providing incentives (e.g., offering family, couple, or small group rates)
			Education about health benefits of exercise, importance of nutrition
	HP → [INT – INT] → IND	Services to link up couples/families/small groups to actually participate in activities together	Technical instruction
			Changing social norms within the group (e.g., putting more emphasis on health, making exercise a family priority)
		Support/discussion groups among families for remaining more active	Group problem-solving techniques
			Social support systems (e.g., buddy system, teaching people how to offer support)
			Modeling (e.g., training peers to act as models for physical activity)
			Providing incentives (e.g., offering family, couple, or small group rates)
			Education about health benefits of exercise, importance of nutrition

Intervention Target	Health Promotion Strategy	Examples of Intervention	Example of Potential Activities That Could Be Used in Varying Combinations to Produce an Intervention
ORG	HP–ORG–IND	Modifying the structure and functioning of an organization	Training for employers/key members of an organization
		Increasing the accessibility of facilities in an organization	Modifying the physical environment (e.g., making stairwells more attractive, visible, accessible)
		Meeting with the head of an organization to encourage employees to become more active	Education for employers about ways to deliver health messages to their employees
		Fostering the creation of new organizations that will offer services directly to the population	Changing social norms within the organization (e.g., putting more emphasis on health, making exercise promotion a priority)
			Providing incentives to organizations (e.g., tax breaks)
	HP–[ORG–ORG]–IND	Creation of community coalitions	Training for key players
			Health education for key players
			Changing social norms within the group (e.g., putting more emphasis on health, making exercise promotion a priority)
			Providing incentives (e.g., pooling of resources)
COM	HP–COM–IND	Modifying the structure and functioning of a community	Changing social norms within the community (e.g., putting more emphasis on health, making exercise promotion a priority)
		Increasing the accessibility of facilities in a community	Modifying the physical environment (e.g., creation of walking/bike path)
		Creation of community supports	Providing a toll-free number for community members looking to access physical activity resources in their community
			Providing incentives (e.g., lower rates for community members to use community pool)
	HP–[COM–COM]–IND	Linking communities together	Intercommunity exercise competitions
			Providing incentives (e.g., pooling of resources)
POL	HP–POL–IND	Influencing political representatives to legislate for the promotion of physical activity	Lobbying activities (e.g., for the development of policies for safer active transportation)
	HP–[POL–POL]–IND	Creation of alliances to promote more effective intergovernmental cooperation	Collaboration among key political players (e.g., Ministry of Education and Ministry of Health joining forces to promote physical activity in the schools and in youth drop-in centers)

HP = health promotion program or intervention; IND = individuals or clients; INT = interpersonal environment; ORG = organizations; COM = community; POL = political actors and processes; → = transformation relationship between the intervention and the target; [ ] = establishment of a network between targets; — = linkage.

optimum conditions," whereas "*effectiveness* trials provide tests of whether a technology, treatment, procedure, intervention, or program does more harm than good when delivered under real-world conditions." More formally defined, an efficacy trial provides "a test of a well-specified and standardized treatment/program that is made available in a uniform fashion, within standardized contexts/settings, to a specified target audience which completely accepts, participates in, complies with, or adheres to the treatment/program as delivered" (p. 452). Efficacy trials usually involve randomized designs and control groups. In comparison, effectiveness trial designs may include randomization and control groups, but a concerted effort to examine variability across contexts/settings is sought. Thus, effectiveness trials may "require assessments of program implementation, availability, and acceptance as well as program effects" (p. 456).

Furthermore, health promotion researchers have provided additional conceptual nuances to the concepts of efficacy and effectiveness. In particular, the notions of what constitutes evidence (McQueen & Anderson, in press) for health promotion programs is currently under discussion. The relevance of randomized trials for testing the efficacy of interventions aimed at targets that, by definition, cannot be fully controlled (i.e., a community, an organization), as is required in randomized trials, is now actively being questioned. The interested reader is referred to McQueen and Anderson (in press), Potvin, Haddad, and Frohlich, (in press), Potvin and Richard (in press), and Susser (1995) for further discussion of these issues. Recently, Glasgow, Vogt, and Boles (1999) suggested that efficacy represents only one dimension needed to gauge the value of interventions for public health. They propose a model, coined RE-AIM (Reach, Efficacy, Adoption, Implementation, and Maintenance), that identifies a series of issues to be examined in assessing the impact of an intervention or policy innovation. The works of these scholars point to the need to examine findings from efficacy trials and effectiveness trials, as well as studies of the acceptability, quality of implementation, and sustainability to understand the impact of physical activity interventions.

Much of the information available on the impact of physical activity interventions has come from randomized trials that were conceptualized, for the most part, as efficacy trials (see Blair & Morrow, 1998). There are few if any effectiveness trials, although there is a trend in the literature to provide far more detailed information regarding intervention activities and implementation (see King, Sallis, et al.'s 1998 description of ACT [Activity Counseling Trial]).

The impact of different interventions designed to promote physical activity is described next. Detailed reviews of the physical activity intervention literature are available elsewhere (see "Theme Issue: Physical Activity Interventions," Volume 15, Number 4 of the *American Journal of Preventive Medicine,* 1998; Dishman & Buckworth, 1996). Therefore, the following subsections contain a recasting of this knowledge within the previously described public health framework, commentary on some of the methodological challenges, and indications of several research directions.

Strategies Focused on Changing the Individual: HP → IND

As seen in Table 28.2, examples of intervention strategies targeting individuals directly include providing activity classes, offering a personal training service, or offering information classes. Intervention activities that could be combined to form an HP → IND physical activity intervention include technical instruction on how to perform different physical activities, leadership during the performance of activities, and a range of more psychosocial or behavioral activities such as cognitive-behavioral treatment, behavioral management activities, goal setting, and self-monitoring activities.

Literature reviews by King, Rejeski, and Buchner (1998), Taylor, Baranowski, and Rohm-Young (1998), and Stone, McKenzie, Welk, and Booth (1998) support the idea that physical activity interventions targeting the individual directly through physical activity classes, cognitive behavioral and behavior management, and health risk appraisal in settings as diverse as schools, fitness centers, and the community can be effective in increasing physical activity behavior. Of interest is the fact that the impact of most interventions is heterogeneous. That is, in a meta-analysis by Dishman and Buckworth (1996), effect sizes ranged from .10 to .92, suggesting that interventions can result in either small (<.25), moderate (.26 to .50), or large (>.51) changes in activity involvement. Interestingly, results also varied as a function of physical activity behaviors pursued, with the smallest effect sizes observed in strength training classes and the largest effects observed in interventions aimed at increasing low- to moderate-intensity activities. In this literature, the impact of interventions targeting the individual is greater when intervention activities are mediated (i.e., delivered through the support of audio or visual media supports).

The particular ideal combination of intervention activities, physical activity goals, and appropriate settings for diverse target groups has proven to be elusive. Furthermore, there is an apparent dearth of effectiveness trials. Notable exceptions include implementation efforts ongoing in Massachussetts and California referred to by King, Rejeski, et al. (1998). From a methodological standpoint, there is a need to develop more detailed descriptions of intervention activities and intervention implementation (King, Rejeski, et al., 1998). Toward this end, qualitative interview methods, archival analysis, and adoption of intervention planning models (e.g., Bartholomew, Parcel, & Kok, 1998; Green & Kreuter, 1999) are appropriate. Particular attention is required to define the intervention activities that compose a given physical activity intervention, as this will allow for an estimation of main effects, synergistic influence effects, and counterproductive effects of activities.

Given the demonstrated feasibility of delivering interventions in a standardized fashion, using randomized trials, and the wealth of information derived from these studies, there is reason to continue using this approach. However, a greater number of effectiveness trials and program evaluations could be included in future research. In particular, the absence of studies to explore the acceptability, feasibility, and value of more widespread implementation of efficacious interventions is apparent. Similarly, evaluations of practitioner-initiated physical activity interventions represent an approach useful for uncovering new perspectives, as many insights can be acquired from persons whose day-to-day tasks involve the promotion of physical activity (cf. McGuire, 1983). Although the practice of documenting input from practitioners has a limited history in the field of physical activity interventions, analysis from the practitioner's perspective in other areas has proven valuable to health promotion efforts (e.g., Paine-Andrews 2000; Richard et al., 2000) and there have been calls to move in this direction in the area of physical activity (see Taylor et al., 1998).

Strategies Focused on Networking Individuals: HP→[IND–IND]

A different strategy for intervention that also reaches individuals involves *networking* rather than *changing* them. Within the public health framework, this type of intervention would be illustrated as follows: HP→[IND–IND] → IND. As seen in Table 28.2, examples of intervention strategies that fall under the umbrella of networking individuals include services designed to link up persons to become physically active as well as support groups for activity. The cornerstone of this type of intervention rests on the idea of creating new social links to facilitate behavior change. Intervention activities that could be combined to form this type of physical activity intervention include, as did the previous type of intervention, technical instruction on how to perform different physical activities and offering group walking opportunities. Also included are activities designed to develop social norms favorable to activity within the network, activities attempting to create a sense of group cohesion, and activities fostering problem solving through the group.

An excellent example of a study that tests the efficacy of an intervention falling under this strategy is provided by Brawley, Rejeski, and Lutes (2000). They developed a physical activity intervention that included group-motivated lifestyle changes. The intervention activities involved creating new groups of seniors interested in becoming more active, applying group development techniques to create a network among participants, having the group engage in discussions, and implementing group problem-solving techniques. They found that persons assigned to the group-motivated lifestyle condition reported more frequent exercise and greater improvements in health-related quality of life than persons assigned to the traditional exercise program.

Extant literature reviews do not specifically address the value of networking individuals together. Hence, generalizations regarding the efficacy of these interventions are difficult. What is of interest, though, is that the one study by Brawley et al. (2000) as well as other studies on social support (Cohen, 1988; Cohen & Lichtenstein, 1990; Thoits, 1995) more generally show that interventions that do not specifically aim to change people but let them work on changing each other can have a significant impact on a host of behavioral and self-regulatory variables. This therefore represents a fruitful area for further research.

There is a need to further develop measures of group processes (Carron, Hausenblas, & Mack, 1996) emerging from the networking situation, as these variables could be mediators of intervention efficacy (Carron & Spink, 1993; Spink & Carron, 1993). The viability of more widespread dissemination also merits further attention, as more people may be reached with fewer interventionists through group-based interaction interventions than one-on-one interventions. Similarly, more detailed descriptions of intervention activities and intervention implementation should be constructed (i.e., what specific activities were undertaken to recruit members, to stimulate group processes, to maintain group activities). These detailed descriptions of intervention activities might serve as a starting point for the examination of intervention acceptability in professional practice settings as well as studies of intervention implementation.

The need for more fine-grained analyses of intervention activities becomes increasingly clear as the direction shifts from individual-level interventions to those that target facets of the interpersonal sphere. That is, the number of potential influencing variables as well as the inherent complexity of nesting people into groups that develop different levels of cohesion, belongingness, and the like increases dramatically. Toward this end, qualitative interview methods, archival analysis, and intervention planning models are appropriate. In addition, sociometric methods and concepts (Bukowski, 1998) used to study group processes should be further integrated into research efforts. Continued efficacy trials, effectiveness trials, and program evaluations are also appropriate.

Strategies Focused on Changing the Interpersonal Environment: HP→INT→IND

As seen in Table 28.2, examples of intervention strategies falling under the umbrella of targeting the interpersonal environment include providing activity classes and information sessions for families or small groups of persons who share friendships. The main focus of these interventions lies in trying to influence physical activity behavior by affecting someone in the person's social network. Whereas in the previous type of intervention there was an attempt to extend to the social network of an individual, in this type of intervention (HP→INT→IND) there is an effort to reach a significant other (e.g., spouse, peers, friends). An example would be the spouse of a post–myocardial infarct patient participating in an intervention to help his or her partner become more physically active. An actual example of an intervention strategy is found in the North Karelia Project, wherein children in schools were given health passports that included their own screening results to take home to their family in an effort to affect family health lifestyles (Puska et al., 1981).

Intervention activities that could be combined to form a physical activity intervention of this type include technical instruction on how to perform different physical activities in a cohesive manner and leadership during actual performance. Other constituent elements include a range of more psychosocial or behavioral activities such as developing family interaction strategies during activities, attempting to increase family norms for physical activity, and developing social support strategies (Berkman, 1995; Thoits, 1995).

Although literature reviews do not specifically address the impact of this type of intervention strategy, there are excellent examples of their successful implementation. Of note is the sustained intervention work by Epstein, Wing, Koeske, and Valoski, (1985; Epstein, Valoski, Wing, & McCurley, 1990; Epstein, Wing, Koeske, Ossip, & Beck, 1982), who developed lifestyle interventions for increasing activity in families of obese children. These authors randomly assigned parent-child clusters to one of three experimental conditions (aerobic exercise plus diet, lifestyle exercise plus diet, and calisthenics plus diet), applied behavior modification principles to instill eating and exercise behavior changes, and conducted follow-up of weight and activity patterns. Participants in the lifestyle plus diet group maintained weight loss after two years in comparison to the other groups. Interestingly, these types of interventions have been shown to have remarkable impact on physical activity and obesity outcomes at least in part because the intervention attempts to change not only individual-level parameters but also family environments (i.e., the INT).

Another example of family-level interventions includes the San Diego Family Health Project, wherein families participated in group problem solving, self-monitoring, family contracting, and exercise and nutrition education (Nader et al., 1989). Though no significant changes in activity levels were observed, the program did result in important changes related to knowledge about diet and exercise.

From a methodological standpoint, there is a wealth of information regarding how to best study families (Copeland & White, 1991). Family dynamics (i.e., whether the family is cohesive or conflictual), family roles (e.g., being a mother in a traditional family; Fisher et al., 1998), and behavior-specific family environments (e.g., social support for physical activity) represent several variables that either have not been examined or have yielded only a limited amount of data. This represents a particularly interesting area for study because of the known gender differences in terms of physical activity involvement. That is, the fact that men typically engage in greater volumes of physical activity than women could be explored in terms of consequences for offspring involvement in similar or different activities. Particular attention is required to define the intervention activities that compose a particular small group or family physical activity intervention, as this will allow for an estimation of main, synergistic, and contradictory effects of activities.

Several comments should also be directed at the role of effectiveness trials in understanding the applicability of HP→INT→IND interventions. Researchers in other areas of public health have shown that health professionals have a propensity to use and exploit intervention strategies that focus directly on the individual (Baum & Sanders, 1995; Beaglehole & Bonita, 1998). Though there is enthusiasm for the implementation of interventions targeting high levels of the human ecology, health professionals often report discomfort and/or lack of knowledge on how to intervene at the interpersonal, organizational, community, or public policy level (Freudenberg, Rogers, & Wallerstein, 1995; Green et al., 1996). As a result, the need for exploring the acceptability and feasibility of implementation of this intervention is more acute than with the two previously described interventions.

Strategies Focused on Networking Interpersonal Environments: HP → [INT–INT] → IND

Examples of intervention strategies that involve networking interpersonal environments include services designed to link up families, couples, or small groups to participate in physical activity in tandem as well as support groups for these socially cohesive groups (see Table 28.2). Intervention activities that could be combined to form this type of physical activity intervention include technical instruction on how to perform different physical activities, offering opportunities to be active, developing favorable social norms, creating a sense of group, and encouraging problem solving within the group. A good example of this type of intervention would be found in trying to link up families to be active together.

Extant literature reviews do not specifically address the value of networking interpersonal environments together. However, it should be noted that one component of the San Diego Family Health Project (Nader et al., 1989) involved organizing meetings where families could get together and discuss family strategies for health. In the context of these meetings, families would discuss problems, offer solutions and suggestions, sometimes attempt implementation, and then apply them in their own family environments. The viability and impact of this type of intervention strategy remain unexplored.

Strategies Focused on Changing Organizations: HP → ORG → IND

HP → ORG → IND intervention strategies do not directly target people. Rather, they focus on organizational change that in turn is hypothesized to influence individuals (Goodman & Steckler, 1989). As seen in Table 28.2, examples of these intervention strategies include modifying the structure and functioning of an organization, fostering the creation of new organizations, meeting with the heads of organizations to encourage them to promote activity, and working with professionals in health care institutions in an effort to encourage them to promote physical activity. Intervention activities that could be combined to form a physical activity intervention no longer involve interactions with the ultimate clients but rather with intermediaries such as physicians, teachers, and organization heads. They include developing persuasive messages for delivery by these intermediaries and teaching intermediaries how to disseminate information or how to deliver intervention activities.

In the physical activity literature, two interventions in this category have been studied extensively. One is curriculum changes in grade school, high school, and post-secondary institutions (see Stone et al., 1998). The intervention activities include implementing physical activity programs before and after school, supplementing or changing the curriculum to include more information about health aspects of diet and exercise, advocacy training, and training of personnel in the schools to deliver the new or modified curriculum. Other more extensively studied physical activity interventions are those consisting of motivating physicians and other health care professionals to promote physical activity with their patients (D. Simons-Morton et al., 1998). The actual intervention activities have included training of physicians, implementation of counseling protocols, delivering information to patients, consultations with fitness professionals, and other training of office staff.

Literature reviews by Stone et al. (1998) and D. Simons-Morton et al. (1998) support the idea that these particular interventions can be effective in increasing physical activity behavior. Although the effects seem to be larger for physician-based counseling than for curriculum changes, there is general agreement that more data are required on the impact of these interventions as well as on the actual organizational dimensions that are changed through these interventions (D. Simons-Morton et al., 1998; Stone et al., 1998). This caution is highlighted by a meta-analytic review of physical activity promotion in workplaces that showed only small effect sizes, many of which were not significantly different from zero (Dishman, Oldenburg, O'Neal, & Shephard, 1998). In this regard, as discussed by Collingwood (1994), the presence of a number of organizational factors is more likely to lead to successful programs: (1) available and convenient activity facilities; (2) programmatic and environmental techniques such as state-of-the-art equipment and policies facilitating activity involvement; and (3) physical activity programs in workplaces wherein facilities access was tied directly to the program (e.g., having an in-house exercise facility, having an outside facility with official links with the workplace).

Studying strategies focused on organizational change will require the application of conceptual models to frame appropriate approaches to couch such interventions. That is, because the interventions target organizational change, concepts and theories pertaining to individual change do not grasp the full reality of the phenomenon of organizational change. In current applications in the physical activity literature, stage theories and organizations change theories (Simnett, 1995) have been applied. These theories represent useful starting points for physical activity intervention development. When dealing with organizations, it is not likely to be feasible to deliver interventions in a fully standardized fashion because organizations are living and self-directed entities that may not submit to the rules of implementation. It seems reasonable to suggest that randomized trials may be more difficult to implement. In this regard, a greater number of effectiveness trials and program evaluations is encouraged.

Strategies Focused on Networking Organizations: HP → [ORG – ORG] → IND

Another intervention type is the HP → [ORG – ORG] → IND intervention. Examples of intervention strategies targeting the networking of organizations revolve mainly around the creation and maintenance of coalitions and intersectorial cooperation (see Table 28.2). Wandersman, Goodman, and Butterfoss (1997) conceptualize coalitions as an interorganizational, cooperative, and synergistic working alliance. They draw from two definitions to identify critical features of coalitions: "The first of these views a coalition as an organization of individuals representing diverse organizations, factions, or constituencies who agree to work together in order to achieve a common goal. The second sees a coalition as an organization of diverse interest groups that combine their human and material resources to effect a specific change that the members are unable to bring about independently" (pp. 262–263).

Although these ideas have much appeal and have received increased attention in the health promotion literature, particularly as they pertain to substance abuse, only two coalitions (i.e., National Coalition to Promote Physical Activity in the United States, and the Coalition for Active Living in Canada) in North America specifically devoted to physical activity promotion have been found. Though there are debates about the impact of such coalitions on health promotion outcomes (Green, 2000), there is interest in documenting their activities and any potential influences on population levels of physical activity.

Strategies Focused on Changing Communities: HP → COM → IND

There have been detailed discussion of promoting physical activity at the community level (King, 1991; USDHHS, 1999), yet only limited research has examined the impact of changing communities on levels of physical activity. It is important to underscore a subtle but important distinction between "interventions in communities" and "community interventions." From the perspective of the public health framework developed above, the former could refer to HP → IND, HP → [IND – IND] → IND, HP → INT → IND, and HP → [INT – INT] → IND interventions delivered in a community setting, whereas the latter would entail HP → COM → IND and HP → [COM–COM] → IND interventions. Thus, when strategies revolve around changing or networking communities, the focus is on modifying characteristics of the community per se rather than simply delivering other types of interventions in a community setting. As seen in Table 28.2, examples of intervention strategies focused on changing communities include modifying the structure and functioning of a community (e.g., creation of organizations, mobilizing the community around a specific health issue), increasing the accessibility of facilities in the community, and creating community supports. Examples of activities include creating walking paths or activities facilities in the community or implementing a toll-free number that community members could phone to find out where they might access physical activity resources in their community.

In the physical activity literature, only a small number of studies is available (Sallis, Bauman, & Pratt, 1998). For example, Linenger, Chesson, and Nice (1991) showed that improvements in bicycle paths and fitness equipment in a military community resulted in increased fitness levels. Another study by Blamey, Mutrie, and Aitchison (1995) involved posting a sign for three weeks in a subway station in Glasgow. Examination of proportions of persons using the stairs rather than the escalators indicated substantial increases in use during the three-week period but quickly returned to baseline on removal of the sign.

The limited data support the idea that it is possible to implement community interventions based on environmental changes and to observe results that are associated with changes. However, as mentioned by Sallis and Owen (1997) and Cheadle, Wagner, Koepsell, Kristal, and Patrick (1992), there is a need to identify the environmental constructs of interest in physical activity promotion and to develop measurement instruments that are valid and reliable. This will open the door to more systematic examination of the influence of community interventions. As with organizations, it is not always feasible to deliver community interventions in a fully standardized fashion. In this regard, the reader is referred to the vast literature on the experience of community heart-health intervention programs (Bracht, 1999; Susser, 1995).

Finally, it should be noted that many scholars (e.g., Green & Kreuter, 1999) currently hold the view that the community should be the main setting for any health promotion efforts. The rationale for this position is founded on the idea that the community is the best place to establish collective priorities and to mobilize persons both collectively and individually because it is close to the homes and the workplaces of citizens. This position is at least partially supported by a wealth of psychological research showing that self-determination (i.e., feeling that one has an impact on the environment and that one is not a pawn) is critical to self-directed action. Others have argued that community participation precedes and feeds sentiments of empowerment (Bandura, 1997; Rappaport, 1987). Examination of the emergence and consequences of community interventions represents a new venue for physical activity promotion research.

Strategies Focused on Networking Communities: HP → [COM – COM] → IND

One type of intervention that has not been systematically examined for the promotion of physical activity pertains to networking of communities. The best example of this type of initiative is the Healthy Cities/Communities Project (Ashton, 1991; Hancock, 1993). As mentioned by Green et al. (1996, p. 276), "the Healthy Cities movement has earlier roots, but for health promotion it was born in 1996 from a small group of professionals brought together to plan a World Health Organization (WHO) Europe Healthy Cities project. Healthy Cities was proposed as a means of furthering the ideals of the new public health proposed by the WHO. One of the central tenets of the Healthy Cities movement is that a person's health is dependent on the quality of the environment in which they live." In this perspective, promoting health necessarily requires commitments from all sectors (e.g., municipal governments, commercial establishments, health care facilities) of a community and targeting of physical, social, and political environments (Flynn, 1996). To become a member of the Healthy Cities Project, an initial commitment from the political actors is required. Subsequently, activities of the communities are identified, formulated, and implemented through community mobilization and intersectorial coop-

eration. In the area of physical activity, this might mean, for example, that the local health committee chooses as one of their priorities the promotion of physical activity throughout the community. Local newspapers might then recruit volunteers to participate in a planning committee that would in turn identify specific activities and make contacts with appropriate community organizations and sectors. This could lead to the offering of new programs, services, and events or to the mobilization of the community toward the development of new exercise facilities.

The ideas have much appeal and have received increased attention in the health promotion arena, yet there are few if any examples of these types of interventions in the physical activity literature. Understanding the emergence of physical activity promotion as a community priority might serve to enhance the understanding of the development of social norms for physical activity and of the maintenance of physical activity patterns through social pathways.

Strategies Targeting Change in the Political Environment: HP → POL → IND

One of the most recent examples of public health efforts to influence the political process occurred in relation to smoking. Legislative initiatives emerging as a result of advocacy activities as well as community mobilization led to the formulation and implementation of laws that prohibit the sale of cigarettes to minors and smoking in workplaces or in public transportation vehicles, and require the obligatory inclusion of messages regarding the health risks of smoking directly on packaging of cigarettes. As seen in Table 28.2, examples of intervention strategies targeting political actors and public policies are still in their infancy in the physical activity intervention literature. In this regard, King et al. (1995) and Blair et al. (1996) have identified several public policies that could allow for increases in physical activity. Similarly, Sallis et al. (1998) describe the success of the Intermodal Surface Transportation Efficiency Act in the United States. This legislative initiative led to the broadening of the mandate for spending in transportation. The policy went from road building and maintenance to include the development and maintenance of pedestrian and cycling routes. There are no data pertaining to the impact of these interventions, however, on physical activity levels. This may in part be due to the fact that the initiative was motivated by a desire to control air pollution and traffic congestion.

Another legislative initiative is found in the advocacy efforts that were deployed over 40 years ago in Canada to implement a law for the promotion of fitness and amateur sport (Glassford, 1992). Specifically, members of Parliament (elected officials) were concerned with the absence of any structures to ensure the promotion of physical activity and opportunities for involvement in amateur sport. The efforts were finally rewarded by the passing of Bill C-131 into law. The Fitness and Amateur Sport Act (see Bouchard, McPherson, & Taylor, 1992) renders the Minister of Health accountable to Parliament as well as to the Canadian people regarding physical activity promotion. The law allows the Minister to expend public funds and endorse activities of civil servants in furtherance of activities designed to promote physical activity and amateur sport in Canada. Unfortunately, there are no documented accounts of the activities that led to the adoption of this law nor of its actual impact on the physical activity levels of Canadians.

Methodologically, planned interventions with political actors will be difficult to implement in a standardized way. However, several health promotion researchers have suggested a number of alternative strategies to document the processes and outcomes of a variety of advocacy activities (see Holtgrave, Doll, & Harrison, 1997). There is great interest in the idea and potential impact of policy and political interventions as they pertain to physical activity interventions. However, little is know about their content, impact, and feasibility.

Strategies Focused on Networking Political Environments: HP → [POL – POL] → IND

Similarly to the previously described intervention, HP → [POL – POL] → IND interventions have a limited history in the physical activity promotion literature. An example of this type of intervention strategy is if the Ministry of Education and the Ministry of Health at one level of government (e.g., state or provincial level) were to network with municipal governments (e.g., municipal leisure departments) to join forces to promote physical activity in the schools and in youth drop-in centers (see Table 28.2 for further examples). Although the ideas have much appeal and have received increased attention in the health promotion literature, there are few if any examples of these types of interventions in the physical activity literature (Blair et al., 1996). There are several initiatives in Canada that involve such intergovernmental cooperation (e.g., Kino-Quebec, 1996; Ministry of Alberta Community Development, 1997; Ontario Ministry of Citizenship, 1995).

Other Comments

The previous selective review of the literature should be supplemented with two additional ideas. First, examination of published research in the area of heart health shows (Lévesque et al., 2000) that there are other even more complicated interventions being implemented. For example, an HP → COM → ORG → IND strategy was noted for an intervention (HP) in which lay leaders (COM) were trained on ways to approach shop owners (ORG) in an effort to get them to display no-smoking signs for the benefit of their clientele (IND) (McAlister, Puska, Salonen, Tuomilehto, & Koskela, 1982). Hence, it is of interest to examine the full breadth of interventions that could be used and those that are in fact implemented by practitioners in their day-to-day activities.

Second, we have attempted to enumerate and illustrate physical activity interventions as they might be conceptualized in an ecological approach: as a function of different targets and general approach to change (i.e., modification vs. networking). However, this enumeration does not highlight a more overriding principle: There is a need to understand how interventions have an influence across levels of intervention. For example, this might mean that if one were to implement an intervention at the level of the interpersonal environment, then one should ascertain its impact simultaneously on the interpersonal and individual levels. Similarly, a community-level intervention should probably be examined from the lens of any changes in community indicators of physical activity as well as organizational indicators, family-level indicators, and individual-level indicators. As mentioned previously, this task has proved elusive as conceptual models typically do not address cross-level influences or interactions and statistical models for the treatment of hierarchically structured data have not, until now, been widely available. We trust that over the next decade researchers will attempt not only to understand physical activity interventions targeted at different levels but also to understand cross-level influences and cross-level interventions.

CONCLUSIONS

Five conclusions can be drawn from the previous discussion. First, research into physical activity interventions can be characterized as emerging mainly from a clinical perspective. That is, most interventions are either HP → IND, HP → [IND – IND] → IND, HP → INT → IND, or HP → [INT – INT] → IND. Comparatively fewer interventions have been aimed at higher levels of the ecology of human functioning (organizations, communities, political actors). Thus, there is comparatively less information on population approaches. This trend parallels the evolution of public health efforts to combat other public health problems, such as diabetes and smoking (Glasgow, Wagner, et al., 1999; Lichtenstein & Glasgow, 1992). It is reasonable to suggest that progress in increasing levels of physical activity in the population could be achieved from the lessons learned in these areas.

Second, there is a need to provide more detailed descriptions of interventions and intervention activities. Physical activity interventions are often complex packages of activities delivered in single settings. A better understanding of intervention efficacy and effectiveness will be gleaned from more detailed descriptive studies. Third, there is a pressing need to develop and refine indicators of intervention outcomes at levels other than the individual level. This means that indicators of physical activity at the interpersonal, organizational, community, and political levels will require conceptualization and measurement. Fourth, more research is required on intervention effectiveness. The availability of effectiveness trials has the potential to pave the way to more extensive and fruitful exchanges between practitioners and researchers.

Finally, above and beyond these comments, the relevance of research into psychosocial factors associated with physical activity interventions should be reiterated. Whether at the individual or population level (see Jeffery, 1989), the focus of these interventions is a behavior. Hence, any full understanding of the manner in which this behavior is elicited should be founded on a thorough understanding of the functioning of the individual (see Bandura, 1998; Baumeister et al., 1994; Carver & Scheier, 1998). In addition and perhaps more critically, the concepts and models emerging from the fields of psychology can be incorporated into studies at various levels of the ecological hierarchy. For example, community psychology has provided many insights into the manner in which communities evolve and change (see Tolan, Keys, Chertok, & Leonard, 1993). On the basis of these ideas, exercise psychology researchers can significantly contribute to the resolution of the public health issue of physical inactivity by contributing to the vast research agenda described above.

REFERENCES

Aguirre-Molina, M., & Gorman, D.M. (1996). Community-based approaches for the prevention of alcohol, tobacco, and other drug use. *Annual Review of Public Health, 17,* 337–358.

American College of Sports Medicine. (1991). Position stand: The recommended quantity of exercise for developing and maintaining cardiorespiratory and muscular fitness in healthy adults. *Medicine and Science in Sports and Exercise, 22,* 265–274.

Ashton, J. (1991). The Healthy Cities Project: A challenge for health education. *Health Education Quarterly, 18,* 39–48.

Ashton, J., & Seymour, H. (1988). *The new public health.* Buckingham, England: Open University Press.

Bandura, A. (1986). *Social foundations of thought and action: A social cognitive theory.* Englewood Cliffs, NJ: Prentice Hall.

Bandura, A. (1997). *Self-efficacy: The exercise of control.* New York: Freeman.

Bandura, A. (1998). Health promotion from the perspective of social cognitive theory. *Psychology & Health, 13,* 623–649.

Baranowski, T., Anderson, C., & Carmack, C. (1998). Mediating variable frameworks in physical activity interventions: How are we doing? How might we do better? *American Journal of Preventive Medicine, 15,* 266–297.

Baranowski, T., Lin, L.S., Wetter, D.W., Resnicow, K., & Davis-Hearn, M. (1997). Theory as mediating variables: Why aren't community interventions working as desired? *Annals of Epidemiology, 57,* 389–595.

Bartholomew, L.K., Parcel, G.S., & Kok, G. (1998). Intervention mapping: A process for developing theory and evidence-based health education programs. *Health Education and Behavior, 25,* 545–563.

Baum, F., & Sanders, D. (1995). Can health promotion and primary health care achieve health for all without a return to their more radical agenda? *Health Promotion International, 10,* 149–160.

Baumeister, R.F., Heatherton, T.F., & Tice, D.M. (1994). *Losing control: How and why people fail at self-regulation.* New York: Academic Press.

Beaglehole, R., & Bonita, R. (1998). Public health at the crossroads: Which way forward? *Lancet, 351,* 590–591.

Berkman, L.F. (1995). The role of social relations in health promotion. *Psychosomatic Medicine, 57,* 245–254.

Blair, S.N., Booth, M., Gyarfas, I., Iwane, H., Mati, B., Matsudo, V., Morrow, M.S., Noakes, T., & Shephard, R. (1996). Development of public policy and physical activity initiatives internationally. *Sports Medicine, 21,* 157–163.

Blair, S.N., Kohl, H.W., & Gordon, N.F. (1992). Physical activity and health: A lifestyle approach. *Medicine, Exercise, Nutrition, and Health, 1,* 54–57.

Blair, S.N., & Morrow, J.R. (1998). Cooper Institute/American College of Sports Medicine: 1997 Physical Activity Interventions conference. *American Journal of Preventive Medicine, 15,* 255–256.

Blamey, A., Mutrie, N., & Aitchison, T. (1995). Health promotion by encouraged use of stairs. *British Medical Journal, 311,* 289–290.

Bouchard, C., McPherson, B.D., & Taylor, A.W. (1992). *Physical activity sciences.* Champaign, IL: Human Kinetics.

Bracht, N. (1999). *Health promotion at the community level: New advances.* (2nd ed.). Newbury Park, CA: Sage.

Brawley, L.R., Rejeski, W.J., & Lutes, L.J. (2000). Group-mediated cognitive-behavioral intervention for increasing adherence to physical activity in older adults. *Journal of Applied Biobehavioral Research, 5,* 47–65.

Breslow, L. (1990). The future of public health: Prospects in the U.S. for the 1990's. *Annual Review of Public Health, 11,* 1–29.

Brownson, R.C., Koffman, D.M., Novotny, T.E., Hughes, R.G., & Eriksen, M.P. (1995). Environmental and policy interventions to control tobacco use and prevent cardiovascular disease. *Health Education Quarterly, 22,* 478–498.

Bryk, T.A., & Raudenbush, S.W. (1992). *Hierarchical linear models.* Newbury Park, CA: Sage.

Bryk, T.A., Raudenbush, S.W., & Congdon, R. (1996). *Hierarchical linear and nonlinear modeling with the HLM/2 and HLM/3 programs.* Chicago: Scientific Software International.

Bukowski, W.M. (Ed.). (1998). *Sociometry then and now: Building on six decades of measuring children's experiences with the peer group.* San Francisco: Jossey-Bass.

Bunton, R., & MacDonald, G. (1992). *Health promotion: Disciplines and diversity.* London: Routledge.

Canadian Fitness and Lifestyle Research Institute. (1996a). How active are Canadians? *Progress in Prevention, 1,* 1–2.

Canadian Fitness and Lifestyle Research Institute. (1996b). Stages of change in physical activity. *Progress in Prevention, 5,* 1–2.

Carron, A.V., Hausenblas, H.A., & Mack, D. (1996). Social influence and exercise: A meta-analysis. *Journal of Sport & Exercise Psychology, 18,* 1–16.

Carron, A.V., & Spink, K.S. (1993). Team building in an exercise setting. *The Sport Psychologist, 7,* 8–18.

Carver, C.S., & Scheier, M.F. (1998). *On the self-regulation of behavior.* Boston: Cambridge University Press.

Caspersen, C.J., Merritt, R.K., & Stephens, T. (1994). International activity patterns: A methodological perspective. In R.K. Dishman (Ed.), *Advances in exercise adherence* (pp. 73–110). Champaign, IL: Human Kinetics.

Cheadle, A., Wagner, E., Koepsell, T., Kristal, A., & Patrick, D. (1992). Environmental indicators: A tool for evaluating community-based health-promotion programs. *American Journal of Preventive Medicine, 8,* 345–350.

Chogahara, M., Cousins, S.O., & Wankel, L.M. (1998). Social influences on physical activity in older adults: A review. *Journal of Aging and Physical Activity, 6,* 1–17.

Cohen, S. (1988). Psychosocial models of social support in the etiology of disease. *Health Psychology, 7,* 269–297.

Cohen, S., & Lichtenstein, E. (1990). Partner behaviors that support quitting smoking. *Journal of Consulting and Clinical Psychology, 58,* 304–309.

Collingwood, T.R. (1994). Fitness programs. In M.P. O'Donnell & J.S. Harris (Eds.), *Health promotion in the workplace* (2nd ed., pp. 240–270). Albany, NY: Delmar.

Copeland, A.P., & White, K.M. (1991). *Studying families: Applied social research methods series* (Vol. 27). Newbury Park, CA: Sage.

Corti, B., Donovan, R.J., & Holman, C.D. (1997). Factors influencing the use of physical activity facilities: Results from qualitative research. *Health Promotion Journal of Australia, 7,* 16–21.

Dishman, R.K. (Ed.). (1994). *Advances in exercise adherence.* Champaign, IL: Human Kinetics.

Dishman, R.K., & Buckworth, J. (1996). Increasing physical activity: A quantitative synthesis. *Medicine and Science in Sports and Exercise, 28,* 706–719.

Dishman, R.K., Oldenburg, B., O'Neal, H., & Shephard, R.J. (1998). Worksite physical activity interventions. *American Journal of Preventive Medicine, 15,* 344–361.

Duncan, C., Jones, K., & Moon, G. (1993). Do places matter: A multi-level analysis of regional variations in health-related behaviour in Britain. *Social Science and Medicine, 37,* 725–733.

Duncan, C., Jones, K., & Moon, G. (1996). Health-related behaviour in context: A multilevel modeling approach. *Social Science and Medicine, 42,* 817–830.

Dunn, A.L., Anderson, R.E., & Jakicic, J.M. (1998). Lifestyle physical activity interventions: History, short- and long-term effects, and recommendations. *American Journal of Preventive Medicine, 15,* 398–412.

Epstein, L.H., Valoski, A., Wing, R.R., & McCurley, J. (1990). Ten-year follow-up of behavioral, family-based treatment for obese children. *Journal of American Medical Association, 264,* 2519–2523.

Epstein, L.H., Wing, R.R., Koeske, R., Ossip, D., & Beck, S.A. (1982). A comparison of lifestyle change and programmed aerobic exercise on weight and fitness changes in obese children. *Behavior Therapy, 13,* 651–665.

Epstein, L.H., Wing, R.R., Koeske, R., & Valoski, A. (1985). A comparison of lifestyle exercise, aerobic exercise, and calisthenics on weight loss in obese children. *Behavior Therapy, 16,* 345–356.

Evans, R.G., Barer, M.L., & Marmor, T.R. (Eds.). (1995). *Why are some people healthy and others not?* New York: Aldine de Gruyter.

Ewart, C.K. (1991). Social action theory for a public health psychology. *American Psychologist, 46,* 931–946.

Fisher, L., Soubhi, H., Mansi, O., Paradis, G., Gauvin, L., & Potvin, L. (1998). Family processes in health research: Extending a family typology to a different cultural context. *Health Psychology, 17,* 358–366.

Flay, B.R. (1986). Efficacy and effectiveness trials (and other phases of research) in the development of health promotion programs. *Preventive Medicine, 15,* 451–474.

Flynn, B.C. (1996). Healthy cities: Toward worldwide health promotion. *Annual Review of Public Health, 17,* 299–309.

Freudenberg, N., Rogers, T., & Wallerstein, N. (1995). Strengthening individual and community capacity to prevent disease and promote health: In search of relevant theories and principles. *Health Education Quarterly, 22,* 290–306.

Glanz, K., Lankenau, B., Forester, S., Temple, S., Mullis, R., & Schmid, T. (1995). Environmental and policy approaches to cardiovascular disease prevention through nutrition: Opportunities for state and local action. *Health Education and Behavior, 22,* 512–527.

Glanz, K., & Mullis, R.M. (1988). Environmental interventions to promote healthy eating: A review of models, programs, and evidence. *Health Education Quarterly, 15,* 395–415.

Glasgow, R.E., Vogt, T.M., & Boles, S.M. (1999). Evaluating the public health impact of health promotion interventions: The RE-AIM framework. *American Journal of Public Health, 89,* 1322–1327.

Glasgow, R.E., Wagner, E.H., Kaplan, R.M., Vinicor, F., Smith, L., & Norman, J. (1999). If diabetes is a public health problem, why not treat it as one? A population-based approach to chronic illness. *Annals of Behavioral Medicine, 21,* 159–170.

Glassford, G.R. (1992). History of the physical activity sciences. In C. Bouchard, B. McPherson, & A.W. Taylor (Eds.), *Physical activity sciences.* Champaign, IL: Human Kinetics.

Goldstein, H., Rasbash, J., Plewis, I., Draper, D., Browne, W., Yang, M., Woodhouse, G., & Healy, M. (1998). *A user's guide to MLwiN.* London: University of London, Institute of Education, Multilevel Models Project.

Goodman, R.M., & Steckler, A.B. (1989). Mobilizing organizations for health enhancement: Theories of organizational change. In K. Glanz, F.M. Lewis, & B.K. Rimer (Eds.), *Health education and health behavior* (pp. 314–341). San Francisco: Jossey-Bass.

Green, L.W. (2000). Caveats on coalitions: In praise of partnerships. *Health Promotion Practice, 1,* 64–65.

Green, L.W., & Kreuter, M.W. (1999). *Health promotion planning: An educational and ecological approach.* Mountain View, CA: Mayfield.

Green, L.W., Richard, L., & Potvin, L. (1996). Ecological foundations of health promotion. *American Journal of Health Promotion, 10,* 270–281.

Hancock, T. (1993). The evolution, impact and significance of the Healthy Cities/Healthy Communities movement. *Journal of Public Health Policy, 14,* 5–18.

Haskell, W.L. (1994). Dose-response issues from a biological perspective. In C. Bouchard, R.J. Shephard, & T. Stephens (Eds.), *Physical activity, fitness, and health: International proceedings and consensus statement* (pp. 1030–1039). Champaign, IL: Human Kinetics.

Holtgrave, D.R., Doll, L.S., & Harrison, J. (1997). Influence of behavioral and social science on public health policymaking. *American Psychologist, 52,* 167–173.

Jeffery, R.W. (1989). Risk behaviors and health: Contrasting individual and population perspectives. *American Psychologist, 44,* 1194–1202.

Karoly, P. (1993). Mechanisms of self-regulation: An overview. *Annual Review of Psychology, 44,* 23–52.

Kickbush, I. (1986). Health promotion: A global perspective. *Canadian Journal of Public Health, 77,* 321–326.

King, A.C. (1991). Community intervention for promotion of physical activity and fitness. *Exercise and Sport Sciences Reviews, 19,* 211–259.

King, A.C. (1994). Community and public health approaches to the promotion of physical activity. *Medicine and Science in Sports and Exercise, 26,* 1405–1412.

King, A.C., Jeffery, R.W., Fridinger, F., Dusenbury, L., Provence, S., Hedlund, S.A., & Spangler, K. (1995). Community and policy approaches to cardiovascular disease prevention through physical activity: Issues and opportunities. *Health Education Quarterly, 22,* 499–511.

King, A.C., Rejeski, W.J., & Buchner, D.M. (1998). Physical activity interventions targeting older adults: A critical review and recommendation. *American Journal of Preventive Medicine, 15,* 316–333.

King, A.C., Sallis, J.F., Dunn, A.L., Simons-Morton, D.G., Albright, C.A., Cohen, S., Rejeski, W.J., Marcus, B.H., & Coday, M.C. (1998). Overview of the Activity Counseling Trial (ACT) intervention for promoting physical activity in primary health care settings. *Medicine and Science in Sports and Exercise, 30,* 1086–1096.

Kino-Québec (1996). *Plan d'action 1996–2000: Ensemble pour un Québec physiquement actif [Action plan 1996–2000: Together for a physically active Quebec].* Montréal, Canada: Bibliothèque nationale du Québec.

Laszlo, E. (1975). The meaning and significance of general system theory. *Behavioral Science, 20,* 9–24.

Lévesque, L., Richard, L., Duplantie, J., Cargo, M., Renaud, L., Gauvin, L., & Potvin, L. (2000). Vers une description et une évaluation du caractère écologique des interventions en promotion de la santé: Le cas de la Carélie du Nord [Toward a description and evaluation of the ecologicalness of health promotion interventions: The North Karelia Project]. *Ruptures, 7,* 114–129.

Lichtenstein, E., & Glasgow, R.E. (1992). Smoking cessation: What have we learned over the past decade? *Journal of Consulting and Clinical Psychology, 60,* 518–527.

Linenger, J.M., Chesson, C.V., & Nice, D.S. (1991). Physical fitness gains following simple environmental changes. *American Journal of Preventive Medicine, 7,* 298–310.

Maddux, J.E., Brawley, L.R., & Boykin, A. (1995). Self-efficacy and healthy behavior: Prevention, promotion, and detection. In J.E. Maddux (Ed.), *Self-efficacy, adaptation, and adjustment: Theory, research, and application* (pp. 123–202). New York: Plenum Press.

McAlister, A., Puska, P., Salonen, J., Tuomilehto, J., & Koskela, K. (1982). Theory and action for health promotion: Illustrations from the North Karelia Project. *American Journal of Public Health, 72,* 43–50.

McGuire, W.J. (1983). A contextualist theory of knowledge: Its implications for innovation and reform in psychological research. In L. Berkowitz (Ed.), *Advances in experimental social psychology* (Vol. 16, pp. 1–47). New York: Academic Press.

McIntyre, S., MacIver, S., & Sooman, A. (1993). Area, class and health: Should we be focusing on places or people? *Journal of Social Policy, 2,* 213–234.

McLeroy, K.R., Bibeau, D., Steckler, A., & Glanz, K. (1988). An ecological perspective on health promotion programs. *Health Education Quarterly, 15,* 351–377.

McQueen, D.V., & Anderson, L.M. (in press). What counts as evidence? Issues and debates on evidence relevant to the evaluation of community health promotion programs. In I. Rootman, M. Goodstadt, B. Hyndman, D.V. McQueen, L. Potvin, J. Springett, & E. Ziglio (Eds.), *Evaluation in health promotion: Principles and perspectives.* Copenhagen, Denmark: World Health Organization.

Miller, J.G. (1978). *Living systems.* New York: McGraw-Hill.

Miller, J.L., & Miller, J.G. (1992). Greater than the sum of its parts: Subsystems which process both matter-energy and information. *Behavioral Science, 37,* 1–9.

Ministry of Alberta Community Development. (1997). *Framework for physical activity: An Alberta Active Living strategy.* Edmonton, Canada: Author.

Montoye, H.J., Kemper, H.C.G., Saris, W.H.M., & Washburn, R.A. (1996). *Measuring physical activity and energy expenditure.* Champaign, IL: Human Kinetics.

Nader, P.R., Sallis, J.F., Patterson, T.L., Abramson, I.S., Rupp, J.W., Senn, K.L., Atkins, C.J., Roppe, B.E., Morris, J.A., Wallace, J.P., & Vega, W.A. (1989). A family approach to cardiovascular risk reduction: Results from the San Diego Family Health Project. *Health Education Quarterly, 16,* 229–244.

Ontario Ministry of Citizenship, Culture, and Recreation and the Ministry of Health. (1995). *Physical Activity Intervention framework.* Ontario, Canada: Author.

Paine-Andrews, A., Fisher, J.L., Harris, K.J., Lewis, R.K., Williams, E.L., Vincent, M.L., Fawcett, E.B., & Campuzano, M.K. (2000). Some experiential lessons in supporting and evaluating community-based initiatives for preventing adolescent pregnancy. *Health Promotion Practice, 1,* 66–76.

Pate, R.R. (1995). Recent statements and initiatives on physical activity and health. *Quest, 47,* 304–310.

Pate, R.R., Pratt, M., Blair, S.N., Haskell, W.L., Macera, C.A., Bouchard, C., Buchner, D., Ettinger, W., Heath, G.W., King, A.C., Kriska, A., Leon, A.S., Marcus, B.H., Morris, J., Paffenbarger, R.S., Patrick, K., Pollock, M.L., Rippe, J.M., Sallis, J.F., & Wilmore, J.H. (1995). Physical activity and public health: A recommendation from the Centers for Disease Control and Prevention and the American College of Sports Medicine. *Journal of American Medical Association, 273,* 402–407.

Pearce, N. (1996). Traditional epidemiology, modern epidemiology, and public health. *American Journal of Public Health, 86,* 678–683.

Pollock, M.L., Gaesser, G.A., Butcher, J.D., Després, J.P., Dishman, R.K., Franklin, B.A., & Garber, C.E. (1998). The recommended quantity and quality of exercise for developing and maintaining cardiorespiratory and muscular fitness, and flexibility in healthy adults. *Medicine and Science in Sports and Exercise, 30,* 975–991.

Potvin, L., Gauvin, L., & Nguyen, N. (1997). Prevalence of stages of change for physical activity in rural, suburban and urban communities. *Journal of Community Health, 22,* 1–13.

Potvin, L., Haddad, S., & Frohlich, K.L. (in press). Beyond process and outcome evaluation: A comprehensive approach for evaluating health promotion programs. In I. Rootman, M. Goodstadt, B. Hyndman, D.V. McQueen, L. Potvin, J. Springett, & E. Ziglio (Eds.), *Evaluation in health promotion: Principles and perspectives.* Copenhagen, Denmark: World Health Organization.

Potvin, L., & Richard, L. (in press). The evaluation of community health promotion programs. In I. Rootman, M. Goodstadt, B. Hyndman, D.V. McQueen, L. Potvin, J. Springett, & E. Ziglio (Eds.), *Evaluation in health promotion: Principles and perspectives.* Copenhagen, Denmark: World Health Organization.

Powell, K.E., Kreuter, M., & Stephens, T. (1991, Winter). The dimensions of health promotion applied to physical activity. *Journal of Public Health Policy,* 492–509.

Puska, P., Vartiainen, E., Pallonen, U., Ruotsalainen, P., Tuomilehto, J., Koskela, K., Lahtinen, A., & Norppa, J. (1981). The North Karelia Youth Project: A community-based intervention study on CVD risk factors among 13- to 15-year-old children: Study design and preliminary findings. *Preventive Medicine, 10,* 133–148.

Raeburn, J., & Beaglehole, R. (1989). Health promotion: Can it redress the health effects of social disadvantage? *Community Health Studies, 13,* 289–293.

Rappaport, J. (1987). Terms of empowerment/exemplars of prevention: Toward a theory for community psychology. *American Journal of Community Psychology, 15,* 121–148.

Richard, L., Potvin, L., Denis, J.L., & Kishchuk, N. (2000). *Integration of the ecological approach in tobacco programs for youth: A survey of Canadian public health organizations.* Manuscript submitted for publication.

Richard, L., Potvin, L., Kishchuk, N., Prlic, H., & Green, L.W. (1996). Assessment of the integration of the ecological approach in health promotion programs. *American Journal of Health Promotion, 10,* 318–328.

Rose, G. (1992). *The strategy of preventive medicine.* New York: Oxford University Press.

Rothman, A.J., & Salovey, P. (1997). Shaping perceptions to motivate healthy behavior: The role of message framing. *Psychological Bulletin, 121,* 3–19.

Sallis, J.F., Bauman, A., & Pratt, M. (1998). Environmental and policy interventions to promote physical activity. *American Journal of Preventive Medicine, 15,* 379–397.

Sallis, J.F., McKenzie, T.L., & Hovell, M.F. (1997). Effects of a 2-year physical education program (SPARK) on physical activity and fitness in elementary school students: SPARK. *American Journal of Public Health, 87,* 1328–1334.

Sallis, J.F., & Owen, N. (1997). Ecological models. In K. Glanz, F.M. Lewis, & B.K. Rimer (Eds.), *Health behavior and health education: Theory, research and practice* (2nd ed., pp. 403–424). San Francisco: Jossey-Bass.

Sallis, J.F., & Owen, N. (1999). *Physical activity and behavioral medicine.* Thousand Oaks, CA: Sage.

Schooler, C. (1995). *Physical activity interventions: Evidence and implications—Physical activity intervention policy framework.* Toronto, Canada: Queen's Printer for Ontario.

Schwab, M., & Syme, L.S. (1997). On paradigms, community participation, and the future of public health. *American Journal of Public Health, 87,* 2049–2051.

Schwartz, R., & Goodman, R.M. (2000). Health promotion practice: Advancing the state of health promotion and education practice. *Health Promotion Practice, 1,* 5–9.

Simnett, I. (1995). *Managing health promotion: Developing healthy organizations and communities.* New York: Wiley.

Simons-Morton, D.G. (1998). The context of the activity counseling trial. *Medicine and Science in Sports and Exercise, 30,* 1084–1085.

Simons-Morton, D.G., Brink, S.G., Simons-Morton, D.G., McIntyre, R., Chapman, M., Longoria, J., & Parcel, G.S. (1989). An ecological approach to the prevention of injuries due to drinking and driving. *Health Education Quarterly, 16,* 397–411.

Simons-Morton, D.G., Simons-Morton, B.G., Parcel, G.S., & Bunker, J.F. (1988). Influencing personal and environmental conditions for community health: A multilevel intervention model. *Family and Community Health, 11,* 25–35.

Spink, K.S., & Carron, A.V. (1993). The effects of team building on the adherence patterns of female exercise participants. *Journal of Sport & Exercise Psychology, 15,* 39–49.

Stephens, T. (1987). Secular trends in physical activity: Exercise boom or bust? *Research Quarterly for Exercise and Sport, 58,* 94–105.

Stephens, T., & Craig, C.L. (1990). *The well-being of Canadians: Highlights of the 1988 Campbell's survey.* Ottawa: Canadian Fitness and Lifestyle Research Institute.

Stokols, D. (1992). Establishing and maintaining healthy environments: Toward a social ecology of health promotion. *American Psychologist, 47,* 6–22.

Stokols, D. (1996). Translating social ecological theory into guidelines for community health promotion. *American Journal of Health Promotion, 10,* 282–298.

Stone, E.J., McKenzie, T.L., Welk, G., & Booth, M. (1998). Effects of physical activity interventions in youth review and synthesis. *American Journal of Preventive Medicine, 15,* 298–315.

Susser, M. (1995). The tribulations of trials: Intervention in communities [Editorial]. *American Journal of Public Health, 85,* 156–158.

Taylor, W., Baranowski, T., & Rohm-Young, D. (1998). Physical activity interventions in low-income, ethnic minority, and populations with disability. *American Journal of Preventive Medicine, 15,* 334–343.

Theme issue: Physical activity interventions. (1998). *American Journal of Preventive Medicine, 15,* 255–432.

Thoits, P. (1995). Stress, coping, and social support processes: Where are we? What next? *Journal of Health and Social Behavior, 36*(Suppl.), 53–79.

Tolan, P.H., Keys, C., Chertok, F., & Leonard, F. (Eds.). (1993). *Researching community psychology: Issues of theory and methods.* Washington, DC: American Psychological Association.

United States Department of Health and Human Services. (1996). *Physical activity and health: A report of the Surgeon General.* Atlanta: U.S. Department of Health and Human Services, Centers for Disease Control and Prevention, National Center for Chronic Disease Prevention and Health Promotion.

United States Department of Health and Human Services. (1999). *Promoting physical activity at the community level: A guide for action.* Champaign, IL: Human Kinetics.

Vogt, T.M. (1993). Paradigms and prevention. *American Journal of Public Health, 83,* 795–796.

Wandersman, A., Goodman, R.M., & Butterfoss, F.D. (1997). Understanding coalitions and how they operate. In M. Minkler (Ed.), *Community organizing and community building for health* (pp. 261–277). New Brunswick, NJ: Rutgers University Press.

CHAPTER 29

Physical Activity and Mental Health

DANIEL M. LANDERS and SHAWN M. ARENT

Although it has been known for some time that exercise is good for one's physical health, it is within the past 10 years that it has become commonplace to read in magazines and health newsletters that exercise can also be of value in promoting sound psychological health. This optimistic appraisal has attracted a great deal of attention among the lay public. However, for the most part, the scientific community has been much more cautious in offering such a blanket endorsement. Until recently, the assessments of the current state of the research literature on psychological outcomes associated with exercise, such as reduced anxiety and depression, have been equivocal.

The conclusions derived from the U.S. Surgeon General's *Report on Physical Activity and Health* (Corbin & Pangrazi, 1996) reflected the state of the literature in 1996. These conclusions were rather tentatively stated such that physical activity appears to relieve symptoms of depression and anxiety and improve moods and that regular physical activity may reduce the risk of developing depression, although further research is needed on this topic (p. 4). The use of carefully chosen words, such as "appears to" and "may," illustrates the caution scientists took in claiming psychological health benefits derived from exercise. More recent reviews of this literature have been more optimistic in concluding that the research evidence for anxiety and depression warrants the firmer conclusion that exercise *is* related to decreases in anxiety and depression (Landers, 1998, 1999; A. Taylor, in press). More recently, Mutrie (in press), in her review of studies that have focused on clinically defined depression, has gone one step further, stating that there is support for a causal link between exercise and decreased depression. An attempt is made in this chapter to discern which of these conclusions is warranted for describing the current state of the literature on exercise and mental health.

The Surgeon General's Report has been extremely important in helping to focus public attention on the role of physical activity in enhancing physical health. However, the statements made in this report regarding the role of physical activity in promoting mental health underestimate the strength of the findings for some topics. The situation is unfortunate and likely resulted from problems the writers of the report had in interpreting the vast scientific literature on exercise and mental health. This would have been particularly difficult for the topics of exercise and anxiety and exercise and depression, for each of which there are well over 100 scientific studies. Adding to the complexity of deriving conclusions from this literature is the fact that some studies show statistically significant benefits with exercise training, whereas others do not.

The paucity of epidemiological and clinical trial studies and the "mixed bag" of significant and nonsignificant findings made it difficult for scientists to give a strong endorsement for the positive influence of exercise on psychological health. One reason for greater optimism in the more recent reviews of the literature (Landers, 1998, 1999; Mutrie, in press; A. Taylor, in press) is the appearance, since 1990, of large-scale epidemiological and experimental studies and quantitative reviews (i.e., meta-analyses) of the literature.

The epidemiological studies that follow cohorts over time allow for the determination of whether activity precedes reductions in anxiety, reductions in depression, or other psychological outcomes. Such evidence is important in establishing the premise that relationships between exercise and psychological outcomes are not due to behavioral artifacts (Morgan, 1997). These studies are limited, however, in the control of all extraneous variables. Experimental studies are designed to control for extraneous variables and thus are vital for determining causation. In the better experimental studies, subjects are randomly assigned to

740

experimental (e.g., exercise training) or control (e.g., no exercise training) groups. For these studies to be useful, however, it is also important that there is low risk of error. This is usually achieved by insisting on a mean difference between groups that would not occur by chance any more than five times in 100 replications, and by having sufficient numbers of participants in each of the groups to minimize the variability. Sackett (1989) established letter grades for levels of evidence derived from empirical studies. Large randomized trials with clear-cut results and low risk of error are considered Grade A studies. Grade B studies are small randomized trials with uncertain results and moderate to high risk of error. Finally, Grade C studies have nonrandomized contemporaneous controls, nonrandomized historical controls (i.e., comparison to previously established norms), or no controls at all (i.e., case studies).

Meta-analytic reviews have also been of value in clarifying the relationships between exercise and various psychological outcomes. These quantitative summaries of results across studies are not experiments and, thus, they lack the control associated with Grade A studies. However, by including all published and unpublished studies and by combining their results and subject pools, statistical power is increased. This is important because most empirical studies dealing with exercise and mental health have insufficient statistical power to detect differences that are significant at the conventional $p < .05$ level of probability. The result has been to increase the potential for making Type II errors, that is, concluding that something is nonsignificant when in fact it is statistically significant. Hart (1994) maintains that the most important aspect of meta-analysis is that combining the results of homogeneous Grade B small-scale experimental studies can provide Grade A evidence.

Considering guidelines that have been established for evaluating overviews of research evidence (Oxman & Guyatt, 1988; see Table 29.1), meta-analyses have distinct advantages. For instance, with meta-analysis, there is a clearly defined sequence of steps that are followed and included in the final report; thus, the meta-analysis is amenable to replication. Two additional advantages that meta-analysis has over traditional narrative reviews are the use of a quantification technique (i.e., effect size) that gives an objective estimate of the magnitude of the exercise treatment effect, and the ability to examine potential moderating variables to determine if they influence exercise–mental health relationships. Although recent reviews (Mutrie, in press) have included the overall results of meta-analyses, they have ignored the conclusions derived from moderating variables.

Table 29.1   Guidelines for Evaluating Overviews and Meta-Analyses

1. Were the questions and methods clearly stated?
2. Were the search methods used to locate relevant studies comprehensive?
3. Were explicit methods used to determine which articles to include in the review?
4. Was the methodologic quality of the primary studies assessed?
5. Were the selection and assessment of the primary studies reproducible and free from bias?
6. Were differences in individual study results adequately explained?
7. Were the results of the primary studies combined appropriately?
8. Were the reviewers' conclusions supported by the data cited?

Source: From Oxman, A.D., & Guyatt, G. (1988). *Canadian Medical Association Journal, 138,* 698. Reprinted by permission.

The primary quantification technique in meta-analysis, the effect size (ES), consists of calculating mean differences of interest (e.g., treatment-control, or pretest-posttest values) and then dividing this difference by an estimate of variability (e.g., pooled standard deviation or standard error). The ESs determined in this manner are considered small if they are below .40, moderate if they range from .41 to .70, and large if they are greater than .71 (J. Cohen, 1992). Given these advantages of using meta-analysis, this chapter focuses primarily on results derived from large-scale epidemiological studies and meta-analytic reviews. Research evidence is applied to the mental health topics of mood state (i.e., anxiety, depression, and positive mood state), stress reactivity, self-esteem, and cognitive functioning. The ES reported show a minus sign to indicate that higher physical activity/fitness are related to lower levels of anxiety, depression, and stress reactivity, and a plus sign if the relationship is intended to show higher positive mood, self-esteem, and cognitive functioning.

ANXIETY REDUCTION FOLLOWING EXERCISE

It is estimated that, in the United States, approximately 7.3% of the adult population has an anxiety disorder that necessitates some form of treatment (Regier et al., 1988). In addition, stress-related emotions, such as anxiety, are common among healthy individuals (S. Cohen, Tyrell, & Smith, 1991). Psychological, psychiatric, and pharmacologic therapies are the major methods by which physicians and mental health practitioners treat anxiety disorders. However, only a small percentage of those afflicted receive any treatment (Bloom, 1985), which leads many to believe that the scope of anxiety and other mental health problems is beyond the capacity of the current health care system (Raglin, 1997). The focus on prevention to reduce health care costs has heightened interest in exercise as an alternative or adjunct to traditional interventions such as psychotherapy or drug therapies.

Anxiety is associated with the emergence of a negative form of cognitive appraisal typified by worry, self-doubt, and apprehension. According to Lazarus and Cohen (1977), "It usually arises . . . in the face of *demands that tax or exceed the resources of the system* or . . . demands to which there are no readily available or automatic adaptive responses" (p. 109). Anxiety is a cognitive phenomenon and is usually measured by questionnaires. However, behavioral measures are used with animals: It is reasoned that nonanxious animals will display less freezing and more free roaming behaviors. The questionnaire measures of anxiety used with human subjects are sometimes accompanied by physiological measures that are associated with heightened arousal/anxiety (e.g., heart rate, blood pressure, skin conductance, muscle tension). A common distinction in this literature is between state and trait questionnaire measures of anxiety. *Trait* anxiety is the general predisposition to respond across many situations with high levels of anxiety. *State* anxiety, on the other hand, is much more specific and refers to the subject's anxiety at a particular moment (Spielberger, Gorsuch, Luschene, Vagg, & Jacobs, 1983). Although trait and state aspects of anxiety are conceptually distinct, the available operational measures show a considerable overlap among these subcomponents of anxiety (Smith, 1989).

For meta-analytic reviews on this topic, the inclusion criterion has been to report only studies examining anxiety measures before and after either acute or chronic exercise. Studies with experiment-imposed psychosocial stressors during the postexercise period have not been included, because this would confound the effects of exercise with the effects of stressors. The problem arises in the interpretations derived from the meta-analytic review by Schlicht (1994), and this has created confusion on the part of subsequent narrative reviewers (Biddle, in press; Raglin, 1997). As Schlicht did not provide a complete listing of studies, Biddle questioned whether the studies in Schlicht's article were the same as in other meta-analyses. However, noting the seeming disparity in meta-analytic findings, Raglin simply concluded that the meta-analytic results were inconsistent and thus of limited value in deriving conclusions. It is important, in this and other comprehensive summaries of the literature, to exclude studies and reviews that contain experiment-imposed psychosocial stressors

because they are beyond the conventional inclusion criteria for this topic.

Overall Effects

In the largest review to date on the topic of exercise and anxiety reduction, Landers and Petruzzello (1994) examined the results of 27 narrative reviews that had been conducted between 1960 and 1992 and found that, in 81% of them, the researchers had concluded that physical activity/physical fitness was related to anxiety reduction following exercise. For the other 19%, they concluded that most of the findings were supportive of exercise being related to a reduction in anxiety, but there were some divergent results. None of these narrative reviews concluded that there was no relationship. These narrative reviews support a more recent comprehensive review on chronic exercise and self-reported anxiety (Leith, 1994) that showed that 73% of the 56 studies reported anxiety-reducing effects.

There have been at least six meta-analyses examining the relationship between exercise and anxiety reduction (Calfas & Taylor, 1994; Kugler, Seelback, & Krüskemper, 1994; Landers & Petruzzello, 1994; Long & van Stavel, 1995; McDonald & Hodgdon, 1991; Petruzzello, Landers, Hatfield, Kubitz, & Salazar, 1991). These meta-analyses ranged from 159 studies in one meta-analysis (Landers & Petruzzello, 1994) to only 11 studies in another (Calfas & Taylor, 1994). All six of these meta-analyses indicated that, across all studies examined, exercise was significantly related to a reduction in anxiety. The ES in these reviews ranged from "small" to "moderate" (ES = −.15 to −.56), and the anxiety reduction was consistent for trait, state, and psychophysiological measures of anxiety (Landers & Petruzzello, 1994; A. Taylor, in press). In terms of psychophysiological changes, another meta-analysis (Kelley & Tran, 1995) has confirmed the results of the Petruzzello et al. meta-analysis. Kelley and Tran examined 35 clinical trial studies involving 1,076 subjects and found small (− 4/ −3 mm Hg) but statistically significant postexercise reductions for both systolic and diastolic blood pressure among normal normotensive adults. In summary, the vast majority of the narrative reviews, and all of the meta-analytic reviews, supported the conclusion that, across studies published between 1960 and 1992, there is a small to moderate relationship showing that both acute and chronic exercise reduce anxiety (Landers & Petruzzello, 1994).

A recent narrative review (A. Taylor, in press) examined 38 chronic and 23 acute exercise studies published since 1989, which was the cut-off point for studies included in the most comprehensive of the previous meta-analyses

(Petruzzello et al., 1991). Unfortunately, Taylor (in press) did not provide an overall ES for these 38 chronic and 23 acute studies, but he did list individual ESs for some of the studies reviewed. Based on his narrative review of these studies, Taylor concluded they showed consistent reductions in state and trait anxiety and that these reductions were low to moderate in size.

Recently, Morgan (1997) and Raglin (1997) have argued that the overall results derived from these meta-analyses could possibly be due to behavioral artifacts, such as demand characteristics, expectancy effects, response distortion, or placebo effects. However, neither Morgan nor Raglin provided any direct evidence that the meta-analytic results were in fact due to behavioral artifacts. Considering the body of evidence on which the relationship between exercise and anxiety reduction has been established, it is highly unlikely that this relationship is due to a behavioral artifact. Behavioral artifacts are more likely to occur if only one operational measure (e.g., questionnaire) is employed. In the exercise and anxiety reduction literature, the same results are found for questionnaire measures, behavioral measures with animals, and psychophysiological measures. The convergence of these multioperational measures, which do not share the same weaknesses, greatly limits the plausibility that behavioral artifacts could be operative (Webb, Campbell, Schwartz, & Sechrest, 1966).

In addition, the greater degree of internal validity present in the higher-quality studies would minimize any effects due to behavioral artifacts. The quality of the studies was examined as a moderating variable in the Petruzzello et al. (1991) meta-analysis. It was found that anxiety was reduced following exercise in both higher- and lower-quality studies. There was also a larger ES when subjects were randomly assigned to treatment conditions than when they were part of an intact group. Similar results were provided by A. Taylor (in press), who concluded that stronger effects are shown by randomized controlled trials. Intervention studies for both acute (Crocker & Grozelle, 1991) and chronic (King, Taylor, & Haskell, 1993) exercise that had the largest number of subjects (Ns = 85 and 357, respectively) also showed that anxiety was reduced following exercise. In addition, there is limited evidence suggesting that the anxiety reduction is not an artifact due more to the cessation of a potentially threatening activity than to the exercise itself (Petruzzello, 1995, p. 109). Given these findings, the most parsimonious explanation is that exercise, rather than behavioral artifacts, is related to the reduction in anxiety.

One question that arises is whether the overall results for exercise are better or worse than the effects for other known anxiety-reducing treatments. This question has important implications in determining if exercise should be used as an adjunct or alternative to other forms of treatment. Although one study (DeVries, 1981) demonstrated that exercise is superior to tranquilizers like meprobamate, most state anxiety studies have not shown that exercise is significantly better or worse than other known anxiety-reducing treatments like meditation, relaxation training, quiet rest, reading, or drugs such as clomipramine and setraline. Petruzzello et al. (1991) showed that, when exercise is compared to other anxiety-reducing treatments, the ES is nearly zero (ES = −.04). There is some support for DeVries's (1981) finding in the trait anxiety literature (Petruzzello et al., 1991) that consists of chronic exercise studies. With trait anxiety, there is a small but meaningful difference (ES = −.31) among the 15 comparisons between exercise and some other anxiety-reducing treatment (e.g., nonaerobic activities like yoga training, group/anxiety therapy, stress inoculation training, adult education, and meditation), indicating that exercise is superior. Studies examined after 1989 (Landers & Petruzzello, 1994; A. Taylor, in press) showed mixed results, suggesting that exercise has comparable anxiety-reducing effects when compared to other medication-free anxiety treatments. The finding that aerobic exercise can produce an anxiety reduction similar in magnitude to other commonly employed anxiety treatments is noteworthy because exercise also has many other health benefits (cardiovascular, muscular, and weight reducing).

Moderator Variables

In addition to these overall effects, some of the meta-analyses (Landers & Petruzzello, 1994; Petruzzello et al., 1991) were able to identify several variables that moderated the relationship between exercise and anxiety reduction. Compared to the overall conclusion noted previously, which is based on hundreds of studies involving thousands of subjects, the findings for each of the moderating variables are based on a much smaller database. Because statistical power is much less for the moderator variables, the conclusions derived from the following moderating variables must be regarded with more caution than is warranted for the overall effects.

Subject Effects

Examination of moderator variables in the larger meta-analytic (Landers & Petruzzello, 1994; Petruzzello et al., 1991) and narrative (A. Taylor, in press) reviews shows that this anxiety reduction occurs for all types of subjects (i.e., male/female, fit/unfit, active/inactive, anxious/nonanxious, healthy/unhealthy, and young/old), although mostly non-clinical subjects were available for inclusion. However, there is now an emerging literature examining exercise in clinically anxious patients. A summary of these empirical studies shows: (1) patients with panic disorder have a lower exercise capacity than physically active controls, but results indicate that they were not more intolerant of exercise than controls (Broocks et al., 1997; Gaffney, Fenton, Lane, & Lake, 1988; Stein et al., 1992; Taylor et al., 1987); (2) exercise is typically avoided by most patients with panic disorder (Broocks et al., 1997); and (3) "reduced aerobic fitness might contribute to the pathophysiology of panic disorder and/or agoraphobia" (Broocks et al., 1997, p. 182). A randomly controlled clinical trial study (Broocks et al., 1998) showed that, in comparison to a placebo condition, a 10-week course of regular endurance running was associated with significant and clinically relevant decreases in anxiety ratings in a group of 46 patients with moderate to severe anxiety disorders (i.e., panic disorder and agoraphobia). The exercise-related decreases in anxiety ($ES = -1.41$) were comparable to a drug treatment (clomipramine; $ES = -1.35$) at the end of the 10-week program, but the drug treatment was superior to exercise earlier (at 4, 6, and 8 weeks) in the training program.

Such results with persons with anxiety disorders do not support the often cited implications derived from early research by Pitts and McClure (1967). They found that anxiety increased in anxious neurotics following the infusion of sodium DL-lactate. This early research led to recommendations that people suffering from anxiety disorders should refrain from vigorous exercise because exercise could increase blood lactate and provoke a panic attack. However, that research has been criticized on methodological grounds (Grosz & Farmer, 1969) in that lactate infusion would result in plasma alkalosis as opposed to acidosis, which occurs with vigorous exercise. It is clear from the results of the Broocks et al. (1998) study that compelling direct evidence now exists to show that people with anxiety disorders can also achieve anxiolytic benefits of exercise.

A related misinterpretation of the scientific findings also exists at the other end of the anxiety spectrum. A common contention is that the anxiolytic effects of exercise are minimal or nonexistent for persons with normal to good mental health (Brown, 1992; Morgan, 1981; Raglin, 1990). In other words, exercise does not make people more normal, it only reduces anxiety in those who are high in anxiety or are clinically anxious. This point of view predates the emergence of meta-analyses of this literature, which show that anxiety scores on questionnaires or psychophysiological measures related to anxiety are reduced regardless

of whether a person is in the normal range of anxiety or high in anxiety. The problem has been that the anxiety reductions experienced by those who are initially high in anxiety are much greater than reductions for people in the normal range and, thus, easier for reviewers to observe.

The meta-analyses (Landers & Petruzzello, 1994; Petruzzello et al., 1991) have clearly revealed (with comparisons within and across trait anxiety studies) that, compared to nonclinical subjects, there is a tendency for higher ES for cardiac rehabilitation patients, psychiatry patients, and highly anxious subjects. Whereas the overall mean ES in meta-analytic reviews for trait anxiety reductions in normal subjects with exercise has been $-.34$, the ES for subjects who are very unfit (i.e., cardiac rehabilitation patients) have been $-.44$, and for psychiatric patients ES has averaged $-.55$ (Landers, 1994). For several of the studies with highly anxious subjects, the ESs are even higher than -1.40 (Broocks et al., 1998; Jette, 1967; Sexton, Maere, & Dahl, 1989; Steptoe, Edwards, Moses, & Mathews, 1989). The results suggest that the anxiolytic effects of exercise may vary in magnitude depending on subjects' initial values of anxiety and their initial state of fitness. Larger effects would be expected for unfit, high anxious subjects, and small but significant effects would be expected for more fit, less anxious subjects (Landers & Petruzzello, 1994).

As mentioned previously, Raglin (1997) has explained that the disparity in reviewers' conclusions regarding anxiolytic effects in normal subjects has stemmed from the failure of investigators to consider behavioral artifacts such as expectancy effects, demand characteristics, and response distortion. This notion ignores the findings derived from more unobtrusive behavioral measures in animals and psychophysiological measures in humans. There is evidence that the demand characteristics of the laboratory environment may have little to do with the anxiolytic effects achieved, because exercising in a laboratory and in a natural environment reduces anxiety (McAuley, Mihalko, & Bane, 1996). Until definitive evidence is produced regarding behavioral artifacts being responsible for the findings in this substantial body of literature, the more parsimonious conclusion is that exercise significantly reduces anxiety, but that the degree of this reduction is greater in low fit or high anxious subjects than in fit subjects or people who are in the normal range of fitness and anxiety.

Exercise Effects

The anxiety reduction following exercise also occurs regardless of the intensity, duration, or type of exercise paradigm (i.e., acute or chronic) employed. However, the meta-analyses (Landers & Petruzzello, 1994; Petruzzello & Landers, 1993) revealed that the larger effects of exercise on anxiety reduction are shown when the exercise is aerobic (e.g., running, swimming, cycling) as opposed to nonaerobic (e.g., handball, strength/flexibility training). This result has held up over time as long as no other variables have been introduced to confound the relationship between exercise and anxiety reduction. Several recent resistance-training studies have either allowed subjects to take a shower or allowed them to leave the laboratory and return later to complete anxiety questionnaires (Focht & Koltyn, 1999; Garvin, Koltyn, & Morgan, 1997; Koltyn, Raglin, O'Connor, & Morgan, 1995; O'Connor, Bryant, Veltri, & Gebhardt, 1993). Any anxiety reductions occurring after showering or leaving the laboratory cannot be clearly attributed to the effects of exercise. It is interesting to note that, in these studies, there were no significant postexercise anxiety-reducing effects resulting from resistance training prior to the time subjects were allowed to shower or leave the laboratory.

A recent study (Bartholomew & Linder, 1998), though, has shown that state anxiety was reduced following 20 minutes of resistance training. However, this effect depended on intensity of the exercise. In this study, the subjects sat quietly in the laboratory for 30 minutes following the exercise. Following low-intensity resistance exercise (40% to 50% of 1 Repetition Maximum), the male and female college students reported a significant decrease in anxiety. This is a potentially important finding and, if confirmed by additional research, may clarify the conditions under which anxiety can be reduced with resistance training.

Bartholomew and Linder (1998) found a short-duration increase in anxiety following 20 minutes of high-intensity exercise (75% to 85% of 1 RM). Post hoc analysis of this increase showed that it was evident for both the arousal and cognitively laden items of the State-Trait Anxiety Inventory, and only those participants who did not reach their preexercise goal for 1 RM reported an increase in anxiety. These results suggest that state anxiety increases following resistance exercise reflect more than merely a change in physiological arousal and that this change could be due to perceptions of success in weight training rather than the bout of exercise per se.

In other studies, the anxiety-reducing effects of exercise were also larger when the length of the aerobic training program was at least 10 weeks and, preferably, greater than 15 weeks (Landers & Petruzzello, 1994; A. Taylor, in press). In addition, in studies where subjects have remained in the exercise testing environment, the time course for postexercise anxiety reduction begins almost immediately after exercise and lasts somewhere between four and six hours before anxiety returns to preexercise levels (Landers & Petruzzello, 1994).

It has commonly been suggested that, to experience anxiolytic benefits from exercise, the exercise needs to be at least 70% to 80% of maximum intensity for a duration of at least 20 minutes (Morgan, 1979, 1981). Although this is a good recommendation to increase one's aerobic capacity, its efficacy for reducing anxiety is not supported by the available scientific evidence. The meta-analyses (Landers & Petruzzello, 1994; Petruzzello et al., 1991) showed that where there were more than 15 ESs for comparisons of varying exercise intensities and durations, the ESs were all significantly different from zero, but there were no differences among the various intensities or durations of exercise (Petruzzello et al., 1991). For the different anxiety measures, there were very few ESs in the meta-analysis for subjects exercising at less than 60% of maximum. In addition, a confound exists in these meta-analytic findings because exercise intensity and duration were not examined together to produce an accurate estimate of work output or total energy consumption. In the meta-analyses, most of the ESs fell in the midrange of work output and, thus, no differences were observed.

More recent research (He, 1998) has systematically varied exercise intensity and duration together and found that, for moderately fit college students, exercise in the midrange of total work output (i.e., 15 and 30 minutes of high-intensity exercise and 30 and 45 minutes of low-intensity exercise) had larger anxiety-reducing effects than aerobic exercise that was outside of this range (i.e., 15 minutes low-intensity and 45 minutes high-intensity exercise). These findings for low- and high-intensity exercise have been confirmed in other studies. Anxiety reductions following exercise were not found for a 60-minute, low-intensity walk (Head, Kendall, Fermer, & Eagles, 1996) or when exercise was greater than 80% of maximum (O'Connor, Petruzzello, Kubitz, & Robinson, 1995). More dose-response research is needed to examine postexercise anxiety reduction as a function of varying exercise intensities and durations for subjects of differing fitness levels.

Explanations for the Anxiety-Reducing Effects of Exercise

Landers (1994) has summarized some of the explanations or mechanisms advanced to account for the effects of exercise or physical fitness on anxiety. These include hypotheses relating to expectations, time-out or distraction, social interaction, self-efficacy, cardiovascular fitness, endorphins, and body temperature. At the present time, some of these explanations (e.g., social interaction and self-efficacy) have very little, if any, scientific support. For the "expectation" explanation, only one study (Petruzzello, 1991, Study 3) was found that examined this. The regular exercisers completed a state anxiety questionnaire based on how they expected to feel before and after exercise, or how they felt after sitting quietly for 15 minutes while imagining a 15-minute bout of exercise. Both of these expectancy conditions revealed that expectations were equivalent to actual self-reported anxiety responses following exercise.

Petruzzello (1991) cautions that these results are correlational and that future researchers need to manipulate expectancies to determine if such a manipulation affects expected responses. It is possible that the subjects in Petruzzello's study were objectively recalling how they felt after exercising, or it could be an artifact related to what they heard from media and other sources. If it is simply an artifact, the expectation hypothesis, like the other psychological hypotheses, fails to provide a convincing explanation that would fit all of the existing data. For example, these psychological explanations may explain self-report data in humans, but they may not easily explain the results derived from behavioral findings in animals or physiological findings in humans. For the anxiety-reducing effects of exercise, these explanations are limited in that they may explain some, but not all, of the findings. The expectation explanation, however, may eventually be one of several psychological, physiological, and perhaps social explanations that receive empirical support in providing a biopsychosocial framework to account for reductions in anxiety following exercise (Gill, 1994; Landers, 1994).

Support for the time-out or distraction explanation has been mixed (Petruzzello & Landers, 1993). Although researchers have not found any difference between anxiety reduction following exercise and meditation (Bahrke & Morgan, 1978), other researchers have observed differences between exercise and activities that would likely serve as a time-out or distraction (e.g., meditation; Petruzzello et al., 1991). One problem with finding no statistical difference between exercise and some other potentially distracting condition (e.g., meditation), and then claiming these data as support for explaining the relationship between exercise and anxiety reduction, is that there may not have been enough statistical power to legitimately test for a difference between these treatment conditions. One advantage of a meta-analysis is the ability to gain statistical power by increasing the number of subjects by combining effects across studies. When meta-analyses have been conducted, exercise

has been shown to produce significantly greater anxiolytic effects than such nonaerobic activities as yoga training and meditation (Petruzzello et al., 1991).

The cardiovascular fitness hypothesis assumes that the reductions in anxiety are associated with changes in aerobic fitness (e.g., VO_2 max). However, there is accumulating evidence that the anxiolytic benefits derived from exercise can be observed even when subjects have not shown increases in aerobic fitness. Studies have shown that even low-intensity or short bouts of walking or stretching can reduce anxiety and produce a sense of calmness (Ekkekakis, Hall, VanLanduyt, & Petruzzello, in press; Head et al., 1996).

The body temperature explanation, which is that the anxiolytic effects following exercise are a result of body heating resulting from exercise, has not received much support. Although this explanation still has some advocates (Koltyn, 1997), most of the studies that have examined core temperature have not provided convincing support for this hypothesis (Petruzzello & Landers, 1993). One problem with this hypothesis is that the research that was the impetus for it has been misreported (Koltyn, 1997; Morgan & O'Connor, 1988; Raglin & Morgan, 1985). What is usually not reported by those who have advanced this hypothesis is that von Euler and Soderberg (1957) found a curvilinear (not linear) relationship between temperature and physiological indicators of relaxation (i.e., neuromuscular activity, EEG) in animals. They noted decreased neuromuscular relaxation when the hypothalamus was heated up to 41 degrees C, but increased neuromuscular activity resulted when heating increased above 41 degrees C. Given that this finding is the basis for the hypothesis, one must wonder why a linear relationship would be expected. Instead, some specified amount of exercise-induced core temperature increase should be needed before anxiolytic effects can be produced. With the currently incomplete understanding of dose-response issues associated with exercise and anxiety reduction, it is important for future researchers to analyze core temperature in situations where anxiety may not be reduced following exercise (e.g., overtraining, or extremely high or low workloads).

Although several biochemical substances increase during prolonged exercise (catecholamines, serotonin, and other neuropeptides), the biochemical substances that have received the most research attention in relation to anxiety reduction following exercise have been endorphins. There is considerable evidence in both the animal and human literature that endogenous opioids, like beta-endorphins, are released into the body as a result of long-duration aerobic exercise (Hoffmann, 1997) as well as high-intensity resistance training (Doiron, Lehnhard, Butterfield, & Whitesides, 1999). It is unlikely that the effects of endorphins act directly on the brain because the blood-brain barrier is rather impermeable to the plasma beta-endorphins in the body. However, plasma beta-endorphins can, on their own, produce behavioral effects that suggest a general calming in animals and humans. Experimental studies in which endorphin blockers, like naloxone, have been administered have produced mixed results (Hoffmann, 1997). In some human studies where attempts have been made to block the effects of endorphins, anxiety reductions following exercise have been attenuated (Allen & Coen, 1987; Daniel, Martin, & Carter, 1992). In other studies, anxiety has either stayed the same as preexercise levels or has decreased (Farrell et al., 1986). Hoffmann suggested that this may be due to the use of low doses of naloxone in studies not showing support for the endorphin hypothesis. Interestingly, researchers who have administered higher doses of naloxone have supported the endorphin hypothesis (Allen & Coen, 1987).

There is also evidence to show that low-frequency peripheral transcutaneous or direct stimulation of afferent nerves, as would occur with skeletal muscle stretch and contraction, has been associated with an analgesic response in rats (Yao, Andersson, & Thoren, 1982a, 1982b). This response consists of a drop in blood pressure lasting as long as 10 hours. In other animal studies, after a cessation of repeated electrical muscle stimulation, blood pressure dropped and this "was accompanied by a behavioral calm with a markedly reduced spontaneous [motor] activity" (Hoffmann, 1997, p. 175). These blood pressure and behavioral effects were reversed with high, but not low, doses of naloxone. These findings strongly support the analgesic effects of beta-endorphins in producing calming effects in humans and animals following exercise.

ANTIDEPRESSANT EFFECTS OF EXERCISE

Depression is a prevalent problem in today's society. Clinical depression affects 2% to 5% of Americans each year (Kessler et al., 1994), and in the most developed countries, it affects 5% to 10% of the population (Weismann & Klerman, 1992). It is estimated that patients suffering from clinical depression make up 6% to 8% of general medical practices (Katon & Schulberg, 1992). Depression is also costly to the health care system in that depressed individuals annually spend 1.5 times more on health care than nondepressed individuals, and those being treated with

antidepressants spend three times more on outpatient pharmacy costs than those not on drug therapy (Simon, VonKorff, & Barlow, 1995). There has been increased governmental pressure to reduce rising health care costs in America. Drugs are currently the preferred method for treating depression, although psychotherapy and electroconvulsive therapy (ECT) are also used (Hale, 1996). The use of drugs, ECT, and weekly sessions of cognitive-behavioral therapy or psychotherapy is costly and often in short supply (Mutrie, in press). Effective, alternative, low-cost therapies that do not have negative side effects need to be incorporated into treatment plans. Exercise has been proposed as an alternative or adjunct to more traditional approaches for treating depression (Hales & Travis, 1987; Martinsen, 1987, 1990).

Overall Effects

Exercise and depression research has a long history. Even before the 1930s, investigators (Franz & Hamilton, 1905; Vaux, 1926) suggested a relationship between exercise and depression. Since the early 1900s, over 100 studies have been published dealing with this relationship, as have many narrative reviews. During the 1990s, at least five meta-analytic reviews (Calfas & Taylor, 1994; Craft & Landers, 1998; Kugler et al., 1994; McDonald & Hodgdon, 1991; North, McCullagh, & Tran, 1990), which have included as few as nine (Calfas & Taylor, 1994) or as many as 80 (North et al., 1990) studies, have been undertaken. Across these five meta-analytic reviews, the results were consistent across different types of depression inventories in showing that both acute and chronic exercise were related to a significant reduction in depression. These effects were generally "moderate" in magnitude for the meta-analyses that included 30 or more studies (ES = −.53 to −.72).

The meta-analyses are inconsistent when comparing exercise to the more traditional treatments for depression, such as psychotherapy and behavioral interventions (e.g., relaxation, meditation). Such findings may be related to the types of subjects employed. In examining all types of subjects, North et al. (1990) found that exercise decreased depression more than relaxation training or engaging in enjoyable activities, but did not produce effects that were different from psychotherapy. In studies with only clinically depressed subjects, exercise produced the same effects as psychotherapy, behavioral interventions, and social contact (Craft & Landers, 1998; Mutrie, in press). Exercise used in combination with individual psychotherapy, or exercise together with drug therapy, produced the largest effects. However, these effects were not significantly different from that produced by exercise alone (Craft & Landers, 1998). Mutrie cautions that the range of psychotherapeutic techniques used in these studies does not always mirror what is considered best practice for depressed patients (i.e., cognitive-behavioral therapy).

Determining that exercise is at least as effective as more traditional therapies is encouraging, especially considering the time and cost involved with treatments such as psychotherapy. Exercise also provides additional health benefits (e.g., increase in muscle tone and decreased incidence of heart disease and obesity) that behavioral interventions do not. Thus, because exercise is cost-effective, has positive health benefits, and is effective in alleviating depression, it is a viable adjunct or alternative to many of the more traditional depression therapies. Although there is a dearth of literature directly comparing exercise to drug treatments for depression, the ESs that do exist for drug treatments are similar to those for behavioral therapies. The efficacy of systematically lowering antidepressant medication dosages while concurrently supplementing the drug treatment with exercise should be of interest to researchers.

Moderating Variables

Moderating variables were also reported in some of the more comprehensive meta-analyses (Craft & Landers, 1998; North et al., 1990) that impacted the previously mentioned results. Many of these moderating effects need to be interpreted cautiously because they are based on far fewer studies and ESs.

Subject Effects

In the most comprehensive of these meta-analyses, North et al. (1990) found that the antidepressive effects of exercise occurred for male and female subjects of various ages. Although most of the subjects in this review were within the normal range on depression scores, they still showed significant decreases in depression scores (ES = −.59). However, the magnitude of these reductions were not as large as those found in meta-analytic studies in which only subjects who were classified as clinically depressed or mentally ill were included (ES = −.72; Craft & Landers, 1998). These reviews show that for subjects who were initially more depressed (e.g., moderately to severely depressed patients, ES = −.88; Craft & Landers, 1998) or less fit (e.g., cardiac rehabilitation patients, ES = −.95; North et al., 1990), exercise produced much larger effects than for subjects who were healthy (ES = −.23) or diagnosed as having mild to moderate levels of depression (ES = −.34). It should be noted that subjects with major or severe depression are rarely studied.

Without a quantitative review, the statistically significant but smaller effects for nondepressed subjects may have been overlooked by narrative reviewers who were able to single out only the larger effects seen in clinically depressed subjects. This may account for many of the earlier narrative reviews on this topic concluding that the antidepressant effects of exercise are associated only with clinical levels of depression (Gleser & Mendelberg, 1990; Martinsen, 1987, 1993, 1994).

More recently, Martinsen and Morgan (1997) have recognized the meta-analytic evidence to the contrary and have suggested that the lowering of depression scores in nondepressed subjects following exercise is likely due to behavioral artifacts. However, like Raglin (1997), Martinsen and Morgan do not provide any research evidence to support the view that behavioral artifacts would produce these results. If true, one might expect to observe larger effects in studies with fewer controls for artifacts (i.e., studies of lower quality). However, meta-analyses (Craft & Landers, 1998; North et al., 1990) indicate that the internal validity of these studies was sometimes related to the magnitude of the findings, but not in the proposed linear fashion (Craft & Landers, 1998; North et al., 1990). Investigations judged to have better quality in the meta-analyses, and "key" studies identified by Mutrie (in press), provide convincing evidence that exercise produces an antidepressant effect.

Consider the logic for the belief that behavioral artifacts explain the findings for nondepressed subjects. The most common way that researchers have operationally defined clinical depression is to identify people who have a score of 16 or above on the Beck Depression Inventory (BDI; Beck, Ward, Mendelsohn, Mock, & Erbaugh, 1961). Consider two people, one clinically depressed (BDI = 19) and the other nondepressed (BDI = 15), who both show a reduction of three points on the BDI following exercise. In the first case, Martinsen and Morgan (1997) argue that this represents a "true" antidepressant effect of exercise, but, in the second case, the reduction in depression scores is interpreted as a behavioral artifact. Note that there is no floor effect for these scores. It would not be very parsimonious, or even logical, to interpret exercise minimal changes in depression scores differently for clinically depressed and nondepressed subjects. In addition, when one considers the accumulating physiological evidence that exercise affects serotonin (Chaouloff, 1997; Jacobs, 1994) and norepinephrine (Dishman, 1997) levels in ways that are known to have antidepressive effects, the behavioral artifact explanation becomes a less plausible account for the findings in nondepressed subjects. It is much more plausible to conclude that, as long as there is room for a reduction in depression scores (i.e., no floor effect), the scores of nonclinically depressed subjects and clinically depressed subjects will be lower following acute or chronic exercise.

The research evidence presented in comprehensive meta-analytic (Craft & Landers, 1998) and narrative (Mutrie, in press) reviews has consistently shown that people diagnosed with clinical depression can reduce their depression with exercise. In addition to reviewing the meta-analytic evidence, Mutrie's review has also examined epidemiological evidence for the antidepressant effects of exercise. The epidemiological studies (Camacho, Roberts, Lazarus, Kaplan, & Cohen, 1991; Farmer et al., 1988; Paffenbarger, Lee, & Leung, 1994; Weyerer, 1992) reviewed were all prospective studies that followed cohorts over time and had samples large enough to control for potentially confounding variables, such as age, physical health status, and socioeconomic status. In all of these studies, there was a significant relationship between physical activity and depression, with less activity being associated with a greater incidence of depression. In three of the four studies, people who were inactive at baseline were the most likely to develop depression at follow-up. These results suggest that inactivity precedes depression and not the other way around. There is also no evidence that increasing physical activity/exercise increases the risk of depression.

The results of a 16-week randomized control trial also support the findings of the meta-analyses and epidemiological studies. Blumenthal et al. (1999) randomly assigned 156 men and women, who suffered from major depressive disorder, to either a supervised aerobic exercise program (three times per week), a medication treatment (Zoloft), or a combined treatment of medication and exercise. The results showed that, after the 16 week intervention period, all three groups significantly reduced depressive symptoms. The exercise and medication effects each elicited comparable changes in depression. These results demonstrate that: (1) in terms of temporal sequencing, exercise precedes changes in depression, and (2) the effects of exercise are comparable to commonly prescribed medications that act to block the reuptake of serotonin into the cell.

Exercise Effects

Exercise produces larger antidepressant effects when (1) the exercise training program is longer than nine weeks and involves a greater number of sessions (Craft & Landers, 1998; North et al., 1990); (2) the exercise is performed in a laboratory as opposed to a treatment center (Craft & Landers, 1998); and (3) the exercise is either aerobic or nonaerobic (e.g., resistance training). Note that

for depression, compared to anxiety, there is much clearer evidence that resistance training is effective in bringing about its reduction. The antidepressant effect of exercise begins as early as the first session of exercise and persists beyond the end of the exercise program (Craft & Landers, 1998; North et al., 1990).

Other than number of weeks or sessions of exercise, none of the other moderating variables associated with dose-response effects of exercise (i.e., average duration, intensity, and number of days per week) were statistically significant (Craft & Landers, 1998). In addition, the magnitude of the ES was large (ES = $-.85$ to $-.94$), regardless of whether there was a training effect or not. As with the anxiety literature, it appears that reductions in depression scores can occur with a variety of exercise conditions and do not depend on a particular level of physical fitness being obtained.

Explanations for the Antidepressant Effects of Exercise

There are both psychological and physiological explanations for the reduction in depression following exercise. Many of the psychological explanations have been previously presented in the discussion of anxiety reduction. Many of the same limitations presented earlier also apply to the depression findings. The primary limitation is that few if any studies have included testing of these psychological explanations with depressed patients. There is more direct evidence from physiological explanations for the antidepressive effects of exercise, namely, the serotonin and norepinephrine hypotheses.

The Serotonin Hypothesis

Drugs that are commonly used in the treatment of depression (Prozac, Zoloft, and Paxil) work by altering the function of neurons that release the neurotransmitter serotonin (Jacobs, 1994). These drugs act to prevent the reuptake of serotonin by the neuron. Thus, because of reduced negative feedback, more serotonin is available to produce heightened nervous system activity. The chronically low levels of serotonin in the nervous systems of depressed patients is associated with their feeling listless, often having trouble simply raising themselves out of bed (Jacobs, 1994).

Presently, data derived from animal and human studies indicate that central serotonergic systems are modified by physical activity (Chaouloff, 1997; Jacobs, 1994). Studies with cats (Jacobs, 1994) show that when awake, the serotonin neural discharge rate is about 3 spikes (or pulses) per second. By systematically increasing motor activity while the animal is awake, the discharge rate of serotonin can increase to 4 or 5 spikes per second (Jacobs, 1994). The frequency of these spikes decreases as the animal becomes drowsy and falls asleep, but falls completely silent during a particular type of sleep called rapid eye movement (REM; Jacobs, 1994).

Exercise increases the amount of serotonin availability in animals and humans and also decreases the amount of REM sleep. REM sleep is a paradoxical form: It is a deep sleep, but it is not as restful as slow-wave sleep. Meta-analytic reviews (Kubitz, Landers, Petruzzello, & Han, 1996; O'Connor & Youngstedt, 1995) have shown that both acute and chronic exercise were related to a significant increase in slow-wave sleep and total sleep time, but was also related to a decrease in sleep-onset latency and REM sleep. In other words, exercisers went to sleep more quickly, slept longer, and had a more restful sleep than untrained subjects or nonexercisers. The increased time that exercisers are in slow-wave sleep relative to REM sleep would, in effect, increase the amount of serotonin available in their nervous system. Likewise, depressed patients can increase serotonin levels by exercising in the awake state, and this exercise would also have the effect of benefiting them during sleep by reducing the time they spent in REM sleep.

The Norepinephrine Hypothesis

Depression is also associated with a lowered synthesis of norepinephrine in the brain. Lowered levels of metabolites of norepinephine are found in the urine of depressed patients and from actions of the drugs that are used to treat depression (Dishman, 1997). Drugs like monoamine oxidase inhibitors and tricyclics block the reuptake of norepinephrine into the neuron, thus increasing the levels of norepinephrine at the synapse (Dishman, 1997).

Dishman (1997) has summarized the research evidence for exercise effects on peripheral and brain levels of norepinephrine. Examination of urinary metabolites of norepinephrine revealed that they either increased or did not change after acute physical activity (Morgan & O'Connor, 1988). Investigators (Sothmann & Ismail, 1985) have reported that, for normal men following rest conditions, there are multivariate relationships among aerobic fitness and urinary epinephrine metabolites, and depression and anxiety. The norepinephrine release also appears to be increased at higher exercise intensities (Kjaer & Galbo, 1988). The levels of norepinephrine in the brain are also raised as a result of treadmill running and chronic activity wheel running (Dishman, 1997). There is also evidence that the stress associated with chronic, unavoidable footshocks to animals produces lowered levels of norepinephrine, which can be attenuated by activity wheel running (Dishman, 1997).

Although the research to date is encouraging, there is much that remains to be determined before the norepinephrine hypothesis can be fully supported. For example, no human evidence exists in which peripheral norepinephrine levels as a function of chronic exercise training have been employed (Dishman, 1997). Likewise, questions remain concerning the interaction of various neuromodulators (norepinephrine, dopamine, gama amino butyric acid, and endorphins) in affecting depression and anxiety.

Does Exercise Cause Decreases in Depression?

A recent case has been made that, for clinically depressed individuals, research evidence is now sufficient to conclude that exercise causes a decrease in depression. Mutrie (in press) used Hill's (1965) classic criteria for determining whether a causal link exists between depression and exercise. Mutrie maintains that the research literature provides support for the following five of Hill's eight criteria: (1) strength of association, (2) consistency, (3) temporal sequence, (4) biological plausibility, and (5) experimental evidence. The meta-analyses reveal a moderate strength of association and consistency of the effects across different types of subjects in a variety of exercise and environmental conditions. The preceding section demonstrated biological plausibility. There are seven experimental studies reviewed by Mutrie, and a more recent experimental study (Blumenthal et al., 1999) also provides support for a causal link. However, only four of these studies could be considered a large randomized trials with clear-cut results (Sackett, 1989). Even the largest of these experimental studies (Blumenthal et al., 1999) had only 39 subjects in the exercise group. Without having studies with much larger samples, Grade A evidence in the medical sciences is lacking (Sackett, 1989).

However, Mutrie (in press) could not show support for three of Hill's (1965) criteria: dose-response, coherence, and specificity. Mutrie concluded "modest" support for a dose-response effect, but she provides very little scientific support for this conclusion. By contrast, the research data derived from meta-analyses that were presented for both reduction of anxiety and depression revealed no consistent evidence for a dose-response effect. This alone should cause major concern about any causal link between exercise and depression. Drugs used in the treatment of anxiety and depression would not be approved by the Federal Food and Drug Administration without an understanding of their dose-response effects. The criterion of specificity suggests that, by demonstrating that exercise is specific in reducing only depression, the argument for causation is strengthened. However, it is obvious that this is not the case because exercise can have many effects on variables that have relevance for physical and mental health. Finally, the criterion of coherence suggests that possible mechanisms should not conflict with what is understood about the natural history and biology of mental illness. The research evidence for epinephrine, serotonin, and endorphins have thus far not presented major obstacles for indicating possible coherence. However, most of the reviews for these physiological mechanisms point out the need for more in-depth research to clarify the interaction of these neuromodulators before one can conclude with greater certainty that coherence exists.

Considering the available research evidence, it seems more plausible to conclude that there is a relationship between exercise and depression. This conclusion may be fairly conservative to some, but is stronger than that contained in the Surgeon General's Report (Corbin & Pangrazi, 1996). It is premature, at this point, to state with certainty that exercise causes reductions in depression or anxiety.

EXERCISE AND STRESS REACTIVITY

The relationship between exercise and stress reactivity is also of interest to researchers concerned with mental health. The research paradigm for stress reactivity is to compare exercisers and nonexercisers in their ability to recover after being subjected to a psychosocial stressor. Stressors, such as frustrating timed cognitive tasks, are given to fit subjects or to subjects following acute exercise to determine the magnitude of their psychological and physiological responses to stressors and the amount of time it takes for them to return to baseline levels. It is believed that exercise may contribute to a "hardy" personality type, which is a person who can transform or buffer stressful events into less stressful forms by altering the appraisals of the stressor (Kobasa, 1979). By contributing to one's hardiness, it is believed that exercise can lead to a reduction in reports of illness by buffering reactions to stressful life events.

Overall Findings

In their stress reactivity meta-analysis, Crews and Landers (1987) found that, across 34 studies involving 1,449 subjects, aerobically fit subjects had significantly reduced psychosocial stress response when compared to either baseline values or a control group. The reduced physiological response to stress and faster physiological recovery resulted in less overall time spent in stress, perhaps at a lower level of stress.

A. Taylor (in press) conducted a narrative review of the stress reactivity literature since 1989 and located 14 cross-sectional, 11 chronic exercise, and 14 acute exercise studies that had not been reported in the Crews and Landers (1987) meta-analysis. Nine of the 14 cross-sectional studies showed that fit and/or active people were less reactive when exposed to psychosocial stressors. For the 11 chronic exercise studies, mixed directional results were obtained. Even though all of the chronic exercise studies led to improvements in aerobic fitness over a period of 5 to 16 weeks, only 5 of these studies showed a positive effect of training for the psychological and physiological measures recorded after a stressor was administered. One of the problems with these studies was that the number of subjects was relatively small and therefore the statistical power was potentially compromised. No statistical differences between trained and untrained people were observed with the other six investigations. The study with the largest number of subjects ($N = 79$; Calvo, Szabo, & Capafons, 1996) showed that, compared to the control group, subjects in the exercise group reduced overt behavior and cognitive/somatic anxiety, and their heart rates showed faster return to baseline following the stressor.

Ten of the 14 studies reviewed by A. Taylor (in press) indicated reduced reactivity to brief passive and active stressors following acute exercise. One of the better-designed studies (Hobson & Rejeski, 1993) with a large number of subjects ($N = 80$) indicated that, with 40 minutes of cycling exercise at 70% of VO_2 max, diastolic blood pressure and mean arterial pressure were reduced following exposure to a stressor. However, no reactivity effects were observed with 10 and 25 minutes of cycling exercise. It is also worth noting that, from these 14 studies, none of the findings that appeared to be directionally opposite from the hypothesis that exercise reduces reactivity to psychosocial stressors was significant. It remains to be seen if these trends in the more recent literature would be significant if meta-analysis would be applied to this set of studies.

Neither the meta-analysis (Crews & Landers, 1987) nor the narrative review (A. Taylor, in press) has included moderator variables. This should be done in future reviews of this area, with particular emphasis on the moderators examining the quality of the studies. Without knowing if there are stress reactivity differences between the better and poorer quality studies, there is the possibility that the overall results are due to behavioral artifacts (Morgan, 1997).

Barring any behavioral artifacts, the results of the meta-analysis, and to a lesser extent the results of the A. Taylor (in press) review, can be interpreted as exercise either acting as a coping strategy or serving as an "inoculator" so as to enable people to more effectively respond to the intrusion of psychosocial stress. Exercise may provide a more efficient system for coping with psychosocial stress by reducing autonomic recovery time. As an inoculator, exercise training bouts may be analogous to repeated psychosocial stress. These training bouts may contribute to the development of a hardy personality by enhancing physical and psychological adaptations to handle stress.

EXERCISE AND POSITIVE MOOD

The aforementioned constructs of anxiety and depression are linked in that they are concepts typically included under the more general rubric of *affect* or *mood* (specifically, negative mood). Other concepts commonly explored and associated with research on mood include anger, vigor, fatigue, confusion, pleasantness, and euphoria (Tuson & Sinyor, 1993). Lazarus (1991) contends that, of the previous constructs, only anxiety, anger, and euphoria represent true affect. Lazarus also maintains that mood and affect do not represent the same thing but, rather, different time periods on the emotional continuum. *Mood,* according to Lazarus, represents a transient state, whereas *affect* represents something more enduring. In an attempt to remain consistent with the current exercise literature, however, in this chapter mood and affect are used interchangeably. Concepts such as depression, anxiety, anger, vigor, fatigue, confusion, pleasantness, and euphoria are included under the rubric of mood. Gauvin and Brawley (1993) argue for this approach when examining exercise and mood along a positive/negative dimension. They suggest that this may be better suited to the understanding of the relationship of affect and exercise because the models that may be derived from it are intended to be broad and encompassing conceptualizations of affective experience. A model of affect that has a wider focus is more likely to capture the nature of exercise-induced affect.

The terms *mood, affect* (positive and negative), *psychological benefits,* and *well-being* are often used interchangeably when assessing the effects of exercise. However, researchers differ greatly with regard to the components and concepts they include under these labels. For example, in the exercise literature, *psychological benefits* often include improvements in cognitive functioning or decreases in stress reactivity (Tuson & Sinyor, 1993). Neither of these concepts is necessarily indicative of improvements in mood or affect, however. *Well-being* also tends to be a rather broad term that can include physical well-being, cognitive functioning, and life satisfaction in addition to those psychological states commonly associated with affect and mood (Tuson & Sinyor, 1993). Although *affect* does appear to be interchangeable with *mood* in most of the exercise literature, this may not always be the case when referring to *psychological benefits* or *well-being*. Therefore, if it is concluded that an exercise treatment did not produce psychological benefits or changes in well-being, this may or may not indicate failure to produce a change in mood state, depending on the constructs included under psychological benefits or well-being.

Overall Effects

The Surgeon General's Report mentions the possibility that exercise improves mood/affect. The cumulative evidence seems to provide considerable support for this effect on negative mood. Unfortunately, though, the area of increased positive mood following exercise has only recently been investigated. However, a meta-analytic review of the effects of exercise on mood states in the elderly (i.e., < 65 years of age) has recently been completed. Arent, Landers, and Etnier (2000) examined 158 ESs derived from 32 studies and found that exercise was associated with significantly enhanced positive mood and reduced negative mood in older adults. The overall ESs were small to moderate, representing approximately two-fifths of a standard deviation improvement of positive mood in the exercise groups. The magnitude of these findings is consistent with the improvements in vigor seen in younger subjects following aerobic exercise (McDonald & Hodgdon, 1991). An analysis of moderating variables indicated that elderly subjects engaging in either cardiovascular or resistance training exercise had greater improvements in positive mood compared to subjects participating in either no-treatment control groups, motivational control groups, or yoga. Furthermore, this effect was noted across levels of intensity of exercise.

Consistent with the Arent et al. (2000) meta-analytic findings, studies with subjects less than 65 years of age revealed a small but consistent increase in positive mood following exercise (Parfitt et al., 1996; Steptoe & Cox, 1988; Tate & Petruzzello, 1995; Treasure & Newberry, 1998; Tuson, Sinyor, & Pelletier, 1995). This effect has also been reported in a review (Stephens, 1988) of four large-scale epidemiological surveys ($N > 55,000$), with positive affect being associated with physical activity. However, this effect was largest for women and for those individuals over

40 years of age. Although many of the preliminary results have been encouraging, it remains to be seen if the additive effects of the data in these studies will result in conclusions that are as robust as the findings for the relationship between exercise and negative mood states such as anxiety and depression.

Possible Moderating Variables

Most of these studies showing elevations in positive mood have demonstrated this effect at low to moderate levels of total work output (He, 1998). However, there appears to be a possible temporal relationship between intensity of exercise and positive mood. Parfitt et al. (1996) indicated that positive affect was higher 5 minutes after exercise than it was during the last 20 seconds of the exercise bout, particularly at the highest level of exercise intensity. Clearly, this temporal relationship warrants further investigation. Furthermore, most researchers interested in the exercise–positive affect relationship have administered an aerobic exercise protocol.

There is evidence, however, that a beneficial mood-enhancing effect might also be obtained from resistance training (Arent et al., 2000). Interestingly, two recent meta-analytic reviews (Ntoumanis & Biddle, 1999, in press) have led to the conclusion that the goal orientation of the individual and the climate of the exercise session influence positive affective reactions. Specifically, larger ESs were associated with individuals adopting a task orientation or perceiving the climate as mastery-oriented compared to individuals adopting an ego orientation or perceiving the climate as performance-oriented. Despite these relatively promising findings, however, it is clear that considerable work remains to be done in the area of exercise and positive mood. This concept of mood enhancement is not unique to exercise. Mood effects have also been investigated with athletes, and this theme will be addressed next.

The Mental Health Model

The literature reviewed up to this point primarily suggests that low to moderate amounts of aerobic exercise have the potential for improving psychological health. Morgan (1985) expanded on this finding through the development of the mental health model. Tests of this model have most often involved the Profile of Mood States (POMS) questionnaire (McNair, Lorr, & Droppleman, 1971/1981). Although a brief version of this questionnaire is now available, the research to date has included the 65-item version to assess tension, depression, anger, vigor, fatigue, and confusion. Most studies have included a global mood measure consisting of the summation of negative mood factors

(tension, depression, anger, fatigue, and confusion) minus the positive mood factor (i.e., vigor); the result is multiplied by 100 to make all scores positive. Athletes completing this questionnaire have been asked to respond with how they "felt during the past week, including today."

Two approaches have been used to study the mental health model with athletes. One approach has been to compare athletes and nonathletes on the six mood factors from the POMS. This between-subjects approach (athletes vs. nonathletes), called the static mental health model, differs from the other approach, called the dynamic mental health model, in that the dynamic model is within-subjects. The dynamic model compares athletes on the POMS scales as they are subjected to dramatic increases in training volume over the course of the training season.

Static Model

The static mental health model states that "positive mental health enhances the likelihood of success in sport, whereas psychopathology is associated with a greater incidence of failure" (Morgan, 1985, p. 79). In a series of research studies, Morgan found that athletes, especially successful ones, possessed a unique mood profile, which he labeled the "Iceberg Profile" (Figure 29.1). This term refers to the graphic picture that raw scores on the POMS create when they are plotted on a profile sheet, with the test norms representing the "water line." In other words, if an athlete scores low on the negative mood scores and high on the positive vigor scale, the plotted curve resembles an iceberg; that is, vigor is above the "water or norm line," and the negative mood items are below this line. Using this terminology, Morgan's hypothesis can be simplified as

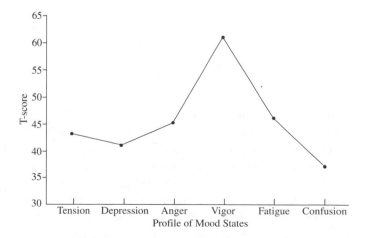

Figure 29.1 The iceberg profile (Morgan, 1985).

follows: Successful athletes possess more of an Iceberg Profile than less successful athletes.

Morgan has claimed that his findings with swimmers, runners, rowers, and wrestlers have consistently supported the Iceberg Profile and the static mental health model (Morgan, Brown, Raglin, O'Connor, & Ellickson, 1987). However, the data from some of Morgan's other studies (Morgan, O'Connor, Sparling, & Pate, 1987; Morgan & Pollock, 1977; Raglin, Morgan, & Luchsinger, 1990) and those of other investigators often show findings that are inconsistent with the Iceberg Profile and predictions derived from the mental health model. Given the conflicting findings and criticisms of the predictive power of the static mental health model (Landers, 1991), a meta-analysis was conducted by Rowley, Landers, Kyllo, and Etnier (1995) on 33 studies comparing the POMS scores of athletes differing in success. The overall effect size was significantly different from zero, but it was also very small (ES = .15). The amount of variance accounted for was less than 1%. With more than 99% of the variance unaccounted for, Rowley et al. pointed out that the meta-analytic findings did not encourage the use of the static mental health model as an instrument to predict which athletes will or will not perform successfully. For other reasons, Renger (1993) has reached the same conclusion. Although Morgan never intended that the Iceberg Profile be used for team selection, there has been the temptation for many coaches to do this. However, Morgan's cautions bear repeating, particularly now that it is known that the effects, although statistically significant, are so small as to be of trivial predictive value.

Dynamic Model

The dynamic model is a within-subjects protocol oriented to assessing the same athletes at multiple times throughout a competitive season. The variable of interest is the overall training volume that athletes are experiencing at different months during a representative season. For example, Morgan, Brown, et al. (1987) studied swimmers and demonstrated that the average yards per day swum was only about 3,000 in September, but increased to approximately 11,000 in January. They then tapered to about 5,200 in February immediately prior to the conference championship. In this example, the highest level of training (i.e., January) is often referred to as a period of overtraining, and the period before the championship is called tapering. When the POMS is administered at these different time periods, Morgan and his colleagues found a total mood disturbance when the subjects were overtrained. In other words, the positive mood factor on the POMS (i.e., vigor) is decreased, and the

five negative factors (i.e., tension, depression, anger, confusion, and fatigue) are increased. These changes are in marked contrast to what the swimmers had reported earlier in the season and, occasionally, these negative factors increase enough to be of clinical significance (Morgan, Brown, et al., 1987). When these mood disturbances appear, Morgan, Brown, et al. claim that "it is not uncommon for 5–10% of the swimmers to experience what we regard as staleness [which is] a state characterized by reduced performance in concert with an inability to train at customary levels" (p. 108). The practical implication of this model is to use the POMS as a marker of impending staleness so that training loads can be adjusted to prevent athletes from developing it.

Morgan and his colleagues (Morgan, Brown, et al., 1987) reviewed several of their own unpublished studies designed within the framework of the dynamic mental health model. Relatively small numbers of athletes ($N < 50$) were analyzed, and the authors pointed out that the considerable variability in the data suggested that major individual differences existed. These series of Grade C studies included the total or global mood measure, which combines the six POMS measures. The problem with this procedure is that the relative contributions of each of the POMS mood measures cannot be determined. As pointed out by O'Connor (1997), the mood states of vigor and fatigue are most sensitive to increases in training. They are the first to reveal a change and lead to the largest change in magnitude. Inspection of two studies (Koutedakis, Budgett, & Faulmann, 1990; Liederbach, Gleim, & Nichoas, 1992) that report data for each of the POMS factors supports O'Connor's observation, as the largest effects were found for fatigue (ES = −2.00 and −3.59) and vigor (ES = −1.45 and −1.85).

Although not mentioned by Morgan and his colleagues, the changes that are readily observed on the POMS vigor and fatigue scales may merely be associated with the subjects' objective assessment of the workload they are experiencing. Instead of a mood disturbance, as many have interpreted, it may merely reflect an outcome of the actual and perceived exertion they are experiencing. If vigor and fatigue are the only measures changing, the total mood scores may have much less psychological significance as markers of mood disturbance and impending staleness than previous supposed.

Of much greater psychological significance for mood disturbances that might be associated with staleness due to overtraining are athletes' scores on the anger, confusion, and depression scales. O'Connor (1997) points out that previous research with athletes (Raglin, Morgan, & O'Connor,

1991) suggests that these POMS measures indicate the smallest mean change in association with overtraining. However, Koutedakis et al. (1990) and Liederbach et al. (1992) reported that the only consistent negative mood reductions were the small effects for anger (ES = −.10 and −.29). The effects for negative mood reductions for depression (ES = −.80 and 2.44) and confusion (ES = −.84 and 1.46) were inconsistent, sometimes showing increases and at other times decreases.

This evidence is in conflict with O'Connor (1997, p. 154), who believes that increases in anger and depression scores "appear to be one of the most effective markers of staleness." He cites two sources for this belief. The first study (O'Connor, Morgan, Raglin, Barksdale, & Kalin, 1989) dealt only with depression. However, it represented little more than a pilot study, with three athletes who were classified as being stale. The swimmers' depression scores were high immediately following the overtraining period and stayed fairly high even after four weeks of reduced training. It is questionable how stable these findings are considering that results are based on only three subjects. When much larger samples are employed (Raglin et al., 1991), relative to normative data for the POMS, swimmers' depression scores show the smallest changes of any of the POMS factors.

The second source of empirical evidence offered by O'Connor (1997) was derived from the work of Raglin and Morgan (1994). It was claimed that five items from the POMS depression scale and two from the anger scale were the most effective in identifying distressed swimmers. Unfortunately, these results are of little value due to major violations of statistical procedures. To produce meaningful results from discriminant function analyses, the number of subjects for each predictor variable considered should be greater than 10 subjects for each variable (ratio of 10:1). In Raglin and Morgan's study, the subject-to-variable ratios in the discriminant analyses conducted were .98:1 and 4.7:1. With these poor subject-to-variable ratios, the information derived is very unstable, and there can be little confidence that these results could be replicated with larger samples and when proper statistical methods are applied.

Although it is clear that vigor and fatigue show large changes that coincide in a dose-response fashion with increases in training load, it is currently unclear if (1) this represents anything more than subjects' objective appraisal of the actual and perceived exertion they are experiencing; (2) other POMS measures having more psychological significance (i.e., anger, tension, depression, and confusion) show similar dose-response changes; and (3) anger, tension, depression, and confusion are linked to mood disturbance and are in some way predictive of staleness in athletes.

Extension of the Dynamic Model

Morgan (1985) has proposed that there is considerable variability in mood scores. This variability is suggestive of individual differences among athletes, and scrutiny of these differences may better account for athletes' mood scores. One study in which individual differences in athletes' responses to the POMS during baseline, overtraining, and tapering stages of swimming training was reported by Goss (1994). Considering that training load is a stressor, it was logical for Goss to examine the personality characteristic of "hardiness." Hardiness can affect stress in the following two ways: by transforming stressful life events into less stressful forms by altering the subject's appraisal of the stressor, and by enabling subjects to utilize more effective coping mechanisms to reduce stress.

Goss (1994) tracked 253 male and female swimmers attending junior high school, high school, and universities in the United States and Canada. It should be pointed out that Goss's study contains far more swimmers than included in previous studies, particularly considering that subjects in other studies were often combined over different competitive seasons and were thus not independent of one another. Swimmers in her study completed the POMS, the 30-item Cognitive Hardiness Inventory, and the 20-item Everly Coping Scale in September, October, November, December, and January. Across these months, there was a threefold increase in training volume.

Consistent with previous studies, Goss (1994) found that, across time, the POMS measures of fatigue and vigor were the only POMS factors to show a significant change (i.e., vigor went down and fatigue went up during the overtraining period). Overall, as scores on the hardiness scale increased, POMS mood disturbances decreased. Swimmers scoring low in hardiness ($n = 36$) had significantly higher POMS scores for depression, anger, fatigue, and confusion than swimmers scoring high in hardiness ($n = 78$). It was also found that "as the level of hardiness increased, adaptive coping behaviors and overall health-enhancing coping behaviors also increased, and maladaptive coping behaviors decreased" (p. 143). It was also interesting that the mood disturbances in Goss's (1994) study were within the normal range for college students and none of them reached the level of clinical significance.

The lack of findings in the clinical range may be due to the training volume not being severe enough in Goss's study

(8,200 yards per day) compared to Morgan, Brown, et al.'s (1987) studies (11,000 yards per day). If any athletes were stale, it would be expected that more clinical depression would have been evident because Morgan, Brown, et al. reported that approximately 80% of stale athletes were clinically depressed. Future research is needed that examines individual differences in hardiness with a focus on all of the POMS mood factors at training volumes in excess of 11,000 yards per day. In this way, it may be determined if mood disturbances of clinical significance exist in swimmers who undergo the rigors of overtraining.

EXERCISE AND SELF-ESTEEM

Related to the study of positive mood states is the theme of physical activity and self-esteem. Self-esteem differs from self-concept in that the latter is a self-description, whereas the former is a self-rating of how the self is doing (Fox, in press). The concept of self-esteem has considerable relevance to one's mental health because it has been shown to be a key indicator of emotional stability and adjustment to life demands and one of the strongest predictors of subjective well-being (Diener, 1984; Fox, in press). It has also been related to other positive qualities (e.g., life satisfaction, positive social adjustment, resilience to stress) and choice and persistence in a range of achievement and health behaviors (Fox, in press).

Operationalizing the concept of self-esteem for scientific measurement has been fraught with problems. Much of the research literature is based on general or global measures of self-esteem. Recent advances have been made in measuring instruments that assess self-ratings in different domains (e.g., work, family, and physical activities). Ratings for the physical self are of particular interest for exercise, and recent models and instruments to test these models have been developed (Fox & Corbin, 1989; Marsh, Richards, Johnson, Roche, & Tremayne, 1994; Sonstroem, Harlow, & Josephs, 1994; Sonstroem & Morgan, 1989). Although these developments are encouraging, they are so recent that they have not as yet assumed a dominant position in the majority of research studies devoted to this topic. Investigations are reviewed and, where possible, distinctions are made between findings derived from measures of global self-esteem and those from measures of physical self-esteem.

Overall Effects

There have been a few comprehensive narrative reviews on physical activity and enhancement of self-esteem. These reviews (Leith, 1994; Sonstroem, 1984) have generally led to the conclusion that approximately half of the experimental, quasi-experimental, and preexperimental studies showed statistically significant improvements in self-esteem. Without a meta-analysis to quantitatively examine these findings, it is possible that small, nonsignificant changes were present that would not be identified in the "vote-counting" method (i.e., statistically significant or not significant) employed by these narrative reviewers. This led narrative reviewers to reach the more conservative conclusions that the results were quite inconsistent (Leith, 1994) or that exercise programs (not exercise per se) were associated with significant increases in participants' self-esteem scores (Sonstroem, 1984). Presently, meta-analytic reviews and reviews of only randomized controlled studies shed new light on the research literature in this area.

There are currently four meta-analytic reviews on self-esteem or physical self-concept (Calfas & Taylor, 1994; Gruber, 1986; McDonald & Hodgdon, 1991; Spence, Poon, & Dyck, 1997). The number of studies in these meta-analyses ranged from 10 (Calfas & Taylor, 1994) to 51 (Spence et al., 1997). In all four of the reviews, physical activity/exercise was determined to bring about small to moderate (ES = .23 to .41) increases in physical self-concept or self-esteem scores.

A recent narrative review of 36 randomized controlled studies published since 1972 was conducted by Fox (in press). He concluded that 78% of these studies yielded positive changes in some aspects of physical self-esteem or self-concept. This is a robust finding that is less susceptible to behavioral artifacts because the studies were experimental. One of the experimental studies (King et al., 1993), the one with the largest number of subjects ($N = 357$) and therefore the greatest statistical power, showed that, compared to inactive controls, subjects in exercise conditions had higher ratings of self-perception of change in health, appearance, fitness, and weight. A clinical control trial by Blumenthal et al. (1999) also found that subjects with major depression had significantly higher self-esteem scores following a 16-week aerobic exercise training program (ES = .50), and that these improvements in self-esteem were roughly the same as those obtained with medication (ES = .59) or a combination of medication and exercise (ES = .48). However, some of the self-esteem studies do not completely eliminate certain types of behavioral artifacts. For instance, social desirability responding on questionnaires has been ruled out in some studies (Sonstroem & Potts, 1996). However, in other studies (Desharnis, Jobin, Côté, Lévesque, & Godin, 1993), an expectancy-modification procedure accounted for differences in self-esteem scores, thus suggesting that exercise may enhance self-esteem by providing a strong placebo effect. The potential for this overall effect to be influenced by subject expectancies or other behavioral artifacts needs to be investigated in the future.

Moderating Variables

Meta-analyses of self-esteem and physical activity have shown that the effects generalize across gender, various ages, and subgroups of the population (Fox, in press). In comparing self-esteem scores in children, Gruber (1986) found that the effect of physical activity was larger for handicapped compared to normal children. In examining eight randomized controlled studies on children, Fox concluded that exercise was particularly effective for children who were initially low in self-esteem. Although positive effects of self-esteem were observed in all age categories, Fox stated that there was currently greater research evidence for this relationship in children and young adults.

Gruber (1986) also reported that aerobic fitness produced much larger effects on children's self-esteem scores than other types of physical education class activities (e.g., learning sports skills or perceptual-motor skills). Fox (in press) noted that for older participants, most of the evidence was in favor of the use of aerobic exercise and weight training, with weight training showing the greatest short-term benefit. Studies that have included other activities like swimming, flexibility training, martial arts, and expressive dance have not revealed significant changes in self-esteem scores. These studies are few in number, however. More research is needed before any firm conclusions can be drawn.

The results for the dose-response effects of exercise on self-esteem scores have been mixed (Fox, in press). Some studies (King et al., 1993) do not indicate any differences in self-esteem scores with exercise of different intensities, whereas other studies (MacMahon & Gross, 1988) find that higher-intensity sports produce larger effects with learning disabled boys. The duration of the exercise program has also been investigated by Leith (1994). He found that exercise programs that were longer than 12 weeks had a greater likelihood of leading to significant self-esteem changes than programs lasting 8 weeks or less.

Explanations for Self-Esteem Changes

Many explanations have been suggested for self-esteem changes due to exercise involvement, but there is very little evidence for any of them. There are some data indicating that self-esteem changes may occur because of a behavioral artifact, such as positive expectancies people associate with exercise (Desharnes et al., 1993). Fox (in press) interprets the inconsistent relationships for global self-esteem as an absence of a generic or generalized psychophysiological or psychobiochemical effect. However, the inconsistent relationship with global self-esteem is probably more a function of the lack of a quantitative literature review. It is also expected that there would be more variability associated with a global self-esteem measure than a measure that is more specific (i.e., physical self-esteem). Given the findings reported by Fox, it is more likely that both global and physical self-esteem measures are affected by exercise, but the effects are probably larger for measures of physical self-esteem. If this hypothesis is correct, then a common psychophysiological mechanism(s) could be mediating these self-esteem findings.

Research suggests that it is not necessary to be physically fit or to have experienced an increase in fitness to have an increase in self-esteem scores (Fox, in press; King et al., 1993). Therefore, the cardiovascular fitness hypothesis, which posits that physiological and biochemical changes associated with improvements in physical fitness are responsible for various mental health benefits, is questioned. The autonomy and personal control that one may gain from participation in exercise programs, or the sense of belonging one may experience from participating in group exercise programs, have been proposed as explanations for increases in self-esteem scores. However, at this time, there is no evidence for either of these social psychological explanations (Fox, in press).

Overall, Fox (in press) maintains that very little is known concerning what it is about exercise or exercise programs that makes people feel better about themselves. He believes that, ultimately, it may be shown that there are several mechanisms operating and that some factors may be necessary and others may not be. Because there is more convincing research evidence that a small to moderate relationship exists between exercise and self-esteem, it is important that future research efforts be directed toward an examination of the proposed explanations and mechanisms underlying this relationship.

EXERCISE AND COGNITIVE FUNCTIONING

The relationship between body and mind has been debated for centuries. During the 20th century, the debate has shifted to questions such as whether exercising the body has a beneficial effect on the functioning of the brain

(Etnier et al., 1997). Theorists such as Piaget (1936) and Kephart (1960), for instance, suggested that opportunities for motor development are important determinants of intellectual development in normal children and children with learning disabilities. With the more recent developments in psychophysiological methodology, evidence indicates that exercise can increase cerebral blood flow, norepinephrine, and dopamine levels and may result in permanent structural changes in the brains of animals (Etnier et al., 1997). Some of these changes associated with exercise can impact the oxygen supply to the brain, and others may have roles in enhancing memory. These research findings have been enlightening and have spawned an expanding amount of behavioral research examining the effect of exercise on the cognitive functioning of humans. This literature will be reviewed next.

Overall Findings

Twelve narrative (e.g., Boutcher, in press; Folkins & Sime, 1981; Spirduso, 1980; Tomporowski & Ellis, 1986) and two meta-analytic reviews (Etnier et al., 1997; Nowell & Landers, 1997) about exercise and cognitive functioning have been produced. The most recent (Boutcher, in press) of the narrative reviews, however, focuses primarily on the cognitive performance and fitness relationship in the elderly. Due to the limited age range in this study, the emphasis of this section is on the findings provided by the most recent and most comprehensive of the reviews of this literature. In a meta-analysis of 134 studies, Etnier et al. concluded that, across tasks such as reaction time, memory, reasoning, and academic achievement tests, the overall effect of exercise showed a small (ES = .29) but significant improvement in cognitive functioning.

Moderating Variables

An analysis of moderating variables by Etnier et al. (1997) indicated that acute exercise produced smaller effects (ES = .16) than chronic (ES = .33) exercise. Also, for acute exercise, having more than 20 people in the exercise group was associated with larger effects (ES = .61); for chronic exercise, having fewer than 10 people in the group led to larger effects (ES = 1.22). For chronic exercise, college-age subjects (ES = .64) had larger ESs than the oldest adults (60 to 90 years, ES = .19). It is also important to note that study quality was associated with a moderating influence on the relationship between exercise and cognitive functioning. For both acute and chronic exercise, better-quality studies produced smaller ESs (ES = < .06) than did the more poorly designed studies (ES = < .57).

This finding allows for the possibility that the observed relationship between exercise and cognitive functioning could be due to behavioral artifacts. In general, the notion of behavioral artifacts could be a viable explanation for the relatively small improvements in cognitive functioning reported with exercise in better-quality studies.

Within cross-sectional and correlational designs, it is possible that the differences in cognitive ability as they relate to fitness are actually preexercise cognitive differences that are inherent to the people who choose to adopt an exercise lifestyle (Etnier et al., 1997). In fact, people who exercise also tend to have a higher level of education. Although this association of fitness and cognition appears to be bolstered by the findings of intervention studies, there may be cause for reluctance in accepting this as a cause-and-effect relationship. For instance, the intervention study with the largest number of subjects (N = 101; Blumenthal et al., 1989) examined pre-post exercise changes in cognitive functioning and found that increases in aerobic power were unrelated to gains in cognitive performance. Furthermore, one requirement for establishing causation is that the participants in a study must be randomly assigned to either a treatment or control condition. However, within the chronic exercise studies analyzed by Etnier et al., the largest ESs were actually found when participants were allowed to self-select their treatment condition or were assigned to treatment conditions as an intact group. Again, these large-scale individual studies and meta-analytic findings do not rule out the possible influence of behavioral artifacts.

Explanations and Mechanisms

Many mechanisms (primarily physiological) have been advanced in an attempt to explain the fitness–cognitive performance relationship. These mechanisms include cerebral circulation, neurotrophic stimulation, neural efficiency, and secondary aging.

Support for the cerebral circulation mechanism is based on evidence that suggests that impaired cerebral circulation is associated with reduced cognitive performance (Chodzko-Zajko & Moore, 1994). Hypoxia has been found to result in a decline on a number of cognitive tasks (Kennedy, Dunlap, Bandert, Smith, & Houston, 1989). Therefore, it is possible that exercise programs (i.e., chronic exercise) help to maintain cerebrovascular integrity by facilitating oxygen delivery to the brain and, thus, positively influence cognitive performance (Boutcher, in press). Proponents of the neurotrophic stimulation mechanism assert that it is conceivable that participation in an exercise regimen may offset changes (such as reduced neurotransmitter synthesis, structural alterations to neurons, and degradation of the central nervous system) associated with aging (Chodzko-Zajko & Moore, 1994). In fact, chronic exercise has been associated with increased brain weight in primates and rats (Boutcher, in press).

A more indirect mechanism than the previous two, the concept of neural efficiency is focused on information processing efficiency of the central nervous system (CNS), which is typically inferred from EEG responses. Most of the research examining this mechanism has been conducted with older adults and has produced at least some evidence that participation in regular aerobic exercise is associated with enhanced processing by the CNS (Boutcher, in press).

A final physiological mechanism that has been proposed is based on the postulation that cardiovascular disease, adult-onset diabetes, and hypertension (all secondary aging phenomena) may impair cognitive functioning (Birren, Woods, & Williams, 1980). The primary role of exercise, then, would be to control these diseases and ultimately reduce their influence on cognitive deterioration.

Although each of these physiological explanations is fundamentally appealing, evidence from the Etnier et al. (1997) meta-analysis suggests that these may not be the most plausible explanations. For example, there was no relationship between ES and any of the moderating variables (i.e., weeks of exercise, days of exercise) that would suggest program efficacy for inducing fitness changes. Furthermore, evidence of a training effect was not related to ES. Because these are fundamental tenets on which the physiological mechanisms are based, support for these mechanisms seems to be questionable. It is more likely, then, that the association between exercise and cognition is explained by one or more of the following: (1) physiological mechanisms independent of cardiovascular fitness; (2) physiological mechanisms related to cardiovascular fitness, but occurring prior to changes in aerobic fitness; or (3) psychological mechanisms (particularly psychosocial mechanisms) independent of cardiovascular fitness (Etnier et al., 1997). This last explanation may be of particular relevance in light of the findings for the moderating effects of group size in both acute and chronic studies.

SUMMARY

The review of various mental health variables that have been related to exercise show overall that exercise is related to, but does not cause, desirable changes to occur in anxiety, depression, stress reactivity, positive mood, self-esteem, and cognitive functioning. The overall magnitude of the effect of exercise on these variables ranges from small to moderate, but in all cases, these effects are statistically significant. The good news is that the research evidence now supports stronger conclusions than presented in the 1996 Surgeon General's Report (Corbin & Pangrazi, 1996). The bad news is that there is still much to learn before the relationship between exercise and these mental health variables can be understood. This is essential in convincing medical health practitioners to increasingly view exercise as an alternative or adjunct to traditional therapies currently used to treat people with problems in these mental health areas.

Although statistically, exercise is related to these variables, some of these relationships have a greater likelihood of being spurious relationships than others. For example, the relationships with anxiety and depression are less likely to be due to behavioral artifacts because they are supported by a convergence of different measures (questionnaire, physiological, behavioral) that do not share the same methodological weaknesses. Where the research evidence consists of only an operational measure (e.g., questionnaire), behavioral artifacts have greater potential for influencing the observed relationships. Researchers should determine the influence of behavioral artifacts, particularly on positive mood, self-esteem, and cognitive functioning. The study of cognitive functioning particularly could be susceptible to contamination by behavioral artifacts because the better-designed investigations did not indicate that exercise was significantly related to cognitive functioning. This is the only area where meta-analysis showed a linear relationship such that the greater the number of threats to internal validity, the stronger was the relationship.

There is evidence from moderating variables that subjects who are extreme responders for these mental health variables at the time of the pretest (e.g., higher in anxiety and depression and lower in positive mood and self-esteem) produce larger effects than subjects who are less extreme. There also appears to be some consistency in chronic exercise producing larger effects than acute exercise, particularly if the chronic exercise program is longer than 12 weeks. Throughout most of the meta-analyses and comprehensive narrative reviews there are no observed effects due to the intensity or duration of the exercise. It is important in future research that dose-response issues (i.e., exercise intensity and duration) be systematically examined for each of these mental health variables. Likewise, the issue of anaerobic training, particularly resistance training, needs to be addressed to determine why it is effective in reducing anxiety only with low-intensity exercise (< 50% of 1 RM), but is effective in reducing depression and increasing positive mood and self-esteem with a much broader range of exercise intensities.

In addition to clarifying issues regarding potential behavioral artifacts and important moderator variables, future research is also needed to evaluate the numerous explanations that have been advanced to account for the relationships between exercise and these mental health variables. Such an examination should, where possible, design studies so that they can test the efficacy of competing explanations. This way these explanations can be directly compared in the contribution they make to explaining the exercise effects on these mental health variables.

REFERENCES

Allen, M.E., & Coen, D. (1987). Naloxone blocking of running-induced mood changes. *Annals of Sports Medicine, 3,* 190–195.

Arent, S.M., Landers, D.M., & Etnier, J.L. (2000). The effects of exercise on mood in older adults: A meta-analytic review. *Journal of Aging and Physical Activity, 8,* 416–439.

Bahrke, M.S., & Morgan, W.P. (1978). Anxiety reduction following exercise and meditation. *Cognitive Therapy and Research, 2,* 323–334.

Bartholomew, J.B., & Linder, D.E. (1998). State anxiety following resistance exercise: The role of gender and exercise intensity. *Journal of Behavioral Medicine, 21,* 205–219.

Beck, A.T., Ward, C.H., Mendelsohn, M., Mock, J., & Erbaugh, H. (1961). An inventory for measuring depression. *Archives of General Psychiatry, 4,* 561–571.

Biddle, S.J.H. (in press). Emotion, mood and physical activity. In S.J.H. Biddle, K.R. Fox, & S.H. Boutcher (Eds.), *Physical activity, mental health, and psychological well-being*. London: Routledge & Kegan Paul.

Birren, J.E., Woods, A.M., & Williams, M.V. (1980). Behavioral slowing with age: Causes, organization, and consequences. In L.W. Poon (Ed.), *Aging in the 1980s: Psychological issues* (pp. 293–308). Washington, DC: American Psychological Association.

Bloom, B.L. (1985). Focal issues in the prevention of mental disorders. In H.H. Goldman & S.E. Goldston (Eds.), *Preventing stress-related psychiatric disorders* (DHHS Publication No. ADM 85–1366). Washington, DC: U.S. Government Printing Office.

Blumenthal, J.A., Babyak, M.A., Moore, K.A., Craighead, W.E., Herman, S., Khatri, P., Waugh, R., Napolitano, M.A., Forman, L.M., Applebaum, M. Doraiswamy, M., & Krishman, R. (1999). Effects of exercise training on older patients with major depression. *Archives of Internal Medicine, 159,* 2349–2356.

Blumenthal, J.A., Emery, C.F., Madden, D.J., George, L.K., Coleman, E., Riddle, M.W., McKee, D.C., Reasoner, J., & Williams, R.S. (1989). Cardiovascular and behavioral effects of aerobic exercise training in healthy older men and women. *Journal of Gerontology: Medical Sciences, 44,* M147–M157.

Boutcher, S.H. (in press). Cognitive performance, fitness, and aging. In S.J.H. Biddle, K.R. Fox, & S.H. Boutcher (Eds.), *Physical activity, mental health, and psychological well-being*. London: Routledge & Kegan Paul.

Broocks, A., Bandelow, D., Pekrun, G., George, A., Meyer, T., Bartmann, U., Hillmer-Vogel, U., & Rüther, E. (1998). Comparison of aerobic exercise, clomipramine, and placebo in the treatment of panic disorder. *The American Journal of Psychiatry, 155,* 603–609.

Broocks, A., Meyer, T., Bandelow, B., George, A., Bartmann, U., Rüther, E., & Hillmer-Vogel, U. (1997). Exercise avoidance and impaired endurance capacity in patients with panic disorder. *Biological Psychology, 36,* 182–187.

Brown, D.R. (1992). Physical activity, aging, and psychological well-being: An overview of the research. *Canadian Journal of Sport Sciences, 17,* 185–193.

Calfas, K.J., & Taylor, W.C. (1994). Effects of physical activity on psychological variables in adolescents. *Pediatric Exercise Science, 6,* 406–423.

Calvo, M.G., Szabo, A., & Capafons, J. (1996). Anxiety and heart rate under psychological stress: The effects of exercise training. *Anxiety, Stress and Coping, 9,* 321–337.

Camacho, T.C., Roberts, R.E., Lazarus, N.B., Kaplan, G.A., & Cohen, R.D. (1991). Physical activity and depression: Evidence from the Alameda County Study. *American Journal of Epidemiology, 134,* 220–231.

Chaouloff, F. (1997). The serotonin hypothesis. In W.P. Morgan (Ed.), *Physical activity and mental health* (pp. 179–198). Washington, DC: Taylor & Francis.

Chodzko-Zajko, W.J., & Moore, K.A. (1994). Physical fitness and cognitive functioning in aging. *Exercise and Sport Science Reviews, 22,* 195–220.

Cohen, J. (1992). A power primer. *Psychological Bulletin, 112,* 155–159.

Cohen, S., Tyrell, D.A.J., & Smith, A.P. (1991). Psychological stress and susceptibility to the common cold. *New England Journal of Medicine, 325,* 606–612.

Corbin, C., & Pangrazi, B. (Eds.). (1996, July). What you need to know about the Surgeon General's report on physical activity and health. *Physical Activity and Fitness Research Digest, 2*(6), 1–8.

Craft, L.L., & Landers, D.M. (1998). The effect of exercise on clinical depression and depression resulting from mental illness: A meta-analysis. *Journal of Sport & Exercise Psychology, 20,* 339–357.

Crews, D.J., & Landers, D.M. (1987). A meta-analytic review of aerobic fitness and reactivity to psychosocial stressors. *Medicine and Science in Sports and Exercise, 19,* S114–S120.

Crocker, P.R., & Grozelle, C. (1991). Reducing induced state anxiety: Effects of acute aerobic exercise and autogenic relaxation. *Journal of Sports Medicine and Physical Fitness, 31,* 277–282.

Daniel, M., Martin, A.D., & Carter, J. (1992). Opiate receptor blockade by naltrexone and mood state after acute physical activity. *British Journal of Sports Medicine, 26,* 111–115.

Desharnis, R., Jobin, J., Côté, C., Lévesque, L., & Godin, G. (1993). Aerobic exercise and the placebo effect: A controlled study. *Psychosomatic Medicine, 55,* 149–154.

DeVries, H.A., Wisell, R.A., Bulbuliam, R., & Moritani, T. (1981). Tranquilizer effect of exercise. *American Journal of Physical Medicine, 60,* 57–60.

Diener, E. (1984). Subjective well-being. *Psychological Bulletin, 95,* 542–575.

Dishman, R.K. (1997). The norepinephrine hypothesis. In W.P. Morgan (Ed.), *Physical activity and mental health* (pp. 199–212). Washington, DC: Taylor & Francis.

Doiron, B.A.H., Lehnhard, R.A., Butterfield, S.A., & Whitesides, J.E. (1999). Beta-endorphin response to high intensity exercise and music in college-age women. *Journal of Strength and Conditioning Research, 13,* 24–28.

Ekkekakis, P., Hall, E.E., VanLanduyt, L.M., & Petruzzello, S.J. (2000). Walking in (affective) circles: Can short walks enhance affect? *Journal of Behavioral Medicine, 23,* 245–275.

Etnier, J.L., Salazar, W., Landers, D.M., Petruzzello, S.J., Han, M.W., & Nowell, P. (1997). The influence of physical activity, fitness, and exercise upon cognitive functioning: A meta-analysis. *Journal of Sport & Exercise Psychology, 19,* 249–277.

Farmer, M.E., Locke, B.Z., Mossicki, E.K., Dannenberg, A.L., Larson, D.B., & Radloff, L.S. (1988). Physical activity and depressive symptoms: The NHANES I epidemiologic follow-up study. *American Journal of Epidemiology, 128,* 1340–1351.

Farrell, P.A., Gustafson, A.B., Garthwaite, T.L., Kalhoff, R.K., Cowley, A.W., & Morgan, W.P. (1986). Influence of endogenous opioids on the response of selected hormones to exercise in man. *Journal of Applied Physiology, 61,* 1051–1057.

Focht, B.C., & Koltyn, K.F. (1999). Influence of resistance exercise of different intensities on state anxiety and blood pressure. *Medicine and Science in Sports and Exercise, 31,* 456–463.

Folkins, C.H., & Sime, W.E. (1981). Physical fitness training and mental health. *American Psychologist, 36,* 373–389.

Fox, K.R. (in press). The effects of exercise on self-perceptions and self-esteem. In S.J.H. Biddle, K.R. Fox, & S.H. Boutcher (Eds.), *Physical activity, mental health, and psychological well-being.* London: Routledge & Kegan Paul.

Fox, K.R., & Corbin, C.B. (1989). The physical self-perception profile: Development and preliminary evaluation. *Journal of Sport & Exercise Psychology, 11,* 408–430.

Franz, S.I., & Hamilton, G.V. (1905). The effects of exercise upon retardation in conditions of depression. *American Journal of Insanity, 62,* 239–256.

Gaffney, F.A., Fenton, B.J., Lane, L.D., & Lake, R. (1988). Hemodynamic, ventilatory, and biochemical responses in panic patients and normal controls with sodium lactate infusion and spontaneous panic attacks. *Archives of General Psychiatry, 45,* 53–60.

Garvin, A.W., Koltyn, K.F., & Morgan, W.P. (1997). Influence of acute physical activity and relaxation on state anxiety and blood lactate in untrained college males. *International Journal of Sports Medicine, 18,* 470–476.

Gauvin, L., & Brawley L.R. (1993). Alternative psychological models and methodologies for the study of exercise and affect. In P. Seraganian (Ed.), *Exercise psychology* (pp. 146–171). New York: Wiley.

Gill, D. (1994). A sport and exercise psychology perspective on stress. *Quest, 46,* 20–27.

Gleser, J., & Mendelberg, H. (1990). Exercise and sport in mental health: A review of the literature. *Israel Journal of Psychiatry and Related Sciences, 27,* 99–112.

Goss, J.D. (1994). Hardiness and mood disturbances in swimmers while overtraining. *Journal of Sport & Exercise Psychology, 16,* 135–149.

Grosz, H.H., & Farmer, B.B. (1969). Blood lactate in the development of anxiety symptoms. *Archives of General Psychiatry, 21,* 611–619.

Gruber, J.J. (1986). Physical activity and self-esteem development in children. In G.A. Stull & H.M. Eckert (Eds.), *Effects of physical activity and self-esteem development in children: Academy papers* (pp. 30–48). Champaign, IL: Human Kinetics.

Hale, A.S. (1996). Recent advances in the treatment of depression. *British Journal of Hospital Medicine, 55,* 183–186.

Hales, R., & Travis, T.W. (1987). Exercise as a treatment option for anxiety and depressive disorders. *Military Medicine, 152,* 299–302.

Hart, L.E. (1994). The role of evidence in promoting consensus in the research literature on physical activity, fitness, and health. In C. Bouchard, R.J. Shephard, & T. Stevens (Eds.), *Physical activity, fitness, and health* (pp. 89–97). Champaign, IL: Human Kinetics.

He, C.X. (1998). *Exercise intensity, duration, and fitness effects on mood and electroencephalographic activity.* Unpublished doctoral dissertation, Arizona State University, Tempe.

Head, A., Kendall, M.J., Fermer, R., & Eagles, C. (1996). Acute effects of beta blockade and exercise on mood and anxiety. *British Journal of Sports Medicine, 30,* 238–242.

Hill, A.B. (1965). The environment and disease: Association or causation? *Proceedings of the Royal Society of Medicine, 58,* 295–300.

Hobson, M.L., & Rejeski, W.J. (1993). Does the dose of acute exercise mediate psychophysiological responses to mental stress? *Journal of Sport & Exercise Psychology, 15,* 77–87.

Hoffmann, P. (1997). The endorphin hypothesis. In W.P. Morgan (Ed.), *Physical activity and mental health* (pp. 163–177). Washington, DC: Taylor & Francis.

Jacobs, B.L. (1994). Serotonin, motor activity and depression-related disorders. *American Scientist, 82,* 456–463.

Jette, M. (1967). *Progressive physical training on anxiety in middle-age men.* Unpublished master's thesis, University of Illinois, Champaign.

Katon, W., & Schulberg, H. (1992). Epidemiology of depression in primary care. *General Hospital Psychiatry, 14,* 237–247.

Kelley, G., & Tran, Z.V. (1995). Aerobic exercise and normotensive adults: A meta-analysis. *Medicine and Science in Sports and Exercise, 27,* 1371–1377.

Kennedy, R.S., Dunlap, W.P., Bandert, L.E., Smith, M.G., & Houston, C.S. (1989). Cognitive performance deficits in a simulated climb of Mount Everest: Operation Everest II. *Aviation, Space and Environmental Medicine, 60,* 99–104.

Kephart, N. (1960). *The slow learner in the classroom.* Columbus, OH: Merrill.

Kessler, R.C., McGonagle, K.A., Zhao, S., Nelson, C.B., Hughes, M., Eshelman, S., Wittchen, H.U., & Kendler, K.S. (1994). Lifetime and 12-month prevalence of *DSM-III-R* psychiatric disorders in the United States: Results from the National Co-Morbidity Survey. *Archives of General Psychiatry, 51,* 8–19.

King, A.C., Taylor, C.B., & Haskell, W.L. (1993). Effects of differing intensities and formats of 12 months of exercise training on psychological outcomes in older adults. *Health Psychology, 12,* 292–300.

Kjaer, M., & Galbo, H. (1988). Effect of physical training on the capacity to secrete epinephrine. *Journal of Applied Physiology, 64,* 11–16.

Klein, M.J., Griest, J.H., Gurman, A.S., Neimeyer, R.A., Lesser, D.P., Bushnell, N.J., & Smith, R.E. (1985). A comparative outcome study of group psychotherapy vs. exercise treatments for depression. *International Journal of Mental Health, 13,* 148–177.

Kobasa, S.C. (1979). Stressful life events, personality and health: An inquiry into hardiness. *Journal of Personality and Social Psychology, 37,* 1–11.

Koltyn, K.F. (1997). The thermogenic hypothesis. In W.P. Morgan (Ed.), *Physical activity and mental health* (pp. 213–226). Washington, DC: Taylor & Francis.

Koltyn, K.F., Raglin, J.S., O'Connor, P.J., & Morgan, W.P. (1995). Influence of weight training on state anxiety, body awareness and blood pressure. *International Journal of Sports Medicine, 16,* 266–269.

Koutedakis, Y., Budgett, R., & Faulmann, L. (1990). Rest in underperforming elite competitors. *British Journal of Sports Medicine, 24,* 248–252.

Kubitz, K.K., Landers, D.M., Petruzzello, S.J., & Han, M.W. (1996). The effects of acute and chronic exercise on sleep. *Sports Medicine, 21,* 277–291.

Kugler, J., Seelback, H., & Krüskemper, G.M. (1994). Effects of rehabilitation exercise programmes on anxiety and depression in coronary patients: A meta-analysis. *British Journal of Clinical Psychology, 33,* 401–410.

Landers, D.M. (1991). Optimizing individual performance. In D. Druckman & R.A. Bjork (Eds.), *In the minds eye: Enhancing human performance* (pp. 193–246). Washington, DC: National Academy Press.

Landers, D.M. (1994). Performance, stress, and health: Overall reaction. *Quest, 46,* 123–135.

Landers, D.M. (1998). Exercise and mental health. *Exercise Science (Journal of the Korea Exercise Science Academy), 7,* 131–146.

Landers, D.M. (1999). The influence of exercise and mental health. In C.B. Corbin & R.P. Pangrazi (Eds.), *Toward a better understanding of physical fitness and activity* (pp. 137–143). Scottsdale, AZ: Holcomb Hathaway.

Landers, D.M., & Petruzzello, S.J. (1994). Physical activity, fitness, and anxiety. In C. Bouchard, R.J. Shephard, & T. Stevens (Eds.), *Physical activity, fitness, and health* (pp. 868–882). Champaign, IL: Human Kinetics.

Lazarus, R.S. (1991). Progress on a cognitive-motivational-relational theory of emotion. *American Psychologist, 46,* 819–834.

Lazarus, R.S., & Cohen, J.P. (1977). Environmental stress. In I. Altman & J.F. Wohlwill (Eds.), *Human behavior and the environment: Current theory and research.* New York: Plenum Press.

Leith, L.M. (1994). *Foundations of exercise and mental health.* Morgantown, WV: Fitness Information Technology.

Liederbach, M., Gleim, G.W., & Nichoas, J.A. (1992). Monitoring training status in professional ballet dancers. *Journal of Sports Medicine and Physical Fitness, 32,* 187–195.

Long, B.C., & van Stavel, R. (1995). Effects of exercise training on anxiety: A meta-analysis. *Journal of Applied Sport Psychology, 7,* 167–189.

MacMahon, J.R., & Gross, R.T. (1988). Physical and psychological effects of aerobic exercise in delinquent males. *American Journal of Delinquency in Children, 142,* 1361–1366.

Marsh, H.W., Richards, G.E., Johnson, S., Roche, L., & Tremayne, P. (1994). Physical self-description questionnaire: Psychometric properties and a multi-trait–multi-method analysis of relationships to existing instruments. *Journal of Sport & Exercise Psychology, 16,* 270–305.

Martinsen, E.W. (1987). The role of aerobic exercise in the treatment of depression. *Stress Medicine, 3,* 93–100.

Martinsen, E.W. (1990). Benefits of exercise for the treatment of depression. *Stress Medicine, 9,* 380–389.

Martinsen, E.W. (1993). Therapeutic implications of exercise for clinically anxious and depressed patients. *International Journal of Sport Psychology, 24,* 185–199.

Martinsen, E.W. (1994). Physical activity and depression: Clinical experience. *Acta Psychiatrica Scandinavica, 377,* 23–27.

Martinsen, E.W., & Morgan, W.P. (1997). Antidepressant effects of physical activity. In W.P. Morgan (Ed.), *Physical activity and mental health* (pp. 93–106). Washington, DC: Taylor & Francis.

McAuley, E., Mihalko, S.L., & Bane, S.M. (1996). Acute exercise and anxiety reduction: Does the environment matter? *Medicine and Science in Sport and Exercise, 11,* 143–182.

McDonald, D.G., & Hodgdon, J.A. (1991). *The psychological effects of aerobic fitness training: Research and theory.* New York: Springer-Verlag.

McNair, D.M., Lorr, M., & Droppleman, L.F. (1981). *Profile of Mood States manual.* San Diego, CA: Educational and Industrial Testing Service. (Original work published in 1971)

Morgan, W.P. (1979). Anxiety reduction following acute physical activity. *Psychiatric Annals, 9,* 141–147.

Morgan, W.P. (1981). Psychological benefits of physical activity. In F.J. Nagel & H.J. Montoye (Eds.), *Exercise in health and disease* (pp. 299–314). Springfield, IL: Thomas.

Morgan, W.P. (1985). Selected psychological factors limiting performance: A mental health model. In D.H. Clarke & H.M. Eckert (Eds.), *Limits of human performance* (pp. 70–80). Champaign, IL: Human Kinetics.

Morgan, W.P. (1997). Methodological considerations. In W.P. Morgan (Ed.), *Physical activity and mental health* (pp. 3–32). Washington, DC: Taylor & Francis.

Morgan, W.P., Brown, D.R., Raglin, J.S., O'Connor, P.J., & Ellickson, K.A. (1987). Psychological monitoring of overtraining and staleness. *British Journal of Sports Medicine, 21,* 107–114.

Morgan, W.P., & O'Connor, P.J. (1988). Exercise and mental health. In R.K. Dishman (Ed.), *Exercise adherence: Its impact on public health* (pp. 91–121). Champaign, IL: Human Kinetics.

Morgan, W.P., O'Connor, P.J., Sparling, P.B., & Pate, R.R. (1987). Psychological characteristics of the elite female distance runner. *International Journal of Sports Medicine, 8*(Suppl.), 124–131.

Morgan, W.P., & Pollock, M.L. (1977). Psychologic characterization of the elite distance runner. *Annals of the New York Academy of Sciences, 301,* 383–403.

Mutrie, N. (in press). The relationship between physical activity and clinically-defined depression. In S.J.H. Biddle, K.R. Fox, & S.H. Boutcher (Eds.), *Physical activity, mental health, and psychological well-being.* London: Routledge & Kegan Paul.

North, T.C., McCullagh, P., & Tran, Z.V. (1990). Effect of exercise on depression. *Exercise and Sport Science Reviews, 18,* 379–415.

Nowell, P.M., & Landers, D.M. (1997, October). *Aerobic fitness and cognition: A meta-analytic examination of the cardiovascular fitness hypothesis.* Paper presented at the IOC World Congress on Sport Sciences, Monte Carlo.

Ntoumanis, N., & Biddle, S.J.H. (1999a). Affect and achievement goals in physical activity: A meta-analysis. *Scandinavian Journal of Medicine and Science in Sports, 9,* 315–332.

Ntoumanis, N., & Biddle, S.J.H. (1999b). A review of motivational climate in physical activity. *Journal of Sports Sciences, 1,* 643–665.

O'Connor, P.J. (1997). Overtraining and staleness. In W.P. Morgan (Ed.), *Physical activity and mental health* (pp. 145–160). Washington, DC: Taylor & Francis.

O'Connor, P.J., Bryant, C.X., Veltri, J.P., & Gebhardt, S.M. (1993). State anxiety and ambulatory blood pressure following resistance exercise in females. *Medicine and Science in Sports and Exercise, 25,* 516–521.

O'Connor, P.J., Morgan, W.P., Raglin, J.S., Barksdale, C.M., & Kalin, N.H. (1989). Mood state and salivary cortisol levels following overtraining in female swimmers. *Psychoneuroendocrinology, 14,* 303–310.

O'Connor, P.J., Petruzzello, S.J., Kubitz, K.A., & Robinson, T.L. (1995). Anxiety responses to maximal exercise testing. *British Journal of Sports Medicine, 29,* 97–102.

O'Connor, P.J., & Youngstedt, M.A. (1995). Influence of exercise on human sleep. *Exercise and Sport Science Reviews, 23,* 105–134.

Oxman, A.D., & Guyatt, G. (1988). Guidelines for reading literature reviews. *Canadian Medical Association Journal, 138,* 697–703.

Paffenbarger, R.S., Lee, I.-M., & Leung, R. (1994). Physical activity and personal characteristics associated with depression and suicide in American college men. *Acta Psychiatrica Scandinavica,* (Suppl. 377), 16–22.

Parfitt, G., Eston, R., & Connolly, D. (1996). Psychological affect at different ratings of perceived exertion in high- and low-active women: A study using a production protocol. *Perceptual and Motor Skills, 82,* 1035–1042.

Petruzzello, S.J. (1991). *An examination of proposed physiological and psychological mechanisms for exercise-related reductions in anxiety.* Unpublished doctoral dissertation, Arizona State University, Tempe.

Petruzzello, S.J. (1995). Anxiety reduction following exercise: Methodological artifact or real phenomenon? *Journal of Sport & Exercise Psychology, 17,* 105–111.

Petruzzello, S.J., & Landers, D.M. (1993). Exercise and anxiety reduction: Examination of temperature as an explanation for affective change. *Journal of Sport & Exercise Psychology, 15,* 63–76.

Petruzzello, S.J., Landers, D.M., Hatfield, B.D., Kubitz, K.A., & Salazar, W. (1991). A meta-analysis on the anxiety-reducing effects of acute and chronic exercise. *Sports Medicine, 11,* 143–182.

Piaget, J. (1936). *The origins of intelligence in children.* New York: New York University Press.

Pitts, F.N., & McClure, J.N. (1967). Lactate metabolism in anxiety neurosis. *New England Journal of Medicine, 277,* 1329–1336.

Raglin, J.S. (1990). Exercise and mental health: Beneficial and detrimental effects. *Sports Medicine, 9,* 323–329.

Raglin, J.S. (1997). Anxiolytic effects of physical activity. In W.P. Morgan (Ed.), *Physical activity and mental health* (pp. 107–126). Washington, DC: Taylor & Francis.

Raglin, J.S., & Morgan, W.P. (1985). Influence of vigorous exercise on mood state. *Behavior Therapist, 8,* 179–183.

Raglin, J.S., & Morgan, W.P. (1994). Development of a scale to use in monitoring training-induced distress in athletes. *International Journal of Sports Medicine, 15,* 84–88.

Raglin, J.S., Morgan, W.P., & Luchsinger, A.E. (1990). Mood and self-motivation in successful and unsuccessful female rowers. *Medicine and Science in Sports and Exercise, 22,* 849–853.

Raglin, J.S., Morgan, W.P., & O'Connor, P.J. (1991). Changes in mood states during training in female and male college swimmers. *International Journal of Sports Medicine, 12,* 585–589.

Regier, D.A., Boyd, J.H., Burke, J.D., Rae, D.S., Myers, J.K., Kramer, M., Robins, L.N., George, L.K., Karno, M., & Locke, B.Z. (1988). One-month prevalence of mental disorders in the United States. *Archives of General Psychiatry, 45,* 977–986.

Renger, R. (1993). A review of the Profile of Mood States (POMS) in the prediction of athletic success. *Journal of Applied Sport Psychology, 5,* 78–84.

Rowley, A.J., Landers, D.M., Kyllo, L.B., & Etnier, J.L. (1995). Does the iceberg profile discriminate between successful and less successful athletes? A meta-analysis. *Journal of Sport & Exercise Psychology, 17,* 185–199.

Sackett, D.L. (1989). Rules of evidence and clinical recommendations on the use of antithrombotic agents. *Chest, 95,* 2S–4S.

Schlicht, W. (1994). Does physical exercise reduce anxious emotions? A meta-analysis. *Anxiety, Stress, and Coping, 6,* 275–288.

Sexton, H., Maere, A., & Dahl, N.H. (1989). Exercise intensity and reduction in neurotic symptoms. *Acta Psychiatrica Scandinavica, 80,* 231–235.

Simon, G.E., VonKorff, M., & Barlow, W. (1995). Health care costs of primary care patients with recognized depression. *Archives of General Psychiatry, 52,* 850–856.

Smith, R.E. (1989). Conceptual and statistical issues in research involving multidimensional anxiety scales. *Journal of Sport & Exercise Psychology, 11,* 452–457.

Sonstroem, R.J. (1984). Exercise and self-esteem. *Exercise and Sport Science Reviews, 12,* 123–155.

Sonstroem, R.J., Harlow, L.L., & Josephs, L. (1994). Exercise and self-esteem: Validity of model expansion and exercise associations. *Journal of Sport & Exercise Psychology, 16,* 29–42.

Sonstroem, R.J., & Morgan, W.P. (1989). Exercise self-esteem: Rationale and model. *Medicine and Science in Sports and Exercise, 21,* 329–337.

Sonstroem, R.J., & Potts, S.A. (1996). Life adjustment correlates of physical self-concepts. *Medicine and Science in Sports and Exercise, 28,* 619–625.

Sothmann, M.S., & Ismail, A.H. (1985). Factor analytic derivation of MHPG/NM ratio: Implications for studying the link between physical fitness and depression. *Biology and Psychiatry, 20,* 570–583.

Spence, J.C., Poon, P., & Dyck, P. (1997). The effect of physical-activity participation on self-concept: A meta-analysis [Abstract]. *Journal of Sport & Exercise Psychology, 19,* S109.

Spielberger, C.D., Gorsuch, R.L., Luschene, R., Vagg, P.R., & Jacobs, G.A. (1983). *Manual for the State-Trait Anxiety Inventory.* Palo Alto, CA: Consulting Psychologists.

Spirduso, W.W. (1980). Physical fitness, aging, and psychomotor speed: A review. *Journal of Gerontology, 35,* 850–865.

Stein, J.M., Papp, L.A., Klein, D.F., Cohen, S., Simon, J., Ross, D., Martinez, J., & Gorman, J.M. (1992). Exercise tolerance in panic disorder patients. *Biological Psychiatry, 32,* 281–287.

Stephens, T. (1988). Physical activity and mental health in the United States and Canada: Evidence from four population surveys. *Preventive Medicine, 17,* 35–47.

Steptoe, A., & Cox, S. (1988). Acute effect of aerobic exercise on mood. *Health Psychology, 7,* 329–340.

Steptoe, A., Edwards, S., Moses, J., & Mathews, A. (1989). The effects of exercise training on mood and perceived coping ability in anxious adults from the general population. *Journal of Psychosomatic Research, 33,* 537–547.

Tate, A.K., & Petruzzello, S.J. (1995). Varying intensity of acute exercise: Implications for changes in affect. *Journal of Sports Medicine and Physical Fitness, 35,* 25–302.

Taylor, A. (in press). Physical activity, anxiety, and stress. In S.J.H. Biddle, K.R. Fox, & S.H. Boutcher (Eds.), *Physical activity, mental health, and psychological well-being.* London: Routledge & Kegan Paul.

Taylor, C.B., King, R., Ehlers, A., Margraf, J., Clark, D., Hayward, C., Roth, W.T., & Agras, S. (1987). Treadmill exercise test and ambulatory measures in panic attacks. *American Journal of Cardiology, 60,* 48J–52J.

Tomporowski, P.D., & Ellis, N.R. (1986). Effects of exercise on cognitive processes: A review. *Psychological Bulletin, 99,* 338–346.

Treasure, D., & Newbery, D. (1998). Relationship between self-efficacy, exercise intensity, and feeling states in a sedentary population during and following an acute bout of exercise. *Journal of Sport & Exercise Psychology, 20,* 1–11.

Tuson, K.M., & Sinyor, D. (1993). On the affective benefits of acute aerobic exercise: Taking stock after twenty years of research. In P. Seraganian (Ed.), *Exercise psychology* (pp. 80–121). New York: Wiley.

Tuson, K.M., Sinyor, D., & Pelletier, L.G. (1995). Acute exercise and positive affect: An investigation of psychological processes leading to affective changes. *International Journal of Sport Psychology, 26,* 138–159.

Vaux, C.L. (1926). A discussion of physical exercise and recreation. *Occupational Therapy and Rehabilitation, 6,* 320–333.

von Euler, C., & Soderberg, U. (1957). The influence of hypothalamic thermoceptive structures on the electroencephalogram and gamma motor activity. *Electroencephalography and Clinical Neurophysiology, 9,* 391–408.

Webb, E.J., Campbell, D.T., Schwartz, R.D., & Sechrest, L. (1966). *Unobtrusive measures: Nonreactive research in the social sciences.* Chicago: Rand McNally.

Weismann, M.M., & Klerman, G.L. (1992). Depression: Current understanding and changing trends. *Annual Review of Public Health, 13,* 319–339.

Weyerer, S. (1992). Physical inactivity and depression in the community: Evidence from the Upper Bavarian Field Study. *International Journal of Sports Medicine, 13,* 492–496.

Yao, T., Andersson, S., & Thoren, P. (1982a). Long-lasting cardiovascular depression induced by acupuncture-like stimulation of the sciatic nerve in unanaesthetized spontaneously hypertensive rats. *Brain Research, 240,* 77–85.

Yao, T., Andersson, S., & Thoren, P. (1982b). Long-lasting cardiovascular depression induced by acupuncture-like stimulation of the sciatic nerve in unanaesthetized spontaneously hypertensive rats: Evidence for the involvement of central endorphin and serotonin systems. *Brain Research, 244,* 295–303.

CHAPTER 30

Psychology of Injury Risk and Prevention

JEAN M. WILLIAMS

Epidemiological studies in the United States indicate that each year more than 70 million injuries occur that require medical attention or at least a day of restricted activity. The incidence of injuries is so serious among children and young adults that injuries have replaced infectious diseases as the leading cause of death and disability (Boyce & Sobolewski, 1989). Within the arena of sport alone, Booth (1987) reports that there are over 17 million sport injuries per year. For example, in Boyce and Sobolewski's study of 55,000 schoolchildren, they found that athletic participation accounted for 44% of the injuries to 14-year-old and older students. Other data indicate that each year nearly half of all amateur athletes suffer an injury that precludes participation (Garrick & Requa, 1978; Hardy & Crace, 1990). According to the Consumer Product Safety Commission, one quarter of these injuries require at least one week of nonparticipation (Hardy & Crace, 1990). The preceding statistics underscore the need for research that delves into both the cause and prevention of sport injuries.

Although many of the causes for injury are undoubtedly physical in nature (e.g., body build, level of conditioning, equipment failures, playing surface, faulty biomechanics) or just plain bad luck, psychosocial factors also play a role. Over the past three decades, growing numbers of sports medicine and sport psychology researchers have tried to determine which psychosocial variables influence vulnerability and resistance to sport and exercise injuries. These researchers have found that athletes who experience many recent stressors and who do not have the personal resources and skills to cope with the stress seem most at risk for injury. This growing body of research as well as efforts to identify mechanisms that might explain why the stress-injury relationship occurs and interventions that will hopefully reduce the injury risk are the areas of focus in this chapter.

Initial attempts to identify psychosocial risk factors were narrow in scope and atheoretical. Researchers tended to look at either personality factors, life event stress, or both, but offered no theoretical foundation to explain how these factors might lead to injury. These limitations led Andersen and Williams in the mid-1980s (Andersen & Williams, 1988; Williams & Andersen, 1986) to develop a multicomponent theoretical model of stress and injury. Their model proposes that most psychological variables, if they impact on injury at all, probably do so through a linkage with stress and a resulting stress response. The model evolved from a synthesis of the stress-illness, stress-injury, and stress-accident literature, and owes much to early stress theorizing by Allen (1983) and Smith (1979).

A recent review and critique of the model found substantial support for the basic facets and hypotheses of the model, but also suggested some minor changes (see Figure 30.1) and words of caution (Williams & Andersen, 1998). Because of the support for the stress-injury model and because the model provides a theoretical base for much of the psychology of injury research, it serves as the foundation in this chapter for organizing and summarizing past injury findings. Future research needs and directions are identified in the discussion of the different facets of the model as well as in a section near the end of the chapter. The chapter concludes with suggestions regarding implications for the practitioner.

The first edition of this chapter (Williams & Roepke, 1993) and earlier stress and injury reviews (Williams, 1996; Williams & Andersen, 1998) helped to provide the content for the present chapter.

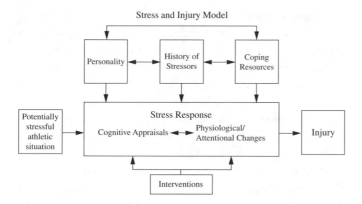

Stress and Injury Model

Personality ↔ History of Stressors ↔ Coping Resources

Potentially stressful athletic situation →

Stress Response

Cognitive Appraisals ↔ Physiological/ Attentional Changes

→ Injury

Interventions

Figure 30.1 Revised version of the stress and injury model. From Williams and Andersen (1998). *Note:* The original model had only directional arrows from personality to history of stressors and from coping resources to history of stressors, and it had no bidirectional arrow between personality and coping resources.

MODEL OF STRESS AND ATHLETIC INJURY

According to the stress-injury model (see Figure 30.1), when sport participants experience stressful situations such as a demanding practice or crucial competition, their history of stressors, personality characteristics, and coping resources contribute interactively or in isolation to the stress response. The central hypothesis of the model is that individuals with a history of many stressors, personality characteristics that tend to exacerbate the stress response, and few coping resources will be more likely, when placed in a stressful situation, to appraise the situation as stressful and to exhibit greater physiological activation and attentional disruptions. The severity of the resulting stress response, caused by the increased stress reactivity of at-risk individuals, is the mechanism proposed to cause the injury risk.

The central core of the model, the stress response, is a bidirectional relationship between the person's cognitive appraisal of a potentially stressful external situation and the physiological and attention aspects of stress (see Figure 30.1). In terms of sport participation, the individual makes some cognitive appraisal of the demands of the practice or competitive situation, the adequacy of his or her ability to meet those demands, and the consequences of failure/success in meeting the demands. For example, if the athlete views competition as challenging, exciting, and fun, the resulting "good" stress (eustress) may help the athlete remain on task, stay focused, and successfully "flow" with the competition. Injury risk in this situation would be lower than when the athlete feels "bad" stress (distress),

such as appraising the competition as ego-threatening or anxiety-producing. Such an interpretation is most likely to occur when athletes perceive that they do not have the resources to meet the demands of the situation and it is important to do so because failure will result in dire consequences.

Whether the cognitive appraisal is accurate or distorted by irrational beliefs or other maladaptive thought patterns is unimportant in the generation of the stress response. If the athlete perceives inadequate resources to meet the demands of the situation and it is important to succeed, the stress response activates and manifests itself physiologically, attentionally, and in the perception of higher state anxiety. Correspondingly, these cognitive appraisals and physiological and attention responses to stress constantly modify and remodify each other. For example, a relaxed body can help calm the mind just as anxious thoughts can activate the sympathetic nervous system. The resulting individual differences in stress responsivity may either inoculate the athlete against injury or exacerbate his or her risk due to psychosocial variables.

The myriad physiological and attentional changes that potentially occur during the stress response led Andersen and Williams (1988) to hypothesize that increases in generalized muscle tension, narrowing of the visual field, and increased distractibility were the primary culprits in the stress-injury relationship. They derived these hypotheses from the recommendations of earlier researchers (e.g., Bramwell, Masuda, Wagner, & Holmes, 1975; Cryan & Alles, 1983; Nideffer, 1983; Williams, Haggert, Tonymon, & Wadsworth, 1986). Unwanted simultaneous contraction of agonist and antagonist muscle groups (often called bracing) is a common response to stressors. This generalized muscle tension can lead to fatigue and reduced flexibility, motor coordination difficulties, and muscle inefficiency. The end result is a greater risk for incurring injuries such as sprains, strains, and other musculoskeletal injuries.

Attention disruptions could result from preoccupation with stressful events and their possible negative consequences or by a blocking of adaptive responses. If such disruptions lead to a narrowing of peripheral vision (e.g., Easterbrook, 1959), potential injury could result by not picking up on or responding in time to dangerous cues in the periphery. For example, an injury to a quarterback from a blindside hit may occur because of not seeing or reacting quickly enough to a defensive player running in from the periphery. Attention disruptions, often due to attention to task-irrelevant cues, may also result in failure to detect or respond quickly enough to relevant cues in the central field of vision. For example, a batter with a high psychosocial risk profile might not see or respond fast enough to avoid a pitch coming directly at his or her head.

Before addressing the research support that exists for the stress response mechanisms proposed in the model, the question of interest is What psychosocial factors influence the stress response? Above the stress response core of the model are three major areas: personality factors, history of stressors, and coping resources (see Figure 30.1). These variables may act in isolation or in combination in influencing the stress response and, ultimately, injury occurrence and severity. The original model hypothesizes that an athlete's history of stressors (life event stress, daily hassles, previous injury) contribute directly to the stress response, whereas personality factors (hardiness, locus of control, sense of coherence, competitive trait anxiety, achievement motivation) and coping resources (general coping behaviors, social support systems, stress management and mental skills) act on the stress response either directly or through a moderating influence on the effects of the history of stressors. For example, the presence of desirable personality and/or coping variables may buffer individuals from stress and injury by helping them to perceive fewer situations and events as stressful or by lessening their susceptibility to the effects of their history of stressors. Conversely, the lack of desirable personality characteristics and coping resources or the presence of undesirable characteristics (e.g., high competitive trait anxiety) may leave individuals vulnerable to higher stress (acute and chronic) and, presumably, greater injury risk.

In addition to the preceding, when Williams and Andersen (1998) critiqued and revised their stress-injury model 10 years after its initial publication, they added bidirectional arrows between personality and history of stressors and between coping resources and history of stressors (see Figure 30.1). The original model had only directional arrows from personality to history of stressors and from coping resources to history of stressors. They proposed adding the bidirectional arrows because there is evidence that the stressors people experience do affect how they develop and characteristically respond or cope. The most dramatic example of this is posttraumatic stress disorder (American Psychiatric Association [APA], 1994). The field of rehabilitation offers plenty of evidence for personality change following injurious events. For example, some individuals who have experienced an amputation or severe burn or a spinal cord injury become withdrawn, agoraphobic, depressed, and sometimes suicidal (e.g., Kishi, Robinson, & Forrester, 1994). Other major life events, such

as a loved one having cancer, can increase general anxiety and depression plus influence coping (Compas, Worsham, Ey, & Howell, 1996). Some support for adding the bidirectional arrows even exists in the earlier stress and sport injury literature (May, Veach, Reed, & Griffey 1985). For example, May et al. suggested that when athletes experience psychological stress, their self-esteem and emotional balance deteriorate.

When Williams and Andersen (1998) modified their model, they also proposed adding a bidirectional arrow between personality and coping resources (see Figure 30.1). The original model had no directional arrow. The personality section later in this chapter provides the rationale for the modification. The proposal of the new bidirectional arrows to the model also is consistent with the transactionist point of view currently espoused for gaining a better understanding of coping (e.g., Aldwin, 1994).

History of Stressors

This category includes major life events, daily hassles, and previous injury history. Of these, life event stress has received the most extensive research. Interest in life event stress evolved initially from the work of Holmes and Rahe (1967). They developed the Social Readjustment Rating Scale (SRRS), a questionnaire that identifies and uniformly ranks the magnitude of 40 life change events found in a general adult population. The scale is based on the assumption that the experiencing of life events causes the body to adapt and, therefore, leads to stress on the body and an increased risk for illness. Examples of life events are incidents such as the breakup of a relationship, taking a vacation, and death of a loved one. On the SRRS, each life event is given a preset, numerical weighting based on the presumed degree of adaptation required for the typical individual in the general population. Individuals indicate the frequency of each event's occurrence during a specified period of time. A total life-change score is tabulated by adding the weighted scores for the checked items. Researchers have supported the relationship of high life event stress to illness and even accidents (e.g., Holmes & Rahe, 1967; T. Miller, 1988; Sarason, Johnson, & Siegel, 1978; Savery & Wooden, 1994; Stuart & Brown, 1981; Theorell, 1992).

In 1970, Holmes administered the SRRS at the start of the football season to players on the University of Washington football team. He then compared the player's life stress scores (tabulated by adding the preset weightings for the life events experienced during the preceding 12 months) to time-loss injury data monitored by athletic trainers throughout the football season. Holmes found that 50% of the athletes who experienced high life stress during the year prior to the football season incurred an athletic injury that required missing at least three days of practice or one game. In contrast, only 9% and 25%, respectively, of athletes with low and moderate levels of life stress experienced equivalent injuries. Holmes concluded that life stress relates to athletic injuries in much the same way it does to the occurrence of illness.

The researchers (Bramwell et al., 1975) who conducted the next life stress–athletic injury study modified the SRRS to make it more appropriate to intercollegiate athletes by deleting the less applicable stressors and adding 20 more appropriate ones for college athletes (e.g., academic eligibility difficulties, trouble with the head coach, change in playing status). Results with the modified tool of 57 life events showed an even stronger relationship between life stress and athletic injuries. When categorized into low, medium, and high life stress groups, 30%, 50%, and 73%, respectively, of the college football players incurred athletic injuries.

Using the same tool, Cryan and Alles (1983) studied the Pennsylvania State University football team and replicated the Bramwell et al. (1975) findings. They also improved on the earlier design by assessing the severity as well as incidence of injuries. The standards of the National Athletic Injury Reporting System (NAIRS) provided the standard for injury severity. A minor injury permitted returning to play within 7 days; moderate and major injuries necessitated, respectively, missing between 8 and 21 days or more than 21 days. They found that life event stress did not differentially affect risk for incurring injuries of varying severity.

In 1983, Passer and Seese advanced the stress–athletic injury research by distinguishing between negative and positive life events and by examining personality variables thought to moderate the influence of life stress. In the earlier studies, life event stress was assessed without tools that distinguished between adaptation required by positive and negative life events. The tools also gave preset weightings to the life events rather than allowing the respondent to indicate the magnitude of effect. Sarason et al. (1978), developers of the Life Experience Survey (LES), contend that the effects from adaptation to negative life change events may differ from those life change events viewed as positive. They also challenged the ability of preset weightings to adequately reflect the interaction between the environment and the individual's perception of the stressfulness of environmental events. Respondents on the LES indicate

whether they perceive a life change event as positive or negative and whether the event had no effect (0 score), a little effect (−1 or +1 score, depending on whether the event is rated negative or positive), a moderate effect (−2 or +2 score), or a great effect (−3 or +3 score). Thus, the LES provides an assessment for negative life events, positive life events, and total life events. As hypothesized, Sarason et al. found that positive life change had either no effect or a less detrimental effect on health-related dependent variables compared to the effects of negative life change. Passer and Seese, using a modified 70-item athletic version of the LES, found that a greater risk of injury occurred for only those football players who reported higher levels of negative life event stress.

Since Holmes conducted the first football investigation, at least 35 studies have examined the relationship of life stress to athletic injury risk. At the time of the writing of the first edition of this chapter, only 20 studies had been identified. In reviewing those studies, Williams and Roepke (1993) concluded that 18 of the 20 studies found a positive relationship between high life stress and injury. The best evidence involved football (six studies), but similar findings had occurred across other sports as diverse as alpine skiing, race walking, figure skating, baseball, gymnastics, soccer, field hockey, wrestling, and track and field. Overall, the risk of injury increased in direct relationship to the level of life event stress. In general, athletes with high life event stress were two to five times more likely to be injured than athletes with low life event stress. Of the 15 life stress studies identified since that review, similar results occurred for 12 of them (Andersen & Williams, 1999; Byrd, 1993; Fawkner, 1995; Kolt & Kirkby, 1996; Meyer, 1995; Patterson, Smith, & Everett, 1998; Perna & McDowell, 1993; Petrie, 1993a, 1993b; Thompson & Morris, 1994; Van Mechelen et al., 1996; Williams & Andersen, 1997). The results of Lavallee and Flint (1996), Petrie and Stoever (1995), and Rider and Hicks (1995), however, failed to determine any relationship between life event stress and injury.

The reported strength of the life stress–injury relationship, and whether the culprit was negative (NLE), positive (PLE), or total life events (TLE), varied considerably across studies. Although the majority of the studies that distinguished between types of life stress indicated that only the *negatively* appraised life events (NLE) put athletes at risk for injury (e.g., Byrd, 1993; Meyer, 1995; Passer & Seese, 1983; Patterson et al., 1998; Petrie, 1992, 1993b; Smith, Ptacek, & Smoll, 1992; Smith, Smoll, & Ptacek 1990a), others found support for TLE and PLE increasing risk of injury. For example, Blackwell and McCullagh (1990) noted that TLE stress contributed the most to injury occurrence and PLE contributed the most to the likelihood of receiving a severe injury. Hanson, McCullagh, and Tonymon (1992) reported that only PLE stress helped to differentiate among injury frequency groups, and Petrie (1993a) observed that PLE was the only life event stressor to predict time loss due to injury. Petrie suggested that the life events athletes might initially rate as positive (e.g., major change in level of responsibility on team, receiving an athletic scholarship) may, in the future, produce considerable stress by putting more pressure on the athlete to perform well or to feel responsible for the team's performance. These changes are likely to lead to negative cognitive appraisal of athletic situations and, thereby, a greater risk for injury.

Hardy and Riehl (1988) found that injured athletes, overall, had significantly higher NLE than noninjured athletes, but injured female athletes reported higher scores on TLE compared to uninjured females. Both TLE and NLE significantly predicted injury across sports, but analyses within sports indicated that injured softball players reported higher TLE, baseball players higher NLE, and track athletes higher object loss (OL; loss of a significant other through death, divorce, separation) compared to equivalent uninjured players. Except for track, none of the stress measures predicted injuries in the specific sports. In track, both TLE and OL predicted injuries. These findings led Hardy and Riehl to conclude that the life stress–injury relationship is influenced by both the athlete's gender and the sport. Hardy, O'Connor, and Geisler's (1990) study of Division I soccer players also supported the conclusion that gender affects the relationship between life stress and injury.

The preceding differences aside, 30 of the 35 studies that assessed life events found at least some significant relationship between life stress and injury. This almost universal finding is itself compelling, but even more so considering it occurred across sports and competitive levels (youth to elite level) and with diverse measures of life stress and definitions of injury. Researchers used eight questionnaires to assess life stress and the criteria for injury varied from requiring treatment from an athletic trainer but no need to reduce practice time or modify activity (e.g., Blackwell & McCullagh, 1990), to time loss requiring missing more than a week of practice (e.g., Coddington & Troxell, 1980). These different operational definitions make it impossible to determine relative injury risk across sports and competitive levels and across positive versus negative stressors. Diverse operational definitions

also contributed to the difficulty in determining the effect of life stress on severity of injury. Approximately two-thirds of the studies found some relationship between life stress and injury severity (Blackwell & McCullagh, 1990; Hanson et al., 1992; Hardy et al., 1990; Hardy & Riehl, 1988; Kerr & Minden, 1988; Meyer, 1995; Petrie, 1992, 1993b) and one third found no effect (Cryan & Alles, 1983; Hardy, Richman, & Rosenfeld, 1991; Lavallee & Flint, 1996; Lysens, Van den Auweele, & Ostyn, 1986; Williams, Tonymon, & Wadsworth, 1986).

The history of stressors portion of the model also includes daily hassles. The stress from many minor daily problems, irritations, or changes may contribute to stress levels and injury risk as much as that encountered from major life event changes. Kanner, Coyne, Schaefer, and Lazarus (1981) suggested that one way major life events influence illness outcome is through all the minor hassles that accompany a major life event. For example, moving to a new city possibly involves loneliness, trying to adjust to a new climate, finding one's way around, and so forth. Daily hassles also occur independent from the experiencing of a major life event (Kanner et al., 1981). Most of the research efforts failed to support daily hassles as a contributor to injury risk (Blackwell & McCullagh, 1990; Hanson et al., 1992; Meyer, 1995; Smith et al., 1990a; Van Mechelen et al., 1996), but the studies had methodological problems that prevented reaching a definitive conclusion. Each measured daily hassles at only one time, either at the start or near the end of the season. Because of their ever changing nature, daily hassles need frequent assessment throughout the athletic season. Researchers can then compare subsequent injuries to the immediately preceding score for stress from minor daily problems/hassles.

In a recent study, Fawkner, McMurray, and Summers (1999) employed such a design (i.e., assessed hassles on a weekly basis) and found that injured athletes had a significant increase in hassles (which they called minor life events) for the week prior to injury, whereas no significant changes occurred for the noninjured athletes. The researchers concluded that their results provided substantial evidence for a link between hassles and athletic injury. Byrd (1993) determined modest support for a relationship between daily hassles and injury. Daily hassles predicted number of injuries in basketball (accounted for 13.1% of the variance) but not volleyball, nor did they predict days lost or modified due to injury. Although Byrd took monthly assessments of daily hassles, it appears the regression analysis included only the initial measure. For the correlation statistics conducted between the four monthly measures of hassles and the injuries for the following month, the only significant correlation was between the preseason measure and the injuries during the first month. Fawkner et al.'s findings suggest that assessing changes in hassles on a weekly basis and noting increases in hassles may yield a more relevant measure of stress and risk for injury. Either way, these two studies offer some support for including daily hassles as an injury vulnerability factor.

Previous injuries, the third component under history of stressors, was included in the stress-injury model for a number of reasons. If the athlete has not recovered enough to return to the sport, but does anyway, the probability of reinjury is high. Also, if the athlete is physically but not psychologically prepared to return to sport participation, problems may arise due to anxiety and negative cognitive appraisals. For example, in their initial stress-injury model paper, Andersen and Williams (1988) conjectured that fear of reinjury may lead to a considerable stress response and, thereby, increase the probability of reinjury. Few researchers have examined the relationship of previous injury history to subsequent injury risk. Hanson et al. (1992) found that time since injury recovery was not related to frequency or severity of injury occurrence. In contrast, Williams, Hogan, and Andersen (1993) observed a positive correlation between prior injury and subsequent injury, and Lysens et al. (1984) found that physical education students with a prior history of injury were at higher risk of recurrence. Van Mechelen et al. (1996) noted that previous injury predicted sport injury better than psychological, psychosocial, physiological, and anthropometrical factors. One limitation of some of the preceding studies is that their design did not permit a distinction between the recurrence of an old injury and the occurrence of a new injury at another location. Another limitation of the Van Mechelen et al. study was that participation rates and injury incidence rates came from the subject's self-report in daily entries on monthly logs kept for 12 months. One strength was that they considered exposure time in their calculations of injury risk.

Personality

Any comprehensive model of the relationship of stress to athletic injury would not be complete without considering personality. The stress-illness literature identifies many personality variables for their role in moderating the stress-illness relationship. Certain personality characteristics may cause some individuals to perceive fewer situations and events as stressful, or they may predispose individuals to be less susceptible to the effects of stressors

such as major life events and daily hassles. Most of the personality variables included in the initial stress-injury model (i.e., hardiness, locus of control, sense of coherence, competitive trait anxiety, achievement motivation) either moderated the stress-illness relationship or were examined in the sport injury literature.

The trait of psychological hardiness is a constellation of characteristics, such as curiosity, willingness to commit, seeing change as a challenge and stimulus to development, and having a sense of control over one's life (Kobasa, 1979). Locus of control (Rotter, 1966) and Antonovsky's (1985) sense of coherence were included in the list of personality factors because of their resemblance to the hardiness concept and because both constructs moderated the relationship between stress and illness. Locus of control is a concept dealing with the degree to which individuals view their lives and environment as under their personal control. An internal orientation is characterized by a belief that one's own actions control personal outcomes in life, whereas an external orientation is indicative of an individual who feels himself or herself a victim of chance or circumstances. Achievement motivation and competitive trait anxiety were included in the model because they were variables that appeared to relate to stress. Achievement motivation addresses both the need to succeed and the need to avoid failure. Trait anxiety is described as a general disposition or tendency to perceive situations as threatening and to react with an anxiety response (Spielberger, 1966). Competitive trait anxiety is anxiety specific to competing in sport. Individuals with a high need to avoid failure or who have high trait anxiety may appraise more situations as stressful and consequently experience an elevated stress response compared to individuals with the opposite profile.

Of the five personality variables proposed in the initial presentation of the stress-injury model, no sport injury researchers assessed hardiness and sense of coherence, and only one study examined achievement motivation. In that study, Van Mechelen et al. (1996) found no relationship between achievement motivation and injury incidence. Mixed results occurred when researchers examined locus of control and trait anxiety. Pargman and Lunt (1989) reported that a higher injury rate correlated with an external locus of control in a sample of freshman college football players. In contrast, Kolt and Kirkby (1996) found no relationship in nonelite gymnasts, but a more internal locus of control significantly predicted injury in elite gymnasts. The other researchers who used nonsport measures to assess locus of control (Blackwell & McCullagh, 1990; Hanson et al., 1992; Kerr & Minden, 1988; McLeod & Kirkby, 1995) and trait anxiety (Kerr & Minden, 1988; Lysens et al., 1986; Passer & Seese, 1983) found no relationship between these variables and the incidence of injury. When researchers used sport-based tools to assess competitive trait anxiety rather than a general trait anxiety tool, athletes who scored high on competitive trait anxiety (Blackwell & McCullagh, 1990; Hanson et al., 1992; Lavallee & Flint, 1996; Passer & Seese, 1983; Petrie, 1993a) had more injuries or more severe injuries.

In Petrie's (1993a) study, the finding that increases in trait anxiety were positively related to injury rate occurred for football starters but not nonstarters. Petrie also found that competitive trait anxiety moderated the effects of positive life stress such that higher levels of anxiety and stress were associated with more days missed due to injury. He conjectured that the combination of starting and having high life stress and competitive trait anxiety "may have negatively influenced these athletes' appraisals such that they either viewed practices and competitions as threatening/uncontrollable or believed they did not have the resources to cope. Such appraisals may have corresponded with attentional and physiological disruptions that would have increased the starters' vulnerability to injury" (p. 272).

Unfortunately, except for Petrie (1993a), none of the preceding studies employed designs that permitted testing whether their personality variables interacted with history of stressors or with other personality and coping variables in influencing injury risk. Such limited designs will not elucidate the potential complexity of the relationship of personality factors to injury vulnerability and resiliency. This limitation and the equivocal preceding findings indicate the need for more research into the relationship of locus of control and competitive trait anxiety to injury vulnerability. It also appears that sport-based instruments might yield more fruitful findings than general instruments.

In addition, when examining competitive trait anxiety, researchers may want to consider using a tool such as the Sport Anxiety Scale (SAS) developed by Smith et al. (1990a) rather than the Sport Competition Anxiety Test (SCAT) used by previous researchers. SCAT employs a unidimensional measure of anxiety, whereas SAS distinguishes between cognitive and somatic trait anxiety. Different levels of these subtypes of anxiety may differentially influence cognitive appraisal and attentional/physiological disruptions when in a stressful practice or competitive situation. Contemporary anxiety researchers (e.g., Jones, 1995) also recommend assessing not merely the intensity of anxiety symptoms (e.g., SCAT and SAS), but

whether athletes interpret their anxiety symptoms as having a facilitative or debilitative effect on performance (referred to as direction of anxiety). The greatest vulnerability to injury may occur with athletes who have high anxiety and who interpret it as having a detrimental effect on performance. See Jones and Leffingwell and Williams (1996) for a more thorough discussion of the conceptual distinctions between intensity and direction of anxiety, and for suggestions to modify current anxiety tools.

Andersen and Williams (1988) proposed that the personality factors they identified in the stress and injury model were merely suggestions for initial research rather than an exhaustive list of potential factors. Recent findings with personality factors not included in the original model indicate merit for the inclusion of other personality factors in the stress and injury model. Although only one study examined the role sensation seeking plays in injury risk, it clearly indicated that sensation seeking can moderate the effect of life event stress (Smith et al., 1992). According to Zuckerman (1979), sensation seeking represents a biologically based dispositional variable that reflects individual differences in optimal levels of arousal. Whereas high sensation seekers love an adrenaline rush, sensation avoiders have a lower tolerance for arousal and, therefore, do not care for change, avoid the unfamiliar, and stay away from risky activities. Smith et al. determined that only athletes who scored low in sensation seeking had a significant positive relationship between major negative sport-specific life events and subsequent injury time-loss. There was no support for a competing hypothesis that the characteristics of high sensation seeking (e.g., more risk-taking behaviors) would constitute an injury vulnerability factor. Also, although they found that sensation avoiders reported poorer stress management coping skills, no support existed for differences in coping skills mediating the injury vulnerability differences. The design of the Smith et al. study, which looked at potential interactions among their variables, provides an excellent prototype for the type of studies needed in future personality research.

Support also exists for adding personality mood states to the list of variables that influence injury data. Williams et al. (1993) concluded that intercollegiate football, volleyball, and cross-country athletes who experienced positive states of mind (e.g., ability to stay focused, keep relaxed, share with others) early in the season incurred significantly fewer injuries during their athletic season compared to athletes who had less positive states of mind. Perhaps even stronger findings might have resulted had they taken multiple assessments for positive states of mind and then compared subsequent injury rates to the immediately preceding positive states of mind measurement.

Whereas positive states of mind might buffer the effects of potentially stressful sport situations, thereby creating less stress and fewer injuries, the presence of negative states might do the opposite. Fawkner (1995) found exactly that when she assessed team and individual sport athletes' mood states (five negative and one positive) over the course of the competitive season. She noted significant increases in mood disturbance in the measurement immediately prior to injury. Lavallee and Flint (1996) also reported a relationship of negative mood states to injury vulnerability. Their significant correlation results indicated that a higher degree of tension/anxiety correlated with a higher rate of injury, and a higher degree of tension/anxiety, anger/hostility, and total negative mood state correlated with higher severity of injury. In a related study, Van Mechelen et al. (1996) stated that persons who reported vital exhaustion, which represented more feelings of depression, malfunctioning, apathy, and anxiety, were more likely to sustain an injury. They "hypothesized that people in such a state may have exhausted their physical and mental resources and will respond inadequately or suboptimally to the physical and mental strain of sports participation" (p. 1177).

In other promising personality research, results indicated that some type of aggression, anger, or dominance measure related to injury risk. Fields, Delaney, and Hinkle (1990) found that runners scoring high (e.g., more aggressive, hard-driving) on a Type A behavior screening questionnaire experienced significantly more injuries, especially multiple injuries, compared to runners scoring lower on this measure. Personality data from Thompson and Morris (1994) indicated that high anger directed outward, but not inward, increases injury risk. Wittig and Schurr (1994) concluded that being tough-minded (i.e., more assertive, independent, and self-assured) predicted the likelihood of more severe injuries, but not the occurrence of injury. They conjectured that an athlete with this type of personality profile might take greater risks and, therefore, incur more severe injuries. Earlier research by Jackson et al. (1978) and Valliant (1981) revealed the opposite (i.e., tender-minded, dependent players received more injuries). Van Mechelen et al. (1996) determined that more dominant persons ran a higher risk of sports injury than those who were less dominant. Dominance was defined as self-reliance, trying to be or play the boss. Similar to the other researchers, they offered the possible explanation that dominant persons tend to play a more central and more intense role in a sports situation and assume more risks to achieve their personal goals than persons with lower dominance.

Other researchers have examined defensive pessimism and obtained mixed results. Perna and McDowell (1993) reported that athletes who scored high on defensive pessimism and who also experienced a high degree of life stress experienced more illness/injury symptoms than did athletes scoring low on defensive pessimism and having fewer stressful life events. Of equal interest is their finding that athletes with the defensive pessimist profile took fewer rest days, especially under the high-stress conditions, than did optimists, even though the pessimists experienced more illness and injury symptoms. Meyer (1995), however, failed in a similar study to replicate their results.

In their critique of the stress and injury model, Williams and Andersen (1998) proposed that more fruitful personality directions might occur from pursuing some of the variables identified in injury research since the development of the initial model. They also concluded that newly identified personality factors, such as positive (Williams et al., 1993) and negative states of mind (Fawkner, 1995), seem intimately tied to coping resources, thereby supporting modification of the stress-injury model to include a bidirectional arrow between personality and coping resources. For example, if athletes experience positive mood states, then it might follow that they could better use their coping resources when dealing with a stressful situation. Conversely, if they had poor cognitive and somatic coping skills, then stressful situations might more likely lead to negative states of mind. Future researchers may wish to examine the interplay between personality and coping resources and how they individually, or interactively, contribute to stress responsivity and, ultimately, injury outcome.

Finally, self-concept was not proposed as a possible personality factor in either the initial or modified stress-injury model, but the first edition of this chapter offered some compelling, although equivocal, evidence for self-concept's potentially influencing injury occurrence. Self-concept is thought to affect the emotional, physical, social, and cognitive life of the individual (Samuels, 1977). As such, differences in self-concept may play a role in injury vulnerability. Using the Tennessee Self-Concept Scale, Young and Cohen (1981) found injured participants ($n = 22$) in a female high school basketball tournament had a higher overall self-concept prior to the tournament than noninjured players ($n = 168$). Injured players also viewed themselves more positively concerning what they were (identity), their state of health and physical appearance and skills (physical self), and their personal worth as seen apart from their body or relationships with others (personal self). The authors conjectured that these self-concept characteristics may have led the injured players to take more risks and thus to find themselves in more situations that could result in injury. The preceding results are counterbalanced by an earlier Young and Cohen (1979) study in which self-concept was not determined to be related to tournament injuries in female collegiate basketball players. The authors proposed that the smaller number of injured college players compared to injured high school players and the age and education differences may have contributed to the different findings between the two studies.

Another study further complicates any definitive conclusions regarding the relationship of self-concept to athletic injury. Lamb (1986) found that female college varsity field hockey players with low self-concept scores, as measured by the Tennessee Self-Concept Scale, tended to have more injuries than players with a higher self-concept. Self-concept was measured at the beginning of the season and injury frequency was recorded throughout the season. Of the 127 injuries sustained by the field hockey team, 23% occurred the day before a game. Of the day-before injuries, 65%, 28%, and 7% were sustained, respectively, by athletes grouped into the lowest, middle, and top third on self-concept. Lamb suggested that the injury rates of the athletes with low self-concepts may have reflected a desire on their part to not play in the upcoming competition or to have a built-in excuse for not playing well, thereby protecting their self-esteem. Although an interesting conjecture, the limited number of subjects ($n = 21$) unfortunately prevents any generalization of such self-handicapping results. Any conclusion regarding whether self-concept affects injury rates, much less how and when it might influence injury, remains impossible without further research.

Coping Resources

Coping resources comprise a wide variety of behaviors and social networks that aid the individual in dealing with the problems, joys, disappointments, and stresses of life. The resources may come from the environment, such as social support, or they may come from personal resources such as emotional control and good nutrition. The presence of good coping resources may directly inoculate the individual against injury or may attenuate the negative effects of stressors and personality traits.

The initial stress-injury model included general coping behaviors, social support systems, stress management and mental skills, and medication (self or prescribed) in the

coping resources section. The general coping behaviors category encompasses such behaviors as sleep patterns, nutritional habits, and taking time for oneself. Agreement on what constitutes social support and the best way to measure it remains illusive. Social support typically considers the presence of others whom we know value and care for us and on whom we can rely (Sarason, Levine, Basham, & Sarason, 1983). The stress management techniques and mental skills (often referred to as psychological coping skills) an individual has at his or her disposal consist of psychological skills such as the ability to control arousal and to concentrate and think effectively under stress.

The last coping resource listed in the initial model was medication, self-selected or prescribed. Drug use is prevalent in society today. Many of these substances influence cognitive perception and physiology and thus could affect the stress response and injury probability. Assessment of drug use is often difficult, if not impossible, because of the frequently clandestine nature of drug use. Unfortunately, researching the medication histories and practices of athletes poses too many problems (e.g., too few athletes taking the relevant drugs, truthful reporting, the clandestine nature of some drug taking) for researchers to have confidence in their results. Therefore, in their critique of the stress-injury model, Williams and Andersen (1998) recommended removal of this item from the model.

A lack of coping resources may easily lead to higher stress and thus greater risk of injury. In contrast, individuals may feel more capable of mastering the demands of stressful athletic environments when they possess one or all of the coping resources. Few researchers have examined whether the various coping resources listed in the model act singly or in combination. One might conjecture that the greatest stress response and stress-injury association would occur among sport participants low in all three variables (general coping behaviors, social support, and psychological coping skills). Correspondingly, the greatest injury resiliency would occur in sport participants possessing high levels of all three.

Considerable evidence exists for an athlete's coping resources either directly affecting injury outcome or moderating the influence life stress has on injury vulnerability. Williams, Tonymon, et al. (1986) found that the only predictor of injury among intercollegiate volleyball players was a low level of coping resources. Their measurement consisted of a rather simplistic but easy-to-administer global measure that included items assessing social support and general coping resources such as eating and sleeping behaviors and taking time for self (L. Miller & Smith, 1982). Blackwell and McCullagh (1990) failed to replicate the Williams, Tonymon, et al. findings when they used the same coping resources questionnaire with intercollegiate football players. However, when Hanson et al. (1992) used a modification of the questionnaire (made it more appropriate for an athlete population), they found that coping resources contributed the most in discriminating group differences in both severity and frequency of injuries. Their injury group had significantly fewer coping resources compared to the no-injury group.

Other researchers have examined social support alone or have separately assessed social support and psychological coping skills. Social support directly influenced sport injuries in three studies (Byrd, 1993; Hardy et al., 1990; Hardy, Prentice, Kirsanoff, Richman, & Rosenfeld, 1987). Athletes with high levels of social support had a lower incidence of injury, and those with low levels of social support had more injuries, regardless of life stress. These findings occurred only for males in the Hardy et al. (1990) study. In addition, Coddington and Troxell (1982), although they did not specifically examine social support, showed more injuries for high school football players who experienced family instabilities from life event stress OL (e.g., separations, divorces, deaths) compared to those players who did not experience such OL. In contrast, Lavallee and Flint (1996) and Rider and Hicks (1995) found no relationship between level of social support and injury vulnerability or resiliency.

Other researchers found social support moderated the life stress–injury relationship, usually in the direction hypothesized by the stress–injury model, but not always. Studying female collegiate gymnasts, Petrie (1992) found that for gymnasts with low social support (bottom third scores on a measure of social support satisfaction), negative life stress accounted for 14% to 24% of the variance in minor, severe, and total injuries. No significant relationships between life stress and injury outcome occurred within any of the gymnasts in the high social support groups. Data on negative life stress alone accounted for only 6% to 12% of the variance in injury outcome. Petrie did not report statistics on whether social support directly influenced injury outcome. He proposed that social support, depending on the level, appears to function in two substantially different ways when athletes experience high negative life stress. High social support seems to protect the athletes from injury, but low social support appears to exacerbate the deleterious effects of life stress such that vulnerability to injury is increased significantly. Patterson et al. (1998) reached a similar conclusion when they studied ballet dancers. Among dancers who reported high levels of social support, negative life events were unrelated to injury, whereas stressful life events accounted for nearly

50% of the injury variance in dancers who reported low levels of social support in their lives.

In a subsequent study, Petrie (1993b) found that playing status moderated the social support–life stress–injury relationship. No relationship emerged for nonstarters, but for football starters, more severe injuries, greater time loss, and more games missed occurred for players with high negative life stress and low social support. These findings replicated Petrie's 1992 findings and support the hypothesized relationship in the stress-injury model. Contrary to the 1992 study and the injury model, however, he also found that under conditions of lower stress, starters who reported high levels of social support were more likely to experience injury than those reporting low levels of support. As a possible explanation for this unexpected finding, he suggested that under conditions of lower stress, high social support may provide athletes with a greater sense of security and confidence. These, in turn, could translate into an increase in sport risk-taking behaviors and greater injury vulnerability.

In two studies, Hardy and colleagues (1990, 1991) found that social support moderated the relationship between life stress and injury depending on gender and the type of life stress. For females in the 1990 study, social support had both a negative and a positive effect on the relationship between life stress and injury. When low in social support (number of people and satisfaction), the event measures accounted for 73% to 92% and 69% to 85%, respectively, of the variance in injury severity depending on whether TLE, NLE, or OL scores were examined. For females high in social support (number of providers), TLE and OB scores accounted for 50% and 55%, respectively, of the variance in injury. The findings may have been an artifact of the small number of female players ($n = 20$) studied. Replication is needed before generalizing the results to other female soccer players.

In their 1991 study, Hardy and his colleagues found that high social support, when combined with high OL or PLE, had a negative rather than positive effect on the well-being of male athletes. In contrast, for male athletes with high negative life events, injury rates decreased when the number of social support providers and the degree of fulfillment for emotional challenge support increased. The researchers concluded that social support was effective with the male athletes only to the degree that a match exists between the stressor and the support type. Hardy et al. also studied female athletes, but found no relationship between social support and injury frequency and severity.

Recently, Andersen and Williams (1999) reported an injury outcome linkage between social support and stress responsivity. They examined the influence of life stress, social support, and stress responsivity (e.g., peripheral narrowing during stress) on injury outcome. For the entire sample of collegiate athletes, only negative life stress predicted injury outcome. When the sample was analyzed after dividing it into participants with high and low social support (median split), social support interacted with negative life stress and stress responsivity to predict injury outcome. For participants with low social support, higher negative life stress and increased peripheral narrowing during stress predicted 26% of injury variance. These results indicate that low levels of social support may directly influence the stress response and act in addition to life stress, leading to greater peripheral narrowing and, thus, greater likelihood of injury.

A major methodological advance occurred when Smith et al. (1990a) studied life stress and two coping resources and then used analyses to determine how the two moderators might interact with one another and life stress to increase or decrease vulnerability to injury. Their two coping resources included social support and psychological coping skills (e.g., the ability to think clearly under stress and to control arousal and concentration). The authors proposed a distinction between conjunctive moderation, in which multiple moderators must co-occur in a specific combination or pattern to maximize a relationship between a predictor (e.g., life events) and an outcome variable (i.e., some aspect of injury outcome), and disjunctive moderation, in which any one of a number of moderators contributes individually to the predictor-criterion relationship.

Smith et al. (1990a) found that coping resources moderated the life stress–injury relationship, but did not directly affect injury occurrence. Athletes who were low in *both* social support and psychological coping skills exhibited the strongest correlation between major negative life events and subsequent injuries. For athletes who scored in the bottom third on both coping resource tools, negative life events (high) accounted for 22% of the injury time-loss variance. The injury variance from life stress increased to more than 30% when comparing more extreme (lower quartile) social support and coping skills athletes. All groups having moderate to high levels of social support or psychological coping skills exhibited a nonsignificant relationship between life stress and injury. The results for athletes with high stress–low coping resources suggest that social support and psychological coping skills operate in a conjunctive manner (need low scores on both) to have maximum injury vulnerability for athletes with high negative life events. In contrast, for athletes with moderate or high scores on social support *or* psychological coping skills,

disjunctive moderation led to a nonsignificant relationship between life stress and injury. That is, having either of the psychological assets reduced injury vulnerability.

The Smith et al. (1990a) study provides an excellent prototype for future injury research. Unfortunately, no other researchers have employed a similar design and statistics, perhaps because of the requirement for a large number of participants (e.g., Smith et al. studied 451 high school varsity athletes). In other studies that examined psychological coping skills using the same questionnaire as did Smith et al. (Byrd, 1993; Lavallee & Flint, 1996; Petrie, 1993a; Rider & Hicks, 1995), no relationship was found to injury outcome. The failure to replicate the Smith et al. findings is not surprising considering the differences in design and statistics among the studies. Byrd's study assessed only a direct relationship to injury vulnerability. The Lavallee and Flint and Rider and Hicks studies computed only a simple correlation between psychological coping skills and injury scores. These studies also suffered from a small number of participants. Although Petrie used regression models that tested for both direct and interaction effects, Smith et al. offered a compelling argument for why this type of analysis might mask significant results when differences are expected primarily because of individuals scoring more on the extreme ends than across the entire continuum of scores. Van Mechelen et al. (1996) also failed to link coping skills with injury. They are the first investigators to use a questionnaire that assesses problem-focused coping and emotion-focused coping.

Injury researchers may not know exactly how each type of coping resource affects injury vulnerability, but most research clearly supports the conclusion that social support either directly affects injury outcome, as hypothesized, or moderates the life stress–injury relationship. Although more modest, support also exists for low levels of general coping behaviors putting athletes at greater risk of injury. Too few studies, however, have investigated general coping behaviors, particularly in terms of whether they might moderate level of stress, to reach any definitive conclusion. Another contaminate for reaching definitive conclusions is that they usually have been studied with a questionnaire that yields a single score for both social support and general coping resources. More research also is needed to reach any definitive conclusions regarding the relationship of psychological coping skills to injury. Although the preponderance of research evidence indicates that psychological coping skills do not influence injury, the strength of the design and the large subject pool in the one study that did find a positive finding (Smith et al., 1990a) indicates that psychological coping skills may influence injury vulnerability. This latter study also illustrates the importance of future researchers examining multiple coping resources and their interrelationships.

The Stress Response

Few researchers have tested the mechanisms proposed to explain how psychosocial factors influence the likelihood of injury. An elevated stress response, particularly the resulting increased muscle tension, narrowing of the visual field, and increased distractibility, is what Andersen and Williams hypothesized to put individuals at greater risk for injuries. With one exception (Andersen & Williams, 1999), none of the studies of the stress response examined the relationship of stress reactivity to injury outcome. Instead, they examined the prediction of what should occur under low and high stress conditions to state anxiety, peripheral narrowing, central vision distractibility, and/or muscle tension for individuals with high compared to low injury-risk profiles.

Only one study examined the connection between psychosocial factors and muscle tension under low and high stress conditions (Andersen, 1988). Andersen found increased muscle tension during the stress condition for the total group, but failed to support the model's hypothesis of even greater muscle tension for high-risk individuals. The failure to do so may have resulted from Andersen's studying the general population rather than a high-risk subpopulation.

When they compared performance under stressful and nonstressful laboratory conditions, Williams, Tonymon, and Andersen (1990, 1991) found that recreational athletes who had experienced many major life events during the preceding year reported higher state anxiety and greater peripheral vision narrowing during the high-stress condition compared to athletes who had experienced few major life events. The high-stress condition consisted of simultaneously performing the peripheral vision task and a Stroop color word task positioned in the central field of focus while listening to a tape that fed loud, distracting phrases into the left ear and white noise and Stroop color words into the right ear. During the low-stress condition, the subjects stayed in a quiet environment and performed just the peripheral vision task. A third study (Andersen, 1988), which used a similar stress manipulation, found the same peripheral narrowing results for participants with high life stress as well as even greater narrowing when the experimenter moved the peripheral targets in slightly faster. The initial assessment moved the targets in as slowly as possible to eliminate any reaction time contaminate. In real-life situations, objects (e.g., people, balls) often approach from the periphery at very fast speeds, suggesting considerably greater deficits than those found in any of the laboratory studies.

The second Williams et al. (1991) study assessed the effects of coping resources (social support and general coping behaviors such as diet, nutrition, and time for self) and daily hassles in addition to the effects of life change events. Coping resources did not affect stress reactivity directly, but moderated the effects of the history of stressors. Recreational athletes with high negative life events or daily hassles, but who also had high coping resources, experienced less self-reported state anxiety during the stress condition compared to athletes with similar high stress but low coping resources. Coping resources, however, had no significant effect on peripheral narrowing.

In a recent study, Williams and Andersen (1997) were the first to determine if, under stressful conditions, performance by athletes with a high injury-risk profile leads to experiencing greater distractibility in the central field of vision. Their measures of central vision deficits included missing or delayed response to important visual cues, responding to irrelevant cues, and lowering of perceptual sensitivity (d', a ratio of missing relative cues and reporting cues not present). They found that performance in the high- compared to low-stress condition led to significant deterioration on all the perceptual variables, but athletes with high negative life event scores experienced even slower central vision reaction time and greater peripheral narrowing than athletes with low life event stress. In addition, males with low versus high social support failed twice as often to detect central cues, and males with high negative life events, low social support, and low coping skills had the lowest perceptual sensitivity. For females, only one significant central vision deficit occurred. Females with high versus low negative life events had twice as many failures to detect central cues, but a significant interaction indicated that this failure occurred only with the group of females who also reported lower psychological coping skills.

None of the preceding studies tested the relationship of stress reactivity to injury outcome. In a recent study, however, Andersen and Williams (1999) gathered relevant psychosocial data, tested their athletes' central and peripheral vision during high- and low-stress conditions, and then recorded the frequency of injuries for the following season. For their entire sample of athletes, only negative life events significantly accounted for variance in injury frequency (19%), but for athletes with low social support, negative life events coupled with changes in peripheral narrowing accounted for 26% of the variance in injury frequency.

Low social support athletes with more negative life events and greater peripheral narrowing during stress incurred more injuries than low social support athletes with fewer negative life events and lesser peripheral narrowing during stress. Although modest, this study did connect the suggested mechanisms to actual injury outcome as proposed in the initial and modified stress and injury model (Andersen & Williams, 1988; Williams & Andersen, 1998).

A completely different line of inquiry offers additional support for attentional disruptions mediating the stress-injury relationship. The Thompson and Morris (1994) study cited under the history of stressors section also determined whether the relationship of stressful life events to injury is mediated by impaired attention, either vigilant (broad, external) or focused (narrow, internal). Using the Symbol Digit Modalities test, they found that injury risk was elevated when recent life event stressors were present and when vigilance decreased, suggesting that stressful life events elevate injury risk by reducing vigilance. In addition, as the players' ability to focus attention increased, their likelihood of injury decreased significantly.

Although they did not study injury or psychosocial variables that might put participants at risk of injury, a recent perception study by Janelle, Singer, and Williams (1999) offers indirect support for the mechanisms proposed in the stress-injury model to explain why injury occurs with an elevated stress response. Janelle et al. examined distraction and attentional narrowing in a dual-task auto racing simulation. Participants assigned to the anxiety conditions were exposed to increasing levels of anxiety. They found that at higher levels of anxiety, the identification of peripheral lights became slower and less accurate and significant performance decrements occurred in central and peripheral tasks. The distraction anxiety group demonstrated the slowest response time and misidentified more peripheral lights than did any other group under high levels of anxiety. Assuming that athletes with a high psychosocial risk profile would respond to anxiety conditions with greater stress reactivity than athletes with a low psychosocial risk profile, these high-risk athletes should experience higher levels of the attention deficits found by Janelle et al., and these in turn could well place the individuals at greater risk of incurring an injury than athletes with a low-risk psychosocial profile.

When they critiqued their stress and injury model, Williams and Andersen (1998) recommended expanding the physiological/attentional aspects of the stress response section of the model to include audition deficits in addition to increased general muscle tension, narrowing of the visual field, and increased distractibility. In support of their recommendation, they cite the work of Landers, Wang, and Courtet (1985), which showed that deficits in audition occur under high-stress conditions in the sport of shooting. Shooters took significantly longer to respond to auditory cues when stressed. Although longer response times or failure to respond to auditory cues has little to do with injury for shooters, in other sports (e.g., contact sports), not responding or responding slowly to auditory warnings of danger could have serious implications for injury risk. Thus, Williams and Andersen believed that merit existed for expanding the model, and the research, into the area of auditory detection during stress.

Interventions to Reduce Injury Vulnerability

The least researched area in the stress-injury model (see Figure 30.1) is the implementation and assessment of interventions that might lessen the stress response and reduce injury vulnerability. The model suggests a two-pronged approach to prevent injuries from the increased stress reactivity of at-risk individuals. One set of interventions aims to change the cognitive appraisal of potentially stressful events; the second set of interventions deals with modifying the physiological/attentional aspects of the stress response. In addition, these interventions and others may be used to directly influence the moderator variables under coping resources and personality factors. Interventions for the cognitive appraisal side of the stress response include techniques to eradicate thinking patterns that create maladaptive responses such as stress. Also included are interventions for fostering realistic expectations, a sense of belonging (e.g., team cohesiveness), and optimal coach-athlete communication. For example, if a sport psychologist can help coaches provide better communication with their athletes regarding their capabilities and potential, then the athletes may have more realistic appraisals of the demands and resources available in potentially stressful athletic situations. Hopefully, a lower maladaptive cognitive response would result from this better coach-athlete communication. Interventions for the attentional/physiological aspects of the stress response would aim at lowering physiological activation and enhancing concentration.

Many sources provide detailed descriptions of the various interventions proposed to reduce the stress response. For example, Zinsser, Bunker, and Williams (1998) describe cognitive techniques such as thought stoppage and cognitive restructuring for both changing dysfunctional thinking and building confidence. Williams and Harris (1998) describe techniques to lower physiological activation levels (e.g., progressive muscle relaxation, meditation, autogenics, breathing exercises). Schmid and Peper (1998) describe numerous concentration training techniques to decrease distractibility and to help keep an appropriate attentional focus.

Partial support for the interventions portion of the model comes from a study in which DeWitt (1980) found that her basketball and football players detected a noticeable decrease in minor injuries after participation in a cognitive and physiological (biofeedback) training program. Unfortunately, DeWitt gathered no objective data regarding physical injuries. Murphy (1988) describes another psychological intervention program in which injuries were not the specific focus, but there may have been some injury benefits from the program. Murphy conducted relaxation sessions with 12 members of a team at the 1987 Olympic Sports Festival, five of whom had minor injuries and two serious injuries. They conducted relaxation sessions after every workout until competition, and found that all 12 athletes were able to compete.

Davis (1991) reported an archival review of injury data collected by athletic trainers before and after two university teams practiced progressive relaxation and technique/strategy imagery during team workouts. Major findings included a 52% reduction in injuries to the swimmers and a 33% reduction in injuries to the football players during the athletic season in which they practiced relaxation and imagery skills. The results of these studies suggest that when sport psychologists initiate performance-enhancement programs, they should include assessment of possible injury reduction benefits in addition to any assessment of improvement in performance.

Another favorable intervention study was conducted by May and Brown (1989), who used such techniques as attention control, imagery, and other mental practice skills in their delivery of interventions to individuals, pairs, and groups of U.S. alpine skiers in the Calgary Olympics. In addition to their mental skills training, they also employed team building, communication, relationship orientations, and crisis interventions. May and Brown reported that their interventions led to reduced injuries, increased self-confidence, and enhanced self-control. The injury benefits from the preceding intervention programs are even more impressive considering that none of them targeted athletes at risk of injury (they targeted athletes in general), and rarely did the intervention programs include cognitive or concentration training interventions.

A recent prospective injury prevention study conducted by Kerr and Goss (1996) offers more experimentally sound

support for reducing life stress and injuries through a stress management program. The participants were 24 gymnasts who competed at the national and international levels. They were matched into pairs according to gender, age, and performance and then randomly assigned to a control or an experimental group. Across an eight-month time period, each experimental gymnast met individually with one of the experimenters for 16 one-hour, biweekly stress management sessions. Meichenbaum's (1985) stress inoculation training program provided the framework for the stress management program, which included skills such as cognitive restructuring, thought control, imagery, and simulations.

From midseason (four months after preintervention assessment) to peak season (four months following midseason and culminating at the National Championships), the stress management group reported significantly less negative athletic stress and total negative stress and a trend toward more positive athletic stress compared to the controls. No differences existed at midseason (after four months). Although not statistically significant, from midseason to the National Championships, the stress management participants spent half the amount of time injured (5 vs. 10 days) compared to the participants in the control group.

When discussing why the injury data did not reach significance, the experimenters speculated that their failure to introduce relaxation and distraction control skills until the fourth month may have meant that the gymnasts did not have the specific skills to cope with increased arousal and distractions soon enough to impact on injuries. In a critique of the study, Andersen and Stoove (1998) proposed that the failure to obtain a significant difference probably had more to do with the small number of participants in each group and the resultant low power than the effectiveness of the intervention. In fact, a substantial effect size of .67 occurred for injury incidence, which is in the high medium effect size range. Thus, the Kerr and Goss (1996) results are encouraging, both in terms of the injury prevention results and the reduction in stress from the psychological interventions.

The results of the earlier stress-injury studies that examined social support variables suggest that resiliency to sport injuries might increase with interventions designed to increase social support in athletes. Based on their disjunctive moderation findings for decreasing injury risk for athletes with high negative life stress, Smith et al. (1990a) propose that, from an intervention perspective, resiliency to athletic injuries could be increased either by increasing social support in the athlete's life or by teaching athletes psychological coping skills. A number of strategies have been proposed for enhancing social support; some involve training of coaches (Smith, Smoll, & Curtis, 1979) and others team building (Nideffer, 1981). A recent article by Richman, Hardy, Rosenfeld, and Callahan (1989) is the best source for a variety of strategies coaches and sport psychologists could implement to affect the type and level of social support in student athletes. To date, no researchers have tried to decrease stress or injuries by improving social support.

In a recent article that included a review of psychological interventions in sport injury prevention, Cupal (1998) concludes that these past intervention studies have been based on cognitive appraisal models and have demonstrated a clear reduction in injuries or time loss due to injuries. She also states that in future intervention research, more sound practices need to be observed. She suggests employing control and placebo groups, prospective longitudinal designs, and appropriate statistical analyses. She also recommends including larger sample sizes, matched participants, homogeneous populations, and randomization to control for extraneous variables that can affect treatment.

SUMMARY OF FUTURE RESEARCH NEEDS AND DIRECTIONS

The complex, interactional stress-injury model proposed by Andersen and Williams (1988) has proven a viable theoretical foundation for conducting research on the psychology of injury risk. Considering the substantial support that exists for the different facets of the stress-injury model and for the hypotheses generated, Williams and Andersen (1998) concluded that no major changes in the model appear warranted. They did, however, offer some words of caution regarding acute and overuse injuries in addition to the minor model changes discussed earlier in this chapter.

According to Williams and Andersen (1998), the stress-injury model, as it stands, is probably most appropriate for acute injuries. For other types of injuries, such as overuse injuries, the causes and the mechanisms are largely known. Overuse injuries result from *overuse* and probably are not, or only minimally, mediated by mechanisms within the stress response. *Why* athletes overuse joints and muscle systems is another matter. Meyer (1995) has suggested that some personality traits may influence overuse injury outcome (e.g., perfectionism). Other chronic injuries, however, may come about through low-grade stress responsivity. In acute high-stress responses, all the attentional and physiological symptoms in the Andersen and Williams (1988) model may become manifest. In low-grade stress,

possibly only generalized muscle tension is present. Some chronic injuries may result from performing with low-level antagonistic and agonistic muscles being simultaneously active, leading to undue strain on muscles and joints. This possibility of the development of chronic injuries through low-level stress responsivity has yet to be explored. Nor have previous researchers adequately assessed the general question of whether the mechanisms leading to an acute injury differ from those leading to overuse injuries.

Future researchers need to study multiple predictor and moderator variables and then determine the varying patterns by which these variables interact with one another to affect the hypothesized stress response and injury vulnerability and resiliency. In addition, the joint influence of social support and psychological coping skills found by Smith and his colleagues (1990a) particularly appears promising as a focus for future research. Whether their disjunctive and conjunctive patterns apply to other sports and age groups (e.g., intercollegiate and professional athletes) and to other personality and coping resources variables remains to be determined. Researchers also should consider measuring their psychosocial variables on multiple occasions across the time period of interest, as recommended by Petrie and Falkstein (1998) in a paper on methodological, measurement, and statistical issues in research on sport injury prediction.

One difficulty in studying multiple predictor and moderator variables and, correspondingly, subgroups of individuals that fall in the extreme on the variables is the need for very large sample sizes. Practical necessity suggests that future researchers should consider involving investigators from a number of geographical areas. An additional benefit from such an approach is enhanced generalizability of the results. Regardless of where the sample of subjects is drawn from, at the start of the study the athletes should be "asymptomatic," that is, free from any time-loss injury or restrictions on type of participation. If researchers fail to follow this protocol, they should separate injured athletes to determine what impact their existing injury has on future injuries and the relationship of predictor and moderator variables to injury outcome. As indicated in the Andersen and Williams (1988) model, prior injuries may be one source of stress within an individual's history of stressors that increases injury vulnerability.

Future researchers also need to determine if sport differences, gender, competitive level, and playing status differentially affect the relationship between psychosocial factors and injury outcome. Although 30 of the 35 studies reviewed in the life event stress–athletic injury area found some association between high life stress and injury outcome, there was considerable variance across studies in the strength of the relationship. Individual differences in relevant psychosocial variables that were not measured probably contributed to some of these differences, but so too may have differences in gender, sport, and competitive level. The risk for different types of injuries and the timing of injuries (e.g., whether before, during, or after competition and whether when winning or losing) also merits investigation when addressing the preceding suggestions.

In implementing the preceding suggestions and others, researchers should continue to use prospective designs and to gather objective injury data (i.e., monitored and recorded by certified athletic trainers or other qualified personnel) rather than a self-determination of injury. Fortunately, fewer than 20% of past stress-injury researchers have reported a retrospective design and/or failed to gather objective injury data.

Another dimension that affects one's ability to accurately make comparisons across studies is the operational definitions for psychosocial variables (particularly life event stress) and injury. As noted earlier, past researchers varied considerably in the tools used to measure life event stress and the criteria for being injured. Future researchers need to determine the optimal tools for measurement of stressors, personality variables, and coping resources as well as the most meaningful criteria for injury outcome. In terms of life event stress, tools that are sport-based and that measure stress through the respondent's perception of the life event's desirability and impact (e.g., Athletic Life Experiences Survey) appear superior to those in which a standardized weighting is given (e.g., Social and Athletic Readjustment Rating Scale). Data shows that the newer Life Events Survey for Collegiate Athletes (LESCA) meets both those criteria, plus it demonstrates excellent content validity and provides a stable measure of life stress (Petrie, 1990b). It also was found to be a better predictor of athletic injury in collegiate gymnasts than the SARRS. Pending replication in other sports, the LESCA may be the best measure of life event stress. In making decisions about instrumentation for personality variables and coping resources, future researchers also should consider whether the questionnaires under consideration are general or sport-based. Sport-based questionnaires appear more effective than general questionnaires in predicting athletic injury. This finding has occurred when measuring trait anxiety and locus of control as well as life event stress.

Regarding assessment of injuries, the most commonly used approach has been some type of time-loss measure. Other approaches have included the number of injuries received, and some researchers have even included injuries that required treatment but no modification of activity. When operationally defining injury, few injury researchers have made a correction to the injury measure based on exposure (i.e., the opportunity to suffer an injury). Both Smith et al. (1990a) and Van Mechelen et al. (1996), who did so, discuss the importance of such an adjustment and illustrate how to operationalize exposure-corrected injuries. See Petrie and Falkstein (1998) for a more complete discussion of measurement issues.

New statistical analyses also might advance the effectiveness of future psychology of injury research. In assessing the effects of moderator variables, Smith et al. (1990a) made a compelling argument for their correlational approach rather than multiple regression analyses. They noted that a moderated regression analysis (Baron & Kenny, 1986; Cronbach, 1987) is the most frequently recommended approach for assessing moderator influences. Such an analysis examines the main effects of the predictor and moderator variables as well as the interactions between and among the variables. Smith et al. and other researchers (e.g., Dunlap & Kemery, 1987; Hedges, 1987), however, note that this type of analysis often fails to reveal moderator effects, particularly when the significant predictor-criterion relation occurs in only a small subsample. A small at-risk subsample may well be the case in athletic injury research (e.g., Smith et al., 1990a).

Petrie (1990a) offers another statistical suggestion for future researchers. He recommends that covariance structure modeling (CSM) be used to determine the validity and practical significance of the Andersen and Williams (1988) theoretical model. CSM allows for the simultaneous specification of the measurement and structural components of theoretical models. After obtaining as much data as possible on the stress history, personality, coping resources, and stress responsivity variables within the model, CSM can determine hypothesized relationships among the variables. The correlations or covariances among the measured variables are used to determine the plausibility of each causal model in the specified population. In addition, Petrie notes that CSM can investigate the psychometric adequacy (in terms of construct validity) of the variables.

Although support exists for the risk factors influencing the mechanisms proposed in the model, particularly peripheral narrowing, more research is needed to determine if experiencing the different perceptual and physiological aspects of the stress response influence the occurrence of injury. Stress responsivity data, when used in conjunction with paper-and-pencil tests, may provide the clearest picture of injury risk and best foundation for designing intervention programs to reduce injury risk. Andersen and

Williams (1993) note that looking at stress reactivity has been used for years in medical research. For example, in assessing risk of cardiac disease, paper-and-pencil tests for Type A behavior and other variables are administered and patients are monitored physiologically during a stress test. It is time for a similar approach to athletic injury research and assessment. See Andersen and Williams (1999) and Williams et al. (1990, 1991) for suggestions of how this might be done. Researchers also should consider simultaneously examining psychosocial variables and physical factors that can contribute to injury risk to determine the relative contribution of psychosocial factors compared to other factors. In one of the few studies in which this was done, Van Mechelen et al. (1996) found that physical fitness and anthropometrical variables were not related to the risk of sustaining a sports injury, whereas psychological factors did have a significant relationship.

One of the most exciting avenues for future research is the implementation and assessment of prospective injury prevention programs. More specifically, with what types of interventions and subpopulations are injury rates and severity of injures most likely to be improved? The variable of primary concern is injury rate, but another approach is to monitor the gains athletes make in controlling stress reactivity by retesting them on the psychophysiological and perceptual stress measures previously described. Moreover, does decreasing stress responsivity improve injury resiliency? Once these questions are answered, practitioners will be able to plan the most feasible, cost-effective, and beneficial interventions for reducing injury vulnerability.

Davis (1991) notes that additional pathways by which interventions might reduce injury vulnerability are through performance enhancement and better pain management. Although not documented, Davis notes that athletic trainers report that athletes are more likely to report injuries following losses and less likely after wins. Regarding the pain management benefits (Kendal & Watson, 1981) of relaxation training, when athletes experience less pain from injuries, they may not complain as much of injuries to athletic trainers or they might recover quicker. At minimum, researchers of injury prevention interventions should consider monitoring potential performance as well as injury benefits, and implementers of performance-enhancement programs should include assessment of possible injury reduction benefits as well as improvements in performance.

IMPLICATIONS FOR THE PRACTITIONER

Injuries contributed to by psychosocial variables need to be recognized and viewed as avoidable rather than unavoidable events. In the same way that coaches and other sports personnel attempt to reduce injury risk through vehicles such as conditioning programs, teaching proper techniques, and providing advances in equipment and facilities design, the time has come to reduce injury risk from psychosocial causes. Some earlier researchers (e.g., Bramwell et al., 1975; Hardy & Riehl, 1988) argued that clinical use of knowledge regarding psychosocial injury risk factors is premature. I argue instead that the monetary, personal, and team/organizational cost of injuries is so serious that we should not overlook any potential means of reducing injuries.

At minimum, sport psychologists should start to educate coaches, athletic trainers, and other sports medicine personnel of psychosocial variables that may impact on injury. Such knowledge might lead to coaches and other relevant personnel increasing their awareness regarding nonsport aspects of an athlete's life that might be causing stress. This increased sensitivity may even lead to providing greater social support, and thus potentially buffering some of the harmful effects of stress. Coaches also may want to consider temporarily modifying training by reducing levels of intensity and risk for athletes whom they know are currently experiencing many disruptive stressors and who do not have adequate coping resources. Other subtle, and not so subtle, modifications can be made to reduce unnecessary sources of psychological stress in the practice and competitive environment.

Ultimately, coaches and sport psychologists should consider implementing intervention programs for athletes with a high injury-risk profile (e.g., many stressors, exacerbating personality characteristics, few coping resources). Learning techniques for changing maladaptive thinking patterns and for recognizing and controlling indicants of physiological arousal should help athletes cope better with stressful events, thereby increasing injury resiliency. Teaching attentional skills designed to increase the ability to focus attention, particularly when under stress, is another potential strategy for injury prevention. Although data to support the injury benefits from such intervention programs are limited, the few relevant studies have yielded only positive results, plus a solid theoretical foundation exists for the recommendations. The worst consequence of implementing such programs is that the athletes may merely experience performance benefits!

A more elaborate approach for identifying at-risk athletes in need of interventions is to include a psychosocial risk assessment as part of the general physical exam at the start of the athletic season. At minimum, assessment should include life events and coping resources. Until researchers can document a stronger and more consistent relationship between injury risk and personality variables and daily hassles, there does not appear to be merit in including these variables in the assessment. As new findings emerge, there also may be merit in including an assessment of stress reactivity.

An important caution in any injury-risk screening is that the information be used merely to design optimal, cost-effective injury prevention interventions and strategies and not for the purpose of excluding an athlete from sport participation (Andersen & Williams, 1993). Practitioners and researchers should never lose sight of the distinction between group and individual prediction. In all studies, there were many athletes with high-risk profiles not being injured and athletes with low-risk profiles being injured. The ultimate value of research dealing with psychosocial risk factors is the potential for using the knowledge to reduce the tragedy and expense caused by avoidable injuries. It is essential that this knowledge is interpreted properly and not used in any way that would prove detrimental to the athlete.

REFERENCES

Aldwin, C.M. (1994). *Stress, coping, and development: An integrative perspective.* New York: Guilford Press.

Allen, R.J. (1983). *Human stress: Its nature and control.* Minneapolis, MN: Burgess International.

American Psychiatric Association. (1994). *Diagnostic and statistical manual of mental disorders* (4th ed.). Washington, DC: Author.

Andersen, M.B. (1988) *Psychosocial factors and changes in peripheral vision, muscle tension, and fine motor skills during stress.* Unpublished doctoral dissertation, University of Arizona, Tucson.

Andersen, M.B., & Stoove, M.A. (1998). The sanctity of *p* < .05 obfuscates good stuff: A comment on Kerr and Goss. *Journal of Applied Sport Psychology, 10,* 168–173.

Andersen, M.B., & Williams, J.M. (1988). A model of stress and athletic injury: Prediction and prevention. *Journal of Sport & Exercise Psychology, 10,* 294–306.

Andersen, M.B., & Williams, J.M. (1993). Psychological risk factors and injury prevention. In J. Heil (Ed.), *The sport psychology of injury* (pp. 49–57). Champaign, IL: Human Kinetics.

Andersen, M.B., & Williams, J.M. (1999). Athletic injury, psychosocial factors, and perceptual changes during stress. *Journal of Sports Sciences, 17,* 735–741.

Antonovsky, A. (1985). The sense of coherence as a determinant of health. In J.D. Matarazzo, S.M. Weiss, J.A. Herd, & N.E. Miller (Eds.), *Behavioral health: A handbook of health enhancement and disease prevention* (pp. 37–50). New York: Wiley.

Baron, R.M., & Kenny, D.A. (1986). The moderator-mediator variable distinction in social psychological research: Conceptual, strategic, and statistical considerations. *Journal of Personality and Social Psychology, 51,* 1173–1182.

Blackwell, B., & McCullagh, P. (1990). The relationship of athletic injury to life stress, competitive anxiety and coping resources. *Athletic Training, 25,* 23–27.

Booth, W. (1987). Arthritis Institute tackles sports. *Science, 237,* 846–847.

Boyce, W.T., & Sobolewski, S. (1989). Recurrent injuries in school children. *American Journal of the Disabled Child, 143,* 338–342.

Bramwell, S.T., Masuda, M., Wagner, N.N., & Holmes, T.H. (1975). Psychological factors in athletic injuries: Development and application of the Social and Athletic Readjustment Rating Scale (SARRS). *Journal of Human Stress, 1,* 6–20.

Byrd, B.J. (1993). *The relationship of history of stressors, personality, and coping resources, with the incidence of athletic injuries.* Unpublished master's thesis, University of Colorado, Boulder.

Coddington, R.D., & Troxell, J.R. (1980). The effect of emotional factors on football injury rates: A pilot study. *Journal of Human Stress, 6,* 3–5.

Compas, B.E., Worsham, N.L., Ey, S., & Howell, D.C. (1996). When Mom or Dad has cancer: II. Coping, cognitive appraisals, and psychological distress in children of cancer patients. *Health Psychology, 15,* 167–175.

Cronbach, L.J. (1987). Statistical tests for moderator variables: Flaws in analyses recently proposed. *Psychological Bulletin, 102,* 114–117.

Cryan, P.O., & Alles, E.F. (1983). The relationship between stress and football injuries. *Journal of Sports Medicine and Physical Fitness, 23,* 52–58.

Cupal, D.D. (1998). Psychological interventions in sport injury prevention and rehabilitation. *Journal of Applied Sport Psychology, 10,* 103–123.

Dalhauser, M., & Thomas, M.B. (1979). Visual disembedding and locus of control as variables associated with high school football injuries. *Perceptual and Motor Skills, 49,* 254.

Davis, J.O. (1991). Sports injuries and stress management: An opportunity for research. *The Sport Psychologist, 5,* 175–182.

DeWitt, D.J. (1980). Cognitive and biofeedback training for stress reduction with university athletes. *Journal of Sport Psychology, 2,* 288–294.

Dunlap, W.P., & Kemery, E.R. (1987). Failure to detect moderating effects: Is multicollinearity the problem? *Psychological Bulletin, 102,* 418–420.

Easterbrook, J.A. (1959). The effect of emotion on cue utilization and the organization of behavior. *Psychological Review, 66,* 183–201.

Fawkner, H.J. (1995). *Predisposition to injury in athletes: The role of psychosocial factors.* Unpublished master's thesis, University of Melbourne, Australia.

Fawkner, H.J., McMurray, N.E., & Summers, J.J. (1999). Athletic injury and minor life events: A prospective study. *Journal of Science and Medicine in Sport, 2,* 117–124.

Fields, K.B., Delaney, M., & Hinkle, S. (1990). A prospective study of Type A behavior and running injuries. *Journal of Family Practice, 30,* 425–429.

Garrick, J.G., & Requa, R.K. (1978). Injuries in high school sports. *Pediatrics, 61,* 465–473.

Hanson, S.J., McCullagh, P., & Tonymon, P. (1992). The relationship of personality characteristics, life stress, and coping resources to athletic injury. *Journal of Sport & Exercise Psychology, 14,* 262–272.

Hardy, C.J., & Crace, R.K. (1990, May/June). Dealing with injury. *Sport Psychology Training Bulletin, 1,* 1–8.

Hardy, C.J., O'Connor, K.A., & Geisler, P.R. (1990). The role of gender and social support in the life stress injury relationship [Abstract]. *Proceedings of the Association for the Advancement of Applied Sport Psychology, fifth annual conference,* 51.

Hardy, C.J., Prentice, W.E., Kirsanoff, M.T., Richman, J.M., & Rosenfeld, L.B. (1987, June). Life stress, social support, and athletic injury; In search of relationships. In J.M. Williams (Chair), *Psychological factors in injury occurrence.* Symposium conducted at the annual meeting of the North American Society for the Psychology of Sport and Physical Activity, Vancouver, Canada.

Hardy, C.J., Richman, J.M., & Rosenfeld, L.B. (1991). The role of social support in the life stress/injury relationship. *The Sport Psychologist, 5,* 128–139.

Hardy, C.J., & Riehl, M.A. (1988). An examination of the life stress-injury relationship among noncontact sport participants. *Behavioral Medicine, 14,* 113–118.

Hedges, L. (1987). The meta-analysis of test validity studies: Some new approaches. In H. Braun & H. Wainer (Eds.), *Test validity for the 1990s and beyond* (pp. 191–212). Hillsdale, NJ: Erlbaum.

Holmes, T.H. (1970). Psychological screening. In *Football injuries: Paper presented at a workshop* (pp. 211–214). Sponsored by Sub-committee on Athletic Injuries, Committee on the Skeletal System, Division of Medical Sciences, National Research Council, February 1969. Washington, DC: National Academy of Sciences.

Holmes, T.H., & Rahe, R.J. (1967). The social readjustment scale. *Journal of Psychosomatic Research, 11,* 213–218.

Jackson, D.W., Jarrett, H., Bailey, D., Kausek, J., Swanson, M.J., & Powell, J.W. (1978). Injury prediction in the young athlete: A preliminary report. *American Journal of Sports Medicine, 6,* 6–12.

Janelle, C.M., Singer, R.N., & Williams, A.M. (1999). External distraction and attentional narrowing: Visual search evidence. *Journal of Sport & Exercise Psychology, 21,* 70–91.

Jones, G. (1995). More than just a game: Research developments and issues in competitive anxiety in sport. *British Journal of Psychology, 86,* 449–478.

Kanner, A.D., Coyne, J.C., Schaefer, C., & Lazarus, R.S. (1981). Comparison of two modes of stress measurement: Daily hassles and uplifts versus major life events. *Journal of Behavioral Medicine, 4,* 1–39.

Kendal, P.C., & Watson, D. (1981). Psychological preparation for stressful medical procedures. In C.K. Prokap & L.A. Bradley (Eds.), *Medical psychology: Contributions to behavioral medicine* (pp. 197–221). New York: Academic Press.

Kerr, G., & Goss, J. (1996). The effects of a stress management program on injuries and stress levels. *Journal of Applied Sport Psychology, 8,* 109–117.

Kerr, G., & Minden, H. (1988). Psychological factors related to the occurrence of athletic injuries. *Journal of Sport & Exercise Psychology, 10,* 167–173.

Kishi, Y., Robinson, R.G., & Forrester, A.W. (1994). Prospective longitudinal study of depression following spinal cord injury. *Journal of Neuropsychiatry and Clinical Neurosciences, 6,* 237–244.

Kobasa, S.C. (1979). Stressful life events, personality and health: An inquiry into hardiness. *Journal of Personality and Social Psychology, 37,* 1–11.

Kolt, G., & Kirkby, R. (1996). Injury in Australian female competitive gymnasts: A psychological perspective. *Australian Physiotherapy, 42,* 121–126.

Lamb, M. (1986). Self-concept and injury frequency among female college field hockey players. *Athletic Training, 21,* 220–224.

Landers, D.M., Wang, M.Q., & Courtet, P. (1985). Peripheral narrowing among experienced and inexperienced rifle shooters under low- and high-stress conditions. *Research Quarterly for Exercise and Sport, 56,* 122–130.

Lavallee, L., & Flint, F. (1996). The relationship of stress, competitive anxiety, mood state, and social support to athletic injury. *Journal of Athletic Training, 31,* 296–299.

Leffingwell, T., & Williams, J.M. (1996). *Measurement of cognitive interpretations of multidimensional competitive trait anxiety symptoms as facilitative or debilitative.* Manuscript submitted for publication.

Lysens, R., Van den Auweele, Y., & Ostyn, M. (1986). The relationship between psychosocial factors and sports injuries. *Journal of Sports Medicine and Physical Fitness, 26,* 77–84.

Lysens, R., Steverlynck, A., Van den Auweele, Y., LeFevre, J., Renson, L., Claessens, A., & Ostyn, M. (1984). The predictability of sports injuries. *Sports Medicine, 1,* 6–10.

May, J.R., & Brown, L. (1989). Delivery of psychological services to the U.S. Alpine ski team prior to and during the Olympics in Calgary. *The Sport Psychologist, 3,* 320–329.

May, J.R., Veach, T.L., Reed, M.W., & Griffey, M.S. (1985). A psychological study of health, injury and performance in athletes on the U.S. Alpine ski team, *Physician and Sportsmedicine, 13,* 111–115.

McLeod, S., & Kirkby, R.J. (1995). Locus of control as a predictor of injury in elite basketball players. *Sports Medicine, Training and Rehabilitation, 6,* 201–206.

Meichenbaum, D. (1985). *Stress inoculation training.* New York: Pergamon Press.

Meyer, K.N. (1995). *The influence of personality factors, life stress, and coping strategies on the incidence of injury in long-distance runners.* Unpublished master's thesis, University of Colorado, Boulder.

Miller, L.H., & Smith, A.D. (1982, December). Stress Audit Questionnaire. *Bostonia. Indepth,* 39–54.

Miller, T.W. (1988). Advances in understanding the impact of stressful life events on health. *Hospital and Community Psychiatry, 39,* 615–622.

Murphy, S.M. (1988). The on-site provision of sport psychology services at the U.S. Olympic Festival. *The Sport Psychologist, 2,* 337–350.

Nideffer, R.M. (1981). *The ethics and practice of applied sport psychology.* Ithaca, NY: Mouvement.

Nideffer, R.M. (1983). The injured athlete: Psychological factors in treatment. *Orthopedic Clinics of North America, 14,* 373–385.

Pargman, D., & Lunt, S.D. (1989). The relationship of self-concept and locus of control to the severity of injury in freshman collegiate football players. *Sports Medicine, Training and Rehabilitation, 1,* 201–208.

Passer, M.W., & Seese, M.D. (1983). Life stress and athletic injury: Examination of positive versus negative events and three moderator variables. *Journal of Human Stress, 9,* 11–16.

Patterson, E.L., Smith, R.E., & Everett, J.J. (1998). Psychosocial factors as predictors of ballet injuries: Interactive effects of life stress and social support. *Journal of Sport Behavior, 21,* 101–112.

Perna, F., & McDowell, S. (1993, October). *The association of stress and coping with illness and injury among elite athletes.* Paper presented at the annual meeting of the Association for the Advancement of Applied Sport Psychology, Montreal, Canada.

Petrie, T.A. (1990a). The application of covariance structure modeling to sport psychology research [Abstract]. *Proceedings of the Association for the Advancement of Applied Sport Psychology, fifth annual conference,* 92.

Petrie, T.A. (1990b). Life stress, social support, and injury in women collegiate gymnasts [Abstract]. *Proceedings of the 98th annual convention of the American Psychological Association,* 230.

Petrie, T.A. (1992). Psychosocial antecedents of athletic injury: The effects of life stress and social support on female collegiate gymnasts. *Behavioral Medicine, 18,* 127–138.

Petrie, T.A. (1993a). Coping skills, competitive trait anxiety, and playing status: Moderating effects of the life stress-injury relationship. *Journal of Sport & Exercise Psychology, 15,* 261–274.

Petrie, T.A. (1993b). The moderating effects of social support and playing status on the life stress-injury relationship. *Journal of Applied Sport Psychology, 5,* 1–16.

Petrie, T.A., & Falkstein, D.L. (1998). Methodological, measurement and statistical issues in research on sport injury prediction. *Journal of Applied Sport Psychology, 10,* 26–45.

Petrie, T., & Stoever, S. (1995). Psychosocial antecedents of athletic injury: A temporal analysis [Abstract]. *Journal of Applied Sport Psychology, 7,* S99.

Richman, J.M., Hardy, C.J., Rosenfeld, L.B., & Callahan, A.E. (1989). Strategies for enhancing social support networks in sport: A brainstorming experience. *Journal of Applied Sport Psychology, 1,* 150–159.

Rider, S.P., & Hicks, R.A. (1995). Stress, coping, and injuries in male and female high school basketball players. *Perceptual and Motor Skills, 81,* 499–503.

Rotter, J.B. (1966). *Generalized expectancies for internal versus external control of Psychological Monographs*80 (Whole).

Samuels, S.C. (1977). *Enhancing self-concept in early childhood,* New York: Human Sciences.

Sarason, I.G., Johnson, J.H., & Siegel, J.M. (1978). Assessing the impact of life changes: Development of the Life Experiences Survey. *Journal of Consulting and Clinical Psychology, 46,* 932–946.

Sarason, I.G., Levine, H.M., Basham, R.B., & Sarason, B.R. (1983). Assessing social support: The Social Support Questionnaire. *Journal of Personality and Social Psychology, 44,* 127–139.

Savery, L.K., & Wooden, M. (1994). The relative influence of life events and hassles on work-related injuries: Some Australian evidence. *Human Relations, 47,* 283–305.

Schmid, A., & Peper, E. (1998). Strategies for training concentration. In J.M. Williams (Ed.), *Applied sport psychology: Personal growth to peak performance* (3rd ed., pp. 316–328). Mountain View, CA: Mayfield.

Smith, R. (1979). A cognitive affective approach to stress management for athletics. In C. Nadeau, W. Halliwell, K. Newell, & G. Roberts (Eds.), *Psychology of motor behavior and sport* (pp. 54–72). Champaign, IL: Human Kinetics.

Smith, R.E., Ptacek, J.T., & Smoll, F.L. (1992). Sensation seeking, stress, and adolescent injuries: A test of stress-buffering, risk-taking, and coping skills hypotheses. *Journal of Personality and Social Psychology, 62,* 1016–1024.

Smith, R.E., Smoll, F.L., & Curtis, B. (1979). Coach effectiveness training: A cognitive-behavioral approach to enhancing relationship skills in youth sports coaches. *Journal of Sport Psychology, 1,* 59–75.

Smith, R.E., Smoll, F.L., & Ptacek, J.T. (1990). Conjunctive moderator variables in vulnerability and resiliency research: Life stress, social support and coping skills, and adolescent sport injuries. *Journal of Personality and Social Psychology, 58,* 360–369.

Smith, R.E., Smoll, F.L., & Schutz, R.W. (1990). Measurement and correlates of sport-specific cognitive and somatic trait anxiety: The Sport Anxiety Scale. *Anxiety Research, 2,* 263–280.

Spielberger, C.D. (1966). *Anxiety and behavior.* New York: Academic Press.

Stuart, J.C., & Brown, B.M. (1981). The relationship of stress and coping ability to incidence of diseases and accidents. *Journal of Psychosomatic Research, 25,* 255–260.

Theorell, T. (1992). Critical life changes: A review of research. *Psychotherapy and Psychosomatics, 57,* 108–117.

Thompson, N.J., & Morris, R.D. (1994). Predicting injury risk in adolescent football players: The importance of psychological variables. *Journal of Pediatric Psychology, 19,* 415–429.

Valliant, P.M. (1981). Personality and injury in competitive runners. *Perceptual and Motor Skills, 53,* 251–253.

Van Mechelen, W., Twisk, J., Molendijk, A., Blom, B., Snel, J., & Kemper, H.C.G. (1996). Subject-related risk factors for sports injuries: A 1-yr prospective study in young adults. *Medicine and Science in Sports and Exercise, 28,* 1171–1179.

Williams, J.M. (1996). Stress, coping resources, and injury risk. *International Journal of Stress Management, 3,* 209–223.

Williams, J.M., & Andersen, M.B. (1986, June). *The relationship between psychological factors and injury occurrence.* Paper presented at the annual meeting of the North American Society for Psychology of Sport and Physical Activity, Scottsdale, AZ.

Williams, J.M., & Andersen, M.B. (1997). Psychosocial influences on central and peripheral vision and reaction time during demanding tasks. *Behavioral Medicine, 26,* 160–167.

Williams, J.M., & Andersen, M.B. (1998). Psychosocial antecedents of sport injury: Review and critique of the stress and injury model. *Journal of Applied Sport Psychology, 10,* 5–25.

Williams, J.M., Haggert, J., Tonymon, P., & Wadsworth, W.A. (1986). Life stress and prediction of athletic injuries in volleyball, basketball, and cross-country running. In L.E. Unestahl (Ed.), *Sport psychology in theory and practice.* Orebro, Sweden: Veje.

Williams, J.M., & Harris, D.V. (1998). Relaxation and energizing techniques for regulation of arousal. In J.M. Williams (Ed.), *Applied sport psychology: Personal growth to peak performance* (3rd ed., pp. 219–236). Mountain View, CA: Mayfield.

Williams, J.M., Hogan, T.D., & Andersen, M.B. (1993). Positive states of mind and athletic injury risk. *Psychosomatic Medicine, 55,* 468–472.

Williams, J.M., & Roepke, N. (1993). Psychology of injury and injury rehabilitation. In R.N. Singer, L.K. Tennant, & M. Murphey (Eds.), *Handbook of research in sport psychology* (pp. 815–839). New York: Macmillan.

Williams, J.M., Tonymon, P., & Andersen, M.B. (1990). Effects of life-event stress on anxiety and peripheral narrowing. *Behavioral Medicine, 16,* 174–181.

Williams, J.M., Tonymon, P., & Andersen, M.B. (1991). Effects of stressors and coping resources on anxiety and peripheral narrowing in recreational athletes. *Journal of Applied Sport Psychology, 3,* 126–141.

Williams, J.M., Tonymon, P., & Wadsworth, W.A. (1986). Relationship of stress to injury in intercollegiate volleyball. *Journal of Human Stress, 12,* 38–43.

Wittig, A.F., & Schurr, K.T. (1994). Psychological characteristics of women volleyball players: Relationships with injuries, rehabilitation, and team success. *Personality and Social Psychology Bulletin, 20,* 322–330.

Young, M.L., & Cohen, D.A. (1979). Self-concept and injuries among female college tournament basketball players. *American Corrective Therapy Journal, 33,* 139–142.

Young, M.L., & Cohen, D.A. (1981). Self-concept and injuries among female high school basketball players. *Journal of Sports Medicine, 21,* 55–59.

Zinsser, N., Bunker, L., & Williams, J.M. (1998). Cognitive techniques for building confidence and enhancing performance. In J.M. Williams (Ed.), *Applied sport psychology: Personal growth to peak performance* (3rd ed., pp. 270–295). Mountain View, CA: Mayfield.

Zuckerman, M. (1979). *Sensation seeking: Beyond the optimal level of arousal.* Hillsdale, NJ: Erlbaum.

CHAPTER 31

Psychology of Sport Injury Rehabilitation

BRITTON W. BREWER

Although sport and exercise participants may reap rewards as a result of their involvement in physical activity, so too may they encounter risks. Physical injury is paramount among these risks. Epidemiological data suggest that sport injury is a pervasive public health problem (Caine, Caine, & Lindner, 1996). In the United Kingdom, sport/exercise was the single leading source of injury in a recent population survey, accounting for approximately 33% of all injuries (Uitenbroek, 1996). In Australia, sport-related injuries were identified as responsible for 20% of child and 18% of adult hospital emergency room visits (Finch, Valuri, & Ozanne-Smith, 1998). In the United States, child and adult participants in sport and recreation sustain an estimated 3 to 17 million injuries (Bijur et al., 1995; Booth, 1987; Kraus & Conroy, 1984), nearly 2 million of which result in hospital emergency room visits (NEISS data highlights, 1998). The personal and societal costs associated with sport injuries are astronomical. During a one-year period in the state of North Carolina, injuries incurred by high school athletes in 12 sports were projected to produce long-term medical costs of $10 million and lost earnings of $19 million (Weaver et al., 1999).

In addition to the adverse impact sport injury can have on physical functioning and, concomitantly, on sport performance, sport injury can exact a psychological toll that is manifested in terms of cognition, affect, and behavior. Despite the traditional focus of sports medicine on identifying physical factors that improve the quality of rehabilitation and hasten the return to sport participation of athletes with injuries, appreciation of the role of psychological factors in sport injury rehabilitation has grown over the past three decades. The purpose of this chapter is to review research addressing the psychology of sport injury rehabilitation. Following a discussion of theoretical perspectives incorporating psychological aspects of sport injury rehabilitation, research on psychological responses to sport injury, psychological factors in sport injury rehabilitation, and patient-practitioner interactions in sport injury rehabilitation is examined. Finally, directions for future psychological research on sport injury rehabilitation are provided.

THEORETICAL PERSPECTIVES

Biopsychosocial Model

To examine psychological factors within the overall context of sport injury rehabilitation, a theoretical framework that merges medical and psychological viewpoints is needed. As with other health outcomes (Cohen & Rodriguez, 1995; Matthews et al., 1997), research on sport injury rehabilitation has given rise to an integrative model that incorporates myriad factors involved in sport injury rehabilitation processes and outcomes. Brewer, Andersen, and Van Raalte (in press) introduced a biopsychosocial model of sport injury rehabilitation designed to widen the focus of sport injury rehabilitation research and provide an integrative framework to incorporate existing models pertaining to sport injury rehabilitation (e.g., Flint, 1998; Leadbetter, 1994; Wiese-Bjornstal, Smith, Shaffer, & Morrey, 1998).

As depicted in Figure 31.1, the model has seven key components: injury, sociodemographic factors, biological factors, psychological factors, social/contextual factors,

Preparation of this chapter was supported in part by grant number R29 AR44484 from the National Institute of Arthritis and Musculoskeletal and Skin Diseases. Its contents are solely the responsibility of the author and do not represent the official views of the National Institute of Arthritis and Musculoskeletal and Skin Diseases.

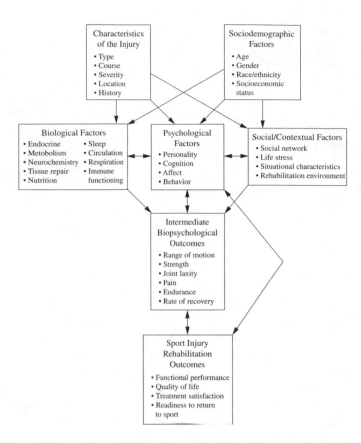

Figure 31.1   A biopsychosocial model of sport injury rehabilitation. From "Psychological aspects of sport injury rehabilitation: Toward a biopsychosocial approach" by B.W. Brewer, M.B. Andersen, and J.L. Van Raalte, *Medical Aspects of Sport and Exercise,* edited by D. Mostofsky and L. Zaichkowsky, in press, Morgantown, WV: Fitness Information Technology.

intermediate biopsychological outcomes, and sport injury rehabilitation outcomes. According to the model, injury (the occurrence of physical damage) initiates the sport injury rehabilitation process. The type, cause, severity, location, and history of injury are thought to influence not only biological factors, but also psychological and social/contextual factors. In providing the background against which sport injury rehabilitation takes place, sociodemographic factors (e.g., age, gender, race/ethnicity, socioeconomic status) are posited to exert a parallel influence on biological, psychological, and social/contextual factors. Occupying a central role in the model, psychological factors are considered to have reciprocal relationships with both biological factors and social/contextual factors. Direct paths to the endpoint of the model, sport injury rehabilitation outcomes, are hypothesized for psychological factors and intermediate biopsychological outcomes (e.g., range of motion, strength, joint laxity, pain, endurance, recovery rate),

the latter of which are thought to be affected by biological and psychological factors. The paths between psychological factors and both intermediate biopsychological outcomes and sport injury rehabilitation outcomes are proposed as bidirectional.

Psychological Models

Although the biopsychosocial model (Brewer et al., in press) provides a broad-based framework for investigating the sport injury rehabilitation process and offers potential explanations for how psychological factors can affect sport injury rehabilitation outcomes, it does not articulate proposed relationships among specific psychological factors. Consequently, to better understand the psychology of sport injury rehabilitation, it is instructive to examine psychological models that elaborate on some of the features of the biopsychosocial model. Most of the extant psychological models in the sport injury rehabilitation literature can be categorized as either stage models or cognitive appraisal models (Brewer, 1994).

Stage Models

Adapted to the context of sport injury from research on psychological reactions to terminal illness and other sources of grief and loss, stage models have been used to describe psychological responses to sport injury. The key assumptions of stage models are that injury constitutes a loss of an aspect of the self (Peretz, 1970) and that psychological responses to sport injury follow a predictable sequence. In applying the model proposed by Kübler-Ross (1969) to sport injury, researchers (e.g., Astle, 1986; Lynch, 1988; Rotella, 1985) have suggested that athletes with injuries pass sequentially through stages of denial, anger, bargaining, and depression before arriving at acceptance of their injuries. Although the Kübler-Ross (1969) model has been especially popular with sport psychologists, other similar models of adjustment to sport injury, varying in number and content of stages, have been proposed (Evans & Hardy, 1995).

As described in the subsequent section on psychological responses to sport injury in this chapter, empirical support has accrued for the premise that sport injury can elicit reactions consistent with a grief response (Macchi & Crossman, 1996; Shelley, 1994). Moreover, as hypothesized by most stage models, emotional responses to sport injury tend to become more adaptive over time (e.g., McDonald & Hardy, 1990; Smith, Scott, O'Fallon, & Young, 1990; Uemukai, 1993). Nevertheless, as with the extensive body of research on psychological reactions to undesirable events (see Silver & Wortman, 1980, for a review), the contention that athletes respond to sport injury in a stereotypic, stage-like manner has not stood up to empirical scrutiny (Brewer, 1994). Research has suggested that the way athletes react psychologically to injury is highly variable across individuals and depends on a variety of factors, including personal characteristics of the athletes and aspects of the situations in which injury and rehabilitation occur (Brewer, 1994; Wiese-Bjornstal et al., 1998).

Recent conceptualizations of the grief response are more dynamic and less stereotypic across individuals than those typically invoked by sport psychologists applying stage models to sport injury (Evans & Hardy, 1995, 1999). Although such theoretical developments weaken the precision and predictive value of stage models (Rape, Bush, & Slavin, 1992), they enable stage models of grief and loss to be integrated with (Evans & Hardy, 1995, 1999) or subsumed by (Wiese-Bjornstal et al., 1998) models that recognize the importance of individual and contextual differences in the psychological consequences of sport injury.

Cognitive Appraisal Models

Constituting the second major category of psychological models of response to sport injury, cognitive appraisal models are a group of related conceptual frameworks that borrow heavily from stress and coping theory and ascribe a central role to cognition in determining psychological reactions to sport injury. Although several cognitive appraisal models have been proposed (e.g., Gordon, 1986; Grove, 1993; Weiss & Troxel, 1986), the "integrated model" set forth by Wiese-Bjornstal et al. (1998) is perhaps the most evolved and well-developed.

As displayed in Figure 31.2, the integrated model holds that responses to injury are influenced by both preinjury variables (i.e., personality, history of stressors, coping resources, interventions) and postinjury variables. Of the postinjury variables, the way the injury and the rehabilitation process are interpreted (or appraised) is thought to affect three interrelated parameters: emotional responses, behavioral responses, and recovery outcomes. Characteristics of the person (i.e., injury attributes, individual difference variables) and the situation (i.e., sport-related variables and aspects of the social and physical environment in which rehabilitation is occurring) are posited to have a direct effect on cognitive appraisals.

Considerable empirical support has amassed for aspects of cognitive appraisal models in general and the integrated model in particular. Research has indicated that sport injury is a significant source of stress (Bianco, Malo, &

Orlick, 1999; Brewer & Petrie, 1995; Ford & Gordon, 1999; Gould, Udry, Bridges, & Beck, 1997b; Heniff et al., 1999), that personal and situational factors are associated with psychological responses to sport injury (Brewer, 1994, 1998, 1999a), and that psychological responses are related to sport injury rehabilitation outcomes (Brewer et al., in press). Although mediational predictions generated from cognitive appraisal models have not been supported in preliminary investigations (Brewer, Van Raalte, et al., 2000; Daly, Brewer, Van Raalte, Petitpas, & Sklar, 1995), the utility of cognitive appraisal models in offering a flexible yet testable conceptual framework has been demonstrated across a growing body of research.

PSYCHOLOGICAL RESPONSES TO SPORT INJURY

Since the publication of a seminal study by Little (1969) reporting that physical injury could precipitate neurotic symptoms in athletic men, the topic within the psychology of sport injury rehabilitation that has attracted the most empirical attention is the impact of sport injury on psychological functioning. In this section of the chapter, research on psychological responses to sport injury is reviewed. Cognitive, emotional, and behavioral responses are examined, consistent with a cognitive appraisal approach to investigating psychological aspects of sport injury rehabilitation.

Cognitive Responses

Given the centrality of cognition to cognitive appraisal models, relatively few studies have addressed cognitive processes in athletes with injuries. Research on cognitive responses to sport injury has focused on four main topics: (1) attributions for injury, (2) self-perceptions following injury, (3) coping strategies, and (4) perceived benefits of injury.

Attributions for Injury

Unexpected events have been shown to stimulate attributional processes (Wong & Weiner, 1981). As a generally unanticipated, sometimes traumatic occurrence, sport injury would be expected to produce attributional cognitive activity. Data in support of this position have been obtained in several studies in which athletes have had little difficulty generating causal attributions for their injuries (Brewer, 1991; Laurence, 1997; Tedder & Biddle, 1998). Interestingly, whereas participants in the Tedder and Biddle study tended to attribute their injuries to behavioral factors, participants in the Brewer and Laurence studies

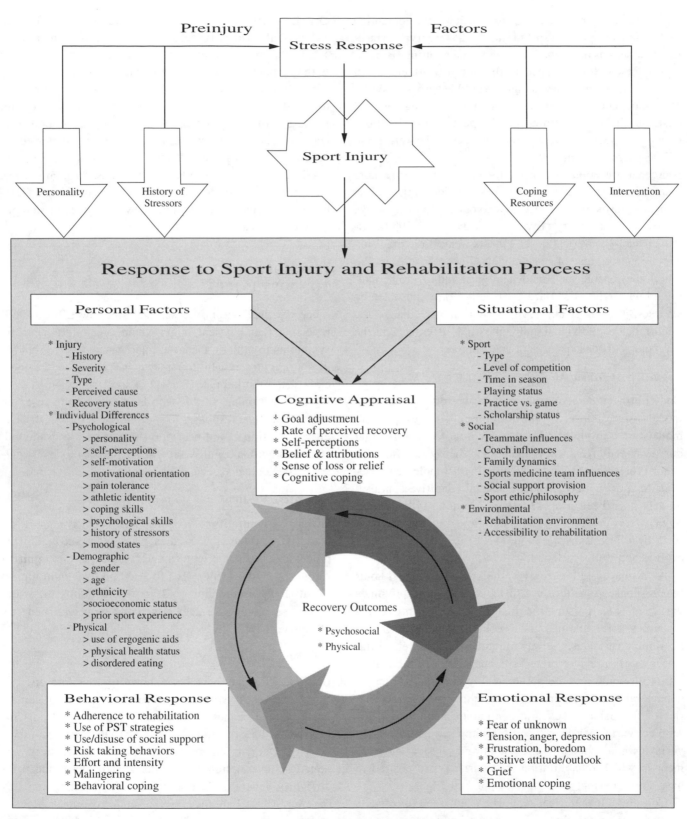

Figure 31.2 Integrated model of psychological response to the sport injury and rehabilitation process. From "An integrated model of response to sport injury: Psychological and sociological dimensions," by D.M. Wiese-Bjornstal, A.M. Smith, S.M. Shaffer, and M.A. Morrey, 1998, *Journal of Applied Sport Psychology, 10,* p. 49. Copyright 1998 by the Association for the Advancement of Applied Sport Psychology. Reprinted with permission.

tended to list mechanical/technical factors as responsible for their injuries. Consistent with a cognitive appraisal approach, it is likely that both personal factors (e.g., attributional style, locus of control) and situational factors (e.g., injury characteristics) contribute to the causal explanations for injury that athletes produce.

Self-Perceptions Following Injury

Recently, researchers have examined self-referent cognition in association with sport injury. They have assessed the self-perceptions (e.g., self-esteem, self-worth) of athletes with injuries both over time following injury and in relation to athletes without injuries. Findings are equivocal with respect to global self-esteem. Although some studies have documented global self-esteem decreases after injury (Leddy, Lambert, & Ogles, 1994) or differences as a function of injured/uninjured status (Chan & Grossman, 1988; Kleiber & Brock, 1992; Leddy et al., 1994; McGowan, Pierce, Williams, & Eastman, 1994), other studies have shown no preinjury-postinjury differences (Connelly, 1991; Smith et al., 1993) or injury status differences (Brewer & Petrie, 1995). Results for domain-specific physical self-esteem have been more consistent, with the two studies on this topic showing preinjury-postinjury decrements (Connelly, 1991; Leddy et al., 1994) and lower scores for athletes with injuries than for athletes without injuries (Leddy et al., 1994). Similarly, a preinjury-postinjury decline in football skills self-efficacy (Connelly, 1991) and lower sport self-confidence in athletes with injuries relative to those without injuries have been reported (LaMott, 1994)

Consistent with what would be predicted from a cognitive appraisal perspective, four studies have documented associations between self-referent cognitions and personal or situational factors. Kleiber and Brock (1992) found that athletes who were highly invested psychologically in playing sport professionally and who had sustained a career-ending injury had lower self-esteem than their counterparts who were less psychologically invested in being a professional athlete. Shaffer (1992) reported that athletes undergoing ankle injury rehabilitation who had successfully rehabilitated an injury in the past had greater rehabilitation self-efficacy than those who had not previously completed injury rehabilitation. Demonstrating the influence of situational factors on self-perception, LaMott (1994) showed that, relative to their presurgery levels of sport self-confidence, athletes had higher self-confidence after reconstructive knee surgery. Quinn and Fallon (1999) also found temporal differences in sport self-confidence over the sport injury rehabilitation period, with athletes

starting rehabilitation high in confidence, experiencing a decline in confidence during rehabilitation, and increasing in confidence on attaining recovery. Other situational factors associated with self-confidence in the Quinn (1996) study (from which the Quinn & Fallon article emerged) included daily hassles and social support. Thus, preliminary data suggest that self-related cognitions may be subject to personal and situational influences.

Coping Strategies

To deal with the physical and psychological trauma that can be associated with incurring a sport injury, athletes with injuries initiate coping efforts. Only recently, however, has the scientific study of coping become a part of the sport injury research agenda. Various methods (i.e., qualitative, quantitative) and measures have been used to investigate coping with sport injury. One regularity to emerge from the early data on coping with sport injury is that cognitive processes are used to combat the intrusive thoughts (Newcomer, Perna, Roh, Maniar, & Stilger, 1999; Newcomer, Roh, Perna, & Etzel, 1998) and other psychological consequences of sport injury.

Qualitative studies, which have been conducted primarily with skiers, offer evidence that the use of cognitive coping strategies by athletes with injuries is common and marked by themes such as accepting injury, focusing on getting better, thinking positively, and using imagery (Bianco, Malo, et al., 1999; Gould, Udry, Bridges, & Beck, 1997a; Rose & Jevne, 1993; Shelley, 1994; Udry, Gould, Bridges, & Beck, 1997). These qualitative findings have been bolstered by the results of quantitative studies, which have substantiated the use of a similar array of cognitive coping strategies by athletes from a wide variety of sports following injury (Grove & Bahnsen, 1997; Morrey, 1997; Quinn & Fallon, 1999; Shelley, 1994; Udry, 1997a).

In line with a cognitive appraisal perspective, associations between reported use of certain coping strategies and selected personal and situational factors have been documented. Grove and Bahnsen (1997) found that athletes high in neuroticism tended to use three emotion-focused coping strategies (denial, emotional focus/venting, mental disengagement) and one problem-focused coping strategy (healing imagery) to deal with their injuries to a greater extent than those low in neuroticism. Several researchers have reported temporal effects in the use of coping strategies, although the use of different coping measures in each study precludes making comparisons across studies. Morrey (1997) observed near significant changes in the pain coping strategies activated by athletes undergoing rehabilitation following knee surgery. Udry (1997a), in examining coping strategies over the course of rehabilitation following knee surgery, found that two emotion-focused coping strategies (negative emotion coping, palliative coping) varied depending on the particular stage of rehabilitation. In contrast to the findings of Morrey and Udry, Quinn and Fallon (1999) reported that athletes did not differ in the use of passive coping and emotion-focused/denial coping strategies across multiple assessments of coping strategies during injury rehabilitation. The results of Quinn and Fallon notwithstanding, it is clear that athletes deploy a common core of strategies to cope with their injuries and that implementation of these strategies varies systematically with individual difference and contextual factors.

Perceived Benefits of Injury

Although the cognitive content of athletes with injuries is often characterized by appraisals of threat or loss (Ford & Gordon, 1999; Gould et al., 1997b; Niedfeldt, 1998), injury may produce more benign thought content in some instances. A growing body of qualitative research suggests that despite the psychological turmoil that can accompany sport injury, perceptions of benefit associated with injury occurrence and rehabilitation can emerge (Ford, 1998; Ford & Gordon, 1999; Niedfeldt, 1998; Rose & Jevne, 1993; Udry, Gould, Bridges, & Beck, 1997). Common benefit-related themes expressed by athletes with injuries include personal growth (e.g., opportunity for reflection, development of interests outside sport), challenge (e.g., test of character), and sport performance enhancement (e.g., increased motivation, physical lessons learned). Perna's (1992) quantitative data indicated that intercollegiate athletes who sustained minor injuries had higher levels of life satisfaction, psychosocial development, and academic performance than those who sustained severe injuries or no injuries. These results bolster the plausibility of the notion that injury can confer benefits on athletes under some circumstances. Further, in a study of athletes who had sustained career-ending injuries (Fisk & King, 1998), perceptions of injury-related growth were greatest for athletes who reported obtaining social and personal growth through sport participation and indicated that they were able to be involved in sport in some way following injury. High levels of perceived growth were also evident for individuals highly self-invested in sport involvement who could describe in detail their desired postinjury lifestyle (Fisk & King, 1998). Additional research is needed, however, to

elucidate the particular personal characteristics and situations that contribute to injury being perceived by athletes as beneficial (Udry, 1999).

Emotional Responses

Emotional reactions constitute the leading target of scientific investigation within the theme of psychological responses to sport injury. Numerous qualitative and quantitative studies have been conducted to examine how athletes' affects, moods, and emotions are influenced by sport injury.

Qualitative Studies

Over the past decade, qualitative inquiry on the emotional consequences of sport injury has become increasingly common. Qualitative research has provided rich descriptions of the emotions experienced by athletes with injuries, the process by which those emotions change over the course of rehabilitation, and factors influencing emotional reactions to sport injury.

Participants in qualitative studies have consistently reported that, in the initial phases of rehabilitation, they experience negative emotions such as depression, frustration, confusion, anger, and fear (Bianco, Malo, et al., 1999; Gordon & Lindgren, 1990; Johnston & Carroll, 1998a; Shelley & Carroll, 1996; Shelley & Sherman, 1996; Sparkes, 1998; Udry, Gould, Bridges, & Beck, 1997). During the middle phases of rehabilitation, reports of depression and frustration have been common, with the source of the dysphoria shifting from injury-related disruption of functioning to rehabilitation-related concerns (Bianco, Malo, et al., 1999; Johnston & Carroll, 1998a). Qualitative data have suggested that as athletes with injury near full recovery and a return to sport, depression and frustration remain salient, with fear of reinjury emerging as a prominent emotion (Bianco, Malo, et al., 1999; Johnston & Carroll, 1998a).

Consistent with cognitive appraisal models of psychological response to sport injury, potential contributors to emotional disturbance following sport injury identified in qualitative investigations include cognitive appraisals (Johnston & Carroll, 1998a) and selected personal and situational factors. Among the personal factors implicated as influencing emotional responses to sport injury are athletic identity (Shelley & Carroll, 1996; Sparkes, 1998) and previous injury experience (Bianco, Malo, et al., 1999). Situational factors reported as affecting emotional adjustment following sport injury include injury severity, injury type, time of the season, and rehabilitation progress (Bianco,

Malo, et al., 1999; Johnston & Carroll, 1998a). Thus, through qualitative inquiry, researchers have documented negative emotional responses to sport injury that seem to vary as a function of personal characteristics and the context in which rehabilitation occurs.

Quantitative Studies

Quantitative investigations, which constitute the bulk of studies examining emotional responses to sport injury, have provided descriptive data on and facilitated identification of factors related to emotional reactions following sport injury. Findings have enabled researchers to estimate the prevalence of clinical levels of psychological distress in athletes with injury and evaluate the utility of psychological models of response to sport injury.

The Profile of Mood States (POMS; McNair, Lorr, & Droppleman, 1971) and the Emotional Responses of Athletes to Injury Questionnaire (ERAIQ; Smith, Scott, & Wiese, 1990) have been used most frequently to assess emotional responses in sport injury research. In convergence with the extant qualitative data, across numerous sport injury studies in which the POMS, the ERAIQ, and other inventories measuring emotions have been administered (for a review, see Wiese-Bjornstal et al., 1998), athletes with injuries have displayed a wide variety of negative emotions and, to a lesser extent, positive emotions. A comparison of the emotions of athletes with injuries to those without injuries indicates that sport injury is associated with emotional disturbance (Brewer & Petrie, 1995; Chan & Grossman, 1988; Johnson, 1997, 1998; Leddy et al., 1994; Miller, 1998; Newcomer, Perna, Maniar, Roh, & Stilger, 1999; Pearson & Jones, 1992; Perna, Roh, Newcomer, & Etzel, 1998; Petrie, Brewer, & Buntrock, 1997; Petrie, Falkstein, & Brewer, 1997; Roh, Newcomer, Perna, & Etzel, 1998; Smith et al., 1993). Similarly, there is evidence that the emotional disturbance of athletes is greater following injury than it is prior to injury (Dubbels, Klein, Ihle, & Wittrock, 1992; Leddy et al., 1994; Miller, 1998; Smith et al., 1993).

As noted by Heil (1993), the majority of psychological distress experienced by individuals with sport injuries is not of sufficient magnitude and duration to approach clinical levels. Nevertheless, epidemiological findings indicate that clinically meaningful levels of emotional disturbance are experienced by 5% to 24% of athletes with injuries (Brewer, Linder, & Phelps, 1995; Brewer, Petitpas, Van Raalte, Sklar, & Ditmar, 1995; Brewer & Petrie, 1995; Leddy et al., 1994; Perna et al., 1998). In cases where the postinjury distress (especially depression) is severe, some

athletes with injuries may even attempt suicide (Smith & Milliner, 1994).

Although there is evidence suggesting that a large portion of athletes experience most of the emotional responses to injury posited to occur by stage models of adjustment (e.g., Astle, 1986; Lynch, 1988; B. Rotella, 1985) at some point during rehabilitation, results of retrospective, cross-sectional, and longitudinal investigations indicate that emotional reactions to injury are more varied and less sequential than those hypothesized by stage models. In particular, the available research data suggest that positive emotions generally increase and negative emotions generally decrease over the course of rehabilitation (Crossman, Gluck, & Jamieson, 1995; Dawes & Roach, 1997; Grove, Stewart, & Gordon, 1990; LaMott, 1994; Laurence, 1997; Leddy et al., 1994; Macchi & Crossman, 1996; McDonald & Hardy, 1990; Miller, 1998; Morrey, 1997; Quackenbush & Crossman, 1994; Quinn & Fallon, 1999; Smith, Scott, O'Fallon, et al., 1990; Uemukai, 1993). An exception to these trends is that positive emotions have been found to decrease slightly and negative emotions to increase slightly as individuals near the end of rehabilitation following reconstructive knee surgery (LaMott, 1994; Morrey, Stuart, Smith, & Wiese-Bjornstal, 1999), perhaps reflecting apprehension about their return to sport activity. In support of this hypothesis, Quinn (1996) found that perceived recovery was negatively correlated with mood disturbance during rehabilitation, but was positively correlated with mood disturbance at the conclusion of rehabilitation.

In addition to analyzing temporal effects, researchers have accounted for some of the variability in emotional responses to sport injury by identifying personal, situational, and cognitive factors associated with athletes' postinjury status. In the integrated model of response to the sport injury and rehabilitation process (Wiese-Bjornstal et al., 1998), the influence of personal and situational factors is thought to be mediated by cognitive appraisals. Most researchers of this topic, however, have not examined the proposed mediational path, but instead have examined direct relationships between the emotional status of athletes with injuries and their personal characteristics and situational aspects, thereby testing indirectly the hypothesized relationships.

Personal factors positively associated with postinjury emotional disturbance include age (Brewer, Linder, et al., 1995; Smith, Scott, O'Fallon, et al., 1990), athletic identity (Brewer, 1993), competitive trait anxiety (Petrie, Falkstein, et al., 1997), investment in playing professional sport (Kleiber & Brock, 1992), level of sport involvement

(Meyers, Sterling, Calvo, Marley, & Duhon, 1991), and pessimistic explanatory style (Grove et al., 1990). Negative correlations have been obtained between emotional distress and hardiness (Grove et al., 1990; Miller, 1998) and, surprisingly, competitive trait anxiety (LaMott, 1994) in athletes with injuries. Further, Meyers et al. (1991) obtained a curvilinear relationship between age and emotional disturbance following knee surgery, with the youngest (age 10 to 19) and oldest (age 40 to 49) participants reporting greater distress than participants of intermediate age (20 to 39).

Situational factors shown to be positively correlated with emotional distress in athletes with injury are current injury status (Alzate, Ramirez, & Lazaro, 1998; Brewer, Linder, et al., 1995; Quinn, 1996), injury severity (Alzate et al., 1998; Pargman & Lunt, 1989; Perna, 1992; Smith, Scott, O'Fallon, et al., 1990; Smith et al., 1993; Uemukai, 1993), impairment of daily activities (Crossman & Jamieson, 1985), life stress (Brewer, 1993; Petrie, Falkstein, et al., 1997; Quinn, 1996), and recovery progress (Quinn, 1996). Impairment of sport performance (Brewer, Linder, et al., 1995), level of sport participation (Crossman et al., 1995), medical prognosis (Gordin, Albert, McShane, & Dobson, 1988), recovery progress (McDonald & Hardy, 1990; Quinn, 1996; Smith, Young, & Scott, 1988), social support for rehabilitation (Brewer, Linder, et al., 1995), and social support satisfaction (Green & Weinberg, 1998; Petrie, Falkstein, et al., 1997; Quinn, 1996) are situational factors that have been negatively associated with emotional disturbance following injury. It should be noted that in the biopsychosocial model, current injury status and recovery progress could be considered intermediate biopsychological outcomes.

As a central feature of the integrated model (Wiese-Bjornstal et al., 1998), cognitive appraisals are posited to influence emotional responses to sport injury. In support of this hypothesis, inverse relationships have been documented between postinjury emotional disturbance and several cognitive variables, including cognitive appraisals of injury coping ability (Daly et al., 1995), confidence in adhering to rehabilitation (Quinn, 1996), confidence in being successful at sport (Quinn, 1996), confidence in recovering fully (Quinn, 1996), physical self-esteem (Brewer, 1993), salience of a hoped-for postinjury possible self (Fisk & King, 1998), self-confidence (Quinn, 1996), self-esteem (Quinn, 1996), and causal attribution of injury to internal and stable factors (Brewer, 1999b). Positive associations have been found between emotional distress following injury and causal attributions of injury to global factors (Brewer, 1991) and, in contrast to the findings of Brewer (1999b), internal factors (Tedder & Biddle, 1998). Thus, a generally consistent pattern of correspondence between

cognitions and emotions has been documented in athletes with injuries.

Behavioral Responses

In addition to eliciting cognitive and emotional reactions, sport injury can trigger behavioral responses. The behavior of athletes with injuries is thought to exert an important influence on the rehabilitation process (Wiese-Bjornstal et al., 1998). This section examines research on adherence to sport injury rehabilitation regimens, the class of behavioral response to sport injury that has generated the most research, and coping behaviors occurring in the aftermath of sport injury.

Adherence to Sport Injury Rehabilitation

Depending on the nature of the injury and the rehabilitation protocol, adherence to sport injury rehabilitation may involve a variety of behaviors in multiple settings. Typical adherence behaviors are participating in clinic-based activities (e.g., exercises, therapy), modifying physical activity (e.g., resting, cross-training), taking medications, and completing home-based activities (e.g., exercises, therapy) in accordance with rehabilitation practitioner recommendations (Brewer, 1998, 1999a). Given the wide range of behaviors involved in adherence to sport injury rehabilitation, researchers have developed numerous measures to assess the construct, the most frequently used of which have been patient attendance at clinic-based rehabilitation sessions, practitioner ratings of adherence during rehabilitation sessions, and patient self-reports of home exercise completion (Brewer, 1999a).

The various types of adherence measures administered across research studies make comparison of prevalence rates for adherence problematic. Some estimates of adherence are based on a percentage of adherent versus nonadherent individuals, whereas other estimates are expressed in terms of percentage of rehabilitation behaviors completed relative to those recommended. Nevertheless, adherence estimates ranging from 40% to 91% have been documented for sport injury rehabilitation regimens (Brewer, 1998, 1999a). Adherence rates tend to be higher for continuous indices of adherence, such as attendance at rehabilitation sessions (e.g., Almekinders & Almekinders, 1994; Daly et al., 1995; Laubach, Brewer, Van Raalte, & Petitpas, 1996) or amount of time spent on home rehabilitation activities (Penpraze & Mutrie, 1999), than for more discrete measures of adherence, which categorize individuals based on their level of adherence (e.g., Taylor & May, 1996).

In keeping with a cognitive appraisal approach to studying psychological responses to sport injury (see

Figure 31.2), it would be expected that personal factors, situational factors, and, more directly, cognitive and emotional responses would be associated with a behavioral response such as adherence to sport injury rehabilitation. Consistent with this expectation, researchers have identified a multitude of variables that are correlated with adherence to sport injury rehabilitation programs.

Personal factors that have been positively correlated with sport injury rehabilitation adherence include internal health locus of control (Murphy, Foreman, Simpson, Molloy, & Molloy, 1999), pain tolerance (Byerly, Worrell, Gahimer, & Domholdt, 1994; Fields, Murphey, Horodyski, & Stopka, 1995; Fisher, Domm, & Wuest, 1988), self-motivation (Brewer, Daly, Van Raalte, Petitpas, & Sklar, 1994; Brewer, Van Raalte, et al., 2000; Culpepper, Masters, & Wittig, 1996; Duda, Smart, & Tappe, 1989; Fields et al., 1995; Fisher et al., 1988; Noyes, Matthews, Mooar, & Grood, 1983), task involvement (Duda et al., 1989), and tough-mindedness (Wittig & Schurr, 1994). Personal factors that have been negatively correlated with adherence to sport injury rehabilitation are ego involvement (Duda et al., 1989) and trait anxiety (Eichenhofer, Wittig, Balogh, & Pisano, 1986).

Numerous situational factors have been found to correlate with adherence to sport injury rehabilitation programs. Positive associations have been documented between adherence and academic class status (Culpepper et al., 1996; Shank, 1988), academic performance level (Shank, 1988), belief in the efficacy of the treatment (Duda et al., 1989; Noyes et al., 1983; Taylor & May, 1996), comfort of the clinical environment (Brewer, Daly, et al., 1994; Fields et al., 1995; Fisher et al., 1988), convenience of rehabilitation scheduling (Fields et al., 1995; Fisher et al., 1988), degree of career goal definition (Shank, 1988), importance or value of rehabilitation to the athlete (Taylor & May, 1996), injury duration (Culpepper et al., 1996), perceived academic load (Shank, 1988), perceived amount of sport participation time (Shank, 1988), perceived availability of time for rehabilitation (Shank, 1988), perceived exertion during rehabilitation activities (Brewer, Daly, et al., 1994; Fisher et al., 1988), perceived injury severity (Taylor & May, 1996), perceived susceptibility to further complications without rehabilitation (Taylor & May, 1996), plans for postcollegiate sport participation (Shank, 1988), rehabilitation practitioner expectancy of patient adherence (Taylor & May, 1995), and social support for rehabilitation (Byerly et al., 1994; Duda et al., 1989; Finnie, 1999; Fisher et al., 1988).

As indicated in Figure 31.1, direct paths between cognitions and behavior are posited in cognitive appraisal models. Consistent with this hypothesis, several cognitive

responses have been associated with sport injury rehabilitation adherence. In particular, individuals who adhere well to sport injury rehabilitation protocols tend to report a high ability to cope with their injuries (Daly et al., 1995), express high rehabilitation self-efficacy (Taylor & May, 1996), have high self-esteem certainty (i.e., do not perceive a threat to their self-esteem) (Lampton, Lambert, & Yost, 1993), attribute their recovery to stable and personally controllable factors (Laubach et al., 1996), set rehabilitation goals, use imagery, and use positive self-talk (Scherzer et al., 1999). Penpraze and Mutrie (1999) provided experimental evidence demonstrating the influence of cognitive factors on sport injury rehabilitation adherence, finding that athletes who were assigned specific rehabilitation goals had greater understanding of and adherence to their injury rehabilitation protocols than athletes who were given nonspecific rehabilitation goals. The quantitative findings of Penpraze and Mutrie dovetail with the qualitative results of Gilbourne and his colleagues (Gilbourne & Taylor, 1995; Gilbourne, Taylor, Downie, & Newton, 1996), who noted that participation in a task-oriented goal-setting program (Gilbourne & Taylor, 1998) was associated with increased perceptions of adherence to the rehabilitation regimen among athletes with injuries.

Few studies have examined the hypothesized relationship between emotional responses and adherence to sport injury rehabilitation. Although Brewer, Van Raalte, et al. (2000) found no correlation between psychological distress and sport injury rehabilitation adherence, mood disturbance has been determined to be related (inversely) to sport injury rehabilitation adherence in other investigations (Alzate et al., 1998; Brickner, 1997; Daly et al., 1995).

As with emotional responses, little research has been conducted on behavioral correlates of sport injury rehabilitation adherence. However, Udry (1997a) did observe that athletes who adhered well to rehabilitation following knee surgery tended to report using instrumental coping behaviors (e.g., asking for additional information about the injury or rehabilitation program) to a greater extent than those who adhered poorly to rehabilitation.

Coping Behaviors

In addition to implementing cognitive coping strategies (discussed in the section on cognitive responses to sport injury), athletes may initiate behavioral efforts to cope with their injuries. Qualitative and quantitative studies have examined the coping behaviors of athletes with injury. In a qualitative investigation of skiers who had sustained season-ending injuries, Gould et al. (1997a) found that the most common coping behaviors were "driving through" (e.g., doing things normally, working hard to achieve rehabilitation goals), distracting oneself (e.g., keeping busy, seeking a change of scenery), seeking/using social resources (e.g., seeking social support), and avoiding others/isolating oneself. Similar qualitative results were obtained by Bianco, Malo, et al. (1999), who determined that skiers with previous injuries reported that they had engaged in such behaviors as adopting an aggressive rehabilitation approach, trying alternative treatments, learning about their injuries, building physical strength, working or training at their own pace, and resting when tired. Bianco et al. noted that the coping behaviors used by the skiers varied over the course of the season.

In a quantitative study involving the COPE inventory (Carver, Scheier, & Weintraub, 1989; Scheier, Carver, & Bridges, 1994) to assess coping strategies and behaviors, Grove and Bahnsen (1997) found that active coping (which involves initiating behavior to deal directly with a stressor or its effects) and instrumental social support (which pertains to the seeking of help or information dealing with a stressor) were the modes of coping endorsed most strongly by a sample of athletes with injuries. Alcohol/drug use and behavioral disengagement (which involves a reduced initiation of behavioral attempts to cope with a stressor) were among the least strongly endorsed modes of coping by the athletes with injuries in the Grove and Bahnsen investigation. In another study with the COPE, Quinn and Fallon (1999) concluded that the coping strategies used by athletes with injuries were stable over time, with the exception of a small but significant trend (i.e., 3% of the variance) for athletes to report making more active coping efforts two-thirds of the way through rehabilitation than they did one-third of the way through rehabilitation. Similar to Grove and Bahnsen's data, instrumental coping was the mode of coping that athletes reported using most frequently throughout rehabilitation following knee surgery (Udry, 1997a). Unlike Quinn and Fallon, however, Udry noted no temporal changes in instrumental coping over the course of rehabilitation. Although insufficient research has been conducted on the coping behaviors of athletes with injuries to draw firm conclusions, the quantitative and qualitative investigations that have been completed provide a strong foundation for further inquiry on the topic.

PSYCHOLOGICAL FACTORS IN SPORT INJURY REHABILITATION

As shown in Figures 31.1 and 31.2, psychological factors are thought to influence sport injury outcomes in both the biopsychosocial model of sport injury rehabilitation (Brewer et al., in press) and the integrated model of psychological response to sport injury (Wiese-Bjornstal et al., 1998). Data from case studies, correlational studies, and experimental studies have provided preliminary support for the hypothesized relationship between psychological factors and recovery from sport injury (Cupal, 1998).

Case Studies

As a research design, the case study is severely limited in terms of generalizability of results and the extent to which findings enable causal inferences to be drawn. Nevertheless, case studies have provided preliminary data on the efficacy of psychological interventions in affecting both psychological and physical processes and outcomes in sport injury rehabilitation. In particular, case reports have suggested that interventions such as counseling, imagery, goal setting, hypnosis, positive self-talk, relaxation, and systematic desensitization may exert a favorable influence on the confidence, perception of pain, motivation, psychological adjustment, physical recovery, reinjury anxiety, and range of motion of athletes with injury (Brewer & Helledy, 1998; Hartman & Finch, 1999; Nicol, 1993; Potter, 1995; R. Rotella & Campbell, 1983; Sthalekar, 1993). Case study data also suggest that failing to adhere to the sport injury rehabilitation protocol can have an adverse effect on rehabilitation outcomes (Hawkins, 1989; Meani, Migliorini, & Tinti, 1986; Satterfield, Dowden, & Yasamura, 1990).

Correlational Studies

As with case studies, causal inferences cannot be made from the results of correlational studies. Because samples are typically larger in correlational studies, however, generalizability of the findings is usually less of an issue. Correlational research designs have been useful in identifying potential psychological antecedents and concomitants of intermediate biopsychological outcomes and sport injury rehabilitation outcomes. Personal, situational, cognitive, emotional, and behavioral correlates of rehabilitation outcomes have been identified for a variety of injury types, consonant with the predictions of the integrated model (Wiese-Bjornstal et al., 1998).

Several personal factors have been linked to sport injury rehabilitation outcomes. In a seminal study, tendencies toward hysteria and hypochondriasis were inversely related to recovery following knee surgery (A. Wise, Jackson, & Rocchio, 1979). In more recent investigations, men have been more likely than women to recover adequately or exceptionally from sport injury (Johnson, 1996, 1997), and athletic identity (Brewer, Van Raalte, et al., 2000) and optimism (LaMott, 1994) have been positively associated with outcome indices following anterior cruciate ligament (ACL) reconstruction. The mechanisms underlying these intriguing associations are not yet known.

The social environment is the situational aspect of sport injury rehabilitation that has received the most empirical attention in relation to rehabilitation outcomes. Results have been inconsistent and difficult to interpret. For example, a positive relationship between social support and rehabilitation outcome has been documented (Tuffey, 1991), a nonsignificant relationship has been reported (Brewer, Van Raalte, et al., 2000), and an inverse relationship has also been obtained (Quinn, 1996). Inconsistencies in the social support–outcome relation may be due to differences across studies in the ways social support and rehabilitation outcome have been measured. Gould et al. (1997b) found that relative to skiers who experienced unsuccessful injury rehabilitation, those who had successful injury rehabilitation were less likely to perceive a lack of attention/empathy from others, less likely to encounter negative social relationships during rehabilitation, and *more* likely to indicate feeling socially isolated during rehabilitation. The disparate findings reviewed in this section suggest that extensive, in-depth investigation is needed to unravel the complexities of social influences on sport injury rehabilitation outcomes.

Numerous cognitive factors have been linked to sport injury rehabilitation outcomes. Positive associations with rehabilitation outcome have been documented for attentional focus on healing (Loundagin & Fisher, 1993), attribution of recovery to stable and personally controllable factors (Brewer, Cornelius, et al., 2000; Laubach et al., 1996), cognitive appraisal of injury coping ability (Niedfeldt, 1998), cognitive appraisal of the injury situation (Johnson, 1996, 1997), denial (Quinn, 1996), emotion-focused coping (Quinn, 1996), expected recovery rate (Laurence, 1997), management of thoughts and emotions (Gould et al., 1997a), number of rehabilitation goals (Johnson, 1996, 1997), positive attitude toward rehabilitation (Johnson, 1996, 1997), recovery confidence (Niedfeldt, 1998; Quinn, 1996), rehabilitation self-efficacy (Shaffer, 1992), self-confidence (Johnson, 1996, 1997), use of goal setting (Gould et al., 1997a; Ievleva & Orlick, 1991; Loundagin & Fisher, 1993), use of healing/recovery imagery (Ievleva & Orlick, 1991; Loundagin & Fisher, 1993), and use of imagery/visualization (Gould et al., 1997a). Inverse relationships with rehabilitation outcome have been found for use of the following coping strategies: mental disengagement, positive reinterpretation, emotional focus/venting, and denial (Grove &

Bahnsen, 1997). Available research suggests that positive cognitions and use of psychological skills are related to enhanced rehabilitation outcome. However, caution is advised in making strong inferences about these findings due to the retrospective nature of some of the studies and inconsistent or nonsignificant results for denial as a coping strategy (Grove & Bahnsen, 1997; Quinn, 1996) and psychological skill usage (Latuda, 1995; Tuffey, 1991).

Associations between emotional variables and sport injury rehabilitation outcomes have been found in four studies. In particular, general well-being (Johnson, 1996, 1997) and vigor (Quinn, 1996) have been positively correlated with rehabilitation outcome. Injury rehabilitation anxiety (Johnson, 1996, 1997), psychological distress (Brewer, Van Raalte, et al., 2000), anger (Alzate et al., 1998; LaMott, 1994), fear, frustration, relief (LaMott, 1994), mood disturbance, depression, fatigue, and tension (Alzate et al., 1998) have been negatively correlated with rehabilitation outcome. Thus, negative emotions seem to be related to a poorer response to rehabilitation.

Adherence to sport injury rehabilitation is the behavioral factor that has been examined most frequently in relation to rehabilitation outcome. Although adherence has been positively associated with outcome in several investigations (Alzate et al., 1998; Brewer, Van Raalte, et al., 2000; Derscheid & Feiring, 1987; Quinn, 1996; Treacy, Barron, Brunet, & Barrack, 1997; Tuffey, 1991), nonsignificant (Brewer, Van Raalte, et al., 2000; Noyes et al., 1983; Quinn, 1996) and negative (Quinn, 1996; Shelbourne & Wilckens, 1990) correlations between adherence and outcome have been obtained in other studies (or analyses within studies). It is likely that the magnitude and direction of the adherence-outcome correlation depends on a variety of factors, including the nature of the injury, the rehabilitation protocol, the phase of rehabilitation, and the particular measures of adherence and outcome (Brewer, 1999a). With regard to behavioral factors other than adherence, better sport injury rehabilitation outcomes have been associated with higher levels of active coping (Quinn, 1996) and lower levels of physical inactivity (Gould et al., 1997a) and seeking social support (Gould et al., 1997a; Johnson, 1996, 1997).

Experimental Studies

The best evidence of causal links between psychological factors and sport injury rehabilitation outcome has been obtained in experimental studies evaluating the effects of psychological interventions on rehabilitation outcomes. As noted by Cupal (1998) in her review of the literature, biofeedback has had, in general, a favorable influence on rehabilitation outcomes among athletes with injuries (Draper, 1990; Draper & Ballard, 1991; Krebs, 1981; Levitt, Deisinger, Wall, Ford, & Cassisi, 1995; H. Wise, Fiebert, & Kates, 1984). Goal setting (Theodorakis, Beneca, Malliou, & Goudas, 1997; Theodorakis, Malliou, Papaioannou, Beneca, & Filactakidou, 1996), imagery/relaxation (Durso-Cupal, 1996), stress inoculation training (Ross & Berger, 1996), and self-talk (Theodorakis, Beneca, Malliou, Antoniou, et al., 1997) have also been effective in enhancing the rate or quality of sport injury rehabilitation. The mechanisms by which the psychological interventions affected sport injury rehabilitation outcomes are not well-understood. From a biopsychosocial perspective (see Figure 31.1), it is likely that the interventions have both direct effects and indirect effects (mediated by biological factors) on rehabilitation outcome. Thus, psychological interventions may elicit changes in psychological (e.g., adherence to rehabilitation) and biological (e.g., circulation) parameters that contribute to therapeutic outcome.

SOCIAL INTERACTIONS IN SPORT INJURY REHABILITATION

Although biological processes are by definition a primary focus of sport injury rehabilitation, rehabilitation is inevitably a social process as well. From the time athletes are injured to the time they conclude rehabilitation, they generally have contact with a number of individuals varying in proximity to the rehabilitation environment (e.g., physicians, physical therapists, athletic trainers, support staff, other athletes with injuries, coaches, teammates, family members, friends). As shown in the preceding sections of this chapter, situational factors (some of which are social variables) have been linked to cognitive, emotional, behavioral, and physical responses to sport injury. Consequently, this section examines social aspects of sport injury rehabilitation in greater detail. Specifically, the oft-researched topic of social support in sport injury rehabilitation is addressed, along with patient-practitioner interactions and referral of athletes with injuries for psychological services.

Social Support in Sport Injury Rehabilitation

In the context of sport injury rehabilitation, social support reflects the quantity, quality, and type of interactions that athletes with injuries have with other people (Udry, 1996). Described next is research on the dimensions of social support experienced by athletes with injury, the providers of support to athletes with injury, and the dynamics of social support in sport injury rehabilitation.

Dimensions of Social Support

Social support is widely recognized as a multidimensional construct (Udry, 1996). Multiple types of social support have been documented in association with sport injury rehabilitation. The social support framework proposed by Richman, Rosenfeld, and Hardy (1993) has been particularly influential in guiding sport injury rehabilitation research (Bianco & Orlick, 1996; Ford, 1998; Ford & Gordon, 1993; Izzo, 1994; Johnston & Carroll, 1998b; LaMott, 1994; Quinn, 1996). Richman et al. identified eight types of social support: listening support, emotional support, emotional challenge, task appreciation, task challenge, reality confirmation, material assistance, and personal assistance. The extent to which these dimensions are salient may vary across both providers and stages of the rehabilitation process.

Social Support Providers

Athletes may receive social support from a variety of individuals while undergoing injury rehabilitation, including coaches, family members, friends, medical personnel, teammates, significant others, and sport administrators (Bianco, Eklund, & Gordon, 1999; Bianco & Orlick, 1996; Ford, 1998; Izzo, 1994; Johnston & Carroll, 1998b; Lewis & LaMott, 1992; Macchi & Crossman, 1996; Peterson, 1997; Udry, 1997b; Udry, Gould, Bridges, & Tuffey, 1997; Udry & Singleton, 1999). Athletes with injuries have reported different levels of satisfaction with the social support that they have received from various sources. In general, family members and teammates have been perceived by athletes with injuries as more supportive than coaches and medical professionals (Finnie, 1999; Lewis & LaMott, 1992; Macchi & Crossman, 1996; Peterson, 1997; Udry, Gould, Bridges, & Tuffey, 1997). Further, some individuals may be more likely than others to provide certain types of social support. Friends, family members, and significant others seem to be the most prevalent providers of emotional support, whereas medical practitioners and coaches have been cited as the most frequent providers of informational and technical support (Ford, 1998; Izzo, 1994; Johnston & Carroll, 1998b; Peterson, 1997; Udry, Gould, Bridges, & Tuffey, 1997). It is interesting to note that although it would be logical for sport psychologists to serve as providers of social support to athletes with injuries, little research has examined this possibility, perhaps reflecting a relatively minor role of sport psychologists in sports medicine service delivery.

Dynamics of Social Support

Temporal variations in types of social support preferred and received over the course of rehabilitation have been observed for athletes with injuries. In a study by LaMott (1994), multiple categories of perceived social support (i.e., listening support, emotional support, task appreciation, task challenge, personal assistance) decreased for athletes undergoing rehabilitation following knee surgery relative to athletes without injuries over a 12-week period. In contrast, Quinn (1996) and Udry (1997a) obtained no significant differences in global social support for athletes with injuries over the course of rehabilitation. Johnston and Carroll (1998b) found that athletes' perceptions of "technical appreciation support received" increased and "listening support received" decreased across the rehabilitation period. These perceptions coincided with the athletes' preferences for social support over the course of rehabilitation. A similar declining pattern in the perceived importance of emotional support (i.e., listening support and emotional comfort) across the rehabilitation period was documented by Ford (1998). Thus, although the findings on changes in social support preferred and received lack consensus, it can be tentatively concluded that the need for emotional support wanes as rehabilitation progresses, with a possible increased need for emotional support as athletes return to sport participation at the end of rehabilitation (Johnston & Carroll, 1998b). The relative salience of various potential providers of social support to athletes with injuries may also vary over the course of rehabilitation, but little systematic research has examined this issue.

Patient-Practitioner Interactions

Paramount among the many social interactions experienced by athletes during the injury rehabilitation process are those with sports medicine practitioners, who not only facilitate physical recovery following sport injury but also provide social support to athletes with injuries (Brewer, Van Raalte, & Petitpas, 1999). Given the high frequency of contact between athletes with injuries and rehabilitation practitioners such as physiotherapists and athletic trainers, it is not surprising that the patient-practitioner dyad has been a topic of scientific inquiry. In particular, researchers have examined concordances and discrepancies in the perceptions held by athletes with injuries and their rehabilitation practitioners.

Consistent with the finding that sport injury rehabilitation professionals tend to provide informational and technical support to a greater extent than they give emotional support (Ford, 1998; Izzo, 1994; Johnston & Carroll, 1998b; Peterson, 1997; Udry, Gould, Bridges, & Tuffey, 1997), Hokanson (1994) presented evidence that the communication of sport physiotherapists and athletic trainers with their patients tended to be predominantly informational and only minimally socioemotional (or empathic). Although the athletes in the Hokanson study were generally satisfied with their communication with sports medicine practitioners, satisfaction with practitioner communication is not tantamount to comprehension of practitioner communication. Indeed, Kahanov and Fairchild (1994) documented discrepancies between athletes with injuries and their athletic trainers in terms of their perceptions of patient-practitioner communication. Approximately one-third of the athletes, for example, reported that they had summarized the explanations for injury given by their athletic trainers when, according to the athletic trainers, no such summary process had taken place. Similarly, results in a recent study indicate that a majority of sport injury clinic patients (77%) misunderstood at least part of their rehabilitation regimen (Webborn, Carbon, & Miller, 1997).

Other discrepancies in patient and practitioner perceptions have been identified in the context of sport injury rehabilitation. Relative to the perceptions of sport rehabilitation practitioners, athletes with injuries tend to overestimate the seriousness of their injuries (Crossman & Jamieson, 1985) and their level of recovery (Van Raalte, Brewer, & Petitpas, 1992), and underestimate the disruptive impact of their injuries (Crossman & Jamieson, 1985; Crossman, Jamieson, & Hume, 1990) and amount of time required to complete their home rehabilitation exercises (May & Taylor, 1994). These discrepancies are noteworthy because misunderstandings between patients and practitioners may contribute to patient pain, emotional distress (Crossman et al., 1985), and nonadherence to the rehabilitation program. Nevertheless, it is important to note that patient and practitioner perceptions of the patient's injury status are generally positively correlated (Brewer, Linder, et al., 1995; Brewer, Van Raalte, Petitpas, Sklar, & Ditmar, 1995b; Crossman & Jamieson, 1985; Van Raalte et al., 1992), although patients and practitioners seem, on occasion, to use different ends of the scale.

Referral for Psychological Services

In circumstances where athletes with injuries display overt signs of psychological distress, report or exhibit difficulty adjusting in important life domains, or experience a particularly difficult course of rehabilitation, it may be appropriate for sport injury rehabilitation practitioners to refer those athletes for counseling or psychotherapy (Brewer,

Petitpas, & Van Raalte, 1999). Although most sports medicine physicians have referred athletes for mental health evaluation or treatment (Brewer, Van Raalte, & Linder, 1991), relatively few athletic trainers have made referrals for psychological services or have established referral procedures (Larson, Starkey, & Zaichkowsky, 1996).

Despite the consistent small percentage of athletes with injuries who experience emotional adjustment difficulties (Brewer, Linder, et al., 1995; Brewer, Petitpas, et al., 1995; Brewer & Petrie, 1995; Leddy et al., 1994; Perna et al., 1998), one factor that may contribute to the lack of psychological referrals generated by typical sport injury rehabilitation professionals is that they have difficulty identifying psychological distress in athletes with injuries. In support of this argument, nonsignificant correlations have been obtained between indices of patient psychological distress and sports medicine practitioner observations or judgments of patient psychological distress (Brewer, Petitpas, et al., 1995; Maniar, Perna, Newcomer, Roh, & Stilger, 1999a). Another possible explanation for the low number of athletic trainer referrals for psychological evaluation and intervention is that although athletes with injuries hold favorable perceptions of psychological treatment in sport injury rehabilitation (Brewer, Jeffers, Petitpas, & Van Raalte, 1994), they find counselors and psychologists less comfortable to talk with than friends and athletic trainers (Maniar, Perna, Newcomer, Roh, & Stilger, 1999b) and voice this opinion to their athletic trainers.

CURRENT TRENDS AND FUTURE RESEARCH DIRECTIONS

Major advances in the quantity and quality of research on psychological aspects of sport injury rehabilitation have occurred over the past three decades. Reflecting on the state of the science in the early 1990s, Williams and Roepke (1993) and Brewer (1994) offered substantive and methodological recommendations for psychological research on sport injury rehabilitation. These recommendations have been heeded to a large extent, contributing greatly to research on this topic. In accord with the suggestions of Williams and Roepke, researchers have (1) identified cognitive and emotional responses to injury that are characteristic of athlete populations (e.g., Leddy et al., 1994; Quinn & Fallon, 1999); (2) investigated the effects of psychological interventions on sport injury rehabilitation (e.g., Durso-Cupal, 1996; Ross & Berger, 1996; Theodorakis, Beneca, Malliou, Antoniu, et al., 1997; Theodorakis, Beneca, Malliou, & Goudas, 1997; Theodorakis et al., 1996); and

(3) initiated education of sports medicine practitioners on the psychological aspects of injury rehabilitation (e.g., Ford & Gordon, 1997, 1998; Gordon, Potter, & Ford, 1998).

Consistent with the recommendations of Brewer (1994), researchers have (1) advanced theory (e.g., Brewer, Andersen, et al., in press; Evans & Hardy, 1995; Johnston & Carroll, 1998a; Wiese-Bjornstal et al., 1998); (2) included both psychological and physical variables in their analyses (e.g., Brewer, Van Raalte, et al., 2000; Durso-Cupal, 1996; LaMott, 1994; Morrey et al., 1999; Niedfeldt, 1998; Ross & Berger, 1996; Theodorakis, Beneca, Malliou, Antoniu, et al., 1997; Theodorakis, Beneca, Malliou, & Goudas, 1997; Theodorakis et al., 1996); (3) assessed the prevalence of clinical levels of psychological distress (Brewer, Linder, et al., 1995; Brewer, Petitpas, et al., 1995; Brewer & Petrie, 1995; Leddy et al., 1994; Perna et al., 1998); (4) implemented prospective, longitudinal research designs (e.g., Brewer, Van Raalte, et al., 2000; LaMott, 1994; Leddy et al., 1994; Morrey, 1997; Morrey et al., 1999; Perna et al., 1998; Petrie, Falkstein, et al., 1997; Roh et al., 1998; Ross & Berger, 1996; Smith et al., 1993; Udry, 1997a); (5) conducted qualitative investigations (e.g., Bianco, Malo, et al., 1999; Gould et al., 1997a, 1997b; Johnston & Carroll, 1998a, 1998b; Shelley, 1994; Udry, Gould, Bridges, & Beck, 1997; Udry, Gould, Bridges, & Tuffey, 1997; (6) used control groups of athletes without injuries (e.g., Brewer & Petrie, 1995; LaMott, 1994; Perna, Ahlgren, & Zaichkowsky, 1999; Petrie, Brewer, et al., 1997); (7) examined groups of athletes that are homogeneous with respect to injury type, severity, and prognosis (e.g., Brewer, Cornelius, et al., 2000; Brewer, Van Raalte, et al., 2000; Durso-Cupal, 1996; LaMott, 1994; Morrey et al., 1999; Ross & Berger, 1996; Theodorakis, Beneca, Malliou, Antoniu, et al., 1997; Theodorakis, Beneca, Malliou, & Goudas, 1997; Theodorakis et al., 1996; Udry, 1997a); and (8) used experimental research designs (e.g., Durso-Cupal, 1996; Ross & Berger, 1996; Theodorakis, Beneca, Malliou, Antoniu, et al., 1997; Theodorakis, Beneca, Malliou, & Goudas, 1997; Theodorakis et al., 1996).

The expansion of research on psychological aspects of sport injury rehabilitation throughout the 1990s and the trend toward increased methodological rigor are encouraging. Nevertheless, continued proliferation of research and attention to methodological details is needed to develop further knowledge on the role of psychological factors in the rehabilitation of sport injuries. As recognition of the diverse array of variables contributing to sport injury rehabilitation processes and outcomes grows, research investigations should become increasingly integrated, including measures of multiple parameters of the biopsychosocial model (see Figure 31.1). In addition, more frequent assessment of psychological factors and intraindividual analyses are needed to capture the dynamic quality of the rehabilitation process (Evans & Hardy, 1999).

Research on psychological aspects of sport injury rehabilitation has, as in many emerging areas of inquiry, been eclectic in orientation and fragmented across studies. There is much to be gained, however, by a more focused and unified research agenda. Greater consistency in the measures and methods used and the research questions asked should help to develop a cohesive foundation of knowledge (Evans & Hardy, 1999). Coping with sport injury, as reviewed in the sections on cognitive and behavioral responses to sport injury, is a prime example of a topic that could benefit markedly from increased standardization of research practices. Due to the heterogeneity of extant research in terms of methods (i.e., qualitative, quantitative) and measures of coping, it is difficult to make meaningful comparisons across studies.

Development of psychological measures specific to the sport injury rehabilitation context may help not only in providing researchers with standardized instruments to measure pertinent constructs, but also in enabling researchers to ask more fine-grained research questions. Examples of psychological measures tailored specifically to sport injury rehabilitation are displayed in Table 31.1. Increased relevance to sport injury rehabilitation is not sufficient, however. As illustrated by studies in which measures specific to sport injury rehabilitation have failed to stand up to psychometric scrutiny (Brewer, Daly, Van Raalte, Petitpas, & Sklar, 1999; Slattery, 1999), establishment of reliability and validity is essential for measures designed for the sport injury rehabilitation context (Evans & Hardy, 1999).

As research on the effects of psychological interventions on sport injury rehabilitation processes and outcomes continues to increase, it will be useful to attempt to identify the degree of effectiveness of the interventions for various medical conditions and explore the mechanisms of effect for the interventions. Such inquiry will enable researchers to better determine "what specific interventions seem to work best under what conditions and with what type of personality characteristics to influence outcomes such as lowering incidences of reinjury, expediting return to previous level of functioning, and restoring confidence" (Williams & Roepke, 1993, p. 835).

Another promising direction for future research is to examine more thoroughly the potential benefits of experiencing sport injury and associated rehabilitation (Udry, 1999). Such inquiry has the potential to enrich and inform the development of psychological interventions for sport injury rehabilitation. Although the bulk of studies on the topic have been qualitative (Ford, 1998; Ford & Gordon, 1999; Niedfeldt, 1998; Rose & Jevne, 1993; Udry, Gould, Bridges, & Beck, 1997), quantitative methodologies are advocated to broaden the study of the benefits of injury (e.g., Park, Cohen, & Murch, 1996; Tedeschi & Calhoun, 1996).

Finally, from a theoretical standpoint, there is much to be gained by developing a comprehensive model of sport injury in an attempt to describe and explain the processes by which

Table 31.1   Examples of Psychological Measures Specific to Sport Injury Rehabilitation

Measure	Author(s)	Construct(s)
Emotional Responses of Athletes to Injury Questionnaire	Smith, Scott & Wiese (1990)	Emotional responses, miscellaneous psychological factors
High School Injured Athlete Perception Inventory	Shelley (1994)	Miscellaneous psychological factors
Injured Athlete Inventory	Slattery (1999)	Alienation
Psychological Responses to Injury Inventory	Evans, Hardy, & Mullen (1996)	Devastation, dispiritedness, rationalization, isolation, reorganization
Rehabilitation Adherence Questionnaire	Fisher, Domm, & Wuest (1988)	Predictors of adherence to rehabilitation
Sport Injury Rehabilitation Adherence Scale	Brewer, Van Raalte, Petitpas, Sklar, & Ditmar (1995a)	Adherence to clinic-based rehabilitation
Sports Injury Clinic Athlete Satisfaction Scale	Taylor & May (1995)	Satisfaction with medical care
Sports Injury Rehabilitation Beliefs Survey	Taylor & May (1996)	Susceptibility, severity, self-efficacy, treatment efficacy
Sports Rehabilitation Locus of Control	Murphy, Foreman, Simpson, Molloy, & Molloy (1999)	Rehabilitation locus of control
Sportsmen's Feelings after Injury Questionnaire	Pearson & Jones (1992)	Emotional responses

athletes incur and recover from injuries. The components and interrelationships among variables in the model of psychological response to sport injury proposed by Wiese-Bjornstal et al. (1998) closely resemble those in the model of sport injury occurrence offered by Williams and Andersen (1998). Presumably, these two models can be integrated to provide a dynamic, psychologically based conceptualization of sport injury from preinjury to postrehabilitation. At a more global level, the biopsychosocial framework depicted in Figure 31.1 can be adapted to accommodate a focus on the antecedents of injury by altering the pathways connecting the injury characteristics box with the biological factors, psychological factors, and social/contextual factors boxes to denote bidirectional relationships. A modification of this sort to the biopsychosocial model would be consistent with research on factors associated with the occurrence of sport injury (Meeuwisse & Fowler, 1988; Williams & Andersen, 1998) and other physical conditions (Cohen & Rodriguez, 1995). By integrating research on the causes and consequences of sport injury, as has been done in several studies (e.g., Henert et al., 1999; Heniff et al., 1999; Petrie, Falkstein, et al., 1997), a more complete picture of sport injury is likely to result.

CONCLUSIONS

A growing, increasingly rigorous body of research has provided strong evidence for the relevance of psychological factors to processes and outcomes in sport injury rehabilitation. Descriptive and inferential studies have presented an emerging picture of the role of cognitive, emotional, and behavioral factors within the broader biological and social contexts in which sport injury rehabilitation occurs. A consequence of research in this area is the development, implementation, and evaluation of psychological interventions that have the potential to enhance the rehabilitation experience of athletes with injury.

REFERENCES

Almekinders, L.C., & Almekinders, S.V. (1994). Outcome in the treatment of chronic overuse sports injuries: A retrospective study. *Journal of Orthopaedic and Sports Physical Therapy, 19,* 157–161.

Alzate, R., Ramirez, A., & Lazaro, I. (1998, August). *Psychological aspect of athletic injury.* Paper presented at the 24th International Congress of Applied Psychology, San Francisco.

Astle, S.J. (1986). The experience of loss in athletes. *Journal of Sports Medicine and Physical Fitness, 26,* 279–284.

Bianco, T.M., Eklund, R.C., & Gordon, S. (1999, September). *Coach support of injured athletes: Coaches and athletes share their views.* Paper presented at the annual meeting of the Association for the Advancement of Applied Sport Psychology, Banff, Canada.

Bianco, T.M., Malo, S., & Orlick, T. (1999). Sport injury and illness: Elite skiers describe their experiences. *Research Quarterly for Exercise and Sport, 70,* 157–169.

Bianco, T.M., & Orlick, T. (1996). Social support influences on recovery from sport injury [Abstract]. *Journal of Applied Sport Psychology, 8*(Suppl.), S57.

Bijur, P.E., Trumble, A., Harel, Y., Overpeck, M.D., Jones, D., & Scheidt, P.C. (1995). Sports and recreation injuries in U.S. children and adolescents. *Archives of Pediatric and Adolescent Medicine, 149,* 1009–1016.

Booth, W. (1987). Arthritis Institute tackles sports. *Science, 237,* 846–847.

Brewer, B.W. (1991, June). *Causal attributions and adjustment to athletic injury.* Paper presented at the annual meeting of the North American Society for the Psychology of Sport and Physical Activity, Pacific Grove, CA.

Brewer, B.W. (1993). Self-identity and specific vulnerability to depressed mood. *Journal of Personality, 61,* 343–364.

Brewer, B.W. (1994). Review and critique of models of psychological adjustment to athletic injury. *Journal of Applied Sport Psychology, 6,* 87–100.

Brewer, B.W. (1998). Adherence to sport injury rehabilitation programs. *Journal of Applied Sport Psychology, 10,* 70–82.

Brewer, B.W. (1999a). Adherence to sport injury rehabilitation regimens. In S.J. Bull (Ed.), *Adherence issues in sport and exercise* (pp. 145–168). Chichester, England: Wiley.

Brewer, B.W. (1999b). Causal attribution dimensions and adjustment to sport injury. *Journal of Personal and Interpersonal Loss, 4,* 215–224.

Brewer, B.W., Andersen, M.B., & Van Raalte, J.L. (in press). Psychological aspects of sport injury rehabilitation: Toward a biopsychosocial approach. In D.I. Mostofsky & L.D. Zaichkowsky (Eds.), *Medical aspects of sport and exercise.* Morgantown, WV: Fitness Information Technology.

Brewer, B.W., Cornelius, A.E., Van Raalte, J.L., Petitpas, A.J., Sklar, J.H., Pohlman, M.H., Krushell, R.J., & Ditmar, T.D. (2000). Attributions for recovery and adherence to rehabilitation following anterior cruciate ligament reconstruction: A prospective analysis. *Psychology & Health, 15,* 283–291.

Brewer, B.W., Daly, J.M., Van Raalte, J.L., Petitpas, A.J., & Sklar, J.H. (1994). A psychometric evaluation of the Rehabilitation Adherence Questionnaire [Abstract]. *Journal of Sport & Exercise Psychology, 16*(Suppl.), S34.

Brewer, B.W., Daly, J.M., Van Raalte, J.L., Petitpas, A.J., & Sklar, J.H. (1999). A psychometric evaluation of the Rehabilitation

Adherence Questionnaire. *Journal of Sport & Exercise Psychology, 21,* 167–173.

Brewer, B.W., & Helledy, K.I. (1998). Off (to) the deep end: Psychological skills training and water running. *Applied Research in Coaching and Athletics Annual, 13,* 99–118.

Brewer, B.W., Jeffers, K.E., Petitpas, A.J., & Van Raalte, J.L. (1994). Perceptions of psychological interventions in the context of sport injury rehabilitation. *The Sport Psychologist, 8,* 176–188.

Brewer, B.W., Linder, D.E., & Phelps, C.M. (1995). Situational correlates of emotional adjustment to athletic injury. *Clinical Journal of Sport Medicine, 5,* 241–245.

Brewer, B.W., Petitpas, A.J., & Van Raalte, J.L. (1999). Referral of injured athletes for counseling and psychotherapy. In R. Ray & D.M. Wiese-Bjornstal (Eds.), *Counseling in sports medicine* (pp. 127–141). Champaign, IL: Human Kinetics.

Brewer, B.W., Petitpas, A.J., Van Raalte, J.L., Sklar, J.H., & Ditmar, T.D. (1995). Prevalence of psychological distress among patients at a physical therapy clinic specializing in sports medicine. *Sports Medicine, Training and Rehabilitation, 6,* 138–145.

Brewer, B.W., & Petrie, T.A. (1995). A comparison between injured and uninjured football players on selected psychosocial variables. *Academic Athletic Journal, 10,* 11–18.

Brewer, B.W., Van Raalte, J.L., Cornelius, A.E., Petitpas, A.J., Sklar, J.H., Pohlman, M.H., Krushell, R.J., & Ditmar, T.D. (2000). Psychological factors, rehabilitation adherence, and rehabilitation outcome following anterior cruciate ligament reconstruction. *Rehabilitation Psychology, 45,* 20–37.

Brewer, B.W., Van Raalte, J.L., & Linder, D.E. (1991). Role of the sport psychologist in treating injured athletes: A survey of sports medicine providers. *Journal of Applied Sport Psychology, 3,* 183–190.

Brewer, B.W., Van Raalte, J.L., & Petitpas, A.J. (1999). Patient-practitioner interactions in sport injury rehabilitation. In D. Pargman (Ed.), *Psychological bases of sport injuries* (2nd ed., pp. 157–174). Morgantown, WV: Fitness Information Technology.

Brewer, B.W., Van Raalte, J.L., Petitpas, A.J., Sklar, J.H., & Ditmar, T.D. (1995a). A brief measure of adherence during sport injury rehabilitation sessions [Abstract]. *Journal of Applied Sport Psychology, 7*(Suppl.), S44.

Brewer, B.W., Van Raalte, J.L., Petitpas, A.J., Sklar, J.H., & Ditmar, T.D. (1995b). Predictors of perceived sport injury rehabilitation status. In R. Vanfraechem-Raway & Y. Vanden Auweele (Eds.), *9th European Congress on Sport Psychology proceedings: Part II* (pp. 606–610). Brussels, Belgium: European Federation of Sports Psychology.

Brickner, J.C. (1997). *Mood states and compliance of patients with orthopedic rehabilitation.* Unpublished master's thesis, Springfield College, MA.

Byerly, P.N., Worrell, T., Gahimer, J., & Domholdt, E. (1994). Rehabilitation compliance in an athletic training environment. *Journal of Athletic Training, 29,* 352–355.

Caine, D.J., Caine, C.G., & Lindner, K.J. (Eds.). (1996). *Epidemiology of sports injuries.* Champaign, IL: Human Kinetics.

Carver, C.S., Scheier, M.F., & Weintraub, J.K. (1989). Assessing coping strategies: A theoretically based approach. *Journal of Personality and Social Psychology, 56,* 267–283.

Chan, C.S., & Grossman, H.Y. (1988). Psychological effects of running loss on consistent runners. *Perceptual and Motor Skills, 66,* 875–883.

Cohen, S., & Rodriguez, M.S. (1995). Pathways linking affective disturbance and physical disorders. *Health Psychology, 14,* 374–380.

Connelly, S.L. (1991). *Injury and self-esteem: A test of Sonstroem and Morgan's model.* Unpublished master's thesis, South Dakota State University, Brookings.

Crossman, J., Gluck, L., & Jamieson, J. (1995). The emotional responses of injured athletes. *New Zealand Journal of Sports Medicine, 23,* 1–2.

Crossman, J., & Jamieson, J. (1985). Differences in perceptions of seriousness and disrupting effects of athletic injury as viewed by athletes and their trainer. *Perceptual and Motor Skills, 61,* 1131–1134.

Crossman, J., Jamieson, J., & Hume, K.M. (1990). Perceptions of athletic injuries by athletes, coaches, and medical professionals. *Perceptual and Motor Skills, 71,* 848–850.

Culpepper, W.L., Masters, K.S., & Wittig, A.F. (1996, August). *Factors influencing injured athletes' adherence to rehabilitation.* Paper presented at the annual meeting of the American Psychological Association, Toronto, Canada.

Cupal, D.D. (1998). Psychological interventions in sport injury prevention and rehabilitation. *Journal of Applied Sport Psychology, 10,* 103–123.

Daly, J.M., Brewer, B.W., Van Raalte, J.L., Petitpas, A.J., & Sklar, J.H. (1995). Cognitive appraisal, emotional adjustment, and adherence to rehabilitation following knee surgery. *Journal of Sport Rehabilitation, 4,* 23–30.

Dawes, H., & Roach, N.K. (1997). Emotional responses of athletes to injury and treatment. *Physiotherapy, 83,* 243–247.

Derscheid, G.L., & Feiring, D.C. (1987). A statistical analysis to characterize treatment adherence of the 18 most common diagnoses seen at a sports medicine clinic. *Journal of Orthopaedic and Sports Physical Therapy, 9,* 40–46.

Draper, V. (1990). Electromyographic biofeedback and recovery of quadriceps femoris muscle function following anterior cruciate ligament reconstruction. *Physical Therapy, 70,* 11–17.

Draper, V., & Ballard, L. (1991). Electrical stimulation versus electromyographic biofeedback in the recovery of quadriceps femoris muscle function following anterior cruciate ligament surgery. *Physical Therapy, 71,* 455–464.

Dubbels, T.K., Klein, J.M., Ihle, K., & Wittrock, D.A. (1992, April). *The psychological effects of injury on college athletes.* Paper presented at the 7th annual Red River Psychology Conference, Fargo, ND.

Duda, J.L., Smart, A.E., & Tappe, M.K. (1989). Predictors of adherence in rehabilitation of athletic injuries: An application of personal investment theory. *Journal of Sport & Exercise Psychology, 11,* 367–381.

Durso-Cupal, D.D. (1996). The efficacy of guided imagery for recovery from anterior cruciate ligament (ACL) replacement [Abstract]. *Journal of Applied Sport Psychology, 8*(Suppl.), S56.

Eichenhofer, R.B., Wittig, A.F., Balogh, D.W., & Pisano, M.D. (1986, May). *Personality indicants of adherence to rehabilitation treatment by injured athletes.* Paper presented at the annual meeting of the Midwestern Psychological Association, Chicago.

Evans, L., & Hardy, L. (1995). Sport injury and grief responses: A review. *Journal of Sport & Exercise Psychology, 17,* 227–245.

Evans, L., & Hardy, L. (1999). Psychological and emotional response to athletic injury: Measurement issues. In D. Pargman (Ed.), *Psychological bases of sport injuries* (2nd ed., pp. 49–64). Morgantown, WV: Fitness Information Technology.

Evans, L., Hardy, L., & Mullen, R. (1996). The development of the Psychological Responses to Injury Inventory [Abstract]. *Journal of Sports Sciences, 14,* 27–28.

Fields, J., Murphey, M., Horodyski, M., & Stopka, C. (1995). Factors associated with adherence to sport injury rehabilitation in college-age recreational athletes. *Journal of Sport Rehabilitation, 4,* 172–180.

Finch, C., Valuri, G., & Ozanne-Smith, J. (1998). Sport and active recreation injuries in Australia: Evidence from emergency department presentations. *British Journal of Sports Medicine, 32,* 220–225.

Finnie, S.B. (1999, September). *The rehabilitation support team: Using social support to aid compliance to sports injury rehabilitation programs.* Paper presented at the annual meeting of the Association for the Advancement of Applied Sport Psychology, Banff, Canada.

Fisher, A.C., Domm, M.A., & Wuest, D.A. (1988). Adherence to sports-injury rehabilitation programs. *Physician and Sportsmedicine, 16*(7), 47–52.

Fisk, L.M., & King, L.A. (1998, August). *Predictors of loss of identity among injured athletes.* Paper presented at the annual meeting of the American Psychological Association, San Francisco.

Flint, F.A. (1998). Integrating sport psychology and sports medicine in research: The dilemmas. *Journal of Applied Sport Psychology, 10,* 83–102.

Ford, I.W. (1998). *Psychosocial processes in sport injury occurrence and rehabilitation.* Unpublished doctoral thesis, University of Western Australia, Nedlands.

Ford, I.W., & Gordon, S. (1993). Social support and athletic injury: The perspective of sport physiotherapists. *Australian Journal of Science and Medicine in Sport, 25,* 17–25.

Ford, I.W., & Gordon, S. (1997). Perspectives of sport physiotherapists on the frequency and significance of psychological factors in professional practice: Implications for curriculum design in professional training. *Australian Journal of Science and Medicine in Sport, 29,* 34–40.

Ford, I.W., & Gordon, S. (1998). Perspectives of sport trainers and athletic therapists on the psychological content of their practice and training. *Journal of Sport Rehabilitation, 7,* 79–94.

Ford, I.W., & Gordon, S. (1999). Coping with sport injury: Resource loss and the role of social support. *Journal of Personal and Interpersonal Loss, 4,* 243–256.

Gilbourne, D., & Taylor, A.H. (1995). Rehabilitation experiences of injured athletes and their perceptions of a task-oriented goal-setting program: The application of an action research design. *Journal of Sports Sciences, 13,* 54–55.

Gilbourne, D., & Taylor, A.H. (1998). From theory to practice: The integration of goal perspective theory and life development approaches within an injury-specific goal-setting program. *Journal of Applied Sport Psychology, 10,* 124–139.

Gilbourne, D., Taylor, A.H., Downie, G., & Newton, P. (1996). Goal-setting during sports injury rehabilitation: A presentation of underlying theory, administration procedure, and an athlete case study. *Sports Exercise and Injury, 2,* 192–201.

Gordin, R., Albert, N.J., McShane, D., & Dobson, W. (1988, September). *The emotional effects of injury on female collegiate gymnasts.* Paper presented at the Seoul Olympic Scientific Congress, South Korea.

Gordon, S. (1986, March). Sport psychology and the injured athlete: A cognitive-behavioral approach to injury response and injury rehabilitation. *Science Periodical on Research and Technology in Sport,* 1–10.

Gordon, S., & Lindgren, S. (1990). Psycho-physical rehabilitation from a serious sport injury: Case study of an elite fast bowler. *Australian Journal of Science and Medicine in Sport, 22,* 71–76.

Gordon, S., Potter, M., & Ford, I. (1998). Toward a psychoeducational curriculum for training sport-injury rehabilitation personnel. *Journal of Applied Sport Psychology, 10,* 140–156.

Gould, D., Udry, E., Bridges, D., & Beck, L. (1997a). Coping with season-ending injuries. *The Sport Psychologist, 11,* 379–399.

Gould, D., Udry, E., Bridges, D., & Beck, L. (1997b). Stress sources encountered when rehabilitating from season-ending ski injuries. *The Sport Psychologist, 11*, 361–378.

Green, S.L., & Weinberg, R.S. (1998). The relationship between athletic identity, coping skills, social support, and the psychological impact of injury [Abstract]. *Journal of Applied Sport Psychology, 10*(Suppl.), S127.

Grove, J.R. (1993). Personality and injury rehabilitation among sport performers. In D. Pargman (Ed.), *Psychological bases of sport injuries* (pp. 99–120). Morgantown, WV: Fitness Information Technology.

Grove, J.R., & Bahnsen, A. (1997). *Personality, injury severity, and coping with rehabilitation.* Unpublished manuscript.

Grove, J.R., Stewart, R.M.L., & Gordon, S. (1990, October). *Emotional reactions of athletes to knee rehabilitation.* Paper presented at the annual meeting of the Australian Sports Medicine Federation, Alice Springs.

Hartman, A., & Finch, L. (1999, September). *A case study to examine the use of goal setting in facilitating social support for injured athletes rehabilitating from injury.* Paper presented at the annual meeting of the Association for the Advancement of Applied Sport Psychology, Banff, Canada.

Hawkins, R.B. (1989). Arthroscopic stapling repair for shoulder instability: A retrospective study of 50 cases. *Arthroscopy: The Journal of Arthroscopic and Related Surgery, 2*, 122–128.

Heil, J. (1993). Sport psychology, the athlete at risk, and the sports medicine team. In J. Heil (Ed.), *Psychology of sport injury* (pp. 1–13). Champaign, IL: Human Kinetics.

Henert, S.E., Wiese-Bjornstal, D.M., Malo, S.A., Schwenz, S., Heniff, C.B., Gardetto, D., & Shaffer, S.M. (1999, September). *Major and minor life event stress, athletic identity, and mood state as predictors of injury in intercollegiate athletes.* Paper presented at the annual meeting of the Association for the Advancement of Applied Sport Psychology, Banff, Canada.

Heniff, C.B., Wiese-Bjornstal, D.M., Henert, S.E., Schwenz, S., Shaffer, S.M., & Gardetto, D. (1999, September). *A comparison between injured and uninjured NCAA Division I female athletes on life event stress, weekly hassles and uplifts, and mood state.* Paper presented at the annual meeting of the Association for the Advancement of Applied Sport Psychology, Banff, Canada.

Hokanson, R.G. (1994). *Relationship between sports rehabilitation practitioners' communication style and athletes' adherence to injury rehabilitation.* Unpublished master's thesis, Springfield College, MA.

Ievleva, L., & Orlick, T. (1991). Mental links to enhanced healing: An exploratory study. *The Sport Psychologist, 5*, 25–40.

Izzo, C.M. (1994). *The relationship between social support and adherence to sport injury rehabilitation.* Unpublished master's thesis, Springfield College, MA.

Johnson, U. (1996). Quality of experience of long-term injury in athletic sports predicts return after rehabilitation. In G. Patriksson (Ed.), *Aktuell beteendevetenskaplig idrottsforskning* (pp. 110–117). Lund, Sweden: SVEBI.

Johnson, U. (1997a). Coping strategies among long-term injured competitive athletes: A study of 81 men and women in team and individual sports. *Scandinavian Journal of Medicine and Science in Sports, 7*, 367–372.

Johnson, U. (1997b). A three-year follow-up of long-term injured competitive athletes: Influence of psychological risk factors on rehabilitation. *Journal of Sport Rehabilitation, 6*, 256–271.

Johnson, U. (1998). Psychological risk factors during the rehabilitation of competitive male soccer players with serious knee injuries [Abstract]. *Journal of Sports Sciences, 16*, 391–392.

Johnston, L.H., & Carroll, D. (1998a). The context of emotional responses to athletic injury: A qualitative analysis. *Journal of Sport Rehabilitation, 7*, 206–220.

Johnston, L.H., & Carroll, D. (1998b). The provision of social support to injured athletes: A qualitative analysis. *Journal of Sport Rehabilitation, 7*, 267–284.

Kahanov, L., & Fairchild, P.C. (1994). Discrepancies in perceptions held by injured athletes and athletic trainers during the initial evaluation. *Journal of Athletic Training, 29*, 70–75.

Kleiber, D.A., & Brock, S.C. (1992). The effect of career-ending injuries on the subsequent well-being of elite college athletes. *Sociology of Sport Journal, 9*, 70–75.

Kraus, J.F., & Conroy, C. (1984). Mortality and morbidity from injury in sports and recreation. *Annual Review of Public Health, 5*, 163–192.

Krebs, D.E. (1981). Clinical EMG feedback following meniscectomy: A multiple regression experimental analysis. *Physical Therapy, 61*, 1017–1021.

Kübler-Ross, E. (1969). *On death and dying.* New York: Macmillan.

LaMott, E.E. (1994). *The anterior cruciate ligament injured athlete: The psychological process.* Unpublished doctoral dissertation, University of Minnesota, Minneapolis.

Lampton, C.C., Lambert, M.E., & Yost, R. (1993). The effects of psychological factors in sports medicine rehabilitation adherence. *Journal of Sports Medicine and Physical Fitness, 33*, 292–299.

Larson, G.A., Starkey, C.A., & Zaichkowsky, L.D. (1996). Psychological aspects of athletic injuries as perceived by athletic trainers. *The Sport Psychologist, 10*, 37–47.

Latuda, L. (1995). The use of psychological skills in enhancing the rehabilitation of injured athletes. *Journal of Sport & Exercise Psychology, 17*(Suppl.), S70.

Laubach, W.J., Brewer, B.W., Van Raalte, J.L., & Petitpas, A.J. (1996). Attributions for recovery and adherence to sport injury rehabilitation. *Australian Journal of Science and Medicine in Sport, 28,* 30–34.

Laurence, C. (1997, September). *Attributional, affective and perceptual processes during injury and rehabilitation in active people.* Paper presented at the 14th World Congress on Psychosomatic Medicine, Cairns, Australia.

Leadbetter, W.B. (1994). Soft tissue athletic injury. In F.H. Fu & D.A. Stone (Eds.), *Sports injuries: Mechanisms, prevention, and treatment* (pp. 733–780). Baltimore: Williams & Wilkins.

Leddy, M.H., Lambert, M.J., & Ogles, B.M. (1994). Psychological consequences of athletic injury among high-level competitors. *Research Quarterly for Exercise and Sport, 65,* 347–354.

Levitt, R., Deisinger, J.A., Wall, J.R., Ford, L., & Cassisi, J.E. (1995). EMG feedback-assisted postoperative rehabilitation of minor arthroscopic knee surgeries. *Journal of Sports Medicine and Physical Fitness, 35,* 218–223.

Lewis, L., & LaMott, E.E. (1992, October). *Psychosocial aspects of the injury response in the pro football: An exploratory study.* Paper presented at the annual meeting of the Association for the Advancement of Applied Sport Psychology, Colorado Springs, CO.

Little, J.C. (1969). The athlete's neurosis: A deprivation crisis. *Acta Psychiatrica Scandinavica, 45,* 187–197.

Loundagin, C., & Fisher, L. (1993, October). *The relationship between mental skills and enhanced athletic injury rehabilitation.* Poster presented at the annual meeting of the Association for the Advancement of Applied Sport Psychology and the Canadian Society for Psychomotor Learning and Sport Psychology, Montreal, Canada.

Lynch, G.P. (1988). Athletic injuries and the practicing sport psychologist: Practical guidelines for assisting athletes. *The Sport Psychologist, 2,* 161–167.

Macchi, R., & Crossman, J. (1996). After the fall: Reflections of injured classical ballet dancers. *Journal of Sport Behavior, 19,* 221–234.

Maniar, S., Perna, F., Newcomer, R., Roh, J., & Stilger, V. (1999a, September). Athletic trainers' recognition of psychological distress following athletic injury: Implications for referral. In F. Perna (Chair), *Pre-injury screening and post-injury assessment: Interactions between sport psychologists and the sports medicine team.* Symposium conducted at the annual meeting of the Association for the Advancement of Applied Sport Psychology, Banff, Canada.

Maniar, S.D., Perna, F.M., Newcomer, R.R., Roh, J.L., & Stilger, V.G. (1999b, August). *Emotional reactions to injury: With whom are athletes comfortable talking?* Paper presented at the annual meeting of the American Psychological Association, Boston.

Matthews, K.A., Shumaker, S.A., Bowen, D.J., Langer, R.D., Hunt, J.R., Kaplan, R.M., Klesges, R.C., & Ritenbaugh, C. (1997). Women's Health Initiative: Why now? What is it? What's new? *American Psychologist, 52,* 101–116.

May, S., & Taylor, A.H. (1994). The development and examination of various measures of patient compliance, for specific use with injured athletes. *Journal of Sports Sciences, 12,* 180–181.

McDonald, S.A., & Hardy, C.J. (1990). Affective response patterns of the injured athlete: An exploratory analysis. *The Sport Psychologist, 4,* 261–274.

McGowan, R.W., Pierce, E.F., Williams, M., & Eastman, N.W. (1994). Athletic injury and self diminution. *Journal of Sports Medicine and Physical Fitness, 34,* 299–304.

McNair, D.M., Lorr, M., & Droppleman, L.F. (1971). *Manual for the Profile of Mood States.* San Diego, CA: Educational and Industrial Testing Service.

Meani, E., Migliorini, S., & Tinti, G. (1986). La patologia de sovraccarico sportivo dei nuclei di accrescimento apofisari [The pathology of apophyseal growth centers caused by overstrain during sports]. *Italian Journal of Sports Traumatology, 8,* 29–38.

Meeuwisse, W.H., & Fowler, P.J. (1988). Frequency and predictability of sports injuries in intercollegiate athletes. *Canadian Journal of Sport Sciences, 13,* 35–42.

Meyers, M.C., Sterling, J.C., Calvo, R.D., Marley, R., & Duhon, T.K. (1991). Mood state of athletes undergoing orthopaedic surgery and rehabilitation: A preliminary report. *Medicine and Science in Sports and Exercise, 23*(Suppl.), S138.

Miller, W.N. (1998). Athletic injury: Mood disturbances and hardiness of intercollegiate athletes [Abstract]. *Journal of Applied Sport Psychology, 10*(Suppl.), S127–128.

Morrey, M.A. (1997). *A longitudinal examination of emotional response, cognitive coping, and physical recovery among athletes undergoing anterior cruciate ligament reconstructive surgery.* Unpublished doctoral dissertation, University of Minnesota, Minneapolis.

Morrey, M.A., Stuart, M.J., Smith, A.M., & Wiese-Bjornstal, D.M. (1999). A longitudinal examination of athletes' emotional and cognitive responses to anterior cruciate ligament injury. *Clinical Journal of Sport Medicine, 9,* 63–69.

Murphy, G.C., Foreman, P.E., Simpson, C.A., Molloy, G.N., & Molloy, E.K. (1999). The development of a locus of control measure predictive of injured athletes' adherence to treatment. *Journal of Science and Medicine in Sport, 2,* 145–152.

NEISS data highlights. (1998). *Consumer Product Safety Review, 3*(1), 4–6.

Newcomer, R., Perna, F., Maniar, S., Roh, J., & Stilger, V. (1999, September). Depressive symptomatology distinguishing injured from non-injured athletes. In F. Perna (Chair),

Preinjury screening and post-injury assessment: Interactions between sport psychologists and the sports medicine team. Symposium conducted at the annual meeting of the Association for the Advancement of Applied Sport Psychology, Banff, Canada.

Newcomer, R.R., Perna, F.M., Roh, J.L., Maniar, S.D., & Stilger, V.G. (1999, August). *Intrusive thoughts and avoidance behaviors following athletic injury among adolescents.* Paper presented at the annual meeting of the American Psychological Association, Boston.

Newcomer, R.R., Roh, J.L., Perna, F.M., & Etzel, E.F. (1998). Injury as a traumatic experience: Intrusive thoughts and avoidance behavior associated with injury among college student-athletes [Abstract]. *Journal of Applied Sport Psychology, 10*(Suppl.), S54.

Nicol, M. (1993). Hypnosis in the treatment of repetitive strain injury. *Australian Journal of Clinical and Experimental Hypnosis, 21,* 121–126.

Niedfeldt, C.E. (1998). *The integration of physical factors into the cognitive appraisal process of injury rehabilitation.* Unpublished master's thesis, University of New Orleans, LA.

Noyes, F.R., Matthews, D.S., Mooar, P.A., & Grood, E.S. (1983). The symptomatic anterior cruciate–deficient knee: Part II. The results of rehabilitation, activity modification, and counseling on functional disability. *Journal of Bone and Joint Surgery, 65–A,* 163–174.

Pargman, D., & Lunt, S.D. (1989). The relationship of self-concept and locus of control to the severity of injury in freshmen collegiate football players. *Sports Training, Medicine and Rehabilitation, 1,* 203–208.

Park, C.L., Cohen, L.H., & Murch, R.L. (1996). Assessment and prediction of stress-related growth. *Journal of Personality, 64,* 71–105.

Pearson, L., & Jones, G. (1992). Emotional effects of sports injuries: Implications for physiotherapists. *Physiotherapy, 78,* 762–770.

Penpraze, P., & Mutrie, N. (1999). Effectiveness of goal setting in an injury rehabilitation programme for increasing patient understanding and compliance [Abstract]. *British Journal of Sports Medicine, 33,* 60.

Peretz, D. (1970). Development, object-relationships, and loss. In B. Schoenberg, A.C. Carr, D. Peretz, & A.H. Kutscher (Eds.), *Loss and grief: Psychological management in medical practice* (pp. 3–19). New York: Columbia University Press.

Perna, F. (1992, October). *A re-examination of injury and post-athletic career adjustment.* Paper presented at the annual meeting of the Association for the Advancement of Applied Sport Psychology, Colorado Springs, CO.

Perna, F.M., Ahlgren, R.L., & Zaichkowsky, L. (1999). The influence of career planning, race, and athletic injury on life

satisfaction among recently retired collegiate male athletes. *Journal of Applied Sport Psychology, 13,* 144–156.

Perna, F.M., Roh, J., Newcomer, R.R., & Etzel, E.F. (1998). Clinical depression among injured athletes: An empirical assessment [Abstract]. *Journal of Applied Sport Psychology, 10*(Suppl.), S54–S55.

Peterson, K. (1997). Role of social support in coping with athletic injury rehabilitation: A longitudinal qualitative investigation [Abstract]. *Journal of Applied Sport Psychology, 9*(Suppl.), S33.

Petrie, T.A., Brewer, B., & Buntrock, C. (1997). A comparison between injured and uninjured NCAA Division I male and female athletes on selected psychosocial variables [Abstract]. *Journal of Applied Sport Psychology, 9*(Suppl.), S144.

Petrie, T.A., Falkstein, D.L., & Brewer, B.W. (1997, August). *Predictors of psychological response to injury in female collegiate athletes.* Paper presented at the annual meeting of the American Psychological Association, Chicago.

Potter, M.J. (1995). *Psychological intervention during rehabilitation case studies of injured athletes.* Unpublished master's thesis, University of Western Australia, Nedlands.

Quackenbush, N., & Crossman, J. (1994). Injured athletes: A study of emotional response. *Journal of Sport Behavior, 17,* 178–187.

Quinn, A.M. (1996). *The psychological factors involved in the recovery of elite athletes from long-term injuries.* Unpublished doctoral dissertation, University of Melbourne, Australia.

Quinn, A.M., & Fallon, B.J. (1999). The changes in psychological characteristics and reactions of elite athletes from injury onset until full recovery. *Journal of Applied Sport Psychology, 11,* 210–229.

Rape, R.N., Bush, J.P., & Slavin, L.A. (1992). Toward a conceptualization of the family's adaptation to a member's head injury: A critique of developmental stage models. *Rehabilitation Psychology, 37,* 3–22.

Richman, J.M., Rosenfeld, L.B., & Hardy, C.J. (1993). The Social Support Survey: A validation study of a clinical measure of the social support process. *Research on Social Work Practice, 3,* 288–311.

Roh, J.L., Newcomer, R.R., Perna, F.M., & Etzel, E.F. (1998). Depressive mood states among college athletes: Pre- and post-injury [Abstract]. *Journal of Applied Sport Psychology, 10*(Suppl.), S54.

Rose, J., & Jevne, R.F.J. (1993). Psychosocial processes associated with sport injuries. *The Sport Psychologist, 7,* 309–328.

Ross, M.J., & Berger, R.S. (1996). Effects of stress inoculation on athletes' postsurgical pain and rehabilitation after orthopedic injury. *Journal of Consulting and Clinical Psychology, 64,* 406–410.

Rotella, B. (1985). The psychological care of the injured athlete. In L.K. Bunker, R.J. Rotella, & A.S. Reilly (Eds.), *Sport psychology: Psychological considerations in maximizing sport performance* (pp. 273–287). Ann Arbor, MI: Mouvement.

Rotella, R.J., & Campbell, M.S. (1983). Systematic desensitization: Psychological rehabilitation of injured athletes. *Athletic Training, 18*, 140–142, 151.

Satterfield, M.J., Dowden, D., & Yasamura, K. (1990). Patient compliance for successful stress fracture rehabilitation. *Journal of Orthopaedic and Sports Physical Therapy, 11*, 321–324.

Scheier, M.F., Carver, C.S., & Bridges, M.W. (1994). Distinguishing optimism from neuroticism (and trait anxiety, self-mastery, and self-esteem): A reevaluation of the Life Orientation Test. *Journal of Personality and Social Psychology, 67*, 1063–1078.

Scherzer, C.B., Brewer, B.W., Cornelius, A.E., Van Raalte, J.L., Petitpas, A.J., Sklar, J.H., Pohlman, M.H., Krushell, R.J., & Ditmar, T. (1999, September). *Self-reported use of psychological skills and adherence to rehabilitation following anterior cruciate ligament reconstruction.* Paper presented at the annual meeting of the Association for the Advancement of Applied Sport Psychology, Banff, Canada.

Shaffer, S.M. (1992). *Attributions and self-efficacy as predictors of rehabilitative success.* Unpublished master's thesis, University of Illinois, Champaign.

Shank, R.H. (1988). *Academic and athletic factors related to predicting compliance by athletes to treatments.* Unpublished doctoral dissertation, University of Virginia, Charlottesville.

Shelbourne, K.D., & Wilckens, J.H. (1990). Current concepts in anterior cruciate ligament rehabilitation. *Orthopaedic Review, 19*, 957–964.

Shelley, G.A. (1994, October). *Athletic injuries: The psychological perspectives of high school athletes.* Poster presented at the annual meeting of the Association for the Advancement of Applied Sport Psychology, Incline Village, NV.

Shelley, G.A., & Carroll, S.A. (1996). Athletic injury: A qualitative, retrospective case study [Abstract]. *Journal of Applied Sport Psychology, 8*(Suppl.), S162.

Shelley, G.A., & Sherman, C.P. (1996). The sport injury experience: A qualitative case study [Abstract]. *Journal of Applied Sport Psychology, 8*(Suppl.), S164.

Silver, R.L., & Wortman, C.B. (1980). Coping with undesirable events. In J. Garber & M.E.P. Seligman (Eds.), *Human helplessness: Theory and applications* (pp. 279–375). New York: Academic Press.

Slattery, M.M. (1999). Construction of an instrument designed to measure alienation in sport of the injured athlete [Abstract]. *Research Quarterly for Exercise and Sport, 70*(Suppl.), A-114.

Smith, A.M., & Milliner, E.K. (1994). Injured athletes and the risk of suicide. *Journal of Athletic Training, 29*, 337–341.

Smith, A.M., Scott, S.G., O'Fallon, W.M., & Young, M.L. (1990). Emotional responses of athletes to injury. *Mayo Clinic Proceedings, 65*, 38–50.

Smith, A.M., Scott, S.G., & Wiese, D.M. (1990). The psychological effects of sports injuries: Coping. *Sports Medicine, 9*, 352–369.

Smith, A.M., Stuart, M.J., Wiese-Bjornstal, D.M., Milliner, E.K., O'Fallon, W.M., & Crowson, C.S. (1993). Competitive athletes: Preinjury and postinjury mood state and self-esteem. *Mayo Clinic Proceedings, 68*, 939–947.

Smith, A.M., Young, M.L., & Scott, S.G. (1988). The emotional responses of athletes to injury. *Canadian Journal of Sport Sciences, 13*(4), 84P–85P.

Sparkes, A.C. (1998). An Achilles heel to the survival of self. *Qualitative Health Research, 8*, 644–664.

Sthalekar, H.A. (1993). Hypnosis for relief of chronic phantom limb pain in a paralysed limb: A case study. *Australian Journal of Clinical Hypnotherapy and Hypnosis, 14*, 75–80.

Taylor, A.H., & May, S. (1995). Development of a Sports Injury Clinic Athlete Satisfaction Scale for auditing patient perceptions. *Physiotherapy Theory and Practice, 11*, 231–238.

Taylor, A.H., & May, S. (1996). Threat and coping appraisal as determinants of compliance to sports injury rehabilitation: An application of protection motivation theory. *Journal of Sports Sciences, 14*, 471–482.

Tedder, S., & Biddle, S.J.H. (1998). Psychological processes involved during sports injury rehabilitation: An attribution-emotion investigation [Abstract]. *Journal of Sports Sciences, 16*, 106–107.

Tedeschi, R.G., & Calhoun, L.G. (1996). The post-traumatic growth inventory: Measuring the positive legacy of trauma. *Journal of Traumatic Stress, 9*, 455–471.

Theodorakis, Y., Beneca, A., Malliou, P., Antoniou, P., Goudas, M., & Laparidis, K. (1997). The effect of a self-talk technique on injury rehabilitation [Abstract]. *Journal of Applied Sport Psychology, 9*(Suppl.), S164.

Theodorakis, Y., Beneca, A., Malliou, P., & Goudas, M. (1997). Examining psychological factors during injury rehabilitation. *Journal of Sport Rehabilitation, 6*, 355–363.

Theodorakis, Y., Malliou, P., Papaioannou, A., Beneca, A., & Filactakidou, A. (1996). The effect of personal goals, self-efficacy, and self-satisfaction on injury rehabilitation. *Journal of Sport Rehabilitation, 5*, 214–223.

Treacy, S.H., Barron, O.A., Brunet, M.E., & Barrack, R.L. (1997). Assessing the need for extensive supervised rehabilitation following arthroscopic surgery. *American Journal of Orthopedics, 26*, 25–29.

Tuffey, S. (1991). *The use of psychological skills to facilitate recovery from athletic injury.* Unpublished master's thesis, University of North Carolina, Greensboro.

Udry, E. (1996). Social support: Exploring its role in the context of athletic injuries. *Journal of Sport Rehabilitation, 5,* 151–163.

Udry, E. (1997a). Coping and social support among injured athletes following surgery. *Journal of Sport & Exercise Psychology, 19,* 71–90.

Udry, E. (1997b). Support providers and injured athletes: A specificity approach [Abstract]. *Journal of Applied Sport Psychology, 9*(Suppl.), S34.

Udry, E. (1999). The paradox of injuries: Unexpected positive consequences. In D. Pargman (Ed.), *Psychological bases of sport injuries* (2nd ed., pp. 79–88). Morgantown, WV: Fitness Information Technology.

Udry, E., Gould, D., Bridges, D., & Beck, L. (1997). Down but not out: Athlete responses to season-ending injuries. *Journal of Sport & Exercise Psychology, 19,* 229–248.

Udry, E., Gould, D., Bridges, D., & Tuffey, S. (1997). People helping people? Examining the social ties of athletes coping with burnout and injury stress. *Journal of Sport & Exercise Psychology, 19,* 368–395.

Udry, E., & Singleton, M. (1999, September). *Views of social support during injuries: Congruence among athletes and coaches?* Paper presented at the annual meeting of the Association for the Advancement of Applied Sport Psychology, Banff, Canada.

Uemukai, K. (1993). Affective responses and the changes in athletes due to injury. In S. Serpa, J. Alves, V. Ferreira, & A. Paula-Brito (Eds.), *Proceedings of the 8th World Congress of Sport Psychology* (pp. 500–503). Lisbon, Portugal: International Society of Sport Psychology.

Uitenbroek, D.G. (1996). Sports, exercise, and other causes of injuries: Results of a population survey. *Research Quarterly for Exercise and Sport, 67,* 380–385.

Van Raalte, J.L., Brewer, B.W., & Petitpas, A.J. (1992). *Correspondence between athlete and trainer appraisals of injury rehabilitation status.* Paper presented at the annual meeting of the Association for the Advancement of Applied Sport Psychology, Colorado Springs, CO.

Weaver, N.L., Marshall, S.W., Spicer, R., Miller, T., Waller, A.E., & Mueller, F.O. (1999). Cost of athletic injuries in 12 North Carolina high school sports [Abstract]. *Medicine and Science in Sports and Exercise, 31*(Suppl.), S93.

Webborn, A.D.J., Carbon, R.J., & Miller, B.P. (1997). Injury rehabilitation programs: "What are we talking about?" *Journal of Sport Rehabilitation, 6,* 54–61.

Weiss, M.R., & Troxel, R.K. (1986). Psychology of the injured athlete. *Athletic Training, 21,* 104–109, 154.

Wiese-Bjornstal, D.M., Smith, A.M., Shaffer, S.M., & Morrey, M.A. (1998). An integrated model of response to sport injury: Psychological and sociological dimensions. *Journal of Applied Sport Psychology, 10,* 46–69.

Williams, J.M., & Andersen, M.B. (1998). Psychosocial antecedents of sport injury: Review and critique of the stress and injury model. *Journal of Applied Sport Psychology, 10,* 5–25.

Williams, J.M., & Roepke, N. (1993). Psychology of injury and injury rehabilitation. In R.N. Singer, M. Murphey, & L.K. Tennant (Eds.), *Handbook of research on sport psychology* (pp. 815–839). New York: Macmillan.

Wise, A., Jackson, D.W., & Rocchio, P. (1979). Preoperative psychologic testing as a predictor of success in knee surgery. *American Journal of Sports Medicine, 7,* 287–292.

Wise, H.H., Fiebert, I.M., & Kates, J.L. (1984). EMG biofeedback as treatment for patellofemoral pain syndrome. *Journal of Orthopaedic and Sports Physical Therapy, 6,* 95–103.

Wittig, A.F., & Schurr, K.T. (1994). Psychological characteristics of women volleyball players: Relationships with injuries, rehabilitation, and team success. *Personality and Social Psychology Bulletin, 20,* 322–330.

Wong, P.T.P., & Weiner, B. (1981). When people ask "why" questions, and the heuristics of attributional search. *Journal of Personality and Social Psychology, 40,* 650–663.

CHAPTER 32

A Social-Cognitive Perspective of Perceived Exertion and Exertion Tolerance

GERSHON TENENBAUM

"Most of the physiological processes that are associated with the perception of effort occur more or less unconsciously, including heart-rate, oxygen consumption, blood pressure, and even lactate production. As exercise intensity grows, so does the possibility that sensation will receive more conscious attention, especially to those variables readily available to consciousness, such as pulmonary ventilation and regionalized pain" (Noble & Robertson, 1996, p. 207) Noble and Robertson defined perceived exertion as a subjective intensity of effort, strain, discomfort, and/or fatigue that is experienced during exercise (i.e., detecting and interpreting sensations arising from the body). The interest in perceived exertion was initiated with the work of Gunnar Borg during the early 1960s. In 1962, Borg viewed "perceived force" as one's perception of exertion in short-time exercise and "perceived fatigue/exertion" as representing exertion during aerobic activities (Noble & Robertson, 1996). In the 1950s and 1960s, perceived exertion was studied using a psychophysiological perspective (i.e., how sensations of exertion are perceived as a function of gradual physiological increase). At the same time, various ratings of perceived exertion scales were developed for various tasks (see Noble & Noble, 1998).

According to Noble and Robertson (1996), of the 450 published articles on perceived exertion, only 39 (8.6%) examined psychological factors. The main areas of research were descriptive studies on how perceived exertion related to physiological factors and conditions, clinical applications, methodical issues, exercise and perception, and environmental factors. Less attention has been given to *exertion tolerance* (i.e., the ability to sustain and cope with feelings of exertion for a period of time). The main purpose of this chapter is to describe the psychological variables that affect perceived exertion and exertion tolerance, from both theoretical and scientific perspectives.

A GUIDING CONCEPTUAL MODEL

Perceived exertion and exertion tolerance are two psychological states that are determined by the interaction of several variables. Perceived exertion and exertion tolerance can be regarded as complex phenomena in which the performer makes attempts to adapt to the social and physical demands imposed on him or her while engaged in exercise. Perceptions of exertion are determined by individual disposition, demographic characteristics, the task (whether aerobic, anaerobic, or both), the intensity level, the conditions under which the task is performed (e.g., temperature, humidity, time of day), and the coping strategies used when experiencing these feelings (see Figure 32.1). The model postulated in Figure 32.1 assumes a mutual relationship between perceived exertion and exertion tolerance. More specifically, when perceived exertion is reported to be low, under any task and environmental condition, the exerciser can adhere to and cope with exertion longer than when perceived exertion is reported to be high.

Dispositional Characteristics

Noble and Robertson (1996) summarized the limited research linking personal dispositions to perceived exertion. They found that (1) the more people desire to impress others, the lower they tend to report their perceived exertion (Boutcher, Fleischer-Curtian, & Gines, 1988); (2) augmenters (i.e., people who exaggerate the importance of events in their life) report greater perceived exertion than do reducers (i.e., people who underestimate

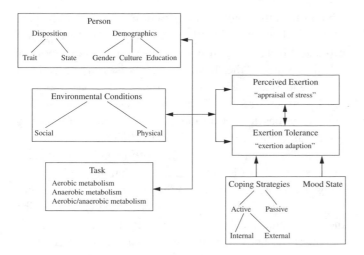

Figure 32.1 A model that postulates the effect of an individual's characteristics, environmental conditions, task characteristics, and coping strategies on both perceived exertion and exertion tolerance. Perceived exertion and exertion tolerance are believed to be independent variables, though strongly related.

the importance of events in their life; Robertson, Gillespie, Hiatt, & Rose, 1977); (3) internal and external locus of control fails to determine perceived exertion (Kohl & Shea, 1988); (4) feminine sex–typed women report greater perceived exertion than do masculine or androgynous women (Hochstetler, Rejeski, & Best, 1985; Rejeski, Best, Griffith, & Kinney, 1985); (5) extroverts suppress painful stimuli and rate their perceived exertion lower than introverts (Morgan, 1973); and (6) task self-efficacy is negatively related to perceived exertion (McAuley & Courneya, 1992). A clear relationship between Type A/B personality and perceived exertion has not been established (DeMeersman, 1988; Hardy, McMurray, & Roberts, 1989; Rejeski, Morley, & Miller, 1983).

In general, the relationships between dispositional variables and perceived exertion are limited. The association found between the desire to impress others, the over/underestimation of life events, femininity/masculinity type, extroversion/introversion, and perceived exertion can be regarded as the effect of social desirability on reported exertion. However, the failure to find any consistent link between locus of control and Type A/B personality with perceived exertion is a consequence of a lack of sound theory (Noble & Robertson, 1996). The result has been a limited selection of psychological constructs with an appropriate methodological plan aimed at verification or modification of these relations. More specifically, the link between motivational components that are responsible for energizing and inhibiting human actions and exertion

components has not been sufficiently postulated and, therefore, not studied. An exception is McAuley and Courneya's (1992) study that linked perceived exertion to task-specific self-efficacy. In line with this study, possible links between motivational variables such as goal orientation, self-efficacy, and task-specific commitment and determination, exertion tolerance, effort investment with perceived exertion, and maintaining an exertive state are discussed in this chapter. These relations are then examined in real-life situations which secure less biased introspective responses of individuals evoked by social desirability (see Tenenbaum & Fogarty, 1998).

Techniques for Coping with Stress

Strategies for coping with physical exertion can take two forms: active (associative) and passive (disassociative; Morgan & Pollack, 1977). As illustrated in Figure 32.1, active strategies are classified as either internal or external to the performer. External strategies are those in which the performer shifts attention to external events to reduce perceptions of neural exertion signals coming from the muscles and joints and the cardiopulmonary systems. Internal strategies are aimed at coping directly with feelings of overuse and exertion through "fighting" against them or other negative events. A passive form of coping with exertion is considered when people do not attempt to do anything that will enable them to better tolerate the sensory signals of fatigue, discomfort, exertion, and pain.

A number of studies have been concerned with the effect of coping strategies on perceived exertion. For example, in the Pennebaker and Lightner (1980) study, attentional focus was manipulated by activating external street sounds while internal attentional focus was manipulated by asking participants to attend to their own breathing while walking on a treadmill. Greater fatigue was experienced when attending to one's own breathing compared to attending to street sounds. Fillingim and Fine (1986) asked participants while running to either count the word dog (external attention) or to focus on their breathing and heartbeat (internal attention). Fewer exercise symptoms were reported under the external attention compared to the internal attention condition. Johnson and Siegel (1987) found that perceived exertion was lower under an active external technique (i.e., problem solving) compared to a passive internal technique. In contrast, Boutcher and Trenske (1990) used visual and auditory stimuli and compared their effects to music and no-stimuli conditions at light, moderate, and high exercise intensities. Under high intensities, no differences in perceived exertion were found. However, under low-intensity exercise, the music condition led to lower perceived exertion as compared to the visual, auditory, or no-stimuli condition. Boutcher and Trenske suggested that the greatest influence from psychological factors is observed at light and moderate intensities rather than high intensities, where salience is provided by physiological inputs.

Morgan and Pollock (1977) studied the strategies used by elite marathoners and recreational long-distance runners in coping with perception of exertion. Marathon runners reported using an association strategy where attention is given to internal sensory cues. In comparison, recreational runners used a dissociation strategy in which they deflected internal bodily signals with various forms of distractive thinking. This finding was expanded by Schomer (1986), who claimed that increases in intensity resulted in a shift from dissociative to associative thinking. Another common technique for coping with aversive stimuli is imagery. Explanations for the effectiveness of imagery in coping with exertive stimuli are based on the premise that a close link exists among emotions, images, and sensations. In the same way that emotions are accompanied by physical sensations, images evoke emotions. Visualization is believed to affect feelings and physical sensations by altering images.

Various relaxation techniques, such as meditation, exercising, rhythmic breathing, and attending to music, are often used to decrease stress symptoms. Progressive relaxation, which consists of active contraction and passive relaxation of gross muscle groups, is a technique frequently used with guided imagery (Edgar & Smith-Hanrahan, 1992). Guided imagery involves the development of mental representations of reality or fantasy. Guided imagery is aimed at reducing the pain and autonomic reactivity. The principle is to hold the image (e.g., a peaceful, pain-free scene) during a painful experience (James, 1992; Taylor, 1995). Imagery can also help to transform pain into numbness or an irrelevant sensation. It may divert attention from internal/external events. In addition, pain can be controlled through somatization (i.e., the focus of attention on the painful area but in a detached manner; Melzack & Wall, 1989).

Images used to cope with aversive stimuli vary. Murphy, Woolfolk, and Budney (1988) manipulated emotive images by instructing participants to develop imagery-arousing specific feelings while performing a strength task with a hand-grip dynamometer. The three feelings were anger, fear (emotional content), and relaxation (nonemotional content). Participants were instructed to imagine a scene in which they felt either angry, afraid, or relaxed. They were then asked to visualize the scene until the feeling was evoked. When feeling fully involved in the scene, they were asked to squeeze the dynamometer as hard as possible. It was found that anger and fear images increased arousal level, but not strength. Relaxation images resulted in decreased strength. Relaxation imagery is more frequently used than emotive imagery in controlling pain and uncomfortable feelings (Taylor, 1995). Both techniques induce a mood state (relaxation or excitement) that may aid in tolerating pain or discomfort. Whereas relaxation imagery improves pain tolerance through physiologically calming the body, emotive imagery increases mental arousal and enhances the body's coping mechanisms to better tolerate exertive experiences. Experimental evidence for this claim is provided later in this chapter.

Environmental Conditions

Perceived exertion and exertion tolerance are directly influenced by the salience of social cues present in the environment (Hardy, Hall, & Prestholdt, 1986). For example, Hardy et al. had participants cycle alone and in the presence of a coactor performing at the same exercise intensities (25%, 50%, and 75% of VO_2max). They found that participants reported lower perceived exertion when cycling at 25% and 50%, but not 75% of VO_2max in the presence of a coactor. Perceived exertion was also lower when instructors were of the opposite gender, but this was less salient for highly trained athletes (Sylva, Boyd, & Magnum, 1990).

The main environmental factors that evoke feelings of exertion are the intensity and duration of a task. "Perceptual responses are an expression of the sensory link between external stimuli arising from physical work and internal responses reflecting physiological function" (Noble, 1977, in Noble & Robertson, 1996, p. 93). Kinsman and Weiser (1976), Weiser and Stamper (1977), and Pandolf (1982) developed a model that postulates the relationship between physiological symptoms occurring during exercise and how they are perceived by the exerciser. There are four levels of subjective reporting of sensory experiences during an ongoing physical exercise, each associated with physiological processes that induce fatigue. The first level, discrete symptoms, is associated with symptoms such as sweating, perspiring, panting, heart pounding, leg aches and cramps, muscle tremors, leg twitching, heavy and shaky legs, tiredness, drive, vigorous mood, and determination. The second level, the subordinate, is associated with cardiopulmonary, leg, and general fatigue. The third level, ordinate, is linked to task aversion and the motivation to adhere in the task. The fourth level, superordinate, is associated with extreme fatigue and/or physical exhaustion. At this stage, one cannot identify specific sensations (i.e., muscle aches, breathing, legs), but rather extreme general fatigue and exhaustion (see Noble & Robertson, 1996, Chap. 4, for a detailed description).

As discussed earlier, the subjective-objective link to exertion is strongly related to the attentional mode of the exerciser. Noble and Robertson (1996) concluded that research has indicated that with an increase in physical load, exertion feelings intensify, and consequently attention shifts from an external-disassociative mode to an internal-associative mode. Under low exertion, perceived exertion can be manipulated by attending to external cues such as music (passive) or problem solving (active). However, diverting attention is much harder to implement when the exerciser is in the superordinate level. At this stage, an exerciser needs a high level of determination and exertion tolerance to persist in the task. The subjective-objective link with respect to attentional mode and perceived exertion manipulation is illustrated in Figure 32.2.

THE SOCIAL-COGNITIVE PERSPECTIVE

In this section, the primary variables studied in the social-cognitive approach in psychology, which are believed to shed new light on perceived exertion and exertion tolerance, are reviewed. The social-cognitive approach, in particular, self-efficacy theory (Bandura, 1982, 1986, 1997),

when applied to exercise behavior, emphasizes the role that task-specific states have on perceiving and coping with exercise stimuli (e.g., physical exertion).

Goal Orientation

Goal orientations reflect individual differences in assigning subjective meaning to outcomes (Ames, 1984; Maer & Braskamp, 1986). The subjective meaning given to success and failure is linked to either a differentiated or an undifferentiated concept of ability. A differentiated concept of ability is determined by comparing one's performance and outcome to others'. This goal orientation is termed *ego orientation* because the person is either motivated by the need to demonstrate competence by comparing his or her performance/outcome to others or by comparative incompetence. An undifferreniated concept of ability is utilized when subjective achievements are compared to self-referenced standards. This orientation is termed *task orientation* and is evoked by the need to meet and improve personal standards (Nicholls, 1984, 1989). Task goal orientation is associated with behaviors such as skill improvement, task mastery, working hard, and persistence. In contrast, ego goal orientation is associated with maladaptive or inhibitive behaviors when social comparisons are avoided. As a consequence, effort and confidence decrease (Jagacinski & Nicholls, 1990).

Task and ego goal orientations are independent of each other and important determinants of motivation (see Duda, 1993, for a review). However, the degree to which one's goal orientation matches situational conditions for an exertive physical task is also an important determinant of self-commitment, motivation, and the amount of effort one is ready to invest to satisfy personal needs. Duda and Hall (this volume) have summarized the literature on the relationship between goal orientation and motivational behaviors, and have concluded that task goal orientation was found to be related to exertion persistence and goal adherence. In contrast, ego goal orientation was associated with lack of persistence. Accordingly, task orientation is associated with a superior level of coping with exertive experience compared to ego goal orientation. This will not necessarily be reflected in perceived exertion, but rather in adherence and tolerance of exertive experiences.

To date, there is a lack of research examining the association between the goal orientations people hold as related to their readiness to invest effort and their commitment during physical exertion. Therefore, sufficient research is required if a comprehensive social-cognitive theory of motivation and exertion perceptions and tolerance is to be

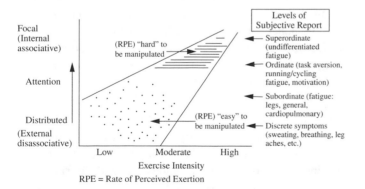

Figure 32.2 Perceived exertion and exertion tolerance as a function of exercise intensity and the physiological substrata. As exercise intensity increases, attention shifts from external and disassociative mode to focal and associative mode. Physiological symptoms are shifted from being discrete to being undifferentiated. As a consequence, manipulation and alteration of perceived exertion and exertion tolerance shifts from "easy" at low physical intensity levels to "very hard" at high intensity level.

established. Presented later in the chapter are recent investigations examining goal orientation, self-efficacy, and other motivational variables that may determine how people can sustain and cope with ongoing strenuous aerobic and anaerobic activity.

Perceived Competence and Self-Efficacy

Competence is a multidimensional construct that is produced by mastery attempts in various tasks, and consequently leads to the development of behaviors and perceptions of control (Harter, 1978). People with similar goal orientations differ from each other in various tasks performed under similar conditions due to their different levels of self-perceived competence. In educational settings, learners with low perceived competence/ability, accompanied with ego goal orientation, were found to reduce their learning effort (Jagacinski & Nicholls, 1990). In football, players with high ego goal orientation exhibited higher competitive anxiety before competitions than did players with greater perceived competence (Boyd, Callaghan, & Yin, 1991). Thus, the greater an individual's perceived competence in a specific task or activity, the better the ability to cope with its physical demands.

Perceived self-efficacy "refers to beliefs in one's power to produce a given level of attainment" (Bandura, 1997, p. 382). It is a cognitive state that has a direct impact on how well actions will be performed. Beliefs of self-efficacy constitute the key factor of human agency. People who lack self-efficacy believe they also lack the power to perform the task. Bandura states that a sense of personal efficacy is represented by prepositional beliefs embedded in a network of functional relationships. An example is coping with aversive experiences in which exertion and discomfort are present.

Self-efficacy expectations differ on three dimensions: magnitude, generality, and strength. The magnitude of self-efficacy can range form simple to challenging tasks. Generality refers to efficacy expectations that may be specific to a task, or a more generalizable sense of efficacy (i.e., related to several tasks). Finally, the strength of expectations refers to the degree to which one will exhibit perseverance when facing aversive and/or frustrating situations such as physical exertion and discomfort.

Turk, Michenbaum, and Genest (1983) studied participants who utilized self-efficacy boosting strategies to tolerate a noxious stimulus (e.g., cold pressure task). They found that participants who could apply efficient coping strategies tolerated the task longer than did those who were unable to apply efficient coping strategies. Litt

(1988) investigated discomfort tolerance caused by a cold pressure task and found that self-efficacy predicted persistence in the task and efficacy expectations strongly determined performance duration. Similarly, Baker and Kirsch (1991) showed that participants who used self-efficacy boosting strategies while immersing their hand in cold water for as long as possible did not decrease in perceived discomfort and only slightly increased discomfort tolerance. Self-efficacy remained a strong predictor of discomfort tolerance but failed to predict reported discomfort.

The effects of both self-efficacy and drugs on tolerating the discomfort of a cold pressure task were investigated by Bandura, O'Leary, Taylor, Gauthier, and Gossard (1987). Participants were given either self-efficacy–related cognitive methods to cope with discomfort tolerance, a placebo, or no intervention control. To test whether changes in discomfort tolerance were mediated by activation of the endorphin system, half the participants in each condition received 10 mg of naloxone, a drug that inhibits the effect of opiates and, therefore, increases the sensation of pain. The other half received 10 mg of a saline solution. Results suggested that those who received cognitive training strengthened their self-efficacy to withstand and reduce pain. The placebo condition resulted in enhanced self-efficacy to withstand pain. However, no significant reductions in actual efficacy emerged. Furthermore, the cognitive training and naloxone group, when compared to the group receiving cognitive training and saline, was less able to tolerate discomfort. However, the cognitive group that received the naloxone was still able to increase discomfort tolerance to some degree. This suggests a nonopioid component in cognitive pain control (Bandura et al., 1987). In conclusion, self-efficacy can be altered, but its effectiveness is accurately assessed only under task-specific conditions.

Bandura (1997), in his extensive literature review, failed to locate any studies that examined perceived self-efficacy and beliefs of control with exertion tolerance. He described, however, the role of cognitive activities in displacing sensations from consciousness and altering their aversiveness: "If aversive sensations are supplanted in consciousness or are construed benignly . . . they become less noticeable and less distressingly intrusive. Research . . . shows that belief that pain is controllable to some extent makes it easier to manage . . . the ameliorative effects of such pain control techniques operate partly through changes in self-efficacy. . . . The stronger the instated perceived coping efficacy, the higher the pain tolerance and the less dysfunction pain produces" (pp. 393–394). Thus, the role that perceived self-efficacy plays in exertion tolerance is to be explored. The experimental results introduced later in this chapter examine this relationship.

Task-Specific Commitment/Determination and Effort

Task-specific commitment/determination and the effort one is ready to invest in and tolerate while experiencing exertion may affect coping and persisting behaviors. The concept of commitment has been conceptualized as a psychological state related to extended engagement in activity over a given period of time that leads to persistence in the face of difficulties or setbacks (Scanlan, Carpenter, Schmidt, Simons, & Keeler, 1993). Commitment is related to the determination, dedication, and effort needed to persist in a particular activity. Scanlan and Simons (1992) further conceptualized commitment as a multidimensional concept, consisting of five main components: enjoyment, personal investment, social constraints, involvement alternatives, and involvement opportunities. Of these five dimensions, only personal investment (i.e., how much effort one is ready to invest in the activity) is relevant to exertion tolerance. Also, commitment can be considered a causing variable rather than an outcome behavior. In other words, a person with more commitment and determination coupled with readiness to invest effort and tolerate exertion will adhere longer to adversive stimuli.

Commitment and exertion tolerance, as psychological states, may be related to task/mastery goal orientation and task-specific self-efficacy. However, each of these variables is believed to account independently for variations in perceived exertion and task-related exertion tolerance. Reported next are research findings in which the separate and combined effects of goal orientation, self-efficacy, and task-specific commitment and exertion tolerance have been related to perceived exertion and performing tasks that require high exertion.

Exertion in Aerobic and Strength Tasks

Tenenbaum et al. (in press) studied 49 participants (M age = 23.01 years): untrained, team sport athletes, and triathletes. The triathletes had significantly greater VO_2max values compared to the other two groups; and were more familiar with running exertion than the other two groups.

Participants completed a goal orientation and physical self-efficacy questionnaire a few days before the exertive task. Two running tasks were conducted. In the first task,

the participants were tested for VO_2max using a direct measure. Exposure to the sensation of exertion was obtained by requesting the participants to run on a motorized treadmill at 90% of their VO_2max one week after their VO_2max was determined. They were then administered the following task-specific questions immediately before they performed the exertive run:

> Specific self-efficacy: "How confident are you in tolerating this exertion and discomfort?"
>
> Degree of commitment/determination: "How committed are you to perform the task?"
>
> Effort investment: "How much effort do you intend to put into the task?"

All questions were rated on a 5-point Likert scale ranging from 1 (not at all) to 5 (very much). The Rating of Perceived Exertion (RPE; Borg, 1982) one-item scale, which has semantic phrases ranging from 0 to 10, was administered at one-minute intervals while the task was performed. The participants were instructed to indicate when they experienced a hard RPE score independently of the one-minute interval ratings. At this time, a blood sample was taken from their index finger to assess their level of lactic acid. Once the participants could no longer tolerate the adverse exertion of the task, they placed their hands on the front railing and the treadmill was brought to a complete stop. Then they completed the three task-specific questions again and a second blood lactate sample was taken. The time lapse from the outset to reporting hard exertion was termed *time to RPE-hard*. The time lapse from reporting hard to full stop was termed *time in exertion*. The summation of these two time lapses was the total time of the run.

Results indicated that triathletes ran significantly longer than both team sport athletes and untrained participants. Times taken to reach RPE-hard and time in exertion were also longer for the triathletes compared to the team sport athletes and untrained participants. These results are depicted in Figure 32.3. Most important to note are the differences among the three groups between the time taken to reach 90% VO_2max and time to report RPE-hard. These differences are presented in Figure 32.4. It is evident that triathletes, who are familiar with exertive feelings, report hard exertion on average 105.63 seconds after reaching the 90% VO_2max level. In contrast, team athletes and untrained participants report hard exertion on average 26.48 to 54.86 seconds prior to reaching this level.

The blood lactic acid concentration at the two time periods, RPE-hard and task completion, are presented in

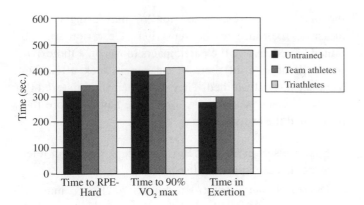

Figure 32.3 Exertion tolerance operationalized as time to RPE-hard and time in exertion (i.e., time interval determined by reporting "hard" and stopping the run) in untrained participants, team players, and triathletes.

Figure 32.5. Though not significantly different, the triathletes terminated the run with lower lactic acid concentration than did both the team athletes and the untrained participants. Running in the "exertion zone" with similar levels of lactic acid is indicative that task familiarity and other psychological variables play an important role in triathletes' exertion tolerance.

The rate of perceived exertion during the run and squeezing a hand dynamometer is shown in Figure 32.6. During the entire running task, the triathletes reported lower perceived exertion than did participants in the other two groups. Indeed, familiarity and repeated exposure to exertive experiences resulted in lower reported exertion during the run. Note that Figure 32.6 does not represent the entire run time because the majority of team sport and untrained participants had terminated the run by 10 minutes.

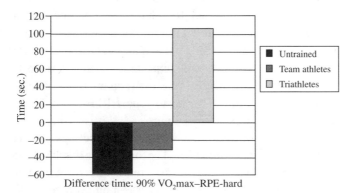

Figure 32.4 Time interval between reaching 90 percent VO_2max and reporting RPE-hard by untrained participants, team players, and triathletes.

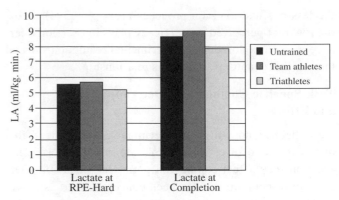

Figure 32.5 Lactic acid (LA) concentration in the blood at two times: when reporting RPE-hard and at task completion in untrained participants, team players, and triathletes.

An important question concerned whether goal orientation, physical and task-specific self-efficacy, task-specific commitment, and effort investment account for exertion tolerance variance over and above the influence of task familiarity. A hierarchical regression in which group type was entered first into the equation, followed by goal orientation, self-efficacy, and task, indicated that 48% of time

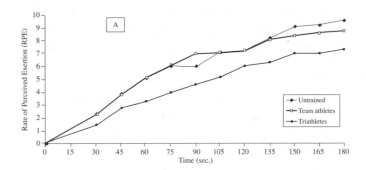

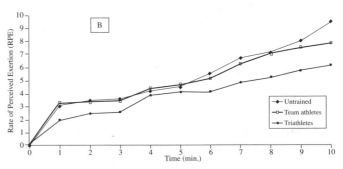

Figure 32.6 Rate of Perceived Exertion (RPE) reported by untrained participants, team players, and triathletes under two conditions: running 90 percent VO_2max, and squeezing a hand dynamometer at 50 percent max.

in exertion variance was accounted for by the four variables. Of the accounted variance, 11% was attributed to task familiarity (triathlete, team sport, and untrained), an additional 20% to goal orientation (task and ego), 7% to physical and task-specific self-efficacy, and 11% to task-specific commitment/determination, discomfort tolerance, and effort investment. In a second study, Tenenbaum et al. (in press) examined 47 male participants (M age = 22.53 years) to determine the effect of the motivational variables on a strength endurance exertion task. The participants were divided into three groups: team sport athletes (basketball, soccer, and field hockey), long-distance runners, and university students who exercised fewer than three times a week. All groups were matched for age and weight but differed in VO_2max (M = 75.69, SD = 2.95; M = 63.96, SD = 8.54; M = 51.97, SD = 8.64 for runners, team sport, and untrained participants, respectively)

Participants were introduced to the dynamometer-squeezing task. Then, separately in an isolated room, each was asked to squeeze the dynamometer's hand bar three times as hard as he could using his dominant hand. One-minute intervals between squeezes were given. The best score was used as a baseline measure. Immediately after completion of this stage, participants were administered the goal orientation, self-efficacy, and task-specific questions used in the previous study. They were then asked to squeeze the dynamometer's hand bar at 50% of their maximum capacity for as long as they could. A decrease in performance by more than 10% of this value terminated the trial. After each 15 seconds, the RPE scale was shown to the performers and they vocally announced their exertion level. Time to RPE-hard and time in exertion were determined as in the previous study. Pretest measures of the dynamometer task revealed no significant group differences. Results indicated that the distance runners and team sport athletes sustained exertion significantly longer than did the untrained participants. Also, it took the distance runners significantly longer to report RPE-hard compared to the team sport athletes and untrained participants. These results are displayed in Figure 32.7.

Similar to the running task, it is evident that people who are familiar with exertion can tolerate and cope with exertion and discomfort longer than those who do not experience these feelings regularly. However, a strength-endurance task showed no significant differences between distance runners and team sport athletes in time in exertion—a clear indication that coping with and sustaining exertion is task-specific. It should be noted that continuous exposure to certain exertion feelings, like those felt by the

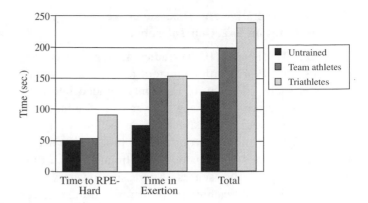

Figure 32.7 Exertion tolerance operationalized as time to RPE-hard and time in exertion (i.e., time interval determined by reporting "hard" and stopping the squeeze).

distance runners, resulted in better capabilities to sustain exertion required by other physical tasks. Figure 32.6 displays the mean rate of perceived exertion, at 15-second intervals, for the three groups. RPE ratings increased in a linear fashion for the three groups, with distance runners displaying considerably lower ratings of perceived exertion than both team sport and untrained participants.

A hierarchical regression with activity type, goal orientation, self-efficacy, and task-specific variables entering in a fixed-order cluster showed that together they accounted for 59% of the time in exertion variance. Of this variance, 10% was attributed to activity type and an additional 6% was accounted for by goal orientations. Physical self-efficacy and task-specific efficacy added 11% to the accounted variance, and, finally, task-specific commitment/determination, effort investment, and exertion tolerance added 32% to the accounted variance. These results can be viewed as strong evidence for the role that task-specific variables play in exertion tolerance.

These two studies demonstrate that self-efficacy and task-specific determination, commitment, effort investment, and exertion tolerance play a major role in determining the variation in people's ability to tolerate both aerobic and anaerobic types of high exertion levels (see Figure 32.1). In another study (Coote & Tenenbaum, 1998), the effect of associative (emotive, imagery) and disassociative (relaxation plus imagery) mental techniques on perceived exertion and exertion tolerance was investigated. The methodology used enabled the examination of the role the social-cognitive variables play in exertion tolerance. The results further confirm the model presented in Figure 32.1.

Effect of Associative and Disassociative Mental States on Exertion Tolerance

Coote and Tenenbaum (1998) studied 48 female university students ($M = 19.42$) with no history of physical or mental health problems. They were randomly divided into three groups. Two groups were taught, over two 45-minute sessions, relaxation or aggressive imagery techniques. Relaxation imagery techniques consisted of progressive muscle relaxation routines accompanied by calm and relaxing images utilizing all five senses. Aggressive imagery techniques consisted of teaching participants to design a scene in which they were angry. They were asked to visualize the angry scene while performing the exertive task for as long as they could. The control participants attended two sessions, each lasting 45 minutes, in which discussion of various irrelevant topics took place.

Exposure to an exertive stimulus was obtained through the use of a handgrip dynamometer mounted on an adjustable stand. A baseline strength measure was recorded from three squeezes of the dominant hand. Participants completed goal orientation, self-efficacy, and task-specific questionnaires. They then squeezed the dynamometer at 50% of the maximal squeeze for as long as they could, until they performed under 10% of their maximum squeeze. The RPE scale was shown to them every 15 seconds. Hard exertion was reported whenever the participant felt hard exertion regardless of the 15-second fixed records. Two sessions of 50% max handgrip were conducted: one prior to teaching the imagery techniques and the other after teaching the techniques.

Analyses indicated that from the first to the second trial, the control group performance declined by 3.7%. In contrast, the aggressive imagery group tolerated exertion at the second trial for 30.5% longer than on its first attempt (no imagery), and the relaxation imagery group improved by 28%. RPE in the first trial (preimagery manipulation) and the second trial (postimagery manipulation) are displayed in Figure 32.8. The three groups were similar in perceived exertion throughout the entire exertive experience. With respect to the role of task-specific and dispositional variables for exertion tolerance, 46% of variance was accounted for in the first exertive trial (prior to imagery manipulation). Goal orientation accounted for 4% of the variance, physical self-efficacy added an additional 12%, and task-specific determination/commitment, exertion tolerance, and effort investment added 21% to the accounted variance. In the second trial, goal orientation accounted for 5% of the exertive tolerance variance, an additional 10%

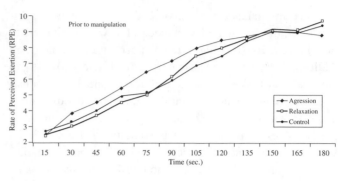

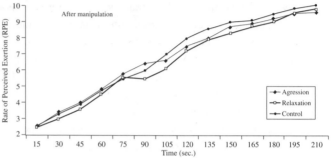

Figure 32.8 RPE in participants of three groups: aggressive imagery, relaxation imagery, and control in 15-second time intervals, prior to and after mental manipulation.

was accounted for by physical self-efficacy, and 25% by task-specific components.

CONCLUSIONS

Psychological components that affect and mediate perceived exertion and exertion tolerance have recently been examined. The literature offers evidence for three conclusions. First, exertion develops in stages with load increase. It starts with discrete symptoms such as sweating, breathing, and leg aches, and ends with an undifferentiated extreme. Second, attention to the exertive symptoms narrows with increase in physical load (i.e., from a distributed mode to a symptom-focused mode). And third, during the exertive experience, dissociative strategies of coping with exertion are more common under low physical load. In contrast, under heavy and continuous loads, associative strategies are more common and perhaps even avoidable. The dispositional characteristics associated with perceived exertion and exertion tolerance were found to be inconsistent, partially because of measurement problems and lack of sound theory to support such relationships.

Social-cognitive theory seems to have much potential in accounting for perceived exertion and exertion tolerance.

Studies indicate that task-specific variables such as determination/commitment, competence in tolerating exertion and discomfort, readiness to invest effort in the task, appropriate goal orientation, and physical self-efficacy, together with task familiarity, account for 50% to 60% of the variance in exertion tolerance. Evidence indicated that (1) psychological variables play a major role in determining how long a person can sustain high exertion under high physical intensity; (2) familiarity with exertion enables persons to sustain exertion for a longer time by reducing their perception of exertion as a consequence of adaptation to similar past experiences; and (3) exertion tolerance can be extended through emotive or relaxation mental techniques even though perceived exertion does not alter. Thus, mental techniques, whether associative (focused on exertion) or dissociative (distracting from exertion), as well as variables such as determination, self-efficacy, and competence in exertion tolerance, strongly determine how long one can tolerate exertion and discomfort. The social-cognitive theory introduced in this chapter in relation to perceived exertion and exertion tolerance reveals new horizons in the study of the psychological states and mechanisms that affect the complex psychophysiological construct of exertion. Innovative methodological designs and paradigms should be initiated to shed new light on this interesting area of study.

REFERENCES

Ames, C. (1984). Competitive, co-operative, and individualistic goal structure: A motivational analysis. In R. Ames & C. Ames (Eds.), *Research on motivation in education: Student motivation* (pp. 177–207). New York: Academic Press.

Baker, S.L., & Kirsch, I. (1991). Cognitive mediators of pain perception and tolerance. *Journal of Personality and Social Psychology 61*, 504–510.

Bandura, A. (1982). Self-efficacy mechanisms in human agency. *American Psychologist 37*, 122–147.

Bandura, A. (1986). *Social foundations of thought and action.* Englewood Cliffs, NJ: Prentice-Hall.

Bandura, A. (1997). *Self-efficacy: The exercise of control,* New York: Freeman.

Bandura, A., O'Leary, A., Taylor, C., Gauthier, J., & Gossard, D. (1987). Perceived self-efficacy and pain control: Opioid and nonopioid mechanisms. *Journal of Personality and Social Psychology, 53*, 563–571.

Borg, G.A.V. (1982). Psychophysiological bases of perceived exertion. *Medicine and Science in Sports and Exercise, 14*, 377–381.

Boutcher, S.H., Fleischer-Curtian, L.A., & Gines, S.D. (1988). The effects of self-presentation on perceived exertion. *Journal of Sport & Exercise Psychology, 10*, 270–280.

Boutcher, S.H., & Trenske, M. (1990). The effects of sensory deprivation and music on perceived exertion and affect during exercise. *Journal of Sport & Exercise Psychology, 12*, 167–176.

Boyd, M., Callaghan, J., & Yin, Z. (1991). *Ego involvement and low competence in sport as a source of competitive trait anxiety.* Paper presented at the North American Society for the Psychology of Sport and Physical Activity, Asilomar, CA

Coote, D., & Tenenbaum, G. (1998). Can emotive imagery aid in tolerating exertion efficiently? *Journal of Sports Medicine and Physical Fitness, 38*, 344–354.

DeMeersman, R.E. (1988). Personality, effort perception and cardiovascular reactivity. *Neuropsychobiology, 19*, 192–194.

Duda, J.L. (1993). Goals: A social-cognitive approach to the study of achievement motivation in sport. In R.N. Singer, M. Murphey, & L.K. Tennant, (Eds.), *Handbook of research on sport psychology* (pp. 421–436). New York: Macmillan.

Edgar, L., & Smith-Hanrahan, C.M. (1992). Nonpharmacological pain management. In J.H. Watt-Watson & M.I. Donovan (Eds.), *Pain management: Nursing perspective* (pp. 162–199). Sydney, Australia: Mosby.

Fillingim, R.B., & Fine, M.A. (1986). The effects of internal versus external information processing on symptom perception in an exercise setting. *Health Psychology, 5*, 115–123.

Hardy, C.J., Hall, E.G., & Prestholdt, P.H. (1986). The mediational role of social influence in the perception of exertion. *Journal of Sport & Exercise Psychology, 8*, 88–104.

Hardy, C.J., McMurray, R.G., & Roberts, S. (1989). A/B types and psychophysiological responses to exercise stress. *Journal of Sport & Exercise Psychology, 11*, 141–151.

Harter, S.E. (1978). Effectance motivation reconsidered: Toward a developmental model. *Human Development, 21* 34–64.

Hochstetler, S.A., Rejeski, W.J., & Best, D.L. (1985). The influence of sex-role orientation on ratings of perceived exertion. *Sex Roles, 12*, 825–835.

Jagacinski, C.W., & Nicholls, J.G. (1990). Reducing effort to protect perceived ability: "They'd do it but I wouldn't." *Journal of Educational Psychology, 82*, 15–21.

James, P.T. (1992). Cognitive therapies. In S. Tyrer (Ed.), *Psychology, psychiatry and chronic pain* (pp. 137–147). Sydney, Australia: Butterworth-Heinemann.

Johnson, J., & Siegel, D. (1987). Active vs. passive attentional manipulation and multidimensional perceptions of exercise intensity. *Canadian Journal of Sport Sciences, 12*, 41–45.

Kinsman, R.A., & Weiser, P.C. (1976). Subjective symptomatology during work and fatigue. In E. Simonson & P.C. Weiser

(Eds.), *Psychological aspects and physiological correlates of work and fatigue* (pp. 336–405). Springfield, IL: Thomas.

Kohl, R.M., & Shea, C.H. (1988). Perceived exertion: Influences of locus of control and expected work intensity and duration. *Journal of Human Movement Studies, 15,* 225–272.

Litt, M.D. (1988). Self efficacy and perceived control: Cognitive mediators of pain tolerance. *Journal of Personality and Social Psychology, 54,* 149–160.

Maehr, M.L., & Braskamp, L. (1986). *The motivation factor: A theory of personal investment.* Lexington, MA: Heath.

McAuley, E., & Courneya, K.S. (1992). Self-efficacy relationships with effective and exertion responses to exercise. *Journal of Applied Social Psychology, 22,* 312–326.

Melzack, R., & Wall, P.D. (1989). *The challenge of pain* (2nd ed). Harmondsworth, England: Penguin.

Morgan, W.P. (1973). Psychological factors influencing perceived exertion. *Medicine and Science in Sports, 5,* 97–103.

Morgan, W.P., & Pollock, M.L. (1977). Psychological characteristics of elite runners. *Annals of the New York Academy of Science, 301,* 382–403.

Murphy, S.M., Woolfolk, R.L., & Budney, A.J. (1988). The effect of emotive imagery on strength performance. *Journal of Sport & Exercise Psychology, 10,* 334–345.

Nicholls, J.G. (1984). Achievement motivation: Conceptions of ability, subjective experience, task choice, and performance. *Psychological Review, 91,* 328–346.

Nicholls, J.G. (1989). *The competitive ethos and democratic education.* Cambridge, MA: Harvard University Press.

Noble, B.J., & Noble, J.M. (1998). Perceived exertion: The measurement. In J.L. Duda (Ed.), *Advances in sport and exercise psychology measurement* (pp. 351–360). Morgantown, WV: Fitness Information Technology.

Noble, B.J., & Robertson, R.J. (1996). *Perceived exertion.* Champaign, IL: Human Kinetics.

Pandolf, K.B. (1982). Differentiated ratings of perceived exertion during physical exercise. *Medicine and Science in Sports and Exercise, 14,* 397–405.

Pennebaker, J.W., & Lightner, J.M. (1980). Competition of internal and external information in an exercise setting. *Journal of Personality and Social Psychology, 39,* 165–174.

Rejeski, W.J., Best, D., Griffith, P., & Kinney, E. (1985). *Feminine males in exercise: Is the inappropriateness of activity the cause of dysfunction in cross-gender behavior?* Unpublished manuscript.

Rejeski, W.J., Morley, D., & Miller, H. (1983). Cardiac rehabilitation: Coronary-prone behavior as a moderator of graded exercise. *Journal of Cardiac Rehabilitation, 3,* 339–346.

Rejeski, W.J., & Sandford, B. (1984). Feminine-typed females: The role of affective schema in the perception of exercise intensity. *Journal of Sport Psychology, 6,* 197–207.

Robertson, R.J., Gillespie, R.L., Hiatt, E., & Rose, K.D. (1977). Perceived exertion and stimulus intensity modulation. *Perceptual and Motor Skills, 45,* 211–218.

Scanlan, T.K., Carpenter, P.J., Schmidt, G.W., Simons, J.P., & Keeler, B. (1993). An introduction to the sport commitment model. *Journal of Sport & Exercise Psychology, 15,* 1–5.

Scanlan, T.K., & Simons, P.J. (1992). The construct of sport enjoyment. In G. Roberts (Ed.), *Motivation in sport and exercise* (pp. 192–215). Champaign, IL: Human Kinetics.

Schomer, H. (1986). Mental strategies and the perception of effort of marathon runners. *International Journal of Sport Psychology, 17,* 41–59.

Sylva, M., Boyd, R., & Mangum, M. (1990). Effects of social influence and sex on rating of perceived exertion in exercising elite athletes. *Perceptual and Motor Skills, 70,* 591–594.

Taylor, S.E. (1995). *Health psychology.* Sydney, Australia: McGraw-Hill.

Tenenbaum, G., & Fogarty, G. (1998). Applications of the Rasch analysis to sport and exercise psychology measurement. In J.L. Duda (Ed), *Advances in sport and exercise psychology measurement* (pp. 409–422). Morgantown, WV: Fitness Information Technology.

Tenenbaum, G., Fogarty, G., Stewart, E., Calcagnini, N., Kirker, B., Thorne, G., & Christensen, S. (1999). Perceived discomfort in running: Scale development and theoretical considerations. *Journal of Sports Sciences, 17,* 183–196.

Tenenbaum, G., Hall, H.K., Calcagnini, V., Lange, R., Freeman, G., & Lloyd, M. (in press). Coping with physical exertion and frustration experiences under competitive and self-standard conditions. *Journal of Applied Social Psychology.*

Turk, D.C., Michenbaum, D., & Genest, M. (1983). *Pain and behavioural medicine: A cognitive-behavioural approach.* Hillsdale, NJ: Earlbaum.

Weiser, P.C., & Stamper, D.A. (1977). Psychophysiological interactions leading to increased effort, leg fatigue, and respiratory distress during prolonged, strenuous bicycle riding. In G. Borg (Ed.), *Physical work and effort,* (pp. 401–416). New York: Pergamon Press.

PART VII

Future Directions

CHAPTER 33

Current Trends and Future Directions in Sport Psychology

JOHN M. SILVA III

What will be the status of the field of sport psychology in 2020 or 2050? Although 20 years may seem like a long way off, asking this question is akin to asking what sport psychology would be like in 2000 back in 1980! Twenty or even 50 years is a short time span when discussing the evolution of a young and dynamic specialization such as sport psychology. Though it is difficult to predict the future of any phenomenon, predicting the complex dynamics of sport psychology, a subdiscipline in development and transition, is an exciting challenge.

Clearly, sport psychology is currently in early adolescence, transitioning from primarily a research-based orientation to a more science practice orientation. The possibility for advancement and continued development is extremely high as scholars, educators, and practitioners discuss and debate many fundamental issues. These issues include establishing a consensus on (1) the definition of sport psychology as an area of study and practice, (2) who can practice sport psychology, (3) how aspiring professionals should be educated and trained, (4) who can properly train the next generation of practicing sport psychologists, and (5) where significant sources of funding will be found to support both basic and applied sport psychology research. Given the importance and volatility of these issues, it is surprising that a search of the literature on the future of sport psychology identified very few publications specifically addressing this topic. Healthy debate has ensued on issues such as graduate training models (Anderson, Van Raalte, & Brewer, 1994; Feltz, 1987; Silva, 1984), the need for certification (Biddle, Bull, & Seheult, 1992; Bond, 1989; Nideffer, 1984; Silva, 1989a, 1989b), the need for accreditation of graduate programs (Selden & Porter 1977; Silva, 1997a, 1997b; Silva, Conroy, & Zizzi, 1999), the use of the title "sport psychologist" (Harrison & Feltz, 1980; Silva, 1989a, 1989c), quantitative versus qualitative

research (Strean & Roberts, 1992), the efficacy of sport psychology interventions (Vealey, 1988, 1994), the role of clinical psychologists in service provision (Nideffer, DuFresne, Nesvig, & Selder, 1980), and the nature of the job market in sport psychology (Andersen, Williams, Aldridge, & Taylor, 1989; Schell, Hunt, & Lloyd, 1984; Silva et al., 1999).

The resolution of these debates will dramatically influence future directions of the field and the very existence of sport psychology as it is known today. This dynamic atmosphere is what makes being a contemporary sport psychologist so exciting! Trails are being blazed and eventually healthy consensus will emerge on the fundamental issues being debated. Once this is achieved, sport psychologists will refocus directly on matters such as funding research programs, marketing sport psychology research and practice, and promoting sport psychology as a legitimate discipline and profession.

To predict future directions, one must carefully examine where the field has been, how it is evolving today, and what forces may shape the new directions that are inevitable in the future. In this chapter, a brief highlight of landmark events in the development of sport psychology is reviewed. However, the main focus and the most significant and exciting aspect of this chapter is to "go on the line" and offer some predictions about the future of sport psychology. Many of the issues addressed will unfold in the next two decades. It will be interesting to revisit this chapter in 2020 and determine the degree of accuracy in forecasting.

LANDMARK EVENTS IN THE DEVELOPMENT OF SPORT PSYCHOLOGY

Although the emphasis of this chapter is not on the history or evolution of sport psychology, it is helpful to briefly emphasize some historical events that have influenced the development of sport psychology. It is extremely important for each generation of sport psychologists to have a perspective of the past and to participate in the continual process of change that shapes the future. There is little doubt that previous events have served as a catalyst for change and will continue to shape the future of sport psychology. Several comprehensive articles have been published detailing with the history and evolution of sport psychology (Alderman, 1980; Hanin, 1979; Silva, 2001; Silva et al., 1999; Wiggins, 1984). These articles very carefully and extensively present the history, development, and current controversies in sport psychology in North America and chronicle important global initiatives. This chapter provides a brief overview of these landmark events, but emphasis is directed toward stimulating thought on the future of sport psychology.

Soviet Influences on the Origin of Sport Psychology

The earliest documentation of systematic research in the field of sport psychology can be traced to the former Soviet Union. As early as 1917, Lenin had identified physical education and training as essential elements in the Soviet way of life (Shteinbakh, 1987). Sport training was taken very seriously in the USSR because of its close relation to the military and its use in helping to prepare the Armed Forces. In 1919, the first Institute for the Study of Sport and Physical Culture was established in St. Petersburg. Within a year, another Institute was quickly established in Moscow. In addition to developing physical education programs and physical training teachers, these Institutes became marked as central facilities for research and application of exercise science principles to sport performance.

Sport psychology played a major role in attempting to understand and develop elite athletic performance. Sport psychologists had direct opportunities to "test" their research and theories with elite athletes who attended or regularly visited the Institutes. This unidimensional focus on the development of elite athlete performance was most recognizable after World War II, when the Soviets increased their world presence not only in the military and political theaters but on the world stage of Olympic competition. The success of athlete development through the "Soviet system" was often attributed to systematic psychological training and intervention provided to Soviet athletes. The success of the Soviet system in athletic competition was not at issue and has seldom been debated. At its peak in the 1980 Moscow Olympics, the Soviets won 80 Gold, 69 Silver, and 46 Bronze medals. The athletic world understood that part of the Soviet success was due to the effective and efficient integration of the sport sciences into their high-level national and Olympic athletic programs. Although many Westerners criticized various aspects of the Soviet delivery system, the use of the sport sciences in general and the mystique that surrounded the use of sport psychology in particular accelerated the attention and interest shown toward sport psychology as an academic area of study by Western counterparts.

Early European Influences on the Development of Sport Psychology

Isolated studies and published articles appeared in the first half of the 20th century in Europe and North America, but it was the success of Soviet athletes in the post–World War II era that drew the interest of fans, sport administrators, and sport psychologists worldwide. Eastern European countries such as the former East Germany, Bulgaria, and the former Czechoslovakia were exposed to the Soviet system in the 1950s and 1960s. This exposure resulted in remarkable success in world competitions for countries with a relatively small population base. These results are particularly impressive when the economic conditions in Eastern Europe in the 1950s and 1960s are considered. These conditions often resulted in spartan training facilities for the athletes representing these countries.

Czechoslovakia is credited for the publication of one of the first theses in sport psychology, entitled "The Psychology of Physical Sciences" and authored by Peclat in 1928 at Charles University in Prague. In the early 1950s, an Institute for Physical Education and Sport was established at the University of Prague (Geron, 1982). Countries such as Bulgaria, Czechoslovakia, and East Germany were involved not only in scientific aspects of sport psychology but also in the application of the research to training. Bulgaria, Czechoslovakia, and East Germany were modeled after the Soviet approach, which emphasized psychological testing, motor testing, and the systematic use of mental training programs. In 1966, laboratories were established in Bulgaria to promote elite athlete development, and according to Salmela (1992), Bulgaria had one of the largest contingents of sport psychologists (127) in Eastern Europe. Eastern Europe played a major role in enhancing the level of awareness of sport psychology and the initial acceptance of the viability of the science of sport psychology to generate meaningful contributions to sport training and competition.

The role of Soviet sport psychology and the subsequent involvement of the Eastern European countries did not go without notice in Western Europe. The most notable sport psychology development in Western Europe was in 1965, when Ferrucciio Antonelli of Italy organized the first International Congress in Sport Psychology in Rome. More than 400 attendees representing 27 countries came to Rome eager to learn more about sport psychology and to generate interest in their native countries (Antonelli, 1989). At this historic meeting, the International Society of Sport Psychology (ISSP) was formed, and sport psychology would soon become an area of interest worldwide. Shortly after the ISSP's first Congress in Rome, the second Congress was held in Washington, D.C., in 1968. European sport psychologists solidified the communication and information exchange process on their continent in 1969 in Vittel, France, by establishing the Fédération Européene de Psychologie des Sports et des Activitiés Corporelles (FEPSAC).

These organizational developments resulted in sport psychology becoming an active discipline in most Western European countries and facilitated the establishment of national professional and research associations in countries such as Italy, Germany, Britain, France, Spain, and Portugal and in all of Scandinavia. The establishment of sport psychology institutes in the Soviet Union and the successful performances of Soviet athletes, along with the formation of the ISSP in Italy, signaled that the organizational development of sport psychology in North America would soon follow.

Sport Psychology in North America

The development of sport psychology in North America is one of the more curious evolutions of the field. Sport psychology was initiated in the United States as early as in any country in the world. The earliest writings addressed psychological aspects of sport and were in the form of essays describing the nature and potential psychological benefits of exercise, spectator attraction to sporting events, and the role that an audience may play in facilitating or inhibiting cycling performance (Patrick, 1903; Scripture, 1899; Triplett, 1897). Although these early writings stimulated a degree of interest, they did not form a coherent, systematic, or sustained attempt to describe or explain the role of psychology in motor learning or sport performance.

It was not until Coleman Roberts Griffith, a University of Illinois professor, established the Athletic Research Laboratory in 1925 on the Illinois campus that sport psychology was truly born in North America. Griffith was an active writer, researcher, and practitioner. He published over 25 articles on sport psychology and motor learning topics in less than 15 years. He also conducted the first applied work documented in North America with a professional baseball team, the Chicago Cubs. He conducted extensive interviews with American football heroes Red Grange and Knute Rockne, but when his laboratory was forced to close due to a lack of financial support, his efforts to research and apply sport psychology were not sustained at Illinois (Kroll & Lewis, 1970).

Although sport psychology faded in North America in the 1930s and 1940s, motor learning laboratories were being established at major universities, such as Pennsylvania State University (John Lawther), the University of Wisconsin (Clarence Ragsdale), and the University of California at Berkeley (Franklin Henry). These motor learning laboratories stimulated interest in psychological aspects of motor learning and motor performance during the 1930s and the 1940s. This is particularly important to North American sport psychology because the advent of World War II resulted in many monetary cuts at universities as money, materials, and human resources were directed toward the war effort. Many academic programs experienced slowdowns or shutdowns, and the funding for sport-related laboratories and research received low priority. Following the end of World War II, a reemergence of interest in topics more akin to contemporary sport psychology was initiated by professors such as Warren Johnson at the University of Maryland. Johnson researched and published a number of articles on aspects of personality and sport performance in *The Research Quarterly* that were widely read and discussed (Johnson & Hutton, 1955; Johnson, Hutton, & Johnson, 1954). *The Research Quarterly* was the major publication outlet in the sport sciences at the time, and sport psychology articles in this journal provided a written forum for the exchange of ideas in the emerging field. The late 1950s and the 1960s were very eventful years for sport psychology. The newly formed North American Society for the Psychology of Sport and Physical Activity (NASPSPA) held its first meeting prior to the 1967 annual meeting of the American Alliance for Health, Physical Education, Recreation, and Dance (AAHPERD) in Las Vegas. Warren Johnson and Arthur Slater-Hammel of Indiana University were instrumental in sponsoring the Second International Congress in Sport Psychology in Washington, D.C., in the fall of 1968, and in the fall of 1969 Robert Wilberg of the University of Alberta joined several Canadian colleagues to form the Canadian Society for Psychomotor Learning and Sport Psychology (CSPLSP; also referred to as SCAPPS to reflect the French translation of the name of the society).

The NASPSPA and CSPLSP organizations reflected the interfacing of motor learning and sport psychology so common in the early development of North American sport psychology. NASPSPA specifically designated three foci of attention: motor learning, motor development, and sport psychology. The first NASPSPA meeting independent from AAHPERD took place in 1973 at the University of Illinois, and the first independent CSPLSP meeting was held in 1977. These meetings are noteworthy because they denoted a trend toward specialization that would affect sport psychology and the study of all the North American sport sciences. The trend toward specialization in focus, graduate training, research, and practice became most pronounced in North American sport psychology during the 1980s and into the 1990s. This trend had an effect on the global development and direction of sport psychology, as communication and the international exchange of ideas became greatly enhanced by the information technology revolution. The events that unfolded during the decade of the 1980s profoundly influenced contemporary issues in the field of sport psychology and will continue to influence the evolution of the science and practice of sport psychology into the foreseeable future.

Contemporary Events Influencing the Future of Sport Psychology

North American sport psychology moved quickly into the world venue with the incorporation of NASPSPA and CSPLSP and with the successful hosting of the 1968 International Congress in Washington, D.C. The decades of the 1960s, 1970s, and early 1980s were characterized by a research orientation that was influenced by motor learning laboratory-type experiments and social psychological research (e.g., Landers, 1975, 1980; Landers, Bauer, & Feltz, 1978; Martens, 1969, 1971, 1974; Martens & Gill, 1976; Scanlan & Passer, 1978; Singer, 1965). Though innovative applications of sport psychology were initiated by individuals such as Bryant Cratty, Warren Johnson, and Bruce Ogilvie, the focus of North American sport psychology was clearly on research and scholarship. The uncompromising focus on scientific and disciplinary aspects of sport psychology was deemed a necessity because sport psychology in North America was emerging from within physical education departments. There was a strong desire to demonstrate to other disciplines the academic viability of this fledging field. Whereas progress was clearly being made in the academic realm of sport psychology, little attention or organizational effort was directed toward the application and professionalization of sport psychology (Martens, 1979; Silva, 1984, 1989a, 1989b).

As sport psychology gained more worldwide visibility, interest in the potential application of sport psychology principles effectively demonstrated in the Soviet Union became popular in North America. The 1980s witnessed

unparalleled interest in sport psychology from a practice and application perspective. As the 1984 Los Angeles Olympics approached, the host country moved to enhance the level of service provision afforded to U.S. athletes in the sport sciences. The U.S. Olympic Committee's (USOC) efforts are of note because the initiative moved the United States to provide an initial level of service provision for athletes participating in the 1984 Olympics.

The integration of sport psychology services in the 1984 Olympics created many positives, such as increased visibility and widespread interest. A troublesome by-product was that many individuals with no training in sport psychology or the sport sciences began to declare themselves "sport psychologists." The opportunity to provide quality services to high-level athletes was at risk as coaches, athletes, and administrators had no guidance pertaining to the expected qualifications and educational background of potential service providers. Clearly, sport psychology in North America had awoken from its quiet existence as a highly specialized academic subdiscipline in departments of physical education to an area of service provision that lacked professional standards and organizational or state regulation.

The professionalization of the field spiked in the 1980s, and without accredited training programs, certification, or licensure, entry into the field and subsequent practice with athletes and athletic teams was unregulated. The gravitation of individuals to sport psychology with no formal exposure or training in the field created not only ethical concerns but concerns for the viability and integrity of the field itself. In an attempt to provide some direction and guidelines to those interested in practicing sport psychology, NASPSPA was informally and formally requested to initiate action that would address regulation. After extensive dialogue from 1982 to 1984, NASPSPA voted in the spring of 1984 not to address the professionalization of sport psychology (Magill, 1984). This vote led to the formation of a new organization, the Association for the Advancement of Applied Sport Psychology (AAASP). The focus of AAASP was to advance organizational development, research, professionalization, and practice in the domain of sport psychology (Silva, 1989a, 1989b, 1989c). The first conference was held in October 1986 with approximately 200 sport psychologists representing several countries in attendance. The immediate success of AAASP in drawing an international membership, and a membership of psychologists as well as exercise scientists trained in sport psychology, indicated the great interest in promoting the orderly regulation of the field. It also demonstrated that sport psychology had sufficient breadth and depth of content to stand independently as an area of inquiry and practice. In 1992, AAASP instituted certification for individuals interested in practicing or applying sport psychology with athletes and sport groups. Currently, the USOC requires consultants who wish to work with Olympic programs to be AAASP-certified.

As the interest and involvement of psychologists increased through interactions in organizations such as AAASP, a special-interest group was formed within the American Psychological Association (APA) that earned divisional status in 1987. Exercise and Sport Psychology (Division 47) provided yet another opportunity to expose and educate individuals from diverse educational and training backgrounds to the field of sport psychology. While members of these organizations have promoted research and the visibility of sport psychology on a global basis, reoccurring and unresolved issues remain in areas as fundamental as (1) a consensus on the focus of the field, (2) promoting certification, (3) regulation of practice or licensure, (4) enhancing graduate education and training, (5) accreditation of graduate training programs in sport psychology, (6) establishing supervised practice experiences for graduate students interested in being eligible for certification or licensure, (7) direct involvement with professional and collegiate sport organizations, and (8) ethical issues such as use of title and limiting practice to one's area of competence (Andersen & Williams-Rice, 1996; Conroy, 1996; Murphy, 1996; Silva, 1992, 1996a, 1996b, 1997a, 1997b, 2000).

Some countries, such as Australia, have forged ahead of North America in resolving these issues by initiating working models that address these controversial areas. Australia has made notable advances in the regulation of service provision and has established certification criteria for individuals interested in working with Australian Olympic athletes. The Australian government has also taken the initiative to provide specific guidelines that regulate the accreditation of coaching programs. Australian sport psychologists affiliated with the Australian Applied Sport Psychology Association, the Sport Psychology Association of Australia and New Zealand, and the Asian and South Pacific Association for Sport Psychology are engaged in the orderly advancement of the professionalization of sport psychology, including title and practice issues (J.W. Bond, personal communication, November 1999). Many countries still struggle with the resolution of these fundamental issues. There is little doubt that the manner in which these difficult issues are resolved will shape the future of sport psychology and the viability of sport psychology as a contributing applied science.

THE FUTURE OF SPORT PSYCHOLOGY: DRAMATIC CHANGES ON THE HORIZON

Considering the current status of sport psychology, what will the future look like and what will be the impact of new developments on current sport psychologists and those interested in entering sport psychology? Given past developments and current academic and professional trends, the following predictions are offered for consideration.

Sport psychology will continue to grow worldwide in the immediate future. Sport psychology is an underdeveloped discipline and profession in all countries, including the United States. Graduate educational models in medicine, business, psychology, and law provide excellent examples of well-conceived and rigorous programs that prepare students for entry into specialized programs of research or practice. There is little debate or argument against sport psychologists acquiring fundamental knowledge in the sport sciences and in psychology. It is important to note, however, that the past 25 years have been characterized by increased specialization and an explosion of information and technology in all science-based fields. The idea that sport psychologists should have advanced expertise in various sport sciences is an antiquated notion and not future-oriented. Failure to specialize and, equally important, failure to strengthen specialized career tracks with a critical mass of faculty and meaningful educational experiences will result in the institutional absorption and eventual extinction of sport psychology as we know it today, and the eventual institutional absorption of all the exercise and sport sciences.

Although some countries have made programmatic advances, many countries are just starting to develop models of training for their sport psychology graduate programs. These countries will provide rich sources of international data on various aspects of sport psychology and will offer alternative models for the development of the discipline and the profession. Several countries currently developing programs will offer comprehensive graduate models designed to accommodate specific career tracks in research, performance enhancement, and clinical aspects of sport psychology. Future growth will be more orderly than past growth, and will be characterized by specificity rather than a generalist orientation in education and training experiences. Sport psychology will continue to grow worldwide, yet one has to question if the window of opportunity for the expansion and development of sport psychology programs in exercise and sport science departments has closed for North American programs.

The number of sport psychology graduate programs in North America will decrease while the number of graduate programs in other countries will increase. Programs in North America will identify themselves as primarily science-oriented or as science-practice-oriented. Programs that are science-oriented will continue to educate and train sport psychologists in the traditional manner common in North America for the past 50 years. Students in science-oriented programs will be engaged in academic course work with a significant component of their preparation involving research. Science-practice programs will extend the graduate education of students by at least one year and will provide similar science experiences provided in traditional programs, along with direct and indirect supervised practica, and course work in counseling and psychology. Practica will provide graduate students opportunities to observe experienced clinicians and work under the supervision of certified or licensed sport psychologists. Students will be given opportunities to apprentice in the areas of intervention, individual counseling, psychological assessment, performance enhancement, and small group counseling.

Upon graduation from an accredited science-practice program, a student will be eligible to sit for licensure in the sport psychology specialization. Due to downsizing, program acquisition, and program merging, several North American science programs in exercise psychology will become obsolete. Due to an inability to make the necessary changes required to meet accreditation standards, several doctoral programs wishing to become science-practice programs will become master's programs in sport psychology. The net effect will be a reduction in the overall and currently inflated number of doctoral programs in sport psychology in North America. The result of this reduction will be a net gain in the clarity of purpose and quality of educational experience offered by the remaining programs.

The number of doctoral programs in Asia will increase, and Australia will continue to refine graduate programs so that students are prepared for current licensure standards in that country. Japan will emerge as a leader in science-practice programs and will establish a model for accreditation of graduate programs and the licensure of individual practitioners. Europe, after much debate, will come to consensus on accrediting programs and there will be one standard for licensure in Europe. The influence of North American sport psychology will lessen in Europe as selective and high-caliber programs develop throughout Europe. The number of programs in Europe will remain small, but the quality of the newly developed programs will be notable.

Interest in applied aspects and the practice of sport psychology will continue to increase. Student interest in applied aspects of sport psychology has grown exponentially during the 1980s and 1990s. This interest will only increase as students trained in the 1980s and 1990s become absorbed into the faculties of universities around the world. These individuals will represent a "new breed" of sport psychologist who have significant interest in practicing with sport teams and athletes. Some will be employed half-time by university and college athletic departments and some may have full-time appointments. These appointments will provide a direct opportunity to serve athletes and to provide supervised experiences to sport psychology graduate students in university programs. The gradual integration of sport psychologists into athletic departments will advance applied aspects of the field at a much faster rate than ever before. These positions will be actively sought by young professionals who have experienced sport psychology internships with athletic departments during their graduate programs.

Sport psychology will be actively marketed to professional and collegiate teams and to the general public. Sport psychology remains a "sleeping giant" in many countries around the world. Debates over proper training, use of title, and right to practice will be settled once proper graduate education and training models are in place. Some of the energy spent on resolution of these issues will be placed into actively marketing sport psychology professionals who are well trained and certified or licensed. As more athletic teams are exposed to competent service provision and as more professional leagues know where to find competent resources in sport psychology, the market will expand to support private practice. Sports medicine clinics in the year 2015 will regularly be composed of a team of specialists—all licensed—who provide service to high school athletes, community and recreational participants, and those requiring rehabilitation from athletic and nonathletic health-related injuries and illnesses. The team of specialists will include applied exercise physiologists, cardiologists, nutritionists, orthopedists, physical therapists, and sport psychologists.

Graduate programs in applied sport psychology will become accredited. A dramatic change in the way applied sport psychologists are trained must occur in the near future. There are many graduate programs in North America offering students a degree in sport psychology without a terminal objective or a program focus. Many students receive a general academic education in sport psychology, which often is insufficient for the practice of sport psychology with athletes and teams. Currently, many North American students complete graduate programs but are not eligible to receive AAASP certification. These students either practice uncertified, often with little or very limited applied training, or they must complete additional work postgraduation (often including supervised practica) to become eligible for certification. Many countries will avoid this pitfall by developing a logical process that accredits graduate programs that adequately prepare students for certification and eventual licensure as a sport psychologist. Such a model will provide clarity of program focus to the student and to the faculty providing graduate education and training experiences.

By 2010, sport psychology graduate programs will become interdisciplinary through the formation of applied curricula at the doctoral level. More counseling and psychology departments will begin to offer specializations in sport psychology. Rather than competing for students and resources, counseling, exercise science, and psychology departments will form curricula in applied sport psychology. These programs will break down artificial barriers between "counselors," "psychologists," and "sport psychologists" and will greatly enhance the training of applied sport psychologists. Students will no longer graduate from a department but from a curriculum. Sport psychology will develop further with professionals specializing in clinical, social, developmental, and human performance domains. The trend toward curricula will extend to all areas of exercise and sport science as economic constraints and the movement toward program consolidation accelerate in higher education. Eventually, this trend will become worldwide and will actually result in better education, training, and funding opportunities as faculty from several departments bring their expertise together to form the curricula.

Most countries will consider and adopt some form of license for individuals interested in practicing sport psychology. The certification of individuals wishing to practice sport psychology was a groundbreaking event by AAASP in 1992. But certification is only the initial step in raising the consciousness of consumers and practitioners. Although there may be some attempt to fractionate or dilute sport psychology by advocating that performance enhancement can be practiced by individuals from eclectic educational backgrounds, the specialization required when providing services to the athletic subculture will be formally recognized and protected through licensing. North America, the leader in promoting the regulation of practice during the 1980s, will eventually follow the advancement of other countries that move to formally regulate training, entrance,

and the right to practice sport psychology, thus providing some protection to the consumer of sport psychology services.

Science-oriented exercise psychology programs will develop a health-related focus. As programs divide along science and science-practice models, science programs will focus on what is currently called "exercise psychology." Psychophysiological aspects of exercise and well-being and the role of exercise in maintaining and promoting health across the age span will receive concentrated attention. Particular interest will be directed to youth and geriatric populations, with attempts to promote healthy lifestyles in early years that will be maintained in the latter years when exercise often decreases. Exercise psychology programs will be dependent on external funding and will by necessity combine basic and applied research in response to funding that mandates social accountability. The majority of funding will come from private companies engaged in health promotion and disease prevention. The body of knowledge for what is known as the exercise and sport sciences today will come from a much larger informational base in the next 15 years. The cost of conducting high-quality research programs on significant psychological and health-related questions will be too high for small exercise psychology specializations. The inability of exercise psychology programs to secure large-scale National Institutes of Health (NIH) and National Science Foundation (NSF)–type funding on a consistent basis will result in a similar type of program merging as will be experienced in the applied sport psychology area. Exercise psychology programs will be absorbed into medical programs in health promotion, disease prevention, and rehabilitation. These changes may initially be resisted by exercise scientists, and they will appear dramatic to traditionalists in the exercise and sport sciences. The net effect of these changes will be a very positive effect on the eventual contributions of applied sport psychology and exercise psychology specializations. Sport psychology service provision and the generation of meaningful research in the areas of health promotion, disease prevention, and the role of exercise and sport in developing and maintaining a healthy lifestyle will be mainstreamed into society and will have greater impact on the mass population.

North America may lose its status as the leader in sport psychology. Sport psychology is developing rapidly in Australia, Japan, and many European countries. As these countries develop sophisticated graduate programs of study in sport psychology, fewer foreign students will perceive a need to come to North America for expert training and supervision. The database for scientific research and application of sport psychology information will explode globally, and international information will be exchanged with much greater ease than it is today. Countries that successfully earn governmental and private industry funding for research and formulate functional models for the delivery of competent service to athletes and sport groups will forge ahead in disciplinary and professional aspects of sport psychology. Sport psychology organizations in several countries outside of North America have already shown an interest in actively promoting a unified approach to education, application, and professional issues. This is perhaps most obvious in Australia, where accreditation of educational programs is in place and use of title is regulated. Japan is currently moving rapidly to unify exercise science and psychology in the areas of education and practice. Organizational leadership may move at a faster and more efficient pace in countries outside North America, resulting in well-conceived programs of graduate education with related yet distinct models in both research and practice.

Technology will play a major role in the practice of sport psychology. The speed at which technology enters daily life will increase at a rate never witnessed before in the history of humanity. While sport psychology will lag behind in bringing the technological revolution into practice, other human factors industries will make a direct entry into sport psychology through professional, Olympic, and collegiate programs. Athletes will train with laser disk simulators that can realistically depict any aspect of their competition. Feedback mechanisms will be developed to help athletes improve their motor skills in activities as diverse as compulsories in figure skating to free-throw shooting in basketball. All training will have a component that involves psychological conditioning and preparation with simulated success and simulated failure components specific to the athlete and the opponent in the upcoming competition.

Equipment will be so portable and miniature that players will be able to use concentration and stress-reducing devices while on the bench or during time-outs in sports such as basketball, football, and soccer. Training in endurance sports, such as swimming and track, will be formulated completely by computer programs. Instant technique feedback will be provided on minicomputers that each athlete owns. These minicomputers will record psychological responses such as arousal level, thought focus, and emotions experienced, along with technique feedback providing the athlete with a composite that shows the optimal psychological, physical, and technical combination for peak performance. The performance matrix will be updated and

modified with each outstanding performance. Each athlete will use this information in an attempt to duplicate the responses most highly related to superior performance.

Decisions made in this decade will determine the future of sport psychology. Some of the most important decisions to confront the field of sport psychology will be made in the decade 2000–2010. We live in an age of specialization, with information exploding at a rate few can keep pace with. The consumer of today and certainly the consumer of tomorrow want competent, efficient, and accountable service in the marketplace. The tendency in many countries toward avoiding important and controversial issues confronting sport psychology will pass. Working models in areas such as graduate program accreditation, marketing, and the licensing of individuals who wish to practice will be adopted. These models will be refined and redesigned as they are tested not in theory but in practice. Without an ability to demonstrate viability in the marketplace, sport psychology will not survive as an esoteric academic discipline in exercise and sport science departments. Sport psychology is at a vital crossroads in many countries. Decisions made in this decade will determine the future health, vitality, and growth of sport psychology on a global level.

SUMMARY: CHANGE IS CONSTANT

Change is a constant in life. The life cycle of academic specializations seldom violates this principle by remaining constant. What did academic and research programs focus on in the 1940s and 1950s? Departments were called physical education, and the exercise sciences as we know them did not exist. That was a mere 40 to 50 years ago! The emphasis was on developing physical education teachers and coaches for the school systems and the universities. This model currently exists in many colleges and universities, and teaching and coaching are important roles to fulfill. Yet any observer of current events in the exercise and sport sciences realizes change has occurred, it is occurring right now, and more change is inevitable in the future.

Does this mean that what the exercise and sport sciences have to offer is not valued or valuable? On the contrary, all of the exercise and sport sciences have much to offer. The challenge for the exercise and sport sciences in general and sport psychology in particular will be to find, nurture, and develop an environment that facilitates the orderly growth of the science and practice of each specialization. Although the present may appear very turbulent to many fellow sport psychology professionals, it is actually the time when the role of sport psychology as a discipline and as a practice is being forged. The success of sport psychology as an emerging field will depend on those who are able to adapt, evolve, integrate, and contribute in the larger context of meaningful science and regulated practice.

REFERENCES

Alderman, R.B. (1980). Sports psychology: Past, present, and future dilemmas. In P. Klavora & K.A.W. Wipper (Eds.), *Psychological and sociological factors in sport* (pp. 3–19). Toronto, Canada: University of Toronto.

Andersen, M.B., Van Raalte, J.L., & Brewer, B.W. (1994). Assessing the skills of sport psychology supervisors. *The Sport Psychologist, 8,* 238–247.

Andersen, M.B., Williams, J.M., Aldridge, T., & Taylor, J. (1997). Tracking the training and careers of advanced degree programs in sport psychology, 1989 to 1994. *The Sport Psychologist, 11,* 326–344.

Andersen, M.B., & Williams-Rice, B.T. (1996). Supervision in the education and training of sport psychology service providers. *The Sport Psychologist, 10,* 278–290.

Antonelli, F. (1989). Applied sport psychology in Italy. *Journal of Applied Sport Psychology, 1,* 45–51.

Biddle, S.J., Bull, S.J., & Seheult, C.L. (1992). Ethical and professional issues in contemporary British sport psychology. *The Sport Psychologist, 6,* 66–76.

Bond, J.W. (1989). Applied sport psychology in Australia: History, current status and future issues. *Journal of Applied Sport Psychology, 1,* 8–22.

Conroy, D.E. (1996). Science-practice and accreditation in applied sport psychology. *Journal of Applied Sport Psychology, 8,* S51.

Feltz, D.L. (1987). The future of graduate education in sport and exercise science: A sport psychology perspective. *Quest, 39,* 217–223.

Geron, E. (1982). History and recent position of sport psychology. In E. Geron (Ed.), *Handbook of sport psychology: Introduction to sport psychology* (Vol. I, pp. 25–44). Netanya, Israel: Wingate Institute for Physical Education and Sport.

Hanin, Y.L. (1979). Applying sport psychology: Past, present, and future. In C.H. Nadeau, W.R. Halliwell, K.M. Newell, & G.C. Roberts (Eds.), *Psychology of motor behavior and sport* (pp. 37–48). Champaign, IL: Human Kinetics.

Harrison, R., & Feltz, D. (1980). The professionalization of sport psychology: Legal considerations. In W.F. Straub (Ed.), *Sport psychology: An analysis of athlete behavior* (2nd ed., pp. 26–34). Ithaca, NY: Mouvement.

Johnson, W.R., & Hutton, D.H. (1955). Effects of a combative sport upon personality dynamics as measured by a projective test. *Research Quarterly, 26,* 49–53.

Johnson, W.R., Hutton, D.H., & Johnson, G.B. (1954). Personality traits of some champion athletes as measured by two projective tests: The Rorschach and H-T-P. *Research Quarterly, 25,* 484–485.

Kroll, W., & Lewis, G. (1970). America's first sport psychologist. *Quest, 13,* 1–4.

Landers, D.M. (1975). Observational learning of a motor skill: Temporal spacing of demonstrations and audience presence. *Journal of Motor Behavior, 7,* 281–287.

Landers, D.M. (1980). The arousal-performance relationship revisited. *Research Quarterly for Exercise and Sport, 51,* 77–90.

Landers, D.M., Bauer, R.S., & Feltz, D.L. (1978). Social facilitation during the initial stage of motor learning: A re-examination of Martens' audience study. *Journal of Motor Behavior, 10,* 325–337.

Magill, R. (1984, Fall). President's message. *North American Society for the Psychology of Sport and Physical Activity Newsletter,* 1.

Martens, R. (1969). Effect of audience on learning and performance of a complex motor skill. *Journal of Personality and Social Psychology, 12,* 252–260.

Martens, R. (1971). Anxiety and motor behavior: A review. *Journal of Motor Behavior, 3,* 151–179.

Martens, R. (1974). Arousal and motor performance. *Exercise and Sport Sciences Reviews, 2,* 155–188.

Martens, R. (1979). About smocks and jocks. *Journal of Sport Psychology, 1,* 94–99.

Martens, R., & Gill, D.L. (1976). State anxiety among successful competitors who differ in competitive trait anxiety. *Research Quarterly, 47,* 698–708.

Murphy, S. (1996). Wither certification? *Journal of Applied Sport Psychology, 8,* S52.

Nideffer, R. (1984). Current concerns in sport psychology. In J.M. Silva & R.S. Weinberg (Eds.), *Psychological foundations of sport* (pp. 35–44). Champaign, IL: Human Kinetics.

Nideffer, R.M., DuFresne, P., Nesvig, D., & Selder, D. (1980). Future of applied sport psychology. *Journal of Sport Psychology, 2,* 170–174.

Patrick, G.T. (1903). The psychology of football. *American Journal of Psychology, 14,* 104–117.

Salmela, J.H. (1992). *The world sport psychology sourcebook.* Champaign, IL: Human Kinetics.

Scanlan, T.K., & Passer, M.W. (1978). Factors related to competitive stress among male youth sport participants. *Medicine and Science in Sports, 10,* 103–108.

Schell, B., Hunt, J., & Lloyd, C. (1984). An investigation of future market opportunities for sport psychologists. *Journal of Sport Psychology, 6,* 335–350.

Scripture, E.W. (1899). Cross-education. *Popular Science Monthly, 56,* 589–596.

Selden, W.K., & Porter, H.V. (1977). *Accreditation: Its purposes and uses*. Washington, DC: Council on Postsecondary Accreditation.

Shteinbakh, V. (1987). *Soviet sport: The success story*. Moscow: Raduga.

Silva, J.M. (1984). The emergence of applied sport psychology: Contemporary trends, future issues. *International Journal of Sport Psychology, 15,* 40–51.

Silva, J.M. (1989a). Establishing professional standards and advancing applied sport psychology research. *Journal of Applied Sport Psychology, 1,* 160–165.

Silva, J.M. (1989b). The evolution of the Association for the Advancement of Applied Sport Psychology and the *Journal of Applied Sport Psychology*. *Journal of Applied Sport Psychology, 1,* 1–3.

Silva, J.M. (1989c). Toward the professionalization of sport psychology. *The Sport Psychologist, 3,* 265–273.

Silva, J.M. (1992). On advancement: An editorial. *Journal of Applied Sport Psychology, 4,* 1–9.

Silva, J.M. (1996a). Current issues confronting the advancement of applied sport psychology. *Journal of Applied Sport Psychology, 8,* S50–S52.

Silva, J.M. (1996b). A second move: Confronting persistent issues that challenge the advancement of applied sport psychology. *Journal of Applied Sport Psychology, 8,* S52.

Silva, J.M. (1997a, August). Advancing progressive training models in applied sport psychology. In C.M. Janelle (Chair), *Training, employment, and accreditation issues in sport psychology: Student perspectives*. Symposium conducted at the meeting of the American Psychological Association, Chicago.

Silva, J.M. (1997b). Initiating program accreditation in sport psychology. *Journal of Applied Sport Psychology, 9,* S47–S49.

Silva, J.M. (2001). The evolution of sport psychology. In J.M. Silva & D.E. Stevens (Eds.), *Psychological foundations of sport*. Needham Heights, MA: Allyn & Bacon.

Silva, J.M., Conroy, D.E., & Zizzi, S.J. (1999). Critical issues confronting the advancement of applied sport psychology. *Journal of Applied Sport Psychology, 11,* 163–197.

Singer, R.N. (1965). Effect of spectators on athletes and nonathletes performing a gross motor task. *Research Quarterly, 36,* 473–482.

Strean, W.B., & Roberts, G.C. (1992). Future directions in applied sport psychology research. *The Sport Psychologist, 6,* 55–65.

Triplett, N. (1897). The dynamogenic factors in pacemaking and competition. *American Journal of Psychology, 9,* 507–553.

Vealey, R. (1988). Future directions in psychological skills training. *The Sport Psychologist, 2,* 318–336.

Vealey, R.S. (1994). Current status and prominent issues in sport psychology interventions. *Medicine and Science in Sports and Exercise, 26,* 495–502.

Wiggins, D.K. (1984). The history of sport psychology in North America. In J.M. Silva & R.S. Weinberg (Eds.), *Psychological foundations of sport* (pp. 9–22). Champaign, IL: Human Kinetics.

Author Index

Abbot, S., 674
Abel, L., 369, 370
Abel, M., 345
Abendroth-Smith, J., 42
Abernethy, B., 3, 4, 6, 7, 8, 9, 10, 12, 25, 41, 44, 45, 54, 55, 58, 60, 61, 68, 70, 74, 75, 76, 144, 154, 163, 164, 174, 176, 177, 179, 180, 182, 183, 184, 190, 212, 223, 275, 277
Ablard, K.E., 432
Abraham, P.C., 33, 35, 39
Abrams, L., 395
Abrams, R.A., 39
Abramson, I.S., 730, 731
Abramson, L.Y., 445, 448, 450, 458, 463, 680
Abrego, P.J., 685
Ackerman, P., 66, 67, 249, 251, 509
Ackland, T.R., 270
Adam, J., 320, 321
Adams, J., 3, 8, 10, 61, 88, 91, 105, 106, 107, 108, 124, 128, 137, 206, 207, 208, 210, 213, 214, 529, 675
Adams, N.E., 680
Adler, P., 615, 616, 625
Adler, T.F., 605, 606, 618, 619, 621, 625, 627
Adler, W., 554
Adolphe, R.M., 184, 378
Adolphe, R.N., 188
Adrian, E.D., 369
Aerts, E., 589
Agras, S., 744
Aguerri, P., 239
Aguirre-Molina, M., 721
Ahlgren, R.L., 682, 800
Aitchison, T., 732
Ajzen, I., 478, 696, 697, 698, 700, 701
Akande, A., 423, 461
Akande, D., 404
Alafat, K.A., 395
Alain, C., 10, 75, 91, 127, 183, 218, 271

Al-Ameer, H., 120
Alamo, L., 306
Albert, N.J., 794
Albinson, J.G., 295, 298, 309
Albrecht, R., 68, 616, 674
Albright, C.A., 728, 729
Alcantara, A.A., 362, 363
Alcaraz, J.E., 659
Alderman, R.B., 243, 824
Aldridge, T., 823
Aldwin, C.M., 768
Alexander, J.F., 246
Alexander, R.A., 508
Alexandris, K., 401
Alfano, P., 672
Alimi, A.M., 39
Allard, F., 3, 6, 8, 9, 13, 45, 68, 74, 117, 130, 174, 175, 176, 177, 179, 182, 185, 186, 187, 190, 223, 277, 278, 279
Allen, B.P., 552
Allen, J.B., 623
Allen, M.E., 747
Allen, R.J., 766
Allen, R.M., 652, 654
Alles, E.F., 767, 769, 770
Allison, M.G., 249
Allison, M.T., 676, 677, 683
Alloy, L.B., 485, 680
Allport, D.A., 12, 56, 62, 63, 65, 66, 73, 76
Allport, G.W., 249
Almekinders, L.C., 794
Almekinders, S.V., 794
Almog, A., 501, 502
Alpert, R., 300, 301
Altmaier, E.M., 463
Alty, P., 164
Alutto, J.A., 486
Alwin, D.F., 682, 684
Alzate, R., 794, 795, 797
Amabile, T.M., 394, 395

Amblard, B., 21, 26
Ames, C., 417, 418, 419, 420, 421, 427, 430, 432, 434, 436, 560, 606, 620, 625, 813
Ammons, R.B., 105
Amorose, A.J., 626, 629
Andersen, M.B., 691, 766, 767, 768, 769, 771, 772, 773, 774, 775, 777, 778, 779, 780, 781, 782, 783, 787, 788, 789, 800, 802, 823, 827
Anderson, B.J., 362, 363
Anderson, C., 709, 712, 714, 715, 720, 725
Anderson, D.C., 504
Anderson, D.F., 226
Anderson, D.I., 26, 107, 130, 164
Anderson, J.A., 328
Anderson, J.R., 3, 4, 128
Anderson, K., 450, 458
Anderson, L.M., 728
Anderson, L.P., 219
Anderson, M., 69
Anderson, P., 369
Anderson, R.E., 720
Andersson, R.L., 135
Andersson, S., 369, 747
Andre, A.D., 212
Andree, K.V., 422
Andrews, F.M., 637
Angus, R., 70
Annesi, J., 87, 97, 329
Annett, J., 69, 87, 93, 105, 222, 529, 532, 538, 539, 540
Ansfield, M., 310
Anshel, M.H., 293, 396, 500, 502, 508, 509, 513, 567, 568, 571, 573, 579
Anson, D., 99
Anson, J.G., 12
Antonelli, F., 825
Antoni, M.H., 643
Antoniou, A., 127
Antoniou, P., 798, 800

833

Antonis, B., 12, 63
Antonovsky, A., 771
Apitzsch, E., 240
Apparies, R.J., 372, 374, 375, 378
Applebaum, M., 749, 750, 756
Apter, M.J., 300, 330
Arbib, M.A., 144, 146, 147, 150, 152, 155, 164
Archer, J., 419, 432, 620
Arent, S.M., 752, 753
Argov, E., 178
Argyle, M., 637, 638
Armitage, C.J., 700
Armony, J., 658
Armor, D.A., 647
Armstrong, C.W., 179
Armstrong, N., 404, 423, 425, 439, 461, 606
Armstrong, T.R., 89
Arnold, C.L., 486
Arnold, R.K., 97, 216
Arond, H., 676, 677, 680, 682, 683, 684
Aronson, R., 68
Arthur, E.J., 135, 212
Arthur, K., 702
Arthur, M.B., 352
Arthur, W., Jr., 219
Arutyunyan, G.H., 164
Arviko, I., 675, 679, 682, 683
Ash, D.W., 122
Ashcroft, M., 404
Asher, S.R., 625, 627, 628
Ashton, J., 721, 733
Assaiante, C., 21, 26
Astle, S.J., 788, 793
Aston, B., 129
Atchley, R.C., 674, 682
Atienza, F.L., 222
Atkins, C.J., 574, 576, 730, 731
Atkinson, J.W., 606
Atkinson, R.C., 24
Attner, P., 362
Aurenty, R., 21, 26
Austin, J.T., 579
Austin, M., 177, 178
Ausubel, D., 678
Avener, M., 282, 301, 304, 536, 558
Avery, C.M., 681
Avison, W.R., 641
Ayllon, T., 249
Azar, B., 284
Azemar, G., 377

Baade, E., 325
Baber, L., 682
Babkes, M.L., 606, 618, 619, 621, 661
Babyak, M.A., 749, 750, 756
Baca, L.D., 475
Bachman, J.C., 6

Back, K., 472
Baddeley, A.D., 135, 161
Badhorn, E., 332
Bagnall, J., 501
Bagozzi, R.P., 574, 576
Bagwell, C.L., 627
Bahill, A.T., 69
Bahnsen, A., 791, 796, 797
Bahrke, M.S., 643, 746
Bailey, D., 773
Bailey, S., 450, 458
Baille, P.H., 685
Baillie, P.H.F., 397
Baines-Preece, J., 38
Baker, C.H., 102
Baker, J., 4, 275, 277
Baker, S.L., 814
Bakker, F.C., 166, 177, 239, 247, 539, 661
Balague, G., 420, 423
Balaguer, I., 222, 420, 434
Baldes, J.J., 519
Baldy, R., 229, 230
Ball, D.W., 674, 683
Ball, J., 485
Ballard, L., 798
Ballon, F., 240, 254
Balogh, D.W., 795
Balsom, P., 38, 185
Baltes, P.B., 270, 284
Bamforth, K., 472
Bandelow, B., 744
Bandelow, D., 744
Bandert, L.E., 758
Bandura, A., 128, 205, 206, 207, 208, 209, 210, 211, 212, 216, 217, 221, 222, 224, 227, 228, 229, 322, 340, 341, 342, 343, 344, 349, 350, 351, 352, 353, 355, 356, 357, 358, 418, 457, 460, 461, 463, 465, 486, 509, 510, 519, 534, 537, 550, 551, 553, 554, 556, 557, 559, 566, 567, 579, 585, 586, 627, 680, 696, 697, 703, 704, 705, 706, 707, 708, 709, 710, 711, 713, 720, 721, 733, 735, 813, 814
Bane, S.M., 744
Banfield, J.T., 460, 461
Banister, H., 180
Bannister, H., 7
Baranowski, T., 696, 709, 712, 714, 715, 720, 725, 728, 729
Barba, D.A., 103, 165, 176, 179, 188
Barber, H., 357
Barber, P.J., 62, 63
Barclay, C.R., 44
Bard, C., 6, 8, 9, 29, 39, 58, 74, 177, 178, 179, 182, 183, 188
Bardy, B.G., 148
Bareket, T., 134

Bar-Eli, M., 178, 250, 251, 500, 501, 502, 503, 505, 510, 571, 577
Barer, M.L., 722
Bargh, J.A., 566, 567
Baria, A., 178, 190
Barksdale, C.M., 755
Barling, J., 345
Barlow, D.H., 247
Barlow, W., 747
Barndollar, K., 566, 567
Barnes, M.W., 303
Barnett, M.L., 500, 503, 517
Barnett, N.P., 622, 623
Barnsley, P.E., 185
Barnsley, R.H., 185
Barnwell, J., 75
Baron, R.A., 216
Baron, R.M., 702, 707, 781
Bar-Or, O., 271
Barr, K., 529, 530, 536, 542, 544
Barrack, R.L., 797
Barresi, J.V., 14, 212
Barrett, S.E., 41
Barrios, B., 247, 249
Barron, O.A., 797
Bar-Tal, D., 618
Bartholomew, J.B., 651, 745
Bartholomew, L.K., 729
Bartlett, C.J., 5
Bartlett, F.C., 74
Bartlett, M.S., 658
Bartmann, U., 744
Bartmus, U., 271, 272, 273, 274
Bartram, D., 304
Bartz, A.E., 180
Basham, R.B., 774
Baskett, G., 591
Basler, M.L., 327
Bateman, J., 41
Batten, J., 672
Battig, W.F., 119
Battista, R., 543
Bauer, R.S., 826
Baum, F., 731
Bauman, A., 659, 732, 733
Baumeister, R.F., 308, 364, 397, 489, 567, 720, 735
Baxter-Jones, A., 38
Beaglehole, R., 722, 731
Beals, R.P., 180
Bear, M.F., 375, 378
Beaton, A.M., 405
Beatty, J., 58
Beauchamp, P.H., 399, 402, 404, 409, 571, 572, 573
Beavers, C., 177, 178
Beazeley, A., 179
Bebeau, M., 591, 599
Bechtel, W., 151
Beck, A.T., 748

Beck, L., 789, 791, 792, 795, 797, 800, 801
Beck, S.A., 730
Becker, S.L., 606, 620
Beckham, J.C., 99, 105
Becklen, R., 68
Beedy, J., 598
Beek, P., 12, 144, 146
Beek, W.J., 143
Beggs, A., 506
Beirinkx, M.B., 98
Beise, D., 181
Beisser, A., 683
Bell, H.H., 134, 135
Bell, M.A., 362, 366
Beller, J., 592, 597
Bem, D., 242, 445
Beneca, A., 527, 798, 800
Benedetti, C., 108
Bengston, V.L., 675
Benguigui, N., 181
Bennett, B., 246, 247, 248, 282, 319, 327, 536, 558
Bennett, S., 144, 145, 148, 152, 158, 159, 160, 162, 163, 165, 166, 167
Bennett, W., 219
Benson, H., 640
Benware, C., 395
Berg, W.P., 6, 12
Berger, B.G., 638, 639, 640, 641, 642, 643, 644, 645, 646, 647, 648, 649, 650, 651, 654, 657, 658, 659, 660, 662, 663
Berger, R.S., 798, 800
Berggren, D., 240
Bergin, A., 680, 685
Bergstrom, B., 327
Berkman, L.F., 730
Berkowitz, L., 643
Berlant, A.R., 215, 223, 230, 231, 341
Berman, P.S., 325
Bernardo, P., 319, 327
Berndt, T.J., 624, 625
Bernoties, L., 533
Bernstein, N., 76, 145, 156, 164, 167, 379
Berntson, G.G., 60
Berry, D.C., 69, 129
Berwind, A., 643, 646, 651
Best, D., 811
Betley, G., 395
Bettes, B.A., 690
Bettinardi, V., 155, 156, 532
Betts, G.H., 529
Beunen, G., 185
Beuter, A., 166
Bhanot, J.L., 74, 180
Bianco, T.M., 789, 791, 792, 793, 796, 798, 800
Bibeau, D., 722, 723, 724

Biddle, S., 396, 399, 401, 403, 404, 407, 420, 421, 425, 426, 428, 430, 434, 435, 437, 439, 446, 448, 449, 450, 452, 456, 457, 458, 460, 461, 462, 463, 464, 574, 576, 696
Biddle, S.J., 262, 419, 423, 425, 427, 433, 444, 448, 457, 458, 461, 462, 465, 606, 639, 742, 753, 789, 794, 823
Bieber, S.L., 659, 662
Bigelow, B.J., 624
Biggs, S.J., 216
Bijlard, M.J., 130, 209
Bijur, P.E., 787
Billing, J., 331, 536
Bilodeau, E.A., 88, 99, 106, 107, 109
Bilodeau, I.M., 88, 99, 106, 107, 108, 109
Binding, M., 180
Binet, A., 53, 54
Bingham, S.M., 502, 504
Bird, A.M., 128, 211, 218, 220
Bird, E., 539, 571, 572, 578
Birkhead-Flight, A.M., 574, 576, 643, 649
Birrell, S., 591
Birren, J.E., 758
Bissonnette, R., 393
Bittner, A.C., 64
Bizot, E., 129
Bizzi, E., 135
Bjork, R.A., 100, 135, 334
Bjorklund, D.F., 182
Black, J.E., 362, 363, 366
Black, P., 58
Black, S.J., 554, 623
Blackburn, J.H., 7
Blackburn, J.M., 180
Blackwell, B., 770, 771, 772, 774
Blahüs, P., 270, 272
Blair, A., 532, 542
Blair, M.S., 642
Blair, S., 591, 696, 709, 712, 718, 719, 720, 728, 733, 734
Blair, V., 346, 349, 351, 476, 486, 504, 571, 572, 573
Blais, M.R., 390, 392, 393, 399, 401, 402, 403, 404, 405, 406, 408, 409, 571, 578
Blakemore, C., 42
Blamey, A., 732
Blanchard, C., 390, 392, 396, 397, 398, 399, 400, 401, 403, 404, 406, 407, 408, 409, 410, 457, 465, 537, 545, 598, 651
Blandin, Y., 161, 162, 218
Blankenbaker, J., 625
Blankendaal, F.C.M., 145
Blanksby, B.A., 270
Blankstein, K.R., 306

Blasi, A., 588
Blatt, M.M., 588
Blatt, S.J., 431
Blinde, E.M., 672, 674, 675, 677, 678, 679, 680, 681, 682, 683, 684, 686
Bliss, C.B., 53
Bliss, J.P., 135
Blom, B., 769, 770, 771, 773, 776, 781, 782
Blomstrand, E., 646
Bloom, B.L., 741
Bloom, B.S., 34, 117, 175, 183, 269, 272, 274, 275, 276, 277, 279, 280, 281
Bloomfield, J., 270
Blumberg, M.S., 147
Blumberg, S.J., 310
Blumenfeld, P.C., 427
Blumenstein, B., 571, 577
Blumenthal, J.A., 749, 750, 756, 758
Blundell, N.L., 181
Boase, P., 306
Bobick, T.M., 702
Bobko, P., 519
Bobrow, D., 60, 63, 65
Bockovan, J., 598, 627
Bodler, N.I., 135
Bohrer, R.E., 368
Boies, S.J., 54
Bojczyk, K.G., 6
Boles, S.M., 728
Bomhoff, G.T., 8, 179
Bompa, T.O., 520
Bond, J.W., 823
Bongaardt, R., 145, 150
Bonita, R., 731
Bonnel, A., 54, 377
Bonner, S., 104, 506
Boone, J., 422
Booth, M., 271, 709, 710, 718, 728, 731, 733, 734
Booth, W., 766, 787
Bootsma, R.J., 8, 12, 75, 166, 179
Borchstead, G.N., 343, 344, 345
Borden, F., 571, 572
Bordiga, M., 181
Borg, G.A.V., 815
Borgeaud, P., 9, 179
Boring, E.G., 53
Borrelli, B., 510
Boschker, M.S.J., 539
Boston, A., 476, 485
Bostrom, A., 597
Bota, J.D., 282
Botterill, C., 672, 681, 689
Bouchard, C., 278, 284, 719, 720, 734
Bouchard, L.J., 132, 176, 179, 188, 222
Bouchard, T.J., Jr., 278
Boucher, J., 38, 108, 185

Bouffard, D.L., 242
Bouffard, M., 229, 230, 659
Boulter, L.R., 106
Boutcher, S., 7, 68, 69, 246, 248, 282, 293, 295, 320, 327, 506, 642, 649, 650, 758, 759, 810, 811
Boutilier, C., 178, 182, 187
Boutmans, J., 177
Bouton, J., 674
Bowen, D.J., 787
Bowers, C.A., 133, 134, 135
Bowers, T.D., 180
Boyce, B.A., 500, 501, 502, 504, 505, 510, 517
Boyce, W.T., 766
Boyd, J.H., 741
Boyd, M., 424, 437, 659, 660, 814
Boyd, R., 812
Boykin, A., 697, 720
Boyle, G.J., 246
Bracht, N., 733
Bradburn, N.M., 636
Bradet, R., 542
Bradford, D.C., 247, 249
Bradley, B., 672
Bradley, P., 284, 328, 365
Bradley, P.W., 248
Bradley, R.D., 216
Bradley, T.A., 518
Brady, F., 163
Bramble, W.J., Jr., 133, 134
Brammer, L.M., 685
Bramwell, S.T., 687, 767, 769, 782
Branta, C., 29, 30, 31, 34, 35
Braskamp, L., 417, 499, 696, 813
Bratton, R.D., 626
Brawley, L.R., 68, 353, 456, 472, 473, 474, 475, 476, 477, 478, 479, 480, 481, 482, 483, 484, 485, 487, 488, 489, 490, 503, 504, 510, 659, 660, 661, 695, 696, 697, 701, 703, 706, 707, 714, 720, 729, 752
Breathnach, S.B., 644
Bredemeier, B., 21, 223, 393, 424, 434, 476, 485, 589, 591, 592, 593, 594, 595, 596, 597, 598, 599, 606, 627
Breger, L., 362
Brehaut, J.C., 41
Brehm, J.W., 320
Brenner, B., 657
Breslow, L., 722
Brewer, B., 249, 653, 787, 788, 789, 791, 793, 794, 795, 796, 797, 799, 800, 801, 802, 823
Brewer, J., 38, 185, 246
Brewer, K., 319
Brewin, C.R., 462
Brickner, J.C., 795
Bridges, D., 789, 791, 792, 795, 797, 798, 799, 800, 801

Bridges, M.W., 796
Brière, N.M., 390, 391, 392, 393, 399, 400, 401, 402, 403, 404, 406, 409, 597, 598
Briggs, G.E., 93, 121, 123
Briggs, J.D., 661
Bright, J.E.H., 309
Briner, R., 517
Brink, S.G., 722
Brisson, G., 641
Brisson, T.A., 106, 127
Britsch, B., 463
Broadbent, D.E., 61, 71, 72, 129
Broadbent, M.H., 129
Broadhurst, C.J., 401
Broadhurst, P.L., 293, 295, 326
Brock, S.C., 791, 793
Brodkin, P., 610, 614
Brody, E.B., 380, 381
Brody, N., 242
Broekoff, J., 38, 39
Broocks, A., 744
Brooke, R., 404
Brooks, D.D., 674
Brooks, R.B., 133
Broom, E.F., 672
Broome, A., 310
Brouwer, W.H., 64
Brower, J.J., 614
Brown, B., 591, 768
Brown, C.J., 99, 105
Brown, D.R., 646, 744, 754, 756
Brown, J.D., 397, 640, 641
Brown, L., 674, 779
Brown, T.L., 65
Browne, M.A., 243, 250
Browne, W., 721
Browning, C.J., 659
Browning, E.R., 680
Brownson, R.C., 723
Brubaker, P.H., 641
Bruce, V., 146
Brunel, P., 427, 428
Brunet, M.E., 797
Bruning, N.S., 680, 681
Brunn, S.E., 511
Brustad, R.J., 402, 409, 606, 607, 611, 615, 616, 617, 618, 619, 621, 624, 661
Bruya, L., 500, 501, 503, 505, 508, 510, 523
Bryan, W.L., 116
Bryant, C.X., 645, 745
Bryk, T.A., 721
Brylinsky, J.A., 252
Btesh, Y., 501, 502
Buchanan, H.T., 625
Buchner, A., 129
Buchner, D., 719, 720, 728, 729
Buchsbaum, M.S., 369, 370

Buckholz, E., 179
Buckolz, E., 530, 531, 535, 540, 541, 543
Buckworth, J., 720, 723, 728
Budgett, R., 754, 755
Budney, A.J., 539, 820
Buekers, M., 95, 96, 195, 220
Bugmann, G., 149
Buhrmann, H.G., 626
Bukowski, B.H., 628
Bukowski, W.M., 447, 624, 625, 730
Bulbuliam, R., 743
Bulgakova, N.S., 271
Bull, S.J., 250, 309, 823
Bullemer, P., 69
Bump, L., 246, 291, 295, 296, 298, 300, 301, 302, 303, 304, 307, 324, 344, 348, 429, 621
Bundrick, C.M., 651, 652, 653, 654, 656
Bungum, T.J., 659
Bunker, J.F., 723, 724
Bunker, L., 559, 560, 778
Bunton, R., 721
Buntrock, C., 793, 800
Bunz, H., 154
Burch, C.D., 211, 216, 230
Burgess-Limerick, R., 12, 154, 164, 190
Burke, J.D., 741
Burke, J.P., 99
Burke, K.L., 497, 501, 502, 507, 509
Burke, T.R., 180
Burley, L.R., 180
Burnett, N., 74, 177
Burns, D.D., 431
Burpee, R.H., 180
Burroughs, W.A., 12, 177
Burton, A.W., 39, 40, 41
Burton, D., 246, 282, 291, 295, 296, 297, 298, 300, 301, 302, 303, 304, 307, 324, 327, 344, 348, 497, 499, 500, 501, 502, 504, 505, 506, 507, 509, 512, 513, 514, 515, 516, 517, 518, 520, 521, 552, 556, 560, 562, 613
Burwitz, L., 70, 74, 144, 163, 164, 166, 179, 182, 188, 209, 213, 214, 221
Bush, J.P., 789
Bushnell, N.J., 762
Busk, J., 366, 373
Buss, A.H., 242
Buss, D.M., 242, 248
Butcher, J., 611, 719, 720
Butki, B.D., 425, 642, 643, 646, 647, 649, 650, 651
Butler, M.S., 95
Butler, R., 225, 231, 608
Butt, D.S., 250
Butterfield, S.A., 747
Butterfoss, F.D., 732
Button, C., 145, 152, 157, 158, 159, 160, 165, 166

Buys, C.J., 484
Byblow, W.D., 58, 154, 160, 161
Byerly, P.N., 795
Byrd, B.J., 769, 770, 775, 776
Byrne, A.T.J., 503, 504, 505, 506, 510, 520
Bysouth-Young, D.F., 58, 154, 161

Cable, N.T., 246, 571, 572, 578
Cacioppo, J.T., 60
Cadopi, M., 211, 229, 230
Cadorette, I., 399, 400, 401
Caherty, F.J., 380
Caicco, M., 178, 182, 187
Caine, C.G., 787
Caine, D.J., 787
Caird, J.K., 206, 214
Calcagnini, N., 820
Calcagnini, V., 817
Caldarone, G., 181
Caldwell, D.S., 99, 105
Cale, A., 293, 296, 302, 304, 501, 503
Calfas, K.J., 659, 742, 747, 756
Calhoun, L.G., 801
Callaghan, J., 424, 814
Callahan, A.E., 780
Callington, B.P., 181
Callow, N., 534, 536, 545
Calvin, W.H., 36, 156
Calvo, M.G., 161, 306, 751
Calvo, R.D., 794
Camacho, T.C., 749
Cameron, R., 680
Campbell, A., 636, 638
Campbell, D., 643
Campbell, D.J., 509
Campbell, D.T., 743
Campbell, J.L., 429, 551, 556, 557
Campbell, M.S., 796
Campbell, R.J., 351
Campos, W., 42
Campuzano, M.K., 729
Camras, L.A., 154
Cancio, L.C., 535
Candee, D., 588
Cannon, W.B., 320
Cantor, N., 254
Cantrell, P., 343, 348, 554
Cantrill, H., 247
Capafons, J., 751
Carbon, R.J., 799
Card, A., 591
Carda, R., 328
Carducci, D., 405
Carello, C., 144
Cargo, M., 734
Carlin, A.S., 136
Carlson, J., 319
Carlson, P., 365, 366
Carlton, L.G., 97

Carlton, M.J., 123, 127
Carmack, C., 720, 725
Carmack, D., 709, 712, 714, 715
Carmack, M.A., 650
Carnahan, H., 94, 101, 120, 218
Carp, F.M., 675
Carpenter, P., 279, 423, 426, 605, 607, 608, 659, 660, 815
Carr, T.H., 65
Carrière, L., 74, 177, 178
Carroll, B., 401
Carroll, C., 534
Carroll, D., 250, 792, 793, 798, 799, 800
Carroll, S.A., 792
Carroll, S.J., 510, 511
Carroll, W.R., 128, 206, 208, 209, 210, 211, 216
Carron, A., 239, 243, 244, 354
Carron, A.C., 447
Carron, A.V., 3, 252, 332, 353, 357, 434, 448, 459, 472, 473, 474, 475, 476, 477, 478, 479, 480, 481, 482, 483, 484, 485, 487, 488, 489, 490, 492, 503, 510, 554, 611, 661, 699, 701, 729
Carruthers, M., 298
Carson, R.C., 145, 146, 168
Carson, R.G., 160
Carter, J., 28, 535, 747
Carter, S., 310
Cartledge, N., 88, 510
Carver, C.S., 301, 307, 557, 567, 579, 720, 735, 796
Casali, J.G., 59
Case, I., 11
Case, R., 586
Cason, H., 88, 93
Caspersen, C.J., 718, 719
Cassisi, J.E., 798
Castelli, J., 643
Castiello, U., 57, 377
Castillo, I., 420
Castracane, V.D., 642
Cater, J.P., 135
Catley, D., 330, 401, 424, 425
Cattaert, D., 160
Cattell, R.B., 324
Caudill, D., 535
Cauraugh, J., 76, 94, 103, 132, 165, 179, 181, 184, 506, 571, 572, 573
Cavill, N., 232, 696, 709, 710, 712
Cazorla, G., 271
Cervello, E.M., 620
Cervone, D., 519
Chaffin, W.M., 165
Chah, D.O., 508
Chahal, P., 574, 575
Challis, R.E., 368
Chamberlin, C.J., 11, 89, 95, 121, 133, 212

Champion, H.R., 133
Chan, C.S., 791, 793
Chandler, C., 457
Chantal, Y., 405
Chaouloff, F., 747, 749
Chapman, M., 722
Charness, N., 46, 117, 175, 186, 189, 269, 270, 278
Chartland, J.M., 281, 673, 681
Chase, L.A., 396
Chase, M.A., 217, 340, 341, 342, 343, 344, 349, 352, 355, 356, 357, 358, 552, 555, 558, 615, 616, 625
Chase, W.G., 6, 9, 25, 43, 74, 117, 186, 193, 278
Chatillon, J.F., 229, 230
Chatzisarantis, N., 437, 461, 462, 465
Chaumeton, N., 614, 625
Cheadle, A., 732
Checa, G., 645
Chemers, M.M., 352, 353, 486
Chen, D., 76, 94, 104, 179, 181, 184
Chen, S.S., 531
Chernick, L., 242
Cherry, E.C., 67, 71
Chertok, F., 735
Chesney, A., 508
Chesson, C.V., 732
Cheyne, D., 156
Chi, D.M., 135
Chi, L., 400, 401, 420, 421, 422, 423, 424, 425, 434
Chi, M.T.H., 24, 25, 40, 41, 42, 43, 179, 182
Chickering, A., 679
Chidester, T.R., 499, 507, 508
Chiesi, H.L., 25, 45, 177
Chiu, C.Y., 460, 461, 462
Chivers, P., 76
Cho, S., 463
Chodzko-Zajko, W.J., 758, 759
Chogahara, M., 723
Choi, J., 212
Christen, J., 574, 575
Christensen, S., 6, 9, 11, 178, 182, 188, 820
Christina, R.W., 5, 12, 13, 14, 58, 212, 380
Chrysler, S.T., 135
Chung, T., 539
Chung, Y., 340, 355, 357
Church, G., 33, 37
Church, M.A., 435, 436
Churchland, P., 147, 156
Cibich, B.J., 67
Claessens, A., 771
Claeys, W., 242
Clark, D., 643, 744
Clark, J.E., 20
Clark, L.A., 406

Clark, R., 129
Clarke, H., 23
Clarke, J.R., 135
Clarke, S.G., 657, 658
Claytor, R.P., 641
Cleeremans, A., 129
Clifton, R.T., 552, 558
Clore, G.L., 643
Coady, W., 218
Coakley, J., 559, 609, 616, 677, 678, 680, 681, 682, 683
Coakley, L., 535
Cockerill, I.M., 7, 180, 181
Cockman, M., 591
Coday, M.C., 728, 729
Coddington, R.D., 770, 775
Coelho, A.J., 212
Coen, D., 747
Cogan, K.D., 535
Cohen, D.A., 773, 774
Cohen, E., 71, 72
Cohen, J., 75, 513, 741, 742
Cohen, L.H., 801
Cohen, M.E., 180
Cohen, M.J., 120
Cohen, N., 687
Cohen, R.D., 749
Cohen, S., 680, 728, 729, 741, 744, 787, 802
Cohn, P.J., 653
Cole, H.W., 69, 369
Colella, A., 518
Coleman, E., 758
Coleman, R., 608, 659
Coles, M.G.H., 367, 375
Colley, A., 145
Collingwood, T.R., 731
Collins, J.P., 132
Collins, R.L., 358
Colvin, C.R., 638
Combs, A., 153
Compas, B.E., 768
Condon, A., 178
Congdon, R., 721
Conkell, C., 661
Conlee, R.K., 676
Connell, J.P., 391, 393, 442
Connelly, S.L., 791
Conner, M., 700
Connolly, D., 752, 753
Connolly, T., 508
Connor, S.A., 59
Connors, B.W., 375, 378
Conrad, D., 164
Conrad, F.G., 128
Conroy, C., 688, 787
Conroy, D.E., 823, 824, 827
Constantine, M.G., 685
Converse, P.E., 636, 638
Conyne, R., 684

Cook, D.L., 254
Cook, M., 178
Cooke, C.J., 282, 558
Cooper, B., 594, 595
Cooper, B.B., 589
Cooper, B.L., 517
Cooper, H., 245, 623
Cooper, L., 243
Coote, D., 817, 818
Copeland, A.P., 730
Copeman, R., 179
Coppell, D.B., 622
Copper, C., 475, 476, 484, 531
Corbett, A.T., 128
Corbin, C., 395, 396, 397, 401, 550, 626, 740, 751, 756, 759
Corcoran, D., 179
Corcos, D.M., 5, 6, 164
Cornelius, A.E., 400, 789, 795, 797, 800
Corr, P.J., 451
Corti, B., 725
Costa, P.T., Jr., 242
Costill, D.L., 298, 363, 647, 650
Cota, A.A., 481, 485
Côté, C., 756, 757
Côté, J., 178, 183, 190, 249, 269, 275, 276, 277, 279, 280
Cotton, D., 625
Couch, J.V., 301
Courneya, K.S., 478, 554, 700, 701, 702, 703, 704, 705, 706, 712, 811
Court, M., 162, 166
Courtet, P., 58, 69, 778
Cousins, S.O., 723
Couture, R.T., 574, 575
Covington, M., 418, 431, 463
Cowart, V.S., 284
Cowden, R.D., 574, 575, 577
Cowen, N., 60
Cowen, R.L., 684
Cowley, A.W., 642, 747
Cox, D.N., 245
Cox, P.D., 215, 217, 230, 231
Cox, R.H., 293, 320, 327, 332
Cox, S., 642, 649, 752
Cox, T., 290, 330
Coyne, J.C., 770
Crace, R.K., 766
Craft, L.L., 639, 747, 748, 749
Craig, C.L., 720
Craig, J.C., 71, 72
Craighead, W.E., 749, 750, 756
Craik, K.H., 242, 248
Crassini, B., 75
Cratty, B.J., 7
Crawford, S., 213
Crespo, M., 434
Crews, D.J., 371, 373, 374, 571, 573, 577, 751

Crews, D.L., 59, 69
Crisp, F., 45, 46, 177, 178, 182, 187, 188, 224, 230
Crocker, P.R., 659, 743
Cronbach, L.J., 781
Crosby, J.V., 64
Cross, C.L., 167, 168
Crossman, E.R.F.W., 4, 66, 116, 117
Crossman, J., 788, 793, 794, 798, 799
Crouch, J.G., 642
Crowell, C.R., 504
Crowne, D.P., 393
Crowson, C.S., 791, 793, 794, 800
Cryan, P.O., 767, 769, 770
Csikszentmihalyi, M., 183, 269, 270, 273, 279, 280, 281, 283, 284, 285, 328, 329, 362, 390, 398, 636, 651, 652, 653, 654, 655, 656, 657, 658
Cuerrier, J.P., 404, 597
Cullen, J., 176, 190, 558
Culos-Reed, S.N., 697, 707
Culpepper, W.L., 795
Cumming, J.L., 536
Cummings, E., 674
Cummings, M.S., 571, 572, 578
Cunningham, S., 120, 218
Cupal, D.D., 530, 780, 796, 797
Curran, T., 69
Curry, L.A., 254
Curtis, B., 622, 685, 712, 713, 780
Curtis, J., 591, 683
Curtis, K.A., 463
Cury, F., 420, 422, 428, 434, 436, 439, 460, 461, 462
Cutrona, C.E., 450
Cuvillier, C., 282

Dacyshyn, A., 678, 679, 684
Dahl, N.H., 744
Dainis, A., 13
Dainty, D., 271
Dalhauser, M., 783
Dalkey, N.C., 636
Dallis, B., 329
Daly, J.M., 789, 794, 795, 801
Damos, D.L., 61, 64
Daniel, M., 747
Daniel, S., 178
Daniels, F.S., 13, 99, 370, 380
Daniels, J., 330, 365, 366, 381, 653, 655, 657
Danish, S., 281, 674
Dannenberg, A.L., 749
Dansereau, F., 486
Dantschik, A., 249
Danziger, K., 262
Darden, G.F., 215
Darlington, P.J., Jr., 36
Darracott, C., 623
Darragh, A., 325

Daugman, J.G., 151
Davey, M.E., 395
Davids, K., 12, 20, 70, 74, 144, 145, 146,
    147, 148, 151, 152, 153, 154, 156,
    157, 158, 159, 160, 161, 162, 163,
    164, 165, 166, 167, 174, 176, 179,
    180, 182, 183, 184, 188, 208, 210
Davidson, C., 452
Davidson, J.W., 117, 185, 269, 270, 272,
    273, 283, 285
Davidson, K.S., 291
Davidson, R.J., 161, 291, 302, 324, 334,
    375, 658
Davis, C., 239
Davis, D., 291, 299
Davis, H., 329, 591
Davis, J., 38, 185, 779, 782
Davis, K.E., 444, 445, 680
Davis, R., 61
Davis Hearn, M., 696, 714, 715, 720, 725
Daw, J., 516, 520
Dawe, S.W.L., 476
Dawes, H., 793
Dawley, D.J., 597
Dawson, K.A., 707
Day, D., 517
Day, E.A., 219
Day, L.J., 179
Deakin, J., 3, 7, 8, 45, 46, 74, 117, 175,
    176, 177, 178, 180, 182, 185, 186,
    187, 188, 190, 223, 224, 230, 277,
    278, 279
Dean, L.R., 674
Dearnaley, E.J., 75
Deaux, K., 447
De Boeck, P., 252, 254, 255, 256, 257,
    259, 261
De Busk, M., 598
DeCarlo, K.J., 657, 659
Decety, J., 125, 155, 156, 167, 532
deCharms, R., 393, 405, 510, 519
Deci, E., 389, 390, 391, 392, 393, 394,
    395, 396, 397, 398, 399, 424, 426,
    427, 465, 510, 519
De Cuyper, B., 239, 240, 245, 246, 254
Deecke, L., 155
Deeter, T.E., 348, 554, 555
Deffenbacher, J.L., 298, 306, 312
Deford, F., 674
DeGrazia, S., 658
De Groot, A.D., 74
De Groot, E.V., 427
De Groot, G., 247, 661
Dehaene, S., 63
Deisenroth, M.P., 69
Deisinger, J.A., 798
DeJaeger, D., 144
DeJong, W., 395
De Knop, P., 400, 561, 604
De Koning, J.J., 247, 661

Delaney, M., 773
Delgado, J., 91
Della-Grasta, M., 6, 12
Delman, R., 680
Del Rey, P., 75, 120
Del Rolan, N., 97
Deluty, R.H., 595
de Marées, H., 271, 272, 273, 274
DeMeersman, R.E., 811
Demorat, M., 463
Dempsey, J.M., 438, 619
Dempster, F.N., 41
den Brinker, B.P.L.M., 127, 130, 209
Denham, C.H., 355
Denis, J.L., 722, 729
Denis, M., 529
Dennis, K.A., 133, 134
Dennis, M.G., 23
Dennis, W., 23
deOliveria, A., 42
Depreeuw, E., 240, 254
Deridder, M., 178
Derri, V., 4, 177, 179, 180, 181, 182
Derrick, W., 59
Derscheid, G.L., 797
Deshaies, P., 181, 245, 246, 404, 597
Desharnis, R., 542, 756, 757
DeShon, R.P., 508
Després, J.P., 719, 720
De Tonac, A., 436
Detterman, D.K., 270, 284
Detweiler, M., 124
Deubel, H., 100
Deutsch, D., 71, 72
Deutsch, J.A., 71, 72
DeVries, H.A., 365, 743
De Vries, M.W., 638
DeWeert, W., 105
Dewey, D., 68
DeWitt, D.J., 779
Dialameh, N., 130
Diana, M., 351, 352
Dickens, T., 133
Dickson, J.F., 7
DiClemente, C.C., 710, 711
Diener, C., 637
Diener, E., 636, 637, 638, 639, 657, 659,
    662, 696, 761
Dienstbier, R., 303, 323, 325, 641
Digman, J.M., 242
Dillon, J.M., 75
DiLorenzo, T.M., 659
Dion, K.L., 481, 485
DiRocco, P., 32
Dishman, R.K., 87, 245, 545, 649, 650,
    651, 696, 711, 718, 719, 720, 723,
    728, 731, 748, 750
Dissanayake, P., 70, 182, 183, 189
Ditmar, T., 789, 793, 795, 797, 799, 800,
    801

Dittus, P., 249
Dixon, R.S., 504
Dixon, W.R., 123
Dobrantu, M., 425
Dobreva-Martinova, T., 405
Dobson, W., 794
Docheff, D.M., 94
Dodder, R., 598
Dodson, J.D., 293, 326, 331
Doffin, J.G., 6, 7
Doil, W., 180
Doiron, B.A.H., 747
Doll, L.S., 734
Dollinger, S.J., 395
Dom, R., 105
Doman, M., 504
Domholdt, E., 795
Domm, M.A., 795, 801
Donahue, J.A., 249
Donchin, E., 59, 124
Donovan, R.J., 725
Doody, S.G., 128, 177, 178, 211, 220
Doraiswamy, M., 749, 750, 756
Dorfman, H.A., 674
Dornier, L.A., 102
Dorsch, K.D., 476, 483
Doubleday, C., 457
Doussard-Roosevelt, J.A., 381
Dove, C., 216, 341
Dover, J., 250
Dowden, D., 796
Downey, P.J., 211, 224
Downie, G., 795
Dowrick, P.W., 205, 216, 231, 341
Doyle, L.A., 13, 380
Draper, D., 721
Draper, V., 798
Dreiling, A., 328
Drexler, J.M., 136
Driskell, J.E., 531
Driver, J., 60
Droppleman, L., 325, 639, 649, 753, 793
Druckman, D., 221, 334
Drummond, J.L., 404
Dubbels, T.K., 793
Ducharme, K., 503
DuCharme, K.A., 703
Duda, J., 166, 241, 246, 247, 254, 330,
    400, 401, 417, 419, 420, 421, 422,
    423, 424, 425, 426, 429, 430, 433,
    434, 435, 460, 461, 482, 506, 554,
    555, 595, 605, 606, 609, 612, 613,
    620, 621, 626, 687, 696, 795, 813
Dudink, A., 185
Duffy, E., 290, 293, 305, 320, 322
DuFresne, P., 823
Duhon, T.K., 794
Dumais, S.T., 309
Dummer, G.M., 615, 616, 625
Duncan, C., 721

Duncan, S.C., 626, 627
Duncan, T.E., 448, 450, 457
Dunham, P., 40, 41, 180
Dunlap, W.P., 758, 781
Dunn, A.L., 720, 728, 729
Dunn, J.C., 595
Dunn, J.G.H., 229, 230, 595
Dunn, T., 70, 182, 183, 189
Duplantie, J., 734
Durand, M., 178, 190, 420, 434, 439,
    460, 461, 462, 530, 531, 532, 541
Durand-Bush, N., 176, 185, 190, 269,
    276, 277, 279, 282, 283
Durkheim, E., 589
Durso-Cupal, D.D., 798, 800
Dusenbury, L., 718, 722, 723, 724, 733
Dutta, A., 121, 123, 124
Dutton, K.A., 397
Dweck, C., 276, 417, 418, 419, 421, 423,
    427, 430, 434, 436, 458, 460, 461,
    462, 463, 499, 523, 606
Dwyer, J.J.M., 396
Dyck, P., 756
d'Ydewalle, G., 177
Dyer, J.B., III, 642
Dyk, R., 75
Dykman, B.M., 432, 434
Dzewaltowski, D.A., 554, 642

Eagles, C., 745, 746
Earle, J.B., 369, 375
Earley, P., 351, 354, 508, 517, 518
Easterbrook, J., 161, 295, 306, 332,
    767
Eastman, C., 250, 534
Eastman, N.W., 791
Eaton, C.A., 712
Eaton, M., 640, 642, 643, 645
Eaton, W.O., 33, 36, 37, 38
Ebbeck, V., 205, 227, 230, 332, 596, 598,
    606, 620, 626, 627, 628
Ebbeling, C.B., 640
Ebersole, P., 652
Eccles, J., 426, 555, 605, 606, 607, 618,
    619, 621
Eccles-Parsons, J., 605, 606, 618, 619,
    621, 625, 627
Eckert, H.M., 29
Edelman, G., 145, 147, 148, 151, 153,
    161, 163, 165
Edgar, L., 812
Edwards, J.M., 120
Edwards, P., 70, 182, 183, 189
Edwards, R., 226, 503, 504, 517
Edwards, S., 185, 649, 744
Edwards, T., 298, 319, 325
Eghan, T., 96, 104
Eghrari, H., 392
Ehlers, A., 744
Eichenhofer, R.B., 795

Eimer, M., 377
Eisenberger, R., 270, 277
Eisman, B., 472
Eisner, E.J., 55
Eitzen, D.S., 625, 687
Ekblom, B., 38
Ekegren, G., 508
Ekkekakis, P., 746
Eklund, R., 213, 282, 290, 292, 429, 621,
    798
Ekman, P., 319, 375, 658
Elbaz, G., 500, 503, 505, 510
Elbert, T., 362, 364, 369
Elig, T., 448
Elkin, D., 677
Elko, P.K., 560
Ellickson, A.E., 248
Ellickson, K., 284, 328, 365, 646, 649,
    754, 756
Elliot, A.J., 435, 436
Elliott, B., 270, 672
Elliott, D., 12, 120, 130, 164, 166,
    178
Elliott, E.S., 499
Ellis, A., 560
Ellis, N.R., 758
Ellis, S.D., 125
Ells, J.G., 57
Elwell, J.L., 87
Emery, C.F., 758
Emmons, R.A., 392, 398, 579, 638, 696
Enberg, M.L., 179
Endler, N.S., 431
Engstrom, L.M., 604
Ennis, R., 683
Enns, L.R., 33, 36, 38
Enright, R., 601
Eom, H.J., 482
Epstein, L.H., 730
Epstein, M.L., 543
Epstein, S., 242, 319, 327, 381
Era, P., 376
Erbaugh, H., 748
Erbaugh, S.J., 503, 517
Érdi, P., 144, 146, 147, 150, 152, 155,
    157, 164
Erez, E., 99
Erez, M., 509, 516, 517
Erffmeyer, E.S., 222
Ericsson, K.A., 4, 46, 117, 174, 175,
    176, 185, 186, 190, 191, 193, 269,
    270, 275, 277, 278, 279, 280, 282,
    283, 362, 533
Eriksen, C.W., 70, 377
Eriksen, M.P., 723
Erikson, E., 678, 679
Erwin, C.I., 5, 12
Escarti, A., 620
Eshelman, S., 747
Espenschade, A.S., 31, 32, 39

Estabrooks, P., 478, 482, 487, 488,
    490
Eston, R., 752, 753
Etnier, J., 245, 373, 651, 752, 753, 758,
    759, 764
Ettinger, W., 719, 720
Etzel, E.F., 500, 503, 674, 791, 793,
    800
Evans, C.R., 481, 485
Evans, F.H., 516
Evans, J., 626
Evans, L., 788, 789, 800, 801
Evans, M.G., 707
Evans, R.G., 722
Everett, J.J., 622, 769, 775
Eves, F., 131
Ewart, C.K., 721
Ewing, M.E., 429, 608
Ey, S., 768
Eysenck, H.J., 243, 245, 585
Eysenck, M.W., 60, 65, 72, 161, 291,
    295, 303, 306, 307, 309
Eysenck, S.B.G., 243

Fabiani, M., 367, 375
Fahrbach, K., 340, 343, 344, 349
Fairall, D.G., 504
Fairchild, P.C., 799
Fairhurst, S.K., 711
Fairs, J., 179
Fairweather, M., 5
Faivre, I.A., 277
Falkstein, D.L., 780, 781, 793, 794, 800,
    802
Fallon, B.J., 791, 792, 793, 796, 800
Fallon, E.A., 372, 375, 378
Faloon, S., 117
Famose, J.P., 420, 428, 434, 439, 460,
    461, 462
Farh, J., 518
Farmer, B.B., 744
Farmer, M.E., 749
Farrell, M., 6, 12
Farrell, P.A., 642, 747
Farrow, D., 76
Faterson, H.F., 75
Faulmann, L., 754, 755
Fawcett, E.B., 729
Fawkner, H.J., 769, 770, 771, 773
Fazey, J., 161, 297, 299, 307
Fazio, F., 155, 156, 532
Fazio, R.H., 241, 242
Fehr, B., 251
Fehrenbach, P.A., 215
Feiring, D.C., 797
Feldman, D.H., 270, 284
Feldman, L., 688
Felner, J.M., 133
Felson, M.B., 619
Feltz, D., 610, 611, 823

Feltz, D.F., 355
Feltz, D.L., 13, 68, 125, 209, 212, 217, 220, 221, 223, 225, 226, 230, 246, 282, 340, 341, 342, 343, 344, 345, 348, 349, 350, 352, 353, 355, 356, 357, 358, 362, 534, 539, 540, 550, 553, 557, 558, 560, 612, 616, 625, 627, 677, 823, 826
Fenigstein, A., 242
Fenker, R.M., 534
Fenton, B.J., 744
Fenz, W.D., 319, 327, 381
Ferguson, R.H., 340, 552, 555, 558
Fermer, R., 745, 746
Fernandez, S.J., 222
Ferrari, M., 188, 230
Ferreira, M.B.R., 608
Festinger, L., 472
Fidell, L.S., 489
Fiebert, I.M., 798
Fields, J., 795
Fields, K.B., 773
Figlerski, L.B., 571, 572, 573
Filactakidou, A., 527, 798, 800
Filarski, K., 365, 366
Filby, W.C.D., 501
Fillingim, R.B., 811
Finch, A.E., 179, 181
Finch, C., 787
Finch, L., 250, 251, 252, 254, 290, 292, 299, 796
Finc, M.A., 811
Finke, R.A., 222
Finnie, S.B., 795, 798
Fiore, C., 713
Fiorito, P., 9, 178, 212
Fischman, M.G., 12, 95, 103
Fishbien, M., 697
Fishburne, G., 540, 543
Fisher, A.C., 13, 239, 242, 243, 244, 327, 795, 801
Fisher, A.G., 676
Fisher, A.T., 123
Fisher, J., 40, 729
Fisher, L., 730, 797
Fishman, S., 92, 96, 104
Fisicaro, S.A., 125
Fisk, A.D., 61
Fisk, L.M., 792, 794
Fiske, S.T., 444, 452
Fitch, H.L., 12
Fitter, M., 71
Fitts, P.M., 3, 4, 5, 10, 24, 39, 44, 128, 362, 367, 371
Fitzgerald, D., 177
Fitzgerald, L.G., 400
Fitzgerald, P., 129
Flanagan, J.C., 638
Flavell, J.H., 24, 224, 226
Flay, B.R., 725

Fleischer-Curtian, L.A., 810
Fleishman, E., 4, 5, 6, 128, 220, 461
Flett, G.L., 306, 431
Fleury, M., 6, 8, 9, 29, 39, 58, 74, 177, 178, 179, 182, 183, 188
Flint, F., 215, 230, 769, 770, 772, 773, 775, 776, 787
Flowers, J.H., 76, 129, 130
Flynn, B.C., 733
Flynn, M.G., 647, 650
Focht, B.C., 745
Fodor, J., 63, 151
Fogarty, G., 811, 820
Fogel, A., 379
Folkins, C.H., 758
Folkman, S., 430, 433, 498, 615, 641, 680
Fomin, V., 379
Ford, D.H., 567
Ford, I., 789, 792, 798, 799, 800, 801
Ford, J.K., 427
Ford, I., 798
Ford, M.E., 389
Ford, S., 55, 60, 68, 330, 402, 655
Foreman, P.E., 795, 801
Forester, S., 723
Forman, L.M., 749, 750, 756
Forrester, A.W., 768
Forsterling, F., 462, 463
Forsyth, L.H., 232, 709, 710, 712
Fortalage, L., 640
Fortier, M.S., 390, 392, 393, 398, 399, 400, 401, 402, 403, 404, 409, 465
Fortney, V.L., 23
Forwell, L., 530
Fournier, J.F., 399, 402, 404, 409, 571, 572, 573
Fowler, C., 66, 99, 501
Fowler, P.J., 802
Fox, K., 239, 396, 399, 400, 401, 407, 423, 425, 439, 450, 457, 458, 460, 461, 462, 574, 576, 606, 626, 756, 757
Fox, N.A., 362, 366
Fox, P.W., 105
Frackowiak, R.S.J., 155, 156
Frank, A.W., 662
Frank, M.G., 658
Franklin, B.A., 719, 720
Franks, I.M., 96, 131, 184, 217, 341
Franz, E.A., 6
Franz, S.I., 747
Frautschi, N.M., 215
Frazer, M.B., 380
Frederick, C.M., 393, 400, 402, 404
Frederick, E., 519
Freedman, O., 309
Freeman, G., 817
Freeman, J., 284
Freeman, W.J., 146, 148, 152, 153, 155, 156, 161

Frehlich, S.G., 103, 165, 176, 179, 184, 188
French, K.E., 4, 5, 10, 11, 12, 20, 33, 34, 35, 38, 41, 43, 44, 45, 46, 177, 179, 182, 189, 190, 191, 223, 224, 225
French, S.N., 571, 578
Freud, S., 389
Freudenberg, N., 731
Frew, D.R., 680, 681
Frey, R.D., 534
Fridinger, F., 232, 709, 710, 712, 718, 722, 723, 724, 733
Fried, R., 643, 646
Friedenreich, C.M., 702
Friedlander, S., 680
Friedman, A., 63
Friedman, E., 640, 642, 643, 645
Friend, R., 291
Frierman, S.H., 501, 503, 505, 510
Friesen, W.V., 319, 375, 658
Frieze, I., 445, 446, 448, 618
Frijda, N.H., 658
Friston, K., 155, 156
Frith, C.D., 155, 156
Frohlich, K.L., 728
Fronske, H., 42
Frost, R.O., 432
Fry, M.D., 423, 606, 609, 626
Fry, R.A., 215
Fuchs, A., 156
Fujita, A., 180
Fukami, K., 180
Fullerton, T.D., 472
Furman, W., 624
Furnham, A., 451
Furrer, D.M., 509
Furst, C.J., 74
Furst, D., 447, 448, 450
Furst, M., 557
Futterman, R., 605, 606, 618, 621, 625, 627

Gaboriault, G., 271
Gabriel, L.T., 270, 284
Gabriel, T.J., 246, 247, 248, 281, 283, 558
Gabriele, T.E., 120, 126, 533
Gaesser, G.A., 719, 720
Gaffney, F.A., 744
Gagné, F., 270
Gagné, R.M., 220
Gagnon, A., 392, 393
Gahimer, J., 795
Gaines, L., 126
Galambos, R., 59
Galanter, E., 567
Galbo, H., 750
Galbraith, G.C., 366, 373
Gallagher, J., 20, 21, 25, 40, 41, 42, 43, 44, 108, 224, 225, 229

Gallahue, D.L., 29
Gallup, G., Jr., 643
Gallwey, W.T., 646
Galvan, Z.J., 504
Gammage, K.L., 311, 529, 537, 541, 542, 543
Gangemi, P.F., 181
Gangestad, S., 243
Gannon, T.L., 373
Gano-Overway, L.A., 423, 433, 435
Gansneder, D., 536
Gara, M., 254
Garber, C.E., 719, 720
Garber, T.B., 301
Garcia, A.W., 344, 348, 349, 659
Garcia-Merita, M.L., 222
Gardetto, D., 789, 802
Gardner, D., 476, 485, 597
Gardner, F., 673, 674
Garfield, S., 680, 685
Garland, H., 500, 501, 503, 508, 523
Garner-Holman, G., 550, 552, 553, 554, 556, 557, 559, 561
Garner-Holman, M., 246, 249, 562
Garrick, J.G., 766
Garstka, M.L., 518
Garthwaite, T.L., 642, 747
Garvin, A.W., 745
Garza, D.L., 342, 343, 345, 350, 560
Gat, I., 239
Gaudette, G.M., 402, 403, 404
Gauthier, J., 814
Gauvin, L., 245, 395, 396, 519, 542, 719, 730, 734, 752
Gayton, W.F., 343, 344, 345, 551
Gearhart, M., 69
Gebhardt, S.M., 645, 745
Gebhart, J.A., 226
Gecas, V., 618
Gehrman, C., 659
Geisler, G.W.W., 345
Geisler, P.R., 770, 775
Gel'fand, I.M., 379
Geller, E.S., 517
Genest, M., 814
Gentile, A.M., 3, 86, 127, 129, 210, 647
Gentner, D.R., 164
George, A., 744
George, L.K., 682, 741, 758
George, T.R., 217, 340, 341, 345, 349, 350, 352, 358, 552, 555, 558
Georgeson, M., 146
Georgiadis, M., 435
Georgiadis, N., 598
Geraci, J.C., 659
Gerkovich, M., 300, 330
Gernigon, C., 422
Geron, E., 271, 824
Gerson, R.F., 647
Gessaroli, M.E., 659

Getty, D., 589
Gevins, A., 362, 363, 369, 375
Ghesquiere, K., 624
Giabrone, C.P., 327
Giacobbi, P., 246, 550, 552, 553, 554, 556, 557, 559, 561
Giacobbi, P.R., Jr., 529, 535, 537
Giannini, J., 355, 502, 503, 506, 554, 559
Gibbons, S., 598, 627, 628
Gibson, C.B., 351, 354
Gibson, E.J., 74
Gibson, J.J., 76
Gilbert, G.G., 33, 37
Gilbourne, D., 795
Gill, D., 293, 295, 298, 299, 343, 346, 347, 348, 350, 403, 552, 554, 555, 558, 571, 573, 577, 610, 746, 826
Gillespie, R.L., 810
Gilley, W.F., 120
Gilligan, C., 591
Gillis, J.H., 249
Gimbel, B., 271
Gines, S.D., 810
Girardin, Y., 10
Girouard, Y., 57, 58
Gladwell, M., 3
Glamser, F.D., 185
Glanz, K., 722, 723, 724
Glaser, R., 182
Glasgow, R.E., 718, 728, 735
Glasser, W., 646, 650
Glassford, G.R., 734
Glassow, R., 23
Gleason, A., 457
Gleim, G.W., 754, 755
Glencross, D., 6, 9, 11, 57, 60, 64, 67, 75, 144, 177, 178, 183
Glenn, S.D., 605, 626, 627
Gleser, J., 748
Globus, G.G., 147, 149, 150, 151, 154, 156, 157, 167
Gloor, P., 369
Gluck, L., 793, 794, 799
Godin, G., 542, 699, 701, 756, 757
Goerner, S., 153
Goff, S.B., 605, 606, 618, 621, 625, 627
Goldberg, L.R., 242, 248, 249, 251
Goldstein, H., 721
Goldstein, M., 89, 713
Goldston, S.E., 644
Goleman, D., 319, 324
Golembiewski, R., 472, 477
Gomez-Mesa, M., 179, 183
Gonda, J., 680
Good, T., 623
Goodale, M.A., 69, 144, 145, 167
Goode, S., 120
Goodenough, D.R., 75
Goodman, R.M., 725, 731, 732

Goodwin, J., 94, 101
Gopher, D., 56, 61, 62, 65, 66, 125
Gopher, L.D., 134
Gorbett, F.J., 679, 680, 681, 685
Gordin, R., 794
Gordon, M.S., 133
Gordon, N.B., 93
Gordon, N.F., 720
Gordon, S., 574, 576, 577, 677, 678, 679, 680, 681, 682, 683, 685, 686, 789, 792, 793, 794, 798, 800, 801
Gorely, T., 574, 576, 577
Gorman, D.M., 721
Gorman, J.M., 744
Gormly, J., 242
Gorsuch, R.I., 291, 302, 308
Gorsuch, R.L., 324, 328, 348, 696, 742
Goss, J., 755, 779
Goss, S., 543
Gossard, D., 814
Gothan, H.J., 659
Gotlib, I.H., 641
Gottfried, A.E., 402
Gottlieb, M.J., 93
Gottsdanker, R., 66
Goudas, M., 396, 399, 401, 403, 404, 407, 420, 434, 439, 452, 574, 576, 798, 800
Gould, D., 161, 205, 211, 216, 217, 230, 250, 251, 252, 254, 282, 290, 292, 293, 294, 295, 296, 297, 298, 299, 303, 304, 306, 319, 320, 321, 322, 325, 327, 328, 329, 331, 332, 340, 355, 357, 389, 398, 429, 506, 507, 509, 535, 552, 554, 558, 559, 610, 611, 612, 614, 615, 616, 621, 623, 673, 674, 789, 791, 792, 795, 797, 798, 799, 800, 801
Goulet, C., 9, 177, 178, 179, 182, 183, 188
Graham, D., 133
Graham, K.C., 10, 11, 45, 177, 182
Graham, S., 6, 9, 45, 74, 176, 177, 182, 223, 457
Granito, V., 475
Grant, A., 167, 184, 212
Grasha, A.F., 68
Gratton, G., 367, 375
Graves, J., 511
Gray, J.A., 451
Gray, S.W., 222
Graybiel, A., 7, 74, 180
Graydon, J., 179, 501
Greathouse, C., 351, 352
Green, L., 530, 719, 721, 722, 723, 724, 729, 731, 732, 733
Green, P.R., 146
Green, S.B., 704
Green, S.L., 794

Green, T.D., 76, 129, 130
Green-Demers, I., 282, 283, 392, 405, 571, 572, 573
Greendorfer, S.L., 617, 672, 674, 675, 677, 678, 679, 680, 681, 682, 683, 684, 686
Greene, D., 390, 395
Greene, P.H., 12
Green-Emrich, A., 463
Greenleaf, C., 282, 340, 355, 357, 435, 558, 560
Greenough, W.T., 362, 363, 366
Greenshields, H., 427
Greenwald, A.G., 62
Greer, N.L., 6, 12
Gregory, M., 61
Grenier, M.N., 403, 404
Grèzes, J., 155, 167
Griest, J.H., 762
Griffee, T.I., 401
Griffey, M.S., 768
Griffin, J., 449
Griffin, N.S., 550
Griffin, S., 638
Griffith, P., 811
Grigsby, W.C., 499, 507, 508
Grindley, G.C., 87
Grolnick, W.S., 391, 393, 442
Grood, E.S., 795
Gross, J., 457
Gross, J.B., 449, 451, 610
Gross, J.D., 649
Gross, N., 472
Gross, R.T., 757
Grossman, H.Y., 791, 793
Grosz, H.H., 744
Grouzet, F.M.E., 390, 398, 401, 409
Grove, J.R., 246, 254, 281, 282, 448, 449, 450, 451, 456, 484, 557, 642, 646, 647, 650, 651, 652, 654, 655, 657, 677, 678, 679, 680, 681, 682, 683, 685, 686, 789, 791, 793, 794, 796, 797
Grove, R., 325, 328, 330, 355, 554, 571, 572, 578
Grozelle, C., 743
Gruber, J.J., 756, 757
Grusec, J., 216, 224
Guadagnoli, M., 100, 102
Guarino, P.A., 457
Guastello, S.J., 299
Guay, F., 392, 393, 397, 398, 401, 405, 406, 408, 409
Guay, M., 102, 103
Guest, M.A., 135
Guézennec, Y., 178
Guillet, E., 422
Guinan, D., 558
Guivernau, M., 423
Gully, S.M., 427

Gurfinkel, V.S., 164, 379
Gurman, A.S., 762
Gushue, N.R., 571, 572, 573
Gustafson, A.B., 642, 747
Gustin, W.C., 278
Gutin, B., 327
Guy, D.E., 108
Guyatt, G., 741
Guzman, J.F., 620
Guzzo, R.A., 351
Gyarfas, I., 718, 733, 734
Gyurcsik, N.C., 696, 701, 706, 707

Haan, N., 589, 590, 592, 627
Haase, H., 178, 246
Haber, R.N., 300, 301
Hackfort, D., 240
Haddad, S., 728
Haddock, G., 433
Haerle, R.K., Jr., 679, 680, 682, 684
Hagen, J., 42
Hager, J.C., 658
Haggard, P., 158
Haggert, J., 767
Hagler, R.W., 90
Hahm, C., 597
Haier, R.J., 369, 370
Haken, H., 12, 154
Hale, A.S., 747
Hale, B.D., 532, 539
Hales, R., 747
Hall, A.K., 219
Hall, C., 120, 126, 222, 311, 334, 529, 530, 531, 532, 533, 534, 535, 536, 537, 538, 540, 541, 542, 543, 544, 545, 557, 560
Hall, E., 591
Hall, E.E., 746
Hall, E.G., 222, 812
Hall, H., 421, 423, 425, 426, 427, 429, 432, 501, 503, 504, 505, 506, 508, 510, 520, 817
Hall, K.G., 89, 95, 120, 129
Hallam, J., 574, 577
Hallden, D., 683
Hallé, M., 74, 178
Haller, S., 99
Halliwell, W., 217, 395
Halliwell, W.L., 245
Halliwell, W.R., 395, 396, 399, 402, 404, 409, 519
Halverson, L.E., 23, 35, 228
Hamacheck, D.E., 431
Hamel, J., 344, 347, 401
Hamill, G., 329
Hamilton, G.V., 747
Hamilton, P., 293, 294, 299, 320
Hamilton, V., 332
Hamilton, W., 53
Hammond, N.V., 131

Hampson, S.E., 248, 249, 251
Han, M., 373, 374, 651, 750, 758, 759
Hancock, P.A., 135, 212
Hancock, T., 733
Hand, M.J., 209, 218
Handel, S., 457
Handford, C., 144, 145, 146, 152, 154, 158, 163, 165, 166, 167
Haney, C.J., 345, 349
Hanin, Y., 239, 240, 241, 260, 294, 295, 304, 319, 320, 325, 328, 329, 824
Hankes, D., 554
Hanks, H., 452, 453, 454, 455
Hanmer, T., 591
Hanrahan, S., 163, 281, 282, 447, 448, 449, 450, 451, 650
Hansen, L., 608
Hanson, A.R., 230, 231
Hanson, D.L., 292
Hanson, R.A., 215, 217, 230, 231
Hanson, S.J., 770, 771, 772, 775
Hansson, T., 239
Hanton, S., 297, 298, 301, 302, 303, 333, 502, 556, 558
Hanvey, T., 184
Harackiewicz, J.M., 395, 397, 510
Harbeson, M.M., 64
Hard, D.H., 452
Harden, R.M., 132
Hardingham, C., 76
Hardman, K., 243, 244, 245
Hardy, C.J., 108, 511, 681, 766, 770, 775, 780, 782, 788, 793, 794, 798, 811, 812
Hardy, J., 311
Hardy, L., 131, 161, 221, 250, 254, 292, 293, 294, 295, 296, 297, 298, 299, 301, 302, 303, 304, 305, 306, 307, 308, 309, 319, 320, 321, 322, 324, 325, 328, 329, 331, 332, 404, 420, 422, 464, 502, 506, 507, 529, 530, 534, 535, 536, 543, 545, 560, 788, 789, 800, 801
Hare, N., 677, 680, 682, 683
Harel, Y., 787
Harger, G., 329
Harkins, S., 475, 508, 511
Harlow, L., 713, 756
Harmer, P., 392, 420
Harold, R., 426, 555, 605, 606, 607, 618, 619, 621
Harper, C.J., 228
Harre, D., 271, 272
Harris, A., 230, 561, 645, 658, 659, 663
Harris, D., 133, 134, 282, 539, 778
Harris, K.J., 729
Harris, K.S., 56, 365
Harris, L.R., 145
Harrison, J., 734

Harrison, R., 823
Harrison, S., 508
Hart, E.A., 662
Hart, J.A., 539
Hart, L.E., 741
Hart, S., 58, 421
Harter, N., 116
Harter, S., 223, 224, 390, 550, 554, 605, 606, 612, 615, 617, 618, 621, 623, 624, 625, 626, 627, 813
Hartlage, S., 458
Hartman, A., 796
Hartman, B.G., 597
Hartman, I., 505, 510
Hartmann, D.P., 247, 249, 624
Hartup, W.W., 624, 625
Harvey, J.H., 444, 683, 685, 686
Harwood, C., 420, 421, 435
Hasbrook, C.A., 554, 606, 618, 624, 626, 627
Haskell, W.L., 719, 720, 743, 756, 757
Haskins, M.J., 179, 597
Haslam, I., 529, 530, 532, 536, 542
Haslam, R.W., 246, 247, 248
Hassmén, P., 239, 646
Hastings, D.W., 189, 190
Hatfield, B.D., 13, 367, 368, 370, 371, 372, 373, 374, 375, 377, 378, 380, 381, 641, 650, 742, 743, 744, 745, 746
Hattie, J.A., 448, 450, 451
Hattrup, K., 352, 486
Hatze, H., 98
Hatzigeorgeadis, A., 430
Haubenstricker, J., 29, 30, 31, 33, 34, 35, 610, 611
Haufler, A.J., 371, 372
Haupt, T.D., 652, 654
Hausenblas, H., 357, 434, 484, 529, 531, 534, 537, 538, 541, 542, 544, 545, 699, 701, 729
Hautala, R.M., 124
Havighurst, R.J., 674
Havlicek, I., 271, 272
Hawkins, B., 12
Hawkins, H.L., 5, 6, 66
Hawkins, R.B., 796
Hawkins, R.P., 249
Haworth, J.T., 657, 658
Hay, J., 183, 270, 275, 276, 277
Hay, L., 29, 39
Hayashi, C.T., 482, 606
Hayashi, S., 246, 356, 550, 552, 553, 554, 556, 557, 559, 561
Hayes, A., 3, 117, 175, 176, 185, 186, 190, 277, 278, 279
Hayes, B.E., 430
Hayes, S.C., 247, 517
Hays, K.F., 639, 640, 643
Hayward, C., 744

Haywood, K.M., 8, 29, 33, 177, 180
Hazeltine, R.E., 6
He, C.X., 745, 753
Head, A., 745, 746
Headrick, B., 677
Healy, M., 721
Heard, N.P., 246, 254, 557
Heath, G.W., 719, 720
Heath, K., 57
Heatherton, T.F., 567, 720, 735
Hebb, D., 293, 320
Hebert, E., 97, 214
Heck, T.A., 661
Hecker, J.E., 535, 539
Heckhausen, H., 518
Hedges, L., 781
Hedlund, S.A., 718, 722, 723, 724, 733
Heemsoth, C., 177
Heft, H., 151
Heider, F., 444, 445, 456
Heil, J., 677, 793
Heitman, R.J., 120
Helledy, K.I., 796
Heller, K.A., 270
Hellickson, R.O., 246
Hellison, D., 598
Hellstedt, J.C., 621
Helms, P., 38
Helsen, W., 46, 70, 74, 96, 117, 175, 176, 177, 179, 181, 182, 183, 184, 185, 186, 188, 190, 195, 270, 277
Hemery, D., 304
Hempel, W.E., 4, 5, 128
Henderson, K.J., 432
Henderson, S.E., 9
Henert, S.E., 789, 802
Heniff, C.B., 789, 802
Henry, F.M., 5, 6, 12
Henschen, K.P., 688
Herald, M.M., 574, 575
Heriza, C.B., 25
Herman, S., 749, 750, 756
Hersen, M., 247
Hesley, J.W., 242
Hettinger, L.J., 133
Heuer, H., 56, 60, 66
Hewitt, J., 657
Hewitt, P.L., 431, 440
Hewstone, M., 444
Heyman, S.R., 243, 672, 677
Heyward, V.H., 449
Hiatt, E., 810
Hick, W.E., 5, 10
Hickey, J., 592
Hicks, R.A., 769, 775, 776
Higgins, A., 588, 592
Higgins, E.T., 455, 483
Higgins, G.A., 133
Higgins, T., 13, 209

Highlen, P., 246, 247, 248, 282, 536, 558
Hill, A.B., 448, 457, 750
Hill, J.O., 659
Hill, K.L., 571, 572
Hill, P., 674, 675, 680, 682, 684
Hill, T., 129
Hillard, N., 674
Hilligan, P., 130
Hillman, C.H., 372, 374, 375, 378
Hillmer-Vogel, U., 744
Hillyard, S.A., 59, 377
Hinkle, S., 773
Hinrichs, R.N., 33, 39
Hinsz, V., 484, 489, 511, 517
Hinton, G.E., 63
Hiralall, A.S., 518
Hirata, C., 300, 330
Hird, J.S., 125, 530, 531, 532
Hirst, W., 64, 65, 66
Hitch, G., 161
Ho, L., 99
Hobson, M.L., 751
Hochstetler, S.A., 811
Hockey, G., 320
Hockey, G.R., 293, 294, 299
Hodgdon, J.A., 742, 747, 752, 756
Hodge, K., 355, 554, 559
Hodge, T., 178, 182, 186
Hodges, L., 354
Hodges, N., 3, 46, 117, 127, 130, 131, 175, 176, 185, 186, 189, 190, 269, 277, 278, 279, 533
Hoffer, R., 672
Hoffman, H.G., 136
Hoffman, J.E., 65
Hoffman, J.J., 363
Hoffman, S., 178, 179, 229
Hoffmann, P., 747
Hogan, J., 107
Hogan, T.D., 771, 772, 773
Hokanson, R.G., 799
Holding, D.H., 122
Holland, G.J., 363
Hollenbeck, J.R., 508, 517
Hollingsworth, B., 500, 503
Holloway, S., 674
Holman, C.D., 725
Holmes, A., 687
Holmes, T.H., 767, 768, 769, 782
Holroyd, K.A., 332
Holroyd, T., 156
Holtgrave, D.R., 734
Holton, J.N., 180
Holtzbauer, R., 509
Hom, H., 423, 425, 606, 620
Hong, Y.Y., 460, 461, 462
Hooper, S.L., 650
Hopson, B., 675
Horan, J.J., 125, 530, 531, 532

Horn, T., 230, 251, 438, 554, 561, 605, 606, 607, 611, 614, 616, 618, 619, 623, 626, 627
Horodyski, M., 795
Horowitz, M.J., 685
Horsfall, J.S., 244
Höss, M., 131
Houck, M.R., 65
Houlston, D.R., 177
House, R.J., 352
Housh, T.J., 365
Housner, L.D., 10, 190, 191, 221
Houston, C.S., 758
Hovell, M.F., 718
Howard, D.V., 128
Howard, G.S., 504
Howard, J.H., Jr., 128
Howarth, C., 9, 179
Howe, B., 458, 505, 510, 623
Howe, M., 117, 185, 269, 270, 272, 273, 283, 285, 672, 673, 674, 675, 676, 677, 678, 679, 683, 685
Howell, D.C., 768
Hoyle, R.H., 427, 621
Hoza, B., 625
Hrycaiko, D., 249, 504
Huang, Y., 284
Huba, G.J., 245
Hubbard, A.W., 8, 10, 12, 177
Huber, V.L., 517
Huddleston, S., 177, 178, 610
Hudley, C., 463
Huether, G., 161
Huffman, S.D., 135
Hughes, B., 11, 53, 54, 61, 63
Hughes, M., 747
Hughes, P.K., 181
Hughes, R., 133, 723
Hulin, C.L., 517
Hull, C.L., 92, 326, 389
Hulse, S.H., 284
Hume, K.M., 799
Humphrey, E., 327, 425, 426
Humphrey, K.G., 145
Humphreys, M.S., 299, 305, 306
Humphries, C.A., 20, 44, 45, 223, 500, 501
Hung, T.M., 367, 368, 377
Hunt, B., 622
Hunt, E., 249
Hunt, J., 787, 823
Hunt, M.B., 181
Hunt, U.V., 332
Hunt, V., 295
Hunter, A., 246
Hunter, J.E., 499, 510
Husak, W.S., 120
Huston, L., 595
Hutchings, C., 291, 299
Hutchinson, S., 518

Hutslar, S., 623
Hutton, D.H., 825
Hyde, J.S., 594
Hyman, R., 10

Ievleva, L., 797
Ihle, K., 793
Imanaka, K., 61
Imber, L.G., 308
Imlay, G., 328
Imwold, C.H., 178
Ingham, A., 511
Ingledew, D., 393, 403, 404, 465
Ingvaldsen, R.P., 167, 168
Ingvar, D., 532
Inomata, K., 220
Irizarry-Lopez, V.M., 12
Irvine, S.H., 270
Isaac, A., 532, 535
Isaac, B., 36
Isaacs, K.R., 362, 363
Isaacs, L.D., 29, 33, 179, 181, 185
Ishikura, T., 220
Ismail, A.H., 750
Iso-Ahola, S.E., 375, 446, 447
Issenberg, S.B., 133
Ivancevich, J.M., 499
Ivry, R., 5, 6, 284
Iwane, H., 718, 733, 734
Izzo, C.M., 798, 799

Jablin, F.M., 681
Jaccard, J., 249
Jack, R., 178
Jackson, A., 355, 396, 497, 500, 501, 502, 503, 505, 506, 507, 508, 509, 510, 513, 523, 535, 554, 557
Jackson, B., 308
Jackson, C., 68
Jackson, D.W., 773, 796
Jackson, J.M., 511
Jackson, M., 179
Jackson, S., 240, 241, 250, 251, 252, 254, 282, 290, 292, 299, 330, 398, 402, 423, 651, 652, 653, 654, 655, 656, 657
Jacobs, B.L., 748, 749, 750
Jacobs, G.A., 696, 742
Jacobs, J.E., 607
Jacobson, E., 282, 539
Jagacinski, C.M., 609, 612
Jagacinski, C.W., 813, 814
Jagacinski, R.J., 121, 123, 124
Jakicic, J.M., 720
Jakubowski, P., 681
Jambor, E.A., 96
James, L.R., 352
James, P.T., 812
James, W., 53, 365, 497
Jamieson, J., 793, 794, 799

Jancarik, A., 272
Jäncke, L., 284
Janelle, C., 3, 67, 103, 117, 165, 166, 176, 179, 185, 188, 269, 278, 279, 310, 333, 372, 374, 375, 378, 778
Janis, I.L., 711
Janssen, J.J., 540
Jaremko, M., 685
Jarrett, H., 773
Jasper, H.H., 367
Jastrow, O., 53
Jeannerod, M., 125, 147, 155, 156, 532
Jeffers, K.E., 800
Jeffery, R.W., 221, 718, 722, 723, 724, 733, 735
Jehn, K., 511
Jenkin, M., 145
Jennings, J.R., 59
Jensen, J.L., 21, 26
Jensen, R.K., 38
Jentsch, F., 134
Jette, M., 744
Jevne, R.F.J., 791, 792, 801
Jick, T., 290
Jin, P., 642, 643, 645, 649
Jobin, J., 756, 757
Joch, V.W., 180
John, E.R., 369
John, O.P., 242, 248, 249, 251, 552
Johns, D.P., 611
Johnson, C., 518
Johnson, G.B., 825
Johnson, H., 325, 680
Johnson, J., 768, 769, 811
Johnson, M.F., 659
Johnson, M.L., 597
Johnson, P., 240, 533
Johnson, S., 245, 503, 756
Johnson, U., 793, 796, 797
Johnson, W.L., 136
Johnson, W.R., 825
Johnson-Laird, P.N., 147
Johnston, B., 333
Johnston, K.A., 637, 638
Johnston, L.H., 792, 793, 798, 799, 800
Johnston, W.L., 180
Johnston-O'Connor, E.J., 509
Jokl, E., 7, 74, 180
Jones, B., 144, 145, 158, 163, 166, 167
Jones, C.M., 8, 179, 212
Jones, D., 787
Jones, E.E., 444, 445, 452, 680
Jones, G., 131, 162, 309, 320, 321, 322, 325, 329, 331, 332, 333, 464, 501, 502, 503, 504, 556, 558, 772, 793, 801
Jones, G.B., 327
Jones, G.J., 250, 254

Jones, J.G., 290, 293, 294, 295, 296, 297, 298, 299, 301, 302, 303, 304, 305, 306, 309, 506
Jones, K., 721
Jones, M.B., 271, 272
Jones, M.G., 71
Jones, R.D., 450
Jones, W., 652, 654
Jonides, J., 66
Jordan, J.A., 219
Jordan, P., 672
Joseph, J., 712, 713
Josephs, L., 756
Jourden, F., 460, 461
Jowdy, D.P., 281, 282, 334

Kabat-Zinn, J., 645
Kaczala, C.M., 605, 606, 618, 619, 621, 625, 627
Kaczor, L.M., 535, 539
Kahanov, L., 799
Kahle, J., 395
Kahn, R., 672, 674, 676
Kahneman, D., 56, 60, 62, 66, 72, 637, 638, 657, 659, 662
Kail, R., 24, 39, 41
Kaiser, R.H., 134
Kakuyama, T., 516
Kalhoff, R.K., 747
Kalin, N.H., 755
Kalinowski, A.G., 278
Kalkhoff, R.K., 642
Kaminski-da-Rosa, V., 684
Kandel, E.R., 379
Kane, J.E., 243
Kane, T.D., 346, 349, 504, 571, 572, 573
Kanfer, F.H., 567
Kanfer, R., 249, 251, 509, 517
Kanner, A.D., 770
Kant, I., 150
Kantowitz, B.H., 62
Kaplan, A., 417, 418, 421, 422, 435, 436
Kaplan, G.A., 749
Kaplan, R.M., 636, 718, 735, 787
Karageorghis, C., 302, 535, 656
Karau, S.J., 475
Karlin, L., 62, 105
Karno, M., 741
Karoly, P., 566, 567, 571, 579, 720
Karp, S.A., 75
Karren, R.J., 499, 507, 508, 518, 520
Karst, T.O., 680
Karteroliotis, C., 295, 299
Kashdan, M.S., 181
Kasimatis, M., 461
Kasper, P., 59
Katch, F.I., 363, 371
Katch, V.L., 363, 371
Kates, J.L., 798
Katon, W., 747

Katzir, T., 270, 284
Kauffmann, S.A., 146, 152, 158
Kaufman, C.R., 133
Kausek, J., 773
Kavussanu, M., 400, 417, 420, 424, 425, 426, 434, 571, 573, 577
Kay, H., 87
Kearsley, N., 642, 649
Keefe, D.E., 430
Keefe, F.J., 99, 105
Keele, S.W., 5, 6, 54, 57, 62, 66, 69, 71, 284, 308
Keeler, B., 279, 605, 607, 815
Keh, N.C., 89, 92
Keil, D., 147, 152
Keller, L.P., 7
Keller, R.T., 472
Kelley, G., 742
Kelley, H.H., 444, 445, 448, 452, 607, 612, 613, 680
Kelly, A.E., 535
Kelso, J.A.S., 56, 130, 132, 144, 146, 147, 148, 152, 154, 155, 156, 157, 158, 160, 164, 167, 365, 379
Kemery, E.R., 781
Kemper, H.C.G., 719, 769, 770, 771, 773, 776, 781, 782
Kendal, P.C., 782
Kendall, M.J., 745, 746
Kendler, K.S., 747
Kendzierski, D., 657, 659
Kennedy, J.A., 40, 44
Kennedy, R.S., 64, 136, 758
Kennedy, T.M., 121, 124
Kenny, D.A., 351, 483, 484, 485, 486, 702, 707, 781
Kenrick, D.T., 242, 249
Keogh, J.F., 550
Kephart, N., 758
Kerick, S.E., 375
Kerlirzin, Y., 177, 183
Kernan, M.G., 507
Kernodle, M.W., 97
Kerr, A., 421, 425, 426, 427, 429, 432
Kerr, B., 4
Kerr, G., 678, 679, 684, 770, 771, 772, 779
Kerr, J., 300, 330, 331, 646
Kerr, N.L., 511
Kerr, R., 40, 41, 271
Kerr, T., 117, 189, 190
Kessler, R.C., 747
Kestenbaum, R., 62
Kettle, R.D., 517
Keutzer, C.S., 654
Keys, C., 735
Khatri, P., 749, 750, 756
Kickbush, I., 721
Kidd, T., 591
Kilik, L., 481, 485

Killpatrick, F.P., 247
Kim, J., 103, 222, 540
Kim, M.-S., 423, 433, 434
Kimble, G.A., 60
Kimiecik, J., 330, 402, 423, 438, 607, 619, 645, 653, 655, 657, 658, 659, 661, 663
Kimmel, S.K., 574, 576
King, A.C., 659, 681, 718, 719, 720, 722, 723, 724, 728, 729, 732, 733, 743, 756, 757
King, K., 249
King, L.A., 792, 794
King, R., 744
Kingston, K.M., 309, 422, 502, 506, 507, 560
Kinney, E., 811
Kino-Québec, 734
Kinsella-Shaw, J., 146, 152, 156, 157
Kinsman, R.A., 812
Kioumourtzoglou, E., 4, 177, 179, 180, 181, 182, 500, 518
Kippers, V., 163
Kirk, D., 657, 678
Kirkby, R., 769, 771
Kirkcaldy, B.D., 574, 575
Kirkendall, D.R., 591
Kirker, B., 820
Kirsanoff, M.T., 775
Kirsch, I., 814
Kirschenbaum, D.S., 509, 510, 516, 519, 521, 567, 571, 572, 573, 574, 578, 695, 715
Kirshenbaum, N., 178
Kirsner, K., 69
Kishchuk, N., 719, 722, 723, 724, 729
Kishi, Y., 768
Kitney, R.I., 368
Kitsantas, A., 502, 506, 518
Kitsantas, A, 573
Kjaer, M., 750
Kjelgaard, M.M., 508
Klapp, S.T., 5, 12, 121, 123, 124
Klavora, P., 319, 327
Kleiber, D., 612, 674, 791, 793
Klein, D.F., 744
Klein, H.J., 351, 508, 517
Klein, J.M., 793
Klein, M.J., 762
Klein, R.M., 61
Klerman, G.L., 747
Klesges, R.C., 787
Kless, S.J., 615, 616, 625
Klimesch, W., 369
Klint, K.A., 42, 226, 227, 229, 230, 344, 348, 606, 611, 612, 614, 616
Knapp, B.N., 73
Knapp, C.G., 123
Knerr, C.S., 510
Knight, B., 556, 562

Knight, P.A., 352
Knoppers, A., 591
Knouse, S.B., 180, 181
Kobasa, S.C., 751, 771
Koch, C., 147, 156
Koeppel, J., 88
Koepsell, T., 732
Koeske, R., 43, 730
Koestner, R., 392, 395, 399, 402, 404, 405, 409, 571, 572, 573
Koffman, D.M., 723
Kohl, H.W., 720
Kohl, R.M., 100, 118, 125, 811
Kohlberg, L., 586, 587, 588, 592, 627
Koivula, N., 239
Kok, G., 699, 701, 729
Kolarz, C.M., 636, 637, 639
Kolbet, L.K., 41
Kolt, G., 769, 771
Koltyn, K.F., 745, 746
Kolyton, K.F., 659
Komadel, L., 271, 272
Komarik, E., 271, 272
Kondoh, A., 180
Kondrasuk, J.N., 510, 511
Koning, P., 182, 190
Konttinen, N., 376
Koob, G., 319, 320, 321
Koonce, J.M., 105, 133, 134
Kordus, R.N., 100
Korn, E., 530
Korn, Z., 517
Kornblum, S., 39
Korteling, J.E., 64
Koskela, K., 730, 734
Kouli, O., 430
Kourtessis, T., 4, 177, 179, 180, 181, 182
Koutedakis, Y., 754, 755
Kovach, R., 104
Kowal, J., 398
Kowalski, E.M., 226
Kowalski, R.M., 493
Kozak, J.J., 135
Kozlowski, S., 352, 486
Kozma, A., 189
Kozub, S.A., 475
Kraemer, R.R., 642
Kraemer, W.J., 365
Krahé, B., 242
Krahenbuhl, G.S., 381
Kramer, A.F., 59
Kramer, J., 676
Kramer, M., 741
Kramer, N.A., 395
Krampe, R., 4, 117, 175, 185, 186, 189, 190, 191, 269, 275, 277, 278, 279, 280, 282, 283, 362, 533
Krampitz, J., 88, 89, 90, 104
Krane, V., 161, 293, 295, 298, 319, 320, 321, 325, 328, 362, 364, 435

Kraus, J.F., 688, 787
Krebs, D.E., 798
Krebs, M.J., 74
Kreighbaum, E., 7, 180
Kreisel, P.S.J., 252, 658, 660
Kreuter, M., 722, 724, 725, 729, 733
Krishman, R., 749, 750, 756
Kriska, A., 719, 720
Kristal, A., 732
Kroll, W., 825
Kruglanski, A.W., 445
Kruse, P., 23
Krushell, R.J., 789, 795, 797, 800
Krüskemper, G.M., 742, 747
Kubitz, K.A., 373, 374, 641, 650, 742, 743, 744, 745, 746
Kubitz, K.K., 750
Kübler-Ross, E., 675, 685, 788
Kugler, J., 742, 747
Kugler, P.N., 144, 146, 152, 156, 157
Kuhlman, W.N., 369
Kuhn, W., 181
Kukla, A., 445, 446
Kulik, J.A., 215
Kumar, M., 643
Kunesh, M.A., 624
Kurth, S.B., 189, 190
Kuypers, J.A., 675
Kyllo, L., 245, 499, 505, 506, 509, 510, 513, 514, 517, 520, 764

Labbé, E.E., 343, 346, 349
LaBerge, D., 61, 62
Labouvie-Vief, G., 680
Lacey, B.C., 69, 325, 380, 381
Lacey, J.I., 69, 294, 298, 320, 325
Lacey, J.L., 380, 381
Lacombe, D., 183
Ladd, G.W., 624
Ladewig, I., 42
La Greca, A.M., 574
LaGuardia, R., 343, 346, 349
Laguna, P., 211, 218
Lahart, C., 432
Lahtinen, A., 730
Lai, Q., 95, 100, 101
Lajoie, Y., 58, 102, 103
Lake, R., 744
Lakie, W.L., 597
Lamb, M., 774
Lamb, R., 325
Lambert, M.E., 795
Lambert, M.J., 791, 793, 800
Lambert, S.M., 504
Lambiotte, J.G., 534
LaMott, E.E., 791, 793, 794, 797, 798, 799, 800
Lampton, C.C., 795
Lancaster, R., 156
Landauer, T.K., 100

Landers, D., 7, 13, 58, 68, 69, 99, 125, 211, 212, 214, 219, 220, 221, 223, 225, 231, 239, 243, 244, 245, 246, 248, 262, 282, 293, 295, 302, 320, 327, 333, 362, 364, 367, 370, 371, 372, 373, 374, 380, 381, 499, 505, 506, 509, 510, 513, 514, 517, 520, 530, 531, 532, 539, 540, 550, 639, 641, 642, 649, 650, 651, 740, 742, 743, 744, 745, 746, 747, 748, 749, 750, 751, 752, 753, 754, 758, 759, 764, 778, 826
Landin, D., 97, 214, 221
Landle, K., 365, 366
Landsman, T., 652, 653
Landy, F., 324
Lane, A.M., 302, 304
Lane, L.D., 744
Lang, P.J., 222, 539, 560
Lange, A.J., 681
Lange, C., 102
Lange, R., 817
Langendorfer, S., 23, 35
Langer, E.J., 308
Langer, R.D., 787
Lanham, D.S., 136
Lankenau, B., 723
Lansing, R.W., 327
Lantero, D.A., 6
Lantis, A., 645
Laparidis, K., 798, 800
LaPlante, G., 184
Larey, T.S., 511
Larish, D.D., 11
LaRitz, T., 69
Larkin, J., 128
Larsen, F., 371
Larson, D.B., 749
Larson, G.A., 800
Larson, R., 638, 656
Laszlo, E., 724
Latane, B., 475, 511
Latash, M.L., 127, 132
Latham, G., 282, 440, 497, 498, 499, 506, 507, 508, 509, 510, 511, 513, 514, 515, 516, 517, 518, 519, 520, 521, 567
Latiri, I., 179, 181
Latuda, L., 797
Laubach, W.J., 794, 795, 797
Lauer, L., 340, 355, 357
Laugier, C., 211
Laurence, C., 789, 793, 797
Laurencelle, L., 57
Laurent, M., 6, 12, 58, 436
Lauterbach, B., 131
Lavallee, D., 677, 678, 679, 680, 681, 682, 683, 685, 686
Lavallee, L., 769, 770, 772, 773, 775, 776

Lavery, J.J., 102, 107
La Voie, L., 351, 483, 484, 485, 486
Lawrence, B.E., 59
Lawton, G.W., 367, 368
Lazaro, I., 794, 795, 797
Lazarus, A., 680
Lazarus, N.B., 749
Lazarus, R.S., 290, 291, 319, 430, 431,
    432, 433, 498, 613, 615, 641, 680,
    742, 752, 770
Leadbetter, W.B., 787
Leary, M.J., 493
Leary, M.R., 397, 489, 615, 662, 696
Leavitt, J., 11, 43, 64, 178, 214
Le Bars, H., 422
Leddy, M.H., 791, 793, 800
LeDoux, J., 322, 658
Lee, A.M., 25, 42, 89, 92, 503, 504, 517
Lee, C., 344, 346, 349, 500, 503, 504,
    518, 519
Lee, D.N., 132
Lee, I.-M., 749
Lee, M., 591
Lee, T.D., 5, 8, 12, 21, 22, 44, 57, 92, 94,
    98, 100, 101, 104, 105, 108, 109,
    115, 116, 118, 119, 120, 121, 126,
    127, 130, 133, 134, 144, 151, 155,
    158, 161, 162, 163, 164, 167, 214,
    215, 218, 219, 533
Lee, T.W., 507, 516
Lee, W., 574, 575
Lees, A., 163, 164, 166
LeFevre, J., 657, 658, 771
Leff, S.S., 621
Leffingwell, T., 772
Legault, P., 185
Leggett, E., 417, 418, 434, 458, 460, 461
Lehmann, A.C., 185, 186, 269, 270, 277
Lehnhard, R.A., 747
Leibowitz, H.W., 70
Leith, L., 333, 345, 448, 449, 639, 645,
    742, 756, 757
Lemire, L., 179
Lemke, J.H., 401
Lenes, H.S., 404
Lenney, E., 555, 558
Lent, R.W., 673, 681
Leon, A.S., 719, 720
Leonard, F., 735
Leone, D.R., 392
Lepes, D., 404
Lepper, M.R., 390, 395
Lerch, S.H., 674, 675, 680, 682, 683, 686
Lerman, D., 457
Lerner, B.S., 500, 501, 503, 509
Lerner, J.D., 282
Lersten, K.C., 121
Leskinen, E., 425, 426, 434, 461, 462
Leslie, E., 659
Lesser, D.P., 762

Lester, D., 675, 678, 685
Leung, R., 749
Leuschen, P.S., 642, 651, 658, 659, 660
Levenson, R.W., 319
Lévesque, L., 104, 734, 756, 757
Levi-Kolker, N., 179
Levine, H.M., 774
Levine, J.M., 55, 479, 483
Levine, S., 325
Levinger, G., 511
Levitt, R., 798
Levitt, S., 327
Levy, C.M., 105
Levy, S.R., 460, 461, 462
Levy-Kolker, N., 178, 500, 502, 505, 510
Lewicki, P., 129
Lewis, G., 825
Lewis, J., 556, 557, 561, 697
Lewis, L., 798
Lewis, M., 330, 655, 657
Lewis, R., 636, 729
Lewis, S., 215, 230
Lewis-Griffith, L., 677
Lewko, J.H., 617, 624
Lewthwaite, R., 252, 397, 614, 615, 616,
    619, 621, 624, 661
Leyshon, G., 532, 542
Li, F., 12, 392, 393, 401, 402, 403, 409,
    420
Li, Y., 218
Libo, L., 472
Lichacz, F.M., 354
Lichtenstein, E., 718, 729, 735
Liddle, P.F., 155, 156
Liden, R.C., 516
Lidor, R., 76, 132, 178, 179, 506, 571,
    572, 573
Lieberman, D., 179
Liebert, R.M., 291, 302
Liederbach, M., 754, 755
Lifka, B., 598
Lighthall, F.F., 291
Lightner, J.M., 811
Liles, L., 558
Lin, D.M.-S., 462
Lin, L.S., 696, 714, 715, 720, 725
Lindahl, L.G., 98
Lindberg, M.A., 40
Linder, D.E., 653, 745, 793, 794, 799,
    800
Lindgren, S., 792
Lindley, S., 45, 46, 70, 76, 177, 178,
    182, 184, 187, 188, 212, 224, 230
Lindner, K.J., 611, 787
Lindsley, D.B., 327
Linenger, J.M., 732
Lintern, G., 91, 93, 105, 121, 122, 123,
    124, 134, 166
Lintunen, T., 425, 426, 434, 461, 462
Linville, P.W., 463

Lirgg, C.D., 225, 230, 340, 341, 349,
    353, 355, 357, 552, 555, 558
Lishman, J.R., 132
Litt, M.D., 814
Little, B.R., 579
Little, J.C., 789
Little, W.S., 87, 88, 209, 220, 223
Lituchy, T., 518
Liu, J., 87, 107
Li-Wei, Z., 222
Llinas, R.R., 369
Lloyd, C., 823
Lloyd, J., 400
Lloyd, M., 817
Lo, S.K., 659
Lobel, M., 608, 659, 660
Lochbaum, M., 294, 295, 325, 328,
    427
Locke, B.Z., 741, 749
Locke, E., 88, 282, 440, 497, 498, 499,
    501, 503, 506, 507, 508, 509, 510,
    511, 512, 513, 514, 515, 516, 517,
    518, 519, 520, 521, 567
Loehr, J., 559
Logan, G.D., 65, 66
Lohasz, P., 333
Lombard, D.N., 712
Lombard, T., 712
Londeree, B., 212
Long, B.C., 345, 349, 639, 641, 643, 645,
    742
Longhurst, K., 610
Longino, J., 503, 505, 510
Longman, D.J.A., 135
Longman, R.S., 481, 485
Longoria, J., 722
Lonky, E., 404
Lopes da Silva, F., 368, 369
Lord, R., 507, 517
Lorge, I., 679, 683
Lorr, M., 325, 639, 649, 753, 793
Losier, G.F., 389, 397, 402, 403, 404,
    405, 409, 426, 465, 597
Lott, A.J., 472, 477
Lott, B.E., 472, 477
Lotter, W.S., 6
Loundagin, C., 797
Lounsbury, J.W., 400
Love, B., 591
Lovett, S.B., 681
Low, D.W., 371
Lowe, B., 674, 675, 680, 682, 684
Lowe, C.A., 472
Lowe, R., 291, 292, 327
Lowes, R., 177
Lox, C.L., 341, 343, 348, 350
Loy, J., 591
Loy, S.F., 363
Lu, S.-E., 434
Lucas, R.E., 637

Luchsinger, A.E., 754
Luck, S.J., 377
Lucker, G.W., 574, 575
Ludwig, D.A., 226
Ludwig, T.D., 517
Lumsdaine, A.A., 220
Lunt, S.D., 771, 794
Luschene, R., 696, 742
Lushene, R.E., 324, 328, 348
Lushene, R.L., 291, 302, 308
Lustgarten, N., 508
Lutes, L., 488, 489, 490, 729
Luzzi, S., 181
Lykken, D.T., 284
Lyle, J., 178
Lynch, G.P., 788, 793
Lyons, N., 591
Lysens, R., 770, 771, 772
Lyytinen, H., 376

Macchi, R., 788, 793, 798
MacDonald, G., 721
Mace, R., 250, 534
Macera, C.A., 719, 720
MacGillivary, W.W., 75
MacIntyre, T., 534
MacIver, D., 230
MacIver, S., 721
Mack, D., 340, 343, 344, 349, 531, 534,
    541, 542, 554, 699, 701, 729
MacKay, D.G., 538, 539
Mackenzie, M.M., 647, 648, 662
Mackinnon, L.T., 163, 641, 650
MacLeod, C., 69
MacMahon, J.R., 757
MacMahon, K., 131
MacQueen, G.M., 41
Macussen, L., 461
Madden, D.J., 758
Madden, L.E., 517
Madden, T.J., 701
Maddox, M.D., 131
Maddux, J.E., 340, 341, 342, 343, 556,
    557, 561, 697, 720
Madigan, R., 534
Madsen, J., 574, 576
Maehr, M.L., 417, 418, 421, 422, 435,
    436, 447, 499, 696, 813
Maere, A., 744
Maffull, N., 38
Magill, R., 26, 67, 76, 89, 92, 93, 95, 96,
    107, 108, 115, 118, 119, 120, 122,
    123, 129, 163, 166, 210, 221, 320,
    826
Magnusson, D., 240, 241, 243, 261,
    262
Mahler, H.I., 215
Mahon, A.D., 381
Mahon, M., 504
Mahoney, K., 516, 518

Mahoney, M.J., 243, 246, 247, 248, 250,
    281, 282, 283, 301, 304, 332, 516,
    518, 536, 558
Maier, S.F., 458
Maile, L.J., 96, 217, 341
Maitlis, S., 517
Maldonado, M., 619
Males, J., 300, 330
Malete, L., 356
Malina, R.M., 27, 28, 30, 38, 39, 278,
    284, 608
Malliou, P., 527, 798, 800
Malmo, R.B., 294, 320, 322
Malo, S., 789, 791, 792, 793, 796, 800,
    802
Malone, L.A., 680, 681, 682
Maloney, T.L., 591
Man, F., 642
Mandell, A., 650
Manderlink, G., 395, 510
Mandler, G., 306
Mané, A.M., 121, 124
Mangum, M., 812
Mangun, G.R., 377
Maniar, S., 793, 800, 806
Manion, U.V., 674, 681, 684
Mann, C.A., 369
Mann, L., 711
Manning, F.J., 472
Manning, T., 402
Mansi, O., 730
Mantel, R.C., 591
Manza, L., 129
Maraj, B., 12, 130, 164
Marañon, G., 312
Marcia, J.E., 678
Marciani, L.M., 185
Marcus, B., 232, 403, 709, 710, 712,
    713, 719, 720, 728, 729
Margraf, J., 744
Maris, E., 259
Markland, D., 309, 393, 403, 404, 465,
    506, 507, 543
Marks, D., 150, 532, 535
Marks, M.A., 346, 349, 504, 571, 572, 573
Markus, H., 242
Marley, R., 794
Marlowe, D., 393
Marmor, T.R., 722
Maroulakis, E., 642
Marsh, H., 245, 330, 398, 402, 652, 653,
    655, 656, 657, 756
Marshall, S.W., 787
Marten, P.A., 432
Marteniuk, R.G., 4, 12, 13, 14, 104, 106,
    327, 529
Martens, B.K., 518
Martens, R., 209, 213, 214, 221, 239,
    243, 244, 246, 250, 274, 284, 291,
    295, 296, 298, 300, 301, 302, 303,

304, 307, 321, 324, 326, 327, 328,
    344, 348, 380, 556, 562, 608, 613,
    614, 615, 650, 826
Martin, A.D., 747
Martin, D., 598, 649
Martin, G., 249, 504
Martin, I., 69
Martin, J.J., 346, 347, 350
Martin, J.W., 433
Martin, K., 534, 544, 545, 554, 557, 560,
    696, 701
Martin, M., 334, 571
Martin, W., 472
Martinek, T.J., 458
Martinez, J., 744
Martinsen, E.W., 640, 747, 748
Marzke, M., 33, 35
Maslow, A., 329, 654
Masser, L.S., 42
Massey, C.J., 136
Masters, K.S., 654, 795
Masters, R., 76, 131, 166, 308, 309, 310
Masuda, M., 687, 767, 769, 782
Mathes, S.A., 543
Mathews, A., 744
Mathiowetz, V., 124
Mati, B., 718, 733, 734
Matlock, T.S., 534
Matschiner, S., 100, 109, 127
Matsui, T., 516
Matsudo, V., 718, 733, 734
Matthews, A., 649
Matthews, B.H.C., 369
Matthews, D.B., 399
Matthews, D.S., 795
Matthews, G.R., 343, 344, 345
Matthews, J., 421, 429, 432
Matthews, K.A., 787
Matzkanin, K., 619
Mausner, B., 216
Mavromatis, G., 500, 518
Maxwell, J., 131
May, J., 672, 674, 768, 779
May, S., 794, 795, 799, 801
Mayberry, M., 69
Mayer, H., 178
Mayer, J.W., 133
Maynard, I.W., 295, 501
Mayocchi, L., 250
Mayr, U., 117, 175, 189
Mayyasi, A.M., 180
Mazziotta, J.C., 155, 156, 369, 532
McAfee, R., 597
McAlister, A., 734
McArdle, W.D., 363, 371
McAuley, E., 212, 340, 343, 347, 392,
    395, 396, 397, 403, 409, 448, 449,
    450, 451, 457, 504, 505, 554, 660,
    700, 701, 703, 704, 705, 706, 744,
    811

McBride, E.R., 531
McCabe, J.F., 66
McCabe, M., 333
McCabe, P.M., 643
McCaffrey, I., 674
McCall, R.B., 46
McCallum, C., 59
McCarrey, M., 451
McCaughan, L., 456
McClelland, J.L., 63
McClenny, B.D., 381
McClosky, D., 57
McClure, J.N., 744
McCracken, H.D., 41, 118
McCrae, R.R., 242
McCrone, J., 146, 151
McCullagh, P., 87, 88, 98, 108, 205, 206,
    209, 211, 214, 215, 216, 217, 219,
    220, 223, 227, 230, 231, 232, 341,
    619, 651, 747, 748, 749, 770, 771,
    772, 774, 775
McCurley, J., 730
McDavid, R.F., 3, 5
McDonald, D.G., 742, 747, 752, 756
McDonald, P.V., 12, 164, 165
McDonald, S.A., 788, 793, 794
McDowell, S., 769, 773
McElroy, M., 591
McEvoy, L.K., 362, 363, 369, 375
McFarquhar, R., 12
McGavern, R., 271
McGinnis, P.M., 99, 126
McGonagle, K.A., 747
McGowan, J., 242
McGowan, R.W., 791
McGrath, J., 291, 292, 321, 472
McGraw, M.B., 23
McGuffin, P., 284
McGuinness, D., 294, 306
McGuire, W.J., 729
McHenry, H.M., 36
McInman, A., 449, 451, 642, 644, 651,
    652, 654
McIntyre, R., 722
McIntyre, S., 721
McKee, D.C., 758
McKelvain, R., 674
McKenzie, I., 165
McKenzie, T.L., 709, 710, 718, 728, 731
McKinney, C.H., 643
McKnight, P., 475, 484
McLaughlin, C., 63
McLean, J.P., 70
McLeod, P., 56, 57, 60, 63, 180
McLeod, S., 771
McLeroy, K.R., 722, 723, 724
McMahan, G.C., 508
McMorris, T., 179
McMurray, N.E., 770, 771
McMurray, R.G., 811

McNair, D., 325, 639, 649, 753, 793
McNair, P.J., 246
McNair, R.J., 571, 572, 578
McNelly, T.L., 219
McNevin, N., 96
McPherson, B.D., 734
McPherson, B.P., 672, 673, 678, 679,
    680, 681, 683
McPherson, S.L., 10, 11, 20, 44, 45, 46,
    177, 179, 182, 189, 190, 223, 225
McQueen, D.V., 728
McShane, D., 794
McWhirter, B.T., 239
Meaney, K.S., 226, 228
Meani, E., 796
Medbery, R., 558
Medley, A.R., 403, 404
Meece, J.L., 427, 605, 606, 618, 621,
    625, 627
Meek, F., 7
Meeuwisse, W.H., 802
Meeuwsen, H., 94, 101
Megaw, E.D., 70
Meichenbaum, D., 362, 680, 685, 779
Meier, L.J., 341, 343
Meijer, O.G., 109, 144, 145, 150, 155,
    164
Meili, L., 372, 375, 378
Melamed, B.G., 539
Melzack, R., 812
Mendelberg, H., 748
Mendelsohn, M., 748
Menickelli, J., 97
Menlove, F.L., 224
Mento, A.J., 499, 507, 508, 513, 518,
    520
Merill, G.L., 133
Mermelstein, R., 510
Merritt, R.K., 718, 719
Mertesdorf, F.L., 649
Mesch, D., 518
Meshkati, N., 59
Messori, A., 181
Mesulam, M.M., 369
Metalsky, G.I., 450, 458
Meugens, P.F., 98
Meyer, C., 676, 677, 683
Meyer, D.E., 39
Meyer, K.N., 214, 769, 770, 773, 780
Meyer, T., 744
Meyers, A., 558, 673
Meyers, M.C., 794
Meyers, W.A., 282
Michael, J.J., 355
Michaels, C.F., 144, 177
Michalopoulou, M., 4, 177, 179, 180,
    181, 182
Michaud, D., 179
Michel, F., 125
Michela, J., 445, 448

Michenbaum, D., 814
Middleton, M.J., 435
Midgley, C., 435, 605, 606, 618, 621,
    625, 627
Migliorini, S., 796
Mihalko, S.L., 340, 704, 705, 706, 744
Mihovilovic, M., 676, 677, 678, 679,
    680, 681, 683, 684
Miles, T.R., 8, 179, 212
Miller, A., 423, 425, 606, 609, 612
Miller, B.P., 799
Miller, D., 7, 451
Miller, G.A., 117, 567
Miller, H., 641, 811
Miller, J.G., 724
Miller, J.L., 724
Miller, J.M., 363
Miller, J.T., 504
Miller, J.W., 180
Miller, K., 68
Miller, L.H., 774
Miller, M., 42, 341, 347, 461
Miller, R., 181, 657
Miller, S., 598
Miller, T., 768, 787
Miller, W.N., 793, 794
Milliner, E.K., 791, 793, 794, 800
Mills, K.D., 534
Millslagle, D., 177
Milner, A.D., 69, 145
Milner, D.A., 144, 145, 167
Mims, V., 395
Minas, C.A., 538
Minas, S.C., 126
Minden, H., 770, 771, 772
Minneo, L., 181
Mirskii, M.L., 164
Mischel, L.J., 351, 358
Mischel, W., 216, 240, 241, 242, 243,
    247, 249, 251, 252, 253, 254, 255,
    261, 552
Miserandino, M., 464
Mitchell, B., 40, 44
Mitchell, S.A., 400
Mitchell, S.K., 486
Mitchell, T.R., 516
Mizusawa, K., 180, 181
Mobily, K.E., 401
Mock, J., 748
Möckel, W., 177
Mogk, J.P., 239
Mohr, K., 624
Molendijk, A., 769, 770, 771, 773, 776,
    781, 782
Moleski, R., 680
Molinek, F.R., Jr., 637, 638
Molloy, E.K., 795, 801
Molloy, G.N., 795, 801
Molotsky, E.J., 400
Monno, A., 58

Monsaas, J.A., 278
Monson, J., 341, 343, 348, 350
Monson, T.C., 242
Monson, W., 509
Montebello, R.A., 7
Montoye, H.J., 719
Montpetit, R., 271
Mooar, P.A., 795
Moon, G., 721
Moore, B., 102
Moore, D., 447, 504
Moore, J., 222, 252, 540
Moore, K.A., 749, 750, 756, 758, 759
Moore, R., 36
Moore, S.P., 13
Moore, W.E., 559, 561
Moos, R., 685
Moran, A., 531, 534
Moray, N., 54, 58, 59, 62, 71
Moreland, J., 99
Moreland, R.L., 479, 483
Morford, L.M., 89
Morgan, D., 365, 366, 381
Morgan, K., 426
Morgan, L.K., 449
Morgan, R.L., 119, 120, 218
Morgan, W., 239, 243, 244, 245, 246,
    247, 284, 294, 328, 365, 381, 639,
    640, 642, 643, 644, 646, 647, 649,
    650, 651, 659, 740, 743, 744, 745,
    746, 747, 748, 750, 751, 753, 754,
    755, 756, 811, 812
Morgan, W.P., 248
Moritani, T., 743
Moritz, S., 334, 340, 343, 344, 349, 352,
    354, 355, 356, 484, 486, 534, 535,
    544, 545, 557, 560
Morley, D., 811
Morrey, M.A., 787, 789, 790, 791, 793,
    794, 796, 800
Morris, D., 180
Morris, G.S.D., 7
Morris, H.H., 244
Morris, J., 719, 720, 730, 731
Morris, L., 291, 299
Morris, L.R., 99, 205, 208, 220
Morris, L.W., 291, 302
Morris, R.D., 769, 773, 778
Morris, W.N., 637
Morrison, C.S., 400, 402
Morrison, G.A., 134
Morrow, J.R., 696, 709, 712, 718, 728
Morrow, L., 672
Morrow, M.S., 718, 733, 734
Mortimer, R.G., 105
Moses, J., 649, 744
Mosher, R., 395
Mossicki, E.K., 749
Motl, R.W., 639, 642, 644, 649, 651,
    658, 659, 660, 662, 663

Mouanda, J., 395
Mountford, S.J., 63
Mowbray, G.H., 10, 65, 67
Mroczek, D.K., 636, 637, 639
Mudrack, P.E., 472
Mueller, C.M., 460
Mueller, F.O., 787
Mugno, D.A., 349, 627
Mullan, E., 393, 465
Mullen, B., 451, 475, 476, 484
Mullen, R., 131, 308, 309, 801
Mullis, R., 722, 723
Mulvey, P.W., 351
Mumford, N.L., 327
Munroe, K., 529, 530, 534, 535, 537,
    538, 541, 542, 544, 545
Munt, E.D., 517
Munton, A.G., 452, 453, 454, 455
Murch, R.L., 801
Murphey, M., 76, 464, 795
Murphy, A., 379
Murphy, G.C., 795, 801
Murphy, L.E., 327
Murphy, S., 282, 334, 535, 539, 560,
    674, 779, 820, 827
Murray, D., 246, 247, 248
Murray, N.P., 372, 375, 378
Murtha, T.C., 249, 251
Musa, D., 185
Mutimer, B., 38, 185
Mutlusoy, F., 105
Mutrie, N., 639, 732, 740, 741, 747, 748,
    749, 750, 794, 795
Mutter, S.A., 128
Myers, J.K., 741

Näätänen, R., 59, 65, 72, 294
Nader, P.R., 730, 731
Nadier, P.R., 574, 576
Nagle, F.J., 246
Nakagawa, A., 9, 178
Nakamura, J., 390
Napolitano, M.A., 749, 750, 756
Narváez, D., 591, 599
Nasco, S.A., 677
Naus, M.J., 24, 43
Naveh-Benjamin, M., 66
Navon, D., 56, 61, 62, 65, 66
Naylor, J.C., 121, 123
Naylor, S., 297, 302, 304
Neal, K., 327
Neal, R.J., 12, 163, 164, 182, 190
Nebeker, D.M., 517
Neil, G.I., 211, 224
Neimeyer, R.A., 762
Neiss, R., 293, 294, 298, 320, 321, 328,
    332
Neisser, U., 64, 65, 66, 68, 72, 151
Nelson, B., 65
Nelson, C.B., 747

Nelson, D., 506, 507
Nelson, E.R., 680, 681, 682
Nelson, J.K., 33, 35, 37, 39, 500, 501
Nelson, J.M., 121, 123, 124
Nelson, K.R., 33, 35, 39
Nelson, L., 557
Nelson, R.O., 247
Ness, R.G., 557
Nessler, J., 181
Nesti, M.S., 304
Nesvig, D., 823
Nettleton, B., 57
Neumaier, A., 178, 179
Neumann, E., 271, 272, 273, 274
Neumann, O., 61, 63
Neuper, C., 368, 369, 372, 374
Nevett, M.E., 4, 5, 10, 11, 12, 45, 177,
    182, 189, 190, 225
Newbery, D., 752
Newcomb, A.F., 624, 627
Newcomb, P.A., 246
Newcomer, R., 791, 793, 800, 806
Newell, D.S., 674
Newell, K.M., 12, 40, 44, 88, 89, 90, 98,
    99, 108, 123, 126, 127, 128, 145,
    152, 153, 154, 163, 164, 165, 166,
    167, 205, 208, 210, 216, 220, 221,
    228
Newland, D.E., 368
Newman, B., 689
Newton, M.L., 401, 421, 423, 424, 425,
    429, 430, 435
Newton, P., 795
Nguyen, N., 719
Nias, D.K.B., 245
Niaura, R.S., 403
Nice, D.S., 732
Nichoas, J.A., 754, 755
Nicholls, J., 417, 418, 419, 420, 421,
    423, 424, 425, 426, 427, 434, 435,
    436, 447, 460, 461, 499, 510, 519,
    551, 554, 595, 605, 606, 609, 612,
    621, 625, 626, 813, 814
Nicholson, C., 591
Nicholson, D.E., 106, 107
Nickless, C.J., 551
Nicol, M., 796
Nida, S.A., 475
Nideffer, R., 68, 246, 282, 333, 767, 780,
    823
Niedfeldt, C.E., 792, 797, 800, 801
Nimmo-Smith, I., 63
Nisbett, R.E., 53, 69, 452
Nissen, M.J., 69
Nix, C., 550
Nixon, H., 591
Noakes, T., 718, 733, 734
Noble, B.J., 696, 810, 811, 812, 813
Noble, J.M., 810
Noel, R.C., 542

Noels, K., 405
Nolen, S., 427
Nolen-Hoeksema, S., 459, 637
Norcross, J.C., 710, 711
Norman, D.A., 60, 61, 63, 65, 66, 72, 73
Norman, J., 718, 735
Norppa, J., 730
North, T.C., 651, 747, 748, 749
Northcraft, G., 351, 358, 518
Noton, D., 70
Nougier, V., 54, 377
Novotny, T.E., 723
Nowell, P., 651, 758, 759
Noyes, F.R., 795
Ntoumanis, N., 421, 430, 433, 434, 753
Nunez, P.L., 369, 378
Nunez, R., 152
Nunnally, J.C., 481, 482
Nygren, T.E., 58
Nyheim, M., 435, 662
Nykodym, N., 675

O'Block, F.R., 516
O'Brien, R.M., 571, 572, 573
O'Brien-Malone, A., 69
O'Connell, E.R., 181
O'Connell, G., 659
O'Connor, B.P., 405
O'Connor, E.A., 571, 572, 573, 574
O'Connor, K.A., 770, 775
O'Connor, P., 284, 294, 328, 365, 643, 645, 646, 647, 648, 650, 745, 746, 750, 754, 755, 756
O'Connor, P.J., 248
O'Donnell, R.D., 60
O'Fallon, W.M., 788, 791, 793, 794, 800
Ogden, G.D., 55
Ogilvie, B., 243, 672, 673, 674, 675, 676, 677, 678, 679, 683, 684, 685, 686
Ogles, B.M., 791, 793, 800
Oishi, S., 637
Ojala, D., 536
Okolo, C.M., 463
Okwumabua, T.M., 347, 349
Oldenburg, B., 731
Oldham, G.R., 516
O'Leary, A., 340, 814
Oliver, S.K., 164, 165
Olivier, G., 284
Olsen, E., 7, 180, 181, 647, 648
Olson, L., 434, 595
Oman, R., 403, 660
Omelich, C., 463
Ommundsen, Y., 423, 426, 428, 431, 434, 660, 661
Oña, A., 91
O'Neal, H., 731
Onestak, D.M., 222

Onglatco, M.L., 516
Orbach, I., 464
Ordman, A.M., 509
Orlebeke, J.F., 69
Orlick, J., 684
Orlick, T., 222, 281, 282, 283, 309, 395, 506, 516, 534, 535, 559, 598, 611, 614, 672, 676, 677, 678, 679, 680, 681, 682, 684, 689, 789, 791, 792, 793, 796, 797, 798, 800
Ornstein, P.A., 24, 43
Ortiz, G.A., 134
Osen, M., 574, 575
Osgood, C.E., 133
Ossip, D., 730
Ostiguy, L.J., 401
Ostrow, A.C., 500, 503, 560, 674
Ostyn, M., 185, 770, 771, 772
Ottinge, D.R., 574
Otto, L.B., 682, 684
Oudejans, R.R.D., 177
Overpeck, M.D., 787
Owen, D.R., 639, 640, 642, 643, 644, 645, 649, 651, 659, 663
Owen, M.J., 284
Owen, N., 232, 659, 709, 710, 712, 719, 722, 723, 725, 732
Owens, D., 571, 572, 573, 574
Oxendine, J.B., 294, 326, 331
Oxman, A.D., 741
Ozanne-Smith, J., 787

Paarsalu, M., 176, 177, 182
Paarsalu, M.E., 6, 9, 45, 223
Paarsalu, M.L., 74
Paas, F., 320, 321
Pabich, P., 658, 660
Paffenbarger, R.S., 647, 648, 719, 720, 749
Paine-Andrews, A., 729
Paivio, A., 222, 531, 534, 536, 539, 541, 542, 543, 560
Paller, K., 327
Pallonen, U., 730
Palmer, J., 66
Pandolf, K.B., 812
Pangrazi, B., 740, 751, 759
Panter, A.T., 245
Pantev, C., 362, 364, 369
Panzarella, R., 652, 657
Papaioannou, A., 400, 420, 430, 527, 798, 800
Papin, J.P., 178
Papp, L.A., 744
Paradis, G., 730
Paradiso, M.A., 375, 378
Parcel, G.S., 722, 723, 724, 729
Parfitt, C.G., 293, 294, 297, 298, 299, 302, 303, 307, 308
Parfitt, G., 321, 324, 325, 752, 753

Pargman, D., 75, 181, 245, 246, 456, 771, 794
Parigi, A., 181
Park, C.L., 801
Parker, H., 7, 64, 65, 178
Parker, J.F., 6
Parker, J.G., 625, 627, 628
Parker, S., 182
Parker, W.D., 432
Parkinson, J.R., 64
Parks, L., 642
Parks, S., 70, 74, 76, 154, 190
Parrish, M.W., 535
Partington, J., 281, 282, 283, 309, 354, 559
Pascoe, C., 40, 41
Pascual-Leone, J., 24, 40
Pascuzzi, D., 447
Paskevich, D.M., 351, 353, 476, 482, 483, 484, 488, 490
Passer, M.W., 26, 225, 291, 292, 550, 608, 615, 616, 621, 769, 772, 826
Pate, R., 33, 37, 294, 328, 718, 719, 720, 754
Pates, J., 298, 299, 303, 308, 321, 324
Patmore, A., 290
Patrick, B.C., 392
Patrick, D., 732
Patrick, G.T., 825
Patrick, J., 105, 179
Patrick, K., 719, 720
Pattee, H.H., 150
Patterson, E.L., 769, 775
Patterson, T.L., 574, 576, 730, 731
Patton, R.W., 557
Paull, G., 11, 75, 177, 183
Paulus, P.B., 511
Pauwels, J.M., 70, 74, 98, 176, 177, 179, 182, 183, 195
Pavot, W., 636, 638
Pawlak, A., 673
Paxton, S.J., 659
Payne, G.V., 29, 33
Payne, R.L., 290
Payne, V.G., 33, 39, 185
Peake, P.K., 242, 249, 253
Pearce, N., 722
Pearson, L., 793, 801
Pearson, R.E., 678, 680, 682, 684, 685
Pease, D., 126, 226, 433
Peaseley, V., 181
Peckham, V., 511
Pedersen, B.H., 431
Pein, R.L., 574, 575
Pekrun, G., 744
Pelletier, L.G., 390, 392, 393, 399, 401, 402, 403, 404, 405, 406, 408, 409, 571, 572, 573, 597, 752
Pendleton, L.R., 178, 182, 187, 188

Pennebaker, J.W., 811
Penpraze, P., 794, 795
Penrose, R., 167
Pensgaard, A.M., 433, 434
Peper, C.E., 75, 144, 146
Peper, E., 779
Perani, D., 155, 156, 532
Peretz, D., 788
Perkins, T.S., 246, 247, 248, 281, 283, 558
Perlini, A., 326, 332
Perlmutter, L.C., 60
Perna, F., 503, 682, 769, 773, 791, 792, 793, 794, 800, 806
Peronnet, F., 641
Perreault, R., 58
Perreault, S., 390, 396, 401, 402, 403, 409
Perry, J.D., 302
Pert, C.B., 642
Pérusse, L., 278, 284
Pervin, L.A., 241, 552
Peterroy, E.T., 472
Peters, D.P., 574, 576, 643, 649
Petersen, S.E., 73, 76
Peterson, C., 351, 450, 451, 458, 476, 486, 690
Peterson, J.R., 10
Peterson, K., 355, 429, 554, 558, 559, 621, 798, 799
Petherick, T., 427
Petitpas, A., 249, 674, 678, 680, 682, 684, 685, 789, 793, 794, 795, 797, 799, 800, 801
Petlichkoff, L., 292, 293, 296, 303, 325, 327, 429, 552, 610, 611, 612, 613, 614, 621, 623, 625
Petosa, R., 574, 577
Petrakis, E., 178, 179
Petrie, B., 591
Petrie, T., 535, 769, 770, 772, 775, 776, 780, 781, 789, 791, 793, 794, 800, 802
Petruzzello, S.J., 373, 374, 641, 650, 651, 742, 743, 744, 745, 746, 750, 752, 758, 759
Petty, R.E., 511
Pew, R.W., 11, 69, 129
Pfurtscheller, G., 368, 369, 372, 374
Pham, L.B., 647
Phelps, C.M., 793, 794, 799, 800
Phelps, M.E., 369
Philipson, L., 532
Phillips, D., 516, 520, 618, 619
Phillips, J.C., 682, 684
Phillips, J.G., 61
Piaget, J., 24, 586, 591, 627, 758
Pickens, C.C., 401
Pickering, J., 147
Pie, J., 501, 502

Pierce, B.E., 502
Pierce, C., 225, 226
Pierce, E.F., 791
Pierson, W.R., 7, 180, 181
Pigott, R.E., 120
Pijpers, J.R., 75
Pilloff, D., 310
Pillsbury, W.B., 53
Pinchas, S., 500, 503, 505, 510
Pinheiro, V., 177
Pinneo, L.R., 327
Pintrich, P., 418, 427
Piotrowski, N.A., 711
Piphers, M., 679
Pisano, M.D., 795
Pittman, T.S., 395, 398
Pitts, F.N., 744
Plake, B., 303
Plamondon, R., 39
Plante, T.G., 645
Pleasants, F., 179, 183
Plett, G.L., 440
Plewis, I., 721
Plimpton, G., 672
Plomin, R., 270, 284
Plowman, S.A., 574, 575, 577
Plutchik, P., 319
Poag, K., 457, 505
Poag-DuCharme, K.A., 504
Podilchak, W., 658
Podsakoff, P., 518
Pohlman, M.H., 789, 795, 797, 800
Pokorny, R.A., 5, 6
Polanyi, M., 129
Polkis, G.A., 44
Pollock, B., 12, 120, 164, 214
Pollock, M.L., 381, 719, 720, 754, 811, 812
Pollock, O., 679, 683
Polman, R.C.J., 131, 158, 159, 160
Polson, C.M., 63
Polson, P.G., 117
Pongrac, J., 535, 543
Poole, R., 505, 510
Poon, P., 177, 178, 182, 188, 756
Populin, L., 57
Porac, J., 395, 516
Porges, S.W., 368, 381
Porter, A., 567, 568, 571, 573, 579
Porter, H.V., 823
Posner, M.I., 3, 4, 5, 8, 24, 44, 53, 54, 57, 63, 73, 76, 128, 362, 367, 371, 377, 378
Post, R.B., 70
Potkay, C.R., 552
Potter, M., 796, 800
Potter, S., 179
Potts, S.A., 756
Potvin, L., 719, 721, 722, 723, 724, 728, 729, 730, 731, 734

Poulin, C., 402, 403
Poulton, E.C., 14, 647
Powell, G.E., 535
Powell, J.W., 773
Powell, K.E., 722, 725
Power, C., 588
Power, F.C., 588, 592
Powers, W.T., 567
Pozos, R.E., 99
Prablanc, C., 125
Pradham, P., 511
Prapavessis, H., 179, 246, 325, 328, 448, 449, 459, 475, 476, 484, 492, 571, 572, 578, 642, 646, 647, 650, 651
Pratt, M., 719, 720, 732, 733
Preece, M., 38
Prentice, W.E., 775
Pressing, J., 145
Pressley, M., 103
Prestholdt, P.H., 812
Pribram, K.H., 294, 306, 567
Price, R.H., 242
Price, S., 464
Prigogine, I., 152
Prinz, W., 131
Privette, G., 329, 651, 652, 653, 654, 655, 656
Prlic, H., 719, 723, 724
Prochaska, J.J., 659
Prochaska, J.O., 710, 711, 713
Proctor, R., 121, 123, 124, 147
Prong, T., 396
Proteau, L., 10, 57, 75, 104, 116, 144, 161, 162, 218, 272
Provence, S., 718, 722, 723, 724, 733
Provencher, P., 397, 400, 404, 407, 408, 409, 410, 598
Ptacek, J.T., 402, 769, 770, 772, 776, 779, 780, 781
Puleo, E., 640
Pullum, B., 370
Purvis, G., 40, 41
Puska, P., 730, 734
Putnam, F.W., 680
Putnam, P., 672

Qi-Wei, M., 222
Quackenbush, N., 793
Quek, J.J., 61
Quinn, A.M., 791, 792, 793, 794, 796, 797, 798, 799, 800
Quinn, J.T., 12
Quinn, J.T., Jr., 90, 98

Racicot, B., 517
Radlo, S.J., 94, 176, 179, 188
Radloff, L.S., 749
Rae, D.S., 741
Raeburn, J., 722
Raedeke, T., 320, 321, 324, 328, 331, 616

Raeder, U., 212
Ragan, J., 327, 332, 390, 395, 396
Raglin, J., 294, 295, 296, 329, 640, 646,
    647, 650, 651, 742, 743, 744, 745,
    746, 748, 754, 755, 756
Ragsdale, M.R., 530, 538, 540, 541
Rahe, R.J., 768
Rahimi, M., 59
Raichle, M., 378
Rainey, D., 475
Rakestraw, T.L., 516
Rakowski, W., 713
Ramirez, A., 794, 795, 797
Ramirez, R.W., 368
Ramos, P.M., 306
Randall, D.M., 700
Randel, A., 351, 354
Randle, S., 295
Rankin, D.B., 624
Ransdell, L.B., 34, 39
Rapagna, S., 211, 224
Rape, R.N., 789
Rappaport, J., 733
Rarick, G.L., 23
Rasbash, J., 721
Rasch, P.S., 181
Ratelle, C.F., 389, 390, 407, 409, 410
Rathunde, K., 183, 269, 279, 280, 281
Raudenbush, S.W., 721
Ravizza, K., 250, 252, 282, 290, 292,
    617, 627, 657, 661, 684
Ravizza, T., 329
Rawlings, E.I., 531
Rawlings, I.L., 531
Ray, W.J., 69, 367, 369, 370, 371, 372,
    373, 374, 380, 381
Reader, M.J., 395
Reason, J.T., 61
Reasoner, J., 758
Reber, A.S., 128, 129
Rebert, C.S., 371
Redding, C., 713
Reed, L., 445, 446
Reed, M., 619, 768
Reed, S.K., 151
Reed, T., 518
Reeds, G.K., 245, 246, 247, 248
Reeve, J., 395, 396
Reeve, T.G., 93, 95
Regian, J.W., 219
Regier, D.A., 741
Régnier, G., 245, 269, 270, 271, 272,
    273
Rehm, M., 254
Reid, D., 40, 41
Reid, G., 43, 58, 389, 395, 397, 402,
    403
Reihman, J.M., 404
Reine, B., 177, 183
Reisser, L., 679

Rejeski, W., 213, 452, 488, 489, 490,
    623, 641, 659, 660, 661, 662, 696,
    728, 729, 751, 811, 820
Remer, R., 681, 684
Remington, R.W., 70
Renaud, L., 734
Renger, R., 245, 246, 247, 754
Renson, L., 771
Renson, R., 185
Requa, R.K., 766
Resnick, L.B., 483
Resnicow, K., 696, 714, 715, 720, 725
Rest, J., 591, 596, 598, 599, 627
Rest, S., 445, 446
Reuschlein, S., 31
Revelle, W., 299, 305, 306
Reynolds, M.J., 675, 681
Reynolds, P., 12, 63
Rhoades, M.U., 10, 65
Rhodenizer, L., 133, 135
Rich, S., 5
Richard, L., 719, 721, 722, 723, 724,
    728, 729, 731, 734
Richards, G.E., 245, 756
Richardson, A., 543
Richardson, J., 70, 219
Richardson, P., 282, 503, 504, 554
Richman, J.M., 681, 770, 775, 780, 798
Richman, J.R., 561
Rickel, J., 136
Riddick, C.C., 646
Riddle, M.W., 758
Rider, S.P., 769, 775, 776
Ridini, L.M., 7, 180, 181
Ridsdale, S., 225, 226
Riedel, J.A., 517
Riehl, M.A., 770, 782
Riek, S., 145, 146, 168
Riessinger, C.A., 341, 342, 534, 553
Riggs, M.L., 352
Rikli, R., 97, 218
Riley, P., 516
Riley, S., 677
Rimer, S., 647
Rinehardt, K.F., 642
Rinfret, N., 409
Riniolo, T.C., 381
Rink, J.E., 10, 11, 45, 177, 182
Riordan, C., 451
Riordan, J., 406
Ripoll, H., 177, 179, 181, 182, 183, 377
Rippe, J.M., 640, 719, 720
Rippere, V., 643
Rippon, G., 532
Ritenbaugh, C., 787
Rittenhouse, C.H., 89
Ritter, W., 59
Ritzdorf, W., 179
Rivera, P.M., 249
Rivkin, F., 291, 302, 348

Rivkin, I.D., 647
Roach, N.K., 221, 793
Roark, A.E., 472
Robbins, M., 343, 348, 554
Roberton, M.A., 23, 29, 31, 32, 33, 35,
    228
Roberts, G., 205, 239, 240, 241, 262,
    330, 400, 417, 420, 422, 423, 424,
    425, 426, 427, 428, 429, 432, 433,
    434, 435, 447, 456, 518, 606, 608,
    612, 620, 626, 653, 655, 662, 823
Roberts, R.E., 749
Roberts, S., 811
Roberts, W., 106, 551, 552, 556, 557,
    558
Robertson, I., 608
Robertson, R.J., 696, 810, 811, 812,
    813
Robertson, S.D., 6
Robins, L.N., 741
Robinson, D.W., 458
Robinson, R.E., 273
Robinson, R.G., 768
Robinson, T., 611
Robinson, T.L., 745
Robinson, T.T., 252
Robinson, W.J., 539
Rocchio, P., 796
Roche, L., 245, 756
Rockstroh, B., 362, 364, 369
Rodgers, R.C., 510
Rodgers, W., 177, 178, 182, 188, 222,
    504, 529, 530, 536, 537, 538, 540,
    541, 542, 543, 544, 545, 651, 701
Rodionov, A.V., 3, 7
Rodrigues, S.T., 183, 188
Rodriguez, M.S., 787, 802
Roenker, D.L., 125
Roepke, N., 766, 769, 800, 801
Rogers, C.A., 108
Rogers, D.E., 5, 12
Rogers, T., 731
Rogers, W.L., 636, 638
Roh, J., 791, 793, 800, 806
Rohm-Young, D., 728, 729
Rohrbaugh, M., 310
Rokeach, M., 591
Romance, T., 598, 627
Romanow, S.K.E., 12
Roper, B.L., 247, 249
Roppe, B.E., 730, 731
Rosblad, B., 21
Rosch, E., 151
Roscoe, S.N., 91, 93, 105, 134
Rose, D., 57, 58, 122, 227, 230, 591
Rose, G., 718
Rose, J., 791, 792, 801
Rose, K.D., 810
Rosenbaum, D.A., 10
Rosenbaum, R.M., 445, 446

Rosenberg, E., 674, 683, 686
Rosenberg, S., 252, 254, 255, 256, 257, 261
Rosenblate, R., 432
Rosenbloom, D., 713
Rosenfarb, I., 517
Rosenfeld, L.B., 561, 681, 770, 775, 780, 798
Rosengren, K.S., 617
Rosenkoetter, M.M., 678
Rosenthal, T.L., 217
Roskin, M., 685
Ross, A., 41, 42
Ross, D., 128, 205, 211, 218, 220, 227, 744
Ross, J.G., 33, 37
Ross, L.E., 180
Ross, M., 451, 798, 800
Rossetti, Y., 61, 69
Rossi, J.S., 403, 713
Rossi, S., 713
Rostad, F.G., 639, 641, 643, 645
Rotella, B., 788, 793
Rotella, R.J., 282, 536, 672, 677, 796
Roth, K., 109, 144
Roth, W.T., 744
Rothengatter, T., 64
Rothman, A.J., 714, 723
Rothman, M., 516
Rothstein, A.L., 97, 216, 531
Rotter, J.B., 771
Rousseau, D.M., 351
Rousseau, F.L., 407, 410
Rowe, D.C., 270, 284
Rowen, R.B., 674, 681
Rowley, A., 245, 764
Rowley, S., 183
Ruark, J.K., 636
Rubin, R.H., 628
Rubin, S., 597
Rubio, N., 404
Ruble, D.N., 608
Ruby, B.C., 254
Rudestam, K.E., 343, 348
Rudisill, M., 456
Rudolph, D.L., 649, 651
Ruebush, B.K., 291
Rumelhart, D.E., 63
Runyan, W.M., 247, 250
Ruotsalainen, P., 730
Rupnow, A.A., 226
Rupp, J.W., 574, 576, 730, 731
Rusbult, C., 607
Rushall, B.S., 222, 243, 244, 249, 284, 534
Rushton, J.P., 585
Russel, J.A., 251
Russell, D., 8, 9, 10, 70, 74, 177, 180, 182, 183, 212, 447, 448, 449, 450, 457

Russell, E., 535
Russell, S., 178, 190, 245, 251, 269, 270, 273
Rusting, C.L., 637
Ruth, W., 508
Rüther, E., 744
Rutherford, W.J., 396
Ruthsatz, J.M., 270, 284
Rutter, B.G., 123
Rutter, M., 36, 270
Rutt Leas, R., 179, 182
Ryan, E.D., 221, 223, 327, 400, 538, 543
Ryan, R.M., 389, 390, 391, 392, 393, 394, 395, 396, 397, 398, 399, 404, 424, 425, 426, 427, 442, 465, 510, 519
Ryan, T.A., 498
Rybczynski, W., 647
Ryckman, R., 343, 344, 347, 348, 401, 554
Ryding, E., 532
Rzewnicki, R., 239, 240, 245, 246, 247, 254

Saarcla, P., 367, 368, 375
Saari, L.M., 497, 498, 507
Sachs, M.L., 654
Sackett, D.L., 741, 750
Sackett, R.S., 538
Sacks, M.H., 657, 660
Sade, S.S., 179
Sagal, M., 282
Sage, G., 319, 320, 327, 591, 687
Salas, E., 133, 135, 427
Salazar, S.J., 373
Salazar, W., 373, 374, 651, 742, 743, 744, 745, 746, 758, 759
Salhani, L., 624
Salizar, W., 641, 650
Sallis, J., 574, 576, 659, 696, 718, 719, 720, 722, 723, 725, 728, 729, 730, 731, 732, 733
Salmela, J., 4, 9, 14, 176, 178, 179, 185, 186, 190, 212, 245, 269, 270, 271, 272, 273, 279, 282, 283, 824
Salmon, J., 529, 530, 536, 542, 659
Salmoni, A., 40, 41, 57, 92, 99, 102, 103, 104, 109
Salonen, J., 734
Salovey, P., 723
Salthouse, T.A., 183
Saltzman, E.L., 158
Salvendy, G., 69, 136
Sammer, G., 59
Samples, P., 677
Samuels, S.C., 773
Sanders, A.F., 62, 290
Sanders, D., 731
Sanderson, D.J., 571, 572, 573, 577
Sanderson, F.H., 180, 181

Sandford, B., 820
Sandman, P.M., 714
Sands, R., 682, 684
Sandvik, E., 638
Sandweiss, J.H., 99
Sanford, B., 213
Sansone, C., 395, 397
Santa Maria, D.L., 371, 372, 377
Sapp, M., 610, 611
Sarason, B.R., 430, 680, 774
Sarason, I.G., 306, 430, 680, 768, 769, 774
Sarason, S.B., 291, 306
Sardinha, L.F., 12
Saris, W.H.M., 719
Saron, C.D., 375
Sarrazin, C., 183
Sarrazin, P., 420, 422, 428, 434, 439, 460, 461, 462
Sasche, S., 76
Satava, R.M., 133
Satterfield, M.J., 796
Saudino, K.J., 284
Saunders, G., 179
Saury, J., 178, 190
Savelsbergh, G.J.P., 75, 158, 159, 160
Savery, L.K., 680, 768
Saxe, G.B., 69
Scammon, R.E., 27
Scanlan, T.K., 250, 252, 279, 282, 290, 291, 292, 397, 550, 605, 607, 608, 614, 615, 616, 617, 619, 621, 627, 645, 658, 659, 660, 661, 662, 684, 815, 826
Schachar, R., 36
Schachter, S., 312, 472
Schacter, S., 445
Schaefer, C., 770
Schaefer, W., 682, 684
Schaik, P., 646
Scharf, P., 592
Scheidt, P.C., 787
Scheier, M.F., 242, 301, 307, 557, 567, 579, 720, 735, 796
Schell, B., 823
Schellenberg, E.G., 270
Scherzer, C.B., 795
Schlattmann, A., 240
Schlaug, G., 284
Schlenker, B.R., 696
Schleser, R., 282
Schlicht, W., 248, 250, 742
Schloder, M., 189, 190
Schlossberg, N., 675, 681
Schmid, A., 779
Schmid, T., 723
Schmidt, D., 530, 531, 533, 541
Schmidt, F.L., 499
Schmidt, G.W., 279, 605, 607, 815

Schmidt, R.A., 5, 8, 9, 12, 21, 22, 44, 57, 66, 88, 91, 92, 98, 99, 100, 101, 102, 103, 104, 106, 107, 109, 115, 116, 118, 121, 127, 133, 144, 151, 155, 158, 163, 164, 166, 167, 207, 208, 210, 211, 214, 218, 462
Schneider, D.J., 310
Schneider, J.K., 574, 575
Schneider, K., 21, 26
Schneider, W., 24, 53, 60, 61, 65, 66, 67, 103, 124, 128, 182, 270, 309
Schneidman, N.N., 7
Schneidt, T., 6
Schoenfelder-Zohdi, B., 102, 208, 221
Scholz, J.P., 157, 160
Schomer, H., 812
Schöner, G., 154, 155, 158
Schönfelder-Zohdi, B., 129
Schooler, C., 718
Schreiber, L.E., 75
Schreiner, W., 63
Schroeder, R.K., 43
Schuiteman, J., 591
Schulberg, H., 747
Schulz, R., 185
Schumsky, D.A., 88
Schunk, D.H., 215, 217, 230, 231, 340, 341, 351, 465, 510
Schurr, K.T., 773, 795
Schutz, R.W., 34, 37, 38, 291, 324, 402, 482, 770, 772, 776, 779, 780, 781
Schwab, M., 721
Schwalbe, M.V., 618
Schwartz, A.J., 399
Schwartz, E., 327
Schwartz, G., 161, 291, 302, 324, 334, 549
Schwartz, J.C., 254
Schwartz, J.H., 379
Schwartz, R., 725, 743
Schwartz, S.G., 641
Schwarz, N., 637, 638, 643, 657, 659, 662
Schwenz, S., 789, 802
Scott, M.A., 12
Scott, S.G., 788, 793, 794, 801
Scripture, E.W., 825
Scully, D.M., 99, 126, 128, 205, 208, 220, 221, 228
Seabourne, T.G., 535
Seat, J.E., 215
Seaward, B.L., 641, 646
Sechrest, L., 743
Seefeldt, V., 29, 30, 31, 33, 34, 35, 272, 608
Seeger, C.M., 5
Seelback, H., 742, 747
Seese, M.D., 769, 772
Sefton, J.M., 658, 660

Segal, L., 105, 134
Seger, C.A., 129
Seheult, C.L., 823
Seifriz, J., 400, 421, 423, 425, 434
Seitz, V., 224, 225, 226
Sejnowski, T., 147, 156, 658
Sekiya, H., 5, 107, 129
Selby, V.C., 403
Selden, W.K., 823
Selder, D., 97, 823
Self, E.A., 320
Seligman, M.E., 445, 448, 450, 458, 459, 463, 690
Selman, R.L., 609
Selye, H., 282, 362, 366, 641, 680
Semjen, A., 58, 154, 160, 161
Semmel, A., 448, 450
Senders, J., 75
Senécal, C., 390, 392, 393, 399, 409
Seng, C.N., 8, 10, 12, 177
Senior, K., 550
Senn, K.L., 574, 576, 730, 731
Senulis, J., 375
Seraganian, P., 641, 695
Serfass, R.C., 246
Serrien, D.J., 98, 105, 214, 215, 219
Sevsek, B., 178, 182, 187
Sewell, D.F., 304
Sexton, H., 744
Seymour, H., 721
Shadmehr, R., 135
Shaffer, L.H., 12, 124
Shaffer, S.M., 787, 789, 790, 791, 793, 794, 796, 797, 800, 802
Shaffner, P., 14, 212
Shake, C.L., 659
Shalley, C., 511, 516
Shallice, T., 66
Shambrook, C.J., 309
Shamir, B., 352
Shank, M.D., 8, 177, 180
Shank, R.H., 795
Shapiro, B.I., 363
Shapiro, D., 57, 102, 106, 107, 118, 120, 327
Sharah, H.S., 472
Sharit, J., 69
Sharp, R.H., 69
Shaw, J.H., 597
Shaw, K.N., 497, 498, 507, 516
Shaw, L.M., 472
Shaw, M.E., 472
Shaw, R.E., 144, 146, 152, 156, 157
Shaw, S., 363, 619
Shay, C.T., 181
Shea, C.H., 11, 95, 100, 101, 109, 118, 127, 210, 219, 221, 811
Shea, G.P., 351
Shea, J.B., 99, 106, 119, 120, 218
Shearin, E.N., 430

Sheath, P., 177, 179, 181
Shebilske, W.L., 219
Sheehan, G., 647
Sheen, R., 133
Sheffield, F.N., 205
Sheikh, A.A., 540
Sheinman, L., 399
Shelbourne, K.D., 797
Sheldon, K.M., 404
Sheldon, R., 679
Shelley, G.A., 788, 791, 792, 800, 801
Shephard, R., 299, 718, 731, 733, 734
Shepp, B.E., 41
Sheridan, T., 55, 136
Sherif, C.W., 473, 479
Sherif, M., 473, 479
Sherman, C.P., 792
Sherman, S.J., 241, 242
Sherman, T.M., 684
Sherman, W.M., 363
Sherrill, C., 226
Sherry, D., 654, 656
Sherwood, D.E., 94, 103, 123
Shewchuk, R., 223, 393, 598, 606, 627
Shields, D., 424, 434, 476, 485, 589, 590, 591, 592, 593, 594, 595, 596, 597, 598, 599, 627
Shiffman, S., 638, 680
Shiffrin, R.M., 24, 53, 60, 61, 65, 66, 71, 72, 128, 309
Shoda, Y., 240, 241, 243, 247, 251, 252, 253, 254, 255, 261
Shoenfelt, E.L., 500, 518
Shoham, V., 310
Shraddhananda, S., 647
Shteinbakh, V., 824
Shulman, G.L., 70
Shulman, H.G., 62
Shultz, B.B., 246, 247, 248
Shumaker, S.A., 787
Shumway-Cook, A., 20, 21, 29, 99
Shurin, C.S., 607, 619
Sidaway, B., 5, 94, 102, 164, 209, 218
Sidhu, L.S., 74, 180
Sieb, G.E., 672
Siegel, B.V., 369, 370
Siegel, D., 125, 211, 216, 230, 811
Siegel, J.M., 641, 768, 769
Siegler, R.S., 103, 185
Signorielli, N., 232
Silva, J., 239, 244, 246, 247, 248, 400, 594, 823, 824, 826, 827
Silver, R.L., 789
Silverman, S., 87, 88, 89, 90, 91, 104
Silvester, J., 453, 454, 455
Sime, W., 303, 758
Simek, T.C., 571, 572, 573
Simkova, N., 271, 272
Simmons, R.W., 99
Simms, S., 530, 541, 542

Simnett, I., 732
Simon, G.E., 747
Simon, H.A., 6, 9, 25, 43, 74, 186, 278
Simon, J., 291, 302, 348, 614, 615, 744
Simon, K.M., 510
Simoneau, J.A., 284
Simonetti, J.L., 675
Simons, J., 185, 221, 223, 279, 296, 303, 325, 327, 538, 543, 552, 605, 607, 608, 645, 658, 659, 660, 815
Simons, P.J., 815
Simons-Morton, B.G., 723, 724
Simons-Morton, D.G., 722, 723, 724, 728, 729, 731
Simonton, D.K., 175, 270
Simpson, C.A., 795, 801
Simpson, R.L., 637, 638
Sinclair, D.A., 551, 558, 677, 678, 681, 682
Singer, J., 312, 445
Singer, R., 3, 67, 76, 103, 104, 117, 126, 132, 165, 166, 176, 179, 180, 181, 184, 185, 188, 222, 241, 243, 246, 247, 254, 269, 278, 279, 310, 333, 456, 464, 506, 529, 540, 571, 572, 573, 647, 659, 778, 826
Singh, M., 574, 575
Singh, P., 117, 189, 190
Singleton, D.A., 341, 348, 350
Singleton, M., 798
Sinnott, K., 396, 463, 464
Sinyor, D., 641, 752
Sistrunk, F., 122, 123
Sivier, J., 91, 105, 134
Sjoberg, L., 327
Sjöholm, H., 532
Skaalvik, E.M., 435
Skinner, B.F., 389
Skinner, E., 444, 464, 465, 466, 701
Skinner, H., 712, 713
Skirstad, B., 604
Sklar, J.H., 789, 793, 794, 795, 797, 799, 800, 801
Skubic, V., 7
Slanger, E., 343, 348
Slater, B.A., 381
Slatt, B., 69
Slattery, M.M., 801
Slavin, L.A., 789
Slifkin, A.B., 154, 164
Sloboda, J.A., 117, 175, 183, 185, 269, 270, 272, 273, 283, 285
Smart, A.E., 687, 696, 795
Smiley-Oyen, A., 42
Smilkstein, G., 614
Smilley-Oyen, A.L., 167, 168
Smith, A., 6, 36
Smith, A.D., 774
Smith, A.L., 215, 230, 231, 341, 624, 625, 626, 627, 628

Smith, A.M., 787, 788, 789, 790, 791, 793, 794, 796, 800, 801
Smith, A.P., 741
Smith, D., 246, 291, 295, 296, 298, 300, 301, 302, 303, 304, 307, 324, 344, 348
Smith, E.M., 427
Smith, G., 97
Smith, J., 39, 174, 176
Smith, K., 99, 249
Smith, L., 153, 155, 718, 735
Smith, M., 500
Smith, M.A., 661
Smith, M.D., 11, 617, 627
Smith, M.E., 362, 363, 369, 375
Smith, M.G., 758
Smith, R., 320, 324, 766
Smith, R.E., 249, 282, 291, 402, 431, 442, 482, 519, 612, 613, 622, 623, 634, 680, 605, 742, 762, 769, 770, 772, 775, 776, 779, 780, 781
Smith, R.J., 509
Smith, T., 463
Smith-Hanrahan, C.M., 812
Smith-Munyon, V.L., 94
Smoll, F., 23, 34, 37, 38, 93, 249, 282, 291, 320, 324, 402, 431, 482, 622, 623, 634, 685, 769, 770, 772, 776, 779, 780, 781
Smyth, M.M., 178, 182, 187, 188
Snel, J., 769, 770, 771, 773, 776, 781, 782
Sneyers, K.M., 96
Snijder, W., 179
Snoddy, G.S., 116
Snow, J., 435
Snowden, S., 102
Snyder, C.R., 254
Snyder, C.W., 9
Snyder, D., 636
Snyder, E., 59, 591, 598, 682
Snyder, M., 242, 243
Sobolewski, S., 766
Soderberg, U., 746
Solmon, M., 40, 44, 422
Solomon, G., 594, 598
Solomons, L., 53, 64
Somsen, R.J.M., 69
Sonneschein, G., 181
Sonneschein, I., 181
Sonstroem, R.J., 319, 327, 756
Sooman, A., 721
Soos, I., 425, 427, 437, 461, 462
Sordoni, C., 530
Sosniak, L.A., 278
Sot, V., 436
Sothmann, M.S., 750
Soubhi, H., 730
Soulière, D., 179
Southard, D., 13, 209

Spalding, T.W., 371, 372, 380, 381
Spangler, K., 718, 722, 723, 724, 733
Sparkes, A.C., 792
Sparling, P.B., 294, 754
Sparrow, W.A., 12, 90, 98, 363, 365
Speelman, C., 69
Spelke, E., 64, 65, 66
Spence, J.C., 756
Spence, J.T., 326
Spence, K.W., 326
Spencer, R.M., 6, 7
Sperandio, J.C., 61
Spicer, R., 787
Spielberger, C.D., 291, 302, 308, 324, 328, 332, 348, 696, 742, 771
Spilich, G.J., 25, 45, 177
Spilker, B., 637, 638
Spink, K.S., 282, 353, 477, 478, 485, 488, 610, 729
Spirduso, W.W., 180, 758
Spoorns, O., 145, 165
Spray, C.M., 462
Spreeman, J., 251, 614, 616
Spreitzer, E., 591, 598
Spurgeon, J.H., 4, 5, 10, 11, 12, 45, 177, 182
Spurgeon, P., 179
Staats, A.W., 247
Stadler, M., 129, 532
Stager, P., 70
Stamper, D.A., 812
Stanbrough, M., 328
Stancak, A., 368, 369, 372, 374
Standage, M., 425, 427
Stanicek, J.A., 500
Stankard, W., 320
Stanley, M.A., 444
Stanney, K., 136
Starek, J., 98, 217
Stark, L., 70
Starkes, J., 3, 6, 7, 8, 9, 13, 45, 46, 57, 70, 74, 76, 117, 174, 175, 176, 177, 178, 179, 180, 181, 182, 183, 184, 185, 186, 187, 188, 189, 190, 191, 212, 223, 224, 230, 269, 270, 277, 278, 279, 533
Starkey, C.A., 800
Start, K.B., 543
Stassen, H., 55
Staszewski, J., 185
Staveland, L.E., 58
Stebelsky, G., 185
Steckler, A., 722, 723, 724, 731
Steel, R.P., 499, 507, 508, 518, 520
Stegeman, D.F., 144, 146
Stein, F., 75
Stein, G., 53, 64, 250, 252, 282, 290, 292, 320, 321, 324, 328, 330, 331, 617, 627, 653, 655, 657, 661, 662, 684

Stein, H., 69
Stein, J., 377
Stein, J.F., 54, 177, 183
Stein, J.M., 744
Steinberg, G.M., 165, 184
Steinmetz, H., 284
Stelmach, G.E., 11, 22, 33, 39, 40, 53, 54, 63, 66, 90, 118
Ste-Marie, D.M., 536
Stenberg, G., 532
Stengers, I., 152
Stennett, R.C., 326
Stephens, D., 595, 596
Stephens, L., 672
Stephens, T., 718, 719, 720, 722, 725, 752
Steptoe, A., 642, 649, 744, 752
Steriade, M., 369
Sterling, J.C., 794
Sterman, M.B., 369
Stern, R., 324, 327
Sternberg, R.J., 3, 270
Stevenson, M., 283
Steverlynck, A., 771
Stewart, D.G., 571, 572, 573
Stewart, E., 177, 179, 181, 820
Stewart, G., 178, 182, 188
Stewart, R.M.L., 793, 794
Sthalekar, H.A., 796
Stiehl, J., 227
Stifter, C.A., 381
Stilger, V., 791, 793, 800, 806
Stipek, D., 230
Stitcher, T., 282, 503, 504
Stoever, S., 769
Stoffregren, T.A., 148
Stokols, D., 721
Stoll, S., 592, 597
Stone, A.A., 638
Stone, B.M., 532
Stone, E.J., 709, 710, 728, 731
Stones, M.J., 189
Stoove, M.A., 779
Stopka, C., 795
Strack, F., 638
Strang, H., 518
Stratton, P., 452, 453, 454, 455
Stratton, R., 42, 180
Straub, W.F., 243, 244
Strayer, D.L., 59
Strean, W.B., 239, 262, 823
Striedter, G.F., 168
Stringfield, D.O., 242
Stroessner, S.J., 460, 461, 462
Stroll, W., 180
Stroop, J.R., 71
Stroup, F., 180
Stuart, J.C., 768
Stuart, M., 596
Stuart, M.E., 627
Stuart, M.J., 791, 793, 794, 800

Stucky-Rupp, R.C., 659
Subramanian, P.R., 87, 90, 91
Suddon, F.H., 107
Sugden, D.A., 41
Suh, E.M., 636, 637
Suinn, R.M., 534, 539
Sullivan, H.S., 624, 625, 626, 628
Sullivan, J.J., 57
Sullivan, P.J., 355, 356
Summers, J., 6, 9, 55, 58, 60, 68, 121, 124, 144, 145, 146, 154, 160, 161, 770, 771
Susser, M., 728, 733
Sussman, M.B., 675, 682
Sutton, S., 699, 701, 714
Svec, O.J., 571, 572, 573, 577
Svoboda, B., 676, 677, 678, 680, 681, 682, 683
Swain, A., 162, 293, 296, 297, 298, 301, 302, 303, 304, 333, 421, 435, 442, 504, 556, 558
Swann, W.B., 398
Swanson, M.J., 773
Sweeney, P.D., 450, 458
Sweeting, R.L., 180, 181
Swets, J.A., 5, 8, 221
Swinnen, S., 86, 98, 102, 104, 105, 106, 107, 108, 109, 116, 214, 215, 219
Sylva, M., 812
Sylvestre, F., 249
Syme, L.S., 721
Syrjä, P., 295, 304, 329
Szabo, A., 751
Szentágothai, J., 144, 146, 147, 150, 152, 155, 164
Szinovacz, M.E., 680

Tabachnick, B.G., 489
Tache, J., 680
Tadary, B., 155, 156, 532
Taggart, P., 298
Takahashi, P.J., 574, 576, 643, 649
Takai, K., 300, 330
Takenaka, K., 282
Takeuchi, A.H., 284
Tammen, V., 392, 395, 396, 397, 409, 674
Tanaka, J.S., 245
Tandy, R.D., 102
Tang, C., 369, 370
Tanner, J.M., 37
Tappe, M.K., 687, 696, 795
Tassone, C., 431
Tate, A.K., 752
Tattersall, A.J., 308
Taub, E., 362, 364, 369
Tayler, M., 158, 159, 160, 166
Taylor, A., 740, 742, 743, 745, 751, 752
Taylor, A.H., 794, 795, 799, 801
Taylor, A.W., 734

Taylor, C., 675, 743, 744, 756, 757, 814
Taylor, H.L., 134
Taylor, J., 672, 673, 674, 675, 676, 681, 685, 686, 823
Taylor, S.E., 444, 452, 647, 812
Taylor, W., 659, 728, 729, 742, 747, 756
Tdlohreg, C.W., 166
Teasdale, J.D., 445, 458, 463, 643
Teasdale, N., 39, 58
Tedder, S., 789, 794
Tedeschi, R.G., 801
Teeken, J., 320, 321
Tegano, C., 684
Tehan, G., 178, 182, 188
Teichner, W.H., 74
Tellegen, A., 406
Temple, J., 41
Temple, S., 723
Templeton, A.E., 180
Templin, D.P., 217
Templin, T., 434, 595
Temprado, J., 6, 12, 58
Tenenbaum, G., 6, 9, 177, 178, 179, 181, 182, 188, 200, 250, 251, 447, 448, 450, 500, 501, 502, 503, 505, 510, 571, 577, 811, 817, 818, 820
Tennant, L.K., 76, 103, 165, 222, 395, 540
Terborg, J.R., 517
Terry, P., 302, 304, 535, 656
Tesch-Römer, C., 4, 117, 175, 185, 186, 190, 191, 269, 270, 275, 277, 278, 279, 280, 282, 283, 533
Tesch-Römer, E., 362
Testerman, E., 25
Thatcher, R.W., 369
Thayer, R.E., 324, 574, 576, 639, 640, 643, 645, 649, 651
Theberge, N., 591
Theeboom, M., 400, 561, 624, 625, 626, 627, 628
Thelen, E., 21, 26, 153, 154, 155, 379
Thelen, M.H., 215
Thelwell, R.C., 295
Theodorakis, Y., 500, 505, 509, 527, 798, 800
Theorell, T., 768
Thibaut, J.W., 607, 612, 613
Thiffault, C., 178, 245, 246
Thill, E., 389, 395, 428, 442
Thirer, J., 7, 74, 180
Thoits, P., 729, 730
Thom, R., 161
Thoma, S., 591, 599
Thomachot, B., 21, 26
Thomas, J., 11, 20, 21, 22, 24, 25, 29, 33, 34, 35, 37, 38, 39, 40, 41, 42, 43, 44, 45, 46, 56, 108, 118, 125, 160, 174, 177, 179, 182, 190, 223, 224,

225, 226, 273, 395, 500, 501, 530, 531, 532
Thomas, K., 20, 21, 22, 25, 33, 38, 39, 40, 41, 42, 43, 44, 45, 46, 118, 174, 190, 224, 225, 273
Thomas, M.B., 783
Thompson, A., 185, 641
Thompson, C.E., 399
Thompson, D.L., 363
Thompson, E., 151
Thompson, J., 598
Thompson, N.J., 769, 773, 778
Thompson, R., 326, 332
Thompson, S., 674
Thompson, T., 463
Thomson, J.A., 132
Thomson, M.A., 99
Thoren, P., 747
Thorkildsen, T., 435
Thorn, I., 681, 684
Thorndike, E.L., 94, 133
Thorne, F.C., 652
Thorne, G., 820
Thornton, B., 343, 348, 554
Thornton, D.C., 59
Thornton, J.S., 676
Thornton, K.M., 459
Thornton, N., 459
Tice, D.M., 567, 720, 735
Tidwell, P.D., 135
Tilson, H.H., 637, 638
Tims, F.C., 643
Tinsdale, R.S., 484, 489
Tinti, G., 796
Tipper, S.P., 41
Titchener, E.B., 53
Tobey, C., 92, 96, 104
Tobias, P.V., 36
Todorov, E., 135
Tolan, P.H., 735
Tolman, E.C., 92
Tomarken, A.J., 509, 510, 519
Tomas, I., 420
Tomporowski, P.D., 758
Toner, B.B., 306
Tongate, R.A., 681, 684
Tonymon, P., 423, 767, 770, 771, 772, 774, 775, 777, 782
Toole, T., 120, 131
Törestad, B., 240, 241, 243, 261, 262
Tosi, E.J., 680
Trachtman, J.N., 180
Tran, Z.V., 651, 742, 747, 748, 749
Trapp, C., 7, 74, 180
Travis, T.W., 747
Treacy, S.H., 797
Treasure, D., 341, 343, 348, 350, 417, 420, 423, 424, 425, 427, 432, 435, 606, 662, 752
Trehub, S.E., 270

Treisman, A., 66, 72
Tremayne, P., 245, 756
Tremblay, L., 144
Trenske, M., 811
Trexler, L.D., 680
Trinity, J., 97
Triplett, N., 219, 825
Trist, E., 472
Trowbridge, M.H., 88, 93
Troxel, R.K., 215, 789, 802
Troxell, J.R., 770, 775
Troyer, M.E., 597
Trudel, P., 178, 190, 249
Trumble, A., 787
Tsetlin, M.L., 379
Tsu, V., 685
Tubbs, M.E., 499, 507, 508
Tuckman, J., 679, 683
Tudor, J., 40
Tuffey, S., 294, 295, 325, 328, 329, 559, 797, 798, 799, 800
Tuller, B., 12, 56, 365
Tully, D.C., 341, 357
Tuomilehto, J., 730, 734
Tupper, R.W., 108
Turek, E., 344, 348, 349
Turk, D.C., 814
Turner, E.E., 659, 660, 661
Turner, P.E., 295
Turner, W.E., 301
Turvey, M.T., 12, 66, 99, 144, 152
Tuson, K.M., 390, 392, 399, 401, 402, 403, 405, 409, 752
Tussing, L., 180, 181
Tuttle, W.W., 180
Twisk, J., 769, 770, 771, 773, 776, 781, 782
Tyldesley, D.A., 8, 11, 179
Tyrell, D.A.J., 741
Tyson, L.A., 88, 89, 90, 104
Tzetzis, G., 500, 518

Udry, E., 295, 304, 319, 320, 321, 322, 535, 559, 789, 791, 792, 795, 796, 797, 798, 799, 800, 801
Uemukai, K., 788, 793, 794
Uitenbroek, D.G., 787
Ulrich, B., 21, 25, 26
Umilta, C., 57, 377
Underwood, G., 53
Underwood, M., 396, 399, 401, 403, 407
Ungerleiter, S., 679, 681, 682, 683
Upton, G., 106
Ursin, H., 320, 325

Vaccoro, P., 381
Vachon, L., 58
Vadocz, E., 534, 535, 557, 560
Vaernes, R., 325
Vagg, P.R., 696, 742

Vaglum, P., 660, 661
Valeriote, T.A., 608
Valkonen, A., 425, 426, 434, 461, 462
Vallerand, R.J., 68, 239, 389, 390, 391, 392, 393, 394, 395, 396, 397, 398, 399, 400, 401, 402, 403, 404, 405, 406, 407, 408, 409, 410, 420, 426, 427, 448, 457, 458, 465, 519, 571, 578, 597, 598
Valliant, P.M., 773
Vallières, E.F., 390, 392, 393
Valois, P., 542
Valoski, A., 730
Valuri, G., 787
Vance, R., 518
Vancouver, J.B., 579
Van den Auweele, Y., 239, 240, 245, 246, 247, 248, 254, 257, 435, 770, 771, 772
van der Brug, H., 239
van der Loo, H., 183
Van der Molen, M.W., 69
Vander Velden, L., 591
Vander Wal, J.S., 659
VanDyne, H.J., 41
Vanek, M., 7, 676, 677, 678, 680, 681, 682, 683
van Emmerik, R.E.A., 12, 130, 164
Van Gelder, T., 144, 151
Van Gerven, D., 185
Van Ingen Schenau, G.J., 247, 661
Vankersschaver, J., 64
VanLanduyt, L.M., 746
Van Loon, E.M., 96
Van Mechelen, I., 252, 254, 257, 261
Van Mechelen, W., 769, 770, 771, 773, 776, 781, 782
Van Mele, V., 239, 240, 245, 246, 247, 251, 254
Van Outryve, D., 177
Van Raalte, J., 249, 449, 653, 787, 788, 789, 793, 794, 795, 797, 799, 800, 801, 823
Van Raalte, N.S., 653
van Rossum, J.H.A., 118, 183
van Santvoord, A.A.M., 12
Van Schoyck, S.R., 68
Van Snippenberg, F.J., 166
van Stavel, R., 639, 641, 643, 645, 742
Vansteelandt, K., 254
VanVlack, S., 680, 681, 682
Van Voorhis, S., 377
van Wieringen, P.C., 12, 75, 145
Van Winckel, J., 185, 186
Van Wolffelaar, P.C., 64
VanYperen, N.W., 422, 423
Varela, F., 151
Vartiainen, E., 730
Vaux, C.L., 747
Veach, T.L., 768

Vealey, R., 239, 240, 241, 244, 246, 249, 254, 262, 282, 291, 295, 296, 298, 300, 301, 302, 303, 304, 307, 324, 343, 344, 348, 420, 429, 534, 538, 539, 550, 551, 552, 553, 554, 555, 556, 557, 558, 559, 560, 561, 562, 823
Vecsey, G., 672
Vega, W.A., 730, 731
Velicier, W.F., 713
Veltri, J.P., 645, 745
Venables, P.H., 69, 319
Vercruyssen, M.J.P., 12
Vereijken, B., 130, 143, 164
Verhulst, J., 185
Vernacchia, R.A., 217
Veroff, J., 608
Verschueren, S.M.P., 105
Verstappen, F., 320, 321
Verstraeten, D., 249, 250
Vesonder, G.T., 177
Vevera, M., 296, 303, 325, 327, 552
Vicente, K.J., 146, 152, 156, 157
Vickers, J.N., 70, 74, 75, 178, 184, 188, 378
Villanova, P., 450
Vincent, M.L., 659, 729
Vincent, W.J., 363
Vincente, K.J., 59
Vinicor, F., 718, 735
Vinnay, G., 683
Vlachopoulos, S., 423, 450, 457, 458, 461, 656
Vlaswinkel, E.H., 330
Vogel, P., 31
Vogt, S., 223, 532
Vogt, T.M., 718, 728
Vollrath, D.A., 484, 489
vonBaeyer, C., 448, 450
von Bertalanfy, L., 566
von Euler, C., 746
Vongjaturapat, S., 420
VonKorff, M., 747
Voroncov, A.R., 271
Vorro, J., 13
Voss, J.F., 25, 45, 177

Waag, W.L., 134, 135
Wade, M.G., 124
Wadsworth, W.A., 767, 770
Wagenaar, R.C., 145
Wagner, E., 718, 732, 735
Wagner, N.N., 687, 767, 769, 782
Wagner, S.L., 400
Wagoner, B.L., 58
Waite, R.R., 291
Wakefield, W.D., 463
Wakelin, D.R., 62
Walker, B.W., 435, 662
Wall, J.R., 798

Wall, P.D., 812
Wallace, C., 366
Wallace, J.P., 730, 731
Wallace, S.A., 90, 160
Waller, A.E., 787
Wallerstein, N., 731
Walling, M., 401, 421, 424, 425
Walsh, V., 148
Walsh, W.D., 9, 179
Walter, C.B., 90, 92, 98, 99, 104, 105, 109
Walter, S.M., 538, 539
Walters, J.M., 181
Walters, L.K., 123
Walters, M.R., 160
Walters, N., 642, 649
Wan, W., 462
Wandersman, A., 732
Wang, J., 462
Wang, L., 184
Wang, M.Q., 7, 58, 68, 69, 246, 248, 778
Wang, Y., 103, 640
Wankel, L., 252, 327, 399, 574, 575, 645, 657, 658, 659, 660, 661, 723
Wanlin, C.M., 504
Wann, D., 319, 320, 321
Wann, J.P., 70, 74
Ward, A., 640
Ward, C.H., 748
Ward, P., 504
Washburn, R.A., 719
Washburn, S.L., 36
Wasserman, E.A., 147
Watchel, P., 70
Waterink, W., 64
Watkins, B., 344, 348, 349
Watkins, D., 104
Watson, C.B., 352, 353, 484, 486
Watson, D., 406, 782
Watson, G.G., 271, 272, 291
Watson, J., 681, 684
Waugh, R., 749, 750, 756
Wayda, V.K., 500, 504, 517
Weary, G., 444
Weaver, N.L., 787
Webb, E.J., 743
Webb, H., 591, 597
Webb, W.M., 677
Webber, B.L., 135
Webborn, A.D.J., 799
Weber, L.J., 684
Weekes, E.M., 96
Weeks, D., 147
Weeks, D.J., 118, 119
Weeks, D.L., 100, 103, 160, 212, 217, 219, 231, 341, 344, 348, 350
Weghorst, S., 136
Wegner, D.M., 309, 310, 311
Wehner, T., 532
Weichman, S.A., 282

Weigand, D.A., 401, 427, 497, 500, 501, 502, 507, 509, 512, 513, 514, 517, 518, 520
Weigelt, C., 76, 130, 131
Weil, M., 125, 134
Weinberg, D.R., 108
Weinberg, H., 156
Weinberg, K., 676, 677, 680, 682, 683, 684
Weinberg, R., 178, 282, 292, 293, 295, 296, 325, 327, 332, 355, 380, 390, 395, 396, 409, 497, 499, 500, 501, 502, 503, 504, 505, 506, 507, 508, 509, 510, 512, 513, 514, 517, 518, 520, 523, 529, 530, 534, 535, 537, 541, 542, 544, 554, 557, 558, 794
Weinbruch, C., 362, 364, 369
Weiner, B., 389, 444, 445, 446, 447, 448, 449, 452, 456, 457, 463, 466, 789
Weingarten, G., 447, 448, 450
Weinstein, N.D., 714
Weintraub, J.K., 796
Weir, P.L., 117, 189, 190, 214
Weisberg, R.W., 270
Weiser, P.C., 812
Weismann, M.M., 747
Weiss, H.M., 516
Weiss, M., 21, 42, 205, 211, 215, 216, 217, 223, 226, 227, 228, 229, 230, 231, 282, 332, 341, 344, 348, 393, 400, 475, 554, 558, 561, 594, 595, 598, 604, 605, 606, 610, 611, 612, 613, 614, 615, 616, 618, 619, 621, 623, 624, 625, 626, 627, 628, 629, 661, 789, 802
Weissbein, D.A., 427
Welch, J.C., 53, 54
Weldon, E., 511
Welford, A.T., 61, 290
Welk, G., 659, 709, 710, 728, 731
Wells, C.L., 34, 39
Wenger, H.A., 327
Wentzell, A.B., 605, 626, 627
Werthner, P., 672, 676, 677, 678, 679, 680, 681, 682, 684
Wessells, M.G., 72
West, R., 42
Westbrook, T., 332
Westerlund, J.H., 180
Westre, K., 475
Wetherill, K.V., 395
Wetter, D.W., 696, 714, 715, 720, 725
Weyerer, S., 749
Whalen, S., 183, 269, 279, 280, 281
Wheeler, B.L., 657
Wheeler, G., 574, 575, 680, 681, 682
Whitacre, C., 219, 221
Whitall, J., 21
White, A., 221, 529, 530, 534, 535, 536
White, C., 672, 680

White, J.L., 9
White, K.A., 625
White, K.M., 730
White, L., 310
White, M.A., 94, 101, 214, 218
White, P.A., 54
White, P.H., 508
White, R.W., 389, 393, 605
White, S.A., 421, 423, 431, 620
Whitehead, J., 246, 395, 397, 401, 417, 420, 421, 422, 606
Whitehurst, M., 75, 120
Whitesides, J.E., 747
Whithey, S.B., 637
Whiting, H.T.A., 75, 126, 127, 130, 143, 144, 158, 159, 160, 164, 167, 168, 180, 181, 208, 209, 239
Whitney, S., 23
Whitwer, S.S., 373
Wickens, C.D., 54, 55, 58, 59, 61, 62, 63, 66, 72
Wickstrom, R.L., 29, 31
Widmeyer, W.N., 353, 472, 473, 474, 475, 476, 477, 478, 479, 480, 481, 483, 484, 485, 487, 488, 489, 503, 510, 661
Wiebe, V.R., 7
Wiechman, S., 320, 324, 431
Wierwille, W.W., 59
Wiese, D.M., 215, 344, 348, 616, 793, 801
Wiese-Bjornstal, D.M., 205, 227, 228, 230, 787, 789, 790, 791, 793, 794, 796, 800, 802
Wiggins, D.K., 614, 824
Wiggins, M.S., 302, 344
Wightman, D.C., 121, 122, 123, 124, 166
Wilckens, J.H., 797
Wild, M.R., 29
Wilkinson, J.G., 649
Wilkinson, J.J., 7
Wilkinson, M.O., 13
Wilks, S., 674, 681
Williams, A.C., 93
Williams, A.M., 20, 67, 70, 74, 144, 145, 146, 151, 153, 154, 156, 157, 161, 162, 164, 165, 166, 167, 174, 176, 178, 179, 182, 183, 184, 188, 208, 210, 212, 310, 778
Williams, C.R., 517
Williams, E.L., 729
Williams, E.S., 298
Williams, H., 28, 29, 41, 180
Williams, J.D., 532
Williams, J.G., 70, 74, 144, 145, 151, 153, 156, 157, 161, 174, 176, 179, 182, 184, 188, 205, 208, 210
Williams, J.M., 7, 74, 282, 293, 302, 362, 364, 475, 484, 559, 560, 625, 691, 766, 767, 768, 769, 770, 771,

772, 773, 774, 775, 777, 778, 780, 781, 782, 783, 800, 801, 802, 823
Williams, K., 35, 475, 511
Williams, L., 246, 248, 249, 403, 421, 554, 606
Williams, M., 333, 758, 791
Williams, R.S., 758
Williams, T.J., 381
Williams-Rice, B.T., 516, 520, 827
Willimczik, K., 273
Willingham, D.B., 137, 144, 146, 147, 148, 149, 151, 155, 167, 223
Willoughby, D., 102
Wills, T.A., 680
Wilmore, J.H., 298, 719, 720
Wilson, F.R., 13
Wilson, G.F., 60
Wilson, K.R., 283
Wilson, T.D., 53, 69, 463
Wilson, T.E., 649
Wilson, V.E., 571, 572, 578
Winborne, W.C., 245
Wine, J.D., 295, 303, 307
Winegardner, D., 675
Winett, R.A., 681, 712
Winfrey, M.L., 217, 231, 341, 344, 348, 350
Wing, A., 56, 60, 158
Wing, R.R., 730
Winner, E., 3, 270
Winograd, S., 7, 180
Winstein, C.J., 91, 99, 100, 102, 104
Winther, K.T., 25, 42
Wippich, W., 129
Wise, A., 796
Wise, H.H., 798
Wisell, R.A., 743
Wishart, L.R., 120, 218
Withers, R.T., 363
Witkin, H.A., 75
Wittchen, H.U., 747
Wittig, A.F., 773, 795
Wittrock, D.A., 509, 567, 793
Wolf, F.M., 245
Wolf, M., 332
Wolf, S., 99, 508
Wolff, J.A., 700
Wolff, R., 675, 678, 685
Wong, K., 130
Wong, P.T.P., 789
Wong, R., 130
Wood, C.A., 93
Wood, J.M., 76, 120, 184
Wood, R., 358, 499, 508, 513, 557, 680
Woodard, R.J., 401
Wooden, M., 768
Woodhouse, G., 721
Woodman, T., 292, 295, 298
Woodman, W., 591

Woods, A.M., 87, 90, 91, 758
Woods, R., 155, 156, 532
Woolfolk, R.L., 535, 539, 820
Woollacott, M.H., 20, 21, 29
Worrell, T., 795
Worringham, C.J., 167, 168
Worsham, N.L., 768
Wortman, C.B., 789
Wraith, S., 457
Wright, C.E., 39
Wright, D., 94, 102, 120, 126, 131, 179, 183, 218, 221
Wright, J.C., 251, 253, 255, 261
Wright, P.M., 508
Wright, W., 597
Wrisberg, C.A., 11, 87, 101, 107, 166, 176, 215, 530, 538, 540, 541, 574, 575
Wuest, D.A., 795, 801
Wughalter, E., 75
Wulf, G., 76, 100, 101, 103, 104, 109, 127, 130, 131, 210, 219, 221
Wulfert, E., 517
Wundt, W., 53
Wurtele, S.K., 343, 349
Wuthnow, R., 657
Wuyts, I.J., 160, 220

Xenikou, A., 451

Yalom, I.D., 685
Yamaji, K., 299
Yamazaki, F., 300, 330
Yammarino, F.J., 486
Yan, J.H., 22, 33, 39, 40, 44, 118
Yancey, G., 327
Yandell, K.M., 180
Yando, R., 224, 225, 226
Yang, M., 721
Yan Lan, L., 295, 299
Yanowitz, B., 107
Yao, T., 747
Yao, W.X., 103
Yarbus, A.L., 70
Yasamura, K., 796
Yates, B., 423
Yates, F.E., 151, 152
Yearta, S., 517
Yeh, Y.Y., 377
Yerkes, R.M., 293, 326, 331
Yerlès, M., 179
Yilk, D., 531
Yin, Z., 421, 437, 659, 660, 814
Yirmiya, N., 457
Yokota, Y., 299
Yoshida, H., 300, 330
Yoshimoto, T., 180
Yost, P.R., 351
Yost, R., 795
Young, B., 186, 190, 277, 279, 280

Young, D.E., 98, 102, 103, 115, 120, 127
Young, M.L., 773, 774, 788, 793, 794
Young, P., 102
Youngen, L., 180
Youngstedt, M.A., 750
Ypelaar, P., 320, 321
Yu, A.P., 37
Yukelson, D., 497, 500, 501, 502, 507, 509, 513, 514, 517, 518, 520, 557
Yukl, G.A., 516
Yura, M.T., 500

Zaccara, G., 181
Zaccaro, S.J., 346, 349, 351, 352, 472, 476, 486, 504, 571, 572, 573

Zagummy, M., 518
Zaichkowsky, L., 68, 282, 329, 682, 800
Zajonc, R.B., 290, 332
Zane, N.S., 622
Zanone, P.G., 58, 132
Zarbatany, L., 624
Zazanis, M., 351, 352, 476, 486
Zeeman, E.C., 298, 299
Zelaznik, H.N., 6, 7, 12, 57
Zellner, S., 431
Zernichke, R.F., 21, 26
Zervas, Y., 642
Zhang, J.J., 433
Zhao, S., 747
Zidon, I., 509

Ziegler, A., 270
Zigler, E., 224, 225, 226
Zimmerman, B., 104, 230, 502, 506, 518, 571, 573
Zimmerman, P., 366
Zimny, S.T., 120
Zinsser, N., 559, 560, 778
Zitzelsberger, L., 222
Zizzi, S.J., 823, 824
Zoeller, M., 128, 211
Zohar, A.H., 270, 284
Zubiaur, M., 91
Zuckerman, J., 209, 213, 214, 221
Zuckerman, M., 772

Subject Index

Ability beliefs, 460–462
Academic Motivation Scale (AMS), 392
Account-making model of coping, 685–686
Achievement goal theory in sport, 417–443, 606
   adaptive/maladaptive patterns, 418–419
   approach/avoidance goal perspectives, 435–436
   behavior, 422–423
   beliefs/values, 423–424
   conceptualization, 417–418
   coping strategies, 432–434
   effort reduction (work avoidance) as goal, 435
   enjoyment and intrinsic motivation, 424–427
   goal orientations, 420
   goal states, 421–422
   interactionist perspective, 434–435
   measurement of sport achievement goals, 420–422
   motivation and, 418–434
   new directions, 434–436
   perfectionism, 431–432
   personality factors, 431–432
   prediction of achievement patterns, 419
   research findings, 422–434
   review of major theoretical constructs/tenets, 417–420
   situational influences, 419–420
   strategy use, 427–428
   stress process, 428–434
Action-language-imagination (ALI) model (imagery), 539–540
Action systems (dynamical systems) perspective, 20
Activation-Deactivation Adjective Check List, 649
Adaptation, specificity of, 363–364
Adolescence. *See also* Youth in sport
   Csikszentmihalyi's view on talented teenagers, 280–281
   motor development and skill acquisition during, 20–52 (*see also* Youth in sport)
Adult exercisers, 661
Aerobic and strength tasks, and exertion tolerance, 815–817
Affect/behavior/cognition (ABC triangle), 556–557
Affective experiences/processes:
   CAPS (Cognitive-Affective Person System) theory, 253–254
   for children in sport, 614–617, 620–621
   correlates of psychomotor skill, 375
   flow, 329–330, 398, 653

   influence of cognitive-affective processes on motor loop, 379
   peers and, 626
Agent-means-ends analysis of attributions, 464–466
Age-related career termination, 676
Age-related changes and gender differences, 26–38
   gender differences, 33–38
   general body development, 27–28
   in growth, 26–39
   in health-related physical fitness, 37–38
   in motor activity level, 36–37
   in motor performance, 33–34
   in motor skill and fitness, 29–33
   running (quantitative/qualitative changes), 30–31
   throwing (gender differences), 33, 34–36
   throwing (quantitative/qualitative changes), 31–33
Alertness, attention as, 54
American Alliance for Health, Physical Education, Recreation, and Dance (AAHPERD), 825, 826
Amotivation, 389
Antidepressant effects of exercise, 747–751
Anxiety, 161–163, 290–318, 319, 614–615, 741–747. *See also* Stress
   antecedents of, 291–293, 311
   arousal and, 290, 293, 319
   catastrophe models of, 297–300
   competitive (model of facilitative/debilitative), 301
   conscious processing hypothesis, 308–309
   definition, 290–291
   hysteresis, 298
   information processing model, 305–306
   interpretation of states of, 300–302
   inverted-U hypothesis, 293
   levels, 614–615
   measurement of, 291, 302–304
   multidimensional theory, 295–297
   performance and, 293–302, 305–312
   processing efficiency theory, 306–308
   reduction following exercise, 741–747
   reversal theory, 300
   as situational constraint, 161–163
   sources of, 291–293, 615–616
   state/trait, 291, 293–302, 311–312, 615–616

Anxiety *(Continued)*
   theory of ironic processes of mental control, 309–311
   youth sport, levels of, 614–616
Arousal, 290, 319–339
   anxiety and, 290, 293, 319
   attentional processes and, 332–333
   cognitive appraisal and, 333
   conceptual model (arousal-performance relationship), 322
   defined, 290, 320–322
   drive theory, 326
   factors mediating arousal and performance, 331–333
   flow and, 329–330
   individual differences and, 332
   inverted-U hypothesis, 326–328
   measuring, 324–325
   neurophysiology of, 320–324
   optimal arousal states, 329–330
   performance measurement issues, 325–326
   regulation of, 333–334
   reversal theory, 330–331
   skill level and, 332
   task complexity and, 331–332
   theories of arousal-performance relationship, 326–331
Association for the Advancement of Applied Sport Psychology
      (AAASP), 826–827, 829
Associative/disassociative mental states and, exertion tolerance,
      818
Athletes:
   high-level performance (*see* Expertise; Psychological
         characteristics of high-level performance)
   multivariate analysis, multidimensional models, and
         multimethodologies in research on, 245–247, 252
   performance enhancement (*see* Psychological techniques for
         individual performance)
   personality, 239–268, 284, 558, 771–774
   retirement (*see* Career termination among athletes)
   self-efficacy research conducted with, 344–351
Athletic Coping Skills Inventory 28, 402
Attention, 53–85, 124–125, 160–161, 206, 332–333
   as alertness, 54
   arousal-performance relationship and, 332–333
   consciousness and, 53–54
   cuing, 124–125
   definitions of, 53
   early works on, 53
   functions of, 76
   observational-learning component, 206
   processes, 160–161, 332–333
   theories of, 76
   uses of term (three: alertness; limited capacity/resource;
         selectivity), 54
Attention, selective, 54, 67–76
   attenuation model of, 72
   changes in (accompanying skill acquisition), 73–75
   expert-novice differences in assignment of pertinence to
         different events and sources of information, 75
   expert-novice differences in performing current perceptual
         analysis, 74–75
   filter models of, 71–72
   methods for determining direction/breadth of, 68–69

   methods for determining relevance of specific cues/
         information sources, 69–70
   neuropsychological models of, 73
   paradigms for studying, 67–70
   performance limitations imposed by, 70–71
   pertinence-based models of, 72–73
   skill acquisition/instruction/practice (implications), 75–76
   theories and models of, 71–73
Attention as limited capacity or resource, 54–67
   changes in capacity/resource allocation accompanying skill
         acquisition, 63–66
   concordance among behavioral/cognitive/physiological
         measures, 59
   connectionist models, 63
   dual task paradigm, 55–58, 63–65
   event-related (evoked) potentials (ERPs), 59
   evidence/mechanisms for improved dual task performance
         with practice, 63–65
   evidence/mechanisms for increased automaticity with
         practice, 65–66
   evidence/mechanisms for reduced PRP delays with practice,
         66
   general, flexible capacity, 62
   heart rate variability, 59
   multiple-resource pools, 62–63
   paradigms for studying capacity/resource limitations, 55–58
   performance limitations, 60–61
   physiological measures of information processing load, 58–59
   primary task demand as limiting factor (on performance),
         60–61
   psychological refractory period (PRP), 61–62, 66
   pupil dilations, 58–59
   single-channel theory, 61–62
   skill acquisition/instruction/practice (implications), 66–67
   strategies for attentional switching and time-sharing as
         limiting factor (on performance), 61
   subjective rating of mental workload, 58
   theories of attentional capacity and resources, 61–63
   total available capacity as limiting factor on performance, 60
Attenuation model of selective attention, 72
Attribution(s), 444–471, 789–791
   actor-observer differences in, 452
   agent-means-ends analysis of, 464–466
   antecedents, 446–447
   assessment of, 447–456
   beliefs about nature of sport ability, 460–462
   cause/outcome elements, 454
   coding dimensions of, 454, 455
   consequences of, 456–464
   depressive attributional style, 448
   emotional reactions, 457
   entity and incremental beliefs, 460–461
   expectancies, 456–457
   extract, 453–454
   founding father of attribution theory (Heider), 444–445
   identifying sources of, 453
   for injury, 789–791
   intentionality, 448
   learned helplessness, 458–462
   retraining, 462–464

revision of basic concepts, 444–446
self-serving bias, 451
speaker/agent/target, 454
spontaneous (naturally occurring), 452–455
style of, 450
Weiner's theory of achievement, 445–446
Attributional Style Questionnaire (ASQ), 450
Attrition, 609–614
Audition, 220–221
Augmented feedback, 86–114, 115, 220–223. *See also* Feedback
  biofeedback, 99
  concurrent, 104–105
  enhancing skill acquisition, 90
  erroneous, 95–96
  error-based (*vs.* correct performance), 93–94
  frequency of presenting, 99–104
  guidance hypothesis explanation of reduced frequency
        effects, 104
  hindering skill acquisition, 90–91
  information provided by, 91–99
  intertrial interval, 109
  knowledge of performance (KP), 86
  knowledge of results (KR), 86
  KR-delay interval, 105–107
  KR *vs.* KP, 91–93
  in motor skill acquisition, 86–114
  movement kinematic information, 98–99
  necessity/non-necessity for, 88–91
  performance-based bandwidths, 94–95, 101–102
  post-KR interval, 107–109
  precision of, 92–93
  reduced frequency effect, 99–101
  role of, in skill acquisition, 87–88
  self-selected frequency technique, 103–104
  technology as source for, 96–99
  terminal, 105–109
  timing of, 104–109
  types of, 86–87
  videotape, 96–98
Automaticity, 11–12, 65–66
Autonomy, 396–397, 401
Avoidance goal perspectives (effort reduction; work avoidance),
        435–436
Awareness-based and metacognitive factors, self-regulation,
        571–572, 574–575

Ball catching, 159–160
Behavior(s)/behavioral:
  ABC triangle (affect/behavior/cognition), 556–557
  adherence, 475
  assessment, 249
  change for health-related purposes, 695–717
  coping, 795–796
  goals and, 422–423
  group-mediated change, 489–490
  implications, public health promotions, 720–721
  intentional movement (integrative modeling approach to
        study of), 144–173
  moral development and, 585–603
  motivated (theories of), 695–717 (*see also* Motivation)
  motor, 146–147, 154–163, 164
  multiple constraints on brain and, 152–154
  neurodynamic theories of processes of brain and, 153–154
  psychological responses to modeling, 209–213
  responses to sport injury rehabilitation, 794–796
  theory of planned (TPB), 697–703
  visuomotor behavior rehearsal (VMBR) treatment, 222
Behavioural Regulation in Exercise Questionnaire (BREQ), 393
Biofeedback, 99. *See also* Augmented feedback
Bioinformational theory (imagery), 539
Biopsychosocial model, sport injury rehabilitation, 787–788
Brain(s):
  and behavior (multiple constraints on), 152–154
  coding, 149–150
  computers and, 148–149
  embodied, 151–152
  neurodynamic theories of processes of, 153–154
Burnout, sport, 616

Canadian Society for Psychomotor Learning and Sport
        Psychology (CSPLSP), 825, 826
CAPS (Cognitive-Affective Person System) theory, 253–254
Cardiac Health and Activity Maintenance Program (CHAMP),
        490
Cardiovascular psychophysiology, 380–381
Career termination among athletes, 672–691
  adaptation factors, 678–680
  adaptation resources, 680–682
  causes of, 675–678
  chronological age and, 676
  coach/organization problems, 678
  conceptual issues, 673–674
  coping strategies, 680–681
  crises of (prevention/treatment), 684–686
  deselection, 676–677
  family reasons, 678
  financial difficulties, 678
  free choice, 677–678
  future research, 686
  grief model and, 675
  historical issues, 673–674
  injury and, 677
  model of, 675–686
  perceptions of control, 679–680
  planning for, 681–682
  quality of adaptation to, 682–684
  self-identity, 678–679
  social gerontology, 674–675
  social identity, 679
  social support, 681
  termination as transition, 675
  thanatology, 674
  theoretical perspectives on, 674–675
Catastrophe models/theory, 297–300, 579
Causal Dimension Scale (CDS), 448–450, 451
Cause/outcome elements, attributions, 454
Change, constancy of, 830–831
Character-building, sport and, 598–599
Childhood/adolescence; motor development and skill
        acquisition during, 20–52. *See also* Youth in sport

Chunking, 12
Closed-loop theory, 207
Coach(es):
    children's psychosocial experiences and, 622–624
    motivation and, 399–400
    problems with, and career termination, 678
    self-efficacy research conducted with, 355–357
    sport confidence and, 554
COBALT (control-based learning theory), 146–148, 149, 150
Cognition:
    exercise and, 757–759
    expertise and, 175–176
    injury rehabilitation, 789–792
    knowledge base, 43–44
    memory, 41–43
    motor skills performance and, 40–44
    perceptual development, 41
    self-regulation, 572, 575–576
    speed of processing, 40–41
    sport injury rehabilitation, 789–792
Cognitive-Affective Person System (CAPS), 253–254
Cognitive appraisal models, 333, 789
Cognitive general (CG) imagery, 533–534
Cognitive-imaginal factors, self-regulation, 572, 575–576
Cognitive readiness, 609
Cognitive science, and intentional movement behavior, 144, 145, 146–152
    abstractness in, 150–151
    computational basis of, 146–152
    dynamical systems modeling, 150–151
Cognitive specific (CS) imagery, 531–533
Cohesion. See Group cohesion in sport/exercise
Collective efficacy, 351–354, 476
Commitment:
    goal, 516–517, 520
    task-specific, and exertion tolerance, 815
Communities, strategies focused on changing/networking, 732–733
Competence, instrumental, 572
Competence, perceptions of:
    exertion tolerance and, 814–815
    motivation and, 396–397, 401
Competence motivation theory, 605–606
Competition:
    goal setting for (vs. for practice), 515–516
    interpersonal, and taxonomy of exercise/physical activity, 646–647
    level of (and group cohesion), 475
    motivation and, 395
    planning skill, 282
    psychological readiness for, 608–609
Competitive anxiety, model of facilitative/debilitative, 301
Competitive Orientation Inventory (COI), 551
Competitive State Anxiety Inventory (CSAI/CSAI-2/CSAI-C), 296, 302, 303, 304, 328, 329, 344, 350, 430, 614
Competitive trait anxiety, 771
Concentration, 282
Conceptions of the Nature of Athletic Ability Questionnaire (CNAAQ), 462
Connectionism, 63, 156

Consciousness and attention, 53–54
Conscious processing hypothesis, 308–309
Continuum of Injurious Acts (CIA), 594
Control-based learning theory (COBALT), 146–148, 149, 150
COPE inventory, 796
Coping, 215–216, 402, 432–434, 680–681, 685–686, 774–777, 791–792, 795–796, 811–812
    account-making model of, 685–686
    Athletic Coping Skills Inventory 28, 402
    behaviors, 795–796
    exertion tolerance, 811–812
    injury rehabilitation, 791–792, 795–796
    marathon running, 812
    motivation and, 402
    resources, 774–777
    strategies/techniques, 432–434, 680–681, 791–792, 811–812
    stress and injury model, 774–777
Covariance structure modeling (CSM), 781
Cusp catastrophe, 579

Dance vs. sport expertise, 186–188
Decision making (and dynamical systems theory), 20
Decision processing, 10–11
Deliberate practice, Ericsson's notion of, 277–280
Demographic characteristics, and sport confidence, 558
Depression: antidepressant effects of exercise, 747–751
Depressive attributional style, 448
Deselection, 676–677
Development. See Life span development; Talent
Developmental considerations in modeling, 224–232
    contemporary modeling studies, 227–230
    early research on children's modeling of motor skills, 225–227
    social psychological effects of modeling, 230–232
    theoretical background, 224–225
Developmental skill acquisition model, 20
Dial-a-Maze, 538
Differentiation, 586
Direct perception interpretation, 208–209
Distraction control, 282
Drive theory, 326
Dual coding theory (imagery), 539–540
Dual task paradigm, 55–58
Dynamical systems modeling/perspective, 20, 25–26, 150–151, 158–160
Dynamic model of mental health, 754–755
Dynamic self-assembly, 144

Effector processing, 5, 11–13
Electroencephalography and skilled psychomotor performance, 366–378
    affective correlates of psychomotor skill, 375
    basic properties of EEG, 367–368
    electrocortical activity and quiet eye period, 378
    event-related potentials (ERPs) and skilled motor performance, 375–378
    international 10–20 standard electrode placements for EEG data collection, 367

intrasubject variability in EEG and performance outcome, 373–375
neurophysiological basis of electrocortical activation, 369–370
spectral differences in expert-novice paradigms, 371–373
spectral EEG and regional cortical specificity, 370–371
Emotion, and arousal, 319
Emotional reactions and attributions, 457
Emotional Responses of Athletes to Injury Questionnaire (ERAIQ), 793, 801
Emotional responses to sport injury rehabilitation, 792–794
Enjoyment, 424–427, 616–617, 657–663
    adherence and, 659
    adult exercisers and, 661
    benefits of, 659
    defining, 657–658
    enhanced mental health and, 659
    vs. fun, 658
    goals and, 424–427
    intrinsic motivation and, 424–427
    measuring, 659
    models describing experience of, 662
    predictors of, 616–617
    sources of, 660–662
    youth sport participants and, 660–661
Environmental engineering/developing action plans, 520–521
European influences, sport psychology, 824–825
Event occlusion studies, 9
Event-related (evoked) potentials (ERPs), 59, 375–378
Exercise compulsion, 643
Exercise Imagery Questionnaire (EIQ), 537, 541
Exercise Motivation Scale (EMS), 393, 407
Exercise/physical activity:
    health and (see Health psychology, and exercise)
    injury and (see Sport injury; Sport injury rehabilitation)
    mental health and, 636–671, 740–765
    peak moments in, 651–657, 663
    possible negative effects, 643
    proposed taxonomy for enhancing psychological benefits of, 644–651, 663
        aerobic quality, 645–646
        closed predictable and temporally and spatially certain activities, 647–648
        mode characteristics, 645–648
        pleasing and enjoyable, 644–645
        practice requirements, 648–651
        relative absence of interpersonal competition, 646–647
        rhythmical abdominal breathing, 645–646
        rhythmical repetitive movements, 648
    public programs (see Public health framework for physical activity promotion research)
    questions about (reflecting research directions), 696
    recommended duration/frequency/intensity, 648–651
    and subjective well-being, 636–671, 752–756
        acute mood changes, 642
        acute mood states, 639–640
        caution (possible mood decrements), 643
        chronic changes, 640
        effectiveness of exercise in comparison to other approaches to enhancing, 643
        exercise compulsion, 643
        injuries, 643
        moderating one's stress response, 640–643
        negative effects of exercise (possible), 643
        normal population, 638–644
        theories of motivated behavior and, 695–717
Exertion/exertion tolerance, 810–820
    in aerobic and strength tasks, 815–817
    associative/disassociative mental states and, 818
    conceptual model, 810–813
    coping techniques, 811–812
    dispositional characteristics, 810–811
    environmental conditions, 812–813
    goal orientation, 813–814
    imagery and, 812
    perceived competence and self-efficacy, 814–815
    Rating of Perceived Exertion (RPE), 815–818
    relaxation techniques, 812
    social-cognitive perspective, 813–818
    stress, 811–812
    task-specific commitment/determination and effort, 815
Expectancy(ies), and attributions, 456–457
Expectancy-value theory (Eccles), 606–607
Expertise, 6, 25, 44–46, 74–75, 174–201, 223–224
    accessing through laboratory tasks, 176
    advance visual cues and probability estimates, 182–183
    approach to study of skill development, 25
    controversial issues in study of, 183–188
    in dance and martial arts vs. sport, 186–188
    defining, 183–184
    early talent and development of, 185–186
    ecological psychology, 190
    expert-novice approach, 6, 74–75, 177–181
    exposure and, 182
    family resources in development of, 183
    future research, 188–191
    gender issues, 190
    generalized visual training programs and athlete performance, 184
    hardware/software, and multitask approach, 176–183
    longitudinal research, 189–190
    modeling and, 223–224
    perception/cognition/strategies differentiating, 175–176
    perceptual analysis and, 75
    practice and, 175–176, 186, 190
    retention, 189
    role of game structure in recall and recognition, 182
    skill/performance/knowledge and, 44–46
    sport-specific perceptual training programs and performance, 184–185
    ten-year rule, 175
    verbal protocols and sport knowledge, 182
Extroversion, 245

Family resources, 183
Feedback, 44, 210, 395, 397, 518. See also Augmented feedback
Filter models of selective attention, 71–72
Flow (affective consequence), 329–330, 398, 653
Friendship and peer acceptance, 624–625

Functional computational modeling, 147
Fun *vs.* enjoyment, 658

Game structure in recall and recognition, 182
Gender differences/issues, 28–39, 190, 542–543, 594
   changes in motor skill and fitness, 29–33
   expertise and, 190
   in growth, 28–29
   in health-related physical fitness, 37–38
   imagery (use of) and, 542–543
   in motor activity level, 36–37
   in motor performance, 33–34
   overhand throwing and, 31–36
   running and, 30–31
Gender Stratification Interview (GSI), 594
General abilities, role of; in skill level, 6–7
Global Motivation Scale (GMS), 393
Goal(s), 417–443, 497–528, 559–560, 572, 576, 595, 813–814
   achievement-goal theory, 417–443
   action plans, 517–518
   as antecedents of adaptive and maladaptive patterns of
       motivation, 418–419
   approach/avoidance perspectives, 435–436
   attribute research, 506–512
   barriers to attainment of, 517
   behavior, 422–423
   beliefs/values and, 423–424
   business settings *vs.* sports (effectiveness), 512–514
   collectivity, 510–512
   commitment, 516–517, 520
   confidence and, 559–560
   definition, 497–499
   difficulty, 508–509, 516, 520
   effectiveness of, 499
   environmental engineering/developing action plans,
       520–521
   evaluating, 518–519, 520
   exertion tolerance and, 813–814
   feedback, 518
   focus, 506–507
   future research, 519–521
   generalization of effects of setting, 521
   mapping, and sports confidence, 559–560
   mechanisms, 498
   monitoring, 520
   optimizing difficulty of, 516, 520
   orientation, 420, 595, 813–814
   practice *vs.* competition, 515–516
   proximity, 509–510
   reinforcing achievement of, 519
   research, 499–512
   self-regulation and, 572, 576
   setting for complex tasks, 521
   specificity, 507–508
   state, 421–422
   state/trait conceptions of, 498–499
   steps in setting process, 514–519
   strategy use and, 427–428
   stress process and, 428–434
   systematic development of, 515

   theory, 499–512
   valence, 509
Graduate programs in sport psychology, 828, 829
Grief model, 675
Group cohesion in sport/exercise, 472–494
   adherence behavior, 475
   advancing research in, 478–484
   collective efficacy, 476
   conceptual model of, 473–474
   consensus *vs.* consistency, 486
   correlates of, 474–478
   definition, 472–473
   dimensions (GI-T/GI-S/ATG-T/ATG-S), 473
   environmental factors, 475
   future directions for research, 484–486, 487–490
   key issues in, 478
   leadership factors, 475–476
   level of competition, 475
   measuring, 473–474
   methodological sophistication, 485
   norms, 476
   performance, 476–477
   personal factors, 475–476
   role involvement, 476
   size of team, 475
   social loafing, 475
   team factors, 476
   topical analysis issues, 485–486
   unit of analysis, 485
   walking clubs, 488–489
Group development continuum, 480
Group Environment Questionnaire (GEQ), 474, 477, 480, 481,
   482
Group-mediated behavior change, 489–490
Growth, 26–39

Haan's theory of moral development, 589–591
Hahm-Beller Values Choice Inventory, 597
Hardware studies (multitask approach), 176, 180–181
Health behavior change, 695–717
   outcome expectations, 707–708
   self-efficacy theory, 703–708
   social-cognitive theory, 708–710
   theory of planned behavior (TPB), 697–703
   transtheoretical model (TTM), 710–714
Health psychology, and exercise:
   mental health and physical activity, 740–765
   psychology of injury risk and prevention, 766–786
   psychology of sport injury rehabilitation, 787–809
   public health framework for physical activity promotion
       research, 718–739
   social-cognitive perspective of perceived exertion and
       exertion tolerance, 810–820
   theories of motivated behavior (perspectives on influence),
       695–717
Heart rate variability, 59
Hierarchical class analysis (HICLAS), 254, 257–259
Hierarchical model of intrinsic/extrinsic motivation, 390–394,
   395, 406–409
Hysteresis, 298

Iceberg Profile of Mood States (POMS), 245, 639, 753, 754
Ideal performance state, 362
Imagery, 125–126, 221–223, 282, 529–549, 560, 812
    action-language-imagination (ALI) model, 539–540
    bioinformational theory, 539
    cognitive general (CG), 533–534
    cognitive specific (CS), 531–533
    dual coding theory, 539–540
    in exercise (where/when/why/what), 537–538
    exertion tolerance and use of, 812
    future directions for research, 544–546
    gender and, 542–543
    how it works, 538–540
    mental practice and, 125–126
    motivational general-arousal (MG-A), 534–535
    motivational general-mastery (MG-M), 534
    motivational specific (MS), 534
    psychoneuromuscular theory, 539
    in sport (where/when/why/what), 530–537
    sports confidence and use of, 560
    symbolic learning theory, 538–539
    variables influencing use of, 540–543
Implicit/explicit learning, 76–77, 128–130
Individual:
    individual-differences approach, 5
    individualized zones of optimal functioning (IZOF),
        294–295, 304, 320, 329
    interindividual vs. intraindividual research, 249–250
    profiling, 164
    public health strategies focused on changing/networking,
        728–730
Information processing, 5–14, 24–25, 305–306
    anxiety model, 305–306
    approach to study of skill development, 24–25
    characteristics of performers at various stages of practice,
        7–13
    decision processing, 10–11
    effector processing, 11–13
    event occlusion studies, 9
    perceptual processing, 8–10
Inheritability of talent, 284–285
Injury. See Sport injury; Sport injury rehabilitation
Intentionality:
    attributions and, 448
    constraints on movement coordination, 155–156
    dynamical movement systems and, 158–160
    intending systems vs. systems exhibiting intentions, 157–158
International Society of Sport Psychology (ISSP), 825
Intrinsic motivation. See Motivation
Intrinsic Motivation Inventory, 392
Inverted-U hypothesis, 293, 326–328
Ironic processes of mental control, theory of, 309–311

Knowledge, sports (development of), 45–46
Knowledge base, 43–44
Knowledge of performance (KP), 86–87, 91–93, 214
Knowledge of results (KR), 86–87, 91–93, 105–109, 213, 214,
    215, 220, 227
    vs. KP, 91–93
Kohlberg's theory of moral development, 587–589

Leadership factors, 475–476
Learned helplessness, 458–462
Learning:
    COBALT (control-based learning theory), 146–148, 149, 150
    defined, 115–116
    feedback and, 44
    implicit/explicit, 76–77, 128–130
    motor learning theories, 207–208
    observational, 206–207, 208, 230
    performance and, 115–116, 211
    practice and, 44
    self-efficacy and, 206–207
    self-regulated strategies, 229, 230
    vs. skill, 115–116
    skill acquisition and, 44
    social learning approach, 585–586
    symbolic learning theory, 538–539
Leeds Attributional Coding System (LACS), 453–454
Licensing, sports psychologists, 829
Life Events Survey for Collegiate Athletes (LESCA), 781
Life Experiences Survey (LES), 769
Life span development:
    adult exercisers, 661
    career termination among athletes, 672–691
    childhood/adolescence; motor development and skill
        acquisition during, 20–52
    growth, 26–39
    moral development and behavior in sport, 585–603
    physical activity and quality of life, 636–671
    teenagers (Csikszentmihalyi's view on talented), 280–281
    youth in sport (psychological considerations), 604–635

Marathon running and coping techniques, 812
Martial arts vs. sport expertise, 186–188
Memory, 41–43
Mental health, and physical activity, 659–660, 740–765
    antidepressant effects, 747–751
    anxiety reduction, 741–747
    cognitive functioning, 757–759
    dynamic/static mental health models, 753–756
    enjoyment, 659–660
    guidelines for evaluating overviews/meta-analyses, 741
    norepinephrine hypothesis, 750
    positive mood, 659–660, 752–756
    self-esteem, 756–757
    serotonin hypothesis, 749–750
    stress reactivity, 751–752
Mental practice, 282
Mental workload, subjective rating of, 58
Metabolic efficiency, psychological states and, 381–382
Modeling (considerations for motor skill performance and
        psychological responses), 205–238
    audition, 220–221
    behavioral and psychological responses to, 209–213
    closed-loop theory, 207
    conceptual considerations, 205–209
    coping and mastery models, 215–216
    demonstration characteristics, 218–223
    developmental considerations in, 224–232
    developmental studies, 227–230

Modeling (considerations for motor skill performance and psychological responses) *(Continued)*
  direct perception interpretation, 208–209
  imagery, 221–223
  learner expertise, 223–224
  model characteristics, 213–218
  motivational orientation, 223
  motor learning theories, 207–208
  observational learning theory, 208
  observer characteristics, 223–224
  physical practice, 221
  practice variables, 218–220
  recall/recognition, 208
  schema theory, 207–208
  self-efficacy (role of, in observational learning), 206–207
  self-modeling, 216–217
  social cognitive approach, 205–206
  social psychological effects of modeling, 230–232
  theoretical background, 224–225
  verbalization, 221
Mood, 639–640, 642. *See also* Exercise/physical activity, and subjective well-being
Moral development, 585–603, 627–628
  assessment of sport-specific moral constructs, 597–598
  comprehensive model, 596–597
  empirical findings, 591–599
  future directions for research, 599
  goal orientation, 595
  Haan's theory of, 589–591
  Kohlberg's theory of, 587–589
  orientations (ego/task), 595
  predicting moral action in sport, 595–596
  social learning approach, 585–586
  sport and character building, 598–599
  sport and moral reasoning, 591–593
  sport and prescriptive moral judgment, 593–595
  sport and prioritizing of moral values, 591
  structural development approach, 586–587
  theoretical approaches to, 585–591
  12-component model of moral action, 596
Motivated behavior, theories of, 695–717
  behavior change for health-related purposes, 695
  common theoretical assumptions and elements, 697
  dilemma facing theoretically based interventions, 714–715
  outcome expectations, 707–708
  questions about exercise that reflect research directions, 696
  self-efficacy theory, 703–708
  social-cognitive theory, 708–710
  sport psychologist and, 695–696
  theory of planned behavior (TPB), 697–703
  theory of reasoned action (TRA), 697
  theory selection, 696–697
  transtheoretical model (TTM), 710–714
Motivation, 389–416
  achievement goal theory, 417–443
  amotivation, 389
  assessing, 392–393
  attributions, 444–471
  attrition and, 609–614
  autonomy, 396

coaches and, 399–400
competition and, 395
consequences, 394, 397–398, 401–405, 406
  at contextual level, 398–405
determinants, 395–397, 398–401, 405–406
  at different levels of generality, 392, 407–409
enjoyment and, 424–427
feedback and, 395, 397
flow (an affective consequence), 398
  at global level, 405–406
goals and, 424–427
group cohesion in sport and exercise, 472–494
hierarchical model, 390–394, 395, 406–407
intrapersonal factors, 397
  as intrapersonal phenomenon, 394
intrinsic, 424–427, 572–573
league organizational patterns, 400
multidimensional perspective of, 390–392
participation/attrition, 609–614
perceived competence/autonomy/relatedness, 396–397, 401
performance, 404
postulates/corollaries (hierarchical model), 395
recursive (bottom-up) effects, 394, 395, 410
research, 394–409, 610–611, 613–614
scholarships, 400
self-determination theory (SDT) and, 390, 396, 397
self-regulation and, 397, 572–573
sequence (determinants/motivation/consequences), 409
situational level of, 394–398
social factors, 395–397
  as social phenomenon, 393–394
team ambience, 400
top-down effect, 395, 401
Motivational general-arousal (MG-A) imagery, 534–535
Motivational general-mastery (MG-M) imagery, 534
Motivational orientation, 223, 595
Motivational readiness, 608
Motivational specific (MS) imagery, 534
Motivation for Physical Activity Measure—Revised, 393
Motor development and skill acquisition (childhood/adolescence), 20–52
  actions systems (dynamical systems) perspective, 20
  age-related changes and gender differences in growth, 26–29
  approaches to study of skill development, 23–26
  cognitive aspects of motor skills performance, 40–44
  decision making (and dynamical systems theory), 20
  developmental control of movement, 39–40
  developmental skill acquisition model, 20
  dynamical systems perspective, 20, 25–26
  expertise, 25, 44–46
  future research recommendations, 46–47
  gender differences, 26–39
  general body development, 27–28
  growth (relationship of to movement), 38–39
  information processing, 24–25
  interventions, longitudinal/cross-sectional research, 23
  learning: practice and feedback, 44
  measurement issues, 21–22
  methodological issues in studying, 21–23

movement characteristics/outcome, 22–23
overhand throwing, 31–33
readiness, 26
running, 30–31
sources of rapid changes, 20
stages of development idea (Piaget), 24
Motor learning theories, 207–208
Movement:
    growth/development and, 38–40
    kinematic information, 98–99
    sequences, 127–128
Movement behavior, intentional (integrative modeling approach
        to study of), 144–173
    abstractness in cognitive science and dynamical systems
            modeling, 150–151
    anxiety as situational constraint, 161–163
    attentional processes and, 160–161
    ball catching, 159–160
    brain, 148–150, 151–154
    coding, 149–150
    cognitive science accounts, 144, 145
    computational basis of cognitive science explanations of
            motor behavior, 146–152
    connectionism and representations, 156
    constraints on self-organization processes, 152–153
    dynamical movement systems, experimental work in,
            158–160
    ecological approach, 144
    functional computational modeling, 147
    intending systems vs. systems exhibiting intentions, 157–158
    intentional constraints on movement coordination, 155–156
    neurodynamic theories (brain/behavior), 153–154
    noncomplementary modeling, 156–158
    perceived weaknesses in the ecological approach to movement
            coordination and control, 145–146
    phenomenological modeling, 144
    practice in sport (searching for "virtual" solutions to
            movement problems), 163–167
    prehension, 158–159
    situational constraints, 154–163
    soccer goalkeeping, 156–157
    structural modeling, 144
Movement Imagery Questionnaire (MIQ), 543
Multidimensional anxiety theory, 295–297
Multidimensional Perfectionism Scale (F-MPS), 432
Multidimensional Sportspersonship Orientation Scale, 404
Multivariate analysis, multidimensional models, and
        multimethodologies in research on elite athlete, 245–247,
        252

NASA Task Load Index (TLX), 58
Neurophysiology:
    of arousal, 320–324
    electromyographic correlates of psychomotor performance,
            379–380
    influence of cognitive-affective processes on motor loop, 379
    neural processes and motor system, 378–381
    neurodynamic theories of processes of brain and behavior,
            153–154
    neuropsychological models of selective attention, 73

Norepinephrine hypothesis, 750
North America, sport psychology in, 825–826, 829–830
North American Society for the Psychology of Sport and
        Physical Activity (NASPSPA), 825, 826

Observational learning theory, 206–207, 208, 230
Optimal arousal states, 329–330
Optimal zone theory, 294–295, 304, 320, 328–329
Order-order transitions, 152
Organization(s):
    culture of, and sport confidence, 552–553, 558
    public health strategies focused on changing/networking,
            731–732
Orientation toward Play Scale, 597
Ottawa Mental Skills Assessment Tool (OMSAT-3),
        282–283
Outcome(s):
    affective, 614–617
    attributions, 454
    expectations, 707–708
    measures, 573, 577
    movement, 22–23
    process and, 209–210

Parental influence, 617–622
Participation motivation research, 609–614. See also
        Motivation
Patient-practitioner interactions, sport injury rehabilitation,
        799
Peak moments in exercise and sport, 651–657, 663
    facilitating, 655–656
    flow, 653
    future research needs, 656–657
    linking to quality of life, 654
    major characteristics of peak moments, 655
    measuring, 656
    peak experience, 654
    peak performance, 653
    running/exercise high, 654
    theories and models, 652–653
Pedestal Sight Manipulation Test (PSMT), 89
Peer influence, youth sport participation, 624–628
    affect and, 626
    context-specific, 624
    friendship and peer acceptance, 624–625
    moral development, 627–628
    self-perceptions, 626
    sport involvement and popularity, 625–626
Peer modeling, 230–232
Perceived Motivational Climate in Sport Questionnaire
        (PMCSQ), 421
Perceptions:
    of autonomy/competence/relatedness, 396–397, 401
    expertise and, 175–176
Perceptions of Success Questionnaire (POSQ), 420, 421
Perceptual development, 41
Perceptual processing, 8–10
Perceptual responses to modeling, 212
Perceptual training programs, 184–185
Perfectionism, 431–432

Performance:
  anxiety affecting, 305–311
  assessing, 188–189
  attention and, 60–61, 70–71
  cohesion relationship and, 476–477
  confidence and, 557–558
  defined, 115
  enhancing (*see* Psychological techniques for individual
      performance)
  goals and, 513
  high-level (*see* Psychological characteristics of high-level
      performance)
  knowledge/skill and, 45–46, 115–116
  levels of skill, 3–19
  measuring, 325–326
  vs. skill/learning/knowledge, 45–46, 115–116
Performance Outcome Survey (POS), 448
Personality, 239–268, 284, 558, 771–774
  behavioral assessment, 249
  cognitive-affective system theory of, 253–254
  conceptual framework for study of, 240–244
  deterministic/probabilistic models, 250–251
  elite performance, and
      predictability/lawfulness/functionality, 240–241
  extroversion, 245
  future research directions, 252–254
  Iceberg Profile of Mood States (POMS), 245
  interactionist situational-dispositional taxonomy of,
      251–252
  interindividual *vs.* intraindividual research, 249–250
  multivariate/multidimensional research, 245–247, 252
  performance and, 248
  situation-related intraindividual personality diagnosis: case
      study, 254–261
  sport confidence and, 558
  stress injury model and, 771–774
  success and, 244–248
  talent development and, 284
Personology, 241, 243–244, 247–252
Pertinence-based models of selective attention, 72–73
Physical activity. *See* Exercise/physical activity
Physical inactivity: population prevalence and demographic
    trends, 719–720
Physical practice, 221
Physical Self-Efficacy Scale (PSE), 343
Physical Self-Presentation Confidence subscale (PSC), 343
Physiological measures of information processing load, 58–59.
    See also Neurophysiology
Pictorial Motivation Scale, 402
Planning and problem solving, self-regulation, 573, 576
Political environment, strategies focused on
    changing/networking, 733–734
POMS. *See* Profile of Mood States (POMS)
Popularity, and sport involvement, 625–626
Practice, 44, 66–67, 75–76, 115–143, 163–167, 175–176, 186,
    190, 218–220, 221, 277–280, 515–516, 648–651
  attentional capacity and, 66–67, 75–76
  augmented feedback, 115
  distinction among performance/skill/learning, 115–116
  in dyads, 219

expertise and, 175–176, 186, 190
goals for (*vs.* competition), 515–516
learning (defined), 115–116
learning and (skill acquisition), 44
manipulating constraints during, 165–166
measurements of skill, 116
modeling variables, 218–220
off-task conditions of, 125–136
  imagery and mental practice, 125–126
  implicit and explicit learning, 128–130
  learning movement sequences, 127–128
  learning novel motor patterns, 130–132
  perspectives, 132
  prepractice instruction and demonstration, 126–132
  role of movement/criterion templates, 127
  simulated reality, 132–136
  simulators, 133–135
  theoretical rationale underlying instructional provision,
      128
  virtual environments, 132–136
  virtual reality, 135–136
on-task conditions of, 116–125
  amount of practice, 116–117
  attention cuing, 124–125
  contextual interference, 119–121
  fractionation, 123–124
  modifying variables, 118–119, 120
  part-task *vs.* whole-task practice, 121–125
  retention effects, 118
  segmentation, 122
  simplification, 124
  theoretical issues, 119–120
  transfer effects, 118
  variability of practice, 117–119
part-task *vs.* whole-task, 121–125
performance/learning/skill (defined), 115–116
physical, 221
scheduling of, 218
searching for "virtual" solutions to movement problems,
    163–167
skill (defined), 115
structural organization of, 166–167
talent and (Ericsson's notion of deliberate practice),
    277–280
Predictive *vs.* descriptive studies, 579
Prehension, 158–159
Prepractice instruction and demonstration, 126–132
Preretirement planning, 681–682
Processing efficiency theory, 306–308
Profile of Mood States (POMS), 245, 261, 639, 640, 651, 753,
    754, 793
Profiling, individual, 164
Psychological:
  hardiness trait, 771
  models, sport injury rehabilitation, 788–789
  readiness for sport competition, 608–609
  responses to modeling, 212–213
  responses to sport injury, 789–796
  services, referral for sport injury rehabilitation, 799–800
  states and metabolic efficiency, 381–382

Psychological characteristics of high-level performance, 319–339
  modeling (considerations for motor skill performance and psychological responses), 205–238
  personality and the athlete, 239–268
  psychophysiology of sport, 362–386
  self-efficacy beliefs of athletes/teams/coaches, 340–361
  stress and anxiety, 290–318
  talent development in sport, 269–289
Psychological refractory period (PRP), 61–62, 66
Psychological Skills Inventory for Sport (PSIS), 281
Psychological techniques for individual performance:
  goal setting in sport, 497–528
  imagery in sport/exercise, 529–549
  self-confidence (understanding/enhancing), 550–565
  self-regulation, 566–581
Psychology of sport/exercise. See Health psychology, and exercise: Sport psychology
Psychoneuromuscular theory (imagery), 539
Psychophysiology of sport, 362–386
  cardiovascular psychophysiology, 380–381
  cognitive-affective processes influencing motor loop, 379
  electroencephalography and skilled psychomotor performance, 366–378
  electromyographic correlates of psychomotor performance, 379–380
  future research, 382
  ideal performance state, 362
  neural processes and motor system, 378–381
  psychological states and metabolic efficiency, 381–382
  psychomotor efficiency, 364–366
  specificity of adaptation, 363–364
Public health framework for physical activity promotion research, 718–739
  behavioral and self-regulatory implications, 720–721
  components of physical activity interventions (descriptions/examples), 726–727
  ecological models, 721–725
  impact of physical activity interventions, 725–734
  intervention settings, 724
  intervention targets, 724–725
  population prevalence and demographic trends of physical inactivity, 719–720
  promoting physical activity, 719–721
  research agenda, 721
  strategies focusing on changing/networking:
    communities, 732–733
    individuals, 728–730
    interpersonal environment, 730–731
    organizations, 731–732
    political environments, 733–734
Pupil dilations, 58–59

Quality of life, 636–671
  adult exercisers, 661
  defined, 636
  enjoyment of physical activity and, 657–662, 663
  factors influencing, 636–637
  measuring, 637–638
  peak moments in exercise and sport, 651–657, 663

  physical activity and, 638, 657–662, 663
  proposed taxonomy for enhancing psychological benefits of physical activity, 644–651, 663
  youth sport participants, 660–661
Quiet eye period, 378

Rating of Perceived Exertion (RPE), 815–818
Reaction-time (RT) paradigm, 5
Readiness approach to study of skill development, 26
Recall/recognition, 208, 210–211
Reciprocal interactionism, 557
Rehabilitation. See Sport injury rehabilitation
Relaxation techniques, exertion tolerance, 812
Representation, 206
Retention, 118, 189, 206
Retraining, attribution, 462–464
Reversal theory, 300, 330–331
Running/exercise high, 654

Schema theory, 207–208
Scholarships, athletic, 400
Science programs and exercise psychology, 829
Selectivity. See Attention, selective
Self-Analysis of Mental Skills questionnaire (SAMS), 281–282
Self-confidence:
  affect/behavior/cognition (ABC triangle), 556–557
  coaches and, 554
  conceptual constructs related to study of, 550
  demographic characteristics, 558
  dispositional/state confidence constructs, 552
  future directions, 561–562
  goal mapping and, 559–560
  historical perspectives, 550–558
  imagery and, 560
  initial conceptual model of sport confidence, 551–552
  integrative model of sport confidence for research/practice, 555–558
  intervention strategies to enhance, 558–561
  organizational culture and, 552–553, 558
  performance and, 557–558
  personality characteristics and, 558
  quality of physical training and perceived achievement, 559
  reciprocal interactionism, 557
  self-regulation, 559, 560
  self-talk, 560
  social climate and, 560–561
  social-cognitive emphasis, 552
  sources of, 553–555, 557
  understanding/enhancing (in athletes), 550–565
Self-determination index, 393
Self-determination theory (SDT), 390, 396, 397
Self-efficacy, 206–207, 340–361, 537, 579, 703–708, 814–815
  athletes and, 344–351
  beliefs (of athletes/teams/coaches), 340–361
  coaches and, 355–357
  collective (groups/teams), 351–354
  exertion tolerance, and, 814–815
  future research, 357–358, 706–707
  imagery and, 537
  measurement of, 343–344

Self-efficacy *(Continued)*
  observational learning and, 206–207
  teams and, 351–354
  theory, 340–343, 703–708
Self-esteem and exercise, 756–757
Self-identity, 678–679
Self-modeling, 216–217
Self-organization, constraints on, 152–153
Self-perceptions:
  injury and, 791
  motivation and, 618–620
  peers and, 626
Self-reaction/self-reward, self-regulation, 573, 577
Self-regulation, 229, 230, 397, 559, 560, 566–581
  awareness-based and metacognitive factors, 571–572,
      574–575
  cognitive-imaginal factors, 572, 575–576
  confidence and, 559, 560
  definitions, 566–567
  emerging complexities, 567–568
  future studies, 578–580
  goal-centered competencies, 572, 576
  hypothesized mechanisms, 569, 571–573, 574–577
  instrumental competence, 572
  intrinsic motivation, 572–573
  learning and, 229
  measures of, 570
  mediator and outcome measures, 573, 577
  model of, 566–567
  organizing assumptions, 568
  planning and problem solving, 573, 576
  processes, 397
  review of research on, 568–578
  self-reactive/self-reward, 573, 577
  skills, 230
  sustained task performance research, 574–577
  task performance research, 571–574
  theories/models of, 571
  training studies, 577–578
Self-serving bias, attributions, 451
Self-talk, and sports confidence, 560
Serotonin hypothesis, 749–750
Simulated reality, 132–136
Single-channel theory, 61–62
Situational constraints (integrated approach to motor behavior),
    154–163
  connectionism/representations, 156
  control parameters (nonspecific/specific), 154–155
  intending systems *vs.* systems exhibiting intentions,
      157–158
  intentional constraints on movement coordination,
      155–156
  intentional movement behavior: noncomplementary
      modeling, 156–158
  soccer goalkeeping, 156–157
Situational Motivation Scale (SIMS), 392, 397, 407
Situation-related intraindividual personality diagnosis: case
    study, 254–261
  data collection, 255–256
  discussion/conclusions, 260–261

  graphic display, 258
  interpretation, 259
  rank and complexity of structure, 258–259
  results, 259–260
Skill(s):
  defined, 115
  high-level *(see* Expertise)
  knowledge/performance, and, 45–46
  measurements of, 116
Skill acquisition:
  attention and, 53–85
  augmented feedback in motor skill acquisition, 86–114
  expert performance in sport and dance, 174–201
  feedback and *(see* Augmented feedback)
  improved dual task performance with practice, 63–65
  increased automaticity with practice, 65–66
  integrative modeling approach to the study of intentional
      movement behavior, 144–173
  motor development in childhood/adolescence, 20–52
  performance skill, levels of, 3–19
  practice, 115–143
  reduced PRP delays with practice, 66
Skill levels, 3–19, 332
  arousal and, 332
  automatization of movement execution, 11–12
  chunking, 12
  decision processing, 10–11
  effector processing, 5, 11–13
  event occlusion studies, 9
  experimental approaches, 4–6
  expert-novice approach, 6
  future research recommendations, 13–14
  general abilities (role of), 6–7
  high *(see* Expertise)
  individual differences approach, 5
  information-processing approach, 5–6, 7–13, 14
  perceptual processing, 8–10
  reaction-time (RT) paradigm, 5
  stages of practice notion, 3–4
  synthesis of research findings, 6–13
Soccer goalkeeping, 156–157
Social and Athletic Readjustment Rating Scale, 781
Social-cognitive theory/perspective:
  exertion tolerance, 813–818
  modeling, 205–206
  motivated behavior and physical activity, 708–710
  sport confidence model, 552
Social gerontology, 674–675
Social identity, 679
Social influence:
  coaches, 622–624
  motivation as social phenomenon, 393–394
  parents, 617–622
  peers, 624–628
  social factors in motivation, 393–397
  sports confidence, 560–561
  in youth sport, 617–628
Social learning approach, moral development, 585–586
Social loafing, 475
Social psychological effects of modeling, 230–232

Social support:
   career termination and, 681
   dimensions of, 798
   dynamics of, 799
   providers of, 798
   in sport injury rehabilitation, 798–800
Software studies (multitask approach), 176, 177–179
Spontaneous attributions, 452–455
Sport Anxiety Scale (SAS), 431, 772
Sport Attributional Style Scale (SASS), 448, 450–451
Sport burnout, 616
Sport commitment model, 607–608
Sport Competition Anxiety Test (SCAT), 772
Sport Confidence Inventory (SCI), 556
Sport expertise. *See* Expertise
Sport Imagery Questionnaire (SIQ), 534–536, 541
Sport injury, 643, 677, 751–752, 766–786, 787–809. *See also*
    Stress and athletic injury model
   athletic career termination caused by, 677
   attributions, 789–791
   psychological responses to, 789–796
   psychology of risk/prevention, 766–786
   quality of life and, 643
Sport injury rehabilitation, 787–809
   adherence to, 794–796
   behavioral responses to, 794–796
   biopsychosocial model, 787–788
   case studies, 796
   cognitive appraisal models, 789
   cognitive responses, 789–792
   coping behaviors, 795–796
   coping strategies, 791–792
   correlational studies, 796–797
   current trends, 800–802
   emotional responses to, 792–794
   experimental studies, 797–798
   future research directions, 800–802
   integrated model of psychological response to, 790
   patient-practitioner interactions, 799
   perceived benefits of injury, 792
   psychological factors in, 796–798
   psychological measures specific to, 801
   psychological models, 788–789
   qualitative/qualitative studies, 792–794
   referral for psychological services, 799–800
   self-perceptions following injury, 791
   social support in, 798–800
   stage models, 788–789
   theoretical perspectives, 787–789
Sport Motivation Scale (SMS), 392, 402, 404, 408
Sport personology, 243–244
Sport psychology, 823–832
   constancy of change, 830–831
   contemporary events influencing future of, 826–827
   current trends in, 823–832
   early European influences on, 824–825
   future of, 827–830
   graduate programs in, 828–829
   growth of, 827–828
   interest in, 828

   landmark events in development of, 823–827
   licensing, 829
   marketing of, 828
   in North America, 825–826, 829–830
   science programs and exercise psychology, 829
   Soviet influence on origin of, 824
   technology and, 830
Stage models:
   development (Piaget), 24
   practice, 3–4
   sport injury rehabilitation, 788–789
   sport participation, 275–277
   talent development, 274–275
State Sport Confidence Inventory (SSCI), 534, 551
State-Trait Anxiety Inventory (STAI), 302, 327, 328
Stress, 290–318, 428–434, 640–643, 751–752, 766–783,
    811–812. *See also* Anxiety
   antecedents of, 311
   applied implications, 311–312
   defined, 290
   exertion tolerance and, 811–812
   future research, 312
   goals and, 428–434
   individualized zones of optimal functioning (IZOF), 294–295
   moderating response, 640–643
   personality factors, 431–432
   physical activity and, 640–643
   sources of, 291–292
Stress and athletic injury model, 767–780
   coping resources, 774–777
   epidemiological studies, 766
   future research needs/directions, 780–782
   history of stressors, 768–771
   implications for practitioner, 782–783
   interventions to reduce injury vulnerability, 778–780
   personality, 771–774
   reactivity, and exercise, 751–752
   stress response, 777–778
Subjective well-being. *See* Exercise/physical activity, and
    subjective well-being; Quality of life
Subjective Workload Assessment Technique (SWAT), 58
Symbolic learning theory, 538–539

Talent, 269–289
   defining, 270
   deliberate practice (Ericsson's notion of), 277–280
   detection methods, 271–274
   development of, in sport, 269–289
   expertise development and, 185–186
   inheritability of, 284, 285
   modern talent development orientations, 274–283
   personality traits and, 284
   psychological characteristics involved in development of,
    281–283
   stages of development of, 274–275
   in teenagers (Csikszentmihalyi's view), 280–281
   traditional development orientations, 270–274
   unresolved issues related to, 283–285
Task and Ego Orientation in Sport Questionnaire (TEOSQ),
    420, 421, 429, 431

Team(s):
   ambience, 400
   self-efficacy, 351–354
   size of, 475
   unity (*see* Group cohesion in sport/exercise)
Technology, 830
Tennessee Self-Concept Scale, 773
Ten-year rule, 175
Thanatology, 674
Theory of planned behavior (TPB), 697–703
Theory of reasoned action (TRA), 697
Thought Occurrence Questionnaire (TOQ), 430
Training studies, self-regulation, 577–578
Trait Sport Confidence Inventory (TSCI), 551
Transfer effects, 118
Transtheoretical model (TTM), 710–714

Validation as process, 482–484
Values:
   beliefs and, 423–424
   goals and, 423–424
   sport and moral reasoning, 591–593
   sport and prescriptive moral judgment, 593–595
   sport and prioritizing of, 591
Verbalization, 221
Verbal protocols and sport knowledge, 182
Videotape, 96–98
Virtual environments, 132–136
Visual training programs, 184

Visuomotor behavior rehearsal (VMBR) treatment, 222
Vividness of Movement Imagery Questionnaire (VMIQ), 535

Walking clubs, 488–489
Wingate Sport Achievement Responsibility Scale (WSARS), 448, 450

Youth in sport, 604–635, 660–661
   achievement goal theory, 606
   affective outcomes, 614–617
   attrition, 609–614
   burnout, 616
   cognitive readiness, 609
   competence motivation theory, 605–606
   enjoyment/quality of life, 616–617, 660–661
   expectancy-value theory (Eccles), 606–607
   future directions in research, 613–614, 617
   motivation, 608, 609–614
   predictors of sport enjoyment, 616–617
   readiness, 608–609
   social influence, 617–628
   sport commitment model, 607–608
   stress/anxiety levels, 614–616
   theoretical perspectives, 605–608, 612–613

Zone of Optimal Functioning (ZOF), 328–329
   Individualized (IZOF), 294–295, 304, 320, 329